Y0-ARB-613

Other Wiley Editorial Offices

John Wiley & Sons Inc., 111 River Street, Hoboken, NJ 07030, USA

Jossey-Bass, 989 Market Street, San Francisco, CA 94103-1741, USA

Wiley-VCH Verlag GmbH, Boschstr. 12, D-69469 Weinheim, Germany

John Wiley & Sons Australia Ltd, 42 McDougall Street, Milton, Queensland 4064, Australia

John Wiley & Sons (Asia) Pte Ltd, 2 Clementi Loop #02-01, Jin Xing Distripark, Singapore 129809

John Wiley & Sons Canada Ltd, 6045 Freemont Blvd, Mississauga, ONT, L5R 4J3, Canada

Wiley also publishes its books in a variety of electronic formats. Some content that appears in print may not be available in electronic books.

British Library Cataloguing in Publication Data

A catalogue record for this book is available from the British Library

ISBN: 978-0-470-99614-0 (PB)

[Ernst & Young personnel only ISBN 978-0-470-75121-3]

Printed and bound in Great Britain by William Clowes Ltd., Beccles, Suffolk.

This book is printed on acid-free paper responsibly manufactured from sustainable forestry in which at least two trees are planted for each one used for paper production.

About this book

This 2008 edition of International GAAP has increased in length by approximately 500 pages since the last edition, due to the fact that it has been revised and expanded substantially in order to:

- deal with all new and amended authoritative pronouncements and exposure drafts, including the new revised standards on business combinations and consolidated financial statements;
- update and expand the extracts from the published accounts of real companies from around the world;
- include an entirely new chapter on accounting for the Extractive Industries; and
- provide insight and guidance in greater detail than ever before on the interpretation and practical application of IFRS from a truly global perspective, based on the authors' experience of dealing with day-to-day practical issues.

As a result, the book is now published in two volumes, comprising 39 Chapters, three indexes, and 90 pages of detailed contents. These are set out over the two volumes as follows:

Volume 1

- Complete set of Detailed Contents
- Chapters 1 to 22
- Index of extracts from financial statements
- Index of standards
- Index

Volume 2

- Complete set of Detailed Contents
- Chapters 23 to 39
- Index of extracts from financial statements
- Index of standards
- Index

Furthermore, for ease of use, the running header of each page of the book now includes a reference to the relevant chapter and section number. For example:

Chapter 28: Revenue recognition *Ch 28: s2.1* 2015

International GAAP® 2008

Generally Accepted Accounting Practice under International Financial Reporting Standards

Mike Bonham
Matthew Curtis
Mike Davies
Pieter Dekker
Tim Denton
Richard Moore
Hedy Richards
Gregory Wilkinson-Riddle
Matt Williams
Allister Wilson

© Cover, cover design and content Copyright Ernst & Young LLP 2007.

The United Kingdom firm of Ernst & Young LLP is a member of Ernst & Young Global.

International GAAP® is a registered trademark of Ernst & Young LLP

http://www.internationalgaap.com

Published in 2008 by John Wiley & Sons, Ltd
The Atrium, Southern Gate, Chichester,
West Sussex PO19 8SQ

Telephone (+44) 1243 779777

Email (for orders and customer service enquiries): cs-books@wiley.co.uk

Visit the Home Page on www.wiley.com

All Rights Reserved. No part of this publication may be reproduced, stored in a retrieval system or transmitted in any form or by any means, electronic, mechanical, photocopying, recording, scanning or otherwise, except under the terms of the Copyright, Designs and Patents Act 1988 or under the terms of a licence issued by the Copyright Licensing Agency Ltd, 90 Tottenham Court Road, London W1T 4LP, UK, without the permission in writing of the Publisher. Requests to the Publisher should be addressed to the Permissions Department, John Wiley & Sons Ltd, The Atrium, Southern Gate, Chichester, West Sussex PO19 8SQ, England, or emailed to permreq@wiley.co.uk, or faxed to (+44) 1243 770620.

Designations used by companies to distinguish their products are often claimed as trademarks. All brand names and product names used in this book are trade names, service marks, trademarks or registered trademarks of their respective owners. The Publisher is not associated with any product or vendor mentioned in this book.

This publication has been carefully prepared, but it necessarily contains information in summary form and is therefore intended for general guidance only, and is not intended to be a substitute for detailed research or the exercise of professional judgement. The publishers, Ernst & Young LLP, Ernst & Young Global or any of its Member Firms can accept no responsibility for loss occasioned to any person acting or refraining from action as a result of any material in this publication. On any specific matter, reference should be made to the appropriate adviser.

Foreword

Philip Laskawy

Chairman of the Trustees
International Accounting Standards Committee Foundation

The movement towards International Financial Reporting Standards (IFRSs) as the leading financial reporting framework for the global capital markets has gathered pace faster than most people expected. This is due to many different factors, including the adoption of and smooth transition to IFRSs in 2005 across Europe and in many other countries around the world. It is due also to the courage, vision and commitment shown not only by the members of the International Accounting Standards Board (IASB) under the outstanding leadership of the Board's Chairman, Sir David Tweedie, but also by national governments, securities' regulators, corporations, the auditing profession and others associated with the adoption.

Naturally, much work remains to be done. Several countries that are major participants in the global economy – such as Brazil, Canada, China, India, Japan and Korea – have announced recently their intention to converge their national standards with IFRSs. As a result, in my view, the single most important challenge now facing standard setters and regulators is to ensure that the application of IFRSs leads to a truly single set of standards used worldwide, and that 'national variations' in the interpretation and application of IFRS do not emerge. I have no doubt that calls will be made for even greater consistency and clarity in the application of IFRSs – both within individual industries and countries and across industries and national borders. Consequently, I believe that if country-specific variations of IFRSs develop, they will be a substantial hindrance to IFRSs becoming a truly global tool of financial communication.

Preventing any fragmentation in the application of IFRSs is particularly important in the light of the recent proposal by the SEC regarding the US GAAP reconciliation requirements relating to foreign private issuers. In one of the most significant moves in support of global standards in recent times, the SEC issued in July 2007 a consultative document that proposes amendments to Form 20-F to accept – without reconciliation to US GAAP – financial statements prepared in accordance with the English language version of IFRS as published by the IASB. Furthermore, the SEC has recently published a Concept Release, asking whether US companies should be able to use IFRSs for their filings with the SEC.

It is important to note that in an effort to create a global system, the SEC is not proposing to change existing reconciliation requirements for foreign private issuers that file financial statements that are not in full compliance with IFRS as published by the IASB. This emphasises the need for jurisdictions to resist the temptation to develop local variations of IFRS in the promulgation, application and regulation of their financial reporting standards.

I warmly welcome the publication of this book, as I believe that it has an important part to play in the process of promoting consistent, comparable and high quality financial reporting under IFRSs. Because IFRSs are principles-based, there is an enormous need for a book such as this; a book that not only provides an analysis of the requirements of the standards and the principles that they expound, but also presents a unique explanation of how the standards should be interpreted and applied in practice. It addresses the main issues in International GAAP by explaining thoroughly the technical aspects of each standard, and providing a detailed analysis of possible solutions to the complex practical issues the application of each standard raises. All this is accompanied by worked examples, a comprehensive discussion of the possible alternative solutions available, and practical illustrations taken from the actual financial statements of companies that report under IFRSs.

October 2007 *Philip Laskawy*

Preface

International accounting standards have come a long way since Henry Benson led the way to the creation, first, of the Accountants International Study Group in 1967 and, thereafter, of the International Accounting Standards Committee in 1973. Perhaps most remarkable is the pace at which the globalisation of accounting standards has moved: from the position only seven years ago where numerous disparate national systems existed, to the position today where IFRS has established itself as the globally accepted passport to capital raising in the world's capital markets.

This represents a considerable achievement by all concerned: the European Union, whose leaders had the vision to set the agenda for a common financial reporting regime across the EU; the former Board of the International Accounting Standards Committee (IASC), who undertook the core standards programme that laid the groundwork for global acceptance of international standards; the many countries throughout the world whose standard-setters have contributed to the work of the IASC and the International Accounting Standards Board (IASB); the members of the IASB, who have worked assiduously over the past seven years under the unstinting leadership of Sir David Tweedie; and the large number of governments that have recognised the value of a common financial reporting regime, and adopted IFRS.

2007 has also seen the significant decision by the US Securities and Exchange Commission to accept from foreign private issuers financial statements prepared in accordance with IFRS as published by the IASB without reconciliation to US GAAP.

However, with the IASB's undeniable success comes considerable responsibility. We believe that the IASB's status as an independent private sector body should be defended vigorously; at the same time, however, given the importance of IFRS in the global capital markets, it is now more important than ever before that the accountability of the IASB to wider society is substantially improved. This implies that the IASB should be the subject of a significantly enhanced system of governance and oversight than is presently the case.

A further duty of the IASB is that it should take heed of the growing concern that is being expressed about certain aspects of the direction in which global financial reporting is moving. Important organisations such as The Corporate Reporting Users' Forum and Columbia Business School's Centre for Excellence in Accounting and Security Analysis are amongst the growing list of institutions that are questioning the IASB's and FASB's pursuit of the fair (exit) value-based balance sheet approach to performance measurement.

Accounting standards should result in corporate reports that are consistent with economic reality. However, in our view, the standard-setters' exit value-based balance sheet approach to performance measurement does not reflect the way in which many businesses operate, are managed or create value. We believe further that a balance sheet dominated approach that is based on exit values can result in information of limited relevance to economic decision making and does not necessarily provide a sound basis for the assessment of value creation. We therefore believe that the standard-setters should, as a matter of priority, explain and justify to their constituencies the position they hold on the conceptual superiority of the balance sheet approach, over the concept of income, as the primary measure of performance and value creation.

****

We are deeply indebted to many of our colleagues within the global organisation of Ernst & Young for their selfless assistance and support in the publication of this book. It has been a truly international effort, with valuable contributions from Ernst & Young people around the globe.

Our thanks go particularly to those who reviewed and edited drafts, most notably: Richard Addison, Justine Belton, Tony Clifford, Michael Elliot, Daniel Feather, Charlie Feeney, Keith Gaebel, Sven Hayn, Mike Herbst, Rich Jones, Vincent de La Bachelerie, David Lindsell, Anne Lockwood, Alan Millings, John O'Grady, Eric Ohlund, Susan Oldmeadow-Hall, Ruth Picker, Chris Schibler, George Schleier, Eric Tarleton, Leo van der Tas, Lynda Tomkins, Dominique Thouvenin, Paul Wallek and Dmitry Weinstein. Within the International Financial Reporting Group itself, our thanks go to everyone who directly and indirectly contributed to the book's creation: Marc Baumgartner, Denise Brand, Robin Chatterjee, Larissa Connor, Richard Crisp, Julie Dempers, Bernd Kremp, Robert Overend, Margaret Pankhurst, Tim Rogerson, Levent Serttas, Amir Shahar, Claire Taylor and Lawrence Wong. We also thank Jeremy Gugenheim for his assistance with the production technology throughout the period of writing.

As authors, however, we take responsibility for all the opinions expressed in the book, and the blame for all its faults.

London,

November 2007

Mike Bonham | *Richard Moore*
Matthew Curtis | *Hedy Richards*
Mike Davies | *Gregory Wilkinson-Riddle*
Pieter Dekker | *Matt Williams*
Tim Denton | *Allister Wilson*

List of chapters

VOLUME 1

The list of chapters in Volume 2 follows overleaf.

VOLUME 2

Detailed contents

VOLUME 1

CHAPTER 1 THE DEVELOPMENT OF INTERNATIONAL GAAP

CHAPTER 2 THE QUEST FOR A CONCEPTUAL FRAMEWORK FOR FINANCIAL REPORTING

CHAPTER 3 PRESENTATION OF FINANCIAL STATEMENTS AND ACCOUNTING POLICIES

CHAPTER 4 NON-CURRENT ASSETS HELD FOR SALE AND DISCONTINUED OPERATIONS

CHAPTER 5 FIRST-TIME ADOPTION

CHAPTER 6 CONSOLIDATED AND SEPARATE FINANCIAL STATEMENTS

CHAPTER 7 BUSINESS COMBINATIONS AND GOODWILL

CHAPTER 8 ASSOCIATES

CHAPTER 9 JOINT VENTURES

CHAPTER 10 FOREIGN EXCHANGE

CHAPTER 11 HYPERINFLATION

CHAPTER 12 INTANGIBLE ASSETS

CHAPTER 13 PROPERTY, PLANT AND EQUIPMENT

CHAPTER 14 INVESTMENT PROPERTY

CHAPTER 15 IMPAIRMENT OF FIXED ASSETS AND GOODWILL

CHAPTER 16 CAPITALISATION OF BORROWING COSTS

CHAPTER 17 FINANCIAL INSTRUMENTS: INTRODUCTION

CHAPTER 18 FINANCIAL INSTRUMENTS: RECOGNITION, DERECOGNITION AND OFFSET

CHAPTER 19 FINANCIAL INSTRUMENTS: FINANCIAL LIABILITIES AND EQUITY

CHAPTER 20 FINANCIAL INSTRUMENTS: MEASUREMENT

CHAPTER 21 FINANCIAL INSTRUMENTS: HEDGE ACCOUNTING

CHAPTER 22 FINANCIAL INSTRUMENTS: DISCLOSURES

The detailed table of contents of Volume 2 follows overleaf.

VOLUME 2

CHAPTER 23 INVENTORIES

CHAPTER 24 CONSTRUCTION CONTRACTS

CHAPTER 25 LEASES

CHAPTER 26 INCOME TAXES

CHAPTER 27 PROVISIONS, CONTINGENT LIABILITIES AND CONTINGENT ASSETS

CHAPTER 28 REVENUE RECOGNITION

CHAPTER 29 TRANSACTIONS WITH GOVERNMENTS: GRANTS AND SERVICE CONCESSION ARRANGEMENTS

CHAPTER 30 SEGMENT REPORTING

CHAPTER 31 SHARE-BASED PAYMENT

CHAPTER 32 EMPLOYEE BENEFITS

CHAPTER 33 EARNINGS PER SHARE

CHAPTER 34 CASH FLOW STATEMENTS

CHAPTER 35 RELATED PARTY DISCLOSURES

CHAPTER 36 EVENTS AFTER THE BALANCE SHEET DATE

CHAPTER 37 INTERIM FINANCIAL REPORTING

CHAPTER 38 AGRICULTURE

CHAPTER 39 EXTRACTIVE INDUSTRIES

Abbreviations

The following abbreviations are used in this book:

Professional and regulatory bodies:

AASB	Australian Accounting Standards Board
AICPA	American Institute of Certified Public Accountants
APB	Accounting Principles Board (of the AICPA, predecessor of the FASB)
ARC	Accounting Regulatory Committee of representatives of EU Member States
ASB	Accounting Standards Board in the UK
ASC	Accounting Standards Committee (the predecessor of the ASB)
CESR	Committee of European Securities Regulators, an independent committee whose members comprise senior representatives from EU securities regulators
CICA	Canadian Institute of Chartered Accountants
EC	European Commission
EFRAG	European Financial Reporting Advisory Group
EITF	Emerging Issues Task Force in the US
EU	European Union
FAF	Financial Accounting Foundation
FASB	Financial Accounting Standards Board in the US
G4+1	The (now disbanded) group of four plus 1, actually with six members, that comprised an informal 'think tank' of staff from the standard setters from Australia, Canada, New Zealand, UK, and USA, plus the IASC
IASB	International Accounting Standards Board
IASC	International Accounting Standards Committee. The former Board of the IASC was the predecessor of the IASB
IASCF	International Accounting Standards Committee Foundation
ICAEW	Institute of Chartered Accountants in England and Wales
ICAS	Institute of Chartered Accountants of Scotland
IFRIC	International Financial Reporting Interpretations Committee of the IASB
IGC	Implementation Guidance Committee on IAS 39 (now disbanded)

IOSCO	International Organisation of Securities Commissions
JWG	Joint Working Group of Standard-setters that comprised representatives from the IASC, the FASB, and eight other international bodies. The purpose of the (now disbanded) group was to develop an integrated and harmonised standard on financial instruments – a task they were unable to complete
SAC	Standards Advisory Council, which provides advice to the IASB on a wide range of issues
SEC	Securities and Exchange Commission (the US securities regulator)
SIC	Standing Interpretations Committee of the IASC (replaced by IFRIC)

Accounting related terms:

ADS	American Depositary Shares
AFS	Available-for-sale investment
ARB	Accounting Research Bulletins (issued by the AICPA)
ARS	Accounting Research Studies (issued by the APB)
CGU	Cash Generating Unit
CIS	Comprehensive Income Statement, as developed by the G4+1 group of accounting standard-setters, and published in June 1999 in the ASB Discussion Paper *Reporting Financial Performance: Proposals for Change*
CU	Currency Unit
CULS	Convertible Unsecured Loan Stock
E	Exposure Draft (of an IAS)
EBIT	Earnings Before Interest and Taxes
EBITDA	Earnings Before Interest, Taxes, Depreciation and Amortisation
ED	Exposure Draft
EPS	Earnings per Share
FAS	Financial Accounting Standards (issued by the FASB)
FC	Foreign currency
FIFO	First-In, First-Out basis of valuation
FRS	Financial Reporting Standard (issued by the ASB)
FTA	First-time Adoption
GAAP	Generally accepted accounting practice (as it applies under IFRS), or generally accepted accounting principles (as it applies to the US)
HTM	Held-to-maturity investment
IAS	International Accounting Standard (issued by the former board of the IASC)

IFAC	International Federation of Accountants
IFRS	International Financial Reporting Standard (issued by the IASB)
IPO	Initial Public Offering
IPR&D	In-process Research and Development
IRR	Internal Rate of Return
JV	Joint Venture
LC	Local Currency
LIBOR	London Inter Bank Offered Rate
LIFO	Last-In, First-Out basis of valuation
NBV	Net Book Value
NRV	Net Realisable Value
PP&E	Property, Plant and Equipment
R&D	Research and development
SFAC	Statement of Financial Accounting Concepts (issued by the FASB as part of its conceptual framework project)
SFAS	Statement of Financial Accounting Standards (issued by the FASB)
SPE	Special Purpose Entity
TSR	Total Shareholder Return
VIU	Value In Use
WACC	Weighted Average Cost of Capital

References to IFRSs, IASs, Interpretations and supporting documentation:

AG	Application Guidance
AV	Alternative View
B, BCZ	Basis for Conclusions on IASs
BC	Basis for Conclusions on IFRSs and IASs
DO	Dissenting Opinion
IE	Illustrative Examples on IFRSs and IASs
IG	Implementation Guidance
IN	Introduction to IFRSs and IASs

Authoritative literature

The content of this book takes into account all accounting standards and other relevant rules issued up to 31 October 2007. Consequently, it covers the IASB's *Framework for the Preparation and Presentation of Financial Statements* and authoritative literature listed below.

Unless otherwise indicated therein, all references in footnotes to the extant pronouncements below are to the versions of those pronouncements as included in the Bound Volume of International Financial Reporting Standards as at 1 January 2007 published by the IASB (ISBN 978-1-905590-26-1).

† The standards and interpretations marked with a dagger have been withdrawn or superseded.

IASB Framework

Framework for the Preparation and Presentation of Financial Statements

International Financial Reporting Standards

IFRS 1	First-time Adoption of International Financial Reporting Standards
IFRS 2	Share-based Payment
IFRS 3	Business Combinations
IFRS 4	Insurance Contracts
IFRS 5	Non-current Assets Held for Sale and Discontinued Operations
IFRS 6	Exploration for and Evaluation of Mineral Resources
IFRS 7	Financial Instruments: Disclosures
IFRS 8	Operating Segments

International Accounting Standards

IAS 1	Presentation of Financial Statements
IAS 2	Inventories
IAS 7	Cash Flow Statements
IAS 8	Accounting Policies, Changes in Accounting Estimates and Errors
IAS 10	Events After the Balance Sheet Date
IAS 11	Construction Contracts
IAS 12	Income Taxes
IAS 14	Segment Reporting
IAS 16	Property, Plant and Equipment
IAS 17	Leases
IAS 18	Revenue
IAS 19	Employee Benefits
IAS 20	Accounting for Government Grants and Disclosure of Government Assistance

	IAS 21	The Effects of Changes in Foreign Exchange Rates
	IAS 23	Borrowing Costs
	IAS 24	Related Party Disclosures
	IAS 26	Accounting and Reporting by Retirement Benefit Plans
	IAS 27	Consolidated and Separate Financial Statements
	IAS 28	Investments in Associates
	IAS 29	Financial Reporting in Hyperinflationary Economies
†	IAS 30	Disclosures in the Financial Statements of Banks and Similar Financial Institutions
	IAS 31	Interests in Joint Ventures
	IAS 32	Financial Instruments: Presentation
	IAS 33	Earnings per Share
	IAS 34	Interim Financial Reporting
	IAS 36	Impairment of Assets
	IAS 37	Provisions, Contingent Liabilities and Contingent Assets
	IAS 38	Intangible Assets
	IAS 39	Financial Instruments: Recognition and Measurement
	IAS 40	Investment Property
	IAS 41	Agriculture

International Financial Reporting Interpretations Committee Interpretations

	IFRIC 1	Changes in Existing Decommissioning, Restoration and Similar Liabilities
	IFRIC 2	Members' Shares in Co-operative Entities and Similar Instruments
†	IFRIC 3	Emission Rights
	IFRIC 4	Determining whether an Arrangement contains a Lease
	IFRIC 5	Rights to Interests arising from Decommissioning, Restoration and Environmental Rehabilitation Funds
	IFRIC 6	Liabilities arising from Participation in a Specific Market – Waste Electrical and Electronic Equipment
	IFRIC 7	Applying the Restatement Approach under IAS 29 – *Financial Reporting in Hyperinflationary Economies*
	IFRIC 8	Scope of IFRS 2
	IFRIC 9	Reassessment of Embedded Derivatives
	IFRIC 10	Interim Financial Reporting and Impairment
	IFRIC 11	IFRS 2 – Group and Treasury Share Transactions
	IFRIC 12	Service Concession Arrangements
	IFRIC 13	Customer Loyalty Programmes
	IFRIC 14	IAS 19 – The Limit on a Defined Benefit Asset, Minimum Funding Requirements and their Interaction

Standing Interpretations Committee Interpretations

SIC-7	Introduction of the Euro
SIC-10	Government Assistance – No Specific Relation to Operating Activities
SIC-12	Consolidation – Special Purpose Entities
SIC-13	Jointly Controlled Entities – Non-Monetary Contributions by Venturers

SIC-15	Operating Leases – Incentives
SIC-21	Income Taxes – Recovery of Revalued Non-Depreciable Assets
SIC-25	Income Taxes – Changes in the Tax Status of an Enterprise or its Shareholders
SIC-27	Evaluating the Substance of Transactions Involving the Legal Form of a Lease
SIC-29	Service Concession Arrangements: Disclosures
SIC-31	Revenue – Barter Transactions Involving Advertising Services
SIC-32	Intangible Assets – Web Site Costs

Other IASB publications

IFRS 3 (Revised)	Near-final draft of the revised IFRS 3, published June 2007.

IASB Exposure Drafts

ED 9	Joint Arrangements
	Amendments to IAS 32 Financial Instruments: Presentation and IAS 1 Presentation of Financial Statements – Financial Instruments Puttable at Fair Value and Obligations Arising on Liquidation
	Amendments to IFRS 2 Share-based Payment – Vesting Conditions and Cancellations
	Amendments to IFRS 3 Business Combinations
	Amendments to IAS 27 Consolidated and Separate Financial Statements
	Amendments to IAS 37 Provisions, Contingent Liabilities and Contingent assets and IAS 19 Employee Benefits
	Amendments to IFRS 1 First-time Adoption of International Financial Reporting Standards – Cost of an Investment in a Subsidiary
	Proposed IFRS for Small and Medium-sized Entities
	Amendments to IAS 24 Related Party Transactions – State-controlled Entities and the Definition of a Related Party.
	Amendments to IAS 39 Financial Instruments Recognition and Measurement – Exposures Qualifying for Hedge Accounting
	Proposed Improvements to International Financial Reporting Standards

IFRIC Exposure Drafts

IFRIC D21	Real Estate Sales
IFRIC D22	Hedges of a Net Investment in a Foreign Operation

Chapter 1 The development of International GAAP

1 THE EVOLUTION OF THE INTERNATIONAL ACCOUNTING STANDARDS BOARD

Globalisation – the removal of barriers to free trade and the closer integration of national economies[1] – is a term now frequently used, when even a decade ago it was relatively rare. With globalisation has come the increasing integration of world markets for goods, services and capital – with the result that companies that traditionally were reliant on their domestic markets for their financing now have substantially increased access to debt and equity capital both inside and outside their national borders.

Yet – perhaps not surprisingly – the world of financial reporting has been slow to respond. Whilst the benefits of adopting common accounting standards for use in the international capital markets appeared obvious to some, vested interest has often seemed to triumph over common sense; people tended to be nationalistic about their accounting standards, and whilst they might have criticised their own rules, they nevertheless believed that they were better than those that existed in other countries. As a result, companies wishing to access the international capital markets were in many cases required either to prepare two sets of financial statements or to reconcile their accounts to the national standards of other countries. This was – until very recently – the case for all non-US companies that are listed on a US stock exchange, as they have to be registered with the US Securities and Exchange Commission (SEC); in turn, the SEC required all foreign companies to file financial statements that disclose information that is substantially similar to US GAAP financial statements.

However, in one of the most significant moves towards convergence and mutual recognition in recent times, the SEC issued in July 2007 a consultative document[2] that proposed amendments to Form 20-F to accept – without reconciliation to US GAAP – financial statements prepared in accordance with International Financial

Reporting Standards (IFRSs) as issued by the International Accounting Standards Board (IASB). In November 2007 the SEC voted unanimously to approve this proposed rule amendment.[3] (The SEC's proposals for the removal of the reconciliation requirement for IFRS reporters are discussed more fully at 3.3.4 below).

Undoubtedly, one of the main advantages of a single set of global accounting standards is that it would enable the international capital markets to assess and compare inter-company performance in a much more meaningful, effective and efficient way than is presently possible. This should increase companies' access to global capital and ultimately reduce the cost thereof; yet it is only in the last five years or so that this has been seen as even a realistic possibility – a possibility that has come about largely as a result of bold action on the part of the European Commission.

In May 1999, the European Commission issued its Financial Services Action Plan.[4] The plan confirmed the Commission's position that comparable, transparent and reliable financial information is fundamental to an efficient and integrated EU capital market, and that International Accounting Standards seemed the most appropriate benchmark for a single set of financial reporting requirements that would be the catalyst for the development of a single EU capital market.

This initiative was given further impetus by the summit of the European Heads of Government held in Lisbon in March 2000, where it was agreed that a single European capital market should be developed as a matter of priority. It was acknowledged further that the adoption of a single financial reporting framework for the European Union was a vital element in that process. The summit conclusions stressed the need to accelerate completion of the internal market for financial services and set a deadline of 2005 to implement the Commission's Financial Services Action Plan.

Following this lead by the European Heads of Government, the Commission announced in June 2000 that it would present proposals to introduce the requirement that all listed EU companies report in accordance with IAS by 2005. This requirement – which was finally adopted in an EU Regulation in 2002[5] – has changed fundamentally not only the face of European financial reporting, but global reporting as well. Largely following Europe's lead, scores of countries have either already adopted IFRS directly, or have aligned their national standards with IFRS, or have committed to do so in the foreseeable future.

Although the European Union is almost certainly the IASB's most significant single constituency for the time being, there are also a number of other economically developed countries that either have already adopted – or will be adopting – IFRS as their primary system of GAAP. Notable examples are Canada, which has announced that Canadian GAAP will be replaced by IFRS from 2011 onwards[6], and Japan where, in August 2007, the Accounting Standards Board of Japan announced an agreement with the IASB to accelerate convergence between Japanese GAAP and IFRSs, with the aim of removing all differences on or before 30 June 2011. Significantly also, countries such as Brazil, China, India and Sri Lanka have made significant progress towards the adoption of IFRS, whilst countries such as Australia and South Africa have already aligned their national standards with IFRS (see section 6 below).

The European Commission's decision to adopt IFRS as the basis of financial reporting for all listed EU companies coincided also with the restructuring of the former International Accounting Standards Committee and the formation on 1 April 2001 of the present day International Accounting Standards Board (IASB), as discussed in section 2 below. Since then, the IASB and the US Financial Accounting Standards Board (FASB) have become increasingly committed to the convergence of IFRS and US GAAP. This is evidenced by the October 2002 Norwalk Agreement and the February 2006 Memorandum of Understanding between the FASB and the IASB, both of which are discussed at 3.3 below. Most significantly, the IASB and FASB have now largely aligned their agendas to the extent that most major projects – such as consolidations, impairment, income taxes, revenue recognition and employee benefit accounting – are now undertaken jointly.

The result is that in the last seven years global financial reporting has ceased to be characterised by numerous disparate national systems to the point at which there are today essentially only two – IFRS and US GAAP. However – perhaps even more remarkably – it now seems feasible that the ultimate goal of a single set of global accounting standards will be reached in the foreseeable future. This chapter is devoted to outlining how this has been achieved.

1.1 The Accountants International Study Group

Whilst many remarkable individuals have featured in the past 40 years' evolution of international accounting, perhaps the single person that stands out as the visionary behind the formation of the International Accounting Standards Committee (IASC) – the predecessor to today's International Accounting Standards Board – is Lord Benson, former President of the Institute of Chartered Accountants in England and Wales (ICAEW) and senior partner in Cooper Brothers & Co.[7] Henry Benson foresaw the importance of international accounting standards and, as President of the ICAEW, pioneered the practical steps that led to the creation, first, of the Accountants International Study Group in 1967 and, ultimately, of the International Accounting Standards Committee in 1973. Henry Benson was the first Chairman of the IASC, serving from 1973 to 1975.

The idea of the Accountants International Study Group was publicly unveiled by Henry Benson during his term as President of the ICAEW, at the Annual Conference of the Canadian Institute of Chartered Accountants (CICA), held in August 1966. Following further discussions with the Presidents of the CICA and the American Institute of Certified Public Accountants (AICPA), the three institutes announced in January 1967 that agreement had been reached for the formation of the Study Group, with AICPA President Robert Trueblood appointed as its first Chairman.

It seems that the formation of the Group may well have been driven by Henry Benson's early conviction of the essential need for harmonised accounting and auditing rules and procedures. The first indication of Henry Benson's understanding of the need for international harmonisation may be found in the Terms of Reference of the Study Group, which read as follows: 'To institute comparative studies as to accounting thought and practice in participating countries, to make reports from time to time, which, subject to the prior approval of the sponsoring Institutes, would be issued to members of those Institutes'.[8] Thus, it seems that Henry Benson believed that the UK, US and Canada should not each be operating in their own technical vacuums without considering developments in the other two.

The Study Group lasted for ten years, and was wound up in 1977. During its existence, it published 20 documents covering a wide range of accounting and auditing topics. These publications were, in effect, comparative studies of existing accepted practice, and the opinions expressed therein were termed 'conclusions'.

1.2 The International Accounting Standards Committee (IASC)

The origins of the IASC can be traced back to the 10th World Congress of Accountants, which was held in September 1972 in Sydney. It was here that Henry Benson – who had been asked by the major accounting Institutes to create an international accounting body based on the Accountants International Study Group – proposed the formation of a new body that would be responsible for the formulation of international accounting standards. Following further meetings between the Presidents of the AICPA, CICA, ICAEW and The Institute of Chartered Accountants of Scotland (ICAS) it was agreed to broaden the participation of countries in the formation of an international accounting body beyond the 'three nations' of the Study Group. Accordingly, invitations were extended to the accounting bodies in Australia, France, Germany, Japan, Mexico and the Netherlands to attend a meeting in London in March 1973.

This meeting led to the formation in June 1973 of the International Accounting Standards Committee as an independent private-sector body through an agreement made by professional accountancy bodies from Australia, Canada, France, Germany, Japan, Mexico, the Netherlands, the United Kingdom and Ireland and the United States of America. From 1983, the IASC's members included all the professional accountancy bodies that were members of the International Federation of Accountants (IFAC). At the time when the Board of the IASC was dissolved in 2001, there were 153 members from 112 countries.

The IASC was founded to formulate and publish, in the public interest, International Accounting Standards (IAS) to be observed in the presentation of published financial statements and to promote their worldwide acceptance and observance.[9] It was envisaged that IAS should be capable of worldwide acceptance and contribute to a significant improvement in the quality and comparability of corporate disclosure.[10]

Although the composition of the IASC Board changed over time, during the last part of its life the business of the IASC was conducted by a Board comprising representatives of accountancy bodies in thirteen countries (or combinations of countries) appointed by the Council of IFAC, and up to four other organisations with an interest in financial reporting. Each Board Member was permitted to nominate up to two representatives and a technical adviser to attend Board meetings. The IASC encouraged each Board Member to include in its delegation at least one person working in industry and one person who was directly involved in the work of the national standard setting body.[11] The Board also had a number of observer members (including representatives of the European Commission, the International Organisation of Securities Commissions (IOSCO) and the FASB) who participated in the debate but did not vote. In 1998, the People's Republic of China became a member of IFAC and joined the IASC Board as an observer member. In 1999, IASC Board meetings were opened up to public observation.

The IASC Board established an international Consultative Group in 1981 that included representatives of international organisations of preparers and users of financial statements, stock exchanges and securities regulators. The Consultative Group met periodically to discuss the technical issues in IASC projects, the IASC's work programme and its strategy. This group played an important part in the IASC's due process for the setting of International Accounting Standards and in gaining acceptance for the resulting standards.

In 1995, the IASC established a high-level international Advisory Council, made up of outstanding individuals in senior positions from the accountancy profession, business and the other users of financial statements. The Advisory Council was responsible for the oversight of the IASC, including finances, and was expected to promote generally the acceptability of International Accounting Standards and enhance the credibility of the IASC's work.

1.2.1 The IASC's Standing Interpretations Committee (SIC)

The IASC Board formed a Standing Interpretations Committee (SIC) in 1997 to consider, on a timely basis, accounting issues that were likely to receive divergent or unacceptable treatment in the absence of authoritative guidance. Its consideration was within the context of existing International Accounting Standards and the IASC *Framework*. In developing interpretations, the SIC consulted similar national committees that had been nominated for that purpose by Member Bodies. The SIC had up to twelve voting members from various countries, including individuals from the accountancy profession, preparer groups, user groups and accounting academics. The European Commission and IOSCO had observer seats. In 2000, SIC meetings were opened up to public observation.

The SIC considered the following criteria for taking issues onto its agenda:

- the issue should involve an interpretation of an existing Standard within the context of the IASC *Framework*;
- the issue should have practical and widespread relevance;
- the issue should relate to a specific fact pattern; and
- significantly divergent interpretations must either be emerging or already exist in practice.

SIC interpretations were published initially in draft form for public comment (usually 60 days), and if no more than three of its voting members voted against an interpretation, the SIC asked the Board to approve the final interpretation for issue; as was the case for International Accounting Standards, this required three-quarters of the Board to vote in favour. The SIC dealt with issues of reasonably widespread importance, not issues of concern to only a small number of businesses. The interpretations that were issued covered both mature issues, where there was unsatisfactory practice within the scope of existing International Accounting Standards, and emerging issues relating to topics not considered when the standards were developed.

The SIC was reconstituted as the International Financial Reporting Interpretations Committee (IFRIC) in December 2001 (see 2.2.6 below).

1.2.2 The IASC's comparability/improvements project

When International Accounting Standards were first issued, they permitted several alternative accounting treatments. The principal reason for this was that the IASC viewed its initial function as prohibiting undesirable accounting practices, whilst acknowledging that there might be more than one acceptable solution to a specific accounting issue.

In 1993, the Board of the IASC completed a major project (known as the comparability/improvements project), which had set out to reduce many of the permitted alternative accounting options. This project took four years to complete and culminated in the publication of a package of ten revised international standards, which became operative for accounting periods beginning on or after 1 January 1995. Unfortunately, this project was less successful than many had hoped it would be, and although the number of permitted alternative options was reduced, not all were eliminated; this meant that international standards still incorporated 'benchmark' treatments and 'allowed alternative' treatments. However, as discussed more fully below, the new International Accounting Standards Board (IASB), through its own Improvements Project, did eliminate a number of the alternative accounting treatments. Where an IAS retains alternative treatments, the IASB removed virtually all references to 'benchmark treatment' and 'allowed alternative treatment', instead using descriptive references, such as 'cost model' and 'revaluation model'.

1.3 The IASC/IOSCO agreement

An increasingly global marketplace brings with it increasing interdependence among regulators. There must be strong links between regulators and the capacity to give effect to those links. Created in 1983, the International Organisation of Securities Commissions (IOSCO) is the world's primary forum of international cooperation for securities regulatory agencies. Its membership comprises national regulatory bodies that have day-to-day responsibility for securities regulation and the administration of securities laws in their countries. The objectives of IOSCO's members are:[12]

- to cooperate together to promote high standards of regulation in order to maintain just, efficient and sound markets;

- to exchange information on their respective experiences in order to promote the development of domestic markets;
- to unite their efforts to establish standards and an effective surveillance of international securities transactions; and
- to provide mutual assistance to promote the integrity of the markets by a rigorous application of the standards and by effective enforcement against offences.

In 1989, IOSCO prepared a report entitled *International Equity Offers*, which noted that cross-border offerings would be facilitated by the development of internationally accepted accounting standards. Rather than attempt to develop those standards itself, IOSCO focused on the efforts of the IASC to provide acceptable international accounting standards for use in multinational securities offerings.

In 1993, IOSCO wrote to the IASC detailing the necessary components of a reasonably complete set of standards to create a comprehensive body of principles for business entities undertaking cross-border securities offerings. In 1994, IOSCO completed a review of the then-current IASC standards and identified a number of issues that would have to be addressed, as well as standards that the IASC would have to improve, before IOSCO could consider recommending IASC standards for use in cross-border listings and offerings. IOSCO divided the issues into three categories:

- issues that required a solution prior to consideration by IOSCO of an endorsement of the IASC standards;
- issues that would not require resolution before IOSCO could consider endorsement, although individual jurisdictions might specify treatments that they would require if those issues were not addressed satisfactorily in the IASC standards; and
- areas where improvements could be made, but that the IASC did not need to address prior to consideration of the IASC standards by IOSCO.

In July 1995, the Board of the IASC and IOSCO's Technical Committee announced that an important milestone had been reached in the development of IAS. The Board had developed a work plan (to become known as 'the core standards work programme') that the Technical Committee agreed would result, upon successful completion, in IAS comprising a comprehensive core set of standards. Completion of comprehensive core standards that were acceptable to the Technical Committee would allow the Technical Committee to recommend the endorsement of IAS by IOSCO for cross-border capital raising and listing purposes in all global markets. IOSCO had already endorsed IAS 7 – *Cash Flow Statements* – and had indicated to the IASC that fourteen of the existing international standards did not require additional improvement, provided that the other core standards were successfully completed.[13]

Both the IASC and IOSCO agreed that there was a compelling need for high quality, comprehensive IAS. The goal of both bodies in reaching this agreement was that financial statements prepared in accordance with IAS could be used worldwide in cross border offerings and listings as an alternative to the use of national accounting standards.

The IASC Board worked extraordinarily hard over the ensuing four and a half years to fulfil its side of the IOSCO agreement. Board meetings were increased both in terms of frequency and duration, several new Steering Committees were formed and several major new projects were placed on the Board's agenda. The Board completed its revised core set of standards at its December 1998 meeting, at which IAS 39 – *Financial Instruments: Recognition and Measurement* – was approved for issue. As a result, the IOSCO review of these core standards began in 1999. In the meantime, IOSCO announced that it wished the issue of accounting for investment properties to be added to the list of core standards, and this matter was dealt with in a new standard, IAS 40 – *Investment Property* – which was approved for issue by the IASC Board at its March 2000 meeting.

So all that remained outstanding was for the IOSCO Technical Committee to announce the result of its assessment of the IASC core standards. However, at the time, many observers felt that the US Securities and Exchange Commission (SEC) was unlikely to allow IOSCO to endorse IASC standards unconditionally unless they corresponded closely to existing US standards. A more likely scenario was that some or all of the IASC standards would be accepted by the SEC only on the basis of additional disclosures and other conditions. Such an attitude was likely to have been reinforced by a FASB publication that claimed to have identified 255 differences between US GAAP and IASC standards.[14]

1.4 The SEC Concept Release on International Accounting Standards

Whilst the financial reporting world was waiting for IOSCO's Technical Committee to complete its assessment of the IASC's core standards and to declare its likely attitude towards recognising the new body of IAS without requiring reconciliation to national standards, the US Securities and Exchange Commission (SEC) appeared to pre-empt what was to come by publishing in February 2000 a 'Concept Release' on International Accounting Standards.[15]

The Concept Release set out the hurdles IAS would have to clear if they were to be deemed acceptable for US filing purposes. The document was mainly in the form of a series of questions apparently seeking opinions about, and experiences of using, IAS. However, although it claimed to be seeking input to determine under what conditions the SEC 'should accept financial statements of foreign private issuers that are prepared using the standards promulgated by the International Accounting Standards Committee', it also set out far broader conditions than the quality of accounting standards for accepting IAS financial statements without reconciliation to US GAAP, including the quality of auditing standards, audit quality assurance, regulation and enforcement.

There is little doubt that the SEC would argue that its Release was objective and fair-minded. Indeed, it started out in a noble enough manner: 'The globalisation of the securities markets has challenged securities regulators around the world to adapt to meet the needs of market participants while maintaining the current high levels of investor protection and market integrity'. This sentence contained two main statements; first, the challenge for securities regulators to adapt and, second, an assertion that, in general, levels of investor protection and market integrity were considered to be high.

However, what followed these encouraging statements was an elaborate exposition of why the SEC should not itself adapt in order to help realise the globalisation aim. Furthermore, it seemed to follow from the SEC's views about the need for changes (i.e. improvements) in what it called 'infrastructure support' that the SEC did not in fact believe that there were high levels of investor protection and market integrity outside the US.

Of course, the essential issue at hand was whether the SEC should accept financial statements prepared under IAS. Instead of responding directly to this question and looking for ways of adapting its own approach as a basis for embracing IAS, the SEC's view seemed to be that the world should adopt its philosophy of regulation. However, it made no suggestions as to how this should be done, or by whom. Although the SEC at one point stated that it was not focusing on differences between IAS and US GAAP, elsewhere it made it clear that differences between IAS and US GAAP were less than desirable, and clearly implied that the benchmark that IAS needed to meet was US GAAP.

Unfortunately, this posture led some commentators to the inescapable conclusion that the SEC was in favour of adaptation – but by everyone except the SEC. It seemed that countries that wished to adapt and progress in relation to IAS should do so separately and apart from the SEC.

The phrase 'high quality' was a recurring theme throughout the Release. No one would disagree with the need for high quality accounting standards in the context of the global financial markets. However, the Release seemed to be based on the premise that the US model met the criteria for high quality, and that any other model, being different, by definition did not. The inference inevitably to be drawn by readers of the Release was that US standards were high quality standards; the US system of formulating and explaining standards was best; any standards that were different, or differently formulated and explained, were lesser quality standards; US standards gave better investor protection than other standards; and regulation and enforcement of standards and the auditing profession was better in the US than anywhere else.

The SEC position centred on investor protection and the pre-eminence of US GAAP, and the regulatory and enforcement regime by which it was underpinned. Therefore, the clear message was that companies had to continue to use US GAAP if they wished to raise capital in the US – at least companies had to produce a US GAAP reconciliation, which was tantamount to the same thing – or else investors would be at risk.

The Concept Release attracted numerous letters of response, many of which expressed views that questioned the general thrust of the document. Although there was never any follow-up to the Release by the SEC, it nevertheless appeared to set the scene for what was to come three months later in IOSCO's Assessment Report on IAS.

1.5 The IOSCO Assessment Report on International Accounting Standards

The IOSCO assessment should be seen in the context of the situation at that time regarding the acceptance of IAS by the international capital markets. The reality was that many of the world's stock exchanges – including the European Union exchanges, Sydney and Zurich – already accepted IAS financial statements for cross-border listing purposes without reconciliation to national GAAP. The only significant exceptions were the exchanges in Canada and the USA. Consequently, a large part of the IOSCO effort was directed towards gaining the acceptance of the North American securities regulators.

In May 2000, IOSCO announced the completion of its assessment of the IASC's core standards through the publication by IOSCO's Technical Committee of a report that summarised its assessment work.[16] In view of the SEC Concept Release that had been issued three months earlier (see 1.4 above), the outcome of the Technical Committee's assessment of the IASC's core standards was perhaps not unexpected. Nevertheless, its content was a great disappointment to many observers and those that had been involved in the core standards programme, who believed that the IASC Board had, in good faith, fulfilled all its obligations under the IOSCO agreement.

The report stated that IOSCO had assessed 30 IASC standards, including their related interpretations (termed 'the IASC 2000 standards'), and considered their suitability for use in cross-border offerings and listings. Although the report recommended that IOSCO members should permit incoming multinational issuers to use the IASC 2000 standards to prepare their financial statements for cross-border offerings and listings, this recommendation was made subject to a significant proviso. The proviso was that each IOSCO member, in deciding how to implement the IASC 2000 standards in its jurisdiction, could choose to mandate one or more of the following 'supplemental treatments':

- *Reconciliation:* this would require reconciliation of the treatment specified in an IASC 2000 standard to another specified accounting treatment (which may be a host country national accounting treatment). This reconciliation would be expected to be presented in a footnote to the financial statements and would quantify the effect of applying the specified alternative accounting treatment;
- *Supplemental disclosure:* this would require supplemental disclosure, either in the form of:
  - more detailed footnote disclosure than an IASC 2000 standard requires; or
  - additional detail on the face of the primary financial statements (e.g. income statement or balance sheet line items) that would have to be presented.
- *Interpretation:* this would require a specific application of an IASC 2000 standard, either:
  - in cases where an IASC 2000 standard permitted different approaches to an issue, generally with one approach identified as a 'benchmark' and

another as an 'allowed alternative', specifying which approach (the 'benchmark' or 'allowed alternative') was accepted in a host jurisdiction; or

- to clarify ambiguity or address silence in an IASC 2000 standard, by specifying a particular interpretation of the IASC 2000 standard that should be used in a host jurisdiction.

If the specified treatment was not followed, it was expected that an IOSCO member would require reconciliation to the specified treatment.

In an Appendix running to more than 100 pages, the report identified numerous 'concerns' raised by IOSCO members during the assessment of the IASC 2000 standards. These 'concerns' included an analysis of outstanding substantive issues relating to the standards, specifying supplemental treatments that might be required in a particular jurisdiction to address each of these concerns.

The effect of this report by the Technical Committee of IOSCO was to negate the intention of the IASC/IOSCO agreement. Its impact was to perpetuate the existing position whereby a company faced the possibility of having to comply with more than one reporting regime in order to obtain a cross-border listing, thereby doing nothing to remove duplication, complication and expense.

Thus, the long-awaited 'endorsement' from IOSCO was, in fact, only a qualified acceptance of IAS that still allowed IOSCO members to request any supplemental treatment that they considered necessary. Whilst one could accept that different regulatory jurisdictions might require additional note disclosures in line with local circumstances, the imposition of any reconciliation requirement mandating different recognition and measurement rules was clearly contrary to any notion of accounting harmonisation. It therefore seemed at the time that any such unconditional endorsement of IAS by IOSCO for cross-border capital raising and listing purposes in all global markets was a long way off, and would require substantial further effort on all sides.

In fact – as discussed at 3.3.4 below – that endorsement has come much quicker than most people expected, with the SEC agreeing in November 2007 to accept from foreign private issuers financial statements prepared in accordance with IFRS as issued by the IASB without reconciliation to US GAAP.[17]

1.6 The influence of the G4+1 Group of standard setters on international accounting

The G4+1 Group of standard setters was an informal grouping of staff members of the accounting standard-setting bodies of Australia, Canada, New Zealand, the United Kingdom, the United States of America and the IASC. Although not an official standard-setting body in its own right, the G4+1 became influential through the publication of discussion papers that dealt with highly topical and usually controversial accounting issues. Examples include: accounting for leases, reporting financial performance and accounting for share-based payments. Although these papers did not reflect the official views of any of the standard-setting bodies represented, the Group was able, through its links with the major Anglo-Saxon standard setters, to set the agenda for the development of new global accounting standards.

Perhaps unfortunately, because of their rather privileged positions and self-referential 'membership' criteria (for example, membership of the Group required acceptance of a conceptual framework similar to that of other members), the Group was something of a closed shop. The result was that much of the output from the Group was predictable, not always of the highest quality and not necessarily informed by practical business considerations.

In any event, at a meeting of the G4+1 held in January 2001, the Group discussed whether its activities should continue given the imminent commencement of activities by the new International Accounting Standards Board (IASB), and agreed to disband and cancel its planned future activities with immediate effect.

2 THE RECONSTITUTION OF THE IASC

2.1 Shaping IASC for the future

Few would disagree that since its formation in 1973, the IASC had achieved a great deal within the limitations of its structure. However, with the globalisation of the world's capital markets, the increasing complexity of business transactions and the growing pressure for a single set of internationally harmonised accounting standards, the IASC Board believed that structural changes were needed for it to anticipate and meet effectively the new challenges that it faced.

Consequently, the IASC Board saw the completion of its core standards programme as an appropriate moment to undertake a review of its strategy. As a result, in 1998 it appointed a Strategy Working Party to conduct a general review of the strategy of the IASC.

The Working Party published its proposals in December 1998 in a Discussion Paper entitled 'Shaping IASC for the future'.[18] The Working Party's proposals were fairly radical, but were framed within the rather nebulous notion of a 'partnership with national standard setters'.[19] The rationale behind this was that the IASC should enter into a partnership with national standard setters enabling the IASC to work with them to accelerate convergence between national standards and International Accounting Standards. However, in order to form this 'partnership', the Working Party proposed the abolition of the IASC Board structure and the establishment of a bicameral system in its place. Under this system, power would be concentrated in a Standards Development Committee (SDC), comprising a small group of select full-time standard setters. It was also proposed that the SDC would replace the IASC's Steering Committee system, under which Standards had been developed. The Working Party's recommendations covered a number of other areas, including the IASC's system of due process, implementation, education, enforcement and funding.

Perhaps not surprisingly, the Working Party's proposals met with considerable opposition, both from within the IASC Board and outside. The principal criticisms of the proposals centred on the bicameral system and the concept of the SDC. One general perception was that the Discussion Paper was aimed at further entrenching the position of the G4+1 group of Anglo-Saxon accounting standard setters (see 1.6 above).[20]

However, many considered the biggest single failing of the Working Party's proposals to be that they did not address adequately the key issue of legitimacy among the IASC's constituencies. So, whilst there was agreement with the objectives identified by the Working Party, there was less support for the structure that was proposed in order to achieve them, since the proposed structure would not have ensured legitimacy. The Discussion Paper contained little elaboration on the details of the proposed 'partnership with national standard setters' and other key constituencies, with the result that their role under the proposed structure was unclear.

Particular concern was expressed also about the representation of users and preparers of accounts in any new standard setting structure. Ultimately, the long-term credibility of International Accounting Standards would depend on their acceptance by the preparer and user communities as well as the international capital markets. Consequently there had to be full participation by all the key players in the marketplace in order to secure the future of IAS.

The IASC Board had a joint meeting on 30 June 1999 with the Strategy Working Party to discuss the comments received on the Discussion Paper. The discussion indicated that the proposed bicameral/SDC system should be abandoned in favour of a single Board structure. There was a general consensus that this single Board should comprise a blend of full and part-time members, although the overall size of the Board and precise proportion of full and part-timers was not agreed. The Strategy Working Party met again during July 1999 in order to develop a new proposal along the lines of its discussions with the IASC Board.

2.2 The new IASC structure

In November 1999, the IASC's Strategy Working Party presented its final report – *Recommendations on Shaping IASC for the Future* – to the IASC Board.[21] In fact, the report was delivered somewhat as a *fait accompli*, and it was clear to the members of the IASC Board that there was little room for discussion: they could either take it or leave it. It seemed to many observers that the process had become highly politicised, and that the influence of the US SEC could be detected in ensuring that the IASB would be constituted as closely as possible in the image of the FASB. Although the Strategy Working Party had seemingly dealt with the objections raised concerning its original bi-cameral structure, a number of fundamental difficulties that many observers and commentators had raised had not been resolved.

From a European perspective, these difficulties surrounded the issue of legitimacy and political accountability that were considered to be vital elements in order to ensure maximum commitment from those constituencies who would have to implement, regulate and enforce the system. The link between legitimacy and enforcement exists because broad support from the key constituencies involved makes it significantly more likely that standards will be applied and enforced, which in turn gives them credibility. However, there was a clear tension between this 'representative' model that was clearly preferred in Europe and elsewhere on the one hand, and the SEC/FASB 'expert' model on the other.

In any event, the Strategy Working Party's proposal was presented to the IASC Board as a non-negotiable agreement with the SEC. This meant that the Board, left with no room to manoeuvre, adopted unanimously the recommendations of the Strategy Working Party. These were then approved by the member bodies of the International Federation of Accountants, under whose patronage the IASC Board operated. The new structure adopted is outlined below.

2.2.1 The IASC Foundation (IASCF)

The governance of the IASC organisation rests with the Trustees of the IASC Foundation who, in turn, act under the terms of the IASC Foundation Constitution.[22] The first Board of Trustees was appointed during the second half of 2000 by a Nominating Committee that was set up for that sole purpose under the Chairmanship of the then US SEC Chairman, Mr. Arthur Levitt. Initially, the Board comprised nineteen Trustees, under the Chairmanship of Mr. Paul A. Volcker, a Former Chairman of the US Federal Reserve Board. However, the number of Trustees was increased to twenty-two, following a review of the Constitution in 2005. It is a requirement of the IASC Foundation Constitution that, in order to ensure a broad international basis, there must be:[23]

- six Trustees appointed from North America;
- six Trustees appointed from Europe;
- six Trustees appointed from the Asia/Oceania region; and
- four Trustees appointed from any area, subject to establishing overall geographical balance.

The appointment of all subsequent Trustees to fill vacancies caused by routine retirement or other reasons is the responsibility of the existing Trustees. The appointment of the Trustees is normally for a term of three years, renewable once.[24]

The IASC Foundation Constitution requires that the Trustees should comprise individuals that, as a group, provide an appropriate balance of professional backgrounds, including auditors, preparers, users, academics, and other officials serving the public interest. Two of the Trustees will normally be senior partners of prominent international accounting firms. To achieve such a balance, Trustees are selected after consultation with national and international organisations of auditors (including the International Federation of Accountants), preparers, users and academics. Although the ultimate decision on Trustee appointments rests with the Trustees themselves, the Constitution further requires the Trustees to establish procedures for inviting suggestions for appointments from these relevant organisations and for allowing individuals to put forward their own names, including advertising vacant positions.[25]

In November 2005, in response to this requirement, the Trustees formed a Trustee Appointments Advisory Group to assist them in nominating and appointing suitably qualified and interested individuals as Trustees. Because the ultimate decision on appointments rests with the Trustees, they are required to explain to the members of the Advisory Group the rationale for any decision contrary to reservations expressed by members of the Advisory Group.

The Constitution provides that 'all Trustees shall be required to show a firm commitment to the IASC Foundation and the IASB as a high quality global standard-setter, to be financially knowledgeable, and to have an ability to meet the time commitment. Each Trustee shall have an understanding of, and be sensitive to the challenges associated with the adoption and application of high quality global accounting standards developed for use in the world's capital markets and by other users.'[26]

The first act of the Board of Trustees in 2000 was to appoint Sir David Tweedie (who had just completed a highly distinguished period of ten years as the Chairman of the UK's Accounting Standards Board) as the first Chairman of the new International Accounting Standards Board (IASB) with effect from 1 January 2001. Subsequently, in January 2001, the Trustees appointed the thirteen other members of the IASB. In December 2005, the Trustees announced that Sir David Tweedie had been re-appointed as IASB Chairman for a further five year term.

The Trustees are responsible also for appointing the members of the International Financial Reporting Interpretations Committee (IFRIC) and Standards Advisory Council (SAC).[27] In addition, their duties include the following:[28]

- assuming responsibility for establishing and maintaining appropriate financing arrangements;
- reviewing annually the strategy of the IASC Foundation and the IASB and their effectiveness, including consideration, but not determination, of the IASB's agenda;
- approving annually the budget of the IASC Foundation and determining the basis for funding;
- reviewing broad strategic issues affecting accounting standards, promoting the IASC Foundation and its work and promoting the objective of rigorous application of International Accounting Standards and International Financial Reporting Standards (the Trustees are, however, excluded from involvement in technical matters relating to accounting standards);
- establishing and amending operating procedures, consultative arrangements and due process for the IASB, the IFRIC and the SAC;
- approving amendments to the Constitution after following a due process, including consultation with the SAC and publication of an Exposure Draft for public comment;
- exercising all powers of the IASC Foundation except for those expressly reserved to the IASB, IFRIC and the SAC; and

- publishing an annual report on the IASC Foundation's activities, including audited financial statements and priorities for the coming year.

With effect from 1 April 2001, the IASB assumed international accounting standard setting responsibilities from its predecessor body, the IASC.

The IASB structure has the following main features: the IASC Foundation is an independent organisation having two main bodies, the Trustees and the IASB, as well as a Standards Advisory Council and the International Financial Reporting Interpretations Committee. The IASC Foundation Trustees appoint the IASB Members, exercise oversight and raise the funds needed, whereas the IASB has sole responsibility for setting accounting standards.

Set out below is a graphical representation of the IASC Foundation structure:[29]

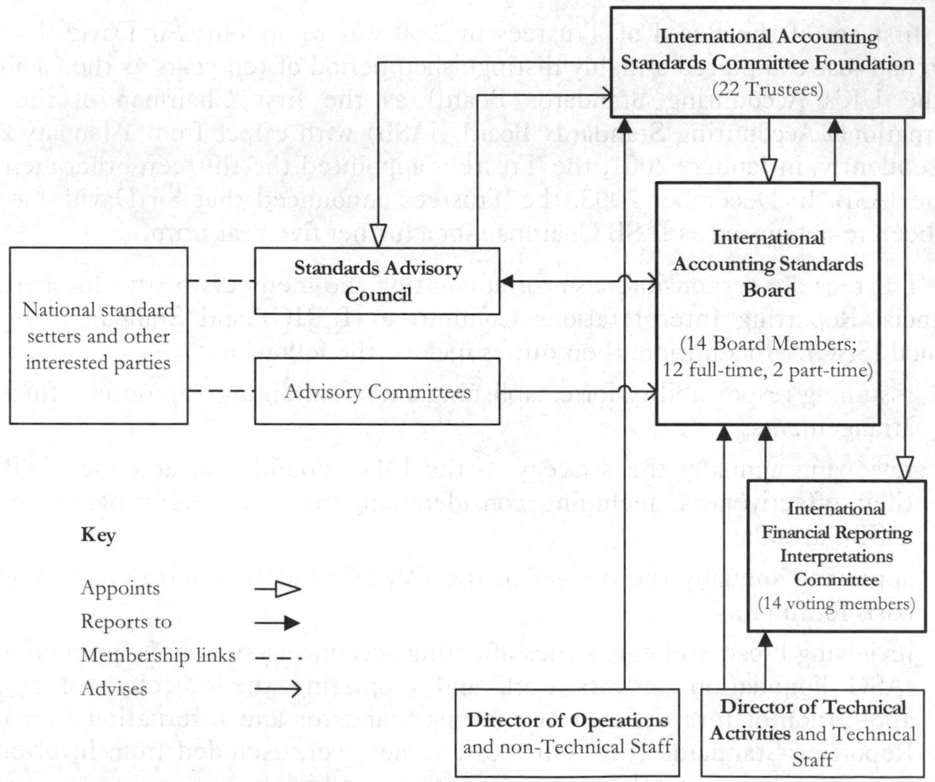

2.2.2 *The IASC Foundation Constitution*[30]

The IASC Foundation Constitution was approved in its original form by the Board of the former International Accounting Standards Committee (IASC) in March 2000 and by the members of IASC at a meeting in Edinburgh on 24 May 2000. At its meeting in December 1999, the IASC Board had appointed a Nominating Committee to select the first Trustees. These Trustees took office in May 2000 as a result of the approval of the Constitution. In execution of their duties under the Constitution, the Trustees formed the International Accounting Standards

Committee Foundation on 6 February 2001. The Foundation was formed as a not-for-profit corporation incorporated in the State of Delaware, USA, and is the parent entity of the IASB, which is based in London.

Each Trustee is required to act in the public interest. In addition, the Trustees are required to undertake, at regular intervals, a review of the entire structure of the IASC Foundation and its effectiveness. These reviews are to include consideration of changing the geographical distribution of Trustees in response to changing global economic conditions, and the proposals of each review are required to be published for public comment. The first such review was required to commence three years after the coming into force of the Constitution, with the objective of implementing any agreed changes by February 2006, five years after the coming into force of the Constitution. Thereafter, the Trustees are required to undertake a similar review every five years.[31]

In accordance with the above commitment, on 12 November 2003, the Trustees announced that they had initiated a review of the Foundation's constitutional arrangements that govern the operating procedures of the Foundation and the IASB. In launching this, the Trustees emphasised that they were willing to examine any aspect of the Constitution and would be consulting a wide range of organisations. To coordinate the process, the Trustees established an internal committee (the 'Constitution Committee'), chaired by Paul Volcker.

Following extensive consultation, the Trustees completed the review in June 2005, and published a revised Constitution with an effective date of 1 July 2005. The Trustees concluded in their review that, having assessed the organisation's progress against the objectives laid out in the constitution, the basic structure set out by the 2000 constitution was sound and therefore did not consider that any fundamental changes to it were necessary. The principal changes of substance were to increase the number of Trustees from 19 to 22, refine the procedures around the appointment of Trustees (which resulted in the establishment of the Trustee Appointments Advisory Group), specify that the Chairman of the Standards Advisory Council would be appointed by the Trustees and would not be a member of the IASB or its staff (previously the IASB chairman was also the SAC Chairman), and increase from eight to nine the number of members of the IASB required to approve the publication of an Exposure Draft, International Accounting Standard, International Financial Reporting Standard, or final Interpretation of the IFRIC.[32]

There were other subtle wording changes and refinements made in the Constitution, for example, the background mix of IASB members: the Constitution now states that 'The Trustees shall select IASB members so that the IASB as a group provides an appropriate mix of recent practical experience among auditors, preparers, users and academics',[33] whereas previously the requirement was for minimums of five practising auditors, three preparers of financial statements, three users of financial statements, and one academic.

The Constitution sets out the basic structural and procedural framework for the various bodies of the IASC Organisation. Article 2 of the Constitution sets the objectives of the IASC Foundation as follows:[34]

(a) to develop, in the public interest, a single set of high quality, understandable and enforceable global accounting standards that require high quality, transparent and comparable information in financial statements and other financial reporting to help participants in the world's capital markets and other users make economic decisions;

(b) to promote the use and rigorous application of those standards;

(c) in fulfilling the objectives associated with (a) and (b), to take account of, as appropriate, the special needs of small and medium-sized entities and emerging economies; and

(d) to bring about convergence of national accounting standards and International Accounting Standards and International Financial Reporting Standards to high quality solutions.

In December 2005, the Trustees announced that Mr. Tommaso Padoa-Schioppa, a founding member of the Executive Board of the European Central Bank, would replace Paul Volcker as Chairman of the Board of Trustees of the IASC Foundation, effective 1 January 2006. Mr Volcker retired from the Board of Trustees, leaving behind an important legacy as its first Chairman. However, Mr Volcker has continued to serve the IASC organisation as Chairman of the Trustee Appointments Advisory Group – an advisory group to help the Trustees in discharging their responsibility for nominating and appointing Trustees. Although the ultimate decision on appointments remains with the Trustees, the Trustees are required to consult the Trustee Appointments Advisory Group before a final decision is made regarding appointments.

Unfortunately, Mr. Padoa-Schioppa's term of office as Chairman of the Board of Trustees lasted only until May 2006, when he stepped down following his appointment to a position in the Government of Italy. Mr Philip Laskawy, a retired Chairman and CEO of Ernst & Young International, was then appointed as a caretaker Chairman during the search for a new high-profile chair. In October 2007, the IASC Foundation announced that Mr Gerrit Zalm, the former Deputy Prime Minister and Finance Minister of the Netherlands, had accepted the Trustees' invitation to become the next Chairman of Trustees for a three-year term beginning on 1 January 2008. Mr Laskawy will then become Vice Chairman of the Trustees from that date.

2.2.3 Trustees' strategy to enhance the IASB's governance arrangements

As IFRSs become more widely adopted by countries as their system of financial reporting, and used throughout the world's capital markets, so has it become necessary to strengthen the institutional framework and accountability of the whole IASC organisation, including the Trustees and the IASB. Consequently, in recent times, the calls for greater governance and accountability around the IASCF have become louder and more frequent. It is therefore timely that, following their meeting at the end of October 2007, the Trustees announced proposals to enhance the IASB's governance arrangements and reinforce the organisation's public accountability.[35] The enhanced governance proposals adopted by the Trustees are as follows:[36]

- Establish a formal reporting link to official organisations: The Trustees should establish a link to a representative group of official organisations, including securities regulators. This body would approve Trustee appointments and review Trustee oversight activities, including the adequacy of the annual funding arrangements as well as the overall budget. The establishment of this 'representative group of official organisations' is discussed at 2.3 below.
- Develop a multi-layered, multi-faceted approach to accountability beyond the formal link to official organisations: The Trustees should intensify and deepen their engagement with key stakeholder groups and develop mechanisms for the Trustees to receive input outside formalised procedures. This would necessarily include mechanisms for meeting with official organisations and policymakers and private sector institutions. Furthermore, such accountability would require consideration of the role and structure of the Standards Advisory Council in the organisation's accountability.
- Create a mechanism for public input to the Trustees outside regularly scheduled meetings with specific stakeholder groups: The Trustees should establish enhanced mechanisms for input from interested parties who wish to comment on the IASC Foundation's and the IASB's policies, processes, and procedures.
- Continue efforts towards a sustained, broad-based funding regime: Having already significantly broadened the funding base through the new approach adopted in 2006, the Trustees should continue their work to broaden the funding base further.

The Trustees will begin a series of consultations with key stakeholders on these proposals in the build up to the Constitution Review, which is scheduled to start no later than July 2008.

2.2.4 The International Accounting Standards Board (IASB)

As stated above, in accordance with Article 18 of the Constitution, the IASC Foundation Trustees appointed twelve full-time IASB Members, including the Chairman and the Vice-Chairman, and two part-time members.

The IASB describes itself in the following terms:[37]

> 'The International Accounting Standards Board is an independent, privately-funded accounting standard-setter based in London, UK. The Board members come from nine countries and have a variety of functional backgrounds.
>
> 'The IASB is committed to developing, in the public interest, a single set of high quality, understandable and enforceable global accounting standards that require transparent and comparable information in general purpose financial statements. In addition, the IASB co-operates with national accounting

standard-setters to achieve convergence in accounting standards around the world.'

The Constitution stipulates that the selection of members of the IASB shall not be based on geographical criteria, but the Trustees shall ensure that the IASB is not dominated by any particular constituency or geographical interest.[38]

The foremost qualifications for membership of the IASB are professional competence and practical experience.[39] The Trustees are required to select IASB members so that the IASB as a group provides an appropriate mix of recent practical experience among auditors, preparers, users and academics. Furthermore, the IASB is, in consultation with the Trustees, expected to establish and maintain liaison with national standard-setters and other official bodies concerned with standard-setting in order to promote the convergence of national accounting standards and IFRSs. However, the requirement of the 2000 Constitution that seven IASB members should be designated as liaisons with major national standard setters was removed from the Constitution when it was revised. No individual can be both a Trustee and an IASB Member at the same time.[40]

The responsibilities of the IASB are listed in Article 31 of the Constitution. Its primary role is to have complete responsibility for all IASB technical matters including the preparation and issuing of International Accounting Standards, International Financial Reporting Standards and Exposure Drafts, each of which shall include any dissenting opinions, and final approval of Interpretations by the IFRIC.[41]

Approval by at least nine of the fourteen members of the IASB is required for the publication of an Exposure Draft, International Accounting Standard, International Financial Reporting Standard, or final Interpretation of the IFRIC (this was previously eight of fourteen in the 2000 Constitution). Other decisions of the IASB, including the publication of a discussion paper, require a simple majority of the members of the IASB present at a meeting that is attended by at least 60% of the members of the IASB.[42] The IASB has full discretion over its technical agenda and over project assignments on technical matters. It must, however, consult the SAC on major projects, agenda decisions and work priorities.[43]

The IASB (whose meetings are open to the public) met in technical session for the first time in April 2001. During this meeting, it approved a resolution to adopt the existing body of International Accounting Standards and Interpretations issued by the former IASC Board and the SIC respectively. The IASB announced also that the IASC Foundation Trustees had agreed that the accounting standards issued by the IASB would be designated 'International Financial Reporting Standards (IFRS)'. The existing pronouncements will, however, continue to be designated 'International Accounting Standards (IAS)'.

2.2.5 The IASB's Due Process Handbook

The Trustees of the IASC Foundation have set up a committee – the Trustees' Procedures Committee – with the task of regularly reviewing and, if necessary, amending the procedures of due process in the light of experience and comments from the IASB and constituents. The Committee reviews proposed procedures for the IASB's due process on new projects and the composition of working groups and ensures that their membership reflects a diversity of views and expertise. The 'Due Process Handbook for the IASB' describes the consultative arrangements of the IASB. It is based on the previously existing framework of due process laid out in the Constitution of the IASC Foundation and the *Preface to International Financial Reporting Standards* issued by the IASB. It also reflects the public consultation conducted by the IASB in 2004 and 2005. The Trustees approved the Handbook in March 2006, following two rounds of public consultations, review by the Standards Advisory Council, and public debate by the Trustees.[44]

The procedures described in the Handbook address the following requirements:[45]

- transparency and accessibility;
- extensive consultation and responsiveness; and
- accountability.

In accordance with the IASC Foundation's Constitution, the IASB has full discretion in developing and pursuing its technical agenda and in organising the conduct of its work. In order to gain a wide range of views from interested parties throughout all stages of a project's development, the Trustees and the IASB have established consultative procedures to govern the standard-setting process.[46]

The IASB's standard-setting process comprises the following six stages, with the Trustees having the opportunity to ensure compliance at various points throughout the process:[47]

- Stage 1: Setting the agenda;
- Stage 2: Project Planning;
- Stage 3: Development and publication of a discussion paper;
- Stage 4: Development and publication of an exposure draft;
- Stage 5: Development and publication of an IFRS;
- Stage 6: Procedures after an IFRS is issued.

It is important to note that the IASB's due process requirements are separated into mandatory and non-mandatory steps under the IASCF Constitution. The following due process steps are mandatory:[48]

- developing and pursuing the IASB's technical agenda;
- preparing and issuing standards and exposure drafts, each of which is to include any dissenting opinions;
- establishing procedures for reviewing comments made within a reasonable period on documents published for comment;
- consulting the SAC on major projects, agenda decisions and work priorities; and
- publishing bases for conclusions with standards and exposure drafts.

The steps specified in the Constitution as being 'non-mandatory' include:[49]

- publishing a discussion document (e.g. a discussion paper);
- establishing working groups or other types of specialist advisory groups;
- holding public hearings;
- undertaking field tests (both in developed countries and in emerging markets).

If the IASB decides not to undertake any of the non-mandatory steps defined by the Constitution, it is required by the Constitution to state its reasons (known as the 'comply or explain' approach). Explanations are normally made at IASB meetings, and are published in the decision summaries and in the basis for conclusions with the exposure draft or standard in question.[50]

In recent times, the IASB has come under criticism for not following some or all of the non-mandatory due process steps, particularly with regard to publishing discussion papers and conducting field tests. A recent example relates to the IASB's June 2005 exposure draft on Business Combinations Phase II,[51] which attracted substantial adverse reaction from respondents. Whilst we support the due process approach taken in the Handbook, requiring explanation of the omission of any 'non-mandatory' procedures, we believe that there should be a presumption that the Board will carry out all the 'non-mandatory' steps outlined in the Handbook for all major projects. Field visits or field tests are the only mechanisms by which the practicality of proposals can be evaluated and should be a presumptive requirement for all major projects.

Only in rare circumstances should field visits or field tests be excluded from the due process procedures for major projects. To improve the utility of field visits, we believe that proposed standards should have longer exposure periods than is currently the case to enable preparers and their auditors to identify any significant implementation issues. Field visits should then involve extensive, in-depth discussions among preparers, Board members and staff regarding the principles of the proposed standard, its implementation and issues encountered by entities in preparing to implement the standard. The longer exposure period and extensive field visits would enable the Board to determine during the exposure period whether amendment or interpretation of the proposed standard is necessary.

Similarly, we consider that public hearings or roundtables should be a presumptive requirement for all major projects. In our view, roundtable discussions will often be more valuable than public hearings in effectively exploring constituents' views and the reasoning behind them. It is therefore encouraging that the IASB has responded positively to the concerns of its constituents regarding its due process procedures.

On 24 July 2006 the IASB announced that, when it had considered its technical plan at its meeting in June, it had concluded that by addressing issues related to the timing of effective dates of IFRSs and consultation, it would continue both to encourage consistent and rigorous application of IFRSs and to facilitate broad input into the IASB's work programme. As a result, following consultation with the Trustees of the IASC Foundation, the Standards Advisory Council, and a wide range of interested parties, the Board announced that it had agreed to the following:[52]

- **Increased lead time to prepare for new standards:** The IASB recognised that many countries require time for translations and implementation of new standards into practice and, where IFRSs are legally binding, into law. To accommodate the time required, the IASB would allow a minimum of one year between the date of the publication of wholly new IFRSs or major amendments to existing IFRSs and the date when implementation is required;
- **Increased opportunity for input on conceptual issues:** The IASB agreed to publish discussion papers, rather than moving directly to exposure drafts, on the individual sections of their Conceptual Framework project;
- **No new major standards to be effective before 2009:** Consistent with the steps described above, the IASB will not require the application of new IFRSs under development or major amendments to existing standards before 1 January 2009. The establishment of 2009 as the first date of required implementation of new standards will both provide some stability in the IFRS platform for those companies that adopted IFRSs in 2005, and provide countries yet to adopt IFRSs with a clear target date for adoption. However, this approach does not preclude the publication of new standards before that date, and companies are permitted to adopt a new standard on a voluntary basis before its effective date. Interpretations and minor amendments to deal with potential issues identified during implementation would not be subject to this approach.

2.2.6 The Standards Advisory Council (SAC)

The primary objective of the SAC (whose members are appointed by the Trustees) is to provide a forum where the IASB consults individuals and representatives of organisations affected by its work, that are committed to the development of high quality IFRSs. As part of that consultative process the SAC gives advice to the IASB on a range of issues which includes, but is not limited to, the following:

- input on the IASB's agenda;
- input on the IASB's project timetable (work programme) including project priorities, and consultation on any changes in agenda and priorities; and
- advice on projects, with particular emphasis on practical application and implementation issues, including matters relating to existing standards that may warrant consideration by the IFRIC.

In view of the importance of the IASB's agenda and priorities, once these have been determined by the IASB, changes thereto are expected to be the subject of consultation with the SAC. When considered appropriate by the members of the SAC, or on the request of the Trustees, the SAC also provides input to the Trustees on matters relating to the activities of the SAC or the IASB and any other relevant issues.[53]

The SAC comprises 'thirty or more members, having a diversity of geographical and professional backgrounds, appointed for renewable terms of three years'.[54] The Chairman of the Council is appointed by the Trustees, and may not be a member of the IASB or a member of its staff.[55] The SAC normally meets at least three times a year, and its meetings are open to the public. The SAC is required to be consulted by the IASB in advance of IASB decisions on major projects and by the Trustees in advance of any proposed changes to the IASC Foundation Constitution.[56]

In June 2001, the Trustees of the IASC Foundation announced the appointment of 49 SAC members, and the SAC met for the first time with the IASB in July 2001. However, as part of the revision of the IASC Foundation Constitution in 2005, the SAC was restructured and, in October 2005, the Trustees of the IASC Foundation announced the membership of the restructured SAC, comprising 41 members under the Chairmanship of Professor Nelson Carvalho, a prominent academic and business leader from Brazil. In addition, the European Commission, the US SEC, and the Financial Services Agency of Japan participate as observers.

The revised structure completed the steps taken by the Trustees to encourage the SAC to be a more effective source of advice both to the Trustees and to the IASB. The membership provides for a broad geographical spread and a range of functional backgrounds that include members drawn from user groups, preparers, financial analysts, academics, auditors, regulators and professional accounting bodies. In addition, certain international organisations may be granted permanent seats on the SAC by the Trustees. Official observer status may also be granted by the Trustees to other bodies and organisations that are influential in the global financial community.[57]

2.2.7 The International Financial Reporting Interpretations Committee (IFRIC)

The International Financial Reporting Interpretations Committee (IFRIC) assists the IASB in improving financial reporting through timely identification, discussion and resolution of financial reporting issues within the framework of IFRSs. The IFRIC was established in December 2001 by the Trustees of the International Accounting Standards Committee Foundation, when it replaced the previous interpretations committee, the SIC (see 1.2.1 above). Mr Robert Garnett, an IASB member, is the non-voting chairman of the IFRIC. The IFRIC currently has twelve voting members, with the European Commission and IOSCO having observer status. However, in April 2007, the Trustees published a consultative document proposing to increase the size of the IFRIC from 12 to 14 voting members.[58] The Trustees are proposing further that the quorum for a meeting of the IFRIC be increased from nine to ten, and that approval of Draft or final Interpretations shall require that not more than four (currently three) voting members vote against the Draft or final Interpretation.

The Trustees believe that enlarging the IFRIC is unlikely to have any significant adverse effect on its work, and that any such effect would be outweighed by the benefit of greater participation by preparers and users of IFRS financial reports.[59] At the meeting of the Trustees held at the end of October 2007, the Trustees approved the proposal to expand the membership of the IFRIC from 12 to 14 members 'in order to broaden IFRS expertise on the committee'.[60]

Initially, the responsibilities and *modus operandi* of the IFRIC were set out in the *Preface to International Financial Reporting Interpretations*. On its own initiative, but with the Trustees' support, the IFRIC undertook an internal review of its operations. In

March 2005 the IASC Foundation published for public comment a consultation paper *IFRIC Review of Operations*. In the light of its consideration of the comments received, the IFRIC developed a draft handbook of its due process. Subsequently, the Trustees considered an analysis of the comment letters, the IFRIC's recommendations and a draft of the handbook. In May 2006, the IASC Foundation published the IFRIC Due Process Handbook in draft for public comment. The final version of the Handbook – which supersedes the *Preface to International Financial Reporting Interpretations* – was approved by the Trustees in January 2007 and published in February 2007.[61]

The IFRIC meets six times a year. All technical decisions are taken at sessions that are open to public observation. The IFRIC reviews newly identified financial reporting issues not specifically addressed in IFRSs or issues where unsatisfactory or conflicting interpretations have developed, or seem likely to develop in the absence of authoritative guidance, with a view to reaching a consensus on the appropriate treatment.[62]

The IFRIC took more than two years to issue its first Interpretation, and has to date (September 2007) issued a total of only 14 Interpretations, one of which (IFRIC 3 on emission rights) was subsequently withdrawn by the Board. As discussed below, the IFRIC spends a significant amount of its time discussing whether or not items submitted to it for consideration should, in fact, be added to its agenda. More often that not, such items are not added to the IFRIC agenda, resulting in the publication of 'rejection notices' in *IFRIC Update*.

A The IFRIC's system of due process

The IFRIC due process comprises the following seven stages:[63]

Stage 1: Identification of issues

The primary responsibility for identifying issues to be considered by the IFRIC is that of its members and appointed observers. Preparers, auditors and others with an interest in financial reporting are encouraged to refer issues to the IFRIC when they believe that divergent practices have emerged regarding the accounting for particular transactions or circumstances or when there is doubt about the appropriate accounting treatment and it is important that a standard treatment is established.

Stage 2: Setting the agenda

The IFRIC decides after debate in a public meeting whether or not to add an issue to its agenda. The Committee assesses proposed agenda items against the criteria listed below. An issue does not have to satisfy all the criteria to qualify for addition to the agenda.

(a) The issue is widespread and has practical relevance.

(b) The issue indicates that there are significantly divergent interpretations (either emerging or already existing in practice). The IFRIC will not add an item to its agenda if IFRSs are clear, with the result that divergent interpretations are not expected in practice.

(c) Financial reporting would be improved through elimination of the diverse reporting methods.

(d) The issue can be resolved efficiently within the confines of existing IFRSs and the *Framework*, and the demands of the interpretation process. The issue should be sufficiently narrow in scope to be capable of interpretation, but not so narrow that it is not cost-effective for the IFRIC and its constituents to undertake the due process associated with an Interpretation.

(e) It is probable that the IFRIC will be able to reach a consensus on the issue on a timely basis.

(f) If the issue relates to a current or planned IASB project, there is a pressing need to provide guidance sooner than would be expected from the IASB's activities. The IFRIC will not add an item to its agenda if an IASB project is expected to resolve the issue in a shorter period than the IFRIC requires to complete its due process.

A consultative period applies to issues that are not added to the agenda. The draft reason for not adding an item to the agenda is published in *IFRIC Update* and electronically on the IASB Website with a comment period of not less than 30 days. The comments received are placed on the public record, unless confidentiality is specifically requested by the commentator (supported by good reason such as commercial confidence), and form part of the deliberation that takes place at the next available IFRIC meeting. At that meeting the IFRIC decides whether to add the issue to its agenda.

A simple majority of IFRIC members present at the meeting can agree to add any issue to the IFRIC agenda. The reasons for not adding an item to the IFRIC agenda are posted on the IASB Website as a historical record of decisions taken. That record is not updated as standards are amended and does not form part of IFRSs.

As a result of this approach, a significant amount of IFRIC meeting time is devoted to discussing whether or not issues should be added to its agenda. In the majority of cases, the decision is not to add items and often results in lengthy debates between IFRIC members and IASB staff over the formulation of the reasons for such decisions – which have become known as 'rejection notices'. The IFRIC has published more than 100 rejection notices since it began the practice in 2005.

In our view, this system of 'non-interpretations' is an effective means of providing helpful guidance to preparers and auditors during a period of widespread adoption of IFRSs in an environment where little authoritative guidance exists. It is still the case that whilst a body of International Financial Reporting Standards exists, no substantial body of custom and practice, – of 'International GAAP' – has yet developed. It will only be after a number of years of full implementation by a representative cross-section of businesses in a number of countries and industries that a consensus will emerge over the way that, in practice and in the context of real commercial transactions, IFRS is actually to be applied. Therefore, the aim of the

IASB should be to promote consistency of application of its standards by whatever means are available, and we believe that the publication by the IFRIC of rejection notices is an efficient and harmless way in helping to achieve this aim.

To ensure that the IFRIC considers only issues on which timely guidance can be provided, over the course of a project it reassesses from time to time whether the issues can be addressed appropriately within the mandate. If an issue has been considered at three meetings and there is still no consensus in prospect for either a draft or final Interpretation, the IFRIC considers whether it should be removed from the agenda. The IFRIC may extend consideration of the issue for an additional period, normally not more than one or two meetings. If the IFRIC has concluded that it will not be able to reach a consensus, it will discontinue work on the issue, inform the IASB and publish the fact that work has been discontinued. The IFRIC may recommend that the matter be taken up by the IASB.

Stage 3: IFRIC meetings and voting

The IFRIC meets in public and follows procedures similar to the IASB's general policy for its Board meetings.

Under recent proposals approved by the Trustees at the end of October 2007, the quorum for a meeting of the IFRIC is ten members, and the approval of Draft or final Interpretations requires that not more than four voting members vote against the Draft or final Interpretation.

Stage 4: Development of a draft Interpretation

The IFRIC reaches its conclusions on the basis of information contained in Issue Summaries that are prepared under the supervision of IASB staff. An Issue Summary describes the issue to be discussed and provides the information necessary for IFRIC members to gain an understanding of the issue and make decisions about it. An Issue Summary is developed for the IFRIC's consideration after a thorough review of the authoritative accounting literature and possible alternatives, including consultation where appropriate with national standard-setters.

Stage 5: The IASB's role in the release of a draft Interpretation

IASB members have access to all IFRIC agenda papers. They are expected to comment on technical matters as the issues are being considered, particularly if they have concerns about alternatives the IFRIC is considering. Thereafter, IASB members are informed when the IFRIC reaches a consensus on a draft Interpretation. The draft Interpretation is released for public comment unless four or more IASB members object within a week of being informed of its completion.

If a draft Interpretation is not released because of IASB members' objections, the issue will be considered at the next IASB meeting. On the basis of discussion at the meeting, the IASB will decide whether the draft Interpretation should be published or whether the matter should be referred back to the IFRIC, added to its own agenda or not be the subject of any further action.

Stage 6: Comment period and deliberation

Draft Interpretations are made available for public comment for not less than 60 days. All comments received during the comment period are considered by the IFRIC before an Interpretation is finalised. Comment letters are made publicly available unless confidentiality is requested by the commentator (supported by good reason such as commercial confidence). A staff summary and analysis of the comment letters are provided to the IFRIC.

If the proposed Interpretation is changed significantly, the IFRIC will consider whether it should be re-exposed. Re-exposure is not required automatically and will depend on the significance of the changes contemplated, whether they were raised in the Basis for Conclusions on the draft Interpretation or in questions posed by the IFRIC, their significance for practice, and what might be learned by the IFRIC from re-exposure.

Stage 7: The IASB's role in an Interpretation

When the IFRIC has reached a consensus on an Interpretation, the Interpretation is put to the IASB for ratification, in a public meeting, before being issued. Approval by the IASB requires at least nine IASB members to be in favour. The IASB votes on the Interpretation as submitted by the IFRIC. If an Interpretation is not approved by the IASB, the IASB provides the IFRIC with an analysis of the objections and concerns of those voting against the Interpretation. On the basis of this analysis, the IASB will decide whether the matter should be referred back to the IFRIC, added to its own agenda or not be the subject of any further action. All approved Interpretations are issued by the IASB.

B The Authority of IFRIC Interpretations[64]

IFRIC Interpretations set out the consensus that entities are required to apply if their financial statements are described as being prepared in accordance with IFRSs. The authoritative text of a draft Interpretation or an Interpretation is that published by the IASB in the English language. IFRIC Interpretations usually apply to periods beginning on or after a specified effective date (usually three months from the date of issue). However, the IFRIC may choose to vary that approach. Transitional provisions that apply on initial application of an IFRIC consensus are specified in the Interpretation. In keeping with IFRSs, the presumption is that IFRIC Interpretations will be applied retrospectively in accordance with IAS 8 – *Accounting Policies, Changes in Accounting Estimates and Errors*. The IFRIC also considers the effect of the transitional provisions on first-time adopters of IFRSs, including the interaction of the transitional provisions with those of IFRS 1 – *First-time Adoption of International Financial Reporting Standards*. An IFRIC Interpretation is withdrawn when an IFRS or other authoritative document issued by the IASB that overrides or confirms a previously issued IFRIC consensus becomes effective. The IFRIC Interpretations that would be affected by an authoritative IASB document are identified in the exposure draft of that document.

2.3 Enhancement the governance of the IASC Foundation[65]

At the beginning of November 2007, the European Commission, the Financial Services Agency of Japan, the International Organization of Securities Commissions (IOSCO) and the US Securities and Exchange Commission issued a combined statement, proposing changes to strengthen the institutional framework of the IASC Foundation and encourage the Foundation's related efforts, while at the same time emphasising the continued importance of an independent standard-setting process. Central to this effort is the establishment of a new monitoring body within the governance structure of the IASC Foundation to reinforce the existing public interest oversight function of the IASC Foundation Trustees. The creation of such a monitoring body would serve to complement the IASC Board of Trustees in its representation of the interest of the global investor community, thereby enhancing public confidence in IFRS.

One key objective is to have the monitoring body meet regularly with IASC Foundation Trustees to discuss, review and comment on the IASB's work program. It is envisaged also that the monitoring body would be responsible for the final approval of Trustee nominees and would have the opportunity to review the Trustees' procedures for overseeing the standard-setting process and ensuring the IASB's proper funding.

This announcement of the establishment of a new monitoring body coincides with the announcement by the IASC Foundation Trustees of proposals to enhance the IASB's governance arrangements and reinforce the organisation's public accountability (see 2.2.3 above).

3 THE IASB'S TECHNICAL AGENDA AND GLOBAL CONVERGENCE

3.1 An initial agenda of twenty-five technical projects

In contemplation of the handover of its functions to the new IASB, the Board of the former International Accounting Standards Committee approved a public Statement at its December 2000 meeting.[66] The purpose of the Statement was to comment on the IASC Board's current work-in-progress and record some of the thinking of the Board resulting from its work on agenda items in progress and other discussions.

In the light of this, and after consultation with the SAC, national accounting standard setters, regulators and other interested parties, the IASB determined an initial agenda of nine technical projects. These were divided into three broad categories:

- Projects intended to provide leadership and promote convergence, which comprised the following:
  - Accounting for insurance contracts;
  - Business combinations;
  - Reporting financial performance;
  - Accounting for share based payments.

- Projects intended to provide for easier application of International Financial Reporting Standards, which comprised the following:
  - Guidance on first-time application of IFRSs;
  - Activities of financial institutions: disclosure and presentation; and
- Projects intended to improve existing standards, which comprised the following:
  - Preface to IFRSs;
  - Improvements to existing IASs (see 3.2 below);
  - Amendments to IAS 39.

In addition to these, sixteen other issues were adopted as 'partner projects' by one or more of the IASB's national standard setting partners. The IASB announced that it would be working with these partners, or at least monitoring their efforts, in order to ensure that any differences between national standard setters or with the IASB would be identified and resolved as quickly as possible. The issues concerned were as follows:

- accounting measurement;
- accounting by extractive industries;
- accounting for financial instruments (i.e. the comprehensive full fair value project);
- accounting for leases;
- accounting by small and medium entities and emerging economies;
- accounting for taxes on income (i.e. dealing with issues of convergence between IAS 12 – *Income Taxes* – and certain national standards such as the UK standard FRS 19);
- business combinations;
- consolidation policy;
- definitions of elements of financial statements;
- derecognition issues, other than those addressed in IAS 39;
- employee benefits (dealing with issues of convergence between IAS 19 – *Employee Benefits* – and certain national standards such as the UK standard FRS 17);
- impairment of assets;
- intangible assets;
- liabilities and revenue recognition;
- Management's Discussion and Analysis (an area not currently dealt with in the IASC literature);
- revaluation of certain assets.

More than six years later, many of these projects are still work-in-progress and at various stages of development. It is for this reason that the IASB has attracted substantial criticism for the way that it has allowed its agenda to lengthen without appropriate prioritisation. Whilst we acknowledge that the Board has set itself some highly ambitious targets, we nevertheless believe that it has failed properly to prioritise its projects according to the needs of preparers and users. As a result, it is trying to do too much too quickly, without appropriate prioritisation and without allowing sufficient time for full consideration of the practical implications and economic impact of its proposals.

3.2 The Improvements Project

In April 2001, the IASB announced the launch of its 'Improvements Project' and called for suggestions as to how existing standards could be improved. The objective of the project was to add clarity and consistency to the requirements of existing IASs issued by the former IASC Board. The specific topics that were addressed came from information already provided to the IASB by sources such as IOSCO, national standard setters, the SIC, major accounting firms and other commentators. The issues addressed were those identified as narrow issues of substance whose resolution could improve the quality of an IAS and/or increase convergence of national and international standards. The Board wished to address these issues immediately, so that companies adopting IAS for the first time would not be faced with significant additional change thereafter.

An Improvements Sub-Committee comprising four Board members was established to consider all the suggestions made for improvement and to make recommendations to the full Board. In May 2002, the Board issued an Exposure Draft proposing amendments to thirteen standards and the withdrawal of one (IAS 15 – *Information reflecting the effect of changing prices*). Eventually, in December 2003, the Board issued the thirteen revised standards in final form, together with 'consequential amendments' to a further seventeen standards. In fact, many of the 'consequential amendments' were somewhat more in the nature of substantive changes (for example, the definition of 'joint control' in IAS 31 – *Interests in Joint Ventures*) – raising questions about the Board's due process. The Improvements Project eliminated some of the alternative accounting treatments in these 'improved' standards. Where an IAS retains alternative treatments, the IASB removed virtually all references to 'benchmark treatment' and 'allowed alternative treatment', instead using descriptive references, such as 'cost model' and 'revaluation model'.

Introducing the revised standards, Sir David Tweedie commented as follows: 'The Improvements Project has raised the quality and enhanced the consistency of international accounting standards. The Board has devoted much time and resources during its first two years of operation to ensuring that we have a solid base on which we can build. From this improved set of standards, we shall move forward on the many complex issues facing accounting today and pursue our longer-term goal of global convergence'.[67]

In reality, the improvements project took more time than originally envisaged (almost three years) to complete, with the result that the Board was not able to devote sufficient time either to dealing with fundamental issues such as measurement, revenue recognition, performance reporting and accounting for common control transactions, or to resolving crucial industry issues such as those relating to the insurance and extractive industries. Consequently, the 2005 landmark was reached with significant gaps in the IASB's authoritative literature, which has, on occasion, required preparers and their auditors to exercise a considerable degree of judgement in determining the appropriate accounting.

3.3 IFRS/US GAAP convergence

'Convergence' is a term used to describe the coming together of national systems of financial reporting and IFRSs. Since its formation in 2001, the IASB has made great strides toward achieving global accounting convergence, with the result that the global acceptance of IFRS is rapidly becoming a reality. All listed EU companies are already required to prepare their consolidated financial statements in accordance with adopted IFRSs. Elsewhere, scores of non-EU countries have either adopted or are in the process of adopting IFRSs or are aligning their national standards with them. For example, in January 2006, Canada's Accounting Standards Board ratified a five-year plan to converge Canadian GAAP with IFRS,[68] and Brazil, China, India, Japan and Sri Lanka are committed to convergence within a similar time frame (see section 6 below).

3.3.1 Convergence with US GAAP: The Norwalk Agreement

For many years, the co-operation between the IASC/IASB and national standard setters had happened – mostly at an informal level – through a variety of bodies such as the G4+1 and the Joint Working Group of Standard Setters.[69] In the US, support for convergence has grown steadily, and in October 2002 the IASB and FASB issued a memorandum of understanding that marked a significant step towards the two Boards formalising their commitment to the convergence of IFRS and US GAAP.[70]

This agreement was reached at a joint meeting held at the FASB's offices in Norwalk, Connecticut, USA in September 2002, where the two Boards each acknowledged their commitment to the development of high-quality, compatible accounting standards that could be used for both domestic and cross-border financial reporting. At that meeting, both Boards pledged to use their best efforts to (a) make their existing financial reporting standards fully compatible as soon as is practicable and (b) to coordinate their future work programmes to ensure that once achieved, compatibility is maintained.[71]

To achieve compatibility, the two Boards agreed, as a matter of high priority, to:

- undertake a short-term project aimed at removing a variety of individual differences between US GAAP and IFRS;
- remove other differences between IFRSs and US GAAP that would remain at 1 January 2005, through coordination of their future work programmes; that is, through the mutual undertaking of discrete, substantial projects that both Boards would address concurrently;
- continue progress on the joint projects that they were currently undertaking; and

- encourage their respective interpretative bodies to coordinate their activities.[72]

The Boards agreed to commit the necessary resources to complete such a major undertaking and to start deliberating differences identified for resolution in the short-term project with the objective of achieving compatibility by identifying common, high-quality solutions. Both Boards agreed also to use their best efforts to issue an exposure draft of proposed changes to US GAAP or IFRSs that reflected common solutions to some, and perhaps all, of the differences identified for inclusion in the short-term project during 2003.[73]

3.3.2 US GAAP convergence and the SEC reconciliation requirement for foreign private issuers: the 2009 'roadmap'

A significant proportion of the world's largest non-US companies are listed on the New York Stock Exchange in addition to their domestic stock exchanges, and are therefore subject to SEC regulation. For those that file a Form 20-F, there is a requirement to provide reconciliations from National GAAP to US GAAP for both income and equity.

Consequently, the Norwalk Agreement was warmly welcomed around the world – particularly by those SEC-registered foreign private issuer companies that are currently required to provide US GAAP reconciliations, who saw this as a means of removing the reconciliation requirement. In addition, a European Commission statement welcomed the IASB/FASB commitment to achieving real convergence between their respective accounting standards by 2005, when listed EU companies would be required to apply IFRS. The EU statement made the point that the announcement heralded a major step towards a global system of accounting standards and hoped that it would, in particular, help the SEC to accept financial statements prepared by EU companies in accordance with IFRS, without reconciliation to US GAAP, for the purposes of listing on the US markets.

Since then, there have been encouraging moves on the part of the SEC towards the elimination of the reconciliation requirement. In April 2005, the then SEC Chairman William Donaldson met with EU Internal Markets Commissioner Charlie McCreevy to discuss a range of topics of mutual interest between the SEC and the EU, including the importance of compatible approaches to furthering investor protection and expanding the use of high-quality global accounting standards. At this meeting, SEC Chairman Donaldson tabled a 'roadmap' developed by SEC staff that highlighted the steps needed to eliminate the US GAAP reconciliation requirement for SEC-registered foreign private issuers that apply IFRSs. The roadmap established a goal of eliminating the requirement as early as possible and by 2009 at the latest. However, it was made clear that achieving this goal would, amongst other things, depend on a detailed analysis of the faithfulness and consistency of the application and interpretation of IFRS in financial statements across companies and jurisdictions, and continued progress on the IASB-FASB convergence project.[74]

Further confirmation that the SEC remained committed to the 'roadmap' was received in the form of a joint statement issued by current SEC Chairman Christopher Cox and EU Internal Markets Commissioner Charlie McCreevy on the occasion of Commissioner McCreevy's visit to Washington in February 2006. In re-affirming the SEC's commitment to the roadmap, SEC Chairman Cox stated the following: 'The SEC is working diligently toward the goal of eliminating the existing IFRS to US GAAP reconciliation requirement. Achieving that goal depends on various factors, as discussed in the April 2005 roadmap, including the effective implementation of IFRS in practice. The ultimate success of IFRS for the benefit of the global capital markets depends on the contributions of many parties, including investors, regulators, auditors, issuers and standard setters.'[75] Again, this statement emphasised the importance that the SEC places on its assessment of how effectively IFRSs are applied in practice.

Nonetheless, as a highly significant sign that the goals of the 'roadmap' have almost been achieved, the SEC agreed in November 2007 to accept from foreign private issuers financial statements prepared in accordance with IFRS as issued by the IASB without reconciliation to US GAAP (see 3.3.4 below).

3.3.3 Memorandum of Understanding between the FASB and the IASB[76]

On 27 February 2006, the FASB and the IASB published a Memorandum of Understanding (MOU) that reaffirmed the two Boards' shared objective of developing high quality, common accounting standards for use in the world's capital markets. The MOU was a further elaboration of the objectives and principles first described in the Boards' Norwalk Agreement published in October 2002 (see 3.3.1 above). While the document did not represent a change in the boards' convergence work programme, it did reflect the context of the 2009 'roadmap' for the removal of the reconciliation requirement for non-US companies that use IFRSs and are registered with the SEC in the United States (see 3.3.2 above). It also reflected the work undertaken by the Committee of European Securities Regulators (CESR) to identify areas for improvement of accounting standards.

Both the FASB and the IASB noted in the MOU that removing the current reconciliation requirements would require continued progress on the two Boards' convergence programme. Accordingly, the MOU set out milestones that the FASB and the IASB believed were achievable.

The Boards agreed that trying to eliminate differences between their respective standards when both were in need of significant improvement was not the best use of resources – instead, new common standards should be developed. Consistent with that principle, convergence work would continue to proceed on the following two tracks:

- first, the Boards would reach a conclusion about whether major differences in focused areas should be eliminated through one or more short-term standard-setting projects, and, if so, would aim to complete or substantially complete work in those areas by 2008; and
- second, the FASB and the IASB would seek to make continued progress on joint projects in other areas identified by both boards where current accounting practices under US GAAP and IFRSs were regarded as candidates for improvement.

The boards pointed out that their work programmes are not limited to the items listed in the MOU. The FASB and the IASB will follow their normal due process when adding items to their agendas.

Topics for short-term convergence included the following:

To be examined by the FASB	To be examined by the IASB
Fair value option*	Borrowing costs
Impairment (jointly with the IASB)	Impairment (jointly with the FASB)
Income tax (jointly with the IASB)	Income tax (jointly with the FASB)
Investment properties**	Government grants
Research and development	Joint ventures
Subsequent events	Segment reporting
FASB Note: * On the active agenda at 1 July 2005. ** To be considered by the FASB as part of the fair value option project.	*IASB Note:* Topics are part of or to be added to the IASB's short-term convergence project, which is already on the agenda.

Other convergence projects that are not part of the short-term agenda are set out under 3.4 below.

3.3.4 SEC proposal to accept IFRS financial statements without reconciliation to US GAAP

Under SEC rules, the term 'foreign private issuer' includes a corporation or other organisation incorporated or organised under the laws of any foreign country. Foreign private issuers that register securities with the SEC are currently required to present audited statements of income, financial position, changes in shareholders' equity and cash flows for each of the past three financial years. Up until now, all foreign private issuers have been required to reconcile to US GAAP the financial statements that they file with the SEC if the financial statements are prepared using any basis of accounting other than US GAAP.

In one of the most significant moves towards convergence and mutual recognition in recent times, the SEC issued in July 2007 a consultative document that proposed amendments to Form 20-F to accept – without reconciliation to US GAAP – financial statements prepared in accordance with IFRS as issued by the IASB.[77] This proposal was approved by the SEC in November 2007, and will apply to financial statements covering years ended after 15 November 2007.[78] The changes will apply to an eligible issuer regardless of whether it is required to prepare such IFRS financial statements by its home country regulator or securities exchange, or whether it simply chooses to do so for the purpose of its Form 20-F.[79]

However, it is important to note that, whilst the revisions will allow a foreign private issuer to file financial statements prepared in accordance with IFRS as issued by the

IASB without reconciliation to US GAAP, the SEC is not proposing to change existing reconciliation requirements for foreign private issuers that file their financial statements under other sets of accounting standards, or that are not in full compliance with IFRS as issued by the IASB. According to the SEC, 'the purpose of the requirement to use the IASB-approved version is to encourage the development of IFRS as a uniform global standard, not a divergent set of standards applied differently in every nation.'[80] Consequently, in order to be eligible to omit the reconciliation, an issuer will be required, in a prominent footnote to its financial statements, to state unreservedly and explicitly that its financial statements are in compliance with IFRS as issued by the IASB. In addition, in its report, the independent auditor will be required to opine similarly on whether or not those financial statements comply with IFRS as issued by the IASB.[81]

This means that the proposed amendments will not be available to an issuer that files financial statements that include deviations from IFRS as issued by the IASB. A foreign private issuer that does not state unreservedly and explicitly that its financial statements are in compliance with IFRS as issued by the IASB, or for which the auditor's report contains any qualification relating to the application of IFRS as issued by the IASB, will continue to be required to provide the US GAAP reconciliation under current rules. Similarly, an issuer that files its financial statements using a set of generally accepted accounting principles of another jurisdiction also will continue to reconcile to US GAAP as under current rules when preparing its financial statements for inclusion in a registration statement or annual report.

Consequently, it seems clear that the proposed amendments will not apply to issuers using a jurisdictional or other variation of IFRS – for example, where an EU company prepares it financial statements in accordance with IFRS as adopted in the EU, where this differs from full IFRS. However, it will be acceptable under the SEC's proposals for an issuer to state compliance with both IFRS as issued by the IASB and a jurisdictional variation of IFRS, and for an audit firm to opine that financial statements comply with IFRS as issued by the IASB and a jurisdictional variation of IFRS, so long as the statement relating to the former was unreserved and explicit.[82]

3.3.5 SEC Concept Release on allowing US issuers to prepare financial statements in accordance with IFRS

The SEC's July 2007 proposal to accept IFRS financial statements without reconciliation to US GAAP raised the question as to whether it also should accept financial statements prepared in accordance with IFRSs from US issuers. Consequently, in August 2007, the SEC published a Concept Release to obtain information about the extent and nature of the public's interest in allowing US issuers to prepare financial statements in accordance with IFRSs for purposes of complying with the rules and regulations of the SEC.[83]

According to the SEC, it has identified at least two market forces that may provide incentives for some market participants to request in the future that the SEC accepts from US issuers financial statements prepared in accordance with IFRSs.[84]

First, as a growing number of jurisdictions move to IFRS, more non-US companies will report their financial results in accordance with IFRS. If a critical mass of non-US companies in a certain industry sector or market reports in accordance with IFRS, then there may be pressure for US issuers in that industry sector or market to likewise report in accordance with IFRS to enable investors to compare US issuers' financial results more efficiently with those of their competitors.

Second, as more jurisdictions accept financial statements prepared in accordance with IFRS for local regulatory or statutory filing purposes, US issuers' subsidiaries based in these jurisdictions may be preparing and filing their local financial statements using IFRS as their basis of accounting. If US issuers have a large number of subsidiaries reporting in this manner, then these US issuers – most likely large, multinational corporations – may incur lower costs in preparing their consolidated financial statements using IFRS rather than US GAAP.

The Commission anticipates that not all US issuers will have incentives to use IFRS. For example, US issuers without significant customers or operations outside the United States – which may tend to be smaller public companies – may not have the market incentives to prepare IFRS financial statements for the foreseeable future. Additionally, the Commission recognises that there may be significant consequences to allowing US issuers to prepare their financial statements in accordance with IFRSs. If the Commission were to accept financial statements prepared in accordance with IFRSs from US issuers, then investors and market participants would have to be able to understand and work with both IFRS and US GAAP when comparing among US issuers, because not all US issuers are likely to elect to prepare IFRS financial statements. On a more practical level, a US issuer may have contracts such as loan agreements that include covenants based on US GAAP financial measures or leases for which rental payments are a function of revenue as determined under US GAAP. Similarly, US issuers may use their financial statements as the basis for filings with other regulators and authorities (for example, local and federal tax authorities, supervisory regulators) that may require US GAAP financial information.

Consequently, the SEC consultation around the Concept Release focused on such matters as:

- Whether market participants believe that the SEC should allow US issuers to prepare financial statements in accordance with IFRSs;
- What the effect would be on the US capital markets of some US issuers reporting in accordance with IFRS and others in accordance with US GAAP;
- What effect the change would have on cost of capital;
- Whether comparative advantages would be conferred on those US issuers who move to IFRS versus those that do not;
- What the effect would be on the US capital markets of not affording the opportunity for US issuers to report in accordance with either IFRS or US GAAP; and

- What immediate, short-term or long-term incentives would a US issuer have to prepare IFRS financial statements and what immediate, short-term or long-term barriers would a US issuer encounter in seeking to prepare IFRS financial statements.

At the time of writing (November 2007), the Concept Release was still under consultation, and would be the subject of roundtables to be held in December 2007. However, in our view, given the SEC's decision in November 2007 to accept IFRS financial statements from foreign private issuers without reconciliation to US GAAP, it seems likely that eventually it will come under considerable pressure to allow US issuers similarly to prepare their financial statements in accordance with IFRSs for SEC filing purposes.

3.4 The IASB's current agenda

The IASB has numerous projects in progress at the moment. These cover a wide range of topics, some of which could potentially have a fundamental impact on financial reporting under IFRS. In addition, it has identified other topics that it may place on its agenda as resources permit.

The IASB's current agenda includes the following:[85]

Short-term convergence projects	Comments
Government Grants (including Emission Rights)	Work on this project has been deferred pending the conclusion of work on other relevant projects, including the revision of IAS 37.
Joint Ventures	Exposure Draft proposing the elimination of the option of proportional consolidation of jointly controlled entities published in September 2007. IFRS expected in the second half of 2008.
Impairment	Joint project with FASB. Staff work in progress.
Income Tax	Joint project with FASB aimed at achieving greater convergence between IAS 12 and FAS 109 – Income Taxes. Exposure Draft expected first quarter 2008, timing of IFRS yet to be determined.

Other convergence projects	Comments
Consolidations, including Special Purpose Entities	Work towards IFRS/US GAAP converged standards. Discussion Paper expected in the first quarter of 2008.
Fair Value Measurement Guidance	This project will provide guidance on how fair value should be determined in those cases where standards require its use. In November 2006 the IASB published a Discussion Paper that set out the Board's preliminary views of the provisions of the FASB's Statement SFAS 157 'Fair Value Measurements' and which principally comprised the full text of that statement. Round-table discussion expected in the second quarter of 2008.
Financial Statement Presentation (formerly known as Performance Reporting)	**Phase A:** On 6 September 2007 the IASB issued a revised version of IAS 1 – *Presentation of Financial Statements*. The changes made are to require information in financial statements to be aggregated on the basis of shared characteristics and to introduce a statement of comprehensive income. **Phase B:** Aimed at developing standards for the presentation of information on the face of financial statements. Discussion Paper expected in the fourth quarter of 2007.
Revenue Recognition	Joint project with FASB. Discussion Paper expected in the first quarter of 2008. Timing of Exposure Draft and IFRS yet to be determined.

Other convergence projects (cont.)	Comments
Post-retirement benefits (including pensions)	In July 2006, the IASB added a project on post-retirement benefits to its agenda (such a project was already on the FASB agenda). The project is to be conducted in two phases, which would involve a fundamental review of all aspects of post-employment benefit accounting. The first phase would consider issues that could be resolved within the next four years, namely: • presentation and disclosure; • definition of defined benefit and defined contribution arrangements and accounting for cash balance plans; • smoothing and deferral mechanisms; and • the treatment of settlements and curtailments. Discussion Paper expected first quarter 2008. Timing of Exposure Draft and IFRS yet to be determined.
Leases	This is a long-term project that is expected to result in a fundamental change in accounting for leases by both lessors and lessees. The project will cover leases of real estate as well as equipment leases. The primary objective of the project is to develop a model for the recognition of assets and liabilities arising under lease contracts, and for the measurement of those assets and liabilities, that is consistent with the *Framework* definitions and other standards. The first step in this process will be the publication of a Discussion Paper, which is expected in the second half of 2008. Timing of Exposure Draft and IFRS yet to be determined.

Conceptual Framework	Comments
Phase A: Objectives and qualitative characteristics	Discussion Paper on Phase A issued in July 2006. ED expected fourth quarter 2007.
Phase B: Elements and recognition Phase C: Measurement	Discussion Paper on Phase B expected in the second half of 2008.
Phase D: Reporting entity	Discussion Paper on Phase D expected in the fourth quarter of 2007.
Phase E: Presentation and disclosure	
Phase F: Purpose and Status (i.e. status of Framework in GAAP hierarchy)	
Phase G: Application to Not-for-Profit Entities	
Phase H: Remaining issues	
Other projects	**Comments**
IFRS for small and medium-sized entities	Exposure Draft published in February 2007. IFRS expected in the second half of 2008.
Insurance Contracts Phase II	Discussion Paper published in May 2007. Timing of Exposure Draft and IFRS yet to be determined.
Liabilities (amendment of IAS 37, formerly known as Non-financial Liabilities project)	Exposure Draft issued June 2005. Roundtable discussions were held in Nov/Dec 2006. Timing of IFRS yet to be determined.
Emission trading schemes	Work on this project has been deferred pending the conclusion of work on other relevant projects, including the revision of IAS 37.

The length and breadth of the IASB's current agenda illustrates the dilemma that the Board currently faces: should its priorities focus on convergence or on the needs of the markets? It is clear that the user community – including regulators – is calling for consistency and comparability in the application of IFRS. However, it is often the case that the time of IASB staff and Board meetings are being dominated by projects that do not address issues that the market sees as priorities in order to achieve greater consistency in the application of IFRSs. For example, issues such as common control transactions, accounting for put options held by minority shareholders and various industry-specific issues are seemingly of lower priority than topics such as segment reporting and borrowing costs, which are not causing difficulty in practice. In our view, the development of high quality principles-based international standards that address today's practical issues is more important in the short term than convergence.

3.5 The IASB's 'Annual Improvements Process'

During 2007, the IASB adopted an annual process to deal with 'non-urgent, minor amendments to IFRSs' (the 'Annual Improvements Process'). Issues dealt with in this process are expected to arise from matters raised by the IFRIC and suggestions from IASB staff or practitioners, and are likely to focus on areas of inconsistency in IFRSs or where clarification of wording is required.

It seems that the premise behind the annual improvements process is to streamline the IASB's standard-setting process. If a number of minor amendments are processed together, there will be benefits both to constituents and the IASB. Agenda proposals and proposed solutions will be presented by IASB staff to the Board in the course of the year. The Board will discuss the proposals and make decisions about the proposed solutions. Subsequently, the decisions of the Board will be published in IASB *Update*, and once the Board has reviewed the amendments, a final draft of these amendments will be published on the IASB Website. In October each year, the amendments will be published in an omnibus Exposure Draft. These Exposure Drafts will have a comment period of 90 days. A final omnibus standard will be issued in April of each year. The effective date of the amendments is expected to be 1 January of the following year. The first omnibus Exposure Draft was published on 11 October 2007, with a comment date of 11 January 2008. The proposed effective date for the proposed amendments, if confirmed, is 1 January 2009.[86]

According to the IASB, the proposals set out in this first Exposure Draft 'range from a restructuring of IFRS 1 – *First-time Adoption of International Financial Reporting Standards*, mainly to remove redundant transitional provisions, to minor changes of wording to clarify the meaning and remove unintended inconsistencies between IFRSs.'[87] However, at first reading, it seems that at least some of the proposed amendments go far beyond minor wording changes and constitute significant changes of substance – for example, the proposals to amend IAS 1 – *Presentation of Financial Statements* (see 7.4 below), and IAS 16 – *Property, Plant and Equipment* (see Chapter 28, section 7.17.2). The issue as to how 'minor' some of the proposed changes really are is perhaps well illustrated by the fact that certain Board members voted against the proposed amendments to three of the standards (IAS 1, IAS 28 and IAS 38) and published alternative views thereon. It will therefore be interesting to see the reaction that the IASB receives to some of these proposals from its constituents through the consultation process.

4 FINANCIAL REPORTING IN COMPLIANCE WITH INTERNATIONAL FINANCIAL REPORTING STANDARDS

4.1 Statement of compliance with IFRS

The year 2005 was a watershed for IFRS with a significant number of countries adopting IFRS as their principal financial reporting regime – either directly (as in the case of the 27 Member States of the European Union), or by aligning their national standards with IFRS (for example, Australia and South Africa).

The main document setting out the basis on which financial statements should be presented under IFRSs, and the required contents of those financial statements, is IAS 1 – *Presentation of Financial Statements*.[88] An entity whose financial statements comply with IFRSs 'shall make an explicit and unreserved statement of such compliance in the notes'.[89] IFRS compliance involves complying with all the recognition, measurement and disclosure provisions of the standards and interpretations. For this reason, IAS 1 states that 'financial statements shall not be described as complying with IFRSs unless they comply with all the requirements of IFRSs'.[90] The IASB has therefore established unambiguously the principle that full application of its standards and related interpretations is necessary for a company to be able to assert that its financial statements comply with IFRS. This requirement means also that it is not acceptable to omit any of the required disclosures of IFRSs on the basis that the information is commercially sensitive or potentially detrimental to the entity.

It is important to note that, at the time of writing (November 2007), the IASB is proposing, as part of its 2007 Annual Improvements Process (see 3.5 above), to insert in IAS 1 disclosure requirements that will oblige entities to describe, in certain circumstances, the differences between IFRSs and the basis on which the financial statements that refer to IFRSs have been prepared.[91] This proposal is discussed in detail at section 7.4 below.

4.2 Fair presentation and compliance with IFRS

Paragraph 13 of IAS 1 states that 'financial statements shall present fairly the financial position, financial performance and cash flows of an entity'. It goes on to state that fair presentation requires the faithful representation of the effects of transactions, other events and conditions in accordance with the definitions and recognition criteria for assets, liabilities, income and expenses set out in the *Framework*. The application of IFRSs, with additional disclosure when necessary, is presumed to result in financial statements that achieve a fair presentation.[92]

IAS 1 states that in virtually all circumstances, a fair presentation is achieved by compliance with applicable IFRSs.[93] A fair presentation under IFRS also requires an entity:

(a) to select and apply accounting policies in accordance with IAS 8 which sets out a hierarchy of authoritative guidance that management considers in the absence of a Standard or an Interpretation that specifically applies to an item;

(b) to present information, including accounting policies, in a manner that provides relevant, reliable, comparable and understandable information; and

(c) to provide additional disclosures when compliance with the specific requirements in IFRSs is insufficient to enable users to understand the impact of particular transactions, other events and conditions on the entity's financial position and financial performance.[94]

4.3 The fair presentation override

IAS 1 makes it clear that inappropriate accounting policies are not rectified either by disclosure of the accounting policies used or by notes or explanatory material.[95] For this reason, IAS 1 had to cater for those situations where compliance with a standard or interpretation would distort fair presentation. Consequently, the standard provides that in the extremely rare circumstances in which management concludes that compliance with a requirement in a Standard or an Interpretation would be so misleading that it would conflict with the objective of financial statements set out in the *Framework*, the entity shall depart from that requirement if the relevant regulatory framework requires, or otherwise does not prohibit, such a departure.[96]

When an entity applies this fair presentation override in these circumstances, it must disclose the following:[97]

(a) that management has concluded that the financial statements present fairly the entity's financial position, financial performance and cash flows;

(b) that it has complied with applicable Standards and Interpretations, except that it has departed from a particular requirement to achieve a fair presentation;

(c) the title of the Standard or Interpretation from which the entity has departed, the nature of the departure, including the treatment that the Standard or Interpretation would require, the reason why that treatment would be so misleading in the circumstances that it would conflict with the objective of financial statements set out in the *Framework*, and the treatment adopted; and

(d) for each period presented, the financial impact of the departure on each item in the financial statements that would have been reported had the treatment required by the Standard or Interpretation been applied.

When an entity has departed from a requirement of a Standard or an Interpretation in a prior period, and that departure affects the amounts recognised in the financial statements for the current period, the standard requires it to make the disclosures set out in (c) and (d) above.[98] Set out below is an example of the application of the fair presentation override, together with all the related disclosures:

Extract 1.1: National Express Group plc (2006)

NOTES TO THE CONSOLIDATED ACCOUNTS
FOR THE YEAR ENDED 31 DECEMBER 2006 [extract]

2 ACCOUNTING POLICIES [extract]

Basis of preparation [extract]

The financial statements have been prepared under the historical cost convention, except for the recognition of derivative financial instruments and available for sale investments detailed below.

As noted above, the Group has taken the extremely rare decision to depart from the requirement of IAS 19 'Retirement Benefits' so as to present fairly its financial performance, position and cash flows in respect of its obligation for the RPS. The details of this departure and impact on the Group's accounts are set out in note 35.

A summary of the Group's accounting policies applied in preparing the accounts for the year ended 31 December 2006 is set out below.

The preparation of accounts in conformity with generally accepted accounting principles requires the use of estimates and assumptions that affect the reported amounts of assets and liabilities at the date of the accounts and the reported amounts of revenues and expenses during the reporting period. Although these estimates are based on management's best knowledge, actual results ultimately may differ from those estimates.

The key sources of estimation uncertainty that have a significant risk of causing material adjustments to the carrying amounts of assets and liabilities within the next financial year are the measurement and impairment of indefinite life intangible assets (including goodwill) and measurement of defined benefit pension obligations. The measurement of intangible assets other than goodwill on a business combination involves estimation of future cash flows and the selection of a suitable discount rate. The Group determines whether indefinite life intangible assets are impaired on an annual basis and this requires an estimation of the value in use of the cash generating units to which the intangible assets are allocated. This requires estimation of future cash flows and choosing a suitable discount rate (see note 14). Measurement of defined benefit pension obligations requires estimation of future changes in salaries and inflation, as well as mortality rates, the expected return on assets and the choice of a suitable discount rate (see note 35).

35 PENSIONS AND OTHER POST-EMPLOYMENT BENEFITS [extract]

b) Accounting for the Railways Pension Scheme

The majority of employees of the UK Train companies are members of the appropriate section of the RPS, a funded defined benefit scheme. The RPS is a shared cost scheme, which means that costs are formally shared 60% employer and 40% employee. To date, the Group has experienced five changes of UK Train franchise ownership where the current owner has funded the scheme during the franchise term and the pension deficit at franchise exist has transferred to the new owner, without cash settlement. However, although the Group's past experience has proven otherwise, our legal advisers have opined that in certain situations, the liability for the deficit on the relevant sections of the RPS could theoretically crystallise for funding by an individual TOC at the end of the franchise. By entering into the franchise contact, the TOC becomes the designated employer for the term of the contract and under the rules of the RPS must fund its share of the pension liability in accordance with the schedule of contributions agreed with the Scheme trustees and actuaries and for which there is no funding cap set out in the franchise contract. We understand that franchise contracts entered into in the future will clarify that RPS pension deficits and surpluses will not be the responsibility of the outgoing franchisee following exit.

To comply with IAS 19, the Group is required to account of its legal obligation under the formal terms of the RPS and its constructive obligation that arises under the terms of each franchise agreement.

In determining the appropriate accounting policy for the RPS to ensure that the Group's accounts present fairly its financial position, financial performance and cash flows, management has consulted with TOC industry peers and has concluded that the Group's constructive but not its legal RPS defined benefit obligations should be accounted for in accordance with IAS 19. This accounting policy, which in all other respects is consistent with that set out in this note for the Group's other defined benefit schemes, means that the Group's accounts reflect that element of the deficits anticipated to be settled by the Group during the franchise term and will prevent gains arising on transfer of the existing RPS deficits to a new owner at franchise exit.

In calculating the Group's constructive obligations in respect of the RPS, the Group has calculated the total pension deficits in each of the RPS sections in accordance with IAS 19 and the assumptions set out above. These deficits are reduced by a 'franchise adjustment' which is that portion of the deficit projected to exist at the end of the franchise and for which the Group will not be required to fund. The franchise adjustment, which has been calculated by the Group's actuaries, is offset against the present value of the RPS liabilities so as to fairly present the financial performance, position and cash flows of the Group's obligations.

The franchise adjustment decreased from £71.0m at 31 December 2005 to £44.4m at 31 December 2006. The decrease is caused by interest on the franchise adjustment of £2.5m offset by net actuarial movements in scheme liabilities of £6.7m and by £22.4m relating to the franchise exits. In the prior year, the franchise adjustment increased by £3.4m from £67.6m at 1 January 2005 to £71.0m at 31 December 2005. The increase was caused by interest on the franchise adjustment of £3.6m offset by net actuarial movements in scheme liabilities of £0.2m.

If the Group has accounted for its legal obligation in respect of the RPS instead of the constructive obligation, the following adjustments would have been made to the financial information:

	2006	2005
	£m	£m
Balance sheet		
Defined benefit pension deficit	**(44.4)**	(71.0)
Deferred tax asset	**13.6**	20.1
Intangible asset	**3.3**	3.4
Net reduction in net assets	**(27.5)**	(47.5)
Statement of recognised income and expense		
Actuarial gains/(losses)	**6.7**	0.2
Tax on actuarial gains and losses	**(0.3)**	0.3
Net increase in actuarial gains	**6.4**	0.5
Income statement		
Interest on franchise adjustment	**(2.5)**	(3.6)
Curtailment gain on franchise exit	**22.4**	–
Intangible asset amortisation	**0.2**	1.1
Deferred tax credit/(charge)	**(6.2)**	0.3
Net increase in income	**13.9**	(2.2)

It should be noted that the fair presentation override is a requirement (not an option) of IAS 1 to be applied only in the extremely rare circumstances in which management concludes – as in the case set out above – that compliance with a requirement in a Standard or an Interpretation would be so misleading that it would conflict with the objective of financial statements set out in the *Framework*.

However, at the same time, the IASB has introduced a somewhat contradictory twist to the application of the override. As noted above, the override can be applied only if 'the relevant regulatory framework requires, or otherwise does not prohibit' its use. This means that the Board has built into IAS 1 the possibility of regulatory intervention in its application. Paragraph 21 of IAS 1 provides for the situation where 'the relevant regulatory framework' prohibits departure from a requirement in a particular standard or interpretation. In such cases, the standard requires an entity, to the maximum extent possible, to reduce the perceived misleading aspects of compliance by disclosing:[99]

(a) the title of the Standard or Interpretation in question, the nature of the requirement, and the reason why management has concluded that complying with that requirement is so misleading in the circumstances that it conflicts with the objective of financial statements set out in the *Framework*; and
(b) for each period presented, the adjustments to each item in the financial statements that management has concluded would be necessary to achieve a fair presentation.

This seems to contradict the clear statement in paragraph 16 of IAS 1 that 'inappropriate accounting policies are not rectified either by disclosure of the accounting policies used or by notes or cxplanatory material'.[100] It seems also to create the unwelcome precedent of a standard formally giving regulators the ability to determine how standards should be applied.

Nevertheless, in our view, the fair presentation override is an important element of financial reporting under IFRSs, as we believe that in any financial reporting regime it is necessary to cater for those extremely rare situations where compliance with a standard or interpretation would distort fair presentation. Interestingly, though, this view is not shared by the staff of the SEC. In a report on the 'Adoption by the United States Financial Reporting System of a Principles-Based Accounting System', the SEC staff state that they do not consider the override to be an appropriate component of principles-bases standard-setting. This view is expressed in the following terms:[101]

'While we believe that it is important for preparers and auditors to determine that the financial statements clearly and transparently provide information to investors that allows them to evaluate the company's financial position, results of operations, and cash flows, we do not believe that a "true and fair override" is a necessary component of a principles-based or objectives-oriented standard setting system. In fact, we would expect that an objectives-oriented standard setting regime should reduce legitimate concerns about the established standards not providing appropriate guidance, as the standards should be based on objectives that would almost certainly not be met by a presentation that was not "true and fair".'

Whilst we can see the logic of the SEC staff's view that in a truly principles-based or objectives-oriented regime the override would not be necessary, the reality is that any system of GAAP will inevitably include a degree of rules-based requirements. It will therefore be interesting to observe whether or not the override survives as part of the IFRS literature as greater IFRS/US GAAP convergence is achieved.

5 THE MOVE TO IFRS IN THE EUROPEAN UNION

5.1 Historical differences in European accounting

European accounting has historically been the product of disparate social, economic and political factors, which have resulted in a number of deep-rooted differences in financial reporting practice throughout the region. The factors that have caused these differences include a variety of legal and tax systems, the perceived objectives of financial reporting and the significance of different sources of finance.

Prior to the adoption of IFRS there was no common broad-based statement of generally accepted theoretical principles that underpinned financial reporting across the individual Member States of the European Union (EU). Clearly, though, it was not the lack of a conceptual framework that caused the differences in European financial reporting practices. European accounting evolved over many centuries, and the differences that exist throughout Europe were shaped by the conditions in each European country.

Until recently, the principal mechanism employed by the European Union to reduce these differences was the adoption of Directives under its company law harmonisation programme. These Directives are not laws that apply directly to companies, but instructions to Member States to alter their own national legislation, if necessary, so as to ensure compliance with the provisions of the Directive. In most cases, the Directives lay down minimum requirements only, so that there is nothing to prevent a Member State from imposing supplementary requirements of a more stringent nature, provided that these are not incompatible with the Directives.

The most significant Directives in the area of financial reporting are the Fourth and Seventh, which were adopted into national legislation by most EU countries during the 1980s.[102] The principal objective of the Fourth Directive was to achieve harmonisation in respect of formats, valuation rules and note disclosure, whilst the Seventh established a requirement for EU companies to prepare consolidated accounts on a common basis.

However, in negotiating the Fourth and Seventh Directives with the EU Member States, the Commission found that the deep-rooted differences in European accounting could be reconciled only through compromise. For example, in the case of the Fourth Directive, this involved a compromise between the German and French desire for certainty and precision in accounts (as reflected in the compulsory charts of accounts in France and the mandatory formats for the balance sheet and profit and loss account in Germany), and the Anglo-Saxon/Dutch desire for a more pragmatic approach requiring the accounts taken as a whole to present a true and fair view. In the case of the Seventh Directive, there was a compromise struck between the economic and legal concepts of a group.

5.2 Harmonisation achieved by the Fourth and Seventh Directives

Historically, the objectives of financial reporting have varied in different countries, and this fact is reflected in the relative importance given to the various parties who have an interest in accounting information. For example, financial reporting in certain countries, such as the UK and The Netherlands, has developed on the basis that shareholders are the most important group entitled to receive financial information. This approach arose from the situation where businesses had historically obtained a substantial proportion of their funds from the public generally and where responsibility for the conduct of the operations of the business was divorced from ownership. Consequently, investors required regular reports to assess the performance achieved by management and future prospects, and annual accounts ensured that the stewardship function was being exercised properly.

In other countries the primary purpose of financial reporting has historically been to provide information for the tax authorities and other government bodies interested in national economic planning. The assessment of liabilities to tax had to be based on standard rules regarding the recognition of income, deduction of expenses and measurement of assets; in this way, all businesses would be subject to tax on the same basis. In Belgium, France, Germany, Greece, Italy, Luxembourg and Portugal, standardised accounts have been used mainly to measure taxable profits. Although in Germany company law has been the principal authority for financial reporting measurement practices, it has historically been based on principles of historical cost and tax-based depreciation.

These contrasting attitudes to the purpose of financial reporting adversely affected the harmonisation of accounting law and practice in the EU, such that the harmonisation programme under the Directives has only been partially successful. This is clearly evidenced by the fact that harmonisation has not been achieved in the areas of recognition and measurement – both of which are fundamental to comparability in financial reporting. Nevertheless, it is clear that the Fourth and Seventh Directives have provided a base level for harmonisation of financial reporting in the EU, and have undoubtedly led to improvements in the quality and comparability of company accounts throughout the Union over the last twenty-five years. They have contributed also to improving the conditions for cross-border business and have allowed the mutual recognition of financial statements for the purposes of quotations on securities exchanges throughout the EU. Moreover, a further important contribution of the Directives has been in the area of creditor protection through the public availability of financial information. In contrast to the US, where only SEC registrant companies are required to publish financial statements, all limited liability companies in the EU are required to produce and publish financial information.

5.3 The European Commission's 1995 Communication on international harmonisation

In 1995 the European Commission issued a Communication (i.e. policy statement)[103] stating that, while EU legislation had improved considerably the quality of financial reporting in the Union, the Directives did not provide answers to all the problems that faced preparers and users of accounts and accounting standard setters. In the Commission's view, the most urgent problem that needed to be addressed concerned European companies with an 'international vocation' (the so-called 'global players') and the need to facilitate the access of such European global players to the international capital markets. The accounts prepared by those companies in accordance with their national legislation (based on the Accounting Directives) were not acceptable for international capital market purposes. These companies were therefore obliged to prepare two sets of accounts, one set which was in conformity with the Accounting Directives and another set required by the international capital markets.

The Commission examined several possible approaches to dealing with the issue of 'upgrading' EU accounting legislation. After careful consideration, the Commission suggested that a closer cooperation between the EU and the IASC, with the objective of ultimately adopting International Accounting Standards at the EU level, was the preferred solution. Referring to the 1995 agreement between IOSCO and the IASC to produce a core set of international accounting standards which would be endorsed by IOSCO (see 1.3 above), the Commission concluded that 'rather than amend the existing Directives, the proposal is to improve the present situation by associating the EU with the efforts undertaken by IASC and IOSCO towards a broader international harmonisation of accounting standards'.

This policy statement of the Commission paved the way for the acceptance of IAS by the EU. Unfortunately, the Commission could not anticipate in 1995 that the ultimate endorsement of IAS by IOSCO in May 2000 would only be a qualified acceptance of the standards. As it turned out, one of the main objectives of the Commission in moving towards IAS (access of European companies to international capital markets without having to provide reconciliations to any National GAAP) was only partly achieved.

5.4 The European Commission's Financial Services Action Plan

Meanwhile, certain EU Member States set about making it easier for their multinational companies to gain access to the international capital markets. In February 1998, new legislation was enacted in Germany to the effect that International Accounting Standards (or indeed other 'internationally recognised accounting principles' such as US GAAP) could be used in the consolidated financial statements of listed groups instead of German law and accounting principles. There was an added proviso that the financial statements must also be 'consistent with' the EU Accounting Directives.

Similar amended legislation was enacted in France in April 1998, allowing French companies whose securities were traded on a regulated market to use IAS or another body of international standards as the sole basis for their consolidated accounts. A number of other European countries (including Italy, Austria, Luxembourg, Belgium and Spain) followed suit. At the time, these were revolutionary changes, and demonstrated the influence of Anglo-American accounting philosophies, at least on those companies that wished either to seek access to the international capital markets, or to achieve greater transparency in their financial reporting. It also raised the stakes for the European Commission, emphasising the need for the Commission to deliver on the strategy set out in its 1995 Communication.

As part of its strategy to embrace IAS, and in response to the growing use of IAS by EU multinational companies, the Commission carried out an ongoing examination of the conformity between the Accounting Directives and IASs and SIC Interpretations.[104] Generally, these comparisons concluded that (with the exception of IAS 39 – see below) there are few conflicts between the Accounting Directives and IAS. Those minor conflicts that did exist would be addressed by the Commission in the context of the modernisation of the Accounting Directives that took place during the next two years or so. The Commission's programme of modernising the Accounting Directives not only removed existing conflicts between IAS and the Directives, but ensured also that all the options then available under IAS would be available to EU companies.

In May 1999, the Commission issued its Financial Services Action Plan.[105] The plan confirmed the Commission's position that comparable, transparent and reliable financial information is fundamental to an efficient and integrated EU capital market, and that International Accounting Standards seemed the most appropriate benchmark for a single set of financial reporting requirements that would be the catalyst for the development of a single EU capital market.

This initiative was given further impetus by the summit of the European Heads of Government held in Lisbon in March 2000, where it was agreed that a single European capital market should be developed as a matter of priority. It was acknowledged further that the adoption of a single financial reporting framework for the European Union was a vital element in that process. The summit conclusions stressed the need to accelerate completion of the internal market for financial services and set a deadline of 2005 to implement the Commission's Financial Services Action Plan.

Following this lead by the European Heads of Government, the Commission announced in June 2000 that it would present proposals to:

- introduce the requirement that all listed EU companies report in accordance with IAS by 2005; and
- modernise the EU Accounting Directives to reduce potential conflicts with IAS and bring the Directives into line with modern accounting developments.[106]

Meanwhile, EU companies reporting at the time under IAS faced an immediate problem as IAS 39, which was due to become operative for 2001 financial statements, required certain financial instruments to be valued at fair value, in some cases with the changes in fair value being recorded in the profit and loss account. These requirements meant that there was a significant conflict between an IAS and the Accounting Directives, with the result that EU companies would not be able to continue to apply IAS unless significant amendments were made to the Directives.

Accordingly, the Commission put forward a proposal to amend the Fourth and Seventh Directives in order to enable EU companies to comply with IAS 39, and therefore prepare their financial statements in conformity with IAS. This was approved by the Council and by the European Parliament in May 2001 in the form of a Directive (the 'Fair Value' Directive) that amended the Fourth, Seventh and Bank Accounts Directives.[107]

Although the Commission wanted to provide more flexibility in the Fair Value Directive in order to anticipate future developments in accounting for financial instruments, the EU Member States insisted on including certain restrictions in the Directive in order to make it as close as possible to the then current version of IAS 39. Unfortunately, as a result, these restrictions meant that the IASB's extension of the fair value provisions in IAS 39 (the 'full fair value option') created new conflicts with the Fourth Directive, which have had to be addressed through further amendments to the Directive. The amendments were published on 16 August 2006 in the Official Journal of the European Union in the form of a new Directive 2006/46/EC, which amended the Fourth and Seventh Company Law Directives, as well as the accounting directives for banks and insurance undertakings.[108] This new Directive deals with a number of financial reporting matters, including:

- establishing collective responsibility of the members of the company body that is responsible for the preparation of the company's financial reports for ensuring that the company's annual report gives a true and fair view;
- requiring companies to provide disclosure about off balance sheet arrangements and related party transactions;
- requiring publicly traded companies to include a corporate governance statement in their annual reports; and
- enabling individual EU Member States to either permit or require companies to apply the relevant IFRSs that deal with financial instruments. This amendment thus deals with the existing conflicts between the Directives and IAS 39, and means that future amendments to any of the IFRSs that address financial instruments will not create any future conflicts with the Directives. In particular, this means that IAS 39's full fair value option is now compatible with the Directives.

EU Member States are required to enact the provisions of the new Directive into their national legislation by 5 September 2008 at the latest.

5.5 The European Commission's Regulation on the application of IAS in the European Union

On 13 February 2001, the European Commission published a draft EU Regulation[109] that would require publicly traded EU incorporated companies[110] to prepare, by 2005 at the latest, their consolidated accounts under IAS 'adopted' (see below) for application within the EU. This was adopted unanimously by the Council, and on 12 March 2002, by a vote of 492 for, 5 against and 29 abstentions, the European Parliament endorsed this proposal. This was adopted as Regulation No. 1606/2002 of the European Parliament and of the Council on 19 July 2002.[111]

An EU Regulation has direct effect on companies, without the need for national legislation. However, the Regulation also provides an option for Member States to permit or require the application of adopted IAS in the preparation of annual (unconsolidated) accounts and to permit or require the application of adopted IAS by unlisted companies. This means that Member States can require the uniform application of adopted IAS by important sectors such as banking or insurance, regardless of whether or not companies are listed.

The Regulation established also the basic rules for the creation of an endorsement mechanism for the adoption of IAS, the timetable for implementation and a review clause to permit an assessment of the overall approach proposed. The endorsement mechanism is discussed below.

Internal Market Commissioner, Frits Bolkestein, commented as follows on the adoption of the Regulation by the Council: 'I am delighted that the IAS Regulation has been adopted in a single reading and am grateful for the positive attitude of both the Parliament and the Council. I believe IAS are the best standards that exist. Applying them throughout the EU will put an end to the current Tower of Babel in financial reporting. It will help protect us against malpractice. It will mean investors and other stakeholders will be able to compare like with like. It will help European firms to compete on equal terms when raising capital on world markets. What is more, during my recent visit to the US, I saw hopeful signs that the US will now work with us towards full convergence of our accounting standards.'

The Regulation provides the facility for individual Member States, at their option, to defer the application of the Regulation until 2007 for those companies publicly traded both in the Community and on a regulated third-country market which are already applying 'another set of internationally accepted standards' (essentially, US GAAP) as the primary basis for their consolidated accounts as well as for companies which have only publicly traded debt securities.[112] However, the Regulation states that it is nonetheless crucial that by 2007 at the latest, IAS are applied by all Community companies publicly traded on a Community regulated market.[113]

There are currently approximately 7,000 companies listed on EU regulated markets that are subject to the Regulation. Only about 275 of these companies applied IAS prior to 2005.

5.6 The EU endorsement mechanism

The Regulation (see 5.5 above) defines the EU endorsement mechanism, which was already foreseen in the Commission's June 2000 Communication. The Commission took the view that an endorsement mechanism was needed to provide the necessary public oversight. The Commission considered also that it was not appropriate, politically or legally, to delegate accounting standard setting unconditionally and irrevocably to a private organisation over which the EU had no influence. In addition, the endorsement mechanism is responsible for examining whether the standards adopted by the IASB satisfy relevant EU public policy criteria.

The role of the endorsement mechanism is not to reformulate or replace IFRSs, but to oversee the adoption of new standards and interpretations, intervening only when these contain material deficiencies or have failed to cater for features specific to the EU economic or legal environments. The central task of this mechanism is to confirm that IFRSs provide a suitable basis for financial reporting by listed EU companies. The mechanism is based on a two-tier structure, combining a regulatory level with an expert level, to assist the Commission in its endorsement role.

The recitals to the Regulation state that the endorsement mechanism should act expeditiously in relation to proposed international accounting standards and also be a means to deliberate, reflect and exchange information on international accounting standards among the main parties concerned, in particular national accounting standard setters, supervisors in the fields of securities, banking and insurance, central banks including the European Central Bank (ECB), the accounting profession and users and preparers of accounts. The mechanism should be a means of fostering common understanding of adopted international accounting standards in the Community.[114]

There are three criteria set out in the Regulation on the application of IAS in the EU with which any individual IAS must comply if it is to be adopted:[115]

- the standard should not be contrary to the principle of true and fair in conformity with the Accounting Directives;
- the standard should be conducive to the European public good; and
- the standard should meet basic criteria as to the quality of information required for financial statements to be useful to users.

These criteria, although wide, do not appear unreasonable or overly burdensome in the light of the substantial power the EU has effectively vested in the IASB, a body not accountable to the EU electorate in any manner. It is important to note that although a standard or interpretation can only be adopted if all three criteria are met, this does not mean that if all three criteria are met a standard or interpretation must necessarily be adopted. However, if a standard or interpretation is not adopted, EU companies are free to apply it, other than in those cases where such application would be in conflict with an accounting standard that has been adopted or with EU law.

5.6.1 The regulatory level of the endorsement mechanism: The Accounting Regulatory Committee

The Accounting Regulatory Committee (ARC) was set up by the European Commission in accordance with the requirements contained in Article 6 of the EC's IAS Regulation (EC/1606/2002). The ARC is composed of representatives from EU Member States and is chaired by the Commission. The function of the Committee is a regulatory one and consists of providing an opinion on Commission proposals to adopt (endorse) an international accounting standard as envisaged under Article 3 of the IAS Regulation. The ARC operates on the basis of appropriate institutional arrangements and under existing comitology[116] rules that will ensure full transparency and accountability towards the Council and the European Parliament.

Under these rules, the Commission presents to the ARC a report that is required to identify the relevant international accounting standard and examine both its conformity with the conditions set out in the Regulation and its suitability as a basis for financial reporting in the EU. The ARC must decide, on the basis of qualified majority voting, whether to recommend to the European Commission that it should adopt or reject the standard for application in the EU. The same procedure applies to the adoption of amendments to previously adopted Standards and of IFRIC Interpretations.

5.6.2 The European Financial Reporting Advisory Group (EFRAG)

The European Financial Reporting Advisory Group (EFRAG), a private-sector initiative, was established by ten key constituents (EFRAG's 'Founding Fathers') interested in financial reporting in Europe, including the European Federation of Accountants (FEE), Business Europe, the European Round Table, the European Banking Federation (EBF), and the Comité Européen des Assurances (CEA).

EFRAG is a two-tier organisation, comprising:

- a group of twelve highly qualified experts (the EFRAG Technical Expert Group), to carry out the technical work; and
- a Supervisory Board of European Organisations (the EFRAG Supervisory Board), to guarantee representation of the full European interest and to enhance the legitimacy and credibility of EFRAG.

The 12 voting members of the Technical Expert Group (TEG) were selected from throughout Europe and come from a variety of backgrounds. The chairmen of the French, German and UK Standard Setters are non-voting members of TEG, and representatives of the European Commission, CESR and the IASB attend TEG meetings as observers.

The members of TEG are appointed by the Supervisory Board, with the assistance of a Nominating Committee, following an open call for candidates. The Supervisory Board looks primarily to the qualifications of the TEG candidates in terms of knowledge and experience and endeavours to ensure a broad geographical balance together with experience from preparers, the accounting profession, users and academics.

The manner in which EFRAG fits into the EC comitology framework of endorsement of IFRS is shown diagrammatically below:

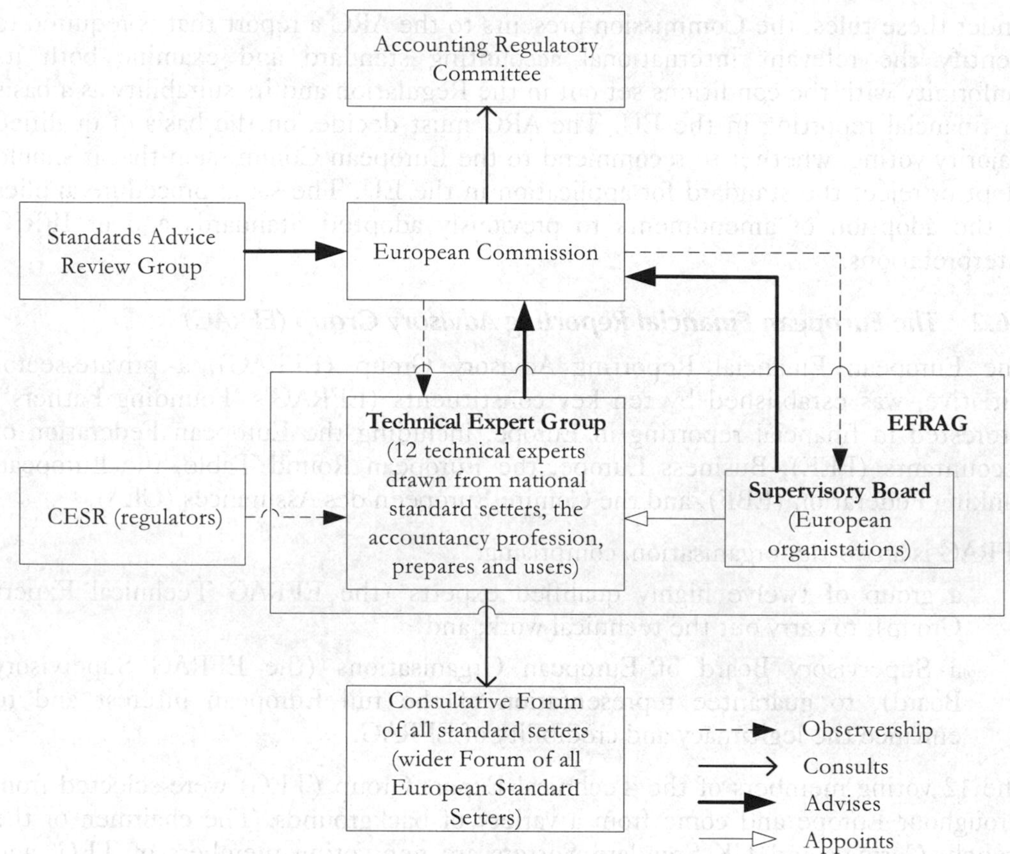

The principal aim of EFRAG is to provide proactive input into the work of the IASB. EFRAG advises the European Commission on the technical assessment of IFRSs and Interpretations, for application in the EU. The technical work of EFRAG is carried out by TEG on the basis of a wide consultation process. National standard setters of Europe have access to EFRAG through a number of routes. In common with other consultative organisations, they receive regular updates of EFRAG agenda items and decisions. Additionally, they comprise EFRAG's Consultative Forum, meeting at least twice a year to engage in technical debate on matters arising from the EFRAG agenda.

TEG was set up by EFRAG on 26 June 2001. Its role is to provide the private sector support and expertise needed to assess the standards and interpretations developed by the IASB on a timely basis. It also has the responsibility to provide input into the IASB standard setting process at all stages of a particular project, and particularly in the early phases. TEG ensures that EU users and preparers are involved in the preparatory discussions of the standards at the international level, and in the technical assessment of the standards, before their adoption by the EU. The role of users has recently received greater prominence through the establishment of a User Panel to assist TEG in its work by providing input from the user community on its comment letters and endorsement advice. In addition the Panel provides input on the long-term proactive work carried out by EFRAG itself. When appropriate, the Panel also assists the user representatives in the various EFRAG working groups.[117]

In an initiative designed to enable Europe as a whole to participate more effectively in the global accounting debate, EFRAG and the European national standard setters agreed to pool some of their resources and work together more closely. It was agreed that this initiative should start by concentrating on long-term pro-active work with the objective of stimulating debate on important items on the IASB agenda at an early stage in the standard-setting process, before the IASB formally issues its proposals. This initiative is known as the 'Proactive Accounting Activities in Europe' (or PAAinE) initiative and has the joint ambitions of representing a European point of view and exercising greater influence on the standard-setting process.

Work carried out under the PAAinE initiative can take a number of different forms and the full objectives of the initiative are:

- to stimulate, carry out and manage pro-active development activities designed to encourage the debate in Europe on accounting matters and to enhance the quality of the pro-active input to the IASB;
- to co-ordinate and resource monitoring work of IASB and FASB projects; and
- to try to ensure, as far as is practicable, that the views that Europe conveys to the IASB are consistent.[118]

TEG – whose meetings are open to public observation – provides advice to the European Commission on the adoption of new and revised IASB standards and IFRIC Interpretations for use in the EU, and it advises the Commission also on whether or not an amendment to the Directives is recommended in the light of international accounting developments. However, TEG has a somewhat uneasy voting arrangement: EFRAG cannot recommend non-endorsement of a standard or interpretation unless there is a two thirds majority vote against the standard. This means that a majority of the Group's members could be against endorsement, yet EFRAG would not be able to recommend non-endorsement unless that majority is at least two-thirds. As the Group comprises twelve members, including the Chairman, this means that at least eight must vote against a particular IFRS or Interpretation in order to recommend non-endorsement.

This uneasiness of this arrangement was manifested in EFRAG's letter of adoption of the amended IAS 39 sent to the Commission on 8 July 2004. In voting on the adoption of IAS 39, five members of the Group voted to support endorsement and six members voted to oppose endorsement (at that time, EFRAG comprised eleven members). As a result, EFRAG's endorsement advice to the Commission read as follows: 'We have decided only to issue a positive endorsement advice if there is a majority supporting endorsement … EFRAG cannot recommend non-endorsement of a standard unless there is a two thirds majority vote against the standard and EFRAG does not support endorsement unless there is majority in favour. Therefore, EFRAG does not issue any advice whether to endorse IAS 39 or not.'[119]

5.6.3 *Standards Advice Review Group*

In July 2006 the European Commission announced the formation of a Standards Advice Review Group for the purpose of ensuring objectivity and proper balance of EFRAG opinions. The Commission appoints the members of the Group from independent experts whose experience and competence in accounting, in particular in financial reporting issues, are widely recognised. The members are appointed in a personal capacity and will advise the Commission independently of any outside influence. The Group's task is to assess whether or not the endorsement advice given by the EFRAG is well balanced and objective. The group is expected to deliver its advice to the Commission within three weeks of EFRAG publishing its endorsement advice.[120]

5.7 Roundtable for the consistent application of IFRS in the EU

In February 2006, the European Commission formed a temporary Roundtable on Consistent Application of IFRSs. The Roundtable met for the first time in May 2006. The function of the Roundtable is set out in its Terms of Reference as follows:[121]

'The function of the Roundtable is to act as a simple and efficient forum for European accounting experts to identify, at an early stage, emerging and potentially problematic accounting issues in relation to consistent application. The Roundtable will thereby complete the existing European infrastructure contributing to a proper and consistent application of IFRS. The Roundtable would gather views in Member States through audit firms, standard setters and other bodies. It could then identify and group together those issues where it is felt there is a real risk of divergence and recommend which of those should be taken up by IFRIC as a matter of urgency. As such the Roundtable would also act as a filter mechanism. It should be underlined that the Roundtable will not be making any interpretations or guidance under IFRS. This is the task of IFRIC. When allowed to do so by their statutory working rules, EU national enforcers of financial information grouped within CESR/EECS[122] will inform the Roundtable about enforcement decisions taken under the Transparency and Prospectus Directives in relation to financial reporting based on IFRS.'

The Roundtable is chaired by the European Commission, and includes all the key EU stakeholders. However, the Commission recognises that for the Roundtable to function effectively, it is vital that the absolute number of participants should be kept as low as practically possible. Of course, a balance must be struck between having, on one hand, a manageable number of participants and, on the other, the need to include the relevant stakeholders. Consequently, in addition to Commission representatives, the Roundtable comprises a total of seventeen representatives from the IASB, CESR, EFRAG, FEE, Business Europe, the audit firms, National-Standard Setters and preparers. However, in addition to the three representatives from the EU National Standard-Setters (France, Germany and the UK), any other national standard-setter can participate by advance notice to the Commission.

It is important to note that the Roundtable is neither a decision-making nor interpretative body. Its function is limited to informal discussion on key topics and it will not develop into any form of interpretative authority on accounting standards. Issues discussed by the Roundtable will, if considered appropriate, be developed into technical papers. Thereafter, if the Roundtable believes that a particular technical paper has highlighted an issue of common concern, the issue will be submitted to IFRIC for consideration.

The output of the meetings of the Roundtable takes the form of a brief, publicly available summary of the meeting by the Chair, setting out the key issues that were discussed and those issues on which common concern was expressed and which therefore warranted referral to the IFRIC.

5.8 Enforcement and regulation in an integrated European capital market

The European Commission has set an ambitious agenda for the European Union to establish an integrated financial and capital market by 2010. However, progress with European capital market integration – a vital ingredient of this agenda – has so far been slow. Nevertheless, the economic gains to be derived from an integrated pan-European financial and capital market are considerable. European companies will have greater access to a deep and liquid market at lower costs of capital; and European consumers will enjoy wider investment choice and increasing net returns on their investments. The macroeconomic benefits could be substantial also, as increased investment implies stronger job creation and GDP growth.

However, the basic structures needed for an integrated market are not yet in place. In Europe, trans-national companies have to report to regulators in twenty-seven member states. They face a wide variety of different rules and regulations and investors have to negotiate fragmented markets that frustrate cross-border trading. Taken together with the differences in regulation, enforcement, taxation, legal systems and bankruptcy laws, this gives a situation that Baron Alexandre Lamfalussy described as 'a remarkable cocktail of Kafkaesque inefficiency that serves no-one – neither consumers, nor investors, nor SMEs, nor large companies, nor governments.' By contrast, the US capital markets provide clear evidence that efficiencies are forced upon businesses when their performances are easily comparable; without these pressures, inefficiency can go unnoticed.

Consequently, the greatest challenge facing Europe in delivering an efficient single capital market is the task of efficient regulation and enforcement. The absence of an effective and coordinated enforcement mechanism severely limits the credibility of any financial reporting regime. Clearly, the adoption of IFRS in Europe will improve the functioning of the securities markets only when it is properly and rigorously enforced. This means that the supervisors of the European capital markets have a crucial role to play in ensuring that companies comply with financial reporting requirements. In our view, this can be achieved only through the establishment of an efficient and lean Europe-wide regulatory system. This implies the co-operative development and implementation of a common EU approach to regulation that would establish a level playing field for EU financial reporting, maintained by rigorous enforcement that will prevent regulatory arbitrage.

In introducing the IAS Regulation, the European Commission stated that one of its key actions would be the development of an enforcement infrastructure that would ensure the rigorous application of IAS by listed companies in the EU. The focus of this initiative would be on disseminating implementation guidance, encouraging high quality auditing, and reinforcing coordinated regulatory oversight. A coordinating body was set up, as described below.

5.8.1 The Committee of European Securities Regulators (CESR)

The Committee of European Securities Regulators (CESR) was established by the European Commission Decision of June 2001.[123] This decision was taken in the light of the recommendation of the Report of the Committee of Wise Men on the Regulation of European Securities Markets (the Lamfalussy Report) as endorsed by the European Council and the European Parliament.[124] CESR is an independent Committee whose members comprise senior representatives from national public authorities competent in the field of securities. CESR has set out its own operational arrangements in its Charter.[125]

The CESR Chair and Vice-Chair are elected from among the Members for a period of two years. The Committee meets at least four times a year. CESR works with the support of a secretariat headed by a Secretary General. A representative of the European Commission is entitled to participate actively in all discussions held by CESR.

CESR submits an Annual Report to the European Commission, which is also sent to the European Parliament and the Council. The Chair of CESR reports regularly to the European Parliament and maintains strong links with the European Securities Committee.

The main tasks of CESR are to:

- advise the European Commission on securities policy issues, either at the European Commission's request or on its own initiative;
- prepare implementing measures as requested by the European Commission;
- foster and review common and uniform day-to-day implementation and application of Community legislation;
- issue guidelines, recommendations and standards that the CESR members introduce in their regulatory practices on a voluntary basis;
- undertake reviews of regulatory and supervisory practices within the single market; for that purpose a Review Panel has been established under the terms specified in a protocol attached to the Charter;
- develop effective operational network mechanisms to enhance day-to-day consistent supervision and enforcement of the Single Market for financial services. The Committee contributes to supervisory convergence through a Mediation Mechanism, established under the terms specified in a protocol attached to the Charter; and

- observe and assess the evolution of financial markets and the global trends in securities regulation and their impact on the regulation of the Single Market for financial services.

In addition, CESR established a sub-group of experts in the field of accounting and auditing, known as CESR-Fin. The principal challenges facing CESR-Fin are to reinforce cooperation among EU national regulators enforcing compliance with IFRS and to deepen the relationship with securities regulators in major third countries on financial reporting matters. This latter challenge is driven by the need to work on the global acceptance of IFRS financial statements prepared by EU entities that are subject to supervision both within and outside Europe.

The tasks of CESR-Fin are set out in its terms of reference as follows:[126]

- to coordinate the operational activities of EU National Enforcers in relation to the enforcement of compliance with IFRS. This includes:
  - the analysis and discussion of individual enforcement decisions under IFRS and emerging financial reporting issues under IFRS;
  - the identification of issues that are not covered by financial reporting standards or which may be affected by conflicting interpretations for referral to standard setting or interpretive bodies such as IASB or IFRIC;
  - the exchange of views and experiences on methods for supervising the financial information of companies offering publicly securities and/or having these securities listed on an EU regulated market;
- to monitor pro-actively and influence the regulatory developments in the area of accounting and auditing, including an active monitoring of the EU endorsement processes of international standards and the work of relevant EU accounting and/or auditing Committees;
- to identify issues in relation to the areas covered above that should be addressed by CESR through appropriate measures such as standards, guidelines or recommendations. CESR-Fin can also make proposals on best enforcement practices or for peer reviews among enforcers;
- to advise other CESR groups, such as the Prospectus Contact Group or the Transparency Expert Group, on technical accounting and auditing issues raised by these groups in relation to their area of activity or as a result of implementation issues identified in connection with CESR-Fin activities;
- to establish and maintain the appropriate relationship with securities regulators from major capital markets outside Europe, in order to foster the operational cooperation between EU and non-EU regulators in the area of financial reporting.

5.8.2 CESR Standard No. 1

During the seventh meeting of CESR held in Paris in March 2003, the first CESR standard on *Financial Information: Enforcement of standards on financial information in Europe*, was approved.[127] The standard represents a significant part of CESR's contribution to the task of developing and implementing a common approach to the enforcement of IFRS in Europe.

The standard sets down 21 principles on which, in CESR's view, harmonisation of the institutional oversight systems in Europe may be achieved. In particular, a definition of enforcement of standards on financial information, its scope, the selection techniques applicable by the enforcers and the responsibilities of the different parties involved are outlined.

The standard states that for financial information other than prospectuses, ex-post enforcement is the normal procedure, whilst for prospectuses ex-ante approval is the norm. Enforcement of all financial information should normally be achieved by selecting a number of issuers and documents to be examined. The preferred models for selecting financial information for enforcement purposes are mixed models whereby a risk-based approach is combined with a rotation and/or a sampling approach.[128]

Where a material misstatement in the financial information is detected, enforcers are required to take appropriate actions to achieve an appropriate disclosure and where relevant, public correction of misstatement.[129] Enforcers should periodically report to the public on their activities providing, as a minimum, information on the enforcement policies adopted and decisions taken in individual cases including accounting and disclosure matters.[130]

5.8.3 CESR Standard No. 2

In April 2004, CESR issued a standard on the organisation of greater co-ordination of enforcement activities by supervisors of financial information in Europe.[131] The standard's aim is further to contribute to the creation within Europe of robust and consistent enforcement of IFRS. The key principles introduced by Standard no. 2 include:

- discussion of enforcement decisions and experiences within a formalised structure;
- the principle that all supervisors should take into account existing decisions taken by EU National Enforcers; and
- the development of a database as a practical reference tool that sets out decisions taken by EU National Enforcers to provide a record of previous decisions reached in particular cases.

The CESR database has now been established, and provides EU securities regulators with the means of sharing with each other their regulatory activity and experiences. In principle, this is a positive development as it will help to promote consistency in the regulation and enforcement of IFRS financial reporting throughout the EU – something that is crucial in the development of an integrated EU capital market.

In addition, extracts from EECS's database of enforcement decisions are now made public on the CESR website (EECS refers to 'European Enforcers Coordination

Sessions', which includes CESR members and non-CESR members who have competences in the enforcement of compliance with IFRS. – see 5.7 above).

5.8.4 CESR/SEC joint work plan

In August 2006 – as part of their ongoing regulatory dialogue – CESR and the SEC published a joint work plan that focuses on three key issues. For each of the following three items, the work plan includes a description of the project goal and the next steps to be taken:[132]

A Implementation of IFRS and US GAAP by internationally active issuers

What this means in practical terms is that, as part of their regular review of corporate filings, the staff of the SEC will review foreign private issuers' implementation of IFRS. Similarly, staff of CESR Members will continue to review US GAAP implementation by US issuers in the European Union. Under the work plan, the output of these reviews will be used in the following ways:

- The staff of the SEC and CESR-Fin will share information about areas of IFRS and US GAAP that are troublesome in terms of high-quality and consistent application.
- Where appropriate, the staff of the SEC and the staff of CESR Members will consult on issuer-specific matters regarding the application of US GAAP and IFRS in order to facilitate a solution that contributes to the consistent application of US GAAP or IFRS by companies that are both listed in the EU and registered with the SEC. Protocols for the sharing of this confidential information between the staff of individual CESR members (e.g. in the UK and Germany) and the staff of the SEC have been established.

These two levels of discussion are aimed at helping to ensure that high standards are maintained and consistent financial reporting is achieved. In addition, they are aimed at ensuring that a single regulator does not act unilaterally or that two individual regulators do not act in an inconsistent manner in relation to companies whose financial statements are subject to review by both.

B Modernization of financial reporting and disclosure

The goal here is to evaluate and identify information technology solutions for disclosure and electronic storage of corporate information (including financial information). The plan is for SEC staff and the relevant CESR expert group (in this case, the Transparency Expert Group, CESR-Tech) to exchange views on policies favouring the use of technology and IT networks in the disclosure and storage of financial information, including the use of interactive data.

C Discussion of risk management practices

In this case, Staff of the SEC and CESR will discuss methodology and tools for prioritising risks they confront as regulators, the risks that have been identified and ranked as high-priority, and the methodology that has resulted in the categorisation of these risks as high-priority. Once common risks are identified, the SEC and CESR will discuss approaches to managing those risks.

6 THE ADOPTION OF IFRS OUTSIDE THE EUROPEAN UNION

A body of generally high quality International Financial Reporting Standards has now been promulgated, and approximately 100 countries have either already adopted IFRS directly, or have aligned their national standards with IFRS, or have committed to do so in the foreseeable future – albeit in many of these 100 countries IFRS is either required only for certain companies (for example, listed companies or financial institutions), or permitted rather than required.

Although the European Union is almost certainly the IASB's most significant single constituency for the time being, there are also a number of other countries that either have already adopted – or will be adopting – IFRS as their primary system of GAAP. Set out below is a brief summary of the basis on which just some of these countries have adopted IFRS.

6.1 Australia

The Australian Financial Reporting Council (FRC) is a statutory body established under the *Australian Securities and Investments Commission Act 2001, as amended by the Corporate Law Economic Reform Program (Audit Reform and Corporate Disclosure) Act 2004*. The FRC is responsible for providing broad oversight of the process for setting accounting and auditing standards as well as monitoring the effectiveness of auditor independence requirements in Australia and providing the Australian Government with reports and advice on these matters. It comprises key stakeholders from the business community, the professional accounting bodies, governments and regulatory agencies.

In July 2002, the Chairman of the FRC announced that the FRC had formalised its support for the adoption by Australia of international accounting standards by 1 January 2005. In accordance with this strategic directive, the Australian Accounting Standards Board (AASB) issued Australian equivalents to IFRSs (AIFRS) on 15 July 2004. Australian Accounting Standards have the force of law for Australian corporations, and therefore the standards issued by the IASB are required to be issued as Australian standards by the AASB. The implementation of the Australian equivalents to international standards has achieved the FRC's strategic directive of ensuring that the financial statements of for-profit entities applying AASB standards are also in compliance with IASB standards.

In adopting the IASB's standards, the AASB's initial approach was to adopt the content and wording of the standards. Words were changed only where there was a need to accommodate the Australian legislative environment. At the time of initial adoption in 2005, in certain AIFRS Standards the AASB permitted only one of certain optional treatments available in the equivalent IASB standards, and retained a number of specific disclosures from domestic GAAP in addition to the disclosure requirements of IFRS. On 30 April 2007, the AASB issued AASB 2007-4 *Amendments to Australian Accounting Standards arising from ED 151 and Other Amendments.* This new standard is a result of an AASB decision that, in principle, Australian equivalents to IFRSs should reflect to the maximum extent possible the requirements and wording of IFRS. AASB 2007-4 is effective for reporting periods beginning on or after 1 July 2007, and has the effect of incorporating all remaining IFRS accounting policy options into AIFRS and removing almost all Australian-specific disclosure requirements from AIFRS.

In some cases, existing AASB standards contained commentary that was not included in the equivalent IASB standards. The AASB has removed all this guidance that was not part of the standards, except where the guidance deals with situations that are commonly encountered in the Australian environment but which are not catered for in the IASB standards.

In 2007, the Australian Auditing and Assurance Standards Board (AUASB) issued a revised auditing standard requiring the auditor to opine on the entity's statement of compliance with IFRS made in accordance with the Australian equivalent of paragraph 14 of IAS 1, if such statement has been made.

The AASB plans to continue to work to maintain consistency with the IASB's standards in order that the FRC's strategic directive continues to be met.

6.2 Brazil

In Brazil, the 'Comissão de Valores Mobiliários' (CVM) is the body responsible for the regulation of the financial statements of publicly listed companies, with the exception of companies in the financial services sector. These financial statements are currently required to be prepared in accordance with Brazilian Corporate Law and local accounting standards. In July 2007, following a period of public consultation, the CVM issued Instruction No. 457, which requires publicly listed companies to publish their consolidated financial statements in accordance with IFRS for periods ending on or after 1 January 2010, with earlier adoption being permitted. At the time of writing (November 2007) there were approximately 640 listed companies in Brazil. Banks and financial institutions are regulated by the Brazilian Central Bank which has also announced the objective of requiring the adoption of IFRS by 2010.[133]

In addition, in 2006 the Brazilian Accounting Standards Committee (Comitê de Pronumciamentos Contábeis – CPC) was established. This Committee was created to give Brazil a single body responsible for issuing accounting standards. There is currently no requirement for non-public companies to publish local GAAP financial statements in Brazil, although a new law (Lei 3741 / 2000) is expected to require this in the future for groups or companies above certain size thresholds. These financial statements will be prepared under 'Brazilian GAAP' which will be regulated by the CPC, and which currently differs in several respects from IFRS. Differences exist in areas where there is no applicable law or accounting standards (for example there is no local guidance regarding accounting for employee share options), or where the current law or accounting standards conflict with IFRS (for example the capitalisation of finance leases is prohibited under Brazilian Corporate Law). However, the stated aim of the CPC is to achieve convergence with IFRS as soon as possible.

6.3 Canada

In Canada the body charged with the responsibility for establishing standards of accounting and reporting for Canadian companies and not-for-profit organisations is the Accounting Standards Board (AcSB). The AcSB derives its authority from the Canadian Institute of Chartered Accountants (CICA). The AcSB is supported in its standard setting role by the Accounting Standards Oversight Committee (AcSOC), which was established in 2000.

In January 2006 the AcSB ratified a new Strategic Plan outlining its direction for financial reporting in Canada for the period 2006 to 2011. Under this plan the AcSB set out its intent to pursue separate strategies for each of the major categories of reporting entities in Canada, which are:

- publicly accountable enterprises,
- non-publicly accountable enterprises and
- not-for-profit organisations.

In so doing, the AcSB recognised that it may not be possible to address the divergent needs of different categories of reporting entities properly within a single strategy. For publicly accountable enterprises, the AcSB has decided to converge Canadian GAAP with IFRSs over a transitional period to an anticipated changeover date in 2011. The term 'publicly accountable enterprises' encompasses public companies and some other classes of enterprise that have relatively large or diverse classes of financial statement users. However, as part of its implementation plan, the AcSB is considering the need for a revised definition of a publicly accountable enterprise. For non-publicly accountable enterprises and not-for-profit organizations the AcSB has undertaken to perform an examination of the needs of users of these enterprise's financial statements before concluding on any action to be taken.

In its plans for publicly accountable enterprises the AcSB has taken into account the experiences of the European Union and the other jurisdictions that have already converted to IFRSs so as to minimise the disruption to business arising from the conversion. The key features of its convergence plan are the relatively long transitional period and a phased adoption of IFRS throughout the transitional period and at the changeover date.

In its strategy document the AcSB explained that its plans for converging Canadian GAAP to IFRSs include:

- adopting standards newly developed by the International Accounting Standards Board (IASB) that are converged with standards issued by the FASB, as these new global standards are issued;

- replacing other Canadian standards with corresponding IFRSs already issued, in accordance with a separate convergence implementation plan developed in consultation with affected stakeholders;
- working with both the IASB and the FASB to ensure that the Canadian perspective is taken into account in their deliberations; and
- working to promote the further convergence of IASB and FASB standards.

The changeover date for conversion to IFRS is provisionally set for 2011 with the new accounting framework being applicable for all reporting periods commencing on or after 1 January 2011. However, the AcSB continues to monitor events in Canada and internationally to identify whether there are any significant changes with respect to the factors that influenced its decision to converge with IFRS. This monitoring process will culminate in a progress review, the results of which are to be published no later than 31 March 2008 at which point the AcSB will set a definitive changeover date.

The adoption of IFRSs in Canada for publicly accountable enterprises will mean that the AcSB will effectively cease to make final decisions on most matters affecting the technical content and timing of implementation of standards applied in Canada. However the AcSB has stated that it will continue to assess and monitor the application of accounting standards. While the AcSB retains the power to modify or add to the requirements of IFRSs, it intends to avoid changing IFRSs when adopting them as Canadian GAAP. Accordingly, the AcSB does not expect to eliminate any options within existing IFRSs. As issues relevant to Canadian users of financial information arise in future the AcSB will work to resolve them through IFRIC – the IASB's interpretive body – and in the event that this is not possible, it will stand ready to develop additional temporary guidance.

6.4 China and Hong Kong

6.4.1 China

The developments in IFRS have been playing an important role in the development of accounting standards and practices in China. The Ministry of Finance (the MOF) – through its Accounting Regulatory Department – is responsible for the promulgation of accounting standards. In 1993, the MOF started a work programme to develop a set of *Accounting Standards for Business Enterprises* (ASBE). Before 2006, China had promulgated and implemented ASBE – *Basic Standard*, with 16 specific ASBE, as well as *Accounting System for Business Enterprises*, *Accounting System for Financial Institutions* and *Accounting System for Small Business Enterprises* which are applicable to various business enterprises.

Representatives of the China Accounting Standards Committee (CASC) – which falls under the Accounting Regulatory Department of the MOF – and the IASB met in Beijing in November 2005 to discuss a range of issues relating to the convergence of Chinese accounting standards with IFRSs. That meeting followed a series of CASC-IASB staff meetings in Beijing in October. At the conclusion of the meeting in

November, the two delegations released a joint statement setting out key points of agreement, including the following:

- China stated that convergence is one of the fundamental goals of their standard-setting programme, with the intention that an enterprise applying ASBE should produce financial statements that are the same as those of an enterprise that applies IFRSs;
- The IASB delegation acknowledged that convergence with IFRSs will take time and how to converge with IFRSs is a matter for China to determine.

In February 2006, the MOF issued a series of new and revised ASBE which included the revised *Basic Standard*, 22 newly-promulgated accounting standards and 16 revised accounting standards. The new and revised ASBE were effective from 1 January 2007 for listed companies. Other companies are also encouraged to adopt them.

The new and revised ASBE, to a large extent, represent convergence with IFRS, with due consideration being given to specific situations in China. The ASBE cover the recognition, measurement, presentation and disclosure of most transactions and events, financial reporting, and nearly all the topics covered by the current IFRS literature. Most of the new and revised ASBE are substantially in line with the corresponding IFRS. For instance, the requirements set out in the standards on revenue, income tax, financial instruments and consolidated financial statements are very similar to those in IAS 18 – *Revenue,* IAS 12 – *Income taxes*, IAS 39 – *Financial Instruments: Recognition and Measurement*, and IAS 27 – *Consolidated and Separate Financial Statements* – respectively. However, there are accounting standards that do not have an IFRS equivalent, such as that on non-monetary transactions, and there are a few standards with requirements that may not be entirely in line with IFRS. A notable example is the accounting standard on impairment of assets, which prohibits the reversal of an impairment loss. Another example is the standard on investment property under which the fair value model can be used only when certain strict criteria are met.

Although at present, only listed companies are required to apply it, the publication of the new and revised ASBE is an important milestone in the convergence process. Thus, although a few exceptions are still acknowledged in certain areas between local and international practices, the convergence process has begun to narrow the gap, particularly over the last few years when significant progress has been made.

6.4.2 Hong Kong

The Hong Kong Institute of Certified Public Accountants (HKICPA), a statutory body established under the Professional Accountants Ordinance, is the principal source of accounting principles in Hong Kong. These include a series of Hong Kong Financial Reporting Standards (HKFRS), accounting standards referred to as Hong Kong Accounting Standards (HKAS) and Interpretations issued by the HKICPA. The term 'Hong Kong Financial Reporting Standards' is deemed to include all of the foregoing. While HKFRS have no direct legal force, they derive their authority from the HKICPA, which may take disciplinary action against any of its members responsible, as preparer or as auditor, for financial statements that do not follow the requirements of the pronouncements.

In 2001, the HKICPA Council mandated a strategy of achieving convergence between its accounting standards and IFRSs issued by the IASB. HKFRSs were fully converged with IFRS with effect from 1 January 2005. The HKICPA Council supports the integration of its standard setting process with that of the IASB.

Although the HKICPA Council has a policy of maintaining convergence of HKFRSs with IFRSs, the HKICPA Council may consider it appropriate to include additional disclosure requirements in a HKFRS or, in some exceptional cases, to deviate from an IFRS. Each HKFRS issued by Council contains information about the extent of compliance with the equivalent IFRS. Where the requirements of a HKFRS and an IFRS differ, the HKFRS should be followed by entities reporting within the area of application of the HKFRSs. However in practice, exceptions to IFRSs are few and relate to certain transitional provisions.

6.5 India

The issue of convergence with IFRS has gained significant momentum in India. At present, the Accounting Standards Board (ASB) of the Institute of Chartered Accountants of India (ICAI) formulates Accounting Standards based on IFRS; however, these standards remain sensitive to local conditions, including the legal and economic environments. Accordingly, the Accounting Standards issued by the ICAI depart from the corresponding IFRSs in order to ensure consistency with the legal, regulatory and economic environments of India. However, it is worth noting that, in some cases, departures are also made on account of conceptual differences with the treatments prescribed in IFRSs.

Although the ICAI is the principal standard-setter, regulators have also set standards for their respective constituencies. The Reserve Bank of India formulates accounting requirements for banks; the Securities and Exchange Board of India, which regulates listed companies, formulates accounting requirements for mutual funds as well as presentation formats for quarterly disclosures by listed companies; it has also formulated accounting rules for employee stock options, which are required to be followed by all listed companies; and the Insurance Regulatory and Development Authority of India formulates accounting requirements for insurance companies. Financial statement presentation requirements are set out in the Companies Act, which also includes other accounting requirements, such as the minimum depreciation rate and accounting for foreign exchange differences.

At its meeting held in May 2006, the Council of the ICAI expressed the view that full IFRS may be adopted at a future date, at least for listed and large entities. The ASB, at its meeting held in August 2006, considered the matter and supported the Council's view that there would be several advantages of converging with IFRS. As a result, in view of the extent of differences between IFRSs and Indian Accounting Standards as well as the fact that convergence with IFRS would be an important policy decision, the ASB decided to form an IFRS Task Force. The objectives of this

Task Force were to: (i) explore the approach for achieving convergence with IFRSs, and (ii) lay down a road map for achieving convergence with IFRSs with a view to making India IFRS-compliant.

Based on the recommendations of the IFRS Task Force, the Council of the ICAI has decided to adopt a 'big bang' approach and fully converge Indian Accounting Standards with IFRSs issued by the IASB for accounting periods commencing on or after 1 April 2011. IFRSs will be adopted for listed and other public interest entities such as banks, insurance companies and large-sized entities.

6.6 Japan[134]

In August 2007, Ikuo Nishikawa, Chairman of the Accounting Standards Board of Japan (ASBJ), and Sir David Tweedie, Chairman of the IASB, jointly announced an agreement (known as 'The Tokyo Agreement') to accelerate convergence between Japanese GAAP and IFRSs, a process that was started in March 2005.

As part of the agreement the two boards will seek to eliminate by 2008 major differences between Japanese GAAP and IFRSs, with the remaining differences being removed on or before 30 June 2011. Whilst the target date of 2011 does not apply to any major new IFRSs now being developed that will become effective after 2011, both boards will work closely to ensure the acceptance of the international approach in Japan when new standards become effective.

Both the ASBJ and IASB share the belief that convergence towards high quality accounting standards will greatly benefit capital markets around the world. They therefore launched a joint project in March 2005 with the final goal of accomplishing convergence between Japanese GAAP and IFRSs. In their discussions in this joint project, the boards identified differences between the two sets of standards and have already made progress towards eliminating those differences.

The ASBJ and the IASB will proceed with the projects in the light of the changing environment surrounding global convergence of accounting standards and will enhance co-operation to facilitate greater input in the international standard-setting process from Japan. For this purpose, in addition to the joint meeting between representatives of the ASBJ and the IASB held semi-annually since 2005, both boards will establish working groups led by project directors in order to discuss further the major issues emerging in the development of accounting standards in a practical manner.

In September 2007, the ASBJ and the IASB held their first two-day meeting since the announcement of 'The Tokyo Agreement'. This meeting had two objectives: first, to review the convergence programme and the shared goal of eliminating major differences between IFRSs and Japanese GAAP by 2008, with the remaining differences being removed on or before 30 June 2011; and, second, to discuss the arrangements for the ASBJ to input its views into the IASB's current work programme. The discussions included a review of short-term convergence projects, where major differences are to be eliminated towards the goal of 2008.[135]

6.7 South Africa

All South African companies are required to prepare annual financial statements which are to be audited. For this purpose, companies use accounting standards issued by the South African standard setting body, the Accounting Practices Board (APB), which is in the process of being replaced as noted below.

In 1994 the APB made the decision to base future accounting standards on international standards. As a result, South African standards issued after that date were generally the same as the equivalent international standards, but with a few minor differences.

In 2003, the APB decided to remove the remaining differences, other than historic differences in effective dates, between IFRS and South African standards. Accordingly in 2004 all IFRS in issue at that time were adopted in South Africa.

With effect from periods beginning on or after 1 January 2005 the South African securities exchange, JSE Limited, required listed companies to prepare financial statements under IFRS.

The Companies Act, together with its Fourth Schedule and the stock exchange's listing requirements, has certain disclosure requirements that are additional to those contained in IFRS. For example, the JSE Listings Requirements require the calculation of headline earnings per share and disclosure of a detailed reconciliation of headline earnings to the earnings numbers used in the calculation of basic earnings per share in accordance with the requirements of IAS 33 – *Earnings per Share*.[136]

South Africa has issued its own interpretations on three issues, as a result of the IASB deciding not to issue opinions on issues that were considered to be specific to South Africa. These deal with an additional tax payable when dividends are declared, the meaning of substantively enacted tax rates and tax laws in a South African context, and accounting for black economic empowerment transactions – which deals with certain issues specific to these types of transactions that are not dealt with in IFRIC 8.

Amendments to the Companies Act were promulgated in 2007 and, at the time of writing (November 2007), these were in the process of being implemented. They make provision for legal backing to accounting standards and the constitution of: (i) a new standard-setting body, the Financial Reporting Standards Council to replace the APB, and (ii) another body to review compliance of financial reporting with accounting standards. Standards that will be issued by the Council for widely held companies, which include listed companies and their subsidiaries, are to be in accordance with IFRSs. In addition, the Companies Act amendments make provision for a separate set of standards for non-widely held companies, which was not previously the case.

7 WHAT CONSTITUTES INTERNATIONAL GAAP?

7.1 Generally Accepted Accounting Practice

It is clear that 2005 was a watershed year for IFRS with a significant number of countries adopting it as their principal financial reporting regime. However, to date, no substantial body of custom, practice or generally accepted ways of employing IFRS has had an opportunity to develop. Indeed, one of the challenges is to put in place a regime under which an 'International GAAP' that is understood and commonly applied throughout the world, can develop.

So what else has to happen before 'International GAAP' can be said to have emerged? The extra element, which only time, practical application, and the inevitable disputes and compromises can supply, is generally accepted practice. It will only be after a number of years of full implementation by a representative cross-section of businesses across all industries in a number of countries, that a consensus will emerge over the way that in practice, and in the context of real commercial transactions, IFRS is actually to be applied.

The term 'generally accepted' does not necessarily imply that there must exist a large number of actual applications of a particular accounting practice. For example, new areas of accounting that have not yet been generally applied may be accepted as part of GAAP. Similarly, alternative accounting treatments for similar items may be generally accepted.

It is our view that in the developing context of IFRS, 'generally accepted' will refer to accounting practices that are regarded as permissible by the accounting profession and regulators internationally – which means a broad consensus will come to exist between users, preparers, auditors, regulators and the markets, across rather than within national boundaries.

In general, any accounting practice that is legitimate in the circumstances under which it has been applied has come to be regarded as GAAP. The acceptability of a particular practice is normally determined by reference to one or more of the following factors, which may therefore be expected to apply as 'International GAAP' emerges:

- Is the practice addressed in accounting standards or other official pronouncements?
- Is the practice addressed in accounting standards that deal with similar and related issues?
- If the practice is not addressed in accounting standards, is it dealt with in the standards of another country that could reasonably be considered to offer authoritative guidance?
- Is the practice consistent with the needs of users and the objectives of financial reporting?
- Does the practice have authoritative support in the accounting literature?

- Is the practice consistent with the underlying conceptual framework document?
- Does the practice meet basic criteria as to the quality of information required for financial statements to be useful to users?
- Does the practice fairly reflect the economic substance of the transaction involved?
- Is the practice consistent with the fundamental concept of 'fair presentation'?
- Are other companies in similar situations generally applying the practice?

In an IFRS context, these factors build on the requirements set out in paragraphs 10 to 12 of IAS 8, which state that, in the absence of a Standard or an Interpretation that specifically applies to a transaction, other event or condition, management is required to use its judgement in developing and applying an accounting policy that results in information that is:

(a) relevant to the economic decision-making needs of users; and

(b) reliable, in that the financial statements:

 (i) represent faithfully the financial position, financial performance and cash flows of the entity;

 (ii) reflect the economic substance of transactions, other events and conditions, and not merely the legal form;

 (iii) are neutral, i.e. free from bias;

 (iv) are prudent; and

 (v) are complete in all material respects.[137]

In support of this primary requirement, the standard gives guidance on how management should apply this judgement. This guidance comes in two 'strengths' – certain things which management 'shall' refer to and consider, and others which it 'may also' consider, as follows:

In making this judgement, management shall refer to, and consider the applicability of, the following sources in descending order:

(a) the requirements and guidance in standards and interpretations dealing with similar and related issues; and

(b) the definitions, recognition criteria and measurement concepts for assets, liabilities, income and expenses in the *Framework*;[138] and

in making this judgement, management may also consider the most recent pronouncements of other standard-setting bodies that use a similar conceptual framework to develop accounting standards, other accounting literature and accepted industry practices, to the extent that these do not conflict with the sources in (a) and (b) above.[139]

7.2 Principles vs. Rules[140]

The question whether accounting standards should be principles or rules-based has been debated for decades. Views are often influenced by historical tradition, legal and regulatory environments and prejudice. However, with IFRS in the process of becoming the accepted global financial reporting framework, and with the growing emphasis on convergence between US GAAP and IFRS, this debate is once again at the forefront of the standard-setting agenda.

The distinction between the two approaches lies precisely where their respective descriptions suggest: principles-based standards are based on a clear hierarchy of overarching principles, contain few or no 'bright line' provisions and rely heavily on the exercise of judgement as to what constitutes fair presentation; rules-based standards are characterised by 'bright line' and anti-abuse provisions and allow relatively less scope for the exercise of judgement in their application. An example of this distinction lies in the requirements for lease classification under IFRS and US GAAP respectively, in so far as IFRS requires a judgement to be formed as to where the risks and rewards incidental to ownership of an asset lie, whereas US GAAP sets down a checklist of rules that must be applied in making this determination. This is not to say that IFRS does not also have rules-based standards, since IAS 39 is almost entirely rules-based.

In fact, IAS 39 provides an instructive example of the differences between rules and principles.[141] In accounting for the hedging of financial risk, a guiding principle might be that the performance statement should reflect the reduction of volatility achieved economically by the hedge. Intuitively, if a company has mitigated the effects of a particular risk – foreign exchange fluctuations for example – it makes sense that this reduction in volatility should flow through to the performance statement in the form of a neutral profit and loss impact (or something which is close to neutral depending on the efficacy of the hedge). It is interesting to note that IAS 39 does not embody such a principle. Rather, there are complex rules that determine whether or not it is acceptable to flow the impact of the hedge and hedged item through the profit and loss account in the same period; and, because the rules include onerous documentation and effectiveness testing requirements, profit and loss neutrality is an outcome that is effectively optional. In other words, if the hedge is not documented and/or the effectiveness tests are not performed, hedge accounting cannot be applied. As a result, it is perfectly possible for the performance statement to report volatility even though economically none exists because a company is hedged perfectly over the term of the hedged instrument. This state of affairs does little for either comparability or faithful representation, even though IAS 39 is so clearly a rules-based standard.

Whether or not IFRS develops into a truly principles-based system will depend largely on the attitudes and approaches of all the participants in the financial reporting process including standard-setters, preparers, auditors, users and regulators. Whilst US GAAP is clearly principles-based (though not based on the same principles throughout, which creates its own problems), it seems that the rules have grown over a number of years due to the demands of preparers and auditors for more detailed guidance and certainty, and the demands from regulators for consistency. There seems, therefore, to be a natural tension between the desire for comparability and the quest for a principles-based system,[142] and it is essential that IFRS does not suffer the growth of rules as US GAAP has. In our view, it is necessary to recognise that complete comparability is never possible in accounting. Instead, more emphasis needs to be placed on explaining the key judgements made by preparers of financial statements, including the sensitivities around those judgements. However, the danger for IFRS is that the demand for implementation guidance may increase as IFRSs become more widely applied and more detailed rules are called for.

Interestingly, the staff of the SEC seem to have come to the view that rules-based standards often provide a vehicle for circumventing the intention of the standards. In a report on the 'Adoption by the United States Financial Reporting System of a Principles-Based Accounting System', the SEC staff have recommended that those involved in the standard-setting process should more consistently develop standards on a principles-based or objectives-oriented basis. In the view of the SEC staff, an optimal accounting standard involves a concise statement of substantive accounting principles with few, if any, exceptions or conceptual inconsistencies in the standard.[143] In this report, the SEC staff made the following observations on the relationship between comparability and principles-based standards:[144]

'We believe that, overall, the movement to an objectives-oriented approach to standard setting should result in increased comparability in terms of economic substance. Indeed, the comparability arguably associated with a rules-based regime is often illusory. This is for four reasons.

'First, complex financial engineering stimulated by and designed to circumvent a rules-based regime reduces transparency and, correspondingly, may reduce genuine comparability of underlying economic circumstances.

'Second, a uniformity of accounting treatment may only result in a superficial kind of comparability if guidance is inappropriately rigid and thereby forces unlike arrangements into the same accounting treatment.

'Third, the clustering of underlying transactions on either side of bright-line rules associated with a rules-based regime results in different accounting treatment being given to arrangements that are fundamentally the same.

'Fourth, it should be noted, of course, that under an objectives-oriented regime, comparability can be achieved as long as there is transparency of method used through disclosure, albeit not necessarily at the same cost to the investor or analyst as under a rules-based regime.

'That being said, there may be some instances in which objectives-oriented accounting standards result in the loss of some degree in the precision of comparability of financial statements across firms and industries in some narrow application contexts, or at least render it more expensive to achieve comparability.

That is, in certain applications, the extra guidance and greater detail provided under a rules-based regime may result in a greater uniformity.'

This clearly highlights the tension between the advantages claimed for rules and those claimed for principles when it comes to how standards should be formulated. At heart, a principles-based system must be underpinned by a degree of trust in the participants, as well as rigorous enforcement. For example, the view is sometimes expressed that standards are set on the basis that Finance Directors or Chief Financial Officers cannot be trusted and need to be policed.[145] Whether or not this is the case, a pre-requisite of principles-based standards is that regulators have to be prepared to accept a range of judgement-based outcomes.[146] Regulators need to trust preparers and auditors, who in turn must be capable of exercising judgement in an appropriate manner. Acceptance of different judgements implies also that the IASB will need to review fundamentally the basis on which note disclosures are presented, and will need to place substantially more emphasis on the provision of information in the notes to the accounts that explains the judgements made by management, together with ranges of possible outcomes and sensitivity analyses. It may be necessary also for regulators and legislators to provide some protection for preparers and auditors against exposure to litigation in the event that disclosed assumptions fail to materialise.

7.3 Practical interpretations of IFRS

In 2005 IFRS became the global standard for financial reporting in the world's capital markets outside North America virtually overnight; therefore, significant questions of interpretation have inevitably arisen. Many of these will be issues of precedent and will have cross-border implications. The biggest challenge facing regulators is to ensure that national variations in the interpretation and application of IFRS do not emerge. Although IFRIC exists as the IASB's interpretations arm, IFRIC is neither able, nor should it be expected, to deal with issues of interpretation that will arise on a day-to-day basis. The need to apply due process and the need to avoid descending into a rules-based system mean that companies cannot expect either IFRIC or the IASB to provide immediate answers to every practical issue that arises.

In reality, the day-to-day issues of interpretation will be decided, initially, by company managements and their auditors. Thereafter, regulators may become influential to a greater or lesser extent. The role of IFRIC and the IASB will principally be to monitor the practical application of standards and, if deemed necessary, issue an interpretation or amend a standard in response to what they consider to be the development of unacceptable treatments or inappropriate practices.

This means that all those involved with the development of IFRS into a global financial reporting framework bear a considerable responsibility to ensure that the development is evolutionary and based on a broad consensus. For the EU in particular, cross-border consistency in regulation and enforcement is essential. Consequently, one of the interesting aspects of financial reporting during the next decade will be to observe how the process of acceptance and implementation of

IFRS across the world generally, and the EU in particular, develops. Put simply, it will be interesting to watch the emergence of 'International GAAP'.

7.4 Who 'owns' International GAAP?

The adoption of IFRS in the European Union as the single financial reporting framework for listed companies, combined with the move to IFRS in many other countries such as Australia, Brazil, Canada, China, India, Japan, South Africa and Switzerland, guarantees that it will not be long before the question of the 'ownership' of International GAAP arises, and who, therefore, is the ultimate authority when the inevitable differences of opinion and judgement occur.

This issue has a number of practical implications for companies applying IFRS; for example, what happens in cases where:

- different (and potentially conflicting) interpretations of the same standard are given by different regulators? or
- there is uncertainty about who has jurisdiction in cases of conflict between two parties on the question of the conformity of a specific set of financial statements with IFRS? For example, what are the roles of the national courts, the European Court of Justice, National Regulators, the IASB, IFRIC etc.?

There is, moreover, the possibility of an even greater level of uncertainty being created as the custom and practice that are an essential part of any GAAP begin to accrue. Hitherto, all standard setting bodies have been given their legitimacy by, and have operated within, national legislative frameworks; by contrast, the IASB is a private sector body, with no political accountability. In theory at least, all it does is set the standards; issues of compliance and enforcement are outside its frame of reference. There is no supreme legislative body or regulator that can decide, for all concerned with applying International GAAP, what does and does not constitute conformity with International GAAP. Rather, pronouncements, rulings, and interpretations issued by others outside the IASB organisation will inevitably become part of International GAAP, although in our view the IASB should make strenuous efforts to monitor and, where relevant, challenge these.

Therefore, it seems that it will only be a matter of time before the ultimate ownership and authority of International GAAP is tested. Paradoxically it may be that the more successful International GAAP becomes as a global financial reporting system, the more its interpretation, integrity and meaning will be disputed.

Perhaps in recognition of this, the IASB is now taking steps to protect the IFRS 'brand' by proposing, as part of its 2007 Annual Improvements Process (see 3.5 above), to insert in IAS 1 – *Presentation of Financial Statements* – disclosure requirements that will oblige entities to describe, in certain circumstances, the differences between IFRSs and the basis on which the financial statements that refer to IFRSs have been prepared.[147]

Paragraph 16 of IAS 1 (as revised in 2007) requires that 'An entity whose financial statements comply with IFRSs shall make an explicit and unreserved statement of such compliance in the notes. An entity shall not describe financial statements as complying with IFRSs unless they comply with all the requirements of IFRSs.'[148] However, an entity might refer to IFRSs in describing the basis on which its financial statements are prepared without describing those statements as complying with IFRSs. For example, the accounting policies may be described as being 'in accordance with IFRSs as adopted by/modified for use in [country X]'. In some situations, a financial reporting framework based on IFRSs and the complete set of current IFRSs may not be significantly different. However, in other cases, the differences may significantly affect the reported financial position or performance of an entity. Consequently, in the view of the IASB, references to IFRSs in describing the basis on which the financial statements are prepared may mislead users. Some users might expect there to be a close relationship between financial statements based on IFRSs and those in compliance with IFRSs. Furthermore, users may be unable to identify the differences between a financial reporting framework based on IFRSs and the complete set of current IFRSs.[149]

Consequently, the IASB is proposing to insert a new paragraph 16A into IAS 1 (as revised in 2007) that will require that:

'When an entity refers to IFRSs in describing the basis on which its financial statements are prepared but is not able to make an explicit and unreserved statement of compliance with IFRSs, the entity shall:

(a) describe each difference between the basis on which its financial statements are prepared and IFRSs that are applicable to its financial statements; and

(b) describe how its reported financial position and performance of the entity would have differed if it had complied with IFRSs.'[150]

In the Board's view, these disclosures would enable users to judge the usefulness of the information presented and the significance of those differences for the financial statements. The Board believes further that the disclosures would also help users to interpret those financial statements and assess their comparability with those of other entities.[151]

At the same time, however, it is interesting to note that the IASB is proposing to introduce these disclosures as part of its 'minor amendments under the first annual improvements project'. Whilst we understand fully the IASB's reasoning behind the inclusion in IAS 1 of the proposed new paragraph 16A, we believe that the proposals go beyond being a minor change of wording and have significant political implications for regulators and technical implications for companies. The issue as to how 'minor' these proposed changes really are is perhaps well illustrated by the fact that two Board members (Messrs Leisenring and McGregor) voted against the proposed amendments to IAS 1 and published the following alternative views thereon:[152]

'[Messrs Leisenring and McGregor] believe it is inappropriate to include a requirement in IFRSs for an entity to disclose that it has not complied with IFRSs. Such a requirement is, in their opinion, tantamount to condoning non-compliance with IFRSs and, as such, undermines the credibility of IFRSs.

'Messrs Leisenring and McGregor also disagree with the proposed disclosure requirement because they believe that the objective of including the requirement is unlikely to be achieved: in their view there is no reason to believe that entities that have failed to comply with other IFRS requirements will comply with this proposed requirement. Moreover, it is hard to imagine an entity disclosing that it has failed to meet this disclosure requirement.'

It will therefore be interesting to see the reaction that the IASB receives to these proposals from its constituents through the consultation process.

8 CONCLUSION

International Accounting Standards have come a long way in the 40 years since the establishment of the Accountants International Study Group by Henry Benson in 1967. When International Accounting Standards were first issued by the former Board of the IASC, some of them permitted alternative accounting treatments. The principal reason for this was that the IASC viewed its initial function as prohibiting undesirable accounting practices, whilst acknowledging that there might be more than one acceptable solution to a specific accounting issue. Today, the focus is on removal of options, consistency and comparability.

The European Commission's Regulation requiring all EU companies listed on a regulated market to prepare their consolidated financial statements in accordance with IFRSs means that the much-discussed notion of globally harmonised financial reporting under a single set of accounting standards is now a real possibility. Europe's decision has encouraged many other countries to adopt a similar path, and even the US SEC is considering whether or not to permit US issuers to prepare IFRS financial statements.

For companies, the requirement to adopt IFRSs has been far more than a technical exercise involving the reordering of information and rearrangement of the financial statements. It has fundamentally affected the way in which they present themselves to investors and other users of their financial statements. For many companies – and to the benefit of users – this has meant that there have been substantially increased levels of transparency – for example, through significantly expanded disclosures and the recognition of derivatives on balance sheets at fair value.

Ultimately, though, the most important challenge in financial reporting during the next decade will be to ensure International GAAP delivers financial reporting that investors and markets can understand and trust. This puts a great burden of responsibility upon all involved – the IASB, securities regulators, national governments, the European Commission and EFRAG, National Standard Setters, professional accountants, analysts, providers of finance, legal advisors and company managements – to work actively and selflessly towards this goal.

References

1 Joseph Stiglitz, *Globalization and its discontents*, Penguin Books, 2002, page ix.

2 Securities and Exchange Commission, 17 CFR Parts 210, 230, 239 and 249, [Release Nos. 33-8818; 34-55998; International Series Release No. 1302; File No. S7-13-07], RIN 3235-AJ90, *Acceptance from Foreign Private Issuers of financial statements prepared in accordance with International Financial Reporting Standards without reconciliation to U.S. GAAP*, July 2, 2007.

3 Press Release, *SEC Takes Action to Improve Consistency of Disclosure to U.S. Investors in Foreign Companies*, U.S. Securities and Exchange Commission, 2007-235, November 15, 2007.

4 European Commission, COM(1999) 232 final of 11.05.1999, *Financial Services: Implementing the Framework for Financial Markets: Action Plan, May* 1999.

5 European Union, *Regulation of the European Parliament and of the Council on the application of international accounting standards*, Regulation No. 1606/2002, 19 July 2002.

6 Chartered Accountants of Canada, Media Release, *Canada's Accounting Standards Board ratifies its strategic plan: Approves convergence with international reporting standards,* Toronto, January 10, 2006.

7 Henry Alexander Benson was a Chartered Accountant who was born and educated in South Africa. He served on the Council of the ICAEW between 1956 and 1975, and as President in 1966-67. He was advisor to the Governor of the Bank of England from 1975 to 1983 and served as Chairman, Royal Commission on Legal Services 1976 to 1979. In his Obituary published in *The Times* on 7 March 1995 it was stated that 'Few men outside Whitehall can have had more influence on public affairs in post-war Britain than Henry Benson. As senior partner in the firm of Coopers & Lybrand, he built up an international reputation as one of the most formidable accountants of his time.' Henry Benson died on 5 March 1995, aged 85.

8 Foreword to *Accounting and Auditing Approaches to Inventories in Three Nations: Stock in Trade and Work in Progress in Canada, the United Kingdom and the United States: a survey*, Accountants International Study Group, Institute of Chartered Accountants in England and Wales, January 1968.

9 IASC, *Preface to Statements of International Accounting Standards*, para. 2.

10 IASC, *Shaping IASC for the future: A Discussion Paper issued for comment by the Strategy Working Party of the International Accounting Standards Committee*, IASC, 7 December 1998, para. 2.

11 At the time of its dissolution on 1 April 2001, the IASC Board members were: Australia, Canada, France, Germany, India, Japan, Malaysia, Mexico, Netherlands, Nordic Federation of Public Accountants, South Africa, United Kingdom, United States of America and representatives of the International Council of Investment Associations (ICIA), the Federation of Swiss Industrial Holding Companies and the International Association of Financial Executives Institutes (IAFEI). The Indian delegation included a representative from Sri Lanka and the South African delegation included a representative from Zimbabwe.

Representatives of the European Commission, the United States Financial Accounting Standards Board (FASB), the International Organisation of Securities Commissions (IOSCO), and the People's Republic of China attended Board meetings as observers.

12 IOSCO Annual Report 2006.

13 IASC Board and IOSCO Technical Committee, *Joint Press Release*, Paris, July 9, 1995.

14 *The IASC-U.S. Comparison Project: A Report on the Similarities and Differences between IASC Standards and U.S. GAAP*, FASB, November 1996.

15 U.S. Securities And Exchange Commission, *SEC Concept Release: International Accounting Standards*, Release Nos. 33-7801, 34-42430; International Series No. 1215 Washington, 18 February 2000.

16 IOSCO, Report of the Technical Committee of the International Organisation of Securities Commissions, *IASC Standards – Assessment Report,* May 2000.

17 Press Release, *SEC Takes Action to Improve Consistency of Disclosure to U.S. Investors in Foreign Companies,* U.S. Securities and Exchange Commission, 2007-235, November 15, 2007. The SEC's reference to IFRS as issued by the IASB is significant, as it excludes those versions of IFRS that contain "local variations" to the official IASB text of IFRS.

18 IASC, *Shaping IASC for the future: A Discussion Paper issued for comment by the Strategy Working Party of the International Accounting Standards Committee*, IASC, 7 December 1998, para. 2.

19 IASC, *Shaping IASC for the future: A Discussion Paper issued for comment by the Strategy Working Party of the International Accounting Standards Committee*, para. 115 *et seq.*

20 The G4+1 was an informal grouping of staff members of the standard-setting bodies of Australia, Canada, New Zealand, the United Kingdom, the United States of America and the IASC. From time to time, the G4+1 published position papers on accounting topics of current interest. These papers did not necessarily reflect the official views of any of the standard-setting bodies represented. At a meeting of the G4+1 held in January 2001, the Group discussed whether its activities should continue given the imminent commencement of activities by the new International Accounting Standards Board (IASB) and agreed to disband and cancel its planned future activities.

21 Report of the IASC's Strategy Working Party, *Recommendations on shaping IASC for the future*, November 1999.

22 IASC Foundation Constitution, approved by the Members of IASC at a meeting in Edinburgh, Scotland on 24 May 2000 and revised by the IASC Foundation Trustees on 5 March and 8 July 2002 and 21 June 2005.

23 IASC Foundation Constitution, Article 6.

24 IASC Foundation Constitution, Article 8. To provide continuity, some of the initial Trustees served staggered terms so as to retire after four or five years.

25 IASC Foundation Constitution, Article 7.

26 IASC Foundation Constitution, Article 6.

27 IASC Foundation Constitution, Article 15(b).

28 IASC Foundation Constitution, Articles 13 and 15.

29 The IASC Foundation structure is depicted in this way on the IASB website at: www.iasb.org/About+Us/About+Us.htm

30 As part of the governance arrangements of the IASCF, the original Constitution required that the Trustees of the IASC Foundation should undertake a review of the entire structure of the IASC Foundation and its effectiveness. The Constitution specified that this review should commence three years after the coming into force of the Constitution, with the objective of implementing any agreed changes five years after the coming into force of the Constitution (i.e. 6 February 2006). At a meeting on 4 November 2003, the Trustees discussed the need to consult interested parties on the full range of issues raised by the Constitution, and agreed on various aspects of the review, including the procedures for conducting the review, the extent of consultation, staffing, and the issues to be discussed. On 12 November 2003, the Trustees announced that they had initiated a review of the Foundation's constitutional arrangements that govern the operating procedures of the Foundation and the IASB. In launching this, the Trustees emphasised that they were willing to examine any aspect of the Constitution and would be consulting a wide range of organisations. To coordinate the process, the Trustees established an internal committee (the 'Constitution Committee'), chaired by Paul Volcker.
Following extensive consultation, the Trustees completed the review in June 2005, and published a revised Constitution with an effective date of 1 July 2005.

31 IASC Foundation Constitution, Article 17.

32 IASC Foundation Constitution, Article 30.

33 IASC Foundation Constitution, Article 21.

34 IASC Foundation Constitution, Article 2.

35 International Accounting Standards Committee Foundation, Press Release, *Trustees announce strategy to enhance governance, report on conclusions at Trustees' meeting*, 6 November 2007.

36 International Accounting Standards Committee Foundation, Press Release, *Trustees announce strategy to enhance governance, report on conclusions at Trustees' meeting,* pages 1 and 2.

37 www.iasb.org/About+Us/About+IASB/About+IASB.htm

38 IASC Foundation Constitution, Article 20.

39 IASC Foundation Constitution, Article 19.

40 IASC Foundation Constitution, Articles 19, 21 and 22.

41 IASC Foundation Constitution, Article 31(a).

42 IASC Foundation Constitution, Article 30.

43 IASC Foundation Constitution, Article 31(d)(iii).

44 Due Process Handbook for the IASB, Approved by the Trustees March 2006, paras. 1 to 3.

45 Due Process Handbook for the IASB, para. 9.

46 Due Process Handbook for the IASB, para. 6.

47 Due Process Handbook for the IASB, paras. 18 to 51.

48 Due Process Handbook for the IASB, para. 110.
49 Due Process Handbook for the IASB, para. 111.
50 Due Process Handbook for the IASB, para. 112.
51 Exposure Draft of Proposed Amendments to IFRS 3 Business Combinations, IASB, June 2005.
52 IASB, Press Release, 'IASB takes steps to assist adoption of IFRSs and reinforce consultation: No new IFRSs effective until 2009', 24 July 2006.
53 Standards Advisory Council Terms of Reference and Operating Procedures, approved by the Trustees in March 2005, para. 1.
54 IASC Foundation Constitution, Article 38.
55 IASC Foundation Constitution, Article 38.
56 IASC Foundation Constitution, Article 39.
57 Standards Advisory Council Terms of Reference and Operating Procedures, para. 3.
58 *Enlarging the IFRIC:* Amendments to the IASC Foundation Constitution and Preface to International Financial Reporting Standards, International Accounting Standards Committee Foundation, April 2007.
59 *Enlarging the IFRIC:* Amendments to the IASC Foundation Constitution and Preface to International Financial Reporting Standards, Introduction and Invitation to Comment.
60 International Accounting Standards Committee Foundation, Press Release, *Trustees announce strategy to enhance governance, report on conclusions at Trustees' meeting,* 6 November 2007.
61 Due Process Handbook for the International Financial Reporting Interpretations Committee, International Accounting Standards Committee Foundation, February 2007, para. 2.
62 Due Process Handbook for the International Financial Reporting Interpretations Committee, para. 5.
63 Due Process Handbook for the International Financial Reporting Interpretations Committee, paras. 17 to 43.
64 Due Process Handbook for the International Financial Reporting Interpretations Committee, paras. 44 to 46.
65 Combined statement of the European Commission, the Financial Services Agency of Japan, the International Organization of Securities Commissions (IOSCO) and the US Securities and Exchange Commission, *Authorities responsible for capital market regulation work to enhance the governance of the IASC Foundation,* November 2007.
66 Statement by the Board of the International Accounting Standards Committee, December 2000.
67 IASB Press Release, *International Accounting Standards Board issues wide-ranging improvements to Standards,* 18 December 2003.
68 Chartered Accountants of Canada, Media Release, *Canada's Accounting Standards Board ratifies its strategic plan: Approves convergence with international reporting standards,* Toronto, January 10, 2006.
69 The Joint Working Group of Standard Setters comprised representatives from the IASC, the FASB and eight other international bodies. The purpose of the Group was to develop an integrated and harmonised standard on financial instruments – a task that they were unable to complete.
70 FASB and IASB joint Press Release, *FASB and IASB Agree to Work Together toward Convergence of Global Accounting Standards,* London, 29 October 2002.
71 Memorandum of Understanding – the Norwalk Agreement.
72 Memorandum of Understanding – the Norwalk Agreement.
73 Memorandum of Understanding – the Norwalk Agreement.
74 U.S. Securities and Exchange Commission, Chairman Donaldson Meets with EU Internal Market Commissioner McCreevy, Washington, D.C., April 21, 2005.
75 U.S. Securities and Exchange Commission, Accounting Standards: SEC Chairman Cox and EU Commissioner McCreevy Affirm Commitment to Elimination of the Need for Reconciliation Requirements, Washington, D.C., Feb. 8, 2006.
76 See FASB and IASB Press Release: 'US FASB and IASB reaffirm commitment to enhance consistency, comparability and efficiency in global capital markets', 27 February 2006 and 'A Roadmap for Convergence between IFRSs and US GAAP – 2006-2008: Memorandum of Understanding between the FASB and the IASB', 27 February 2006.
77 Securities and Exchange Commission, 17 CFR Parts 210, 230, 239 and 249, [Release Nos. 33-8818; 34-55998; International Series Release No. 1302; File No. S7-13-07], RIN 3235-AJ90, *Acceptance from Foreign Private Issuers of financial statements prepared in accordance with International Financial Reporting Standards without reconciliation to U.S. GAAP.*

78 Press Release, *SEC Takes Action to Improve Consistency of Disclosure to U.S. Investors in Foreign Companies,* U.S. Securities and Exchange Commission, 2007-235, November 15, 2007.

79 Securities and Exchange Commission, 17 CFR Parts 210, 230, 239 and 249, [Release Nos. 33-8818; 34-55998; International Series Release No. 1302; File No. S7-13-07], RIN 3235-AJ90, *Acceptance from Foreign Private Issuers of financial statements prepared in accordance with International Financial Reporting Standards without reconciliation to U.S. GAAP*, page 39.

80 Press Release, *SEC Takes Action to Improve Consistency of Disclosure to U.S. Investors in Foreign Companies,* U.S. Securities and Exchange Commission, 2007-235, November 15, 2007.

81 Securities and Exchange Commission, 17 CFR Parts 210, 230, 239 and 249, [Release Nos. 33-8818; 34-55998; International Series Release No. 1302; File No. S7-13-07], RIN 3235-AJ90, *Acceptance from Foreign Private Issuers of financial statements prepared in accordance with International Financial Reporting Standards without reconciliation to U.S. GAAP*, page 39.

82 Securities and Exchange Commission, 17 CFR Parts 210, 230, 239 and 249, [Release Nos. 33-8818; 34-55998; International Series Release No. 1302; File No. S7-13-07], RIN 3235-AJ90, *Acceptance from Foreign Private Issuers of financial statements prepared in accordance with International Financial Reporting Standards without reconciliation to U.S. GAAP*, pages 39 and 40.

83 Securities and Exchange Commission, 17 CFR Parts 210, 228, 229, 230, 239, 240 and 249 [Release No. 33-8831; 34-56217; IC-27924; File No. S7-20-07] RIN 3235-AJ93, Concept Release on allowing U.S. issuers to prepare financial statements in accordance with International Financial Reporting Standards, August 7, 2007. The comment date of this Concept Release was 13 November 2007.

84 Securities and Exchange Commission, 17 CFR Parts 210, 228, 229, 230, 239, 240 and 249 [Release No. 33-8831; 34-56217; IC-27924; File No. S7-20-07] RIN 3235-AJ93, Concept Release on allowing U.S. issuers to prepare financial statements in accordance with International Financial Reporting Standards, pages 12 and 13.

85 Prepared on the basis of: *IASB Work Plan – projected timetable as at 30 September 2007.*

86 IASB, Exposure Draft of Proposed Improvements to International Financial Reporting Standards, October 2007.

87 IASB Press Release, *IASB publishes proposals for minor amendments under the first annual improvements project*, 11 October 2007.

88 IAS 1, *Presentation of financial statements*, IASC Foundation, Revised 2004.

89 IAS 1, para. 14.

90 IAS 1, para. 14.

91 IASB, Exposure Draft of Proposed Improvements to International Financial Reporting Standards, pages 55, 57 and 60.

92 IAS 1, para. 13.

93 IAS 1, para. 15.

94 IAS 1, para. 15.

95 IAS 1, para. 16.

96 IAS 1, para. 17.

97 IAS 1, para. 18.

98 IAS 1, para. 19.

99 IAS 1, para. 21.

100 IAS 1, para. 16.

101 Study Pursuant to Section 108(d) of the Sarbanes-Oxley Act of 2002 on the Adoption by the United States Financial Reporting System of a Principles-Based Accounting System. Submitted to Committee on Banking, Housing, and Urban Affairs of the United States Senate and Committee on Financial Services of the United States House of Representatives, Office of the Chief Accountant Office of Economic Analysis United States Securities and Exchange Commission, Section III. Components of Objectives-Oriented Standard Setting, G. No True and Fair Override

102 Fourth Council Directive 78/660/EEC of 25 July 1978 based on Article 54 (3) (g) of the Treaty on the annual accounts of certain types of companies; Seventh Council Directive 83/349/EEC of 13 June 1983 based on the Article 54 (3) (g) of the Treaty on consolidated accounts.

103 Communication from the European Commission, *Accounting harmonisation: a new strategy vis-à-vis international harmonisation,* 1995.

104 See for example, European Commission, *Examination of the conformity between International Accounting Standards applicable to accounting periods beginning before 1 July 1999 and the European Accounting Directives*, February 2000; European Commission, *Examination of the Conformity between SIC-1 to SIC-25 and the European Accounting Directives*, February 2001. The full set of these comparisons may be found on the EC website:

http://europa.eu.int/comm/internal_market/en/company/account/index.htm

105 European Commission, COM(1999) 232 final of 11.05.1999, *Financial Services: Implementing the Framework for Financial Markets : Action Plan*, May 1999.

106 European Commission, *EU Financial Reporting Strategy: the way forward*, June 2000.

107 European Union, *Directive of the European Parliament and of the Council amending Directives 78/660/EEC, 83/349/EEC and 86/635/EEC as regards the valuation rules for the annual accounts and consolidated accounts of certain types of companies as well as of banks and other financial institutions*, PE-CONS 3624/01, Brussels, 22 May 2001.

108 Directive 2006/46/EC of the European Parliament and of the Council of 14 June 2006 amending Council Directives 78/660/EEC on the annual accounts of certain types of companies, 83/349/EEC on consolidated accounts, 86/635/EEC on the annual accounts and consolidated accounts of banks and other financial institutions and 91/674/EEC on the annual accounts and consolidated accounts of insurance undertakings.

109 European Commission, *Proposal for a Regulation of the Parliament and of the Council on the Application of International Accounting Standards*, COM(2001) 80, February 2001.

110 This means those with their securities admitted to trading on a regulated market within the meaning of Article 1(13) of Council Directive 93/22/EEC (on investment services in the securities field) or those offered to the public in view of their admission to such trading under Council Directive 80/390/EEC (co-ordinating the requirements for the drawing up, scrutiny and distribution of the listing particulars to be published for the admission of securities to official stock exchange listing).

111 European Union, *Regulation of the European Parliament and of the Council on the application of international accounting standards*, Regulation No. 1606/2002, 19 July 2002.

112 EU IAS Regulation, Article 9.

113 EU IAS Regulation, Recital 17.

114 EU IAS Regulation, Recital 11.

115 EU IAS Regulation, Article 3.

116 The term 'comitology' is essentially jargon meaning 'committee procedure'. It describes a process under which the European Commission, when implementing EU law, has to consult special advisory committees made up of experts from the EU Member States.

117 EFRAG, User Panel: Terms of Reference, 20 August 2006.

118 www.efrag.org/content/default.asp?id=4109

119 EFRAG, letter to Dr. Alexander Schaub, Director General, Internal Market, European Commission, *Adoption of the amended IAS 39 Financial Instruments: Recognition and Measurement.*

120 European Commission, Accounting: new Commission expert group to ensure balanced advice on accounting standards, Brussels, 17 July 2006.

121 European Commission Internal Market and Services DG, 'Consistent IFRS application: Roundtable'.

122 EECS refers to 'European Enforcers Coordination Sessions', which includes CESR members and non-CESR members who have competences in the enforcement of compliance with IFRS.

123 Commission of the European Communities, *Establishing the Committee of European Securities Regulators*, Commission Decision of 6 June 2001.

124 The Lamfalussy Report, *Final Report of the Committee of Wise Men on The Regulation of European Securities Markets,* Brussels, 15 February 2001.

125 The Committee of European Securities Regulators, *Charter of the Committee of European Securities Regulators*. The Charter took effect on 11 September 2001, and was amended in July 2006.

126 The Committee of European Securities Regulators, Terms of Reference on the Organisation and Functioning of CESR-Fin, 17 May 2006, para. 1.

127 The Committee of European Securities Regulators, Standard No. 1 on Financial Information: *Enforcement of standards on financial information in Europe*, CESR/03-073, 12 March 2003.

128 CESR Standard No.1, Principles 11 to 13.

129 CESR Standard No.1, Principle 16.

130 CESR Standard No.1, Principle 21.

131 The Committee of European Securities Regulators, Standard No. 2, *Co-ordination of Enforcement Activities*, CESR/03-317c, 22 April 2004.

132 US Securities and Exchange Commission: SEC and CESR Launch Work Plan Focused on Financial Reporting: Developing Cross Atlantic Financial Markets, Washington, D.C., Aug. 2, 2006.

133 Brazilian Central Bank, Communication 14.259/06.

134 Press Release, *The ASBJ and the IASB announce Tokyo Agreement on achieving convergence of accounting standards by 2011*, IASB, 8 August 2007.

135 International Accounting Standards Board, Press Release, *ASBJ and IASB make continued progress towards goal of convergence in accounting standards by 2011*, 2 October 2007.

136 The South African Institute of Chartered Accountants, *Headline Earnings,* Circular 8/2007, July 2007. 'Headline earnings' is an additional earnings number that is permitted by IAS 33. The starting point is earnings as determined in IAS 33, excluding certain *'separately identifiable re-measurements'*, net of related tax (both current and deferred) and minority interest. An example of an item that would be excluded in the calculation of headline earnings is any impairment and subsequent reversal of an impairment covered by IAS 36.

137 IAS 8 (Revised 2003), *Accounting Policies, Changes in Accounting Estimates and Errors,* IASCF, December 2003, para, 10.

138 IAS 8, para. 11.

139 IAS 8, para. 12.

140 This section draws heavily from 'Rules Not Principles – A Question of Judgement', The Institute of Chartered Accountants of Scotland, April 2006. This document was published by the Technical Policy Board of The Institute of Chartered Accountants of Scotland (ICAS). The views expressed in this document are those of the members of the Principles versus Rules Working Group and do not necessarily represent the views of the Board or of the Council of the Institute.

141 This example is taken from The Institute of Chartered Accountants of Scotland, 'Rules Not Principles – A Question of Judgement', page 6.

142 A view expressed also by The Institute of Chartered Accountants of Scotland in 'Rules Not Principles – A Question of Judgement', page 5.

143 *Study Pursuant to Section 108(d) of the Sarbanes-Oxley Act of 2002 on the Adoption by the United States Financial Reporting System of a Principles-Based Accounting System.* Submitted to Committee on Banking, Housing, and Urban Affairs of the United States Senate and Committee on Financial Services of the United States House of Representatives, Office of the Chief Accountant Office of Economic Analysis United States Securities and Exchange Commission, Executive Summary.

144 *Study Pursuant to Section 108(d) of the Sarbanes-Oxley Act of 2002 on the Adoption by the United States Financial Reporting System of a Principles-Based Accounting System.* Submitted to Committee on Banking, Housing, and Urban Affairs of the United States Senate and Committee on Financial Services of the United States House of Representatives, Office of the Chief Accountant Office of Economic Analysis United States Securities and Exchange Commission, Section V, Economic and Policy Analysis: H Comparability Issues.

145 See, for example, The Institute of Chartered Accountants of Scotland, 'Rules Not Principles – A Question of Judgement', page 10.

146 This is one of the 10 recommendations of The Institute of Chartered Accountants of Scotland, 'Rules Not Principles – A Question of Judgement', page 3.

147 IASB, Exposure Draft of Proposed Improvements to International Financial Reporting Standards, pages 55, 57 and 60.

148 IAS 1 (as revised in 2007), para. 16.

149 IASB, Exposure Draft of Proposed Improvements to International Financial Reporting Standards, page 60, BC2.

150 IASB, Exposure Draft of Proposed Improvements to International Financial Reporting Standards, page 57: proposed new paragraph 16A to be inserted in IAS 1 (as revised in 2007).

151 IASB, Exposure Draft of Proposed Improvements to International Financial Reporting Standards, page 60, BC3.

152 IASB, Exposure Draft of Proposed Improvements to International Financial Reporting Standards, page 62, AV2 and AV3.

Chapter 2 The quest for a conceptual framework for financial reporting

1 INTRODUCTION

There have been numerous attempts over many decades to define the purpose and nature of accounting. These are to be found in countless writings on accounting theory, the authors of which have considered many of the conceptual issues that require resolution in the development of a conceptual framework for financial reporting. Perhaps not surprisingly, most of the earlier studies were carried out by individual academics and academic committees in the US; for example, the writings in 1940 of Paton and Littleton[1] were intended to present a framework of accounting theory that would be regarded as a coherent and consistent foundation for the development of accounting standards, whilst the studies carried out over the years by various committees of the American Accounting Association have made a significant contribution to accounting theory.[2] In addition to the research carried out by individuals and academic committees, professional accounting bodies around the world have also, from time to time, issued statements that deal with various aspects of accounting theory. These can be seen as the first attempts at developing some form of conceptual framework, some of which are discussed later in this chapter.

However, the position today is very different from that which existed even ten years ago: with the globalisation of business and the increased access to the world's capital markets that goes with it, there are essentially only two global-scale systems of financial reporting – IFRS and US GAAP. As these two systems converge, it is logical to think that the development of a single agreed conceptual framework is a precondition for the convergence of the two systems. Whilst discussing the many international endeavours undertaken over the past 50 years in the quest for a conceptual framework for financial reporting, this chapter focuses on the existing conceptual frameworks of the IASB and FASB, as well as their joint project currently under way to develop a single agreed conceptual framework for global financial reporting.

1.1 What is a conceptual framework?

In general terms, a conceptual framework is a statement of generally accepted theoretical principles which form the frame of reference for a particular field of enquiry. In terms of financial reporting, these theoretical principles provide the basis for both the development of new reporting practices and the evaluation of existing ones. Since the financial reporting process is concerned with the provision of information that is useful in making business and economic decisions, a conceptual framework will form the theoretical basis for determining which events should be accounted for, how they should be measured and how they should be communicated to the user. Therefore, although it is theoretical in nature, a conceptual framework for financial reporting has a highly practical end in view.

1.2 Why is a conceptual framework necessary?

A conceptual framework for financial reporting should therefore be a theory of accounting against which practical problems can be tested objectively, the utility of which is decided by the adequacy of the practical solutions it provides. However, the various standard-setting bodies around the world initially often attempted to resolve practical accounting and reporting problems through the development of accounting standards, without such an accepted theoretical frame of reference. The end result was that standard-setters determined the form and content of external financial reports, without resolving such fundamental issues as:

- what are the objectives of these reports?
- who are the users of these reports?
- what are the informational needs of these users?
- what types of report will best satisfy their needs?

Consequently, standards were often produced on a haphazard and 'fire-fighting' basis with the danger of mutual inconsistencies. On the other hand, if an agreed framework were to exist, the role of the standard-setters would be changed from that of fireman to that of architect, as the framework would provide them with a basis for designing external financial reports that meet the needs of the user.

Perhaps the word 'agreed' is the key qualification in this argument. The IASB's conceptual framework was clearly derived from the FASB framework, which was developed much earlier. Not surprisingly therefore, the IASB framework (although substantially less detailed) has many aspects in common with the FASB equivalent. The resulting underlying similarity between the FASB and IASB conceptual frameworks is explained within this chapter. However, the way these principles are translated into detailed rules within the accounting standards issued by each of the standard-setters can result in very different financial reports.[3]

Furthermore, the existence of a given conceptual framework can be used as a lever to alter the basis of actual financial reporting towards the type of measurement base chosen in that framework – the full implications of which may not be understood by accountants generally. At times, also, standard-setters adopt strategies that are absent from their frameworks – the current policy of the IASB towards the use of fair values in asset and liability measurement is a case in point.

Equally, experience of the last thirty years shows that, in the absence of an agreed comprehensive conceptual framework, the same theoretical issues are revisited on numerous occasions by different standard-setting working parties. This inevitably sometimes resulted in the development of standards that were internally inconsistent and inconsistent with each other, or which were founded on incompatible concepts. For example, inconsistencies and conflicts have existed between and within individual standards concerning the emphasis placed on substance versus form; matching versus prudence; and whether earnings should be determined through balance sheet measurements or by matching costs and revenue. Some standard-setters have permitted two or more methods of accounting for the same set of circumstances, whilst others permitted certain accounting practices to be followed on an arbitrary or unspecified basis. These inconsistencies and irrationalities perhaps reflect the difficulty of determining what is 'truc and fair'.

There have been differences also in the tactics adopted by standard setters concerning how the tenets of a conceptual framework become realised in actual financial reports. There are significant differences between the tactics adopted by the FASB on the one hand, and the IASB on the other. In the US the FASB, in spite of its pioneering work on a conceptual framework, has also produced a large number of highly detailed accounting rules. Clearly, the proliferation of accounting standards in the US stems from many factors, including the legal and regulatory environment; however, a more satisfactory conceptual framework might reduce the need for such a large number of highly detailed standards, since more emphasis could be placed on general principles rather than specific rules. Indeed this change of emphasis has been specifically considered by the US authorities following the reporting problems that led to the creation of the Sarbanes-Oxley Act and the setting up of the Public Company Accounting Oversight Board in the USA. This is not to say that the more 'general principles' based IASB approach to standard setting is necessarily more satisfactory than the FASB's; rather that the legal and regulatory environment within which non-US businesses habitually work is quite different from that of the USA.

The political and economic environment not only influences the approach taken to standard setting, but also the nature of the conceptual framework on which standards are based. Following the European Union's decision to require listed entities to apply adopted IFRS in their consolidated financial statements and the widespread incorporation of IFRS into the national GAAPs of many other countries, the IASB is faced with a considerable number and variety of stakeholders. These different stakeholders are likely to express differing views on proposals issued by the IASB and will certainly want their views to be taken into account. Under these circumstances, an agreed conceptual framework is of great value, though standard-setters' best bulwark against undue interference in the standard-setting process is the capital markets' need for financial reporting that is a sound basis for decision making, which in turn implies relevance, reliability, practicality and understandability. While it is probable that these characteristics are more likely to be achieved using a sound theoretical foundation, the converse also applies: namely that the framework must result in standards that account appropriately for actual business practice and economic reality. Otherwise how, for example, is an industry to be persuaded that a particular accounting treatment perceived as adversely affecting its economic interests is better than one which does not?[4]

An agreed framework is therefore not the panacea for all accounting problems. Nor does it obviate the need for judgement to be exercised in the process of resolving accounting issues. What it can provide is a framework within which those judgements can be made. Indeed this is happening, as the principles expressed in the IASB's *Framework for the Preparation and Presentation of Financial Statements* are frequently referred to in IFRSs and during the process of their development. Unfortunately there is clear evidence also of the IASB issuing standards that contravene its own conceptual framework. For example IAS 38 – *Intangible Assets* – requires the capitalisation of goodwill as an asset, despite the fact that goodwill does not meet the definition of an asset in the IASB's conceptual framework. Similarly IAS 12 – *Income Taxes* – requires recognition of deferred tax assets and liabilities that do not meet the asset and liability definitions under the framework.

As discussed more fully in section 5 of this chapter, the IASB and the FASB are currently engaged in the development of a new joint conceptual framework. To date, only preliminary drafts of part of the proposed joint framework document have been published, together with discussion papers on measurement. The accounts of IASB discussions and the various documents that have been published so far, do not indicate that any radical new approaches are under consideration. They do, however, suggest that the IASB and the FASB are intent on widening the application of fair values in the valuation of both assets and liabilities within financial statements; this, in turn, is causing the two boards to change the way in which they articulate the objectives of financial reporting and the qualitative characteristics of financial reports that are needed to meet those objectives (see 5.2 below).

1.3 Accounting and the globalisation of economic activity

A further dimension to any consideration of the development of a conceptual framework must be the economic background to this process. Globalisation – the global interdependence, cultural homogeneity, integration of ownership and use, and depersonalisation of economic assets – is a term now frequently used, when even a decade ago it was relatively rare. The process of globalisation has been happening for centuries if not millennia – arguably since the first empires started to spread their core cultural and economic systems. However, it has now become obvious that since the 1960s the huge growth in telecommunications; the ease, speed and low cost of physical travel; the economic growth experienced by many countries throughout the world together with the spread of the 'western' business culture, has resulted in globalisation on an unprecedented scale.

Financial reporting has not been insulated from this process. As discussed below, during the last fifty years the development of a conceptual framework has increasingly preoccupied standard-setting bodies. To start with, these were mainly single-country initiatives, the first modern work being undertaken in the US in the 1970s and 80s. The FASB framework subsequently formed the basis of the framework developed by the former board of the IASC (which was adopted in 2001 by the IASB), as well as the frameworks of various national standard-setters, such as those of the UK, Canada, Australia and New Zealand.

Reflecting economic globalisation, the world now finds itself with only two principal sets of accounting standards: IFRS and US GAAP, a state of affairs that seemed unlikely even 10 years ago. With the benefit of hindsight it seems obvious that globalisation would require harmonisation of financial reporting; nevertheless the speed with which it has occurred has been remarkable, greatly assisted by the European Union's bold decision to harmonise financial reporting for listed EU entities under the IFRS umbrella. Furthermore, the integration process has not stopped, as in September 2002 the FASB and the IASB signed the Norwalk Agreement that commits both standard setters further to converge and harmonise their respective regimes. Since that time a number of IASB standards have indeed been (or are in the process of being) altered to align them with their US equivalents. The objectives and principles of the Norwalk Agreement have since been re-affirmed and elaborated upon in a Memorandum of Understanding that was entered into by the IASB and the FASB in February 2006 (see Chapter 1 at 3.3.3).

These developments illustrate the paradoxical nature of the search for a conceptual framework. The idea of a framework is to have a set of principles that guide the detailed requirements of individual standards, yet those principles are influenced by practical global economic and political reality. Ultimately, economic forces and the needs of the capital markets for useful information will be the context in which standard-setters operate. Arguably, their frameworks, or even as seems possible now, their framework, will always be as much practice into theory, as the reverse.

2 THE DEVELOPMENT OF A US CONCEPTUAL FRAMEWORK

2.1 Accounting Research Studies

The Accounting Principles Board (APB) of the American Institute of Certified Public Accountants (AICPA) was formed in 1959 to replace the former Committee on Accounting Procedure and the Committee on Terminology. During its existence, the Committee on Accounting Procedure had issued a series of Accounting Research Bulletins (ARBs). In 1953, the first 42 ARBs (eight of which dealt solely with terminology) were revised and restated as a consolidated ARB No. 43 and Accounting Terminology Bulletin No. 1; thereafter, a further eight ARBs were issued. The ARBs were supposedly aimed at the development of generally accepted accounting principles; however, the Committee met with considerable criticism over its failure to deal with contemporary accounting issues (such as leasing and business combinations), which could not be solved from precedents and required the development of accounting principles through pure accounting research.

As a direct response to this, the President of the AICPA set up the Special Committee on Research Program in 1957; in 1958 the Committee recommended the formation of the APB, and the appointment of a director of research with a permanent research staff. The Special Committee also recommended that 'an immediate project of the accounting research staff should be a study of the basic postulates underlying accounting principles generally, and the preparation of a brief statement thereof. There should be also a study of the broad principles of accounting. … The results of these, as adopted by the [Accounting Principles] Board, should serve as the foundation for the entire body of future pronouncements by the Institute on accounting matters, to which each new release should be related.'[5]

This, therefore, was probably the first mandate given by a professional body for the development of a conceptual framework. The AICPA appointed Maurice Moonitz as its first Director of Accounting Research; Moonitz started work on the postulates study, and appointed Robert Sprouse to work with him on the study of broad accounting principles. The products of the research were contained in Accounting Research Study No. 1 – *The Basic Postulates of Accounting*[6] – and Accounting Research Study No. 3 – *A Tentative Set of Broad Accounting Principles for Business Enterprises* – which were published in 1961 and 1962 respectively.[7]

These studies, however, caused a storm of controversy. Instead of establishing a sound foundation of accounting theory through rigorous argument based on deductive reasoning, Moonitz and Sprouse attempted to persuade the accounting profession to accept a new system of financial reporting based on current values. Furthermore, the realisation principle was discarded on the basis of the assertion that 'profit is attributable to the whole process of business activity, not just to the moment of sale.'[8] This was reflected, for example, in the statement that 'inventories which are readily saleable at known prices with negligible costs of disposal, or with known or readily predictable costs of disposal, should be measured at net realizable value.'[9]

However, the criticism that was levelled at these studies appeared to be based more on the fear of the unknown, rather than on any intellectual shortcomings. Consequently, they were viewed as being too radically different from contemporary generally accepted accounting practice to be accepted, and were rejected by the APB. This resulted in the commissioning of Grady's Accounting Research Study No. 7 – *Inventory of Generally Accepted Accounting Principles for Business Enterprises* – which was published in 1965 and which catalogued the various accounting methods that had been approved by ARBs, APB Opinions or some other precedent.

In all, 15 Accounting Research Studies were published during the life of the APB. However, following the rejection of ARS Nos. 1 and 3, the studies tended to be carried out on an ad hoc basis and without the support of a common foundation. Furthermore, the recommendations contained in the research studies appeared to have been largely ignored in the drafting of the 31 Opinions that the APB issued between 1962 and 1973. Consequently, generally accepted accounting principles in the US were continuing to be formulated without the benefit of research or the foundation of an agreed theoretical framework and, to all intents and purposes, the APB slowly resorted to the position of its predecessor, the Committee on Accounting Procedure.

2.2 APB Statement No. 4

In 1965 the APB made a further attempt to provide a basis for guiding the future development of accounting by establishing a committee to carry out a study that could be used as a basis for understanding the broad fundamentals of accounting. In 1970, the APB approved Statement No. 4 – *Basic Concepts and Accounting Principles Underlying Financial Statements of Business Enterprises.*[10] The statement contained a description of (1) the environment of financial accounting, (2) the objectives of financial statements, (3) the basic features and basic elements of financial accounting and (4) a summary of existing generally accepted accounting principles.

Therefore, it was (on its own admission)[11] a descriptive statement, not prescriptive. For example, assets and liabilities were defined as economic resources and obligations 'that are recognised and measured in conformity with generally accepted accounting principles',[12] which meant that the definitions failed to provide a theoretical basis for the development of generally accepted principles. As a result APB No. 4 was deficient as a theory of accounting and did not respond to the problems that were facing the profession at the time and which had been brought about by the inconsistencies and inadequacies of financial reporting practice.

2.3 The Wheat and Trueblood Committees

In 1971, in response to continued criticism from both within the profession and from the SEC about its inability to establish sound accounting principles, the AICPA announced the formation of two study groups: the *Study Group on Establishment of Accounting Principles*, to be chaired by Francis Wheat, and the *Study Group on Objectives of Financial Statements*, to be chaired by Robert Trueblood. The Wheat Committee published its report in 1972, resulting in the establishment of the Financial Accounting Standards Board (FASB) in 1973 as the successor to the APB. This had the effect of taking the responsibility for setting accounting standards away from the accounting profession and placing it in the hands of an independent body in the private sector. The FASB comprises seven members appointed by the Financial Accounting Foundation (FAF), and is funded by the sale of publications and from contributions made to the FAF. The Board of Trustees of the FAF is appointed by its eight sponsoring organisations, which include, inter alia, the American Accounting Association, the AICPA and two organisations which represent government.

The study carried out by the Trueblood Committee represents the next significant step in the attempt to develop a conceptual framework. In setting the terms of reference of the study group, the Board of Directors of the AICPA stated that the main purpose of the study was 'to refine the objectives of financial statements'.[13]

They went on to suggest that APB Statement No. 4 would be a logical starting point for the study, whilst at the same time noting that APB 4 'contains objectives in terms of what is considered acceptable today rather than in terms of what is needed and what is attainable to meet these needs.'[14] The study group was asked to consider at least the following questions:

- Who needs financial statements?
- What information do they need?
- How much of the needed information can be provided by accounting?
- What framework is required to provide the needed information?[15]

The Trueblood Report[16] was published in October 1973 and developed twelve objectives of financial statements. The principal objective was stated in the following terms: 'the basic objective of financial statements is to provide information useful for making economic decisions.'[17] Having established its twelve objectives of financial statements, the report then discussed seven qualitative characteristics which information contained in financial statements should possess in order to satisfy the needs of users.[18] As will be seen below, the Trueblood Report's objectives of financial statements formed the basis for the development of the FASB's first concepts statement, whilst the qualitative characteristics identified were amongst those discussed in the second concepts statement.

2.4 The FASB conceptual framework

The Trueblood Committee was at work on its report when the FASB came into existence. Consequently, the Trueblood Report was effectively passed on to the FASB for consideration, thus signalling the beginnings of the FASB's Conceptual Framework Project. The FASB duly considered the report and in June 1974 published a Discussion Memorandum – *Conceptual Framework for Accounting and Reporting: Consideration of the Report of the Study Group on the Objectives of Financial Statements* – which asked for comments on the issues raised.[19] A public hearing was held during September 1974, and in December 1976 the FASB published its *Tentative Conclusions on Objectives of Financial Statements of Business Enterprises*. In December 1976 the FASB also published a paper – *Scope and Implications of the Conceptual Framework Project* – which summarised its aims for the project, the expected benefits to be derived and the main areas which were expected to be covered.[20]

Following the criticism and eventual replacement of first the Committee on Accounting Procedure, followed by the APB, the FASB was seen by many commentators to be the last opportunity of keeping accounting standard-setting in the private sector. The FASB was clearly aware that accounting standards had to regain the credibility of public opinion which had been lost as a result of the many perceived abuses of financial reporting during the 1960s. The FASB referred to this lack of public confidence, and the possible consequences thereof, as follows: 'skepticism about financial reporting has adverse effects on businesses, on business leaders, and on the public at large. One of these effects is the risk of imposition of government reporting and other regulatory requirements that are not justified –

requirements that are not in the public interest because the perceived benefits do not exist or are more than offset by costly interference with the orderly operation of the economy. Skepticism creates adverse public opinion, which may be the antecedent of unjustified government regulation. Every company, every industry stands to suffer because of skepticism about financial reporting.'[21] The FASB, therefore, saw its conceptual framework project as the means of enhancing the credibility of financial statements in the eyes of the public.

The FASB also recognised that although there had been many attempts by individuals and organisations (such as the American Accounting Association) to develop a theory of accounting, none of these individual theories had become universally accepted or relied on in practice. They therefore expressed a need for a '*constitution*, a coherent system of interrelated objectives and fundamentals that can lead to consistent standards and that prescribes the nature, function, and limits of financial accounting and financial statements.'[22] The conceptual framework was expected to:

(a) guide the body responsible for establishing standards;
(b) provide a frame of reference for resolving accounting questions in the absence of a specific promulgated standard;
(c) determine bounds for judgement in preparing financial statements;
(d) increase financial statement users' understanding of and confidence in financial statements; and
(e) enhance comparability.[23]

To date the FASB has issued seven concepts statements, of which one (SFAC No. 4) deals with the objectives of financial reporting by non-business organisations and is beyond the scope of this book, whilst another (SFAC No. 3 – *Elements of Financial Statements of Business Enterprises*) dealt with elements of financial statements by business enterprises, and was superseded by SFAC No. 6 – *Elements of Financial Statements* – which expanded the scope of SFAC No. 3 to encompass not-for-profit organisations. The remaining five are discussed in the sections which follow.

2.5 The objectives of financial reporting

The first phase of the FASB's conceptual framework project was to develop a statement of the objectives of financial reporting. Clearly, some pioneering work in this area had been done by the Trueblood Committee (see 2.3 above), and this formed the basis of the FASB's first concepts statement. Nevertheless, it was not until 1978 that the FASB finally published this statement.

SFAC No. 1 – *Objectives of Financial Reporting by Business Enterprises* – starts off by making the point that financial reporting includes not only financial statements, but also incorporates other means of communicating financial and non-financial information; this may be achieved, for example, through the medium of stock exchange documents, news releases, management forecasts etc.[24] Having said this, the statement stresses that 'financial reporting is not an end in itself but is intended to provide information that is useful in making business and economic decisions.'[25]

This, however, is no new revelation; it is the type of broad generalisation that has characterised numerous previous attempts at establishing a conceptual framework. On the other hand, what it does do is raise all the same issues which the Trueblood Committee had been asked to consider seven years previously, such as: For whom is this information intended? What types of 'business and economic decisions' do they make? What information do they need to enable them to make these decisions? What framework is required to provide this needed information?

The statement details an extensive list of potential users, distinguishing between those with a direct interest and those with an indirect interest in the information provided by financial reporting.[26] The groups of user which have a direct interest include owners, management, creditors and employees; whilst user groups such as financial analysts and advisers, journalists, regulatory authorities and trade unions are deemed to have an indirect interest, since they advise or represent those who have a direct interest. However, having identified this wide range of users, the statement focuses on the information needs of investors and creditors. These are encompassed in the first of three primary objectives identified in the statement: 'financial reporting should provide information that is useful to present and potential investors and creditors and other users in making rational investment, credit, and similar decisions.'[27]

This objective leads to the first of the two most significant and far-reaching conclusions in the statement, namely that 'financial reporting should provide information to help investors, creditors, and others assess the amounts, timing, and uncertainty of prospective net cash inflows to the related enterprise.'[28] The statement articulated its reasoning behind this conclusion as follows: 'Potential users of financial information most directly concerned with a particular business enterprise are generally interested in its ability to generate favourable cash flows, because their decisions relate to amounts, timing, and uncertainties of expected cash flows. To investors, lenders, suppliers, and employees, a business enterprise is a source of cash in the form of dividends or interest and perhaps appreciated market prices, repayment of borrowing, payment for goods or services, or salaries and wages. They invest cash, goods, or services in an enterprise and expect to obtain sufficient cash in return to make the investment worthwhile. They are directly concerned with the ability of the enterprise to generate favourable cash flows and may also be concerned with how the market's perception of that ability affects the relative prices of its securities. To customers, a business enterprise is a source of goods or services, but only by obtaining sufficient cash to pay for the resources it uses and to meet its other obligations can the enterprise provide those goods or services. To managers, the cash flows of a business enterprise are a significant part of their management responsibilities, including their accountability to directors and owners. Many, if not most, of their decisions have cash flow consequences for the enterprise. Thus, investors, creditors, employees, customers, and managers significantly share a common interest in an enterprise's ability to generate favourable cash flows. Other potential users of financial information share the same interest, derived from investors, creditors, employees, customers, or managers whom they advise or represent or derived from an interest in how those groups (and especially stockholders) are faring.'[29]

In reaching this conclusion, the FASB was aware of the fact that it might precipitate an adverse reaction leading to the possible rejection of the statement through what might have been seen as an objective that would ultimately result in companies being required to present cash flow, management forecast or current value information. The FASB pre-empted this potential adverse reaction by stating that 'the objective focuses on the purpose for which information provided should be useful ... rather than the kinds of information that may be useful for that purpose. The objective neither requires nor prohibits 'cash flow information', 'current value information', 'management forecast information', or any other specific information. Conclusions about 'current value information' and 'management forecast information' are beyond the scope of this Statement. Paragraphs 42-44 [of SFAC No. 1] note that information about cash receipts and disbursements is not usually considered to be the most useful information for the purposes described in this objective.'[30]

The second fundamental conclusion reached in SFAC No. 1 that has far-reaching implications for the future development of accounting standards is concerned with the primary focus of financial reporting. During the early stages of the development of accounting rules in the first half of this century, the primary focus of financial statements was based on the principle of 'stewardship'. This arose from the fact that the management of an enterprise were primarily seen to be accountable to the owners for safeguarding the assets which had been entrusted to them, leading to a balance sheet emphasis in financial reporting. However, the focus has gradually shifted away from the notion of the balance sheet reporting on the custodianship of assets, to an earnings emphasis based on the principle that the income statement should present 'decision-useful' information. This is encapsulated in the statement in SFAC No. 1 that 'the primary focus of financial reporting is information about an enterprise's performance provided by measures of earnings and its components. Investors, creditors, and others who are concerned with assessing the prospects for enterprise net cash inflows are especially interested in that information.'[31]

SFAC No. 1 still recognises the fact that financial reporting should provide information about how the management of an enterprise has discharged its stewardship responsibility.[32] However, it goes on to say that 'earnings information is commonly the focus for assessing management's stewardship or accountability. Management, owners, and others emphasize enterprise performance or profitability in describing how management has discharged its stewardship accountability.'[33]

In other words, the statement is asserting that the measurement of earnings in the income statement should take precedence over the measurement of assets and liabilities in the balance sheet. This is an important principle which should have had an important impact on the principles laid down in the development of future accounting standards. However, as will be seen below, the FASB's subsequent concepts statements have essentially avoided the issue of how to determine net income. Furthermore, more recent statements issued by the FASB tend to suggest an uncertainty as to whether an earnings or balance sheet approach should be followed (for example, SFAS 109 – *Accounting for Income Taxes* – would appear to view the balance sheet as the primary statement).

This tension between income statement and balance sheet primacy has swayed towards the balance sheet, at least as far as recent IASB standards indicate. As is more fully described at 3 below, the IASB's conceptual framework adopts a balance sheet approach to recognition, whereby all the elements of financial statements are defined in terms of assets and liabilities, with the consequence that income recognition is a function of increases and decreases in net assets rather than the completion of acts of performance.

Consequently, despite the focus of the capital markets on performance measurement, the conceptual underpinning for financial reporting adopted by the FASB and the IASB appears to be focusing principally on the recognition and derecognition of assets and liabilities. Further evidence for this view is provided by the drafts published to date concerning the new IASB-FASB joint conceptual framework project, described in section 5 below. As will be seen also, both the FASB and IASB are seeking to marginalise the stewardship objective and establish decision-usefulness as the single objective of financial reporting.

2.6 The qualitative characteristics of accounting information

The FASB's second Concepts Statement – *Qualitative Characteristics of Accounting Information* – examines the characteristics that make accounting information useful to the users of that information. The statement views these characteristics as 'a hierarchy of accounting qualities', which then form the basis for selecting and evaluating information for inclusion in financial reports. The hierarchy is represented in Figure 1 below:[34]

Figure 1

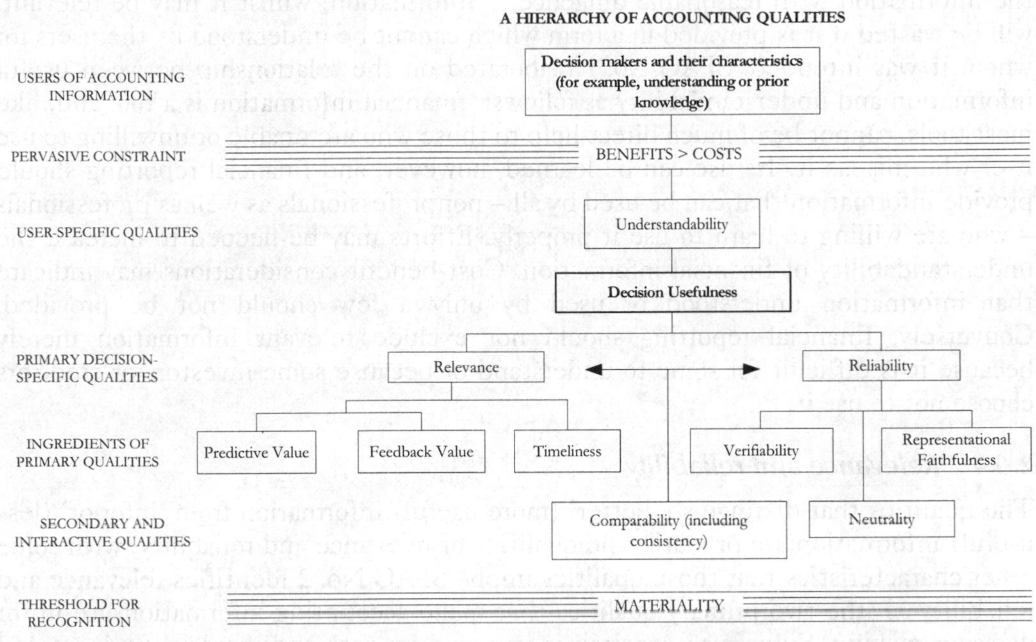

2.6.1 *The decision-makers*

The decision-makers (users) appear at the top of the hierarchy against the background of their own specific characteristics. Whilst usefulness for decision-making is the most important quality that accounting information should possess, each decision-maker has to judge what information is useful for a specific decision. This judgement would be based on such factors as the nature of the decision to be made, the information already in the individual's possession or available from other sources, the decision-making process employed and the decision maker's capacity to process all the information obtained.

2.6.2 *The cost/benefit constraint*

Since information should be provided only if the benefits to be derived from that information outweigh the costs of providing it, the cost/benefit constraint pervades the hierarchy. However, the application of this constraint may cause a certain amount of difficulty, since the costs of providing financial information are normally borne by the enterprise (and ultimately passed on to its customers), whilst the users reap the benefits. For this reason, the normal forces of demand and supply will not prevail in the market of financial information, since the external user will almost always view the benefits of additional information as outweighing the costs.

2.6.3 *Understandability*

The hierarchy depicts understandability as being the key quality for accounting information to achieve 'decision usefulness'. SFAC No. 1 stated that the information provided by financial reporting 'should be comprehensible to those who have a reasonable understanding of business and economic activities and are willing to study the information with reasonable diligence.'[35] Information, whilst it may be relevant, will be wasted if it is provided in a form which cannot be understood by the users for whom it was intended. SFAC No. 1 elaborated on the relationship between useful information and understandability as follows: 'financial information is a tool and, like most tools, cannot be of much direct help to those who are unable or unwilling to use it or who misuse it. Its use can be learned, however, and financial reporting should provide information that can be used by all – nonprofessionals as well as professionals – who are willing to learn to use it properly. Efforts may be needed to increase the understandability of financial information. Cost-benefit considerations may indicate that information understood or used by only a few should not be provided. Conversely, financial reporting should not exclude relevant information merely because it is difficult for some to understand or because some investors or creditors choose not to use it.'[36]

2.6.4 Relevance and reliability

The qualities that distinguish 'better' (more useful) information from 'inferior' (less useful) information are primarily the qualities of relevance and reliability, with some other characteristics that those qualities imply. SFAC No. 2 identifies relevance and reliability as 'the two primary qualities that make accounting information useful for decision making. Subject to constraints imposed by cost and materiality, increased relevance and increased reliability are the characteristics that make information a more desirable commodity – that is, one useful in making decisions.'[37] However, this was not new – the qualitative characteristics of relevance and reliability had been discussed in several preceding studies (such as the Trueblood and Corporate Reports). What was new (and probably the most significant aspect of SFAC No. 2), was the explicit recognition of the fact that 'reliability and relevance often impinge on each other'.[38] Consequently, whenever accounting standards are set, decisions have to be made concerning the relative importance of these two characteristics, often resulting in trade-offs being made between them.

In today's context, where standard-setting bodies seem intent on replacing the historical cost system by an income and measurement system based on fair values, deciding the relative weight to be attributed to relevance and to reliability when presenting information is increasingly pertinent. It is worth noting, therefore, that in their joint conceptual framework project, the FASB and IASB are proposing to remove reliability as a primary quality for decision-useful information. One possible explanation for this might be that the retention of reliability as a specific qualitative characteristic might be an impediment to the further extension of fair value measurement in financial reporting. This is discussed in more detail at 5.2.2 below.

A Relevance

SFAC No. 2 defines relevant accounting information as being information that is 'capable of making a difference in a decision by helping users to form predictions about the outcomes of past, present, and future events or to confirm or correct prior expectations.'[39] The statement further describes 'timeliness' as an 'ancillary aspect of relevance. If information is not available when it is needed or becomes available only so long after the reported events that it has no value for future action, it lacks relevance and is of little or no use.'[40] Therefore, in the context of financial reporting, the characteristic of timeliness means that information must be made available to users before it loses its capacity to influence their decisions. However, while timeliness alone cannot make information relevant, a lack of timeliness can result in information losing a degree of relevance which it once had.[41] On the other hand, in many instances there also has to be a trade-off between timeliness and reliability, since generally the more timely the information the less reliable it is.

The hierarchy identifies 'predictive value' and 'feedback value' as the other components of relevance on the basis that 'information can make a difference to decisions by improving decision makers' capacities to predict or by confirming or correcting their earlier expectations'.[42] Predictive value is defined as 'the quality of information that helps users to increase the likelihood of correctly forecasting the outcome of past or present events',[43] whilst feedback value is defined as 'the quality of information that enables users to confirm or correct prior expectations.'[44] Clearly, however, in saying that accounting information has predictive value, it is not suggesting that it is itself a prediction.

B Reliability

Reliability is the second of the primary qualities, and is ascribed three attributes in the hierarchy. The statement asserts that the 'reliability of a measure rests on the faithfulness with which it represents what it purports to represent, coupled with an assurance for the user, which comes through verification, that it has that representational quality.'[45] This definition gives rise to the three subsidiary qualities of 'representational faithfulness', 'verifiability', and 'neutrality'. Representational faithfulness is an unnecessary piece of jargon introduced into accounting terminology by SFAC No. 2; what it essentially means is that information included in financial reports should represent what it purports to represent. In other words, financial reporting should be truthful. For example, if a group's consolidated balance sheet discloses cash and bank balances, users would be justified in assuming that, in the absence of any statement to the contrary, the financial statements were truthful, and that these represented cash resources freely available to the group; however, if the reality of the situation was that the cash resources were situated in countries which had severe exchange control restrictions, and were, therefore, not available to the group, some might hold the view that the financial statements would not be entirely 'representationally faithful'.

It should be noted, however, that there are degrees of representational faithfulness. Because the financial reporting process involves allocations, estimations and subjective judgements, it cannot produce an 'exact' result; consequently, the trade-off between relevance and reliability will often apply, resulting in the presentation of information that is assigned a high degree of relevance, but which sacrifices representational faithfulness. An example of where this might apply is in fair value accounting for an acquisition, where fair values have to be assigned to the separable net assets acquired.

Reliable information should also be verifiable and neutral so that neither measurement nor measurer bias results in the information being presented in such a way that it unjustifiably influences the particular decision being made. Verifiability is a quality of representational faithfulness in that it excludes the possibility of measurement bias, whilst neutrality implies the provision of all relevant and reliable information – irrespective of the effects that the information will have on the entity or a particular user group.

2.6.5 Comparability

The hierarchy lists comparability as an additional quality that financial information should possess in order to achieve relevance and reliability. The quality of comparability includes the fundamental accounting concept of consistency, since the usefulness of information is greatly enhanced if it is prepared on a consistent basis from one period to the next, and can be compared with corresponding information of the same enterprise for some other period, or with similar information about some other enterprise.

2.6.6 Materiality

All the qualitative criteria discussed in SFAC No. 2 are subject to a materiality threshold, since only material information will have an impact on the decision-making process. However, the statement provides no quantitative guidelines for materiality, and it will be a matter of judgement for the providers of information to determine whether or not an item of information has crossed the materiality threshold for recognition. Materiality is closely related to the characteristic of relevance, since both are defined in terms of what influences or makes a difference to an investor or other decision-maker. On the other hand, the two concepts can be distinguished; a decision by management not to disclose certain information may be made because users have no interest in that kind of information (i.e. it is not relevant to their specific needs), or because the amounts involved are too small to make a difference to the users' decisions (i.e. they are not material).

However, if the preparers of financial statements are to decide on what to include in their reporting package, they must have a clear understanding of the users of their reports and their specific information and decision-making needs. In so doing, they should be aware of the types of information likely to influence their decisions (i.e. relevance) as well as the associated magnitude of this information (i.e. materiality). Consequently, financial reporting will focus generally on information that is regarded as relevant, and specifically on that which is material. The principal difficulty with this, however, is that the materiality thresholds of users vary from class to class and amongst individual users in the same class.

2.6.7 Conservatism

SFAC No. 2 includes an interesting discussion on the convention of 'conservatism' (i.e. prudence).[46] In so doing, it draws a distinction between the 'deliberate, consistent understatement of net assets and profits',[47] and the practice of ensuring that 'uncertainties and risks inherent in business situations are adequately considered'.[48] The statement recognised the fact that, in the eyes of bankers and other lenders, deliberate understatement of assets was desirable, since it increased their margin of safety on assets pledged as security for debts. On the other hand, it was also recognised that consistent understatement was difficult to maintain over a period of any length, and that understated assets would clearly lead to overstated income in later periods when the assets were ultimately realised. Consequently, unwarranted and deliberate conservatism in financial reporting would lead to a contravention of certain of the qualitative characteristics, such as neutrality and representational faithfulness. The new IASB-FASB conceptual framework project, discussed at 5 below, has further elevated representational faithfulness and downgraded conservatism as a qualitative characteristic of financial statements.

2.7 The elements of financial statements

SFAC No. 6 was issued in 1985 as a replacement to SFAC No. 3 having expanded its scope to encompass non-profit organisations. The statement defines ten 'elements' of financial statements that are directly related to the measurement of performance and financial status of an entity. However, the elements are very much interrelated, as six of them are arithmetically derived from the definitions of assets and liabilities.

2.7.1 Assets

Assets are defined as being 'probable future economic benefits obtained or controlled by a particular entity as a result of past transactions or events.'[49] However, the statement then goes on to say that the kinds of items that qualify as assets under this definition are also commonly called 'economic resources'. They are the scarce means that are useful for carrying out economic activities, such as consumption, production and exchange.[50] The common characteristic possessed by all assets is 'service potential' or 'future economic benefit' which eventually results in net cash inflows to the enterprise.[51]

The adequacy of this definition today is discussed in more detail at 5 below. Under historical cost accounting a non-monetary asset is no more than a deferred cost; a cost which has been incurred before the balance sheet date and, in terms of the accruals concept, relates to future periods beyond the balance sheet date, thereby justifying it being carried forward as an asset. This applies to all non-monetary assets that are recognised in an historical cost balance sheet – whether they be tangible fixed assets, stock, prepayments or deferred development expenditure. Consequently, there are certain occasions when items will be recognised as assets under the traditional historical cost system, but which will not fit the SFAC No. 6 definition of an asset. For example the spreading of certain pension-related expenses over the service lives of employees is seemingly in conflict with this definition because an unexpensed pension cost, if carried forward in the balance sheet, would fail to conform to the 'economic resource with future benefits' definition of an asset.

The selection of this definition has also embedded a deep-rooted problem within the FASB's existing conceptual framework. First, as far as SFAC No. 6 is concerned, since most of the elements defined in the statement are derived from the definition of an asset, any inadequacy in this definition inevitably affects the validity of the definitions of other elements. Second, in identifying the elements of financial statements before addressing the fundamental issues of how they are to be measured and on what basis of capital maintenance profit is to be determined, the FASB seriously limited its ability to address the issues of recognition and measurement properly. The result of this is that SFAC No. 5 – *Recognition and Measurement in Financial Statements of Business Enterprises* – has serious shortcomings (see 2.8 below).

2.7.2 Liabilities

Liabilities are defined as 'probable future sacrifices of economic benefits arising from present obligations of a particular entity to transfer assets or provide services to other entities in the future as a result of past transactions or events.'[52] The statement goes on to say that a liability has three essential characteristics:

(a) it embodies a present duty or responsibility to one or more other entities that entails settlement by probable future transfer or use of assets at a specified or determinable date, on occurrence of a specified event, or on demand;

(b) the duty or responsibility obligates the entity, leaving it little or no discretion to avoid the future sacrifice; and

(c) the transaction or other event obligating the entity has already happened.[53]

Thus, in terms of this definition, liabilities represent the amounts of obligations – giving rise to a problem similar to that outlined above in respect of the definition of assets. There are certain items which have traditionally been recognised as liabilities, but which do not meet the statement's definition. This is because they are deferred credits awaiting recognition in the profit and loss account, rather than obligations to other entities. This has led to quite tortuous methods of accounting for what are straightforward matters under traditional historic cost accounting.

2.7.3 Equity

Equity is defined as 'the residual interest in the assets of an entity that remains after deducting its liabilities.'[54] This is a somewhat tautological definition arising from the accounting equation that assets minus liabilities equals equity, but it avoids the potential problem of having non-equity items that are neither assets nor liabilities. Equity is, in fact, the sum of the equity investments made by the entity's owners, and the entity's earnings retained from its profit-making activities. Because of the way in which the definitions of the various elements are interrelated, it might appear to some that the FASB have taken the easy route in defining equity as net assets, rather than in terms of capital contributions plus retained earnings; a possible explanation for this might be that it enabled the FASB to define income in terms of changes in equity.

2.7.4 Investments by owners

Investments by owners are defined as being 'increases in equity of a particular business enterprise resulting from transfers to it from other entities of something valuable to obtain or increase ownership interests (or equity) in it.'[55] The statement goes on to say that although investments by owners are most commonly made in the form of assets, the investments can also be represented by services, or the settlement or conversion of liabilities of the enterprise.[56]

2.7.5 Distributions to owners

Distributions to owners are defined as 'decreases in equity of a particular business enterprise resulting from transferring assets, rendering services, or incurring liabilities by the enterprise to owners.'[57] Distributions to owners, therefore, incorporate all forms of capital distributions which result in a decrease in net assets.

2.7.6 Comprehensive income

Comprehensive income is defined as 'the change in equity of a business enterprise during a period from transactions and other events and circumstances from nonowner sources. It includes all changes in equity during a period except those resulting from investments by owners and distributions to owners.'[58] On its own, the term 'comprehensive income' is somewhat meaningless; for example, how does it tie in with the statement in SFAC No. 1[59] that 'the primary focus of financial reporting is information about an enterprise's performance provided by measures of earnings and its components'? Clearly, the FASB was keeping its options open by not defining earnings; in fact, it explained (in a footnote to SFAC No. 6) that whilst 'comprehensive income' is the term used in the statement for the concept that was called 'earnings' in SFAC No. 1, SFAC No. 5 had described earnings for a period as excluding certain cumulative accounting adjustments and other non-owner changes in equity that are included in comprehensive income for a period.[60]

The FASB issued a standard on this topic in June 1997, SFAS 130 – *Reporting Comprehensive Income* – however a generally accepted standard based on the concept continues to elude standard-setters. The IASB in 2003 decided to postpone its project to produce an exposure draft on the topic, and at the IASB-FASB joint meeting in April 2004 the joint boards gave every impression that the difficulties of defining and accounting for comprehensive income continue to remain formidable.

2.7.7 Revenues, expenses, gains and losses

SFAC No. 6 identifies the remaining four elements as those which constitute the basic components of 'comprehensive income':

Revenues, which are 'inflows or other enhancements of assets of an entity or settlements of its liabilities (or a combination of both) from delivering or producing goods, rendering services, or other activities that constitute the entity's ongoing major central operations.'[61]

Expenses, which are 'outflows or other using up of assets or incurrences of liabilities (or a combination of both) from delivering or producing goods, rendering services, or carrying out other activities that constitute the entity's ongoing major or central operations.'[62]

Gains, which are 'increases in equity (net assets) from peripheral or incidental transactions of an entity and from all other transactions and other events and circumstances affecting the entity except those that result from revenues or investments by owners.'[63]

Losses, which are 'decreases in equity (net assets) from peripheral or incidental transactions of an entity and from all other transactions and other events and circumstances affecting the entity except those that result from expenses or distributions to owners.'[64]

Therefore, comprehensive income equals revenues minus expenses plus gains minus losses; however, although the statement states that revenues, expenses, gains and losses can be combined in various ways to obtain various measures of enterprise performance,[65] it fails to define net income.

The difficulty surrounding the FASB's definitions of the ten elements is that they are so interrelated, that in attempting to piece them together into a meaningful accounting framework, one gets caught up in a tautology of terms which all lead back to the definitions of assets and liabilities. Essentially, what the FASB is saying is that assets minus liabilities equals equity and comprehensive income equals changes in equity (excluding transactions with owners), therefore comprehensive income equals the change in net assets. Consequently, the definition of comprehensive income would incorporate items such as capital contributions from non-owners, government grants for capital expenditure and unrealised holding gains. This would be all very well, if the issues of measurement and capital maintenance had already been settled. However, this is not the case, with the result that the FASB is either restricting itself in the future development of different accounting models for different purposes, or it might have to develop different definitions of the elements of financial statements as different models are developed.

In fact it now seems that the FASB and IASB have concluded that the definitions of the elements of financial statements are, indeed, deficient and require reconsideration. This view was confirmed by the IASB announcement in July 2001 that it has placed the definitions of the elements of financial statements on its agenda of technical projects. Further confirmation is provided by the decision taken at the April 2004 FASB/IASB joint board meeting to begin work on a new conceptual framework project, Phase B of which will deal with elements.

2.8 Recognition and measurement

Throughout the framework project, the FASB had avoided dealing with certain fundamental issues on the basis that they were the 'subject of another project'.[66] The result was the publication in December 1984 of SFAC No. 5 which attempted to deal with all the previously unresolved issues. However, the statement was somewhat inconclusive – possibly as a consequence of both its self-imposed restrictions discussed above, and the need to reach compromises in order to complete this phase of the project. The statement tends to describe practices current at the time, rather than indicate preferences or propose improvements; for example, in dealing with the issue of measurement attributes, the statement merely states that 'items currently reported in financial statements are measured by different attributes, depending on the nature of the item and the relevance and reliability of the attribute measured.'[67] Then, instead of either prescribing a particular measurement attribute, or discussing the circumstances under which particular attributes should apply, the statement discusses five different attributes which 'are used in present practice' – historical cost, current cost, current market value, net realisable value and present value of future cash flows – and concludes that 'the use of different attributes will continue'.[68] Furthermore, the statement fails to prescribe a particular concept of capital maintenance that should be adopted by an entity, although the FASB bases its discussions on the concept of financial capital maintenance.[69]

The statement defines recognition as 'the process of formally recording or incorporating an item into the financial statements of an entity as an asset, liability, revenue, expense, or the like.'[70] It goes on to discuss four 'fundamental recognition criteria' which any item should meet in order for it to be recognised in the financial statements of an entity. These criteria, which are subject to a cost-benefit constraint and a materiality threshold, are described as follows:

Definitions – the item meets the definition of an element of financial statements.

Measurability – the item has a relevant attribute measurable with sufficient reliability.

Relevance – the information about the item is capable of making a difference in user decisions.

Reliability – the information is representationally faithful, verifiable and neutral.[71]

Although it was probably worth setting out these criteria, they are no more than an encapsulation of certain criteria already contained in Concepts Statements 2 and 6.

SFAC No. 5 does make some progress in distinguishing between comprehensive income, earnings and net income. It states that the concept of earnings is similar to net income in present practice, and that a statement of earnings will be much like a present income statement, although 'earnings' does not include the cumulative effect of certain accounting adjustments of earlier periods that are recognised in the current period.[72] However, the statement goes on to say that the FASB 'expects the concept of earnings to be subject to the process of gradual change or evolution that has characterised the development of net income.'[73] Whilst many would agree with the principle that gradual change is the best approach towards gaining general acceptance, one of the problems with SFAC No. 5 is that the FASB does not indicate what it considers to be the desirable direction for this gradual change to follow. Furthermore, the FASB seems to be saying that concepts will evolve as accounting standards are developed – instead of the other way around.

In an evaluation of the FASB's conceptual framework, Professor David Solomons (who, incidentally, was the principal author of SFAC No. 2) took a distinctly critical view of this 'evolutionary' view of the emergence of concepts, stating the following: 'These appeals to evolution should be seen as what they are – a cop-out. If all that is needed to improve our accounting model is reliance on evolution … why was an expensive and protracted conceptual framework project necessary in the first place? … And, for that matter, if progress is simply a matter of waiting for evolution, who needs the FASB?'[74] Professor Solomons came to the following conclusions about SFAC No. 5: 'Under a rigorous grading system I would give Concepts Statement No. 5 an F and require the board to take the course over again – that is, to scrap the statement and start afresh.'[75] This led Solomons to conclude ultimately that 'my judgment of the project as a whole must be that it has failed.'[76]

Interestingly, the FASB's own special report on its conceptual framework makes the point that although SFAC No. 5's name implies that it gives conceptual guidance on recognition and measurement, its conceptual contributions to financial reporting are not really in those areas.[77] The report goes on to say that 'as a result of compromises necessary to issue it, much of Concepts Statement 5 merely describes present practice and some of the reasons that have been used to support or explain it but provides little or no conceptual basis for analyzing and attempting to resolve the controversial issues of recognition and measurement about which accountants have disagreed for years.'[78] The concluding sentence of the FASB's report sums up elegantly the views that have long been expressed by critics of SFAC No. 5: 'Concepts Statement 5 does make some noteworthy conceptual contributions – they are just not on recognition and measurement.'[79]

2.9 Using cash flow information in accounting measurements (discounting)

In February 2000 the FASB issued a new Statement of Financial Accounting Concepts, SFAC 7 – *Using cash flow information and present value in accounting measurements*. The finalised statement resulted from drafts published in 1999 and 1997. The purpose of the statement is to provide a framework for using future cash flows as the basis for accounting measurement. It aims to provide general principles governing the use of present value, especially when the amounts of future cash flows and/or their timing are uncertain. The proposals are limited to issues of measurement and do not address recognition questions.

Present values are used to incorporate the time value of money in a measurement. In their simplest form, present value techniques capture the amount that an entity demands (or that others demand from it) for money that it will receive (or pay) in the future.[80] The FASB's objective of using present value in an accounting measurement is to capture, to the extent possible, the economic difference between sets of estimated future cash flows, taking into account their uncertainty as well as their timing differences. Normal discounting distinguishes between a cash flow of €1,000 due in one day and a cash flow of €1,000 due in ten years, although both have an undiscounted measurement of €1,000. SFAC 7 seeks to distinguish additionally between cash flows based upon their different risks. For example to distinguish between two identical inflows due in (say) five years time, but which have different risks attached to them because of the relative uncertainties of their being received. Consequently, SFAC 7 postulates that a present value measurement which incorporates the uncertainty in estimated future cash flows always provides more relevant information than a measurement based on the undiscounted sum of those cash flows or a discounted measurement that ignores uncertainty.[81]

Any combination of cash flows and interest rates could be used to compute a present value, at least in the broadest sense of the term. However, present value is not an end in itself. Simply applying an arbitrary interest rate to a series of cash flows provides limited information to financial statement users, and may mislead rather than assist. To provide relevant information in financial reporting, present value must represent some observable measurement attribute of assets or liabilities. The statement identifies the following characteristics of a present value measurement that would capture fully the economic differences between various future cash flows:

- An estimate of the future cash flow;
- Expectations about possible variations in amount or timing of those cash flows;
- The time value of money, represented by the risk free rate of interest;
- The price for bearing the uncertainty inherent in the asset or liability;
- Other, sometimes unidentifiable, factors including illiquidity and market imperfections.[82]

SFAC 7 selects fair value as the sole measurement attribute that incorporates all the above aspects, and rejects the possible alternatives of value in use, effective settlement and cost-accumulation as being less satisfactory. The FASB holds that each of the rejected measurement attributes (a) adds factors that are not contemplated in the price of a market transaction for the asset or liability in question, (b) inserts assumptions made by the entity's management in the place of those the market would make, and/or (c) excludes factors that would be contemplated in the price of a market transaction. Consequently fair value represents a price and, as such, provides an unambiguous objective for the development of the cash flows and interest rates used in present value measurement.[83]

The statement sets out the following four general principles that, it considers, govern any application of present value techniques in measuring assets:

- To the extent possible, estimated cash flows and interest rates should reflect assumptions about all future events and uncertainties that would be considered in deciding whether to acquire an asset or group of assets in an arm's-length transaction for cash;
- Interest rates used to discount cash flows should reflect assumptions that are consistent with those inherent in the estimated cash flows. Otherwise, the effect of some assumptions will be double counted or ignored. For example, an interest rate of 12 per cent might be applied to contractual cash flows of a loan. That rate reflects expectations about future defaults from loans with particular characteristics. That same 12 per cent rate should not be used to discount expected cash flows because those cash flows already reflect assumptions about future defaults;
- Estimated cash flows and interest rates should be free from both bias and factors unrelated to the asset or group of assets in question. For example,

deliberately understating estimated net cash flows to enhance the apparent future profitability of an asset introduces a bias into the measurement;

- Estimated cash flows or interest rates should reflect the range of possible outcomes rather than a single most likely, minimum, or maximum possible amount.[84]

The stance adopted by SFAC 7 on the measurement of liabilities is consistent with its conclusion on assets. Thus fair value is the single measurement objective when present value is to be used in measuring liabilities, although the statement is not particularly specific as to how fair value is to be determined, stating that the measurement of liabilities 'may require different techniques in arriving at fair value'. However it does state that the objective of using present value techniques to estimate the fair value of a liability is to estimate the value of assets required currently to (a) settle the liability or (b) transfer the liability to an entity of comparable credit standing.[85] The difficulty of defining and identifying fair value remains a problem for any conceptual framework that relies upon the notion, and is further discussed at 3 below in relation to the IASB's framework.

The most significant element of SFAC 7 as concerns liabilities, centres around the incorporation of the entity's own credit standing into the measurement. Fair value in settlement as described above implies that the credit standing of the entity must be taken into account in arriving at the fair value of its liabilities. Accordingly, the fair value in settlement of an entity's liability should assume settlement with an entity of comparable, rather than superior, credit standing. Consequently, as the entity's credit standing affects the interest rate at which it borrows in the market place, it therefore affects the fair value of its liabilities.

This view entails the FASB adopting a quite complex form of discounting in SFAC 7, to facilitate which it has defined for its purposes a number of terms that are not necessarily used in their normal everyday sense. Instead of discounting the best estimate of any future cash flow (i.e. the most likely amount), the statement insists that the 'expected' cash flows should be discounted. The 'expected' cash flow to be used is defined as the sum of probability-weighted amounts in a range of possible estimated amounts.[86] Therefore, SFAC 7 requires the estimation of the likelihood of a range of outcomes (for example, for the repayment of a debt); the probability weighting of each; the calculation of each probability weighted amount; their summation and finally the calculation of the present value of that derived total. The statement does not define the rate to be used in any discounting but appears to indicate that a risk free rate is often the appropriate rate to use.

The statement implies a number of practical results, which many will find odd. For instance the fair valuation of warranty obligations, if not calculated on a cost accumulation (incremental) basis, could result in the liability being overstated. It is probable that the market's rate for performing warranty work would involve overhead costs not incurred by the entity itself, which would incur only incremental costs. This could result in the understatement of current profits and the overstatement of subsequent ones, as the extra cost factored into the (market price based) fair value warranty obligations and charged as an expense at the time of sale, was subsequently written back (usually referred to as 'unwound').

The inclusion of the credit standing of entities in the calculations can produce unwanted results. The lower the credit rating of a business, the higher the interest rate it will have to pay. Therefore, after discounting, the obligation of a low credit rated firm (using the higher discount rate its higher borrowing rate implies) will produce a lower net present value than that of a firm with an identical obligation and a better credit rating. This produces the extraordinary result whereby a poorer credit-rated, less safe firm, shows a significantly lower liability than a higher rated, safer firm – despite the fact that both have an identical settlement payment to make. Nevertheless, this is the position that the IASB has taken in its standard on the recognition and measurement of financial instruments, IAS 39 – *Financial Instruments: Recognition and Measurement*. This standard requires that, in determining the fair value of its liabilities, an entity should take account of its own credit risk.[87]

All in all, SFAC 7 comes across as no more than an overview of the issues surrounding the use of present values in accounting measurement. In spite of choosing fair values as the sole allowable measurement base, it leaves the door open to a fairly wide range of discounting practices, which can be applied as and when the FASB so decides. It is unfortunate that the statement contains no explanation in plain English of what its practical ramifications are and where, if it were to be adopted, financial reporting would be heading. It is therefore possible that the FASB has deliberately adopted a SFAC that will seemingly provide conceptual support for the introduction of an ever widening variety of discounting practices into US financial reporting, and further extend the notion of fair value.

2.10 Concluding remarks on the FASB conceptual framework

In order to be able to assess the success or failure of the FASB's conceptual framework project, one must refer back to the originally perceived benefits of the project and evaluate whether or not any of them has been achieved (see 2.4 above). Perhaps the acid test may be found in analysing the extent to which the FASB has used the framework in the development of accounting standards. Possibly the best example of where the framework has been used as the basis for an accounting standard is in the development of SFAS 95 – *Statement of Cash Flows* – however, this is clearly the exception. An analysis of the Appendices headed 'Basis for Conclusions' in the more recently issued SFASs, reveals few references to the fact that the members of the FASB have used the concepts statements to guide their thinking – and where reference is made it is generally to broad objectives or qualitative characteristics. On the other hand, it might be argued that the concepts statements have guided the thinking of FASB members without it being expressly stated. However, if this were the case, why is it that the FASB has, for example, issued a statement on reporting comprehensive income (SFAS 130) that seemingly lacks any conceptual integrity and is in conflict with the framework? The same might be said of the standard on deferred tax (SFAS 109) that similarly lacks any discernible conceptual underpinning.

The weakness of the FASB's conceptual framework project may be attributed to a number of factors; however, the most significant reason will probably be shown to be the Board's failure to deal with the fundamental issues of recognition and measurement. To a certain extent, the FASB has fallen into the same trap as the AICPA did in APB Statement No. 4, in that SFAC No. 5 is a descriptive rather than a prescriptive statement; a statement of accounting concepts should provide a frame of reference for the formulation of financial reporting practice, and not be a description of what current reporting practices are. In the words of Professor Stephen Zeff, 'the FASB's conceptual framework failed to fulfil expectations that it might constitute a powerful intellectual force for improving financial reporting.'[88]

Underlying the entire issue of developing a conceptual framework is the unspoken yet pervasive view of the project's authors that the logical structure for the framework should be a highly deductive one whereby the entire schema follows from a number of definitional assertions. To the practically minded accountant the problem of (for instance) ensuring worthless research and development expenditure is not carried forward, is one of determining whether the expenditure in question is likely to result in profitable sales in the future. By contrast, this precise problem is cited in the FASB special report as a prime reason for adopting a definition that excludes all deferred charges. This desire for an entirely deductive system amounts to a view of what accounting is that may not coincide with reality. Accounting is an activity born out of the needs of society (principally the needs of industrialised nations) that responds to those needs as and when conditions alter. The fact that the framework project has not obviously impinged upon the thinking behind a number of standards seems to be evidence for this view. It may not be a fault that accounting lacks a set of principles that accurately and inescapably predict the future in the way that scientific laws do; rather it may be a necessary attribute of accounting continuing to be useful to society.[89]

This is not to say that the FASB's project has been ineffective; it contains some outstanding work, particularly in the area of qualitative characteristics, and has fundamentally influenced the thinking and output of other standard setters, most notably the Board of the IASC and its successor, the IASB. As discussed below, the definitions adopted in the conceptual framework of the IASB are taken essentially unchanged from the FASB's concept statements. Thus, intentionally or not, the FASB's framework project has created a global language and definitional structure used by the only two standard-setting bodies currently involved with global-scale financial reporting.

However, both for the FASB and for the IASB, if the deductive model is to be maintained, a way must be found to address the fundamental issues of recognition and measurement that does not involve both attempting to maintain the truth of the framework's definitions while quietly compromising them when events require it. As discussed in 5 below, the IASB and the FASB are in the process of formulating a new joint Framework and it is to be hoped that the opportunity will be taken both to acknowledge and address the inconsistencies and difficulties that currently exist.

3 THE IASB'S CONCEPTUAL FRAMEWORK

3.1 Introduction

In May 1988, the Board of the IASC (before it was reconstituted as the IASB) issued an exposure draft – *Framework for the Preparation and Presentation of Financial Statements* – which set out its understanding of 'the conceptual framework that underlies the preparation and presentation of financial statements'.[90] This was converted without major change into a final statement in September 1989, although it is stressed within the statement that it will be revised from time to time in the light of the Board's experience in working with it.[91] The statement is not an accounting standard and does not override any specific international accounting standard or interpretation.[92] Whilst it therefore has much the same status as the FASB's concepts statements, unlike those statements, the IASB's framework does have a formal place in the IFRS hierarchy to which reference should be made when selecting accounting policies in the absence of a specific standard or interpretation. This is set out in paragraph 11 of IAS 8 – *Accounting Policies, Changes in Accounting Estimates and Errors* – and is discussed in Chapter 3.

In April 2001 the newly constituted IASB formally adopted the Framework, and it is the most recently published version of it that is referred to in this section. The Framework is a short document at 35 pages and 110 numbered paragraphs, and clearly is derived from the FASB's first six concepts statements. It is therefore open to the same criticisms and contains the same flaws as the FASB's concepts, which are discussed at 2.4 to 2.10 above.

The IASB and the FASB are currently undertaking the development of a new joint framework. A number of preliminary documents have been published and discussions have taken place at IASB open meetings, though it does not appear that any fundamentally new approach is being contemplated. The joint IASB-FASB framework project is discussed at 5 below.

3.2 The contents of the IASB's Framework

The Framework sets out in its introduction that its purpose is to:

'(a) assist the Board of IASC in the development of future International Accounting Standards and in its review of existing International Accounting Standards;

(b) assist the Board of IASC in promoting harmonisation of regulations, accounting standards and procedures relating to the presentation of financial statements by providing a basis for reducing the number of alternative accounting treatments permitted by International Accounting Standards;

(c) assist national standard-setting bodies in developing national standards;

(d) assist preparers of financial statements in applying International Accounting Standards and in dealing with topics that have yet to form the subject of an International Accounting Standard;

(e) assist auditors in forming an opinion as to whether financial statements conform with International Accounting Standards;

(f) assist users of financial statements in interpreting the information contained in financial statements prepared in conformity with International Accounting Standards; and

(g) provide those who are interested in the work of IASC with information about its approach to the formulation of International Accounting Standards.'[93]

The Board accepts that there may be conflicts between the Framework and the provisions of individual standards, but states that these are expected to diminish over time as standards are reviewed or replaced.

Perhaps inevitably the reporting status quo seems to be taken as read by the Framework; as evidenced, for example, by the statement in the introduction to the effect that financial statements normally include a balance sheet, a profit and loss statement, a statement of changes in financial position and notes.[94] The document is then devoted to applying its discussion to this traditional financial reporting package, without, for example, following or apparently even considering the possibility of an entirely new package.

Following the Introduction, the IASB's *Framework* is divided into the following seven major sections that are discussed below:

- The objective of financial statements;
- Underlying assumptions;
- Qualitative characteristics of financial statements;
- The elements of financial statements;
- Recognition of the elements of financial statements;
- Measurement of the elements of financial statements;
- Concepts of capital and capital maintenance.

3.2.1 The objective and underlying assumptions of financial statements

The objective of financial statements set out in the IASB's Framework is described in terms of decision-usefulness and will be quite familiar to readers of the FASB equivalent:

> 'to provide information about the financial position, performance and changes in financial position of an enterprise that is useful to a wide range of users in making economic decisions.'[95]

Stewardship is specifically referred to in a paragraph elaborating upon the objective of financial statements, and refers to the fact that there are decisions to be made by users of financial statements that require the management's stewardship to be assessed. The framework states this objective as follows:

> 'Financial statements also show the results of the stewardship of management, or the accountability of management for the resources entrusted to it. Those users who wish to assess the stewardship or accountability of management do

> so in order that they may make economic decisions; these decisions may include, for example, whether to hold or sell their investment in the entity or whether to reappoint or replace the management.'[96]

As discussed more fully at 5.2.1 below, both the FASB and IASB are seeking to marginalise the stewardship objective and establish decision-usefulness as the single objective of financial reporting.

Users are listed in the Introduction as investors, employees, lenders, suppliers and trade creditors, customers, governments and their agencies, and the public – a list that excludes nobody; however, it has to be admitted that the needs of all these groups cannot be met. Therefore financial statements that meet the needs of investors who 'are providers of risk capital' are stated to satisfy also 'most of the needs of other users that financial statements can satisfy'.[97] Perhaps it may be indicative of the derivative nature of the Framework that the phrase 'that financial statements can satisfy' is used. If an examination of a subject starts with preconceptions of what can and cannot be done, it is unlikely that much in the way of new insights or approaches will emerge. In any event, the investor's perspective is chosen as the one most likely to be useful in the preparation of what will remain general purpose financial statements.

The remainder of this part of the Framework contains a range of assertions, also quite familiar, covering how users need to know about the performance, financial position, cash generation, and liquidity and solvency of an entity, including changes in them.

The Framework sets out two 'underlying assumptions': the accruals basis of accounting and the going concern basis. Accruals is described as follows, significantly omitting matching from the concept:

> 'effects of transactions and other events are recognised when they occur (and not as cash or its equivalent is received or paid) and they are recorded in the accounting records and reported in the financial statements of the periods to which they relate.'[98]

Later on in the Framework, in the section on recognition, the point is specifically made that 'the application of the matching concept under this framework does not allow the recognition of items in the balance sheet which do not meet the definition of assets and liabilities.'[99] Equally significantly, prudence is not an underlying assumption of the Framework, but is relegated to being a subsidiary quality of reliability.

The going concern assumption is quite conventionally stated as follows:

> 'financial statements are normally prepared on the assumption that an enterprise is a going concern and will continue in operation for the foreseeable future. Hence, it is assumed that the enterprise has neither the intention nor the need to liquidate or curtail materially the scale of its operations.'[100]

3.2.2 The qualitative characteristics of financial statements

The Framework explains that qualitative characteristics are the attributes that make the information provided in financial statements useful to users.[101] The qualitative characteristics set out in the document are also taken directly from the FASB conceptual framework project. The familiar list of understandability, relevance, reliability and comparability is advanced.

A Understandability

One of the factors that all framework attempts have paid lip-service to is understandability, which is dealt with in its entirety in the IASB's Framework as follows:

> 'An essential quality of the information provided in financial statements is that it is readily understandable by users. For this purpose, users are assumed to have a reasonable knowledge of business and economic activities and accounting and a willingness to study the information with reasonable diligence. However, information about complex matters that should be included in the financial statements because of its relevance to the economic decision-making needs of users should not be excluded merely on the grounds that it may be too difficult for certain users to understand.'[102]

The Framework has advanced as an essential quality in the above paragraph that the 'information provided in financial statements … is readily understandable by users'; however, this is significantly different from financial statements actually *being* understood. The paragraph goes on to specify the required capabilities of users as having 'a reasonable knowledge of business and economic activities and accounting and a willingness to study the information with reasonable diligence.' This assertion, whilst similar to those in other frameworks, avoids the understandability problem in two ways.

First the phrase 'reasonable knowledge … of accounting' is entirely open-ended. It is highly unlikely that this could possibly be interpreted to mean 'a complete technical understanding of all the nuances involved with the intricacies of the many accounting rules and regulations', for example. In which case it is clear that much of what the IASB promulgates is not, in this sense, understandable.

Second, the capabilities required would probably reduce the 'allowable' users to a small set of professional analysts, accountants, academics, and the odd graduate of the subject. When this constituency is contrasted with the many types of people who actually own shares, the extremely diverse individual capabilities of even this 'providers of risk capital' user group, and with the very wide definition of users in the Framework, it becomes apparent that the issue of understandability remains considerable and cannot comfortably be defined away in the manner attempted.

B Relevance

Relevance is the second principal qualitative characteristic put forward. The Framework asserts that 'Information has the quality of relevance when it influences the economic decisions of users by helping them evaluate past, present or future events or confirming, or correcting, their past evaluations.'[103] The predictive value of relevant information is emphasised. Not that financial statements should be predictions in the sense of forecasts, but that the information they contain should be relevant to predictions that users might make for themselves about the 'ability of the enterprise to take advantage of opportunities and its ability to react to adverse situations.'[104]

Materiality is discussed as a subsection of relevance, in terms of providing a threshold point below which relevance does not exist. Information is stated to be material 'if its omission or misstatement could influence the economic decisions of users taken on the basis of the financial statements.'[105] The important question, however, is against which yardstick information should be judged to be material or immaterial, and for whom, but the Framework provides no further discussion of, or guidance about, identifying material items. In practice materiality is both a qualitative as well as a quantitative concept, mere small size would not necessarily make an item immaterial. Thus in this matter the Framework seems more superficial than would be expected.

C *Reliability*

Reliability is the third primary qualitative characteristic. Information is reliable if 'it is free from material error and bias and can be depended upon by users to represent faithfully that which it either purports to represent or could reasonably be expected to represent.'[106] Importantly, the Framework highlights the trade-off between reliability and relevance, stating that 'information may be relevant but so unreliable in nature or representation that its recognition may be potentially misleading.'[107] This is significant as the IASB and FASB have decided, as part of their joint framework project, to remove reliability – once thought of by both boards as a primary decision-specific quality – from the framework (see 5.2.2 below).

Faithful representation is used by the Framework as a term that can explain and clarify the notion of reliability. It states that 'Most financial information is subject to some risk of being less than a faithful representation of that which it purports to portray.'[108] This is a considerable admission and either is an overstatement of the case (i.e. there is no material risk in most cases) or if considered true, calls into question why the IASB has accepted it as a satisfactory state of affairs. More importantly, 'faithful representation' assumes satisfactory answers exist to fundamental questions. In particular, answers about what a given item in a set of financial statements might 'purport to represent'. Fundamentally this is taking as solved and understood the entire set of difficulties that the accounting profession and the many framework attempts have, and are still, grappling with.

Substance over form, neutrality, prudence and completeness are cited as four other characteristics that along with representational faithfulness, contribute to the principal qualitative characteristic of reliability. Substance over form is well understood in some jurisdictions, but not in others. In the USA, for example, it does not appear to be considered a useful concept, whereas in the UK and certain other countries throughout the world, it is clearly understood and applied. Essentially, substance over form relies upon accepting the possibility that the economic reality of a transaction can be disguised by its legal form. This doctrine means that any transactions structured to give a legal form that does not reflect the underlying economic reality, should be accounted for in accordance with that economic reality rather than the legal form. Thus a sale of a property would not be considered to result in an immediate profit to an entity if the entity simultaneously entered into a leasing agreement that had all the characteristics of a secured loan on that property. This is a key concept in the Framework that in our view is of great importance to the reliability and utility of financial statements if applied wisely in accounting standards.

The Framework defines neutrality as freedom from bias. There is no discussion of neutrality in the Framework, other than the statement that 'financial statements are not neutral if, by the selection or presentation of information, they influence the making of a decision or judgement in order to achieve a predetermined result or outcome.'[109]

Prudence (conservatism) is dealt with slightly more fully. Prudence is characterised as follows:

> 'Prudence is the inclusion of a degree of caution in the exercise of the judgements needed in making the estimates required under conditions of uncertainty, such that assets or income are not overstated and liabilities or expenses are not understated. However, the exercise of prudence does not allow, for example, the creation of hidden reserves or excessive provisions, the deliberate understatement of assets or income, or the deliberate overstatement of liabilities or expenses, because the financial statements would not be neutral and, therefore, not have the quality of reliability.'[110]

This statement is of considerable importance in the understanding of the IASB's deliberate move towards financial statements based on fair values. Prudence is characterised here as (a) to be exercised only when uncertainty exists, and (b) not to include 'income smoothing' – characterised as overstatement of provisions or liabilities or understatement of assets. Under an historical cost system this is not what prudence means. Rather it means the necessary caution, once thought fundamental to financial reporting, whereby profit is not taken until it is earned. Under the prudence concept, revenue and profits are not anticipated but are recognised by inclusion in the profit and loss account only when realised in the form of cash or of other assets the ultimate cash realisation of which can be assessed with reasonable certainty. On the other hand, provision is made for all known liabilities whether the amount of these is known with certainty or is a best estimate in the light of the information available.

Completeness, the fourth sub-characteristic of reliability, means 'the financial statements must be complete within the bounds of materiality and cost.'[111]

D Comparability

Comparability is the fourth principal qualitative characteristic in the Framework, which is an uncontroversial characteristic shared by all conceptual frameworks. Additionally, the IASB includes in the discussion the importance of disclosing accounting policies as an essential part of comparability:

> 'An important implication of the qualitative characteristic of comparability is that users be informed of the accounting policies employed in the preparation of the financial statements, any changes in those policies and the effects of such changes. Users need to be able to identify differences between the accounting policies for like transactions and other events used by the same enterprise from period to period and by different enterprises.'[112]

The point is made, however, that comparability does not extend to preventing the improvement of accounting standards. Comparability also entails the provision of comparative figures for the corresponding preceding accounting periods.

There follows a discussion under the heading 'Timeliness' that recognises that there is an element of conflict between two of the principal qualitative characteristics: relevance and reliability:

> 'To provide information on a timely basis it may often be necessary to report before all aspects of a transaction or other event are known, thus impairing reliability. Conversely, if reporting is delayed until all aspects are known, the information may be highly reliable but of little use to users who have had to make decisions in the interim.'[113]

The Framework indicates that this conflict is to be resolved by considering 'how best to satisfy the economic decision-making needs of users'[114] although how these are to be identified in any particular case is not discussed. The first point to make is that the conflict between relevance and reliability is an entirely self-inflicted problem, caused by the downgrading of the prudence concept as explained above, because the IASB wishes to incorporate fair values (that are inherently less reliable than realised profits) into financial statements. Secondly, the advice that this conflict should be resolved by determining 'how best to satisfy the economic decision-making needs of users' is utterly vacuous. It is unclear what this can mean in practice, and how it can assist a preparer, other than by a circular appeal to produce relevant and reliable financial statements. Probably in recognition of this difficulty, paragraph 45 of the Framework acknowledges that a 'trade-off between qualitative characteristics is often necessary' and that their relative importance 'is a matter of professional judgement'.

3.2.3 The elements of financial statements

A Assets

The section of the Framework that deals with the elements of financial statements is also derived from its FASB equivalent. Assets are defined as:

'(a) An asset is a resource controlled by the enterprise as a result of past events and from which future economic benefits are expected to flow to the enterprise.'[115]

The definition of an asset used by the Framework is adopted wholesale from the FASB framework, with one important difference. Under SFAC 6 the discussion is in the context of benefits 'obtained or controlled', while the Framework definition refers solely to resources 'controlled' by the enterprise. This is a fundamental difference that has significant implications in practice – for example goodwill falls within the definition of an asset under the FASB concepts, but falls outside the definition under the IASB's Framework, as it fails to meet the 'controlled' requirement. The problem the IASB's Framework therefore has is that it fails to include within its asset definition an asset that all accountants in practice, and the IASB itself, acknowledge *is* an asset. The same problem occurred in the UK's framework project (see 4.6 below for a further discussion of this point).

This definition also has to contend with the problem that future economic benefits may not materialise. Consequently, for an item to be recognised as an asset it must be 'probable that any future economic benefit associated with the item will flow to ... the enterprise.'[116] The question therefore arises: what is a future economic benefit? Future economic benefits are obviously other items of property, near cash such as debtors, or cash itself. The logical problem in the absence of any other meaning being given to the phrase 'future economic benefits' is that the asset definition is completely circular. It has no explanatory power, but is precisely logically equivalent to: 'an asset is a resource controlled by the enterprise from which assets are expected to be gained by the enterprise in the future'.

Thus both the FASB and the IASB have a flawed definition at the heart of their conceptual frameworks. If the definition of assets is flawed the entire logical structure derived from it is too, including all the remaining definitions of the elements of financial statements that depend upon the asset definition.

Paragraph 50 of the Framework makes it clear that because something meets the definition of an asset or liability, it does not imply it will necessarily be included ('recognised') in the balance sheet. That is, meeting the definition is a necessary but not a sufficient condition for inclusion in the financial statements. The IASB's recognition criteria are discussed in the following section. Once again, and importantly, the Framework emphasises that:

> 'In assessing whether an item meets the definition of an asset, liability or equity, attention needs to be given to its underlying substance and economic reality and not merely its legal form.'[117]

The emphasis on substance over form is a key practical difference between the IASB conceptual framework and that of the FASB. It is potentially immensely powerful and of great importance to users, in that it requires preparers to produce financial statements that clearly report on the underlying economic reality of the transactions an entity has undertaken.

B Liabilities

In the IASB's Framework a liability is defined as:

> 'a present obligation of the enterprise arising from past events, the settlement of which is expected to result in an outflow from the enterprise of resources embodying economic benefits.'[118]

The 'present obligation arising from a past event' definition of a liability is also adopted from the FASB equivalent, with the same consequences for recognising provisions which, if based solely on the basis of a management decision, will not qualify under this definition. For example, IAS 37 – *Provisions, Contingent Liabilities and Contingent Assets* – relies heavily on this definition to restrict severely the circumstances under which provisions can be recognised. This is because provisions are not seen as a separate element of financial statements and, instead, are defined as being a subset of liabilities (see Chapter 27). The concept of the 'constructive obligation' used in IAS 37 as a sub-set of the term present obligation, is not referred to in the Framework.

Assets and liabilities are therefore characterised as rights and obligations – rights to receive future economic benefits in the form of cash inflows and obligations to transfer out economic benefits in the form of cash outflows. The remaining definitions are derived from these definitions of assets and liabilities.

C Equity

Equity is defined as follows:

> 'Equity is the residual interest in the assets of the enterprise after deducting all its liabilities.'[119]

Again the wording is similar to that used in SFAC 6. The logic of the definition is identical, and follows from the equation that assets minus liabilities equals equity.

D Income and expenses

Income and expenses definitions rely directly upon the balance sheet approach outlined above., and are defined in terms of the changes to assets and liabilities as follows:

> 'Income is increases in economic benefits during the accounting period in the form of inflows or enhancements of assets or decreases of liabilities that result in increases in equity, other than those relating to contributions from equity participants.
>
> 'Expenses are decreases in economic benefits during the accounting period in the form of outflows or depletions of assets or incurrences of liabilities that result in decreases in equity, other than those relating to distributions to equity participants.'[120]

Although income and expenses are defined in terms of balance sheet recognition criteria in the same manner as adopted by the FASB, the Framework has adopted a simpler approach as it uses a single element to cover what SFAC 6 describes separately as revenues and gains (see 2.7.7 above). The distinction is that the US definitions differentiate between gains arising from central operations and those which do not, whereas the IASB Framework uses a single definition for both. This is explained as follows: 'Gains represent other items that meet the definition of income and may, or may not, arise in the course of the ordinary activities of an entity. Gains represent increases in economic benefits and as such are no different in nature from revenue. Hence, they are not regarded as constituting a separate element in this Framework.'[121]

Similarly, the definition of expenses embraces both expenses and losses[122] as the terms are used in SFAC 6 (see 2.7.7 above).

The realisation principle is not discussed in the Framework, except to the extent that it is made clear that income and expenses include both realised and unrealised gains and losses. This is expressed as follows: 'The definition of income also includes unrealised gains; for example, those arising on the revaluation of marketable securities and those resulting from increases in the carrying amount of long-term assets. ... The definition of expenses also includes unrealised losses, for example, those arising from the effects of increases in the rate of exchange for a foreign currency in respect of the borrowings of an entity in that currency.'[123]

3.2.4 *Recognition of the elements of financial statements*

The recognition criteria adopted in the Framework are also entirely familiar from other conceptual framework projects. Thus an asset will be recognised if 'it is probable that the future economic benefits will flow to the enterprise and the asset has a cost or value that can be measured reliably.'[124] A liability is recognised 'when it is probable that an outflow of resources embodying economic benefits will result from the settlement of a present obligation and the amount at which the settlement will take place can be measured reliably.'[125] As with its US equivalents, the recognition criteria for income and expenses are derived by deduction from these definitions.

The balance sheet approach to income and expense recognition is absolutely explicit in the Framework, as demonstrated by paragraph 92:

> 'Income is recognised in the income statement when an increase in future economic benefits related to an increase in an asset or a decrease of a liability has arisen that can be measured reliably. This means, in effect, that recognition of income occurs simultaneously with the recognition of increases in assets or decreases in liabilities.'

Paragraph 94 contains similar wording relating to expense recognition.

3.2.5 *Measurement of the elements of financial statements*

This is the third stage of the IASB's process of inclusion of an item into the financial statements. First there is definition (e.g. of an asset); if an item meets the definition, then comes recognition; if an item can be recognised (i.e. it is probable that economic benefits will come to the enterprise and that cost or value can be measured reliably); the final stage is measurement. However, despite the importance of measurement to any conceptual framework, the IASB's framework provides no conceptual guidance whatsoever in this area.

Measurement is defined as:

> 'the process of determining the monetary amounts at which the elements of the financial statements are to be recognised and carried in the balance sheet and income statement. This involves the selection of the particular basis of measurement.'[126]

The Framework lists four 'basis of measurement' possibilities: historical cost; current cost; realisable (settlement) value; and present value. Present value means that assets are carried at the present value of their expected future cash flows, while liabilities are carried at the present value of the amount that will be required to settle the liability in the future. In spite of its frequent use in the IASB's standards, fair value is not among the measurement bases listed in the Framework and is not in fact mentioned in it at all. However, in its current standards the IASB defines fair value as 'the amount for which an asset could be exchanged between knowledgeable, willing parties in an arm's length transaction', which essentially means that the term fair value has been adopted to mean what the Framework refers to as realisable value. There is no further discussion of which measurement basis might be preferable. The subject is dealt with in its entirety in a solely descriptive manner in three paragraphs, and ends with the statement that historical cost is most commonly adopted.

3.2.6 Concepts of capital and capital maintenance

Finally, there is a short section dealing with concepts of capital maintenance. This summarises the concepts of physical and financial capital maintenance as follows:

> 'Under a financial concept of capital, such as invested money or invested purchasing power, capital is synonymous with the net assets or equity of the enterprise. Under a physical concept of capital, such as operating capability, capital is regarded as the productive capacity of the enterprise based on, for example, units of output per day.'[127]

No attempt is made to examine or discuss the adequacy of each concept or how their use might contribute to improving financial reporting. Even recommending one or the other is avoided by the customary and in effect empty formula of 'selection of the appropriate concept of capital by an enterprise should be based on the needs of the users of its financial statements'.[128]

This final section ends with the entirely unsupported assertion that the Framework is applicable to any chosen accounting model, in that it is 'applicable to a range of accounting models and provides guidance on preparing and presenting the financial statements constructed under the [any] chosen model.'[129] This is unlikely to be the case as, for example, even a brief reading of section 4 below shows that there are a number of alternative conceptual framework possibilities in respect of which the IASB's Framework would have little or no obvious application or relevance. Finally the Framework ends on a rather open ended note as follows:

> 'At the present time, it is not the intention of the Board of IASC to prescribe a particular model other than in exceptional circumstances, such as for those enterprises reporting in the currency of a hyperinflationary economy. This intention will, however, be reviewed in the light of world developments.'[130]

3.3 Assessment of the IASB's Framework

There is no really fundamental difference in substance between the IASB and FASB conceptual frameworks, apart from the fact that the FASB statements are more voluminous and detailed than the IASB equivalent. The IASB document clearly derives from the original FASB work embodied in its concepts statements, and in truth the IASB's Framework is little more than a synopsis of the FASB conceptual statements and shares their shortcomings. It is perhaps unfortunate, and certainly was a lost opportunity, that the IASB did not take the chance presented by the publication of a conceptual framework document to explore more fundamentally the questions posed by such an endeavour. A conceptual framework should be more than an *ex post facto* justification of an already chosen approach, in our view.

The fundamental problem with the Framework is that we do not believe that it is possible to develop general purpose rules on the recognition of elements of financial statements, whilst simultaneously leaving open the questions of how they are to be measured and against what capital maintenance yardstick profit is to be determined. We do not suggest that any one system is necessarily superior to another, but it is not possible to fit all possible systems of accounting into one framework of rules on the elements of financial statements and their recognition. We believe that lack of clarity on this point has led to constant confusion on accounting concepts, where ideas which belong in discrete methodologies are used interchangeably and lead to a result that lacks any cohesion. It should be the role of a conceptual framework study to unravel this tangle, but in this respect at least we believe that the IASB Framework document simply compounds the confusion by failing to distinguish the essential features that make different approaches mutually incompatible.

We therefore hope that, in seeking to develop a new conceptual framework jointly with the FASB, the IASB finds it possible to differentiate the features of alternative approaches which require the development of distinct principles on identification, recognition and measurement of the individual elements.

4 OTHER FRAMEWORK ENDEAVOURS

For those concerned with understanding the process by which the IASB has arrived at many of its standards, or with making a contribution to the development of future IFRSs through Exposure Draft responses, an understanding of how the profession has moved from uncritical use of historical cost in the 1960s to a mix of cost and fair value today, is valuable. The IASB and many national equivalents developed their views in response to the appearance of practical financial reporting problems that caused users and others to require change. In the past this imperative triggered fundamental work by a number of accounting bodies and standard setters from different nations, and their contributions to the development of financial reporting are outlined below. This work taken together, has contributed consciously or not to the development of the IASB's own framework, and the thinking that underlies it.

4.1 The Corporate Report

The first real attempt by the accounting profession in Europe to develop a conceptual framework is to be found in a discussion paper issued by the UK accounting profession in 1975 by the then-styled Accounting Standards Steering Committee and entitled *The Corporate Report*.[131]

The discussion paper dealt with 'the fundamental aims of published financial reports and the means by which these aims can be achieved'[132] and used the term 'corporate report' to mean 'the comprehensive package of information of all kinds which most completely describes an organisation's economic activity.'[133] It was suggested that this 'comprehensive package' should include more than the 'basic financial statements' (i.e. the balance sheet, profit and loss account and funds statement), and should incorporate additional narrative and descriptive statements.[134] The discussion paper centred on three main elements: 'the types of organisation which should be expected to publish regular financial information; the main users of such information and their needs; and the form of report which will best meet those needs.'[135]

The discussion paper followed the basic approach that corporate reports should seek to satisfy, as far as possible, the information needs of users.[136] The Committee argued that every economic entity of significant size has an implicit responsibility to report publicly, and concluded that general purpose reports designed for general purpose use are the primary means by which this public accountability is fulfilled. Users were defined 'as those having a reasonable right to information concerning the reporting entity',[137] a right that arises from the entity's public accountability.

The paper identified seven user groups[138] as having a reasonable right to information, and discussed the basis of the rights of each group and their information needs. Not surprisingly, the Committee identified a considerable overlap of interest between each of the user groups, including items such as 'evaluating the performance of the entity', 'estimating the future prospects of the entity', 'evaluating managerial performance', 'assessing the liquidity of the entity, its present or future requirements for additional fixed or working capital, and its ability to raise long and short term finance.'[139]

On this basis the Committee concluded that 'the fundamental objective of corporate reports is to communicate economic measurements of and information about the resources and performance of the reporting entity useful to those having reasonable rights to such information.'[140] They went on to say that in order to fulfil this objective and be useful, corporate reports should be relevant, understandable, reliable, complete, objective, timely and comparable[141] (these qualitative characteristics identified were similar to those discussed in the Trueblood Report).

The discussion paper then reviewed the conventional thinking on the aim of published reports together with the then-existing features of published financial statements of UK companies. The Committee also conducted a survey of corporate objectives amongst the chairmen of 300 of the largest UK listed companies, and concluded that 'distributable profit can no longer be regarded as the sole or premier indicator of performance.'[142] Consequently, it was suggested that there was a need for additional indicators of performance in the corporate reports of all entities.[143]

Part II of the study considered the 'measurement and method' of achieving the above aims. Since the Committee had concluded that current reporting practices did not fully satisfy the needs of users, it was suggested that the following additional statements should be published in the corporate report: a statement of value added, an employment report, a statement of money exchanges with government, a statement of transactions in foreign currency, a statement of future prospects and a statement of corporate objectives.[144] In addition, the Committee recommended further study into methods of social accounting as well as the disaggregation of certain financial information.[145]

Finally, the Committee discussed the concepts and measurements employed in the 'basic financial statements'. In considering the purpose of profit measurement, it concluded that income statements 'should be concerned with the measurement of performance although they may also be used in the measurement of capital maintenance and income distributability.'[146] It was, however, recognised that this dual purpose of income statements often gave rise to conflict in the application of accounting concepts – particularly the fundamental concepts of prudence and matching. Various measurement bases were then discussed in the context of the inadequacies of the historical cost system. The Committee stated that 'the usefulness of financial statements in fulfilling user needs is restricted at the present time because of the defects of the basis of measurement generally used. Historical cost accounting fails, in times of rapidly changing prices and values, to ensure that sufficient provision is made for capital maintenance.'[147]

The committee then briefly surveyed several bases of measurement, including historical cost, current purchasing power (CPP) and various current value bases such as replacement cost and net realisable value. The conclusion reached was that no one system of measurement is capable of satisfying the user needs identified in the study, and that, therefore, research should be undertaken into the feasibility of multi-column reporting, as well as into the development of a standardised system of current value accounting.[148]

It is probable that the business community were concerned about the possibility of their reporting responsibility being extended through the development of the Committee's concept of public accountability. Although this aspect of the Corporate Report has largely been absent from all further conceptual framework documents, arguably it was a far-sighted approach. The rise of public interest in, and of academic research into, alternative reports dealing with areas such as the environment and corporate social responsibility,, may indicate that the public accountability aspect of corporate reporting will have to become more formally recognised. Indeed, this is the case already with the prominence now being attached to corporate governance disclosures by a number of listing authorities.

4.2 Financial reporting in times of high inflation

Through most of the 1970s and early 1980s, inflation was an intractable problem in the UK and in certain other countries, with rates of inflation well above 10% common, and on occasion over 20%. Inflation poses insoluble problems for historical cost based financial statements because the buying-power of a monetary unit from one accounting period to the next is so different. Outlining the findings of a UK Government committee set up to consider this problem provides a useful way of considering the alternative systems of accounting that have been put forward, as opposed to the more evolutionary nature of the FASB's approach.

The UK Government announced the creation of an Inflation Accounting Committee, subsequently referred to as the Sandilands Committee after its chairman, 'to consider whether, and if so how, company accounts should allow for changes (including relative changes) in costs and prices'.[149] The Sandilands Report is dealt with here in some detail, as it was, and remains, the most comprehensive summary of the many different approaches that have been taken by academic and professional accountants, prompted by a variety of economic conditions, to solving the problems that have surrounded the development of a conceptual framework.

The Sandilands Report followed a similar approach to that of the Corporate Report to the extent that it focused on the information needs of users. The report stated that 'the requirements of users of accounts should be the fundamental consideration in deciding the information to be disclosed in company accounts.'[150]

The report proposed the development of a system of accounting for inflation that would evolve towards a system of current cost accounting, the essential features of which are:

(a) money is the unit of measurement (as opposed to the 'current purchasing power' basis of expressing financial information in terms of a unit of measurement of constant value when prices change);

(b) assets and liabilities should be shown in the balance sheet at their 'value to the business'; and

(c) operating profit (to be known as 'current cost profit') would be calculated after charging the 'value to the business' of the assets consumed during the period, thereby excluding holding gains and showing them separately.[151]

4.2.1 Current Purchasing Power accounting

In formulating its system of current cost accounting, the Committee examined three alternative accounting systems that had been developed in an attempt to overcome the deficiencies of historical cost accounting. The first of these systems studied was a 'current purchasing power' (CPP) method of inflation accounting, whereby supplementary information would be given in addition to the historical cost financial statements. The main features of the CPP approach were:

(a) companies would continue to keep their records and present their basic annual accounts in historical pounds, i.e. in terms of the value of the pound at the time of each transaction or revaluation;

(b) in addition, all listed companies should present to their shareholders a supplementary statement in terms of the value of the pound at the end of the period to which the accounts relate;

(c) the conversion of the figures in the basic accounts into the figures in the supplementary statement should be by means of a general index of the purchasing power of the pound;[152] and

(d) the directors would be required to provide in a note to the supplementary statement an explanation of the basis on which it has been prepared and it was considered desirable that directors should comment on the significance of the figures.[153]

The Committee concluded that the CPP method 'does not remedy the main deficiencies of historic cost accounting during a time of changing costs and prices and we do not recommend it as the best long-term solution to the problem of accounting for inflation.'[154] Numerous arguments were put forward to support this conclusion, for example:

- since, during a period of changing prices, historical cost figures expressed in terms of monetary units do not show the 'value to the business' of assets, a CPP supplementary statement will show the historic cost figures restated in units of current purchasing power, not the 'value to the business' of assets.[155] Thus, a major deficiency of historical cost accounts would not be overcome;
- since companies were required to express their CPP supplementary statements in terms of the current purchasing power of the pound at the closing balance sheet date, the unit of measurement in the supplementary statement would change from year to year. This was likely to cause confusion, compounded by the fact that companies which had different accounting dates would be preparing supplementary statements in terms of different units, resulting in a lack of comparability;[156] and
- since a unit of measurement with an absolute value through time is unattainable, there is no advantage in preparing financial statements in CPP units rather than in units of money.[157]

4.2.2 Value accounting

The Committee then examined three forms of 'value accounting' – a term used to describe a wide range of different accounting systems which measure net assets by reference to their 'value' rather than their cost. The three value accounting systems examined were: replacement cost accounting; present value accounting; and continuously contemporary accounting.

A Replacement cost accounting based on current entry values

'Replacement cost' is the price which will have to be paid to replace an asset used or given up in exchange for another asset. Consequently, the basic principle underlying replacement cost accounting is that, since a business has to replace its assets over time in order to continue in operational existence, charges for the consumption or exchange of an asset should be based on the cost of replacing it. Consequently, assets are valued at the balance sheet date by reference to the price which would have to be paid at that date to purchase a similar asset in a similar condition – i.e. the replacement cost of the assets. This system, therefore, adopts a method of income determination that reflects changes in capital both at the point of realisation of assets and, before realisation, while holding assets.

The pioneers of an income and value model based on replacement costs (entry values) were Edwards and Bell,[158] who attempted to interpret accounting concepts in terms of economic concepts. Their theory abandoned both the realisation principle and the idea of the 'unitary income statement' which does not separate operating profit from holding gains. They introduced a new concept of 'business profit', which was made up of current operating profit of the current period, realised holding gains of the same period and unrealised holding gains.

A major disadvantage of the replacement cost model is the difficulty and subjectivity involved in assigning replacement costs; for example, are replacement costs based on identical or equivalent replacements, and how is technological obsolescence dealt with? However, the Sandilands Committee took the view that this disadvantage was far outweighed by the usefulness of the information provided by the system in the form of meaningful balance sheet values and a segregated business profit figure. The Sandilands Committee concluded that the replacement cost accounting system 'comes close to meeting the dominant requirements of users of accounts and the Committee's own proposals have many similarities with certain forms of this system of accounting.'[159]

B Present value accounting

Present value accounting is based on the economic concept of income, and values an asset on the basis of the present value of the cash flows that are expected to be derived from that asset. In order to maintain the capital of the entity, an amount at least equal to the original investment should be reinvested, whilst the remaining cash flows are treated as realised. For example, if the discounted net present value of all expected future cash flows of an entity are €100,000 at the beginning of the year and €115,000 at the end of the year, and if the net cash flows arising during the year were €10,000, then the profit for the year will be €25,000, since this amount could be distributed whilst maintaining the original capital base of €100,000.

Whilst this approach might have some degree of theoretical soundness, the Sandilands Committee considered it to be totally impracticable. The Committee believed that issues such as risk, the determination of discount rates, changes in interest rates and the uncertainty of future cash flows presented virtually insurmountable problems. The Sandilands Committee therefore rejected present value accounting on the grounds that use of economic value as the basis of valuation of an asset would not meet the needs of users, as it would only be in comparatively few cases that this would represent the value of an asset to a business.[160]

C Continuously Contemporary Accounting (CoCoA)

The current value income model based on exit prices or realisable market values was first advocated by MacNeal in a book published by him in 1939 which dealt, inter alia, with the ethical issue of 'truth' in accounting.[161] MacNeal maintained that financial statements could only present the 'truth' if assets were stated at their current value and the profit and losses accruing from the changes in these values are included in income, and classified as either realised or unrealised. MacNeal did, however, concede that under certain circumstances the use of net realisable values was not appropriate, and that in such cases current replacement costs should be used.

The system known as continuously contemporary accounting (CoCoA) was formally introduced by Chambers in a book published in 1966,[162] and the case for exit value accounting was further developed by Sterling.[163] Chambers' theory is based on the premise that entities must be able to choose between alternative courses of action and, because resources are limited, they need to know what resources are available to enable them to engage in exchanges. Consequently, Chambers asserts that this capacity to engage in exchanges is measured by the opportunity cost of holding assets in their existing form, and that this opportunity cost is represented by the current cash equivalent of assets – which Chambers defines as being their current sales value. Initially, Chambers did not apply this principle rigorously and proposed that stocks should be valued at current replacement cost. However, he subsequently amended his view and advocated that exit values should be applied to the valuation of all assets. A difference in the theories of Chambers and Sterling is, for example, that Chambers believed that net realisable values should be based on the assumption that assets are realised in an orderly manner based on sensible adaptations to changing circumstances; Sterling, on the other hand, believed that net realisable values should be based on immediate liquidation prices.

The capital maintenance concept adopted by CoCoA is based on the preservation of the purchasing power of shareholders' equity (using the monetary unit as the unit of measurement, and not the current purchasing power unit used in CPP accounting). Consequently, since all assets (both monetary and non-monetary) are measured at net realisable value, income is defined as the difference between opening and closing equity after maintaining the purchasing power or cash equivalent of such equity. Income for the year, therefore, will comprise (1) the net profit/loss on business operations, (2) the accrued profit/loss arising from the change in the current cash equivalent of assets and (3) the effect on the capital of the entity brought about by the change in the purchasing power of money.

However, despite the widespread publication of his theories, Chambers failed to gain any measure of support for CoCoA outside academic circles.

There is no doubt that there are some compelling theoretical arguments for the presentation of financial statements based on net realisable values; for example, they provide useful information in the assessment of liquidity and financial flexibility. However, net realisable value is unlikely to reflect an asset's 'value to the business', since, for instance, an item of plant might have negligible net realisable value but substantial use value. Therefore, whilst the disclosure of net realisable values might provide useful supplementary information, the arguments in favour of CoCoA as the primary basis of accounting are unconvincing. CoCoA was rejected by the Sandilands Committee on the basis that, as a whole, it did not satisfy the information needs of users which they had identified.[164] It is, however, noteworthy that in its discussion document – *Making Corporate Reports Valuable* – the Research Committee of the ICAS advocated a reporting system based on net realisable values[165] (see 4.4 below). Rather interestingly, the measurement ideas underlining the FASB's standard on fair value measurement, SFAS 157, published in 2006, bear a striking resemblance to Chambers' ideas. SFAS 157 is further discussed at 6.2 below.

4.2.3 Cash flow accounting

Finally the Sandilands Committee considered cash flow accounting. The principal proponents of cash flow reporting were Lee[166] and Lawson,[167] although there are several other advocates of various approaches to cash flow reporting. Lee's system of cash flow reporting relied heavily on exit value theory and aimed to report both actual and potential cash flows. Assets are classified according to their realisability, based on Chambers' principle of orderly liquidation. If a sale price does not exist, assets are to be accounted for as having a zero cash equivalent.[168] Lee suggested the following four asset classifications for his statement of financial position:

1. realised assets (e.g. bank balances);
2. readily-realisable assets (i.e. assets which have a ready market and sale price, such as listed securities, debtors and stocks of finished goods);
3. non-readily-realisable assets (i.e. assets which do have a market and sale price, but which would not be quickly realised because of the limited nature of the market, such as certain items of plant and work-in-progress); and
4. not-realisable assets (i.e. assets which have no known sales price and no market, and would therefore be ascribed a zero value, such as highly specialised or obsolete plant).[169]

Liabilities are classified according to maturity, in line with conventional accounting practice.

Lee proposed that, in addition to a 'statement of financial position', the cash flow reporting system should present a 'statement of realised cash flow', a 'statement of realisable earnings' and a 'statement of changes in financial position'.[170] The statement of realised cash flow would report an entity's actual cash inflows and outflows during a particular period; it is noteworthy that the information contained in this statement would be broadly equivalent to that which would be presented in a statement of cash flows under IAS 7 – *Cash Flow Statements* – (see Chapter 34). The statement of realisable earnings would report periodic profit similar to that provided by a net realisable value accounting system, except that it is described in terms of realised and realisable cash flows. The statement would provide an analysis of realised earnings (derived from the entity's operating cash flow), and unrealised earnings (which represent potential cash flows that have accrued during the period as a result of changes in the realisable values of assets, net of the changes in liabilities). The statement of changes in financial position was effectively a conventional funds statement presented on an exit value basis.

Although there are a number of practical accounting and disclosure problems in cash flow reporting, it does have considerable merit. However, one difficulty which does exist is caused by the artificial 12 month reporting period and the necessity to measure 'profitability' over that period and from one period to the next. The principal reason for the development of the accrual basis of accounting was that financial statements prepared on a cash basis (which was probably the oldest form of presentation) provided distorted profit figures from one period to the next.

Although the Sandilands Committee stated that there was 'much of value in the cash flow accounting principle',[171] it was felt that cash flow accounting would rekindle all the 'old difficulties of assessing the profit or loss for the year when the accounting system does not match revenues against costs incurred in their generation.'[172] The Committee therefore concluded that the abandonment of the existing concept of the profit and loss account in favour of a cash flow statement would result in the information needs of users not being met. Clearly, however, the Committee had not considered the possibility of the presentation of a 'statement of realisable earnings' as advocated by Lee, which would provide a more stable basis for reporting profit than the statement of receipts and payments the Committee apparently envisaged. Lee, however, recognised the problems created by the traditional 12 month reporting period, and suggested that a solution might be found in the use of multi-period aggregates for analysis purposes.

4.2.4 Current cost accounting (CCA)

The Sandilands Committee recommended the development of a system of current cost accounting that used the monetary unit as the unit of measurement and dealt with the effects of specific price changes (as opposed to changes in the general purchasing power of money) on individual businesses. The Committee recommended that the balance sheet should present the 'value to the business' of the company's assets, which was equated with the amount of the loss that would be suffered by an entity if the asset were to be lost or destroyed. Whilst it was stated that the 'value to the business' of an asset might, under certain circumstances, be its net realisable value or economic value, it would normally be based on its replacement cost. Because the Committee recommended that financial statements be drawn up in terms of the monetary unit, no adjustment would be made for monetary items.[173] However, it is arguable that current cost accounting does not produce a balance sheet which seeks to be a statement of values of the resources of the company; it simply updates the costs at which they are recorded. This distinction can be illustrated by looking at the financial statements of an oil and gas exploration company. Even on a current cost basis, the carrying value of its principal assets is still based on the (backward-looking) cost of exploration expenditure incurred, not the (forward-looking) value of the oil and gas it has found.

Under the Sandilands system, an entity's 'current cost profit' for a period would be calculated by charging against income 'the value to the business' of assets consumed during the year. In simple terms, therefore, the current cost profit could be derived from the historical cost profit by means of an adjustment to depreciation and a cost of sales adjustment. The Committee also recommended the presentation of a summary statement of total gains or losses for the period, which would present the entity's total gains/losses in terms of three classifications: operating gains/losses (i.e. current cost profit/loss), extraordinary gains/losses and holding gains/losses. An interesting observation regarding these two statements recommended by the Committee is that they are based on a different capital maintenance concepts. The calculation of current cost profit was based on the concept of physical capital maintenance, whilst the summary statement of total gains was concerned with the maintenance of financial capital. However, because the calculation of current cost profit subsequently received greater prominence than the summary of total gains, it is generally thought that the Sandilands proposals were based on the concept of physical capital maintenance.[174]

The Committee recommended that current cost accounting should replace historical cost accounting, and that its proposals should be incorporated in an accounting standard. Its recommendations met with little support, which was attributed at the time to the fact that there was considerable objection to the replacement of historical cost accounting by a new untested system; the proposals were considered too complicated; and the profit figure was considered misleading without adjustment for monetary items.

Subsequently, a further UK study – The Hyde Guidelines – recommended that three adjustments should be made to the historical cost results: in addition to the depreciation and cost of sales adjustments proposed by Sandilands, it was recommended that a 'gearing adjustment' be made as an interim solution to dealing with monetary items in inflation-adjusted financial statements. Since no account of the existence of borrowings was taken in calculating current cost operating profit, the implication was that operating capability had to be maintained entirely out of the generation of revenues. However, the reality is clearly that this could be financed partly by borrowings; consequently, the gearing adjustment was designed to take account of the extent to which fixed assets and working capital were financed by borrowings.

Following these efforts a standard, SSAP 16 – *Current cost accounting* – was issued in the UK in 1980 that:[175]

(a) introduced a fourth adjustment, called the 'monetary working capital adjustment', which effectively extended the cost of sales adjustment (which allowed for increases in the investment needed to maintain stocks when prices were increasing) to the other working capital items. Consequently, the monetary working capital adjustment represented an estimate of the extra investment in debtors, creditors and liquid resources required to maintain operations when prices were increasing;

(b) proposed the presentation of a current cost balance sheet, in which fixed assets and stock would be measured on a current cost basis; and

(c) proposed that listed companies disclose current cost earnings per share.

SSAP 16 perpetuated the concept of current cost operating profit based on the maintenance of physical capital, which had been extended to monetary working capital through the monetary working capital adjustment. The associated gearing adjustment probably arose as a result of the need to compromise with critics of the entire process in order to find an acceptable solution – as opposed to having any theoretically sound justification.

It is worthy of note, given our view that ultimately any accounting theoretical framework will be subject to the rigorous test of whether it is applicable and useful in practice, that SSAP 16 suffered a very low level of compliance until it was eventually withdrawn.

It might be argued that the activities described in this section provide evidence for the view that accounting standard setting is a process of establishing convention in response to the needs of the times. The high inflation rates of the late 1970s and early 1980s drove both practitioners and academics to undertake various studies and produce a number of recommendations. Since inflation has ceased to be a concern, interest in this problem has noticeably waned.

4.3 Canada: The Stamp Report

In 1980, Professor Edward Stamp produced a research study primarily for the Canadian Institute of Chartered Accountants which was 'intended to provide a Canadian solution to the problem of improving the quality of corporate financial reporting standards.'[176] Stamp adopted a similar approach to that of other studies (such as the Corporate Report and Trueblood) by looking at users, their needs, their rights to information and the qualitative characteristics of that information. Stamp identified a more detailed list of users (15 in all) than did, for example, the Corporate or Sandilands Reports.

Stamp developed a set of 20 qualitative criteria which could be used as yardsticks whereby standard-setters, as well as the preparers and users of published financial statements, can decide whether or not the financial statements are meeting the objectives of financial reporting and the needs of users. An interesting rider to this aspect of Stamp's study was that he subsequently used his list of qualitative criteria as the basis of an empirical study of the relative importance of each of the criteria.[177] Stamp supplied each member of the UK's standard setting body (the ASC at that time) with a copy of Chapter 7 of his CICA research study in which the significance and meaning of each of the 20 criteria were discussed. He also gave them each a questionnaire in which they were asked to rank the 20 criteria in order of importance.[178] Although the ranking revealed 'relevance' as the most important criterion and 'conservatism' as the least important, this in itself was not the most significant aspect of Stamp's study. The real significance was that he demonstrated it would be possible to establish rankings of characteristics of accounting information for each category of user.

In his CICA research study, Stamp also devoted a considerable amount of effort towards discussing certain fundamental conceptual issues such as problems of allocation, income measurement, capital maintenance, the proprietary versus the entity theory, and the question of which attribute accounting should measure.[179] These issues are all fundamental to the development of a conceptual framework for financial reporting; yet they have not been resolved unequivocally by the conceptual frameworks of the two most influential global standard setting bodies – the FASB and the IASB.

4.4 Discussion document: 'Making Corporate Reports Valuable'

4.4.1 Background

This discussion document, which was issued in 1988, was the product of a major research project undertaken by the Research Committee of the Institute of Chartered Accountants of Scotland, and included David Tweedie (now Sir David Tweedie, Chairman of the IASB) among its project members. The reason why this paper was so refreshing at the time was principally because the research committee started from the basis of a 'clean sheet'. In other words, the members were able to ignore existing laws, accounting rules, terminology and all other constraints in order to try and achieve what they believed to be the best result. The Committee started off by explaining what motivated it to reconsider the nature of corporate reporting. The reasons which were given included the following basic conclusions:

- all financial reports ought to reflect economic reality;
- the information which investors need is the same in kind, but not in volume, as the information which managements need to run their entities;
- some of the information that management has but does not normally communicate comes out into the open when management wants something – such as additional capital or to be able to defend a hostile take-over bid;
- present-day financial reports are deficient in that they are based on legal form rather than economic substance, on cost rather than value, on the past rather than the future, and on 'profit' rather than 'wealth';
- there is no consistent conceptual basis underlying the production of either the profit and loss account or the balance sheet, and some of the concepts used appear to defy normal understanding of financial affairs;
- corporate reports are not made public sufficiently speedily; and
- the audit report is insufficiently informative and is often incomprehensible to non-auditors.[180]

The Committee then discussed various bases for applying values to assets, focusing on historical cost, current replacement cost, current net realisable values and economic values. Having discussed what it saw as the deficiencies of historical cost and economic value, the Committee noted that current replacement cost and net realisable value both met its criteria of economic reality and 'additivity' (i.e. the total number in a statement should not mean something different in kind from its constituent numbers). Nevertheless, the Committee expressed a preference for net realisable value as the basis for applying values to assets, 'principally because it is value-based whereas replacement cost is cost-based',[181] and it was felt that 'value rather than cost is important in assessing financial wealth.'[182]

4.4.2 The proposed information package

The Committee proposed what was then an entirely new information package, using net realisable values as the basis of valuation. In order to present the financial wealth of an entity, the Committee proposed that the following four basic statements should replace the existing financial statements:

(a) *Assets and Liabilities Statement*, which would present the assets and liabilities of the entity at the reporting date, each stated at its net realisable value. Net realisable values would normally be determined according to the principle of orderly disposal, unless the entity is in financial trouble, in which case 'a more appropriate method' (such as break-up values) should be used;[183]

(b) *Operations Statement*, which calculates the financial wealth added to the entity by trading and by its operations generally. It differs from the present form of profit and loss account in that:
   (i) there would be no depreciation charge;
   (ii) the stock would be accounted for at net realisable value; and
   (iii) the only exceptional or extraordinary items would be those arising out of unusual events of a revenue nature; exceptional or extraordinary gains or losses on fixed assets would be dealt with in the Statement of Changes in Financial Wealth outlined at (c) below;[184]

(c) *Statement of Changes in Financial Wealth*, which shows the change in the worth of the business for the period under consideration, such change being split into its main components with an indication of how each of these arose. The Committee proposed that the change in wealth would be measured in terms of year-end pounds, although 'in times of significant inflation it may be helpful if investors can be given an indication of the real change in financial wealth over the period concerned by applying the retail price index';[185] and

(d) *Distributions Statement*, which reflects the distributable change in financial wealth for the period plus any surpluses retained from previous periods, less dividends paid and proposed. In times of rising prices the 'real value' of capital should be maintained by an inflation adjustment which should be shown in the distributions statement and might be computed by applying the retail price index to the value of shareholders' contributed capital as at the start of the period. The paper went on to say that entities wishing to maintain their operating capability in physical terms could make a further appropriation to maintain the asset portfolio or to provide for the replacement of the services which these assets have been supplying.[186]

In addition to the four basic statements and information relating to corporate objectives and future financial plans, the Committee suggested the inclusion of the following additional information in the reporting package:

(a) a cash flow statement;

(b) segmental information;[187]

(c) information on related parties;

(d) information on accounting areas subject to uncertainty, for example management's view on the margin of error in accounting estimates;

(e) a statement on relative innovation which would illustrate the stance that the company is adopting in relation to innovation;

(f) information on effectiveness and lead-time of research and development;

(g) information on the economic environment within which the entity operates, including an analysis of facts such as market share, market strength, market size, the activities of competitors etc.;

(h) comparative operational statistics contrasting the reporting firm with its competitors;[188]

(i) information on staff resources; and

(j) information on ownership, management and their responsibilities.

4.4.3 Conclusion

At the time this was one of the boldest, most innovative and refreshing discussion documents ever to be published by a professional accounting body anywhere in the world. Of course it had flaws and can be criticised for either failing to address or inadequately addressing certain issues; however, it should be seen for what it was – a document designed to stimulate discussion, experimentation and further research. Although there was always the danger that the document would be regarded as too revolutionary in its approach, and be dismissed as an amusing intellectual exercise, it is now clear that the IASB's agenda of accounting change and development draws heavily on MCRV. For example the list of supplementary information above no longer looks innovative because so much of its suggested contents now appears in the financial reports of companies.

4.5 The Solomons Report

In May 1987, the Research Board of the ICAEW announced that it had decided to sponsor a project to address the need for guidelines for decisions in financial reporting. Professor David Solomons, a recently retired academic who in his lifetime was president of both the American Accounting Association and the British Accounting Association, agreed to carry out the study.

Solomons followed an approach to the subject that was almost identical to that taken by the FASB (see 2 above), perhaps not surprisingly considering that he acted as consultant to the FASB on its conceptual framework project and was principal author of SFAC No. 2. He started by examining the purposes of financial reporting, identifying users and how their needs were at present being met. His report then discussed the elements of financial statements and decided upon the asset and liability, rather than the revenue and expense, approach to financial accounting.[189]

Solomons' principal argument against the revenue and expense view of income determination was that it 'opens the door to all kinds of income smoothing'[190] and that it 'threatens the integrity of the balance sheet and its value as a useful financial statement. Its value is maximized if it can be seen as a statement of financial position; but it can only be that if all the items in it are truly assets, liabilities, and equity, and not other bits left over from the profit and loss account, and if all such items that are capable of being recognised are included in it.'[191] This attitude of Solomons has obviously been influential in the thinking of the IASB subsequently.

Solomons then set about defining the elements of financial statements on much the same basis as was done in SFAC No. 6 (see 2.4 above). Assets are defined as 'resources or rights incontestably controlled by an entity at the accounting date that are expected to yield it future economic benefits',[192] whilst liabilities are defined as 'obligations of an entity at the accounting date to make future transfers of assets or services (sometimes uncertain as to timing and amount) to other entities.'[193] As with the FASB and IASB concepts, all the other elements are then derived from these basic definitions; for example, owners' equity comprises net assets and income is the change in net assets.[194]

The Report focused attention on the issues of recognition and measurement and the choice of an accounting model for use in preparing general purpose financial statements. In view of the fact that Solomons' guidelines are based on the asset and liability view, it is not surprising that his recognition criteria concentrate on these two elements. Consequently, under Solomons' approach, an item should only be recognised in financial statements if:

'(a) it conforms to the definition of an asset or liability or of one of the sub-elements derived therefrom; and

(b) its magnitude as specified by the accounting model being used can be measured and verified with reasonable certainty; and

(c) the magnitude so arrived at is material in amount.'[195]

Solomons, having rejected the historical cost model generally in use at the time, set about devising an improved model for general purpose financial reporting, and listed the following five criteria that such an improved model should possess:

(a) the balance sheet should be a true and fair statement of an entity's financial condition, showing all its assets and liabilities that satisfy the above recognition criteria and conform with the asset and liability definitions;

(b) the entity's assets and liabilities should be carried in the balance sheet at their value to a going concern at the balance sheet date;

(c) profits or losses should mean increases or decreases of real financial capital as compared with the amount at the beginning of the year;

(d) the results shown by the financial statements should be measured consistently and should therefore be comparable from year to year, both in periods of fluctuating prices and stable prices; and

(e) all the information given by the financial statements should be verifiable and cost-effective.[196]

(In a subsequent posthumous publication entitled *Commentary: criteria for choosing an accounting model*[197] the number of criteria is expanded to seven, the extra two being essentially clarifications of the meanings of the original five.)

Solomons then attempted to prove that the model that best satisfies these requirements rests on two concepts: value to the business (as espoused by the Corporate Report and Sandilands Committee) and the maintenance of real financial capital. Although these may have some intellectual appeal, it is difficult to see whether either of them has any practical meaning. Solomons identified an asset's value to the business as being the loss that the business would suffer if it were deprived of the asset. He argued that since if deprived of an asset, the business would normally seek to replace it, replacement cost would determine value to the business.

However, Solomons recognised that circumstances exist where an asset's value to the business might be less than its replacement cost; for example, in the circumstances where a plant asset is technologically inferior to an equivalent new asset, the current cost of replacing the services rendered by the existing asset should be used. Furthermore, where an asset would not be replaced by a business if it were lost, its value to the business would be its recoverable amount, which is the higher of the asset's present value and its net realisable value. Therefore, Solomons' final formula for 'value to the business' is that it is equal to 'current cost or recoverable amount, if that is lower.'[198] It is interesting to note that this approach is almost identical to the criteria specified in IAS 36 – *Impairment of assets* – for identifying if an asset is impaired (see Chapter 15).

In the case of liabilities, the Solomons' equivalent to an asset's deprival value is a liability's relief value. In other words, liabilities would be valued at the amount that the entity 'could currently raise by the issue of a precisely similar debt security or the cost of discharging the liability by the most economical means, whichever is the higher.'[199] The view advanced in the late 1990s by the G4+1, is very similar to the Solomons approach and is clearly still influential in the thinking of the IASB today.

As mentioned above, Solomons' model is based on the maintenance of real financial capital, with income being defined in terms of the change in net worth. He took the view that because of the uncertainty surrounding the measurement and verification of intangible assets, the changes in such assets cannot be recognised in financial statements; consequently, income will only include changes in recognised tangible assets minus changes in recognised liabilities.[200] This view seems untenable today in view of the important role intangibles play in business and commerce, and provides another interesting example of the influence that business practice has on accounting theory, as at the time Solomons wrote, his views on the recognition of intangibles were not considered obviously flawed.

Solomons recommended a 'current-cost-constant-purchasing-power model' that recognised both changes in the general level of prices and changes in specific prices, and was based on the maintenance of real financial capital, not operating capacity.[201]

The following pro forma profit and loss account illustrates how Solomons' version of real income is derived:[202]

Pro forma profit and loss account as proposed by Solomons

		£
Sales revenue		xxx
Current cost (or lower recoverable amount) of goods sold		xxx
		xxx
Depreciation at current cost	xxx	
Other expenses	xxx	
		xxx
Current operating profit		xxx
Add:		
Holding gains less losses on non-monetary assets (net of inflation)	xxx	
Purchasing power gains on monetary liabilities less purchasing power losses on monetary assets	xxx	
		xxx
Real income		xxx

However it is the views expressed by Solomons on pensions that seem extraordinarily prescient and influential to the present day reader. For example he recommended if all or most of the assets of a pension plan can be moved freely back to the employer from the plan by a vote of the trustees, then the affairs of the plan should be consolidated with those of the employer. This approach is based on the view that a pension fund is, in effect, an off balance sheet vehicle set up to meet a company's future obligations. Solomons' proposal was extremely close to the approach adopted by the IASB in IAS 19 (Revised) – *Employee Benefits* – which is discussed in Chapter 32.

On the subject of goodwill, Solomons states that non-purchased goodwill should not be recognised; his reason for this being that 'determining the value of goodwill where it is not the subject of a purchase and sale transaction and in the presence of a highly imperfect market is too subjective to yield a reliable measure for the purpose of recognition.'[203] What he is saying is that since non-purchased goodwill does not have an historical cost, it is not possible to update an unknown cost in order to determine its current cost. The same argument applies to all internally generated intangibles, such as brand names. This remains a considerable problem for standard setters, in view of the commercial importance of intangible assets.

4.6 The UK's conceptual framework

The United Kingdom's conceptual framework document is interesting as it was the most recently published and also because the then Chairman of the UK's Accounting Standards Board, Sir David Tweedie, is currently Chairman of the IASB. The finalised version of the UK's Accounting Standards Board's *Statement of Principles for Financial Reporting* was published in December 1999 and the abbreviation 'SoP' is used hereafter.[204] The SoP is now somewhat redundant in the context of EU reporting under IFRS, and is therefore very briefly outlined below; although in view of the involvement of Sir David Tweedie, and its relatively recent publication, it may subsequently be seen as having been influential on the new IASB-FASB framework project's outcome.

The SoP comprised a compendium of eight 'chapters', with titles that owe much to the US and IASC's framework projects:

1. The objective of financial statements
2. The reporting entity
3. The qualitative characteristics of financial information
4. The elements of financial statements
5. Recognition in financial statements
6. Measurement in financial statements
7. Presentation of financial information
8. Accounting for interests in other entities

The ASB acknowledged that, in drafting the SoP it was drawing heavily on the work of previous projects in other countries, notably the FASB concept statements discussed at 2 above and the IASC Framework discussed at 3 above. The objectives ascribed to financial statements are therefore quite familiar.[205]

As in the IASB's Framework, the investor's perspective is deemed to represent the user's needs. Having established this generalisation, the SoP then goes on to assert that investors need information about the generation and use of cash in order to assess the entity's: liquidity and solvency; the relationship between profits and cash flows; the implications that financial performance has for future cash flows; and other aspects of financial adaptability.[206] Therefore, the academic stance that predicting future cash flows is the objective of reporting is endorsed.

The SoP also selects relevance and reliability as the two primary characteristics of accounting information, and again recognises that they are sometimes in conflict, so as to require a trade-off between them. In this case the choice is to be resolved as follows:

> 'if a choice exists between relevant and reliable approaches that are mutually exclusive, the approach chosen needs to be the one that results in the relevance of the information provided being maximised.'[207]

Therefore, the SoP takes the view that relevance takes priority over reliability and states that relevant information has the ability to 'influence the economic decisions of users and is provided in time to influence those decisions.'[208] This assertion of the priority of relevance over reliability was a substantial departure from the traditional view of prudence (conservatism), and was a harbinger of what has emerged from the first stage of the joint IASB-FASB framework project (discussed at 5.2 below). However it is a departure that is not altogether surprising, given the move towards fair value accounting that is predicated on the view that fair values are more relevant than cost, even if they are somewhat unreliable. This view overlooks that fact that users find information relevant only if it is reliable, and there is a threshold of reliability below which relevance ceases.

Thereafter the discussion of qualitative characteristics follows closely the IASB's Framework discussed above, including the unsatisfactory defining away of the problem of understandability.

Seven elements of financial statements are defined: Assets, Liabilities, Ownership Interest, Gains, Losses, Contributions from Owners, Distributions to Owners. The definitions and their deductive structure closely follow the IASB's Framework, starting with a near-identical asset definition. A definitional refinement is added however, namely that for a future economic benefit to be an asset it must also be 'controlled independently of the business as a whole.'[209] This new concept of independence from the business as a whole is only illustrated, not defined, although examples are given: 'market share, superior management or good labour relations ... cannot be controlled independently of the business as a whole.'[210] In this way, the SoP intends to prevent certain types of expenditure from being deferred and carried forward in the balance sheet as an asset.

Revenue recognition (which is not characterised as such) is referred to as follows:

> 'In a transaction involving the provision of services or goods for a net gain, the recognition criteria described above [i.e. the asset/liability criteria above] will be met on the occurrence of the critical event in the operating cycle involved.'[211]

By including this paragraph, the UK framework document seems to be fending off any potential criticism of its asset/liability approach to revenue recognition. In defending the approach that gains and losses are merely increases and decreases in net assets, other than those resulting from transactions with shareholders, the ASB is attempting to assert that both an asset/liability approach and a critical event approach to revenue recognition end up with the same answer. What the above paragraph is saying is that a net gain that is recognised on the basis of the critical event approach will necessarily result in an increase in net assets, with the result that the asset/liability recognition criteria will also be met.

However, while this is so, the converse is not. The implication is that irrespective of whether one follows a balance sheet approach to income recognition or a transactions-based income statement approach, one will always get to the same end-result. This is patently not true. Just because all revenue recognised under an income statement based transactions system will satisfy the asset/liability recognition criteria, it does not follow that all increases and decreases in net assets relate to revenue arising 'on the occurrence of the critical event in the operating cycle involved'. Revenue recognition criteria are more demanding than those for recognising changes in assets and liabilities, since in our view they should embody the concept of the revenue having been earned, based on performance by the reporting company. The issue of revenue recognition is discussed in detail in Chapter 28.

The SoP settles for a traditional approach to the statements that should be included in financial reports. However its discussion of how to account for investments in other entities acknowledges a difficulty inherent in both the UK's and IASB's framework documents. This difficulty is that the definition of assets excludes goodwill (because goodwill cannot meet the 'controlled' part of the definition), which creates a particular problem for the presentation of group accounts. This is acknowledged in the SoP, which seeks to justify the departure from the principle as follows:

> 'Purchased goodwill ... is not an asset in itself ... [but] if the parent's investment is to be fully reflected in the group's financial statements and the parent is to be held accountable for its investment ... purchased goodwill needs to be recognised as if it were an asset.'[212]

Perhaps this admission illustrates how standard setters often will, when practical considerations require it, quietly ignore the fundamental principles their standards are stated to rest upon. It is to be hoped that the decision by the IASB and the FASB in April 2004 to cooperate on a new framework document will result in such anomalies being resolved.

4.7 Conclusion

It can be seen that much of the academic and professionally sponsored research described above has been influential in shaping the underlying thinking in, and the practical requirements of, the IASB's accounting standards. Equally it is clear that much of this research has been influenced by the economic circumstances of the periods in which it took place. For example, inflation is no longer a preoccupation either of the profession or of economists, yet it was the phenomenon that drove much of the work described above. Somewhat paradoxically, historical cost accounting with its inherent simplicity, certainty and understandability, although easily dismissed as inadequate in inflationary times, becomes increasingly viable in the current low-inflation environment. It is one of those historical 'what-if' questions, but whether the IASB would be moving towards a full fair-value system had the current low-inflationary economic environment existed for the last 40 years, is an interesting moot point.

It is also interesting to note that a number of concepts used in current IASB standards (e.g. fair value, value in use) are really applications of concepts already extant in the academic literature. Value to the business as described by Solomons (see 4.5 above) equates to value in use; while fair value, as used by the IASB, is really sometimes an entry value, as discussed by Edwards and Bell (see 4.2.2 A above) and sometimes an exit value as discussed by Chambers, Sterling and Lee (see 4.2.2 C and 4.2.3 above).

5 CONVERGENCE AND THE IASB-FASB FRAMEWORK PROJECT

5.1 Introduction

The IASB and the FASB have a stated policy of working towards the convergence of International GAAP and US GAAP. This had been happening at an informal level for many years through a variety of bodies such as the G4+1 and the Joint Working Group on Financial Instruments. However, as described in Chapter 1, in September 2002 at a formal meeting between the IASB and the FASB, held at Norwalk, Connecticut, USA, this cooperation was placed on a more formal footing. Consequently in April 2004 at a joint meeting the FASB and the IASB agreed that their underlying conceptual frameworks should be revisited and, if possible, an agreed single conceptual framework produced. This endeavour is now a formal IASB-FASB joint project and is well under way.

The joint framework project is planned to be developed over a number of phases as follows:

Phase A: Objectives and Qualitative Characteristics

Phase B: Elements: Recognition and Measurement Attributes

Phase C: Initial and Subsequent Measurement

Phase D: Reporting Entity

Phase E: Presentation and Disclosure

Phase F: Purpose and Status (i.e. status of Framework in GAAP hierarchy)

Phase G: Application to Not-for-Profit Entities

Phase H: Finalisation (i.e. consideration by the IASB and FASB of how the project should be finalised once all phases have been exposed for public comment)

At the time of writing, September 2007, Phase A has been published by both the IASB and the FASB as a discussion paper, and an Exposure Draft is anticipated in 2008. The discussion paper is considered below. A discussion paper on Phase D is planned for late 2007 and round table discussions have been held on Phase C during the first half of 2007.

5.2 IASB-FASB Discussion paper – Preliminary views on an improved conceptual framework for financial reporting

In July 2006 the IASB published a Discussion paper – *Preliminary views on an improved conceptual framework for financial reporting: The objective of financial reporting and qualitative characteristics of decision-useful financial reporting information* – which appears to be a relatively advanced draft of the two chapters of its proposed new framework.[213] It is made clear that the paper has been prepared jointly with the FASB and represents the Boards' joint views.

The core of the discussion paper is a draft of the first two chapters of a new conceptual framework:

Chapter 1: The objective of financial reporting

Chapter 2: Qualitative characteristics of decision-useful financial reporting information

In addition, it contains an explanatory preface setting out why the Boards are undertaking the project and their approach to it and a summary of the draft chapters. The Boards have elected not to conduct a full review of their existing versions, as explained in the Preface:

> 'The boards concluded that a comprehensive reconsideration of all concepts would not be an efficient use of their resources. Many aspects of their frameworks are consistent with each other and, pending comments on the preliminary views set out in this Discussion Paper, do not seem to need fundamental revision. Instead, the boards adopted an approach that focuses mainly on improving the framework, giving priority to issues that are likely to yield standard-setting benefits in the near term.'[214]

The two draft chapters of the new IASB-FASB conceptual framework are discussed in the following sections.

5.2.1 The objective of financial reporting

The objective of financial reporting has been revised and is stated as follows:

> 'The objective of general purpose external financial reporting is to provide information that is useful to present and potential investors and creditors and others in making investment, credit, and similar resource allocation decisions.'[215]

The meaning of the phrase 'information that is useful' is further clarified in the draft as follows:

> 'financial reporting should provide information to help present and potential investors and creditors and others to assess the amounts, timing, and uncertainty of the entity's future cash inflows and outflows (the entity's future cash flows). That information is essential in assessing an entity's ability to generate net cash inflows and thus to provide returns to investors and creditors.'[216]

Therefore the position clearly adopted in the draft of the new joint conceptual framework is that it is the principal purpose of financial statements to enable users to assess the future cash flows of the entity concerned.

The objective has been subtly narrowed, as in contrast to the current IASB framework (see above at 3.2.1) stewardship is not mentioned as part of the objective of financial reporting. This represents a move by the IASB towards the FASB position (see 2.5 above) that has always considered that stewardship is principally assessed through the earnings information within financial statements.

A Stewardship

The removal of stewardship as an objective is specifically referred to in Chapter 1 of the discussion paper and is justified by the statement that an assessment of stewardship is to be derived from assessing future cash flows. Stewardship is thus acknowledged, but is held to be of consequence only because of its impact on an entity's ability to generate cash, and not as an important aspect in its own right:

> 'Because management's performance in discharging its stewardship responsibilities significantly affects an entity's ability to generate net cash inflows, management's stewardship is of significant interest to users of financial reports who are interested in making resource allocation decisions.' …
>
> 'Thus, the objective of financial reporting stated in paragraph OB2 encompasses providing information useful in assessing management's stewardship.'[217]

What this is saying is that the only reason why users are interested in stewardship is because of the effect it has on the generation of cash flows. This doubtful reasoning prompted two of the IASB's members to vote against the proposal to subsume stewardship within the decision-usefulness objective. In a separate Alternative View, the two members' draw a very important distinction between users' decisions concerning the *competence* of the stewards of the entity, and those concerning their *integrity*.[218] The point is developed as follows:

> 'It is accepted that information relevant to predicting future flows of economic benefit is relevant to this stewardship process, but it will not provide a complete set of information for stewardship purposes. For example, stewardship may require more emphasis on related party transactions, and generally on past rather than future transactions and events, than would be required by the primary focus on future cash flows. Thus, stewardship and decision-usefulness for investors are parallel objectives which do not necessarily conflict, but which have different emphases. They should therefore be defined as separate objectives.
>
> 'The two IASB members do not agree that stewardship requires management performance to be separated from entity performance [as stated in paragraphs BC1.35, BC1.37 and BC1.38]. The stewardship responsibility of the management board extends to all of the activities of the entity. Even if some risks are out of the control of management, the decision to be exposed to those risks (by the choice of activities, investments and hedging and insurance strategies) is within management control.
>
> 'Paragraph BC1.41 also states that 'Financial reports generally are useful to those with the responsibility for making decisions about management remuneration and monitoring management's dealings with an entity's owners because financial reports include the effects of all transactions engaged in by management on behalf of owners, as well as transactions between the entity and members of its management.' Although this statement is correct, the two IASB members believe that, as described in paragraph BC1.34, such information, produced as a by-product of the decision-usefulness objective,

> may be inadequate to meet the objective of stewardship. In order to meet that objective, a greater amount of disaggregation of information may be required. In particular, the level of materiality for reporting dealings with management should, for stewardship purposes, be determined by reference to the individual rather than the entity. A payment that may appear to have little significance in relation to the entity as a whole may assume much greater significance when viewed as a transaction with an individual manager.'[219]

At a narrow level, a stewardship objective would have been essential had not the draft framework specifically restricted its definition of users to loan creditors and investors. Additionally, the discussion paper asserts that financial reports should 'reflect the perspective of the entity rather than only the perspective of the entity's owners'.[220] Thus stewardship, which is in part an objective concerning the responsibility of managers to owners, is defined away as a secondary consideration.

More broadly, in a global context where ethical trading, ecological considerations, and efficient energy use are major and growing concerns, it is not tenable to maintain that the prediction of future cash flows is the only consideration of interest to users, whoever they are, and it is certainly not the case that a company's performance concerning such matters can be determined and assessed from cash flow information.

This is a powerful example at a fundamental level of the extent to which the FASB's original conceptual framework project has influenced the IASB-FASB joint project. The FASB's SFAC No. 1, while recognising the fact that financial reporting should provide information about how the management of an enterprise has discharged its stewardship responsibility,[221] goes on to say that 'earnings information is commonly the focus for assessing management's stewardship or accountability. Management, owners, and others emphasize enterprise performance or profitability in describing how management has discharged its stewardship accountability.'[222]

The draft states that the Boards have deferred consideration of 'the boundaries of financial reporting' until a later phase of the project; however given the relegation of the stewardship objective to a matter of cash flow performance, the IASB will have little difficulty, if it so wishes, in rejecting any wider considerations.

B Users of financial reports

The statement that the objective of financial statements is to provide information that is useful in assessing 'an entity's ability to generate net cash inflows and thus to provide returns to investors and creditors'[223] also contains a subtle difference of meaning compared with the IASB's current framework. The draft framework includes a list of potential users that contains literally everyone: equity investors, loan creditors and trade suppliers (i.e. trade creditors), employees, customers, governments, government agencies, regulatory bodies, members of the public.[224] However, the subtlety is that the draft framework specifically redefines, and thereby restricts the use of, the term creditors to: 'present and potential institutional and individual lenders and their advisers.'[225] The reason given for this restriction is that loan creditors expect a return on, as well as a return of the cash provided, whereas (for example) trade creditors do not. It is further asserted that suppliers, employees, customers, governmental agencies, or others have a 'dual role in relation to the entity. For instance, customers' rights to receive goods or services may be more important to them than any right to receive a cash refund or other cash payment'.[226] The draft contents itself with the assertion that 'Nevertheless, information that satisfies the needs of investors and creditors [as defined specially] is likely to be useful to those [other] parties as well.'[227]

It is not further explained what the dual role of trade creditors is, or why if it exists, it precludes them from being considered creditors by the proposed framework. Certainly there is no basis in law for such a distinction. One consequence of this proposed change is that it will only be necessary for financial statements to be comprehensible to investors, lenders and their respective advisors for the qualitative characteristic of understandability to be achieved. Thus the Boards' are implicitly asserting that financial statements only need to be understandable by a small number of specialists. Therefore it seems likely that trade creditors and others have been excluded by definition from the users for whom financial statements are intended because it is necessary to restrict 'allowable' users to participants in the capital markets, i.e. to experts, if lip service is to be paid to understandability.

C Financial performance

The draft framework makes it explicit that financial performance is secondary to, and derived from, balance sheet changes between the start and end of an accounting period, 'Information about an entity's financial performance during a period *measured by changes in its resources and the claims on them other than claims resulting from transactions with owners as owners*, as well as the components of the total change, is critical in assessing the entity's ability to generate net cash inflows'[228] (emphasis added).

This statement confirms and makes entirely explicit the Boards' commitment to the balance sheet approach to measuring performance, and its acceptance is critical to the justification and adoption of the Boards' fair value measurement agenda (see 6 below). If performance is defined in terms of changes in wealth between t1 and t2, the definition logically implies current valuations are required – otherwise the data would not be comparable. The Boards are thus explicitly rejecting in their new framework document any more rigorous measure of performance, such as one that would require a sales transaction, or a realised profit.

5.2.2 The qualitative characteristics of decision-useful financial reporting information

Chapter 2 of the draft framework deals with qualitative characteristics. The draft lists the following four principal qualitative characteristics of decision-useful financial reporting information:

- relevance;
- faithful representation;
- comparability; and
- understandability.

The four are subject to two 'pervasive constraints':

- Materiality; and
- Benefits that justify costs.[229]

One of the four principal qualitative characteristics has been considerably altered when compared with the existing frameworks of both Boards, and the hierarchy within which the characteristics are set has been changed also. Relevance, comparability and understandability are carried over with their meanings essentially unchanged from the previous framework, but reliability has been changed.

The IASB's existing framework document states that 'information has the quality of reliability when it is free from material error and bias and can be depended upon by users to represent faithfully that which it either purports to represent or could reasonably be expected to represent.'[230] It goes on to state that 'information may be relevant but so unreliable in nature or representation that its recognition may be potentially misleading.'[231] However, the IASB has decided that the existing framework does not convey 'the meaning of reliability clearly enough to avoid misunderstandings',[232] and is therefore proposing to remove reliability from the framework and to replace it with the qualitative characteristic of 'faithful representation'. It is open to question whether this is the underlying reason for proposing to remove the qualitative characteristic of reliability from the framework. After all, if the IASB believes that its meaning is not conveyed clearly enough in the existing framework it could provide the necessary degree of clarity in the revised one. An alternative explanation might be that the retention of reliability as a specific qualitative characteristic could be an impediment to the further extension of fair value measurement in IFRSs – particularly in those areas where reliable market-based fair value estimates are not obtainable.

In any event, the IASB has concluded that faithful representation, which is described as being 'correspondence or agreement between the accounting measures or descriptions in financial reports and the economic phenomena they purport to represent'[233] encompasses all of the qualities that the previous framework included as aspects of reliability. The practical effect of this statement is that reliability – instead of being identified separately as a primary decision-specific quality – is subsumed within the qualitative characteristics of verifiability, neutrality and completeness.

In the FASB's second Concepts Statement (see 2.6 above and figure 1 at 2.6) a hierarchy of qualitative characteristics is set out and shown diagrammatically. In this hierarchy, understandability is the paramount characteristic, followed by the two primary decision-specific qualities of relevance and reliability that are equal, and below these comes comparability together with a number of other sub-characteristics such as representational faithfulness, timeliness, verifiability, predictive value and neutrality. The Boards' new draft makes no such hierarchical distinctions between the four principal qualitative characteristics. Therefore, the level of importance given to reliability in the FASB's existing conceptual framework has been somewhat reduced in the draft of the new one.

A Faithful representation, verifiability and precision

As stated above, the definition of faithful representation offered in the draft framework is that it 'must be a *faithful representation* of the real-world economic phenomena that it purports to represent.'[234] As an explanation, this tautology is on par with that in Molière's famous satire of the medical profession *Le Malade imaginaire* – opium makes you sleepy because it has the power to put you to sleep. Fortunately, the draft further expands upon what is meant by 'faithful representation' by stating that 'to be a faithful representation of ... economic phenomena, information must be verifiable, neutral and complete.'[235]

The draft framework redefines verifiability and in doing so alters its normal meaning, as follows:

> 'To assure users that information faithfully represents the economic phenomena that it purports to represent, the information must be verifiable. *Verifiability* implies that different knowledgeable and independent observers would reach general consensus, although not necessarily complete agreement, either:
>
> (a) that the information represents the economic phenomena that it purports to represent without material error or bias (by direct verification); or
>
> (b) that the chosen recognition or measurement method has been applied without material error or bias (by indirect verification).
>
> To be verifiable, information need not be a single point estimate. A range of possible amounts and the related probabilities can also be verified.'[236]

One is prompted to ask why the Boards have chosen to define 'verify' in such a way that it could actually mean unverified information, or even unverifiable information, that has been arrived at by a *method* that has been applied correctly, with no requirement that the method is appropriate or applied to reliable data. One IASB board member disagreed with the draft framework's redefinition of verifiability, stating in an Alterative view:

> 'that the description of verifiability in paragraph QC23 should additionally specify that the consensus between knowledgeable and independent observers should be based on reliable evidence. Consensus that is not based on reliable evidence does not constitute verification', and
>
> 'that the description of indirect verification in paragraph QC23 should include a requirement that the method used should be one that may be expected to yield an estimate of the economic phenomenon that is free from material error or bias. Establishing that an inappropriate method has been applied without material error or bias does not constitute verification of the resulting estimate.'[237]

As part of the draft framework's discussion of faithful representation, the discussion paper states:

> 'Determining how best to depict in financial terms the machine as it currently exists in the real world is the role of faithful representation. The machine's original cost is a real-world economic phenomenon, and reporting that amount would be one way to faithfully represent the machine. However, if the machine is three years old, reporting it at original cost would not be a faithful representation of the machine as it now exists. In that situation, reporting the machine at an amount based on allocating its original cost over its useful life (amortised or depreciated cost) rather than at its original cost would better represent the machine as it currently exists. Another method, such as reporting the machine at an amount based on what it would cost to replace it in its current condition (replacement cost) might provide an even better representation of the machine as it now exists in the real world. Another method of representing the machine in its current condition would be to report the amount that would be received for the machine in a current exchange between a willing buyer and willing seller (fair value).'[238]

A new phrase, 'real world economic phenomenon' has been introduced by the draft framework as a type of filter for what should and should not be included in a financial report. It is explained thus:

> 'The phrase *real-world economic phenomena* deserves emphasis because its implications have often been overlooked. The phenomena depicted in financial reports are *real-world* because they exist now or have already occurred. ... The phenomena to be represented in financial reports are *economic* because they are relating to the production and distribution of material wealth.'[239]

At the purely logical level, this is insufficiently discriminatory. A financial report itself falls within the definition, as it is clearly 'relating to the production and distribution of wealth'. To what extent other real world *non-economic* phenomena – such as legal rights and duties – fail the real world economic phenomena test is a further question, but it seems unlikely that their effects will be excluded from financial reporting.

In the Basis for Conclusions attached to Chapter 2 of the draft framework there is further discussion of the notion of representational faithfulness and real-world economic phenomena. Paragraph BC2.28 states:

> 'In addition, elevating faithful representation helps to emphasise that the goal of financial reporting is to faithfully represent real-world economic phenomena and changes in them – whatever they may be. For example, representations of fair values should change when the values change, and the changes should reflect the degree of volatility in those changes. To depict a lack of volatility if the values are, in fact, volatile would not faithfully represent the economic phenomenon.'

This statement perhaps reflects the underlying purpose of the Boards, and equally illustrates a degree of confusion and lack of rigour in the draft framework. If the Boards believe that financial statements should depict fair values, that view should be explicit and should be justified. Instead, the draft framework drifts towards that stance by way of 'real world economic phenomena'-type justifications, without properly stating it.

The key question is what exactly is meant by 'real-world economic phenomena'. For instance, since 1950, the fundamental real-world economic phenomena have been extremely un-volatile: during this period the western economies have normally recorded annualized GDP growth of between 2% and 3%. This is not to be confused with short term economic data, such as stock exchange prices, exchange rates, interest rates and commodity prices, that have indeed seen large fluctuations. If the Boards want financial reports to reflect short term volatility that is unrelated to output, economic activity levels or the cash generating powers of the business concerned, it should be explicit, and be prepared to justify that view. However, it is not obvious that balance sheet exit price valuations in financial statements should generally reflect fluctuations in such short term data, or would be improved if they did.

Finally the draft makes it clear that information can be a faithful representation without being precisely so. To a degree, it seems that precision is not considered to be of paramount importance:

> 'Accuracy of estimates is desirable, of course, and some minimum level of accuracy (precision) is necessary for an estimate to be a faithful representation of an economic phenomenon. However, faithful representation implies neither absolute precision in the estimate nor certainty about the outcome. To imply a degree of precision or certainty of information that it does not possess would diminish the extent to which the information faithfully represents the economic phenomena that it purports to represent.'[240]

This statement needs more explanation and justification in our view. If the real-world economic phenomena being depicted are such short term phenomena as interest rates, commodity prices or exchange rates, then they are capable of precise determination. If, by contrast, the Boards are seeking to allow the use of types of valuations (such as mark-to-model valuations) that are inherently incapable of precise determination, allowing a degree of imprecision into the qualitative characteristic of faithful representation may be essential for such valuations to be legitimately used in financial reporting.

B Neutrality and conservatism

Chapter 2 of the draft framework states that neutrality is 'the absence of bias intended to attain a predetermined result or induce a particular behaviour.'[241] As such it is stated to be an essential aspect of representational faithfulness. Neutrality features in both Boards' existing framework documents; however in these earlier documents neutrality co-existed with conservatism (see 2.6.7 and 3.2.2C above). The draft takes a more robust line in relation to the two, and states that 'conservatism is incompatible with neutrality which implies a bias in financial reporting information.'[242]

It is clear from paragraph BC2.22 of the Basis for Conclusions of the discussion paper that the Boards regard 'conservatism' and 'prudence' as synonymous. This is not the case and in our view reflects a misunderstanding of the concept of prudence, which in fact implies – in general – caution over the use of unreliable, unverifiable data in financial reporting. In the specific context of performance, it implies that profit has not been earned until it has been realised. These two statements seem so sensible that we would welcome a proper justification for the rejection of the concept of prudence.

C Understandability

The qualitative characteristic of understandability is once more listed as an essential property of financial reporting. In common with all previous framework attempts, the normal meaning of the word is defined away. Thus:

> 'In developing financial reporting standards, standard-setters presume that those who use the resulting information will have a reasonable knowledge of business and economic activities and be able to read a financial report. Standard-setters also presume that users of financial reporting information will review and analyse the information with reasonable diligence. Financial reporting is a means of communicating information and, like most other types of information, cannot be of much direct help to those who are unable or unwilling to use it or who misuse it. One does not need to be a cartographer to use a map to get to an unfamiliar location. But it is necessary to know how to read a map, including understanding the concepts and symbols used in preparing it, and one must study the map carefully to get to the desired location. Likewise, one does not need to be an accountant or a professional investor to use financial reporting information, but it is necessary to learn how to read a financial report.'[243]

The map reading analogy is quite misleading, as most people can read a map after a few minutes tuition. The point is that some financial statements have become so complex and compendious that very few people indeed, regardless of the efforts they may make, can understand them. Indeed, even those whom the Boards would admit to be qualified map-readers were misled in a number of cases of sudden corporate failure in the early 2000s. The draft framework contains nothing seeking to alter the extremely exclusive meaning previously attached to understandability, and by incorporating advisors into its restrictive definition of eligible users (see 5.2.1B above) arguably further retreats from giving the characteristic any real effect.

D Substance over form

Finally, the notion of 'substance over form' – such a powerful inhibitor of synthetic schemes to hide the real extent of an entity's obligations – has been omitted from the draft framework, even though it has considerable prominence in the IASB's current document. The justification is as follows:

> 'the quality of faithful representation is incompatible with representations that subordinate substance to form. Accordingly, the proposed framework does not identify *substance over form* as a component of faithful representation because to do so would be redundant.'[244]

This is a similar line of reasoning to that advanced (see 5.2.1A above) to justify the absence of stewardship as an explicit objective in the draft. The justification that a specific rule is not needed because the matter is implied by a general rule, is analogous to a government saying a law prohibiting bad behaviour exists, so there is no need for a law prohibiting stealing. In our view a definite commitment to the well understood and frequently expressed principle of substance over form would have been much more reassuring in a framework document, and would be to the benefit of financial reporting. It may well be that the notion is a casualty of the IASB-FASB joint project, as it is not necessarily considered to be a useful, or legally easy to explain, concept in the USA. It would be an interesting challenge also for the IASB to explain how IAS 39 – a standard that is widely accepted as being form-based – is consistent with the assertion that 'the quality of faithful representation is incompatible with representations that subordinate substance to form'.

5.2.3 Current discussions

A The revised definition of an asset, recognition and derecognition

At the time of writing, it is not expected that further draft chapters of the proposed new joint IASB-FASB conceptual framework will be published until late2007, when a discussion paper on Phase D: Reporting entity is currently planned (see 5.1 above). As noted below, at its July 2007 meeting the Board decided to suspend staff work on Phase B: Elements and recognition, and a discussion paper on this topic will not appear before late 2008 at the earliest. Nevertheless the Boards regularly discuss the conceptual framework at open meetings and the IASB provides reports of these discussions in its various publications. The definition of assets, a core part of Phase B of the project was the focus of Board discussions in late 2006 and early 2007. It is accepted that the definition is by no means finalised, and it is greatly to the Boards' credit that such difficult discussions are so openly conducted.

A report in the IASB's Update publication issued in June 2006 indicated that the IASB-FASB joint conceptual framework project is considering revising the definition of an asset. The definition being considered is:

> 'An *asset* is a present economic resource of an entity. An asset of an entity has three essential characteristics:
>
> - There is an underlying economic resource;
> - The entity has rights or other privileged access to the economic resource;
> - The economic resource and the rights or other privileged access both exist at the financial statement date.'

This definition was further amplified, as reported in the November 2006 issue of Update as follows:

'An asset is a present economic resource to which the entity has a present right or other privileged access.

Present means that both the economic resource and the right or other privileged access to it exist on the date of the financial statements.

An *economic resource* is something that has positive economic value. It is scarce and capable of being used to carry out economic activities such as production and exchange. An economic resource can contribute to producing cash inflows or reducing cash outflows, directly or indirectly, alone or together with other economic resources. Economic resources include non-conditional contractual promises that others make to the entity, such as promises to pay cash, deliver goods, or render services. Rendering services includes standing ready to perform or refraining from engaging in activities that the entity could otherwise undertake.

A right or other privileged access enables the entity to use the present economic resource directly or indirectly and precludes or limits its use by others. *Rights* are legally enforceable or enforceable by equivalent means (such as by a professional association). Other privileged access is not enforceable, but is otherwise protected by secrecy or other barriers to access.'

The June definition seems to be somewhat circular, as it states both that an asset is an economic resource, and that it is essential that there is an economic resource underlying the economic resource. It is not at all clear what is meant by 'economic resource' and the November amplification of its meaning is so vague and wordy as to be insufficiently discriminatory to merit the term 'definition'. Additionally, the proposed definition includes two other terms, 'rights' and 'privileged access' to describe the entity's relationship with the asset; neither of these is easy to define, yet both are crucial to the application of the definition in practice. For example, it is difficult to understand how goodwill arising on consolidation is an 'economic resource' without a much fuller explanation of the term.

It appears from the published discussions and from accounts of the discussions at open IASB meetings that the definition adopted has to be able to explain a forward contract between a farmer and a buyer of corn, as for reasons that are not quite clear, this arrangement must fit into the definition. A common-sense view of such an arrangement might be that nobody has an asset, just a contract, and that when delivery is effected the transaction would be recorded by the entities concerned. Apparently, in open discussion, project staff members have advanced the view that the right to obtain delivery is the asset, not the corn itself – the existence of which is irrelevant – even though this view would seem to conflict with the requirement for there to be an underlying economic resource. It may also be fallacious to argue that because something can be sold there must be an asset in any objective accounting sense – after all, lottery tickets are sold.

Such difficulties of definition, and the reliance upon undefined and unexplained 'concepts' such as privileged access, perhaps best illustrate the conceptual problems that the Boards' exclusively balance sheet orientated view of financial reporting involve. For example, whether a promise is an economic resource in the 'real-world economic phenomenon' sense used in Chapter 2 of their draft framework (discussed in 5.2.2 above) is debatable. This is not to say that promises *cannot* be assets – indeed the business of banks is to lend against contractual undertakings to repay, and of entities generally to conclude sales contracts that involve undertakings to pay for goods and services supplied – it is to say that requiring all possible contractual arrangements to be encompassed by a single asset definition might be unnecessary if, for example, a more straightforward transaction performance approach were to be adopted.

In the IASB Update published in July 2007, it was stated that the Boards have instructed staff to cease further consideration of the definition of assets and liabilities, and for the immediate future decided staff time should be spent on considering criteria for recognition, derecognition and identifying the 'unit of account'.

B Measurement

The Board discussed a preliminary staff paper on this fundamental area in July 2007, at which meeting the Board also decided to ask staff to concentrate upon measurement, rather than finalising the definitions of the elements of financial accounting. It is clear from observers' reports that there is a considerable divergence of views on how the measurement phase of the conceptual framework should be progressed. A discussion paper is not planned in the immediate future – the Board discussed 2009 as being the earliest likely date. However, the IASB has sponsored and published, a measurement discussion paper written for the Canadian Accounting Standards Board (discussed at 6.1 below) that unequivocally recommended the measurement of assets upon initial recognition at fair value. It is not known whether this paper reflects the IASB's current views, though in an interview in the IASB publication Insight in August 2007, Sir David Tweedie, and other IASB members appeared to indicate an acceptance of mixed measurement – some items at historic cost, some at exit valuations – in the balance sheets of entities.

5.2.4 The status of the framework

The IASB's current reasons for having a framework at all are set out in the preface to the Discussion Paper as follows:

'P3 A common goal of the boards – a goal shared by their constituents – is for their standards to be clearly based on consistent principles. To be consistent, principles must be rooted in fundamental concepts rather than being a collection of conventions. For the body of standards taken as a whole to result in coherent financial reporting, the fundamental concepts need to constitute a framework that is sound, comprehensive, and internally consistent;

'P4 The IASB's *Framework* and the FASB's Concepts Statements articulate concepts that go a long way towards being an adequate foundation for consistent standards, and the boards have used them for that purpose. For example, the bases for conclusions of most of the boards' standards discuss how their conclusions are consistent with the applicable concepts;

> 'P5 Another common goal of the boards is to bring their standards into convergence. The boards are aligning their agendas more closely to achieve convergence in future standards, but they will encounter difficulties in doing that if they base their decisions on different frameworks.'[245]

The problem with this statement is that it does not actually commit the IASB to any sort of deductive process, or indeed any rational process at all. The phrases '*based on* consistent principles', '*rooted in* fundamental concepts', 'a framework *that is sound*', '*a long way towards being* an adequate foundation' [emphases added] are meaningless if there is no rational process to ensure consistent application. This concern is reinforced by the following paragraph from the section of the paper entitled 'Introduction to the [draft] framework':

> 'The [draft] framework does not establish standards for particular financial reporting issues. Some existing standards may be inconsistent with the concepts set forth in this [draft] framework. The [draft] framework does not override those standards, nor does it constitute support for providing financial reports that do not comply with them. The boards may reconsider such standards in the future, depending on the extent to which the topics satisfy the criteria for adding a project to the respective board's agenda. In addition, financial reporting is not static; it evolves over time. Financial reporting standards developed in response to changes in business practices and the economic environment may help in continuing the development of the [proposed] framework.'[246]

What is explicit, therefore, is that the IASB does not undertake to produce standards that logically follow from its concepts or principles, or that are logically consistent with them. In fact, it even suggests that the continued development of the framework may be driven by new standards, rather than the reverse. A legitimate question, therefore, is what is the status of this new framework? In a further paragraph from the Introduction the Board states:

> 'Without the guidance provided by an established framework, standard-setting would be based on the personal financial reporting frameworks developed by each member of the standard-setting body. Standard-setting based on such personal frameworks can produce agreement on specific standard-setting issues only if enough of those frameworks happen to intersect on those issues. Even those agreements might prove transitory because, as the membership of the standard-setting body changes over time, the mix of personal conceptual frameworks changes as well.'[247]

It seems that the new framework is proposed as a sort of *aide memoire* for the Board, to remind them, as individuals, of current policy, and as an indication to new members of what the club rules are. These rules will be changed as required, according to pragmatic developments such as changes in business practices and the economic environment. This would be quite acceptable if it were unequivocally presented as such; however, in our view, it is not. Rather, the discussion paper is presented as a rigorously deductive exercise starting from fundamental principles, with all the credibility that process endows; yet at the same time, the Boards seek to excuse themselves from adhering to that approach. Neither does it make any commitment to demonstrate that its conclusions actually do follow from its principles, whereas other possible alternatives do not.

These methodological points are not merely academic, they go to the centre of the standard-setting process. Standard setters frequently ignore comments on draft pronouncements on the basis of their lack of adherence to that body's principles. Workable, practical, obvious solutions are rejected by standard setters because they are not in conformity with their 'principles'. If it transpires that these 'principles' are actually arbitrary and subject to change, it is questionable whether they can be described as principles at all. The Boards, by not accepting the discipline of a deductive process, weaken their claims to be basing their standards on principle. This methodological ambiguity is also evident in the measurement discussion paper discussed at 6.1 below.

6 MEASUREMENT

Measurement – how to express in monetary terms the asset or liability depicted in financial statements – is perhaps the most fundamental aspect of accounting currently under consideration. For many decades historical cost, or modified historical cost, has been used as the basis for measuring assets or liabilities. Gradually over the last decade or so, this has changed as more complex types of financial instruments and methods of financing businesses have emerged. Currently, most financial statements contain assets and liabilities that are measured using a variety of measurement methods, depending upon the type of asset or liability concerned. A typical modern financial statement in compliance with IFRS might include, for example, assets measured in all of the following ways: historical cost, depreciated historical cost, market value, calculated fair value, valuations by actuaries or other specialists, and measurements modified by impairment tests.

There appears to be a desire by both the FASB and the IASB to move balance sheet valuations generally away from historical cost-based measurements towards what is termed in a number of their standards 'fair value'. Both the manner in which the new draft conceptual framework has been expressed and the accommodations made in its definitions, confirm this view. The possible general application of fair value measurements to all assets and liabilities in the foreseeable future – as distinct from its application to certain types such as financial instruments only – would represent an alteration to financial statements of the most fundamental kind. Three recent publications on the subject of measurement – an IASB discussion paper on measurement; a FASB standard on fair value measurement; and an IASB discussion paper based on that FASB standard – are discussed at 6.1, 6.2 and 6.3 below, and a general discussion on the use of fair values in financial reporting is included at 6.4.

6.1 Discussion paper: Measurement bases for financial accounting – measurement on initial recognition

In November 2005 the IASB published a Discussion Paper entitled *Measurement bases for financial accounting – measurement on initial recognition*. This paper represents the output of a research project that was undertaken by the staff of the Canadian Accounting Standards Board at the request of the IASB and on the basis of input from, and discussions with, individual members of the IASB and their staff. However, its content has not been formally deliberated by the IASB.

'Measurement' in the context of this paper refers to whether the actual cost, or fair value, or some other method is the best measurement basis to use in considering the values at which assets are to be recognised initially and carried in the balance sheet. The paper is quite extensive, running to some 140 pages, and contains the following major sections:

Summary

Part I: Measurement bases project

Chapter 1	Purpose of project and scope
Chapter 2	Criteria for evaluation

Part II: Measurement on initial recognition

Chapter 3	Possible bases for measurement on initial recognition
Chapter 4	General conceptual analysis – market versus entity-specific measurement objectives
Chapter 5	General conceptual analysis – value-affecting properties and market sources
Chapter 6	General conceptual analysis – reliability
Chapter 7	Analysis of alternative measurement bases
Chapter 8	A synthesis of some consequential recommendations

The purpose of the project is stated as follows:

> 'The project is intended to provide the International Accounting Standards Board (IASB) and national standard setters with a sound conceptual basis for:
>
> (a) revising and expanding the measurement aspects of their conceptual frameworks; and
>
> (b) improving the measurement requirements of their financial reporting standards.
>
> 'In regard to (a), the IASB and the Financial Accounting Standards Board (FASB) in the United States have initiated a joint project to converge and improve their conceptual frameworks, including the measurement aspects. For the IASB, the discussion paper represents the first step of its due process for the measurement aspects within the broader conceptual framework project.'[248]

It is difficult to gauge the extent to which the paper – which, after all, is published by the IASB as an IASB Discussion Paper – actually reflects the views of the IASB. In our view it is reasonable to assume that the IASB would not have published the paper under its banner if it did not broadly support the views expressed therein.

The project was undertaken 'because existing measurement standards and practices are inconsistent, and a number of major measurement issues remain unsettled. Some existing standards reflect more or less arbitrary mixed measurement compromises, pending resolution of conflicting views on appropriate measurement bases. The coverage of the measurement component of existing conceptual frameworks is very limited and out of date. Major developments have taken place since these frameworks were put in place that have significant implications for accounting measurement. These include developments in finance theory and capital markets, the application of present value and statistical probability principles, fair value measurement practices, and computer and information technology.'[249]

6.1.1 The 'cash-equivalent expectations attribute' of assets and liabilities

The analysis in the paper starts with a discussion of the evaluation criteria that should be applied to each possible measurement basis and 'proceeds on the basis that these criteria should be developed from, and be consistent with, the objectives of financial reporting, qualitative characteristics, and definitions of the elements of financial statements that are contained in the existing conceptual frameworks of accounting standard setters.'[250] Consequently, the paper provides a brief analysis based mainly on the IASB's conceptual framework, with the aim of establishing the necessary 'evaluation criteria'.

The conclusion of this analysis is that the primary criteria for evaluating possible measurement bases, derived from the conceptual frameworks, are:[251]

(a) Decision usefulness;

(b) Qualitative characteristics of useful information:
  - Understandability;
  - Relevance – predictive value, feedback value, timeliness;
  - Reliability – representational faithfulness, neutrality, verifiability;
  - Comparability.

(c) Concepts of assets and liabilities:
  - How the expected cash-equivalent flow attribute of assets and liabilities is measured.

(d) Cost/benefit considerations.

The paper concludes that these aspects of the frameworks 'narrow the rationally acceptable possibilities, but they are not sufficient, in themselves, for achieving agreement on a single measurement basis or how to choose between different bases in different circumstances.'[252] Since the existing IASB Framework makes no attempt to relate measurement to other parts of the framework, but simply lists indiscriminately some of the measurement bases that are employed in financial statements, we do not believe the Framework can even be said to 'narrow the rationally acceptable possibilities'.

Nevertheless, whilst the paper's analysis of the IASB Framework provides no great conceptual insight, the authors of the paper use it to conclude that 'the information on the amounts (value), timing and uncertainty of cash-equivalent flows is considered to be the primary focus of financial accounting.'[253] This leads to the statement 'that 'assets' (economic resources ultimately reflecting expected direct or indirect cash flows or cash-equivalent benefits) and 'liabilities' (present obligations reflecting expected outflows of economic resources, ultimately cash or cash-equivalent outflows) are the basic subject matter of financial accounting measurement. Since it is the cash-equivalent expectations attribute of assets and liabilities that is the primary focus of business activities, it seems appropriate to conclude that this attribute should be the primary focus of accounting measurement.'[254] As will be seen below, the unsupported assertion that 'the cash-equivalent expectations attribute of an asset is the primary focus of accounting measurement' enables the paper to conclude that fair value is the most relevant measure of an asset or liability on initial recognition.

6.1.2 Possible bases for measurement on initial recognition

The paper analyses possible bases of measurement for assets and liabilities on initial recognition only – i.e. when assets and liabilities are first recognised in the financial statements of an entity. Issues relating to re-measurement, including impairment, will be dealt with in subsequent papers. The conclusions reached are described as being 'tentative' and will be re-assessed when their potential implications for re-measurement are considered in subsequent papers.

The paper does not deal generally with the timing of when initial recognition of an asset or a liability should occur. The paper does, however, propose that initial measurement should be determined as at the date of initial recognition. This has important implications. For example, if prices change between the date when a fixed cash price is negotiated and the initial recognition of the asset acquired, then, in accordance with some measurement bases, the asset would be measured based on prices at the later date. Furthermore, the paper proposes that the initial recognition of a non-contractual asset that is developed over a period of time should be considered to occur, for purposes of initial measurement, when the asset becomes ready to contribute to the generation of future cash flows.

The paper proposes that the following are the possible bases for measurement on initial recognition, and proposes working definitions, based as a starting reference point on those currently being used in IFRSs:[255]

(a) *Historical cost*: Assets are recorded at the fair value of the consideration given to acquire them at the time of their acquisition. Liabilities are recorded at the fair value of the consideration received in exchange for incurring the obligations at the time they were incurred.

This is based on the definition of historical cost in the IASB *Framework* at paragraph 100(a), with the following changes:

(i) The IASB definition states that 'Assets are recorded at the amount of cash or cash equivalents paid or the fair value of the consideration given ...', whilst the paper asserts that the words 'cash or cash equivalents paid' are redundant because the amount of cash or cash equivalents paid should always equal the fair value of consideration given;

(ii) The IASB definition states that 'Liabilities are recorded at the amount of proceeds received in exchange for the obligation.' In the Discussion Paper, the words 'amount of proceeds' are replaced by 'fair value of the consideration'. This change is made ostensibly in order to be more precise and consistent with the definition of historical cost for assets;

(iii) The IASB definition goes on to add that '... or in some circumstances (for example, income taxes), at the amounts of cash or cash equivalents to be paid to satisfy the liability in the normal course of business.' This phrase has been omitted from the above definition because it seems – to the paper's authors – to be describing an expected value measurement rather than one that is consistent with the historical cost objective.

(b) *Current Cost – Reproduction Cost and Replacement Cost:* The reproduction cost of an asset is defined as 'the most economic current cost of replacing an existing asset with an identical one', whilst the replacement cost of an asset is defined as 'the most economic current cost of replacing an existing asset with an asset of equivalent productive capacity or service potential.'[256]

International standards had formerly defined replacement cost as '... the current acquisition cost of a similar asset, new or used, or of an equivalent productive capacity or service potential.'[257] This is commonly known as 'current cost'. Current cost is defined for the purposes of the paper as the most economic cost of an asset or of its equivalent productive capacity or service potential. This definition embodies reproduction cost and replacement cost, which are usually separately defined in the authoritative literature of other standard setters.

The liability equivalent of replacement and reproduction cost is not defined in IFRSs. However, for the purposes of the paper, it has been presumed to be 'the fair value of the consideration that the owing entity would have received if the liability had been incurred by it on the measurement date';[258]

(c) *Net realizable value (of an asset):* The estimated selling price in the ordinary course of business less the estimated costs of completion and the estimated costs necessary to make the sale.

This is the definition found in IAS 2 – *Inventories*. Again, the equivalent liability definition does not seem to have formally been defined in accounting literature, but the paper proposes that it may be defined as 'the estimated amount that would be incurred in the ordinary course of business to be released from the liability on the measurement date plus the estimated costs necessary to secure that release';[259]

(d) *Value in use (of an asset):* The present value of estimated future cash flows expected to arise from the continuing use of an asset and from its disposal at the end of its useful life. This is the definition found in IAS 36. This definition does not state whose expectations should be the basis for determining value in use, although it is clear from IAS 36 that the objective is to reflect the reporting entity management's best estimates of future cash flows;

(e) *Fair value*: The amount for which an asset or liability could be exchanged between knowledgeable, willing parties in an arm's length transaction. This is the existing IFRS definition that is consistently used in its standards (for example, in IAS 39), with one change. The IFRS definition states '... asset could be exchanged, or a liability settled ...', whereas the definition above defines fair value in terms of the amount for which either an asset or a liability could be exchanged. In the view of the paper's authors, this change avoids the implication that the fair value of a liability is necessarily the amount for which it could be settled, that is, its exit value. In other words, the paper – in the view of its authors – adopts a working definition of the fair value measurement basis expressed in neutral terms as the amount that could be exchanged for an asset or liability, without seeming to be limited to an exit, as opposed to an entry, market price;[260]

(f) *Deprival value*: The loss that an entity would suffer if it were deprived of an asset. It is the lower of replacement cost and recoverable amount on the measurement date, with recoverable amount being the higher of value in use and net realizable value.[261] The paper notes that some people do not consider deprival value to be a separate measurement basis, but rather a decision rule for selecting between three of the above measurement bases (replacement cost, net realizable value, and value in use). However, the paper argues that deprival value is based on an overarching theory of management behaviour that adds an important dimension that integrates the three bases into a distinct measurement approach.[262]

The paper explains that 'present value' does not appear on this list of measurement bases because it is not a measurement basis in itself. Rather, it is a measurement technique that can be applied to make estimates under several of the above measurement bases. The present value measurement technique is important because it provides the mathematical structure for valuing expected future cash flows, taking into account the time value of money and attendant risks.[263]

6.1.3 Market vs. entity-specific measurement objectives

The paper proposes that differences between bases for measuring assets and liabilities on initial recognition arise from two fundamental sources:

- Market versus entity-specific measurement objectives; and
- Differences in defining the properties that affect the values of assets and liabilities.

The market value measurement objective is to measure an asset or liability at the price for which it would be exchanged under competitive market conditions, reflecting the market's expectations as to the amounts, timing and uncertainty of future cash flows discounted at market rates of return for commensurate risk. The paper analyses the essential properties of market value, and addresses its relationship to fair value.

An entity-specific measurement objective looks to the expectations of the reporting entity, which may differ significantly from those implicit in a market price. Any measure of an asset or liability that differs from its market value must be based, explicitly or implicitly, on entity-specific expectations that differ from those of the market.

The paper concludes that, for external financial reporting purposes, the market measurement objective has important qualities that make it superior to entity-specific measurement objectives, at least on initial recognition. In particular, the paper asserts that the more relevant financial statement measurement objective on initial recognition for investors and other external users is that entities be measured against market values and subject to the discipline of the marketplace, rather than to entities' individual expectations.

However, this proposed conclusion presumes the existence of a market for an asset or liability on initial recognition, or failing the existence of an observable market, the ability to estimate reliably what the market price would be if a market did exist. It is proposed that the objective of the fair value measurement basis is to represent the properties of market value.

In fact, in the absence of any evaluation of the relative merits of the two approaches, the discussion in the paper provides at least as much support for the views of those who favour an entity-specific approach as it does for those who favour a market-based approach. The proposition that the market value objective is superior to an entity-specific measurement is little more than an unsubstantiated assertion, rather than, as the paper states, a conclusion that has been reached 'on the basis of [the paper's] conceptual analysis.'[264] The limited 'conceptual analysis' that the paper does contain in fact points to 'the cash-equivalent expectations attribute of assets and liabilities' being more appropriately reflected in the measurement of cash generating units on the basis of value to the business (VTB), rather than on the basis of an exit value for individual assets and liabilities, which would in most cases be calculated based on the assumptions of a hypothetical market comprising hypothetical buyers and sellers. Indeed, the implication in the paper that entity-specific measures are non-market based is pejorative: it is often the case that a VTB measurement provides a greater indication of market conditions (and hence the 'cash-equivalent expectations attribute of assets and liabilities') than is the case with many so-called exit values.

6.1.4 *Value-affecting properties of assets and liabilities*

The paper argues that, traditionally, measurement bases have been classified and evaluated in terms of whether they are 'entry' or 'exit' values. An entry value is a measure of the amount for which an asset could be bought or a liability could be incurred. An exit value is a measure of the amount for which an asset could be realized or a liability could be settled.

However, the paper presents an entirely different perspective of the entry-exit value debate, and argues that the market value measurement objective does not envisage that there could be different entry and exit market (fair) values for the same asset or liability at the same time. We believe that this assertion is open to challenge. For example, the replacement cost (entry value) of a specialised production asset may well be different from its net realisable (exit) value – for example, in the case of an oil refinery. Nevertheless, the paper asserts that differences between apparent market values of seemingly identical assets or liabilities, for example between their exit and entry values, may be attributable to one or both of the following sources:

(a) Differences between the assets and liabilities traded in different markets. Apparently different entry and exit prices for an asset or liability may be due to, sometimes subtle, differences between the asset or liability that is traded in an 'entry' market and the asset or liability that is traded in an 'exit' market;

(b) Entity-specific charges or credits. Some differences between exit and entry values of assets and liabilities are due to entity-specific charges or credits. Under the market value measurement objective, these would be treated as expenses or income (or perhaps, in some cases, as direct charges or credits to equity) on recognition. Under an entity-specific measurement objective, they might qualify for inclusion in the measurement of the asset or liability depending on management's expectations, intentions, and assumptions. An example of this might be transaction costs, which the paper believes should be expensed and not included in the initial measurement of an asset.

6.1.5 *Fair value*

Having put forward the proposition that the market value measurement objective provides superior information, the paper (almost inevitably) concludes that fair value is more relevant than the other identified bases on initial recognition. This determination is made on the basis of the assertion that all of the alternative measurement bases other than fair value directly or indirectly incorporate entity-specific measurements. For this reason, the paper proposes that fair value should be used to measure assets and liabilities on initial recognition, provided it can be measured reliably.

Nevertheless, the paper does acknowledge that significant measurement uncertainty in measuring fair value exists in some common situations. Some of the problems identified include determining what constitutes a market and understanding what data inputs market participants would likely use when a market does not exist for the item in question.

The paper then considers which measurement bases are acceptable substitutes for fair value when fair value cannot be measured reliably on initial recognition. Consistent with the fundamental proposition that the market value measurement objective provides superior information, the paper proposes that the alternative measurement basis used should be the one that is most consistent with the market value measurement objective, provided it can be measured reliably and, when cost bases are used, the amount is expected to be recoverable.

In evaluating cost bases as possible substitutes for fair value on initial recognition, replacement cost is considered to be more relevant than reproduction cost, and both are considered more relevant than historical cost.

Net realizable value and value in use are considered and rejected as substitutes for fair value on initial recognition. However, redefined concepts of realizable value and present value, applied as consistently as possible with the fair value measurement objective, are considered as possible estimates of, or substitutes for, fair value. The analysis indicates that replacement cost is unlikely to be capable of reliable estimation in many cases, and that reproduction cost may be reliably estimable in some situations in which replacement cost is not. The paper asserts that there are also significant reliability limitations with historical cost measurements, notably the indeterminacy inherent in any one-to-many cost allocations, and the failure to include costs that were incurred before the asset or liability qualified for initial recognition. Nonetheless, the paper accepts that historical cost can be an appropriate substitute in some cases. The paper acknowledges that deprival value overcomes some of the potential weaknesses of each of its component measurement bases evaluated individually and proposes a refinement of the deprival value decision rule in light of the analysis of the alternative measurement bases.

On the basis of this analysis, the paper proposes a four-level measurement hierarchy for assets and liabilities when they are initially recognized:[265]

Level 1 – observable market prices; any adjustments are consistent with those that market participants can be expected to make;

Level 2 – accepted valuation models or techniques; all significant inputs are consistent with those that market participants can be expected to use;

Level 3 – current cost (i.e. reproduction cost and replacement cost); with the possibility of substituting historical cost, provided a reliable estimate can be made and the amount can be expected to be recoverable;

Level 4 – models and techniques that use entity-specific inputs only; when unavoidable and when not demonstrably inconsistent with those that market participants can be expected to use.

The paper notes that only Level 1 and 2 measurements should be described as 'fair value'. Level 3 and 4 measurement bases have sufficient relevance and reliability to be used as substitutes for fair value, but are not sufficiently based on market expectations to be described as 'fair value'. Importantly, the paper notes that if none of the above measurement alternatives is feasible, the item in question fails to meet the conditions for recognition as an asset or liability.

It is worth noting that this proposed hierarchy differs in some important respects from the fair value hierarchy in the FASB draft standard on fair value measurements (see 6.2 below).

6.1.6 Efficient market price

The paper includes lengthy discussion and analysis of market and entity-specific measurement objectives and a comparison of the two. The discussion and analysis is almost entirely based on finance literature and assumes that an 'efficient market price' (unaffected by entity-specific factors) can be determined for all assets and liabilities. Indeed, the Paper refers to an 'a priori expectation reasoned from the market value measurement objective … that there can be only one fair value for a particular asset or liability on a measurement date.'[266] However, in the real world few assets and liabilities are traded on active markets and therefore few assets and liabilities have real market values.

Furthermore, we have no confidence that a deductive approach to the practice of financial reporting will yield satisfactory outcomes when those deductions are based upon *a priori*, rather than *a posteriori*, premises. The paper claims that a deductive approach will be 'most useful in developing conceptual theories and hypotheses concerning the various possible measurement bases', and it expects 'inductive analysis' to act as a 'reality check'.[267] As no empirical evidence is cited by the paper in support of any of its conclusions, in the face of considerable evidence to the contrary and the (to us) insuperable logical difficulties inherent in its assertions, we question whether the methodology adopted by the authors has, in fact, included such a 'reality check' in practice.

The paper takes this further, stating that 'competitive market forces work to resolve diverse expectations of various entities' managements to a single price that impartially reflects all publicly available information… .'[268] Therefore, where there is more than one market in which an asset or liability is traded, the problem of different prices is to be dealt with by the simple expedient of '…[excluding the differences] from the determination of fair value.'[269] This assumes that it is possible firstly to identify the nature and then to quantify the effect of the particular differences that are responsible for causing the market price in a particular market to deviate from pure fair value and that when these differences are stripped away, the one fair value of similar assets or liabilities will be revealed. We do not believe this to be realistic.

Similarly, the paper goes on to presume that if a market does not exist, it is nevertheless possible to estimate reliably what the market price would be were a market to exist, which seems contradictory and illogical. Since, according to the paper, it takes competitive market forces to resolve diverse expectations of various entities' managements to a single price,[270] how can there be such a single price for a particular asset or liability if there is no active market with 'competitive market forces'? If there is no market, how can such a market be assumed to exist and how could anyone arrive at a single price that is reliable? In short, in the absence of a market it is a logical impossibility to be able either to identify the fair value from a range of possible options or to prove that the value selected is the 'true' one.

The analysis in the paper is based solely on the premise that this 'one fair value' characteristic 'gives [market value] measurements a quality of comparability over time and as between entities' whereas 'an entity-specific measurement ... is subject to the vagaries of individual entity expectations, intentions and assumptions'[271] and is therefore less relevant. As we believe there is neither in theory nor in practice 'one fair value' that can be demonstrated logically to be such in the face of alternative fair values, we believe that the analysis in the paper is fundamentally flawed.

In our view, the conceptual analysis on which the paper is based is simplistic. It adopts a dualistic approach under which every market imperfection or inefficiency is attributed to 'entity-specific' factors. However, whilst it is true that markets will tend to 'work to resolve diverse expectations ... to a single price', it is also the very essence of dynamic markets that new diverse expectations are constantly being created based on new information or differences in the information known to market participants. This will particularly be the case with assets and liabilities that are not actively traded because there are insufficient knowledgeable, willing buyers and willing sellers to arbitrage away price differences.

We therefore do not believe that market value measurement in practice has the qualities of reliability and relevance that the paper claims, except where there is an efficient/perfect market for the asset or liability *and* where market value measurement provides the most useful insight into the value, timing and uncertainty of cash-equivalent flows. The items for which the efficient market and usefulness criteria are met include some financial instruments and investment properties, which are already required or permitted to be measured at market value in IFRS financial statements. We believe that the discussion paper should have approached the subject of measurement by considering the nature and purpose of particular assets and liabilities in entities with different activities.

6.2 The FASB Statement of Financial Accounting Standards No.157 – Fair Value Measurements

In September 2006 the FASB published Statement of Financial Accounting Standards No. 157 – *Fair value measurements.*[272] This statement becomes effective for financial statements issued for fiscal years beginning after 15 November 2007 and interim periods within those years. The statement provides guidance on how to arrive at fair values under those FASB standards that already require a fair value measurement to be made; it does not extend the scope of fair value measurement in US GAAP. This FASB standard is significant for IFRS, as the IASB issued it unchanged in November 2006 in the form of a Discussion Paper. This is discussed at 6.3 below.

The changes to current US practice that will result from the application of SFAS 157 relate to the definition of fair value, the methods used to measure fair value, and the expanded disclosures about fair value measurements.

The SFAS clarifies that the meaning it ascribes to fair value is an exit price:

> 'The definition of fair value retains the exchange price notion in earlier definitions of fair value. This Statement clarifies that the exchange price is the price in an orderly transaction between market participants to sell the asset or transfer the liability in the market in which the reporting entity would transact for the asset or liability, that is, the principal or most advantageous market for the asset or liability. The transaction to sell the asset or transfer the liability is a hypothetical transaction at the measurement date, considered from the perspective of a market participant that holds the asset or owes the liability. Therefore, the definition focuses on the price that would be received to sell the asset or paid to transfer the liability (an exit price), not the price that would be paid to acquire the asset or received to assume the liability (an entry price).'[273]

The SFAS states further that:[274]

- fair value is a market measurement, not an entity-specific one (consistent with the stance taken in the measurement paper discussed at 6.1 above). Therefore, a fair value measurement should be determined based on the assumptions that market participants would use in pricing the asset or liability. As a basis for considering market participant assumptions in fair value measurements, SFAS 157 establishes a fair value hierarchy (see below) that distinguishes between (1) market participant assumptions developed based on market data obtained from sources independent of the reporting entity (observable inputs) and (2) the reporting entity's own assumptions about market participant assumptions developed based on the best information available in the circumstances (unobservable inputs). The notion of unobservable inputs is intended to allow for situations in which there is little, if any, market activity for the asset or liability at the measurement date. In those situations, the reporting entity need not undertake all possible efforts to obtain information about market participant assumptions. However, the reporting entity must not ignore information about market participant assumptions that is reasonably obtainable without undue cost and effort;
- market participant assumptions must include assumptions about risk (for example, the risk inherent in using a valuation technique to measure fair value rather than an observable market price) and/or the risk inherent in the inputs to the valuation technique. A fair value measurement should include an adjustment for risk if market participants would include one in pricing the related asset or liability, even if the adjustment is difficult to determine. Therefore, a measurement (for example, a 'mark-to-model' measurement) that does not include an adjustment for risk would not represent a fair value measurement if market participants would include one in pricing the related asset or liability;

- market participant assumptions must also include assumptions about the effect of a restriction on the sale or use of an asset. A fair value measurement for a restricted asset should consider the effect of the restriction if market participants would consider the effect of the restriction in pricing the asset;
- a fair value measurement for a liability must reflect its non-performance risk (the risk that the obligation will not be fulfilled). Because non-performance risk includes the reporting entity's credit risk, the reporting entity should consider the effect of its credit risk (credit standing) on the fair value of the liability in all periods in which the liability is measured at fair value under other accounting pronouncements (such as FAS 133). Whilst this requirement has the counterintuitive effect of producing 'gains' when an entity's credit worthiness deteriorates – because the liability is reduced – and 'losses' when it improves – because the liability increases, it should be noted that it is already a requirement under IAS 39 that the credit risk relating to a financial liability is included in the fair value measurement of that liability.[275]

Fair value is defined in the standard as 'the price that would be received to sell an asset or paid to transfer a liability in an orderly transaction between market participants at the measurement date.'[276] The fair value arrived at must take into consideration the condition and location of the asset at the measurement date,[277] which means that entity-specific considerations must play a part, although the SFAS states that fair value is not an entity specific measurement.[278] Market participants are defined as 'buyers and sellers in the principal (or most advantageous) market … that are:

a. Independent of the reporting entity; that is, they are not related parties
b. Knowledgeable, having a reasonable understanding about the asset or liability and the transaction based on all available information, including information that might be obtained through due diligence efforts that are usual and customary
c. Able to transact for the asset or liability
d. Willing to transact for the asset or liability; that is, they are motivated but not forced or otherwise compelled to do so.'[279]

The SFAS states that a fair value measurement assumes that the transaction to sell the asset or transfer the liability occurs in the principal market, or in the absence of a principal market in the most advantageous market.[280] The principal market is 'the market in which the reporting entity would sell the asset or transfer the liability with the greatest volume and level of activity for the asset or liability'.[281] The most advantageous market is the market in which the reporting entity would sell the asset of transfer the liability with the price that maximises the amount that would be received for the asset or minimises the amount to be paid to transfer the liability considering transaction costs. If there is a principal market, the fair value measurement shall represent the price in that market, even if the price in a different market is potentially more advantageous.[282]

The SFAS includes the concept of 'highest and best use'. One reason this is necessary is because often an asset is used in conjunction with others and its worth on its own is not representative of its worth within the asset group. The SFAS states that 'In broad terms, highest and best use refers to the use of an asset by market participants that would maximize the value of the asset or group of assets within which the asset would be used'.[283] The measurement to determine fair value must take into account both the use to which the asset is being put or will be put by the entity (fair value in-use), and the most advantageous price that could be obtained for that asset if its use were to be changed (fair value in-exchange). This is explained as follows:

'The highest and best use of the asset establishes the valuation premise used to measure the fair value of the asset. Specifically:

a. *In-use.* The highest and best use of the asset is in-use if the asset would provide maximum value to market participants principally through its use in combination with other assets as a group (as installed or otherwise configured for use). For example, that might be the case for certain nonfinancial assets. If the highest and best use of the asset is in-use, the fair value of the asset shall be measured using an in-use valuation premise. When using an in-use valuation premise, the fair value of the asset is determined based on the price that would be received in a current transaction to sell the asset assuming that the asset would be used with other assets as a group and that those assets would be available to market participants. Generally, assumptions about the highest and best use of the asset should be consistent for all of the assets of the group within which it would be used.

b. *In-exchange.* The highest and best use of the asset is in-exchange if the asset would provide maximum value to market participants principally on a standalone basis. For example, that might be the case for a financial asset. If the highest and best use of the asset is in-exchange, the fair value of the asset shall be measured using an in-exchange valuation premise. When using an in-exchange valuation premise, the fair value of the asset is determined based on the price that would be received in a current transaction to sell the asset standalone.'[284]

The notion of 'highest and best use' is not an easy one to explain in principle, and it is not completely obvious how it should be identified or used in practice. It appears to imply a partial acceptance of entity-specific considerations, as the group of assets to be taken into account in an in-use valuation must inevitably be those actually being used by the entity in conjunction with the asset being valued.

The SFAS states that valuation techniques consistent with a market approach, an income approach or a cost approach shall be used to measure fair value.[285] These are, respectively in brief, actual market prices, or prices modelled on market data; discounted future cash flows or option pricing models such as the Black-Scholes-Merton formula or a binomial model; and the cost of what would be required to replace the service capacity of an asset (current replacement cost).[286]

There is a section of the SFAS that deals with the 'inputs' that may be used to arrive at fair value. These are (i) observable inputs: i.e. inputs that reflect the assumptions market participants would use in pricing assets or liabilities based on market data obtained from sources independent of the reporting entity; and (ii) unobservable inputs: i.e. inputs that reflect the entity's own assumptions about the assumptions market participants would use in pricing the asset or liability.[287] To further clarify this notion, the SFAS includes a fair value hierarchy, which is illustrated in Figure 2 below:

Figure 2

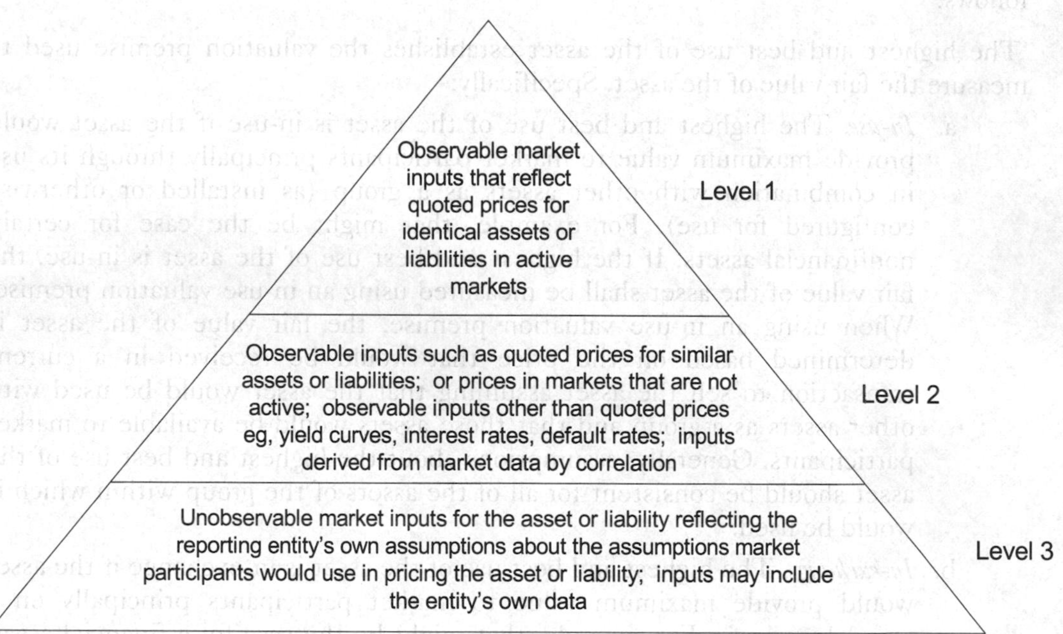

Observable market inputs that reflect quoted prices for identical assets or liabilities in active markets
Level 1
Observable inputs such as quoted prices for similar assets or liabilities; or prices in markets that are not active; observable inputs other than quoted prices eg, yield curves, interest rates, default rates; inputs derived from market data by correlation
Level 2
Unobservable market inputs for the asset or liability reflecting the reporting entity's own assumptions about the assumptions market participants would use in pricing the asset or liability; inputs may include the entity's own data
Level 3

Level 1 inputs represent quoted market prices for identical assets; level 2 inputs are either quoted market prices for similar assets or liabilities, or market inputs such as interest rates, yield curves and default rates.[288] Level 3 unobservable market inputs are less clear, and the SFAS explains them as follows:

> 'Unobservable inputs shall be used to measure fair value to the extent that observable inputs are not available, thereby allowing for situations in which there is little, if any, market activity for the asset or liability at the measurement date. However, the fair value measurement objective remains the same, that is, an exit price from the perspective of a market participant that holds the asset or owes the liability. Therefore, unobservable inputs shall reflect the reporting entity's own assumptions about the assumptions that market participants would use in pricing the asset or liability (including assumptions about risk). Unobservable inputs shall be developed based on the best information available in the circumstances, which might include the reporting entity's own data. In developing unobservable inputs, the reporting entity need not undertake all possible efforts to obtain information about

> market participant assumptions. However, the reporting entity shall not ignore information about market participant assumptions that is reasonably available without undue cost and effort. Therefore, the reporting entity's own data used to develop unobservable inputs shall be adjusted if information is reasonably available without undue cost and effort that indicates that market participants would use different assumptions.'[289]

The difficulty is that the SFAS has had to finesse the fact that market prices do not exist for a number of the assets and liabilities that are required to be measured at fair value by existing FASB standards. This difficulty is similar to that faced by the Measurement discussion paper considered at 6.1 above, which recommends the universal use of fair values for initial recognition of assets and liabilities. At the heart of this approach is the assumption that such prices can be synthesised reliably; whether this is the case in fact, remains unresolved.

The disclosure requirements of SFAS 157 to an extent reflect the importance of users being aware of the magnitude of the fair value measurements that are not based on market prices. There is a specific requirement in SFAS 157 to make disclosures segregating the fair value measurements at the reporting date into those derived from using each of the three levels in the hierarchy. Furthermore, Level 3-based fair value measurements are subject to more detailed disclosure requirements, as follows:

'c. For fair value measurements using significant unobservable inputs (Level 3), a reconciliation of the beginning and ending balances, separately presenting changes during the period attributable to the following:

(1) Total gains or losses for the period (realized and unrealized), segregating those gains or losses included in earnings (or changes in net assets), and description of where those gains or losses included in earnings (or changes in net assets) are reported in the statement of income (or activities)

(2) Purchases, sales, issuances, and settlements (net)

(3) Transfers in and/or out of Level 3 (for example, transfers due to changes in the observability of significant inputs)

d. The amount of the total gains or losses for the period in subparagraph (c)(1) above included in earnings (or changes in net assets) that are attributable to the change in unrealized gains or losses relating to those assets and liabilities still held at the reporting date and a description of where those unrealized gains or losses are reported in the statement of income (or activities)'.[290]

The SFAS includes substantial implementation guidance and discussion of present value techniques in its appendices.

6.2.1 The conceptual significance of FAS 57

The importance of SFAS 157 for a discussion of conceptual frameworks is twofold: (i) it codifies the way one influential standard setter considers that a fair value can be synthesised reliably in the absence of market prices; and (ii) it thereby opens the way for an extension of the application of fair value measurements to a more general use, as most assets and liabilities do not have observable market prices.

It is instructive to note that the basis of valuation put forward in SFAS 157 is in fact almost identical to that advanced by Chambers in the 1960s as set out in 4.2.2 C above. Chambers advocated 'continuously contemporary accounting' (CoCoA). The theory was based on the premise that entities must be able to choose between alternative courses of action and, because resources are limited, they need to know what resources are available to enable them to engage in exchanges. The theory further stated that this capacity to engage in exchanges is measured by the opportunity cost of holding assets in their existing form, and that this opportunity cost is represented by the current cash equivalent of assets – which Chambers defined as being their current sales value. He advocated further that exit values should be determined on the assumption that assets are realised in an orderly manner, based on sensible adaptations to changing circumstances. This notion is seemingly identical to SFAS 157's notion of the highest and best use.

Whether such a measurement basis is accurately described as a fair value, and whether it is suitable for general use throughout financial reporting, are matters that we consider should be addressed specifically and agreed upon. Consequently, we were pleased that in late 2006 the IASB published SFAS 157 in the form of a Discussion Paper for public comment amongst its constituency. Certain key assumptions made in this discussion paper are considered below.

6.3 The IASB's Discussion Paper: Fair value measurements

In November 2006 the IASB published the full text of SFAS 157 in the form of a Discussion Paper, under the title *Fair value measurements*.[291] The paper consists principally of the text of SFAS 157, with a 16 page Invitation to Comment that provides context for each of 27 individual questions ranged across 13 'issues' specifically identified by the Board.

The purpose of the Discussion Paper is to indicate the Board's preliminary view of the provisions of SFAS 157 and its effect on existing fair value measurement guidance in IFRSs. The Board invited respondents to comment on the Board's preliminary views as well as the provisions of SFAS 157. Round table discussions on the subject of the measurement phase of the proposed new framework (see 5.1 above) were also held by the Board in early 2007. The feedback from these discussions, though ostensibly not held on the subject of the discussion paper, seems to have been influential in the Board's thinking, as explained at 6.3.1 below.

The feedback from written comments will be considered as part of the development of an IASB Exposure Draft on fair value measurements, which is not planned until the second half of 2008 at the earliest. As the text of SFAS 157 is discussed in detail above at 6.2, this section confines itself to discussing the broader issues that are raised by the publication of this standard in the form of a discussion paper by the IASB.

We consider that it is both timely and of fundamental importance that a full public debate on measurement in financial statements is held. The stated objectives of the discussion paper are to 'codify, clarify and simplify' existing guidance for fair value measurements where they are allowed or required under IFRS, not to extend their use.[292] Even so, when considered in conjunction with the Board's publication of the Canadian paper on initial measurement, see 6.1 above, and with its current work on measurement as part of the joint IASB/FASB conceptual framework project, discussed at 5 above, it is clear that the Board is at the centre of a wide-ranging debate on measurement. It is our view that specifying the measurement bases available under IFRS and when they should be used is an essential preliminary to the issuance of a standard based on SFAS 157 or indeed any substantive changes to the measurement requirements of current standards. The principal assumptions in the discussion paper that we consider need explicit examination are discussed below.

A   Fair value-based information is the most useful

The view expressed in the discussion paper is that the majority of IASB members believe an 'exit price' provides the most useful information for non-financial assets and liabilities, because 'it reflects current market-based expectations of economic benefits into or out of the entity'.[293] As set out in 6.2 above, fair values as defined under SFAS 157 are exit prices. This view has never been justified other than in the case of assets or liabilities that are readily realisable or that an entity intends to sell or transfer; therefore we do not think the board is justified in assuming it is a universally accepted or self-evidently true proposition.

The market-based exit price methodology in SFAS 157 employs a number of assumptions or conventions, such as principal or most advantageous market and market participants, that are very difficult if not impossible to apply meaningfully in valuing assets and liabilities other than those for which markets exist. Since active markets and therefore market participants do not exist for most assets and liabilities, the application of SFAS 157 to most assets and liabilities would involve piling hypothesis upon hypothesis and we question whether information which is so detached both from actual transactions and from real future cash flows is either relevant or reliable. It is not clear to us why (other than in the case of assets that will be settled or transferred for cash or another financial instrument and assets that are leased or subject to licensing agreements and that therefore directly generate cash flows) the exit price of assets as defined in the guidance provides more useful information about the timing, amount and uncertainty of cash flows than their value in use.

B   The fair value of a liability should be measured on the basis of transferring that liability

There is an assumption in SFAS 157 that the fair value of a liability should be measured on the basis of transferring the liability. In reality, liabilities are rarely transferred. We cannot see the relevance of including in the measurement of a liability the profit and risk margin that a counterparty would demand in order to accept the transfer of a liability when there is no likelihood at all that the liability will be transferred and such costs are not incurred when the liability is settled.

The rationale for the approach in SFAS 157 is made clear in its Basis for Conclusions: despite what is said elsewhere in SFAS 157 and the discussion paper's Invitation to Comment, the objective of fair value measurement in SFAS 157 is not in fact to provide information about the amount, timing and uncertainty of future cash flows. Rather, fair value measurement 'provides a benchmark to use as a basis for assessing the reporting entity's advantages (or disadvantages) in performance or settlement relative to the market'.[294] The Board has not previously exposed this notion to public debate. The measurement of assets and liabilities at hypothetical exit values, in the knowledge that the assets concerned will continue to be held and not disposed of and the liabilities concerned will be settled and not transferred, represents a form of 'discarded opportunity'-based accounting whereby the opportunity cost or benefit is the (generally hypothetical) market-based exit value. Performance reporting then becomes a matter of out-performance or under-performance against that benchmark. As SFAS 157 explains, 'specifically, when a liability is measured at fair value, the relative efficiency of the reporting entity in settling the liability using its own resources appears in earnings over the course of its settlement, not before'.[295] This is a true statement but the question of whether it is appropriate for performance to be measured relative to a purely hypothetical benchmark is not addressed at all in the discussion paper. This approach to financial reporting is fundamentally different from the approach currently applied by users and preparers of financial statements

The Invitation to Comment states that 'although IFRSs use the term 'settlement' in the definition of fair value, the IASB's preliminary view is that the term 'transfer' more accurately describes the fair value measurement objective in IFRSs'. This may or may not be the case but in our experience a settlement approach is in practice generally and quite legitimately applied in measuring liabilities. In our view, such a major potential change in approach should not be introduced in a cursory manner in a highly 'technical' document like this Fair Value Measurement Discussion Paper but should rather be the subject of a detailed paper as part of the Framework project setting out, in terms that the vast majority of the Board's constituents can understand, the full implications of the proposed approach.

C 'Fair value' is a useful term

The term 'fair value' is not informative when used as a label for a particular measurement basis. The term encompasses a number of current value measurement bases and therefore does not assist users of financial statements to understand the basis on which any particular item has been measured. In our view the Board should cease using the term 'fair value' and it should be expunged from the IFRS literature. The basis of measurement in SFAS 157 is best described as 'market-based exit price' and we suggest that this term be used where appropriate. Clear and unambiguous distinction can then be made between current entry value, market-based exit value, and value in use.

6.3.1 *Constituents' views of the fair value agenda*

A number of 'round table' discussions on the subject of the measurement phase of the proposed new framework (see 5.1 above) were held by the IASB with representatives from many preparers, users and other interested parties in the first half of 2007. While these round tables were not held directly on the discussion paper, it is clear that during them the entire fair value agenda of the IASB came in for substantial criticism. The somewhat unusual statements made in the August 2007 edition of the IASB publication Insight, may indicate the tone of the feedback received by the IASB to date. It contains denials from Sir David Tweedie that the Board is 'fair value obsessed' and he states that 'It is simply not true that we want to put everything at fair value'. In the same publication Elizabeth Hickey, IASB Director of Technical Activities, denies that the IASB has 'a secret agenda to impose fair value'. These denials are perhaps a sign that the Board's constituency is becoming uneasy about the direction of the Board's published matter, aware of the issues involved, and unprepared to accept them.

Sir David Tweedie commented specifically on the round table discussions in the August 2007 edition of Insight. Interviewed by respected British financial journalist Robert Bruce, he commented on 'myths' surrounding the IASB's views as follows:

> 'The first [myth] is that we are obsessed with fair value', said Tweedie. 'The fair value myth came in with IAS 39. The standard existed before the IASB was set up. People didn't like it. They probably didn't pay enough attention to it when IASC produced it', he said. 'But we were tarred with the fair value brush. Our supposed obsession is grossly overstated. People assume that IAS 39 was all our work, when it certainly wasn't. The only major fair value changes we've brought in are the valuation of share options and the fair value option, which makes hedging easier.'
>
> But the fair value myth stuck. 'What we tried to do at the round tables we held earlier this year', he said, 'was show that what exists in the balance sheet at present is a mixture of value and cost. Very few people think that we should only use fair value in the balance sheet and very few want only historical cost. So what people want is a mixture and the only decision is where do we cut it? There didn't seem to be a huge desire to value operational assets. People were quite happy with cost. There were mixed views on financial instruments, and as for surplus assets, many people thought they should be at value.'

It is to be hoped that the IASB will take to heart the views of their constituents. It may be the case that this interview heralds a change of course, and that the many published indications of the IASB's intentions, set out in sections 5 and 6 of this chapter, fall victim to a changed strategy. We sincerely hope that the extension of market-based exit values to all assets and liabilities is not the aim of the IASB, and that a sensible middle course can be adopted in which appropriate measurement methods are permitted according to the type of asset or liability concerned.

6.4 Measurement: current state

The IASB's joint project with the FASB to revise their respective conceptual frameworks is far from complete, and crucial issues of the definition of the elements of financial statements and their recognition and measurement are still outstanding. As the IASB's published material consistently shows – with the sole exception of the informal denials referred to above at 6.3.1 – a reasonable inference from the IASB's work programme is that the board has already made up its mind to adopt fair value as its measurement base.

It is already the case that a substantial portion of a reporting entity's assets and liabilities are stated in the balance sheet at 'fair value' – including pension assets and liabilities, derivative financial instruments, certain other financial assets and financial liabilities, tangible and intangible fixed assets that have been acquired in a business combination, impaired or revalued, assets held for disposal, share-based payment liabilities, investment properties, provisions and biological assets. In addition, a number of the IASB's current projects in progress – such as business combinations and financial instruments – are aimed at extending fair value measurement even further.

Consequently, it has become a matter of importance that, before this process goes any further, consensus is reached amongst preparers, users, auditors and regulators regarding the relevance and applicability of fair value measurement.

There are only three alternative general bases that could be applied in the determination of the current value of an asset: the entry value (replacement cost), exit value (net realisable value) and value in use (present value of the expected future earnings from the asset). These three bases describe the range of values that reflect the fact that an asset might be bought, sold or held. Therefore, fair value – which is defined by the IASB as being the amount for which an asset could be exchanged between knowledgeable, willing parties in an arm's length transaction – is not a new or different fourth measurement basis; it is merely a term adopted by standard-setters to describe exit value. In other words, fair value is simply an exit price determined at the balance sheet date from the perspective of the reporting entity.

The IASB advocates its fair value approach on the grounds of relevance: the board quite simply considers fair value to be the most relevant measurement basis. However, the board's arguments to support this position are generally limited and are usually based on unsubstantiated assertion, rather than a conclusion that has been reached on the basis of conceptual analysis, a deficiency illustrated by the measurement discussion paper considered at 6.1 above. Moreover, the conclusion that fair value is superior to other measurement bases cannot be accepted until all the assertions concerning fair value have been subjected to intellectually rigorous analysis.

This is important because, as discussed above at 5.2.1C, the IASB believes that all movements in fair value from one balance sheet to the next (other than transactions with shareholders as shareholders) deserve to be regarded as components of a company's performance – with the result that changes in fair value translate directly into performance gains and losses.

Consequently, the relevance of fair value should be tested against the objectives of financial reporting, which, as discussed above at 5.2.1, surround decision-usefulness achieved through the predictability of the amounts, timing, and uncertainty of an entity's future cash inflows and outflows. This means that the following question needs to be addressed: is fair value (i.e. exit value) the most relevant measure to enable users to predict the amounts, timing and uncertainty of an entity's future cash inflows and outflows?

In our view, the answer to this question is 'No'. With the exception of assets that are equivalent to cash because they are traded in highly liquid and deep markets, there is minimal predictive value in the fair value of a single asset. This is because the whole economic rationale for a particular business enterprise is that cash flows are generated not by individual assets but by the unique combination of assets used in its production and delivery processes. Very often, because no deep and liquid markets exist for most assets, the fair value of an asset will be an hypothetical price calculated on the basis of hypothetical markets, with hypothetical buyers and sellers. It is therefore far from clear how the balance sheet presentation of these hypothetical market values of individual assets will enable users of accounts to predict the amounts, timing, and uncertainty of an entity's future cash inflows and outflows.

Nor is it clear how the reporting of changes in hypothetical fair values as gains and losses provides a true and fair view of a business entity's performance. The fair value approach to performance reporting suffers from a major theoretical flaw: it fails to recognise that a market value, however 'fair', is a theoretical price at a single point in time that simply represents an opportunity. If the opportunity is not taken, then it is a rejected opportunity and, however good or bad it might have been, it has little economic relevance once it has been rejected.[296] This means that whilst there might be some relevance, decision-usefulness and predictive value in knowing the market value of an asset that is held for disposal, there is little predictive value in the exit price of an individual asset that is part of a unique combination of assets used by a business in its production and delivery processes.

However, it is important to note that, just because the relevance of fair value measurement based on exit value is open to question, it does not mean that other forms of current valuation should be rejected as well. For example, it may be that the IASB's stated objective of financial reporting would be reflected more appropriately in the measurement of cash generating units on the basis of value to the business (i.e. the lower of replacement cost and recoverable amount), rather than on the basis of an hypothetical exit value for individual assets. Indeed, it may be the case that a value to the business measurement provides greater insight into trading conditions (and hence the predictability of future cash flows) than many exit values.

Nevertheless, the fact that the IASB has yet to articulate conceptually robust arguments to support fair value changes as the basis for performance reporting does not rule out the financial statement disclosure of fair values. However, any such disclosure should explain the basis on which the amount was arrived at, including the principal assumptions used, the reasons those assumptions were selected, and a sensitivity analysis of changes in the assumptions.

At the practical level, even under the IASB's proposed new framework, it seems that mark-to-model fair values calculated by company management may in some cases be incompatible with the qualitative characteristic of representational faithfulness. This is because 'neutrality' is described as being 'the absence of bias intended to attain a predetermined result or to induce a particular behaviour.' It goes on to state that 'neutrality is an essential aspect of faithful representation because biased financial reporting information cannot faithfully represent economic phenomena.'[297] Often, mathematical models of the type required to determine fair values may give very different results when quite small adjustments are made to the underlying assumptions and predictions. It is submitted that it is, at best, unrealistic to expect company management to set their assumptions and apply these models in a neutral and unbiased way.

These concerns have been expressed by others as well. On 22nd November 2004, at the 13th Central Banking Conference held in London, England, Sir Andrew Large, Deputy Governor of the Bank of England, drew attention to a number of concerns at the regulatory level over the use of non-market-based fair values in the case of financial instruments. Amongst other remarks he said:

'First, there is a question as to how one can obtain robust fair values for instruments which are not priced, even indirectly, in reasonably deep and liquid markets. Model-based valuation techniques may be used, but they may not be analogous to genuine market clearing prices. The issues here include determining the conceptual basis for valuation ('the model'), obtaining the necessary inputs, and avoiding slavish adherence to a model which may in some circumstances deliver misleading results. In other words how, and to what extent, can human judgement properly be used to modify the model?

'Second, there is the question of the economic relevance of unrealised gains and losses – particularly if they are not immediately realisable. For example, while information on changes in the fair value of bank loans conveys useful economic insights, it needs to be interpreted carefully. In many cases, a gain cannot be realised 'up front' given the absence at present of developed secondary markets in bank loans – even if securitisations may be increasing in that area.'

Sir Andrew went on to express concern that 'The potential for opacity has therefore increased, so it is essential that accounting standards are clear and capture the economic substance. This is important for the various stakeholders and for financial stability generally.'

More recently on July 21 2007 the Economist published an article entitled 'Bearing it all' that drew attention to the dangers of mark-to-model based fair values, in the particular context of difficulties experienced at that time by hedge funds with investments associated with US 'sub prime' mortgages.

'... many complex derivatives, such as mortgage-backed securities, do not trade smoothly and frequently in arm's length markets. This makes it impossible for book-keepers to 'mark' them to market. Instead they resort to 'mark-to-model' accounting, entering values based on the output of a computer.

'Unfortunately, the market does not always resemble the model. When the ... funds ran into trouble, their bankers tried to sell their collateral, which was mostly in the form of mortgage-backed derivatives. As well as raising cash, such a sale would have had the side-effect of setting a true market price for these hard-to-value instruments. But the bankers worried that if the derivatives were sold into a falling market, the low price would set an ugly precedent for their own portfolios. The disclosure of fire-sale prices could force them to slash carrying values on their own books. This in turn would spur more selling, driving prices further down in a vicious cycle. In the end, the bankers decided that they would rather hold the toxic investment.

'Situations like this, says Ray Beier at PricewaterhouseCoopers, reach 'the heart of the fundamental challenge in fair-value accounting'. Models are supposed to show the price an asset would fetch in a sale. But in an illiquid market, a big sale can itself drive down prices. This can sometimes create a sizeable difference between 'mark-to-model' valuations and true market prices.

'That is not the only problem with fair-value accounting. According to Richard Herring, a finance professor at the Wharton School, 'models are easy to manipulate'. RiskData, a consultancy, studied more than 1,000 hedge funds and concluded that nearly a third of funds trading illiquid securities were smoothing the results of their models, so as to iron out too much volatility in their books.'

7 CONCLUSION

This chapter provides an outline of the immense amount of energy that has been expended (both on the part of individuals and by specifically constituted committees) in attempting to establish an agreed conceptual framework for financial reporting. It has also highlighted the irreconcilable differences and logical difficulties that exist in the various accounting theories that have been developed over the years. The existence of such framework documents might have raised the prospect of a degree of rigour and consistency being applied to accounting standards issued by the various standard-setting bodies. In practice, however, standard setters have made more use of these documents to prevent practices they dislike, and framework documents have, on occasion, been conveniently ignored when a standard is required that conflicts with them. Inconsistencies of this nature are probably inevitable whilst matters that are fundamental to their resolution remain unresolved. Since Edwards and Bell and Maurice Moonitz (see 4.2.2A and 2.1 above respectively) published their work in the early 1960s, there has been controversy over, and disagreement about, the valuation basis to be used in financial reporting. These disagreements have been over whether current values should be used in place of historical costs at all, and if so what type of current value system is to be used. Further disagreement surrounds the way current values are to be determined even if a given system is selected.

What has emerged is the adoption of a particular balance sheet-orientated model by the IASB and the FASB, and what has been published so far of their new conceptual framework document (see 5 above) seems to indicate that this approach is unlikely to change. At the same time, it is clear that many users may not understand fully the asset/liability fair value model either, and that many of those that do are not convinced about its appropriateness as the basis for financial reporting. It is worth noting that, although the extent of the information provided in the preliminary results announcements of IFRS-reporting companies varies greatly in practice, it is almost always the case that such announcements focus on performance (i.e. the income statement) rather than financial condition (i.e. the balance sheet). In our view, this speaks volumes about the preparer and user communities' opinion of the relative importance of transactions-based performance as opposed to changes in balance sheet fair values.

We therefore welcome the fact that the IASB-FASB joint conceptual framework project will present the financial community with the opportunity to subject the IASB Framework to the specific scrutiny and debate that it has so far avoided.

At the global level, the process of reporting harmonisation continues strongly, following the lead of the EU in 2005 when all listed EU companies adopted IFRS in the preparation of their consolidated accounts. As set out in Chapter 1, many countries throughout the world have embarked on a process of either adopting IFRS, or aligning their accounting standards with it. This harmonisation process is an important development in world financial reporting that we strongly support, and that we hope will contribute to the development of an eventual global GAAP –which must be the ultimate goal of the IASB-FASB cooperation agreements. If it becomes a reality, the SEC's recent moves to abolish the reconciliation requirement for IFRS-reporting companies listed on US stock exchanges, will mark the advent of Global GAAP. This will be a considerable achievement that even ten years ago seemed unattainable in the foreseeable future.

We hope also that the IASB and the FASB will make every effort to be sensitive to the concerns of users, preparers and regulators throughout the intended global constituency, and be sure that they give sufficient consideration to the coherence and practicality of their agenda. A prerequisite for this is that their standards must be based upon a conceptual framework that has received specific approval from all involved with business endeavour.

References

1 W. A. Paton and A. C. Littleton, *An Introduction to Corporate Accounting Standards*, Monograph No. 3, American Accounting Association, 1940.

2 See, for example: American Accounting Association, Executive Committee, 'A Tentative Statement of Accounting Principles Affecting Corporate Reports', *Accounting Review*, June 1936, pp. 187-191; American Accounting Association, Executive Committee, 'Accounting Principles Underlying Corporate Financial Statements', *Accounting Review*, June 1941, pp. 133-139; American Accounting Association, Committee to Prepare a Statement of Basic Accounting Theory, *A Statement of Basic Accounting Theory*, 1966; American Accounting Association, Committee on Concepts and Standards for External Financial Reports, *Statement on Accounting Theory and Theory Acceptance*, 1977. The 1977 report concluded that closure on the debate was not feasible, which is perhaps indicative of the complexity of the problem.

3 As can be seen, for example, in the way that asset impairment is measured and accounted for under IFRS and US GAAP. It is for this reason that the IASB and FASB have embarked on a project to develop an agreed single conceptual framework – see section 5 of this chapter.

4 For a full discussion on the politicisation of accounting see: David Solomons, '*The Politicization of Accounting*', Journal of Accountancy, November 1978, p. 71.

5 Maurice Moonitz, *The Basic Postulates of Accounting*, Accounting Research Study No. 1, AICPA, 1961, Preface.

6 The basic postulates of accounting.

7 Robert T. Sprouse and Maurice Moonitz, *A Tentative Set of Broad Accounting Principles for Business Enterprises*, Accounting Research Study No. 3, AICPA, 1962.

8 A Tentative Set of Broad Accounting Principles for Business Enterprises, p. 14.

9 A Tentative Set of Broad Accounting Principles for Business Enterprises, p. 27.

10 APB Statement No. 4, *Basic Concepts and Accounting Principles Underlying Financial Statements of Business Enterprises*, AICPA, October 1970.

11 APB Statement No. 4, para. 3.

12 APB Statement No. 4, para. 132.

13 Report of the Study Group on the Objectives of Financial Statements, *Objectives of Financial Statements*, AICPA, October 1973, p. 65.

14 *Objectives of Financial Statements*, AICPA.

15 *Objectives of Financial Statements*, AICPA.

16 *Objectives of Financial Statements*, AICPA.

17 *Objectives of Financial Statements*, AICPA p. 13.

18 *Objectives of Financial Statements*, AICPA pp. 57-60.

19 FASB Discussion Memorandum, *Conceptual Framework for Accounting and Reporting: Consideration of the Report of the Study Group on the Objectives of Financial Statements*, FASB, June 6, 1974.

20 FASB, Scope and Implications of the Conceptual Framework Project, FASB, December 2, 1976.

21 FASB, Scope and Implications of the Conceptual Framework Project, p. 5.

22 FASB, Scope and Implications of the Conceptual Framework Project, p. 2.

23 FASB, Scope and Implications of the Conceptual Framework Project, pp. 5 and 6.

24 SFAC No. 1, *Objectives of Financial Reporting by Business Enterprises*, FASB, November 1978, para. 7.

25 SFAC No. 1, para. 9.

26 SFAC No. 1, para. 24.

27 SFAC No. 1, para. 34.

28 SFAC No. 1, para. 37.

29 SFAC No. 1, para. 24.

30 SFAC No. 1, footnote 6.

31 SFAC No. 1, para. 43.

32 SFAC No. 1, para. 50.

33 SFAC No. 1, para. 51.

34 SFAC No. 2, *Qualitative Characteristics of Accounting Information*, FASB, May 1980, Figure 1.

35 SFAC No. 1, para. 34.

36 SFAC No. 2, para. 36.

37 SFAC No. 2, p. x.

38 SFAC No. 2, para. 90.

39 SFAC No. 2, p. xi.

40 SFAC No. 2, para. 56.

41 SFAC No. 2.

42 SFAC No. 2, para. 51.

43 SFAC No. 2, p. xvi.

44 SFAC No. 2.

45 SFAC No. 2, para. 59.

46 SFAC No. 2, paras. 91-97.

47 SFAC No. 2, para. 93.

48 SFAC No. 2, para. 95.

49 SFAC No. 6, *Elements of Financial Statements*, a replacement of FASB Concepts Statement No. 3, FASB, December 1985, para. 25.
50 SFAC No. 6, para. 27.
51 SFAC No. 6, para. 28.
52 SFAC No. 6, para. 35.
53 SFAC No. 6, para. 36.
54 SFAC No. 6, para. 49.
55 SFAC No. 6, para. 66.
56 SFAC No. 6.
57 SFAC No. 6, para. 67.
58 SFAC No. 6, para. 70.
59 SFAC No. 1, para. 43.
60 SFAC No. 6, p. 1, footnote 1.
61 SFAC No. 6, para. 78.
62 SFAC No. 6, para. 80.
63 SFAC No. 6, para. 82.
64 SFAC No. 6, para. 83.
65 SFAC No. 6, para. 77.
66 See, for example, SFAC No. 3, *Elements of Financial Statements of Business Enterprises*, FASB, December 1980, para. 58.
67 SFAC No. 5, *Recognition and Measurement in Financial Statements of Business Enterprises*, FASB, December 1984, para. 66.
68 SFAC No. 5, paras. 66-70.
69 SFAC No. 5, paras. 45-48.
70 SFAC No. 5, para. 58.
71 SFAC No. 5, para. 63.
72 SFAC No. 5, paras. 33 and 34.
73 SFAC No. 5, para. 35.
74 David Solomons, '*The FASB's Conceptual Framework: An evaluation*', Journal of Accountancy, June 1986, pp. 114-124, at p. 122.
75 The FASB's Conceptual Framework: An evaluation, p. 124.
76 The FASB's Conceptual Framework: An evaluation.
77 Special Report: The Framework of Financial Accounting Concepts and Standards, p. 158.
78 Special Report: The Framework of Financial Accounting Concepts and Standards, p. 158.
79 Special Report: The Framework of Financial Accounting Concepts and Standards, p. 160.
80 Statement of Financial Accounting Concepts 7, *Using Cash Flow Information and Present Value in Accounting Measurements*, FASB, February 2000, para. 19.
81 SFAC No. 7, para. 21.
82 SFAC No. 7, para. 23.
83 SFAC No. 7, paras. 31 and 37.
84 SFAC No. 7, para. 41.
85 SFAC No. 7, para. 75.
86 SFAC No. 7, Glossary of terms.
87 IAS 39, *Financial Instruments: Recognition and Measurement,* IASB, December 2003 (amended March 2004), para. BC89.
88 Stephen A. Zeff, Accounting Horizons, '*A Perspective on the U.S. Public/Private-Sector Approach to the Regulation of Financial Reporting*', Vol. 9 No. 1, March 1995, p. 60.
89 See Steinar Sars Kvifte, *The Usefulness of the Asset-Liability View – An Analysis of Conceptual Frameworks and the Implications for Norwegian Accounting Regulation.* PhD Dissertation in Accounting, The Norwegian School of Economics and Business Administration, the Department of Accounting, Auditing and Law, Bergen, Norway. In this dissertation, Dr. Kvifte provides substantial evidence to support the conclusion that the asset/liability definitions of the FASB conceptual framework have been ineffective tools in accounting standard-setting in the US. Similar evidence is provided in the case of the IASB Framework.
90 Exposure Draft, *Framework for the Preparation and Presentation of Financial Statements*, IASC, May 1988.
91 *Framework for the Preparation and Presentation of Financial Statements*, IASB, September 1989, para. 4.
92 Framework, para. 2.
93 Framework, para. 1.
94 Framework, para. 7.
95 Framework, para. 12.
96 Framework, para. 14.
97 Framework, para. 10.
98 Framework, para. 22.
99 Framework, para. 95.
100 Framework, para. 23.
101 Framework, para. 24.
102 Framework, para. 25.
103 Framework, para. 26.
104 Framework, para. 27.
105 Framework, para. 30.
106 Framework, para. 31.
107 Framework, para. 32.
108 Framework, para. 33.
109 Framework, para. 36.
110 Framework, para. 37.
111 Framework, para. 38.
112 Framework, para. 40.
113 Framework, para. 43.
114 Framework, para. 43.
115 Framework, para. 25.
116 Framework, para. 83.
117 Framework, para. 51.
118 Framework, para. 25.
119 Framework, para. 25.
120 Framework, para. 70.
121 Framework, para. 75.
122 Framework, para. 79.
123 Framework, paras. 76 and 79.
124 Framework, para. 88.

125 Framework, para. 91.
126 Framework, para. 99.
127 Framework, para. 102.
128 Framework, para. 103.
129 Framework, para. 110.
130 Framework, para. 110.
131 *The Corporate Report*, A discussion paper published for comment by the Accounting Standards Steering Committee, London, 1975.
132 The Corporate Report, para. 0.1.
133 The Corporate Report, para. 0.2.
134 The committee's recommended package of information which should be contained in the annual corporate reports of business enterprises is listed in Appendix 2 of the discussion paper.
135 The Corporate Report, para. 0.3.
136 The Corporate Report, para. 1.1.
137 The Corporate Report, para. 1.8.
138 The Corporate Report, para. 1.9. The seven user groups identified were: (a) the equity investor group, (b) the loan creditor group, (c) the employee group, (d) the analyst-adviser group, (e) the business contact group, (f) the government and (g) the public.
139 The Corporate Report, paras. 2.1-2.40.
140 The Corporate Report, para. 3.2.
141 The Corporate Report, para. 3.3.
142 The Corporate Report, para. 4.30.
143 The Corporate Report, para. 4.40.
144 The Corporate Report, para. 6.56.
145 The Corporate Report, paras. 6.56 and 6.57.
146 The Corporate Report, para. 7.4.
147 The Corporate Report, para. 7.15.
148 The Corporate Report, paras. 7.40 and 7.43.
149 Report of the Inflation Accounting Committee, *Inflation Accounting*, Cmnd. 6225, London: HMSO, 1975, (the Sandilands Report), p. iv.
150 Inflation Accounting, para. 144.
151 Inflation Accounting, Chapter 12.
152 SSAP 7 (Provisional) *Accounting for the changes in the purchasing power of money*, May 1974 recommended that the RPI should be used for this purpose.
153 SSAP 7, para. 12.
154 The Sandilands Report, para. 20.
155 The Sandilands Report, para. 422.
156 The Sandilands Report, paras. 411 and 412.
157 The Sandilands Report, para. 415.
158 Edwards and Bell have made significant contributions in the areas of income determination and value measurement – however, it is beyond the scope of this book to provide a detailed analysis of their theories. Their case for income and value measurement based on replacement costs may be found in their classic work: E. O. Edwards and P. W. Bell, *The Theory and Measurement of Business Income*, University of California Press, 1961.
159 The Sandilands Report, para. 453.
160 The Sandilands Report, para. 499.
161 Kenneth MacNeal, *Truth in Accounting*, Philadelphia: University of Pennsylvania Press, 1939.
162 R. J. Chambers, *Accounting, Evaluation and Economic Behaviour*, Prentice-Hall, 1966.
163 R. R. Sterling, *Theory of the Measurement of Enterprise Income*, University of Kansas Press, 1970.
164 The Sandilands Report, para. 510.
165 The Institute of Chartered Accountants of Scotland, *Making Corporate Reports Valuable*, London: Kogan Page, 1988, paras. 6.20-6.23.
166 Lee has published numerous papers on the subject of cash flow accounting, the ideas of which have been drawn together in his book: Tom Lee, *Cash Flow Accounting*, Wokingham, Van Nostrand Reinhold (UK), 1984.
167 Lawson has published widely on the subject of cash flow accounting – see, for example: G. H. Lawson, '*Cash-flow Accounting*', The Accountant, October 28th, 1971, pp. 586-589; G. H. Lawson, '*The Measurement of Corporate Profitability on a Cash-flow Basis*', The International Journal of Accounting Education and Research, Vol. 16, No. 1, pp. 11-46.
168 Tom Lee, *op. cit.*, p. 51.
169 Tom Lee, *op. cit.*, pp. 51-52.
170 Lee presents a quantified example of his proposed cash flow reporting system, Tom Lee, *op. cit.*, pp. 57-72.
171 The Sandilands Report, para. 518.
172 The Sandilands Report, para. 517.
173 The Sandilands Report, para. 537.
174 For a detailed discussion of the capital maintenance concepts which apply in the Sandilands proposals, see: H. C. Edey, '*Sandilands and the Logic of Current Cost*', Accounting and Business Research, Volume 9, No. 35, Summer 1979, pp. 191-200.
175 SSAP 16, *Current cost accounting*, March 1980, para. 9.
176 Edward Stamp, *Corporate Reporting: Its Future Evolution*, a research study published by the Canadian Institute of Chartered Accountants, 1980, (the Stamp Report), Ch. 1, para. 3.
177 Edward Stamp, '*First steps towards a British conceptual framework*', Accountancy, March 1982, pp. 123-130.

178 Stamp's qualitative criteria were ranked (from most important to least important) by the ASC members as follows (*'First steps towards a British conceptual framework'*, Accountancy, March 1982, Figure 2, p. 126): relevance, clarity, substance over form, timeliness, comparability, materiality, freedom from bias, objectivity, rationality, full disclosure, consistency, isomorphism, verifiability, cost/benefit effectiveness, non-arbitrariness, data availability, flexibility, uniformity, precision, conservatism.
179 The Stamp Report, Chapter 2.
180 Making Corporate Reports Valuable, paras. 1.1-1.20, *passim*.
181 Making Corporate Reports Valuable, para. 6.36.
182 Making Corporate Reports Valuable, para. 6.36.
183 Making Corporate Reports Valuable, paras. 7.12-7.20, *passim*.
184 Making Corporate Reports Valuable, para. 7.21.
185 Making Corporate Reports Valuable, paras. 7.23-7.26, *passim*.
186 Making Corporate Reports Valuable, paras. 7.27-7.32, *passim*.
187 Making Corporate Reports Valuable, para. 7.39.
188 Making Corporate Reports Valuable, para. 5.44.
189 David Solomons, *Guidelines for Financial Reporting Standards*, A Paper Prepared for The Research Board of the Institute of Chartered Accountants in England and Wales and addressed to the Accounting Standards Committee, ICAEW, 1989, (the Solomons Report), p. 17.
190 Guidelines for Financial Reporting Standards, p. 18.
191 Guidelines for Financial Reporting Standards, p. 18.
192 Guidelines for Financial Reporting Standards, p. 20.
193 Guidelines for Financial Reporting Standards, p. 21.
194 Guidelines for Financial Reporting Standards, pp. 23-28.
195 Guidelines for Financial Reporting Standards, p. 43.
196 Guidelines for Financial Reporting Standards, pp. 51-52.
197 Accounting Horizons, vol. 9 no. 1, pp. 42-51.
198 Guidelines for Financial Reporting Standards, p. 53.
199 Guidelines for Financial Reporting Standards, p. 53.
200 Guidelines for Financial Reporting Standards, p. 54.
201 Guidelines for Financial Reporting Standards, p. 55.
202 Guidelines for Financial Reporting Standards, p. 56.
203 Guidelines for Financial Reporting Standards, p. 69.
204 Statement of Principles for Financial Reporting, ASB, December 1999.
205 Statement of Principles for Financial Reporting Chapter 1, Principles.
206 Statement of Principles for Financial Reporting para. 1.18
207 Statement of Principles for Financial Reporting Chapter 3, Principles.
208 Statement of Principles for Financial Reporting Chapter 3, Principles.
209 Statement of Principles for Financial Reporting para. 4.21.
210 Statement of Principles for Financial Reporting para. 4.21.
211 Statement of Principles for Financial Reporting Chapter 5, Principles.
212 Statement of Principles for Financial Reporting para. 8.13.
213 Discussion paper, *Preliminary views on an improved conceptual framework for financial reporting: The objective of financial reporting and Qualitative characteristics of decision-useful financial reporting information*, IASB, July 2006.
214 Preliminary views on an improved conceptual framework for financial reporting, OB2.
215 Preliminary views on an improved conceptual framework for financial reporting, OB2.
216 Preliminary views on an improved conceptual framework for financial reporting, OB3.
217 Preliminary views on an improved conceptual framework for financial reporting, OB27, 28.
218 Preliminary views on an improved conceptual framework for financial reporting, AV1.3.
219 Preliminary views on an improved conceptual framework for financial reporting, AV1.4, 1.5, 1.7.
220 Preliminary views on an improved conceptual framework for financial reporting, OB 10.
221 SFAC No. 1, para. 50.
222 SFAC No. 1, para. 51.
223 Preliminary views on an improved conceptual framework for financial reporting, OB3.
224 Preliminary views on an improved conceptual framework for financial reporting, OB6.
225 Preliminary views on an improved conceptual framework for financial reporting, OB7.
226 Preliminary views on an improved conceptual framework for financial reporting, OB8.
227 Preliminary views on an improved conceptual framework for financial reporting, OB8.

228 Preliminary views on an improved conceptual framework for financial reporting, OB23.
229 Preliminary views on an improved conceptual framework for financial reporting, QC7.
230 Framework, para. 31.
231 Framework, para. 32.
232 Preliminary views on an improved conceptual framework for financial reporting, BC2.13.
233 Preliminary views on an improved conceptual framework for financial reporting, BC2.28.
234 Preliminary views on an improved conceptual framework for financial reporting, QC16.
235 Preliminary views on an improved conceptual framework for financial reporting, QC16.
236 Preliminary views on an improved conceptual framework for financial reporting, QC23.
237 Preliminary views on an improved conceptual framework for financial reporting, AV2.1, 2.2.
238 Preliminary views on an improved conceptual framework for financial reporting, QC18.
239 Preliminary views on an improved conceptual framework for financial reporting, QC18.
240 Preliminary views on an improved conceptual framework for financial reporting, QC21.
241 Preliminary views on an improved conceptual framework for financial reporting, QC27.
242 Preliminary views on an improved conceptual framework for financial reporting, QC28.
243 Preliminary views on an improved conceptual framework for financial reporting, QC4.
244 Preliminary views on an improved conceptual framework for financial reporting, BC2.18.
245 Preliminary views on an improved conceptual framework for financial reporting, Preface.
246 Preliminary views on an improved conceptual framework for financial reporting, Introduction IN5.
247 Preliminary views on an improved conceptual framework for financial reporting, Introduction IN5.
248 Discussion paper, *Measurement bases for financial accounting – measurement on initial recognition*, IASB, November 2005, Introduction p6.
249 Measurement bases for financial accounting – measurement on initial recognition, Summary, p7.
250 Measurement bases for financial accounting – measurement on initial recognition, para. 29.
251 Measurement bases for financial accounting – measurement on initial recognition, para. 54.
252 Measurement bases for financial accounting – measurement on initial recognition, para. 55.
253 Measurement bases for financial accounting – measurement on initial recognition, para. 48.
254 Measurement bases for financial accounting – measurement on initial recognition, para. 48.
255 Measurement bases for financial accounting – measurement on initial recognition, paras. 69 to 96.
256 Measurement bases for financial accounting – measurement on initial recognition, para. 81.
257 IAS 15, para. 13. IAS 15 was withdrawn by the IASB with effect from 1 January, 2005, with the result that, as of that date, the term is no longer defined in IASB standards.
258 Measurement bases for financial accounting – measurement on initial recognition, para. 83.
259 Measurement bases for financial accounting – measurement on initial recognition, para. 85.
260 Measurement bases for financial accounting – measurement on initial recognition, para. 89.
261 Measurement bases for financial accounting – measurement on initial recognition, para. 94.
262 Measurement bases for financial accounting – measurement on initial recognition, para. 73.
263 Measurement bases for financial accounting – measurement on initial recognition, para. 71.
264 Measurement bases for financial accounting – measurement on initial recognition, para. 128.
265 Measurement bases for financial accounting – measurement on initial recognition, Chapters 7 and 8 generally.
266 Measurement bases for financial accounting – measurement on initial recognition, para. 135.
267 Measurement bases for financial accounting – measurement on initial recognition, para. 26.
268 Measurement bases for financial accounting – measurement on initial recognition, para. 128.
269 Measurement bases for financial accounting – measurement on initial recognition, para. 180.
270 Measurement bases for financial accounting – measurement on initial recognition, para. 128.
271 Measurement bases for financial accounting – measurement on initial recognition, para. 128.

272 Statement of Financial Accounting Standards No.157 – *Fair Value Measurements*, FASB, September 2006.
273 SFAS 157, Summary.
274 SFAS 157, Summary.
275 IAS 39, AG82.
276 SFAS 157, para. 5.
277 SFAS 157, para. 6.
278 SFAS 157, Summary.
279 SFAS 157, para. 10.
280 SFAS 157, para. 8.
281 SFAS 157, para. 8.
282 SFAS 157, para. 10.
283 SFAS 157, para. 12.
284 SFAS 157, para. 13.
285 SFAS 157, para. 18.
286 SFAS 157, para. 18.
287 SFAS 157, para. 21.
288 SFAS 157, paras. 24-29.
289 SFAS 157, para. 30.
290 SFAS 157, para. 32.
291 Discussion paper, *Fair value measurements*, IASB, November 2007,
292 Fair value measurements. Part 1 Invitation to comment, para. 7.
293 Fair value measurements. Part 1 Invitation to comment, para. 13.
294 SFAS 157, Background information and basis for conclusions, para. C40.
295 SFAS 157, Background information and basis for conclusions, para. C40.
296 The irrelevance of fair value change is discussed at length in *Accounting Standards: True or False?*, Dr. R.A. Rayman, Routledge, Abingdon, Oxon, 2006. See Chapter 9, *Fair value accounting: a dead end?*
297 Preliminary views on an improved conceptual framework for financial reporting, Ch.2, QC27.

Chapter 3 Presentation of financial statements and accounting policies

1 INTRODUCTION

There is no single standard dealing with the form, content and structure of financial statements and the accounting policies to be applied in their preparation. Of course, all international accounting standards specify some required disclosures and many mention the level of prominence required (such as on the face of a primary statement rather than in the notes). The subject of just what financial statements are, their purpose, contents and presentation is addressed principally by three standards.

IAS 1 – *Presentation of Financial Statements* – is the main standard dealing with the overall requirements for the presentation of financial statements, including their purpose, form, content and structure.[1] IAS 8 – *Accounting Policies, Changes in Accounting Estimates and Errors* – deals with the requirements for the selection and application of accounting policies.[2] It also deals with the requirements as to when changes in accounting policies should be made, and how such changes should be accounted for and disclosed. This chapter deals with the requirements of IAS 1 and IAS 8, including the requirements of the latter dealing with changes in accounting estimates and errors. Chapter 4 discusses the requirements of IFRS 5 – *Non-current Assets Held for Sale and Discontinued Operations*.[3] That standard principally deals with the classification and presentation of non-current assets held for sale in the balance sheet, and the presentation of discontinued operations in the income statement, although it also sets out the measurement requirements for such items.

1.1 IAS 1

1.1.1 Background to IAS 1

In August 1997, the IASC issued IAS 1 (revised) – *Presentation of Financial Statements* – which consolidated and replaced IAS 1 – *Disclosure of Accounting Policies* (originally published in 1974), IAS 5 – *Information to be Disclosed in Financial Statements* (originally published in 1974), and IAS 13 – *Presentation of Current Assets and Current Liabilities* (originally published in 1979). In December 2003 the standard was updated as part of the IASB's improvements project and some further revisions were made in March 2004 by IFRS 5. This version of IAS 1 came into force for periods beginning on or after 1 January 2005. The Board's main objectives in updating IAS 1 were (without reconsidering the fundamental approach to the presentation of financial statements):

(a) to provide a framework within which an entity assesses how to present fairly the effects of transactions and other events, and assesses whether the result of complying with a requirement in a standard or an interpretation would be so misleading that it would not give a fair presentation;

(b) to base the criteria for classifying liabilities as current or non-current solely on the conditions existing at the balance sheet date;

(c) to prohibit the presentation of items of income and expense as 'extraordinary items';

(d) to specify disclosures about the judgements management has made in the process of applying the entity's accounting policies, apart from those involving estimations, that have the most significant effect on the amounts recognised in the financial statements; and

(e) to specify disclosures about key sources of estimation uncertainty at the balance sheet date that have a significant risk of causing a material adjustment to the carrying amounts of assets and liabilities within the next financial year.[4]

In December 2004 a revision to IAS 19 – *Employee benefits* – relating to the recognition of actuarial gains and losses made consequential amendments to IAS 1 relating to the presentation of a statement of recognised income and expense (see 3.3 below).[5] The changes apply to periods beginning on or after 1 January 2006, with early adoption encouraged.

In August 2005, IFRS 7 – *Financial Instruments: Disclosures* – was published by the IASB. This made some minor consequential amendments to IAS 1, effective for periods beginning on or after 1 January 2007. Published at the same time was an amendment to IAS 1 introducing further disclosure about capital (see 5.4 below).[6] This is also effective for periods beginning on or after 1 January 2007 with early application encouraged.

For readers approaching the topic from an EU background, IAS 1 can best be described as the IASB's version of the EU Fourth Directive. It deals with the components of financial statements, fair presentation, fundamental accounting concepts, disclosure of accounting policies, the structure and content of financial statements and the statement of changes in equity.

1.1.2 Objective and scope of IAS 1

IAS 1 applies to what it calls 'general purpose financial statements', that is those intended to meet the needs of users who are not in a position to demand reports tailored to meet their particular information needs, and it should be applied to all such financial statements prepared in accordance with International Financial Reporting Standards.[7] Although International Financial Reporting Standards (IFRSs) is probably a self explanatory phrase, both IAS 1 and IAS 8 define it as 'Standards and Interpretations adopted by the International Accounting Standards Board (IASB). They comprise:

(a) International Financial Reporting Standards;
(b) International Accounting Standards; and
(c) Interpretations originated by the International Financial Reporting Interpretations Committee (IFRIC) or the former Standing Interpretations Committee (SIC).'[8]

An important point here is that implementation guidance for standards issued by the IASB does not form part of those standards, and therefore does not contain requirements for financial statements.[9] Accordingly, the often voluminous implementation guidance accompanying standards is not, strictly speaking, part of 'IFRS'. We would generally be surprised, though, at entities not following such guidance without valid reason.

General purpose financial statements include those that are presented separately or within another public document such as an annual report or a prospectus. The standard applies equally to all entities and whether or not they need to prepare consolidated financial statements or separate financial statements, as defined in IAS 27 – *Consolidated and Separate Financial Statements* (discussed in Chapter 6).[10] IAS 1 does not apply to the structure and content of condensed interim financial statements prepared in accordance with IAS 34 – *Interim Financial Reporting* (discussed in Chapter 37),[11] although its provisions relating to fair presentation, compliance with IFRS and fundamental accounting principles do apply to interims.[12] These provisions of IAS 1 are discussed at 4.1 below.

The objective of the standard is to prescribe the basis for presentation of general purpose financial statements, and by doing so to ensure comparability both with the entity's financial statements of previous periods and with the financial statements of other entities. To achieve this objective, the standard sets out overall requirements for the presentation of financial statements, guidelines for their structure and minimum requirements for their content. The recognition, measurement and disclosure of specific transactions and other events are dealt with in other standards and in interpretations.[13]

IAS 1 is primarily directed at profit oriented entities (including public sector business entities), and this is reflected in the terminology it uses and its requirements. It acknowledges that entities with not-for-profit activities in the private sector, public sector or government may want to apply the standard and that such entities may need to amend the descriptions used for particular line items in the financial statements and for the financial statements themselves.[14] Furthermore, IAS 1 is a general standard that does not address issues specific to particular industries. It does observe, though, that entities without equity (such as some mutual funds) or whose share capital is not equity (such as some co-operative entities) may need to adapt the presentation of members' or unit holders' interests.[15]

1.2 IAS 8

1.2.1 Background to IAS 8

IAS 8 has a long history, and the evolution of its title alone says much about the changing focus of the standard. In October 1976 the IASC issued its eighth exposure draft, E8 – *The Treatment in the Income Statement of Unusual Items and Changes in Accounting Estimates and Accounting Policies*. This led, in February 1978 to the publication of IAS 8 – *Unusual and Prior Period Items and Changes in Accounting Policies*.

July 1992 saw the publication of E46 – *Extraordinary Items, Fundamental Errors and Changes in Accounting Policies* which resulted in December 1993 with a revised version of the standard: IAS 8 (Revised 1993) – *Net Profit or Loss for the Period, Fundamental Errors and Changes in Accounting Policies*.

In December 2003, the IASB's improvements project revised the standard again and re-titled it IAS 8 – *Accounting Policies, Changes in Accounting Estimates and Errors*. This revision also superseded the following two interpretations:

(a) SIC-2 – *Consistency – Capitalisation of Borrowing Costs*; and

(b) SIC-18 – *Consistency – Alternative Methods*.[16]

This version applies to periods beginning on or after 1 January 2005. Earlier application is encouraged and if it is applied early that fact should be disclosed.[17]

The Board's main objectives in updating IAS 8 were:

(a) to remove the allowed alternative to retrospective application of voluntary changes in accounting policies and retrospective restatement to correct prior period errors;

(b) to eliminate the concept of a fundamental error;

(c) to articulate the hierarchy of guidance to which management refers, whose applicability it considers when selecting accounting policies in the absence of standards and interpretations that specifically apply;

(d) to define material omissions or misstatements, and describe how to apply the concept of materiality when applying accounting policies and correcting errors; and

(e) to incorporate the consensus in SIC-2 and in SIC-18.[18]

The above represent some of the main changes from the previous version of IAS 8.[19] Others identified by the standard include:

- more detailed guidance on materiality;[20]
- more detailed guidance on the impracticability of restatement of prior periods for changes in accounting policies and the correction of errors;[21]
- a requirement (rather than just encouragement) to disclose an impending change in accounting policy due to a new standard or interpretation;[22]
- a definition of a change in accounting estimate;[23]
- some further disclosure requirements;[24] and
- reallocating the guidance of various topics between IAS 1 and IAS 8.[25]

1.2.2 Objective and scope of IAS 8

IAS 8 applies to selecting and applying accounting policies, and accounting for changes in accounting policies, changes in accounting estimates and corrections of prior period errors.[26] Its objective is to prescribe the criteria for selecting and changing accounting policies, together with the accounting treatment and disclosure of changes in accounting policies, changes in accounting estimates and corrections of errors. The standard's intention is to enhance the relevance and reliability of an entity's financial statements, and the comparability of those financial statements over time and with the financial statements of other entities.[27]

Two particular issues which one might expect to be dealt with regarding the above are discussed in other standards and cross-referred to by IAS 8:

- disclosure requirements for accounting policies, except those for changes in accounting policies, are dealt with in IAS 1;[28] and
- accounting and disclosure requirements regarding the tax effects of corrections of prior period errors and of retrospective adjustments made to apply changes in accounting policies are dealt with in IAS 12 – *Income Taxes* (discussed in Chapter 26).[29]

2 THE PURPOSE AND COMPOSITION OF FINANCIAL STATEMENTS

What financial statements are and what they are for are clearly important basic questions for any body of accounting literature, and answering them is the main purpose of IAS 1.

2.1 The purpose of financial statements

IAS 1 describes financial statements as a structured representation of the financial position and financial performance of an entity. It states that the objective of general purpose financial statements is to provide information about the financial position, financial performance and cash flows of an entity that is useful to a wide range of users in making economic decisions. A focus on assisting decision making by the users of financial statements is seeking (at least in part) a forward looking or predictive quality. This is reflected by some requirements of accounting standards (for example, the disclosure of discontinued operations (discussed in Chapter 4), and the use of profit from continuing operations as the control number in calculating diluted earnings per share (discussed at 6.3.1 in Chapter 33)) and also the desire of some entities to present performance measures excluding what they see as unusual, infrequent or just historic items (discussed at 3.2.4 below).

IAS 1 also acknowledges a second important role of financial statements. That is, that they also show the results of management's stewardship of the resources entrusted to it. To meet this objective, IAS 1 requires financial statements provide information about an entity's:

(a) assets;

(b) liabilities;

(c) equity;

(d) income and expenses, including gains and losses;

(e) other changes in equity; and

(f) cash flows.

The standard observes that this information, along with other information in the notes, assists users of financial statements in predicting the entity's future cash flows and, in particular, their timing and certainty.[30]

2.2 Frequency of reporting and period covered

IAS 1 requires that financial statements be presented 'at least annually'. Whilst this drafting is not exactly precise, it does not seem to mean that financial statements must never be more than a year apart (which is perhaps the most natural meaning of the phrase). This is because the standard goes on to mention that an entity's balance sheet date may change, and that the annual financial statements are therefore presented for a period *longer* or shorter than one year. When this is the case, IAS 1 requires disclosure of, in addition to the period covered by the financial statements:

(a) the reason for using a longer or shorter period; and

(b) the fact that comparative amounts for the income statement, statement of changes in equity, cash flow statement and related notes are not entirely comparable.[31]

Some entities, particularly in the retail sector, traditionally present financial statements for a 52 week period. IAS 1 does not preclude this practice. Whilst it notes that normally financial statements are consistently prepared covering a one year period, it states that a 52 week period is unlikely to produce materially different results.[32]

2.3 The components of financial statements

A complete set of financial statements under IAS 1 comprises:

(a) a balance sheet;

(b) an income statement;

(c) a statement of changes in equity showing either:

  (i) all changes in equity, or

(ii) changes in equity other than those arising from transactions with equity holders acting in their capacity as such. In such a case, the statement is titled a 'statement of recognised income and expense';

(d) a cash flow statement; and

(e) notes, comprising a summary of significant accounting policies and other explanatory notes.[33] The standard explains that notes contain information in addition to that presented in the balance sheet, income statement, statement of changes in equity and cash flow statement, and provide narrative descriptions or disaggregations of items disclosed in those statements and information about items that do not qualify for recognition in those statements.[34]

In addition to information about the reporting period, IAS 1 also requires information about the preceding period. Comparative information is discussed at 2.4 below.

Financial statements are usually published as part of a larger annual report, with the accompanying discussions and analyses often being more voluminous than the financial statements themselves. IAS 1 acknowledges this, but makes clear that such reports and statements (including financial reviews, environmental reports and value added statements) presented outside financial statements are outside the scope of IFRSs.[35]

Notwithstanding that this type of information is not within the scope of IFRSs, IAS 1 devotes two paragraphs to discussing what this information may comprise, observing that:

- a financial review by management may describe and explain the main features of the entity's financial performance and financial position and the principal uncertainties it faces and that it may include a review of:
  (a) the main factors and influences determining financial performance, including changes in the environment in which the entity operates, the entity's response to those changes and their effect, and the entity's policy for investment to maintain and enhance financial performance, including its dividend policy;
  (b) the entity's sources of funding and its targeted ratio of liabilities to equity; and
  (c) the entity's resources not recognised in the balance sheet in accordance with IFRS.[36]
- reports and statements such as environmental reports and value added statements may be presented, particularly in industries in which environmental factors are significant and when employees are regarded as an important user group.[37]

It strikes us as strange that an accounting standard would concern itself with a discussion of matters outside its scope in this way. However, discursive reports accompanying financial statements are not just common (indeed, required by most markets) but also clearly useful, so perhaps the IASB's discussion is attempting to encourage and support their preparation. In October 2005 the IASB published a discussion paper on management commentary. The paper assesses the role the IASB could play in improving the quality of the management commentary that frequently accompanies financial statements. The IASB sets out its view that management commentary is widely regarded as an important part of companies' annual reports and many jurisdictions have developed requirements or principles on management commentary. The Paper reviews those requirements and offers recommendations on how the IASB might promote the wider adoption of best practice in the interests of investors and others who use financial reports. The paper does not properly address the key question as to whether financial statements can achieve a 'fair presentation' on their own, or whether a management commentary is needed to do so. Notwithstanding the clear usefulness of management commentaries, we believe that it has historically been recognised that financial statements can stand alone and achieve a fair presentation without a supporting commentary. Accordingly, we question the IASB's mandate to develop guidance (whether a mandatory revision to IAS 1 or some kind of 'persuasive' non-mandatory guidance) in this area.

2.4 Comparative information

IAS 1 requires, except when a standard or an interpretation permits or requires otherwise, comparative information to be disclosed in respect of the previous period for all amounts reported in the financial statements. If any information is voluntarily presented, there will by definition be no standard or interpretation providing a dispensation from comparatives. Accordingly, comparative information is necessary for any voluntarily presented current period disclosure.

Comparative information is also required for narrative and descriptive information when it is relevant to an understanding of the current period's financial statements.[38] The standard illustrates the current year relevance of the previous year's narratives with a legal dispute, the outcome of which is was uncertain at the last balance sheet date and is yet to be resolved (the disclosure of contingent liabilities is discussed in Chapter 27). It observes that users benefit from information that the uncertainty existed at the last balance sheet date, and about the steps that have been taken during the period to resolve the uncertainty.[39]

Another example would be the required disclosure of material items, which would include items commonly called exceptional items, although that expression is not used by the standard (see 3.2.4 below). IAS 1 requires that the nature and amount of such items be disclosed separately.[40] Often a simple caption or line item heading will be sufficient to convey the 'nature' of material items. Sometimes, though a more extensive description in the notes may be needed to do this. In that case, the same information is likely to be relevant the following year.

As noted at 1.1.2 above, one of the objectives of IAS 1 is to ensure the comparability of financial statements with previous periods. The standard notes that enhancing the inter-period comparability of information assists users in making economic decisions, especially by allowing the assessment of trends in financial information for predictive purposes.[41] Requiring the presentation of comparatives allows such a comparison to be made within one set of financial statements. For a comparison to be meaningful, the amounts for prior periods need to be reclassified whenever the presentation or classification of items in the financial statements is amended. When this is the case, disclosure is required of the nature, amount and reasons for the reclassification.[42]

The standard acknowledges, though, that in some circumstances it is impracticable to reclassify comparative information for a particular prior period to achieve comparability with the current period. For these purposes, reclassification is impracticable when it cannot be done after making every reasonable effort to do so.[43] An example given by the standard is that data may not have been collected in the prior period(s) in a way that allows reclassification, and it may not be practicable to recreate the information.[44] When it proves impracticable to reclassify comparative data, IAS 1 requires disclosure of the reason for this and also the nature of the adjustments that would have been made if the amounts had been reclassified.[45]

As well as reclassification to reflect current period classifications as required by IAS 1, a change to comparatives as they were originally reported could be necessary:

(a) following a change in accounting policy (discussed at 4.4 below);

(b) to correct an error discovered in previous financial statements (discussed at 4.6 below); or

(c) in relation to non-current assets held for sale, disposal groups and discontinued operations (discussed in Chapter 4).

2.5 Identification of the financial statements and accompanying information

2.5.1 *Identification of financial statements*

It is commonly the case that financial statements will form only part of a larger annual report or other document. As IFRSs only apply to financial statements, it is important that the financial statements are clearly identified so that users of the report can distinguish information that is prepared using IFRSs from other information that may be useful but is not the subject of those requirements.[46]

As well as requiring that the financial statements be clearly distinguished, IAS 1 also requires that each component of the financial statements be identified clearly. Furthermore, the following information is required to be displayed prominently, and repeated when it is necessary for a proper understanding of the information presented:

(a) the name of the reporting entity or other means of identification, and any change in that information from the preceding balance sheet date;

(b) whether the financial statements cover the individual entity or a group of entities;

(c) the balance sheet date or the period covered by the financial statements, whichever is appropriate to that component of the financial statements;

(d) the presentation currency, as defined in IAS 21 – *The Effects of Changes in Foreign Exchange Rates* (discussed in Chapter 10); and

(e) the level of rounding used in presenting amounts in the financial statements.[47]

These requirements are normally met by the use of page headings and abbreviated column headings on each page of the financial statements. The standard notes that judgement is required in determining the best way of presenting such information. For example, when the financial statements are presented electronically, separate pages are not always used; the above items then need to be presented frequently enough to ensure a proper understanding of the information included in the financial statements.[48] IAS 1 considers that financial statements are often made more understandable by presenting information in thousands or millions of units of the presentation currency. It considers this acceptable as long as the level of rounding in presentation is disclosed and material information is not omitted.[49]

2.5.2 *Statement of compliance with IFRS*

As well as identifying which particular part of any larger document constitutes the financial statements, IAS 1 also requires that financial statements complying with IFRSs make an explicit and unreserved statement of such compliance in the notes.[50] As this statement itself is required for full compliance, its absence would render the whole financial statements non-compliant, even if there was otherwise full compliance. In a curious twist, the standard goes on to say that financial statements 'shall not be described as complying with IFRSs unless they comply with all the requirements of IFRSs.'[51] It is one thing for a standard setter to say what is necessary to comply with its rules. However, it is quite another thing to try and prescribe what an entity (which is, by definition, *not* complying with its rules) may or may not say.

The issue of financial statements prepared on a basis similar to, but not in compliance with, IFRS evidently continues to concern the IASB and at the time of writing the Board currently consulting on a change to IAS 1 relating to this issue. The proposed amendment would require that when an entity refers to IFRSs in describing the basis on which its financial statements are prepared but is not able to make an explicit and unreserved statement of compliance with IFRSs, the entity should:

(a) describe each difference between the basis on which its financial statements are prepared and IFRSs that are applicable to its financial statements; and

(b) describe how its reported financial position and performance of the entity would have differed if it had complied with IFRSs.[52]

3 THE STRUCTURE OF FINANCIAL STATEMENTS

As noted at 2.3 above, a complete set of financial statements under IAS 1 comprises:

(a) a balance sheet;

(b) an income statement;

(c) a statement of changes in equity showing either:

 (i) all changes in equity; or

(ii) changes in equity other than those arising from transactions with equity holders acting in their capacity as equity holders;

(d) a cash flow statement; and

(e) notes, comprising a summary of significant accounting policies and other explanatory notes.

The standard adopts a generally permissive stance, by setting out minimum levels of required items to be shown in each statement (sometimes specifically on the face of the statement, and sometimes either on the face or in the notes) whilst allowing great flexibility of order and layout.[53] The standard notes that sometimes it uses the term 'disclosure' in a broad sense, encompassing items presented on the face of the balance sheet, income statement, statement of changes in equity and cash flow statement, as well as in the notes. Other standards and interpretations also require 'disclosures'. IAS 1 makes clear that unless specified to the contrary in IAS 1, or in another standard or interpretation, such disclosures can be made either on the face of the balance sheet, income statement, statement of changes in equity or cash flow statement (whichever is relevant), or in the notes.[54]

IAS 1 observes that cash flow information provides users of financial statements with a basis to assess the ability of the entity to generate cash and cash equivalents and the needs of the entity to utilise those cash flows. Requirements for the presentation of the cash flow statement and related disclosures are set out IAS 7 – *Cash Flow Statements*.[55] Cash flow statements are discussed in Chapter 34, each of the other primary statements listed above is discussed in the following sections.

3.1 The balance sheet

3.1.1 The distinction between current/non-current assets and liabilities

A General

In most situations (but see the exception discussed below, and the treatment of non-current assets held for sale discussed in Chapter 4) IAS 1 requires balance sheets to distinguish current assets and liabilities from non-current ones.[56] The standard uses the term 'non-current' to include tangible, intangible and financial assets of a long-term nature. It does not prohibit the use of alternative descriptions as long as the meaning is clear.[57] A common alternative description seen in practice is the term fixed assets.

The standard explains the requirement to present current and non-current items separately by observing that when an entity supplies goods or services within a clearly identifiable operating cycle, separate classification of current and non-current assets and liabilities on the face of the balance sheet will provide useful information by distinguishing the net assets that are continuously circulating as working capital from those used in long-term operations. Furthermore, the analysis will also highlight assets that are expected to be realised within the current operating cycle, and liabilities that are due for settlement within the same period.[58] The distinction between current and non-current items therefore depends on the length of the entity's operating cycle. The standard states that the operating cycle of an entity is the time between the acquisition of assets for processing and their realisation in cash or cash equivalents. However, when the entity's normal operating cycle is not clearly identifiable, its duration is assumed to be twelve months.[59]

Once assets have been classified as non-current they should not be reclassified as current assets until they meet the criteria to be classified as held for sale in accordance with IFRS 5 (see Chapter 4). Assets of a class that an entity would normally regard as non-current that are acquired exclusively with a view to resale also should not be classified as current unless they meet those criteria.[60]

The basic requirement of the standard is that current and non-current assets, and current and non-current liabilities, should be presented as separate classifications on the face of its balance sheet.[61] The standard defines current assets and current liabilities (discussed at 3.1.3 and 3.1.4 below), with the non-current category being the residual.[62] Example 3.1 at 3.1.7 below provides an illustration of a balance sheet presenting this classification.

An exception to this requirement is when a presentation based on liquidity provides information that is reliable and is more relevant. When that exception applies, all assets and liabilities are required to be presented broadly in order of liquidity.[63] The reason for this exception given by the standard is that some entities (such as financial institutions) do not supply goods or services within a clearly identifiable operating cycle, and for these entities a presentation of assets and liabilities in increasing or decreasing order of liquidity provides information that is reliable and is more relevant than a current/non-current presentation.[64]

The standard also makes clear that an entity is permitted to present some of its assets and liabilities using a current/non-current classification and others in order of liquidity when this provides information that is reliable and is more relevant. It goes on to observe that the need for a mixed basis of presentation might arise when an entity has diverse operations.[65]

Whichever method of presentation is adopted, IAS 1 requires for each asset and liability line item that combines amounts expected to be recovered or settled:

(a) no more than twelve months after the balance sheet date; and

(b) more than twelve months after the balance sheet date;

disclosure of the amount expected to be recovered or settled after more than twelve months.[66]

The standard explains this requirement by noting that information about expected dates of realisation of assets and liabilities is useful in assessing the liquidity and solvency of an entity. In this vein, IAS 1 contains a reminder that IFRS 7 requires disclosure of the maturity dates of financial assets (including trade and other receivables) and financial liabilities (including trade and other payables) – see Chapter 22 (formerly these were requirements of IAS 32 – *Financial Instruments: Disclosure and Presentation*). This assertion in IAS 1 is not strictly correct, as IFRS 7 in fact only requires a maturity *analysis* (rather than maturity dates) and only requires this for financial liabilities. IFRS 7 is discussed in Chapter 22. Similarly, IAS 1 views information on the expected date of recovery and settlement of non-monetary assets and liabilities such as inventories and provisions as also useful, whether or not assets and liabilities are classified as current or non-current. An example of this given by the standard is that an entity should disclose the amount of inventories that are expected to be recovered more than twelve months after the balance sheet date.[67]

B *Classification of derivatives to which hedge accounting is not applied*

The classification of assets and liabilities as current is discussed at 3.1.3 and 3.1.4 below. One issue of note is the classification of derivatives to which hedge accounting is not applied.

As discussed below, IAS 1 requires that derivative assets and liabilities be classified as current if they are 'held primarily for the purpose of being traded'. For current assets, this is reiterated in the non-bold explanatory text. However, for current liabilities the non-bold explanatory text includes 'Examples [of items held primarily for trading] include financial liabilities classified as held for trading in accordance with IAS 39 ...' As discussed in Chapter 21, derivatives are classified as held for trading if they fail to qualify for hedge accounting. This could be for a number of reasons, for example:

(a) the entity is genuinely actively trading in derivatives;

(b) the entity has achieved an effective economic hedge but chooses not to apply hedge accounting, perhaps on the grounds that the requirements for designation, documentation and effectiveness testing are considered overly onerous;

(c) whilst the entity expects some degree of economic hedge, the derivative is not expected to be 'highly effective' in accordance with IAS 39 or

(d) the derivative is embedded in another instrument and, whilst not qualifying for hedge accounting, was taken out for commercial reasons unrelated to speculative hedging.

Based on the natural meaning of the words, (b), (c) and (d) could be viewed as not being 'held primarily for trading', as that was not the entity's motive for entering into them. However, they certainly are *classified* as such in accordance with IAS 39. The ambiguity in the standard has inevitably resulted in a variety of practice. Many entities have opted to present as current all derivatives which are not accounted for as hedges. Others have taken the view that derivatives which do not qualify for hedge accounting need not necessarily be regarded as held primarily for trading. Unless and until the issue is clarified by IFRIC or the IASB we expect practice will remain mixed. This issue was discussed by IFRIC in May 2007, but it decided not to take the issue onto its agenda. However, it noted that 'some believe that IAS 1 paragraph 62 could be read as implying that financial liabilities that are classified as held for trading in accordance with IAS 39 are required to be presented as current.' In light of this, IFRIC decided to recommend to the IASB that IAS 1 be amended to remove that implication.[68]

An example of a company classifying some such items as non-current and others as current is shown in the extract below.

Extract 3.1: Suez Group (2005)

Note 1 Summary of significant accounting policies [extract]

M. Derivatives and hedge accounting [extract]

4. Derivative instruments not qualifying for hedge accounting: recognition and presentation [extract]

These items mainly concern derivative financial instruments used in economic hedges that have not been – or are no longer – documented, as well as derivatives entered into by the Group in connection with proprietary energy trading activities and energy trading on behalf of its customers.

When a derivative financial instrument does not qualify or no longer qualifies for hedge accounting, changes in fair value are recognized directly in income, under "Changes in fair value of commodity derivative instruments," in operating income for derivative instruments with nonfinancial assets as the underlying, and in financial income or expense for currency, interest rate and equity derivatives.

Derivative instruments used by the Group in connection with proprietary energy trading activities and energy trading on behalf of customers and other derivatives expiring in less than 12 months are recognized in the consolidated balance sheet in current assets and liabilities. All other derivative financial instruments are recognized in non-current assets and liabilities.

C Settlement of a liability by issuing of equity

As discussed at 3.1.4 below, a liability will fall to be classified as current if an entity does not have an unconditional right to defer settlement for at least twelve months after the balance sheet date. IAS 1 does not elaborate further the meaning of 'settlement' and in particular does not restrict the word to mean only those forms of settlement which involve a net outflow of resources. Furthermore, the Framework indicates that the conversion of a liability into equity is a form of settlement.[69] One consequence of this is that if the conversion option in convertible debt is exercisable by the holder at any time then the liability component would fall to be classified as current even if the maturity for cash settlement is greater than one year. The accounting treatment for convertible debt is discussed in Chapter 19.

The IASB considered this issue and in particular considered the relevance of equity settlement to the notion in the Framework that information about liquidity and solvency is useful to users of financial statements. The Board concluded that classifying liabilities based on the requirements to transfer cash or other assets better reflects the liquidity and solvency position of an entity. Accordingly, the IASB intends to amend IAS 1 as part of the 2007 annual improvements process. The proposed amendment will clarify that an entity needs an unconditional right to defer settlement *by the transfer of cash or other assets* for more than a year in order to classify a liability as non-current.[70]

3.1.2 Non-current assets and disposal groups held for sale

The general requirement to classify balance sheet items as current or non-current (or present them broadly in order of liquidity) is overlaid with further requirements by IFRS 5 regarding non-current assets held for sale and disposal groups (discussed in Chapter 4). IFRS 5's aim is that entities should present and disclose information that enables users of the financial statements to evaluate the financial effects of disposals of non-current assets (or disposal groups).[71] In pursuit of this aim, IFRS 5 requires:

- non-current assets classified as held for sale and the assets of a disposal group classified as held for sale to be presented separately from other assets in the balance sheet; and
- the liabilities of a disposal group classified as held for sale to be presented separately from other liabilities in the balance sheet.

These assets and liabilities should not be offset and presented as a single amount. In addition:

(a) major classes of assets and liabilities classified as held for sale should generally be separately disclosed either on the face of the balance sheet or in the notes (see 3.1.6 below). However, this is not necessary for a disposal group if it is a subsidiary that met the criteria to be classified as held for sale on acquisition; and

(b) any cumulative income or expense recognised directly in equity relating to a non-current asset (or disposal group) classified as held for sale should be presented separately.[72]

3.1.3 Current assets

IAS 1 requires an asset to be classified as current when it satisfies any of the following criteria, with all other assets classified as non-current. The criteria are:

(a) it is expected to be realised in, or is intended for sale or consumption in, the entity's normal operating cycle (discussed at 3.1.1 above);

(b) it is held primarily for the purpose of being traded;

(c) it is expected to be realised within twelve months after the balance sheet date; or

(d) it is cash or a cash equivalent (as defined in IAS 7, discussed in Chapter 34) unless it is restricted from being exchanged or used to settle a liability for at least twelve months after the balance sheet date.[73]

As an exception to this, deferred tax assets are never allowed to be classified as current.[74]

Current assets include assets (such as inventories and trade receivables) that are sold, consumed or realised as part of the normal operating cycle even when they are not expected to be realised within twelve months after the balance sheet date. Current assets also include assets held primarily for the purpose of being traded (financial assets within this category would be classified as held for trading in accordance with IAS 39 discussed in Chapter 17 at 7.1.1) and the current portion of non-current financial assets.[75]

3.1.4 Current liabilities

IAS 1 requires a liability to be classified as current when it satisfies any of the following criteria, with all other liabilities classified as non-current. The criteria are:

(a) it is expected to be settled in the entity's normal operating cycle (discussed at 3.1.1 above);

(b) it is held primarily for the purpose of being traded;

(c) it is due to be settled within twelve months after the balance sheet date; or

(d) the entity does not have an unconditional right to defer settlement of the liability for at least twelve months after the balance sheet date.[76]

As an exception to this, deferred tax liabilities are never allowed to be classified as current.[77]

The standard notes that some current liabilities, such as trade payables and some accruals for employee and other operating costs, are part of the working capital used in the entity's normal operating cycle. Such operating items are classified as current liabilities even if they are due to be settled more than twelve months after the balance sheet date.[78]

However, neither IAS 19 nor IAS 1 specifies where in the balance sheet an asset or liability in respect of a defined benefit plan should be presented, nor whether such balances should be shown separately on the face of the balance sheet or only in the notes – this is left to the judgement of the reporting entity (see 3.1.5 below). When the format of balance sheet distinguishes current assets and liabilities from non-current ones, the question arises as to whether this split needs also to be made for defined benefit plan balances. IAS 19 does not specify whether such a split should be made, on the grounds that it may sometimes be arbitrary.[79]

Some current liabilities are not settled as part of the normal operating cycle, but are due for settlement within twelve months after the balance sheet date or held primarily for the purpose of being traded. Examples given by the standard are financial liabilities classified as held for trading in accordance with IAS 39, bank overdrafts, and the current portion of non-current financial liabilities, dividends payable, income taxes and other non-trade payables. Financial liabilities that provide financing on a long-term basis (i.e. are not part of the working capital used in the entity's normal operating cycle) and are not due for settlement within twelve months after the balance sheet date are non-current liabilities.[80]

The assessment of a liability as current or non-current is applied very strictly in IAS 1. In particular, a liability should be classified as current:

(a) when it is due to be settled within twelve months after the balance sheet date, even if:

  (i) the original term was for a period longer than twelve months; and

  (ii) an agreement to refinance, or to reschedule payments, on a long-term basis is completed after the balance sheet date and before the financial statements are authorised for issue (although disclosure of the post balance sheet refinancing would be required);[81] or

(b) when an entity breaches an undertaking under a long-term loan agreement on or before the balance sheet date with the effect that the liability becomes payable on demand. This is the case even if the lender has agreed, after the balance sheet date and before the authorisation of the financial statements for issue, not to demand payment as a consequence of the breach (although the post balance sheet agreement would be disclosed). The meaning of the term 'authorised for issue' is discussed in Chapter 36 at 2.1. The standard explains that the liability should be classified as current because, at the balance sheet date, the entity does not have an unconditional right to defer its settlement for at least twelve months after that date.[82] However, the liability would be classified as non-current if the lender agreed by the balance sheet date to provide a period of grace ending at least twelve months after the balance sheet date, within which the entity can rectify the breach and during which the lender cannot demand immediate repayment.[83]

The key point here is that for a liability to be classified as non-current requires that the entity has *at the balance sheet date* an unconditional right to defer its settlement for at least twelve months after the balance sheet date. Accordingly, the standard explains that liabilities would be non-current if an entity expects, and has the discretion, to refinance or roll over an obligation for at least twelve months after the balance sheet date under an existing loan facility, even if it would otherwise be due within a shorter period. However, when refinancing or rolling over the obligation is not at the discretion of the entity the obligation is classified as current.[84]

At the time of writing the IASB is proposing an amendment to IAS 1 relating to convertible debt. The proposed amendment will make clear that the ability to defer settlement by at least a year in order to classify a liability as non-current relates to settlement by way of transferring assets. Holder settlement options to be satisfied by the issue of equity would be disregarded. This is discussed further at 3.1.1 C above.

3.1.5 Information required on the face of the balance sheet

IAS 1 does not contain a prescriptive format or order for the balance sheet.[85] Rather, it contains two mechanisms which require certain information to be shown on the face of the balance sheet. First, it contains a list of specific items for which this is required, on the basis that they are sufficiently different in nature or function to warrant separate presentation.[86] Second, it stipulates that additional line items, headings and subtotals should be presented on the face of the balance sheet when such presentation is relevant to an understanding of the entity's financial position.[87] Clearly this is a highly judgemental decision for entities to make when preparing a balance sheet, and allows a wide variety of possible presentations. The judgement as to whether additional items should be presented separately is based on an assessment of:

(a) the nature and liquidity of assets;

(b) the function of assets within the entity; and

(c) the amounts, nature and timing of liabilities.[88]

IAS 1 indicates that the use of different measurement bases for different classes of assets suggests that their nature or function differs and, therefore, that they should be presented as separate line items. For example, different classes of property, plant and equipment can be carried at cost or revalued amounts in accordance with IAS 16 – *Property, Plant and Equipment*.[89]

As a minimum, the face of the balance sheet should include line items that present the following amounts:

(a) property, plant and equipment;
(b) investment property;
(c) intangible assets;
(d) financial assets (excluding amounts shown under (e), (h) and (i));
(e) investments accounted for using the equity method;
(f) biological assets;
(g) inventories;
(h) trade and other receivables;
(i) cash and cash equivalents;
(j) trade and other payables;
(k) provisions;
(l) financial liabilities (excluding amounts shown under (j) and (k));
(m) liabilities and assets for current tax, as defined in IAS 12;
(n) deferred tax liabilities and deferred tax assets, as defined in IAS 12;
(o) minority interest, presented within equity;
(p) issued capital and reserves attributable to equity holders of the parent;
(q) the total of assets classified as held for sale and assets included in disposal groups classified as held for sale in accordance with IFRS 5; and
(r) liabilities included in disposal groups classified as held for sale in accordance with IFRS 5.

Those items covered by (q) and (r) should be excluded from all other captions.[90]

The standard notes that items (a) to (p) above represent a list of items that are sufficiently different in nature or function to warrant separate presentation on the face of the balance sheet. Items (q) and (r) were introduced by IFRS 5, presumably for the same reason. In addition:

(a) line items should be included when the size, nature or function of an item or aggregation of similar items is such that separate presentation is relevant to an understanding of the entity's financial position; and
(b) the descriptions used and the ordering of items or aggregation of similar items may be amended according to the nature of the entity and its transactions, to provide information that is relevant to an understanding of the entity's

financial position. For example, a financial institution may amend the above descriptions to provide information that is relevant to the operations of a financial institution.[91]

3.1.6 Information required either on the face of the balance sheet or in the notes

IAS 1 requires further sub-classifications of the line items shown on the face of the balance sheet to be presented either on the face of the balance sheet or in the notes. The requirements for these further sub-classifications are approached by the standard in a similar manner to those for line items on the face of the balance sheet. There is a prescriptive list of items required (see below) and also a more general requirement that the sub-classifications should be made in a manner appropriate to the entity's operations.[92] The standard notes that the detail provided in sub-classifications depends on the requirements of IFRSs (as numerous disclosures are required by other standards) and on the size, nature and function of the amounts involved.[93]

Aside of the specific requirements, deciding what level of detailed disclosure is necessary is clearly a judgemental exercise. As is the case for items on the face of the balance sheet, IAS 1 requires that the judgement as to whether additional items should be presented separately should be based on an assessment of:

(a) the nature and liquidity of assets;

(b) the function of assets within the entity; and

(c) the amounts, nature and timing of liabilities.[94]

The disclosures will also vary for each item, examples given by the standard are:

(a) items of property, plant and equipment are disaggregated into classes in accordance with IAS 16;

(b) receivables are disaggregated into amounts receivable from trade customers, receivables from related parties, prepayments and other amounts;

(c) inventories are sub-classified, in accordance with IAS 2 – *Inventories*, into classifications such as merchandise, production supplies, materials, work in progress and finished goods;

(d) provisions are disaggregated into provisions for employee benefits and other items; and

(e) equity capital and reserves are disaggregated into various classes, such as paid-in capital, share premium and reserves.[95]

IAS 1 specifically requires the following information regarding equity and share capital to be shown either on the face of the balance sheet or in the notes:

(a) for each class of share capital:

  (i) the number of shares authorised;

  (ii) the number of shares issued and fully paid, and issued but not fully paid;

  (iii) par value per share, or that the shares have no par value;

(iv) a reconciliation of the number of shares outstanding at the beginning and at the end of the period;

(v) the rights, preferences and restrictions attaching to that class including restrictions on the distribution of dividends and the repayment of capital;

(vi) shares in the entity held by the entity or by its subsidiaries or associates; and

(vii) shares reserved for issue under options and contracts for the sale of shares, including the terms and amounts; and

(b) a description of the nature and purpose of each reserve within equity.[96]

An entity without share capital (such as a partnership or trust) should disclose information equivalent to that required by (a) above, showing changes during the period in each category of equity interest, and the rights, preferences and restrictions attaching to each category of equity interest.[97]

3.1.7 Illustrative balance sheets

The implementation guidance accompanying IAS 1 provides an illustration of a balance sheet presented to distinguish current and non-current items. It makes clear that other formats may be equally appropriate, as long as the distinction is clear.[98] As discussed in Chapter 4, IFRS 5 provides further guidance relating to the presentation of non-current assets and disposal groups held for sale.

Example 3.1: *Illustrative balance sheet*[99]

XYZ GROUP – BALANCE SHEET AS AT 31 DECEMBER 2008

(in thousands of Euros)

	2008	**2007**
ASSETS		
Non-current assets		
Property, plant and equipment	×	×
Goodwill	×	×
Other intangible assets	×	×
Investments in associates	×	×
Available-for-sale investments	×	×
	×	×
Current assets		
Inventories	×	×
Trade receivables	×	×
Other current assets	×	×
Cash and cash equivalents	×	×
	×	×
Total assets	×	×

EQUITY AND LIABILITIES		
Equity attributable to equity holders of the parent		
Share capital	×	×
Other reserves	×	×
Retained earnings	×	×
	×	×
Minority interest	×	×
Total equity	×	×
Non-current liabilities		
Long-term borrowings	×	×
Deferred tax	×	×
Long-term provisions	×	×
Total non-current liabilities	×	×
Current liabilities		
Trade and other payables	×	×
Short-term borrowings	×	×
Current portion of long-term borrowings	×	×
Current tax payable	×	×
Short-term provisions	×	×
Total current liabilities	×	×
Total liabilities	×	×
Total equity and liabilities	×	×

3.2 The income statement

IAS 1 adopts an essentially permissive approach to the format of the income statement. It observes that, because the effects of an entity's various activities, transactions and other events differ in frequency, potential for gain or loss and predictability, disclosing the components of financial performance assists in an understanding of the financial performance achieved and in making projections of future results.[100] In other words, some analysis of the make-up of net profit is needed, but a wide variety of presentations would all be acceptable. The general rule is that income and expense items are not offset unless certain criteria are met, this is discussed at 4.1.5 B below.

As is the case for the balance sheet, IAS 1 sets out certain items which must appear on the face of the income statement and other required disclosures which may be made either on the face or in the notes.

3.2.1 Information required on the face of the income statement

IAS 1 requires certain specific items to appear on the face of the income statement and then supplements this with a more general requirement that additional line items, headings and subtotals should be presented on the face of the statement when such presentation is relevant to an understanding of the entity's financial performance.[101] The standard explains that additional line items should be included on the face of the income statement, and the descriptions used and the ordering of items are amended when this is necessary to explain the elements of financial performance. Factors to be considered would include materiality and the nature and function of the components of income and expenses. An example of this is that a financial institution may amend the descriptions to provide information that is relevant to the operations of a financial institution.[102]

As a minimum, the face of the income statement should include line items that present the following amounts (although as noted above, the order and description of the items should be amended as necessary):

(a) revenue;

(b) finance costs;

(c) share of the profit or loss of associates and joint ventures accounted for using the equity method;

(d) tax expense;

(e) a single amount comprising the total of:

  (i) the post-tax profit or loss of discontinued operations; and

  (ii) the post-tax gain or loss recognised on the measurement to fair value less costs to sell or on the disposal of the assets or disposal group(s) constituting the discontinued operation;

(f) profit or loss;[103] and

(g) the following as allocations of profit or loss for the period:

  (i) profit or loss attributable to minority interest; and

  (ii) profit or loss attributable to equity holders of the parent.[104]

As discussed at 3.2.2 below, an analysis of expenses is required based either on their nature or their function. IAS 1 encourages, but does not require this to be shown on the face of the income statement.[105]

The standard also requires the disclosure of the amount of dividends recognised as distributions to equity holders during the period, and the related amount per share. This may be shown either on the face of the income statement or the statement of changes in equity, or in the notes.[106]

Subsequent to the 2003 improvements project, IAS 1 has omitted the requirement in the previous version to disclose the results of operating activities as a line item on the face of the income statement. The reason given for this in the Basis for Conclusions to the standard is that 'Operating activities' are not defined in the standard, and the Board decided not to require disclosure of an undefined item.[107]

The Basis for Conclusions to IAS 1 goes on to state that 'The Board recognises that an entity may elect to disclose the results of operating activities, or a similar line item, even though this term is not defined. In such cases, the Board notes that the entity should ensure the amount disclosed is representative of activities that would normally be considered to be 'operating'.

'In the Board's view, it would be misleading and would impair the comparability of financial statements if items of an operating nature were excluded from the results of operating activities, even if that had been industry practice. For example, it would be inappropriate to exclude items clearly related to operations (such as inventory write-downs and restructuring and relocation expenses) because they occur irregularly or infrequently or are unusual in amount. Similarly, it would be inappropriate to exclude items on the grounds that they do not involve cash flows, such as depreciation and amortisation expenses.'[108]

Whilst we agree with the sentiments in the second paragraph, in our view it is regrettable that the IASB has approached this issue by presenting its opinions *outside* of IFRS about something not required by IFRS but which it thinks some entities may choose to do. As it has, though, we question how the authority of this 'guidance' will be viewed. However, in our view the general requirement for a fair presentation (discussed at 4.1.1 below) would seem to prohibit the exclusion from any voluntarily presented 'operating' result of items which reasonable users of the financial statements would generally consider to be 'operating' in nature.

The implementation guidance accompanying the standard provides illustrative examples of an income statement (see 3.2.2 below).

3.2.2 Classification of expenses by nature or function

IAS 1 states that components of financial performance may differ in terms of frequency, potential for gain or loss and predictability, and requires that expenses should be sub-classified to highlight this.[109] To achieve this, the standard requires the presentation of an analysis of expenses using a classification based on either the nature of expenses or their function within the entity, whichever provides information that is reliable and more relevant.[110] It is because each method of presentation has merit for different types of entities, that the standard requires management to select the most relevant and reliable presentation. As noted at 3.2.1 above IAS 1 encourages, but does not require the chosen analysis to be shown on the face of the income statement.[111] This means that entities are permitted to disclose the classification on the face on a mixed basis, as long as the required classification is provided in the notes. Indeed, the IASB itself produces an example of such an income statement in an appendix to IAS 7.[112]

The standard also notes that the choice between the function of expense method and the nature of expense method will depend on historical and industry factors and the nature of the entity. Both methods provide an indication of those costs that might vary, directly or indirectly, with the level of sales or production of the entity. However, because information on the nature of expenses is useful in predicting future cash flows, additional disclosure is required when the function of expense classification is used (see B below).[113]

A Analysis of expenses by nature

For some entities, 'more reliable and relevant information' may be achieved by aggregating expenses for display in the income statement according to their nature (for example, depreciation, purchases of materials, transport costs, employee benefits and advertising costs), and not reallocating them among various functions within the entity. IAS 1 observes that this method may be simple to apply because no allocations of expenses to functional classifications are necessary. The standard illustrates a classification using the nature of expense method is as follows:

Example 3.2: Example of classification of expenses by nature[114]

Revenue		×
Other income		×
Changes in inventories of finished goods and work in progress	×	
Raw materials and consumables used	×	
Employee benefits costs	×	
Depreciation and amortisation expense	×	
Other expenses	×	
Total expenses		(×)
Profit		×

The implementation guidance accompanying the standard provides a further example of an income statement analysing expenses by nature. Whilst very similar to the above, it is expanded to show further captions as follows:[115]

XYZ GROUP – INCOME STATEMENT FOR THE YEAR ENDED 31 DECEMBER 2008

(in thousands of Euro)

	2008	**2007**
Revenue	×	×
Other income	×	×
Changes in inventories of finished goods and work in progress	(×)	×
Work performed by the entity and capitalised	×	×
Raw material and consumables used	(×)	(×)
Employee benefits expense	(×)	(×)
Depreciation and amortisation expense	(×)	(×)
Impairment of property, plant and equipment	(×)	(×)
Other expenses	(×)	(×)
Finance costs	(×)	(×)
Share of profit of associates	×	×
Profit before tax	×	×
Income tax expense	(×)	(×)
Profit for the period	×	×
Attributable to:		
Equity holders of the parent	×	×
Minority interest	×	×
	×	×

The guidance observes that in an income statement in which expenses are classified by nature, an impairment of property, plant and equipment is shown as a separate line item. By contrast, if expenses are classified by function, the impairment is included in the function(s) to which it relates. The guidance also notes that the line item relating to associates means the share of associates' profit attributable to equity holders of the associates, i.e. it is after tax and minority interests in the associates.

B Analysis of expenses by function

For some entities, 'more reliable and relevant information' may be achieved by aggregating expenses for display in the income statement according to their function for example, as part of cost of sales, the costs of distribution or administrative activities. Under this method, IAS 1 requires as a minimum, disclosure of cost of sales separately from other expenses (although it does not specify whether this should be on the face of the statement or in the notes). The standard observes that this method can provide more relevant information to users than the classification of expenses by nature, but that allocating costs to functions may require arbitrary allocations and involve considerable judgement. Examples of classification using the function of expense method given by the standard are as follows:

Example 3.3: Example of classification by function[116]

Revenue	×
Cost of sales	(×)
Gross profit	×
Other income	×
Distribution costs	(×)
Administrative expenses	(×)
Other expenses	(×)
Profit	×

The implementation guidance accompanying the standard provides a further example of an income statement analysing expenses by nature. Whilst very similar to the above, it is expanded to show further captions as follows.[117]

XYZ GROUP – INCOME STATEMENT FOR THE YEAR ENDED 31 DECEMBER 2008

(illustrating the classification of expenses by function)
(in thousands of Euros)

	2008	**2007**
Revenue	×	×
Cost of sales	(×)	(×)
Gross profit	×	×
Other income	×	×
Distribution costs	(×)	(×)
Administrative expenses	(×)	(×)
Other expenses	(×)	(×)
Finance costs	(×)	(×)
Share of profit of associates	×	×
Profit before tax	×	×
Income tax expense	(×)	(×)
Profit for the period	×	×

Attributable to:		
Equity holders of the parent	×	×
Minority interest	×	×
	×	×

The guidance notes that the line item relating to associates means the share of associates' profit attributable to equity holders of the associates, i.e. it is after tax and minority interests in the associates.

Entities classifying expenses by function are required by IAS 1 to disclose additional information on the nature of expenses, and this must include depreciation and amortisation expense and employee benefits expense.[118] This requirement of IAS 1 strikes us as unnecessary as the disclosure of these items (broken down into their components) is specifically required by IAS 16, IAS 19 and IAS 38 – *Intangible Assets*.

3.2.3 Discontinued operations

As discussed in Chapter 4, IFRS 5 requires the presentation of a single amount on the face of the income statement relating to discontinued operations, with further analysis either on the face of the income statement or in the notes.

3.2.4 Material, exceptional and extraordinary items

A Exceptional or material items

IAS 1 does not use the phrase exceptional items. However, it does require that when items of income and expense are material, their nature and amount should be disclosed separately.[119] Materiality is discussed at 4.1.5 A below. The standard goes on to suggest that circumstances that would give rise to the separate disclosure of items of income and expense include:

(a) write-downs of inventories to net realisable value or of property, plant and equipment to recoverable amount, as well as reversals of such write-downs;

(b) restructurings of the activities of an entity and reversals of any provisions for the costs of restructuring;

(c) disposals of items of property, plant and equipment;

(d) disposals of investments;

(e) discontinued operations;

(f) litigation settlements; and

(g) other reversals of provisions.[120]

This information may be given on the face of the income statement or in the notes. In line with the permissive approach taken to the format of the income statement discussed above, the level of prominence given to such items is left to the judgement of the entity concerned. However, regarding (e) above, IFRS 5 requires certain information to be presented on the face of the income statement (see Chapter 4).

B Ordinary activities and extraordinary items

There is a certain amount of tension (or at least of ongoing evolution) in the IFRS literature concerning results from ordinary activities, and in particular the categorisation of certain items as falling outwith them – that is extraordinary items.

The IASB's *Framework* seems to consider the distinction a useful one, and states 'Income and expenses may be presented in the income statement in different ways so as to provide information that is relevant for economic decision-making. For example, it is common practice to distinguish between those items of income and expenses that arise in the course of the ordinary activities of the enterprise and those that do not. This distinction is made on the basis that the source of an item is relevant in evaluating the ability of the enterprise to generate cash and cash equivalents in the future; for example, incidental activities such as the disposal of a long-term investment are unlikely to recur on a regular basis. When distinguishing between items in this way consideration needs to be given to the nature of the enterprise and its operations. Items that arise from the ordinary activities of one enterprise may be unusual in respect of another.'[121] This was reflected in the requirement in the pre- December 2003 version of IAS 8 to present this distinction on the face of the income statement supported by a definition of ordinary activities and extraordinary items.[122]

The IASB's improvements project took a different view of the ordinary/extraordinary distinction, perhaps due to a feeling that it was being abused. The 'improved' IAS 1 and IAS 8 prohibit entities making this distinction, IAS 1 now stating that an entity 'shall not present any items of income and expense as extraordinary items, either on the face of the income statement or in the notes.'[123] Also, definitions of ordinary activities and extraordinary items have been removed. The IASB explains its decision to eliminate the concept of extraordinary items as follows 'The Board decided that items treated as extraordinary result from the normal business risks faced by an entity and do not warrant presentation in a separate component of the income statement. The nature or function of a transaction or other event, rather than its frequency, should determine its presentation within the income statement. Items currently classified as 'extraordinary' are only a subset of the items of income and expense that may warrant disclosure to assist users in predicting an entity's future performance.'[124]

We do not expect that the changes will have any real impact on the prominence given to items in the income statement and the earnings measures which entities choose to focus on when discussing their performance. This is because the whole approach to the content and layout of the income statement is permissive. Certain items must be shown on the face, yet the order of them and their captions are left to the judgement of the entity. Furthermore, additional items can (indeed, must) be introduced where necessary. Against that backdrop banning extraordinary items seems to us like mere semantics.

3.3 The statement of changes in equity

The net assets of an entity (its equity) can change for various reasons, principally income and expenses reported in the income statement and the introduction by or return of capital to shareholders, although in addition some items of income and expense are required to bypass the income statement.

IAS 1 requires all items of income and expense recognised in a period to be included in profit or loss unless another standard or an interpretation requires otherwise (discussed at 4.1.6 below).[125] Other standards require some gains and losses (such as revaluation increases and decreases, particular foreign exchange differences, gains or losses on remeasuring available-for-sale financial assets, and related amounts of current tax and deferred tax) to be recognised directly as changes in equity. The standard asserts that, because it is important to consider all items of income and expense in assessing changes in an entity's financial position between two balance sheet dates, the presentation of a statement of changes in equity is required that highlights an entity's total income and expenses, including those that are recognised directly in equity.[126] Accordingly, IAS 1 requires the presentation of a statement of changes in equity showing on the face of the statement:

(a) profit or loss for the period;

(b) each item of income and expense for the period that, as required by other standards or by interpretations, is recognised directly in equity, and the total of these items;

(c) total income and expense for the period (calculated as the sum of (a) and (b)), showing separately the total amounts attributable to equity holders of the parent and to minority interest; and

(d) for each component of equity, the effects of changes in accounting policies and corrections of errors recognised in accordance with IAS 8 (discussed at 4.4 and 4.6 below).

As discussed below, the statement may contain further items. If it only contains the above items it must be titled 'statement of recognised income and expense'.[127]

Items (a) to (c) above reflect the focus of the IASB on the balance sheet – whereby any changes in net assets (aside of those arising from transactions with shareholders) are gains and losses, regarded as performance. In this vein, IAS 1 observes that changes in an entity's equity between two balance sheet dates reflect the increase or decrease in its net assets during the period. Except for changes resulting from transactions with equity holders acting in their capacity as equity holders (such as equity contributions, reacquisitions of the entity's own equity instruments and dividends) and transaction costs directly related to such transactions, the overall change in equity during a period represents the total amount of income and expenses, including gains and losses, generated by the entity's activities during that period (whether those items of income and expenses are recognised in profit or loss or directly as changes in equity).[128]

After taking account of total gains and losses in this way, any other changes in equity will result from either:

- the restatement of prior periods; or
- transactions with owners in their capacity as such (for example, the issue and redemption of shares, distributions, and the credit entry relating to equity settled share based payment charges).

Point (d) above reflects the first of these. IAS 8 requires retrospective adjustments to effect changes in accounting policies, to the extent practicable, except when the transitional provisions in another standard or an interpretation require otherwise. IAS 8 also requires that restatements to correct errors are made retrospectively, to the extent practicable. Retrospective adjustments and retrospective restatements should be made to the balance of retained earnings, except when a standard or an interpretation requires retrospective adjustment of another component of equity. Point (d) above therefore requires disclosure in the statement of changes in equity of the total adjustment to each component of equity resulting, separately, from changes in accounting policies and from corrections of errors. These adjustments should be disclosed for each prior period and the beginning of the period.[129]

At this point, entities have a choice as regards the second bullet above. IAS 1 requires the presentation either on the face of the statement of changes in equity or in the notes of:

(a) the amounts of transactions with equity holders acting in their capacity as equity holders, showing separately distributions to equity holders (although, as noted at 3.2.1 above, distributions may be presented on the face of the income statement);

(b) the balance of retained earnings (i.e. accumulated profit or loss) at the beginning of the period and at the balance sheet date, and the changes during the period; and

(c) a reconciliation between the carrying amount of each class of contributed equity and each reserve at the beginning and the end of the period, separately disclosing each change.[130]

The standard notes that the above requirements may be met in various ways. One example would be a columnar format that reconciles the opening and closing balances of each element within equity on the face of the statement. An alternative would be to present the items set out (a) to (c) above in the notes.[131] In other words, the statement of changes in equity could be left as a kind of 'performance statement' excluding transactions with owners, or it could be presented as a combined statement of all changes in equity.

Entities electing to recognise all actuarial gains and losses outside of the income statement are required to present a statement of recognised income and expense which excludes transactions with owner in their capacity as such.[132] This accounting option is discussed in Chapter 32 at 5.3.1 A II.

The implementation guidance accompanying the IAS 1 provides two illustrations of how its requirements could be met reflecting the two choices described above.

First, the full reconciliation of each component of equity in a columnar format is illustrated as follows.

Example 3.4: Combined statement of all changes in equity.[133]

XYZ GROUP – STATEMENT OF CHANGES IN EQUITY FOR THE YEAR ENDED 31 DECEMBER 2008

(in thousands of Euros)

	Attributable to equity holders of the parent						
	Share capital	Other reserves*	Translation reserve	Retained earnings	Total	Minority interest	Total equity
Balance at 31 December 2006	×	×	(×)	×	×	×	×
Changes in accounting policy				(×)	(×)	(×)	(×)
Restated balance	×	×	(×)	×	×	×	×
Changes in equity for 2007							
Gain on property revaluation		×			×	×	×
Available-for-sale investments:							
Valuation gains/(losses) taken to equity		(×)			(×)		(×)
Transferred to profit or loss on sale		(×)			(×)		(×)
Cash flow hedges:							
Gains/(losses) taken to equity		×			×	×	×
Transferred to profit or loss for the period		×			×	×	×
Transferred to initial carrying amount of hedged items		(×)			(×)		(×)
Exchange differences on translating foreign operations			(×)		(×)	(×)	(×)
Tax on items taken directly to or transferred from equity		(×)	×		(×)	(×)	(×)
Net income recognised directly in equity		×	(×)		×	×	×
Profit for the period				×	×	×	×
Total recognised income and expense for the period		×	(×)	×	×	×	×
Dividends				(×)	(×)	(×)	(×)
Issue of share capital	×				×		×
Equity share options issued		×			×		×
Balance at 31 December 2007 carried forward	×	×	(×)	×	×	×	×

* Other reserves are analysed into their components, if material.

XYZ GROUP – STATEMENT OF CHANGES IN EQUITY FOR THE YEAR ENDED 31 DECEMBER 2008 (continued)

(in thousands of Euros)

	Attributable to equity holders of the parent						
	Share capital	Other reserves*	Trans-lation reserve	Retained earnings	Total	Minority interest	Total equity
Balance at 31 December 2007 brought forward	×	×	(×)	×	×	×	×
Changes in equity for 2008							
Loss on property revaluation		(×)			(×)	(×)	(×)
Available-for-sale investments:							
Valuation gains/(losses) taken to equity		(×)			(×)		(×)
Transferred to profit or loss on sale		×			×		×
Cash flow hedges:							
Gains/(losses) taken to equity		×			×		×
Transferred to profit or loss for the period		(×)			(×)	(×)	(×)
Transferred to initial carrying amount of hedged items		(×)			(×)		(×)
Exchange differences on translating foreign operations			(×)		(×)	(×)	(×)
Tax on items taken directly to or transferred from equity		×	×		×	×	×
Net income recognised directly in equity		(×)	(×)		(×)	(×)	(×)
Profit for the period				×	×	×	×
Total recognised income and expense for the period		(×)	(×)	×	×	×	×
Dividends				(×)	(×)	(×)	(×)
Issue of share capital	×				×		×
Balance at 31 December 2008	×	×	(×)	×	×	×	×

* Other reserves are analysed into their components, if material.

Second, the guidance illustrates a statement of recognised income and expense as follows.

Example 3.5: Statement of recognised income and expense[134]

XYZ GROUP – STATEMENT OF RECOGNISED INCOME AND EXPENSE FOR THE YEAR ENDED 31 DECEMBER 2008

(in thousands of Euro)

	2008	**2007**
Gain/(loss) on revaluation of properties	(×)	×
Available-for-sale investments:		
Valuation gains/(losses) taken to equity	(×)	(×)
Transferred to profit or loss on sale	×	(×)
Cash flow hedges:		
Gains/(losses) taken to equity	×	×
Transferred to profit or loss for the period	(×)	×
Transferred to the initial carrying amount of hedged items	(×)	(×)
Exchange differences on translation of foreign operations	(×)	(×)
Actuarial gains (losses) on defined benefit plans	(×)	(×)
Tax on items taken directly to or transferred from equity	×	(×)
Net income recognised directly in equity	(×)	×
Profit for the period	×	×
Total recognised income and expense for the period	×	×
Attributable to:		
Equity holders of the parent	×	×
Minority interest	×	×
	×	×
Effect of changes in accounting policy:		
Equity holders of the parent		(×)
Minority interest		(×)
		(×)

This example illustrates an approach that presents changes in equity representing income and expense in a separate component of the financial statements. Under this approach, a reconciliation of opening and closing balances of share capital, reserves and accumulated profit would be given in the notes.

3.4 The notes to the financial statements

IAS 1 requires the presentation of notes to the financial statements that:

(a) present information about the basis of preparation of the financial statements and the specific accounting policies used (see 5.1 below);

(b) disclose the information required by IFRSs that is not presented on the face of the balance sheet, income statement, statement of changes in equity or cash flow statement; and

(c) provide additional information that is not presented on the face of the balance sheet, income statement, statement of changes in equity or cash flow statement, but is relevant to an understanding of any of them.[135]

An example of information under (c) relates to service concession agreements. SIC-29 *Service Concession Arrangements: Disclosure* sets out some detailed requirements for the type of disclosures required for such arrangements to satisfy the requirement of IAS 1. This is discussed in Chapter 29.

The notes should, as far as practicable, be presented in a systematic manner. Each item on the face of the balance sheet, income statement, statement of changes in equity and cash flow statement should be cross-referenced to any related information in the notes.[136]

The notes are normally presented in the following order, which is intended to assist users in understanding the financial statements and comparing them with financial statements of other entities:

(a) a statement of compliance with IFRSs (see 5.1 below);

(b) a summary of significant accounting policies applied (see 5.1 below);

(c) supporting information for items presented on the face of the balance sheet, income statement, statement of changes in equity and cash flow statement, in the order in which each statement and each line item is presented; and

(d) other disclosures, including:

  (i) contingent liabilities (discussed in Chapter 27) and unrecognised contractual commitments; and

  (ii) non-financial disclosures, e.g. the entity's financial risk management objectives and policies (discussed in Chapter 22).[137]

However, the standard allows that notes providing information about the basis of preparation of the financial statements and specific accounting policies may be presented as a separate component of the financial statements.[138]

Although the above represents the normal arrangement of the notes, in some circumstances it may be necessary or desirable to vary the ordering of specific items within the notes. An example given by the standard is that information on changes in fair value recognised in profit or loss may be combined with information on maturities of financial instruments, although the former disclosures relate to the income statement and the latter relate to the balance sheet. Nevertheless, a systematic structure for the notes should be retained as far as practicable.[139]

4 ACCOUNTING POLICIES

The selection and application of accounting policies is obviously crucial in the preparation of financial statements. As a general premise, the whole purpose of accounting standards is to specify required accounting policies, presentation and disclosure. However, judgement will always remain; many standards may allow choices to accommodate different views, and no body of accounting literature could hope to prescribe precise treatments for all possible situations.

In the broadest sense, accounting policies are discussed by both IAS 1 and IAS 8. Whilst, as its title suggest, IAS 8 deals explicitly with accounting policies, IAS 1 deals with what one might describe as overarching or general principles.

4.1 General principles

IAS 1 deals with some general principles relating to accounting policies, with IAS 8 discussing the detail of selection and application of individual accounting policies and their disclosure.

The general principles discussed by IAS 1 can be described as follows:

- fair presentation and compliance with accounting standards;
- going concern;
- the accrual basis of accounting;
- consistency;
- materiality and aggregation;
- offsetting; and
- profit or loss for the period.

These are discussed in the sections that follow.

4.1.1 Fair presentation

A Fair presentation and compliance with IFRS

Consistent with its objective and statement of the purpose of financial statements, IAS 1 requires that financial statements present fairly the financial position, financial performance and cash flows of an entity. Fair presentation for these purposes requires the faithful representation of the effects of transactions, other events and conditions in accordance with the definitions and recognition criteria for assets, liabilities, income and expenses set out in the Framework (discussed in Chapter 2).

The main premise of the standard is that application of IFRSs, with additional disclosure when necessary, is presumed to result in financial statements that achieve a fair presentation.[140] As noted at 1.1.2 above, an important point here is that implementation guidance for standards issued by the IASB does not form part of those standards, and therefore does not contain requirements for financial statements.[141] Accordingly, the often voluminous implementation guidance accompanying standards is not, strictly speaking, part of 'IFRS'. We would generally be surprised, though, at entities not following such guidance without valid reason. The presumption that application of IFRS (with any necessary additional disclosure) results in a fair presentation is potentially rebuttable, as discussed at B below.

To reflect this presumption, as discussed at 2.5.2 above, the standard requires an explicit and unreserved statement of compliance to be included in the notes. A fair presentation also requires an entity to:

(a) select and apply accounting policies in accordance with IAS 8, which also sets out a hierarchy of authoritative guidance that should be considered in the absence of a standard or an interpretation that specifically applies to an item;

(b) present information, including accounting policies, in a manner that provides relevant, reliable, comparable and understandable information; and

(c) provide additional disclosures when compliance with the specific requirements in IFRSs is insufficient to enable users to understand the impact of particular transactions, other events and conditions on the entity's financial position and financial performance.[142]

However, the standard makes clear that inappropriate accounting policies are not rectified either by disclosure of the accounting policies used or by notes or explanatory material.[143] We support this position, however the IASB has (admittedly only in rare situations) essentially delegated standard setting to the authors of 'relevant regulatory frameworks' in this regard. As discussed at B below, it is possible that a rare circumstance arises where departure from a provision of IFRS is needed to achieve fair presentation. This is only allowed by IAS 1, however, if permitted by such a regulatory framework. If it is not, then it seems the fairest presentation politically possible for the IASB is indeed achieved through additional disclosure in the face of inappropriate accounting policies.

B The fair presentation override

The presumption that the application of IFRSs, with additional disclosure when necessary, results in financial statements that achieve a fair presentation is a rebutabble one, although the standard makes clear that in virtually all situations a fair presentation is achieved through compliance.[144]

The standard observes that an item of information would conflict with the objective of financial statements when it does not represent faithfully the transactions, other events and conditions that it either purports to represent or could reasonably be expected to represent and, consequently, it would be likely to influence economic decisions made by users of financial statements. When assessing whether complying with a specific requirement in a standard or an interpretation would be so misleading that it would conflict with the objective of financial statements, IAS 1 requires consideration of:

(a) why the objective of financial statements is not achieved in the particular circumstances; and

(b) how the entity's circumstances differ from those of other entities that comply with the requirement. If other entities in similar circumstances comply with the requirement, there is a rebuttable presumption that the entity's compliance with the requirement would not be so misleading that it would conflict with the objective of financial statements.[145]

In the extremely rare circumstances in which management concludes that compliance with a requirement in a standard or an interpretation would be so misleading that it would conflict with the objective of financial statements, IAS 1 requires departure from that requirement. However, this is only permitted if the 'relevant regulatory framework requires, or otherwise does not prohibit, such a departure', which is discussed further below.[146]

When the relevant regulatory framework allows a departure, an entity should make it and also disclose:

(a) that management has concluded that the financial statements present fairly the entity's financial position, financial performance and cash flows;

(b) that it has complied with applicable standards and interpretations, except that it has departed from a particular requirement to achieve a fair presentation;

(c) the title of the standard or interpretation from which the entity has departed, the nature of the departure, including:

  (i) the treatment that the standard or interpretation would require,

  (ii) the reason why that treatment would be so misleading in the circumstances that it would conflict with the objective of financial statements set out in the Framework; and

  (iii) the treatment adopted;

(d) for each period presented, the financial impact of the departure on each item in the financial statements that would have been reported in complying with the requirement; and

(e) when there has been a departure from a requirement of a standard or an interpretation in a prior period, and that departure affects the amounts recognised in the financial statements for the current period, the disclosures set out in (c) and (d) above.[147]

Regarding (e) above, the standard explains that the requirement could apply, for example, when an entity departed in a prior period from a requirement in a standard or an interpretation for the measurement of assets or liabilities and that departure affects the measurement of changes in assets and liabilities recognised in the current period's financial statements.[148]

An example of a company adopting the fair presentation override is shown in Extract 1.1 in Chapter 1.

When the relevant regulatory framework does not allow a departure from IFRS, IAS 1 accepts that, notwithstanding the failure to achieve fair presentation, that it should not be made. Although intended to occur only in extremely rare circumstances, this is a very important provision of the standard as it allows a 'relevant regulatory framework' to override a requirement of IFRS which is specifically necessary to achieve a fair presentation. In that light, it is perhaps surprising that there is no definition or discussion in the standard of just what a relevant regulatory framework may be.

When a departure otherwise required by IAS 1 is not allowed by the relevant regulatory framework, the standard requires that the perceived misleading aspects of compliance are reduced, to the maximum extent possible, by the disclosure of:

(a) the title of the standard or interpretation in question, the nature of the requirement, and the reason why management has concluded that complying with that requirement is so misleading in the circumstances that it conflicts with the objective of financial statements set out in the Framework; and

(b) for each period presented, the adjustments to each item in the financial statements that management has concluded would be necessary to achieve a fair presentation.[149]

Overall, this strikes us as a fairly uncomfortable compromise, as it involves:

- the entity stating publicly that it considers its financial statements fail to achieve a fair presentation;
- the IASB essentially allowing unspecified regulators to overrule it; and
- an accounting standard that contradicts itself.

However, the rule is reasonably clear and in our view such a circumstance will indeed be a rare one.

4.1.2 Going concern

When preparing financial statements, IAS 1 requires management to make an assessment of an entity's ability to continue as a going concern. This term is not defined, but its meaning is implicit in the requirement of the standard that financial statements should be prepared on a going concern basis unless management either intends to liquidate the entity or to cease trading, or has no realistic alternative but to do so. The standard goes on to require that when management is aware, in making its assessment, of material uncertainties related to events or conditions that may cast significant doubt upon the entity's ability to continue as a going concern, those uncertainties shall be disclosed. When financial statements are not prepared on a going concern basis, that fact should be disclosed, together with the basis on which the financial statements are prepared and the reason why the entity is not regarded as a going concern.[150]

In assessing whether the going concern assumption is appropriate, the standard requires that all available information about the future, which is at least, but is not limited to, twelve months from the balance sheet date should be taken into account. The degree of consideration required will depend on the facts in each case. When an entity has a history of profitable operations and ready access to financial resources, a conclusion that the going concern basis of accounting is appropriate may be reached without detailed analysis. In other cases, management may need to consider a wide range of factors relating to current and expected profitability, debt repayment schedules and potential sources of replacement financing before it can satisfy itself that the going concern basis is appropriate.[151]

There is no guidance in the standard concerning what impact there should be on the financial statements if it is determined that the going concern basis is not appropriate. Accordingly, entities will need to consider carefully their individual circumstances to arrive at an appropriate basis.

4.1.3 The accrual basis of accounting

IAS 1 requires that financial statements be prepared, except for cash flow information, using the accrual basis of accounting.[152] No definition of this is given by the standard, but an explanation is presented that 'When the accrual basis of accounting is used, items are recognised as assets, liabilities, equity, income and expenses (the elements of financial statements) when they satisfy the definitions and recognition criteria for those elements in the Framework.'[153]

The Framework itself is a little more helpful, explaining the accruals basis as follows. 'Under this basis, the effects of transactions and other events are recognised when they occur (and not as cash or its equivalent is received or paid) and they are recorded in the accounting records and reported in the financial statements of the periods to which they relate. Financial statements prepared on the accrual basis inform users not only of past transactions involving the payment and receipt of cash but also of obligations to pay cash in the future and of resources that represent cash to be received in the future. Hence, they provide the type of information about past transactions and other events that is most useful to users in making economic decisions.'[154]

The requirements of the framework are discussed in more detail in Chapter 2.

4.1.4 Consistency

As noted at 1.1.2 and 1.2.2 above, one of the objectives of both IAS 1 and IAS 8 is to ensure the comparability of financial statements with those of previous periods. To this end, each standard addresses the principle of consistency.

IAS 1 requires that the 'presentation and classification' of items in the financial statements be retained from one period to the next unless:

(a) it is apparent, following a significant change in the nature of the entity's operations or a review of its financial statements, that another presentation or classification would be more appropriate having regard to the criteria for the selection and application of accounting policies in IAS 8 (see 4.3 below); or

(b) a standard or an interpretation requires a change in presentation.[155]

The standard goes on to amplify this by explaining that a significant acquisition or disposal, or a review of the presentation of the financial statements, might suggest that the financial statements need to be presented differently. An entity should change the presentation of its financial statements only if the changed presentation provides information that is reliable and is more relevant to users of the financial statements and the revised structure is likely to continue, so that comparability is not impaired. When making such changes in presentation, an entity will need to reclassify its comparative information as discussed at 2.4 above.[156]

IAS 8 addresses consistency of accounting policies and observes that users of financial statements need to be able to compare the financial statements of an entity over time to identify trends in its financial position, financial performance and cash flows. For this reason, the same accounting policies need to be applied within each period and from one period to the next unless a change in accounting policy meets certain criteria (changes in accounting policy are discussed at 4.4 below).[157] Accordingly, the standard requires that accounting policies be selected and applied consistently for similar transactions, other events and conditions, unless a standard or an interpretation specifically requires or permits categorisation of items for which different policies may be appropriate. If a standard or an interpretation requires or permits such categorisation, an appropriate accounting policy should be selected and applied consistently to each category.[158]

4.1.5 Materiality, aggregation and offset

A Materiality and aggregation

Financial statements result from processing large numbers of transactions or other events that are aggregated into classes according to their nature or function. The final stage in the process of aggregation and classification is the presentation of condensed and classified data, which form line items on the face of the balance sheet, income statement, statement of changes in equity and cash flow statement, or in the notes.[159] The extent of aggregation versus detailed analysis is clearly a judgemental one, with either extreme eroding the usefulness of the information.

IAS 1 resolves this issue with the concept of materiality, by requiring:

- each material class of similar items to be presented separately in the financial statements; and
- items of a dissimilar nature or function to be presented separately unless they arc immatcrial.[160]

Materiality is defined by both IAS 1 and IAS 8 as follows. 'Omissions or misstatements of items are material if they could, individually or collectively, influence the economic decisions of users taken on the basis of the financial statements. Materiality depends on the size and nature of the omission or misstatement judged in the surrounding circumstances. The size or nature of the item, or a combination of both, could be the determining factor.'[161] At a general level, applying the concept of materiality means that a specific disclosure requirement in a standard or an interpretation need not be satisfied if the information is not material.[162]

IAS 1 and IAS 8 go on to observe that assessing whether an omission or misstatement could influence economic decisions of users, and so be material, requires consideration of the characteristics of those users. For these purposes users are assumed to have a reasonable knowledge of business and economic activities and accounting and a willingness to study the information with reasonable diligence. Therefore, the assessment of materiality needs to take into account how users with such attributes could reasonably be expected to be influenced in making economic decisions.[163]

Regarding the presentation of financial statements, IAS 1 requires that if a line item is not individually material, it should be aggregated with other items either on the face of those statements or in the notes. The standard also states that an item that is not sufficiently material to warrant separate presentation on the face of those statements may nevertheless be sufficiently material for it to be presented separately in the notes.[164]

B Offset

IAS 1 considers it important that assets and liabilities, and income and expenses, are reported separately. This is because offsetting in the income statement or the balance sheet, except when offsetting reflects the substance of the transaction or other event, detracts from the ability of users both to understand the transactions, other events and conditions that have occurred and to assess the entity's future cash flows. It clarifies, though, that measuring assets net of valuation allowances – for example, obsolescence allowances on inventories and doubtful debts allowances on receivables – is not offsetting.[165]

Accordingly, IAS 1 requires that assets and liabilities, and income and expenses, should not be offset unless required or permitted by a standard or an interpretation.[166]

Just what constitutes offsetting, particularly given the rider noted above of 'reflecting the substance of the transaction' is not always obvious. IAS 1 expands on its meaning as follows. It notes that:

(a) IAS 18 – *Revenue* – defines revenue and requires it to be measured at the fair value of the consideration received or receivable, taking into account the amount of any trade discounts and volume rebates allowed by the entity – in other words a notional 'gross' revenue and a discount should not be shown separately, but should be offset. Revenue is discussed in Chapter 28;

(b) entities can undertake, in the course of their ordinary activities, other transactions that do not generate revenue but are incidental to the main revenue-generating activities. The results of such transactions should be presented, when this presentation reflects the substance of the transaction or other event, by netting any income with related expenses arising on the same transaction. For example:

    (i) gains and losses on the disposal of non-current assets, including investments and operating assets, should be reported by deducting from the proceeds on disposal the carrying amount of the asset and related selling expenses; and

    (ii) expenditure related to a provision that is recognised in accordance with IAS 37 – *Provisions, Contingent Liabilities and Contingent Assets* – and reimbursed under a contractual arrangement with a third party (for example, a supplier's warranty agreement) may be netted against the related reimbursement;[167] and

(c) gains and losses arising from a group of similar transactions should be reported on a net basis, for example, foreign exchange gains and losses or gains and losses arising on financial instruments held for trading. However, such gains and losses should be reported separately if they are material.[168]

The offset of finance items in the income statement was discussed in 2006 by IFRIC and then by the IASB. IFRIC asked the Board to consider an apparent conflict between the requirements of IAS 1 and IFRS 7 regarding the presentation of finance costs. IFRIC observed that paragraphs 32 and 81 of IAS 1 preclude presenting 'net finance costs' on the face of the income statement without showing separately the finance costs and finance revenue included in the net amount. However, paragraph IG13 of IFRS 7 states that total interest income and total income expense are components of finance costs. This indicates a net presentation in the income statement. The Board decided to resolve this conflict by deleting paragraph IG13.[169] An amendment to IFRS 7 has been proposed as part of the Board's 2007 annual improvements project.[170]

4.1.6 Profit or loss for the period

The final provision of IAS 1 which we term a general principle is a very important one. It is that, unless a standard or an interpretation requires otherwise, all items of income and expense recognised in a period should be included in profit or loss.[171]

Income and expense are not defined by the standard, but they are defined by the Framework as follows:

(a) income is increases in economic benefits during the accounting period in the form of inflows or enhancements of assets or decreases of liabilities that result in increases in equity, other than those relating to contributions from equity participants; and

(b) expenses are decreases in economic benefits during the accounting period in the form of outflows or depletions of assets or incurrences of liabilities that result in decreases in equity, other than those relating to distributions to equity participants.[172]

This clearly indicates to us that the terms do not have what many would consider their natural meaning, as they encompass all gains and losses (for example, capital appreciation in a non-current asset like property). As discussed in Chapter 2, how to present financial performance, including all gains and losses, is currently being debated by the Board and key to this is the meaning of an income statement. As things stand now, there is a somewhat awkward compromise with various gains and losses either required or permitted to bypass the income statement and be reported directly in equity.

IAS 1 notes that normally, all items of income and expense recognised in a period are included in profit or loss, and that this includes the effects of changes in accounting estimates. However, circumstances may exist when particular items may be excluded from profit or loss for the current period. IAS 8 deals with two such circumstances: the correction of errors and the effect of changes in accounting policies (discussed at 4.4 and 4.6 below).[173] Other standards deal with items that may meet the Framework's definitions of income or expense but are usually excluded from profit or loss. Examples include revaluation surpluses (discussed in Chapter 13), particular gains and losses arising on translating the financial statements of a foreign operation (discussed in Chapter 10) and gains or losses on remeasuring available-for-sale financial assets (discussed in Chapter 20).[174]

4.2 The distinction between accounting policies and accounting estimates

IAS 8 defines accounting policies as 'the specific principles, bases, conventions, rules and practices applied by an entity in preparing and presenting financial statements.'[175] In particular, IAS 8 considers a change in 'measurement basis' to be a change in accounting policy (rather than a change in estimate).[176] Although not a defined term, IAS 1 (when requiring disclosure of them) gives examples of measurement bases as follows:

- historical cost;
- current cost;
- net realisable value;
- fair value; and
- recoverable amount.[177]

'Accounting estimates' is not a term defined directly by the standards. However, it is indirectly defined by the definition in IAS 8 of a change in an accounting estimate as follows. A change in accounting estimate is an adjustment of the carrying amount of an asset or a liability, or the amount of the periodic consumption of an asset, that results from the assessment of the present status of, and expected future benefits and obligations associated with, assets and liabilities. Changes in accounting estimates result from new information or new developments and, accordingly, are not corrections of errors.[178] Examples given by the IASB are estimates of bad debts and the estimated useful life of, or the expected pattern of consumption of the future economic benefits embodied in, a depreciable asset.[179]

The standard also notes that corrections of errors should be distinguished from changes in accounting estimates. Accounting estimates by their nature are approximations that may need revision as additional information becomes known. For example, the gain or loss recognised on the outcome of a contingency is not the correction of an error.[180]

The distinction between an accounting policy and an accounting estimate is particularly important because a very different treatment is required when there are changes in accounting policies or accounting estimates (discussed at 4.4 and 4.5 below). When it is difficult to distinguish a change in an accounting policy from a change in an accounting estimate, IAS 8 requires the change to be treated as a change in an accounting estimate.[181]

4.3 The selection and application of accounting policies

Entities complying with IFRS (which is a defined term, discussed at 1.1.2 above) do not have a free hand in selecting accounting policies, indeed the very purpose of a body of accounting literature is to confine such choices.

IFRS set out accounting policies that the IASB has concluded result in financial statements containing relevant and reliable information about the transactions, other events and conditions to which they apply.[182]

To this end, IAS 8's starting point is that when a standard or an interpretation specifically applies to a transaction, other event or condition, the accounting policy or policies applied to that item should be determined by applying the standard or interpretation and considering any relevant implementation guidance issued by the IASB for the standard or interpretation.[183] This draws out the distinction that IFRS must be *applied* whereas implementation guidance (which, as discussed at 1.1.2 above, is not part of IFRS) must be *considered*. As noted earlier, though, we would generally be surprised at entities not following such guidance without good reason.

Those policies need not be applied when the effect of applying them is immaterial. However, it is inappropriate to make, or leave uncorrected, immaterial departures from IFRSs to achieve a particular presentation of an entity's financial position, financial performance or cash flows.[184] The concept of materiality is discussed at 4.1.5 above.

There will be circumstances where a particular event, transaction or other condition is not specifically addressed by IFRS. When this is the case, IAS 8 sets out a hierarchy of guidance to be considered in the selection of an accounting policy.

The primary requirement of the standard is that management should use its judgement in developing and applying an accounting policy that results in information that is:

(a) relevant to the economic decision-making needs of users; and
(b) reliable, in that the financial statements:
    (i) represent faithfully the financial position, financial performance and cash flows of the entity;
    (ii) reflect the economic substance of transactions, other events and conditions, and not merely the legal form;
    (iii) are neutral, i.e. free from bias;
    (iv) are prudent; and
    (v) are complete in all material respects.[185]

There is, in our view, clearly a tension between (b) (iii) and (b) (iv) above. Prudence and neutrality are not defined or otherwise discussed by IAS 8. However, the Framework discusses them and goes some way to addressing this tension as follows. 'To be reliable, the information contained in financial statements must be neutral, that is, free from bias. Financial statements are not neutral if, by the selection or presentation of information, they influence the making of a decision or judgement in order to achieve a predetermined result or outcome.

'The preparers of financial statements do, however, have to contend with the uncertainties that inevitably surround many events and circumstances, such as the collectability of doubtful receivables, the probable useful life of plant and equipment and the number of warranty claims that may occur. Such uncertainties are recognised by the disclosure of their nature and extent and by the exercise of prudence in the preparation of the financial statements. Prudence is the inclusion of a degree of caution in the exercise of the judgements needed in making the estimates required under conditions of uncertainty, such that assets or income are not overstated and liabilities or expenses are not understated. However, the exercise of prudence does not allow, for example, the creation of hidden reserves or excessive provisions, the deliberate understatement of assets or income, or the deliberate overstatement of liabilities or expenses, because the financial statements would not be neutral and, therefore, not have the quality of reliability.'[186]

In support of this primary requirement, the standard gives guidance on how management should apply this judgement. This guidance comes in two 'strengths' – certain things which management is required to consider, and others which it 'may' consider, as follows.

In making this judgement, management *should* refer to, and consider the applicability of, the following sources in descending order:

(a) the requirements and guidance in standards and interpretations dealing with similar and related issues; and

(b) the definitions, recognition criteria and measurement concepts for assets, liabilities, income and expenses in the Framework;[187] and

in making this judgement, management *may* also consider the most recent pronouncements of other standard-setting bodies that use a similar conceptual framework to develop accounting standards, other accounting literature and accepted industry practices, to the extent that these do not conflict with the sources in (a) and (b) above.[188]

4.4 Changes in accounting policies

As discussed at 4.1.4 above, consistency of accounting policies and presentation is a basic principle in both IAS 1 and IAS 8. Accordingly, IAS 8 only permits a change in accounting policies if the change:

(a) is required by a standard or an interpretation; or

(b) results in the financial statements providing reliable and more relevant information about the effects of transactions, other events or conditions on the entity's financial position, financial performance or cash flows.[189]

IAS 8 addresses changes of accounting policy arising from three sources:

(a) the initial application (including early application) of a standard or interpretation containing specific transitional provisions;

(b) the initial application of a standard or interpretation which does not contain specific transitional provisions; and

(c) voluntary changes in accounting policy.

Policy changes under (a) should be accounted for in accordance with the specific transitional provisions of that standard or interpretation.

A change of accounting policy under (b) or (c) should be applied retrospectively, that is applied to transactions, other events and conditions as if it had always been applied.[190] The standard goes on to explain that retrospective application requires adjustment of the opening balance of each affected component of equity for the earliest prior period presented and the other comparative amounts disclosed for each prior period presented as if the new accounting policy had always been applied.[191] The standard observes that the amount of the resulting adjustment relating to periods before those presented in the financial statements (which is made to the opening balance of each affected component of equity of the earliest prior period presented) will usually be made to retained earnings. However, it goes on to note that the adjustment may be made to another component of equity (for example, to comply with a standard or an interpretation). IAS 8 also makes clear that any other information about prior periods, such as historical summaries of financial data, should be also adjusted.[192]

Frequently it will be straightforward to apply a change in accounting policy retrospectively. However, the standard accepts that sometimes it may be impractical to do so. Accordingly, retrospective application of a change in accounting policy is not required to the extent that it is impracticable to determine either the period-specific effects or the cumulative effect of the change.[193] This is discussed further at 4.7 below. As noted at 4.3 above, in the absence of a specifically applicable standard or an interpretation an entity may apply an accounting policy from the most recent pronouncements of another standard-setting body that use a similar conceptual framework. The standard makes clear that a change in accounting policy reflecting a change in such a pronouncement is a voluntary change in accounting policy which should be accounted for and disclosed as such.[194]

Perhaps unnecessarily, the standard clarifies that the following are not changes in accounting policy:

- the application of an accounting policy for transactions, other events or conditions that differ in substance from those previously occurring; and
- the application of a new accounting policy for transactions, other events or conditions that did not occur previously or were immaterial.[195]

More importantly, the standard requires that a change to a policy of revaluing intangible assets or property plant and equipment in accordance with IAS 38 and IAS 16 respectively is not to be accounted for under IAS 8 as a change in accounting policy. Rather, the change should be dealt with as revaluations in accordance with the relevant standards (discussed in Chapter 12 and Chapter 13).[196] What this means is that it is not necessary to restate prior periods for the carrying value and depreciation charge of the assets concerned. Aside of this particular exception, the standard makes clear that a change in measurement basis is a change in an accounting policy, and is not a change in an accounting estimate. However, when it is difficult to distinguish a change in an accounting policy from a change in an accounting estimate, the standard requires it to be treated as a change in an accounting estimate, discussed in 4.5 below.[197]

The implementation guidance accompanying the standard provides an illustration of the retrospective application of a change in accounting policy as follows.

Example 3.6: Change in accounting policy with retrospective application[198]

During 2008, Gamma Co changed its accounting policy for the treatment of borrowing costs that are directly attributable to the acquisition of a hydro-electric power station under construction for use by Gamma. In previous periods, Gamma had capitalised such costs. Gamma has now decided to treat these costs as an expense, rather than capitalise them. Management judges that the new policy is preferable because it results in a more transparent treatment of finance costs and is consistent with local industry practice, making Gamma's financial statements more comparable.

Gamma capitalised borrowing costs incurred of €2,600 during 2007 and €5,200 in periods before 2007. All borrowing costs incurred in previous years in respect of the acquisition of the power station were capitalised.

Gamma's accounting records for 2008 show profit before interest and income taxes of €30,000; interest expense of €3,000 (which relates only to 2008); and income taxes of €8,100.

Gamma has not yet recognised any depreciation on the power station because it is not yet in use.

In 2007, Gamma reported:

	€
Profit before interest and income taxes	18,000
Interest expense	–
Profit before income taxes	18,000
Income taxes	(5,400)
Profit	12,600

The 2007 opening retained earnings was €20,000 and closing retained earnings was €32,600.

Gamma's tax rate was 30 per cent for 2008, 2007 and prior periods.

Gamma had €10,000 of share capital throughout, and no other components of equity except for retained earnings. Its shares are not publicly traded and it does not disclose earnings per share.

Gamma Co
Extract from the Income Statement

	2008 €	(restated) 2007 €
Profit before interest and income taxes	30,000	18,000
Interest expense	(3,000)	(2,600)
Profit before income taxes	27,000	15,400
Income taxes	(8,100)	(4,620)
Profit	18,900	10,780

Gamma Co
Statement of Changes in Equity

	Share capital €	(restated) Retained earnings €	Total €
Balance at 31 December 2006 as previously reported	10,000	20,000	30,000
Change in accounting policy for the capitalisation of interest (net of income taxes of €1,560) (Note 1)	–	(3,640)	(3,640)
Balance at 31 December 2006 as restated	10,000	16,360	26,360
Profit for the year ended 31 December 2007 (restated)		10,780	10,780
Balance at 31 December 2007	10,000	27,140	37,140
Profit for the year ended 31 December 2008	–	18,900	18,900
Balance at 31 December 2008	10,000	46,040	56,040

Extracts from the Notes

1 During 2008, Gamma changed its accounting policy for the treatment of borrowing costs related to a hydro-electric power station under construction for use by Gamma. Previously, Gamma capitalised such costs. They are now written off as expenses as incurred. Management judges that this policy provides reliable and more relevant information because it results in a more transparent treatment of finance costs and is consistent with local industry practice, making Gamma's financial statements more comparable. This change in accounting policy has been accounted for retrospectively, and the comparative statements for 2007 have been restated. The effect of the change on 2007 is tabulated below. Opening retained earnings for 2007 have been reduced by €3,640, which is the amount of the adjustment relating to periods prior to 2007.

Effect on 2007	€
(Increase) in interest expense	(2,600)
Decrease in income tax expense	780
(Decrease) in profit	(1,820)
Effect on periods prior to 2007	
(Decrease) in profit (€5,200 interest expense less tax of €1,560)	(3,640)
(Decrease) in assets in the course of construction and in retained earnings at 31 December 2007	(5,460)

4.5 Changes in accounting estimates

The making of estimates is a fundamental feature of financial reporting reflecting the uncertainties inherent in business activities. IAS 8 notes that the use of reasonable estimates is an essential part of the preparation of financial statements and it does not undermine their reliability. Examples of estimates given by the standard are:

- bad debts;
- inventory obsolescence;
- the fair value of financial assets or financial liabilities;
- the useful lives of, or expected pattern of consumption of the future economic benefits embodied in, depreciable assets; and
- warranty obligations.[199]

Of course there are many others, some of the more subjective relating to share-based payments and post-retirement benefits.

Estimates will need revision as changes occur in the circumstances on which they are based or as a result of new information or more experience. The standard observes that, by its nature, the revision of an estimate does not relate to prior periods and is not the correction of an error.[200] Accordingly, IAS 8 requires that changes in estimate be accounted for prospectively;[201] defined as recognising the effect of the change in the accounting estimate in the current and future periods affected by the change.[202] The standard goes on to explain that this will mean (as appropriate):

- adjusting the carrying amount of an asset, liability or item of equity in the balance sheet in the period of change; and
- recognising the change by including it in profit and loss in:
  - the period of change, if it affects that period only (for example, a change in estimate of bad debts); or
  - the period of change and future periods, if it affects both (for example, a change in estimated useful life of a depreciable asset or the expected pattern of consumption of the economic benefits embodied in it).[203]

4.6 Correction of errors

Errors can arise in respect of the recognition, measurement, presentation or disclosure of elements of financial statements. IAS 8 states that financial statements do not comply with IFRS if they contain errors that are:

(a) material; or

(b) immaterial but are made intentionally to achieve a particular presentation of an entities financial position, financial performance or cash flows.[204]

The concept in (b) is a little curious. As discussed at 4.1.5 above, an error is material if it could influence the economic decisions of users taken on the basis of the financial statements. We find it difficult to imagine a scenario where an entity would deliberately seek to misstate its financial statements to achieve a particular presentation of its financial position, performance or cash flows but only in such a way that *did not* influence the decisions of users. In any event, and perhaps somewhat unnecessarily, IAS 8 notes that potential current period errors detected before the financial statements are authorised for issue should be corrected in those financial statements. This requirement is phrased so as to apply to all potential errors, not just material ones.[205] The standard notes that corrections of errors are distinguished from changes in accounting estimates. Accounting estimates by their nature are approximations that may need revision as additional information becomes known. For example, the gain or loss recognised on the outcome of a contingency is not the correction of an error.[206]

As with all things, financial reporting is not immune to error and sometimes financial statements can be published which, whether by accident or design, contain errors. IAS 8 defines prior period errors as omissions from, and misstatements in, an entity's financial statements for one or more prior periods (including the effects of mathematical mistakes, mistakes in applying accounting policies, oversights or misinterpretations of facts, and fraud) arising from a failure to use, or misuse of, reliable information that:

(a) was available when financial statements for those periods were authorised for issue; and

(b) could reasonably be expected to have been obtained and taken into account in the preparation and presentation of those financial statements.[207]

When it is discovered that material prior period errors have occurred, IAS 8 requires that they be corrected in the first set of financial statements prepared after their discovery.[208] The correction should be excluded from profit or loss for the period in which the error is discovered. Rather, any information presented about prior periods (including any historical summaries of financial data) should be restated as far back as practicable.[209] This should be done by:

(a) restating the comparative amounts for the prior period(s) presented in which the error occurred; or

(b) if the error occurred before the earliest prior period presented, restating the opening balances of assets, liabilities and equity for the earliest prior period presented.[210]

This process is described by the standard as retrospective restatement, which it also defines as correcting the recognition, measurement and disclosure of amounts of elements of financial statements as if a prior period error had never occurred.[211]

The implementation guidance accompanying the standard provides an example of the retrospective restatement of errors as follows.

Example 3.7: Retrospective restatement of errors[212]

During 2008, Beta Co discovered that some products that had been sold during 2007 were incorrectly included in inventory at 31 December 2007 at €6,500.

Beta's accounting records for 2008 show sales of €104,000, cost of goods sold of €86,500 (including €6,500 for the error in opening inventory), and income taxes of €5,250.

In 2007, Beta reported:

	€
Sales	73,500
Cost of goods sold	(53,500)
Profit before income taxes	20,000
Income taxes	(6,000)
Profit	14,000

The 2007 opening retained earnings was €20,000 and closing retained earnings was €34,000.

Beta's income tax rate was 30 per cent for 2008 and 2007. It had no other income or expenses.

Beta had €5,000 of share capital throughout, and no other components of equity except for retained earnings. Its shares are not publicly traded and it does not disclose earnings per share.

Beta Co
Extract from the Income Statement

	2008 €	(restated) 2007 €
Sales	104,000	73,500
Cost of goods sold	(80,000)	(60,000)
Profit before income taxes	24,000	13,500
Income taxes	(7,200)	(4,050)
Profit	16,800	9,450

Beta Co
Statement of Changes in Equity

	Share capital €	Retained earnings €	Total €
Balance at 31 December 2006	5,000	20,000	25,000
Profit for the year ended 31 December 2007 as restated	–	9,450	9,450
Balance at 31 December 2007	5,000	29,450	34,450
Profit for the year ended 31 December 2008	–	16,800	16,800
Balance at 31 December 2008	5,000	46,250	51,250

Extracts from the Notes

1. Some products that had been sold in 2007 were incorrectly included in inventory at 31 December 2007 at €6,500. The financial statements of 2007 have been restated to correct this error. The effect of the restatement on those financial statements is summarised below. There is no effect in 2008.

	Effect on 2007 €
(Increase) in cost of goods sold	(6,500)
Decrease in income tax expense	1,950
(Decrease) in profit	(4,550)
(Decrease) in inventory	(6,500)
Decrease in income tax payable	1,950
(Decrease) in equity	(4,550)

As is the case for the retrospective application of a change in accounting policy, retrospective restatement for the correction of prior period material errors is not required to the extent that it is impracticable to determine either the period-specific effects or the cumulative effect of the error.[213] This is discussed further at 4.7 below.

4.7 Impracticability of restatement

As noted at 4.4 and 4.6 above, IAS 8 does not require the restatement of prior periods following a change in accounting policy or the correction of material errors if such a restatement is impracticable.

The standard devotes a considerable amount of guidance to discussing what 'impracticable' means for these purposes.

The standard states that applying a requirement is impracticable when an entity cannot apply it after making every reasonable effort to do so. It goes on to note that, for a particular prior period, it is impracticable to apply a change in an accounting policy retrospectively or to make a retrospective restatement to correct an error if:

(a) the effects of the retrospective application or retrospective restatement are not determinable;

(b) the retrospective application or retrospective restatement requires assumptions about what management's intent would have been in that period; or

(c) the retrospective application or retrospective restatement requires significant estimates of amounts and it is impossible to distinguish objectively information about those estimates that:

   (i) provides evidence of circumstances that existed on the date(s) as at which those amounts are to be recognised, measured or disclosed; and

   (ii) would have been available when the financial statements for that prior period were authorised for issue,

   from other information.[214]

An example of a scenario covered by (a) above given by the standard is that in some circumstances it may impracticable to adjust comparative information for one or more prior periods to achieve comparability with the current period because data may not have been collected in the prior period(s) in a way that allows either retrospective application of a new accounting policy (or its prospective application to prior periods) or retrospective restatement to correct a prior period error, and it may be impracticable to recreate the information.[215]

IAS 8 observes that it is frequently necessary to make estimates in applying an accounting policy and that estimation is inherently subjective, and that estimates may be developed after the balance sheet date. Developing estimates is potentially more difficult when retrospectively applying an accounting policy or making a retrospective restatement to correct a prior period error, because of the longer period of time that might have passed since the affected transaction, other event or condition occurred.

However, the objective of estimates related to prior periods remains the same as for estimates made in the current period, namely, for the estimate to reflect the circumstances that existed when the transaction, other event or condition occurred.[216] Hindsight should not be used when applying a new accounting policy to, or correcting amounts for, a prior period, either in making assumptions about what management's intentions would have been in a prior period or estimating the amounts recognised, measured or disclosed in a prior period. For example, if an entity corrects a prior period error in measuring financial assets previously classified as held-to-maturity investments in accordance with IAS 39, it should not change their basis of measurement for that period if management decided later not to hold them to maturity. In addition, if an entity corrects a prior period error in calculating its liability for employees' accumulated sick leave in accordance with IAS 19, it would disregard information about an unusually severe influenza season during the next period that became available after the financial statements for the prior period were authorised for issue. However, the fact that significant estimates are frequently required when amending comparative information presented for prior periods does not prevent reliable adjustment or correction of the comparative information.[217]
Therefore, retrospectively applying a new accounting policy or correcting a prior period error requires distinguishing information that:

(a) provides evidence of circumstances that existed on the date(s) as at which the transaction, other event or condition occurred; and

(b) would have been available when the financial statements for that prior period were authorised for issue,

from other information. The standard states that for some types of estimates (e.g. an estimate of fair value not based on an observable price or observable inputs), it is impracticable to distinguish these types of information. When retrospective application or retrospective restatement would require making a significant estimate for which it is impossible to distinguish these two types of information, it is impracticable to apply the new accounting policy or correct the prior period error retrospectively.[218]

IAS 8 addresses the impracticability of restatement separately (although similarly) for changes in accounting policy and the correction of material errors.

4.7.1 Impracticability of restatement for a change in accounting policy.

When retrospective application of a change in accounting policy is required, the change in policy should be applied retrospectively except to the extent that it is impracticable to determine either the period-specific effects or the cumulative effect of the change.[219] When an entity applies a new accounting policy retrospectively, the standard requires it to be applied to comparative information for prior periods as far back as is practicable. Retrospective application to a prior period is not practicable for these purposes unless it is practicable to determine the cumulative effect on the amounts in both the opening and closing balance sheets for that period.[220]

When it is impracticable to determine the period-specific effects of changing an accounting policy on comparative information for one or more prior periods presented, the new accounting policy should be applied to the carrying amounts of assets and liabilities as at the beginning of the earliest period for which retrospective application is practicable and a corresponding adjustment to the opening balance of each affected component of equity for that period should be made. The standard notes that this may be the current period.[221]

When it is impracticable to determine the cumulative effect, at the beginning of the current period, of applying a new accounting policy to all prior periods, the standard requires an adjustment to the comparative information to apply the new accounting policy prospectively from the earliest date practicable.[222] Prospective application is defined by the standard as applying the new accounting policy to transactions, other events and conditions occurring after the date as at which the policy is changed.[223] This means that the portion of the cumulative adjustment to assets, liabilities and equity arising before that date is disregarded. Changing an accounting policy is permitted by IAS 8 even if it is impracticable to apply the policy prospectively for any prior period.[224]

The implementation guidance accompanying the standard illustrates the prospective application of a change in accounting policy as follows.

Example 3.8: Prospective application of a change in accounting policy when retrospective application is not practicable[225]

During 2008, Delta Co changed its accounting policy for depreciating property, plant and equipment, so as to apply much more fully a components approach, whilst at the same time adopting the revaluation model.

In years before 2008, Delta's asset records were not sufficiently detailed to apply a components approach fully. At the end of 2007, management commissioned an engineering survey, which provided information on the components held and their fair values, useful lives, estimated residual values and depreciable amounts at the beginning of 2008. However, the survey did not provide a sufficient basis for reliably estimating the cost of those components that had not previously been accounted for separately, and the existing records before the survey did not permit this information to be reconstructed.

Delta's management considered how to account for each of the two aspects of the accounting change. They determined that it was not practicable to account for the change to a fuller components approach retrospectively, or to account for that change prospectively from any earlier date than the start of 2008. Also, the change from a cost model to a revaluation model is required to be accounted for prospectively (see 4.4 above). Therefore, management concluded that it should apply Delta's new policy prospectively from the start of 2008.

Additional information:

Delta's tax rate is 30 per cent.

	€
Property, plant and equipment at the end of 2007:	
Cost	25,000
Depreciation	(14,000)
Net book value	11,000
Prospective depreciation expense for 2008 (old basis)	1,500
Some results of the engineering survey:	
Valuation	17,000
Estimated residual value	3,000
Average remaining asset life (years)	7
Depreciation expense on existing property, plant and equipment for 2008 (new basis)	2,000

Extract from the Notes

1 From the start of 2008, Delta changed its accounting policy for depreciating property, plant and equipment, so as to apply much more fully a components approach, whilst at the same time adopting the revaluation model. Management takes the view that this policy provides reliable and more relevant information because it deals more accurately with the components of property, plant and equipment and is based on up-to-date values. The policy has been applied prospectively from the start of 2008 because it was not practicable to estimate the effects of applying the policy either retrospectively, or prospectively from any earlier date. Accordingly, the adoption of the new policy has no effect on prior years. The effect on the current year is to increase the carrying amount of property, plant and equipment at the start of the year by €6,000; increase the opening deferred tax provision by €1,800; create a revaluation reserve at the start of the year of €4,200; increase depreciation expense by €500; and reduce tax expense by €150.

4.7.2 *Impracticability of restatement for a material error*

IAS 8 requires that a prior period error should be corrected by retrospective restatement except to the extent that it is impracticable to determine either the period-specific effects or the cumulative effect of the error.[226]

When it is impracticable to determine the period-specific effects of an error on comparative information for one or more prior periods presented, the opening balances of assets, liabilities and equity should be restated for the earliest period for which retrospective restatement is practicable (which the standard notes may be the current period).[227]

When it is impracticable to determine the cumulative effect, at the beginning of the current period, of an error on all prior periods, the comparative information should be restated to correct the error prospectively from the earliest date practicable.[228] The standard explains that this will mean disregarding the portion of the cumulative restatement of assets, liabilities and equity arising before that date.[229]

5 DISCLOSURE REQUIREMENTS

5.1 Disclosures relating to accounting policies

5.1.1 Disclosure of accounting policies

A Summary of significant accounting policies

IAS 1 makes the valid observation that it is important for users to be informed of the measurement basis or bases used in the financial statements (for example, historical cost, current cost, net realisable value, fair value or recoverable amount) because the basis on which the financial statements are prepared significantly affects their analysis.[230]

Accordingly, the standard requires disclosure in a summary of significant accounting policies of:

(a) the measurement basis (or bases) used in preparing the financial statements; and

(b) the other accounting policies used that are relevant to an understanding of the financial statements.[231]

When more than one measurement basis is used in the financial statements, for example when particular classes of assets are revalued, it is sufficient to provide an indication of the categories of assets and liabilities to which each measurement basis is applied.[232]

It is clearly necessary to apply judgement when deciding on the level of detail required in a summary of accounting policies. However, the general tone of IAS 1 suggests a quite detailed analysis is necessary. Of particular note, is that the decision as to whether to disclose a policy should not just be a function of the magnitude of the sums involved. The standard states that an accounting policy may be significant because of the nature of the entity's operations even if amounts for current and prior periods are not material. It is also appropriate to disclose each significant accounting policy that is not specifically required by IFRSs, but is selected and applied in accordance with IAS 8 (discussed at 4.3 above).[233]

In deciding whether a particular accounting policy should be disclosed, IAS 1 requires consideration of whether disclosure would assist users in understanding how transactions, other events and conditions are reflected in the reported financial performance and financial position. Disclosure of particular accounting policies is especially useful to users when those policies are selected from alternatives allowed in standards and interpretations. An example is disclosure of whether a venturer recognises its interest in a jointly controlled entity using proportionate consolidation or the equity method (discussed in Chapter 9). Some standards specifically require disclosure of particular accounting policies, including choices made by management between different policies they allow. For example:

- IAS 16 requires disclosure of the measurement bases used for classes of property, plant and equipment (discussed in Chapter 13); and

- IAS 23 – *Borrowing Costs* – requires disclosure of whether borrowing costs are recognised immediately as an expense or capitalised as part of the cost of qualifying assets.[234]

Each entity is required to consider the nature of its operations and the policies that the users of its financial statements would expect to be disclosed for that type of entity. For example:

- an entity subject to income taxes would be expected to disclose its accounting policies for income taxes, including those applicable to deferred tax liabilities and assets;
- when an entity has significant foreign operations or transactions in foreign currencies, disclosure of accounting policies for the recognition of foreign exchange gains and losses would be expected; and
- when business combinations have occurred, the policies used for measuring goodwill and minority interest should be disclosed.[235]

B Judgements made in applying accounting policies

The process of applying an entity's accounting policies, requires various judgements, apart from those involving estimations, that can significantly affect the amounts recognised in the financial statements. For example, judgements are required in determining:

(a) whether financial assets are held-to-maturity investments;

(b) when substantially all the significant risks and rewards of ownership of financial assets and lease assets are transferred to other entities;

(c) whether, in substance, particular sales of goods are financing arrangements and therefore do not give rise to revenue; and

(d) whether the substance of the relationship between the entity and a special purpose entity indicates that the special purpose entity is controlled by the entity.[236]

IAS 1 requires disclosure, in the summary of significant accounting policies or other notes, of the judgements (apart from those involving estimations, see 5.2.1 below) management has made in the process of applying the entity's accounting policies that have the most significant effect on the amounts recognised in the financial statements.[237]

Some of these disclosures are required by other standards. For example:

- IAS 27 requires an entity to disclose the reasons why the entity's ownership interest does not constitute control, in respect of an investee that is not a subsidiary even though more than half of its voting or potential voting power is owned directly or indirectly through subsidiaries; and
- IAS 40 – *Investment Property* – requires disclosure of the criteria developed by the entity to distinguish investment property from owner-occupied property and from property held for sale in the ordinary course of business, when classification of the property is difficult.[238]

5.1.2 Disclosure of changes in accounting policies

IAS 8 distinguishes between accounting policy changes made pursuant to the initial application of a standard or interpretation from voluntary changes in accounting policy (discussed at 4.4 above). It sets out different disclosure requirements for each, as set out in A and B below. Also, if a standard or interpretation is in issue but is not yet effective and has not been applied certain disclosures of its likely impact are required. These are set out in C below.

A Accounting policy changes pursuant to the initial application of a standard or interpretation

When initial application of a standard or an interpretation has an effect on the current period or any prior period, would have such an effect except that it is impracticable to determine the amount of the adjustment, or might have an effect on future periods, an entity should disclose:

(a) the title of the standard or interpretation;

(b) when applicable, that the change in accounting policy is made in accordance with its transitional provisions;

(c) the nature of the change in accounting policy;

(d) when applicable, a description of the transitional provisions;

(e) when applicable, the transitional provisions that might have an effect on future periods;

(f) for the current period and each prior period presented, to the extent practicable, the amount of the adjustment:

  (i) for each financial statement line item affected; and

  (ii) if IAS 33 – *Earnings per Share* – applies to the entity, for basic and diluted earnings per share;

(g) the amount of the adjustment relating to periods before those presented, to the extent practicable; and

(h) if retrospective application required by IAS 8 is impracticable for a particular prior period, or for periods before those presented, the circumstances that led to the existence of that condition and a description of how and from when the change in accounting policy has been applied.

Impracticability of restatement is discussed at 4.7 above. Financial statements of subsequent periods need not repeat these disclosures.[239]

B Voluntary changes in accounting policy

When a voluntary change in accounting policy has an effect on the current period or any prior period, would have an effect on that period except that it is impracticable to determine the amount of the adjustment, or might have an effect on future periods, an entity should disclose:

(a) the nature of the change in accounting policy;

(b) the reasons why applying the new accounting policy provides reliable and more relevant information;

(c) for the current period and each prior period presented, to the extent practicable, the amount of the adjustment:

   (i) for each financial statement line item affected; and

   (ii) if IAS 33 applies to the entity, for basic and diluted earnings per share;

(d) the amount of the adjustment relating to periods before those presented, to the extent practicable; and

(e) if retrospective application is impracticable for a particular prior period, or for periods before those presented, the circumstances that led to the existence of that condition and a description of how and from when the change in accounting policy has been applied.

Financial statements of subsequent periods need not repeat these disclosures.[240]

Impracticability of restatement is discussed at 4.7 above. Example 3.8 therein illustrates the above disclosure requirements.

C Future impact of a new standard or interpretation

When an entity has not applied a new standard or interpretation that has been issued but is not yet effective, it should disclose:

(a) that fact; and

(b) known or reasonably estimable information relevant to assessing the possible impact that application of the new standard or interpretation will have on the financial statements in the period of initial application.[241]

In producing the above disclosure, the standard requires that an entity should consider disclosing:

(a) the title of the new standard or interpretation;

(b) the nature of the impending change or changes in accounting policy;

(c) the date by which application of the standard or interpretation is required;

(d) the date as at which it plans to apply the standard or interpretation initially; and

(e) either:

   (i) a discussion of the impact that initial application of the standard or interpretation is expected to have on the entity's financial statements; or

   (ii) if that impact is not known or reasonably estimable, a statement to that effect.[242]

5.2 Disclosure of estimation uncertainty and changes in estimates

5.2.1 Key sources of estimation uncertainty

Determining the carrying amounts of some assets and liabilities requires estimation of the effects of uncertain future events on those assets and liabilities at the balance sheet date. Examples given by IAS 1 are that, in the absence of recently observed market prices used to measure them, the following assets and liabilities require future-oriented estimates to measure them:

- the recoverable amount of classes of property, plant and equipment;
- the effect of technological obsolescence on inventories;
- provisions subject to the future outcome of litigation in progress; and
- long-term employee benefit liabilities such as pension obligations.

These estimates involve assumptions about such items as the risk adjustment to cash flows or discount rates used, future changes in salaries and future changes in prices affecting other costs.[243]

In light of this, IAS 1 requires disclosure in the notes of information about the key assumptions concerning the future, and other key sources of estimation uncertainty at the balance sheet date, that have a significant risk of causing a material adjustment to the carrying amounts of assets and liabilities *within the next financial year*. In respect of those assets and liabilities, the notes must include details of:

(a) their nature; and

(b) their carrying amount as at the balance sheet date.[244]

IAS 1 goes on to observe that these key assumptions and other key sources of estimation uncertainty relate to the estimates that require management's most difficult, subjective or complex judgements. As the number of variables and assumptions affecting the possible future resolution of the uncertainties increases, those judgements become more subjective and complex, and the potential for a consequential material adjustment to the carrying amounts of assets and liabilities normally increases accordingly.[245]

The disclosures are required to be presented in a manner that helps users of financial statements to understand the judgements management makes about the future and about other key sources of estimation uncertainty. The nature and extent of the information provided will vary according to the nature of the assumption and other circumstances. Examples given by the standard of the types of disclosures to be made are:

(a) the nature of the assumption or other estimation uncertainty;

(b) the sensitivity of carrying amounts to the methods, assumptions and estimates underlying their calculation, including the reasons for the sensitivity;

(c) the expected resolution of an uncertainty and the range of reasonably possible outcomes within the next financial year in respect of the carrying amounts of the assets and liabilities affected; and

(d) an explanation of changes made to past assumptions concerning those assets and liabilities, if the uncertainty remains unresolved.[246]

The disclosure of some of these key assumptions is required by other standards. IAS 1 notes the following examples:

- IAS 37 requires disclosure, in specified circumstances, of major assumptions concerning future events affecting classes of provisions;
- IFRS 7 requires disclosure of significant assumptions applied in estimating fair values of financial assets and financial liabilities that are carried at fair value (formerly required by IAS 32); and
- IAS 16 requires disclosure of significant assumptions applied in estimating fair values of revalued items of property, plant and equipment.[247]

Other examples would include:

- IAS 19 requires disclosure of actuarial assumptions;
- IFRS 2 – *Share-based Payment* – requires disclosure, in certain circumstances, of: the option pricing model used, and the method used and the assumptions made to incorporate the effects of early exercise; and
- IAS 36 – *Impairment of Assets* – requires disclosure, in certain circumstances, of each key assumption on which management has based its cash flow projections.

These key assumptions and other key sources of estimation uncertainty are not required to be disclosed for assets and liabilities with a significant risk that their carrying amounts might change materially within the next financial year if, at the balance sheet date, they are measured at fair value based on recently observed market prices. This is because, whilst their fair values might change materially within the next financial year those changes would not arise from assumptions or other sources of estimation uncertainty at the balance sheet date.[248] Also, it is not necessary to disclose budget information or forecasts in making the disclosures.[249] Furthermore, the disclosures of particular judgements management made in the process of applying the entity's accounting policies (discussed at 5.1.1 B above) do not relate to the disclosures of key sources of estimation uncertainty.[250]

When it is impracticable to disclose the extent of the possible effects of a key assumption or another key source of estimation uncertainty at the balance sheet date, the entity should disclose that it is reasonably possible, based on existing knowledge, that outcomes within the next financial year that are different from assumptions could require a material adjustment to the carrying amount of the asset or liability affected. In all cases, the entity should disclose the nature and carrying amount of the specific asset or liability (or class of assets or liabilities) affected by the assumption.[251]

In our view, these requirements of IAS 1 represent potentially highly onerous disclosures. The extensive judgements required in deciding the level of detail to be given has resulted in a wide variety of disclosure in practice. The Basis for Conclusions to the standard reveals that the Board was aware that the requirement could potentially require quite extensive disclosures and explains its attempt to limit this as follows. 'The revised Standard limits the scope of the disclosures to items that have a significant risk of causing a material adjustment to the carrying amounts of assets and liabilities *within the next financial year*. The longer the future period to which the disclosures relate, the greater the range of items that would qualify for disclosure, and the less specific the disclosures that could be made about particular assets or liabilities. A period longer than the next financial year might obscure the most relevant information with other disclosures.'[252]

5.2.2 Changes in accounting estimates

IAS 8 requires disclosure of the nature and amount of a change in an accounting estimate that has an effect in the current period or is expected to have an effect in future periods, except for the disclosure of the effect on future periods when it is impracticable to estimate that effect.[253] If the amount of the effect in future periods is not disclosed because estimating it is impracticable, that fact should be disclosed.[254]

5.3 Disclosure of prior period errors

When correction has been made for a material prior period error, IAS 8 requires disclosure of the following:

(a) the nature of the prior period error;

(b) for each prior period presented, to the extent practicable, the amount of the correction:
   (i) for each financial statement line item affected; and
   (ii) if IAS 33 applies to the entity, for basic and diluted earnings per share;

(c) the amount of the correction at the beginning of the earliest prior period presented; and

(d) if retrospective restatement is impracticable for a particular prior period, the circumstances that led to the existence of that condition and a description of how and from when the error has been corrected.

Financial statements of subsequent periods need not repeat these disclosures.[255]

Example 3.7 at 4.6 above illustrates these disclosure requirements.

5.4 Disclosures about capital

The IASB believes that the level of an entity's capital and how it manages it are important factors for users to consider in assessing the risk profile of an entity and its ability to withstand unexpected adverse events. Furthermore, the level of capital might also affect the entity's ability to pay dividends.[256] For these reasons, in August 2005 IAS 1 was updated to require (for period starting on or after 1 January 2007) disclosure of information that enables users of financial statements to evaluate an entity's objectives, policies and processes for managing capital.[257]

To achieve this, IAS 1 requires disclosure of the following, which should be based on the information provided internally to the entity's key management personnel:[258]

(a) qualitative information about its objectives, policies and processes for managing capital, including (but not limited to):
   (i) a description of what it manages as capital;

(ii) when an entity is subject to externally imposed capital requirements, the nature of those requirements and how those requirements are incorporated into the management of capital; and

(iii) how it is meeting its objectives for managing capital;

(b) summary quantitative data about what it manages as capital;

Some entities regard some financial liabilities (e.g. some forms of subordinated debt) as part of capital. Other entities regard capital as excluding some components of equity (e.g. components arising from cash flow hedges).

(c) any changes in (a) and (b) from the previous period;

(d) whether during the period it complied with any externally imposed capital requirements to which it is subject; and

(e) when the entity has not complied with such externally imposed capital requirements, the consequences of such non-compliance.

IAS 1 observes that capital may be managed in a number of ways and be subject to a number of different capital requirements. For example, a conglomerate may include entities that undertake insurance activities and banking activities, and those entities may also operate in several jurisdictions. When an aggregate disclosure of capital requirements and how capital is managed would not provide useful information or distorts a financial statement user's understanding of an entity's capital resources, the standard requires disclosure of separate information for each capital requirement to which the entity is subject.[259]

Examples 3.9 and 3.10 below are based on the illustrative examples of capital disclosures contained in the implementation guidance accompanying IAS 1.

Example 3.9: Illustrative capital disclosures: An entity that is not a regulated financial institution[260]

The following example illustrates the application of the requirements discussed above for an entity that is not a financial institution and is not subject to an externally imposed capital requirement. In this example, the entity monitors capital using a debt-to-adjusted capital ratio. Other entities may use different methods to monitor capital. The example is also relatively simple. An entity should decide, in the light of its circumstances, how much detail to provide.

Facts

Group A manufactures and sells cars. It includes a finance subsidiary that provides finance to customers, primarily in the form of leases. Group A is not subject to any externally imposed capital requirements.

Example disclosure

The Group's objectives when managing capital are:

- to safeguard the entity's ability to continue as a going concern, so that it can continue to provide returns for shareholders and benefits for other stakeholders; and
- to provide an adequate return to shareholders by pricing products and services commensurately with the level of risk.

The Group sets the amount of capital in proportion to risk. The Group manages the capital structure and makes adjustments to it in the light of changes in economic conditions and the risk characteristics of the underlying assets. In order to maintain or adjust the capital structure, the Group may adjust the amount of dividends paid to shareholders, return capital to shareholders, issue new shares, or sell assets to reduce debt.

Consistently with others in the industry, the Group monitors capital on the basis of the debt-to-adjusted capital ratio. This ratio is calculated as net debt ÷ adjusted capital. Net debt is calculated as total debt (as shown in the balance sheet) less cash and cash equivalents. Adjusted capital comprises all components of equity (i.e. share capital, share premium, minority interest, retained earnings, and revaluation reserve) other than amounts recognised in equity relating to cash flow hedges, and includes some forms of subordinated debt.

During 2008, the Group's strategy, which was unchanged from 2007, was to maintain the debt-to-adjusted capital ratio at the lower end of the range 6:1 to 7:1, in order to secure access to finance at a reasonable cost by maintaining a BB credit rating. The debt-to-adjusted capital ratios at 31 December 2008 and at 31 December 2007 were as follows:

	2008 €million	2007 €million
Total debt	1,000	1,100
Less: cash and cash equivalents	(90)	(150)
Net debt	910	950
Total equity	110	105
Add: subordinated debt instruments	38	38
Less: amounts recognised in equity relating to cash flow hedges	(10)	(5)
Adjusted capital	138	138
Debt-to-adjusted capital ratio	6.6	6.9

The decrease in the debt-to-adjusted capital ratio during 2008 resulted primarily from the reduction in net debt that occurred on the sale of subsidiary Z. As a result of this reduction in net debt, improved profitability and lower levels of managed receivables, the dividend payment was increased to €2.8 million for 2008 (from €2.5 million for 2007).

Example 3.10: Illustrative capital disclosures: An entity that has not complied with externally imposed capital requirements[261]

The following example illustrates the application of the requirement to disclose when an entity has not complied with externally imposed capital requirements during the period. Other disclosures would be provided to comply with the other requirements relating to capital.

Facts

Entity A provides financial services to its customers and is subject to capital requirements imposed by Regulator B. During the year ended 31 December 2008, Entity A did not comply with the capital requirements imposed by Regulator B. In its financial statements for the year ended 31 December 2008, Entity A provides the following disclosure relating to its non-compliance.

Example disclosure

Entity A filed its quarterly regulatory capital return for 30 September 2008 on 20 October 2008. At that date, Entity A's regulatory capital was below the capital requirement imposed by Regulator B by $1 million. As a result, Entity A was required to submit a plan to the regulator indicating how it would increase its regulatory capital to the amount required. Entity A submitted a plan that entailed selling part of its unquoted equities portfolio with a carrying amount of $11.5 million in the fourth quarter of 2008. In the fourth quarter of 2008, Entity A sold its fixed interest investment portfolio for $12.6 million and met its regulatory capital requirement.

5.5 Other disclosures

IAS 1 also requires disclosure:

(a) in the notes of:

  (i) the amount of dividends proposed or declared before the financial statements were authorised for issue but not recognised as a distribution to equity holders during the period, and the related amount per share; and

  (ii) the amount of any cumulative preference dividends not recognised;[262]

(b) either on the face of the income statement or the statement of changes in equity, or in the notes, the amount of dividends recognised as distributions to equity holders during the period, and the related amount per share;[263]

(c) in accordance with IAS 10 – *Events after the Balance Sheet Date* – the following non-adjusting events in respect of loans classified as current liabilities, if they occur between the balance sheet date and the date the financial statements are authorised for issue (see Chapter 36) :

  (i) refinancing on a long-term basis;

  (ii) rectification of a breach of a long-term loan agreement; and

  (iii) the receipt from the lender of a period of grace to rectify a breach of a long-term loan agreement ending at least twelve months after the balance sheet date;[264]

(d) the following, if not disclosed elsewhere in information published with the financial statements:

  (i) the domicile and legal form of the entity, its country of incorporation and the address of its registered office (or principal place of business, if different from the registered office);

  (ii) a description of the nature of the entity's operations and its principal activities; and

  (iii) the name of the parent and the ultimate parent of the group.[265]

6 FUTURE DEVELOPMENTS

6.1 The IASB's joint project on financial statement presentation

The IASB is currently pursuing a project which it terms 'financial statement presentation'. Although the project began as a consideration of the presentation of gains and losses, its has evolved to have a much wider scope. The current intention of the IASB is to pursue the project jointly with the FASB. The IASB/FASB Boards' stated objectives in this project are to present information in the individual financial statements (and among the financial statements) in ways that improve the ability of investors, creditors, and other financial statement users to:

(a) understand an entity's present and past financial position;

(b) understand the past operating, financing, and other activities that caused an entity's financial position to change and the components of those changes; and

(c) use that financial statement information (along with information from other sources) to assess the amounts, timing, and uncertainty of an entity's future cash flows.

The project is divided into the following three phases:

- Phase A addresses what constitutes a complete set of financial statements and requirements to present comparative information. The IASB and FASB have completed deliberations on this phase;
- Phase B addresses more fundamental issues for presentation of information on the face of the financial statements; and
- Phase C (which has not yet begun) will address interim financial reporting.[266]

6.2 Financial statement presentation project Phase A

Phase A of the project resulted in the publication in March 2006 of an exposure draft of proposed amendments to IAS 1.[267] In September 2007 a revised standard was published, it applies to annual periods beginning on or after 1 January 2009. Earlier application is permitted but must be disclosed. The main changes to IAS 1 in the revision are as follows:

(a) The current version of IAS 1 uses the titles 'balance sheet' and 'cash flow statement' to describe two of the statements within a complete set of financial statements. The revised version uses 'statement of financial position' and 'statement of cash flows' for those statements.[268] The Board believes these new titles reflect more closely the function of those statements, as described in the Framework.[269] However, the revision makes these new titles optional, meaning an entity could continue to use the familiar titles should it wish to;[270]

(b) IAS 1 currently requires an entity to disclose comparative information in respect of the previous period – that is, to disclose as a minimum two of each of the statements and related notes. The revised standard introduces a requirement to include a statement of financial position as at the beginning of the earliest comparative period whenever the entity retrospectively applies an accounting policy or makes a retrospective restatement of items in its financial statements, or when it reclassifies items in its financial statements.[271] The purpose is to provide information that the Board considers useful in analysing an entity's financial statements;[272]

(c) As discussed at 3.3 above, IAS 1 currently allows (in most circumstances, although the choice may be constrained depending on the accounting policy selected for any actuarial gains and losses) an entity to choose to present a statement of all changes in equity or a statement of recognised income and expense. If the latter is chosen, other changes in equity are disclosed in the notes. The revised version of IAS 1 requires:

(i) all income and expenses (that is, changes in equity other than those arising on transactions with owners in their capacity as such) to be presented in one statement (a statement of comprehensive income) or in two statements (an income statement and a statement of comprehensive income), separately from owner changes in equity;[273]

(ii) whatever option is taken in (i) above, total comprehensive income must be presented in the financial statements;[274]

(iii) all changes in equity arising from transactions with owners in their capacity as owners to be presented separately from non-owner changes in equity in a statement of changes in equity.[275] The purpose of this is to provide what the Board believes to be better information to users by requiring aggregation of items with shared characteristics and separation of items with different characteristics.[276]

(d) A requirement to disclose income tax relating to each component of other comprehensive income has been introduced.[277] The current version of IAS 1 does not include such a requirement. The purpose of this is to provide users with tax information relating to these components because they often have tax rates different from those applied to profit or loss;[278]

(e) The revised IAS 1 requires an entity to disclose reclassification adjustments relating to components of other comprehensive income. Reclassification adjustments are amounts reclassified to profit or loss in the current period that were recognised in other comprehensive income in previous periods.[279] The purpose is to provide users with information to assess the effect of reclassifications on profit or loss;[280]

(f) A requirement has been introduced to disclose the amount of dividends recognised as distributions to equity holders (now referred to as 'owners') and the related amount per share in the statement of changes in equity or in the notes.[281] Currently, IAS 1 requires this information either on the face of the income statement or the statement of changes in equity or in the notes.

In a separate project the IASB published, in June 2006, an exposure draft of proposed amendments to IAS 32. The proposals relate to the classification within equity (rather than liabilities) of instruments puttable at fair value (discussed in Chapter 19 at 3.2.2. The exposure draft also proposes some amendments to IAS 1 to require further disclosures in these circumstances.[282]

7 CONCLUSION

IAS 1 and IAS 8 deal with overlapping issues and together run to over 180 detailed paragraphs, along with extensive further material in appendices. In our view their usefulness could be greatly enhanced by combining them in one standard and reducing repetition. Notwithstanding this and the occasional lack of clarity, they provide a workable backbone for IFRS.

References

1 IAS 1, *Presentation of Financial Statements*, IASB.
2 IAS 8, *Accounting Policies, Changes in Accounting Estimates and Errors*, IASB.
3 IFRS 5, *Non-current Assets Held for Sale and Discontinued Operations*, IASB.
4 IAS 1, paras. IN3-IN4.
5 *Amendment to international accounting standard IAS 19 Employee Benefits: Actuarial Gains and Losses, Group Plans and Disclosures*, IASB, December 2004.
6 *Amendment to international accounting standard, IAS 1 Presentation of Financial Statements: Capital Disclosures*, IASB, August 2005.
7 IAS 1, paras. 2-3.
8 IAS 1, para. 11 and IAS 8, para. 5.
9 IAS 8, para. 9.
10 IAS 27, *Consolidated and Separate Financial Statements*, IASB.
11 IAS 34, *Interim Financial Reporting*, IASB.
12 IAS 1, para. 3.
13 IAS 1, para. 1.
14 IAS 1, para. 5.
15 IAS 1, para. 6.
16 IAS 8, para. 56.
17 IAS 8, para. 54.
18 IAS 8, para. IN3.
19 IAS 8, paras. IN7-IN9, IN12 and IN16.
20 IAS 8, para. IN7.
21 IAS 8, paras. IN10-IN11.
22 IAS 8, para. IN14.
23 IAS 8, para. IN17.
24 IAS 8, para. IN14.
25 IAS 8, paras. IN6 and IN15.
26 IAS 8, para. 3.
27 IAS 8, para. 1.
28 IAS 8, para. 2.
29 IAS 8, para. 4.
30 IAS 1, para. 7.
31 IAS 1, para. 49.
32 IAS 1, para. 50.
33 IAS 1, para. 8.
34 IAS 1, para. 11.
35 IAS 1, para. 10.
36 IAS 1, para. 9.
37 IAS 1, para. 10.
38 IAS 1, para. 36.
39 IAS 1, para. 37.
40 IAS 1, para. 86.
41 IAS 1, para. 40.
42 IAS 1, para. 38.
43 IAS 1, para. 11.
44 IAS 1, para. 40.
45 IAS 1, para. 39.
46 IAS 1, paras. 44-45.
47 IAS 1, para. 46.
48 IAS 1, para. 47.
49 IAS 1, para. 48.
50 IAS 1, para. 14.
51 IAS 1, para. 14.
52 ED amendment to IAS 1, IASB website, July 2007, proposed new paragraph 14A.
53 IAS 1, para. 42.
54 IAS 1, para. 43.
55 IAS 1, para. 102.
56 IAS 1, para. 51.
57 IAS 1, para. 58.
58 IAS 1, para. 53.
59 IAS 1, paras. 59 and 61.
60 IFRS 5, para. 3.
61 IAS 1, para. 51.
62 IAS 1, paras. 57 and 60.
63 IAS 1, para. 51.
64 IAS 1, para. 54.
65 IAS 1, para. 55.
66 IAS 1, para. 52.
67 IAS 1, para. 56.
68 *IFRIC Update*, IFRIC, May 2007, page 5.
69 *Framework for the preparation and presentation of financial statements*, IASB, para 62(e).
70 Near final draft of amendment to IAS 1 – Classification of the liability component of a convertible instrument, IASB, website version July 2007.
71 IFRS 5, para. 30.
72 IFRS 5, paras. 38-39.
73 IAS 1, para. 57.
74 IAS 1, para. 70.
75 IAS 1, para. 59.
76 IAS 1, para. 60.
77 IAS 1, para. 70.
78 IAS 1, para. 61.
79 IAS 19, *Employee Benefits*, IASB, para. 118 and Basis for Conclusions, para. 81.
80 IAS 1, para. 62.
81 IAS 1, paras. 63 and 67.
82 IAS 1, paras. 65 and 67.
83 IAS 1, para. 66.
84 IAS 1, para. 64.
85 IAS 1, para. 71.
86 IAS 1, paras. 68 and 71.
87 IAS 1, para. 69.
88 IAS 1, para. 72.
89 IAS 1, para. 73.
90 IAS 1, paras. 68 and 68A.
91 IAS 1, para. 71.
92 IAS 1, para. 74.
93 IAS 1, para. 75.

94 IAS 1, paras. 72 and 75.
95 IAS 1, para. 75.
96 IAS 1, para. 76.
97 IAS 1, para. 77.
98 IAS 1, para. IG2.
99 IAS 1, para. IG4.
100 IAS 1, para. 84.
101 IAS 1, para. 83.
102 IAS 1, para. 84.
103 IAS 1, para. 81.
104 IAS 1, para. 82.
105 IAS 1, para. 89.
106 IAS 1, para. 95.
107 IAS 1, para. BC12.
108 IAS 1, para. BC13.
109 IAS 1, para. 90.
110 IAS 1, para. 88.
111 IAS 1, para. 89.
112 IAS 7 (amended 2003), *Cash flow statements*, IASB, Appendix A.
113 IAS 1, para. 94.
114 IAS 1, para. 91.
115 IAS 1, para. IG4.
116 IAS 1, para. 92.
117 IAS 1, para. IG4.
118 IAS 1, para. 93.
119 IAS 1, para. 86.
120 IAS 1, para. 87.
121 *Framework for the Preparation and Presentation of Financial Statements*, IASB, para. 72.
122 IAS 8 (revised 1993), *Net Profit or Loss for the period, Fundamental Errors and Changes in Accounting Policies*, IASC, December 1993, paras. 6 and 10-15.
123 IAS 1, para. 85.
124 IAS 1, para. BC17.
125 IAS 1, paras. 78 and 99.
126 IAS 1, para. 99.
127 IAS 1, para. 96.
128 IAS 1, para. 98.
129 IAS 1, para. 100.
130 IAS 1, para. 97.
131 IAS 1, para. 101.
132 IAS 19, para 93B.
133 IAS 1, para. IG4.
134 IAS 1, para. IG4.
135 IAS 1, para. 103.
136 IAS 1, para. 104.
137 IAS 1, para. 105.
138 IAS 1, para. 107.
139 IAS 1, para. 106.
140 IAS 1, para. 13.
141 IAS 8, para. 9.
142 IAS 1, para. 15.
143 IAS 1, para. 16.
144 IAS 1, para. 15.
145 IAS 1, para. 22.
146 IAS 1, para. 17.
147 IAS 1, paras. 18-19.
148 IAS 1, para. 20.
149 IAS 1, para. 21.
150 IAS 1, para. 23.
151 IAS 1, para. 24.
152 IAS 1, para. 25.
153 IAS 1, para. 26.
154 Framework, para. 22.
155 IAS 1, para. 27.
156 IAS 1, para. 28.
157 IAS 8, para. 15.
158 IAS 8, para. 13.
159 IAS 1, para. 30.
160 IAS 1, para. 29.
161 IAS 1, para. 11 and IAS 8, para. 5.
162 IAS 1, para. 31.
163 IAS 1, para. 12 and IAS 8, para. 6.
164 IAS 1, para. 30.
165 IAS 1, para. 33.
166 IAS 1, para. 32.
167 IAS 1, para. 34.
168 IAS 1, para. 35.
169 *IASB Update*, IASB, November 2006, page 3.
170 Near final draft of amendment to IFRS 7 – Net finance costs, IASB, website version July 2007.
171 IAS 1, para. 78.
172 Framework, para. 70.
173 IAS 1, para. 79.
174 IAS 1, para. 80.
175 IAS 8, para. 5.
176 IAS 8, para. 35.
177 IAS 1, para. 109.
178 IAS 8, para. 5.
179 IAS 8, para. 38.
180 IAS 8, para. 48.
181 IAS 8, para. 35.
182 IAS 8, para. 8.
183 IAS 8, para. 7.
184 IAS 8, para. 8.
185 IAS 8, para. 10.
186 Framework, paras. 36-37.
187 IAS 8, para. 11.
188 IAS 8, para. 12.
189 IAS 8, para. 14.
190 IAS 8, paras. 5 and 19-20.
191 IAS 8, para. 22.
192 IAS 8, para. 26.
193 IAS 8, para. 23.
194 IAS 8, para. 21.
195 IAS 8, para. 16.
196 IAS 8, paras. 17-18.
197 IAS 8, para. 35.
198 IAS 8, Implementation Guidance, Example 2.
199 IAS 8, paras. 32-33.
200 IAS 8, para. 34.

201 IAS 8, para. 36.
202 IAS 8, para. 5.
203 IAS 8, paras. 36-38.
204 IAS 8, para. 41.
205 IAS 8, para. 41.
206 IAS 8, para. 48.
207 IAS 8, para. 5.
208 IAS 8, para. 42.
209 IAS 8, para. 46.
210 IAS 8, para. 42.
211 IAS 8, para. 5.
212 IAS 8, Implementation Guidance, Example 1.
213 IAS 8, para. 43.
214 IAS 8, para. 5.
215 IAS 8, para. 50.
216 IAS 8, para. 51.
217 IAS 8, para. 53.
218 IAS 8, para. 52.
219 IAS 8, para. 23.
220 IAS 8, para. 26.
221 IAS 8, para. 24.
222 IAS 8, para. 25.
223 IAS 8, para. 5.
224 IAS 8, para. 27.
225 IAS 8, Implementation Guidancc, Example 3.
226 IAS 8, para. 43.
227 IAS 8, para. 44.
228 IAS 8, para. 45.
229 IAS 8, para. 47.
230 IAS 1, para. 109.
231 IAS 1, para. 108.
232 IAS 1, para. 109.
233 IAS 1, para. 112.
234 IAS 1, para. 110.
235 IAS 1, para. 111.
236 IAS 1, para. 114.
237 IAS 1, para. 113.
238 IAS 1, para. 115.
239 IAS 8, para. 28.
240 IAS 8, para. 29.
241 IAS 8, para. 30.
242 IAS 8, para. 31.
243 IAS 1, para. 117.
244 IAS 1, para. 116.
245 IAS 1, para. 118.
246 IAS 1, para. 120.
247 IAS 1, para. 124.
248 IAS 1, para. 119.
249 IAS 1, para. 121.
250 IAS 1, para. 123.
251 IAS 1, para. 122.
252 IAS 1, para. BC37.
253 IAS 8, para. 39.
254 IAS 8, para. 40.
255 IAS 8, para. 49.
256 IAS 1, para BC42
257 IAS 1, para 124A
258 IAS 1, para 124B
259 IAS 1, para 124C
260 IAS 1, Implementation Guidance, para IG5
261 IAS 1, Implementation Guidance, para IG6.
262 IAS 1, para. 125.
263 IAS 1, para. 95.
264 IAS 1, para. 67.
265 IAS 1, para. 126.
266 *IASB website project summary,* IASB, August 2006.
267 IAS 1 (ED), *Exposure draft of proposes amendments to IAS 1 Presentation of Financial Statements: A Revised Presentation,* IASB, March 2006.
268 IAS 1(Revised 2007) para. 10, IASB, September 2007.
269 IAS 1(Revised 2007), paras. BC 14-21.
270 IAS 1(Revised 2007), para. 10.
271 IAS 1(Revised 2007), para. 39.
272 IAS 1(Revised 2007), paras. BC 31 and 32.
273 IAS IAS 1(Revised 2007), para. 81.
274 IAS 1(Revised 2007), para. 83.
275 IAS 1(Revised 2007), Para 106.
276 IAS 1(Revised 2007), Para BC 37 and 38.
277 IAS 1 IAS 1(Revised 2007), para. 90.
278 IAS 1 IAS 1(Revised 2007), paras. BC 65-68.
279 IAS 1 IAS 1(Revised 2007), paras. 92 and 93.
280 IAS 1 IAS 1(Revised 2007), paras. BC 69-73.
281 IAS 1 IAS 1(Revised 2007), para. 107.
282 *Exposure Draft of Proposed Amendments to IAS 32 Financial Instruments: Presentation and IAS 1 Presentation of Financial Statements: Financial Instruments Puttable at Fair Value and Obligations Arising on Liquidation*, IASB, 2006.

Chapter 4 Non-current assets held for sale and discontinued operations

1 INTRODUCTION

1.1 Background to IFRS 5

The IASC issued IAS 35 – *Discontinuing Operations* – in June 1998, which was concerned with the presentation and disclosures relating to *discontinuing* operations. It contained no recognition or measurement rules of its own. In March 2004 IAS 35 was replaced by IFRS 5 – *Non-current Assets Held for Sale and Discontinued Operations.*[1]

IFRS 5 was developed as part of the IASB's convergence project and arises from the IASB's consideration of FASB Statement No. 144 – *Accounting for the Impairment or Disposal of Long-Lived Assets* (SFAS 144), which was issued in 2001.[2] SFAS 144 addresses three areas:

(a) the impairment of long-lived assets to be held and used;

(b) the classification, measurement and presentation of long-lived assets held for sale; and

(c) the classification and presentation of discontinued operations.

The IASB concluded that there were extensive differences between IFRSs and US GAAP as regards (a) above, which it did not think capable of resolution in a relatively short time. However, convergence on the other two areas was thought to be worth pursuing within the context of the short-term convergence project.[3] Accordingly, IFRS 5 was published, which achieves substantial convergence with the requirements of SFAS 144 relating to assets held for sale, the timing of the classification of operations as discontinued and the presentation of such operations.[4] However, there are still differences between the two. For example, the definition of a discontinued operation in IFRS 5 is narrower. The IASB used a different definition to the one contained in SFAS 144 on the grounds that the size of the operation which would meet SFAS 144's definition was too small and that this was causing practical problems. Accordingly, the IASB 'intends to work with the FASB to arrive at a converged definition within a relatively short time.'[5]

1.2 Objective and scope of IFRS 5

The objective of IFRS 5 is to specify the accounting for assets held for sale, and the presentation and disclosure of discontinued operations. In particular, the standard requires that non-current assets (and, in a 'disposal group', liabilities and current assets, discussed at 2.1.1 below) meeting its criteria to be classified as held for sale:

(a) be measured at the lower of carrying amount and fair value less costs to sell, with depreciation on them ceasing; and

(b) be presented separately on the face of the balance sheet with the results of discontinued operations presented separately in the income statement.[6]

The classification and presentation requirements apply to all recognised non-current assets and disposal groups, while there are certain exceptions to the measurement provisions of the standard.[7] These issues are discussed further at 2.2 below.

1.3 Effective date and transitional provisions

IFRS 5 is mandatory for annual periods beginning on or after 1 January 2005, with earlier application encouraged. If it was applied for a period beginning before 1 January 2005, that fact was required to be disclosed.[8]

1.3.1 Transitional arrangements for entities already reporting under IFRS

The standard was to be applied prospectively to non-current assets (or disposal groups) that met the criteria to be classified as held for sale and operations that met the criteria to be classified as discontinued after the effective date of the IFRS. The requirements could be applied to all non-current assets (or disposal groups) that met the criteria to be classified as held for sale and operations that met the criteria to be classified as discontinued after any date before the effective date of the IFRS, provided the valuations and other information needed to apply the standard were obtained at the time those criteria were originally met.[9]

1.3.2 First-time adoption issues

IFRS 1 – *First-time Adoption of International Financial Reporting Standards* – requires an entity with a date of transition to IFRS before 1 January 2005 to apply the transitional provisions of IFRS 5 described above. For an entity with a date of transition to IFRSs on or after 1 January 2005 IFRS 5 is required to be applied retrospectively.[10]

2 NON-CURRENT ASSETS (AND DISPOSAL GROUPS) HELD FOR SALE

2.1 Classification of non-current assets (and disposal groups) held for sale

IFRS 5 frequently refers to current assets and non-current assets. It provides a definition of each term as follows:

A current asset is 'an asset that satisfies any of the following criteria:

(a) it is expected to be realised in, or is intended for sale or consumption in, the entity's normal operating cycle;

(b) it is held primarily for the purpose of being traded;

(c) it is expected to be realised within twelve months after the balance sheet date; or

(d) it is cash or a cash equivalent asset unless it is restricted from being exchanged or used to settle a liability for at least twelve months after the balance sheet date.'

A non-current asset is 'an asset that does not meet the definition of a current asset.'[11]

These definitions are essentially the same as those in IAS 1 – *Presentation of Financial Statements* (discussed in Chapter 3 at 3.1.1). There is one minor difference, in that the IAS 1 definition of a current asset makes explicit that 'cash or a cash equivalent' should have the meaning defined in IAS 7 – *Cash Flow Statements*. However, we do not think this is intended to produce a difference in practice.

2.1.1 The concept of a disposal group

As its title suggests, IFRS 5 addresses the accounting treatment of non-current assets held for sale, that is assets whose carrying amount will be recovered principally through sale rather than continuing use in the business.[12] However, the standard also applies to certain liabilities and current assets where they form part of a 'disposal group'.

The standard observes that sometimes an entity will dispose of a group of assets, possibly with some directly associated liabilities, together in a single transaction.[13] A common example would be the disposal of a subsidiary. For these circumstances, IFRS 5 introduces the concept of a disposal group, which it defines as 'a group of assets to be disposed of, by sale or otherwise, together as a group in a single transaction, and liabilities directly associated with those assets that will be transferred in the transaction. The group includes goodwill acquired in a business combination if the group is a cash-generating unit to which goodwill has been allocated in accordance with the requirements of paragraphs 80-87 of IAS 36 – *Impairment of Assets* (as revised in 2004) or if it is an operation within such a cash-generating unit.'[14]

The use of the phrase 'together in a single transaction' indicates that the only liabilities that can be included in the group are those assumed by the purchaser.

Accordingly, any borrowings of the entity which are to be repaid out of the sales proceeds would be excluded from the disposal group.

The standard goes on to explain that a disposal group:

- may be a group of cash-generating units, a single cash-generating unit, or part of a cash-generating unit. However, once the cash flows from an asset or group of assets are expected to arise principally from sale rather than continuing use, they become less dependent on cash flows arising from other assets, and a disposal group that was part of a cash-generating unit becomes a separate cash-generating unit; and
- may include any assets and any liabilities of the entity, including current assets, current liabilities and assets outside the scope of the measurement requirements of this IFRS (see 2.2 below).[15]

Discontinued operations are discussed at 3 below. As noted there, it seems highly unlikely that the definition of a discontinued operation would ever be met by a single non-current asset. Accordingly, a discontinued operation will also be a disposal group.

2.1.2 *Classification as held for sale*

IFRS 5 requires a non-current asset (or disposal group) to be classified as held for sale if its carrying amount will be recovered principally through a sale transaction rather than through continuing use.[16] For these purposes, sale transactions include exchanges of non-current assets for other non-current assets when the exchange has commercial substance in accordance with IAS 16 – *Property, Plant and Equipment* (discussed in Chapter 13).[17] For assets classified according to a liquidity presentation (see Chapter 3 at 3.1.1), non-current assets are taken to be assets that include amounts expected to be recovered more than twelve months after the balance sheet date.[18]

Determining whether (and when) an asset stops being recovered principally through use and becomes recoverable principally through sale is clearly the critical distinction, and much of the standard is devoted to explaining how to make the determination.

For an asset (or disposal group) to be classified as held for sale:

(a) it must be available for immediate sale in its present condition, subject only to terms that are usual and customary for sales of such assets (or disposal groups);

(b) its sale must be highly probable;[19] and

(c) it must genuinely be sold, not abandoned.[20]

These criteria are discussed further below. If an asset (or disposal group) has been classified as held for sale, but these criteria cease to be met, an entity should cease to classify the asset (or disposal group) as held for sale.[21] Changes in plan are discussed at 2.2.5 below.

Slightly different criteria apply when an entity acquires a non-current asset (or disposal group) exclusively with a view to its subsequent disposal. In that case it should only classify the non-current asset (or disposal group) as held for sale at the acquisition date if:

- the 'one-year requirement' is met subject to its one exception (this is part of being 'highly probable', discussed at B below); and
- it is highly probable that any other criteria in (a) and (b) above that are not met at that date will be met within a short period following the acquisition (usually within three months).[22]

The standard also makes clear that the criteria in (a) and (b) above must be met at the balance sheet date for a non-current asset (or disposal group) to be classified as held for sale in those financial statements when issued. However, if those criteria are met after the balance sheet date but before the authorisation of the financial statements for issue, the standard requires certain additional disclosures (discussed at 5 below).[23]

A Meaning of available for immediate sale

To qualify for classification as held for sale, a non-current asset (or disposal group) must be available for immediate sale in its present condition subject only to terms that are usual and customary for sales of such assets (or disposal groups). This is taken to mean that an entity currently has the intention and ability to transfer the asset (or disposal group) to a buyer in its present condition. The standard illustrates this concept with the following examples.

Example 4.1: Non-current assets and disposal groups available for immediate sale[24]

1 Disposal of a headquarters building

An entity is committed to a plan to sell its headquarters building and has initiated actions to locate a buyer.

(a) The entity intends to transfer the building to a buyer after it vacates the building. The time necessary to vacate the building is usual and customary for sales of such assets. The criterion of being available for immediate sale would therefore be met at the plan commitment date.

(b) The entity will continue to use the building until construction of a new headquarters building is completed. The entity does not intend to transfer the existing building to a buyer until after construction of the new building is completed (and it vacates the existing building). The delay in the timing of the transfer of the existing building imposed by the entity (seller) demonstrates that the building is not available for immediate sale. The criterion would not be met until construction of the new building is completed, even if a firm purchase commitment for the future transfer of the existing building is obtained earlier.

2 Sale of a manufacturing facility

An entity is committed to a plan to sell a manufacturing facility and has initiated actions to locate a buyer. At the plan commitment date, there is a backlog of uncompleted customer orders.

(a) The entity intends to sell the manufacturing facility with its operations. Any uncompleted customer orders at the sale date will be transferred to the buyer. The transfer of uncompleted customer orders at the sale date will not affect the timing of the transfer of the facility. The criterion of being available for immediate sale would therefore be met at the plan commitment date.

(b) The entity intends to sell the manufacturing facility, but without its operations. The entity does not intend to transfer the facility to a buyer until after it ceases all operations of the facility and eliminates the backlog of uncompleted customer orders. The delay in the timing of the transfer of the facility imposed by the entity (seller) demonstrates that the facility is not available for immediate sale. The criterion would not be met until the operations of the facility cease, even if a firm purchase commitment for the future transfer of the facility were obtained earlier.

3 Land and buildings acquired through foreclosure

An entity acquires through foreclosure a property comprising land and buildings that it intends to sell.

(a) The entity does not intend to transfer the property to a buyer until after it completes renovations to increase the property's sales value. The delay in the timing of the transfer of the property imposed by the entity (seller) demonstrates that the property is not available for immediate sale. The criterion of being available for immediate sale would therefore not be met until the renovations are completed.

(b) After the renovations are completed and the property is classified as held for sale but before a firm purchase commitment is obtained, the entity becomes aware of environmental damage requiring remediation. The entity still intends to sell the property. However, the entity does not have the ability to transfer the property to a buyer until after the remediation is completed. The delay in the timing of the transfer of the property imposed by others *before* a firm purchase commitment is obtained demonstrates that the property is not available for immediate sale (different requirements could apply if this happened *after* a firm commitment is obtained, as illustrated in scenario (b) of Example 4.2 below). The criterion would not continue to be met. The property would be reclassified as held and used in accordance with the requirements discussed at 2.2.5 below.

B Meaning of highly probable

Many observers may consider the meaning of 'highly probable' to be reasonably self-evident, albeit highly judgemental. However, IFRS 5 provides extensive discussion of the topic. As a first step, the term is defined by the standard as meaning 'significantly more likely than probable'. This is supplemented by a second definition – probable is defined as 'more likely than not'.[25] Substituting the latter into the former leads to a definition of highly probable as meaning 'significantly more likely than more likely than not'. This is reassuringly close to (but, a little surprisingly, not the same as) the meaning given to the term in IAS 39 – *Financial Instruments: Recognition and Measurement* – which observes that 'The term 'highly probable' indicates a much greater likelihood of happening than the term 'more likely than not'.'[26]

In the particular context of classification as held for sale, the IASB evidently did not consider that 'significantly more likely than more likely than not' was an adequate definition of the phrase, so the standard goes on to elaborate as follows.

For the sale to be highly probable:

- the appropriate level of management must be committed to a plan to sell the asset (or disposal group);

- an active programme to locate a buyer and complete the plan must have been initiated;
- the asset (or disposal group) must be actively marketed for sale at a price that is reasonable in relation to its current fair value;
- the sale should be expected to qualify for recognition as a completed sale within one year from the date of classification (although in certain circumstances this period may be extended as discussed below); and
- actions required to complete the plan should indicate that it is unlikely that significant changes to the plan will be made or that the plan will be withdrawn.[27]

The basic rule above that for qualification as held for sale the sale should be expected to qualify for recognition as a completed sale within one year from the date of classification (the 'one year rule') is applied quite strictly by the standard. In particular, that criterion would not be met if:

(a) an entity that is a commercial leasing and finance company is holding for sale or lease equipment that has recently ceased to be leased and the ultimate form of a future transaction (sale or lease) has not yet been determined;

(b) an entity is committed to a plan to 'sell' a property that is in use, and the transfer of the property will be accounted for as a sale and finance leaseback.[28]

In (a), the entity does not yet know whether the asset will be sold at all and hence may not presume that it will be sold within a year. In (b), whilst in legal form the asset has been sold it will not be *recognised* as sold in the financial statements.

As indicated above, the standard contains an exception to the one year rule. It states that events or circumstances may extend the period to complete the sale beyond one year. Such an extension would not preclude an asset (or disposal group) from being classified as held for sale if the delay is caused by events or circumstances beyond the entity's control and there is sufficient evidence that the entity remains committed to its plan to sell the asset (or disposal group). This will be the case in the following situations:[29]

(a) at the date an entity commits itself to a plan to sell a non-current asset (or disposal group) it reasonably expects that others (not a buyer) will impose conditions on the transfer of the asset (or disposal group) that will extend the period required to complete the sale; and:

  (i) actions necessary to respond to those conditions cannot be initiated until after a firm purchase commitment is obtained; and

  (ii) a firm purchase commitment is highly probable within one year;

(b) an entity obtains a firm purchase commitment and, as a result, a buyer or others unexpectedly impose conditions on the transfer of a non-current asset (or disposal group) previously classified as held for sale that will extend the period required to complete the sale; and:

  (i) timely actions necessary to respond to the conditions have been taken; and

(ii) a favourable resolution of the delaying factors is expected;

(c) during the initial one year period, circumstances arise that were previously considered unlikely and, as a result, a non-current asset (or disposal group) previously classified as held for sale is not sold by the end of that period; and

(i) during the initial one year period the entity took action necessary to respond to the change in circumstances;

(ii) the non-current asset (or disposal group) is being actively marketed at a price that is reasonable, given the change in circumstances; and

(iii) the non-current asset (or disposal group) remains available for immediate sale and the sale is highly probable.[30]

Firm purchase commitment is a defined term in IFRS 5, meaning an agreement with an unrelated party, binding on both parties and usually legally enforceable, that:

- specifies all significant terms, including the price and timing of the transactions; and
- includes a disincentive for non-performance that is sufficiently large to make performance highly probable.[31]

The word 'binding' in this definition seems to envisage an agreement still being subject to contingencies. The standard provides an example where a 'firm purchase commitment' exists but is subject to regulatory approval (see scenario (a) in Example 4.2 below). In our view, to be 'binding' in this sense a contingent agreement should be only subject to contingencies outside the control of both parties.

The standard illustrates each of these exceptions to the one year rule with the following examples.

Example 4.2: Exceptions to the 'one year rule'

Scenario illustrating (a) above[32]

An entity in the power generating industry is committed to a plan to sell a disposal group that represents a significant portion of its regulated operations. The sale requires regulatory approval, which could extend the period required to complete the sale beyond one year. Actions necessary to obtain that approval cannot be initiated until after a buyer is known and a firm purchase commitment is obtained. However, a firm purchase commitment is highly probable within one year. In that situation, the conditions for an exception to the one year requirement would be met.

Scenario illustrating (b) above[33]

An entity is committed to a plan to sell a manufacturing facility in its present condition and classifies the facility as held for sale at that date. After a firm purchase commitment is obtained, the buyer's inspection of the property identifies environmental damage not previously known to exist. The entity is required by the buyer to make good the damage, which will extend the period required to complete the sale beyond one year. However, the entity has initiated actions to make good the damage, and satisfactory rectification of the damage is highly probable. In that situation, the conditions for an exception to the one year requirement would be met.

Scenario illustrating (c) above[34]

An entity is committed to a plan to sell a non-current asset and classifies the asset as held for sale at that date.

(a) During the initial one year period, the market conditions that existed at the date the asset was classified initially as held for sale deteriorate and, as a result, the asset is not sold by the end of that period. During that period, the entity actively solicited but did not receive any reasonable offers to purchase the asset and, in response, reduced the price. The asset continues to be actively marketed at a price that is reasonable given the change in market conditions, and the criteria regarding availability for immediate sale which is highly probable are therefore met. In that situation, the conditions for an exception to the one year requirement would be met. At the end of the initial one year period, the asset would continue to be classified as held for sale.

(b) During the following one year period, market conditions deteriorate further, and the asset is not sold by the end of that period. The entity believes that the market conditions will improve and has not further reduced the price of the asset. The asset continues to be held for sale, but at a price in excess of its current fair value. In that situation, the absence of a price reduction demonstrates that the asset is not available for immediate sale. In addition, to meet the condition that a sale be highly probable also requires an asset to be marketed at a price that is reasonable in relation to its current fair value. Therefore, the conditions for an exception to the one year requirement would not be met. The asset would be reclassified as held and used in accordance with the requirements discussed at 2.2.5 below.

C Abandonment

IFRS 5 stipulates that a non-current asset (or disposal group) that is to be abandoned should not be classified as held for sale. This includes non-current assets (or disposal groups) that are to be used to the end of their economic life and non-current assets (or disposal groups) that arc to bc closcd rather than sold. The standard explains that this is because its carrying amount will be recovered principally through continuing use.[35]

If the disposal group to be abandoned meets the criteria for being a discontinued operation the standard requires it to be treated as such in the income statement and relevant notes.[36] This is discussed at 3.1 below. However, a non-current asset that has been temporarily taken out of use should not be accounted for as if it had been abandoned.[37] An example given by the standard is of a manufacturing plant that ceases to be used because demand for its product has declined but which is maintained in workable condition and is expected to be brought back into use if demand picks up. The plant is not regarded as abandoned.[38] However, in these circumstances an impairment loss may need to be recognised in accordance with IAS 36 (discussed in Chapter 15).

2.1.3 Partial disposals of operations

IFRS 5 provides no guidance relating to a partial disposal of an operation for determining whether the definition of held for sale is met. Key here is exactly what is meant by the phrase 'carrying amount will be recovered principally through a sale transaction rather than through continuing use.' An entity could sell some, but not all, of its interest in an operation such that the balance retained is:

(a) still a subsidiary;

(b) an available for sale investment accounted for under IAS 39;

(c) an associate or jointly controlled entity accounted for using the equity method; or

(d) a joint venture accounted for by proportionate consolidation.

The question arises as to whether, other things aside, it is appropriate to consider the operation's assets and liabilities to be held for sale.

The two extremes (a) and (b) above are not contentious. If the operation remains a subsidiary (and the assets and liabilities of it therefore remain fully consolidated) it is hard to argue that the assets and liabilities are recovered principally though sale. If the stake retained is a simple minority investment (subsequently carried at fair value as an available for sale investment) it is equally clear that the assets and liabilities concerned have indeed been recovered principally through sale. The doubt lies in the middle of these extremes where the selling entity's share of the assets and liabilities are still reflected in its balance sheet, either as one line or through proportionate consolidation.

One analysis would be that recovery principally through sale means that more than half of the original stake is disposed of. For example, if 51% of a wholly owned subsidiary is disposed of (leaving a 49% associate) all of the subsidiary's assets and liabilities could be considered to be classified as held for sale.

This ostensibly sensible analysis can be challenged on the grounds that there is an arbitrary point of inflection. Extending the example above (with a 49% stake retained):

- original holdings of greater that 98% result in a disposal of greater than 50%;
- original holdings of less than 98% result in a disposal of less than 50%; and
- original holdings of exactly 98% result in a disposal of exactly 50%.

It would be arbitrary in the extreme to consider the first category to be recovered through sale and the second one not. Furthermore, the analysis provides no answer regarding the third category.

Another approach to analyse the problem would be to consider the nature of the retained stake. If the retained stake is of a different nature to the original holding (say, a subsidiary becoming an associate or an associate becoming an available for sale investment) it could be argued that the operation's assets have been recovered principally through sale. Those supporting this analysis would argue that such transactions are essentially the disposal of 100% of the original holding followed by the re-acquisition of the retained stake which comprises something quite different in nature. Whilst this may have some intellectual appeal, it still suffers from the same problem mentioned above. If a holding in an operation moves from, say, a 60% subsidiary to a 40% associate it remains quite hard to accept that the assets have been recovered principally through sale when only one third of the economic stake in the operation has actually been sold. That problem would be even more stark in the extreme example of a 51% subsidiary becoming a 49% associate.

A further consideration would be to consider the accounting consequences of classification of held for sale. If the retained stake is an associate or joint venture, the underlying assets and liabilities are still reflected in the group balance sheet, albeit now only the group's share, either condensed into one line or on a line by line basis. Once the transaction completes the non-current assets will be depreciated and that depreciation will flow into the group financial statements either through equity accounting or proportionate consolidation. On that basis, it seems questionable to temporarily suspend depreciation for the period that the stake being sold is held for sale (potentially up to a year, and in some circumstances even longer). Furthermore, classification as held for sale raises the question of how to compute the opening carrying value for equity accounting purposes, to which there is no satisfactory answer. For example, should the depreciation 'holiday' be reversed? Should any impairment to fair value less costs to sell be reversed (see 2.2.2 below)? If a provision was recognised because there were no qualifying assets to absorb an impairment write-down (see 2.2.3 below), how should the retained element be dealt with?

There seems to be no obvious conclusion to deal satisfactorily with the various issues discussed above. In light of this and the lack of clarity in the standard we expect a variety of approaches could be acceptable, based on the individual facts and circumstances and on the judgement of the entity concerned.

This issue was discussed by IFRIC in its March 2007 meeting. At the time of writing IFRIC has yet to decide whether to include the topic on its agenda.[39] Following IFRIC's deliberations the IASB also discussed this issue. It tentatively decided that an entity that is committed to a sale plan that meets the conditions in IFRS 5 and involves loss of control of a subsidiary should classify the subsidiary's assets and liabilities as held for sale, regardless of whether the entity will retain a non-controlling interest in its former subsidiary after the sale.[40] This tentative decision has yet to be progressed to an amendment to the standard.

2.2 Measurement of non-current assets (and disposal groups) held for sale

2.2.1 *Scope of the measurement requirements*

IFRS 5's classification and presentation requirements apply to all recognised non-current assets (which is defined in the same way as in IAS 1, discussed at 2.1 above) and disposal groups. However, the measurement provisions of the standard do not apply to the following assets (which remain covered by the standards listed) either as individual assets or as part of a disposal group:[41]

(a) deferred tax assets (dealt with in IAS 12 – *Income Taxes*);

(b) assets arising from employee benefits (dealt with in IAS 19 – *Employee Benefits*);

(c) financial assets within the scope of IAS 39;

(d) non-current assets that are accounted for in accordance with the fair value model in IAS 40 – *Investment Property*;

(e) non-current assets that are measured at fair value less estimated point-of-sale costs in accordance with IAS 41 – *Agriculture*; and

(f) contractual rights under insurance contracts as defined in IFRS 4 – *Insurance Contracts*.

2.2.2 Measurement of non-current assets and disposal groups held for sale

A Measurement on initial classification as held for sale

IFRS 5 requires that immediately before the initial classification of an asset (or disposal group) as held for sale, the carrying amount of the asset (or all the assets and liabilities in the group) should be measured in accordance with applicable IFRSs.[42] In other words, an entity should apply its usual accounting policies up until the criteria for classification as held for sale are met.

Thereafter a non-current asset (or disposal group) classified as held for sale should be measured at the lower of its carrying amount and fair value less costs to sell.[43] Fair value is defined as 'the amount for which an asset could be exchanged, or a liability settled, between knowledgeable, willing parties in an arm's length transaction.' Costs to sell are defined as 'the incremental costs directly attributable to the disposal of an asset (or disposal group), excluding finance costs and income tax expense.'[44] When the sale is expected to occur beyond one year, the costs to sell should be measured at their present value. Any increase in the present value of the costs to sell that arises from the passage of time should be presented in profit or loss as a financing cost.[45] There is no similar requirement to present that element of an increase in fair value which also relates to just the passage of time as finance income.

For disposal groups, the standard adopts a portfolio approach. It requires that if a non-current asset within the scope of its measurement requirements is part of a disposal group, the measurement requirements should apply to the group as a whole, so that the group is measured at the lower of its carrying amount and fair value less costs to sell.[46] It will still be necessary to apportion any write down to the underlying assets of the disposal group, but no element is apportioned to items outside the scope of the standard's measurement provisions. This is discussed further at 2.2.3 below.

If a newly acquired asset (or disposal group) meets the criteria to be classified as held for sale (which, as discussed at 2.1.2 above are subtly different for assets acquired exclusively with a view to subsequent disposal), applying the above requirements will result in the asset (or disposal group) being measured on initial recognition at the lower of its carrying amount had it not been so classified (for example, cost) and fair value less costs to sell. This means that, if the asset (or disposal group) is acquired as part of a business combination, it will be measured at fair value less costs to sell.[47]

The implementation guidance accompanying the standard provides the following illustration of a subsidiary acquired with a view to sale.

Example 4.3: Measuring and presenting subsidiaries acquired with a view to sale and classified as held for sale[48]

Entity A acquires an entity H, which is a holding company with two subsidiaries, S1 and S2. S2 is acquired exclusively with a view to sale and meets the criteria to be classified as held for sale. Accordingly, S2 is also a discontinued operation (see 3.1 below).

The estimated fair value less costs to sell of S2 is €135. A accounts for S2 as follows:

- initially, A measures the identifiable liabilities of S2 at fair value, say at €40;
- initially, A measures the acquired assets as the fair value less costs to sell of S2 (€135) plus the fair value of the identifiable liabilities (€40), i.e. at €175;
- at the balance sheet date, A remeasures the disposal group at the lower of its cost and fair value less costs to sell, say at €130. The liabilities are remeasured in accordance with applicable IFRSs, say at €35. The total assets are measured at €130 + €35, i.e. at €165;
- at the balance sheet date, A presents the assets and liabilities separately from other assets and liabilities in its consolidated financial statements as illustrated in Example 4.5 at 2.2.4 below; and
- in the income statement, A presents the total of the post-tax profit or loss of S2 and the post-tax gain or loss recognised on the subsequent remeasurement of S2, which equals the remeasurement of the disposal group from €135 to €130.

Further analysis of the assets and liabilities or of the change in value of the disposal group is not required.

The final sentence in the IASB's above example is somewhat misleading. It is true to say that IFRS 5 requires no further disclosures that would involve further analysis. However, there are other accounting standards where the disclosure requirements have not been 'switched-off' and accordingly still apply. For example, disclosures for the whole entity would still appear to be required in respect of financial instruments, income tax and pensions. It is fair to say that some confusion exists in practice in this area. In particular, some IFRS reporters consider that the various disclosures required by other standards should reflect only the continuing operations of the group. Furthermore, a detailed purchase price analysis and tracking of the acquired entity is still needed, notwithstanding a partial relaxation of what is required to be disclosed by IFRS 5. This is needed not just for the disclosures in other standards but also to be able to determine the split between gross assets and liabilities and how movements in the carrying amounts are reflected in income or equity.

B Subsequent remeasurement

While a non-current asset is classified as held for sale or while it is part of a disposal group classified as held for sale it should not be depreciated or amortised. Interest and other expenses attributable to the liabilities of a disposal group classified as held for sale should continue to be recognised.[49]

On subsequent remeasurement of a disposal group, the standard requires that the carrying amounts of any assets and liabilities that are not within the scope of its measurement requirements, be remeasured in accordance with applicable IFRSs before the fair value less costs to sell of the disposal group is remeasured.[50]

2.2.3 *Impairments and reversals of impairment*

The requirement to measure a non-current asset or disposal group held for sale at the lower of carrying amount less costs to sell may give rise to a write down in value (impairment loss) and possibly its subsequent reversal. As noted above, the first step is to account for any items outwith the scope of the standard's measurement rules in the normal way. After that, any excess of carrying value over fair value less costs to sell should be recognised as an impairment.[51]

Any subsequent increase in fair value less costs to sell of an asset up to the cumulative impairment loss previously recognised either in accordance with IFRS 5 or in accordance with IAS 36 should be recognised as a gain.[52] In the case of a disposal group, any subsequent increase in fair value less costs to sell should be recognised:

(a) to the extent that it has not been recognised under another standard in relation to those assets outside the scope of IFRS 5's measurement requirements; but

(b) not in excess of the cumulative amount of losses previously recognised under IFRS 5 or before that under IAS 36 in respect of the non-current assets in the group which are within the scope of the measurement rules of IFRS 5.[53]

Any impairment loss (or any subsequent gain) recognised for a disposal group should be allocated to the non-current assets in the group that are within the scope of the measurement requirements of IFRS 5. The order of allocation should be:

- first, to reduce the carrying amount of any goodwill in the group; and
- then, to the other non-current assets of the group pro rata on the basis of the carrying amount of each asset in the group.[54]

This is illustrated by the standard with the following example.

Example 4.4: Allocation of impairment loss to the components of a disposal group[55]

An entity plans to dispose of a group of its assets (as an asset sale). The assets form a disposal group, and are measured as follows:

	Carrying amount at the reporting date before classification as held for sale	Carrying amount as remeasured immediately before classification as held for sale
	€	€
Goodwill	1,500	1,500
Property, plant and equipment (carried at revalued amounts)	4,600	4,000
Property, plant and equipment (carried at cost)	5,700	5,700
Inventory	2,400	2,200
Available for sale financial assets	1,800	1,500
Total	16,000	14,900

The entity recognises the loss of €1,100 (€16,000 – €14,900) immediately before classifying the disposal group as held for sale. The entity estimates that fair value less costs to sell of the disposal group amounts to €13,000. Because an entity measures a disposal group classified as held for sale at the lower of its carrying amount and fair value less costs to sell, the entity recognises an impairment loss of €1,900 (€14,900 – €13,000) when the group is initially classified as held for sale. The impairment loss is allocated to non-current assets to which the measurement requirements of the IFRS are applicable. Therefore, no impairment loss is allocated to inventory and AFS financial assets. The loss is allocated to the other assets in the order of allocation described above.

The allocation can be illustrated as follows:

First, the impairment loss reduces any amount of goodwill. Then, the residual loss is allocated to other assets pro rata based on the carrying amounts of those assets.

	Carrying amount as remeasured immediately before classification as held for sale	Allocated impairment loss	Carrying amount after allocation of impairment loss
	€	€	€
Goodwill	1,500	(1,500)	–
Property, plant and equipment (carried at revalued amounts)	4,000	(165)	3,835
Property, plant and equipment (carried at cost)	5,700	(235)	5,465
Inventory	2,200	–	2,200
AFS financial assets	1,500	–	1,500
Total	14,900	(1,900)	13,000

In the first table of this example, it is not particularly clear what the meaning and purpose of the left hand column is. The fact that some of the figures are different in each column, seems to indicate that the column header 'Carrying amount at the reporting date before classification as held for sale' is referring to the opening balance sheet at the beginning of the period in which the classification is made. As noted at 2.2.2 A above, an entity is required to remeasure the assets as normal under the relevant standards immediately before classifying them as held for sale. This would mean the difference of €1,100 reflects routine accounting entries (such as depreciation and revaluation) from the start of the period to the date of classification as held to sale. Also worthy of note is that the example does not say where the entity recognises the loss of €1,100. Given that the disposal group contains available for sale financial assets, some of this amount would probably be recorded in equity rather than the income statement. Similarly, movements in property plant and equipment held at revalued amounts may fall to be recorded directly in equity.

The standard contains a reminder that requirements relating to derecognition are set out in IAS 16 for property, plant and equipment (discussed in Chapter 13), and IAS 38 – *Intangible Assets* – for intangible assets (discussed in Chapter 12) and notes that a gain or loss not previously recognised by the date of the sale of a non-current asset (or disposal group) should be recognised at the date of derecognition.[56]

One thing which the example above fails to illustrate is a logical flaw in the standard's measurement requirements. It is quite possible that the required impairment exceeds the carrying value of the non-current assets within the scope of the standard's measurement rules. IFRS 5 is silent on what to do in such circumstances. Possible approaches would be:

(a) to apply the impairment to current assets;

(b) to apply the impairment to non-current assets outside the scope of the standard's measurement rules; or

(c) to recognise a separate provision.

In general, we would expect (c) to be the most appropriate approach.

2.2.4 Balance sheet presentation of non-current assets and disposal groups held for sale

The general requirement, discussed in Chapter 3 at 3.1.1, to classify balance sheet items as current or non-current (or present them broadly in order of liquidity) is overlaid with further requirements by IFRS 5 regarding non-current assets held for sale and disposal groups. IFRS 5's aim is that entities should present and disclose information that enables users of the financial statements to evaluate the financial effects of disposals of non-current assets (or disposal groups).[57] In pursuit of this aim, IFRS 5 requires:

- non-current assets classified as held for sale and the assets of a disposal group classified as held for sale to be presented separately from other assets in the balance sheet; and
- the liabilities of a disposal group classified as held for sale to be presented separately from other liabilities in the balance sheet.

These assets and liabilities should not be offset and presented as a single amount. In addition:

(a) major classes of assets and liabilities classified as held for sale should generally be separately disclosed either on the face of the balance sheet or in the notes. However, this is not necessary for a disposal group if it is a subsidiary that met the criteria to be classified as held for sale on acquisition; and

(b) any cumulative income or expense recognised directly in equity relating to a non-current asset (or disposal group) classified as held for sale should be presented separately.[58]

The requirement in (b) was included in response to comments made to the IASB during the development of the standard. The Board describes the development as follows. 'Respondents to ED 4 noted that the separate presentation within equity of amounts relating to assets and disposal groups classified as held for sale (such as, for example, unrealised gains and losses on available-for-sale assets and foreign currency translation adjustments) would also provide useful information. The Board agreed and has added such a requirement to the IFRS.'[59] On that basis, it might be considered that any minority interest relating to non-current assets (or disposal groups) held for sale should also be presented separately as it would seem to represent equally useful information about amounts within equity. However, such disclosure of minority interests is not specifically required by the standard so would remain voluntary,

IFRS 5 is silent as to whether the information specified in (b) above should be on the face of the balance sheet or in a note. However, the implementation guidance to IFRS 5 shows a caption called 'Amounts recognised directly in equity in relation to non-current assets held for sale' and illustrates the requirements as follows.

Example 4.5: Presenting non-current assets or disposal groups classified as held for sale[60]

At the end of 2008, an entity decides to dispose of part of its assets (and directly associated liabilities). The disposal, which meets the criteria to be classified as held for sale, takes the form of two disposal groups, as follows:

	Carrying amount after classification as held for sale	
	Disposal group I	Disposal group II
	€	€
Property, plant and equipment	4,900	1,700
AFS financial asset	*1,400	–
Liabilities	(2,400)	(900)
Net carrying amount of disposal group	3,900	800

* An amount of €400 relating to these assets has been recognised directly in equity.

The presentation in the entity's balance sheet of the disposal groups classified as held for sale can be shown as follows:

	2008	2007
	€	€
ASSETS		
Non-current assets	×	×
AAA	×	×
BBB	×	×
CCC	×	×
	×	×
Current assets		
DDD	×	×
EEE	×	×
	×	×
Non-current assets classified as held for sale	8,000	–
Total assets	×	×

EQUITY AND LIABILITIES		
Equity attributable to equity holders of the parent		
FFF	×	×
GGG	×	×
Amounts recognised directly in equity relating to non-current assets held for sale	400	–
	×	×
Minority interest	×	×
Total equity	×	×
Non-current liabilities		
HHH	×	×
III	×	×
JJJ	×	×
	×	×
Current liabilities		
KKK	×	×
LLL	×	×
MMM	×	×
	×	×
Liabilities directly associated with non-current assets classified as held for sale	3,300	–
	×	×
Total liabilities	×	×
Total equity and liabilities	×	×

The presentation requirements for assets (or disposal groups) classified as held for sale at the end of the reporting period do not apply retrospectively. The comparative balance sheets for any previous periods are therefore not re-presented.

Once assets have been classified as non-current they should not be reclassified as current assets until they meet the criteria to be classified as held for sale in accordance with IFRS 5. Assets of a class that an entity would normally regard as non-current that are acquired exclusively with a view to resale also should not be classified as current unless they meet those criteria.[61]

The treatment of comparatives when the classification as held for sale commences or ceases is discussed at 4 below.

2.2.5 Changes to a plan of sale

An asset (or disposal group) should cease to be classified as held for sale if the criteria discussed in 2.1.2 are no longer met.[62]

If an individual asset or liability is removed from a disposal group classified as held for sale, the remaining assets and liabilities of the disposal group to be sold should only continue to be measured as a group if the group still meets these criteria. Otherwise, the remaining non-current assets of the group that individually meet the criteria should be measured individually at the lower of their carrying amounts and fair values less costs to sell at that date. Any that do not meet the criteria should cease to be classified as held for sale.[63]

A non-current asset that ceases to be classified as held for sale (or ceases to be included in a disposal group classified as held for sale) should be measured at the lower of:

(a) its carrying amount before the asset (or disposal group) was classified as held for sale, adjusted for any depreciation, amortisation or revaluations that would have been recognised had the asset (or disposal group) not been classified as held for sale; and

(b) its recoverable amount at the date of the subsequent decision not to sell.

Regarding (b) above, the standard notes that if the non-current asset is part of a cash-generating unit, its recoverable amount is the carrying amount that would have been recognised after the allocation of any impairment loss arising on that cash-generating unit in accordance with IAS 36.[64] Recoverable amount is defined as the higher of:

- an asset's fair value less costs to sell; and
- its value in use.

Value in use is defined as 'the present value of estimated future cash flows expected to arise from the continuing use of an asset and from its disposal at the end of its useful life.'[65]

Any required adjustment to the carrying amount of a non-current asset that ceases to be classified as held for sale should be included

- in income from continuing operations in the period in which the criteria are no longer met (unless the asset had been revalued in accordance with IAS 16 or IAS 38 before classification as held for sale, in which case the adjustment should be treated as a revaluation increase or decrease); and
- in the same income statement caption used to present any gain or loss recognised in relation to remeasuring non-current assets (or disposal groups) held for sale but not meeting the definition of a discontinued operation.[66]

3 DISCONTINUED OPERATIONS

As discussed at 3.2 below, IFRS 5 requires the presentation of a single amount on the face of the income statement relating to discontinued operations, with further analysis either on the face of the income statement or in the notes.

3.1 Definition of a discontinued operation

IFRS 5 defines a discontinued operation as 'a component of an entity that either has been disposed of, or is classified as held for sale, and

(a) represents a separate major line of business or geographical area of operations;

(b) is part of a single co-ordinated plan to dispose of a separate major line of business or geographical area of operations; or

(c) is a subsidiary acquired exclusively with a view to resale.'[67]

Classification as held for sale is discussed at 2.1 above. For the purposes of the above definition, a 'component of an entity' is also defined by the standard as comprising 'operations and cash flows that can be clearly distinguished, operationally and for financial reporting purposes, from the rest of the entity. In other words, a component of an entity will have been a cash-generating unit or a group of cash-generating units while being held for use.'[68] IFRS 5 defines cash generating unit in the same way as IAS 36, that is as 'the smallest identifiable group of assets that generates cash inflows that are largely independent of the cash inflows from other assets or groups of assets.'[69] Cash generating units are discussed in Chapter 15.

It seems highly unlikely that this definition of a discontinued operation would ever be met by a single non-current asset. Accordingly, a discontinued operation will also be a 'disposal group' which is a group of assets to be disposed of, by sale or otherwise, together as a group in a single transaction, and liabilities directly associated with those assets that will be transferred in the transaction (discussed at 2.1.1 above). In our view, the definition of a discontinued operation is somewhat vague, and in particular much will depend on the interpretation of 'a separate major line of business or geographical area of business'. We think this will inevitably mean different things to different people, and that comparability in financial reporting will suffer as a result. However, it is only an interim measure. The IASB used this definition in preference to the one contained in SFAS 144, on the grounds that the size of the operation which would meet SFAS 144's definition was too small and that this was causing practical problems. Accordingly, the IASB noted in the standard that it 'intends to work with the FASB to arrive at a converged definition within a relatively short time.'[70] In April 2007, the IASB agreed to add to its agenda a project to re-consider the definition of discontinued operations through a joint project with the FASB.[71] This project is to be progressed separately from the ongoing project dealing with financial statement presentation. The Board had earlier tentatively agreed that the definition of a discontinued operation should be based on the operating segment notion, as provided by IFRS 8 – *Operating Segments*.[72] IFRS 8 is discussed in Chapter 30 at 4.

As discussed at 2.1.2 C above, IFRS 5 stipulates that a non-current asset (or disposal group) that is to be abandoned should not be classified as held for sale. This includes non-current assets (or disposal groups) that are to be used to the end of their economic life and non-current assets (or disposal groups) that are to be closed rather than sold. However, if the disposal group to be abandoned meets the criteria above for being a discontinued operation the standard requires it to be treated as such in the income statement and relevant notes 'at the date on which it ceases to be used.'[73] In other words, the treatment as discontinued in the income statement only starts in the period when abandonment actually occurs (see Example 4.6 below).

A non-current asset that has been temporarily taken out of use should not be accounted for as if it had been abandoned.[74] Accordingly it would not be disclosed as a discontinued operation. The standard provides an illustration of a discontinued operation arising from abandonment upon which the following example is based.

Example 4.6: Discontinued operation arising from abandonment[75]

In October 2008 an entity decides to abandon all of its cotton mills, which constitute a major line of business. All work stops at the cotton mills during the year ended 31 December 2009. In the financial statements for the year ended 31 December 2008, results and cash flows of the cotton mills are treated as continuing operations. In the financial statements for the year ended 31 December 2009, the results and cash flows of the cotton mills are treated as discontinued operations and the entity makes the disclosures required (see 3.2 below).

An issue not considered by IFRS 5 is a partial disposal of an operation. This is discussed at 2.1.3 above in the context of meeting the criteria of being held for sale.

3.2 Presentation of discontinued operations

IFRS 5 requires the presentation of a single amount on the face of the income statement comprising:

(a) the post-tax profit or loss of discontinued operations; and

(b) the post-tax gain or loss recognised on the measurement to fair value less costs to sell or on the disposal of the assets or disposal group(s) constituting the discontinued operation.[76]

This single amount should be further analysed (either on the face of the income statement or in the notes) into:

(a) the revenue, expenses and pre-tax profit or loss of discontinued operations;

(b) the gain or loss recognised on the measurement to fair value less costs to sell or on the disposal of the assets or disposal group(s) constituting the discontinued operation; and

(c) separately for each of (a) and (b) the related income tax expense as required IAS 12 (see Chapter 26).

The analysis is not required for disposal groups that are newly acquired subsidiaries that meet the criteria to be classified as held for sale on acquisition (see 2.2.2 above).[77] However, in either case it should be remembered that any disclosures that might be required by other IFRSs about amounts recognised in the income statement need to include any relevant amounts relating to the discontinued operations.

If the required analysis is presented on the face of the income statement it should be presented in a section identified as relating to discontinued operations, i.e. separately from continuing operations. One possibility would be a columnar approach. The standard also makes clear that any gain or loss on the remeasurement of a non-current asset (or disposal group) classified as held for sale that does not meet the definition of a discontinued operation should not be included within these amounts for discontinued operations, but be included in profit or loss from continuing operations.[78]

IFRS 5 requires that these disclosures be re-presented for prior periods presented in the financial statements so that the disclosures relate to all operations that have been discontinued by the balance sheet date for the latest period presented.[79] Accordingly, adjustments to the comparative information as originally reported will be necessary for those disposal groups categorised as discontinued operations. Comparative information relating to discontinued operations is discussed further at 4 below.

The implementation guidance accompanying IFRS 5 provides the following illustration of the presentation of discontinued operations.

Example 4.7: Presenting discontinued operations[80]

XYZ GROUP – INCOME STATEMENT FOR THE YEAR ENDED 31 DECEMBER 2008
(illustrating the classification of expenses by function)

(in thousands of Euros)

	2008	2007
Continuing operations		
Revenue	×	×
Cost of sales	(×)	(×)
Gross profit	×	×
Other income	×	×
Distribution costs	(×)	(×)
Administrative expenses	(×)	(×)
Other expenses	(×)	(×)
Finance costs	(×)	(×)
Share of profit of associates	×	×
Profit before tax	×	×
Income tax expense	(×)	(×)
Profit for the period from continuing operations	×	×
Discontinued operations		
Profit for the period from discontinued operations*	×	×
Profit for the period	×	×
Attributable to:		
Equity holders of the parent	×	×
Minority interest	×	×
	×	×

* The required analysis would be given in the notes.

Adjustments in the current period to amounts previously presented in discontinued operations that are directly related to the disposal of a discontinued operation in a prior period should be classified separately in discontinued operations. The nature and amount of the adjustments should be disclosed. Examples given by the standard of circumstances in which these adjustments may arise include the following:

(a) the resolution of uncertainties that arise from the terms of the disposal transaction, such as the resolution of purchase price adjustments and indemnification issues with the purchaser;

(b) the resolution of uncertainties that arise from and are directly related to the operations of the component before its disposal, such as environmental and product warranty obligations retained by the seller; and

(c) the settlement of employee benefit plan obligations, provided that the settlement is directly related to the disposal transaction.[81]

In addition, IFRS 5 requires disclosure of the net cash flows attributable to the operating, investing and financing activities of discontinued operations. The standard allows that these disclosures may be presented either in the notes or on the face of the financial statements. It is not readily clear what 'on the face of the financial statements' is intended to mean, but it seems likely that this data would be presented on the face of the cash flow statement. These disclosures are not required for disposal groups that are newly acquired subsidiaries that meet the criteria to be classified as held for sale on acquisition (see 2.2.2 above).[82]

3.3 Trading between continuing and discontinued operations

Notwithstanding the one line income statement presentation discussed above, discontinued operations remain consolidated in group financial statements. That means any transactions between discontinued and continuing operations are eliminated as usual in the consolidation. As a consequence, the amounts ascribed to the continuing and discontinued operations will be income and expense only from transactions with counterparties external to the group. Importantly, this means the results presented on the face of the income statement will not represent the activities of the operations as individual entities. One company which decided to explain and quantify this was BP, as shown in the following extract.

Extract 4.1: BP p.l.c. (2006)

Notes to the Financial Statements [extract]

7 Segmental analysis [extract]

									$million 2005
By business	Exploration and production	Refining and Marketing	Gas, Power and Re-newables	Other businesses and corporate	Consolid-ation adjustment and elimin-ations	Total group	Innovene operations	Consolid-ation adjustment and elimin-ations[a]	Total continuing operations
Sales and other operating revenues									
Segment sales and other operating revenues	47,210	213,326	25,696	21,295	(55,359)	252,168	(20,627)	8,251	239,792
Less: sales between businesses	(32,606)	(11,407)	(3,095)	(8,251)	55,359	–	8,251	(8,251)	–
Third party sales	14,604	201,919	22,601	13,044	–	252,168	(12,376)	–	239,792
Equity-accounted earnings	3,232	249	62	(14)	–	3,529	14	–	3,543
Segment revenues	17,836	202,168	22,663	13,030	–	255,697	(12,362)	–	243,335
Interest and other revenues	–	–	–	–	689	689	(76)	–	613
Total revenues	17,836	202,168	22,663	13,030	689	256,386	(12,438)	–	243,948
Segment results									
Profit (loss) before interest and tax	25,502	6,926	1,172	(569)	(208)	32,823	(668)	527	32,682
Finance costs and other finance expense	–	–	–	–	(758)	(758)	(3)	–	(761)
Profit (loss) before taxation	25,502	6,296	1,172	(569)	(966)	32,065	(671)	527	31,921
Taxation	–	–	–	–	(9,433)	(9,433)	133	(173)	(9,473)
Profit (loss) for the year	25,502	6,926	1,172	(569)	(10,399)	22,632	(538)	354	22,448

[a]In the circumstances of discontinued operations, IFRS requires that the profits earned by the discontinued operations, in this case the Innovene operations, on sales to the continuing operations be eliminated on consolidation from the discontinued operations and attributed to the continuing operations and vice versa. This adjustment has two offsetting elements: the net margin on crude refined by Innovene as substantially all crude for its refineries was supplied by BP and most of the refined products manufactured were taken by BP; and the margin on sales of feedstock from BP's US refineries to Innovene's manufacturing plants. The profits attributable to individual segments are not affected by this adjustment. This representation does not indicate the profits earned by continuing or Innovene operations, as if they were standalone entities, for past periods or likely to be earned in future periods.

4 COMPARATIVE INFORMATION

As discussed in Chapter 3 at 2.4, IAS 1 requires the presentation of comparative information. IFRS 5 deals with the particular requirements for non-current assets held for sale (and disposal groups) and discontinued operations. However, in our view, the way it does so is somewhat muddled.

Entities will need to consider whether any (and if so what) changes are necessary to comparative information as previously reported whenever:

- non-current assets or disposal groups first become classified as such; and
- that classification ceases.

This will need to be considered in terms of both the income statement and balance sheet and separately (for the income statement) for those components falling to be treated as discontinued operations.

4.1 Treatment of comparative information on initial classification as held for sale

4.1.1 The income statement

For non-current assets and disposal groups not qualifying as discontinued operations there are no special requirements relating to income statement presentation, accordingly no restatement of comparative amounts would be relevant.

When a component of an entity becomes classified as a discontinued operation, separate presentation of the total of its results for the period and any gain or loss on remeasurement is required on the face of the income statement (see 3.2 above). IFRS 5 requires that these disclosures be re-presented for prior periods presented in the financial statements so that the disclosures relate to all operations that have been discontinued by the balance sheet date for the latest period presented.[83] Accordingly, adjustments to the comparative information as originally reported will be necessary for those disposal groups categorised as discontinued operations.

4.1.2 The balance sheet

IFRS 5 states that 'An entity shall not reclassify or re-present amounts presented for non-current assets or for the assets and liabilities of disposal groups classified as held for sale in the balance sheets for prior periods to reflect the classification in the balance sheet for the latest period presented.'[84] The exact meaning of this is imprecise, and would be clarified if the sentence contained some punctuation. In particular, it is unclear whether the prohibition is aimed at the commencement or cessation of the held for sale classification or both. The implementation guidance accompanying the standard contains an example of a disposal group becoming classified as held for sale (see Example 4.5 at 2.2.4 above), and states that the presentation requirements for assets (or disposal groups) classified as held for sale at the end of the reporting period do not apply retrospectively. The comparative balance sheets for any previous periods are therefore not re-presented.[85] In our view, comparatives should not be re-presented when the classification as held for sale ceases.

The standard has no separate requirements relating to the balance sheet for a disposal group also qualifying as a discontinued operation.

4.2 Treatment of comparative information on the cessation of classification as held for sale

4.2.1 General requirements

As discussed at 2.2.5 above, when a non-current asset ceases to be classified as held for sale the measurement basis for it reverts to what it would have been if it had not been so classified at all (or recoverable amount if lower). Typically this would require a 'catch-up' depreciation charge as depreciation would not have been accounted for while it was held for sale. The standard explicitly requires this to be a current year charge.[86] This seems to indicate that for non-current assets and disposal groups ceasing to be so classified the *measurement* of items in comparative information (income statement and balance sheet) should not be revisited. This requirement applies equally to discontinued operations. However, as discussed at 4.2.2 below, this is not the case for associates and joint ventures.

Regarding the treatment of discontinued operations in the income statement, the standard states that if an entity ceases to classify a component as held for sale, the results of operations of the component previously presented in discontinued operations should be reclassified and included in income from continuing operations for all periods presented. The amounts for prior periods should be described as having been re-presented.[87]

As discussed at 4.1.2 above, the amounts presented for non-current assets or for the assets and liabilities of disposal groups classified as held for sale in the comparative balance sheet should not be reclassified or re-presented.

4.2.2 The treatment of associates and joint ventures

Somewhat perplexingly, both IAS 28 – *Investments in Associates* – and IAS 31 – *Interests in Joint Ventures* – require a different approach to that discussed above. When an investment in an associate or an interest in a jointly controlled entity previously classified as held for sale (and hence accounted for in accordance with IFRS 5) ceases to be so classified they are required to be accounted for using the equity method or proportionate consolidation (as appropriate) *as from the date of classification as held for sale*.[88] Both standards also state that financial statements for the periods since classification as held for sale should be amended accordingly.

5 DISCLOSURE REQUIREMENTS

As discussed at 2.2.4 and 3.2 above, IFRS 5 sets out detailed requirements for the prominent presentation of amounts relating to non-current assets held for resale, disposal groups and discontinued operations. In addition, disclosure is required in the notes in the period in which a non-current asset (or disposal group) has been either classified as held for sale or sold of:

(a) a description of the non-current asset (or disposal group);

(b) a description of the facts and circumstances of the sale, or leading to the expected disposal, and the expected manner and timing of that disposal;

(c) the gain or loss recognised as a result of measuring the non-current asset (or disposal group) at fair value less costs to sell (discussed at 2 above) and, if not separately presented on the face of the income statement, the caption in the income statement that includes that gain or loss; and

(d) if applicable, the segment in which the non-current asset (or disposal group) is presented in accordance with IAS 14 – *Segment Reporting* (discussed in Chapter 30).[89]

If a non-current asset (or disposal group) meets the criteria to be classified as held for sale after the balance sheet date but before the financial statements are authorised for issue, the information specified in (a), (b) and (d) above should also be disclosed in the notes.[90]

Further, should:

- a non-current asset (or disposal group) cease to be classified as held for sale; or
- an individual asset or liability be removed from a disposal group,

IFRS 5 requires disclosure, in the period of the decision to change the plan to sell the non-current asset (or disposal group), a description of the facts and circumstances leading to the decision and the effect of the decision on the results of operations for the period and any prior periods presented.[91]

6 CONCLUSION

In our view, IFRS 5 is not particularly well drafted nor well conceived. The definition of a discontinued operation is vague, and in particular the meaning of 'a separate major line of business' will inevitably mean different things to different people. The requirement not to depreciate assets which are still actively used (for periods which could exceed a year) introduces a conflict with how assets which are not intended to be sold are treated – although the requirements for impairment and the use of current price residuals may limit the practical impact of this on the balance sheet. Also, the portfolio approach to measuring disposal groups conflicts with the general requirements for separate determination used elsewhere in IFRS and sits particularly awkwardly with the components approach of IAS 16.

References

1 IFRS 5, *Non-current Assets Held for Sale and Discontinued Operations*, IASB, March 2004, para. 45.
2 IFRS 5, paras. IN2-IN3.
3 IFRS 5, para. IN4.
4 IFRS 5, para. IN5.
5 IFRS 5, paras. BC67-BC71.
6 IFRS 5, para. 1.
7 IFRS 5, paras. 2 and 5.
8 IFRS 5, para. 44.
9 IFRS 5, para. 43.
10 IFRS 1, *First-time Adoption of International Financial Reporting Standards*, IASB, 2006

Bound Volume International Financial Reporting Standards, para. 34B.
11 IFRS 5, Appendix A.
12 IFRS 5, para. 6.
13 IFRS 5, para. 4.
14 IFRS 5, Appendix A.
15 IFRS 5, para. 4.
16 IFRS 5, para. 6.
17 IFRS 5, para. 10.
18 IFRS 5, para. 2.
19 IFRS 5, para. 7.
20 IFRS 5, para. 13.
21 IFRS 5, para. 26.
22 IFRS 5, para. 11.
23 IFRS 5, para. 12.
24 IFRS 5, Implementation Guidance, Examples 1-3.
25 IFRS 5, Appendix A.
26 IAS 39, *Financial Instruments: Recognition and Measurement*, IASB, December 2003 (amended March 2004), para. F.3.7.
27 IFRS 5, para. 8.
28 IFRS 5, Implementation Guidance, Example 4.
29 IFRS 5, para. 9.
30 IFRS 5, Appendix B.
31 IFRS 5, Appendix A.
32 IFRS 5, Implementation Guidance, Example 5.
33 IFRS 5, Implementation Guidance, Example 6.
34 IFRS 5, Implementation Guidance, Example 7.
35 IFRS 5, para. 13.
36 IFRS 5, para. 13.
37 IFRS 5, para. 14.
38 IFRS 5, Implementation Guidance, Example 8.
39 IFRIC UPDATE, IFRIC, March 2007, p 3.
40 IASB UPDATE, IASB, July 2007, p 3.
41 IFRS 5, paras. 2 and 5.
42 IFRS 5, para. 18.
43 IFRS 5, para. 15.
44 IFRS 5, Appendix A.
45 IFRS 5, para. 17.
46 IFRS 5, para. 4.
47 IFRS 5, para. 16.
48 IFRS 5, Implementation Guidance, Example 13.
49 IFRS 5, para. 25.
50 IFRS 5, para. 19.
51 IFRS 5, para. 20.
52 IFRS 5, para. 21.
53 IFRS 5, para. 22.
54 IFRS 5, para. 23.
55 IFRS 5, Implementation Guidance, Example 10.
56 IFRS 5, para. 24.
57 IFRS 5, para. 30.
58 IFRS 5, paras. 38-39.
59 IFRS 5, para. BC58.
60 IFRS 5, Implementation Guidance, Example 12.
61 IFRS 5, para. 3.
62 IFRS 5, para. 26.
63 IFRS 5, para. 29.
64 IFRS 5, para. 27.
65 IFRS 5, Appendix A.
66 IFRS 5, paras. 28 and 37.
67 IFRS 5, para. 32 and Appendix A.
68 IFRS 5, para. 31 and Appendix A.
69 IFRS 5, Appendix A.
70 IFRS 5, paras. BC67-BC71.
71 IASB UPDATE, IASB, April 2007, page 3.
72 IASB UPDATE, IASB, January 2007, page 3.
73 IFRS 5, para. 13.
74 IFRS 5, para. 14.
75 IFRS 5, Implementation Guidance, Example 9.
76 IFRS 5, para. 33(a).
77 IFRS 5, para. 33(b).
78 IFRS 5, para. 37.
79 IFRS 5, para. 34.
80 IFRS 5, Implementation Guidance, Example 11.
81 IFRS 5, para. 35.
82 IFRS 5, para. 33(c).
83 IFRS 5, para. 34.
84 IFRS 5, para. 40.
85 IFRS 5, Implementation Guidance, Example 13.
86 IFRS 5, para. 28.
87 IFRS 5, para. 36.
88 IAS 28, *Investments in Associates*, IASB, December 2003 (amended March 2004), para. 15 and IAS 31, *Interests in Joint Ventures*, IASB, December 2003 (amend. March 2004), para. 43.
89 IFRS 5, para. 41.
90 IFRS 5, para. 12.
91 IFRS 5, para. 42.

Chapter 5 First-time adoption

1 INTRODUCTION

1.1 Background

IFRS 1 – *First-time Adoption of International Financial Reporting Standards* – is a unique standard. It owes its existence primarily to the 2005 adoption of IFRS by EU companies whose securities are traded on a EU regulated market.[1] Also, following the EU's lead, entities in many other jurisdictions will be required by their governments to adopt IFRS. It is the radically different nature of IFRS compared with many national GAAPs that necessitated IFRS 1.

Although entities are frequently required to adopt new accounting standards under their national GAAP, adopting IFRS, an entirely different basis of accounting, poses a distinct set of problems:

- the sheer magnitude of the effort involved in adopting a large number of new accounting standards;
- the requirements of individual standards will often differ significantly from those under an entity's previous GAAP;
- information may need to be collected that was not required under the previous GAAP; and
- practical experience of applying a principles-based system of financial reporting standards such as IFRS does not exist in many entities.

1.2 Development of IFRS 1

1.2.1 SIC-8

In 1997 the former IASC Board asked its Standing Interpretations Committee to address the issue of how first-time adopters should account for the transition to IFRS. This resulted, in July 1998, in the adoption of SIC-8 – *First-Time Application of IASs as the Primary Basis of Accounting*. SIC-8 required that 'in the period when IASs are applied in full for the first time as the primary accounting basis, the financial statements of an enterprise should be prepared and presented as if the financial statements had always been prepared in accordance with the Standards and

Interpretations effective for the period of first-time application.'[2] It became clear shortly after SIC-8 was issued that, although theoretically sound, the approach taken by the interpretation could give rise to substantial practical difficulties for entities adopting IFRS for the first time. For example, it required all prior business combinations to be restated on an IFRS basis, which would have been wholly impracticable.

1.2.2 The need for IFRS 1

The spotlight was placed firmly on first-time adoption of IFRS when the European Commission proposed to require all publicly traded EU incorporated companies to prepare their consolidated accounts under IFRS, by 2005 at the latest. After the IASB had been made aware of the considerable practical difficulties surrounding first-time application under SIC-8, it announced that it would undertake a separate project on this subject. Consequently, in July 2002, the IASB published ED 1 – *First-time Application of International Financial Reporting Standards*.[3] The Board made significant changes to the exposure draft before finalising it in June 2003 as IFRS 1 – *First-time Adoption of International Financial Reporting Standards*.

In the introduction to the standard, the IASB cites the following reasons for replacing SIC-8 by IFRS 1:[4]

- SIC-8 required full retrospective application that could cause costs that exceeded the likely benefits for users of financial statements;
- although SIC-8 did not require retrospective application when this would be impracticable, it did not define 'impracticable' leaving it unclear whether it should be interpreted as a high hurdle or a low hurdle;
- SIC-8 could require a first-time adopter to apply two different versions of a Standard if a new version were introduced during the periods covered by its first financial statements prepared under IASs and the new version prohibited retrospective application;
- SIC-8 did not state clearly whether a first-time adopter should use hindsight in applying recognition and measurement decisions retrospectively; and
- there was some doubt about how SIC-8 interacted with specific transitional provisions in individual Standards.

IFRS 1 offers many significant improvements over SIC-8, but it also has a number of weaknesses. Firstly, given the IASB's worldwide constituency, IFRS 1 had to be written in a way that completely ignores a first-time adopter's previous GAAP. One of the IASB's aims in developing IFRS 1 was 'to find solutions that will be appropriate for any entity, in any part of the world, regardless of whether adoption occurs in 2005 or at a different time'.[5] Consequently, first-time adoption exemptions are made available to all first-time adopters, even those first-time adopters whose previous GAAP was very close to IFRS. A first-time adopter will be able to make considerable adjustments to its opening IFRS balance sheet, using the available exemptions in IFRS 1, even if the difference between its previous GAAP and IFRS was only minor. It may even be required to make considerable adjustments due to the exemptions and exceptions.

Secondly, in its basis for conclusions, the IASB notes that ideally a regime for the first-time adoption of IFRS would achieve comparability between the financial statements of an entity over time, between different first-time adopters, and between first-time adopters and entities already applying IFRS.[6] SIC-8 gave priority to ensuring comparability between a first-time adopter and entities already reporting under IFRS. Inevitably there are tensions between these objectives, and IFRS 1 gives priority to achieving 'comparability over time within a first-time adopter's first IFRS financial statements and between different entities adopting IFRS for the first time at a given date; achieving comparability between first-time adopters and entities that already apply IFRS is a secondary objective.'[7]

1.2.3 Amendments to IFRS 1

When it issues a new IFRS, the IASB considers whether a first-time adopter should apply that IFRS retrospectively or prospectively. In the limited number of cases that the IASB considers prospective application more appropriate it will amend IFRS 1.[8] Furthermore, the IASB also amended IFRS 1 to introduce a special first-time adoption regime for IAS 32 – *Financial Instruments: Disclosure and Presentation*,[9] IAS 39 – *Financial Instruments: Recognition and Measurement* – and IFRS 4 – *Insurance Contracts* (see 2.6.1 below).

The IASB's desire to ensure that IFRS 1 comprises all first-time adoption rules has meant that IFRS 1 has been amended by standards and interpretations that the Board has subsequently issued. This approach always carried the risk that its complexity might eventually overwhelm its practical application. Therefore, it was perhaps not surprising when the Board directed its staff in February 2007 to draft a restructured version of IFRS 1 to deal with the issues arising from the fact that 'IFRS 1 has been amended several times to accommodate first-time adoption requirements resulting from new standards or amendments to standards. Because of the way IFRS 1 is structured, such amendments are making the standard more complex and less clear. As more amendments become necessary, this problem will become worse.'[10]

The detailed requirements of the standard are discussed below. The practical application of the standard is illustrated by worked examples throughout this chapter, by comprehensive extracts from the financial statements of a number of companies applying IFRS 1 and by a discussion of practical issues at 3 below.

2 REQUIREMENTS OF IFRS 1

2.1 Objective

The underlying principle in IFRS 1 is that a first-time adopter should prepare financial statements as if it had always applied IFRS, but there are a number of exemptions and exceptions that allow or require a first-time adopter to deviate from the general rule. The objective of IFRS 1 is to ensure that an entity's first IFRS financial statements and its first IFRS interim financial statements contain high quality financial information that:[11]

(a) is transparent for users and comparable over all periods presented;

(b) provides a suitable starting point for accounting under IFRS; and

(c) can be generated at a cost that does not exceed the benefits to users.

2.2 Scope and definitions

2.2.1 *What counts as first-time adoption?*

Clearly, given the differing regimes applicable to first-time adopters and entities already using IFRS, what counts as first-time adoption is a question of some importance. The standard defines an entity's first IFRS financial statements as being the first annual financial statements in which an entity adopts IFRS by an 'explicit and unreserved statement' of compliance with IFRS in those financial statements.[12] The decisive factor is whether or not the entity made that explicit and unreserved statement. An entity is *not* considered to be a first-time adopter if it departed from certain IFRS (whether recognition, measurement or disclosure) in its previous financial statements but still made an explicit and unreserved statement of compliance. Accordingly, such an entity is not allowed to apply IFRS 1 in accounting for changes in its accounting policies. Instead, it is required to apply IAS 8 – *Accounting Policies, Changes in Accounting Estimates and Errors* – in making any corrections or changes.

IFRS 1 states that an entity's first IFRS financial statements will be subject to IFRS 1 even if it presented its most recent previous financial statements in conformity with IFRS in all respects except that they did not contain an explicit and unreserved statement.[13] An entity's financial statements are considered its first IFRS financial statements, and thus fall within the scope of IFRS 1, when it:

'(a) presented its most recent previous financial statements:
  - (i) under national requirements that are not consistent with IFRSs in all respects;
  - (ii) in conformity with IFRSs in all respects, except that the financial statements did not contain an explicit and unreserved statement that they complied with IFRSs;
  - (iii) containing an explicit statement of compliance with some, but not all, IFRSs;
  - (iv) under national requirements inconsistent with IFRSs, using some individual IFRSs to account for items for which national requirements did not exist; or
  - (v) under national requirements, with a reconciliation of some amounts to the amounts determined under IFRSs;

(b) prepared financial statements under IFRSs for internal use only, without making them available to the entity's owners or any other external users;

(c) prepared a reporting package under IFRSs for consolidation purposes without preparing a complete set of financial statements as defined in IAS 1 – *Presentation of Financial Statements*; or

(d) did not present financial statements for previous periods.'[14]

Therefore, an entity whose most recent previous financial statements contained an explicit and unreserved statement of compliance with IFRS can never be considered a first-time adopter. This is the case even in the following circumstances:

(a) the entity issued financial statements claiming to comply both with national GAAP and IFRS, and subsequently drops the national GAAP compliance claim; or

(b) the entity issued financial statements containing an explicit and unreserved statement of compliance with IFRS despite the fact that the auditors issued a qualified audit report on those IFRS financial statements; or

(c) the entity stops presenting a separate set of financial statements under national requirements.[15]

The IASB could have introduced special rules that would have required an entity that significantly departed from IFRS to apply IFRS 1. However, the IASB considered that such rules would lead to 'complexity and uncertainty'.[16] In addition, this would have given entities applying 'IFRS-lite' (i.e. entities not applying IFRS rigorously in all respects) an option to side step the requirements of IAS 8.[17]

It is clear that the scope of IFRS 1 is very much rule-based, which, as the example below illustrates, can lead to different answers in similar situations and sometimes to counter-intuitive answers.

Example 5.1: Scope of application of IFRS 1

Entity A applied IFRS in its previous financial statements, but stated that it 'applied IFRS except for SIC-12 – *Consolidation – Special Purpose Entities.*'

Entity A is a first-time adopter because its financial statements did not contain an unreserved statement of compliance with IFRS. It is irrelevant whether the auditors' report was qualified or not.

Entity B applied IFRS in its previous financial statements and stated that the 'financial statements are prepared in conformity with IFRS.' Despite that statement, B had not applied SIC-12.

Entity B is not a first-time adopter because its financial statements contained an unreserved statement of compliance with IFRS. Even if the auditors had qualified their report, the entity would still not be a first-time adopter.

Example 5.2: Entity applying national GAAP and IFRS

Entity C prepares two sets of financial statements, one set of financial statements based on its national GAAP and the other set based on IFRS. The IFRS financial statements contained an explicit and unreserved statement of compliance with IFRS and were made available externally. From 2007 onwards, C stops presenting financial statements based on its national GAAP.

Entity C is not a first-time adopter because it already published financial statements that contained an explicit and unreserved statement of compliance with IFRS.

Example 5.3: Entity not applying IFRS for one year

Entity D prepared IFRS financial statements in 2005 and 2006 that contained an unreserved statement of compliance with IFRS. However, in 2007 Entity D did not make an unreserved statement of compliance with IFRS.

Entity D would be considered a first-time adopter for the purposes of its 2008 financial statements because its most recent financial statements did not contain an unreserved statement of compliance with IFRS. This is the case even though Entity D produced IFRS financial statements prior to 2007.

An entity that is not a first-time adopter cannot apply IFRS 1 to changes in its accounting policies. Instead, such an entity should apply:

- the requirements of IAS 8; and
- specific transitional requirements in other IFRS.[18]

2.2.2 When should IFRS 1 be applied?

An entity that presents its first IFRS financial statements is a first-time adopter[19] and should apply IFRS 1 in preparing those financial statements.[20] It should also apply the standard in each interim financial report that it presents under IAS 34 – *Interim Financial Reporting* – for a part of the period covered by its first IFRS financial statements.[21] However, a first-time adopter that only issues a 'trading statement' at its interim reporting dates, which is not described as complying with IAS 34 or IFRS, is not required to apply IAS 34.[22] Therefore, IFRS 1 does not apply to such interim reports.

2.2.3 First-time adoption timeline

IFRS 1 defines the following terms in connection with the transition to IFRS:[23]

Date of transition to IFRS: The beginning of the earliest period for which an entity presents full comparative information under IFRS in its first IFRS financial statements.

Reporting date: The end of the latest period covered by financial statements or by an interim financial report.

First IFRS financial statements: The first annual financial statements in which an entity adopts International Financial Reporting Standards, by an explicit and unreserved statement of compliance with IFRS.

First IFRS reporting period: The reporting period ending on the reporting date of an entity's first IFRS financial statements.

Opening IFRS balance sheet: An entity's balance sheet (published or unpublished) at the date of transition to IFRS.

International Financial Reporting Standards: Standards and Interpretations adopted by the International Accounting Standards Board (IASB). They comprise:

(a) International Financial Reporting Standards;

(b) International Accounting Standards; and

(c) Interpretations originated by the International Financial Reporting Interpretations Committee (IFRIC) or the former Standing Interpretations Committee (SIC).

Previous GAAP: The basis of accounting that a first-time adopter used immediately before adopting IFRS.

An entity's first IFRS financial statements must include at least one comparative period, but an entity may elect or be required to provide more than one comparative period.[24] The beginning of the earliest comparative period for which the entity presents full comparative information under IFRS will be treated as its date of transition to IFRS. The diagram below shows how for an entity with a December year-end the above terms are related:

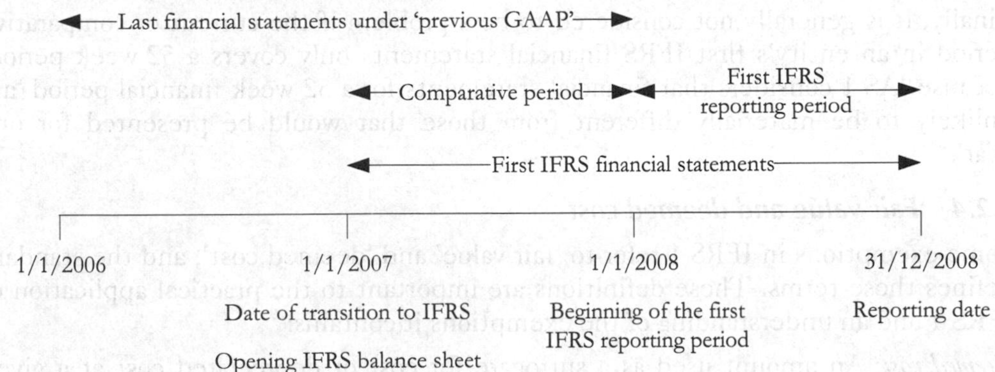

The diagram above also illustrates that there is a period of overlap, for the financial year 2007, which is reported first under the entity's previous GAAP and then as a comparative period under IFRS. The following examples illustrate how an entity should determine its date of transition to IFRS.

Example 5.4: Determining the date of transition to IFRS

Entity D's year-end is 31 December and it presents financial statements that include one comparative period. D is required to produce IFRS financial statements for the first accounting period starting on or after 1 January 2008.

D's first reporting date under IFRS is 31 December 2008. Its date of transition to IFRS is 1 January 2007, which is the beginning of the first comparative period included in its IFRS financial statements.

Entity E's year-end is 31 July and it presents financial statements that include two comparative periods. E is required to produce IFRS financial statements for the first accounting period starting on or after 1 January 2008.

E's first reporting date under IFRS is 31 July 2009. Its date of transition to IFRS is 1 August 2006, which is the beginning of the first comparative period included in its IFRS financial statements.

IFRS 1 does not specifically address how these requirements apply to an entity whose current or comparative financial period is not exactly equal to one year. Paragraph 36 of IFRS 1 states that in order to comply with the requirements of IAS 1, an entity's first IFRS financial statements should include 'at least one year of comparative information under IFRSs.'[25] However, IAS 1 itself only requires disclosure of comparative information 'in respect of the previous period for all amounts reported in the financial statements.'[26] The difference in the drafting appears to be inadvertent as the IASB decided that a first-time adopter need not 'present more comparative information than IAS 1 requires, because such a requirement would impose costs out of proportion to the benefits to users, and increase the risk that preparers might need to make arbitrary assumptions in applying hindsight.'[27] In our view, as IAS 1 does not require the comparative period to be exactly one year when an entity changes its financial reporting period, it logically follows that the same applies to a comparative period presented by a first-time adopter. Thus, the entity's date of transition will be the beginning of the comparative period, irrespective of the length of that period.

Finally, it is generally not considered to be a problem if the current or comparative period in an entity's first IFRS financial statements only covers a 52 week period, because IAS 1 considers that financial statements for a 52 week financial period 'are unlikely to be materially different from those that would be presented for one year'.[28]

2.2.4 *Fair value and deemed cost*

Some exemptions in IFRS 1 refer to 'fair value' and 'deemed cost', and the standard defines these terms. These definitions are important to the practical application of IFRS 1 and an understanding of the exemptions it contains:[29]

Deemed cost: An amount used as a surrogate for cost or depreciated cost at a given date. Subsequent depreciation or amortisation assumes that the entity had initially recognised the asset or liability at the given date and that its cost was equal to the deemed cost.

Fair value: The amount for which an asset could be exchanged, or a liability settled, between knowledgeable, willing parties in an arm's length transaction.

In determining the fair value of items, a first-time adopter should use the guidance in IFRS 3 – *Business Combinations* (see Chapter 7) unless 'another IFRS contains more specific guidance on the determination of fair values for the asset or liability in question'. The fair values determined by a first-time adopter should reflect the conditions that existed at the date for which they were determined,[30] i.e. the first-time adopter should not apply hindsight in measuring the fair value at an earlier date (see Chapter 7 at 2.3.3).

2.3 Recognition and measurement principles

2.3.1 *Opening IFRS balance sheet and accounting policies*

At the date of transition to IFRS (e.g. 1 January 2007 for an entity presenting one year of comparative figures and reporting at 31 December 2008) an entity should prepare an opening IFRS balance sheet that is the starting point for its accounting under IFRS. This opening balance sheet does not have to be published in the first IFRS financial statements.[31] In practice, the opening balance sheet is often presented as it is required for, and integral to, the equity reconciliation that has to be presented in an entity's first IFRS financial statements (see 2.10.2 below).

The requirement to prepare an opening IFRS balance sheet and 'reset the clock' at that date poses a number of challenges for first-time adopters. Even a first-time adopter that already applies a standard that is directly based on IFRS may need to restate items in its opening IFRS balance sheet. This happens, for example, in the case of an entity applying a pensions standard that is based on IAS 19 – *Employee Benefits* – before an entity's date of transition to IFRS (see 2.7.1 below).

With the exception of financial instruments and insurance contracts (see 2.6.1 below), IFRS 1 requires a first-time adopter to use the same accounting policies in its opening IFRS balance sheet and all periods presented in its first IFRS financial statements. However, this will not happen quite so straightforwardly, since to achieve this, the entity should comply with each IFRS effective at the reporting date for its first IFRS financial statements, and should take into account a number of exemptions from certain IFRS and exceptions to retrospective application of other IFRS allowed by IFRS 1 (see 2.3.3 below).[32] In other words, the fundamental principle of IFRS 1 is to require full retrospective application of the standards in force at an entity's reporting date, but with limited exceptions. The IASB initially entertained a suggestion to restrict retrospective application of IFRS to a limited 'look back' period of three to five years – to avoid the cost of investigating very old transactions – but concluded that this approach could lead to the omission of material assets or liabilities from an entity's opening IFRS balance sheet.[33] The diagram below shows how the process of selecting IFRS accounting policies operates.

The requirement to apply the same accounting policies to all periods also prohibits a first-time adopter from applying previous versions of standards that were effective at earlier dates.[34] The IASB believes that this:

- enhances comparability because the first IFRS financial statements are prepared on a consistent basis over time;
- gives users comparative information that is based on IFRS that are superior to superseded versions of those standards; and
- avoids unnecessary costs.[35]

For similar reasons, IFRS 1 also permits an entity to apply a new IFRS that is not yet mandatory if that standard allows early application.[36] Users of financial statements should be aware that, depending on an entity's reporting date, it may or may not have the option to choose which version of a particular standard it may apply, as can be seen in the example below.

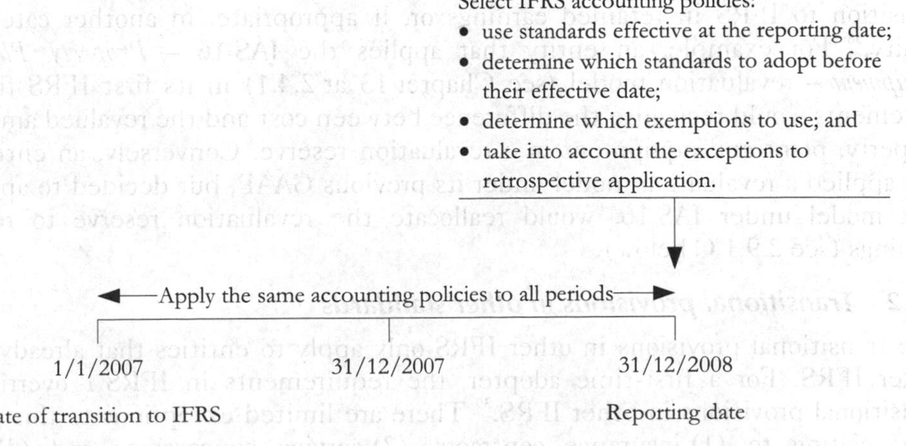

Example 5.5: Prohibition from applying superseded IFRS

Entity F's date of transition to IFRS is 1 January 2003 and its first reporting date under IFRS is 31 December 2005. Should F apply IAS 35 – *Discontinuing Operations* – in its first comparative period or should it apply IFRS 5 – *Non-current Assets Held for Sale and Discontinued Operations* – to all periods presented?

IFRS 1 prohibits F from applying IAS 35 in its first IFRS financial statements because IFRS 5, which is only effective for financial periods starting on or after 1 January 2005, is effective at its first IFRS reporting date. However, the transitional provisions of IFRS 5 only permit earlier application provided that the valuations and other information needed to apply the standard were obtained contemporaneously. Consequently F would not need to apply IAS 35 or IFRS 5 in 2003 or 2004.

Entity G's date of transition to IFRS is 1 January 2007 and its first reporting date under IFRS is 31 December 2008. Should G make segmental information disclosures under IAS 14 – *Segment Reporting* – or IFRS 8 – *Operating Segments* – in its first IFRS financial statements?

IFRS 1 allows G to disclose the information required by IAS 14. IFRS 1 also allows G to disclose the information required by IFRS 8 because although it is only mandatory for periods starting on or after 1 January 2009, that standard also permits early application. However, IFRS 1 prohibits an entity from applying IAS 14 in 2007 while applying IFRS 8 in 2008.

Apart from when the exceptions at 2.3.3 below apply, an entity should in preparing its opening IFRS balance sheet:

'(a) recognise all assets and liabilities whose recognition is required by IFRSs;

(b) not recognise items as assets or liabilities if IFRSs do not permit such recognition;

(c) reclassify items that it recognised under previous GAAP as one type of asset, liability or component of equity, but are a different type of asset, liability or component of equity under IFRSs; and

(d) apply IFRSs in measuring all recognised assets and liabilities.'[37]

Any change in accounting policies on adoption of IFRS may cause changes in the amounts previously recorded in respect of events and transactions that occurred before the date of transition. These adjustments should be recognised at the date of transition to IFRS in retained earnings or, if appropriate, in another category of equity.[38] For example, an entity that applies the IAS 16 – *Property, Plant and Equipment* – revaluation model (see Chapter 13 at 2.4.1) in its first IFRS financial statements would recognise the difference between cost and the revalued amount of property, plant and equipment in a revaluation reserve. Conversely, an entity that had applied a revaluation model under its previous GAAP, but decided to apply the cost model under IAS 16, would reallocate the revaluation reserve to retained earnings (see 2.9.1 C below).

2.3.2 *Transitional provisions in other standards*

The transitional provisions in other IFRS only apply to entities that already report under IFRS. For a first-time adopter, the requirements in IFRS 1 override the transitional provisions in other IFRS.[39] There are limited exceptions to this general rule relating to (1) insurance contracts, (2) service concessions and (3) assets classified as held for sale and discontinued operations. In these cases IFRS 1 specifically requires application of the transitional rules in the relevant IFRS (see 2.7.4, 2.7.6 and 2.8.2 below). It is important to note that the transition rules for first-time adopters and entities that already report under IFRS may differ significantly.

2.3.3 Departures from full retrospective application of IFRS

The IASB's *Framework* recognises the necessity to balance the cost and benefit of information as a constraint that may limit the provision of relevant and reliable information in financial reporting.[40] In developing IFRS 1 the IASB specifically considered this cost-benefit constraint, which resulted in a number of exceptions from the general principle of retrospective application. It is worthwhile noting that the IASB 'expects that most first-time adopters will begin planning on a timely basis for the transition to IFRSs. Accordingly, in balancing benefits and costs, the Board took as its benchmark an entity that plans the transition well in advance and can collect most information needed for its opening IFRS balance sheet at, or very soon after, the date of transition to IFRSs.'[41]

IFRS 1 establishes two types of departure from the principle of full retrospective application of standards in force at the first reporting date under IFRS:[42]

- it allows a number of optional exemptions from some of the requirements of certain IFRS;[43] and
- it requires a number of mandatory exceptions from the requirement for the retrospective application of other IFRS.[44]

A Optional exemptions from the requirements of certain IFRS

IFRS 1 grants limited *exemptions* from the general requirement of full retrospective application of the standards in force at an entity's reporting date 'where the cost of complying with them would be likely to exceed the benefits to users of financial statements.'[45] The standard establishes exemptions in relation to:[46]

(a) business combinations (see 2.4 below);

(b) the use of fair value or revaluation as deemed cost of property, plant and equipment, investment properties and certain intangible assets (see 2.5 below);

(c) financial instruments:
- restatement of comparative information (see 2.6.1 below);
- designation of previously recognised financial instruments (see 2.6.2 below);
- compound financial instruments (see 2.6.3 below);
- fair value measurement of financial assets or financial liabilities at initial recognition (see 2.6.6 below);

(d) employee benefits (see 2.7.1 below);

(e) cumulative translation differences (see 2.7.2 below);

(f) share-based payment transactions (see 2.7.3 below);

(g) insurance contracts (see 2.7.4 below);

(h) assets and liabilities of subsidiaries, associates and joint ventures (see 2.7.5 below). Some commentators have argued that this is not really an exemption, because it is not optional and actually requires a parent to use the IFRS measurements already used in a subsidiary's separate IFRS financial statements;

(i) service concessions (see 2.7.6 below);

(j) decommissioning liabilities included in the cost of property, plant and equipment (see 2.9.1.D below);

(k) leases (see 2.9.2 below);

(l) comparative information for IFRS 6 – *Exploration for and Evaluation of Mineral Resources* (see 2.9.8 below); and

(m) borrowing costs (see 2.9.7 below).

It is specifically prohibited under IFRS 1 to apply these exemptions by analogy to other items.[47]

Application of these exemptions is entirely optional, i.e. a first-time adopter can pick and choose the exemptions that it wants to apply. Importantly, the IASB did not establish a hierarchy of exemptions. Therefore, when an item is covered by more than one exemption, a first-time adopter has a free choice in determining the order in which it applies the exemptions.

Example 5.6: Order of application of exemptions

Entity H acquired a building in a business combination. If H applied the business combinations exemption it would have to value the building at €120. However, if it used fair value as the deemed cost of the building it would have to value it at €150. Which value should H use?

H can choose whether it wants to value the building at €120 or €150 in its opening IFRS balance sheet. The fact that H uses the business combinations exemption does not prohibit it from applying the 'fair value as deemed cost' exemption in relation to the same assets.

B Exceptions to retrospective application of other IFRS

In addition to the optional *exemptions* discussed above, IFRS 1 also defines a number of mandatory *exceptions* that prohibit 'retrospective application of IFRSs in some areas, particularly where retrospective application would require judgements by management about past conditions after the outcome of a particular transaction is already known.'[48] The mandatory *exceptions* in the standard cover the following situations:[49]

(a) financial instruments:

- derecognition of financial assets and financial liabilities (see 2.6.4 below);
- hedge accounting (see 2.6.5 below);

(b) estimates (see 2.8.1 below); and

(c) assets classified as held for sale and discontinued operations (see 2.8.2 below).

The reasoning behind these exceptions is that retrospective application of IFRS in these situations could easily result in an unacceptable use of hindsight and lead to arbitrary or biased restatements, which would be neither relevant nor reliable.

2.4 Business combinations exemption

The business combinations exemption in IFRS 1 is probably the single most important exemption in the standard, as it permits a first-time adopter not to restate business combinations prior to its date of transition to IFRS. The detailed guidance on the application of the business combinations exemption is contained in a separate appendix to IFRS 1 and is described below.[50]

2.4.1 Option to restate business combinations retrospectively

A first-time adopter must account for business combinations after its date of transition to IFRS under IFRS 3 (see Chapter 7). Thus, any business combinations during the comparative periods presented by an entity will need to be restated in accordance with the standard. An entity may elect not to apply IFRS 3 to any business combination before the date of transition, but may do so if it so chooses. However, if a first-time adopter restates any business combination prior to its date of transition to comply with IFRS 3 it must also restate all subsequent business combinations under IFRS 3 and apply both IAS 36 (revised 2004) – *Impairment of Assets* – and IAS 38 (revised 2004) – *Intangible Assets* – from that date onwards.[51] In other words, as shown on the time line below, a first-time adopter is allowed to choose any date in the past and account for business combinations going forward under IFRS 3 without having to restate business combinations prior to the earliest IFRS 3 restatement.

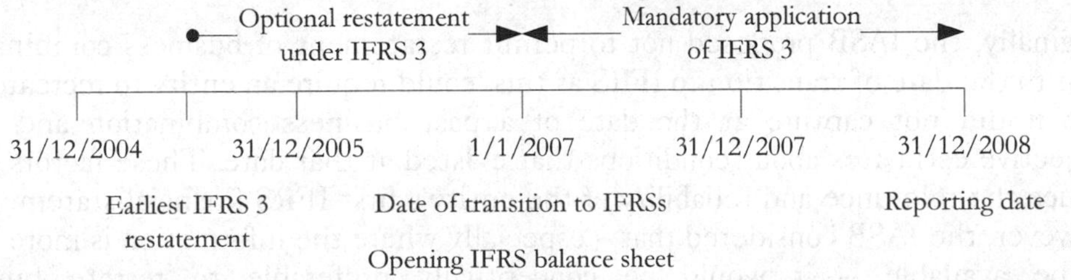

This exemption for past business combinations applies also to past acquisitions of associates and interests in joint ventures. However, it is important to note that the date selected for the first restatement of business combinations should also be applied to the restatement of acquisitions of associates and interests in joint ventures.[52]

This leaves the question of whether the exemption for past business combinations also covers acquisitions of minority interests that have been accounted for under previous GAAP. Restatement of such transactions is likely to be highly impracticable for the same reasons that requiring restatement of past business combinations would be impracticable. Therefore, in our opinion, had the Board explicitly considered this transitional issue, it would have given an exemption from the requirement to restate. Accordingly, in our view, a first-time adopter is not required to restate acquisitions of minority interests which have been accounted for under previous GAAP. However, a first-time adopter could restate the previous accounting, if it so wished, by applying the policy adopted under IFRS for the accounting of minority interests (see Chapter 7 at 2.3.7 A).

Extract 5.1 and Extracts 5.5 and 5.6 at 2.10.2 below illustrate the typical disclosure made by entities that opted not to restate business combinations before their date of transition to IFRS.

Extract 5.1: HSBC Holdings plc (2005)

Notes on the Financial Statements [extract]

1 **Basis of preparation** [extract]

In accordance with IFRS 1, HSBC has chosen not to restate business combinations that took place prior to 1 January 2004, the date of transition to IFRSs.

46 **Transition to IFRSs** [extract]

(a) Transitional exemptions [extract]

(i) Business combinations

HSBC has elected not to restate business combinations that took place prior to the 1 January 2004 transition date. Had this exemption not been taken the main effects would have been to recognise additional deferred tax on fair value adjustments made at the date of acquisition and to recognise additional intangible assets with consequential adjustments to the carrying value of goodwill and retained earnings as at 1 January 2004.

The recognition of additional intangibles with a definite life would have given rise to an increased amortisation charge, which would have reduced IFRSs net income prospectively with a consequential reduction in total shareholders' equity. The restatement of goodwill would have had no impact on prospective net income unless it was written off following a subsequent impairment review.

Originally, the IASB proposed not to permit restatement of business combinations prior to the date of transition to IFRS as this 'could require an entity to recreate data that it did not capture at the date of a past business combination and make subjective estimates about conditions that existed at that date. These factors could reduce the relevance and reliability of the entity's first IFRS financial statements.'[53] However, the IASB considered that – especially where the information is more likely to be available – it would be conceptually preferable to restate business combinations as the 'effects of business combination accounting can last for many years' and 'previous GAAP may differ significantly from IFRS.'[54] Therefore, the IASB concluded that although it could not require restatement of business combinations for cost-benefit reasons, it should at least permit restatement on condition that all subsequent business combinations are also restated.[55]

It is remarkable that availability of reliable contemporaneous information necessary for the application of IFRS 3 is not an explicit condition for retrospective application of IFRS 3 by first-time adopters; especially because this was a condition that existing IFRS-reporting entities had to meet.[56] In our opinion, a first-time adopter should not restate business combinations before the date of transition when this would require undue use of hindsight, even though this is not specifically prohibited.

2.4.2 Classification of business combinations

IFRS 3 mandates that business combinations should be accounted for as acquisitions or reverse acquisitions. An entity's previous GAAP may be based on a different definition of, for example, a business combination, an acquisition, a merger and a reverse acquisition. An important benefit of the business combinations exemption is that a first-time adopter will not have to determine the classification of past business combinations in accordance with IFRS 3.[57] For example, a transaction that was accounted for as a merger or uniting of interests using the pooling-of-interests method under an entity's previous GAAP will not have to be reclassified and accounted for under the IFRS 3 purchase method. However, an entity may still elect to do so if it so wishes – subject, of course, to the conditions set out under 2.4.1 above.

The business combinations exemption applies only to 'business combinations that the entity recognised before the date of transition to IFRSs.'[58] Consequently, the business combinations exemption does not apply to a transaction that IFRS considers to be an acquisition of an asset. First-time adopters will therefore have to consider whether past transactions would qualify as business combinations under IFRS, which are defined as 'the bringing together of separate entities or businesses into one reporting entity.'[59] A business is defined as follows:[60]

> 'An integrated set of activities and assets conducted and managed for the purpose of providing:
>
> (a) a return to investors; or
>
> (b) lower costs or other economic benefits directly and proportionately to policyholders or participants. A business generally consists of inputs, processes applied to those inputs, and resulting outputs that are, or will be, used to generate revenues. If goodwill is present in a transferred set of activities and assets, the transferred set shall be presumed to be a business.'

Furthermore, IFRS 3 states that 'if an entity obtains control of one or more other entities that are not businesses, the bringing together of those entities is not a business combination.'[61] Therefore, it is possible that under some national GAAPs, transactions that are not business combinations under IFRS 3, such as asset purchases, may have been accounted for as if they were business combinations. A first-time adopter will need to restate any transactions that it accounted for as business combinations under its previous GAAP, but which are not business combinations under IFRS.

Example 5.7: Acquisition of an asset

Entity J acquired a holding company that held several assets at the time of acquisition. That holding company had no employees and the asset itself was not in use at the date of acquisition. J accounted for the transaction under its previous GAAP using the purchase method, which resulted in goodwill. Can J apply the business combinations exemption to the acquisition of these assets?

If J concludes that the asset is not a business as defined in IFRS 3, it will not be able to apply the business combinations exemption to the acquisition of the asset. Instead, it should apply the guidance in paragraph 4 of IFRS 3, which requires it to allocate the cost 'between the individual identifiable assets and liabilities in the group based on their relative fair values at the date of acquisition'.[62]

2.4.3 Recognition and measurement of assets and liabilities

A Derecognition of assets and liabilities

A first-time adopter should exclude from its opening IFRS balance sheet any items it recognised under its previous GAAP that do not qualify for recognition as an asset or liability under IFRS. If the first-time adopter previously recognised an intangible asset, as part of a business combination, that does not qualify for recognition as an asset under IAS 38, it should reclassify that item and the related deferred tax and minority interests as part of goodwill (unless it previously deducted goodwill directly from equity under its previous GAAP) (see 2.4.4 below). All other changes resulting from derecognition of such assets and liabilities should be accounted for as adjustments of retained earnings.[63]

B Recognition of assets and liabilities

In its opening IFRS balance sheet, a first-time adopter should recognise all assets and liabilities that were acquired or assumed in a past business combination, with the exception of:

- certain financial assets and liabilities that were derecognised and that fall under the derecognition exception (see 2.6.4 below); and
- assets (including goodwill) and liabilities that were not recognised in the acquirer's consolidated balance sheet under its previous GAAP that would not qualify for recognition under IFRS in the separate balance sheet of the acquiree (see Example 5.13 below).[64]

The change resulting from the recognition of such assets and liabilities should be accounted for as an adjustment of retained earnings or another category of equity, if appropriate. However, if the change results from the recognition of an intangible asset that was previously subsumed in goodwill, it should be accounted for as an adjustment of that goodwill (see 2.4.4 A below).[65] As indicated at E below, the recognition of such intangibles will be rare.

The following examples, which are based on the guidance on implementation of IFRS 1, illustrate how a first-time adopter would apply these requirements. Further examples can be found at 2.4.3 E below.

Example 5.8: Finance lease not capitalised under previous GAAP[66]

Background

Parent L's date of transition to IFRS is 1 January 2007. Parent L acquired subsidiary M on 15 January 2004 and did not capitalise subsidiary M's finance leases. If subsidiary M prepared separate financial statements under IFRS, it would recognise finance lease obligations of 300 and leased assets of 250 at 1 January 2007.

Application of requirements

In its consolidated opening IFRS balance sheet, parent L recognises finance lease obligations of 300 and leased assets of 250, and charges 50 to retained earnings.

Example 5.9: Restructuring provision[67]

Background

Entity D's first IFRS financial statements have a reporting date of 31 December 2008 and include comparative information for 2007 only. It chooses not to restate previous business combinations for IFRS 3. On 1 July 2006, entity D acquired 100 per cent of subsidiary E. Under its previous GAAP, entity D recognised an (undiscounted) restructuring provision of 100 that would not have qualified as an identifiable liability under IFRS 3. The recognition of this restructuring provision increased goodwill by 100. At 31 December 2006 (date of transition to IFRSs), entity D:

(a) had paid restructuring costs of 60; and

(b) estimated that it would pay further costs of 40 in 2007, and that the effects of discounting were immaterial. At 31 December 2006, those further costs did not qualify for recognition as a provision under IAS 37 – *Provisions, Contingent Liabilities and Contingent Assets.*

Application of requirements

In its opening IFRS balance sheet, entity D:

(a) does not recognise a restructuring provision.

(b) does not adjust the amount assigned to goodwill. However, entity D tests the goodwill for impairment under IAS 36, and recognises any resulting impairment loss.

(c) as a result of (a) and (b), reports retained earnings in its opening IFRS balance sheet that are higher by 40 (before income taxes, and before recognising any impairment loss) than in the balance sheet at the same date under previous GAAP.

C Subsequent measurement under IFRS not based on cost

IFRS requires subsequent measurement of some assets and liabilities on a basis other than original cost, such as fair value. When a first-time adopter does not apply IFRS 3 retrospectively to a business combination, such assets and liabilities must be measured on that other basis in its opening IFRS balance sheet. Any change in the carrying amount of those assets and liabilities should be accounted for as an adjustment of retained earnings, or other appropriate category of equity, rather than as an adjustment of goodwill.[68]

Example 5.10: Items not measured at original cost

Entity K acquired in a business combination a trading portfolio of equity securities and a number of investment properties. Under its previous GAAP, K initially measured these assets at cost (i.e. their fair value at the date of acquisition).

Upon adoption of IFRS, K measures the trading portfolio of equity securities and the investment properties (under the IAS 40 – *Investment Properties* – fair value model) at fair value in its opening IFRS balance sheet. The resulting adjustment to these assets at the date of transition is reflected in retained earnings.

D Subsequent measurement on a cost basis under IFRS

For assets and liabilities that are accounted for on a cost basis under IFRS, the standard stipulates that 'immediately after the business combination, the carrying amount under previous GAAP, of assets acquired and liabilities assumed in that business combination shall be their deemed cost under IFRSs at that date. If IFRSs require a cost-based measurement of those assets and liabilities at a later date, that deemed cost shall be the basis for cost-based depreciation or amortisation from the date of the business combination.'[69]

The standard does not specifically define 'immediately after a business combination', but it is commonly understood that this takes account of the completion of purchase accounting. In other words, a first-time adopter would not use the provisionally determined fair values of assets acquired and liabilities assumed.

Example 5.11: Provisionally determined fair values

Parent A acquired subsidiary B in August 2006 and made a provisional assessment of subsidiary B's identifiable net assets in its 31 December 2006 consolidated financial statements under its previous GAAP. In its 31 December 2007 consolidated financial statements – its last financial statements under previous GAAP – parent A completed the initial accounting for the business combination and adjusted the provisional values of the identifiable net assets and the corresponding goodwill. Upon first-time adoption of IFRS, parent A elects not to restate past business combinations.

In preparing its opening IFRS balance sheet, parent A should use the adjusted carrying amounts of the identifiable net assets as determined in its 2007 financial statements rather than the provisional carrying amounts of the identifiable net assets and goodwill at 31 December 2006.

IFRS 1 is silent as to whether the relevant carrying amounts of the identifiable net assets and goodwill are those that appeared in the financial statements drawn up immediately before the transition date (31 December 2006 in this case) or any restated balance appearing in a later set of previous GAAP accounts. Since the adjustments that were made under previous GAAP effectively resulted in a restatement of the balances at the transition date in a manner that is consistent with the approach permitted by IFRS 3, it is in our opinion appropriate to reflect those adjustments in the opening IFRS balance sheet. Since the adjustments are effectively made as at the transition date it is also appropriate to use the window period permitted by previous GAAP provided that this does not extend into the first IFRS reporting period since any restatements in that period can only be made in accordance with IFRS 3.

In effect, the phrase 'immediately after the business combination' in paragraph B2(e) of IFRS 1 should be interpreted as including a window period that ends at the earlier of the end of the window period allowed by the previous GAAP and the beginning of the first IFRS reporting period.

Cost basis, being based on previous GAAP, might be considered as inconsistent with the requirements of IFRS for assets and liabilities that were *not* acquired in a business combination. However, the IASB did not identify any situations in which 'it would not be acceptable to bring forward cost-based measurements made under previous GAAP.'[70]

Example 5.12: Items measured on a cost basis

Entity L applies the business combination exemption under IFRS 1. In a business combination L acquired property, plant and equipment, inventory and accounts receivable. Under its previous GAAP, L initially measured these assets at cost (i.e. their fair value at the date of acquisition).

Upon adoption of IFRS, L determines that its accounting policy for these assets under its previous GAAP complied with the requirements of IFRS. Therefore, property, plant and equipment, inventory and accounts receivable are not adjusted, but recognised in the opening IFRS balance sheet at the carrying amount under the previous GAAP.

E Measurement of items not recognised under previous GAAP

An asset acquired or a liability assumed in a past business combination may not have been recognised under the entity's previous GAAP. However, this does not mean that such items have a deemed cost of zero in the opening IFRS balance sheet. Instead, the acquirer recognises and measures those items in its opening IFRS balance sheet on the basis that IFRS would require in the balance sheet of the acquiree.[71] The change resulting from the recognition of such assets and liabilities should be accounted for as an adjustment of retained earnings or another category of equity, if appropriate. The IASB included this requirement to avoid 'an unjustifiable departure from the principle that the opening IFRS balance sheet should include all assets and liabilities.'[72]

A first-time adopter that restates previous business combinations under IFRS 3 will recognise the intangible assets held by acquired subsidiaries. However, intangible assets acquired as part of a business combination that were not recognised under a first-time adopter's previous GAAP, will rarely be recognised in the opening IFRS balance sheet of a first-time adopter that applies the business combinations exemption because either (1) they cannot be capitalised in the acquiree's own balance sheet or (2) capitalisation would require the use of hindsight which is not permitted under IAS 38 (see 2.9.5 below).

Example 5.13: Items not recognised under previous GAAP

Entity K acquired Entity L but did not capitalise L's finance leases and internally generated customer lists under its previous GAAP.

Upon first-time adoption of IFRS, K recognises the finance leases in its opening IFRS balance sheet using the amounts that L would recognise in its IFRS balance sheet. The resulting adjustment to the net assets at the date of transition is reflected in retained earnings; goodwill is not restated to reflect the net assets that would have been recognised at the date of acquisition (see 2.4.4 below). However, K does not recognise the customer lists in its opening IFRS balance sheet, because L is not permitted to capitalise internally generated customer lists. Any value that might have been attributable to the customer lists would remain subsumed in goodwill in K's opening IFRS balance sheet.

Entity M acquired Entity N but did not recognise N's brand name as a separate intangible asset under its previous GAAP.

Upon first-time adoption of IFRS, M will not recognise N's brand name in its opening IFRS balance sheet because N would not have been permitted under IAS 38 to recognise it as an asset in its own separate balance sheet. Again, any value that might have been attributable to the brand name would remain subsumed in goodwill in M's opening IFRS balance sheet.

F Summary of recognition and measurement requirements

The following diagram summarises the recognition and measurement rules – that are discussed above – for assets acquired and liabilities assumed in a business combination that is accounted for under the business combinations exemption.

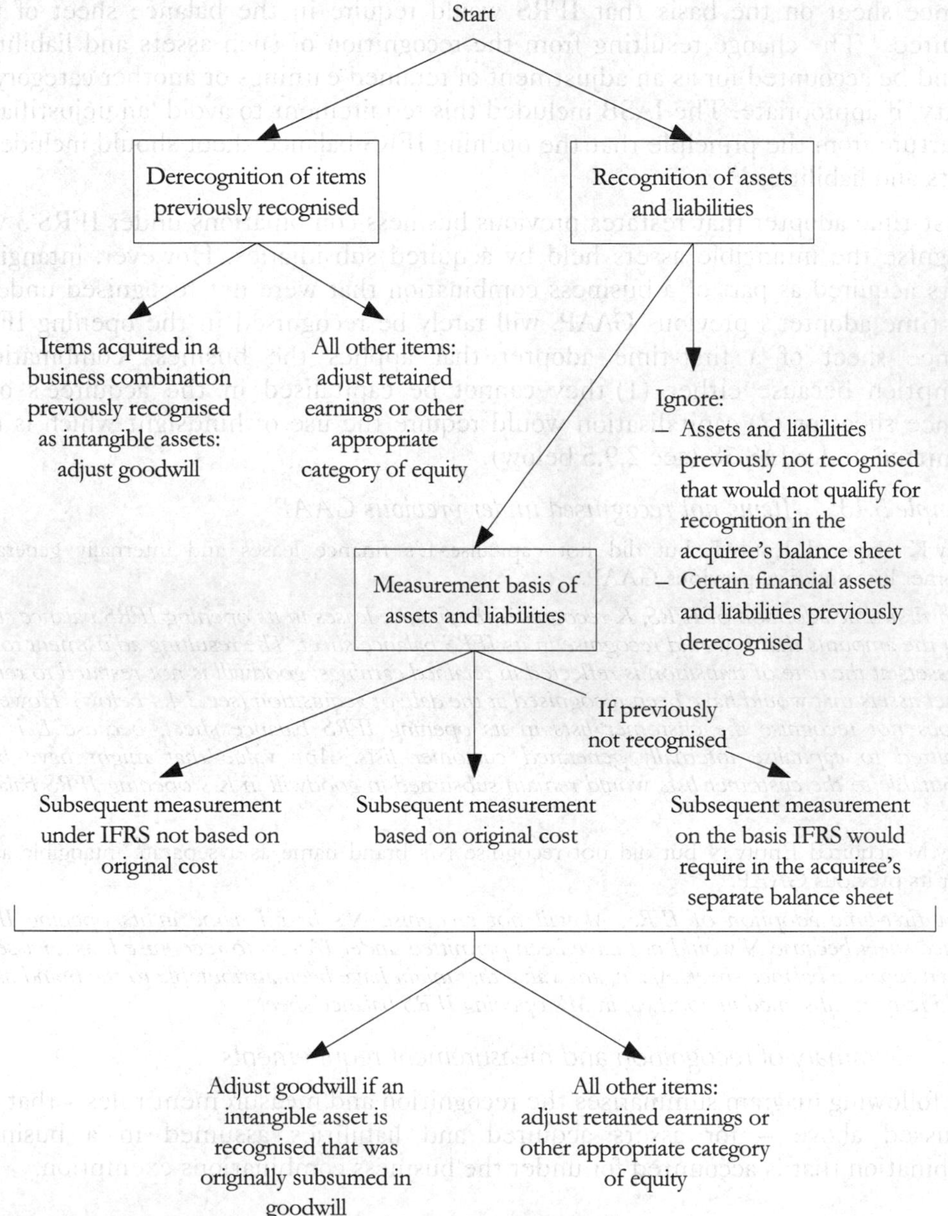

The guidance on implementation of IFRS 1 contains the following example that illustrates many of the requirements discussed above.[73]

Example 5.14: Business combination example

Background

Entity B's first IFRS financial statements have a reporting date of 31 December 2005 and include comparative information for 2004 only. On 1 July 2001, entity B acquired 100 per cent of subsidiary C. Under its previous GAAP, entity B:

(a) classified the business combination as an acquisition by entity B;

(b) measured the assets acquired and liabilities assumed at the following amounts under previous GAAP at 31 December 2003 (date of transition to IFRSs):

  (i) identifiable assets less liabilities for which IFRSs require cost-based measurement at a date after the business combination: 200 (with a tax base of 150 and an applicable tax rate of 30 per cent);

  (ii) pension liability (for which the present value of the defined benefit obligation measured under IAS 19 is 130 and the fair value of plan assets is 100): nil (because entity B used a pay-as-you-go cash method of accounting for pensions under its previous GAAP). The tax base of the pension liability is also nil;

  (iii) goodwill: 180;

(c) did not, at the date of acquisition, recognise deferred tax arising from temporary differences associated with the identifiable assets acquired and liabilities assumed.

Application of requirements

In its opening (consolidated) IFRS balance sheet, entity B:

(a) classifies the business combination as an acquisition by entity B even if the business combination would have qualified under IFRS 3 as a reverse acquisition by subsidiary C (paragraph B2(a) of IFRS 1);

(b) does not adjust the accumulated amortisation of goodwill. Entity B tests the goodwill for impairment under IAS 36 and recognises any resulting impairment loss, based on conditions that existed at the date of transition to IFRSs. If no impairment exists, the carrying amount of the goodwill remains at 180 (paragraph B2(g) of IFRS 1);

(c) for those net identifiable assets acquired for which IFRSs require cost-based measurement at a date after the business combination, treats their carrying amount under previous GAAP immediately after the business combination as their deemed cost at that date (paragraph B2(e) of IFRS 1);

(d) does not restate the accumulated depreciation and amortisation of the net identifiable assets in (c) above, unless the depreciation methods and rates under previous GAAP result in amounts that differ materially from those required under IFRSs (for example, if they were adopted solely for tax purposes and do not reflect a reasonable estimate of the asset's useful life under IFRSs). If no such restatement is made, the carrying amount of those assets in the opening IFRS balance sheet equals their carrying amount under previous GAAP at the date of transition to IFRSs (200) (paragraph IG7 of IFRS 1);

(e) if there is any indication that identifiable assets are impaired, tests those assets for impairment, based on conditions that existed at the date of transition to IFRSs (see IAS 36);

(f) recognises the pension liability, and measures it, at the present value of the defined benefit obligation (130) less the fair value of the plan assets (100), giving a carrying amount of 30, with a corresponding debit of 30 to retained earnings (paragraph B2(d) of IFRS 1). However, if subsidiary C had already adopted IFRSs in an earlier period, entity B would measure the pension liability at the same amount as in subsidiary C's separate financial statements (paragraph 25 of IFRS 1 and IG Example 9);

(g) recognises a net deferred tax liability of 6 (20 at 30 per cent) arising from:

  (i) the taxable temporary difference of 50 (200 less 150) associated with the identifiable assets acquired and non-pension liabilities assumed; less

  (ii) the deductible temporary difference of 30 (30 less nil) associated with the pension liability.

  The entity recognises the resulting increase in the deferred tax liability as a deduction from retained earnings (paragraph B2(k) of IFRS 1). If a taxable temporary difference arises from the initial recognition of the goodwill, entity B does not recognise the resulting deferred tax liability (paragraph 15(a) of IAS 12 – *Income Taxes*).

2.4.4 Restatement of goodwill

A Mandatory adjustments of goodwill

Under the business combinations exemption, a first-time adopter takes the carrying amount of goodwill under its previous GAAP at the date of transition to IFRS as a starting point and only adjusts it as follows:[74]

- A first-time adopter increases goodwill at the date of transition by an amount equal to the carrying amount of an item that it recognised as an intangible asset acquired in a business combination under its previous GAAP (less any related deferred tax and minority interests), but which does not meet the recognition criteria under IFRS. That is, the first-time adopter accounts for the change in classification prospectively and does not, for example, reverse the cumulative amortisation on the item that it recognised as an intangible asset under its previous GAAP;
- If a first-time adopter is required to recognise an intangible asset under IFRS that was subsumed in goodwill under its previous GAAP, it decreases goodwill accordingly and adjusts deferred tax and minority interests;
- 'A contingency affecting the amount of the purchase consideration for a past business combination may have been resolved before the date of transition to IFRS. If a reliable estimate of the contingent adjustment can be made and its payment is probable, the first-time adopter shall adjust the goodwill by that amount. Similarly, the first-time adopter shall adjust the carrying amount of goodwill if a previously recognised contingent adjustment can no longer be measured reliably or its payment is no longer probable';[75] and
- 'Regardless of whether there is any indication that the goodwill may be impaired, the first-time adopter shall apply IAS 36 – *Impairment of Assets* – in testing the goodwill for impairment at the date of transition to IFRS and in recognising any resulting impairment loss in retained earnings (or, if so required by IAS 36, in revaluation surplus). The impairment test shall be based on conditions at the date of transition to IFRS.'[76]

  The estimates used to determine whether a first-time adopter recognises an impairment loss or provision at the date of transition to IFRS should be consistent with estimates made for the same date under previous GAAP (after adjustments to reflect any difference in accounting policies), unless there is objective evidence that those estimates were in error.[77] If a first-time adopter needs to make estimates for that date that were not necessary under its previous GAAP, such estimates and assumptions should not reflect conditions that arose after the date of transition to IFRS.[78]

  If a first-time adopter's opening IFRS balance sheet reflects impairment losses, it recognises any later reversal of those impairment losses in the income statement unless IAS 36 requires that reversal to be treated as a revaluation. This applies to both impairment losses recognised under previous GAAP and additional impairment losses recognised on transition to IFRS.[79]

Under IFRS 1, assets acquired and liabilities assumed in a business combination prior to the date of transition to IFRS are not necessarily valued on a basis that is consistent with IFRS 3. This can lead to 'double counting' in the carrying amount of assets and goodwill as is illustrated in the example below.

Example 5.15: Impairment testing of goodwill on first-time adoption

Entity P acquired a business before its date of transition to IFRS. The cost of acquisition was €530 and P allocated the purchase price as follows:

	€
Properties, at carry-over cost	450
Liabilities, at amortised cost	(180)
Goodwill	260
Purchase price	530

The goodwill under P's previous GAAP relates entirely to the properties that had a fair value at date of acquisition that was significantly in excess of their value on a carry-over cost basis. In P's opening IFRS balance sheet the same assets, liabilities and goodwill are valued as follows:

	€
Properties, at fair value	750
Liabilities, at amortised cost	(200)
Provisional IFRS goodwill (before impairment test)	260
Total carrying amount	810

P used the option to measure the properties at fair value at its date of transition in its opening IFRS balance sheet. However, IFRS 1 does not permit goodwill to be adjusted to reflect the extent to which the increase in fair value relates to the time of the acquisition. The total carrying amount of the acquired net assets including goodwill of €810 may now exceed the recoverable amount. When P tests the 'provisional IFRS goodwill' for impairment on first-time adoption of IFRS, the recoverable amount of the business is determined to be €600. Accordingly, it will have to recognise an impairment of goodwill of €210 and disclose this impairment under IFRS 1.

In some cases the write-off will completely eliminate the goodwill and thereby any 'double counting'. However, in this particular case the remaining goodwill of €50 in truth represents goodwill that was internally generated between the date of acquisition and the date of transition to IFRS.

The IASB accepted that IFRS 1 'does not prevent the implicit recognition of internally generated goodwill that arose after the date of the business combination. However, the Board concluded that an attempt to exclude such internally generated goodwill would be costly and lead to arbitrary results.'[80]

B Prohibition of other adjustments of goodwill

The IASB concluded that 'to avoid costs that would exceed the likely benefits to users', IFRS 1 should prohibit 'restatement of goodwill for most other adjustments reflected in the opening IFRS balance sheet, unless a first-time adopter elects to apply IFRS 3 retrospectively.'[81] Therefore, a first-time adopter electing not to apply IFRS 3 retrospectively is not permitted to make any adjustments to goodwill other than those described at 2.4.4 A above. For example, such a first-time adopter should not restate the carrying amount of goodwill:[82]

'(i) to exclude in-process research and development acquired in that business combination (unless the related intangible asset would qualify for recognition under IAS 38 in the balance sheet of the acquiree);

(ii) to adjust previous amortisation of goodwill;

(iii) to reverse adjustments to goodwill that IFRS 3 would not permit, but were made under previous GAAP because of adjustments to assets and liabilities between the date of the business combination and the date of transition to IFRS.'

Although IFRS 1 specifically prohibits other adjustments to goodwill, differences between the goodwill amount in the opening IFRS balance sheet and that in the financial statements under previous GAAP may arise because:

(a) goodwill may have to be restated as a result of a retrospective application of IAS 21 – *The Effects of Changes in Foreign Exchange Rates* (see 2.4.5 below);

(b) goodwill in relation to previously unconsolidated subsidiaries will have to be recognised (see 2.4.6 below);

(c) goodwill in relation to transactions that do not qualify as business combinations under IFRS must be derecognised (see 2.4.2 above); and

(d) 'negative goodwill' that may have been included within goodwill under previous GAAP should be derecognised under IFRS (see C below).

Example 5.16: Adjusting goodwill

Entity R acquired Entity S but under its previous GAAP it did not recognise the following items:

- S's customer lists which had a fair value of ¥1,100 at the date of the acquisition and ¥1,500 at the date of transition to IFRS; and
- Deferred tax liabilities related to the fair value adjustment of S's property, plant and equipment, which amounted to ¥9,500 at the date of the acquisition and ¥7,800 at the date of transition to IFRS.

What adjustment should R make to goodwill to account for the customer lists and deferred tax liabilities at its date of transition to IFRS?

As explained at 2.4.3 E above, R cannot recognise the customer lists when it uses the business combinations exemption. Accordingly, R cannot adjust goodwill for the customer lists.

R must recognise the deferred tax liability at its date of transition under IAS 12 because there is no exemption from recognising deferred taxation under IFRS 1. However, R is not permitted to adjust goodwill for the deferred tax liability that would have been recognised at the date of acquisition. Instead, R should recognise the change in deferred tax in retained earnings or other category of equity, if appropriate.

C Derecognition of negative goodwill

IFRS 3 specifically requires derecognition of negative goodwill (which IFRS 3 calls 'excess of acquirer's interest in the net fair value of acquiree's identifiable assets, liabilities and contingent liabilities over cost') with a corresponding adjustment to the opening balance of retained earnings on adoption of the standard (see Chapter 7 at 4.2.1).[83] Although IFRS 1 does not specifically address accounting for negative goodwill recognised under a previous GAAP, negative goodwill should be derecognised by a first-time adopter because it is not permitted 'to recognise items or liabilities if IFRS do not permit such recognition.'[84] Negative goodwill clearly does not meet the definition of a liability under the IASB's *Framework* and its recognition is not permitted under IFRS 3.

D Goodwill previously deducted from equity

If a first-time adopter deducted goodwill from equity under its previous GAAP then 'it shall not recognise that goodwill in its opening IFRS balance sheet. Furthermore, it shall not transfer that goodwill to the income statement if it disposes of the subsidiary or if the investment in the subsidiary becomes impaired.'[85] Effectively, under IFRS such goodwill ceases to exist.

Example 5.17: Goodwill deducted from equity and treatment of related intangible assets[86]

Entity H acquired a subsidiary before the date of transition to IFRS. Under its previous GAAP, H:

(a) recognised goodwill as an immediate deduction from equity;

(b) recognised an intangible asset of the subsidiary that does not qualify for recognition as an asset under IAS 38; and

(c) did not recognise an intangible asset of the subsidiary that would qualify under IAS 38 for recognition as an asset in the financial statements of the subsidiary. The subsidiary held the asset at the date of its acquisition by H.

In its opening IFRS balance sheet, H:

(a) does not recognise the goodwill, as it did not recognise the goodwill as an asset under previous GAAP;

(b) does not recognise the intangible asset that does not qualify for recognition as an asset under IAS 38. Because H deducted goodwill from equity under its previous GAAP, the elimination of this intangible asset reduces retained earnings (see 2.4.3 A above); and

(c) recognises the intangible asset that qualifies under IAS 38 for recognition as an asset in the financial statements of the subsidiary, even though the amount assigned to it under previous GAAP in H's consolidated financial statements was nil (see 2.4.3 E above)). The recognition criteria in IAS 38 include the availability of a reliable measurement of cost and H measures the asset at cost less accumulated depreciation and less any impairment losses identified under IAS 36 (see 2.9.5 below). Because H deducted goodwill from equity under its previous GAAP, the recognition of this intangible asset increases retained earnings. However, if this intangible asset had been subsumed in goodwill recognised as an asset under previous GAAP, H would have decreased the carrying amount of that goodwill accordingly (and, if applicable, adjusted deferred tax and minority interests) (see 2.4.4 A above).

The prohibition to reinstate goodwill that was deducted from equity may have a significant impact on first-time adopters that hedge their foreign net investments.

Example 5.18: Goodwill related to foreign net investments

Entity T, which uses the euro (€) as its functional currency, acquired a subsidiary in the United States whose functional currency is the US dollar ($). The goodwill on the acquisition of $2,100 was deducted from equity, but under its previous GAAP Entity T hedged the currency exposure on the goodwill because it would be required to recognise the goodwill as an expense upon disposal of the subsidiary.

IFRS 1 does not permit reinstatement of goodwill deducted from equity nor does it permit transfer of goodwill to the income statement upon disposal of the investment of the subsidiary. Under IFRS, goodwill deducted from equity ceases to exist and T can no longer hedge the currency exposure on that goodwill.

If a first-time adopter deducted goodwill from equity under its previous GAAP then 'adjustments resulting from the subsequent resolution of a contingency affecting the purchase consideration shall be recognised in retained earnings.'[87] Effectively, the adjustment is being accounted for in the same way as the original goodwill that arose on the acquisition, rather than having to be adjusted against capitalised goodwill under IFRS 3. This requirement could affect, for example, the way a first-time adopter accounts for earn-out clauses relating to business combinations prior to its date of transition to IFRS.

Example 5.19: Earn-out clause in acquisition

Entity U acquired a business before its date of transition to IFRS and agreed to make an initial payment to the vendor together with further payments based on a multiple of future profits of the acquiree. The fair value of the earn-out is contingent on future profits and could not be determined reliably at the date of transition to IFRS. Under U's previous GAAP any goodwill was written off against equity as incurred.

After its date of transition to IFRS, U will account for the earn-out as a change in purchase consideration and recognise it in retained earnings.

2.4.5 Currency adjustments to goodwill

IAS 21 requires that 'any goodwill arising on the acquisition of a foreign operation and any fair value adjustments to the carrying amounts of assets and liabilities arising on the acquisition of that foreign operation shall be treated as assets and liabilities of the foreign operation.'[88] For a first-time adopter it may be impracticable, especially after a corporate restructuring, to determine retrospectively the currency in which goodwill and fair value adjustments should be expressed. Consequently, under IFRS 1, a first-time adopter need not apply this requirement of IAS 21 'retrospectively to fair value adjustments and goodwill arising in business combinations that occurred before the date of transition to IFRSs.'[89] If IAS 21 is not applied retrospectively, a first-time adopter should treat such fair value adjustments and goodwill 'as assets and liabilities of the entity rather than as assets and liabilities of the acquiree. Therefore, those goodwill and fair value adjustments either are already expressed in the entity's functional currency or are non-monetary foreign currency items, which are reported using the exchange rate applied under previous GAAP.'[90]

If a first-time adopter chooses not to take the full exemption, it must apply IAS 21 retrospectively to fair value adjustments and goodwill arising in either:

'(a) all business combinations that occurred before the date of transition to IFRSs; or

(b) all business combinations that the entity elects to restate to comply with IFRS 3.'[91]

The decision to treat goodwill and fair value adjustments as either items denominated in the parent's or the acquiree's functional currency will also affect the extent to which the net investment in those foreign subsidiaries can be hedged (see also 2.4.4 D above).

Despite this exemption, there are a number of significant practical issues relating to currency adjustments to goodwill that are discussed at 3.5 below. It should also be noted that the above exemption is different from the 'cumulative translation differences' exemption, which is discussed at 2.7.2 below.

2.4.6 Previously unconsolidated subsidiaries

Under its previous GAAP a first-time adopter may not have consolidated a subsidiary acquired in a past business combination. In that case, a first-time adopter applying the business combinations exemption should 'adjust the carrying amounts of the subsidiary's assets and liabilities to the amounts that IFRSs would require in the subsidiary's balance sheet. The deemed cost of goodwill equals the difference at the date of transition to IFRSs between:

(i) the parent's interest in those adjusted carrying amounts; and

(ii) the cost in the parent's separate financial statements of its investment in the subsidiary.'[92]

The cost of a subsidiary in the parent's separate financial statements should be determined under the cost method of accounting under IAS 27 – *Consolidated and Separate Financial Statements* (see Chapter 6 at 7.3). Thus, a first-time adopter does not have to calculate what the goodwill would have been at the date of the original acquisition. The deemed cost of goodwill will, however, be capitalised as an asset in the opening IFRS balance sheet. The guidance on the implementation of IFRS 1 contains the following example that illustrates this.

Example 5.20: Subsidiary not consolidated under previous GAAP[93]

Background

Parent J's date of transition to IFRSs is 1 January 2004. Under its previous GAAP, parent J did not consolidate its 75 per cent subsidiary K, acquired in a business combination on 15 July 2001. On 1 January 2004:

(a) the cost of parent J's investment in subsidiary K is 180.

(b) under IFRSs, subsidiary K would measure its assets at 500 and its liabilities (including deferred tax under IAS 12) at 300. On this basis, subsidiary K's net assets are 200 under IFRSs.

Application of requirements

Parent J consolidates subsidiary K. The consolidated balance sheet at 1 January 2004 includes:

(a) subsidiary K's assets at 500 and liabilities at 300;

(b) minority interests of 50 (25 per cent of [500 – 300]); and

(c) goodwill of 30 (cost of 180 less 75 per cent of [500 – 300]). Parent J tests the goodwill for impairment under IAS 36 and recognises any resulting impairment loss, based on conditions that existed at the date of transition to IFRSs.

If the original acquisition cost is lower than the net asset value at the date of transition to IFRS, the difference is taken to retained earnings.

Slightly different rules apply to all other subsidiaries (i.e. those not acquired in a business combination) that an entity did not consolidate under its previous GAAP, the main difference being that goodwill should not be recognised in relation to those subsidiaries (see 2.9.3 below).

It should be noted that in calculating the deemed cost of the goodwill, the first-time adopter is required to compare the historical cost of the investment to its share of the carrying amount of the net assets determined on a different date. In the case of a highly profitable subsidiary this could give rise to the following anomaly:

Example 5.21: Calculation of deemed goodwill

Parent L acquired subsidiary M before the date of transition for $500. The net assets of M would have been $220 under IFRS at the date of acquisition. M makes on average an annual net profit of $60, which it does not distribute to L.

At the date of transition to IFRS, the cost of L's investment in M is still $500. However, the net assets of M have increased to $460. Therefore, under IFRS 1 the deemed cost of goodwill is $40.

The deemed goodwill is much lower than the goodwill that was paid at the date of acquisition because M did not distribute its profits. In fact, if M had distributed a dividend to its parent just before the date of transition, the deemed goodwill would have been significantly higher.

2.4.7 Previously consolidated entities that are not subsidiaries

A first-time adopter may have consolidated an investment under its previous GAAP that does not meet the definition of a subsidiary under IFRS. In this case the entity should first determine the appropriate classification of the investment under IFRS and then apply the first-time adoption rules in IFRS 1. Generally such previously consolidated investments should be accounted for as either:

- *an associate:* First-time adopters applying the business combinations exemption should also apply that exemption to past acquisitions of investments in associates. If the business combinations exemption is not applicable or the entity did not acquire the investment in the associate, IAS 28 – *Investments in Associates* – should be applied retrospectively;
- *a joint venture:* First-time adopters applying the business combinations exemption should also apply that exemption to past acquisitions of investments in joint ventures. If the business combinations exemption is not applicable or the entity did not acquire the investment in the joint venture, IAS 31 – *Interests in Joint Ventures* – should be applied retrospectively;
- *an investment under IAS 39* (see 2.6.2 below); or
- *an executory contract or service concession arrangement:* There are no first-time adoption exemptions that apply; therefore, IFRS should be applied retrospectively.

2.4.8 Measurement of deferred taxation and minority interests

Deferred taxation is calculated based on the difference between the carrying amount of assets and liabilities and their respective tax base. Therefore, deferred taxation should be calculated after all assets acquired and liabilities assumed have been adjusted under IFRS 1.[94]

Minority interest is defined in IAS 27 as 'that portion of the profit or loss and net assets of a subsidiary attributable to equity interests that are not owned, directly or indirectly through subsidiaries, by the parent.'[95] Minority interests related to subsidiaries acquired in a business combination should be calculated after all assets acquired, liabilities assumed and deferred taxation have been adjusted under IFRS 1.[96]

Any resulting change in the carrying amount of deferred taxation and minority interests should be recognised by adjusting retained earnings (or, if appropriate, another category of equity), unless they relate to adjustments to intangible assets that are adjusted against goodwill.

Example 5.22: Restatement of intangible assets, deferred tax and minority interests[97]

Entity V's first IFRS financial statements have a reporting date of 31 December 2005 and include comparative information for 2004 only. On 1 July 2001, V acquired 75% of subsidiary W. Under its previous GAAP, V assigned an initial carrying amount of 200 to intangible assets that would not have qualified for recognition under IAS 38. The tax base of the intangible assets was nil, giving rise to a deferred tax liability (at 30%) of 60. V measured minority interests as the minority's share of the fair value of the identifiable net assets acquired. Goodwill arising on the acquisition was capitalised as an asset in V's consolidated financial statements.

On 1 January 2004 (the date of transition to IFRS), the carrying amount of the intangible assets under previous GAAP was 160, and the carrying amount of the related deferred tax liability was 48 (30% of 160).

Under IFRS 1, V reclassifies intangible assets that do not qualify for recognition as separate assets under IAS 38, together with the related deferred tax liability of 48 and minority interests, as part of goodwill (see 2.4.4 A above). The related minority interests amount to 28 (25% of 112 (160 minus 48)). V makes the following adjustment in its opening IFRS balance sheet:

Goodwill	84	
Deferred tax liability	48	
Minority interests	28	
Intangible assets		160

V tests the goodwill for impairment under IAS 36 and recognises any resulting impairment loss, based on conditions that existed at the date of transition to IFRS.

Under IFRS 1, a first-time adopter is required to 'adjust opening retained earnings if, on transition to IFRSs, it recognises for the first time a deferred tax liability relating to an acquired intangible asset recognised in accordance with its previous GAAP. In contrast, if the entity had subsumed the intangible asset in recognised goodwill in accordance with its previous GAAP, it would be required to decrease the carrying amount of goodwill accordingly and, if applicable, adjust deferred tax and minority interests.'[98] The IASB discussed this issue in October 2005, but decided not to propose an amendment to address this inconsistency.

2.5 'Fair value or revaluation as deemed cost' exemption

2.5.1 Background

IFRS 1 requires full retrospective application of standards extant at a first-time adopter's first IFRS reporting date. Therefore, in the absence of the deemed cost exemption, the requirements of IAS 16, IAS 38 and IAS 40 would have to be applied as if the first-time adopter had always applied these standards. This could be quite onerous because:

- these items are long-lived which means that accounting records for the period of acquisition may not be available anymore. In the case of formerly state-owned businesses, the required accounting records possibly never even existed;

- the entity may have revalued the items in the past as a matter of accounting policy or because this was required under national law; or
- even if the items were carried at depreciated cost, the accounting policy for recognition and depreciation may not have been IFRS compliant.

Given the significance of property, plant and equipment in particular in the balance sheet of most first-time adopters (and the sheer number of transactions affecting property, plant and equipment), restatement is not only difficult but would often also involve undue cost and effort. Nevertheless, a first-time adopter needs a cost basis for the assets in its opening IFRS balance sheet. Therefore, the IASB decided to introduce the notion of a 'deemed cost' that is not the 'true' IFRS compliant cost basis of an asset, but a surrogate that is deemed to be a suitable starting point.

In its deliberations on IFRS 1, the IASB noted that 'reconstructed cost data might be less relevant to users, and less reliable, than current fair value data. ... Therefore, the IFRS permits an entity to use fair value as deemed cost in some cases without any need to demonstrate undue cost or effort.'[99]

2.5.2 *Scope of 'fair value or revaluation as deemed cost' exemption*

To deal with the problem of restatement of long-lived assets upon first-time adoption of IFRS, the standard permits a first-time adopter – for the categories of assets listed below – to measure an item in its opening IFRS balance sheet using an amount that is based on its deemed cost:[100]

- property, plant and equipment (see 2.9.1);[101]
- investment property, if an entity elects to use the cost model in IAS 40. The fact that the exemption can only be applied to investment property accounted for under the cost model will not pose any problems in practice as the fair value model under IAS 40 requires an entity to measure its investment property at fair value at its date of transition to IFRS;[102] and
- intangible assets (see 2.9.5) that meet:
  - the recognition criteria in IAS 38 (including reliable measurement of original cost); and
  - the criteria in IAS 38 for revaluation (including the existence of an active market).[103]

A first-time adopter cannot use a deemed cost approach for any other assets or liabilities.[104]

The use of fair value or revaluation as deemed cost for intangible assets will be very limited in practice because of the very restrictive definition of an active market in IAS 38 (see Chapter 12 at 2.4.2 A).[105] It is therefore unlikely that a first-time adopter will be able to apply this exemption to any intangible assets.

It is important to note that the deemed cost exemption in IFRS 1 does not take classes or categories of assets as its unit of measure, but refers to 'an item of property, plant and equipment'.[106] The same exemption is available for investment property and intangible assets. IAS 16 does not 'prescribe the unit of measure for recognition, i.e. what constitutes an item of property, plant and equipment. Thus, judgement is required in applying the recognition criteria to an entity's specific circumstances' (see Chapter 12 at 2.3.2).[107] A first-time adopter can therefore apply the deemed cost exemption to only some of its assets. For example, it could apply the exemption only to:

- a selection of properties;
- part of a factory; or
- some of the assets leased under a single finance lease.

The IASB argued that it is not necessary to restrict application of the exemption to classes of assets to prevent selective revaluations, because 'IAS 36 requires an impairment test if there is any indication that an asset is impaired. Thus, if an entity uses fair value as deemed cost for assets whose fair value is above cost, it cannot ignore indications that the recoverable amount of other assets may have fallen below their carrying amount. Therefore, the IFRS does not restrict the use of fair value as deemed cost to entire classes of asset.'[108] Nevertheless, it seems doubtful that the quality of financial information would benefit from a revaluation of a haphazard selection of items of property, plant and equipment. Therefore, a first-time adopter should exercise judgment in selecting the items to which it believes it is appropriate to apply the exemption.

Extracts 5.2 and 5.3 below are typical disclosures of the use of the 'fair value as deemed cost' exemption.

Extract 5.2: Publicis Groupe SA (2005)

Notes to the consolidated financial statements [extract]

Note 32.2 Accounting options related to first-time application of IFRS [extract]

Measurement of certain tangible assets at fair value as deemed cost

Publicis opted to revalue its building at 133, avenue des Champs Elysées in Paris at its fair value and to consider this value as being the deemed cost at the transition date. The fair value of this building at the transition date amounts to €164 M, which represents an adjustment of €159 M compared to its carrying amount under previous accounting standards. The valuation was performed by an independent expert using the rent capitalization method.

Extract 5.3: BAA plc (2005)

Accounting policies [extract]

Property, plant and equipment [extract]

Operational assets [extract]

Terminal complexes, airfield assets, plant and equipment, rail assets, and Group occupied properties are stated at cost less accumulated depreciation and impairment losses. At the date of transition to IFRS, the Group elected to measure the majority of operational land at fair value and to use these fair values as deemed cost at that date. This excludes land acquired in 2002 for the construction of Terminal 5, as its carrying value is considered to be at an appropriate value given the recent acquisition of the land.

2.5.3 Determining deemed cost

The deemed cost that a first-time adopter uses is either:

(1) the fair value of the item at the date of transition to IFRS (see 2.2.4 above);[109]

(2) a revaluation under its previous GAAP at or before the date of transition to IFRS, if the revaluation was, at the date of the revaluation, broadly comparable to:[110]

'(a) fair value; or

(b) cost or depreciated cost under IFRS, adjusted to reflect, for example, changes in a general or specific price index'; or

(3) the deemed cost under its previous GAAP that was established by measuring items at their fair value at one particular date because of an event such as a privatisation or initial public offering.[111]

The revaluations referred to in (2) above need only be 'broadly comparable to fair value or reflect an index applied to a cost that is broadly comparable to cost determined under IFRSs.'[112] It appears that in the interest of practicality the IASB is allowing a good deal of flexibility in this matter. The IASB explains in the basis for conclusions that 'it may not always be clear whether a previous revaluation was intended as a measure of fair value or differs materially from fair value. The flexibility in this area permits a cost-effective solution for the unique problem of transition to IFRS. It allows a first-time adopter to establish a deemed cost using a measurement that is already available and is a reasonable starting point for a cost-based measurement.'[113]

If the deemed cost of an asset was determined before the date of transition to IFRS then an IFRS accounting policy needs to be applied to that deemed cost in the intervening period to determine what the carrying amount of the asset is in the opening IFRS balance sheet, as is illustrated in the example below.

Example 5.23: Deemed cost of property, plant and equipment

Entity A used to revalue items of property, plant and equipment to fair value under its previous GAAP, but changed its accounting policy on 1 January 2001 when it adopted a different accounting policy. Under that accounting policy, entity A did not depreciate the asset and only recognised the maintenance costs as an expense. Entity A's date of transition to IFRS is 1 January 2007.

In its balance sheet under previous GAAP the carrying amount of the asset is £80 at the date of transition to IFRS, which is equal to the last revaluation. Entity A can use the last revalued amount as the deemed cost of the asset on 1 January 2001. However, Entity A will need to apply IAS 16 to the period after 1 January 2001 because the accounting policy under its previous GAAP is not permitted under IFRS. Assuming that the economic life of the asset is 40 years and that the residual value is nil, Entity A would account for the asset at £68 in its opening IFRS balance sheet, which represents the deemed cost minus 6 years of depreciation.

In summary, at its date of transition to IFRS, a first-time adopter is allowed under IFRS 1 to measure property, plant and equipment, investment properties and intangible assets at an amount based on either:

- historical cost determined in accordance with IAS 16, IAS 38 and IAS 40;
- fair value at the date of transition to IFRS;

- a revalued amount that is equal to:
  - fair value at the date of revaluation;
  - cost adjusted for changes in a general or specific index; or
  - an event-driven fair value, for example, at the date of an initial public offering or privatisation; or
- in the case of an item acquired in a business combination:
  - carrying amount under previous GAAP immediately after acquisition; or
  - if the item was not recognised under previous GAAP, the carrying amount on the basis that IFRS would require in the separate balance sheet of the acquiree.

The fact that IFRS 1 offers so many different bases for valuation does not disturb the IASB as it reasons that 'cost is generally equivalent to fair value at the date of acquisition. Therefore, the use of fair value as the deemed cost of an asset means that an entity will report the same cost data as if it had acquired an asset with the same remaining service potential at the date of transition to IFRSs. If there is any lack of comparability, it arises from the aggregation of costs incurred at different dates, rather than from the targeted use of fair value as deemed cost for some assets. The Board regarded this approach as justified to solve the unique problem of introducing IFRSs in a cost-effective way without damaging transparency.'[114] Although this is valid, it still means that an individual first-time adopter can greatly influence its future reported performance by carefully selecting a first-time adoption policy for the valuation of its assets. Users of the financial statements of a first-time adopter should therefore be mindful that historical trends under the previous GAAP might no longer be present in an entity's IFRS financial statements.

2.6 Financial instruments

2.6.1 Exemption from the requirement to restate comparative information

The IASB issued a revised version of IAS 32 and IAS 39 in December 2003 and an amendment to IAS 39 – *Fair Value Hedge Accounting for a Portfolio Hedge of Interest Rate Risk* – in March 2004. To allow entities adopting IFRS for the first time before 1 January 2006 sufficient time to comply with the requirements of those standards, the IASB decided not to require them to prepare comparative information under IAS 32, IAS 39 and IFRS 4 (see 2.7.4).[115]

The fact that the IASB did not use the defined terms 'date of transition', 'reporting date' or 'first IFRS reporting period' in drafting the scope of the exemption, is generally interpreted as meaning that the IASB intended the exemption to apply to entities whose first IFRS reporting period started before 1 January 2006. The example below illustrates that this exemption is not available to entities that are transitioning to IFRS in 2007 or later.

Example 5.24: Applicability to entity transitioning to IFRS in 2007

Entity B's year-end is 31 December and it presents financial statements that include one comparative period. B is required to produce IFRS financial statements for the first accounting period starting on or after 1 January 2007.

B's first reporting date under IFRS is 31 December 2007 and the start of its first IFRS reporting period is 1 January 2007. Therefore, B cannot make use of the exemption and will need to present comparative information prepared in accordance with IAS 32, IAS 39 and IFRS 4.

2.6.2 Designation of previously recognised financial instruments

IAS 39 permits a financial instrument to be designated on initial recognition as a *financial asset or financial liability at fair value through profit or loss* or as an *available-for-sale financial asset*, subject to the criteria in that standard.[116] Retrospective designation of financial instruments as available-for-sale financial assets 'requires a first-time adopter to recognise the cumulative fair value changes in a separate component of equity in the opening IFRS balance sheet, and transfer those fair value changes to the income statement on subsequent disposal or impairment of the asset'.[117] The IASB recognised that this could give rise to a selective approach, whereby first-time adopters would only designate financial instruments with cumulative gains as available-for-sale, but it noted that a first-time adopter could achieve similar results by selectively disposing of some financial assets before the date of transition to IFRS.[118] Therefore, IFRS 1 does not impose any additional restrictions on first-time adopters regarding the designation of financial instruments as available-for-sale financial assets.

In June 2005, the IASB published *Amendments to International Accounting Standard 39 Financial Instruments: Recognition and Measurement – The Fair Value Option*. These amendments to IAS 39 gave rise to a number of consequential changes to IFRS 1 that should be applied for annual periods beginning on or after 1 January 2006, or earlier period in which an entity applies these amendments to IAS 39 (see Chapter 17 at 7.1.2 B). The exact first-time adoption requirements now depend on whether an entity's first IFRS reporting period starts before or after 1 January 2006, as discussed under A and B below.

A Periods beginning before 1 January 2006

A first-time adopter with a first IFRS reporting period beginning before 1 January 2006 that was not adopting the fair value option amendment early, was allowed to designate a financial instrument at the date of transition to IFRS as a 'financial asset or financial liability at fair value through profit or loss' or as available-for-sale.[119] This exemption is not available to first-time adopters that are adopting IFRS in 2008.

B Periods beginning on or after 1 January 2006 and early adopters

A first-time adopter, whose first IFRS reporting period begins after 1 January 2006, is allowed to designate a financial asset on initial recognition as available-for-sale or designate a financial instrument (provided it meets certain criteria) as a 'financial asset or financial liability at fair value through profit or loss'. Although any entity is permitted to make an available-for-sale designation at the date of transition to IFRS, there are restrictions in relation to designation as 'financial asset or financial liability at fair value through profit or loss' in the following circumstances:[120]

'(b) *an entity that presents its first IFRS financial statements for an annual period beginning on or after 1 September 2006* – such an entity is permitted to designate, at the date of transition to IFRSs, any financial asset or financial liability as at fair value through profit or loss provided the asset or liability meets the criteria in paragraph 9(b)(i), 9(b)(ii) or 11A of IAS 39 at that date;

(c) *an entity that presents its first IFRS financial statements for an annual period beginning on or after 1 January 2006 and before 1 September 2006* – such an entity is permitted to designate, at the date of transition to IFRSs, any financial asset or financial liability as at fair value through profit or loss provided the asset or liability meets the criteria in paragraph 9(b)(i), 9(b)(ii) or 11A of IAS 39 at that date. When the date of transition to IFRSs is before 1 September 2005, such designations need not be completed until 1 September 2005 and may also include financial assets and financial liabilities recognised between the date of transition to IFRSs and 1 September 2005;

(d) *an entity that presents its first IFRS financial statements for an annual period beginning before 1 January 2006 and applies paragraphs 11A, 48A, AG4B–AG4K, AG33A and AG33B and the 2005 amendments in paragraphs 9, 12 and 13 of IAS 39* – [The guidance from IFRS 1, has not been repeated here as the exemption is not available to first-time adopters that are adopting IFRS in 2008];

(e) *for an entity that presents its first IFRS financial statements for an annual period beginning before 1 September 2006* – notwithstanding paragraph 91 of IAS 39, any financial assets and financial liabilities such an entity designated as at fair value through profit or loss in accordance with subparagraph (c) or (d) above that were previously designated as the hedged item in fair value hedge accounting relationships shall be de-designated from those relationships at the same time they are designated as at fair value through profit or loss.'

This rather complicated exemption is based on the transitional rules that apply to entities that already report under IFRS.[121] An entity may, under its previous GAAP, have measured investments at fair value and recognised the revaluation gain directly in equity.[122] Therefore, if upon initial application of IAS 39 the investment is classified as:[123]

- *at fair value through profit or loss*, any pre-IAS 39 revaluation gain that had been recognised in equity is reclassified into retained earnings on initial application of IAS 39;
- *available-for-sale*, then any pre-IAS 39 revaluation gain is recognised in a separate component of equity. Subsequently, the entity recognises gains and losses on the available-for-sale financial asset in that separate component of equity until the investment is impaired, sold, collected or otherwise disposed of. On subsequent derecognition or impairment of the available-for-sale financial asset, the first-time adopter transfers to profit or loss the cumulative gain or loss remaining in equity.

A first-time adopter that applies this exemption needs to make certain additional disclosures (see 2.10.2 B below).[124]

C Implementation guidance on other categories of financial instruments

The implementation guidance to IFRS 1 clarifies how, in preparing its opening IFRS balance sheet, an entity should apply the criteria in IAS 39 to identify those financial assets and financial liabilities that are measured at fair value and those that are measured at amortised cost:

- *held-to-maturity investments* – 'classification of financial assets as held-to-maturity investments relies on a designation made by the entity in applying IAS 39 reflecting the entity's intention and ability at the date of transition to IFRSs.'[125] In other words, sales or transfers of held-to-maturity investments before the date of transition to IFRS do not trigger the 'tainting' rules in IAS 39;
- *loans and receivables* – the category of 'loans and receivables' refers to the circumstances when the financial asset first satisfied the recognition criteria in IAS 39;[126]
- *financial assets and financial liabilities measured at amortised cost* – the cost of financial assets and financial liabilities measured at amortised cost in the opening IFRS balance sheet should be determined on the basis of circumstances existing when the assets and liabilities first satisfied the recognition criteria in IAS 39, unless they were acquired in a past business combination in which case their carrying amount under previous GAAP immediately following the business combination is their deemed cost under IFRSs at that date (see 2.4.3 D above); and[127]
- *loan impairments* – an entity's estimates of loan impairments at the date of transition to IFRS should be consistent with estimates made for the same date under previous GAAP (after adjustments to reflect any difference in accounting policies), unless there is objective evidence that those assumptions were in error. Any later revisions to those estimates should be treated as impairment losses (or reversals of impairment losses) of the period in which it makes the revisions.[128]

2.6.3 Compound financial instruments

IAS 32 requires compound financial instruments (such as a convertible bond) to be split at inception into separate equity and liability components. If the liability component is no longer outstanding, a full retrospective application of IAS 32 would involve identifying two components, one representing the original equity component and the other representing the cumulative interest on the liability component, both of which are accounted for in equity (see Chapter 19 at 8). A first-time adopter does not need to make this allocation if the liability component is no longer outstanding at the date of transition to IFRS (or the beginning of the first IFRS reporting period, if comparatives are not restated).[129] For example, in the case of a convertible bond that has been converted into equity, it is not necessary to make this split.

A first-time adopter applying this exemption can therefore avoid the possibly complex allocation process that would be involved. However, if the liability component of the compound instrument is still outstanding at the date of transition to IFRS (or the beginning of the first IFRS reporting period, if comparatives are not restated), then a split will need to be made (see Chapter 19).[130] In practice this exemption is of limited value because the number of different compound financial instruments that were outstanding before the date of transition to IFRS (or the beginning of the first IFRS reporting period, if comparatives are not restated) is bound to be limited for any given first-time adopter.

2.6.4 Derecognition of financial assets and financial liabilities

A first-time adopter should apply the derecognition requirements in IAS 39 prospectively to transactions occurring on or after 1 January 2004. Therefore, if a first-time adopter derecognised non-derivative financial assets or non-derivative financial liabilities under its previous GAAP as a result of a transaction that occurred before 1 January 2004, it should not recognise those assets and liabilities under IFRS (unless they qualify for recognition as a result of a later transaction or event).[131] A first-time adopter that wants to apply the derecognition requirements in IAS 39 retrospectively from a date of the entity's choosing can only do so 'provided that the information needed to apply IAS 39 to financial assets and financial liabilities derecognised as a result of past transactions was obtained at the time of initially accounting for those transactions.'[132] This will effectively ban most first-time adopters from restating transactions that occurred before 1 January 2004.

A first-time adopter that derecognised non-derivative financial assets and liabilities under its previous GAAP before 1 January 2004 will not have to recognise these items under IFRS even if they meet the IAS 39 recognition criteria.[133] However, a first-time adopter is not exempt from SIC-12 – *Consolidation – Special Purpose Entities* – which requires consolidation of all special purpose entities. Therefore, not all previously derecognised items will remain off-balance sheet upon adoption of IFRS. Extract 5.5 at 2.10.2 below illustrates how an entity might disclose the fact that it has made use of this exemption.

2.6.5 Hedge accounting

Hedge accounting is dealt with comprehensively in Chapter 21. The discussion below of first-time adoption issues relating to hedge accounting can also be found in Chapter 21 at 7.3.1 to 7.3.4. Detailed worked examples illustrating the first-time adoption requirements in IFRS 1 can be found in Chapter 21 at 7.3.5.

A Prohibition on retrospective application

IFRS 1 explains that entities are prohibited from applying retrospectively some of the hedge accounting provisions of IAS 39.[134] In the basis for conclusions, it is explained that:

> '... it is unlikely that most entities would have adopted IAS 39's criteria for (a) documenting hedges at their inception and (b) testing the hedges for effectiveness, even if they intended to continue the same hedging strategies after adopting IAS 39. Furthermore, retrospective designation of hedges (or retrospective reversal of their designation) could lead to selective designation of some hedges to report a particular result.[135]
>
> To overcome these problems, the transitional requirements in IAS 39 require an entity already applying IFRS to apply the hedging requirements prospectively when it adopts IAS 39. As the same problems arise for a first-

> time adopter, the IFRS requires prospective application by a first-time adopter.'[136]

Unfortunately, there is only a limited amount of guidance in IFRS 1 regarding hedge accounting and therefore it is not entirely clear what applying these requirements of IAS 39 'prospectively' actually involves, especially insofar as the opening IFRS balance sheet is concerned. However, the basis for conclusions continues:

> 'ED 1 included a redrafted version of the transitional provisions in IAS 39 and related Questions and Answers (Q&As) developed by the IAS 39 Implementation Guidance Committee. The Board confirmed in the Basis for Conclusions published with ED 1 that it did not intend the redrafting to create substantive changes. However, in the light of responses to ED 1, the Board decided in finalising IFRS 1 that the redrafting would not make it easier for first-time adopters and others to understand and apply the transition provisions and Q&As. However, the project to improve IAS 32 and IAS 39 resulted in certain amendments to the transition requirements. In addition, this project incorporated selected other Q&As (i.e. not on transition) into IAS 39. The Board therefore took this opportunity to consolidate all the guidance for first-time adopters in one place, by incorporating the Q&As on transition into IFRS 1.'[137]

This indicates that the transitional provisions set out in the previous version of IAS 39 and IGC Q&As, ED 1 and IFRS 1 are intended to be broadly consistent. Consequently, the fact that all three sources are expressed in different ways can be useful in interpreting this aspect of IFRS 1. These documents are referred to at B below where they assist in understanding the requirements set out in IFRS 1.

B Hedge accounting: opening IFRS balance sheet

I Measurement of derivatives and elimination of deferred gains and losses

Under its previous GAAP an entity's accounting policies might have included a number of accounting treatments for derivatives that formed part of a hedge relationship. For example, accounting policies might have included those where the derivative was:

- not explicitly recognised as an asset or liability (e.g. in the case of a forward contract used to hedge an expected but uncontracted future transaction);
- recognised as an asset or liability but at an amount different from its fair value (e.g. a purchased option recognised at its original cost, perhaps less amortisation; or an interest rate swap accounted for by accruing the periodic interest payments and receipts); or
- subsumed within the accounting for another asset or liability (e.g. a foreign currency denominated monetary item and a matching forward contract or swap accounted for as a 'synthetic' functional currency denominated monetary item).

Whatever the previous accounting treatment, a first-time adopter should isolate and separately account for all derivatives in its opening IFRS balance sheet as assets or liabilities measured at fair value.[138]

The implementation guidance explains that all derivatives, other than those that are designated and effective hedging instruments, are classified as held for trading. Accordingly, the difference between the previous carrying amount of a derivative (which may have been zero) and its fair value should be recognised as an adjustment of the balance of retained earnings at the beginning of the financial year in which IFRS 1 is initially applied (other than for a derivative that is a designated and effective hedging instrument).[139] In addition, IFRS 1 would require an entity that is unable to determine whether a particular portion of an adjustment is a transitional adjustment or a change in estimate, to treat that portion as a change in accounting estimate under IAS 8, with appropriate disclosures as required by paragraphs 32 to 40 of IAS 8.[140]

Hedge accounting policies under an entity's previous GAAP might also have included one or both of the following accounting treatments:

- derivatives were measured at fair value but, to the extent they were regarded as hedging future transactions, the gain (or loss) arising was reported as a liability (or asset) such as deferred (or accrued) income;
- realised gains or losses arising on the termination of a previously unrecognised derivative used in a hedge relationship (such as an interest rate swap hedging a borrowing) were included in the balance sheet as deferred or accrued income and amortised over the remaining term of the hedged exposure.

In all cases an entity is required to eliminate deferred gains and losses arising on derivatives 'that were reported under previous GAAP as if they were assets or liabilities.'[141] Essentially this is because deferred gains and losses do not meet the definition of assets or liabilities under the IASB's *Framework*. In contrast to adjustments made to restate derivatives at fair value, the implementation guidance in IFRS 1 does not specify in general terms how to deal with adjustments to eliminate deferred gains or losses.

The requirement to eliminate deferred gains and losses does not appear to extend to those that have been included in the carrying amount of other assets or liabilities that will continue to be recognised under IFRS. For example, under an entity's previous GAAP, the carrying amount of non-financial assets such as inventories or property, plant and equipment might have included the equivalent of a basis adjustment (i.e. hedging gains or losses were considered an integral part of the asset's cost). In fact carrying forward this treatment into an entity's first set of IFRS financial statements would be consistent with the transitional provisions of the revised IAS 39 (see Chapter 21 at 7.2). Of course entities should also consider any other provisions of IFRS 1 that apply to those hedged items.

The way in which an entity accounts for these adjustments will, to a large extent, dictate how its existing hedge relationships will be reflected in its ongoing IFRS financial statements. Particularly, an entity's future results will be different depending on whether the adjustments are taken to retained earnings or to a separate component of equity – in the latter case they would be recycled to profit or loss at a later date but would not in the former. Similarly, its future results would be affected if the carrying amounts of related assets or liabilities are changed to reflect these adjustments (as opposed to the adjustments being made to retained earnings). For short-term hedges (e.g. of sales and inventory purchases) these effects are likely to work their way out of the IFRS financial statements relatively quickly. However for other hedges (e.g. of long term borrowings) an entity's results may be affected for many years. The question of which hedge relationships should be reflected in an entity's opening IFRS balance sheet is dealt with at II to IV below.

II Hedge relationships reflected in the opening IFRS balance sheet

The standard states that a first-time adopter *should not* reflect a hedging relationship in its opening IFRS balance sheet (or the balance sheet at the beginning of its first IFRS reporting period, if comparatives are not restated) if that hedging relationship is of a type that *does not* qualify for hedge accounting under IAS 39. As examples of this it cites many hedging relationships where the hedging instrument is a cash instrument or written option; where the hedged item is a net position; or where the hedge covers interest risk in a held-to-maturity investment.[142]

However, if an entity had designated a net position as a hedged item under its previous GAAP, the IASB decided that an individual item within that net position *may* be designated as a hedged item under IFRS, provided that it does so no later than the date of transition to IFRS (or the beginning of the first IFRS reporting period, if comparatives are not restated).[143] In other words, such designation could allow the hedge relationship to be reflected in the opening IFRS balance sheet (or the balance sheet at the beginning of its first IFRS reporting period, if comparatives are not restated).

Further, a first-time adopter is not permitted to designate hedges retrospectively in relation to transactions entered into before the date of transition to IFRS (or the beginning of the first IFRS reporting period, if comparatives are not restated).[144] This would appear to prevent an entity from reflecting hedge relationships in its opening balance sheet that it did not identify as such under its previous GAAP.

Assuming that an eligible IAS 39 hedge relationship existed under previous GAAP that was accounted for as such, it would appear that there is no restriction on testing hedge effectiveness based on the effectiveness of the hedge for its entire life – which may include a start date well before transition – rather than from the date of transition. Under IAS 39, the hedge documentation should state specifically whether the expected hedge effectiveness will be assessed either cumulatively over the life of the hedge from inception *or* separately for each reporting period.[145]

It might seem to follow that a hedge relationship designated under an entity's previous GAAP *should* be reflected in its opening IFRS balance sheet (or the balance sheet at the beginning of its first IFRS reporting period, if comparatives are not restated) if that hedging relationship *is* of a type that *does* qualify for hedge accounting under IAS 39. In fact, if an entity was allowed not to reflect such a hedge in its opening IFRS balance sheet (or the balance sheet at the beginning of its first IFRS reporting period, if comparatives are not restated) this would effectively allow the retrospective reversal of the hedge designation. As noted at I above, this is something the IASB has sought to avoid.[146] However, while such a 'principle' seems to be implied by the implementation guidance (see III and IV below), the IASB has not actually articulated it in these terms.

There are, perhaps, a number of reasons for the IASB's reticence. For example, under an entity's previous GAAP, it might not have been clear whether a derivative instrument was actually designated as a hedge. Further, even if it were clear that a derivative had previously been designated as a hedge, the hedged item might not have been identified with sufficient specificity to allow the effects of the hedge to be reflected in the opening IFRS balance sheet and/or, thereafter, to be 'unwound' at the appropriate time. Nevertheless, if (1) a hedge relationship can be specifically identified under an entity's previous GAAP and (2) that hedge relationship is eligible for hedge accounting under IFRS then the entity must account for the hedge relationship upon transition, regardless of whether the hedge relationship is effective or not. However, if the hedge relationship does not meet the requirements in IAS 39 prospectively then hedge discontinuation rules in that standard apply immediately after transition.

III Reflecting cash flow hedges in the opening IFRS balance sheet

The implementation guidance to IFRS 1 explains that a first-time adopter may, under its previous GAAP, have deferred gains and losses on a cash flow hedge of a forecast transaction. If, at the date of transition to IFRS (or the beginning of the first IFRS reporting period, if comparatives are not restated), the hedged forecast transaction is not highly probable, but is expected to occur, the entire deferred gain or loss should be recognised in equity.[147] To be consistent, this would be included in the same component of equity an entity would use to record future gains and losses on cash flow hedges.

This raises the question of how to deal with such a hedge if, at the date of transition to IFRS (or the beginning of the first IFRS reporting period, if comparatives are not restated), the forecast transaction *was* highly probable. It would make no sense if the former was required to be reflected in the opening IFRS balance sheet, but the latter (which is clearly a 'better' hedge) was not. Therefore, it must follow that a cash flow hedge should be reflected in the opening IFRS balance sheet in the way set out above if the hedged item is a forecast transaction that is highly probable. Similarly, it follows that a cash flow hedge of the variability in cash flows attributable to a particular risk associated with a recognised asset or liability (such as all or some future interest payments on variable rate debt) should also be reflected in the opening balance sheet.

If, at the date of transition to IFRS (or the beginning of the first IFRS reporting period, if comparatives are not restated), the forecast transaction was *not* expected to occur, this would be a relationship of a type that does not qualify for hedge accounting under IAS 39. Therefore the hedging relationship should not be reflected in the opening IFRS balance sheet. In fact ED 1 was explicit on this point.[148]

There are various ways in which gains or losses might have been deferred under an entity's previous GAAP. ED 1 explained that, in this context, deferral included:

- treating deferred gains as if they were liabilities and deferred losses as if they were assets; and

- not recognising changes in the fair value of the hedging instrument.[149]

Even though this explanation was not incorporated into IFRS 1, at a conceptual level there is scarce reason why it should not apply under the standard. However, it is possible to read parts of the implementation guidance as preventing this treatment if the hedge has not been designated in an effective hedge under IAS 39 by the date of transition (or the beginning of the first IFRS reporting period, if comparatives are not restated). The following example highlights this issue.

Example 5.25: Unrecognised gains and losses on existing cash flow hedge

Company T has the euro as its functional currency. In September 2005 it entered into a forward currency contract to sell dollars for euros in twelve months to hedge dollar denominated sales it forecasts are highly probable to occur in September 2006. T will apply IAS 39 from 1 January 2006, its date of transition to IFRS. The historical cost of the forward contract is €nil and at the date of transition it had a positive fair value of €100.

Case 1: Gains and losses deferred

Under T's previous GAAP, until the sales occurred the forward contract was recognised in the balance sheet at its fair value and the resulting gain or loss was deferred in the balance sheet as a liability or asset. When the sale occurred any deferred gain or loss was recognised in profit or loss as an offset to the revenue recognised on the hedged sales.

Case 2: Gains and losses unrecognised

Under T's previous GAAP the contract was not recognised in the balance sheet. When the sale occurred any unrecognised gain or loss was recognised in profit or loss as an offset to the revenue recognised on the hedged sales.

In Case 1 the relationship can clearly be reflected in T's opening IFRS balance sheet whether or not it is designated as an effective hedge in accordance with IAS 39 at the date of transition: there is no restriction on transferring the deferred gain to a separate component of equity and there is no adjustment to the carrying amount of the forward contract.

Case 2 is slightly more problematic. As noted at I above, the implementation guidance explains that the difference between the previous carrying amount of a derivative and its fair value should be recognised as an adjustment of the balance of retained earnings (other than for a derivative that is a designated and effective hedging instrument).[150] Read literally, if T had not designated the relationship as an effective hedge in accordance with IAS 39 at the date of transition, this implementation guidance could prevent the relationship from being reflected in T's opening IFRS balance sheet. This is because the adjustment to the carrying amount of the forward would be recorded in retained earnings rather than a separate component of equity.

Such an interpretation would allow T to choose not to designate (in accordance with IAS 39) certain cash flow hedges, say those that are in a loss position, until one day after its date of transition, thereby allowing associated hedging losses to bypass profit or loss completely. Notwithstanding this, some have suggested the literal interpretation is appropriate. However, this would effectively result in the retrospective de-designation of hedges to achieve a desired result, thereby breaching this general principle of IFRS 1. Arguably this general principle of the standard should take precedence over the implementation guidance.

IV Reflecting fair value hedges in the opening IFRS balance sheet

The implementation guidance to IFRS 1 explains that a first-time adopter may, under its previous GAAP, have deferred or not recognised gains and losses on a fair value hedge of a hedged item that is not measured at fair value. For such a fair value hedge, the entity should adjust the carrying amount of the hedged item at the date of transition to IFRS (or the beginning of the first IFRS reporting period, if comparatives are not restated). The adjustment, which is essentially the effective part of the hedge that was not recognised in the carrying amount of the hedged item under the previous GAAP, should be calculated as the lower of:

(a) that portion of the cumulative change in the fair value of the hedged item that reflects the designated hedged risk and was not recognised under previous GAAP; and

(b) that portion of the cumulative change in the fair value of the hedging instrument that reflects the designated hedged risk and, under previous GAAP, was either (i) not recognised or (ii) deferred in the balance sheet as an asset or liability.[151]

This is consistent with the requirement in the previous version of IAS 39 (and the proposals in ED 1) under which any balance sheet positions in fair value hedges of existing assets and liabilities would be accounted for in the opening balance sheet in (broadly) the same manner as above.[152]

Available-for-sale assets are measured at fair value, so the guidance above would not appear to apply to fair value hedges of such instruments. However, it would be logical to apply an equivalent adjustment to the cost or amortised cost of such assets.

C Hedge accounting: subsequent treatment

The implementation guidance explains that hedge accounting can be applied prospectively only from the date the hedge relationship is fully designated and documented. Therefore, if the hedging instrument is still held at the date of transition to IFRS (or the beginning of the first IFRS reporting period, if comparatives are not restated), the designation and documentation of a hedge relationship must be completed on or before that date if the hedge relationship is to qualify for hedge accounting on an ongoing basis from that date.[153]

An entity may, before the date of transition to IFRS (or the beginning of the first IFRS reporting period, if comparatives are not restated), have designated a transaction as a hedge that does not meet the conditions for hedge accounting in IAS 39. In these cases it should follow the general requirements in IAS 39 for discontinuing hedge accounting – these are dealt with in Chapter 21 at 4.1.3 for fair value hedges and in Chapter 21 at 4.2.3 for cash flow hedges.[154]

For cash flow hedges, any net cumulative gain or loss that was reclassified to equity on initial application of IAS 39 (see 2.6.5 B III above) should remain in equity until:

(a) the forecast transaction subsequently results in the recognition of a non-financial asset or non-financial liability;

(b) the forecast transaction affects profit or loss; or

(c) subsequently circumstances change and the forecast transaction is no longer expected to occur, in which case any related net cumulative gain or loss that had been recognised directly in equity is recognised in profit or loss.[155]

The requirements above do little more than reiterate the general requirements of IAS 39, i.e. that hedge accounting can only be applied prospectively if the qualifying conditions are met, and entities should experience few interpretative problems in dealing with this aspect of the hedge accounting requirements.

2.6.6 Fair value measurement of financial instruments at initial recognition

In December 2004, the IASB issued an amendment to IAS 39 – *Transition and Initial Recognition of Financial Assets and Financial Liabilities* – which clarifies that the application of paragraph AG76 of IAS 39 should not give rise to a 'Day 1' gain or loss upon initial recognition of a financial asset or financial liability (see Chapter 20 at 4.7). This amendment would have been applicable retrospectively to all first-time adopters after 1 January 2005.[156] However, given the concerns of the IASB's constituents that 'retrospective application would diverge from the requirements of US GAAP',[157] the Board decided to allow first-time adopters to apply the requirements of paragraphs AG76 and AG76A of IAS 39 in any of the following ways:[158]

(a) retrospectively;

(b) prospectively to transactions entered into after 25 October 2002; or

(c) prospectively to transactions entered into after 1 January 2004.

2.6.7 Derivatives, embedded derivatives and transaction costs

At the date of transition to IFRS (or the beginning of the first IFRS reporting period, if comparatives are not restated), IAS 39 requires a first-time adopter to measure all derivatives at fair value and to eliminate deferred gains and losses arising 'on derivatives that were reported under previous GAAP as if they were assets or liabilities.'[159]

A Derivatives

All derivatives, except for those that are designated and effective hedging instruments, are classified as held for trading under IAS 39. Therefore, the difference between their fair value and their previous carrying amount should be recognised as an adjustment to retained earnings at the beginning of the financial year in which IAS 39 is initially applied (other than for a derivative that is a designated and effective hedging instrument).[160]

B Embedded derivatives

IAS 39 requires an entity to account separately for some embedded derivatives at fair value (see Chapter 17 at 5). Under US GAAP, the transitional provisions of SFAS 133 – *Accounting for Derivative Instruments and Hedging Activities* – exempt an entity from having to account for some pre-existing embedded derivatives separately. The IASB considered this and the fact that full retrospective accounting for embedded derivatives might be costly, but concluded 'that the failure to measure embedded derivatives at fair value would diminish the relevance and reliability of an entity's first IFRS financial statements.'[161] A first-time adopter will therefore have to consider all contracts existing at its date of transition to IFRS (or the beginning of the first IFRS reporting period, if comparatives are not restated) and decide whether or not they contain embedded derivatives. Any embedded derivatives that are identified and have to be accounted for separately should be recognised as assets or liabilities, and be measured at their fair value. If an entity 'cannot determine the initial carrying amounts of the embedded derivative and host contract reliably, it treats the entire combined contract as a financial instrument held for trading.'[162]

C Transaction costs

To determine the amortised cost of a financial asset or liability using the effective interest rate method, a first-time adopter needs to establish the transaction costs incurred when the instrument was originated. Despite arguments by some commentators that this might involve unduc cost or effort, the IASB concluded that 'the unamortised portion of transaction costs at the date of transition to IFRSs [or the beginning of the first IFRS reporting period, if comparatives are not restated] is unlikely to be material for most financial assets and financial liabilities' and therefore presumably does not require restatement.[163] The IASB presumes that 'even when the unamortised portion is material, reasonable estimates should be possible.'[164]

2.7 Other exemptions

As discussed at 2.3.3 A above, IFRS 1 establishes exemptions from the requirements of other IFRS. Those exemptions not already dealt with above are discussed at 2.7.1 to 2.7.5 below.

2.7.1 Employee benefits

Under IAS 19 an entity is allowed to use a 'corridor' approach that leaves some actuarial gains and losses on defined benefit plans unrecognised.[165] To calculate the net cumulative unrecognised gains or losses at the date of transition to IFRS, a first-time adopter would need to determine actuarial gains or losses for each year since inception (or later date of acquisition of the subsidiary to which the defined benefit plan relates) of each defined benefit plan. It is obvious that a full retrospective application of IAS 19 would be costly (if not impossible to achieve) and not benefit users of the financial statements.[166] Therefore, the IASB introduced an exemption that allows a first-time adopter 'to recognise all cumulative actuarial gains and losses at the date of transition to IFRS, even if it uses the corridor approach for later actuarial gains and losses'. If a first-time adopter uses this exemption it will have to apply the exemption to all its defined benefit plans.[167]

In the extract below an entity discloses that it used the employee benefits exemption in IFRS 1.

Extract 5.4: Fortis SA/NV (2005)

2 Accounting principles [extract]

2.3 First-Time Adoption of IFRS [extract]

Employee Benefits: Under IAS 19, Employee Benefits, entities may elect to use a 'corridor' approach that leaves some actuarial gains and losses within defined limits unrecognised. Retrospective application of this approach requires an entity to split the cumulative actuarial gains and losses from the inception of the plan until the date of transition to IFRS into a recognised portion and an unrecognised portion. However, entities may elect to recognise all cumulative actuarial gains and losses at the date of transition to IFRS. Fortis has decided to take advantage of this exemption and therefore doesn't apply IAS 19 retrospectively, and recognises all actuarial gains and losses on the opening balance sheet on 1 January 2004. Fortis applies the corridor approach prospectively from this date.

A Full actuarial valuations

An entity's first IFRS financial statements may reflect its defined benefit liabilities at three different dates, that is, the reporting date, the end of the comparative period and the date of transition to IFRS. An entity that presents two comparative periods would have to calculate its defined benefits liabilities at four different dates. Clearly, it is quite costly to require a first-time adopter to perform three, or possibly even four, actuarial valuations. However, the IASB decided against permitting 'an entity to use a single actuarial valuation, based, for example, on assumptions valid at the reporting date, with service costs and interest costs based on those assumptions for each of the periods presented.'[168] The IASB's main objection to such an exemption was that it 'would conflict with the objective of providing understandable, relevant, reliable and comparable information for users.'[169] Nevertheless, the IASB agreed to the compromise position that if an entity obtains a full actuarial valuation at one or two dates, it is allowed to roll forward (or roll back) to another date but only as long as the roll forward (or roll back) reflects material transactions and other material events between those dates (including changes in market prices and interest rates).[170]

B Actuarial assumptions

A first-time adopter's actuarial assumptions at its date of transition to IFRS should be consistent with the ones it used for the same date under its previous GAAP, unless there is objective evidence that those assumptions were in error (see 2.8.1 below). The impact of any later revisions to those assumptions is an actuarial gain or loss of the period in which the entity makes the revisions.[171] If a first-time adopter needs 'to make actuarial assumptions at the date of transition to IFRSs that were not necessary under its previous GAAP' these actuarial assumptions should 'not reflect conditions that arose after the date of transition to IFRS. In particular, discount rates and the fair value of plan assets at the date of transition to IFRSs reflect market conditions at that date. Similarly, the entity's actuarial assumptions at the date of transition to IFRSs about future employee turnover rates do not reflect a significant increase in estimated employee turnover rates as a result of a curtailment of the pension plan that occurred after the date of transition to IFRSs.'[172]

C Unrecognised past service costs

It is worth mentioning that the employee benefits exemption only applies to unrecognised actuarial gains or losses, it does not apply to 'unrecognised past service costs' that relate to unvested benefits. The IASB decided that an exemption for past service cost was not justified because a full retrospective application of IAS 19 to unrecognised past service costs 'is less onerous than the retrospective application of the corridor for actuarial gains and losses because it does not require the recreation of data since the inception of the plan.'[173] A first-time adopter therefore needs to look at periods before its date of transition to IFRS to determine the amount of unrecognised past service costs that relate to unvested benefits in accordance with IAS 19.

D Exemption from presenting historical summary information

When IAS 19 was amended in December 2004, the IASB introduced a requirement in paragraph 120A(p) of IAS 19 to disclose the amounts for the current annual period and previous four annual periods of (see Chapter 32 at 7.2.2):

- the present value of the defined benefit obligation, the fair value of the plan assets and the surplus or deficit in the plan; and
- the experience adjustments arising on:
  - the plan liabilities expressed either as (1) an amount or (2) a percentage of the plan liabilities at the balance sheet date; and
  - the plan assets expressed either as (1) an amount or (2) a percentage of the plan assets at the balance sheet date.

Obviously, an entity that applied the employee benefits exemption above will not be able to comply with this requirement for periods prior to its date of transition. An entity is therefore permitted to disclose the above information for each accounting period prospectively from the transition date.[174]

2.7.2 Cumulative translation differences

Exchange differences arising on a monetary item that forms part of a reporting entity's net investment in a foreign operation are recognised in a separate component of equity under IAS 21.[175] IAS 21 and IAS 39 require that, on disposal of a foreign operation, the cumulative amount of the exchange differences deferred in the separate component of equity relating to that foreign operation (which includes, for example, the cumulative translation difference for that foreign operation, the exchange differences arising on certain translations to a different presentation currency and any gains and losses on related hedges) should be recognised in profit or loss when the gain or loss on disposal is recognised.[176]

Full retrospective application of IAS 21 would require a first-time adopter to restate all financial statements of its foreign operations to IFRS from their date of inception or later acquisition onwards, and then determine the cumulative translation differences arising in relation to each of these foreign operations. The costs of this restatement are likely to exceed the benefits to users of financial statements. For this reason 'a first-time adopter need not comply with these requirements for cumulative translation differences that existed at the date of transition to IFRSs. If a first-time adopter uses this exemption:

(a) the cumulative translation differences for all foreign operations are deemed to be zero at the date of transition to IFRSs; and

(b) the gain or loss on a subsequent disposal of any foreign operation shall exclude translation differences that arose before the date of transition to IFRS and shall include later translation differences.'[177]

As discussed in Chapter 21 at 7.3.1, IFRS 1 is unfortunately not entirely clear as to whether the exemption extends to similar gains and losses arising on related hedges. Therefore, entities will need to apply judgement in determining how and when the cumulative gains and losses on net investment hedges are reset to zero.

Extract 5.5 at 2.10.2 below illustrates how companies typically disclose the fact that they have made use of this exemption.

As discussed at 3.4 below, IFRS 1 requires full retrospective application of IAS 21. Consequently, a first-time adopter that measured transactions in a currency that was not its functional currency will need to restate its financial statements.

2.7.3 *Share-based payment transactions*

IFRS 2 applies to accounting for the acquisition of goods or services in equity-settled share-based payment transactions, cash-settled share-based payment transactions and transactions in which the entity or the counter-party has the option to choose between settlement in cash or equity. Although the transitional rules for first-time adopters are based on the transitional rules for existing IFRS reporting entities, the IASB specifically added the following exemptions for first-time adopters:[178]

- a first-time adopter is not required to apply IFRS 2 to equity instruments that were granted after 7 November 2002 but that vested before the date of transition to IFRS; and
- a first-time adopter is not required to apply IFRS 2 to liabilities arising from cash-settled share-based payment transactions if those liabilities were settled before 1 January 2005 or before the date of transition to IFRS.

IFRS 1 contains the following exemptions and requirements regarding share-based payment transactions:

(a) only if a first-time adopter 'has disclosed publicly the fair value of those equity instruments, determined at the measurement date, as defined in IFRS 2' is it encouraged but not required to apply IFRS 2 to:[179]

   (i) equity instruments that were granted on or before 7 November 2002;

   (ii) equity instruments that were granted after 7 November 2002 but vested before the later of (1) the date of transition to IFRS and (2) 1 January 2005.

   Many first-time adopters will not have published the fair value of equity instruments granted and are, therefore, not allowed to apply IFRS 2 retrospectively to those share-based transactions;

(b) for all grants of equity instruments to which IFRS 2 has not been applied a first-time adopter shall nevertheless disclose the information required by paragraphs 44 and 45 of IFRS 2;[180] and

(c) if a first-time adopter modifies the terms or conditions of a grant of equity instruments to which IFRS 2 has not been applied, the entity is not required to apply paragraphs 26–29 of IFRS 2 if the modification occurred before the later of (1) the date of transition to IFRS and (2) 1 January 2005.[181]

Furthermore, if share-based payments give rise to liabilities, a first-time adopter is:[182]

(d) 'encouraged, but not required, to apply IFRS 2 to liabilities arising from share-based payment transactions that were settled before the date of transition to IFRS';

(e) 'also encouraged, but not required, to apply IFRS 2 to liabilities that were settled before 1 January 2005' and

(f) 'for liabilities to which IFRS 2 is applied … not required to restate comparative information to the extent that the information relates to a period or date that is earlier than 7 November 2002'.

IFRS 1 allows a first-time adopter to pick and choose from these options as it sees fit, i.e. it does not encourage or require a first-time adopter to make logical use of the options. However, the qualitative characteristics of financial statements as set out in the *Framework* would seem to dictate that a first-time adopter should not apply the above exemptions in a random fashion.[183]

Extract 5.5 at 2.10.2 below provides an illustration of typical disclosures made in relation to the share-based payments exemption.

A Meaning of 'disclosed publicly'

IFRS 1 only permits retrospective application of IFRS 2 to the extent that the entity has 'disclosed publicly' the fair value of those equity instruments, but IFRS does not define what is meant by 'disclosed publicly'. However, the basis for conclusions to IAS 40 – which also uses the phrase 'disclosed publicly' – states that 'there is a risk that restatement of prior periods might allow entities to manipulate their reported profit or loss for the period by selective use of hindsight in determining fair values in prior periods. Accordingly, the Board decided to prohibit restatement in the fair value model, except where an entity has already publicly disclosed fair values for prior periods …'.[184] It is therefore likely that the IASB introduced the same wording in relation to share-based payments to ensure that only entities that contemporaneously calculated and publicly disclosed the fair value of their share-based payments would be able to apply IFRS 2 retrospectively. Although IFRS 1 does not specifically require public disclosure of the fair value of an entity's share-based payments in its previous financial statements, in our opinion it does seem clear that IFRS 1 would require that fair value to have been published contemporaneously.

B Restatement of costs recognised under previous GAAP?

A first-time adopter may elect to take advantage of the transitional provisions in IFRS 1 which allow it not to apply IFRS 2 to certain share-based payments whether or not it recognised a cost for those transactions in accordance with its previous GAAP. Neither IFRS 1 nor IFRS 2 clearly indicates the appropriate treatment of the costs of share-based payments that were recognised under the previous GAAP. In practice, either of the following approaches is considered acceptable, provided that the treatment chosen is disclosed in the financial statements if the previously recognised costs are material:

- *previous GAAP share-based payment charge* – For transactions covered by the share-based payments exemption, a share-based payment expense determined in accordance with the previous GAAP is recognised in the first IFRS financial statements; or
- *recognise no share-based payment expense* – No share-based payment expense is recognised for those transactions that are covered by the share-based payments exemption.

Under both approaches the comparability between reporting periods is somewhat limited. Full comparability can only be achieved if the first-time adopter is capable of opting not to make use of the share-based payment exemption.

2.7.4 Insurance contracts

A first-time adopter may apply the transitional provisions in IFRS 4. That standard limits an insurer to changing 'its accounting policies for insurance contracts if, and only if, the change makes the financial statements more relevant to the economic decision-making needs of users and no less reliable, or more reliable and no less relevant to those needs. An insurer shall judge relevance and reliability by the criteria in IAS 8.'[185]

The option not to present comparative information in accordance with IFRS 4 was only available to first-time adopters that adopted IFRS for the first time before 1 January 2006 and is therefore no longer relevant.[186]

2.7.5 Assets and liabilities of subsidiaries, associates and joint ventures

A Subsidiary becomes a first-time adopter later than its parent

Within groups, some subsidiaries, associates and joint ventures may have a different date of transition to IFRS than the parent/investor (for example, national legislation required IFRS after, or prohibited IFRS at, the date of transition to IFRS of the parent/investor). This could result in permanent differences between the IFRS figures in a subsidiary's own financial statements and those it reports to its parent. In turn this could force a subsidiary to keep two parallel sets of accounting records based on different dates of transition to IFRS.[187] To mitigate this difficulty, the IASB introduced a special exemption regarding the assets and liabilities of subsidiaries, associates and joint ventures.

If a subsidiary becomes a first-time adopter later than its parent, it should in its financial statements measure its assets and liabilities at either:

'(a) the carrying amounts that would be included in the parent's consolidated financial statements, based on the parent's date of transition to IFRSs, if no adjustments were made for consolidation procedures and for the effects of the business combination in which the parent acquired the subsidiary; or

(b) the carrying amounts required by the rest of this IFRS [IFRS 1], based on the subsidiary's date of transition to IFRSs. These carrying amounts could differ from those described in (a):

  (i) when the exemptions in this IFRS result in measurements that depend on the date of transition to IFRSs;

  (ii) when the accounting policies used in the subsidiary's financial statements differ from those in the consolidated financial statements. For example, the subsidiary may use as its accounting policy the cost model in IAS 16, whereas the group may use the revaluation model.'[188]

A similar election is available to an associate or joint venture that becomes a first-time adopter later than an entity that has significant influence or joint control over it.[189] The following example, which is taken from the guidance on implementation of IFRS 1, illustrates how an entity should apply these requirements.

Example 5.26: Parent adopts IFRSs before subsidiary[190]

Background

Parent N presents its (consolidated) first IFRS financial statements in 2005. Its foreign subsidiary O, wholly owned by parent N since formation, prepares information under IFRSs for internal consolidation purposes from that date, but subsidiary O will not present its first IFRS financial statements until 2007.

Application of requirements

If subsidiary O applies paragraph 24(a) of the IFRS, the carrying amounts of its assets and liabilities are the same in both its opening IFRS balance sheet at 1 January 2006 and parent N's consolidated balance sheet (except for adjustments for consolidation procedures) and are based on parent N's date of transition to IFRSs.

Alternatively, subsidiary O may, under paragraph 24(b) of the IFRS, measure all its assets or liabilities based on its own date of transition to IFRSs (1 January 2006). However, the fact that subsidiary O becomes a first-time adopter in 2007 does not change the carrying amounts of its assets and liabilities in parent N's consolidated financial statements.

Under option (b) a subsidiary would prepare its own IFRS financial statements, completely ignoring the IFRS reports that its parent uses in preparing its consolidated financial statements. Under option (a) the numbers in a subsidiary's IFRS financial statements will be as close to those used by its parent as possible. However, differences other than those arising from consolidation procedures and business combinations will still exist in many cases, for example:

- a subsidiary may have hedged an exposure by entering into a transaction with a fellow subsidiary. Such transaction could qualify for hedge accounting in the subsidiary's own financial statements but not in the parent's consolidated financial statements; or

- a pension plan may have to be classified as a defined contribution plan from the subsidiary's point of view, but is accounted for as a defined benefit plan in the parent's consolidated financial statements.

The IASB seems content with the fact that the exemption 'will ease some practical problems', though it will rarely succeed in achieving more than a moderate reduction of the number of reconciling differences between a subsidiary's own reporting and the numbers used by its parent.[191]

Application of option (a) would be more difficult when a parent and its subsidiary (joint venture or associate) have different financial years. In that case, IFRS 1 would seem to require the IFRS information for the subsidiary (joint venture or associate) to be based on the parent's date of transition to IFRS, which may not even coincide with an interim reporting date of the subsidiary (joint venture or associate).

A subsidiary may become a first-time adopter later than its parent, because it previously prepared a reporting package under IFRS for consolidation purposes but did not present a full set of financial statements under IFRS. The above election may be 'relevant not only when a subsidiary's reporting package complies fully with the recognition and measurement requirements of IFRSs, but also when it is adjusted centrally for matters such as post-balance sheet events review and central allocation of pension costs.'[192] Adjustments made centrally to an unpublished reporting package are not considered to be corrections of errors for the purposes of the disclosure requirements in IFRS 1. However, a subsidiary is not permitted to ignore misstatements that are immaterial to the consolidated financial statements of its parent but material to its own financial statements.

If a subsidiary was acquired after the parent's date of transition to IFRS, it seems that the subsidiary cannot apply option (a) because 'the carrying amounts that would be included in the parent's consolidated financial statements, based on the parent's date of transition to IFRS' would not exist.[193]

The exemption is also available to associates and joint ventures. This means that in many cases an associate or joint venture that wants to apply option (a) will need to choose which shareholder it considers its 'parent' for IFRS 1 purposes and determine the IFRS carrying amount of its assets and liabilities by reference to that parent's date of transition to IFRS.

B Parent becomes a first-time adopter later than its subsidiary

If an entity becomes a first-time adopter later than its subsidiary, associate or joint venture the entity should 'in its consolidated financial statements, measure the assets and liabilities of the subsidiary (or associate or joint venture) at the same carrying amounts as in the financial statements of the subsidiary (or associate or joint venture), after adjusting for consolidation and equity accounting adjustments and for the effects of the business combination in which the entity acquired the subsidiary.'[194]

Whereas a subsidiary can choose to prepare its first IFRS financial statements by reference to its own date of transition to IFRS or that of its parent, the parent itself must use the IFRS measurements already used in the subsidiary's separate financial statements, except to adjust for consolidation procedures and for the effects of the business combination in which the parent acquired the subsidiary.[195]

The following example, which is taken from the guidance on implementation of IFRS 1, illustrates how an entity should apply these requirements.

Example 5.27: Subsidiary adopts IFRS before parent[196]

Background

Parent P presents its (consolidated) first IFRS financial statements in 2007. Its foreign subsidiary Q, wholly owned by parent P since formation, presented its first IFRS financial statements in 2005. Until 2007, subsidiary Q prepared information for internal consolidation purposes under parent P's previous GAAP.

Application of requirements

The carrying amounts of subsidiary Q's assets and liabilities at 1 January 2006 are the same in both parent P's (consolidated) opening IFRS balance sheet and subsidiary Q's separate financial statements (except for adjustments for consolidation procedures) and are based on subsidiary Q's date of transition to IFRSs. The fact that parent P becomes a first-time adopter in 2007 does not change those carrying amounts.

IFRS 1 does not elaborate on exactly what constitute 'consolidation adjustments' but in our view it would encompass adjustments required in order to harmonise Q's accounting policies with those of P as well as purely 'mechanical' consolidation adjustments such as the elimination of intragroup balances, profits and losses.

When a subsidiary adopts IFRS before its parent, this will limit the parent's ability to choose first-time adoption exemptions in IFRS 1 freely, as illustrated in the example below.

Example 5.28: Limited ability to choose first-time adoption exemptions

Parent A will adopt IFRS for the first time in 2007 and its date of transition is 1 January 2006. Subsidiary B adopted IFRS in 2004 and its date of transition was 1 January 2003:

(a) Subsidiary B and Parent A both account for their property, plant and equipment at historical cost under IAS 16. Upon first-time adoption, Parent A may only adjust carrying amounts of subsidiary B's assets and liabilities to adjust for the effects of consolidation, equity accounting and business combinations. Parent A can therefore not apply the exemption to use fair value as deemed cost of subsidiary B's property, plant and equipment as at its own date of transition (1 January 2006);

(b) Subsidiary B accounts for its property, plant and equipment at revalued amounts under IAS 16, while parent A accounts for its property, plant and equipment at historical cost under IAS 16. In this case, parent A would not be allowed to apply the exemption to use fair value as deemed cost of subsidiary B's property, plant and equipment because paragraph 25 of IFRS 1 would only permit adjustments for the effects of consolidation, equity accounting and business combinations Although a consolidation adjustment would be necessary, this would only be to adjust Subsidiary B's revalued amounts to figures based on historical cost.

However, this does not mean that the parent's ability to choose first-time adoption exemptions will always be limited. For example, Subsidiary B may have deemed the cumulative translation difference for all its foreign subsidiaries to be zero at its date of transition (1 January 2003). When Parent A adopts IFRS it can deem subsidiary B's cumulative translation differences to be zero at its date of transition (1 January 2006), because paragraph 22 of IFRS 1 specifically states that under the option 'the cumulative translation differences for *all* [emphasis added] foreign operations are deemed to be zero at the date of transition to IFRSs'.

C *Implementation guidance on accounting for assets and liabilities of subsidiaries, associates and joint ventures*

When an entity applies the rules discussed under A and B above, these do not override the requirements:

'(a) to apply Appendix B of the IFRS to assets acquired, and liabilities assumed, in a business combination that occurred before the acquirer's date of transition to IFRSs. However, the acquirer applies paragraph 25 [of IFRS 1] to new assets acquired, and liabilities assumed, by the acquiree after that business combination and still held at the acquirer's date of transition to IFRSs;

(b) to apply the rest of the IFRS in measuring all assets and liabilities for which paragraphs 24 and 25 [of IFRS 1] are not relevant;

(c) to give all disclosures required by the IFRS as of the first-time adopter's own date of transition to IFRSs.'[197]

D *Adoption of IFRS on different dates in separate and consolidated financial statements*

If a parent adopts IFRS in its 'separate financial statements earlier or later than for its consolidated financial statements, it shall measure its assets and liabilities at the same amounts in both financial statements, except for consolidation adjustments.'[198]

As drafted, the requirement is merely that the 'same' basis be used, without being explicit as to which set of financial statements should be used as the benchmark. However, it seems clear from the context that the IASB intends that the measurement basis used in whichever set of financial statements first comply with IFRS must also be used when IFRS are subsequently adopted in the other set.

2.7.6 *Service concession arrangements*

A first-time adopter may apply the transitional provision in IFRIC 12.[199] That interpretation requires retrospective application unless it is, for any particular service arrangement, impracticable for the operator to apply IFRIC 12 retrospectively at the start of the earliest period presented, in which case it should:[200]

'(a) recognise financial assets and intangible assets that existed at the start of the earliest period presented;

(b) use the previous carrying amounts of those financial and intangible assets (however previously classified) as their carrying amounts as at that date; and

(c) test financial and intangible assets recognised at that date for impairment, unless this is not practicable, in which case the amounts shall be tested for impairment as at the start of the current period.'

2.8 Other exceptions to retrospective application of other IFRSs

As discussed at 2.3.3 B above, IFRS 1 specifically prohibits retrospective application of IFRS in a number of situations. The exceptions that have not been covered at 2.6.4 and 2.6.5 above are discussed below.

2.8.1 Estimates

IFRS 1 requires an entity to use estimates under IFRS that are consistent with the estimates made for the same date under its previous GAAP – after adjusting for any difference in accounting policy – unless there is objective evidence that those estimates were in error.[201] IAS 8 defines prior period errors as:

> 'omissions from, and misstatements in, the entity's financial statements for one or more prior periods arising from a failure to use, or misuse of, reliable information that:
>
> (a) was available when financial statements for those periods were authorised for issue; and
>
> (b) could reasonably be expected to have been obtained and taken into account in the preparation and presentation of those financial statements.
>
> Such errors include the effects of mathematical mistakes, mistakes in applying accounting policies, oversights or misinterpretations of facts, and fraud.'[202]

In October 2004, the IFRIC considered whether the 'impracticability' exception under IAS 8 should also apply to first-time adopters. The IFRIC agreed 'that there were potential issues, especially with respect to 'old' items, such as property, plant and equipment. However, those issues could usually be resolved by using one of the transition options available in IFRS 1'.[203]

Under IFRS 1 an entity cannot apply hindsight and make 'better' estimates when it prepares its first IFRS financial statements. This also means that an entity is not allowed to take account of any subsequent events that provide evidence of conditions that existed at that date, but that came to light after the date of its previous GAAP financial statements were finalised. The IASB considers that although 'some of those events might qualify as adjusting events under IAS 10 – *Events After the Balance Sheet Date* ... if the entity made those estimates on a basis consistent with IFRSs ... it would be more helpful to users – and more consistent with IAS 8 to recognise the revision of those estimates as income or expense in the period when the entity made the revision, rather than in preparing the opening IFRS balance sheet.'[204] Effectively, the IASB wishes to prevent entities using hindsight to 'clean up' their balance sheets by direct write-offs to equity as part of the opening IFRS balance sheet exercise. As discussed at 2.6.5 B I in relation to financial instruments, IFRS 1 would require an entity that is unable to determine whether a particular portion of an adjustment is a transitional adjustment or a change in estimate, to treat that portion as a change in accounting estimate under IAS 8, with appropriate disclosures as required by paragraphs 32 to 40 of IAS 8.[205]

The requirement that an entity should use estimates consistent with those made under its previous GAAP applies both to estimates made in respect of the date of transition to IFRS and to those in respect of the end of any comparative period.[206] IFRS 1 provides the following guidance on how an entity should put this requirement into practice:

- When an entity receives information after the relevant date about estimates that it had made under previous GAAP, it treats this information in the same way as a non-adjusting event after the balance sheet date under IAS 10.[207] An entity can be in one of the following two positions:[208]
  - its previous GAAP accounting policy was consistent with IFRS, in which case the adjustment is reflected in the period in which the revision is made; or
  - its previous GAAP accounting policy was not consistent with IFRS, in which case it will need to adjust the estimate for the difference in accounting policies.

  In both situations, if an entity later adjusts those estimates, it accounts for the revisions to those estimates as events of the period in which it makes the revisions;[209]
- When an entity needs to make estimates under IFRS at the relevant date that were not required under its previous GAAP, those estimates should be consistent with IAS 10 and reflect conditions that existed at the relevant date. This means, for example, that estimates of market prices, interest rates or foreign exchange rates should reflect market conditions at that date;[210] and
- IFRS 1 does not override the requirements in other IFRS that base classifications or measurements on circumstances existing at a particular date, such as for example:
  - the distinction between finance leases and operating leases;
  - the restrictions in IAS 38 that prohibit capitalisation of expenditure on an internally generated intangible asset if the asset did not qualify for recognition when the expenditure was incurred; and
  - the distinction between financial liabilities and equity instruments (see IAS 32).[211]

The flowchart below shows the decision-making process that an entity needs to apply in dealing with estimates under its previous GAAP.

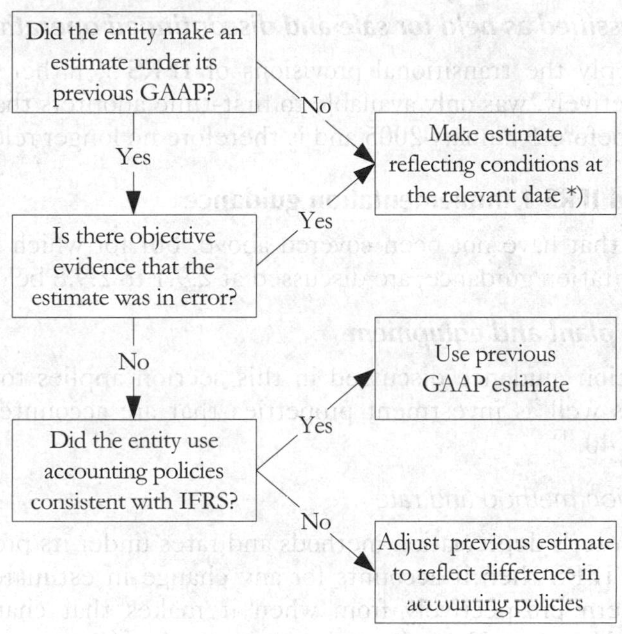

*) the relevant date is the date to which the estimate relates

The example below illustrates how an entity should deal with estimates under its previous GAAP.

Example 5.29: Application of IFRS 1 to estimates

Entity A previously accounted for its pension plan on a cash basis. However, under IAS 19 the plan is classified as a defined benefit plan and actuarial estimates are required.

A will need to make estimates under IFRS at the relevant date that reflect conditions that existed at the relevant date. This means, for example, that it needs to use a discount rate that would have been used at that time, ignoring any developments after that date.

Entity B accounted for inventories at the lower of cost and net realisable value under it previous GAAP. B's accounting policy is consistent with the requirements of IAS 2 – *Inventories*. Under previous GAAP, the goods were accounted for at a price of £1.25/kg. Due to changes in market circumstances, B ultimately could only sell the goods in the following period for £0.90/kg.

Assuming that B's estimate of the net realisable value was not in error, it will account for the goods at £1.25/kg upon transition to IFRS and makes no adjustments because the estimate was not in error and its accounting policy was consistent with IFRS. The effect of selling the goods for £0.90/kg will be reflected in the period in which they were sold.

Entity C accounted for a provision of $125,000 in connection with a court case. C's accounting policy was consistent with the requirements of IAS 37 except for the fact that C did not discount the provision for the time value of money. The discounted value of the provision would have been $90,000. The case was settled for $190,000 several months after the date of C's IFRS opening balance sheet.

In its opening IFRS balance sheet C will measure the provision at $90,000. IFRS 1 does not permit an entity to adjust the estimate itself, unless it was in error, but does require an adjustment to reflect the difference in accounting policies.

2.8.2 *Assets classified as held for sale and discontinued operations*

The option to apply the transitional provisions of IFRS 5, rather than apply that standard retrospectively, was only available to first-time adopters that adopted IFRS for the first time before 1 January 2005 and is therefore no longer relevant.[212]

2.9 Additional IFRS 1 implementation guidance

Accounting areas that have not been covered above, but for which IFRS 1 provides specific implementation guidance, are discussed at 2.9.1 to 2.9.8 below.

2.9.1 *Property, plant and equipment*

The implementation guidance discussed in this section applies to property, plant and equipment as well as investment properties that are accounted for under the cost model in IAS 40.[213]

A Depreciation method and rate

If a first-time adopter's depreciation methods and rates under its previous GAAP are acceptable under IFRS then it accounts for any change in estimated useful life or depreciation pattern prospectively from when it makes that change in estimate (see 2.8.1 above). However, if the depreciation methods and rates are not acceptable under IFRS and the difference has a material impact on the financial statements, a first-time adopter should adjust the accumulated depreciation in its opening IFRS balance sheet retrospectively.[214] If a restatement of the depreciation methods and rates would be too onerous, a first-time adopter could opt instead to use fair value as the deemed cost.

B Use of fair value or revaluation as deemed cost

As discussed at 2.5 above, a first-time adopter may elect to use fair value or a revaluation as the deemed cost of an item of property, plant and equipment. When a first-time adopter uses a fair value or a revaluation as the deemed cost of an item of property, plant and equipment it will need to start depreciating the item 'from the date for which the entity established the fair value measurement or revaluation' and not from its date of transition to IFRS (see Example 5.23 at 2.5.3 above).[215]

C Revaluation model

A first-time adopter that chooses to account for some or all classes of property, plant and equipment under the revaluation model needs to present the cumulative revaluation surplus as a separate component of equity. However, IFRS 1 requires that 'the revaluation surplus at the date of transition to IFRS is based on a comparison of the carrying amount of the asset at that date with its cost or deemed cost.'[216] If revaluations under previous GAAP did not satisfy the criteria in IFRS 1, a first-time adopter measures the revalued assets in its opening balance sheet on one of the following bases:[217]

(a) cost (or deemed cost) less any accumulated depreciation and any accumulated impairment losses under the cost model in IAS 16;

(b) deemed cost, being the fair value at the date of transition to IFRS; or

(c) revalued amount, if the entity adopts the revaluation model in IAS 16 as its accounting policy under IFRS for all items of property, plant and equipment in the same class.

A first-time adopter that uses fair value as the deemed cost for those classes of property, plant and equipment would be required to reset the cumulative revaluation surplus to zero.

D Decommissioning provisions

Under IAS 16 the cost of an item of property, plant and equipment includes 'the initial estimate of the costs of dismantling and removing the item and restoring the site on which it is located, the obligation for which an entity incurs either when the item is acquired or as a consequence of having used the item during a particular period for purposes other than to produce inventories during that period.'[218] Therefore, a first-time adopter needs to ensure that cost includes an item representing the decommissioning provision as determined under IAS 37.[219]

An entity should apply IAS 16 in determining the resulting amount included in the cost of the asset, before depreciation and impairment losses. Items such as depreciation and impairment losses cause differences between the carrying amount of the liability and the amount related to decommissioning costs included in the carrying amount of the asset. An entity accounts for changes in decommissioning provisions in accordance with IFRIC 1 – *Changes in Existing Decommissioning, Restoration and Similar Liabilities* – but IFRS 1 provides an exemption for changes that occurred before the date of transition to IFRS and prescribes an alternative treatment if the exemption is used. In such cases, a first-time adopter should:[220]

'(a) measure the [decommissioning] liability as at the date of transition to IFRSs in accordance with IAS 37;

(b) to the extent that the liability is within the scope of IFRIC 1, estimate the amount that would have been included in the cost of the related asset when the liability first arose, by discounting the liability to that date using its best estimate of the historical risk-adjusted discount rate(s) that would have applied for that liability over the intervening period; and

(c) calculate the accumulated depreciation on that amount, as at the date of transition to IFRSs, on the basis of the current estimate of the useful life of the asset, using the depreciation policy adopted by the entity under IFRSs.'[221]

Example 5.30: Decommissioning component in property, plant and equipment

Entity D's date of transition to IFRS is 1 January 2007 and its first IFRS reporting date is 31 December 2008. D built a factory that was completed and ready for use on 1 January 2002. Under its previous GAAP, D accrued a decommissioning provision over the expected life of the plant. The facts can be summarised as follows:

Cost of the plant	€1,400
Residual value	€200
Economic life	20 years
Original estimate of decommissioning cost in year 20	€175
Revised estimate at 2004 of decommissioning cost in year 20	€300
Discount rate applicable to decommissioning liability (the discount rate is assumed to be constant)	5.65%
Discounted value of original decommissioning liability on 1 January 2002	€58
Discounted value of revised decommissioning liability on 1 January 2002	€100
Discounted value of revised decommissioning liability on 1 January 2007	€131

If D applies the exemption from full retrospective application, what are the carrying amounts of the factory and the decommissioning liability in D's opening IFRS balance sheet?

The tables below show how D accounts for the decommissioning liability and the factory under its previous GAAP, under IFRS 1 using the exemption and under IFRS 1 applying IFRIC 1 retrospectively.

	Decommissioning liability		
	Previous GAAP	*Exemption IFRS 1*	*Retrospective application of IFRIC 1*
1 January 2002	–	100	58
Decommissioning costs €175 ÷ 20 years × 2 =	17.5		
Decommissioning costs €100 × (1.0565^2 – 1) =		12	
Decommissioning costs €58 × (1.0565^2 – 1) =			7
1 January 2004	17.5	112	65
Revised estimate of decommissioning provision	12.5		47
1 January 2004	30	112	112
Decommissioning costs €300 ÷ 20 years × 3 =	45		
Decommissioning costs €112 × (1.0565^3 – 1) =		19	
Decommissioning costs €112 × (1.0565^3 – 1) =			19
1 January 2007	75	131	131
Decommissioning costs €300 ÷ 20 years × 2 =	30		
Decommissioning costs €131 × (1.0565^2 – 1) =		16	
Decommissioning costs €131 × (1.0565^2 – 1) =			16
31 December 2008	105	147	147

In calculating the decommissioning provision, it makes no difference whether D goes back in time and tracks the history of the decommissioning provision or whether it just calculates the decommissioning provision at its date of transition to IFRS. This is not the case for the calculation of the related asset, as can be seen below.

	Factory		
	Previous GAAP	*Exemption IFRS 1*	*Retrospective application of IFRIC 1*
1 January 2002	1,400	1,500	1,458
Depreciation (€1,400 – €200) ÷ 20 years × 2 =	(120)		
Depreciation (€1,500 – €200) ÷ 20 years × 2 =		(130)	
Depreciation (€1,458 – €200) ÷ 20 years × 2 =			(126)
1 January 2004			1,332
Revised estimate of decommissioning provision			47
1 January 2004			1,379
Depreciation (€1,400 – €200) ÷ 20 years × 3 =	(180)		
Depreciation (€1,500 – €200) ÷ 20 years × 3 =		(195)	
Depreciation (€1,379 – €200) ÷ 18 years × 3 =			(197)
1 January 2007	1,100	1,175	1,182
Depreciation (€1,400 – €200) ÷ 20 years × 2 =	(120)		
Depreciation (€1,500 – €200) ÷ 20 years × 2 =		(130)	
Depreciation (€1,379 – €200) ÷ 18 years × 2 =			(131)
31 December 2008	980	1,045	1,051

As can be seen above, a full retrospective application of IFRIC 1 would require an entity to go back in time and account for each revision of the decommissioning provision in accordance with IFRIC 1. In the case of a long-lived asset there could be a significant number of revisions that a first-time adopter would need to account for. It should also be noted that despite the significant revision of the decommissioning costs, the impact on the carrying amount of the factory is quite modest.

At its date of transition to IFRS (1 January 2007), D makes the following adjustments:

- the decommissioning liability is increased by €56 (= €131 – €75) to reflect the difference in accounting policy, irrespective of whether D applies the exemption or not; and
- if D applies the exemption it increases the carrying amount of the factory by €75. Whereas if D applies IFRIC 1 retrospectively, the carrying amount of the factory would increase by €82.

It is important to note that in both cases the decommissioning component of the factory will be significantly lower than the decommissioning liability itself.

From the above example it is clear that the exemption reduces the amount of effort required to restate items of property, plant and equipment with a decommissioning component. In many cases the difference between the two methods will be insignificant, except where an entity had to make major adjustments to the estimate of the decommissioning costs near the end of the life of the related assets.

2.9.2 *Leases*

IFRS 1 requires a first-time adopter to classify leases as operating or finance leases based on the circumstances existing at the inception of the lease and not those existing at the date of transition to IFRS.[222] However, if 'at any time the lessee and the lessor agree to change the provisions of the lease, other than by renewing the lease, in a manner that would have resulted in a different classification of the lease ... if the changed terms had been in effect at the inception of the lease, the revised agreement is regarded as a new agreement over its term.'[223] In other words, an entity classifies a lease based on the lease terms that are in force at its date of transition to IFRS; the lease classification is not based on lease terms that are no longer in force.

In December 2004, the IASB issued IFRIC 4 – *Determining whether an Arrangement contains a Lease* – which contains guidance on determining whether an arrangement contains a lease. Given the practical difficulties in going back potentially many years, first-time adopters may apply the transitional provisions in IFRIC 4, which allow them to apply the interpretation to arrangements existing at their date of transition on the basis of facts and circumstances existing at that date.[224]

A first-time adopter should apply SIC-15 – *Operating Leases – Incentives (amended 2003)* – retrospectively to all leases.[225]

2.9.3 Subsidiaries and Special Purpose Entities

A first-time adopter should consolidate all subsidiaries and Special Purpose Entities, except when IAS 27 requires otherwise.[226] If a first-time adopter did not consolidate a subsidiary under its previous GAAP, it should in its opening IFRS balance sheet measure the subsidiary's assets and liabilities at either:[227]

- the same carrying amounts as in the separate IFRS financial statements of the subsidiary, after adjusting for consolidation procedures and for the effects of the business combination in which it acquired the subsidiary;[228] or
- if the subsidiary has not adopted IFRS, the carrying amounts that IFRS would require in the subsidiary's separate balance sheet.

If the parent acquired the subsidiary in a business combination it should recognise goodwill as explained at 2.4.6 above. If the parent created the subsidiary it should not recognise goodwill.[229] The adjustment of the carrying amounts of assets and liabilities of a first-time adopter's subsidiaries may affect minority interests and deferred tax.[230]

A Future developments

At its meeting in March 2006, the IASB added a project to its agenda to address various difficulties that, it had been noted, could arise from a fully retrospective application of IAS 27 in separate financial statements. This project resulted, in January 2007, in the issuance of an exposure draft of proposed amendments to IFRS 1.[231]

I Cost of investment

The exposure draft proposes to provide first-time adopters with an exemption from the requirement of IAS 27 related to the measurement of investments in subsidiaries. The amendments will allow entities to measure some or all investments in subsidiaries, at the date of transition, at a deemed cost (rather than cost), being either:[232]

- the carrying amount of the net assets, in accordance with IFRSs, of the subsidiary at the date of the parent's transition to IFRS; or
- the fair value of the subsidiary at the date of the parent's transition to IFRSs.

A first-time adopter may choose which measurement to use for each individual investment in a subsidiary.

The Board decided to allow these two options because the 'net asset deemed cost would provide relevant information to users about the subsidiary's financial position at the date of transition to IFRSs and would be relatively easy for an entity to determine'.[233] The fair value deemed cost, on the other hand, would provide information about the underlying market value of a subsidiary at the date of transition to IFRSs, but might be more costly and difficult to determine. The Board rejected the use of a deemed cost based on the previous GAAP cost because it bears little resemblance to cost in accordance with IAS 27 and would provide less useful information than the other two methods proposed.[234]

II Pre-acquisition distributions

When an entity applies the amendment to measure an investment in subsidiary on transition at a 'deemed cost', the accumulated profits of that subsidiary as calculated in accordance with IFRS at the date of transition will be deemed to be pre-acquisition profits.[235] This will result in any future dividends paid that are greater than future profits being treated as a return on investment, which may in turn have implications for the ability of the parent to remit dividends to its shareholders.

Where an entity does not apply the relief from determining the cost of an investment in subsidiary on transition, an entity may use either (1) the previous GAAP value of pre-acquisition profits or (2) the value as calculated in accordance with IFRS as the pre-acquisition profits under IFRS.[236]

III Impact of the proposed amendment

Whilst the amendments proposed in the exposure draft will overcome one of the practical problems that often arise on the adoption of IFRS for the separate financial statements of a parent, other, more fundamental difficulties that impede entities from adopting IFRS arise from IAS 27 are not addressed by the amendment and we believe these need to also be addressed.

Firstly, IAS 27 does not define 'cost' (see Chapter 6 at 7.3.1). A clear definition of cost in IAS 27 would also enable entities to assess more easily whether there is a difference between the carrying amount of an investment in a subsidiary under previous GAAP and that under IAS 27. This, in turn, would assist an entity to determine whether or not it should use deemed cost as proposed in the exposure draft.

Secondly, the requirement to recognise dividends received from investments that are paid from pre-acquisition profits as a reduction of the cost of the investment reflects an outdated model of capital maintenance which is difficult to align with the principles in the *Framework*. When a group carries out an internal restructuring in which the ownership of individual subsidiaries within the group changes, a literal application of the definition of 'cost method' in IAS 27 results in profits that are, from the perspective of the group, post-acquisition, being treated as pre-acquisition by the new intermediate parent, thereby preventing the ultimate parent from distributing such profits as dividends to shareholders.

The problems being addressed by the amendment to IFRS 1 are relevant not only to the measurement of investments in subsidiaries but also to the measurement of investments in associates and joint ventures in the separate financial statements of the investor.

IV Response to the exposure draft

In September 2007, the IASB determined – in the light of comments from respondents on the exposure draft – that if a net assets measure was to be used it should be the amounts that the parent incorporates in its consolidated financial statements (rather than the amounts recognised in the separate or individual financial statements of the subsidiary). The Board asked the staff to consult respondents to the exposure draft to establish whether the revised net assets measure would resolve their concerns.[237] The Board tentatively decided:

- that unless its net asset approach addresses the concerns of respondents, deemed cost could be measured as the carrying amount of the investment under previous GAAP;
- to extend the deemed cost exemption on transition to IFRSs to the initial measurement in the parent's separate financial statements of investments in associates and interests in joint ventures; and
- to amend IAS 27:
    - to remove the definition of the cost method from paragraph 4 of IAS 27; and
    - to require a parent to recognise as income in its separate financial statements all dividends it receives from a subsidiary and to assess the carrying amount of its investment in that subsidiary for impairment in accordance with IAS 36 upon receipt of such a dividend.

The Board decided that the proposed changes should be re-exposed.[238]

2.9.4 Hyperinflation

The IASB decided not to exempt first-time adopters from retrospective application of IAS 29 – *Financial Reporting in Hyperinflationary Economies*. Although the cost of restating financial statements for the effects of hyperinflation in periods before the date of transition to IFRS might exceed the benefits, particularly if the currency is no longer hyperinflationary, the IASB concluded that a full retrospective 'restatement should be required, because hyperinflation can make unadjusted financial statements meaningless or misleading.'[239]

In preparing its opening IFRS balance sheet a first-time adopter should apply 'IAS 29 to any periods during which the economy of the functional currency or presentation currency was hyperinflationary.'[240] To make the restatement process less onerous, a first-time adopter may want to consider using fair value as deemed cost for long-lived assets such as property, plant and equipment, investment properties and certain intangible assets (see 2.5 above).[241] If a first-time adopter applies the exemption to use fair value or a revaluation as deemed cost, 'it applies

IAS 29 to periods after the date for which the revalued amount or fair value was determined.'[242]

2.9.5 Intangible assets

In its opening IFRS balance sheet a first-time adopter:

'(a) excludes all intangible assets and other intangible items that do not meet the criteria for recognition under IAS 38 at the date of transition to IFRSs; and

(b) includes all intangible assets that meet the recognition criteria in IAS 38 at that date, except for intangible assets acquired in a business combination that were not recognised in the acquirer's consolidated balance sheet under previous GAAP and also would not qualify for recognition under IAS 38 in the separate balance sheet of the acquiree.'[243]

An intangible asset is only capable of capitalisation under IAS 38 if it is probable that the future economic benefits attributable to the asset will flow to the entity and the cost of the asset can be measured reliably.[244] IAS 38 imposes a number of additional criteria that further restrict capitalisation of internally generated intangible assets. An important restriction is the prohibition from using hindsight to conclude retrospectively that recognition criteria are met.[245] Therefore, a first-time adopter is only permitted to capitalise the costs of internally generated intangible assets when it:[246]

'(a) concludes, based on an assessment made and documented at the date of that conclusion, that it is probable that future economic benefits from the asset will flow to the entity; and

(b) has a reliable system for accumulating the costs of internally generated intangible assets when, or shortly after, they are incurred.'

In other words, it is not permitted under IFRS 1 to reconstruct retrospectively the costs of intangible assets. If an internally generated intangible asset qualifies for recognition at the date of transition to IFRS, a first-time adopter recognises the asset in its opening IFRS balance sheet even if it had recognised the related expenditure as an expense under its previous GAAP.[247] However, first-time adopters that did not capitalise internally generated intangible assets are unlikely to have the type of documentation and systems required by IFRS 1 and will therefore not be able to capitalise these items in their opening IFRS balance sheet. Furthermore, if the asset does not qualify 'for recognition under IAS 38 until a later date, its cost is the sum of the expenditure incurred from that later date.'[248] Nonetheless, going forward, first-time adopters will need to implement the internal systems and procedures that enable them to determine whether or not any future internally generated intangible assets should be capitalised (for example, in the case of development costs).

Capitalisation of separately acquired intangible assets will generally be easier because contemporaneous documentation that was prepared to support the investment decisions often exists.[249] However, if an entity did not recognise an intangible asset acquired in a business combination under its previous GAAP, it would only be able to do so upon first-time adoption if the intangible asset met the

IAS 38 recognition criteria in the balance sheet of the acquiree (see 2.4.3 E above).[250]

If a first-time adopter's 'amortisation methods and rates under previous GAAP would be acceptable under IFRSs, the entity does not restate the accumulated amortisation in its opening IFRS balance sheet. Instead, the entity accounts for any change in estimated useful life or amortisation pattern prospectively from the period when it makes that change in estimate ... However, in some cases, an entity's amortisation methods and rates under previous GAAP may differ from those that would be acceptable under IFRSs ... If those differences have a material effect on the financial statements, the entity adjusts the accumulated amortisation in its opening IFRS balance sheet retrospectively so that it complies with IFRSs.'[251]

2.9.6 Revenue recognition

If a first-time adopter 'has received amounts that do not yet qualify for recognition as revenue under IAS 18 (for example, the proceeds of a sale that does not qualify for revenue recognition), [it] recognises the amounts received as a liability in its opening IFRS balance sheet and measures that liability at the amount received.'[252] It is therefore possible that revenue that was already recognised under a first-time adopter's previous GAAP, will need to be deferred in its opening IFRS balance sheet and recognised again (this time under IFRS) as revenue at a later date.

2.9.7 Borrowing costs

If on first-time adoption of IFRS an entity 'adopts a policy of capitalising borrowing costs ... or not capitalising them ... The entity applies that policy consistently in its opening IFRS balance sheet and in all periods presented in its first IFRS financial statements.'[253] It is therefore not possible to capitalise borrowing costs prospectively from the date of transition. Instead, a first-time adopter that applies IAS 23's – *Borrowing Costs* – allowed alternative treatment to capitalise borrowing costs, should apply that treatment retrospectively, even for periods before the effective date of the standard.[254] However, if the entity established a deemed cost for an asset, it does not capitalise borrowing costs incurred before the date of the measurement that established the deemed cost.

In March 2007, the IASB issued an amended version of IAS 23 that eliminates the option to expense borrowing costs as incurred. The consequential amendments to IFRS 1 allow a first-time adopter to 'apply the transitional provisions set out in paragraphs 27 and 28 of IAS 23 *Borrowing Costs*, as revised in 2007. In those paragraphs references to the effective date shall be interpreted as 1 January 2009 or the date of transition to IFRSs, whichever is later'.[255] If a first-time adopter applies IAS 23 (revised 2007) for an annual period beginning before 1 January 2009 then it should also apply the consequential amendment to IFRS 1 for that earlier period.[256]

2.9.8 Comparative information under IFRS 6

The option not to present comparative information in accordance with IFRS 6 was only available to first-time adopters that adopted IFRS for the first time before 1 January 2006 and is therefore no longer relevant.[257]

2.10 Presentation and disclosure

As a general principle, IFRS 1 does not exempt a first-time adopter from any of the presentation and disclosure requirements in other standards.

If an entity adopts IFRS 1 early, i.e. in its first IFRS financial statements for a period beginning before 1 January 2004, it should disclose the fact that it applies IFRS 1 and not SIC-8.[258]

2.10.1 Comparative information

IAS 1 requires (except where a standard or interpretation permits or requires otherwise) comparative information 'in respect of the previous period for all amounts reported in the financial statements' and 'for narrative and descriptive information when it is relevant to an understanding of the current period's financial statements.'[259] Accordingly, an entity's first IFRS financial statements should include at least one year of comparative information under IFRS.[260] It is however not required to present its opening IFRS balance sheet in its first IFRS financial statements, although it is integral to the equity reconciliation at the date of transition that has to be presented in the entity's first IFRS financial statements (see 2.10.2 below).[261] The IASB does not require a first-time adopter to present more than one comparative period under IFRS because 'such a requirement would impose costs out of proportion to the benefits to users, and increase the risk that preparers might need to make arbitrary assumptions in applying hindsight.'[262]

A Exemption from the requirement to restate comparative information for IAS 32, IAS 39, IFRS 4 and IFRS 7

I Disclosure of financial instruments under IAS 32, IAS 39 and IFRS 4

As discussed at 2.6.1 above, an entity adopting IFRS for the first time before 1 January 2006 may elect to present comparative information that does not comply with IAS 32, IAS 39 and IFRS 4, in which case it needs to:[263]

- disclose that the comparative information does not comply with IAS 32, IAS 39 and IFRS 4 together with the basis used under the previous GAAP to prepare the information;
- disclose the nature of the main adjustments that would make the information comply with IAS 32, IAS 39 and IFRS 4. The entity need not quantify those adjustments; and
- treat any adjustment between the balance sheet at the comparative period's reporting date and the start of the first IFRS reporting period as arising from a change in accounting policy. This difference is accounted for as an 'adjustment to the opening balance of each affected component of equity' at the start of the first IFRS reporting period.[264] The entity is required to make the disclosures prescribed by paragraphs 28(a)–(e) and (f)(i) of IAS 8 (see Chapter 3 at 5.1.2 A).[265]

Originally IFRS 1 required all first-time adopters to prepare comparative information that complied with IAS 32 and IAS 39 because this improved 'comparability within the first IFRS financial statements' and because the IASB believed that this should not be a problem for entities that planned the adoption of IFRS in a timely manner.[266] Unfortunately, the less-than-timely publication of the revised IAS 32 and IAS 39 obliged the IASB to exempt entities adopting IFRS before 1 January 2006 from applying these standards in preparing comparative information.

IFRS 7 introduces the requirement, for periods beginning on or after the earlier of 1 January 2007 or the date of adoption of IFRS 7, for an entity:

> '...to comply with paragraph 15(c) of IAS 1 to provide additional disclosures when compliance with the specific requirements in IFRSs is insufficient to enable users to understand the impact of particular transactions, other events and conditions on the entity's financial position and financial performance.'[267]

Although, as discussed at 2.6.1 above, the amendment itself only applies to entities that adopt IFRS and IFRS 7 before 1 January 2006, the requirement to comply with paragraph 15(c) of IAS 1 applies in any event.

II Disclosure of financial instruments under IFRS 7

An entity that adopts IFRS before 1 January 2006 and chooses to adopt IFRS 7 in its first IFRS financial statements is not required to present the comparative disclosures required by IFRS 7.[268] This exemption is similar to the one available to entities which present financial instrument disclosures in accordance with IAS 32.

B Non-IFRS comparative information and historical summaries

Normally IFRS requires comparative information that is prepared on the same basis as information relating to the current reporting period. However, when an entity presents 'historical summaries of selected data for periods before the first period for which they present full comparative information under IFRS', the standard does not 'require such summaries to comply with the recognition and measurement requirements of IFRS.'[269]

As an entity is only allowed to apply IFRS 1 in its first IFRS financial statements, a literal reading of IFRS 1 would seem to suggest that the above exemption is not available to an entity that prepares its second IFRS financial statements. In practice this is not likely to cause a significant problem because this type of information is generally presented outside the financial statements where it is not covered by the requirements of IFRS.

If an entity presents comparative information under its previous GAAP in addition to the comparative information required by IFRS it should:

'(a) label the previous GAAP information prominently as not being prepared under IFRSs; and

(b) disclose the nature of the main adjustments that would make it comply with IFRSs. An entity need not quantify those adjustments.'[270]

Although IFRS 1 does not specifically require disclosure of this information when the historical summaries are presented outside the financial statements, such disclosure would be of benefit to users of such historical summaries.

2.10.2 Explanation of transition to IFRS

A first-time adopter is required to explain how the transition from its previous GAAP to IFRS affected its reported financial position, financial performance and cash flows.[271] The IASB decided 'that such disclosures are essential … because they help users understand the effect and implications of the transition to IFRS and how they need to change their analytical models to make the best use of information presented using IFRS.'[272]

As indicated at 2.3.3 A above, IFRS 1 offers a wide range of exemptions that a first-time adopter may elect to apply. However, somewhat curiously, the standard does not explicitly require an entity to disclose which exemptions it has applied and how it applied them. In the case of, for example, the exemptions relating to employee benefits and cumulative translation differences, it will be rather obvious whether or not an entity has chosen to apply the exemption. In other cases, users will have to rely on a first-time adopter disclosing those transitional accounting policies that are 'relevant to an understanding of the financial statements'.[273] In practice most first-time adopters voluntarily disclose which IFRS 1 exemptions they elected to apply and which exceptions apply to them, as is illustrated below by Extracts 5.5 and 5.6.

Extract 5.5: TNT N.V. (2005)

Notes to the consolidated financial statements [extract]

TRANSITION TO INTERNATIONAL FINANCIAL REPORTING STANDARDS AS ADOPTED BY THE EUROPEAN UNION [extract]

Our financial statements for the year ended 31 December 2005 are the first annual financial statements that comply with IFRS as adopted by the EU. References to IFRS Standards throughout this document refer to the application of IAS and related Interpretations of IFRIC and Interpretations of the SIC. We have applied IFRS 1, *First-time Adoption of International Financial Reporting Standards*, in preparing these consolidated financial statements. Since TNT is also listed on the New York Stock Exchange, it has to meet the requirements of the SEC. On 13 April 2005 the SEC adopted amendments to Form 20-F for foreign private issuers related to the first-time adoption of IFRS. Under this amendment TNT is permitted to provide only one year of comparative IFRS balances in the consolidated financial statements for the year 2005.

Our transition date to IFRS is 1 January 2004. We prepared our opening IFRS balance sheet at that date. The reporting date of these consolidated financial statements is 31 December 2005 and our IFRS adoption date is 1 January 2005. In preparing these consolidated financial statements in accordance with IFRS 1, we have applied the mandatory exceptions and certain of the optional exemptions from full retrospective application of IFRS.

We have elected to apply the following optional exemptions from full retrospective application:

Business combinations exemption

We have applied the business combinations exemption in IFRS 1. We have not restated business combinations that took place prior to the 1 January 2004 transition date.

Employee benefits exemption

Until 31 December 2004 we applied SFAS 87, *Employers accounting for pensions*, as permitted under Dutch GAAP. As permitted under IFRS 1, we have elected to recognise all cumulative actuarial gains and losses as at 1 January 2004. The unrecognised prior year service costs reported under SFAS 87 at the date of transition to IFRS are treated as a curtailment result under IAS 19 and have been adjusted against shareholders' equity.

Cumulative translation differences exemption

We have elected to set the previously accumulated cumulative translation to zero at 1 January 2004. This exemption has been applied to all subsidiaries in accordance with IFRS 1. As a result the gain or loss on a subsequent disposal of any foreign operation shall exclude translation differences that arose prior to 1 January 2004 and shall include translation differences that will arise subsequent to this date.

Exemption from restatement of comparatives for IAS 32 and IAS 39

We have elected to apply this exemption. We apply previous GAAP rules to derivatives, financial assets and financial liabilities and to hedging relationships for the 2004 comparative information. The adjustments required for differences between previous GAAP and IAS 32 and IAS 39 are determined and recognised at 1 January 2005.

Designation of financial assets and financial liabilities exemption

We have reclassified various securities as available-for-sale investments and as financial assts at fair value through profit and loss. The adjustments relating to IAS 32 and IAS 39 at the opening balance sheet date of 1 January 2005, the IAS 32/39 transition date, are detailed in Note "Adoption of New IFRS Pronouncements".

Shares based payment transaction exemption

We have elected to apply the share based payment exemption. We have applied IFRS 2 from 1 January 2004 to those options that were issued after 7 November 2002 but that have not vested by 1 January 2005.

Fair value measurement of financial assts or liabilities at initial recognition

We have not applied the exemption offered by the revision of IAS 39 on the initial recognition of the financial instruments measured at fair value through profit and loss where there is no active market. This exemption is therefore not applicable.

Assets held for sale and discounted operations exception

Although the effective date for adopting IFRS 5 – *Assets Held for Sale and Discontinued Operations Exception*, was 1 January 2005, as permitted under IFRS 5, we have applied the requirements of IFRS 5 prospectively from 1 January 2004. Assets held for sale or discontinued operations are recognised in accordance with IFRS 5 from 1 January 2004.

We have applied the following mandatory exceptions from retrospective application:

Derecognition of financial assets and liabilities exception

Financial assets and liabilities derecognised before 1 January 2004 are not rerecognised under IFRS. The application of the exemption from restating comparatives for IAS 32 and IAS 39 means that we recognised from 1 January 2005 any financial assets and financial liabilities derecognised since 1 January 2004 that do not meet the IAS 39 derecognition criteria. Management did not choose to apply the IAS 39 derecognition criteria to an earlier date.

Hedge accounting exception

Management has claimed hedge accounting from 1 January 2005 only if the hedge relationship meets all hedge accounting criteria under IAS 39.

Estimates exception

Estimates under IFRS at 1 January 2004 should be consistent with estimates made for the same date under previous GAAP, unless there is evidence that those estimates were in error.

Extract 5.6: GlaxoSmithKline plc (2005)

Notes to the consolidated financial statements [extract]

40 Transition to IFRS [extract]

IFRS 1 exemptions and elections

IFRS 1, First-Time Adoption of International Financial Reporting Standards, permits those companies adopting IFRS for the first time to take some exemptions from the full requirements of IFRS in the transition period or to make elections to apply IFRS with full retrospective effect where not required to do so. GSK has adopted the following key exemptions and elections:

- Business combinations: Business combinations prior to the transition date (1st January 2003) have not been restated onto an IFRS basis. If the merger of Glaxo Wellcome and SmithKline Beecham in 2000 had been restated onto an IFRS basis it would have been accounted for as an acquisition. Fair value adjustments to the net assets of the acquired company would have been required, including the recognition of significant intangible asset balances for product rights relating to both marketed products and in-process R&D, which were not recognised under merger accounting. A significant goodwill balance would also have been recorded
- Goodwill written off to reserves prior to 1998 under old UK GAAP is not written back to goodwill. If the business combinations exemption had not been taken, additional goodwill balances relating to acquisitions prior to 1998 would have been recognised on the IFRS balance sheet
- Amortisation of goodwill under UK GAAP prior to the date of transition to IFRS, 1st January 2003, has not been reversed. Accordingly, goodwill recognised on the IFRS balance sheet is lower in this respect than it would have been if GSK had not taken advantage of the business combinations exemption
- Share-based payments: IFRS 2, Share-based Payment, applies to equity instruments, such as share options granted since 7th November 2002, but GlaxoSmithKline has elected to adopt full retrospective application of the standard
- Financial instruments: Financial instruments in the comparative periods presented in the Annual Report 2005 (i.e. 2004 and 2003) are recognised and measured on the UK GAAP basis applicable in those years, rather than in accordance with IAS 39 'Financial Instruments: Recognition and Measurement'. As a result, certain derivative instruments, are not recognised in the comparative periods. IFRS hedge accounting is not applied in the comparative periods so hedged borrowings are recorded at amortised cost rather than at fair value. Also, available-for-sale financial assets such as equity investments and liquid investments are recorded at cost less impairments rather than at fair value.

If a first-time adopter did not present financial statements for previous periods this fact should be disclosed.[274] For example, in practice this disclosure is sometimes made by entities that did not prepare consolidated accounts under their previous GAAP. In such cases and others, an explanation of how the transition to IFRS affected the entity's reported financial position, financial performance and cash flows cannot be presented, because relevant comparative information under the entity's previous GAAP does not exist.

A Reconciliations

A first-time adopter is required to present:

- reconciliations of its equity reported under previous GAAP to its equity under IFRS at:[275]
  - the date of transition to IFRS; and
  - the end of the latest period presented in the entity's most recent annual financial statements under previous GAAP;

- a reconciliation of the profit or loss reported under previous GAAP for the latest period in the entity's most recent annual financial statements to its profit or loss under IFRS for the same period; and[276]
- an explanation of the material adjustments to the cash flow statement, if it presented one under its previous GAAP.[277]

First-time adopters should not apply the requirements of IAS 8 relating to the disclosure of changes in accounting policies because that standard 'does not deal with changes in accounting policies that occur when an entity first adopts IFRS.'[278]

The example below illustrates how these requirements apply to an entity whose first IFRS reporting date is 31 December 2008 and date of transition to IFRS is 1 January 2007.

Example 5.31: Reconciliations to be presented in first IFRS financial statements

Entity E's date of transition to IFRS is 1 January 2007 and its reporting date is 31 December 2008. Which primary financial statements and reconciliations should E present in its first IFRS financial statements?

	1 January 2007	*31 December 2007*	*31 December 2008*
Balance sheet		•	•
Reconciliation of equity	•	•	
For the period ending			
Income statement		•	•
Cash flow statement		•	•
Statement of changes in equity *		•	•
Reconciliation of profit or loss		•	
Explanation of material adjustments to cash flow statement		•	

* or alternatively the entity's statement of recognised income and expense

These reconciliations should be sufficiently detailed 'to enable users to understand the material adjustments to the balance sheet and income statement'[279] and the entity should 'distinguish the correction of ... errors from changes in accounting policies.'[280] While the standard does not prescribe a layout for these reconciliations, the implementation guidance contains an example of a reconciliation of equity and profit or loss that contains a line-by-line reconciliation of both balance sheet and income statement.[281] Such a presentation may be particularly appropriate when a first-time adopter needs to make transitional adjustments that affect a significant number of line items in the primary financial statements. If the adjustments are less pervasive a straightforward reconciliation of the equity and profit or loss figures may be able to provide an equally effective explanation of how the adoption of IFRS affects the reported financial position, financial performance and cash flows.

The extracts below show how a first-time adopter might present the reconciliations required by IFRS 1.

Extract 5.7: Vodafone Group Plc (2005)

Notes to the Consolidated Financial Statements [extract]

40 Transition to IFRS on first-time adoption [extract]

Basis of preparation of IFRS financial information

The Group's Annual Report for the year ended 31 March 2006 is the first annual Consolidated Financial Statements that comply with IFRS. The Consolidated Financial Statements have been prepared in accordance with the significant accounting policies described in note 2. The Group has applied IFRS 1, "First-time Adoption of International Financial Reporting Standards" in preparing these statements.

IFRS 1 exemptions

IFRS 1 sets out the procedures that the Group must follow when it adopts IFRS for the first time as the basis for preparing its Consolidated Financial Statements. The Group is required to establish its IFRS accounting policies as at 31 March 2006 and, in general, apply these retrospectively to determine the IFRS opening balance sheet at its date of transition, 1 April 2004. This standard provides a number of optional exemptions to this general principle. These are set out below, together with a description in each case of the exemption adopted by the Group.

Business combinations that occurred before the opening IFRS balance sheet date (IFRS 3, "Business Combinations")

The Group has elected not to apply IFRS 3 retrospectively to business combinations that took place before the date of transition. As a result, in the opening balance sheet, goodwill arising from past business combinations remains as stated under UK GAAP at 31 March 2004.

If the Group had elected to apply IFRS 3 retrospectively, the purchase consideration would have been allocated to the following major categories of acquired intangible assets and liabilities based on their fair values: licence and spectrum fees, brands, customer bases, and deferred tax liabilities. Goodwill would have been recognised as the excess of the purchase consideration over the fair values of acquired assets and liabilities – retrospective application may have resulted in an increase or decrease to goodwill. The fair values of the acquired intangible assets would have been amortised over their respective useful lives.

Employee benefits – actuarial gains and losses (IAS 19, "Employee Benefits")

The Group has elected to recognise all cumulative actuarial gains and losses in relation to employee benefit schemes at the date of transition.

Share-based payments (IFRS 2, "Share-based Payment")

The Group has elected to apply IFRS 2 to all relevant share-based payment transactions granted but not fully vested at 1 April 2004.

Financial instruments (IAS 39, "Financial Instruments: Recognition and Measurement" and IFRS 7, "Financial Instruments: Disclosures")

The Group has applied IAS 32 and IAS 39 for all periods presented and has therefore not taken advantage of the exemption in IFRS 1 that would enable the Group to only apply these standards from 1 April 2005.

Cumulative translation differences (IAS 21, "The Effects of Changes in Foreign Exchange Rates")

The Group has deemed the cumulative translation differences at the date of transition to IFRS to be zero. As a result, the gain or loss of a subsequent disposal of any foreign operation will exclude the translation differences that arose before the date of transition to IFRS.

If the Group had not applied the exemption, the gain or loss on any disposals after the transition date would include additional cumulative transaction differences relating to the business disposed of.

Fair value or revaluation as deemed cost (IAS 16, "Property, Plant and Equipment" and IAS 38, "Intangible Assets")

The Group has not elected to measure any item of property, plant and equipment or intangible asset at the date of transition to IFRS at its fair value.

Impact of transition to IFRS

The following is a summary of the effects of the differences between IFRS and UK GAAP on the Group's total equity shareholders' funds and profit for the financial year for the years previously reported under UK GAAP following the date of transition to IFRS.

Total equity shareholders' funds

	Note	1 April 2004 £m	31 March 2005 £m
Total equity shareholders' funds (UK GAAP)		111,924	99,317
Measurement and recognition differences:			
Intangible assets	a	(164)	13,986
Proposed dividends	b	728	1,395
Financial instruments	c	385	350
Share-based payments	d	12	63
Defined benefit pension schemes	e	(257)	(361)
Deferred and current taxes	f	(1,011)	(774)
Other		(66)	(176)
Total equity shareholders' funds (IFRS)		111,551	113,800

Profit for the year ended 31 March 2005	Note	£m
Loss on ordinary activities after taxation (UK GAAP)		(6,938)
Measurement and recognition differences:		
Intangible assets	a	14,263
Financial instruments	c	(174)
Share-based payments	d	(91)
Defined benefit pension schemes	e	7
Deferred and current taxes	f	10
Other		(130)
Presentation differences:		
Presentation of equity accounted investments	g	(45)
Presentation of joint ventures	h	(384)
Profit for the financial year (IFRS)		6,518

There were no significant differences between IFRS and UK GAAP on the Group's cash flow statement for the year ended 31 March 2005.

Measurement and recognition differences

a. Intangible assets

IAS 38, "Intangible Assets" requires that goodwill is not amortised. Instead it is subject to an annual impairment review. As the Group has elected not to apply IFRS 3 retrospectively to business combinations prior to the opening balance sheet date under IFRS, the UK GAAP goodwill balance, after adjusting for items including the impact of proportionate consolidation of joint ventures, at 31 March 2004 (£78,753 million) has been included in the opening IFRS consolidated balance sheet and is no longer amortised.

Under IAS 38, capitalised payments for licences and spectrum fees are amortised on a straight line basis over their useful economic life. Amortisation is charged from the commencement of service of the network. Under UK GAAP, the Group's policy was to amortise such costs in proportion to the capacity of the network during the start up period and then on a straight-line basis thereafter.

b. Proposed dividends

IAS 10, "Events after the Balance Sheet Date" requires that dividends declared after the balance sheet date should not be recognised as a liability at that balance sheet date as the liability does not represent obligation as defined by IAS 37, "Provisions, Contingent Liabilities and Contingent Assets".

c. Financial instruments

IAS 32, "Financial Instruments: Disclosure and Presentation" and IAS 39, "Financial Instruments: Recognition and Measurement" address the accounting for, and reporting of, financial instruments. IAS 39 sets out detailed accounting requirements in relation to financial assets and liabilities.

All derivative financial instruments are accounted for at fair market value whilst other financial instruments are accounted for either at amortised cost or at fair value depending on their classification. Subject to certain criteria, financial assets and financial liabilities may be designated as forming hedge relationships as a result of which fair value changes are offset in the income statement or charged/credited to equity depending on the nature of the hedge relationship.

d. Share-based payments

IFRS 2, "Share-based Payment" requires that an expense for equity instruments granted be recognised in the financial statements based on their fair value at the date of grant. This expense, which is primarily in relation to employee option and performance share schemes, is recognised over the vesting period of the scheme.

While IFRS 2 allows the measurement of this expense to be calculated only on options granted after 7 November 2002, the Group has applied IFRS 2 to all instruments granted but not fully vested as at 1 April 2004. The Group has adopted the binomial model for the purposes of calculating fair value under IFRS, calibrated using a Black-Scholes framework.

e. Defined benefit pension schemes

The Group elected to adopt early the amendment to IAS 19, "Employee Benefits" issued by the IASB on 16 December 2004 which allows all actuarial gains and losses to be charged or credited to equity.

The Group's opening IFRS balance sheet at 1 April 2004 reflects the assets and liabilities of the Group's defined benefit schemes totalling a net liability of £154 million. The transitional adjustment of £257 million to opening reserves comprises the reversal of entries in relation to UK GAAP accounting under SSAP 24 less the recognition of the net liabilities of the Group's and associated undertakings' defined benefit schemes.

f. Deferred and current taxes

The scope of IAS 12, "Income Taxes" is wider than the corresponding UK GAAP standards, and requires deferred tax to be provided on all temporary differences rather than just timing differences under UK GAAP.

As a result, taxes in the Group's IFRS opening balance sheet at 1 April 2004 were adjusted by £1.0 billion. This includes an additional deferred tax liability of £1.8 billion in respect of the differences between the carrying value and tax written down value of the Group's investments in associated undertakings and joint ventures. This comprises £13 billion in respect of differences that arose when US investments were acquired and £0.5 billion is respect of undistributed earnings of certain associated undertakings and joint ventures, principally Vodafone Italy. UK GAAP does not permit deferred tax to be provided on the undistributed earnings of the Group's associated undertakings and joint ventures until there is a binding obligation to distribute those earnings.

IAS 12 also requires deferred tax to be provided in respect of the Group's liabilities under its post employment benefit arrangements and on other employee benefits such as share and share option schemes.

g. Presentation of equity accounted investments

Under IFRS, in accordance with IAS 1, "Presentation of Financial Statements", "Tax on profit" on the face of the consolidated income statement comprises the tax charge of the Company, its subsidiaries and its share of the tax charge of joint ventures. The Group's share of its associated undertakings' tax charges is shown as part of "Share of result in associated undertakings" rather than being disclosed as part of the tax charge under UK GAAP.

In respect of the Verizon Wireless partnership, the line "Share of result in associated undertakings" includes the Group's share of pre-tax partnership income and the Group's share of the post-tax income attributable to corporate entities (as determined for US corporate income tax purposes) held by the partnership. The tax attributable to the Group's share of allocable partnership income is included as part of "Tax on profit" in the consolidated income statement. This treatment reflects the fact that tax on allocable partnership income is, for US corporate income tax purposes, a liability of the partners and not the partnership. Under UK GAAP, the Group's share of minority interests in associated undertakings was reported in minority interests, under IFRS this is reported within investments in associated undertakings.

h. Presentation of joint ventures

IAS 31, "Interests in Joint Ventures" defines a jointly controlled entity a an entity where unanimous consent over the strategic financial and operating decisions is required between the parties sharing control. Control is defined as the power to govern the financial and operating decisions of an entity so as to obtain economic benefit from it.

The Group has reviewed the classification of its investments and concluded that the Group's 76.9% (31 March 2005: 76.8%) interest in Vodafone Italy, classified as a subsidiary undertaking under UK GAAP, should be accounted for as a joint venture under IFRS. In addition, the Group's interests in South Africa, Poland, Kenya and Fiji, which were classified as associated undertakings under UK GAAP, have been classified as joint ventures under IFRS as a result of the contractual rights held by the Group. The Group's interest in Romania was classified as a joint venture until the acquisition of the controlling stake from Telesystem International Wireless Inc. of Canada completed on 31 May 2005. The Group has adopted proportionate consolidation as the method of accounting for these six entities.

Under UK GAAP, the revenue, operating profit, net financing costs and taxation of Vodafone Italy were consolidated in full in the income statement with a corresponding allocation to minority interest. Under proportionate consolidation, the Group recognises its share of all income statement lines with no allocation to minority interest. There is no effect on the result for a financial period from this adjustment.

Under UK GAAP, the Group's interests in South Africa, Poland, Romania, Kenya and Fiji were accounted for under the equity method, with the Group's share of operating profit, interest and tax being recognised separately in the consolidated income statement. Under proportionate consolidation, the Group recognises its share of all income statement lines. There is no effect on the result for a financial period from this adjustment.

Under UK GAAP, the Group fully consolidated the cash flows of Vodafone Italy, but did not consolidate the cash flows of its associated undertakings. The IFRS consolidated cash flow statement reflects the Group's share of cash flows relating to its joint ventures on a line by line basis, with a corresponding recognition of the Group's share of net debt for each of the proportionately consolidated entities.

Other differences

i. Reclassification of non-equity minority interests to liabilities

The primary impact of the implementation of IAS 32 is the reclassification of the $1.65 billion preferred shares issued by the Group's subsidiary. Vodafone Americas Inc., from non-equity minority interests to liabilities. The reclassification at 1 April 2004 was £875 million. Dividend payments by this subsidiary, which were previously reported in the Group's income statement as non-equity minority interests, have been reclassified to financing costs.

j. Fair value of available-for-sale financial assets

The Group has classified certain of its cost-based investments as available-for-sale financial assets as defined in IAS 39. This classification does not reflect the intentions of management in relation to these investments. These assets are measured at fair value at each reporting date with movements in fair value taken to equity. At 1 April 2004, a cumulative increase of £233 million in the fair value over the carrying value of these investments was recognised.

Reconciliation of the UK GAAP consolidated profit and loss account to the IFRS consolidated income statement

Year ended 31 March 2005

UK GAAP format	UK GAAP £m	Presentation differences £m	Measurement and recognition differences £m	Discontinued operations £m	IFRS £m	IFRS format
Turnover	34,133	–	(60)	(7,395)	26,678	Revenue
Cost of sales	(20,733)	–	(711)	5,664	(15,800)	Cost of sales
Gross profit	13,380	–	(771)	(1,731)	10,878	Gross profit
Selling and distribution costs	(2,031)	–	(15)	397	(1,649)	Selling and distribution expenses
Administrative expenses	(16,653)	315	12,812	670	(2,856)	Administrative expenses
		404	1,576	–	1,980	Share of result in associated undertakings
		(315)	(160)	–	(475)	Other income and expense
Operating loss	(5,304)	404	13,442	664)	7,878	Operating profit
Share of result in associated undertakings	1,193	(1,193)				
Exceptional non-operating items	13	(13)				
		8	(2)	(13)	(7)	Non-operating income and expense
		324	(21)	(9)	294	Investment income
Net interest payable and similar items	(604)	(113)	(183)	20	(880)	Financing costs
Loss on ordinary activities before taxation	(4,702)	(583)	13,236	(666)	7,285	Profit before taxation
Tax on loss on ordinary activities	(2,236)	538	265	(436)	(1,869)	Tax on profit
Loss on ordinary activities after taxation	(6,938)	(45)	13,501	(1,102)	5,416	Profit on ordinary activities after taxation from continuing operations
	–	–	–	1,102	1,102	Profit on ordinary activities after taxation from discontinued operations
	(6,938)	(45)	13,501	–	6,518	Profit for the financial year
Minority interest	(602)	45	449	–	(108)	Profit for the financial year attributable to minority interests
Loss for the financial year	(7,540)	–	13,950	–	6,410	Profit for the financial year attributable to equity shareholders

Reconciliation of the UK GAAP consolidated balance sheet to the IFRS consolidated balance sheet

1 April 2004

UK GAAP format	UK GAAP £m	Presentation differences £m	Measurement and recognition differences £m	IFRS £m	IFRS format
Fixed assets:					Non-current assets:
Intangible assets	93,622	–	1,002	94,624	Intangible assets
Tangible assets	18,083	–	(971)	17,112	Property, plant and equipment
Investments in associated undertakings	21,226	–	(800)	20,426	Investments in associated undertakings
Other investments	1,049	–	233	1,282	Other investments
		671	136	807	Deferred tax assets
		221	(9)	212	Trade and other receivables
	133,980	892	(409)	134,463	

Current assets:					Current assets:
Stocks	458	–	10	468	Inventory
Debtors	6,901	(6,901)			
		372	(103)	269	Taxation recoverable
		5,148	305	5,453	Trade and other receivables
Investments	4,381	(4,381)			
Cash at bank and in hand	1,409	4,381	61	5,851	Cash and cash equivalents
	13,149	(1,381)	273	12,041	
Total assets	147,129	(489)	(136)	146,504	Total assets
Capital and reserves:					Equity:
Called up share capital	4,280	–	–	4,280	Called up share capital
Share premium account	52,154	–	–	52,154	Share premium account
Own shares held	(1,136)	–	–	(1,136)	Own shares held
Other reserve	99,640	–	310	99,950	Additional paid-in capital
		–	233	233	Other reserve
Profit and loss account	(43,014)	–	(916)	(43,930)	Retained losses
Total equity shareholders' funds	111,924	–	(373)	111,551	Total equity shareholders' funds
Minority interests	3,007	–	(2,198)	809	Minority interests
	114,931	–	(2,571)	112,360	
Creditors – amounts falling due after more than one year	12,975	(12,975)			Non-current liabilities
		12,224	1,859	14,083	Long-term borrowings
		3,314	1,421	4,735	Deferred tax liabilities
		(73)	227	154	Post employment benefits
Provisions for liabilities and charges	4,197	(3,858)	5	344	Provisions for liabilities and charges
		751	(449)	302	Trade and other payables
	17,172	(617)	3,063	19,618	
Creditors – amounts falling due within one year	15,026	(15,026)			Current liabilities:
		2,054	788	2,842	Short-term borrowings
		4,275	(356)	3,919	Current taxation liabilities
		8,643	(1,068)	7,575	Trade and other payables
		182	8	190	Provisions for liabilities and charges
	15,026	128	(628)	14,526	
	147,129	(489)	(136)	146,504	Total equity and liabilities

31 March 2005

UK GAAP format	UK GAAP	Presentation differences	Measurement and recognition differences	IFRS	IFRS format
	£m	£m	£m	£m	
Fixed assets:					Non-current assets:
		68,673	12,326	80,999	Goodwill
Intangible assets	83,464	(68,673)	1,358	16,149	Other intangible assets
Tangible assets	18,398	–	(956)	17,442	Property, plant and equipment
Investments in associated undertakings	19,398	–	836	20,234	Investment in associated undertakings
Other investment	852	–	329	1,181	Other investments
		1,084	100	1,184	Deferred tax assets
		12	–	12	Post employment benefits
		613	(28)	585	Trade and other receivables
	122,112	1,709	13,965	137,786	

Current assets:					Current assets:
Stocks	430	–	10	440	Inventory
Debtors	7,698	(7,698)			
		268	(230)	38	Taxation receivables
		5,049	115	5,164	Trade and other receivables
Investments	816	(816)			
Cash at bank and in hand	2,850	816	103	3,759	Cash and cash equivalents
	11,794	(2,381)	(2)	9,411	
	133,906	(672)	13,963	147,197	Total assets
Capital and reserves:					Equity:
Called up share capital	4,286	–	–	4,286	Called up share capital
Share premium account	52,284	–	–	52,284	Share premium account
Own shares held	(5,121)	–		(5,121)	Own shares held
Other reserve	99,556	–	525	100,081	Additional paid-in capital
		–	1,781	1,781	Accumulated other recognised income and expense
Profit and loss account	(51,688)	–	12,177	(39,511)	Retained losses
Total equity shareholders' funds	99,317	–	14,483	113,800	Total equity shareholders' funds
Minority interests	2,818	–	(2,970)	(152)	Minority interests
	102,135	–	11,513	113,648	
Creditors – amounts falling due after more than one year	12,382	(12,382)			Non-current liabilities:
		11,613	1,577	13,190	Long term borrowings
		3,481	1,368	4,849	Deferred tax liabilities
		(171)	307	136	Post employment benefits
Provisions for liabilities and charges	4,552	(4,235)	2	319	Provisions for other liabilities and charges
		797	(359)	438	Trade and other payables
	16,934	(897)	2,895	18,932	
Creditors – amounts falling due within one year	14,837	(14,837)			Current liabilities:
		392	1,611	2,003	Short-term borrowings
		4,759	(406)	4,353	Current taxation liabilities
		9,717	(1,694)	8,033	Trade and other payables
		194	34	228	Provisions for other liabilities and charges
	14,837	225	(445)	14,617	
	133,906	(672)	13,963	147,196	Total equity and liabilities

In its first IFRS financial statements GlaxoSmithKline presented the following detailed descriptions of the reconciling differences between IFRS and its previous GAAP. Its detailed reconciliations for its balance sheet, income statement and statement of recognised income and expense have not been reproduced here.

Extract 5.8: GlaxoSmithKline plc (2005)

Notes to the consolidated financial statements [extract]

40 Transition to IFRS [extract]

Background

The IFRS Project

In June 2002, the Council of the European Union adopted a Regulation requiring listed companies in its Member States to prepare their consolidated financial statements in accordance with International Financial Reporting Standards (IFRS) from 2005.

The GlaxoSmithKline Annual Report for the year ending 31st December 2005 is the first Annual Report prepared under IFRS.

As 2003 is the earliest year for which full IFRS financial statements are presented in the Annual report 2005, the transition date to IFRS for GlaxoSmithKline is 1st January 2003. Normally, accounting changes of this nature would require full retrospective application, but GSK has taken advantage of exemptions available under the IFRS transitional rules to apply certain requirements only with effect from the transition date of 1st January 2003 or, in the case of financial instruments, from 1st January 2005.

Financial instruments

GSK has adopted IAS 39 as endorsed by the European Union. However, one of the exemptions available under IFRS 1 relaxes the requirement for comparative information presented in the Annual Report 2005 to comply with IAS 32 and IAS 39. GlaxoSmithKline has taken advantage of this exemption, and so, in 2003 and 2004, financial instruments are accounted for and presented on a UK GAAP basis.

On 1st January 2005 there was an adjustment of £12 million to the opening balance sheet to reflect the movements from the UK GAAP carrying values to the IAS 39 values, which for many financial instruments will be fair value.

The financial instruments concerned are:

- Held at fair value under IFRS with movements recorded in equity:
  - Equity investments
  - Liquid investments
  - Derivatives classified as cash flow hedging instruments
- Held at fair value under IFRS with movements recorded in the income statement:
  - Equity collar linked to the Group's investment in Quest Diagnostics Inc.
  - Put and call options linked to the Group strategic alliance with Theravance Inc.
  - Other derivatives not classified as hedging instruments, including embedded derivatives
  - Derivatives classified as fair value hedges together with the hedged element of the relevant asset or liability
- Presentation differences only:
  - Non-equity minority interests (repaid during 2004).

If the IAS 39 valuation rules had been applied in 2004 there would have been a charge to profit before tax the largest elements of which arise from the Quest collar (£42 million; 2003 – £42 million) and the Theravance put and call options (£53 million; 2003 – nil). Valuations are inherently unpredictable and changes in the fair value of financial instruments could have a material impact on the future results and financial position of GSK.

IFRS adjustments

A summary of the principal differences between UK GAAP and IFRS as they apply to GSK is set out below and the financial effect is shown on pages 153 to 156.

Customer allowances

This adjustment is a reclassification between turnover and expenses with no profit or cash flow effect. IFRS has no detailed rules in relation to when certain marketing and promotional expenditure should be deducted from turnover rather than recorded as an expense. However, these rules do exist under US GAAP in EITF 01-09, 'Accounting for Consideration Given by a Vendor to a Customer', which requires most marketing, advertising, and promotion payments made to customers to be deducted from turnover. This has the most significant impact in the Consumer Healthcare business where payments to large retailers for in-store advertising, preferential shelf-space, product listings etc. are commonplace.

GSK believes that this reflects best practice in revenue recognition and hence, in the absence of detailed guidance under IFRS, has decided to adopt a revenue recognition policy under IFRS in line with EITF 01-09. Therefore there is not expected to be any difference between turnover reported under IFRS and turnover reported under US GAAP. This adjustment has no impact on profit before tax or EPS.

Share-based payments

The previous UK GAAP approach to share-based payments was to record any intrinsic loss on grant suffered by the company. This means that for share options granted at the market price, there was no charge to the income statement. Where shares or options were granted at no cost to the employee (e.g. under long-term incentive plans) the income statement was charged with an amount equal to the market price on the date of the award, spread over the performance period (usually three years).

IFRS 2, 'Share-based Payment', and its UK GAAP equivalent FRS 20, 'Share-based Payment', both of which came into force in 2005, require the fair value of the equity instruments issued to be charged to the income statement. The Group has chosen to recognise all unvested options and awards retrospectively.

GSK receives a tax credit, as appropriate, which relates to share options and awards when exercised, based on the gains the holders make and dependent on the tax rules in the country in which the deduction is claimed. The deferred tax asset represents an estimate of future tax relief for this gain and is based on the potential gains available to the option or award holders at the balance sheet date. The movement in deferred tax asset from one balance sheet to the next may result in either a tax credit or a tax charge recorded in the income statement is capped at the cumulative amount of the tax effect of the share-based payment charge. Any excess credit is taken to equity.

This adjustment reduced profit before tax in 2004 by £309 million (2003 – £368 million), earnings by £314 million (2003 – £344 million) and EPS by 5.5 pence (2003 – 5.9 pence).

The share-based payments charge reduced to a more normal level of £236 million in 2005. The considerably higher charge in 2004 and 2003 arises from two main factors. Relatively few share options were granted during 2000 when the GW/SB merger was being finalised, but then in 2001 there was a full "catch-up" grant early in the year followed by the normal annual grant in November 2001. In addition, the grants in 2001 were made at an average share price in excess of £18. These share options became exercisable in 2004 and therefore fell out of the charge in 2005, which now reflects more current share prices and more normal grant levels.

Coreg capitalisation and amortisation

The North American rights to *Coreg* were acquired at the time of the GW/SB merger as partial consideration for the required disposal of Kytril to Roche. Under UK GAAP this was accounted for as an exchange of assets with no value being attributed to *Coreg* on the balance sheet. IFRS, however, requires the acquired rights to *Coreg* to be added to intangible assets at their fair value on the date of acquisition of $400 million, and then amortised over their remaining useful life of eight years. This adjustment reduces 2004 profit before tax by £27 million (2003 – £31 million) and EPS by 0.3 pence (2003 – 0.3 pence).

Other intangible assets amortisation

Under UK GAAP, GSK amortised intangible assets over their estimated expected useful lives from acquisition, which was up to a maximum of 15 years. IFRS only permits amortisation to commence when the asset becomes available for use, with annual impairment testing required before this point. GSK has determined that the point at which amortisation of product-related assets commences under IFRS will normally be regulatory approval. The majority of the Group's intangible assets relates to the acquisition of rights to compounds in development and so has not reached the point at which amortisation commences. This has led to a reduction in the amortisation charge, which is likely to reverse in the future as these compounds reach regulatory approval and amortisation is then charged over a shorter period. Profit before tax in 2004 increased by £43 million (2003 – £43 million) and EPS by 0.5 pence (2003 – 0.5 pence).

Goodwill amortisation

UK GAAP required goodwill to be amortised over its estimated expected useful like, which GSK has determined to be normally no longer than 20 years. Under IFRS, however, goodwill is considered to have an indefinite life and so is not amortised, but is subject to annual impairment testing. This adjustment therefore reverses the goodwill amortisation charged under UK GAAP, including that recorded in the profit on share of associates line relating to the acquisition of the Group's interest in Quest Diagnostics Inc. Under the business combinations exemption of IFRS 1, goodwill previously written off direct to reserves under UK GAAP is not recycled to the income statement on the disposal or part-disposal of the subsidiary or associate, as it would be under UK GAAP. The adjustment increases 2004 profit before tax by £37 million (2003 – £26 million) and EPS by 0.7 pence (2003 – 0.4 pence).

Pensions and other post-employment benefits

GlaxoSmithKline accounted under UK GAAP for pensions and other post-employment benefits (OPEBs) in accordance with SSAP 24, which spread the costs of providing the benefits over the estimated average service lives of the employees.

IAS 19, 'Employee Benefits', recognises surpluses and deficits in the accounts, and in accordance with the transitional provisions of IFRS 1, the surpluses and deficits have been recognised in full on the balance sheet at the transition date of 1st January 2003. In addition, following an amendment to IAS 19 issued by the IASB in December 2004, it is permitted to recognise any movements in the surpluses or deficits immediately in the balance sheet, but outside the income statement, in the Statement of recognised income and expense. This means that, in most cases, the balance sheet reflects the full surplus or deficit positions of the funds.

The Group's policy is to charge out to the operating businesses the service cost element of the pension charge, which then gets reported within cost of sales, selling, general and administrative expenditure or research and development as appropriate, but not to charge out the element related to the funding deficit, which is all reported in selling, general and administrative expenditure. Under IAS 19, the service cost element of the total charge is considerably higher then under SSAP 24 and the funding deficit element lower. This has led to an additional reclassification adjustment between the income statement expense headings.

The overall impact of the adjustments to pensions and OPEBs in 2004 was a decrease in profit before tax of £36 million (2003 – increase of £11 million) and a decrease in EPS of 0.4 pence (2003 – nil).

Share of profits of associates

Under UK GAAP the share of profits of associates was reported within profit before tax for the Group. However, IFRS requires this share of profits to be the net profit attributable to the Group, i.e. after interest, tax and minority interests of the associate. This has led to a reclassification adjustment removing the share of the associates' interest, tax and minority interests from those lines in the income statement and netting them all together in the share of profits of associates line. This adjustment reduced 2004 profit before tax by £42 million (2003 – £42 million) but did not affect EPS.

Deferred tax on intercompany profit

Under UK GAAP, deferred tax on the provision for intercompany profit held in inventory is calculated at the supplying company's effective tax rate. IFRS, however, takes a balance sheet approach to the recognition of deferred tax which results in the tax rate of the company holding the inventory at the balance sheet date being applied to the provision. If the proportions of the Group's inventory held in specific locations change significantly from one balance sheet date to the next there could be a significant change in the value of the deferred tax asset, which is reflected through the tax change for the year.

Other adjustments

There are a number of other minor adjustments and reclassifications, including:

- Computer software, which is recorded as an intangible asset unless it forms an integral part of the operating system of a tangible fixed asset
- Deferred tax on brands acquired with a company, where if there is a difference between the fair value of the brands on acquisition and the tax value, a taxable temporary difference arises
- Cash equivalents reclassification, where liquid investments with maturities of less than three months at acquisition are included within cash and cash equivalents
- Provisions reclassification, where the elements of provision expected to be paid within one year of the balance sheet date, with the exception of pensions and OPEBs, are presented within current liabilities.

Cash flow statement

The move from UK GAAP to IFRS does not change any of the cash flows of the Group. The IFRS cash flow format is similar to UK GAAP but presents various cash flows in different categories and in a different order from the UK GAAP cash flow statement. All of the IFRS accounting adjustments net out within cash generated from operations except for the intangible assets reclassification and the inclusion of liquid investments with a maturity of less than three months on acquisition, together with related exchange adjustments, within cash and cash equivalents under IFRS.

If a first-time adopter recognised or reversed any impairment losses on transition to IFRS it should disclose the information that IAS 36 would have required 'if the entity had recognised those impairment losses or reversals in the period beginning with the date of transition to IFRS' (see Chapter 15 at 3).[282] The purpose of this disclosure requirement is that while 'there is inevitably subjectivity about impairment losses [the] disclosure provides transparency about impairment losses recognised on transition to IFRS. These losses might otherwise receive less attention than impairment losses recognised in earlier or later periods.'[283]

B Designation of financial assets and financial liabilities

IAS 39 permits a financial instrument to be designated on initial recognition as a *financial asset or financial liability at fair value through profit or loss* or as an *available-for-sale financial asset*, subject to the criteria in that standard.[284] If a first-time adopter designates a previously recognised financial asset or financial liability as a 'financial asset or financial liability at fair value through profit or loss' or a financial asset as available-for-sale (see 2.6.2 above), it should disclose for each category:[285]

- the fair value of any financial assets or financial liabilities designated into it at the date of designation; and
- their classification and carrying amount in the previous financial statements.

The extract below illustrates the above disclosure requirement.

Extract 5.9: Aegon N.V. (2005)

Notes to the consolidated financial statements of AEGON Group [extract]

56 First-time adoption of IFRS [extract]

DESIGNATION OF FINANCIAL ASSETS AND FINANCIAL LIABILITIES AS FINANCIAL ASSETS OR FINANCIAL LIABILITIES AT FAIR VALUE THROUGH PROFIT OR LOSS OR AS AVAILABLE-FOR-SALE FINANCIAL ASSET

The following table provides a summary of the fair value of financial assets and financial liabilities designated into each of these categories as at January 1, 2004, and their classification and carrying amount in the previous financial statements:

FINANCIAL ASSETS DESIGNATED AS AT FAIR VALUE THROUGH PROFIT OR LOSS AT JANUARY 1, 2004

	Carrying value under DAP	Fair value 1 January 2004
CLASSIFICATION UNDER DAP		
General account investments		
Other financial investments	9,489	9,803
Investments for account of policyholders	99,868	99,868
	109,357	109,671

FINANCIAL LIABILITIES DESIGNATED AS AT FAIR VALUE THROUGH PROFIT OR LOSS AT JANUARY 1, 2004

	Carrying value under DAP	Fair value 1 January 2004
CLASSIFICATION UNDER DAP		
General account liabilities		
Technical provisions	638	638
Technical provisions with investments for account of policyholders	42,506	42,539
	43,144	43,177

FINANCIAL ASSETS CLASSIFIED AS AVAILABLE-FOR-SALE AT JANUARY 1, 2004	Carrying value under DAP	Fair value 1 January 2004
CLASSIFICATION UNDER DAP		
General account investments		
Other financial investments	88,183	91,831
	88,183	91,831

C Use of fair value as deemed cost

If a first-time adopter uses 'fair value in its opening IFRS balance sheet as deemed cost for an item of property, plant and equipment, an investment property or an intangible asset' (see 2.5 above), it should disclose for each line item in the opening IFRS balance sheet:[286]

- the aggregate of those fair values; and
- the aggregate adjustment to the carrying amounts reported under previous GAAP.

2.10.3 Interim financial reports

If a first-time adopter presents an interim financial report under IAS 34 for part of the period covered by its first IFRS financial statements, that report should:[287]

(a) include reconciliations of:
- its equity under previous GAAP at the end of that comparable interim period to its equity under IFRS at that date; and
- its profit or loss under previous GAAP for that comparable interim period, both on a current and year-to-date basis, to its profit or loss under IFRS for that period; and

(b) include the reconciliations described at 2.10.2 A above or a cross-reference to another published document that includes these reconciliations.

For an entity presenting annual financial statements under IFRS it is not compulsory to prepare interim financial reports under IAS 34. Therefore, the above requirements only apply to first-time adopters that prepare interim reports under IAS 34 on a voluntary basis or that are required to do so by a regulator or other party.[288] However, even if an entity does not present interim financial reports prepared in accordance with IAS 34, the accounting policies applied in preparing its interim financial statements should still be IFRS compliant.

Example 5.32: Reconciliations to be presented in IFRS half-year reports

As in Example 5.31 at 2.10.2 A above, Entity E's date of transition to IFRS is 1 January 2007, its reporting date is 31 December 2008 and it publishes a half-year report as at 30 June under IAS 34. Which primary financial statements and reconciliations should E present in its first IFRS half-year report?

	1 January 2007	*30 June 2007*	*31 December 2007*	*30 June 2008*
Balance sheet			●	●
Reconciliation of equity	● *	●	● *	
For the period ending				
Income statement		●		●
Cash flow statement		●		●
Statement of changes in equity		●		●
Reconciliation of profit or loss		●	● *	
Explanation of material adjustments to cash flow statement			● *	

* Additional reconciliations required under paragraph 39 of IFRS 1.

The IAS 34 requirements regarding the disclosure of primary financial statements in interim reports are discussed in Chapter 37.

As can be seen from the table in Example 5.32, the additional reconciliations and explanations required under (b) above would be presented out of context, i.e. without the balance sheet, income statement and cash flow statement that they relate to. For this reason a first-time adopter may want either (1) to include the primary financial statements to which these reconciliations relate or (2) to refer to another document that includes these reconciliations.

Example 5.33: Reconciliations to be presented in first IFRS financial statement and interim reports[289]

Entity F's date of transition to IFRS is 1 January 2007, its reporting date is 31 December 2008 and it publishes quarterly reports under IAS 34. Which reconciliations should F present in its 2008 interim reports and in its first IFRS financial statements?

	Reconciliation of equity	*Reconciliation of profit or loss*	*Explanation of material adjustments to cash flow statement*
First quarter			
1 January 2007	○		
31 December 2007	○	○	○
31 March 2007			
– 3 months ending	●	●	
Second quarter			
30 June 2007			
– 3 months ending		●	
– 6 months ending	●	●	
Third quarter			
30 September 2007			
– 3 months ending		●	
– 9 months ending	●	●	

First IFRS financial statements			
1 January 2007	●		
31 December 2007	●	●	●

- ● Mandatory disclosures required to be included in the interim report.
- ○ These reconciliations are only required to be presented in an entity's *first* interim financial report under IAS 34 and may be included by way of a cross-reference to another published document in which these reconciliations are presented.

Interim financial reports under IAS 34 contain considerably less detail than annual financial statements because they 'are based on the assumption that users of the interim financial report also have access to the most recent annual financial statements.'[290] Therefore, a first-time adopter will have to ensure that its first interim financial report contains sufficient information about events or transactions that are material to an understanding of the current interim period. Hence it may be necessary for a first-time adopter to include in its first IFRS interim report significantly more information that it would normally include in an interim report; alternatively it could include a cross-reference to another published document that includes such information.[291]

2.11 Effective date

IFRS 1 is mandatory for an entity's first IFRS financial statements for a period beginning on or after 1 January 2004, although early application was encouraged. If an entity applied IFRS 1 early, it had to disclose this fact (see 2.10 above).[292]

As mentioned earlier (see 2.3.2), the IASB's desire to ensure that IFRS 1 comprises all first-time adoption rules has meant that IFRS 1 has been amended a number of times. Unavoidably the effective dates of each of these amendments are different, which has given rise to the following, rather complicated, situation:[293]

Standard or interpretation	**Effective date †**	**Amendment**
IFRIC 1 – *Changes in Existing Decommissioning, Restoration and Similar Liabilities*	1 September 2004	IFRS 1.25E
IFRIC 4 – *Determining whether an Arrangement contains a Lease*	1 January 2006	IFRS 1.25F
IFRS 6 – *Exploration for and Evaluation of Mineral Resources*	1 January 2006	IFRS 1.36B
IFRS 7 – *Financial Instruments: Disclosures*	1 January 2006	IFRS 1.36C
Amendment to IAS 19 – *Employee Benefits – Actuarial Gains and Losses, Group Plans and Disclosures*	1 January 2006	IFRS 1.20A
Amendment to IAS 39 – *Financial Instruments: Recognition and Measurement – Transition and Initial Recognition of Financial Assets and Financial Liabilities*	1 January 2005	IFRS 1.25G
IFRIC 12 – *Service Concession Arrangements*	1 January 2008	IFRS 1.25H
IAS 23 – *Borrowing Costs*	1 January 2009	IFRS 1.25I

† The amendments apply to periods starting on or after the effective date.

If an entity applies any of the above standards or interpretations before its effective date, it should apply the corresponding paragraphs in IFRS 1 from the same date onwards.

3 PRACTICAL ISSUES

3.1 First-time adoption by SEC registrants

An entity that is registered with the US Securities and Exchange Commission (SEC) is normally required to present two comparative periods for its income statement, cash flow statement and statement of changes in equity. Converting two comparative periods to IFRS was considered to be a considerable burden to companies. Therefore, in April 2005, SEC published amendments to Form 20-F that changed the filing requirements for foreign private issuers that are first-time adopters of IFRS.[294]

The amendments permit 'eligible foreign private issuers for their first year of reporting under IFRS to file two years rather than three years of statements of income, changes in shareholders' equity and cash flows prepared in accordance with IFRS, with appropriate related disclosure. The accommodation retains current requirements regarding the reconciliation of financial statement items to generally accepted accounting principles as used in the United States ("U.S. GAAP"). In addition, the amendments require certain disclosures of all foreign private issuers that change their basis of accounting to IFRS.'[295]

A foreign private issuer is eligible to exclude IFRS financial statements for the third financial year from its annual report on Form 20-F if:[296]

- the annual report relates to the first financial year starting on or after 1 January 2007 or an earlier financial year;
- the issuer adopts IFRS for the first time by an explicit and unreserved statement of compliance with IFRS; and
- the audited financial statements for the financial year to which the annual report relates are prepared in accordance with IFRS.

The accommodation is only available to a company that is able to state 'unreservedly and explicitly that its financial statements comply with IFRS, and if its audited financial statements are not subject to any qualification regarding compliance with IFRS, including any qualification of the report of the independent auditor relating to the application of IFRS. A foreign private issuer that had not complied with all IFRSs in effect as published by the IASB, or IFRS as "adopted for use in the European Union" ("EU GAAP"), would not be able to make the required unreserved statement of compliance with IFRS and would not be eligible to rely on the accommodation the Commission has adopted.'[297]

First-time adopters that rely on the accommodation are allowed, but not required, to include any financial statements, discussions or other financial information based on their previous GAAP. If first-time adopters do include such information, they should prominently disclose cautionary language to avoid inappropriate comparison with information presented under IFRS. The SEC did not mandate a specific location for any previous GAAP information but did prohibit presentation of previous GAAP information in a side-by-side columnar format with IFRS financial information.

In addition, the accommodation only requires entities to provide selected historical financial data based on IFRS for the two most recent financial years. Selected historical financial data based on US GAAP would continue to be required for the five most recent financial years. Although the SEC does not prohibit entities from including selected financial data based on previous GAAP in their annual reports, side-by-side presentation of data prepared under IFRS and data prepared under previous GAAP is prohibited.

Where a narrative discussion of its financial condition is provided, the accommodation requires management to focus on the financial statements prepared under IFRS and the reconciliation to US GAAP for the past two financial years. In addition, management should explain any differences between IFRS and US GAAP that are not otherwise discussed in the reconciliation necessary for an understanding of the financial statements as a whole.

IFRS 1 requires a first-time adopter to present a reconciliation from its previous GAAP to IFRS in the notes to its financial statements and allows certain exceptions from full retrospective application of IFRS in deriving the relevant data. Under the SEC's accommodation, any issuer relying on any of the elective or mandatory exceptions from IFRS that are contained within IFRS 1 will have to disclose additional information which includes:[298]

- to the extent the primary financial statements reflect the use of exceptions permitted or required by IFRS 1:
  - detailed information for each exception used, including:
    - an indication of the items or class of items to which the exception was applied; and
    - a description of what accounting principle was used and how it was applied; and
  - where material, qualitative disclosure of the impact on financial condition, changes in financial condition and results of operations that the treatment specified by IFRS would have had absent the election to rely on the exception.

The accommodation requires an entity that adopts IFRS 'adopted for use in the European Union' to provide the following additional information:

- an audited reconciliation to IFRS as published by the IASB that contains information relating to financial statement line items and footnote disclosure equivalent to that required under IFRS as published by the IASB;
- an audited reconciliation to US GAAP that must begin either with IFRS as published by the IASB or with EU GAAP;
- additional selected financial data based on (1) IFRS as published by the IASB and (2) US GAAP; and

- Operating and Financial Review and Prospects focused on the EU GAAP financial statements, with a discussion of any differences between EU GAAP, IFRS as published by the IASB, and US GAAP not otherwise discussed in the reconciliation footnote, to the extent necessary to understand the financial statements as a whole.

Currently, the accommodation to first-time adopters of IFRS expires after the first financial year starting on or after 1 January 2007. That timing was intended to comport with the requirements of the EU Regulation relating to the transition to IFRS of European companies, although the accommodation is available to an eligible first-time adopter of IFRS issuer from any jurisdiction. The SEC is aware that several countries will be changing their national accounting standards to IFRS, and is therefore proposing to extend the accommodation for five years, to cover financial statements for the 2012 financial year or earlier that are included in annual reports or registration statements.

3.2 Income taxes

IFRS 1 requires full retrospective application of IAS 12. A first-time adopter needs to apply IAS 12 to 'temporary differences between the carrying amount of the assets and liabilities in its opening IFRS balance sheet and their tax bases.'[299] This poses several problems that may not be immediately obvious at first sight. First of all, IAS 12 does not require an entity to account for all temporary differences. For example, an entity is not required under IAS 12 to recognise deferred tax for temporary differences relating to:

- the initial recognition of goodwill; and[300]
- the initial recognition of an asset or liability in a transaction that is not a business combination and that affected neither accounting profit nor taxable profit.[301]

Secondly, a change in deferred tax should be accounted for in equity, instead of income, when the tax relates to an item that was originally accounted for in equity. Thirdly, IAS 12 requires that goodwill be adjusted through the income statement when deferred tax assets, that did not satisfy the criteria in IFRS 3 for separate recognition when a business combination was initially accounted for, are subsequently realised.[302]

Therefore, full retrospective application of IAS 12 requires a first-time adopter to establish the history of the items that give rise to temporary differences because, depending on the type of transaction, it may not be necessary to account for deferred tax, or changes in the deferred tax may need to be accounted for in equity.

The goodwill on a business combination that is not restated would not be adjusted for deferred taxation that arises on the acquired intangible assets if those intangible assets were separately recognised under the previous GAAP (see 2.4.8 above).

3.2.1 Previously revalued plant, property and equipment treated as deemed cost on transition

In some cases IFRS 1 allows an entity, on transition to IFRS, to treat the carrying amount of plant, property and equipment revalued under its previous GAAP as a deemed cost for the purposes of IFRS (see 2.5 above).

Where an asset is carried at deemed cost on transition to IFRS, but the tax base of the asset remains at original cost (or an amount based on original cost), the pre-transition revaluation will give rise to a temporary difference (typically, a taxable temporary difference) associated with the asset. IAS 12 requires deferred tax to be recognised on any such temporary difference at transition.

If, after transition, the deferred tax is required to be remeasured (e.g. because of a change in tax rate, or a re-basing of the asset for tax purposes), and the asset concerned was revalued through equity under the previous GAAP, the question arises as to whether the resulting deferred tax income or expense should be recognised in the income statement or in equity.

The argument for recognising such income or expense in the income statement is essentially that the reference in paragraph 61 of IAS 12 to the tax effects of 'items charged or credited … directly to equity' must mean items accounted for in equity under IFRS, not under previous GAAP. An asset carried at deemed cost on transition is not otherwise treated as a revalued asset for the purposes of IFRS. For example, any impairment of such an asset must be accounted for in the income statement. By contrast, any impairment of plant, property and equipment treated as a revalued asset under IAS 16 would be accounted for in equity up to the amount of the cumulative revaluation gain previously recognised.

The argument for recognising such income or expense in equity is essentially that the reference in paragraph 61 of IAS 12 to the tax effects of 'items charged or credited … directly to equity' need not be read as referring only to items accounted for in equity under IFRS. Those who hold this view may do so in the context that the entity's previous GAAP required tax income and expense to be allocated between the income statement and equity in a manner similar to that required by IAS 12. It is argued that it is inappropriate that the effect of transitioning from the previous GAAP to IFRS, either of which, if applied continuously, would have required an item to be recognised in equity, is to require that item to be recognised in the income statement.

On balance, we believe that the first approach is preferable, but either approach is acceptable, so long as it is applied consistently.

If the IASB's proposals for the allocation of tax charges and credits between the income statement and equity are put into effect, all such differences would be accounted for in the income statement (see Chapter 26).

3.2.2 Share-based payment transactions subject to transitional provisions of IFRS 1 and IFRS 2

As discussed at 2.7.3 above, IFRS 1 provides first-time adopters with some transitional exemptions from accounting for share-based payment transactions.

However, there are no transitional or first-time adoption exemptions for the provisions of IAS 12 relating to share-based payment transactions. These were originally inserted into IAS 12 by Appendix C of IFRS 2. That appendix is not subject to any transitional provisions of IFRS 2, and IAS 12 is subject to no transitional provisions in IFRS 1.

Accordingly the provisions of IAS 12 relating to share-based payment transactions are applicable to all share-based payment transactions, whether accounted for in accordance with IFRS 2 or not. A tax-deductible share-based payment is treated as having a carrying amount equivalent to the total cumulative expense recognised in respect of it, irrespective of how, or indeed whether, the share-based payment is itself accounted for.

This means that on transition to IFRS, and subject to the restrictions on recognition of deferred tax assets (see Chapter 26 at 4.2.3), a deferred tax asset should be established for all share-based payment transactions, including those not accounted for under the transitional provisions.

Where such an asset is remeasured or recognised after transition to IFRS, the general rule regarding the 'capping' of the amount of any tax relief recognised in the income statement to the amount charged to the income statement applies. Therefore, if, as is likely to be the case, there was no income statement charge for share-based payment transactions under previous national GAAP, all tax effects of share-based payment transactions not accounted for under IFRS 2 should be dealt with in equity.

3.3 Property, plant and equipment

3.3.1 Parts approach

IAS 16 requires a 'parts approach' to the recognition of property, plant and equipment. Thus a large item such as an aircraft is recognised as a series of 'parts' that may have different useful lives. An engine of an aircraft may be a part. IAS 16 does not prescribe the physical unit of measure (the 'part') for recognition or what constitutes an item of property, plant and equipment. Instead the standard relies on judgement 'in applying the recognition criteria to an entity's specific circumstances.'[303] However, the standard does require an entity to:

- apply a very restrictive definition of maintenance costs (or costs of day-to-day servicing) which it describes as 'primarily the costs of labour and consumables, and may include the cost of small parts. The purpose of these expenditures is often described as for the 'repairs and maintenance' of the item of property, plant and equipment';[304]
- derecognise the carrying amount of the parts that are replaced; and[305]
- depreciate separately each part of an item of property, plant and equipment with a cost that is significant in relation to the total cost of the item.[306]

Based on this, it is reasonable to surmise that parts can be relatively small units. Therefore, it is possible that even if a first-time adopter's depreciation methods and rates are acceptable under IFRS, it may have to restate property, plant and equipment because its unit of measure was based on physical units significantly larger than IAS 16's parts.

3.3.2 Estimates of useful life and residual value

An entity may use fair value as deemed cost for an item of property, plant and equipment that it had depreciated to zero under its previous GAAP (i.e. the asset has already reached the end of its originally assessed economic life). Although IFRS 1 requires an entity to use estimates made under its previous GAAP, paragraph 51 of IAS 16 would require the entity to re-assess the remaining useful life and residual value at least annually. Therefore, the asset's deemed cost should be depreciated over its re-assessed economic life and taking into account its re-assessed residual value.

The same applies when an entity does not use fair value or revaluation as deemed cost. If there were indicators in the past that the useful life or residual value changed but those changes were not required to be recognised under previous GAAP, the IFRS carrying amount as of the date of transition should be determined by taking into account the re-assessed economic life and the re-assessed residual value.

3.4 Functional currency

Under IAS 21 an entity is required to record a foreign currency transaction 'on initial recognition in the functional currency, by applying to the foreign currency amount the spot exchange rate between the functional currency and the foreign currency at the date of the transaction.'[307] The standard defines an entity's functional currency as 'the currency of the primary economic environment in which the entity operates' and contains detailed guidance on determining the functional currency.[308]

Many national GAAPs do not specifically define the concept of functional currency, or they may contain guidance on identifying the functional currency that differs from that in IAS 21. Consequently, a first-time adopter that measured transactions in a currency that was not its functional currency will need to restate its financial statements. Full retrospective application of IAS 21 is extremely onerous as it affects measurement of all non-monetary items in a first-time adopter's opening IFRS balance sheet. The exemption that allows a first-time adopter to reset the cumulative exchange differences in equity to zero cannot be applied to assets or liabilities (see 2.7.2 above). In October 2004, the IFRIC considered whether 'a specific exception should be granted to first-time adopters to permit entities to translate all assets and liabilities at the transition date exchange rate rather than applying the functional currency approach in IAS 21 … The IFRIC agreed that the position under IFRS 1 and IAS 21 was clear, and that there was no scope for an Interpretation on this topic that would provide any relief.'[309]

Therefore, a restatement cannot be avoided because IFRS 1 does not contain an exemption that would allow a first-time adopter to use a currency other than the functional currency in determining the cost of assets and liabilities. The only possible mitigation would be if a first-time adopter chose to use fair value or a revaluation as deemed cost for property, plant and equipment.

3.5 Currency adjustments to goodwill

Under IFRS 1, a first-time adopter need not apply this requirement of IAS 21 retrospectively to fair value adjustments and goodwill arising in business combinations that occurred before the date of transition to IFRS. However, in practice that exemption may be of limited use for a number of reasons.

First, the exemption permits 'goodwill and fair value adjustments' to be treated as assets and liabilities of the entity rather than as assets and liabilities of the acquiree. Implicit in the exemption is the requirement to treat goodwill and fair value adjustments consistently. However, the IASB apparently did not consider that many first-time adopters, under their previous GAAP, will have treated fair value adjustments as assets or liabilities of the acquiree, while at the same time treating goodwill as an asset of the acquirer. As the exemption under IFRS 1 did not foresee this particular situation, those first-time adopters will need to restate either their goodwill or fair value adjustments. In many cases restatement of goodwill is less onerous than restatement of fair value adjustments.

Secondly, the paragraphs in IFRS 1 that introduce the exemption were drafted at a later date than the rest of the Appendix that they form part of. Instead of referring to 'first-time adopter' these paragraphs refer to 'entity'. Nevertheless, it is clear from the context that 'entity' should be read as 'first-time adopter'. This means that the exemption only permits goodwill and fair value adjustments to be treated as assets of the first-time adopter (i.e. ultimate parent). In practice, however, many groups have treated goodwill (and fair value adjustments) as an asset of an intermediate parent. Where the intermediate parent has a functional currency that is different from that of the ultimate parent or the acquiree, it will be necessary to restate goodwill (and fair value adjustments).

Thirdly, the exemption only applies to goodwill that arose before the entity's date of transition. Additional goodwill that arises on a step-acquisition after the date of transition should therefore be treated as an asset of the acquiree.[310] Under this approach 'new' goodwill would be expressed in a different currency than the previous goodwill, which will cause complications in performing an IAS 36 impairment test.

3.6 Changes in IFRS accounting policies before first IFRS financial statements

Some first-time adopters find that they need to change their IFRS accounting policies after they have prepared an IFRS interim report but before their first IFRS financial statements. Normally when an entity changes an accounting policy, it should apply IAS 8 to such a change. However, IFRS 1 specifically states that 'IAS 8 does not deal with changes in accounting policies that occur when an entity first adopts IFRSs.'[311] Instead, the standard requires that a first-time adopter should apply 'the same accounting policies in its opening IFRS balance sheet and throughout all periods presented in its first IFRS financial statements.'[312] Therefore, the change in accounting policies should be treated as a change in the entity's IFRS opening balance sheet and the policy should be applied consistently in all periods presented under IFRS. In our view, additional disclosures about the nature of the change in accounting policies would generally be appropriate under IAS 1.

3.7 Disclosure of IFRS information in financial statements for periods prior to an entity's first IFRS reporting period

3.7.1 CESR recommendation

In December 2003, the Committee of European Securities Regulators (CESR) published a recommendation that encourages European listed companies 'to provide markets with appropriate and useful information during the transition phase from local accounting standards to International Financial Reporting Standards', which a first-time adopter may want to follow.[313] The recommendation provides helpful guidance about disclosures that an entity may want to include in its financial statements and interim reports just before and just after its transition to IFRS. The key recommendations are as follows:

- in its previous GAAP financial statements for the period prior to its date of transition, an entity should disclose its plan and degree of achievement in its move towards IFRS;
- in its last financial statements under its previous GAAP an entity should present the reconciliations from previous GAAP to IFRS and an explanatory note to explain the effect of the transition;
- in its IFRS interim reporting before its first full IFRS financial statement, an entity should present the primary financial statements for the most recent comparative period both under IFRS and its previous GAAP (the so-called 'bridge approach'); and
- in its first IFRS financial statements, an entity should present the disclosures required by IFRS 1 (see 2.10.2 above). In addition, CESR also considers the 'bridge approach' equally acceptable for the annual financial statements.

3.7.2 IFRS guidance

Although IFRS 1 provides detailed rules on disclosures to be made in an entity's first IFRS financial statements and in interim reports covering part of its first IFRS reporting period, it does not provide any guidance on presenting a reconciliation to IFRS in financial reports before the start of the first IFRS reporting period. An entity wishing to disclose information on the impact of IFRS in its last financial statements under its previous GAAP cannot claim that such information was prepared and presented in accordance with IFRS because it does not disclose all information required in full IFRS financial statements and it does not disclose comparative information.

As the extract below illustrates, in practice, some entities get around this problem by disclosing pro forma IFRS information and stating that the pro forma information does not comply with IFRS.

Extract 5.10: ARINSO International SA (2003)

2003 IFRS Consolidated Financial Information [extract]

1. OPENING BALANCE AT JANUARY 1, 2003 [extract]

In 2003, ARINSO decided to anticipate the adoption of the International Financial Reporting Standards (earlier called International Accounting Standards (IAS)). These standards will become mandatory in 2005 for the consolidated financial statements of all companies listed on stock exchanges within the European Union.

As of 2004 ARINSO will publish quarterly reports in full compliance with IFRS. In order to have comparable figures as requested by IFRS, the 2003 financial statements were already prepared on an IFRS basis. In 2003, the impact of the IFRS conversion on the quarterly figures was published in our press releases.

The main differences between Belgian Generally Accepted Accounting Principles (GAAP) and IFRS as well as a reconciliation of the equity to IFRS at the date of conversion are presented hereunder.

3. IFRS VALUATION RULES [extract]

3.2 Adoption of the IFRS

The IFRS standards will be adopted for the first time in the consolidated financial statements for the year ended December 31, 2004. The standard for the first time application of the IFRS, published by the IASB in June 2003, was utilized in the pro forma consolidated IFRS balance sheet, income statement and cash flow statement published for the year ended December 31, 2003.

The information related to accounting year 2003 was converted from Belgian GAAP to IFRS in view of the comparison of information next year. The 2004 annual report will include all necessary comparable information.

Free translation of the Statutory Auditor's Report submitted to the shareholders, originally prepared in Dutch, on the restatement of the consolidated balance sheet, the profit and loss account and cash flow statement from accounting principles generally accepted in Belgium into IFRS [extract]

The financial statements provided, which do not include all notes to the financial statements in accordance with IFRS, have been prepared under the responsibility of the company's management, and do not comply with IFRS.

3.8 Transition to IFRS after 2005

Understandably much attention has been given to entities transitioning to IFRS in 2005, but there is also a considerable population of entities that will be adopting IFRS after 2005. Although IFRS 1 will apply to first-time adoption by those entities, not all of the exemptions in IFRS 1 will be available to them. Whether the following exemptions are available will depend on the entity's date of transition:

- *Exemption from the requirement to restate comparative information for IAS 32 (or IFRS 7), IAS 39 and IFRS 4* – An entity that adopts IFRS on or after 1 January 2006 cannot make use of this exemption and will need to present comparative information that complies with IAS 32 (or IFRS 7, if adopted early), IAS 39 and IFRS 4 (see 2.6.1 above);
- *Designation of previously recognised financial instruments* – The transitional regime depends on whether an entity adopts IFRS (1) before 1 January 2006, (2) between 1 January 2006 and 1 September 2006, or (3) after 1 September 2006 (see 2.6.2 above);

- *Derecognition of financial assets and financial liabilities* – The importance of this exemption will reduce over time because, at a minimum, IFRS must be applied to all transactions entered into after 1 January 2004 (see 2.6.4 above);
- *Fair value measurement of financial assets or financial liabilities at initial recognition* – The importance of this exemption will reduce over time because, at a minimum, IFRS must be applied to all transactions entered into after 1 January 2004 (see 2.6.6 above);
- *Share-based payments* – The exemption from application of IFRS 2 in respect of share-based payments granted before 7 November 2002 will gradually diminish in importance. However, first-time adopters will continue to be able to apply the exemption in respect of share-based payments that were granted after 7 November 2002 that vested before an entity's date of transition to IFRS do not need to be restated to IFRS (see 2.7.3 above);
- *Assets classified as held for sale and discontinued operations* – An entity with a date of transition after 1 January 2005 cannot make use of this exemption and should apply IFRS 5 fully retrospectively (see 2.8.2 above); and
- *Exemptions from the requirement to present comparative information for IFRS 6* – An entity that adopts IFRS on or after 1 January 2006 cannot make use of this exemption and will need to present comparative information that complies with IFRS 6 (see 2.9.8 above).

Some amendments to IFRS 1 are not mandatory for first-time adopters whose date of transition is before the effective date of the amendment, unless the entity adopts the amending standard or interpretation early (see 2.11 above).

4 CONCLUSION

It was always clear that a first-time adoption standard driven by the desire to avoid undue cost and effort would have to include exemptions that would permit first-time adopters to apply IFRS in a practical manner. The objectives that the IASB sets out in the standard are to ensure that an entity's first IFRS financial statements and its first IFRS interim financial reports contain high quality financial information that:[314]

'(a) is transparent for users and comparable over all periods presented;

(b) provides a suitable starting point for accounting under IFRS; and

(c) can be generated at a cost that does not exceed the benefits to users.'

It seemed unavoidable that these objectives would be subject to practical reality. Inevitably, the range of options available in IFRS 1 has meant that similar entities have produced dissimilar IFRS financial statements. For example, the first-time adoption rules on hedge accounting, derecognition and estimates have resulted in financial statements that still owe much to the first-time adopter's previous GAAP. Nevertheless, the effect of these exemptions and exceptions fades quickly once an entity has been reporting under IFRS for a number of years.

In the long run, only the effect of the business combinations and 'fair value or revaluation as deemed cost' exemptions will be enduring. However, even the impact of those exemptions will be relatively insignificant compared with, for example, the effect an acquisition can have on the comparability of financial statements from one period to another.

IFRS 1 may not quite meet the lofty goals set by the IASB, but five years from now this will probably be long forgotten. In the meantime, for first-time adopters, IFRS 1 has made the transition to IFRS much more straightforward than would ever have been possible under the theoretically pure, but practically unworkable, SIC-8. Still, some first-time adopters of IFRS will have concerns about, for example, the complexity of the first-time adoption exemption for share-based payments. Others will complain about the unfairness of a business combination exemption that does not allow an adjustment to goodwill for items other than intangible assets, contingencies and impairments.

Overall the IASB is to be complimented for taking a practical approach to first-time adoption. It has steered a reasonable course between practicality and theoretical perfection that most preparers will, with effort, be able to follow. However, IFRS 1 has become more complex than necessary because of exemptions that have been added and ones that have expired. We, therefore, believe that the IASB's project to restructure the standard is both helpful and timely.

References

1 Regulation (EC) No 1606/2002 of the European Parliament and of the Council of 19 July 2002 on the application of international accounting standards, article 4 defines these companies as follows: 'For each financial year starting on or after 1 January 2005, companies governed by the law of a Member State shall prepare their consolidated accounts in conformity with the international accounting standards adopted in accordance with the procedure laid down in Article 6(2) if, at their balance sheet date, their securities are admitted to trading on a regulated market of any Member State within the meaning of Article 1(13) of Council Directive 93/22/EEC of 10 May 1993 on investment services in the securities field.'
2 SIC-8, *First-Time Application of IASs as the Primary Basis of Accounting*, SIC, July 1998, para. 3.
3 ED 1, *First-time Application of International Financial Reporting Standards*, IASB, July 2002.
4 IFRS 1, *First-time Adoption of International Financial Reporting Standards*, para. IN1.
5 IFRS 1, para. BC3.
6 IFRS 1, para. BC9.
7 IFRS 1, para. BC10.
8 IFRS 1, para. BC14.
9 With effect from 1 January 2007, the title of IAS 32 will be 'Financial Instruments: Presentation', this as a result of the amendments introduced by IFRS 7.
10 *IASB Update*, IASB, February 2007, p. 3.
11 IFRS 1, para. 1.
12 IFRS 1, para. 3 and Appendix A.
13 IFRS 1, para. 3.
14 IFRS 1, para. 3.
15 IFRS 1, para. 4.
16 IFRS 1, para. BC5.
17 IFRS 1, para. BC6.
18 IFRS 1, para. 5.
19 IFRS 1, Appendix A.
20 IFRS 1, para. 2.
21 IFRS 1, para. 2.
22 IAS 34, *Interim Financial Reporting*, para. 3.
23 IFRS 1, Appendix A.
24 IFRS 1, para. 36.
25 IFRS 1, para. 36.
26 IAS 1, *Presentation of Financial Statements*, para. 36.
27 IFRS 1, para. BC86.
28 IAS 1, para. 50.

29 IFRS 1, Appendix A.
30 IFRS 1, para. 14.
31 IFRS 1, para. 6.
32 IFRS 1, para. 7.
33 IFRS 1, paras. BC17-BC18.
34 IFRS 1, para. 8.
35 IFRS 1, para. BC11.
36 IFRS 1, para. 8.
37 IFRS 1, para. 10.
38 IFRS 1, para. 11.
39 IFRS 1, para. 9.
40 Framework, *Framework for the Preparation and Presentation of Financial Statements*, para. 44.
41 IFRS 1, para. BC27.
42 IFRS 1, para. 12.
43 IFRS 1, para. 13.
44 IFRS 1, para. 26.
45 IFRS 1, para. IN4.
46 IFRS 1, paras. 13 and 36A.
47 IFRS 1, para. 13.
48 IFRS 1, para. IN4.
49 IFRS 1, para. 26.
50 IFRS 1, para. 15 and Appendix B.
51 IFRS 1, para. B1.
52 IFRS 1, para. B3.
53 IFRS 1, para. BC32.
54 IFRS 1, paras. BC33-BC34.
55 IFRS 1, para. BC34.
56 IFRS 3, *Business Combinations*, para. 85.
57 IFRS 1, para. B2(a).
58 IFRS 1, para. 15.
59 IFRS 3, Appendix A.
60 IFRS 3, Appendix A.
61 IFRS 3, para. 4.
62 IFRS 3, para. 4.
63 IFRS 1, para. B2(c).
64 IFRS 1, para. B2(b).
65 IFRS 1, para. B2(b).
66 IFRS 1, IG Example 7.
67 IFRS 1, IG Example 3.
68 IFRS 1, para. B2(d).
69 IFRS 1, para. B2(e).
70 IFRS 1, para. BC36.
71 IFRS 1, para. B2(f).
72 IFRS 1, para. BC35.
73 IFRS 1, IG Example 2.
74 IFRS 1, para. B2(g).
75 IFRS 1, para. B2(g).
76 IFRS 1, para. B2(g).
77 IFRS 1, para. IG40.
78 IFRS 1, para. IG41.
79 IFRS 1, para. IG43.
80 IFRS 1, para. BC39.
81 IFRS 1, para. BC38.
82 IFRS 1, para. B2(h).
83 IFRS 3, para. 81.
84 IFRS 1, para. 10.
85 IFRS 1, para. B2(i).
86 IFRS 1, IG Example 5.
87 IFRS 1, para. B2(i).
88 IAS 21, *The Effects of Changes in Foreign Exchange Rates*, para. 47.
89 IFRS 1, paras. B1A and IG21A.
90 IFRS 1, para. B1A.
91 IFRS 1, para. B1B.
92 IFRS 1, para. B2(j).
93 IFRS 1, IG Example 6.
94 IFRS 1, para. B2(k).
95 IAS 27, *Consolidated and Separate Financial Statements*, para. 4.
96 IFRS 1, para. B2(k).
97 IFRS 1, IG Example 4.
98 *IASB Update*, IASB, October 2005, p. 1.
99 IFRS 1, para. BC42.
100 IFRS 1, paras. 16-17.
101 IFRS 1, para. 16.
102 IFRS 1, para. 18.
103 IFRS 1, para. 18.
104 IFRS 1, para. 18.
105 IFRS 1, para. IG50.
106 IFRS 1, para. 16.
107 IAS 16, *Property, Plant and Equipment*, para. 9.
108 IFRS 1, para. BC45.
109 IFRS 1, para. 16.
110 IFRS 1, para. 17.
111 IFRS 1, para. 19.
112 IFRS 1, para. BC47.
113 IFRS 1, para. BC47.
114 IFRS 1, para. BC43.
115 IFRS 1, para. BC89A.
116 IAS 39, *Financial Instruments: Recognition and Measurement*, para. 9.
117 IFRS 1, para. BC81.
118 IFRS 1, paras. BC81-BC82.
119 IFRS 1 (2005 Bound Volume), para. 25A.
120 IFRS 1, para. 25A.
121 IFRS 1, para. BC63A.
122 IFRS 1, para. IG59.
123 IFRS 1, para. IG59.
124 IFRS 1, para. 43A.
125 IFRS 1, para. IG56(a).
126 IFRS 1, para. IG56(b).
127 IFRS 1, para. IG57.
128 IFRS 1, para. IG58.
129 IFRS 1, para. 23.
130 IFRS 1, paras. IG35-IG36.
131 IFRS 1, para. 27.
132 IFRS 1, para. 27A.
133 IFRS 1, paras. IG53-IG54.
134 IFRS 1, para. 26(c).
135 IFRS 1, para. BC75.
136 IFRS 1, para. BC76.
137 IFRS 1, para. BC77.
138 IFRS 1, para. 28.

139 IFRS 1, para. IG58A.
140 IFRS 1, para. IG58B.
141 IFRS 1, para. 28.
142 IFRS 1, para. 29.
143 IFRS 1, para. 29.
144 IFRS 1, para. 30.
145 IAS 39, para. F.4.2.
146 IFRS 1, para. BC75.
147 IFRS 1, para. IG60B.
148 ED 1, para. C3(c)(i).
149 ED 1, para. C4.
150 IFRS 1, para. IG58A.
151 IFRS 1, para. IG60A.
152 IAS 39, *Financial Instruments: Recognition and Measurement*, IASB, December 1998 (amended 2000), para. 172(e) and ED 1, para. C3(b).
153 IFRS 1, paras. IG60 and IG60B.
154 IFRS 1, para. 30.
155 IFRS 1, para. IG60B.
156 *Amendment to International Accounting Standard IAS 39 Financial Instruments: Recognition and Measurement Transition and Initial Recognition of Financial Assets and Financial Liabilities*, IASB, December 2004, Appendix.
157 IFRS 1, para. BC83A.
158 IFRS 1, para. 25G.
159 IFRS 1, para. 28.
160 IFRS 1, para. IG58A.
161 IFRS 1, paras. BC65-BC66.
162 IFRS 1, para. IG55.
163 IFRS 1, para. BC73.
164 IFRS 1, para. BC73.
165 IFRS 1, para. 20.
166 IFRS 1, para. BC48.
167 IFRS 1, paras. 20 and IG18.
168 IFRS 1, paras. BC50-BC51.
169 IFRS 1, para. BC51.
170 IFRS 1, paras. BC51 and IG21.
171 IFRS 1, para. IG19.
172 IFRS 1, para. IG20.
173 IFRS 1, para. BC52.
174 IFRS 1, para. 20A.
175 IAS 21, paras. 32 and 39 and IFRS 1, para. 21.
176 IAS 21, para. 48 and IFRS 1, para. 21.
177 IFRS 1, para. 22.
178 IFRS 1, para. BC63B.
179 IFRS 1, para. 25B.
180 IFRS 1, para. 25B.
181 IFRS 1, para. 25B.
182 IFRS 1, para. 25C.
183 Framework, paras. 25-28.
184 IAS 40, *Investment Property*, para. B67(h).
185 IFRS 1, para. 25D and IFRS 4, para. 22.
186 IFRS 1, para. 36A.
187 IFRS 1, para. BC59.
188 IFRS 1, para. 24.
189 IFRS 1, para. 24.
190 IFRS 1, IG Example 8.
191 IFRS 1, para. BC62.
192 IFRS 1, para. IG31.
193 IFRS 1, para. 24.
194 IFRS 1, para. 25.
195 IFRS 1, para. BC63.
196 IFRS 1, IG Example 9.
197 IFRS 1, para. IG30.
198 IFRS 1, para. 25.
199 IFRS 1, para. 25H.
200 IFRIC 12, *Service Concession Arrangements*, para. 29 and 30.
201 IFRS 1, para. 31.
202 IAS 8, *Accounting Policies, Changes in Accounting Estimates and Errors*, para. 5.
203 *IFRIC Update*, IFRIC, October 2004, p. 3.
204 IFRS 1, para. BC84.
205 IFRS 1, para. IG58B.
206 IFRS 1, para. 34.
207 IFRS 1, paras. 32 and IG2.
208 IFRS 1, para. IG3.
209 IFRS 1, para. IG3.
210 IFRS 1, paras. 33 and IG3.
211 IFRS 1, para. IG4.
212 IFRS 1, paras. 34A-34B.
213 IFRS 1, para. IG62.
214 IFRS 1, para. IG7.
215 IFRS 1, paras. IG8-IG9.
216 IFRS 1, para. IG10.
217 IFRS 1, para. IG11.
218 IAS 16, para. 16.
219 IFRS 1, para. IG13.
220 IFRS 1, paras. 25E and IG201-IG203.
221 IFRS 1, para. 25E.
222 IFRS 1, para. IG14.
223 IAS 17, *Leases*, para. 13.
224 IFRIC 4, *Determining whether an Arrangement contains a Lease*, para. 17 and IFRS 1, paras. 25F and BC63D.
225 IFRS 1, para. IG16.
226 IFRS 1, para. IG26.
227 IFRS 1, para. IG27.
228 IFRS 1, para. 25.
229 IFRS 1, para. IG27.
230 IFRS 1, para. IG28.
231 IFRS 1 (ED), *Exposure Draft of Proposed Amendments to IFRS 1 First-Time Adoption of International Financial Reporting Standards – Cost of an Investment in a Subsidiary*, IASB, January 2007.
232 IFRS 1 (ED), para. B5.
233 IFRS 1 (ED), para. BC4.
234 IFRS 1 (ED), para. BC4.
235 IFRS 1 (ED), para. B6(a).
236 IFRS 1 (ED), para. B6(b).
237 *IASB Update*, IASB, September 2007, p. 4.

238 *IASB Update*, IASB, September 2007, p. 4.
239 IFRS 1, para. BC67.
240 IFRS 1, para. IG32.
241 IFRS 1, para. IG33.
242 IFRS 1, para. IG34.
243 IFRS 1, para. IG44.
244 IAS 38, *Intangible Assets*, para. 21.
245 IAS 38, para. 71.
246 IFRS 1, para. IG46.
247 IFRS 1, para. IG47.
248 IFRS 1, para. IG47.
249 IFRS 1, para. IG48.
250 IFRS 1, para. IG49.
251 IFRS 1, para. IG51.
252 IFRS 1, para. IG17.
253 IFRS 1, para. IG23.
254 IFRS 1, para. IG25.
255 IFRS 1, para. 25I.
256 IFRS 1, para. 47G.
257 IFRS 1, para. 36B.
258 IFRS 1, para. 47.
259 IAS 1, para. 36.
260 IFRS 1, para. 36.
261 IFRS 1, para. 6.
262 IFRS 1, para. BC86.
263 IFRS 1, para. 36A.
264 IAS 8, para. 24.
265 IAS 8, para. 28.
266 IFRS 1, para. BC89.
267 IFRS 7, para. C9.
268 IFRS 1, para. 36C.
269 IFRS 1, para. 37.
270 IFRS 1, para. 37.
271 IFRS 1, para. 38.
272 IFRS 1, para. BC91.
273 IAS 1, para. 108.
274 IFRS 1, para. 43.
275 IFRS 1, para. 39.
276 IFRS 1, para. 39.
277 IFRS 1, para. 40.
278 IFRS 1, para. 42.
279 IFRS 1, para. 40.
280 IFRS 1, para. 41.
281 IFRS 1, para. IG63.
282 IFRS 1, para. 39.
283 IFRS 1, para. BC94.
284 IAS 39, para. 9.
285 IFRS 1, para. 43A.
286 IFRS 1, para. 44.
287 IFRS 1, para. 45.
288 IFRS 1, para. IG37.
289 IFRS 1, IG Example 10.
290 IFRS 1, para. 46.
291 IFRS 1, para. 46.
292 IFRS 1, para. 47.
293 IFRS 1, paras. 47A-47E.
294 Release No. 33-8567, *First-Time Application of International Financial Reporting Standards*, Securities and Exchange Commission (SEC), 12 April 2005.
295 Release No. 33-8567.
296 Release No. 33-8567.
297 Release No. 33-8567.
298 Release No. 33-8567.
299 IFRS 1, para. IG5.
300 IAS 12, *Income Taxes*, para. 15.
301 IAS 12, paras. 15 and 24.
302 IAS 12, para. 68.
303 IAS 16, para. 9.
304 IAS 16, para. 12.
305 IAS 16, para. 13.
306 IAS 16, para. 43.
307 IAS 21, para. 21.
308 IAS 21, paras. 8-14.
309 *IFRIC Update*, IASB, October 2004, p. 3.
310 IAS 21, para. 47.
311 IFRS 1, paras. 5 and 42.
312 IFRS 1, para. 7.
313 *European Regulation on the Application of IFRS in 2005 – Recommendation for Additional Guidance Regarding the Transition to IFRS (CESR/03-323e)*, Committee of European Securities Regulators (CESR), December 2003.
314 IFRS 1, para. 1.

Chapter 6 Consolidated and separate financial statements

1 THE CONCEPT OF A GROUP

1.1 Background

It is a commercial practice of long standing for an entity to conduct its business not only directly but also through strategic investments in other entities. IFRS, and most national GAAPs, broadly distinguish three types of such strategic investment:

- entities controlled by the reporting entity (subsidiaries). These include entities that, although not owned by the reporting entity, are operating for its benefit (special purpose entities);
- entities jointly controlled by the reporting entity and one or more third parties (joint ventures);[1] and
- entities that, while not controlled or jointly controlled by the reporting entity, are subject to significant influence by it (associates).

This raises the question of how such strategic investments should be accounted for. There is a consensus that it is not adequate to account for such entities merely by recording income received from them, and that some mechanism is required to reflect their activities directly in the financial statements of reporting entities that hold them. Under IFRS:

- an entity and its subsidiaries are collectively referred to as a 'group', and accounted for in accordance with IAS 27 – *Consolidated and Separate Financial Statements* – using consolidated financial statements (which are addressed in the remainder of this chapter);[2]
- associates are accounted for in accordance with IAS 28 – *Investments in Associates* – using equity accounting (which is addressed in Chapter 8); and

- joint ventures are accounted for in accordance with IAS 31 – *Interests in Joint Ventures* – using a variety of methods, depending on their structure (see Chapter 9).

IFRS also acknowledges that entities may wish (or be obliged by local legal requirements) to present additional financial statements in which such strategic investments are accounted for on some other basis, such as cost or valuation. Whilst IFRS does not require the preparation of such additional financial statements (referred to as 'separate financial statements'), it does prescribe the accounting treatment to be followed where they are prepared and stated to be in compliance with IFRS.[3] Separate financial statements are discussed further at 7 below.

1.2 The objectives of consolidated financial statements

Consolidated financial statements are designed to extend the reporting entity so as to embrace other entities which are subject to its control. They involve treating the net assets and activities of subsidiaries held by a reporting entity as if they were part of the holding entity's own net assets and activities. The overall aim is to present the results and state of affairs of the reporting entity and its subsidiaries (referred to as a group) as if they were those of a single entity.

As noted above, the standard dealing with this topic under IFRS is IAS 27, which requires a parent (i.e. an entity with one or more subsidiaries)[4] to present consolidated financial statements in which all subsidiaries are included.[5]

1.3 What is a subsidiary?

The definition of a subsidiary is fundamental to any discussion of consolidated financial statements, since this determines the scope and extent of the reporting entity which is the subject of the consolidated financial statements. When the concept of consolidated financial statements was originally introduced in the first half of the last century, the question of whether or not an entity was a subsidiary was generally determined by legal ownership. In other words, any entity in which the reporting entity held more than half the equity would be regarded as subject to the reporting entity's control (and therefore a subsidiary), whereas any entity in which the reporting entity held half or less of the equity would be regarded as not subject to the reporting entity's control (and therefore a not subsidiary).

However, this 'ownership' model proved increasingly inadequate, particularly with the growth of 'off-balance sheet' financing from the 1970s onwards. It proved relatively easy for a reporting entity to set up another entity in which it had little or no legal ownership interest, but which it effectively controlled (for example, because the shares were owned by parties who could be expected to act in accordance with the reporting entity's wishes). It became common for companies to use such entities as vehicles for making borrowings that did not appear in the consolidated financial statements, because the borrowing entity, although controlled by the reporting entity, did not meet the definition of a subsidiary under the ownership model.

As a result, there emerged a new concept: the question of whether or not an entity is a subsidiary for consolidation purposes should be determined not by legal ownership, but by the existence of economic control. The first major codification of an 'economic control' model for consolidated financial statements was in the EU Seventh Company Law Directive in 1983.

However, the concept of economic control in the Seventh Directive was widely drawn. For example, the Directive allowed (but did not require) consolidation of an entity by a shareholder that in practice appointed the majority of the board, even if it did not have the majority of the voting rights. This was to cater with the situation where, due to the wide dispersal of the majority of shareholdings, a significant minority shareholder can exercise *de facto* control. The Directive also permitted, but did not require, a further extension of the 'economic control' model to so-called 'horizontal' groups – i.e. entities with no shareholding relationship but under common control (e.g. because they are owned by the same individual). IAS 27 does not require consolidation of 'horizontal' groups, but the treatment of entities over which there is *de facto* control is somewhat more ambiguous.

The consolidation model in IAS 27 is based primarily on the legal and contractual rights of shareholders, rather than on a pure 'ownership' model or 'economic control' model. However, aspects of an 'economic control' model are also in evidence, particularly in the SIC interpretation SIC-12 – *Consolidation – Special Purpose Entities* (see 3 below).[6]

1.4 Consolidating partly owned subsidiaries

Various alternative ways of looking at a group become relevant when there are subsidiary companies which are not wholly owned by the holding entity. The particular matters which are affected are:

- the elimination of the effects of intragroup transactions;
- the calculation and treatment of minority interests, i.e. the interests of shareholders other than the controlling shareholder. (The term 'minority' is strictly a legacy from the 'ownership' model of consolidation. Under a 'legal and contractual' model or an 'economic control' model it is quite possible for the 'minority' shareholders to own more than half the shares in a subsidiary); and
- the treatment of changes in stake in the subsidiary.

There are two widely accepted concepts, referred to respectively as the entity concept and the proprietary concept, although the latter has a number of further variants.

1.4.1 The entity concept

The entity concept focuses on the existence of the group as an economic unit, rather than looking at it only through the eyes of the dominant shareholder group. It concentrates on the resources controlled by the entity, and regards the identity of owners with claims on these resources as being of secondary importance. It therefore makes no distinction between the treatment given to different classes of shareholders, whether majority or minority, and all transactions between the shareholders are regarded as internal to the group.

1.4.2 The proprietary (parent entity) concept

The proprietary concept emphasises ownership through a controlling shareholding interest, and regards the consolidated financial statements as being principally for the information of the shareholders of the holding entity. Its primary concern is not to present financial statements which are relevant to the minority shareholders. This is achieved either by treating the minority shareholders as 'outsiders' and reflecting their interests as quasi-liabilities or by leaving them out of the group financial statements entirely, thereby consolidating only the parent's percentage interest in the assets and liabilities of the subsidiary (the 'proportionate consolidation' method). The proprietary concept is sometimes referred to as the 'parent entity' concept, and there is a variant of it known as the 'parent entity extension' concept, which leans more towards the entity concept described above.

IFRS (IAS 27 together with IFRS 3 – *Business Combinations* – discussed in Chapter 7) is currently most closely aligned to the 'parent entity extension' concept, whereby the net identifiable assets (i.e. other than goodwill) of the group are reported without regard to the underlying ownership (as in the entity concept), whilst goodwill is recognised only to the extent of the controlling shareholder's interest (as in the proprietary concept). However, as discussed in Chapter 7 at 2.3.7 A and at 6.7.4 below, IFRS currently allows certain transactions involving minority interests to be accounted for in a manner more closely related to the entity concept, or by using a hybrid method that draws on aspects of both the entity and proprietary concepts.

The IASB, as part of its Business Combinations (Phase II) project undertaken jointly with the FASB, has leant towards requiring an approach much more akin to the entity concept whereby goodwill would be calculated for an acquired business as a whole and allocated between the controlling shareholder and any minority. However, the Board decided not to make this approach mandatory. IFRS 3 – *Near-final draft of IFRS 3 Business Combinations* – therefore permits an acquirer to measure any non-controlling interest in an acquiree at the acquisition date either at fair value or as the non-controlling interest's proportionate share of the acquiree's net identifiable assets, on a transaction-by-transaction basis.[7] The Basis for Conclusions to IFRS 3 (near-final) observes that the 'IASB reluctantly concluded that the only way the IFRS would receive sufficient votes to be issued was if it permitted an acquirer to measure a noncontrolling interest either at fair value or at its proportionate share of the acquiree's net identifiable assets, on a transaction-by-transaction basis'.[8]

In addition, IAS 27 – *Near-final draft of IAS 27 Consolidated and Separate Financial Statements* – proposes that 'changes in a parent's ownership interest in a subsidiary that do not result in a loss of control are accounted for as equity transactions (i.e. transactions with owners acting in their capacity as owners)',[9] which is also akin to the entity concept.

The revised standards are discussed in Chapter 7 at 5.1 to the extent that they relate to business combinations and in this chapter to the extent that they relate to consolidation techniques and disposals. The revised standards are expected to be effective for business combinations where the acquisition date is on or after the beginning of annual periods starting on or after 1 July 2009, although earlier application will be permitted.

It will become apparent from the discussion in 1.4.3 and following, below, that the current approach of IFRS actually contains elements of each of these different concepts rather than following any one on a consistent basis.

1.4.3 Comparison between the different concepts of a group

The distinction between the different methods in practice can best be illustrated by an example:

Example 6.1: Comparison between the different concepts of a group

Assume that entity A buys 75% of entity B for €1,200 when entity B has total net assets with a fair value of €1,000 and a carrying amount of €800. Under the various concepts described above, the consolidated balance sheet of entity A would incorporate the effects of the acquisition calculated as follows:

	Entity concept €	Proprietary concept €	Parent entity extension concept €
Net assets of B	1,000	950	1,000
Goodwill	600	450	450
	1,600	1,400	1,450
Investor interest	1,200	1,200	1,200
Minority interest	400	200	250
	1,600	1,400	1,450

Entity concept

Both the net identifiable assets and goodwill are reported in the balance sheet at the full amount of their fair value as determined by the transaction involving the majority shareholder. These amounts are then apportioned between the majority and minority shareholders.

Proprietary concept

The proprietary concept leaves the minority interest unaffected by the transaction of the majority shareholder. It is shown simply as their proportionate share of the carrying values of the net assets of the entity. This means that the goodwill is stated at a figure which represents the difference between the cost of the 75% investment (€1,200) and 75% of the fair value of the assets (€750). Perhaps more disturbingly, the assets are carried on a mixed basis which represents 75% of their fair value and 25% of their book value.

This feature is eliminated if proportionate consolidation is adopted, since the minority interest is disregarded altogether, being set against the assets and liabilities of the subsidiary on a line by line basis, so that only the majority investor's share of the subsidiary's assets is consolidated. This would result in the consolidation of assets of €750 and goodwill of €450, representing the total of the investment of €1,200. However, IFRS does not allow proportionate consolidation for subsidiaries, although it is one of the permitted treatments for certain types of joint venture (see Chapter 8).

Parent entity extension concept

The mixed basis for the carrying amount of net identifiable assets is also avoided in the parent entity extension concept, which includes the net identifiable assets at the whole amount of their fair value and apportions that between the majority and minority interests, but includes goodwill only as it relates to the majority investor.

A Intragroup transactions

The different concepts are also relevant to the calculation of the adjustments made to eliminate the effects of intragroup transactions (i.e. those between entities within the same group). If entity A in Example 6.1 sold an item of inventory to entity B for a profit of €100, and entity B still held the inventory at the year end, it would be necessary to make an adjustment on consolidation to eliminate what was an unrealised profit from the group point of view.

Under the proprietary concept, the minority shareholders are regarded as outsiders, and therefore there is a case for saying that 25% of the profit *has* been realised; this would be done by limiting the elimination of intragroup profit to €75.

Under the proportionate consolidation method, only 75% of the inventory would appear in the consolidated balance sheet in the first place, so the adjustment would simply be to deduct €75 from both the group profit and loss account and from the inventory.

Under the entity concept, as it is the parent which has made the sale, the whole write-down of inventory of €100 would be charged against the group profit and loss account, with no amount attributed to the minority interest. This is the approach adopted in IAS 27.

A further possible approach is the separate entities approach,[10] whereby the adjustment is effected by apportioning the €100 between the group profit and loss account and the minority interest in the ratio 75:25.

B Loss-making subsidiaries

A further practical situation where differences between the concepts emerge is when the partly-owned subsidiary makes losses which put it into overall deficit. Under the entity concept, the consolidated financial statements would continue to account for these losses and apportion them between the majority and minority interests in proportion to their holdings, even if this created a debit balance for the minority interest in the balance sheet.

A proprietary concept would not normally permit the minority interest to be shown as a debit balance, because it could not usually be regarded as a recoverable asset from the point of view of the majority interest, which is the orientation of the financial statements under the proprietary concept. This is the approach adopted in IAS 27 (see 6.7.2 below). As discussed at 6.7.2 B below, the IASB is proposing as part of its Business Combinations (Phase II) project to require that total comprehensive income be attributed to the owners of the parent and to the non-controlling interests even if this results in the non-controlling interests having a deficit balance.

1.5 Other issues

The composition of a group may change, either through entities joining or leaving the group, or by the parent's increasing or decreasing its stake in existing subsidiaries. Currently IFRS does not address many of these issues, which will be dealt with in the IASB's Business Combinations (Phase II) project. Some aspects of accounting for an increase in stake in an existing subsidiary are discussed in Chapter 7 at 2.3.7, whilst those relating to a decrease in stake are dealt with at 6.6.2, 6.6.3 and 6.7.4 below.

There are some situations where it is considered unnecessary for a parent to prepare consolidated financial statements, particularly where the parent is itself a subsidiary of another entity. The exemptions given by IAS 27 are dealt with at 4 below.

2 DEVELOPMENT OF IAS 27

IAS 27 was originally issued in April 1989 and has since been subject to various amendments, most significantly in December 2003 as part of the IASB's improvements project, when the previous version of IAS 27 was withdrawn and superseded by a substantially revised version.

Since its publication in December 2003, IAS 27 has been further amended, notably by IFRS 3 and IFRS 5 – *Non-current Assets Held for Sale and Discontinued Operations.*[11] As a result, the previous requirements regarding investments that are intended to be held on a temporary basis have been removed from IAS 27 although the introduction to the standard still refers to it.[12] Such investments will now generally be accounted for under IFRS 5 (see Chapter 4).[13]

The IASB has the following projects on its agenda, which may result in changes to IAS 27:

- Accounting in separate financial statements for the formation of a new parent (see 7.3.1 C below);
- Application of the cost method in separate financial statements (see 9.4.1 below);
- Business Combinations (Phase II) (see 10.1 below);
- Consolidation (see 10.2 below); and
- Plans to sell the controlling interest in a subsidiary (see 10.3 below).

3 DEFINITION OF SUBSIDIARY

As indicated at 1.3 above, the definition of 'subsidiary' is fundamental to any discussion of consolidated financial statements. The question is also relevant to the subject of off-balance sheet financing, because frequently this definition determines whether the group balance sheet should include the accounts of an entity which holds certain assets and liabilities which management may not wish to include in the consolidated financial statements.

IAS 27 uses the following definition of subsidiary and related terms.

A *parent* is an entity with one or more subsidiaries.[14]

A *subsidiary* is an entity, including an unincorporated entity such as a partnership, that is controlled by another entity (known as the parent).[15]

A *group* is a parent and all its subsidiaries.[16]

Control is the power to govern the financial and operating policies of an entity so as to obtain benefits from its activities.[17]

3.1 Control

As can be seen, the definition of control effectively underpins the definition of parent and subsidiary, and IAS 27 therefore elaborates on it further.

3.1.1 Primary indicators of control

IAS 27 states that control is presumed to exist if the parent owns, directly or indirectly through subsidiaries, more than half of the voting power of an entity unless, in exceptional circumstances, it can be clearly demonstrated that such ownership does not constitute control. Control is also considered to exist even when the parent does not own a majority of the voting rights when there is:

(a) power over more than half of the voting rights by virtue of an agreement with other investors;

(b) power to govern the financial and operating policies of the entity under a statute or an agreement;

(c) power to appoint or remove the majority of the members of the board of directors or equivalent governing body and control of the entity is by that board or body; or

(d) power to cast the majority of votes at meetings of the board of directors or equivalent governing body and control of the entity is by that board or body.[18]

IAS 27 does not elaborate on the situations in which it might be 'clearly demonstrated' that ownership of more than half the voting power does not constitute control. The most obvious, and common, example will be where, by virtue of one or more of (a) to (d) above, an entity is a subsidiary of another shareholder owning half or less of the voting power. Similarly, if another party has veto rights over, or the ability to block, substantive decisions of the majority holder that may mean that the majority holder effectively cannot exercise control. In this context, substantive decisions are the significant decisions made in the ordinary course of business that are normally expected to arise in directing and carrying out the entity's current business activities (e.g. the approval of the annual operating budget is expected to be in the ordinary course of business, and therefore the minority party's ability to veto that decision is likely to provide them with effective participation, provided that the right is substantive and that such veto results in the entity having to redraft and re-propose a new budget).

In complex situations where minority shareholders have rights of veto or approval over certain issues, it may be helpful to have regard to the analysis, for the purposes of US GAAP, in EITF 96-16 – *Investor's Accounting for an Investee When the Investor Has a Majority of the Voting Interest but the Minority Shareholder or Shareholders Have Certain Approval or Veto Rights*.[19] Broadly, EITF 96-16 draws a distinction between minority rights that essentially exist to protect the minority from potentially damaging actions by the majority shareholders (which would not normally impact on the control exercised by majority shareholders) and minority rights that result in active participation in day-to-day decisions of the entity (which may result in a rebuttal of the presumption that the majority shareholder has control). In some cases, the effect might be that the entity is in fact a joint venture between the majority and minority shareholder which should be accounted for in accordance with IAS 31 (see Chapter 9). However, minority rights giving rise only to *de facto* control, as opposed to a legal or contractual right to control, will not necessarily amount to control for the purposes of IAS 27. This is discussed further at 3.1.3 below.

The implementation guidance to IAS 27 notes that it is inherent in the definition of control than an entity cannot be controlled by more than one party (although it might be jointly controlled by more than one party). Accordingly, when two or more entities each hold significant voting rights (whether actual rights or potential rights – see 3.1.2 below), the factors in (a) to (d) above should be reassessed into order to determine which entity (if any) actually has control.[20]

IAS 27 emphasises that the reference to 'power' in the definition of 'control' above means the ability to do or affect something. Consequently, an entity has control over another entity when it currently has the ability to exercise that power, regardless of whether control is actively demonstrated or is passive in nature.[21] Passive control may be exercised over another entity through potential voting rights (see 3.1.2 below).

3.1.2 Potential voting rights

An entity may own share warrants, share call options, debt or equity instruments that are convertible into ordinary shares, or other similar instruments that have the potential, if exercised or converted, to give the entity voting power or reduce another party's voting power over the financial and operating policies of another entity (potential voting rights).[22]

IAS 27 requires an entity to consider the existence and effect of potential voting rights that are currently exercisable or convertible, including potential voting rights held by another entity (see B below), when assessing whether an entity has the power to govern the financial and operating policies of another entity.[23] As discussed further at B below, IAS 27 takes a very strict and, some might argue, rather form-based approach to determining what potential voting rights should be taken into account for this purpose.

A Interaction with IAS 28 and IAS 31

IAS 28 and IAS 31 also require the existence and effect of potential voting rights to be taken into account in assessing whether an entity has, respectively, significant influence over, or joint control of, another entity. Accordingly, the guidance in IAS 27 on this issue, summarised below, is also relevant to IAS 28 and IAS 31.[24] However, IAS 27 notes that its guidance may be less relevant to IAS 31, since the issue of whether or not an entity is a joint venture depends primarily on the contractual relationship between the parties[25] (which would not typically be affected by the existence of potential voting rights).

B What rights are 'currently exercisable'?

Potential voting rights are not currently exercisable or convertible when they cannot be exercised or converted until a future date or until the occurrence of a future event.[26] The effect of this requirement is illustrated by Example 6.2 below.

Example 6.2: Potential voting rights (1)

An entity (A) holds 40% of another entity (B), together with loan notes in B convertible, at A's option, into further shares in B which, if issued, would give A a 60% interest in B. A can require conversion of its loan notes into shares at any time on or after the fifth anniversary of their issue.

Until that fifth anniversary occurs, A cannot exercise its conversion rights. They are therefore ignored, such that B would not (absent other circumstances) be a subsidiary of A. Once the fifth anniversary has occurred, A can exercise its option to convert and is therefore regarded as having the majority of the voting rights of B, such that B would (absent exceptional circumstances) become a subsidiary of A for the purposes of IAS 27.

The implementation guidance indicates that potential voting rights include not only those actually held by an entity (as in Example 6.2 above), but also those to which the entity currently has the right of access, as illustrated by Example 6.3 below.[27]

Example 6.3: Potential voting rights (2)

Entities A, B and C own 25%, 35% and 40% respectively of the ordinary shares that carry voting rights at a general meeting of shareholders of entity D. B and C also have share warrants that are exercisable at any time at a fixed price and provide potential voting rights. A has a call option to purchase these share warrants at any time for a nominal amount. If the call option is exercised, A would have the potential to increase its ownership interest, and thereby its voting rights, in D to 51% and dilute B's and C's interests to 23% and 26% respectively.

Although the share warrants are not owned by A, they are considered in assessing control because they are currently exercisable by B and C. Normally, if an action (e.g. purchase or exercise of another right) is required before an entity has ownership of a potential voting right, the potential voting right is not regarded as held by the entity. However, the share warrants are, in substance, held by A, because the terms of the call option are designed to ensure A's position. The combination of the call option and share warrants gives A the power to set the operating and financial policies of D, because A could currently exercise the option and share warrants.

Example 6.3 also illustrates the requirement of IAS 27 that the reporting entity must have regard not only to its own potential voting rights in an investee, but also to those of other shareholders. A potential practical issue here is that, in some more secretive jurisdictions, it might be difficult to obtain information about the potential voting power of other shareholders.

C *Management intention and ability to exercise potential ownership rights*

IAS 27 adds some further points of clarification. In assessing whether potential voting rights contribute to control, an entity must examine all facts and circumstances (including the terms of exercise of the potential voting rights and any other contractual arrangements whether considered individually or in combination) that affect potential voting rights, except the intention of management and the financial ability to exercise or convert.[28]

The implementation guidance expands on this point at some length, but in the process adds some confusion. On the one hand, it gives some illustrative examples (the substance of which is reproduced as Examples 5.4 to 5.6 below) which suggest that this requirement is to be interpreted very strictly.[29]

Example 6.4: Potential voting rights (3)

Entities A and B own 80% and 20% respectively of the ordinary shares that carry voting rights at a general meeting of shareholders of entity C. A sells one half of its interest to D and buys call options from D that are exercisable at any time at a premium to the market price when issued and, if exercised, would return to A its original 80% ownership interest and voting rights. Although the options are out of the money, they are currently exercisable and give A the power to continue to set the operating and financial policies of C, because A could exercise its options now. The existence of the potential voting rights is considered, and it is determined (absent other special circumstances) that A controls C.

Example 6.5: Potential voting rights (4)

Entities A, B and C each own one third of the ordinary shares that carry voting rights at a general meeting of shareholders of entity D. A, B and C each have the right to appoint two directors to the board of D. A also owns call options that are exercisable at a fixed price at any time and, if exercised, would give it all the voting rights in D. The management of A does not intend to exercise the call options, even if B and C do not vote in the same manner as A. The existence of the potential voting rights is considered and it is determined (absent other special circumstances) that A controls D. The intention of A's management does not influence the assessment.

Example 6.6: Potential voting rights (5)

Entities A and B own 55% and 45% respectively of the ordinary shares that carry voting rights at a general meeting of shareholders of entity C. B also holds debt instruments that are convertible into ordinary shares of C. The debt can be converted, on payment of a substantial exercise price in comparison with B's net assets, at any time and, if converted, would require B to borrow additional funds to make the payment. If the debt were to be converted, B would hold 70% of the voting rights and A's interest would reduce to 30%. Although the debt instruments are convertible at a substantial price, they are currently convertible and the conversion feature gives B the power to set the operating and financial policies of C. The existence of the potential voting rights, as well as the other factors described at 3.1.1 above, is considered and it is determined (absent other special circumstances) that B, not A, controls C. The financial ability of B to pay the conversion price does not influence the assessment.

On the other hand, the guidance states, somewhat contradictorily, that potential voting rights should be ignored where they lack economic substance '(e.g. where the exercise price is set in a manner that precludes exercise in any feasible scenario).'[30] The use of the word 'feasible' is rather curious, but may have been used in deliberate distinction from the more expected 'foreseeable' – in other words exercise has to be impossible rather than merely highly unlikely. However, this is somewhat contradicted by Example 6.6 above, which stresses that B's financial inability to exercise its conversion rights is irrelevant, and by the overall emphasis on the importance of there being a currently exercisable right.

This almost casual reference to economic substance in the implementation guidance together with the requirement in the main body of IAS 27 (and IAS 28) to examine 'all facts and circumstances' surrounding potential voting rights is no doubt in part an attempt to prevent potential abuses by the use of contrived agreements to deconsolidate loss-making or highly-geared subsidiaries.

However, in our view, the IASB has been so preoccupied by an understandable anxiety to prevent deconsolidation of subsidiaries through contrived sales (as in Example 6.4 above) that it has, particularly through the explicit prohibition on having regard to 'the intention of management and the financial ability to exercise or convert', created the real risk of entities achieving deconsolidation through contrived option arrangements, as illustrated in Example 6.7 below.

Example 6.7: Potential voting rights (6)

A parent (P) wishes to deconsolidate its loss-making subsidiary (S). It grants immediately exercisable options at an uneconomically high price to a friendly third party (F) which, if exercised, would give F ownership of more than half of the voting power of S. It is known by all concerned that F has no intention of actually exercising its options, and that it would not be in its financial interest to do so. Yet IAS 27 appears to require P to ignore these very pertinent facts in its assessment of whether or not S should continue to be treated as a subsidiary of P.

However, this is not the end of the matter. It might well be that P would continue to be regarded as the parent on the basis that it had an (unwritten) agreement with F that F would never actually exercise its options, thus falling within condition (a) in 3.1.1 above. Moreover, the provisions of SIC-12 could well be relevant (see 3.2 below). Most importantly perhaps, F would be unlikely to enter into such a transaction if it were subject to IAS 27 or a broadly comparable national standard.

Whilst fully exercisable potential voting rights may give rise to situations where an entity becomes (or ceases to be) a subsidiary, the proportion of the entity that is accounted for depends on the actual ownership interests at each reporting date (see 6.2 below).

3.1.3 De facto control

De facto control over an entity by a minority shareholder may arise in a number of ways. Two common examples are when other shareholdings are widely dispersed, or when a sufficient number of other shareholders regularly fail to exercise their rights as shareholders (e.g. to vote at general meetings) that the minority shareholder wields the majority of votes actually cast.

In our view IAS 27 as currently drafted would not necessarily require consolidation of entities subject only to *de facto* control since the definition of control refers to the 'power' to govern the financial and operating policies of an entity (see 3 above) and power is explained as representing the ability to do or effect something, whether actively or passively (see 3.1.1 above). In our view, this wording, as reinforced by the implementation guidance in the standard, refers to powers arising from the contractual rights of shareholders in relation to the entity and to each other, rather than to an ability to control arising as a result of particular circumstances.

A IASB statement on de facto control

However, the IASB evidently thought otherwise, and in October 2005 it was reported in *IASB Update* that it had recently become aware of differences in how IAS 27 might be applied in the circumstances in which an entity owns less than half the voting power in an entity. As result the IASB discussed the definition of control in IAS 27 and decided to make a statement outlining its views on *de facto* control, in the following terms:

> 'IAS 27 contemplates that there are circumstances in which one entity can control another entity without owning more than half the voting power.[31]
>
> During its deliberations on its control project, the Board confirmed its view that an entity holding a minority interest can control another entity in the absence of any formal arrangements that would give it a majority of the voting rights. For example, control is achievable if the balance of holdings is dispersed and the other shareholders have not organised their interests in such a way that they exercise more votes than the minority holder. This is sometimes referred to as 'de facto control'.
>
> 'During those deliberations, the Board has made it clear that, in its view, the control concept in IAS 27 includes de facto control. The Board also acknowledged that professional skill and judgement is required in applying the control concept including determining if de facto control exists. The Board has recently become aware that some who apply IFRSs hold the view that, in the circumstances described, IAS 27 requires an entity to have legal control over a majority of the voting rights to consolidate another entity.
>
> 'The Board accepts that it would have been helpful if IAS 27 had included guidance to assist preparers in exercising the judgement to apply the control concept. Without that guidance there is a greater risk that two entities faced with the same set of circumstances might reach different conclusions on whether they control another entity. The Board is aware that differences in

> the application of IAS 27 might also be influenced by the practices followed in jurisdictions before adopting IFRSs.'

B Implications of the IASB's statement

In our view, any determination of whether *de facto* control exists will always have to be based on the particular circumstances and it is unlikely to be sufficiently certain that *de facto* control exists until actions have been taken that provide evidence of control – i.e. control must have been actively exercised. In general, the more the legal or contractually-based powers that are held in relation to an entity fall short of 50% of the total, the greater will be the need for evidence of actively exercised de facto control.

As noted at 3 above, IAS 27 defines control as 'the power to govern the financial and operating policies of an entity so as to obtain benefits from its activities.' It follows from this definition that control involves the ability:

- to make decisions without the support or consent of other shareholders; and
- to give directions with respect to the operating and financial policies of the entity concerned, with which directions the entity's directors are obliged to comply.

Accordingly, a parent-subsidiary relationship does not exist where an investor must obtain the consent of one or more other shareholders in order to govern the policies of the investee.

In order to have the ability to govern the financial and operating policies of an entity, an investor must be able to hold the management of the entity accountable. It is therefore unlikely that *de facto* control over an entity can exist unless the investor has the power to appoint and remove a majority of its governing body (i.e. normally the board of directors in the case of a company). This power is normally exercisable by holders of the voting shares in general meeting.

In practice, *de facto* control is most likely to be evidenced where a minority voting interest holder is able to have its chosen candidates (re)nominated for election to an entity's board of directors and its votes exceed 50% of the votes typically cast in the entity's election of directors. For example, if only 70% of the eligible votes are typically cast on resolutions for the appointment of directors, a minority holding of 40% might give *de facto* control. For this to be the case, however, the remaining shares would have to be widely held, such that no party has an interest of sufficient size to block, either by itself or with a small number of others, the wishes of the minority voting interest holder.

The question may also arise as to whether *de facto* control can exist where a minority voting interest represents less than 50% of votes typically cast in elections of directors, for example a voting interest of 30% where, typically, 70% of the eligible votes are cast in elections. This is highly unlikely to be the case. As control is unilateral, no account should be taken in assessing whether *de facto* control exists of the possibility that other shareholders will cast their votes in the same way as the holder of a substantial minority interest.

As the IASB has acknowledged, until such time as the IASB issues guidance to assist preparers in exercising the judgement required to apply the control concept, there will be differences in how IAS 27 is applied. Accordingly, we do not believe that the IASB's statement on *de facto* control obliged companies to change any pre-existing accounting policy with regard to the scope of the consolidated financial statements.

One practical issue that will need to be addressed by any guidance that the IASB may issue in due course is the accounting treatment required when an entity shifts between being under the *de facto* control of the investor (and therefore a subsidiary) and being subject only to the investor's significant influence (and therefore an associate).

3.1.4 Investments held in a fiduciary capacity

An entity (A) such as a fund-manager may hold, on behalf of investors in the fund, an interest in another entity (B) that either on its own or, when combined with any interest held by A on its own account, gives A control of the majority of the voting rights in, or the ability to appoint or remove a majority of the members of the board of, B. This raises the question of whether B should be regarded as a subsidiary of A.

In our view, it generally should not. IAS 27 defines control as 'the power to govern the financial and operating policies of an entity *so as to obtain benefits from its activities* ' (our emphasis added). A trustee or other fiduciary exercises any decision making powers relating to assets under its management so as obtain benefits not for itself but for those on whose behalf it exercises the powers.

3.2 Special Purpose Entities

Like many national standard setters before it, the IASB (strictly, its predecessor the IASC) has had to address the issue of an entity conducting its affairs through a vehicle that, though not meeting the definition of a subsidiary, is still controlled by the entity. In principle, there should be less need for such guidance under IFRS (which defines a subsidiary simply as a controlled entity) as compared to other national GAAPs where subsidiary is defined by reference to a number of more specific, or more legally framed, indicators (so that further guidance is required in order to establish an over-riding control test).

In practice, however, the off-balance sheet industry proved no less active under IFRS than elsewhere, so that the SIC felt compelled to issue SIC-12. This requires an entity to consolidate a 'special purpose entity' ('SPE') when the substance of the relationship between them indicates that the entity controls the SPE.[32]

3.2.1 Definition of SPE

SIC-12 is in fact careful *not* to define an SPE, so as to minimise the possibility of avoiding its requirements through exploitation of a loophole in the drafting. Instead an SPE is described as an entity 'created to accomplish a narrow and well-defined objective (e.g. to effect a lease, research and development activities or a securitisation of financial assets).' An SPE may take the form of a corporation, trust, partnership or unincorporated entity. SPEs are often created with legal arrangements that impose strict and sometimes permanent limits on the decision-making powers of their governing board, trustee or management over the operations of the SPE that cannot be modified, other than perhaps by the creator or sponsor of the SPE (i.e. they operate on 'autopilot').[33]

This description is extremely wide and could, in our view, encompass not only a separate legal entity, but also an economic entity represented by a parcel of 'ring fenced' assets and liabilities within a larger legal entity, such as a cell in a protected cell entity (see Chapter 9 at 2.5), or a portfolio of securitised assets and the related borrowings.

The sponsor (or entity on whose behalf the SPE was created) frequently transfers assets to the SPE, obtains the right to use assets held by the SPE or performs services for the SPE, while other parties ('capital providers') may provide the funding to the SPE. An entity that engages in transactions with an SPE (frequently the creator or sponsor) may in substance control the SPE.[34] A beneficial interest in an SPE may, for example, take the form of a debt instrument, an equity instrument, a participation right, a residual interest or a lease. Some beneficial interests may simply provide the holder with a fixed or stated rate of return, while others give the holder rights or access to other future economic benefits of the SPE's activities. In most cases, the creator or sponsor (or the entity on whose behalf the SPE was created) retains a significant beneficial interest in the SPE's activities, even though it may own little or none of the SPE's equity.[35]

SIC-12 does not apply to post-employment benefit plans or other long-term employee benefit plans accounted for under IAS 19 – *Employee Benefits*. It does, however, apply to share-based payment plans.[36] The accounting for post-employment plans and share-based payment plans is dealt with in Chapters 32 and 31 respectively.

3.2.2 Determining whether an entity is an SPE

SIC-12 notes that control of an SPE may arise through the predetermination of its activities so that it operates on 'autopilot', or otherwise. It emphasises those provisions of IAS 27 that indicate that an entity has control over another entity, even though it owns one half or less (or even none) of the voting power in that other entity (see 3.1 above).[37]

In particular, SIC-12 points out that, under IAS 27, control of an entity comprises the ability to control the entity's decision making with a view to obtaining benefits from the entity. The ability to control decision-making alone is not sufficient to establish control for accounting purposes, but must be accompanied by the objective of obtaining benefits from the entity's activities.[38]

These reminders are doubtless made in the context that the first line of defence for those seeking to establish an off-balance sheet SPE tends to be to argue that some third party (such as a charitable trust) owns all the voting rights. However, if the trust (as is typically the case) does not obtain any real benefit from the SPE, this indicates that it is not the SPE's parent for accounting purposes.

SIC-12 states that determining whether or not an entity controls an SPE is a matter of judgement on the facts of each case. However, one or more of the circumstances set out in (a) to (d) below may indicate that an entity controls an SPE:[39]

(a) In substance, the activities of the SPE are being conducted on behalf of the entity according to its specific business needs so that the entity obtains benefits from the SPE's operation. This is particularly likely to be the case where the SPE was directly or indirectly created by the reporting entity. Examples are where the SPE:

    (i) is principally engaged in providing a source of long-term capital to an entity or funding to support an entity's ongoing major or central operations; or

    (ii) provides a supply of goods or services that is consistent with an entity's ongoing major or central operations which, without the existence of the SPE, would have to be provided by the entity itself.

    However, economic dependence of an entity on the reporting entity (such as the relationship of a supplier to a significant customer) does not, by itself, lead to control;

(b) In substance, the entity has the decision-making powers (including those coming into existence after the formation of the SPE) to obtain the majority of the benefits of the activities of the SPE or, by setting up an 'autopilot' mechanism, the entity has delegated these decision-making powers. Examples of such powers are:

    (i) power unilaterally to dissolve an SPE; or

    (ii) power to change, or veto proposed changes to, the SPE's charter or bylaws.

(c) In substance, the entity has the rights to obtain the majority of the benefits of the SPE and therefore may be exposed to risks incident to the activities of the SPE. These rights may arise through a statute, contract, agreement, or trust deed, or any other scheme, arrangement or device. Such rights to benefits in the SPE may be indicators of control when they are specified in favour of an entity that is engaged in transactions with an SPE and that entity stands to gain those benefits from the financial performance of the SPE. Examples are:

    (i) rights to a majority of any economic benefits distributed by an entity in the form of future net cash flows, earnings, net assets, or other economic benefits; or

    (ii) rights to majority residual interests in scheduled residual distributions or in a liquidation of the SPE.

(d) In substance, the entity retains the majority of the residual or ownership risks related to the SPE or its assets in order to obtain benefits from its activities. Frequently, the reporting entity guarantees a return or credit protection directly or indirectly through the SPE to outside investors who provide substantially all of the capital to the SPE. As a result of the guarantee, the entity retains residual or ownership risks and the investors are, in substance, only lenders because their exposure to gains and losses is limited. Examples are:

(i) the capital providers do not have a significant interest in the underlying net assets of the SPE;

(ii) the capital providers do not have rights to the future economic benefits of the SPE;

(iii) the capital providers are not substantively exposed to the inherent risks of the underlying net assets or operations of the SPE; or

(iv) in substance, the capital providers receive mainly consideration equivalent to a lender's return through a debt or equity interest.

3.2.3 *Practical interpretation issues*

A Securitisation transactions

SPEs are most commonly found in, but are not unique to, the financial services sector, where they are used as vehicles for securitisation of financial assets such as mortgages or credit card receivables. The effect of SIC-12, combined with the derecognition provisions of IAS 39 – *Financial Instruments: Recognition and Measurement* – may be that:

- a securitisation transaction qualifies as a sale of the financial asset concerned (which is thus, in principle, derecognised, or removed from the financial statements); but
- the 'buyer' is an SPE, so that the asset is immediately re-recognised through consolidation of the SPE.

This is discussed further in Chapter 18 at 4.

B Majority of the benefits and risks

In our view, the reference to the majority of benefits and risks in criteria (c) and (d) in 3.2.2 above should be read as referring to the majority of benefits and risks that are likely to arise in practice than to the majority of all theoretically possible benefits and risks as illustrated by Example 6.8 below.

Example 6.8: Assessment of majority of benefits and risks of an SPE

An SPE is established to undertake a securitisation of financial assets. The SPE has only nominal equity, but issues €1,000 of debt – €100 subordinated debt to the reporting entity and €900 senior debt to a financial institution. The SPE buys €1,000 of receivables from the reporting entity.

The terms of the two classes of debt have the effect that the reporting entity bears the first €100 of any credit losses and the financial institution the remainder. This could suggest that the financial institution is bearing the majority of the risks, since it has €900 of the possible €1,000 bad debt risk. However, if (as is likely to be the case) bad debt risk is in the order of, say, 5% to 7%, all the losses that are in fact likely to occur will be borne by the reporting entity as the holder of the subordinated debt. This would lead to the conclusion that the SPE should be consolidated by the reporting entity.

This analysis is consistent with the approach to assessing risks and benefits under the rules for the derecognition of financial assets in IAS 39, where more weight is required to be given to those risks and benefits that are more likely to occur (see Chapter 18 at 4.5).

C Benefits not necessarily financial

As discussed at 3.2.2 above, the first of the indicators of whether an entity is an SPE is that its activities are being conducted on behalf of the entity according to its specific business needs so that the entity obtains benefits from the SPE's operation. In our view this does not necessarily require that the reporting entity has any direct financial benefit, as illustrated by Example 6.9 below.

Example 6.9: SPE with no direct financial benefit for the reporting entity

The reporting entity wishes to issue debt, the coupons on which are linked to the price of a commodity (to which the entity's revenue is strongly correlated), to a provider of finance that wants to lend fixed rate debt. The solution in most cases would be for the entity to issue fixed rate debt to the lender and then hedge it by entering into a swap under which it pays index-linked interest and receives fixed rate interest.

Such a swap would not qualify as a hedging instrument under IAS 39 and would therefore, if entered into directly by the entity, be required to be recorded at fair value through profit or loss, resulting in potentially significant volatility in the financial statements. To avoid this, the entity sets up an SPE, to which it issues floating rate debt. The SPE then issues fixed rate debt to the lender and enters into a pay index-linked/receive fixed interest rate swap on arm's-length terms with a third party.

The financial risks and rewards of the SPE are shared by the lender and the counterparty to the swap. The entity might therefore argue that, as it has no financial risks or rewards, it should not consolidate the SPE. However, in our view, it could be argued that the SPE was set up according to the entity's business needs – i.e. to achieve financial 'engineering', by avoiding the potential volatility that would arise from accounting for the swap under IAS 39 – and should therefore be consolidated by the reporting entity.

An argument that the SPE was set up for the benefit of the lender – on the grounds that this enables it to lend fixed rate rather than the index-linked rate required by the entity – does not, in our view, have merit. If, as is likely, there is no shortage of potential lenders seeking to borrow at fixed rate, the SPE is not required in order to fulfil the lender's commercial needs.

The extract below from the financial statements of Barclays illustrates some of the accounting issues discussed above.

Extract 6.1: Barclays PLC (2006)

Significant Accounting Policies [extract]

4. Consolidation [extract]

Subsidiaries [extract]

The consolidated financial statements combine the financial statements of Barclays PLC and all its subsidiaries, including certain special purpose entities where appropriate, made up to 31st December. Entities qualify as subsidiaries where the Group has the power to govern the financial and operating policies of the entity so as to obtain benefits from its activities, generally accompanying a shareholding of more than one half of the voting rights. The existence and effect of potential voting rights that are currently exercisable or convertible are considered in assessing whether the Group controls another entity. Details of the principal subsidiaries are given in Note 47.

34 Securitisations

During the year, the Group has engaged in securitisation transactions involving Barclays residential mortgage loans, business loans and credit card balances. In addition, the Group acts as a conduit for commercial paper, whereby it acquires static pools of residential mortgage loans from other lending institutions for securitisation transactions.

In these transactions, the assets, or interests in the assets, or beneficial interests in the cash flows arising from the assets, are transferred to a special purpose entity, or to a trust which then transfers its beneficial interests to a special purpose entity, which then issues floating rate debt securities to third-party investors.

Securitisations may, depending on the individual arrangement: result in continued recognition of the securitised assets and the recognition of the debt securities issued in the transaction; partial continued recognition of the assets to the extent of the Group's continuing involvement in those assets; or derecognition of the assets and the separate recognition, as assets or liabilities, of any rights and obligations created or retained in the transfer. Full derecognition only occurs when the Group transfers both its contractual right to receive cash flows from the financial assets and substantially all the risks and rewards of ownership, including credit risk, prepayment risk and interest rate risk.

The following table shows the carrying amount of securitised assets, stated at the amount of the Group's continuing involvement where appropriate, together with the associated liabilities, for each category of asset in the balance sheet:

	2006		2005	
	Carrying amount of assets £m	Associated liabilities £m	Carrying amount of assets £m	Associated liabilities £m
Loans and advances to customers (Note 16)				
Residential mortgage loans	12,577	13,271	6,779	6,861
Commercial loans	6,081	5,558	5,000	4,760
Credit card receivables	5,700	5,195	6,815	6,799
Total	24,358	24,024	18,594	18,420
Assets designated at fair value through profit or loss (Note 13)				
Retained interest in residential mortgage loans	628	–	175	–

Retained interests in residential mortgage loans include interest only strips which represent a continuing exposure to the prepayment and credit risk in the underlying securitised assets, the total amount of which was £15,063m (2005: £6,291m). These are initially recorded as an allocation of the original carrying amount based on the relative fair values of the portion derecognised and the portion retained.

48 Other entities [extract]

There are a number of entities that do not qualify as subsidiaries under UK Law but which are consolidated under IAS 27 (SIC-12) when the substance of the relationship between the Group and the entity (usually a Special Purpose Entity (SPE)) indicates that the entity is controlled by the Group. Such entities are deemed to be controlled by the Group when relationships with such entities gives rise to benefits that are in substance no different from those that would arise were the entity a subsidiary.

The consolidation of such entities may be appropriate in a number of situations, but primarily when:

- the operating and financial polices of the entity are closely defined from the outset (i.e. it operates on an 'autopilot' basis) with such policies being largely determined by the Group;
- the Group has rights to obtain the majority of the benefits of the entity and/or retains the majority of the residual or ownership risks related to the entity; or
- the activities of the entity are being conducted largely on behalf of the Group according to its specific business objectives.

> Such entities are created for a variety of purposes including securitisation, structuring, asset realisation, intermediation and management.
>
> Entities may have a different reporting date from that of the parent of 31st December. Dates may differ for a variety of reasons including local reporting regulations or tax laws. In accordance with our accounting policies, for the purpose of inclusion in the consolidated financial statements of Barclays PLC, entities with different reporting dates are made up until 31st December.
>
> Entities may have restrictions placed on their ability to transfer funds, including payment of dividends and repayment of loans, to their parent entity.
> Reasons for the restrictions include:
>
> - Central bank restrictions relating to local exchange control laws.
> - Central bank capital adequacy requirements.
> - Company law restrictions relating to treatment of the entities as going concerns.
>
> Although the Group's interest in the equity voting rights in certain entities exceeds 50%, these entities are excluded from consolidation because the Group either does not direct the financial and operating policies of these entities, or on the ground that another group has a superior economic interest in such entities. Consequently, these entities are not deemed to be controlled by Barclays under IAS 27 (SIC-12).

3.3 Future developments

The IASB is undertaking a project on consolidation that is intended to lead to a new IFRS replacing IAS 27 with significant changes to the criteria for consolidation. This is discussed further at 10.2 below.

4 REQUIREMENT TO PREPARE CONSOLIDATED FINANCIAL STATEMENTS

IAS 27 requires a parent to prepare consolidated financial statements – i.e. financial statements of a group presented as those of a single economic entity,[40] unless it avails itself the exemption discussed in 4.1 below.[41] The consolidated financial statements of a parent that is an investor in an associate must also comply with IAS 28 (see Chapter 8), and the consolidated financial statements of a parent that is a venturer in a jointly controlled entity must also comply with IAS 31 (see Chapter 9).[42]

4.1 Exemption from preparing consolidated financial statements

A parent should present consolidated financial statements in which it consolidates its investments in subsidiaries in accordance with IAS 27.[43] A parent need not present consolidated financial statements if and only if:[44]

(a) the parent is itself a wholly-owned subsidiary, or is a partially-owned subsidiary of another entity and its other owners, including those not otherwise entitled to vote, have been informed about, and do not object to, the parent not presenting consolidated financial statements;

(b) the parent's debt or equity instruments are not traded in a public market (a domestic or foreign stock exchange or an over-the-counter market, including local and regional markets);

(c) the parent did not file, nor is it in the process of filing, its financial statements with a securities commission or other regulatory organisation for the purpose of issuing any class of instruments in a public market; and

(d) the ultimate or any intermediate parent of the parent produces consolidated financial statements available for public use that comply with International Financial Reporting Standards.

Where an entity avails itself of this exemption, it may, but is not required, to prepare separate financial statements (see 7 below) as its only financial statements.[45] If separate financial statements are prepared, however, they must comply with the provisions of IAS 27 for such statements.[46]

The conditions for exemption from preparing consolidated financial statements, although mostly self-explanatory, raise a number of detailed issues of interpretation as follows.

4.1.1 Condition (a) – consent of minority shareholders

IAS 27 requires that, where the parent is itself a partly-owned subsidiary, any minority shareholders are actively informed of the parent's intention not to prepare consolidated financial statements. The minority do not have to give explicit consent – the absence of dissent is sufficient. Interestingly, however, IAS 27 sets no limit on when the minority can register any objection. Thus, in principle, it would be open to a minority to object to a parent's election not to prepare consolidated financial statements not merely at the eleventh hour before the accounts are printed but even after they have been issued. Parents that are partly-owned subsidiaries and wish to take the exemption from preparing consolidated financial statements might therefore be well-advised to obtain explicit written consent from minority shareholders in advance.

IAS 27 also requires all minority owners 'including those not otherwise entitled to vote' to be informed of the parent's intention not to prepare consolidated financial statements. Thus, for example, any the holders of any non-voting preference shares must be notified of, and consent (or not object) to, the entity's intention to take the exemption.

As drafted, the requirement to inform the minority where the parent 'is a partially-owned subsidiary of another entity' is slightly ambiguous, as illustrated by Examples 6.10 and 6.11 below.

Example 6.10: Minority consent for not preparing consolidated financial statements (1)

A parent wishing to claim the exemption (P) is owned 60% by entity A and 40% by entity B. Entity A and entity B are both wholly-owned by entity C. In this case, in our view, P would not be obliged to inform its minority shareholder B of any intention not to prepare consolidated financial statements since, although it is a partly-owned subsidiary of A, it is a wholly-owned subsidiary of C (and therefore satisfies condition (a) without regard to its immediate owners).

Example 6.11: Minority consent for not preparing consolidated financial statements (2)

The facts are as in Example 6.8 above, except that A and B were both owned by an individual (Mr X). P is not a wholly-owned subsidiary of any other entity, and therefore the rules applicable to partly-owned subsidiaries apply. Thus, it appears that in such a case IAS 27 requires P to inform B of any intention not to prepare consolidated financial statements.

4.1.2 Condition (b) – securities not traded in a public market

The potential source of confusion here is what exactly constitutes a 'public market'. It is clear that, where quoted prices are available for any of the parent's securities on a generally recognised stock exchange, it cannot avoid the requirement to prepare consolidated financial statements. However, what is the position of a parent with securities for which there are no quoted prices but which are occasionally traded, for example on a matched bargain basis, through an exchange (as opposed to by private treaty between individual buyers and sellers)?

It is clear from the Basis for Conclusions for IAS 27 that the IASB regarded conditions (b) and (c) above as linked, in other words that an entity would fall within (c) before falling within (b).[47] It will be seen that condition (c) refers to the filing of financial statements with a securities commission or regulator as a precursor to public listing of securities. In our view, therefore, it may reasonably be inferred that any security that is traded in circumstances where it is necessary to have filed financial statements with a securities commission or regulator should be regarded as 'traded in a public market' for the purposes of condition (b).

4.1.3 Condition (c) – no filing of financial statements for the purpose of listing securities

The difficulties here arise from the less than clear drafting.

Firstly, it is not clear whether the 'financial statements' referred to are only those prepared under IFRS or include those prepared in pursuance of local requirements. In our view, the phrase is intended to mean any financial statements filed in connection with the public trading of securities. This is because the Basis for Conclusions for IAS 27 makes clear the IASB's view that the information needs of users of financial statements of entities whose debt or equity instruments are traded in a public market are best served when investments in subsidiaries, associates and jointly controlled entities are accounted for in accordance with IAS 27, IAS 28 and IAS 31. The Board therefore decided that the exemption from preparing such consolidated financial statements should not be available to such entities or to entities in the process of issuing instruments in a public market.[48] In other words, the key test is that the entity's securities are, or are about to be, publicly traded.

Secondly, IAS 27 allows an exemption from preparing consolidated financial statements only to an entity that 'did' not file financial statements in connection with the public trading of securities, without any reference to the period to which those financial statements relate. Thus, if read literally, IAS 27 would deny the exemption to any parent that has ever had publicly traded securities, which would include those hundreds of previously listed entities that are now wholly-owned subsidiaries as a result of takeover activity or group reorganisations. This, we suggest, is a nonsense that the IASB cannot have intended. On the other hand, the use of the word 'did' means that, again if read literally, IAS 27 cannot be referring to already filed financial statements for the current period, since an entity that had already prepared its financial statements for the current period would have no reason to be considering IAS 27 in respect of that period. In our view, condition (c) makes sense only if 'did' is regarded as a drafting slip for 'does'. In other words, the test is whether the entity currently has, or shortly will have, an ongoing obligation to file financial statements with a regulator in connection with the public trading of any of its securities.

4.1.4 Condition (d) – IFRS financial statements of parent's parent publicly available

A possible issue here might be whether the exemption can be claimed only where a parent of the parent prepares consolidated financial statements under IFRS that are publicly available through some form of national or regional public filing requirement, or whether it also applies where those consolidated financial statements are available on request.

The disclosure requirements in respect of entities that have taken advantage of the exemption from preparing consolidated financial statements make it clear that either route is acceptable, provided that the source for obtaining the consolidated financial statements of the relevant parent of the parent is disclosed (see 8.2 below).

4.2 Entity no longer a parent at the balance sheet date

IAS 27 simply states that a parent must prepare consolidated financial statements (unless exempt under the criteria discussed in 4.1 above). By contrast, national law, or other regulations, may require an entity that is a parent at its balance sheet date to prepare consolidated financial statements. This begs the question of whether IAS 27 requires an entity to prepare consolidated financial statements only if it is a parent at the balance sheet date, or also if it was a parent at any time during the period.

In our view, the requirement of IAS 27 for a parent to consolidate a subsidiary until the date on which the parent ceases to control the subsidiary (see 6.6 below) indicates that consolidated financial statements should be prepared by an entity that was a parent during the period, even if it is no longer at the balance sheet date, for example because it has disposed of all its subsidiaries. This will mean that, if a parent does not prepare consolidated financial statements in these circumstances pursuant to a concession in local law – see 4.3 below), it will not be able present separate financial statements (see 7 below) in purported compliance with IFRS.

Likewise, we believe that an entity not preparing consolidated financial statements which had an associate, or in interest in a joint venture, during the reporting period but no longer does so at the year end should apply IAS 28 or IAS 31, as the case may be, to those investments in its financial statements for the period, if not otherwise exempt from doing so.

4.3 Interaction of IAS 27 and EU law

For entities incorporated in the European Union (EU), there may in some cases be a subtle interaction between the requirements of IAS 27 and the EU Regulation on International Accounting Standards (see Chapter 1 at 5.5). The Regulation requires IFRS to be applied by entities in their consolidated financial statements. However, the determination of whether or not consolidated financial statements are required is to be made under the relevant national legislation based on the EU Seventh Directive and not IAS 27.[49]

In the majority of cases this is a technicality with little practical effect. In some cases, however, there will be differences. For example, it may be that an entity has an investment in an SPE that is not a subsidiary undertaking under the Seventh Directive. The entity is therefore not explicitly required to prepare consolidated financial statements under the Regulation, even though it would be under application of 'pure' IFRS.

However, this means that, as in 4.2 above, such an entity may not present separate financial statements in purported compliance with IFRS (because the group accounts required by IAS 27 have not been prepared). Thus, in member state counties where entities are required to apply IFRS as opposed to local GAAP in separate financial statements, it may well be that such an entity is effectively compelled to prepare consolidated financial statements, since it will not satisfy the requirements of IAS 27 for not doing so.

4.4 Combined financial statements

Consolidated financial statements are sometimes prepared under IFRS for a reporting 'entity' that does not comprise a group under IAS 27. Examples might be:

- two or more legal entities under common control of the same individual or group of individuals;
- a group of business units that are intended to become a group for the purposes of IAS 27 in the future (e.g. following an initial public offering or demerger).

This raises the question as to whether such financial statements, even if they fully comply with all other aspects of IFRS, can be stated to be in compliance with IFRS, on the basis that they are prepared in respect of a reporting entity not recognised as such by IFRS.

In our view, there are very limited circumstances in which such combined financial statements can give a true and fair view in accordance with IFRS. As a minimum it would be necessary for there to be:

- a common ownership structure for all entities within the whole 'group';
- a common board of directors for all material operational, financing and investing decisions; and
- evidence of the integration of the 'group' for operational purposes (e.g. budgetary control purposes, financing structure, operation as an unified business).

This is not an exclusive 'checklist' and it would be necessary for each such 'group' to be considered on its own merits. We also consider it essential that the combined financial statements of such a 'group' include:

- all entities that are part of the 'group' for operational purposes (including any associates and joint ventures);
- all normal consolidation entries (such as elimination of intra-'group' transactions and intra-'group' profits and losses);
- a comprehensive list of all entities that have been combined in the financial statements and the beneficial ownership of these entities; and
- comprehensive related party disclosures.

In those very rare cases where full compliance with IFRS is possible, the reporting entity would effectively be invoking the fair presentation over-ride in IAS 1 – *Presentation of Financial Statements* (see Chapter 3 at 4.1.1 B), so as to prepare consolidated financial statements for an entity not considered a group under IAS 27.

In most cases this will not be justified, but it may well be possible to assert that the various financial statements included in the combined financial statements individually comply with IFRS, and then explain the basis on which they have been combined.

5 SCOPE OF CONSOLIDATED FINANCIAL STATEMENTS

Consolidated financial statements must include all subsidiaries of the parent,[50] including SPEs (see 3.2 above). An accounting policy stating that 'all material subsidiaries are consolidated' or 'all subsidiaries are consolidated except for immaterial subsidiaries' would not be in accordance with IFRS, because materiality is not an accounting policy. However, materiality can be invoked in applying accounting policies (i.e. financial statements might still be in compliance with IFRS if certain immaterial subsidiaries are not consolidated).

Although consolidated financial statements must include all subsidiaries of the parent, if on acquisition a subsidiary meets the criteria to be classified as held for sale in accordance with IFRS 5, it is accounted for in accordance with IFRS 5 (see Chapter 4),[51] rather than following the consolidation procedures discussed at 6 below. The exemption in the previous version of IAS 27 from consolidating certain subsidiaries held for sale is no longer available.

5.1 Venture capital organisations and similar entities

IAS 27 specifically notes that a subsidiary is not excluded from consolidation simply because the investor is a venture capital organisation, mutual fund, unit trust or similar entity.[52] The intention here is to emphasise that, although certain associates and joint ventures held by such investors are exempt from the general requirements of IAS 28 and IAS 31 (see Chapters 8 and 9), there is no such exemption for investments in subsidiaries under IAS 27.

A number of commentators on the exposure draft of the improved IAS 27 expressed the view that it was inconsistent to allow venture capitalists and similar entities to use fair value accounting for their portfolio investments in associates and joint ventures, but not for their investments in subsidiaries. The IASB rejects this view at some length in the Basis for Conclusions by drawing a clear distinction, in its mind, between investments in controlled entities (i.e. subsidiaries) and those in uncontrolled entities. Essentially, the IASB sees the fact that a subsidiary is controlled as more significant than the fact that it may be held as part of a portfolio of investments, and believes that a consistent accounting approach (i.e. consolidation) should be applied to all controlled entities by all investors, irrespective of their industry, or the strategy for holding the investment.[53]

5.2 Subsidiaries with dissimilar activities

A subsidiary cannot be excluded from consolidation because its business activities are dissimilar from those of the other entities within the group. Instead, relevant information is provided by consolidating such subsidiaries and disclosing additional information in the consolidated financial statements about the different business activities of subsidiaries. IAS 27 clarifies that the disclosures required by IAS 14 – *Segment Reporting* – or those required by IFRS 8 – *Operating Segments* (see Chapter 30) help to explain the significance of different business activities within the group.[54]

5.3 Subsidiaries subject to restrictions

It is noted in the introduction to IAS 27 that an entity is not permitted to exclude from consolidation an entity that it continues to control simply because that entity is operating under severe long-term restrictions that significantly impair its ability to transfer funds to the parent. Control must be lost for exclusion to occur.[55]

In fact, such a requirement does not appear explicitly in the main body of IAS 27, but it is broadly consistent with the fact that the standard notes that a parent loses control when it loses the power to govern the financial and operating policies of an investee so as to obtain benefit from its activities. The loss of control can occur with or without a change in absolute or relative ownership levels. It could occur, for example, when a subsidiary becomes subject to the control of a government, court, administrator or regulator. It could also occur as a result of a contractual agreement.[56]

However, there is a certain lack of clarity as to the IASB's precise intentions here. On the one hand, the previous paragraph suggests that control of a subsidiary is lost (other than through disposal or reduction of ownership) only when a third party actively manages the subsidiary. However, the basic definition of a subsidiary is an entity that is subject to control, defined as the power to govern the financial and operating policies of an entity 'so as to obtain benefits from its activities'. If an investor is unable through exchange controls or other restrictions to obtain any benefits from another entity – even an entity that it owns and manages on a day-to-day basis – is there not an argument that, since the investor is unable 'to obtain benefits from its activities', the investor does not have control of the entity as defined by IAS 27?

Perhaps the distinction that the IASB is intending to draw is between:

- restrictions, that 'significantly impair' the ability of a subsidiary to transfer funds to its parent (which do not result in a loss of control as defined in IAS 27), such as
  - exchange controls; or
  - in the case of a US-registered subsidiary, filing for protection from creditors under Chapter 11 of the United States Bankruptcy Code (and similar arrangements in other jurisdictions); and
- restrictions which completely prevent such transfers (which do result in a loss of control as defined in IAS 27).

6 CONSOLIDATION PROCEDURES

It is beyond the scope of this chapter to discuss the detailed mechanics of the consolidation process, for which reference should be made to the various specialised texts which give a full exposition of this subject. The analysis below essentially deals only with those areas where IAS 27 prescribes one of a number of possible treatments.

6.1 Basic principles

In preparing consolidated financial statements, an entity first combines the financial statements of the parent and its subsidiaries on a 'line-by-line' basis by adding together like items of assets, liabilities, equity, income and expenses. In order that the consolidated financial statements present financial information about the group as that of a single economic entity, the following adjustments are made:

(a) the carrying amount of the parent's investment in each subsidiary and the parent's portion of equity of each subsidiary are eliminated. Any difference (representing either goodwill if positive or, if negative, the excess of the acquirer's interest in the net fair value of the acquiree's identifiable assets, liabilities and contingent liabilities over cost) is accounted for in accordance with IFRS 3 (see Chapter 7);

(b) minority interests (see below) in the profit or loss of consolidated subsidiaries for the reporting period are identified; and

(c) minority interests in the net assets of consolidated subsidiaries are identified separately from the parent shareholders' equity in them. Minority interests in the net assets consist of:

  (i) the amount of those minority interests at the date of the original combination calculated in accordance with IFRS 3; and

  (ii) the minority's share of changes in equity since the date of the combination.[57]

Minority interest is that portion of the profit or loss and net assets of a subsidiary attributable to equity interests that are not owned, directly or indirectly through subsidiaries, by the parent.[58] The accounting treatment for minority interests is discussed in more detail at 6.7 below.

6.1.1 *Acquisition of a subsidiary that is not a business*

The above basic principles should also be applied when a parent acquires an interest in an entity that is not a business, as illustrated in the example below.

Example 6.12: Acquisition of a majority interest in a single asset entity

Entity A pays £160,000 to acquire an 80% controlling interest in entity B, which holds a single property that does not constitute a business. The remaining 20% interest is held by an unrelated third party. How should entity A account for its interest in entity B?

Under IAS 27, entity A is required to consolidate entity B and recognise a minority interest in accordance with IFRS 3.[59] That standard states that 'when an entity acquires a group of assets or net assets that does not constitute a business, it shall allocate the cost of the group between the individual identifiable assets and liabilities in the group based on their relative fair values at the date of acquisition.'[60] Therefore, after entity A allocates its purchase consideration to the individual assets acquired, it notionally grosses up those assets and recognises the difference as minority interest:

	£m	£m
Investment property (£160,000 ÷ 80%)	200,000	
Minority interest (£200,000 × 20%)		40,000
Cash		160,000

The minority interests are stated at their proportion of the relative fair values of the assets

If, however, in the above example there was an arrangement between entity A and the minority interest resulting in joint control, IAS 31 would be applied (see Chapter 9 at 3.3), and the investment in entity B would be recognised and measured using proportionate consolidation or the equity method.

6.2 Proportion consolidated

As discussed at 3.1.2 above, IAS 27 requires that, where an investor has currently exercisable contingent rights over shares (such as options or conversion rights) in another entity, those rights should be taken into account in determining whether or not the investor controls that other entity.

However, when potential voting rights exist, the proportions of profit or loss and changes in equity allocated to the parent and minority interests are determined on the basis of present ownership interests and do not reflect the possible exercise or conversion of potential voting rights.[61] These provisions are equally applicable to determining what share of an associate or joint venture should be accounted for under, respectively IAS 28 and IAS 31.[62]

The basic principle is illustrated by Example 6.13 below.

Example 6.13: Potential voting rights (7)

Entities A and B hold 40% and 60% respectively of the equity of entity C. A also holds a currently exercisable option over one third of B's shares, which, if exercised, would give A a 60% interest in C. This would, absent exceptional circumstances, lead to the conclusion that C was a subsidiary of A. However, in preparing its consolidated financial statements, A would attribute 60% of the results and net assets of C to minority interests.

However, simply to allocate the proportions of profit or loss and changes in equity on the basis of present legal ownership interests might not always be appropriate. This treatment would be appropriate if the options in Example 6.13 above contained one or more of the following features:

- the option price has not yet been determined;
- the option price is based on the expected future results or net assets of the subsidiary at the date of exercise; or
- it has been agreed between A and B that, prior to the exercise of the option, all retained profits may be freely distributed to the existing shareholders according to their current shareholdings.

The implementation guidance to IAS 27 clarifies that, in determining the level of present ownership interest, an entity should have regard to the eventual exercise of potential rights and other derivatives that give the entity access to the economic benefits at present.[63]

It may well be that, as part of a business combination, put and call options are created over minority interests. The issues raised by such arrangements are discussed further in Chapter 7 at 2.3.9. Finally, the proportion consolidated might be different when a subsidiary is loss-making (see 6.7.2 below) or when cumulative preference shares are held by minority shareholders (see 6.7.3 below).

6.2.1 *Interaction with IAS 39*

Interests in subsidiaries, associates or joint ventures are normally accounted for in accordance with, respectively, IAS 27, IAS 28 and IAS 31, while derivatives over such interests are normally accounted for in accordance with IAS 39 (see Chapter 17 at 3.1). Where, however, the effect of a derivative is taken into account in determining not merely the existence of control (or of significant influence or joint control) but also the share of the investment to be accounted for, it ceases to be within the scope of IAS 39.[64] This is entirely appropriate, since, if IAS 39 continued to be applied, there would clearly be an element of double counting by an entity that accounted both for changes in the fair value of such a derivative under IAS 39 and for the effective interest created by the derivative in the underlying investment under IAS 27, IAS 28 or IAS 31.

6.3 Intragroup eliminations

IAS 27 requires intragroup balances, transactions, income, expenses and dividends to be eliminated in full.[65] Profits and losses resulting from intragroup transactions that are recognised in assets, such as inventory and fixed assets, are eliminated in full.[66]

Example 6.14: Transactions with a partly owned subsidiary

A parent entity sells a 100% owned subsidiary to another subsidiary in which it holds only an 80% interest. The fair value of the consideration received is in excess of the carrying amount of the net assets of the 100% subsidiary that it sold. Should the parent entity eliminate the gain in its consolidated accounts?

Under the proprietary concept, the minority shareholders are regarded as outsiders, and hence it might be thought that there is a case for saying that 20% of the gain has been realised (see 1.4.3 A above). However, the transaction is not a transaction with minority interests as there has been no issue, transfer or purchase of shares or other equity instruments to or from minority interests. Accordingly, the transaction cannot be considered to be a partial disposal of an interest in a subsidiary and accounted for as such (see 6.7.4 below). Instead, irrespective of whether the parent applies the entity concept or the proprietary concept, IAS 27 specifically requires gains on intragroup transactions to be eliminated in full. As a consequence, no gain or loss is recognised in the consolidated income statement.

Although losses on intragroup transactions are to be eliminated in full, such losses may indicate an impairment that requires recognition in the consolidated financial statements.[67] For example, if one member of a group sells a property to another at a price intended to replicate an arm's-length price which is lower than the carrying value of the asset, the transfer may well indicate that the property is no longer part of a larger cash-generating unit whose value in use is not sensitive to the shortfall in the individual asset's fair value. The property may now be impaired from the perspective of the consolidated financial statements (see Chapter 15).

Moreover, intragroup transactions, although eliminated, may, under IAS 12 – *Income Taxes* – give rise to a tax charge or credit in the consolidated financial statements if they result in a change in the tax base of the item that is the subject of the transaction.[68] This is discussed in Chapter 26 at 5.5.

6.4 Non-coterminous accounting periods

It is implicit in the objective of consolidated financial statements (i.e. that they should be prepared as if the group were a single entity) that the financial statements of the various members of the group incorporated in the consolidated financial statements should cover the same accounting period.

Accordingly, IAS 27 requires the financial statements of the parent and its subsidiaries used in the preparation of the consolidated financial statements to be prepared as at the same reporting date. When the reporting dates of the parent and a subsidiary are different, the subsidiary prepares, for consolidation purposes, additional financial statements as of the same date as the financial statements of the parent unless it is impracticable to do so.[69] IAS 27 does not clarify what is meant by 'impracticable' in this context, but it may reasonably be assumed that the IASB intended the same meaning as in IAS 1, i.e. that the entity cannot comply with the requirement after making every effort to do so (see Chapter 3 at 2.4).[70]

When the financial statements of a subsidiary used in the preparation of consolidated financial statements are prepared as of a reporting date different from that of the parent, adjustments must be made for the effects of significant transactions or events that occur between that date and the date of the parent's financial statements. In any case, the difference between the reporting date of the subsidiary and that of the parent must be no more than three months. The length of the reporting periods and any difference in the reporting dates must be the same from period to period.[71] This implies that where a subsidiary previously consolidated on the basis of non-coterminous financial statements is consolidated using coterminous financial statements, it is necessary to restate comparative information so that financial information in respect of the subsidiary is included in the consolidated financial statements for an equivalent period in each period presented.

IAS 27 requires merely that a non-coterminous accounting period of a subsidiary used for consolidation purposes ends within three months of that of the parent. It is not necessary (as in some current national GAAPs) for such a period to end before that of the parent.

The accounting policy of Prudential illustrates the treatment of entities with non-coterminous year-ends.

Extract 6.2: Prudential plc (2006)

Notes on the Group financial statements [extract]

A: Background and adoption of International Financial Reporting Standards (IFRS) [extract]

A4: Significant accounting policies [extract]

(c) Other assets, liabilities, income and expenditure [extract]

Basis of consolidation [extract]

The consolidated financial statements of the Group include the assets, liabilities and results of the Company and subsidiary undertakings in which Prudential has a controlling interest, using accounts drawn up to 31 December 2006 except where entities have non-coterminous year ends. In such cases, the information consolidated is based on the accounting period of these entities and is adjusted for material changes up to 31 December. Accordingly, the information consolidated is deemed to cover the same period for all entities throughout the Group. The results of subsidiaries are included in the financial statements from the date acquired to the effective date of disposal. All inter-company transactions are eliminated on consolidation. Results of investment management activities include those for managing internal funds.

6.5 Consistent accounting policies

The objective that consolidated financial statements should be prepared as if the group were a single entity also implies that the financial statements being aggregated in the consolidation process have been compiled on a consistent basis and, therefore, that uniform accounting policies have been adopted by all the members of the group. Of course, local reporting requirements for each subsidiary might dictate that different policies must be used for domestic purposes. Where this occurs it is necessary to ensure that appropriate adjustments are made in the course of the consolidation process to eliminate the effects of such differences.

IAS 27 requires consolidated financial statements to be prepared using uniform accounting policies for like transactions and other events in similar circumstances.[72] Accordingly, if a member of the group uses accounting policies other than those adopted in the consolidated financial statements for like transactions and events in similar circumstances, appropriate adjustments must be made to its financial statements in preparing the consolidated financial statements.[73]

6.6 Date of commencement and cessation of consolidation

It is inherent in the definition of a subsidiary (i.e. an entity controlled by the parent) that it should be consolidated from the date on which the parent first achieves control to the date on which control is lost. As IAS 27 does not deal with methods of accounting for business combinations and their effects on consolidation, the determination of the date of acquisition (i.e. the date on which control is first obtained) is discussed in IFRS 3 (see Chapter 7 at 2.3).[74]

IAS 27 notes that the income and expenses of a subsidiary are included from the date of acquisition until the date on which the parent ceases to control the subsidiary.[75] This also applies to a subsidiary held for sale accounted for under IFRS 5 (see Chapter 4).

When a subsidiary is disposed of, a gain or loss on disposal is recognised in the income statement comprising the difference between any proceeds on disposal of the subsidiary and its carrying amount (i.e. net assets and recognised goodwill) as at the date of disposal, including the cumulative amount of any exchange differences relating to the subsidiary that have previously been recognised in equity in accordance with IAS 21 – *The Effects of Foreign Exchange Rates* (see Chapter 10 at 2.7.3 and 6.6.1 below).[76]

As drafted, IAS 27 could be literally construed as drawing a distinction between, on the one hand, the parent losing control of a subsidiary (at which point consolidation ceases) and the requirement to account for a gain or loss 'on disposal' of a subsidiary – the implication being that a gain or loss is recognised only on the outright disposal of a subsidiary and not, for example, when a holding is reduced below a controlling interest through a partial disposal or deemed disposal. In our view this is not the intention of IAS 27, and a gain or loss should be recognised on all reductions in the investor's interest, whether arising from disposal or deemed disposal (see the further discussion at 6.6.3 and 6.7.4 below).

A Future developments

The IASB's Business Combinations Phase II project is proposing a number of changes in accounting for a loss of control. At the time of writing, it is expected that the final versions of the revised IAS 27 and IFRS 3 will be published in late 2007 or early 2008. The revised standards are expected to be effective for business combinations where the acquisition date is on or after the beginning of annual periods starting on or after 1 July 2009, although earlier application will be permitted. The revised IAS 27 states that a parent can lose control of a subsidiary with or without a change in absolute or relative ownership levels.[77] When a parent loses control of a subsidiary as a result of two or more arrangements, the revised IAS 27 requires it to consider all of the terms and conditions of the arrangements and their economic effects in determining whether it should account for them as a single transaction.[78] One or more of the following may indicate that the parent should account for those arrangements as a single transaction:[79]

(a) they are entered into at the same time or in contemplation of each other;

(b) they form a single transaction designed to achieve an overall commercial effect;

(c) the occurrence of one arrangement is dependent on the occurrence of at least one other arrangement; and

(d) one arrangement considered on its own is not economically justified, but it is economically justified when considered together with other arrangements.

6.6.1 *Cumulative gains and losses reflected in equity*

A Cumulative exchange gains and losses

IAS 27 requires cumulative foreign exchange differences relating to subsidiaries to be 'recycled' in the income statement only on a disposal of the investment in the subsidiary. IAS 21 clarifies that disposal of a foreign operation may occur through sale, liquidation, repayment of share capital, abandonment or receipt of a dividend out of pre-acquisition profits (see 7.2.1 below). When a partial disposal occurs, only the proportionate share of the related accumulated exchange difference is included in profit or loss.

IAS 21 further clarifies that a write-down of a foreign operation does not constitute a partial disposal, and accordingly no part of the deferred foreign exchange gain or loss is recognised in profit or loss at the time of the such a write-down,[80] unless of course the write-down is consequent upon an event of 'disposal' as described in the previous paragraph. Moreover, it is implicit in the requirement of IFRS 5 for separate disclosure of cumulative gains and losses recognised in equity relating to a disposal group (see Chapter 4) that the classification of a subsidiary as held for sale under IFRS 5 does not give rise to recycling of foreign exchange differences.

However, the IASB has proposed significant changes in this area as part of its Business Combinations (Phase II) project (see C below)

B Other cumulative gains and losses previously recognised in equity

IAS 27 as currently drafted does not specifically address the accounting treatment, on disposal of a subsidiary, of other cumulative gains and losses previously accounted for in equity relating to assets and liabilities of the disposed subsidiary. Such cumulative gains and losses, which would be recycled in profit or loss if those assets and liabilities had been disposed of separately, could include:

- accumulated hedging gains and losses accounted for under IAS 39 (see Chapter 21); and
- any other amounts previously recognised in equity that would have been recognised in profit or loss if the group had directly disposed of the assets to which they relate, such as gains or losses on available-for-sale financial assets accounted for under IAS 39 (see Chapter 20 at 3.4).

IAS 39 does not specifically address this issue either. However, in our view, recycling is appropriate, since the disposal of a subsidiary results in the derecognition of the separate assets and liabilities of that subsidiary just as if they had been disposed of separately. Moreover, this is the underlying rationale for the IASB's proposal to amend IAS 27 so as explicitly to require gains and losses to be recycled on disposal of a subsidiary (see C below).

C *Future developments*

The IASB's Business Combinations Phase II project is proposing a number of changes in accounting for a loss of control. The revised IAS 27 proposes the following amendment:

'If a parent loses control of a subsidiary, it:

(a) derecognises the assets (including any goodwill) and liabilities of the subsidiary at their carrying amounts at the date control is lost;

(b) derecognises the carrying amount of any non-controlling interest in the former subsidiary at the date control is lost (including any components of other comprehensive income attributable to it);

(c) recognises the fair value of the proceeds, if any, from the transaction, event or circumstances that resulted in the loss of control;

(d) if the transaction that resulted in the loss of control involves a distribution of shares of the subsidiary to owners in their capacity as owners, recognises that distribution;

(e) recognises any investment retained in the former subsidiary at its fair value at the date when control is lost; and

(f) recognises any resulting difference as a gain or loss in profit or loss attributable to the parent.'[81]

In addition, if a parent loses control of a subsidiary, it should recognise any components of other comprehensive income related to that subsidiary on the same basis that would be required if the parent had directly disposed of the related assets or liabilities. This includes the parent's share of any gains or losses:[82]

(a) on exchange differences that were recognised as components of other comprehensive income in accordance with IAS 21;

(b) related to the effective portion of hedging instruments designated as cash flow hedges recognised as components of other comprehensive income in accordance with IAS 39; and

(c) related to the assets and liabilities: for example, available-for-sale financial assets previously recognised as components of other comprehensive income.

In other words, the revised IAS 27 requires the entire amount of such gains and losses to be 'recycled' on a loss of control, even if the reporting entity retains an investment in its former subsidiary (including an investment accounted for as an associate or joint venture). The Board reached this conclusion because it believes that the approach adopted in these amendments is consistent with its previous decision that non-controlling interests are a separate component of equity – this point is illustrated by the discussion at 6.6.2 A below.[83]

At the time of writing, it is expected that the final versions of the revised IFRS 3 and IAS 27 will be published in late 2007 or early 2008. The revised standards are expected to be effective for business combinations where the acquisition date is on or after the beginning of annual periods starting on or after 1 July 2009, although earlier application will be permitted.

6.6.2 Group investment ceasing to be subsidiary

Where an investment ceases to be a subsidiary, and does not become either an associate as defined in IAS 28 (see Chapter 8) or a joint venture as defined in IAS 31 (see Chapter 9), it must be accounted for in accordance with IAS 39.[84]

The measurement rules in IAS 39 are complex and discussed in detail in Chapter 20. In brief, however, they will entail the former subsidiary being recorded initially at 'cost' (which is deemed to be its carrying amount on the date that it ceases to be a subsidiary)[85] and then classified as either a 'financial asset at fair value through profit or loss' or an 'available-for-sale' financial asset. In either case, the investment will be immediately remeasured at fair value, and continuously remeasured at fair value thereafter, with gains and losses arising on revaluation accounted for in the income statement, in the case of as asset classified as a 'financial asset at fair value through profit or loss' or in equity, in the case of an 'available-for-sale' financial asset.

Under the revised IAS 27, a former subsidiary in which the group retains an interest would be initially recorded at fair value rather than cost, with the valuation movement effectively being included as part of the gain or loss on disposal (see Example 6.15 at 6.6.3 below).[86]

A Cumulative exchange differences on former subsidiaries

As noted above, IAS 27 requires the cost of an investment formerly a subsidiary to be treated as its 'carrying amount', which excludes, in the case of a foreign subsidiary, the cumulative amount of any exchange differences relating to the subsidiary that have previously been recognised in equity in accordance with IAS 21. This begs the question of how such differences are to be dealt with. The question is only one of time – it is clearly a fundamental principle of IAS 21, IAS 27 and IAS 39 that such differences must at some point be recognised in the income statement.

In our view, the provisions of IAS 21, as currently drafted, summarised in 6.6.1 above indicate that cumulative foreign exchange differences are 'recycled' only when the reporting entity's interest in the relevant investment is disposed of, not when its status changes (e.g. because of changes in the relative voting powers of the owners of the investment). However, this does create the slight anomaly in the case of a former subsidiary which is to be accounted for as 'at fair value through profit or loss' that some part of the gains or losses related to that subsidiary will have been accounted for in equity, and not in profit or loss, until ultimate disposal of the investment.

However, as noted at 6.6.1 C above, the IASB has proposed significant changes in this area as part of its Business Combinations (Phase II) project, such that the entire amount of exchange differences is recycled upon the loss of control of the subsidiary.

6.6.3 Deemed disposals

A subsidiary may cease to be subsidiary, or the group may reduce its interest in that subsidiary, other than by actual disposal. Such a reduction in interest is commonly referred to as a 'deemed disposal'. Deemed disposals may arise for a number of reasons, including:

- the group does not take up its full allocation in a rights issue by the subsidiary;
- the subsidiary declares scrip dividends which are not taken up by the parent so that its proportional interest is diminished;
- another party exercises its options or warrants issued by the subsidiary; or
- the subsidiary issues shares to third parties.

An illustration of such a transaction is given in Example 6.15 below. The more specialised case of a deemed disposal that reduces the parent's stake without resulting in a loss of overall control is discussed at 6.7.4 below.

Example 6.15: Deemed disposal through share issue by subsidiary

A parent entity P owns 600,000 of the 1,000,000 shares issued by its subsidiary S, giving it a 60% interest. The carrying value of S's net identifiable assets in the consolidated financial statements of P is £120 million. In addition, goodwill of £15 million arose on the original acquisition of S, and has not subsequently been impaired. S issues 500,000 shares to a new investor for £80 million, as a result of which P's 600,000 shares represent 40% of the 1,500,000 shares issued by S, which becomes as associate of P. This transaction implies a fair value for S (excluding any control premium) of £240 million (the £80 million share issue proceeds give the new shareholder a one-third interest in S – £80m × 3 = £240m).

In our view, a deemed disposal that results in a loss of control of a subsidiary gives rise to a gain or loss. Whilst IAS 27 does not currently prescribe how this should be calculated, in our view the most appropriate result is obtained by comparing the carrying value of P's effective interest in S before and after the transaction, as follows:

	£m
P's effective interest in S after S's share issue *	90
Less: P's effective interest in S before S's share issue †	(87)
Gain on deemed disposal	3

* 40% of €200m net identifiable assets (£120m original net identifiable assets + £80m cash raised by S's share issue) = £80m + £10m goodwill (40/60 ×£15m original goodwill) = £90m. It could be argued that the amount of goodwill to be recognised is only 40/60 of the original goodwill excluding any control premium.

† 60% of £120m original net identifiable assets = £72m + £15m goodwill = £87m.

This gives rise to the following journal entry on the deemed disposal:

	£m	£m
Interest in P (see above)	90	
Minority interest *	48	
Profit on disposal (see above)		3
Net assets of S (previously consolidated)		120
Goodwill (previously shown separately)		15

* As previously recognised, 40% of £120m = £48m.

Future developments

As part of its business combinations (Phase II) project, the IASB proposes in the revised IAS 27 to require the remaining interest in the former subsidiary to be recorded at fair value.[87] Therefore, the profit or loss recognised on the loss of control of a subsidiary will take account of the fair value of new holding. As noted above, the implied fair value of S following the new share issue is £240 million, of which P's 40% share is £96 million. This would give rise to a profit of £9 million on disposal, recorded as follows:

	£m	£m
Interest in P (see above)	96	
Minority interest (see above)	48	
Profit on disposal (see above)		9
Net assets of S (previously consolidated)		120
Goodwill (previously shown separately)		15

6.6.4 *Presentation of comparative information for a former subsidiary*

In cases, such as that in Example 6.15 above, where a subsidiary becomes an associate accounted for under the equity method, the effect will be that the reporting entity's interest in the investee will be reported:

- under the equity method from the date on which control is lost in the current period; and
- for any earlier part of the current period, and of any earlier period, during which the investee was controlled using full consolidation.

There is no question of restating financial information for periods prior to the loss of control using the equity method so as to provide some form of comparability with the new presentation. IAS 27 is explicit that consolidation continues until control is lost (see 6.6 above), and IAS 28 is equally clear that equity accounting commences only from the date on which an entity becomes an associate (see Chapter 8).

6.6.5 *Demergers*

Groups may dispose of subsidiaries by way of a demerger. This typically involves the transfer of the subsidiaries to be disposed of, either:

- directly to shareholders, by way of a dividend in kind; or
- (more usually) to a newly formed company in exchange for the issue of shares by that company to the shareholders of the disposing entity.

This raises the question of how the disposing entity should account for the disposal of the demerged assets.

There are broadly three views as to how a demerger should be accounted for.

A Distribution at carrying amount

Some take the view that the most appropriate approach is to record the demerger as a distribution to shareholders at the carrying amount, in the consolidated financial statements, of the net assets and goodwill attributable to the demerged business. This is consistent with the treatment of cash dividends under IAS 32 (see Chapter 19 at 5). Those who support this approach argue that, as a demerger is not an exchange transaction, there is no need to measure it at the fair value of the net assets and goodwill transferred.

B Distribution at fair value with gain recognised in equity

Others take the view that a demerger, whilst essentially a distribution to shareholders, is an economic event of unusual significance, and it is therefore most appropriately recorded at fair value, in order to show the true value returned to shareholders. If this approach is adopted, it will be necessary to record an offsetting credit within equity (equivalent to a gain on revaluation of the net assets and goodwill disposed). The net of this gain and the demerger dividend at fair value will of course be the same as the amount shown as a distribution at carrying amount under the approach in A above.

C Distribution at fair value with gain recognised in profit or loss

Some take the view that a demerger should be considered as the equivalent of two transactions – a cash dividend (of the fair value of the demerger dividend) to shareholders, who then use that cash to acquire the demerged net assets and goodwill, giving rise to a gain for the reporting entity.

D Conclusion

In our view, the approach in C above is not appropriate (even though we have noted in practice that securities regulators in some jurisdictions contend that it must be applied, whilst others insist with equal vigour that it must not!). A demerger is effectively a distribution of assets to shareholders, and therefore gives rise to no gain or loss under the *Framework*. However, we consider that there are arguments for recording a demerger at either the carrying amount of the net assets and goodwill of the subsidiaries disposed of (as in A above), or at fair value (as in B above). Accordingly, in our view, either approach may be adopted as a matter of accounting policy.

E Future developments

This issue had been brought to the agenda committee of the IFRIC in July 2006, but further discussion was postponed pending the IASB's Business Combinations (Phase II) project. The Board decided in March 2007 not to address the measurement basis of distributions to owners in its business combinations project. In May 2007, the IFRIC decided that the issue should be taken on to its agenda and noted that 'the issue was widespread and that significant diversity in practice existed with the assets or businesses distributed being measured by some entities at their carrying amounts and by others at fair value. Those that used fair value recognised the difference between the carrying amount and fair value either in profit or loss or directly in equity'.[88] In July 2007, the IFRIC tentatively agreed that its project should

- 'define in-specie distributions as unconditional non-reciprocal transfers of assets by an entity to its equity holders acting in their capacity as equity holders;
- address all non-cash distributions; and
- focus on the financial statements of the entity that makes the distribution.'[89]

However, in September 2007, the IFRIC decided that the scope of the project should:[90]

- not include distributions that involve entities under common control;
- not address how an entity should account for any difference between the carrying amount of the dividend payable and the adjustment to the non-controlling interest in the consolidated financial statements if it retains control over a subsidiary after the distribution; and
- should not address when an entity should recognise a dividend payable.

The IFRIC also decided that:[91]

- accounting for all dividends payable should be determined by one standard, regardless of the types of the assets to be distributed. The IFRIC concluded that IAS 37 – *Provisions, Contingent Liabilities and Contingent Assets* – was the most relevant standard. Therefore, an entity would be required to consider the fair value of the assets to be distributed in determining the best estimate of the dividend payable;
- when an entity makes the distribution that settles the liability and results in its losing control over the assets distributed, any difference between the carrying amount of the liability for the dividend payable and the carrying amount of the assets distributed should be recognised in comprehensive income; and
- no exceptions should be made to the requirement that all dividends payable should be measured in accordance with IAS 37.

The IFRIC concluded that while IFRS 5 disclosures would be useful to users of financial statements, that standard needs to be amended as it currently only applies to non-current assets (or disposal groups) that will be sold.

6.7 Minority interests

IAS 27 requires minority interests to be presented in the consolidated balance sheet within equity, separately from the parent shareholders' equity. Minority interests in the profit or loss of the group must also be separately disclosed.[92] The profit or loss is attributed to the parent shareholders and minority interests (see also 6.1 above). Because the interest of parent shareholders and minority interests are both equity, the amount attributed to minority interests is not income or expense.[93]

This requirement caused one member of the IASB (Tatsumi Yamada) to dissent from the improved version of IAS 27. The main grounds for Mr Yamada's dissent were a concern that this presentation effectively pre-empted the outcome of the IASB's broader debate as to whether to require the entity model or the parent company model (see 1.4 above) for consolidated financial statements, and should not therefore be mandated until that debate has been concluded.[94] As noted at 1.4 above, this debate has now moved on with the issue of the near-final version of IAS 27, which requires transactions with minority interest to be accounted for as transactions with other equity holders (see 6.7.4 C below).

6.7.1 Interaction with IAS 32

Notwithstanding the general requirement of IAS 27 to treat minority interests as equity, there are some circumstances – essentially where the minority have a claim on the group more akin to that of a creditor than that of an equity shareholder – where minority interests are required to be classified as financial liabilities (and payments to them as interest expense) by IAS 32 – *Financial Instruments: Presentation*. This is discussed further in Chapter 19 at 3.6.

However, where a minority interest is treated as equity in consolidated financial statements, in our view, it is subject to all the requirements of IAS 32 relating to own equity. For example, put or call options over minority interests accounted for as equity should be accounted for in consolidated financial statements as contracts over own equity instruments under IAS 32 (see Chapter 19 at 7).

In some cases, however, the effect of options over what are in law minority interests may be such that no minority interest is reflected in the financial statements, particularly when such options are put in place as part of a business combination transaction. This is discussed further in Chapter 7 at 2.3.9.

6.7.2 Loss-making subsidiaries

Where losses attributable to the minority in a consolidated subsidiary exceed the minority interest in the subsidiary's equity, the excess, and any further losses applicable to the minority, are allocated against the majority interest except to the extent that the minority has a binding obligation, and is able, to make an additional investment to cover the losses. If the subsidiary subsequently reports profits, such profits are allocated to the majority interest until the minority's share of losses previously absorbed by the majority has been recovered.[95]

This treatment, sometimes referred to as 'waterline accounting', is illustrated by Example 6.16 below.

Example 6.16: Minority interest in loss-making subsidiary ('waterline accounting')

The reporting entity (P) sets up a subsidiary (S) with another party (M). P owns 70%, and M 30%, of the equity, and the terms of the arrangement are such that S is a subsidiary of P (rather than a joint venture of P and M), and M has no obligation to make additional investment to cover any losses.

The initial investment of the parties is €700,000 by P and €300,000 by M. Further finance is provided by way of a bank loan. The first five years' results of S are as follows:

Year	Profit/(loss) (€)	Shareholders' equity (€)
0		1,000,000
1	(700,000)	300,000
2	(800,000)	(500,000)
3	400,000	(100,000)
4	500,000	400,000
5	750,000	1,150,000

The allocation of each year's result between P and M would be as follows.

Year	Profit/(loss) (€)	P's share of result (€)	P's share of net equity (€)	M's share of result (€)	M's share of net equity (€)
0			700,000		300,000
1	(700,000)	(490,000)	210,000	(210,000)	90,000
2	(800,000)	(710,000)	(500,000)	(90,000)	–
3	400,000	400,000	(100,000)	–	–
4	500,000	380,000	280,000	120,000	120,000
5	750,000	525,000	805,000	225,000	345,000

In year 1 the loss does not reduce shareholders' equity to zero, and is therefore allocated 70/30 according the relative shareholdings of P and M. By year 2 the cumulative losses of €1,500,000 are greater than P's and M's initial investment, so that the share of the loss allocated to M is restricted to the amount needed to write its investment down to zero, with the balance of the loss being borne by P. In year 3, the profit is insufficient to return the shareholders' equity of S to more than zero, so that P takes credit for the full profit. At the end of year 4, shareholders' equity, though less than P's and M's initial investment, is €400,000, of which M's 30% share is €120,000. Accordingly, M's share of the year 4 profit is restricted to €120,000. In year 5, P and M once more participate in the result according to their relative shareholdings.

A Future developments

As part of the IASB's Business Combinations (Phase II) project, the revised IAS 27 requires total comprehensive income to be attributed to the owners of the parent and to the non-controlling interests even if this results in the non-controlling interests having a deficit balance.[96] The revised IAS 27 also requires that if the parent and the non-controlling interest have entered into an arrangement that determines the attribution of profit or loss and other comprehensive income, the attribution should be based on the terms of the arrangement.[97] At the time of writing, it is expected that the final versions of the revised IFRS 3 and IAS 27 will be published in late 2007 or early 2008. The revised standards are expected to be effective for business combinations where the acquisition date is on or after the beginning of annual periods starting on or after 1 July 2009, although earlier application will be permitted.

6.7.3 *Cumulative preference shares held by minority interests*

If a subsidiary has outstanding cumulative preference shares that are held by minority interests and classified as equity, the parent is required to compute its share of profits or losses after adjusting for the dividends on such shares, whether or not dividends have been declared.[98]

6.7.4 *Part disposals with no loss of control*

A True disposals

The reporting entity may dispose of part of its interest in a subsidiary, but still retain overall control of that subsidiary. IAS 27 is currently silent on this issue, as is IFRS 3 on the related issue of accounting for increases in a stake in a partly-owned subsidiary.

As discussed in Chapter 7 at 2.3.7 A, we believe that there are three acceptable approaches to acquisitions of minority interests (the 'parent entity extension method', the 'entity method' and the 'hybrid entity concept/parent entity method'), but that an entity should apply one of these conceptual approaches consistently as a matter of accounting policy.

In our view, an entity should adopt an accounting policy for reductions in its interest in a subsidiary consistent with its policy for increases in its interest in a subsidiary. This will leave the entity with a broad choice between:

- calculating a gain or loss on disposal and reflecting it in the income statement, where the 'parent entity extension method' is applied; or
- treating the entire transaction as a transaction with other equity shareholders, where either of the other methods is applied.

These broad approaches are illustrated in Example 6.17 below.

Example 6.17: Partial disposal of subsidiary

As in Example 6.15 above, a parent entity P owns 600,000 of the 1,000,000 shares issued by its subsidiary S, giving it a 60% interest. The carrying value of S's net identifiable assets in the consolidated financial statements of P is £120 million. In addition, goodwill of £15 million arose on the original acquisition of S, and has not subsequently been impaired. P disposes of 50,000 of its shares for £10 million, leaving it with a 55% interest in S.

Parent entity extension method

If P accounts for acquisitions of minority interests using the parent entity extension method, it will recognise a gain on disposal in its consolidated financial statements calculated as follows:

	£m
Proceeds received	10.00
Share of identifiable net assets and goodwill disposed of *	7.25
Gain on disposal	2.75

* £6m identifiable net assets (5% of £120m) + £1.25m goodwill (5/60 of £15m) = £7.25m.

This gives rise to the following journal entry to record the disposal in P's consolidated financial statements:

	£m	£m
Cash	10.00	
Minority interest *		6.00
Goodwill (as above)		1.25
Gain on disposal (as above)		2.75

* Previously 40% of £120m = £48m, now 45% of £120m = £54m – increase of £6m.

Entity method

If P's policy is to recognise such disposals as transactions with shareholders, no gain or loss is recognised, nor is there any adjustment to goodwill, and the required journal entry in P's consolidated financial statements would be:

	£m	£m
Cash	10.00	
Minority interest (as above)		6.00
Equity		4.00

It is consistent with the underlying concept of the entity method that this is a transaction with shareholders rather than a disposal not to adjust the carrying amount of goodwill. However, in some cases the effect might be that, since the goodwill relates only to the parent's interest in its subsidiary, it has become diluted to the extent that the goodwill relating to its original investment has effectively become impaired (e.g. because the control premium paid for a 100% interest is higher than that for a 55% interest). In such a case IAS 36 – *Impairment of Assets* – would require a charge to be recognised in the income statement (see Chapter 15).

Hybrid method

If P accounts for acquisitions of minority interests using the hybrid method, it will make the same adjustments to the carrying amounts of net assets, goodwill and minority interests as under the parent entity extension method above, but will record an adjustment to equity rather than a gain or loss on disposal, as follows:

	£m	£m
Cash	10.00	
Minority interest (as above)		6.00
Goodwill (as above)		1.25
Equity		2.75

An alternative analysis might be that in effect £1.25 million of goodwill has been transferred from the controlling shareholder to the minority interest, suggesting the accounting entry:

	£m	£m
Cash	10.00	
Minority interest *		7.25
Equity		2.75

* £6m (as above) + £1.25m goodwill (as above) no longer attributed to controlling shareholder.

Some might question whether it is appropriate to attribute goodwill to the minority in this way, given that the current model of consolidation does not do so on initial acquisition of a subsidiary. Those who support the approach above would presumably counter this by arguing that, in contrast to the initial acquisition of a subsidiary, in which the minority shareholders do not participate, in this case the minority shareholders are parties to the transaction, and it is therefore appropriate for some part of the goodwill to be allocated to them.

B Deemed disposals

In our view, an entity should account for deemed disposals not resulting in a loss of control using the same policy as is used for actual disposals not resulting in a loss of control, as illustrated by Example 6.18 below.

Example 6.18: Deemed partial disposal of subsidiary

As in Example 6.15 above, a parent entity P owns 600,000 of the 1,000,000 shares issued by its subsidiary S, giving it a 60% interest. The carrying value of S's net identifiable assets in the consolidated financial statements of P is £120 million. In addition, goodwill of £15 million arose on the original acquisition of S, and has not subsequently been impaired. However, in this case S issues 90,909 shares to a new investor for parties other than P for £18.18 million, as a result of which P's 600,000 shares represent 55% of the 1,090,909 shares issued by S.

Parent entity extension method

If P accounts for acquisitions of minority interests using the parent entity extension method, it will recognise a gain on disposal in its consolidated financial statements calculated as follows:

	£m
P's effective interest in S after S's share issue *	89.75
Less: P's effective interest in S before S's share issue †	(87.00)
Gain on deemed disposal	2.75

* 55% of £138.18m net identifiable assets (£120m original net identifiable assets + £18.18m cash raised by S's share issue) = £76.00m + £13.75m goodwill (55/60 × £15m) =£89.75m.

† 60% of £120m net identifiable assets = £72m + £15m goodwill = £87m .

This gives rise to the following journal entry to record the disposal in P's consolidated financial statements:

	£m	£m
Cash	18.18	
Minority interest *		14.18
Goodwill †		1.25
Gain on deemed disposal (as above)		2.75

* Previously 40% of £120m = £48m, now 45% of £138.18m (£120m + £18.18m share issue proceeds) = £62.18m – increase of £14.18m.

† Originally £15m less amount retained £13.75m (see above) = £1.25m

Entity method

If P's policy is to recognise such disposals as transactions with shareholders, no gain or loss is recognised, nor is there any adjustment to goodwill, and the required journal entry in P's consolidated financial statements would be:

	£m	£m
Cash	18.18	
Minority interest (as above)		14.18
Equity		4.00

It is consistent with the underlying concept of the entity method that this is a transaction with shareholders rather than a disposal not to adjust the carrying amount of goodwill. However, in some cases the effect might be that, since the goodwill is relates only to the parent's interest in its subsidiary, it has become diluted to the extent that the goodwill relating to its original investment has effectively become impaired (e.g. because the control premium paid for a 100% interest is higher than that for a 55% interest). In such a case IAS 36 – *Impairment of Assets* – would require a charge to be recognised in the income statement (see Chapter 15).

Hybrid method

If P accounts for acquisitions of minority interests using the hybrid method, it will make the same adjustments to the carrying amounts of net assets, goodwill and minority interests as under the parent entity extension method above, but will record an adjustment to equity rather than a gain or loss on disposal, as follows:

	£m	£m
Cash	18.18	
Minority interest (as above)		14.18
Goodwill (as above)		1.25
Equity		2.75

An alternative analysis might be that in effect £1.25 million of goodwill has been transferred from the controlling shareholder to the minority interest, suggesting the accounting entry:

	£m	£m
Cash	18.18	
Minority interest *		15.43
Equity		2.75

* £14.18m (as above) + £1.25m goodwill (as above) no longer attributed to controlling shareholder.

Some might question whether it is appropriate to attribute goodwill to the minority in this way, given that the current model of consolidation does not do so on initial acquisition of a subsidiary. Those who support the approach above would presumably counter this by arguing that, in contrast to the initial acquisition of a subsidiary, in which the minority shareholders do not participate, in this case the minority shareholders are parties to the transaction, and it is therefore appropriate for some part of the goodwill to be allocated to them.

C Future developments

As noted at 1.4.2 above, the IASB proposes to amend IAS 27 so as to require a partial disposal or deemed disposal that does not result in a loss of overall control to be accounted for as an equity transaction. In addition, the IASB decided to permit an acquirer to measure any non-controlling interest in an acquiree at the acquisition date either at fair value or as the non-controlling interest's proportionate share of the acquiree's net identifiable assets, on a transaction-by-transaction basis.

The exposure draft of IAS 27, proposed that goodwill should allocated to both the parent shareholders and the minority interest on initial acquisition, and should therefore be reallocated on a disposal or deemed disposal.[99] However, now that the IASB has decided to introduce an option in IFRS 3 regarding the measurement of any non-controlling interest in an acquiree, the accounting for partial disposals and deemed disposals it is not clear from the near-final draft of IAS 27.

7 SEPARATE FINANCIAL STATEMENTS

7.1 What are 'separate financial statements'?

IAS 27 defines 'separate financial statements' as those presented by a parent, an investor in an associate or a venturer in a jointly controlled entity, in which the investments are accounted for on the basis of the direct equity interest rather than on the basis of the reported results and net assets of the investees.[100] It follows from this definition that the financial statements of an entity that does not have a subsidiary, associate or joint venture are not 'separate financial statements'.[101]

As noted in 4 above, the consolidated financial statements of a parent that is an investor in an associate must also comply with IAS 28 and the consolidated financial statements of a parent that is a venturer in a jointly controlled entity must also comply with IAS 31. Any other financial statements prepared by such a parent are separate financial statements.[102] There is no requirement for such a parent to prepare separate financial statements, or for any separate financial statements that are voluntarily prepared to be appended to, or accompany, the consolidated financial statements.[103]

The IASB takes the view that the needs of users of financial statements are fully met by requiring entities to consolidate subsidiaries, equity account for associates, and proportionately consolidate or equity account for jointly controlled entities. However, it is recognised that entities with subsidiaries, associates or joint ventures may wish, or may be required by local law, to present financial statements in which their investments are accounted for simply as equity investments.[104]

Accordingly, IFRS does not require the preparation of separate financial statements. However, where an investor with subsidiaries, associates or joint ventures does prepare separate financial statements purporting to comply with IFRS, they must be prepared in accordance with IAS 27.[105]

7.1.1 *Practical implications*

As noted above, IAS 27:

- requires consolidated financial statements of a parent that is also an investor in an associate or a venturer in a jointly controlled entity to comply with IAS 28 and/or IAS 31;
- defines separate financial statements as those presented by a parent, an investor in an associate or a venturer in a jointly controlled entity, in which the investments are accounted for on the basis of the direct equity interest rather than on the basis of the reported results and net assets of the investees.

These requirements have the effect that a parent cannot prepare financial statements in purported compliance with IFRS in which subsidiaries are consolidated, but associates and joint ventures are not accounted for under, respectively, IAS 28 and IAS 31 but on some other basis (e.g. at cost). Financial statements prepared on such a basis would be neither consolidated financial statements (because of the failure to apply IAS 28 and IAS 31) nor separate financial statements (because of the failure to account for subsidiaries on the basis of the direct equity interest).

Moreover, 'separate financial statements' as defined in IAS 27 are not, other than by coincidence, equivalent to what is meant in some jurisdictions by terms such as 'single entity accounts', 'solus accounts', 'parent entity accounts', 'entity-only accounts', 'stand-alone accounts', which are used to refer to the accounts of an entity other than its consolidated accounts.

The main difference arises from the fact that, in some national GAAPs, investors that have no subsidiaries (and therefore do not prepare consolidated accounts), but do have associates or joint ventures, are not required to account for their share of the profits and net assets of associates or joint ventures in their 'single entity accounts'.

By contrast, as discussed further in Chapters 8 and 9, IFRS may well require an investor in an associate, or a venturer in a jointly controlled entity, to account for its share of the net assets and profits of its investee even though it is not preparing consolidated financial statements. Such non-consolidated financial statements prepared by an investor in an associate or a venturer in a jointly controlled entity include the investment in the associate or joint venture on the basis of the reported results and net assets of the investment, and are thus *not* 'separate financial statements' as defined in IAS 27 (see definition above).

7.1.2 Publication requirements

IAS 27 does not directly address the publication requirements for separate financial statements. In some jurisdictions, an entity which prepares consolidated financial statements is prohibited from publishing its separate financial statements without also publishing its consolidated financial statements.

However, in our view, IAS 27 does not prohibit an entity which prepares consolidated financial statements from publishing its separate financial statements without also publishing its consolidated financial statements, provided that:

- the separate financial statements give all the disclosures required by IAS 27 in respect of the consolidated financial statements (see 8.3 below);
- the consolidated financial statements have been prepared no later than the date on which the separate financial statements have been approved. However, it is apparently not possible to publish the separate financial statements before the consolidated financial statements have been finalised (see 8.3 below); and
- the separate financial statements include a note advising users how they can obtain a copy of the consolidated financial statements. Paragraph 9 of IAS 27 requires an entity to produce consolidated financial statements that are available for public use, unless the exemption provided in paragraph 10 of the standard is applicable.

7.2 Requirements for separate financial statements

In separate financial statements, investments in subsidiaries, associates and joint ventures that are classified as held for sale (or included in a disposal group that is classified as held for sale) in accordance with IFRS 5 are accounted for in accordance with IFRS 5 (see Chapter 4).[106]

All other investments are accounted for either at cost (see 7.3 below) or in accordance with IAS 39 (see 7.4 below). Each 'category' of investments must be accounted for consistently.[107] While 'category' is not defined, we take this to mean, for example, that, while all subsidiaries must be accounted for at cost or in accordance with IAS 39, it would be permissible (if perhaps rather strange) to account for all subsidiaries at cost and all associates under IAS 39.

Where an investment in a subsidiary, associate or jointly controlled entity is accounted for in accordance with IAS 39 in the consolidated financial statements, it must also be accounted for in accordance with IAS 39 in the separate financial statements.[108] In fact, following the amendments to IAS 27 by IFRS 3 and IFRS 5, there appear to be no circumstances in which an investment in a *subsidiary* (as opposed to an investment formerly treated as a subsidiary) is accounted for in accordance with IAS 39 in consolidated financial statements. The circumstances in which investments in associates or jointly controlled entities are accounted for in accordance with IAS 39 in consolidated financial statements are discussed in, respectively, Chapter 8 at 2.1 and Chapter 9 at 2.1.

Whilst IAS 27 does not say so explicitly, it seems clear that not only must such investments be accounted for in accordance with IAS 39 in both the consolidated and separate financial statements, but they must also follow the same accounting model in IAS 39. In other words, the same investment cannot be treated as a 'financial asset at fair value through profit or loss' in one set of financial statements and as an 'available-for-sale financial asset' in the other.

7.3 Cost method

IAS 27 describes the cost method as 'a method of accounting for an investment whereby the investment is recognised at cost. The investor recognises income from the investment only to the extent that the investor receives distributions from accumulated profits of the investee arising after the date of acquisition. Distributions received in excess of such profits are regarded as a recovery of investment and are recognised as a reduction of the cost of the investment.'[109] This reinforces the requirement of IAS 18 – *Revenue* – to treat dividends made out of pre-acquisition profits as a return of the initial investment (see Chapter 28 at 3.12).

This raises the following issues of interpretation:

- the meaning of 'cost' (see 7.3.1 below); and
- the meaning of 'profits ... arising after the date of acquisition' in the context of the treatment of dividend income (see 7.3.2 below).

7.3.1 Cost of investment

IAS 27 does not define what is meant by 'cost'. As discussed further in Chapter 3 at 4.3, IAS 8 – *Accounting Policies, Changes in Estimates and Errors* – requires that, in the absence of specific guidance in IFRS, management should first refer to the requirements and guidance in IFRS dealing with similar and related issues.

Where the acquisition of a subsidiary is treated as a business combination (or part of a business combination) in the consolidated financial statements, it would in our view be appropriate for the cost of the subsidiary in the separate financial statements to be based on the cost attributed to the acquisition of the business (or the relevant part of it) in the consolidated financial statements under IFRS 3.

When a subsidiary is acquired in a common control transaction, which is not accounted for as a business combination under IFRS 3 in consolidated financial statements (e.g. in a group reconstruction), the cost should be measured at the fair value of the consideration given (be it cash, other assets or additional shares) plus, where applicable any costs directly attributable to the acquisition, rather than at the cost in the books of the transferring entity or the acquired subsidiary's net book value. Although the common control exemption in IFRS 3 provides relief from the application of the purchase method, there is no corresponding relief from IAS 27 in determining the cost of an investment in the separate financial statements. Accounting in separate financial statements for the formation of a new parent, which was discussed by the IASB in July 2007, is discussed in detailed at C below.

Another point of reference might be IAS 32 and IAS 39. Investments in subsidiaries, associates and joint ventures, while outside the scope of IAS 32 and IAS 39, are clearly financial assets (and therefore financial instruments) as defined in those standards. IAS 39 requires financial assets to be initially recognised at fair value together with transaction costs that are directly attributable (see Chapter 20 at 2).

A Investments acquired for shares or other equity instruments

A transaction in which an investment in a subsidiary, associate or joint venture is acquired in exchange for an issue of shares or other equity instruments is not specifically addressed under IFRS, since it falls outside the scope of both IAS 39 (see above) and IFRS 2 – *Share-based Payment* (see Chapter 31 at 2.2.3).

Moreover, IFRS has no general requirements for accounting of the issue of equity instruments. Rather, consistent with the position taken by the *Framework* that equity is a residual rather than an item 'in its own right', the amount of an equity instrument is normally measured by reference to the item (expense or asset) in consideration for which the equity is issued, as determined in accordance with IFRS applicable to that other item. Again, however, we believe that it would be appropriate, by analogy with IFRS on related areas, to account for such a transaction at the fair value of the investment acquired (together with directly attributable acquisition costs).

In some jurisdictions, local law may permit investments acquired for an issue of shares to be recorded at a notional value (for example, the nominal value of the shares issued). In our view, this is not an appropriate measure of cost under IFRS.

B Cost of subsidiary acquired in stages

It may be that a subsidiary was acquired in stages so that, up to the date on which control was first achieved, the initial investment was accounted for at fair value under IAS 39. In the consolidated financial statements, the cost of the subsidiary is the actual amount paid (see Chapter 7 at 2.3). This raises the question of what the carrying amount should be in the separate financial statements when the cost method is applied.

In our view, the cost of such a subsidiary should be the sum of the actual amounts paid. Accordingly, any accumulated fair value changes relating to the investment should be reversed when control is obtained. The reversal will be an adjustment to the component of equity containing the cumulative valuation gains and losses, i.e. retained earnings where the investment has been treated as at fair value through profit or loss, or the 'available-for-sale reserve' where the investment has been treated as available-for-sale. However, any impairment recognised before control was obtained should not be reversed unless the conditions required for reversal under IAS 39 (see Chapter 20 at 6.2.5) have been satisfied.

C Accounting in separate financial statements for the formation of a new parent

IAS 27 requires that investments in subsidiaries are accounted for in the separate financial statements either at cost or in accordance with IAS 39. In July 2007, the IASB discussed the issue that IFRS is being interpreted as always 'requiring a newly formed parent entity to measure its investment in the previous parent at fair value'.[110] The Board concluded that when a new holding company is established that becomes the parent of the existing parent in a one-for-one share exchange, there are no changes in substance resulting from such a revision of the organisation structure. The Board directed its staff to draft an amendment to paragraph 37 of IAS 27 that clarifies that that paragraph does not apply to such transactions. Furthermore, the Board tentatively decided that such reorganisations should be accounted for by reference to the existing carrying amounts.[111]

7.3.2 'Pre-acquisition' profits

As noted above, IAS 27 requires distributions received in excess of profits arising after the date of acquisition (sometimes referred to as dividends out of 'pre-acquisition' profits) to be regarded as a recovery of the investment and therefore accounted for as a reduction of the cost of the investment.

A What are 'profits'?

The underlying principle is clear – namely that if an investor receives income in the form of a dividend of 'pre-acquisition' profits, in reality that 'income' is no more than a return of some part of the initial investment. However, the drafting of IAS 27 creates potential difficulties by referring specifically to distributions in excess of post-acquisition *profits*, since situations arise under IFRS where:

- expenses are recognised in the income statement, with a corresponding credit to equity (such that the expense does not represent a reduction in the investor's initial investment); or
- income or expenditure is recognised directly in equity (such that there is an increase or decrease in the investor's initial investment, but no corresponding increase or decrease in accumulated *profits*).

It is also possible that a gain recognised in the post-acquisition income statement of the investee in fact represents the realisation of a latent unrecognised pre-acquisition gain (such that its payment by way of dividend would effectively represent a return of the investor's investment).

Examples of these situations are discussed below.

I Share-based payment transactions

If an investee enters into an equity-settled share-based payment transaction as defined in IFRS 2, IFRS 2 requires the investee to account for the transaction by recording a charge in the income statement with a corresponding credit to equity (see Chapter 31 at 4). In some jurisdictions, the credit will be made to a component of equity comprising part of the entity's distributable reserves, so that the accounting entry will have no overall effect on either the profits available for distribution or the net worth of the investee.

Moreover, if the investee receives tax relief on the share-based payment transaction, IAS 12 may require some element of that tax relief to be credited directly to equity (see Chapter 26 at 6.3). In some jurisdictions, such tax relief will increase distributable profits. Thus, the increase in the investee's post-acquisition distributable reserves and net worth may exceed its post-acquisition reported profits.

II Recycled gains and losses

It may be that in the post-acquisition period an amount is recognised in the investee's income statement that represents the 'recycling' of a pre-acquisition gain or loss previously recognised in equity (e.g. on an available-for-sale financial asset or a cash flow hedge). Whilst this is, literally speaking, a post-acquisition profit or loss, it clearly represents the realisation of a position reflected in the investor's purchase price. Accordingly, we believe that gains and losses held in equity as at the date of acquisition, and reflected in the fair value exercise undertaken for the purpose of the consolidated financial statements, should be treated as if they were pre-acquisition profits or losses when they are recycled in the post-acquisition period.

III Latent gains and losses

It may be that, at the date of acquisition, a subsidiary held assets carried at an historic or amortised cost below fair value. For example, it might be that, at the date of acquisition, a subsidiary held land with a carrying value of £1 million and a fair value of £2 million.

Five years later the land is sold for £3.5 million. The subsidiary would record a gain on sale of £2.5 million which, literally speaking, is a post-acquisition profit, However, as in II above, the first £1 million of that profit clearly represents the realisation of a position reflected in the investor's purchase price. Accordingly, we believe that it should be treated as if it were a pre-acquisition profit.

IV PPE accounted for under the revaluation model in IAS 16

The revaluation model for accounting for property, plant and equipment under IAS 16 – *Property, Plant and Equipment* (see Chapter 12 at 2.4.2) also highlights the anomalies in the required treatment of dividends under the cost method in IAS 27.

Under IAS 16 any gains on revaluation are recorded in equity and never subsequently recycled through the income statement. Moreover, any depreciation charge recognised in the income statement is based on the revalued amount, not the historical cost, of the asset.

In many jurisdictions, however, the revaluation gains may become realised (and hence available for distribution) as the assets to which they relate are sold or consumed in the business. Some of these realised gains may relate to revaluation gains that have arisen since the acquisition of the subsidiary. Thus, again, the increase in the investee's post-acquisition distributable reserves may exceed its post-acquisition reported profits, as illustrated by Example 6.19 below.

Example 6.19: Post-acquisition profits

On 1 January 2008, H acquires a subsidiary S. Shortly afterwards, S acquires land for €1 million. S adopts the revaluation model under IAS 16 and over the five years to 31 December 2012 it revalues the land to €2.8 million and sells it for that amount shortly thereafter. Clearly S has made a profit of €1.8 million on the land which in many jurisdictions would be available for distribution. However, this amount has never been reported as a post-acquisition 'profit', but as a post-acquisition revaluation gain.

If the investee were to pay a dividend equivalent to the post-acquisition increase in its distributable reserves in such cases, it would not in any sense represent a return of the investor's initial investment. However, IAS 27 as drafted requires any excess over reported 'profits' to be treated as such.

In our view, entities must adopt some pragmatism in applying the cost method. We suggest that it remains within the spirit and intention of IAS 27 for an investor to treat dividends representing a post-acquisition increase in the net assets of an investee (other than one arising from further investment by the investor) as income whether or not that increase was accounted for as a profit by the investee.

The accounting treatment currently applied under some national GAAPs is to treat all dividends from an investment as income and then, as a separate exercise, to determine whether or not the investment has been impaired as a result. Even where dividends are received out of 'pre-acquisition' profits, it might be possible to conclude that the investment is not impaired because it is worth at least its carrying amount, for example as the result of a post-acquisition increase in the goodwill of the investment, which is not recognised in its financial statements under IFRS.

IAS 27 does not permit this treatment, but requires all dividends of 'pre-acquisition' profits to be treated as a reduction in the cost of investment, irrespective of whether the investment has been impaired. This approach is arguably not consistent with the treatment of goodwill under IFRS 3, which effectively, albeit not explicitly, permits reductions in the value of acquired goodwill to be offset by new goodwill arising after the acquisition.[112]

However, the IASB could argue that an approach of treating all dividends as income and then, as a separate exercise, determining whether or not the investment has been impaired as a result, is a hybrid accounting model which, however pragmatic, is built on dubious conceptual foundations. It effectively offsets partial realisations of the initial investment against (unrecognised) post-acquisition increases in its value. By contrast, IAS 27 requires entities to choose between a true cost or valuation model.

B Group reconstructions

It is very common for entities to be moved around a group for a number of valid commercial reasons. However, groups containing entities:

- incorporated in a jurisdiction where distributable profits are determined by reference to the separate financial statements, and
- preparing their separate financial statements under IFRS, applying the cost method under IAS 27

may find their distributable profits reduced after a group reconstruction.

This is because, when one member of a group (A) acquires another (B), A can treat dividends received from B as income only when they arise out of profits made after the acquisition of B by A, not after its (earlier) date of acquisition by the group. Example 6.20 illustrates the point.

Example 6.20: Group distributable profits 'lost' on group reconstruction

Assume that a parent company (P) acquired a subsidiary S1 (itself the parent of a number of subsidiaries) in 2006 for £100,000. By 2008, S1 had made post-acquisition profits of £30,000. P decided that it would be a more appropriate group structure if the S1 sub-group were directly held by S2 (a subsidiary originally acquired in 1993) rather than P. Therefore P sold S1 to S2 for £100,000 (its original cost to the P group).

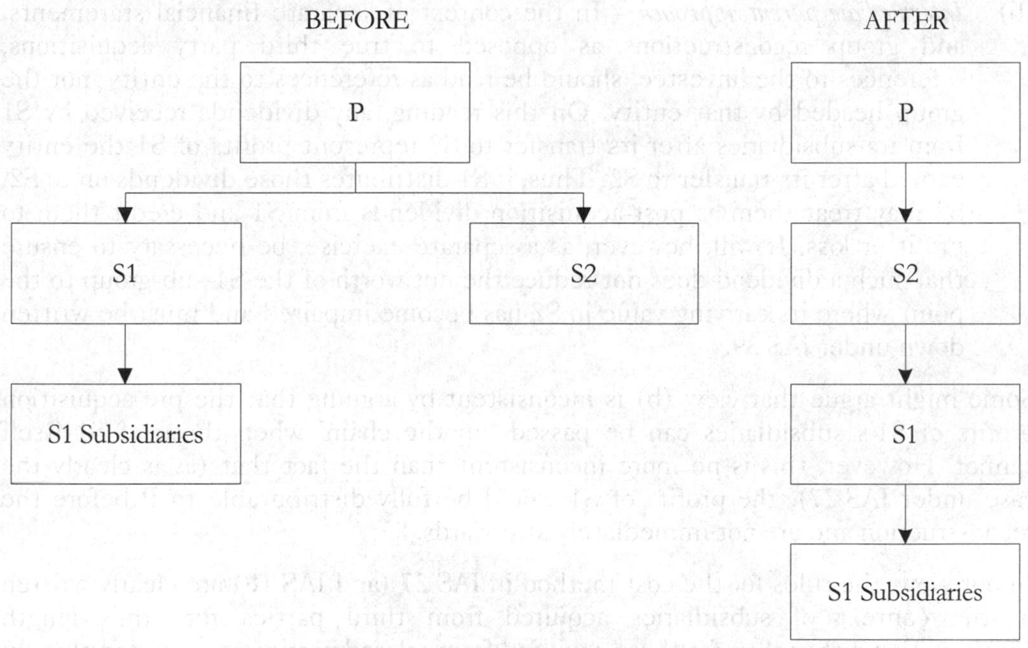

This may well have been a transaction at an undervalue, but this is not unusual in the case of group reorganisations. Under IAS 27, S1's retained profit of £30,000 becomes pre-acquisition to S2, notwithstanding that:

- it would have been post-acquisition to P if it had been distributed to P before the sale of S1 to S2; and
- even if the £30,000 were paid up in full to the new parent S2, S2's £100,000 investment in S1 is still supported by the underlying net assets and goodwill of S1 (since it was acquired at an undervalue – i.e. the original cost to the group).

The net effect is that the £30,000 of post-acquisition profits which S1 could have distributed to P prior to its sale to S2 is effectively lost to P, as it cannot be passed up beyond S2 until the investment in S1 is liquidated.

For future group reorganisations it might be possible to mitigate some of these problems. In the example above, S1 could have paid a dividend of £30,000 to P before its sale to S2. Alternatively, it might sell S1 to S2 for at least £130,000 so as to create a profit for P equivalent to the pre-acquisition reserves 'lost' in the transfer. Whilst it would be appropriate to recognise an accounting profit on such a transaction (as it simply replicates the dividend that could have been paid by S1 before the transfer), in some jurisdictions, the nature of the consideration given might call into question whether such an accounting profit was realised, and therefore available for distribution.

A further point is the effect on any retained profits of the subsidiaries of S1 transferred with S1 to S2. There are two ways of looking at the profits of S1's subsidiaries:

(a) *Subgroup approach* – Treat all profits of the sub-group at the date of transfer as pre-acquisition profits from the perspective of S2; or

(b) *Intermediate parent approach* – In the context of separate financial statements, and group reconstructions as opposed to true third party acquisitions, references to the 'investee' should be read as references to the entity, not the group headed by that entity. On this reading, any dividends received by S1 from its subsidiaries after its transfer to S2 represent profits of S1 the entity earned after its transfer to S2. Thus, if S1 distributes those dividends on to S2, S2 may treat them as post-acquisition dividends from S1 and credit them to profit or loss. It will, however, as a separate exercise, be necessary to ensure that such a dividend does not reduce the net worth of the S1 sub-group to the point where its carrying value in S2 has become impaired and must be written down under IAS 39.

Some might argue that view (b) is inconsistent by arguing that the pre-acquisition profits of S1's subsidiaries can be passed 'up the chain' when those of S1 itself cannot. However, this is no more inconsistent than the fact that (as is clearly the case under IAS 27), the profits of S1 would be fully distributable to P before the reconstruction and are not immediately afterwards.

In our view, the rules for the cost method in IAS 27 (and IAS 18) are clearly written in the context of subsidiaries acquired from third parties for arm's length consideration rather than for those acquired from related parties at an undervalue. In our view, the underlying rationale for the method must be that, where a subsidiary is acquired for fair value, any dividend out of pre-acquisition profits represents a partial return of that value to the investor. It would therefore seem reasonable to take the view that, where the transaction is undertaken at an undervalue, any dividend from pre-acquisition profits that represents a return of value not reflected in the purchase price represents revenue. However, the current drafting of the method in IAS 27 and IAS 18, as a 'blanket' prohibition on the recognition by an investor of all distributions from pre-acquisition earnings as income, makes such an interpretation difficult.

Ultimately the question whether view (a) or view (b) is considered to be most appropriate will depend on the legal and regulatory environment in the jurisdiction in which the entities are based.

IFRS may originally have been written for the financial markets rather than for regulatory reasons. However, as IFRS gain wider acceptance, they will become increasingly relevant for purposes and users for which they may not have been intended. Therefore, it is helpful that to address these issues the IASB tentatively decided (1) to extend the deemed cost exemption on transition to IFRSs and (2) to amend IAS 27 (see 9.4.1 D below).

In some jurisdictions it may be the case that the payment of such a 'pre-acquisition' dividend, although not giving rise to income under IAS 27 and IAS 18, may have the effect of converting an equivalent amount of equity reserves from undistributable to distributable reserves, so that there is no overall loss of distributable reserves to the group as a whole. These issues often require specialist legal and financial reporting advice in the context of specific local laws and regulations.

7.4 IAS 39 method

The measurement rules in IAS 39 are complex and discussed in detail in Chapter 20. In brief, however, they will entail the subsidiary being recorded initially at cost and then classified as either a 'financial asset at fair value through profit or loss' or an 'available-for-sale financial asset'. In either case, the investment will be measured at fair value. However, the gains and losses arising on periodic remeasurement are accounted for:

- in the case of a financial asset at fair value through profit or loss, in the income statement; and
- in the case of an available-for-sale financial asset, in equity.

8 DISCLOSURE

8.1 Consolidated financial statements

The following disclosures are required in consolidated financial statements:[113]

(a) the nature of the relationship between the parent and a subsidiary when the parent does not own, directly or indirectly through subsidiaries, more than half of the voting power;

(b) the reasons why the ownership, directly or indirectly through subsidiaries, of more than half of the voting or potential voting power of an investee does not constitute control;

(c) where the reporting date or period of the financial statements of a subsidiary used to prepare consolidated financial statements is different from the reporting date or period of the parent:
   (i) the reporting date of that subsidiary's financial statements; and
   (ii) the reason for using a different reporting date or period; and

(d) the nature and extent of any significant restrictions (e.g. resulting from borrowing arrangements or regulatory requirements) on the ability of subsidiaries to transfer funds to the parent in the form of cash dividends or to repay loans or advances.

8.2 Separate financial statements prepared by parent electing not to prepare consolidated financial statements

When separate financial statements are prepared for a parent that, in accordance with the exemption discussed at 4 above, elects not to prepare consolidated financial statements, those separate financial statements shall disclose:[114]

(a) the fact that the financial statements are separate financial statements;

(b) that the exemption from consolidation has been used;

(c) the name and country of incorporation or residence of the entity whose consolidated financial statements that comply with International Financial Reporting Standards have been produced for public use and the address where those consolidated financial statements are obtainable;

(d) a list of significant investments in subsidiaries, jointly controlled entities and associates, including for each such investment its:
   (i) name;
   (ii) country of incorporation or residence; and
   (iii) proportion of ownership interest and, if different, proportion of voting power held; and

(e) a description of the method used to account for the investments listed under (d).

These disclosure requirements are illustrated in the extract below.

Extract 6.3: Lifetime Group Limited (2005)

Accounting policies [extract]

(A) Basis of presentation [extract]

As permitted under IAS 27, *Consolidated and Separate Financial Statements*, the Company has elected in accordance with paragraph 10 not to present consolidated financial statements. These financial statements present information about the Company as an individual undertaking and not about its Group. Information on the ultimate controlling parent and immediate parent can be found on page 25.

(E) Subsidiary undertakings

Investments held as fixed assets are stated at fair value. For all subsidiaries, fair value is based on net asset value. Impairments in value are charged to the income statement.

9. Investments in subsidiary undertakings

	£
Fair value	
At 1 April 2004 and 31 December 2004	11
Additions	2,249,999
Fair value losses	(565,190)
At 31 December 2005	**1,684,820**

The Company's principal subsidiaries at 31 December 2005 were:

Name of company	Principal activity	Percentage of equity held	Country of registration
Lifetime Investment Management Limited	Dormant	100%	England & Wales
Lifetime Marketing Services Limited	Financial services	100%	England & Wales
Lifetime Portfolio Services Limited	Dormant	100%	England & Wales
Lifetrack Portfolio Services Limited	Dormant	100%	England & Wales
Lifeguard Portfolio Services Limited	Dormant	100%	England & Wales
Lifestyle Portfolio Services Limited	Dormant	100%	England & Wales
Lifetime Group Trustees Limited	Dormant	100%	England & Wales
Lifetime Nominees Limited	Dormant	100%*	England & Wales
Lifewrap Limited	Dormant	100%	England & Wales
Lifeportfolio Limited	Dormant	100%	England & Wales
The Bigger Picture Limited	Dormant	100%	England & Wales
Lifetime Online Solutions Pty Limited	IT development	100%	Australia

(* -100% subsidiary of Lifetime Marketing Services Limited)

> **18. Related party transactions** [extract]
>
> **(d) Parent entity**
>
> The immediate holding entity is Norwich Union Life & Pension Limited, a company registered in England.
>
> **(e) Ultimate controlling entity**
>
> The ultimate controlling entity is Aviva plc, a company registered in England. Its Group financial statements, which are both the largest and smallest group in which the results of the Company are consolidated, are available on application to the Group Company Secretary, Aviva plc, St Helen's, 1 Undershaft, London EC3P 3DQ.

These disclosures are given only where the parent has taken advantage of the exemption from preparing consolidated financial statements. Where the parent has not taken advantage of the exemption, and also prepares separate financial statements, it gives the disclosures at 8.3 below in respect of those separate financial statements.

8.3 Separate financial statements prepared by an entity other than a parent electing not to prepare consolidated financial statements

As drafted, IAS 27 requires these disclosures to be given by:

- a parent preparing separate financial statements in addition to consolidated financial statements (i.e. whether or not it is required to prepare consolidated financial statements – the disclosures in 8.2 apply only when the parent has actually taken advantage of the exemption, not merely when it is eligible to do so); and
- an entity (not being a parent) that is an investor in an associate or a venturer in joint venture in respect of any separate financial statements that it prepares, i.e. whether:
  - (i) as its only financial statements (if permitted by IAS 28 or IAS 31), or
  - (ii) in addition to financial statements in which the results and net assets of associates or joint ventures are included.

  However, the relevance of certain of these disclosures to financial statements falling within (i) above is not immediately obvious – see 8.3.1 below.

Where an entity is both a parent and either an investor in an associate or a venturer in a joint venture, it should follow the disclosure requirements governing parents – in other words, it complies with the disclosures in 8.2 above if electing not to prepare consolidated financial statements and otherwise with the disclosures below.

Separate financial statements prepared by an entity other than a parent electing not to prepare consolidated financial must disclose:[115]

(a) the fact that the statements are separate financial statements and the reasons why those statements are prepared if not required by law;

(b) a list of significant investments in subsidiaries, jointly controlled entities and associates, including for including for each such investment its:

(i) name;

(ii) country of incorporation or residence; and

(iii) proportion of ownership interest and, if different, proportion of voting power held; and

(c) a description of the method used to account for the investments listed under (b).

The separate financial statements must also identify the financial statements prepared in accordance with the requirements of paragraph 9 of IAS 27 (requirement to prepare consolidated financial statements), IAS 28 and IAS 31 to which they relate.[116] In other words, they must draw attention to the fact that the entity also prepares consolidated financial statements or, as the case may be, financial statements in which the results and net assets of associates or joint ventures are included.

The implication of this disclosure requirement is that an entity which publishes both separate and consolidated financial statements cannot issue the separate financial statements before the consolidated financial statements, since there would not be, at the date of issue of the separate financial statements, any consolidated financial statements 'to which they relate'. There might well be consolidated financial statements for a *previous* period, but it is difficult, on a natural construction of the words of the standard, to assert that the separate financial statements of the current period 'relate' to consolidated financial statements of a prior period. The IFRIC has also considered this issue and reached the same conclusion.[117]

8.3.1 Entities with no subsidiaries but exempt from applying IAS 28 or IAS 31

Entities which have no subsidiaries, but which have investments in associates or jointly controlled entities are permitted by IAS 28 and IAS 31 to prepare separate financial statements as their only financial statements if they satisfy criteria broadly similar to those in 4 above (see Chapter 8 at 2.4 and Chapter 9 at 2.4).

As drafted, IAS 27 requires such entities to make the disclosures above, even though some of them are nonsensical – in particular the requirement to identify the 'full' financial statements (which, under the exemptions in IAS 28 and IAS 31, are not required to be prepared) to which the separate financial statements relate. It would be far more relevant for entities with no subsidiaries that qualify for the exemptions in IAS 28 and IAS 31 to be required to make disclosures equivalent to those in 8.2 above. On the face of it, this appears to be a drafting error by the IASB.

9 TRANSITIONAL AND FIRST-TIME ADOPTION ISSUES

IAS 27 had to be applied for accounting periods beginning on or after 1 January 2005. Entities were encouraged to adopt the revised version of IAS 27 for earlier periods, but were required to disclose that they had done so.[118] There were no transitional provisions, so that an existing IFRS user had to apply the revised version of IAS 27 with full retrospective effect.

For first-time adopters of IFRS, IFRS 1 – *First-time Adoption of International Financial Reporting Standards* – together with its implementation guidance, identifies a number of issues in relation to IAS 27, as discussed in 9.1 to 9.3 below.

A first-time adopter that is a parent must consolidate all subsidiaries that it controls, unless IAS 27 'requires' otherwise.[119] Despite this wording, we presume that it is acceptable for a first-time adopter to avail itself of the exemption in IAS 27 from preparing consolidated financial statements (see 4 above), even though the use of this exemption is merely permitted, and not 'required', by IAS 27.

There may be implications for the separate financial statements of an entity that, under its previous GAAP, recorded as income dividends received out of the pre-acquisition earnings of subsidiaries that under IAS 27 (and IAS 18) are required to be accounted for as a reduction in the cost of the investment (see 9.4 below).

9.1 Subsidiaries consolidated for the first time on first-time adoption

First-time adoption of IFRS may result in the consolidation for the first time of a subsidiary not consolidated under previous GAAP, either because the subsidiary was not regarded as such under previous GAAP, or because the parent did not prepare consolidated financial statements under previous GAAP. In that case, the first time adopter should recognise the assets and liabilities of that subsidiary in its consolidated financial statements at the date of transition at either:

(a) if the subsidiary prepares financial statements in accordance with IFRS, the amounts at which they are recorded in the subsidiary's financial statements; or

(b) if the subsidiary does not prepare financial statements in accordance with IFRS, the amounts at which they would be recorded if it did so,

in either case after adjusting for consolidation procedures and for the effects of the business combination in which the subsidiary was acquired.[120]

If the newly-consolidated subsidiary was acquired in a business combination before the date of the parent's transition to IFRS, it calculates goodwill as the difference between the carrying amount determined under either (a) or (b) above and the cost in the parent's separate financial statements of its investment in the subsidiary.[121] 'Goodwill' calculated on this basis is no more than a pragmatic 'plug' in order to facilitate the consolidation process and does not represent the true goodwill that might have been recorded if IFRS had been applied at the date of the original business combination. IFRS 1 provides further guidance on this, which is discussed in Chapter 7 at 4.2.

If the parent did not acquire the subsidiary, but established it, it does not recognise goodwill.[122] Any difference between the carrying amount of the subsidiary and the net identifiable assets as determined in (a) or (b) above would be treated as an adjustment to equity, representing the accumulated profits or losses that would have been recognised had the subsidiary been consolidated *ab initio*.

9.2 Subsidiaries consolidated under previous GAAP

IFRS 1 contains extensive exemptions from the requirement to apply the provisions of IFRS 3 to subsidiaries already consolidated under previous GAAP. These are discussed in more detail in Chapter 5 at 2.4 and Chapter 7 at 4.2.

IFRS 1 reminds first-time adopters that adjustments to the assets and liabilities of consolidated subsidiaries may well require consequential adjustments to minority interests and deferred tax.[123]

9.3 Parents and subsidiaries and with different dates of adoption of IFRS

IFRS 1 contains quite extensive guidance on the approach to be adopted where a parent adopts IFRS before its subsidiary (see 9.3.1 below) and where a subsidiary adopts IFRS before its parent (see 9.3.2 below). These provisions also apply when IFRS is adopted at different dates by:

- an investor in an associate and the associate; or
- a venturer in a jointly controlled entity and the jointly controlled entity.[124]

In the discussion that follows 'parent' should be therefore read as including an investor in an associate or a venturer in a jointly controlled entity, and 'subsidiary' as including an associate or a jointly controlled entity. Additionally, references to consolidation adjustments should be read as including similar adjustments made when applying equity accounting (see Chapter 8) or proportionate consolidation (see Chapter 9).

IFRS 1 also addresses the requirements for a parent that adopts IFRS at different dates for the purposes of its consolidated and its separate financial statements (see 9.3.3 below).

More discussion of these aspects of first-time adoption may be found in Chapter 5 at 2.7.5.

9.3.1 Subsidiary adopting IFRS after parent

If a subsidiary becomes a first-time adopter later than its parent, IFRS 1 allows the subsidiary, in its financial statements, to measure its assets and liabilities at either:

(a) the carrying amounts that would be included in the parent's consolidated financial statements, based on the parent's date of transition to IFRS, if no adjustments were made for consolidation procedures and for the effects of the business combination in which the parent acquired the subsidiary; or

(b) the carrying amounts otherwise required by IFRS 1 (see Chapter 5), based on the subsidiary's date of transition to IFRS. These carrying amounts could differ from those in (a) above when:

  (i) the exemptions in IFRS 1 result in measurements that depend on the date of transition to IFRS (see Chapter 5); or

  (ii) the accounting policies used in the subsidiary's financial statements differ from those in the consolidated financial statements. For example, in accounting for property, plant and equipment, the subsidiary may use the cost model in IAS 16, whereas the group may use the revaluation model.[125]

Example 6.21 illustrates the effect of these provisions.[126]

Example 6.21: Subsidiary adopting IFRS after parent

A parent (P) presents its first consolidated IFRS financial statements in 2005. Its foreign subsidiary (S), wholly-owned since its formation, prepares information under IFRS for internal consolidation purposes from that date, but S does not present its (separate) first IFRS financial statements until the year ended 31 December 2008.

If S adopts alternative (a) above, the carrying amounts of its assets and liabilities are the same in both S's (separate) opening IFRS balance sheet at 1 January 2006 and P's consolidated balance sheet (except for adjustments for consolidation procedures) and are based on P's date of transition to IFRS.

Alternatively, S may, under alternative (b) above, measure all its assets or liabilities based on its own date of transition to IFRS (1 January 2006). However, the fact that S becomes a first-time adopter in 2008 does not change the carrying amounts of S's assets and liabilities in P's consolidated financial statements.

For the purposes of the reconciliation disclosures required to be made by a first-time adopter (see Chapter 5 at 2.10.2 A), a subsidiary cannot ignore previous misstatements that are material to its own financial statements, even if they are not material to the consolidated financial statements of its parent.[127]

A Subsidiaries preparing consolidation reporting packs under IFRS

A subsidiary may have prepared a reporting pack for consolidation purposes either in full compliance with IFRS, or in compliance with IFRS but subject to central adjustments. In either case, the subsidiary is not regarded as having adopted IFRS – it does so only when it first presents full financial statements with an explicit and unreserved statement of compliance with IFRS as required by IFRS 1 (see Chapter 5 at 2.2.1). For the purposes of the reconciliation disclosures required by a first-time adopter (see Chapter 5 at 2.10.2 A), central adjustments made to consolidation packs, such as post-balance sheet events and the allocation of pension costs, are not regarded as corrections of errors.[128]

9.3.2 Parent adopting IFRS after its subsidiary

If a parent becomes a first-time adopter later than its subsidiary, IFRS 1 requires the parent, in its consolidated financial statements, to measure the assets and liabilities of the subsidiary at the same carrying amounts as in the separate financial statements of the subsidiary, after adjusting for consolidation adjustments and for the effects of the business combination in which the entity acquired the subsidiary.[129]

Example 6.22 illustrates the effect of these provisions.[130]

Example 6.22: Parent adopting IFRS after subsidiary

A parent (P) presents its first consolidated IFRS financial statements in 2008. Its foreign subsidiary S, wholly-owned by P since formation, presented its first (separate) IFRS financial statements in the year ended 31 December 2005. Until 2008, S prepares information for internal consolidation purposes under parent P's previous GAAP.

The carrying amounts of S's assets and liabilities at 1 January 2006 are the same in both parent P's (consolidated) opening IFRS balance sheet and S's separate financial statements (except for adjustments for consolidation procedures) and are based on S's date of transition to IFRSs (1 January 2004). The fact that P becomes a first-time adopter in 2008 does not change those carrying amounts.

IFRS 1 does not elaborate on exactly what constitute 'consolidation adjustments' but in our view it would encompass adjustments required in order to harmonise S's accounting policies with those of P as well as purely 'mechanical' consolidation adjustments such as the elimination of intragroup balances, profits and losses.

9.3.3 Parent adopting IFRS at different dates in consolidated and separate financial statements

If a parent becomes a first-time adopter for its separate financial statements earlier or later than for its consolidated financial statements, it must measure its assets and liabilities at the same amounts in both financial statements, except for consolidation adjustments.[131] As drafted, the requirement is merely that the 'same' basis be used, without being explicit as to which set of financial statements should be used as the benchmark. However, it seems clear from the context that the IASB intends that the measurement basis used in whichever set of financial statements first comply with IFRS must also be used when IFRS are subsequently adopted in the other set.

9.3.4 Interaction with other requirements of IFRS 1

The implementation guidance to IFRS 1 clarifies that the provisions summarised in 9.3.1 to 9.3.3 above do not override the following requirements of IFRS 1:[132]

- the business combinations exemption in Appendix B to IFRS 1 (see Chapter 5 at 2.4) applies in respect of assets and liabilities of a subsidiary acquired and assumed in a business combination that occurred before the parent's date of transition to IFRS. The rules summarised in 9.3.2 above (parent adopting IFRS after subsidiary) apply only to assets and liabilities acquired and assumed by the subsidiary after the business combination and still held and owed by it at the parent's date of transition to IFRS;
- the requirements in IFRS 1 other than the provisions summarised in 9.3.1 to 9.3.3 above apply in full to assets and liabilities to which those provisions are not relevant; and
- a first-time adopter must give all the disclosures required by IFRS 1 as of its own date of transition to IFRS.

9.4 Separate financial statements – cost method

Where an entity applies IAS 27 in its separate financial statements and adopts the cost method for accounting for investments in subsidiaries and associates and interests in joint ventures, there is no transitional relief from the requirement to regard distributions received out of pre-acquisition profits as a return of part of the cost of the investment rather than as income (see 7.3.2 above).

This means that, where an entity has received such a distribution at any time in the past, it must transfer the amount of the dividend out of retained earnings and reduce the carrying amount of the relevant investment by the same amount (possibly offset by the reversal of any impairment charge recognised as a result of the receipt of such dividend). In cases where the receiving company has already paid on any such dividends received by way of dividend to its own shareholders, the effect may be to create a deficit on retained earnings. In some jurisdictions, this may prevent the payment of any future dividends until the deficit is made good by new profits.

In groups where there have been a number of reorganisations of the group structure since an investment was originally acquired by the group, it will be necessary to investigate the history of such reorganisations to ensure that the potential problems discussed at 7.3.2 B above have been addressed.

9.4.1 *Future developments*

At its meeting in March 2006, the IASB added a project to its agenda to address various difficulties that, it had been noted, could arise from a fully retrospective application of IAS 27 in separate financial statements. This project resulted, in January 2007, in the issuance of an exposure draft of proposed amendments to IFRS 1.[133]

A Cost of investment

The exposure draft proposes to provide entities with an exemption from the requirement of IAS 27 related to the measurement of investments in subsidiaries. The amendments will allow entities to measure an investment in a subsidiary, at the date of transition, at a deemed cost (rather than cost), being either:[134]

- the carrying amount of the net assets, in accordance with IFRSs, of the subsidiary at the date of the parent's transition to IFRSs; or
- the fair value of the subsidiary at the date of the parent's transition to IFRSs.

This election can be made separately for each subsidiary.

The Board decided to allow these two options because the 'net asset deemed cost would provide relevant information to users about the subsidiary's financial position at the date of transition to IFRSs and would be relatively easy for an entity to determine'.[135] The fair value deemed cost, on the other hand, would provide information about the underlying market value of a subsidiary at the date of transition to IFRSs, but might be more costly and difficult to determine. The Board rejected the use of a deemed cost based on the previous GAAP cost because it bears little resemblance to cost in accordance with IAS 27 and would provide less useful information than the other two methods proposed.[136]

B Pre-acquisition distributions

When an entity applies the amendment to measure an investment in subsidiary on transition at a 'deemed cost', the accumulated profits of that subsidiary as calculated in accordance with IFRS at the date of transition will be deemed to be pre-acquisition profits.[137] This will result in any future dividends paid that are greater than future profits being treated as a return on investment, which may in turn have implications for the ability of the parent to remit dividends to its shareholders.

Where an entity does not apply the relief from determining the cost of an investment in subsidiary on transition, an entity may use either (1) the previous GAAP value of pre-acquisition profits or (2) the value as calculated in accordance with IFRS as the pre-acquisition profits under IFRS.[138]

C Impact of the proposed amendment

Whilst the amendments proposed in the exposure draft will overcome one of the practical problems that often arise on the adoption of IFRS for the separate financial statements of a parent, other, more fundamental difficulties that impede entities from adopting IFRS arise from IAS 27 are not addressed by the amendment and we believe these need to also be addressed.

Firstly, IAS 27 does not define 'cost' (see 7.3.1 above). A clear definition of cost in IAS 27 would also enable entities to assess more easily whether there is a difference between the carrying amount of an investment in a subsidiary under previous GAAP and that under IAS 27. This, in turn, would assist an entity to determine whether or not it should use deemed cost as proposed in the exposure draft.

Secondly, the requirement to recognise dividends received from investments that are paid from pre-acquisition profits as a reduction of the cost of the investment reflects an outdated model of capital maintenance which is difficult to align with the principles in the *Framework*. When a group carries out an internal restructuring in which the ownership of individual subsidiaries within the group changes, a literal application of the definition of 'cost method' in IAS 27 results in profits that are, from the perspective of the group, post-acquisition, being treated as pre-acquisition by the new intermediate parent, thereby preventing the ultimate parent from distributing such profits as dividends to shareholders. We believe the Board should review this requirement as a separate and urgent project as it has wide-reaching commercial implications and is a major disincentive to the preparation of IFRS financial statements by individual companies.

The problems being addressed by the amendment to IFRS 1 are relevant not only to the measurement of investments in subsidiaries but also to the measurement of investments in associates and joint ventures in the separate financial statements of the investor.

D Response to the exposure draft

In September 2007, the IASB determined – in the light of comments from respondents on the exposure draft – that if a net assets measure was to be used it should be the amounts that the parent incorporates in its consolidated financial statements (rather than the amounts recognised in the separate or individual financial statements of the subsidiary). The Board asked the staff to consult respondents to the exposure draft to establish whether the revised net assets measure would resolve their concerns.[139] The Board tentatively decided:

- that unless its net asset approach addresses the concerns of respondents, deemed cost could be measured as the carrying amount of the investment under previous GAAP;
- to extend the deemed cost exemption on transition to IFRSs to the initial measurement in the parent's separate financial statements of investments in associates and interests in joint ventures; and
- to amend IAS 27:
  - to remove the definition of the cost method from paragraph 4 of IAS 27; and
  - to require a parent to recognise as income in its separate financial statements all dividends it receives from a subsidiary and to assess the carrying amount of its investment in that subsidiary for impairment in accordance with IAS 36 upon receipt of such a dividend.

The Board decided that the proposed changes should be re-exposed.[140]

10 FUTURE DEVELOPMENTS

Apart from any changes to IAS 27 that may result from the IASB's deliberations discussed at 7.3.1 C and 9.4.1 above relating to the cost method in separate financial statements, the IASB and IFRIC are engaged in several projects that will affect the accounting treatment of subsidiaries:

- Business Combinations (Phase II) (see 10.1 below);
- Consolidation (see 10.2 below); and
- Plans to sell the controlling interest in a subsidiary (see 10.3 below).

10.1 Business Combinations (Phase II)

This is principally discussed in Chapter 7 at 5. However, as noted at 1.4 above, one of the proposed changes is to treat minority shareholders (or 'non-controlling interests' as they will now be called) as part of the equity of the consolidated group such that *inter alia*:

- an acquirer is permitted to measure any non-controlling interest in an acquiree either at fair value *or* as the non-controlling interest's proportionate share of the acquiree's net identifiable assets;

- the non-controlling interest would bear their proportionate share of losses even if this reduced their interest below zero; and
- transactions between the majority shareholders and non-controlling interests (not resulting in a loss of control over the subsidiary) would be treated as equity transactions not giving rise to a profit or loss.

The effects of these provisions have been summarised at various points in the Chapter, particularly sections 6.6 and 6.7 above.

At the time of writing, it is expected that the final versions of the revised IFRS 3 and IAS 27 will be published in late 2007 or early 2008. The revised standards are expected to be effective for business combinations where the acquisition date is on or after the beginning of annual periods starting on or after 1 July 2009, although earlier application will be permitted.

10.2 Consolidation

The ultimate aim of the consolidation project is to issue a new IFRS to replace IAS 27 and SIC-12.[141] Like IAS 27, the new IFRS will require consolidation to be based on control. However, it is likely that there will be significant changes to the criteria giving rise to a presumption of control. The IASB's thinking has been focused on the following key principles:[142]

- consolidation should be driven by the principle of reporting a parent and its subsidiaries as if it were a single economic entity;
- identifying whether an entity is a subsidiary should be based on the notion of control – i.e. an entity's control of another entity should be used as a proxy for identifying the assets controlled by the first entity. Thus the concept is linked to access to economic benefits, and associated exposure to risks;
- only one entity can control another entity. In other words, control must be unilateral or non-shared;
- there should be no exemption from consolidation because a subsidiary's operations are dissimilar to those of its controller or because an entity adopts measurement models different to those of the controller; and
- consistent control criteria should be developed for all entities, including SPEs.

10.2.1 Tentative decisions to date

The IASB has tentatively agreed that the concept of control should require satisfaction of three tests by the potential controller:[143]

- *Power Criterion* (the ability to direct the strategic financing and operating policies of the entity);
- *Benefits Criterion* (the ability to access benefits flowing from the entity); and
- the ability to use its power so as to increase, protect or maintain the amount of those benefits.

The IASB has also tentatively concluded that:

- the holdings or interests of parties effectively acting as agent for another entity should be considered in assessing whether that other entity is a controller;[144]
- an investor's unexercised, but presently exercisable, holdings of options or convertible securities that give the holder the right to obtain other instruments are relevant in assessing whether the investor satisfies the Power Criterion in respect of the investee. For example, if A has a 100% ownership interest in B, but C holds currently exercisable options over all of the equity instruments in B, then C rather than A would, in the absence of other factors, satisfy the Power Criterion in relation to B;[145]
- it is not relevant to the assessment of whether the Power Criterion is satisfied whether or not exercise of potential voting rights is economically favourable to the holder of those rights;[146]
- there should be clarification in respect of fiduciary holdings, specifying those aspects of a fiduciary relationship that differentiate the particular circumstances of a fiduciary from those of a controller (see 3.1.4 above);[147]
- the fact that control of an entity might be temporary does not of itself change the assets controlled by an entity. During the time that control is held and until such time as control ceases, the controlled assets are part of the economic entity and should be recognised as such;[148]
- an entity should recognise the assets it controls through another entity until such time as control over the underlying assets is lost;[149]
- veto rights, even if limited to the ability to block actions, may negate control if those rights relate to operating and financing policies. However, to negate control those veto rights must also relate to decisions in the ordinary course of business, rather than being limited to fundamental changes in the organisation (such as disposals of business units or acquisitions of significant assets);[150] and
- veto rights may in some circumstances be sufficient to enable holders to exercise control.[151]

The Board also affirmed that investment companies such as private equity entities and venture capital organisations should not be excluded from the scope of the proposed standard because the information needs of users are best served by financial statements that consolidate investments under the control of the reporting entity.[152]

As noted at 3.1.3 above, the IASB also intends to issue guidance on *de facto* control so as to give effect to the its view that the control concept in IAS 27 can include *de facto* control.[153]

10.2.2 Matters to be discussed

The IASB has still to reach a decision on the following issues.

A 'Autopilot' SPEs

Many SPEs (see 3.2 above) set up to undertake predefined transactions are 'autopilot' entities (i.e. their activities are largely predetermined). Such entities (which are often components of financial products devised by banks and similar financial institutions for their clients) present a problem in terms of the IASB's proposed new consolidation model, in that the SPE's operating policies may be determined by the bank, but the SPE operates for the benefit of the client. Such an arrangement breaks the link between the Power Criterion and the Benefits Criterion, implying that the SPE is not a subsidiary of either the bank or its client – a somewhat counter-intuitive outcome.

The IASB has recognised that there is a conflict between the control model of IAS 27 and the risks and rewards model of SIC-12, and are developing an integrated model that will reconcile the control model and the risks and rewards models, as far as possible. It is unlikely that one attribute or feature will be an appropriate determinant of control in all circumstances.

B Recognition and derecognition

The IASB is keen to ensure that there are no inconsistencies between the approaches of IAS 27 and IAS 39 to recognition and derecognition, particularly in respect of assets subject to option. It would be anomalous, for example, if an entity were not able to recognise an asset subject to an option under IAS 39, but required under IAS 27 to consolidate an entity holding that asset as a result of a similar option over the equity of the entity.

C Attribution of profits or losses in the context of potential voting rights

As discussed at 6.2 above, IAS 27 may require contingent rights over shares to be taken into account in determining whether an entity should be consolidated as a subsidiary, but requires the consolidation to be based on present ownership interests.

The IASB has tentatively rejected an approach where the accounting is based on a hypothetical exercise of the potential voting rights ('as if' the options have been exercised). Proposals being considered are based on *present* ownership interests such that:

- the shares to which the option relates are recognised as the non-controlling interest in the subsidiary;
- any option premium reduces the carrying amount of the non-controlling interest; and
- the group does not report any increase in the fair value of the option during the exercise period, because the consideration for the subsidiary was established at the date control was established.

The IASB has noted that, applying the tentative decisions, a group that is consolidated as a result of an out-of-the-money option might report profits or losses during the period the option is exercisable, even if the option lapses and the non-controlling interests are derecognised.[154]

D Economic dependence

The IASB has agreed that economic dependence would not normally, of itself, satisfy the Power Criterion. However, assessing control in such circumstances can be difficult. The IASB has therefore decided to consider this issue further.

E Disclosure

The proposed standard will avoid 'bright-line' tests of when control exists, but will instead provide principles and guidance to help an entity decide whether it controls another entity. Some decisions will require the exercise of more judgement than others, such as where control is as a result of *de facto* rather than legal power over voting rights. It is inevitable that two entities faced with the same set of circumstances could reach different conclusions as to whether they control another entity more often than they would under a 'bright-line' test.

The IASB will therefore develop disclosures designed to enhance the ability of users to compare entities.

10.2.3 Next steps

At the time of writing, the IASB expects to publish a discussion paper on consolidation in the first quarter of 2008, which is to be followed by an exposure draft. Hence the project will not result a in a standard that will be effective for financial periods beginning 1 January 2009.

10.3 Plans to sell the controlling interest in a subsidiary

In July 2007, the IFRIC discussed whether it should provide 'guidance on applying IFRS 5 when an entity is committed to a plan to sell the controlling interest in a subsidiary'.[155] The IFRIC decided to recommend to the Board that it amend IFRS 5 to clarify:

- 'whether the criteria for classification as held for sale are met for all of a subsidiary's assets and liabilities when the parent is committed to a plan that involves loss of control over the subsidiary';[156] and
- 'that having a plan that meets the conditions in IFRS 5 involving loss of control over a subsidiary should trigger classification as held for sale of all the subsidiary's assets and liabilities'.[157]

The IFRIC decided not to address the question whether classification as a discontinued operation is relevant when the entity plans to retain significant influence over its former subsidiary after the sale, as it did not expect divergence in practice.[158]

In July 2007, the IASB tentatively decided that 'an entity that is committed to a sale plan that meets the conditions in IFRS 5 ... and involves loss of control of a subsidiary should classify the subsidiary's assets and liabilities as held for sale, regardless of whether the entity will retain a non-controlling interest in its former subsidiary after the sale'.[159]

References

1 A joint venture need not take the form of a separate entity (see Chapter 8).
2 IAS 27, *Consolidated and Separate Financial Statements,* IASB, para. 1.
3 IAS 27, para. 3.
4 IAS 27, para. 4.
5 IAS 27, paras. 9 and 12.
6 SIC-12, *Consolidation – Special Purpose Entities*, IASB.
7 IFRS 3 (near-final), *Near-final draft of IFRS 3 Business Combinations*, IASB, June 2007, para. 33.
8 IFRS 3 (near-final), para. B218.
9 IAS 27 (near-final), *Near-final draft of IAS 27 Consolidated and Separate Financial Statements*, IASB, June 2007, para. 36A.
10 R. M. Wilkins, *Group Accounts*, Second edition, London: ICAEW, 1979, p.170.
11 IFRS 3, *Business Combinations,* IASB; IFRS 5, *Non-current Assets Held for Sale and Discontinued Operations.*
12 IAS 27, para. IN7.
13 IFRS 3, para. 36.
14 IAS 27, para. 4.
15 IAS 27, para. 4.
16 IAS 27, para. 4.
17 IAS 27, para. 4.
18 IAS 27, para. 13.
19 EITF 96-16, *Investor's Accounting for an Investee When the Investor Has a Majority of the Voting Interest but the Minority Shareholder or Shareholders Have Certain Approval or Veto Rights*, EITF, July 1998.
20 IAS 27, para. IG4.
21 IAS 27, para. IG2.
22 IAS 27, para. 14.
23 IAS 27, paras. 14 and IG1-IG4.
24 IAS 27, paras. 14 and IG1.
25 IAS 27, para. IG3.
26 IAS 27, para. 14.
27 IAS 27, para. IG8 (Example 3).
28 IAS 27, para. 15.
29 IAS 27, para. IG8 (Examples 1, 4 and 5).
30 IAS 27, para. IG2.
31 For example, IAS 27 requires disclosure of the reason for consolidating an entity in which the reporting entity does not own more than one-half of the voting power (see 8.1 above).
32 SIC-12, para. 8.
33 SIC-12, para. 1.
34 SIC-12, para. 2.
35 SIC-12, para. 3.
36 SIC-12, paras. 6, 15A-E.
37 SIC-12, para. 9.
38 SIC-12, para. 13.
39 SIC-12, para. 10 and Appendix.
40 IAS 27, para. 4.
41 IAS 27, para. 10.
42 IAS 27, para. 5.
43 IAS 27, para. 9.
44 IAS 27, para. 10
45 IAS 27, para. 8.
46 IAS 27, para. 11.
47 IAS 27, para. BC10.
48 IAS 27, para. BC10.
49 EU Regulation 1606/2002, preamble para. (3).
50 IAS 27, para. 12.
51 IFRS 3, para. 36.
52 IAS 27, para. 19.
53 IAS 27, paras. BC16-BC22.
54 IAS 27, para. 20.
55 IAS 27, para. IN9.
56 IAS 27, para. 21.
57 IAS 27, para. 22.
58 IAS 27, para. 4.
59 IAS 27, para. 22.
60 IFRS 3, para. 4.
61 IAS 27, para. 23.
62 IAS 27, paras. IG1-IG8
63 IAS 27, para. IG6.
64 IAS 27, para. IG7.
65 IAS 27, para. 24.
66 IAS 27, para. 25.
67 IAS 27, para. 25.
68 IAS 27, para. 25.
69 IAS 27, para. 26.
70 IAS 1, *Presentation of Financial Statements*, IASB, para. 11.
71 IAS 27, para. 27.
72 IAS 27, para. 28.
73 IAS 27, para. 29.
74 IAS 27, para. 2.
75 IAS 27, para. 30.
76 IAS 27, para. 30.
77 IAS 27 (near-final), para. 36C.
78 IAS 27 (near-final), para. 36D.
79 IAS 27 (near-final), para. 36D.
80 IAS 21, *The Effects of Changes in Foreign Exchange Rates*, IASB, para. 49.
81 IAS 27 (near-final), para. 36E.
82 IAS 27 (near-final), para. 36F.
83 IAS 27 (near-final), para. BC27J.
84 IAS 27, para. 31.
85 IAS 27, para. 32.
86 IAS 27 (near-final), para. 36E.
87 IAS 27 (near-final), para. 36H.

88 *IFRIC Update*, IFRIC, May 2007, p. 4.
89 *IFRIC Update*, IFRIC, July 2007, p. 2.
90 *IASB Update*, IASB, September 2007, p. 2.
91 *IASB Update*, IASB, September 2007, p. 2.
92 IAS 27, para. 33.
93 IAS 27, para. 34.
94 IAS 27, paras. DO1-DO3.
95 IAS 27, para. 35.
96 IAS 27 (near-final), para. 35.
97 IAS 27 (near-final), para. 34.
98 IAS 27, para. 36.
99 IAS 27 (ED), IAS 27 as proposed to be amended by *Exposure Draft of Proposed Amendments to IAS 27*, IASB, June 2005, paras. 30A-30B.
100 IAS 27, para. 4.
101 IAS 27, para. 7.
102 IAS 27, paras. 5-6.
103 IAS 27, paras. 6 and 38.
104 IAS 27, paras. IN13 and BC10.
105 IAS 27, para. 38.
106 IAS 27, para. 37.
107 IAS 27, para. 37.
108 IAS 27, para. 39.
109 IAS 27, para. 4.
110 IASB Agenda Paper 6, *IAS 27 – Accounting in the separate financial statements for the formation of a new parent*, IASB, 19 July 2007, para. 1.
111 *IASB Update*, IASB, July 2007, p. 4.
112 IFRS 3, para. BC140.
113 IAS 27, para. 40.
114 IAS 27, para. 41.
115 IAS 27, para. 42.
116 IAS 27, para. 42.
117 *IFRIC Update*, IFRIC, March 2006.
118 IAS 27, para. 43.
119 IFRS 1, *First-time Adoption of International Financial Reporting Standards*, IASB, para. IG26.
120 IFRS 1, para. IG27(a).
121 IFRS 1, paras. B2(j) and IG27(b).
122 IFRS 1, para. IG27(c).
123 IFRS 1, paras. B2(k) and IG28.
124 IFRS 1, paras. 24-25.
125 IFRS 1, para. 24.
126 IFRS 1, para. IG29 (IG Example 8).
127 IFRS 1, para. IG31
128 IFRS 1, para. IG31.
129 IFRS 1, para. 25.
130 IFRS 1, para. IG29 (IG Example 9).
131 IFRS 1, para. 25.
132 IFRS 1, para. IG30.
133 IFRS 1 (ED), *Exposure Draft of Proposed Amendments to IFRS 1 First-Time Adoption of International Financial Reporting Standards – Cost of an Investment in a Subsidiary*, IASB, January 2007.
134 IFRS 1 (ED), para. B5.
135 IFRS 1 (ED), para. BC4.
136 IFRS 1 (ED), para. BC4.
137 IFRS 1 (ED), para. B6(a).
138 IFRS 1 (ED), para. B6(b).
139 *IASB Update*, IASB, September 2007, p. 4.
140 *IASB Update*, IASB, September 2007, p. 4.
141 IASB project summary *Consolidation (including special purpose entities)*, IASB, June 2007 version.
142 IASB project summary *Consolidation (including special purpose entities)*, para. 17.
143 IASB project summary *Consolidation (including special purpose entities)*, para. 18.
144 IASB project summary *Consolidation (including special purpose entities)*, para. 25.
145 IASB project summary *Consolidation (including special purpose entities)*, para. 21.
146 IASB project summary *Consolidation (including special purpose entities)*, para. 22.
147 IASB project summary *Consolidation (including special purpose entities)*, para. 26.
148 IASB project summary *Consolidation (including special purpose entities)*, para. 28.
149 IASB project summary *Consolidation (including special purpose entities)*, para. 29.
150 IASB project summary *Consolidation (including special purpose entities)*, para. 23.
151 IASB project summary *Consolidation (including special purpose entities)*, para. 24.
152 IASB project summary *Consolidation (including special purpose entities)*, para. 27.
153 IASB project summary *Consolidation (including special purpose entities)*, para. 20.
154 *IASB Update*, IASB, September 2005, p. 3.
155 *IFRIC Update*, IFRIC, July 2007, p. 4.
156 *IFRIC Update*, IFRIC, July 2007, p. 4.
157 *IFRIC Update*, IFRIC, July 2007, p. 4.
158 *IFRIC Update*, IFRIC, July 2007, p. 4.
159 *IASB Update*, IASB, July 2007, p. 3.

Chapter 7 Business combinations and goodwill

1 INTRODUCTION

1.1 Background

A business combination is defined by the IASB as 'the bringing together of separate entities or businesses into one reporting entity'.[1] This applies not only when an entity becomes a subsidiary of a parent but also where an entity purchases a business comprising the net assets, including any goodwill, of another entity.[2]

In accounting terms there have traditionally been two distinctly different forms of reporting the effects of a business combination; the purchase method of accounting (or acquisition accounting) and the pooling of interests method (or merger accounting).

The two methods of accounting look at business combinations through quite different eyes. An acquisition is seen as the absorption of the target into the clutches of the predator; there is continuity only of the acquiring entity, in the sense that only the post-acquisition results of the target are reported as earnings of the acquiring entity, and the comparative figures remain those of the acquiring entity. In contrast, a uniting of interests is seen as the pooling together of two formerly distinct shareholder groups, and in order to present continuity of both entities there is retrospective restatement to show the enlarged entity as if the two entities had always been together, by combining the results of both entities pre- and post-combination and also by restatement of the comparatives. The difficulty for accountants, however, has been how to translate this difference in philosophy into criteria which permit particular transactions to be categorised as being of one type or the other.

The other main issues facing accountants have been in relation to accounting for an acquisition. In order to do so, the acquiring entity has to determine the cost of its acquisition and then allocate that cost between the identifiable assets and liabilities of the target. Depending on what items are included within this allocation process and what values are placed on them, this will invariably result in a difference that has to be accounted for. Where the amounts allocated to the assets and liabilities are less than the overall cost, the difference is accounted for as goodwill. Over the years there have been different views on how goodwill should be accounted for, but the general method has been to deal with it as an asset. The question then has been: should it be amortised over its economic life (whatever that may be thought to be) or should it not be amortised at all, but subjected to some form of impairment test? Where the cost has been less than the values allocated to the identifiable assets and liabilities, then this has traditionally been treated as negative goodwill. The issue has then been how such a credit should be released to the income statement.

1.2 Development of an international standard

1.2.1 IAS 22 and related SIC Interpretations

Until recently, the relevant international standard was IAS 22 – *Business Combinations*. The original standard was issued in November 1983, but had been revised and amended on a number of occasions since then.[3]

The SIC issued 3 interpretations relating to IAS 22: SIC-9 – *Business Combinations – Classification either as Acquisitions or Unitings of Interests*, SIC-22 – *Business Combinations – Subsequent Adjustment of Fair Values and Goodwill Initially Reported* – and SIC-28 – *Business Combinations – "Date of Exchange" and Fair Value of Equity Instruments*.

A summary of the requirements of these pronouncements can be found in section 1.2 of Chapter 6 of a previous edition of this book, *International GAAP 2005*.

1.2.2 IASB's project

In 2001 the IASB began a project to review IAS 22 as part of its initial agenda, with the objective of improving the quality of, and seeking international convergence on, the accounting for business combinations. The project on business combinations was originally considered to have two phases.

As part of phase I, the IASB published in December 2002 ED 3 – *Business Combinations*, together with an exposure draft of proposed related amendments to IAS 38 – *Intangible Assets* – and IAS 36 – *Impairment of Assets*.[4] The Board's intention in developing an IFRS as part of the first phase of the project was not to reconsider all of the requirements in IAS 22. Instead, the Board's primary focus was on:

(a) the method of accounting for business combinations;

(b) the initial measurement of the identifiable assets acquired and liabilities and contingent liabilities assumed in a business combination;

(c) the recognition of liabilities for terminating or reducing the activities of an acquiree;

(d) the treatment of any excess of the acquirer's interest in the fair value of identifiable net assets acquired in a business combination over the cost of the combination; and

(e) the accounting for goodwill and intangible assets acquired in a business combination.[5]

Phase II of the project was considered to have three aspects:[6]

- issues related to the application of the purchase method. This is being conducted as a joint project with the FASB;
- the accounting for business combinations in which separate entities or operations of entities are brought together to form a joint venture, including possible applications for 'fresh start' accounting. 'Fresh-start' accounting derives from the view that a new entity emerges as a result of a business combination. Therefore, the assets and liabilities of each of the combining entities, including assets and liabilities not previously recognised, are recorded by the new entity at their fair values; and
- the accounting for business combinations excluded from phase I, i.e.:
  - business combination involving entities (or operations of entities) under common control;
  - business combinations involving two or more mutual entities (such as mutual insurance companies or mutual cooperative entities); and
  - business combinations in which separate entities are brought together to form a reporting entity by contract only without the obtaining of an ownership interest (for example, business combinations in which separate entities are brought together by contract to form a dual listed company).

However, as the project has developed, what was regarded as being phase II is now being done as a number of separate phases.

1.2.3 IFRS 3

The first phase of the IASB's project resulted in the Board issuing, simultaneously in March 2004, IFRS 3 – *Business Combinations* – and revised versions of IAS 36 and IAS 38. The requirements of IFRS 3 are principally dealt with at 2 below. The requirements of IAS 36 relating specifically to the impairment of goodwill are dealt with at 3 below; the general requirements of IAS 36 are covered in Chapter 15. The specific requirements of IAS 38 relating to intangible assets acquired as part of a business combination are dealt with at 2.3.3 B below; the other requirements of IAS 38 are covered in Chapter 12.

A Reasons for revising IAS 22

The IASB's reasons for revising IAS 22 are set out in the introduction to IFRS 3.

IAS 22 permitted business combinations to be accounted for using one of two methods: the pooling of interests method or the purchase method. Although IAS 22 restricted the use of the pooling of interests method to business combinations classified as unitings of interests, the IASB stated that 'analysts and other users of financial statements indicated that permitting two methods of accounting for substantially similar transactions impaired the comparability of financial statements. Others argued that requiring more than one method of accounting for such transactions created incentives for structuring those transactions to achieve a desired accounting result, particularly given that the two methods produce quite different results.'[7]

The IASB went on to say that 'these factors, combined with the prohibition of the pooling of interests method in Australia, Canada and the United States, prompted the International Accounting Standards Board to examine whether, given that few combinations were understood to be accounted for in accordance with IAS 22 using the pooling of interests method, it would be advantageous for international standards to converge with those in Australia and North America by also prohibiting the method'.[8]

It is also noted that 'accounting for business combinations varied across jurisdictions in other respects as well. These included the accounting for goodwill and intangible assets acquired in a business combination, the treatment of any excess of the acquirer's interest in the fair values of identifiable net assets acquired over the cost of the business combination, and the recognition of liabilities for terminating or reducing the activities of an acquiree.'[9]

Where an acquirer purchased less than 100% of the acquiree, IAS 22 contained an option in respect of how the purchase method could be applied. The IASB 'believes that permitting similar transactions to be accounted for in dissimilar ways impairs the usefulness of the information provided to users of financial statements, because both comparability and reliability are diminished'.[10]

The IASB stated therefore that IFRS 3 had 'been issued to improve the quality of, and seek international convergence on, the accounting for business combinations' including those areas that were the primary focus of phase I of the project (see 1.2.2 above).[11]

B Main changes from IAS 22

The main changes from IAS 22 as described by the IASB are set out below.

I Method of accounting

IFRS 3 requires all business combinations within its scope to be accounted for using the purchase method, whereas IAS 22 permitted business combinations to be accounted for using one of two methods: the pooling of interests method for combinations classified as unitings of interests and the purchase method for combinations classified as acquisitions.[12]

II Recognising the identifiable assets acquired and liabilities and contingent liabilities assumed

IFRS 3 changed the requirements in IAS 22 for separately recognising the identifiable assets acquired and liabilities and contingent liabilities assumed as part of allocating the cost of a business combination.

The standard clarifies the criteria for separately recognising intangible assets of the acquiree as part of allocating the cost of a combination, such that more intangible assets will now be recognised separately from goodwill. IAS 22 required an intangible asset to be recognised if, and only if, it was probable that the future economic benefits attributable to the asset would flow to the entity, and its cost could be measured reliably. The probability recognition criterion is not included in IFRS 3 because it is always considered to be satisfied for intangible assets acquired in business combinations.[13] The effect of probability is reflected in the fair value measurement of the intangible asset.[14] Additionally, the standard includes guidance clarifying that the fair value of an intangible asset acquired in a business combination can normally be measured with sufficient reliability to qualify for recognition separately from goodwill. If an intangible asset acquired in a business combination has a finite useful life, there is a rebuttable presumption that its fair value can be measured reliably.[15] IFRS 3 also provides a large list of examples of items that meet the definition of an intangible asset and are therefore to be recognised separately from goodwill (see 2.3.3 below).

IFRS 3 restricts the recognition of restructuring or reorganisation provisions as part of allocating the cost of the combination such that they can only be made when the acquiree has, at the acquisition date, an existing liability for restructuring recognised in accordance with IAS 37 – *Provisions, Contingent Liabilities and Contingent Assets*. IAS 22 required an acquirer to recognise as part of allocating the cost of a business combination a provision for terminating or reducing the activities of the acquiree that was not a liability of the acquiree at the acquisition date, provided the acquirer satisfied specified criteria.[16]

IFRS 3 requires an acquirer to recognise separately the acquiree's contingent liabilities (as defined in IAS 37) at the acquisition date as part of allocating the cost of a business combination, provided their fair values can be measured reliably. Such contingent liabilities were, in accordance with IAS 22, subsumed within the amount recognised as goodwill or negative goodwill.[17]

III *Measuring the identifiable assets acquired and liabilities and contingent liabilities assumed*

Where an acquirer purchases less than 100% of the acquiree so that a minority interest has a stake in the identifiable assets and liabilities, IAS 22 included a benchmark and an allowed alternative treatment for the initial measurement of the identifiable net assets acquired in a business combination, and therefore for the initial measurement of any minority interests. IFRS 3 requires the acquiree's identifiable assets, liabilities and contingent liabilities recognised as part of allocating the cost of the combination to be measured initially by the acquirer at their fair values at the acquisition date. Therefore, any minority interest in the acquiree is stated at the minority's proportion of the net fair values of those items. This is consistent with IAS 22's allowed alternative treatment.[18]

IV *Subsequent accounting for goodwill*

IFRS 3 requires goodwill acquired in a business combination to be measured after initial recognition at cost less any accumulated impairment losses. Therefore, the goodwill is not amortised and instead must be tested for impairment annually, or more frequently if events or changes in circumstances indicate that it might be impaired. IAS 22 required acquired goodwill to be systematically amortised over its useful life, and included a rebuttable presumption that its useful life could not exceed twenty years from initial recognition.[19]

V Excess of acquirer's interest in the net fair value of acquiree's identifiable assets, liabilities and contingent liabilities over cost

IFRS 3 requires the acquirer to reassess the identification and measurement of the acquiree's identifiable assets, liabilities and contingent liabilities and the measurement of the cost of the combination if, at the acquisition date, the acquirer's interest in the net fair value of those items exceeds the cost of the combination. Any excess remaining after that reassessment must be recognised by the acquirer immediately in profit or loss.[20] IAS 22 required such 'negative goodwill', to be recognised in income depending on whether it related to identifiable expected future losses and expenses which did not represent liabilities at the date of the acquisition and the extent of any identifiable acquired depreciable/amortisable assets.

1.2.4 Future developments

As indicated at 1.2.2 above, the IASB is considering a number of other issues relating to business combinations in what was originally phase II of its project.

In April 2004, the IASB issued an exposure draft of proposed amendments to IFRS 3 to remove the scope exceptions for combinations by contract alone or involving mutual entities (see 2.2.2 below). This was only an interim solution and proposed that in applying the purchase method of accounting, the acquirer measures the cost of such combinations in such a way that no goodwill would be recognised in the former type of combination and that goodwill would only be recognised in the latter situation to the extent that consideration was given by the acquirer in exchange for control of the acquiree. However, the accounting for such combinations is now being addressed as part of the joint project with the FASB in dealing with issues related to the application of the purchase method.[21]

This second phase of the project involves a broad reconsideration of the requirements in IFRSs and US GAAP on applying the purchase method (which the draft revised IFRS 3 refers to as the acquisition method). An objective of the second phase of the project is to reconsider existing guidance on the application of the acquisition method in order to improve the completeness, relevance, and comparability of financial information about business combinations that is provided in financial statements. Another objective of this phase is to achieve convergence of IFRSs and US GAAP on how the acquisition method is applied.[22]

The second phase has resulted in the IASB publishing simultaneously in June 2005 a draft revised IFRS, which proposes to replace IFRS 3, together with exposure drafts proposing amendments to IAS 27 and IAS 37.[23] The comment period for the exposure drafts ended in October 2005, and the Boards also held public round-table discussions on the IFRS 3/IAS 27 proposals in late October and early November of that year. In January 2006, the Boards began their redeliberations on the proposed requirements based on the comments received. These continued over the next 18 months or so, and during that time the IASB agreed to make some changes to the original proposals contained in the exposure drafts. In July 2007, the IASB made available near-final drafts of both the revised IFRS 3 and the revised IAS 27.[24] At the time of writing, it is expected that the final versions of these revised standards will be published in late 2007 or early 2008. The revised standards are expected to be effective for business combinations where the acquisition date is on or after the beginning of annual periods starting on or after 1 July 2009, although earlier application will be permitted.[25] A summary of the expected revised IFRS 3, based on the near-final draft, is discussed at 5.1 below, whilst the expected revised IAS 27 is dealt with in Chapter 6 at 10.1.

As indicated above, the IASB had also issued an exposure draft proposing amendments to IAS 37. At that time, the IASB expected that the effective date of the revised IAS 37 would be the same as the effective date of the revised IFRS 3. However, the IASB is still redeliberating its proposals and has yet to determine the timing for the publication of a revised IAS 37. Consequently, the IASB has not reflected in the expected revised IFRS 3 its original proposals for dealing with contingencies, but has indicated that it expects to reconsider the requirements within the revised IFRS 3 when it issues the revised IAS 37.[26] The IASB proposals for revising IAS 37 are discussed in Chapter 27 at 8.1.

In the June 2005 exposure draft of the revised IFRS 3, the IASB indicated that it would consider the following issues as part of future phases of its project on business combinations:[27]

(a) the accounting for business combinations in which separate entities or businesses are brought together to form a joint venture, including possible applications of 'fresh start' accounting.

(b) the accounting for business combinations involving entities under common control.

However, the IASB's latest work plan no longer includes a project on business combinations on its agenda.[28] The expected revised IFRS 3 also indicates that neither the FASB nor the IASB currently has on its agenda a project to consider the 'fresh start' method of accounting, although they might at some future date undertake a joint project to consider the issues.[29]

2 BUSINESS COMBINATIONS

IFRS 3 does not have an effective date in the sense that it is applicable for accounting periods commencing on or after a certain date. Instead, the standard applies to the accounting for business combinations for which the agreement date is on or after 31 March 2004 (the date of issue of the standard). It also applies to the accounting for:

(a) goodwill arising from a business combination for which the agreement date is on or after 31 March 2004; or

(b) any excess of the acquirer's interest in the net fair value of the acquiree's identifiable assets, liabilities and contingent liabilities over the cost of a business combination for which the agreement date is on or after 31 March 2004.[30]

As far as previously recognised goodwill, negative goodwill and intangibles in respect of business combinations for which the agreement date was before 31 March 2004 was concerned, the standard had transitional provisions that were to be applied from the beginning of the first annual period beginning on or after 31 March 2004.[31]

Entities, however, were permitted to apply the requirements of the standard to goodwill existing at or acquired after, and to business combinations occurring from, any date before the effective dates outlined above, provided certain conditions were met.[32]

These transitional arrangements for existing IFRS adopters are no longer relevant. A discussion of the arrangements can be found in section 4.1 of Chapter 7 of the previous edition of this book, *International GAAP 2007*.

First-time adopters must account for business combinations after their date of transition to IFRS under IFRS 3. However, IFRS 1 – *First-time Adoption of International Financial Reporting Standards* – provides an exemption that permits a first-time adopter not to restate business combinations prior to its date of transition to IFRS. This is discussed at 4.2 below.

2.1 Objective of IFRS 3

IFRS 3 states that its objective 'is to specify the financial reporting by an entity when it undertakes a business combination. In particular, it specifies that all business combinations should be accounted for by applying the purchase method. Therefore, the acquirer recognises the acquiree's identifiable assets, liabilities and contingent liabilities at their fair values at the acquisition date, and also recognises goodwill, which is subsequently tested for impairment rather than amortised.'[33]

2.2 Scope of IFRS 3

Entities are required to apply the provisions of IFRS 3 when accounting for all business combinations, except for those that are specifically excluded as set out at 2.2.2 below.[34] These types of business combination that are excluded will be dealt with later as part of the IASB's ongoing project on business combinations.

2.2.1 Identifying a business combination

IFRS 3 defines a business combination as 'the bringing together of separate entities or businesses into one reporting entity'.[35] The standard then goes on to say that 'the result of nearly all business combinations is that one entity, the acquirer, obtains control of one or more other businesses, the acquiree'.[36]

For this purpose, IFRS 3 defines a 'business' as 'an integrated set of activities and assets conducted and managed for the purpose of providing:

(a) a return to investors; or

(b) lower costs or other economic benefits directly and proportionately to policyholders or participants'.[37]

It goes on to say that 'a business generally consists of inputs, processes applied to those inputs, and resulting outputs that are, or will be, used to generate revenues. If goodwill is present in a transferred set of activities and assets, the transferred set shall be presumed to be a business.'[38]

If an entity obtains control of one or more other entities that are not businesses, the bringing together of those entities is not a business combination.[39] Thus, it would seem that the requirements of IFRS 3 do not apply. However, the standard states that 'when an entity acquires a group of assets or net assets that does not constitute a business, it shall allocate the cost of the group between the individual identifiable assets and liabilities in the group based on their relative fair values at the date of acquisition'.[40] Thus, existing book values or values in the acquisition agreement may not be appropriate, and no goodwill can be recognised in such an asset deal. Where an entity acquires a controlling interest in an entity that is not a business, but obtains less than 100% of the entity, after it has allocated its purchase consideration to the individual assets acquired, it notionally grosses up those assets and recognises the difference as minority interest (see Chapter 6 at 6.1.1).

In some situations, there may be difficulties in determining whether or not an acquisition of a group of assets constitutes a business, and judgement will be required to be exercised based on the particular circumstances.

IFRS 3 indicates that a business combination may be structured in a variety of ways for legal, taxation or other reasons. It may involve the purchase by an entity of the equity of another entity, the purchase of all the net assets of another entity, the assumption of the liabilities of another entity, or the purchase of some of the net assets of another entity that together form one or more businesses. It may be effected by the issue of equity instruments, the transfer of cash, cash equivalents or other assets, or a combination thereof. The transaction may be between the shareholders of the combining entities or between one entity and the shareholders of another entity. It may involve the establishment of a new entity to control the combining entities or net assets transferred, or the restructuring of one or more of the combining entities.[41] Whatever the legal structure, if it is a 'business combination' then the requirements of IFRS 3 apply (unless it is specifically excluded by the standard).

The standard notes that a business combination may result in a parent-subsidiary relationship in which the acquirer is the parent and the acquiree a subsidiary of the acquirer. In such circumstances, the acquirer applies IFRS 3 in its consolidated financial statements. It includes its interest in the acquiree in any separate financial statements it issues as an investment in a subsidiary under IAS 27 (see Chapter 6 at 7.2).[42]

As indicated above, a business combination may involve the purchase of the net assets, including any goodwill, of another entity rather than the purchase of the equity of the other entity. The standard notes that such a combination does not result in a parent-subsidiary relationship.[43] Nevertheless, the acquirer (even if it is a single entity) will account for such a business combination under the standard in its individual or separate financial statements and consequently in any consolidated financial statements.

The standard emphasises that, included within the definition of a business combination, and therefore the scope of IFRS 3, are business combinations in which one entity obtains control of another entity but for which the date of obtaining control (i.e. the acquisition date) does not coincide with the date or dates of acquiring an ownership interest (i.e. the date or dates of exchange). This situation may arise, for example, when an investee enters into share buy-back arrangements with some of its investors and, as a result, control of the investee changes.[44] Although not explicitly discussed in the standard, it would seem that the accounting for such a business combination would be done in a similar manner to that for business combinations achieved in stages (see 2.3.7 below).

2.2.2 *Exclusions*

The standard excludes the following types of business combinations from its scope:[45]

(a) business combinations in which separate entities or businesses are brought together to form a joint venture.

(b) business combinations involving entities or businesses under common control.

(c) business combinations involving two or more mutual entities.

(d) business combinations in which separate entities or businesses are brought together to form a reporting entity by contract alone without the obtaining of an ownership interest (for example, combinations in which separate entities are brought together by contract alone to form a dual listed corporation).

These exclusions are only intended to be a temporary measure while the IASB considers the issues relating to such combinations under the later phases of its business combinations project. As discussed at 5 below, in April 2004, the IASB issued an exposure draft of proposed amendments to IFRS 3 to remove the scope exclusions (c) and (d) above. The intention being that by the time entities had to apply IFRS 3, it would already have been revised with these exclusions removed from the standard. However, this did not happen since the IASB subsequently decided that this would be dealt with as part of the joint project with the FASB in dealing with issues related to the application of the purchase method, so the exemptions remain in place in the meantime.

The exclusion in (b) above for business combinations involving entities or businesses under common control is discussed further at 2.4 below.

2.3 Purchase method of accounting

All business combinations (apart from those excluded from the scope of the standard) are accounted for by applying the purchase method.[46]

The purchase method views a business combination from the perspective of the combining entity that is identified as the acquirer. The acquirer purchases net assets and recognises the assets acquired and the liabilities and contingent liabilities assumed, including those not previously recognised by the acquiree. The measurement of the acquirer's assets and liabilities is not affected by the transaction, nor are any additional assets or liabilities of the acquirer recognised as a result of the transaction, because they are not the subjects of the transaction.[47] For example, if as a result of the business combination the acquirer is able to recognise a previously unrecognised tax asset of its own, this is not included as part of the accounting for the business combination and thus impact on the calculation of goodwill; the recognition of such an asset will be accounted for as income.

Application of the purchase method starts from the acquisition date, which is the date on which the acquirer effectively obtains control of the acquiree (see 2.3.1 below). Because control is the power to govern the financial and operating policies of an entity or business so as to obtain benefits from its activities, it is not necessary for a transaction to be closed or finalised at law before the acquirer obtains control. All pertinent facts and circumstances surrounding a business combination are considered in assessing when the acquirer has obtained control.[48]

No further guidance is given in IFRS 3 as to how to determine the acquisition date, but it is clearly a matter of fact. It cannot be artificially backdated or otherwise altered, for example, by the inclusion of terms in the agreement indicating that the acquisition is to be effective as of an earlier date, with the acquirer being entitled to profits arising after that date, even if the purchase price is based on the net asset position of the acquiree at that date.

The date control is obtained will be dependent on a number of factors, including whether the acquisition arises from a public offer or a private deal, is subject to approval by other parties, or is effected by the issue of shares.

For an acquisition by way of a public offer, the date of acquisition could be when the offer has become unconditional as a result of a sufficient number of acceptances being received or at the date that the offer closes. As noted at 2 above, IFRS 3 used the term 'agreement date' for the purposes of determining the date from which the standard was applicable, and in that context indicates that in the case of a hostile takeover, the earliest date this could be would be the date 'that a sufficient number of the acquiree's owners have accepted the acquirer's offer for the acquirer to obtain control of the acquiree'.[49] In a private deal, the date would generally be when an unconditional offer has been accepted by the vendors.

It can be seen from the above that one of the key factors is that the offer is 'unconditional'. Thus, where an offer is conditional on the approval of the acquiring entity's shareholders then until that has been received, it is unlikely that control will have been obtained. Where the offer is conditional upon receiving some form of regulatory approval, then it will depend on the nature of that approval. Where it is a substantive hurdle, such as obtaining the approval of a competition authority, it is unlikely that control could have been obtained prior to that approval. However, where the approval is merely a formality, or 'rubber-stamping' exercise, then this would not preclude control having been obtained at an earlier date.

Where the acquisition is effected by the issue of shares, then the date of control will generally be when the exchange of shares takes place.

However, as indicated above, whether control has been obtained by a certain date is a matter of fact, and all pertinent facts and circumstances surrounding a business combination need to be considered in assessing when the acquirer has obtained control.

Applying the purchase method involves the following steps:[50]

(a) identifying an acquirer;

(b) measuring the cost of the business combination; and

(c) allocating, at the acquisition date, the cost of the business combination to the assets acquired and liabilities and contingent liabilities assumed.

These steps are discussed below.

2.3.1 *Identifying the acquirer*

Since the purchase method views a business combination from the acquirer's perspective, it assumes that one of the parties to the transaction can be identified as the acquirer.[51]

IFRS 3 therefore requires that an acquirer must be identified for all business combinations. The acquirer is the combining entity that obtains control of the other combining entities or businesses.[52]

Control is defined as 'the power to govern the financial and operating policies of an entity or business so as to obtain benefits from its activities'.[53] The standard states that 'a combining entity shall be presumed to have obtained control of another combining entity when it acquires more than one-half of that other entity's voting rights, unless it can be demonstrated that such ownership does not constitute control. Even if one of the combining entities does not acquire more than one-half of the voting rights of another combining entity, it might have obtained control of that other entity if, as a result of the combination, it obtains:

(a) power over more than one-half of the voting rights of the other entity by virtue of an agreement with other investors; or

(b) power to govern the financial and operating policies of the other entity under a statute or an agreement; or

(c) power to appoint or remove the majority of the members of the board of directors or equivalent governing body of the other entity; or

(d) power to cast the majority of votes at meetings of the board of directors or equivalent governing body of the other entity.'[54]

These provisions about 'control' are equivalent to those in IAS 27 with respect to the identification of subsidiaries for the purposes of consolidation. (See Chapter 6 at 3.1)

The standard notes that although sometimes it may be difficult to identify an acquirer, there are usually indications that one exists. For example:

(a) if the fair value of one of the combining entities is significantly greater than that of the other combining entity, the entity with the greater fair value is likely to be the acquirer;

(b) if the business combination is effected through an exchange of voting ordinary equity instruments for cash or other assets, the entity giving up cash or other assets is likely to be the acquirer; and

(c) if the business combination results in the management of one of the combining entities being able to dominate the selection of the management team of the resulting combined entity, the entity whose management is able so to dominate is likely to be the acquirer.[55]

In a business combination effected through an exchange of equity interests, the standard takes the view that the entity that issues the equity interests is normally the acquirer. However, it emphasises that all pertinent facts and circumstances must be considered to determine which of the combining entities has the power to govern the financial and operating policies of the other entity (or entities) so as to obtain benefits from its (or their) activities. The standard recognises that in some business combinations, commonly referred to as reverse acquisitions, the acquirer is the entity whose equity interests have been acquired and the issuing entity is the acquiree. This might be the case when, for example, a private entity arranges to have itself 'acquired' by a smaller public entity as a means of obtaining a stock exchange listing[56] and, as part of the agreement, the directors of the public entity resign and are replaced with directors appointed by the private entity and its former owners.[57] Although legally the issuing public entity is regarded as the parent and the private entity is regarded as the subsidiary, the legal subsidiary is the acquirer if it has the power to govern the financial and operating policies of the legal parent so as to obtain benefits from its activities. Guidance on the accounting for reverse acquisitions is provided in Appendix B to IFRS 3 (see 2.3.8 below).[58]

Occasionally, a new entity is formed to issue equity instruments to effect a business combination between, for example, two other entities. In that situation, paragraph 22 of IFRS 3 requires that one of the combining entities that existed before the combination to be identified as the acquirer on the basis of the evidence available;[59] the new entity formed to effect the combination cannot be the acquirer.[60] In such a transaction, the combination between the new entity and the identified acquirer is effectively the same as if a new entity had been inserted above an existing entity. As discussed at 2.4.2 B below, such a transaction should be accounted for either as a reverse acquisition or under the pooling of interests method.

An example of such a business combination is illustrated in the 2005 financial statements of Group 4 Securicor as seen below.

Extract 7.1: Group 4 Securicor plc (2005)

Notes to the consolidated financial statements [extract]

1 **General information** [extract]

Group 4 Securicor plc is a company incorporated in the United Kingdom under the Companies Act 1985. As a result of a Scheme of Arrangement of Securicor plc, which became effective on 19 July 2004, Group 4 Securicor plc became the ultimate holding company of the Securicor plc group of companies and, on the same date, and as a result of a recommended offer for its shares, acquired Group 4 A/S, the holding company of the former security businesses of Group 4 Falck A/S. On the basis that the transaction was effected by using a new parent, Group 4 A/S was identified as the acquirer. The comparative results for the year to 31 December 2004 are therefore those of the full year of trading of the security businesses of the former Group 4 Falck A/S and the trading of the businesses of Securicor plc for the period from 20 July 2004 to 31 December 2004.

Similarly, when a business combination involves more than two combining entities, one of the combining entities that existed before the combination is identified as the acquirer on the basis of the evidence available. Determining the acquirer in such cases shall include a consideration of, amongst other things, which of the combining entities initiated the combination and whether the assets or revenues of one of the combining entities significantly exceed those of the others.[61]

An issue considered by IFRIC was whether a new entity formed to effect a business combination in which it pays cash as consideration for the business acquired could be identified as the acquirer. In March 2006, IFRIC decided that it is clear that paragraph 22 of IFRS 3 does not prohibit a newly formed entity that pays cash to effect a business combination from being identified as the acquirer; accordingly, it would not expect diversity in practice and did not take this item onto its agenda.[62]

One situation where we believe this would be appropriate is where the newly formed entity (hereafter referred to as 'Newco') is established and used on behalf of a group of investors or another entity to acquire a controlling interest in a 'target entity' in an arm's length transaction.

Example 7.1: Business combination effected by a Newco for cash consideration (1)

Entity A intends to acquire the voting shares (and therefore obtain control) of Target Entity. Entity A incorporates Newco and uses this entity to effect the business combination. Entity A provides a loan at commercial interest rates to Newco. The loan funds are used by Newco to acquire 100% of the voting shares of Target Entity in an arm's length transaction.

The group structure post-transaction is as follows:

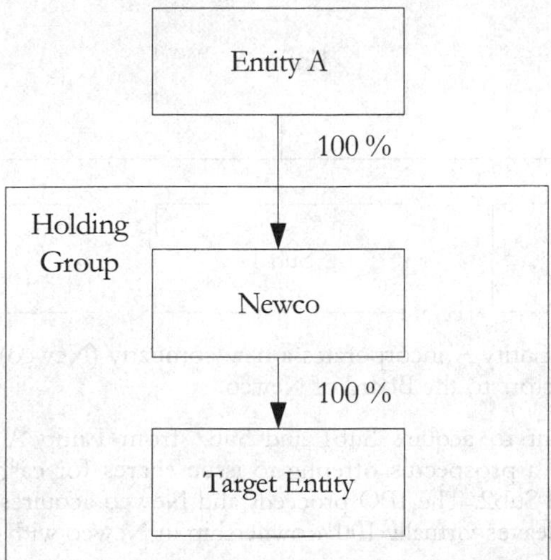

Under its local regulations, Newco is required to prepare IFRS-compliant consolidated financial statements for the Holding Group (the reporting entity). (In most situations like this, Newco would be exempt from preparing consolidated financial statements – see Chapter 6 at 4.1.)

As indicated above, under IFRS 3, the acquirer is 'the combining entity that obtains control of the other combining entities or businesses'. Whenever a new entity is formed to effect a business combination other than through the issue of shares, it is appropriate to consider that Newco as being an extension of one of the transacting parties. Where the Newco is considered to be an extension of the transacting party (or parties) that ultimately gain control of the other combining entities, the Newco would be identified as the acquirer.

In this situation, Parent Entity has obtained control of Target Entity in an arm's length transaction, using Newco to effect the acquisition. The transaction has resulted in a change in control of Target Entity and Newco is in effect an extension of Parent Entity acting at its direction to obtain control for Parent Entity. Accordingly, Newco would be identified as the acquirer at the Holding Group level.

If, rather than Parent Entity establishing Newco, a group of investors had established it as the acquiring vehicle through which they obtained control of Target Entity then again it would be appropriate for Newco to be regarded as the acquirer since it is an extension of the group of investors.

Another situation where we believe it is appropriate for a Newco to be identified as the acquirer is illustrated below.

Example 7.2: Business combination effected by a Newco for cash consideration (2)

Entity A proposes to spin-off two of its existing businesses (currently housed in two separate entities, Sub1 and Sub2) as part of an initial public offering (IPO). The existing group structure is as follows:

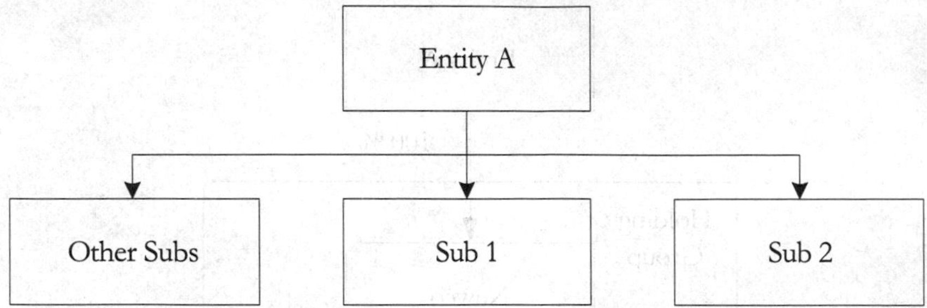

To facilitate the spin-off, Entity A incorporates a new company (Newco) with nominal equity and appoints independent directors to the Board of Newco.

Newco signs an agreement to acquire Sub1 and Sub2 from Entity A conditional on the IPO proceeding. Newco issues a prospectus offering to issue shares for cash to provide Newco with funds to acquire Sub1 and Sub2. The IPO proceeds and Newco acquires Sub1 and Sub2 for cash. Entity A's nominal equity leaves virtually 100% ownership in Newco with the new investors.

Following the IPO, the respective group structures of Entity A and Newco appear as follows:

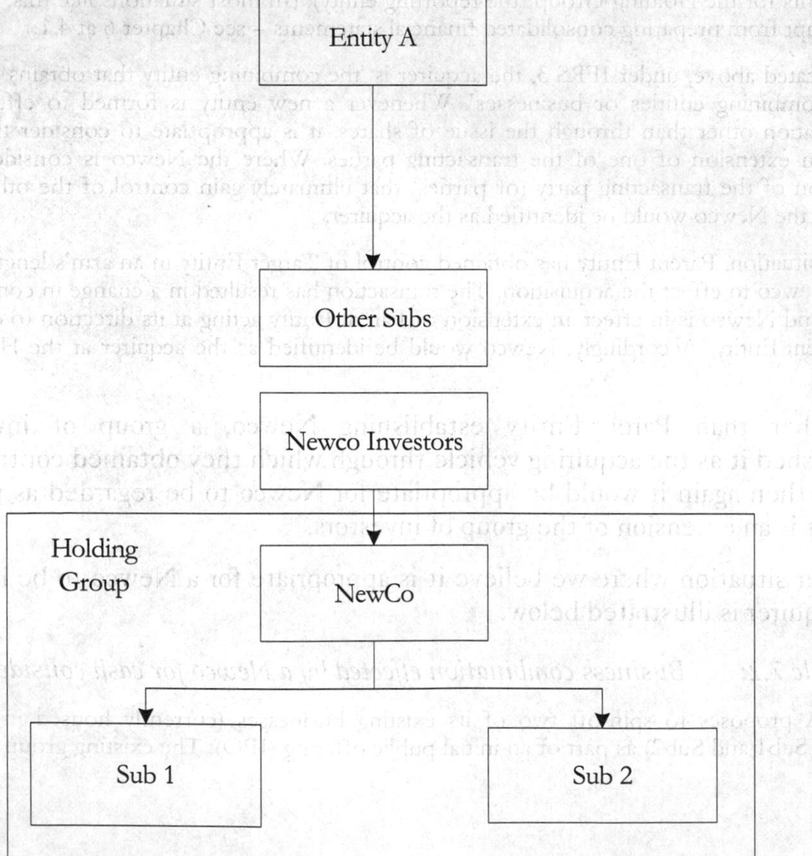

In this case, we believe it is appropriate that Newco should be identified as the acquirer. The Newco investors have obtained control and virtually 100% ownership of Sub1 and Sub2 in an arm's length transaction, using Newco to effect the acquisition. The transaction has resulted in a change in control of Sub1 and Sub2 (i.e. Entity A losing control and Newco investors, via Newco, obtaining control). Newco is in effect an extension of the Newco investors since:

- the acquisition of Sub1 and Sub2 was conditional on the IPO proceeding so that the IPO is an integral part of the transaction as a whole evidencing that Entity A did not have control of the transaction/entities; and
- there being a substantial change in the ownership of Sub1 and Sub2 by virtue of the IPO (i.e. Entity A only retains a negligible ownership interest in Newco).

Accordingly, Newco should be identified as the acquirer at the Holding Group level.

Whether a Newco formed to facilitate an IPO is capable of being identified as an acquirer depends on the facts and circumstances and ultimately requires judgement. Changes to the fact pattern could result in a different assessment. For example, where Entity A incorporates Newco and arranges for it to acquire Sub1 and Sub2 prior to the IPO proceeding (in other words, remove the conditionality element), it is likely that Newco would be viewed as an extension of Entity A or possibly an extension of Sub1 or Sub2. This is because the IPO and the reorganisation may not be seen as being part of the one integral transaction.

2.3.2 *Cost of a business combination*

Having identified the acquirer, the next step is for the acquirer to measure the cost of the business combination. IFRS 3 requires this to be the aggregate of:

(a) the fair values, at the date of exchange, of assets given, liabilities incurred or assumed, and equity instruments issued by the acquirer, in exchange for control of the acquiree; plus

(b) any costs directly attributable to the business combination.[63]

These requirements are essentially the same as those in IAS 22 and SIC-28, without reconsideration, but the IASB will be reconsidering these requirements as part of the second phase of its project.[64]

A *Date of exchange*

When a business combination is achieved in a single exchange transaction, the date of exchange coincides with the acquisition date (see 2.3 above). However, a business combination may involve more than one exchange transaction, for example when it is achieved in stages by successive share purchases. When this occurs:

(a) the cost of the combination is the aggregate cost of the individual transactions; and

(b) the date of exchange is the date of each exchange transaction (i.e. the date that each individual investment is recognised in the financial statements of the acquirer), whereas the acquisition date is the date on which the acquirer obtains control of the acquiree.[65]

The accounting for business combinations achieved in stages is discussed at 2.3.7 below.

B Assets given and liabilities incurred or assumed by the acquirer

Assets given and liabilities incurred or assumed by the acquirer in exchange for control of the acquiree are required by paragraph 24 of the standard to be measured at their fair values at the date of exchange. Fair value is defined as 'the amount for which an asset could be exchanged, or a liability settled, between knowledgeable, willing parties in an arm's length transaction'.[66] The standard gives no guidance as to how such fair values might be arrived at, other than to say that when settlement of all or any part of the cost of a business combination is deferred, the fair value of that deferred component is determined by discounting the amounts payable to their present value at the date of exchange, taking into account any premium or discount likely to be incurred in settlement.[67] No guidance is given as to what an appropriate discount rate would be. However, IAS 39 – *Financial Instruments: Recognition and Measurement* – would suggest using a rate currently charged by others for similar debt instruments (i.e. similar remaining maturity, cash flow pattern, currency, credit risk, collateral and interest basis).[68] Where the assets given as consideration or the liabilities incurred or assumed by the acquirer are financial assets or financial liabilities under IAS 39, then it would seem appropriate that the guidance in determining the fair values of such financial instruments should be followed (see Chapter 20 at 4).

An example of a company giving an investment in another entity as part of the consideration for the acquisition of a business is Reuters as shown in the following extract.

Extract 7.2: Reuters Group plc (2005)

Notes to the financial statements [extract]

36 **Acquisitions** [extract]

On 3 June 2005, Reuters purchased the trade and assets of Telerate and 100% of the share capital of three of Telerate's subsidiaries in exchange for cash and the Group's 14% holding in Savvis convertible preference shares. In addition, on 6 June 2005, Reuters carried out a merger with Quick Telerate, the distributor of Telerate's products in Japan. All of these purchases have been accounted for as acquisitions. As a result of this acquisition, Reuters disposed of its 4.85% holding in Quick Corporation, the parent of Quick Telerate. The profit on disposal is detailed within note 37.

	Book value £m	Fair value adjustments £m	Provisional fair value £m
Non-current assets:			
Intangible assets	7	49	56
Property, plant and equipment	3	(1)	2
Current assets:			
Cash and cash equivalents	16	–	16
Other current assets	19	–	19
Current liabilities	(31)	1	(30)
Non-current liabilities	(3)	(2)	(5)
Net assets acquired	**11**	**47**	**58**
Goodwill			72
Total consideration			**130**

Consideration satisfied by:	
Cash (including £8 million of transaction fees)	99
Fair value of investment in Savvis convertible preference shares	31
Total consideration	**130**

The fair value adjustments in respect of intangible assets are due to the recognition of £2 million is respect of trademarks and £53 million in respect of customer relationships, which have been independently valued, partly offset by the write-off of £6 million of intangibles that were recorded on Telerate's balance sheet prior to the acquisition. Goodwill represents the value of synergies arising from the acquisition and the acquiree's assembled work force. The adjustments to property, plant and equipment, current assets, current liabilities and non-current liabilities relate to valuation adjustments and are provisional, based on management's best estimates. The fair values adjustments relating to the Telerate acquisition will be finalised in the 2006 financial statements.

The outflow of cash and cash equivalents on the acquisition can be calculated as follows:

	£m
Cash consideration	99
Cash acquired	(16)
Total outflow of cash and cash equivalents	**83**

From the date of acquisition to 31 December 2005, the acquisition contributed £74 million to turnover, £5 million loss before interest and amortisation of intangibles and £5 million loss before amortisation, but after interest.

If the acquisitions had been made at the beginning of the financial year, Telerate would have contributed £133 million to revenue and incurred a £21 million loss. This information takes into account the amortisation of acquired intangible assets, together with related income tax effects and should not be viewed as indicative of the results of operations that would have occurred if the acquisitions had been made at the beginning of the year.

In business combinations where some of the consideration is deferred, it may be that this will not be settled by cash, but by shares. IFRS 3 makes no explicit reference to such a situation, and IFRS 2 – *Share-based Payment* – explicitly scopes out from its provisions 'transactions in which an entity acquires goods as part of the net assets acquired in a business combination to which IFRS 3' applies. It also goes on to say that 'equity instruments issued in a business combination in exchange for control of the acquiree are not within the scope of' IFRS 2.[69] However, the contractual obligation will be a financial instrument within the scope of IAS 32 – *Financial Instruments: Presentation*. In relation to the acquirer in a business combination, IAS 32 only scopes out of its provisions 'contracts for contingent consideration' (see E below).[70]

Accordingly, the determination of the fair value of deferred consideration that is to be settled by shares will depend on whether it is an equity instrument or a financial liability under IAS 32 (see Chapter 19). In many situations, the consideration to be given will be fixed as a monetary amount, with the number of shares to be issued varying based on the share price at the date of their ultimate issue. In that case, the deferred consideration is a financial liability, and should be valued as outlined above. When the liability is ultimately settled by the issue of the shares, then the entity will derecognise the financial liability and credit equity with the then carrying amount of the liability. On the other hand, where the consideration will be settled by a fixed number of shares, then it will qualify as an equity instrument under

IAS 32. In that case, the fair value of such deferred consideration should be based on the guidance in C below, rather than outlined above for deferred consideration. However, in this situation the fair value of the 'equity instrument' at the date of exchange would need to take into account, for example, an allowance for any estimated dividends on the shares that will not be payable during the deferral period. The amount attributed should be included within equity, possibly under a caption of 'shares to be issued'.

The cost of a business combination includes liabilities incurred or assumed by the acquirer in exchange for control of the acquiree. IFRS 3 states explicitly that future losses or other costs expected to be incurred as a result of a combination are not liabilities incurred or assumed by the acquirer in exchange for control of the acquiree, and are not, therefore, included as part of the cost of the combination.[71] The very restricted circumstances in which future losses or other costs may be recognised as part of the liabilities of the acquired entity are described at 2.3.3 A below.

C *Equity instruments issued by the acquirer*

Where equity instruments issued by the acquirer are given as consideration, IFRS 3 states that the published price at the date of exchange of a quoted equity instrument provides the best evidence of the instrument's fair value and is used, except in rare circumstances.[72] This value should be used even if a different share price was used in agreeing the terms of the business combination. Although IFRS 3 refers to the 'published price' it does not explicitly say whether this should be the 'bid' price, 'offer' price or 'mid' price at that date. However, as noted below, it does refer to the guidance on determining the fair value of equity instruments (held as investments) set out in IAS 39 which would indicate that the 'bid' price should be used. Other evidence and valuation methods are considered only in the rare circumstances when the acquirer can demonstrate that the published price at the date of exchange is an unreliable indicator of fair value, and that the other evidence and valuation methods provide a more reliable measure of the equity instrument's fair value. The standard takes the view that the published price at the date of exchange is an unreliable indicator only when it has been affected by the thinness of the market.[73] The fact that the price may have been affected by an undue price fluctuation is not considered by the IASB to be a justification for not using the published price at the date of exchange.[74] Also, the Basis for Conclusions indicates that 'estimates of premiums for large, and discounts for small, blocks of equity instruments issued in comparison to that exchanged in observable transactions are not considered'.[75]

If the published price at the date of exchange is an unreliable indicator or if a published price does not exist for equity instruments issued by the acquirer, the standard states that the fair value of those instruments could, for example, be estimated by reference to their proportional interest in the fair value of the acquirer or by reference to the proportional interest in the fair value of the acquiree obtained, whichever is the more clearly evident. The fair value at the date of exchange of monetary assets given to equity holders of the acquiree as an alternative to equity instruments may also provide evidence of the total fair value given by the acquirer in exchange for control of the acquiree. In any event, the standard requires that all aspects of the combination, including significant factors influencing the negotiations, are to be considered. Reference is also made to the further guidance on determining the fair value of equity instruments (held as investments) set out in IAS 39 (see Chapter 20 at 4).[76]

D Costs directly attributable to the business combination

The cost of a business combination includes any costs directly attributable to the combination, such as professional fees paid to accountants, legal advisers, valuers and other consultants to effect the combination. General administrative costs, including the costs of maintaining an acquisitions department, and other costs that cannot be directly attributed to the particular combination being accounted for are not included in the cost of the combination: they are recognised as an expense when incurred.[77] Although not explicitly stated in IFRS 3, it would appear that it is only incremental costs that should be included.

It may be that an entity engages another party to investigate or assist in identifying a potential target. Whether any fee payable to such a party can be included as part of the cost of a business combination will depend on whether the work performed can be regarded as directly attributable to that particular business combination. Where the fee is payable only if the combination takes place then it should be included as part of the cost.

In some jurisdictions, tax relief may be given in respect of certain of the costs included as part of the cost of a business combination. In our view, any related taxes should not be netted against the costs in line with the 'no offsetting' principle in IAS 1 – *Presentation of Financial Statements*.[78] The implications for deferred taxation are discussed in Chapter 26 at 6.2.4.

IFRS 3 requires the costs of arranging and issuing financial liabilities to be an integral part of the liability issue transaction, even when the liabilities are issued to effect a business combination, rather than costs directly attributable to the combination. Therefore, entities shall not include such costs in the cost of a business combination. In accordance with IAS 39, such costs are to be included in the initial measurement of the liability (see Chapter 20 at 2.3).[79]

Similarly, the costs of issuing equity instruments are an integral part of the equity issue transaction, even when the equity instruments are issued to effect a business combination, rather than costs directly attributable to the combination. Therefore, entities shall not include such costs in the cost of a business combination. In accordance with IAS 32, such costs reduce the proceeds from the equity issue.[80] While these requirements will affect the amount at which the entity's liabilities and equity are recorded in the consolidated financial statements, they do not affect the measurement of goodwill in the business combination.

When professional advisors provide advice on all aspects of the business combination, including the arranging and issuing of financial liabilities and/or issuing equity instruments, it will be necessary for some allocation of the fees payable to be made, possibly by obtaining a breakdown from the relevant advisor.

It may be that an entity at its balance sheet date is in the process of acquiring another business and has incurred costs that are considered to be directly attributable to that expected business combination. At the balance sheet date, the entity has not yet obtained control over the business. In this situation how should the costs be accounted for? One view would be that the costs have to be expensed since at the balance sheet date there has been no business combination. However, we believe that since directly attributable costs are to be included in the cost of a business combination, then the costs should be carried forward as an asset from the date that is considered probable that the business combination will be completed. Any costs incurred prior to the date that it is considered probable that the business combination will be completed should be expensed, and remain written off regardless of whether the acquisition takes place; they cannot be reinstated and capitalised at a later date. In the subsequent period when the business combination is completed, the costs carried forward will be reclassified as part of the cost of the business combination (and therefore into goodwill). If in the subsequent period it is no longer considered probable that the business combination will be completed, then the costs initially recognised as an asset will be expensed in the income statement.

E Adjustments to the cost of a business combination contingent on future events ('Contingent consideration')

IFRS 3 recognises that the terms of a business combination agreement may provide for an adjustment to the cost of the combination contingent on future events, such as a specified level of profit being maintained or achieved in future periods, or on the market price of the instruments issued being maintained.[81]

When a business combination agreement provides for an adjustment to the cost of the business combination contingent on future events, IFRS 3 requires the acquirer to include the amount of the adjustment in the cost of the combination at the acquisition date if the adjustment is probable and can be measured reliably.[82] If the future events do not occur or the estimate needs to be revised, the cost of the business combination is to be adjusted accordingly,[83] (unless the payment to the seller is compensation for a reduction in value of consideration received as discussed below).

The standard states that 'it is usually possible to estimate the amount of any such adjustment at the time of initially accounting for the combination without impairing the reliability of the information, even though some uncertainty exists'.[84] This is more likely to be the case in those situations where the contingent consideration is based on the acquiree maintaining a level of profits which it is currently earning (either for a particular period or as an average over a set period) or achieving profits which it is currently budgeting.

However, when a business combination agreement provides for such an adjustment, that adjustment is not included in the cost of the combination at the time of initially accounting for the combination if it either is not probable or cannot be measured reliably. If that adjustment subsequently becomes probable and can be measured reliably, the additional consideration shall be treated as an adjustment to the cost of the combination.[85]

Any subsequent adjustments in respect of such contingent consideration will consequently be reflected in the carrying amount of goodwill. However, if an impairment loss has already been recognised in respect of the goodwill (see 3 below), this is likely to require a further impairment loss to be recognised.

Where contingent consideration for a business combination does become probable after the date of acquisition, what amount should be recognised as the adjustment to the cost of acquisition and how should the adjustment be reflected in the financial statements?

Example 7.3: Contingent consideration subsequently recognised

Entity A acquires Entity B on 31 December 2006 where consideration of $8 million is contingent on meeting a profit target by 31 December 2009.

At the date of acquisition it is not considered probable that the acquiree will meet the profit target. Accordingly, no amount is recognised as part of the cost of the acquisition in the financial statements for 31 December 2006. However, at 31 December 2007 it is considered probable that Entity B will meet the profit target.

Assuming a discount rate of 8% as at the date of acquisition (31 December 2006) and a discount rate of 7% as at the date of probability of meeting conditions (31 December 2007) the relevant present values are as follows:

	PV at 8%	PV at 7%
	$	$
31 December 2006	6,350,658	6,530,383
Interest for 2007	508,053	457,127
31 December 2007	6,858,711	6,987,510
Interest for 2008	548,696	489,126
31 December 2008	7,407,407	7,476,636
Interest for 2009	592,593	523,364
31 December 2009	8,000,000	8,000,000

What amount should be recognised as the adjustment to the cost of the combination at 31 December 2007 and how should it be reflected in the financial statements?

One view is that the adjustment should be calculated retrospectively, as if it had occurred as at the date of acquisition. Accordingly, the cost of the investment and goodwill would be adjusted by $6,350,658 (being the present value at the date of acquisition), with interest charged since the date of acquisition of $508,053.

However, we do not consider this view appropriate. The adjustment is due to a change in probability which is generally considered to be a change in estimate. As discussed in Chapter 3, changes in estimates are recognised prospectively from the date of change. Therefore at the date that the contingent event becomes probable it should be recognised as a change in estimate and measured at that date, taking into account the period in which the expected payment will be made. It is, therefore, discounted at the rate determined at the date that the contingent consideration is recognised to reflect the fair value of the consideration expected to be given. Accordingly, an adjustment of $6,987,510 to the purchase price and therefore goodwill is recognised at 31 December 2007. The unwinding of the discount will be reflected in the income statement in 2008 and 2009. However, the resulting liability should continue to be reassessed at each reporting date thereafter for changes in estimated cash flows, including changes in discount rates, and any necessary adjustment made to the cost of the combination (and therefore goodwill).

Paragraph 35 of IFRS 3 also recognises that in some circumstances, the acquirer may be required to make a subsequent payment to the seller as compensation for a reduction in the value of the assets given, equity instruments issued or liabilities incurred or assumed by the acquirer in exchange for control of the acquiree. For example, the acquirer may guarantee the market price of equity or debt instruments issued as part of the cost of the business combination and is required to issue additional equity or debt instruments to restore the originally determined cost. In such cases, no increase in the cost of the business combination is recognised. In the case of equity instruments, the fair value of the additional payment is offset by an equal reduction in the value attributed to the instruments initially issued.[86] Thus, it would appear that any increase reflected in equity for the extra equity instruments issued is offset by a corresponding debit to equity. In the case of debt instruments, the additional payment is regarded as a reduction in the premium or an increase in the discount on the initial issue.[87] The extra payment will be taken to the income statement as part of an increased interest expense over the period of the debt instrument.

I Distinguishing 'contingent consideration' from other arrangements

The requirements of IFRS 3 discussed above set out the accounting for 'contingent consideration' under the standard but the term is not defined. It is important to be able to identify those arrangements that represent contingent consideration and those that do not as contingent consideration generally results in some form of adjustment to the accounting for a business combination,.

In our view, an arrangement that provides for additional payments to be made to the vendors of an acquiree should be accounted for as contingent consideration if the payment:

(a) is made as consideration for the acquisition of a controlling interest in the acquiree (based on the substance of the arrangement); *and*

(b) is contingent on future events that relate to either:

  (i) the value of the acquiree (for example, an acquirer makes an additional cash payment if the acquiree achieves a profit target); *or*

  (ii) the value of the purchase consideration (specifically in terms of the acquirer compensating the vendor for a reduction in the value of the consideration previously given, for example, an acquirer issues additional shares in order to compensate for a loss in value of the shares that were issued at the acquisition date).

These criteria are discussed below. However, as indicated earlier, accounting for contingencies of type (i) and (ii) is quite different. Contingencies that relate to the value of the acquiree result in an adjustment to the cost of the combination (and goodwill). However, where the contingency relates to the value of the purchase consideration, the fair value of the additional amount paid is offset by an equal reduction in the value of that initial consideration. Accordingly, there is no change in the total cost of the combination (nor to goodwill).

It is necessary to consider the substance of the arrangement to determine whether additional payments are made as consideration of the acquisition of a controlling interest in the acquiree (criterion (a) above). Where a vendor has a continuing relationship with the acquirer (for example, an on-going customer or supplier relationship) it is necessary to determine in what capacity payments are made to the vendor. As there is no specific guidance, the following factors may be considered in evaluating the substance of the arrangement:

- whether the additional payments are linked to the on-going relationship;
- what are the reasons for the contingent payments; and
- the nature of the formula for determining the contingent payments.

A particular example of this type of situation is where the vendors become or continue to be key employees of the acquiree subsequent to the acquisition. This is discussed further at II below.

Criterion (b) above involves a consideration of whether the contingency relates to either the value of the acquiree or the value of the purchase consideration. Whilst contingent consideration is not defined in IFRS 3, the examples given in IFRS 3 are of contingencies relating to either the value of the business acquired or the value of the purchase consideration (the latter in terms of the acquirer being obliged to make additional payments to compensate the vendor for a reduction in the value of the consideration given). If it is not clear what the contingency relates to, it will be necessary to consider its nature carefully in order to determine whether it should be accounted for as contingent consideration or separately from the business combination.

Examples of 'contingent consideration' relating to the value of the acquiree

Arrangements that provide for additional payments to be made to the vendors of an acquiree that are contingent on future events relating to the value of the acquiree, and thus will result in adjustments to the cost of the business combination, can take a number of forms. Examples would include:

- an additional payment of €1m if the acquiree's profit in the year after acquisition exceeds €2m;
- an additional payment of $1m if a drug currently under development receives regulatory approval at a later date; and
- an additional payment of X% of actual EBITDA of the acquiree in the year after acquisition.

The first example of an 'earn-out' clause – whereby the acquirer agrees to pay additional amounts if the future earnings of the acquiree exceed specified amounts – is a typical example of contingent consideration relating to the value of the acquiree.

The second example is where the contingency relates to a key business-related milestone that will have an impact on the value of the acquiree.

In both of these examples, there is uncertainty linked to a specific event as to whether an additional payment will be made (profit exceeding X or drug approval). In the third case, which also relates to the value of the acquiree, there will be an additional payment (on the assumption that a negative EBITDA is highly unlikely for that business) but there is uncertainty as to how much the payment will be.

In our view, IFRS 3 requires an adjustment to the cost of the business combination in all of these situations. 'Future events' should include events that affect the amount of the payment and not just those that affect whether a specified payment is required or not. Thus, any consideration for a business combination where the amount or the timing is unknown with certainty is contingent consideration.

Examples of 'contingent consideration' relating to the value of the purchase consideration

Arrangements that represent contingent consideration relating to the value of the purchase consideration are illustrated below.

Example 7.4: Acquirer guarantees the value of shares issued as consideration

Acquirer, a listed entity, acquires 100% of the issued shares of Target. The consideration is 10,000 shares of Acquirer that have a fair value of £100 each (i.e. a total value of £1m) at the date of acquisition. Under the terms of the purchase agreement, Acquirer guarantees that the value of the shares will not be less than £100 each one year after the acquisition date. If the share price is below £100 at that time, Acquirer will issue sufficient additional shares so that the total value of all shares given is £1m.

The guarantee satisfies the criteria for classification as contingent consideration. It is issued in exchange for the ownership of Target and does not relate to any other arrangement with the vendor. It relates specifically to the value of the 10,000 shares issued as consideration. Although the guarantee meets the definition of a financial liability it is also contingent consideration and is, therefore, accounted for under IFRS 3 rather than IAS 39.

In this case, no increase in the cost of the business combination is recognised – the contingent payment is effectively regarded as an adjustment to the original consideration. So, if Acquirer's share price has fallen to £80 one year after the acquisition date, then the 10,000 shares issued are now only worth £800,000. Under the agreement, Acquirer is obliged to issue a further 2,500 shares (worth £200,000 at the current price) so that a total of 12,500 shares have been issued that are now worth £1m. The value of the new shares is offset by an equal reduction in the value attributed to the shares originally issued i.e. the first 10,000 shares are now regarded as having been issued at a price of £80, being £800,000. The total cost of the combination remains £1m.

Example 7.5: Acquirer issues a put option on its shares that will be settled net in cash

Acquirer acquires 100% of the issued shares of Target. The consideration consists of 10,000 shares of the Acquirer that have a fair value of £100 each (i.e. a total value of £1m) at the date of acquisition. In addition, as part of the business combination agreement, Acquirer issues to the vendor a put option on 10,000 of its shares that will be settled net in cash. That is, Acquirer gives the vendor the right to receive and Acquirer the obligation to pay the shortfall of the fair value of the 10,000 Acquirer's shares at the exercise date compared to a fixed amount (the 'exercise price') representing the value of the shares at the date of the business combination, if vendor exercises that right. The cash settled put option can be exercised one year after the acquisition date. Any payments made by Acquirer under the put option are contingent on the vendor exercising its right under the put option.

The put option satisfies the criteria for classification as contingent consideration. It is issued as part of the consideration for a controlling interest in Target and does not relate to any other arrangement with the vendor. It relates specifically to the value of the 10,000 shares issued as consideration. Although the put option meets the definition of a financial liability it is also contingent consideration and is, therefore, accounted for under IFRS 3 rather than IAS 39.

The contingent payment is effectively regarded as an adjustment to the original consideration and no increase in the cost of the business combination is recognised. If Acquirer's share price has fallen to £80 then the 10,000 shares issued are now worth £800,000. Vendor exercises the rights under the put options and Acquirer is obliged to pay £200,000. The original consideration in shares is now considered to have been only £800,000 rather than £1m. This is corrected by debiting equity and crediting liability at £200,000. The total cost of the combination remains £1m.

Examples of arrangements that are not 'contingent consideration'

The following examples illustrate arrangements where the additional payments that may be made to the vendors under the business combination agreement should not be accounted for as 'contingent consideration' under IFRS 3.

Example 7.6: Business combination agreement commits acquirer to undertake capital expenditure

Target is a State-owned organisation that is in the process of being privatised. Acquirer acquires 100% of the issued shares of Target. The privatisation agreement with the State commits Acquirer to undertake capital expenditure in connection with the activities of Target; otherwise, Acquirer has to pay a penalty to the state equivalent to the unfulfilled capital expenditure. However, Acquirer expects to carry out the capital expenditure and the obligation is not onerous.

The penalty arrangement does not satisfy the criteria for classification as contingent consideration.

Firstly, the contingent penalty payments are not made as consideration for the acquisition of an interest in Target. Acquirer will only be required to pay the penalty in the event that it fails to meet the capital expenditure commitments. The penalty arrangement is, in substance, an incentive to Acquirer to undertake the capital expenditure. Further, the formula for determining the contingent payment is by reference to the capital expenditure not undertaken, as opposed to the value of Target.

This is also consistent with paragraph 28 of IFRS 3 which states that 'future losses or other costs expected to be incurred *as a result of* a business combination *are not liabilities incurred or assumed by the acquirer in exchange for control of the acquiree*, and are not, therefore, included as part of the cost of the combination.' [emphasis added] That is, whilst the payment of the penalty may arise as a result of Acquirer having acquired Target (and as a result of Acquirer failing to undertake the capital expenditure commitments), any such penalty payment is not made as consideration for the acquisition of a controlling interest in Target.

Secondly, the contingency relates neither to the value of the business acquired nor to the value of the consideration given (i.e. payment is contingent on Acquirer failing to undertake the capital expenditure commitments).

However, if Acquirer knew at the time of the acquisition that the capital expenditure would not be undertaken, or if the obligation to undertake the capital expenditure would have been onerous at the date of the business combination, then the Acquirer would have a liability at that time which would form part of the cost of the combination.

Example 7.7: Vendor retains a customer relationship with acquiree and is entitled to volume rebates on purchases it makes

Target is a subsidiary of Vendor Entity. Target provides goods and services to Vendor Entity that represent a significant portion of Target's business. Acquirer acquires 100% of the issued shares of Target. The purchase price is considered to represent the fair value of Target.

As part of the business combination agreement, Acquirer agrees to pay Vendor Entity a volume rebate for the next 5 years if Vendor Entity's purchases from Target exceed a specified amount in each of those years). The volume rebate offered is consistent with terms offered to other customers.

The volume rebate arrangement with the Vendor should not be accounted for as contingent consideration as it does not satisfy the criteria.

Firstly, it is not consideration for the acquisition of a controlling interest in Target:

- The purchase price paid for the issued shares of Target is considered to represent fair value of Target; and
- Acquirer will only be required to pay the volume rebates in the event that Vendor Entity's purchases exceed a specified amount. The volume rebate arrangement is merely a means of securing Vendor Entity's custom for the next 5 years. Therefore, whilst the volume rebate arrangement arises by virtue of Acquirer having acquired Target, it does not represent additional consideration for the acquisition of a controlling interest in Target.

This is also consistent with paragraph 28 of IFRS 3 (see Example 7.6 above).

Secondly, the contingency relates neither to the value of the business acquired nor to the value of the consideration given because payment is contingent on Vendor Entity's future purchases exceeding a specified amount.

Example 7.8: Acquirer issues to the vendor a call option on its shares that will be settled net in cash

Acquirer acquires 100% of the issued shares of Target. The consideration consists of 10,000 shares of the Acquirer. In addition, as part of the business combination agreement, Acquirer issues to the vendor call options on 1,000 of its shares exercisable at a fixed price that will be settled net in cash. That is, Acquirer gives the vendor the right to receive and Acquirer the obligation to pay the excess of the fair value of 1,000 of Acquirer's shares at the exercise date over the exercise price, if the vendor exercises that right. The cash settled call option can be exercised at anytime up until maturity date. Any payments made by Acquirer under the call option are contingent on the vendor exercising its right under the call option.

In this situation, the call option should not be accounted for as contingent consideration. Whilst it is granted as part of the consideration for acquisition of a controlling interest in Target (and therefore satisfies the first criterion for classification as contingent consideration) it does not satisfy the second criterion. This is because the contingency ultimately relates to the market price of Acquirer's own ordinary shares. As such, the contingency does not relate to the value of the acquiree (i.e. Target). Obviously since Target is now part of the Acquirer group, there will be some link between the value of Target and the value of the option issued by Acquirer. However, normally this indirect link would not justify treating the option as contingent consideration as the value of the option is likely to be much more directly affected by the performance of the Acquirer rather than the Target group.

Further, any payment made by Acquirer under the call option is not made to 'restore' the value of consideration previously given. Rather, the Acquirer's payments, if any, under the call option will increase as the value of its shares goes up and will decrease as the value of its shares goes down. Therefore, there is no element of compensation or restoration of value in the event that the value of the 10,000 shares issued as consideration goes down. As such, the contingency does not relate to the value of the share consideration given.

The call option represents a financial liability as at the acquisition date. It should therefore be accounted for consistent with all other liabilities incurred/assumed in exchange for control of the acquiree (see 2.3.2 B above). That is, the fair value of the call option at the date of the business combination will be included in the cost of the combination. The call option obligation is a derivative that will be remeasured to fair value throughout its life, with fair value remeasurements recognised in profit or loss for the period.

II Contingent consideration relating to future services

A particular example of a situation where vendors may have a continuing relationship with the acquirer is where they become or continue to be key employees of the acquiree subsequent to the acquisition with positions that may affect the financial results of the acquiree.

IFRS 3 does not distinguish between contingent consideration that, in substance, is additional purchase price and contingent consideration that, in substance, represents compensation for future services. However, consistent with the discussion at I above, we believe that an acquirer must make such a distinction and therefore identify contingent consideration that is, in substance, compensation for future services, and account for this separately from the cost of the combination. This is because the IASB's *Framework* requires that in order for the information to represent faithfully the transactions, they should be accounted for in accordance with their substance, rather than their legal form, which may not be consistent with the substance and economic reality.[88] Therefore, where a vendor is also a continuing employee it is necessary to determine whether payments are made to them in their capacity as vendor or as employee.

If, for example, the consideration takes the form of share-based payments, it is necessary to determine how much of the share-based payment relates to the acquisition of control (which forms part of the cost of combination, accounted for under IFRS 3) and how much relates to the provision of future services (which is a post-combination operating expense accounted for under IFRS 2). This would be the case if, for example, the vendor of an acquired entity receives a share-based payment for transferring control of the entity and for remaining in continuing employment.

There is currently no IFRS or interpretation containing guidance for evaluating the substance of the contingent consideration or determining an appropriate split. However, under the hierarchy set out in IAS 8 – *Accounting Policies, Changes in Accounting Estimates and Errors* (see Chapter 3 at 4.3) further guidance for making such an evaluation can be found in US GAAP where under EITF 95-8 – *Accounting for Contingent Consideration Paid to the Shareholders for an Acquired Enterprise in a Purchase Business Combination* – the following factors are considered:

(a) whether the consideration is linked to continuing employment or not;

(b) whether payments made to vendors who are employees are comparable with payments to vendors who are not employees or to employees who are not vendors;

(c) what the reasons are for the contingent payments; and

(d) the nature of the formula for determining contingent consideration.

III Contingent transaction costs

As indicated at I above, one of the examples of contingent consideration is where an additional payment is made if the acquiree's profits exceed a certain amount. In some business combinations an entity may agree to pay an adviser a fee for services relating to a business combination. If that fee is contingent on the acquiree achieving a specified profit hurdle can this be accounted for as contingent consideration arising on the business combination?

Example 7.9: Contingent transaction costs

Entity A engages Entity X, which has specific technical knowledge, to assist in identifying an investment target. Entity X recommends that Entity A purchase Entity B. Entity A has agreed to pay Entity X a performance fee in the event that the return from its investment in Entity B exceeds a specified target. Can such a fee be regarded as 'contingent consideration' and therefore any reassessment of the fee payable accounted for as an adjustment to the cost of the business combination, and therefore adjusted against goodwill?

The contingent consideration requirements of IFRS 3 only apply 'when a business combination agreement provides for an adjustment to the cost of the combination'. By its nature, a business combination agreement is an agreement between the vendor and the purchaser – it does not include agreements between the purchaser and third parties unconnected with the vendor. Thus, in our view, the payment to Entity X is not contingent consideration as it is not part of the agreement between the vendor and the purchaser. It arises from a separate agreement with the third party adviser.

Accordingly, whilst the payment to Entity X is part of the cost of the combination it must be measured as at the date of acquisition. Any subsequent remeasurement cannot be adjusted against the cost of the combination except where it is an adjustment upon completion of the initial accounting (see 2.3.6 A below). However, an adjustment to the initial accounting must reflect conditions as they existed at the date of the combination and does not take into account subsequent events.

IV Contingent consideration to be settled by equity instruments

In some business combination agreements involving contingent consideration, it may be that additional consideration will not be settled by cash, but by shares. IFRS 3 makes no explicit reference to such a situation, and IFRS 2 explicitly scopes out from its provisions 'transactions in which an entity acquires goods as part of the net assets acquired in a business combination to which IFRS 3' applies. It also goes on to say that 'equity instruments issued in a business combination in exchange for control of the acquiree are not within the scope of' IFRS 2.[89] In addition, IAS 32 also scopes out of its provisions 'contracts for contingent consideration'.[90]

In practice, there is a wide variety of share-settled contingent consideration arrangements, but they are generally based on one of two models:

- Arrangements whereby shares are issued to a particular value based on certain conditions being met, e.g. if profits are €A then additional consideration of €M will be given, to be satisfied by shares based on the share price at date of issue.

- Arrangements whereby a particular number of shares are issued if certain conditions are met, e.g. if profits are €A then X shares will be issued, but if profits are €B then Y shares will be issued.

The issues that need to be considered in accounting for such arrangements are:

- If the consideration is recognised, should it be classified as a liability or as equity?
- How should the consideration be valued, both on initial recognition and if re-assessed at a later date?

Example 7.10: Share-settled contingent consideration (1)

Entity P acquires a 100% interest in Entity S on 31 December 2008. As part of the consideration arrangements, additional consideration will be payable on 1 January 2012, based on Entity S meeting certain profit targets over the 3 years ended 31 December 2011, as follows:

Profit target (average profits over 3 year period)	*Additional consideration*
€1m but less than €1.25m	€5m
€1.25m but less than €1.5m	€6m
€1.5m+	€7.5m

Any additional consideration will be satisfied by issuing the appropriate number of shares with a value equivalent to the additional consideration payable based on Entity P's share price at 1 January 2012.

At the date of acquisition, Entity P considers that it is probable that Entity S will meet the first profit target, but not the others.

How should Entity P classify the additional consideration in its financial statements for the year ended 31 December 2008, and what amount should be recognised in respect of it?

Contracts for contingent consideration are specifically scoped out of both IFRS 2 and IAS 32. IFRS 2 requires equity-settled share-based payment transactions to be reflected in equity (see Chapter 31 at 4). However, in our view the principles of IAS 32 appear more relevant than those of IFRS 2 in determining the appropriate classification of such arrangements. On that basis, the contingent consideration in this situation is of the type of arrangement considered in paragraph 21 of IAS 32 whereby an 'entity may have a contractual right or obligation to receive or deliver a number of its own shares or other equity instruments that varies so that the fair value of the entity's own equity instruments to be received or delivered equals the amount of the contractual right or obligation'. Accordingly, classification as a liability seems appropriate.

On the basis that the consideration is reflected as a liability then, as with contingent consideration payable in cash, the amount to be recognised at 31 December 2008 should be the present value of the €5m consideration expected to be payable on 1 January 2012.

If at 31 December 2009, Entity P considers that is it is probable that Entity S will now meet the second target, it should remeasure the liability at that date to the present value of the €6m that is now expected to be payable on 1 January 2012 with a corresponding adjustment to goodwill, having reflected the unwinding of the discount on the original €5m in the income statement (see Example 7.3 above).

In the above example, the arrangement was of the type where the shares issued to settle the consideration were equivalent to a particular value. However, what if the arrangement was of the type where a particular number of shares are to be issued to satisfy the consideration?

Example 7.11: Share-settled contingent consideration (2)

Assume the same facts as in Example 7.10 above, except that the additional consideration will be payable as follows:

Profit target (average profits over 3 year period)	*Additional consideration*
€1m but less than €1.25m	100,000 shares
€1.25m but less than €1.5m	150,000 shares
€1.5m+	200,000 shares

How should Entity P classify the additional consideration in its financial statements for the year ended 31 December 2008, and what amount should be recognised in respect of it?

As with Example 7.10 above, in our view the principles of IAS 32 appear more relevant than those of IFRS 2 in determining the appropriate classification of such arrangements. However, it is highly questionable whether the contingent consideration in this situation is of the type of arrangement considered in paragraph 21 of IAS 32 whereby an 'entity may have a contractual right or obligation to receive or deliver a number of its own shares or other equity instruments that varies so that the fair value of the entity's own equity instruments to be received or delivered equals the amount of the contractual right or obligation'. One view would be that on the basis that the number of shares to be issued does vary (depending on profit) and that the fair value of the shares to be issued does always equal the fair value of the obligation – by definition the two must always be the same – such an arrangement constitutes a liability. However this analysis does not seem entirely satisfactory.

In determining the contingent consideration to be recorded under IFRS 3, Entity P has to estimate what level of profit it anticipates Entity S will achieve and the relevant number of shares to be issued as a result. At 31 December 2008, Entity P has determined that it is probable that Entity S will meet the first target level, and as a result Entity P will issue 100,000 shares on 1 January 2012. Thereafter, if that level of profit is achieved there will no variation in the number of shares issued. Clearly Entity P may reassess the level of profit it expects to be achieved and revise the number of shares it expects to issue, but again once that determination is made if the revised estimate is achieved there is no variation in the number of shares to be issued.

Fundamentally, paragraph 21 of IAS 32 appears to be addressing situations where shares to be issued vary such that they are equal in value to a fixed or variable, but determinable, monetary amount. That is not the case in this situation. Accordingly, we believe that it is appropriate that the consideration is classified as an equity instrument.

On the basis that the consideration is reflected as equity, we believe that the amount recognised for the consideration should be based on the requirements of IFRS 3 in respect of equity instruments issued as consideration (see C above), i.e. at the fair value at the date of exchange (31 December 2008). However, in this situation the fair value of the 'equity instrument' at the date of exchange would need to take into account, for example, an allowance for any estimated dividends on the shares that will not be payable during the period until they are issued on 1 January 2012.

One other issue that arises in this situation is whether adjustments should be made to the consideration, and thus goodwill, to reflect subsequent changes in the fair value of the shares such that the consideration is ultimately measured at Entity P's share price at the date the shares are finally issued. Although the requirements for contingent consideration would generally require subsequent changes in the estimate of the consideration that will ultimately be given to be recognised, we do not believe that this should reflect such changes in fair value. Since the consideration is regarded as equity, then consistent with the requirements of paragraph 22 of IAS 32, 'changes in the fair value of an equity instrument are not recognised in the financial statements'.

If at 31 December 2009, Entity P considers that is it is probable that Entity S will now meet the second target, then the financial statements at that date need to reflect that Entity P now expects to issue 150,000 shares. As discussed above, we do not believe that any change should be made to reflect changes in the value of Entity P's shares since the date of exchange (31 December 2008), and so the additional consideration of 50,000 shares should be valued using the same value per share as the original estimated consideration of 100,000 shares.

V *Indemnities given by vendor to the acquirer in respect of contingencies of acquiree*

In some business combinations, it may be identified that the acquiree has a specific contingency for which no liability has been recognised as the acquiree did not consider that it was probable that any liability would crystallise. Consequently, the business combination agreement may provide for the vendor to indemnify the acquirer in the event that the acquiree has to make a payment in respect of the contingency by way of a refund of the consideration paid by the acquirer.

As discussed at 2.3.3 C below, the acquirer will be required to recognise a liability for the contingency at its fair value, despite the fact that the acquiree has not recognised any liability for that contingency.

However, how should the acquirer account for the indemnity given by the vendor in relation to the contingency?

Example 7.12: Indemnity given by vendor to the acquirer in respect of a contingent liability of the acquiree

Entity A intends to acquire Entity B. It is considered by both Entity A and the vendor of Entity B that the value of Entity B's business is $150m. As part of due diligence, Entity A identifies that Entity B has a contingent liability in respect of a claim by a third party that has not been recognised by Entity B as a liability on the basis that was not considered probable that any amount would be payable by Entity B. The maximum amount payable in respect of the claim is $60m, and the vendor is still of the view that no amount will ultimately be payable by Entity B.

Accordingly, the purchase agreement includes the following terms:

- $150m is to be paid upfront (being the value of Entity B excluding the contingent liability).
- The vendor agrees to pay an amount to the acquirer, Entity A, by way of a refund of the purchase price in the event that the contingent liability crystallises and is settled by Entity B.

The intention of these terms is that the impact of the contingent liability on the results reported in Entity A's consolidated financial statements should be the same, regardless of the outcome of the contingent liability.

The fair value of Entity B's net assets (excluding the contingent liability) is $50m, and the fair value of the contingent liability is determined to be $20m.

In the absence of the contingent liability, goodwill of $100m would be recognised, being the difference between the consideration paid ($150m) and the fair value of the net assets acquired ($50m). As indicated above, IFRS 3 requires the contingent liability to be recognised as a liability at its fair value of $20m; based on consideration of $150m this would mean that goodwill of $120m is recognised.

However, how should the indemnity be accounted for?

A literal application of IFRS 3 results in any reimbursement by the vendor being accounted for as 'negative' contingent consideration since the agreement provides for an adjustment to the cost of the combination contingent on a future event. On this basis, no adjustment would be made at the acquisition date (since it is not probable that any amount would be received), and thus goodwill of $120m would be recognised as indicated above. If at a later date, the contingent liability crystallised at its maximum amount of $60m, then the consolidated financial statements would recognise this increased liability of $60m, resulting in a loss of $40m in the income statement. The refund received by Entity A of $60m would be recognised as an adjustment to the consideration, resulting in a reduction of the goodwill by that amount. On the other hand, if at a later date, the uncertainty about the contingent liability was resolved such that no amount was payable by Entity B, then the consolidated financial statements would recognise the release of the original liability of $20m, resulting in a gain in the income statement. There would no adjustment to the goodwill. This does not seem a particularly sensible result.

Another approach might be to view the transaction as having two components – the business combination and the purchase of an indemnity asset. On this basis, therefore, the total price of $150m comprises two distinct elements: $130m representing the cost of the business combination, and the remaining $20m representing an additional payment to receive the indemnity from the vendor in relation to the contingent liability acquired. Therefore, based on the cost of the business combination of $130m, goodwill of $100m is recognised. A separate 'indemnity' asset of $20m is recognised (effectively Entity A has purchased a reimbursement right relating to the contingent liability). Any amount received under the indemnity is a realisation of that asset and is not adjusted against the cost of the business combination which remains $130m.

Proponents of this approach argue that contingent consideration is not defined in IFRS 3 and the examples given are for contingencies relating either to the value of the business acquired or the value of the consideration provided. For these contingencies there is a logical link to the combination accounting and, accordingly, these give rise to contingent consideration. In the case of the indemnity, it is argued that the contingency does not relate either to the value of the business (it only relates to one element) nor to the value of the consideration. In these circumstances, it is thought appropriate to consider the substance of the arrangement to determine whether or not it should be accounted for as contingent consideration.

In support of this approach, proponents would argue that in any event it would seem inappropriate to adjust any amount received against the cost of the combination (and goodwill). As noted earlier, paragraph 35 of IFRS 3 requires a different approach to accounting for contingencies when the acquirer guarantees the value of equity or debt instruments issued as consideration and must issue additional equity or debt instruments to restore the originally determined cost. In such cases, no increase in the cost of the business combination (or adjustment to goodwill) is recognised and the adjustment is reflected instead in the equity or debt instruments. Therefore, the accounting for the contingent consideration is determined by the nature of the contingency and the nature of the adjustment follows from this. This is thought to further support the view that the nature of the contingency needs to be considered to determine the appropriate accounting. For the indemnity, the contingency also does not relate to the value of the business acquired – rather it relates to the value of one of the specific liabilities acquired. Therefore, consistent with the approach in paragraph 35, it is argued that no adjustment should be made to the cost of the business combination as a result of any payment received under the indemnity. Subsequent movements in the value of the separate asset and contingent liability are adjusted for in the income statement.

We can see some merit in this 'indemnity asset' approach and consider it an acceptable way of accounting for such an indemnity. Under this approach, if at a later date, the contingent liability crystallised at its maximum amount of $60m, then the consolidated financial statements would recognise this increased liability of $60m, resulting in a loss of $40m in the income statement. However, this would be offset by an equivalent amount being the refund received by Entity A of $60m less the cost of 'indemnity' asset. On the other hand, if at a later date, the uncertainty about the contingent liability was resolved such that no amount was payable by Entity B, then the consolidated financial statements would recognise the release of the original liability of $20m, resulting in a gain in the income statement. This would then be offset by Entity A writing off its 'indemnity' asset.

2.3.3 Allocating the cost to the assets acquired and liabilities and contingent liabilities assumed

Having determined the cost of the business combination, the next stage is to allocate that cost to the assets acquired and liabilities and contingent liabilities assumed.

IFRS 3 requires that the acquirer shall, at the acquisition date, allocate the cost of a business combination by recognising the acquiree's identifiable assets, liabilities and contingent liabilities that satisfy the recognition criteria in paragraph 37 of the standard at their fair values at that date, except for non-current assets (or disposal groups) that are classified as held for sale in accordance with IFRS 5 – *Non-current Assets Held for Sale and Discontinued Operations*, which are recognised at fair value less costs to sell. Any difference between the cost of the business combination and the acquirer's interest in the net fair value of the identifiable assets, liabilities and contingent liabilities so recognised is accounted for as goodwill or 'negative goodwill' (see 2.3.4 and 2.3.5 below respectively).[91]

Paragraph 37 of IFRS 3 states that the acquirer shall recognise separately the acquiree's identifiable assets, liabilities and contingent liabilities at the acquisition date only if they satisfy the following criteria at that date:

(a) in the case of an asset other than an intangible asset, it is probable that any associated future economic benefits will flow to the acquirer, and its fair value can be measured reliably;

(b) in the case of a liability other than a contingent liability, it is probable that an outflow of resources embodying economic benefits will be required to settle the obligation, and its fair value can be measured reliably;

(c) in the case of an intangible asset or a contingent liability, its fair value can be measured reliably.[92]

It can be seen that the recognition criteria for intangible assets and contingent liabilities are different from those of other assets and liabilities. In the case of intangible assets, the IASB has taken the view that the probability recognition criterion is always considered to be satisfied for such assets acquired in a business combination. In developing the standard, the Board observed that the fair value of an intangible asset reflects market expectations about the probability that the future economic benefits associated with the intangible asset will flow to the acquirer. In other words, the effect of probability is reflected in the fair value measurement of an intangible asset. The IASB notes that this highlights a general inconsistency between the recognition criteria for assets and liabilities in its *Framework* (see Chapter 2 at 3.2.4) and the fair value measurements required in a business combination, but has concluded that the role of probability as a criterion for recognition in the *Framework* should be considered more generally as part of a forthcoming Concepts project.[93] The allocation of the cost of the business combination to intangible assets is discussed further at 2.3.3 B below.

Similarly, in the case of contingent liabilities, the IASB takes the view that although a contingent liability of the acquiree is not recognised by the acquiree before the business combination, that contingent liability has a fair value, the amount of which reflects market expectations about any uncertainty surrounding the possibility that an outflow of resources embodying economic benefits will be required to settle the possible or present obligation. Again, the IASB notes that this highlights an inconsistency between the recognition criteria applying to liabilities and contingent liabilities in IAS 37 (see Chapter 27 at 3) and the *Framework* and the fair value measurement cost of a business combination, and that the role of probability should be considered more generally as part of a forthcoming Concepts project.[94] The allocation of the cost of the business combination to contingent liabilities is discussed further at 2.3.3 C below.

The recognition criteria in paragraph 37 of the standard set out above makes no reference to contingent assets of the acquiree. We believe that, consistent with the treatment of contingent liabilities, IFRS 3 should have required an acquirer to recognise an acquiree's contingent assets at their fair value as part of allocating the cost of the business combination provided their fair values can be measured reliably. We see no conceptual justification to include only contingent liabilities but not contingent assets in the cost allocation process of a business combination, as both are likely to have had an impact on the purchase price and the contingent asset is as much an asset as the contingent liability is a liability. Arguably, a contingent asset that has not been recognised as an asset by the acquiree on the basis that the inflow of benefits is not virtually certain (see Chapter 27 at 3.2.2), but it is probable that the benefits will arise, is covered by criterion (a) above. However, it appears that this is not the case as at the time of issuing IFRS 3 the IASB indicated that it would consider as part of the second phase of its business combinations project whether items meeting the definition of contingent assets in IAS 37 should be recognised separately as part of allocating the cost of a business combination.[95]

The allocation of the cost of the business combination to the assets acquired and liabilities and contingent liabilities assumed is critical to the reporting of the post-acquisition performance relating to the business combination. As indicated in the standard, the acquirer's income statement shall incorporate the acquiree's profits and losses after the acquisition date by including the acquiree's income and expenses based on that allocation. For example, depreciation expense included after the acquisition date in the acquirer's income statement that relates to the acquiree's depreciable assets is based on the fair values of those depreciable assets at the acquisition date, i.e. their cost to the acquirer.[96] However, of more importance, is the fact that the subsequent accounting for the items that are being recognised separately will in most cases be different from that required for goodwill. For example, the requirement to recognise intangible assets with finite useful lives separately (rather than subsuming them within goodwill), will mean that the values attributed will be amortised over that useful life (see Chapter 12 at 2.4 and 2.5) whereas the goodwill will not be amortised, but subjected to an impairment test (see 3 below).

Further explanation as to how the recognition requirements for other assets and liabilities, principally liabilities, are to be applied is given in the standard. This is discussed at 2.3.3 A below.

Guidance on determining the fair values of the acquiree's identifiable assets, liabilities and contingent liabilities for the purpose of allocating the cost of a business combination is discussed at 2.3.3 D below.

As the acquirer recognises the acquiree's identifiable assets, liabilities and contingent liabilities that satisfy the recognition criteria in paragraph 37 at their fair values at the acquisition date, any minority interest in the acquiree is stated at the minority's proportion of the net fair value of those items.[97]

A Acquiree's identifiable assets and liabilities

As indicated above, further explanation about how the recognition requirements for other assets and liabilities, principally liabilities, are to be applied is given in the standard.

Firstly, IFRS 3 makes it clear that the acquirer, when allocating the cost of the combination, shall not recognise liabilities for future losses or other costs expected to be incurred as a result of the business combination.[98]

Secondly, the standard severely restricts the ability of an acquirer to recognise a liability for reorganisation or restructuring costs resulting from the business combination. The standard states that 'the acquirer shall recognise liabilities for terminating or reducing the activities of the acquiree as part of allocating the cost of the combination only when the acquiree has, at the acquisition date, an existing liability for restructuring recognised in accordance with IAS 37'.[99] The requirements for the recognition of restructuring provisions under IAS 37 are discussed in Chapter 27 at 5.1.

The Basis for Conclusions accompanying IFRS 3 considers a number of ways that it might be thought possible to get around this requirement, for example, by the acquiree, on instructions of the acquirer, entering into obligations to restructure the business before the formal transfer of control.[100] It indicates that 'if the acquirer can compel the acquiree to incur obligations, then it is likely that the acquirer already controls the acquiree, given that control is the power to govern the financial and operating policies of an entity so as to obtain benefits from its activities'.[101] In that situation, the date of acquisition would be date the acquirer effectively obtained control, and at that time the acquiree would not have had an existing liability under IAS 37. However, the Basis for Conclusions does state that 'if, alternatively, the acquirer suggests that negotiations cannot proceed until the acquiree arranges, for example, to restructure its workforce, and the acquiree takes the steps necessary to satisfy the recognition criteria for restructuring provisions in IAS 37, then those obligations are pre-combination obligations of the acquiree and, in the Board's view, should be recognised as part of allocating the cost of the combination'.[102] In that situation, the acquiree has a liability for the restructuring irrespective of whether the business combination takes place or not, and is taking the risk that having made that commitment the acquirer may not complete the acquisition.

The IASB also considered the situation whereby the acquiree and the acquirer could agree for the acquiree to take the steps necessary to satisfy the recognition requirements of the standard, but to make the execution of the plan conditional on the acquiree being acquired in a business combination.[103] However, the standard clarifies that an acquiree's restructuring plan whose execution is conditional upon its being acquired in a business combination is not, immediately before the business combination, a present obligation of the acquiree.[104] The reason being that even if the main features of the plan were announced to those that would be affected by it, the entity has not raised the 'valid expectation' that it will be carried out since it is conditional on the entity being acquired in a business combination.[105] Nor is it a contingent liability of the acquiree immediately before the combination because it is not a possible obligation arising from a past event whose existence will be confirmed only by the occurrence or non-occurrence of one or more uncertain future events not wholly within the control of the acquiree.[106] The reason being that the uncertain future event (i.e. being acquired in a business combination) is generally within the acquiree's control.[107] Therefore, an acquirer shall not recognise a liability for such restructuring plans as part of allocating the cost of the combination.[108]

Thirdly, IFRS 3 states that a payment that an entity is contractually required to make, for example, to its employees or suppliers in the event that it is acquired in a business combination is a present obligation of the entity that is regarded as a contingent liability until it becomes probable that a business combination will take place. The contractual obligation is recognised as a liability by that entity in accordance with IAS 37 when a business combination becomes probable and the liability can be measured reliably. Therefore, when the business combination is effected, that liability of the acquiree is recognised by the acquirer as part of allocating the cost of the combination.[109]

Lastly, the standard states that the identifiable assets and liabilities that are recognised in accordance with paragraph 36 of the standard include all of the acquiree's assets and liabilities that the acquirer purchases or assumes, including all of its financial assets and financial liabilities. They might also include assets and liabilities not previously recognised in the acquiree's financial statements, e.g. because they did not qualify for recognition before the acquisition. For example, a tax benefit arising from the acquiree's tax losses that was not recognised by the acquiree before the business combination qualifies for recognition as an identifiable asset in accordance with paragraph 36 if it is probable that the acquirer will have future taxable profits against which the unrecognised tax benefit can be applied.[110]

B Acquiree's intangible assets

As indicated at 2.3.3 above, the allocation of the cost of the business combination includes the separate recognition of the acquiree's intangible assets. This is irrespective of whether the asset had been recognised by the acquiree before the business combination.[111] IFRS 3 requires the acquirer to recognise separately an intangible asset of the acquiree at the acquisition date only if:

- it meets the definition of an intangible asset in IAS 38; and
- its fair value can be measured reliably.[112]

IAS 38 includes equivalent requirements, and also emphasises that the probability recognition criterion in paragraph 21(a) of IAS 38 (see Chapter 12 at 2.2) is always considered to be satisfied for an intangible asset acquired in a business combination, the effect of probability being taken into account in the determination of fair value.[113]

IFRS 3 refers to the guidance provided within IAS 38 on determining whether the fair value of an intangible asset acquired in a business combination can be measured reliably.[114]

I What is an intangible asset?

IAS 38 defines an 'intangible asset' as 'an identifiable non-monetary asset without physical substance'.[115] IFRS 3 states that in accordance with IAS 38, an asset meets the identifiability criterion in the definition of an intangible asset only if it:

(a) is separable, i.e. capable of being separated or divided from the entity and sold, transferred, licensed, rented or exchanged, either individually or together with a related contract, asset or liability; or

(b) arises from contractual or other legal rights, regardless of whether those rights are transferable or separable from the entity or from other rights and obligations.[116]

Both IFRS 3 and IAS 38 explicitly refer to the fact that this means that the acquirer recognises as an asset separately from goodwill an in-process research and development project of the acquiree (if the project meets the definition of an intangible asset and its fair value can be measured reliably).[117] This is discussed further below. IFRS 3 gives guidance in an Illustrative Example that provides a large list of examples of items acquired in a business combination that meet the definition of an intangible asset and are therefore to be recognised separately from goodwill, provided that their fair values can be measured reliably, whilst noting that they are not intended to be an exhaustive list of items acquired in a business combination that meet the definition of an intangible asset.[118] A non-monetary asset without physical substance acquired in a business combination might meet the identifiability criterion for identification as an intangible asset but not be included in the guidance.

The guidance designates the assets listed with symbols to identify those that meet part (a) of the definition and those that meet part (b) of the definition, whilst noting that those designated as meeting part (b) might also be separable. However, it emphasises that separability is not a necessary condition for an asset to meet the contractual-legal criterion.

The table below summarises the items included in the Illustrative Example that the IASB regard as meeting the definition of an intangible asset and are therefore to be recognised separately from goodwill, provided that their fair values can be measured reliably. Reference should be made to the Illustrative Example for any further explanation about some of these items.

Intangible assets arising from contractual or other legal rights (regardless of being separable)	Other intangible assets that are separable
Marketing-related	
– Trademarks, trade names, service marks, collective marks and certification marks	
– Internet domain names	
– Trade dress (unique colour, shape or package design)	
– Newspaper mastheads	
– Non-competition agreements	
Customer-related	
– Order or production backlogs	– Customer lists
– Customer contracts and the related customer relationships	– Non-contractual customer relationships
Artistic-related	
– Plays, operas and ballets	
– Books, magazines, newspapers and other literary works	
– Musical works such as compositions, song lyrics and advertising jingles	
– Pictures and photographs	
– Video and audiovisual material, including films, music videos and television programmes	
Contract-based	
– Licensing, royalty and standstill agreements	
– Advertising, construction, management, service or supply contracts	
– Lease agreements	
– Construction permits	
– Franchise agreements	
– Operating and broadcasting rights	
– Use rights such as drilling, water, air, mineral, timber-cutting and route authorities	
– Servicing contracts such as mortgage servicing contracts	
– Employment contracts that are beneficial contracts from the perspective of the employer because the pricing of those contracts is below their current market value	
Technology-based	
– Patented technology	– Unpatented technology
– Computer software and mask works	– Databases
– Trade secrets such as secret formulas, processes or recipes	

It can be seen from the table that customer relationships can potentially fall under either category. Where relationships are established with customers through contracts, those customer relationships arise from contractual rights, regardless of whether a contract exists, or there is any backlog of orders, at the date of acquisition. In such cases, it does not matter that the relationship is separable. It would only be if the relationship did not arise from a contract that the recognition depends on the separability criterion.

It is clear from the table above that the IASB envisages a wide range of items meeting the definition of an intangible asset, and therefore potentially being recognised separately from goodwill. Whether they are recognised separately or not will depend on whether their fair values can be measured reliably.

One company that has recognised numerous intangible assets as a result of business combinations is ITV as illustrated in the following extract.

Extract 7.3: ITV plc (2005)

Notes to the accounts [extract]

28 Acquisitions and disposals of business

Acquisition and disposals in 2005

SDN

On 27 April 2005, the Group acquired 50.1% of the shares in SDN Ltd and 100% of the shares in United Media & Information Ltd (which held the remaining shares in SDN Ltd) for a total consideration of £83 million in cash. As part of the acquisition, loan amounts due by these companies, totalling £53 million, were repaid bringing the total cash outflow of the Group to £136 million. SDN holds the licence to operate Multiplex A on digital terrestrial television.

In the period to 31 December 2005 SDN contributed £8 million to the consolidated operating profit of the Group (before additional amortisation of £4 million). Had the acquisition occurred on 1 January 2005, the estimated revenue for the Group would have been £7 million higher at £2,184 million and operating profit before amortisation and exceptional items £2 million higher at £462 million (additional amortisation is £2 million) for the year ended 31 December 2005. The acquired net assets of SDN are set out in the table below.

	Book value before acquisition £m	Fair value adjustments £m	Fair value to ITV plc £m
Intangible assets	–	82	82
Trade and other receivables	6	–	6
Borrowings	(53)	–	(53)
Trade and other payables	(7)	3	(4)
Deferred tax liability	–	(25)	(25)
Net assets and liabilities	(54)	60	6
Goodwill on acquisition			77
Consideration paid			83
Borrowings settled at date of acquisition			53
Total cash outflow			136

The intangible assets recognised at a fair value of £82 million include the Multiplex licence and customer contracts. A deferred tax liability of £25 million has been recognised in respect of these intangible assets.

The goodwill recognised represents the wider strategic benefits of the acquisition to ITV plc and the value of those assets not requiring valuation under IFRS 3 (Business combinations). The strategic benefits are principally the enhanced ability to promote Freeview as a platform, business relationships with the channels which are on Multiplex A and the additional capacity available from 2010. These, in combination with existing Group assets including the ITV brand and programming, generate the goodwill on acquisition.

Friends Reunited

On 6 December 2005, the Group agreed to acquire 100% of the shares in Friends Reunited Holdings Limited for a total initial consideration of £120 million and deferred consideration of up to £55 million payable in 2009 contingent upon the future performance of the acquired business. The initial consideration consisted of £75 million cash, £21 million loan notes and £24 million ITV plc shares. Of the initial consideration £94 million was paid in 2005 with the balance of £26 million paid in 2006 (being the 21 million (£24 million) ITV plc shares and £2 million loan notes).

The fair value of the consideration is £145 million. This takes into account the initial consideration, the present value of the expected deferred consideration and other costs associated with the acquisition.

Had the acquisition occurred on 1 January 2005, the estimated revenue for the Group would have been £12 million higher at £2,189 million and operating profit before amortisation and exceptional items £6 million higher at £466 million (additional amortisation would have been £4 million) for the year ended 31 December 2005.

The acquired net assets of Friends Reunited are set out in the table below.

	Book value before acquisition £m	Fair value adjustments £m	Fair value to ITV plc £m
Intangible assets	4	34	38
Cash and cash equivalents	3	–	3
Trade and other receivables	1	–	1
Borrowings	(2)	–	(2)
Trade and other payables	(5)	–	(5)
Current tax (liability)/asset	(1)	3	2
Deferred tax asset	–	8	8
Net assets and liabilities	–	45	45
Goodwill on acquisition			100
Fair value of consideration			145

The intangible assets recognised at fair value include the brands and customer relationships. A deferred tax liability of £10 million has been recognised in respect of these intangible assets. A current tax asset of £3 million and a deferred tax asset of £18 million has been recognised in respect of the exercise of share options.

The goodwill recognised represents the benefits of the acquisition across the Group when combined with existing Group assets and businesses and the value of those assets not requiring valuation under IFRS 3 (Business combinations).

Valuation of acquired intangible assets methodology

Valuation of acquired intangibles has been performed in accordance with industry standard practice. Methods applied are designed to isolate the value of each intangible asset separately from the other assets of the business. The value of brands are assessed by applying a royalty rate to the expected future revenues over the life of the brand. Licences are valued on a start-up basis. Customer relationships and controls are valued based on expected future cash flows from those existing at the date of acquisition. Contributory charges from other assets are taken as appropriate with post tax cash flows then being discounted back to their present value. Typical discount rates applied in the valuation of intangible assets acquired in the period are 8% – 11%.

Disposal

During the year the Group disposed of Superhire Ltd for gross consideration of £2 million.

Acquisition and disposals in 2004

Summary of the effect of the acquisition of new businesses:

	Carlton		GMTV/GSkyB			
	Book value before acquisition	Fair value to ITV plc	Book value before acquisition	Fair value to ITV plc	Reclass-ifications*	Total
	£m	£m	£m	£m	£m	£m
Intangible assets	87	583	–	31	–	614
Fixed assets	81	86	3	3	7	96
Investments	96	122	–	–	(36)	86
Distribution rights	13	13	–	–	–	13
Deferred tax	29	(106)	–	(9)	3	(112)
Programme rights and other inventory	106	96	7	1	6	103
Trade and other receivables	155	149	14	13	45	207
Current asset investments	182	178	–	–	–	178
Assets held for sale	–	59	–	–	–	59
Cash and cash equivalents	410	410	19	19	59	488
Trade and other payables, provisions and borrowings	(1,204)	(1,245)	(29)	(32)	(111)	(1,388)
Pensions	(129)	(129)	–	–	(9)	(138)
Current tax	(62)	(62)	–	–	–	(62)
	(236)	154	14	26	(36)	144
Share of net assets within equity accounted investments plus minority interest		(168)		(8)	(3)	(179)
Goodwill on acquisition		1,932		33	39	2,004
Revaluation reserve adjustment		–		(6)		(6)
		1,918		45	–	1,963
Fair value of consideration paid		1,897		45		1,942
Acquisition costs		21		–		21
		1,918		45		1,963

*Reclassification of ITV 2, LNN, ITFC, ITV News Channel and ITV Network Limited to subsidiaries on combination of Granada and Carlton. These were previously held within investments in joint ventures and associates.

The most material acquisition accounted for during 2004 results from acquisition accounting for the combination with Carlton Communications Plc on 2 February 2004. Consideration comprised 1,308 million ordinary shares and 124 million convertible shares in ITV plc. The fair value of the consideration at the date of merger was £1,897 million.

In the period to 31 December 2004 Carlton contributed £82 million to the consolidated operating profit of the Group (before additional amortisation of £101 million). Had the acquisition occurred on 1 January 2004, the estimated revenue for the Group would have been £30 million higher at £2,083 million and operating profit before amortisation and exceptional items £1 million higher at £325 million for the year ended 31 December 2004.

The principal fair value adjustments to the book values (under IFRS) of the acquired assets and liabilities are as follows:

- Recognition of acquired intangible assets at fair value. These are principally brands, customer contracts, customer relationships, licences and acquired film libraries.
- Acquired properties stated at market value.
- Revaluation of investments to estimated market value.
- Write down of inventories to estimated selling price less reasonable profit margin.
- Assets held for sale shown at expected net proceeds discounted back to their present value at the date of acquisition.
- Revaluation of financial instruments to market value.
- Deferred tax provided on acquisition accounting adjustments as appropriate.

Disposals

During 2004 the Group disposed of The Moving Picture Company Holdings Ltd and Carlton Books Ltd (which were classified as held for resale) for respective gross considerations of £59 million and £nil.

II Customer relationship intangible assets acquired in a business combination

Further guidance on customer relationships acquired in a business combination is provided by IFRS 3 in the Illustrative Examples (which are reproduced in the example below) that demonstrate how an entity should interpret the contractual-legal and separability criteria in the context of acquired customer relationships.[119]

Example 7.13: Customer relationship intangible assets acquired in a business combination

Supply agreement

Parent obtained control of Supplier in a business combination. Supplier has a five-year agreement to supply goods to Buyer. Both Supplier and Parent believe that Buyer will renew the supply agreement at the end of the current contract. The supply agreement is not separable.

The supply agreement (whether cancellable or not) meets the contractual-legal criterion for identification as an intangible asset, and therefore is recognised separately from goodwill, provided its fair value can be measured reliably. Additionally, because Supplier establishes its relationship with Buyer through a contract, the customer relationship with Buyer meets the contractual-legal criterion for identification as an intangible asset. Therefore, the customer relationship intangible asset is also recognised separately from goodwill provided its fair value can be measured reliably. In determining the fair value of the customer relationship, Parent considers assumptions such as the expected renewal of the supply agreement.

Sporting goods and electronics

Parent obtained control of Subsidiary in a business combination. Subsidiary manufactures goods in two distinct lines of business: sporting goods and electronics. Customer purchases from Subsidiary both sporting goods and electronics. Subsidiary has a contract with Customer to be its exclusive provider of sporting goods. However, there is no contract for the supply of electronics to Customer. Both Subsidiary and Parent believe that there is only one overall customer relationship between Subsidiary and Customer.

The contract to be Customer's exclusive supplier of sporting goods (whether cancellable or not) meets the contractual-legal criterion for identification as an intangible asset, and is therefore recognised separately from goodwill, provided its fair value can be measured reliably. Additionally, because Subsidiary establishes its relationship with Customer through a contract, the customer relationship with Customer meets the contractual-legal criterion for identification as an intangible asset. Therefore, the customer relationship intangible asset is also recognised separately from goodwill, provided its fair value can be measured reliably. Because there is only one customer relationship with Customer, the fair value of that relationship incorporates assumptions regarding Subsidiary's relationship with Customer related to both sporting goods and electronics.

However, if both Parent and Subsidiary believed there were separate customer relationships with Customer – one for sporting goods and another for electronics – the customer relationship with respect to electronics would be assessed by Parent to determine whether it meets the separability criterion for identification as an intangible asset.

Order backlog and recurring customers

Entity A obtained control of Entity B in a business combination on 31 December 2004. Entity B does business with its customers solely through purchase and sales orders. At 31 December 2004, Entity B has a backlog of customer purchase orders from 60 per cent of its customers, all of whom are recurring customers. The other 40 per cent of Entity B's customers are also recurring customers. However, as of 31 December 2004, Entity B does not have any open purchase orders or other contracts with those customers.

The purchase orders from 60 per cent of Entity B's customers (whether cancellable or not) meet the contractual-legal criterion for identification as intangible assets, and are therefore recognised separately from goodwill, provided their fair values can be measured reliably. Additionally, because Entity B has established its relationship with 60 per cent of its customers through contracts, those customer relationships meet the contractual-legal criterion for identification as an intangible asset. Therefore, the customer relationship intangible asset is also recognised separately from goodwill provided its fair value can be measured reliably.

Because Entity B has a practice of establishing contracts with the remaining 40 per cent of its customers, its relationship with those customers also arises through contractual rights, and therefore meets the contractual-legal criterion for identification as an intangible asset. Entity A recognises this customer relationship separately from goodwill, provided its fair value can be measured reliably, even though Entity B does not have contracts with those customers at 31 December 2004.

Motor insurance contracts

Parent obtained control of Insurer in a business combination. Insurer has a portfolio of one-year motor insurance contracts that are cancellable by policyholders. A reasonably predictable number of policyholders renew their insurance contracts each year.

Because Insurer establishes its relationships with policyholders through insurance contracts, the customer relationship with policyholders meets the contractual-legal criterion for identification as an intangible asset. Therefore, the customer relationship intangible asset is recognised separately from goodwill, provided its fair value can be measured reliably. In determining the fair value of the customer relationship intangible asset, Parent considers estimates of renewals and cross-selling. IAS 36 and IAS 38 apply to the customer relationship intangible asset.

In determining the fair value of the liability relating to the portfolio of insurance contracts, Parent considers estimates of cancellations by policyholders. IFRS 4 – *Insurance Contracts* – provides further guidance on accounting for the acquired contracts.

An example of a company recognising customer contracts and customer relationship intangible assets is ITV as illustrated in Extract 7.3 above. Another example is Reuters as shown in Extract 7.2 at 2.3.2 B above.

One particular type of customer relationship intangible asset that should be recognised (as indicated by the last scenario in Example 7.13 above) is the value of the future profit of businesses acquired (VOBA) relating to insurance contracts or investment contracts, notwithstanding the fact that it is the customer or policyholder that decides on the continuation of the relationship. One company recognising such intangibles is Sanlam as shown below.

> *Extract 7.4: Sanlam Limited (2006)*
>
> **Basis of Presentation and Accounting Policies** [extract]
>
> **Valuation of insurance and investment business acquired**
>
> The value of insurance and investment contract business acquired (VOBA) in a business combination is recognised as an intangible asset. VOBA, at initial recognition is equal to the discounted value, using a risk-adjusted discount rate, of the projected stream of future after-tax profit that is expected to flow from the book of in-force business acquired, after allowing for the cost of capital supporting the business. The valuation is based on the Group's actuarial principles and assumptions in respect of future premium income, investment return, policy benefits, costs, taxation, mortality, morbidity and surrenders.
>
> VOBA is amortised on a straight-line basis over the expected life of the client relationships underlying the book of in-force business acquired. VOBA is tested for impairment on a bi-annual basis and written down for impairment where this is considered necessary. The gain or loss on disposal of a subsidiary or business includes the carrying amount of VOBA attributable to the entity or business sold. VOBA is derecognised when the related contracts are settled or disposed of.

III Can fair value be measured reliably?

IFRS 3 itself provides no guidance on whether the fair value of an intangible asset can be measured reliably. Instead, it refers to the guidance contained in IAS 38.[120]

IAS 38 states that the fair value of intangible assets acquired in business combinations can normally be measured with sufficient reliability to be recognised separately from goodwill.[121] As noted earlier, IAS 38 indicates that the fair value of an intangible asset reflects market expectations about the probability that the future economic benefits embodied in the asset will flow to the entity. In other words, the effect of probability is reflected in the fair value measurement of the intangible asset.[122]

When, for the estimates used to measure an intangible asset's fair value, there is a range of possible outcomes with different probabilities, that uncertainty is factored into the measurement of the asset's fair value, rather than demonstrating an inability to measure fair value reliably.

If an intangible asset acquired in a business combination has a finite useful life, there is a rebuttable presumption in IAS 38 that its fair value can be measured reliably.[123]

In developing its proposals, the IASB had originally concluded that, except for an assembled workforce, sufficient information could reasonably be expected to exist to measure reliably the fair value of all intangible assets. However, after considering respondents' comments and the experiences of field visit and round-table participants, it concluded that, in some instances, there might not be sufficient information to measure reliably the fair value of an intangible asset separately from goodwill, notwithstanding that the asset is 'identifiable'.[124]

IAS 38 therefore states that 'the only circumstances in which it might not be possible to measure reliably the fair value of an intangible asset acquired in a business combination are when the intangible asset arises from legal or other contractual rights and either:

(a) is not separable; or

(b) is separable, but there is no history or evidence of exchange transactions for the same or similar assets, and otherwise estimating fair value would be dependent on immeasurable variables.'[125]

It is clear that the IASB envisages that most intangible assets should be accounted for separately from goodwill. Possibly as an anti-avoidance measure, the IASB has introduced a specific disclosure requirement to give a description of each intangible asset that was not recognised separately from goodwill and an explanation of why the intangible asset's fair value could not be measured reliably (see item (h) at 2.3.10 A below).

The IASB has recognised that an intangible asset acquired in a business combination might be separable, but only together with a related tangible or intangible asset. For example, a magazine's publishing title might not be able to be sold separately from a related subscriber database, or a trademark for natural spring water might relate to a particular spring and could not be sold separately from the spring. In such cases IAS 38 requires the acquirer to recognise the group of assets as a single asset separately from goodwill if the individual fair values of the assets in the group are not reliably measurable.[126] In practice, where the other asset is a tangible asset it is likely that its fair value can be determined.

IAS 38 notes that the terms 'brand' and 'brand name' are often used as synonyms for trademarks and other marks. However, the former are regarded as general marketing terms that are typically used to refer to a group of complementary assets such as a trademark (or service mark) and its related trade name, formulas, recipes and technological expertise. Accordingly, IAS 38 requires the acquirer to recognise as a single asset a group of complementary intangible assets comprising a brand if the individual fair values of the complementary assets are not reliably measurable. If the individual fair values of the complementary assets are reliably measurable, an acquirer may nevertheless still recognise them as a single asset provided the individual assets have similar useful lives.[127] Guidance on the determination of asset lives of intangible assets is discussed in Chapter 12 at 2.5.

Heineken, for example, combines the carrying amount of brands and customer bases acquired in business combinations, as shown below in extract 7.5.

Extract 7.5: Heineken N.V. (2006)

Notes to the consolidated financial statements [extract]
Significant accounting policies [extract]
(f) Intangible assets [extract]
(ii) Brands

Brands acquired, separately, or as part of a business combination are capitalised as part of a brand portfolio if the portfolio meets the definition of an intangible asset and the recognition criteria are satisfied. Brand portfolios acquired as part of a business combination include the customer base related to the brand because it is assumed that brands have no value without customer base and vice versa. Brand portfolios acquired as part of a business combination are valued at fair value based on the royalty relief method. Brands and brand portfolios acquired separately are measured at cost. Brands and brand portfolios are amortised on a straight-line basis over their estimated useful life.

IV *In-process research or development project expenditure*

Both IFRS 3 and IAS 38 explicitly refer to the fact that the acquirer recognises as an asset separately from goodwill an in-process research and development project of the acquiree (if the project meets the definition of an intangible asset and its fair value can be measured reliably).[128] It is worth considering further the meaning of the words in parentheses.

An intangible asset meets the identifiability criterion under IAS 38 when it:

'(a) is separable, i.e. is capable of being separated or divided from the entity and sold, transferred, licensed, rented or exchanged, either individually or together with a related contract, asset or liability; or

(b) arises from contractual or other legal rights, regardless of whether those rights are transferable or separable from the entity or from other rights and obligations'.[129]

In-process research and development projects, whether or not recognised by the acquiree, are protected by legal rights and are on occasion bought and sold by entities without there being a business acquisition. Therefore, they are intangible assets as defined by IAS 38. Moreover, because they are separable and there is evidence of exchange transactions, the standard assumes that the fair value can be measured reliably. In addition, under IFRS 3 the probability criterion for recognition of an intangible asset is deemed to be met as long as its fair value can be measured reliably.

Therefore, the recognition of in-process research and development as an asset on acquisition applies different criteria to those that are required for internal projects. The research costs of internal projects may under no circumstances be capitalised.[130] Before capitalising development expenditure, entities must meet a series of exacting requirements. They must demonstrate the intangible assets' technical feasibility, their ability to complete the assets and use them or sell them and must be able to measure reliably the attributable expenditure.[131] The probable future economic benefits must be assessed using the principles in IAS 36 which means that they have to be calculated as the net present value of the cash flows generated by the asset or, if it can only generate cash flows in conjunction with other assets, of the cash-generating unit of which it is a part.[132] This process is described further in Chapter 15.

What this means is that entities will be required to recognise on acquisition some research and development expenditure that they would not have been able to recognise if it had been an internal project. The IASB was aware of this inconsistency but concluded that this did not provide a basis for subsuming in-process research and development within goodwill. It has considered the alternative (a reconsideration of the conditions for recognition of research and development costs) as being outwith the scope of the business combinations project.[133]

Although the amount attributed to the project is accounted for as an asset, IAS 38 goes on to require that any subsequent expenditure incurred after the acquisition of the project is to be accounted for in accordance with paragraphs 54-62 of IAS 38.[134] These requirements are discussed in Chapter 12 at 2.3.6.

In summary, this means that the subsequent expenditure is:

(a) recognised as an expense when incurred if it is research expenditure;

(b) recognised as an expense when incurred if it is development expenditure that does not satisfy the criteria for recognition as an intangible asset in paragraph 57; and

(c) added to the carrying amount of the acquired in-process research or development project if it is development expenditure that satisfies the recognition criteria in paragraph 57.[135]

The inference is that the in-process research and development expenditure recognised as an asset on acquisition that never progresses to the stage of satisfying the recognition criteria for an internal project will ultimately be impaired, although it may be that this impairment will not arise until the entity is satisfied that the project will not continue. However, since it is an intangible asset not yet available for use, it will need to be tested for impairment annually by comparing its carrying amount with its recoverable amount.[136] Any impairment loss will be reflected in the entity's income statement as a post-acquisition event.

V Emission rights acquired in a business combination

If an acquiree has been granted emission rights or allowances under a cap and trade emission rights scheme (see Chapter 12 at 3.3), how should an acquirer recognise these rights and associated liabilities?

Emission rights meet the definition of an intangible asset and should therefore be recognised at the acquisition date at their fair value. Likewise, the acquirer is required to recognise a liability at fair value for the actual emissions made at the acquisition date.

As discussed in Chapter 12 at 3.3.2 B one approach that may be adopted in accounting for such rights is the 'net liability approach' whereby the emission rights are recorded at a nominal amount and the entity will only record a liability once the actual emissions exceed the emission rights granted and still held. Where the acquiree has adopted such an approach, it may be that at the date of acquisition it has not recognised an asset or liability. Nevertheless, the acquirer should recognise the emission rights as intangible assets at their fair value and a liability at fair value for the actual emissions made at the acquisition date. As discussed in Chapter 12 at 3.3.2, the net liability approach is not permitted for purchased emission rights and therefore is also not permitted to be applied to emission rights of the acquiree in a business combination.

Example 7.14: Emission rights acquired in a business combination under the 'net liability approach'

Entity A acquires all of the shares in Entity B. Entity B had been granted emission rights for free and adopted the net liability approach for recognition of emission rights prior to the acquisition. At acquisition date the emission rights held exceed the actual emissions made and hence no asset or provision is recognised in the financial statements of Entity B in respect of emissions.

Entity A also adopts the net liability approach for emission rights granted.

In a business combination, the emission rights of the acquiree, regardless of how the acquiree received these rights, are considered to be rights purchased by the Entity A group. Accordingly, they should be treated in the same manner as emission rights purchased directly by the group.

At the acquisition date Entity A recognises the emission rights held by Entity B as intangible assets at fair value and recognises a provision for the actual emissions made up to that date at fair value.

One impact of this is that subsequent to the acquisition, the consolidated income statement will show an expense for the actual emissions made thereafter as a provision will have to be recognised on an ongoing basis. As discussed in Chapter 12 at 3.3.2 B II, there are different views of the impact that such 'purchased' emission rights have on the measurement of the provision.

The emission rights held by the acquiree will relate to specific items of property, plant and equipment. Therefore when determining the fair value of these assets, care needs to be taken to ensure that there is no double counting of the rights held.

C *Acquiree's contingent liabilities*

As indicated at 2.3.3 above, the allocation of the cost of the business combination includes the separate recognition of the acquiree's contingent liabilities, if its fair value can be measured reliably, despite the fact that the acquiree has not recognised any liability for that contingency and that the recognition as a liability by the acquirer in accounting for the business combination is inconsistent with the recognition criteria in IAS 37. As indicated earlier, the IASB takes the view that the fair value of a contingent liability reflects market expectations about any uncertainty surrounding the possibility that an outflow of resources embodying economic benefits will be required to settle the possible or present obligation.

Since the recognition of this liability is not what would be required by IAS 37, IFRS 3 therefore includes requirements for the subsequent measurement of such liabilities. Accordingly, after their initial recognition, the acquirer shall measure contingent liabilities that are recognised separately in accordance with paragraph 36 of the standard at the higher of:

(a) the amount that would be recognised in accordance with IAS 37, and

(b) the amount initially recognised less, when appropriate, cumulative amortisation recognised in accordance with IAS 18 – *Revenue*.[137]

In developing the requirements the IASB had originally proposed that the amount should be remeasured at fair value, with any changes recognised in profit or loss until settled or the uncertain future event resolved. However, in considering respondents' comments, the IASB noted that the proposal was inconsistent with the accounting for financial guarantees and commitments to provide loans at below-market interest rates under IAS 39 (see Chapter 20 at 3.7 and Chapter 17 at 3.4) and so decided to amend its proposals for consistency with IAS 39.[138]

The implications of part (a) of the requirement are clear. If the acquiree has to recognise a provision in respect of the former contingent liability, and the best estimate of this liability is higher than the original fair value attributed by the acquirer, then the greater liability should now be recognised by the acquirer with the difference taken to the income statement. It would now be a provision to be measured and recognised in accordance with IAS 37. What is less clear is part (b) of the requirement. The reference to 'amortisation recognised in accordance with IAS 18' might relate to the recognition of income in respect of those loan commitments that are contingent liabilities of the acquiree, but have been recognised at fair value at date of acquisition. The implication of the requirement would appear to mean that the amount of the liability cannot be reduced below its originally attributed fair value except in restrictive circumstances. It would also seem to imply that the liability could not be derecognised even if the contingency were resolved without an outflow of economic benefits or the item has been settled at a lower amount, which clearly could not have been what was intended.

We consider that it is important to bear in mind that the contingent liabilities have not been recognised by the acquiree because they are either:

- possible obligations, as it has yet to be confirmed whether the entity has a present obligation that could lead to an outflow of resources embodying economic benefits; or
- present obligations that do not meet the recognition criteria in IAS 37 (because either it is not probable that an outflow of resources embodying economic benefits will be required to settle the obligation, or a sufficiently reliable estimate of the amount of the obligation cannot be made).[139]

In many instances, therefore, these contingent liabilities will never become liabilities under IAS 37 or be settled (in cash or other resources) by the entities. Therefore, it must be acceptable to write back the contingent liability if the uncertainty is resolved (whether by payment or otherwise) and it is clear that there is no remaining obligation on the part of the entity.

Despite the fact that the requirement for subsequent measurement discussed above was introduced for consistency with IAS 39, the standard makes it clear that the requirement does not apply to contracts accounted for in accordance with IAS 39. However, loan commitments excluded from the scope of IAS 39 (other than those that are commitments to provide loans at below-market interest rates) will fall within the requirements of IFRS 3. Such loan commitments are to be regarded as contingent liabilities of the acquiree if, at the acquisition date, it is not probable that an outflow of resources embodying economic benefits will be required to settle the obligation or if the amount of the obligation cannot be measured with sufficient reliability. As with other contingent liabilities of the acquiree, such a loan commitment is recognised separately as part of allocating the cost of a combination only if its fair value can be measured reliably.[140]

IFRS 3 notes that contingent liabilities recognised separately as part of allocating the cost of a business combination are excluded from the scope of IAS 37. Nevertheless, the acquirer has to disclose for those contingent liabilities the information required to be disclosed by IAS 37 for each class of provision (see Chapter 27 at 6.1).[141]

If the fair value of a contingent liability cannot be measured reliably then the standard notes that this will affect the amount recognised as goodwill or 'negative goodwill' (see 2.3.4 and 2.3.5 below). In that case, the acquirer shall disclose the information about that contingent liability required to be disclosed by IAS 37 (see Chapter 27 at 6.2).[142]

D Determining the fair values of the acquiree's identifiable assets, liabilities and contingent liabilities

IFRS 3 requires an acquirer to recognise the acquiree's identifiable assets, liabilities and contingent liabilities that satisfy the relevant recognition criteria at their fair values at the acquisition date (except for non-current assets (or disposal groups) that are classified as held for sale in accordance with IFRS 5 which are recognised at fair value less costs to sell). Fair value is defined as 'the amount for which an asset could be exchanged, or a liability settled, between knowledgeable, willing parties in an arm's length transaction'.[143] Appendix B to IFRS 3, which is an integral part of the standard, gives guidance on the measures that should be used in determining the fair values of various items. It also notes that if the guidance for a particular item does not refer to the use of present value techniques, such techniques may be used in estimating the fair value of that item.[144] In addition, IAS 38 contains specific guidance on measuring the fair values of intangible assets. The guidance for particular items is discussed below.

I Financial instruments

Financial instruments traded in an active market should be valued at their current market values. For financial instruments not traded in an active market estimated values should be used taking into consideration features such as price-earnings ratios, dividend yields and expected growth rates of comparable instruments of entities with similar characteristics.[145] This guidance reflects the fact that its origin comes from IAS 22, which only referred to 'securities' rather than financial instruments. For other types of financial instruments that are not traded on an active market, fair values may need to be estimated using present value techniques. Further guidance on the fair values of financial instruments is discussed in Chapter 20 at 4.

Although investments in associates are scoped out of IAS 39 they meet the definition of a 'financial instrument'. Accordingly, where as part of a business combination one of the identified assets is an investment in an associate, then the fair value of the associate should be determined in accordance with the above guidance, rather than calculating a fair value based on the appropriate share of the fair values of the identifiable assets, liabilities and contingent liabilities of the associate. By doing so, any goodwill relating to the associate is subsumed within the carrying amount for the associate rather than within the goodwill arising on the overall business combination. Nevertheless, although this fair value is effectively the 'cost' to the group to which equity accounting is applied, the underlying fair values of the identifiable assets, liabilities and contingent liabilities also need to be determined to apply equity accounting (see Chapter 8 at 3.2).

If the fair value exercise results in an excess of assets over the fair value of the consideration (commonly referred to as 'negative goodwill'), in accordance with the requirements of IFRS 3 discussed at 2.3.5 below, the acquirer should challenge the fair value placed on the associate as it rechallenges the values place on all of the assets, liabilities and contingent liabilities of the acquiree to ensure that the value has not been overstated.

II Receivables, beneficial contracts and other identifiable assets

Receivables, beneficial contracts and other identifiable assets should be valued based on the present values of the amounts to be received, determined at appropriate current interest rates, less allowances for uncollectibility and collection costs, if necessary. However, discounting is not required for short-term receivables, beneficial contracts and other identifiable assets when the difference between the nominal and discounted amounts is not material.[146]

III Inventories

Finished goods and merchandise should be valued using selling prices less the costs of disposal and a reasonable profit allowance for the selling effort of the acquirer based on profit for similar finished goods and merchandise. Work in progress should be valued using selling prices of finished goods less the sum of the costs to complete, the costs of disposal and a reasonable profit allowance for the completing and selling effort based on profit for similar finished goods. Raw materials should be valued using current replacement costs.[147]

Example 7.15: Fair value of work in progress

Entity A acquires Entity B on 30 June 2008. Entity B operates a dairy business and included in its inventory at the date of acquisition was work in progress being inventory of cheddar cheese in the cellars of the dairy left to mature for a year. The carrying amount of this inventory, being the costs incurred to the date of acquisition, is €400,000.

The intention is to sell the cheese once it has matured. The sales price of fully-matured cheese of the same quality at 30 June 2008 is €900,000. Future storage, marketing and selling expenses required to complete the process and market the product to retailers are estimated at €185,000.

How should the fair value of the work in progress be determined?

The guidance in IFRS 3 requires that work in progress should be valued using the selling prices of finished goods less the sum of costs to complete, the cost of disposal and a reasonable profit allowance for completing and selling effort based on the profit for similar finished goods. This effectively means that the overall profit made as a result of manufacturing and selling the cheese is split between the pre-acquisition effort of the acquiree and the post-acquisition effort of the group. However, the standard does not define how to calculate the reasonable profit allowance to be related to the completing and selling efforts. Clearly, judgement will be required by entities in making such a determination.

Assuming that there are no significant inefficiencies in the business processes, one approach would be to use the cost structure of Entity B to determine the reasonable profit allowance for subsequent costs to be incurred. Accordingly, it may be concluded that if Entity B had not been acquired by Entity A, it would have incurred total costs of €585,000. Based on the estimated selling price of €900,000, this would result in an overall profit of €315,000. Consequently, the profit allowance to be made for the completing and selling effort would be €100,000 (being €315,000 × €185,000/€585,000). On this basis, the fair value of the work in progress would be €615,000 (being €900,000 – €185,000 – €100,000).

IV Land and buildings

These should be valued using market values.[148] Like plant and equipment below, these will probably need to be determined by appraisal. Also, in our view if there is no market-based evidence of fair value because of the specialised nature of the property, the fair value may need to be estimated using an income or a depreciated replacement cost approach.

V Plant and equipment

Again, these should be valued using market values, normally determined by appraisal. If there is no market-based evidence of fair value because of the specialised nature of the item of plant and equipment and the item is rarely sold, except as part of a continuing business, an acquirer may need to estimate fair value using an income or a depreciated replacement cost approach.[149]

VI Intangible assets

Intangible assets should be valued by reference to an active market as defined in IAS 38 (see Chapter 12 at 2.3.2 A).[150] IAS 38 states that 'quoted market prices in an active market provide the most reliable estimate of the fair value of an intangible asset'. It goes on to say that 'the appropriate market price is usually the current bid price. If current bid prices are unavailable, the price of the most recent similar transaction may provide a basis from which to estimate fair value, provided that there has not been a significant change in economic circumstances between the transaction date and the date at which the asset's fair value is estimated.'[151]

However, IAS 38 also notes that it is uncommon for an active market to exist for intangible assets and that such a market cannot exist for brands, newspaper mastheads, music and publishing rights, patents or trademarks,[152] i.e. many of the intangible assets that IFRS 3 and IAS 38 require an acquirer to recognise as part of the allocation process. Accordingly, if no active market exists, the intangible assets should be valued on a basis that reflects the amounts the acquirer would have paid for the assets in arm's length transactions between knowledgeable willing parties, based on the best information available.[153] In determining this amount, an entity considers the outcome of recent transactions for similar assets.[154]

IAS 38 acknowledges that entities that are regularly involved in the purchase and sale of unique intangible assets may have developed techniques for estimating their fair values indirectly. Accordingly, it allows these techniques to be used for initial measurement of an intangible asset acquired in a business combination if their objective is to estimate fair value and if they reflect current transactions and practices in the industry to which the asset belongs. These techniques include, when appropriate:

(a) applying multiples reflecting current market transactions to indicators that drive the profitability of the asset (such as revenue, market shares and operating profit) or to the royalty stream that could be obtained from licensing the intangible asset to another party in an arm's length transaction (as in the 'relief from royalty' approach); or

(b) discounting estimated future net cash flows from the asset.[155]

It is generally considered that there are three broad approaches to valuing intangible assets as shown in the diagram below.

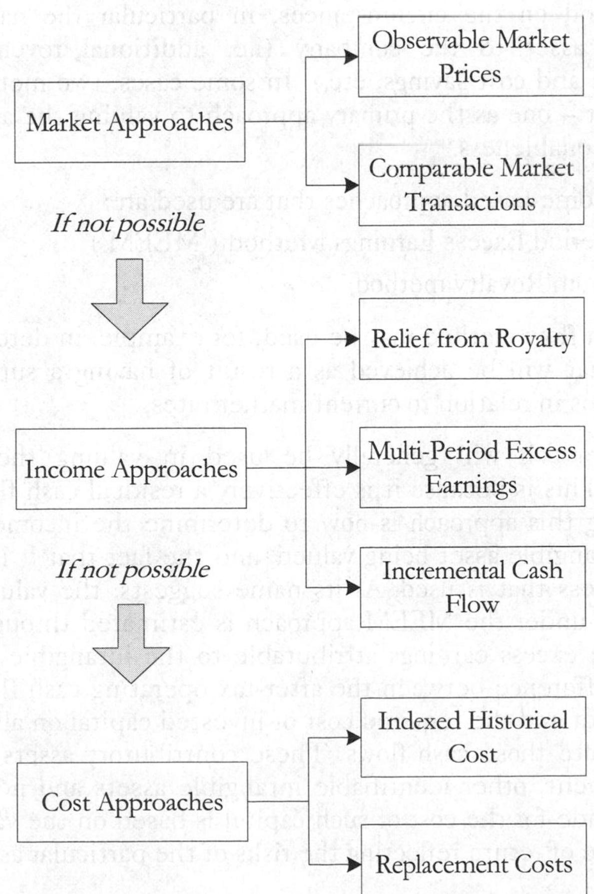

Under a market-based approach, if no actual market prices are available for the respective asset, the fair value of the intangible is derived by analysing similar intangible assets that have recently been sold or licensed, and then comparing these transactions to the intangible asset that needs to be valued. This approach is regarded as preferable where an active market for the assets exist. However, in practice, the ability to use such an approach is very limited. Intangible assets are generally unique, and there is rarely an active market to examine.

A cost-based approach is generally regarded as having limited application and difficult to use in many cases. The premise of the cost approach is that an investor would pay no more for an intangible asset than the cost to recreate it. However, for most intangibles, cost approaches are rarely consistent with the definition of 'fair value'.

Income-based approaches are much more commonly used. These involve identifying the expected economic benefits to be derived from the ownership of the particular intangible asset, and calculating the fair value of an intangible asset at the present value of those benefits. These are discussed further below.

For each asset, there are often several methodologies which can be applied. The choice will depend on the circumstances, in particular the nature of the value brought by the asset to the company (i.e. additional revenue, cost savings, replacement time and cost savings, etc.). In some cases, two methods may be used for the same asset – one as the primary approach to valuing the asset and the other as a check for reasonableness.

The two main income-based approaches that are used are:

- the Multi Period Excess Earnings Method ('MEEM')
- the Relief from Royalty method.

A discounted cash flow method may be used, for example, in determining the value of cost-savings that will be achieved as a result of having a supply contract with advantageous terms in relation to current market rates.

The MEEM approach will generally be used in valuing the most important intangible asset. This is because it is effectively a residual cash flow approach. The key issue in using this approach is how to determine the income/cash flow that is related to the intangible asset being valued, and the fact that it is not the full cash flow of the business that is used. As its name suggests, the value of an intangible asset determined under the MEEM approach is estimated through the sum of the discounted future excess earnings attributable to the intangible asset. The excess earnings is the difference between the after-tax operating cash flow attributable to the intangible asset and the required cost of invested capital on all other assets used in order to generate those cash flows. These contributory assets include property, plant and equipment, other identifiable intangible assets and net working capital. The allowance made for the cost of such capital is based on the value of such assets and a required rate of return reflecting the risks of the particular assets.

The Relief from Royalty method is used in many cases to calculate the value of a trademark or trade name. This approach is based on the concept that if an entity owns a trademark, it does not have to pay for the use of it and therefore is relieved from paying a royalty. The amount of that theoretical payment is used as a surrogate for income attributable to the trademark. The valuation is arrived at computing the present value of the after-tax royalty savings using an appropriate discount rate. The after-tax royalty savings are calculating by applying an appropriate royalty rate to the projected revenue, deducting the legal protection expenses relating to the trademark, and an allowance for tax at the appropriate rate.

Companies will generally use more than one of the above approaches in attributing fair values to intangible assets in a business combination as illustrated in the following extract.

Extract 7.6: Bayer AG (2005)

Notes to the Consolidated Financial Statements of the Bayer Group [extract]

5. Critical accounting policies

Acquisition accounting [extract]

We account for the acquired businesses using the purchase method of accounting which requires that the assets acquired and the liabilities assumed be recorded at the date of acquisition at their respective fair values.

The application of the purchase method requires certain estimates and assumptions especially concerning the determination of the fair values of acquired intangible assets and property, plant and equipment as well as liabilities assumed at the date of the acquisition. Moreover the useful lives of the acquired intangible assets, property, plant and equipment have to be determined. The judgments made in the context of the purchase price allocation can materially impact our future results of operations. Accordingly, for significant acquisitions, we obtain assistance from third party valuation specialists. The valuations are based on information available at the acquisition date.

Significant judgments and assumptions made regarding the purchase price allocation in the course of the acquisition of Schering AG, Berlin, Germany, included the following:

For intangible assets associated with products, product related technology, and qualified in-process research and development (IPR&D) we base our valuation on the expected future cash flows using the Multi-Period Excess Earnings approach. This method employs a discounted cash flow analysis using the present value of the estimated after-tax cash flows expected to be generated from the purchased intangible asset using risk adjusted discount rates and revenue forecasts as appropriate. The period of expected cash flows was based on the individual patent protection, taking into account the term of the product's main patent protection and essential extension of patent protection, as well as market entry of generics, considering sales, volume, potential defense strategies and market development at patent expiry.

For the valuation of brands, the relief-from-royalty method was applied which includes estimating the cost savings that result from the company's ownership of trademarks and licenses on which it does not have to pay royalties to a licensor. The intangible asset is then recognized at the present value of these savings. The brand-specific royalty rates were calculated using a product-specific scoring model. The corporate brands "Schering" and "Medrad" were assumed to have an unlimited life. (Please note that the rights to the name "Schering" in the United States and Canada do not belong to us but to Schering-Plough Corporation, New Jersey. Schering-Plough Corporation and the company acquired by Bayer in June 2006, i.e. Bayer Schering Pharma AG (formerly named Schering AGI, Berlin, Germany, are unaffiliated companies that have been totally independent of each other for many years.) Product brands, however, were assumed to have limited lives depending on the respective products' life cycles. The expected amortization of these assets is determined on the basis of expected product-specific revenues.

Another example is ITV as shown in Extract 7.3 at 2.3.3 .B I above.

In some situations, it may be that the value of an intangible asset will reflect not only the present value of the future post-tax cash flows as indicated above, but also the value of any tax benefits (sometimes called 'tax amortisation benefits') that the owner might have obtained if the asset had been bought separately, i.e. not as part of a business combination. Whether such tax benefits are included will depend on nature of the intangible asset and the relevant tax jurisdiction. Where such a value is included in the fair value of the intangible asset, an asset that has been purchased as part of a business combination may be one that is wholly or in part not actually tax-deductible by the entity. This therefore raises a potential impairment issue that is discussed in Chapter 15 at 5.2.2.

Another issue relating to the valuation of intangible assets is whether the acquirer's intention in relation to those assets should be taken into account in attributing a fair value, for example, where the acquirer does not intend to use an intangible asset of the acquiree.

Example 7.16: Impact of acquirer's intention on fair value of intangible asset

Entity A acquires a competitor, Entity B. One of the identifiable intangible assets of Entity B is the trade name of one of Entity B's branded products. However, since Entity A has a similar product, it does not intend to use that trade name post-acquisition. Entity A will discontinue sales of Entity B's product, thereby eliminating competition and enhancing the value of its own branded product. The cash flows relating to the acquired trade name are therefore expected to be nil.

Given that the cash flows relating to that trade name will be nil, can Entity A attribute a fair value of nil to that trade name?

In our view, the answer is no. As indicated at 2.3.3 D above, IFRS 3 defines fair value as 'the amount for which an asset could be exchanged, or a liability settled, between knowledgeable, willing parties in an arm's length transaction'. Accordingly, Entity A's future intentions about the asset should only be reflected in determining the fair value if that is what other knowledgeable willing buyers would do. In most situations, this will not be the case and therefore it is likely that the trade name does have a value. In fact, Entity A could probably have sold the trade name post-acquisition, but it has chosen not to do that to protect its own branded product. Accordingly, a fair value is attributed to that trade name. Only if it was not possible to reliably measure the fair value would no amount be recognised for the trade name (see 2.3.3 B III above).

This does raise an issue as to whether an immediate impairment loss should be reflected in respect of the trade name since the expected cash flows relating to it are nil. Again, in our view the answer is no – there is no immediate impairment loss. As discussed at 3.3 of Chapter 15, for the purposes of the impairment test under IAS 36, the recoverable amount of an asset is the higher of its value in use (VIU) and its fair value less costs to sell (FV). The FV of the trade name will initially not be materially different from the fair value attributed to it, and therefore unlikely to be impaired.

However, since Entity A is not intending to use the trade name to generate cash flows, it is unlikely that it could be regarded as having an indefinite life for the purposes of IAS 38, and therefore it should be amortised over its expected useful life. The estimate of the life should reflect the use to which Entity A is putting the trade name, which is as a means of eliminating competition for its own product. This is likely to be a relatively short period as the impact of the absence of that particular trade name in the market will not last for long, and any value that it did have will quickly reduce.

Where the above situation arises, consideration should also be given as to whether all intangible assets of the acquiree have been identified, and an appropriate fair value attributed to them. For example, it may be that what is thought to be the value of a brand or trade name actually comprises of other rights connected to the business acquired such as customer relationships, distribution networks, etc. As indicated at 2.3.3 B above, IFRS 3 requires such intangibles to be recognised separately.

VII Defined benefit plans

Net employee benefit assets or liabilities for defined benefit plans should be valued using the present value of the defined benefit obligation less the fair value of any plan assets. However, an asset is recognised only to the extent that it is probable it will be available to the acquirer in the form of refunds from the plan or a reduction in future contributions.[156] In computing the present value of the obligation, IAS 19 – *Employee Benefits* – states that any items such as actuarial gains and losses (whether or not within the 10% corridor allowed by IAS 19), past service costs and amounts not yet recognised by the acquiree under the transitional provisions of IAS 19 at the date of the acquisition should be included.[157] This means that there are no exemptions for the acquirer from recognising the full defined benefit obligation on acquisition.

VIII Tax assets and liabilities

Tax assets and liabilities should be valued using the amount of the tax benefit arising from tax losses or the taxes payable in respect of profit or loss in accordance with IAS 12 – *Income Taxes*, assessed from the perspective of the combined entity. The tax asset or liability is determined after allowing for the tax effect of restating identifiable assets, liabilities and contingent liabilities to their fair values and is not discounted.[158] The deferred tax consequences of business combinations are discussed further in Chapter 26 at 6.2.

IX Payables

Accounts and notes payable, long-term debt, liabilities, accruals and other claims payable should be valued using the present values of amounts to be disbursed in settling the liabilities determined at appropriate current interest rates. However, discounting is not required for short-term liabilities when the difference between the nominal and discounted amounts is not material.[159]

X Onerous contracts and other identifiable liabilities

Onerous contracts and other identifiable liabilities of the acquiree the acquirer shall use the present values of amounts to be disbursed in settling the obligations determined at appropriate current interest rates.[160]

IFRS 3 contains no further reference to 'onerous contracts', nor does it give any examples. Clearly, any provisions for onerous contracts that would be recognised under IAS 37 will require to be recognised and measured at their fair value under IFRS 3. As discussed in Chapter 27 at 5.3, IAS 37 defines on onerous contract as 'a contract in which the unavoidable costs of meeting the obligations exceed the economic benefits expected to be received under it', i.e. one that is directly loss-making, not simply uneconomic by reference to current prices.

Accordingly, it might be thought that onerous contracts recognised under IFRS 3 should only encompass those that would be recognised under IAS 37, and therefore no liability should be recognised, for example, for leases at an unfavourable rental or for an excessive amount of space, or for contracts to provide services in an area of business which is uneconomic. However, as discussed at 2.3.3 above, IFRS 3 envisages liabilities being recognised at the date of acquisition that were not previously recognised by the acquiree before the acquisition. Also, much of the guidance in other areas in the standard require fair values to be based on market conditions at the acquisition date. Therefore, we believe that contracts that are 'onerous' by reference to market conditions at the date of acquisitions should be recognised as liabilities. This is consistent with the IFRS 3 requirements for intangible assets. As discussed at B above, IFRS 3 includes within its list of examples of intangible assets that should be recognised, includes contract-based intangibles such as lease agreements. Thus, any leases that are 'favourable' by reference to market conditions would be recognised as assets at their fair value.

XI Contingent liabilities

Contingent liabilities of the acquiree should be valued using the amounts that a third party would charge to assume those contingent liabilities. Such an amount shall reflect all expectations about possible cash flows and not the single most likely or the expected maximum or minimum cash flow.[161] This is especially relevant given that many contingent liabilities are so defined as it is not probable that an outflow of resources embodying economic benefits will be required to settle the obligation[162] – even though the minimum cash flow may be zero, a third party would still charge a sum to assume the contingent liability.

E Reassessment of the acquiree's classification of assets, liabilities, equity and relationships acquired in a business combination

As discussed at 2.3.3 A above, IFRS 3 states that the identifiable assets and liabilities that are recognised in accordance with paragraph 36 of the standard include all of the acquiree's assets and liabilities that the acquirer purchases or assumes, including all of its financial assets and financial liabilities. They might also include assets and liabilities not previously recognised in the acquiree's financial statements, e.g. because they did not qualify for recognition before the acquisition.[163] It is irrelevant whether or not the acquiree had previously recognised those assets and liabilities; the acquirer makes a new assessment of what should be recognised based on conditions at the date of the business combination. The acquirer now controls the assets acquired and the liabilities assumed, and recognises them on this basis.

Although IFRS 3 is explicit on recognition, it is silent on classification. This issue was considered by the IFRIC in March 2007 when it was asked to provide guidance on whether, and in what circumstances, a business combination triggers reassessment of the acquiree's classification or designation of assets, liabilities, equity and relationships acquired in a business combination. Reassessment issues include, for instance, whether embedded derivatives should be separated from the host contract, the continuation or de-designation of hedge relationships and the classification of leases as operating or finance leases. The IFRIC noted that the IASB, at its meeting in February 2007, decided that the issue should be dealt with in Business Combinations phase II. Given that decision, the IFRIC decided not to take this item on to its agenda.[164]

In the meantime, since IFRS 3 does not contain a general principle regarding whether reassessment of the acquiree's classification of assets, liabilities and equity is allowed, required or prohibited in a business combination, we believe that the treatment should be based on the requirements of the particular IFRS relevant to the items concerned.

Example 7.17: Reassessment of the acquiree's classification of assets, liabilities, equity and relationships acquired in a business combination

Entity A obtains control of Entity B in a business combination. Entity B is a party to a number of contracts such that included within the assets and liabilities of Entity B are the following:

(a) Lease contracts, some of which are classified as operating leases and some of which are classified as finance leases in accordance with paragraph 4 of IAS 17;

(b) Some financial guarantee contracts are classified as insurance contracts and have been accounted for under IFRS 4;

(c) Certain hedge relationships have been designated at the inception of the hedges such that they qualify for hedge accounting in accordance with paragraph 88 of IAS 39;

(d) Financial assets and liabilities have been classified upon initial recognition in accordance with paragraph 9 of IAS 39, including items designated as at fair value through profit or loss and items as held-to-maturity; and

(e) Embedded derivatives, some of which have been separated from the host contract and some of which have not at the date of inception of the contracts in accordance with paragraph 11 of IAS 39.

Based on the requirements of the particular IFRS relevant to these items, whether Entity A is allowed or required to reassess the classification of such items is as follows:

(a) As discussed in Chapter 25 at 2.3.3, IAS 17 requires that lease classification is made at the inception of the lease. A change in classification only arises if the lessee and the lessor agree to change the provisions of the lease. Thus, in the absence of such changes, Entity A cannot reassess the classification of the leases.

(b) As discussed in Chapter 17 at 3.4.2, the election to classify financial guarantee contracts as insurance contracts and account for them under IFRS 4 is irrevocable. Also, paragraph B30 of IFRS 4 states that 'a contract that qualifies as an insurance contract remains an insurance contract until all rights and obligations are extinguished or expire'. Thus, Entity A cannot reassess the classification of these financial guarantee contracts.

(c) As discussed in Chapter 21 at 5, there are a number of conditions that need to be met for hedge relationships to qualify for hedge accounting, in particular formal documentation and an ongoing assessment of the designated hedge. As long as the documentation of Entity B is consistent with the risk management strategy of the Entity A group, the documentation can be carried over for both cash flow hedges and fair value hedges. However, we believe that there should exist some evidence of re-affirmation of the hedge relationship upon 'carry-over' of the hedge documentation. It should be noted that the documentation may differ depending upon the level of the entity (parent company, subsidiary, or consolidation) at which the hedge relationship exists.

Similar to the documentation requirements, the hedge effectiveness testing may also be carried forward. If effectiveness changes upon 'carry-over', the documentation will need to change. However, if it is a cash flow hedge, the Entity A group does not inherit Entity B's existing cash flow hedge reserve, as this clearly represents cumulative pre-acquisition gains and losses. This has implications for the assessment of hedge effectiveness and the measurement of ineffectiveness because, so far as the Entity A group is concerned, it has started a new hedge relationship with a hedging instrument that is likely to have a non-zero fair value (see Chapter 21 at 4.2.4).

Thus, Entity A effectively needs to reassess the hedging relationships, even if in some situations it may only be reaffirming what Entity B has done.

(d) The requirements for the classification of financial assets and liabilities are discussed in Chapter 17 at 7. The classification is made upon initial recognition and the categories identified are: financial assets and liabilities at fair value through profit or loss, held-to-maturity investments, loans and receivables, available-for-sale financial assets, and other financial liabilities. As indicated at 7.5 in Chapter 17, financial assets and financial liabilities cannot be reclassified into or out of the fair value through profit or loss category. However, reclassifications are permitted, and in some situations required, between held-to-maturity investments and available-for-sale assets. Although IAS 39 would appear to prohibit the reclassification of items into or out of the fair value through profit or loss category, arguably this does not apply to the Entity A group, since from the perspective of Entity A, initial recognition only takes place at the date of the business combination. Also, if Entity A already has an accounting policy for like transactions, IAS 27 requires the Entity A consolidated financial statements to use uniform accounting policies. Thus, it would be appropriate for Entity A to reassess the designation of such financial assets and financial liabilities.

(e) The requirements for the reassessment of embedded derivatives are discussed in Chapter 17 at 5.4. Whereas IAS 39 requires an entity to assess whether an embedded derivative needs to be separated from the host contract and accounted for a derivative when it first becomes a party to that contract, IFRIC 9 explains that during the life of the contract subsequent reassessment is prohibited. However, as indicated at 5.4.3 in Chapter 17, IFRIC makes it clear that it does not address the acquisition of contracts with embedded derivatives in a business combination nor their possible reassessment at the date of acquisition. Consequently, Entity A appears to have a choice of two accounting policies for such contracts: either reassess the contracts based on the terms of the contract and the economic circumstances at the date of the business combination or do not reassess the contracts and continue with the classification made by Entity B when it first became a party to the contracts. Whichever policy is adopted, it should be applied consistently.

As indicated above, in February 2007 the IASB decided to deal with this issue in its forthcoming revision of IFRS 3 (see 5.1 below). Following its joint meeting with the FASB in April 2007, it was decided to include in the final standard a principle that an acquirer should classify or designate the assets, liabilities and equity instruments acquired or assumed on the basis of the conditions that exist at the acquisition date. However, the Boards also tentatively decided that the revised business combinations standard should include exceptions to that principle for leases and insurance contracts acquired in a business combination. Leases and insurance contracts should be classified on the basis of the terms and conditions that existed at their inception (or at the date of the last substantive modification).[165]

F Pre-existing relationships with an acquiree

In some business combinations an acquirer and an acquiree have a relationship that predates the business combination. Often the effect of consolidating the acquiree is that the pre-existing relationship is settled or extinguished. In such cases, should this be accounted for as part of the business combination or as a separate transaction?

Although IFRS currently has no specific guidance on accounting for pre-existing relationships between an acquirer and acquiree the fact that the business combination has two economic effects – the acquisition of a business and the effective settlement of the pre-existing arrangement – indicates that there are two components to be accounted for separately. This is consistent with existing guidance in US GAAP in EITF 04-1 – *Accounting for Pre-existing Relationships between the Parties to a Business Combination* – as well as the guidance in the IASB's exposure draft of its Phase II Business Combinations proposals (see 5.x below).

In our view such pre-existing relationships should be accounted for separately from the business combination by:

(a) allocating the cost of the combination to all acquired assets and liabilities including those that reflect pre-existing relationships, and

(b) treating this as an effective settlement of the pre-existing relationship by applying the same accounting treatment that would have applied if the settlement had occurred as a stand alone transaction. This 'settlement' will generally result automatically through the application of normal consolidation elimination principles as required by IAS 27 (see Chapter 6 at 6.3).

The following table illustrates how the acquirer would account for the settlement of common pre-existing relationships in its consolidated financial statements:

Acquiree holds the following:	Acquirer accounts for as:
A receivable from / payable to the acquirer	Extinguishment of the acquirer's payable / receivable
Shares in the acquirer	Acquisition of treasury shares
Shares in a subsidiary of the acquirer	Acquisition of minority interest
Shares in an associate of the acquirer	Step acquisition of associate (or possibly a subsidiary)
A supply contract with the acquirer	Termination of the contract
Contractual rights to use an intangible asset of the acquirer (e.g. licence of trade name)	Repurchase of the contractual right

For financial assets and liabilities, such as receivables or payables, it can generally be presumed that they would be settled at fair value when undertaking an arms' length transaction. Accordingly, the allocated value would be equal to their fair value assessed by reference to the guidance in IAS 39 (see Chapter 20 at 4). Where this value is different from the acquirer's carrying value of the corresponding asset or liability, there is a resulting gain or loss on consolidation when the asset and liability are eliminated.

Similarly, the allocated value for shares in the acquirer, subsidiary of the acquirer or an associate of the acquirer would be equal to their fair value assessed by reference to the guidance in IAS 39. Where the asset held is shares in the acquirer, the effective settlement is accounted for as an acquisition of treasury shares, so the value attributed will be deducted from equity (see Chapter 19 at 6). Where the asset held is shares in a subsidiary of the acquirer, the value attributed will be treated as the cost of acquisition of a minority interest in that subsidiary (see 2.3.7 A below for guidance on the acquisition of minority interests). Where the asset held is shares in an associate of the acquirer, the value attributed will be treated as the cost in a step-acquisition of an associate (see Chapter 8 at 3.2.2 for guidance on such transactions) or possibly the cost in a step-acquisition of a subsidiary (if the additional shares together with the existing shares held now mean that the associate becomes a subsidiary) – see 2.3.7 below for guidance on such business combinations achieved in stages.

For supply and other executory contracts there is no explicit guidance in the current IFRS 3 regarding how to measure the effective settlement value. In our view it would be acceptable to measure this at either:

(a) the least cost of exiting the contract i.e. the lesser of:
   (i) the amount by which the contract is favourable or unfavourable by reference to current market pricing for similar transactions; and
   (ii) any explicit settlement terms in the contract available to the party to which the contract is unfavourable; or
(b) the total fair value of the contract which may also reflect the value associated with the selling effort in acquiring the contract and any related customer relationship.

This will result in a gain or loss on settlement equal to the settlement value less any amount that has already been recorded by the acquirer in relation to the contract.

Example 7.18: Effective settlement of a supply contract with the acquirer

An acquirer pays €50m to acquire a business that has other identifiable net assets of €40m in addition to a supply contract. The contract is a fixed price contract for the acquiree to supply goods to the acquirer for a further three years. Current market prices are less than the contract price. The fair value of the contract is assessed as €6m comprising (i) €2m reflecting the value of an 'at market' three year contract (e.g. this could reflect the value of the selling effort in securing such a contract); and (ii) €4m reflecting the unfavourable pricing.

One approach is that the acquirer would assign a settlement value of €4m for the contract, being the amount reflecting the unfavourable pricing. Therefore, the acquirer would:

(a) allocate the total cost of the combination (€50m) to (i) the contract (€4m); (ii) other identifiable net assets (€40m); and (iii) goodwill (€6m); and
(b) eliminate the contract and thus recognise a settlement loss of €4m (less any amount that had already been recognised as a liability by the acquirer).

This approach reflects an expectation that if parties are acting rationally they ought to be prepared to settle based upon current market pricing (€4m in the example). However, if the contract contains explicit settlement terms then the party to whom the contract is unfavourable would be expected to exit on those terms where this is less than the 'off-market' value of the contract. So, if the acquirer was permitted to terminate the contract early upon payment of a penalty of, say, €3m then this value would be the settlement value. Thus, goodwill of €7m would be recognised.

As indicated above, the settlement value of a contract is not necessarily equal to its fair value since fair value will also reflect the value associated with the selling effort in acquiring the contract. Similarly, the settlement value does not include the value of any related customer relationship intangible that may arise from the contractual relationship between the parties. Since the consolidated entity cannot have a contractual relationship with itself no asset is recorded in relation to the contract or the relationship. This means that any such value is effectively subsumed within goodwill.

The alternative approach would be to measure the settlement value at the total fair value of the contract rather than just the off-market pricing. This is not the approach that is proposed in the guidance in the IASB's exposure draft of its revised IFRS 3 (see 5.x below). However, in the absence of explicit guidance in the current IFRS 3 this approach would also be considered acceptable since the amount attributed to the contract asset is its fair value. On this basis €6m would be allocated to the contract, thus resulting in a settlement loss of €6m and a correspondingly lower amount for goodwill of €4m.

IFRS is currently silent on the accounting for the repurchase of contractual rights to use an intangible asset – such as the grant of a right to use a brand name or a franchise agreement. As with executory contracts, repurchased contractual rights may also give rise to a gain or loss on settlement due to any 'off-market' pricing value. For any remaining value of the repurchased right, i.e. the 'on-market' element, the accounting should be consistent with the accounting that would be adopted for the purchase of contractual rights outside of a business combination. Provided that the underlying intangible asset is capable of separate recognition as an asset any remaining value is accounted for by recognising a separate intangible asset for the repurchased right that is amortised over the original contract term.

Note that the repurchase of a contractual right can be distinguished from executory contracts such as supply agreements. In the case of a supply agreement all of the rights and benefits are created by the agreement itself. In contrast, a contractual right to use an asset is the right to use an existing asset of the grantor i.e. a right that exists and is capable of being recognised independently of the contractual right to use. Accordingly, it is appropriate for the grantor in its consolidated financial statements to recognise an asset upon repurchase as it gives the grantor the ability to use those repurchased rights.

2.3.4 Goodwill

IFRS 3 defines 'goodwill' in terms of its nature, rather than in terms of its measurement.[166] It is defined as 'future economic benefits arising from assets that are not capable of being individually identified and separately recognised'.[167]

Accordingly, the standard requires that an acquirer shall, at the acquisition date, recognise goodwill acquired in a business combination as an asset. However, rather than attributing a fair value to the goodwill directly, the standard requires that the initial measurement of goodwill is its cost, being the excess of the cost of the business combination (as determined in 2.3.2 above) over the acquirer's interest in the net fair value of the identifiable assets, liabilities and contingent liabilities recognised in accordance with the standard (as determined in 2.3.3 above).[168]

Thus, although any minority interest in the acquiree will reflect the minority's proportion of net fair value of those net assets, no amount is included for any goodwill relating to the minority interest.

IFRS 3 thus considers goodwill acquired in a business combination to represent a payment made by the acquirer in anticipation of future economic benefits from assets that are not capable of being individually identified and separately recognised.[169]

Since goodwill is measured as the residual cost of the business combination after recognising the acquiree's identifiable assets, liabilities and contingent liabilities, then to the extent that the acquiree's identifiable assets, liabilities or contingent liabilities do not satisfy the criteria in IFRS 3 for separate recognition at the acquisition date (see 2.3.3 above), there is a resulting effect on the amount recognised as goodwill.[170]

The IASB in developing the standard observed that 'when goodwill is measured as a residual it could comprise the following components:

(a) the fair value of the "going concern" element of the acquiree. The going concern element represents the ability of the acquiree to earn a higher rate of return on an assembled collection of net assets than would be expected from those net assets operating separately. That value stems from the synergies of the net assets of the acquiree, as well as from other benefits such as factors related to market imperfections, including the ability to earn monopoly profits and barriers to market entry.

(b) the fair value of the expected synergies and other benefits from combining the acquiree's net assets with those of the acquirer. Those synergies and other benefits are unique to each business combination, and different combinations produce different synergies and, hence, different values.

(c) overpayments by the acquirer.

(d) errors in measuring and recognising the fair value of either the cost of the business combination or the acquiree's identifiable assets, liabilities or contingent liabilities, or a requirement in an accounting standard to measure those identifiable items at an amount that is not fair value.'[171]

The Board regards components (a) and (b) as being 'core goodwill' and conceptually part of goodwill that should be recognised as an asset, whereas components (c) and (d) are not. However, it took the view that it would not be feasible to determine the amount attributable to each component and, since the residual amount is likely to consist primarily of core goodwill, concluded it should be recognised as an asset.[172] Any overpayment logically would be exposed by the impairment test required in the subsequent accounting for goodwill discussed at 3 below.

2.3.5 *Excess of acquirer's interest in the net fair value of acquiree's identifiable assets, liabilities and contingent liabilities over cost*

IFRS 3 recognises that in some business combinations, the acquirer's interest in the net fair value of the acquiree's identifiable assets, liabilities and contingent liabilities exceeds the cost of the combination. Traditionally, that excess has been commonly referred to as 'negative goodwill' (although IFRS 3 does not use this term).

Where such an excess arises, IFRS 3 requires the acquirer to reassess the identification and measurement of the acquiree's identifiable assets, liabilities and contingent liabilities and the measurement of the cost of the combination.[173] This is because the existence of this excess might indicate that:

(a) the values attributed to the acquiree's identifiable assets have been overstated;

(b) identifiable liabilities and/or contingent liabilities of the acquiree have been omitted or the values attributed to those items have been understated; or

(c) the values assigned to the items comprising the cost of the business combination have been understated.[174]

The IASB considers that the excess cannot come about because there is an expectation of future losses and expenses. Instead, it considers that the expectation of such losses and expenses will depress the fair value of the acquiree's identifiable assets, liabilities and contingent liabilities.[175] As future losses and restructuring expenses are expressly prohibited from recognition as liabilities of the acquiree (see 2.3.3 A above), there would appear to be many occasions where the acquirer will have to perform an impairment exercise of the assets or cash generating assets that it has acquired in order to reflect their fair values.

Having undertaken that reassessment, the standard then requires that any excess remaining after that reassessment is recognised immediately in profit or loss.[176]

The standard notes that a gain recognised in accordance with the above requirement could comprise one or more of the following components:

(a) errors in measuring the fair value of either the cost of the combination or the acquiree's identifiable assets, liabilities or contingent liabilities, notwithstanding the reassessment. Possible future costs arising in respect of the acquiree that have not been reflected correctly in the fair value of the acquiree's identifiable assets, liabilities or contingent liabilities are a potential cause of such errors.

(b) a requirement in an accounting standard to measure identifiable net assets acquired at an amount that is not fair value, but is treated as though it is fair value for the purpose of allocating the cost of the combination. For example, the guidance in Appendix B to the standard (see 2.3.3 D above) on determining the fair values of the acquiree's identifiable assets and liabilities requires the amount assigned to tax assets and liabilities to be undiscounted.

(c) a bargain purchase.[177] This might occur, for example, when the seller of a business wishes to exit from that business for other than economic reasons and is prepared to accept less than its fair value as consideration;[178] this is particularly common if there is a distressed or 'fire' sale.

In developing the standard, the IASB considered whether the appropriate treatment for these components should be to recognise it as a reduction in the values attributed to the identifiable net asset, as a separate liability or immediately in profit or loss. However, the Board rejected the first two treatments and decided that the immediate recognition of a gain was the most faithful treatment of the part of the excess arising from a bargain purchase and that it would not be feasible to identify separately the amounts that are attributable to components (a) and (b) above.[179]

2.3.6 Subsequent adjustments to fair values

The initial accounting for a business combination under IFRS 3 involves identifying and determining the fair values to be assigned to the acquiree's identifiable assets, liabilities and contingent liabilities and the cost of the combination.[180]

The fact that the fair value process is inevitably, to some degree, a rationalisation of the price paid after the event means that an accounting issue arises: how much hindsight can the acquirer impute into the values assigned, or must the allocation be based solely on the information which it had at the time when it was making the bid? There is a theoretical argument for the latter, which is that if the acquirer was unaware of a particular matter, such as the fact that there was a deficiency in the pension fund of the target, then it cannot have influenced the acquisition price and thus should not feature in any allocation of that price.

Whatever the merits of that view in theory, however, it cannot be used in practice. If the acquirer was only able to assign values to items that it knew about at the time of the acquisition, the exercise would in many cases be completely impossible, because most acquisitions are not primarily based on an assessment of the value of the assets and liabilities of the target entity, but on an assessment of future earnings and cash flows. It is therefore necessary to allow the acquirer a reasonable period of time in which to investigate the assets and liabilities that have been acquired and make a reasoned allocation of values to them. The remaining question is, how much time should be allowed?

IFRS 3 effectively requires the acquirer to complete the allocation of the cost of the business combination to the acquiree's assets, liabilities and contingent liabilities within a period of twelve months of the acquisition date.[181] The important practical point for an acquirer is that it will have to demonstrate that any subsequent adjustments were in fact made by this date and not at its subsequent period end date.

If the initial accounting for a business combination can be determined only provisionally by the end of the period in which the combination is effected because either the fair values to be assigned to the acquiree's identifiable assets, liabilities or contingent liabilities or the cost of the combination can be determined only provisionally, the acquirer shall account for the combination using those provisional values.[182] IFRS 3 requires disclosure of the fact that it has only been determined provisionally, with an explanation as to why that has been case (see 2.3.10 below).

A Adjustments upon completion of initial accounting

Where as a result of completing the initial accounting within twelve months from the acquisition date adjustments to the provisional values have been found to be necessary, IFRS 3 requires them to be recognised from the acquisition date. This means, therefore, that:

(a) the carrying amount of an identifiable asset, liability or contingent liability that is recognised or adjusted as a result of completing the initial accounting is calculated as if its fair value at the acquisition date had been recognised from that date;

(b) goodwill or any gain recognised in accordance with paragraph 56 of the standard is adjusted from the acquisition date by an amount equal to the adjustment to the fair value at the acquisition date of the identifiable asset, liability or contingent liability being recognised or adjusted; and

(c) comparative information presented for the periods before the initial accounting for the combination is complete is presented as if the initial accounting had been completed from the acquisition date. This includes any additional depreciation, amortisation or other profit or loss effect recognised as a result of completing the initial accounting.[183]

These requirements are illustrated in the following example, which is based on Example 7 included within the Illustrative Examples accompanying IFRS 3. The deferred tax implications have been ignored.

Example 7.19: Finalisation of provisional values upon completion of initial accounting

Entity A prepares financial statements for annual periods ending on 31 December and does not prepare interim financial statements. The entity acquired another entity on 30 September 2007. Entity A sought an independent appraisal for an item of property, plant and equipment acquired in the combination. However, the appraisal was not finalised by the time the entity completed its 2007 annual financial statements. Entity A recognised in its 2007 annual financial statements a provisional fair value for the asset of €30,000, and a provisional value for acquired goodwill of €100,000. The item of property, plant and equipment had a remaining useful life at the acquisition date of five years.

Six months after the acquisition date, the entity received the independent appraisal, which estimated the asset's fair value at the acquisition date at €40,000.

In preparing its 2008 financial statements, Entity A is required to recognise any adjustments to provisional values as a result of completing the initial accounting from the acquisition date.

Part (a) of the requirement means that an adjustment is made to the carrying amount of the item of property, plant and equipment. That adjustment is measured as the fair value adjustment at the acquisition date of €10,000, less the additional depreciation that would have been recognised had the asset's fair value at the acquisition date been recognised from that date (€500 for three months' depreciation to 31 December 2007), i.e. an increase of €9,500. Part (b) requires the carrying amount of goodwill to be adjusted for the increase in value of the asset at the acquisition date of €10,000. Part (c) requires the 2007 comparative information to be restated to reflect these adjustments. Accordingly, the 2007 balance sheet is restated by increasing the carrying amount of property, plant and equipment by €9,500, reducing goodwill by €10,000 and retained earnings by €500. The 2007 income statement is restated to include additional depreciation of €500.

Entity A will disclose in its 2007 financial statements that the initial accounting for the business combination has been determined only provisionally, and explain why this is the case. In its 2008 financial statements it will disclose the amounts and explanations of the adjustments to the provisional values recognised during the current reporting period. Therefore, Entity A will disclose that:

- the fair value of the item of property, plant and equipment at the acquisition date has been increased by €10,000 with a corresponding decrease in goodwill; and

- the 2007 comparative information is restated to reflect this adjustment, including additional depreciation of €500 relating to the year ended 31 December 2007.

The above example illustrates a situation where a provisional value of an asset was finalised at a different amount as part of the completion of the initial accounting.

Example 7.20: Identification of an asset upon completion of initial accounting

Entity C prepares financial statements for annual periods ending on 31 December and does not prepare interim financial statements. The entity acquired another entity on 30 November 2007. Entity C engaged an independent appraiser to assist with the identification and determination of fair values to be assigned to the acquiree's assets, liabilities and contingent liabilities and the cost of the business combination. However, the appraisal was not finalised by the time the entity completed its 2007 annual financial statements, and therefore the amounts recognised in its 2007 annual financial statements were on a provisional basis.

As part of the work carried out in finalising the initial accounting, it was identified by the independent appraiser that the acquiree had an intangible asset (meeting all of the IAS 38 recognition and identification criteria) with a fair value at the date of acquisition of €20,000. However, this had not been identified at the time when Entity C was preparing its 2007 annual financial statements. Thus, no value had been included for this intangible asset.

In preparing its 2008 financial statements, Entity C is required to recognise any adjustments to provisional values as a result of completing the initial accounting from the acquisition date. In this case, no value had been recognised, and indeed, the intangible asset had not even been identified at the time of preparing its 2007 financial statements. So, can an adjustment be made under these provisions of IFRS 3?

In our view, an adjustment is appropriate. The requirements are not limited to measurement adjustments (although a literal reading of the first sentence of paragraph 62 could imply that to be the case). Adjustments to recognise subsequently identified assets or liabilities are permitted as a result of completing the initial accounting. The initial accounting involves the identification as well as the measurement of the acquiree's assets, liabilities and contingent liabilities, and it is clear from (a) above that adjustments are to be made for items that are *recognised* as a result of completing the exercise.

Although IFRS 3 allows this period of hindsight to be used, it is important that any adjustments to the provisional allocation reflect conditions as they existed at the date of the acquisition, rather than being affected by subsequent events; the objective is to determine the fair values of the items at the date of acquisition. There is a parallel to be drawn here with the accounting treatment of events after the balance sheet date. Only those events which provide further evidence of conditions as they existed at the acquisition date should be taken into account.

B Adjustments after the initial accounting is complete

With three exceptions (see C below), after the initial accounting is complete, IFRS 3 only allows adjustments to the initial accounting for a business combination to be made to correct an error in accordance with IAS 8 (see Chapter 3 at 4.6).[184] This would probably be the case only if the original allocation was based on a complete misinterpretation of the facts which were available at the time; it would not apply simply because new information had come to light which changed the acquiring management's view of the value of the item in question.

Adjustments to the initial accounting for a business combination after it is complete are not made for the effect of changes in estimates. In accordance with IAS 8, the effect of a change in estimates is recognised in the current and future periods (see Chapter 3 at 4.5).[185]

Where it is determined that an error has been made, IFRS 3 notes that IAS 8 requires an entity to account for an error correction retrospectively, and to present financial statements as if the error had never occurred by restating the comparative information for the prior period(s) in which the error occurred.[186] The accounting is similar to that outlined above for adjustments upon completion of initial accounting. The only difference being there is no time limit as to when such adjustments may be required.

These requirements are illustrated in Examples 7.21 and 7.22 below, which are based on Examples 8 and 9 included within the Illustrative Examples accompanying IFRS 3. The deferred tax implications have been ignored.

Example 7.21: Error resulting in an increase in identifiable assets leading to a decrease in goodwill

Entity A prepares financial statements for annual periods ending on 31 December and does not prepare interim financial statements. The entity acquired another entity on 30 September 2007. As part of the initial accounting for that combination, Entity A recognised goodwill of €100,000 in its 2007 financial statements. No impairment was recognised for this goodwill, so the carrying amount of goodwill at 31 December 2006 was €100,000.

During 2008, Entity A becomes aware of an error relating to the amount initially allocated to property, plant and equipment assets acquired in the business combination. In particular, €20,000 of the €100,000 initially allocated to goodwill should have been allocated to property, plant and equipment assets that had a remaining useful life at the acquisition date of five years, with an assumed residual value of nil.

In preparing its 2008 financial statements, Entity A is required to account for the correction of the error retrospectively, and for the financial statements to be presented as if the error had never occurred by correcting the error in the comparative information for the prior period in which it occurred.

Therefore, in the 2008 financial statements, an adjustment is made to the carrying amount of property, plant and equipment assets at 31 December 2007. The adjustment is measured as the fair value adjustment at the acquisition date of €20,000 less the amount that would have been recognised as depreciation of the fair value adjustment (€1,000 for three months' depreciation to 31 December 2007); i.e. property, plant and equipment is increased by €19,000. The carrying amount of goodwill is also adjusted for the reduction in its value at the acquisition date of €20,000. Accordingly, retained earnings at 31 December 2007 are reduced by €1,000. The 2007 income statement is restated to include additional depreciation of €1,000.

In accordance with IAS 8, Entity A will disclose in its 2008 financial statements the nature of the error and that, as a result of correcting that error, an adjustment was made to the carrying amount of property, plant and equipment. It will also disclose that:

- the fair value of property, plant and equipment assets at the acquisition date has been increased by €20,000 with a corresponding decrease in goodwill; and
- the 2007 comparative information is restated to reflect this adjustment, including additional depreciation of €1,000 for the year ended 31 December 2007.

Example 7.22: Error resulting in a decrease in identifiable assets leading to an increase in goodwill

This example assumes the same facts as in Example 7.21 above, except that the amount initially allocated to property, plant and equipment assets is decreased by €20,000 to correct the error, rather than increased by €20,000. This example also assumes that Entity A determines that the recoverable amount of the additional goodwill is only €17,000 at 31 December 2007.

Therefore, in the 2008 financial statements, an adjustment is made to the carrying amount of property, plant and equipment assets at 31 December 2007. The adjustment is measured as the fair value adjustment at the acquisition date of €20,000 less the amount that should not have been recognised as depreciation of the fair value adjustment (€1,000 for three months' depreciation to 31 December 2007); i.e. property, plant and equipment is reduced by €19,000. The carrying amount of goodwill is increased by €17,000, being the increase in value at the acquisition date of €20,000 less a €3,000 impairment loss to reflect that the carrying amount of the adjustment exceeds its recoverable amount. Accordingly, retained earnings at 31 December 2007 are reduced by €2,000. The 2007 income statement is restated to reflect these adjustments; i.e. it includes the €3,000 impairment loss but excludes the €1,000 depreciation.

C Recognition of deferred tax assets after the initial accounting is complete

IFRS 3 makes three exceptions to this requirement of only allowing adjustments for errors once the initial accounting is complete. The first two relate to adjustments to the cost of a business combination that was contingent on future events (see 2.3.2 E above). The other exception relates to the recognition of deferred tax assets. This exception was carried forward from IAS 22 without reconsideration by the IASB, and will be reconsidered as part of phase II of its business combinations project (as are the other two exceptions).

If the potential benefit of the acquiree's income tax loss carry-forwards or other deferred tax assets did not satisfy the criteria in paragraph 37 of IFRS 3 for separate recognition when a business combination is initially accounted for but is subsequently realised, IFRS 3 states that the acquirer recognises that benefit as income in accordance with IAS 12. However, in addition, the acquirer:

(a) reduces the carrying amount of goodwill to the amount that would have been recognised if the deferred tax asset had been recognised as an identifiable asset from the acquisition date; and

(b) recognises the reduction in the carrying amount of the goodwill as an expense.

The standard goes on to say that this procedure is not to result in the creation of an excess as described in paragraph 56 of the standard (see 2.3.5 above), nor is it to increase the amount of any gain previously recognised in accordance with paragraph 56.[187]

These requirements are discussed further in Chapter 26 at 6.2.2 B to D.

2.3.7 Business combinations achieved in stages

So far, this chapter has discussed the application of the purchase method of accounting in the context of business combinations that result from a single exchange transaction. However, in practice some subsidiaries are acquired in a series of steps which can take place over an extended period, during which the underlying value of the subsidiary is likely to change, both because of the trading profits (or losses) which it retains and because of other movements in the fair values of its assets and liabilities. The accounting problems which this creates are therefore how to establish the cost of the business combination, the fair values of the net assets acquired, and therefore the amount of goodwill arising. It also has implications for the impact of the business combination on the post-acquisition reserves in the consolidated financial statements of the acquirer.

IFRS 3 recognises that a business combination may involve more than one exchange transaction, for example when it occurs in stages by successive share purchases. The requirements of the standard have principally been carried forward from IAS 22 and they will be reconsidered as part of the second phase of the business combinations project.[188]

Where a business combination does involve more than one exchange transaction, the standard requires that each exchange transaction shall be treated separately by the acquirer; i.e. by using the cost of the transaction and fair value information at the date of each exchange transaction, to determine the amount of any goodwill associated with that transaction. This results in a step-by-step comparison of the cost of the individual investments with the acquirer's interest in the fair values of the acquiree's identifiable assets, liabilities and contingent liabilities at each step.[189] (It has to be said that this actually contradicts the requirement of paragraph 36 of the standard (see 2.3.3 above) which is to allocate the cost of the business combination (this is the same under both requirements) to the acquiree's identifiable assets, liabilities and contingent liabilities at their fair values at the date of acquisition (i.e. the date that it obtains control), with any difference between the cost and the acquirer's interest in those net fair values being accounted for as goodwill or a gain in profit or loss. This is because the methodology in paragraph 36 would otherwise result in the share of reserves and asset revaluation reserves relating to the interest in the associate being rolled into the calculation of goodwill, as can be seen in the following examples.)

Where a subsidiary has been acquired by successive share purchases, then theoretically the standard would require separate comparisons, even if the shares were purchased over a short period of time. However, it may that in such a situation that the fair values of the acquiree's identifiable assets, liabilities and contingent liabilities at the date of acquisition could be used, as long as the values are unlikely to have been materially different during the period the shares were being purchased.

The standard notes that when a business combination involves more than one exchange transaction, the fair values of the acquiree's identifiable assets, liabilities and contingent liabilities may be different at the date of each exchange transaction.[190] This is likely to be the case where the transactions have taken place over an extended period. The standard states that because:

(a) the acquiree's identifiable assets, liabilities and contingent liabilities are notionally restated to their fair values at the date of each exchange transaction to determine the amount of any goodwill associated with each transaction; and

(b) the acquiree's identifiable assets, liabilities and contingent liabilities must then be recognised by the acquirer at their fair values at the acquisition date,

any adjustment to those fair values relating to previously held interests of the acquirer is a revaluation to be accounted for as such. However, it goes on to say that because this revaluation arises on the initial recognition by the acquirer of the acquiree's assets, liabilities and contingent liabilities, it does not signify that the acquirer has elected to apply an accounting policy of revaluing those items after initial recognition in accordance with, for example, IAS 16 – *Property, Plant and Equipment*.[191]

Before qualifying as a business combination, a transaction may qualify as an investment in an associate and be accounted for in accordance with IAS 28 – *Investments in Associates* – using the equity method. If so, the fair values of the investee's identifiable net assets at the date of each earlier exchange transaction will have been determined previously in applying the equity method to the investment (see Chapter 8 at 3.2).[192]

These requirements are illustrated in the following examples which are based on Example 6 included within the Illustrative Examples accompanying IFRS 3, except that in Example 7.23 below the acquirer has reflected the changes in value of its original investment in equity rather than in profit or loss.

Example 7.23: Business combination achieved in stages – original investment treated as an available-for-sale investment under IAS 39

Investor acquires a 20 per cent ownership interest in Investee (a service company) on 1 January 2006 for £3,500,000 cash. At that date, the fair value of Investee's identifiable assets is £10,000,000, and the carrying amount of those assets is £8,000,000. Investee has no liabilities or contingent liabilities at that date. The following shows Investee's balance sheet at 1 January 2006 together with the fair values of the identifiable assets:

Investee's balance sheet at 1 January 2006	Carrying amounts £'000	Fair values £'000
Cash and receivables	2,000	2,000
Land	6,000	8,000
	8,000	10,000
Issued equity: 1,000,000 ordinary shares	5,000	
Retained earnings	3,000	
	8,000	

During the year ended 31 December 2006, Investee reports a profit of £6,000,000 but does not pay any dividends. In addition, the fair value of Investee's land increases by £3,000,000 to £11,000,000. However, the amount recognised by Investee in respect of the land remains unchanged at £6,000,000. The following shows Investee's balance sheet at 31 December 2006 together with the fair values of the identifiable assets:

Investee's balance sheet at 31 December 2006	Carrying amounts	Fair values
	£'000	£'000
Cash and receivables	8,000	8,000
Land	6,000	11,000
	14,000	19,000
Issued equity: 1,000,000 ordinary shares	5,000	
Retained earnings	9,000	
	14,000	

On 1 January 2007, Investor acquires a further 60 per cent ownership interest in Investee for £22,000,000 cash, thereby obtaining control. Before obtaining control, Investor does not have significant influence over Investee, and accounts for its initial 20 per cent investment at fair value with changes in value taken to equity. Investee's ordinary shares have a quoted market price at 31 December 2006 of £30 per share.

Throughout the period 1 January 2006 to 1 January 2007, Investor's issued equity was £30,000,000. Investor's only asset apart from its investment in Investee is cash.

Accounting for the initial investment before obtaining control

Investor's initial 20 per cent investment in Investee is measured at its cost of £3,500,000. However, Investee's 1,000,000 ordinary shares have a quoted market price at 31 December 2006 of £30 per share. Therefore, the carrying amount of Investor's initial 20 per cent investment is remeasured in Investor's financial statements to £6,000,000 at 31 December 2006, with the £2,500,000 increase recognised in equity. Therefore, Investor's balance sheet at 31 December 2006, before the acquisition of the additional 60 per cent ownership interest, is as follows:

Investor's balance sheet at 31 December 2006	£'000
Cash	26,500
Investment in Investee	6,000
	32,500
Issued equity	30,000
Gain on available-for-sale investment	2,500
	32,500

Accounting for the business combination

Paragraph 25 of IFRS 3 (see 2.3.2 A above) states that when a business combination involves more than one exchange transaction, the cost of the combination is the aggregate cost of the individual transactions, with the cost of each individual transaction determined at the date of each exchange transaction, i.e. the date that each individual investment is recognised in the acquirer's financial statements). This means that for this example, the cost to Investor of the business combination is the aggregate of the cost of the initial 20 per cent ownership interest (£3,500,000) plus the cost of the subsequent 60 per cent ownership interest (£22,000,000), irrespective of the fact that the carrying amount of the initial 20 per cent interest has changed.

In addition, and in accordance with paragraph 58 of IFRS 3, each transaction must be treated separately to determine the goodwill on that transaction, using cost and fair value information at the date of each exchange transaction. Therefore, Investor recognises the following amounts for goodwill in its consolidated financial statements:

	£'000	Goodwill £'000
Acquisition of 20% interest on 1 January 2006		
Cost	3,500	
Share of fair values at that date (20% × £10,000,000)	2,000	
		1,500
Acquisition of 60% interest on 1 January 2007		
Cost	22,000	
Share of fair values at that date (60% × £19,000,000)	11,400	
		10,600
		12,100

The following shows Investor's consolidation worksheet immediately after the acquisition of the additional 60 per cent ownership interest in Investee, together with consolidation adjustments and associated explanations:

	Investor	Investee	Consolidation adjustments Dr	Cr	Consolidated
	£'000	£'000	£'000	£'000	£'000
Cash and receivables	4,500	8,000			12,500
Investment in investee	28,000	–		2,500 (2) 3,500 (3) 22,000 (4)	–
Land		6,000	5,000 (1)		11,000 (a)
Goodwill			1,500 (3) 10,600 (4)		12,100 (b)
	32,500	14,000			35,600
Issued equity	30,000	5,000	1,000 (3) 3,000 (4) 1,000 (5)		30,000 (c)
Asset revaluation surplus			400 (3) 3,000 (4) 1,000 (5)	5,000 (1)	600 (d)
Gain on available-for-sale investment	2,500		2,500 (2)		
Retained earnings		9,000	600 (3) 5,400 (4) 1,800 (5)		1,200 (e)
Minority interest				3,800 (5)	3,800 (a)
	32,500	14,000			35,600

Consolidation Adjustments

		£'000	£'000
(1)	Land	5,000	
	Asset revaluation surplus		5,000
	To recognise Investee's identifiable assets at fair values at the acquisition date		

		£'000	£'000
(2)	Gain on available-for-sale investment	2,500	
	Investment in Investee		2,500
	To restate the initial 20 per cent investment in Investee to cost		

		£'000	£'000
(3)	Issued equity [20% × 5,000,000]	1,000	
	Asset revaluation surplus [20% × 2,000,000]	400	
	Retained earnings [20% × 3,000,000]	600	
	Goodwill	1,500	
	Investment in investee		3,500
	To recognise goodwill on the initial 20 per cent investment in Investee and record the elimination of that investment against associated equity balances		

		£'000	£'000
(4)	Issued equity [60% × 5,000,000]	3,000	
	Asset revaluation surplus [60% × 5,000,000]	3,000	
	Retained earnings [60% × 9,000,000]	5,400	
	Goodwill	10,600	
	Investment in investee		22,000
	To recognise goodwill on the subsequent 60 per cent investment in Investee and record elimination of that investment against associated equity balances		

		£'000	£'000
(5)	Issued equity [20% × 5,000,000]	1,000	
	Asset revaluation surplus [20% × 5,000,000]	1,000	
	Retained earnings [20% × 9,000,000]	1,800	
	Minority interest (in issued equity)		1,000
	Minority interest (in asset revaluation surplus)		1,000
	Minority interest (in retained earnings)		1,800
	To recognise the minority interest in the Investee		

Notes

The above consolidation adjustments result in:

(a) Investee's identifiable net assets being stated at their full fair values at the date Investor obtains control of Investee, i.e. £19,000,000. This means that the 20 per cent minority interest in Investee also is stated at the minority's 20 per cent share of the fair values of Investee's identifiable net assets.

(b) goodwill being recognised from the acquisition date at an amount based on treating each exchange transaction separately and using cost and fair value information at the date of each exchange transaction.

(c) issued equity of £30,000,000 comprising the issued equity of Investor of£30,000,000.

(d) an asset revaluation surplus of £600,000. This amount reflects that part of the increase in the fair value of Investee's identifiable net assets after the acquisition of the initial 20 per cent interest that is attributable to that initial 20 per cent interest [20% × £3,000,000].

(e) a retained earnings balance of £1,200,000. This amount reflects the changes in Investee's retained earnings after Investor acquired its initial 20 per cent interest that is attributable to that 20 per cent interest [20% × £6,000,000].

Therefore, the effect of applying the requirements in IFRS 3 to business combinations involving successive share purchases for which the investment was previously accounted for at fair value with changes in value taken to equity is to cause:

- changes in the fair value of previously held ownership interests to be reversed (so that the carrying amounts of those ownership interests are restated to cost).
- changes in the investee's retained earnings and other equity balances after each exchange transaction to be included in the post-combination consolidated financial statements to the extent that they relate to the previously held ownership interests.

Theses changes will need to be reflected in the statement of changes in equity.

As noted earlier, these requirements contradict the requirements of paragraph 36 of the standard. If that paragraph had been applied literally, the goodwill would have been £10,300,000, being the total cost of investment of £25,500,000 less £15,200,000 (being Investor's interest of 80% of the fair value of Investee's assets of £19,000,000 at the date of acquisition). The difference of £1,800,000 between this figure and goodwill as calculated above on each exchange transaction is the asset revaluation surplus of £600,000 ((d) above) and the share of reserves of £1,200,000 ((e) above), both of which would be subsumed within goodwill calculated solely as at the date that Investee became a subsidiary.

If the investor in the above example had accounted for its original investment of 20% as an associate using the equity method under IAS 28, then the accounting would have been as follows:

Example 7.24: Business combination achieved in stages – original investment treated as an associate under IAS 28

This example uses the same facts as in Example 7.23 above, except that Investor does have significant influence over Investee following its initial 20 per cent investment.

Accounting for the initial investment before obtaining control

Investor's initial 20 per cent investment in Investee is included in Investor's consolidated financial statements under the equity method (see Chapter 8 at 3). Accordingly, it is initially recognised at its cost of £3,500,000 and adjusted thereafter for its share of the profits of Investee after the date of acquisition of £1,200,000 (being 20% × £6,000,000). Investor's policy for property, plant and equipment is to use the cost model under IAS 16 (see Chapter 13 at 2.4), therefore in applying the equity method it does not include its share of the increased value of the land held by Investee. IAS 28 requires that on the acquisition of an associate, any difference between the cost of the acquisition and its share of the fair values of the associate's identifiable assets, liabilities and contingent liabilities is accounted for under IFRS 3, although any goodwill is included within the carrying amount of the investment in the associate. Accordingly, Investor has already calculated the goodwill of £1,500,000 arising on its original investment of 20%. Therefore, Investor's consolidated balance sheet at 31 December 2006, before the acquisition of the additional 60 per cent ownership interest, is as follows:

Investor's consolidated balance sheet at 31 December 2006	£'000
Cash	26,500
Investment in associate	4,700
	31,200
Issued equity	30,000
Retained earnings	1,200
	31,200

In its separate financial statements, Investor includes its investment in the associate at its cost of £3,500,000.

Accounting for the business combination

As in Example 7.23, the cost of the combination is the aggregate cost of the individual transactions, with the cost of each individual transaction determined at the date of each exchange transaction, i.e. the date that each individual investment is recognised in the acquirer's financial statements), and each transaction must be treated separately to determine the goodwill on that transaction, using cost and fair value information at the date of each exchange transaction. Therefore, Investor recognises the following amounts for goodwill in its consolidated financial statements:

	£'000	Goodwill £'000
Acquisition of 20% interest on 1 January 2006		
Cost	3,500	
Share of fair values at that date (20% × £10,000,000)	2,000	
		1,500
Acquisition of 60% interest on 1 January 2007		
Cost	22,000	
Share of fair values at that date (60% × £19,000,000)	11,400	
		10,600
		12,100

As indicated above, Investor will have already calculated the goodwill arising on its original investment, but not recognised it separately.

The following shows Investor's consolidation worksheet immediately after the acquisition of the additional 60 per cent ownership interest in Investee, together with consolidation adjustments and associated explanations.

	Investor	Investee	Consolidation adjustments		Consolidated
			Dr	Cr	
	£'000	£'000	£'000	£'000	£'000
Cash and receivables	4,500	8,000			12,500
Investment in investee	25,500	–			–
				3,500 (3)	
				22,000 (4)	
Land		6,000	5,000 (1)		11,000 (a)
Goodwill			1,500 (3)		12,100 (b)
			10,600 (4)		
	30,000	14,000			35,600

Issued equity	30,000	5,000	1,000 (3) 3,000 (4) 1,000 (5)		30,000 (c)
Asset revaluation surplus			400 (3) 3,000 (4) 1,000 (5)	5,000 (1)	600 (d)
Retained earnings		9,000	600 (3) 5,400 (4) 1,800 (5)		1,200 (e)
Minority interest				3,800 (5)	3,800 (a)
	30,000	14,000			35,600

The consolidation adjustments are exactly the same as in Example 7.23, except that there was no need for adjustment (2) since the investment of 20% was already included at cost.

The notes in Example 7.23 also apply to this example. The only difference is that the retained earnings balance has already been reflected in the consolidated balance sheet of Investor at 31 December 2006.

Therefore, the effect of applying the requirements in IFRS 3 to business combinations involving successive share purchases for which the investment was previously accounted for under the equity method is to cause changes in the investee's equity balances after each exchange transaction that result from changes in fair values to be included in the post-combination consolidated financial statements to the extent that they relate to the previously held ownership interests (and have not already been recognised).

In this example, the £600,000 asset revaluation surplus will be recognised in the statement of changes in equity in Investor's consolidated financial statements for 2007.

Overall, therefore, the effect of applying IFRS 3 to any business combination involving successive share purchases is to cause:

- any changes in the carrying amount of previously held ownership interests to be reversed (so that the carrying amounts of those ownership interests are restated to cost).
- changes in the investee's retained earnings and other equity balances after each exchange transaction to be included in the post-combination consolidated financial statements to the extent that they relate to the previously held ownership interests.

Consequently, the consolidated financial statements immediately after Investor acquires the additional 60 per cent ownership interest and obtains control of Investee would be the same irrespective of the method used to account for the initial 20 per cent investment in Investee before obtaining control.

As indicated earlier, the standard states that the adjustment to those fair values relating to previously held interests of the acquirer is a revaluation to be accounted for as such.[193] However, the standard is silent as to whether any such revaluation gain (or loss) can be recycled into profit or loss at a later date. IAS 27 – *Consolidated and Separate Financial Statements* – also does not make any reference to such items being taken into account in calculating the gain or loss on disposal of a subsidiary (see Chapter 6 at 6.6). Although in the above examples, the revaluation gain arose on land, in practice, any revaluation gain or loss is likely to arise on various assets or liabilities of the acquiree. It will therefore depend on the facts and circumstances whether revaluation amounts arising on business combinations achieved in stages are recycled through profit or loss on subsequent disposal of the underlying assets (or liabilities) or businesses concerned. In many cases, the revaluation amounts are likely to arise on items such as intangible assets and property, plant and equipment, where under the relevant standard for such items, revaluations gains and losses are not recycled upon disposal of the related asset. Accordingly, revaluation amounts in respect of such items that arise from a business combination involving successive share purchases should not be recycled into profit or loss, either on disposal of the underlying assets or the business concerned. However, where the revaluation amounts relate specifically to items where the relevant accounting standard would require recycling, such as available-for-sale investments under IAS 39, then gains on such items should be treated no differently from any other subsequent gains or losses for such items that are taken to equity. Thus, they may be recycled into the profit or loss, either on disposal of the underlying assets or the business concerned.

If the revaluation surplus in equity relates directly to an identifiable fixed asset, whether intangible or an item of property, plant and equipment, it may be transferred directly to retained earnings when the asset is derecognised, in whole on disposal or as the asset concerned is depreciated or amortised.[194] If, as may well be the case, the revaluation relates to fair value adjustments on a bundle of assets and liabilities, the reserve will only be transferred to retained earnings on derecognition of the interest in the subsidiary.

In situations such as that illustrated in Example 7.24 above, where the equity method of accounting has been applied to the original investments, the requirements of IFRS 3 do not appear to create any additional practical difficulties over and above those that arose when the acquirer had to allocate the cost of the associate originally to the fair values of the acquiree's assets, liabilities and contingent liabilities. The main practical difficulty will be where equity accounting has not been applied to earlier stages of the business combination, such as in Example 7.23 above. In that case, the acquirer has to calculate goodwill based on fair values at the time of that original acquisition, yet will not have had to carry out such an exercise at that time. This situation is similar in many ways to that considered by the IASB in relation to the transitional provisions of IFRS 3 where it was decided that applying the standard retrospectively would be problematic, particularly in relation to the role of hindsight, and may even be impossible because the information needed may not exist or may no longer be obtainable. As discussed at 4.1.5 below the IASB only allows retrospective application of the standard where valuations and other information were obtained at the time the business combinations were initially accounted for. Where entities are contemplating making initial investments in other entities with a view to possibly obtaining a controlling stake in the entity in the future, they should consider carrying out a fair value exercise at that time, albeit that it may have to be done on a broad brush basis due to the lack of detailed information.

Although the requirements discussed above, and Example 7.24 above, deal with an associate becoming a subsidiary, the same accounting treatment applies when a jointly controlled entity becomes a subsidiary.

Example 7.25: Business combination achieved in stages – jointly controlled entity becoming a subsidiary

Entity M and Entity P currently operate a joint venture, Entity J, with Entity M holding a 75% interest and Entity P a 25% interest, each party having joint control. Entity M accounts for Entity J's activities as a jointly controlled entity according to IAS 31 – *Interests in Joint Ventures* (see Chapter 9).

Entity M now buys out Entity P's 25% interest in Entity J and as a result, obtains control over Entity J's activities.

Consequently, the acquisition of the remaining 25% of Entity J gives rise to a business combination. Therefore, at the date control is obtained, Entity M accounts for the transaction as a step acquisition, and thus:

- determines goodwill for the newly acquired 25% interest using the cost of that transaction and the fair value of Entity J's identifiable net assets at the date control is obtained;
- recognises the assets and liabilities at 100% of their fair value at the date of control; and
- treats any adjustment to those fair values relating to previously held interests as a revaluation.

This applies irrespective of whether Entity M equity accounted for its 75% interest in the joint venture or dealt with it by way of proportionate consolidation.

A Acquisitions of minority interests

The requirements discussed above deal only with those situations where there have been earlier exchange transactions prior to the one that has resulted in a business combination, such as the acquisition of a subsidiary, whereby the acquirer now has control over that business. However, the standard is silent on how later exchange transactions should be accounted for, such as the acquisition of some or all of the minority interest in a subsidiary.

Example 7.26: Acquisition of minority interest

Following on from Example 7.23 above, during the year ended 31 December 2007, Investee, now an 80% subsidiary of Investor, reports a profit of £8,000,000 but does not pay any dividends. In addition, the fair value of Investee's land increases by a further £4,000,000 to £15,000,000. However, the amount recognised by Investee in respect of the land remains unchanged at £6,000,000. The following shows Investee's balance sheet at 31 December 2007 together with the fair values of the identifiable assets:

Investee's balance sheet at 31 December 2007	Carrying amounts £'000	Fair values £'000
Cash and receivables	16,000	16,000
Land	6,000	15,000
	22,000	31,000
Issued equity: 1,000,000 ordinary shares	5,000	
Retained earnings	17,000	
	22,000	

Investor's issued equity remains at £30,000,000 and has not reported any profits for the year ended 31 December 2007.

The following shows Investor's consolidation worksheet as at 31 December 2007, together with consolidation adjustments and associated explanations:

	Investor	Investee	Consolidation adjustments Dr	Consolidation adjustments Cr	Consolidated
	£'000	£'000	£'000	£'000	£'000
Cash and receivables	4,500	16,000			20,500
Investment in investee	28,000	–		2,500 (2) 3,500 (3) 22,000 (4)	–
Land		6,000	5,000 (1)		11,000 (a)
Goodwill			1,500 (3) 10,600 (4)		12,100 (b)
	32,500	22,000			43,600
Issued equity	30,000	5,000	1,000 (3) 3,000 (4) 1,000 (5)		30,000 (c)
Asset revaluation surplus			400 (3) 3,000 (4) 1,000 (5)	5,000 (1)	600 (d)
Gain on available-for-sale investment	2,500		2,500 (2)		
Retained earnings		17,000	600 (3) 5,400 (4) 1,800 (5) 1,600 (5)		7,600 (e)
Minority interest				5,400 (5)	5,400 (a)
	32,500	22,000			43,600

Consolidation Adjustments

The consolidation adjustments are the same as in Example 7.23, except that consolidation adjustment (5) reflects an additional adjustment of:

		£'000	£'000
(5)	Retained earnings [20% × 8,000,000]	1,600	
	Minority interest (in retained earnings)		1,600
	To recognise the minority interest in Investee's results for 2007		

Notes

The consolidation adjustments result in:

(a) Investee's identifiable net assets being stated at their full fair values at the date Investor obtains control of Investee, i.e. £19,000,000, plus the profits for the year of £8,000,000. This means that the 20 per cent minority interest in Investee is stated at the minority's 20 per cent share of £27,000,000.

(e) a retained earnings balance of £7,600,000, being the £1,200,000 as in Example 7.23 together with £6,400,000 being Investor's 80% share of Investee's profits of £8,000,000.

Notes (b), (c) and (d) in Example 7.23 also apply to this example.

On 1 January 2008, Investor acquires the remaining 20 per cent ownership interest in Investee for £6,500,000 cash. How should this be accounted for?

In accounting for the acquisition of the minority interest there are two main issues that need to be considered:

- are the acquiree's net assets restated – either in full or in part – to their fair values at the date the minority interest is acquired?
- how is any difference between the cost of acquisition and the minority interest acquired accounted for?

As far as the first issue is concerned, in our view the acquiree's net assets must not be restated, either in full or in part, to their fair value at the date the minority interest is acquired. Fair value adjustments are made only at the date of the business combination, and the acquisition of a minority interest is not considered a business combination under IFRS 3. This would also apply if an acquirer had previously adopted IAS 22's benchmark treatment whereby fair value adjustments were not recognised for the minority's ownership interest.

As far as the second issue is concerned, as the acquisition of a minority interest is not a business combination there is no specific accounting prescribed in IFRS for such a transaction. Accordingly, Investor must, therefore, apply the hierarchy in IAS 8 (see Chapter 3) to develop an appropriate accounting policy for such a transaction. Several conceptual approaches may be acceptable but the approach chosen should be consistently applied. In our view, the following are acceptable methods of accounting for the difference between the cost of acquisition and the minority interest acquired:

(a) the entire difference may be reflected as goodwill (the 'Parent entity extension method' – see Chapter 6 at 1.4.2)

Under this method, the entire difference between the cost of the additional interest in the subsidiary and the minority interest's share of the assets and liabilities reflected in the consolidated balance sheet at the date of the acquisition of the minority interest is reflected as goodwill. The assets and liabilities of the subsidiary would not be remeasured to reflect their fair values at the date of the transaction. In this case, Investor would recognise additional goodwill of £1,100,000 being the difference between the cost of £6,500,000 and £5,400,000 (the minority interest's 20% share in the net assets of Investee). The drawback with this method is that it results in a figure for goodwill for that particular transaction that is not based on fair values at the date of that transaction.

(b) the entire difference may be reflected as an equity transaction (the 'Entity concept method' – see Chapter 6 at 1.4.1)

Under this method, the entire difference between the cost of the additional interest in the subsidiary and the minority interest's share of the assets and liabilities reflected in the consolidated balance sheet at the date of the acquisition of the minority interest is reflected as being a transaction between owners. In this case, Investor would recognise the £1,100,000 as an equity transaction. This method is supported by the fact IAS 27 requires minority interests to be presented in the consolidated balance sheet within equity, separately from the parent shareholders' equity (see Chapter 6 at 6.7). The drawback with this method is that the entity concept on which it is based, is not presently used under IFRS 3 for determining goodwill. As indicated below, this is the method that the IASB is proposing as part of phase II of its business combinations project.

(c) the difference may be reflected partly as goodwill – measured using IFRS 3's principles – and partly as equity (effectively a 'Hybrid entity concept/parent entity method')

Under this method, the difference between the cost of the additional interest in the subsidiary and the minority interest's share of the assets and liabilities reflected in the consolidated balance sheet at the date of the acquisition of the minority interest is reflected partly as goodwill (measured using IFRS 3 principles) and partly as an equity transaction. In this case, the share of fair values of Investee at 1 January 2008 is £6,200,000 (being 20% of £31,000,000), thus resulting in additional goodwill of £300,000 (£6,500,000 – £6,200,000), and the balance of

£800,000 would be recognised directly in equity. As with the entity concept method, this approach is supported by the equity classification of minority interests and remains consistent with the purchased goodwill methodology required by IFRS 3. The drawback is that it does not consistently adopt one conceptual approach or the other.

As indicated above in respect of the first issue, we believe that the following methods that are sometimes advocated for dealing with this issue are not acceptable under IFRS:

- Full step-up
  This method would adopt the same treatment in IFRS 3, i.e. recording a full step up in values and using the cost of the transaction and fair value information at the date of this exchange transaction to determine the amount of any goodwill associated with this transaction. In this case the share of fair values at 1 January 2008 is £6,200,000 (being 20% of £31,000,000), thus resulting in additional goodwill of £300,000. The land is included in the consolidated financial statements at its full fair value of £15,000,000 at 1 January 2008, resulting in a further asset revaluation surplus of £3,200,000, being 80% of £4,000,000. The £800,000 attributable to the minority interest's share is eliminated as part of the calculation of goodwill relating to the acquisition of the minority interest. In our view, this method is unacceptable because this revaluation does not arise on the initial recognition by the acquirer of the acquiree's assets, and IFRS 3 only permits the remeasurement of existing assets and liabilities, including the recognition of identifiable intangible assets and contingent liabilities when there has been a business combination with a change in control. Further, there is no other IFRS that allows or requires recognition of contingent liabilities or the remeasurement of all internally generated intangible assets.
- Partial step-up (US GAAP)
  This method would adopt a similar approach to that in IFRS 3, but restricting the step-up in fair values to the amounts used for the purpose of determining the amount of any goodwill associated with that particular transaction. However, no adjustments are made to incorporate any revaluations in respect of the interest in the subsidiary that was already held. This is the treatment that would be required by US GAAP.[195] In this case, Investor would still recognise goodwill of £300,000 but, in order to do so, it would need to reflect the land at £11,800,000. This would effectively represent £8,800,000 (being 80% of £11,000,000, the fair value at the date Investee became a subsidiary) and £3,000,000 (being 20% of £15,000,000, the fair value at the date of acquiring the minority interest). Although this method may result in a more meaningful figure for the goodwill arising on this transaction, in our view it is also unacceptable for the same reasons as for the full step-up method above. Whilst the method may be permitted by US GAAP, IFRS only permits entities to look to another framework when IFRS is silent, and where the method does not conflict with the requirements of IFRS. As already noted, a step-up would conflict with the requirements of IFRS in several areas such as the recognition or remeasurements of certain intangible assets.

It is clear from the above example that the three methods that we regard as being acceptable have drawbacks and that none of them are ideal. However, whatever conceptual approach is adopted, it should be applied consistently. So, for example, the 'Entity concept method' is acceptable but only if an entity follows that approach consistently, with any disposals of less than a controlling interest in a subsidiary by a parent to a minority shareholder also being recorded as an equity transaction.

An example of a company adopting the 'parent entity extension method' is Swisscom as shown in the following extract.

Extract 7.7: Swisscom AG (2006)

Notes to the consolidated financial statements [extract]

29 Repurchase of a share of 25% in Swisscom Mobile AG [extract]

On December 20, 2006, Swisscom bought back a minority share of 25% in Swisscom Mobile from Vodafone for CHF 4,258 million including transaction costs of CHF 8 million. On the date of acquisition the carrying amount of Vodafone's minority interest in Swisscom Mobile of CHF 565 million was removed from equity and offset against the purchasing price. The difference of CHF 3,693 million between the carrying amount of the minority interest and the purchase price was recorded as goodwill.

One company that states explicitly that it adopts such a method for both acquisitions and disposals in transactions with minority interests is Svenska Cellulosa as shown by the following extract from its accounting policies.

Extract 7.8: Svenska Cellulosa Aktiebolaget SCA (2006)

Notes [extract]

NOTE 1 Accounting principles [extract]

Consolidated accounts [extract]

Minority interests

Minority share in a subsidiary's net assets is reported as a separate item in the Group's equity. In the consolidated income statement, minority share is included in net profit. Transactions with minority interests are handled in the same way as transactions with external parties. Sale of participations to minority interests result in a gain or loss that is recognized in the consolidated income statement. Acquisition of minority shares can result in goodwill if the cost exceeds the carrying amount of the acquired net assets.

In February 2005, IFRIC discussed a potential agenda item regarding the accounting for the acquisition of a minority interest in an existing subsidiary by a reporting entity. Although IFRIC recognised this is an urgent issue and that there is wide divergence in current practice, it noted that it is being addressed by the IASB as part of phase II of its business combinations project. IFRIC concluded that it would monitor the progress of the Board's project, and reconsider whether to add the issue to the agenda later in 2005.[196] At the date of writing, no such item has been added to IFRIC's agenda.

As noted above, the Board is dealing with this issue as part of phase II of its business combinations project (see 5.1 below). Under the proposed revised IAS 27, after a parent obtains control of a subsidiary, subsequent increases in the ownership interest in the subsidiary are to be accounted for as transactions between equity holders. Accordingly, any premium or discount on subsequent purchases from minority interests ('non-controlling interests') is to be recognised directly in equity. However, this reflects the IASB's proposed 'full goodwill' approach whereby all of the goodwill of the acquiree (including that attributable to minority interests) is recognised at the date of the original business combination.

2.3.8 *Reverse acquisitions*

As discussed at 2.3.1 above, in some business combinations, commonly referred to as reverse acquisitions, the acquirer is the entity whose equity interests have been acquired and the issuing entity is the acquiree. This might be the case when, for example, a private entity arranges to have itself 'acquired' by a smaller public entity as a means of obtaining a stock exchange listing. Although legally the issuing public entity is regarded as the parent and the private entity is regarded as the subsidiary, the legal subsidiary is the acquirer if it has the power to govern the financial and operating policies of the legal parent so as to obtain benefits from its activities.

Appendix B to IFRS 3, which is an integral part of the standard, gives guidance on the accounting for reverse acquisitions. It notes that reverse acquisition accounting determines the allocation of the cost of the business combination as at the acquisition date and does not apply to transactions after the combination.[197]

A Cost of the business combination

When equity instruments are issued as part of the cost of the business combination, paragraph 24 of the standard requires the cost of the combination to include the fair value of those equity instruments at the date of exchange (see 2.3.2 above). Paragraph 27 notes that, in the absence of a reliable published price, the fair value of the equity instruments can be estimated by reference to the fair value of the acquirer or the fair value of the acquiree, whichever is more clearly evident (see 2.3.2 C above).[198]

In a reverse acquisition, the cost of the business combination is deemed to have been incurred by the legal subsidiary (i.e. the acquirer for accounting purposes) in the form of equity instruments issued to the owners of the legal parent (i.e. the acquiree for accounting purposes). If the published price of the equity instruments of the legal subsidiary is used to determine the cost of the combination, a calculation shall be made to determine the number of equity instruments the legal subsidiary would have had to issue to provide the same percentage ownership interest of the combined entity to the owners of the legal parent as they have in the combined entity as a result of the reverse acquisition. The fair value of the number of equity instruments so calculated shall be used as the cost of the combination.[199]

On the other hand, if the fair value of the equity instruments of the legal subsidiary is not otherwise clearly evident, the total fair value of all the issued equity instruments of the legal parent before the business combination shall be used as the basis for determining the cost of the combination.[200] The following example illustrates the application of this guidance. It is based on Example 5 within the Illustrative Examples accompanying IFRS 3.

Example 7.27: Reverse acquisition – calculating the cost of the business combination using the fair value of the equity shares of the legal subsidiary

Entity A, the entity issuing equity instruments and therefore the legal parent, is acquired in a reverse acquisition by Entity B, the legal subsidiary, on 30 September 2007. The accounting for any income tax effects is ignored.

Balance sheets of Entity A and Entity B immediately before the business combination

	Entity A	Entity B
	€	€
Current assets	500	700
Non-current assets	1,300	3,000
	1,800	3,700
Current liabilities	300	600
Non-current liabilities	400	1,100
	700	1,700
Owner's equity		
Issued equity		
100 ordinary shares	300	
60 Ordinary shares		600
Retained earnings	800	1,400
	1,100	2,000

Other information

(a) On 30 September 2007, Entity A issues 2½ shares in exchange for each ordinary share of Entity B. All of Entity B's shareholders exchange their shares in Entity B. Therefore, Entity A issues 150 ordinary shares in exchange for all 60 ordinary shares of Entity B.

(b) The fair value of each ordinary share of Entity B at 30 September 2007 is €40. The quoted market price of Entity A's ordinary shares at that date is €12.

(c) The fair values of Entity A's identifiable assets and liabilities at 30 September 2007 are the same as their carrying amounts, with the exception of non-current assets. The fair value of Entity A's non-current assets at 30 September 2007 is €1,500.

Calculating the cost of the business combination

As a result of the issue of 150 ordinary shares by Entity A, Entity B's shareholders own 60 per cent of the issued shares of the combined entity (i.e. 150 shares out of 250 issued shares). The remaining 40 per cent are owned by Entity A's shareholders. If the business combination had taken place in the form of Entity B issuing additional ordinary shares to Entity A's shareholders in exchange for their ordinary shares in Entity A, Entity B would have had to issue 40 shares for the ratio of ownership interest in the combined entity to be the same. Entity B's shareholders would then own 60 out of the 100 issued shares of Entity B and therefore 60 per cent of the combined entity.

As a result, the cost of the business combination is €1,600 (i.e. 40 shares each with a fair value of €40).

In the above example, the fair value of the ordinary shares was evident. However, in those situations where a private entity arranges to have itself 'acquired' by a smaller public entity as a means of obtaining a stock exchange listing, it may be that this will not be the case. In which case, the fair value of the shares of the legal parent should be used.

Example 7.28: Reverse acquisition – calculating the cost of the business combination using the fair value of the shares of the legal parent

If in the above example, the fair value of the ordinary shares of Entity B was not clearly evident, the total fair value of all the issued equity instruments of the Entity A before the business combination would be used as the basis for determining the cost of the combination.

The total fair value of all of Entity A's shares before the business combination was €1,200 (i.e. 100 shares each with a fair value of €12). Since Entity B is treated as having acquired a 100% interest in Entity A, then the cost of the business combination would be €1,200.

B Preparation and presentation of consolidated financial statements

Since the legal parent is the acquiree for accounting purposes, the consolidated financial statements prepared following a reverse acquisition reflect the fair values of the assets, liabilities and contingent liabilities of the legal parent, not those of the legal subsidiary. Therefore, the cost of the business combination (as determined under 2.3.8 A above) is allocated by measuring the identifiable assets, liabilities and contingent liabilities of the legal parent that satisfy the recognition criteria in paragraph 37 of the standard at their fair values at the acquisition date (see 2.3.3 above). Any excess of the cost of the combination over the acquirer's interest in the net fair value of those items is then accounted for as goodwill (see 2.3.4 above). Any excess of the acquirer's interest in the net fair value of those items over the cost of the combination is accounted for as an immediate gain in profit or loss (after having reassessed the fair value of those items and the measurement of the cost of the business combination) (see 2.3.5 above).[201]

Example 7.29: Reverse acquisition – allocating the cost of the business combination to the assets acquired and liabilities and contingent liabilities assumed

Using the facts in Example 7.27 above, the acquirer, Entity B, has to allocate the cost of the business combination of €1,600 to the net fair value of Entity A's identifiable assets and liabilities. This results in goodwill of €300, measured as follows:

	€	€
Cost of the business combination		1,600
Net fair value of Entity A's identifiable assets and liabilities:		
Current assets	500	
Non-current assets	1,500	
Current liabilities	(300)	
Non-current liabilities	(400)	
		1,300
Goodwill		300

If the cost of the business combination had been determined as in Example 7.28 above, i.e. €1,200, then no goodwill would have arisen and, assuming no adjustments were required as a result of the re-assessment of that cost or of the net fair values of Entity A's net assets, a gain of €100 would be recognised immediately in profit or loss.

Although the accounting for the reverse acquisition reflects the legal subsidiary as being the acquirer, the consolidated financial statements prepared following a reverse acquisition are issued under the name of the legal parent. Consequently they have to be described in the notes as a continuation of the financial statements of the legal subsidiary, since it is the acquirer for accounting purposes. Because such consolidated financial statements represent a continuation of the financial statements of the legal subsidiary:

(a) the assets and liabilities of the legal subsidiary are recognised and measured in those consolidated financial statements at their pre-combination carrying amounts; i.e. no fair value adjustments are made to the assets and liabilities of the legal subsidiary;

(b) the retained earnings and other equity balances recognised in those consolidated financial statements are the retained earnings and other equity balances of the legal subsidiary immediately before the business combination, not those of the legal parent;

(c) the amount recognised as issued equity instruments in those consolidated financial statements are determined by adding to the issued equity of the legal subsidiary immediately before the business combination the cost of the combination determined as discussed at 2.3.8 A above. However, the equity structure appearing in those consolidated financial statements (i.e. the number and type of equity instruments issued) reflects the equity structure of the legal parent, including the equity instruments issued by the legal parent to effect the combination;

(d) the comparative information presented in those consolidated financial statements is that of the legal subsidiary, not that originally presented in the previous financial statements of the legal parent;[202] and

(e) the income statement for the current period reflects that of the legal subsidiary for the full period together with the post-acquisition results of the legal parent (based on the attributed fair values).

Continuing with Example 7.27 above, this results in the following consolidated balance sheet.

Example 7.30: Reverse acquisition – consolidated balance sheet

Using the facts in Example 7.27 above, this results in the following consolidated balance sheet at the date of the business combination (the intermediate columns for Entity B and Entity A are included to show the workings):

	Entity B Book values	Entity A Fair values	Consolidated
	€	€	€
Current assets	700	500	1,200
Non-current assets	3,000	1,500	4,500
Goodwill		300	300
	3,700	2,300	6,000
Current liabilities	600	300	900
Non-current liabilities	1,100	400	1,500
	1,700	700	2,400
Owner's equity			
Issued equity			
250 ordinary shares	600	1,600	2,200
Retained earnings	1,400	–	1,400
	2,000	1,600	3,600

Although reverse acquisition accounting is applied in the consolidated financial statements, in the legal parent's separate financial statements, if any, the investment in the legal subsidiary is accounted for in accordance with the requirements in IAS 27 on accounting for investments in an investor's separate financial statements.[203]

Example 7.31: Reverse acquisition – legal parent's balance sheet in separate financial statements

Using the facts in Example 7.27 above, the balance sheet of Entity A, the legal parent, in its separate financial statements immediately following the business combination will be as follows:

	Entity A
	€
Current assets	500
Non-current assets	1,300
Investment in subsidiary (Entity B)	1,800
	3,600
Current liabilities	300
Non-current liabilities	400
	700
Owner's equity	
Issued equity	
250 ordinary shares	2,100
Retained earnings	800
	2,900

The investment in the subsidiary is included at its cost of €1,800, being the fair value of the shares issued by Entity A (150 × €12). It can be seen that the issued equity is different from that in the consolidated financial statements and its non-current assets remain at their carrying amounts before the business combination.

C Minority interest

In some reverse acquisitions, some of the owners of the legal subsidiary do not exchange their equity instruments for equity instruments of the legal parent. Although reverse acquisition accounting regards the entity in which those owners hold equity instruments (the legal subsidiary) as having acquired another entity (the legal parent), those owners are required to be treated as a minority interest in the consolidated financial statements prepared after the reverse acquisition. This is because the owners of the legal subsidiary that do not exchange their equity instruments for equity instruments of the legal parent have an interest only in the results and net assets of the legal subsidiary, and not in the results and net assets of the combined entity. Conversely, all of the owners of the legal parent, notwithstanding that the legal parent is regarded as the acquiree, have an interest in the results and net assets of the combined entity.[204]

Because the assets and liabilities of the legal subsidiary are recognised and measured in the consolidated financial statements at their pre-combination carrying amounts, the minority interest shall reflect the minority shareholders' proportionate interest in the pre-combination carrying amounts of the legal subsidiary's net assets.[205]

These requirements are illustrated in the following example.

Example 7.32: Reverse acquisition – minority interest

This example uses the same facts in Example 7.27 above, except that in this case only 56 of Entity B's ordinary shares are tendered for exchange rather than all 60. Because Entity A issues 2½ shares in exchange for each ordinary share of Entity B, Entity A issues only 140 (rather than 150) shares. As a result, Entity B's shareholders own 58.3 per cent of the issued shares of the combined entity (i.e. 140 shares out of 240 issued shares).

As in Example 7.27 above, the cost of the business combination is calculated by assuming that the combination had taken place in the form of Entity B issuing additional ordinary shares to the shareholders of Entity A in exchange for their ordinary shares in Entity A. In calculating the number of shares that would have to be issued by Entity B, the minority interest is ignored. The majority shareholders own 56 shares of Entity B. For this to represent a 58.3 per cent ownership interest, Entity B would have had to issue an additional 40 shares. The majority shareholders would then own 56 out of the 96 issued shares of Entity B and therefore 58.3 per cent of the combined entity.

As a result, the cost of the business combination is €1,600 (i.e. 40 shares each with a fair value of €40). This is the same amount as when all 60 of Entity B's ordinary shares are tendered for exchange (see Example 7.27 above). The cost of the combination does not change simply because some of Entity B's shareholders do not participate in the exchange.

The minority interest is represented by the 4 shares of the total 60 shares of Entity B that are not exchanged for shares of Entity A. Therefore, the minority interest is 6.7 per cent. The minority interest reflects the minority shareholders' proportionate interest in the pre-combination carrying amounts of the net assets of the legal subsidiary. Therefore, the consolidated balance sheet is adjusted to show a minority interest of 6.7 per cent of the pre-combination carrying amounts of Entity B's net assets (i.e. €134 or 6.7 per cent of €2,000).

The consolidated balance sheet at 30 September 2007 (the date of the business combination) reflecting the minority interest is as follows (the intermediate columns for Entity B, minority interest and Entity A are included to show the workings):

	Entity B Book values €	Minority interest €	Entity A Fair values €	Consolidated €
Current assets	700		500	1,200
Non-current assets	3,000		1,500	4,500
Goodwill			300	300
	3,700		2,300	6,000
Current liabilities	600		300	900
Non-current liabilities	1,100		400	1,500
	1,700		700	2,400
Owner's equity				
Issued equity				
240 ordinary shares	600	(40)	1,600	2,160
Retained earnings	1,400	(94)	–	1,306
Minority interest	–	134	–	134
	2,000	–	1,600	3,600

D Earnings per share

As indicated at 2.3.8 B above the equity structure appearing in the consolidated financial statements prepared following a reverse acquisition reflects the equity structure of the legal parent, including the equity instruments issued by the legal parent to effect the business combination.[206]

Where the legal parent is required by IAS 33 – *Earnings per Share* – to disclose earnings per share information (see Chapter 33), then for the purpose of calculating the weighted average number of ordinary shares outstanding (the denominator) during the period in which the reverse acquisition occurs:

(a) the number of ordinary shares outstanding from the beginning of that period to the acquisition date is deemed to be the number of ordinary shares issued by the legal parent to the owners of the legal subsidiary (rather than the actual number of shares of the legal parent during that period); and

(b) the number of ordinary shares outstanding from the acquisition date to the end of that period is the actual number of ordinary shares of the legal parent outstanding during that period.[207]

The basic earnings per share disclosed for each comparative period before the acquisition date that is presented in the consolidated financial statements following a reverse acquisition is calculated by dividing the profit or loss of the legal subsidiary attributable to ordinary shareholders in each of those periods by the number of ordinary shares issued by the legal parent to the owners of the legal subsidiary in the reverse acquisition.[208]

The calculations outlined above assume that there were no changes in the number of the legal subsidiary's issued ordinary shares during the comparative periods and during the period from the beginning of the period in which the reverse acquisition occurred to the acquisition date. The calculation of earnings per share is appropriately adjusted to take into account the effect of a change in the number of the legal subsidiary's issued ordinary shares during those periods.[209]

These requirements are illustrated in the following example.

Example 7.33: Reverse acquisition – earnings per share

This example uses the same facts in Example 7.27 above. Assume that Entity B's profit for the annual period ending 31 December 2006 was €600, and that the consolidated profit for the annual period ending 31 December 2007 is €800. Assume also that there was no change in the number of ordinary shares issued by Entity B during the annual period ending 31 December 2006 and during the period from 1 January 2007 to the date of the reverse acquisition (30 September 2007).

Earnings per share for the annual period ending 31 December 2007 is calculated as follows:

Number of shares deemed to be outstanding for the period from 1 January 2007 to the acquisition date (30 September 2007), being the number of ordinary shares issued by Entity A in the reverse acquisition	150
Number of shares outstanding from the acquisition date to 31 December 2007	250
Weighted average number of share outstanding (150 × 9/12) + (250 × 3/12)	175
Earnings per share €800/175	€4.57

The restated earnings per share for the annual period ending 31 December 2006 is €4.00 (being €600/150, i.e. the profit of Entity B for that period divided by the number of ordinary shares issued by Entity A in the reverse acquisition). Any earnings per share information for that period disclosed by either Entity A or Entity B is irrelevant.

E Cash consideration

Typically, a reverse acquisition occurs where the legal acquirer (Entity A) issues new shares to 'acquire' shares in the legal acquiree (Entity B). However, in some circumstances the combination may be effected whereby some or all of the consideration given by Entity A to acquire the shares in Entity B is cash.

In such circumstances, can the combination be accounted for as a reverse acquisition of Entity A by Entity B despite some or all of the consideration being in the form of cash?

Normally, the entity issuing cash consideration would be considered to be the acquirer. However, despite the form of the consideration, the key determinant in identifying an acquirer remains the power of one party to control the other (see 2.3.1 above).

Therefore, where there is clear evidence demonstrating that the legal acquiree, Entity B, has obtained the power to govern the financial and operating policies of Entity A, for example, through domination of the selection of management (a control indicator under paragraph 20(c) of IFRS3), this will overcome the presumption that Entity A is the acquirer and the combination should be accounted for as a reverse acquisition.

In that case, how should any cash paid be accounted for?

One approach might be to treat the payment as a pre-acquisition transaction with a resulting reduction in the consideration and in net assets acquired (with no net impact on goodwill). However, we do not believe this to be appropriate. Any consideration, whether cash or shares, paid by Entity A cannot form part of the cost of the business combination as Entity A is the deemed acquiree. As discussed at B above, although the consolidated financial statements prepared following a reverse acquisition are issued under the name of the legal parent, they are to be described in the notes as a continuation of the financial statements of the legal subsidiary. Therefore, since the consolidated financial statements are a continuation of Entity B's financial statements, in our view the cash consideration paid from Entity A (the deemed acquiree) should be accounted for as a distribution from the consolidated group to the acquirer's (Entity B's) shareholders as at the combination date.

However, where a cash payment is made to effect the combination, then the requirements of Appendix B to IFRS 3 need to be applied with care as illustrated in the following example.

Example 7.34: Reverse acquisition effected with cash consideration

Entity A has 100,000 ordinary shares in issue, with a market price of £2.00 per share, giving a market capitalisation of £200,000. It acquires all of the shares in Entity B for a consideration of £500,000 satisfied by the issue of 200,000 shares (with a value of £400,000) and a cash payment of £100,000 to Entity B's shareholders. Entity B has 200,000 shares in issue, with an estimated fair value of £2.50 per share.

After the combination Entity B's shareholders control the voting of Entity A and, as a result, have been able to appoint Entity B's directors and key executives to replace their Entity A counterparts. Accordingly, the combination must be accounted for as a reverse acquisition, i.e. Entity B is taken to have acquired Entity A since it has the power to govern the financial and operating policies of Entity A.

How should the cost of the combination be calculated?

Applying the requirements of paragraph B5 of IFRS 3 (discussed at A above) to the transaction might lead to the following conclusion. Entity A has had to issue 200,000 shares to Entity B's shareholders, resulting in Entity B's shareholders having 66.67% (200,000/300,000) of the equity and Entity A's shareholders 33.33% (100,000/300,000). If Entity B's share price is used to determine the cost of the acquisition, then under paragraph B5, Entity B would have had to issue 100,000 shares to Entity A's shareholders to result in the same % shareholdings (200,000/300,000 = 66.67%). This would apparently give a cost of 100,000 @ £2.50 = £250,000. This does not seem correct.

If there had been no cash consideration at all, then Entity A would have issued 250,000 shares to Entity B's shareholders, resulting in Entity B's shareholders having 71.43% (250,000/350,000) of the equity and Entity A's shareholders 28.57% (100,000/350,000). If Entity B's share price is used to determine the cost of the acquisition, then under paragraph B5, Entity B would have had to issue 80,000 shares to Entity A's shareholders to result in the same % shareholdings (200,000/280,000 = 71.43%). This would give a cost of 80,000 @ £2.50 = £200,000. If it is thought that the fair value of Entity B's shares is not otherwise clearly evident, paragraph B6 of IFRS 3 would require the total value of Entity A to be used instead. As Entity B has effectively acquired 100% of Entity A, the cost of the investment would be£200,000 (the same as under paragraph B5).

In our view, the proper analysis of the paragraph B5 calculation in this case is that of the 100,000 shares that Entity B is deemed to have issued, only 80,000 of them are to acquire Entity A's shares, resulting in a cost of £200,000. The extra 20,000 shares are to compensate Entity A's shareholders for the fact that Entity B's shareholders have received a cash distribution of £100,000, and is effectively a stock distribution to Entity A's shareholders of £50,000 (20,000 @ £2.50), being their share (33.33%) of a total distribution of £150,000. However, since the equity structure (i.e. the number and type of shares) appearing in the consolidated financial statements reflects that of the legal parent, Entity A, this 'stock distribution' will not actually be apparent. The only distribution that will be shown as a movement in equity is the £100,000 cash paid to Entity B's shareholders.

2.3.9 *Call and put options over minority interests*

Where, in a business combination, the acquirer obtains less than a 100% interest in the acquiree, this will be accounted for by recognising at the date of acquisition:

- All of the identifiable assets, liabilities and contingent liabilities of the acquiree recognised in accordance with the standard at their fair values (as determined in 2.3.3 above).
- Goodwill being the excess of the cost of the business combination (as determined in 2.3.2 above) over the acquirer's interest in those net assets.

- A minority interest in the acquiree reflecting the minority's proportion of the net identifiable assets, liabilities and contingent liabilities of the acquiree at their attributed fair values; no amount is included for any goodwill relating to the minority interest.

Minority interest is defined in both IFRS 3 and IAS 27 as 'that portion of the profit or loss and net assets of a subsidiary attributable to equity interests that are not owned, directly or indirectly through subsidiaries, by the parent'.[210]

In most business combinations where less than 100% of the equity shares have been acquired, the determination of the acquirer's share of the net assets of the acquiree (and, thus the amount of the minority interest) is straightforward. If an entity acquires 60% of the equity shares of the acquiree then goodwill will be based on 60% of the net assets of the acquiree and a minority interest representing 40% of the net assets of the acquiree will be recognised. As discussed in Chapter 6 at 6.7, the minority interest will be presented in the consolidated balance sheet within equity, separately from the parent shareholders' equity.

However, in some business combinations where less than 100% of the equity shares are acquired, it may be that the transaction also involves options over some or all of the outstanding shares. It may that the acquirer has a call option, i.e. a right to acquire the outstanding shares at a future date for cash at a particular price. Alternatively, it may be that the acquirer has granted a put option to the other shareholders whereby they have the right to sell their shares to the acquirer at a future date for cash at a particular price. Indeed in some cases, there may be a combination of such call and put options, the terms of which may be equivalent or may be different.

IFRS 3 gives no guidance as to how such options should impact on the accounting for a business combination. However, in determining the appropriate accounting in such situations, the implications of a number of other IFRSs need to be considered; these are IAS 27, IAS 32 and IAS 39.

Although the discussion below deals with options, similar considerations to those discussed at B below will apply in situations where the transaction means that the acquirer has entered into a forward purchase contract in respect of the shares held by the other shareholders (see C below).

A Call options only

As discussed in Chapter 6 at 3.1.2, IAS 27 requires that where an entity has call options over shares in another entity that are currently exercisable, then the potential voting rights attaching to those shares are taken into account in determining whether the entity has control over that other entity. In the context of a business combination where an entity has acquired, say, a 60% interest in the shares of another entity, but also has a call option over the remaining shares, the option will be irrelevant in determining control, since the entity has obtained control through the acquisition of the 60% interest. However, where an interest of, say, only 40% has been acquired, but the entity also has a call option over a further 20%, then the existence of the call option may mean that it has acquired a subsidiary that needs to be accounted for as a business combination under IFRS 3.

Although such call options are taken into account in determining whether the entity has obtained control, as discussed at 6.2 of Chapter 6, IAS 27 requires that the proportions allocated to the parent and minority interests are determined on the basis of present ownership interests. However, the proportion allocated would be determined taking into account the eventual exercise of potential voting rights under the call option, if in substance the entity had access at present to the economic benefits associated with that ownership interest.[211]

I Options giving the acquirer present access to benefits associated with ownership interest

Whether the call options, in substance, give the acquiring entity present access to such benefits will depend on the terms of the call option. This is likely to be the case if the option price is fixed (or determinable) and it is agreed between the parties that no dividends will be paid to the other shareholders, or the terms are set such that the other shareholders effectively receive only a lender's return. Accordingly, if the call option is over all of the other shares, then no minority interest would be reflected in equity. Thus, the business combination would be accounted for on the basis that a 100% interest had been acquired. Since the accounting reflects the 'eventual exercise' of the option, the cost of the business combination should include an amount representing the fair value of the 'liability' to the 'minority interest' shareholders under the call option (effectively, the present value of the exercise price payable under the option). The unwinding of the discount will be reflected in the income statement. In the event that the call option is not ultimately exercised, then the entity has effectively disposed of a partial interest in its subsidiary in return for the amount recognised as the 'liability' at the date of expiry and should account for the transaction as discussed in Chapter 6 at 6.7.4.

II Options not giving the acquirer present access to benefits associated with ownership interest

On the other hand, the call option may not give the acquiring entity present access to the benefits associated with the ownership interest. This might be the case if the terms of the option contain one or more of the following features:

- the option price has not yet been determined or will be the fair value of the shares at the date of exercise;
- the option price is based on expected future results or net assets of the subsidiary at the date of exercise; or
- it has been agreed between the parties that, prior to the exercise of the option, all retained profits may be freely distributed to the existing shareholders according to their current shareholdings.

Where it considered that the call option does not give access to the benefits associated with the ownership interest, then the implementation guidance in IAS 27 states that in such situations the 'instruments containing the potential voting rights are accounted for in accordance with IAS 39'.[212] This would appear to be based on paragraph 2(a) of IAS 39 which states that entities shall apply that standard 'to derivatives on an interest in a subsidiary ... unless the derivative meets the definition of an equity instrument of the entity in IAS 32'. Clearly, in the separate financial statements of the acquirer, this means that the call option over the shares in the subsidiary will be initially recognised as a financial asset at its fair value (which, in the case of a call option exercisable at the fair value at the date of exercise, or at an amount intended to be a surrogate for such a value, may not be material), with any subsequent changes in its fair value reflected in the income statement.

Such a treatment would also apply in the consolidated financial statements of the acquirer if the call option does not meet the definition of an equity instrument of the entity. This would be the case if the terms of the option were such that it did not involve an exercise price that was a fixed amount. In the event that the call option is exercised, the fair value of the option at that date will be included as part of the cost of the acquisition of the minority interest, the accounting for which will depend on the acquirer's chosen policy for such acquisitions (see 2.3.7 A above). In the event that the option lapses unexercised, any carrying amount for the option will be expensed in the income statement.

However, if the exercise price under the option was a fixed amount then as it is an option over the minority interest in the consolidated financial statements, and as indicated earlier IAS 27 regards the minority interest as 'equity' in those financial statements, it would seem that the call option should be accounted for in a similar fashion to that for a call option over an entity's own equity shares as discussed in Example 19.15 in 7.2.1 of Chapter 19. As the call option over the minority interest's shares will be gross-settled, this means that the initial fair value of the option is not accounted for as a financial asset, but is taken to equity. In the event that the call option is exercised, this initial fair value will be included as part of the cost of the acquisition of the minority interest, the accounting for which will depend on the acquirer's chosen policy for such acquisitions (see 2.3.7 A above).

B Put options only

Suppose, in the context of a business combination where an entity has acquired, say, a 60% interest in the shares of another entity, the acquirer, rather than having a call option over the remaining shares, has granted a put option to the other shareholders whereby they have the right to sell their shares to the acquirer at a future date for cash at a particular price. As with call options discussed above, the price to be paid under the put option might be fixed, based on the fair value of the shares at the date of exercise, or determined by way of a formula based on expected future results or net assets of the subsidiary.

This is an area that IFRIC considered during 2006, not only in the context of put options negotiated at the time of the acquisition of the majority interest but also at a later date. In May 2006, it was reported that:[213]

> 'IFRIC considered the treatment under IAS 32 and IFRS 3 of puts and forwards held by minority interests in response to a request to the IFRIC related to situations where a parent enters into a commitment through a written put or a forward purchase to acquire shares in a subsidiary held by a third party. The settlement amount might be fixed, based on fair value of the shares at the settlement date or based on a formula, such as a multiple of EBITDA or net income. This type of contract might be negotiated as part of the purchase of the majority interest or negotiated independently at a later date. Two issues that arise regularly in practice are whether the parent must recognise a liability for the amount potentially payable under the contract and whether the minority interest continues to be recognised for the minority's shares that are subject to the agreement.
>
> The IFRIC tentatively decided not to take the item onto its agenda but deferred publishing formal wording for this until the following meeting, when it intended to address the related issue, whether puts or forwards received by minority interests in a business combination are contingent consideration.'

At the next meeting in July 2006, IFRIC considered this related issue and tentatively decided not to take it onto its agenda either, commenting that the 'accounting for these arrangements, including the circumstances considered by the IFRIC, is being considered by the Board as part of the current redeliberations on the proposed revised IFRS 3 … The IFRIC therefore believed that it could not develop guidance more quickly than is likely to be developed in the business combinations project and [decided] not to take a project on this issue onto its agenda.'[214]

At the same meeting, in relation to the original issue, IFRIC again tentatively decided not to take it onto its agenda, commenting that:[215]

> 'Paragraph 23 of IAS 32 states that a parent must recognise a financial liability when it has an obligation to pay cash in the future to purchase the minority's shares, even if the payment of that cash is conditional on the option being exercised by the holder. After initial recognition any liability to which IFRS 3 is not being applied will be accounted for in accordance with IAS 39. The parent will reclassify the liability to equity if a put expires unexercised.
>
> The IFRIC agreed that there is likely to be divergence in practice in how the related equity is reclassified. However, the IFRIC did not believe that it could reach a consensus view on this matter on a timely basis.'

In November 2006, IFRIC confirmed these decisions not to take these items onto its agenda.[216]

So, how should put options, granted to holders of minority interest at the date of acquiring control of a subsidiary, be accounted for?

It is quite clear from paragraph 23 of IAS 32 that a written put option over an entity's own equity instruments that is to be gross-settled (i.e. the entity pays cash in return for the counterparty delivering shares), whether for a fixed or variable amount, should be recognised as a financial liability at its fair value, being the present value of the amount payable (see Chapter 19 at 3.3.3 and 7.3.2). As indicated earlier IAS 27 regards the minority interest as 'equity' for the purpose of the consolidated financial statements. Thus, any put options granted to minority interests give rise to a financial liability to be recognised initially at the present value of the amount payable upon exercise of the option. The liability is subsequently remeasured at each reporting date to the present value of the amount payable on exercise. The fact that such a financial liability should be recognised is confirmed by the IFRIC rejection notice quoted above.

However, we believe that the accounting for the remaining aspects of the put option depends in part upon an assessment of the terms of the transaction and, in some areas, involves a choice of accounting policy, which once selected, must be applied consistently. These choices arise because of the lack of explicit guidance in IFRS and potential contradictions between the requirements of IAS 27 and IAS 32 and the related guidance within those standards, reinforced by the fact that IFRIC decided not to take the issue on to its agenda despite the fact that it agreed that there is likely to be divergence in practice. Accordingly, a number of alternatives exist.

As with call options above, consideration needs to be given as to whether or not the terms of the transaction give the acquirer present access to the economic benefits associated with the ownership interest that is the subject of the put option. In addition, key policy decisions that management must make in order to conclude an accounting approach, are:

- given potential contradictions between IAS 32 and IAS 27, which standard takes precedence;
- whether the liability arising from 'acquiring' shares held by the minority interest is to be an IFRS 3 liability (with elements of contingent consideration) or an IAS 39 financial liability;
- if minority interest is recognised on initial acquisition – whether it continues to be recognised or not;
- if minority interest is subsequently derecognised – whether it is to be accounted for as an acquisition of minority interest or not
- the accounting policy for acquisition of minority interest (see 2.3.7 A above).

The following diagram summarises the analysis that we believe should be performed, the questions to be addressed and the alternatives that apply, which are discussed further below.

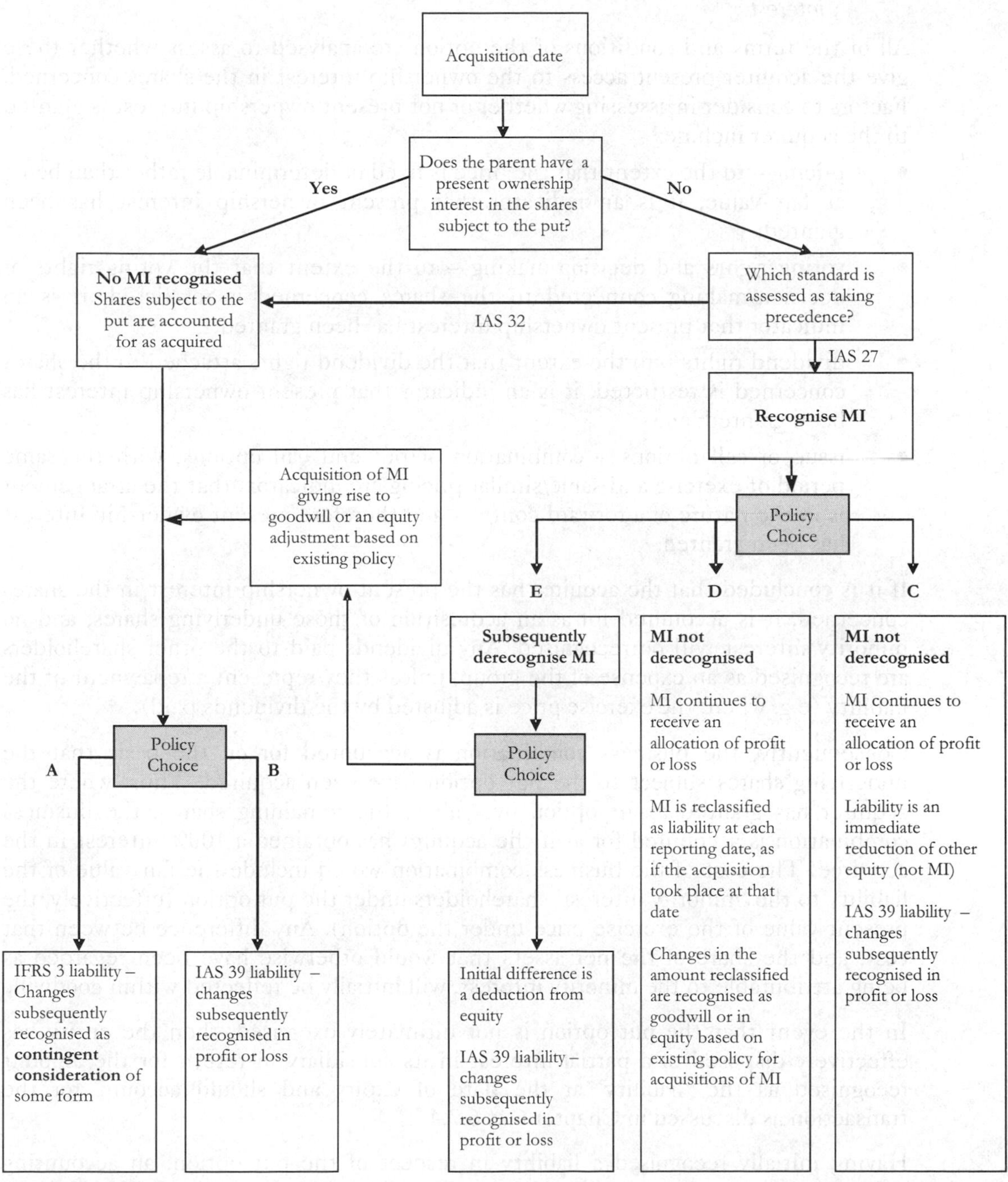

Note
MI: minority interests

I Options giving the acquirer present access to benefits associated with ownership interest

All of the terms and conditions of the option are analysed to assess whether these give the acquirer present access to the ownership interest in the shares concerned. Factors to consider in assessing whether or not present ownership interest is granted to the acquirer include:

- pricing – to the extent that the price is fixed or determinable rather than being at fair value, it is an indicator that present ownership interest has been granted;
- voting rights and decision-making – to the extent that the voting rights or decision-making connected to the shares concerned is restricted, it is an indicator that present ownership interest has been granted;
- dividend rights – to the extent that the dividend rights attached to the shares concerned is restricted, it is an indicator that present ownership interest has been granted; and
- issue of call options – combination of put and call options, with the same period of exercise and same/similar pricing are indicators that the arrangement is in the nature of a forward contract and therefore present ownership interest has been granted.

If it is concluded that the acquirer has the present ownership interest in the shares concerned, it is accounted for as an acquisition of those underlying shares, and no minority interest will be recognised. Any dividends paid to the other shareholders are recognised as an expense of the group, unless they represent a repayment of the liability (e.g. where the exercise price is adjusted by the dividends paid).

Consequently, the business combination is accounted for on the basis that the underlying shares subject to the put option have been acquired. Thus, where the acquirer has granted a put option over all of the remaining shares, the business combination is accounted for as if the acquirer has obtained a 100% interest in the acquiree. The cost of the business combination would include the fair value of the liability to the 'minority interest' shareholders under the put option (effectively, the present value of the exercise price under the option). Any difference between that cost, and the share of the net assets that would otherwise have been regarded as being attributable to the minority interest, will initially be reflected within goodwill.

In the event that the put option is not ultimately exercised, then the entity has effectively disposed of a partial interest in its subsidiary in return for the amount recognised as the 'liability' at the date of expiry and should account for the transaction as discussed in Chapter 6 at 6.7.4.

Having initially recognised a liability in respect of the put option, an accounting policy choice is then available as to the type of liability that exists, affecting how subsequent changes in the liability are accounted for.

Alternative A – IFRS 3 liability

The liability, in some form, relates to contingent consideration for the purchase of the shares subject to the put option, and can be accounted for as such under IFRS 3. As indicated earlier, IFRIC decided not to take this issue onto its agenda, but stated that 'after initial recognition [of the financial liability for the put option] any liability to which IFRS 3 is not being applied will be accounted for in accordance with IAS 39'. Thus, it would appear that IFRIC does not preclude that some or all of the financial liability can be accounted for as contingent consideration under IFRS 3.

Under IFRS 3, changes in the liability relating to a business combination only affect the accounting for the combination if it is contingent on a future event. Paragraph 32 of IFRS 3 states 'When a business combination agreement provides for an adjustment to the cost of the combination contingent on future events, the acquirer shall include the amount of that adjustment in the cost of the combination at the acquisition date if the adjustment is probable and can be measured reliably.' Paragraph 33 of IFRS 3 further states 'If the future events do not occur or the estimate needs to be revised, the cost of the business combination shall be adjusted accordingly.' The treatment of contingent consideration is discussed at 2.3.2 E above.

However, it is not clear in the context of the liability for the put option, what element of the amount payable may be considered to be contingent on future events. Three possible views exist so, accordingly, we believe there is then a further choice as to which view to adopt to determine the amount of the liability that represents contingent consideration:

(a) All of the liability is regarded as contingent consideration as the entire payment is conditional upon the put being exercised.

This is based on the view that any eventual payment under the option is contingent on a future event, being the decision by the other shareholders to exercise their rights under the put option or not. In this case, all changes in the carrying amount of the liability are adjusted against goodwill, except for the unwinding of the discount due to the passage of time which is recognised in the income statement.

(b) All of the liability is regarded as contingent consideration only if exercise of the put is also conditional on certain criterion being met or there is a variable exercise price.

This is based on the view that it is only if the terms of the put option are such that there are other future events that mean that there will be an adjustment to the amount of the cost of the business combination. On this basis, a put option that is merely exercisable at a fixed price would not qualify as contingent consideration; the liability for such a put option would be accounted for under Alternative B below. However, one with terms based on, say, achievement of a specified level of profits would qualify, as would put options exercisable at fair value at the date of exercise or at a price based on expected future results or net assets at the date of exercise. In this case, all changes in the carrying amount of the liability are adjusted against goodwill, except for the unwinding of the discount due to the passage of time which is recognised in the income statement.

(c) Contingent consideration exists only to the extent that the exercise price is *not* at fair value or is based on a formula that will not reflect fair value.

This is based on the view that put options exercisable at fair value at the date of exercise, or at an exercise price based on a formula that is intended to be a proxy for such fair value, should not be regarded as contingent consideration. Changes in value of the liability should be taken to the income statement as this reflects the gain/loss of entering into the put option itself rather than being linked to a future event. Only to the extent that the exercise price was different from such fair value, such that it reflects an adjustment from market, would there be an element of contingent consideration.

To that extent, any changes in the liability are adjusted against goodwill, except for the unwinding of the discount due to the passage of time. The unwinding of the discount is recognised in the income statement. To the extent the liability does not qualify to be contingent consideration, it would be accounted for under Alternative B below.

Alternative B – IAS 39 liability

The liability under the put option is a financial liability that is to be accounted for under IAS 39. This is based on the view that future events that are a choice given to the other party, cannot be included in contingent consideration, as the future events being contemplated in paragraph 32 of IFRS 3 are events which change the amount of the consideration for an agreed purchase, rather than being contingent on whether or not the purchase actually occurs.

Accordingly, the financial liability is subsequently measured in accordance with the requirements of IAS 39. Where the price under the option is based on the fair value of the underlying shares at the date of exercise, this means that the financial liability will be remeasured at each reporting date based on the fair value of the shares at that date, with any change in that value reflected in the income statement, normally as a finance charge or credit. On the other hand, where the price is fixed, any unwinding of the discount will be reflected in the income statement as a finance charge.

Where the put option is ultimately exercised, the amount recognised as the financial liability at that date will be extinguished by the payment of the exercise price. Where the put option expires unexercised, the entity has effectively disposed of a partial interest in its subsidiary in return for the amount recognised as the financial liability at the date of expiry and should account for the transaction as discussed in Chapter 6 at 6.7.4.

II Options not giving the acquirer present access to benefits associated with ownership interest

If having considered the factors set out in I above, it is concluded that the acquirer does *not* have the present ownership interest in the shares concerned, we consider that there is a choice of policy available as to which standard takes precedence.

IAS 32 takes precedence over IAS 27

By recognising the liability in respect of the put option over the shares held by the minority shareholders there is no minority interest recognised at all. This is based on the requirements and guidance within IAS 32. In addition to the requirements of paragraph 23 of IAS 32 discussed above, paragraph AG29 of IAS 32 indicates that when a subsidiary in a group issues a financial instrument and a parent or other group entity agrees additional terms directly with the holders of the instrument, the group may not have discretion over distributions or redemption. Although the subsidiary may appropriately classify the instrument without regard to these additional terms in its individual financial statements, the effect of other agreements between members of the group and the holders of the instrument is considered in order to ensure that consolidated financial statements reflect the contracts and transactions entered into by the group as a whole. To the extent that there is such an obligation or settlement provision, the instrument (or the component of it that is subject to the obligation) is classified as a financial liability in the consolidated financial statements. Since this suggests that it is the financial instrument itself (i.e. the shares in the subsidiary) that is subject to the obligation that is classified as a financial liability, this means that the minority interest shareholders rights are represented by the financial liability. Accordingly, since their rights are not regarded as equity interests in the consolidated financial statements, there is no minority interest that has to be accounted for under IAS 27.

Consequently, the business combination is accounted for on the basis that the underlying shares subject to the put option have been acquired. Thus, where the acquirer has granted a put option over all of the remaining shares, the business combination is accounted for as if the acquirer has obtained a 100% interest in the acquiree. The cost of the business combination would include the fair value of the liability to the 'minority interest' shareholders under the put option (effectively, the present value of the exercise price under the option). Any difference between that cost, and the share of the net assets that would otherwise have been regarded as being attributable to the minority interest, will initially be reflected within goodwill.

In the event that the put option is not ultimately exercised, then the entity has effectively disposed of a partial interest in its subsidiary in return for the amount recognised as the 'liability' at the date of expiry and should account for the transaction as discussed in Chapter 6 at 6.7.4.

Having initially recognised a liability in respect of the put option, the same accounting policy choice as set out in I above (Alternative A or Alternative B) is then available as to the type of liability that exists, affecting how subsequent changes in the liability are accounted for.

IAS 27 takes precedence over IAS 32

A minority interest in the acquiree is recognised as, having considered the terms of the put option in light of the guidance within IAS 27, it is determined that the minority interest shareholders have a present ownership interest in the underlying shares. Consequently, the business combination is accounted for on the basis that the acquirer has obtained a less than 100% interest in the acquiree by reflecting the minority's proportion of the net identifiable assets, liabilities and contingent liabilities of the acquiree at their attributed fair values. No amount is included for any goodwill relating to the minority interest.

As in the previous analysis, we believe that there is then a further choice of policy available as to whether the minority interest that has initially been recognised should continue to be recognised or not. As a result, a number of alternatives exist depending on how the interaction between the requirements of IAS 27 and IAS 32 is accounted for.

Alternative C – Minority interest is not derecognised – full recognition of minority interest

This takes the view that the requirements of IAS 27 continue to take precedence and therefore minority interest continues to be recognised in accordance with IAS 27, since it has been determined that the minority interest shareholders have a present ownership interest in the underlying shares. The minority interest is accounted for subsequently under IAS 27 (see Chapter 6 at 6.7) until the put is exercised.

As far as the financial liability in respect of the put option is concerned, this is accounted for under IAS 39 like any other written put option on equity instruments. Thus, as discussed in Chapter 19 at 3.3.3 and 7.3.2, on initial recognition of the financial liability the other side of the journal entry is reflected as a reduction in equity. However, since IAS 27 requires the minority interest to be presented separately within equity, the reduction needs to be reflected in another component of equity.

Subsequently, the financial liability is measured in accordance with the requirements of IAS 39. Where the price under the option is based on the fair value of the underlying shares at the date of exercise, this means that the financial liability will be remeasured at each reporting date based on the fair value of the shares at that date, with any change in that value reflected in the income statement, normally as a finance charge or credit. Where the price is fixed, any unwinding of the discount will be reflected in the income statement as a finance charge. These changes in the amount of the financial liability that are recognised in the income statement are considered to be consolidation adjustments against the parent's income, so are not included as part of the minority interest share of the income of the subsidiary.

Where the put option is ultimately exercised, the entity will account for the acquisition of the minority interest in accordance with its chosen policy for such acquisitions (see 2.3.7 A above). At the same time, a credit entry equivalent to the financial liability will also need to be reflected in equity. Where the put option expires unexercised, the financial liability will be transferred to equity. In both situations, it would seem appropriate to use the same component of equity that was previously reduced.

Alternative D – Minority interest is not derecognised – partial recognition of minority interest

This takes the view that the requirements of IAS 27 initially take precedence, such that the minority interest is still attributed its share of profits and losses (and other changes in equity) of acquiree after the business combination as required by IAS 27 (see Chapter 6 at 6.7).

However, based on the requirements of AG29 of IAS 32 discussed earlier, the impact of the put option is that the amount of the minority interest that would have been included within equity at the balance sheet date has to be reclassified as a financial liability. This means that the minority interest that has been reclassified is deemed to have been derecognised as it if had been acquired at the balance sheet date. Effectively, the eventual acquisition of the minority interest is being anticipated, and therefore the accounting at the balance sheet date should replicate the accounting that would be adopted as if the option had been exercised at that date.

Accordingly, any difference between the present value of the amount payable under the put option at the balance sheet date and the minority interest reclassified and deemed to have been derecognised at that date is accounted for in accordance with the entity's chosen policy for acquisitions of minority interests (see 2.3.7 A above). Where the entity's policy for such acquisitions is to use the 'Parent entity extension method', then this means that the difference is taken to goodwill. Otherwise some or all of the difference between the initial fair value of the liability and the minority interest will be taken to equity.

Under this alternative, no amount is recognised in the income statement for the financial liability or separate accounting for the unwinding of any discount in respect of the liability.

While the put option remains unexercised, at each reporting date the amount that would have been recognised within equity for the minority interest is updated to reflect its share of profits and losses (and other changes in equity) of the acquiree for the period, and this is accounted for as if it had been acquired for the present value of the amount payable under the put option at that balance sheet date. Where the put option is ultimately exercised, the same treatment will be applied up to the date of exercise. The amount recognised as the financial liability at that date will be extinguished by the payment of the exercise price. Where the put option expires unexercised, the position will be unwound such that the minority interest at that date is reclassified back to equity, the financial liability is derecognised, and any difference taken to goodwill or equity to negate the entries made under their policy for acquisitions of minority interests.

Alternative E – Minority interest is subsequently derecognised

This takes the view that, based on the requirements of paragraph 23 and AG29 of IAS 32 discussed earlier, the recognition of the financial liability in respect of the put option results in derecognition of the minority interest initially recognised. However, we consider that the entity has a choice of policy available as to how the derecognition of the minority interest is accounted for. These are either (a) as an acquisition of the minority interest or (b) as part of the equity elimination resulting from the recognition of the financial liability in respect of the put option.

(a) Immediate acquisition of minority interest

Under this view, the minority interest that has initially been recognised as part of the business combination is treated as having been acquired. Consequently, any difference between the minority interest and the initial liability recognised in respect of the put option will be accounted for in accordance with the acquirer's chosen policy for the acquisition of the minority interests (see 2.3.7 A above).

The same accounting policy choice as set out in I above (Alternative A or Alternative B) is then available as to the type of liability that exists, affecting how subsequent changes in the liability are accounted for.

Where Alternative A is selected, any adjustments to the consideration will be recognised as an adjustment to goodwill or equity (depending on the entity's policy for accounting for the acquisition of minority interest).

(b) Minority interest eliminated as part of equity deduction for financial liability

Under this view, the derecognition of the minority interest is reflected in the accounting for the written put option. As with Alternative C, as far as the financial liability in respect of the put option is concerned, this is accounted for under IAS 39 like any other written put option on equity instruments. Thus, as discussed in Chapter 19 at 3.3.3 and 7.3.2, on initial recognition of the financial liability the other side of the journal entry is reflected as a reduction in equity. However, in this instance the reduction in equity is reflected partially against minority interest on the basis that paragraph AG29 of IAS 32 requires the financial instrument (i.e. the shares held by the minority shareholder) to be reclassified from equity, with the remaining amount against another component of equity.

Subsequently, the financial liability is measured in accordance with the requirements of IAS 39. Where the price under the option is based on the fair value of the underlying shares at the date of exercise, this means that the financial liability will be remeasured at each reporting date based on the fair value of the shares at that date, with any change in that value reflected in the income statement, normally as a finance charge or credit. On the other hand, where the price is fixed, any unwinding of the discount will be reflected in the income statement as a finance charge.

Where the put option is ultimately exercised, the amount recognised as the financial liability at that date will be extinguished by the payment of the exercise price. Where the put option expires unexercised, in accordance with paragraph 23 of IAS 32, the financial liability will be reclassified back to equity, partly by recognising the minority interest at an amount that reflects the minority's share of the net assets of the acquiree at that date, with any remaining amount taken to another component of equity. It would seem appropriate to use the same component of equity that was previously reduced.

C Combination of call and put options

In some business combinations where an entity has acquired, say, a 60% interest in the shares of another entity, it may be that as part of the transaction there is a combination of call and put options, the terms of which may be equivalent or may be different.

The determination of the appropriate accounting for such options should be based on the discussions in 2.3.9 A and B above. However, where there is a call and put option with equivalent terms, particularly at a fixed price, the combination of the options is more likely to mean that they give the acquirer present access to the economic benefits associated with the ownership interest that is the subject of the put option, such that the acquirer has effectively acquired a 100% interest in the subsidiary at the date of the business combination, and thus the accounting discussed in 2.3.9 B I above should be followed. In such situations, the entity may be in a similar position as if it had acquired a 100% interest in the subsidiary with either deferred consideration (where the exercise price is fixed) or contingent consideration (where the settlement amount is not fixed, but is dependent upon a future event).

Where the transaction does not involve options, but instead the acquirer has entered into a forward purchase contract in respect of the shares held by the other shareholders, it would seem appropriate that the accounting should be the same as for a combination of call and put options with equivalent terms.

D Call and put options entered into in relation to existing minority interests

The discussion above has focused on call and put options entered into at the same time as the acquisition of the subsidiary. It may be that an entity enters into such options with the minority shareholders some time after the business combination. Again, the determination of the appropriate accounting for such options should be based on the discussions in 2.3.9 A and B above.

The main difference in such situations, particularly in relation to put options, is where it is considered that the minority interest should no longer be recognised within equity, and the transaction is being accounted for as an acquisition of the minority interest. In this instance, since such acquisitions are not business combinations under IFRS 3, whether any goodwill is recognised on the acquisition of such minority interest will depend on the entity's accounting policy for such transactions as discussed at 2.3.7 A above.

2.3.10 Disclosure requirements relating to business combinations

In developing the disclosure requirements of IFRS 3, the IASB identified three disclosure objectives that should be met.[217] Accordingly the standard sets out three principles of disclosure dealing with these objectives, and supplements them with specific disclosure requirements. The first two principles relate to business combinations generally, while the third deals with goodwill. The disclosure requirements of the standard relating to goodwill are discussed at 3.10 below; the other requirements relating to business combinations generally are dealt with below.

A Nature and financial effect of business combinations

The first disclosure principle is that an acquirer discloses information that enables users of its financial statements to evaluate the nature and financial effect of business combinations that were effected:

(a) during the period, or

(b) after the balance sheet date but before the financial statements are authorised for issue.[218]

I Business combinations during the period

To give effect to this principle, the acquirer is required to disclose the following information for *each* business combination that was effected during the period:

(a) the names and descriptions of the combining entities or businesses;

(b) the acquisition date;

(c) the percentage of voting equity instruments acquired;

(d) the cost of the combination and a description of the components of that cost, including any costs directly attributable to the combination.

When equity instruments are issued or issuable as part of the cost, the following shall also be disclosed:

(i) the number of equity instruments issued or issuable; and

(ii) the fair value of those instruments and the basis for determining that fair value.

If a published price does not exist for the instruments at the date of exchange, the significant assumptions used to determine fair value shall be disclosed.

If a published price exists at the date of exchange but was not used as the basis for determining the cost of the combination, that fact shall be disclosed together with:

- the reasons the published price was not used;
- the method and significant assumptions used to attribute a value to the equity instruments; and
- the aggregate amount of the difference between the value attributed to, and the published price of, the equity instruments;

(e) details of any operations the entity has decided to dispose of as a result of the combination;

(f) the amounts recognised at the acquisition date for each class of the acquiree's assets, liabilities and contingent liabilities, and, unless disclosure would be impracticable, the carrying amounts of each of those classes, determined in accordance with IFRSs, immediately before the combination.

If such disclosure about the carrying amounts would be impracticable, that fact shall be disclosed, together with an explanation of why this is the case;

(g) the amount of any excess recognised in profit or loss in accordance with paragraph 56 of the standard (see 2.3.5 above), and the line item in the income statement in which the excess is recognised;

(h) a description of the factors that contributed to a cost that results in the recognition of goodwill, including a description of each intangible asset that was not recognised separately from goodwill and an explanation of why the intangible asset's fair value could not be measured reliably – or a description of the nature of any excess recognised in profit or loss in accordance with paragraph 56 of the standard; and

(i) the amount of the acquiree's profit or loss since the acquisition date included in the acquirer's profit or loss for the period, unless disclosure would be impracticable.

If such disclosure would be impracticable, that fact shall be disclosed, together with an explanation of why this is the case.[219]

The above information is required to be disclosed for each material business combination. For business combinations effected during the reporting period that are individually immaterial, the standard requires that the above information is disclosed in aggregate.[220]

If the initial accounting for a business combination that was effected during the period was determined only provisionally (see 2.3.6 above), that fact must be disclosed together with an explanation of why this is the case.[221]

To give effect to the principle, the acquirer discloses the following information, unless such disclosure would be impracticable:

(a) the revenue of the combined entity for the period as though the acquisition date for all business combinations effected during the period had been the beginning of that period; and

(b) the profit or loss of the combined entity for the period as though the acquisition date for all business combinations effected during the period had been the beginning of the period.

If disclosure of this information would be impracticable, that fact must be disclosed, together with an explanation of why this is the case.[222]

A number of the requirements allow the information not to be disclosed if disclosure would be impracticable. Whether an entity is justified to omit the disclosure on these grounds will depend on the particular circumstances. As discussed in Chapter 3 at 2.4 and 4.7, IAS 1 and IAS 8 both regard a requirement as being impracticable when the entity cannot apply it after making every reasonable effort to do so.

II Business combinations effected after the balance sheet date

To give effect to the principle set out above, the acquirer is required to disclose the information under items (a) to (i) above for each business combination effected after the balance sheet date but before the financial statements are authorised for issue, unless such disclosure would be impracticable. If disclosure of any of that information would be impracticable, that fact must be disclosed, together with an explanation of why this is the case.[223]

B Effects of gains, losses, error corrections and other adjustments recognised in the current period relating to business combinations

The second disclosure principle is that an acquirer discloses information that enables users of its financial statements to evaluate the financial effects of gains, losses, error corrections and other adjustments recognised in the current period that relate to business combinations that were effected in the current or in previous periods.[224]

To give effect to this principle, the acquirer is required to disclose the following information:

(a) the amount and an explanation of any gain or loss recognised in the current period that:
   (i) relates to the identifiable assets acquired or liabilities or contingent liabilities assumed in a business combination that was effected in the current or a previous period; and
   (ii) is of such size, nature or incidence that disclosure is relevant to an understanding of the combined entity's financial performance;

(b) if the initial accounting for a business combination that was effected in the immediately preceding period was determined only provisionally at the end of that period, the amounts and explanations of the adjustments to the provisional values recognised during the current period (see 2.3.6 A above); and

(c) the information about error corrections required to be disclosed by IAS 8 for any of the acquiree's identifiable assets, liabilities or contingent liabilities, or changes in the values assigned to those items, that the acquirer recognises during the current period (see 2.3.6 B above).[225]

Item (a) has been included as an aid in meeting the objective of the second disclosure principle,[226] but does not really add anything to the requirement within IAS 1 to disclose the nature and amount of items of income and expenditure when they are material (see Chapter 3 at 3.2.4). Similarly, item (c) merely appears to repeat the requirements of IAS 8 (see Chapter 3 at 5.3).

C Other necessary information

The standard includes a catch-all disclosure requirement, that if in any situation the information required to be disclosed set out above does not satisfy the objectives of the disclosure principles, the entity shall disclose such additional information as is necessary to meet those objectives.[227] Possible disclosures under this requirement could be information relating to the cost of a business combination that is contingent on future events and any adjustments made thereto (see 2.3.2 E above).

In addition to the disclosures required by IFRS 3 discussed above, IAS 7 – *Cash Flow Statements* – requires disclosures in respect of acquisitions of subsidiaries and other business units (see Chapter 34 at 2.4.2).[228]

2.4 Common control transactions and group reorganisations

2.4.1 Common control exemption

As indicated at 2.2.2 above, IFRS 3 excludes business combinations involving entities or businesses under common control from its scope. For this purpose, a business combination involving entities or businesses under common control 'is a business combination in which all of the combining entities or businesses are ultimately controlled by the same party or parties both before and after the business combination, and that control is not transitory'.[229] This will include transactions, such as the transfer of subsidiarics or businesses, between entities within a group.

The extent of minority interests in each of the combining entities before and after the business combination is not relevant to determining whether the combination involves entities under common control.[230] This is because a partially-owned subsidiary is nevertheless under the control of the parent entity. Therefore transactions involving partially-owned subsidiaries would be outside the scope of the standard. Similarly, the fact that one of the combining entities is a subsidiary that has been excluded from the consolidated financial statements of the group in accordance with IAS 27 is not relevant to determining whether a combination involves entities under common control.[231]

A Common control by an individual or group of individuals

The exclusion is not, however, restricted to transactions between entities within a group. The standard notes that an entity can be controlled by an individual, or by a group of individuals acting together under a contractual arrangement, and that individual or group of individuals may not be subject to the financial reporting requirements of IFRSs.[232] Thus a transaction involving entities controlled by the same individual, including one that results in a new parent entity, would be outwith the scope of the standard. It is not necessary for combining entities to be included as part of the same consolidated financial statements for a business combination to be regarded as one involving entities under common control.[233]

A group of individuals shall be regarded as controlling an entity when, as a result of contractual arrangements, they collectively have the power to govern its financial and operating policies so as to obtain benefits from its activities. Therefore, a business combination is outside the scope of IFRS 3 when the same group of individuals has, as a result of contractual arrangements, ultimate collective power to govern the financial and operating policies of each of the combining entities so as to obtain benefits from their activities, and that ultimate collective power is not transitory.[234]

It can be seen that for the exemption to apply when a group of individuals are involved there has to be a 'contractual arrangement' between them such that they have control over the entities involved in the transaction. IFRS 3 does not indicate what form such an arrangement should take. However, IAS 31 in determining what is a 'joint venture' states that '... whatever its form, the contractual arrangement is usually in writing ...'.[235] Although it is acknowledged that a contractual arrangement is usually in writing, this also implies that it is possible for a contractual arrangement to be in non-written form. Clearly, where the arrangement is not in writing, consideration needs to be given to all of the facts and circumstances to determine whether it is appropriate to apply the exemption.

Example 7.35: Common control involving individuals

Entity A has 3 shareholders Mr W, Mr X, and Mr Y. Mr X and Mr Y are family members who each hold a 30% interest in Entity A. Mr X and Mr Y also each hold a 30% interest in Entity B. There is no written contractual arrangement between Mr X and Mr Y requiring them to act collectively as shareholders in Entity A and Entity B.

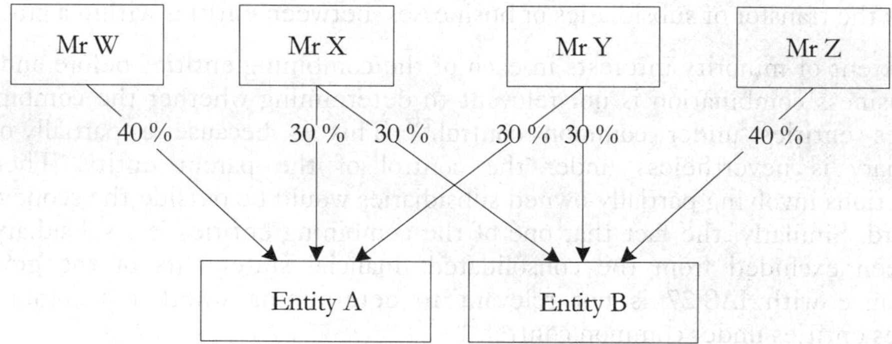

If Entity A acquires 100% of Entity B, is this a business combination involving entities under common control as a result of the joint holdings of Mr X and Mr Y, and therefore outside the scope of IFRS 3, where the nature of the family relationship is:

(a) Mr X is the father and Mr Y is his young dependent son?; or

(b) Mr X is a patriarchal father and, as a result of his highly influential standing, his adult son Mr Y has traditionally followed his father's decisions?; or

(c) Mr X and Mr Y are adult siblings?

Whether common control exists between family members very much depends on the specific facts and circumstances. In the case of family members it is unlikely that there will be any written agreement between them. However, the influence that normally arises within relationships between 'close members of the family' as defined in IAS 24 – *Related Parties* (see Chapter 35 at 2.3.7) means that it is possible, but no means assured, that an unwritten arrangement may exist that they will act collectively such that there is common control, and thus the business combination can be considered to be outwith the scope of IFRS 3.

This may be the case in scenario (a), where the father, Mr X, may effectively control the voting of his dependent son (particularly a young dependant) by acting on his behalf and thus vote the entire 60% combined holding collectively. It may also be possible in scenario (b) as a highly influential parent may be able to ensure that the adult family members act collectively. However, there would need to be clear evidence that the family influence has resulted in a pattern of collective family decisions. Nevertheless, if there was any evidence to indicate that Mr X and Mr Y actually act independently (e.g. by voting differently at shareholder or board meetings), then the common control exemption would not apply since they have not been acting collectively to control the entities.

However, common control is unlikely to exist in scenario (c). Where the family members are not 'close members of the family', there is likely to be far less influence between them. Therefore, in scenario (c) where Mr X and Mr Y are adult siblings, it is far less likely that an unwritten agreement will exist as adult siblings generally would be expected to have less influence over each other and are more likely to act independently. Accordingly, we believe that there should be a presumption that common control does not exist between non-close family members and a high level of evidence that they act collectively, rather than independently, would need to exist to overcome this presumption.

If in the above example, Mr X and Mr Y had been unrelated, then in the absence of a written agreement, consideration would need to be given to all of the facts and circumstances to determine whether it is appropriate to apply the exemption. In our view, there would need to be a high level of evidence of them acting together to control both entities in a collective manner in order to demonstrate than a written contractual agreement really exists, and that such control is not transitory.

B Transitory control

The inclusion of the condition that the 'control is not transitory' is intended to deal with concerns expressed by some commentators that business combinations between parties acting at arm's length could be structured through the use of 'grooming' transactions so that, for a brief period immediately before the combination, the combining entities or businesses are under common control. In this way, it might have been possible for combinations that would otherwise be accounted for in accordance with IFRS 3 using the purchase method to be accounted for using some other method.[236]

An issue considered by IFRIC was whether a reorganisation involving the formation of a new entity (Newco) to facilitate the sale of part of an organisation is a business combination within the scope of IFRS 3. It had been suggested to IFRIC that, because control of the new entity is transitory, a combination involving that newly formed entity would be within the scope of IFRS 3.

As discussed at 2.3.1 above, IFRS 3 states that when an entity is formed to issue equity instruments to effect a business combination, one of the combining entities that existed before the combination must be identified as the acquirer on the basis of the evidence available. IFRIC noted that, to be consistent, the question of whether the entities or businesses are under common control applies to the combining entities that existed before the combination, excluding the newly formed entity. Accordingly, IFRIC decided not to add this topic to its agenda.[237]

Example 7.36: Formation of Newco to facilitate disposal of businesses

Entity A currently has two business operated through Entity X and Entity Y. The group structure (ignoring other entities within the group) is as follows:

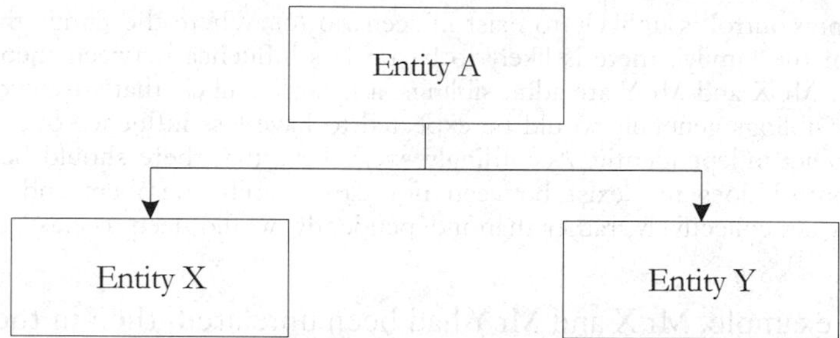

Entity A proposes to combine the two businesses (currently operated by Entity X and Entity Y) into the one entity and then spin-off the combined entity as part of an initial public offering (IPO). Both of the businesses have been owned by Entity A for several years. The internal reconstruction will be structured such that Entity A will establish a new entity (Newco) and transfer its interests in Entity X and Entity Y to Newco, resulting in the following group structure:

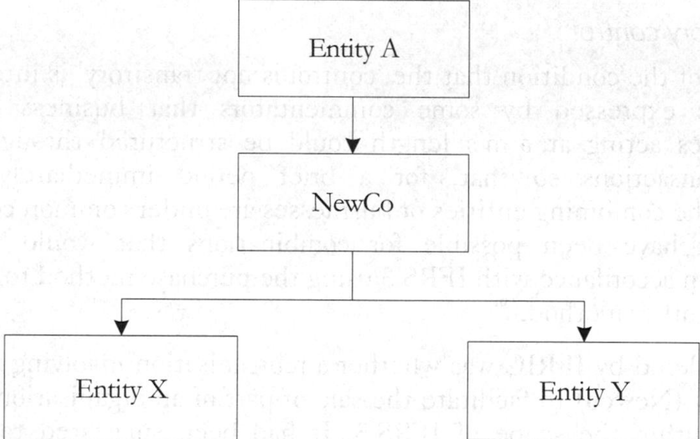

After the IPO, Newco will no longer be under the control of Entity A.

If Newco were to prepare consolidated financial statements, is it entitled to the 'common control' exemption?

As indicated by IFRIC, the question of whether the entities or businesses are under common control applies to the combining entities that existed before the combination, excluding the newly formed entity. In this situation, the combining entities that existed before the combination were Entity X and Entity Y, and these clearly are entities that have been under the common control of Entity A, and are still under the common control of Entity A after the transfer. Clearly, if Newco were preparing consolidated financial statements without there being an intended IPO, it would be entitled to the exemption. However, given that the purpose of the transaction was to facilitate the disposal of the businesses by way of the IPO, such that Entity A no longer has control over Entity X and Entity Y, does this mean that common control is 'transitory'?

In our view, the answer is 'no'. Common control is not considered to be transitory and therefore the reorganisation is excluded from the scope of IFRS 3. As indicated above, the reason for the requirement 'that control is not transitory' is intended as an anti-avoidance mechanism to prevent business combinations between parties acting at arm's length from being structured through the use of 'grooming' transactions so that, *for a brief period immediately before the combination*, the combining entities or businesses are under common control. Whether or not control is 'transitory' should be assessed by looking at the duration of control in the period both before and after the transaction – it is not limited to an assessment of the duration of control only after the transaction.

This is consistent with the ordinary meaning of 'transitory' being something which is fleeting, brief or temporary. The common control of Entity X and Entity Y was not fleeting in the fact pattern as both entities had been controlled by Entity A for several years. By contrast, if Entity Y had only recently come into the group, this may well indicate that control is transitory.

Therefore, an intention to sell the business or go to an IPO shortly after the restructure does not, by itself, prevent the use of the common control exemption.

This is consistent with the views expressed by IFRIC. Although the focus of the issue was on the fact that there was a new entity involved, the decision confirmed the point that the intended sale did not mean control was transitory and that 'control of the combining entities that existed before the combination' must be considered.

Although the above example involved a new entity, the same considerations apply regardless of the manner in which the internal reconstruction may have been structured prior to the IPO. For example, Entity X may have acquired Entity Y (or the net assets and trade of Entity Y), with Entity X then being the subject to an IPO. In such a situation, Entity X would be entitled to the common control exemption with respect to the business combination.

C *Accounting for business combinations involving entities or businesses under common control*

IFRIC also considered a request for guidance on how to apply IFRS 3 to reorganisations in which control remains within the original group. However, IFRIC decided not to add this topic to the agenda, since it was unlikely that it would reach agreement in a reasonable period, in the light of existing diversity in practice and the explicit exclusion of common control transactions from the scope of IFRS 3.[238]

As discussed in 5.3 below, the IASB has stated that it will consider as part of phase II of its project, the treatment of business combinations involving entities or businesses under common control. In the meantime, IFRS 3 only prescribes the purchase method for combinations that are within its scope and does not describe any other methods; it does not address at all the methods of accounting that may be appropriate when a business combination involves entities under common control.

As discussed further in Chapter 3 at 4.3, IAS 8 requires that in the absence of specific guidance in IFRS, management shall use its judgement in developing and applying an accounting policy that is relevant and reliable.[239] In making that judgement, in the absence of IFRS dealing with similar or related issues or guidance within the IASB *Framework*, management may also consider the most recent pronouncements of other standard-setting bodies that use a similar conceptual framework to develop accounting standards, to the extent that these do not conflict with the *Framework* or any other IFRS or Interpretation.[240] Several such bodies have issued guidance and some allow or require the pooling of interests method in accounting for business combinations involving entities under common control.

Accordingly, until such time as the IASB publishes its conclusions, we believe that entities should apply either:

(a) the pooling of interest method; or

(b) the purchase method (as in IFRS 3)

in accounting for business combinations involving entities under common control.

Although the pooling of interest method is not referred to in IFRS 3 (except in the context of eliminating it as a method for accounting for business combinations generally), since IFRS 3 scopes out common control transactions it is therefore not prescriptive as to what method must be followed in such transactions. Therefore, an entity can choose either method for common control transactions. The fact that IFRS 3 scopes out common control business combinations does not emanate from the fact that the Board felt either method was inappropriate, but that it wanted to address common control transactions as a separate issue in the business combination project. The Board did not want to prescribe or ban either of these methods in the meantime. However, we do not consider that 'fresh start accounting', whereby all combining businesses are restated to fair value, is an appropriate method for accounting for combinations between entities under common control.

Whichever policy is adopted should be applied consistently. However, in our view, where the purchase method of accounting is selected, the transaction must have substance from the perspective of the reporting entity. This is because the purchase method results in a reassessment of the value of the net assets of one or more of the entities involved and/or the recognition of goodwill. IFRS contains limited circumstances when net assets may be restated to fair value and restricts the recognition of internally generated goodwill, and a common control transaction should not be used to circumvent these limitations. Careful consideration is required of all of the facts and circumstances from the perspective of each entity, before it is concluded that a transaction has substance. If there is no substance to the transaction, the pooling of interests method is the only method that may be applied to that transaction.

When evaluating whether the transaction has substance, the following factors should all be taken into account:

- the purpose of the transaction;
- the involvement of outside parties in the transaction, such as minority interests or other third parties;
- whether or not the transaction is conducted at fair value;
- the existing activities of the entities involved in the transactions;
- whether or not it is bringing entities together into a 'reporting entity' that did not exist before; and
- where a Newco is established, whether it is undertaken in connection with an IPO or spin-off or other change in control and significant change in ownership.

Example 7.37: Accounting for common control transactions (1)

Entity A currently has two business operated through two wholly-owned subsidiaries, Entity B and Entity C. The group structure (ignoring other entities within the group) is as follows:

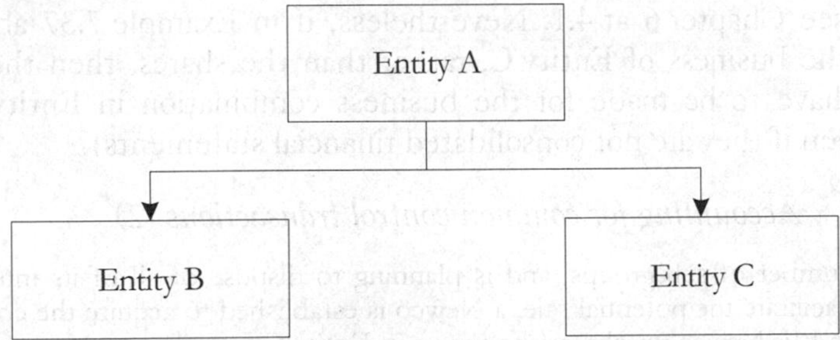

Entity A proposes to combine the two businesses (currently operated by Entity B and Entity C) into the one entity in anticipation of spinning-off the combined entity as part of an initial public offering (IPO). Both of the businesses have been owned by Entity A for several years. The internal reconstruction will be structured such that Entity B will acquire the shares of the much smaller Entity C from Entity A for cash at its fair value of £1,000. The carrying value of the net assets of Entity C is £200. This also represents the carrying amount of Entity C's net assets in the consolidated financial statements of Entity A. The fair values of Entity C's identifiable assets, liabilities and contingent liabilities are £600.

Assuming that the policy is to apply the purchase method of accounting to such transactions, how should this business combination be accounted for in the consolidated financial statements of both Entity B and Entity A?

As far as Entity B is concerned, there does appear to be substance to this transaction from its perspective. There is a business purpose to the transaction; it has been conducted at fair value; both Entity B and Entity C have existing activities; and they have been brought together to create a reporting entity that did not exist before. Accordingly, since Entity B now controls Entity C, it can apply the purchase method of accounting (as discussed at 2.3 above) to its acquisition of its new subsidiary in its consolidated financial statements. In summary, this will mean that Entity C's identifiable assets, liabilities and contingent liabilities will be initially reflected at their fair values of £600, together with goodwill of £400 (£1,000 less £600), in the consolidated balance sheet, with only the post-acquisition results of Entity C reflected in the consolidated income statement.

As far as Entity A is concerned, there is no substance to this transaction from the perspective of the Entity A group – all that has happened is that Entity C, rather than being directly held and controlled by Entity A, is now indirectly held and controlled through Entity B. Accordingly, this has no impact on the consolidated financial statements of Entity A. Thus, the carrying amounts for Entity C's net assets included in those consolidated financial statements do not change. Even if it was thought that there was substance to the transaction from the perspective of the Entity A group, and there was another national GAAP that would allow the purchase method to be applied (with the net assets reflected at their fair values of £600 together with goodwill of £400), and a gain recognised on the transaction (effectively for the uplift in the value of the assets, including goodwill), in our view it could not be adopted since it conflicts with guidance in other IFRS. IFRS 3 only permits the remeasurement of existing assets and liabilities, including the recognition of identifiable intangible assets and contingent liabilities when there has been a business combination with a change in control. In this situation, there is no change in control from Entity A's perspective. In addition, IAS 27 requires the elimination of intragroup transactions, including any resulting profits and losses (see Chapter 6 at 6.3).

In the above example, Entity B had to account for its acquisition of its new subsidiary, Entity C, as it was preparing consolidated financial statements. This may only be required when the new Entity B group is being demerged or spun-off as part of an IPO as in the example. In some situations, Entity B would not need to account for the business combination at all, as it may be exempt from preparing consolidated financial statements – see Chapter 6 at 4.1. Nevertheless, if in Example 7.37 above, Entity B had acquired the business of Entity C, rather than the shares, then the same policy choice would have to be made for the business combination in Entity B's financial statements (even if they are not consolidated financial statements).

Example 7.38: Accounting for common control transactions (2)

Entity A has a number of sub-groups, and is planning to dispose of all of its interests in certain subsidiaries. To facilitate the potential sale, a Newco is established to acquire the entities to be sold – Subgroups C and E. Newco purchases the shares in Entity C from Entity A for cash from a bank loan. The group structure before and after this transaction is as follows:

Before

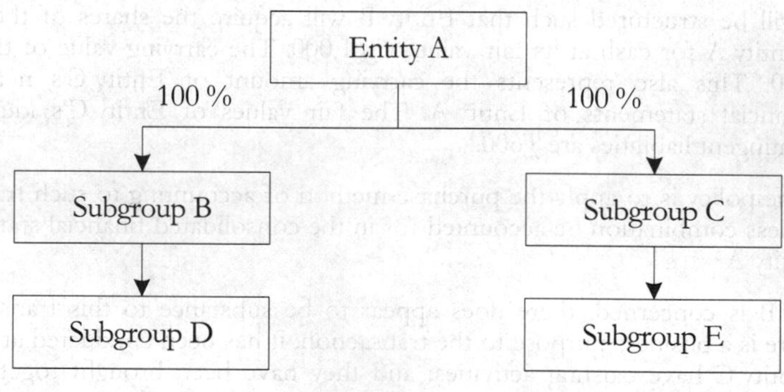

After

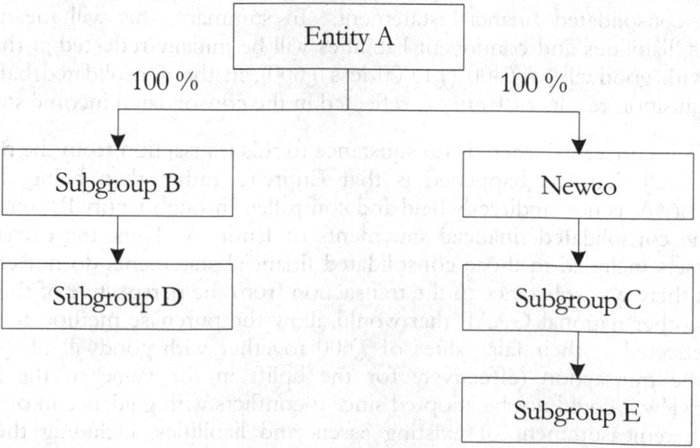

In this situation, there is no substance to the transaction from Newco's perspective as the Newco group is simply a continuation of the existing subgroup comprising Subgroup C and Subgroup E's activities. Newco is essentially an extension of the parent as it does not have its own operations. The change in control is only planned, and it is not an integral part of the transaction. Thus, Newco cannot apply the purchase method of accounting in preparing its consolidated financial statements. It would have to apply the pooling of interest method. However, if such a restructuring was linked to another transaction such as a sale or disposal via an IPO, the circumstances may be such that Newco could be regarded as the acquirer if it is considered to be effectively an extension of the new owners (see Example 7.2 at 2.3.1 above).

I Application of the purchase method

When the purchase method is being applied to business combinations involving entities under common control, then as indicated above entities need to follow the requirements of IFRS 3. As indicated at 2.3 above, applying the purchase method in IFRS 3 involves the following steps:[241]

(a) identifying an acquirer (see 2.3.1 above);
(b) measuring the cost of the business combination (see 2.3.2 above); and
(c) allocating, at the acquisition date, the cost of the business combination to the assets acquired and liabilities and contingent liabilities assumed (see 2.3.3 to 2.3.6 above).

As far as (a) is concerned, it may be that in some situations that the identification of the acquirer may mean that the business combination needs to be accounted for as a reverse acquisition (see 2.3.8 above). This is likely to be the case when new entities are involved (see 2.4.2 below).

As far as the other requirements of IFRS 3 in relation to the purchase method are concerned, they have clearly been developed for dealing with business combinations between parties on an arms' length basis. For business combinations involving entities under common control, this may not be the case. Consider the following example.

Example 7.39: Cash consideration less than the fair value of business acquired

Assume the same facts as in Example 7.37 above, except that Entity B, rather than acquiring Entity C from Entity A for cash at its fair value of £1,000, only pays cash of £700. How should this be reflected by Entity B when applying the purchase method for its acquisition of Entity C?

In our view, there are two acceptable ways of accounting for this. Either:

(a) the cost of the business combination is the fair value of the cash given as consideration, i.e. £700. Accordingly, goodwill of only £100 (£700 less £600) is recognised; or
(b) the cost of the business combination is the fair value of the cash given as consideration (£700), together with a deemed capital contribution received from Entity A for the difference up to the fair value of the business of Entity C, i.e. £300 (£1,000 less £700), giving a total consideration of £1,000. Accordingly, goodwill of £400 is recognised. The capital contribution of £300 would be reflected in equity.

Whichever method is adopted should be applied on a consistent basis.

If Entity B only paid cash of £500, then the impact under (a) and (b) above would be:

(a) Since the cost is only £500, then no goodwill is recognised. However, £100 (being the excess of the fair values of the identifiable assets, liabilities and contingent liabilities (£600) over the cost of £500) is recognised in the income statement (see 2.3.5 above).
(b) As before, goodwill of £400 is recognised, but a capital contribution of £500 would be reflected in equity.

In Example 7.37 and Example 7.39 above, the consideration paid by Entity B was in cash. However, what if Entity B issued shares to Entity A to effect the business combination?

Where equity instruments are issued by an acquirer to effect a business combination, IFRS 3 requires the cost of the business combination to be based on the fair value of the equity instruments issued. As indicated at 2.3.2 C above, for quoted equity instruments, IFRS 3 regards the published price at the date of exchange as providing the best estimate of the instrument's fair value. In situations such as this, where the business combination is between entities under common control, there is unlikely to be a published price for the acquirer's shares. Where this is the case, IFRS 3 states that 'if a published price does not exist for equity instruments issued by the acquirer, the fair value of those instruments could, for example, be estimated by reference to their proportional interest in the fair value of the acquirer or by reference to the proportional interest in the fair value of the acquiree obtained, whichever is the more clearly evident'.[242]

In Example 7.39 above, if Entity B issued shares to Entity A to acquire Entity C, and there is no quoted price for Entity B's shares, then the fair value of the shares issued would need to be based on either the fair value of Entity B or the fair value of Entity C, whichever is the more clearly evident. If the fair value of Entity B was more clearly evident, and the value of the shares issued as consideration was only £700, then as with cash consideration less than the fair value of the business acquired, Entity B would apply whichever method in Example 7.39 it has adopted for such transactions. However, in the absence of a 'more clearly evident' fair value for Entity B, the cost would be based on the fair value of Entity C, i.e. £1,000. Thus, goodwill of £400 would be recognised, with the £1,000 cost reflected in equity.

II Application of the pooling of interest method

As indicated above, we believe that where entities do not adopt a policy of using the purchase method under IFRS 3, then they should apply the pooling of interest method when accounting for business combinations between entities under common control. IFRS 3 makes no reference to the pooling of interest method (except in the context of eliminating it as a method for accounting for business combinations generally). However, the pooling of interests method (or merger accounting as it is known in some jurisdictions) is generally considered to involve the following:[243]

- The assets and liabilities of the combining entities are reflected at their carrying amounts.

  No adjustments are made to reflect fair values, or recognise any new assets or liabilities, that would otherwise be done under the purchase method. The only adjustments that are made are to harmonise accounting policies.
- No 'new' goodwill is recognised as a result of the combination.

  The only goodwill that is recognised is any existing goodwill relating to either of the combining entities. Any difference between the consideration paid and the equity 'acquired' is reflected within equity.
- The income statement reflects the results of the combining entities for the full year, irrespective of when the combination took place.
- Comparatives are presented as if the entities had always been combined.

In some jurisdictions, regulators take the view that comparatives cannot be restated as such a treatment is inconsistent with IAS 27. This appears to be on the basis that a parent's consolidated financial statements can only include the income and expenses of a subsidiary from the acquisition date as defined in IFRS 3, i.e. the date it acquires control of the subsidiary. Such a view would also appear to mean that, when applying the pooling of interests method, the pre-acquisition income and expenses of a subsidiary in the current year should also not be included. We believe that such a view is a narrow interpretation of IFRS, and that the general requirements outlined above should all be applied when using the pooling of interests method.

The application of these general requirements for the pooling of interests method in the context of business combinations involving entities under common control can sometimes raise particular issues as discussed below.

In general, no adjustments would be expected to be made to harmonise accounting policies of the entities involved in a business combination between entities under common control. This is because in the preparation of the consolidated financial statements of the ultimate parent entity under IFRS, uniform accounting policies should have been adopted by all members of the group. However, it may be necessary to make adjustments where the combining entities have used different accounting policies when preparing their own financial statements. Nevertheless, the main issue relating to the use of carrying amounts when applying the pooling of interest method for common control combinations is whether the amounts should be based on:

(a) the carrying values reported in the consolidated financial statements of the parent; or

(b) the carrying values reported in the standalone financial statements of the combining entities.

Consider the following example.

Example 7.40: Carrying amounts of assets and liabilities

Entity A currently has two business operated through two wholly-owned subsidiaries, Entity B and Entity C. The group structure (ignoring other entities within the group) is as follows:

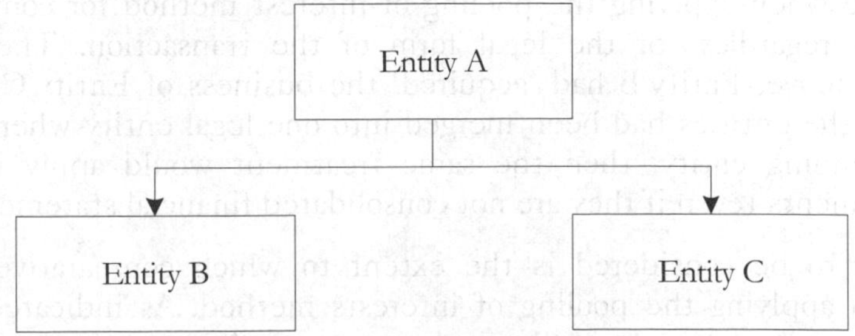

Both entities have been owned by Entity A for a number of years.

On 1 July 2008, Entity A restructures the group by transferring its investment in Entity C to Entity B, such that Entity C becomes a subsidiary of Entity B. The policy adopted for business combinations involving entities under common control is to apply the pooling of interest method.

In Entity B's consolidated financial statements for the year ended 31 December 2008, what values should be reflected in respect of Entity C?

In our view, Entity B can elect to use either:

(a) the carrying values reported in Entity A's consolidated financial statements; or

(b) the carrying values reported in Entity C's own financial statements.

Once an option is selected by an entity, the method should be applied consistently to all transactions of this type.

Under option (a) the value of the assets and liabilities of Entity C in Entity B's consolidated financial statements will be the carrying values that were used in Entity A's consolidated financial statements. Accordingly, they will be based on the fair value as at the date Entity C became part of the Entity A group and adjusted for subsequent transactions. Any goodwill relating to Entity C that was recognised in Entity A's consolidated financial statements will also be recognised. The carrying values of the assets of Entity B will remain as before.

The rationale for this approach is that the transaction is essentially a transfer of the assets and liabilities of Entity C from the consolidated financial statements of Entity A to the financial statements of Entity B. From a group perspective of Entity B's shareholder, nothing has changed except the location of those assets and liabilities. Entity B has effectively taken the group's ownership on. Therefore the values used in the consolidated financial statements are appropriate values to apply to the assets and liabilities, as they represent the carrying values to the Entity A group.

Under option (b) the carrying value of the assets and liabilities of Entity C in Entity B's consolidated financial statements will be the carrying values reported in Entity C's own financial statements. (Entity A will therefore still be required to make any necessary consolidation adjustments in preparing its own consolidated financial statements.)

Under this approach, the transaction is considered from the perspective of the reporting entity (Entity B sub-group), and the Entity A group's perspective is ignored in accounting for the transaction. Therefore the carrying value in Entity C's own financial statements will be relevant. The consolidated financial statements of Entity B after the transfer are effectively a combination of the financial statements of both entities. The shareholder, Entity A, is thus receiving the same financial information as before, but in one set of financial statements rather than two.

In our view, an entity should elect to apply either of the methods outlined in the above example when applying the pooling of interest method for common control transactions – regardless of the legal form of the transaction. Therefore, if in Example 7.40 above, Entity B had 'acquired' the business of Entity C, rather than the shares, or the entities had been merged into one legal entity whereby Entity B was the continuing entity, then the same treatment would apply in Entity B's financial statements (even if they are not consolidated financial statements).

Another issue to be considered is the extent to which comparatives should be restated when applying the pooling of interests method. As indicated above, the pooling of interests method generally involves comparatives to be presented as it the entities had always been combined.

Example 7.41: Restatement of comparatives (1)

Assume the same facts as in Example 7.40 above.

In preparing its consolidated financial statements for the year ended 31 December 2008, should Entity B restate the 2007 comparatives in its consolidated financial statements as if the business combination (and the investment in Entity C) took place as from 1 January 2007?

Since Entity C has been part of the Entity A group for a number of years, then Entity B should restate the 2007 comparatives in its consolidated financial statements for 2008. Restatement is required to reflect the combination as if it had occurred from the beginning of the earliest period presented in the financial statements, regardless of the actual date of the combination. In common control situations the logic of pooling is that there has been no change in control the ultimate controlling party (in this case, Entity A) has had over the combined resources – it has merely changed the location of its resources. Accordingly, if the ultimate controlling party had control of these resources in the comparative period then the comparatives should be restated.

In the above example, Entity C had been part of the Entity A group for a number of years. What if this had not been the case?

Example 7.42: Restatement of comparatives (2)

Assume the same facts as in Example 7.40 above, except that in this situation Entity A only acquired Entity C on 1 January 2008 (i.e. the transaction is still considered to be under common control at the date of Entity B's acquisition of Entity C, but Entity B and Entity C were not under common control during the comparative period).

In preparing its consolidated financial statements for the year ended 31 December 2008, should Entity B restate the 2007 comparatives in its consolidated financial statements as if the business combination (and the investment in Entity C) took place as from 1 January 2007?

In this situation, the pooling of interests method is applied from the date that the entities came under common control. Therefore, this would be 1 January 2008. In our view restatement of prior periods should not be made when adopting the pooling of interests method of accounting if the entities were not under common control during that comparative period.

As indicated above, in common control situations, the logic of pooling is that there has been no change in control the ultimate controlling party has had over the combined resources – it has merely changed the location of its resources. Accordingly, if the ultimate controlling party had control of these resources in the comparative period then the comparatives should be restated. However, where there is a change in control, the ultimate controlling party has not always had control over these combined resources, and application of the pooling of interests method should reflect that – that is, it cannot be applied during the period that common control did not exist.

If Entity A had only acquired Entity C on 1 July 2007, such that Entity B and Entity C had come under common control as at that date, then Entity B would restate its comparatives but only to reflect the assets, liabilities and results of Entity C from 1 July 2007.

2.4.2 Group reorganisations

A Introduction

Group reorganisations may be undertaken for a number of reasons, for example, to improve the co-ordination of diverse businesses possibly so that the different businesses are conducted through directly owned subsidiaries, or to create a tax grouping in a particular jurisdiction. In some cases, it may be to split up an existing group of companies into two or more separate groups of companies, in order to separate their different trades, possibly as a prelude to the disposal of part of the group either by way of sale or by way of an IPO. Similarly, the introduction of a new holding company may be undertaken as part of an IPO of the group.

Group reorganisations involve the restructuring of the relationships between companies in a group (or under common control) and can take many forms. For example, setting up a new holding company, changing the direct ownership of subsidiaries within the group (possibly involving the creation of new intermediate holding company), or transferring businesses from one company to another. In principle, most such changes should have no impact on the consolidated financial statements of an existing group (provided there are no minority interests affected), because they are purely internal and cannot affect the group when it is being portrayed as a single entity. Some reorganisations may involve transferring businesses outwith the group (possibly involving the creation of a new holding company for those businesses).

For some of the entities involved in the reorganisation, there may well be a business combination that needs to be accounted for. The sections which follow consider only this particular aspect of the transaction in the context of the forms of reorganisations that are illustrated, based on the discussion contained in 2.4.1 above with respect to the common control exemption in IFRS 3. Some other forms of reorganisation have already been considered in 2.4.1 above. The accounting for disposals of subsidiaries is discussed in Chapter 6 at 6.6. All of the examples that follow involve a new entity (Newco) and assume that all entities are owned 100% by the entity at the top of the particular structure.

B Setting up a new top holding company

Example 7.43: Newco inserted at the top of an existing group

A Newco is incorporated and inserted at the top of an existing group. Newco issues shares to the existing shareholders of Entity A in exchange for the shares already held in that entity. There are no changes to the shareholder group. The group structure before and after this transaction is as follows:

Before

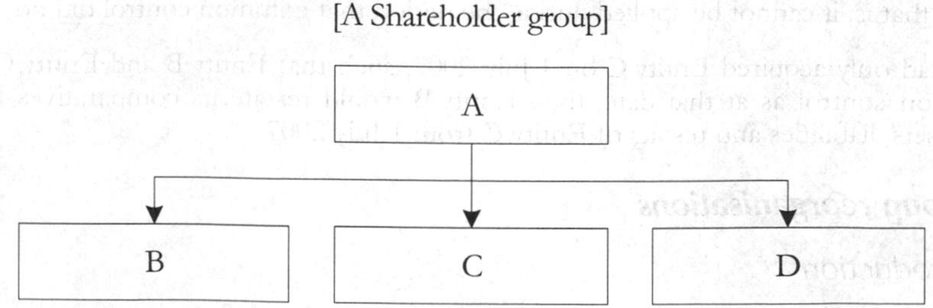

After

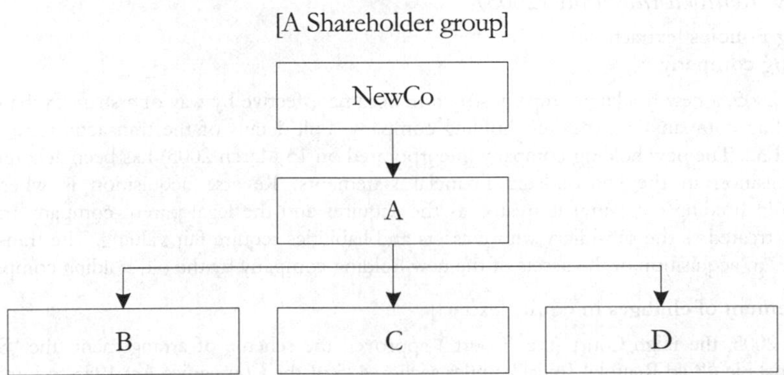

In this situation, the first question to be asked is whether it within the scope of IFRS 3 at all?

One view is that it does not represent a business combination at all, since a Newco that issues shares to effect a business combination can never be identified as the acquirer (see 2.3.1 above), and A has not combined with any other business. On this basis, although outwith the scope of IFRS 3, the purchase method in IFRS cannot be applied, therefore the pooling of interest method should be used (see 2.4.1 C II above). In this situation, the consolidated financial statements are effectively those that were presented by A. The only difference is that the share capital will be that of Newco, and to the extent that this is different from that of A, then an adjustment needs to be made to equity. Where the share capital of Newco is greater than that of A, then this will require a debit adjustment to be made to equity. In our view, this should not be taken to any component of equity of the A group that may require to be recycled to the income statement under IFRS at a later date. For example, reserves representing gains on available-for sale investments under IAS 39 or exchange gains on foreign operations under IAS 21 – *The Effects of Changes in Foreign Exchange Rates*. However, any other equity balance such as a share premium account or additional paid-in capital account could be used.

An alternative view is that this is a 'business combination' which is defined in paragraph 4 of IFRS 3 as 'the bringing together of separate entities or businesses into one reporting entity'. In this case, Newco and the A group are separate entities that have been brought together. Accordingly, it is within the scope of IFRS 3 unless otherwise exempt. In most situations this type of reorganisation will not qualify for the 'common control exemption' since there will be no contractual arrangement between the shareholders (see 2.4.1 A above). As a result, the purchase method in IFRS 3 needs to be applied. However, since Newco cannot be the acquirer, the transaction needs to be accounted for as a reverse acquisition of Newco by A (see 2.3.8 above). As Newco did not have any existing assets or business, this results in the same reported income and net assets as under the pooling of interest method. The only difference is that the equity balances are those that were reported in A's consolidated financial statements (see 2.3.8 B above). Thus, there is no equity adjustment to be made as required by the pooling of interest method.

We believe that both views are acceptable, but as indicated above the consolidated financial statements are effectively the same.

In the event that the 'common control exemption' was applicable because there was one shareholder, or a group of the shareholders who did have some contractual arrangement, then under the alternative view, either the pooling of interest method or reverse acquisition accounting would be applied.

One company that has accounted for such a transaction as a reverse acquisition is Rentokil Initial as shown in the following extract.

Extract 7.9: Rentokil Initial plc (2005)

Accounting Policies [extract]

New holding company

On 21 June 2005, a new holding company structure became effective by way of a share exchange between the old holding company and the new holding company. Full details of the transaction are disclosed in notes 27 and 32. The new holding company (incorporated on 15 March 2005) has been accounted for as a reverse acquisition in the consolidated financial statements. Reverse acquisition is where the legal subsidiary (old holding company) is treated as the acquirer and the legal parent company (new holding company) is treated as the subsidiary whose assets and liabilities require fair valuing. The transaction was, in substance, an acquisition of the assets of the new holding company by the old holding company.

27. Statement of changes in equity [extract]

On 20 June 2005, the High Court (the "Court") approved the scheme of arrangement (the "Scheme") of Rentokil Initial plc ("Old Rentokil Initial") under section 425 of the Companies Act 1985 to introduce a new listed group holding company, Rentokil Initial 2005 plc ("New Rentokil Initial"). The Scheme became effective on 21 June 2005 and New Rentokil Initial changed its name to Rentokil Initial plc and Old Rentokil Initial changed its name to Rentokil Initial 1927 plc at that time. Under the terms of the Scheme, holders of Old Rentokil Initial shares received one New Rentokil Initial share for each Old Rentokil Initial share.

On 22 June 2005, the Court approved the reduction of capital of Rentokil Initial plc, whereby the nominal value of each ordinary share was reduced from 100p to 1p. The reduction of capital became effective on 23 June 2005. As shown above, the effect of the scheme of arrangement and the subsequent reduction in capital has increased distributable reserves by £1,792.3m. The capital reorganisation transaction has been treated as a reverse acquisition in the consolidated financial accounts.

32. Business combinations [extract]

On 21 June 2005, the legal parent company (new holding company) acquired the entire share capital of the old holding company. This has been treated as a reverse acquisition in accordance with IFRS 3 "Business Combinations". The book value and fair value of the net assets of the legal parent prior to acquisition were £50,002. The legal parent company did not trade prior to acquisition. See note 27 for further details.

In Example 7.43 above, the reorganisation was effected by Newco issuing shares. If Newco gave cash consideration as part of the transaction, then in most situations this will not affect the analysis above. Any cash paid will be treated as an equity transaction, either as part of the equity elimination under the pooling of interest method or as part of the reverse acquisition accounting (see 2.3.8 E above). As discussed at 2.4.1 C above, it would only be if the facts and circumstances meant that there was substance to the transaction such that Newco could be regarded as the acquirer that the purchase method would result in fair values being attributed to the assets, liabilities and contingent liabilities of the A group, and the recognition of goodwill. For example, where the transaction was contingent on completion of an IPO that resulted in a change in control of the A group.

Example 7.44: Newco inserted at the top of entities owned by the same shareholders thereby creating a new reporting group

A Newco is incorporated and inserted at the top of a number of entities owned by the same shareholders. Newco issues shares to the existing shareholders of entities B, C and D in exchange for the shares already held in those entities. The group structure before and after this transaction is as follows:

Before

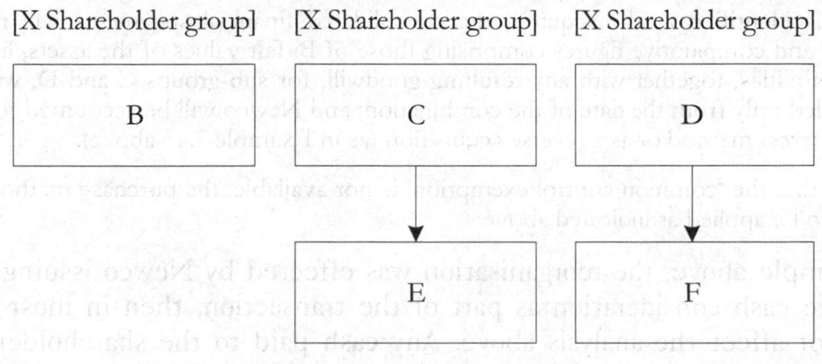

After

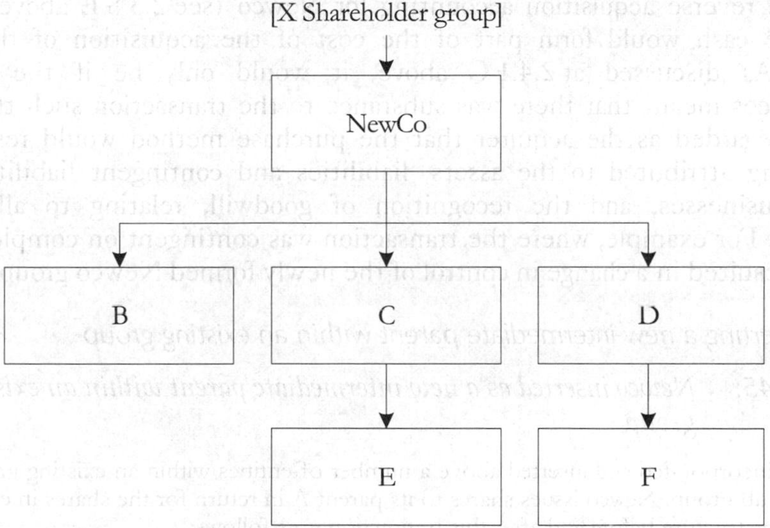

Unlike the situation in Example 7.43 above, this is clearly a business combination as defined by IFRS 3 since B and sub-groups C and D have been brought together to form a new reporting entity under a new parent entity, Newco. Accordingly, it is within the scope of IFRS 3 unless otherwise exempt.

It may be that this type of reorganisation will qualify for the 'common control exemption' (see 2.4.1 A above) since the number of shareholders will generally be relatively few. Accordingly, there may well be one individual, or a sub-group of the shareholders with a contractual arrangement, who controls entities B, C and D. The exemption will apply as long as the common control is not transitory (see 2.4.1 B above). In that case, a policy choice should be made as to whether the pooling of interest method or the purchase method is adopted (see 2.4.1 C above).

If the pooling of interest method is used, as discussed at 2.4.1 C II above, the consolidated financial statements will be presented as if the entities had always been combined, reflecting the carrying values of each of the entities (although since in this case the entities did not comprise a formal group before, it may be necessary to harmonise accounting policies) and including comparative figures for all of the entities 'acquired by Newco' (although this will depend on whether all of those entities were under common control for all of the periods presented).

If the purchase method in IFRS 3 is to be used, since Newco cannot be the acquirer, one of the existing entities (either B, C or D) will need to be identified as the acquirer (see 2.3.1 above), If, for example, B is identified as the acquirer, the consolidated financial statements will reflect book values for B, and comparative figures comprising those of B; fair values of the assets, liabilities and contingent liabilities, together with any resulting goodwill, for sub-groups C and D, whose results will be included only from the date of the combination; and Newco will be accounted for under the pooling of interest method or as a reverse acquisition (as in Example 7.43 above).

In the event that the 'common control exemption' is not available, the purchase method in IFRS 3 would have to be applied as indicated above.

In the example above, the reorganisation was effected by Newco issuing shares. If Newco gave cash consideration as part of the transaction, then in most situations this will not affect the analysis above. Any cash paid to the shareholders in their capacity as owners of the identified acquirer will be treated as an equity transaction, either as part of the equity elimination under the pooling of interest method or as part of the reverse acquisition accounting for Newco (see 2.3.8 E above), and the rest of the cash would form part of the cost of the acquisition of the entities acquired. As discussed at 2.4.1 C above, it would only be if the facts and circumstances meant that there was substance to the transaction such that Newco could be regarded as the acquirer that the purchase method would result in fair values being attributed to the assets, liabilities and contingent liabilities of the existing businesses, and the recognition of goodwill, relating to all of those businesses. For example, where the transaction was contingent on completion of an IPO that resulted in a change in control of the newly formed Newco group.

C Inserting a new intermediate parent within an existing group

Example 7.45: Newco inserted as a new intermediate parent within an existing group

A Newco is incorporated and inserted above a number of entities within an existing group so as to form a new sub-group. Newco issues shares to its parent A in return for the shares in entities C and D. The group structure before and after this transaction is as follows:

Before

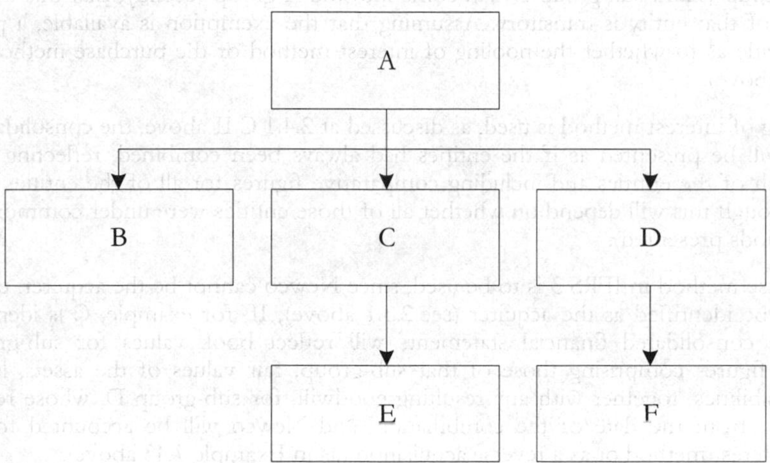

After

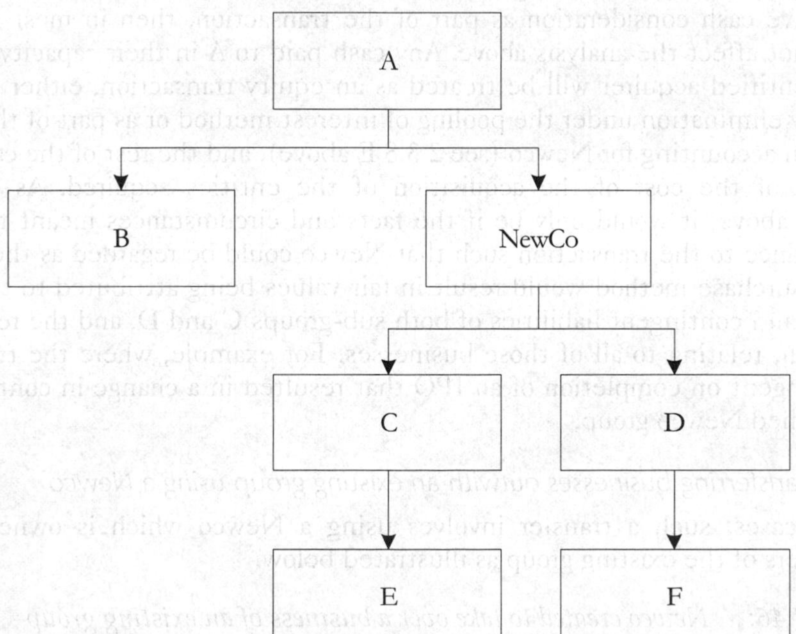

In most situations, Newco will be exempt from preparing consolidated financial statements (see Chapter 6 at 4.1). However, if it chooses to prepare such financial statements, or loses the right to the exemption due to, say, an IPO of the Newco group, then the implications of IFRS 3 need to be considered.

This type of reorganisation will generally qualify for the 'common control exemption' in IFRS 3 since sub-group C and sub-group D are controlled by entity A. As discussed at 2.4.1 B above, the exemption will apply as long as the common control is not transitory, and in making that assessment the newly formed entity Newco is excluded. It would only be if any of the entities within sub-group C and sub-group D had come into the A group recently, that this might indicate that control of that entity is transitory. Assuming that the exemption is available, a policy choice should be made as to whether the pooling of interest method or the purchase method is adopted (see 2.4.1 C above).

If the pooling of interest method is used, as discussed at 2.4.1 C II above, the consolidated financial statements will be presented as if the entities had always been combined, reflecting the carrying values of each of the entities and including comparative figures for all of the entities 'acquired by Newco' (although this will depend on whether all of those entities were under common control for all of the periods presented).

If the purchase method in IFRS 3 is to be used, since Newco cannot be the acquirer, either C or D will need to be identified as the acquirer (see 2.3.1 above), If, for example, C is identified as the acquirer, the consolidated financial statements will reflect book values for sub-group C, and comparative figures comprising those of that sub-group; fair values of the assets, liabilities and contingent liabilities, together with any resulting goodwill, for sub-group D, whose results will be included only from the date of the combination; and Newco will be accounted for under the pooling of interest method or as a reverse acquisition (as in Example 7.43 above).

In the event that the 'common control exemption' is not available, the purchase method in IFRS 3 would have to be applied as indicated above.

In the example above, the reorganisation was effected by Newco issuing shares. If Newco gave cash consideration as part of the transaction, then in most situations this will not affect the analysis above. Any cash paid to A in their capacity as owner of the identified acquirer will be treated as an equity transaction, either as part of the equity elimination under the pooling of interest method or as part of the reverse acquisition accounting for Newco (see 2.3.8 E above), and the rest of the cash would form part of the cost of the acquisition of the entities acquired. As discussed at 2.4.1 C above, it would only be if the facts and circumstances meant that there was substance to the transaction such that Newco could be regarded as the acquirer that the purchase method would result in fair values being attributed to the assets, liabilities and contingent liabilities of both sub-groups C and D, and the recognition of goodwill, relating to all of those businesses. For example, where the transaction was contingent on completion of an IPO that resulted in a change in control of the newly formed Newco group.

D Transferring businesses outwith an existing group using a Newco

In some cases, such a transfer involves using a Newco which is owned by the shareholders of the existing group as illustrated below.

Example 7.46: Newco created to take over a business of an existing group

Entity C, a subsidiary of Parent A, transfers the shares held in its subsidiary, Entity E, to a newly formed entity, Newco. In return, Newco issues shares to the existing shareholders of Parent A. The group structure before and after this transaction is as follows:

Before

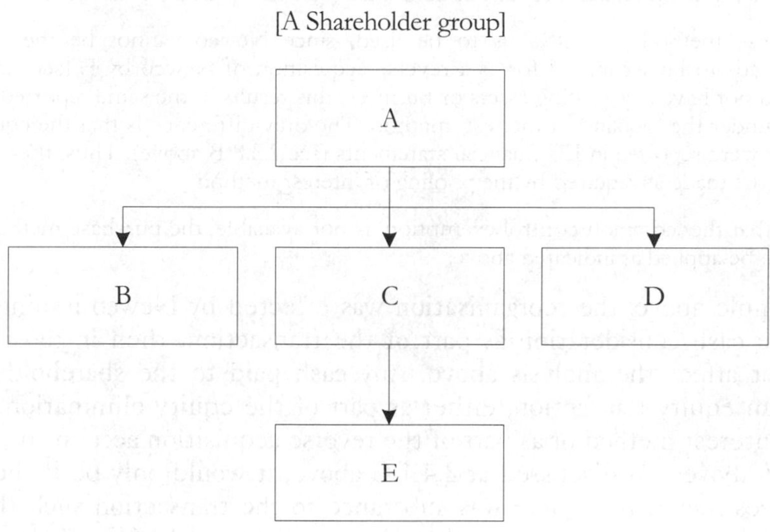

After

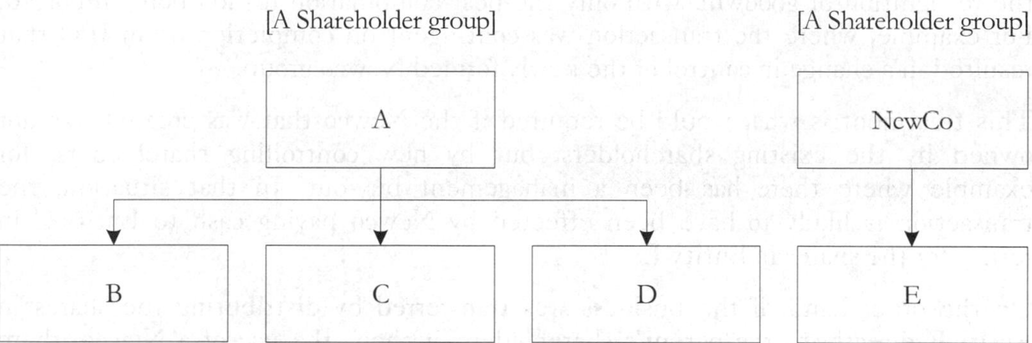

This would appear to be a business combination as defined by IFRS 3 since Newco and Entity E have been brought together to form a new reporting entity, the Newco group. Accordingly, it is within the scope of IFRS 3 unless otherwise exempt.

It may be that this type of reorganisation will qualify for the 'common control exemption' (see 2.4.1 A above). This will be case if there is one individual, or a sub-group of the shareholders with a contractual arrangement, who controls entity A and the new Newco group. The exemption will apply as long as the common control is not transitory (see 2.4.1 B above). In that case, a policy choice should be made as to whether the pooling of interest method or the purchase method is adopted (see 2.4.1 C above).

If the pooling of interest method is used, as discussed at 2.4.1 C II above, the consolidated financial statements are effectively those that were presented by E. The only difference is that the share capital will be that of Newco, and to the extent that this is different from that of E, then an adjustment needs to be made to equity. Where the share capital of Newco is greater than that of E, then this will require a debit adjustment to be made to equity. In our view, this should not be taken to any component of equity of E that may require to be recycled to the income statement under IFRS at a later date. For example, reserves representing gains on available-for sale investments under IAS 39 or exchange gains on foreign operations under IAS 21. However, any other equity balance such as a share premium account or additional paid-in capital account could be used.

If the purchase method in IFRS 3 is to be used, since Newco cannot be the acquirer, the transaction needs to be accounted for as a reverse acquisition of Newco by E (see 2.3.8 E above) As Newco did not have any existing assets or business, this results in the same reported income and net assets as under the 'pooling of interest' method. The only difference is that the equity balances are those that were reported in E's financial statements (see 2.3.8 B above). Thus, there is no equity adjustment to be made as required by the pooling of interest method.

In the event that the 'common control exemption' is not available, the purchase method in IFRS 3 would have to be applied as indicated above.

In the example above, the reorganisation was effected by Newco issuing shares. If Newco gave cash consideration as part of the transaction, then in most situations this will not affect the analysis above. Any cash paid to the shareholders will be treated as an equity transaction, either as part of the equity elimination under the pooling of interest method or as part of the reverse acquisition accounting for Newco (see 2.3.8 E above). As discussed at 2.4.1 C above, it would only be if the facts and circumstances meant that there was substance to the transaction such that Newco could be regarded as the acquirer that the purchase method would result in fair values being attributed to the assets, liabilities and contingent liabilities of E, and the recognition of goodwill, with only the post-combination results being reported. For example, where the transaction was contingent on completion of an IPO that resulted in a change in control of the newly formed Newco group.

This treatment is what would be required if the Newco that was created was not owned by the existing shareholders, but by new controlling shareholders, for example where there has been a management buy-out. In that situation, the transaction is likely to have been effected by Newco paying cash to Entity C in return for the shares in Entity E.

On the other hand, if the business was transferred by distributing the shares in Entity E directly to the parent's shareholders, without the use of a Newco, there would be no business combination at all. Entity E would not reflect any changes in its financial statements. The only impact for Entity E is that rather than only having one shareholder, Entity C, it now has a number of shareholders.

3 GOODWILL

The initial recognition and measurement of the goodwill acquired in a business combination as an asset was discussed at 2.3.4 above. The main issue relating to such goodwill is then how it should be subsequently accounted for. The requirements of IFRS 3 in this respect are straightforward; but that is only because the detailed requirements in relation to the subsequent accounting for goodwill are dealt with in IAS 36.

3.1 Subsequent accounting for goodwill

IFRS 3 requires that, after initial recognition, the acquirer measures goodwill acquired in a business combination at cost less any accumulated impairment losses.[244]

Goodwill acquired in a business combination is not to be amortised (as was the treatment under IAS 22). Instead, the acquirer has to test it for impairment annually, or more frequently if events or changes in circumstances indicate that it might be impaired, in accordance with IAS 36.[245] The requirements of IAS 36 relating specifically to the impairment of goodwill are dealt with below; the general requirements of IAS 36 are covered in Chapter 15.

3.2 Allocation of goodwill to cash-generating units

As indicated at 2.3.4 above, IFRS 3 considers goodwill acquired in a business combination to represent a payment made by an acquirer in anticipation of future economic benefits from assets that are not capable of being individually identified and separately recognised. Thus, an impairment test cannot be carried out on goodwill alone, since it does not generate cash flows independently of other assets. Therefore to test goodwill for impairment necessitates its allocation to a cash-generating unit (CGU) of the acquirer or to a group of CGUs. The concept of a CGU is discussed in Chapter 15 at 3.3.2.

IAS 36 requires that, for the purpose of impairment testing, goodwill acquired in a business combination is, from the acquisition date, to be allocated to each of the acquirer's CGUs, or to a group of CGUs, that are expected to benefit from the synergies of the combination. This is irrespective of whether other assets or liabilities of the acquiree are assigned to those CGUs or group of CGUs. The standard recognises that goodwill sometimes cannot be allocated on a non-arbitrary basis to an individual CGU, so permits it to be allocated to a group of CGUs. However, each CGU or group of CGUs to which the goodwill is so allocated must:

(a) represent the lowest level within the entity at which the goodwill is monitored for internal management purposes; and
(b) not be larger than a segment based on either the entity's primary or the entity's secondary reporting format determined in accordance with IAS 14 – *Segment Reporting*.[246]

IFRS 8 – *Operating Segments* – issued by the IASB in November 2006, will replace IAS 14 and will change the basis for identifying segments starting in financial statements from 1 January 2009. Under IFRS 8 an 'operating segment' is identified on the basis of internal reports that are regularly reviewed by the entity's chief operating decision maker in order to allocate resources to the segment and assess its performance.[247] As a result, IAS 36 has been amended and as from 1 January 2009, goodwill to be tested for impairment cannot be allocated to a CGU or CGU group larger than an *operating* segment. IFRS 8 is discussed in Chapter 30.

As the adoption of IFRS 8 might result in a change in the identification of the entity's segments, some groups or entities will have to face the issue of validating the previous goodwill allocation to CGUs or group of CGUs or of reallocating goodwill to the new operating segments it has identified when performing the impairment test. This is discussed further at 3.9 below.

All CGUs or group of CGUs to which goodwill has been allocated have to be tested for impairment on an annual basis.

The standard takes the view that applying the above requirements results in goodwill being tested for impairment at a level that reflects the way an entity manages its operations and with which the goodwill would naturally be associated. Therefore, the development of additional reporting systems is typically not necessary.[248] It would only be if an entity did not monitor goodwill at or below the segment level that it would be necessary to develop new or additional reporting systems in order to comply with the standard.[249]

It can be seen from (b) above that the segment level is based on either the entity's primary or secondary reporting under IAS 14 (see Chapter 30 at 2.3). This is to ensure that entities that are managed on a matrix basis are able to test goodwill for impairment at the level of internal reporting that reflects the way they manage their operations.[250]

IAS 36 emphasises that a CGU to which goodwill is allocated for the purpose of impairment testing may not coincide with the level at which goodwill is allocated in accordance with IAS 21 for the purpose of measuring foreign currency gains and losses (see Chapter 10 at 3.3.4).[251] In many cases the allocation under IAS 21 will be at a lower level. This will apply not only on the acquisition of a multinational operation but could also apply on the acquisition of a single operation where the goodwill is allocated to a larger cash generating unit under IAS 36 that is made up of businesses with different functional currencies. However, IAS 36 clarifies that the entity is not required to test the goodwill for impairment at that same level unless it also monitors the goodwill at that level for internal management purposes.[252]

3.3 Goodwill initially unallocated to cash-generating units

As discussed at 2.3.6 above, the initial accounting for a business combination may only been determined provisionally by the end of the period in which the combination is effected. IAS 36 recognises that in such circumstances, it might also not be possible to complete the initial allocation of the goodwill to a CGU (or group of CGUs) for impairment purposes before the end of the annual period in which the combination is effected.[253]

Where this is the case, IAS 36 does not require a provisional allocation to be made, but the goodwill (or a portion thereof) is left unallocated for that period. However, the standard requires disclosure of the amount of the unallocated goodwill together with an explanation as to why that is the case (see 3.10 below).

The initial allocation has to be completed before the end of the first annual period beginning after the acquisition date.[254] Note that this period differs from that required by IFRS 3 for finalisation of the allocation of the cost of the business combination (and hence the initial measurement of goodwill), which is twelve months after the acquisition date. The reason for this is that the IASB's view is that acquirers should be allowed a longer period to complete the goodwill allocation, because that allocation might not be able to be performed until after the initial allocating is complete.[255] However, where an entity was to change its annual reporting date, it could mean that it is in fact a shorter period.

Example 7.47: Impact of shortened accounting period

Entity A prepares its financial statements for annual periods ending on 31 December. It acquired Entity B on 30 September 2007. In accounting for this business combination in its financial statements for the year ended 31 December 2007, Entity A has only been able to determine the fair values to be assigned to Entity B's assets, liabilities and contingent liabilities on a provisional basis and has not allocated the resulting provisional amount of goodwill arising on the acquisition to any CGU (or group of CGUs). During 2008, Entity A changes its annual reporting date to June and is preparing its financial statements as at its new period end of 30 June 2008. IFRS 3 does not require the fair values assigned to Entity B's net assets (and therefore the initial amount of goodwill) to be finalised by that period end, since Entity A has until 30 September 2008 to finalise the values. However, IAS 36 would appear to require the allocation of the goodwill to CGUs for impairment purposes be completed by the date of those financial statements since these are for the first annual period beginning after the acquisition date, despite the fact that the initial accounting under IFRS 3 is not yet complete.

3.4 Testing cash-generating units with goodwill for impairment

IAS 36 requires a CGU (or group of CGUs) to which goodwill has been allocated to be tested for impairment annually by comparing the carrying amount of the CGU (or group of CGUs), including the goodwill, with its recoverable amount.[256] The requirements of the standard in relation to the timing of such an annual impairment test are discussed at 3.4.2 below. However, this annual impairment test is not a substitute for management being aware of events occurring or circumstances changing between annual tests indicating a possible impairment of goodwill.[257] IAS 36 requires an entity to assess at each reporting date whether there is an indication that a CGU may be impaired.[258] So, whenever there is an indication that a CGU (or group of CGUs) to which goodwill has been allocated may be impaired (see Chapter 15 at 3.2 for a discussion of what constitutes an indication of impairment), it shall be tested for impairment by comparing the carrying amount of the CGU (or group of CGUs), including the goodwill, with its recoverable amount.[259]

The determination of what is the carrying amount of a CGU is discussed in Chapter 15 at 3.3.2. The measurement of the recoverable amount of a CGU is discussed at 3.3 of that Chapter. If the recoverable amount of the CGU (or group of CGUs) exceeds the carrying amount of the CGU (or group of CGUs), including the goodwill, the CGU (or group of CGUs), and the goodwill allocated to that CGU (or group of CGUs), are not regarded as being impaired. If the carrying amount of the CGU (or group of CGUs), including the goodwill, exceeds the recoverable amount of the CGU (or group of CGUs), then an impairment loss has to be recognised in accordance with paragraph 104 of the standard (see 3.5 below).[260]

3.4.1 Minority interest

Under IFRS 3, goodwill recognised in a business combination only represents the goodwill acquired by a parent based on the parent's ownership interest, rather than the amount of goodwill controlled by the parent as a result of the business combination (see 2.3.4 above). Therefore, goodwill attributable to a minority interest is not recognised in the parent's consolidated financial statements (as noted at 2.3.3 above, the minority interest is stated at the minority's proportion of the net fair value of the acquiree). Accordingly, if there is a minority interest in a CGU to which goodwill has been allocated, the carrying amount of that CGU comprises:

(a) both the parent's interest and the minority interest in the identifiable net assets of the CGU; and

(b) the parent's interest in goodwill.

However, part of the recoverable amount of the CGU determined in accordance with IAS 36 is attributable to the minority interest in goodwill.[261]

Consequently, to enable a like-for-like comparison, for the purpose of impairment testing a non-wholly-owned CGU with goodwill, IAS 36 requires the carrying amount of that CGU to be notionally adjusted, before being compared with its recoverable amount. This is accomplished by grossing up the carrying amount of goodwill allocated to the CGU to include the goodwill attributable to the minority interest. This notionally adjusted carrying amount is then compared with the recoverable amount of the CGU to determine whether the CGU (including the goodwill) is impaired. If it is, the entity allocates the impairment loss in accordance with paragraph 104 of the standard first to reduce the carrying amount of goodwill allocated to the CGU (see 3.5 below).[262]

However, because goodwill is recognised only to the extent of the parent's ownership interest, any impairment loss relating to the goodwill is apportioned between that attributable to the parent and that attributable to the minority interest, with only the former being recognised as a goodwill impairment loss.[263]

If the total impairment loss relating to goodwill is less than the amount by which the notionally adjusted carrying amount of the CGU exceeds its recoverable amount, paragraph 104 of the standard requires the remaining excess to be allocated to the other assets of the CGU pro rata on the basis of the carrying amount of each asset in the CGU.[264]

These requirements are illustrated in the following example which is based on Example 7 included within the Illustrative Examples accompanying IAS 36. In the examples, tax effects are ignored.

Example 7.48: Impairment testing of a CGU with goodwill and minority interests (1)

Entity X acquires an 80 per cent ownership interest in Entity Y for €1,600 on 1 January 2008. At that date, Entity Y's identifiable net assets have a fair value of €1,500. Entity Y has no contingent liabilities. Therefore, Entity X recognises in its consolidated financial statements:

(a) goodwill of €400, being the difference between the cost of the business combination of €1,600 and Entity X's 80 per cent interest in Entity Y's identifiable net assets;

(b) Entity Y's identifiable net assets at their fair value of €1,500; and

(c) a minority interest of €300, being the 20 per cent interest in Entity Y's identifiable net assets held by parties outside Entity X.

The assets of Entity Y together are the smallest group of assets that generate cash inflows that are largely independent of the cash inflows from other assets or groups of assets. Therefore Entity Y is a CGU. Because this CGU includes goodwill within its carrying amount, it must be tested for impairment annually, or more frequently if there is an indication that it may be impaired (see paragraph 90 of IAS 36).

At the end of 2008, the carrying amount of Entity Y's identifiable assets has reduced to €1,350 and Entity X determines that the recoverable amount of CGU Y is €1,000.

Testing CGU Y for Impairment

A portion of CGU Y's recoverable amount of €1,000 is attributable to the unrecognised minority interest in goodwill. Therefore, in accordance with paragraph 92 of IAS 36, the carrying amount of CGU Y must be notionally adjusted to include goodwill attributable to the minority interest, before being compared with the recoverable amount of €1,000. Testing CGU Y for impairment at the end of 2008 gives rise to an impairment loss of €850 calculated as follows:

	Goodwill	Identifiable net assets	Total
	€	€	€
Carrying amount	400	1,350	1,750
Unrecognised minority interest*	100	–	100
Notionally adjusted carrying amount	500	1,350	1,850
Recoverable amount			1,000
Impairment loss			850

* Goodwill attributable to Entity X's 80% interest in Entity Y at the acquisition date is €400. Therefore, goodwill notionally attributable to the 20% minority interest in Entity Y at the acquisition date is €100, being €400 × 20/80.

In accordance with paragraph 104 of IAS 36, the impairment loss of €850 is allocated to the assets in the CGU by first reducing the carrying amount of goodwill to zero.

Therefore, €500 of the €850 impairment loss for the CGU is allocated to the goodwill. However, because the goodwill is recognised only to the extent of Entity X's 80 per cent ownership interest in Entity Y, Entity X recognises only 80 per cent of that goodwill impairment loss (i.e. €400).

The remaining impairment loss of €350 is recognised by reducing the carrying amounts of Entity Y's identifiable assets.

This allocation of the impairment loss results in the following carrying amounts for CGU Y in the financial statements of Entity X at the end of 2008.

	Goodwill	Identifiable net assets	Total
	€	€	€
Carrying amount	400	1,350	1,750
Impairment loss	(400)	(350)	(750)
Carrying amount after impairment loss	–	1,000	1,000

Of the impairment loss of €350 relating to Entity Y's identifiable assets, €70 (i.e. 20% thereof) would be attributed to the minority interest.

It can be seen from the above example that in that situation the total carrying amount of the identifiable net assets and the goodwill has been reduced to the recoverable amount of €1,000. In fact the same result would have been achieved by just comparing the recoverable amount of €1,000 with the carrying amount of €1,750. However, what if the recoverable amount of the CGU had been greater than the carrying amount of the identifiable net assets prior to recognising the impairment loss?

Example 7.49: Impairment testing of a CGU with goodwill and minority interests (2)

This example is based on the same facts as Example 7.48 above, except that at the end of 2008, Entity X determines that the recoverable amount of CGU Y is €1,400.

Testing CGU Y for impairment

In this case, testing CGU Y for impairment at the end of 2008 gives rise to an impairment loss of €450 calculated as follows:

	Goodwill	Identifiable net assets	Total
	€	€	€
Carrying amount	400	1,350	1,750
Unrecognised minority interest	100	–	100
Notionally adjusted carrying amount	500	1,350	1,850
Recoverable amount			1,400
Impairment loss			450

As in Example 7.48 the impairment loss of €450 is allocated to the assets in the CGU by first reducing the carrying amount of goodwill.

Therefore, all of the €450 impairment loss for the CGU is allocated to the goodwill. However, because the goodwill is recognised only to the extent of Entity X's 80 per cent ownership interest in Entity Y, Entity X recognises only 80 per cent of that goodwill impairment loss (i.e. €360).

This allocation of the impairment loss results in the following carrying amounts for CGU Y in the financial statements of Entity X at the end of 2008.

	Goodwill	Identifiable net assets	Total
	€	€	€
Carrying amount	400	1,350	1,750
Impairment loss	(360)	–	(360)
Carrying amount after impairment loss	40	1,350	1,390

Of the impairment loss of €360, none of it is attributable to the minority interest since it all relates to the majority shareholder's goodwill.

It can be seen from the above example that in this situation the total carrying amount of the identifiable net assets and the goodwill has not been reduced to the recoverable amount of €1,400, but is actually less than the recoverable amount. This is because the recoverable amount of goodwill relating to the minority interest (20% of [€500 – €450]) is not recognised in the consolidated financial statements. If a direct comparison of the recoverable amount of €1,400 with the carrying amount of €1,750 was made, an impairment loss of €350 would have been recognised against goodwill. However, this would have meant that the goodwill would only have been reduced to €50, which would be overstated by €10 being the recoverable amount that is actually attributable to the minority interest.

3.4.2 Timing of impairment tests

As indicated at 3.4 above, IAS 36 requires a CGU or a group of CGUs to which goodwill has been allocated to be tested for impairment annually. It might be thought that this means that the impairment test has to be carried out at the end of the reporting period. However, the standard permits the annual impairment test to be performed at any time during an annual period, provided the test is performed at the same time every year. Indeed, different CGUs may be tested for impairment at different times.

However, if some or all of the goodwill allocated to a CGU (or group of CGUs) was acquired in a business combination during the current annual period, that unit shall be tested for impairment before the end of the current annual period.[265]

The reason for this last requirement is that the IASB 'observed that acquirers can sometimes "overpay" for an acquiree, resulting in the amount initially recognised for the business combination and the resulting goodwill exceeding the recoverable amount of the investment. The Board concluded that the users of an entity's financial statements are provided with representationally faithful, and therefore useful, information about a business combination if such an impairment loss is recognised by the acquirer in the annual period in which the business combination occurs.'[266] The Board was concerned that without this requirement it might be possible for entities to delay recognising such an impairment loss until the annual period after the business combination if the standard included only a requirement to impairment test CGUs (or groups of CGUs) to which goodwill has been allocated on an annual basis at any time during a period.[267]

It has to be said that the wording of the requirement may not achieve that result, since the goodwill may not have been allocated to a CGU in the period in which the business combination occurs (see 3.3 above). Consider the following example.

Example 7.50: Timing of annual impairment test of goodwill

Entity A prepares its financial statements for annual periods ending on 31 December. It carries out its annual impairment tests for all the CGUs to which it has allocated goodwill at the end of September. On 30 October 2007 Entity A acquires Entity B. In accounting for this business combination in its financial statements for the year ended 31 December 2007, Entity A has only been able to determine the fair values to be assigned to Entity B's assets, liabilities and contingent liabilities on a provisional basis and has not allocated the resulting provisional amount of goodwill arising on the acquisition to any CGU (or group of CGUs).

During 2008, as permitted by IFRS 3, Entity A does not finalise the fair values assigned to Entity B's net assets (and therefore the initial amount of goodwill) until 30 October 2008. Also,

IAS 36 only requires Entity A to allocate the goodwill to CGUs by the end of the financial year. It does this in December.

In this case, at the time of carrying out its annual impairment tests at 30 September 2008, Entity A has not yet allocated the goodwill relating to Entity B, therefore no impairment test of that goodwill should be carried out at that time. When it does allocate the goodwill in December, the requirement to perform an impairment test for the CGUs to which this goodwill is allocated does not seem to be applicable since the goodwill does not relate to a business combination during the current annual period. It actually relates to a business combination in the previous period; it is just that it has only been allocated for impairment purposes in the current period. Nevertheless we believe that Entity A should perform an updated impairment test for the CGUs to which this goodwill is allocated for the purposes of its financial statements ended 31 December 2008 since this would seem to be the intention of the IASB. Not to do so, would mean that the impairment of this goodwill would not be tested until September 2009, nearly 2 years after the business combination.

3.4.3 Sequence of impairment tests

At the time of impairment testing a CGU to which goodwill has been allocated, there may be an indication of an impairment of an asset within the unit containing the goodwill. In such circumstances, IAS 36 requires the entity to test the asset for impairment first, and recognise any impairment loss for that asset before testing for impairment the CGU containing the goodwill. Similarly, there may be an indication of an impairment of a CGU within a group of CGUs containing the goodwill. In such circumstances, the standard requires the entity to test the CGU for impairment first, and recognise any impairment loss for that CGU, before testing for impairment the group of CGUs to which the goodwill is allocated.[268]

3.4.4 Carry-forward of a previous impairment test calculation

IAS 36 permits the most recent detailed calculation of the recoverable amount of a CGU (or group of CGUs) to which goodwill has been allocated to be carried forward from a preceding period for use in the current period's impairment provided all of the following criteria are met:

(a) the assets and liabilities making up the CGU (or group of CGUs) have not changed significantly since the most recent recoverable amount calculation;

(b) the most recent recoverable amount calculation resulted in an amount that exceeded the carrying amount of the CGU (or group of CGUs) by a substantial margin; and

(c) based on an analysis of events that have occurred and circumstances that have changed since the most recent recoverable amount calculation, the likelihood that a current recoverable amount determination would be less than the current carrying amount of the CGU (or group of CGUs) is remote.[269]

The Basis for Conclusions accompanying IAS 36 indicates that the reason for this dispensation is to reduce the costs of applying the impairment test, without compromising its integrity.[270] However, clearly it is a matter of considerable judgement as to whether each of the criteria is actually met.

3.4.5 *Acquisition of minority interest*

As discussed at 2.3.7 A above, when an entity acquires an existing minority interest in a subsidiary, we believe that there are three acceptable treatments for accounting for the difference between the cost of acquisition and the minority interest acquired:

(a) the entire difference may be reflected as goodwill (the 'Parent entity extension method');

(b) the entire difference may be reflected as an equity transaction (the 'Entity concept method'); or

(c) the difference may be reflected partly as goodwill – measured using IFRS 3's principles – and partly as equity (the 'Hybrid entity concept/parent entity method').

Where an entity adopts either (b) or (c) in accounting for such a transaction, this raises the issue as to whether any notional adjustment needs to be made to gross-up the carrying the amount of goodwill in carrying out the impairment test of goodwill, similar to that discussed at 3.4.1 above.

In our view, where all of the minority interest has been acquired such that the subsidiary is now wholly-owned, no notional adjustment should be made, and the carrying amount of the CGU to which the goodwill has been allocated only needs to reflect the amount of goodwill that has been recognised as an asset. A notional adjustment is only required where there is still a minority interest in the CGU.

3.5 Impairment loss for a cash-generating unit to which goodwill has been allocated

As indicated at 3.4 above, if the carrying amount of the CGU (or group of CGUs), including the goodwill, exceeds the recoverable amount of the CGU (or group of CGUs), then an impairment loss has to be recognised in accordance with paragraph 104 of the standard.[271]

That paragraph requires that the impairment loss is allocated to reduce the carrying amount of the assets of the CGU (or group of CGUs) in the following order:

(a) first, to reduce the carrying amount of the allocated goodwill; and

(b) then, to the other assets of the CGU (or group of CGUs) on a pro rata basis.

This is illustrated in Examples 7.48 and 7.49 at 3.4.1 above.

The impairment loss for goodwill is recognised in accordance with paragraph 60 of the standard, which is to recognise it immediately in profit or loss.[272] The recognition of the impairment loss under (b) above is discussed in detail in Chapter 15 at 3.3.3 B.

3.6 Reversing an impairment loss for goodwill

Once an impairment loss has been recognised for goodwill, IAS 36 prohibits its reversal in a subsequent period.[273] The standard justifies this on the grounds that any reversal 'is likely to be an increase in internally generated goodwill, rather than a reversal of the impairment loss recognised for the acquired goodwill', and IAS 38 prohibits the recognition of internally generated goodwill.[274]

3.7 Disposal of operation within a cash-generating unit to which goodwill has been allocated

If goodwill has been allocated to a CGU (or a group of CGUs) and the entity disposes of an operation within that CGU, IAS 36 requires that the goodwill associated with the operation disposed of is included in the carrying amount of the operation when determining the gain or loss on disposal. For that purpose, the standard requires that the amount to be included is measured on the basis of the relative values of the operation disposed of and the portion of the CGU retained, unless the entity can demonstrate that some other method better reflects the goodwill associated with the operation disposed of.[275]

Example 7.51: Goodwill attributable to the disposal of an operation based on relative values

An entity sells for €100 an operation that was part of a CGU to which goodwill of €60 has been allocated. The goodwill allocated to the CGU cannot be identified or associated with an asset group at a level lower than that CGU, except arbitrarily. The recoverable amount of the portion of the CGU retained is €300. Because the goodwill allocated to the CGU cannot be non-arbitrarily identified or associated with an asset group at a level lower than that CGU, the goodwill associated with the operation disposed of is measured on the basis of the relative values of the operation disposed of and the portion of the CGU retained. Therefore, 25 per cent of the goodwill allocated to the CGU, i.e. €15 is included in the carrying amount of the operation that is sold.

The standard refers to the 'relative values' of the parts without specifying how these are to be calculated. The recoverable amount of the part that it has retained will be based on the principles of IAS 36, i.e. at the higher of fair value less costs to sell and value in use. In most circumstances, it will be its value in use, rather than its fair value less costs to sell. This means that the value in use of the part retained may have to be calculated as part of the allocation exercise on disposal (see Chapter 15 at 3.3.2 for a discussion of the calculation of the value in use).

In addition, the value in use and fair value less costs to sell of the part disposed of will be materially the same. This is because the value in use will consist mainly of the net disposal proceeds; it cannot be based on the assumption that the sale would not take place.

It will not necessarily follow, for example, that the business disposed of generated 25% of the net cash flows of the combined CGU. Therefore, the method advocated by the standard to be applied in most circumstances will most likely be based on a mismatch in the valuation bases used on the different parts of the business, reflecting the purchaser's assessment of the value of the part disposed of at the point of sale rather than that of the vendor at purchase.

The standard allows the use of some other method if it better reflects the goodwill associated with the part disposed of. The IASB had in mind a scenario in which an entity buys a business, integrates it with an existing CGU that does not include any goodwill in its carrying amount and immediately sells a loss-making part of the combined CGU. It is accepted that in these circumstances it may be reasonable to conclude that no part of the carrying amount of the goodwill has been disposed of.[276] The loss-making business being disposed of could, of course, have been owned by the entity before the acquisition or it could be part of the acquired business.

Where the operation disposed of is a foreign operation for the purposes of IAS 21, another possibility might be to use the goodwill allocated to that foreign operation for the purpose of measuring foreign currency gains and losses (see Chapter 10 at 3.3.4), particularly as the exchange gains and losses on that amount of goodwill will also be taken to profit or loss on disposal of that foreign operation (see Chapter 10 at 2.7.3). Even then, this might only be a better method if there has been no previous impairments recognised in respect of goodwill allocated to the CGU including that foreign operation since it was acquired.

One has to bear in mind that any basis of allocation of goodwill on disposal other than that recommended by the standard could be an indication that goodwill should have been allocated on a different basis on acquisition, i.e. there may have been some basis of allocating goodwill within the CGU/CGU group that was not arbitrary.

3.8 Changes in composition of cash-generating units

If an entity reorganises its reporting structure in a way that changes the composition of one or more CGUs to which goodwill has been allocated, IAS 36 requires that the goodwill shall be reallocated to the units affected. For this purpose, the standard requires that this reallocation is performed using a relative value approach similar to that discussed at 3.7 above when an entity disposes of an operation within a CGU, unless the entity can demonstrate that some other method better reflects the goodwill associated with the reorganised units.[277]

Example 7.52: Reallocation of goodwill to CGUs based on relative values

Goodwill of €160 had previously been allocated to CGU A. The goodwill allocated to A cannot be identified or associated with an asset group at a level lower than A, except arbitrarily. A is to be divided and integrated into three other CGUs, B, C and D. Because the goodwill allocated to A cannot be non-arbitrarily identified or associated with an asset group at a level lower than A, it is reallocated to CGUs B, C and D on the basis of the relative values of the three portions of A before those portions are integrated with B, C and D. The recoverable amounts of these portions of A before integration with the other CGUs are €200, €300 and €500 respectively. Accordingly, the amounts of goodwill reallocated to CGUs B, C and D are €32, €48 and €80 respectively.

Again, the standard gives no indication as to what other methods might better reflect the goodwill associated with the reorganised units.

In this situation as well, the recoverable amount of the CGUs will be based on the principles of IAS 36. Accordingly, it will often be necessary in practice to assess the value in use of all of the CGUs to which the goodwill is to be allocated.

In practice, situations may be considerably more complex than Examples 7.51 and 7.52 above. Elements of both may arise following an acquisition whereby there are disposals of acquired businesses, reorganisations and integrations. The entity may sell some parts of its acquired business immediately but may also use the acquisition in order to replace part of its existing capacity, disposing of existing elements. In addition, groups frequently undertake reorganisations of their statutory entities. It is often the case that CGUs do not correspond to these individual entities and the reorganisations may be undertaken for taxation reasons so the ownership structure within a group may not correspond to its CGUs. This makes it clear how important it is that entities identify their CGUs and the allocation of goodwill to them, so that they already have a basis for making any necessary allocations when an impairment issue arises or there is a disposal.

3.9 The effect of IFRS 8 – *Operating Segments* – on the allocation of goodwill

IAS 36 states that goodwill must be allocated to a CGU or group of CGUs that is no larger than a segment based on either the entity's primary or the entity's secondary reporting format determined in accordance with IAS 14 – *Segment Reporting*.[278] IAS 36 will be amended when IAS 14 is replaced by IFRS 8 – *Operating Segments*; in financial statements from 1 January 2009, goodwill to be tested for impairment cannot be allocated to a CGU or CGU group larger than an *operating* segment as defined by the new standard. IFRS 8 is discussed in Chapter 30.

If the different basis of segmentation under IFRS 8 results in different segments being reported than were reported under IAS 14, it follows that there will be differences between the CGUs that make up an IFRS 8 segment and those that made up an IAS 14 segment. As a result, the CGUs supporting goodwill may no longer be in the same segment under IFRS 8 as under IAS 14. This could occur, in particular, where goodwill has been allocated to groups of CGUs at or close to the level of an IAS 14 segment. It may therefore be necessary to reallocate goodwill. It is possible that this reallocation of goodwill could 'expose' CGUs for which the carrying amount, including the allocated goodwill exceeds the recoverable amount, thereby giving rise to an impairment loss.

Example 7.53: Implementing IFRS 8 affects the allocation of goodwill to segments

An entity has a single reportable segment under IAS 14, consisting of CGU A and CGU B. Goodwill of €100 is allocated at the segment level. Following the implementation of IFRS 8, the entity determines that CGU A and CGU B are separate reportable segments and goodwill of €30 is allocable to CGU A and €70 to CGU B. An impairment loss is triggered on the implementation of IFRS 8, as follows:

	Single segment under IAS 14	
	CGU A under IFRS 8	CGU B under IFRS 8
	€	€
Carrying amount (including goodwill)	100	130
Recoverable amount	80	200
Excess of recoverable amount over carrying amount of CGU	(20)	70
Impairment loss under IAS 14	nil	nil
Impairment loss under IFRS 8	(20)	nil

In practice, the lowest level within the entity at which goodwill is monitored for internal purposes is unlikely to be larger than an operating segment under IFRS 8. However, it is possible that the detailed requirements in IFRS 8 could result in an entity changing its segments in such a way that the CGUs supporting goodwill are no longer in the same segment. There are no transitional rules for an entity that finds itself in this situation. In our view, an entity that finds itself in this situation ought to be able to reallocate goodwill for the purposes of testing it for impairment but how, in the absence of guidance, would an entity go about reallocating goodwill?

In two situations, the disposal of an operation within a CGU and a change in the composition of CGUs due to a reorganisation, which are described at 3.7 and 3.8 above, IAS 36 allows a reallocation based on relative values. A reallocation of goodwill driven by the identification of new operating segments has some similarities to a reorganisation of the reporting structure.

Additional difficulties may arise because it is difficult to reconstruct conditions that existed at the time of the past acquisition so it may no longer be clear what the acquired goodwill originally related to. The reallocation of the goodwill to the operating segment level will be more difficult and arbitrary when the acquired business has lost its separate identity as a result of post-acquisition integration with pre-existing operations or other reorganisations. Thus, when information relating to the goodwill allocation is not available, the entity will have no alternative to allocating goodwill based on the current segment reporting structure.

It would be unusual for the fair value less costs to sell of a segment to be determinable, as no sale transaction will have occurred. Accordingly, it will often be necessary in practice to assess the value in use of all the operating segments to which goodwill is to be allocated.

IAS 36 allows the use of a method other than relative values if it better reflects the goodwill associated with the part disposed of or with the reorganised units, but it does not give any indication as to what such a method might be.

Whatever allocation methodology is used, goodwill can be allocated only to operating segments that benefit from the synergies of the business combination concerned.

3.10 Disclosure requirements relating to goodwill

As indicated at 2.3.10 above, in developing the disclosure requirements of IFRS 3 in respect of business combinations, the IASB identified disclosure objectives that should be met.[279] The principle relating to goodwill is that 'an entity shall disclose information that enables users of its financial statements to evaluate changes in the carrying amount of goodwill during the period'.[280]

To give effect to this principle, the entity is required to disclose a reconciliation of the carrying amount of goodwill at the beginning and end of the period, showing separately:

(a) the gross amount and accumulated impairment losses at the beginning of the period;

(b) additional goodwill recognised during the period (except goodwill included in a disposal group that, on acquisition, meets the criteria to be classified as held for sale in accordance with IFRS 5 – see Chapter 4 at 2.1);

(c) adjustments resulting from the subsequent recognition of deferred tax assets during the period (see 2.3.6 C above);

(d) goodwill included in a disposal group classified as held for sale in accordance with IFRS 5 and goodwill derecognised during the period without having previously been included in a disposal group classified as held for sale;

(e) impairment losses recognised during the period in accordance with IAS 36;

(f) net exchange differences arising during the period in accordance with IAS 21 (see Chapter 10 at 3.3.4);

(g) any other changes in the carrying amount during the period; and

(h) the gross amount and accumulated impairment losses at the end of the period.[281]

As with the other disclosure requirements relating to business combinations dealt with at 2.3.10 above, IFRS 3 includes a catch-all disclosure requirement, that if in any situation the information required to be disclosed set out above does not satisfy the objectives of the disclosure principle, the entity shall disclose such additional information as is necessary to meet those objectives.[282]

IFRS 3 emphasises that in addition to the information required by (e) above, the entity also discloses information about the recoverable amount and impairment of goodwill in accordance with IAS 36.[283] These requirements are dealt with in Chapter 15 at 4.2.

As discussed at 3.3 above, a portion of the goodwill acquired in a business combination during the period may not been allocated to a CGU (or group of CGUs) at the reporting date. If that is the case, IAS 36 requires that the amount of the unallocated goodwill to be disclosed together with the reasons why that amount remains unallocated.[284]

4 TRANSITIONAL ARRANGEMENTS AND FIRST-TIME ADOPTION ISSUES

4.1 Transitional arrangements for entities already reporting under IFRS

As discussed at 2 above, IFRS 3 does not have an effective date in the sense that it is applicable for accounting periods commencing on or after a certain date. Instead, the standard applies to the accounting for business combinations for which the agreement date is on or after 31 March 2004 (the date of issue of the standard). It also applies to the accounting for:

(a) goodwill arising from a business combination for which the agreement date is on or after 31 March 2004; or

(b) any excess of the acquirer's interest in the net fair value of the acquiree's identifiable assets, liabilities and contingent liabilities over the cost of a business combination for which the agreement date is on or after 31 March 2004.[285]

Although the IASB observed that requiring the standard to be applied retrospectively to all business combinations might improve the comparability of financial information, it considered that such an approach would be problematic for the following reasons:

(a) it is likely to be impossible for many business combinations because the information needed may not exist or may no longer be obtainable.

(b) it requires the determination of estimates that would have been made at a prior date, and therefore raises problems in relation to the role of hindsight – in particular, whether the benefit of hindsight should be included or excluded from those estimates and, if excluded, how the effect of hindsight can be separated from the other factors existing at the date for which the estimates are required.

The IASB therefore concluded that the problems associated with applying the standard retrospectively, on balance, outweighed the benefit of improved comparability of financial information.[286]

As far as previously recognised goodwill, negative goodwill and intangibles in respect of business combinations for which the agreement date was before 31 March 2004 was concerned, the standard had transitional provisions that were to be applied from the beginning of the first annual period beginning on or after 31 March 2004.[287] The standard also dealt with the implications for equity accounted investments.

Entities, however, were permitted to apply the requirements of the standard to goodwill existing at or acquired after, and to business combinations occurring from, any date before the effective dates outlined above, provided certain conditions were met.[288]

These transitional arrangements for existing IFRS adopters are no longer relevant. A discussion of the arrangements can be found in section 4.1 of Chapter 7 of the previous edition of this book, *International GAAP 2007*.

4.2 First-time adoption issues

As discussed in Chapter 5 at 2.4, IFRS 1 provides an exemption from full retrospective application of IFRS 3 on transition to IFRS for first-time adopters. The exemption permits a first-time adopter not to restate business combinations prior to its date of transition to IFRS. The detailed requirements on the application of the exemption are contained in Appendix B to IFRS 1,[289] with examples illustrating its effect given in the implementation guidance to IFRS 1,[290] and are discussed below.

4.2.1 Option to restate business combinations retrospectively

A first-time adopter must account for business combinations after its date of transition to IFRS under IFRS 3. Thus, any business combinations during the comparative periods presented by an entity will need to be restated in accordance with the standard. An entity may elect not to apply IFRS 3 to any business combination before that date, but may do so if it so chooses. However, if a first-time adopter restates any business combination prior to its date of transition to comply with IFRS 3 it must also restate all subsequent business combinations under IFRS 3 and apply both IAS 36 and IAS 38 from that date onwards.[291] In other words, as shown on the time line below, a first-time adopter is allowed to choose any date in the past and account for business combinations going forward under IFRS 3 without having to restate business combinations prior to the earliest IFRS 3 restatement.

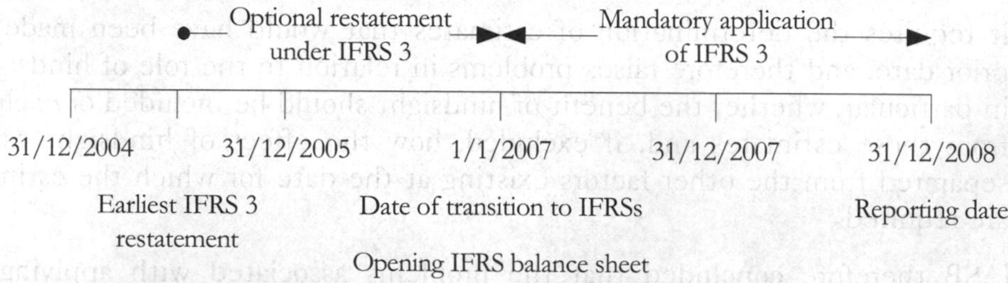

This exemption for past business combinations applies also to past acquisitions of associates and interests in joint ventures. However, it is important to note that the date selected for the first restatement of business combinations should also be applied to the restatement of acquisitions of associates and interests in joint ventures.[292]

This leaves the question whether the exemption for past business combinations also covers acquisitions of minority interests that have been accounted for under previous GAAP. Restatement of such transactions is likely to be highly impracticable for the same reasons that requiring restatement of past business combinations would be impracticable. Therefore, we believe that had the Board explicitly considered this transitional issue, it would have given an exemption from the requirement to restate. Accordingly, in our view, a first-time adopter is not required to restate acquisitions of minority interests which have been accounted for under previous GAAP. However, a first-time adopter could restate the previous accounting, if it so wished, by applying the policy adopted under IFRS for the accounting of minority interests (see 2.3.7 A above).

Originally, the IASB proposed not to permit restatement of business combinations prior to the date of transition to IFRS as this 'could require an entity to recreate data that it did not capture at the date of a past business combination and make subjective estimates about conditions that existed at that date. These factors could reduce the relevance and reliability of the entity's first IFRS financial statements.'[293] However, the IASB considered that – especially where the information is more likely to be available – it would be conceptually preferable to restate business combinations as the 'effects of business combination accounting can last for many years' and 'previous GAAP may differ significantly from IFRS'.[294] Therefore, the IASB concluded that although it could not require restatement of business combinations for cost-benefit reasons, it should at least permit restatement on condition that all subsequent business combinations are also restated.[295]

It is remarkable that availability of reliable contemporaneous information necessary for the application of IFRS 3 is not an explicit condition for retrospective application of IFRS 3 by first-time adopters; especially because this was a condition that existing IFRS-reporting entities had to meet. In our opinion, a first-time adopter should not restate business combinations before the date of transition when this would require undue use of hindsight, even though this is not specifically prohibited.

4.2.2 Classification of business combinations

IFRS 3 mandates that business combinations should be accounted for as acquisitions or reverse acquisitions. An entity's previous GAAP may be based on a different definition of, for example, a business combination, an acquisition, a merger and a reverse acquisition. An important benefit of the business combinations exemption is that a first-time adopter will not have to determine the classification of business combinations in accordance with IFRS 3 for transactions prior to the date of transition to IFRS.[296] For example, a transaction that was accounted as a merger or uniting of interests using the pooling-of-interests method under an entity's previous GAAP will not have to reclassified and accounted for under the IFRS 3 purchase method. However, an entity may still elect to do so if it so wishes – subject, of course, to the conditions set out under 4.2.1 above.

The business combinations exemption only applies to 'business combinations that the entity recognised before the date of transition to IFRSs'.[297] Consequently, the business combinations exemption does not apply to a transaction that IFRS considers to be an acquisition of an asset. First-time adopters will therefore have to consider whether past transactions would qualify as business combinations under IFRS 3 (see 2.2.1 above).

It is possible that under some national GAAPs, transactions that are not business combinations, such as asset purchases, may have been accounted for as if they were business combinations. A first-time adopter will need to restate any transactions that it accounted for as a business combination under its previous GAAP, but which are not business combinations under IFRS 3.

Example 7.54: Acquisition of an asset

Entity J acquired a holding company that held a single asset at the time of acquisition. That holding company had no employees and the asset itself was not in use at the date of acquisition. J accounted for the transaction under its previous GAAP using the purchase method, which resulted in goodwill. Can J apply the business combinations exemption to the acquisition of the asset?

If J concludes that the asset is not a business, as defined in IFRS 3, it will not be able to apply the business combination exemption to the acquisition of the asset.

4.2.3 Recognition and measurement of assets and liabilities

A Derecognition of assets and liabilities

A first-time adopter should exclude from its opening IFRS balance sheet any items it recognised under its previous GAAP that do not qualify for recognition as an asset or liability under IFRS. If the first-time adopter previously recognised an intangible asset as part of a business combination that does not qualify for recognition as an asset under IAS 38, it should reclassify that item and the related deferred tax and minority interests as part of goodwill (unless it previously deducted goodwill directly from equity under its previous GAAP) (see 4.2.4 below). All other changes resulting from derecognition of such assets and liabilities should be accounted for as adjustments of retained earnings.[298]

B Recognition of assets and liabilities

In its opening IFRS balance sheet, a first-time adopter should recognise all assets and liabilities that were acquired or assumed in a past business combination, with the exception of:

- certain financial assets and liabilities that were derecognised and that fall under the derecognition exception (see Chapter 5 at 2.6.4); and
- assets (including goodwill) and liabilities that were not recognised in the acquirer's consolidated balance sheet under its previous GAAP that would not qualify for recognition under IFRS in the separate balance sheet of the acquiree (see Example 7.60 below).[299]

The change resulting from the recognition of such assets and liabilities should be accounted for as an adjustment of retained earnings or another category of equity, if appropriate. However, if the change results from the recognition of an intangible asset that was previously subsumed in goodwill, it should be accounted for as an adjustment of that goodwill (see 4.2.4 A below).[300] As indicated at E below, the recognition of such intangibles will be rare.

The following examples, which are based on equivalent examples within the guidance on implementation of IFRS 1, illustrate how a first-time adopter would apply these requirements (further examples can be found at E below).

Example 7.55: Finance lease not capitalised under previous GAAP[301]

Background

Parent L's date of transition to IFRSs is 1 January 2007. Parent L acquired subsidiary M on 15 January 2004 and did not capitalise subsidiary M's finance leases. If subsidiary M prepared separate financial statements under IFRSs, it would recognise finance lease obligations of 300 and leased assets of 250 at 1 January 2007.

Application of requirements

In its consolidated opening IFRS balance sheet, parent L recognises finance lease obligations of 300 and leased assets of 250, and charges 50 to retained earnings.

Example 7.56: Restructuring provision[302]

Background

Entity D's first IFRS financial statements have a reporting date of 31 December 2008 and include comparative information for 2007 only. It chooses not to restate previous business combinations for IFRS 3. On 1 July 2006, entity D acquired 100 per cent of subsidiary E. Under its previous GAAP, entity D recognised an (undiscounted) restructuring provision of 100 that would not have qualified as an identifiable liability under IFRS 3. The recognition of this restructuring provision increased goodwill by 100. At 31 December 2006 (date of transition to IFRSs), entity D:

(a) had paid restructuring costs of 60; and

(b) estimated that it would pay further costs of 40 in 2007, and that the effects of discounting were immaterial. At 31 December 2006, those further costs did not qualify for recognition as a provision under IAS 37.

Application of requirements

In its opening IFRS balance sheet, entity D:

(a) does not recognise a restructuring provision.

(b) does not adjust the amount assigned to goodwill. However, entity D tests the goodwill for impairment under IAS 36, and recognises any resulting impairment loss.

(c) as a result of (a) and (b), reports retained earnings in its opening IFRS balance sheet that are higher by 40 (before income taxes, and before recognising any impairment loss) than in the balance sheet at the same date under previous GAAP.

C Subsequent measurement under IFRS not based on cost

IFRS requires subsequent measurement of some assets and liabilities on a basis other than original cost, such as fair value. When a first-time adopter does not apply IFRS 3 retrospectively to a business combination, such assets and liabilities must be measured on that other basis in its opening IFRS balance sheet. Any change in the carrying amount of those assets and liabilities should be accounted for as an adjustment of retained earnings, or other appropriate category of equity, rather than as an adjustment of goodwill.[303]

Example 7.57: Items not measured at original cost

Entity K acquired in a business combination a trading portfolio of equity securities and a number of investment properties. Under its previous GAAP, K initially measured these assets at cost (i.e. their fair value at the date of acquisition).

Upon adoption of IFRS, K measures the trading portfolio of equity securities and the investment properties (under the IAS 40 – *Investment Properties* – fair value model) at fair value on the date of transition in its opening IFRS balance sheet. The resulting adjustment to these assets at the date of transition is reflected in retained earnings.

D Subsequent measurement on a cost basis under IFRS

For assets and liabilities that are accounted for on a cost basis under IFRS, IFRS 1 stipulates that 'immediately after the business combination, the carrying amount under previous GAAP of assets acquired and liabilities assumed in that business combination shall be their deemed cost under IFRSs at that date. If IFRSs require a cost-based measurement of those assets and liabilities at a later date, that deemed cost shall be the basis for cost-based depreciation or amortisation from the date of the business combination.'[304]

IFRS 1 does not specifically define 'immediately after a business combination', but it is commonly understood that this takes account of the completion of purchase accounting. In other words, a first-time adopter would not use the provisionally determined fair values of assets acquired and liabilities assumed.

Example 7.58: Provisionally determined fair values

Parent A acquired subsidiary B in August 2006 and made a provisional assessment of subsidiary B's identifiable net assets in its 31 December 2006 consolidated financial statements under its previous GAAP. In its 31 December 2007 consolidated financial statements – its last financial statements under previous GAAP – parent A completed the initial accounting for the business combination and adjusted the provisional values of the identifiable net assets and the corresponding goodwill. Upon first-time adoption of IFRS, parent A elects not to restate past business combinations.

In preparing its opening IFRS balance sheet, parent A should use the adjusted carrying amounts of the identifiable net assets as determined in its 2007 financial statements rather than the provisional carrying amounts of the identifiable net assets and goodwill at 31 December 2006.

IFRS 1 is silent as to whether the relevant carrying amounts of the identifiable net assets and goodwill are those that appeared in the financial statements drawn up immediately before the transition date (31 December 2006 in this case) or any restated balance appearing in a later set of previous GAAP accounts. Since the adjustments that were made under previous GAAP effectively resulted in a restatement of the balances at the transition date in a manner that is consistent with the approach permitted by IFRS 3, it is in our opinion appropriate to reflect those adjustments in the transition date balance sheet. Since the adjustments are effectively made as at the transition date it is also appropriate to use the window period permitted by previous GAAP provided that this does not extend into the first IFRS reporting period since any restatements in that period can only be made in accordance with IFRS 3.

In effect, the phrase 'immediately after the business combination' in paragraph B2(e) of IFRS 1 should be interpreted as including a window period that ends at the earlier of the window period allowed by the previous GAAP and the beginning of the first IFRS reporting period.

Cost basis, being based on previous GAAP, might be considered as inconsistent with the requirements of IFRS for assets and liabilities that were *not* acquired in a business combination. However, the IASB did not any identify any situations in which 'it would not be acceptable to bring forward cost-based measurements made under previous GAAP'.[305]

Example 7.59: Items measured on a cost basis

Entity L applies the business combination exemption under IFRS 1. In a business combination L acquired property, plant and equipment, inventory and accounts receivable. Under its previous GAAP, L initially measured these assets at cost (i.e. their fair value at the date of acquisition).

Upon adoption of IFRS, L determines that its accounting policy for these assets under its previous GAAP complied with the requirements of IFRS. Therefore, property, plant and equipment, inventory and accounts receivable are not adjusted, but recognised in the opening IFRS balance sheet at the carrying amount under the previous GAAP.

E Measurement of items not recognised under previous GAAP

An asset acquired or a liability assumed in a past business combination may not have been recognised under the entity's previous GAAP. However, this does not mean that such items have a deemed cost of zero in the opening IFRS balance sheet. Instead, the acquirer recognises and measures those items in its opening IFRS balance sheet on the basis that IFRS would require in the balance sheet of the acquiree.[306] The change resulting from the recognition of such assets and liabilities should be accounted for as an adjustment of retained earnings or another category of equity, if appropriate. The IASB included this requirement to avoid 'an unjustifiable departure from the principle that the opening IFRS balance sheet should include all assets and liabilities'.[307]

A first-time adopter that restates previous business combinations under IFRS 3 will recognise the intangible assets held by acquired subsidiaries. However, intangible assets acquired as part of a business combination that were not recognised under a first-time adopter's previous GAAP, will rarely be recognised in the opening IFRS balance sheet of a first-time adopter that applies the business combinations exemption because either (1) they cannot be capitalised in the acquiree's own balance sheet or (2) capitalisation would require the use of hindsight which is not permitted under IAS 38 (see Chapter 5 at 2.9.5).

Example 7.60: Items not recognised under previous GAAP

Entity K acquired Entity L but did not capitalise L's finance leases and internally generated customer lists under its previous GAAP.

Upon first-time adoption of IFRS, K recognises the finance leases in its opening IFRS balance sheet using the amounts that L would recognise in its IFRS balance sheet. The resulting adjustment to the net assets at the date of transition is reflected in retained earnings; goodwill is not restated to reflect the net assets that would have been recognised at the date of acquisition (see 4.2.4 below). However, K does not recognise the customer lists in its opening IFRS balance sheet, because L is not permitted to capitalise internally generated customer lists. Any value that might have been attributable to the customer lists would remain subsumed in goodwill in K's opening IFRS balance sheet.

Entity M acquired Entity N but did not recognise N's brand name as a separate intangible asset under its previous GAAP.

Upon first-time adoption of IFRS, M will not recognise N's brand name in its opening IFRS balance sheet because N would not have been permitted under IAS 38 to recognise it as an asset in its own separate balance sheet. Again, any value that might have been attributable to the brand name would remain subsumed in goodwill in M's opening IFRS balance sheet.

F Summary of recognition and measurement requirements

The following diagram summarises the recognition and measurement rules – that are discussed above – for assets acquired and liabilities assumed in a business combination that is accounted for under the business combinations exemption.

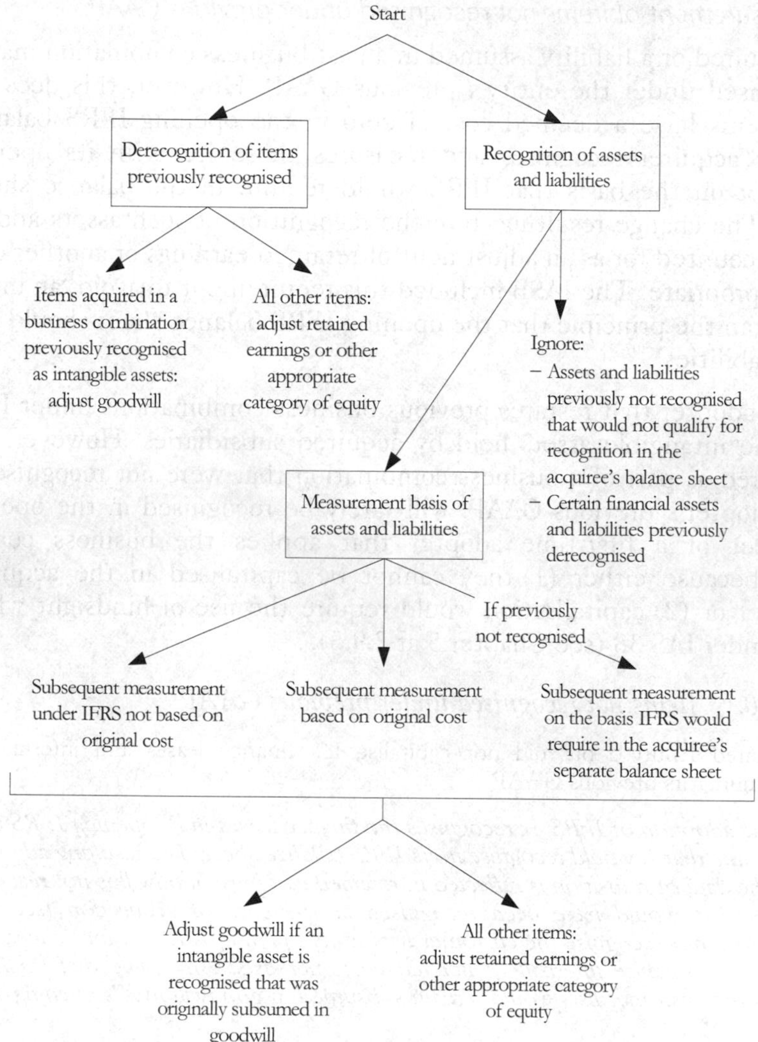

The guidance on implementation of IFRS 1 contains the following example that illustrates many of the requirements discussed above.[308]

Example 7.61: Business combination example

Background

Entity B's first IFRS financial statements have a reporting date of 31 December 2005 and include comparative information for 2004 only. On 1 July 2001, entity B acquired 100 per cent of subsidiary C. Under its previous GAAP, entity B:

(a) classified the business combination as an acquisition by entity B;

(b) measured the assets acquired and liabilities assumed at the following amounts under previous GAAP at 31 December 2003 (date of transition to IFRSs):

(i) identifiable assets less liabilities for which IFRSs require cost-based measurement at a date after the business combination: 200 (with a tax base of 150 and an applicable tax rate of 30 per cent);

(ii) pension liability (for which the present value of the defined benefit obligation measured under IAS 19 is 130 and the fair value of plan assets is 100): nil (because entity B used a pay-as-you-go cash method of accounting for pensions under its previous GAAP). The tax base of the pension liability is also nil;

(iii) goodwill: 180;

(c) did not, at the date of acquisition, recognise deferred tax arising from temporary differences associated with the identifiable assets acquired and liabilities assumed.

Application of requirements

In its opening (consolidated) IFRS balance sheet, entity B:

(a) classifies the business combination as an acquisition by entity B even if the business combination would have qualified under IFRS 3 as a reverse acquisition by subsidiary C (paragraph B2(a) of IFRS 1);

(b) does not adjust the accumulated amortisation of goodwill. Entity B tests the goodwill for impairment under IAS 36 and recognises any resulting impairment loss, based on conditions that existed at the date of transition to IFRSs. If no impairment exists, the carrying amount of the goodwill remains at 180 (paragraph B2(g) of IFRS 1);

(c) for those net identifiable assets acquired for which IFRSs require cost-based measurement at a date after the business combination, treats their carrying amount under previous GAAP immediately after the business combination as their deemed cost at that date (paragraph B2(e) of IFRS 1);

(d) does not restate the accumulated depreciation and amortisation of the net identifiable assets in (c) above, unless the depreciation methods and rates under previous GAAP result in amounts that differ materially from those required under IFRSs (for example, if they were adopted solely for tax purposes and do not reflect a reasonable estimate of the asset's useful life under IFRSs). If no such restatement is made, the carrying amount of those assets in the opening IFRS balance sheet equals their carrying amount under previous GAAP at the date of transition to IFRSs (200) (paragraph IG7 of IFRS 1);

(e) if there is any indication that identifiable assets are impaired, tests those assets for impairment, based on conditions that existed at the date of transition to IFRSs (see IAS 36);

(f) recognises the pension liability, and measures it, at the present value of the defined benefit obligation (130) less the fair value of the plan assets (100), giving a carrying amount of 30, with a corresponding debit of 30 to retained earnings (paragraph B2(d) of IFRS 1). However, if subsidiary C had already adopted IFRSs in an earlier period, entity B would measure the pension liability at the same amount as in subsidiary C's separate financial statements (paragraph 25 of IFRS 1 and IG Example 9);

(g) recognises a net deferred tax liability of 6 (20 at 30 per cent) arising from:

(i) the taxable temporary difference of 50 (200 less 150) associated with the identifiable assets acquired and non-pension liabilities assumed, less

(ii) the deductible temporary difference of 30 (30 less nil) associated with the pension liability.

The entity recognises the resulting increase in the deferred tax liability as a deduction from retained earnings (paragraph B2(k) of IFRS 1). If a taxable temporary difference arises from the initial recognition of the goodwill, entity B does not recognise the resulting deferred tax liability (paragraph 15(a) of IAS 12).

4.2.4 Restatement of goodwill

A Mandatory adjustments of goodwill

Under the business combinations exemption, a first-time adopter takes the carrying amount of goodwill under its previous GAAP at the date of transition to IFRS as a starting point and only adjusts it as follows:[309]

- a first-time adopter increases goodwill by an amount equal to the carrying amount of an item that it recognised as an intangible asset under its previous GAAP (less any related deferred tax and minority interests), but which does not meet the recognition criteria under IFRS. That is, the first-time adopter accounts for the change in classification prospectively and does not, for example, reverse the cumulative amortisation on the item that it recognised as an intangible asset under its previous GAAP;
- if a first-time adopter is required to recognise an intangible asset under IFRS that was subsumed in goodwill under its previous GAAP, it decreases goodwill accordingly and adjusts deferred tax and minority interests;
- a contingency affecting the amount of the purchase consideration for a past business combination may have been resolved before the date of transition to IFRS. If a reliable estimate of the contingent adjustment can be made and its payment is probable, the first-time adopter shall adjust the goodwill by that amount. Similarly, the first-time adopter shall adjust the carrying amount of goodwill if a previously recognised contingent adjustment can no longer be measured reliably or its payment is no longer probable;[310] and
- regardless of whether there is any indication that the goodwill may be impaired, the first-time adopter shall apply IAS 36 in testing the goodwill for impairment at the date of transition to IFRS and in recognising any resulting impairment loss in retained earnings (or, if so required by IAS 36, in revaluation surplus). The impairment test shall be based on conditions at the date of transition to IFRS.[311]

Example 7.62: Restatement of goodwill[312]

Entity V's first IFRS financial statements have a reporting date of 31 December 2005 and include comparative information for 2004 only. On 1 July 2001, V acquired 75% of subsidiary W. Under its previous GAAP, V assigned an initial carrying amount of 200 to intangible assets that would not have qualified for recognition under IAS 38. The tax base of the intangible assets was nil, giving rise to a deferred tax liability (at 30%) of 60. V measured minority interests at the minority's share of the fair value of the identifiable net assets acquired. Goodwill arising on the acquisition was capitalised as an asset in V's consolidated financial statements.

On 1 January 2004 (the date of transition to IFRS), the carrying amount of the intangible assets under previous GAAP was 160, and the carrying amount of the related deferred tax liability was 48 (30% of 160).

Under IFRS 1, V reclassifies intangible assets that do not qualify for recognition as separate assets under IAS 38, together with the related deferred tax liability of 48 and minority interests, as part of goodwill. The related minority interests amount to 28 (25% of 112 (160 minus 48)). V makes the following adjustment in its opening IFRS balance sheet:

Goodwill	84	
Deferred tax liability	48	
Minority interests	28	
Intangible assets		160

V tests the goodwill for impairment under IAS 36 and recognises any resulting impairment loss, based on conditions that existed at the date of transition to IFRS.

The main implication for first-time adopters will clearly be the requirement to carry out an impairment test of goodwill at the date of transition to IFRS. The requirements of IAS 36 relating specifically to the impairment of goodwill are dealt with at 3 above. The estimates used to determine whether a first-time adopter recognises an impairment loss or provision at the date of transition to IFRS should be consistent with estimates made for the same date under previous GAAP (after adjustments to reflect any difference in accounting policies), unless there is objective evidence that those estimates were in error.[313] If a first-time adopter needs to make estimates for that date that were not necessary under its previous GAAP, such estimates and assumptions should not reflect conditions that arose after the date of transition to IFRS.[314]

If a first-time adopter's opening IFRS balance sheet reflects impairment losses, it recognises any later reversal of those impairment losses in the income statement unless IAS 36 requires that reversal to be treated as a revaluation. This applies to both impairment losses recognised under previous GAAP and additional impairment losses recognised on transition to IFRS.[315]

Under IFRS 1, assets acquired and liabilities assumed in a business combination prior to the date of transition to IFRS are not necessarily valued on a basis that is consistent with IFRS 3. This can lead to 'double counting' in the carrying amount of assets and goodwill as is illustrated in the example below.

Example 7.63: Impairment testing of goodwill on first-time adoption

Entity P acquired a business before its date of transition to IFRS. The cost of acquisition was €530 and P allocated the purchase price as follows:

	€
Properties, at carry-over cost	450
Liabilities, at amortised cost	(180)
Goodwill	260
Purchase price	530

The goodwill under P's previous GAAP relates entirely to the properties that had a fair value at date of acquisition that was significantly in excess of their value on a carry-over cost basis. In P's opening IFRS balance sheet the same assets, liabilities and goodwill are valued as follows:

	€
Properties, at fair value	750
Liabilities, at amortised cost	(200)
Provisional IFRS goodwill (before impairment test)	260
Total carrying amount	810

P used the option to measure the properties at fair value at its date of transition in its opening IFRS balance sheet. However, IFRS 1 does not permit goodwill to be adjusted to reflect the extent to which the increase in fair value relates to the time of the acquisition. The total carrying amount of the acquired net assets including goodwill of €810 may now exceed the recoverable amount. When P tests the 'provisional IFRS goodwill' for impairment on first-time adoption of IFRS, the recoverable amount of the business is determined to be €600. Accordingly, it will have to recognise an impairment of goodwill of €210 and disclose this impairment under IFRS 1.

In some cases the write-off will completely eliminate the goodwill and thereby any 'double counting'. However, in this particular case the remaining goodwill of €50 in truth represents goodwill that was internally generated between the date of acquisition and the date of transition to IFRS.

The IASB accepted that IFRS 1 'does not prevent the implicit recognition of internally generated goodwill that arose after the date of the business combination. However, the Board concluded that an attempt to exclude such internally generated goodwill would be costly and lead to arbitrary results.'[316]

B Prohibition of other adjustments of goodwill

The IASB concluded that 'to avoid costs that would exceed the likely benefits to users', IFRS 1 should prohibit 'restatement of goodwill for most other adjustments reflected in the opening IFRS balance sheet, unless a first-time adopter elects to apply IFRS 3 retrospectively'.[317] Therefore, a first-time adopter electing not to apply IFRS 3 retrospectively is not permitted to make any adjustments to goodwill other than those described at 4.2.4 A above. For example, a first-time adopter should not restate the carrying amount of goodwill:[318]

'(i) to exclude in-process research and development acquired in that business combination (unless the related intangible asset would qualify for recognition under IAS 38 in the balance sheet of the acquiree);

(ii) to adjust previous amortisation of goodwill;

(iii) to reverse adjustments to goodwill that IFRS 3 would not permit, but were made under previous GAAP because of adjustments to assets and liabilities between the date of the business combination and the date of transition to IFRS'.

Although IFRS 1 specifically prohibits other adjustments of goodwill, differences between the goodwill amount in the opening IFRS balance sheet and that in the financial statements under previous GAAP may arise because:

(a) goodwill may have been restated as a result of a retrospective application of IAS 21 (see Chapter 10 at 4.2.2);

(b) goodwill in relation to previously unconsolidated subsidiaries will have to be recognised (see 4.2.5 below);

(c) goodwill in relation to transactions that do not qualify as business combinations under IFRS must be derecognised (see 4.2.2 above); and

(d) 'negative goodwill' that may have been included within goodwill under previous GAAP should be derecognised under IFRS (see C below).

Example 7.64: Adjusting goodwill

Entity R acquired Entity S but under its previous GAAP it did not recognise the following items:

- S's customer lists which had a fair value of ¥1,100 at the date of the acquisition and ¥1,500 at the date of transition to IFRS; and
- Deferred tax liabilities related to the fair value adjustment of S's property, plant and equipment, which amounted to ¥9,500 at the date of the acquisition and ¥7,800 at the date of transition to IFRS.

What adjustment should R make to goodwill to account for the customer lists and deferred tax liabilities at its date of transition to IFRS?

As explained at 4.2.3 E above, R cannot recognise the customer lists when it uses the business combinations exemption. Accordingly, R cannot adjust goodwill for the customer lists.

R must recognise the deferred tax liability at its date of transition under IAS 12 because there is no exemption from recognising deferred taxation under IFRS 1. However, R is not permitted to adjust goodwill for the deferred tax liability that would have been recognised at the date of acquisition. Instead, R should recognise the change in deferred tax in retained earnings or other category of equity, if appropriate.

C Derecognition of negative goodwill

IFRS 3 specifically requires derecognition of negative goodwill with a corresponding adjustment to the opening balance of retained earnings on adoption of the standard by entities already reporting under IFRS. Although IFRS 1 does not specifically address accounting for negative goodwill recognised under a previous GAAP, negative goodwill should be derecognised by a first-time adopter because it is not permitted 'to recognise items or liabilities if IFRS do not permit such recognition'.[319] Negative goodwill clearly does not meet the definition of a liability under the IASB's *Framework* and its recognition is not permitted under IFRS 3.

D Goodwill previously deducted from equity

If a first-time adopter deducted goodwill from equity under its previous GAAP then 'it shall not recognise that goodwill in its opening IFRS balance sheet. Furthermore, it shall not transfer that goodwill to the income statement if it disposes of the subsidiary or if the investment in the subsidiary becomes impaired.'[320] Effectively, under IFRS such goodwill ceases to exist.

Example 7.65: Goodwill deducted from equity and treatment of related intangible assets[321]

Entity H acquired a subsidiary before the date of transition to IFRSs. Under its previous GAAP, entity H:

(a) recognised goodwill as an immediate deduction from equity;

(b) recognised an intangible asset of the subsidiary that does not qualify for recognition as an asset under IAS 38; and

(c) did not recognise an intangible asset of the subsidiary that would qualify under IAS 38 for recognition as an asset in the financial statements of the subsidiary. The subsidiary held the asset at the date of its acquisition by entity H.

In its opening IFRS balance sheet, entity H:

(a) does not recognise the goodwill, as it did not recognise the goodwill as an asset under previous GAAP;

(b) does not recognise the intangible asset that does not qualify for recognition as an asset under IAS 38. Because entity H deducted goodwill from equity under its previous GAAP, the elimination of this intangible asset reduces retained earnings (see 4.2.3 A above); and

(c) recognises the intangible asset that qualifies under IAS 38 for recognition as an asset in the financial statements of the subsidiary, even though the amount assigned to it under previous GAAP in entity H's consolidated financial statements was nil (see 4.2.3 E above)). The recognition criteria in IAS 38 include the availability of a reliable measurement of cost and entity H measures the asset at cost less accumulated depreciation and less any impairment losses identified under IAS 36 (see Chapter 5 at 2.9.5). Because entity H deducted goodwill from equity under its previous GAAP, the recognition of this intangible asset increases retained earnings. However, if this intangible asset had been subsumed in goodwill recognised as an asset under previous GAAP, entity H would have decreased the carrying amount of that goodwill accordingly (and, if applicable, adjusted deferred tax and minority interests) (see 4.2.4 A above).

If a first-time adopter deducted goodwill from equity under its previous GAAP then 'adjustments resulting from the subsequent resolution of a contingency affecting the purchase consideration shall be recognised in retained earnings'.[322] Effectively, the adjustment is being accounted for in the same way as the original goodwill that arose on the acquisition, rather than having to be adjusted against capitalised goodwill under IFRS 3. This requirement could affect, for example, the way a first-time adopter accounts for earn-out clauses relating to business combinations prior to its date of transition to IFRS.

Example 7.66: Earn-out clause in acquisition

Entity U acquired a business before its date of transition to IFRS and agreed to make an initial payment to the vendor together with further payments based on a multiple of future profits of the acquiree. The fair value of the earn-out is contingent on future profits and could not be determined reliably at the date of transition to IFRS. Under U's previous GAAP any goodwill was written off against equity as incurred.

After its date of transition to IFRS, U will account for the earn-out as a change in purchase consideration and recognise it in retained earnings.

4.2.5 *Previously unconsolidated subsidiaries*

Under its previous GAAP a first-time adopter may not have consolidated a subsidiary acquired in a past business combination. In that case a first-time adopter applying the business combinations exemption should 'adjust the carrying amounts of the subsidiary's assets and liabilities to the amounts that IFRSs would require in the subsidiary's balance sheet. The deemed cost of goodwill equals the difference at the date of transition to IFRSs between:

(i) the parent's interest in those adjusted carrying amounts; and

(ii) the cost in the parent's separate financial statements of its investment in the subsidiary.'[323]

The cost of a subsidiary in the parent's separate financial statements should be determined under the cost method of accounting under IAS 27 (see Chapter 6 at 7.3.1). Thus, a first-time adopter does not have to calculate what the goodwill would have been at the date of the original acquisition. The deemed cost of goodwill will, however, be capitalised as an asset in the opening IFRS balance sheet. The guidance on the implementation of IFRS 1 contains the following example that illustrates this.[324]

Example 7.67: Subsidiary not consolidated under previous GAAP

Background

Parent J's date of transition to IFRSs is 1 January 2004. Under its previous GAAP, parent J did not consolidate its 75 per cent subsidiary K, acquired in a business combination on 15 July 2001. On 1 January 2004:

(a) the cost of parent J's investment in subsidiary K is 180.

(b) under IFRSs, subsidiary K would measure its assets at 500 and its liabilities (including deferred tax under IAS 12) at 300. On this basis, subsidiary K's net assets are 200 under IFRSs.

Application of requirements

Parent J consolidates subsidiary K. The consolidated balance sheet at 1 January 2004 includes:

(a) subsidiary K's assets at 500 and liabilities at 300;

(b) minority interests of 50 (25 per cent of [500 – 300]); and

(c) goodwill of 30 (cost of 180 less 75 per cent of [500 – 300]). Parent J tests the goodwill for impairment under IAS 36 and recognises any resulting impairment loss, based on conditions that existed at the date of transition to IFRSs.

If the original acquisition cost is lower than the net asset value at the date of transition to IFRS, the difference is taken to retained earnings.

Slightly different rules apply to all other subsidiaries (i.e. those not acquired in a business combination) that an entity did not consolidate under its previous GAAP, the main difference being that goodwill should not be recognised in relation to those subsidiaries (see Chapter 5 at 2.9.3).

Note that in calculating the deemed cost of the goodwill, the first-time adopter is required to compare the historical cost of the investment to its share of the carrying amount of the net assets determined on a different date. In the case of a highly profitable subsidiary this could give rise to the following anomaly:

Example 7.68: Calculation of deemed goodwill

Parent L acquired subsidiary M before the date of transition for $500. The net assets of M would have been $220 under IFRS at the date of acquisition. M makes on average an annual net profit of $60, which it does not distribute to L.

At the date of transition to IFRS, the cost of L's investment in M is still $500. However, the net assets of M have increased to $460. Therefore, under IFRS 1 the deemed cost of goodwill is $40.

The deemed goodwill is much lower than the goodwill that was paid at the date of acquisition because M did not distribute its profits. In fact, if M had distributed a dividend to its parent just before the date of transition, the deemed goodwill would have been significantly higher.

5 FUTURE DEVELOPMENTS

As indicated at 1.2.2 above, the IASB is considering a number of other issues relating to business combinations in what was originally phase II of its project.

In April 2004, the IASB issued an exposure draft of proposed amendments to IFRS 3 to remove the scope exceptions for combinations by contract alone or involving mutual entities (see 2.2.2 above). This was only an interim solution and proposed that in applying the purchase method of accounting, the acquirer measures the cost of such combinations in such a way that no goodwill would be recognised in the former type of combination and that goodwill would only be recognised in the latter situation to the extent that consideration was given by the acquirer in exchange for control of the acquiree. However, the accounting for such combinations is now being addressed as part of the joint project with the FASB in dealing with issues related to the application of the purchase method.[325]

This second phase of the project involves a broad reconsideration of the requirements in IFRSs and US GAAP on applying the purchase method (which the draft revised IFRS 3 refers to as the acquisition method). An objective of the second phase of the project is to reconsider existing guidance on the application of the acquisition method in order to improve the completeness, relevance, and comparability of financial information about business combinations that is provided in financial statements. Another objective of this phase is to achieve convergence of IFRSs and US GAAP on how the acquisition method is applied.[326]

The second phase has resulted in the IASB publishing simultaneously in June 2005 a draft revised IFRS, which proposes to replace IFRS 3, together with exposure drafts proposing amendments to IAS 27 and IAS 37.[327] The comment period for the exposure drafts ended in October 2005, and the Boards also held public round-table discussions on the IFRS 3/IAS 27 proposals in late October and early November of that year. In January 2006, the Boards began their redeliberations on the proposed requirements based on the comments received. These continued over the next 18 months or so, and during that time the IASB agreed to make some changes to the original proposals contained in the exposure drafts. In July 2007, the IASB made available near-final drafts of both the revised IFRS 3 and the revised IAS 27.[328] At the time of writing, it is expected that the final versions of these revised standards will be published in November. The revised standards are expected to be effective for annual periods beginning on or after 1 January 2009, although earlier application will be permitted.[329] A summary of the expected revised IFRS 3, based on the near-final draft, is discussed at 5.1 below, whilst the expected revised IAS 27 is dealt with in Chapter 6 at 10.1.

As indicated above, the IASB had also issued an exposure draft proposing amendments to IAS 37. At that time, the IASB expected that the effective date of the revised IAS 37 would be the same as the effective date of the revised IFRS 3. However, the IASB is still redeliberating its proposals and has yet to determine the timing for the publication of a revised IAS 37. Consequently, the IASB has not reflected in the expected revised IFRS 3 its original proposals for dealing with contingencies, but has indicated that it expects to reconsider the requirements within the revised IFRS 3 when it issues the revised IAS 37.[330] The IASB proposals for revising IAS 37 are discussed in Chapter 27 at 8.1.

In the June 2005 exposure draft of the revised IFRS 3, the IASB indicated that it would consider the following issues as part of future phases of its project on business combinations:[331]

(a) the accounting for business combinations in which separate entities or businesses are brought together to form a joint venture, including possible applications of 'fresh start' accounting.

(b) the accounting for business combinations involving entities under common control.

However, the IASB's latest work plan no longer includes a project on business combinations on its agenda.[332] The expected revised IFRS 3 also indicates that neither the FASB nor the IASB currently has on its agenda a project to consider the 'fresh start' method of accounting, although they might at some future date undertake a joint project to consider the issues.[333]

5.1 Summary of the expected revised IFRS 3

5.1.1 Introduction

The revised IFRS 3 is expected to change significantly the accounting for business combinations. At the time of writing, it is expected that the final version of the revised standard will be published in late 2007 or early 2008. The revised standard is expected to be effective for business combinations where the acquisition date is on or after the beginning of annual periods starting on or after 1 July 2009. The most significant of the changes proposed would result in:

- a possible change in approach in acquisitions involving less than a 100% interest. Any minority interest (or 'non-controlling interest' as it will now be termed) can be measured at its fair value at the date of acquisition rather than its proportionate share of net assets. This could result in substantial grossing-up of goodwill and related minority interests in acquisitions involving less than 100%.
- recognising contingent consideration obligations at their acquisition-date fair values, with subsequent changes in fair value generally reflected in profit and loss. This represents a significant change from the current practice of recognising contingent consideration obligations only when the contingency is probable and can be measured reliably, with subsequent adjustments generally reflected in goodwill.

- expensing acquisition-related transaction costs rather than treating them as part of the consideration for the acquisition and reflected within goodwill.
- recognising gains and losses in initial equity holdings for step acquisition transactions (with corresponding adjustments to goodwill).

The current practice of accounting for business combinations under IFRS is a cost-based approach, whereby the cost of the acquired entity is allocated to the assets acquired and liabilities (and contingent liabilities) assumed. In contrast, the revised IFRS 3 is adopting an approach whereby the various components of a business combination are measured at their acquisition-date fair values (albeit with a number of exceptions including that relating to the measurement of any non-controlling interest). This represents a change from that originally proposed in the June 2005 exposure draft which was adopting an approach whereby the acquirer should recognise the fair value of the business acquired, regardless of the acquirer's percentage ownership, with any goodwill then being allocated between the acquirer and any non-controlling interest. The June 2005 exposure draft adopted the working principle that a business combination is an exchange of equal values and that the exchange should be measured based on the fair value of the consideration transferred or the fair value of the business (net assets) acquired, whichever is more reliably measurable.

Under the approach in the expected revised IFRS 3, the acquirer would measure and recognise the assets and liabilities of an acquired business similarly, regardless of whether some or all of the equity interests are acquired or how the acquisition was achieved (e.g. a step acquisition, a single purchase resulting in control, or a change in control without a purchase of equity interests).

The revised IFRS 3 also clarifies a number of issues where the current IFRS 3 was either silent or needed improvement. For example, it is to be clarified that it is only transactions that are part of the exchange for the acquiree that should be included in the accounting for a business combination. Any assets acquired, liabilities assumed, or portions of the consideration transferred for the acquiree, that are not part of the exchange for the acquiree, would not to be included in applying the acquisition method, but should instead be accounted for as separate transactions in accordance with relevant IFRSs.

5.1.2 Scope

As indicated at 5 above, the IASB has added into the scope of the revised IFRS 3 the acquisition method of accounting for combinations involving only mutual entities (e.g. credit unions, cooperatives, etc.) and combinations in which separate entities are brought together by contract alone (e.g. dual listed corporations and stapled entity structures).[334] Despite respondents' concerns, the Board considers that the attributes of mutual entities are not sufficiently different from those of investor-owned entities to justify a different method of accounting for business combinations between two mutual entities. It also considers that such combinations are economically similar to business combinations involving two investor-owned entities, and should be similarly reported.[335] Similarly, although the Board understands that difficulties may arise in applying the acquisition method to combinations achieved by contract alone, in particular the absence of the payment of any readily measurable consideration, it has concluded that the acquisition method should be applied for such transactions.[336] However, additional guidance is expected to be given in the revised IFRS 3 for applying the acquisition method to such business combinations (see 5.1.9 D and E below).

The formation of a joint venture and combinations involving entities under common control (as in the current IFRS 3) are to be excluded from the scope of the revised standard.[337]

5.1.3 Identifying a business combination

The revised IFRS 3 is expected to require an entity to determine whether a transaction or event is a *business combination* by applying the definition in the standard, which requires that the assets acquired and liabilities assumed constitute a *business*. If the assets acquired and liabilities assumed do not constitute a business, the transaction would be accounted for as an asset acquisition.[338]

A Definition of a business combination

Under the current IFRS 3, a business combination is defined as 'the bringing together of separate entities or businesses into one reporting entity' (see 2.2.1 above). This definition of a business combination was considered to be too broad and that it could be read to include circumstances in which there may be no triggering economic event or transaction and thus no change in an economic entity, per se.[339] Therefore, the revised IFRS 3 is expected to now define a business combination as a 'transaction or other event in which an acquirer obtains control of one or more businesses'.[340]

By emphasising the obtaining of control, the revised IFRS 3 will apparently narrow the current IFRS 3 definition of a business combination, which used the term 'bringing together' rather than 'obtaining control'. Notwithstanding this, the IASB states in the Basis for Conclusions accompanying the revised IFRS 3 that the revised definition includes all transactions and events initially included in the scope of the current IFRS 3.[341]

B Definition of a business

The existing definition of a business in IFRS 3 is expected to be revised such that it now means 'an integrated set of activities and assets that is capable of being conducted and managed for the purpose of providing a return in the form of dividends, lower costs, increased share prices, or other economic benefits to investors or other owners, members or participants'.[342]

As discussed at 2.2.1 above, the current IFRS 3 indicates that a business generally consists of three different elements – (1) inputs, (2) processes that are applied to those inputs, and (3) resulting outputs that are, or will be, used to generate revenues. The revised IFRS 3 would provide definitions of each of these elements and clarify that a business would only be required to have the first two of these three elements (i.e. inputs and processes), which together have the ability to create outputs. Although businesses usually have outputs, they would not need to be present for an integrated set of assets and activities to be a business.[343]

The revised IFRS 3 is also expected to clarify that a transferred set of activities and assets need not be self-sustaining (i.e. contain all of the inputs and processes necessary for it to conduct normal operations after it is separated from the transferor) in order to be considered a business. The determination of whether a particular set of activities and assets is a business would be based on whether others are capable of acquiring the business and continuing to produce outputs (e.g. by integrating the acquired business with their own inputs and processes). In evaluating whether a particular set of activities and assets is a business, it is not relevant whether the seller had historically operated the transferred set as a business or whether the acquirer intends to operate the set as a business.[344]

Additionally, the revised IFRS 3 is expected to contain guidance on assessing whether development stage entities are businesses. In these situations, various factors would need to be assessed to determine whether the transferred set of assets and activities is a business, including whether the set has begun its planned principal activities, has employees, intellectual property, and other inputs and processes that can be applied to those inputs, is pursuing a plan to produce outputs, and has the ability to obtain access to customers that will purchase those outputs. Not all of these factors would need to be present for a particular integrated set of activities and assets in the development stage to qualify as a business.[345]

The revised IFRS 3 is expected to retain the presumption in the current IFRS 3 that if goodwill is present in a transferred set of activities and assets, the transferred set is presumed to be a business.[346]

The acquisition of a non-producing oil field (or perhaps a single piece of real estate) would currently not be treated as a business combination, whether it is acquired directly or via a corporate entity. However, based on a literal reading of the expected revised IFRS 3, it may be that such single asset acquisitions are now to be treated as business combinations.

5.1.4 The acquisition method

The revised IFRS 3 will require that a business combination is accounted for by applying the acquisition method.[347] The change in terminology from the purchase method (as used in the current IFRS 3) is due to the fact that a business combination can arise in the absence of a purchase transaction.[348]

Applying the acquisition method will involve the following steps:[349]

(a) identifying an acquirer;

(b) determining the acquisition date

(c) recognising and measuring the identifiable assets acquired, the liabilities assumed, and any non-controlling interest in the acquiree; and

(d) recognising and measuring goodwill or a gain in a bargain purchase.

Steps (c) and (d) reflect the change in approach in the revised IFRS 3 from the cost-based approach, whereby the cost of the acquired entity is allocated to the assets acquired and liabilities (and contingent liabilities) assumed. They also represent a change from those in the June 2005 exposure draft whereby goodwill was to be measured by reference to the fair value of the acquiree, as a whole, including goodwill attributable to any non-controlling interest. As indicated at 5.1.1 above, the reason for this change is due to the decision to focus on measuring the components of the business combination, including any non-controlling interest in the acquiree, rather than measuring the fair value of the acquiree as a whole.[350]

The above steps are discussed below.

5.1.5 *Identifying the acquirer*

As with the current IFRS 3, one of the combining entities must be identified as the acquirer and guidance is given in making that determination.[351] Although changes will be made to the wording of the guidance in order to clarify some of the intentions of the IASB, and to conform with that used in the equivalent US standard, the guidance in the revised IFRS 3 for identifying the acquirer is considered by the IASB to be, in substance, the same as that in the current IFRS 3,[352] and will require significant judgement, particularly in reverse acquisitions.

Application guidance, including an illustrative example, on the accounting for reverse acquisitions will be given in the revised IFRS 3.[353] This is expected to be broadly similar to that in the current IFRS 3 discussed at 2.3.8 above.

5.1.6 *Determining the acquisition date*

The acquisition date is expected to be defined in the same way as in the current IFRS 3, i.e. it is the date on which the acquirer obtains control of the acquiree.[354] The expected revised IFRS 3 indicates that this will generally be the closing date – the date on which consideration is transferred, assets are acquired and liabilities assumed. However, the revised standard is expected to acknowledge that the acquirer might obtain control on a date that is either earlier or later than the closing date and, therefore, will emphasise that all pertinent facts and circumstances in assessing the acquisition date must be considered.[355]

5.1.7 *Recognising and measuring the identifiable assets acquired, the liabilities assumed, and any non-controlling interest in the acquiree*

A General principles

The general principles of the revised IFRS 3 are expected to be that the identifiable assets acquired and liabilities assumed of the acquiree are recognised as of the acquisition date and measured at fair value as at that date, with certain limited exceptions.[356] Any non-controlling interest in the acquiree would be recognised at the acquisition date, however, the acquirer can measure this either at fair value at that date or at the non-controlling interest's proportionate share of the acquiree's net identifiable assets as measured at the acquisition date.[357] The accounting for any non-controlling interest at the acquisition date is discussed further at 5.1.10 below.

To be included in the accounting for the business combination, the identifiable assets acquired and liabilities assumed must be part of the exchange for the acquiree, rather than as a result of separate transactions.[358] Explicit guidance is expected to be given in the revised IFRS 3 for making such an assessment as discussed at 5.1.13 below.

The revised IFRS 3 is expected to provide guidance for recognising and measuring particular assets acquired and liabilities assumed as at the acquisition date.[359] However, it is expected that much of the guidance relating to fair value (which remains defined as the amount for which an asset could be exchanged, or a liability settled, between knowledgeable, willing parties in an arm's length transaction)[360] that is contained in the current IFRS 3 (see 2.3.3 D above) would no longer be included. This is due to the IASB's current project on fair value measurement (see Chapter 2 at 6.3). In addition, the proposed guidance on how to measure fair value contained in Appendix E of the June 2005 exposure draft, including the 'fair value hierarchy', is also not expected to be included in the revised IFRS 3.

In addition, although the objective of the second phase of the business combinations project was not focused on issues related to the 'day-two' accounting for assets acquired and liabilities assumed, the revised IFRS 3 is expected to provide guidance on the accounting for certain acquired assets and assumed liabilities subsequent to a business combination.[361]

B Classifying or designating identifiable assets acquired and liabilities assumed

As discussed at 2.3.3 E above, the current IFRS 3 is silent on whether, and in what circumstances, a business combination triggers reassessment of the acquiree's classification or designation of assets, liabilities, equity and relationships acquired in a business combination. The IFRIC considered this issue but decided not to take this item on to its agenda as it noted that the IASB, at its meeting in February 2007, decided that the issue should be dealt with in Business Combinations phase II.[362]

Accordingly, the revised IFRS 3 is expected to include the principle that any classifications, designations or assessments for all assets acquired and liabilities assumed are made by the acquirer at the date of acquisition, based on the contractual terms, economic conditions, policies of the acquirer and any other relevant factors as at that date. However, the standard would provide for two exceptions to this principle:[363]

- Classification of leases in accordance with IAS 17 – classification is to be determined based on the contractual terms and factors at inception of the contract, unless the contract terms are modified at the date of acquisition.
- Classification of a contract as an insurance contract in accordance with IFRS 4 – classification is to be determined based on the contractual terms and factors at inception of the contract, unless the contract terms are modified at the date of acquisition.

As a result of this principle, therefore, all financial instruments of the acquiree would have to be carefully reviewed to determine how they should be classified or designated and therefore subsequently accounted for. For example, the accounting for particular financial assets and liabilities differs depending on whether they are classified at fair value through profit or loss, available for sale, or held to maturity in accordance with IAS 39. Hedging relationships would need to be reassessed as hedge accounting depends on whether a hedge is designated, the type of hedge designated and the assessment of hedge effectiveness. There would also need to be a reassessment as to whether any embedded derivatives exist in any contracts that relate to the assets acquired and liabilities assumed that should be separated from the host contract. It would not be appropriate to assume that the acquirer will simply take on the classification previously adopted by the acquiree. Such an assessment can be time consuming and may result in additional assets or liabilities that require measurement to fair value.

C Recognising and measuring particular assets acquired and liabilities assumed

The revised IFRS 3 is expected to give the following guidance on recognising and measuring particular assets acquired and liabilities assumed:

I Operating leases

As indicated above, although existing leases of the acquiree are new leases from the perspective of the acquirer, the classification of the leases between operating and finance is not revisited. If the acquiree is the lessee to an operating lease, the acquirer does not recognise the acquiree's rights under the operating lease separately from its obligations as part of the purchase price allocation (i.e. the asset and liability arising from the operating lease is not recognised on a gross basis). However, the acquirer would be required to recognise operating leases in which the acquiree is the lessee as either intangible assets or liabilities if the terms of the lease are favourable (asset) or unfavourable (liability) relative to market terms and prices.[364]

The revised IFRS 3 is also expected to indicate that an operating lease contract, even one that is at market terms, may have value because the lease provides future economic benefits such that an identifiable intangible asset should be recognised. For example, a lease of gates at an airport or of retail space in a prime shopping centre may provide entry into a market or other future economic benefits.[365]

However, where the acquiree is a lessor in an operating lease, the acquirer is not expected to separately recognise an intangible asset or liability where the terms of the lease are favourable or unfavourable relative to market terms and prices. The extent of any off-market terms would instead be reflected in the carrying value of the asset subject to lease.[366] This is to avoid any inconsistency with IAS 40 which requires the fair value of investment property to take into account rental income from current leases, and the IASB understands that practice is to measure the fair value of investment property taking into account the contractual terms of the leases and other contracts in place relating to the asset.[367]

II Intangible assets

The current IFRS 3 states that any asset acquired or liability assumed in a business combination must be able to be measured reliably to be recognised. The inclusion in

IFRS 3 of the reliability of measurement criterion was the result of extensive field tests conducted by the IASB on the proposals in the exposure draft preceding IFRS 3 (ED 3). Those field visits, which included discussions with accountants and valuation professionals, highlighted that there were certain circumstances in which an intangible asset acquired in a business combination might have a value that could not be measured reliably.

Despite this, and in the interest of convergence with US GAAP, the Board has decided not to include an equivalent statement in the revised IFRS 3.[368]

Accordingly, under the expected revised IFRS 3, identifiable intangible assets are recognised separately from goodwill if they are either separable or arise from contractual or other legal rights.[369] It would no longer be necessary that the intangible asset must be capable of reliable measurement in order for it to be recognised, despite the reasons for including this criterion in the current IFRS 3. Therefore, whenever an intangible asset can be separately identified it would now be recognised and a measure assigned to it.

The revised IFRS 3 is expected to give guidance for applying the definition of 'identifiable' to intangible assets, including examples of identifiable intangible assets[370] as done in the current IFRS 3 (see 2.3.3 B I above).

One particular intangible asset that the revised IFRS 3 is expected to require an acquirer to recognise is that of a reacquired right (see 5.1.7 D V below).

III Valuation allowances

An acquirer may not recognise a separate provision or valuation allowance as of the acquisition date for assets acquired in a business combination that are initially recognised at fair value. For example, as receivables (including loans) that are acquired in a business combination would be recognised and measured at fair value at the acquisition date, any uncertainty about collections and future cash flows would be included in the fair value measure. Accordingly, the acquiring entity would not recognise a separate provision or valuation allowance for uncollectible amounts at the acquisition date.[371]

IV Assets that the acquirer intends not to use or to use in a way that is different from other market participants

As discussed in Example 7.16 at 2.3.3 D IV above, one issue relating to the valuation of intangible assets under the current IFRS 3 is whether the acquirer's intention in relation to those assets should be taken into account in attributing a fair value, for example, where the acquirer does not intend to use an intangible asset of the acquiree. The revised IFRS 3 is expected to explicitly deal with this issue and clarify that the acquirer's intention is ignored. The asset has to be measured at a fair value that reflects how it would be used by other market participants.[372]

D Exceptions to the recognition and/or measurement principles

The IASB is also expected to make a number of exceptions to the principles in the revised IFRS 3 that all assets acquired and liabilities assumed should be recognised and measured at fair value.

I Contingent liabilities

Like the current IFRS 3 (see 2.3.3 above), the revised IFRS 3 is expected to require that for contingent liabilities assumed in a business combination a liability is recognised at its fair value if there is a present obligation arising from a past event that can be reliably measured, even if it is not probable that an outflow of resources will be required to settle the obligation.[373] However, for a contingent liability that only represents a possible obligation that arises from a past event, whose existence will be confirmed only by the occurrence or non-occurrence of one or more uncertain future events not wholly within the control of the entity, no liability is to recognised under the expected revised IFRS 3 (unlike the current IFRS 3).[374]

Where a liability is recognised for a contingent liability, since this is not what would be required under IAS 37, the revised IFRS 3 is expected to retain the existing requirements for the subsequent measurement of such liabilities (see 2.3.3 C above).[375]

As far as contingent assets are concerned, the IASB is expected to clarify in the Basis for Conclusions that under the revised IFRS 3 these should not be recognised. This also appears to be the case even if it is virtually certain that they will become unconditional or non-contingent. It would only be if the entity determined that an asset exists at the acquisition date (that is, that it has an unconditional right at the acquisition date) that an asset would be recognised.[376] This does appear to be inconsistent with the requirements of IAS 37 which states that, when the realisation of income is virtually certain, then the related asset is no longer regarded as contingent and recognition is appropriate (see Chapter 27 at 3.2.2).[377]

The above requirements of the expected revised IFRS 3 differ from those proposed in the June 2005 exposure draft which reflected changes to the requirements of IAS 37 contained in another exposure draft issued at the same time (see Chapter 27 at 8 for a discussion of those proposals). At that time, the IASB expected that the effective date of the revised IAS 37 would be the same as the effective date for the revised IFRS 3. The IASB has yet to determine when it might eventually issue a revised IAS 37, but it expects to reconsider and, if necessary, amend the requirements of the revised IFRS 3 when it does so.[378]

II Income taxes

As with the current IFRS 3, deferred income tax assets and liabilities are expected to continue to be recognised and measured in accordance with IAS 12, rather than at their acquisition-date fair values.[379] However, IAS 12 is also expected to be amended so as to change the accounting for deferred tax benefits that did not meet the recognition criteria at the date of acquisition, but are subsequently recognised. IAS 12 would now require that:[380]

(a) acquired deferred tax benefits recognised within the measurement period (see 5.1.14 below) that result from new information obtained about facts and circumstances existing at the acquisition date would result in a reduction of goodwill related to that acquisition. If the carrying amount of goodwill is zero, any remaining deferred tax benefits would be recognised in profit or loss; and

(b) all other acquired tax benefits realised would be recognised in profit or loss.

It will therefore be necessary to carefully assess the reasons for changes in the assessment of deferred tax made during the measurement period to determine whether it relates to facts and circumstances at the acquisition date or if it is a change in facts and circumstances since acquisition date.

This differs from the treatment under the current IFRS 3 of deferred tax benefits subsequently recognised, whereby the carrying amount of goodwill is reduced for the subsequent recognition of such deferred tax benefits. Further, the current IFRS 3 does not impose a time limit in terms of adjusting goodwill for the subsequent realisation of deferred tax benefits acquired in a business combination (see 2.3.6 C above).

The above new requirements in IAS 12 are expected to be applied prospectively from the effective date of the revised IFRS 3 (see 5.1.16 below) to the recognition of deferred tax assets acquired in business combinations effected before the revised IFRS 3 is applied. Therefore, an acquirer would not adjust the accounting for prior business combinations if the deferred tax benefits failed to satisfy the criteria for separate recognition as of the acquisition date and are subsequently recognised, unless the benefits are recognised within the measurement period and result from new information about facts and circumstances that existed at the acquisition date.[381]

IAS 12 is also expected to be amended so as to require tax benefits arising from the excess of tax-deductible goodwill over goodwill for financial reporting purposes to be accounted for at the acquisition date as a deferred tax asset similar to the accounting for other temporary differences.[382]

The expected amendments to IAS 12 are discussed further in Chapter 26 at 10.

III Indemnification assets

In certain situations, primarily those related to uncertainties as to the outcome of pre-acquisition contingencies (e.g. uncertain tax positions, environmental liabilities, or legal matters), the seller might provide an indemnification to the acquirer. The indemnification typically requires the acquiree's selling shareholders to reimburse the acquirer for some or all of the costs incurred by the acquirer in connection with the assumed pre-acquisition contingency. As discussed at 2.3.2 E IV above, such indemnities are not explicitly addressed in the current IFRS 3 but are either treated as 'negative' contingent consideration or as a separate 'indemnity asset'.

Such indemnities are now expected to be addressed in the revised IFRS 3. From the acquirer's perspective, the indemnification is an acquired asset to be recognised at its acquisition-date fair value. However, in order to avoid 'recognition or measurement' anomalies for indemnifications related to items for which liabilities are not required to be measured at fair value (e.g. uncertain tax positions), the revised IFRS 3 is expected to make an exception to the general principles of recognising the indemnification asset at its acquisition-date fair values.[383] If the indemnified item is recognised as a liability at the acquisition date, the asset would be recognised and measured according to the contractual terms of the agreement, using assumptions consistent with those used to measure the indemnified item, subject to management's assessment of collectability. Thus, if the agreement fully indemnifies the acquirer, the asset would be recognised and measured at the same amount as the liability. If the indemnification only relates to a portion of the liability, then the asset would be limited to that indemnified portion. However, if no liability is recognised for the indemnified item at the date of acquisition, an indemnification asset would also not recognised.[384]

Subsequent to the business combination, it is expected that the indemnification asset is measured using the same assumptions used to calculate the liability, subject to management's assessment of collectability.[385] Any changes in the value recognised as an asset would be recognised in the profit or loss, where the change in the value of the related liability would also be recognised.

IV Employee benefits

As with the current IFRS 3, it is expected that assets or liabilities relating to an acquiree's employee benefit plans are recognised and measured in accordance with IAS 19, i.e. at the present value of the obligation, less the fair value of any plan assets, rather than at their acquisition-date fair values.[386] The same would apply for all employee benefit arrangements accounted for under IAS 19.[387]

V Reacquired rights

As indicated earlier at 5.1.7 C II above, if the assets of the acquiree include a right previously granted to it, allowing use of the acquirer's assets – a reacquired right – the revised IFRS 3 is expected to require it to be recognised as an identifiable intangible asset. For example, a right to use the acquirer's trade name under a franchise agreement or a right to use the acquirer's technology under a technology licensing agreement.[388] However, rather than valuing the intangible asset at its acquisition-date fair value, it is to be valued on the basis of the remaining contractual term of the related contract, regardless of whether market participants would consider potential contractual renewals in determining its fair value.[389]

If the terms of the right are favourable or unfavourable compared to the market terms and prices at the date of acquisition, a settlement gain or loss is expected to be recognised in the profit or loss.[390]

After acquisition, the intangible asset would be amortised over the remaining contractual period of the contract, and would not include any renewal periods.[391]

As discussed at 2.3.3 F above, the current IFRS 3 is silent in this area.

VI Assets held for sale

As with the current IFRS 3, it is expected that non-current assets (or disposal groups) classified as held for sale at the acquisition date in accordance with IFRS 5 are measured at fair value less costs to sell.[392] This exception is to avoid the need to recognise a loss for the selling costs immediately after a business, if the assets had initially been measured at their fair value at the acquisition date. Subsequent to the issue of the June 2005 exposure draft, the Board tentatively decided to remove the proposed exception and amend IFRS 5 by replacing the words 'fair value less costs to sell' with 'fair value'. However, this has not yet been done, but the IASB intends that the eventual amendment to IFRS 5 is effective at the same time as the revised IFRS 3, at which time this exception will be removed.[393]

VII Share-based payment awards

The revised IFRS 3 is also expected to provide an exception that, a liability or an equity instrument related to the replacement of an acquiree's share-based payment award is measured in accordance with IFRS 2 (referred to as the 'fair-value based method), rather than at fair value.[394] Additional guidance, expected to be given in the revised IFRS 3 for accounting for replacement of share-based payment awards in a business combination, is discussed at 5.1.9 B below.

5.1.8 Recognising and measuring goodwill or a gain in a bargain purchase

As indicated at 5.1.1 above, the current IFRS 3 adopts a cost-based approach, whereby the cost of the acquired entity is allocated to the assets and liabilities (and contingent liabilities) assumed. Goodwill is recognised as an asset and measured at its cost, being the excess of the cost of the acquirer's interest in the acquiree over the acquirer's interest in assets and liabilities of the acquiree. No amount is included for any goodwill relating to any minority interest (now termed 'non-controlling interests'. Accordingly, goodwill is not measured at its fair value, but is measured as a residual.

Under the revised IFRS 3, it is expected that goodwill is still measured as a residual. However, due to the expected change in focus on measuring the various components of the business combination at their acquisition-date fair values (albeit with a number of exceptions including that relating to the measurement of any non-controlling interest), the calculation of goodwill (or a gain) would be computed as the difference between:[395]

(a) the aggregate of:
   (i) the acquisition-date fair value of the consideration transferred;
   (ii) the amount of any non-controlling interest in the acquiree; and
   (iii) the acquisition-date fair value of the acquirer's previously held equity interest in the acquiree; and

(b) the net of the acquisition-date fair values (or other amounts recognised in accordance with the requirements of the revised standard) of the identifiable assets acquired and the liabilities assumed.

Goodwill arises where (a) exceeds (b). A gain on a bargain purchase arises when (b) exceeds (a). Bargain purchase transactions are discussed further at 5.1.12 below.

(b) has been discussed at 5.1.7 above. The items included within (a) are discussed below.

5.1.9 Consideration transferred

The consideration transferred is comprised of the acquisition-date fair values of assets transferred by the acquirer, liabilities incurred by the acquirer to the former owners of the acquiree, and equity interests issued by the acquirer. The consideration may take many forms, including cash, other assets, a business or subsidiary of the acquirer, and securities of the acquirer (e.g. ordinary shares, preferred shares, options, warrants, and debt instruments).

It is expected that the consideration transferred will also include the fair value of any contingent consideration and may also include some or all of any acquirer's share-based payment awards exchanged for awards held by the acquiree's employees. These are discussed further below.[396]

When the consideration transferred includes assets or liabilities with carrying amounts that differ from the acquisition-date fair values, it is expected that the acquirer should remeasure the transferred assets or liabilities at their acquisition-date fair values and recognise any resulting gains or losses in profit or loss. However, it may be that the transferred assets or liabilities remain within the combined entity after the acquisition date (for example, they were transferred to the acquiree rather than to its former owners), and therefore the acquirer retains control of them. In that case, it is expected they are measured at their existing carrying amounts immediately before the acquisition, and therefore no gain or loss is recognised.[397]

Where the acquirer and the acquiree exchange only equity interests, the acquisition-date fair value of the acquiree's equity interests may be more reliably measurable than that of the acquirer's equity interests. In that case, the revised IFRS 3 is expected to require that the calculation of goodwill should use the acquisition-date fair value of the acquiree's equity interests rather than the acquisition-date fair value of the consideration transferred.[398]

Where no consideration is transferred by the acquirer, the revised IFRS 3 is expected to give additional guidance for such situations. This is discussed at 5.1.9 D below.

A Contingent consideration

The acquirer may agree to transfer additional equity interests, cash, or other assets to the former owners of the acquired business after the acquisition date if certain specified events occur or conditions are met in the future. Such arrangements are commonly used by buyers and sellers when there are differences in view as to the fair value of the acquired business. It is expected that, under the revised IFRS 3, the acquirer recognises the acquisition-date fair value of any contingent consideration as part of the consideration transferred in exchange for the acquiree.[399] This represents a significant change from the practice under the current IFRS 3 of recognising contingent consideration obligations only when the contingency is probable and can be measured reliably.

The initial measurement of contingent consideration at the fair value of the obligation is to be based on an assessment of the facts and circumstances that exist at the acquisition date. Classification of a contingent consideration obligation as either a liability or equity would be based on the definitions of an equity instrument and a financial liability in IAS 32 (see Chapter 19) or other applicable accounting standards.[400]

Another expected significant change from current practice is that subsequent changes in the value of contingent consideration would no longer be accounted for as adjustments to the consideration transferred in the business combination (and would therefore no longer result in changes to goodwill) as required under the current IFRS 3 (see 2.3.2 E above).

The IASB is expected to conclude that subsequent changes in the fair value of a contingent consideration obligation generally do not affect the acquisition-date fair value of the consideration transferred to the acquiree. Instead, those subsequent changes in value are related to post-combination events and changes in circumstances of the combined entity. Thus, the Board believes that subsequent changes in value for post-combination events and circumstances should not affect the measurement of the consideration transferred or goodwill on the acquisition date.[401] Accordingly, the revised IFRS 3 is expected to require that after initial recognition, changes in the fair value of contingent consideration resulting from events after the acquisition date such as meeting an earnings target, reaching a specified share price, or meeting a milestone on a research and development project are accounted for as follows:[402]

- Contingent consideration classified as equity is not subsequently remeasured (consistent with the accounting for equity instruments generally), and settlement is accounted for within equity.
- Contingent consideration classified as a liability that:
    - is a financial instrument and within the scope of IAS 39 is remeasured at fair value, with any resulting gain or loss recognised in either profit or other comprehensive income in accordance with IAS 39;
    - is not within the scope of IAS 39 is accounted for in accordance with IAS 37 or other standards as appropriate.

It is unclear what contingent consideration classified as a liability would not be within the scope of IAS 39, and would therefore be accounted for under IAS 37 or another standard, but even where that is the case, any changes in the fair value of the liability would be recognised in profit or loss.

The revised IFRS 3 is expected to include one exception to the above requirement for accounting for changes in the fair value of contingent consideration, and that is where the changes are the result of additional information about the facts and circumstances that existed at the acquisition date that the acquirer obtained after that date.[403] Such changes are measurement period adjustments and are to be accounted for as discussed at 5.1.14 below.

It is expected that the revised IFRS 3 will also recognise that, in some situations, the agreement may give the acquirer the right to the return of previously transferred consideration if specified future events occur or conditions are met. Such a right would fall within the definition of 'contingent consideration', and would be accounted for as such by recognising an asset at its acquisition-date fair value.[404]

B Share-based payment awards exchanged for awards held by the acquiree's employees

Acquirers often exchange share-based payment awards (i.e. replacement awards) for awards held by employees of the acquiree. These exchanges frequently occur because the acquirer wants to avoid the effect of having minority interests in the acquiree represented by the shares that are ultimately held by employees, the acquirer's shares are often more liquid than the shares of the acquired business after the acquisition, and/or to motivate former employees of the acquiree toward the overall performance of the combined, post-acquisition business. Such exchanges are accounted for in accordance with IFRS 2. As discussed in Chapter 31 at 10.1.1, there is currently no explicit guidance for such replacement awards and different treatments are possible.

It is expected that the revised IFRS 3 will now deal with issue and, as indicated at 5.1.9 above, the consideration transferred may include some or all of any acquirer's share-based payment awards exchanged for awards held by the acquiree's employees. Such exchanges are modifications of share-based payment awards in accordance with IFRS 2.

The revised IFRS 3 is expected to require that where the acquirer is obligated to issue replacement awards in exchange for acquiree share-based payment awards held by employees of the acquiree, then all or a portion of the fair-value based measure of the acquirer's replacement awards is included as part of the consideration transferred by the acquirer. The acquirer would be considered to have an obligation to replace the acquiree awards if the employees or the acquiree can enforce replacement, and generally arises from the terms of the acquisition agreement, the acquiree's plan or legislation.[405]

The portion of the replacement award that is part of the consideration transferred would be the amount that is attributable to past service that the employee has provided to the acquiree.[406] Where additional service conditions are imposed by the acquirer, a portion of the replacement award would be considered as being in respect of post-combination services and therefore an expense would be recognised. This is expected to be regardless of whether employees had rendered all of the service required for their acquiree awards to vest before the acquisition date.[407] The portion of the fair value of the replacement award included as part of the consideration transferred (i.e. the portion related to past services) is expected to be determined as follows:[408]

$$\text{Fair value on the acquisition date of the replaced (i.e. acquiree) award} \times \frac{\text{Vesting period completed}}{\text{Greater of total vesting period and original vesting period}}$$

It is expected that the difference between the fair value on the acquisition date of the replacement (i.e. acquirer) award and the amount allocated to consideration transferred would be included as compensation cost over the period from the acquisition date until the service period ends. This effectively means the excess of the fair value of the replacement awards over the fair value of the replaced award, if any, would be recognised as compensation cost in the acquirer's post-combination financial statements over the period from the acquisition date until the service period ends.[409] If no post-combination service is required, the excess of the fair value of the replacement awards over the fair value of the replaced award would, therefore, be an immediate post-combination expense.

Additional guidance is expected to be given on distinguishing between the portion of a replacement award that is attributable to pre-combination service (which the acquirer would include in the consideration transferred in a business combination) and the portion that is attributed to post-combination service (which the acquirer would recognise as a post-combination expense) by way of a number of illustrative examples.[410]

The revised IFRS 3 is expected to require that if the acquirer is not obligated to issue replacement awards, but elects to do so, none of the replacement awards are to be included as part of the consideration transferred. In that case, the acquirer would apply the requirements of IFRS 2 for accounting for modifications to determine how much post-compensation expense is recognised as a result of granting the replacement awards.[411]

C Acquisition-related costs

An acquirer generally incurs various acquisition-related costs in connection with a business combination, including:

- direct costs of the transaction, such as (i) costs for the services of lawyers, investment bankers, accountants, and other third parties and (ii) costs to issue debt or equity instruments used to effect the business combination (i.e. issuance costs); and
- indirect costs of the transaction, such as recurring internal costs (e.g. the cost of maintaining an acquisition department).

Under the current IFRS 3, payments made to third parties for services that are directly related to a business combination are currently included as part of the cost of the acquisition (see 2.3.2 D above). Debt issuance costs and the costs of registering and issuing equity securities are treated as a reduction of the proceeds of the debt or securities issued (see Chapter 19 at 5.1 and Chapter 20 at 2.3). The indirect costs of an acquisition are expensed in the period incurred.

The IASB is expected to conclude that acquisition-related costs, whether for services performed by external parties or internal staff of the acquirer, are not part of the fair value exchange between the buyer and seller for the acquired business. Rather, they are separate transactions in which the buyer makes payments in exchange for the services received. Thus, under the revised IFRS 3, it is expected that the acquirer accounts for acquisition-related costs separately from the business combination. The Board noted that acquisition-related costs generally do not represent assets of the acquirer at the acquisition date as they are consumed as the services are rendered.[412] Thus, with the exception of the costs of registering and issuing debt and securities that are recognised in accordance with IAS 39, acquisition-related costs are expected to be accounted for as expenses in the periods in which the costs are incurred and the related services are received.[413]

In addition, in order to mitigate concerns about potential abuse, e.g. where a buyer might ask a seller to make payments to third parties on its behalf, but the consideration to be paid for the business is sufficient to reimburse the seller for making such payments, the revised IFRS 3 is expected to require that a transaction that reimburses the acquiree or its former owners for paying the acquirer's acquisition-related costs is not to be included in applying the acquisition method (see 5.1.13 below).[414]

D Business combinations achieved without the transfer of consideration

An acquirer sometimes obtains control of an acquiree without transferring consideration. The revised IFRS 3 is expected to say that such circumstances include:[415]

(a) the acquiree repurchasing a sufficient number of its own shares for an existing investor (the acquirer) to obtain control.

(b) minority veto rights that previously kept the acquirer from controlling an acquiree in which the acquirer held the majority voting rights lapsing;

(c) the acquirer and the acquiree agreeing to combine their businesses by contract alone. In that case, the acquirer transfers no consideration in exchange for control of an acquiree and holds no equity interests in the acquiree, either on the acquisition date or previously. Examples of business combinations achieved by contract alone include bringing two businesses together in a stapling arrangement or forming a dual listed corporation.

The acquisition method, as described in the revised IFRS 3, is expected to apply to a business combination achieved without the transfer of consideration.[416] To determine the amount of goodwill in such a business combination, it is expected that the acquirer is required to use the acquisition-date fair value of the acquirer's interest in the acquiree instead of the acquisition-date fair value of the consideration transferred.[417] The acquisition-date fair value of the acquirer's interest in the acquiree is expected to be determined using one or more valuation techniques that are appropriate in the circumstances and for which sufficient data is available. If more than one valuation technique is used, the acquirer should evaluate the results of the techniques, considering the relevance and reliability of the inputs used and the extent of the available data.[418]

In a business combination achieved by contract alone, since the acquirer does not have an interest in the equity in the acquiree, it would appear that no amount is included in the calculation of goodwill. However, in such a business combination, the revised IFRS 3 is expected to require that the acquirer attributes to the equity holders of the acquiree the amount of the acquiree's net assets recognised under the standard (see 5.1.7 above). In other words, the equity interests in the acquiree held by parties other than the acquirer are a non-controlling interest in the acquirer's consolidated financial statements, even if it results in all of the equity interests in the acquiree being attributed to the non-controlling interest.[419] This would appear to suggest that no goodwill is to be recognised in a business combination achieved by contract alone. It is unclear, however, how this fits in with the option discussed at 5.1.10 below in measuring non-controlling interests in an acquiree at its acquisition-date fair value. If this were done, goodwill would be recognised.

E Combinations involving mutual entities

As indicated at 5.1.2 above, combinations involving mutual entities are within the scope of the revised IFRS 3 and the standard is expected to provide some guidance in applying its requirements when two mutual entities combine. The revised IFRS 3 is expected to note that the fair value of the acquiree may be more reliably measurable than the fair value of the member interests transferred by the acquirer. It is expected that the standard will take the view that, in the absence of evidence to the contrary, these values are presumed to be equal. An example of evidence to the contrary would be that the acquirer has made a bargain purchase because the seller is acting under duress (see 5.1.12 below). However, it is expected that the revised IFRS 3 will require that in no event is the acquirer to recognise the entire amount of the acquiree's net assets recognised in accordance with the standard (see 5.1.7 above) as a gain resulting from a bargain purchase. In addition, as in other business combinations, the acquirer in a combination of mutual entities would recognise an amount equal to the recognised amounts of the acquiree's net assets as a direct addition to capital or equity, not as an addition to retained earnings.[420]

The revised IFRS 3 is expected to recognise that mutual entities, although similar in many ways to other businesses, have distinct characteristics that arise because their members are both customers and owners. Members generally expect to receive benefits for their membership, often in the form of reduced fees charged for goods and services or patronage dividends (the portion of such dividends allocated to each member is often based on the amount of business the member did with the mutual entity during the year).

In arriving at a fair value measurement of a mutual entity, the standard is expected to state, therefore, that the assumptions that market participants make about the entity are to include assumptions that the market participants would make about future member benefits. For example, where an estimated cash flow model is used to determine the fair value of the mutual entity, the cash flows used as inputs to the model should be based on the expected cash flows of the mutual entity, which are likely to reflect reductions for member benefits, such as reduced fees charged for goods and services.[421]

5.1.10 Recognising and measuring non-controlling interests in acquiree

Under the current IFRS 3, where the acquirer obtains less than a 100% interest in the acquiree, a minority interest in the acquiree is recognised reflecting the minority's proportion of the net identifiable assets, liabilities and contingent liabilities of the acquiree at their attributed fair values at the date of acquisition; no amount is included for any goodwill relating to the minority interest.

Under the June 2005 exposure draft, the IASB proposed that in a business combination in which the acquirer holds less than 100% of the equity interests in the acquiree at the acquisition date, the acquirer would recognise the acquiree, as a whole, and the assets acquired and liabilities assumed at the full amount of their fair values as of that date, regardless of the percentage ownership in the acquiree. The excess of the fair value of the business acquired over the net amount of the recognised identifiable assets acquired and liabilities assumed would be measured and recognised as goodwill. Thus, all of the goodwill of the acquired business, not only the acquirer's share, would be recognised under this 'full-goodwill' approach. The amount of goodwill would then be allocated to the controlling and non-controlling interests.[422]

In redeliberating the exposure draft, the Board observed that it had specified the mechanics of determining the reported amount of a non-controlling interest, but had not identified its measurement attribute. The result of those mechanics would have been that the non-controlling interest was effectively measured as the 'final residual' in a business combination. As goodwill is also measured as a residual, the Board concluded that it is undesirable to have two residual amounts in accounting for a business combination. Accordingly, it was concluded that, in concept, the non-controlling interest, like other components of the business combination, should be measured at fair value.[423] However, the IASB was unable to agree on a single measurement basis for non-controlling interests because neither of the alternatives (fair value or proportionate share of the acquiree's net identifiable assets) received sufficient Board support to enable a revised business combinations standard to be issued.[424]

Consequently, the revised IFRS 3 is expected to require any non-controlling interest in an acquiree to be recognised,[425] but provide a choice of two methods in measuring non-controlling interests arising in a business combination:

- Option 1, to measure the non-controlling interest at its acquisition-date fair value (consistent with the measurement principle for other components of the business combination)
- Option 2, to measure the non-controlling interest at the proportionate share of the value of net identifiable assets acquired (see 5.1.7 above).[426]

It is expected that the choice of method is made for each business combination, rather than being a policy choice, and will require management to carefully consider their future intentions about acquiring the non-controlling interest, as each option, combined with the revisions to accounting for changes in ownership interest of a subsidiary introduced in the revised IAS 27 (see Chapter 6 at 10.1) will potentially have a significant effect on the amount recognised for goodwill.

A Option 1 – Measuring non-controlling interest at acquisition-date fair value

Where this option is applied, the revised IFRS 3 is expected to state that an acquirer will sometimes be able to measure the acquisition-date fair value of a non-controlling interest on the basis of market prices for equity shares not held by the acquirer. However, in other situations where the shares are not publicly traded, a market price may not be available, so the acquirer will need to measure the fair value of the non-controlling interest by using a valuation technique.[427]

The expected revised IFRS 3 goes on to say that the fair value of the acquirer's interest in the acquiree and the non-controlling interest on a per-share basis might differ. This is likely to be because the consideration transferred by the acquirer will generally include a control premium, or conversely, the inclusion of a discount for lack of control in the per-share value of the non-controlling interest.[428] Therefore, it may not be appropriate to extrapolate the fair value of an acquirer's interest to determine the fair value of the non-controlling interests.

B Option 2 – Measuring non-controlling interest at the proportionate share of the value of net identifiable assets acquired

Under this option, the non-controlling interest is measured at the share of the value of the net assets acquired and liabilities assumed of the acquiree (see 5.1.7 above), consistent with the current requirements of IFRS 3. The result is that the amount recognised for goodwill is the equivalent of only the acquirer's share, as is the case under the current IFRS 3. However, where the outstanding non-controlling interest is subsequently acquired, no additional goodwill is recorded since under the revised IAS 27 this is an equity transaction (see Chapter 6 at 10.1).

The following example illustrates the impact of these options.

Example 7.69: Measurement of non-controlling interests

Entity B has 40% of its shares publicly traded on an exchange. Entity A purchases the 60% non-publicly traded shares in one transaction, paying €630. Based on the trading price of the shares of entity B at the date of gaining control a value of €400 is assigned to the 40% non-controlling interest, indicating that entity A has paid a control premium of €30. The fair value of entity B's identifiable net assets is €700.

Option 1

Entity A accounts for the acquisition as follows:

	€	€
Fair value of identifiable net assets acquired	700	
Goodwill	330	
Cash		630
Non-controlling interest in entity B		400

Option 2

Entity A accounts for the acquisition as follows:

	€	€
Fair value of identifiable net assets acquired	700	
Goodwill	210	
Cash		630
Non-controlling interest in entity B (€700 × 40%)		280

The IASB has noted that there are likely to be three main differences arising from measuring the non-controlling interest at its proportionate share of the acquiree's net identifiable assets, rather than at fair value. First, the amounts recognised in a business combination for the non-controlling interest and goodwill are likely to be lower (as illustrated in the above example).

Second, if a cash generating unit to which the goodwill has been allocated is subsequently impaired, any resulting impairment of goodwill recognised through income is likely to be lower than it would have been if the non-controlling interest had been measured at fair value. The IASB states that it will not affect the impairment loss attributable to the controlling interest,[429] however, based on the expected consequential amendments made to IAS 36, this is not the case (see C below).[430]

The third difference noted by the IASB is that which arises if the acquirer subsequently purchases some (or all) of the shares held by the non-controlling shareholders. Under the revised IAS 27, such a transaction is to be accounted for as an equity transaction (see Chapter 6 at 10.1). By acquiring the non-controlling interest, presumably at fair value, the equity of the group is reduced by the non-controlling interest's share of any unrecognised changes in fair value of the net assets of the business, including goodwill. By measuring the non-controlling interest initially as a proportionate share of the acquiree's net identifiable assets, rather than at fair value, that reduction in the reported equity attributable to the acquirer is likely to be larger.[431] If in Example 7.69 above, entity A were to subsequently acquire all of the non-controlling interest for, say, €500, then assuming that there had been no changes in the carrying amounts for the net identifiable assets and the goodwill, entity A would reduce its equity by €220 (€500 – €280) if option 2 had been adopted, whereas the reduction would only be €100 (€500 – €400) if option 1 had been adopted.

C Impairment testing cash-generation units with goodwill and non-controlling interests

As a result of the above choice for measuring non-controlling interests, the IASB is amending IAS 36 to reflect the different treatments. It is also expected that amendments will be made to clarify the existing requirements of IAS 36 to reflect the fact that not all of the goodwill arising will necessarily be allocated to a CGU or group of CGUs which includes the subsidiary with the non-controlling interest – the existing Example 7 is being modified to reflect this. That example continues to illustrate the requirement to calculate a notionally adjusted carrying amount of goodwill where the non-controlling interest was initially measured at the proportionate share of assets.[432]

Guidance is also expected to be given on how to allocate impairment losses in respect of a larger CGU to those parts of that CGU that contain a subsidiary with a non-controlling interest. This would be done based on the relative values of the goodwill prior to the impairment. Any goodwill impairment losses in respect of a subsidiary that is itself a CGU, or that have been allocated to that part of a larger CGU that contain a subsidiary with a non-controlling interest, is attributed between the parent and the non-controlling interest on the same basis that profit or loss is allocated. A new Example 7A, based on the non-controlling interest initially measured at fair value, would be given that illustrated these requirements.[433]

5.1.11 Business combinations achieved in stages ('step acquisitions')

An acquirer may obtain control of an acquiree through a series of acquisitions of two or more different investments (commonly referred to as a 'step acquisition'). Under the current IFRS 3, an acquirer is required to treat each exchange transaction separately for the purpose of measuring goodwill (this results in a step-by-step comparison of the cost of the individual investments with the acquirer's interest in the net fair value of the acquiree's identifiable assets and liabilities at each step) – see 2.3.7 above.

The revised IFRS 3 is expected to take a completely different approach. It is expected to require that, if the acquirer holds a non-controlling equity investment in the acquiree immediately before obtaining control, the acquirer remeasures that investment at its acquisition-date fair value and recognise any resulting gain or loss in profit and loss.[434] The Board has concluded that a change from holding a non-controlling equity investment in an entity to obtaining control of that entity is a significant change in the nature of and economic circumstances surrounding that investment. That change warrants a change in the investment's classification and measurement (i.e. a remeasurement event).[435] In addition, if the acquirer had recognised changes in the value of its equity interest in the acquiree directly in equity (i.e. the investment was classified as available-for-sale in accordance with IAS 39), it is expected that the amount in equity is to be recognised on the same basis that would be required if the acquirer had directly disposed of the previously held investment, i.e. the amount at the acquisition date is recycled into profit or loss.[436]

The acquirer's non-controlling equity investment in the acquiree prior to obtaining control, after remeasurement to its acquisition-date fair value, would then be a component of the fair value of the consideration transferred by the acquirer in the business combination (see 5.1.8 above).

5.1.12 Bargain purchase transactions

IFRS 3 is currently based on a cost allocation model and presumes that, with one exception, the fair value of the acquirer's interest in the business acquired is equivalent to the fair value of the consideration transferred for that interest. In other words, with one exception, IFRS 3 presumes that there are no bargain purchases. The exception arises only when the consideration transferred is less than the fair value of the acquirer's interest in the identifiable net assets. When this is the case, IFRS 3 currently requires a gain to be recognised for the excess of the fair value of the acquirer's interest in the identifiable net assets acquired over the consideration transferred (having first reassessed the identification and measurement of the acquiree's identifiable assets, liabilities and contingent liabilities and the measurement of the cost of the combination) – see 2.3.5 above.

The revised IFRS 3 is expected to adopt a similar approach. A bargain purchase is considered to arise when the aggregate of the amounts specified in paragraph 49(b) exceeds the amount in paragraph 49(a) and, as indicated at 5.1.8 above, a gain is to be recognised in profit or loss on the acquisition date. All of the gain is attributed to the acquirer. A bargain purchase might happen, for example, in a business combination that is a forced sale in which the seller is acting under compulsion. However, the standard is also expected to acknowledge that the requirements to measure particular assets acquired or liabilities assumed in accordance with other IFRSs, rather than fair value, also may result in an apparent bargain purchase.[437] As with the current IFRS 3, the revised standard would require that before recognising such a gain, the acquirer should reassess all components of the calculation. This is to ensure that the measurements appropriately reflect consideration of all available information as of the acquisition date.[438]

Additional guidance is expected to be provided by way of an illustrative example. This indicates that the amount of the gain recognised is affected by the choice of measuring any non-controlling interest.[439] Indeed, it might be that if the non-controlling interest is measured at its acquisition-date fair value, goodwill is recognised rather than a gain.

5.1.13 Assessing what is part of the exchange for the acquiree

The current IFRS 3 has no specific guidance on accounting for pre-existing relationships between an acquirer and an acquiree (although, as discussed at 2.3.3 F above, in our view such relationships should be accounted for separately from the business combination. Similarly, the current IFRS 3 does not distinguish between contingent consideration that, in substance, is part of the cost of the business combination and contingent consideration that, in substance represents compensation for future services (although as discussed at 2.3.3 E II above, we believe that such a distinction should be made). These are issues that are now expected to be explicitly addressed in the revised IFRS 3.

As indicated at 5.1.7 A above, to be included in the accounting for the business combination, the identifiable assets acquired and liabilities assumed must be part of the exchange for the acquiree, rather than as a result of separate transactions.[440]

The expected revised IFRS 3 recognises that the acquirer and the acquiree may have a pre-existing relationship or other arrangement before the negotiations for the business combination, or they may enter into an arrangement during the negotiations that is separate from the business combination. In either situation, the acquirer would be required to identify any amounts that are separate from the business combination and thus are not part of what the acquirer and the acquiree (or its former owners) exchanged in the business combination, that is, amounts that are not part of the exchange for the acquiree. Accordingly, the acquirer would have to assess if any assets acquired, liabilities assumed, or portions of the consideration transferred for the acquiree, are not part of the exchange for the acquiree to be included in applying the acquisition method, but should instead be accounted for as separate transactions in accordance with relevant IFRSs.[441] This would require the acquirer to evaluate the substance of transactions entered into by the parties to determine whether those transactions or arrangements were designed primarily for the economic benefit of the acquirer or the combined entity, rather than primarily for the economic benefit of the acquiree (or its former owners) before the transaction. The former are not part of the business combination transaction, and are likely to be accounted for as separate transactions.[442] It is expected that factors such as reasons for the other aspects of the transaction, the party initiating the transaction or event, the nature and extent of pre-existing relationships between the acquirer and the acquiree or its former owners, and the timing of the overall transaction should be considered in completing the assessment.[443]

Examples of transactions that the revised IFRS 3 is expected to regard as substantively separate and would not be considered part of the exchange for the acquiree are as follows:[444]

- A transaction that effectively settles pre-existing relationships between the acquirer and acquiree. For example, a lawsuit, supply contract, franchising or licensing arrangement.
- A transaction that compensates employees or former owners of the acquiree for future services.
- A transaction that reimburses the acquiree or its former owners for paying the acquirer's acquisition-related costs (see 5.1.9 C above).

The revised IFRS 3 is expected to provide further detailed guidance for determining whether a transaction is separate from a business combination, including a number of worked examples.[445]

A Effective settlement of pre-existing relationships

If the business combination results in the effective settlement of a pre-existing relationship, it is expected that the acquirer will be required to recognise a gain or a loss, measured on the following bases.

For a pre-existing non-contractual relationship, such as a lawsuit, the gain or loss is measured at its fair value. For a pre-existing contractual relationship, such as a supply contract, the gain or loss is measured as the lesser of:

(a) the amount by which the contract is favourable or unfavourable from the perspective of the acquirer when compared with pricing for current market transactions for the same or similar terms. (It is emphasised that an unfavourable contract is not necessarily an onerous contract.); and

(b) the amount of any stated settlement provisions in the contract available to the counterparty to whom the contract is unfavourable.

If (b) is less than (a), the difference is included as part of the business combination accounting.

The requirements for contractual relationships are expected to be illustrated by 2 examples in the Application Guidance to the revised IFRS 3.[446]

B Arrangements for contingent payments to employees

Whether arrangement for contingent payments to employees are contingent consideration to be included in the measure of the consideration transferred (see 5.1.9 A above) or are separate transactions would depend on the nature of the arrangements.[447] If it is not clear whether an arrangement for payments to employees is part of the exchange for the acquiree or is a transaction separate from the business combination, it is expected that the acquirer should consider the following indicators:

- Continuing employment
- Duration of continuing employment
- Level of compensation
- Incremental payments to employees
- Number of shares owned
- Linkage to the valuation
- Formula for determining consideration
- Other agreements and issues

Although the expected guidance says that the acquirer should consider the above factors in determining whether the arrangement is part of the business combination or not, it is categorically stated that 'a contingent consideration arrangement in which the payments are automatically forfeited if employment terminates is compensation for post-combination services'.[448]

These requirements are expected to be illustrated by an example in the application guidance to the revised IFRS 3.[449]

5.1.14 Measurement period

As discussed at 2.3.6 above, the current IFRS 3 allows an acquirer a reasonable period of time to identify and determine appropriate fair values for the acquiree's identifiable assets, liabilities and contingent liabilities, and the cost of the business combination. If at the period end after the acquisition the initial accounting can only be determined provisionally, the acquirer accounts for the combination on that basis, making the necessary disclosures. The initial accounting is effectively required to be completed within twelve months of the acquisition, and any adjustments found necessary are to be accounted from the acquisition date.

The revised IFRS 3 is also expected to contain provisions in respect of a 'measurement period', which although quite similar to those in the current IFRS 3, are not identical. Under the revised IFRS 3, if the initial accounting in a business combination is incomplete by the end of the reporting period in which the combination occurs, it is expected that the acquirer would report in its financial statements provisional amounts for the items for which the accounting is incomplete. During the measurement period, it is expected that the acquirer retrospectively adjusts the provisional amounts recognised at the acquisition date to reflect new information obtained about facts and circumstances that existed as of the acquisition date that, if known, would have affected the measurement of the amounts recognised as of that date. Also, during the measurement period, the acquirer would recognise additional assets or liabilities if new information is obtained about facts and circumstances that existed at the acquisition date that, if known, would have resulted in the recognition of those assets and liabilities as of that date. It is expected that the measurement period ends as soon as the acquirer receives the information it was seeking about facts and circumstances that existed as of the acquisition date or learns that more information is not obtainable. However, it is expected that the measurement period is not to exceed one year from the acquisition date.[450]

The measurement period is to provide the acquirer with a reasonable time to obtain the information necessary to identify and measure all of the various components of the business combination.[451]

It is expected that the acquirer would be required to consider all pertinent factors in determining whether information obtained after the acquisition date should result in an adjustment to the provisional amounts recognised or whether the information results from events that occurred after the acquisition date. Pertinent factors include the time at which the additional information is obtained and whether the acquirer can identify a reason for a change to provisional amounts. The standard is expected to consider that information obtained shortly after the acquisition date is more likely than information obtained several months later to reflect circumstances that existed at the acquisition date. For example, the sale of an asset to a third party shortly after the acquisition date for an amount that differs significantly from its provisional fair value determined at that date is likely to indicate an error in the provisional amount unless an intervening event that changes its fair value can be identified.[452]

Although an increase/(decrease) in the provisional amount recognised for an identifiable asset will usually mean a corresponding decrease/(increase) in goodwill, the revised IFRS 3 is expected to note that part of the adjustment may be to another identifiable asset or liability rather than to goodwill. For example, the amount of an acquirer's obligation to pay contingent consideration might be directly related to the value of an acquired intangible asset. If the acquirer obtains new information during the measurement period about the fair value of the intangible asset as of the acquisition date, the adjustment to the asset may be offset (in whole or in part) by a corresponding adjustment to the provisional amount recognised for the contingent consideration liability.[453] Similarly, if there is a non-controlling interest in the acquiree, and this is measured based on the proportionate share of the net identifiable assets of the acquiree, any adjustments to those assets that had initially been determined on a provisional basis will be offset by the proportionate share attributable to the non-controlling interest.

It is expected that adjustments to provisional amounts that are made during the measurement period are recognised as if the accounting for the business combination had been completed at the acquisition date. Thus, the acquirer would revise comparative information for prior periods presented in financial statements as needed, including making any change in depreciation, amortisation or other income effects recognised in completing the acquisition accounting.[454] These requirements are expected to be illustrated by an example in the application guidance to the revised IFRS 3.[455]

Under the revised IFRS 3, after the measurement period ends, it is expected that the acquirer can only revise the accounting for a business combination to correct an error in accordance with IAS 8.[456]

5.1.15 Disclosures

The current IFRS 3 identifies three disclosure objectives and specifies particular disclosures that should be made to meet those objectives (see 2.3.10 and 3.10 above). The revised IFRS 3 is expected to take a similar approach, but would incorporate the objective dealing with goodwill within the objective to provide information that enables users to evaluate the financial effects of adjustments recognised in the current period that relate to business combinations that occurred in the current or previous reporting periods.

Many of the specific disclosures required by the current IFRS 3 are expected to be included within the revised IFRS 3, although some of them would be modified to reflect the acquisition-date fair value approach of the revised IFRS 3 rather than the cost-based approach of the current IFRS 3. It is expected that some additional disclosures would now be required (principally as a result of new explicit guidance for particular issues).[457] The main items for which new or specific information is expected to be required are listed below:

- contingent consideration (see 5.1.9 A above)[458]
- acquired receivables[459]
- transactions recognised separately from the business combination (see 5.1.13 above)[460]
- acquisition-related costs (see 5.1.9 C above)[461]
- non-controlling interests (see 5.1.10 above)[462]
- business combinations achieved in stages (see 5.1.11 above)[463]
- revenue of the acquiree and of the combined entity[464]
- provisional amounts and measurement period adjustments (see 5.1.14 above)[465]

One item of the current disclosure requirements that is expected to be deleted in the revised IFRS 3 is the disclosure of the acquiree's carrying amounts for each class of assets and liabilities immediately before the combination.[466]

An illustration of the disclosure requirements of the revised IFRS 3 is expected to be given in the Application Guidance to the standard.[467]

5.1.16 Effective date and transition

At the time of writing, it is expected that the final version of the revised standards will be published in late 2007 or early 2008. The revised standard is expected to be effective for business combinations where the acquisition date is on or after the beginning of annual periods starting on or after 1 July 2009. It is expected that earlier adoption will be permitted, although it may only be applied as early as periods beginning on or after 30 June 2007. However, if the revised IFRS 3 is adopted early, it is expected that fact must be disclosed, and the revised IAS 27 must be applied at the same time.

The revised IFRS 3 is expected to be applied prospectively to business combinations for which the acquisition date is on or after the beginning of the annual period in which the standard is adopted.[468] It is expected that assets and liabilities that arose from business combinations whose acquisition dates preceded the adoption of the revised IFRS 3 would not be adjusted upon application of the standard.[469] As a result, the current version of IFRS 3 will continue to apply to business combinations effected before the adoption date of the revised IFRS 3, with one exception relating to changes in deferred tax of the acquiree.

The revised IAS 12 (as amended by the revised IFRS 3) is expected to be applied prospectively. Therefore, for such earlier business combinations, it is expected that goodwill would not be adjusted for the subsequent recognition of deferred tax benefits that failed to satisfy the criteria for separate recognition as of the acquisition date.[470]

An entity, such as a mutual entity, that has not yet applied the current IFRS 3 and had one or more business combinations that were accounted for using the purchase method is to apply certain transitional provisions expected to be included in the Application Guidance in the revised IFRS 3.[471]

6 CONCLUSION

The IASB clearly saw business combinations and goodwill as an area of considerable divergence across jurisdictions and one that was to be given priority in its initial agenda, but in splitting its project into two phases recognised that it would be a major task to deal with all of the issues.

The first phase of the project resulted in the publication in March 2004 of IFRS 3, together with revised versions of IAS 36 and IAS 38, which introduced a number of significant changes in accounting for business combinations and goodwill from that required by the previous standard, IAS 22.

One of the major implications of IFRS 3 has been the need for acquirers to recognise, separate from goodwill, the identifiable intangible assets of the acquiree and to attribute a fair value to them, assuming that the value can be measured reliably. The guidance for valuing intangibles is effectively contained in IAS 38, but in our view more detailed guidance is required. The fact that for most of the intangible assets that need to be valued there will be no quoted market price, means that entities have to determine the value 'based on the best information available'. Unless an entity has developed valuation techniques in valuing such assets, in many cases specialists are needed to assist in determining the appropriate fair values.

The other major change brought about by IFRS 3 has been the treatment of goodwill, whereby it is no longer amortised but is subject to an annual impairment test under IAS 36 (see Chapter 15). Although we agree with the IASB's view that annual impairment testing of goodwill may better reflect the value of purchased goodwill as an asset, we consider that the cost of performing such a test, rather than systematic amortisation, may outweigh the benefits derived from it.

However, it should be recognised that IFRS 3 is not the last word on accounting for business combinations. As indicated at 5 above, the IASB has been developing a revised standard as part of phase II of its project. As outlined at 5.1 above, in conjunction with the FASB in the US, it is expected that in November 2007 the IASB will issue a revised IFRS 3 that will change significantly the accounting for business combinations in the future.

References

1 IFRS 3, *Business Combinations*, IASB, Appendix A.
2 IFRS 3, paras. 6-7.
3 See the introductory pages of IAS 22, *Business Combinations*, IASC, September 1998 (superseded March 2004), for a summary of the changes.
4 IFRS 3, para. BC2.
5 IFRS 3, para. BC3.

6 Project Summary, *Business Combinations (Phase II) – Application of the Purchase Method*, IASB, 26 January 2004, pp. 1 and 2.
7 IFRS 3, para. IN2.
8 IFRS 3, para. IN3.
9 IFRS 3, para. IN4.
10 IFRS 3, para. IN5.
11 IFRS 3, para. IN6.
12 IFRS 3, para. IN9.
13 IFRS 3, para. IN13.
14 IFRS 3, para. BC96.
15 IFRS 3, para. IN13.
16 IFRS 3, para. IN11.
17 IFRS 3, para. IN12.
18 IFRS 3, para. IN14.
19 IFRS 3, para. IN15.
20 IFRS 3, para. IN16.
21 *Exposure Draft of Proposed Amendments to IFRS 3 Business Combinations* ('IFRS 3 ED'), IASB, June 2005, para. BC5.
22 IFRS 3 ED, para. BC4.
23 IFRS 3 ED, para. BC7.
24 *Near-final draft of IFRS 3 Business Combinations* ('Near-final IFRS 3R'), IASB, June 2007; *Near-final draft of IAS 27 Consolidated and Separate Financial Statements* ('Near-final IAS 27R'), IASB, June 2007.
25 Near-final IFRS 3R, para. 88; IAS 27, para. 43A.
26 Near-final IFRS 3R, para. B272-B273.
27 IFRS 3 ED, para. BC9.
28 *IASB Work Plan – projected timetable as at 30 September 2007*, IASB.
29 Near-final IFRS 3R, para. B59.
30 IFRS 3, para. 78.
31 IFRS 3, paras. 79-84.
32 IFRS 3, para. 85.
33 IFRS 3, para. 1.
34 IFRS 3, para. 2.
35 IFRS 3, para. 4.
36 IFRS 3, para. 4.
37 IFRS 3, Appendix A.
38 IFRS 3, Appendix A.
39 IFRS 3, para. 4.
40 IFRS 3, para. 4.
41 IFRS 3, para. 5.
42 IFRS 3, para. 6.
43 IFRS 3, para. 7.
44 IFRS 3, para. 8.
45 IFRS 3, para. 3.
46 IFRS 3, para. 14.
47 IFRS 3, para. 15.
48 IFRS 3, para. 39.
49 IFRS 3, Appendix A.
50 IFRS 3, para. 16.
51 IFRS 3, para. 18.
52 IFRS 3, para. 17.
53 IFRS 3, Appendix A.
54 IFRS 3, para. 19.
55 IFRS 3, para. 20.
56 IFRS 3, para. 21.
57 IFRS 3, para. BC59.
58 IFRS 3, para. 21.
59 IFRS 3, para. 22.
60 IFRS 3, para. BC66.
61 IFRS 3, para. 23.
62 *IFRIC Update*, IASB, March 2006, p. 6.
63 IFRS 3, para. 24.
64 IFRS 3, para. BC67.
65 IFRS 3, para. 25.
66 IFRS 3, Appendix A.
67 IFRS 3, para. 26.
68 IAS 39, *Financial Instruments: Recognition and Measurement*, IASB, para. AG77.
69 IFRS 2, *Share-based Payment*, IASB, para. 5.
70 IAS 32, *Financial Instruments: Presentation*, IASB, para. 4.
71 IFRS 3, para. 28.
72 IFRS 3, para. 27.
73 IFRS 3, para. 27.
74 IFRS 3, para. BC69.
75 IFRS 3, para. BC68.
76 IFRS 3, para. 27.
77 IFRS 3, para. 29.
78 IAS 1, *Presentation of Financial Statements*, IASB, para. 32.
79 IFRS 3, para. 30.
80 IFRS 3, para. 31.
81 IFRS 3, para. 33.
82 IFRS 3, para. 32.
83 IFRS 3, para. 33.
84 IFRS 3, para. 33.
85 IFRS 3, para. 34.
86 IFRS 3, para. 35.
87 IFRS 3, para. 35.
88 *Framework for the Preparation and Presentation of Financial Statements*, IASB, para. 35.
89 IFRS 2, para. 5.
90 IAS 32, para. 4.
91 IFRS 3, para. 36.
92 IFRS 3, para. 37.
93 IFRS 3, paras. BC95-BC96.
94 IFRS 3, paras. BC111-BC112.
95 IFRS 3, para. BC117.
96 IFRS 3, para. 38.
97 IFRS 3, para. 40.
98 IFRS 3, para. 41.
99 IFRS 3, para. 41.
100 IFRS 3, paras. BC83-87.
101 IFRS 3, para. BC85.
102 IFRS 3, para. BC85.
103 IFRS 3, paras. BC108-BC110.
104 IFRS 3, para. 43.
105 IFRS 3, para. BC109.

106 IFRS 3, para. 43.
107 IFRS 3, para. BC109.
108 IFRS 3, para. 43.
109 IFRS 3, para. 42.
110 IFRS 3, para. 44.
111 IAS 38, *Intangible Assets*, IASB, para. 34.
112 IFRS 3, para. 45.
113 IAS 38, paras. 33-34.
114 IFRS 3, para. 45.
115 IAS 38, para. 8.
116 IFRS 3, para. 46 and IAS 38, para. 12.
117 IFRS 3, para. 45 and IAS 38, para. 34.
118 IFRS 3, Illustrative Examples, *Examples of items acquired in a business combination that meet the definition of an intangible asset*.
119 IFRS 3, Illustrative Examples, *Customer relationship intangible assets acquired in a business combination*.
120 IFRS 3, para. 45.
121 IAS 38, para. 35.
122 IAS 38, para. 33.
123 IAS 38, para. 35.
124 IFRS 3, paras. BC97-BC101.
125 IAS 38, para. 38.
126 IAS 38, para. 36.
127 IAS 38, para. 37.
128 IFRS 3, para. 45 and IAS 38, para. 34.
129 IAS 38, para. 12.
130 IAS 38, para. 54.
131 IAS 38, para. 57.
132 IAS 38, para. 60.
133 IFRS 3, BC106.
134 IAS 38, para. 42.
135 IAS 38, para. 43.
136 IAS 36, *Impairment of Assets*, IASB, para. 10.
137 IFRS 3, para. 48.
138 IFRS 3, paras. BC114-BC115.
139 IAS 37, *Provisions, Contingent Liabilities and Contingent Assets*, IASB, para. 13.
140 IFRS 3, para. 49.
141 IFRS 3, para. 50.
142 IFRS 3, para. 47.
143 IFRS 3, Appendix A.
144 IFRS 3, para. B17.
145 IFRS 3, para. B16.
146 IFRS 3, para. B16.
147 IFRS 3, para. B16.
148 IFRS 3, para. B16.
149 IFRS 3, para. B16.
150 IFRS 3, para. B16.
151 IAS 38, para. 39.
152 IAS 38, para. 78.
153 IFRS 3, para. B16 and IAS 38, para. 40.
154 IAS 38, para. 40.
155 IAS 38, para. 41.
156 IFRS 3, para. B16.
157 IAS 19, *Employee Benefits*, IASB, para. 108.
158 IFRS 3, para. B16.
159 IFRS 3, para. B16.
160 IFRS 3, para. B16.
161 IFRS 3, para. B16.
162 IAS 37, para. 13.
163 IFRS 3, para. 44.
164 *IFRIC Update*, IASB, May 2007, p. 5.
165 *IASB Update*, IASB, April 2007, pp. 5-6.
166 IFRS 3, para. BC129.
167 IFRS 3, Appendix A.
168 IFRS 3, para. 51.
169 IFRS 3, para. 52.
170 IFRS 3, para. 53.
171 IFRS 3, para. BC130.
172 IFRS 3, paras. BC131-BC135.
173 IFRS 3, para. 56.
174 IFRS 3, para. BC146.
175 IFRS 3, para. BC149.
176 IFRS 3, para. 56.
177 IFRS 3, para. 57.
178 IFRS 3, para. BC148.
179 IFRS 3, paras. BC148-BC156.
180 IFRS 3, para. 61.
181 IFRS 3, para. 62.
182 IFRS 3, para. 62.
183 IFRS 3, para. 62.
184 IFRS 3, para. 63.
185 IFRS 3, para. 63.
186 IFRS 3, para. 64.
187 IFRS 3, para. 65.
188 IFRS 3, para. BC157.
189 IFRS 3, para. 58.
190 IFRS 3, para. 59.
191 IFRS 3, para. 59.
192 IFRS 3, para. 60.
193 IFRS 3, para. 59.
194 IAS 16, *Property, Plant and Equipment*, IASB, para. 41 and IAS 38, para. 87.
195 SFAS 141, *Business Combinations*, FASB, June 2001, para. 14 and Appendix A.
196 *IFRIC Update*, IASB, February 2005, p. 5.
197 IFRS 3, paras. B1-B3.
198 IFRS 3, para. B4.
199 IFRS 3, para. B5.
200 IFRS 3, para. B6.
201 IFRS 3, para. B9.
202 IFRS 3, para. B7.
203 IFRS 3, para. B8.
204 IFRS 3, para. B10.
205 IFRS 3, para. B11.
206 IFRS 3, para. B12.
207 IFRS 3, para. B13.
208 IFRS 3, para. B14.
209 IFRS 3, para. B15.
210 IFRS 3, Appendix A and IAS 27, para. 4.
211 IAS 27, paras. 23 and IG5-IG6.
212 IAS 27, para. IG7.

213 *IFRIC Update*, IASB, May 2006, p. 5.
214 *IFRIC Update*, IASB, July 2006, p. 6.
215 *IFRIC Update*, IASB, July 2006, p. 6.
216 *IFRIC Update*, IASB, November 2006, pp. 8 and 10.
217 IFRS 3, para. BC170.
218 IFRS 3, para. 66.
219 IFRS 3, para. 67.
220 IFRS 3, para. 68.
221 IFRS 3, para. 69.
222 IFRS 3, para. 70.
223 IFRS 3, para. 71.
224 IFRS 3, para. 72.
225 IFRS 3, para. 73.
226 IFRS 3, para. BC175.
227 IFRS 3, para. 77.
228 IAS 7, *Cash Flow Statements*, IASB, paras. 39-42.
229 IFRS 3, para. 10.
230 IFRS 3, para. 13.
231 IFRS 3, para. 13.
232 IFRS 3, para. 12.
233 IFRS 3, para. 12.
234 IFRS 3, para. 11.
235 IAS 31, *Interests in Joint Ventures*, IASB, para. 10.
236 IFRS 3, para. BC28.
237 *IFRIC Update*, IASB, March 2006, p. 6.
238 *IFRIC Update*, IASB, March 2006, p. 6.
239 IAS 8, *Accounting Policies, Changes in Accounting Estimates and Errors*, IASB, para. 10.
240 IAS 8, paras. 11-12.
241 IFRS 3, para. 16.
242 IFRS 3, para. 27.
243 For example, see SFAS 141, paras. D15-D17 and F1; and FRS 6, *Acquisitions and Mergers*, ASB, September 1994, paras. 16-19.
244 IFRS 3, para. 54.
245 IFRS 3, para. 55.
246 IAS 36, paras. 80-81.
247 IFRS 8, *Operating Segments*, IASB, November 2006, para. 5.
248 IAS 36, para. 82.
249 IAS 36, para. BC140.
250 IAS 36, paras. BC143-BC144.
251 IAS 36, para. 83.
252 IAS 36, para. 83.
253 IAS 36, para. 85.
254 IAS 36, para. 84.
255 IAS 36, para. BC152.
256 IAS 36, para. 90.
257 IAS 36, para. BC162.
258 IAS 36, para. 9.
259 IAS 36, para. 90.
260 IAS 36, para. 90.
261 IAS 36, para. 91.
262 IAS 36, para. 92.
263 IAS 36, para. 93.
264 IAS 36, para. 94.
265 IAS 36, para. 96.
266 IAS 36, para. BC172.
267 IAS 36, para. BC173.
268 IAS 36, paras. 97-98.
269 IAS 36, para. 99.
270 IAS 36, para. BC177.
271 IAS 36, para. 90.
272 IAS 36, para. 104.
273 IAS 36, para. 124.
274 IAS 36, para. 125.
275 IAS 36, para. 86.
276 IAS 36, para. BC156.
277 IAS 36, para. 87.
278 IAS 36, paras. 80-81.
279 IFRS 3, para. BC170.
280 IFRS 3, para. 74.
281 IFRS 3, para. 75.
282 IFRS 3, para. 77.
283 IFRS 3, para. 76.
284 IAS 36, para. 133.
285 IFRS 3, para. 78.
286 IFRS 3, para. BC180.
287 IFRS 3, paras. 79-84.
288 IFRS 3, para. 85.
289 IFRS 1, *First-time Adoption of International Financial Reporting Standards*, IASB, para. 15 and Appendix B.
290 IFRS 1, para. IG22.
291 IFRS 1, para. B1.
292 IFRS 1, para. B3.
293 IFRS 1, para. BC32.
294 IFRS 1, paras. BC33-BC34.
295 IFRS 1, para. BC34.
296 IFRS 1, para. B2(a).
297 IFRS 1, para. 15.
298 IFRS 1, para. B2(c).
299 IFRS 1, para. B2(b).
300 IFRS 1, para. B2(b).
301 IFRS 1, IG Example 7.
302 IFRS 1, IG Example 3.
303 IFRS 1, para. B2(d).
304 IFRS 1, para. B2(e).
305 IFRS 1, para. BC36.
306 IFRS 1, para. B2(f).
307 IFRS 1, para. BC35.
308 IFRS 1, IG Example 2.
309 IFRS 1, para. B2(g).
310 IFRS 1, para. B2(g).
311 IFRS 1, para. B2(g).
312 IFRS 1, IG Example 4.
313 IFRS 1, para. IG40.
314 IFRS 1, para. IG41.
315 IFRS 1, para. IG43.
316 IFRS 1, para. BC39.
317 IFRS 1, para. BC38.

318 IFRS 1, para. B2(h).
319 IFRS 1, para. 10.
320 IFRS 1, para. B2(i).
321 IFRS 1, IG Example 5.
322 IFRS 1, para. B2(i).
323 IFRS 1, para. B2(j).
324 IFRS 1, IG Example 6.
325 IFRS 3 ED, para. BC5.
326 IFRS 3 ED, para. BC4.
327 IFRS 3 ED, para. BC7.
328 *Near-final draft of IFRS 3 Business Combinations* ('Near-final IFRS 3R'), IASB, June 2007; *Near-final draft of IAS 27 Consolidated and Separate Financial Statements* ('Near-final IAS 27R'), IASB, June 2007.
329 Near-final IFRS 3R, para. 88; IAS 27, para. 43A.
330 Near-final IFRS 3R, para. B272-B273.
331 IFRS 3 ED, para. BC9.
332 *IASB Work Plan – projected timetable as at 30 September 2007*, IASB.
333 Near-final IFRS 3R, para. B59.
334 Near-final IFRS 3R, para. B60.
335 Near-final IFRS 3R, para. B75-B76.
336 Near-final IFRS 3R, para. B83.
337 Near-final IFRS 3R, para. 2.
338 Near-final IFRS 3R, para. 4.
339 Near-final IFRS 3R, paras. B8-B10.
340 Near-final IFRS 3R, para. 3.
341 Near-final IFRS 3R, para. B11.
342 Near-final IFRS 3R, para. 3.
343 Near-final IFRS 3R, para. A2.
344 Near-final IFRS 3R, para. A3-6.
345 Near-final IFRS 3R, para. A5.
346 Near-final IFRS 3R, para. A7.
347 Near-final IFRS 3R, para. 8.
348 Near-final IFRS 3R, para. B14.
349 Near-final IFRS 3R, para. 9.
350 Near-final IFRS 3R, paras. B84-B85.
351 Near-final IFRS 3R, paras. 10-16.
352 Near-final IFRS 3R, para. B106.
353 Near-final IFRS 3R, paras. A90-A111.
354 Near-final IFRS 3R, para. 3.
355 Near-final IFRS 3R, paras. 17-18.
356 Near-final IFRS 3R, paras. 19, 20, 33 and 34.
357 Near-final IFRS 3R, paras. 19 and 33.
358 Near-final IFRS 3R, para. 22.
359 Near-final IFRS 3R, paras. 27-32 and 35-37.
360 Near-final IFRS 3R, para. 3.
361 Near-final IFRS 3R, paras. 75-78.
362 *IFRIC Update*, IASB, May 2007, p. 5.
363 Near-final IFRS 3R, paras. 24-26.
364 Near-final IFRS 3R, paras. 27-28.
365 Near-final IFRS 3R, para. 29.
366 Near-final IFRS 3R, paras. 28 and 36.
367 Near-final IFRS 3R, para. B155.
368 Near-final IFRS 3R, paras. B180-181.
369 Near-final IFRS 3R, para. 30.
370 Near-final IFRS 3R, paras. A8-A43.
371 Near-final IFRS 3R, para. 35.
372 Near-final IFRS 3R, para. 37.
373 Near-final IFRS 3R, para. 40.
374 Near-final IFRS 3R, para. B275.
375 Near-final IFRS 3R, para. 77.
376 Near-final IFRS 3R, para. B276.
377 IAS 37, para. 33.
378 Near-final IFRS 3R, para. B273.
379 Near-final IFRS 3R, paras. 42 and B281.
380 Near-final IFRS 3R, para. D4 (IAS 12, para. 68).
381 Near-final IFRS 3R, para. D4 (IAS 12, paras. 92-93).
382 Near-final IFRS 3R, para. D4 (IAS 12, para. 32).
383 Near-final IFRS 3R, paras. B302-303.
384 Near-final IFRS 3R, para. 44.
385 Near-final IFRS 3R, para. 78.
386 Near-final IFRS 3R, paras. 45 and B299.
387 Near-final IFRS 3R, paras. 45 and B300.
388 Near-final IFRS 3R, para. 31.
389 Near-final IFRS 3R, para. 46.
390 Near-final IFRS 3R, para. 32.
391 Near-final IFRS 3R, para. 76.
392 Near-final IFRS 3R, para. 48.
393 Near-final IFRS 3R, paras. B305-307.
394 Near-final IFRS 3R, paras. 47 and B311.
395 Near-final IFRS 3R, paras. 49 and B328-B329.
396 Near-final IFRS 3R, para. 54.
397 Near-final IFRS 3R, para. 55.
398 Near-final IFRS 3R, para. 50.
399 Near-final IFRS 3R, para. 56.
400 Near-final IFRS 3R, para. 57.
401 Near-final IFRS 3R, para. B357.
402 Near-final IFRS 3R, para. 79.
403 Near-final IFRS 3R, para. 79.
404 Near-final IFRS 3R, para. 3, 56 and 57.
405 Near-final IFRS 3R, para. 58.
406 Near-final IFRS 3R, para. 59.
407 Near-final IFRS 3R, para. 60.
408 Near-final IFRS 3R, para. A75.
409 Near-final IFRS 3R, para. A76.
410 Near-final IFRS 3R, para. A82-A88.
411 Near-final IFRS 3R, para. 58.
412 Near-final IFRS 3R, paras. 74, B365-B367.
413 Near-final IFRS 3R, para. 74.
414 Near-final IFRS 3R, paras. 72-74 and B370.
415 Near-final IFRS 3R, para. 64.
416 Near-final IFRS 3R, para. 65.
417 Near-final IFRS 3R, para. 50.
418 Near-final IFRS 3R, para. A48.
419 Near-final IFRS 3R, para. 65.
420 Near-final IFRS 3R, para. A49.
421 Near-final IFRS 3R, para. A50-A51.

422 IFRS 3 ED, paras. 49 and 58.
423 Near-final IFRS 3R, paras. B208-B209.
424 Near-final IFRS 3R, para. B212.
425 Near-final IFRS 3R, para. 19.
426 Near-final IFRS 3R, para. 33.
427 Near-final IFRS 3R, para. 38.
428 Near-final IFRS 3R, para. 39.
429 Near-final IFRS 3R, para. B219.
430 Examples 7 and 7A in Near-final IFRS 3R, para. IGA3 are based on the same facts, except for the method used in measuring the non-controlling interest and the recoverable amount of the subsidiary. If Example 7 was based on the same recoverable amount of CU1,650 used in Example 7A, then the impairment loss on the notionally adjusted carrying amount of CU1,850 would be CU200, of which only 80% would be recognised, i.e. CU160. All of which would be attributed to the parent. This is greater than the total impairment loss in Example 7A of CU150, of which only CU120 is attributed to the parent.
If, on the other hand, Example 7A was based on the same recoverable amount of CU1,000 used in Example 7, then the impairment loss would be CU800, of which 80%, i.e. CU640 would be attributed to the parent. Although the overall impairment loss is greater than the CU750 in Example 7, it is less than the amount attributable to the parent of CU680 (CU400 + (80% of CU350)).
431 Near-final IFRS 3R, para. B220.
432 Near-final IFRS 3R, para. D10 (IAS 36, paras. C2-C4) and para. IGA3.
433 Near-final IFRS 3R, para. D10 (IAS 36, paras. C5-C10) and para. IGA3.
434 Near-final IFRS 3R, para. 63.
435 Near-final IFRS 3R, para. B385.
436 Near-final IFRS 3R, para. 63.
437 Near-final IFRS 3R, paras. 51 and 53.
438 Near-final IFRS 3R, para. 52.
439 Near-final IFRS 3R, paras. A52-A54.
440 Near-final IFRS 3R, para. 22.
441 Near-final IFRS 3R, para. 72.
442 Near-final IFRS 3R, paras. 73.
443 Near-final IFRS 3R, paras. A59-A60.
444 Near-final IFRS 3R, para. 73.
445 Near-final IFRS 3R, paras. A59-A88.
446 Near-final IFRS 3R, paras. A61-A67.
447 Near-final IFRS 3R, para. A68.
448 Near-final IFRS 3R, para. A69.
449 Near-final IFRS 3R, paras. A70-A72.
450 Near-final IFRS 3R, para. 66.
451 Near-final IFRS 3R, para. 67.
452 Near-final IFRS 3R, para. 68.
453 Near-final IFRS 3R, para. 69.
454 Near-final IFRS 3R, para. 70.
455 Near-final IFRS 3R, paras. A55-A58.
456 Near-final IFRS 3R, para. 71.
457 Near-final IFRS 3R, paras. B418-421.
458 Near-final IFRS 3R, para. 82(g) and 86(b).
459 Near-final IFRS 3R, para. 82(h).
460 Near-final IFRS 3R, para. 82(m).
461 Near-final IFRS 3R, para. 82(n).
462 Near-final IFRS 3R, para. 82(p).
463 Near-final IFRS 3R, para. 82(q).
464 Near-final IFRS 3R, para. 82(r).
465 Near-final IFRS 3R, para. 86(a).
466 Near-final IFRS 3R, para. B421(n).
467 Near-final IFRS 3R, para. A89.
468 Near-final IFRS 3R, para. 88.
469 Near-final IFRS 3R, para. 89.
470 Near-final IFRS 3R, para. 91.
471 Near-final IFRS 3R, paras. 90 and A112-A113.

Chapter 8 Associates

1 INTRODUCTION

1.1 The origins of equity accounting

As noted in the introduction to Chapter 6, an entity may conduct its business not only directly but also through strategic investments in other entities. IFRS, and most national GAAPs, broadly distinguish three types of such strategic investment:

- entities controlled by the reporting entity (subsidiaries – see Chapter 6);
- entities jointly controlled by the reporting entity and one or more third parties (joint ventures – see Chapter 9); and
- entities that, while not controlled or jointly controlled by the reporting entity, are subject to significant influence by it (associates – the subject of this Chapter).

In the early days of consolidated financial statements, investments in entities which did not satisfy the criteria for classification as subsidiaries were carried at cost, and the revenue from them was recognised only on the basis of dividends received. However, during the 1960s it was recognised that there was a case for an intermediate form of accounting, since there was a growing tendency for groups to conduct part of their activities by taking substantial minority stakes in other entities and exercising a degree of influence over their business which, although falling short of complete control, was nevertheless significant. Mere recognition of dividends was seen to be an inadequate measure of the results of this activity (and one which could be manipulated by the investor, where it could influence the investee's distribution policy). Moreover, since it was unlikely that the investee would fully distribute its earnings, the cost of the investment would give an increasingly unrealistic indication of its underlying value.

This intermediate form of accounting, equity accounting, was first used by the Royal Dutch Shell group in 1964. It involves a modified form of consolidation of the results and assets of investees in the investor's financial statements when the investor exercises 'significant influence', but not control, over the management of the investee. The essence of equity accounting is that, rather than full scale consolidation on a line-by-line basis, it requires incorporation of the investor's share of net assets of the investee in one line in the investor's consolidated balance sheet and the share of its results at only one level of the income statement (although some national standards require equity accounting at more than one level of the income statement).

Another form of 'intermediate consolidation' used by some entities, particularly in certain industries, was proportional consolidation (now referred to under IFRS as 'proportionate' consolidation). As its name implies, this involves including the results and assets and liabilities of an investment on a line-by-line basis, but only to the extent of the investor's share, rather than, as under normal consolidation, in full with credit given for any minority interest. However, under IFRS currently, proportionate consolidation can be adopted only for certain types of joint venture, although the IASB has plans to eliminate the option of proportionate consolidation altogether (see Chapter 9 at 3.3.7).

1.2 Development of IAS 28

Under IFRS accounting for associates is dealt with principally by IAS 28 – *Investments in Associates*. This was originally issued in April 1989 and has since been subject to a number of amendments, most significantly in December 2003 as part of the IASB's improvements project, when the previous version of IAS 28 was withdrawn and replaced by a significantly revised version that became effective for accounting periods beginning on or after 1 January 2005. IAS 28 has been subject to further amendment by IFRSs issued since December 2003.

1.3 Other applicable IFRSs

In addition to IAS 28, the following pronouncements are relevant to accounting for associates:

- IAS 27 – *Consolidated and Separate Financial Statements*;
- IFRS 5 – *Non-current Assets Held for Sale and Discontinued Operations*;
- IAS 1 – *Presentation of Financial Statements*;
- IFRS 1 – *First-time Adoption of International Financial Reporting Standards*; and
- IAS 39 – *Financial Instruments: Recognition and Measurement*.

2 SCOPE OF IAS 28

2.1 General

IAS 28 must be applied in accounting for investments in associates (see 2.2 below). However, it does not apply to investments in associates held by:

(a) venture capital organisations, or
(b) mutual funds, unit trusts and similar entities including investment-linked insurance funds

that upon initial recognition are designated as financial assets 'at fair value through profit or loss' or are classified as financial assets held for trading and accounted for in accordance with IAS 39. Such investments are measured at fair value in accordance with IAS 39, with changes in fair value recognised in profit or loss in the period of the change (see Chapter 20).[1] This exemption is discussed further at 2.1.1 below.

A venturer with an interest in a jointly controlled entity within the scope of IAS 31 – *Interests in Joint Ventures* (see Chapter 9) that elects (as permitted by IAS 31) to account for that interest using the equity method should comply with the requirements of IAS 28 relating to the equity method of accounting (see 3 below).[2]

2.1.1 Exemption for venture capital organisations and similar entities

The exemption for venture capital organisations and other similar financial institutions raises a number of questions of interpretation. The first is exactly what entities comprise those described in (a) and (b) in 2.1 above, since they are not defined in IAS 28 – a deliberate decision by the IASB given the difficulty of crafting a definition.[3] The experience of similar exemptions in some national GAAPs has been that it can be difficult to limit precisely the entities to which they apply. The IASB no doubt hopes that preparers and their auditors can be relied upon not to abuse the scope of the exemption without the need for further intervention.

As discussed more fully in Chapter 6 at 5.1, IAS 27 does not exempt venture capital organisations and other similar financial institutions from consolidating investments in subsidiaries, a source of some controversy during the exposure period of the IASB's improvements project standard (which included the revised versions of IAS 27 and IAS 28).

A Application of IAS 39 to associates exempt from IAS 28

The reason for introducing the exemption was that the IASB considered that for venture capital organisations, mutual funds, unit trusts and similar entities the application of the equity method often produces information that is not relevant to their management and investors. As they often manage their investments on the basis of fair values, the application of IAS 39 would produce more relevant information. Furthermore, the financial statements would be less useful if changes in the level of ownership in an investment resulted in frequent changes in the method of accounting for the investment.[4] 3i Group plc applies this exemption as illustrated in the extract below.

Extract 8.1: 3i Group plc (2007)

Significant accounting policies [extract]

C Basis of consolidation [extract]

(ii) Associates [extract]

Associates are those entities in which the Group has significant influence, but not control, over the financial and operating policies. Investments that are held as part of the Group's investment portfolio are carried in the balance sheet at fair value even though the Group may have significant influence over those companies. This treatment is permitted by IAS 28 Investment in Associates, which requires investments held by venture capital organisations to be excluded from its scope where those investments are designated, upon initial recognition, as at fair value through profit or loss and accounted for in accordance with IAS 39, with changes in fair value recognised in the income statement in the period of the change. The Group has no interests in associates through which it carries on its business.

I Venture capital organisations with a mix of activities

The exemption clearly applies to venture capital organisations and other similar financial institutions whose main activities consist of managing an investment portfolio comprising investments unrelated to the investor's business. Although the exemption is not intended to apply to trading companies that hold investments in a number of associates, there are cases in which entities have significant venture capital activities as well as significant trading activities. In those cases the entity should consider whether:[5]

- the venture capital activities are managed separately on the basis of fair values; and
- there are frequent changes in the level of ownership of investments.

In making this assessment it is not relevant whether or not a venture capital activity is contained within a separate legal entity. Rather, the venture capital activity needs to be a separate part of the organisation – with its own objectives – that manages its investment portfolio.

Example 8.1: Entity owning a discrete venture capital organisation

Parent P operates a construction business and owns a venture capital organisation (subsidiary V) that invests in the telecommunications industry. Even though P itself is not a venture capital organisation, subsidiary V would be able to apply the exemption and account for its investments at fair value under IAS 39. In the consolidated accounts of P, the investments held by V would also be accounted for at fair value under IAS 39.

Example 8.2: Entity owning an integrated venture capital organisation

Parent P is a software company and owns a venture capital organisation (subsidiary V) that invests in the software industry. Subsidiary V provides advisory services to some of its investees and is sometimes has significant involvement in management of the investees. As both P and V are active in the software industry, the activities of V may not be entirely separate from P. In addition, the activities of V in relation to its investments go beyond those of an ordinary investor. For those reasons the exemption from application of the equity method may not be available to V.

HSBC is an example of a large bank that reports an interest in an associate that it holds as part of its venture capital activities.

Extract 8.2: HSBC Holdings plc (2006)

Notes on the Financial Statements [extract]

24 Investments in subsidiaries [extract]

Investments where HSBC owns 20 per cent or more of the voting rights but does not classify the investment as a subsidiary, joint venture or associate

Investment	**HSBC's interest in equity capital**	**Description of relationship that results in HSBC accounting for entity as an investment**
2005	%	
Zhong-Run Company Limited	25.0	Entity is held by a venture capital organisation which is exempt from classifying investments as associates under IAS 28.

In 2006 there were no significant investments where HSBC owned 20 per cent or more of the voting rights but did not classify the investment as a subsidiary, joint venture or associate.

II Designation of investments as 'at fair value through profit or loss'

As noted above, venture capital organisations and other similar financial institutions which use the exemption in IAS 28 for their investments in associates are required to apply IAS 39 to those investments. The exemption is available only where the associates are either (as defined under IAS 39) held for trading, or, if not, are designated upon initial recognition as investments to be accounted for 'at fair value through profit or loss' under IAS 39.[6] Designation at a later date is not possible. Whilst IAS 28 does not say so explicitly, we consider that such designation is irrevocable, as there is no provision in IAS 39 for investments that have been designated in this way to be subsequently de-designated.

IAS 28 does not explicitly require venture capital organisations and other similar financial institutions consistently to designate all their associates (other than those defined as held for trading) as 'at fair value through profit or loss' under IAS 39. However, such entities need to balance the free choice apparently given by IAS 28 with the requirement of IAS 8 – *Accounting Policies, Changes in Accounting Estimates and Errors* – for the adoption of consistent accounting policies for similar transactions. The freedom of choice may have been given so as to allow such entities to apply IAS 39 to their own portfolio investments but to apply IAS 28 to any strategic investments in similar entities which act as an extension of their own business.

The recognition, measurement and disclosure requirements of IAS 39 for items classified as held for trading or designated as at fair value through profit or loss are discussed in Chapters 17, 20 and 22.

III Availability of fair value information

In the Basis for Conclusion of IAS 28 the IASB states that fair value information is often readily available because fair value measurement is a well-established practice in these industries including for investments in entities in the early stages of their development or in non-listed entities.[7] However, designation of investments as 'at fair value through profit or loss' is prohibited under IAS 39 for investments in equity instruments that (1) do not have a quoted market price in an active market and (2) for which the range of reasonable fair value estimates is significant and the probabilities of the various estimates cannot be reasonably assessed.[8] If reliable fair value information is not available the equity method should be applied.

IV Disclosure of interests in associates

An entity accounting for an interest in an associate using IAS 39 should still apparently disclose the information required by IAS 28 (see 5.2.1 below). This is because IAS 32 – *Financial Instruments: Disclosure and Presentation* – and IFRS 7 – *Financial Instruments: Disclosures* – specifically call for the IAS 28 disclosures to be made in addition to the disclosures required by the standards themselves,[9] despite the fact that, as indicated at 2.1 above, IAS 28 does not apply to the entity.

In May 2007, the IASB tentatively decided to deal with this inconsistency by deleting the general IAS 28 disclosure requirements from IAS 32 and IFRS 7 for associates that are accounted for at fair value through profit or loss, but to retain the disclosure in paragraph 37(f) of IAS 28 regarding restrictions on the ability of associates to transfer funds to the investor.[10] An exposure containing this amendment is expected to be published in October 2007.

2.2 Definition of 'associate' and related terms

An *associate* is an entity, including an unincorporated entity such as a partnership, over which the investor has significant influence and that is neither a subsidiary nor an interest in a joint venture (see below).[11]

A *subsidiary* is an entity, including an unincorporated entity such as a partnership, that is controlled by another entity (known as the parent). *Control* is the power to govern the financial and operating policies of an entity so as to obtain benefits from its activities.[12] Although IFRS does not define what financial and operating policies are, these are generally presumed to include areas such as budgeting, capital expenditures, treasury management, dividend policy, production, marketing, sales and human resources. The definitions of 'subsidiary' and 'control' are the same as those in IAS 27 and are discussed in more detail in Chapter 6 at 3.

IAS 28 does not define *joint venture*, but the definition in IAS 31 is presumably intended to apply, namely a contractual arrangement whereby two or more parties undertake an economic activity that is subject to joint control.[13] *Joint control* is defined by IAS 28, albeit in the same terms as IAS 31, as contractually agreed sharing of control over an economic activity, which exists only when the strategic financial and operating decisions relating to the activity require the unanimous consent of the parties sharing control (the venturers).[14] The definitions of joint venture and joint control are discussed in more detail in Chapter 9 at 2.2.

Significant influence is the power to participate in the financial and operating policy decisions of the investee but is not control or joint control over those policies,[15] and is discussed further at 2.2.1 below.

2.2.1 Significant influence

Under IAS 28, a holding of 20% or more of the voting power of the investee is presumed to give rise to significant influence, unless it can be clearly demonstrated that this is not the case. Conversely, a holding of less than 20% of the voting power is presumed not to give rise to significant influence, unless it can be clearly demonstrated that there is in fact significant influence. The existence of a substantial or majority interest of another investor does not necessarily preclude the investor from having significant influence.[16] In calculating the interest of a group, account should be taken of shares held directly by the parent and those held indirectly through subsidiaries, but holdings by other associates or joint ventures of the group are ignored.[17] However, an entity should consider both ordinary shares and other categories of shares in determining its voting rights.

IAS 28 states that the exercise of significant influence will usually be evidenced in one or more of the following ways:

(a) representation on the board of directors or equivalent governing body of the investee;

(b) participation in policy-making processes, including participation in decisions about dividends and other distributions;

(c) material transactions between the investor and the investee;

(d) interchange of managerial personnel; or

(e) provision of essential technical information.[18]

An entity loses significant influence over an investee when it loses the power to participate in the financial and operating policy decisions of that investee. The loss of significant influence can occur with or without a change in absolute or relative ownership levels. It could occur as a result of a contractual agreement. It could also occur, for example, when an associate becomes subject to the control of a government, court, administrator or regulator.[19] Loss of significant influence may therefore be an indicator of impairment also.

In some jurisdictions entities are able to seek protection from creditors without this resulting in the appointment of an administrator (e.g. under Chapter 11 of the Bankruptcy Code in the United States). Instead, existing management is given more time to reorganise the entity while enjoying protection from creditors. An investor in such an entity could still be able to exercise significant influence over the financial and operating policies.

Many of the factors relevant in assessing whether or not significant influence exists over another entity are also relevant to an assessment of whether control exists. Accordingly much of the implementation guidance to IAS 27 (discussed in Chapter 6 at 3.1) is also relevant to associates accounted for under IAS 28.[20]

In particular, IAS 27 notes that the reference to 'power' in the definition of 'significant influence' above means the ability to do or affect something. Consequently, an entity has significant influence over another entity when it currently has the ability to exercise that power, regardless of whether significant influence is actively demonstrated or is passive in nature.[21] Passive significant influence may be exercised over another entity through potential voting rights (see D below).

A Lack of significant influence

The presumption of significant influence may sometimes be overcome in the following circumstances:

- the investor has failed to obtain representation on the investee's board of directors;
- the investee is opposing the investor's attempts to exercise significant influence;
- the investor is unable to obtain timely financial information or cannot obtain more information – required to apply the equity method – than shareholders that do not have significant influence; or
- a group of shareholders that holds the majority ownership of the investee operates without regard to the views of the investor.

B Holdings of less than 20% of the voting power

As noted above, there is a presumption that an investor that holds less than 20% of the voting power in an investee cannot exercise significant influence.[22] In our view, however, investments that give rise to only slightly less than 20% of the voting rights (e.g. 19.9% of the voting rights) should also generally be presumed to give rise to significant influence.

In some cases an investor may have an investment that gives rise to significantly less than 20% of the voting power. The investor may still be able to exercise significant influence in the following circumstances:

- the investor's voting power is much larger than that of any other shareholder of the investee;
- the corporate governance arrangements may be such that the investor is able to appoint members to the board, supervisory board or significant committees of the investee; or
- the investor has the power to veto significant financial and operating decisions. Determining which policies are significant requires considerable judgement.

Extract 8.3: GlaxoSmithKline plc (2006)

Notes to the financial statements [extract]

18 Investments in associates and joint ventures [extract]

The principal associated undertaking is Quest Diagnostics Inc. a US clinical laboratory business listed on the New York Stock Exchange. The investment had a book value at 31st December 2006 of £262 million (2005 – £244 million) and a market value of £987 million (2005 – £1,093 million).

At 31st December 2006, the Group owned 18.7% of Quest (2005 – 18.4%). Although the Group holds less than 20% of the ownership interest and voting control in Quest, the Group has the ability to exercise significant influence through both its significant shareholding and its nominated director's active participation on the Quest Board of Directors and Board sub-committees.

C *Holdings of more than 50% of the voting power*

Control is presumed to exist under IAS 27 when the parent owns, directly or indirectly through subsidiaries, more than half of the voting power of an entity unless, in exceptional circumstances, it can be clearly demonstrated that such ownership does not constitute control (see Chapter 6 at 3.1.1).[23] An investor that does not have control despite holding more than 50% of the voting power, will typically be able to exercise significant influence and treat the investee as an associate.

Extract 8.4: BP p.l.c. (2005)

Accounting policies [extract]

Interests in associates [extract]

An associate is an entity over which the group is in a position to exercise significant influence through participation in the financial and operating policy decisions of the investee, but which is not a subsidiary or a jointly controlled entity.

51 Subsidiaries, jointly controlled entities and associates [extract]

...

Associates	%	Country of incorporation	Principal activities
Abu Dhabi			
Abu Dhabi Marine Areas	37	England	Crude oil production
Abu Dhabi Petroleum Co.	24	England	Crude oil production
Azerbaijan			
The Baku-Tbilisi-Ceyhan Pipeline Co.	30	Cayman Islands	Pipelines
Korea			
Samsung Petrochemical Co.	47	England	Petrochemicals
Taiwan			
China American Petrochemical Co.	61	Taiwan	Petrochemicals
Trinidad and Tobago			
Atlantic LNG Company of Trinidad and Tobago	34	Trinidad and Tobago	LNG manufacture
Atlantic LNG 2/3 Company of Trinidad and Tobago	43	Trinidad and Tobago	LNG manufacture

D *Potential voting rights*

An entity may own share warrants, share call options, debt or equity instruments that are convertible into ordinary shares, or other similar instruments that have the potential, if exercised or converted, to give the entity voting power or reduce another party's voting power over the financial and operating policies of another entity (potential voting rights).[24]

IAS 28 requires an entity to consider the existence and effect of potential voting rights that are currently exercisable or convertible, including potential voting rights held by another entity, when assessing whether an entity has significant influence over the financial and operating policies of another entity.[25]

Potential voting rights are not currently exercisable or convertible when they cannot be exercised or converted until a future date or until the occurrence of a future event.[26]

IAS 28 adds some further points of clarification. In assessing whether potential voting rights contribute to significant influence, an entity must examine all facts and circumstances (including the terms of exercise of the potential voting rights and any other contractual arrangements whether considered individually or in combination) that affect potential voting rights, except the intention of management and the financial ability to exercise or convert.[27]

The implementation guidance in IAS 27[28] elaborates on the above requirements in some detail, and reference should be made to the further discussion in Chapter 6 at 3.1.2.

E Voting rights held in a fiduciary capacity

Voting rights on shares held as security remain the rights of the provider of the security, and are generally not taken into account if the rights are only exercisable in accordance with instructions from the provider of the security or in his interest. Similarly, voting rights that are held in a fiduciary capacity may not be those of the entity itself. However, if voting rights are held by a nominee on behalf of the entity, they should be taken into account.

F Long-term restrictions over associate's ability to transfer funds to investor

Previous versions of IAS 28 contained an exemption from applying the equity method in accounting for an associate when severe long-term restrictions impaired an associate's ability to transfer funds to the investor. This exemption no longer applies.[29] The IASB indicates that it removed the exemption because such restrictions may not in fact affect the investor's significant influence over the associate. Whilst an investor should, when assessing its ability to exercise significant influence over an entity, consider restrictions on the transfer of funds from the associate to the investor, such restrictions do not in themselves preclude the exercise of significant influence.[30]

However, the nature and extent of any significant restrictions on the ability of associates to transfer funds to the investor in the form of cash dividends, or repayment of loans or advances should be disclosed (see 5.2 below).[31]

2.3 Requirement to apply the equity method

An investment in an associate must be accounted for using the equity method (see 3 below), except when:[32]

(a) the investment is classified as held for sale in accordance with IFRS 5,[33] in which case it is accounted for under that standard (see 2.3.1 below);

(b) the reporting entity is a parent (i.e. an entity with one or more subsidiaries)[34] exempt from preparing consolidated financial statements under IAS 27 (see Chapter 6 at 4.1); or

(c) all of the following apply:

(i) the investor is a wholly-owned subsidiary, or is a partially-owned subsidiary of another entity and its other owners, including those not otherwise entitled to vote, have been informed about, and do not object to, the investor not applying the equity method;

(ii) the investor's debt or equity instruments are not traded in a public market (a domestic or foreign stock exchange or an over-the-counter market, including local and regional markets);

(iii) the investor did not file, nor is it in the process of filing, its financial statements with a securities commission or other regulatory organisation, for the purpose of issuing any class of instruments in a public market; and

(iv) the ultimate or any intermediate parent of the investor produces consolidated financial statements available for public use that comply with International Financial Reporting Standards.

Exemption (c) above will apply only where the investor in an associate is not also a parent. If it is a parent, it must look to the similar exemption from preparation of consolidated financial statements in IAS 27 (see Chapter 6 at 4). In fact, however, the conditions (i) to (iv) in (c) above are identical to the criteria that must be satisfied by a parent in order to be exempt from preparing consolidated financial statements under IAS 27. Further discussion of the meaning and interpretation of these conditions may be found in Chapter 6 at 4.1.

The exemption in (c) above is available only to entities that are themselves either wholly-owned subsidiaries or whose minority shareholders consent to the presentation of financial statements that do not include associates using the equity method. Some of these 'intermediate' entities will not be exempt, for example if none of their parent companies prepares consolidated financial statements in accordance with IFRS. A typical example is that of an entity that is a subsidiary of a US group that prepares consolidated accounts in accordance with US GAAP only. In addition, any entity that has publicly traded debt or equity, or is in the process of obtaining a listing for such instruments, will not satisfy the criteria for exemption.

The effect of the above requirements is that a reporting entity that has associates, but no subsidiaries, and does not meet all the criteria above, is required to apply equity accounting for its associates in its own (non-consolidated) financial statements (not to be confused with its 'separate financial statements' – see 2.4 below). This may be a significant change from many national GAAPs, where equity accounting for associates is required (or indeed permitted) only in consolidated financial statements.

As drafted, IAS 28 *requires*, rather than merely permits, an investor that meets the criteria in (b) or (c) above not to apply equity accounting. By contrast, the equivalent exemptions in IAS 27 (see Chapter 6 at 4) and IAS 31 (see Chapter 9 at 2.3) are drafted so as to be permissive rather than compulsory. We take the view that this was an unintentional drafting error, and that the exemption from equity accounting in IAS 28 is intended to be optional, not compulsory.

2.3.1 Associates held for sale

IAS 28 requires an investment in an associate to be accounted for under IFRS 5 and classified as held for sale if its carrying amount will be recovered principally through a sale transaction rather than through continuing use.[35] Although the introduction to IAS 28 still makes reference to disposals within twelve months of acquisition,[36] the corresponding guidance in the standard has been superseded by IFRS 5. The detailed IFRS requirements for classification as held for sale are discussed in Chapter 4 at 2.1.2.

From the date that an associate is classified as held for sale the investor ceases to apply the equity method, instead the associate is then measured at the lower of its carrying amount and fair value less cost to sell.[37] The measurement requirements as set out in IFRS 5 are discussed in detail in Chapter 4 at 2.2.

When an investment in an associate no longer meets the criteria to be classified as held for sale, it should be accounted for under the equity method from the date of its classification as held for sale. The financial statements of any prior periods since that classification must be restated.[38] The reason for requiring such restatement is not entirely clear (after all, the change in circumstances will often be the result of a non-adjusting event after the balance sheet date), but it may well be intended to avoid abuse.

2.4 Separate financial statements

Separate financial statements are defined by IAS 28, consistent with IAS 27, as those presented by a parent, an investor in an associate or a venturer in a jointly controlled entity, in which the investments are accounted for on the basis of the direct equity interest rather than on the basis of the reported results and net assets of the investees.[39] IAS 27 requires that, in separate financial statements, investments in associates that are not classified as held for sale (or included in a disposal group that is classified as held for sale) in accordance with IFRS 5 should be accounted for either:[40]

- at cost;[41] or
- in accordance with IAS 39.

The detailed IFRS requirements for separate financial statements are set out in IAS 27[42] and are discussed more fully in Chapter 6 at 7.

It follows from the definition of separate financial statements above that financial statements (including non-consolidated financial statements) in which the equity method is applied are not separate financial statements; neither are the financial statements of an entity that does not have a subsidiary, associate or venturer's interest in a joint venture.[43]

Separate financial statements are financial statements presented in addition to:[44]

- consolidated financial statements;
- financial statements in which investments are accounted for using the equity method; and

- financial statements in which venturers' interests in joint ventures are proportionately consolidated.

There is no requirement for any entity to prepare separate financial statements, or for any separate financial statements that are voluntarily prepared to be appended to, or accompany, the 'main' financial statements.[45]

An entity may present separate financial statements as its only financial statements if it satisfies the conditions for exemption from:[46]

- preparing consolidated financial statements under paragraph 10 of IAS 27 (see Chapter 6 at 4.1);
- equity accounting for associates under paragraph 13(c) of IAS 28 (see (c) under 2.3 above); and
- proportionately consolidating (or equity accounting for) jointly controlled entities under paragraph 2 of IAS 31 (see Chapter 9 at 2.4).

As drafted, this exemption makes a curious distinction between an entity with associates and one with jointly controlled entities only.

An entity with associates may prepare separate financial statements as its only financial statements only if it satisfies the exemption in 'paragraph 13(c)' of IAS 28. In other words, if an entity has associates, but is exempt from equity accounting for all of them under paragraph 13(a) – i.e. because they are all accounted for under IFRS 5 – it may apparently not present separate financial statements as its only financial statements. However, an entity with jointly controlled entities may prepare separate financial statements as its only financial statements if it satisfies the exemption in 'paragraph 2' of IAS 31, which includes jointly controlled entities accounted for under IFRS 5.

In our view, it can be assumed that this inconsistency was unintentional, but it is less obvious as to which exemption is correct and which incorrect. On balance, our view is that it is the exemption in relation to joint ventures which is incorrect. In other words, the IASB intended to give the exemption only to 'non-public interest' companies and should have referred to 'paragraph 2(c)' of IAS 31.

3 APPLICATION OF THE EQUITY METHOD

3.1 Overview

IAS 28 defines the equity method as 'a method of accounting whereby the investment is initially recorded at cost and adjusted thereafter for the post acquisition change in the investor's share of net assets of the investee. The profit or loss of the investor includes the investor's share of the results of operations of the investee.'[47] Distributions received from an investee reduce the carrying amount of the investment. Adjustments to the carrying amount may also be necessary for changes in the investor's proportionate interest in the investee arising from changes in the investee's equity that have not been recognised in the investee's profit or loss. Such changes include those arising from the revaluation of property, plant and equipment and from foreign exchange translation differences. The investor's share of any such changes is recognised directly in equity of the investor.[48]

Example 8.3: Application of the equity method

On 1 January 2008 entity A acquires a 35% interest in entity B, over which it is able to exercise significant influence. Entity A paid €475,000 for its interest in B. At that date the book value of B's net assets was €900,000, and their fair value €1,100,000, the difference of €200,000 relates entirely to an item of property, plant and equipment with a remaining useful life of 10 years. During the year B made a profit of €80,000 and paid a dividend of €120,000 on 31 December 2008. Entity B also owned an investment in securities classified as available-for-sale that increased in value by €20,000 during the year.

Entity A accounts for its investment in B under the equity method as follows:

	€	€
Acquisition of investment in B		
Share in book value of B's net assets: 35% of €900,000	315,000	
Share in fair valuation of B's net assets: 35% of (€1,100,000 – €900,000) *	70,000	
Goodwill on investment in B: €475,000 – €315,000 – €70,000	90,000	
Cost of investment		475,000
Profit during the year		
Share in the profit reported by B: 35% of €80,000	28,000	
Adjustment to reflect effect of fair valuation *		
35% of ((€1,100,000 – €900,000) ÷ 10 years)	(7,000)	
Share of profit in B recognised in income by A		21,000
Revaluation of available-for-sale asset		
Share in revaluation recognised in equity by A: 35% of €20,000		7,000
Dividend received by A during the year		(42,000)
Share in book value of B's net assets:		
€315,000 + 35% (€80,000 – €120,000 + €20,000)	308,000	
Share in fair valuation of B's net assets: €70,000 – €7,000 *	63,000	
Goodwill on investment in B	90,000	
Closing balance of A's investment in B		461,000

* These line items are normally not presented separately, but are combined with the ones immediately above.

IAS 28 explains that equity accounting is necessary because to recognise income simply on the basis of distributions received may not be an adequate measure of the income earned by an investor on an investment in an associate, since distributions received may bear little relation to the performance of the associate. Through its significant influence over the associate, the investor has an interest in the associate's performance and, as a result, the return on its investment. The investor accounts for this interest by extending the scope of its financial statements so as to include its share of profits or losses of such an associate. As a result, application of the equity method provides more informative reporting of the net assets and profit or loss of the investor.[49]

3.2 Similarities of equity accounting and consolidation

IAS 28 notes that many procedures appropriate for the application of the equity method, and described in more detail in 3.3 to 3.8 below, are similar to the consolidation procedures described in IAS 27 (see Chapter 6 at 6). Furthermore the concepts underlying the procedures used in accounting for the acquisition of a subsidiary are also adopted in accounting for the acquisition of an investment in an associate.[50]

In particular, on acquisition of an investment in an associate, any difference between the cost of the investment and the investor's share of the net fair value of the associate's identifiable assets, liabilities and contingent liabilities is accounted for in accordance with IFRS 3 – *Business Combinations* (see Chapter 7 at 2.3.3). This has the effect that:

- Goodwill relating to an associate is included in the carrying amount of the investment (and not as a separate item, as would be the case in respect of goodwill relating to the acquisition of a subsidiary). Amortisation of that goodwill is not permitted and is therefore not included in the determination of the investor's share of the associate's profits or losses (see 4.2 below);
- Any excess of the investor's share of the net fair value of the associate's identifiable assets, liabilities and contingent liabilities over the cost of the investment is excluded from the carrying amount of the investment and is instead included as income in the determination of the investor's share of the associate's profit or loss in the period in which the investment is acquired.

IAS 28 states that appropriate adjustments to the investor's share of the associate's profits or losses after acquisition are also made to account, for example, for depreciation of the depreciable assets based on their fair values at the acquisition date. Similarly, appropriate adjustments to the investor's share of the associate's profits or losses after acquisition are made for impairment losses recognised by the associate, such as for goodwill or property, plant and equipment (see 4.1 below).[51]

However, an investor will not necessarily simply recognise impairment losses in respect of an associate equivalent to its share of the impairment losses recognised by the associate itself (even after fair value and other consolidation adjustments). This is discussed further at 4 below.

Moreover, it may be necessary to make adjustments for transactions between the investor and its associates (see 3.4 below).

3.2.1 *Differences between equity accounting and consolidation*

An investor that controls a subsidiary has control over the assets and liabilities of that subsidiary. While an investor that has significant influence over an associate controls its holding in the shares of the associate, it does not control the assets and liabilities of that associate. Therefore, the investor does not account for the assets and the liabilities of the associate, but only accounts for its investment in the associate as a whole. This subtle difference means, for example, that an investor cannot capitalise its own borrowing costs in respect of an associate's assets under construction (an investment in an associate is not a qualifying asset under IAS 23 – *Borrowing Costs* – regardless of the associate's activities or assets). Similarly, difficulties would arise if an investor wanted to designate a financial instrument as a hedge of an associate's transactions, assets or liabilities (see Chapter 9 at 3.3.2 A III for more details).

3.2.2 Piecemeal acquisition of an associate

A Step increase in an existing associate

Accounting for an increase of an interest in an associate is not specifically addressed by IAS 28. However, that standard does require the requirements of IFRS 3 to be applied in accounting for the acquisition of an investment in an associate.[52] IFRS 3 acknowledges that before qualifying as a business combination, a transaction may qualify as an investment in an associate and be accounted for in accordance with IAS 28, which means that the fair values of the investee's identifiable net assets at the date of each earlier exchange transaction should have been determined previously in applying the equity method to the investment.[53] This means that a step-by-step comparison of the cost of the individual investments with the acquirer's interest in the fair values of the acquiree's identifiable assets, liabilities and contingent liabilities at each step is required.[54] The requirement in IFRS 3 to revalue previously held interests of the investor to fair value only applies when the investor obtains control over the investment.[55] Therefore, in our view, when an additional interest is acquired in an associate that continues to be accounted for under the equity method, the existing interest in the associate should not be remeasured to take into account previously unrecognised changes in the fair value of the investor's share in the identifiable net assets.

B Financial instrument becoming an associate

A step acquisition also arises when an entity gains significant influence over an existing investment upon acquisition of a further interest or due to a change in circumstances. IAS 28 is unclear on how an investor should account for an existing investment, which is accounted for under IAS 39, that subsequently becomes an associate that should be accounted for under the equity method. In practice, there are three acceptable methods that are explained below. However, in our view Method A is most consistent with the principles underlying the equity method of accounting – namely, applying consolidation and business combination principles as well as accounting for the investor's share of associate's results after the date of acquisition. Nevertheless, there is also some support within IAS 28 for methods B and C. The method that an entity selects should however be applied consistently.

I Method A

Method A requires the investor to revert to its original cost and then recognise a 'catch up' equity method adjustment for its share of post acquisition profits and reserves since the original acquisition date. Dividend income continues to be recognised in the income statement up to the date the entity becomes an associate.

IAS 28 notes that the concepts underlying the procedures used in accounting for the acquisition of a subsidiary should also be adopted in accounting for the acquisition of an associate.[56] Furthermore, the standard notes that 'on acquisition of the investment any difference between the cost of the investment and the investor's share of the net fair value of the associate's identifiable assets, liabilities and contingent liabilities is accounted for in accordance with IFRS 3'.[57] Although IFRS 3 only deals with business combinations that are achieved in stages, it does contain guidance that can be applied by analogy.[58] In particular, it notes that cost should be determined at the date of each exchange transaction irrespective of the fact that the carrying amount has changed. Example 6 in IFRS 3's Illustrative Examples shows that the post-acquisition changes in *retained earnings* relating to each 'tranche' of a step acquisition should be included in retained earnings rather than being eliminated.[59] Therefore, on initial application of the equity method it is appropriate to recognise the investor's share of the investee's earnings on the existing tranches of its investment. This adjustment will, by necessity, be net of dividend income already recorded. This approach is consistent with the description of the equity method in paragraph 11 of IAS 28.

Example 6 in IFRS 3's Illustrative Examples also shows that that the post-acquisition changes in *fair value* relating to each tranche are also included in equity rather than being eliminated.[60]

Similarly, goodwill is also calculated separately for each tranche in accordance with IFRS 3.[61] IAS 22 – *Business Combinations* – specifically required that when an investment 'did not qualify previously as an associate, the fair values of the identifiable assets and liabilities are determined as at the date of each significant step and goodwill or negative goodwill is recognised from the date of acquisition'.[62] Although an identical requirement does not appear in IFRS 3, its basis for conclusions indicates that the requirements of IAS 22 dealing with step acquisitions were not intended to be changed.[63] Therefore, we consider it appropriate to determine the fair values as at the date of each individual acquisition.

II Method B

Method B requires the investor to revert to its original cost, but not to recognise a 'catch up' adjustment. Dividend income continues to be recognised in the income statement up to the date the entity becomes an associate.

This method uses the same underlying logic as method A for determining cost and goodwill. However, IAS 28 states that 'an investment in an associate is accounted for using the equity method from the date on which it becomes an associate'.[64] To avoid contradicting this specific requirement in IAS 28, method B does not recognise a cumulative adjustment for prior periods.

However, it should be emphasised that if the ownership interest increases further and the investment becomes a subsidiary, the full step acquisition guidance of IFRS 3 would apply, hence the cumulative results that are ignored by method B would need to be recognised at that point.

III Method C

Method C uses fair value as deemed cost and does not require recognition of a 'catch up' adjustment. Dividend income continues to be recognised in the income statement up to the date the entity becomes an associate. This may be a pragmatic approach where it is difficult to obtain the information required for the other methods.

Under IAS 28 an investor should 'discontinue the use of the equity method from the date that it ceases to have significant influence over an associate and [should] account for the investment in accordance with IAS 39 from that date, provided the associate does not become a subsidiary or a joint venture as defined in IAS 31.[65] In addition, the 'carrying amount of the investment at the date that it ceases to be an associate shall be regarded as its cost on initial measurement as a financial asset in accordance with IAS 39'.[66] As IAS 28 is not clear as to how cost is determined in a step acquisition, it could be argued that the above guidance could be applied by analogy. Thus, if an investment changes from an investment to an associate it is also appropriate to take its carrying value as its deemed cost.

Similar to method B, if the ownership interest increases further and the investment becomes a subsidiary, the full step acquisition guidance of IFRS 3 would apply, hence the cumulative results that are ignored by method C will have to be recognised at that point. Likewise, any fair value adjustments that are not reversed should be reversed at that point.

IV Practical example

The application of methods A, B and C is illustrated in the example below.

Example 8.4: Accounting for existing financial instruments on the step-acquisition of an associate

In 2005, an investor acquired a 10% interest in an investee for $100. Three years later, in 2008, the investor acquired a further 15% interest in the investee for $225. The investor now holds a 25% interest and is able to exercise significant influence.

The investor had been accounting for its initial 10% interest at fair value in accordance with IAS 39. The financial information relating to the investee can be summarised as follows:

	2005		**2008**	
	100%	**10%**	**100%**	**15%**
	$	*$*	*$*	*$*
Purchase consideration		100		225
Change in fair value		50		
Fair value of shares in 2008		150		
Book value of net assets of investee	600		900	
Fair value of net assets of investee *)	800	80	1,200	180
Profit since acquisition in 2005	500	50		
Dividends declared between 2005 and 2008	–200	–20		
Increase in fair value of net assets of investee	100	10		
Cost plus post-acquisition changes in net assets		140		
Other changes in fair value of the investee		10		

*) The fair value uplift from $600 to $800 entirely relates to non-depreciable assets.

How should the investor account for the acquisition of the additional 15% interest?

Method A

Under this method, cost is the sum of the consideration paid for the two tranches. Therefore, the investor should account for the following:

- If the original investment had been fair valued through profit or loss, the change in fair value previously recognised through profit or loss (excluding dividend income) is reversed through retained earnings to bring the asset back to its original cost; or
- If the original investment had been fair valued through equity, the change in fair value in equity is reversed so as to bring the asset back to its original cost.

Goodwill is calculated as the difference between the cost of each tranche and the share of the fair value of the assets and liabilities acquired in each tranche. Dividend income continues to be recognised in the income statement up to the date the entity becomes an associate. However, at that date an adjustment will also be made through retained earnings to recognise the investor's share of post acquisition profits or losses, net of (1) any dividends receivable and (2) any changes in fair value of the underlying assets since the acquisition of the first tranche.

Therefore, in the above example the total cost is $325. The change in the fair value of $50 relating to the initial 10% investment is reversed through retained earnings or the revaluation reserves as appropriate. The investor's share of the equity method profits of $50 earned on this investment and a share of the change in fair values of $10 is recognised. The investment balance is therefore:

	First tranche	Second tranche	Total
	$	*$*	*$*
Cost	100	225	325
Profit since acquisition in 2005	50		
Dividends declared between 2005 and 2008	–20		
Increase in fair value of assets of investee	10		
Total investment	140	225	365
Goodwill included in the investment:			
– First tranche: $100 – $80 =			20
– Second tranche: $225 – $180 =			45
			65

Method B

Method B gives the same goodwill as method A, but there is no adjustment made to recognise the investor's share of profits or changes in fair value of underlying assets up to the date of gaining significant influence. In other words, the investment balance is the original cost of $325.

Method C

The carrying value of the investment at the date it becomes an associate is considered to be its 'cost'. Consequently no adjustment is made to reverse previous fair value adjustments. If the investment was previously accounted for as an available-for-sale investment, the gain recognised within equity remains there until the associated is either impaired or disposed of.

Goodwill is calculated based on the difference between this 'cost' and the share of the fair value of the assets and liabilities acquired at the date of becoming an associate. Equity accounting is applied to profits or losses arising subsequent to the investment becoming an associate. The investment balance is therefore:

	First tranche	Second tranche	Total
	$	$	$
Cost	150	225	375
Goodwill included in the investment:			
– First tranche: $150 – 10% of $1,200 =			30
– Second tranche: $225 – 15% of $1,200 =			45
			75

Finally, it should be noted that under methods A, B and C the 'cost' in the separate financial statements of the investor would be $325 in each case.

C Future developments

The IASB's Business Combinations Phase II project is proposing to change the requirements in IAS 28 relating to the acquisition of associates. IFRS 3 – *Near-final draft of IFRS 3 Business Combinations* – amends paragraph 23 of IAS 28 so that it will read as follows:

> 'An investment in an associate is accounted for using the equity method from the date on which it becomes an associate. On acquisition of the investment any difference between the cost of the investment and the investor's share of the net fair value of the associate's identifiable assets and liabilities is accounted for as:
>
> (a) goodwill relating to an associate is included in the carrying amount of the investment. Amortisation of that goodwill is not permitted.
>
> (b) any excess of the investor's share of the net fair value of the associate's identifiable assets and liabilities over the cost of the investment is included as income in the determination of the investor's share of the associate's profit or loss in the period in which the investment is acquired.
>
> Appropriate adjustments to the investor's share of the associate's profits or losses after acquisition are also made to account, for example, for depreciation of the depreciable assets based on their fair values at the acquisition date. Similarly, appropriate adjustments to the investor's share of the associate's profits or losses after acquisition are made for impairment losses recognised by the associate, such as for goodwill or property, plant and equipment.'[67]

This means that accounting for situations in which an investor obtains significant influence over an investee will change considerably when IAS 28 (revised) comes into effect.

3.3 Share accounted for

3.3.1 Contingent voting rights

As noted at 2.2.1 A above, an entity is required to consider currently exercisable potential voting rights in determining whether it has significant influence over an investee such that the investee is an associate. However, when applying the equity method, the investor determines its share of the profit or loss of the investee, and of changes in the investee's equity, by reference to its current ownership interest and does not reflect the possible exercise or conversion of potential voting rights.[68]

However, the implementation guidance on potential voting rights in IAS 27, which applies also to IAS 28, recognises that in some rare cases potential voting rights actually give rise to present access to the economic benefits inherent in those rights. An example might be a presently exercisable option over shares in the investee at a fixed price combined with the right to veto any distribution by the investee before the option is exercised. In these rare cases, it might be appropriate to equity account for the share that would be held if the option were exercised. This is discussed further in Chapter 6 at 6.2.

3.3.2 Where the reporting entity or the associate is a group

As noted at 2.2.1 above, a group's share in an associate is the aggregate of the holdings in that associate by the parent and its subsidiaries. The holdings of the group's other associates or joint ventures are ignored for this purpose. When an associate itself has subsidiaries, associates, or joint ventures, the profits or losses and net assets taken into account in applying the equity method are those recognised in the associate's financial statements (including the associate's share of the profits or losses and net assets of its associates and joint ventures), but after any adjustments necessary to give effect to uniform accounting policies (see 3.6 below).[69]

Example 8.5: Share in an associate

Parent A holds a 95% investment in subsidiary B, which in turn holds 25% investment in associate Z. In addition, parent A also holds a 30% investment in associate C and a 50% investment in joint venture D, each of which hold a 10% investment in associate Z.

In its consolidated financial statements parent A accounts for a 25% investment in associate Z under the equity method because:

- the investments in associate Z held by associate C and joint venture D should not be taken into account; and
- parent A fully consolidates the assets of subsidiary B, which include a 25% investment in associate Z.

3.3.3 Cumulative preference shares held by parties other than the investor

If an associate has outstanding cumulative preference shares that are held by parties other than the investor and that are classified as equity, the investor computes its share of profits or losses after adjusting for the dividends on such shares, whether or not the dividends have been declared.[70]

Example 8.6: Cumulative preference shares issued by an associate

An entity holds an investment of 30% in the common shares of an associate that has net assets of £200,000. The associate has issued 5,000 9% cumulative preference shares with a nominal value of £10. The cumulative preference shares are classified by the associate as equity in accordance with the requirements of IAS 32. The associate has not declared dividends on the cumulative preference shares in the past two years.

The investor calculates its share of the associate's net assets and net profit as follows:

	£
Net assets	200,000
9% Cumulative preference shares	(50,000)
Undeclared dividend on cumulative preference shares	
2 years × 9% × £50,000 =	(9,000)
Net assets value attributable to common shareholders	141,000
Investor's 30% share of the net assets	42,300
Net profit for the year	24,500
Share of profit of holders of cumulative preference shares	
9% of £50,000 =	(4,500)
Net profit attributable to common shareholders	20,000
Investor's 30% share of the net profit	6,000

If the investor also owned all of the cumulative preference shares then its share in the net assets of the associate would be £42,300 + £50,000 + £9,000 = £101,300. Its share in the net profit would be £6,000 + £4,500 = £10,500.

3.3.4 *Several classes of equity*

When an associate has a complicated equity structure with several classes of equity shares that have varying entitlements to net profits and equity, the investor needs to assess carefully the rights attaching to each class of equity share in determining the appropriate percentage of ownership interest.

Example 8.7: Preference shares with a liquidation preference

Entity A has issued 10,000 preference shares with a nominal value of €0.10. The preference shareholders are entitled to a cumulative dividend equal to 25% of the net profits, 35% of the equity upon liquidation and have a liquidation preference in respect of the nominal value of the shares. Entity A has also issued ordinary shares that are entitled to the remainder of the net profits and equity upon liquidation.

An investor that holds 40% of the ordinary shares of Entity A will need to assess carefully what its appropriate share in the profits and equity of Entity A is. The investor would take the liquidation preference into account in calculating its interest in the associate to the extent that there is economic substance to that right.

3.4 Transactions between the reporting entity and associates

3.4.1 Elimination of 'upstream' and 'downstream' transactions

IAS 28 requires profits and losses resulting from what it refers to as 'upstream' and 'downstream' transactions between an investor (including its consolidated subsidiaries) and an associate to be recognised in the investor's financial statements only to the extent of unrelated investors' interests in the associate. 'Upstream' transactions are, for example, sales of assets from an associate to the investor. 'Downstream' transactions are, for example, sales of assets from the investor to an associate. The investor's share in the associate's profits and losses resulting from these transactions is eliminated.[71]

IAS 28 is not entirely clear as to how this very generally expressed requirement translates into accounting entries, but we suggest that an appropriate approach might be to proceed as follows:

- In the income statement, the adjustment should be taken against either the investor's profit or the share of the associate's profit, according to whether the investor or the associate recorded the profit on the transaction, respectively;
- In the balance sheet, the adjustment should be made against the asset which was the subject of the transaction if it is held by the investor or against the carrying amount for the associate if the asset is held by the associate.

This is consistent with the approach required by SIC–13 in dealing with the related area of the contribution of assets by venturers to joint ventures (see Chapter 9 at 3.4.3).

Extract 8.5: Nokia Corporation (2006)

Notes to the Consolidated Financial Statements [extract]

1. Accounting principles [extract]

Principles of consolidation [extract]

Profits realized in connection with the sale of fixed assets between the Group and associated companies are eliminated in proportion to share ownership. Such profits are deducted from the Group's equity and fixed assets and released in the Group accounts over the same period as depreciation is charged.

Examples 8.8 and 8.9 below illustrate our interpretation of this treatment. Both examples deal with the reporting entity H and its 40% associate A. The journal entries are based on the premise that H's financial statements are initially prepared as a simple aggregation of H and the relevant share of its associates. The entries below would then be applied to the numbers at that stage of the process.

Example 8.8: Elimination of profit on sale by investor to associate

On 1 December 2007 H sells inventory costing £750,000 to A for £1 million. On 10 January 2008, A sells the inventory to a third party for £1.2 million. What adjustments are made in the group financial statements of H at 31 December 2007 and 31 December 2008?

In the year ended 31 December 2007, H has recorded revenue of £1 million and cost of sales of £750,000. However since, at the balance sheet date, the inventory is still held by A, only 60% of this transaction is regarded by IAS 28 as having taken place (in effect with the other shareholders of A). This is reflected by the consolidation entry:

	£	£
Revenue	400,000	
Cost of sales		300,000
Investment in A		100,000

This effectively defers recognition of 40% of the sale and offsets the deferred profit against the carrying amount of H's investment in A.

During 2008, when the inventory is sold on by A, this deferred profit can be released to the group income statement, reflected by the following accounting entry.

	£	£
Opening reserves	100,000	
Cost of sales	300,000	
Revenue		400,000

Opening reserves are adjusted because the financial statement working papers (if prepared as assumed above) will already include this profit in opening reserves, since it forms part of H's opening reserves.

An alternative approach would be to eliminate the profit on 40% of the sale against the cost of sales, as follows:

	£	£
Cost of sales	100,000	
Investment in A		100,000

An argument in favour of this approach is that the revenue figures should not be adjusted because the sales to associates need to be disclosed as related party transactions. However, in our view, this is more than outweighed by the drawback of the approach, namely that it causes volatility in H's reported gross margin as revenue and the related net margin are not necessarily recognised in the same accounting period.

Example 8.9: Elimination of profit on sale by associate to reporting entity

This is the mirror image of the transaction in Example 8.1 above. On 1 December 2007 A sells inventory costing £750,000 to H for £1,000,000. On 10 January 2008, H sells the inventory to a third party for £1.2 million. What adjustments are made in the group financial statements of H at 31 December 2007 and 31 December 2008?

H's share of the profit of A as included on the financial statement working papers at 31 December 2007 will include a profit of £250,000 (£1,000,000 – £750,000), 40% of which (£100,000) is regarded under IAS 28 as unrealised by H, and is therefore deferred and offset against closing inventory:

	£	£
Share of A's result (income statement)	100,000	
Inventory		100,000

In the following period when the inventory is sold H's separate financial statements will record a profit of £200,000, which must be increased on consolidation by the £100,000 deferred from the previous period. The entry is:

	£	£
Opening reserves	100,000	
Share of A's result (income statement)		100,000

Again, opening reserves are adjusted because the financial statement working papers (if prepared as assumed above) will already include this profit in opening reserves, this time, however, as part of H's share of the opening reserves of A.

A slightly counter-intuitive consequence of this treatment is that at the end of 2007 the investment in A in H's consolidated balance sheet will have increased by £100,000 more than the share of profit of associates as reported in the group income statement (and in 2008 by £100,000 less). This is because the balance sheet adjustment at the end of 2007 is made against inventory rather than the carrying value of the investment in A, which could be seen as reflecting the fact that A has, indeed, made a profit. It might therefore be necessary to indicate in the notes to the financial statements that part of the profit made by A is regarded as unrealised by the group in 2007 and has therefore been deferred until 2008 by offsetting it against inventory.

It may be that a transaction between an associate and its investor indicates an impairment of the asset that is the subject of the transaction. IAS 28 does not specifically address this issue. However, IAS 31 indicates that where a transaction between a venturer and a joint venture indicates an impairment of the asset that is the subject of the transaction, the venturer should recognise the full impairment loss and not merely its share.[72] In our view, this treatment should also be adopted when a transaction between and an investor its associate indicates an impairment of the investor's asset. Further discussion, and examples, of this treatment may be found in Chapter 9 at 3.4.2.

A *Elimination of 'downstream' unrealised gains in excess of the investment*

Occasionally an investor's share of the unrealised profit on the sale of an asset to an associate exceeds the carrying value of the investment held, as illustrated in the following example.

Example 8.10: Elimination of unrealised gains in excess of the investment

An investor has a 40% investment in an associate, which it carries in its balance sheet at €800,000. The investor sells a property to the associate in exchange for cash, which results in a profit of €3 million. After the sale, 40% of that profit (i.e. €1.2 million) is unrealised from the investor's perspective.

There are two approaches for determining to what extent a profit in excess of the carrying value of the investment should be eliminated.

Preferred approach

Our preferred approach is to apply the requirements in paragraph 22 of IAS 28 literally, which is also consistent with the general requirement to apply IAS 27 consolidation elimination principles.[73] Furthermore, the requirement in IAS 28 to discontinue application of the equity method when an investor's share of losses equals or exceeds it interest in the associate (see 3.7 below), should not apply as the elimination does not represent a real 'loss' to the investor but is simply the non-recognition of a gain as a result of normal consolidation principles.[74] In other words, paragraph 29 of IAS 28 should not override the requirement to eliminate unrealised profits. Therefore, under the preferred approach the investor would eliminate the unrealised gain by reducing the investment in the associate to zero, with the excess deferred through the creation of a 'deferred income' or similar balance, as follows:

	€	€
Gain on sale of property	1,200,000	
Investment in associate		800,000
'Deferred income'		400,000

Acceptable alternative

There has been ongoing debate about whether the equity method of accounting is a consolidation method or a measurement method. Although IAS 28 generally adopts consolidation principles it nevertheless retains features of a valuation methodology – such as the one line nature of the income statement and balance sheet entries and the requirement to discontinue the equity method where losses would otherwise reduce the investment below zero (see 3.7 below). Therefore, it is considered an acceptable alternative to apply the principles of paragraph 29 of IAS 28 and not recognise elimination entries to the extent that the elimination exceeds the carrying amount of the investment in the associate, provided that the investor does not have any further legal or constructive obligations in relation to the asset or the associate. Under the alternative approach the investor would eliminate the unrealised gain as follows:

	€	€
Gain on sale of property	800,000	
Investment in associate		800,000

Future profits of the associate are not recognised until they exceed the unrecognised unrealised profits of €400,000.

Conclusion

An investor should apply its accounting policy choice consistently to all associates and should consistently treat the equity method as either a consolidation method or a measurement method. Furthermore, if an investor has any continuing involvement with a transferred asset caution needs to be exercised as this may indicate that no revenue or gain should be recognised in the first place.

B Transactions between associates and/or joint ventures

When transactions take place between associates and/or joint ventures, which are accounted for under the equity method, the investor should apply the requirements of IAS 27 and IAS 28 by analogy and eliminate its share of the profits.[75] In practice it may be difficult though to determine whether such transactions have taken place.

3.4.2 Reciprocal interests

Reciprocal interests (or 'cross-holdings') arise when an associate itself holds an investment in the reporting entity. The reciprocal interests can give rise to a measure of double counting of profits and net assets between the investor and its associate. Paragraph 20 of IAS 28 states that many of the procedures appropriate for the application of the equity method are similar to the consolidation procedures described in IAS 27. Therefore, the requirement in paragraph 24 of IAS 27 to eliminate intragroup balances, transactions, income and expenses should be applied by analogy.

What is unfortunately not clear from either IAS 27 or IAS 28 is exactly how an entity should go about eliminating the double counting that arises from reciprocal holdings. In theory there are a number of methods that may seem attractive in dealing with reciprocal interests:

(1) *Full gross up without elimination* – In this case the profit and net assets of both the investor and its associate are determined using a simultaneous equations method;

(2) *Economic interest of 'outside' shareholders* – This method would take the outcome from the above method as its starting point and eliminate profits attributable to reciprocally held shares; and

(3) *Direct holding only* – Under this method the profit of the investor is calculated by adding to its trading profits only its direct investment in the associate.

On balance we consider the 'direct holding only' method to be preferable for the reasons explained in the example below.

Example 8.11: Elimination of reciprocal interests in the income statement[76]

To effect a strategic alliance and profit sharing arrangement entity A has taken a 40% equity interest in entity B and conversely, entity B has taken a 30% interest in entity A. How should entity A and entity B account for their reciprocal investment?

The structure of the reciprocal holdings is shown in the diagram below:

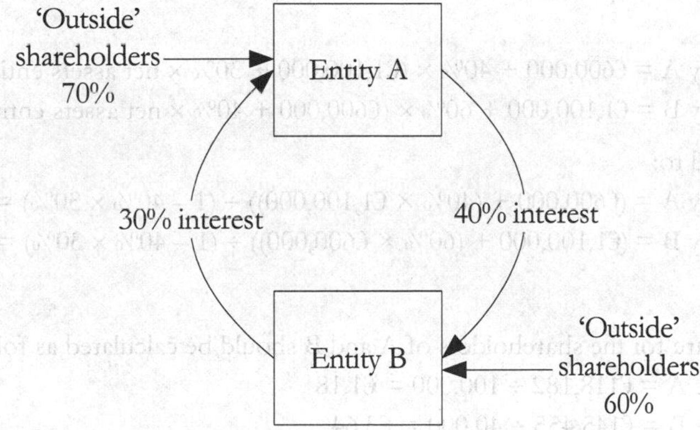

Entity A

Share in equity of B	40%
Shares in A held by 'outside' shareholders	70%
Trading profit of A (before share in profit of B)	€60,000
Net assets of A (before share in net assets of B)	€600,000
Number of shares in issue	100,000

Entity B

Share in equity of A	30%
Shares in B held by 'outside' shareholders	60%
Trading profit of B (before share in profit of A)	€110,000
Net assets of B (before share in net assets of A)	€1,100,000
Number of shares in issue	40,000

Method 1 – Full gross up without elimination

Income

The profit for the period is calculated by solving the simultaneous equations below:

Profit entity A = €60,000 + 40% × profit entity B
Profit entity B = €110,000 + 30% × profit entity A

by substitution:

Profit entity A = €60,000 + 40% × (€110,000 + 30% × profit entity A)
Profit entity B = €110,000 + 30% × (€60,000 + 40% × profit entity B)

this can be simplified to:

Profit entity A = (€60,000 + (40% × €110,000)) ÷ (1 – 40% × 30%) = €118,182
Profit entity B = (€110,000 + (30% × €60,000)) ÷ (1 – 40% × 30%) = €145,455

Balance sheet

A similar approach can be applied to calculate the net assets of A and B:

Net assets of entity A = €600,000 + 40% × net assets entity B
Net assets of entity B = €1,100,000 + 30% × net assets entity A

by substitution:

Net assets of entity A = €600,000 + 40% × (€1,100,000 + 30% × net assets entity A)
Net assets of entity B = €1,100,000 + 60% × (€600,000 + 40% × net assets entity B)

this can be simplified to:

Net assets of entity A = (€600,000 + (40% × €1,100,000)) ÷ (1 – 40% × 30%) = €1,181,818
Net assets of entity B = (€1,100,000 + (60% × €600,000)) ÷ (1 – 40% × 30%) = €1,454,545

Earnings per share

The earnings per share for the shareholders of A and B should be calculated as follows:

Earnings per share A = €118,182 ÷ 100,000 = €1.18
Earnings per share B = €145,455 ÷ 40,000 = €3.64

Under this method, it is not necessary to adjust the number of shares in issue as the net profit number relates to all shares in issue, rather than just those shares that are not held reciprocally.

It can be shown that, if both A and B were to distribute their entire profits – which would require a number of iterations because of their reciprocal interests – each share in A would, in fact, attract €1.18 in dividends, while each share in B would attract €3.64 in dividends.

Conclusion

It is questionable whether the 'full gross up without elimination' method complies with the spirit of the IAS 27 consolidation rules – or the IAS 32 rules on treasury shares – which would require elimination of an entity's holdings of its own shares.

It is worthwhile noting that the combined underlying trading profit of A and B is only €170,000 (i.e. €60,000 + €110,000), whereas their combined reported profit is €263,637 (i.e. €118,182 + €145,455). Similarly, the combined underlying net assets of A and B are only €1,700,000, whereas the combined reported net assets are €2,636,363.

Method 2 – Economic interest of 'outside' shareholders

Income

The profit for the period is calculated by taking the profit calculated under Method 1 above and eliminating the profits attributable to reciprocally held shares:

Profit entity A = (100% – 30%) × €118,182 = €82,727

Profit entity B = (100% – 40%) × €145,455 = €87,273

Balance sheet

A similar approach can be applied to calculate the net assets of A and B:

Net assets of A attributable to 'outside' shareholders = €827,272

Net assets of B attributable to 'outside' shareholders = €872,727

Earnings per share

The profit figure calculated above only related to the 'outside' shareholders in A and B and should therefore by divided by the number of 'outside' shares, as follows:

Earnings per share A = €82,727 ÷ 70,000 = €1.18

Earnings per share B = €87,273 ÷ 24,000 = €3.64

Conclusion

An advantage of this method is that the combined reported profit of A and B is €170,000 (= €82,727 + €87,273), which is equal to the combined underlying trading profit of A and B. In addition, the outcome of this method is very similar to that which would have arisen if A and B had entered into a regular profit sharing contract.

This method does, however, produce outcomes that, at first sight, seem somewhat counterintuitive, but do in fact reflect the economic reality that, in this example, the cross-holding is to A's advantage. For example, entity B's income statement would look as follows:

	€
Trading profit of B	110,000
Share in profit of associate A after elimination of reciprocal interests	(22,727)
Net profit for the period	87,273

The net profit for the period of €87,273 is actually less than its trading profit of €110,000, because the impact of the reciprocal interests is clearly not neutral. In this particular example the reciprocal relationship is disadvantageous for 'outside' shareholders of B which has a 30% interest in A which is not very profitable, while the 'outside' shareholders of A benefit from A's 40% interest in B which is very profitable. In other words, the profit sharing arrangement is unfavourable from B's point of view.

This method eliminates all shares that are not held by 'outside' shareholders, as it treats the combined reciprocal interests as if they were a single profit sharing arrangement. To achieve this, the method offsets (1) A's right to dividends from B against (2) A's obligation to pay dividends to B. This seems to go beyond the elimination requirements in IAS 27 in that it eliminates the interests that B shareholders have in A.

Method 3 – Direct holding only

Income

The profit for the period is calculated by adding the direct interest in the associate's profit:

Profit entity A = €60,000 + 40% × trading profit entity B = €60,000 + 40% × €110,000 = €104,000

Profit entity B = €110,000 + 30% × trading profit entity A = €110,000 + 30% × €60,000 = €128,000

Balance sheet

A similar approach can be applied to calculate the net assets of A and B:

Net assets of A including share in B without eliminations = €1,040,000

Net assets of B including share in A without eliminations = €1,280,000

Earnings per share

Under this method the profits related to the reciprocal interests have been ignored. Therefore, in calculating the earnings per share it is necessary to adjust the number of shares to eliminate the reciprocal holdings: For entity A it can be argued that it indirectly owns 40% of B's 30% interest, i.e. entity A indirectly owns 12% (= 40% × 30%) of its own shares. Those shares should therefore be treated as being equivalent to 'treasury shares' and be ignored for the purposes of the EPS calculation.

Number of A shares after elimination of 'treasury shares' = 100,000 × (100% – 12%) = 88,000 shares

While entity B indirectly owns 30% of A's 40% interest, i.e. entity B indirectly owns 12% (= 30% × 40%) of its own shares.

Number of B shares after elimination of 'treasury shares' = 40,000 × (100% – 12%) = 35,200 shares

The earnings per share for the shareholders of A and B should be calculated as follows:

Earnings per share A = €104,000 ÷ 88,000 = €1.18

Earnings per share B = €128,000 ÷ 35,200 = €3.64

As before, the earnings per share would be equivalent to the hypothetical dividend per share in the case of full distribution of all profits as discussed in Method 1 above.

Conclusion

Rather than treating the reciprocal holdings as a single profit sharing arrangement, this method only eliminates the effects of an entity's indirect investment in its own shares. The financial statements therefore reflect both the interests of the 'outside' shareholders and the interests that B shareholders have in A. On balance we believe that this method is therefore preferable.

It is worthwhile noting that the combined underlying trading profit of A and B is only €170,000 (i.e. €60,000 + €110,000), whereas their combined reported profit is €232,000 (i.e. €104,000 + €128,000). Similarly, the combined underlying net assets of A and B are only €1,700,000, whereas the combined reported net assets are €2,320,000.

From the above it seems that the elimination of reciprocal interests is somewhat more complicated than it might have appeared to the IFRIC in August 2002. The IFRIC agreed not to require publication of an Interpretation on this issue, but did state that 'like the consolidation procedures applied when a subsidiary is consolidated, the equity method requires reciprocal interests to be eliminated.'[77]

3.4.3 Loans and borrowings between the reporting entity and associates

IAS 28's requirement to eliminate partially unrealised profits or losses on transactions with associates is expressed in terms of transactions involving the transfer of assets. In our view, the requirement for partial elimination of profits does not apply to items such as interest paid on loans and borrowings between associates and the reporting entity, since such loans and borrowings do not involve the transfer of assets giving rise to gains or losses. Moreover, they are not normally regarded as part of the investor's share of the net assets of the associate, but as separate transactions, except in the case of loss-making associates, where interests in long-term loans and borrowings may be required to be accounted for as if they were part of the reporting entity's equity investment in determining the carrying value of the associate against which losses may be offset (see 3.7 below). Likewise, loans and borrowings between the reporting entity and associates should not be eliminated in the reporting entity's consolidated accounts because associates are not part of the group.

Finally, if the associate had a policy of capitalising borrowing costs then the investor would need to eliminate a relevant share of the profit, in the same way it would eliminate a share of the capitalised management or advisory fees charged to an associate.

3.4.4 Cash flow statement

In the cash flow statement (whether in the consolidated or separate financial statements) no adjustment is made in respect of the cash flows relating to transactions with associates, whereas in consolidated cash flow statements cash flows between members of the group are eliminated in the same way as intragroup transactions are eliminated in the profit and loss account and balance sheet.

3.4.5 Contributions of non-monetary assets to an associate

It is fairly common for an entity to create or change its interest in an associate by contributing some of the entity's existing non-monetary assets to that associate. This raises a number of issues as to how such transactions should be accounted for, in particular whether they should be accounted for at book value or fair value. There is no explicit guidance on this issue in IFRS as regards the formation of associates. However, the SIC considered the issue in connection with the contribution of assets to joint ventures, and contributions of non-monetary assets are also addressed by IAS 16 – *Property, Plant and Equipment* – and IAS 38 – *Intangible Assets* (see Chapter 9 at 3.4.3). In our view, it would be appropriate to consider this guidance when accounting for contributions of assets to associates.

3.5 Non-coterminous accounting periods

In applying the equity method, the investor should use the most recent financial statements of the associate. Where the reporting dates of the investor and the associate are different, IAS 28 requires the associate to prepare, for the use of the investor, financial statements as of the same date as those of the investor unless it is impracticable to do so.[78]

When the financial statements of an associate used in applying the equity method are prepared as of a different reporting date from that of the investor, adjustments must be made for the effects of significant transactions or events that occurred between that date and the date of the investor's financial statements. In no case can the difference between the reporting date of the associate and that of the investor be more than three months.[79] There are no exemptions from this requirement despite the fact that it may be quite onerous in practice, for example, because:

- the associate might need to produce interim financial statements so that the investor can comply with this requirement; or
- the associate may be a listed company in its own right whose financial information is considered price-sensitive, which means that the associate may not be able to provide detailed financial information to one investor without providing equivalent information to all other investors at the same time.

The length of the reporting periods and any difference in the reporting dates must be the same from period to period.[80] This implies that where an associate previously equity accounted for on the basis of non-coterminous financial statements is equity accounted for using coterminous financial statements, it is necessary to restate comparative information so that financial information in respect of the associate is included in the investor's financial statements for an equivalent period in each period presented.

IAS 28 requires merely that a non-coterminous accounting period of an associate used for equity accounting purposes ends within three months of that of the investor. It is not necessary for such a non-coterminous period to end before that of the investor.

3.6 Consistent accounting policies

IAS 28 requires the investor's financial statements to be prepared using uniform accounting policies for like transactions and events in similar circumstances.[81] If an associate uses accounting policies different from those of the investor for like transactions and events in similar circumstances, adjustments must be made to conform the associate's accounting policies to those of the investor when the associate's financial statements are used by the investor in applying the equity method.[82]

In practice, this may be easier said than done, since an investor's influence over an associate, although significant, may still not be sufficient to secure access to the relevant underlying information in sufficient detail to make such adjustments with certainty. Restating the financial statements of an associate to IFRS may require, extensive detailed information that may simply not be required under the associate's local GAAP (for example, in respect of business combinations, share-based payments, financial instruments and revenue recognition).

3.7 Loss-making associates

An investor in an associate should recognise its share of the losses of an associate until its share of losses equals or exceeds its interest in the associate, at which point the investor discontinues recognising its share of further losses. For this purpose, the investor's interest in an associate is the carrying amount of the investment in the associate under the equity method together with any long-term interests that, in substance, form part of the investor's net investment in the associate. For example, an item for which settlement is neither planned nor likely to occur in the foreseeable future is, in substance, an extension of the entity's investment in that associate. The IASB argued that this requirement ensures that investors are not able to avoid recognising the loss of an associate by restructuring their investment to provide the majority of funding through non-equity investments.[83]

Such items include:

- preference shares; or
- long-term receivables or loans (unless supported by adequate collateral),

but do not include:

- trade receivables;
- trade payables; or
- any long-term receivables for which adequate collateral exists, such as secured loans.

Once the investor's share of losses recognised under the equity method has reduced the investor's investment in ordinary shares to zero, its share of any further losses is applied so as to reduce the other components of the investor's interest in an associate in the reverse order of their seniority (i.e. priority in liquidation).[84]

Once the investor's interest is reduced to zero, additional losses are provided for, and a liability is recognised, only to the extent that the investor has incurred legal or constructive obligations or made payments on behalf of the associate. The investor would account for such losses as a liability under IAS 37 – *Provisions, Contingent Liabilities and Contingent Assets*. If the associate subsequently reports profits, the investor resumes recognising its share of those profits only after its share of the profits equals the share of losses not recognised.[85] Whilst IAS 28 does not say so explicitly, it is presumably envisaged that, when profits begin to be recognised again, they are applied to write back the various components of the investor's interest in the associate (see previous paragraph) in the reverse order to that in which they were written down (i.e. in order of their priority in a liquidation).

This method of accounting, sometimes referred to as 'waterline accounting', is broadly equivalent to the requirements of IAS 27 for the attribution of losses of partially-owned subsidiaries to the minority shareholders. An example of 'waterline accounting' may be found as Example 6.11 in Chapter 6 at 6.7.2. An investor in an associate would account for its share of the associate's losses in the same way that the losses of entity S in that example are allocated to the minority shareholder M.

In addition to the recognition of losses arising from application of the equity method, an investor in an associate must consider the additional requirements of IAS 28 in respect of impairment losses (see 4 below).

Example 8.12: Accounting for a loss-making associate

At the beginning of the year entity H invests €5 million to acquire a 30% equity interest in an associate, entity A. In addition, H lends €9 million to the associate, but does not provide any guarantees or commit itself to provide further funding. How should H account for the €20 million loss that the associate made during the year?

H's share in A's loss is €20 million × 30% = €6 million. If H's loan to A is considered part of the net investment in the associate then the carrying amount of the associate is reduced by €6 million, from €14 million (= €5 million + €9 million) to €8 million. That is, the equity interest is reduced to nil and the loan is reduced to €8 million. However, if the loan is not part of the net investment in the associate then H accounts for the loss as follows:

- the equity interest in the associate is reduced from €5 million to zero;
- a loss of €1 million remains unrecognised because H did not provide any guarantees and has no commitments to provide further funding. If in the second year, however, A were to make a profit of €10 million then H would only recognise a profit of €2 million (= €10 million × 30% – €1 million). However, if in the second year H were to provide a €1.5 million guarantee to A and A's net profit were nil, then H would need to recognise an immediate loss of €1 million (i.e. the lower of the unrecognised loss of €1 million and the guarantee of €1.5 million) because it now has a legal obligation pay A's debts; and
- as there are a number of indicators of impairment, the loan from H to A should be tested for impairment in accordance with IAS 39.

3.8 Date of commencement and cessation of equity accounting

Under the general requirements for equity accounting discussed at 2.3 above, an investor will begin equity accounting for an associate from the date on which it has significant influence over it (and is not otherwise exempt from equity accounting for it).[86]

Where an investor has not been equity accounting for an associate on the basis that it is classified as held for sale under IFRS 5 (see 2.3 above), and the investment ceases to be so classified, the investor must apply equity accounting retrospectively as from the date on which the investment was originally classified as held for sale. The financial statements of any prior periods since that classification must be restated.[87]

An investor ceases to account for an investment using the equity method on the date that it ceases to have significant influence over it. If the investment becomes a subsidiary or joint venture, it will be accounted for in accordance with, respectively, IAS 27 (see Chapter 6) or IAS 31 (see Chapter 9). Otherwise it will be accounted for in accordance with IAS 39.[88]

The measurement rules in IAS 39 are complex and discussed in detail in Chapter 20. In brief, however, they will entail the former associate being recorded initially at fair value,[89] but its cost is deemed to be its carrying amount on the date that it ceases to be an associate.[90] Therefore, if the investment is subsequently accounted for as an 'available-for-sale' financial asset the difference between its cost and fair value should be accounted for within equity. If the investment is subsequently accounted for as a 'financial asset at fair value through profit or loss' then the difference is recognised in net profit for the period. In either case, the investment will subsequently be measured at fair value – what differs is whether the gains and losses arising on revaluation are accounted for in the income statement or in equity.

However, the IASB has proposed significant changes in this area as part of its Business Combinations (Phase II) project (see 3.8.1 B below).

3.8.1 Cumulative exchange differences on associates

IAS 27 (see Chapter 6 at 6.6.1) specifically reinforces the requirement of IAS 21 – *The Effects of Foreign Exchange Rates* (see Chapter 10 at 2.7.3) that, when an investment in a foreign operation is disposed of, the gain or loss on disposal should include the 'recycling' of the cumulative exchange gains and losses that have, in accordance with IAS 21, been recognised in equity in respect of that operation. Whilst there is no such explicit reinforcement of IAS 21 in IAS 28, it seems clear that the same principle should apply on disposal of an associate.

IAS 21 clarifies that disposal of a foreign operation may occur through sale, liquidation, repayment of share capital, abandonment or receipt of a dividend out of pre-acquisition profits. When a partial disposal occurs, only the proportionate share of the related accumulated exchange difference is included in profit or loss. IAS 21 further clarifies that a write-down of a foreign operation does not constitute a partial disposal, and accordingly no part of the deferred foreign exchange gain or loss is recognised in profit or loss at the time of such a write-down,[91] unless the write-down is consequent upon an event of 'disposal' as just described.

This begs the further question of the appropriate treatment of any cumulative exchange gains and losses on a former associate which becomes subject to IAS 39 as described above. The issues here are very similar to those arising in respect of a former subsidiary which becomes subject to IAS 39, which are discussed in Chapter 6 at 6.6.2 A.

A Other cumulative gains and losses previously recognised in equity

Like IAS 27, IAS 28 does not specifically address the accounting treatment, on disposal of an associate, of the investor's share of other cumulative gains and losses previously accounted for in equity relating to assets and liabilities of the disposed associate. Such cumulative gains and losses, which would be recycled in profit or loss if those assets and liabilities had been disposed of separately by the associate, could include:

- accumulated hedging gains and losses accounted for under IAS 39 (see Chapter 21); and
- any other amounts previously recognised in equity that would have been recognised in profit or loss if the associate had directly disposed of the assets to which they relate, such as gains or losses on available-for-sale financial assets accounted for under IAS 39 (see Chapter 20 at 3.4).

IAS 39 does not specifically address this issue either. However, it would appear that recycling is appropriate, since the disposal of an associate does give rise to the derecognition of the investor's share of the separate assets and liabilities of that associate just as if they had been disposed of separately. Moreover, the IASB's proposals for amendments to IAS 28 (see B below) strongly indicate that this is the preferred approach.

B Future developments

The IASB's Business Combinations Phase II project is proposing a number of changes in accounting for a loss of significant influence. IAS 27 – *Near-final draft of IAS 27 Consolidated and Separate Financial Statements* – amends paragraph 18 of IAS 28 so that it will read as follows:

> 'An investor shall discontinue the use of the equity method from the date that it ceases to have significant influence over an associate and shall account for the investment in accordance with IAS 39 from that date, provided the associate does not become a subsidiary or a jointly controlled entity as defined in IAS 31. On loss of significant influence, the investor shall measure at fair value any investment the investor retains in the former associate. The investor shall recognise in profit or loss any difference between:
>
> (a) the fair value of the retained investment and any proceeds from disposing of the part interest in the associate; and
>
> (b) the carrying amount of the investment at the date significant influence is lost.'[92]

Furthermore, IAS 28 will be amended to require that if an investor loses significant influence over an associate, all amounts recognised in other comprehensive income in relation to that associate should be recognised by the investor on the same basis that would be required if the associate had directly disposed of the related assets or liabilities.[93] Similarly, IAS 21 will be amended to require that upon loss of significant influence the cumulative amount of the exchange differences deferred in the separate component of equity relating to that associate be recognised in profit or loss.[94] In practice that would mean that a gain or loss should be recognised upon loss of significant influence, even if a former associate is subsequently accounted for as an available-for-sale financial asset.

When an investor's interest in an associate is reduced (but the investee remains an associate), then the investor should 'reclassify to profit or loss only a proportionate amount of the gain or loss previously recognised in other comprehensive income'[95] and 'reclassify to profit or loss only the proportionate share of the cumulative amount of the exchange differences recognised in other comprehensive income'.[96] That means that the investor should recognise in profit or loss a proportion of:

- foreign exchange differences recognised in equity under IAS 21,
- accumulated hedging gains and losses recognised in equity under IAS 39 (see Chapter 21), and

- any other amounts previously recognised in equity that would have been recognised in profit or loss if the associate had directly disposed of the assets to which they relate, such as gains or losses on available-for-sale financial assets accounted for under IAS 39 (see Chapter 20 at 3.4),

in each case proportionate to the interest disposed of.

The above amendments are expected to be effective for annual periods beginning on or after 1 January 2009.[97]

3.8.2 Deemed disposals

An investor's interest in an associate may be reduced other than by an actual disposal. Such a reduction in interest, which is commonly referred to as a 'deemed disposal', gives rise to a 'dilution' gain or loss. Deemed disposals may arise for a number of reasons, including:

- the investor does not take up its full allocation in a rights issue by the associate;
- the associate declares scrip dividends which are not taken up by the investor so that its proportional interest is diminished;
- another party exercises its options or warrants issued by the associate; or
- the associate issues shares to third parties.

An illustration of such a transaction is given in Example 8.13 below.

Example 8.13: Deemed disposal of an associate

On 1 January 2006 investor A acquired a 30% interest in entity B at a cost of £500,000. Investor A has significant influence over entity B and accounts for its investment in the associate under the equity method. The associate has net assets of £1,000,000 at the date of acquisition, which have a fair value of £1,200,000. During the year ended 31 December 2006 entity B recognised a post-tax profit of £200,000, and paid a dividend of £18,000. Entity B also recognised foreign exchange losses of £40,000 directly in equity.

Entity B's net assets at 31 December 2006 can be determined as follows:

	£
Net assets 1 January 2006	1,000,000
Profit for year	200,000
Dividends paid	(18,000)
Foreign exchange losses	(40,000)
B's net assets at 31 December 2006	1,142,000

Investor A's interest in entity B at 31 December 2006 is calculated as follows:

	£
On acquisition (including goodwill of £500,000 – (30% × £1,200,000) = £140,000):	500,000
Share of after tax profit (30% × £200,000)	60,000
Elimination of dividend (30% of £18,000)	(5,400)
A's share of exchange differences (30% × £40,000)	(12,000)
A's interest in B at 31 December 2006 under the equity method	542,600

which can also be determined as follows:

	£
A's share of B's net assets (30% × £1,142,000)	342,600
Goodwill	140,000
A's share of fair value uplift (30% × £200,000) †	60,000
A's interest in B at 31 December 2006	542,600

† This assumes that none of the uplift related to depreciable assets, such that the £200,000 did not diminish after the acquisition.

On 1 January 2007, entity B has a rights issue that investor A does not participate in. The rights issue brings in an additional £150,000 in cash, and dilutes investor A's interest in entity B to 25%.

Consequently, entity B's net assets at 1 January 2007 are:

	£
Entity B's net assets at 31 December 2006	1,142,000
Additional cash	150,000
Entity B's net assets at 1 January 2007	1,292,000

Considering the facts above, how should investor A account for the dilution of its investment in entity B?

Method A

IAS 28 defines the equity method as 'a method of accounting whereby the investment is initially recognised at cost and adjusted thereafter for the post acquisition change in the investor's share of net assets of the investee. The profit or loss of the investor includes the investor's share of the profit or loss of the investee'.[98] A literal reading of this definition suggests that in calculating the loss on dilution, investor A should only take account of the change in its share of entity B's net assets but not account for a change in the notional goodwill component:

	£	£
Carrying amount of the investment before the deemed disposal		542,600
Cost of deemed disposal ([£542,600 – £140,000 †] × (30% – 25%) / 30%)	(67,100)	
Share of the contribution (£150,000 × 25%)	37,500	
Reduction in carrying amount of associate	(29,600)	(29,600)
Recycling of share in currency translation: (£40,000 × 30% × (25% – 30%) / 30%)	(2,000)	
Loss on deemed disposal	(31,600)	
Carrying amount of the investment after the deemed disposal		513,000

Whilst goodwill (†) is included in the carrying amount of the investment, it is not separately recognised nor tested separately for impairment. However, it could be argued that the dilution of the shareholding and the recognition of an initial loss of £31,600 provide objective evidence of impairment, requiring the carrying amount of £513,000 to be tested for impairment under IAS 36.

Method B

Others consider that deemed disposals should be accounted for in the same way as 'true' disposals. That is, the entire carrying amount of the equity investment – including goodwill – should be taken into account. Thus the loss on the deemed disposal is calculated as follows:

	£	£
Carrying amount of the investment before the deemed disposal		542,600
Cost of deemed disposal (£542,600 × (30% – 25%) / 30%)	(90,433)	
Share of the contribution (£150,000 × 25%)	37,500	
Reduction in carrying amount of associate	(52,933)	(52,933)
Recycling of share in currency translation: (£40,000 × 30% × (25% – 30%) / 30%)	(2,000)	
Loss on deemed disposal	(54,933)	
Carrying amount of the investment after the deemed disposal		489,667

Paragraph 33 of IAS 28 specifically states that goodwill included in the carrying amount of an investment in an associate is not separately recognised. Hence, there is a strong argument that it should not be excluded from the cost of a deemed disposal either.

Although the IASB did not explicitly consider accounting for deemed disposals of associates in drafting IAS 28, the standard requires application of IFRS 3 in accounting for acquisitions of interests in associates. Therefore, rather than relying on a literal reading of the definition of the equity method, it is more appropriate to account for deemed disposals of associates in the same way as deemed disposals of subsidiaries (see Chapter 6 at 6.7.4).

Finally, in the absence of a Standard or an Interpretation that specifically applies to a transaction, other event or condition, IAS 8 requires management to consider pronouncements of other standard-setting bodies that use a similar conceptual framework to develop accounting standards. Several standard-setters (e.g. in the United Kingdom and United States) specifically require the goodwill component of an investment in an associate to be included in the cost of a deemed disposal.

Conclusion

In summary, on the strength of the above arguments, we believe that the method B is generally more appropriate than method A. However, it should be noted that when the SIC discussed accounting for dilution gains and losses on deemed disposals of subsidiaries, joint ventures and associates in 1997, it was unable to reach a consensus on both:

– how dilution gains and losses should be calculated; and
– whether dilution gains and losses should be recognised directly in equity or in the income statement.

3.9 Income taxes

Income taxes arising from investments in associates are accounted for in accordance with IAS 12 – *Income Taxes*. This will often lead to full provision for deferred tax on temporary differences relating to associates (see Chapter 26 at 4.2.6).

3.10 Distributions received in excess of the carrying amount

When an associate makes dividend distributions to the investor in excess of the investor's carrying amount it is not immediately clear how the excess should be accounted for. A liability under IAS 37 (see 3.7 above) should only be recognised if the investor is obliged to refund the dividend, has incurred a legal or constructive obligation or made payments on behalf of the associate. In the absence of such obligations, it would seem that the investor could recognise the excess in net profit for the period. When the associate subsequently makes profits, the investor should only start recognising profits when they exceed the excess cash distributions recognised in net profit plus any previously unrecognised losses (see 3.7 above).

4 IMPAIRMENT LOSSES

4.1 General

Determining whether an investment in an associate is impaired may be more complicated than is apparent at first sight, as it involves carrying out several separate impairment assessments:

- *Assets of the associate*

  It is generally not appropriate for the investor to simply multiply the amount of the impairment recognised in the investee's own books by the investor's percentage of ownership, because the investor should measure its interest in an associate's identifiable net assets at fair value at the date of acquisition of an associate (see 3.2 above). Therefore, if the value that the investor attributes to the associate's net assets differs from the carrying amount of those net assets in the associate's own books, the investor should restate any impairment losses recognised by the associate and also needs to consider whether it needs to recognise any impairments that the associate itself did not recognise in its own books.

  Any goodwill recognised by an associate needs to be separated into two elements. Goodwill that existed at the date the investor acquired its interest in the associate is not an identifiable asset of the associate from the perspective of the investor. That goodwill should be combined with the investor's goodwill on the acquisition of its interest in the associate. However, goodwill that arises on subsequent acquisitions by the associate should be accounted for as such in the books of the associate and is tested for impairment in accordance with IAS 36 – *Impairment of Assets* – by the associate. The investor should not make any adjustments to the associate's accounting for that goodwill.

- *Investment in the associate*

  As well as applying the equity method as summarised in 3 above, including the recognition of losses (see 3.7 above), IAS 28 requires an investor to apply the requirements of IAS 39 (which are discussed below and in Chapter 20 at 6) in order to determine whether it is necessary to recognise any additional impairment loss with respect to the investor's net investment in the associate.[99] Whilst IAS 39 is used to determine whether it is necessary to recognise any further impairment, the amount of any impairment is calculated in accordance with IAS 36 (see Chapter 15 and below);[100]

- *Loans that are not part of the net investment in the associate*

  The investor must also apply IAS 39 in order to determine whether it is necessary to recognise any additional impairment loss with respect to that part of the investor's interest in the associate that does not comprise its net investment in the associate. This would include, for example, trade receivables and payables, and collateralised long-term receivables (see 3.7 above). In this case, however, the impairment is calculated in accordance with IAS 39, and not IAS 36.[101]

This has the effect that it is extremely unlikely any impairment charge recognised in respect of an associate will simply be the investor's share of any impairment charge recognised by the associate itself, even when the associate complies with IFRS.

The requirement of IAS 28 to apply both IAS 36 and IAS 39 perhaps indicates ambivalence on the part of the IASB about whether associates are similar to subsidiaries (in which case information about goodwill and the cash generating units to which it is attributed ought to be available) or are, in fact, a type of financial asset.

IAS 28 requires the recoverable amount of an investment in an associate to be assessed individually, unless the associate does not generate cash inflows from continuing use that are largely independent of those from other assets of the entity.[102]

4.2 Goodwill

The requirements of IFRS 3 with respect to the fair value exercise mean that any goodwill that an associate may have recognised in its own financial statements at the date of its acquisition is not considered an identifiable asset from the investor's point of view. Rather, the investor recognises goodwill on its investment in the associate in accordance with IAS 28. Goodwill arising on the acquisition of an associate is not separately recognised, but is included in the carrying value of that associate (see 3.2 above).[103] Accordingly such goodwill, unlike that separately recognised, is not separately tested for impairment on an annual basis under IAS 36. Generally, impairment losses of goodwill recognised in the financial statements of an associate should be reversed when the investor applies the equity method. However, impairment losses that relate to goodwill on the associate's own business combinations, after the investor acquired its interest in that associate, should be taken into account in determining the investor's share of the associate's profits or losses (see 4.1 above).

Whenever application of the requirements in IAS 39 indicates that the investment may be impaired (see below), the entire carrying amount of the investment is tested under IAS 36 for impairment, by comparing its recoverable amount (the higher of value in use and fair value less costs to sell) with its carrying amount. In determining the value in use of the investment, an entity estimates:[104]

- its share of the present value of the estimated future cash flows expected to be generated by the associate, including the cash flows from the operations of the associate and the proceeds on the ultimate disposal of the investment; or
- the present value of the estimated future cash flows expected to arise from dividends to be received from the investment and from its ultimate disposal.

IAS 28 notes that, under 'appropriate assumptions', both methods give the same result. In effect, IAS 28 requires the investor to regard its investment in an associate as a single cash-generating unit, rather than 'drilling down' into the separate cash-generating units determined by the associate itself for the purposes of its own financial statements. The IASB does not explain why it adopted this approach, although we imagine that it may have been for the very practical reason that an investor's influence over an associate, although significant, may still not be sufficient to secure access to the relevant underlying information. Furthermore, the standard requires the investment as a whole to be reviewed for impairment as if it were a financial asset.

IAS 39 states that financial assets are not impaired unless there is 'objective evidence' that one or more events occurring after the initial recognition of the asset ('loss events') have had an impact on the estimated future cash flows of the financial asset or group of financial assets that can be reliably estimated.

Such 'objective evidence' that a financial asset or group of assets is impaired includes observable data that comes to the attention of the holder of the asset about the following loss events:

(a) significant financial difficulty of the issuer or obligor;

(b) a breach of contract, such as a default or delinquency in interest or principal payments;

(c) the lender, for economic or legal reasons relating to the borrower's financial difficulty, granting to the borrower a concession that the lender would not otherwise consider;

(d) it becoming probable that the borrower will enter bankruptcy or other financial reorganisation;

(e) the disappearance of an active market for that financial asset because of financial difficulties; or

(f) observable data indicating that there is a measurable decrease in the estimated future cash flows from a group of financial assets since the initial recognition of those assets, although the decrease cannot yet be identified with the individual financial assets in the group, including:

  (i) adverse changes in the payment status of borrowers in the group (e.g. an increased number of delayed payments or an increased number of credit card borrowers who have reached their credit limit and are paying the minimum monthly amount); or

  (ii) national or local economic conditions that correlate with defaults on the assets in the group (e.g. an increase in the unemployment rate in the geographical area of the borrowers, a decrease in property prices for mortgages in the relevant area, a decrease in oil prices for loan assets to oil producers, or adverse changes in industry conditions that affect the borrowers in the group).[105]

Many of these considerations can only be applied with difficulty to an investment in an associate.

We consider that the only practical way in which entities can assess whether interests in associates need to be tested for impairment is by focusing on the cash flow assumptions, in the two bullets above, on which the value in use is to be based. IAS 28 appears to allow entities to estimate the present value of all cash flows that it expects to receive from the associate, no matter when it expects to get them. Only in that case could any entity expect the present value of its share of the cash flows generated by the associate to be equal to the dividends it expects to receive (in both cases aggregated with the proceeds of ultimate disposal). Such an approach is consistent with impairment reviews of financial assets under IAS 39.

It is important to note that these cash flows are not estimated in accordance with IAS 36. IAS 36 imposes a restricted time horizon on cash flow estimates based on the entity's own budgets and forecasts, which can only cover a maximum period of five years. Cash flow projections beyond this are extrapolated using a steady or declining growth rate. A longer period or a higher rate may be justified only in specific circumstances.[106] Other aspects of the impairment review, such as selection of the discount rate, will be conducted in accordance with IAS 36 (see Chapter 15 for a description of impairment reviews under IAS 36).

Moreover, in contrast to the requirement in IAS 36 for continuous annual testing of goodwill relating to subsidiaries, an entity will have to test its associate for impairment only if an event has occurred that indicates that it will not recover its carrying value. The most common of these events, trading losses, will (subject to the requirement to adopt 'waterline accounting' – see 3.7 above) have automatically been taken into account in determining the carrying value of the investment, leaving only the remaining net carrying amount (i.e. after deducting the share of trading losses) to be assessed for impairment.

4.3 Allocation of impairment

In May 2007 the IASB discussed impairment testing of investments in associates. The Board noted that IAS 28 is 'unclear whether an impairment recognised against an investment in an associate should be allocated against the goodwill included in the investment, and thus whether the impairment can be reversed subsequently. The Board noted that applying the equity method includes reflecting the impact of acquisition date fair values on the investor's share of impairment losses recognised by the associate against assets such as goodwill or property, plant and equipment.'[107] The Board decided that any further impairment recognised by an investor after applying the equity method should not be allocated against goodwill included in the carrying amount of the associate. In addition, such an impairment charge 'should therefore be reversed in a subsequent period to the extent that the recoverable amount of the associate increases'.[108] The Board decided to amend the standard accordingly and expects to publish an exposure draft in October 2007.

Still, even under the current wording of IFRS we believe that an associate should be treated as a single asset for impairment testing purposes. Therefore, if an investor concludes that the associate is impaired, the impairment should not be allocated to the underlying assets or goodwill of the associate. Instead, the carrying amount of the associate as a whole is considered to be impaired and the investor's share of profits under the equity method should not be adjusted to reflect the impaired value of the underlying assets.

4.4 Reversal of impairment

IAS 28 as currently drafted does not address reversal of impairments, which raises the question whether an investor can recognise reversals of impairment losses on associates.

Example 8.14: Impairment and reversal of impairment

On 1 January 2006 an investor acquired a 25% interest in an associate for €1,000. The investor has identified goodwill of €125, which is included in the carrying amount of the associate.

During 2006 the associate makes a profit of €400, the investor's share in this profit is €100. In 2007 the associate reports a loss of €400, which reduces the carrying amount of the associate to €1,000 in the books of the investor. Based on its estimates of future cash flows to be received from the associate, the investor records an impairment of €200 and reduces the carrying amount of the associate to €800.

In 2008 the investor recalculates the value in use of the associate and determines that the recoverable amount has increased and is now in excess of €1,000. How should the investor account for the reversal of the impairment:

(a) reverse the entire €200 impairment;

(b) reverse €75, which is the amount by which the impairment exceeded the goodwill; or

(c) not reverse the impairment as this issue is not addressed by IAS 28?

Under IAS 28 an investor applies the requirements in IAS 39 to determine whether it is necessary to recognise impairment losses on its investment in associates.[109] However, other guidance on accounting for impairment of financial assets in IAS 39 does not apply to associates accounted for under the equity method.

Goodwill included in the carrying amount of an investment in an associate is not separately tested for impairment under IAS 36 because it is not a separately recognised asset in the balance sheet.[110] Consequently, in our view, the IAS 36 prohibition on the reversal of impairment losses on goodwill would not apply either.[111] Financial assets classified as associates are specifically included within the scope of IAS 36.[112] Therefore, with the exception of the rules for identifying impairment and reversal of impairment of separable goodwill, all other provisions of IAS 36 – including those on reversal of impairment – apply to investments in associates. In our opinion, a previously recognised impairment of an investment in an associate is therefore fully reversible under IFRS as currently drafted, i.e. in the example above the entity should reverse the entire €200 impairment. As noted at 4.3 above, the IASB is planning to amend IAS 28 to make this an explicit requirement.

5 PRESENTATION AND DISCLOSURE

5.1 Presentation

5.1.1 Balance sheet

In the balance sheet, investments in associates accounted for using the equity method are classified as non-current assets,[113] within financial assets.[114]

IAS 28 does not explicitly define what is meant by 'investment in an associate'. However, paragraph 29 states that 'the interest in an associate is the carrying amount of the investment in the associate under the equity method together with any long-term interests that, in substance, form part of the investor's net investment in the associate. ... Such items may include preference shares and long-term receivables or loans but do not include trade receivables, trade payables or any long-term receivables for which adequate collateral exists, such as secured loans.'[115] Some have interpreted this as a requirement to present the investment in ordinary shares and other long-term interests in associates within the same line item.

Yet, when associates are profitable, long-term interests such as loans are normally accounted for under IAS 39 rather than under the equity method. Therefore, it generally considered acceptable to present the investment in ordinary shares and other long-term interests in associates in separate line items.

Goodwill relating to an associate is included in the carrying amount of the investment, as is illustrated by Anglo American below.[116]

Extract 8.6: Anglo American plc (2006)

Notes to financial statements [extract]

1. Accounting policies [extract]

Business combinations and goodwill arising thereon [extract]

Goodwill in respect of subsidiaries and joint ventures is included within intangible assets. Goodwill relating to associates is included within the carrying value of the associate.

5.1.2 Income statement

In the income statement, the aggregate of the investor's share of the profit or loss of associates and joint ventures accounted for using the equity method must be shown.[117] 'Profit or loss' in this context is interpreted in the implementation guidance to IAS 1 as meaning the 'profit attributable to equity holders of the associates, i.e. it is after tax and minority interests in the associates.'[118]

There is no requirement as to where in the income statement the investor's share of the profit or loss of associates and joint ventures accounted for using the equity method should be shown, and different approaches are therefore seen in practice. Nokia includes its share of the (post-tax) results of associates after operating profit, but before pre-tax profit, as shown in Extract 8.5 below.

Extract 8.7: Nokia Corporation (2006)

Consolidated profit and loss accounts, IFRS [extract]

		Financial year ended December 31		
		2006	2005	2004
Financial year ended Dec. 31	Notes	**EURm**	EURm	EURm
Net sales		**41,121**	34,191	29,371
Cost of sales		**(27,742)**	(22,209)	(18,179)
Gross profit		**13,379**	11,982	11,192
Research and development expenses		**(3,897)**	(3,825)	(3,776)
Selling and marketing expenses	6	**(3,314)**	(2,961)	(2,564)
Administrative and general expenses		**(666)**	(609)	(611)
Other income	7	**522**	285	343
Other expenses	7,8	**(536)**	(233)	(162)
Amortization of goodwill	10	**–**	–	(96)
Operating profit	2-10	**5,488**	4,639	4,326
Share of results of associated companies	15,33	**28**	10	(26)
Financial income and expenses	11	**207**	322	405
Profit before tax		**5,723**	4,971	4,705

By contrast, Nestlé includes its share of the post-tax results of associates as the final item in its profit and loss account.

Extract 8.8: Nestlé S.A. (2005)

Consolidated income statement
For the year ended 31st December 2005 [extract]

In millions of CHF	Notes	**2005**	2004 (a)
Profit before taxes		**10,226**	7,818
Taxes	5	**(2,597)**	(2,404)
Profit of consolidated companies before discontinued operations		**7,629**	5,414
Net profit/(loss) on discontinued operations	30	**(7)**	29
Profit of consolidated companies		**7,622**	5,443
Share of results of associates		**6,896**	1,588
Profit for the period		**8,518**	7,031
of which attributable to minority interests		**523**	410
of which attributable to the Group (Net profit)		**7,995**	6,621

(a) Restated following first application of IFRS 2 – *Share-based Payment* – and the discontinued operation resulting from the announcement made in December 2005 for the Chilled dairy activities in Europe.

A *Impairment of associates*

It is unclear where impairments of associates should be presented in the income statement. IAS 28 requires an impairment test to be performed 'after application of the equity method',[119] which could be read as implying that impairment of an associate is not part of the investor's share of the profit or loss of an associate accounted for using the equity method. On the other hand, the guidance on accounting for impairment losses on associates is presented under the heading 'application of the equity method' in IAS 28, which suggests that accounting for impairments of associates is part of the equity method. In practice, both interpretations appear to have gained a degree of acceptance.

RWE reports impairment losses on associates within income from investments accounted for using the equity method.

> *Extract 8.9: RWE Aktiengesellschaft (2006)*
>
> **Notes** [extract]
>
> **Consolidation principles** [extract]
>
> These consolidation principles also apply to investments accounted for using the equity method, in respect of which recognized goodwill is reported on the balance sheet under investments. This goodwill is not amortized either. If necessary, impairment losses on the equity value are reported under income from investments accounted for using the equity method. The financial statements of investments accounted for using the equity method are also prepared using uniform accounting policies.

5.1.3 *Statement of changes in equity*

The investor's share of items recognised directly in the equity of the associate is recognised directly in the investor's equity and separately disclosed on the face of the statement of changes in equity required by IAS 1.[120]

5.2 Disclosures

5.2.1 *Requirements of IAS 28*

As stated above, investments in associates accounted for using the equity method are classified in the balance sheet as non-current assets,[121] within financial assets.[122]

IAS 28 requires the following disclosures:

(a) the investor's share of the profits or losses of associates accounted for using the equity method;[123]

(b) the carrying amount of investments in associates accounted for using the equity method;[124]

(c) the investor's share of any discontinued operations of associates accounted for using the equity method;[125]

(d) the fair value of investments in associates for which there are published price quotations;[126]

(e) summarised financial information of associates, including the aggregated amounts of assets, liabilities, revenues and profit or loss (see A below);[127]

(f) if applicable, the reasons why the presumption that an investor does not have significant influence is overcome if the investor holds, directly or indirectly through subsidiaries, less than 20% of the voting or potential voting power of the investee but concludes that it has significant influence;[128]

(g) the reasons why the presumption that an investor has significant influence is overcome if the investor holds, directly or indirectly through subsidiaries, 20% or more of the voting or potential voting power of the investee but concludes that it does not have significant influence;[129]

(h) the reporting date of the financial statements of an associate, when such financial statements are used in applying the equity method and are as of a reporting date or for a period that is different from that of the investor, and the reason for using a different reporting date or different period;[130]

(i) the nature and extent of any significant restrictions (e.g. resulting from borrowing arrangements or regulatory requirements) on the ability of associates to transfer funds to the investor in the form of cash dividends, or repayment of loans or advances;[131]

(j) the unrecognised share of losses of an associate, both for the period and cumulatively, if an investor has discontinued recognition of its share of losses of an associate;[132]

(k) the fact that an associate is not accounted for using the equity method in accordance with paragraph 13 of IAS 28 (i.e. the exemptions summarised at 2.3 above);[133] and

(l) summarised financial information of associates, either individually or in groups, that are not accounted for using the equity method, including the amounts of total assets, total liabilities, revenues and profit or loss.[134]

The information required under (a), (b) and (c) should be presented in the notes in the event that associates and jointly controlled entities are presented together on the face of the primary financial statements.

Some of these disclosures can be seen in the financial statements of Barclays, as illustrated in Extract 8.10 below.

Extract 8.10: Barclays PLC (2006)

22 Investment in associated and joint ventures [extract]

Share of net assets

	Associates		Joint ventures		Total	
	2006	2005	2006	2005	2006	2005
	£m	£m	£m	£m	£m	£m
At beginning of year	427	399	119	30	546	429
Share of results before tax	63	63	(6)	(12)	57	51
Share of tax	(10)	(10)	(1)	4	(11)	(6)
Share of post-tax results	53	53	(7)	(8)	46	45
Dividends paid	(17)	(23)	–	–	(17)	(23)
New investments	2	–	7	81	9	81
Acquisitions	51	72	102	23	153	95
Disposals	(404)	(39)	(72)	(1)	(476)	(40)
Exchange and other adjustments	(38)	(35)	5	(6)	(33)	(41)
At end of year	74	427	154	119	228	546

Goodwill included above:

	Associates		Joint ventures		Total	
	2006	2005	2006	2005	2006	2005
	£m	£m	£m	£m	£m	£m
Cost						
At beginning of year	122	122	83	–	205	122
Acquisitions	–	–	–	83	–	83
Disposals	(121)	–	–	–	(121)	–
Transfer	–	–	(43)	–	(43)	–
At end of year	1	122	40	83	41	205

The fair value of the investment in Gabetti Holding SpA, which is listed on the Milan stock exchange, is £16m (2005: 315m).

Disposal of FirstCaribbean International Bank

On 22nd December 2006 the Group disposed of its investment in FirstCaribbean International Bank, its former principal associate, for cash consideration, net of transaction costs of £583m, which, after deducting the Group's share of its net assets on the date of disposal, resulted in a profit of £247.

Following this transaction, there were no individually significant associates or joint ventures.

Of the £46m share of post-tax results of associates and joint ventures, FirstCaribbean International Bank contributed £41m (2005:£37m).

The table below provides summarised financial information of the Group's associates and joint ventures (the entities' entire financial position and results of operations are presented, not the Group's share).

	2006			2005		
	FirstCaribbean International Bank	Other associates	Joint ventures	FirstCaribbean International Bank	Other associates	Joint ventures
	£m	£m	£m	£m	£m	£m
Property, plant and equipment	–	599	142	86	454	119
Financial investments	–	4	2	376	66	24
Trading portfolio assets	–	1	–	389	–	–
Loans to banks and customers	–	1,378	797	4,379	1,575	393
Other assets	–	541	199	267	226	16
Total assets	–	2,523	1,140	5,497	2,321	552
Deposits from banks and customers	–	1,421	769	4,519	1,527	369
Trading portfolio liabilities	–	1	–	115	–	–
Other liabilities	–	887	187	270	572	188
Shareholders' equity	–	214	184	593	222	(5)
Total liabilities	–	2,523	1,140	5,497	2,321	552
Net income	274	264	178	234	213	176
Operating expenses	(167)	(167)	(178)	(148)	(161)	(213)
Profit/(loss) before tax	107	97	–	86	52	(37)
Profit/(loss) after tax	96	90	(2)	76	37	(26)

The amounts included above are based on accounts made up to 31st December 2006 with the exception of FirstCaribbean International Bank and certain undertakings included within the Other associates category for which the amounts are based on accounts made up to dates not earlier than three months before the balance sheet date.

Other associates in 2006 includes £1,525m (2005: £1,885m) of assets, £1,380m (2005: £1,741,) of liabilities and £25m (2005: £20m) of profit after tax in associates within the Absa Group.

The Group's share of commitments and contingencies incurred in relation to its joint ventures is £nil (2005: £1m) and its share of contingent liabilities of an associate or joint venture for which it is contingently liable is £nil (2005: £252m).

It is worth noting that Barclays' disclosure of summarised financial information of associates and joint ventures in which the Group has an interest is prepared on the basis of the relevant entities' entire financial position and results of operations, and not on the basis of Barclays' share thereof. Once again, the standard is unclear as to whether this information is to be shown on the basis of the associates' entire financial position and results of operations (as Barclays have done), or on the basis of the investor's share thereof. In our view, both approaches are acceptable, and we believe that it is more important that companies disclose which approach they have followed.

A Summarised financial information of associates

IAS 28 is not clear about the basis on which the information required under (e) above should be presented. That is, it is not clear whether the information should:

- conform with IFRS as applied by the investor or should be based on the associate's own financial statements that may not even be prepared under IFRS;
- include the effects of the fair value exercise carried out by the investor; and
- be based on the investor's share of the associate or 100% of the associate's figures.

Two approaches, which both require the information to be presented in accordance with IFRS, are considered acceptable provided that they are applied consistently and are appropriately disclosed in the financial statements. The first approach is based on the view that the information disclosed should reflect the information that the investor uses in applying the equity method (i.e. reflecting the investor's accounting policies and its fair value exercise). If the information were to be measured on any other basis, its usefulness would be diminished considerably. The second approach is based on the argument that the whole purpose of the disclosure is for the reporting entity to present users with unadjusted summarised financial information of its associates. Nevertheless, we believe that this information would be most helpful to the user if it were to be presented based on the first approach. In fact, some may argue that only the first approach complies with the spirit of the requirements in IFRS, because:

- IAS 28 requires an associate to use the same accounting policies as the investor (see 3.6 above);[135]
- IAS 1 requires that financial statements and the notes thereto should be prepared on the same basis (see Chapter 3 at 2.3); and[136]
- any references to assets, liabilities, revenues and profit or loss in IAS 28 must logically be references to those terms as defined under IFRS.

However, it needs to be made clear that our comments regarding this lack of clarity in the standard apply only to the disclosures required about summarised financial information under paragraph 37(b) of IAS 28. The standard is clear that, in the case of both recognition and measurement, investments in associates must be accounted for on the basis of the investor's uniform accounting policies and must reflect appropriate fair value adjustments on acquisition (see 3.2 and 3.6 above).

5.2.2 *IAS 37 – Provisions, Contingent Liabilities and Contingent Assets*

In accordance with IAS 37[137] an investor must disclose:

- its share of the contingent liabilities of an associate incurred jointly with other investors; and
- those contingent liabilities that arise because the investor is severally liable for all or part of the liabilities of the associate.[138]

6 TRANSITIONAL AND FIRST-TIME ADOPTION ISSUES

6.1 General

As noted at 1.2 above, the December 2003 revised version of IAS 28 had to be applied for accounting periods beginning on or after 1 January 2005. Entities were encouraged to adopt this revised version of IAS 28 for earlier periods, but were required to disclose that they had done so.[139] There were no transitional provisions. Accordingly, an existing IFRS user had to apply the revised version of IAS 28 with full retrospective effect.

For first-time adopters there are a number of special provisions in IFRS 1. Most significant is the business combinations exemption, which also applies to past acquisitions of investments in associates (see 6.1.1 below).[140] In addition, there are separate rules that deal with situations in which an investor adopts IFRS before or after an associate does so (see 6.1.2 below).[141]

Otherwise there are no specific first-time adoption provisions in IAS 28, which means that a first-time adopter of IFRS is effectively required to apply IAS 28 as if it had always done so. For some first-time adopters, this may mean application of the equity method for the first time. For the majority of first time adopters, however, the issue is that they are already applying the equity method under national GAAP, and will now need to identify the potentially significant differences between the methodology of the equity method under their predecessor GAAP and under IAS 28.

In particular there may be differences between:

- the criteria used to determine which investments are associates;
- the elimination of transactions between investors and associates;
- the treatment of loss-making associates;
- the permitted interval between the reporting dates of an investor and an associate with non-coterminous year-ends; and
- the treatment of investments in entities formerly classified as associates.

6.1.1 Transition impairment review

A first-time adopter of IFRS is required by IFRS 1 to apply an impairment test in accordance with IAS 36 to any goodwill recognised at the date of transition to IFRS, regardless of whether there is any indication of impairment.[142] IFRS 1 specifically notes that its provisions with regard to past business combinations apply also to past acquisitions of investments in associates (see Chapter 5 at 2.4).[143] Therefore, a transition impairment review must be undertaken in accordance with the requirements of paragraphs B2(g) and B2(h) of IFRS 1 for investments in associates whose carrying value includes an element of goodwill. This impairment review will, however, need to be carried out on the basis required by IAS 28 as described in 4.1 above.

6.2 Investor and associate with different dates of first-time adoption of IFRS

IFRS 1 addresses in some detail the accounting treatment to be adopted when an investor in an associate adopts IFRS for the first time before its associate and where an associate adopts IFRS for the first time before its investor. This is discussed in Chapter 6 at 9.3.

7 CONCLUSION

IAS 28 is a standard that was issued in its original form nearly 20 years ago; it applies to all investments in associates – except for investments held by a venture capital organisation, mutual fund, unit trust or similar entity that are accounted for as financial assets under IAS 39 at fair value, with changes in fair value recognised in profit or loss.

However, despite its prolonged existence as a method of accounting, equity accounting is not necessarily accepted by all as the most appropriate approach to accounting for investments in entities that are currently defined as associates. For example, there is still no general agreement as to whether equity accounting itself is a form of one-line consolidation, or whether it is a form of valuation methodology. Of those that take the view that it is a form of valuation methodology, there are some that believe that all associates should be accounted for as financial assets at fair value under IAS 39. Indeed, IAS 28's option that allows venture capital organisations, mutual funds, unit trusts and similar entity to elect to account for their associates under IAS 39 implies that the IASB may not be averse to this approach.

In the meantime, the IASB intends to eliminate the option in IAS 31 of proportionate consolidation of jointly controlled entities, which means that joint venture entities will in the future all have to be accounted for under the equity method. It is possible that, once this has been achieved, the IASB may turn its attention to considering whether all investments in associates – and not just those held by venture capital organisations etc. – should be accounted for at fair value under IAS 39, thereby leaving equity accounting as a method that applies solely to certain joint venture arrangements.

References

1 IAS 28, *Investments in associates*, IASB, para. 1.
2 IAS 31, *Interests in Joint Ventures*, IASB, para. 38.
3 IAS 28, para. BC12.
4 IAS 28, paras. BC5-BC6.
5 IAS 28, paras. BC5-BC6.
6 IAS 28, para. BC8-BC9.
7 IAS 28, para. BC7.
8 IAS 39, *Financial Instruments: Recognition and Measurement*, IASB, paras. 9 and AG80-AG81.
9 IAS 32, *Financial Instruments: Disclosure and Presentation*, IASB, para. 4(a) and IFRS 7, *Financial Instruments: Disclosures*, IASB, para. 3(a).
10 *IASB Update*, IASB, May 2007, p. 4.
11 IAS 28, para. 2.

12 IAS 28, para. 2.
13 IAS 31, para. 2.
14 IAS 28, para. 2.
15 IAS 28, para. 2.
16 IAS 28, para. 6.
17 IAS 28, para. 21.
18 IAS 28, para. 7.
19 IAS 28, para. 10.
20 IAS 27, *Consolidated and Separate Financial Statements*, IASB, paras. 14 and IG1.
21 IAS 27, para. IG2.
22 IAS 28, para. 6.
23 IAS 27, para. 13.
24 IAS 28, para. 8.
25 IAS 28, para. 8.
26 IAS 28, para. 8.
27 IAS 28, para. 9.
28 IAS 27, paras. IG1-IG4.
29 IAS 28, para. IN10.
30 IAS 28, para. BC15.
31 IAS 28, para. 37(f).
32 IAS 28, para. 13.
33 IAS 28, para. 14.
34 IAS 27, para. 4.
35 IAS 28, para. 14.
36 IAS 28, para. IN9.
37 IFRS 5, *Non-current Assets Held for Sale and Discontinued Operations*, IASB, para. 15.
38 IAS 28, para. 15.
39 IAS 28, para. 2.
40 IAS 27, para. 37.
41 IAS 27, para. 4.
42 IAS 28, para. 35 and IAS 27, paras. 37-42.
43 IAS 28, para. 3.
44 IAS 28, para. 4.
45 IAS 28, para. 36.
46 IAS 28, para. 5.
47 IAS 28, para. 2.
48 IAS 28, para. 11.
49 IAS 28, para. 17.
50 IAS 28, para. 20.
51 IAS 28, para. 23.
52 IAS 28, para. 23.
53 IFRS 3, *Business Combinations*, IASB, para. 60.
54 IFRS 3, para. 58.
55 IFRS 3, para. 59.
56 IAS 28, para. 20.
57 IAS 28, para. 23.
58 IFRS 3, paras. 58-60.
59 IFRS 3, Illustrative Examples, Example 6.
60 IFRS 3, Illustrative Examples, Example 6.
61 IFRS 3, para. 58.
62 IAS 22, *Business Combinations*, IASC, Revised 1998, para. 38.
63 IFRS 3, paras. BC157-BC158.
64 IAS 28, para. 23.
65 IAS 28, para. 18.
66 IAS 28, para. 19.
67 IFRS 3 (near-final), *Near-final draft of IFRS 3 Business Combinations*, IASB, June 2007, para. D6.
68 IAS 28, para. 12.
69 IAS 28, para. 21.
70 IAS 28, para. 28.
71 IAS 28, para. 22.
72 There is a similar provision in IAS 27 (see Chapter 7 at 6.2).
73 IAS 28, para. 20.
74 IAS 28, para. 29.
75 IAS 27, para. 24 and IAS 28, paras. 20 and 22.
76 Detailed worked examples on the elimination cross-holdings in subsidiaries and associates can be found in *Bogie on group accounts*, John C. Shaw (editor), Bristol, 1973.
77 *IFRIC Update*, IFRIC, August 2002, p. 3.
78 IAS 28, para. 24.
79 IAS 28, paras. 25 and BC16.
80 IAS 28, para. 25.
81 IAS 28, para. 26.
82 IAS 28, para. 27.
83 IAS 28, paras. BC18-BC19.
84 IAS 28, para. 29.
85 IAS 28, para. 30.
86 IAS 28, para. 23.
87 IAS 28, para. 15.
88 IAS 28, para. 18.
89 IAS 39, para. 43.
90 IAS 28, para. 19.
91 IAS 21, *The Effects of Changes in Foreign Exchange Rates*, IASB, para. 49.
92 IAS 27 (near-final), *Near-final draft of IAS 27 Consolidated and Separate Financial Statements*, IASB, June 2007, para. A7 (IAS 28, para. 18).
93 IAS 27 (near-final), para. A7 (IAS 28, para. 19A).
94 IAS 27 (near-final), para. A6 (IAS 21, para. 48A).
95 IAS 27 (near-final), para. A7 (IAS 28, para. 19A).
96 IAS 27 (near-final), para. A6 (IAS 21, para. 48C).
97 IAS 27 (near-final), para. 43A.
98 IAS 28, para. 2.
99 IAS 28, para. 31.
100 IAS 28, para. 33.
101 IAS 28, para. 32.
102 IAS 28, para. 34.
103 IAS 28, para. 23.
104 IAS 28, para. 33.
105 IAS 39, para. 59.
106 IAS 36, *Impairment of Assets*, IASB, para. 33.
107 *IASB Update*, IASB, May 2007, p. 4.
108 *IASB Update*, IASB, May 2007, p. 4.
109 IAS 28, para. 31.

110 IAS 28, para. 33.
111 IAS 36, paras. 124-125.
112 IAS 36, para. 4.
113 IAS 28, para. 38.
114 IAS 1, *Presentation of Financial Statements*, IASB, para. 68(d).
115 IAS 28, para. 29.
116 IAS 28, para. 23.
117 IAS 1, para. 81(c).
118 IAS 1, para. IG4 'XYZ Group – Income statement for the year ended 31 December 20X2 (illustrating the classification of expenses by function)'.
119 IAS 28, para. 31.
120 IAS 1, para. 96 and IAS 28, para. 39.
121 IAS 28, para. 38.
122 IAS 1, para. 68(d).
123 IAS 28, para. 38.
124 IAS 28, para. 38.
125 IAS 28, para. 38.
126 IAS 28, para. 37(a).
127 IAS 28, para. 37(b).
128 IAS 28, para. 37(c).
129 IAS 28, para. 37(d).
130 IAS 28, para. 37(e).
131 IAS 28, para. 37(f).
132 IAS 28, para. 37(g).
133 IAS 28, para. 37(h).
134 IAS 28, para. 37(i).
135 IAS 28, para. 27.
136 IAS 1, para. 11.
137 The disclosure of contingent liabilities and contingent assets is dealt with in paragraphs 86 to 92 of IAS 37.
138 IAS 28, para. 40.
139 IAS 28, para. 41.
140 IFRS 1, *First-time Adoption of International Financial Reporting Standards*, IASB, para. B3.
141 IFRS 1, paras. 24-25.
142 IFRS 1, para. B2(g)(iii).
143 IFRS 1, para. B3.

110 IAS 28, para. 33.
111 IAS 36, paras. 124-125.
112 IAS 36, para. 4.
113 IAS 28, para. 38.
114 IAS 1, *Presentation of Financial Statements*, IASB, para. 68(b).
115 IAS 28, para. 29.
116 IAS 28, para. 28.
117 IAS 1, para. 81(c).
118 IAS 1, para. IG4 'XYZ Group – Income statement for the year ended 31 December 20X2 (illustrating the classification of expenses by function)'.
119 IAS 28, para. 31.
120 IAS 1, para. 76 and IAS 28, para. 39.
121 IAS 28, para. 38.
122 IAS 1, para. 68(e).
123 IAS 28, para. 38.
124 IAS 28, para. 38.
125 IAS 28, para. 38.
126 IAS 28, para. 37(a).
127 IAS 28, para. 37(b).
128 IAS 28, para. 37(c).
129 IAS 28, para. 37(d).
130 IAS 28, para. 37(e).
131 IAS 28, para. 37(f).
132 IAS 28, para. 37(g).
133 IAS 28, para. 37(h).
134 IAS 28, para. 37(i).
135 IAS 28, para. [illegible]
136 IAS 1, para. 11.
137 The disclosure of contingent liabilities and contingent assets is dealt with in paragraphs 86 to 92 of IAS 37.
138 IAS 28, para. 40.
139 IAS 28, para. 41.
140 IFRS 1, *First-time Adoption of International Financial Reporting Standards*, IASB, para. B5.
141 IFRS 1, paras. 24-25.
142 IFRS 1, para. B2(j)(ii).
143 IFRS 1, para. B5.

Chapter 9 Joint ventures

1 INTRODUCTION

1.1 The nature of joint ventures

As noted in the introduction to Chapter 6, an entity may conduct its business not only directly but also through strategic investments in other entities. IFRS, and most national GAAPs, broadly distinguish three types of such strategic investment:

- entities controlled by the reporting entity (subsidiaries – see Chapter 6);
- entities jointly controlled by the reporting entity and one or more third parties (joint ventures, the subject of this Chapter); and
- entities that, while not controlled or jointly controlled by the reporting entity, are subject to significant influence by it (associates – see Chapter 8).

There is a key distinction, both for the purposes of IFRS and commercially, between, on the one hand, subsidiaries and associates and, on the other hand, joint ventures. An interest in a subsidiary or an associate normally entails the acquisition or formation of a separate legal or economic entity. By contrast, a joint venture is essentially created by a legal or contractual relationship between the parties to the venture. Whilst many joint ventures do result in the creation of a separate legal entity to house the activities that are the subject of the venture, this is not a critical feature, and indeed many joint ventures result from direct joint ownership and control of assets, as opposed to joint ownership and control of an entity that in turn owns the assets.

Accounting for interests in joint ventures under IFRS is dealt with in IAS 31 – *Interests in Joint Ventures*. This is somewhat more complex than its 'sister' standards IAS 27 – *Consolidated and Separate Financial Statements* – and IAS 28 – *Investments in Associates* (which are discussed, respectively, in Chapters 6 and 8) in two respects.

Firstly, IAS 31 distinguishes between three types of joint venture (jointly controlled operations, jointly controlled assets, and jointly controlled entities) and prescribes different accounting treatments for each. Secondly, it allows two rather different accounting treatments (proportionate consolidation and equity accounting) for accounting for jointly controlled entities.

This choice of accounting treatment is somewhat unusual, given the IASB's efforts during its improvements project to eliminate alternative accounting treatments within IFRS, but must be seen against the following background. Joint ventures comprise a major part – sometimes all – of the activities of entities in some sectors (particularly extractive industries, property and construction). Over the years, these sectors have developed generally accepted 'industry GAAPs' that result in similar arrangements being accounted for differently in different sectors.

The IASB itself is still in the process of debating the merits of equity accounting and proportionate consolidation, not merely in the context of accounting for interests in joint ventures but also more generally. To have prescribed one or other method in IAS 31 could have been seen as pre-empting the outcome of those discussions. However, the IASB does intend to move to remove the option of proportionate consolidation for jointly controlled entities (see 3.3.8 and 7 below).

1.2 Development of IAS 31

Under IFRS accounting for joint ventures is dealt with principally by IAS 31. This was originally issued in December 1990 and has since been subject to a number of amendments, most notably in December 2003 as part of the IASB's improvements project, when the previous version of IAS 31 was withdrawn and replaced by a significantly revised version that became effective for accounting periods beginning on or after 1 January 2005. IAS 28 has been subject to further amendment by IFRSs issued since December 2003.

The SIC has issued an interpretation of IAS 31, SIC-13 – *Jointly Controlled Entities – Non-monetary Contributions by Venturers*.

1.3 Other applicable IFRS

In addition to IAS 31, the following pronouncements are relevant to accounting for joint ventures:

- IAS 27 – *Consolidated and Separate Financial Statements*;
- IAS 28 – *Investments in Associates*;
- IFRS 5 – *Non-current Assets Held for Sale and Discontinued Operations*;
- IFRS 1 – *First-time Adoption of International Financial Reporting Standards*;
- IAS 1 – *Presentation of Financial Statements*; and
- IAS 39 – *Financial Instruments: Recognition and Measurement*.

2 SCOPE OF IAS 31

2.1 General

IAS 31 must be applied in accounting for interests in joint ventures (see 2.2 below) and the reporting of joint venture assets, liabilities, income and expenses in the financial statements of venturers and investors, regardless of the structures or forms under which the joint venture activities take place.

However, IAS 31 does not apply to venturers' interests (see 2.2.1 below) in jointly controlled entities (see 3.3.1 below) held by:

(a) venture capital organisations, or

(b) mutual funds, unit trusts and similar entities including investment-linked insurance funds

that upon initial recognition are designated as 'at fair value through profit or loss' or are classified as 'held for trading' and accounted for in accordance with IAS 39. Such investments are measured at fair value in accordance with IAS 39, with changes in fair value recognised in profit or loss in the period of the change.[1]

The exemption for venture capital organisations and other similar financial institutions raises the question of exactly what entities comprise those described in (a) and (b), since they are not defined. Essentially the same issues arise in respect of the equivalent exemption in IAS 28 for investments in associates held by such entities, which is discussed in Chapter 8 at 2.1.1.

2.1.1 Disclosures of venturers' interests

An entity accounting for an interest in a joint controlled entity using IAS 39 should still disclose the information required by IAS 31 (see 4.2.2 and 4.2.3 below). This is because IAS 32 – *Financial Instruments: Disclosure and Presentation* – and IFRS 7 – *Financial Instruments: Disclosures* – specifically call for the IAS 31 disclosures to be made in addition to the disclosures required by the standards themselves[2], despite the fact that, as indicated at 2.1 above, IAS 31 does not apply to the entity.

In May 2007, the IASB tentatively decided to deal with this inconsistency by deleting the general IAS 31 disclosure requirements from IAS 32 and IFRS 7, but to retain the more burdensome disclosures required by paragraphs 55 and 56 of the standard.[3] Therefore, the amendment will not significantly reduce the disclosures required. An exposure containing this amendment is expected to be published in October 2007.

2.2 Definition of 'joint venture' and related terms

A *joint venture* is a contractual arrangement whereby two or more parties undertake an economic activity that is subject to joint control.[4]

Joint control is the contractually agreed sharing of control over an economic activity, and exists only when the strategic financial and operating decisions relating to the activity require the unanimous consent of the parties sharing control (the venturers).[5] Although IFRS does not define what financial and operating policies are, these are generally understood to include areas such as budgeting, capital expenditures, treasury management, dividend policy, production, marketing, sales and human resources.

An *investor* in a joint venture is a party to a joint venture and does not have joint control over that joint venture.[6]

A *venturer* is a party to a joint venture and has joint control over that joint venture.[7]

2.2.1 'Venturer' versus 'investor'

The definitions of 'investor' and 'venturer' above draw a distinction between participants in a joint venture who also participate in the joint control of that venture and more passive investors, as illustrated by Example 9.1.

Example 9.1: 'Venturer' versus 'investor'

A, B and C establish a fourth entity D, of which A owns 40%, B 11% and C 49%. A and B enter into a contractual arrangement whereby any financial and operating decisions taken by A and B relating to the activity of D require the unanimous consent of A and B. In the jurisdiction where D is incorporated a simple majority of shareholders only is required for all major decisions. IAS 31 would regard A and B as being 'venturers', and C as an 'investor', in D.

The interest of an 'investor' in a jointly controlled entity should be treated as:

(a) an associate within the scope of IAS 28 if the investor has significant influence over the entity (see Chapter 8); or

(b) otherwise as a financial asset within the scope of IAS 39 (see Chapter 20).[8]

2.2.2 Joint control

As noted in 1.1 above, joint ventures take many different forms and structures. However, IAS 31 identifies three broad types:

- jointly controlled operations (see 3.1 below);
- jointly controlled assets (see 3.2 below); and
- jointly controlled entities (see 3.3 below).

Under IAS 31, the following characteristics are common to all joint ventures:

(a) two or more venturers are bound by a contractual arrangement (see A below); and

(b) the contractual arrangement establishes joint control.[9]

A Contractual arrangement

IAS 31 emphasises that it is the existence of a contractual arrangement that distinguishes interests that involve joint control from investments in associates in which the investor has significant influence[10] (i.e. the power to participate in the financial and operating policy decisions of the investee but not amounting to control or joint control over those policies).[11]

Activities that have no contractual arrangement to establish joint control are not joint ventures for the purposes of IAS 31.[12] In other words, if two entities A and B set up a third entity C in which A and B each hold 50% of the equity, C will not, by virtue of the relative shareholdings *alone*, be a joint venture of A and B for the purposes of IAS 31. There needs to be an agreement for unanimous decision making on key matters – although this might automatically flow from the general provisions of corporate law in the jurisdiction concerned.

A contractual arrangement between venturers may be evidenced in a number of ways. There might be a separate contract between the venturers or minutes of discussions between them. In some cases, the arrangement is incorporated in the articles or other by-laws of the joint venture. Whatever its form, the contractual arrangement is usually in writing and deals with such matters as:

(a) the activity, duration and reporting obligations of the joint venture;

(b) the appointment of the board of directors or equivalent governing body of the joint venture and the voting rights of the venturers;

(c) capital contributions by the venturers; and

(d) the sharing by the venturers of the output, income, expenses or results of the joint venture.[13]

The effect of a contractual arrangement is to establish joint control over the joint venture, ensuring that no single venturer is in a position to control the activity unilaterally.[14] That means, for example, that none of the parties to the contractual arrangement should have a casting vote that enables it to resolve a deadlock, as that would constitute a form of unilateral control.

A contractual arrangement may identify one venturer as the operator or manager of the joint venture. The operator does not control the joint venture but acts within the financial and operating policies agreed by the venturers in accordance with the contractual arrangement and delegated to the operator. If the operator does have the power to govern (i.e. not merely to execute) the financial and operating policies of the economic activity, the operator controls the venture and the venture is a subsidiary of the operator and not a joint venture.[15]

B Legal and other restrictions on investee

IAS 31 notes that joint control may be precluded when an investee is in legal reorganisation or in bankruptcy, or operates under severe long-term restrictions on its ability to transfer funds to the venturer. However, if joint control continues, these events are not enough in themselves to justify not accounting for the investee as a joint venture in accordance with IAS 31.[16] This issue is discussed further (in the context of loss of control over subsidiaries) in Chapter 6 at 5.3.

C Potential voting rights

An entity may own share warrants, share call options, debt or equity instruments that are convertible into ordinary shares, or other similar instruments that have the potential, if exercised or converted, to give the entity voting power or reduce another party's voting power over the financial and operating policies of another entity (potential voting rights).

Potential voting rights are not directly addressed in IAS 31. However, the application guidance on potential voting rights in IAS 27 (see Chapter 6 at 3.1.2) indicates that it may also be relevant to the determination of joint control under IAS 31, while at the same time acknowledging that a contractual arrangement giving rise to joint control will tend to over-ride relative ownership interests (see 3.3.1 below). This is an issue that will need to be addressed in the light of individual facts and circumstances.

2.3 Requirement to apply IAS 31 to jointly controlled entities

There are no exemptions from applying IAS 31 to jointly controlled operations (see 3.1 below) or jointly controlled assets (see 3.2 below). Nevertheless, IFRS 5 would apply to jointly controlled operations and jointly controlled assets that meet the definition of an asset held for sale (disposal group) or discontinued operation

A venturer with an interest in a jointly controlled entity need not account for its interest using proportionate consolidation or equity accounting (see 3.3 below) if:[17]

(a) the interest is classified as held for sale in accordance with IFRS 5, in which case it is accounted for under that standard (see Chapter 4 at 2.1);[18]

(b) the venturer is a parent exempt from preparing consolidated financial statements under IAS 27 (see Chapter 6 at 4.1); or

(c) all of the following apply:

  (i) the venturer is a wholly-owned subsidiary, or is a partially-owned subsidiary of another entity and its other owners, including those not otherwise entitled to vote, have been informed about, and do not object to, the investor not applying proportionate consolidation or the equity method;

  (ii) the venturer's debt or equity instruments are not traded in a public market (a domestic or foreign stock exchange or an over-the-counter market, including local and regional markets);

  (iii) the venturer did not file, nor is it in the process of filing, its financial statements with a securities commission or other regulatory organisation, for the purpose of issuing any class of instruments in a public market; and

  (iv) the ultimate or any intermediate parent of the venturer produces consolidated financial statements available for public use that comply with International Financial Reporting Standards.

Conditions (i) to (iv) in (c) above are identical to the criteria that must be satisfied by:

- a parent in order to be exempt from preparing consolidated financial statements under IAS 27; or
- an investor in an associate that is not a parent in order to be exempt from equity accounting for its investment under IAS 28.

Further discussion of the meaning and interpretation of these conditions may be found in Chapter 6 at 4.1 and Chapter 8 at 2.3.

Essentially, exemption (c) is only available to entities that are themselves either wholly-owned subsidiaries or whose minority shareholders approve the presentation of financial statements that do not include jointly controlled entities using proportionate consolidation or the equity method. Some of these 'intermediate' entities will not be exempt, for example if none of their parents prepares consolidated financial statements in accordance with IFRS. A typical example is that of an entity that is a subsidiary of a US group that prepares consolidated accounts in accordance with US GAAP only. In addition, any entity that has publicly traded debt or equity, or is in the process of obtaining a listing for such instruments, will not meet the exemptions.

The effect of the above requirements is that a reporting entity that has jointly controlled entities, but no subsidiaries, and does not meet all the criteria in (c), is required to apply proportionate consolidation or equity accounting to its jointly controlled entities in its own (non-consolidated) financial statements (not to be confused with its 'separate financial statements' – see 2.4 below). This is significantly different from the requirement of many national GAAPs, where proportionate consolidation or equity accounting for jointly controlled entities is required (or indeed permitted) only in consolidated financial statements.

2.4 Separate financial statements

Separate financial statements are defined by IAS 31, consistent with IAS 27, as those presented by a parent, an investor in an associate or a venturer in a jointly controlled entity, in which the investments are accounted for on the basis of the direct equity interest rather than on the basis of the reported results and net assets of the investees.[19] The detailed IFRS requirements for separate financial statements are set out in IAS 27 and are discussed more fully in Chapter 6 at 7.[20]

It follows from the definition of separate financial statements above that financial statements (including non-consolidated financial statements) in which proportionate consolidation or the equity method is applied are not separate financial statements; neither are the financial statements of an entity that does not have a subsidiary, associate or venturer's interest in a joint venture.[21]

Separate financial statements are any financial statements presented in addition to:

- consolidated financial statements;
- financial statements in which investments are accounted for using the equity method; and
- financial statements in which venturers' interests in joint ventures are proportionately consolidated.

There is no requirement for an entity to prepare separate financial statements, or for any separate financial statements that are voluntarily prepared to be appended to, or accompany, the 'main' financial statements.[22]

An entity may present separate financial statements as its only financial statements if it satisfies the conditions for exemption from:[23]

- preparing consolidated financial statements under paragraph 10 of IAS 27 (see Chapter 6 at 4.1);
- equity accounting for associates under paragraph 13(c) of IAS 28 (see Chapter 8 at 2.3); and
- proportionately consolidating (or equity accounting for) jointly controlled entities under paragraph 2 of IAS 31 (see above).

As drafted this exemption makes a curious distinction between an entity with associates only and one with jointly controlled entities only.

An entity with associates may prepare separate financial statements as its only financial statements only if it satisfies the exemption in paragraph 13(c) of IAS 28. In other words, if an entity has associates, but is exempt from equity accounting for all of them under paragraph 13(a) – i.e. because they are all accounted for under IFRS 5 – it may apparently not present separate financial statements as its only financial statements. However, an entity with jointly controlled entities may prepare separate financial statements as its only financial statements if it satisfies the exemption in paragraph 2 of IAS 31, which includes jointly controlled entities accounted for under IFRS 5.

It can safely be assumed that this inconsistency was unintentional, but it is less obvious as to which exemption is correct and which incorrect. On balance, our view is that it is the exemption in relation to joint ventures which is incorrect. In other words, the IASB intended to give the exemption only to 'non-public interest' companies and should have referred to paragraph 2(c) of IAS 31.

2.5 'Pseudo' joint ventures

Some entities may have certain general characteristics of joint ventures, but not in fact be joint ventures. A particular example is the protected cell entity.

Example 9.2: Is it a joint venture? – Protected cell entity

Some jurisdictions permit the formation of so called 'protected cell' entities. Essentially these are entities which have a number of 'cells', with the assets and liabilities of each cell being completely ring-fenced – in other words the creditors of a particular cell have recourse only to the assets of that cell. In addition to the cells, each one of which has its own capital, there is a so-called 'core', whose shareholders may manage the activities of the cells on behalf of their owners. Diagrammatically, the structure can be portrayed as follows:

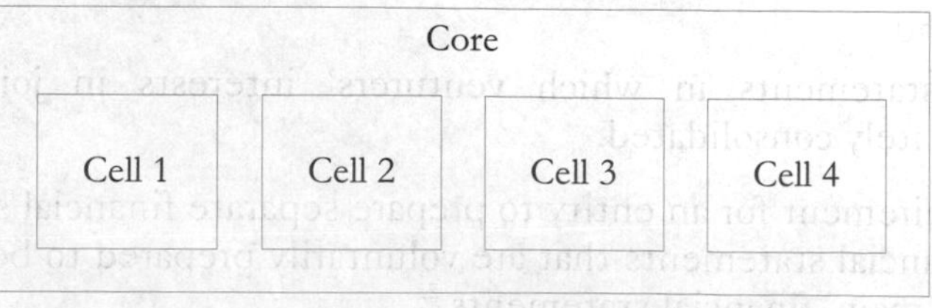

An original intention of this structure was to allow a fund-manager (who would hold the core shares) to run a number of independent funds (whose investors would hold the shares in the particular cell(s) concerned), with the incorporation of a single legal entity, as compared to the traditional position where each managed fund, and the management company, would be a separate legal entity, with all the attendant administrative costs and burdens.

Such a structure may give the superficial appearance of being a joint activity, but this is not the case. In most cases, it is extremely unlikely to be appropriate for an entity to regard an investment in a cell as a joint venture (or an associate). This is because the 'ring-fencing' of the assets and liabilities of each cell means that there is a direct linkage between the reporting entity and one or more particular cells, rather than that the reporting entity has some share of the profits or losses of the cell entity as a whole. The most likely conclusion is that each cell is a special purpose entity (SPE) of another entity (see Chapter 6 at 3.2).

3 ACCOUNTING REQUIREMENTS

3.1 Jointly controlled operations

A jointly controlled operation is one which involves the use of assets and other resources of the venturers, rather than the establishment of a corporation, partnership of other entity, or a financial structure, separate from the venturers themselves. Each venturer uses its own property, plant and equipment and carries its own inventories. It also incurs its own expenses and liabilities and raises its own finance, which represent its own obligations. The joint venture activities may be carried out by the venturer's employees alongside similar activities of the venturer. The joint venture agreement usually provides the basis for sharing among the venturers the revenue sales of the joint product and any common expenses incurred.[24]

An example of a jointly controlled operation might be that two or more venturers combine their operations, resources and expertise in order to jointly manufacture, market and distribute a particular product, such as an aircraft, with each venturer undertaking different parts of the manufacturing process. Each venturer bears its own costs and takes a share of the revenue from the sale of the aircraft, such share being determined in accordance with the contractual arrangement.[25]

In respect of its interest in a jointly controlled operation, IAS 31 requires a venturer to recognise in its financial statements:

- the assets that it controls and the liabilities that it incurs; and
- the expenses that it incurs and its share of the income that it earns from the sale of goods or services by the joint venture.[26]

IAS 31 notes that, because the assets, liabilities, income and expenses are already recognised in the financial statements of the venturer, no adjustments or other consolidation procedures are required in respect of these items when the venturer presents consolidated financial statements. Separate accounting records may not be required, nor financial statements prepared, for the joint venture itself, although the venturers may prepare management accounts so that they may assess the performance of the joint venture.[27]

When venturers are funding the operations of a jointly controlled operation they may need to account for a receivable or payable from other venturers, as illustrated in Example 9.3 below.

Example 9.3: Loans to jointly controlled operations

Two entities – A and B – each own half of a jointly controlled operation. Entity A has lent €400 to the jointly controlled operation, while entity B has lent €300. How should entity A account for its loan?

The jointly controlled operation has total borrowings of €400 + €300 = €700. A's share in the borrowings of €350 (=50% of €700) should be offset against its receivable of €400. Entity A should, therefore, account for a net receivable from its joint venture partner of €50 (=€400 – €350).

The jointly controlled operation is not a separate legal entity and under the joint venture agreement A has a business relationship only with B. Gross presentation of a receivable of €200 (=€400 – 50% of €400) and a liability of €150 (=50% of €300) would therefore not be appropriate.

The extract below shows a typical accounting policy for jointly controlled operations.

Extract 9.1: Xstrata plc (2006)

Notes to the Financial Statements [extract]
6. Principal Accounting Policies [extract]
Jointly controlled operations
A jointly controlled operation involves the use of assets and other resources of the Group and other venturers rather than the establishment of a corporation, partnership or other entity.
The Group accounts for the assets it controls and the liabilities it incurs, the expenses it incurs and the share of income that it earns from the sale of goods or services by the joint venture.

3.2 Jointly controlled assets

Some joint ventures involve the joint control, and often the joint ownership, of one or more assets contributed to, or acquired for, and dedicated to the purposes of, the joint venture. The assets are used to obtain benefits for the venturers, who may each take a share of the output from the assets and bear an agreed share of the expenses incurred. Such ventures do not involve the establishment of an entity or financial structure separate from the venturers themselves, so that each venturer has control over its share of future economic benefits through its share in the jointly controlled asset.[28]

IAS 31 notes that joint ventures of this type are particularly common in extractive industries. For example, a number of oil companies may jointly control and operate an oil pipeline. Each venturer uses the pipeline to transport its own product in return for which it bears an agreed proportion of the operating expenses of the pipeline. Another example of a jointly controlled asset could be that two entities jointly control a property, each taking a share of the rents received and bearing a share of the expenses.[29]

In respect of its interest in jointly controlled assets, IAS 31 requires a venturer to recognise in its financial statements:

- its share of the jointly controlled assets, classified according to the nature of the assets (i.e. a share in a jointly controlled pipeline should be shown within property, plant and equipment rather than as an investment);
- any liabilities which it has incurred;
- its share of any liabilities incurred jointly with the other venturers;
- any income from the sale or use of its share of the output of the joint venture;
- its share of any expenses incurred by the joint venture; and
- any expenses which it has incurred in respect of its interest in the joint venture (e.g. those relating to financing the venturer's interest in the assets and selling its share of the output).[30]

The IASB believes that this treatment reflects the substance and economic reality and, usually, the legal form of the joint venture.[31] However, it should be noted that, as Example 9.4 at 3.3.1 below illustrates, the classification of a joint venture as either a jointly controlled asset or a jointly controlled entity is largely form driven.

As in the case of jointly controlled operations (see 3.1 above), no adjustments or other consolidation procedures are required when the venturer presents consolidated financial statements, because the relevant assets, liabilities, income and expenses are already recognised in the financial statements of the venturer.[32]

IAS 31 notes that the accounting records of the joint venture itself may be limited to a record of the expenses incurred in common by the venturers, and ultimately borne by them according to their agreed shares. Financial statements may not be prepared for the joint venture, although the venturers may prepare management accounts so that they may assess the performance of the joint venture.[33]

Extract 9.2 below shows a typical accounting policy for jointly controlled assets.

Extract 9.2: Xstrata plc (2006)

Notes to the Financial Statements [extract]

6. Principal Accounting Policies [extract]

Jointly controlled assets

A jointly controlled asset involves joint control and offers joint ownership by the Group and other venturers of assets contributed to or acquired for the purpose of the joint venture, without the formation of a corporation, partnership or other entity.

The Group accounts for its share of the jointly controlled assets, any liabilities it has incurred, its share of any liabilities jointly incurred with other ventures, income from the sale or use of its share of the joint venture's output, together with its share of the expenses incurred by the joint venture, and any expenses it incurs in relation to its interest in the joint venture.

Extract 9.3 below illustrates an example of a company contributing its own assets to joint ventures that are accounted for as jointly controlled assets.

Extract 9.3: Anglo Platinum Limited (2006)

NOTES TO THE CONSOLIDATED FINANCIAL STATEMENTS [extract]

17 Joint ventures [extract]

Jointly controlled assets

Bafokeng-Rasimone Platinum Mine (BRPM) Joint Venture

The Group and Royal Bafokeng Resources (Pty) Limited (RBR) have entered into a 50:50 joint venture. In terms of the agreement, the Group contributes the operating Bafokeng-Rasimone Platinum Mine (BRPM) and the related mineral rights to the venture, while RBR contributes certain mineral rights and has to compensate the Group for the net cash spent on the development of BRPM, plus interest.

Mototolo Joint Venture

The Group and Xstrata South Africa (Pty) Limited have entered into a 50:50 joint venture. In terms of the agreement, each party will contribute a similar amount of in situ PGM reserves and resources from Xstrata's Thorncliffe farm, adjacent to its Thorncliffe chrome mine and the Group's bordering farm, part of its Der Brochen project area. This joint venture became unconditional during October 2005.

3.3 Jointly controlled entities

3.3.1 Definition

In contrast to a jointly controlled operation or jointly controlled asset, a jointly controlled entity is a joint venture that involves the establishment of a corporation, partnership or other entity in which each venturer has an interest. The entity operates in the same way as any other entity, except that a contractual arrangement between the venturers establishes joint control over the economic activity of the entity.[34]

A jointly controlled entity controls the assets of the joint venture, incurs liabilities and expenses and earns income. It may enter into contracts in its own name and raise finance for the purposes of the joint venture activity. IAS 31 notes that 'each venturer is entitled to a share of the results of the jointly controlled entity, although some jointly controlled entities also involve a sharing of output.'[35]

IAS 31's reference to the fact that a venturer's interest in a jointly controlled entity may be in its 'output' rather than its results, suggests that, once a separate legal entity is involved, one is dealing with a jointly controlled entity and not a jointly controlled asset, even if the economic substance appears very similar. Example 9.4 illustrates the point.

Example 9.4: Jointly controlled asset or jointly controlled entity?

If three entities – A, B and C – each own one-third of a pipeline (and enter into a contractual agreement giving each party joint control), the venture is a jointly controlled asset. If, however, A, B and C each own one-third of a fourth entity D which owns the pipeline (and enter into a contractual agreement giving each party joint control), the venture is considered to be a jointly controlled entity.

This suggests that a venturer's share of the output of an asset may be accounted for differently depending on whether the share in the asset is held directly or through a separate legal entity, particularly when it is borne in mind that IAS 31 gives an exemption in respect of accounting for a jointly controlled entity (see 2.3 above), but not in respect of a jointly controlled asset.

However, it could be said that these different outcomes are no different to the fact that, if a company owns a property, it shows a property in its separate financial statements whereas, if it incorporates a subsidiary to hold the property, it shows an investment in subsidiary in its separate financial statements.

IAS 31 goes on to say that many jointly controlled entities are similar in substance to jointly controlled operations or jointly controlled assets. For example, the venturers may transfer a jointly controlled asset, such as an oil pipeline, into a jointly controlled entity, for tax or other reasons. Similarly, the venturers may contribute into a jointly controlled entity assets which will be operated jointly. Some jointly controlled operations also involve the establishment of a jointly controlled entity to deal with particular aspects of the activity, for example, the design, marketing, distribution or after-sales service of the product.[36]

This emphasises the fact that, whilst the economic substance of a jointly controlled asset and a jointly controlled entity may in fact be similar, the difference in form does matter in determining the accounting treatment. This is articulated in paragraph 32 of the standard (which deals with proportionate consolidation – see 3.3.3 below), as follows:[37]

> 'when recognising an interest in a jointly controlled entity, it is essential that a venturer reflects the substance and economic reality of the arrangement, rather than the joint venture's particular structure or form. In a jointly controlled entity, a venturer has control over its share of future economic benefits through its share of the assets and liabilities of the venture. This substance and economic reality are reflected in the consolidated financial statements of the venturer when the venturer recognises its interests in the assets, liabilities, income and expenses of the jointly controlled entity by using one of the two reporting formats for proportionate consolidation described [below].'

This indicates that, in the IASB's view, the substance of a joint venture is determined by its legal form and that, once joint ventures are enveloped in a separate legal entity, they become jointly controlled entities under IAS 31. Therefore a contractual arrangement that involves the establishment of a legal entity under joint control would be a jointly controlled entity, even if the entity does not carry on a trade or business of its own and merely owns a group of assets.

IAS 31 notes that a common example of a jointly controlled entity is when two entities combine their activities in a particular line of business by transferring the relevant assets and liabilities into a jointly controlled entity. Another example might be that an entity, in order to commence a business in a foreign country in conjunction with the government or other agency in that country, establishes a separate entity which is jointly controlled by the entity and the government or a government agency.[38]

IAS 31 adds that another feature of a jointly controlled entity is that it maintains its own accounting records and prepares and presents financial statements in the same way as other entities in conformity with IFRS.[39] This again reinforces the message that the classification of joint ventures as jointly controlled entities is, in fact, rather form-based. Whether or not an entity keeps its own books is arguably more a reflection of local legal requirements than of the economic substance of its activities.

IAS 31 notes that each venturer usually contributes cash or other resources to the jointly controlled entity. These contributions are included in the accounting records of the venturer and recognised in its separate financial statements as an investment in the jointly controlled entity.[40]

3.3.2 Accounting treatment – summary

IAS 31 permits two methods of accounting for jointly controlled entities:

- proportionate consolidation (see 3.3.3 below), using one of two permitted formats; and
- the equity method (see 3.3.4 below).[41]

Subject to the exemption discussed at 2.3 above, the venturer must apply whichever method it selects irrespective of whether it also has investments in subsidiaries or whether it describes its financial statements as 'consolidated financial statements'.[42] This requirement in IAS 31 is intended to emphasise that proportionate consolidation (or equity accounting) for jointly controlled entities may be required even for an entity that is not preparing consolidated financial statements.

A Difference between allowed treatments

In many cases the essential difference between the two methods is simply one of presentation – i.e. whether items are shown on a 'line-by-line' basis (in the case of proportionate consolidation) or a 'one line' basis (in the case of equity accounting). However, this is not always the case as is discussed at I to IV below.

I Loss-making joint ventures

The treatment of a loss-making jointly controlled entity may differ significantly under each method. Where proportionate consolidation is used, the venturer will simply pick up its share of all losses as they arise. Whereas under the equity method, the reporting entity will apply 'waterline accounting' (see Chapter 8 at 3.7), so that the carrying amount of its interest in the joint venture never falls below zero, except to the extent that the investor has incurred legal or constructive obligations or made payments on behalf of the joint venture. Of course, it is in the nature of joint ventures that a venturer in a joint venture is more likely to have such legal or constructive obligations than an investor in an associate. Therefore, in some cases there is no difference between equity accounting for, and proportionate consolidation of, loss-making jointly controlled entities.

II Capitalisation of borrowing costs

A difference between proportionate consolidation and equity accounting may arise when the venturer capitalises borrowing costs that are directly attributable to the acquisition, construction or production of a qualifying asset. A qualifying asset is defined by IAS 23 – *Borrowing Costs* – as 'an asset that necessarily takes a substantial period of time to get ready for its intended use or sale.'[43]

If the jointly controlled entity itself did not incur any borrowing costs then the venturer would capitalise its own borrowing costs in respect of all qualifying assets of a proportionately consolidated jointly controlled entity. However, a venturer applying the equity method to such joint ventures would not be able to capitalise its borrowing costs because investments accounted for under the equity method are not qualifying assets.[44]

III Hedging of the joint ventures

Another difference relates to the application of hedge accounting. A venturer that proportionately consolidates its investments in jointly controlled entities may be able to apply hedge accounting to assets, liabilities, firm commitments and highly probable forecast transactions of the joint venture. Whereas a venturer applying the equity method to similar joint ventures would only be able to apply hedge accounting to the equity accounted investment as a whole.

IV Impairment of a jointly controlled entity

IAS 28 contains special impairment testing rules that apply to investments accounted for under the equity method (see Chapter 8 at 4). This involves applying the requirements of IAS 39 to determine whether an impairment exists, followed by an impairment test under IAS 36 – *Impairment of Assets* – of the investment as a whole. That is, the cash generating units and goodwill of the joint venture would not be tested separately for impairment under IAS 36. Consequently, in our view, the IAS 36 prohibition on the reversal of impairment losses on goodwill would not apply either, and a previously recognised impairment of an investment that is accounted for under the equity method is fully reversible (see Chapter 8 at 4.4).

Venturers that proportionately consolidate their investments under IAS 31 would be required to test the cash generating units and goodwill of the joint venture separately for impairment under IAS 36, which means that impairment of goodwill is irreversible. However, it is not necessary to carry out an additional impairment test as envisioned under IAS 28.

B Consistency of treatment

As drafted, IAS 31 requires a venturer to apply either proportionate consolidation or equity accounting to its interest in 'a' jointly controlled entity.[45] This could be interpreted as suggesting that the venturer can make the choice of accounting treatment for each jointly controlled entity individually.

However, the disclosure provisions of IAS 31 (see 4.2.2 below) require a venturer to disclose 'the' method used to account for 'its interests in jointly controlled entities'.[46] In our view, this, together with:

- the use of similar wording in another disclosure requirement in IAS 31;
- the statement that IAS 8 – *Accounting Policies, Changes in Accounting Estimates and Errors* – incorporates the consensus in SIC-18 – *Consistency – Alternative Methods* – which specifically required consistent application of the option in IAS 31; and[47]
- the overall requirement of IAS 1 for the use of consistent accounting policies for similar transactions (see Chapter 3 at 4.1.4),

clearly indicates that the IASB expects a venturer to account for all jointly controlled entities on a consistent basis.

3.3.3 Proportionate consolidation

IAS 31 defines proportionate consolidation as 'a method of accounting whereby a venturer's share of each of the assets, liabilities, income and expenses of a jointly controlled entity is combined line by line with similar items in the venturer's financial statements or reported as separate line items in the venturer's financial statements.'[48]

As noted in the discussion at 3.3.1 above, IAS 31 asserts that this method of accounting is necessary in order to capture the substance and economic reality of a venturer's interest in a jointly controlled entity.[49]

The application of proportionate consolidation means that the balance sheet of the venturer includes its share of the assets that it controls jointly and its share of the liabilities for which it is jointly responsible. The income statement of the venturer includes its share of the income and expenses of the jointly controlled entity.[50] In effect, the end result is equivalent to accounting for a partly-owned subsidiary, but excluding net assets attributable to the minority interest. IAS 31 notes that the procedures for consolidation of subsidiaries set out in IAS 27 (see Chapter 6 at 6) will generally be appropriate for the proportionate consolidation of joint ventures.[51]

Proportionate consolidation should be carried out using one of two permitted formats.

- *Line-by-line presentation*

  The jointly controlled entity is consolidated on an aggregated line-by-line basis (i.e. the venturer combines its share of the assets, liabilities, income and expenditure of the jointly controlled entity within the similar items in its own financial statements);

- *Presentation as separate line items*

  The venturer includes separate line items for its share of the total assets, liabilities, income and expenditure of the jointly controlled entity in its own consolidated accounts. Thus for example the item 'debtors' in the venturer's own financial statements would include a sub-heading 'share of debtors of joint ventures'.

The difference between the formats is clearly one of presentation only. Both formats result in the reporting of identical amounts of profit or loss and of each major classification of assets, liabilities, income and expenses.[52] In practice though, few companies present their investment in jointly controlled entities as separate line items.

IAS 31 states that, whatever format is used to give effect to proportionate consolidation, it is inappropriate to offset any assets or liabilities by the deduction of other liabilities or assets or any income or expenses by the deduction of other expenses or income, unless a legal right of set-off exists and the offsetting represents the expectation as to the realisation of the asset or the settlement of the liability.[53] It is not entirely clear what IAS 31 means by this. We take it to mean that, whereas a balance between two members of a group would always be eliminated in consolidated financial statements as a matter of general consolidation practice (i.e. regardless of whether or not the balances are as a matter of law offsettable and intended to be settled net), a balance between a venturer and a joint venture is eliminated only where there exists a legal right of set-off, and an intention to settle net.

Proportionate consolidation of a jointly controlled entity should cease on the date that the venturer ceases to have joint control over the entity. This may occur either when the venturer disposes of its interest or when such external restrictions are placed on the jointly controlled entity that the venturer no longer has joint control.[54] See also 3.3.6 below.

Under proportionate consolidation, the venturer simply accounts for its share of the jointly controlled entity. It does not, for example, treat the interests of any passive investors (see 2.2 above) as some form of minority interest.

Extract 9.4 below shows a typical accounting policy for the proportionate consolidation of jointly controlled entities.

Extract 9.4: ABN AMRO NV (2006)

Accounting policies [extract]

Basis of consolidation [extract]

Jointly controlled entities

Jointly controlled entities are those enterprises over whose activities the Group has joint control, established by contractual agreement. The consolidated financial statements include the Group's proportionate share of these enterprises' assets, liabilities, equity, income and expenses on a line-by-line basis, from the date on which joint control commences until the date on which joint control ceases.

3.3.4 *Equity method*

The equity method is defined as in IAS 28 as a method of accounting whereby an interest in a jointly controlled entity is initially recorded at cost and adjusted thereafter for the post-acquisition change in the venturer's share of net assets of the jointly controlled entity. The profit or loss of the venturer includes the venturer's share of the profit or loss of the jointly controlled entity.[55]

Where a venturer accounts for its interest in jointly controlled entities using equity accounting, it follows the requirements of IAS 28 with regard to the application of the equity method (see Chapter 8 at 3).[56]

IAS 31 states that the use of the equity method is supported by:

(a) those who argue that it is inappropriate to combine controlled items with jointly controlled items; and

(b) those who believe that venturers have significant influence, rather than joint control, in a jointly controlled entity.[57]

Both these arguments are somewhat difficult to understand, at least as expressed here. The objection raised by the argument in (a) would be met by presenting the share of the jointly controlled entity's assets, liabilities, income and expenditure alongside, but not aggregated with, those of the venturer (see 'Presentation as separate line items' at 3.3.3 above).

The argument in (b) above makes little sense at all, since, as a matter of definition in IAS 28 and IAS 31, it is impossible for an entity over which the investor has only 'significant influence' to be a 'jointly controlled entity'. In effect, such an argument implies a belief that the definitions of 'significant influence' and 'joint control' are themselves wrong, and it therefore surprising that the IASB should permit an accounting treatment based on such a premise.

Rather curiously, IAS 31 does not acknowledge the real conceptual objection to proportionate consolidation, which is that in many cases 'joint control' is not the same as having an interest in part of the individual assets and liabilities; rather, it is a share in the venture as a whole. Indeed, those who hold this view often consider that there are circumstances in which it is appropriate to use equity accounting and others where proportionate consolidation may better represent the entity's interests in the underlying venture, so that it is not appropriate to prescribe a single accounting treatment for all joint ventures.

IAS 31 does not recommend the use of the equity method because, in its view, proportionate consolidation better reflects the substance and economic reality of a venturer's interest in a jointly controlled entity, that is to say, control over the venturer's share of the future economic benefits. Nevertheless, IAS 31 permits the use of the equity method, as an alternative treatment, when recognising interests in jointly controlled entities.[58]

As noted in 1.1 above, the choice of accounting treatment permitted by IAS 31 in all probability owes as much to 'political' as to technical considerations.

A venturer that applies the equity method to its interest in a jointly controlled entity discontinues this accounting treatment from the date on which it ceases to have joint control over the entity, unless the entity becomes an associate under IAS 28, in which case the equity method is continued, but pursuant to IAS 28 rather than IAS 31 (see also 3.3.6 below).[59]

The extract below shows a detailed accounting policy for jointly controlled entities that are accounted for under the equity method.

Extract 9.5: BP p.l.c. (2006)

Notes on financial statements [extract]

1 Significant accounting policies [extract]

Interests in joint ventures

A joint venture is a contractual arrangement whereby two or more parties (venturers) undertake an economic activity that is subject to joint control. Joint control exists only when the strategic financial and operating decisions relating to the activity require the unanimous consent of the venturers. A jointly controlled entity is a joint venture that involves the establishment of a company, partnership or other entity to engage in economic activity that the group jointly controls with its fellow venturers.

The results, assets and liabilities of a jointly controlled entity are incorporated in these financial statements using the equity method of accounting. Under the equity method, the investment in a jointly controlled entity is carried in the balance sheet at cost plus post-acquisition changes in the group's share of net assets of the jointly controlled entity, less distributions received and less any impairment in value of the investment. The group income statement reflects the group's share of the results after tax of the jointly controlled entity. The group statement of recognized income and expense reflects the group's share of any income and expense recognized by the jointly controlled entity outside profit and loss.

Financial statements of jointly controlled entities are prepared for the same reporting year as the group. Where necessary, adjustments are made to those financial statements to bring the accounting policies used into line with those of the group.

Unrealized gains on transactions between the group and its jointly controlled entities are eliminated to the extent of the group's interest in the jointly controlled entities. Unrealized losses are also eliminated unless the transaction provides evidence of an impairment of the asset transferred. The group assesses at each balance sheet date whether an investment in a jointly controlled entity is impaired. If there is objective evidence that an impairment loss has been incurred, the carrying amount of the investment is compared with its recoverable amount, being the higher of its fair value less costs to sell and value in use. Where the carrying amount exceeds the recoverable amount, the investment is written down to its recoverable amount.

The group ceases to use the equity method of accounting on the date from which it no longer has joint control over, or significant influence in the joint venture, or when the interest becomes held for sale.

Certain of the group's activities, particularly in the Exploration and Production segment, are conducted through joint ventures where the venturers have a direct ownership interest in and jointly control the assets of the venture. The income, expenses, assets and liabilities of these jointly controlled assets are included in the consolidated financial statements in proportion to the group's interest.

3.3.5 *Jointly controlled entity previously accounted for under IFRS 5*

Where an investor has not been proportionately consolidating, or equity accounting for, an interest in a jointly controlled entity on the basis that it is classified as held for sale under IFRS 5 (see 2.3 above), and the investment ceases to be so classified, the investor must apply proportionate consolidation or equity accounting retrospectively as from the date on which the investment was originally classified as held for sale. The financial statements of any prior periods since that classification must be restated.[60]

3.3.6 *Jointly controlled entity ceasing to be jointly controlled entity*

If a jointly controlled entity becomes a subsidiary, it should be accounted for, from the date that it does so, in accordance with IAS 27 (see Chapter 6). If a jointly controlled entity becomes an associate, it should be accounted for, from the date that it does so, in accordance with IAS 28 (see Chapter 8).[61]

Unlike IAS 27 and IAS 28, IAS 31 does not specifically provide any guidance on the treatment of an interest a jointly controlled entity that ceases to be so, and becomes neither a subsidiary nor an associate, but an investment. However, the clear inference is that:

- a former jointly controlled entity that has been accounted for using proportionate consolidation should be accounted for under the requirements of IAS 27 in respect of former subsidiaries that become investments (see Chapter 6 at 6.6.2); and
- a former jointly controlled entity that has been accounted for using equity accounting should be accounted for under the requirements of IAS 28 in respect of former associates that become investments (see Chapter 8 at 3.8).

In effect, the former jointly controlled entity will ultimately be accounted for in accordance with IAS 39. The measurement rules in IAS 39 are complex and are discussed in detail in Chapter 20. In brief, however, they will entail the former associate being recorded initially at 'fair value',[62] but its cost is deemed to be its carrying amount on the date that it ceases to be an associate.[63] Therefore, if the investment is subsequently accounted for as an 'available-for-sale' financial asset the difference between its cost and fair value should be accounted for within equity. If the investment is subsequently accounted for as a 'financial asset at fair value through profit or loss' then the difference is recognised in net profit for the period. In either case, the investment will subsequently be measured at fair value – what differs is whether the gains and losses arising on revaluation are accounted for in the income statement or in equity.

However, the IASB has proposed significant changes in this area as part of its Business Combinations (Phase II) project (see C below).

A Cumulative exchange differences on jointly controlled entities

IAS 27 (see Chapter 6 at 6.6.1) specifically reinforces the requirement of IAS 21 – *The Effects of Foreign Exchange Rates* (see Chapter 10 at 2.7.3) that, when an investment in a foreign operation is disposed of, the gain or loss on disposal should include the 'recycling' of the cumulative exchange gains and losses that have, in accordance with IAS 21, been recognised in equity in respect of that operation. Whilst there is no such explicit reinforcement of IAS 21 in IAS 31, it seems clear that the same principle should apply on disposal of a jointly controlled entity.

IAS 21 clarifies that disposal of a foreign operation may occur through sale, liquidation, repayment of share capital, abandonment or receipt of a dividend out of pre-acquisition profits. When a partial disposal occurs, only the proportionate share of the related accumulated exchange difference is included in profit or loss. IAS 21 further clarifies that a write-down of a foreign operation does not constitute a partial disposal, and accordingly no part of the deferred foreign exchange gain or loss is recognised in profit or loss at the time of the such a write-down,[64] unless of course the write-down is consequent upon an event of 'disposal' as just described.

This begs the further question as to the appropriate treatment of any cumulative exchange gains and losses on a former jointly controlled entity which becomes subject to IAS 39, as described above. The issues here are very similar to those arising in respect of a former subsidiary which becomes subject to IAS 39, which are discussed in Chapter 6 at 6.6.2 A.

However, the IASB has proposed significant changes in this area as part of its Business Combinations (Phase II) project (see C below).

B Other cumulative gains and losses previously recognised in equity

Like IAS 27, IAS 31 does not specifically address the accounting treatment, on disposal of a jointly controlled entity, of the venturer's share of other cumulative gains and losses previously accounted for in equity relating to assets and liabilities of the disposed jointly controlled entity. Such cumulative gains and losses, which would be recycled in profit or loss if those assets and liabilities had been disposed of separately by the jointly controlled entity, could include:

- accumulated hedging gains and losses accounted for under IAS 39 (see Chapter 21), and
- any other amounts previously recognised in equity that would have been recognised in profit or loss if the jointly controlled entity had directly disposed of the assets to which they relate, such as gains or losses on available-for-sale financial assets accounted for under IAS 39 (see Chapter 20 at 3.4).

IAS 39 does not specifically address this issue either. However, it would appear that recycling is appropriate, since the disposal of a jointly controlled entity does give rise to the derecognition of the venturer's share of the separate assets and liabilities of that jointly controlled entity just as if they had been disposed of separately. Moreover, the changes that the IASB proposes to make to IAS 31 (see C below) appear to assume that it is clear that such gains and losses should be recycled on disposal of a jointly controlled entity.

C Future developments: Business Combinations Phase II

The IASB's Business Combinations Phase II project is proposing a number of changes in accounting for a loss of joint control. IAS 27 – *Near-final draft of IAS 27 Consolidated and Separate Financial Statements* – amends paragraph 45 of IAS 31 so that it will read as follows:

> 'When an investor ceases to have joint control over an entity, it shall account for any remaining investment in accordance with IAS 39 from that date, provided that the former jointly controlled entity does not become a subsidiary or associate. From the date on which a jointly controlled entity becomes a subsidiary of an investor, the investor shall account for its interest in accordance with IAS 27 and IFRS 3 (where applicable). From the date on which a jointly controlled entity becomes an associate of an investor, the investor shall account for its interest in accordance with IAS 28. On the loss of joint control, the investor shall measure at fair value any investment the

investor retains in the former jointly controlled entity. The investor shall recognise in profit or loss any difference between:

(a) the fair value of the retained investment and any proceeds from disposing of the part interest in the jointly controlled entity; and

(b) the carrying amount of the investment at the date joint control is lost.'[65]

Furthermore, IAS 28 will be amended to require that if an investor loses joint control of an entity, all amounts recognised in other comprehensive income and accumulated as a separate component of equity in relation to that entity should be recognised by the investor on the same basis that would be required if the jointly controlled entity had directly disposed of the related assets or liabilities.[66] Similarly, IAS 21 will be amended to require that upon loss of joint control the cumulative amount of the exchange differences deferred in the separate component of equity relating to that jointly controlled entity be recognised in profit or loss.[67] In practice that would mean that a gain or loss should be recognised upon loss of joint control, even if a former jointly controlled entity is subsequently accounted for as an available-for-sale financial asset.

When an investor's interest in a jointly controlled entity is reduced (but the investee remains a jointly controlled entity), then the investor should 'reclassify to profit or loss only a proportionate amount of the gain or loss previously recognised in other comprehensive income'[68] and 'reclassify to profit or loss only the proportionate share of the cumulative amount of the exchange differences recognised in other comprehensive income'.[69] That means that the investor should recognise in profit or loss a proportion of:

- foreign exchange differences recognised in equity under IAS 21,
- accumulated hedging gains and losses recognised in equity under IAS 39 (see Chapter 21), and
- any other amounts previously recognised in equity that would have been recognised in profit or loss if the jointly controlled entity had directly disposed of the assets to which they relate, such as gains or losses on available-for-sale financial assets accounted for under IAS 39 (see Chapter 20 at 3.4),

in each case proportionate to the interest disposed of.

The above amendments are expected to be effective for annual periods beginning on or after 1 January 2009.[70]

3.3.7 Step acquisition of a joint venture

It is not clear under IFRS how an investor should account for a situation in which it obtains joint control over an associate because of an additional investment and new contractual arrangements. Example 9.5 below describes two methods of accounting for such transactions.

Example 9.5: Associate becoming a joint venture after an increase in ownership

In 2005, Entity A acquired a 20% interest in Entity B. Entity A is able to exercise significant influence and accounts for its investment under the equity method. In 2007, A acquired an additional 30% interest in B, thereby increasing its total interest in B to 50%. At the time of the acquisition, A enters into a joint venture agreement that gives it joint control over B. Entity A accounts for its 50% interest in B using proportionate consolidation under IAS 31.

This raises the question whether A, in applying proportionate consolidation for the first time to its investment in B, should recognise its existing 20% interest in the net assets of B at (1) the amounts that it used in applying the equity method or (2) their fair value at the date that A obtained joint control. In our view, re-measurement of the existing 20% interest is only appropriate when A applies proportionate consolidation in accounting for its interests in jointly controlled entities and there is:

- a change in the relationship between A and B, that is, from one in which A can exercise significant influence to one in which A has joint control; and
- a simultaneous change in the method of accounting for the investment from the equity method to proportionate consolidation.

Where these conditions apply, we consider it acceptable to view this as analogous to the initial application of the consolidation method so that the revaluation provisions of paragraph 59 of IFRS 3 could be applied. However, if Entity A's policy is to apply the equity method in accounting for its interests in joint ventures, the existing interest should not be re-measured. In addition, it would not be appropriate for the investor to change its policy from the equity method to proportionate consolidation to facilitate the re-measurement of its existing interest to fair value.

A Future developments

The IASB's Business Combinations Phase II project is proposing changes to IFRS 3 (see Chapter 7 at 5.1) and IAS 28 (see Chapter 8 at 3.2.2 C) that will affect the way that step acquisitions of joint ventures should be accounted for.

3.4 Transactions between a venturer and a joint venture

3.4.1 Background

It is common for venturers to transact with the joint venture, in particular on the formation of the venture. Typical transactions include:

- The venturers contribute cash to the venture in proportion to their agreed relative shares. The venture then uses some or all of the cash to acquire assets from the venturers for use in the venture;
- The venturers contribute other assets (or a mixture of cash and other assets) to the joint venture with fair values, as agreed between the venturers, in proportion to the venturers' agreed relative shares in the venture;
- The venturers contribute other assets to the joint venture with fair values, as agreed between the venturers, not in proportion to the venturers' agreed relative shares. Cash 'equalisation' payments are then made between the venturers so that the overall financial position of the venturer does correspond to their agreed relative shares in the venture.

A further complication is that some of these assets that are the subject of such transactions may be intangible assets not recognised under IFRS in the financial statements of the contributing venturers (e.g. internally generated brands and know-how).

IAS 31, together with SIC–13, provides broad overall principles as to the treatment of such transactions, but no specific indication of the accounting entries required to give effect to those principles. Moreover, SIC–13 applies strictly only to transactions involving the transfer of assets to jointly controlled entities (and not to other types of joint venture).

3.4.2 IAS 31 requirements

When a venturer contributes or sells assets to a joint venture, IAS 31 requires that the recognition of any gain or loss should reflect the substance of the transaction. While the assets are retained by the joint venture, and provided that the venturer has transferred the significant risks and rewards of ownership, the venturer should recognise only that portion of the gain or loss which is attributable to the interests of the other venturers. However, the venturer should recognise the full amount of any loss when the contribution or sale provides evidence of a reduction in the net realisable value of current assets or an impairment loss. Where non-monetary assets are contributed to a jointly controlled entity, the additional guidance in SIC–13 must also be considered (see 3.4.3 below).[71]

When a venturer purchases assets from a joint venture, the venturer must not recognise its share of the profits of the joint venture from the transaction until it resells the assets to an unrelated third party. A venturer recognises its share of the losses resulting from these transactions in the same way as profits, except that (as in the case of sales to the joint venture) losses should be recognised immediately when they represent a reduction in the net realisable value of current assets or an impairment loss.[72]

The venturer should assess whether a transaction between itself and a joint venture provides evidence of impairment of any asset transferred in accordance with IAS 36 which is discussed in Chapter 15 at 3.[73]

The effect of these requirements is illustrated in Examples 9.5 to 9.8 below. It should be noted that these requirements appear to apply to all transactions with joint ventures, irrespective of whether the venturer has availed itself of IAS 31's exemption from proportionate consolidation or equity accounting for joint ventures (see 2.3 above). They also appear to apply to the separate financial statements of a venturer.

Example 9.6: Sale of asset from venturer to joint venture at a profit

Two entities A and B establish a joint venture involving the creation of a jointly controlled entity C in which A and B each hold 50%. A and B each contribute €5 million in cash to the joint venture in exchange for equity shares. C then uses €8 million of its €10 million cash to acquire from A a property recorded in the financial statements of A at €6 million. It is agreed that €8 million is the fair market value of the property. How should A account for these transactions?

The required accounting entry if A accounts for its interest in C using proportionate consolidation is:

	€m	€m
Cash (1)	3	
Share of cash of C (2)	1	
Share of property of C (3)	3	
Property (4)		6
Gain on sale (5)		1

(1) €8 million received from C less €5 million contributed to C.

(2) 50% of C's cash of €2 million [€10 million received from A and B less €8 million paid to A]

(3) 50% of €8 million (carrying value in books of C), less €1 million (share of profit eliminated – see (5) below). In effect, this treatment represents that A still holds 50% of the property at its original carrying value to A (50% of €6 million = €3 million).

(4) Derecognition of A's original property.

(5) Gain on sale of property €2 million (€8 million received from C less €6 million carrying value = €2 million), less 50% eliminated (so as to reflect only profit attributable to interest of other venturer B) = €1 million.

If A accounted for C using equity accounting the accounting would be identical, except that it would show simply 'Investment in C' of €4 million rather than the €1 million share of C's cash and €3 million share of C's property.

Example 9.7: Sale of asset from venturer to joint venture at a loss

Two entities A and B establish a joint venture involving the creation of a jointly controlled entity C in which A and B each hold 50%. A and B each contribute €5 million in cash to the joint venture in exchange for equity shares. C then uses €8 million of its €10 million cash to acquire from A a property recorded in the financial statements of A at €10 million. €8 million is agreed to be the fair market value of the property. How should A account for these transactions?

The required accounting entry if A accounts for its interest in C using proportionate consolidation is:

	€m	€m
Cash (1)	3	
Share of cash of C (2)	1	
Share of property of C (3)	4	
Loss on sale (4)	2	
Property (5)		10

(1) €8 million received from C less €5 million contributed to C.

(2) 50% of C's cash €2 million (€10 million from A and B minus €8 million to A)

(3) 50% of €8 million (carrying value in books of C), not adjusted since the transaction indicated an impairment of A's asset.

(4) Loss on sale of property €2 million (€8 million received from C less €10 million carrying value = €2 million) not adjusted since the transaction indicated an impairment of the property. In effect, it is the result that would have been obtained if A had recognised an impairment charge immediately prior to the sale and then recognised no gain or loss on the sale.

(5) Derecognition of A's original property.

If A accounted for C using equity accounting the accounting would be identical, except that it would show simply 'Investment in C' of €5 million rather than the €1 million share of C's cash and €4 million share of C's property.

Example 9.8: Sale of asset from joint venture to venturer at a profit

Two entities A and B establish a joint venture involving the creation of a jointly controlled entity C in which A and B each hold 50%. A and B each contribute €5 million in cash to the joint venture in exchange for equity shares. C then uses €8 million of its €10 million cash to acquire a property from an independent third party D. The property is later sold to A for €12 million, which is agreed to be its market value. How should A account for these transactions?

The required accounting entry if A accounts for its interest in C using proportionate consolidation is:

	€m	€m
Property (1)	10	
Share of cash of C (2)	7	
Cash (3)		17

(1) €12 million paid to C less elimination of A's share of the profit made by C €2 million (50% of [€12 million sales proceeds less €8 million cost to C]).

(2) 50% of C's cash €14 million (€10 million from A and B minus €8 million to D plus €12 million from A).

(3) €5 million cash contributed to C plus €12 million consideration paid for property

If A accounted for C using equity accounting the accounting would be identical, except that it would show 'Investment in C' of €7 million rather than the €7 million share of C's cash.

Example 9.9: Sale of asset from joint venture to venturer at a loss

Two entities A and B establish a joint venture involving the creation of a jointly controlled entity C in which A and B each hold 50%. A and B each contribute €5 million in cash to the joint venture in exchange for equity shares. C then uses €8 million of its €10 million cash to acquire a property from an independent third party D. The property is then sold to A for €7 million, which is agreed to be its market value. How should A account for these transactions?

The required accounting entry if A accounts for its interest in C using proportionate consolidation is:

	€m	€m
Property (1)	7.0	
Share of cash of C (2)	4.5	
Share of loss of C (3)	0.5	
Cash (4)		12.0

(1) €7 million paid to C not adjusted since the transaction indicated an impairment of C's asset.

(2) 50% of C's cash €9 million (€10 million from A and B minus €8 million to D plus €7 million received from A).

(3) Loss in C's books is €1 million (€8 million cost of property less €7 million proceeds of sale). A recognises its 50% share because the transaction indicates an impairment of the asset. In effect, it is the result that would have been obtained if C had recognised an impairment charge immediately prior to the sale and then recognised no gain or loss on the sale.

(4) €5 million cash contributed to C plus €7 million consideration for property.

If A accounted for C using equity accounting the accounting would be identical, except that it would show 'Investment in C' of €4.5 million rather than the €4.5 million share of C's cash.

It may be that transactions occur between a venturer and a joint venture in assets, such as inventories, which are destined for onward sale in the normal course of business by the buying party. The accounting adjustments required are essentially the same as those for similar transactions between an investor and its associate, examples of which are given in Chapter 8 at 3.4.

3.4.3 Non-monetary contributions to joint ventures

SIC-13 provides guidance on the application of these general principles to the specific situation of a transfer of non-monetary assets to a jointly controlled entity in exchange for equity. This states that the venturer should recognise in its income statement the portion of any gain or loss arising on the transfer attributable to the other venturers unless:

- significant risks and rewards of ownership of the contributed non-monetary asset(s) have not been transferred to the jointly controlled entity; or
- the gain or loss on the non-monetary contribution cannot be measured reliably; or
- the contribution lacks commercial substance, as that term is described in IAS 16 – *Property, Plant and Equipment* (see A below and Chapter 13 at 2.3.3).[74]

If any of the above conditions applies, the gain or loss arising would be considered 'unrealised' (and therefore not recognised in the income statement), unless in addition to receiving an equity interest in the entity, a venturer receives monetary or non-monetary assets, in which case an 'appropriate portion' of the gain or loss on the transaction should be recognised by the venturer. SIC-13 does not elaborate on what would constitute an appropriate portion of the gain or loss in such circumstances.[75]

Where the venturer accounts for the jointly controlled entity using proportionate consolidation, any unrealised gains or losses should be eliminated against the venturer's share of the underlying assets of the entity. Where equity accounting is used, the elimination should be against the carrying value of the investment in the entity. Unrealised gains or losses should not be accounted for as deferred income or expenditure.[76] Where 'unrealised' losses are eliminated in this way, the effect will be to apply what is sometimes referred to as 'asset swap' accounting. In other words, the carrying value of the investment in the jointly controlled entity will be the same as the carrying value of the non-monetary assets transferred in exchange for it, subject of course to any necessary provision for impairment uncovered by the transaction.

A 'Commercial substance'

As noted above, SIC–13 requires that a transaction should not be treated as realised when, inter alia, it lacks commercial substance as described in IAS 16. That standard states that an exchange of assets has 'commercial substance' when:

(a) either:

(i) the configuration (risk, timing and amount) of the cash flows of the asset received differs from the configuration of the cash flows of the asset transferred; or

(ii) the entity-specific value of the portion of the entity's operations affected by the transaction changes as a result of the exchange; and

(b) the difference in (i) or (ii) above is significant relative to the fair value of the assets exchanged.[77]

IAS 16's 'commercial substance' test is designed to enable an entity to measure, with reasonable objectivity, whether the asset that it has acquired in a non-monetary exchange is different to the asset it has given up.

The first stage is to determine the cash flows both of the asset given up and of the asset acquired (the latter being, of course, the interest in the jointly controlled entity). This determination may be sufficient by itself to satisfy (a) above, as it may be obvious that there are significant differences in the configuration of the cash flows. The type of income may have changed. For example, if the entity contributed a non-monetary asset such as a property or intangible asset to the jointly controlled entity, the reporting entity may now be receiving a rental or royalty stream from the jointly controlled entity, whereas previously the asset contributed to the cash flows of the cash-generating unit of which it was a part.

However, determining the cash flows may not result in a clear-cut conclusion, in which case the entity-specific value will have to be calculated. This is not the same as a value in use calculation under IAS 36, in that the entity is allowed to use a discount rate based on its own assessment of the risks specific to the operations, not those that reflect current market assessments[78] and post-tax cash flows.[79] The transaction will have commercial substance if these entity-specific values are not only different to one another but also significant compared to the fair values of the assets exchanged.

The calculation may not be highly sensitive to the discount rate as the same rate is used to calculate the entity-specific value of both the asset surrendered and the entity's interest in the jointly controlled entity. However, if the entity considers that a high discount rate is appropriate, this will have an impact on whether or not the difference is significant relative to the fair value of the assets exchanged. It is also necessary to consider the significance of:

(a) the requirement above that the entity should recognise in its income statement the portion of any gain or loss arising on the transfer attributable to the other venturers;

(b) the general requirements of IAS 31 in respect of transactions between venturers and their joint ventures; and

(c) the general requirement of IFRS 3 – *Business Combinations* – to recognise assets acquired in a business combination at fair value (see Chapter 7).

As a result, we consider that it is likely that transactions entered into with genuine commercial purposes in mind are likely to pass the 'commercial substance' tests outlined above. However, these rules are designed to prevent the recognition of gains where an entity enters into an artificial transaction with the intention of manufacturing a gain by attributing inflated values to the assets exchanged.[80]

B Applying SIC–13 in practice

SIC–13 does not give an example of the accounting treatment that it envisages when a gain is treated as 'realised'. However, we believe that the intended approach is that set out in Example 9.10 below. In essence, this approach reflects the fact that the reporting entity has:

(a) acquired an interest in a jointly controlled entity that must be accounted for at fair value under IFRS 3; but

(b) is required to restrict any gain arising as a result of the exchange relating to its own assets to the extent that the gain is attributable to the other party to the joint venture. This leads to an adjustment of the carrying amount of the assets of the joint venture (as in Example 9.6 at 3.4.2 above).

Example 9.10: Contribution of non-monetary assets to form joint venture

A and B are two major pharmaceutical companies, which agree to form a joint venture (JV Co) in respect of a particular part of each of their businesses. A will own 40% of the joint venture, and B 60%. The parties agree that the total value of the new business is £250 million.

A's contribution to the venture is one of its subsidiaries, in respect of which A's consolidated balance sheet reflects separable net assets of £50 million and goodwill of £10 million. The fair value of the separable net assets of the subsidiary contributed by A is considered to be £80 million. The implicit fair value of the business contributed is £100 million (40% of the total fair value of £250 million).

B also contributes a subsidiary, in respect of which B's consolidated balance sheet reflects separable net assets of £85 million and goodwill of £15 million. The fair value of the separable net assets is considered to be £120 million. The implicit fair value of the business contributed is £150 million (60% of total fair value of £250 million).

The book and fair values of the businesses contributed by A and B can therefore be summarised as follows:

	A		B	
(in £m)	Book value	Fair value	Book value	Fair value
Separable net assets	50	80	85	120
Goodwill	10	20	15	30
Total	60	100	100	150

How should A apply SIC–13 in accounting for the set-up of the joint venture?

The general principles of IFRS 3 require that A should account at fair value for the acquisition of its 40% interest in the new venture. However, as noted above, any gain or loss recognised by A must reflect only the extent to which it has disposed of the assets to the other partners in the venture (i.e. in this case, 60% – the extent to which A's former subsidiary is effectively transferred to B through B's 60% interest in the new venture).

This gives rise to the following accounting entry.

	£m	£m
Share of net assets of JV Co (1)	68	
Goodwill (2)	16	
Separable net assets and goodwill contributed to JV Co (3)		60
Gain on disposal (4)		24

(1) 40% of fair value of separable net assets of new entity £80 million (40% of [£80 million + £120 million] as in table above) less elimination of 40% of gain on disposal £12 million (40% of £30 million, being the difference between the book value [£50 million] and fair value [£80 million] of A's separable net assets, as in table above, contributed to JV Co) = £68 million.

This is equivalent to, and perhaps more easily calculated as, 40% of [book value of A's separable net assets + fair value of B's separable net assets], i.e. 40% × [£50 million + £120 million] = £68 million.

If A adopted proportionate consolidation, this £68 million would naturally be allocated to the relevant balance sheet headings.

(2) Fair value of consideration given £100 million (as in table above) less fair value of 40% share of separable net assets of JV Co acquired £80 million (see (1) above) = £20 million, less elimination of 40% gain on disposal £4 million (40% of £10 million, being the difference between the book value [£10 million] and fair value [£20 million] of A's goodwill, as in table above, contributed to JV Co) = £16 million.

This is equivalent to, and perhaps more easily calculated as, 40% of [book value of A's goodwill + fair value of B's goodwill], i.e. 40% × [£10 million + £30 million] = £16 million.

(3) Previous carrying amount of net assets contributed by A, now deconsolidated. In reality there would be a number of entries to deconsolidate these on a line-by-line basis.

(4) Fair value of business acquired £100 million (as in table above) less book value of assets disposed of £60 million (as in table above) = £40 million, less 40% of gain eliminated (£16 million) = £24 million. The £16 million eliminated reduces A's share of JV Co's separable net assets by £12 million (see (1) above) and its share of JV Co's goodwill by £4 million (see (2) above).

As noted in the introductory remarks above, it is common when joint ventures are set up in this way for the fair value of the assets contributed not to be exactly in proportion to the fair values venturers' agreed relative shares. Cash 'equalisation' payments are then made between the venturers so that the overall financial position of the venturer does correspond to their agreed relative shares in the venture (see Extract 9.6 below). Our suggested treatment of such payments in the context of a transaction within the scope of SIC–13 is illustrated in Example 9.11 below.

Example 9.11: Contribution of non-monetary assets to form joint venture with cash equalisation payment between venturers

Suppose that the transaction in Example 9.10 was varied so that A is to have only a 36% interest in JV Co. However, as shown by the introductory table in Example 9.10, A is contributing a business worth 40% of the total fair value of JV Co. Accordingly, B makes good the shortfall by making a cash payment to A equivalent to 4% of the fair value of JV Co, i.e. £10 million (4% of £250 million).

This would require A to make the following accounting entries.

	£m	£m
Share of net assets of JV Co (1)	61.2	
Cash (equalisation payment from B)	10.0	
Goodwill (2)	14.4	
Separable net assets and goodwill contributed to JV Co (3)		60.0
Gain on disposal (4)		25.6

(1) 36% of fair value of separable net assets of new entity £72 million (36% of [£80 million + £120 million] as in table above) less elimination of 36% of gain on disposal £10.8 million (36% of £30 million, being the difference between the book value [£50 million] and fair value

[£80 million] of A's separable net assets, as in table above, contributed to JV Co) = £61.2 million.

This is equivalent to, and perhaps more easily calculated as, 36% of [book value of A's separable net assets + fair value of B's separable net assets], i.e. 36% × [£50 million + £120 million] = £61.2 million.

If A adopted proportionate consolidation, this £61.2 million would naturally be allocated to the relevant balance sheet headings.

(2) Fair value of consideration given £100 million (as in table above), less cash equalisation payment received £10 million = £90 million less fair value of 36% share of separable net assets of JV Co acquired £72 million (see (1) above) = £18 million, less elimination of 36% gain on disposal £3.6 million (36% of £10 million, being the difference between the book value [£10 million] and fair value [£20 million] of A's goodwill, as in table above, contributed to JV Co) = £14.4 million.

This is equivalent to, and perhaps more easily calculated as, 36% of [book value of A's goodwill + fair value of B's goodwill], i.e. 36% × [£10 million + £30 million] = £14.4 million.

(3) Previous carrying amount of net assets (excluding goodwill) contributed by A, now deconsolidated. In reality there would be a number of entries to deconsolidate these on a line-by-line basis.

(4) Fair value of business acquired £90 million (36% of £250 million) plus cash equalisation payment £10 million = £100 million, less book value of assets disposed of £60 million (as in table above) = £40 million, less 36% of gain eliminated (£14.4 million) = £25.6 million. The £14.4 million eliminated reduces A's share of JV Co's separable net assets by £10.8 million (see (1) above) and its share of JV Co's goodwill by £3.6 million (see (2) above).

The extract below shows how a company might in practice want to disclose the effect of the application of SIC-13.

Extract 9.6: Alcatel-Lucent (2006)

Notes to consolidated financial statements [extract]

Note 3 – Changes in consolidated companies [extract]

On July 1, 2005, Alcatel and Finmeccanica announced the successful creation of two joint ventures that had been described in a memorandum of understanding signed by the parties on June 24, 2004: Alcatel Alenia Space (Alcatel-Lucent holds 67% and Finmeccanica 33%) and Telespazio Holding (Finmeccanica holds 67% and Alcatel 33%). These joint ventures are consolidated using the proportionate consolidation method starting July 1, 2005.

Alcatel analyzed this transaction as a sale to Finmeccanica of 33% of Alcatel Space's satellite industrial activity and 67% of its service activity and as an acquisition of 67% of Alenia Spazio (the industrial space systems of Finmeccanica) and of 33% of Telespazio (service activities for Finmeccanica's space systems).

The values assigned to this transaction were €1,530 million for Alenia Space and €215 million for Telespazio, resulting in a gain to Alcatel on the sale before tax of €129 million in 2005 and in goodwill not yet allocated of €143 million. Alcatel received from Finmeccanica an equalization payment of €109 million. Net cash resulting from the activities acquired and disposed of is €15 million at the transaction date. Due to the existence of price adjustment clauses in the agreement between Alcatel and Finmeccanica, adjustments to the above amounts were made during the third quarter 2006 (see above).

Proportionately consolidating the combined space activities of the two partners did not have a significant impact on Alcatel's revenues, operating margin and total balance sheet. However, this consolidation method resulted in recognizing a deferred tax charge of €38 million due to the removal from the French tax consolidation of the companies transferred to the joint ventures in the context of the transaction described above.

Note 38 – Summary of differences between accounting principles followed by Alcatel-Lucent and U.S. GAAP [extract]

(a) Differences in accounting for business combinations [extract]

Contribution of Space businesses by Alcatel and Alenia to two jointly controlled joint ventures [extract]

As described in Note 3 to the financial statements, on July 1, 2005, Alcatel and Finmeccanica announced the creation of two joint ventures that had been described in a memorandum of understanding signed by the parties on June 24, 2004: Alcatel Alenia Space (Alcatel holds 67% and Finmeccanica 33%) and Telespazio Holding (Finmeccanica holds 67% and Alcatel 33%). These joint ventures are jointly controlled, as defined by IAS 31 *Joint Ventures* and are therefore consolidated using the proportionate method of consolidation starting July 1, 2005.

Under IFRS, in accordance with the guidance provided by SIC 13 *Jointly Controlled Entities – Non-Monetary Contributions by Venturers*, the recognition of any portion of a gain or loss from the transaction shall reflect the substance of the transaction. While the assets are retained by the joint venture, and provided the venturer has transferred the significant risks and rewards of ownership, the venturer shall recognise only that portion of the gain or loss that is attributable to the interests of the other venturers. Therefore a gain related to the contributed business was accounted for amounting to €129 million as of December 31, 2005.

Under U.S. GAAP, contributing assets to a joint venture does not usually result in the culmination of the earnings process. However, similar to the guidance in Statement of Position 78-9, *Accounting for Investments in Real Estate Ventures*, when cash is paid to one of the joint venturers in order to balance the fair market value of assets contributed by each venturer, gain recognition is allowed insofar as such gain is limited to the lesser of the computed gain or the amount of cash received, provided the recipient has no refund or continuing support obligation. As indicated in Note 3, Alcatel received from Finmeccanica a payment of €109 million upon creation of the joint venture.

Further, the gain on contributed assets differs under U.S. GAAP from the gain accounted for under IFRS due to differences between the net book value of the contributed assets under both standards, mainly related to the amortization of goodwill (see Note 38b) and accounting treatment of pensions (see Note 38f). As a consequence of the above, the gain related to the contributed business accounted for under U.S. GAAP in 2005 amounts to €72 million.

I 'Artificial' transactions

A concern with transactions such as this is that it is the relative, rather than the absolute, value of the transaction that is of concern to the parties. In other words, in Example 9.10 above, it could be argued that the only clear inference that can be drawn is that A and B have agreed that the ratio of the fair values of the businesses they have each contributed is 40:60, rather than that the business as a whole is worth £250 million. Thus it might be open to A and B, without altering the substance of the transaction, to assert that the value of the combined operations is £500 million (with a view to enlarging their balance sheets) or £200 million, (with a view to increasing future profitability).

Another way in which the valuation of the transaction might be distorted is through disaggregation of the consideration. Suppose that the £60 million net assets contributed by A in Example 9.10 above comprised:

	£m
Cash	12
Other net current assets	13
Property, plant and equipment	25
Goodwill	10
	60

Further suppose that, for tax reasons, the transaction was structured such that A was issued with 4% of the shares of JV Co in exchange for the cash and 36% in exchange for the remaining assets. This could lead to the suggestion that, as there can be no doubt as to the fair value of the cash, A's entire investment must be worth £120 million (i.e. £12 million × 40/4). Testing transactions for their commercial substance will require entities to focus on the fair value of the transaction as a whole and not to follow the strict legal form.

Of course, once cash equalisation payments are introduced, as in Example 9.11 above, the transaction terms provide evidence as to both the relative and absolute fair values of the assets contributed by each party.

II Accounts of JV Co

IFRS 3 does not apply to business combinations in which separate entities or businesses are brought together to form a joint venture.[81] Therefore, it is not clear under IFRS how the acquisition of the former businesses of both A and B by JV Co should be accounted for. We consider that under the GAAP hierarchy in IAS 8 the pooling of interests method is still available when accounting for the formation of a joint venture and there may be other approaches (including the purchase method) that will be considered to give a fair presentation in particular circumstances.

If JV Co were to apply the purchase method, which it could justify under the GAAP hierarchy in paragraph 11 of IAS 8 (see Chapter 3 at 4.3), it would mean that the amounts taken up in the accounts of A and B may bear little relation to either party's share of the net assets of the joint venture as reported in the underlying financial statements of the investee. For example, A's share of any depreciation charge recorded by JV Co must be based on the carrying amount of A's share of JV Co's PPE, not as recorded in JV Co's books (i.e. at fair value) but as recorded in A's books, which will be based on book value as regards PPE contributed by A and at fair value as regards PPE contributed by B. Accordingly it may be necessary for both A and B to keep a 'memorandum' set of books for consolidation purposes reflecting their share of assets originally their own at book value and those originally of the other party at fair value.

Alternatively, if JV Co were to apply the pooling of interest method, both A and B would still need to keep a 'memorandum' set of books for consolidation purposes because their share of assets that were originally of the other party should be carried at fair value rather than carry-over cost.

In practice, however, keeping a set of 'memorandum' books may be easier said than done, and a fairly broad brush approach may be unavoidable.

3.4.4 Loans and borrowings between the reporting entity and joint ventures

IAS 31's requirement to eliminate partially unrealised profits or losses on transactions with joint ventures is expressed in terms of transactions involving the transfer of assets. This raises the question of whether this requirement is generally intended to items such as interest paid on loans between joint ventures and the reporting entity.

Where a jointly controlled entity is accounted for using proportionate consolidation, we believe that the requirement for partial elimination of profits is generally intended to be extended to loans and related items, but subject to the general restrictions on offset that IAS 31 requires when proportionate consolidation is adopted (see 3.3.3 above).

Where a jointly controlled entity is accounted for using equity accounting, however, we do not believe that the requirement for partial elimination of profits is generally intended to be extended to loans and related items, since such loans do not involve the transfer of assets giving rise to gains or losses. Moreover, they are not normally regarded as part of the investor's share of the net assets of the investee, but as separate transactions, except in the case of loss-making investees, where interests in long-term loans may be required to be accounted for as if they were part of the reporting entity's equity investment in determining the carrying value of the joint venture against which losses may be offset (see Chapter 8 at 3.7).

3.5 Income Taxes

Income taxes arising from interests in joint ventures are accounted for in accordance with IAS 12 – *Income Taxes*. In cases where joint control does not give joint control over the distribution policy of the joint venture, the venturer may be required to provide in full for deferred tax on temporary differences relating to joint ventures.

Some might question whether the lack of joint control over distribution policy suggests that in fact the venturer does not exert joint control sufficient for the investment to be treated as a joint venture under IAS 31. However, IAS 12 notes that a joint venture agreement will 'usually' give joint control over distribution policy, but does not appear to regard it as an essential feature of such an agreement.[82] This is discussed further in Chapter 26 at 4.2.6.

3.6 Operators of joint ventures

One or more venturers may act as the operator or manager of a joint venture. Operators are usually paid a management fee for such duties. The fees are accounted for by the joint venture as an expense. IAS 31 requires the operators or managers of a joint venture to account for any such fees in accordance with IAS 18 – *Revenue* (see Chapter 28).[83]

An operator will often act as an agent and pay for specific costs on behalf of the joint venture (i.e. the principal). Such payments should not be accounted for as costs in the income statement of the operator and the reimbursement by the joint venture should not be presented as revenue. However, an operator that charges a management fee, which is intended to defray unspecified overhead costs, cannot be said to act as an agent. Therefore the operator should account for the management fee income and overhead costs in it income statement on a gross basis as it is not acting as an agent and does not meet the offset criteria in IAS 1.[84]

4 PRESENTATION AND DISCLOSURE

4.1 Presentation

4.1.1 Jointly controlled operations and jointly controlled assets

IFRS does not prescribe how jointly controlled operations and jointly controlled assets should be presented in the balance sheet or income statement of an entity. In practice few companies disclose details of those types of joint ventures on the face of their balance sheets or income statements.

4.1.2 Jointly controlled entities

An entity that proportionately consolidates its investments in jointly controlled entities can elect to use one of two permitted formats (see 3.3.3 above):

- *Line-by-line presentation* – The jointly controlled entity is consolidated on an aggregated line-by-line basis; or
- *Presentation as separate line items* – The venturer includes separate line items for its share of the total assets, liabilities, income and expenditure of the jointly controlled entity in its own consolidated accounts.

On the other hand, an entity that accounts for its investments in jointly controlled entities under the equity method is required to present:

- its aggregate share of the profit or loss of associates and joint ventures accounted for using the equity method on the face of its income statement (see Chapter 8 at 5.1.2); and[85]
- its investments accounted for using the equity method as non-current assets[86] on the face of its balance sheet.[87] The entity would be permitted to combine its investments in jointly controlled entities and associates into one line item.

4.2 Disclosure

4.2.1 Interests in joint ventures

A venturer should disclose a listing and description of interests in significant joint ventures and the proportion of ownership interest held in jointly controlled entities.[88]

A venturer which reports its interests in jointly controlled entities using the line-by-line reporting format for proportionate consolidation or the equity method should disclose the aggregate amounts of each of:

- current assets;
- long-term assets;
- current liabilities;
- long-term liabilities;
- income; and
- expenses

related to its interests in joint ventures.[89] An example of this disclosure is found in the financial statements of Scottish & Newcastle.

Extract 9.7: Scottish & Newcastle plc (2006)

Notes to the accounts [extract]

17. Investment in joint ventures

The main joint venture investments are in the following brewers:

50% holding in Baltic Beverages Holding (BBH) which operates in Russia, Ukraine, the Baltic countries and Kazakhstan. 40% holding in Millennium Alcobev which operates in India. 37.5% holding in United Breweries Limited which operates in India. The holding was acquired in May 2005, and: 45% holding in Serviced Dispense Equipment (Holdings) Limited which provides dispense equipment in the UK. 50% holding in Kuehne + Nagel Drinkflow Logistics Limited which provides logistical services in the UK.

The Group's share of joint ventures' assets and liabilities are as follows:

	2006 £m	2005 £m
Non current assets	1,798	1,713
Current assets	295	213
Current liabilities	(236)	(415)
Non current liabilities	(434)	(173)
Minority interest	(77)	(70)
Share of net assets of joint ventures	1,346	1,268

The Group's share of joint ventures' profits are as follows:

		2006				2005
	Before exceptional items	Exceptional items	After exceptional items	Before exceptional items	Exceptional items	After exceptional items
Revenue	804	–	804	645	–	645
Net operating costs	(628)	14	(614)	(519)	(4)	(523)
Operating profit	176	14	190	126	(4)	122
Net finance costs	(18)	4	(14)	(13)	(12)	(25)
Profit before tax	158	18	176	113	(16)	97
Tax	(44)	–	(44)	(28)	–	(28)
Minorities	(21)	–	(21)	(19)	–	(19)
Share of profit of joint ventures	93	18	111	66	(16)	50

The Group's share of the capital commitments of joint ventures in respect of property, plant and equipment was £41m (2005 – £14m).

4.2.2 *Accounting policy for jointly controlled entities*

A venturer must disclose the method that it uses to recognise its interests in jointly controlled entities[90] (i.e. proportionate consolidation or the equity method – see 3.3 above).

4.2.3 *Contingencies and commitments*

IAS 31 requires a venturer to disclose the aggregate amount of the following contingent liabilities, unless the probability of loss is remote, separately from the amount of other contingent liabilities:

- any contingent liabilities that the venturer has incurred in relation to its interests in joint ventures and its share in each of the contingent liabilities that have been incurred jointly with other venturers;
- its share of the contingent liabilities of the joint ventures themselves for which it is contingently liable; and
- those contingent liabilities that arise because the venturer is contingently liable for the liabilities of the other venturers of a joint venture.[91]

A venturer must also disclose the aggregate amount of the following commitments in respect of its interests in joint ventures separately from other commitments:

- any capital commitments of the venturer in relation to its interests in joint ventures and its share in the capital commitments that have been incurred jointly with other venturers; and
- its share of the capital commitments of the joint ventures themselves.[92]

5 PRACTICAL ISSUES

5.1 Variable profit share

Venturers may not always be entitled to a fixed proportion of the profit of a jointly controlled entity. Venturers that each have a 50% interest in a joint venture may, for example, agree that;

- in the initial three years of operation one of the venturers will be entitled to 75% of the profits in order to recover its investment quicker; or
- the venturers are entitled to a fixed proportion of cash flows 'as defined in the joint venture agreement'; or
- distribute the profit of the joint venture based on an alternative measure of profitability such as EBITDA.

It may not be appropriate in those cases for the venturers to account for 50% of the profit of the joint venture. Instead, they would need to take into account the substance of the profit sharing arrangements that apply in each reporting period, in determining their share of the profits and net assets of the joint venture. A venturer's profit share may therefore differ from its share in the net assets of the joint venture. This situation is not unlike the situation that arises in the case of an investment in an associate that has different classes of equity (see Chapter 8 at 3.3.4).

5.2 Related party disclosures

IAS 24 – *Related Party Disclosures* – treats joint ventures in which an entity is a venturer as related parties. Transactions with a jointly controlled entity would therefore need to be disclosed as related party transactions, at least to the extent that they are not eliminated as intercompany transactions under proportionate consolidation.

It is less obvious how this requirement should be applied in the case of jointly controlled operations and jointly controlled assets, because in those cases there is no separate legal entity that could be described as a related party. Since a venturer only has a contractual arrangement with the other venturers, one might argue that the other venturers should be treated as related parties. However, we believe that IAS 24 does not require respective venturers to be treated as related parties (see Chapter 35 at 2.3.5).

6 TRANSITIONAL AND FIRST-TIME ADOPTION ISSUES

6.1 General

The December 2003 revised version of IAS 31 had to be applied for accounting periods beginning on or after 1 January 2005. Entities were encouraged to adopt this revised version of IAS 31 for earlier periods, but were required to disclose that they had done so.[93] There were no transitional provisions. Accordingly, an existing IFRS user had to apply the revised version of IAS 31 with full retrospective effect.

For first-time adopters there are a number of special provisions in IFRS 1. Most significant is the business combinations exemption, which also applies to past acquisitions of investments in joint ventures (see 6.1.1 below).[94] In addition, there are separate rules that deal with situations in which a venturer adopts IFRS before or after a joint venture does so (see 6.1.2 below).[95]

Otherwise, there are no specific first-time adoption provisions in IFRS 1, which means that a first-time adopter of IFRS is required to apply IAS 31 as if it had always done so. For some first-time adopters, this may mean application of proportionate consolidation or the equity method for the first time. For the majority of first time adopters, however, we anticipate that the issue is that they are already applying proportionate consolidation or the equity method under national GAAP, and will now need to identify the, potentially significant, differences between the methodology under their predecessor GAAP and under IAS 31.

In particular there may be differences between:

- the criteria used to determine what interests are joint ventures;
- the elimination of transactions between venturers and joint ventures;
- the treatment of loss-making jointly controlled entities;
- the permitted interval between the reporting dates of a venturer and a joint venture with non-coterminous year-ends; and
- the treatment of investments in entities formerly classified as joint ventures.

The requirements for 'jointly controlled operations' and 'jointly controlled assets' may result in assets that were previously derecognised under predecessor GAAP and reclassified as investments in joint ventures being re-recognised, so as to reflect the requirement of IAS 31 to treat assets used in such joint ventures as assets of the venturers themselves rather than of the venture.

6.1.1 Transition impairment review

A first-time adopter of IFRS is required by IFRS 1 to apply an impairment test in accordance with IAS 36 to any goodwill recognised at the date of transition to IFRS, regardless of whether there is any indication of impairment.[96] IFRS 1 specifically notes that its provisions with regard to past business combinations apply also to past acquisitions of investments in joint ventures (see Chapter 5 at 2.4).[97] Therefore, a transition impairment review must be undertaken in accordance with the requirements of paragraphs B2(g) and B2(h) of IFRS 1 for investments in joint ventures whose carrying value includes an element of goodwill. This impairment review will, however, need to be carried out on the basis required by IAS 28 as described in Chapter 8 at 4.1.

6.2 Venturer and joint venture with different dates of first-time adoption of IFRS

IFRS 1 addresses in some detail the accounting treatment to be adopted when a venturer in a joint venture adopts IFRS for the first time before the joint venture and vice-versa. This is discussed in Chapter 6 at 9.3.

7 FUTURE DEVELOPMENTS IN JOINT VENTURE ACCOUNTING

At its meeting in December 2005, the IASB agreed to consider the accounting for interests in joint ventures within the short-term convergence project. In September 2007, the IASB issued Exposure Draft 9 (ED 9) – *Joint Arrangements*, which is intended to replace IAS 31 and SIC-13. ED 9 is another step in the short-term conversion project between the IASB and the Financial Accounting Standards Board (FASB).

ED 9 establishes a core principle that parties in a joint arrangement are to recognise their contractual rights and obligations arising from the arrangement.

The types of arrangement addressed by ED 9 are essentially the same as those covered by IAS 31, although some of the terminology has been changed. The principal change to IAS 31 is that proportionate consolidation of jointly controlled entities will no longer be allowed. Therefore, the equity method will have to be used to account for all interests in jointly controlled entities. In this regard, the proposals in ED 9 would bring IFRS into line with US GAAP. Under US GAAP, proportionate gross financial statement presentation (i.e. proportionate consolidation) is 'not appropriate for an investment in an unincorporated legal entity accounted for by the equity method of accounting unless the investee is in either the construction industry or an extractive industry where there is a longstanding practice of its use'.[98]

ED 9 defines a joint arrangement as a contractual arrangement whereby two or more parties undertake an economic activity together and share decision-making relating to that activity. Joint arrangements are to be classified into three types (i.e. joint operations, joint assets and joint ventures) based on the rights and obligations that arise from the contractual arrangement:

- 'Joint operation' will replace the term 'jointly controlled operation' used in IAS 31. A joint operation is one in which the parties to the arrangement use their own assets and other resources, and share revenues and expenses incurred in common in undertaking an activity. As each party controls its own assets and incurs its own obligations, it accounts for those assets and liabilities in accordance with applicable IFRS, together with its share of revenue and expenses from the activities.
- 'Joint asset' will replace the term 'jointly controlled asset' used in IAS 31. A joint asset is an asset to which each party has rights, often with joint ownership. Each party takes a share of the output from and shares the costs of operating the asset. Each party recognises its share of the joint asset in accordance with applicable IFRS, any liabilities it incurs, together with its share of any liabilities incurred jointly with the other parties, revenue from the sale of its share of the output of the asset and expenses incurred in respect of its interest in the joint arrangement.
- 'Joint venture' will replace the term 'jointly controlled entity' used in IAS 31. A joint venture is an arrangement that is jointly controlled by the venturers. In other words, a contractually agreed sharing of the power to govern the operating and financial policies of the venture to obtain benefits. In a joint venture, the venturers do not have direct rights to individual assets or direct obligations for expenses of the venture. Instead, each party shares in the outcome (e.g. profit or loss) of the activity. Such arrangements will be accounted for using the equity method – proportionate consolidation will no longer be available.

As in the case of IAS 31, ED 9 will not apply to interests in jointly controlled entities held by venture capital organisations and certain other investment vehicles that are measured at fair value through profit and loss.

The type of joint arrangement an entity is party to depends on the rights and obligations that arise from the contractual terms of the arrangement. The legal form of the arrangement is only one of the factors to be considered in assessing the rights and obligations, and does not itself determine the type of arrangement. Under IAS 31, the substance of a joint venture is determined by its legal form and, once joint ventures are enveloped in a separate legal entity, they become jointly controlled entities under the standard.

ED 9 also proposes how the loss of control of an interest in a joint venture is to be accounted for. Where joint control is lost and the investment does not become an associate, any retained investment is measured at fair value. The gain or loss on the loss of control is then calculated as the difference between:

(a) the sum of fair value of the interest retained and the proceeds from the interest disposed of; and

(b) the carrying value of the interest in the joint venture.

In such circumstances, any amounts included in 'other comprehensive income' or another component of equity in relation to the joint venture are to be recognised on the same basis as if the joint venture had disposed of the related assets and liabilities directly. Any amount that, as a result, is taken to profit or loss is a reclassification adjustment in accordance with the revised IAS 1 that was issued in September 2007.

If adopted by the IASB as a standard, ED 9 would require entities that currently account for their jointly-controlled entities using the proportionate consolidation method to change their accounting policies. Rather than simply switch to equity accounting, however, the contractual arrangements would need to be examined to ascertain whether the parties have contractual rights and obligations relating to individual assets and liabilities of the joint arrangement concerned – if so, those assets and liabilities would have to be recognised directly in the financial statements.

Since the effective dates of amendments or new standards is 6 to 18 months after publication,[99] it would seem that the earliest effective date may be for financial periods beginning 1 January 2010.

References

1 IAS 31, *Interests in Joint Ventures*, para. 1.
2 IAS 32, *Financial Instruments: Disclosure and Presentation*, para. 4(a) and IFRS 7, *Financial Instruments: Disclosures*, para. 3(a).
3 *IASB Update*, IASB, May 2007, p. 4.
4 IAS 31, para. 3.
5 IAS 31, para. 3.
6 IAS 31, para. 3.
7 IAS 31, para. 3.
8 IAS 31, para. 51.
9 IAS 31, para. 7.
10 IAS 31, para. 9.
11 IAS 31, para. 3.
12 IAS 28, *Investments in Associates*, para. 9.
13 IAS 31, para. 10.
14 IAS 31, para. 11.
15 IAS 31, para. 12.
16 IAS 31, para. 8.
17 IAS 31, para. 2.
18 IAS 31, para. 42.
19 IAS 31, para. 3.
20 IAS 31, para. 46.
21 IAS 31, para. 4.
22 IAS 31, paras. 5 and 47.
23 IAS 31, para. 6.
24 IAS 31, para. 13.
25 IAS 31, para. 14.
26 IAS 31, para. 15.
27 IAS 31, paras. 16-17.
28 IAS 31, paras. 18-19.
29 IAS 31, para. 20.
30 IAS 31, paras. 21-22.
31 IAS 31, para. 23.
32 IAS 31, para. 22.
33 IAS 31, para. 23.
34 IAS 31, para. 24.
35 IAS 31, para. 25.
36 IAS 31, para. 27.
37 IAS 31, para. 32.
38 IAS 31, para. 26.
39 IAS 31, para. 28.
40 IAS 31, para. 29.
41 IAS 31, paras. 30 and 38.
42 IAS 31, paras. 31 and 39.
43 IAS 23, *Borrowing Costs*, para. 4.
44 IAS 23, para. 6.
45 IAS 31, paras. 30 and 38.
46 IAS 31, para. 57.
47 IAS 8, *Accounting Policies, Changes in Accounting Estimates and Errors*, para. IN16.
48 IAS 31, para. 3.
49 IAS 31, para. 32.
50 IAS 31, para. 33.
51 IAS 31, para. 33.
52 IAS 31, para. 34.
53 IAS 31, para. 35.
54 IAS 31, paras. 36-37.
55 IAS 31, para. 3.
56 IAS 31, para. 40.
57 IAS 31, para. 40.
58 IAS 31, para. 40.
59 IAS 31, para. 41.

60 IAS 31, para. 43.
61 IAS 31, para. 45.
62 IAS 39, *Financial Instruments: Recognition and Measurement*, para. 43.
63 IAS 28, para. 19.
64 IAS 21, *The Effects of Changes in Foreign Exchange Rates*, para. 49.
65 IAS 27 (near-final), *Near-final draft of IAS 27 Consolidated and Separate Financial Statements*, IASB, June 2007, para. A8 (IAS 31, para. 45).
66 IAS 27 (near-final), para. A8 (IAS 31, para. 45B).
67 IAS 27 (near-final), para. A6 (IAS 21, para. 48A).
68 IAS 27 (near-final), para. A8 (IAS 31, para. 45B).
69 IAS 27 (near-final), para. A6 (IAS 21, para. 48C).
70 IAS 27 (near-final), para. 43A.
71 IAS 31, para. 48.
72 IAS 31, para. 49.
73 IAS 31, para. 50.
74 SIC-13, *Jointly Controlled Entities – Non-monetary Contributions by Venturers*, para. 5.
75 SIC-13, para. 6.
76 SIC-13, para. 7.
77 IAS 16, *Property, Plant and Equipment*, para. 25.
78 IAS 16, para. BC22.
79 IAS 16, para. 25.
80 IAS 16, para. BC23.
81 IFRS 3, *Business Combinations*, para. 3(a).
82 IAS 12, *Income Taxes*, para. 43.
83 IAS 31, paras. 52-53.
84 IAS 1, *Presentation of Financial Statements*, paras. 32-35.
85 IAS 1, para. 81(c).
86 IAS 28, para. 38.
87 IAS 1, para. 68(d).
88 IAS 31, para. 56.
89 IAS 31, para. 56.
90 IAS 31, para. 57.
91 IAS 31, para. 54.
92 IAS 31, para. 55.
93 IAS 31, para. 58.
94 IFRS 1, *First-time Adoption of International Financial Reporting Standards*, para. B3.
95 IFRS 1, paras. 24-25.
96 IFRS 1, para. B2(g)(iii).
97 IFRS 1, para. B3.
98 EITF 00-1, *Investor Balance Sheet and Income Statement Display under the Equity Method for Investments in Certain Partnerships and Other Ventures*, EITF, July 2000, para. 4.
99 *IASB Work Plan – projected timetable as at 31 March 2007*, IASB.

Chapter 10 Foreign exchange

1 INTRODUCTION

1.1 Background

An entity can engage in foreign currency activities in two ways. It may enter directly into transactions which are denominated in foreign currencies, the results of which need to be translated into the currency in which the company measures its results and financial position. Alternatively, it may conduct foreign operations through a foreign entity, such as a subsidiary, associate, joint venture or branch which keeps its accounting records in terms of its own currency. In this case it will need to translate the financial statements of the foreign entity for the purposes of inclusion in the consolidated financial statements.

Before an international standard was developed, there were four distinct methods which could be used in the translation process:

(a) *current rate method* – all assets and liabilities are translated at the current rate of exchange, i.e. the exchange rate at the balance sheet date;

(b) *temporal method* – assets and liabilities carried at current prices (e.g. cash, receivables, payables, and investments at market value) are translated at the current rate of exchange. Assets and liabilities carried at past prices (e.g. property, investments at cost, prepayments) are translated at the rate of exchange in effect at the dates to which the prices pertain;

(c) *current/non-current method* – all current assets and current liabilities are translated at the current rate of exchange. Non-current assets and liabilities are translated at historical rates, i.e. the exchange rate in effect at the time the asset was acquired or the liability incurred; and

(d) *monetary/non-monetary method* – monetary assets and liabilities, i.e. items which represent the right to receive or the obligation to pay a fixed amount of money, are translated at the current rate of exchange. Non-monetary assets and liabilities are translated at the historical rate.

There was no consensus internationally on the best theoretical approach to adopt. In essence, the arguments surround the choice of exchange rates to be used in the translation process and the subsequent treatment of the exchange differences which arise.

1.2 Development of an international standard

1.2.1 IAS 21

The principal international standard dealing with this topic is IAS 21 – *The Effects of Changes in Foreign Exchange Rates*. The original standard was issued by the IASC in July 1983. Equivalent standards in the UK, US and Canada had already been issued following a long period of consultation between the ASC, the FASB and the CICA. The reason for the consultation was that it was considered that there was a need for international harmonisation in this field. IAS 21 followed the same general approach as its international counterparts in that it was based on a closing rate/net investment concept and an approach to translation which is related to the cash flow consequences of exchange movements. Exchange differences which give rise to cash flows, i.e. those resulting from business transactions, were to be reported as part of the profit or loss for the period. Other exchange differences which do not give rise to cash flows, because they result from retranslations of the holding company's long-term investment in the foreign subsidiary, were reported as reserve movements.

The standard therefore required that the procedures to be adopted when accounting for foreign operations should be considered in two stages, namely the preparation of the financial statements of the individual company and the preparation of the consolidated financial statements. The method used to translate the financial statements of a foreign operation for inclusion in consolidated financial statements depended on the way in which it was financed and operated in relation to the reporting entity. For this purpose, foreign operations were classified as either 'foreign entities' or 'foreign operations that are integral to the operations of the reporting enterprise'.[1] In the former case, the closing rate method of translation was used[2] and in the latter case the temporal method was used.[3] Although a revised version of IAS 21 was published in December 1993, it followed the same general approach as its predecessor.

1.2.2 IAS 21 (Revised 2003)

In December 2003, the IASB issued a revised version of IAS 21 to replace the earlier version issued by the IASC.

The IASB developed this revised IAS 21 as part of its project on Improvements to International Accounting Standards. The project was undertaken in the light of queries and criticisms raised in relation to the standards by securities regulators, professional accountants and other interested parties. The objectives of the project were to reduce or eliminate alternatives, redundancies and conflicts within the standards, to deal with some convergence issues and to make other improvements.[4]

For IAS 21 the Board's main objective was to provide additional guidance on the translation method and on determining the functional and presentation currencies. The Board did not reconsider the fundamental approach to accounting for the effects of changes in foreign exchange rates contained in IAS 21.[5]

This revised version of the standard applied to annual periods beginning on or after 1 January 2005, although earlier application was encouraged.[6]

1.2.3 IAS 21 Amendment – Net Investment in a Foreign Operation

After this revised version of IAS 21 was issued in December 2003, constituents raised a number of concerns with respect to the requirements for monetary items included as part of the net investment in a foreign operation (see 3.4.1 below). Following a proposal to deal with this issue by means of a 'Technical Correction',[7] the IASB published an Amendment to IAS 21 in December 2005.[8] The amendments (which added a new paragraph 15A and an amended paragraph 33) are discussed at 3.4.1 below, and were to be applied for annual periods beginning on or after 1 January 2006, although earlier application was encouraged.[9]

1.2.4 SIC pronouncements

The SIC had issued four interpretations of IAS 21 prior to its revision in 2003; SIC-7 – *Introduction of the Euro*, SIC-11 – *Foreign Exchange – Capitalisation of Losses Resulting from Severe Currency Devaluations*, SIC-19 – *Reporting Currency – Measurement and Presentation of Financial Statements under IAS 21 and IAS 29* – and SIC-30 – *Reporting Currency – Translation from Measurement Currency to Presentation Currency.*

SIC-7 deals with the application of IAS 21 to the changeover from the national currencies of participating Member States of the European Union to the euro and is covered at 3.5 below.

The other interpretations, SIC-11, SIC-19 and SIC-30, are no longer relevant following the revision to the standard in 2003.[10]

2 REQUIREMENTS OF IAS 21

As noted at 1.2.2 above, the 2003 version of IAS 21 was mandatory for annual periods beginning on or after 1 January 2005, although earlier application was encouraged.[11] As indicated at 1.2.3 above, the December 2005 Amendment was to be applied for annual periods beginning on or after 1 January 2006, although earlier application was encouraged.[12]

Apart from its requirements relating to goodwill and fair value adjustments, all changes resulting from the application of the standard (including the 2005 Amendment) were to be accounted for in accordance with the requirements of IAS 8 – *Accounting Policies, Changes in Accounting Estimates and Errors* (see Chapter 3 at 4.4),[13] i.e. by retrospective application of the new requirements. The transitional arrangements relating to goodwill and fair value adjustments for entities already reporting under IFRS, and the specific arrangements for first time adopters under

IFRS 1 – *First-time Adoption of International Financial Reporting Standards* – are discussed at 4 below.

2.1 Objective of the standard

As indicated at 1.1 above, an entity may carry on foreign activities in two ways. It may have transactions in foreign currencies or it may have foreign operations. In addition, an entity may present its financial statements in a foreign currency. IAS 21 does not set out what the objective of foreign currency translation should be, but just states that the objective of the standard is 'to prescribe how to include foreign currency transactions and foreign operations in the financial statements of an entity and how to translate financial statements into a presentation currency'.[14]

It also indicates that the principal issues to be addressed are 'which exchange rate(s) to use and how to report the effects of changes in exchange rates in the financial statements'.[15]

2.2 Scope

IAS 21 shall be applied:[16]

(a) in accounting for transactions and balances in foreign currencies, except for those derivative transactions and balances that are within the scope of IAS 39 – *Financial Instruments: Recognition and Measurement;*

(b) in translating the results and financial position of foreign operations that are included in the financial statements of the entity by consolidation, proportionate consolidation or the equity method; and

(c) in translating an entity's results and financial position into a presentation currency.

The standard explains that IAS 39 applies to many foreign currency derivatives and, accordingly, these are excluded from the scope of this standard. However, it goes on to say that those foreign currency derivatives that are not within the scope of IAS 39 (e.g. some foreign currency derivatives that are embedded in other contracts) are within the scope of IAS 21. In addition, it also states that IAS 21 applies when an entity translates amounts relating to derivatives from its functional currency to its presentation currency.[17]

IAS 21 also does not apply to hedge accounting for foreign currency items, including the hedging of a net investment in a foreign operation.[18] This is dealt with in IAS 39, which has detailed rules on hedging (see Chapter 21).

The standard explains that its requirements are applicable to an entity's statements that are to be described as complying with International Financial Reporting Standards. They do not apply to translations of financial information into a foreign currency that do not meet these requirements, although the standard does specify information to be disclosed in respect of such 'convenience translations'.[19]

IAS 21 does not apply to the presentation in a cash flow statement of cash flows arising from transactions in a foreign currency, or to the translation of cash flows of a foreign operation.[20] These are dealt with in IAS 7 – *Cash Flow Statements* (see Chapter 34 at 2.5.2).

2.3 Definitions of terms

The definitions of terms which are contained in IAS 21 are as follows:[21]

Closing rate is the spot exchange rate at the balance sheet date.

Exchange difference is the difference resulting from translating a given number of units of one currency into another currency at different exchange rates.

Exchange rate is the ratio of exchange for two currencies.

Fair value is the amount for which an asset could be exchanged, or a liability settled, between knowledgeable, willing parties in an arm's length transaction.

Foreign currency is a currency other than the functional currency of the entity.

Foreign operation is an entity that is a subsidiary, associate, joint venture or branch of a reporting entity, the activities of which are based or conducted in a country or currency other than those of the reporting entity.

Functional currency is the currency of the primary economic environment in which the entity operates.

A *group* is a parent and all its subsidiaries.

Monetary items are units of currency held and assets and liabilities to be received or paid in a fixed or determinable number of units of currency.

Net investment in a foreign operation is the amount of the reporting entity's interest in the net assets of that operation.

Presentation currency is the currency in which the financial statements are presented.

Spot exchange rate is the exchange rate for immediate delivery.

The terms 'functional currency', 'monetary items' and 'net investment in a foreign operation' are elaborated on further within the standard. These are discussed at 2.5, 3.2.4 and 3.4.1 below.

2.4 Summary of the approach required by the standard

In preparing financial statements, each entity – whether a stand-alone entity, an entity with foreign operations (such as a parent) or a foreign operation (such as a subsidiary or branch) – determines its functional currency.[22] This is discussed at 2.5 below. In the case of group financial statements, it should be emphasised that there is not a 'group' functional currency; each entity included within the group financial statements, be it the parent, subsidiary, associate, joint venture or branch, has its own functional currency. Where an entity enters into a transaction denominated in a currency other than its functional currency, then it translates those foreign currency items into its functional currency and reports the effects of such translation in accordance with the provisions of IAS 21 discussed at 2.6 below.[23]

Many reporting entities comprise a number of individual entities (e.g. a group is made up of a parent and one or more subsidiaries). Various types of entities, whether members of a group or otherwise, may have investments in associates or joint ventures. They may also have branches. It is necessary for the results and financial position of each individual entity included in the reporting entity to be translated into the currency in which the reporting entity presents its financial statements (if this presentation currency is different from the individual entity's functional currency). The results and financial position of any individual entity within the reporting entity whose functional currency differs from the presentation currency are translated in accordance with the provisions of IAS 21 discussed at 2.7 below.[24] Since IAS 21 permits the presentation currency of a reporting entity to be any currency (or currencies), this translation process will also apply to the parent's figures if its functional currency is different from the presentation currency.

The standard also permits a stand-alone entity preparing financial statements or an entity preparing separate financial statements in accordance with IAS 27 – *Consolidated and Separate Financial Statements* – to present its financial statements in any currency (or currencies). If the entity's presentation currency differs from its functional currency, its results and financial position are also translated into the presentation currency in accordance with the provisions of IAS 21 discussed at 2.7 below.[25]

2.5 Determination of an entity's functional currency

As indicated at 2.3 above, functional currency is defined as the currency of 'the primary economic environment in which the entity operates'. This will normally be the one in which it primarily generates and expends cash.[26]

IAS 21 sets out a number of factors or indicators that any entity should or may need to consider in determining its functional currency. When the factors or indicators are mixed and the functional currency is not obvious, the standard requires management to use its judgement to determine the functional currency that most faithfully represents the economic effects of the underlying transactions, events and conditions. As part of this approach, management gives priority to the following primary indicators before considering the other indicators set out in the standard, which are designed to provide additional supporting evidence to determine an entity's functional currency.[27]

The primary factors that IAS 21 requires an entity to consider in determining its functional currency are as follows:[28]

(a) the currency:
   (i) that mainly influences sales prices for goods and services (this will often be the currency in which sales prices for its goods and services are denominated and settled); and
   (ii) of the country whose competitive forces and regulations mainly determine the sales prices of its goods and services.

(b) the currency that mainly influences labour, material and other costs of providing goods or services (this will often be the currency in which such costs are denominated and settled).

Where the functional currency of the entity is not obvious from the above, then the standard indicates that the following factors may also provide evidence of an entity's functional currency:[29]

(a) the currency in which funds from financing activities (i.e. issuing debt and equity instruments) are generated;

(b) the currency in which receipts from operating activities are usually retained.

The standard also says that the following additional factors are considered in determining the functional currency of a foreign operation, and whether its functional currency is the same as that of the reporting entity (the reporting entity, in this context, being the entity that has the foreign operation as its subsidiary, branch, associate or joint venture):[30]

(a) whether the activities of the foreign operation are carried out as an extension of the reporting entity, rather than being carried out with a significant degree of autonomy. An example of the former is when the foreign operation only sells goods imported from the reporting entity and remits the proceeds to it. An example of the latter is when the operation accumulates cash and other monetary items, incurs expenses, generates income and arranges borrowings, all substantially in its local currency;

(b) whether transactions with the reporting entity are a high or a low proportion of the foreign operation's activities;

(c) whether cash flows from the activities of the foreign operation directly affect the cash flows of the reporting entity and are readily available for remittance to it;

(d) whether cash flows from the activities of the foreign operation are sufficient to service existing and normally expected debt obligations without funds being made available by the reporting entity.

Although the standard says that these factors 'are' considered in determining the functional currency of a foreign operation, this contradicts the requirement in the standard that management gives priority to the primary indicators before considering the other indicators. If it is obvious from the primary indicators what the entity's functional currency is, then there is no need to consider any of the other factors.

Example 10.1: Factors to be considered when determining the functional currency

A French entity (Parent A) has a US subsidiary (Subsidiary B) that produces and sells knitwear in the United States.

It is clear from the primary factors in paragraph 9 of IAS 21 described above that Subsidiary B's functional currency is the US dollar, because the US dollar mainly influences sales prices for goods, labour, material and other costs of providing goods, and the competitive forces and regulations that mainly determine the sales prices of the goods are located in the United States.

However, suppose Subsidiary B is financed by an inter-company loan denominated in euros granted from Parent A and the cash flows generated by Subsidiary B are transferred to Parent A on a regular basis. Should these additional factors be taken into account in determining the functional currency of Subsidiary B?

In our view, they should not. These additional factors only have to be considered when it is not obvious from the primary factors in paragraph 9 what Subsidiary B's functional currency is.

However, if Subsidiary B was not producing the knitwear itself, but purchasing it from sources in Europe (such that its operating costs were predominantly in euros, and this meant that it was no longer obvious based on the primary factors in paragraph 9 that its functional currency was the US dollar), then the additional factors would be taken into account in determining Subsidiary B's functional currency.

Since an entity's functional currency reflects the underlying transactions, events and conditions that are relevant to it, once it is determined, IAS 21 requires that the functional currency is not changed unless there is a change in those underlying transactions, events and conditions.[31] The implication of this is that management of an entity cannot decree what the functional currency is – it is a matter of fact, albeit subjectively determined fact based on management's judgement of all the circumstances.

For some entities the determination of functional currency may be relatively straightforward. However, for many entities, particularly entities within a group, this may not be the case. This is discussed further at 3.1 below.

2.6 Reporting foreign currency transactions in the functional currency of an entity

As indicated at 1.1 above, an entity may carry on foreign activities in two ways. It may have transactions in foreign currencies or it may have foreign operations. Where an entity enters into a transaction denominated in a currency other than its functional currency then it will have to translate those foreign currency items into its functional currency and report the effects of such translation.

The general requirements of IAS 21 are as follows.

2.6.1 *Initial recognition*

A foreign currency transaction is a transaction that is denominated or requires settlement in a foreign currency, including transactions arising when an entity:[32]

(a) buys or sells goods or services whose price is denominated in a foreign currency;

(b) borrows or lends funds when the amounts payable or receivable are denominated in a foreign currency; or
(c) otherwise acquires or disposes of assets, or incurs or settles liabilities, denominated in a foreign currency.

On initial recognition, foreign currency transactions shall be translated into the functional currency using the spot exchange rate between the foreign currency and the functional currency on the date of the transaction.[33] The date of a transaction is the date on which it first qualifies for recognition in accordance with IFRS. For convenience, an average rate for a week or month may be used for all foreign currency transactions occurring during that period, if the exchange rate does not fluctuate significantly.[34]

2.6.2 *Reporting at subsequent balance sheet dates*

At each balance sheet date:[35]

(a) foreign currency monetary items shall be translated using the closing rate;
(b) non-monetary items that are measured in terms of historical cost in a foreign currency shall be translated using the exchange rate at the date of the transaction; and
(c) non-monetary items that are measured at fair value in a foreign currency shall be translated using the exchange rate at the date when the fair value was determined.

2.6.3 *Treatment of exchange differences*

A *Monetary items*

The general rule in IAS 21 is that exchange differences on the settlement or retranslation of monetary items shall be recognised in profit or loss in the period in which they arise.[36]

As the standard explains 'when monetary items arise from a foreign currency transaction and there is a change in the exchange rate between the transaction date and the date of settlement, an exchange difference results. When the transaction is settled within the same accounting period as that in which it occurred, all the exchange difference is recognised in that period. However, when the transaction is settled in a subsequent accounting period, the exchange difference recognised in each period up to the date of settlement is determined by the change in exchange rates during each period.'[37]

The above general requirements can be illustrated in the following examples:

Example 10.2: Reporting a foreign currency transaction in the functional currency

A French entity purchases plant and equipment on credit from a Canadian supplier for C$328,000 in January 2008 when the exchange rate is €1=C$1.64. The entity records the asset at a cost of €200,000. At the French entity's year end at 31 March 2008 the account has not yet been settled. The closing rate is €1=C$1.61. The amount payable would be retranslated at €203,727 in the balance sheet and an exchange loss of €3,727 would be reported as part of the profit or loss for the period. The cost of the asset would remain as €200,000.

Example 10.3: Reporting a foreign currency transaction in the functional currency

A UK entity sells goods to a German entity for €87,000 on 28 February 2008 when the exchange rate is £1=€1.45. It receives payment on 31 March 2008 when the exchange rate is £1=€1.50. On 28 February the UK entity will record a sale and corresponding receivable of £60,000. When payment is received on 31 March the actual amount received is only £58,000. The loss on exchange of £2,000 would be reported as part of the profit or loss for the period.

IAS 21 does not specify where any exchange differences on monetary items should be presented in the income statement. As indicated at 2.9.1 below, we recommend that entities in disclosing the amount of such exchange differences should indicate the line item(s) in which they are included. Further, the classification of exchange differences (both gains and losses) arising from transactions of a similar nature should be classified consistently throughout the periods presented.

However, there are situations where the above general rule will not be applied. The first exception to the general rule identified in IAS 21 relates to exchange differences arising on a monetary item that, in substance, forms part of an entity's net investment in a foreign operation (see 3.4.1 below). In this situation the exchange differences shall be recognised initially in a separate component of equity until the disposal of the investment (see 2.7.3 below). However, this treatment only applies in the financial statements that include the foreign operation and the reporting entity (i.e. financial statements in which the foreign operation is consolidated, proportionately consolidated or accounted for using the equity method). It does not apply to the reporting entity's separate financial statements or the financial statements of the foreign operation; the exchange differences will be recognised in profit or loss in the period in which they arise in the financial statements of the entity that has the foreign currency exposure.[38] This is discussed further at 3.4.1 below.

The next exception relates to hedge accounting. As noted at 2.2 above, IAS 39 applies to hedge accounting for foreign currency items. The application of hedge accounting requires an entity to account for some exchange differences differently from the treatment of exchange differences required by IAS 21. For example, IAS 39 requires that exchange differences on monetary items that qualify as hedging instruments in a cash flow hedge or a hedge of a net investment in a foreign operation are reported initially in equity to the extent the hedge is effective (see Chapter 21).

In addition to the above exceptions identified in IAS 21, as discussed at 3.2.5 below, there can be other situations where exchange differences on monetary items are not taken to the income statement in the period they arise.

B Non-monetary items

When non-monetary items that are measured at fair value in a foreign currency are translated using the exchange rate as at the date when the fair value was determined, any re-measurement gain or loss will include an element relating to the change on exchange rates. In this situation, the exchange differences are recognised as part of the gain or loss arising on the fair value re-measurement.

When a gain or loss on a non-monetary item is recognised directly in equity, any exchange component of that gain or loss shall be recognised directly in equity.[39] For example, IAS 16 – *Property, Plant and Equipment* – requires some gains and losses arising on a revaluation of property, plant and equipment to be recognised directly in equity (see Chapter 13 at 2.4.1). When such an asset is measured in a foreign currency, the revalued amount has to be translated using the rate at the date the value is determined, resulting in an exchange difference that is also recognised in equity.[40]

Conversely, when a gain or loss on a non-monetary item is recognised in profit or loss (e.g. financial instruments that are measured at fair value through profit or loss in accordance with IAS 39 – see Chapter 20 at 3.1), any exchange component of that gain or loss shall be recognised in profit or loss.[41]

An example of an accounting policy dealing with the reporting of foreign currency transactions in the functional currency of an entity is illustrated below.

Extract 10.1: ING Groep N.V. (2006)

FOREIGN CURRENCY TRANSLATION [extract]

Functional and presentation currency

Items included in the financial statements of each of the Group's entities are measured using the currency of the primary economic environment in which the entity operates ('the functional currency'). The consolidated financial statements are presented in euro, which is the Company's functional and presentation currency.

Transactions and balances

Foreign currency transactions are translated into the functional currency using the exchange rates prevailing at the dates of the transactions. Foreign exchange gains and losses resulting from the settlement of such transactions and from the translation at year-end exchange rates of monetary assets and liabilities denominated in foreign currencies are recognised in the profit and loss account, except when deferred in equity as part of qualifying cash flow hedges and qualifying net investment hedges.

Translation differences on non-monetary items, measured at fair value through profit and loss are reported as part of the fair value gain or loss. Non-monetary items are retranslated at the date fair value is determined. Translation differences on non-monetary items measured at fair value through the revaluation reserve are included in the revaluation reserve in equity.

2.6.4 Change in functional currency

As indicated at 2.5 above, IAS 21 requires management to use its judgment to determine the entity's functional currency such that it most faithfully represents the economic effects of the underlying transactions, events and conditions that are relevant to the entity. Accordingly, once the functional currency is determined, the standard only allows it to be changed if there is a change to those underlying transactions, events and conditions. For example, a change in the currency that mainly influences the sales prices of goods and services may lead to a change in an entity's functional currency.[42]

When there is a change in an entity's functional currency, the entity shall apply the translation procedures applicable to the new functional currency prospectively from the date of the change.[43]

In other words, an entity translates all items into the new functional currency using the exchange rate at the date of the change. The resulting translated amounts for non-monetary items are treated as their historical cost. Exchange differences arising from the translation of a foreign operation previously classified in equity are not recognised in profit or loss until the disposal of the operation (see 2.7.3 below).[44]

Example 10.4: Change in functional currency

The management of Entity A has considered the functional currency of the entity to be the euro. However, as a result of change in circumstances affecting the operations of the entity, management determines that on 1 January 2008 the functional currency of the entity is now the US dollar. The exchange rate at that date is €1=US$1.20. The balance sheet of Entity A at 1 January 2008 in its old functional currency is as follows:

	€
Property, plant and equipment	200,000
Current assets	
Inventories	10,000
Receivables	20,000
Cash	5,000
	35,000
Current liabilities	
Payables	15,000
Taxation	3,000
	18,000
Net current assets	17,000
	217,000
Long-term loans	120,000
	97,000
Share capital	50,000
Retained profits	47,000
	97,000

Included within the balance sheet at 1 January 2008 are the following items:

- Equipment with a cost of €33,000 and a net book value of €16,500. This equipment was originally purchased for £20,000 in 2004 and has been translated at the rate ruling at the date of purchase of £1=€1.65.
- Inventories with a cost of €6,000. These were purchased for US$6,000 and have been translated at the rate ruling at the date of purchase of €1=US$1.00.
- Payables of €5,000 representing the US$6,000 due in respect of the above inventories, translated at the rate ruling at 1 January 2008.

- Long-term loans of €15,000 representing the outstanding balance of £10,000 on a loan originally taken out to finance the acquisition of the above equipment, translated at £1=€1.50, the rate ruling at 1 January 2008.

Entity A applies the translational procedures applicable to its new functional currency prospectively from the date of change. Accordingly, all items in its balance sheet at 1 January 2008 are translated at the rate of €1=US$1.20 giving rise to the following amounts:

	$
Property, plant and equipment	240,000
Current assets	
Inventories	12,000
Receivables	24,000
Cash	6,000
	42,000
Current liabilities	
Payables	18,000
Taxation	3,600
	21,600
Net current assets	20,400
	260,400
Long-term loans	144,000
	116,400
Share capital	60,000
Retained profits	56,400
	116,400

As far as the equipment that was originally purchased for £20,000 is concerned, the cost and net book value in terms of Entity A's new functional currency are US$39,600 and US$19,800 respectively, being €33,000 and €16,500 translated at €1=US$1.20. Entity A does not go back and translate the £20,000 cost at whatever the £ sterling/US dollar exchange rate was at the date of purchase and calculate a revised net book value on that basis.

Similarly, the inventories purchased in US dollars are included at $7,200, being €6,000 translated at €1=US$1.20. This is despite the fact that Entity A knows that the original cost was $6,000.

As far as the payables in respect of the inventories are concerned, these are included at $6,000, being €5,000 translated at €1=US$1.20. This represents the original amount payable in US dollars. However, this is as it should be since the original payable had been translated into euros at the rate ruling at 1 January 2008 and has just been translated back into US dollars at the same rate. The impact of the change in functional currency is that whereas Entity A had recorded an exchange gain of €1,000 while the functional currency was the euro, no further exchange difference will be recorded in respect of this amount payable. Exchange differences will now arise from 1 January 2008 on those payables denominated in euros, whereas no such differences would have arisen on such items prior to that date.

Similarly, the £10,000 amount outstanding on the loan will be included at $18,000, being €15,000 translated at €1=US$1.20. This is equivalent to the translation of the £10,000 at a rate of £1=US$1.80, being the direct exchange rate between the two currencies at 1 January 2008. In this case, whereas previously exchange gains and losses would have been recognised on this loan balance based on movements of the £/€ exchange rate, as from 1 January 2008 the exchange gains and losses will be recognised based on the £/$ exchange rate.

2.7 Use of a presentation currency other than the functional currency

As indicated at 2.4 above, an entity may present its financial statements in any currency (or currencies). If the presentation currency differs from the entity's functional currency, it needs to translate its results and financial position into the presentation currency. For example, when a group contains individual entities with different functional currencies, the results and financial position of each entity are expressed in a common currency so that consolidated financial statements may be presented.[45] As noted earlier, there is no concept of a 'group' functional currency. Each entity within the group has its own functional currency, and the results and financial position of each entity have to be translated into the presentation currency that is used for the consolidated financial statements.[46]

The requirements of IAS 21 in respect of this translation process are discussed below. The procedures to be adopted apply not only to the inclusion of foreign subsidiaries in consolidated financial statements but also to the incorporation of the results of associates and joint ventures.[47] They also apply when the results of a foreign branch are to be incorporated into the financial statements of an individual entity or a stand-alone entity preparing financial statements or when an entity preparing separate financial statements in accordance with IAS 27 presents its financial statements in a currency other than its functional currency.

2.7.1 *Translation to the presentation currency*

Under IAS 21, the method of translation depends on whether the entity's functional currency is that of a hyperinflationary economy or not, and if it is, whether it is being translated into a presentation currency which is that of a hyperinflationary economy or not. A hyperinflationary economy is defined in IAS 29 (see Chapter 11 at 2.3.1). The requirements of IAS 21 discussed below can be summarised as follows:

	Presentation currency	
	Non-hyperinflationary	**Hyperinflationary**
Non-hyperinflationary functional currency		
Assets/liabilities		
– current period	Closing rate (current B/S date)	Closing rate (current B/S date)
– comparative period	Closing rate (comparative B/S date)	Closing rate (comparative B/S date)
Equity items		
– current period	Not specified	Not specified
– comparative period	Not specified	Not specified
Income/expenses (including those recognised directly in equity)		
– current period	Actual rates (or appropriate average for current period)	Actual rates (or appropriate average for current period)
– comparative period	Actual rates (or appropriate average for comparative period)	Actual rates (or appropriate average for comparative period)
Exchange differences	Separate component of equity	Separate component of equity

Hyperinflationary functional currency		
Assets/liabilities		
– current period	Closing rate (current B/S date)	Closing rate (current B/S date)
– comparative period	Closing rate (comparative B/S date)	Closing rate (current B/S date)
Equity items		
– current period	Closing rate (current B/S date)	Closing rate (current B/S date)
– comparative period	Closing rate (comparative B/S date)	Closing rate (current B/S date)
Income/expenses (including those recognised directly in equity)		
– current period	Closing rate (current B/S date)	Closing rate (current B/S date)
– comparative period	Closing rate (comparative B/S date)	Closing rate (current B/S date)
Exchange differences	Not specified	Not applicable

A *Functional currency is not that of a hyperinflationary economy*

The results and financial position of an entity whose functional currency is not the currency of a hyperinflationary economy shall be translated into a different presentation currency using the following procedures:[48]

(a) assets and liabilities for each balance sheet presented (i.e. including comparatives) shall be translated at the closing rate at the date of that balance sheet;

(b) income and expenses for each income statement (i.e. including comparatives) shall be translated at exchange rates at the dates of the transactions; and

(c) all resulting exchange differences shall be recognised as a separate component of equity.

For practical reasons, the reporting entity may use a rate that approximates the actual exchange rate, e.g. an average rate for the period, to translate income and expense items. However, if exchange rates fluctuate significantly, the use of the average rate for a period is inappropriate.[49]

The translational process above makes no reference to the translation of equity items. The treatment of such items is discussed at 3.3.3 below.

IAS 21 indicates that the exchange differences referred to in item (c) above result from:[50]

- translating income and expenses at the exchange rates at the dates of the transactions and assets and liabilities at the closing rate. Such exchange differences arise both on income and expense items recognised in profit or loss and on those recognised directly in equity; and
- translating the opening net assets at a closing rate that differs from the previous closing rate.

This is not in fact completely accurate since if the entity has had any transactions with equity holders that have resulted in a change in the net assets during the period there are likely to be further exchange differences that need to be recognised to the extent that the closing rate differs from the rate used to translate the transaction. This will particularly be the case where a parent has subscribed for further equity shares in a subsidiary.

The reason why these exchange differences are not recognised in profit or loss is because the changes in exchange rates have little or no direct effect on the present and future cash flows from operations.[51]

The application of these procedures is illustrated in the following example.

Example 10.5: Translation of a non-hyperinflationary functional currency to a non-hyperinflationary presentation currency

An Australian entity owns 100% of the share capital of a foreign entity which was set up a number of years ago when the exchange rate was A$1=FC2. It is consolidating the financial statements of the subsidiary in its consolidated financial statements for the year ended 31 December 2008. The exchange rate at the year-end is A$1=FC4 (2007: A$1=FC3). For the purposes of illustration, it is assumed that exchange rates have not fluctuated significantly and the appropriate weighted average rate for the year was A$1=FC3.5, and that the currency of the foreign entity is not that of a hyperinflationary economy. The income statement of the subsidiary for that year and its balance sheet at the beginning and end of the year in its functional currency and translated into Australian dollars are as follows:

Income statement

	FC	A$
Sales	35,000	10,000
Cost of sales	(33,190)	(9,483)
Depreciation	(500)	(143)
Interest	(350)	(100)
Profit before taxation	960	274
Taxation	(460)	(131)
Profit after taxation	500	143

Balance sheets	2007 FC	2008 FC	2007 A$	2008 A$
Property, plant and equipment	6,000	5,500	2,000	1,375
Current assets				
Inventories	2,700	3,000	900	750
Receivables	4,800	4,000	1,600	1,000
Cash	200	600	67	150
	7,700	7,600	2,567	1,900
Current liabilities				
Payables	4,530	3,840	1,510	960
Taxation	870	460	290	115
	5,400	4,300	1,800	1,075
Net current assets	2,300	3,300	767	825
	8,300	8,800	2,767	2,200
Long-term loans	3,600	3,600	1,200	900
	4,700	5,200	1,567	1,300
Share capital	1,000	1,000	500	500
Retained profits*	3,700	4,200	1,500	1,643
Exchange reserve*			(433)	(843)
	4,700	5,200	1,567	1,300

* The opening balances for 2007 in A$ have been assumed and represent cumulative amounts since the foreign entity was set up.

The movement of A$(410) in the exchange reserve included as a separate component of equity is made up as follows:

(i) the exchange loss of A$392 on the opening net investment in the subsidiary, calculated as follows:

Opening net assets at opening rate	– FC4,700 at FC3 = A$1 =	A$1,567
Opening net assets at closing rate	– FC4,700 at FC4 = A$1 =	A$1,175
Exchange loss on net assets		A$392

(ii) the exchange loss of A$18, being the difference between the income account translated at an average rate, i.e. £143, and at the closing rate, i.e. £125.

When the exchange differences relate to a foreign operation that is consolidated but not wholly-owned, accumulated exchange differences arising from translation and attributable to minority interests are allocated to, and recognised as part of, minority interest in the consolidated balance sheet.[52]

An example of an accounting policy dealing with the translation of entities whose functional currency is not that of a hyperinflationary economy is illustrated in the following extract.

Extract 10.2: Lloyds TSB Group plc (2006)

1 Accounting policies [extract]

(s) Foreign currency translation

(1) Functional and presentation currency

Items included in the financial statements of each of the Group's entities are measured using the currency of the primary economic environment in which the entity operates ('the functional currency'). The consolidated financial statements are presented in sterling, which is the Company's functional and presentation currency.

(2) Transactions and balances

Foreign currency transactions are translated into the functional currency using the exchange rates prevailing at the dates of the transactions. Foreign exchange gains and losses resulting from the settlement of such transactions and from the translation at year end exchange rates of monetary assets and liabilities denominated in foreign currencies are recognised in the income statement, except when deferred in equity as qualifying cash flow or net investment hedges. Non-monetary assets that are measured at fair value are translated using the exchange rate at the date that the fair value was determined. Translation differences on equities and similar non-monetary items measured at fair value are recognised in profit or loss, except for differences on available-for-sale non-monetary financial assets such as equity shares, which are included in the fair value reserve in equity unless the asset is a hedged item in a fair value hedge.

(3) Group companies

The results and financial position of all the Group entities (none of which has the currency of a hyperinflationary economy) that have a functional currency different from the presentation currency are translated into the presentation currency as follows:

(i) assets and liabilities for each balance sheet presented are translated at the closing rate at the date of that balance sheet;

(ii) income and expenses for each income statement are translated at average exchange rates (unless this average is not a reasonable approximation of the cumulative effect of the rates prevailing on the transaction dates, in which case income and expenses are translated at the dates of the transactions); and

(iii) all resulting exchange differences are recognised as a separate component of equity.

> On consolidation, exchange differences arising from the translation of the net investment in foreign entities are taken to shareholders' equity. When a foreign operation is sold, such exchange differences are recognised in the income statement as part of the gain or loss on sale.
>
> Goodwill and fair value adjustments arising on the acquisition of a foreign entity are treated as assets and liabilities of the foreign entity and translated at the closing rate.

The IASB had considered an alternative translation method, which would have been to translate all amounts (including comparatives) at the most recent closing rate. This was considered to have several advantages: it is simple to apply; it does not generate any new gains and losses; and it does not change ratios such as return on assets. Supporters of this method believed that the process of merely expressing amounts in a different currency should preserve the same relationships among amounts as measured in the functional currency.[53] These views were probably based more on the IASB's proposals for allowing an entity to present its financial statements in a currency other than its functional currency, rather than the translation of foreign operations for inclusion in consolidated financial statements. Such an approach does have theoretical appeal. However, the major drawback is that it would require the comparatives to be restated from those previously reported.

The IASB rejected this alternative and decided to require the method that the previous version of IAS 21 required for translation the financial statements of a foreign operation.[54] It is asserted that this method results in the same amounts in the presentation currency regardless of whether the financial statements of a foreign operation are first translated into the functional currency of another group entity and then into the presentation currency or translated directly into the presentation currency.[55] We agree that it will result in the same amounts for the balance sheet, regardless of whether the translation process is a single or two-stage process. However, it does not necessarily hold true for income and expense items particularly if an average rate is used, although any difference is likely to be insignificant.

The IASB states that the method chosen avoids the need to decide the currency in which to express the financial statements of a multinational group before they are translated into the presentation currency. In addition, it produces the same amounts in the presentation currency for a stand-alone entity as for an identical subsidiary of a parent whose functional currency is the presentation currency.[56] For example, if a Swiss entity with the Swiss franc as its functional currency wishes to present its financial statements in euros, the translated amounts in euros should be the same as those for an identical entity with the Swiss franc as its functional currency that are included within the consolidated financial statements of its parent that presents its financial statements in euros.

Although the above discussion about the IASB's reasons for the choice of translation method suggests that the translation process can be either a single or a two-stage process, we believe that various requirements of the standard effectively mean that a single stage process will probably need to be used when translating foreign operations for the purposes of consolidated financial statements. This is discussed further at 3.3.5 below.

B Functional currency is that of a hyperinflationary economy

The results and financial position of an entity whose functional currency is the currency of a hyperinflationary economy shall be translated into a different presentation currency using the following procedures:[57]

(a) all amounts (i.e. assets, liabilities, equity items, income and expenses, including comparatives) shall be translated at the closing rate at the date of the most recent balance sheet, except that

(b) when amounts are translated into the currency of a non-hyperinflationary economy, comparative amounts shall be those that were presented as current year amounts in the relevant prior year financial statements (i.e. not adjusted for subsequent changes in the price level or subsequent changes in exchange rates).

When an entity's functional currency is the currency of a hyperinflationary economy, the entity shall restate its financial statements in accordance with IAS 29 before applying the translation method set out above, except for comparative amounts that are translated into a currency of a non-hyperinflationary economy (see (b) above).[58]

When the economy ceases to be hyperinflationary and the entity no longer restates its financial statements in accordance with IAS 29, it shall use as the historical costs for translation into the presentation currency the amounts restated to the price level at the date the entity ceased restating its financial statements.[59]

Example 10.6: Translation of a hyperinflationary functional currency to a non-hyperinflationary presentation currency

Using the same basic facts as Example 10.5 above, but assuming that the functional currency of the subsidiary is that of a hyperinflationary economy, the income account of the subsidiary for that year and its balance sheet at the beginning and end of the year in its functional currency and translated into Australian dollars are as shown below. For the purposes of illustration, any adjustments resulting from the restatement in accordance with IAS 29 have been ignored. See Chapter 11 for a discussion of such adjustments.

Income statement

	FC	A$
Sales	35,000	8,750
Cost of sales	(33,190)	(8,298)
Depreciation	(500)	(125)
Interest	(350)	(75)
Profit before taxation	960	240
Taxation	(460)	(115)
Profit after taxation	500	125

Balance sheets	2007 FC	2008 FC	2007 A$	2008 A$
Property, plant and equipment	6,000	5,500	2,000	1,375
Current assets				
Inventories	2,700	3,000	900	750
Receivables	4,800	4,000	1,600	1,000
Cash	200	600	67	150
	7,700	7,600	2,567	1,900
Current liabilities				
Payables	4,530	3,840	1,510	960
Taxation	870	460	290	115
	5,400	4,300	1,800	1,075
Net current assets	2,300	3,300	767	825
	8,300	8,800	2,767	2,200
Long-term loans	3,600	3,600	1,200	900
	4,700	5,200	1,567	1,300
Share capital	1,000	1,000	333	250
Retained profits*	3,700	4,200	1,234	1,050
	4,700	5,200	1,567	1,300

*The movement in retained profits is as follows:

	A$
Balance brought forward	1,234
Profit for year	125
Exchange difference	(309)
	1,050

The exchange loss of A$309 represents the reduction in retained profits due the movements in exchange, calculated as follows:

Opening balance at opening rate	– FC3,700 at FC3 = A$1 =	A$1,234
Opening balance at closing rate	– FC3,700 at FC4 = A$1 =	A$925
Exchange loss		A$(309)

It is unclear what should happen to such an exchange difference (and also the movement in share capital caused by the change in exchange rates) since paragraph 42 of IAS 21 makes no reference any possible exchange differences arising from this process. However, in the absence of any requirement to take them to a separate component of equity (as in Example 10.5 above) or to the income statement, it would seem that they are to be included as movements in the equity balances to which they relate.

An example of an accounting policy dealing with the translation of entities whose functional currency is that of a hyperinflationary economy is illustrated in the following extract.

Extract 10.3: France Telecom S.A. (2005)

2.1 SIGNIFICANT ACCOUNTING POLICIES [extract]

2.1.7 Effect of changes in foreign exchange rates [extract]

Translation of financial statements of foreign subsidiaries

The financial statements of foreign subsidiaries whose functional currency is not the euro or the currency of a hyperinflationary economy are translated into France Telecom's presentation currency (euros) as follows:

– assets and liabilities are translated at the year-end rate;

– items in the statement of income are translated at the average rate for the year;

– the translation adjustment resulting from the use of these different rates is included as a separate component of shareholders' equity.

Hyperinflationary economies

The financial statements of subsidiaries whose functional currency is the currency of a hyperinflationary economy are adjusted for the effects of inflation prior to translation into euros as follows:

– non-monetary balance sheet, statement of income and cash flow items are adjusted for inflation based on the change in a general price index from the date of acquisition to the balance sheet date;

– the exchange gain or loss on the subsidiary's net monetary position during the period (determined based on the change in the general price index over the same period) is recognized in the income statement under exchange gains and losses;

– the differences resulting from the application of the index of prices in force at the balance sheet date to monetary and non-monetary items reflected in the opening balance sheet are recorded as a separate component of shareholders' equity.

The financial statements of foreign subsidiaries previously adjusted for inflation as described above are subsequently translated into euros as follows:

– assets, liabilities, statement of income and cash flow items are translated at the year-end rate;

– the translation gains and losses resulting from the use of the year-end exchange rate to translate assets and liabilities presented in the opening balance sheet are recorded as a separate component of shareholders' equity.

Another example is shown in Extract 10.7 at 3.4.1 D II below.

2.7.2 *Translation of a foreign operation*

In addition to the procedures discussed at 2.7.1 above, IAS 21 has additional provisions that apply when the results and financial position of a foreign operation are translated into a presentation currency so that the foreign operation can be included in the financial statements of the reporting entity by consolidation, proportionate consolidation or the equity method.[60]

A *Exchange differences on intragroup balances*

The standard states that 'the incorporation of the results and financial position of a foreign operation with those of the reporting entity follows normal consolidation procedures, such as the elimination of intragroup balances and intragroup transactions of a subsidiary'.[61] However, an intragroup monetary asset (or liability), whether short-term or long-term, cannot be eliminated against the corresponding intragroup liability (or asset) without the entity with the currency exposure recognising an exchange difference on the intragroup balance. As indicated at 2.6.3 A above this will be reflected in that entity's profit or loss for the period. Except as indicated below, IAS 21 requires this exchange difference to continue to be included in profit or loss in the consolidated financial statements. This is because the monetary item represents a commitment to convert one currency into another and exposes the reporting entity to a gain or loss through currency fluctuations. However, where the exchange difference arises on an intragroup balance that, in substance, forms part of an entity's net investment in a foreign operation (see 3.4.1 below), then the exchange difference is not to be taken to profit or loss in the consolidated financial statements, but is classified as equity until the disposal of the foreign operation (see 2.7.3 below).[62]

B Non-coterminous period ends

IAS 21 recognises that in preparing consolidated financial statements it may be that a foreign operation is consolidated on the basis of financial statements made up to a different date from that of the reporting entity (see Chapter 6 at 6.4). In such a case, the standard initially states that the assets and liabilities of the foreign operation are to be translated at the exchange rate at the balance sheet date of the foreign operation rather than that at the date of the consolidated financial statements. However, it then goes on to say that adjustments are made for significant changes in exchange rates up to the balance sheet date of the reporting entity in accordance with IAS 27. The same approach is used in applying the equity method to associates and joint ventures and in applying proportionate consolidation to joint ventures in accordance with IAS 28 – *Investments in Associates* – and IAS 31 – *Interests in Joint Ventures* (see Chapters 8 and 9 respectively).[63]

The rationale for this approach is not explained in IAS 21. The initial treatment is that required by SFAS 52 and the reason given in that standard is that this presents the functional currency performance of the subsidiary during the subsidiary's financial year and its position at the end of that period in terms of the parent company's reporting (presentation) currency.[64] The subsidiary may have entered into transactions in other currencies, including the functional currency of the parent, and monetary items in these currencies will have been translated using rates ruling at the subsidiary's balance sheet date. The income statement of the subsidiary will reflect the economic consequences of carrying out these transactions during the period ended on that date. In order that the effects of these transactions in the subsidiary's financial statements are not distorted, the financial statements should be translated using the closing rate at the subsidiary's balance sheet date.

However, an alternative argument could have been advanced for using the closing rate ruling at the parent's balance sheet date. All subsidiaries within a group should normally prepare financial statements up to the same date as the parent entity so that the parent can prepare consolidated financial statements that present fairly the financial performance and financial position about the group as that of a single entity. The use of financial statements of a subsidiary made up to a date earlier than that of the parent is only an administrative convenience and a surrogate for financial statements made up to the proper date. Arguably, therefore the closing rate that should have been used is that which would have been used if the financial statements were made up to the proper date, i.e. that ruling at the date of the balance sheet date of the parent. Another reason for using this rate is that there may be subsidiaries that have the same functional currency as the subsidiary with the non-coterminous year end that do make up their financial statements to the same date as the parent company and therefore in order to be consistent with them the same rate should be used.

C *Goodwill and fair value adjustments*

The previous version of IAS 21 allowed these items to be translated at historical rates.[65] In revising the standard, the IASB decided that the treatment of such items depends on whether they are part of:[66]

(a) the assets and liabilities of the acquired entity (which would imply translating them at the closing rate); or

(b) the assets and liabilities of the parent (which would imply translating them at the historical rate).

In the case of fair value adjustments these clearly relate to the acquired entity. However, in the case of goodwill there were different views expressed by commentators.

Example 10.7: Translation of goodwill

A UK company acquires all of the share capital of an Australian company on 30 June 2008 at a cost of A$3m. The fair value of the net assets of the Australian company at that date was A$2.1m. In the consolidated financial statements at 31 December 2008 the goodwill is recognised as an asset in accordance with IFRS 3 – *Business Combinations.* The relevant exchange rates at 30 June 2008 and 31 December 2008 are £1=A$2.61 and £1=A$2.43 respectively. At what amount should the goodwill on consolidation be included in the balance sheet?

	A$	(i) £	(ii) £
Goodwill	900,000	344,828	370,370

(i) This method regards goodwill as being an asset of the parent and therefore translated at the historical rate. Supporters of this view believe that, in economic terms, the goodwill is an asset of the parent because it is part of the acquisition price paid by the parent, particularly in situations where the parent acquires a multinational operation comprising businesses with many different functional currencies.[67]

(ii) This method regards goodwill as being part of the parent's net investment in the acquired entity and therefore translated at the closing rate. Supporters of this view believe that goodwill should be treated no differently from other assets of the acquired entity, in particular intangible assets, because a significant part of the goodwill is likely to comprise intangible assets that do not qualify for separate recognition; the goodwill arises only because of the investment in the foreign entity and has no existence apart from that entity; and the cash flows that support the continued recognition of the goodwill are generated in the entity's functional currency.[68]

The IASB was persuaded by the arguments set out in (ii) above.[69] Accordingly, IAS 21 requires that any goodwill arising on the acquisition of a foreign operation and any fair value adjustments to the carrying amounts of assets and liabilities arising on the acquisition of that foreign operation shall be treated as assets and liabilities of the foreign operation. Thus they shall be expressed in the functional currency of the foreign operation and shall be translated at the closing rate in accordance with the requirements discussed at 2.7.1 above.[70] However, for entities affected by this change in requirement, transitional arrangements on implementation of the new standard were introduced as discussed at 4 below.

Clearly, if an entity acquires a single foreign entity this will be a straightforward exercise. Where, however, the acquisition is of a multinational operation comprising a number of businesses with different functional currencies this will not be the case. This is discussed at 3.3.4 below.

2.7.3 Disposal of a foreign operation

As discussed at 2.7.1 above, all resulting exchange differences on the translation of a foreign operation to a different presentation currency are to be recognised within a separate component of equity.

On the disposal of a foreign operation, IAS 21 requires the cumulative amount of the exchange differences deferred in the separate component of equity relating to that foreign operation to be recognised in profit or loss when the gain or loss on disposal is recognised.[71] As indicated at 2.7.2 A above, this will include exchange differences arising on an intragroup balance that, in substance, forms part of an entity's net investment in a foreign operation.

Example 10.8: Disposal of a foreign operation

A German entity has a Swiss subsidiary which was set up on 1 January 2005 with a share capital of CHF200,000 when the exchange rate was €1=CHF1.55. The subsidiary is included in the parent's separate financial statements at its original cost of €129,032. The profits of the subsidiary, all of which have been retained by the subsidiary, for each of the three years ended 31 December 2007 were CHF40,000, CHF50,000 and CHF60,000 respectively, so that the net assets at 31 December 2007 are CHF350,000. In the consolidated financial statements the results of the subsidiary have been translated at the respective average rates of €1=CHF1.60, €1=CHF1.68 and €1=CHF1.70 and the net assets at the respective closing rates of €1=CHF1.71, €1=CHF1.65 and €1=CHF1.66. All exchange differences have been taken to a separate exchange reserve. The consolidated reserves have therefore included the following amounts in respect of the subsidiary:

	Retained profit	Exchange reserve
	€	€
1 January 2005	–	–
Movement during 2005	25,000	(13,681)
31 December 2005	25,000	(13,681)
Movement during 2006	29,762	5,645
31 December 2006	54,762	(8,036)
Movement during 2007	35,294	(209)
31 December 2007	90,056	(8,245)

The net assets at 31 December 2007 of CHF350,000 are included in the consolidated financial statements at €210,843.

On 1 January 2008 the subsidiary is sold for CHF400,000 (€240,964), thus resulting in a gain on disposal in the parent entity's books of €111,932, i.e. €240,964 less €129,032.

In the consolidated financial statements for 2008, IAS 21 requires the cumulative exchange losses of €8,245 to be recognised in profit or loss for that year. Indeed, IAS 27 requires them to be included as part of the gain on disposal which is reduced to €21,876, being €30,121 (the difference between the proceeds of €240,964 and net asset value of €210,843 at the date of disposal) together with the cumulative exchange losses of €8,245.[72]

In this example, this gain on disposal of €21,876 represents the parent's profit of €111,932 less the cumulative profits already taken in the group income statement of €90,056.

The following accounting policies of Pearson reflect these requirements as shown below.

Extract 10.4: Pearson plc (2006)

1 **Accounting policies** [extract]

c. **Foreign currency translation** [extract]

(3) Group companies – The results and financial position of all Group entities that have a functional currency different from the presentation currency are translated into the presentation currency as follows:

i) assets and liabilities are translated at the closing rate at the date of the balance sheet;

ii) income and expenses are translated at average exchange rates;

iii) all resulting exchange differences are recognised as a separate component of equity.

On consolidation, exchange differences arising from the translation of the net investment in foreign entities, and of borrowings and other currency instruments designated as hedges of such investments, are taken to shareholders' equity. The Group treats specific inter-company loan balances, which are not intended to be repaid for the foreseeable future, as part of its net investment. When a foreign entity is sold, such exchange differences are recognised in the income statement as part of the gain or loss on sale.

At the date of transition to IFRS the cumulative translation differences for foreign operations have been deemed to be zero. Any gains and losses on disposals of foreign operations will exclude translation differences arising prior to the transition date.

The principal overseas currency for the Group is the US Dollar. The average rate for the year against Sterling was $1.84 (2005: $1.81) and the year end rate was $1.96 (2005: $1.72).

The treatment in IAS 21 is to be adopted not only when an entity sells an interest in a foreign entity, but also when it disposes of its interest through liquidation, repayment of share capital, or abandonment of that entity. It also applies for partial disposals, in which case, only the proportionate share of the related accumulated exchange differences is included in the gain or loss. The payment of a dividend, however, is part of a disposal only when it constitutes a return of the investment, e.g. when the dividend is paid out of pre-acquisition profits. A write-down of the carrying amount of a foreign operation does not constitute a partial disposal, therefore no deferred exchange difference should be recognised in income at the time of the write-down.[73] Similarly, it is implicit in the requirement of IFRS 5 – *Non-current Assets Held for Sale and Discontinued Operations* – for separate disclosure of cumulative gains and losses recognised in equity relating to a disposal group (see Chapter 4 at 2.2.4) that the classification of a foreign operation as held for sale under IFRS 5 does not give rise to recycling of foreign exchange differences at that time.

There are a number of practical issues relating to the application of these requirements. These are discussed at 3.3.6 and 3.4.1 F below.

A Future developments

It should be noted, however, that the IASB has proposed changes in this area as part of Phase II of its business combinations project. In June 2005 the IASB issued an exposure draft proposing a number of amendments to IAS 27 that includes a number of consequential amendments to IAS 21.[74] In July 2007, the IASB made available a near-final draft of the revised IAS 27.[75] At the time of writing, it is expected that the final version of the revised standard will be published in November. The consequential amendments to IAS 21 are expected to be effective for annual periods beginning on or after 1 January 2009, although if the revised IAS 27 is applied for an earlier period, the IAS 21 amendments also would have to be applied from that earlier period.[76] The main change expected is that loss of control, joint control or significant influence of a foreign operation is a disposal for the purposes of IAS 21. On the loss of control of a subsidiary, the *entire* cumulative amount of exchange differences relating to the foreign operation that is attributable to the equity holders of the parent is recycled to the income statement. Similarly, when an investee ceases to be a foreign operation because it is no longer an associate or joint venture, the entire accumulated exchange differences relating to that foreign operation is recycled. This is irrespective of any remaining interest held.[77] Where an entity's proportionate ownership interest in a foreign operation that is an associate or joint venture is reduced, without there being any loss of significant influence or joint control, then only the proportionate share of the related accumulated foreign exchange differences are recycled to the income statement. However, when there has been a partial disposal or a reduction in a proportionate interest in a subsidiary, without any loss of control, none of the accumulated exchange differences relating to that subsidiary would be recycled at that time. Instead, the proportionate share of the accumulated exchange differences is re-attributed to the non-controlling interests (the new term for 'minority interests').[78]

2.8 Tax effects of all exchange differences

IAS 21 merely states that 'gains and losses on foreign currency transactions and exchange differences arising on translating the results and financial position of an entity (including a foreign operation) into a different currency may have tax effects' and that IAS 12 – *Income Taxes* – applies to these tax effects.[79] The requirements of IAS 12 are discussed in Chapter 26.

2.9 Disclosure requirements

2.9.1 Exchange differences

IAS 21 requires the amount of exchange differences recognised in profit or loss (except for those arising on financial instruments measured at fair value through profit or loss in accordance with IAS 39) to be disclosed.[80] Since IAS 21 does not specify where such exchange differences are presented in the income statement, we recommend that entities in disclosing the amount of such exchange differences indicate the line item(s) in which they are included. Further, the classification of exchange differences (both gains and losses) arising from transactions of a similar nature should be classified consistently throughout the periods presented.

The standard also requires the net exchange differences classified in a separate component of equity, and a reconciliation of the amount of such exchange differences at the beginning and end of the period, to be disclosed.[81]

2.9.2 Presentation and functional currency

When the presentation currency is different from the functional currency, that fact shall be stated, together with disclosure of the functional currency and the reason for using a different presentation currency.[82] For this purpose, in the case of a group, the references to 'functional currency' are to that of the parent.[83]

When there is a change in the functional currency of either the reporting entity or a significant foreign operation, that fact and the reason for the change in functional currency shall be disclosed.[84]

2.9.3 Convenience translations of financial statements or other financial information

Paragraph 55 of IAS 21 indicates that when an entity presents its financial statements in a currency that is different from its functional currency, it shall describe the financial statements as complying with IFRS only if they comply with all the requirements of each applicable standard and interpretation of those standards, including the translation method set out in IAS 21 (see 2.7.1 above).[85]

However, the standard recognises that an entity sometimes presents its financial statements or other financial information in a currency that is not its functional currency without meeting the above requirements. Examples noted by IAS 21 are where an entity converts into another currency only selected items from its financial statements or where an entity whose functional currency is not the currency of a hyperinflationary economy converts the financial statements into another currency by translating all items at the most recent closing rate. Such conversions are not in accordance with IFRS; nevertheless IAS 21 requires disclosures to be made.[86]

The standard requires that when an entity displays its financial statements or other financial information in a currency that is different from either its functional currency or its presentation currency and the requirements of paragraph 55 are not met, it shall:[87]

(a) clearly identify the information as supplementary information to distinguish it from the information that complies with IFRS;

(b) disclose the currency in which the supplementary information is displayed; and

(c) disclose the entity's functional currency and the method of translation used to determine the supplementary information.

For the purpose of these requirements, in the case of a group, the references to 'functional currency' are to that of the parent.[88]

3 PRACTICAL ISSUES

3.1 Determination of functional currency

3.1.1 General

As indicated earlier, an entity is required to determine its functional currency using the guidance discussed at 2.5 above. For some entities that determination may be relatively straightforward. However, for many entities, particularly entities within a group, this may not be the case. As indicated earlier, when the factors or indicators set out at 2.5 above are mixed and the functional currency is not obvious, the standard requires management to use its judgement to determine the functional currency that most faithfully represents the economic effects of the underlying transactions, events and conditions.

Since the determination of an entity's functional currency is critical to the translation process under IAS 21, we believe that an entity should clearly document its decision about its functional currency, setting out the factors taken into account in making that determination, particularly where it is not obvious from the primary factors set out in paragraph 9 of the standard. We recommend that the ultimate parent entity of a group should do this for each entity within the group and agree that determination with the local management of those entities, particularly where those entities are presenting financial statements in accordance with IFRS. Although the determination of functional currency is a judgemental issue, it would be expected that within the group the same determination would be made as to the functional currency of a particular entity. If local management has come up with a different analysis of the facts from that of the parent, it should be discussed to ensure that both parties have considered all the relevant facts and circumstances and a final determination made.

By documenting the decision about the functional currency of each entity, and the factors taken into account in making that determination, the reporting entity will be better placed in the future to determine whether a change in the underlying transactions, events and conditions relating to that entity warrant a change in its functional currency.

3.1.2 Intermediate holding companies or finance subsidiaries

One particular difficulty is the determination of the functional currency of an intermediate holding company or finance subsidiary within an international group.

Example 10.9: Functional currency of intermediate holding companies or finance subsidiaries

An international group is headquartered in the UK. The UK parent entity has a functional currency of pound sterling, which is also the group's presentation currency. The group has three international sub-operations, structured as follows:

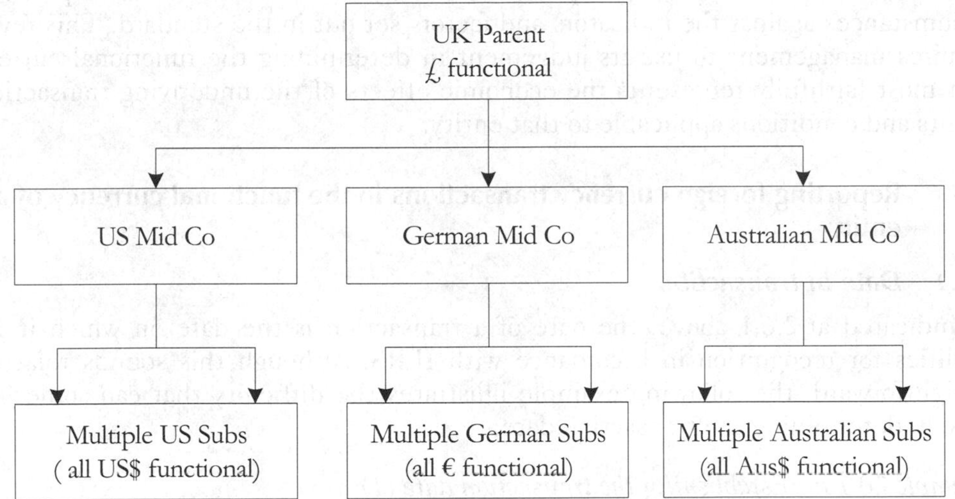

What is the functional currency of the 3 Mid Cos?

There are a variety of factors to be considered for intermediate holding companies or finance subsidiaries when deciding on the appropriate functional currency. Therefore, there will not be a single analysis applicable to all such entities.

As indicated at 2.3 above IAS 21 defines a 'foreign operation' as 'an entity that is a subsidiary…the activities of which are based or conducted in a country or currency other than those of the reporting entity'. This definition would seem to suggest that a foreign operation must have its own 'activities'.

Also, paragraph 9 of the standard states that the functional currency is 'the currency of the primary economic environment in which the entity operates'. However, as discussed at 2.5 above, under paragraph 9 this is determined by reference to the currency that mainly influences sales prices and the operation's costs, and is therefore not directly relevant to intermediate holding companies or finance subsidiaries. Paragraphs 10 and 11 set out a number of factors to consider in determining the functional currency of a foreign operation. The theme running through these factors is the extent to which the activities and cash flows of the foreign operation are independent of those of the reporting entity.

In the case of an intermediate holding company or finance subsidiary, the acid-test question to consider is whether it is an extension of the parent and performing the functions of the parent – i.e. whether its role is simply to hold the investment in, or provide finance to, the foreign operation on behalf of the parent company or whether its functions are essentially an extension of a local operation (e.g. performing selling, payroll or similar activities for that operation) or indeed it is undertaking activities on its own account.

This means that subsidiaries that do nothing but hold investments or borrow money on behalf of the parent will normally have the functional currency of the parent. The borrowings of such companies are frequently guaranteed by the parent, which is itself likely to be a relevant factor. In other words, on whose credit is the lender relying? If the lender is looking to the ultimate parent, then the functional currency is likely to be that of the ultimate parent. However, if the lender is looking to the sub-group, then the functional currency of the companies in the sub-group will be relevant. Accordingly, any analysis that such a company has a functional currency other than that of the parent will require careful consideration of the features of the entity which give rise to that conclusion. Complex situations are likely to require the application of careful management judgement as indicated by the standard.

As for other entities within a group, each entity should be reviewed for its particular circumstances against the indicators and factors set out in the standard. This review requires management to use its judgement in determining the functional currency that most faithfully represents the economic effects of the underlying transactions, events and conditions applicable to that entity.

3.2 Reporting foreign currency transactions in the functional currency of an entity

3.2.1 *Date of transaction*

As indicated at 2.6.1 above, the date of a transaction is the date on which it first qualifies for recognition in accordance with IFRS. Although this sounds relatively straightforward, the following example illustrates the difficulty that can sometimes arise in determining the transaction date:

Example 10.10: Establishing the transaction date (1)

A Belgian entity buys an item of inventory from a Canadian supplier. The dates relating to the transaction, and the relevant exchange rates, are as follows:

Date	Event	€1=C$
14 April 2008	Goods are ordered	1.50
5 May 2008	Goods are shipped from Canada and invoice dated that day	1.53
7 May 2008	Invoice is received	1.51
10 May 2008	Goods are received	1.54
14 May 2008	Invoice is recorded	1.56
7 June 2008	Invoice is paid	1.60

IAS 2 – *Inventories* – does not make any reference to the date of initial recognition of inventory. However, IAS 39 deals with the initial recognition of financial liabilities. It requires the financial liability to be recognised when, and only when, the entity becomes a party to the contractual provisions of the instrument.[89] In discussing firm commitments to purchase goods, it indicates that an entity placing the order does not recognise the liability at the time of the commitment, but delays recognition until the ordered goods have been shipped or delivered,[90] i.e. the date that the risks and rewards of ownership have passed.

Accordingly, it is unlikely that the date the goods are ordered should be used as the date of the transaction.

If the goods are shipped free on board (f.o.b.) then as the risks and rewards of ownership pass on shipment then this date should be used.

If, however, the goods are not shipped f.o.b. then the risks and rewards of ownership normally pass on delivery and therefore the date the goods are received should be treated as the date of the transaction.

The dates on which the invoice is received and is recorded are irrelevant to when the risks and rewards of ownership pass and therefore should not in principle be considered to be the date of the transaction. In practice, it may be acceptable that as a matter of administrative convenience that the exchange rate at the date the invoice is recorded is used, particularly if there is no undue delay in processing the invoice. If this is done then care should be taken to ensure that the exchange rate used is not significantly different from that ruling on the 'true' date of the transaction.

It is clear from IAS 21 that the date the invoice is paid is not the date of the transaction because if it were then no exchange differences would arise on unsettled transactions.

The above example illustrated that the date that a transaction is recorded in an entity's books and records is not necessarily the same as the date at which it qualifies for recognition under IFRS. Other situations where this is likely to arise is where an entity is recording a transaction that relates to a period, rather than one being recognised at a single point in time, as illustrated below:

Example 10.11: Establishing the transaction date (2)

On 30 September 2008 Company A, whose functional currency is the euro, acquires a US dollar bond for US$8,000. The bond carries fixed interest of 5% per annum paid quarterly, i.e. US$100 per quarter. The exchange rate at that date is US$1 to €1.50.

On 31 December 2008, the US dollar has appreciated and the exchange rate is US$1 to €2.00. Interest received on the bond on 31 December 2008 is US$100 (= €200).

Although the interest may only be being recorded at that date, the rate at 31 December 2008 is not the spot rate ruling at the date of the transaction. Since the interest has accrued over the 3 month period, it should be translated at the spot rates applicable to the accrual of interest during the 3 month period. Accordingly, a weighted average rate for the 3 month period should be used. Assuming that the appropriate average rate is US$1 to €1.75 the interest income is €175 (= US$100 × 1.75).

Accordingly, there is also an exchange gain on the interest receivable of €25 (= US$100 × [2.00 – 1.75]) to be reflected in the income statement. The journal entry for recording the receipt of the interest on 31 December 2008 is therefore as follows:

	€	€
Cash	200	
Interest income (income statement)		175
Exchange gain (income statement)		25

3.2.2 Use of average rate

As indicated at 2.6.1 above, rather than using the actual rate ruling at the date of the transaction 'an average rate for a week or month may be used for all foreign currency transactions occurring during that period', if the exchange rate does not fluctuate significantly.[91] For entities which engage in a large number of foreign currency transactions it will be more convenient for them to use an average rate rather than using the exact rate for each transaction. If an average rate is to be used, what guidance can be given in choosing and using such a rate?

(a) Length of period

As an average rate should only be used as an approximation of actual rates then care has to be taken that significant fluctuations in the day-to-day exchange rates do not arise in the period selected. For this reason the period chosen should not be too long. We believe that the period should be no longer than one month and where there is volatility of exchange rates it will be better to set rates on a more frequent basis, say, a weekly basis, especially where the value of transactions is significant;

(b) Estimate of average rate relevant to date of transaction

The estimation of the appropriate average rate will depend on whether the rate is to be applied to transactions which have already occurred or to transactions which will occur after setting the rate. Obviously, if the transactions have already occurred then the average rate used should relate to the period during which those transactions occurred; e.g. purchase transactions for the previous week should be translated using the average rate for that week, not an average rate for the week the invoices are being recorded;

If the rate is being set for the following period the rate selected should be a reasonable estimate of the expected exchange rate during that period. This could be done by using the closing rate at the end of the previous period or by using the actual average rate for the previous period. We would suggest that the former be used. Whatever means is used to estimate the average rate, the actual rates during the period should be monitored and if there is a significant move in the exchange rate away from the average rate then the rate being applied should be revised;

(c) Application of average rate to type of item

We believe that average rates should be used only as a matter of convenience where there are a large number of transactions. Even where an average rate is used, we recommend that the actual rate should be used for large one-off transactions such as the purchase of a fixed asset or an overseas investment or taking out a foreign loan. Where the number of foreign currency transactions is small it will probably not be worthwhile setting and monitoring average rates and therefore actual rates should be used.

3.2.3 *Dual rates or suspension of rates*

One practical difficulty in translating foreign currency amounts is where there is more than one exchange rate for that particular currency depending on the nature of the transaction. In some cases the difference between the exchange rates can be small and therefore it probably does not matter which rate is actually used. However, in other situations the difference can be quite significant. In these circumstances, what rate should be used? IAS 21 states that 'when several exchange rates are available, the rate used is that at which the future cash flows represented by the transaction or balance could have been settled if those cash flows had occurred at the measurement date'.[92] Companies should therefore look at the nature of the transaction and apply the appropriate exchange rate.

Another practical difficulty which could arise is where for some reason exchangeability between two currencies is temporarily lacking at the transaction date or at the subsequent balance sheet date. In this case, IAS 21 requires that the rate to be used is 'the first subsequent rate at which exchanges could be made'.[93]

3.2.4 *Monetary or non-monetary?*

As indicated in 2.6.2 above, IAS 21 generally requires that monetary items denominated in foreign currencies be retranslated using closing rates at each balance sheet date and non-monetary items should not be retranslated. Monetary items are defined as 'units of currency held and assets and liabilities to be received or paid in a fixed or determinable number of units of currency'.[94] The standard elaborates further on this by stating that 'the essential feature of a monetary item is a right to receive (or an obligation to deliver) a fixed or determinable number of units of currency'. Examples given by IAS 21 are pensions and other employee benefits to be paid in cash; provisions that are to be settled in cash; and cash dividends that are recognised as a liability.[95] More obvious examples are cash and bank balances; trade receivables and payables; and loan receivables and payables. IAS 39 also indicates that where a foreign currency bond is held as an available-for-sale financial asset, then it should first be accounted for at amortised cost in the underlying currency, thus effectively treating that amount as if it was a monetary item. This is discussed further in Chapter 20 at 7.1. This suggests that foreign currency bonds that are classified as held-to-maturity investments under IAS 39 are monetary items.

The following extract from Aviva's 2005 financial statements illustrates the IAS 39 treatment for monetary financial assets designated as available-for-sale.

Extract 10.5: Aviva plc (2006)

Accounting policies [extract]

(D) Foreign currency translation

Income statements and cash flows of foreign entities are translated into the Group's presentation currency at average exchange rates for the year while their balance sheets are translated at the year end exchange rates. Exchange differences arising from the translation of the net investment in foreign subsidiaries, associates and joint ventures, and of borrowings and other currency instruments designated as hedges of such investments, are taken to the currency translation reserve within equity. On disposal of a foreign entity, such exchange differences are transferred out of this reserve and are recognised in the income statement as part of the gain or loss on sale. The cumulative translation differences were deemed to be zero at the transition date to IFRS.

Foreign currency transactions are accounted for at the exchange rates prevailing at the date of the transactions. Gains and losses resulting from the settlement of such transactions, and from the translation of monetary assets and liabilities denominated in foreign currencies, are recognised in the income statement.

Translation differences on debt securities and other monetary financial assets measured at fair value and designated as held at fair value through profit or loss (FV) (see policy R) are included in foreign exchange gains and losses in the income statement. For monetary financial assets designated as AFS, translation differences are calculated as if they were carried at amortised cost and so are recognised in the income statement, whilst foreign exchange differences arising from fair value gains and losses are included in the investment valuation reserve within equity. Translation differences on non-monetary items, such as equities which are designated as FV, are reported as part of the fair value gain or loss, whereas such differences on AFS equities are included in the investment valuation reserve.

IAS 21 also states that 'a contract to receive (or deliver) a variable number of the entity's own equity instruments or a variable amount of assets in which the fair value to be received (or delivered) equals a fixed or determinable number of units of currency is a monetary item'.[96] No examples of such contracts are given in IAS 21.

However, it would seem to embrace those contracts settled in the entity's own equity shares that under IAS 32 – *Financial Instruments: Disclosure and Presentation* – would be presented as financial assets or liabilities (see Chapter 19 at 3.3.2 A).

Conversely, the essential feature of a non-monetary item is the absence of a right to receive (or an obligation to deliver) a fixed or determinable number of units of currency. Examples given by the standard are amounts prepaid for goods and services (e.g. prepaid rent); goodwill; intangible assets; inventories; property, plant and equipment; and provisions that are to be settled by the delivery of a non-monetary asset.[97] IAS 39 also indicates that equity instruments that are held as available-for-sale financial assets are non-monetary items.[98] This suggests that equity investments in subsidiaries, associates or joint ventures are non-monetary items.

Even with this guidance there will clearly be a number of situations where the distinction may not be altogether clear.

A Deposits or progress payments

Entities may be required to pay deposits or progress payments when acquiring certain assets, such as property, plant and equipment or inventories, from foreign suppliers. The question then arises as to whether such payments should be retranslated as monetary items or not.

Example 10.12: Deposits or progress payments

A Dutch entity contracts to purchase an item of plant and machinery for US$10,000 on the following terms:

Payable on signing contract (1 August 2008)	– 10%
Payable on delivery (19 December 2008)	– 40%
Payable on installation (7 January 2008)	– 50%

At 31 December 2008 the entity has paid the first two amounts on the due dates when the respective exchange rates were €1=US$1.25 and €1=US$1.20. The closing rate at its balance sheet date, 31 December 2008, is €1=US$1.15.

		(i) €	(ii) €
First payment	– US$1,000	800	870
Second payment	– US$4,000	3,333	3,478
		4,133	4,348

(i) If the payments made are regarded as prepayments or as progress payments then the amounts should be treated as non-monetary items and included in the balance sheet at €4,133. This would appear to be consistent with SFAS 52 which in defining 'transaction date' states: 'A long-term commitment may have more than one transaction date (for example, the due date of each progress payment under a construction contract is an anticipated transaction date).'[99]

(ii) If the payments made are regarded as deposits, and are refundable, then the amounts could possibly be treated as monetary items and included in the balance sheet at €4,348 and an exchange gain of €215 recorded in the income statement. A variant of this would be to only treat the first payment as a deposit until the second payment is made, since once delivery is made it is less likely that the asset will be returned and a refund sought from the supplier.

In practice, it will often be necessary to consider the terms of the contract to ascertain the nature of the payments made in order to determine the appropriate accounting treatment.

B Investments in preference shares

Entities may invest in preference shares of other entities. Whether such shares are monetary items or not will depend on the rights attaching to the shares. As noted at 3.2.4 above, IAS 39 indicates that equity instruments that are held as available-for-sale financial assets are non-monetary items.[100] Thus, it appears that if the terms of the preference shares are such that they are classified by the issuer as equity, rather than as a financial liability, then they are non-monetary items. However, if the terms of the preference shares are such that they are classified by the issuer as a financial liability (e.g. a preference share that provides for mandatory redemption by the issue for a fixed or determinable amount at a fixed or determinable future date), then it would appear that they should be treated as monetary items. Indeed, IAS 39 would allow such an instrument to be classified within loans and receivables by the holder provided the definition in IAS 39 is otherwise met (see Chapter 17 at 7.3). However, even where an investment in such redeemable preference shares is not classified within loans and receivables, but as a held-to-maturity investment or as an available-for-sale financial asset, then it would seem that it should be treated as a monetary item (in the latter case, to the extent that it would be measured at amortised cost, similar to an investment in a bond as discussed at 3.2.4 above).

C Foreign currency share capital

Entities may issue share capital denominated in a currency that is not its functional currency or, due to changes in circumstances that result in a re-determination of its functional currency, may find that its share capital is no longer denominated in its functional currency. Neither IAS 21 nor IAS 39 addresses the treatment of translation of share capital denominated in a currency other than the functional currency. In theory two treatments are possible: the foreign currency share capital (and any related share premium or additional paid-in capital) could be maintained at a fixed amount by being translated at a historical rate of exchange, or it could be retranslated annually at the closing rate as if it were a monetary amount. In the latter case a second question would arise: whether to take the difference arising on translation to the income statement or deal with it within equity.

Where the shares denominated in a foreign currency are ordinary shares, or are otherwise irredeemable and classified as equity instruments, our preferred view is that the shares should be translated at historical rates and not remeasured, because the effect of rate changes is not expected to have an impact on the entity's cash flows. Such capital items are included within the examples of non-monetary items listed in SFAS 52 as accounts to be remeasured using historical exchange rates when the temporal method is being applied.[101] As noted at 2.6.2 above, IAS 21 requires non-monetary items that are measured at historical cost in a foreign currency shall be translated using the historical rate. This is also the treatment required by the equivalent Canadian standard.[102]

Where such share capital is retranslated at closing rate, we do not believe that it is appropriate for the exchange differences to be taken to the income statement, since they do not affect the cash flows of the entity; the exchange differences should be taken to equity. Consequently, whether such share capital is maintained at a historical rate, or is dealt with in this way, the treatment has no impact on the overall equity of the entity.

Where the shares are not classified as equity instruments, but as financial liabilities, under IAS 32, e.g. preference shares that provide for mandatory redemption by the issue for a fixed or determinable amount at a fixed or determinable future date, then, as with investments in such shares discussed at 3.2.4 B above, they should be treated as monetary items and translated at closing rate. Any exchange differences will be taken to profit or loss, unless the shares form part of a hedging relationship and IAS 39 would account for the exchange differences differently (see Chapter 21).

D Deferred tax

One of the examples of a monetary item included within the exposure draft that preceded IAS 21 was deferred tax.[103] However, this has been dropped from the list of examples in the final standard. No explanation is given in IAS 21 as to why this is the case. Nevertheless, IAS 12 suggests that any deferred foreign tax assets or liabilities are monetary items since it states that 'where exchange differences on deferred foreign tax liabilities or assets are recognised in the income statement, such differences may be classified as deferred tax expense (income) if that presentation is considered to be the most useful to financial statement users'.[104]

E Post-employment benefit plans

As noted above, one of the examples of a monetary item given by IAS 21 is 'pensions and other employee benefits to be paid in cash'. For most entities, this will not be an issue because any pension benefits payable under a post-employment benefit plan that is a defined benefit plan will be payable in the functional currency of the entity. However, it may be that the plan has assets that are denominated in a foreign currency. Since IAS 19 – *Employee Benefits* – requires these to be measured at their fair value at the balance sheet date, then IAS 21 requires such assets to be translated at closing rate. How should the entity deal with any exchange differences arising on such assets held by a defined benefit plan?

I Foreign currency assets

One approach would be to follow the normal treatment within IAS 21. Accordingly, any exchange differences on non-monetary items such as investments in equity or property would go the statement of recognised income and expense since that is where the valuation gains and losses are taken. For investments in currency bonds, as noted above, IAS 39 indicates these are first accounted for at 'amortised cost' i.e. as a monetary item with exchange differences on that amount going to the income statement. Any further exchange differences due to being valued at fair value would be treated in the same way as those arising on the equity and property investments. However, the accounting for defined benefit schemes under IAS 19 requires an entity to reflect the expected return on any plan assets as part of the annual pension cost in the income statement. As discussed in Chapter 32 at 5.4.3, this 'expected return' is a forward-looking expectation or estimate based on market expectations at the beginning of the period for returns over the entire life of the related obligation. Although IAS 19 is silent on the matter, it would seem that such an estimate should reflect the effect of any exchange risk relating to the assets that are in a foreign currency. On that basis, although the assets at the balance sheet date would be translated at closing rate, the effect of doing so would be reflected as part of the actuarial gain or loss, being the difference between the actual return and the expected return, and accounted for in accordance with the entity's accounting policy for dealing with actuarial gains and losses (see Chapter 32 at 5.3.1 A).

II Foreign currency plans?

For some entities it may be that the pension benefits payable under a post-employment benefit plan will not be payable in the functional currency of the entity. For example, a UK entity in the oil and gas industry may determine that its functional currency is the US dollar, but its employee costs including the pension benefits are payable in sterling. How should such an entity account for its post-employment benefit plan?

As noted above, one of the examples of a monetary item given by IAS 21 are 'pensions and other employee benefits to be paid in cash'. However, the standard does not expand on this, and does not appear to make any distinction between pensions provided by defined contribution plans or defined benefit plans. Clearly for pensions that are payable under a post-employment benefit plan that is a defined contribution plan (or is accounted for as such) this is straightforward. Any liability for outstanding contributions at the balance sheet date is a monetary item that should be translated at closing rate, with any resulting exchange differences taken to the income statement. It would appear that IAS 21 envisages that the defined benefit obligation under a defined benefit plan at the balance sheet date should also to be treated as a monetary item, and therefore translated at closing rate.

As far as the assets held by the plan are concerned, these will predominantly be non-monetary items, but since IAS 19 requires these to be measured at their fair value at the balance sheet date, then IAS 21 requires such assets also to be translated at closing rate. However, as discussed at 2.6.3 above, exchange differences on monetary items are generally taken to the income statement, whereas the exchange differences on non-monetary assets are taken to the income statement only when valuation gains and losses are recognised in profit or loss. This clearly results in a mismatch since, under IAS 19, the valuation gains and losses will be actuarial gains and losses that are either immediately recognised in the statement of total recognised gains and losses or only recognised under the IAS 19 corridor approach (see Chapter 32 at 5.3.1 A). Is there any way in which this can be mitigated?

One approach would be to argue that the exchange differences relating to the defined benefit obligation are similar to actuarial gains and losses. The calculation of the obligation under IAS 19 will be based on actuarial assumptions that reflect the currency of the obligation to the employee (for example, the discount rate used 'shall be consistent with the currency and estimated term' of the obligation[105]). Any variations from those assumptions on both the obligation and the assets are dealt with in the same way under IAS 19. Actuarial assumptions are 'an entity's best estimates of the variables that will determine the ultimate cost of providing post-employment benefits' and include financial assumptions.[106] Although IAS 19 does not refer to exchange rates, it is clearly a variable that will determine the ultimate cost to the entity of providing the post-employment benefits. On that basis, it would seem reasonable for the effect of exchange rate differences on both the assets and the obligations of the fund to be accounted for in a similar manner to actuarial gains and losses, based on the entity's accounting policy for dealing with actuarial gains and losses (see Chapter 32 at 5.3.1 A).

It might be argued that the plan should be regarded as a 'foreign operation' under IAS 21 (see 2.3 above). However, in this situation it is very difficult to say that its 'functional currency' can be regarded as being different from that of the reporting entity given the relationship between the plan and the reporting entity (see 2.5 above). Thus, it would appear that the entity cannot treat the plan as a foreign operation with a different functional currency from its own.

3.2.5 Treatment of exchange differences

The general rule in IAS 21 is that exchange differences on the settlement or retranslation of monetary items shall be recognised in profit or loss in the period in which they arise.[107] However, as noted at 2.6.3 A above, the standard identifies two exceptions to this rule – monetary items forming part of an entity's net investment in a foreign operation (see 3.4.1 below) and hedge accounting under IAS 39 (see Chapter 21). Apart from these, are there any other circumstances where it is possible for exchange differences not to be taken to the income statement in the period they arise?

One situation would be where an entity capitalises borrowing costs under IAS 23 – *Borrowing Costs* – since that standard allows exchange differences arising from foreign currency borrowings to be capitalised, but only to the extent that they are regarded as an adjustment to interest costs (see Chapter 16).[108]

As discussed at 3.2.4 E above, another situation might be in relation to the exchange differences on a defined benefit obligation where they are treated as being similar to the actuarial gains and losses on the obligation.

One example of a monetary item given by IAS 21 is 'provisions that are to be settled in cash'. In most cases it will be appropriate for the exchange differences arising on provisions to be taken to the income statement in the period they arise. However, it may be that an entity has recognised a decommissioning provision under IAS 37 – *Provisions, Contingent Liabilities and Contingent Assets*. One practical difficulty with such a provision is that due to the long timescale of when the actual cash outflows will arise, an entity may not be able to say with any certainty the currency in which the transaction will actually be settled. Nevertheless if it is determined that it is expected to be settled in a foreign currency it will be a monetary item. The main issue then is what should happen to any exchange differences. As discussed in Chapter 27 at 5.4.2 A, IFRIC 1 – *Changes in existing decommissioning, restoration and similar liabilities* – applies to any decommissioning or similar liability that has been both included as part of an asset measured as a liability in accordance with IAS 37. IFRIC 1 requires, *inter alia*, that any adjustment to such a provision resulting from changes in the estimated outflow of resources embodying economic benefits (e.g. cash flows) required to settle the obligation should not be taken to the income statement as it occurs, but should be added to or deducted from the cost of the asset to which it relates. The requirement of IAS 21 to take the exchange differences arising on the provision to the income statement in the period in which they arise conflicts with this requirement in IFRIC 1. Accordingly, we believe that it would be more logical for the exchange differences not to be taken to the income statement, but dealt with in accordance with IFRIC 1.

3.2.6 Books and records not kept in functional currency

Occasionally, an entity may keep its underlying books and records in a currency that is not its functional currency under IAS 21. For example, it could record its transactions in terms of the local currency of the country in which it is located, possibly as a result of local requirements.

When an entity keeps its books and records in a currency other than its functional currency, then IAS 21 requires that at the time the entity prepares its financial statements all amounts are translated into the functional currency in accordance with paragraphs 20-26 of the standard,[109] i.e. those discussed at 2.6.1, 2.6.2 and 3.2.1 to 3.2.4 above. The standard goes on to say that 'this produces the same amounts in the functional currency as would have occurred had the items been recorded initially in the functional currency. For example, monetary items are translated into the functional currency using the closing rate, and non-monetary items that are measured on a historical cost basis are translated using the exchange rate at the date of the transaction that resulted in their recognition.'[110] This presupposes that the initial recording of transactions in foreign currencies (including the entity's functional currency), and any subsequent retranslation of the resulting balance sheet items, have been translated into the recording currency in accordance with those paragraphs. For example, all foreign currency monetary items have been translated into the recording currency at the closing rate at the balance sheet date. It is only if this has been done that the subsequent translation of those monetary items to the functional currency using the closing rate between the recording currency and the functional currency will result in the same amounts that would have occurred if the foreign currency amounts had been translated directly into the functional currency at their respective closing rates. However, if the foreign currency monetary items have been retained at their original historical rate in the books and records, then the subsequent translation of those monetary items to the functional currency using the closing rate between the recording currency and the functional currency will *not* result in the same amounts that would have occurred if the foreign currency amounts had been translated directly into the functional currency at their respective closing rates.

Accordingly, when an entity keeps its books and records in a currency other than its functional currency, it will be necessary to obtain an understanding about the underlying translation process before applying these requirements of the standard to ensure that the resulting amounts are the same amounts in the functional currency as would have occurred had the items been recorded initially in the functional currency.

As indicated above, IAS 21 only refers to the translation into the functional currency in accordance with paragraphs 20-26 of the standard. These paragraphs do not include those relating to the treatment of exchange differences arising from that translation process. However, we believe that any resulting exchange differences should be recognised as discussed at 2.6.3 above.

3.3 Translation to a different presentation currency

3.3.1 Dual rates or suspension of rates

The problems of dual rates and suspension of rates in relation to the translation of foreign currency transactions and balances into an entity's functional currency and the related requirements of IAS 21 dealing with such issues have already been discussed in 3.2.3 above. However, the standard makes no reference to them in the context of translating the results and financial position of an entity into a different presentation currency, particularly where the results and financial position of a foreign operation are being translated for inclusion in the financial statements of the reporting entity by consolidation, proportionate consolidation or the equity method.

Where the problem is one of suspension of rates, then we believe that the requirement in IAS 21 relating to transactions and balances should be followed; i.e. the rate to be used is 'the first subsequent rate at which exchanges could be made'.[111] However, the requirement in IAS 21 relating to dual rates is not entirely relevant in this context. Again, guidance can be sought from SFAS 52 which states that the rate to be used to translate foreign financial statements should be, in the absence of unusual circumstances, the rate applicable to dividend remittances.[112] The reason for this is that the use of that rate is more meaningful than any other rate because cash flows to the parent company from the foreign entity can be converted only at that rate, and realisation of a net investment in the foreign entity will ultimately be in the form of cash flows from that entity.[113]

3.3.2 Calculation of average rate

As indicated at 2.7.1 A above, when translating the results of an entity whose functional currency is not that of a hyperinflationary economy, for practical reasons, the reporting entity may use a rate that approximates the actual exchange rate, e.g. an average rate for the period, to translate income and expense items.[114]

The standard does not give any guidance on the factors that should be taken into account in determining what may be an appropriate average rate for the period – it merely says that 'if exchange rates fluctuate significantly, the use of the average rate for the period is inappropriate'.[115] What methods are, therefore, available to entities to use in calculating an appropriate average rate? Possible methods might be:

(a) mid-year rate;

(b) average of opening and closing rates;

(c) average of month end/quarter end rates;

(d) average of monthly average rates;

(e) monthly/quarterly results at month end/quarter end rates; or

(f) monthly/quarterly results at monthly/quarterly averages.

Example 10.13: Calculation of average rate

A Spanish entity has a foreign subsidiary and is preparing its consolidated financial statements for the year ended 30 April 2008. It intends to use an average rate for translating the results of the subsidiary. The relevant exchange rates for €1=FC are as follows:

Month	Month end	Average for month	Average for quarter	Average for year
April 2007	1.67			
May 2007	1.63	1.67		
June 2007	1.67	1.64		
July 2007	1.64	1.65	1.65	
August 2007	1.67	1.64		
September 2007	1.70	1.63		
October 2007	1.67	1.68	1.65	
November 2007	1.65	1.70		
December 2007	1.66	1.66		
January 2008	1.64	1.67	1.68	
February 2008	1.60	1.65		
March 2008	1.61	1.63		
April 2008	1.61	1.62	1.63	1.65

Average of month end rates – 1.65

Average of quarter end rates – 1.64

The results of the subsidiary for each of the 12 months to 30 April 2008 and the translation thereof under each of the above methods (using monthly figures where appropriate) are shown below:

Method (a)	FC31,050 @ 1.67 = €18,593
Method (b)	FC31,050 @ 1.64 = €18,933
Method (c) – monthly	FC31,050 @ 1.65 = €18,818
Method (c) – quarterly	FC31,050 @ 1.64 = €18,933
Method (d)	FC31,050 @ 1.65 = €18,818

Month	FC	(e) quarterly €	(e) monthly €	(f) quarterly €	(f) monthly €
May 2007	1,000		613		599
June 2007	1,100		659		671
July 2007	1,200	2,012	732	2,000	727
August 2007	1,300		778		793
September 2007	1,300		765		798
October 2007	1,350	2,365	808	2,394	804
November 2007	1,400		848		824
December 2007	1,400		843		843
January 2008	2,000	2,927	1,220	2,857	1,198
February 2008	5,000		3,125		3,030
March 2008	10,000		6,211		6,135
April 2008	4,000	11,801	2,484	11,656	2,469
Total	31,050	19,105	19,086	18,907	18,891

It can be seen that by far the simplest methods to use are the methods (a) to (d).

In our view methods (a) and (b) should not normally be used as it is unlikely in times of volatile exchange rates that they will give appropriate weighting to the exchange rates which have been in existence throughout the period in question. They are only likely to give an acceptable answer if the exchange rate has been static or steadily increasing or decreasing throughout the period.

Method (c) based on quarter end rates has similar drawbacks and therefore should not normally be used.

Method (c) based on month end rates and method (d) are better than the previous methods as they do take into account more exchange rates which have applied throughout the year, with method (d) being preferable, as this will have taken account of daily exchange rates. Average monthly rates for most major currencies are likely to be given in publications issued by the government, banks and other sources and therefore it is unnecessary for entities to calculate their own. The work involved in calculating an average for the year, therefore, is not very onerous. Method (d) will normally give reasonable and acceptable results when there are no seasonal variations in items of income and expenditure.

Where there are seasonal variations in items of income and expenditure then this may not be the case. In these situations appropriate exchange rates should be applied to the appropriate items. This can be done by using either of methods (e) or (f) preferably using figures and rates for each month. Where such a method is being used care should be taken to ensure that the periodic accounts are accurate and that cut-off procedures have been adequate, otherwise significant items may be translated at the wrong average rate.

Where there are significant one-off items of income and expenses then it is likely that actual rates at the date of the transaction should be used to translate such items.

3.3.3 Translation of equity items

The method of translation of the results and financial position of an entity whose functional currency is not the currency of a hyperinflationary economy is discussed at 2.7.1 A above. The translation process makes no reference to the translation of equity items. The exposure draft that preceded the standard had proposed that '… equity items other than those resulting from income and expense recognised in the period … shall be translated at the closing rate'. However, the IASB decided not to specify in the standard the translation rate for equity items,[116] but no explanation has been given in the Basis of Conclusions about this matter.

So how should entities deal with the translation of equity items?

A Share capital

Where an entity is presenting its financial statements in a currency other than its functional currency, it would seem more appropriate that its share capital (whether they are ordinary shares, or are otherwise irredeemable and classified as equity instruments) should be translated at historical rates of exchange. As noted at 3.2.4 C above, such capital items are included within the examples of non-monetary items listed in SFAS 52 as accounts to be remeasured using historical exchange rates when the temporal method is being applied.[117] As noted at 2.6.2 above, IAS 21 requires non-monetary items that are measured at historical cost in a foreign currency to be translated using the historical rate. This is also the treatment required by the equivalent Canadian standard.[118] Translation at a historical rate would imply using the rate ruling at the date of the issue of the shares. However, where a subsidiary is presenting its financial statements in the currency of its parent, it may be that the more appropriate historical rate for share capital that was in issue at the date it became a subsidiary would be that ruling at the date it became a subsidiary of the parent, rather than at earlier dates of issue.

Where such share capital is retranslated at closing rate, we do not believe that it is appropriate for the exchange differences to be taken to the separate component of equity required by IAS 21 (since to do so could result in them being recycled to the income statement upon disposal of part of the entity's operations in the future), but should either be taken to retained earnings or some other reserve. Consequently, whether such share capital is maintained at a historical rate, or is dealt with in this way, the treatment has no impact on the overall equity of the entity.

B Other equity balances resulting from transactions with equity holders

In addition to share capital, an entity may have other equity balances resulting from the issue of shares, such as a share premium account (additional paid-in capital). Like share capital, the translation of such balances could be done at either historical rates or at closing rate. However, we believe that whichever method is adopted is consistent with the treatment used for share capital. Again, where exchange differences arise through using the closing rate, we believe that it is not appropriate for them to be taken to the separate component of equity required by IAS 21.

A similar approach should be adopted where an entity has acquired its own equity shares and has deducted those 'treasury shares' from equity as required by IAS 32 (see Chapter 19 at 6).

C Other equity balances resulting from income and expenses being taken direct to equity

Although IAS 21 makes no reference to equity items in its translation process, the standard does suggest, however, that income and expenses that are recognised directly in equity will have been translated at the exchange rates ruling at the dates of the transaction, since it is only by doing so, and translating the period end assets and liabilities at closing rates, that exchange differences will arise on such items so that they get recognised within the separate component of equity.[119] Examples of such items of income and expense are certain revaluation gains and losses on property, plant and equipment under IAS 16 (see Chapter 13 at 2.4.1) and on certain intangible assets under IAS 38 – *Intangible Assets* (see Chapter 12 at 2.4.2), gains and losses on available-for-sale financial assets under IAS 39 (see Chapter 20 at 3.4), gains and losses on cash flow hedges under IAS 39 (see Chapter 21 at 4.2.1), and any amounts of current and deferred tax taken to equity under IAS 12 (see Chapter 26 at 6.1). This would suggest that where these gains and losses are taken to a separate reserve or component of equity, then any period-end balance should represent the cumulative translated amounts of such gains and losses. However, as IAS 21 is silent on the matter it would seem that it would be acceptable to translate these equity balances at closing rate, as long as the exchange differences arising are not taken to the separate component of equity required by IAS 21. The differences would have to be taken to retained earnings or some other reserve, effectively as a transfer between the reserves. Consequently, whether such balances are maintained at the original translated rates, or are translated at closing rates, the treatment has no impact on the overall equity of the entity.

3.3.4 Goodwill

As discussed at 2.7.2 C above, IAS 21 requires that any goodwill arising on the acquisition of a foreign operation shall be expressed in the functional currency of the foreign operation and shall be translated at the closing rate in accordance with the requirements discussed at 2.7.1 above.[120] Clearly, if an entity acquires a single foreign entity this will be a straightforward exercise. Where, however, the acquisition is of a multinational operation comprising a number of businesses with different functional currencies this will not be the case. The goodwill needs to be allocated to the level of each functional currency of the acquired operation. However, the standard gives no guidance on how this should be done.

In our view, the preferred basis of allocating goodwill to different functional currencies would be an economic value approach. This approach effectively calculates the goodwill relating to each different functional currency operation by allocating the cost of the acquisition to the different functional currency operations on the basis of the relative economic values of those businesses and then deducting the fair values that have been attributed to the net assets of those businesses as part of the fair value exercise in accounting for the business combination (see Chapter 7 at 2.3.3). We consider that any other basis for allocating goodwill to different functional currencies would need to be substantiated.

The Basis of Conclusions issued by the IASB notes that the level to which goodwill is allocated for foreign currency translation purpose may be different from the level at which the goodwill is tested for impairment under IAS 36 – *Impairment of Assets* (see Chapter 7 at 3.2).[121] In many cases the allocation under IAS 21 will be at a lower level. This will apply not only on the acquisition of a multinational operation but could also apply on the acquisition of a single operation where the goodwill is allocated to a larger cash generating unit under IAS 36 that is made up of businesses with different functional currencies.

As a consequence of this different level of allocation one particular difficulty that entities are likely to face is how to deal with an impairment loss that is recognised in respect of goodwill under IAS 36. If the impairment loss relates to a larger cash generating unit made up of businesses with different functional currencies, again some allocation of this impairment loss will be required to determine the amount of the remaining carrying amount of goodwill in each of the functional currencies for the purposes of translation under IAS 21.

3.3.5 Accounting for foreign operations where sub-groups exist

The method required by IAS 21 for the translation of a foreign operation whose functional currency is not that of a hyperinflationary economy to a different presentation currency was adopted by the IASB for reasons discussed at 2.7.1 A above. Although the discussion about the IASB's reasons for the choice of translation method suggests that the translation process can be a single or two-stage process, we believe that various requirements of the standard effectively mean that a single stage process will probably need to be used when translating foreign operations for the purposes of consolidated financial statements.

Example 10.14: Accounting for sub-groups

Parent A's functional currency is the US dollar and prepares its consolidated financial statements in US dollars. It has a 100% investment in Subsidiary A, the functional currency of which is the euro. Subsidiary A has a 100% investment in Subsidiary B, the functional currency of which is pound sterling.

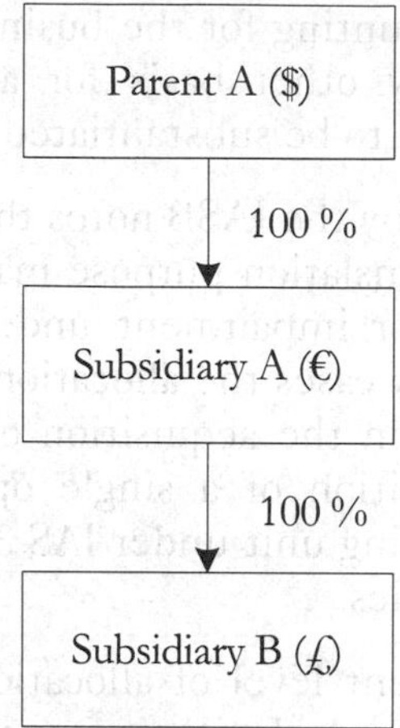

Should Parent A prepare consolidated financial statements by including the consolidated position of Subsidiary A (including Subsidiary B), or consolidate Subsidiary A and Subsidiary B as standalone entities?

In our view it is more consistent with various requirements of IAS 21 that each entity in a group should be consolidated individually, ignoring sub-groups and sub-consolidations. Under IAS 21, it makes no difference whether the reporting entity holds the foreign operation directly or whether there is an intermediate holding entity between the reporting entity and the foreign operation. This is made clear in paragraph 18 of the standard which states that 'it is necessary for the results and financial position of each individual entity included in the reporting entity to be translated into the currency in which the reporting entity presents its financial statements. … The results and financial position of any individual entity within the reporting entity whose functional currency differs from the presentation currency are translated in accordance with paragraphs 38-50.'

Paragraph 38 states that 'An entity may present its financial statements in any currency (or currencies). If the presentation currency differs from the entity's functional currency, it translates its results and financial position into the presentation currency. For example, when a group contains individual entities with different functional currencies, the results and financial position of each entity are expressed in a common currency so that consolidated financial statements may be presented.'

Paragraph 45 continues by stating that 'The incorporation of the results and financial position of a foreign operation with those of the reporting entity follows normal consolidation procedures, such as the elimination of intragroup balances and intragroup transactions of a subsidiary (see IAS 27 and IAS 31). However, an intragroup monetary asset (or liability), whether short-term or long-term, cannot be eliminated against the corresponding intragroup liability (or asset) without showing the results of currency fluctuations in the consolidated financial statements. This is because the monetary item represents a commitment to convert one currency into another and exposes the reporting entity to a gain or loss through currency fluctuations. Accordingly, in the consolidated financial statements of the reporting entity, such an exchange difference continues to be recognised in profit or loss or, if it arises from the circumstances described in paragraph 32, it is classified as equity until the disposal of the foreign operation.' Paragraph 32 is discussed at 3.4.1 below.

Furthermore paragraph 48 confirms that 'On the disposal of a foreign operation, the cumulative amount of the exchange differences deferred in the separate component of equity relating to that foreign operation shall be recognised in profit or loss when the gain or loss on disposal is recognised.' This requirement is discussed further at 3.3.6 below.

The above-mentioned paragraphs refer to an *individual* entity being translated to the presentation currency, with the exchange differences arising from that process (i.e. between its functional currency and the presentation currency) being taken to equity, and for those cumulative exchange differences to be taken to the income statement upon the disposal of that foreign operation.

This is an aspect of IAS 21 that has been discussed by the IFRIC in developing IFRIC Draft Interpretation D22 – *Hedges of a Net Investment in a Foreign Operation* – published in July 2007 (see Chapter 21 at 3.6.3 for a discussion of this issue). In November 2006, the IFRIC considered whether IAS 21 presumes certain mechanics of consolidation (i.e. either consolidation of each individual subsidiary directly to the ultimate parent or a step-by-step series of sub-consolidations by immediate parent entities up to a final consolidation at the ultimate parent level). It was noted that IAS 21 did not presume any particular mechanics of consolidation, but that the IASB staff should consider whether clarifying this point would resolve most of the diversity occurring in practice.[122]

In January 2007, the IFRIC decided that an Interpretation on the mechanics of consolidation would not resolve the issues in the project.[123] The relevant agenda paper for that meeting indicated that the staff considered that IAS 21 did not specify the mechanics of consolidation. It was also noted that, as indicated in paragraph BC18 of the standard, the translation method in IAS 21 results in the same amounts in the presentation currency regardless of whether the financial statements of a foreign operation are first translated into the functional currency of another group entity and then into the presentation currency or translated directly into the presentation currency. Thus, it was concluded that both the direct method and the step-by-step method will result in the same amounts shown in the presentation currency on consolidation of the financial statements.[124]

We agree that it will result in the same amounts for the balance sheet, regardless of whether the translation process is a single or two-stage process or the consolidation is done using the direct or step-by-step method. However, it does not necessarily hold true for income and expense items particularly if an average rate is used, although any difference is likely to be insignificant. Nevertheless, the main reason why we believe that the direct method should be used whereby each entity in a group should be consolidated individually, rather than the step-by-step method using sub-groups and sub-consolidations, is that it is more consistent with various requirements of IAS 21 as explained in Example 10.14 above. The latter method may mean that any exchange differences that should be recycled on the disposal of a foreign operation as required by paragraph 48 of IAS 21 may not be identified or computed correctly as discussed and illustrated in Example 10.15 below.

3.3.6 Disposal of a foreign operation

As discussed at 2.7.3 above, on the disposal of a foreign operation, paragraph 48 of IAS 21 requires the cumulative amount of the exchange differences deferred in the separate component of equity relating to a foreign operation to be recognised in profit or loss when the gain or loss on disposal is recognised.[125] This will include exchange differences arising on an intragroup balance that, in substance, forms part of an entity's net investment in a foreign operation.

Paragraph 49 of IAS 21 requires that this recycling of exchange differences is to be adopted not only when an entity sells an interest in a foreign entity, but also when it disposes of its interest through liquidation, repayment of share capital, or abandonment of that entity. It also applies for partial disposals, in which case only the proportionate share of the related accumulated exchange differences is included in the gain or loss. The payment of a dividend, however, is part of a disposal only when it constitutes a return of the investment, e.g. when the dividend is paid out of pre-acquisition profits. A write-down of the carrying amount of a foreign operation does not constitute a partial disposal, therefore no deferred exchange difference should be recognised in income at the time of the write-down.[126] Similarly, it is implicit in the requirement of IFRS 5 – *Non-current Assets Held for Sale and Discontinued Operations* – for separate disclosure of cumulative gains and losses recognised in equity relating to a disposal group (see Chapter 4 at 2.2.4) that the classification of a foreign operation as held for sale under IFRS 5 does not give rise to recycling of foreign exchange differences at that time.

There are a number of practical issues relating to the application of these requirements in IAS 21.

Whilst the reference to repayment of share capital might suggest that any such repayment could trigger a recycling of exchange differences, we believe that, like the payment of dividends, such a transaction should only result in recycling of exchange differences where the payment represents a return of the investment. This is discussed further in Example 10.23 at 3.4.1 F below which also discusses the recycling of exchange differences on the settlement of an intragroup balance that, in substance, formed part of an entity's net investment in a foreign operation.

The requirement to recycle the cumulative exchange differences cannot be avoided, for example, by an entity merely disposing of the net assets and business of the foreign operation, rather than disposing of its interest in the legal entity that is the foreign operation. This is because paragraph 49 refers to the disposal of a foreign operation, and a foreign operation as defined by IAS 21 must have 'activities' (see 2.3 above). Following the disposal of the net assets and business, there no longer are 'activities'. Furthermore, a foreign operation need not be an incorporated entity but may be a branch, the disposal of which would necessarily take the form of an asset sale. The legal form of the entity should make no difference to the accounting treatment of exchange differences, including the recycling of cumulative exchange differences from equity.

We illustrated the basic requirement to recycle cumulative exchange differences on the disposal of a foreign operation in Example 10.8 at 2.7.3 above where a parent sold a direct interest in a subsidiary. In our view, it is more consistent with various requirements of IAS 21 (as explained in Example 10.14 at 3.3.5 above) that the requirement to recycle such exchange differences applies not only on the disposal of a direct interest in a foreign operation, but also on the disposal of an indirect interest. Under IAS 21, it should make no difference whether the reporting entity holds the foreign operation directly or whether there is an intermediate holding entity between the reporting entity and the foreign operation. For example, on the disposal of a US subsidiary by a US intermediate holding company within a group headed by a UK parent, any exchange differences deferred in the separate component of equity relating to the US subsidiary should be recognised in profit or loss on its disposal. Paragraphs 48 and 49 of the standard require recycling of the cumulative exchange differences from equity to profit or loss when the gain or loss on the disposal of the foreign operation is recognised. This is irrespective of whether or not the ultimate parent has been a party to the disposal. It is mainly for this reason why, as discussed at 3.3.5 above, we believe that it is more consistent with various requirements of IAS 21 that the direct method should be used whereby each entity in a group is consolidated individually, rather than the step-by-step method using sub-groups and sub-consolidations. If, in this example, the consolidated financial statements for the UK parent were prepared by incorporating consolidated financial information of the US intermediate holding company sub-group, including the US subsidiary that had been sold, that consolidated information would not include any exchange differences relating to that subsidiary as part of the consolidated profit or loss of the US sub-group. Accordingly, any exchange differences that should be recycled on the disposal of that US subsidiary as required by paragraph 48 of IAS 21 may not be identified.

Where the intermediate holding company and the subsidiary each have different functional currencies, the sub-consolidation will include within profit or loss an amount relating to the recycling of exchange differences on the disposal of the subsidiary. However, this amount will have been measured based on the functional currencies of the intermediate holding company and the subsidiary. The translation of that amount into the presentation currency of the ultimate parent will not be the same as if the ultimate parent had consolidated the subsidiary individually. In that case, the exchange differences on translation of the subsidiary would have been measured based on the functional currency of the subsidiary and the presentation currency used by the ultimate parent. It is these exchange differences that the translation process in paragraph 39 of IAS 21 requires to be recognised as a separate component of equity, and that paragraph 48 requires to be recognised in profit or loss on the disposal of the foreign operation. This is illustrated in the following example.

Example 10.15: Disposal of an indirectly held foreign operation

On 1 January 2007, Entity A is incorporated in the UK with share capital of £300m. It sets up a wholly-owned Swiss subsidiary, Entity B, on the same day with share capital of CHF200m. Entity B in turn sets up a wholly-owned German subsidiary, Entity C, with share capital of €45m. All of the capital subscribed in each of the entities, to the extent that it has not been invested in a subsidiary, is used to acquire operating assets in their country of incorporation. The functional currency of each of the entities is therefore pound sterling, the Swiss franc and the euro respectively. The relevant exchange rates at 1 January 2007 are £1=CHF2.50=€1.50.

For the purposes of the example, it is assumed that in the year ended 31 December 2007 each of the entities made no profit or loss. The relevant exchange rates at that date were £1=CHF3.00=€1.25.

On 1 January 2008, the German subsidiary, Entity C, is sold by Entity B for €45m.

The exchange differences relating to Entity C that will be recycled into the consolidated income statement of the Entity A group for the year ended 31 December 2008 on the basis that each of the subsidiaries are consolidated individually (the direct method) will be as follows:

Consolidating each subsidiary individually (the direct method)

The opening consolidated balance sheet of the Entity A group at 1 January 2007 is as follows:

	Entity A	Entity B		Entity C		Adjustments	Consolidated
Millions	£	CHF	£	€	£	£	£
Investment in B	80.0					(80.0)	
Investment in C		75.0	30.0			(30.0)	
Other net assets	220.0	125.0	50.0	45.0	30.0		300.0
	300.0	200.0	80.0	45.0	30.0		300.0
Share capital	300.0						300.0
Share capital		200.0	80.0			(80.0)	
Share capital				45.0	30.0	(30.0)	

The consolidated balance sheet of the Entity A group at 31 December 2007 is as follows:

	Entity A	Entity B		Entity C		Adjustments	Consolidated
Millions	£	CHF	£	€	£	£	£
Investment in B	80.0					(80.0)	
Investment in C		75.0	25.0			(25.0)	
Other net assets	220.0	125.0	41.7	45.0	36.0		297.7
	300.0	200.0	66.7	45.0	36.0		297.7
Share capital	300.0						300.0
Share capital		200.0	80.0			(80.0)	
Share capital				45.0	30.0	(30.0)	
Exchange – B			(13.3)			5.0	(8.3)
Exchange – C					6.0		6.0
	300.0	200.0	66.7	45.0	36.0		297.7

The exchange differences in respect of Entity B and Entity C are only shown for illustration purposes; the consolidated balance sheet would only show the net amount of £(2.3)m as a separate component of equity. The exchange difference of £6.0m in respect of Entity C is that arising on the translation of its opening net assets of €45m into the presentation currency of pound sterling based on the opening and closing exchange rates of £1=€1.50 and £1=€1.25 respectively, as required by paragraph 39 of IAS 21. Accordingly, it is this amount of £6.0m that will be recycled into the income statement for the year ended 31 December 2008 upon the disposal of Entity C as required by paragraph 48 of IAS 21.

If the consolidated balance sheet for the Entity A group at 31 December 2007 had been prepared on the basis of a sub-consolidation of the Entity B sub-group incorporating Entity C, the position would have been as follows.

Consolidating using a sub-group consolidation (the step-by-step method)

The exchange rates at 1 January 2007 and 31 December 2007 are the equivalent of €1=CHF1.667 and €1=CHF2.400.

The sub-consolidation of Entity B and Entity C at 31 December 2007 is as follows:

Millions	Entity B CHF	Entity C €	CHF	Adjustments CHF	Consolidated CHF
Investment in C	75.0			(75.0)	
Other net assets	125.0	45.0	108.0		233.0
	200.0	45.0	108.0		233.0
Share capital	200.0				200.0
Share capital		45.0	75.0	(75.0)	
Exchange – C			33.0		33.0
	200.0	45.0	108.0		233.0

The exchange difference of CHF33.0m in respect of Entity C is that arising on the translation of its opening net assets of €45m into the functional currency of that of Entity B, the Swiss franc, based on the opening and closing exchange rates of €1=CHF1.667 and €1=CHF2.400 respectively.

In the consolidated income statement of the Entity B sub-group for the year ended 31 December 2008, it is this amount of CHF33.0m that would be recycled upon the disposal of Entity C.

The consolidated balance sheet of the Entity A group at 31 December 2007 prepared using this sub-consolidation would be as follows:

Millions	Entity A £	Entity B sub-group CHF	£	Adjustments £	Consolidated £
Investment in B	80.0			(80.0)	
Other net assets	220.0	233.0	77.7		297.7
	300.0	233.0	77.7		297.7
Share capital	300.0				200.0
Share capital		200.0	80.0	(80.0)	
Exchange – C		33.0	11.0		11.0
Exchange – B group			(13.3)		(13.3)
	300.0	233.0	77.7		297.7

The exchange differences in respect of Entity C and that for the Entity B sub-group are only shown for illustration purposes; the consolidated balance sheet would only show the net amount of £(2.3)m as a separate component of equity. As can be seen, the consolidated position for the Entity A group is the same as that using the direct method. However, using the step-by-step method, the exchange difference of £11.0m in respect of Entity C is the exchange difference of CHF33.0 included in the Entity B sub-consolidation translated into the presentation currency used in the Entity A consolidated financial statements.

As indicated above, it is this amount of CHF33.0m that would be recycled upon the disposal of Entity C in the consolidated income statement of the Entity B sub-group for the year ended 31 December 2008. In the consolidated income statement of the Entity A group for the year ended 31 December 2008, it would be the translated amount of £11.0m that would be included as the recycled amount of exchange differences on the disposal of Entity C.

It can be seen from the above example, that the amount of exchange differences computed as being those to be recycled under paragraph 48 of IAS 21 under the step-by-step method using a sub-consolidation is different from that computed under the direct method by consolidating each entity individually. In our view, the step-by-step method does not arguably result in the correct amount of exchange differences to be recycled that relate to the disposed entity, which should be measured based on the translation requirements of paragraph 39 of IAS 21, i.e. as a result of translating the functional currency figures for the entity into the presentation currency of the ultimate parent. In Example 10.15 above, it would have been relatively easy to identify the exchange differences that related to Entity C contained within the overall exchange differences that arose on the translation of the Entity B sub-group into the presentation currency used for the consolidated financial statements of Entity A so as to compute the total amount of exchange differences that related to Entity C. However, in practice, in a more complex group with a number of sub-groups each containing a number of subsidiaries, it would be more difficult. It is mainly for this reason why, as discussed at 3.3.5 above, we believe that it is more consistent with various requirements of IAS 21 that the direct method should be used whereby each entity in a group should be consolidated individually, rather than the step-by-step method using sub-groups and sub-consolidations.

3.4 Intragroup transactions

The standard states that 'the incorporation of the results and financial position of a foreign operation with those of the reporting entity follows normal consolidation procedures, such as the elimination of intragroup balances and intragroup transactions of a subsidiary'.[127] On this basis, there is a tendency sometimes to assume that exchange differences on intragroup balances should not impact on the reported profit or loss for the group in the consolidated financial statements. However, as discussed at 2.7.2 A above, that is not the case. The general requirement of IAS 21 is that exchange differences arising on intragroup balances continue to be reflected in profit or loss in the consolidated financial statements, effectively treating them in the same way as exchange differences on monetary items resulting from transactions with third parties.

Nevertheless, the standard makes an exception to this requirement where the exchange difference arises on an intragroup balance that, in substance, forms part of an entity's net investment in a foreign operation. In that case, the exchange difference is not to be taken to profit or loss in the consolidated financial statements, but is classified as equity until the disposal of the foreign operation (see 2.7.3 above).[128]

3.4.1 Monetary items included as part of the net investment in a foreign operation

A General

The 'net investment in a foreign operation' is defined as being 'the amount of the reporting entity's interest in the net assets of that operation'.[129] The standard elaborates on this by stating that 'an entity may have a monetary item that is receivable from or payable to a foreign operation. An item for which settlement is neither planned nor likely to occur in the foreseeable future is, in substance, a part of the entity's net investment in that foreign operation'. Such monetary items may include long-term receivables or loans. They do not include trade receivables or trade payables.[130]

Under what circumstances can receivables/payables be included as part of an entity's net investment in a foreign operation? Consider the following example:

Example 10.16: Receivables/payables included as part of net investment in a foreign operation?

A UK entity, A, has a Belgian subsidiary, B. A has a receivable due from B amounting to £1,000,000.

In each of the following scenarios, could the receivable be included as part of A's net investment in B?

Scenario 1

The receivable arises from the sale of goods, together with interest payments and dividend payments which have not been paid in cash but have been accumulated in the inter-company account. A and B agree that A can claim at any time the repayment of this receivable. It is likely that there will be a settlement of the receivable in the foreseeable future.

Although the standard states that trade receivables and payables are not included, we do not believe that it necessarily precludes deferred trading balances from being included. In our view, such balances can be included as part of the net investment in the foreign operation, but only if cash settlement is not made or planned to be made in the foreseeable future.

In this scenario, the settlement of A's receivable due from B is not planned; however, it is likely that a settlement will occur in the foreseeable future. Accordingly, the receivable does not qualify to be treated as part of A's net investment in B. The term 'foreseeable future' is not defined and no specific time period is implied. It could be argued that the receivable should only be considered as part of the net investment if it will be repaid only when the reporting entity disinvests from the foreign operation. However, it is recognised that in most circumstances this would be unrealistic and therefore a shorter time span should be considered in determining the foreseeable future.

Scenario 2

The receivable represents a loan made by A to B and it is agreed that the receivable will be repaid in 20 years.

In this scenario, A's receivable due from B has a specified term for repayment. This suggests that settlement is planned. Accordingly, the receivable does not qualify to be treated as part of A's investment in B.

Scenario 3

A and B have previously agreed that the receivable under scenario 2 will be repaid in 20 years but A now decides that it will replace the loan on maturity either with a further inter-company loan or with an injection of equity. This approach is consistent with A's intention to maintain the strategic long-term investment in B.

In this scenario, the words from paragraph 15 of IAS 21 '… settlement is neither planned nor likely to occur in the foreseeable future …' are potentially problematic, since a loan with a fixed maturity must, prima facie, have a planned settlement. However, from the date A decides that it will re-finance the inter-company debt upon maturity with a further long-term instrument, or replace it with equity, the substance of the inter-company loan is that it is part of the entity's net investment in the foreign operation, and there is no actual 'intent' to settle the investment without replacement. On this basis, loans with a stated maturity may qualify to be treated in accordance with paragraph 32 of IAS 21, with foreign currency gains and losses recorded in a separate component of equity in the consolidated financial statements. However, in our view, management's intention to refinance the loan must be documented appropriately, for example in the form of a minute of a meeting of the management board or board of directors or letter of representation. In addition, there should not be any established historical pattern of the entity demanding repayment of such inter-company debt without replacement.

Consequently, when the purpose of the loan is to fund a long-term strategic investment then it is the entity's overall intention with regard to the investment and ultimate funding thereof, rather than the specific terms of the inter-company loan funding the investment, that should be considered.

Scenario 4

The receivable arises from the sale of goods, together with interest payments and dividend payments which have not been paid in cash but have been accumulated in the inter-company account. However, in this scenario, A and B agree that A can claim the repayment of this receivable only in the event that the subsidiary is disposed of. A has no plans to dispose of entity B.

In this scenario, the settlement of A's receivable due from B is not planned nor is it likely to occur in the foreseeable future. Although the term 'foreseeable future' is not defined, it will not go beyond a point of time after the disposal of a foreign operation. Accordingly, the receivable does qualify for being treated as part of a net investment in a foreign operation.

As indicated in scenario 1 in the above example, in our view trade receivables and payables can be included as part of the net investment in the foreign operation, but only if cash settlement is not made or planned to be made in the foreseeable future. However, if a subsidiary makes payment for purchases from its parent, but is continually indebted to the parent as a result of new purchases, then in these circumstances, since individual transactions are settled, no part of the inter-company balance should be regarded as part of the net investment in the subsidiary. Accordingly, such exchange differences should be taken to the consolidated income account.

B Monetary item denominated in functional currency of either the reporting entity or the foreign operation

When a monetary item is considered to form part of a reporting entity's net investment in a foreign operation and is denominated in the functional currency of the reporting entity, an exchange difference will be recognised in profit or loss for the period when it arises in the foreign operation's individual financial statements. If the item is denominated in the functional currency of the foreign operation, an exchange difference will be recognised in profit or loss for the period when it arises in the reporting entity's separate financial statements. Such exchange differences are only reclassified to the separate component of equity in the financial statements that include the foreign operation and the reporting entity (i.e. financial statements in which the foreign operation is consolidated, proportionately consolidated or accounted for using the equity method).[131]

Example 10.17: Monetary item in functional currency of either the reporting entity or the foreign operation

A UK entity has a Belgian subsidiary. On the last day of its financial year, 31 March 2007, the UK entity lends the subsidiary £1,000,000. Settlement of the loan is neither planned nor likely to occur in the foreseeable future, so the UK entity regards the loan as part of its net investment in the Belgian subsidiary. The exchange rate at 31 March 2007 was £1=€1.40. Since the loan was made on the last day of the year there are no exchange differences to recognise for that year. At 31 March

2008, the loan has not been repaid and is still regarded as part of the net investment in the Belgian subsidiary. The relevant exchange rate at that date was £1=€1.50. The average exchange rate for the year ended 31 March 2008 was £1=€1.45.

In the UK entity's separate financial statements no exchange difference is recognised since the loan is denominated in its functional currency of pound sterling. In the Belgian subsidiary's financial statements, the liability to the parent is translated into the subsidiary's functional currency of euros at the closing rate at €1,500,000, giving rise to an exchange loss of €100,000, i.e. €1,500,000 less €1,400,000 (£1,000,000 @ £1=€1.40). This exchange loss is reflected in the Belgian subsidiary's profit or loss for that year. In the UK entity's consolidated financial statements, this exchange loss included in the subsidiary's profit or loss for the year will be translated at the average rate for the year, giving rise a loss of £68,966 (€100,000@ £1=€1.45). This will be taken to the separate component of equity together with an exchange gain of £2,299, being the difference between the amount included in the Belgian subsidiary's income statement translated at average rate, i.e. £68,966, and at the closing rate, i.e. £66,667 (€100,000@ £1=€1.50). The overall exchange loss taken to equity is £66,667. This represents the exchange loss on the increased net investment of €1,400,000 in the subsidiary made at 31 March 2007, i.e. £1,000,000 (€1,400,000 @ £1=€1.40) less £933,333 (€1,400,000 @ £1=€1.50).

If, on the other hand, the loan made to the Belgian subsidiary had been denominated in the equivalent amount of euros at 31 March 2007, i.e. €1,400,000, the treatment would have been as follows:

In the UK entity's separate financial statements, the amount receivable from the Belgian subsidiary would be translated at the closing rate at £933,333 (€1,400,000 @ £1=€1.50), giving rise to an exchange loss of £66,667, i.e. £1,000,000 (€1,400,000 @ £1=€1.40) less £933,333, which is included in its profit or loss for the year. In the Belgian subsidiary's financial statements, no exchange difference is recognised since the loan is denominated in its functional currency of euros. In the UK entity's consolidated financial statements, the exchange loss included in its profit or loss for the year in its separate financial statements will be taken to the separate component of equity. As before, this represents the exchange loss on the increased net investment of €1,400,000 in the subsidiary made at 31 March 2007, i.e. £1,000,000 (€1,400,000 @ £1=€1.40) less £933,333 (€1,400,000 @ £1=€1.40).

C Monetary item denominated in functional currency that is not that of either the reporting entity or the foreign operation

I IAS 21 (Revised 2003) – before 2005 amendment

In most situations, such an intragroup balance will be denominated in the functional currency of either the reporting entity or the foreign operation. However, IAS 21 indicates that this will not always be the case, and a monetary item that forms part of the reporting entity's net investment in a foreign operation may be denominated in a currency other than the functional currency of either the reporting entity or the foreign operation. In this situation, the revised version of IAS 21 issued in December 2003 required that the exchange differences arising on translating the monetary item into the functional currencies of the reporting entity and the foreign operation were not to be reclassified to the separate component of equity in the financial statements that include the foreign operation and the reporting entity (i.e. they were to remain recognised in profit or loss).[132]

Example 10.18: Monetary item in functional currency that is not that of either the reporting entity or the foreign operation

Suppose in Example 10.16 above, the loan made to the Belgian subsidiary had been denominated in the equivalent amount of US dollars at 31 March 2007. The relevant exchange rates at that date were £1=US$1.54, €1=US$1.10 and £1=€1.40. The loan would therefore have been $1,540,000, which is equivalent to £1,000,000 (US$1,540,000 @ £1=$1.54) and €1,400,000 (US$1,540,000 @ €1=US$1.10). The relevant exchange rates at 31 March 2008 were £1=US$1.80, €1=US$1.20 and £1=€1.50. The average exchange rates for the year ended 31 March 2008 were £1=US$1.656, €1=US$1.15 and £1=€1.45.

In the UK entity's separate financial statements, the amount receivable from the Belgian subsidiary would be translated at the closing rate at £855,555 (US$1,540,000 @ £1=$1.80), giving rise to an exchange loss of £144,445, i.e. £1,000,000 less £855,555. In the Belgian subsidiary's financial statements, the liability to the parent is translated into the subsidiary's functional currency of euros at the closing rate at €1,283,333 (US$1,540,000 @ €1=US$1.20), giving rise to an exchange gain of €116,667, i.e. €1,400,000 less €1,283,333. This exchange gain is reflected in the Belgian subsidiary's profit or loss for that year. In the UK entity's consolidated financial statements, this exchange gain included in the subsidiary's profit or loss for the year will be translated at the average rate for the year, giving rise a translated gain of £80,460 (€116,667@ £1=€1.45). Prior to the amendment made in December 2005 (see II below), IAS 21 required that this gain of £80,460 together with the exchange loss of £144,445 in the parent's profit or loss were not to be reclassified as part of the separate component of equity, but were to remain in the consolidated profit or loss for the year, i.e. a net loss of £63,985. The gain recognised by the Belgian subsidiary of €116,667 would give rise to an exchange loss of £2,682, being the difference between the amount included in the Belgian subsidiary's income statement translated at average rate, i.e. £80,460, and at the closing rate, i.e. £77,778 (€116,667@ £1=€1.50). This loss of £2,682 would be taken to the separate component of equity. The liability included in the Belgian subsidiary's balance sheet at €1,283,333 will be translated at the closing exchange rate of £1=€1.50, giving rise to a liability of £855,555 which will be eliminated against the receivable included in the UK entity's balance sheet.

The example above illustrates that the overall impact of this requirement in such a situation as this, is that it made no difference as to whether the intragroup loan was regarded as forming part of the net investment in the foreign operation; the accounting was the same as it would have been if the intragroup loan had not been so regarded.

II IAS 21 Amendment (December 2005)

Clearly, this is not what the IASB intended. As noted at 1.2.3 above, the IASB made amendments to IAS 21 in December 2005 after constituents raised a number of concerns with respect to these requirements for monetary items included as part of the net investment in a foreign operation. The amendments were to be applied for annual periods beginning on or after 1 January 2006, although earlier application was encouraged.[133]

The concerns raised by constituents in respect of the currency of the monetary item were as follows:[134]

- It is common practice for a monetary item that forms part of an entity's investment in a foreign operation to be denominated in a currency that is not the functional currency of either the reporting entity or the foreign operation. An example is a monetary item denominated in a currency that is more readily convertible than the local domestic currency of the foreign operation;

- An investment in a foreign operation denominated in a currency that is not the functional currency of the reporting entity or the foreign operation does not expose the group as a whole to a greater foreign currency exchange difference than arises when the investment is denominated in the functional currency of the reporting entity or the foreign operation. It simply results in exchange differences arising in both the foreign operation's individual financial statements and the reporting entity's separate financial statements, rather than in only one of them.

The Board noted that the nature of the monetary item referred to in paragraph 15 of IAS 21 is similar to an equity investment in a foreign operation, i.e. settlement of the monetary item is neither planned nor likely to occur in the foreseeable future. Therefore, the principle in paragraph 32 to recognise exchange differences arising on a monetary item initially in a separate component of equity effectively results in the monetary item being accounted for in the same way as an equity investment in the foreign operation when consolidated financial statements are prepared. The Board concluded that the accounting treatment in the consolidated financial statements should not be dependent on the currency in which the monetary item is denominated, nor on which entity within the group conducts the transaction with the foreign operation.[135]

Accordingly, paragraph 33 of IAS 21 was amended. If a monetary item is denominated in a currency other than the functional currency of either the reporting entity or the foreign operation, an exchange difference arises in the reporting entity's separate financial statements and in the foreign operation's individual financial statements. Such exchange differences are reclassified to the separate component of equity in the financial statements that include the foreign operation and the reporting entity (i.e. financial statements in which the foreign operation is consolidated, proportionately consolidated or accounted for using the equity method).[136] Thus, the requirement in IAS 21 applies irrespective of the currency of the monetary item.

Therefore, in Example 10.18 above, the net loss of £63,985 (being the parent's loss of £144,445 less the translated gain of the subsidiary of £80,460) would be reclassified to equity under the amended version of the standard.

One company that has now been able to take exchange differences on such intragroup loans to equity instead of its income statement is British American Tobacco as shown below.

Extract 10.6: British American Tobacco p.l.c. (2006)

1 Accounting policies [extract]

Foreign currencies

The income and cash flow statements of Group undertakings expressed in currencies other than sterling are translated to sterling at average rates of exchange in each year, provided that the average rate approximates the exchange rate at the date of the underlying transactions. Assets and liabilities of these undertakings are translated at rates of exchange at the end of each year. For high inflation countries, the translation from local currencies to sterling makes allowance for the impact of inflation on the local currency results.

The differences between retained profits of overseas subsidiary and associated undertakings translated at average and closing rates of exchange are taken to reserves, as are differences arising on the retranslation to sterling (using closing rate of exchange) of overseas net assets at the beginning of the year. Any differences that have arisen since 1 January 2004 are presented as a separate component of equity. As permitted under IFRS1, any differences prior to that date are not included in this separate component of equity. On the disposal of an overseas undertaking, the cumulative amount of the related exchange differences deferred in the separate component of equity are recognised in the income statement when the gain or loss on disposal is recognised.

Foreign currency transactions are initially recorded at the exchange rate ruling at the date of the transaction. Foreign exchange gains and losses resulting from the settlement of such transactions and from the translation of foreign currency assets and liabilities at year end rates of exchange are recognised in the income statement, except when deferred in equity as qualifying cash flow hedges, qualifying net investment hedges and on inter company quasi-equity loans. Foreign exchange gains or losses recognised in the income statement are included in profit from operations or net finance costs depending on the underlying transactions that gave rise to these exchange differences.

4 Net finance costs [extract]

In December 2005, the International Accounting Standards Board issued an amendment to IAS21 on foreign currency rates. The amendment to IAS21 allowed inter company balances that form part of a reporting entity's net investment in a foreign operation to be denominated in a currency other than the functional currency of either the ultimate parent or the foreign operation itself. This means that certain exchange differences previously taken to the income statement are instead reflected directly in total equity. However, this amendment was only adopted by the EU in 2006. Therefore the previously published results for 2005 have been restated accordingly, which has resulted in an increase in net finance costs above of £4 million and a corresponding reduction in differences on exchange in equity movements (page 112 note 20).

It is emphasised that the exception for exchange differences on monetary items forming part of the net investment in a foreign operation applies only in the consolidated financial statements. In the individual financial statements of the entity (or entities) with the currency exposure the exchange differences have to be reflected in that entity's profit or loss for the period. It is unclear why this should be the case since the standard does not acknowledge that this represents a change from the version of IAS 21 prior to its revision in 2003.

We see no reason why such exchange differences should have to be taken to the income statement. As indicated above, when the Board amended IAS 21 in December 2005 it noted that the nature of the monetary item referred to in paragraph 15 is similar to an equity investment in a foreign operation, i.e. settlement of the monetary item is neither planned nor likely to occur in the foreseeable future. Therefore, the principle in paragraph 32 to recognise exchange differences arising on a monetary item initially in a separate component of equity effectively results in the monetary item being accounted for in the same way as an equity investment in the foreign operation when consolidated financial statements are prepared. Accordingly, the exchange differences are treated in the same way as the exchange differences on the net assets of the foreign operation. The stated reason within the standard as to why the exchange differences on the net assets of the foreign operation are not recognised in profit or loss is because the changes in exchange rates have little or no direct effect on the present and future cash flows from operations.[137] On that basis, the same would hold true for the separate financial statements of the reporting entity. Indeed, since the item is considered to be, in substance, part of the net investment, in our view it would have been more appropriate to treat it as such, and therefore consider it to be a 'non-monetary item' under the standard. Thus, either no exchange differences would have been recognised or they would have been reflected in equity.

D Monetary items transacted by other members of the group

As illustrated in the examples above, the requirements of IAS 21 whereby exchange differences on a monetary item that forms part of the net investment in a foreign operation are classified in equity until disposal of the foreign operation for the purposes of the consolidated financial statements clearly apply where the monetary item is transacted between the parent preparing the consolidated financial statements and the subsidiary that is the foreign operation. What was less clear from the December 2003 version of the standard was whether the same treatment was applicable when the monetary item was transacted by other members of the group, such as an intermediate parent or a sister subsidiary, rather than by the ultimate parent.

I IAS 21 (Revised 2003) – before 2005 amendment

Some commentators believed it was not possible for such a treatment to be adopted for such transactions.

However, in our view it was possible for exchange differences on such inter-company loans to be classified in equity until disposal, provided that the loan was denominated in the same functional currency as that of either the ultimate parent or the ultimate borrower as illustrated in the following scenarios.

Example 10.19: Loan from intermediate parent to its subsidiary

Parent A's functional currency is the US dollar, which is also the presentation currency of the group (Group A). Parent A has a direct investment in an intermediate holding company (Company B), whose functional currency is also the US dollar. Company B, in turn, has a subsidiary (Company C), whose functional currency is pound sterling. Company B lends $100m to Company C.

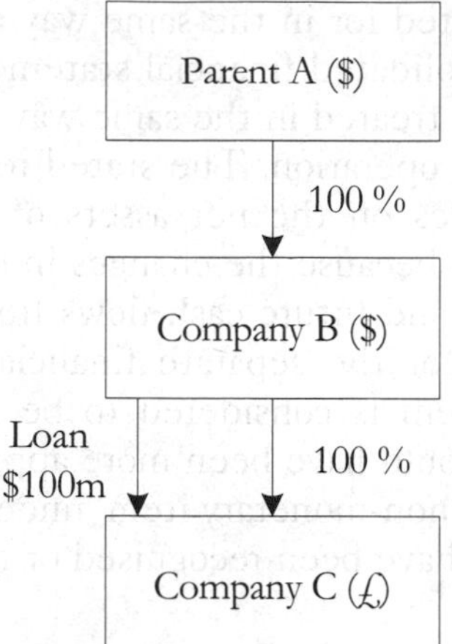

In the consolidated financial statements of Group A, could the loan be accounted for as part of Group A's net investment in Company C?

In our view, it could. Based on paragraphs 32 and 33 of IAS 21 (Revised 2003), we believed that the following principle should be applied in all cases: In the financial statements of the entity that is the foreign operation, the exchange differences arising on the translation of the loan would be shown in that entity's income statement. On consolidation, whether these differences remained in profit and loss or were transferred to equity depended on the currencies of the loan and the functional currencies of the reporting entity and ultimate borrower. Accordingly, our view was that, in order to be permitted to reflect the exchange difference in equity on consolidation, the loan must be denominated in the same currency as *either* the reporting entity *or* the ultimate borrower. In the scenario above, because the loan is denominated in US$, which is the same currency as the functional currency of Parent A, the transfer to equity was permitted on consolidation. This position held true irrespective of the functional currency of Company B.

Example 10.20: Loan from one sister subsidiary to another

Parent A's functional currency is the US dollar, which is also the presentation currency of the group (Group A). Parent A has two 100% owned subsidiaries, Sister X, whose functional currency is the US dollar and Sister Y, whose functional currency is pound sterling.

Sister X has excess funds of $100m. It lends the funds to Sister Y, with the expectation that the funds will not be returned for some time.

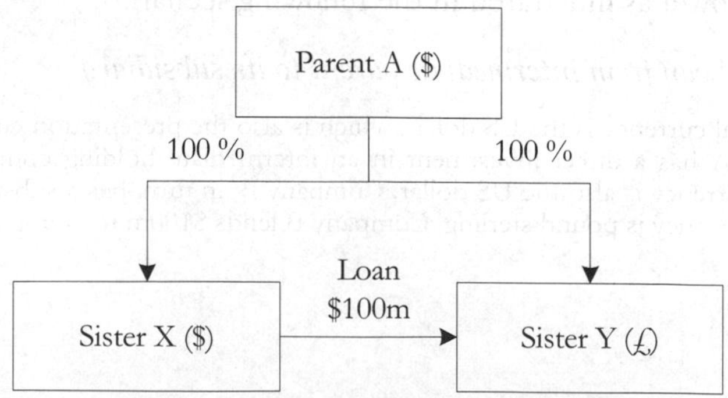

In the consolidated financial statements of Group A, could the sister-to-sister loan be accounted for as part of Group A's net investment in Sister Y?

For the reasons set out in Example 10.19 above, we believed that it could. In the scenario above, because the loan is denominated in US$, which is the same currency as the functional currency of Parent A, the transfer to equity was permitted on consolidation. This position held true irrespective of the functional currency of Sister X.

In Examples 10.19 and 10.20 above, the loan was denominated in the functional currency of the ultimate parent company. Did it make any difference if the functional currency of the ultimate parent company was different to that of the lending company?

Example 10.21: Loans not in functional currency of the reporting entity

Assume the same fact patterns as Examples 10.19 and 10.20 above, except that the functional currency of Parent A is the euro. Did this have any impact as to whether or not net investment accounting was permitted?

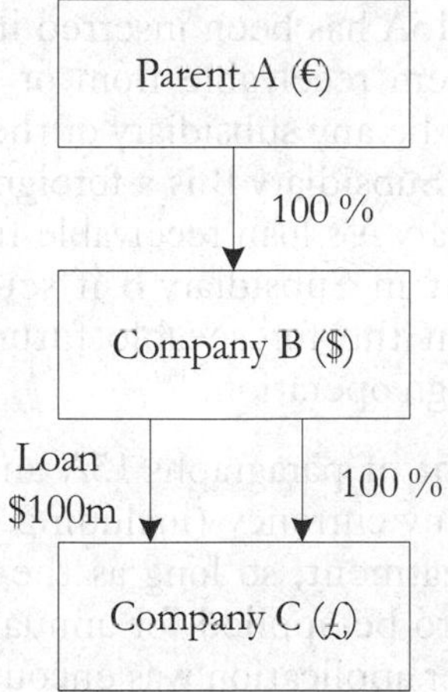

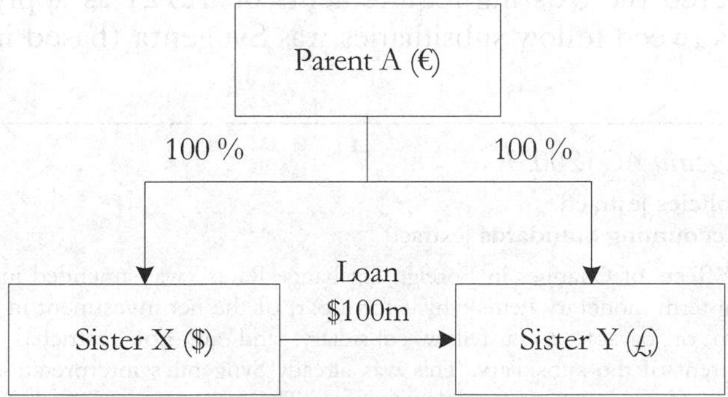

For the reasons set out in Example 10.19 above, in our view, it did have an impact and the exchange differences could not be taken to equity. Under the principle set out in Example 10.19 above, the exchange difference in both cases would have to remain in profit and loss on consolidation, since the US$ loan is denominated in a currency that is different to the functional currencies of both the ultimate parent (€) and the ultimate borrower (£).

II IAS 21 Amendment (December 2005)

The IASB has addressed this issue in its December 2005 amendment of IAS 21. The Board noted that it was not clear whether the term 'reporting entity' in paragraph 32 in IAS 21 should be interpreted as the single entity or the group comprising a parent and all its subsidiaries. As a result, constituents questioned whether the monetary item must be transacted between the foreign operation and the reporting entity, or whether it could be transacted between the foreign operation and any member of the consolidated group, i.e. the reporting entity or any of its subsidiaries.[138]

As noted in 3.4.1 C II above, the Board concluded that the accounting treatment in the consolidated financial statements should not be dependent on the currency in which the monetary item is denominated, nor on which entity within the group conducts the transaction with the foreign operation.[139]

Accordingly, a new paragraph 15A has been inserted in IAS 21. This states that 'The entity that has a monetary item receivable from or payable to a foreign operation described in paragraph 15 may be any subsidiary of the group. For example, an entity has two subsidiaries, A and B. Subsidiary B is a foreign operation. Subsidiary A grants a loan to Subsidiary B. Subsidiary A's loan receivable from Subsidiary B would be part of the entity's net investment in Subsidiary B if settlement of the loan is neither planned nor likely to occur in the foreseeable future. This would also be true if Subsidiary A were itself a foreign operation.'[140]

In the light of the amendment of paragraphs 15A and 33 of IAS 21, it is clear that loans from any entity and in any currency (including those in Example 10.20 above) qualify for net investment treatment, so long as the conditions of paragraph 15 are met. The amendments were to be applied for annual periods beginning on or after 1 January 2006, although earlier application was encouraged.[141]

One company that adopted the amendment in 2005, but was unaffected by it since it already interpreted the existing requirements of IAS 21 as applying to long-term monetary items between fellow subsidiaries was Syngenta (based in Switzerland) as illustrated below.

Extract 10.7: Syngenta AG (2005)

2. Accounting policies [extract]

Adoption of new Accounting Standards [extract]

– IAS 21, "The Effects of Changes in Foreign Exchange Rates" was amended in December 2005 to clarify that long-term monetary items which form part of the net investment in a subsidiary may be receivable from or payable to a fellow subsidiary, and are not restricted to the ultimate or intermediate parent of the subsidiary. This was already Syngenta's interpretation of IAS 21 and its adoption had no effect on these financial statements. The amendment also allows the monetary item to be denominated in any currency. Before the amendment, IAS 21 (revised December 2003) required the item to be denominated in the functional currency of the subsidiary or of the reporting entity. Adoption of this change had no effect on these financial statements.

Foreign currencies

The consolidated financial statements are expressed in US dollars, however the local currency has primarily been used as the measurement currency by each operating unit.

In the respective local financial statements used to prepare these consolidated financial statements, monetary assets and liabilities denominated in foreign currencies are translated at the rate prevailing at the balance sheet date. Non-monetary assets and liabilities denominated in foreign currencies, which are stated at historical cost, are translated into local currency at the foreign exchange rate ruling at the date of the transaction. Foreign currency transactions are translated to the relevant local currency at the exchange rate prevailing at the date of the transaction. With the exception of unrealized gains or losses related to equity loans, and hedging arrangements for which reserve accounting is permitted under IAS 39, all resulting foreign exchange transaction gains and losses are recognized in the local income statements. Equity loans are inter-company monetary items which form part of Syngenta's net investment in the borrowing subsidiary.

Income, expense and cash flows of foreign operations included in the consolidated financial statements whose measurement currency is that of a hyperinflationary economy have been translated into US dollars using exchange rates prevailing at the balance sheet date. Income, expense and cash flows of other foreign operations included in the consolidated financial statements have been translated into US dollars using average exchange rates prevailing during the period. The assets and liabilities of foreign operations are translated to US dollars at foreign exchange rates prevailing at the balance sheet date. Foreign exchange differences arising on these translations are recognized directly in equity.

Syngenta denominates goodwill and fair value adjustments arising on acquisitions in the functional currency(ies) of the acquired entity(ies).

Rio Tinto in its 2005 financial statements revised its treatment of such loans following the clarification in the amendment as indicated below:

Extract 10.8: Rio Tinto plc and Rio Tinto Limited (2005)

1 PRINCIPAL ACCOUNTING POLICIES [extract]

Basis of preparation [extract]

In preparing the financial information presented in these financial statements, certain exchange gains/losses which were included in the income statement in the announcement of results for the six months ended 30 June 2005, as published on 3 August 2005, have been reclassified to equity. In December 2005, the IASB issued a clarification to IAS 21, 'The effects of changes in foreign exchange rates', relating to the treatment of exchange gains and losses on balances between fellow subsidiary companies. The clarification means that, in certain circumstances, such loans can now be included as part of the reporting entity's net investment in foreign operations. For the year ended 31 December 2004, the amount reclassified was a net exchange loss of US$85 million (US$79 million net of tax). Net exchange gains of US$25 million (US$25 million net of tax) have been reclassified in respect of the six months ended 30 June 2005.

(d) Currency translation

The functional currency for each entity in the Group, and for jointly controlled entities and associates, is determined as the currency of the primary economic environment in which it operates. For most entities, this is the local currency of the country in which it operates. Transactions denominated in currencies other than the functional currency of the entity are translated at the exchange rate ruling at the date of the transaction. Monetary assets and liabilities denominated in foreign currencies are retranslated at year end exchange rates.

The US dollar is the currency in which the Group's Financial statements are presented, as it most reliably reflects the global business performance of the Group as a whole.

On consolidation, income statement items are translated into US dollars at average rates of exchange. Balance sheet items are translated into US dollars at year end exchange rates. Exchange differences on the translation of the net assets of entities with functional currencies other than the US dollar, and any offsetting exchange differences on net debt hedging those net assets, are dealt with through equity.

> Exchange gains and losses which arise on balances between Group entities are taken to equity where that balance is, in substance, part of the Group's net investment in the subsidiary and the balance is denominated in the functional currency of one party to the loan.
>
> The Group finances its operations primarily in US dollars and a substantial part of the Group's US dollar debt is located in subsidiaries having functional currencies other than the US dollar. Except as noted above, exchange gains and losses relating to such US dollar debt are charged or credited to the Group's income statement in the year in which they arise. This means that the impact of financing in US dollars on the Group's income statement is dependent on the functional currency of the particular subsidiary where the debt is located.
>
> Except as noted above, or in Note (p) below relating to derivative contracts, all exchange differences are charged or credited to the income statement in the year in which they arise.

E Monetary items becoming part of the net investment in a foreign operation

It may happen that a parent will decide that its subsidiary requires to be refinanced and instead of investing more equity capital in the subsidiary decides that an existing inter-company account, which has previously been regarded as a normal monetary item, should become a long-term deferred trading balance and no repayment of such amount will be requested within the foreseeable future. How should the parent treat the exchange differences relating to the inter-company account in the consolidated financial statements in the year it was so designated?

Example 10.22: Monetary item becoming part of the net investment in a foreign operation

A UK entity has a wholly owned Canadian subsidiary whose net assets at 31 December 2007 were C$2,000,000. These net assets were arrived at after taking account of a liability to the UK parent of £250,000. Using the closing exchange rate of £1=C$2.35 this liability was included in the Canadian company's balance sheet at that date at C$587,500. On 30 June 2008, when the exchange rate was £1=C$2.45, the parent decided that in order to refinance the Canadian subsidiary it would regard the liability of £250,000 as a long-term liability which would not be called for repayment in the foreseeable future. Consequently, the parent thereafter regarded the loan as being part of its net investment in the subsidiary. In the year ended 31 December 2008 the Canadian company made no profit or loss other than any exchange difference to be recognised on its liability to its parent. The relevant exchange rate at that date was £1=C$2.56. The average exchange rate for the year ended 31 December 2008 was £1=C$2.50.

The financial statements of the subsidiary in C$ and translated using the closing rate are as follows:

Balance sheet	31 December 2008		31 December 2007	
	C$	£	C$	£
Assets	2,587,500	1,010,742	2,587,500	1,101,064
Amount due to parent	640,000	250,000	587,500	250,000
Net assets	1,947,500	760,742	2,000,000	851,064
Income statement				
Exchange difference	(52,500)			

If the amount due to the parent is not part of the parent's net investment in the foreign operation, this exchange loss would be translated at the average rate and included in the consolidated profit and loss account as £21,000. As the net investment was C$2,000,000 then there would have been an exchange loss taken to equity of £69,814, i.e. £851,064 less £781,250 (C$2,000,000 @ £1=C$2.56), together with an exchange gain of £492, being the difference between the income statement translated at average rate, i.e. £21,000, and at the closing rate, i.e. £20,508.

However, the parent now regards the amount due as being part of the net investment in the subsidiary. The question then arises as to when this should be regarded as having happened and how the exchange difference on it should be calculated. No guidance is given in IAS 21.

In our view, the 'capital injection' should be regarded as having occurred at the time it is decided to redesignate the inter-company account. The exchange differences arising on the account up to that date should be included in the income statement. Only the exchange difference arising thereafter would be taken to equity on consolidation. The inter-company account that was converted into a long-term loan becomes part of the entity's (UK parent's) net investment in the foreign operation (Canadian subsidiary) at the moment in time when the entity decides that settlement is neither planned nor likely to occur in the foreseeable future, i.e. 30 June 2008. Accordingly, exchange differences arising on the long-term loan are recognised in a separate component of equity from that date. The same accounting treatment would have been applied if a capital injection had taken place at the date of redesignation.

At 30 June 2008 the subsidiary would have translated the inter-company account as C$612,500 (£250,000 @ £1=C$2.45) and therefore the exchange loss up to that date was C$25,000. Translated at the average rate this amount would be included in the consolidated income statement as £10,000, with only an exchange gain of £234 taken to equity, being the difference between the income statement translated at average rate, i.e. £10,000, and at the closing rate, i.e. £9,766. Accordingly, £11,000 (£21,000 less £10,000) offset by a reduction in the exchange gain on the translation of the income statement of £258 (£492 less £234) would be taken to equity. This amount represents the exchange loss on the 'capital injection' of C$612,500. Translated at the closing rate this amounts to £239,258 which is £10,742 less than the original £250,000.

Some might argue that an approach of regarding the 'capital injection' as having occurred at the beginning of the accounting period would have the merit of treating all of the exchange differences for this year in the same way. However, for the reasons provided above we do not regard such an approach as being acceptable.

Suppose, instead of the inter-company account being £250,000, it was denominated in dollars at C$587,500. In this case the parent would be exposed to the exchange risk; what would be the position?

The subsidiary's net assets at both 31 December 2007 and 2008 would be:

Assets	C$2,587,500
Amount due to parent	587,500
Net assets	C$2,000,000

As the inter-company account is expressed in Canadian dollars, there will be no exchange difference thereon in the subsidiary's income statement.

There will, however, be an exchange loss in the parent as follows:

C$587,500	@ 2.35 =	£250,000
	@ 2.56 =	£229,492
		£20,508

Again, in the consolidated financial statements as the inter-company account is now regarded as part of the equity investment some of this amount should be taken to equity. For the reasons stated above, in our view it is only the exchange differences that have arisen after the date of redesignation, i.e. 30 June 2008, that should be taken to equity.

On this basis, the exchange loss would be split as follows:

C$587,500	@ 2.35 =	£250,000	
	@ 2.45 =	£239,796	
			£10,204
	@ 2.45 =	£239,796	
	@ 2.56 =	£229,492	
			£10,304

The exchange loss up to 30 June 2008 of £10,204 would be taken to the consolidated income statement and the exchange loss thereafter of £10,304 would be taken to equity. This is different from when the account was expressed in sterling because the 'capital injection' in this case is C$587,500 whereas before it was effectively C$612,500.

F *Monetary items ceasing to be part of the net investment in a foreign operation*

The previous section dealt with the situation where a monetary item is now considered to form part of the net investment in a foreign operation. However, what happens where a monetary item that was considered to be part of the net investment in a foreign operation is no longer the case, either because the circumstances have changed such that it is now planned or is likely to be settled in the foreseeable future or indeed that the monetary item is in fact settled?

Where the circumstances have changed such that the monetary item is now planned or is likely to be settled in the foreseeable future, then similar issues to those discussed at 3.4.1 A above apply; i.e. are the exchange differences on the intragroup balance to be taken to the income statement only from the date of change or from the beginning of the financial year? For the same reasons set out in Example 10.22 above, in our view, the monetary item ceases to form part of the net investment in the foreign operation at the moment in time when the entity decides that settlement is planned or is likely to occur in the foreseeable future. Accordingly, exchange differences arising on the monetary item up to that date are recognised in a separate component of equity. The exchange differences that arise after that date are taken to the income statement.

However, in this situation consideration also needs to be given as to the treatment of the cumulative exchange differences on the monetary item that have been taken to equity, including those that had been taken to equity in prior years.

As indicated at 3.4 above, the treatment of these exchange differences is to classify them as equity until the disposal of the foreign operation (see 2.7.3 and 3.3.6 above).[142] Accordingly, the exchange differences should remain in the separate component of equity.

However, where the intragroup balance is actually settled in cash, consideration needs to be given as to whether the cumulative exchange differences that relate to the amount repaid should be recognised in profit or loss at the time of the repayment. In our view, this will depend on whether the settlement constitutes a return of the net investment in the foreign operation. This is because the requirement to recycle the exchange differences applies when an entity partially disposes of its foreign operation thereby recovering part of its investment in the operation (see 2.7.3 and 3.3.6 above). Thus, since the repayment of the intragroup balance is akin to the repayment of share capital, if it constitutes a partial return of the investment then a proportion of the cumulative exchange differences relating to the investment in the foreign operation should be recycled and recognised in profit or loss at the time of the repayment. Otherwise, the exchange differences should remain in the separate component of equity. This is illustrated in the following example.

Example 10.23: Recycling of exchange differences on settlement of monetary items included as part of the net investment in a foreign operation

The following scenarios consider a simple group as follows: Entity H, the parent, has the euro as its functional currency and presents its consolidated financial statements in euro. Entity S is Entity H's wholly owned subsidiary and has the US dollar as its functional currency. Both companies have substantive operations.

In each case the question addressed is whether or not any of the transactions identified should trigger a recycling of exchange differences from the separate component of equity to profit or loss in the consolidated financial statements.

Scenario 1

On 1 January 2005, Entity H establishes Entity S, subscribes US$50m for its entire share capital and makes a loan to it of US$50m. The loan is considered to form part of Entity H's net investment in Entity S.

During the next three years, Entity S makes profits of US$10m per year and retains them.

In 2008, it is decided that Entity S should repatriate US$30m (its retained profits) to Entity H which it can do in one of three ways:

(a) payment of a dividend of US$30m;

(b) partial redemption of share capital for US$30m; or

(c) repayment of US$30m of the loan that was considered to be part of Entity H's net investment in Entity S.

Analysis

(a) As indicated at 2.7.3 and 3.3.6 above, paragraph 49 of IAS 21 states that 'the payment of a dividend is part of a disposal only when it constitutes a return of the investment, for example when the dividend is paid out of pre-acquisition profits.' This makes it clear that this dividend payment should not trigger any recycling. However, any additional distributions would trigger a recycling unless they were represented by profits of Entity S that had been made subsequent to the first dividend.

(b) As indicated at 2.7.3 and 3.3.6 above, paragraph 49 of IAS 21 states that 'an entity may dispose of its interest in a foreign operation through sale, liquidation, repayment of share capital or abandonment of all, or part of, that entity.' Whilst the reference to repayment of share capital might suggest that this transaction could trigger a recycling of exchange differences, more clarity as to the underlying principle of IAS 21 can be found in the sentence referred to in (a) above, i.e. that the payment represents a return of the investment.

Therefore, because the repayment of share capital does not reduce the overall net investment in Entity S below the amount of the original investment, this transaction should not be seen as a return of Entity H's investment in Entity S and should not result in the recycling of any gains or losses from equity.

As in (a) above, any additional distributions or repayments of share capital would trigger a recycling unless they were represented by profits of Entity S that had been made subsequent to this repayment.

This analysis effectively regards two of the components of Entity H's net investment in Entity S, i.e. its retained earnings and share capital as fungible, which seems entirely appropriate, since the net investment in a foreign operation is the amount of the reporting entity's interest in the net assets of that operation.

(c) It might be thought this transaction should trigger a recycling of the gain or loss in equity that is associated with that loan, since cash has been received in settlement of the loan. This analysis implies that the component of Entity H's net investment represented by the loan is somehow different to the other components. However, this seems contrary to the notion in paragraph 15 of IAS 21 (see 3.4.1 above) that the loan is *in substance* part of the net investment in Entity S. The analysis in (b) seems more appropriate, i.e. to regard the loan as a fungible part of Entity H's net investment in Entity S.

Therefore, because the repayment of the loan does not reduce the overall net investment in Entity S below the amount of the original investment, this transaction should not be seen as a return of Entity H's investment in Entity S and should not result in the recycling of any gains or losses from equity.

Scenario 2

On 1 January 2005, Entity H establishes Entity S, subscribes US$50m for its entire share capital and makes a loan to it of US$50m. The loan is considered to form part of Entity H's net investment in Entity S.

During the next three years, Entity S makes profits of US$10m per year and distributes them to Entity H at the end of each year.

In 2008, Entity S borrows US$40m from a third party and uses the proceeds to repay US$40m of the loan that was considered to be part of Entity H's net investment in Entity S.

Analysis

For the same reasons as set out in Scenario 1 above, the distribution of profits in 2005 to 2007 do not trigger any recycling. The transaction in 2008 clearly reduces the initial net investment in Entity S from US$100m to US$60m and so is akin to a return of the investment in Entity S per paragraph 49 of IAS 21 and should trigger recycling.

Following the analysis in Scenario 1 above, recycling would also be required if, instead of repaying US$40 of the loan, Entity S repatriated US$40m by way of a dividend or repayment of share capital.

Scenario 3

On 1 January 2005, Entity H establishes Entity S and subscribes US$100m for its entire share capital. However, this is more capital than Entity S requires for the foreseeable future, so it immediately lends $30m back to Entity H and the loan is considered to form part of Entity H's net investment in Entity S.

During the next three years, Entity S makes profits of US$10m per year and distributes them to Entity H at the end of each year.

In 2008, due to previously unidentified opportunities, Entity H decides the operations of Entity S should be expanded. To do this, Entity S will need an extra US$30m of capital which Entity H can provide in one of two ways:

(a) subscribing for US$30m of additional share capital; or

(b) settling the US$30m loan that was considered to be part of Entity H's net investment in Entity S.

Analysis

(a) It is clear that this transaction, which results in an *increase* in Entity H's net investment in Entity S, should not trigger a recycling.

(b) It might be thought this transaction should trigger a recycling of the gain or loss in equity that is associated with that loan, since cash has been received in settlement of the loan. Again, this analysis implies that the (negative) component of Entity H's net investment represented by the loan is somehow different to the other components. However, as in Scenario 1 above, this seems contrary to the notion in paragraph 15 of IAS 21 (see 3.4.1 above) that the loan is *in substance* part of the net investment in Entity S. Furthermore, it seems entirely contrary to the general principle in paragraph 48 of IAS 21 that recycling occurs on a disposal of a net investment when this transaction results in an *increase* in Entity H's net investment in Entity S.

Therefore, because the repayment of the loan increases the net investment in Entity S above the amount of the original net investment of US$50m, this transaction should not result in the recycling of any gains or losses from equity.

3.4.2 Other intragroup transactions

As indicated in 3.4 above, exchange differences on intragroup transactions should normally be treated in the same way as if they arose on transactions with third parties. However, there are two further problem areas that arise when preparing the consolidated financial statements.

A Dividends

The first area relates to dividends payable by a foreign subsidiary to its parent.

If a subsidiary pays a dividend to the parent during the year the parent should record the dividend at the rate ruling when the dividend was declared. An exchange difference will arise in the parent's own financial statements if the exchange rate moves between the declaration date and the date the dividend is actually received. This exchange difference requires to be taken to the income statement and will remain there on consolidation.

The same will apply if the subsidiary declares a dividend to its parent on the last day of its financial year and this is recorded at the year-end in both entities' financial statements. There is no problem in that year as both the intragroup balances and the dividends will eliminate on consolidation with no exchange differences arising. However, as the dividend will not be received until the following year an exchange difference will arise in the parent's financial statements in that year if exchange rates have moved in the meantime. Again, this exchange difference should remain in the consolidated income statement as it is no different from any other exchange difference arising on intragroup balances resulting from other types of intragroup transactions. It should not be taken to equity.

It may seem odd that the consolidated results can be affected by exchange differences on inter-company dividends. However, once the dividend has been declared, the parent now effectively has a functional currency exposure to assets that were previously regarded as part of the net investment. In order to minimise the effect of exchange rate movements entities should, therefore, arrange for inter-company dividends to be paid on the same day the dividend is declared, or as soon after the dividend is declared as possible.

B Unrealised profits on intragroup transactions

The other problem area is the elimination of unrealised profits resulting from intragroup transactions when one of the parties to the transaction is a foreign subsidiary.

Example 10.24: Unrealised profits on intragroup transaction

An Italian parent has a wholly owned Swiss subsidiary. On 30 November 2008 the subsidiary sold goods to the parent for CHF1,000. The cost of the goods to the subsidiary was CHF700. The goods were recorded by the parent at €685 based on the exchange rate ruling on 30 November 2008 of €1=CHF1.46. All of the goods are unsold by the year-end, 31 December 2008. The exchange rate at that date was €1=CHF1.52. How should the intragroup profit be eliminated?

IAS 21 contains no specific guidance on this matter. However, SFAS 52 requires the rate ruling at the date of the transaction to be used.[143]

The profit shown by the subsidiary is CHF300 which translated at the rate ruling on the transaction of €1=CHF1.46 equals €205. Consequently, the goods will be included in the balance sheet at:

Per parent company balance sheet	€685
Less unrealised profit eliminated	205
	€480

It can be seen that the resulting figure for inventory is equivalent to the original euro cost translated at the rate ruling on the date of the transaction. Whereas if the subsidiary still held the inventory it would be included at €461 (CHF700 @ €1=CHF1.52).

If in the above example the goods had been sold by the Italian parent to the Swiss subsidiary then we believe the amount to be eliminated is the amount of profit shown in the Italian entity's financial statements. Again, this will not necessarily result in the goods being carried in the consolidated financial statements at their original cost to the group.

3.5 Introduction of the euro

From 1 January 1999, the effective start of Economic and Monetary Union (EMU), the euro became a currency in its own right and the conversion rates between the euro and the national currencies of those countries who were going to participate in the first phase were irrevocably fixed, such that the risk of subsequent exchange differences related to these currencies was eliminated from that date on.

In October 1997, the SIC issued SIC-7 which deals with the application of IAS 21 to the changeover from the national currencies of participating Member States of the European Union to the euro. Consequential amendments have been made to this interpretation as a result of the IASB's revised version of IAS 21.

Although the Interpretation is no longer relevant with respect to the national currencies of those countries that participated in the first phase, SIC-7 makes it clear that the same rationale applies to the fixing of exchange rates when countries join EMU at later stages.[144]

Under SIC-7, the requirements of IAS 21 regarding the translation of foreign currency transactions and financial statements of foreign operations should be strictly applied to the changeover.[145]

This means that, in particular:

(a) Foreign currency monetary assets and liabilities resulting from transactions shall continue to be translated into the functional currency at the closing rate. Any resultant exchange differences shall be recognised as income or expense immediately, except that an entity shall continue to apply its existing accounting policy for exchange gains and losses related to hedges of the currency risk of a forecast transaction.[146]

The effective start of the EMU after the balance sheet date does not change the application of these requirements at the balance sheet date; in accordance with IAS 10 – *Events after the Balance Sheet Date* – it is not relevant whether or not the closing rate can fluctuate after the balance sheet date.[147]

Like IAS 21, the Interpretation does not address how foreign currency hedges should be accounted for. The effective start of EMU, of itself, does not justify a change to an entity's established accounting policy related to hedges of forecast transactions because the changeover does not affect the economic rationale of such hedges. Therefore, the changeover should not alter the accounting policy where gains and losses on financial instruments used as hedges of forecast transactions are initially recognised in equity and matched with the related income or expense in a future period;[148]

(b) Cumulative exchange differences relating to the translation of financial statements of foreign operations shall continue to be classified as equity and shall be recognised as income or expense only on the disposal of the net investment in the foreign operation.[149]

The fact that the cumulative amount of exchange differences will be fixed under EMU does not justify immediate recognition as income or expenses since the wording and the rationale of IAS 21 clearly preclude such a treatment.[150]

4 TRANSITIONAL ARRANGEMENTS AND FIRST-TIME ADOPTION ISSUES

4.1 Transitional arrangements for entities already reporting under IFRS

As indicated at 2 above, most changes resulting from the application of the standard were to be accounted for in accordance with the requirements of IAS 8 (see Chapter 3 at 4.4),[151] i.e. by retrospective application of the new requirements. However, in a change from the proposals in the exposure draft that preceded the standard, the IASB made an exception from this requirement in respect of its new requirements for goodwill and fair value adjustments.

The standard required that an entity applied the requirements for goodwill and fair value adjustments (i.e. expressed in the functional currency of the acquired entity and therefore translated at closing rate) prospectively to all acquisitions occurring after the beginning of the financial reporting period in which IAS 21 was first applied. However, retrospective application of the new requirements to earlier acquisitions was permitted.[152] The standard goes on to say that 'for an acquisition of a foreign operation treated prospectively but which occurred before the date on which this Standard is first applied, the entity shall not restate prior years and accordingly may, when appropriate, treat goodwill and fair value adjustments arising on that acquisition as assets and liabilities of the entity rather than as assets and liabilities of the foreign operation. Therefore, those goodwill and fair value adjustments either are already expressed in the entity's functional currency or are non-monetary foreign currency items, which are reported using the exchange rate at the date of the acquisition.'[153] Accordingly, those entities that used the option allowed under the previous version of the standard to translate goodwill and fair value adjustments in respect of earlier acquisitions at historical rates could continue to do so. It is unclear why this transitional arrangement was included in the standard since the Basis of Conclusions issued with the standard makes no reference to it, but it was presumably based on comments that entities may have had difficulty in restating old transactions.

One company that took advantage of these transitional arrangements was AngloGold Ashanti as shown below.

Extract 10.9: AngloGold Ashanti Limited (2005)

1.2 Changes in accounting policies [extract]

IAS 21 (revised) "The effects of changes in foreign exchange rates" and IAS 21 Amendment – "Net investment in foreign operation" [extract]

As of 1 January 2005, the group adopted IAS 21 (revised). As a result, any goodwill arising on the acquisition of a foreign operation and any fair value adjustments to the carrying amounts of assets and liabilities arising on the acquisition are now treated as assets and liabilities of the foreign operation and translated at closing rate. In accordance with the transitional provisions of IAS 21 this change is applied prospectively. This change in accounting policy had no impact as at 31 December 2005.

4.2 First-time adoption issues

As discussed in Chapter 5 at 2.4.5 and 2.7.2, IFRS 1 provides 2 optional exemptions from full retrospective application of IAS 21 on transition to IFRS for first time adopters.

4.2.1 *Cumulative translation differences*

The first exemption relates to the requirements in IAS 21:[154]

(a) to recognise some translation differences (principally those resulting from the process of translating the results and financial position of an entity whose functional currency is not that the currency of a hyperinflationary economy into a different presentation currency) as a separate component of equity (see 2.7.1 above); and

(b) on disposal of a foreign operation, to transfer the cumulative translation differences included within that separate component of equity relating to that operation to the income statement as part of the gain or loss on disposal (see 2.7.3 above).

Under its previous GAAP, an entity may never have recorded such exchange differences as a separate component of equity. Clearly, it could be extremely onerous for an entity to compile such information. Even if under its previous GAAP, an entity did recognise such exchange differences as a separate component of equity, these might be affected by adjustments made on transition to IFRS to the recognised net assets of the foreign operation. Also, an entity might not have the information to determine how much of that separate component of equity related to individual foreign operations to make the necessary transfer on the disposal of a particular operation. Accordingly, the IASB considered that it would be more transparent and comparable to exempt an entity from the requirement to identify the cumulative translation differences at the date of transition to IFRS.[155]

Therefore, under IFRS 1, a first time adopter need not comply with these requirements for the cumulative exchange differences that existed at the date of transition to IFRS. Instead, it shall deem the cumulative translation differences for foreign operations to be zero at the date of transition and the gain or loss on a subsequent disposal shall exclude translation differences that arose before the date of transition and only include later translation differences.[156]

If a first time adopter chooses to use this exemption, it should apply it to all foreign operations at the date of transition to IFRS. If that entity has an existing separate component of equity relating to such translation differences at the date of transition then it should it transfer this reserve to retained earnings at that date.

Since there is no requirement to justify the use of the exemption on grounds of impracticality or undue cost or effort, an entity that already has a separate component of equity and the necessary information to determine how much of it relates to each foreign operation in accordance with IAS 21 (or can do so without much effort) is still able to use the exemption. Accordingly, an entity that has cumulative exchange losses in respect of foreign operations, may consider it advantageous to use the exemption so as to avoid having to recognise these losses in the event of the foreign operation being sold at some time in the future.

Many companies have taken this exemption. One such company is Pearson as illustrated in Extract 10.4 at 2.7.3 above.

4.2.2 Goodwill and fair value adjustments

As a result of the transitional arrangement introduced in IAS 21 discussed at 4.1 above, a similar transitional arrangement was included with IFRS 1. Accordingly, a first time adopter need not apply the requirements of IAS 21 retrospectively to fair value adjustments and goodwill arising on business combinations that occurred before the date of transition to IFRS. If IAS 21 is not applied retrospectively a first-time adopter should treat such fair value adjustments and goodwill 'as assets and liabilities of the entity rather than as assets and liabilities of the acquiree. Therefore, those goodwill and fair value adjustments either are already expressed in the entity's functional currency or are non-monetary foreign currency items, which are reported using the exchange rate applied under previous GAAP.'[157]

If a first-time adopter chooses not to take the exemption, it must apply the requirements of IAS 21 retrospectively to fair value adjustments and goodwill arising in either:[158]

(a) all business combinations that occurred before the date of transition to IFRS; or

(b) all business combinations that the entity elects to restate to comply with IFRS 3, as permitted by IFRS 1 (see Chapter 7 at 4.2.1).

However, in practice the exemption may be of limited use for a number of reasons.

First, the exemption permits 'goodwill and fair value adjustments' to be treated as assets and liabilities of the entity rather than as assets and liabilities of the acquiree. Implicit in the exemption is the requirement to treat goodwill and fair value adjustments consistently. However, the IASB apparently did not consider that many first-time adopters, under their previous GAAP, will have treated fair value adjustments as assets or liabilities of the acquiree, while at the same time treating goodwill as an asset of the acquirer. As the exemption under IFRS 1 did not foresee this particular situation, those first-time adopters will need to restate either their goodwill or fair value adjustments. In many cases restatement of goodwill is less onerous than restatement of fair value adjustments.

Secondly, the paragraphs in IFRS 1 that introduce the exemption were drafted at a later date than the rest of the Appendix that they form part of. Instead of referring to 'first-time adopter' these paragraphs refer to 'entity'. Nevertheless, it is clear from the context that 'entity' should be read as 'first-time adopter'. This means that the exemption only permits goodwill and fair value adjustments to be treated as assets of the first-time adopter (i.e. ultimate parent). In practice, however, many groups have treated goodwill (and fair value adjustments) as an asset of an intermediate parent. Where the intermediate parent has a functional currency that is different from that of the ultimate parent or the acquiree, it will be necessary to restate goodwill (and fair value adjustments).

4.2.3 Other practical issues

These are the only exemptions allowed by IFRS 1 in relation to the requirements of IAS 21.

Companies will need to confirm whether all entities included within the financial statements are accounted for in the appropriate functional currency.

One other difficulty that an entity may face in preparing its opening IFRS balance sheet is that the guidance in IAS 21 in relation to the determination of the functional currency of each of the entities within the group (see 2.5 above) may mean that there has been a change in the functional currency of an entity from that which had been used under its previous GAAP. This will need to be accounted for by restating the assets and liabilities of the entity at the date of transition to IFRS, rather than prospectively from the date of transition as would be the case on an ongoing basis under IAS 21 (as discussed at 2.6.4 above). The translation of monetary items, or non-monetary assets included at valuation at the balance sheet date, are unlikely to cause much of a problem. Since these are likely to have been translated into the 'old' functional currency at a closing rate, the retranslation into the IAS 21 functional currency will be done at the exchange rate for those currencies at the date of transition. The principal difficulty relates to non-monetary items that are measured on the basis of historical cost, particularly property, plant and machinery, since these will need to be re-measured in terms of the IAS 21 functional currency at the rates of exchange applying at the date of acquisition of the assets concerned, and recalculating cumulative depreciation or amortisation charges accordingly. It may be that to circumvent this difficulty an entity should consider using the option in IFRS 1 whereby the fair value of such assets at the date of transition is treated as being the deemed cost of those assets (see Chapter 5 at 2.5).

Some of the practical issues discussed at 3 above may have to be considered in accounting for foreign exchange in the periods after the date of transition in preparing the first IFRS financial statements, including the comparatives.

5 CONCLUSION

The issues relating to the accounting for foreign currency activities, whether through having transactions in another currency or through foreign operations, generally come down to two choices – the exchange rate to be used in the translation process and the subsequent treatment of the exchange differences that arise. The changes made by the IASB to IAS 21 in December 2003 have, in general, resulted in a better standard, and the revised version provides a workable basis for dealing with these issues.

The accounting for transactions in a currency other than the functional currency of an entity required by the standard is basically the same as that in the original standard, and as such, is well understood and does not give rise to too many difficulties. The critical issue is the determination of an entity's functional currency, since it is by reference to that currency that transactions and balances will be regarded as being 'foreign' and thus give rise to foreign exchange differences. The other main issue is that for certain items, the distinction as to whether it is a monetary item or not may not be clear cut; the importance being that it is only monetary items that are translated at closing rates and thus result in exchange differences being taken to profit or loss.

As far as the translation of foreign operations is concerned, the standard deals with this as part of the process of an entity presenting its financial statements in a currency other than its functional currency or the functional currencies of the individual entities included in consolidated financial statements. However, for most situations, this translation process is effectively based on that in the previous version of the standard for translating foreign operations in consolidated financial statements, i.e. assets and liabilities translated at closing rates, income and expenses at actual rates (or an appropriate average rate), and resulting exchange differences taken to equity to be recycled to profit or loss upon disposal of the operation. Again, this process is well understood and does not give rise to too many difficulties that are not addressed by the standard. The main area that is not addressed is the translation of equity items where the IASB has deliberately remained silent.

One aspect of the revised standard that we consider was given inadequate attention by the IASB is that relating to monetary items forming part of the net investment in a foreign operation (see 3.4.1 above). As before, the standard allows exchange differences on such monetary items to be taken to equity in the consolidated financial statements. However, such a treatment can no longer be adopted in the separate financial statements of the entity with the foreign currency exposure; it has to take the exchange differences to its income statement, despite the fact that these are not expected to have any impact of the entity's cash flows. In addition, where the monetary item is denominated in a currency that is not the functional currency of either entity, the exchange differences reflected in the individual entities' financial statements was also to remain in the consolidated financial statements, thus treating the item like any other intragroup balance. We therefore welcome the amendment made in December 2005 such that the requirement in the consolidated financial statements applies irrespective of the currency of the monetary item and of whether the monetary item results from a transaction with the reporting entity or any of its subsidiaries. However, it is still unclear what the rationale is for requiring the exchange differences to be recognised in profit or loss in the separate financial statements of the entity with the foreign currency exposure.

References

1 IAS 21 (revised 1993), *The Effects of Changes in Foreign Exchange Rates*, IASC, Revised 1993, para. 23.
2 IAS 21 (revised 1993), paras. 30-31.
3 IAS 21 (revised 1993), paras. 27-29.
4 IAS 21, *The Effects of Changes in Foreign Exchange Rates*, IASB, para. IN2.
5 IAS 21, para. IN3.
6 IAS 21, para. IN1.
7 Draft Technical Correction 1, *Proposed Amendments to IAS 21 The Effects of Changes in Foreign Exchange Rates – Net Investment in a Foreign Operation*, IASB, October 2005.
8 Amendment to IAS 21, *The Effects of Changes in Foreign Exchange Rates – Net Investment in a Foreign Operation*, IASB, December 2005.
9 IAS 21, para. 58A.
10 IAS 21, para. IN1.
11 IAS 21, para. 58.
12 IAS 21, para. 58A.
13 IAS 21, paras. 59-60.
14 IAS 21, para. 1.
15 IAS 21, para. 2.
16 IAS 21, para. 3.
17 IAS 21, para. 4.
18 IAS 21, para. 5.
19 IAS 21, para. 6.
20 IAS 21, para. 7.
21 IAS 21, para. 8.
22 IAS 21, para. 17.
23 IAS 21, para. 17.
24 IAS 21, para. 18.
25 IAS 21, para. 19.
26 IAS 21, para. 9.
27 IAS 21, para. 12.
28 IAS 21, para. 9.
29 IAS 21, para. 10.
30 IAS 21, para. 11.
31 IAS 21, para. 13.
32 IAS 21, para. 20.

33 IAS 21, para. 21.
34 IAS 21, para. 22.
35 IAS 21, para. 23.
36 IAS 21, para. 28.
37 IAS 21, para. 29.
38 IAS 21, para. 32.
39 IAS 21, para. 30.
40 IAS 21, para. 31.
41 IAS 21, para. 30.
42 IAS 21, para. 36.
43 IAS 21, para. 35.
44 IAS 21, para. 37.
45 IAS 21, para. 38.
46 IAS 21, para. 18.
47 IAS 21, para. 44.
48 IAS 21, para. 39.
49 IAS 21, para. 40.
50 IAS 21, para. 41.
51 IAS 21, para. 41.
52 IAS 21, para. 41.
53 IAS 21, para. BC17.
54 IAS 21, para. BC20.
55 IAS 21, para. BC18.
56 IAS 21, para. BC19.
57 IAS 21, para. 42.
58 IAS 21, para. 43.
59 IAS 21, para. 43.
60 IAS 21, para. 44.
61 IAS 21, para. 45.
62 IAS 21, para. 45.
63 IAS 21, para. 46.
64 SFAS 52, *Foreign Currency Translation*, FASB, December 1981, para. 139.
65 IAS 21 (revised 1993), para. 33.
66 IAS 21, para. BC27.
67 IAS 21, para. BC30.
68 IAS 21, para. BC31.
69 IAS 21, para. BC32.
70 IAS 21, para. 47.
71 IAS 21, para. 48.
72 IAS 27, *Consolidated and Separate Financial Statements*, IASB, para. 30.
73 IAS 21, para. 49.
74 *Exposure Draft of Proposed Amendments to IAS 27 Consolidated and Separate Financial Statements*, IASB, June 2005.
75 *Near-final draft of IAS 27 Consolidated and Separate Financial Statements* ('Near-final IAS 27R'), IASB, June 2007.
76 Near-final IAS 27, para. A6 (IAS 21, para. 58X).
77 Near-final IAS 27, para. A6 (IAS 21, paras. 48A-48B), para. BCA1 (IAS 21, paras. BC33-34).
78 Near-final IAS 27, para. A6 (IAS 21, para. 48C).
79 IAS 21, para. 50.
80 IAS 21, para. 52.
81 IAS 21, para. 52.
82 IAS 21, para. 53.
83 IAS 21, para. 51.
84 IAS 21, para. 54.
85 IAS 21, para. 55.
86 IAS 21, para. 56.
87 IAS 21, para. 57.
88 IAS 21, para. 51.
89 IAS 39, *Financial Instruments: Recognition and Measurement*, IASB, para. 14.
90 IAS 39, para. AG35.
91 IAS 21, para. 22.
92 IAS 21, para. 26.
93 IAS 21, para. 26.
94 IAS 21, para. 8.
95 IAS 21, para. 16.
96 IAS 21, para. 16.
97 IAS 21, para. 16.
98 IAS 39, para. AG83.
99 SFAS 52, para. 162.
100 IAS 39, para. AG83.
101 SFAS 52, para. 48.
102 CICA Handbook, Section 1651, Foreign currency translation, para. 47.
103 *Exposure Draft of Revised IAS 21*, IASB, May 2002, para. 14.
104 IAS 12, *Income Taxes*, IASB, para. 78.
105 IAS 19, para. 78.
106 IAS 19, para. 73.
107 IAS 21, para. 28.
108 IAS 23, *Borrowing Costs*, IASB, para. 5.
109 IAS 21, para. 34.
110 IAS 21, para. 34.
111 IAS 21, para. 26.
112 SFAS 52, para. 27.
113 SFAS 52, para. 138.
114 IAS 21, para. 40.
115 IAS 21, para. 40.
116 *IASB Update*, IASB, February 2003, p.5.
117 SFAS 52, para. 48.
118 CICA 1651, para. 47.
119 IAS 21, para. 41.
120 IAS 21, para. 47.
121 IAS 21, para. BC32.
122 *IFRIC Update*, IASB, November 2006, pp. 5-6.
123 *IFRIC Update*, IASB, January 2007, p. 3.
124 Agenda Paper 11, *Hedging of a Net Investment in a Foreign Operation*, IFRIC Meeting, January 2007, paras. 5-9.
125 IAS 21, para. 48.
126 IAS 21, para. 49.
127 IAS 21, para. 45.
128 IAS 21, para. 45.
129 IAS 21, para. 8.
130 IAS 21, para. 15.

131 IAS 21, paras. 32-33.
132 IAS 21 (revised 2003), *The Effects of Changes in Foreign Exchange Rates,* IASB, December 2003, para. 33.
133 IAS 21, para. 58A.
134 IAS 21, para. BC25C.
135 IAS 21, para. BC25D.
136 IAS 21, para. 33.
137 IAS 21, para. 41.
138 IAS 21, para. BC25C.
139 IAS 21, para. BC25D.
140 IAS 21, para. 15A.
141 IAS 21, para. 58A.
142 IAS 21, para. 45.
143 SFAS 52, para. 25.
144 SIC-7, *Introduction of the Euro*, IASB, para. 3.
145 SIC-7, para. 3.
146 SIC-7, para. 4.
147 SIC-7, para. 5.
148 SIC-7, para. 6.
149 SIC-7, para. 4.
150 SIC-7, para. 7.
151 IAS 21, para. 60.
152 IAS 21, para. 59.
153 IAS 21, para. 59.
154 IFRS 1, *First-time Adoption of International Financial Reporting Standards*, IASB, para. 21.
155 IFRS 1, paras. BC54-BC55.
156 IFRS 1, para. 22.
157 IFRS 1, para. B1A.
158 IFRS 1, para. B1B.

Chapter 11 Hyperinflation

1 INTRODUCTION

Accounting standards generally assume that the value of money (the unit of measurement) is constant over time, which normally is an acceptable practical assumption. However, when the effect of inflation on the value of money is no longer negligible, the usefulness of historical cost based financial reporting is often significantly reduced. High rates of inflation give rise to a number of problems for entities that prepare their financial statements on a historical cost basis, for example:

- historical cost figures expressed in terms of monetary units do not show the 'value to the business' of assets;
- holding gains on non-monetary assets that are reported as operating profits do not represent real economic gains;
- financial information presented for the current period is not comparable with that presented for the prior periods; and
- 'real' capital can be reduced because profits reported do not take account of the higher replacement costs of resources used in the period. Therefore, if in calculating profit 'return on capital' is not distinguished properly from 'return of capital', the erosion of 'real' capital may go unnoticed in the financial statements. This is the underlying point in the concept of capital maintenance.

Rates of inflation well in excess of 10% during most of the 1970s and early 1980s in most of the world brought these and other shortcomings of historical cost based financial reporting in an inflationary environment to prominence. Though methods of inflation accounting were extensively debated, interest in the subject dissipated quickly in the late 1980s when inflation all but disappeared in the US and Western Europe. Moreover, the discussions about inflation accounting and concepts of capital maintenance, undeservingly, have left little traces in modern accounting standards. The IASB's *Framework* mentions the existence of different concepts of capital maintenance but is ultimately based on the financial capital maintenance concept (see Chapter 2 at 3.2.6). Under this concept the capital of the entity will be maintained if the amount of gains during a period is at least equal to the amount of losses in that period. The IASB's Framework describes the concept of physical capital maintenance under which 'a profit is earned only if the physical productive capacity (or operating capability) of the entity (or the resources or funds needed to achieve that capacity) at the end of the period exceeds the physical productive capacity at the beginning of the period, after excluding any distributions to, and contributions from, owners during the period'.[1] However, the IASB did not really develop the physical capital maintenance concept in its Framework or any of its standards.[2] The financial capital maintenance concept on which International Financial Reporting Standards are based is only satisfactory under conditions of stable prices.

1.1 Hyperinflationary economies

From a Western European perspective it is easy to overlook that there are countries where inflation is still a major economic concern. In some of these countries, inflation has reached such levels – hyperinflation – that (1) the local currency is no longer a useful measure of value in the economy and (2) the general population may prefer not to hold its wealth in the local currency. Instead, they hold their wealth in a stable foreign currency or non-monetary assets. Under US accounting standards hyperinflation is deemed to exist when the cumulative rate of inflation over a three-year period exceeds 100%. As discussed at 2.3.1 below, there are several additional criteria that need to be taken into account under IFRS to determine whether hyperinflation exists.[3] Countries that are generally considered hyperinflationary, because they have recently had three-year cumulative inflation of 100% or more, include Angola, Myanmar and Zimbabwe.[4] Information on inflation rates in various countries is available in *International Financial Statistics*, published monthly by the International Monetary Fund.

1.2 Adjustment approaches

The historical cost based financial reporting problems reach such a magnitude under hyperinflationary circumstances that financial reporting in the hyperinflationary currency is all but meaningless. Therefore, a solution is needed to allow meaningful financial reporting by entities that operate in hyperinflationary economies. Two solutions to accounting for hyperinflation that have traditionally been applied can be summarised as follows:

- *Restatement approach* – Financial information recorded in the hyperinflationary currency is adjusted by applying a general price index and expressed in the measuring unit (the hyperinflationary currency) current at the balance sheet date;
- *Stable foreign currency* – The entity uses a relatively stable currency, for example the presentation currency of its parent, as the currency in which it measures items in its financial statements. If the transactions of the operation are not recorded initially in that stable currency, then they are remeasured into the stable currency by applying the temporal method of translation (see Chapter 10 at 1.1 and 1.2.1).

The relevant international standard, IAS 29 – *Financial Reporting in Hyperinflationary Economies*, only permits the restatement approach. Entities operating in a hyperinflationary economy are prohibited under IFRS from selecting a stable currency as their unit of accounting if that currency is not its functional currency under IAS 21 – *The Effects of Changes in Foreign Exchange Rates*, i.e. 'the currency of the primary economic environment in which the entity operates' (see Chapter 10 at 2.5).[5]

2 REQUIREMENTS OF IAS 29

2.1 History

The (then) IASC adopted IAS 29 in April 1989 and has only addressed the subject of hyperinflation since to clarify the provisions of the standard. This is not surprising as memories of high inflation rapidly receded from the collective conscious of most of the IASC's more influential constituents in the 1990s.

In February 2000, SIC-19 – *Reporting Currency – Measurement and Presentation of Financial Statements under IAS 21 and IAS 29* – was adopted, which provided rules on the selection of a measurement currency. Before the adoption of SIC-19 it was possible for entities operating in hyperinflationary economies to use any measurement currency of their liking, which allowed them to avoid using a hyperinflationary measurement currency and thereby to sidestep the requirements of IAS 29. As a result of the IASB's Improvements Project, the rules in SIC-19 have now been incorporated in IAS 21, which specifically prohibits an entity from avoiding 'restatement in accordance with IAS 29 by, for example, adopting as its functional currency a currency other than the functional currency determined in accordance with this Standard'.[6]

In March 2004, IFRIC issued Draft Interpretation D5 – *Applying IAS 29 Financial Reporting Hyperinflationary Economies for the First Time* – which proposed specific guidance to facilitate the first time application of IAS 29.[7] After a number of changes the draft interpretation was issued in its final form in November 2005 as IFRIC Interpretation 7 – *Applying the Restatement Approach under IAS 29 Financial Reporting in Hyperinflationary Economies*, which is effective for annual periods beginning on or after 1 March 2006.[8]

The IFRS literature defines the following currency related notions:

- *Functional currency* is defined in IAS 21 as the currency of the primary economic environment in which the entity operates;[9]
- *Measurement currency* was defined in SIC-19 as the currency in which the entity measures the items in the financial statements.[10] This notion has now been replaced by 'functional currency' (see above) which is more commonly used and, according to the IASB, has 'essentially the same meaning';[11]
- *Presentation currency* is defined in IAS 21 as the currency in which the financial statements are presented;[12]

- *Reporting currency* was defined in IAS 21 (revised 1993) as the currency used in presenting the financial statements.[13] The standard did not specify the currency in which an entity presented its financial statements, although it noted that an entity would normally use the currency of the country in which it was domiciled.[14] However, the choice of reporting currency established that all other currencies were treated as foreign currencies for the purposes of IAS 21 (revised 1993) and therefore would affect the financial statements. IAS 21 (revised 2003) replaced the notion of 'reporting currency' with two notions 'functional currency' and 'presentation currency'.[15]

2.2 Objective

The underlying premise of IAS 29 is that 'reporting of operating results and financial position in the local [hyperinflationary] currency without restatement is not useful'.[16] The standard's approach is therefore to require that:[17]

(a) the financial statements of an entity whose functional currency is the currency of a hyperinflationary economy, whether they are based on a historical cost approach or a current cost approach, should be stated in terms of the measuring unit current at the balance sheet date;

(b) the corresponding figures for the previous period required by IAS 1 – *Presentation of Financial Statements* – and any information in respect of earlier periods shall also be stated in terms of the measuring unit current at the balance sheet date; and

(c) the gain or loss on the net monetary position should be included in net income and separately disclosed.

IAS 29 requires 'balance sheet amounts not already expressed in terms of the measuring unit current at the balance sheet date' to be restated in terms of the measuring unit current at the balance sheet date, by applying a general price index.[18] The example below illustrates how this would apply to the balance sheet of an entity (for a detailed discussion of IAS 29 and the restatement process see 2.4 below):

Example 11.1: Accounting for hyperinflation under IAS 29

An entity that operates in a hyperinflationary economy is required under IAS 29 to restate all non-monetary items in its balance sheet to the measuring unit at balance sheet date by applying a general price index as follows:

	Before restatement (HC)	Historical general price index	Year-end general price index	After restatement (HC)
Plant and equipment	225	* 150	600	900
Inventory	250	500	600	300
Cash	100			100
Total assets	575			1,300
Accounts payable	180			180
Long-term debt	250			250
Equity **	145			870
	575			1,300

* General price index at the date of purchase
** The restatement of equity is not illustrated here, but discussed at 2.4.2 G below.

The simplified example above already raises a number of questions, such as:

- Which balance sheet items are monetary and which are non-monetary?
- How does the entity select the appropriate general price index?
- What was the general price index when the assets were acquired?

The standard provides guidance on the restatement to the measuring unit current at the balance sheet date, but concedes that 'the consistent application of these [inflation accounting] procedures and judgements from period to period is more important than the precise accuracy of the resulting amounts included in the restated financial statements'.[19] The requirements of the standard look deceptively straightforward but their application may represent a considerable challenge. These difficulties and other aspects of the practical application of the IAS 29 method of accounting for hyperinflation are discussed at 2.4.2 and 4 below.

Apart from the more technical reservations that exist about IAS 29, the concept of restating financial information to the measuring units current at the balance sheet date could have been articulated more clearly. Given the choice between (1) restating financial information for hyperinflation after the balance sheet date or (2) financial statements expressed in a stable foreign currency, some users might prefer the latter. Nevertheless, even when translated to a stable foreign currency, difficulties remain because of the complexities of the economic phenomenon of hyperinflation. Additionally, expressing financial statements of entities operating in hyperinflationary economies in a stable currency might give users a false sense of security.

2.3 Scope

IAS 29 should be applied by all entities whose functional currency is the currency of a hyperinflationary economy because 'money loses purchasing power at such a rate that comparison of amounts from transactions and other events that have occurred at different times, even within the same accounting period, is misleading'.[20] The standard should be applied in an entity's separate financial statements and its consolidated financial statements, as well as by parents that include such an entity in their consolidated financial statements. Financial statements of entities whose functional currency is that of a hyperinflationary economy first have to be restated under IAS 29 and then, if their parent has a different functional currency, translated under IAS 21 before they can be incorporated within the consolidated financial statements of the parent entity.

Almost all entities operating in hyperinflationary economies will be subject to the accounting regime of IAS 29, unless they can legitimately argue that the local hyperinflationary currency is not their functional currency as defined by IAS 21 (see Chapter 10 at 2.5).

2.3.1 *Definition of hyperinflation*

Determining whether an economy is hyperinflationary in accordance with IAS 29 requires judgement. The standard does not establish an absolute rate at which hyperinflation is deemed to arise. Instead, it considers the following characteristics of the economic environment of a country to be strong indicators of the existence of hyperinflation:[21]

(a) the general population prefers to keep its wealth in non-monetary assets or in a relatively stable foreign currency. Amounts of local currency held are immediately invested to maintain purchasing power;

(b) the general population regards monetary amounts not in terms of the local currency but in terms of a relatively stable foreign currency. Prices may be quoted in that currency;

(c) sales and purchases on credit take place at prices that compensate for the expected loss of purchasing power during the credit period, even if the period is short;

(d) interest rates, wages and prices are linked to a price index; and

(e) the cumulative inflation rate over three years is approaching, or exceeds, 100%.

The above list is not exhaustive and there may be other indicators that an economy is hyperinflationary, such as the existence of price controls and restrictive exchange controls. In determining whether an economy is hyperinflationary, condition (e) is quantitatively measurable while the other indicators require reliance on more qualitative, often anecdotal, evidence. For the purposes of testing condition (e), reference should be made to authoritative sources such as the International Monetary Fund's *International Financial Statistics Book, World Economic Outlook and International Financial Statistics*, though too-mechanical an application of the 100% criterion is not necessarily advisable. Despite the fact that IAS 29 expresses a preference 'that all entities that report in the currency of the same hyperinflationary economy apply this Standard from the same date',[22] that is in practice often an unrealistic wish given the way it defines hyperinflation. In any event, once an entity has identified the existence of hyperinflation, it should apply IAS 29 from the beginning of the reporting period in which it identified the existence of hyperinflation.[23]

Identifying when a currency becomes hyperinflationary, and as importantly when it ceases to be so, is not easy in practice. The consideration of trends, and the application of common sense, is important in this judgement, as are consistency of measurement and of presentation (see 2.7 below).

2.4 The IAS 29 restatement process

Restatement of financial statements in accordance with IAS 29 can be seen as a process comprising the following steps:

(a) selection of a general price index (see 2.4.1 below);

(b) analysis and restatement of assets and liabilities (see 2.4.2 below);

(c) restatement of the income statement (see 2.4.3 below);

(d) calculation of the gain or loss on the net monetary position (see 2.4.4 below);

(e) restatement of the cash flow statement (see 2.4.5 below); and

(f) restatement of the corresponding figures (see 2.4.6 below).

These steps are discussed below.

2.4.1 Selection of a general price index

The standard requires entities to use 'a general price index that reflects changes in general purchasing power', preferably the same price index should be used by all entities in the same hyperinflationary currency (see 4.1 below).[24]

Sometimes the general price index chosen by the entity is not available for all periods for which the restatement of long-lived assets is required. In that case, the entity will need to make an estimate of the price index based, for example, on 'the movements in the exchange rate between the functional currency and a relatively stable foreign currency' (see 4.2 below).[25]

2.4.2 *Analysis and restatement of balance sheet items*

A broad outline of the process to restate assets and liabilities in accordance with the requirements of IAS 29 is shown in the diagram below:

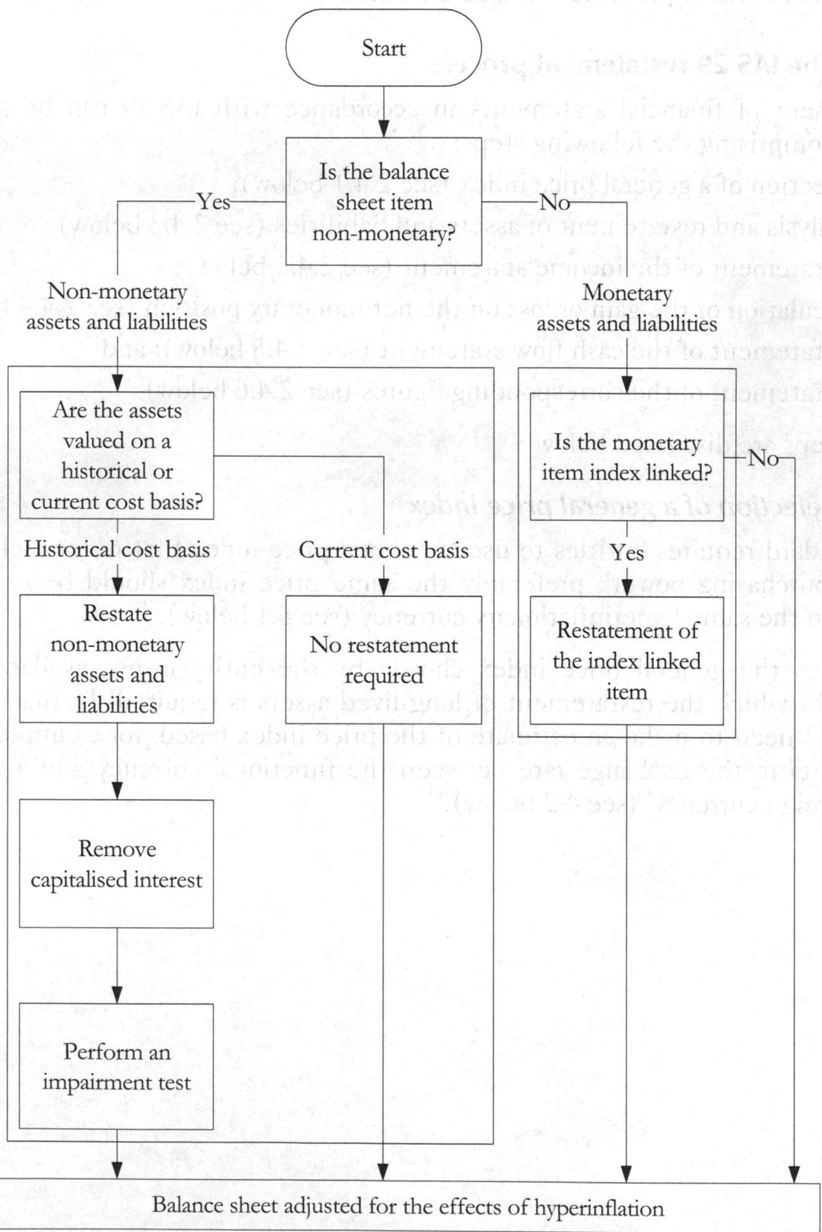

In many hyperinflationary economies, national legislation may require entities to adjust historical cost based financial information in a way that is not in accordance with IAS 29 (for example, national legislation may require entities to adjust the carrying amount of tangible fixed assets by applying a multiplier). Though financial information adjusted in accordance with national legislation is sometimes described as 'current cost' information, it will often not meet the definition of current cost in accordance with the IASB's Framework (see C below).[26] Where this is the case, entities must first determine the real historical cost basis of assets and liabilities before applying the requirements of IAS 29.

The above flowchart does not illustrate the restatement of investees and subsidiaries (see E below), deferred taxation (see F below) and equity (see G below).

A Monetary or non-monetary

The first question to be addressed in the restatement of the balance sheet is which items are monetary and which are not. This is because monetary items normally need not be restated as they are already expressed in the measurement unit current at the balance sheet date. Most balance sheet items are readily classified as either monetary or non-monetary as is shown in the table below:

Monetary items	Non-monetary items
Assets	**Assets**
Cash and cash equivalents	Property, plant and equipment
Debt securities	Intangible assets
Loans	Investments in equity securities
Trade and other receivables	Assets held for sale
	Inventories
	Construction contract work-in-progress
	Prepaid costs
	Investment properties
Liabilities	**Liabilities**
Trade and other payables	Warranty provision
Borrowings	
Other liabilities	
Tax payable	

Classification of items as either monetary or non-monetary is not always straightforward. Monetary items are defined in IAS 29 as 'money held and items to be received or paid in money'.[27] IAS 21 expands somewhat on this definition by defining monetary items as 'units of currency held and assets and liabilities to be received or paid in a fixed or determinable number of units of currency'.[28] The standard elaborates further on this by stating that 'the essential feature of a monetary item is a right to receive (or an obligation to deliver) a fixed or determinable number of units of currency'. Examples given by IAS 21 are pensions and other employee benefits to be paid in cash, provisions that are to be settled in cash, and cash dividends that are recognised as a liability.[29] More obvious examples are cash and bank balances, trade receivables and payables, and loan receivables and payables.

IAS 21 states that 'a contract to receive (or deliver) a variable number of the entity's own equity instruments or a variable amount of assets in which the fair value to be received (or delivered) equals a fixed or determinable number of units of currency is a monetary item.'[30] Although no examples of such contracts are given in IAS 21, it would seem to include those contracts settled in the entity's own equity shares that under IAS 32 – *Financial Instruments: Disclosure and Presentation* – would be presented as financial assets or liabilities.

Conversely, the essential feature of a non-monetary item is the absence of a right to receive (or an obligation to deliver) a fixed or determinable number of units of currency. Examples given by the standard are amounts prepaid for goods and services (e.g. prepaid rent); goodwill; intangible assets; inventories; property, plant and equipment; and provisions that are to be settled by the delivery of a non-monetary asset.[31] IAS 39 – *Financial Instruments: Recognition and Measurement* – indicates that equity instruments that are held as available-for-sale financial assets are non-monetary items.[32] This implies that equity investments in subsidiaries, associates or joint ventures are also non-monetary items.

Even with this guidance there will clearly be a number of situations where the distinction may not be altogether clear (see also Chapter 10 at 3.2.4). Certain assets and liabilities may require careful analysis before they can be classified, and even then their classification is not entirely satisfactory. Examples of items that are not easily classified as either monetary or non-monetary include:

(a) *provisions for liabilities:* these can be monetary, non-monetary or partly monetary. For example, a warranty provision would be:

   (i) entirely monetary when customers only have a right to return the product and obtain a cash refund equal to the amount they originally paid;

   (ii) non-monetary when customers have the right to have any defective product replaced; and

   (iii) partly monetary if customers can choose between a refund and a replacement of the defect product.

   Obviously, classification as either monetary or non-monetary is not very satisfactory in (iii) above. In the spirit of the IAS 29 requirements, part of the provision should be treated as a non-monetary item and the remainder as a monetary item;

(b) *deferred tax assets and liabilities:* characterising these as monetary or non-monetary is fraught with difficulties, which are explained in F below;

(c) *associates and joint ventures:* these are most likely to be at least partly monetary in nature, depending on the degree to which they themselves hold monetary items or non-monetary items. Whatever the case may be, IAS 29 provides separate rules on restatement of investees that do not rely on the distinction between monetary and non-monetary (see E below);

(d) *deposits or progress payments paid or received:* if the payments made are regarded as prepayments or as progress payments then the amounts should be treated as non-monetary items. However, if the payments made are regarded as deposits, and are refundable, then the amounts should probably be treated as monetary items; and

(e) *index-linked assets and liabilities:* classification is particularly difficult when interest rates, lease payments or prices are linked to a price index.

In summary, the practical application of the monetary/non-monetary distinction is beset with difficulties and, after the classification of the more obvious items, judgement on the part of preparers of financial statements is required.[33] Further examples of problem areas in the application of the monetary/non-monetary distinction are discussed in Chapter 10 at 3.2.4.

B Monetary items

Generally, monetary items need not be restated to reflect the effect of inflation. However, monetary assets and liabilities linked by agreement to changes in prices – such as index-linked bonds and loans – should be adjusted in accordance with the underlying agreement to show the repayment obligation in accordance with the terms of the agreement at the balance sheet date.[34] This adjustment should be offset against the gain or loss on the net monetary position (see 2.4.4 below). This type of restatement is in fact not an inflation accounting adjustment, but rather a gain or loss on a financial instrument. Accounting for inflation linked bonds and loans under IAS 39 may well lead to very complicated financial reporting. Depending on the specific wording of the inflation adjustment clause, such contracts may give rise to embedded derivatives and gains or losses will have to be recorded either in income or equity depending on how the instrument is classified for IAS 39 purposes (see Chapter 17 at 5.1.2 C and 5.1.3 B).

C Non-monetary items carried at current cost

Non-monetary items carried at current cost are not restated because they are already expressed in terms of the measuring unit current at the balance sheet date.[35] Current cost is not defined by the standard, but the Framework provides the following definition: 'Assets are carried at the amount of cash or cash equivalents that would have to be paid if the same or an equivalent asset was acquired currently. Liabilities are carried at the undiscounted amount of cash or cash equivalents that would be required to settle the obligation currently'.[36] For the purposes of restating historical cost financial statements, IAS 29 expands this definition by including net realisable value and market value into the concept of 'amounts current at the balance sheet date'.[37] Similarly, non-monetary items valued at fair value are included in IAS 29's current cost concept.

It is important to note that non-monetary items that were revalued at some earlier date, are not necessarily carried at current cost and need to be restated from the date of their latest revaluation.[38]

D Non-monetary items carried at historical cost

Non-monetary items carried at historical cost, or cost less depreciation, are stated at amounts that were current at the date of their acquisition. The restated cost, or cost less depreciation, of those items is calculated as follows:

$$\text{net book value restated for hyperinflation} = \text{historical cost} \times \frac{\text{general price index at the balance sheet date}}{\text{general price index at the date of acquisition}}$$

Application of this formula to property, plant and equipment, investments, inventories of raw materials and merchandise, goodwill, patents, trademarks and similar assets appears to be straightforward, but does require detailed records of their acquisition dates and accurate price indices at those dates.[39] It should be noted though that IAS 29 permits certain approximations as long as the procedures and judgements are consistent from period to period.[40] Where sufficiently detailed records are not available or capable of estimation, IAS 29 suggests that it may be necessary to obtain 'an independent professional assessment of the value of the items as the basis for their restatement' in the first period of application of the standard.[41]

Example 11.2: Restatement of property, plant and equipment

The table below illustrates how the restatement of a non-monetary item (for example, property, plant and equipment) would be calculated in accordance with the requirements of IAS 29.

Net book value of property, plant and equipment	Historical movements	Conversion factor	Restated for hyperinflation	
Opening balance, 1 January	510	2.40	1,224	(a)
– Additions (May)	360	1.80	648	(b)
– Disposals (March)	(120)	2.10	(252)	(c)
– Depreciation	(200)		(448)	(d)
Closing balance, 31 December	550		1,172	(e)

(a) The opening balance is restated by adjusting the historical balance for the increase in the price index between the opening balance sheet date and closing balance sheet date;

(b) The additions are restated for the increase in the price index from May to December;

(c) The disposals are restated for the increase in the price index between the opening balance sheet date and closing balance sheet date;

(d) Depreciation has been recalculated using the cost balance restated for hyperinflation as a starting point. The alternative approach, to restate the depreciation charge by applying the appropriate conversion factor, could be easier to apply but may not be accurate enough when there is a significant level of additions and disposals during the reporting period;

(e) The closing balance is in practice determined by adding up items (a)-(d). Alternatively, the entity could calculate the closing balance by restating the acquisition cost of the individual assets for the change in the price index during the period of ownership.

The calculations described under (a)-(e) all require estimates regarding the general price index at given dates and are sometimes based on averages or best estimates of the actual date of the transaction.

Inventories of finished and partly finished goods should be restated from the dates on which the costs of purchase and of conversion were incurred.[42] This means that the individual components of finished goods should be restated from their respective purchase dates. Similarly, if assembly takes place in several distinct phases, the cost of each of those phases should be restated from the date that the cost was incurred.

When an entity purchases an asset and payment is deferred beyond normal credit terms, it would normally recognise the present value of the cash payment as its cost.[43] When it is impracticable to determine the amount of interest, IAS 29 provides relief by allowing such assets to be restated from the payment date rather than the date of purchase.[44]

In order to arrive at the restated cost of the non-monetary items, the provisional restated cost needs to be adjusted as follows:[45]

	net book value		borrowing costs that		adjustment to
restated costs =	restated for	–	compensate for inflation	–	recoverable
	hyperinflation		capitalised under IAS 23		amount

Capitalisation of all borrowing costs (see Chapter 16) is not considered appropriate under IAS 29 because of the risk of double counting as the entity would both 'restate the capital expenditure financed by borrowing and ... capitalise that part of the borrowing costs that compensates for the inflation during the same period'.[46] Application of the allowed alternative treatment under IAS 23 – *Borrowing Costs*, which requires capitalisation of borrowing costs, is permitted when an entity falls within the scope of IAS 29 if the entity only capitalises borrowing costs to the extent that they do not compensate for inflation. Unfortunately, the standard does not provide any guidance on how an entity should go about determining the component of borrowing costs that compensates for the effects of inflation. In practice many entities operating in hyperinflationary economies have found the IAS 23 benchmark treatment, which requires borrowings costs to be expensed, to be more attractive. However, in March 2007, the IASB issued a revised version of IAS 23 that abolishes the benchmark treatment for financial periods starting on or after 1 January 2009.[47]

It is possible that an IAS 29 inflation adjustment based on the general price index leads to non-monetary assets being stated above their net realisable value. Therefore, IAS 29 requires that 'the restated amount of a non-monetary item is reduced, in accordance with appropriate International Financial Reporting Standards, when it exceeds the amount recoverable from the item's future use (including sale or other disposal)'.[48] This requirement should be taken to mean that overstated inventories should be written down to net realisable value under IAS 2 – *Inventories* – and that any overstatement of non-monetary assets not within the scope of IAS 39 should be calculated in accordance with IAS 36 – *Impairment of Assets*.

The following Example 11.3, illustrates how, after the entity has restated the historical cost based carrying amount of property, plant and equipment by applying the general price index, it can adjust the net book value restated for hyperinflation:

Example 11.3: Borrowing costs and net realisable value adjustments

After the entity has restated the historical cost based carrying amount of property, plant and equipment by applying the general price index, it needs to adjust the net book value restated for hyperinflation as follows:

Net book value restated for hyperinflation		1,725	
Borrowing costs capitalised at historical cost under IAS 23	42		
Borrowing costs that compensated for inflation	(30)		
Borrowing costs permitted to be capitalised under IAS 29	12		
Borrowing costs that compensated for inflation	(30)		
Relevant conversion factor for the borrowing costs	2.10 ×		
		(63)	(a)
Net book value restated for hyperinflation and after adjustment of capitalised borrowing costs		1,662	
Net book value restated for hyperinflation and after adjustment of capitalised borrowing costs	1,662		
Amount recoverable from the item's future use	1,750		
	(88)		
Adjustment to lower recoverable amount		–	(b)
Carrying amount restated under IAS 29		1,662	

(a) The borrowing costs capitalised in the original historical cost financial statements are reversed, as they are not permitted under IAS 29;

(b) To the extent that the 'net book value restated for hyperinflation and after adjustment of capitalised borrowing costs' exceeds the 'amount recoverable from the item's future use', the restated amount should be reduced to the lower 'amount recoverable from the item's future use'.

E *Restatement of investees and subsidiaries*

IAS 29 provides separate rules for the restatement of investees (i.e. associates and joint ventures) that are accounted for under the equity method. If the investee itself operates in the same currency, the entity should restate the balance sheet and income statement of the investee in accordance with the requirements of IAS 29 in order to calculate its share of the investee's net assets and results of operations. If the restated financial statements of the investee are expressed in a foreign currency – that is either hyperinflationary or a non-hyperinflationary – they should be translated at the closing rate.[49] IAS 21 contains a similar provision that requires that all current year amounts related to an entity (i.e. investee), whose functional currency is the currency of a hyperinflationary economy, to be translated at the closing rate at the date of the most recent balance sheet (see Chapter 10 at 2.7.1 B).[50]

If a parent that reports in the currency of a hyperinflationary economy has a subsidiary that also reports in the currency of a hyperinflationary economy, then the financial statements of that subsidiary must first be 'restated by applying a general price index of the country in whose currency it reports before they are included in the consolidated financial statements issued by its parent'.[51] IAS 21 further clarifies that all current year amounts related to an entity (i.e. subsidiary), whose functional currency is the currency of a hyperinflationary economy, should be translated at the closing rate at the date of the most recent balance sheet (see Chapter 10 at 2.7.1 B).[52]

If a parent that reports in the currency of a hyperinflationary economy has a subsidiary that reports in a currency that is not hyperinflationary, the financial statements of that subsidiary should be translated in accordance with paragraph 39 of IAS 21 (see Chapter 10 at 2.7.1 A).[53]

Finally, IAS 29 requires that when 'financial statements with different reporting dates are consolidated, all items, whether non-monetary or monetary, ... be restated into the measuring unit current at the date of the consolidated financial statements'.[54]

F Calculation of deferred taxation

Determining whether deferred tax assets and liabilities are monetary or non-monetary is difficult because:

- deferred taxation could be seen as a valuation adjustment that is either monetary or non-monetary depending on the asset or liability it relates to, but
- it could also be argued that any deferred taxation payable or receivable in the very near future is almost identical to current tax payable and receivable. Therefore, at least the short-term portion of deferred taxation, if payable or receivable, should be treated as if it were monetary.

There continues to be a difference of opinion as to whether deferred taxation is monetary or non-monetary.[55] In any event, the debate has been settled for practical purposes because:

- IAS 12 – *Income Taxes* – requires deferred taxation in the closing balance sheet for the year to be calculated based on the difference between the carrying amount and the tax base of assets and liabilities, irrespective of the monetary/non-monetary distinction; and
- IFRIC 7 requires an entity to remeasure the deferred tax items in any comparative period in accordance with IAS 12 after it has restated the nominal carrying amounts of its non-monetary items at the date of the opening balance sheet of the reporting period by applying the measuring unit at that date. These remeasured deferred tax items are then restated for the change in the measuring unit from the date of the opening balance sheet of the reporting period to the closing balance sheet date of that period.[56]

The following example, which is based on the illustrative example in IFRIC 7, shows how an entity should restate its deferred taxation in the comparative period.[57]

Example 11.4: Restatement of deferred taxation

Entity A owns a building that it acquired in December 2002. The carrying amount and tax base of the building, and the deferred tax liability are as follows:

Before IAS 29 restatement	2004	2003
Building (unrestated)	€300	€400
Tax basis	€200	€333
Tax rate	30%	30%
Deferred tax liability:		
(€300 – €200) × 30% =	€30	
(€400 – €333) × 30% =		€20

Entity A has identified the existence of hyperinflation in 2004 and therefore applies IAS 29 from the beginning of 2004. Entity A will use the following general price index and conversion factors to restate its financial statements:

	General price index
December 2002	95
December 2003	135
December 2004	223

Before adoption of IFRIC 7 it was not clear from IAS 29 how deferred tax in the comparative period should be restated. A common method for restating deferred taxation, which is no longer allowed under IFRS 7, was to treat it as a monetary item and adjust the balance for hyperinflation during the year, which would result in a restated balance of €20 × 223 ÷ 135 = €33. The table below shows the method prescribed by IFRS 7:

	2004	2003
Building (unrestated)	€300	€400
Building (restated in 2004 financial statements):		
€300×(223 ÷ 95) =	€704	
€400×(223 ÷ 95) =		€939
Building (restated in 2003 financial statements):		
€400 × (135 ÷ 95) =		€568 (a)
Tax basis	€200	€333 (b)
Tax rate	30%	30%
Deferred tax liability (restated in 2004 financial statements):		
(€704 – €200) × 30% =	151	
(€568 – €333) × 30% × (223 ÷ 135) =		117

Entity A measures the temporary difference at the end of 2003 by comparing (a) the restated carrying amount of the building in 2003 accounts to (b) its tax base at that date. The temporary difference calculated in that manner is then multiplied by the applicable tax rate and the resulting amount is then adjusted for the hyperinflation during 2004, resulting in a deferred tax liability of 117.

After entity A has restated its financial statements, all corresponding figures in the financial statements for a subsequent reporting period, including deferred tax items, are restated by applying the change in the measuring unit for that subsequent reporting period only to the restated financial statements for the previous reporting period.[58]

IAS 29 refers to IAS 12 for guidance on the calculation of deferred taxation by entities operating in hyperinflationary economies.[59] IAS 12 recognises that IAS 29 restatements of assets and liabilities may give rise to temporary differences when equivalent adjustments are not allowed for tax purposes.[60] Where IAS 29 adjustments give rise to temporary differences, IAS 12 requires the following accounting treatment:

'(1) the deferred taxation is charged in the income statement; and

(2) if, in addition to the restatement, the non-monetary assets are also revalued, the deferred tax relating to the revaluation is charged to equity and the deferred tax relating to the restatement is charged in the income statement'.[61]

For example, deferred taxation arising on *revaluation* of property, plant and equipment should be recognised in equity, just as it would be if the entity were not operating in a hyperinflationary economy. On the other hand, *restatement* in accordance with IAS 29 of property, plant and equipment that is measured at historical cost should be recognised in the income statement. Thus the treatment of deferred taxation related to non-monetary assets valued at historical cost and those that are revalued, is consistent with the general requirements of IAS 12.

G Restatement of equity

At the beginning of the first period when an entity applies IAS 29, because the economy in which it is operating has become hyperinflationary, it should restate the components of owners' equity as follows:[62]

- the components of owners' equity, except retained earnings and any revaluation surplus, are restated by applying a general price index from the dates the components were contributed or otherwise arose;
- any revaluation surplus that arose in previous periods is eliminated; and
- restated retained earnings are derived from all the other amounts in the restated balance sheet.

At the end of the first period and in subsequent periods, all components of owners' equity are restated by applying a general price index from the beginning of the period or the date of contribution, if later.[63] It may seem anomalous that the restatement of a historical cost balance sheet for hyperinflationary conditions may possibly result in an increase in retained earnings. However, this may well be the effect of the transfer of revaluation reserve to retained earnings implicit in the second bullet point above. Finally, elimination of the revaluation surplus is only required when IAS 29 is first applied. Subsequent revaluations may therefore give rise to a revaluation surplus within equity.

Though IAS 29 provides guidance on the restatement of assets, liabilities and individual components of shareholders' equity, it should be noted that national laws and regulations with which the entity needs to comply might not permit such revaluations. This can mean that IAS 29 may require restatement of distributable reserves, but that from the legal point of view in the jurisdiction concerned, those same reserves remain unchanged. That is, it is possible that 'restated retained earnings' under IAS 29 will not all be legally distributable.

Example 11.5: Restatement of equity

The table below shows the effect of a hypothetical IAS 29 restatement on individual components of equity. Issued share capital and share premium increase by applying the general price index, the revaluation reserve is eliminated as required, and retained earnings is the balancing figure derived from all other amounts in the restated balance sheet.

	Amounts before restatement	Amounts after IAS 29 restatement	Components of equity under national law
Issued capital and share premium	1,500	3,150	1,500
Revaluation reserve	800	–	800
Retained earnings	350	1,600	350
Total equity	2,650	4,750	2,650

A user of the financial statements of the entity might get the impression, based on the information restated in accordance with IAS 29, that distributable reserves have increased from 350 to 1,600. However, if national law does not permit revaluation of assets, liabilities and components of equity then distributable reserves remain unchanged.

Users of financial statements restated under IAS 29 may for that reason be misled about the extent to which components of equity are distributable. Entities reporting under IAS 29 should therefore disclose the extent to which components of equity are distributable where this is not obvious from the financial statements. In our view it is important for entities to give supplementary information in the circumstances where the IAS 29 adjustments have produced large apparently distributable reserves that are in fact not distributable.

Because of its global constituency, the IASB's standards cannot deal with specific national legal requirements relating to a legal entity's equity. Therefore, instead of prescribing an accounting treatment for individual components of equity, we consider that the IASB would be better advised to recognise the wide variety in national legislation, and prescribe disclosure requirements that ensure users of financial statements are not misled.

2.4.3 Restatement of the income statement

IAS 29 requires that all items in historical cost based income statements be expressed in terms of the measuring unit current at the balance sheet date.[64] The standard contains a similar requirement for current cost based income statements, because the underlying transactions or events are recorded at current cost at the time they occurred rather than in the measuring unit current at the balance sheet date.[65] Therefore, all amounts in the income statement need to be restated as follows:

$$\text{restated amount} = \text{amount before restatement} \times \frac{\text{general price index at the balance sheet date}}{\text{general price index when the underlying income or expenses were initially recorded}}$$

Actually performing the above calculation on a real set of financial statements is often difficult because an entity would need to keep a very detailed record of when it entered into transactions and when it incurred expenses. Instead of using the exact price index for a transaction it may be more practical to use an average price index that approximates the actual rate at the date of the transaction. For example, an average rate for a week or a month might be used for all transactions occurring during that period. However, it must be stressed that if price indices fluctuate significantly, the use of an average for the period is inappropriate.

There may be items in the income statement (e.g. interest income and expense) that comprise an element that is intended to compensate for the effect of hyperinflation. However, even those items need to be restated as IAS 29 specifically requires that 'all amounts need to be restated' (see 4.5 below).[66]

Example 11.6 illustrates how an entity might, for example, restate its revenue to the measuring unit current at the balance sheet date. A similar calculation would work well for other items in the income statement, with the exception of:

(a) depreciation and amortisation charges which are often easier to restate by using the cost balance restated for hyperinflation as a starting point;

(b) deferred taxation which should be based on the temporary differences between the carrying amount and tax base of assets and liabilities, the restated carrying amount of balance sheet items, and the underlying tax base of those items; and

(c) the net monetary gain or loss which results from the IAS 29 restatements (see 2.4.4 below).

Example 11.6: Restatement of historical cost income statement

An entity would restate its revenue for the period ending 31 December 2007, when the general price index was 2,880, as shown in the table below.

	General price index	Conversion factor	Revenue before restatement	Restated revenue
31 January 2007	1,315	(2,880 ÷ 1,315) = 2.19	40	87.6
28 February 2007	1,345	(2,880 ÷ 1,345) = 2.14	35	74.9
31 March 2007	1,371	etc. = 2.10	45	94.5
30 April 2007	1,490	1.93	45	87.0
31 May 2007	1,600	1.80	65	117.0
30 June 2007	1,846	1.56	70	109.2
31 July 2007	1,923	1.50	70	104.8
31 August 2007	2,071	1.39	65	90.4
30 September 2007	2,163	1.33	75	99.9
31 October 2007	2,511	1.15	75	86.0
30 November 2007	2,599	1.11	80	88.6
31 December 2007	2,880	1.00	80	80.0
			745	1,119.9

A similar calculation can be made for other items in the income statement. Inevitably, in practice there is some approximation because of the assumptions that the entity is required to make, for example:

(a) the use of weighted averages rather than more detailed calculations; and

(b) assumptions as to the timing of the underlying transactions (e.g. the calculation above assumes the revenues for the month are earned on the final day of the month, which is not realistic).

2.4.4 Calculation of the gain or loss on the net monetary position

In theory, hyperinflation only affects the value of money and monetary items and does not affect the value, as distinct from the price, of non-monetary items. Therefore, any gain or loss because of hyperinflation will be the gain or loss on the net monetary position of the entity. By arranging the items in an ordinary balance sheet, it can be shown that the monetary position minus the non-monetary position is always equal to zero:

	Total	Monetary items	Non-monetary items
Monetary assets	280	280	
Non-monetary assets	170		170
Monetary liabilities	(200)	(200)	
Non-monetary liabilities	(110)		(110)
Assets minus liabilities	140		
Shareholders' equity	(140)		(140)
Net position	0	80	(80)

Theoretically, the gain or loss on the net monetary position can be calculated by applying the general price index to the entity's monetary assets and liabilities. This would require the entity to determine its net monetary position on a daily basis, which would be entirely impracticable given the difficulties in making the monetary/non-monetary distinction (see 2.4.2 A above). The standard therefore allows the gain or loss on the net monetary position to 'be estimated by applying the change in a general price index to the weighted average for the period of the difference between monetary assets and monetary liabilities'.[67] Due care should be exercised in estimating the gain or loss on the net monetary position, as a calculation based on averages for the period (or monthly averages) can be unreliable if addressed without accurate consideration of the pattern of hyperinflation and the volatility of the net monetary position.

However, as shown in the above table, any restatement of the non-monetary items must be met by an equal restatement of the monetary items. Therefore, in preparing financial statements it is more practical to assume that the gain or loss on the net monetary position is exactly the reverse of the restatement of the non-monetary items. A stand-alone calculation of the net gain or loss can, however, be used to verify the reasonableness of the restatement of the non-monetary items.

The gain or loss on the net monetary position should be included in net income and disclosed separately. It may be helpful to present it together with items that are also associated with the net monetary position such as 'interest income and expense, and foreign exchange differences related to invested or borrowed funds'.[68]

2.4.5 Restatement of the cash flow statement

The standard also requires that all items in the cash flow statement be expressed in terms of the measuring unit current at the balance sheet date.[69] This is a most difficult requirement to fulfil in practice.

An understanding of the complication inherent in this requirement of IAS 29 becomes apparent when the restatement of a cash flow is actually contemplated. IAS 7 – *Cash Flow Statements* – requires the following information to be presented:[70]

(a) cash flows from operating activities, which are the principal revenue-producing activities of the entity and other activities that are not investing or financing activities;

(b) cash flows from investing activities, which are the acquisition and disposal of long-term assets and other investments not included in cash equivalents; and

(c) cash flows from financing activities, which are activities that result in changes in the size and composition of the equity capital and borrowings of the entity.

In effect IAS 29 requires restatement of most items in a cash flow statement, implying that therefore the actual cash flows at the time of the transactions will be different from the numbers presented in the cash flow statement itself. However, not all items are restated using the same method and many of the restatements are based on estimates. For example, items in the income statement are to be restated using an estimate of the general price index at the time that the revenues were earned and the costs incurred. Unavoidably this will give rise to some inconsistencies. Similarly, the restatement of balance sheet items will give rise to discrepancies because some items are not easily classified as either monetary or non-monetary. This raises the question how an entity should classify the monetary gain or loss relating to a balance sheet item in its cash flow statement.

It is not clear from IAS 29 how a monetary gain or loss should be presented in the cash flow statements. In practice different approaches have been adopted such as:

(a) presenting the effect of inflation on operating, investing and financing cash flows separately for each of these activities and present the net monetary gain or loss as a reconciling item in the cash and cash equivalents reconciliation;

(b) presenting the monetary gain or loss on cash and cash equivalents and the effect of inflation on operating, investing and financing cash flows as one number; and

(c) attributing the effect of inflation on operating, investing and financing cash flows to the underlying item and presenting the monetary gain or loss on cash and cash equivalents separately.

Irrespective of the method chosen, users of cash flow statements prepared in the currency of a hyperinflationary economy should be mindful of the fact that figures presented in the cash flow statement may have been restated in accordance with IAS 29 and may differ from the actual underlying cash flows.

2.4.6 *Restatement of the corresponding figures*

The standard requires that all financial information be presented in terms of the measurement unit current at the balance sheet date, therefore:[71]

- corresponding figures for the previous reporting period, whether they were based on a historical cost approach or a current cost approach, are restated by applying a general price index; and
- information that is disclosed in respect of earlier periods is also expressed in terms of the measuring unit current at the end of the reporting period.

2.5 Interim reporting

Appendix B to IAS 34 – *Interim Financial Reporting* – requires that 'interim financial reports in hyperinflationary economies are prepared by the same principles as at financial year end'. This means that the financial statements must be stated in terms of the measuring unit current at the end of the interim period and that the gain or loss on the net monetary position is included in net income.[72] The comparative financial information reported for prior periods must also be restated to the current measuring unit.[73] An entity that reports quarterly information must restate the comparative balance sheets and income statements each quarter.

In restating its financial information an entity is not allowed to 'annualise the recognition of the gain or loss' on the net monetary position or to 'use an estimated annual inflation rate in preparing an interim financial report in a hyperinflationary economy'.[74]

2.6 Economies becoming hyperinflationary

When the functional currency of an entity becomes hyperinflationary it must start applying IAS 29. The standard requires that the financial statements and any information in respect of earlier periods 'should be stated in terms of the measuring unit current at the balance sheet date'.[75] The standard does not explicitly state:[76]

(a) whether restatement should be fully retrospective, i.e. items should be restated from the date of their acquisition or last revaluation; or

(b) whether restatements should be prospective from the date that the economy became hyperinflationary.

IFRIC considered that the wording of paragraph 4 of IAS 29 was not sufficiently clear and that there was therefore 'uncertainty whether the opening balance sheet at the beginning of the reporting period should be restated to reflect changes in prices before that date'.[77] IFRIC 7 removes this ambiguity by requiring that items should be restated fully retrospectively. In the first year in which the entity identifies the existence of hyperinflation the requirements of IAS 29 should be applied as if the economy had always been hyperinflationary. The opening balance sheet at the beginning of the earliest period presented in the financial statements should be restated as follows:[78]

- non-monetary items measured at historical cost should be restated to reflect the effect of inflation from the date the assets were acquired and the liabilities were incurred or assumed; and
- non-monetary items carried at amounts current at dates other than those of acquisition or incurrence should be restated to reflect the effect of inflation from the dates those carrying amounts were determined.

What is less obvious is how an entity (a parent), which does not operate in a hyperinflationary economy, should account for the restatement of an entity (a subsidiary) that operates in an economy that became hyperinflationary in the current reporting period when incorporating it within its consolidated financial statements. This issue has been clarified by paragraph 42(b) of IAS 21 which specifically prohibits restatement of comparative figures when the reporting currency is not hyperinflationary. This means that when the financial statements of a hyperinflationary subsidiary are translated into the non-hyperinflationary reporting currency of the parent, the comparative amounts are not adjusted.

2.7 Economies ceasing to be hyperinflationary

When an economy ceases to be hyperinflationary, entities should discontinue preparation and presentation of financial statements in accordance with IAS 29. The amounts expressed in the measuring unit current at the end of the previous reporting period will be treated as the deemed cost of the items in the balance sheet.[79]

Determining when a currency stops being hyperinflationary is not easy in practice. It is important to review trends, not just at the balance sheet date but also subsequently. In addition, consistency demands that the financial statements do not unnecessarily 'yo-yo' in and out of a hyperinflationary presentation, where a more careful judgement would have avoided it.

It is possible or even likely that an economy becomes hyperinflationary sometime during an entity's financial year. Therefore, it would be reasonable and sensible that as soon as an entity determines that it is operating in hyperinflation it starts preparing its interim reports using the principles underlying IAS 29. The standard should be applied from the beginning of the reporting period in which the existence of hyperinflation is identified.[80] Equally, it is possible that an economy ceases to be hyperinflationary during the year. If an entity concludes that the economy ceases to be hyperinflationary during the year, the standard requires that the entity should stop applying IAS 29 at that point. It should be noted that, an amalgamation of interim periods during which IAS 29 was applied with those where it was not, may result in financial statements that are difficult to interpret.

2.8 Translation to a different presentation currency

An entity is permitted to present its financial statements in any presentation currency it chooses. However, a change in presentation currency will not alter the entity's functional currency or the requirement to apply IAS 29.

If an entity, whose functional currency is hyperinflationary, wants to translate its financial statements into a different presentation currency it must first restate its financial statements in accordance with IAS 29 and then apply the following procedures under IAS 21:

'(a) all amounts (i.e. assets, liabilities, equity items, income and expenses, including comparatives) shall be translated at the closing rate at the date of the most recent balance sheet, except that

(b) when amounts are translated into the currency of a non-hyperinflationary economy, comparative amounts shall be those that were presented as current year amounts in the relevant prior year financial statements (i.e. not adjusted for subsequent changes in the price level or subsequent changes in exchange rates).'[81]

In other words, when an entity that applies IAS 29 translates its financial statements into a non-hyperinflationary presentation currency the comparative information should not be restated under IAS 29, instead IAS 21 should be applied (i.e. the comparative amounts should be those that were presented as current year amounts in the prior period). For a more detailed discussion of these requirements reference is made to Chapter 10 at 2.7.1 B.

When the economy ceases to be hyperinflationary, and restatement in accordance with IAS 29 is no longer required, an entity uses the amounts restated to the price level at the date it ceased restating its financial statements as the historical costs for translation into the presentation currency.[82]

2.9 Disclosures

IAS 29 requires that entities should disclose the following information when they apply the provisions of the standard:[83]

(a) the fact that the financial statements and the corresponding figures for previous periods have been restated for the changes in the general purchasing power of the functional currency and, as a result, are stated in terms of the measuring unit current at the balance sheet date;

(b) whether the financial statements are based on a historical cost approach or a current cost approach; and

(c) the identity and level of the price index at the balance sheet date and the movement in the index during the current and the previous reporting period.

An entity that applies IFRIC 7 to financial statements for a period beginning before 1 March 2006 should disclose that fact.[84]

It should be noted that disclosure of financial information that is restated under IAS 29 as a supplement to unrestated financial information is not permitted. This is to prevent entities from giving the historical cost based financial information greater prominence than the information that is restated under IAS 29. The standard also discourages separate presentation of unrestated financial information, but does not explicitly prohibit it.[85] However, such unrestated financial statements would not be in accordance with IFRS.

An entity that is required (for example by local tax authorities or stock exchange regulators) to present unrestated financial statements needs to ensure that the IFRS financial statements are perceived to be the main financial statements rather than mere supplemental information. This means, for example, that an entity reporting under IAS 29 should refrain from presenting historical cost information on the face of the primary financial statements because this would not result in a fair presentation as required by paragraph 13 of IAS 1.

Tofaş Türk Otomobil Fabrikası discloses that they operate in a hyperinflationary economy and make the appropriate disclosures:

Extract 11.1: Tofaş Türk Otomobil Fabrikası A.Ş. (2005)

CONSOLIDATED CASH FLOW STATEMENT [extract]
For the year ended December 31, 2005
(Currency – Thousands of YTL in equivalent purchasing power at December 31, 2005, unless otherwise indicated)

…		
Monetary loss on cash and cash equivalents	(14,761)	(14,574)
Net change in cash and cash equivalents	166,744	(19,675)
Cash and cash equivalents at the beginning of the year	291,982	311,657
Cash and cash equivalents at the end of the year	**458,726**	**291,982**

2. Summary of significant accounting policies [extract]

Measurement Currency and Reporting Currency

IAS 29 requires that financial statements prepared in the currency of a hyperinflationary economy be stated in terms of the measuring unit current at the balance sheet date and the corresponding figures for previous periods be restated in the same terms. Determining whether an economy is hyperinflationary in accordance with IAS 29 requires judgment as the standard does not establish an absolute rate, instead it considers the following characteristics of the economic environment of a country to be strong indicators of the existence of hyperinflation: (a) the general population prefers to keep its wealth in non monetary assets or in a relatively stable currency; amounts of local currency held are immediately invested to maintain purchasing power, (b) the general population regards monetary amounts not in terms of local currency but in terms of a relatively stable currency; prices may be quoted in that currency, (c) sales and purchases on credit take place at prices that compensate for the expected loss of purchasing power during the credit period, even if the period is short, (d) interest rates, wages and prices are linked to a price index and (e) the cumulative inflation rate over three years is approaching, or exceeds 100%. Although as of December 31, 2005, the three-year cumulative rate has been 35.6% (December 31, 2004 – 69.7 %) based on the **Turkish countrywide wholesale price index** published by the State Institute of Statistics, considering the economic characteristics indicated above, IAS 29 is continued to be applied in the preparation of the current period financial statements. Such index and conversion factors as of the end of the three year period ended December 31, 2005 are given below:

Dates	Index	Conversion Factors
December 31, 2002	6,478.8	1.356
December 31, 2003	7,382.1	1.190
December 31, 2004	8,403.8	1.045
December 31, 2005	8,785.7	1.000

The main guidelines for the above mentioned restatement are as follows:

- The consolidated financial statements of prior year, including monetary assets and liabilities reported therein, which were previously reported in terms of the measuring unit current at the end of that year are restated in their entirety to the measuring unit current at December 31, 2005.
- Monetary assets and liabilities reported in the consolidated balance sheet as of December 31, 2005 are not restated because they are already expressed in terms of the monetary unit current at that balance sheet date.
- The inflation adjusted issued share capital was derived by indexing cash contributions, transfers from statutory retained earnings and income from sale of investments and property, transferred to issued share capital from the date they were contributed.
- Non-monetary assets and liabilities which are not carried at amounts current at the balance sheet date and other components of equity (except for the statutory revaluation adjustment which is eliminated) are restated by applying the relevant conversion factors.
- The effect of general inflation on the net monetary position is included in the income statement as monetary gain / (loss).
- All items in the income statement are restated by applying appropriate average conversion factors with the exception of depreciation, amortization, gain or loss on disposal of non-monetary assets.

Restatement of balance sheet and income statement items through the use of a general price index and relevant conversion factors does not necessarily mean that the Group could realize or settle the same values of assets and liabilities as indicated in the consolidated balance sheets. Similarly, it does not necessarily mean that the Group could return or settle the same values of equity to its shareholders.

10. Property, plant and equipment (PP&E), net [extract]

	Land, Land Improvements and Buildings
At January 1, 2005, net of accumulated depreciation	103,956
Additions	1,439
Disposals	(14,392)
Transfers	–
Depreciation charge for the period	(6,518)
Accumulated depreciation of disposals	14,376
At December 31, 2005, net of accumulated depreciation	**98,861**

15. Warranty provisions

Movements in the warranty provision for the years ended 2005 and 2004 are as follows:

	2005	2004
January 1	**46,238**	25,484
Amounts utilised	**(20,934)**	(15,674)
Current year provision	**30,141**	40,662
Monetary gain	**(2,100)**	(4,234)
December 31	**53,345**	46,238

Tofaş Türk Otomobil Fabrikası is required under IAS 29 to restate its comparative amounts of property, plant and equipment and therefore does not present the impact of the hyperinflation adjustments in the movement schedule. While Carlsberg, which has a number of subsidiaries that operate in countries with hyperinflationary economies, is not permitted to restate the comparative amounts and therefore reports a reconciling item for the effect of hyperinflation adjustments.

Extract 11.2: Carlsberg A/S (2005)

Accounting policies [extract]

Prior to translation of the financial statements of foreign entities in countries with hyperinflation, the statements (including comparative figures) are inflation-adjusted for changes in purchasing power in the local currency. Inflation adjustment is based on relevant price indexes at the balance sheet date.

Note 15 Property, plant and equipment [extract]

DKK million	2005 Land and buildings
Cost:	
Cost at 1 January 2005	13,187
Acquisition of subsidiaries	67
Divestment of subsidiaries	–
Additions during the year	167
Disposals during the year	–1,092
Currency translation adjustments etc.	315
Transfers to assets held for sale	–260
Transfers	221
Effect of hyperinflation adjustments	55
Cost at 31 December 2005	12,660

3 TRANSITIONAL ARRANGEMENTS AND FIRST-TIME ADOPTION ISSUES

The requirements of IAS 29 must be observed initially in the following circumstances:

- First-time IFRS adopters that operate in hyperinflationary economies need to apply IAS 29 immediately (see 3.2 below); and
- When economies become hyperinflationary existing IFRS reporting entities must start applying IAS 29 (see 2.6 above).

3.1 Transition

IAS 29 became effective 'for financial statements covering periods beginning on or after 1 January 1990' and did not provide for a transitional regime for existing IFRS reporting companies.[86]

IFRIC 7 should be applied for annual periods beginning on or after 1 March 2006, though earlier application is encouraged (see 2.9 above).[87]

3.2 First-time adoption of IFRS

IFRS 1 – *First-time Adoption of International Financial Reporting Standards* – requires full retrospective application of IAS 29 'to any periods during which the economy of the functional currency or presentation currency was hyperinflationary'.[88] As discussed at 2.6 above, this requires that non-monetary items measured at historical cost should be restated to reflect the effect of inflation from the date the assets were acquired and the liabilities were incurred or assumed. However, the option to use the fair value of an item of property, plant and equipment at the date of transition to IFRS (see Chapter 5 at 2.5), which is also available to entities operating in hyperinflationary economies, may be the most practical way of reducing the burden of complying with the standard's requirements.[89]

The implementation guidance to IFRS 1 states that 'if an entity elects to use the exemptions in paragraphs 16-19 of the IFRS, it applies IAS 29 to periods after the date for which the revalued amount or fair value was determined.'[90] The basis for conclusions to IFRS 1 makes clear that the IASB expects that items not covered by the IFRS 1 exemptions to be restated under IAS 29.[91]

4 PRACTICAL PROBLEMS

4.1 Selecting a general price index

Selecting an appropriate general price index is fraught with difficulties in many cases. IAS 29 requires entities to use a general price index that reflects changes in general purchasing power.[92] It is generally accepted practice to use a Consumer Price Index (CPI) for this purpose, unless that index is clearly flawed. National statistical offices in most countries issue several price indices that potentially could be used for the purposes of IAS 29. Important characteristics of a good general price index include the following:

- a wide range of goods and services has been included in the price index;
- continuity and consistency of measurement techniques and underlying assumptions;
- free from bias;
- frequently updated; and
- available for a long period.

The entity should use the above criteria to choose the most reliable and most readily available general price index and use that index consistently. It is important that the index selected is representative of the real position of the hyperinflationary currency concerned.

4.2 General price index not available for all periods

IAS 29 requires an entity to make an estimate of the price index if the general price index is not available for all periods for which the restatement of long-lived assets is required. The entity could base the estimate, for example, on the movements in the exchange rate between the functional currency and a relatively stable foreign currency.[93] It should be noted that this method is only acceptable if the currency of the hyperinflationary economy is freely exchangeable, i.e. not subject to currency controls and 'official' exchange rates. Entities should be mindful that, especially in the short term, the exchange rate may fluctuate significantly in response to factors other than changes in the domestic price level.

Entities could use a similar approach when they cannot find a general price index that meets its minimum criteria for reliability (e.g. because the national statistical office in the hyperinflationary economy may be subject to significant political bias). However, this would only be acceptable if all available general price indices are fatally flawed.

4.3 Inventories

To restate the balance sheet under IAS 29 an entity needs to exercise judgement and make assumptions regarding:

- whether balance sheet items are monetary or non-monetary in nature;
- the date of acquisition of items; and
- the level of the general price index at the date of acquisition.

Given the large number of transactions affecting an entity's inventory position, it is often a challenge to determine the date of acquisition of inventory. Therefore, entities commonly approximate the ageing of inventories by basing it on inventory turnover. In a similar vein, the level of the general price index at the date of acquisition is often determined at the average level for the month because an up-to-date price index is not available for each day of the month. Determining the appropriate level of the general price index can be particularly challenging when the price index is updated relatively infrequently and the entity's business is highly seasonal.

IAS 29 requires restatement of inventory by applying a general price index, which could result in an overvaluation when the price of inventory items increases at a different rate from the general price index. At the end of each period it is therefore essential to ensure that items of inventory are not valued in excess of their net realisable value.

4.4 Investees accounted for under the equity method

IAS 29 requires restatement of such investees that also operate in hyperinflationary economies 'in accordance with this Standard in order to calculate the investor's share of its net assets and results of operations'.[94] The standard specifically requires that the balance sheet and income statement of an investee to be restated in accordance with IAS 29 in order to calculate the investor's share of the net assets and results of operations, i.e. the standard does not permit the investment in the investee to be treated as a single indivisible item for the purposes of the IAS 29 restatement.

Restating the financial statements of an associate before application of the equity method will often be difficult because the investor may not have access to the detailed information required. The fact that the investor can exercise significant influence or has joint control over an investee often does not mean that the investor has unrestricted access to the investee's books and records at all times.

4.5 Restatement of interest and exchange differences

A common question is whether an entity should restate exchange differences under IAS 29, because the standard considers that 'foreign exchange differences related to invested or borrowed funds ... are also associated with the net monetary position'.[95] Nevertheless, the standard requires that 'all items in the income statement are expressed in terms of the measuring unit current at the balance sheet date. Therefore all amounts need to be restated by applying the change in the general price index from the dates when the items of income and expenses were initially recorded in the financial statements'.[96] Interest and exchange differences should therefore be restated for the effect of inflation as all the other items in the income statement and be presented on a gross basis though 'it may be helpful if they are presented together with the gain or loss on net monetary position in the income statement'.[97]

References

1 Framework, *Framework for the Preparation and Presentation of Financial Statements*, para. 104.
2 IAS 29, *Financial Reporting in Hyperinflationary Economies*, para. 6.
3 It should be noted that the definition of hyperinflation used in financial reporting does not have a solid theoretical basis. In fact, economists researching hyperinflation often use Cagan's definition which defines hyperinflation as consumer price increases of more than 50% per month. International Monetary Fund, *World Economic Outlook – Fiscal Policy and Macroeconomic Stability*, May 2001. Cagan, Phillip. *op. cit.*, 'The Monetary Dynamics of Hyperinflation.' In Studies in the Quantity Theory of Money, ed. by Milton Friedman, pp. 25-117. Chicago: University of Chicago Press.
4 Based on information published by the AICPA, *Highlights*, AICPA International Practices Task Force, 24 April 2007. The Dominican Republic is no longer considered to be hyperinflationary by the AICPA IPTF from 15 March 2007 onwards. Countries that have a 'three-year cumulative inflation rate in excess of 70%' or 'significant inflation in the current or prior year' are Eritrea, Guinea, Haiti, Iran, Venezuela and Zambia.
5 IAS 21, *The Effects of Changes in Foreign Exchange Rates*, paras. 8-14.
6 IAS 21, para. 14.
7 IFRIC D5, *Applying IAS 29 Financial Reporting in Hyperinflationary Economies for the first time*.
8 IFRIC 7, *Applying the Restatement Approach under IAS 29 Financial Reporting in Hyperinflationary Economies*.
9 IAS 21, para. 8.
10 SIC-19, *Reporting Currency – Measurement and Presentation of Financial Statements under IAS 21 and IAS 29*, SIC, November 2000 (superseded December 2003).
11 IAS 21, para. IN6.
12 IAS 21, para. 8.
13 IAS 21 (revised 1993), *The Effects of Changes in Foreign Exchange Rates*, IASB, December 1993, para. 7.
14 IAS 21 (revised 1993), para. 4.
15 IAS 21, para. IN6.
16 IAS 29, para. 2.
17 IAS 29, paras. 8-9.
18 IAS 29, para. 11.
19 IAS 29, para. 10.
20 IAS 29, paras. 1-2.
21 IAS 29, para. 3.
22 IAS 29, para. 4.
23 IAS 29, para. 4.

24 IAS 29, para. 37.
25 IAS 29, para. 17.
26 Framework, para. 100(b).
27 IAS 29, para. 12.
28 IAS 21, para. 8.
29 IAS 21, para. 16.
30 IAS 21, para. 16.
31 IAS 21, para. 16.
32 IAS 39, para. AG83.
33 *IFRIC Update*, IFRIC, October 2003, p. 2. IFRIC concluded in its October 2003 meeting that 'it is not clear how an entity should restate items that are neither monetary nor non-monetary in nature, e.g. deferred tax assets and deferred tax liabilities'.
34 IAS 29, para. 13.
35 IAS 29, para. 29.
36 Framework, para. 100(b).
37 IAS 29, para. 14.
38 IAS 29, para. 18.
39 IAS 29, para. 15.
40 IAS 29, para. 10.
41 IAS 29, para. 16.
42 IAS 29, para. 15.
43 IAS 16, *Property, Plant and Equipment*, para. 23.
44 IAS 29, para. 22.
45 IAS 29, paras. 19 and 21.
46 IAS 29, para. 21.
47 IAS 23 (revised 2007), *Borrowing Costs*, IASB, March 2007.
48 IAS 29, para. 19.
49 IAS 29, para. 20.
50 IAS 21, para. 42.
51 IAS 29, para. 35.
52 IAS 21, para. 42.
53 IAS 29, para. 35.
54 IAS 29, para. 36.
55 IFRIC 7, paras. BC21-BC22.
56 IFRIC 7, para. 4.
57 IFRIC 7, paras. IE1-IE6.
58 IFRIC 7, para. 5.
59 IAS 29, para. 32.
60 IAS 12, *Income Taxes*, Appendix A, para. 18.
61 IAS 12, Appendix A, para. 18.
62 IAS 29, para. 24.
63 IAS 29, para. 25.
64 IAS 29, para. 26.
65 IAS 29, para. 30.
66 IAS 29, paras. 26 and 30.
67 IAS 29, paras. 27 and 31.
68 IAS 29, para. 28.
69 IAS 29, para. 33.
70 IAS 7, *Cash Flow Statements*, paras. 6 and 10.
71 IAS 29, para. 34.
72 IAS 34, *Interim Financial Reporting*, Appendix B, para. 33.
73 IAS 34, Appendix B, para. 32.
74 IAS 34, Appendix B, para. 34.
75 IAS 29, para. 8.
76 IAS 29, paras. 11-36.
77 IFRIC 7, para. BC2.
78 IFRIC 7, para. 3.
79 IAS 29, para. 38.
80 IAS 29, para. 4.
81 IAS 21, para. 42.
82 IAS 21, para. 43.
83 IAS 29, para. 39.
84 IFRIC 7, para. 6.
85 IAS 29, para. 7.
86 IAS 29, para. 41.
87 IFRIC 7, para. 6.
88 IFRS 1, *First-time Adoption of International Financial Reporting Standards*, para. IG32.
89 IFRS 1, para. IG33.
90 IFRS 1, para. IG34.
91 IFRS 1, para. BC67.
92 IAS 29, para. 37.
93 IAS 29, para. 17.
94 IAS 29, para. 20.
95 IAS 29, para. 28.
96 IAS 29, para. 26.
97 IAS 29, para. 28.

Chapter 12 Intangible assets

1 INTRODUCTION

1.1 The incidence of intangible assets

Economic, commercial and marketing imperatives in the more developed world economies, particularly over the last twenty years, have driven many businesses to invest substantial sums in ways that were not previously commonplace. It is not unusual for the premium paid to acquire a business to be greater than the balance sheet value of net assets acquired. The commercial importance of brands that are attractive to consumers, and the cost and uncertainty of attempting to develop them from scratch, has partly fuelled this trend. Equally, businesses that own successful brands spend large sums in maintaining consumer awareness of, and loyalty to them.

As time goes by new types of business asset come into being. Over the last fifteen years or so, entities had to consider how to account for software and related expenditure on computerised sales and marketing systems and website development. More recently, entities have emerged whose principal revenues come from the exchange of intangible rights, businesses are acquiring and developing intellectual property rights and governments are raising revenues from the sale of broadcasting rights and telecommunications licences. As with goodwill and brands, these types of expenditure were not unknown before. It is the commercial imperative brought about by much higher levels of spending on these items, and larger numbers of businesses incurring it, that has forced the topic into prominence.

These relatively high levels of expenditure on intangible aspects of commerce have inevitably resulted in companies wanting to account for it in various different ways. As the incidence and magnitude of such expenditure increased, it became necessary for the IASB, and the accounting profession generally, to develop common rules for its recognition and treatment in financial statements.

1.2 Background to accounting for intangible assets

1.2.1 Development of IAS 9, IAS 22, IAS 38 and SIC-32

The main debate surrounding the accounting treatment of expenditure on intangibles has centred on whether such expenditure should be written off immediately as incurred, or whether it should be capitalised in the balance sheet as a type of asset. A secondary consideration, if the decision to write off the expenditure was taken, was the manner of any write-off. For example was goodwill to be written off directly to reserves, rather than through the profit and loss account? If expenditure on intangibles was to be capitalised, there were a number of matters to be considered further. For example, could expenditure on creating a new brand from scratch (i.e. an internally developed intangible) be capitalised? Over what period would such expenditure be written off, if at all? Could such assets be revalued and if so, on what basis would they be valued?

The situation by the early 1990s was that there were well-established ways of accounting for goodwill (IAS 22 (revised 1993) – *Accounting for Business Combinations)* – and for research and development costs (IAS 9 (revised 1993) – *Accounting for Research and Development Activities*). At that time there was relatively little incidence of 'traditional' intangibles such as patents and licenses, though 'new' intangibles such as brands were appearing on an increasing number of entity balance sheets. There were no specific rules governing expenditure on intangibles such as brands, and the most common method of accounting for goodwill (writing it off directly against reserves) began to seem inappropriate for the large goodwill figures being generated by acquisitions.

This unsatisfactory situation was resolved by the (then) IASC standardising the basis on which goodwill arising on acquisitions, and any other types of intangible asset, were to be treated by entities reporting under International Accounting Standards. This led in September 1998 to the adoption of IAS 22 (revised 1998) and IAS 38 (1998) – *Intangible Assets*. Under these standards there were now definite criteria that had to be met before any expenditure could be considered to have given rise to an intangible asset and definite requirements governing the amortisation and revaluation of such assets.

The accounting treatment of software-related expenditure is not quite so clear under IFRS. There is an inherent difficulty in deciding if such expenditures should be recognised as intangible assets or expenses. This is particularly so in relation to the costs of developing web-based marketing and information systems. The late 1990s saw very large sums spent on the operation and development of websites and this led to the issue of SIC-32 (amended 2003) – *Intangible Assets – Web Site Costs* – that is discussed at 2.3.6 D below.

1.2.2 IFRS 3 and IAS 38 (as revised in 2004)

In 2001 the IASB began a project to review its prescribed accounting for business combinations, which it is pursuing in two phases. Obviously therefore, this project will affect the accounting treatment of intangible assets and goodwill.[1] As part of the first phase, the IASB published in December 2002 ED 3 – *Business Combinations* – together with an exposure draft of proposed related amendments to IAS 38 and IAS 36 – *Impairment of Assets*.[2] The IASB's intention in the first phase was not wholesale change to the existing provisions of IAS 38; rather it was to clarify the following matters:

(a) the treatment of any excess of the acquirer's interest in the fair value of identifiable net assets acquired in a business combination over the cost of the combination;[3]

(b) the accounting for goodwill and intangible assets acquired in a business combination;[4]

(c) the notion of 'identifiability' as it relates to intangible assets;[5]

(d) the useful life and amortisation of intangible assets;[6] and

(e) the accounting for in-process research and development projects acquired in business combinations.[7]

The first phase of the project resulted in the IASB issuing in March 2004 IFRS 3 – *Business Combinations* – and revised versions of IAS 36 and IAS 38. This has significantly broadened the range of intangible assets that an entity is required to recognise in accounting for business combinations.

The second phase of the business combinations project resulted in June 2005 in the publication of an exposure draft of amendments to IFRS 3, which proposed a number of limited amendments to IAS 38. The IASB issued a near-final draft of the revised IFRS 3 in June 2007. However, at the time of writing it is not expected that a final standard will be issued until November 2007.[8]

The requirements of IFRS 3 are principally dealt with in Chapter 7 at 2; the requirements of IAS 36 relating specifically to the impairment of goodwill are dealt with in Chapter 7 at 3; and the general requirements of IAS 36 are covered in Chapter 15. The specific requirements of IAS 38 relating to intangible assets are dealt with at 2 below; while the requirements relating to intangible assets acquired as part of a business combination are covered both at 2.3.2 below and in Chapter 7 at 2.3.3 B. The proposed revision to IFRS 3 is discussed in Chapter 7 at 5.

2 THE REQUIREMENTS OF IAS 38

2.1 Scope and definitions

2.1.1 *Scope*

The objective of IAS 38 is to prescribe the accounting treatment for all intangible assets that are not specifically dealt with in another standard.[9] Hence, IAS 38 does not apply to accounting for:[10]

(a) intangible assets that are within the scope of another standard;

(b) financial assets, as defined in IAS 32 – *Financial Instruments: Presentation*;

(c) the recognition and measurement of exploration and evaluation assets within the scope of IFRS 6 – *Exploration for and Evaluation of Mineral Resources*; and
(d) expenditure on the development and extraction of, minerals, oil, natural gas and similar non-regenerative resources.

Examples of specific types of intangible asset that fall within the scope of another standard include:[11]

(a) intangible assets held by an entity for sale in the ordinary course of business, to which IAS 2 – *Inventories* – or IAS 11 – *Construction Contracts* – applies (see Chapters 23 and 24);
(b) deferred tax assets, which are governed by IAS 12 – *Income Taxes* (see Chapter 26);
(c) leases that are within the scope of IAS 17 – *Leases* (see Chapter 25). However, an entity that leases an intangible asset under a finance lease should apply IAS 38 to account for the underlying asset after its initial recognition.[12] Leases that are outside the scope of IAS 17 such as 'licensing agreements for such items as motion picture films, video recordings, plays, manuscripts, patents and copyrights'[13] are within the scope of IAS 38;[14]
(d) assets arising from employee benefits, for which IAS 19 – *Employee Benefits* – is relevant (see Chapter 32);
(e) financial assets as defined in IAS 32. The recognition and measurement of some financial assets are covered by IAS 27 – *Consolidated and Separate Financial Statements*, IAS 28 – *Investments in Associates* – and IAS 31 – *Interests in Joint Ventures* (see Chapters 6, 8, 9 and 17 to 22);
(f) goodwill acquired in a business combination, which is determined under IFRS 3 (see Chapter 7);
(g) deferred acquisition costs, and intangible assets, arising from an insurer's contractual rights under insurance contracts within the scope of IFRS 4 – *Insurance Contracts*. IFRS 4 sets out specific disclosure requirements for those deferred acquisition costs but not for those intangible assets. Therefore, the disclosure requirements in this standard apply to those intangible assets; and
(h) non-current intangible assets classified as held for sale, or included in a disposal group that is classified as held for sale, in accordance with IFRS 5 – *Non-current Assets Held for Sale and Discontinued Operations* (see Chapter 4).

IAS 38 states that insurance contracts and expenditure on the exploration for, or development and extraction of, oil, gas and mineral deposits in extractive industries are excluded from its scope. Activities or transactions in these areas are so specialised that they give rise to accounting issues that need to be dealt with in a different way. However, the standard does apply 'to other intangible assets used (such as computer software), and other expenditure incurred (such as start-up costs), in extractive industries or by insurers'.[15]

Finally, the standard makes it clear that it does apply to expenditure on advertising, training, start-up and research and development activities.[16]

2.1.2 *What is an intangible asset?*

IAS 38 defines an asset as 'a resource controlled by an entity as a result of past events; and from which future economic benefits are expected to flow to the entity'.[17] Intangible assets form a sub-section of this group and are further defined as 'identifiable non-monetary assets without physical substance'.[18] It is important to note that the revised IAS 38 no longer requires that an intangible asset be 'held for use in the production or supply of goods or services, for rental to others, or for administrative services', because the IASB considers that 'the purpose for which an entity holds an item with these characteristics is not relevant to its classification as an intangible asset, and that all such items should be within the scope of the Standard'.[19] However, there is one caveat, intangible assets held for sale (either in the ordinary course of business or as part of a disposal group) that are accounted for under IAS 2, IAS 11 or IFRS 5 are specifically excluded from the scope of IAS 38.[20]

Businesses frequently incur expenditure on all sorts of intangible resources such as scientific or technical knowledge, design and implementation of new processes or systems, licences, intellectual property, market knowledge, trademarks, brand names and publishing titles. Examples that fall under these headings are computer software, patents, copyrights, motion picture films, customer lists, licences, quotas and many others.[21]

However, although these items are covered by the standard, not all of them will meet the standard's criteria for treatment as an intangible asset, which requires identifiability, control and the existence of future economic benefits. Expenditure on items that do not meet all three criteria will be expensed when incurred, unless they have arisen in the context of a business combination, where they will form part of the calculation of goodwill.[22]

A Identifiability

An intangible asset needs to be identifiable to distinguish it from goodwill. IFRS 3 defines goodwill as the 'future economic benefits arising from assets that are not capable of being individually identified and separately recognised.'[23] For example, the future economic benefits may result from synergy between the identifiable assets acquired or from assets that, individually, do not qualify for recognition in the financial statements but for which the acquirer is prepared to make a payment in the business combination.[24]

When the IASB was revising IAS 38 and developing IFRS 3 it observed that intangible assets acquired in a business combination were often included in the amount recognised as goodwill, despite the requirements for separate recognition.[25] The Board therefore concluded that the concept of identifiability needed to be articulated more clearly.[26] Under the revised IAS 38 an intangible asset meets the identifiability criterion when it:[27]

(a) is separable, meaning that it is capable of being separated or divided from the entity and sold, transferred, licensed, rented or exchanged, either individually or together with a related contract, asset or liability; or

(b) arises from contractual or other legal rights, regardless of whether those rights are transferable or separable from the entity or from other rights and obligations.

This definition of identifiability requires preparers of financial statements to recognise more than those intangible resources that are obviously separable. The definition is consistent with guidance from the previous version of the standard that separability is not the only indication of identifiability and confirms the IASB's position that the existence of contractual or legal rights is a characteristic that distinguishes an intangible asset from goodwill, even if those rights are not readily separable from the entity as a whole. The Board cites as an example of such an intangible asset a licence that is not transferable except by sale of the entity as a whole.[28]

Equally, however, preparers should not restrict their search for intangible assets to those embodied in contractual or other legal rights, since the definition of identifiability merely requires such rights to be *capable* of separation. In considering the responses to ED 3 – *Business Combinations* – the Board observed that 'if an entity separately acquires a non-contractual customer relationship, the existence of an exchange transaction for that relationship provides evidence both that the item is separable, and that the entity is able to control the expected future economic benefits flowing from the relationship. Therefore, the relationship would meet the intangible asset definition and be recognised as such.' In the absence of exchange transactions for the same or similar non-contractual customer relationships, an entity would not be able to demonstrate that such relationships are separable or that it is able to control the expected future economic benefits flowing from those relationships[29] (see B below).

The extract below provides an example of a situation in which the existence of an exchange transaction provides evidence that the item is separable and that the entity has the ability to control the expected future economic benefits.

Extract 12.1: Aegon N.V. (2006)

Notes to the consolidated financial statements of AEGON Group [extract]
2 Summary of significant accounting policies [extract]
2.7 Intangible assets [extract]
B. Value of Business Acquired

When a portfolio of insurance contracts is acquired, whether directly from another insurance company or as part of a business combination, the difference between the fair value and the carrying amount of the insurance liabilities is recognized as value of business acquired (VOBA). The Group also recognizes VOBA when it acquires a portfolio of investment contracts with discretionary participation features.

VOBA is amortized over the useful life of the acquired contracts, based on either the expected future premiums or the expected gross profit margins. For products sold in the United States and Canada, with amortization based on expected gross profit margins, the amortization period and pattern are reviewed at each reporting date. Any change in estimates is recorded in the income statement. For all products, VOBA is assessed for recoverability at least annually on a country-by-country basis and the portion determined not to be recoverable is charged to the income statement. VOBA is considered in the liability adequacy test for each reporting period.

When unrealized gains or losses arise on available-for-sale assets, VOBA is adjusted to equal the effect that the realization of the gains or losses would have had on VOBA. The adjustment is recognized directly in equity. VOBA is derecognized when the related contracts are settled or disposed of.

B Control

Control is defined as the power to obtain the future economic benefits generated by the resource and the ability to restrict access to those benefits to others. While control normally results from legal rights, it may also be demonstrated in the absence of legal enforceability by factors such as market and technical knowledge.[30] Although legal enforceability of a right is not a necessary condition for control, because an entity may be able to control the future economic benefits in some other way, it will be more difficult to demonstrate control in its absence.[31]

An entity usually has insufficient control over the future economic benefits arising from an assembled workforce (i.e. a team of skilled workers, or specific management or technical talent) for these items to meet the definition of an intangible asset.[32] Therefore, if an entity acquires a pharmaceutical company, it is most unlikely that it will be able to recognise as an intangible asset the acquiree's team of research chemists. By contrast, a football club may pay a certain amount to a player's previous club in connection with the transfer of the player's registration, which enables the club to negotiate a playing contract with the footballer that covers a number of seasons and prevent other clubs from using that player's services. This may give the entity sufficient control to enable it to recognise the payment as an intangible asset. In this case, of course, the transfer fee is a stand-alone payment and not part of a business combination; when an entity separately acquires an intangible resource it is much more likely that it can demonstrate that its purchase meets the definition of an asset (see 2.3.1 below).

Similarly, an entity 'may have a portfolio of customers or a market share and expect that, because of its efforts in building customer relationships and loyalty, the customers will continue to trade with the entity. However, in the absence of legal rights to protect or control the relationship or loyalty of customers, the entity usually has insufficient control over these items to meet the definition of intangible assets.'[33] Nevertheless, exchange transactions involving the same or similar non-contractual customer relationships may provide evidence that the entity is able to control the expected future economic benefits even in the absence of legal rights. Where this is the case, those customer relationships could meet the definition of an intangible asset.[34] IFRS 3 includes a number of examples of customer-related intangible assets acquired in business combinations that meet the definition of an intangible asset, which are discussed in more detail at 2.3.3 below.[35] It is worthwhile noting here that intangible assets should only be recognised when they meet (1) the definition of an intangible asset and (2) the applicable recognition criteria in IAS 38,[36] which are discussed at 2.2.1 below.

The extract below illustrates the range of intangible assets that require recognition under IAS 38.

Extract 12.2: Reed Elsevier (2006)

Accounting policies [extract]
Intangible assets [extract]

Intangible assets acquired as part of business combinations comprise: market related assets (e.g. trade marks, imprints, brands); customer related assets (e.g. subscription bases, customer lists, customer relationships); editorial content; software and systems (e.g. application infrastructure, product delivery platforms, in-process research and development); contract based assets (e.g. publishing rights, exhibition rights, supply contracts); and other intangible assets. Internally generated intangible assets typically comprise software and systems development where an identifiable asset is created that is probable to generate future economic benefits.

C Future economic benefits

Future economic benefits include not only future revenues from the sale of products or services but also cost savings. For example, the use of intellectual property in a production process may reduce future production costs rather than increase future revenues.[37]

2.1.3 Tangible and intangible assets

Before the advent of IAS 38 many entities used to account for assets without physical substance in the same way as property, plant and equipment. Indeed, many intangible assets are 'contained in or on a physical substance such as a compact disc (in the case of computer software), legal documentation (in the case of a licence or patent) or film'.[38] An entity therefore needs to exercise judgement in determining whether an 'asset that incorporates both intangible and tangible elements should be treated under IAS 16 – *Property, Plant and Equipment* – or as an intangible asset' under IAS 38, for example:[39]

- software that is embedded in computer-controlled equipment that cannot operate without that specific software is an integral part of the related hardware and is treated as property, plant and equipment;
- application software that is being used on a computer is generally easily replaced and is not an integral part of the related hardware is treated as an intangible asset, whereas the operating system normally is integral to the computer and is included in property, plant and equipment;
- a database that is stored on a compact disc is considered to be an intangible asset because the value of the physical medium is wholly insignificant compared to that of the data collection; and
- research and development expenditure may result in an asset with physical substance (e.g. a prototype), but as the physical element is secondary to its intangible component, the related knowledge, it is treated as an intangible asset.[40]

It is worthwhile noting that the 'parts approach' in IAS 16 requires an entity to account for significant parts of an asset separately because they have a different economic life or are often replaced[41] (see Chapter 13). This raises 'boundary' problems between IAS 16 and IAS 38 when software and similar expenditure is involved. We believe that where IAS 16 requires an entity to identify parts of an asset and account for them separately, the entity needs to evaluate whether any intangible-type part is actually integral to the larger asset or whether it is really a separate asset in its own right. The intangible part is more likely to be an asset in its own right if it was developed separately or if it can be used independently of the item of property, plant and equipment of which it apparently forms part.

2.2 Recognition and measurement

2.2.1 Recognition

Recognition of intangible assets under IAS 38 is based on a general principle that 'applies to costs incurred initially to acquire or internally generate an intangible asset and those incurred subsequently to add to, replace part of, or service it'.[42] An item that meets the definition of an intangible asset should only be recognised if:[43]

'(a) it is probable that the expected future economic benefits that are attributable to the asset will flow to the entity; and

(b) the cost of the asset can be measured reliably.'

Although IAS 38 does not define 'probable', it is defined in several other International Financial Reporting Standards as 'more likely than not'.[44] In measuring the probability of expected future economic benefits, the entity should use 'reasonable and supportable assumptions that represent management's best estimate of the set of economic conditions that will exist over the useful life of the asset'.[45] In making the above judgement the entity should assess the degree of certainty attached to the flow of future economic benefits based on the evidence available at the time of initial recognition, giving greater weight to external evidence.[46] The difficulties that may arise in applying these criteria when an entity enters into a contract to buy an intangible asset for delivery in some future period are discussed in detail at 3.4.2 below.

The guidance in IAS 38 on the recognition and initial measurement of intangible assets takes account of the way in which an entity obtained the asset. Separate rules for recognition and initial measurement exist for intangible assets depending on whether they were:

- acquired separately (see 2.3.1 below);
- acquired as part of a business combination (see 2.3.2 below);
- acquired by way of government grant (see 2.3.3 below);
- obtained in an exchange of assets (see 2.3.4 below); and
- generated internally (see 2.3.6 below).

It is important to note here that for recognition purposes IAS 38 does not distinguish between an internally and an externally developed intangible asset (other than when considering the treatment of goodwill). When the definition of an intangible asset and the relevant recognition criteria are met, all such assets should be recognised.[47] Preparers do not have the option to decide, as a matter of policy, that costs relating to internally generated intangible assets are expensed.[48]

2.2.2 Measurement

Upon initial recognition an intangible asset should be measured at cost.[49] The standard defines this as 'the amount of cash or cash equivalents paid or the fair value of other consideration given to acquire an asset at the time of its acquisition or construction, or, when applicable, the amount attributed to that asset when initially recognised in accordance with the specific requirements of other IFRSs, e.g. IFRS 2 – *Share-based Payment*.'[50]

The components of the cost of an internally generated intangible asset are discussed in more detail at 2.3.7 below.

2.2.3 Subsequent expenditure

Although IAS 38 is based on a general recognition principle that applies to both initial acquisition and subsequent expenditures, the hurdle for the recognition of subsequent expenditure as an addition to an intangible asset is set higher, because it must first be confirmed that the expenditure is not associated with the replacement of an existing asset (see 2.9 below) or the creation of an internally generated intangible that would not be eligible for recognition under the standard (see 2.3.6 below). The standard argues that 'the nature of intangible assets is such that, in many cases, there are no additions to such an asset or replacements of part of it. Accordingly, most subsequent expenditures are likely to maintain the expected future economic benefits embodied in an existing intangible asset rather than meet the definition of an intangible asset and the recognition criteria in this Standard. In addition, it is often difficult to attribute subsequent expenditure directly to a particular intangible asset rather than to the business as a whole.'[51]

The standard therefore presumes that only rarely will subsequent expenditure-expenditure incurred after the initial recognition of an acquired intangible asset or after completion of an internally generated intangible asset be recognised in the carrying amount of an asset.[52] Capitalisation of subsequent expenditure on brands, mastheads, publishing titles, customer lists and similar items is expressly forbidden even if they were initially acquired externally, which is consistent with the general prohibition on recognising them if internally generated. This is because the standard argues that such expenditure cannot be distinguished from the cost of developing the business of which they are a part.[53] Thus, at best such expenditure creates internally generated goodwill.

2.3 Specific recognition and measurement requirements

2.3.1 Separate acquisition

A Recognition

Separately acquired intangible assets should normally be recognised as assets. IAS 38 assumes that the price paid to acquire an intangible asset separately usually reflects expectations about the probability that the future economic benefits embodied in it will flow to the entity. In other words, the effect of probability is reflected in the cost of the intangible asset.[54] Therefore, when an entity separately acquires an intangible asset the standard:

- considers future economic benefits to be probable;[55] and
- assumes that the cost of a separately acquired intangible asset can usually be measured reliably, especially in the case of a monetary purchase consideration.[56]

In its basis for conclusions on IAS 38, the IASB observed that 'this highlights a general inconsistency between the recognition criteria for assets and liabilities in the *Framework* (which states that an item meeting the definition of an element should be recognised only if it is probable that any future economic benefits associated with the item will flow to or from the entity, and the item can be measured reliably) and the fair value measurements required in, for example, a business combination. However, the Board concluded that the role of probability as a criterion for recognition in the *Framework* should be considered more generally as part of a forthcoming Concepts project.'[57]

Not all external costs incurred to secure intangible rights automatically qualify for capitalisation as a separately acquired asset. An entity that subcontracts the development of intangible assets (e.g. development-and-supply contracts or R&D contracts) to other parties, must exercise judgement in determining whether it is acquiring an intangible asset or whether it is obtaining goods and services that are being used in the development of an intangible asset by the entity itself. For example, when a supplier is paid upfront or milestone payments during the course of a project, the entity should capitalise only those costs that are incurred after it becomes probable that economic benefits are expected to flow to the entity and, in the case of a supplier working on an internal project, after the criteria have been met for recognising an internally developed intangible asset (see 2.3.6 below).

In determining whether a supplier is providing services to develop an internally generated intangible asset, it can be useful to consider the terms of the supply agreement, in particular whether the supplier is bearing a significant proportion of the risks associated with a failure of the project. For example, if the supplier is always compensated under a development-and-supply contract for development services and tool costs irrespective of the project's outcome, the entity on whose behalf the development is undertaken should account for those activities as its own.

B Components of cost

The cost of a separately acquired intangible asset comprises:[58]

- its purchase price, including import duties and non-refundable purchase taxes, after deducting trade discounts and rebates; and
- any directly attributable cost of preparing the asset for its intended use, for example:[59]
  - costs of employee benefits arising directly from bringing the asset to its working condition;
  - professional fees arising directly from bringing the asset to its working condition; and

- costs of testing whether the asset is functioning properly.

Capitalisation of expenditure ceases when the asset is in the condition necessary for it to be capable of operating in the manner intended by management.[60] This may well be before the date on which it is brought into use.

If payment for an intangible asset is deferred beyond normal credit terms, its cost is the cash price equivalent. The difference between this amount and the total payments is recognised as interest expense over the period of credit unless the criteria in IAS 23 – *Borrowing Costs* – are met.[61]

C Costs to be expensed

The following types of expenditure are not considered to be part of the cost of a separately acquired intangible asset:[62]

- costs of introducing a new product or service, including costs of advertising and promotional activities;
- costs of conducting business in a new location or with a new class of customer, including costs of staff training;
- administration and other general overhead costs;
- costs incurred in using or redeploying an intangible asset;
- costs incurred while an asset capable of operating in the manner intended by management has yet to be brought into use; and
- initial operating losses, such as those incurred while demand for the asset's output builds up.

In addition, start-up costs, training costs, advertising and promotional activities, and relocation or reorganisation costs should be expensed (see 2.3.8 below).

D Incidental operations

When an entity generates income while it is developing or constructing an asset, the question arises as to whether this income should reduce the initial carrying value of the asset being developed or be recognised in profit or loss. In September 2000, the (then) IASC issued draft interpretation SIC-D26 – *Property, Plant and Equipment – Results of Incidental Operations* – which proposed that an entity should recognise the results of incidental operations in profit or loss for the period. However, the IASB decided that it would be better to address this issue as part of its improvements project. It was therefore only in December 2003 that the IASB issued guidance on accounting for the results of incidental operations as part of IAS 16.[63] Identical guidance on accounting for the results of incidental operations is incorporated in IAS 38, which was issued several months later in March 2004.

When an entity engages in operations in connection with the development of an intangible asset that are 'not necessary to bring the asset to the condition necessary for it to be capable of operating in the manner intended by management', the entity should recognise the income and related expenses of incidental operations 'immediately in profit or loss ... in their respective classifications of income and expense'.[64] Such incidental operations can occur before or during the development activities. The example below illustrates these requirements.

Example 12.1: Incidental operations

Entity A is pioneering a new process for the production of a certain type of chemical. Entity A will be able to patent the new production process. During the development phase, A is selling quantities of the chemical that are produced as a by-product of the development activities that are taking place. The expenditure incurred comprises labour, raw materials, assembly costs, costs of equipment and professional fees.

The revenues and costs associated with the production and sale of the chemical are accounted for in profit or loss for the period, while the development costs that meet the strict recognition criteria of IAS 38 are recognised as an intangible asset. Development costs that fail the IAS 38 recognition test are also expensed.

As the above example suggests, identifying the revenue from incidental operations will often be much easier than allocating costs to incidental operations. Furthermore, it will often be challenging to determine when exactly a project moves from the development phase into its start-up phase.

2.3.2 Acquisition as part of a business combination

Chapter 7 at 2.3.3 discusses in detail the requirements regarding recognition and initial measurement of assets acquired and liabilities and contingent liabilities assumed in a business combination. A summary of requirements regarding intangible assets acquired in a business combination is provided at A to C below. However, it is worth noting that the effect of the requirement in IFRS 3 to recognise intangible assets when their fair value can be measured reliably,[65] has been to extend the range of intangible assets that should be recognised following a business combination, rather than being subsumed within goodwill. The illustrative examples in IFRS 3 state that, for example, the following types of intangible assets should be recognised separately if they meet the criteria in IAS 38: trademarks, trade names, internet domain names, non-competition agreements, customer lists, non-contractual customer relationships, films, music videos, television programmes, franchise agreements, unpatented technology and databases.[66]

This list is virtually the same as the list of examples of intangible assets that meet the criteria for separate recognition in FAS 141 – *Business Combinations*.[67] The original list of intangible assets included in the 1999 exposure draft included the following additional items, which the FASB decided to exclude as they do not generally meet the recognition criteria in FAS 141: customer base, customer service capability, presence in geographic markets or locations, non-union status or strong labour relations, ongoing training or recruiting programs, outstanding credit ratings and access to capital markets, favourable government relations, and assembled workforce.[68]

A Recognition of intangible assets acquired in a business combination

At the acquisition date, an acquirer should separately recognise, under IFRS 3, an intangible asset of the acquiree if:[69]

- it meets the definition of an intangible asset in IAS 38; and
- its fair value can be measured reliably.

For such item to be recognised as an intangible asset, it must also be probable that the expected future benefits that are attributable to the asset will flow to the entity.[70]

The cost of an intangible asset acquired in a business combination is its fair value at the acquisition date (see Chapter 7 at 2.3.3).[71] As with separately acquired intangible rights, the standard indicates that the fair value of an intangible asset reflects market expectations about the probability that the future economic benefits embodied in the asset will flow to the entity. In other words, the effect of probability is reflected in the fair value measurement of the intangible asset. Therefore, in the case of intangible assets acquired in a business combination, the probability recognition criterion is always considered to be satisfied.[72]

An intangible asset is recognised at the acquisition date irrespective of whether it had been reflected in the acquiree's financial statements before the business combination. If its fair value can be measured reliably, an acquirer should recognise an intangible asset separately from goodwill.[73]

In developing IAS 38 the IASB originally took the position that sufficient information should exist to measure reliably the fair value of intangible assets that have an underlying contractual or legal basis, or that are capable of being separated from the entity.[74] During its field visits and round-table discussions with auditors, preparers, accounting standard-setters and regulators the IASB was presented with numerous examples of acquired intangible assets whose fair value could not be measured reliably.[75] These included many forms of permit allocated by governments. It is often a feature of such assets that the entity has legal rights, they are clearly valuable but they cannot legally be bought and sold. Presumably if an airline were to buy a smaller competitor and then close its business, retaining only its landing slots, it might be able to establish reliably what it had paid for them. However, in some cases, when a business is closed such rights are lost and together with the lack of a secondary market, even if prices were available on a 'grey' market of dubious legality, there may not be a good basis for establishing fair value. Nevertheless, the Board remained concerned that entities might use the reliability of measurement criterion to avoid recognising intangible assets separately from goodwill.[76] Therefore, the standard is quite restrictive and states that 'the only circumstances in which it might not be possible to measure reliably the fair value of an intangible asset acquired in a business combination are when the intangible asset arises from legal or other contractual rights and either:[77]

(a) is not separable; or

(b) is separable, but there is no history or evidence of exchange transactions for the same or similar assets, and otherwise estimating fair value would be dependent on immeasurable variables.'

The IASB recognised that an intangible asset acquired in a business combination might be separable, but only together with a related tangible or intangible asset. For example, a magazine's publishing title might not be able to be sold separately from a related subscriber database. Therefore, IAS 38 requires the acquirer to recognise the group of assets as a single asset, separately from goodwill, if the individual fair values of the assets in the group are not reliably measurable.[78] This is to prevent an entity from having to allocate cash flows on an arbitrary basis between individual items in a group of assets.[79]

The standard notes that the terms 'brand' and 'brand name' are often used as synonyms for trademarks and other marks. However, the former are regarded as general marketing terms that are typically used to refer to a group of complementary assets such as a trademark (or service mark) and its related trade name, formulas, recipes and technological expertise. Accordingly, IAS 38 requires the acquirer to recognise a group of complementary intangible assets as a single asset comprising a brand if the individual fair values of the complementary assets are not reliably measurable. If the individual fair values of the complementary assets are reliably measurable, an acquirer may recognise them as a single asset provided the individual assets have similar useful lives.[80] Heineken, for example, combines the carrying amount of brands and customer bases acquired in business combinations.

Extract 12.3: Heineken N.V. (2006)

Notes to the consolidated financial statements [extract]
Significant accounting policies [extract]
(f) Intangible assets [extract]
(ii) Brands

Brands acquired, separately, or as part of a business combination are capitalised as part of a brand portfolio if the portfolio meets the definition of an intangible asset and the recognition criteria are satisfied. Brand portfolios acquired as part of a business combination include the customer base related to the brand because it is assumed that brands have no value without a customer base and vice versa. Brand portfolios acquired as part of a business combination are valued at fair value based on the royalty relief method. Brands and brand portfolios acquired separately are measured at cost. Brands and brand portfolios are amortised on a straight-line basis over their estimated useful life.

B IFRS 3 examples of intangible assets acquired in a business combination

IFRS 3 gives guidance in an Illustrative Example that provides a long list of examples of items acquired in a business combination that meet the definition of an intangible asset and should therefore be recognised separately from goodwill, provided that their fair values can be measured reliably. The list is not intended to be exhaustive and other items acquired in a business combination might still meet the definition of an intangible asset.[81]

The table below summarises the items included in the IASB's Illustrative Example. Reference should be made to the Illustrative Example itself for any further explanation about some of these items.

Intangible assets arising from contractual or other legal rights (regardless of being separable)	**Other intangible assets that are separable**
Marketing-related	
– Trademarks, trade names, service marks, collective marks and certification marks	
– Internet domain names	
– Trade dress (unique colour, shape or package design)	
– Newspaper mastheads	
– Non-competition agreements	
Customer-related	
– Order or production backlogs	– Customer lists
– Customer contracts and the related customer relationships	– Non-contractual customer relationships
Artistic-related	
– Plays, operas and ballets	
– Books, magazines, newspapers and other literary works	
– Musical works such as compositions, song lyrics and advertising jingles	
– Pictures and photographs	
– Video and audiovisual material, including films, music videos and television programmes	
Contract-based	
– Licensing, royalty and standstill agreements	
– Advertising, construction, management, service or supply contracts	
– Lease agreements	
– Construction permits	
– Franchise agreements	
– Operating and broadcasting rights	
– Use rights such as drilling, water, air, mineral, timber-cutting and route authorities	
– Servicing contracts such as mortgage servicing contracts	
– Employment contracts that are beneficial contracts from the perspective of the employer because the pricing of those contracts is below their current market value	
Technology-based	
– Patented technology	– Unpatented technology
– Computer software and mask works	– Databases
– Trade secrets such as secret formulas, processes or recipes	

It is clear from the table above that the IASB envisages a wide range of items meeting the definition of an intangible asset, and therefore potentially being recognised separately from goodwill. Whether they are recognised separately or not will depend on whether their fair values can be measured reliably.

Further details on the requirements relating to intangible assets acquired as part of a business combination are covered in Chapter 7 at 2.3.3 B.

C *Measuring fair value of intangible assets acquired in a business combination*

IAS 38 presumes that the fair value of intangible assets acquired in business combinations can normally be measured with sufficient reliability to be recognised separately from goodwill. The existence of uncertainty in measurement does not prevent separate recognition. When there is a range of possible outcomes with different probabilities, that uncertainty is a component of the estimate used to determine the intangible asset's fair value, rather than demonstrating an inability to measure fair value reliably. If an intangible asset acquired in a business combination has a finite useful life, there is a rebuttable presumption in the standard that its fair value can be measured reliably.[82] This demonstrates the change to the way in which goodwill and intangible assets have been classified and distinguished in accounting standards. A characteristic of goodwill used to be the acquiring entity's ability to earn superprofits from an acquired business. Now, if that acquired business has a finite life, e.g. it is based on a contract or a franchise, this 'goodwill' must presumably now be defined as an intangible asset, because it arises from contractual rights and has a finite life, even though it is clearly not separable.

The standard sets out a hierarchy for reliability of measurement, stating that quoted market prices in an active market provide the most reliable estimate of the fair value of an intangible asset and that the appropriate market price is usually the current bid price. If current bid prices are unavailable, the price of the most recent similar transaction may provide a basis from which to estimate fair value, provided that there has not been a significant change in economic circumstances between the transaction date and the date at which the asset's fair value is estimated.[83]

As the standard itself notes, although intangible assets are bought and sold, it is uncommon for an active market to exist for intangible assets. The value of many intangible assets such as brands, newspaper mastheads, music and film publishing rights, patents or trademarks depends on the fact that they are unique. Sale and purchase contracts are negotiated between individual buyers and sellers and transactions are relatively infrequent. Accordingly an active market cannot exist for many of the intangible assets that IFRS 3 and IAS 38 require an acquirer to recognise as part of the allocation process.[84] Therefore the standard requires that in the absence of an active market, intangible assets are valued on a basis that reflects the amounts the acquirer would have paid for the assets in an arm's length transaction between knowledgeable willing parties, based on the best information available. In determining this amount, an entity should consider recent transactions for similar assets.[85] However, since many intangible assets are unique by nature, the consideration of transactions for similar assets is aimed at understanding the method used to determine fair value for that type of asset rather than at applying the actual price agreed in that case.

IAS 38 acknowledges that entities that are regularly involved in the purchase and sale of unique intangible assets may have developed techniques for estimating their fair values indirectly. Therefore, it allows these techniques to be used for initial measurement of an intangible asset acquired in a business combination if their objective is to estimate fair value and if they reflect current transactions and practices in the industry to which the asset belongs. These techniques include, when appropriate:[86]

(a) applying multiples reflecting current market transactions to indicators that drive the profitability of the asset (such as revenue, market shares and operating profit) or to the royalty stream that could be obtained from licensing the intangible asset to another party in an arm's length transaction (as in the 'relief from royalty' approach); or

(b) discounting estimated future net cash flows from the asset.

Newspaper and magazine titles frequently change hands based on multiples of revenue. Here, of course, it may be a challenge (if the acquisition is of another publishing entity) to establish the boundaries between the intangible titles and goodwill arising on the acquired entity as a whole.

In summary, the fair value of an intangible asset acquired in a business combination is usually determined by hypothesising what a market price would be if there was a market, based on management assumptions about the future and using a valuation model. The issues underlying the initial measurement of these intangible assets are discussed further at 3.5.2 below.

D Customer relationship intangible assets acquired in a business combination

Further guidance on customer relationships acquired in a business combination is provided by IFRS 3 in the Illustrative Examples (which are reproduced in the example below). These demonstrate how the contractual-legal and separability criteria, discussed in 2.1.2 above, interact in the context of acquired customer relationships.[87]

Example 12.2: Customer relationship intangible assets acquired in a business combination

Supply agreement

Parent obtained control of Supplier in a business combination. Supplier has a five-year agreement to supply goods to Buyer. Both Supplier and Parent believe that Buyer will renew the supply agreement at the end of the current contract. The supply agreement is not separable.

The supply agreement (whether cancellable or not) meets the contractual-legal criterion for identification as an intangible asset, and therefore is recognised separately from goodwill, provided its fair value can be measured reliably. Additionally, because Supplier establishes its relationship with Buyer through a contract, the customer relationship with Buyer meets the contractual-legal criterion for identification as an intangible asset. Therefore, the customer relationship intangible asset is also recognised separately from goodwill provided its fair value can be measured reliably. In determining the fair value of the customer relationship, Parent considers assumptions such as the expected renewal of the supply agreement.

Sporting goods and electronics

Parent obtained control of Subsidiary in a business combination. Subsidiary manufactures goods in two distinct lines of business: sporting goods and electronics. Customer purchases from Subsidiary both sporting goods and electronics. Subsidiary has a contract with Customer to be its exclusive provider of sporting goods. However, there is no contract for the supply of electronics to Customer. Both Subsidiary and Parent believe that there is only one overall customer relationship between Subsidiary and Customer.

The contract to be Customer's exclusive supplier of sporting goods (whether cancellable or not) meets the contractual-legal criterion for identification as an intangible asset, and is therefore recognised separately from goodwill, provided its fair value can be measured reliably. Additionally, because Subsidiary establishes its relationship with Customer through a contract, the customer relationship with Customer meets the contractual-legal criterion for identification as an intangible asset. Therefore, the customer relationship intangible asset is also recognised separately from goodwill, provided its fair value can be measured reliably. Because there is only one customer relationship with Customer, the fair value of that relationship incorporates assumptions regarding Subsidiary's relationship with Customer related to both sporting goods and electronics.

However, if both Parent and Subsidiary believed there were separate customer relationships with Customer – one for sporting goods and another for electronics – the customer relationship with respect to electronics would be assessed by Parent to determine whether it meets the separability criterion for identification as an intangible asset.

Order backlog and recurring customers

Entity A obtained control of Entity B in a business combination on 31 December 2004. Entity B does business with its customers solely through purchase and sales orders. At 31 December 2004, Entity B has a backlog of customer purchase orders from 60 per cent of its customers, all of whom are recurring customers. The other 40 per cent of Entity B's customers are also recurring customers. However, as of 31 December 2004, Entity B does not have any open purchase orders or other contracts with those customers.

The purchase orders from 60 per cent of Entity B's customers (whether cancellable or not) meet the contractual-legal criterion for identification as intangible assets, and are therefore recognised separately from goodwill, provided their fair values can be measured reliably. Additionally, because Entity B has established its relationship with 60 per cent of its customers through contracts, those customer relationships meet the contractual-legal criterion for identification as an intangible asset. Therefore, the customer relationship intangible asset is also recognised separately from goodwill provided its fair value can be measured reliably.

Because Entity B has a practice of establishing contracts with the remaining 40 per cent of its customers, its relationship with those customers also arises through contractual rights, and therefore meets the contractual-legal criterion for identification as an intangible asset. Entity A recognises this customer relationship separately from goodwill, provided its fair value can be measured reliably, even though Entity B does not have contracts with those customers at 31 December 2004.

Motor insurance contracts

Parent obtained control of Insurer in a business combination. Insurer has a portfolio of one-year motor insurance contracts that are cancellable by policyholders. A reasonably predictable number of policyholders renew their insurance contracts each year.

Because Insurer establishes its relationships with policyholders through insurance contracts, the customer relationship with policyholders meets the contractual-legal criterion for identification as an intangible asset. Therefore, the customer relationship intangible asset is recognised separately from goodwill, provided its fair value can be measured reliably. In determining the fair value of the customer relationship intangible asset, Parent considers estimates of renewals and cross-selling. IAS 36 and IAS 38 apply to the customer relationship intangible asset.

In determining the fair value of the liability relating to the portfolio of insurance contracts, Parent considers estimates of cancellations by policyholders. IFRS 4 provides further guidance on accounting for the acquired contracts.

E In-process research and development

The term 'in-process research and development' (IPR&D) refers to those identifiable intangible assets resulting from research and development activities that are acquired in a business combination. An acquirer should recognise IPR&D separately from goodwill if the project meets the definition of an intangible asset and its fair value can be measured reliably. This is the case when the IPR&D project:

(a) meets the definition of an asset; and
(b) is identifiable, i.e. is separable or arises from contractual or other legal rights.'[88]

Any subsequent expenditure incurred on the project after its acquisition should be accounted for in accordance with the general rules in IAS 38 on internally generated intangible assets which are discussed at 2.3.6 below.[89] In summary, this means that the subsequent expenditure is accounted for as follows:

- research expenditure is recognised as an expense when incurred;
- development expenditure that does not satisfy the criteria for recognition as an intangible asset is recognised as an expense when incurred; and
- development expenditure that satisfies the recognition criteria is added to the carrying value of the acquired in-process research or development project.[90]

Critics of the above approach have pointed out in the past that it results in some IPR&D projects acquired in business combinations being treated differently from similar projects started internally. The IASB acknowledges this criticism but decided that it could not support a treatment that allowed acquired IPR&D to be subsumed within goodwill and it would not extend the scope of its project to revise IAS 38 to reconsider the treatment of projects started internally.[91] Until the Board finds time to address this issue, users of financial statements will have to live with the problem that an asset can be recognised for acquired research and development projects despite the fact that the entity might recognise as an expense the costs of projects at a similar stage of development but started internally.

The implication is that if an acquired project never achieves the recognition criteria for an internal project, the asset recognised for in-process research and development expenditure will ultimately be impaired, although it may be that this impairment will not arise until the entity is satisfied that the project will not continue. However, since it is an intangible asset not yet available for use, such an evaluation cannot be significantly delayed as the entity will need to test the asset for impairment annually by comparing its carrying amount with its recoverable amount (see Chapter 15 at 3.4).[92] Any impairment loss will be reflected in the entity's income statement as a post-acquisition event. Hence accounting for IPR&D under IFRS is significantly different from US GAAP, which requires it to be expensed at the acquisition date.

2.3.3 Acquisition by way of government grant

An intangible asset may sometimes 'be acquired free of charge, or for nominal consideration, by way of a government grant'.[93] Examples of intangible assets that governments frequently allocate to entities include airport-landing rights, licences to operate radio or television stations, emission rights (see 3.3 below), import licences or quotas, or rights to access other restricted resources.[94]

Government grants should be accounted for under IAS 20 – *Accounting for Government Grants and Disclosure of Government Assistance* – which permits initial recognition of intangible assets received at either:[95]

- fair value; or
- a nominal amount plus any expenditure that is directly attributable to preparing the asset for its intended use.

The accounting policy for intangible assets acquired by way of government grant should be applied consistently to all intangible assets acquired in this manner.

It is not possible to measure reliably the fair value of all of the permits allocated by governments because they may have been allocated for nil consideration, may not be transferable and may only be bought and sold as part of a business. Some of the issues surrounding the fair values of airline landing slots were considered under 2.3.2.A above. On the other hand, other allocated permits such as milk quotas are freely traded and therefore do have a readily ascertainable fair value.

2.3.4 Exchanges of assets

Asset exchanges are transactions that have preoccupied standard-setters for a number of years. For example, an entity might swap certain intangible assets that it does not require or is no longer allowed to use for those of a counterparty that has other surplus assets. It is not uncommon for airlines and newspaper chains to exchange landing slots and newspaper titles, respectively, to meet demands of competition authorities. The question arises whether such transactions should be recorded at cost or fair value, which would give rise to a gain in the circumstances where the fair value of the incoming asset exceeds the carrying amount of the outgoing one. Equally, it is possible that a transaction could be arranged with no real commercial substance, solely to boost apparent profits.

Three separate international accounting standards contain virtually identical guidance on accounting for exchanges of assets: IAS 16 (see Chapter 13), IAS 40 – *Investment Property* (also see Chapter 14) and IAS 38 (which is discussed below).

A Measurement of assets exchanged

IAS 38 requires all acquisitions of intangible assets in exchange for non-monetary assets, or a combination of monetary and non-monetary assets, to be measured at fair value. The acquired intangible asset is measured at fair value unless:[96]

(a) the exchange transaction lacks commercial substance; or

(b) the fair value of neither the asset received nor the asset given up is reliably measurable.

The acquired asset is measured in this way even if an entity cannot immediately derecognise the asset given up. If an entity is able to determine reliably the fair value of either the asset received or the asset given up, then it uses the fair value of the asset given up to measure cost unless the fair value of the asset received is more clearly evident.[97] If the fair value of neither the asset given up, nor the asset received can be measured reliably the acquired intangible asset is measured at the carrying amount of the asset given up.[98]

B Commercial substance

The commercial substance test for asset exchanges was put in place to prevent gains in income being recognised when the transaction had no 'discernable effect on the entity's economics'.[99] The commercial substance of an exchange is to be determined by forecasting and comparing the future cash flows budgeted to be generated by the incoming and outgoing assets. For commercial substance to be present there must be a significant difference between the two forecasts. The standard sets out this requirement as follows:[100]

> 'An entity determines whether an exchange transaction has commercial substance by considering the extent to which its future cash flows are expected to change as a result of the transaction. An exchange transaction has commercial substance if:
>
> (a) the configuration (i.e. risk, timing and amount) of the cash flows of the asset received differs from the configuration of the cash flows of the asset transferred; or
>
> (b) the entity-specific value of the portion of the entity's operations affected by the transaction changes as a result of the exchange; and
>
> (c) the difference in (a) or (b) is significant relative to the fair value of the assets exchanged.'

IAS 38 defines the 'entity-specific value' of an intangible asset as 'the present value of the cash flows an entity expects to arise from the continuing use of an asset and from its disposal at the end of its useful life or expects to incur when settling a liability'.[101] In determining whether an exchange transaction has commercial substance, the entity-specific value of the portion of the entity's operations affected by the transaction should reflect post-tax cash flows.[102] This is somewhat different from the calculation of an asset's value in use under IAS 36 (see Chapter 15), as it uses a post-tax discount rate based on the entity's own risks rather than IAS 36's use of the pre-tax rate that the market would apply to a similar asset.

It should be noted that the above commercial substance test relies on a prediction of future cash flows in the determination of the carrying amount of some intangible assets. The standard states that 'the fair value of an intangible asset for which comparable market transactions do not exist is reliably measurable if (a) the variability in the range of reasonable fair value estimates is not significant for that asset or (b) the probabilities of the various estimates within the range can be reasonably assessed and used in estimating fair value.'[103] The standard allows an entity to forego the effort of performing these detailed calculations when the outcome would be clear in advance[104] – perhaps if it is obvious that there is no 'commercial substance' in this very restricted sense.

2.3.5 *Internally generated goodwill*

IAS 38 explicitly prohibits the recognition of internally generated goodwill as an asset[105], because internally generated goodwill is neither separable nor does it arise from contractual or legal rights and, as such, is not an identifiable resource controlled by the entity that can be measured reliably at cost.[106] It therefore does not meet the definition of an intangible asset under the standard or that of an asset under the IASB's *Framework*. The standard maintains that the difference between the market value of an entity and the carrying amount of its identifiable net assets at any time may capture a range of factors that affect the value of the entity, but that such differences do not represent the cost of intangible assets controlled by the entity.[107]

2.3.6 Internally generated intangible assets

The IASB recognises that it may be difficult to decide whether an internally generated intangible asset qualifies for recognition because of problems in:[108]

(a) confirming whether and when there is an identifiable asset that will generate expected future economic benefits; and

(b) determining the cost of the asset reliably, especially in cases where the cost of generating an intangible asset internally cannot be distinguished from the cost of maintaining or enhancing the entity's internally generated goodwill or of running day-to-day operations.

To avoid the inappropriate recognition of an asset, IAS 38 requires that internally generated intangible assets are not only tested against the general requirements for recognition and initial measurement, but also meet criteria which confirm that the related internal development project is at a sufficiently advanced stage; is economically viable; and includes only directly attributable costs.[109] Those criteria comprise detailed guidance on accounting for intangible assets in the research phase (see A below), the development phase (see B below) and on components of cost of an internally generated intangible asset (see 2.3.7 below).

Having established that the general recognition and initial measurement requirements of the standard are met, the entity classifies the generation of the internally developed asset into a research phase and a development phase.[110] The standard defines research and development activities as follows:

Research is original and planned investigation undertaken with the prospect of gaining new scientific or technical knowledge and understanding.[111]

The standard gives the following examples of research activities:[112]

(a) activities aimed at obtaining new knowledge;

(b) the search for, evaluation and final selection of, applications of research findings or other knowledge;

(c) the search for alternatives for materials, devices, products, processes, systems or services; and

(d) the formulation, design, evaluation and final selection of possible alternatives for new or improved materials, devices, products, processes, systems or services.

Development is the application of research findings or other knowledge to a plan or design for the production of new or substantially improved materials, devices, products, processes, systems or services before the start of commercial production or use.[113]

The standard gives the following examples of development activities:[114]

(a) the design, construction and testing of pre-production or pre-use prototypes and models;

(b) the design of tools, jigs, moulds and dies involving new technology;

(c) the design, construction and operation of a pilot plant that is not of a scale economically feasible for commercial production; and

(d) the design, construction and testing of a chosen alternative for new or improved materials, devices, products, processes, systems or services.

A Research phase

An entity cannot recognise an intangible asset arising from research or from the research phase of an internal project. Instead, any expenditure on research or the research phase of an internal project should be expensed as incurred because the entity cannot demonstrate that an intangible asset exists that will generate probable future economic benefits.[115]

B Development phase

An intangible asset arising from development or from the development phase of an internal project should be recognised as an internally generated intangible if, and only if, an entity can demonstrate all of the following:[116]

(a) the technical feasibility of completing the intangible asset so that it will be available for use or sale;

(b) its intention to complete the intangible asset and use or sell it;

(c) its ability to use or sell the intangible asset;

(d) how the intangible asset will generate probable future economic benefits. Among other things, the entity can demonstrate the existence of a market for the output of the intangible asset or the intangible asset itself or, if it is to be used internally, the usefulness of the intangible asset;

(e) the availability of adequate technical, financial and other resources to complete the development and to use or sell the intangible asset;

(f) its ability to measure reliably the expenditure attributable to the intangible asset during its development.

The standard requires recognition of a qualifying intangible asset in the development phase because the development phase of a project is further advanced than the research phase and an entity may be able to demonstrate that the asset will generate probable future economic benefits.[117]

It may be challenging to obtain objective evidence on each of the above conditions because:

- condition (b) relies on management intent;
- conditions (c), (e) and (f) are entity-specific, i.e. whether development expenditure meets any of these conditions depends both on the development activity itself and the entity; and

- condition (d) above is more restrictive than is immediately apparent because the entity needs to assess the probable future economic benefits using the principles in IAS 36, i.e. using discounted cash flows. If the asset will generate economic benefits only in conjunction with other assets, the entity should apply the concept of cash-generating units.[118] The requirements of the IAS 36 are discussed in Chapter 15.

IAS 38 indicates that evidence may be available in the form of:

- a business plan showing the technical, financial and other resources needed and the entity's ability to secure those resources;[119]
- a lender's indication of its willingness to fund the plan confirming the availability of external finance;[120] and
- detailed project information demonstrating that an entity's costing systems can measure reliably the cost of generating an intangible asset internally, such as salary and other expenditure incurred in securing copyrights or licences or developing computer software.[121]

In any case, an entity should maintain books and records that allow it to prove whether it meets the conditions set out by IAS 38.

Certain types of product (e.g. pharmaceuticals, aircraft and electrical equipment) require regulatory approval before they can be sold. Regulatory approval is not one of the criteria for recognition under IAS 38. Therefore, when regulatory approval for a product under development has not yet been obtained, an entity would not necessarily be prohibited from capitalising its development costs. However, in the case of a totally new product, the absence of regulatory approval may indicate significant uncertainty around the possible future economic benefits. The practical impact of regulatory approval on pharmaceuticals is shown in Extract 12.5 below.

The standard does not define the terms 'research phase' and 'development phase' but explains that they should be interpreted more broadly than 'research' and 'development' which it does define.[122] The features characterising the research phase have less to do with what activities are performed, but relate more to an inability to demonstrate at that time that an intangible asset exists that will generate probable future benefits.[123] This means that the research phase may include activities that do not necessarily meet the definition of 'research'. For example, the research phase for IAS 38 purposes may extend to the whole period preceding a product launch, regardless of the fact that activities that would otherwise characterise development are taking place at the same time, because certain features that would mean the project has entered its development phase are still absent (such as confirming an ability to use or sell the asset; demonstrating sufficient market demand for a product; or uncertainty regarding the source of funds to complete the project). As a result, an entity might not be able to distinguish the research phase from the development phase of an internal project to create an intangible asset, in which case it should treat the expenditure on that project as if it were incurred in the research phase only and recognise an expense accordingly.[124] It also means that the development phase may include activities that do not necessarily meet the definition of 'development'. The example below explains how an entity would apply these rules in practice.

Example 12.3: Research phase and development phase under IAS 38

Entity K is working on a project to create a database containing images and articles from newspapers around the world, which it intends to sell to customers over the internet. K has identified the following stages in its project:

(a) Research stage – gaining the technical knowledge necessary to transfer images to customers and assessing whether the project is feasible from a technological point of view;

(b) Development stage – performing market analysis to identify potential demand and customer requirements; developing the ability to exploit the image capture technology including configuration of the required database software and acquiring the required data to populate the database, designing the customer interface and testing a prototype of the system; and

(c) Production stage – before and after the commercial launch of the service, debugging the system and improving functionality to service higher user volumes; updating and managing the database to ensure its currency.

The above can be summarised as follows:

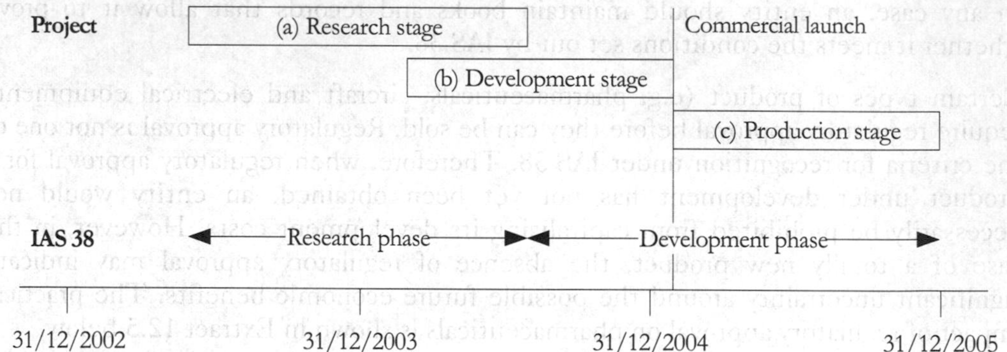

The activities in the research stage included under (a) meet the definition of research under IAS 38 and would be accounted for as part of the research phase of the project.

The activities in the development stage included under (b) meet the definition of development under IAS 38. However, whilst K has started to plan the commercial exploitation of its image and data capture technology, it will not be immediately apparent that the project is economically viable. Until this point is reached, for example when the entity has established there is demand for the database and it is likely that a working prototype of the system will be available, the development activities cannot be distinguished from the research activities taking place at the same time. Accordingly, the initial development activities are accounted for as if they were incurred in the research phase. Only once it becomes possible to demonstrate the existence of an intangible asset that will generate future income streams, can project expenditure be accounted for under IAS 38 as part of the development phase.

There may be a period after the commercial launch of the service that would still be accounted for as part of the development phase. For example, activities to improve functionality to deal with higher actual customer volumes could constitute development. This does not necessarily mean that K can capitalise all this expenditure because it needs pass the double hurdle of:

- the presumption in paragraph 20 of IAS 38 that 'there are no additions to such an asset or replacements of part of it' (see 2.2.3 above); and
- the six criteria in paragraph 57 for recognition of development costs (see above).

Activity to ensure that the database is up-to-date is a routine process that does not involve major innovations or new technologies. Therefore, these activities in the production stage do not meet the definition of 'research' or 'development' and the related costs are recognised as an expense.

As the above example illustrates, the guidance in IAS 38 seems to take a somewhat out-of-date view as to how internally generated intangible assets are created and managed in practice, as well as what types of internally generated intangible assets there can be. It requires activity to be classified into research and development phases, but this methodology does not easily fit with intangible assets that are created for use by the entity itself. The standard therefore ignores the everyday reality for software companies, television production companies, newspapers and data vendors that produce intangible assets in industrial-scale routine processes.

Many of the intangible assets produced in routine processes – e.g. software, television programmes, newspaper content and databases – meet the recognition criteria in the standard, but no specific guidance is available that could help an entity in dealing with the practical problems that arise when accounting for them. Such guidance does not appear to be forthcoming. In February 2002, the IFRIC concluded that it would not be necessary to develop specific guidance on accounting for the 'costs of acquiring or developing content for electronic databases' as it considered that IAS 38 and SIC-32 provide sufficient guidance.[125]

On the one hand the standard requires recognition of an intangible asset arising from development (or the development phase of an internal project), while on the other hand it imposes stringent conditions that restrict recognition. For an entity that wants to recognise development expenditure as an intangible asset these tests create a sensible balance, ensuring that the entity does not recognise unrecoverable costs as an asset. It should be noted that the (then) IASC considered the argument that 'comparability of financial statements will not be achieved … because the judgement involved in determining whether it is probable that future economic benefits will flow from internally generated intangible assets is too subjective to result in similar accounting under similar circumstances',[126] but ultimately decided that there 'should be no difference between the requirement for (a) intangible assets that are acquired externally and (b) internally generated intangible assets, whether they arise from development activities or other types of activities'.[127] They concluded that the recognition criteria are met implicitly for acquired intangible assets and, therefore, it is for the entity to demonstrate explicitly that they are met in the case of the internally generated assets.

Extract 12.4 shows how Air Liquide navigates the distinction between the definitions of research and development and the broader interpretation applied for determining whether projects are classified as research phase or development phase activities in designing its accounting policies for research and development costs and for the treatment of other internally generated intangible assets.

Extract 12.4: Air Liquide S.A. (2006)

Accounting principles

4. Accounting policies [extract]

4.5 Non-current assets [extract]

b/ Research and Development expenditures

Research and Development expenditures include all costs relating to the scientific and technical activities, patent work, education and training necessary to assure the development, manufacturing, start-up, and market research of new or improved products or processes.

According to IAS38, development costs shall be recognized as assets if and only if the Group can demonstrate all the following:

- the project is clearly identified and the related costs are individualized and reliably monitored,
- the technical feasibility of completing the intangible asset so that it will be available for use or sale,
- there is a clear intention to complete the intangible asset and use or sell it,
- the Group can demonstrate how the intangible asset will generate future economic benefits.

Research expenditures are recognized as an expense when incurred. The Group did not capitalize Research and Development expenditures as it as it considers that the conditions required by IFRS standards for the capitalization of development costs were not met, since expenditures do not systematically result in the completion of an intangible asset that will be available for use or sale. As a result, the Development costs incurred by the Group in its Research and Development projects are expensed.

c/ Internally generated intangible assets

Other internally generated intangible assets mainly represent the development costs of information management systems. These costs are capitalized only if they satisfy the criteria defined by IAS38 and described above.

Internal and external development costs on management information systems arising from the development phase are capitalized. Significant maintenance and improvement costs are added to the initial cost of assets if they specifically meet the capitalization criteria.

Internally generated intangible assets are amortized over their useful life.

The extract below illustrates some of the difficulty in applying the IAS 38 recognition criteria for development costs in the pharmaceutical industry. Typically, technical and economic feasibility are established very late in the process of developing a new product, which means that usually only a small proportion of the development costs is capitalised (see 3.2 below).

Extract 12.5: Merck KGaA (2006)

Accounting Policies [extract]

Research and development

The breakdown of research and development by business sectors and regions is presented under "Segment Reporting". In addition to the costs of research departments and process development, this item also includes the cost of purchased services and the cost of clinical trials. The costs of research and development are expensed in full in the period in which they are incurred. Development expenses in the Pharmaceuticals business sector cannot be capitalized since the high level of risk up to the time that pharmaceutical products are marketed means that the requirements of IAS 38 are not satisfied in full. Costs incurred after regulatory approval are insignificant. In the same way, the risks involved until products are marketed means that development expenses in the Chemicals business sector cannot be capitalized. In addition to our own research and development, Merck is also a partner in collaborations aimed at developing marketable products. These collaborations typically involve payments for the achievements of certain milestones. With respect to this situation, an assessment is required as to whether these upfront or milestone payments represent ongoing research and development expense or whether these payments represent the acquisition of the right to capitalize the R&D expense. Reimbursements for R&D are offset against research and development costs.

C Internally generated brands, mastheads, publishing titles and customer lists

IAS 38 prohibits recognition of such items as intangible assets,[128] because it considers internally generated brands, mastheads, publishing titles, customer lists and items similar in substance to be indistinguishable from the cost of developing a business as a whole.[129] As discussed at 2.2.3 above, the same applies to subsequent expenditures incurred in connection with such intangible assets.[130] For example, expenditure incurred in redesigning the layout of newspapers or magazines, which represent subsequent expenditure on publishing titles and mastheads, should not be capitalised.

The (then) IASC set out this explicit prohibition so as to remove any room for misunderstanding, but believed that in any event an entity would interpret the criteria in IAS 38 to determine that internally generated intangible items of this kind would rarely, and perhaps never, qualify for recognition.[131]

D Website costs

In May 2001, the IASB issued SIC-32 (amended 2003) in reaction to the very large sums that were being spent at the time on the operation and development of websites. An entity's own website that arises from development and is for internal or external access is an internally generated intangible asset that is subject to the requirements of IAS 38.[132] SIC-32 clarifies how IAS 38 applies to accounting for costs in relation to websites designed for use by the entity in its business, but does not apply to items that are accounted for under another standard, such as the development or operation of a website (or website software) for sale to another entity (IAS 2 and IAS 11); acquiring or developing hardware supporting a website (IAS 16); or in determining the initial recognition of an asset for a website subject to a leasing arrangement (IAS 17). However, SIC-32 should be applied by lessors providing a website under an operating lease and by lessees considering the treatment of subsequent expenditure relating to a website asset leased under a finance lease.[133]

The interpretation recognises that a website may be used for various purposes such as to promote and advertise an entity's own products and services, provide electronic services to customers, and sell products and services. A website may be used within the entity to give staff access to company policies and customer details, and allow them to search relevant information.[134]

Under SIC-32, an intangible asset should be recognised for website development costs if and only if, in addition to complying with the general recognition requirements in IAS 38 (see 2.2.1 above), the six conditions for the recognition of development costs are met in full (see 2.3.6 B above).[135] The interpretation deems that an entity is not able to demonstrate how a web site developed solely or primarily for promoting and advertising its own products and services will generate probable future economic benefits, and consequently all expenditure on developing such a web site should be recognised as an expense when incurred. Accordingly, it is unlikely that costs will be eligible for capitalisation unless an entity can demonstrate that the website is used directly in the income generating process, for example where customers can place orders on the entity's website.[136]

The following stages of a website's development are identified by the interpretation:[137]

(a) *planning* includes undertaking feasibility studies, defining objectives and specifications, evaluating alternatives and selecting preferences. Expenditure incurred in this stage is similar in nature to the research phase and should be recognised as an expense when it is incurred;

(b) *application and infrastructure development* includes obtaining a domain name, purchasing and developing hardware and operating software, installing developed applications and stress testing. The requirements of IAS 16 are applied to expenditure on physical assets. Other costs are recognised as an expense, unless they can be directly attributed, or allocated on a reasonable and consistent basis, to preparing the website for its intended use and the project to develop the website meets the SIC-12 criteria for recognition as an intangible asset;

(c) *graphical design development* includes designing the appearance of web pages. Costs incurred at this stage should be accounted for in the same way as expenditure incurred in the 'application and infrastructure development' stage described under (b) above;

(d) *content development* includes creating, purchasing, preparing and uploading information, either textual or graphical in nature, on the website before the completion of the website's development. An expense is always recognised for the costs of content that is developed to advertise and promote an entity's own products and services. Other costs incurred in this stage should be recognised as an expense unless the criteria for recognition as an asset described in (b) above are satisfied;

(e) the *operating stage*, which starts after completion of the development of a website, when an entity maintains and enhances the applications, infrastructure, graphical design and content of the website.[138] Expenditure incurred in this stage should be recognised as an expense when it is incurred unless it meets the asset recognition criteria in IAS 38.

In making the above assessments, the entity should evaluate the nature of each activity for which expenditure is incurred, independently of its consideration of the website's stage of development. Additional guidance is provided in the Appendix to SIC-32.[139] This means that even where a project has been determined to qualify for recognition as an intangible asset, not all costs incurred in relation to a qualifying stage of development are eligible for capitalisation. For example, whilst the direct costs of developing an online ordering system might qualify for recognition as an asset, the costs of training staff to operate that system should be expensed because training costs are not deemed necessary to creating, producing or preparing the website for it to be capable of operating (see 2.3.7 below).[140]

A website that is recognised as an intangible asset should be measured after initial recognition by applying the cost model or the revaluation model in IAS 38 as discussed at 2.4 and 2.5 below. The IASB requires an entity to be prudent in assessing the useful life of website assets, by stating it should be short.[141]

Extract 12.6: France Telecom S.A. (2006)

Note 2 – SIGNIFICANT ACCOUNTING POLICIES AND CHANGES IN ESTIMATES [extract]

2.3 Significant accounting policies [extract]

2.3.8 Intangible assets [extract]

Other development costs

Website development costs are capitalized when all of the following conditions are met:

– it is probable that the website will be successfully developed, the Group has adequate technical, financial and other resources to complete the development and has the intention of and ability to complete the site and use or sell it;
– the website will generate future economic benefits;
– the Group has the ability to reliably measure the expenditure attributable to the website during its development.

Website development costs are expensed as incurred or recognized as an intangible asset depending on the phase:

– initial design costs are expensed as incurred;
– qualifying development and graphic design costs are recognized as an intangible asset;
– expenditure incurred after the website has been completed is recorded as an expense, except where it enables the website to generate future additional economic benefits, and if it can be reliably estimated and attributed to the website.

2.3.7 *Cost of an internally generated intangible asset*

As discussed at 2.2 above, upon initial recognition an intangible asset should be measured at cost,[142] which the standard defines as 'the amount of cash or cash equivalents paid or the fair value of other consideration given to acquire an asset at the time of its acquisition or construction, or, when applicable, the amount attributed to that asset when initially recognised in accordance with the specific requirements of other IFRSs, e.g. IFRS 2.'[143] For internally generated intangible assets, it is important to ensure that cost includes only the expenditure incurred after the recognition criteria are met and to confirm that only costs directly related to the creation of the asset are capitalised.

A Establishing the time from which costs can be capitalised

The cost of an internally generated intangible asset is the sum of the expenditure incurred from the date when the intangible asset first meets the recognition criteria of the standard,[144] that is:

(a) it is probable that the expected future economic benefits that are attributable to the asset will flow to the entity, using reasonable and supportable assumptions that represent management's best estimate of the set of economic conditions that will exist over the useful life of the asset;[145]

(b) the cost of the asset can be measured reliably;[146]

(c) the asset meets the detailed conditions for recognition of development phase costs as an asset from paragraph 57 of the standard (see 2.3.6 B above); and

Costs incurred before these criteria are met are recognised as an expense[147] and cannot be reinstated retrospectively,[148] because IAS 38 does not permit recognition of past expenses as an intangible asset at a later date.[149]

The following example, which is taken from IAS 38, illustrates how these above rules should be applied in practice.[150]

Example 12.4: Recognition of internally generated intangible assets

An entity is developing a new production process. During 2005, expenditure incurred was €1,000, of which €900 was incurred before 1 December 2005 and €100 was incurred between 1 December 2005 and 31 December 2005. The entity is able to demonstrate that, at 1 December 2005, the production process met the criteria for recognition as an intangible asset. The recoverable amount of the know-how embodied in the process (including future cash outflows to complete the process before it is available for use) is estimated to be €500.

At the end of 2005, the production process is recognised as an intangible asset at a cost of €100 (expenditure incurred since the date when the recognition criteria were met, i.e. 1 December 2005). The €900 expenditure incurred before 1 December 2005 is recognised as an expense because the recognition criteria were not met until 1 December 2005. This expenditure does not form part of the cost of the production process recognised in the balance sheet.

During 2006, expenditure incurred is €2,000. At the end of 2006, the recoverable amount of the know-how embodied in the process (including future cash outflows to complete the process before it is available for use) is estimated to be €1,900.

At the end of 2006, the cost of the production process is €2,100 (€100 expenditure recognised at the end of 2005 plus €2,000 expenditure recognised in 2006). The entity recognises an impairment loss of €200 to adjust the carrying amount of the process before impairment loss (€2,100) to its recoverable amount (€1,900). This impairment loss will be reversed in a subsequent period if the requirements for the reversal of an impairment loss in IAS 36 are met.

B Determining the costs eligible for capitalisation

The cost of an internally generated intangible asset comprises all directly attributable costs necessary to create, produce, and prepare the asset to be capable of operating in the manner intended by management. Examples of directly attributable costs are:[151]

- costs of materials and services used or consumed in generating the intangible asset;
- costs of employee benefits arising from the generation of the intangible asset;
- fees to register a legal right;
- amortisation of patents and licences that are used to generate the intangible asset; and
- borrowing costs that meet the criteria under IAS 23 for recognition as an element of cost.

Indirect costs and general overheads, even if they can be allocated on a reasonable and consistent basis, can no longer be recognised as part of the cost of the asset, as was possible under the previous version of IAS 38 which permitted this. The standard also specifically prohibits recognition of the following items as a component of cost:[152]

- selling, administrative and other general overhead expenditure unless this expenditure can be directly attributed to preparing the asset for use;
- identified inefficiencies and initial operating losses incurred before the asset achieves planned performance; and
- expenditure on training staff to operate the asset.

2.3.8 Recognition of an expense

Unless expenditure is incurred in connection with an intangible item that the standard requires to be recognised, and is an eligible component of cost, it should be expensed. The only exception is in connection with a business combination, where the costs associated with an intangible that cannot be recognised will form part of the carrying amount of goodwill.[153]

Some of the ineligible components of cost were identified in 2.3.7 above. Sometimes expenditure is incurred to provide future economic benefits to an entity, but no intangible asset or other asset is acquired or created that can be recognised. In these cases, the expenditure is recognised as an expense when it is incurred. IAS 38 provides other examples of expenditure that is recognised as an expense when incurred:[154]

(a) start-up costs, unless they qualify for recognition as part of the cost of property, plant and equipment under IAS 16 (see Chapter 13 at 2.3.1) Start-up costs recognised as an expense may consist of establishment costs such as legal and secretarial costs incurred in establishing a legal entity, expenditure to open a new facility or business or expenditures for starting new operations or launching new products or processes;

(b) training costs;

(c) advertising and promotional activities; and
(d) relocation or reorganisation costs.

The standard does not preclude an entity recognising a prepayment as an asset when payment for the delivery of goods or services has been made in advance of the delivery of goods or the rendering of services.[155] However, once an entity receives those goods or services, it should recognise an expense if the related intangible asset does not meet the recognition criteria.

A Catalogues and other advertising costs

In September 2006 the IFRIC discussed accounting for catalogues and other advertising costs. The IFRIC thought 'it likely that divergence exists in practice with some entities accounting for catalogues as inventory, some as a prepayment, and some recognising the costs in profit or loss immediately. Where costs are deferred, the IFRIC considered that divergence may exist in the way that the costs are subsequently recognised as an expense, with some being recognised as an expense when the catalogues are distributed, and others amortised over the life of the catalogues'.[156] It therefore agreed to initiate a project to consider when costs incurred for advertising and promotional activities (including catalogues) may be carried forward in the balance sheet. As part of this project, the IFRIC decided to 'pay particular attention to paragraphs 68-70 of IAS 38, which state that advertising and promotional expenditure must be recognised as an expense when incurred but do not preclude recognising a prepayment when payment for the goods or services has been made in advance of the delivery of goods or rendering of services'.[157]

Over the next six months, the IFRIC considered a number of alternative milestones beyond which deferral should cease and at which an expense should be recognised:

- when the entity recognises a liability to pay for the advertising or promotional activities;
- when the entity takes delivery of the advertising or promotional materials;
- when the entity delivers the advertising to its customers; or
- when the entity receives the benefit of its advertising by way of increased sales revenue.

The IFRIC initially reached a consensus only on the fourth option, agreeing that it was not appropriate to capitalise advertising and promotion costs and amortise them over the expected period of benefit.[158] It later rejected the option to recognise an expense when the entity delivers the advertising to its customers, because the implication of this proposal would have been that start-up costs could be deferred until the start-up event occurred.[159] In March 2007, the IFRIC asked the IASB to consider the matter as part of its annual improvements process.[160]

The proposal submitted to the IASB was that a prepayment can be recognised only until the related goods and services are received by the entity, except in the case of advertising and promotional or training activities in which case deferral continues until the first time as the activities take place. The Board concluded that the question contained two elements, the treatment of the cost of developing content (advertising and training content or materials); and the treatment of costs relating to communication (delivery of that content, for example using television airtime).[161]

An entity takes delivery of the content when it has physical access to it, so the cost of catalogues or the promotional recording for later transmission is recognised as an expense when they are received by the entity. Only if the item had an alternative use that directly generates revenue would there be a case for recognising an asset such as inventory at this point. The costs of communication (the cost of despatching catalogues or for television airtime) are expensed when the entity receives those services, being when its catalogues are uplifted for despatch or the time at which television airtime is granted.

In May 2007, the Board tentatively decided that the annual improvements process would include proposals to amend paragraphs 68-70 of IAS 38, such that the cost of advertising and promotional content and materials is expensed when the entity takes delivery of those goods and services.[162] The Board confirmed this view at its June 2007 meeting and indicated that an exposure draft would be published in October 2007.[163]

2.4 Measurement after initial recognition

IAS 38, in common with a number of other international standards, provides an entity the option to choose between two alternative treatments that may be summarised as follows:[164]

- the *cost model*, which requires measurement at cost less any accumulated amortisation and any accumulated impairment losses[165] (see 2.4.1 below); and
- the *revaluation model*, which requires measurement at a revalued amount (based on fair value) less any subsequent accumulated amortisation and any subsequent accumulated impairment losses[166] (see 2.4.2 below).

The revaluation option is only available if an active market exists for the intangible asset.[167] There are no provisions in IAS 38 allowing fair value in this situation to be determined indirectly, for example by using the techniques and financial models applied to estimate the fair value of intangible assets acquired in a business combination (see 2.3.2 above). When an entity chooses to measure an intangible asset at valuation, it must apply the revaluation model to all the assets in that class, unless there is no active market for those other assets.[168] A class of intangible assets is defined as 'a grouping of assets of a similar nature and use in an entity's operations'.[169] Examples of separate classes of intangible asset include:[170]

(a) brand names;

(b) mastheads and publishing titles;

(c) computer software;

(d) licences and franchises;

(e) copyrights, patents and other industrial property rights, service and operating rights;

(f) recipes, formulae, models, designs and prototypes; and

(g) intangible assets under development.

The standard requires assets in the same class to be revalued at the same time, 'to avoid selective revaluation of assets and the reporting of amounts in the financial statements representing a mixture of costs and values as at different dates'.[171]

2.4.1 Cost model

Under the cost model, after initial recognition the carrying amount of an intangible asset is its cost less any accumulated amortisation and accumulated impairment losses.[172] The rules on amortisation of intangible assets are discussed at 2.6 and 2.7 below; and impairment is discussed at 2.8 below.

2.4.2 Revaluation model

Under the revaluation model, after initial recognition an intangible asset should be carried at a revalued amount, which is its fair value at the date of the revaluation less any subsequent accumulated amortisation and any subsequent accumulated impairment losses.[173] An entity can only elect to apply the revaluation model if the fair value can be determined by reference to an active market for the intangible asset.[174] To prevent an entity from circumventing the recognition rules of the standard, the revaluation model does not allow:[175]

- the revaluation of intangible assets that have not previously been recognised as assets; or
- the initial recognition of intangible assets at amounts other than cost.

However, it is permitted to apply the revaluation model to the whole of an intangible asset even if only part of its cost is recognised as an asset because it did not meet the criteria for recognition until part of the way through the process.[176] These rules are designed to prevent an entity from recognising at a 'revalued' amount an intangible asset that was never recorded because its costs were expensed as they did not at the time meet the recognition rules. As these rules would also prohibit the revaluation of quotas and permits allocated by governments and similar bodies – which are amongst the few intangible assets that do have an active market – the standard specifically makes an exception and allows the revaluation model to be applied to 'an intangible asset that was received by way of a government grant and recognised at a nominal amount'.[177]

The example below illustrates how this would work in practice.

Example 12.5: Application of revaluation model to intangible assets that are partially recognised or received by way of government grant

Entity C spent ¥12,000,000 in preparing its application for a number of taxi licenses, which it expensed because of the uncertain outcome of the process. The application was successful and C was granted a number of freely transferable taxi licenses and paid a nominal registration fee of ¥50,000, which it recognised as an asset. There is an active and liquid market in these taxi licenses.

C can apply the revaluation model under IAS 38 to these taxi licenses, because it previously recognised the license (even if it only recognised part of the costs as an asset) and there is an active market in these licenses.

Entity D obtained a number of freely transferable fishing quotas free of charge, which it recognised at a nominal amount as permitted under IAS 20. There is an active and liquid market in these quotas.

D can apply the revaluation model under IAS 38 to these fishing quotas, because it previously recognised the license (even if it only recognised it at a nominal amount) and there is an active market in these licenses.

A Active market

As mentioned above, an entity can only elect to apply the revaluation model if the fair value can be determined by reference to an active market for the intangible asset.[178] IAS 38 defines an active market as one in which all the following conditions exist:[179]

(a) the items traded in the market are homogeneous;

(b) willing buyers and sellers can normally be found at any time; and

(c) prices are available to the public.

The fact that all these criteria must be met means that few intangible assets will be eligible for revaluation and indeed the standard concedes that such an active market would be uncommon. Nevertheless it is possible for a class of intangible assets to be regarded as homogeneous. For example, in some jurisdictions, an active market may exist for freely transferable taxi licences, fishing licences or production quotas.[180] However, by their very nature most intangible assets are somehow unique or entity-specific. For example, the standard lists brands, newspaper mastheads, music and film publishing rights, patents or trademarks, as ineligible for revaluation because each such asset is unique.[181] In other words, 'homogeneous' in the definition of an active market is to be interpreted as meaning 'identical' or 'virtually identical'. It is not enough for intangible assets merely to be very similar in use or function.

The term 'homogeneous' in the definition applies not only to the nature of the asset, but also to the manner in which it is traded. Even if the intangible assets traded can be regarded as identical in nature, the existence of a previous sale and purchase transaction is not sufficient evidence for the market to be regarded as active. The standard notes that where contracts are negotiated between individual buyers and sellers or when transactions are relatively infrequent, the price of a previous transaction for *one* intangible asset may not provide sufficient evidence of the fair value of another. In addition, if prices are not available to the public, this is taken as evidence that an active market does *not* exist.[182]

B Frequency of revaluations

If an entity manages to satisfy itself that an active market exists, IAS 38 requires revaluation to be performed 'with such regularity that at the balance sheet date the carrying amount of the asset does not differ materially from its fair value'.[183] The standard lets entities judge for themselves the frequency of revaluations depending on the volatility of the fair values of the underlying intangible assets, though it does add that 'some intangible assets may experience significant and volatile movements in fair value, thus necessitating annual revaluation. Such frequent revaluations are unnecessary for intangible assets with only insignificant movements in fair value.'[184]

Nevertheless, considering the narrow definition of an 'active market' and the definition of 'material' in IAS 1 – *Presentation of Financial Statements* – an entity should err on the side of caution and revalue frequently because there is normally no excuse for ignoring price information that the standard requires to be available to the public. As noted above, when an entity has a number of items in the same class of intangible assets, the standard requires that they are all valued at the same time.[185]

C Accounting for revaluations

Increases in an intangible asset's carrying amount as a result of a revaluation should be credited directly to equity under the heading of revaluation surplus, unless the revaluation reverses a revaluation decrease of the same asset that was previously recognised in profit or loss.[186] Conversely, decreases in an intangible asset's carrying amount as a result of a revaluation should be recognised in profit or loss, unless the revaluation reverses an earlier revaluation increase, in which case the decrease should first be debited directly to equity to extinguish the revaluation surplus in respect of the asset.[187] The example below illustrates how this works.

Example 12.6: Accounting for upward and downward revaluations

Entity E acquired an intangible asset that it accounts for under the revaluation model. The fair value of the asset changes as follows:

	£
Acquisition	530
A	550
B	520
C	510
D	555

The diagram below summarises this information (the impact of amortisation on the carrying amount and revaluation surplus has been ignored in this example for the sake of simplicity).

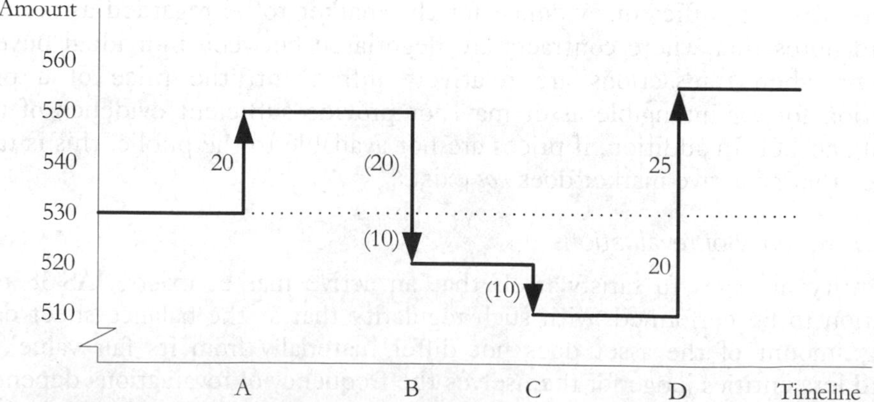

The table below shows how entity E should account for the upward and downward revaluations.

	Value of asset	Cumulative revaluation reserve	Revaluation recognised in equity	Revaluation recognised in profit or loss
	£	£	£	£
Acquisition	530	–	–	–
A	550	20	20	–
B	520	–	(20)	(10)
C	510	–	–	(10)
D	555	25	25	20

The upward revaluation at A is accounted for in equity. The downward revaluation at B first reduces the revaluation reserve for that asset to nil and the excess of £10 is recognised as a loss in income. The second downward revaluation at C is recognised as a loss in income. The upward revaluation at D first reverses the cumulative loss recognised in income and the excess is accounted for in the revaluation reserve.

In the example above the impact of amortisation on the carrying amount of the assets and the revaluation surplus was ignored for the sake of simplicity. However, the cumulative revaluation surplus included in equity may be transferred directly to retained earnings when the surplus is realised, which happens either (1) on the retirement or disposal of the asset or (2) as the asset is used by the entity.[188] In the latter case, the 'amount of the surplus realised is the difference between amortisation based on the revalued carrying amount of the asset and amortisation that would have been recognised based on the asset's historical cost'.[189] In practice this means two things:

- an entity applying the revaluation model would need to track both the historical cost and revalued amount of an asset to determine how much of the revaluation surplus has been realised; and
- any revaluation surplus is amortised over the life of the related asset. Therefore, in the case of a significant downward revaluation there is a smaller revaluation surplus available against which the downward revaluation can be offset.

The transfer from revaluation surplus to retained earnings is not made through the income statement.[190]

If an intangible asset is revalued, the standard allows an entity to account for the accumulated amortisation at the date of revaluation by either:[191]

(a) restating it proportionately with the change in the gross carrying amount of the asset so that the carrying amount of the asset after revaluation equals its revalued amount; or

(b) eliminating it against the gross carrying amount of the asset and the net amount restated to the revalued amount of the asset.

The proportionate method is rarely used unless the asset's net carrying amount is being revalued to depreciated replacement cost using an index, which will rarely be the case for an intangible asset.

Example 12.7: Restatement of accumulated amortisation after a revaluation

Entity F revalued an intangible asset from its carrying amount of £120 to its fair value of £150. The proportionate restatement approach (in the middle column) leads to grossing up of both gross carrying amount and the accumulated amortisation. The elimination approach (in the right-hand column) results in elimination of the accumulated amortisation.

		After revaluation	
	Before revaluation	*Proportionate restatement*	*Eliminating amortisation*
	£	£	£
Gross carrying amount	300	375	150
Accumulated amortisation	(180)	(225)	–
Net carrying amount	120	150	150

D No active market

The standard requires an entity to apply the revaluation model to entire classes of intangible assets,[192] but if there is no active market for an item in a class of revalued intangible assets, the asset is carried at its cost less any accumulated amortisation and impairment losses'.[193]

Similarly, an entity should stop revaluing an asset if the market used to determine its fair value ceases to meet the criteria for an active market. The valuation is 'frozen' from that date, and reduced thereafter by subsequent amortisation and any subsequent impairment losses.[194] The IASB believes that such a lack of a previously active market may indicate that the asset needs to be tested for impairment in accordance with IAS 36.[195]

If an active market for the previously revalued asset emerges at a later date, the entity is required to apply the revaluation model from that date.[196]

2.5 Assessing the useful life of an intangible asset

IAS 38 defines the useful life of an intangible asset as:[197]

(a) the period over which an asset is expected to be available for use by an entity; or

(b) the number of production or similar units expected to be obtained from the asset by an entity.

Thus in some cases the useful life of an intangible asset should be expressed as a number of production or similar units rather than a period of time.

The standard requires an entity to assess whether the useful life of an intangible asset is finite or indefinite.[198] If an entity concludes that the useful life of an intangible asset is finite, it estimates the length of its useful life or the number of production units (or similar units) constituting that useful life.[199] An intangible asset with a finite useful life is amortised, whereas an intangible asset with an indefinite useful life is not.[200]

For this purpose the term 'indefinite' does not mean 'infinite'.[201] The standard requires an intangible asset to be classified as having an indefinite useful life 'when, based on an analysis of all of the relevant factors, there is no foreseeable limit to the period over which the asset is expected to generate net cash inflows for the entity'.[202]

The previous version of IAS 38 prescribed a presumptive maximum useful life for intangible assets of 20 years.[203] However, the IASB observed that 'some intangible assets are based on legal rights that are conveyed in perpetuity rather than for finite terms. ... The Board concluded that if the cash flows are expected to continue for a finite period, the useful life of the asset is limited to that finite period. However, if the cash flows are expected to continue indefinitely, the useful life is indefinite.'[204] The IASB decided to remove the presumptive maximum useful life for intangible assets, because it is 'inconsistent with the view that the amortisation period for an intangible asset should, to be representationally faithful, reflect its useful life and, by extension, the cash flow streams associated with the asset'.[205]

This means that under IAS 38 it is now possible to account for intangible assets without amortising them at all. However, an important underlying assumption in making the assessment of the useful life of an intangible asset is that it 'reflects only that level of future maintenance expenditure required to maintain the asset at its standard of performance assessed at the time of estimating the asset's useful life, and the entity's ability and intention to reach such a level. A conclusion that the useful life of an intangible asset is indefinite should not depend on planned future expenditure in excess of that required to maintain the asset at that standard of performance.'[206]

The standard identifies a number of factors that may affect the useful life of an intangible asset:[207]

(a) the expected usage of the asset by the entity and whether the asset could be managed efficiently by another management team;
(b) typical product life cycles for the asset and public information on estimates of useful lives of similar assets that are used in a similar way;
(c) technical, technological, commercial or other types of obsolescence;
(d) the stability of the industry in which the asset operates and changes in the market demand for the products or services output from the asset;
(e) expected actions by competitors or potential competitors;
(f) the level of maintenance expenditure required to obtain the expected future economic benefits from the asset and the entity's ability and intention to reach such a level;
(g) the period of control over the asset and legal or similar limits on the use of the asset, such as the expiry dates of related leases; and
(h) whether the useful life of the asset is dependent on the useful life of other assets of the entity.

Further guidance is provided by IAS 38 in the form of Illustrative Examples (which are reproduced in the example below) that demonstrate how an entity would go about determining the useful life for different intangible assets and the subsequent accounting for those assets based on the useful life determinations.[208]

Example 12.8: Assessing the useful life of an intangible asset

Acquired customer list

A direct-mail marketing company acquires a customer list and expects that it will be able to derive benefit from the information on the list for at least one year, but no more than three years.

The customer list would be amortised over management's best estimate of its useful life, say 18 months. Although the direct-mail marketing company may intend to add customer names and other information to the list in the future, the expected benefits of the acquired customer list relate only to the customers on that list at the date it was acquired. The customer list also would be reviewed for impairment in accordance with IAS 36 by assessing at each reporting date whether there is any indication that the customer list may be impaired.

An acquired patent that expires in 15 years

The product protected by the patented technology is expected to be a source of net cash inflows for at least 15 years. The entity has a commitment from a third party to purchase that patent in five years for 60 per cent of the fair value of the patent at the date it was acquired, and the entity intends to sell the patent in five years.

The patent would be amortised over its five-year useful life to the entity, with a residual value equal to the present value of 60 per cent of the patent's fair value at the date it was acquired. The patent would also be reviewed for impairment in accordance with IAS 36 by assessing at each reporting date whether there is any indication that it may be impaired.

An acquired copyright that has a remaining legal life of 50 years

An analysis of consumer habits and market trends provides evidence that the copyrighted material will generate net cash inflows for only 30 more years.

The copyright would be amortised over its 30-year estimated useful life. The copyright also would be reviewed for impairment in accordance with IAS 36 by assessing at each reporting date whether there is any indication that it may be impaired.

An acquired broadcasting licence that expires in five years

The broadcasting licence is renewable every 10 years if the entity provides at least an average level of service to its customers and complies with the relevant legislative requirements. The licence may be renewed indefinitely at little cost and has been renewed twice before the most recent acquisition. The acquiring entity intends to renew the licence indefinitely and evidence supports its ability to do so. Historically, there has been no compelling challenge to the licence renewal. The technology used in broadcasting is not expected to be replaced by another technology at any time in the foreseeable future. Therefore, the licence is expected to contribute to the entity's net cash inflows indefinitely.

The broadcasting licence would be treated as having an indefinite useful life because it is expected to contribute to the entity's net cash inflows indefinitely. Therefore, the licence would not be amortised until its useful life is determined to be finite. The licence would be tested for impairment in accordance with IAS 36 annually and whenever there is an indication that it may be impaired.

The broadcasting licence in the example above

The licensing authority subsequently decides that it will no longer renew broadcasting licences, but rather will auction the licences. At the time the licensing authority's decision is made, the entity's broadcasting licence has three years until it expires. The entity expects that the licence will continue to contribute to net cash inflows until the licence expires.

Because the broadcasting licence can no longer be renewed, its useful life is no longer indefinite. Thus, the acquired licence would be amortised over its remaining three-year useful life and immediately tested for impairment in accordance with IAS 36.

An acquired airline route authority between two European cities that expires in three years

The route authority may be renewed every five years, and the acquiring entity intends to comply with the applicable rules and regulations surrounding renewal. Route authority renewals are routinely granted at a minimal cost and historically have been renewed when the airline has complied with the applicable rules and regulations. The acquiring entity expects to provide service indefinitely between the two cities from its hub airports and expects that the related supporting infrastructure (airport gates, slots, and terminal facility leases) will remain in place at those airports for as long as it has the route authority. An analysis of demand and cash flows supports those assumptions.

Because the facts and circumstances support the acquiring entity's ability to continue providing air service indefinitely between the two cities, the intangible asset related to the route authority is treated as having an indefinite useful life. Therefore, the route authority would not be amortised until its useful life is determined to be finite. It would be tested for impairment in accordance with IAS 36 annually and whenever there is an indication that it may be impaired.

An acquired trademark used to identify and distinguish a leading consumer product that has been a market-share leader for the past eight years

The trademark has a remaining legal life of five years but is renewable every 10 years at little cost. The acquiring entity intends to renew the trademark continuously and evidence supports its ability to do so. An analysis of (1) product life cycle studies, (2) market, competitive and environmental trends, and (3) brand extension opportunities provides evidence that the trademarked product will generate net cash inflows for the acquiring entity for an indefinite period.

The trademark would be treated as having an indefinite useful life because it is expected to contribute to net cash inflows indefinitely. Therefore, the trademark would not be amortised until its useful life is determined to be finite. It would be tested for impairment in accordance with IAS 36 annually and whenever there is an indication that it may be impaired.

A trademark acquired 10 years ago that distinguishes a leading consumer product

The trademark was regarded as having an indefinite useful life when it was acquired because the trademarked product was expected to generate net cash inflows indefinitely. However, unexpected competition has recently entered the market and will reduce future sales of the product. Management estimates that net cash inflows generated by the product will be 20 per cent less for the foreseeable future. However, management expects that the product will continue to generate net cash inflows indefinitely at those reduced amounts.

As a result of the projected decrease in future net cash inflows, the entity determines that the estimated recoverable amount of the trademark is less than its carrying amount, and an impairment loss is recognised. Because it is still regarded as having an indefinite useful life, the trademark would continue not to be amortised but would be tested for impairment in accordance with IAS 36 annually and whenever there is an indication that it may be impaired.

A trademark for a line of products acquired several years ago in a business combination

At the time of the business combination the acquiree had been producing the line of products for 35 years with many new models developed under the trademark. At the acquisition date the acquirer expected to continue producing the line, and an analysis of various economic factors indicated there was no limit to the period the trademark would contribute to net cash inflows. Consequently, the trademark was not amortised by the acquirer. However, management has recently decided that production of the product line will be discontinued over the next four years.

Because the useful life of the acquired trademark is no longer regarded as indefinite, the carrying amount of the trademark would be tested for impairment in accordance with IAS 36 and amortised over its remaining four-year useful life.

The standard explicitly warns against both:

- overestimating the useful life of an intangible asset. For example, 'given the history of rapid changes in technology, computer software and many other intangible assets are susceptible to technological obsolescence. Therefore, it is likely that their useful life is short.';[209] and
- underestimating the useful life. For example, 'the useful life of an intangible asset may be very long or even indefinite. Uncertainty justifies estimating the useful life of an intangible asset on a prudent basis, but it does not justify choosing a life that is unrealistically short.'[210]

It may be clear from the above discussion that despite the fairly detailed guidance in the standard an entity will need to exercise judgement in estimating the useful life of intangible assets.

2.5.1 Useful life of contractual or other legal rights

Where an intangible asset arises from contractual or other legal rights, the standard requires an entity to take account of both economic and legal factors influencing its useful life and determine the useful life as the shorter of:[211]

- the period of the contractual or other legal rights; and
- the period (determined by economic factors) over which the entity expects to obtain economic benefits from the asset.

If the contractual or other legal rights are conveyed for a limited term that can be renewed, the useful life of the intangible asset should include the renewal period only if there is evidence to support renewal by the entity without significant cost.[212] The existence of the following factors may indicate that an entity is able to renew the contractual or other legal rights without significant cost:[213]

(a) there is evidence, possibly based on experience, that the contractual or other legal rights will be renewed. If renewal is contingent upon the consent of a third party, this includes evidence that the third party will give its consent;

(b) there is evidence that any conditions necessary to obtain renewal will be satisfied; and

(c) the cost to the entity of renewal is not significant when compared with the future economic benefits expected to flow to the entity from renewal.

A renewal period is only added to the estimate of useful life if its cost is insignificant when compared with the future economic benefits expected to flow to the entity from renewal.[214] If this is not the case, then the original asset's useful life ends at the contracted renewal date and the renewal cost is treated as the cost to acquire a new intangible asset.[215] An entity needs to exercise judgement in assessing what it regards as a significant cost.

2.6 Intangible assets with a finite useful life

2.6.1 Amortisation period and method

Amortisation is the systematic allocation of the depreciable amount of an intangible asset over its useful life. The depreciable amount is the cost of an asset, or other amount substituted for cost (e.g. revaluation), less its residual value.[216] The depreciable amount of an intangible asset with a finite useful life should be allocated on a systematic basis over its useful life in the following manner:[217]

- amortisation should begin when the asset is available for use, i.e. when it is in the location and condition necessary for it to be capable of operating in the manner intended by management. Therefore, even if an entity is not using the asset, it should still be amortised because it is available for use, although there may be exceptions from this general rule (see 2.6.2 below);
- amortisation should cease at the earlier of:
  - the date that the asset is classified as held for sale, or included in a disposal group that is classified as held for sale, in accordance with IFRS 5; and
  - the date that the asset is derecognised.
- the amortisation method should reflect the pattern of consumption of the economic benefits that the intangible asset provides. If that pattern cannot be reliably determined, a straight-line basis should be used.

Amortisation of an intangible asset with a finite useful life continues until the asset has been fully depreciated or is classified as held for sale, as noted above, or derecognised. Amortisation does not cease simply because an asset is not being used,[218] although this fact might give rise to an indicator of impairment.

Although the standard allows a variety of amortisation methods to be used to depreciate the asset on a systematic basis over its useful life (such as the straight-line method, the diminishing balance method and the unit of production method), it states that 'there is rarely, if ever, persuasive evidence to support an amortisation method for intangible assets with finite useful lives that results in a lower amount of accumulated amortisation than under the straight-line method'.[219] This requires entities to seriously challenge the use of amortisation methods that indicate a pattern of consumption that is weighted towards the later period of an intangible asset's estimated useful life. However, this does not mean that such methods are prohibited and the IASB proposes as part of its 2007 annual improvements process to delete this sentence, thereby clarifying that such methods can be applied when determined to be the most appropriate.[220]

The amortisation charge for each period should be recognised in profit or loss unless IFRS specifically permits or requires it to be capitalised as part of the carrying amount of another asset (e.g. inventory or work in progress).[221]

2.6.2 Review of amortisation period and amortisation method

An entity should review the amortisation period and the amortisation method for an intangible asset with a finite useful life at least at each financial year-end. If the expected useful life of the asset has changed, the amortisation period should be changed accordingly.[222] An entity may, for example, consider its previous estimate of the useful life of an intangible asset inappropriate upon recognition of an impairment loss on the asset.[223]

If the expected pattern of consumption of the future economic benefits embodied in the asset has changed, the amortisation method should be changed to reflect the changed pattern.[224] The standard provides two examples of when this might happen:

- if it becomes apparent that a diminishing balance method of amortisation is appropriate rather than a straight-line method;[225] and
- if use of the rights represented by a licence is deferred pending action on other components of the business plan. In this case, economic benefits that flow from the asset may not be received until later periods.[226] This implies that circumstances may exist in which it is appropriate not to recognise an amortisation charge in relation to an intangible asset, because the entity may not be ready to use the intangible asset (e.g. as happens in the case of telecommunication companies that have acquired Universal Mobile Telecommunications System (UMTS) licenses, but that have not completed the physical network to use the license. Note that an entity must perform an impairment test at least annually for any intangible asset that has not yet been brought into use: see 2.8 below).

Both changes in the amortisation period and the amortisation method should be accounted for as changes in accounting estimates in accordance with IAS 8 – *Accounting Policies, Changes in Accounting Estimates and Errors*[227] – which requires such changes to be recognised prospectively.[228]

2.6.3 Residual value

The residual value of an intangible asset is the estimated amount that an entity would currently obtain from disposal of the asset, after deducting the estimated costs of disposal, if the asset were already of the age and in the condition expected at the end of its useful life.[229]

IAS 38 requires entities to assume a residual value of zero for an intangible asset with a finite useful life, unless there is a commitment by a third party to purchase the asset at the end of its useful life *or* there is an active market for the asset from which to determine its residual value and it is probable that such a market will exist at the end of the asset's useful life.[230] The presumption that the residual value of an intangible asset is normally zero was included in the previous version of IAS 38 as an anti-abuse measure to prevent entities from circumventing the requirement to amortise all intangible assets. It was retained in the amended standard for similar anti-avoidance reasons,[231] but its effectiveness is much reduced as an entity can avoid amortisation altogether on intangible assets with an indefinite useful life.

Given the very restrictive definition of 'active market' (see 2.4.2 A above) it seems highly unlikely that – in the absence of a commitment by a third party to buy the asset – an entity will ever be able to prove that the residual value is other than zero. A residual value other than zero implies that the entity intends to dispose of the asset before the end of its useful life.[232]

If an entity can demonstrate a case for estimating a residual value other than zero, its estimate should be based on 'the amount recoverable from disposal using prices prevailing at the date of the estimate for the sale of a similar asset that has reached the end of its useful life and has operated under conditions similar to those in which the asset will be used'.[233] Contrary to what was required by the previous version of IAS 38, the standard now requires a review of the residual value at each financial year-end. This review can result in an upward or downward revision of the estimated residual value and thereby affect the depreciable amount of the asset; that change to depreciation should be accounted for as a change in an accounting estimate in accordance with IAS 8.[234]

The standard does not permit negative amortisation in the event that the residual value of an intangible asset increases to an amount greater than the asset's carrying amount. Instead, the asset's amortisation charge would be 'zero unless and until its residual value subsequently decreases to an amount below the asset's carrying amount'.[235]

2.7 Intangible assets with an indefinite useful life

IAS 38 prohibits amortisation of an intangible asset with an indefinite useful life.[236] Instead, such an intangible asset should be tested for impairment under IAS 36 by comparing its recoverable amount with its carrying amount:[237]

(a) annually, and

(b) whenever there is an indication that the intangible asset may be impaired.

In other words, intangible assets with an indefinite useful life should be tested for impairment annually, irrespective of whether there exists an impairment trigger that warrants impairment testing (see Chapter 15).

An entity should review and validate at each reporting date its decision to classify the useful life of an intangible asset as indefinite.[238] If events and circumstances no longer support an indefinite useful life, the change from indefinite to finite should be accounted for under IAS 8,[239] which requires such changes to be recognised prospectively.[240] Furthermore, reassessing the useful life of an intangible asset as finite rather than indefinite is an indicator that the asset may be impaired.[241]

2.8 Impairment losses

An impairment loss is the amount by which the carrying amount of an asset exceeds its recoverable amount.[242] An entity applies IAS 36 in determining whether an intangible asset is impaired (see Chapter 15 at 3.3).[243]

It is important to note that IAS 36 requires an entity to perform an annual impairment test on every intangible asset that has an indefinite useful life and every intangible asset that is not yet available for use (see Chapter 15 at 3.4.1).[244] The previous version of IAS 38 also required an annual impairment test of intangible assets that had a useful life of over twenty years, irrespective of whether there were any indications of impairment. In its deliberations on the revised IAS 38, the IASB concluded that it 'could see no conceptual reason for requiring the recoverable amounts of some identifiable assets being amortised over very long periods to be determined more regularly than for other identifiable assets being amortised or depreciated over similar periods. ... Consequently, the Board decided to remove the requirement in the previous version of IAS 38 for the recoverable amount of such an intangible asset to be measured at least at each financial year-end.'[245] This reduces the administrative burden for entities somewhat, because the recoverable amount of such intangible assets only needs to be calculated under IAS 36 if there is an impairment indicator.

2.9 Retirements and disposals

An intangible asset should be derecognised on disposal *or* when no future economic benefits are expected from its use or disposal.[246] Although gains on disposal should not be classified as revenue,[247] an entity should apply the criteria for recognising revenue in IAS 18 – *Revenue* – in determining the date of disposal of an intangible asset (see Chapter 28). In the case of a disposal by a sale and leaseback, an entity should apply IAS 17.[248]

The gain or loss on derecognition, which is determined as the difference between the net disposal proceeds and the carrying amount of the asset, should be accounted for in profit or loss unless IAS 17 requires otherwise on a sale and leaseback. Gains on disposal should not be presented as revenue, because they are incidental to the entity's main revenue-generating activities.[249]

The consideration receivable on disposal of an intangible asset is recognised initially at its fair value. This means that, if payment for the intangible asset is deferred, the consideration received is recognised initially at the cash price equivalent. The difference between the nominal amount of the consideration and the cash price equivalent is recognised as interest using the effective interest method under IAS 18.[250]

The standard requires an entity to recognise in the carrying amount of an asset the cost of a replacement for part of an intangible asset and to derecognise the carrying amount of the replaced part. 'If it is not practicable for an entity to determine the carrying amount of the replaced part, it may use the cost of the replacement as an indication of what the cost of the replaced part was at the time it was acquired or internally generated.'[251] However, as noted by the standard, the nature of intangible assets is such that that, in many cases, there are no additions or replacements that would meet its recognition criteria, so this should be an unlikely event (see 2.2.3 above).[252]

2.10 Disclosure

IAS 38 contains a clear and well laid out disclosure section that is easy to use and understand. The main requirements are set out below, but it might also be appropriate to refer to the disclosure requirements of IFRS 5 in Chapter 4 and the disclosure requirements of IAS 36 in Chapter 15.

2.10.1 General disclosures

IAS 38 requires certain disclosures to be presented by class of intangible assets. A class of intangible assets is defined as a grouping of assets of a similar nature and use in an entity's operations. The standard provides examples of classes of assets, which may be 'disaggregated (aggregated) into smaller (larger) classes if this results in more relevant information for the users of the financial statements' (see 2.4 above for examples of classes of intangible assets).[253] Although separate information is required for internally generated intangible assets and other intangible assets, these categories are not considered to be separate classes when they relate to intangible assets of a similar nature and use in an entity's operations. Hence the standard requires the following disclosures to be given for each class of intangible assets – distinguishing between internally generated intangible assets and other intangible assets:[254]

(a) whether the useful lives are indefinite or finite and, if finite, the useful lives or the amortisation rates used;

(b) the amortisation methods used for intangible assets with finite useful lives;

(c) the gross carrying amount and any accumulated amortisation (aggregated with accumulated impairment losses) at the beginning and end of the period;

(d) the line item(s) of the income statement in which any amortisation of intangible assets is included;

(e) a reconciliation of the carrying amount at the beginning and end of the period showing:

  (i) additions, indicating separately those from internal development, those acquired separately, and those acquired through business combinations;

  (ii) assets classified as held for sale or included in a disposal group classified as held for sale in accordance with IFRS 5 and other disposals;

  (iii) increases or decreases during the period resulting from revaluations under paragraphs 75, 85 and 86 and from impairment losses recognised or reversed directly in equity in accordance with IAS 36 (if any);

  (iv) impairment losses recognised in profit or loss during the period in accordance with IAS 36 (if any);

  (v) impairment losses reversed in profit or loss during the period in accordance with IAS 36 (if any);

  (vi) any amortisation recognised during the period;

  (vii) net exchange differences arising on the translation of the financial statements into the presentation currency, and on the translation of a foreign operation into the presentation currency of the entity; and

(viii) other changes in the carrying amount during the period.

The standard permits an entity to present the reconciliation required under (e) above either for the net carrying amount or separately for (1) the gross carrying amount and (2) the accumulated amortisation and impairments (see Extract 12.7 below).

An entity may want to consider separate disclosure of intangible assets acquired by way of government grant or obtained in an exchange of assets, even though disclosure is not specifically required under (e)(i) above.

The current version of IAS 38 requires comparative information for the reconciliation in (e) above, the exemption in the earlier versions of the standard being withdrawn.

The extract below provides a typical example of the disclosures for goodwill and intangible assets, including the reconciliation, under IFRS.

Extract 12.7: Unilever Group (2006)

Notes to the consolidated accounts [extract]

9 Goodwill and intangible assets [extract]

Indefinite-lived intangible assets principally comprise those trademarks for which there is no foreseeable limit to the period over which they are expected to generate net cash inflows. These are considered to have an indefinite life, given the strength and durability of our brands and the level of marketing support. Brands that are classified as indefinite have been in the market for many years, and the nature of the industry we operate in is such that brand obsolescence is not common, if appropriately supported by advertising and marketing spend. Finite-lived intangible assets, which primarily comprise patented and non-patented technology, know-how, and software, are capitalised and amortised in operating profit on a straight-line basis over the period of their expected useful lives, none of which exceeds ten years. The level of amortisation for finite-lived intangible assets is not expected to change materially over the next five years.

At cost less amortisation and impairment	**€ million 2006**	€ million 2005
Goodwill	**12 425**	12 963
Indefinite-lived intangible assets	**4 174**	4 450
Finite-lived intangible assets	**343**	416
Software	**264**	226
	17 206	18 055

Movements during 2006	**€ million Goodwill**	**€ million Indefinite-lived intangible assets**	**€ million Finite-lived intangible assets**	**€ million Software**	**€ million Total**
Cost					
1 January 2006	**14 080**	**4 713**	**631**	**291**	**19 715**
Acquisitions of group companies	**60**	**8**	**1**	**–**	**69**
Disposals of group companies	**(1)**	**–**	**–**	**–**	**(1)**
Change in useful life assumptions	**–**	**(32)**	**32**	**–**	**–**
Additions	**–**	**–**	**3**	**110**	**113**
Currency retranslation	**(685)**	**(280)**	**(25)**	**(9)**	**(999)**
31 December 2006	**13 454**	**4 409**	**642**	**392**	**18 897**

Amortisation and impairment					
1 January 2006	**(1 117)**	**(263)**	**(215)**	**(65)**	**(1 660)**
Amortisation for the year	**–**	**–**	**(94)**	**(63)**	**(157)**
Impairment	**(12)**	**–**	**–**	**(2)**	**(14)**
Currency retranslation	**100**	**28**	**10**	**2**	**140**
31 December 2006	**(1 029)**	**(235)**	**(299)**	**(128)**	**(1 691)**
Net book value 31 December 2006	**12 425**	**4 174**	**343**	**264**	**17 206**

Movements during 2005	€ million Goodwill	€ million Indefinite-lived intangible assets	€ million Finite-lived intangible assets	€ million Software	€ million Total
Cost					
1 January 2005	12 887	4 251	597	193	17 928
Acquisitions of group companies	13	–	–	–	13
Disposals of group companies	(49)	(6)	(16)	(4)	(75)
Additions	–	2	4	86	92
Reversal of assets held for sale not included in final disposal	15	55	–	–	70
Currency retranslation	1 214	411	46	16	1 687
31 December 2005	14 080	4 713	631	291	19 715
Amortisation and impairment					
1 January 2005	(937)	–	(150)	(27)	(1 114)
Disposals of group companies	42	1	3	2	48
Amortisation for the year (a)	–	–	(62)	(38)	(100)
Impairment losses	(131)	(251)	–	–	(382)
Currency retranslation	(91)	(13)	(6)	(2)	(112)
31 December 2005	(1 117)	(263)	(215)	(65)	(1 660)
Net book value 31 December 2005	12 963	4 450	416	226	18 055

(a) Includes €(1) million relating to discontinued operations.

There are no significant carrying amounts of goodwill and intangible assets that are allocated across multiple cash generating units (CGUs).

Any impairment of intangibles is to be disclosed in accordance with IAS 36, which is discussed in Chapter 15 at 4,[255] while any changes in useful life, amortisation method or residual value estimates should be disclosed in accordance with the provisions of IAS 8.[256]

There are a number of additional disclosure requirements, some of which only apply in certain circumstances:[257]

'(a) for an intangible asset assessed as having an indefinite useful life, the carrying amount of that asset and the reasons supporting the assessment of an indefinite useful life. In giving these reasons, the entity shall describe the factor(s) that played a significant role in determining that the asset has an indefinite useful life;

(b) a description, the carrying amount and remaining amortisation period of any individual intangible asset that is material to the entity's financial statements;

(c) for intangible assets acquired by way of a government grant and initially recognised at fair value (see paragraph 44):
   (i) the fair value initially recognised for these assets;
   (ii) their carrying amount; and
   (iii) whether they are measured after recognition under the cost model or the revaluation model.

(d) the existence and carrying amounts of intangible assets whose title is restricted and the carrying amounts of intangible assets pledged as security for liabilities;

(e) the amount of contractual commitments for the acquisition of intangible assets.'

In describing the factors (as required under (a) above) that played a significant role in determining that the useful life of an intangible asset is indefinite, an entity considers the list of factors in paragraph 90 of IAS 38 (see 2.5 above).[258]

Finally, an entity is encouraged to disclose the following information:[259]

'(a) a description of any fully amortised intangible asset that is still in use; and

(b) a brief description of significant intangible assets controlled by the entity but not recognised as assets because they did not meet the recognition criteria in this Standard or because they were acquired or generated before the version of IAS 38 issued in 1998 was effective.'

2.10.2 Balance sheet presentation

IAS 1 does not use the term fixed assets, which is used in accounting standards under many other GAAPs. Instead it draws a distinction between current and non-current assets. IAS 1 uses the term 'non-current' to include tangible, intangible and financial assets of a long-term nature, although it 'does not prohibit the use of alternative descriptions as long as the meaning is clear'.[260] Although most intangible assets are non-current, an intangible asset may meet the definition of a current asset (i.e. it has an economic life of less than 12 months) when it is acquired and should be classified accordingly.

IAS 1 requires intangible assets to be shown as a separate category of asset on the face of the balance sheet.[261] Intangible assets will, therefore, normally appear as a separate category of asset in the balance sheet at a suitable point within non-current assets, or at a point in an undifferentiated balance sheet that reflects their relative liquidity[262] – that is the time over which they are to be amortised or sold. An entity that holds a wide variety of different intangible assets may need to present these in separate line items on the face of the balance sheet if such presentation is relevant to an understanding of the entity's financial position.[263]

While the balance sheet figure for intangible assets may include goodwill, the relevant standards require more detailed disclosures of the constituent elements of the balance sheet figure to be included in the notes to the financial statements.

The extract below shows how GN Store Nord discloses no less than six different types of intangible asset on the face of its balance sheet.

Extract 12.8: GN Store Nord A/S (2006)

BALANCE SHEET AT DECEMBER 31 – ASSETS [extract]

	Consolidated	
(DKK millions)	**2006**	**2005**
Non-current assets		
Goodwill	455	3,044
Development projects, developed in-house	115	445
Software	66	107
Patents and rights	4	69
Telecommunications systems	27	33
Other intangible assets	79	366
Total intangible assets	**746**	**4,064**

In many cases though, entities will be able to aggregate the intangible assets into slightly broader categories in order to reduce the number of lines items on the face of their balance sheets.

2.10.3 Income statement presentation

Only limited guidance is available on the presentation of amortisation, impairment, and gains or losses related to intangible assets:

- Gains on the sale of intangible assets should not be presented within revenue;[264] and
- An entity should disclose the line item(s) of the income statement in which any amortisation of intangible assets is included.[265]

In the absence of detailed guidance on how to present such items in the income statement, it will in practice usually be appropriate to present them in a similar way as those related to property, plant and equipment.

2.10.4 Additional disclosures under the revaluation model

IAS 38 requires an entity, which accounts for intangible assets at revalued amounts, to disclose the following additional information:[266]

'(a) by class of intangible assets:

(i) the effective date of the revaluation;

(ii) the carrying amount of revalued intangible assets; and

(iii) the carrying amount that would have been recognised had the revalued class of intangible assets been measured after recognition using the cost model in paragraph 74 (see 2.4.1 above);

(b) the amount of the revaluation surplus that relates to intangible assets at the beginning and end of the period, indicating the changes during the period and any restrictions on the distribution of the balance to shareholders; and

(c) the methods and significant assumptions applied in estimating the assets' fair values.'

Classes of revalued assets should only be aggregated for disclosure purposes to the extent that this does not result 'in the combination of a class of intangible assets that includes amounts measured under both the cost and revaluation models'.[267]

2.10.5 Research and development expenditure

An entity should disclose the aggregate total amount of all expenditure that is directly attributable to research or development activities that is recognised as an expense during the period.[268] Development expenditure that is capitalised during the period should be excluded for the purposes of this disclosure.

3 PRACTICAL ISSUES

3.1 Regulatory assets

In many countries the provision of utilities (e.g. water, natural gas or electricity) to consumers is regulated by the national government. Regulations differ between countries but often regulators operate a cost-plus system under which a utility is allowed to make a fixed return on investment. Similarly, a regulator may allow a utility to recoup its investment by increasing the prices over a defined period.

Consequently, the future price that a utility is allowed to charge its customer may be influenced by past cost levels and investment levels. Under many national GAAPs accounting practices have been developed that allow an entity to account for the effects of regulation by recognising a 'regulatory' asset (or liability) that reflects the increase (or decrease) in future prices approved by the regulator. Such 'regulatory assets' may have been classified as intangible assets under national GAAPs.

Most 'regulatory assets' of this kind do not meet the definition of intangible assets under IFRS, because they are not 'a resource controlled by an entity as a result of past events; and from which future economic benefits are expected to flow to the entity'.[269] The economic benefits arising from a right to charge a higher price can only flow to the entity as a result of future sales to those customers. The economic benefits from sales to customers should be recognised in accordance with IAS 18, which requires delivery of the goods or services to the customers.

Many would argue that 'regulatory assets' are better described simply as past costs, which the regulator allows the entity to recover through higher sales prices in the future. Instead of arguing that 'regulatory assets' result from the right to charge a higher price in the future, they would argue that these debits are 'regulatory losses' resulting from a price cap imposed by the regulator in the past.

It is worth considering also the situation when the opposite occurs and the entity is required by its regulator to reduce prices in the subsequent period. In most circumstances this would not give rise to a liability under IAS 37 – *Provisions, Contingent Liabilities and Contingent Assets* – as it is not a 'present obligation of the entity arising from past events, the settlement of which is expected to result in an outflow from the entity of resources embodying economic benefits';[270] what it means is that the entity will charge less, and receive less from individual customers in the subsequent period. This reinforces the argument that the 'regulatory asset' should not be carried forward in the balance sheet, whether as an intangible asset or as a prepayment. (Regulatory liabilities are discussed in Chapter 28 at 7.18.)

3.1.1 SFAS 71 – Accounting for the effects of certain types of regulation

In August 2005, the IFRIC considered the question whether an entity reporting under IFRS could apply SFAS 71 – *Accounting for the Effects of Certain Types of Regulation* – in the absence of specific guidance in IFRS.[271]

The IFRIC noted that 'it had previously discussed whether a regulatory asset should be recognised in the context of service concession arrangements, either as deferred costs or as an intangible asset to reflect an expectation that the entity will recover these costs as part of the price charged in future periods. It had concluded that entities applying IFRSs should recognise only assets that qualified for recognition in accordance with the IASB's *Framework for the Preparation and Presentation of Financial Statements* and relevant accounting standards'.[272]

The IFRIC concluded that the recognition criteria in SFAS 71 are not fully consistent with the recognition criteria under IFRS. Therefore, the special regulatory asset model of SFAS 71 cannot be used under IFRS without modification and expenses incurred in performing price-regulated activities should be recognised in accordance with the applicable standards under IFRS.

3.2 Research and development in the pharmaceutical industry

Entities in the pharmaceutical industry consider research and development to be of primary importance to their business. Consequently, these entities spend a considerable amount on research and development every year. Therefore, one would expect pharmaceutical companies to carry internally generated development intangible assets on their balance sheets. However, a review of the financial statements of pharmaceutical companies reveals that they often consider the uncertainties in the development of pharmaceuticals to be too great to permit capitalisation of development costs. Extracts 11.9 and 11.10 and the extracts below illustrate this.

Extract 12.9: Bayer AG (2006)

Notes to the Consolidated Financial Statements of the Bayer Group [extract]

[4] Basic principles of the consolidated financial statements [extract]

Research and development expenses

A substantial proportion of the Bayer Group's financial resources is invested in research and development. In addition to in-house research and development activities, especially in the health care business, various research and development collaborations and alliances are maintained with third parties involving the provision of funding and/or payments for the achievement of performance milestones.

For accounting purposes, research expenses are defined as costs incurred for current or planned investigations undertaken with the prospect of gaining new scientific or technical knowledge and understanding.

> Development expenses are defined as costs incurred for the application of research findings or specialist knowledge to production, production methods, services or goods prior to the commencement of commercial production or use.
>
> According to IAS 38 (Intangible Assets), research costs cannot be capitalized; development costs must be capitalized if, and only if, specific, narrowly defined conditions are fulfilled. Development costs must be capitalized if it is sufficiently certain that the future economic benefits to the company will also cover the respective development costs. Since development projects are often subject to regulatory approval procedures and other uncertainties, the conditions for the capitalization of costs incurred before approvals are received are not normally satisfied.
>
> With respect to costs incurred in collaborations and alliances with third parties, considerable judgment is involved in assessing whether milestone-based payments simply reflect the funding of research, in which case expensing is always required, or whether, by making a milestone payment, an asset is acquired. In the latter case, the relevant costs are to be capitalized.
>
> The following costs in particular, by their very nature, constitute research and development expenses: the appropriate allocations of direct personnel and material costs and related overheads for internal or external application technology, engineering and other departments that provide the respective services; costs for experimental and pilot facilities (including depreciation of buildings or parts of buildings used for research or development purposes); costs for clinical research; regular costs for the utilization of third parties' patents for research and development purposes; other taxes related to research facilities; and fees for the filing and registration of self-generated patents that are not capitalized.
>
> The Bayer Group capitalizes the costs incurred in the application development phase of in-house software development. These costs are amortized over the useful life of the software from the date it is placed in service.

> *Extract 12.10: Syngenta AG (2006)*
>
> **2. Accounting policies** [extract]
>
> **Research and development**
>
> Research and development expenses are charged to the income statement when incurred. Syngenta considers that the regulatory and other uncertainties inherent in the development of its key new products preclude it from capitalizing development costs.
>
> Costs of purchasing patent rights are capitalized as intangible assets. Costs of applying for patents for internally developed products, costs of defending existing patents and costs of challenging patents held by third parties where these are considered invalid, are considered part of development expense and expensed as incurred.

One of the problems of course is that in the case of true 'development' activities in the pharmaceutical industry the technical and economic feasibility are typically established very late in the development phase, which means that only a small proportion of the development costs can ever be capitalised. In particular, many drugs require approval by a regulator such as the US Food and Drug Administration (FDA) before they can be put on the market and until that time the entity may be uncertain of their success. After approval, of course, there is little in the way of expenditure other than on advertising and entities are precluded from capitalising this as part of the asset.

In our opinion, in the pharmaceutical sector, the capitalisation of development costs for new drugs would in most cases begin at the date on which the product receives regulatory approval. In most cases that is when the IAS 38 criteria for recognition of intangible assets are met. It is unlikely that these criteria will have been met before the request for new drug approval is filed.

As noted at 2.3.2 E above, there is an inconsistency at the heart of IAS 38 that results in a different treatment of acquired versus internally generated intangible assets. Intangible assets acquired in a separate transaction or business combinations must be recognised while future economic benefits are deemed to be probable, whereas internally developed intangible assets can only be recognised when they meet the strict (and somewhat subjective) recognition criteria in IAS 38.

3.3 Emission rights

A number of countries around the world either have, or are in the process of developing, schemes to encourage reduced emissions of pollutants, in particular of greenhouse gases. Some schemes are based on a 'cap and trade' model whereby participants are allocated emission rights or allowances equal to a cap (i.e. target level of emissions) and are permitted to trade those allowances. A cap and trade emission rights scheme typically has the following features:

- an entity participating in the scheme (participant) is set a target to reduce its emissions to a specified level (the cap). The participant is issued allowances equal in number to its cap by a government or government agency. Allowances may be issued free of charge, or participants may pay the government for them;
- the scheme operates for defined compliance periods;
- participants are free to buy and sell allowances at any time;
- if at the end of the compliance period a participant's actual emissions exceeded its emission rights, the participant will have to buy additional rights in the market or it will incur a penalty;
- in some schemes emission rights surpluses and deficits may be carried forward to future periods; and
- the scheme may provide for brokers – who are not themselves participants – to buy and sell emission rights.

3.3.1 Development of IFRIC 3

As there was no guidance on the accounting for cap and trade emission rights schemes and no consensus had emerged among market participants on what the accounting treatment should be, the IFRIC concluded that an interpretation should be issued to explain how IFRS should be applied to such schemes.

Accordingly, in December 2004 the IASB issued IFRIC 3 – *Emission Rights* – which addresses accounting for emission rights that arise from cap and trade emission rights schemes. However, the interpretation met with significant resistance because application of IFRIC 3 (which is discussed in more detail at 3.3.2 A below) would result in a number of mismatches:[273]

- a measurement mismatch between the assets and liabilities recognised in accordance with IFRIC 3;

- a mismatch in the location in which the gains and losses on those assets are reported; and
- a possible timing mismatch because allowances would be recognised when they are obtained – typically at the start of the year – whereas the emission liability would be recognised during the year as it is incurred.

Consequently, the IASB decided in June 2005 to withdraw IFRIC 3 despite the fact that it considers it to be 'an appropriate interpretation of existing IFRSs'.[274] The IASB also decided to reconsider the accounting for cap and trade emission right schemes itself rather than ask the IFRIC to continue its work, because developing an approach that eliminates the mismatches will require the amendment of one or more standards. However, work on emission rights and government grants has been deferred pending conclusion of work on other relevant projects, in particular the project to amend IAS 37.[275]

3.3.2 Accounting for emission rights by participants in cap and trade schemes

Until the IASB issues definitive guidance on accounting for cap and trade emission rights schemes, an entity has the option either:

(a) to apply IFRIC 3, which despite having been withdrawn, is considered to be an appropriate interpretation of existing IFRS (see A below); or

(b) to develop its own accounting policy for cap and trade schemes based on the hierarchy of authoritative guidance in IAS 8 (see B below).

A IFRIC 3

IFRIC 3 dealt with accounting for cap and trade schemes by entities that participated in them. It did not address accounting by entities that were not yet subject to a scheme (even if they expected to be subject to one in the future) and brokers that were not themselves participants.[276] The provisions of the interpretation were also considered to be relevant to other schemes designed to encourage reduced levels of emissions and share some of the features outlined above.[277]

IFRIC 3 took the view that a cap and trade scheme did not give rise to a net asset or liability, but that it gave rise to various items that were to be accounted for separately:[278]

(a) *an asset for allowances held* – Allowances, whether allocated by government or purchased, were to be regarded as intangible assets and accounted for under IAS 38. Allowances issued for less than fair value were to be measured initially at their fair value;[279]

(b) *a government grant* – When allowances are issued for less than fair value, the difference between the amount paid and fair value was a government grant that should be accounted for under IAS 20. Initially the grant was to be recognised as deferred income in the balance sheet and subsequently recognised as income on a systematic basis over the compliance period for which the allowances were issued, regardless of whether the allowances were held or sold;[280]

(c) *a liability for the obligation to deliver allowances equal to emissions that have been made* – As emissions are made, a liability was to be recognised as a provision that falls within the scope of IAS 37. The liability was to be measured at the best estimate of the expenditure required to settle the present obligation at the balance sheet date. This would usually be the present market price of the number of allowances required to cover emissions made up to the balance sheet date.[281]

The interpretation also noted that 'the existence or requirements of an emission rights scheme may cause a reduction in the cash flows expected to be generated by certain assets. Such a reduction is an indication that those assets may be impaired and hence requires those assets to be tested for impairment in accordance with IAS 36.'[282]

B Application of the IAS 8 hierarchy of authoritative guidance

In light of the mismatches resulting from the application of IFRIC 3 (see 3.3.1 above), it is perhaps no surprise that in practice very few companies have applied IFRIC 3 on a voluntary basis. Instead companies have developed a range of different approaches in accounting for cap and trade emission rights schemes, which are discussed below:

- 'net liability' approaches (see I and II below);
- 'government grants' approach (see III below),

I Net liability approach

Under the 'net liability' approach emission allowances received by way of grant are recorded at a nominal amount and the entity will only record a liability once the actual emissions exceed the emission rights granted and still held.

We believe that an entity can apply a 'net liability' approach, because there is no specific guidance on the accounting for emission rights, and IAS 20 allows non-monetary government grants and the related asset (emission rights) received to be measured at a nominal amount (i.e. nil).[283]

Under IAS 37, a provision can only be recognised if the recognition criteria in the standard are met (see Chapter 27 at 3.1). As far as emissions are concerned, the 'obligating event' is the emission itself, therefore a provision is recognised as emissions are made, but only when the reporting entity has made emissions in excess of rights held. This means that an entity should not recognise a full provision for an expected shortfall immediately when the expectation arises; nor should it accrete a provision over the period of the expected shortfall.

Under IAS 37 the entire obligation to deliver allowances should be measured at 'the best estimate of the expenditure required to settle the present obligation at the balance sheet date' (see Chapter 27 at 4.1).[284] In this situation, an outflow of cash or other resources only occurs if and when the entity's emissions exceed the emission rights that it holds. The allocated emission rights are not recognised as assets and therefore are not considered to be part of the expenditure.

Critics of the 'net liability' approach have noted that under IAS 20 the emission rights are always recognised, either at their fair value or at a nominal amount.[285] Furthermore, they point out that IAS 37 requires that the best estimate of the expenditure required to settle the present obligation to be determined by reference to 'the amount that an entity would rationally pay to settle the obligation at the balance sheet date or to transfer it to a third party at that time'.[286] Therefore, they would consider it more appropriate to recognise the entire obligation at its present fair value (i.e. the approach under IFRIC 3). Nevertheless, the 'net liability' approach appears to have gained acceptance in practice.

Example 12.9: Application of 'net liability' approach

Company A received allowances representing the right to produce 10,000 tons of CO_2 for the year to 31 December 2008. The expected emissions for the full year are 12,000 tons of CO_2. At the end of the third quarter, it has emitted 9,000 tons of CO_2. The market price of the allowances at the end of the each quarter is €10/ton, €12/ton, €14/ton and €16/ton respectively.

Under the 'net liability' approach, the provision at the end of the first, second and third quarters would be nil, because the company has not yet exceeded its emissions target. Only in the fourth quarter is a provision recognised, for the excess tonnage emitted, at 2,000 tons × €16/ton = €32,000.

The company cannot anticipate the future shortfall of 2,000 tons on day one by accreting the provision over the year, nor can it recognise on day one the full provision for the 2,000 ton expected shortfall.

Some schemes cover a period of more than one year, such that the entity is unconditionally entitled to receive allowances for, say, a 3-year period, and it is possible to carry-over emission rights from one year to the next. In our view, this provides a basis for applying the net liability approach for the entire period concerned, not just the period for which emission rights have been transferred to the entity physically. Accordingly, when applying the net liability approach, an entity may choose a system that measures deficits on the basis of:

- an annual allocation of emission rights, or
- an allocation that covers the entire first 3-year period of the scheme (provided that the entity is unconditionally entitled to all the allowances for the first period concerned).

For such schemes, the entity must apply the chosen method consistently at every reporting date. If the entity chooses the annual allocation basis, a deficit is measured on that basis and there can be no carrying over of rights from one year to the next or back to the previous year.

II Impact of purchased emission rights on the 'net liability' approach

In Example 12.9 above, the entity had an expected shortfall of 2,000 tons. Suppose that during the year it had purchased emission rights to cover some or all of the expected shortfall. How should these be accounted for?

Example 12.10: Impact of purchased emission rights on the application of 'net liability' approach

In Example 12.9 above, Company A had an expected shortfall of 2,000 tons. The same facts apply, except that at the end of the second quarter, it purchases emission rights for 1,000 tons at €12/ton, i.e. a cost of €12,000. It records these as an intangible asset at cost. No impairment has been necessary.

In recognising the provision for its excess emissions of 2,000 tons at the end of the year, can the entity apply a method whereby the provision is based on the carrying amount of the emission rights it already owns (the 'carrying value method'), with the balance based on the market price at the year end? That is, can the entity recognise a provision of €28,000, being €12,000 (1,000 tons at €12/ton) plus €16,000 (1,000 tons at €16/ton)?

One view is that this is indeed appropriate. As discussed in Chapter 27 at 4.1, IAS 37 requires the amount of a provision to be measured at 'the best estimate of the expenditure required to settle the present obligation at the balance sheet date'. The standard equates this estimate with 'the amount that an entity would rationally pay to settle the obligation at the balance sheet date or to transfer it to a third party at that time'.[287] Proponents of this view argue that this cannot be applied in measuring liabilities for emissions as an entity cannot settle the obligation other than by delivering allowances and is not permitted to pay someone to assume the obligation. For this reason, it is argued, the provision can be measured at the cost of settling the obligation, and that the cost to the entity is the current carrying value of the emission rights held.

Another view is that this in an incorrect interpretation of paragraph 37 of IAS 37 as the cost of settlement must be measured at the best estimate of the expenditure required to settle the obligation. The fact that assets that are currently being held may be used to settle the obligation is not relevant in measuring the provision. In accordance with this view, the provision has to be measured as in Example 12.9, i.e. at €32,000 (based on the market value of emission rights at the year end). However, although the measurement of the liability cannot be linked to the measurement of an asset, one could argue that the measurement of the asset could be linked to the measurement of the liability. In other words, IAS 37 allows for reimbursement rights to be measured based upon the measurement of the liability, and actually capped to that amount (see Chapter 27 at 4.4).

Under this 'net liability / reimbursement rights' approach, the entity may consider the emission rights it has as a reimbursement right in respect of the liability, which means it can re-measure to fair value the emission rights that are reimbursements against the liability caused by actual emissions that are measured at fair value. So although Company A has recognised a provision (and an expense) of €32,000, at the same time it would revalue its emission rights, as a reimbursement right, from €12/ton to €16/ton. It would thus recognise a gain of 1,000 tons × €4/ton = €4,000. This leads to a net expense of €28,000 in the income statement. This is the same as the income statement effect of the method whereby the provision is partly measured based on the cost of the asset held.

We believe that both approaches are acceptable, although the reimbursement rights approach is, in our opinion, preferable to the carrying value method.

In practice both the 'net liability' approach and the 'net liability / reimbursement rights' approach have gained acceptance as is illustrated in Extracts 12.11 and 12.12 below.

Centrica applies a 'net liability' approach, i.e. emission rights granted free of charge are accounted for at their nominal value of zero and no government grant is recognised. A liability for the obligation to deliver allowances is only recognised when the level of emissions exceed the level of allowances granted. Centrica measures the liability at the cost of purchased allowances up to the level of purchased allowances

extent that emissions are not covered by emission rights, the liability is recognised at the fair value of such allowances at the balance sheet date. Similar to Stora Enso, the grant of emission rights is treated as government grant under IAS 20.

Extract 12.14: Repsol YPF, S.A. (2006)

Notes to the consolidated financial statements for 2005 [extract]
3. Accounting Policies [extract]
3.7. Other intangible assets [extract]
f) Emission allowances

Emission allowances are recognised as an intangible asset and are measured at acquisition cost.

Allowances received for no consideration under the National Emission Allowance Assignment Plan, are initially recognised at the market price prevailing at the beginning of the year in which they are issued, and a balancing item is recognised as a grant for the same amount under deferred income.

As the emissions are made, the Group recognises a provision on the basis of the tonnes of CO_2 emissions, which is measured as follows: (i) the emission allowances assigned for no consideration, at the lower of the original price and the quoted price at year-end; (ii) the emission allowances purchased in the market, at the lower of average purchases price and quoted price at year-end, and (iii) emissions made in the period for which the Company does not have emission allowances, at the quoted price at year-end.

The deferred income recognised for the emission allowances received for no consideration are taken to income as the CO_2 emissions are made.

The net effect on the Group's income statement of transactions relating to emission allowances amounted to a net expense of EUR 4 million and EUR 2 million in 2006 and 2005, respectively.

Emissions allowances are derecognised when they are delivered, transferred to third parties or meet the conditions established for their expiry.

In determining the fair value upon initial recognition of emission rights that are accounted as intangible assets an entity should take account of the guidance in IAS 38.[289] However, if no active market in emission rights exists, an entity may want to refer to the application guidance in IAS 39 which addresses the issue valuation in the absence of an active market.[290]

IV Amortisation and impairment testing of emission rights

In principle it is possible to amortise emission rights that are accounted for as intangible assets, but their expected residual value, at least at inception, will be equal to their fair value. Subsequently, the residual value of emission rights is equal to their market value. In the case of cap and trade schemes, however, there is no consumption of economic benefit while the emission right is held. Instead, the economic benefits are realised by surrendering the rights to settle obligations under the scheme for emissions made, or by selling rights to another party. Therefore, the amount to be amortised will in many circumstances be nil. However, it is necessary to perform an IAS 36 impairment test whenever there is an indication of impairment. Nevertheless, when the market value of an emission right drops below its carrying amount, this does not automatically result in an impairment charge because emission rights are often tested for impairment as part of a larger cash generating unit.

V Emission rights acquired in a business combination

Complications in accounting for emission rights also arise in the context of business combinations. At the date of acquisition of a business, an acquirer is required to recognise the acquiree's identifiable intangible assets (e.g. emission rights) at their fair values, when that value can be measured reliably.[291] However, an acquirer should only recognise a provision for actual emissions that have occurred up to that date.

Accordingly, an acquirer cannot apply the 'net liability' approach to emission rights acquired in a business combination. Instead, such an acquirer should treat acquired emission rights in the same way as purchased emission rights (see II above). An acquirer that applies IFRIC 3 or the 'government grant' approach would recognise acquired emission rights at their fair value, but cannot recognise a deferred credit for a 'government grant' as it acquired the emission rights by way of a business combination.

Consequently, an acquirer may report a higher emission expense in its income statement in the compliance period in which it acquires a business.

VI Sale of emission rights

The sale of emission rights that are accounted for as intangible assets should be recognised in accordance with IAS 38. This means that they should be derecognised on disposal or when no future economic benefits are expected from their use or disposal (see 2.9 above).[292] The gain or loss arising from derecognition of the emission rights should be determined as the difference between the net disposal proceeds and the carrying amount of emission rights.[293]

Prior to the sale the entity may not have recognised the obligation, to deliver allowances equal to the emissions caused, at its fair value at the date of derecognition. If that were the case then the entity would need to ensure that the liability in excess of the emission rights held by the company after the sale is recognised at the present fair value of the emission rights.

Both the gain or loss on the derecognition of the emission rights and the adjustment of the liability should be recognised when the emission rights are derecognised. Any gain should not be classified as revenue.[294]

If an entity that applies the 'net liability' approach were to sell all its emission rights at the start of the compliance period, it would not be permitted to defer the gain on that sale even if it was certain that the entity would need to repurchase emission rights later in the year to cover actual emissions. A gain is recognised immediately on the sale and a provision is recognised as gases are emitted.

VII Disclosure

It is clear that the interpretation of the hierarchy of authoritative guidance in IAS 8 has led to a number of methods of accounting for emission rights, each with its own merits. In the absence of more detailed IFRS guidance, companies should disclose their accounting policies regarding grants of emission rights, the emission rights themselves, the liability for the obligation to deliver allowances equal to emissions that have been made and the presentation in the income statement.[295]

3.3.3 Accounting for emission rights by brokers and traders

As mentioned above, IFRIC 3 does not address accounting by brokers and traders that are not themselves participants in a cap and trade scheme. However, in their case emission rights are assets held for sale in the ordinary course of business, which means that they meet the definition of inventories in IAS 2.[296] Under that standard a broker-trader may choose between measuring emission rights at the lower of cost and net realisable value or at fair value less costs to sell. Commodity broker-traders who measure their inventories at fair value less costs to sell may recognise changes in fair value less costs in profit or loss in the period of the change.[297]

When a company trades derivatives based on the emission rights, they fall within the scope of IAS 39 and are accounted for at fair value through profit or loss unless they hedge the fair value of the emission rights granted to the company or qualify for the 'own use exemption'.

When an entity holds emission rights for own use and has a trading department trading in emission rights, the company should split the books between emission rights held for own use and those held for trading. The emission rights should be treated as intangible assets and inventory respectively.

3.3.4 Accounting for green certificates or renewable energy certificates

Some governments have launched schemes to promote power production from renewable sources, based on green certificates, also known as renewable energy certificates, green tags or tradable renewable certificates. There are similarities between green certificates and emission rights, except that whilst emission rights are granted to reflect a future limit on emissions, green certificates are awarded on the basis of the amount of green energy already produced.

In a typical scheme, producers of electricity are granted certificates by the government based on the power output (kWh) derived from renewable sources. Entities distributing electricity (produced from both renewable and traditional sources) are required to hand over to the government a number of certificates based on the total kWh of electricity sold to consumers during the year, or pay a penalty to the extent that an insufficient number of certificates is rendered. It is this requirement that creates a valuable market for the certificates, allowing producers to sell their certificates to distributors, using the income to subsidise in effect the higher cost of generation from renewable sources.

I Accounting by producers using renewable energy sources

As in the case of emission rights, the award of green certificates is treated as a government grant by a producer. An intangible asset representing an entitlement to that grant is recognised at the point in time when the green electricity is produced. As with any government grant, the entitlement is initially measured at either fair value or a nominal amount.

Where the entitlement asset is initially recognised at fair value, a credit entry is recorded in the income statement as either a reduction in production costs for the period (on the basis that the purpose of the grant is to compensate the producer for the higher cost of using renewable energy sources) or as other income. Subsequent revaluation of the intangible asset is only allowed if an active market exists for the green certificates, and the other requirements of IAS 38 are applied (see 2.4.2 above). The intangible is derecognised when the certificate is sold by the producer.

II Accounting by distributors of renewable energy

When the distributor is also a producer of renewable energy, it has the option to use certificates granted to it or to sell them in the market. Accordingly, the permissible accounting treatments of green certificates are in principle the same as those discussed at 3.3.2 above for emission rights. The distributor is obliged to remit certificates and therefore recognises a provision as sales are recorded (in the same way that a provision for emission rights is recognised as emissions are made). As discussed at 3.3.2 above, the distributor might apply a 'net liability' approach, and only start to recognise a provision once it has achieved a level of sales exceeding that covered by certificates granted to the entity in its capacity as a producer.

Where a distributor is not also a producer of renewable energy, it recognises a provision as sales are made, measured at the fair value of green certificates to be remitted. A corresponding cost is included in cost of sales. The provision is remeasured to fair value at each reporting date. If such an entity purchases certificates in the market, they are recognised as an intangible asset and initially measured at cost. Subsequent revaluation is only allowed if an active market exists for the green certificates, and the other requirements of IAS 38 are applied (see 2.4.2 above).

Alternatively, as discussed in Example 12.10 above, the asset held may be designated by management as a reimbursement right in respect of the associated liability, allowing remeasurement to fair value. Similarly, although a less preferable approach in our view, the entity could apply a carrying value method, measuring the provision based on the value and extent of certificates already held and applying fair value only to the extent that it has an obligation to make further purchases in the market or to incur a penalty if it fails to do so.

III Accounting by brokers and traders

As discussed at 3.3.3 above, brokers and traders should apply IAS 2 where green certificates are held for sale in the ordinary course of business; account for derivatives based on green certificates in accordance with IAS 39; and properly distinguish those held for own use (carried within intangible assets) from certificates held for trading (included in inventory).

3.4 Television and programme rights

A number of accounting issues arise for television stations and other media companies that produce, own or broadcast programmes on television or otherwise:

- classification of programme rights (see 3.4.1 below);
- recognition of programme rights that have not been paid for (see 3.4.2 below); and
- amortisation of programme rights (see 3.4.3 below).

3.4.1 Classification of programme rights

Programme rights meet the definition of intangible assets because they are identifiable non-monetary assets without physical substance. Earlier versions of IAS 38 required intangible assets to be 'held for use in the production or supply of goods or services, for rental to others, or for administrative purposes' in order to meet the definition of an intangible asset.[298] The amendment of IAS 38 in 2003 broadened the definition of an intangible asset and it now covers both programme rights that are 'held for use in the production or supply of goods or services, for rental to others, or for administrative purposes' and all other programme rights that are not specifically covered by another standard.

Programme rights that are held or developed for sale in the ordinary course of business also meet the definition of inventory and are therefore within the scope of IAS 2.[299] When an entity holds the rights to programmes exclusively with a view to selling those rights to other parties, they evidently meet the definition of inventory.

In the case of programmes held with a view to broadcasting them to an audience, it is possible to argue that they are comparable to 'materials or supplies to be consumed in the production process or in the rendering of services',[300] which would mean that they could also be treated as inventory. Equally, it can be argued that such programme rights are intangible assets as they are used in the production or supply of services.

Ultimately, the appropriate classification of programme rights will depend on the particular facts and circumstances as they apply to an entity. However, it is clearly possible for an entity to conclude that some of its programme rights are intangible assets while others should be treated as inventory.

In practice, companies either classify programme rights as intangible assets or as inventories. Vivendi accounts for its film and television rights catalogues as intangible assets (see Extract 12.16 below). ITV on the other hand, presents its programme rights as current assets under the caption 'Programme rights and other inventory'.

Extract 12.15: ITV plc (2006)

Notes to the accounts[extract]

1 Accounting policies[extract]

l) Programme rights [extract]

Where programming, sports rights and film rights are acquired for the primary purpose of broadcasting, these are recognised within current assets. An asset is recognised when the Group controls, in substance, the respective assets and the risks and rewards associated with them. For acquired programme rights an asset is recognised as payments are made and is recognised in full when the acquired programming is available for transmission. Programming produced internally either for the purpose of broadcasting or to be sold in the normal course of the Group's operating cycle is recognised within current assets at production cost.

Programme costs and rights, including those acquired under sale and leaseback arrangements, are written off to operating costs in full on first transmission except certain film rights which are written off over a number of transmissions. Programme costs and rights not yet written off at the balance sheet date are included on the balance sheet at the lower of cost and net realisable value.

17 Programme rights and other inventory

	2006	2005
	£m	£m
Commissions	**106**	99
Sports rights	**20**	25
Acquired films	**184**	104
Production	**48**	74
Prepayments	**41**	85
Other	**1**	1
	400	388

Net programme rights and other inventory written off in the year, included within operating costs analysed in note 4, was £12 million (2005: £28 million).

3.4.2 Recognition of programme rights

Television stations frequently enter into contracts to buy programme rights related to long-running televisions series or future sports events that are not yet available for broadcast, which raises the question when those programme rights should be recognised in the balance sheet.

The IASB's Framework recognises that in practice 'obligations under contracts that are equally proportionately unperformed (for example, liabilities for inventory ordered but not yet received) are generally not recognised as liabilities in the financial statements'.[301] For example, liabilities in connection with non-cancellable orders of inventory or items of property, plant and equipment are generally not recognised in an entity's balance sheet until the goods have been delivered. The same approach can also be applied to programme rights as is illustrated in the extract from Vivendi below.

Extract 12.16: Vivendi S.A. (2006)

NOTES TO THE CONSOLIDATED FINANCIAL STATEMENTS [extract]
10.2. Contractual content commitments as at December 31, 2006 and December 31, 2005 [extract]
Commitments given recorded in the Statement of Financial Position: content liabilities [extract]

(in millions of euros)	Total as at December 31, 2006	Payments due in 2007	2008-2011	After 2011	Total as at December 31, 2005
Music royalties to artists and repertoire owners	1,334	1,279	55	–	1,514
Film and television rights (a)	116	116	–	–	63
Sport rights	500	482	18	–	445
Creative talent and employment agreements (b)	201	30	135	36	196
Total content liabilities	**2,151**	**1,907**	**208**	**36**	**2,218**

Off balance sheet commitments given/received

(in millions of euros)	Total as at December 31, 2006	Payments due in 2007	2008-2011	After 2011	Total as at December 31, 2005
Film and television rights (a)	2,672	840	1,236	596	2,412
Sport rights	748	677	71	–	1,377
Creative talent and employment agreements (b)	979	462	462	55	930
TOTAL GIVEN	**4,399**	**1,979**	**1,769**	**651**	**4,719**
Film and television rights (a)	(118)	(69)	(49)	–	(111)
Sport rights	(29)	(19)	(10)	–	(48)
Creative talent and employment agreements (b)			not available		
TOTAL RECEIVED	**(147)**	**(88)**	**(59)**	**–**	**(159)**
Total net	**4,252**	**1,891**	**1,710**	**651**	**4,560**

The amount presented above for off balance sheet commitments given is the minimum amount guaranteed to third parties.

(a) Includes primarily contracts valid over several years relating to the broadcast of future film and TV productions (mainly exclusivity contracts with major US studios and pre-purchases in the French movie industry), StudioCanal film coproduction commitments (given and received) and broadcasting rights of CanalSat and Cyfra+ multichannel digital TV packages. They are recorded as content assets when the broadcast is available for initial release.

(b) UMG routinely commits to artists and other parties to pay agreed amounts upon delivery of content or other product ("Creative talent and employment agreements"). Until the artist or other party has delivered his or her content, UMG discloses its obligation as an off balance sheet commitment. While the artist or other party is also obligated to deliver his or her content or other product to UMG (these arrangements are generally exclusive), UMG does not report these obligations (or the likelihood of the other party's failure to meet its obligations) as an offset to its off balance sheet commitments.

As illustrated in Extract 12.15 above, ITV follows a similar type of approach for acquired programme rights under which an asset is recognised as payments are made and is recognised in full when the acquired programming is available for transmission.

3.4.3 Amortisation of programme rights

The value of programme rights diminishes because the programmes have been broadcast to the same audience before and as result of the passage of time (e.g. the right is for a limited period or audiences loose interest in old programmes). In accounting for this diminution in value, in practice, entities usually take into account how often a programme has been broadcast and, less frequently, the passage of time as such.

When an entity accounts for programme rights as inventory, the problem arises that IAS 2 requires valuation 'at the lower of cost and net realisable value' and does not appear to recognise the concept of amortisation of inventories.[302] However, it has been argued that a programme right embodies a series of identifiable components (i.e. first transmission, second transmission, etc.), which an entity should account for separately. This appears to be the approach that ITV applies in writing off its programme rights (see Extract 12.15 above).

An entity that accounts for programme rights as intangible assets would need to comply with the requirements of IAS 38, which requires that the amortisation method reflects the pattern in which the asset's future economic benefits are expected to be consumed by the entity.[303] Although the standard permits a range of amortisation methods (e.g. the straight-line method, the diminishing balance method and the unit of production method), it cautions that 'there is rarely, if ever, persuasive evidence to support an amortisation method for intangible assets with finite useful lives that results in a lower amount of accumulated amortisation than under the straight-line method.'[304] An entity that applies any method other than straight-line amortisation of programme rights would need to be able to prove that that method reflects the pattern in which the asset's future economic benefits are expected to be consumed.

The extract from Antena 3's financial statements below, illustrates a commonly used method of amortisation of programme rights that is based on the number of showings.

Extract 12.17: Antena 3 de Televisión, S.A. (2006)

NOTES TO THE 2006 AND 2005 CONSOLIDATED FINANCIAL STATEMENTS [extract]

3. Accounting policies [extract]

D) Programme rights [extract]

Programme rights are valued, based on their nature, as follows:

1. Inventoriable in-house productions (programmes produced to be re-run, such as series) are measured at acquisition and/or production cost, which includes both external costs billed by third parties for programme production and for the acquisition of resources, and internal production costs, which are calculated by applying preset internal rates on the basis of the time during which operating resources are used in production. The costs incurred in producing the programmes are recognised, based on their nature, under the appropriate headings in the consolidated income statement and are included under "Programme Rights" in the consolidated balance sheet with a credit to "Inclusion in Programme Rights" under "Programme Amortisation and Other Procurements" in the accompanying consolidated income statement.

   Amortisation of these programmes is recorded under "Programme Amortisation and Other Procurements" in the consolidated income statement, on the basis of the number of showings, in accordance with the rates shown below:

	Amortisation Rate
1st showing	90%
2nd showing	10%

   The maximum period for amortisation of series is three years, after which the unamortised amount is written off.

   Given their special nature, the series which are broadcast daily are amortised in full when the first showing of each episode is broadcast.

2. Non-inventoriable in-house productions (programmes produced to be shown only once) are valued by the same methods and procedures as those used to value inventoriable in-house productions. Programmes produced and not shown are recognised at year-end under "Programme Rights – In-House Productions and Productions in Process" in the consolidated balance sheet. The cost of these programmes is recognised as an expense under "Programme Amortisation and Other Procurements" in the consolidated income statement at the time of the first showing.

Mediaset is an example of a company that amortises some of its programme rights on a straight line basis.

Extract 12.18: Mediaset S.p.A. (2006)

Explanatory notes [extract]

3. Summary of significant accounting policies and valuation criteria [extract]

Intangible assets [extract]

Assets with defined useful life are amortised on a straight-line basis starting from the moment when the asset is available for use for the period of their expected use; the possibility to recover their value is assessed according to the criteria envisaged by IAS 36, described in the next section impairment of assets.

This principle is also used for multi-annual licences regarding **television rights**, which are generally amortised on a straight-line basis unless a different principle can be determined that can reasonably and reliably reflect the correlation between costs, audience and advertising revenues.

In particular, for the library of television rights available for broadcasting on multiple networks, the straight-line amortisation method was generally adopted, calculated over the period of the relevant contract and, in any event, over a period not exceeding 120 months, a method which reflects greater opportunities to exploit television rights, also in the light of the difficulty in identifying objective components for making a correlation between advertising revenues and the amortisation of rights. Regardless of the amortisation already recognised, if all showings made available under rights contracts have been used up, the residual value is fully expensed.

Sports, news and entertainment programmes rights are amortised almost entirely (90%) in the year the rights run, with the remainder being expensed the following year; rights to long-series dramas are amortised in the first year starting from their availability (70%) and in the following twelve months (30%).

For the library of television rights available for broadcasting on a single network, a generally decreasing amortisation model is used, connected with the number of showings available by contract and their actual broadcasting.

Sports rights acquired for *Pay Per View* on digital terrestrial technology are amortised at 100% when the event is broadcasted.

3.5 Measurement of intangible assets acquired in a business combination

3.5.1 Identifying intangible assets

The process of identifying intangible assets acquired in a business combination can be broken down into a number of steps as illustrated in the flow chart below, which reflects the recognition criteria in IAS 38 as discussed at 2.1.2, 2.2.1 and 2.3.2 above.

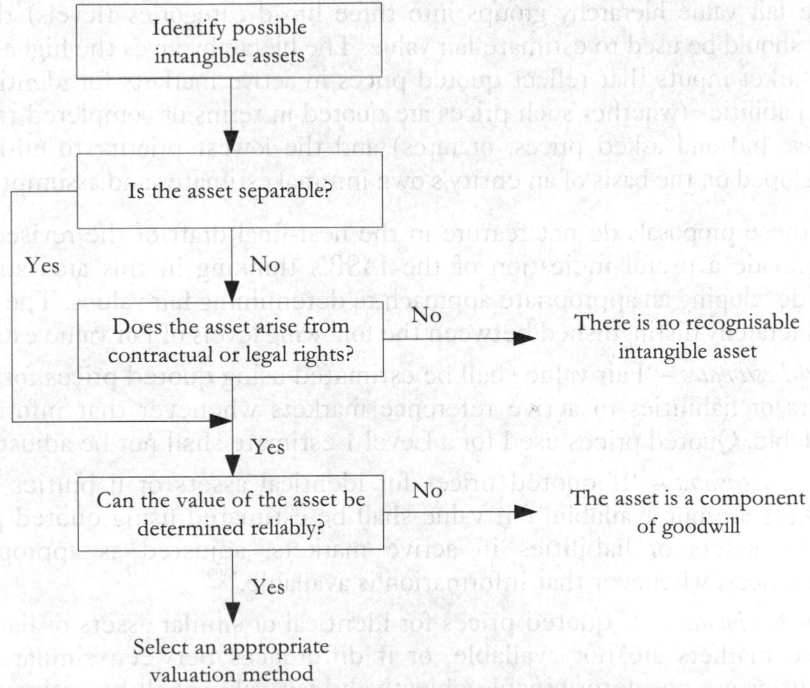

Identifying the intangible assets that possibly exist might involve, for example:

- reviewing the list of items acquired in a business combination that meet the definition of an intangible asset in IFRS 3 (see 2.3.2 B above);

- review of documents such as those related to the acquisition, other internal documents produced by the entity, public filings, press releases, analysts' reports, and other externally available documents; and
- comparing the acquired business to similar businesses and their intangible assets.

The intangible assets that are used will differ considerably between industries and between individual entities. Therefore, considerable expertise and careful judgement is required in determining whether there are intangible assets that need to be recognised and valued separately.

3.5.2 Valuing the intangible assets

Fair value is defined as 'the amount for which an asset could be exchanged, or a liability settled, between knowledgeable, willing parties in an arm's length transaction.'[305] The fair value of an intangible should reflect 'market expectations about the probability that the future economic benefits associated with the intangible asset will flow to the acquirer'.[306]

Currently IFRS does not offer detailed guidance on determining fair values. However, the exposure draft issued in June 2005 out of the second phase of the business combinations project proposed to introduce a 'fair value hierarchy':

> 'The fair value hierarchy groups into three broad categories (levels) the inputs that should be used to estimate fair value. The hierarchy gives the highest priority to market inputs that reflect quoted prices in active markets for identical assets and liabilities (whether such prices are quoted in terms of completed transaction prices, bid and asked prices, or rates) and the lowest priority to entity inputs developed on the basis of an entity's own internal estimates and assumptions.'[307]

Although these proposals do not feature in the near-final draft of the revised IFRS 3, they do provide a useful indication of the IASB's thinking in this area and can be helpful in developing an appropriate approach to determining fair values. The proposed fair value hierarchy distinguished between the following levels of fair value estimates:

(a) *Level 1 estimates* – 'Fair value shall be estimated using quoted prices for identical assets or liabilities in active reference markets whenever that information is available. Quoted prices used for a Level 1 estimate shall not be adjusted.'[308]

(b) *Level 2 estimates* – 'If quoted prices for identical assets or liabilities in active markets are not available, fair value shall be estimated using quoted prices for similar assets or liabilities in active markets, adjusted as appropriate for differences, whenever that information is available.'[309]

(c) *Level 3 estimates* – 'If quoted prices for identical or similar assets or liabilities in active markets are not available, or if differences between similar assets or liabilities are not determinable objectively, fair value shall be estimated using multiple valuation techniques consistent with the market approach, income approach, and cost approach whenever the information necessary to apply those multiple techniques is available without undue cost and effort.'[310]

The practical reality is that a Level 3 assessment would be necessary for most intangible assets acquired in a business combination. 'Fair values' would be determined by estimating what the market price would be if there were a market.

There are a number of approaches that could be used to value intangible assets:

(a) *Market approach* – The fair value of an intangible asset is derived by analysing similar intangible assets that have recently been sold or licensed, and then comparing these transactions to the intangible asset that needs to be valued. This approach corresponds to Levels 1 and 2 of the fair value hierarchy;

(b) *Income approach* – The fair value of an intangible asset is calculated as the present value of the expected economic income to be earned from the ownership of a particular intangible asset. Entities commonly use either a discounted cash flow calculation based on estimated net cash flows or the 'relief from royalty' method. The income approach corresponds to Level 3 of the fair value hierarchy; and

(c) *Cost approach* – The premise of the cost approach is that an investor would pay no more for an intangible asset than its replacement cost. Under IFRS, application of a cost approach may not always be appropriate as 'replacement cost measures the cost of an asset and not the future economic benefits recoverable from its use and/or disposal'.[311]

The extract below illustrates that many companies use more than one approach in calculating the fair value of intangible assets.

Extract 12.19: Bayer AG (2006)

Notes to the Consolidated Financial Statements of the Bayer Group [extract]

5. Critical accounting policies

Acquisition accounting [extract]

For intangible assets associated with products, product related technology, and qualified in-process research and development (IPR&D) we base our valuation on the expected future cash flows using the Multi-Period Excess Earnings approach. This method employs a discounted cash flow analysis using the present value of the estimated after-tax cash flows expected to be generated from the purchased intangible asset using risk adjusted discount rates and revenue forecasts as appropriate. The period of expected cash flows was based on the individual patent protection, taking into account the term of the product's main patent protection and essential extension of patent protection, as well as market entry of generics, considering sales, volume, prices, potential defense strategies and market development at patent expiry.

For the valuation of brands, the relief-from-royalty method was applied which includes estimating the cost savings that result from the company's ownership of trademarks and licenses on which it does not have to pay royalties to a licensor. The intangible asset is then recognized at the present value of these savings. The brand-specific royalty rates were calculated using a product-specific scoring model. The corporate brands "Schering" and "Medrad" were assumed to have an unlimited life. (Please note that the rights to the name "Schering" in the United States and Canada do not belong to us but to Schering-Plough Corporation, New Jersey. Schering-Plough Corporation and the company acquired by Bayer in June 2006, i.e. Bayer Schering Pharma AG [formerly named Schering AG], Berlin, Germany, are unaffiliated companies that have been totally independent of each other for many years.) Product brands, however, were assumed to have limited lives depending on the respective products' life cycles. The expected amortization of these assets is determined on the basis of expected product-specific revenues.

4 TRANSITION AND FIRST-TIME ADOPTION

4.1 Transitional arrangements for entities already reporting under IFRS

An entity should apply IAS 38 (as revised in 2004) to 'the accounting for intangible assets acquired in business combinations for which the agreement date is on or after 31 March 2004'.[312] The agreement date for a business combination is defined by the standard as 'the date that a substantive agreement between the combining parties is reached and, in the case of publicly listed entities, announced to the public. In the case of a hostile takeover, the earliest date that a substantive agreement between the combining parties is reached is the date that a sufficient number of the acquiree's owners have accepted the acquirer's offer for the acquirer to obtain control of the acquiree.'[313]

An entity should apply IAS 38 (as revised in 2004) to 'the accounting for all other intangible assets prospectively from the beginning of the first annual period beginning on or after 31 March 2004'.[314] The entity should not adjust the carrying amount of intangible assets recognised at that date, but should reassess the useful lives of such intangible assets. Any change in the assessment of the useful life of an asset should be accounted for as a change in an accounting estimate in accordance with IAS 8,[315] which requires such changes to be recognised prospectively.[316]

Early adoption of IAS 38 (as revised in 2004) is encouraged, but 'if an entity applies this Standard before those effective dates, it also shall apply IFRS 3 and IAS 36 (as revised in 2004) at the same time'.[317]

An entity should apply the amendments to the scope of IAS 38 (in paragraph 2) for annual periods beginning on or after 1 January 2006. However, if an entity applies IFRS 6 for an earlier period, those amendments should be applied for that earlier period.[318]

4.1.1 Early adoption of IFRS 3

If an entity applies IFRS 3 early, it should also apply IAS 38 (as revised in 2004) prospectively from the same date. The entity should not adjust the carrying amount of intangible assets recognised at that date, but should reassess the useful lives of such intangible assets. Any change in the assessment of the useful life of an asset should be accounted for as a change in an accounting estimate in accordance with IAS 8,[319] which requires such changes to be recognised prospectively.[320]

4.1.2 Exchanges of similar assets

IAS 38 (as revised in 2004) should be applied prospectively to exchanges of assets: 'if an exchange of assets was measured before the effective date of this Standard on the basis of the carrying amount of the asset given up, the entity does not restate the carrying amount of the asset acquired to reflect its fair value at the acquisition date'.[321] Therefore, an entity that already reports under IFRS is not required to restate prior exchanges of assets in accordance with the revised rules in IAS 38.

4.2 First-time adoption

4.2.1 Retrospective application of IAS 38

Entities applying IFRS for the first time must comply with the requirements of IFRS 1 – *First-time Adoption of International Financial Reporting Standards* – rather than the transitional provisions referred to at 4.1 above.[322] An intangible asset is only capable of capitalisation under IAS 38 if it is probable that the future economic benefits attributable to the asset will flow to the entity and the cost of the asset can be measured reliably.[323] Accordingly, an entity's opening IFRS balance sheet:[324]

'(a) excludes all intangible assets and other intangible items that do not meet the criteria for recognition under IAS 38 at the date of transition to IFRSs; and

(b) includes all intangible assets that meet the recognition criteria in IAS 38 at that date, except for intangible assets acquired in a business combination that were not recognised in the acquirer's consolidated balance sheet under previous GAAP and also would not qualify for recognition under IAS 38 in the separate balance sheet of the acquiree'.

As discussed at 2.3.6 above, IAS 38 imposes a number of additional criteria that further restrict capitalisation of internally generated intangible assets. An important restriction is the prohibition from using hindsight to conclude retrospectively that the recognition criteria are met, thereby capitalising an amount previously recognised as an expense.[325] A first-time adopter of IFRS must be particularly careful that, in applying IAS 38 retrospectively as at the date of transition, it does not capitalise costs incurred before the standard's recognition criteria were met. Therefore, a first-time adopter is only permitted to capitalise the costs of internally generated intangible assets when it:[326]

'(a) concludes, based on an assessment made and documented at the date of that conclusion, that it is probable that future economic benefits from the asset will flow to the entity; and

(b) has a reliable system for accumulating the costs of internally generated intangible assets when, or shortly after, they are incurred.'

In other words, an entity is not permitted under IFRS 1 to use evidence that was only available after its date of transition to retrospectively reconstruct the costs of intangible assets. First-time adopters that did not capitalise internally generated intangible assets under their previous GAAP will often not have the type of documentation and systems required by IFRS 1 and will therefore only be able to capitalise these items in their opening IFRS balance sheet if they had anticipated its requirements and established their intangible assets contemporaneously. However, going forward they will need to implement internal systems and procedures that enable them to determine whether any future internally generated intangible assets should be capitalised or not. If an internal project does not qualify for recognition until after the entity's date of transition, then the cost of the related intangible asset contains only the expenditure incurred from that later date.[327] Capitalisation of separately acquired intangible assets will generally be easier because contemporaneous documentation that was prepared to support the investment decisions often exists.[328]

4.2.2 Using fair value or revaluation as deemed cost

To deal with the problem of restatement of long-lived intangible assets upon first-time adoption of IFRS, IFRS 1 permits a first-time adopter to measure an intangible asset in its opening IFRS balance sheet at an amount that is based on its deemed cost. By using deemed cost – which is a surrogate for cost or depreciated cost at a given date[329] – for an intangible asset a first-time adopter can avoid a potentially onerous exercise to reconstruct the true historical cost of that asset. A first-time adopter is allowed to measure an intangible asset in its opening IFRS balance sheet at deemed cost if it meets:[330]

- the recognition criteria in IAS 38 (including reliable measurement of original cost); and
- the criteria in IAS 38 for revaluation (including the existence of an active market).

The use of fair value or revaluation as deemed cost for intangible assets will be very limited in practice, because of the very restrictive definition of an active market in IAS 38 (see 2.4.2 A above).[331] It is therefore unlikely that a first-time adopter will be able to apply this exemption to any intangible assets.[332]

It is important to note that the deemed cost exemption in IFRS 1 does not take classes or categories of assets as its unit of measure, but refers to individual items.[333] As discussed at 2.4 above, IAS 38 usually requires a policy of revaluation to be applied to a whole class of assets.[334] However, the IASB argued that it is not necessary to restrict application of the deemed cost exemption to classes of assets to prevent selective revaluations, because 'IAS 36 requires an impairment test if there is any indication that an asset is impaired. Thus, if an entity uses fair value as deemed cost for assets whose fair value is above cost, it cannot ignore indications that the recoverable amount of other assets may have fallen below their carrying amount. Therefore, the IFRS does not restrict the use of fair value as deemed cost to entire classes of asset.'[335] Nevertheless, it seems doubtful that the quality of financial information would benefit from a revaluation of a haphazard selection of intangible assets. Therefore, a first-time adopter should exercise judgment in selecting the items that it wants the exemption to apply to.

In summary, at its date of transition to IFRS a first-time adopter is allowed under IFRS 1 to value intangible assets at either:

- historical cost determined in accordance with IAS 38;
- fair value at the date of transition to IFRS;
- a revalued amount that is equal to:
  - fair value at the date of revaluation;
  - cost adjusted for changes in a general or specific index; or

  - an event-driven fair value, for example, at the date of an initial public offering or privatisation; or
- in the case of an item acquired in a business combination:
  - carrying amount under previous GAAP immediately after acquisition; or
  - if the item was not recognised under previous GAAP, the carrying amount on the basis that IFRS would require in the separate balance sheet of the acquiree.

The fact that IFRS 1 offers seven different bases for valuation does not disturb the IASB as it reasons that 'cost is generally equivalent to fair value at the date of acquisition. Therefore, the use of fair value as the deemed cost of an asset means that an entity will report the same cost data as if it had acquired an asset with the same remaining service potential at the date of transition to IFRSs. If there is any lack of comparability, it arises from the aggregation of costs incurred at different dates, rather than from the targeted use of fair value as deemed cost for some assets. The Board regarded this approach as justified to solve the unique problem of introducing IFRS in a cost-effective way without damaging transparency.'[336] Users of the financial statements of a first-time adopter should therefore be mindful that historical trends under the previous GAAP might no longer be present in an entity's IFRS financial statements.

5 CONCLUSION

Throughout the last decade there has been a gradual shift in the emphasis of what financial statements are meant to portray, from a transactions-based, performance-orientated model in which the profit and loss account is the most important statement towards a balance sheet-orientated model based on fair values.

This approach has not made the treatment of intangible assets in the balance sheet at the conceptual level any easier. The IASB has promulgated standards that have greatly reduced the scope for creative accounting as far as intangibles are concerned, as well as producing standards that are as unambiguously drafted as may reasonably be expected. It is also true that, in spite of the considerable effort put into its conceptual framework, the IASB has not come up with a conceptually integrated or logically consistent treatment of intangible assets.

The virtual prohibition on the recognition of many internally generated intangibles, is a tacit admission of the limits of our ability to deal with such items, rather than a deductive consequence of the reasons offered in the standards themselves. Thus it appears that accounting for intangible assets is at the stage of having a workable but imperfect set of rules which falls well short of consistency.

If the move towards an accounting model based on recording the entire balance sheet at fair values continues, the challenge will be to find an acceptable, logically consistent method that can value all intangibles that have worth, without arbitrarily scoping out those that present too many difficulties.

References

1 IAS 38, *Intangible Assets*, IASB, para. IN2.
2 IAS 38, para. IN3.
3 IAS 38, para. IN3.
4 IAS 38, para. IN3.
5 IAS 38, para. BC2.
6 IAS 38, para. BC2.
7 IAS 38, para. BC2.
8 Project Updates, *Business Combinations: Applying the Acquisition Method – Joint Project of the IASB and FASB*, FASB, 25 October 2007, Immediate Plans.
9 IAS 38, para. 1.
10 IAS 38, para. 2.
11 IAS 38, para. 3.
12 IAS 38, para. 6.
13 IAS 17, *Leases*, IASB, para. 2.
14 IAS 38, para. 6.
15 IAS 38, para. 7.
16 IAS 38, para. 5.
17 IAS 38, para. 8.
18 IAS 38, para. 8.
19 IAS 38, paras. BC4-BC5.
20 IAS 38, para. 3.
21 IAS 38, para. 9.
22 IAS 38, para. 10.
23 IFRS 3, *Business Combinations*, IASB, Appendix A.
24 IAS 38, para. 11.
25 IAS 38, para. BC7.
26 IAS 38, para. BC8.
27 IAS 38, para. 12.
28 IAS 38, para. BC10.
29 IAS 38, para. BC13.
30 IAS 38, paras. 13-14.
31 IAS 38, para. 13.
32 IAS 38, para. 15.
33 IAS 38, para. 16.
34 IAS 38, para. 16.
35 IFRS 3, Illustrative Examples, Examples of items acquired in a business combination that meet the definition of an intangible asset.
36 IAS 38, para. 18.
37 IAS 38, para. 17.
38 IAS 38, para. 4.
39 IAS 38, para. 4.
40 IAS 38, para. 5.
41 IAS 16, *Property, Plant and Equipment*, IASB, paras. 43-47.
42 IAS 38, para. 18.
43 IAS 38, para. 21.
44 IFRS 3, Appendix A and IFRS 5, *Non-current Assets Held for Sale and Discontinued Operations*, Appendix A.
45 IAS 38, para. 22.
46 IAS 38, para. 23.
47 IAS 38, paras. BCZ39-BCZ40.
48 IAS 38, para. BCZ41.
49 IAS 38, para. 24.
50 IAS 38, para. 8.
51 IAS 38, para. 20.
52 IAS 38, para. 20.
53 IAS 38, para. 20 and paras. 63-64.
54 IAS 38, para. 25.
55 IAS 38, para. 25.
56 IAS 38, para. 26.
57 IAS 38, para. BC18.
58 IAS 38, para. 27.
59 IAS 38, para. 28.
60 IAS 38, para. 30.
61 IAS 38, para. 32.
62 IAS 38, paras. 29-30.
63 IAS 16, para. 21.
64 IAS 38, para. 31.
65 IFRS 3, para. 37.
66 IFRS 3, Illustrative Examples.
67 SFAS 141, *Business Combinations*, FASB, June 2001, para. A14.
68 SFAS 141, paras. BC165 and BC169.
69 IFRS 3, para. 45.
70 IAS 38, para. 21
71 IAS 38, para. 33.
72 IAS 38, para. 33.
73 IAS 38, para. 34.
74 IAS 38, para. BC19.
75 IAS 38, para. BC21.
76 IAS 38, para. BC23.
77 IAS 38, para. 38.
78 IAS 38, para. 36.
79 IAS 38, para. BC25.
80 IAS 38, para. 37.
81 IFRS 3, Illustrative Examples, *Examples of items acquired in a business combination that meet the definition of an intangible asset*.
82 IAS 38, para. 35.
83 IAS 38, para. 39.
84 IAS 38, para. 78.
85 IAS 38, para. 40.
86 IAS 38, para. 41.
87 IFRS 3, Illustrative Examples, *Customer relationship intangible assets acquired in a business combination*.
88 IAS 38, para. 34.
89 IAS 38, para. 42.
90 IAS 38, para. 43.
91 IAS 38, para. BC82.
92 IAS 36, *Impairment of Assets*, IASB, para. 10.

93 IAS 38, para. 44.
94 IAS 38, para. 44.
95 IAS 20, *Accounting for Government Grants and Disclosure of Government Assistance*, IASB, para. 23.
96 IAS 38, para. 45.
97 IAS 38, para. 47.
98 IAS 38, para. 45.
99 IAS 16, para. BC21.
100 IAS 38, para. 46.
101 IAS 38, para. 8.
102 IAS 38, para. 46.
103 IAS 38, para. 47.
104 IAS 38, para. 46.
105 IAS 38, para. 48.
106 IAS 38, para. 49.
107 IAS 38, para. 50.
108 IAS 38, para. 51.
109 IAS 38, para. 51.
110 IAS 38, para. 52.
111 IAS 38, para. 8.
112 IAS 38, para. 56.
113 IAS 38, para. 8.
114 IAS 38, para. 59.
115 IAS 38, paras. 54-55.
116 IAS 38, para. 57.
117 IAS 38, para. 58.
118 IAS 38, para. 60.
119 IAS 38, para. 61.
120 IAS 38, para. 61.
121 IAS 38, para. 62.
122 IAS 38, para. 52.
123 IAS 38, para. 55.
124 IAS 38, para. 53.
125 *IFRIC Update*, IFRIC, February 2002, p.2.
126 IAS 38, para. BCZ38.
127 IAS 38, para. BCZ40.
128 IAS 38, para. 63.
129 IAS 38, para. 64.
130 IAS 38, para. 20.
131 IAS 38, para. BCZ45.
132 SIC-32, *Intangible Assets – Web Site Costs*, IASB, para. 7.
133 SIC-32, paras. 5-6.
134 SIC-32, para. 1.
135 SIC-32, para. 8.
136 SIC-32, para. 8.
137 SIC-32, paras. 2 and 9.
138 SIC-32, para. 3.
139 SIC-32, para. 9.
140 IAS 38, para. 67.
141 SIC-32, para. 10.
142 IAS 38, para. 24.
143 IAS 38, para. 8.
144 IAS 38, para. 65.
145 IAS 38, paras. 21-22.
146 IAS 38, para. 21.
147 IAS 38, para. 68.
148 IAS 38, para. 65.
149 IAS 38, para. 71.
150 IAS 38, Example Illustrating paragraph 65.
151 IAS 38, para. 66.
152 IAS 38, para. 67.
153 IAS 38, para. 68.
154 IAS 38, para. 69.
155 IAS 38, para. 70.
156 *IFRIC Update*, IFRIC, September 2006, p. 4.
157 *IFRIC Update*, IFRIC, September 2006, p. 4.
158 *IFRIC Update*, IFRIC, November 2006, p. 4.
159 *IFRIC Update*, IFRIC, January 2007, p. 4.
160 *IFRIC Update*, IFRIC, March 2007, p. 3.
161 *IASB Update*, IASB, April 2007, p. 4.
162 *IASB Update*, IASB, May 2007, p. 4.
163 *IASB Update*, IASB, June 2007, p. 4.
164 IAS 38, para. 72.
165 IAS 38, para. 74.
166 IAS 38, para. 75.
167 IAS 38, paras. 75, 81 and 82.
168 IAS 38, para. 72.
169 IAS 38, para. 73.
170 IAS 38, para. 119.
171 IAS 38, para. 73.
172 IAS 38, para. 74.
173 IAS 38, para. 75.
174 IAS 38, paras. 75, 81 and 82.
175 IAS 38, para. 76.
176 IAS 38, para. 77.
177 IAS 38, para. 77.
178 IAS 38, paras. 75, 81 and 82.
179 IAS 38, para. 8.
180 IAS 38, para. 78.
181 IAS 38, para. 78.
182 IAS 38, para. 78.
183 IAS 38, para. 75.
184 IAS 38, para. 79.
185 IAS 38, para. 73.
186 IAS 38, para. 85.
187 IAS 38, para. 86.
188 IAS 38, para. 87.
189 IAS 38, para. 87.
190 IAS 38, para. 87.
191 IAS 38, para. 80.
192 IAS 38, para. 72.
193 IAS 38, para. 81.
194 IAS 38, para. 82.
195 IAS 38, para. 83.
196 IAS 38, para. 84.
197 IAS 38, para. 8.
198 IAS 38, para. 88.
199 IAS 38, para. 88.
200 IAS 38, para. 89.
201 IAS 38, para. 91.
202 IAS 38, para. 88.
203 IAS 38, para. BC63.

204 IAS 38, para. BC62.
205 IAS 38, para. BC63.
206 IAS 38, para. 91.
207 IAS 38, para. 90.
208 IAS 38, para. 89 and Illustrative Examples.
209 IAS 38, para. 92.
210 IAS 38, para. 93.
211 IAS 38, paras. 94-95.
212 IAS 38, para. 94.
213 IAS 38, para. 96.
214 IAS 38, para. 94.
215 IAS 38, para. 96.
216 IAS 38, para. 8.
217 IAS 38, para. 97.
218 IAS 38, para. 117.
219 IAS 38, para. 98.
220 *Exposure Draft of Proposed Improvements to Financial Reporting Standards, IASB, October 2007, Proposed Amendments to IAS 38*, para. BC5.
221 IAS 38, paras. 97 and 99.
222 IAS 38, para. 104.
223 IAS 38, para. 105.
224 IAS 38, para. 104.
225 IAS 38, para. 106.
226 IAS 38, para. 106.
227 IAS 38, para. 104.
228 IAS 8, *Accounting Policies, Changes in Accounting Estimates and Errors*, IASB, para. 36.
229 IAS 38, para. 8.
230 IAS 38, para. 100.
231 IAS 38, para. BC59.
232 IAS 38, para. 101.
233 IAS 38, para. 102.
234 IAS 38, para. 102.
235 IAS 38, para. 103.
236 IAS 38, para. 107.
237 IAS 38, para. 108.
238 IAS 38, para. 109.
239 IAS 38, para. 109.
240 IAS 8, para. 36.
241 IAS 38, para. 110
242 IAS 38, para. 8.
243 IAS 38, para. 111.
244 IAS 36, para. 10.
245 IAS 38, para. BC55.
246 IAS 38, para. 112.
247 IAS 38, para. 113.
248 IAS 38, para. 114.
249 IAS 38, para. 113.
250 IAS 38, para. 116.
251 IAS 38, para. 115.
252 IAS 38, para. 20.
253 IAS 38, para. 119.
254 IAS 38, para. 118.
255 IAS 38, para. 120.
256 IAS 38, para. 121.
257 IAS 38, para. 122.
258 IAS 38, para. 123.
259 IAS 38, para. 128.
260 IAS 1, *Presentation of Financial Statements*, IASB, para. 58.
261 IAS 1, para. 68.
262 IAS 1, para. 51.
263 IAS 1, para. 69.
264 IAS 38, para. 113.
265 IAS 38, para. 118(d).
266 IAS 38, para. 124.
267 IAS 38, para. 125.
268 IAS 38, paras. 126-127.
269 IAS 38, para. 8.
270 IAS 37, *Provisions, Contingent Liabilities and Contingent Assets*, IASB, para. 10.
271 *IFRIC Update*, IFRIC, August 2005, p. 6.
272 *IFRIC Update*, IFRIC, August 2005, p. 6.
273 *IASB Update*, IASB, June 2005, p. 1.
274 *IASB Update*, IASB, June 2005, p. 1.
275 *IASB Insight*, IASB, May 2006, p. 13.
276 IFRIC 3, *Emission Rights*, 2005 Bound Volume of International Financial Reporting Standards, IASB, para. 2.
277 IFRIC 3, para. 3.
278 IFRIC 3, para. 5.
279 IFRIC 3, para. 6.
280 IFRIC 3, para. 7.
281 IFRIC 3, para. 8.
282 IFRIC 3, para. 9.
283 IAS 20, para. 23.
284 IAS 37, para. 36.
285 IAS 20, para. 23.
286 IAS 37, para. 37.
287 IAS 37, para. 37.
288 IAS 37, para. 37.
289 IAS 38, para. 75.
290 IAS 39, *Financial Instruments: Recognition and Measurement*, IASB, paras. AG74-AG79.
291 IFRS 3, paras. 36-37.
292 IAS 38, para. 112.
293 IAS 38, para. 113.
294 IAS 38, para. 113.
295 IAS 1, paras. 108 and 112.
296 IAS 2, *Inventories*, IASB, para. 6.
297 IAS 2, para. 3.
298 IAS 38 (1998), *Intangible Assets*, IASB, September 1998, para. 7.
299 IAS 38, para. 3.
300 IAS 2, para. 6.
301 Framework, *Framework for the Preparation and Presentation of Financial Statements*, IASB, para. 91.
302 IAS 2, para. 9.
303 IAS 38, para. 97.
304 IAS 38, para. 98.
305 IAS 38, para. 8.

306 IFRS 3, para. BC96.
307 IFRS 3 (ED), *Exposure Draft of Amendments to IFRS 3 Business Combinations*, IASB, June 2005, para. E11.
308 IFRS 3 (ED), para. E13.
309 IFRS 3 (ED), para. E17.
310 IFRS 3 (ED), para. E19.
311 IAS 36, para. BCZ29.
312 IAS 38, para. 130.
313 IAS 38, para. 8.
314 IAS 38, para. 130.
315 IAS 38, para. 130.
316 IAS 8, para. 36.
317 IAS 38, para. 132.
318 IAS 38, para. 130A.
319 IAS 38, para. 129.
320 IAS 8, para. 36.
321 IAS 38, para. 131.
322 IFRS 1, *First-time Adoption of International Financial Reporting Standards*, IASB, para. 9.
323 IAS 38, para. 21. and IFRS 1, para. IG45.
324 IFRS 1, para. IG44.
325 IAS 38, para. 71.
326 IFRS 1, para. IG46.
327 IFRS 1, para. IG47.
328 IFRS 1, para. IG48.
329 IFRS 1, Appendix A.
330 IFRS 1, paras. 16-18.
331 IAS 38, para. 8.
332 IAS 38, para. 78.
333 IFRS 1, para. 16.
334 IAS 38, para. 72.
335 IFRS 1, para. BC45.
336 IFRS 1, para. BC43.

Chapter 13 Property, plant and equipment

1 INTRODUCTION

One fundamental problem in financial reporting is how to account annually for performance when many of the expenditures an entity incurs in the current period also contribute to future accounting periods. Expenditure on property, plant and equipment (hereafter abbreviated to PP&E, but also known as fixed assets in many jurisdictions) is the best example of this difficulty. The accounting conventions permitted by the IASB to solve it are the subject of this chapter, although the underlying broad principles involved are among the first that accountants and business people learn in their business life. The cost of an item of PP&E is capitalised when acquired (i.e. recorded in the balance sheet as an asset); then subsequently a proportion of the cost is charged each year to profit or loss (i.e. the cost is spread out over the future accounting periods expected to benefit). Ideally, at the end of the item's working life the cost remaining in the balance sheet should be equal to the disposal proceeds of the item, or be zero if there are none.

Basic prudence dictates that during the life of the item any uncharged cost remaining in the balance sheet should be written down if it is not fully recoverable. Finally, when an item of PP&E is sold or scrapped, the difference between the written down value and any proceeds is recorded as the gain or loss on disposal.

There are inevitably some detailed rules required to apply these principles in practice, such as precisely when PP&E should initially be recognised, and how its cost should be measured. Additionally, it is not always obvious if an item is PP&E or not, nor, if a policy of revaluation is adopted, how the PP&E should be accounted for. Thus, although the basic principles are generally well understood, as in most other areas of financial reporting, the development of more detailed requirements has necessitated an accounting standard.

Under IFRS the main standard is IAS 16 – *Property, Plant and Equipment*. Impairment is covered by IAS 36 – *Impairment of Assets* – and dealt with as a separate topic in Chapter 15. Impairment is a major consideration in accounting for PP&E, as this procedure is intended to ensure PP&E costs that are not fully recoverable are immediately written down to a level that is. In addition, there is a separate standard, IAS 40 – *Investment Property* – that deals with that particular category of PP&E which is discussed in Chapter 14. Finally, IFRS 5 – *Non-current Assets Held for Sale and Discontinued Operations* – that deals with the accounting required when items of PP&E are held for sale, is discussed in Chapter 4.

IAS 16 was revised in 1998 and became operative for annual financial statements covering periods beginning on or after 1 July 1999. Further revisions were made in late 2003 and early 2004, as a result of the IASB's Improvements project and the publication of other new IFRSs. The most recent version of IAS 16, published in March 2004 and which became effective for periods beginning on or after 1 January 2005, is discussed in this chapter.

2 THE REQUIREMENTS OF IAS 16

2.1 Introduction

One of the objectives of the IASB's Improvements project was to reduce the number of alternative treatments allowed by then existing IAS. However, in IAS 16 there remain two very different alternative accounting treatments that may be chosen to account for PP&E: items may be carried at either cost less depreciation, or at their fair value. Other than this, IAS 16 is a fairly straightforward standard that attempts to delineate the boundaries of what may, and may not, be considered part of the cost of an item of PP&E.

2.2 Scope, definition and recognition

All PP&E is within the scope of IAS 16 except as follows:

- when another standard requires or permits a different accounting treatment (e.g. IAS 40 for investment properties);
- PP&E classified as held for sale in accordance with IFRS 5;
- biological assets related to agricultural activity (covered by IAS 41 – *Agriculture*); and
- mineral rights and mineral reserves such as oil, gas, and similar 'non-regenerative' resources.[1]

Note that although the standard scopes out biological assets and mineral resources, it includes any PP&E used in developing or maintaining such resources. Therefore, exploration PP&E is included in the scope of the standard, as is agricultural PP&E. It is important also to note that although completed investment property is subject to IAS 40, currently IAS 16 applies during the time investment property is in the course of construction, or while property is being developed for future use as investment property (although, if the IASB exposure draft issued as part of the annual improvement process is finalised as currently drafted, then from 1 January 2009 investment property under construction will be dealt with under IAS 40 see Chapter 14 at 2.2.5). However, if existing investment property is being redeveloped for the continuing use as investment property in the future, it remains subject to IAS 40 during its redevelopment.[2]

Other standards may require an item of PP&E to be recognised on a basis different from that required by IAS 16. For example IAS 17 – *Leases* – has its own rules regarding recognition and measurement; see Chapter 25 for a description of how an item of PP&E held under a finance lease is recognised and measured. However, once an item of PP&E has been recognised as a finance lease under IAS 17, its treatment thereafter is in accordance with IAS 16.[3]

2.2.1 Definitions

IAS 16 defines the main terms it uses throughout thc standard as follows:

Carrying amount is the amount at which an asset is recognised after deducting any accumulated depreciation and accumulated impairment losses.

Cost is the amount of cash or cash equivalents paid or the fair value of other consideration given to acquire an asset at thc timc of its acquisition or construction or, where applicable, the amount attributed to that asset when initially recognised in accordance with the specific requirements of other IFRSs, e.g. IFRS 2 – *Share-based Payment*.

Depreciable amount is the cost of an asset, or other amount substituted for cost, less its residual value.

Depreciation is the systematic allocation of the depreciable amount of an asset over its useful life.

Entity-specific value is the present value of the cash flows an entity expects to arise from the continuing use of an asset and from its disposal at the end of its useful life or expects to incur when settling a liability.

Fair value is the amount for which an asset could be exchanged between knowledgeable, willing parties in an arm's length transaction.

An *impairment loss* is the amount by which the carrying amount of an asset exceeds its recoverable amount.

Property, plant and equipment are tangible items that:

(a) are held for use in the production or supply of goods or services, for rental to others, or for administrative purposes; and

(b) are expected to be used during more than one period.

Recoverable amount is the higher of an asset's net selling price and its value in use.

The *residual value* of an asset is the estimated amount that an entity would currently obtain from disposal of the asset, after deducting the estimated costs of disposal, if the asset were already of the age and in the condition expected at the end of its useful life.

Useful life is:

(a) the period over which an asset is expected to be available for use by an entity; or

(b) the number of production or similar units expected to be obtained from the asset by an entity.[4]

These definitions are discussed in the relevant sections below.

2.2.2 Recognition

An item of PP&E should be recognised, i.e. its cost included in the balance sheet as an asset, only if its cost can be measured reliably and it is probable that future economic benefits associated with the item will flow to the entity.[5] This requirement for recognition is directly taken from the IASB's Framework, which is discussed in some detail in Chapter 2. It follows from the Framework's characterisation of an asset as future economic benefits, rather than the item of property itself, that to be recognised the economic benefits must be forthcoming, or at least probable.

There are materiality judgements to be considered when deciding how an item of PP&E should be accounted for. Major spare parts, for example, qualify as PP&E, while smaller spares would be carried as inventory, and as a practical matter many companies have a minimum value for capitalising assets (see Extract 13.1 below). However if a set of spares can only be used on one item of PP&E, then they should be accounted for as PP&E.[6]

Extract 13.1: BMW AG (2006)

Notes to the Group Financial Statements [extract]
Accounting Principles and Policies [extract]
Property, plant and equipment [extract]

Expenditure on low value non-current assets is written off in full in the year of acquisition.

Some types of business may have a very large number of minor fixed assets such as spare parts, tools, pallets and returnable containers, which nevertheless are used in more than one accounting period. There are practical problems in recording them on an asset-by-asset basis in an asset register; they are difficult to control and frequently lost. The main consequence is that it becomes very difficult to provide depreciation on them. The standard notes that there are issues concerning what actually constitutes a single item of PP&E to be individually recognised. The 'unit of measurement for recognition' is not prescribed and entities have to apply judgement in defining PP&E in their individual circumstances. The standard suggests that some parts such as tools, moulds and dies should be aggregated and the standard applied to the aggregate amount (presumably without having to identify the individual assets).[7]

The standard acknowledges that there may be expenditures forced upon an entity by legislation that require it to buy 'assets' that do not meet the recognition criteria because the expenditure does not directly increase the expected future benefits expected to flow from the asset.[8] Examples would be safety or environmental protection equipment. IAS 16 explains that these expenditures do qualify for recognition as they allow future benefits in excess of those that would flow if the expenditure had not been made; for example a plant might have to be closed down if the expenditures were not made.

In our view this approach is sensible (even if it is indicative of a deficiency in the recognition criteria) and has no more significance, and is in the same category as, the cost of fitting guards to machinery at original manufacture.

An entity may voluntarily invest in environmental equipment even though it is not required by law to do so. We consider that the entity should expense those investments in environmental and safety equipment as incurred, unless either it can demonstrate that the equipment is likely to increase the economic life of the related assets or that it can demonstrate all of the following:

- the entity can prove that a constructive obligation exists to invest in environmental and safety equipment (e.g. it is standard practice in the industry, environmental groups are likely to raise issues or employees demand certain equipment to be present);
- the expenditure is directly related to improvement of the asset's environmental and safety standards; and
- the expenditure is not related to repairs and maintenance or forms part of period costs or operational costs.

Whenever safety and environmental assets are capitalised, the standard requires the resulting carrying amount of the asset and any related asset to be reviewed in accordance with IAS 36 (see Chapter 15).[9]

Extract 13.2 below describes Skanska AB's criteria for the recognition of PP&E:

Extract 13.2: Skanska AB (2006)

Note 1 Accounting and Valuation principles [extract]
IAS 16, "Property, Plant and Equipment" [extract]

Property, plant and equipment are recognized as assets in the balance sheet if it is probable that the Group will derive future economic benefits from them and the cost of an asset can be reliably estimated. Property, plant and equipment are recognized at cost minus accumulated depreciation and any impairment losses. Cost includes purchase price plus expenses directly attributable to the asset in order to bring it to the location and condition to be operated in the intended manner. Examples of directly attributable expenses are delivery and handling costs, installation, ownership documents, consultant fees and legal services. Borrowing costs are included in the cost of self-constructed property, plant and equipment. Impairment losses are applied in compliance with IAS 36, "Impairment of assets."

The cost of self-constructed property, plant and equipment includes expenditures for materials and compensation to employees, plus other applicable manufacturing costs that are considered attributable to the asset.

> Further expenditures are added to cost only if it is probable that the Group will enjoy future economic benefits associated with the asset and the cost can be reliably estimated. All other further expenditures are recognized as expenses in the period when they arise.
>
> What is decisive in determining when a further expenditure is added to cost is whether the expenditure is related to replacement of identified components, or their parts, at which time such expenditures are capitalized. In cases where a new component is created, this expenditure is also added to cost. Any undepreciated carrying amounts for replaced components, or their parts, are disposed of and recognized as an expense at the time of replacement. If the cost of the removed component cannot be determined directly, its cost is estimated as the cost of the new component adjusted by a suitable price index to take into account inflation. Repairs are recognised as expenses continuously.

IAS 16 makes no distinction in principle between the initial costs of acquiring an asset and any subsequent expenditure upon it. In both cases any and all expenditure has to meet the recognition rules, and be expensed in the income statement if it does not. IAS 16 states:

> 'An entity evaluates under this recognition principle all its property, plant and equipment costs at the time they are incurred. These costs include costs incurred initially to acquire or construct an item of property, plant and equipment and costs incurred subsequently to add to, replace part of, or service it.'[10]

The standard draws a distinction between servicing and more major expenditure. Day-to-day servicing, by which is meant the repair and maintenance of PP&E, and which largely comprises labour costs and minor parts, should be recognised in the income statement as incurred.[11] However, if the expenditure involves replacing a significant part of the asset, this part should be recognised, i.e. capitalised as part of the fixed asset, if the recognition criteria are met. The carrying amount of the part that has been replaced should be derecognised, as described in 2.6 below. An example of this treatment of major maintenance expenditure is shown in Extract 13.3 below:

> *Extract 13.3: Akzo Nobel N.V. (2006)*
>
> **Summary of significant accounting policies** [extract]
> **Property, Plant and Equipment** [extract]
>
> Cost of major maintenance activities are capitalized as a separate component of property, plant and equipment, and depreciated over the estimated useful life. Maintenance costs which cannot be separately defined as a component of property, plant and equipment are expensed in the period in which they occur.

IAS 16 identifies two particular types of parts of assets. The first is an item that requires replacement at regular intervals during the life of the asset. For example a furnace may require relining after a specified number of hours of use, or aircraft interiors such as seats and galleys may require replacement several times during the life of the airframe. The second type involves less frequently recurring replacements, such as replacing the interior walls of a building. The standard proposes that under the recognition principle described above, an entity recognises in the carrying amount of an item of property, plant and equipment the cost of replacing part of such an item when that cost is incurred while derecognising the carrying amount of the parts that have been replaced.[12]

IAS 16 does not state that these expenditures necessarily qualify for recognition. Some of its examples, such as aircraft engines that require regular overhaul, are clearly best treated as separate assets as they have a useful life different from that of the asset of which they are part. With others, such as interior walls, it is less clear why they meet the recognition criteria. However, replacing internal walls or similar expenditure may extend the useful life of a building while upgrading machinery may increase its capacity, improve the quality of its output or reduce operating costs. Hence, this type of expenditure may give rise to future economic benefits.

This parts approach is illustrated by British Airways plc in Extract 13.4 below.

Extract 13.4: British Airways plc (2007)

Notes to the accounts [extract]

2 **Accounting policies** [extract]

Property, plant and equipment [extract]

b Fleet

All aircraft are stated at the fair value of the consideration given after taking account of manufacturers' credits. Fleet assets owned, or held on finance lease or hire purchase arrangements, are depreciated at rates calculated to write down the cost to the estimated residual value at the end of their planned operational lives on a straight line basis.

Cabin interior modifications, including those required for brand changes and relaunches, are depreciated over the lower of five years and the remaining life of the aircraft.

Aircraft and engine spares acquired on the introduction or expansion of a fleet, as well as rotable spares purchased separately, are carried as tangible fixed assets and generally depreciated in line with the fleet to which they relate.

Major overhaul expenditure, including replacement spares and labour costs, is capitalised and amortised over the average expected life between major overhauls. All other replacement spares and other costs relating to maintenance of fleet assets (including maintenance provided under 'power-by-the-hour' contracts) are charged to the income statement on consumption or as incurred respectively.

Accounting for parts of assets is discussed in greater detail in 2.8.1 below.

The standard also allows a separate part to be recognised if an entity is required to perform regular major inspections for faults, regardless of whether any physical parts of the asset are replaced.

The reason for this approach is to maintain a degree of consistency with IAS 37 – *Provisions, Contingent Liabilities and Contingent Assets* – which forbids an entity to make provisions that are not obligations. Therefore an entity is prohibited by IAS 37 from making a provision to overhaul (say) an aircraft engine by providing a quarter of the cost for four years and then utilising the provision when the engine is overhauled in year four. This had been a common practice in the airline and oil refining industries, although it had never been universally applied in either sector; some companies accounted for the expenditure when incurred, others capitalised the cost and depreciated it over the period until the next major overhaul. IAS 37 proposed that the entity's results could be largely insulated from the effects of any change in the policy of providing for repair costs over time by adjusting the asset's carrying value and depreciation charge.[13] IAS 16 now applies the same recognition criteria to the cost of major inspections. Inspection costs are added to the asset's cost and any amount remaining from the previous inspection is derecognised. This process of recognition and derecognition should take place regardless of whether the cost of the previous inspection was identified (and considered a separate part) when the asset was originally acquired or constructed. Therefore, if the element relating to the inspection had previously been identified, it would have been depreciated between that time and the current overhaul. However, if it had not previously been identified, the recognition and derecognition rules still apply, but the standard allows the estimated cost of a future similar inspection to be used as an indication of the cost of the existing inspection component that must be derecognised.[14] This appears to allow the entity to reconstruct the carrying amount of the previous inspection (i.e. to estimate the net depreciated carrying value of the previous inspection that will be derecognised) rather than simply using a depreciated replacement cost approach.

2.3 Measurement at recognition

IAS 16 draws a distinction between measurement at recognition (i.e. the initial recognition of an item of PP&E on acquisition) and measurement after recognition (i.e. the subsequent treatment of the item). Measurement after recognition is discussed at 2.4 below.

The standard states that 'An item of property, plant and equipment that qualifies for recognition as an asset shall be measured at its cost.'[15] Therefore the question arises as to what may be included in the cost of an item, and the standard contains considerable guidance on this matter, under the heading 'Elements of cost'.

2.3.1 Elements of cost and cost measurement

Paragraph 18 of IAS 16 sets out the constituents of the cost of an item of PP&E on its initial recognition, as follows:

'The cost of an item of property, plant and equipment comprises:

(a) its purchase price, including import duties and non-refundable purchase taxes, after deducting trade discounts and rebates.

(b) any costs directly attributable to bringing the asset to the location and condition necessary for it to be capable of operating in the manner intended by management.

(c) the initial estimate of the costs of dismantling and removing the item and restoring the site on which it is located, the obligation for which an entity incurs either when the item is acquired or as a consequence of having used the item during a particular period for purposes other than to produce inventories during that period.'[16] The costs of obligations to dismantle, remove or restore an asset that is used to produce inventories are dealt with in accordance with IAS 2 – *Inventories* – as dealt with in Chapter 23.[17]

Note that all site restoration costs and other environmental restoration and similar costs must be estimated and capitalised at initial recognition, in order that such costs can be recovered over the life of the item of PP&E, even if the expenditure will only be incurred at the end of the item's life. The obligations are calculated in accordance with IAS 37.[18] This treatment is illustrated in Extract 13.5 below:

Extract 13.5: L'Air Liquide S.A (2006)

Accounting principles [extract]

4 Accounting policies [extract]

4.5 Non current assets [extract]

e/ Property, plant and equipment [extract]

Land, buildings and equipment are carried at cost less any accumulated depreciation and any accumulated impairment losses.

In the case of mandatory dismantling or asset removals, the related costs are added to the initial cost of the relevant assets and provisions are recognized to cover these costs.

A common instance of (c) above is dilapidation obligations in lease agreements, under which a lessee is obliged to return premises to the landlord in an agreed condition. Arguably, a provision is required whenever the 'damage' is incurred. Therefore, if a retailer rents two adjoining premises and knocks them into one and has an obligation to make good the party wall at the end of the lease term, he should immediately provide for the costs of so doing. The 'other side' of the provision entry is an asset that will be amortised over the lease term – notwithstanding the fact that some of the costs of modifying the premises may also have been capitalised as assets.

A 'Directly attributable' costs

This is the key issue in the measurement of cost. The standard gives examples of types of expenditure that are, and are not, considered to be directly attributable. The following examples are given of those types of expenditure that are considered to be directly attributable, and hence may be included in cost at initial recognition:

(a) costs of employee benefits (as defined in IAS 19 – *Employee Benefits*) arising directly from the construction or acquisition of the item of property, plant and equipment. This means that the labour costs of an entity's own employees (e.g. site workers, in-house architects and surveyors) arising directly from the construction, or acquisition, of the specific item of PP&E may be recognised;

(b) costs of site preparation;

(c) initial delivery and handling costs;

(d) installation and assembly costs;

(e) costs of testing whether the asset is functioning properly, after deducting the net proceeds from selling any items produced while bringing the asset to that location and condition (such as samples produced when testing equipment); and

(f) professional fees.[19]

B Borrowing costs

If directly attributable to the item, borrowing costs may be included in the cost of PP&E, but are not currently required to be included. However, capitalisation of borrowing costs is mandated for accounting periods beginning on or after 1 January 2009 and earlier implementation is permitted. The treatment of borrowing costs is the subject of IAS 23 – *Borrowing Costs* – which is discussed separately in Chapter 16.

C Administration and other general overheads

Administration and other general overhead costs are not costs of an item of PP&E. This means that employee costs not related to a specific asset, such as site selection activities, and general management time do not qualify for capitalisation. Entities are also not allowed to recognise so-called 'start up costs' as part of the item of PP&E. These include costs related to opening a new facility, introducing a new product or service (including costs of advertising and promotional activities), conducting business in a new territory or with a new class of customer (including costs of staff training) and similar items.[20] These costs should be accounted for in the same way as similar costs incurred as part of the entity's on-going activities.

D Cessation of capitalisation

Once an item of PP&E is in the location and condition necessary for it to be capable of operating in the manner intended by management, which will usually be the date of practical completion of the physical asset, cost recognition ceases. IAS 16 therefore prohibits the recognition of relocation and reorganisation costs, costs incurred during the run up to full use once an item is ready to be used, and any initial operating losses.[21]An entity is not precluded from continuing to capitalise costs during an initial commissioning period that is necessary for running in machinery or testing equipment. By contrast no further costs should be capitalised if the asset is fully operational but is not yet achieving its targeted profitability because demand is still building up, for example in a new hotel or bookstore. In this case, the asset is clearly in the location and condition necessary for it to be capable of operating in the manner intended by management.

E Incidental and non-incidental income

Under IAS 16, the cost of an item of PP&E includes any costs directly attributable to bringing the asset to the location and condition necessary for it to be capable of operating in the manner intended by management.[22] However, during the construction of an asset, an entity may enter into incidental operations that are not, in themselves, necessary to bring the asset itself into the location and condition necessary for it to be capable of operating in the manner intended by management. The standard gives the example of income earned by using a building site as a car park prior to starting construction. Because incidental operations such as these are not necessary to bring an item to the location and condition necessary for it to be capable of operating in the manner intended by management, the income and related expenses of incidental operations are recognised in profit or loss and included in their respective classifications of income and expense.[23] Such incidental income is not offset against the cost of the asset.

If, however, some income is generated wholly and necessarily as a result of the process of bringing the asset into the location and condition for its intended use, for example from the sale of samples produced when testing the equipment concerned, then the income should be credited to the cost of the asset (see F below).

On the other hand, if the asset is *already in* the location and condition necessary for it to be capable of being used in the manner intended by management then IAS 16 requires capitalisation to cease and depreciation to start.[24] In these circumstances all income earned from using the asset must be recognised as revenue in the income statement and the related costs of the activity should include an element of depreciation of the asset.

F Proceeds from selling items produced while bringing the asset to the location and condition intended by management

As noted above at A, the directly attributable costs of an item of PP&E include the costs of testing whether the asset is functioning properly, after deducting the net proceeds from selling any items produced while bringing the asset to that location and condition.[25] The standard gives the example of samples produced when testing equipment.

There are other situations in which income may be earned whilst bringing the asset to the intended location and condition. For example, the mining industry is highly capital intensive – particularly so in the case of deep level mining – and a mining operation may extract some saleable 'product' during the phase of its operation to sink mine shafts that reach the intended depth where the main ore-bearing rock is located. During the evaluation and construction phases, income can be earned by an entity in various ways. For example, during the evaluation phase – i.e. when the technical feasibility and commercial viability are being determined – an entity may 'trial mine', to determine which method would be the most profitable and efficient in the circumstances, and which metallurgical process is the most efficient. Ore mined through trial mining may be processed and sold during the evaluation phase. At the other end of the spectrum, income may be earned from the sale of product from 'ramping up' the mine to full production at commercial levels.

It will be a matter of judgement as to when the asset is in the location and condition intended by management, but as noted in D above, capitalisation (including the recording of income as a credit to the cost of the mine) ceases when the asset is fully operational, regardless of whether or not it is yet achieving its targeted levels of production or profitability.

G Other forms of income

Income may arise in other ways, for example, liquidated damages received as a result of delays by a contractor constructing an asset. Normally such damages received should be set off against the asset cost. If however, the settlement specifically refers to damages as compensation for loss of revenue arising as a consequence of contract delays, and the basis is clearly related to income lost, then the damages received should be recognised in the income statement.

Compensation for impairment (for example insurance proceeds) is dealt with at 2.5.1 below.

H Self-built assets

If an asset is self-built by the entity, the same general principles apply as for an acquired asset. If the same type of asset is made for resale by the business, it should be recognised at cost of production, without including any profit element – this allows self-constructed assets to include attributable overheads in accordance with IAS 2 (see Chapter 23). Abnormal amounts of wasted resources, whether labour, materials or other resources, may not be included in the cost of self-built assets. IAS 23, discussed in Chapter 16, contains criteria relating to the recognition of any interest as a component of a self-built item of PP&E.[26] Kazakhmys PLC provides an example of an accounting policy for self-built assets:

> *Extract 13.6: Kazakhmys Plc (2006)*
>
> **NOTES TO THE CONSOLIDATED FINANCIAL STATEMENTS** [extract]
> **3. SUMMARY OF SIGNIFICANT ACCOUNTING POLICIES** [extract]
> **(d) TANGIBLE ASSETS** [extract]
> **(i) Property, plant and equipment** [extract]
>
> Property, plant and equipment is stated at cost less accumulated depreciation and impairment losses. The cost of self-constructed assets includes the cost of materials, direct labour and an appropriate proportion of production overheads.

I Deferred payment

IAS 16 specifically eliminates the capitalisation of 'hidden' credit charges as part of the cost of an item of PP&E, so the cost of an item of PP&E is its 'cash price equivalent' at the recognition date. This means that if payment is made in some other manner, the cost to be capitalised is the normal cash price. Thus, if the payment terms are extended beyond 'normal' credit terms, the cost to be recognised must be the cash price equivalent, and any difference must be treated as an interest expense.[27] Assets partly paid for by government grants, and those held under finance leases are discussed in Chapters 29 and 25, respectively.

J Land and buildings to be redeveloped

It is common for property developers to acquire land with an existing building where the planned redevelopment necessitates the demolition of that building and its replacement with a new building that is to be held to earn rentals (and will therefore fall under IAS 40 when it is complete) or will be owner occupied. Whilst IAS 16 requires that the building and land be classified as two separate items[28], in our view it is appropriate, if the existing building is unusable or likely to be demolished by any party acquiring it, that the entire purchase price be allocated to the land. Similarly, subsequent demolition costs should be treated as being attributable to the cost of the land.

Owner-occupiers may also replace existing buildings with new facilities for their own use or to rent to others. Here the consequences are different and the carrying of the existing building cannot be rolled into the costs of the new development. The existing building must be depreciated over its remaining useful life to reduce the carrying amount of the asset to its residual value (presumably nil) at the point at which it is demolished. Consideration will have to be given as to whether the asset is impaired in value in accordance with IAS 36. However, many properties do not directly generate independent cash inflows (i.e. they are part of a cash-generating unit) and reducing the useful life will not necessarily lead to an impairment of the cash-generating unit(see Chapter 15).

Developers or owner-occupiers replacing an existing building with a building to be sold in the ordinary course of their business will deal with the land and buildings under IAS 2 (see Chapter 23).

K Tooling contributions when the supplier owns the tooling equipment

A supplier may receive a contribution to the development costs of specific tooling equipment from another manufacturer to whom the supplier will sell parts using that specific tooling equipment under a supply agreement.

Currently, our preferred approach would be to recognise the contribution as income over the same period as the useful life of the tooling equipment, with income not yet taken to the income statement classified as deferred income. We believe it is also currently permissible to deduct the contribution from the cost of the equipment. In these circumstances the tooling contribution is recognised over the useful life of the tooling equipment by way of a reduced depreciation charge.

However, it should be noted that, at the time of writing, the IFRIC are considering how an entity should account for the receipt of a customer contribution in the form of an asset that is then used to deliver an ongoing service to that customer. The IFRIC has initially concluded the following:

- On receipt of a customer contribution an entity should assess whether:
  - it has received an asset that meets the recognition criteria in IFRS; and
  - the related service arrangement contains a lease (using IFRIC 4 – *Determining whether an Arrangement contains a Lease*[29] – see Chapter 25). The IFRIC concluded that if an entity determines there is a finance leaseback the entity should reconsider whether the asset meets the recognition criteria and noted that if the entity considered the arrangement as a whole, it would assess that no asset has been transferred and that neither a finance lease receivable nor liability should be recognised.
- The customer contribution should be recorded at fair value on initial recognition;
- The resultant credit is a liability representing the obligation to provide an ongoing service. This credit should be recognised in income as access to that service is given. Recognising income over the period of a related contract may

not be appropriate in all cases as an entity may be obliged to provide access to an ongoing service for reasons other than the existence of a contract. The IFRIC asked its staff to develop guidance to help identify an appropriate period but noted that the period would be unlikely to exceed the useful economic life of the asset; and

- The receipt of a cash contribution should be accounted for in the same way as the receipt of an item of PP&E since both produce substantially similar economic effects.

The IFRIC has asked its staff to develop a draft Interpretation reflecting these conclusions.

2.3.2 *Accounting for changes in decommissioning and restoration costs*

IAS 16 is unclear about the extent to which an item's carrying amount should be affected by changes in the estimated amount of dismantling and site restoration costs that occur *after* the estimate made upon initial measurement. This issue is the subject of IFRIC 1 – *Changes in Existing Decommissioning, Restoration and Similar Liabilities* – issued in May 2004.

IFRIC 1 applies to any decommissioning or similar liability that has both been included as part of an asset measured in accordance with IAS 16 and measured as a liability in accordance with IAS 37.[30] It deals with the impact of events that change the measurement of an existing liability. Such events include a change in the estimated cash flows, the discount rate and the unwinding of the discount.[31]

IFRIC 1 differentiates between the treatment required depending upon whether the items of PP&E concerned are valued under the cost or under the valuation model of IAS 16 (these models are discussed at 2.4 below). If the asset is carried at cost, changes in the liability are added to, or deducted from, the cost of the asset. This deduction may not exceed the carrying amount of the asset and any excess over the carrying value is taken immediately to profit or loss. If the change in estimate results in an addition to the carrying value, the entity is required to consider whether this is an indication of impairment of the asset as a whole and test for impairment in accordance with IAS 36 (see Chapter 15).[32]

If the related asset is carried at valuation and changes in the estimated liability alter the valuation surplus (i.e. the re-estimation takes place independently of the valuation of the asset), then a decrease in the liability is credited directly to the revaluation surplus in equity, unless it reverses a revaluation deficit on the asset that was previously recognised in profit or loss, in which case it may be taken to the income statement. Similarly, an increase in the liability is taken straight to profit or loss, unless there is a revaluation surplus existing in respect of that asset.[33]

If the liability decreases and the deduction exceeds the amount that the asset would have been carried at under the cost model (e.g. its depreciated cost), the amount by which the asset is reduced is capped at this amount. Any excess is taken immediately to the income statement.[34] This means that the maximum amount by which an asset can be reduced is the same whether it is carried at cost or valuation.

This change in the revalued amount must be assessed against the requirements in IAS 16 regarding revalued assets, particularly the requirement that they must be carried at an amount that does not differ materially from fair value (see 2.4.1 below for the standard's rules regarding revaluations of assets). Such an adjustment is an indication that the carrying amount may differ from fair value and the asset may have to be revalued. Any such revaluation must, of course, take account of the adjustment of the estimated liability. If a revaluation is necessary, all assets of the same class must be revalued.[35]

Any changes in estimate taken to equity must be disclosed on the face of the statement of changes in equity in accordance with IAS 1 – *Presentation of Financial statements* – (see Chapter 3).[36] Depreciation of the 'decommissioning asset' and any changes thereto are covered by 2.4.2 below. The unwinding of the discount must be recognised in profit or loss as a finance cost as it occurs. The allowed alternative treatment of capitalisation under IAS 23 is not permitted.[37]

2.3.3 Exchanges of assets

Asset exchanges are transactions that have been discussed intermittently by standard setters over a number of years. For example, an entity might swap a facility it does not require in a particular area, for one it does in another – the opposite being the case for the counterparty. Such exchanges are not uncommon in the hotel, retail and leisure businesses, particularly after an acquisition. Indeed, governmental or EU competition rules may even require such exchanges in certain cases. The question arises whether such transactions give rise to a profit in circumstances where the carrying value of the outgoing facility is less than the incoming one. This can occur when carrying values are less than market values. Equally, it is possible that a transaction with no real commercial substance could be arranged solely to boost apparent profits.

IAS 16 requires all acquisitions of PP&E in exchange for non-monetary assets, or a combination of monetary and non-monetary assets, to be measured at fair value, subject to the following conditions:

'The cost of such an item of property, plant and equipment is measured at fair value unless (a) the exchange transaction lacks commercial substance or (b) the fair value of neither the asset received nor the asset given up is reliably measurable. The acquired item is measured in this way even if an entity cannot immediately derecognise the asset given up.'[38]

If the fair value of neither the asset given up nor the asset received can be measured reliably, the cost of the asset is measured at the carrying amount of the asset given up[39] and there is no gain on the transaction. That is, if at least one of the two fair values can be measured reliably, that value is used for measuring the exchange transaction; if not, then the exchange is measured at the carrying value of the asset the entity no longer owns. However, this relatively understandable requirement (leaving aside how straightforward determining a reliable fair value will actually be) is qualified by a 'commercial substance' test.[40] The commercial substance test was put in place as an anti-abuse provision to prevent gains in income being recognised when the transaction had no discernable effect on the entity's economics.[41] The commercial substance of an exchange is to be determined by forecasting and comparing the future cash flows budgeted to be generated by the incoming and outgoing assets. For commercial substance to be present, there must be a significant difference between the two forecasts. The standard sets out this requirement as follows:

'An entity determines whether an exchange transaction has commercial substance by considering the extent to which its future cash flows are expected to change as a result of the transaction. An exchange transaction has commercial substance if:

(a) the configuration (risk, timing and amount) of the cash flows of the asset received differs from the configuration of the cash flows of the asset transferred; or

(b) the entity-specific value of the portion of the entity's operations affected by the transaction changes as a result of the exchange; and

(c) the difference in (a) or (b) is significant relative to the fair value of the assets exchanged.'[42]

As set out in the definitions of the standard, see 2.2.1 above, entity-specific value is the net present value of the future predicted cash flows from continuing use and disposal of the asset. Post-tax cash flows should be used for this calculation. The standard contains no guidance on the discount rate to be used for this exercise, nor on any of the other parameters involved, but it does suggest that the result of these analyses might be clear without having to perform detailed calculations.[43]

The IASB has concluded that the recognition of income from an exchange of assets does not depend on whether the assets exchanged are dissimilar.[44] Care will have to be taken to ensure that the transaction has commercial substance as defined in the standard if an entity receives a similar item of property, plant and equipment in exchange for a similar asset of its own. Commercial substance may be difficult to demonstrate if the entity is exchanging a piece of land for a similar one in a similar location. However, in the latter case, the risk, timing and amount of cash flows could differ if one asset were available for sale and the entity intended to sell it whereas the previous asset could not be realised by sale or only sold in a much longer timescale. It is feasible that such a transaction could meet conditions (a) and (c) above. Similarly, it would be unusual if the entity-specific values of similar assets differed enough in any arm's length exchange transaction to meet condition (c). However, many exchanges are more likely to pass the 'commercial substance' test, for example:

- exchanging an interest in an investment property for one that the entity uses for its own purposes. The entity has exchanged a rental stream and instead has an asset that contributes to the cash flows of the cash-generating unit of which it is a part; or
- exchanging a property for a stake in a jointly controlled entity. The entity will now receive a rental or royalty stream from an asset that was previously part of a cash-generating unit.

In both of these cases it is possible that the risk, timing and amount of the cash flows of the asset received would differ from the configuration of the cash flows of the asset transferred.

In the context of asset exchanges, the standard contains guidance on the reliable determination of fair values in the circumstances where market values do not exist:

'The fair value of an asset for which comparable market transactions do not exist is reliably measurable if (a) the variability in the range of reasonable fair value estimates is not significant for that asset or (b) the probabilities of the various estimates within the range can be reasonably assessed and used in estimating fair value. If an entity is able to determine reliably the fair value of either the asset received or the asset given up, then the fair value of the asset given up is used to measure the cost of the asset received unless the fair value of the asset received is more clearly evident.'[45]

No guidance is given on how to assemble a 'range of reasonable fair value estimates'. IAS 16 itself permits the estimation of the fair value using income or depreciated replacement cost bases (see 2.8.3B below) but the latter hardly seems relevant to an exchange transaction. Another way would be to base fair value on the 'entity-specific value' – i.e. on the discounted budgeted cash flows of the entity. This is a technique used for valuing investment properties in thin markets (see Chapter 14 at 3.2). However, if the fair value *is* the entity-specific value, how can the difference between it and the fair value be significant?

The term 'commercial substance' is used by the standard in a particular sense only, as in practice commercial substance can exist (in the sense that an entity has a good reason for the exchange) even if forecast cash flows are similar. If it is not possible to demonstrate that the transaction has commercial substance as defined by the standard, assets received in exchange transactions will be recorded at the carrying value of the asset given up.

If the transaction passes the 'commercial substance' test then IAS 16 requires the exchanged asset to be recorded at its fair value. As discussed in 2.6 below, the standard requires gains or losses on items that have been derecognised to be included in profit or loss in the period of derecognition but does not allow gains on derecognition to be classified as revenue.[46] It gives no further indication regarding their classification in the income statement It should be noted that the exchange of goods and services is dealt with in IAS 18 – *Revenue* – which takes a different approach from IAS16 with respect to exchanges of PP&E (see Chapter 28 at 3.9).

2.3.4 Assets held under finance leases

The cost at initial recognition of assets held under finance leases is determined in accordance with IAS 17,[47] as described in Chapter 25.

2.3.5 Assets acquired with the assistance of government grants

The carrying amount of an item of PP&E may be reduced by government grants in accordance with IAS 20 – *Accounting for Government Grants and Disclosure of Government Assistance.*[48] The requirements of this standard are discussed in Chapter 29.

2.4 Measurement after recognition

IAS 16 allows one of two alternatives to be chosen as the accounting policy for measurement of PP&E after initial recognition. The choice made must be applied to an entire class of PP&E, but all classes are not required to have the same policy.[49]

The first alternative is the 'cost model' (in fact the traditional way PP&E has been accounted for) whereby the item is carried at cost less accumulated depreciation and less any impairment losses.[50] The requirements of IAS 16 concerning depreciation are dealt with at 2.4.2 below. The second alternative, the revaluation model, is discussed below at 2.4.1.

2.4.1 Revaluation model

If the revaluation model is adopted, PP&E is to be carried at fair value less subsequent accumulated depreciation or impairment losses.[51] 'Fair value' will usually be the market value of the asset. In the case of land and buildings the standard states that this will be 'determined from market based evidence', which is normally to be determined by professional valuers, though there is no requirement for a professional external valuation or even for a professionally qualified valuer to perform the appraisal. The fair value of other items of PP&E is usually their appraised market value.[52] Although market value is not discussed further, fair value is defined (see 2.2.1 above) as the amount at which an asset could be exchanged between knowledgeable, willing parties in an arm's length transaction.

If there is no market-based evidence of fair value because of the specialised nature of the items, or because they are rarely sold, a depreciated replacement cost approach or an 'income' approach is to be used.[53] Neither of these terms is explained further. These valuation issues are discussed further at 2.8.3 below.

Valuation frequency is not laid down precisely by IAS 16, which states that revaluations are to be made with sufficient regularity to ensure that the carrying amount does not differ materially from the fair value at the balance sheet date.[54] When the fair value of a revalued asset differs materially from its carrying amount, a further revaluation is necessary. The standard suggests that some items of property, plant and equipment have frequent and volatile changes in fair value and these should be revalued annually. This is true of property assets in many jurisdictions, but even in such cases there may be much quieter periods also with little movement in values. If there are only insignificant movements it may only be necessary to perform valuations at three or five year intervals.[55]

If the revaluation model is adopted, IAS 16 specifies that all items within a class of asset are to be revalued simultaneously to prevent selective revaluations. A class of PP&E is a grouping of assets of a similar nature and use in an entity's operations.

This is not a precise definition. The following are examples of separate classes of asset given in IAS 16:

(i) land;
(ii) land and buildings;
(iii) machinery;
(iv) ships;
(v) aircraft;
(vi) motor vehicles;
(vii) furniture and fixtures; and
(viii) office equipment.[56]

These are very broad categories of asset and it is possible for them to be classified further into groupings of assets of a similar nature and use. Office buildings and factories or hotels and fitness centres, could be separate classes of asset. If the entity used the same type of asset in two different geographical locations, e.g. clothing manufacturing facilities for similar products or products with similar markets, say footwear in Sri Lanka and knitwear in Guatemala, it is likely that these would be seen as part of the same class of asset. However, if the entity manufactured pharmaceuticals and clothing, both in European facilities, then arguably these could be assets with a sufficiently different nature and use to be a separate class. Ultimately it must be a matter of judgement in the context of the specific operations of individual entities.

IAS 16 does permit a rolling valuation of a class of assets, whereby the class is revalued over an (undefined) short period of time, 'provided the valuations are kept up to date'.[57] This final condition makes it difficult to see how rolling valuations can be performed unless the value of the assets changes very little (in which case the standard states that valuations need only be performed every three to five years), or if a large change is revealed, then presumably a wholesale revaluation is required.

A Accounting for valuation surpluses and deficits

Increases in a valuation should be credited to a revaluation surplus within equity. If a revaluation increase reverses a decrease that was recognised as an expense, it may be credited to income. Decreases in valuation should be charged to the income statement, except to the extent that they reverse an existing revaluation surplus on the same asset.[58] This means that it is not permissible under the standard to carry a negative revaluation reserve in respect of any asset.

IAS 16 generally retains a model in which the revalued amount substitutes for cost in both balance sheet and income statement and there is no recycling of amounts taken directly to equity. This is unlike the treatment subsequently adopted by the IASB in relation to available for sale financial assets, in which gains and losses initially taken to equity on remeasurement to fair value are taken to income when the asset is derecognised (see Chapter 20 at 3.4). Different rules apply to impairment losses. An impairment loss on a revalued asset is first used to reduce the revaluation surplus for that asset. Only when the impairment loss exceeds the amount in the revaluation surplus for that same asset is any further impairment loss recognised in profit or loss (see Chapter 15 at 3.3.3).[59] The revaluation surplus included in equity may be transferred directly to retained earnings as the surplus is realised, and all of it may be transferred when the asset is disposed of. However, the difference between depreciation based on the revalued carrying amount of the asset and depreciation based on its original cost may be transferred as the asset is used by the entity. This is illustrated in Example 13.1 below. This provision recognises that any depreciation on the revalued part of an asset's carrying value has been realised by being charged to income. Thus a transfer can be made of an equivalent amount from the revaluation surplus in equity to retained profits. However any transfer is made directly from revaluation surplus to retained earnings and not through the income statement.[60]

Example 13.1: Effect of depreciation on the revaluation reserve

On 1 January 2003 an entity acquired an asset for €1,000. The asset has an economic life of ten years and is depreciated on a straight-line basis. The residual value is assumed to be €nil. At 31 December 2007 (when the cost net of accumulated depreciation is €600) the asset is valued at €900. The entity accounts for the revaluation by debiting accumulated depreciation €300 and crediting €300 to the revaluation reserve. At 31 December 2007 the economic life of the asset is considered to be the remainder of its original life, i.e. six years, and its residual value is still considered to be €nil. In the year ended 31 December 2008 and in later years, the depreciation charged to the income statement is €150.

The usual treatment thereafter for each of the remaining 6 years of the asset's life, is to transfer €50 p.a. from the revaluation reserve to retained earnings (not through the income statement). This avoids the revaluation reserve being maintained indefinitely even after the asset ceases to exist, which does not seem sensible.

The effect on taxation, both current and deferred, of a policy of revaluing assets is dealt with in Chapter 26.

B Adopting a policy of revaluation

Although the adoption of a policy of revaluation by an entity that has previously used the cost model is a change in accounting policy, it is not dealt with as a prior year adjustment in accordance with IAS 8 – *Accounting policies, changes in accounting estimates and errors*, but instead is treated as a revaluation during the year.[61]

C Assets held under finance leases

Once assets held under finance leases have been capitalised as items of PP&E, their subsequent accounting is the same as for any other asset. Therefore:

- they may also be revalued using the revaluation model but, if the revaluation model is used, then the entire class of assets (both owned and those held under finance lease) must be revalued;
- they should be considered to be the same class of asset as those with a similar nature that are owned. Consequently, there is no need to provide separate reconciliations of movements in owned assets from assets held under finance leases (see 2.7.1 (e) below).

2.4.2 Depreciation

IAS 16 links its recognition concept of a 'part' of an asset, discussed at 2.2.2 above, with the analysis of assets for the purpose of depreciation. Each part of an asset with a cost that is significant in relation to the total cost of the item must be depreciated separately,[62] which means that the initial cost must be allocated between the significant parts by the entity. The standard's example is again that of the airframe and engines of an aircraft.[63]

However, because parts are identified by their significant cost rather than their effect on depreciation, they may have the same useful lives and depreciation method and the standard allows them to be grouped for depreciation purposes.[64] It also identifies other circumstances in which the significant parts do not correspond to the depreciable components within the asset. The remainder of an asset that has not separately been identified into parts may consist of other parts that are individually not significant and the entity may need to use approximation techniques to calculate an appropriate depreciation method for all of these parts.[65] The standard also allows an entity to depreciate separately parts that are not significant in relation to the whole.[66]

The depreciation charge is recognised in the income statement unless it forms part of the cost of another asset, e.g. as part of the cost of finished manufactured goods held in inventory in accordance with IAS 2.[67]

Accounting for parts of assets is discussed further at 2.6 and 2.8.1 below.

A Depreciable amount, useful life and residual values

As noted in 2.2.1 above, the depreciable amount of an item of PP&E is its cost or valuation less its estimated residual value. The standard states that an entity must review the residual values of all its items of PP&E, and therefore all parts of them, at least at each financial year-end. If the estimated residual value differs from previous estimates, changes must be accounted for prospectively as a change in accounting estimate in accordance with IAS 8.[68] Although not expressly stated, this passage in the standard applies only to material differences.

As the definition (see 2.2.1 above) implies, the residual value of an item of PP&E today is to be calculated by taking the price such an asset would fetch today, but assuming that it was already in the condition it will be in at the end of its useful life. Therefore IAS 16 contains an element of continuous updating of one component of an asset's carrying value.

As any change in the residual value directly affects the depreciable amount, it may also affect the depreciation charge. This is because the depreciable amount (i.e. the amount actually charged to the income statement over the life of the asset) is calculated by deducting the residual value from the cost or valuation of the asset, although for these purposes the residual value is capped at the asset's carrying amount.[69] Although many items of PP&E have a negligible residual value because they are kept for significantly all of their useful lives, there are a number of types of asset where this requirement could have a significant effect, and conceivably cause noticeable volatility in the depreciation charge. The residual values, and hence depreciation charges, of ships, aircraft, hotels and other assets of this nature, could potentially be affected by this requirement.

In addition, the standard requires year-end reviews of an asset's useful life, and, if expectations differ from previous estimates, the depreciation charge should be adjusted prospectively.[70] Factors that may affect the useful life are discussed at C below.

The requirement concerning the residual values of assets highlights how important it is that residual values are considered and reviewed in conjunction with the review of useful lives. The useful life is the period over which the entity expects to use the asset, not the asset's economic life. Residual values are of no relevance if the entity intends to keep the asset until it is of no use to anyone else. If an entity points to the prices fetched in the market by a type of asset that it holds, it must also demonstrate an intention to dispose of it before the end of its economic life.

B Depreciation charge

The standard requires the depreciable amount of an asset to be allocated on a systematic basis over its useful life.[71]

The standard makes it clear that depreciation must be charged on all items of PP&E, including those carried under the revaluation model, even if the fair value of the asset at the year-end is higher than the carrying amount,[72] as long as the residual value of the item is lower than the carrying amount. If the residual value exceeds the carrying amount, no depreciation is charged until the residual value once again decreases to less than the carrying amount.[73] IAS 16 makes it clear that the repair and maintenance of an asset does not of itself negate the need to depreciate it.[74] This is discussed further below.

There is no requirement in IAS 16 for an automatic impairment review if no depreciation is charged.

C Useful lives

The judgement that entities must make is how long the useful life of an item of PP&E will be. IAS 16 provides the following guidance about the factors to be considered when estimating the useful life of an asset:

'(a) expected usage of the asset. Usage is assessed by reference to the asset's expected capacity or physical output;

(b) expected physical wear and tear, which depends on operational factors such as the number of shifts for which the asset is to be used and the repair and maintenance programme, and the care and maintenance of the asset while idle;

(c) technical or commercial obsolescence arising from changes or improvements in production, or from a change in the market demand for the product or service output of the asset;

(d) legal or similar limits on the use of the asset, such as the expiry dates of related leases.'[75]

Arcelor is an example of an entity depreciating an asset over its expected usage by reference to the production period.

> *Extract 13.7: Arcelor SA (2006)*
> **Notes to the Consolidated Financial Statements** [extract]
> **Note 2 ACCOUNTING POLICIES** [extract]
> **7) Property, plant and equipment** [extract]
>
> The cost of the periodic relining of blast furnaces is capitalised and depreciated over the expected production period.

The initial assessment of the useful life of the asset will take account of the expected routine spending on repairs and expenditure necessary for it to achieve that life. Although (b) above implies an item of plant and machinery, care and maintenance programmes are relevant to assessing the useful lives of many other types of asset. For example, an entity may assess the useful life of a railway engine at thirty-five years on the assumption that it has a major overhaul every seven years. Without this expenditure, the life of the engine would be much less certain and could be much shorter. Maintenance necessary to support the fabric of a building and its service potential will also be taken into account in assessing its useful life. Eventually, it will always become uneconomic for the entity to continue to maintain the asset so, while the expenditure may lengthen the useful life, it is unlikely to make it indefinite. However, as the maintenance spend may affect the residual value, it may indirectly reduce the depreciable amount to zero.

The useful life of an asset is defined in terms of its use to the business, not its economic life, so it is quite possible that an asset's useful life will be shorter than its economic life. Many entities have a policy of disposing of assets when they still have a residual value, which means that another user will benefit from the asset.[76] This is particularly common with property and motor vehicles, where there are effective second-hand markets, but less usual for plant and machinery. The standard requires the land and the building elements of property to be accounted for as separate components. Land, which usually has an unlimited life, is not depreciated, while buildings are depreciable assets. IAS 16 states that the useful life of a building is not affected by an increase in the value of the land on which it stands.[77]

There are circumstances in which depreciation may be applied to land. In those instances in which land does have a finite life it will be either used for extractive purposes (a quarry or mine) or for some purpose such as landfill; it will be depreciated in an appropriate manner (but it is highly unlikely that there will be any issue regarding separating the interest in land from any building element). However, the cost of such land may include an element for site dismantlement or restoration (see 2.3.1 above), in which case this element will have to be depreciated over an appropriate period. The standard describes this as 'the period of benefits obtained by incurring these costs';[78] which will often be the estimated useful life of the site for its purpose and function. So, for example, an entity engaged in landfill on a new site may make a provision for restoring it as soon as it starts preparation by removing the overburden. It will depreciate this 'restoration asset' over the landfill site's estimated useful life. If the land has an infinite useful life, an appropriate depreciation basis will have to be chosen that reflects the period of benefits obtained from the restoration asset.

If the estimated costs are revised in accordance with IFRIC 1, the adjusted depreciable amount of the asset is depreciated over its useful life. Therefore, once the related asset has reached the end of its useful life, all subsequent changes in the liability shall be recognised in profit or loss as they occur, irrespective of whether the entity applies the cost or revaluation model.[79]

D When depreciation starts

The standard is clear on when deprecation should start and finish, and sets out the requirements succinctly as follows:

- depreciation of an asset begins when it is available for use, which is defined by the standard as occurring when the asset is in the location and condition necessary for it to be capable of operating in the manner intended by management. This is the point at which capitalisation of costs relating to the asset cease;
- depreciation of an asset ceases at the earlier of the date that the asset is classified as held for sale (or included in a disposal group that is classified as held for sale) in accordance with IFRS 5 and the date that the asset is derecognised.[80]

Therefore, an entity does not stop depreciating an asset merely because it has become idle or has been retired from active use (unless, of course, the asset is fully depreciated). However, if the entity is using a usage method of depreciation the charge can be zero while there is no production.[81] Of course, a prolonged period in which there is no production may raise questions as to whether the asset is impaired: an asset becoming idle is a specific example of an indication of impairment in IAS 36 (see Chapter 15).[82]

Assets held for sale under IFRS 5 are discussed below at 2.6.1.

E Depreciation methods

The standard is not prescriptive about methods of depreciation, mentioning straight line, diminishing balance and units of production as possibilities. The overriding requirement is that the depreciation charge reflects the pattern of consumption of the benefits the asset brings over its useful life, and is applied consistently from period to period.[83] IAS 16 contains an explicit requirement for the depreciation method to be reviewed at least at each period end to determine if there has been a significant change in the pattern of consumption of an asset's benefits. This would be unusual; it would mean, for example, concluding that the unit of production method was no longer appropriate and changing to a straight line or diminishing balance method. Nevertheless, if there has been such a change, the depreciation method should be changed to reflect it. However, under IAS 8, this change is a change in accounting estimate and not a change in accounting policy.[84] This means that the consequent depreciation adjustment should be made prospectively, that is the asset's depreciable amount should be written off over current and future periods.[85] See 2.8.6 below for a discussion of depreciation methods in practice.

2.5 Impairment

All items of PP&E accounted for under IAS 16 are subject to the impairment requirements of IAS 36. Impairment is discussed in Chapter 15.[86]

2.5.1 Compensation for impairment

The question has arisen about the treatment of any compensation an entity may be due to receive as a result of an asset being impaired. For example an asset that is insured might be destroyed in a fire, so repayment from an insurance company might be expected. IAS 16 states that these two events – the impairment and any compensation – are 'separate economic events' and should be accounted for separately as follows:

- impairments of PP&E are recognised in accordance with IAS 36 (see Chapter 15);
- derecognition of items retired or disposed of should be recognised in accordance with IAS 16 (derecognition is discussed below); and
- compensation from third parties for PP&E that is impaired lost or given up is included in profit and loss when it becomes receivable.[87]

Therefore any compensation is accounted for separately from any impairment. Although the question as to when 'compensation becomes receivable' is not discussed further in the standard, IAS 37 requires that reimbursements from third parties should be recognised as a separate asset when it is 'virtually certain' that the reimbursement will be received.[88]

2.6 Derecognition and disposal

Derecognition (i.e. removal of the carrying amount of the item from the financial statements of the entity) occurs when an item of PP&E is either disposed of, or when no further economic benefits are expected to flow from its use or disposal.[89] The actual date of disposal is determined in accordance with the criteria in IAS 18 for the recognition of revenue from the sale of goods[90] (revenue recognition is discussed in Chapter 28). All gains and losses on derecognition must be included in profit and loss for the period when the item is derecognised, unless another standard applies – for example under IAS 17 a sale and leaseback transaction might not give rise to a gain.

Gains are not to be classified as revenue, although in some limited circumstances presenting gross revenue on the sale of certain assets may be appropriate (see 2.6.2 below).[91] Gains and losses are to be calculated as the difference between any net disposal proceeds and the carrying value of the item of PP&E[92] – this means that any revaluation surplus relating to the asset disposed of is transferred directly to equity when the asset is derecognised and not reflected in profit or loss.[93]

Replacement of 'parts' of an asset requires derecognition of the carrying value of the original part, even if that part was not being depreciated separately. Under these circumstances, the standard allows the cost of a replacement part to be a guide to the original cost of the replaced part, if that cannot be determined.[94]

Any consideration received on the disposal of an item should be recognised at its fair value. If deferred credit terms are given, the consideration for the sale is the cash price equivalent, and any surplus is treated as interest revenue using the effective yield method as required by IAS 18 (see Chapter 28 at 3.3).[95]

2.6.1 IFRS 5 – Non-current assets held for sale and discontinued operations

IFRS 5 introduced a new category of asset, 'held for sale', and PP&E within this category is outside the scope of IAS 16, although IAS 16 requires certain disclosures about assets held for sale to be made, as set out at 2.7 below.

IFRS 5 requires that an item of PP&E should be classified as held for sale if its carrying amount will be recovered principally though a sale transaction rather then continuing use, though continuing use is not in itself precluded for assets classified as held for sale.[96] An asset can also be part of a 'disposal group' (that is a group of assets that are to be disposed of together), in which case the group can be treated as a whole. Once this classification has been made, depreciation ceases, even if the asset is still being used, but the assets must be carried at the lower of their previous carrying amount and fair value less costs to sell. For assets to be classified as held for sale, they must be available for immediate sale in their present condition, and the sale must be highly probable.[97]

Additionally, the sale should be completed within one year from the date of classification as held for sale, management at an 'appropriate level' must be committed to the plan, and an active programme of marketing the assets must have been started.[98]

The requirements of IFRS 5 are dealt with in Chapter 4.

2.6.2 Sale of assets held for rental

In their May 2007 meeting the IFRIC discussed a request for guidance on the accounting for sales of assets that were previously held for rental. For example, car rental companies may acquire vehicles with the intention of holding them as rental cars for limited period and then selling them.

The issue that arises is whether the sale of such assets (which arguably have a dual purpose of being rented out and then sold) should be presented gross (revenue and cost of sales) or net (gain or loss) in the income statement.

The IFRIC noted the requirement in paragraph 68 of IAS 16 that disposals of PP&E should not be classified as revenue. However, the IFRIC also considered that in some limited circumstances reporting gross revenue would be consistent with the Framework and certain other International Financial Reporting Standards and for this reason the IFRIC decided to draw the issue to the attention of the IASB and not to take the item on to its own agenda.

In considering this request from the IFRIC the IASB noted at their June 2007 meeting that:

- Paragraph BC35 of IAS 16 explains the reason for the 'net' treatment of gains on sale of PP&E is that 'users of financial statements would consider these gains and the proceeds from an entity's sale of goods in the course of its ordinary activities differently in their evaluation of an entity's past results and their projections of future cash flows.'
- The notion 'in the course of its ordinary activities' appears in IAS 18 Revenue, IAS 2 Inventories and the Framework.

The IASB therefore took the view that the presentation of gross revenue (rather than a net gain or loss) would better reflect the ordinary activities of some such entities and therefore tentatively decided that if an entity, in the course of its ordinary activities, routinely sells property, plant and equipment that it has held for rental to others, it should transfer such assets to inventories at their carrying amount when they cease to be rented and held for sale. The proceeds from the sale of such assets should be recognised as revenue.

The IASB decided to prepare an amendment to IAS 16 to reflect this decision and would further consider the need for additional disclosures and the effects on the cash flow statement (to avoid initial expenditure on purchases of assets being classified as investing activities while inflows from sales are recorded within operating activities).

This treatment should not be adopted until this proposed amendment to IAS 16 is effective.

2.7 IAS 16 disclosure requirements

IAS 16 contains a clear and well laid out disclosure section that is easy to use and understand. The main requirements are set out below, but note that the related disclosure requirements of IAS 36 are relevant also in the case of PP&E that is impaired. IAS 36 is dealt with in Chapter 15.

2.7.1 General disclosures

For each class of property plant and equipment the following should be disclosed in the financial statements:

(a) the measurement bases used for determining the gross carrying amount (for example, cost, fair value). When more than one basis has been used, the gross carrying amount for that basis in each category should be disclosed (however the standard requires that if revaluation is adopted the entire class of assets must be revalued);

(b) the depreciation methods used;

(c) the useful lives or the depreciation rates used;

(d) the gross carrying amount and the accumulated depreciation (aggregated with accumulated impairment losses) at the beginning and end of the period;

(e) a reconciliation of the carrying amount at the beginning and end of the period showing:

(i) additions;

(ii) disposals,

(iii) assets classified as held for sale, or included in a disposal group held for sale;

(iv) acquisitions through business combinations;

(v) increases or decreases during the period resulting from revaluations and from impairment losses recognised or reversed directly in equity under IAS 36 (if any);

(vi) impairment losses recognised in the income statement during the period under IAS 36 (if any);

(vii) impairment losses reversed in the income statement during the period under IAS 36 (if any);

(viii) depreciation for the period;

(ix) the net exchange differences arising on the translation of the financial statements from the functional currency into a different presentation currency, including the translation of a foreign operation into the presentation currency of the reporting entity; and

(x) other changes.

Under the previous version of IAS 16, it was not required to provide comparative information for the reconciliation in (e) above, because the standard offered a specific exemption from the requirement in IAS 1 to disclose 'comparative information ... in respect of the previous period for all amounts reported in the financial statements'.[99] However, the current version of IAS 16 does not contain this exemption, thereby making it necessary to include comparative information for this reconciliation.

Extract 13.8 illustrates a PP&E accounting policy together with the movement and reconciliation note (a comparative is provided in the financial statements but is not reproduced here).

Extract 13.8: Volkswagen Aktiengesellschaft (2006)

Notes to the consolidated financial statements of the Volkswagen Group for the Fiscal Year ended December 31, 2006 [extract]

PROPERTY, PLANT AND EQUIPMENT [extract]

Property, plant and equipment is carried at cost less depreciation and – where necessary – write-downs for impairment. Investment grants are generally deducted from cost. Cost is determined on the basis of the direct costs as well as proportionate material and production overheads, including depreciation. The cost of repairs and borrowing costs are recorded as current expenses. Property, plant and equipment is depreciated using the straight-line method over its estimated useful life. The useful lives of items of property, plant and equipment are reviewed at each balance sheet date and adjusted if required.

Depreciation is based mainly on the following useful lives:

	Useful life
Buildings	25 to 50 years
Site improvements	10 to 18 years
Technical equipment and machinery	6 to 12 years
Other equipment, operating and office equipment, including special tools	3 to 15 years

[11] PROPERTY, PLANT AND EQUIPMENT [extract]
CHANGES IN PROPERTY, PLANT AND EQUIPMENT
BETWEEN JANUARY 1 AND DECEMBER 31, 2006

€ million	**Land, land rights and buildings, including buildings on third-party land**	**Technical equipment and machinery**	**Other equipment operating and office equipment**	**Payments on account and assets under construction**	**Total**
Historical cost					
Balance at Jan. 1, 2006	**13,897**	**24,525**	**31,120**	**1,330**	**70,872**
Foreign exchange differences	–38	–59	–180	–11	–288
Changes in consolidated Group	–61	–12	–261	–15	–349
Additions	338	585	1,439	1,234	3,596
Transfers	133	397	449	–997	–18
Disposals	128	898	1,256	23	2,305
Balance at Dec. 31, 2006	**14,141**	**24,538**	**31,311**	**1,518**	**71,508**
Depreciation and impairment					
Balance at Jan. 1, 2006	**6,820**	**17,865**	**23,303**	**0**	**47,988**
Foreign exchange differences	–32	–39	–127	0	–198
Changes in consolidated Group	–22	–6	–192	–	–220
Additions to cumulative depreciation	480	1,814	2,965	–	5,259
Additions to cumulative impairment losses	47	63	353	10	473
Transfers	–4	6	–3	–3	–4
Disposals	69	877	1,153	–	2,099
Reversal of impairment losses	–6	–25	0	–	–31
Balance at Dec. 31, 2006	**7,214**	**18,801**	**25,146**	**7**	**51,168**
Carrying amount at Dec. 31, 2006	**6,927**	**5,737**	**6,165**	**1,511**	**20,340**
Of which assets leased under finance lease contracts					
Carrying amount at Dec. 31, 2006	203	1	16	–	220

IAS 16 also requires the disclosure of the following information, which is useful to gain a fuller understanding of the entire position of the entity's holdings of and its commitments to purchase property plant and equipment:

(a) the existence and amounts of restrictions on title, and property, plant and equipment pledged as security for liabilities;
(b) the amount of expenditures recognised in the carrying amount of property, plant and equipment in the course of construction;
(c) the amount of contractual commitments for the acquisition of property, plant and equipment; and
(d) if it is not disclosed separately on the face of the income statement, the amount of compensation from third parties for items of property, plant and equipment that were impaired, lost or given up that is included in profit or loss.[100]

In addition there is a reminder in the standard that, in accordance with IAS 8, any changes in accounting estimate (e.g. depreciation methods, useful lives, residual values) that have a material effect on the current or future periods must be disclosed.[101]

2.7.2 Additional disclosures for revalued assets

The IASB has gone to some lengths in IAS 16 to ensure that if the revaluation model is adopted, users of the financial statements should have enough information to clearly see its effects. The additional requirements if the revaluation basis is adopted are:

(a) the effective date of the revaluation;
(b) whether an independent valuer was involved;
(c) the methods and significant assumptions applied in estimating the items' fair values;
(d) the extent to which the items' fair values were determined directly by reference to observable prices in an active market or recent market transactions on arm's length terms or were estimated using other valuation techniques;
(e) for each revalued class of property, plant and equipment, the carrying amount that would have been recognised had the assets been carried under the cost model; and
(f) the revaluation surplus, indicating the change for the period and any restrictions on the distribution of the balance to shareholders.[102]

In particular the requirement under (e) is quite onerous for entities, as it entails their keeping asset register information in some detail in order to meet it.

Extract 13.9 below from Aegon NV shows disclosures relating to PP&E held at a valuation – in this case real estate held for own use – together with the policies adopted by the group for investment property.

Extract 13.9: Aegon N.V. (2006)

NOTES TO THE CONSOLIDATED FINANCIAL STATEMENTS OF AEGON GROUP [extract]

2 SUMMARY OF SIGNIFICANT ACCOUNTING PRINCIPLES [extract]

2.8 INVESTMENTS [extract]

Investments for general account comprise financial assets, excluding derivatives, as well as investments in real estate and real estate held for own use.

B. Real estate [extract]

Real estate held for own use is carried at its revalued amount, which is the fair value at the date of revaluation less subsequent accumulated depreciation and impairment losses. Depreciation is calculated on a straight line basis over the useful life of a building. Land is not depreciated. On revaluation the accumulated depreciation is eliminated against the gross carrying amount of the asset and the net amount is restated to the revalued amount. Increases in the net carrying amount are recognized in the related revaluation reserve in shareholders' equity and are released to retained earnings over the remaining useful life of the property.

Valuations of both investments in real estate and real estate held for own use are conducted with sufficient regularity to ensure the value correctly reflects the fair value at the balance sheet date. Valuations are mostly based on active market prices, adjusted for any difference in the nature, location or condition of the specific property. If such information is not available, other valuation methods are applied, considering the current cost of reproducing or replacing the property, the value that the property's net earning power will support and the value indicated by recent sales of comparable properties. For properly held for own use, valuers may also consider the present value of the future rental income cash flows that could be achieved had the real estate been let out.

On disposal of an asset, the difference between the net proceeds received and the carrying amount is recognized in the income statement. Any remaining surplus attributable to real estate in own use in the revaluation reserve is transferred to retained earnings.

7.6 REAL ESTATE HELD FOR OWN USE

Net book value		
At January 1, 2005		328
At December 31, 2005		355
AT DECEMBER 31, 2006		**313**
Cost		
At January 1	377	347
Additions	90	162
Acquired through business combinations	18	–
Capitalized subsequent expenditure	5	1
Disposals	(3)	(46)
Unrealised gains/(losses) through equity	16	(1)
Realised gains/(losses) through income statement	(5)	1
Transfers to investments in real estate	(136)	(108)
Net exchange differences	(21)	26
Other	–	(5)
AT DECEMBER 31	341	377
Accumulated depreciation, and impairment losses		
At January 1	22	19
Depreciation through income statement	8	7
Disposals	(1)	–
Net exchange differences	(1)	1
Other	–	(5)
AT DECEMBER 31	28	22

> General account real estate held for own use are mainly held by AEGON USA and AEGON The Netherlands, with relatively smaller holdings in Hungary and Spain and are carried at revalued amounts. The carrying value under a historical cost model amounts to EUR 169 million (2005: EUR 152 million).
>
> 61% of the real estate held for own use was last revalued in 2006, based on market value appraisals by qualified internal and external appraisers. Approximately 75% of the appraisals in 2006 were performed by independent external appraisers.
>
> Real estate held for own use has not been pledged as security for liabilities, nor are there any restrictions on title.
>
> Depreciation expenses are charged in 'Commissions and expenses' in the income statement. The useful lives of buildings range between 40 and 50 years.
>
> Refer to note 49 for a summary of contractual commitments for the acquisition of real estate held for own use.

2.7.3 *Other disclosures*

The standard emphasises that entities are also required to disclose information about impairment in accordance with IAS 36, in addition to the disclosures on this matter required by IAS 16.

The standard encourages, but does not require, entities to disclose other additional information such as the carrying amount of any idle assets, the gross amount of any fully depreciated assets in use, and any held for disposal. For any property plant and equipment held at cost less depreciation, the disclosure of its fair value is also encouraged if it is materially different from the carrying amount.[103]

2.8 Practical issues

2.8.1 *Accounting for parts of assets*

IAS 16 has a single set of recognition criteria, which means that subsequent expenditure must also meet these criteria before it is recognised.

Parts of an asset are to be identified so that the cost of replacing a part may be recognised (i.e. capitalised as part of the asset) and the previous part derecognised. 'Parts' are distinguished from day-to-day servicing but they are not otherwise identified and defined; moreover, the unit of measurement to which the standard applies (i.e. what comprises an item of PP&E) is not itself defined.

IAS 16 requires 'significant parts' of an asset to be depreciated separately.[104] These are parts that have a cost that is significant in relation to the total cost of the asset. An entity will have to identify the significant parts of the asset on initial recognition in order for it to depreciate the asset properly. There is no requirement to identify all parts. IAS 16 requires entities to derecognise an existing part when it is replaced, regardless of whether it has been depreciated separately, and allows the carrying value of the part that has been replaced to be estimated if necessary:

'If it is not practicable for an entity to determine the carrying amount of the replaced part, it may use the cost of the replacement as an indication of what the cost of the replaced part was at the time it was acquired or constructed.'[105]

As a consequence, an entity may not actually identify the parts of an asset until it incurs the replacement expenditure, as in the following example.

Example 13.2: Recognition and derecognition of parts

An entity buys a piece of machinery with an estimated useful life of ten years for €10 million. The asset contains two identical pumps, which are assumed to have the same useful life as the machine of which they are a part. After seven years one of the pumps fails and is replaced at a cost of €200,000. The entity had not identified the pumps as separate parts and does not know the original cost. It uses the cost of the replacement part to estimate the carrying value of the original pump. With the help of the supplier, it estimates that the cost would have been approximately €170,000 and that this would have a remaining carrying value after seven year's depreciation of €51,000. Accordingly it derecognises €51,000 and capitalises the cost of the replacement.

It may be that the entity has no better information than the cost of the replacement part, in which case it appears that the entity is permitted to use a depreciated replacement cost basis to calculate the amount derecognised in respect of the original asset.

2.8.2 Useful life

One of the critical assumptions on which the depreciation charge depends is the useful economic life of the asset. The useful economic life is the period over which the present owner will benefit and not the total potential life of the asset; the two will often not be the same. For example, an entity may have a policy of replacing all of its motor vehicles after three years, so this will be their estimated useful life for depreciation purposes. The entity will depreciate them over this period down to the estimated residual value. The residual values of motor vehicles are often easy to obtain and the entity will be able to reassess these residuals in line with the requirements of the standard.

The effects of technological change are often underestimated. It affects many assets, not only high technology plant and equipment such as computer systems. For example, many offices that have been purpose-built can become obsolete long before their fabric has physically deteriorated, for reasons such as the difficulty of introducing computer network infrastructures or air conditioning, poor environmental performance or an inability to meet new legislative requirements such as access for people with disabilities.

As explained above, the standard requires asset lives to be estimated on a realistic basis and reviewed at the end of each reporting period. The effects of changes in estimated life are to be recognised prospectively, over the remaining life of the asset. In practice, many entities have previously tended to use quite a 'broad brush' approach to estimating asset lives, often based on perceived norms (for example, 50 years for freehold buildings) rather than a close analysis of their own expectations. The requirements of IAS 16 will necessitate more attention being paid to asset lives and residual values.

2.8.3 The meaning of fair value

A Fair value or market value

IAS 16 describes the process of determining fair value. For land and buildings, which are almost the only assets ever revalued, fair value should be 'determined from market-based evidence' (although income or depreciated replacement cost approaches are permitted if no such evidence is available).[106] The standard does not imply that fair value and market value are synonymous.

This allows a broader meaning of the term 'fair value'. The term can certainly be interpreted as encompassing the following two commonly used, market derived, valuation bases:

- market value in existing use, an entry value for property in continuing use in the business which is based on the concept of net current replacement cost; and
- open market value, which is an exit value and based on the amount that a property that is surplus to requirements could reach when sold.

Both of these bases are market derived, yet they can differ for a variety of reasons. A property may have a higher value on the open market if it could be redeployed to a more valuable use. On the other hand, the present owner may enjoy some benefits that could not be passed on in a sale, such as planning consents that are personal to the present occupier. Market valuation issues are further discussed in the context of Investment Property in Chapter 14 at 3.2.

The IASB has conceded that a lack of codified and consistent guidance has contributed to inconsistency in measuring fair value. In consequence a Fair Value Measurements project was added to the their agenda in order to develop a single standard that provides guidance to entities on measuring the fair value of assets and liabilities when required by IFRS.

However, the IASB, noting that the Financial Accounting Standards Board (FASB) was nearing completion of its fair value measurements project, tentatively decided to issue the FASB's final fair value measurement standard as an IASB Exposure Draft. The FASB Statement of Financial Accounting Standard No. 157 – *Fair value measurements* – was subsequently published in September 2006 and was issued by the IASB, actually in the form of a Discussion Paper, in the fourth quarter of 2006.

FASB Statement of Financial Accounting Standard No. 157 and the IASB Discussion Paper is further discussed in Chapter 2 at 6.2 and 6.3.

In the mean time, IAS 16 requires detailed disclosures regarding the methods and significant assumptions applied in estimating the items' fair values.[107] This means that the basis or bases that an entity has applied in valuing its assets will have to be disclosed in the accounts, including the extent to which it has applied either or both of the bases described above.

B Other methods of calculating fair value

IAS 16 allows other methods of deriving the fair value of assets in the absence of market-based evidence. If there is no market-based evidence because of the specialised nature of the asset and because it is rarely sold except as part of a continuing business, the entity is allowed to base fair value on an income or a depreciated replacement cost (DRC) approach.[108]

I Income approaches

The standard does not define what it means by an income approach. There are a number of techniques that may be used. The valuation may be based on transactions in an active market for dissimilar assets as adjusted to reflect the differences, or on transactions on less active markets if they have been adjusted to take account of subsequent changes in economic conditions. Both of these are allowed methods of calculating the fair value of investment property (see Chapter 14 at 3.2). Presumably income approaches could include use of discounted cash flow projections based on estimated future cash flows that will be generated by the asset. Care would have to be taken as the asset may not generate income by itself, being instead part of a cash generating unit (see Chapter 15); obviously, cash flows generated by other assets are not relevant to the valuation of the asset in question. Other methods that are encountered in practice include valuation methods based on factors such as notional rentals or multiples reflecting current transactions of indicators such as revenue or profits, which may be relevant for certain assets.

An entity must disclose the extent to which it has determined fair value using a valuation technique that is not based on observable process in an active market or recent market transactions.[109]

II Depreciated replacement cost

IAS 16 states that the alternative basis for valuing assets when they are rarely sold except as part of a continuing business is a depreciated replacement cost (DRC) approach.[110] The basis underlying DRC is that the asset is so specialised that there is no market value for it. There are three main subsets of such assets: (a) those that are only ever sold as part of a business; (b) assets primarily used to provide services to the public (whether on a paying or non-paying basis); and (c) assets that are so specialised by nature of their size or location or similar features that there is no market for them.

Examples of specialised properties include:

- oil refineries and chemical works where, usually, the buildings are no more than housings or cladding for highly specialised plant;
- power stations and dock installations where the building and site engineering works are related directly to the business of the owner, it being highly unlikely that they would have a value to anyone other than a company acquiring the undertaking;

- schools, colleges, universities and research establishments where there is no competing market demand from other organisations using these types of property in the locality;
- hospitals, other specialised health care premises and leisure centres where there is no competing market demand from other organisations wishing to use these types of property in the locality; and
- museums, libraries, and other similar premises provided by the public sector.

In addition, there may be no market-based evidence for properties of such specialised construction, arrangement, size or specification that it is unlikely that there would be a single purchaser. The same may be the case even for standard properties in geographical areas remote from main business centres (perhaps originally located there for operational or business reasons that no longer exist). This could occur if the buildings were of such an abnormal size for the district that no market for them would exist.

DRC is considered to be the aggregate amount of the value of the land for the existing use or a notional replacement site in the same locality, and the gross replacement cost of the buildings and other site works, from which appropriate deductions may then be made to allow for the age, condition, economic or functional obsolescence and environmental factors. The objective of DRC is to make a realistic estimate of the current cost of constructing an asset that has the same service potential as the existing asset.

DRC is inevitably rather an unsatisfactory valuation basis at the theoretical level, as it is represented as a valuation of property, but in circumstances where, by definition, the asset has no market value. Moreover, because a DRC valuation is based on replacement cost, it is often likely to give a higher valuation than one using market-based evidence that reflects the actual current condition of the asset. For this reason, it is necessary to ensure that the property really is so specialised that such evidence cannot be obtained. It is also necessary to be satisfied that the potential profitability of the business is adequate to support the value derived on a DRC basis.

DRC approaches are often applied also to the valuation of plant and machinery (as distinct from property assets) where there is rarely a market from which to derive a fair value.

2.8.4 Reversals of downward valuations

IAS 16 says that if an asset's carrying amount is increased as a result of a revaluation, the increase shall be credited directly to equity under the heading of revaluation surplus. However, the increase shall be recognised in profit or loss to the extent that it reverses a revaluation decrease of the same asset previously recognised in profit or loss.[111]

If the revalued asset is being depreciated we consider that the full amount of any reversal should not be taken to the income statement. Rather it should take account of the depreciation that would have been charged on the previously higher book value. This is required by IAS 36 when impairment losses are reversed, that standard stating:

> 'The increased carrying amount of an asset other than goodwill attributable to a reversal of an impairment loss shall not exceed the carrying amount that would have been determined for the asset in prior years'.[112]

The following example demonstrates a way in which this could be applied:

Example 13.3: Reversal of a downward valuation

An asset has a cost of £1,000,000, a life of 10 years and a residual value of £nil. At the end of year 3, when the asset's NBV is £700,000, it is revalued to £350,000. This write down below cost of £350,000 is taken through the income statement.

The entity then depreciated its asset by £50,000 per annum, so as to write off the carrying value of £350,000 over the remaining 7 years.

At the end of year 6, the asset is revalued to £500,000. The effect on the entity's asset is as follows:

	£000
Valuation	
At the beginning of year 6	350
Surplus on revaluation	150
At the end of the year	500
Accumulated depreciation	
At beginning of year 6*	100
Charge for the year	50
Accumulated depreciation written back on revaluation	(150)
At the end of the year	–
Net book value at the end of year 6	500
Net book value at the beginning of year 6	250

* Two year's depreciation (years 4 and 5) at £50,000 per annum.

Upon the revaluation in year 6 the total credit is £300,000. However, only £200,000 is taken through the income statement. £100,000 represents depreciation that would otherwise have been charged to the income statement in years 4 and 5. This will be taken directly to the revaluation surplus in equity.

From the beginning of year 7 the asset will be written off over the remaining four years at £125,000 per annum.

In the example the amount of the revaluation that is credited to the revaluation surplus in equity represents the difference between the net book value that would have resulted had the asset been held on a cost basis (£400,000) and the net book value on a revalued basis (£500,000).

Of course this is an extreme example. Most assets that are subject to a policy of revaluation would not show such marked changes in value and it would be expected that there would be valuation movements in the intervening years rather than dramatic losses and gains in years 3 and 6. However, we consider that in principle this is the way in which downward valuations should be effected.

There may be major practical difficulties for any entity that finds itself in the position of reversing revaluation deficits on depreciating assets, although whether in practice this eventuality often occurs is open to doubt. If it were to occur though, the business would need to continue to maintain asset registers on the original, pre-write down basis.

2.8.5 Depreciation of infrastructure assets

In some jurisdictions, under their former national GAAPs, infrastructure assets such as electricity distribution networks have been dealt with on a renewals accounting basis. Under renewals accounting, the level of annual expenditure required to maintain the operating capacity of the infrastructure asset is treated as the depreciation charged for the period and is deducted from the carrying amount of the asset (as part of accumulated depreciation). Actual expenditure is capitalised (as part of the cost of the asset) as incurred. IAS 16 makes no mention of renewals accounting, which does not appear to be allowable under the standard.

2.8.6 Depreciation methods

There is little discussion of depreciation methods in IAS 16, which simply says that 'the depreciation method shall reflect the pattern in which the asset's future economic benefits are expected to be consumed by the entity'.[113]

IAS 16 mentions only three depreciation methods, straight line and diminishing (reducing) balance, and units of production. The straight line and reducing balance methods are well known and understood. It may be appropriate to use other methods with particular assets and, for reference purposes, some are illustrated below. However, it is worth noting that IAS 16 does not contain the restriction in IAS 38 – *Intangible Assets* – that there is rarely, if ever, persuasive evidence to support an amortisation method that results in a lower amount of accumulated amortisation than under the straight line method.

A Double declining balance

This method is sometimes applied in the US, where it has corresponded to tax allowances on assets. The method involves determining the asset's depreciation on a straight-line basis over its useful life. This annual amount is multiplied by an appropriate factor (it does not have to be doubled) to give the first year's charge and depreciation at the same percentage rate is charged on the reducing balance in subsequent years.

Example 13.4: Double declining balance depreciation

An asset costs €6,000 and has a life of ten years, which means that, calculated on the straight-line basis, the annual depreciation charge would be €600. On the double declining balance method (assuming a factor of two), the depreciation charge for the first year would be €1,200 and depreciation would continue to be charged at 20% on the reducing balance thereafter.

B Sum of the digits

This is another form of the reducing balance method, but one that is based on the estimated life of the asset and which can therefore easily be applied if the asset has a residual value. If an asset has an estimated useful life of four years then the digits 1, 2, 3, and 4 are added together, giving a total of 10. Depreciation of four-tenths, three-tenths and so on, of the cost of the asset, less any residual value, will be charged in the respective years. The method is sometimes called the 'rule of 78', 78 being the sum of the digits 1 to 12.

Example 13.5: Sum of the digits depreciation

An asset costs €10,000 and is expected to be sold for €2,000 after four years. Depreciation is to be provided over four years using the sum of the digits method.

		€
Year 1	Cost	10,000
	Depreciation at 4/10 of €8,000	3,200
	Net book value	6,800
Year 2	Depreciation at 3/10 of €8,000	2,400
	Net book value	4,400
Year 3	Depreciation at 2/10 of €8,000	1,600
	Net book value	2,800
Year 4	Depreciation at 1/10 of €8,000	800
	Net book value	2,000

C Unit of production method

Under this method, the asset is written off in line with its estimated total output. By relating depreciation to the proportion of productive capacity utilised to date, it reflects the fact that the useful economic life of certain assets, principally machinery, is more closely linked to its usage and output than to time. This method is normally used in extractive industries, for example, to amortise the costs of development of productive oil and gas facilities.

The essence of choosing a fair depreciation method is to reflect the consumption of economic benefits provided by the asset concerned. In most cases the straight-line basis will give perfectly acceptable results, and the vast majority of entities use this method. Where there are instances, such as the extraction of a known proportion of a mineral resource, or the use of a certain amount of the total available number of working hours of a machine, it may be that a unit of production method will give fairer results.

2.8.7 Tangible or intangible assets – the issue of new technology costs

IAS 38's restrictions on capitalising certain internally-generated intangible assets has focused attention on the treatment of many internal costs. In practice, items such as computer software purchased by entities are frequently capitalised as part of a tangible asset, for example as part of an accounting or communications infrastructure. Equally, internally written software may be capitalised as part of a tangible production facility, and so on. Judgement must be exercised in deciding whether such items are to be accounted for under IAS 16 or IAS 38 and this distinction becomes increasingly important if the two standards would prescribe differing treatments in any particular case. IAS 16 does not refer to this type of asset, but IAS 38 does: it states that an entity needs to exercise judgment in determining whether an asset that incorporates both intangible and tangible elements should be treated under IAS 16 or as an intangible asset under IAS 38, for example:

- computer software that is embedded in computer-controlled equipment that cannot operate without that specific software is an integral part of the related hardware and is treated as property, plant and equipment;
- application software that is being used on a computer is generally easily replaced and is not an integral part of the related hardware, whereas the operating system normally is; and
- a database that is stored on a compact disc is considered to be an intangible asset because the value of the physical medium is wholly insignificant compared to that of the data collection.[114]

It is worthwhile noting that as the 'parts approach' in IAS 16 requires an entity to account for significant parts of an asset separately, this raises 'boundary' problems between IAS 16 and IAS 38 when software and similar expenditure are involved. We believe that where IAS 16 requires an entity to identify significant parts of an asset and account for them separately, the entity needs to evaluate whether any software-type intangible part is actually integral to the larger asset or whether it is really a separate asset in its own right. The intangible part is more likely to be an asset in its own right if it was developed separately or if it can be used independently of the item of property, plant and equipment that it apparently forms part of.

2.8.8 *Amounts charged under operating leases during the construction of an asset*

It is our opinion that amounts charged under operating leases during the construction period of an asset may be included as part of the cost of the PP&E if those lease costs are 'directly attributable to bringing the asset to the location and condition necessary for it to be capable of operating in the manner intended by management'.[115] This may be the case, for example, where a building is constructed on land that is leased under an operating lease. This approach must be applied consistently.

3 TRANSITIONAL PROVISIONS AND FIRST-TIME ADOPTION OF IAS 16

3.1 First-time adoption of IAS 16

For first time adopters of IFRS, the main difficulty with the general approach of IFRS 1 – *First-time Adoption of International Financial Reporting Standards* – is that it requires full retrospective application of IAS 16, which entails choosing one of the two measurement bases the standard permits: cost or fair value. Whichever is chosen, the valuation will have to be adjusted for depreciation and impairment as appropriate, which will in turn involve the identification of the significant parts of the assets concerned. However, this would be extremely difficult to achieve in many cases, as the original cost of many long-lived items of PP&E might be very costly, if not impossible to determine. Consequently, the IASB decided to permit the use of 'deemed cost' in place of actual cost in the opening IFRS balance sheet. Under IFRS 1, deemed cost can be:

(1) the fair value of the item at the date of transition to IFRS;[116]

(2) a revaluation under its previous GAAP at or before the date of transition to IFRS, if the revaluation was at the date of the revaluation broadly comparable to:[117]

'(a) fair value; or

(b) cost or depreciated cost under IFRS, adjusted to reflect, for example, changes in a general or specific price index'; or

(3) the deemed cost under its previous GAAP that was established by measuring items at their fair value at one particular date because of an event such as a privatisation or initial public offering.[118]

In addition, if the asset was acquired as part of a business combination, deemed cost can be the carrying amount under the previous GAAP immediately after acquisition, or, if the item was not recognised under a previous GAAP, the carrying amount on the basis that IFRS would require in the separate balance sheet of the acquiree.

Note that these alternatives are freely available to the entity, although obviously it will need to take its future IFRS accounting policy into account. This means that an entity that has previously carried its properties at fair value may use that fair value as deemed cost as at the date of transition to IFRS and thereafter apply the cost model.

This alternative is also available for investment properties (see Chapter 14).

In addition, an entity is permitted to bring forward assets on different bases, so, for example, it could bring into its IFRS accounts some assets of the same class at cost and others at a deemed cost based on a valuation under previous GAAP undertaken several years before.

Entities will have to ensure that they have adequately identified the significant parts of the asset at transition and that they have been depreciated on an appropriate basis. The same rules regarding deemed cost are available to significant parts.

These provisions are a sensible compromise by the IASB and will enable many of the initial difficulties in the area of PP&E on adoption of IFRS to be overcome. A full explanation of the provisions of IFRS 1 for first-time application of IAS 16 and IAS 40 is set out in Chapter 5 at 2.5.

3.2 First-time adoption of IFRIC 1

A first-time adopter is not required to restate the carrying amount included in an asset in respect of decommissioning that occurred before the date of transition to IFRSs, e.g. those changes in respect of estimated cash outflows, discount rate and unwinding discount that are described in 2.3.1 above. Instead, the exemption allows the entity to estimate the liability by calculating it at the transition date in accordance with IAS 37 and adjusting this amount by discounting it at its best estimate of the historical risk-adjusted discount rate(s) that would have applied over the intervening period. Accumulated depreciation as at the transition date is then based on the current estimate of the useful life of the asset, using the depreciation policy adopted by the entity under IFRSs.[119]

4 CONCLUSION

In principle, accounting for PP&E is straightforward; the essential purpose is to allocate expenditure which provides enduring benefits against the revenues of the periods that enjoy those benefits. The meaning of 'PP&E' is deeply rooted in the manufacturing tradition and the conventional model still works well for machinery assets that wear out reasonably predictably.

However the position is complicated by revaluations of assets. This practice poses a number of accounting questions; for example, how to treat the revaluation surplus, whether depreciation is necessary if assets are carried at a valuation and, more fundamentally, what the balance sheet is meant to portray. The surreptitious 'stretching' by the IASB of the meaning of fair value from a market price-based concept to include a mark-to-model valuation (if a market price is not available) has only added further complexity. How these matters might be resolved is the subject of much of the discussion concerning a new conceptual framework, a project currently being undertaken jointly by the FASB and the IASB, and fully discussed in Chapter 2 at 5.

References

1 IAS 16, *Property, Plant and Equipment*, IASB, paras. 2-3.
2 IAS 16, para. 5.
3 IAS 16, para. 4.
4 IAS 16, para. 6.
5 IAS 16, para. 7.
6 IAS 16, para. 8.
7 IAS 16, para. 9.
8 IAS 16, para. 11.
9 IAS 16, para. 11.
10 IAS 16, para. 10.
11 IAS 16, para. 12.
12 IAS 16, para. 13.
13 IAS 37, *Provisions, Contingent Liabilities and Contingent Assets*, IASB, Appendix C, Examples 11A and 11B.
14 IAS 16, para. 14.
15 IAS 16, para. 15.
16 IAS 16, para. 16.
17 IAS 16, para. 18.
18 IAS 16, para. 18.
19 IAS 16, para. 17.
20 IAS 16, para. 19.
21 IAS 16, para. 20.
22 IAS 16, para. 16(b).
23 IAS 16, para. 21.
24 IAS 16, para. 20.
25 IAS 16, para. 17(e).
26 IAS 16, para. 22.
27 IAS 16, para. 23.
28 IAS 16, para. 58.
29 IFRIC 4, *Determining whether an Arrangement contains a Lease* , IFRIC.

30 IFRIC 1, *Changes in Existing Decommissioning, Restoration and Similar Liabilities*, IFRIC, para. 2.
31 IFRIC 1, para. 3.
32 IFRIC 1, para. 5.
33 IFRIC 1, para. 6.
34 IFRIC 1, para. 7.
35 IFRIC 1, para. 7.
36 IFRIC 1, para. 6.
37 IFRIC 1, para. 8.
38 IAS 16, para. 24.
39 IAS 16, para. 24.
40 IAS 16, para. 24.
41 IAS 16, para. BC21.
42 IAS 16, para. 25.
43 IAS 16, para. 25.
44 IAS 16, para. BC19.
45 IAS 16, para. 26.
46 IAS 16, para. 68.
47 IAS 16, para. 27.
48 IAS 16, para. 28.
49 IAS 16, para. 29.
50 IAS 16, para. 30.
51 IAS 16, para. 31.
52 IAS 16, para. 32.
53 IAS 16, para. 33.
54 IAS 16, para. 31.
55 IAS 16, para. 34.
56 IAS 16, para. 37.
57 IAS 16, para. 38.
58 IAS 16, paras. 39-40.
59 IAS 36, *Impairment of assets*, IASB, para. 61.
60 IAS 16, para. 41.
61 IAS 8, *Accounting Policies, Changes in Accounting Estimates and Errors*, IASB, para. 17.
62 IAS 16, para. 43.
63 IAS 16, para. 44.
64 IAS 16, para. 45.
65 IAS 16, para. 46.
66 IAS 16, para. 47.
67 IAS 16, paras. 48-49.
68 IAS 16, para. 51.
69 IAS 16, paras. 53-54.
70 IAS 16, para. 51.
71 IAS 16, para. 50.
72 IAS 16, para. 52.
73 IAS 16, para. 54.
74 IAS 16, para. 52.
75 IAS 16, para. 56.
76 IAS 16, para. 57.
77 IAS 16, para. 58.
78 IAS 36, para. 12(f).
79 IAS 36, para. 12(f).
80 IAS 16, para. 55.
81 IAS 16, para. 55.
82 IFRIC 1, para. 7.
83 IAS 16, paras. 60-62.
84 IAS 8, para. 32 (d).
85 IAS 8, para. 36.
86 IAS 16, para. 63.
87 IAS 16, paras. 65-66.
88 IAS 37, para 53.
89 IAS 16, para. 67.
90 IAS 16, para. 69.
91 IAS 16, para. 68.
92 IAS 16, para. 71.
93 IAS 16, para. 41.
94 IAS 16, para. 70.
95 IAS 16, para. 72.
96 IFRS 5, *Non-current Assets Held for Sale and Discontinued Operations*, IASB, para. 6.
97 IFRS 5, para. 7.
98 IFRS 5, para. 8.
99 IAS 1, *Presentation of Financial Statements*, IASB, para. 36.
100 IAS 16, para. 74.
101 IAS 16, para. 76.
102 IAS 16, para. 77.
103 IAS 16, para. 79.
104 IAS 16, paras. 43-44.
105 IAS 16, para. 70.
106 IAS 16, para. 32.
107 IAS 16, para. 77(c).
108 IAS 16, para. 33.
109 IAS 16, para. 77(d).
110 IAS 16, para. 33.
111 IAS 16, para. 39.
112 IAS 36, para. 117.
113 IAS 16, para. 60.
114 IAS 38, para. 4.
115 IAS 16, para. 16b.
116 IFRS 1, *First-time Adoption of International Financial Reporting Standards*, IASB, para. 16.
117 IFRS 1, para. 17.
118 IFRS 1, para. 19.
119 IFRS 1, para. 25E.

30 IFRIC 1, *Changes in Existing Decommissioning, Restoration and Similar Liabilities*, IFRIC, para. 2.
31 IFRIC 1, para. 5.
32 IFRIC 1, para. 5.
33 IFRIC 1, para. 6.
34 IFRIC 1, para. 7.
35 IFRIC 1, para. 7.
36 IFRIC 1, para. 6.
37 IFRIC 1, para. 8.
38 IAS 16, para. 24.
39 IAS 16, para. 24.
40 IAS 16, para. 24.
41 IAS 16, para. BC22.
42 IAS 16, para. 25.
43 IAS 16, para. 25.
44 IAS 16, para. BC19.
45 IAS 16, para. 26.
46 IAS 16, para. 6.
47 IAS 16, para. 27.
48 IAS 16, para. 28.
49 IAS 16, para. 29.
50 IAS 16, para. 30.
51 IAS 16, para. 31.
52 IAS 16, para. 32.
53 IAS 16, para. 33.
54 IAS 16, para. [illegible]
55 IAS 16, para. 34.
56 IAS 16, para. 35.
57 IAS 16, para. 36.
58 IAS 16, paras. 39–40.
59 IAS 36, *Impairment of Assets*, IASB, para. 61.
60 IAS 16, para. 41.
61 IAS 8, *Accounting Policies, Changes in Accounting Estimates and Errors*, IASB, para. 17.
62 IAS 16, para. 43.
63 IAS 16, para. 44.
64 IAS 16, para. 45.
65 IAS 16, para. 46.
66 IAS 16, para. 47.
67 IAS 16, paras. 48–49.
68 IAS 16, para. 51.
69 IAS 16, paras. 52–54.
70 IAS 16, para. 61.
71 IAS 16, para. 50.
72 IAS 16, para. 53.
73 IAS 16, para. 54.
74 IAS 16, para. 55.
75 IAS 16, para. 56.
76 IAS 16, para. 57.
77 IAS 16, para. 58.
78 IAS 36, para. 126(f).
79 IAS 36, para. 126(f).
80 IAS 16, para. 55.
81 IAS 16, para. 55.
82 IFRIC 1, para. 7.
83 IAS 16, paras. 60–62.
84 IAS 8, para. 32(d).
85 IAS 8, para. 36.
86 IAS 16, para. 63.
87 IAS 16, paras. 65–66.
88 IAS 37, para. 53.
89 IAS 16, para. 67.
90 IAS 16, para. 69.
91 IAS 16, para. 68.
92 IAS 16, para. 71.
93 IAS 16, para. 41.
94 IAS 16, para. 70.
95 IAS 16, para. 72.
96 IFRS 5, *Non-current Assets Held for Sale and Discontinued Operations*, IASB, para. 6.
97 IFRS 5, para. 7.
98 IFRS 5, para. 8.
99 IAS 1, *Presentation of Financial Statements*, IASB, para. 36.
100 IAS 16, para. 74.
101 IAS 16, para. 76.
102 IAS 16, para. 77.
103 IAS 16, para. 79.
104 IAS 16, paras. 43–44.
105 IAS 16, para. 70.
106 IAS 16, para. 32.
107 IAS 16, para. 77(c).
108 IAS 16, para. 33.
109 IAS 16, para. 77(d).
110 IAS 16, para. 35.
111 IAS 16, para. 39.
112 IAS 36, para. 117.
113 IAS 16, para. 60.
114 IAS 38, para. 4.
115 IAS 16, para. 16b.
116 IFRS 1, *First-time Adoption of International Financial Reporting Standards*, IASB, para. 16.
117 IFRS 1, para. 1[illegible]
118 IFRS 1, para. 1[illegible]
119 IFRS 1, para. 25E.

Chapter 14 Investment property

1 INTRODUCTION

IAS 40 – *Investment property* – is a rare example of the particular commercial characteristics of an industry resulting in the special treatment of a certain category of property (investment properties), even though the assets themselves are not intrinsically different from those within the scope of IAS 16 – *Property Plant and Equipment*. Nevertheless, despite being focused on the needs of the investment property industry, the standard allows entities a free choice between two measurement models: historic cost and fair value. It should be borne in mind also that it is not only investment property companies that hold investment property; any property that meets the investment property definition is so classified, irrespective of the nature of the business of the reporting entity.

The original standard, which was approved in March 2000 by the Board of the former IASC as part of the IOSCO core standards programme (see Chapter 1 at 1.3), represented a major conceptual shift, as it was the first international standard to introduce the possibility of applying a full fair value model when accounting for non-financial assets. Under this option the asset is neither depreciated nor subject to impairment testing, and all valuation changes (i.e. fair value changes) from one period to the next are treated as gains and losses and reported in the income statement. Consequently, the fair value option of IAS 40 means that the income statement will contain a mixture of realised gains and losses (for example rental income and maintenance costs) and unrealised fair value changes. This contrasts with the revaluation approach allowed under IAS 16 (see Chapter 13 at 2.4.1) where increases above cost, and their reversals, are recognised directly in equity through the statement of recognised income and expense.

IAS 40 also allows investment property to be accounted for more conventionally, by being carried at cost less depreciation, under the cost model set out in IAS 16.

The exposure draft that preceded IAS 40 proposed that fair value should be the sole measurement model for investment property. However, in the light of comments received from respondents, several members of the Board of the former IASC were concerned that, in certain parts of the world, property markets were not sufficiently liquid to support fair value measurement for financial reporting purposes. Consequently, the cost option was introduced into the standard, together with the following explanation:

> 'This is the first time that the Board has proposed requiring a fair value accounting model for non-financial assets. The comment letters on E64 showed that although many support this step, many others still have significant conceptual and practical reservations about extending a fair value model to non-financial assets, particularly (but not exclusively) for entities whose main activity is not to hold property for capital appreciation. Also, some entities feel that certain property markets are not yet sufficiently mature for a fair value model to work satisfactorily. Furthermore, some believe that it is impossible to create a rigorous definition of investment property and that this makes it impracticable to require a fair value model at present.
>
> For those reasons the Board believes that it is impracticable, at this stage, to require a fair value model for all investment property. At the same time, the Board believes that it is desirable to permit a fair value model. This evolutionary step forward will allow preparers and users to gain greater experience working with a fair value model and will allow time for certain property markets to achieve greater maturity'.[1]

The treatment of investment property under the fair value model is significantly different from the treatment of trading properties held for sale in the ordinary course of business, which are accounted for as inventory under IAS 2's cost model, even though the latter are likely to be more liquid assets. However, this is not necessarily an issue in practice, as trading properties are generally held for a relatively short period of time, whilst investment properties are generally held for the longer term.

2 DEFINITIONS AND SCOPE

An investment property is defined in IAS 40 as a:

> 'property (land or a building – or part of a building – or both) held (by the owner or by the lessee under a finance lease) to earn rentals or for capital appreciation or both, rather than for:
>
> (a) use in the production or supply of goods or services or for administrative purposes; or
>
> (b) sale in the ordinary course of business.'[2]

As stated above, this means that any entity, whatever the underlying nature of its business, can hold investment property assets.

In contrast, 'owner-occupied' property is defined as 'property held (by the owner or by the lessee under a finance lease) for use in the production or supply of goods or services or for administrative purposes'.[3] Such property falls outside the scope of IAS 40 and is accounted for under IAS 16, together with IAS 17 – *Leases* – if relevant.

IAS 40 does not apply to:[4]

(a) Biological assets related to agricultural activities. Under IAS 41 – *Agriculture* – biological assets that are physically attached to land (for example, trees in a plantation forest) are measured at their fair value less estimated point-of-sale costs separately from the land.[5] The land related to the agricultural activity is accounted for either as property under IAS 16 or investment property under IAS 40.[6]

(b) Mineral rights and mineral revenues such as oil, natural gas and similar non-regenerative resources.

2.1 Property interests held under operating leases

Entities are permitted to treat interests held under operating leases as investment properties – providing that they would otherwise meet the standard's investment property definition and that the fair value model is applied. This situation arises where, for example, an entity acquires an operating leasehold interest as an investment property by effectively prepaying a certain number of years' operating lease rentals. This classification alternative is available on a property-by-property basis so that the entity need not classify all property interests held under operating leases as investment properties. However, IAS 40 requires that once one operating leasehold interest is classified as an investment property, all property classified as investment property must be accounted for under the fair value method. These leasehold interests are subject also to the same disclosure requirements as other investment properties (see 6.2 below).[7]

IAS 17 requires leases to be separated into land and building components, subject to this being possible or the land element being material (see Chapter 25). If the interest is to be an investment property carried at fair value in accordance with IAS 40, there is no requirement to separate the land and buildings elements of the lease.[8]

2.2 Identifying investment property

What primarily distinguishes investment property from other types of property interest is that its cash flows (from rental or sale) are largely independent of those from other assets held by the entity. By contrast, property used by an entity for administrative purposes or for the production or supply of goods or services do not generate cash flows themselves but do so only in conjunction with other assets.[9]

However, even with this distinction, it may not be easy to distinguish investment property from owner-occupied property to which IAS 16 applies. The standard therefore gives guidance to help determine whether or not an asset is an investment property.[10]

2.2.1 Land

Land is an investment property if it is either held for long-term capital appreciation or for a currently undetermined future use. This is in contrast to land that is held for sale in the short term in the ordinary course of business. If the entity has not determined whether it will use the land as owner-occupied property or for short-term sale in the ordinary course of business, it is deemed to be held for capital appreciation and must be classified as an investment property.[11]

2.2.2 *Buildings leased to others*

Buildings leased out under one or more operating leases are generally investment properties, whether they are owned by the reporting entity or held under finance leases. This will also apply if the building is currently vacant while tenants are being sought.[12]

However, in our opinion, an exception should be made in those cases where, despite being leased out, properties are held for sale in the ordinary course of business. Leasing of properties prior to sale is a common practice in the real estate industry in order to minimise cash outflows and because prospective buyers may view the existence of lease contracts positively, especially those that wish to acquire property for investment purposes.

In those circumstances, and notwithstanding that they are leased to tenants under operating leases, the intention to hold property for short-term sale dictates that they should be accounted for as inventory under IAS 2 (see 2.2.3 below).

Property that is leased to another entity under a finance lease is not an investment property but is accounted for under IAS 17 (see Chapter 25).[13]

2.2.3 *Property held for trading or being constructed for resale*

Property held for trading purposes or being constructed for resale is not investment property. This includes property held in the following circumstances:

(a) property intended for sale in the ordinary course of business, including property in the process of construction or development. This includes property acquired exclusively for sale in the near future or for development and resale. These are accounted for as inventory under IAS 2 (see Chapter 23); and

(b) property being built or developed under a construction contract for third parties. These are covered by IAS 11 – *Construction Contracts* – which is discussed in Chapter 24.[14]

2.2.4 *Owner occupation*

As stated above, owner-occupied property, that is property held for use in the production or supply of goods or services or for administrative purposes,[15] is specifically excluded from being treated as investment property and is subject to the provisions of IAS 16. Owner-occupied property includes:

(a) property that is going to be owner-occupied in the future (whether or not it has first to be redeveloped);

(b) property occupied by employees, whether or not they pay rent at market rates; and

(c) owner-occupied property awaiting disposal.[16]

Swiss Property Group discloses how it deals with own-use property below:

Extract 14.1: PSP Swiss Property Ltd (2006)

Accounting and Valuation Principles [extract]
Own-used real estate [extract]

In accordance with IAS 16, properties used by the Company itself are stated at historical cost and depreciated over their economically useful life, divided according to their significant parts. Depreciable life is 40 years for buildings and 20 years for facilities (such as air-conditioning, elevators, ventilation, etc.). Land belonging to the property is not depreciated. Where the Company uses only part of a property it owns, utilisation of less than 25 % is regarded as immaterial, which means that the whole property is stated at market value as an investment property.

Note that the treatment in the consolidated accounts does not necessarily determine the treatment by individual group entities. For example, it may be the case that a property is held by one group company for occupation by another group company. This will be owner-occupied from the perspective of the group as a whole but classified as an investment property in the accounts of the individual entity that owns it.[17] This classification in the individual entity's financial statements will apply even if the rental is not at arm's length and the individual entity is not in a position to benefit from capital appreciation. The IASB has concluded that it is more significant that the property itself will still generate largely independent cash flows.

Associates and joint ventures are not part of the group, so properties occupied by such entities would be accounted for as investment properties in the consolidated financial statements (provided, of course, they meet the investment property definition). This is the case, even if the property is occupied by a jointly controlled entity that is proportionately consolidated under paragraph 30 of IAS 31 – *Interests in Joint Ventures.*

2.2.5 Property in the course of construction and redevelopment

IAS 16 applies to property that is being constructed or developed for future use as investment property until construction or development is complete, at which time the property becomes investment property. This relaxation of the approach in the standard is primarily because, when IAS 40 was being developed, the IASB considered that fair values of incomplete investment properties were difficult to obtain.[18] The effect is that IAS 16's rules regarding the recognition of costs apply during the construction period (see Chapter 13 at 2.3).

In contrast, IAS 40 must be applied to existing investment property that is being redeveloped for continued future use as investment property. In this case it appears the IASB was satisfied that a fair value could be obtained for incomplete developments simply because they were previously classified as investment property. Whilst this means that entities applying IAS 40's fair value option will not have to reclassify such investment properties while they are being redeveloped, they will still have to revalue them to fair value during the redevelopment period.

However, in their July 2006 meeting[19] the IFRIC discussed whether or not to take on a project to consider whether the revaluation model in IAS 16 is available for investment property under construction. The IFRIC noted that whilst the Basis for

Conclusions to IAS 40 implies that investment property under construction may not be revalued,[20] IAS 16 does not preclude accounting for such property using the revaluation model. The IFRIC did note that there may be 'practical issues in practice' in applying the revaluation model to investment property under construction.

The IFRIC deferred its discussion on these potential issues and on whether to take the issue onto its agenda at all. Instead the IFRIC noted that, since IAS 40 was written, the use of fair values in accounting has become more widespread and valuation techniques have become more robust. The IFRIC therefore considered that the requirement that investment property under construction be accounted for under IAS 16 might no longer be necessary and agreed to ask the Board whether it would consider amending IAS 40 to state that investment property under construction should be accounted for under that Standard.

In their October 2006 meeting the Board tentatively decided to amend IAS 40 and IAS 16 to include investment property under construction within the scope of IAS 40. Consequently, as part of their annual improvement process, the Board has issued an Exposure Draft which would, if finalised as drafted, bring such a change into effect from 1 January 2009.

In the meantime, we consider that the IAS 16 revaluation model is still available for investment property under construction and one entity that has adopted the revaluation model is Liberty International PLC, which notes that it considers that reliable estimates are available.

Extract 14.2: Liberty International PLC (2006)

Development properties [extract]

The group has elected to use the fair value model as reliable estimates are available. Property under development and land are initially recognised at cost and subsequently revalued at the balance sheet date to fair value as determined by professionally qualified external valuers. Cost includes interest and other directly attributable outgoings, except in the case of properties and land where no development is imminent, in which case no interest is included. In accordance with IAS 16 – "Property, Plant and Equipment", gains or losses arising from changes in the fair value of development property are dealt with in reserves to the extent that fair value exceeds cost and are otherwise recognised in the income statement. Upon completion, development properties to be held for long-term rental income and capital appreciation are transferred to investment property.

Judgement is required in determining whether and when the redevelopment of an existing investment property becomes, instead, the development of an entirely new one; this judgement will, in turn, dictate whether IAS 16 or IAS 40 applies during the redevelopment period. One entity that discloses the criteria for such a judgement is Rodamco Europe – see Extract 14.3 below.

Extract 14.3: Rodamco Europe, NV (2006)

Significant accounting policies [extract]

(h) Pipeline projects

A property is transferred from 'investment property' to 'pipeline project' at its carrying value only in case of major reconstruction whereby starting the project results in a reduction of nearly all net rental income and the projected capital expenditure more or less equals or exceeds the carrying value. Any other reconstruction is accounted for as renovation projects.

Furthermore, where an entity carries its investment properties in the course of development using IAS 16's revaluation model, the question arises as to the amount at which the asset should be stated when it is reclassified. This is addressed in 2.4 below.

2.2.6 Properties with dual uses

IAS 40 states that if a property has both investment property and non-investment property uses, providing the parts of the property could be sold or leased under a finance lease separately, they should be accounted for separately.[21]

However, to meet this requirement we consider that a property must actually be in a state and condition to enable it to be disposed of separately at the balance sheet date. The fact that a property could be divided in future periods if the owner so chose is insufficient to conclude that the portions can be accounted for separately. Consequently, if a property requires sub-division before the portions could be disposed of separately, then those parts should, in our view, not be accounted for as separate portions until such sub-divisions occur.

In the event that no separation is possible, the property is an investment property only if an insignificant proportion is used for non-investment property purposes.[22]

2.2.7 Provision of services

If the owner supplies ancillary services to the user of the investment property, the property will not qualify as an investment property unless the value of these services is an insignificant component of the arrangement as a whole.[23]

Security and maintenance services are described by the standard as being insignificant.[24] It becomes more difficult to make the analysis when the building itself is used to generate the revenues. The crucial issue is the extent to which the owner retains significant exposure to the risks of running a business.[25] The standard uses the example of a hotel. An owner-managed hotel, for example, would be precluded from being an investment property as the services provided to guests are a significant component of the commercial arrangements.

The standard admits that this distinction can require judgements to be made, and specifies that businesses should develop consistent criteria for use in such instances that reflect the spirit of the provisions described above. These criteria must be disclosed in those cases where classification is difficult.[26]

One entity that does make such a distinction is Mapeley Limited as set out in their accounting policy below. The lack of detailed criteria may suggest that the directors did not consider this classification to be difficult.

> *Extract 14.4: Mapeley Limited (2006)*
>
> **Property, plant and equipment** [extract]
>
> ***Property***
>
> Where the Group provides significant levels of ancillary services to the occupiers of its property, this property is not classified as investment property. Such freehold property and property held under finance leases are revalued to fair value annually and depreciated in accordance with IAS 16 Property, Plant and Equipment.

2.2.8 *Group of assets leased out under a single operating lease*

It is sometimes the case in practice that a group of assets comprising land, buildings and 'other assets' is leased out by a lessor under a single operating lease contract in order to earn rentals. In such a case, the 'other assets' would generally comprise assets that relate to the manner in which the land and buildings are used under the lease. The issue that arises is under what circumstances should the 'other assets' be regarded by the lessor as part of an investment property rather than as a separate item of property, plant and equipment? This is illustrated in the following real-life example:

Example 14.1: Definition of an investment property: a group of assets leased out under a single operating lease

A lessor enters into the following two single contract leases in order to earn rentals. All the individual assets subject to the leases meet the test of being classified as an operating lease. The lessor applies the fair value measurement model for subsequent measurement of investment property.

Lease 1: Vineyard and winery

A vineyard including a winery is leased out under an operating lease. The vineyard comprises the following assets:

- Land
- Vineyard infrastructure (e.g. trellises)
- Winery building structures
- Winery plant and machinery (crushing equipment, distilling equipment)
- Vines (grapes are excluded, as they belong to the lessee).

Lease 2: Port

A port is leased out under an operating lease. The port comprises the following assets:

- Land
- Warehouses
- Transport infrastructure to and from the port (roads, rail tracks, bridges)
- Wharves
- Light towers (that enable the 24 hour operation of the port)

- Specialised container cranes.

To what extent can the 'other assets' included in the leases (but which are not considered to constitute a piece of land or a building) be included in the investment property definition under IAS 40?

This is an important issue, as the consequence of including plant and equipment in the definition of investment property is that if the investment property is accounted for at fair value, changes in the fair value of that plant and equipment will be recognised in the income statement.

From a literal reading of the definition of an investment property as set out in paragraph 5 of IAS 40 it could be argued that an investment property can consist only of a building (or part of a building), a piece of land, or both and cannot include 'other assets'. However, such a reading of paragraph 5 of IAS 40 is inconsistent with paragraph 50 of IAS 40, which implies that a broader interpretation is more appropriate. Paragraphs 50(a) and (b) of IAS 40 read as follows:

'In determining the fair value of investment property, an entity does not double-count assets or liabilities that are recognised as separate assets or liabilities. For example:

(a) equipment such as lifts or air-conditioning is often an integral part of a building and is generally included in the fair value of the investment property, rather than recognised separately as property, plant and equipment.

(b) if an office is leased on a furnished basis, the fair value of the office generally includes the fair value of the furniture, because the rental income relates to the furnished office. When furniture is included in the fair value of investment property, an entity does not recognise that furniture as a separate asset.'[27]

Although paragraph 50 addresses the fair valuation of investment property, it nevertheless implies that other assets that are integral to the land and buildings should also be regarded as being part of the investment property.

Consequently, in our view, an item other than a piece of land or a building should be regarded by a lessor as being part of an investment property if this item is an integral part of it, that is, it is necessary for the land and buildings to be used by a lessee in the intended way and is leased to the lessee on the same basis (e.g. over the same the lease term) as the land and buildings. The determination as to whether or not an item constitutes an integral part of an investment property requires judgement and will depend on the particular facts and circumstances. However, it is our view that in order for all the assets to be classified as investment property, the following conditions should be present:

- the land and buildings should be the 'dominant assets' that form the investment property;
- the 'other assets' are leased to the lessee together with the land and building as a whole; and
- the entire group of assets is generating the income stream from the lease contract.

This means that, in the case of Lease 1, the investment property comprises the land, the vineyard infrastructure, the winery building structures and the winery plant and machinery. Vines, which meet the definition of biological assets, are subject to the requirements of IAS 41 – *Agriculture*. This is because 'biological assets related to agricultural activity' are outside the scope of IAS 40.[28]

In the case of Lease 2, the investment property comprises all of the assets – i.e. the land, the warehouses, the transport infrastructure, the wharves, the light towers, and the specialised container cranes.

2.3 Recognition

An investment property should be recognised as an asset when it is probable that the future economic benefits that are associated with the investment property will flow to the entity and its cost can be measured reliably.[29]

Like IAS 16, IAS 40 has a single set of recognition criteria for any costs incurred, whether initially or subsequently. This means that all investment property costs, whether on initial recognition or thereafter (for example, to add to or replace part of a property) must meet the recognition criteria at the point at which the expenditure is incurred if they are to be capitalised.[30]

The standard expands on this point. Day-to-day servicing, by which it means the repairs and maintenance of the property which largely comprises labour costs and minor parts, should be recognised in the income statement as incurred.[31] However, the treatment is different if larger parts of the building have been replaced – the standard cites the example of interior walls that are replacements of the original walls. In this case, the cost of replacing the part will be recognised, while the carrying amount of the original part is derecognised.[32] The inference is that by restoring the asset to its originally assessed standard of performance, the new part will meet the recognition criteria and future economic benefits will flow to the entity once the old part is replaced. The inference is also that replacement is needed for the total asset to be operative. This being the case, the new walls will therefore meet the recognition criteria and the cost will therefore be capitalised.

Other than interior walls (also quoted in IAS 16 as an example of an item that might require infrequent but recurring replacement), large parts that might have to be replaced include elements such as lifts, escalators, air conditioning equipment and the like.

IAS 40 does not explicitly require an analysis of investment properties into parts. However, this analysis is needed for the purposes of recognition and derecognition (see Chapter 13 at 2.6) of all expenditure after the asset has initially been recognised and (if the parts are significant) for depreciation of those parts. Some of this is not relevant to assets held under the fair value model that are not depreciated because the standard expects the necessary adjustments to the carrying value of the asset as a whole to be made via the fair value mechanism (see 3.2 and 5.1 below). However, entities that adopt the cost model are obliged to account for them after initial recognition in accordance with the requirements of IAS 16. The cost model is discussed further at 3.4 below.

2.4 Initial measurement

IAS 40 requires an investment property to be measured initially at cost, which includes transaction costs.[33] If a property is purchased, cost means purchase price and any directly attributable expenditure such as professional fees, property transfer taxes and other transaction costs.[34]

As noted in 2.2.5, self-constructed investment property during construction is currently subject to IAS 16. Once it is completed it becomes investment property to which IAS 40 applies.[35] This means that only those elements of cost that are allowed by IAS 16 may be capitalised and that capitalisation ceases when the asset has reached the condition necessary for it to be capable of operating in the manner intended by management (see also Chapter 13 at 2.3.1).[36] Abnormal wastage of resources in constructing an investment property is not part of its cost. IAS 40 also specifies that start up costs (unless necessary to bring the property into working condition) and operating losses before the investment property achieves the planned occupancy level, are not to be capitalised.[37] IAS 40 therefore prohibits the practice of capitalising costs until a particular level of occupation or rental income is achieved; this point normally would be reached considerably later than the date of physical completion – at which earlier time the asset would be *capable* of operating in the manner intended by management. This forestalls an argument, sometimes advanced in the past, that the asset being constructed was not simply the physical structure of the building but a fully tenanted investment property, and its cost correspondingly included not simply the construction period but also the letting period.

As noted at 2.2.5 above, the revaluation model in IAS 16 can be used for properties under development that were not previously investment properties. When completed, such properties should be reclassified as investment properties. IAS 40 requires an entity to treat any difference between the fair value at the date of completion and the previous carrying amount to be recognised in profit and loss.[38]

IAS 40 is silent in respect of the treatment of any accumulated revaluation surplus in equity in respect of such properties. In our view, it is appropriate, in order to be consistent with the treatment of revaluation surpluses under IAS 16 (see Chapter 13 at 2.4.1 A), for any surplus to be transferred directly to retained earnings (not through the income statement) upon reclassification. Hammerson PLC has described this approach in their accounting policies, as follows:

Extract 14.5: Hammerson PLC (2006)

Development properties [extract]

When development properties are completed, they are reclassified as investment properties and any accumulated revaluation surplus or deficit is transferred to retained earnings.

Finally, if payment for the property is deferred, the cost to be recognised is the cash price equivalent. Any difference between the cash price and the total payment to be made is recognised as interest over the credit period.[39]

2.5 Initial measurement of property held under finance or operating leases

The same accounting is applied both to property acquired under finance leases and to operating leases where the property interests otherwise meet the definition as investment properties and have been classified as such. This means that a property interest that is held by a lessee under an operating lease and classified as an investment property must be accounted for as if it were a finance lease.

At the commencement of the lease term, the entity recognises the property asset and related liability in its balance sheet in accordance with IAS 17, at amounts equal at the inception of the lease to the fair value of the leased item or, if lower, at the present value of the minimum lease payments (see Chapter 25).[40] If the interest is held under an operating lease, then it must be recorded at the present value of the minimum lease payments. The entity's initial direct costs are added to the asset[41] – these might include similar costs to those described in 2.4 above such as professional fees for legal services.

If the entity pays a premium for the lease, this is part of the minimum lease payments and is included in the cost of the asset; however, it does, of course, reduce the amount of the liability.[42]

The standard emphasises that the property interest, the fair value of which is to be determined, is the leasehold interest and not the underlying property. Guidance on fair values of property interests, which is also relevant for fair values used for initial recognition under the cost model, is described at 3.2 below.

2.6 Initial measurement of assets acquired in exchange transactions

The requirements of IAS 40 for investment properties acquired in exchange for non-monetary assets, or a combination or monetary and non-monetary assets, are the same as those of IAS 16.[43] These provisions are discussed in detail in Chapter 13 at 2.3.3.

3 MEASUREMENT AFTER INITIAL RECOGNITION

Once recognised, IAS 40 allows entities to choose between one of two methods of accounting for investment property: the 'fair value model' or the 'cost model'. The standard does not identify a preferred alternative. There is, however, one exception to the choice of measurement: a property interest that is held by a lessee under an operating lease may be classified as an investment property – provided that the fair value model is applied for the asset recognised and, therefore, for all investment properties.

An entity has to choose one model or the other, and apply it to all its investment property (unless the entity is an insurer or similar, in which case there are exemptions that are described briefly below at 3.1).[44] The standard discourages changes from the fair value model to the cost model, stating that it is highly unlikely that this will result in a more appropriate presentation, which is a requirement of IAS 8 for any change in accounting policy.[45]

All entities, regardless of which measurement option is chosen, are required to determine the fair value of their investment properties, because even those entities that use the cost model are required to disclose the fair value. Use of an independent valuer with a recognised qualification and recent experience is encouraged, but not required.[46]

3.1 Measurement by insurers and similar entities

The only exception to the requirement that an entity must apply either the fair value or the cost model to all its investment properties, is in respect of insurance companies and other entities that hold investment properties whose return is directly linked to the return paid on specific liabilities. These entities are permitted to choose either the fair value or the cost model for such properties without it affecting the choice available for any other investment properties that they may hold. However, all properties within a given fund must be held on the same basis and transfers between funds are to be made at fair value.[47]

3.2 The fair value model

Under this model all investment property is included in the balance sheet at its fair value at the balance sheet date, and all changes in the fair value from one balance sheet to the next are included in the income statement for the period.[48] However, as stated above, an entity must use the fair value model if it wishes to classify interests held under operating leases as investment properties.[49]

The standard defines fair value as 'the amount for which an asset could be exchanged between knowledgeable, willing parties in an arm's length transaction'.[50] Fair value specifically excludes an estimated price inflated or deflated by special terms or circumstances such as atypical financing, sale and leaseback arrangements that are not at market rates or special considerations or concessions granted by anyone associated with the sale.[51] Transaction costs which may be incurred by the vendor on sale are not deducted.[52]

A Transaction costs incurred by the purchaser

An issue that arises in practice is whether transaction costs that have been incurred by the purchaser of an investment property be taken into account in determining the subsequent fair value of the property when applying the fair value model. This is illustrated in the following example:

Example 14.2: The fair value model and transaction costs incurred at acquisition

On 1 January 2007 Entity A acquired an investment property for a purchase price of €10,000. In addition, A incurred legal costs of €200 in connection with the purchase and paid property transfer tax of €400. Accordingly, the investment property was initially recorded at €10,600. Company A applies the fair value model for subsequent measurement of investment property. At the next reporting date the following different scenarios are considered:

	Development of prices in property market	Appraised market value of property €	Cost of property initially recognised €	Difference €
Scenario 1	unchanged	10,000	10,600	(600)
Scenario 2	slightly increased	10,250	10,600	(350)
Scenario 3	significantly increased	11,000	10,600	400
Scenario 4	decreased	9,500	10,600	(1,100)

The issue that arises in practice is whether or not the purchase transaction costs that were incurred by Company A on 1 January 2007 can be considered in determining the fair value of the investment property at the next reporting date.

In our view, the purchase transaction costs incurred by Company A may not be considered separately in determining the fair value of an investment property. In the example above, on the next reporting date the carrying value to be recorded in the balance sheet is its fair value, which is the appraised market value at the reporting date. Changes from the initial carrying amount to the appraised market value at the sequent reporting date (reflected in the 'Difference' column in the table) are recognised in the income statement.

Although paragraph 21 of IAS 40 states that transaction costs incurred by a purchaser on the acquisition of an investment property are included in the cost of the investment property at initial recognition, if an entity applies the fair value model, the same investment property that was recorded at cost on initial recognition is subsequently measured at fair value. The fact that the cost of the investment property recorded on initial recognition included legal and other transaction costs is irrelevant to the subsequent fair valuation of the asset.

Professional valuers of investment property generally determine the *market value* of an investment property in an appraisal. International Valuation Standards state: '*The expression Market Value and the term Fair Value as it commonly appears in accounting standards are generally compatible, if not in every instance exactly equivalent concepts. Fair Value, an accounting concept, is defined in IFRS and other accounting standards as the amount for which an asset could be exchanged, or a liability settled, between knowledgeable, willing parties in an arm's-length transaction. Fair Value is generally used for both Market and Non-Market Values in financial statements. Where the Market Value of an asset can be established, this value will equate to Fair Value.*'[53]

Consequently, when the market value has been established for an investment property it is not, in our view, appropriate to add to this market value the transaction costs incurred by the purchaser, as these have no relevance to the market value of the property.

B Determining fair value

Paragraphs 38 to 52 of IAS 40 contain a substantial amount of guidance on the methodology of valuations in practice, necessitated by the number of jurisdictions to which the standard may apply. Fair value reflects market conditions as at the balance sheet date and is a valuation as at a specific moment in time. It assumes simultaneous exchange and completion, to avoid the variations in price that might otherwise take place.[54] The fair value of the property is driven, at least in part, by the rental income from tenants and, if appropriate, outflows such as rental payments. It is further assumed that the valuation is based on assumptions that would be considered to be reasonable and supportable by willing and knowledgeable parties.[55] For example, the buyer and seller must be 'knowledgeable', which means that they are reasonably informed about the property and the market at the date of the transaction; neither is under any compulsion to buy or sell; the buyer will not pay more than a knowledgeable, willing buyer; and the seller is not a forced seller.[56] The transaction is presumed to be at arm's length between unrelated parties.[57]

The standard states that the best evidence of fair value will be given by actual transactions in similar property in a similar location and condition.[58] However, it allows the fair value to be estimated by using other information when market values are not available. This means that gains and losses may be recorded in the income statement where there is no market value for the property and its fair value has been constructed from a variety of other sources.

The other information that an entity may draw on includes:

(a) transactions in an active market for dissimilar property (e.g. property of a different nature, condition or location, or subject to a different type of lease), as adjusted to reflect the differences;

(b) transactions in less active markets if they have been adjusted to take account of subsequent changes in economic conditions; or

(c) discounted cash flow projections based on estimated future cash flows (as long as these are reliable). These should be supported by existing leases and current market rents for similar properties in the same location and condition. The discount rate should reflect current market assessments of the uncertainty and timing of the cash flows.[59]

The technique suggested in (c) above is not dissimilar to a valuation using property yields (a basis on which properties commonly are bought and sold) except that yields already assume rental growth that would have to be separately factored into a discounted cash flow calculation. Future capital expenditure that will enhance the benefits may not be taken into account in determining the fair value, nor may the income that might arise from this expenditure.[60]

The standard notes that the fair value of a leased asset at acquisition is zero ('acquisition' means the commencement of the lease as defined by IAS 17, which is before any lease payments are due or any other accounting entries are required to be made, see Chapter 25). This applies regardless of whether the asset is brought in at fair value (as is usually the case with a finance lease) or at the present value of the minimum lease payments (for an interest under an operating lease). Consequently, re-measuring an interest in a lease to fair value will only give rise to a gain or loss if the fair value model is applied, and only upon subsequent remeasurement after initial measurement.[61]

As these various bases may result in a range of valuations, the entity must consider the underlying reasons for the variation in order to determine the most reliable estimate, within a range of 'reasonable' estimates of fair value.[62] The fair value will not be determinable reliably on a continuing basis if the range is too wide and the probabilities of various outcomes are too difficult to assess.[63]

Fair value is based on a hypothetical transaction. It is not the same as value in use as defined in IAS 36 – *Impairment of Assets*. In particular, it does not take account of additional value derived from holding a portfolio of assets, synergies between the investment properties and other assets or legal rights or tax benefits or burdens pertaining to the current owner.[64] Fair value is also not the same as net realisable value. It is a valuation as at a specific point in time rather than at a time at which the entity may realistically have expected to sell the property. It assumes circumstances that rarely apply in practice such as simultaneous exchange (i.e. contractual commitment) and completion.[65]

Finally, an entity must also take care not to double-count assets and liabilities, and paragraph 50 of the standard describes a number of specific situations where this might otherwise happen. These are discussed in sections 3.2.1 to 3.2.3 below.

C The fair value discussion paper

The IASB has conceded that a lack of codified and consistent guidance across IFRS has contributed to inconsistency in measuring fair value. In consequence a Fair Value Measurements project was added to the Board's agenda in order to develop a single standard that provides guidance to entities on measuring the fair value of assets and liabilities when required by IFRS.

However, the IASB, noting that the Financial Accounting Standards Board (FASB) was nearing completion of its fair value measurements project, decided to issue the FASB's final fair value measurement standard as an IASB Exposure Draft. The FASB Statement of Financial Accounting Standard No. 157 – *Fair value measurements* – was subsequently published in September 2006 and was issued by the IASB, actually in the form of a Discussion Paper, in the fourth quarter of 2006.

FASB Statement of Financial Accounting Standard No. 157 and the IASB Discussion Paper are discussed further in Chapter 2 at 6.2 and 6.3.

3.2.1 Assets and liabilities subsumed within fair value

Fixtures and fittings such as lifts or air conditioning units are usually reflected within the fair value of the investment property rather than being accounted for separately.[66] In other cases, additional assets may be necessary in order that the property can be used for its specific purposes. The standard refers to furniture within a property that is being let as furnished offices, and argues that this should not be recognised as a separate asset if it has been included in the fair value of the investment property.[67]

The entity may have other assets that have not been included within the valuation, in which case these will be recognised separately and accounted for in accordance with IAS 16.

3.2.2 Prepaid or accrued operating lease income

The requirement in IAS 40 not to double-count assets or liabilities recognised separately, is usually interpreted as a requirement to reduce the carrying value of an investment property below its fair value to the extent that an asset arises under SIC-15 – *Operating Leases – Incentives*. For example, when an entity offers an initial rent-free period to a lessee, it will build up an asset over the rent free period and amortise it over the remaining lease term, thereby spreading the reduction in rental income over the duration of the lease. This procedure is further described in Chapter 25.

One entity following this interpretation, The British Land Company PLC, explains the treatment in its accounting policies as shown below.

Extract 14.6: The British Land Company PLC (2007)

Net rental income [extract]

Rental income from fixed and minimum guaranteed rent reviews is recognised on a straight-line basis over the shorter of the entire lease term or the period to the first break option. Where such rental income is recognised ahead of the related cash flow, an adjustment is made to ensure the carrying value of the related property including the accrued rent does not exceed the external valuation.

This treatment can also be seen in Extracts 14.7 and 14.8 below.

3.2.3 The fair value of properties held under a lease

The standard points out that the fair value of a lease interest takes account of all rental payments, including contingent rents, that an entity is expected to make. Therefore, if the entity obtains a property valuation net of the valuer's estimate of the present value of future lease obligations, which is usual practice, to the extent that the lease obligations have already been accounted for as a finance lease obligation an amount is to be added back to arrive at the fair value of the investment property for the purposes of the financial statements.

A Methods currently available

We consider that, at present (see B below), this can be achieved in two ways:

- adjusting for the valuer's assessment of the present value of the lease obligations (Method 1); or
- adjusting for the finance lease obligation recognised in the financial statements (Method 2).

This is illustrated using the information in the following example:

Example 14.3: Valuation of a property held under a finance lease

Company A pays €991,000 for a 50 year leasehold interest in a property which is classified as an investment property using the fair value model. In addition a ground rent of €10,000 is payable annually during the lease term, the present value of which is calculated at €99,000 using a discount rate of 10% which reflects the market required yield at that time. The company has initially recognised the investment property at the following amount:

	€'000
Amount paid	991
Present value of the ground rent obligation on acquisition	99
Cost recorded	1,090

At the next reporting date the leasehold interest in the property has been assessed to have a fair value of €1,006,000 calculated as follows:

	€'000
Present value of estimated future lease income	1,089
Less: Present value of the ground rent obligation at the reporting date *	(83)
Assessed fair value	1,006

* at the next reporting date the market required yield has increased to 12%. Therefore the present value of the ground rent obligations of €10,000 per annum for the remaining 49 years is now

€83,000. At the same time the ground rent finance lease liability has reduced to €98,000 as payments are made.

The two methods referred to above would give the following results:

		Method 1	Method 2
		€'000	€'000
Assessed fair value		1,006	1,006
Add:	- assessed present value of the ground rent obligation at the reporting date; or	83	–
	- recognised finance lease liability	–	98
		1,089	1,104

Which ever method is used, it should be consistently applied.

Method 1: Adjusting by the valuer's assessment of the present value of the lease obligations

Using this approach the property asset is recorded at a fair value €1,089,000 as the valuer's assessment of the present value of the remaining lease obligations of €83,000 is added back (the cash flows this represents have already been taken into account as a finance lease liability). As the lease liability is recorded at €98,000 the net carrying amount of the two related balances is €991,000 (€1,089,000 minus €98,000).

If this approach is taken, the effect of IAS 40 is that, because the finance lease liability is not reassessed as market rates of return change, the net carrying values of investment property assets and related finance lease obligations (in the above example €991,000) may differ from the assessed fair value of the investment property (in the above example €1,006,000). However, in the event that the net of the carrying value of the investment property and related finance lease liability exceed the appraised market value, consideration should be given as to whether the carrying value of the investment property should be reduced by that excess.

Occasionally a ground rent or head lease payment has a fixed amount but also a contingent element – for example based on the turnover of the business using the property. In these situations, when assessing the fair value of such a property, a valuer would typically estimate the likely future amounts of such contingent lease payments. As contingent lease payments are not included in the minimum lease payments when the finance lease obligation is calculated, the valuer's estimate of the contingent element of future head lease or ground rent payments should not be added back to obtain the carrying value of an investment property for financial reporting purposes.

Method 2: Adjusting by the finance lease obligation recognised in the financial statements

Here, the property asset would be recorded at fair value of €1,104,000 as the recognised finance lease liability is added back.

If this approach is taken, the effect of IAS 40 is that the aggregate carrying value of investment property net of the related finance lease liability is the same as assessed fair value of the investment property.

Examples of this method can be seen in the Extracts below:

Extract 14.7: Liberty International PLC (2005)

10 Investment and development properties [extract]

The group's interests in investment and development properties were valued as at 31 December 2005 by external valuers in accordance with the Appraisal and Valuation Manual of RICS, on the basis of Market Value. Market Value represents the figure that would appear in a hypothetical contract of sale between a willing buyer and a willing seller.

In the UK, properties were valued by either DTZ Debenham Tie Leung, Chartered Surveyors, Knight Frank LLP, CB Richard Ellis or Matthews & Goodman LLP. In the United States, properties were valued by Cushman and Wakefield California, Inc.

A reconciliation of investment and development property valuations to the balance sheet carrying value of property is shown below:

	2005 £m	2004 £m
Investment and development property at market value as determined by external valuers	**6,936.3**	5,309.7
Add minimum payment under head leases separately included as a creditor in the balance sheet	**53.9**	31.9
Less accrued incentives separately included as a debtor in the balance sheet	**(52.4)**	(44.0)
Balance sheet carrying value of investment and development property	**6,937.8**	5,297.6

Extract 14.8: Land Securities Group PLC (2007)

Notes to the Financial Statements [extract]

13. Non-current assets [extract]

The following table reconciles the net book value of the investment properties (excluding those within Land Securities Trillium) to the market value. The components of the reconciliation are included within their relevant balance sheet headings.

	Property investment		
	Portfolio management £m	Development programme £m	Total investment properties £m
Net book value at 31 March 2006	10,211.2	1,229.3	11,440.5
Plus: amount included in prepayments in respect of lease incentives	76.8	4.6	81.4
Less: head leases capitalised (note 28)	(66.1)	(8.5)	(74.6)
Plus: properties treated as finance leases	171.7	–	171.7
Market value at 31 March 2006			
– Group	10,393.6	1,225.4	11,619.0
– Plus: share of joint ventures (note 17)			1,273.9
Market value at 31 March 2006			
– Group and share of joint ventures			12,892.9
Net book value at 31 March 2007	10,607.4	2,284.3	12,891.7
Plus: amount included in prepayments in respect of lease incentives	93.6	37.4	131.0
Less: head leases capitalised (note 28)	(61.6)	(9.4)	(71.0)
Plus: properties treated as finance leases	163.1	–	163.1
Market value at 31 March 2007			
– Group	10,802.5	2,312.3	13,114.8
– Plus: share of joint ventures (note 17)			1,637.7
Market value at 31 March 2007			
– Group and share of joint ventures			14,752.5

B Future changes

As part of the IASB annual improvement process, paragraph 50(d) of IAS 40 is proposed to be amended to say 'if a valuation obtained for a property is net of all payments expected to be made, it will be necessary to add back any recognised lease liability, to arrive at the carrying amount of the investment property using the fair value model'. If the standard is amended as proposed, Method 1 as described above would no longer be available.

3.3 Inability to determine fair value

It is a rebuttable presumption that an entity can determine the fair value of a property reliably on a continuing basis, that is, on each subsequent occasion in which it records the investment property in its financial statements. The standard stresses that it is only in exceptional cases that the entity will be able to conclude, when it first recognises a particular investment property, that it will not be able to determine its fair value in the future. Additionally, entities are strongly discouraged from arguing that fair value cannot be reliably measured. It would only be an acceptable argument if there were infrequent market transactions and, either that the entity was unable to construct a fair value using the alternative measures allowed by the standard, or that the range of fair value estimates was too great to establish a reliable value. In such cases, the property should be treated under the cost model of IAS 16 and assumed to have a nil residual value.[68] This means that it has to be carried at cost and the building and its component parts depreciated over their useful lives. In these circumstances IAS 16's revaluation model, under which assets may be revalued to fair value, is specifically ruled out. If this situation occurs, the cost model of IAS 16 should continue to be applied until disposal. Even if an entity is 'compelled' to carry an individual property at cost, all other investment property must continue to be carried at fair value.[69]

In addition, once a property is initially recognised at its fair value, it must always be so recognised until disposed of or reclassified for owner-occupation or development, even if comparable market transactions become less frequent or market prices become less easily available.[70] This is to prevent a switch to the cost model if there were a property price collapse when there would be few transactions and the fair value could become uncomfortably low or volatile.

3.4 The cost model

The cost model requires that all investment property be measured after initial recognition under the cost model treatment of IAS 16. This means that the asset must be recognised at cost and depreciated systematically over its useful life.[71] The residual value and useful life of each investment property must be reviewed at least at each financial year-end and, if expectations differ from previous estimates, the changes must be accounted for as a change in accounting estimate in accordance with IAS 8.[72] The property has to be analysed into appropriate significant parts, each of which will have to be depreciated separately (see also Chapter 13 at 2.4.2).

The analysis into significant parts is not a straightforward exercise since properties typically contain a large number of components with varying useful lives. Klépierre disclose their approach to this exercise below:

Extract 14.9: Klépierre (2006)

Financial Statements [extract]

Components method [extract]

The application of the components method is based on the recommendations issued by the *Fédération des Sociétés Immobiliéres et Foncières* regarding components and useful lives:

– concerning buildings developed by the companies themselves, precise analysis of assets by component type and posting at realization cost;

– concerning buildings held in portfolio, sometimes for a long time, components identification was based on four property asset types: business premises, shopping centers, offices and residential property.

Four components were identified for each of these asset types in addition to the land:

- o Structure
- o Facades, waterproofing and roofing;
- o General and technical installations(IGT);
- o Fittings

The components are broken down by history and the technical aspects specific to each building.

For the first-time adoption of the components method, the historic cost of buildings has been reconstituted according to the percentages allocated to each component using the reappraisal values retained as the presumed cost at January 1, 2003.

	Office buildings		Shopping centers	
	Period	**Portion**	**Period**	**Portion**
Structure	60 years	60%	35 to 50 years	50%
Facades	30 years	15%	25 years	15%
IGT	20 years	15%	20 years	25%
Fittings	12 years	10%	10 to 15 years	10%

The components matrix is a new "matrix". As a result, Klépierre determined the portions at January 1, 2003 of the components of "Fittings", "Technical installations" and "Cladding" according to the periods outlined in the matrix applied from the construction date or the last major renovation for fixed assets. The portion of structure component is deducted from the portion of other components and is amortized over the residual period as fixed in 2003 by the appraisers.

Acquisition costs are allocated between land and construction. The portion assigned to construction is amortized over the amortization period of the structure.

The residual value is equal to the current estimate of the amount which the company would obtain if the asset were already old and in the condition at the end of it useful life, after deducting disposal costs. Given the selected useful lives, the residual value of the components is nil.

The entity is also be required to recognise replacement parts and derecognise the replaced part as described in Chapter 13 at 2.6. The revaluation model of IAS 16 is not available for investment property.

IVG Immobilien AG adopted the cost model and made the following statement in their 2005 financial statements:

Extract 14.10: IVG Immobilien AG (2005)

5.2 Investment properties [extract]

Investment properties are carried at depreciated cost (see 5.1) in accordance with IAS 40.56 and not at market value. As industry standards with regard to choice of accounting policy for investment property are still evolving, IVG opted to apply the cost model in its consolidated financial statements from 2004. This has the advantage that it is possible to change to the fair value model should this be adopted as best practice by the capital markets. A switch in the other direction from the fair value model to the cost model is not permitted.

However, this policy choice will apparently be short lived as can be seen from the following statement in their 2006 financial statements:

Extract 14.11: IVG Immobilien AG (2006)

5. Accounting principles [extract]

2006 is the last year in which investment properties will be carried at depreciated cost (see 5.1) and depreciated on a flat-line basis according to IAS 40.56. The fair value of investment properties is given separately in the notes. It is calculated using internationally recognized valuation methods (for details see section 7.2).

As the fair value method is now accepted by the capital markets as best practice for measuring investment properties, IVG will switch to the fair value method in 2007. In the future this will mean that fluctuations in the market value of these properties will be recognized in income.

If an entity adopts the cost model, the fair value of its investment property has to be disclosed (see 6.4 below). Entities may have limited internal resources and consequently may need to obtain professional assistance in order to meet the disclosure requirements. In the past, such entities may have chosen the cost model in part to avoid the cost of an annual valuation. This benefit of using the cost model may no longer be so evident. Under the cost model, investment properties that meet the criteria to be classified as held for sale, or that are included within a disposal group classified as held for sale, are measured in accordance with IFRS 5 – *Non-current Assets Held for Sale and Discontinued Operations*.[73] This means that they will be held at the lower of carrying amount and fair value less costs to sell, and so depreciation of the asset will cease. This topic is fully discussed in Chapter 4.

3.5 IFRS 5 and investment properties measured at fair value

As set out in Chapter 4 at 2.2.1, investment property measured at fair value is not subject to the measurement requirements of IFRS 5. However, such property is subject to the presentation requirement of that standard. Consequently investment property that meets the definition of held for sale is required to be presented separately from other assets in the balance sheet. This does not mean that such property should be presented within current assets.

An example of an entity applying the presentation requirements of IFRS 5 to investment property measured at fair value is Development Securities plc.

Extract 14.12: Development Securities PLC (2006)

Financial Statements [extract]
Consolidated balance sheet [extract]
As at 31 December 2006

	Notes	£'000	2006 £'000	£'000	2005 restated* £'000
Non-current assets					
Property, plant and equipment					
– Operating properties	10	**8,090**		9,000	
– Other property, plant and equipment	10	**3,618**		3,776	
Investment properties	11	**139,461**		159,568	
Financial assets	12	**5,881**		755	
Investments in joint ventures	12	**20,464**		–	
Investment in associates	12	**673**		1,165	
Trade and other receivables	14	**1,468**		1,420	
Deferred tax assets	17	**5,619**		4,387	
			185,274		180,071
Investment property – held for sale	11		**5,299**		–
Current assets					
Inventory – developments and trading properties	13	**74,663**		56,479	
Trade and other receivables	14	**10,014**		9,677	
Cash and short-term deposits		**88,536**		73,094	
			173,213		139,250
Total assets			**363,786**		319,321

Investment properties measured using the cost method are subject to both the measurement and presentation requirements of IFRS 5.

4 TRANSFER OF ASSETS INTO OR FROM INVESTMENT PROPERTY

The standard specifies the circumstances in which a property becomes, or ceases to be, an investment property. There must be a change in use, evidenced by:

(a) the commencement or end of owner-occupation;

(b) the commencement of development with a view to sale, at which point an investment property would be transferred to inventory. The standard allows a transfer to inventory only when there is a change of use evidenced by the start of a development with a view to subsequent sale (see Extract 14.13 below);

(c) entering into an operating lease to another party which would generally require a transfer from inventory to investment property (but see 2.2.2 above); or

(d) the end of construction or development, when a property in the course of construction or development is transferred to investment property. IAS 16 currently (see 2.2.5) covers properties in the course of construction.[74]

Extract 14.13: Land Securities Group PLC (2006)

2. Significant accounting policies [extract]

(d) Investment properties

When the Group begins to redevelop an existing investment property with a view to sale, the property is transferred to trading properties and held as a current asset. The property is re-measured to fair value as at the date of the transfer with any gain or loss being taken to profit or loss. The re-measured amount becomes the deemed cost at which the property is then carried in trading properties.

However, some changes in status do not result in transfers:

(a) If an entity decides to dispose of an investment property without development with a view to sale, it may not be transferred to inventory;

(b) An existing investment property that is being redeveloped for continued future use as an investment property by the entity must remain classified as an investment property and is not reclassified as owner-occupied property during the redevelopment.[75]

Transfers to and from the status of investment property under the fair value model are accounted for as follows:

- *Transfers to inventory or owner-occupation*: the cost for subsequent accounting under IAS 16 or IAS 2 should be its fair value at the date the use changed.[76]
- *Transfers from owner-occupation*: IAS 16 will be applied up to the time that the use changed. At that date any difference between the IAS 16 carrying amount and the fair value is to be treated in the same way as a revaluation under IAS 16.[77]

Up until the time that an owner occupied property becomes an investment property carried at fair value, depreciation under IAS 16 continues and any impairment losses up to the date of change of use must be recognised in accordance with IAS 36. The difference between the carrying value under IAS 16 and the fair value under IAS 40 is accounted for in the same way as a revaluation under IAS 16. If the owner occupied property had not previously been revalued, the transfer does not imply that the entity has now chosen a policy of revaluation for other property accounted for under IAS 16 in the same class. The treatment depends on whether it is a decrease or increase in value and whether the asset had previously been revalued or impaired in value (as described at 2.4). Paragraph 62 of the standard sets out the treatment as follows:[78]

'Up to the date when an owner-occupied property becomes an investment property carried at fair value, an entity depreciates the property and recognises any impairment losses that have occurred. The entity treats any difference at that date between the carrying amount of the property in accordance with IAS 16 and its fair value in the same way as a revaluation in accordance with IAS 16. In other words:

(a) any resulting decrease in the carrying amount of the property is recognised in profit or loss. However, to the extent that an amount is included in revaluation surplus for that property, the decrease is charged against that revaluation surplus.

(b) any resulting increase in the carrying amount is treated as follows:

  (i) to the extent that the increase reverses a previous impairment loss for that property, the increase is recognised in profit or loss. The amount recognised in profit or loss does not exceed the amount needed to restore the carrying amount to the carrying amount that would have been determined (net of depreciation) had no impairment loss been recognised.

  (ii) any remaining part of the increase is credited directly to equity in revaluation surplus. On subsequent disposal of the investment property, the revaluation surplus included in equity may be transferred to retained earnings. The transfer from revaluation surplus to retained earnings is not made through profit or loss.'

When the business uses the cost model for investment property, transfers between investment property, inventory and owner occupation do not change the carrying amount of the property transferred.[79]

4.1 Transfers of investment property held under operating leases

An entity applying the fair value model is allowed to classify interests held under operating leases as investment properties in the same manner as if they were held under finance leases. In these circumstances, neither IAS 17 nor IAS 40 requires the entity to separate the land value from the value of the buildings. IAS 17 allows this treatment to continue even if the property interest ceases to be classified as an investment property by the lessee and gives two examples:

- the lessee occupies the property, in which case it is transferred to owner-occupied property at fair value at the date of change of use; or
- the lessee grants a sublease over substantially all of its property interest to an unrelated third party. It will treat the sublease as a finance lease to the third party even though the interest may well be accounted for as an operating lease by that party.[80]

Therefore, on transfer the treatment of interests held under operating leases mirrors that of other ownership interests.

5 DISPOSAL OF INVESTMENT PROPERTY

IAS 40 requires that an investment property should be removed from the balance sheet ('derecognised') on disposal or when it is permanently withdrawn from use and no further economic benefits are expected from its disposal.[81]

A disposal of an investment property is achieved upon a sale or:

- when it becomes the subject of a finance lease (the owner becoming the lessor); or
- when it becomes the subject of a sale and leaseback deal (the original owner becoming the lessee); [82]

IAS 17 applies if a property is disposed of by the owner becoming a finance lessor, or if a property is the subject of a sale and leaseback transaction.[83]

These derecognition rules also apply to a part of the investment property that has been replaced, as discussed below.

IAS 18 – *Revenue* – applies on a sale.[84] IAS 18 allows that while revenue would normally be recognised when legal title passes, in some jurisdictions the risks and rewards of ownership may pass to the buyer before legal title has passed. In such cases, provided that the seller has no further substantial acts to complete under the contract, it may be appropriate to recognise revenue. Brixton plc has taken this approach.

Extract 14.14: Brixton plc (2006)

1 Statement of significant accounting policies [extract]

n Revenue recognition

A property is regarded as sold when the significant risks and returns have been transferred to the buyer, which is normally on unconditional exchange of contracts. For conditional exchanges, sales are recognised as the conditions are satisfied.

An example given in IAS 18 of such a 'substantial act' is the completion of construction.[85] Another example of a 'substantial act' that has to be completed before a sale can be recognised is if formal shareholder approval is required before a property can be sold.

Gains and losses are calculated based on the difference between the net disposal proceeds and the carrying amount of the asset. This is recognised in the income statement unless it is a sale and leaseback and IAS 17 requires a different treatment.[86] IAS 17 allows only the immediate recognition of profits and losses on a sale and operating leaseback if the transaction is established at fair value; no gains would be recognised if the transaction resulted in a finance leaseback. Refer to Chapter 25 for a discussion of sale and leaseback under IAS 17.

The proceeds of sale are recognised at their fair value. If the sale proceeds are deferred (deferral is not defined but it must mean beyond normal credit terms) the consideration recognised on the disposal will be the cash price equivalent. Any difference between the total payments received and the cash equivalent will be treated as interest receivable under IAS 18 using the effective interest method.[87]

If an entity retains any liabilities after disposing of an investment property these are measured and accounted for in accordance with IAS 37 – *Provisions, Contingent Liabilities and Contingent Assets* – or other relevant standards.[88]

Finally, it is also of note that, in their July 2006 meeting[89] the IFRIC decided to take onto its agenda a project to clarify the requirements of IAS 18 for real estate sales in which an agreement for sale is reached before the construction of property is complete. The project was triggered by the guidance set out in section 9 of the Appendix to IAS 18, which the IFRIC believed to be contradictory with the other requirements of IAS 18.

Consequently, in its May 2007 meeting, the IFRIC announced its intention to provide guidance on determining whether such a sale agreement is:

- a construction contract within the scope of IAS 11 Construction Contracts, or
- an agreement for the sale of goods within the scope of IAS 18 Revenue.

The draft Interpretation (IFRIC D21), issued in July 2007, therefore proposes that IAS 11 is applicable only if the sale agreement is a contract to provide construction services to the buyers' specifications, as opposed to selling completed buildings or units thereof. D21 lists features of a contract that indicate the seller is providing construction services to the buyers' specifications. The proposed Interpretation may require developers that are currently applying IAS 11 to apply IAS 18 instead, with a consequent deferral in the recognition of revenue.

Property that is subject to sale prior to completion of construction, if not previously classified as investment property, is likely to be property intended for sale in the ordinary course of business (see 2.2.3 above) and is therefore not investment property. This issue is discussed in more detail in Chapter 28 at 7.17.

5.1 Replacement of parts of investment property

When an entity that applies the fair value model wishes to capitalise a replacement part, the question arises of how to deal with the cost of the new part and the carrying value of the original. The basic principle in IAS 40 is that the entity derecognises the carrying value of the replaced part. However the problem arises that even if the cost of the old part may be known, its carrying value – at fair value – is usually by no means clear. It is possible also that the fair value may already reflect the loss in value of the part to be replaced, because the valuation reflected the fact that an acquirer would reduce the price accordingly.

As all fair value changes are taken to the income statement, the standard concludes that it is not necessary to identify separately the elements that relate to replacements from other fair value movements. Therefore, if it is not practical to identify the amount by which fair value should be reduced for the part replaced, the cost of the replacement is added to the carrying amount of the asset and the fair value of the investment property as a whole is reassessed. The standard notes that this is the treatment that would be applied to additions that did not involve replacing any existing part of the property.

If the investment property is carried under the cost model, then the entity should derecognise the carrying amount of the original part. A replaced part may not have been depreciated separately, in which case the standard allows the entity to use the cost of the replacement as an indication of an appropriate carrying value.[90] This does not mean that the entity has to apply depreciated replacement cost, rather that it can use the cost of the replacement as an indication of the original cost of the replaced part in order to reconstruct a suitable net present value for the replaced part.

5.2 Compensation from third parties

IAS 40 applies the same rules as IAS 16 to the treatment of compensation from third parties if property has been impaired, lost or given up. It stresses that impairments or losses of investment property, related claims for or payments of compensation from third parties and any subsequent purchase or construction of replacement parts are separate economic events that have to be accounted for separately.

Impairment of investment property will be recorded automatically if the fair value model is used; but if the property is accounted for using the cost model, it is to be calculated in accordance with IAS 36. If the entity no longer owns the asset, for example because it has been destroyed or subject to a compulsory purchase order, it will be derecognised as described in 5 above. Compensation (for example from an insurance company) is recognised in income when it is receivable. The cost of any replacement asset is accounted for wholly on its own merits according to the recognition rules covered in 2.3 above.[91]

6 THE DISCLOSURE REQUIREMENTS OF IAS 40

6.1 Introduction

For businesses that adopt the fair value option in IAS 40, attention will focus on the judgmental and subjective aspects of property valuations, because they will be reported in the income statement. If a counter-intuitive failure were to occur (for instance a company that had reported large profits soon afterwards ran out of cash) this type of income statement could be discredited. Possibly as a consequence of these considerations, IAS 40 requires significant amounts of information to be disclosed about the judgements involved and the cash-related performance of the investment property, as set out below.

6.2 Disclosures under both fair value and cost models

Whichever model is chosen, fair value or cost, IAS 40 requires all companies to disclose the fair value of their investment property. Therefore the following disclosures are required in both instances:

(a) whether it applies the cost model or the fair value model;

(b) if it applies the fair value model, whether, and in what circumstances, property interests held under operating leases are classified and accounted for as investment property;

(c) when classification is difficult (see 2.2 above), the criteria it uses to distinguish investment property from owner occupied property and from property held for sale in the ordinary course of business;

(d) the methods and significant assumptions applied in determining the fair value of investment property, including a statement whether the determination of fair value was supported by market evidence or was more heavily based on other factors (which the entity shall disclose) because of the nature of the property and lack of comparable market data;

(e) the extent to which the fair value of investment property (as measured or disclosed in the financial statements) is based on a valuation by an independent valuer who holds a recognised and relevant professional qualification and has recent experience in the location and category of the investment property being valued. If there has been no such valuation, that fact shall be disclosed;

(f) the amounts recognised in profit or loss for:

   (i) rental income from investment property;

   (ii) direct operating expenses (including repairs and maintenance) arising from investment property that generated rental income during the period; and

   (iii) direct operating expenses (including repairs and maintenance) arising from investment property that did not generate rental income during the period;

   (iv) the cumulative change in fair value recognised in profit or loss on sale of an investment property from a pool of assets in which the cost model is used into a pool in which the fair value model is used (see 3.4 above).

(g) the existence and amounts of restrictions on the realisability of investment property or the remittance of income and proceeds of disposal;

(h) contractual obligations to purchase, construct or develop investment property or for repairs, maintenance or enhancements.[92]

Describing the methods and significant assumptions applied in determining the fair value adequately can result in some lengthy disclosures, as shown in the Extract from Castellum AS below.

Extract 14.15: Castellum AS (2006)

Note 11 Investment properties [extract]

Valuation model

According to accepted theory, the value of an asset consists of the net present value of the future cash flows that the asset is expected to generate. This section aims to describe and illustrate Castellum's cash flow-based model for the calculation of the value of the real estate portfolio.

The value of the real estate portfolio is calculated in this model as the total present value of net operating income minus remaining investments on ongoing projects, during the next nine years and the present value of the estimated residual value in year ten. The residual value in year ten consists of the total present value of net operating income during the remaining economic life span. The estimated market value of undeveloped land is added to this.

The required yield and the assumption regarding future real growth are of crucial importance for the calculated value of the real estate portfolio, as they are the most important value-driving factors in the valuation model. The required yield is the weighted cost of borrowed capital and equity. The cost of borrowed capital is based on the market interest rate for loans. The cost of equity is based on a "risk-free interest rate" equivalent to the long-term government bond rate with the addition of a "risk premium". The risk premium is unique to each investment and depends on the investor's perception of future risk and potential.

To illustrate the model, the following example is provided. It should be noted that assumptions regarding cash flow growth and other assumptions included in the model are only intended to illustrate the model. The examples should thus not be regarded as a forecast of the company's expected earnings.

Assumptions in the example:

- The economic occupancy rate is assumed to increase in order to reach a long-term level of 95% in the year 2011.
- Net operating income for 2006 is based on the result for the investment properties, with an assumed cost of SEK 30/sq.m. for pure property administration.
- Growth in rental value and property costs has been assumed to 1% per annum during the calculation period.
- The average economic life of the real estate portfolio has been assumed to be 50 years.
- Projects and land have been assumed to be SEKm 846.
- The required yield is calculated according to the following assumptions:

	Required yield	Percentage of capital	Weighted required yield
Equity	7.0% – 20.5%	30%	2.1% – 6.1%
Borrowed capital	5.5%	70%	3.9%
Weighted required yield		100%	6.0% – 10.0%

Example – calculation of the value of the real estate portfolio

SEKm	2006	2007	2008	2009	2010	2011	2012	2013	2014	2015	2016
Rental value	**2387**	2411	2435	2459	2484	2509	2534	2559	2585	2611	2637
Rental income	**2078**	2146	2216	2272	2335	2383	2407	2431	2456	2480	2505
Economic occupancy rate	**87.1%**	89%	91%	92%	94%	95%	95%	95%	95%	95%	95%
Property costs	**-682**	–689	–696	–703	–710	–717	–724	–731	–739	–746	–753
Net operating income=cash flow	**1396**	**1457**	**1520**	**1569**	**1625**	**1666**	**1683**	**1700**	**1717**	**1734**	**1752**
Discounted cash flow, years 1-9	**10511**					Discounted cash flow					
Discounted cash flow, year 10	**12769**					Discounted residual value					25314
Assumed value, projects and land	**846**										
Total property value	**24126**										

Castellum records the investment properties at fair value and has made an internal valuation of all properties as of December 31, 2006. The valuation was carried out in a uniform manner, and was based on a ten-year cash flow model, which was described in principle above. The internal valuation was based on an individual assessment for each property of both its future earnings capacity and its required yield. In assessing a property's future earnings capacity we took into account an assumed level of inflation of 1.5% and potential changes in rental levels from each contract's rent and expiry date compared with the estimated current market rent, as well as changes in occupancy rate and property costs. Included in property costs are operating expenses, maintenance, ground rent, real estate tax, and leasing and property management. Possible premiums paid on portfolios have not been taken into account.

Assumptions on the required yield

The required yield on equity is different for each property, and is based on assumptions regarding real interest rate, inflation and risk premium. The risk premium is different for each property and can be divided into two parts – general risk and individual risk. The general risk adjusts for the fact that a real estate investment is not as liquid as a bond, and that the asset is affected by the general economic situation. The general risk has assumed to be 3.0%. The individual risk is specific to each property, and comprises a weighted assessment of; the property's category, the town/city in which the property is located, the property's location within the town/city with reference to the property's category, if the property has the right design, is appropriate and makes efficient use of space, the property's technical standard with regard to such criteria as the choice of material, the quality of public installations, furnishing and equipment on the premises and apartments and the nature of the lease agreement, with regard to such issues as the length, size and number of agreements.

In order to calculate the required yield on total capital, an assumption has been made about the cost of borrowed capital of 5.5%. The required yield of borrowed capital comprises the real interest rate and inflation. The equity/assets ratio is assumed to be 20% – 45%, depending on the property category.

The required yield on total capital is calculated by weighting the required yield on equity and the cost of borrowing on the basis of the equity/assets ratio. The required yield on total capital is used to discount the expected 10-year future cash flow, while the residual value is discounted by calculating the return on total capital minus growth which is set equal to the inflation.

The assumptions that form the basis for Castellum's valuation are shown in the table below.

Assumptions per property category 31-12-2006	Office/Retail	Warehouse/ Industrial
Real interest rate	3.0%	3.0%
Inflation	1.5%	1.5%
Risk	5.0% – 12.3%	6.7% – 13.8%
Return on equity	9.5% –16.8%	11.2% – 18.3%
Interest rate	5.5%	5.5%
Equity/assets ratio	35%	45%
Return on total capital	6.9% – 9.5%	8.1% – 11.2%
Required yield minus growth equal to inflation	5.4% – 8.0%	6.6% – 9.7%

Compared to previous year the required yield has been reduced by approx. 0.4 percentage units in order to reflect the increase in prices seen on the real estate market.

Development projects and building permissions

Projects in progress have been valued using the same principle, but with deductions for remaining investment. Sites with building permission and land have been valued on the basis of an estimated market value per square metre.

The value of the real estate portfolio and calculated net asset value

The internal valuation shows a fair value of SEKm 24,238 (21,270), which is an increase in value of approx. 5% (4%).

The table below shows the fair value distributed by property category and region.

Property value, SEKm 31-12-2006	Office/ Retail	Warehouse/ Industrial	Projects and Land	Total
Greater Gothenburg	4491	3339	273	8103
Öresund Region	4537	1633	29	6199
Greater Stockholm	3286	1231	253	4770
Mälardalen	1889	709	285	2883
Western Småland	1668	609	6	2283
Total	15871	7521	846	24238

External valuation

In order to provide further assurance and validation of the valuation more than 100 properties, representing 51% of the value of the portfolio, were valued by NAI Svefa. The properties were selected on the basis of the largest properties in terms of value, but also in order to reflect the composition of the portfolio as a whole in terms of category and geographical location of the properties. NAI Svefa's valuation of the selected properties amounted to SEKm 12,499, within an uncertainty range of +/- 5% - 10% on property level. The size of the uncertainty range varies depending on each property's category and location. Castellum's valuation of the same properties amounted to SEKm 12,314. It can be noted that, at portfolio level, the external and internal valuations correspond well, although there are individual differences.

Net asset value and uncertainty range

When assets and liabilities are valued at fair value the net asset value can be calculated using shareholders' equity in the balance sheet. However, consideration should be taken to the value range of +/- 5% - 10% used in property valuations in order to reflect the uncertainty that exists in the assumptions and calculations made. Further, the effective tax can be expected to be lower than the reported 28% nominal tax rate, in part due to the possibility to sell properties in a tax efficient way, and in part due to the time factor for which the tax should be discounted.

In all this gives, with the assumption of a value range of +/– 5% on property level and with the assumption of a calculated effective tax rate of 10%, a net asset value in the range below.

Net asset value – sensitivity analysis	SEKm	Uncertainty range
Equity according to the balance sheet	10184	
Reversed 28% deferred tax	2723	
Net asset value excluding tax	12907	(+/– 9%)
SEK/share	79	*(SEK 86 – 71)*
Calculated deferred tax 10%	–972	
Net asset value after 10% tax	11935	(+/– 9%)
SEK/share	73	*(SEK 79 – 66)*

6.3 Additional disclosures for the fair value model

A reconciliation of the carrying amounts of investment property at the start and finish of the period must be given showing the following:

(a) additions, disclosing separately those additions resulting from acquisitions and those resulting from subsequent expenditure recognised in the carrying amount of an asset;

(b) additions resulting from acquisitions through business combinations;

(c) disposals;
(d) net gains or losses from fair value adjustments;
(e) the net exchange differences arising on the translation of the financial statements into a different presentation currency, and on translation of a foreign operation into the presentation currency of the reporting entity;
(f) transfers to and from inventories and owner-occupied property; and
(g) other changes.[93]

When a valuation obtained for investment property is adjusted significantly for the purpose of the financial statements, for example to avoid double-counting of assets or liabilities that are recognised separately as required by paragraph 50 of the standard, the entity must disclose a reconciliation between the valuation obtained and the adjusted valuation included in the financial statements, showing separately the aggregate amount of any recognised lease obligations that have been added back, and any other significant adjustments.[94] Extracts 14.7 and 14.8 above provide examples of such disclosure.

6.3.1 *Presentation of changes in fair value in the income statement*

IAS 40 does not specify how changes in the fair value of investment property should be presented in the income statement. The Extracts below show two different approaches. In Extract 14.16 the change in fair value (here referred to as a gain on revaluation) is presented together with the profit or loss on disposal of properties with an analysis of the components included in the notes to the accounts. By contrast, in Extract 14.17, the change in fair value is analysed and presented separately from the profit or loss on disposal of properties on the face of the income statement.

Both companies include the change in fair value within their definition of operating profit.

Extract 14.16: Liberty International plc (2006)

Consolidated Income Statement for the year ended 31 December 2006 [extract]

	Notes	**2006 £m**	2005 £m
Revenue	1	**562.8**	434.3
Rental income		**493.1**	417.1
Rental expenses		**(152.5)**	(117.0)
Net rental income	1	**340.6**	300.1
Other income		**34.8**	14.2
Gain on revaluation and sale of investment and development property	3	**586.5**	565.5
		961.9	879.8
Administration expenses		**(34.2)**	(29.2)
Operating profit		**927.7**	850.6

Extract 14.17: Rodamco Europe, NV (2006)

Consolidated Profit and Loss Account for the year ended December 31, 2006 [extract]
In €millions

	Notes	**2006**	2005
Gross rental income	4	652	594
Service charge income	5	98	83
Revenues		**750**	**677**
Service charge expenses	5	(103)	(89)
Property operating expenses	6	(84)	(85)
Net rental income		**563**	**503**
Valuation result investment property	7	1,270	965
Valuation result renovation projects	7	–	–
Valuation result pipeline projects	7	37	63
Valuation result		**1,307**	**1,028**
Result on disposal of investment property and pipeline	7	27	10
Administrative expenses	8	(52)	(44)
Other income and expenses	9	–	2
Operating profit		**1,845**	1,499

6.3.2 *Extra disclosures where fair value cannot be determined reliably*

If fair value cannot be measured reliably and the asset is accounted for under the provisions of the cost model of IAS 16, the reconciliations described under 6.3 above should separately disclose the amounts for such investment property. In addition to this the following should be disclosed:

(a) a description of the investment property;

(b) an explanation of why fair value cannot be determined reliably;

(c) if possible, the range of estimates within which fair value is highly likely to lie; and

(d) on disposal of investment property not carried at fair value:

  (i) the fact that the entity has disposed of investment property not carried at fair value;

  (ii) the carrying amount of that investment property at the time of sale; and

  (iii) the amount of gain or loss recognised.[95]

The standard makes it clear that this situation would be exceptional (see 3.3.3 above).

6.4 Additional disclosures for the cost model

In the event that investment property is carried at cost less depreciation, the following disclosures are required by IAS 40:

(a) the depreciation methods used;

(b) the useful lives or the depreciation rates used;

(c) the gross carrying amount and the accumulated depreciation (aggregated with accumulated impairment losses) at the beginning and end of the period;

(d) a reconciliation of the carrying amount of investment property at the beginning and end of the period, showing the following:
   (i) additions, disclosing separately those additions resulting from acquisitions and those resulting from subsequent expenditure recognised as an asset;
   (ii) additions resulting from acquisitions through business combinations;
   (iii) disposals;
   (iv) depreciation;
   (v) the amount of impairment losses recognised, and the amount of impairment losses reversed, during the period in accordance with IAS 36;
   (vi) the net exchange differences arising on the translation of the financial statements into a different presentation currency, and on translation of a foreign operation into the presentation currency of the reporting entity;
   (vii) transfers to and from inventories and owner-occupied property; and
   (viii) other changes; and

(e) the fair value of investment property. In the exceptional cases when an entity cannot determine the fair value of the investment property reliably (see 3.3 above), it shall disclose:
   (i) a description of the investment property;
   (ii) an explanation of why fair value cannot be determined reliably; and
   (iii) if possible, the range of estimates within which fair value is highly likely to lie.'[96]

7 FIRST-TIME ADOPTION

IFRS 1 – *First-time Adoption of International Financial Reporting Standards* – permits the use of 'deemed cost' in place of actual cost in the opening IFRS balance sheet (see Chapter 13 at 3.1). This alternative is available for investment properties, which could enable an entity to change from a valuation model under its previous GAAP to the cost model under IAS 40. This might be an attractive option for entities with only a few properties that meet the IAS 40 definition, especially if the residual values of its properties were so high that there was little depreciable amount. By adopting a new policy under IFRS, the entity would be exposed in the short term to a small amount of depreciation rather than the risk of taking valuation changes to the income statement.

A full explanation of the provisions of IFRS 1 for first time application of IAS 40 is set out in Chapter 5 at 2.5.

8 FUTURE DEVELOPMENTS

8.1 Measurement of investment property under construction

As noted in 2.2.5 above, as part of their annual improvement process, the Board has issued an Exposure Draft which would, if finalised as drafted, mean that investment property under construction would not be dealt with IAS 16 but under IAS 40. The effect is that entities that choose the revaluation model will take gains and losses on revaluation during the construction period to income. The change to the standard is expected to take effect from 1 January 2009.

8.2 Revenue

As noted in section 5 above the IFRIC has taken onto its agenda a project to clarify the requirements of IAS 18 for real estate sales in which an agreement for sale is reached before the construction of property is complete.

The draft Interpretation (IFRIC D21) issued in July 2007 proposes that IAS 11 is the applicable Standard if the sale agreement is a contract to provide construction services to the buyers' specifications, as opposed to selling. The proposed Interpretation may require developers that are currently applying IAS 11 to apply IAS 18 instead - with a consequent deferral in the recognition of revenue.

Of course, property that is subject to sale prior to completion of construction that has not been previously classified as investment property is likely to be property intended for sale in the ordinary course of business (see 2.2.3 above), and is therefore not investment property. This issue is discussed in more detail in Chapter 28 at 7.17.

9 CONCLUSION

For many, IAS 40 has been the harbinger of a wholesale shift to fair values in the balance sheet, and of a performance statement in which realised profits and unrealised gains are not distinguished. Consequently, it is inevitable that the volatility of reported assets and profits will increase vastly.

It is therefore relevant to ask whether such fair values do provide the user of the financial statements with relevant, reliable and understandable information. Many would argue that the use of the fair value model for investment property does properly reflect the focus of the real estate sector on net asset performance. This view is reinforced by what appears to be the widespread, if not universal, use of the fair value model by investing entities. Perhaps, therefore, to the users of such financial statements it is of little consequence how the resulting fair value gain or loss is reported in the performance statements.

However, the move to fair value accounting does require that users understand, both what mark-to-model asset valuations really are, and the implications in terms of cash generation of a fair value based 'profit'.

References

1 IAS 40, *Investment Property*, IASB, para. B4.
2 IAS 40, para. 5.
3 IAS 40, para. 5.
4 IAS 40, para. 4.
5 IAS 41, *Agriculture*, para. 12.
6 IAS 41, para. 2.
7 IAS 40, para. 6.
8 IAS 17, *Leases*, para. 18.
9 IAS 40, para. 7.
10 IAS 40, paras. 8-15.
11 IAS 40, para. 8.
12 IAS 40, para. 8.
13 IAS 40, para. 9.
14 IAS 40, para. 9.
15 IAS 40, para. 5.
16 IAS 40, para. 9.
17 IAS 40, para. 15.
18 IAS 40, paras. B16-B18.
19 IFRIC Update, IFRIC, July 2006.
20 IAS 40, paras. B16-B18.
21 IAS 40, para. 10.
22 IAS 40, para. 10.
23 IAS 40, para. 11.
24 IAS 40, para. 11.
25 IAS 40, paras. 12-13.
26 IAS 40, para. 14.
27 IAS 40, paras. 50(a) and (b).
28 IAS 40, para. 4(a).
29 IAS 40, para. 16.
30 IAS 40, para. 17.
31 IAS 40, para. 18.
32 IAS 40, para. 19.
33 IAS 40, para. 20.
34 IAS 40, para. 21.
35 IAS 40, para. 22.
36 IAS 16, *Property, Plant and Equipment*, IASB, para. 16(b).
37 IAS 40, para. 23.
38 IAS 40, para. 65.
39 IAS 40, para. 24.
40 IAS 40, para. 25.
41 IAS 17, para. 20.
42 IAS 40, para. 26.
43 IAS 40, para. 29.
44 IAS 40, para. 30.
45 IAS 40, para. 31.
46 IAS 40, para. 32.
47 IAS 40, paras. 32A-32C.
48 IAS 40, paras. 33-35.
49 IAS 40, para. 34.
50 IAS 40, para. 5.
51 IAS 40, para. 36.
52 IAS 40, para. 37.
53 International Valuation Standards, General Valuation Concepts and Principles, Chapter 8.0.
54 IAS 40, paras. 38-39.
55 IAS 40, para. 40.
56 IAS 40, paras. 42-43.
57 IAS 40, para. 44.
58 IAS 40, para. 45.
59 IAS 40, para. 46.
60 IAS 40, para. 51.
61 IAS 40, para. 41.
62 IAS 40, para. 47.
63 IAS 40, para. 48.
64 IAS 40, para. 49.
65 IAS 40, para. 39.
66 IAS 40, para. 50.
67 IAS 40, para. 50.
68 IAS 40, para. 53.
69 IAS 40, para. 54.
70 IAS 40, para. 55.
71 IAS 40, para. 56.
72 IAS 16, para. 51.
73 IAS 40, para. 56.
74 IAS 40, para. 57.
75 IAS 40, para. 58.
76 IAS 40, para. 60.
77 IAS 40, para. 61.
78 IAS 40, para. 62.
79 IAS 40, para. 59.
80 IAS 17, para. 19.
81 IAS 40, paras. 66-67.
82 IAS 40, paras. 66-67.
83 IAS 40, para. 67.
84 IAS 40, para. 67.
85 IAS 18, *Revenue*, IASB, Appendix, para. 9.
86 IAS 40, para. 69.
87 IAS 40, para. 70.
88 IAS 40, para. 71.
89 IFRIC Update, IFRIC, March 2006.
90 IAS 40, para. 68.
91 IAS 40, para. 72.
92 IAS 40, para. 75.
93 IAS 40, para. 76.
94 IAS 40, para. 77.
95 IAS 40, para. 78.
96 IAS 40, para. 79.

Chapter 15 Impairment of fixed assets and goodwill

1 INTRODUCTION

Impairment, as a procedure, is an essential element in the IASB's strategy of moving financial reporting from historical cost to a fair value basis, as discussed in Chapter 2. When prudence ceases to be an underlying principle and is replaced by fair values – often arrived at after the application of a valuation model, rather than resulting from observable market prices – there has to be a control mechanism to prevent unduly optimistic valuations. In a fair value world, the impairment test performs this necessary function. Under a reporting system that increasingly relies on fair values, the impairment test is the 'new prudence'. Notwithstanding these strategic considerations, under IFRS the relevant standard, IAS 36 – *Impairment of Assets* – applies to most assets held by an entity regardless of the valuation basis used.

In principle an asset is impaired when an entity will not be able to recover that asset's balance sheet carrying value, either through using it or selling it. The (then) IASC introduced IAS 36 in 1998 and it applied to periods beginning on or after 1 July 1999. At the time the point was made that writing down impaired assets is not in principle a new requirement, and prudence apart, in many jurisdictions provisions for diminution in value are required to be made for assets if a reduction in value is expected to be permanent.

However, prior to IAS 36 there was little detailed guidance to support this broad principle, though the principle was either explicit or implicit in a number of standards. The position now is that the impairment provisions of IFRS are explicit and, to summarise, if circumstances arise which indicate assets might be impaired, a review should be undertaken of their cash generating abilities either through use or sale. This review will produce an amount which should be compared with the assets' carrying value, and if the carrying value is higher, the difference must be written off as an impairment adjustment in the income statement. The provisions within the standard that set out exactly how this is to be done, and how the figures involved are to be calculated, are detailed and quite complex. Therefore, as a preliminary introduction to the detail, the following section explains the theory underlying the type of impairment review adopted by the IASB in IAS 36.

2 THE THEORY BEHIND THE IMPAIRMENT REVIEW

The purpose of the review is to ensure that intangible and tangible assets, and goodwill are not carried at a figure greater than their *recoverable amount*. This recoverable amount is compared with the carrying value of the asset to determine if the asset is impaired. The definition of recoverable amount, therefore, is key. It is defined as the higher of *fair value less costs to sell* (FV) and *value in use* (VIU); the underlying concept being that an asset should not be carried at more than the amount it will raise, either from selling it now or from using it in the future.

Fair value less costs to sell essentially means what the asset could be sold for, having deducted *costs of disposal* (incrementally incurred direct selling costs). *Value in use* is defined in terms of discounted future cash flows, as the present value of the cash flows expected from the future use and eventual sale of the asset at the end of its useful life. As the recoverable amount is to be expressed as a present value, not in actual terms, discounting is a central feature of the impairment test.

Diagrammatically, this comparison between carrying value and recoverable amount, and the definition of recoverable amount, can be portrayed as follows:

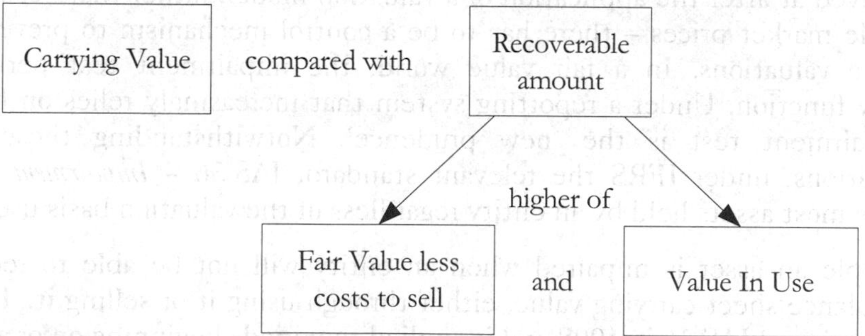

It may not always be necessary to identify both VIU and FV, as if either of VIU or FV is higher than the carrying amount then there is no impairment and no write-down is necessary. Thus, if FV is greater than the carrying amount then no further consideration need be given to VIU, or to the need for an impairment write down. The more complex issues arise when the FV is not greater than the carrying value, and so a VIU calculation is necessary. Typically for property plant and equipment used in manufacturing, this will be the case.

Although an impairment review might theoretically be conducted by looking at individual assets, this is likely to be a rare occurrence. It may not be possible to obtain reliable FV estimates for all assets and some, such as goodwill or certain intangible assets, may not have a separate FV at all. Even if FVs can be obtained for individual items of property plant and equipment, estimates of VIUs usually cannot be. This is because the cash flows necessary for the VIU calculation are not usually generated by single assets, but by groups of assets being used together.

Often, therefore, the impairment review cannot be done at the level of the individual asset and it must be done at what might be termed an operating unit level. IAS 36 uses the term *cash generating unit* (CGU) for the smallest identifiable group of assets that together have cash inflows that are largely independent of the cash inflows from other assets and that therefore can be the subject of a VIU calculation. CGU basically means a part of the business that generates income and which is largely independent of other parts of the business. This focus on the CGU is fundamental, as it has the effect of making the review essentially a business-value test, in as much as the assets of a business unit cannot usually be carried at an amount greater than the value of that business unit.

As it would be unduly onerous for all fixed assets and goodwill to be reviewed for impairment every year, IAS 36 in the main requires property, plant and equipment to be reviewed only if there is some indication that impairment may have occurred. If there are indications that the carrying amount of an asset may not be recoverable, a review for impairment should be carried out. The 'indications' of impairment may relate to either the assets themselves or to the economic environment in which they are operated. IAS 36 gives examples of indications of impairment, but makes it clear this is not an exhaustive list, and states explicitly that the entity may identify other indications that an asset is impaired, that would equally trigger an impairment review.[1]

The following section discusses in detail the individual provisions of IAS 36.

3 THE REQUIREMENTS OF IAS 36

3.1 Scope and definitions

IAS 36 was originally published in April 1998. A revised version of the standard was published in 2003 and amended variously in 2004, principally because of scope changes, as a result of the publication of IFRS 3 – *Business Combinations*, IFRS 4 – *Insurance Contracts*, IFRS 5 – *Non-current Assets Held for Sale and Discontinued Operations* – and as a result of the improvements project to existing standards, including IAS 38 – *Intangible Assets* – completed by the IASB in December 2003. For those already applying IFRS the implementation date of IAS 36 (revised), IAS 38 (revised) and IFRS 3 is 31 March 2004, and it applies as follows:

(a) to goodwill and intangible assets acquired in business combinations for which the agreement date is on or after 31 March 2004; and

(b) to all other assets prospectively from the beginning of the first annual period beginning on or after 31 March 2004.[2]

However if an entity adopted IFRS 3 early then IAS 36 and IAS 38 as revised also had to be applied prospectively from that date.

The specific inclusion of business combinations within the scope of the standard represents a considerable extension of the application of the methodology – this is because under IFRS 3 goodwill is not to be systematically depreciated, but instead subject to an annual impairment test – however the basic methodology of the original standard remains unchanged. In this chapter it is the revised and amended version of IAS 36 that is referred to. The standard is a general impairment standard and its provisions are referred to in other standards, for example IAS 16, IAS 38 and IFRS 3, where impairment is to be considered.

The objective of the standard is to ensure that assets are not carried at more than their recoverable amount (the principles underlying the term recoverable amount and other terms are explained in 2 above). If the carrying amount is higher than the amount estimated to be able to be recovered by use or sale of the asset, then the entity should recognise an impairment loss.[3]

The standard has a general application to all assets, but the following are outside its scope: inventories, assets arising from construction contracts, deferred tax assets, assets arising from employee benefits, financial assets that are included in the scope of IAS 39 – *Financial Instruments: Recognition and Measurement* – investment property that is measured at fair value, biological assets under IAS 41 – *Agriculture* – deferred acquisition costs and intangible assets arising from an insurer's contractual rights under insurance contracts within the scope of IFRS 4, and non-current assets (or disposal groups) classified as held for sale in accordance with IFRS 5.[4] This, the standard states, is because these issues are subject to specific recognition and measurement rules.[5] The effect of these exclusions is to reduce the scope of IAS 36; however, it does not exempt investment properties not carried at fair value, oil and mineral exploration and evaluation assets or an entity's own shares held by a share trust. Investments in subsidiaries, joint ventures and associates in the separate financial statements of the parent are within its scope.[6]

The standard does apply to assets carried at valuation under IAS 16 – *Property, Plant and Equipment*. It is explained that there are two reasons for this. First, the only difference between fair value based on market value and fair value less costs to sell is the costs of disposal. Therefore, if these are not negligible, the entity may have to consider the asset's value in use. Second, in the absence of market values, the entity may have constructed a fair value using a technique acceptable under IAS 16 (see Chapter 13), in which case it would be quite possible for the asset to be impaired.[7] A specific example of a situation in which this might happen is if the asset is valued using depreciated replacement cost, a valuation method that often gives a higher valuation than one using market-based evidence.

The key definitions used in IAS 36 are:

'An *active market* is a market in which all the following conditions exist:

(a) the items traded within the market are homogeneous;

(b) willing buyers and sellers can normally be found at any time; and

(c) prices are available to the public.

The *agreement date* for a business combination is the date that a substantive agreement between the combining parties is reached and, in the case of publicly listed entities, announced to the public. In the case of a hostile takeover, the earliest date that a substantive agreement between the combining parties is reached is the date that a sufficient number of the acquiree's owners have accepted the acquirer's offer for the acquirer to obtain control of the acquiree;

Carrying amount is the amount at which an asset is recognised after deducting any accumulated depreciation (amortisation) and accumulated impairment losses thereon;

A *cash-generating unit* is the smallest identifiable group of assets that generates cash inflows that are largely independent of the cash inflows from other assets or groups of assets;

Corporate assets are assets other than goodwill that contribute to the future cash flows of both the cash-generating unit under review and other cash-generating units;

Costs of disposal are incremental costs directly attributable to the disposal of an asset or cash-generating unit, excluding finance costs and income tax expense;

Depreciable amount is the cost of an asset, or other amount substituted for cost in the financial statements, less its residual value;

Depreciation (Amortisation) is the systematic allocation of the depreciable amount of an asset over its useful life;

Fair value less costs to sell is the amount obtainable from the sale of an asset or cash-generating unit in an arm's length transaction between knowledgeable, willing parties, less the costs of disposal;

An *impairment loss* is the amount by which the carrying amount of an asset or a cash-generating unit exceeds its recoverable amount;

The *recoverable amount* of an asset or a cash-generating unit is the higher of its fair value less costs to sell and its value in use;

Useful life is either:

(a) the period of time over which an asset is expected to be used by the entity; or

(b) the number of production or similar units expected to be obtained from the asset by the entity.

Value in use is the present value of the future cash flows expected to be derived from an asset or cash-generating unit.'[8]

These definitions will be referred to when discussing the provisions of the standard in the remainder of the chapter.

3.2 When an impairment test is required

There is an important distinction in IAS 36 between (a) assessing whether there are indications of impairment, and (b) actually carrying out an impairment test. The standard has two different general requirements governing when an impairment test should be carried out:

- For all intangible assets with an indefinite life and goodwill (which as a result of the provisions of IFRS 3 will not be subject to systematic annual depreciation) the standard requires that an annual impairment test must be performed. The impairment test may be performed at any time in the annual reporting period, but it must be performed at the same time every year;[9]
- For all other classes of assets within the scope of IAS 36, the entity is required to assess at each balance sheet date whether there are any 'indications of impairment'. Only if indications of impairment are present will the impairment test itself have to be carried out.[10]

In addition, the carrying amount of an intangible asset that has not yet been brought into use must be tested at least annually. This, the standard argues, is because intangible assets are intrinsically subject to greater uncertainty before they are brought into use.[11]

The particular requirements of IAS 36 concerning the impairment testing of intangible assets with an indefinite life and goodwill are discussed separately at 3.4 below, however the methodology used is identical for all types of assets.

If indications of impairment exist, then an impairment test that estimates the asset's recoverable amount must be performed, using the method required by the standard unless there was sufficient headroom in a previous impairment calculation that would not have been eroded by subsequent events or the asset or CGU is not sensitive to a particular indicator; these exceptions are discussed further below.[12]

Normally however, if there are indications of impairment an impairment test (i.e. a formal estimate of the asset's recoverable amount as set out in the standard) must be undertaken.[13] Consequently the identification of indications of impairment becomes a crucial stage in the process.

IAS 36 lists examples of indications of impairment. The standard states that the examples represent the minimum indications that should be considered by the entity, and that the list is not exhaustive.[14] They are divided into external and internal indications as follows:

External sources of information

(a) a decline in an asset's market value during the period that is significantly more than would be expected from normal use;

(b) significant adverse changes that have taken place during the period, or will take place in the near future, in the technological, market, economic or legal environment in which the entity operates or in the market to which an asset is dedicated;

(c) an increase in the period in market interest rates or other market rates of return on investments if these increases are likely to affect the discount rate used in calculating an asset's value in use and decrease the asset's recoverable amount materially;

(d) the carrying amount of the net assets of the entity exceeds its market capitalisation.

Internal sources of information:

(e) evidence of obsolescence or physical damage of an asset;

(f) significant changes in the extent to which, or manner in which, an asset is used or is expected to be used, that have taken place in the period or soon thereafter and that will have an adverse effect on it. These changes include the asset becoming idle, plans to dispose of an asset sooner than expected, reassessing its useful life as finite rather than indefinite or plans to restructure the operation to which the asset belongs;

(g) internal reports that indicates that the economic performance of an asset is, or will be, worse than expected.[15]

The standard amplifies and explains what is relevant evidence from internal reporting that indicates that an asset may be impaired as follows:

(a) cash flows for acquiring the asset, or subsequent cash needs for operating or maintaining it, are significantly higher than originally budgeted;

(b) operating profit or loss or actual net cash flows are significantly worse than those budgeted;

(c) a significant decline in budgeted net cash flows or operating profit, or a significant increase in budgeted loss; or

(d) operating losses or net cash outflows for the asset, if current period amounts are aggregated with budgeted amounts for the future.[16]

The presence of indicators or impairment will not necessarily mean that the entity has to calculate the recoverable amount of the asset in accordance with IAS 36. A previous calculation may have shown that an asset's recoverable amount was significantly greater than its carrying amount and it may be clear that subsequent events have been insufficient to eliminate this headroom. Similarly, previous analysis may show that an asset's recoverable amount is not sensitive to one or more of these indicators.[17]

There are two particularly significant elements in this list of indications. The first is the inclusion of market capitalisation as an external indication of impairment. Market capitalisation is, potentially, a powerful indicator as, if it shows a lower figure than the book value of shareholders' funds, it inescapably suggests the market considers that the business is overvalued. However, the market may have taken account of factors other than the return that the entity is generating on its assets (for example, the entity may have a high level of debt that it is unable to service fully) and a market capitalisation below shareholders' funds will not necessarily be reflected in an equivalent impairment loss. In these circumstances, entities will have to review their assets and CGUs for impairment but it is possible that not all assets or CGUs are sensitive to market capitalisation as an indicator. The second significant element is an explicit reference in (b), (c) and (d) above to internal evidence that future performance will be worse than expected. Thus IAS 36 requires that an impairment review should be undertaken if performance is or will be significantly below that previously budgeted. In particular, there may be indicators of impairment even if the asset is profitable in the current period if budgeted results for the future indicate that there will be losses or net cash outflows when these are aggregated with the current period results.

Some of the indicators are aimed at individual fixed assets rather than the CGU of which they are a part, for example a decline in the market value of an asset or evidence that it is obsolete or damaged. However, they may also imply that a wider review of the business or CGU is required. For example, if there is a property slump and the market value of the entity's new head office falls below its carrying value this would constitute an indicator of impairment and trigger a review. At the level of the individual asset, as FV is below carrying amount this might indicate that a write-down is necessary. However, the building's recoverable amount may have to be considered in the context of a CGU of which it is a part and if it is, the recoverable amount will be based on VIU, not FV. This is an example of a situation where it may not be necessary to re-estimate an asset's recoverable amount because it may be obvious that the CGU has suffered no impairment. In short, it may be irrelevant to the recoverable amount of the CGU that it contains a head office whose market value has fallen.

The inclusion of interest rates as an indicator of impairment could imply that assets are judged to be impaired if they are no longer expected to earn a market rate of return, even though they may generate the same cash flows as before. However, it may well be that an upward movement in general interest rates will not give rise to a write-down in assets because they may not affect the rate of return expected from the asset itself. The standard indicates that this may be another instance where the asset's recoverable amount is not sensitive to a particular indicator.

An entity is not required to make a formal estimate of an asset's recoverable amount if the discount rate used in calculating the asset's VIU is unlikely to be affected by the increase in market rates. The discount rate used in a VIU calculation should be based on the rate specific for the asset, and if the asset has a long remaining useful life this may not be materially affected by increases in short-term rates. Previous sensitivity analyses of the recoverable amount may show that it is unlikely that there will be a material decrease because future cash flows are also likely to increase to compensate. Consequently, the potential decrease in recoverable amount may simply be unlikely to be material.[18]

If there are indications that the asset is impaired, it may also be necessary to examine the remaining useful life of the asset, its residual value and the depreciation method used, as these may also need to be adjusted even if no impairment loss is recognised.[19]

3.3 The impairment test

The standard requires the carrying amount to be compared with the recoverable amount. The recoverable amount is the higher of VIU and FV, both terms are defined in 3.1 above.[20]

Estimating the VIU of an asset involves estimating the future cash inflows and outflows that will be derived from the use of the asset and from its ultimate disposal, and discounting them at an appropriate rate.[21] There are complex issues involved in determining the cash flows and choosing a discount rate and often there is no agreed methodology to follow (refer to 3.3.2 below for a discussion of some of these difficulties). However, broadly the requirement means that the recoverable amount is the higher of the net sale proceeds and the discounted future cash flows, where a discounting rate is used that is reasonable for the type of business and risks involved. If either the FV or the VIU is higher than the carrying amount, no further action is necessary as the asset is not impaired.[22] It may be possible to estimate the net selling price even in the absence of an active market but if it cannot be estimated satisfactorily then the value of an asset must be based on its VIU.[23] The practical point to emphasise is that if the FV is greater than the asset's carrying value, no VIU calculation is necessary.

The standard describes other circumstances in which it may be appropriate to use an asset's FV, rather than VIU, as the measure of an asset's recoverable amount. There may be no significant difference between FV and VIU, in which case the asset's FV may be used as its recoverable amount.[24] This would be the case for example, if management were intending to dispose of the asset, as apart from its disposal proceeds there would be few if any cash flows from further use. Therefore there would be no significant difference between the asset's FV and VIU. The asset may also be held for sale as defined by IFRS 5, by which stage it will be outside the scope of IAS 36, although it should be noted that IFRS 5 also requires such assets to be measured immediately before their initial classification as held for sale 'in accordance with applicable IFRSs'.[25] A decision to sell is a triggering event for an impairment review, which means that any existing impairment will be recognised at the point of classification and not be rolled into the gain or loss on disposal of the asset. See Chapter 4 for a description of the subsequent measurement of the carrying amounts of the assets.

Clearly IFRS 5's requirement to test for impairment prior to redesignation is intended to avoid impairment losses being recognised as losses on disposal. However, one effect is that this rule may require the recognition of impairment losses on individual assets that form part of a single disposal group subsequently sold at a profit, as in the following example.

Example 15.1: Impairment of assets held for sale

Entity A decided to sell a group of three assets in one transaction to the same acquirer. Each asset had been part of a different CGU. The decision to sell was made on 20 December 2005, just prior to Entity A's year end on 31 December. The assets met IFRS 5's requirements for classification as a disposal group on 10 January 2006.

The information about the carrying amounts and fair values less cost to sell of individual assets at 20 December 2005 and the disposal group on 10 January 2005 is summarised below. There was no change in the fair values of the assets between the two dates.

Asset	*Carrying amount*	*FV of separate assets*	*Aggregate of the lower of the carrying amount and FV*	*Fair value of the group*
	€	€	€	€
X	4,600	4,300	4,300	
Y	5,700	5,800	5,700	
Z	2,400	2,500	2,400	
Total	12,700	12,600	12,400	12,600

Although these assets were classified as held for sale subsequent to the year end, the decision to sell them was an indicator of impairment. Accordingly, it is necessary to determine whether the three assets together comprise a new CGU. If so, impairment would be assessed on the three assets together initially, prior to reclassification and remeasurement under IFRS 5.

If the three assets together do not comprise a CGU, they would have to be tested for impairment individually at the year end, which would result in an impairment loss on Asset X of €300. As there is no change in the recoverable amount between the year end and immediately before the classification under IFRS 5, the aggregate value of these assets prior to classification under IFRS 5 would be €12,400 (4,300 + 5,700 + 2,400). The fair value less costs to sell of the disposal group at the date of the first application of IFRS 5 (10 January 2005) is €12,600. Therefore according to the measurement criteria under IFRS 5 the carrying amount of the disposal group remains at €12,400 and the impairment loss previously recognised on Asset A would only be reversed, should the fair value less costs to sell of the disposal group exceed €12,600.

In different circumstances the requirement to take an impairment write down on reclassification may be far less clear-cut. Assets no longer form part of their original CGU once they have been designated for disposal. It is possible that a group of assets could comprise a new CGU if they are to be sold to a single purchaser as part of an arrangement. Their individual FVs may be uncertain if they are sold as a parcel, as the seller receives aggregate proceeds for the group of assets (this could be the case whether the sale is of a CGU or a group of assets). There may be little separation in time between the decision to sell and designation as held for sale.

The basic requirement of IAS 36 is that recoverable amount is calculated for an individual asset, unless that asset does not generate cash inflows that are largely independent of those from other assets or groups of assets. In this case, recoverable amount is determined for the CGU to which the asset belongs unless either:

(a) the asset's FV is higher than its carrying amount; or

(b) the asset's VIU can be estimated to be close to its FV and its FV can be determined.[26]

If either of (a) or (b) apply, then even if the asset generates cash flows in conjunction with other assets, and it would normally be necessary to calculate the VIU of the cash generating unit to which it belongs, it may in some circumstances be appropriate to base the recoverable amount of the asset on its FV. If for example, the CGU to which the asset belongs has been impaired, the asset's own carrying value could be based on its FV. Or if an asset is held for resale it would be carried at its estimated FV even though it only generates operating cash flows in conjunction with other assets.

IAS 36 allows the use of estimates, averages and computational shortcuts to provide a reasonable approximation of FV or VIU.[27]

3.3.1 Fair value less costs to sell

The standard goes into considerable detail regarding the estimation of an asset's FV.

The best evidence is the sales price of the asset in question, based on a binding sale agreement negotiated at arm's length, less incremental costs directly attributable to the sale.[28] If there is a binding sale agreement, the asset is either already classified as held for sale, in which case IFRS 5's measurement rules apply (see Chapter 4), or it is about to be reclassified and must be tested for impairment as described above.

If there is no binding sale agreement for the asset in question, but there is an active market for assets of this type, net realisable value may be estimated from current or recent bid prices. If there are no current bid prices, the price may be estimated from the most recent transaction provided there has been no significant change in economic circumstances in the intervening period.[29]

In reality there are few active markets for tangible and intangible assets, given that IFRSs define an active market as one in which all of the items traded are homogeneous, that has a constant supply of willing buyers and sellers. and prices that are available to the public. Consequently, most estimates of fair value will be based on estimates of the market price of the asset in an arm's length transaction. This will involve consideration of the outcome of recent transactions for similar assets in the same industry. The entity will use the best information it has available at the balance sheet date to construct the price payable in an arm's length transaction between knowledgeable, willing parties.[30]

FV does not reflect a forced sale unless the management is compelled to sell immediately.[31] In all cases, FV should take account of estimated disposal costs. These include legal costs, stamp duty and other transaction taxes, costs of moving the asset and other direct incremental costs. Business reorganisation costs and employee termination costs (as defined in IAS 19 – *Employee Benefits* – see Chapter 32) may not be treated as costs of disposal.[32]

If the disposal of an asset would entail the buyer assuming a liability, then this liability should be deducted from the FV in arriving at the relevant amount for determining the recoverable amount.[33] The obligation must also be taken into account in calculating the carrying value of the asset to enable a meaningful comparison.

3.3.2 Determining value in use (VIU)

IAS 36 requires the following elements to be reflected in the VIU calculation:

'(a) an estimate of the future cash flows the entity expects to derive from the asset;

(b) expectations about possible variations in the amount or timing of those future cash flows;

(c) the time value of money, represented by the current market risk-free rate of interest;

(d) the price for bearing the uncertainty inherent in the asset; and

(e) other factors, such as illiquidity, that market participants would reflect in pricing the future cash flows the entity expects to derive from the asset.' [34]

The calculation requires the entity to estimate the future cash flows and discount them at an appropriate rate.[35] It also requires uncertainty as to the timing of cash flows or the market's assessment of risk in those assets ((d) and (e) above) to be taken into account either by adjusting the cash flows or the discount rate. The intention is that the VIU should be the expected present value of those future cash flows.

If possible, recoverable amount is calculated for individual assets.[36]

If an impairment review has to be carried out then it will frequently be necessary to calculate the VIU of the CGU of which it is a part. This is because:

- it is unlikely that a single asset generates sufficiently independent cash inflows,[37] and
- in the case of the possible impairment of a single asset, FV will frequently be lower than the carrying amount.

Where a CGU is being reviewed for impairment, this will involve calculation of the VIU of the CGU as a whole unless a reliable estimate of the CGU's FV can be made. In general, the FVs of CGUs are far less reliable because they are far less homogeneous than individual assets and bought and sold far less often. If no such FV is identifiable, or if it is below the total of the CGU's net assets, VIU will have to be calculated.

VIU calculations at the level of the CGU will thus be required when:

- goodwill is suspected of being impaired;
- a CGU itself is suspected of being impaired (and no satisfactory FV is available); or
- intangible assets or other fixed assets are suspected of being impaired, individual future cash flows cannot be identified for them, and either no reliable FV is available or the FV is below carrying amount.

The standard contains detailed requirements concerning the data to be assembled to calculate VIU that can best be explained and set out as a series of steps. These are set out in subsections 1 to 5 below that also contain a discussion of the practicalities and difficulties in determining the VIU of an asset. The steps in the process are:

Step 1: Dividing the entity into cash-generating units (CGUs)

Step 2: Identifying the carrying amount of CGU assets

Step 3: Estimating the future pre-tax cash flows of the CGU under review

Step 4: Identifying an appropriate discount rate and discounting the future cash flows

Step 5: Comparing carrying value with VIU and recognising impairment losses

Although this process describes the determination of the VIU of a CGU, steps 2 to 5 are the same as those that would be applied to an individual asset if it generated cash inflows independently of other assets.

Step 1 Dividing the entity into cash-generating units (CGUs)

If a calculation of VIU is required, one of the early tasks will be to identify the individual assets affected and if those assets do not have individually identifiable cash flows, divide the entity into CGUs i.e. groups of assets as defined in 3.1 above. The group of assets that is considered together should be as small as is reasonably practicable, i.e. the entity should be divided into as many CGUs as possible – an entity must identify the lowest aggregation of assets that generate largely independent cash inflows.[38]

Example 15.2: Identification of CGUs and largely independent cash flows

An entity obtains a contract to deliver mail to all users within a region, for a price that depends solely on the weight of the item, regardless of the distance between sender and recipient. It makes a significant loss in deliveries to outlying regions. Because of the entity's service obligations, the CGU is the whole region covered by its mail services.

That said, the division should not go beyond the level at which each income stream is capable of being separately monitored and not beyond the point at which it would become necessary to start allocating direct costs between CGUs. For example, it may be difficult to identify a level below an individual factory as a CGU but of course an individual factory may or may not be a CGU. A practical approach to identifying CGUs involves two stages, the first being to work down to the smallest group of assets for which a stream of cash inflows can be identified. These groups of assets will be CGUs unless the performance of their cash inflow-generating assets are dependent on those generated by other assets, or *vice versa* their cash inflows are affected by those of other assets. If the cash inflows generated by the group of assets are not largely independent of those generated by other assets, the second stage is to add the other assets to the group to form the smallest collection of assets that generates largely independent cash inflows. This approach might be characterised as a 'bottom-up' approach to identifying CGUs and is illustrated in Example 15.3 below. The existence of a degree of flexibility over what constitutes a CGU is obvious. Indeed, the standard acknowledges that the identification of CGUs involves judgement.[39] The key guidance offered by the standard is that CGU selection will be influenced by 'how management monitors the entity's operations (such as by product lines, businesses, individual locations, districts or regional areas) or how management makes decisions about continuing or disposing of the entity's assets and operations'.[40]

While monitoring by management may help identify CGUs, it does not override the requirement that the identification of CGUs is based on largely independent cash inflows.

Example 15.3: Identification of cash-generating units

Example A – newspapers

An entity publishes 10 suburban newspapers, each with a different mast-head, across 4 distinct regions within a major city. The price paid for a purchased mast-head is recognised as an intangible asset. The newspapers are distributed to residents free of charge. No newspaper is distributed outside its region. All of the revenue generated by each newspaper comes from advertising sales. An analysis of advertising sales shows that for each mast-head:

- Approximately 90% of sales come from advertisers purchasing 'bundled' advertisements that appear in all those newspapers published in one particular region of the city;
- Approximately 6% of sales come from advertisers purchasing 'bundled' advertisements that appear in all 10 newspapers in the major city; and
- Approximately 4% of sales come from advertisers purchasing advertisements that appear in one newspaper only.

What is the cash-generating unit for an individual mast-head?

Stage 1: Identify the smallest aggregation of assets for which a stream of cash inflows can be identified.

The fact that it is possible to use a pro-rata allocation basis to determine the cash inflows attributable to each newspaper means that each mast-head is likely to represent the smallest aggregation of assets for which a stream of cash inflows can be identified.

Stage 2: Are the cash inflows generated by an individual mast-head largely independent of those of other mast-heads and, conversely, is that individual mast-head affecting the cash inflows generated by other mast-heads?

As approximately 96% of cash inflows for each mast-head arise from 'bundled' advertising sales across multiple mast-heads, the cash inflows generated by an individual mast-head are not largely independent.

Therefore, the individual mast-heads would most likely need to be aggregated to form the smallest collection of assets that generates largely independent cash inflows. On the basis that approximately 90% of cash inflows for each mast-head arise from 'bundled' advertising sales across all of the newspapers published in a particular region, it is likely that those mast-heads published in one region will together form a cash-generating unit.

Example B – retail outlets

An entity has a chain of retail outlets located in the same country. The business model of the entity is highly integrated and the majority of the entity's revenue generating decisions, such as decisions about investments and monitoring of performance, are carried out at an entity level by the executive committee, with some decisions (such as product range and marketing) delegated to the regional or store levels. The majority of the operations, such as purchasing, are centralised. Management operates its business on a regional basis; but sales are monitored at the individual store level.

The outlets are usually bought and sold in packages of outlets that are subject to common economic characteristics e.g. outlets of similar size or location such as a shopping centre or city or region. Only in rare situations has the entity sold or closed down an individual outlet.

The determining factor for CGUs is the level at which largely independent cash inflows are generated, and not the manner in which the entity's operations are organised and monitored. The fact that operations and costs are managed centrally does not of itself impact the source and independence of the cash inflows. The interdependence of cash outflows is unlikely to be relevant to the identification of CGUs.

The key issue in deciding whether CGUs should be identified at the level of the individual store as opposed to a group of stores is whether, if a store is closed down, all the customers of that store would seek out another of the entity's stores such that there is no overall 'leakage' of custom from the store closure. In the highly likely event that all the customers would not do this, the individual stores are separate CGUs.

Example B above illustrates a very important point. Management may consider that the primary way in which they monitor their business is on a regional or segmental basis, but crucially, cash flows are monitored at the level of an individual store and closure decisions are made at this level. In other cases it may be that the entity is capable of monitoring individual cash flows from assets but this is not the most relevant feature in determining the composition of its CGUs.

Example 15.4: Identification of cash-generating units – grouping of assets

A tour operator's hotels

A tour operator owns three hotels of a similar class near the beach at a large holiday resort. These hotels are advertised as alternatives in the operator's brochure, at the same price. Holidaymakers are frequently transferred from one to another and there is a central booking system for independent travellers. In this case, it may be that the hotels can be regarded as offering genuinely substitutable products by a sufficiently high proportion of potential guests and can be grouped together as a single cash-generating unit. Effectively, the hotels are being run as a single hotel on three sites. The entity will have to bear in mind that disposal decisions may still be made on a hotel-by-hotel basis and have to weight this appropriately in its determination of its CGUs.

The standard allows reasonable approximations and one way in which entities may apply this in practice is to group together assets that are separate CGUs, but which if considered individually for impairment would not be material. Retail outlets may be grouped on a geographical basis (e.g. all of the retail outlets in a city centre owned by a branded clothes retailer) because they are all subject to the same economic circumstances and individually will have an immaterial effect. However, the entity will still have to scrutinise the individual CGUs to ensure that those that it intends to sell or that have significantly underperformed the others with which they are grouped are identified and dealt with individually.

In practice different entities will inevitably have varying approaches to determining their CGUs. There is judgement to be exercised in determining an income stream and in determining whether it is largely independent of other streams. Given this, therefore, entities may tend towards larger rather than smaller CGUs, to keep the complexity of the process within reasonable bounds.

The standard stresses the significance of an active market for the output of an asset in identifying a CGU. If there is an active market for the output produced by an asset or group of assets, the assets concerned are identified as a cash-generating unit, even if some or all of the output is used internally. If the cash inflows generated by the asset or CGU are based on internal transfer pricing, the best estimate of an external arm's length transaction price should be used in estimating the future cash flows to determine the asset's CGU's or VIU.[41]

The reason given for this rule is that the existence of an active market means that the assets or CGU could generate cash inflows independently from the rest of the business by selling on the active market.[42] There are active markets, as defined at 3.1 above, for many metals, energy products (various grades of oil product, natural gas) and other commodities that are freely traded.

Example A below, based on Example 1 in IAS 36's accompanying section of illustrative examples, illustrates the point. Example B describes circumstances in which the existence of an active market does not necessarily lead to the identification of a separate CGU.

Example 15.5: Identification of cash-generating units – internally-used products

Example A – Plant for an Intermediate Step in a Production Process

A significant raw material used for plant Y's final production is an intermediate product bought from plant X of the same entity. X's products are sold to Y at a transfer price that passes all margins to X. 60 per cent of X's final production is sold to Y and the remaining 40 per cent is sold to customers outside of the entity. Y sells 80 per cent of its products to customers outside of the entity

If X can sell its products in an active market and generate cash inflows that are largely independent of the cash inflows from Y, it is likely that X is a CGU even though part of its production is used by Y. Therefore, its cash inflows can be regarded as being largely independent. It is likely that Y is also a separate CGU. However, internal transfer prices do not reflect market prices for X's output. Therefore, in determining value in use of both X and Y, the entity adjusts financial budgets/forecasts to reflect management's best estimate of future prices that could be achieved in arm's length transactions for those of X's products that are used internally.

If, on the other hand, there is no active market, it is likely that the recoverable amount of each plant cannot be assessed independently of the recoverable amount of the other plant. The majority of X's production is used internally and could not be sold in an active market. Cash inflows of X depend on demand for Y's products. Therefore, X cannot be considered to generate cash inflows that are largely independent of those of Y. In addition, the two plants are managed together. As a consequence, it is likely that X and Y together are the smallest group of assets that generates cash inflows that are largely independent.[43]

Example B – 'Market' for intermediate product not relevant to identification of a separate CGU

A vertically integrated operation located in Australia produces an intermediate product that is fully used internally to manufacture the end product. There is no active market for the intermediate product in Australia. The entity has only one other competitor in Australia, which is also vertically integrated and, likewise, uses the intermediate product internally. Both entities are, and have always been, very profitable when looking at their vertically integrated manufacturing processes to the end-stage product.

There is an active market for the intermediate product in China, but the prices at which the product can be sold are so low that a company based in Australia whose sole activity is to sell the intermediate product into China would never be profitable and a company would never set up manufacturing operations in Australia in order to sell into China.

Each of the Australian companies will occasionally sell small surpluses of their intermediate products into the active market in China, rather than make that product available to their competitor in Australia.

The existence of an active market for the intermediate product in China might suggest that the operations involved in it should be treated as a separate CGU. However, the mere existence of an active market somewhere in the world does not mean that the asset or CGU could realistically generate cash inflows independently from the rest of the business by selling on that active market. If such sales are a genuine incidental activity (i.e. if it is genuinely a case of obtaining some proceeds from excess product that would otherwise be scrapped), it may be appropriate not to regard that market as an active market for the intermediate product for IAS 36 purposes.

If the market is not regarded as an active market for IAS 36 purposes, the assets/operations involved in producing the intermediate product will not be treated as a separate CGU.

IAS 36 also requires that the identification of cash generating units shall be consistent from period to period unless the change is justified; if changes are made disclosures are required.[44]

Assets held for resale cannot be subsumed within a larger CGU and their impairment or otherwise should be judged solely by the cash flows expected to be generated by sale. Once they are classified as held for sale they will be accounted for in accordance with IFRS 5 and carried at an amount that may not exceed their FV less costs to sell (see Chapter 4 for a further discussion of IFRS 5's requirements).

Step 2 Identifying the carrying amount of CGU assets

The recoverable amount of a CGU is determined in the same way as for an individual asset and its carrying amount must be determined on a basis that is consistent with the way in which its recoverable amount is determined.[45]

The carrying amount of a CGU includes only those assets that can be attributed directly, or allocated on a reasonable and consistent basis. These must be the assets that will generate the future cash inflows used in determining the CGU's value in use. It does not include the carrying amount of any recognised liability, unless the recoverable amount of the cash-generating unit cannot be determined without taking it into account. Both FV and VIU of a CGU are determined excluding cash flows that relate to assets that are not part of the cash-generating unit and liabilities that have been recognised.[46]

The standard emphasises the importance of completeness in the allocation of assets to CGUs. Every asset used in generating the cash flow being tested must be included in the CGU; otherwise an impaired CGU might appear to be unimpaired, as its carrying value would be understated by having missed out assets.[47]

There are exceptions allowed to the rule that recognised liabilities are not included in arriving at the CGU's carrying value or VIU. Paragraph 78 makes it clear that if the disposal of an asset would entail the buyer assuming a liability, then this liability should be deducted from the CGU's carrying amount and VIU in order to perform a meaningful comparison.[48]

The second exception occurs if it is only practicable to determine the recoverable amount of a CGU after taking into account assets and liabilities such as, receivables, or other financial assets, trade payables, pensions and other provisions that are outside the scope of IAS 36.[49] Essentially this seems to mean that if the cash flows of a CGU or its FV can only be sensibly determined taking into account these sorts of items, then the entity should include them. If it is only possible to determine cash flows that include receipts from trade debtors or payments to trade creditors, then these balances should be reflected in the carrying amount of the CGU. It is essential that cash flows and assets and liabilities within CGUs are prepared on a consistent basis.

Other assets such as goodwill and corporate assets may not be able to be attributed on a reasonable and consistent basis and the standard has separate rules regarding their treatment. Goodwill is dealt with separately at 3.4 below in detail, and also in Chapter 7 in relation to business combinations.

I Corporate assets

An entity may have assets that are inherently incapable of generating cash inflows independently, such as headquarters buildings or central IT facilities. IAS 36 characterises this type of asset as 'corporate assets' and they are defined in 3.1 above. Paragraph 100 points out that 'the distinctive characteristics of corporate assets are that they do not generate cash inflows independently of other assets or groups of assets and their carrying amount cannot be fully attributed to the cash-generating unit under review.' [50] As the definition makes clear, the characteristic of a corporate asset is that it contributes to more than one CGU.

This lack of cash flow generation by corporate assets presents a problem in the event of those assets showing indications of impairment. It also raises a question of what those indications might actually be, in the absence of cash inflows directly relating to this type of asset. Some, but not all, of these assets may have relatively easily determinable FVs. However, while this is usually true of a headquarters building, the same could not be said for a central IT facility. We have already noted in 3.2 above that a decline in market value of itself may not trigger a need for an impairment review, if it is obvious that the CGUs of which corporate assets are a part are not showing any indications of impairment – unless, of course, management has decided to dispose of the asset. Therefore, it is most likely that a corporate asset will show indications of impairment if the CGU or group of CGUs it relates to are showing indications of it. It is this type of eventuality that requires rules for allocating the carrying values of corporate assets to individual CGUs or to groups of CGUs.

Therefore it is necessary, if there are indications of impairment of a corporate asset and its VIU needs to be determined, for the corporate asset's carrying value to be allocated to CGUs. This allocation allows the recoverable amount of all of the assets involved, both CGU and corporate ones, to be considered.[51]

The standard sets out the procedure as follows. If possible, the corporate assets are to be allocated to individual CGUs on a 'reasonable and consistent basis'.[52] This is not expanded upon and affords some flexibility, although plainly consistency is vital

– the same criteria must be applied at all times. Therefore if the carrying value of a corporate asset can be allocated on a reasonable and consistent basis between individual CGUs, each CGU has its impairment test done separately and its carrying value includes its share of the corporate asset. If the corporate asset's carrying value cannot be allocated to an individual CGU, there are three steps. First the individual CGU is impairment tested and any impairment written off. Then as a second step a group of CGUs is identified to which, as a group, all or part of the carrying value of the corporate asset can be allocated. This group must include the individual CGU that was the subject of the first test. Finally, all CGUs in this group have to be tested to determine if the group's carrying value (including the allocation of the corporate asset's carrying value) is in excess of the group's VIU.[53] If it is not sufficient, the impairment loss will be allocated pro-rata to all assets in the group of CGUs and the allocated portion of the corporate asset, as described under 3.3.3 below.

In IAS 36's accompanying section of illustrative examples, Example 8 has a fully worked example of the allocation and calculation of a VIU involving corporate assets.[54] The table below is included in it, and serves to illustrate the allocation of the corporate asset to CGUs:

Example 15.6: Allocation of corporate assets

An entity comprises three CGUs and a headquarters building. The carrying amount of the headquarters building of 150 is allocated to the carrying amount of each individual cash-generating unit. A weighted allocation basis is used because the estimated remaining useful life of A's cash-generating unit is 10 years, whereas the estimated remaining useful lives of B and C's cash-generating units are 20 years.

Schedule 1. Calculation of a weighted allocation of the carrying amount of the headquarter building

End of 20X0	**A**	**B**	**C**	**Total**
Carrying amount	100	150	200	450
Useful life	10 years	20 years	20 years	
Weighting based on useful life	1	2	2	
Carrying amount after weighting	100	300	400	800
Pro-rata allocation of the building	(100/800)= 12%	(300/800)= 38%	(400/800)= 50%	100%
Allocation of the carrying amount of the building (based on pro-rata above)	19	56	75	(150)
Carrying amount (after allocation of the building)	119	206	275	600

The allocation need not be made on carrying value or financial measures such as turnover – employee numbers or a time basis might be a valid basis in certain circumstances.

One effect of this pro-rata process is that the amount of the head office allocated to each CGU will change as the useful lives and carrying values change. In the above example, the allocation of the head office to CGU A will be redistributed to CGUs B and C as A's remaining life shortens. The entity will have to ensure that B and C can support an increased head office allocation. Similar effects will be observed if the sizes of any other factor on which the allocation to the CGUs is made change relative to one another.

Step 3 Estimating the future pre-tax cash flows of the CGU under review

This step needs to be performed only if the CGU concerned either has no identifiable FV, or a FV that is lower than its carrying value, and it shows indications of impairment. In order to calculate the VIU the entity needs to estimate the future cash flows that it will derive from its use and consider possible variations in their amount or timing.[55] In estimating future cash flows the entity should:

'(a) base cash flow projections on reasonable and supportable assumptions that represent management's best estimate of the range of economic conditions that will exist over the remaining useful life of the asset. Greater weight shall be given to external evidence;

(b) base cash flow projections on the most recent financial budgets/forecasts approved by management, but shall exclude any estimated future cash inflows or outflows expected to arise from future restructurings or from improving or enhancing the asset's performance. Projections based on these budgets/forecasts shall cover a maximum period of five years, unless a longer period can be justified;

(c) estimate cash flow projections beyond the period covered by the most recent budgets/forecasts by extrapolating the projections based on the budgets/forecasts using a steady or declining growth rate for subsequent years, unless an increasing rate can be justified. This growth rate shall not exceed the long-term average growth rate for the products, industries, or country or countries in which the entity operates, or for the market in which the asset is used, unless a higher rate can be justified.'[56]

The standard describes the responsibilities of management towards the estimation of cash flows in some detail. Management are required to ensure that the assumptions on which its current cash flow projections are based are consistent with past actual outcomes by examining the causes of differences between past cash flow projections and actual cash flows. They can, of course, take account of the effects of subsequent events or circumstances that did not exist when those actual cash flows were generated.[57]

IAS 36 states that the cash flows should be based on the most recent budgets and forecasts for a maximum of five years because reliable forecasts are rarely available for a longer period. If management is confident that its projections are reliable and can demonstrate this from past experience, it may use a longer period.[58] In using budgets and forecasts, management is required to consider whether these really are the best estimate of economic conditions that will exist over the remaining useful life of the asset.[59] Cash flows for the period beyond that covered by the forecasts or budgets assume a steady, declining or even negative rate of growth. An increase in the rate may be used if it is supported by objective information.[60]

Therefore only in exceptional circumstances should an increasing growth rate be used, or should the period before a steady or declining growth rate is assumed extend to more than five years. This five year rule is based on general economic theory that postulates above-average growth rates will only be achievable in the short-term, because such above-average growth will lead to competitors entering the market. This increased competition will, over a period of time, lead to a reduction of the growth rate, towards the average for the economy as a whole. IAS 36 suggests that entities will find it difficult to exceed the average historical growth rate for the products, countries or markets over the long term, say twenty years.[61]

This stage of the impairment review illustrates the point that it is not only fixed assets that are being assessed. The future cash flow to be forecast is *all* cash flows – receipts from sales, purchases, administrative expenses, etc. It is akin to a free cash flow valuation of a business with the resulting valuation then being compared to the carrying value of the assets in the CGU.

The cash flow forecast should include three elements:

- cash inflows from the continuing use of the asset;
- the cash outflows necessary to generate these cash inflows, including cash outflows to prepare the asset for use, that can either be directly attributed, or allocated on a reasonable and consistent basis; and
- the net cash flows, if any, that the entity may receive or pay for the disposal of the asset at the end of its useful life.[62]

Cash flows can be estimated by taking into account general price changes caused by inflation, or on the basis of stable prices. If inflation is built into the cash flow then the discount rate selected must also be adjusted to remove the inflationary effect.[63] Generally entities will use whichever method is most convenient to them that is consistent with the method they use in their budgets and forecasts and it is, of course, fundamental that cash flows and discount rate are both estimated on a consistent basis.

To avoid the danger of double counting, the future cash flows exclude those relating to financial assets, including receivables and liabilities such as payables, pensions and provisions.[64] However, see Step 1 above: paragraph 79 allows the inclusion of such assets and liabilities for practical reasons if the entity is unable to determine the recoverable amount without including them.

Projections in the cash flow should include costs of day-to-day servicing as well as overheads that can be reasonably attributed to the use of the asset.[65] Whilst a part-completed asset must have the costs to complete it included in the cash flow,[66] the general rule is that future cash flows should be forecast for CGUs or assets in their current condition. Forecasts should not include estimated future cash inflows or outflows that are expected to arise from improving or enhancing the asset's performance.[67]

While the restriction on enhanced performance may be understandable, it adds an element of unreality that is hard to reconcile with other assumptions made in the

VIU process. For example, the underlying forecast cash flows that the standard makes the foundation of the procedure will obviously be based on the business as it is actually expected to develop in the future, growth, improvements and all. Producing a special forecast based on unrealistic assumptions, even for this limited purpose, may be difficult.

Nevertheless, paragraph 48 explicitly states that improvements to the current performance of an asset may not be included in the estimates of future cash flows until the expenditure that provides those improvements is incurred. The treatment of such expenditure is illustrated in Example 6 in the standard's accompanying section of illustrative examples.[68] The implication of this requirement is that if an asset is impaired, and even if the entity is going to make the future expenditure to reverse that impairment, the asset will still have to be written down. Subsequently, the impairment can be reversed, to the degree appropriate, after the expenditure has taken place.

This restriction may stop optimistic forecasts, but an assumption of new capital investment is in practice intrinsic to the VIU test. What has to be assessed is the future cash flows of a productive unit, such as a factory or hotel. The cash flows, out into the far future, will include the sales of product, cost of sales, administrative expenses, etc. They must necessarily include capital expenditure as well, at least to the extent required to keep the CGU functioning as forecast. This is explicitly acknowledged as follows:

> 'Estimates of future cash flows include future cash outflows necessary to maintain the level of economic benefits expected to arise from the asset in its current condition. When a cash-generating unit consists of assets with different estimated useful lives, all of which are essential to the ongoing operation of the unit, the replacement of assets with shorter lives is considered to be part of the day-to-day servicing of the unit when estimating the future cash flows associated with the unit. Similarly, when a single asset consists of components with different estimated useful lives, the replacement of components with shorter lives is considered to be part of the day-to-day servicing of the asset when estimating the future cash flows generated by the asset.'[69]

Accordingly, *some* capital expenditure cash flows must be built into the forecast cash flows. Whilst improving capital expenditure may not be recognised, routine or replacement capital expenditure necessary to maintain the function of the asset or assets in the CGU has to be included. This distinction may not be easy to draw in practice. Some of the practical difficulties in determining the amount of capital expenditure are described at 5.3 below.

The standard contains similar rules with regard to any future restructuring that may affect the VIU of the asset or CGU. The prohibition on including the results of restructuring applies only to those plans to which the entity is not committed. Again, this is because of the general rule that the cash flows must be based on the asset in its current condition and therefore future events that may change that condition are not to be taken into account.[70] When an entity becomes committed to a restructuring (as set out in IAS 37 – *Provisions, Contingent Assets and Contingent Liabilities* – see

Chapter 27) IAS 36 then allows an entity's estimates of future cash inflows and outflows to reflect the cost savings and other benefits from the restructuring (based on the most recent financial budgets/forecasts approved by management).[71] Treatment of such a future restructuring is illustrated by Example 5 in the standard's accompanying section of illustrative examples. The standard specifically points out that the increase in cash inflows as a result of such a restructuring may not be taken into account until after the entity is committed to the restructuring.[72] Entities will sometimes be required to recognise impairment losses that will be reversed once the expenditure has been incurred and the restructuring completed.

The expected future cash flows of the CGU being assessed for impairment should not include cash inflows or outflows from financing activities or tax receipts or payments. This is because the discount rate used and the future cash flows are themselves to be determined on a pre-tax basis.[73]

The inclusion of the disposal proceeds and costs at the end of the useful life of the asset should be based on current prices and costs for similar assets, adjusted if necessary for price level changes if the entity has chosen to include this factor in its forecasts and selection of a discount rate. The entity must take care that its estimate is based on a proper assessment of the amount that would be received in an arm's length transaction.[74]

Foreign currency cash flows should first be estimated in the currency in which they will be generated and then discounted using a discount rate appropriate for that currency. An entity should translate the present value calculated in the foreign currency using the spot exchange rate at the date of the value in use calculation.[75] Significantly, this could well be a different rate from that used to translate the foreign currency assets, goodwill and liabilities of a subsidiary at the period end. For example, a non-monetary asset such as an item of property, plant and equipment may be carried at an amount based on exchange rates on the date on which it was acquired but generates foreign currency cash flows. In order to determine its carrying amount if there are indicators of impairment, IAS 21 – *The Effects of Changes in Foreign Exchange Rates* – states that the recoverable amount will be calculated in accordance with IAS 36, and the cash flows translated at the exchange rate at the date when that value was determined.[76] IAS 21 notes that this may be the rate at the balance sheet date. The VIU is then compared to the carrying value and the item is then carried forward at the lower of these two values. Similarly, different rates may be used if the impairment review is of goodwill or an intangible asset with indefinite life, where the review need not be carried out at the year-end.

Finally, although probably inherent in their identification, the forecast cash flows of the CGU have to be allocated to different periods for the purpose of the discounting step, discussed next.

Step 4 Identifying an appropriate discount rate and discounting the future cash flows

When the future cash flows have been estimated and allocated to different periods, the present value of these cash flows should then be calculated by discounting them. The standard expresses this as follows:

'The discount rate (rates) shall be a pre-tax rate (rates) that reflect(s) current market assessments of:

(a) the time value of money; and

(b) the risks specific to the asset for which the future cash flow estimates have not been adjusted.' [77]

This means the discount rate to be applied should be an estimate of the rate that the market would expect on an equally risky investment. The standard states:

'A rate that reflects current market assessments of the time value of money and the risks specific to the asset is the return that investors would require if they were to choose an investment that would generate cash flows of amounts, timing and risk profile equivalent to those that the entity expects to derive from the asset.' [78]

Therefore, if at all possible, the rate is to be obtained from market transactions or market rates. It should be the rate implicit in current market transactions for similar assets or the weighted average cost of capital (WACC) of a listed entity that has a single asset (or a portfolio of assets) with similar service potential and risks to the asset under review.[79] Even if such a listed entity could be found, care would have to be taken in using its WACC as the standard specifies that the discount rate is independent of the entity's capital structure and the way it financed the purchase of the asset (see below). The effect of gearing and its effect on calculating an appropriate WACC are discussed further in Example 15.7 and there is more discussion on the use of the WACC in 5.1 below.

It is only in rare cases (e.g. property assets) that such market rates can be obtained. In the event of an asset-specific rate not being available from the market, 'surrogates' should be used which are set out in Appendix A of IAS 36. The discount rate that 'investors would require if they were to choose an investment that would generate cash flows of amounts, timing and risk profile equivalent to those that the entity expects to derive from the asset' will not be easy to determine in many cases, but what guidance IAS 36 provides is as follows:

'As a starting point, the entity may take into account the following rates:

(a) the entity's weighted average cost of capital determined using techniques such as the Capital Asset Pricing Model;

(b) the entity's incremental borrowing rate; and

(c) other market borrowing rates.' [80]

Appendix A also gives the following guidelines for selecting the appropriate discount rate:

- it should be adjusted to reflect the specific risks associated with the projected cash flows (such as country, currency, price and cash flow risks) and to exclude risks that are not relevant;[81]
- to avoid double counting, the discount rate does not reflect risks for which future cash flow estimates have been adjusted;[82]

- the discount rate is independent of the entity's capital structure and the way it financed the purchase of the asset;[83]
- if the basis for the rate is post-tax (such as a weighted average cost of capital), it is adjusted to reflect a pre-tax rate;[84] and
- normally the entity uses a single discount rate for the estimation of an asset's VIU but it should use separate discount rates for different future periods if the VIU is sensitive to different risks or the terms structure of interest rates.[85]

Under IAS 36, therefore, assets are judged to be impaired if they are no longer expected to earn a current market rate of return. However, we have already seen that the IASB argues that the discount rate specific for the asset may not be sensitive to increases in short-term rates – this is discussed in 3.2 above.[86]

It is suggested that the incremental borrowing rate of the business is relevant to the selection of a discount rate. This could only be a starting point as the appropriate discount rate should be independent of the entity's capital structure or the way in which it financed the purchase of the asset. The incremental borrowing rate must be used with extreme caution as it might, for example, include an element of default risk for the entity as a whole, which is not relevant in assessing the return expected from the assets.

It is likely that in practice an estimate of the appropriate discount rate will have to be made using the concept of the WACC. Since most VIU calculations are done in the context of a CGU, and only rarely is there likely to be a market in similar CGUs, it is unlikely the discount rate can be calculated in any other way.

The appropriate way to calculate WACC is an extremely technical subject, and one about which there is much academic literature and no general agreement. The selection of the rate is obviously a crucial part of the impairment testing process and in practice it will probably not be possible to obtain a theoretically perfect rate. The objective, therefore, must be to obtain a rate which is sensible and justifiable. There are probably a number of acceptable methods of arriving at the appropriate rate and one method is set out below. While this illustration may appear to be quite complex, it has been written at a fairly general level. In practice, the calculation of the appropriate discount rate may be extremely complex and specialist advice may be needed.[87]

Example 15.7: Calculating a discount rate

This example is based on determining the WACC for a listed company with a similar risk profile to the CGU in question. Because it is highly unlikely that such a company will exist, it will usually have to be simulated by looking at a hypothetical company with a similar risk profile.

The following three elements need to be estimated for the hypothetical listed company with a similar risk profile:

- gearing, i.e. the ratio of market value of debt to market value of equity
- cost of debt; and
- cost of equity.

Gearing can best be obtained by reviewing quoted companies operating predominantly in the same industry as the CGU and identifying an average level of gearing for such companies. The companies need to be quoted so that the market value of equity can be readily determined.

Where companies in the sector typically have quoted debt, the cost of such debt can be determined directly. In order to calculate the cost of debt for bank loans and borrowings more generally, one method is to take the rate implicit in fixed interest government bonds – with a period to maturity similar to the expected life of the assets being reviewed for impairment – and to add to this rate a bank's margin, i.e. the commercial premium that would be added to the bond rate by a bank lending to the hypothetical listed company. In some cases, the margin being charged on existing borrowings to the company in question will provide evidence to help with establishing the bank's margin. Obviously, the appropriateness of this will depend upon the extent to which the risks facing the CGU being tested are similar to the risks facing the company or group as a whole.

If goodwill or intangible assets with an indefinite life were being included in a CGU reviewed for impairment (see 3.4 below) the appropriate gilt-edged bond rate to use might have to be adjusted towards that for irredeemable bonds. The additional bank's margin to add would be a matter for judgement but would vary according to the ease with which the sector under review was generally able to obtain bank finance and, as noted above, there might be evidence from the borrowings actually in place of the likely margin that would be chargeable. Sectors that invest significantly in tangible assets such as properties that are readily available as security for borrowings, would require a lower margin than other sectors where such security could not be found so easily.

Cost of equity is the hardest component of the cost of capital to determine. One technique referred to in the standard, frequently used in practice and written up in numerous textbooks is the 'Capital Asset Pricing Model' (CAPM). The theory underlying this model is that the cost of equity is equal to the risk-free rate plus a multiple, known as the beta, of the market risk premium. The risk-free rate is the same as that used to determine the nominal cost of debt and described above as being obtainable from government bond yields with an appropriate period to redemption. The market risk premium is the premium that investors require for investing in equities rather than government bonds. There are also reasons why this rate may be loaded in certain cases, for instance to take account of specific risks in the CGU in question that are not reflected in its market sector generally. Loadings are typically made when determining the cost of equity for a small company. The beta for a quoted company is a number that is greater or less than one according to whether market movements generally are reflected in a proportionately greater (beta more than one) or smaller (beta less than one) movement in the particular stock in question. Most betas fall into the range 0.4 to 1.5.

Various bodies, such as The London Business School, publish betas on a regular basis both for individual stocks and for industry sectors in general. Published betas are levered, i.e. they reflect the level of gearing in the company or sector concerned.

The cost of equity for the hypothetical company having a similar risk profile to the CGU is:

Cost of equity = risk-free rate + (levered beta × market risk premium)

Having determined the component costs of debt and equity and the appropriate level of gearing, the WACC for the hypothetical company having a similar risk profile to the CGU in question is:

$$\text{WACC} = (1 - t) \times D \times \frac{g}{(1 + g)} + E \times \left[1 - \frac{g}{(1 + g)}\right]$$

where:

D is the cost of debt;
E is the cost of equity
g is the gearing level (i.e. the ratio of debt to equity) for the sector; and
t is the rate of tax relief available on the debt servicing payments.

IAS 36 requires that the forecast cash flows are before tax and finance costs, though it is more common in discounted cash flow valuations to use cash flows after tax. However, as pre-tax cash flows are being used, the standard requires a pre-tax discount rate to be used.[88] This will theoretically involve discounting higher future cash flows (before deduction of tax) with a higher discount rate. This higher discount rate is the post-tax rate adjusted to reflect the specific amount and timing of the future tax flows. In other words, the pre-tax discount rate is the rate that gives the same present value when discounting the pre-tax cash flows as the post-tax cash flows discounted at the post-tax rate of return.[89]

Once the WACC has been calculated, the pre-tax WACC can be calculated. In those circumstances where a simple gross up is appropriate, it can be calculated by applying the fraction 1/(1–t). Thus, if the WACC comes out at, say, 12% the pre-tax WACC will be 12% divided by 0.7 (assuming a corporation tax rate of 30% to be the appropriate rate in the context of the reporting entity), which would give a pre-tax rate of 17.1%.

However, the pre-tax discount rate is generally not the post-tax rate grossed up by a standard rate of tax. It also depends on the timing of future tax cash flows and the useful life of the asset; these tax flows can be scheduled and an iterative process used to calculate the pre-tax discount rate.[90] The timing of tax cash flows can be extremely important if the CGU has tax losses that mean that there will be no payment of tax for a number of years, perhaps not until after the five year time horizon covered by budgets and forecasts. The effect of the tax cash flows on the VIU will have to be estimated and it may be necessary to consult a valuations expert on these more complex matters. These matters are discussed further in 5.1 below.

The selection of discount rates leaves considerable room for judgement in the absence of more specific guidance, and it is likely that many very different approaches will be applied in practice, even though this may not always be evident from the financial statements. However, once the discount rate has been chosen, the future cash flows are discounted in order to produce a present value figure representing the VIU of the CGU or individual asset that is the subject of the impairment test. The final step in the impairment review can now be taken.

Step 5 Comparing carrying value with VIU and recognising impairment losses

If the carrying value of an individual asset or of a CGU is less than (or equal to) its calculated VIU, there is no impairment. On the other hand, if the carrying value of the CGU is greater than its VIU, an impairment write-down should be recognised. IAS 36 has rules on the allocation of impairment losses, depending upon whether an individual asset, an individual CGU, or a group of CGUs with goodwill or corporate assets allocated to the group as a whole, is involved. These aspects are discussed below.

3.3.3 Recognition of impairment losses

If the VIU calculation has produced an impairment loss, then IAS 36 sets out how such losses should be recognised. There are three cases involved, an impairment loss on an individual asset, an impairment loss on an individual CGU and an impairment loss on a group of CGUs. The latter may occur where there are corporate assets (see 3.3.1 Step 2 above) or goodwill (see 3.4 below) that have been allocated to a group of CGUs rather than to individual ones.

A Impairment losses on individual assets

For individual assets IAS 36 states:

> 'If, and only if, the recoverable amount of an asset is less than its carrying amount, the carrying amount of the asset shall be reduced to its recoverable amount. That reduction is an impairment loss.[91]
>
> An impairment loss shall be recognised immediately in profit or loss, unless the asset is carried at revalued amount in accordance with another Standard (for example, in accordance with the revaluation model in IAS 16). Any impairment loss of a revalued asset shall be treated as a revaluation decrease in accordance with that other Standard' [92]

If there is an impairment loss on a non-revalued asset it is recognised in profit or loss. However, an impairment loss on a revalued asset is first used to reduce the revaluation surplus for that asset. Only when the impairment loss exceeds the amount in the revaluation surplus for that same asset is any further impairment loss recognised in the profit and loss.[93] IAS 36 does not state a particular position in the income statement for impairment losses to be shown. Neither does it address whether any amounts written off a fixed asset should be treated as (i) a deduction from the gross amount (cost or valuation) or (ii) as an increase in cumulative depreciation, in the reconciliation required by IAS 16 between the carrying amounts at the beginning and end of the year.[94] If the asset is carried at cost, we consider that it is more appropriate to carry an impairment write down within cumulative depreciation. If the asset is held at valuation then there is less of an issue and the impairment will be reflected in the revalued carrying amount.

An impairment loss greater than the carrying value of the asset does not give rise to a liability unless another standard requires it, presumably as this would be tantamount to providing for future losses.[95] An impairment loss will reduce the depreciable amount of an asset and the revised amount will be written off prospectively over the remaining life.[96] However, an entity ought also to review the useful life and residual value of its impaired asset, as both of these may need to be revised. The circumstances that give rise to impairments frequently impact these as well. Finally, an impairment loss will have implications for any deferred tax calculation involving the asset and in the standard's accompanying section of illustrative examples Example 3, on which the following is based, illustrates the possible effects.

Example 15.8: Recognition of an impairment loss creates a deferred tax asset

An entity has an asset with a carrying amount of €2,000 whose recoverable amount is €1300. The tax rate is 30% and the tax base of the asset is €1,500. Impairment losses are not deductible for tax purposes. The effect of the impairment loss is as follows:

	Before impairment €	Effect of impairment €	After impairment €
Carrying amount	2,000	(700)	1,300
Tax base	1,500	–	1,500
Taxable (deductible) temporary difference	500	(700)	(200)
Deferred tax liability (asset) at 30%	150	(210)	(60)

The entity will recognise the deferred tax asset to the extent that it is probable that there will be available taxable profits against which the deductible temporary difference can be utilised.

B Impairment losses and CGUs

Impairment losses in a CGU can occur in two ways:

(i) an impairment loss is incurred in a CGU on its own, and that CGU may or may not have corporate assets or goodwill included in its carrying value;

(ii) an impairment loss is identified that must be allocated across a group of CGUs because a corporate asset or goodwill is involved whose carrying value could only be allocated to a group of CGUs as a whole, rather than to individual ones (the allocation of corporate assets to CGUs is discussed in 3.3.1 Step 2 above, and goodwill is discussed at 3.4 below).

The relevant paragraphs from the standard deal with both instances but are readily understandable only if the above distinction is appreciated. The standard lays down that impairment losses in CGUs should be recognised to reduce the carrying amount of the assets of the unit (group of units) in the following order:

(a) first, to reduce the carrying amount of any goodwill allocated to the CGU or group of units.; and

(b) if the goodwill has been written off, to reduce the other assets of the CGU (or group of CGUs) pro rata to their carrying amount.[97]

Note that if there are indicators of impairment in connection with a CGU to which goodwill has been allocated, this CGU should be tested and any necessary impairment loss taken, prior to performing an impairment test for goodwill (see 3.4.2A below).[98] These impairment losses and consequent reductions in carrying values are treated in exactly the same way as those for individual assets, in accordance with paragraph 60 of IAS 36, as explained above.

The important point is to be clear about the order set out above. This requires any goodwill to be written down first, and thereafter if an impairment loss remains, the other assets in the CGU or group of CGUs are written down pro-rata to their carrying values. This pro-rating is in two stages if a group of CGUs is involved:

(i) the loss is eliminated against goodwill (which by definition in this instance is unallocated to individual CGUs in the group);

(ii) any remaining loss is pro-rated between the carrying values of the individual CGUs in the group; and

(iii) within each individual CGU the loss is again pro-rated between the individual assets' carrying values.

Unless it is possible to estimate the recoverable amount of each individual asset within a CGU, it is necessary to allocate impairment losses to individual assets in such a way that the revised carrying amounts of these assets correspond with the requirements of the standard. Therefore, the entity does not reduce the carrying amount of an individual asset below the highest of its FV or VIU (if these can be established), or zero. The amount of the impairment loss that would otherwise have been allocated to the asset is then allocated pro rata to the other assets of the CGU or CGU group.[99] The standard argues that this arbitrary allocation to individual assets when their recoverable amount cannot be individually assessed is appropriate because all assets of a CGU 'work together'.[100]

If corporate assets are allocated to a CGU or group of CGUs, then any remaining loss at (ii) above (i.e. after allocation to goodwill) is pro-rated against the allocated share of the corporate asset and the other assets in the CGU.

This process, then, writes down the carrying value attributed or allocated to a CGU until the carrying value of the net assets is not more than the computed VIU. As is recognised in paragraph 105 of IAS 36, set out above, it is logically possible, after all assets and goodwill are either written off or down to their FV, for the carrying value of the CGU to be higher than the computed VIU. There is no suggestion that the net assets should be reduced any further because at this point the FV would be the relevant impairment figure. The remaining amount will only be recognised as a liability if that is a requirement of another standard.[101]

IAS 36 includes in the standard's accompanying section of illustrative examples Example 2 which illustrates the calculation, recognition and allocation of an impairment loss across CGUs.

However, the standard stresses that no impairment loss should be reflected against an individual asset if the CGU to which it belongs has not been impaired, even if its carrying value exceeds its FV. This is expanded in the following example, based on that in paragraph 107 of the standard:

Example 15.9: Individually impaired assets within CGUs

A machine has suffered physical damage but is still working, although not as well as before it was damaged. The machine's FV less costs to sell is less than its carrying amount. The machine does not generate independent cash inflows. The smallest identifiable group of assets that includes the machine and generates cash inflows that are largely independent of the cash inflows from other assets is the production line to which the machine belongs. The recoverable amount of the production line shows that the production line taken as a whole is not impaired.

Assumption 1: budgets/forecasts approved by management reflect no commitment of management to replace the machine.

The recoverable amount of the machine alone cannot be estimated because its VIU may be different from its FV less costs to sell (because the entity is going to continue to use it) and can be determined only for the CGU to which it belongs (the production line).

As the production line is not impaired, no impairment loss is recognised for the machine. Nevertheless, the entity may need to reassess the depreciation period or the depreciation method for the machine. Perhaps a shorter depreciation period or a faster depreciation method is required to reflect the expected remaining useful life of the machine or the pattern in which economic benefits are expected to be consumed by the entity.

Assumption 2: budgets/forecasts approved by management reflect a commitment of management to replace the machine and sell it in the near future.

Cash flows from continuing use of the machine until its disposal are estimated to be negligible. The machine's VIU can be estimated to be close to its FV less costs to sell. Therefore, the recoverable amount of the machine can be determined and no consideration is given to the CGU (the production line) to which it belongs. As the machine's carrying amount exceeds its FV less costs to sell, an impairment loss is recognised to write it down to FV less costs to sell.[102]

Note that it is assumed that the asset is still useable (otherwise it would not be contributing to the cash flows of the CGU and would have to be written off) and not held for sale as defined by IFRS 5, whose requirements are discussed further in Chapter 4.

Once the impairment write-down has been made, henceforth the entity will theoretically be able to make the rate of return on its assets which the providers of its capital are looking to see on their funds invested. This is the rate implicit in the calculation that forms the basis of the discount rate chosen for the impairment calculations. An implication of the standard therefore, but not one that we have seen much evidence of in those jurisdictions that have been operating similar impairment standards so far, is that no entities should be reporting materially sub-standard returns on an ongoing basis – at least not those in which an impairment review has been triggered by an 'indicator of impairment'.

The fact that in reality entities continue to report sub-market returns in jurisdictions where similar impairment rules apply, has implications for the practical efficacy of impairment as the check and balance against undue optimism about asset values in the IASB's intended fair-value based accounting future. Whether impairment as a system will actually be the effective safeguard it is intended to be in a fair-value future, is far from obvious. As noted in the introduction to this chapter, impairment in a fair value world takes on the role of prudence under historical cost systems. The effectiveness of this 'new prudence' is only a theoretical hope so far; whether it turns out to be a sensible alternative to traditional prudence is an open question. Particularly as it must be remembered that the appearance of an 'indicator of impairment' is required before an impairment review is required at all.

3.4 Impairment of intangible assets with an indefinite life and goodwill

With the publication of IFRS 3 came a change to the treatment of goodwill previously required by IFRS. Hitherto, entities were required to systematically depreciate goodwill, with a very strong presumption that its useful life would not exceed twenty years. As a result of the IASB's strategy of converging towards US GAAP, this position has changed considerably.

Under IFRS 3, effective from 1 January 2005, goodwill may not be systematically depreciated; instead it is required to be subject to an annual impairment review.[103] As a consequence of the change to the treatment of goodwill, the revised IAS 38 now allows that intangible assets may also have indefinite useful lives. IAS 38 makes a distinction between intangible assets with finite useful lives and those with indefinite useful lives. The former must be depreciated systematically over their useful lives; however intangible assets with an indefinite useful life may not be systematically depreciated, but must also be subject to an annual impairment test.[104]

An objective observer would probably be less than convinced that the changes to IFRS to accommodate convergence with US GAAP, described above, were an unquestioned improvement. The rather unconvincing record of impairment testing, which has not produced consistent effects, must mean that there is a degree of risk involved with the change. Certainly, volatility must accompany it. These considerations make it probable that if an impairment becomes necessary it is highly likely to involve a very considerable portion of the intangible asset or goodwill sum involved – all of which will be reported in profit and loss immediately.

The impairment tests required for goodwill and intangible assets with an indefinite life must be performed annually, but not necessarily at the period end balance sheet date. This is in contrast to the impairment tests for other assets described in 3.2 and 3.3 above that are required only if there are indications of impairment, but which must be performed at the period end. The detailed requirements of IAS 36 concerning goodwill and intangible assets with an indefinite life are discussed below; however the assumption is made that the reader is conversant with the previously described impairment test procedures.

3.4.1 Impairment of intangible assets with an indefinite useful life

IAS 38 makes the point that 'indefinite' does not mean 'infinite', and unforeseeable factors may affect the entity's ability and intention to maintain the asset at its standard of performance assessed at the time of estimating the asset's useful life.[105] An intangible asset with an indefinite useful life needs to be impairment tested annually, and at the same time each year but not necessarily the year-end, even though it is not subject to systematic depreciation.[106] However intangible assets with an indefinite useful life are not exempted from the normal requirements of IAS 36, so if there are any indications of impairment, an impairment test must be performed at the period end as set out in the standard and described in 3.1 to 3.3 above. This is in addition to the annual test unless, of course, that test indicated that there was sufficient headroom.

The requirements of IAS 36 for this type of asset can be summarised as follows:

1. All intangible assets with indefinite useful lives must be tested for impairment at least once per year and at the same time each year;[107]
2. Any intangible asset with an indefinite useful life recognised during the reporting period must be tested for impairment before the end of the period;[108]
3. Any intangible asset (regardless of whether it has an indefinite useful life or not) *that is not yet available for use* recognised during the reporting period must be impairment tested before the end of the period;[109]
4. If an intangible asset that has an indefinite useful life or is not yet available for use can only be tested for impairment as part of a CGU, then that CGU must be tested for impairment at least annually;[110]
5. If there are indicators of impairment a year end test must also be performed.

The reason given for the annual requirement to test any intangible asset not yet ready for use is as follows:

> 'The ability of an intangible asset to generate sufficient future economic benefits to recover its carrying amount is usually subject to greater uncertainty before the asset is available for use than after it is available for use. Therefore, this Standard requires an entity to test for impairment, at least annually, the carrying amount of an intangible asset that is not yet available for use.'[111]

This will obviously have a major impact on any entity that capitalises development expenditure in accordance with IAS 38 where the period of development may straddle more than one accounting period.

A Measuring the recoverable amount of an intangible asset with an indefinite useful life

An intangible asset with an indefinite useful life may generate independent cash inflows as an individual asset, in which case the impairment testing procedure as set out in 3.2 and 3.3 above for a single asset applies. Additionally an intangible asset may form part of the assets within a CGU, in which case the procedures relevant to testing a CGU as set out above apply. In particular IAS 36 makes it clear that if an intangible asset with an indefinite useful life, or any intangible asset not yet ready for use, is included in the assets of a CGU, then that CGU has to be tested for impairment annually.[112]

However, IAS 36 allows a concession that only applies to those intangible assets with an indefinite useful life that form part of a CGU. It allows the most recent detailed calculation of such an asset's recoverable amount made in a preceding period to be used in the impairment test in the current period if all of the following criteria are met:

(a) if the intangible asset is part of a CGU and the assets and liabilities making up that unit have not changed significantly since the most recent recoverable amount calculation;

(b) that calculation of the asset's recoverable amount exceeded its carrying amount by a substantial margin; and

(c) the likelihood that an updated calculation of the recoverable amount would be less than the asset's carrying amount is remote, based on an analysis of events and circumstances since the most recent calculation of the recoverable amount.[113]

Thus if there was sufficient headroom on the last calculation and little has changed in the CGU to which the asset belongs, it can be revisited and re-used rather than having to be entirely restarted from scratch, which considerably reduces the work involved in the annual test. The impairment test cannot be rolled forward forever, of course, and an entity will have to take a cautious approach to estimating when circumstances have changed sufficiently to require a new test.

Impairment losses experienced on intangible assets with an indefinite useful life are recognised exactly as set out above in 3.3.2, either as an individual asset or as part of a CGU, depending upon whether the intangible concerned is part of a CGU or not. Note that there is an important distinction concerning the allocation of losses in a CGU between the treatment of goodwill and intangible assets with an indefinite useful life. As set out above in 3.3.2, if goodwill forms part of the assets of a CGU, any impairment loss first reduces the goodwill and thereafter the remaining assets are reduced pro-rata. However, if an intangible asset is part of a CGU that is impaired, there is no requirement to write down the intangible before the other assets in the CGU, rather all are written down pro-rata.

3.4.2 Impairment of goodwill

This topic is dealt with in detail in Chapter 7.

Under IFRS, only goodwill acquired in a business combination can be recognised. Inherently, goodwill cannot produce cash flows independently of other groups of assets; therefore to test it for impairment necessitates its allocation to CGUs (or groups of CGUs).

The standard does not require goodwill to be allocated between every CGU that is identified by the business. Rather it allows goodwill to be allocated to groups of CGUs, as it does corporate assets. In fact the only requirement is that goodwill is allocated to groups of CGUs that together are not larger than the 'lowest level within the entity at which the goodwill is monitored for internal management purposes' with the only proviso being that such groups should 'not be larger than a segment based on either the entity's primary or … secondary reporting format determined in accordance with IAS 14 – *Segment Reporting*.'[114] The allocation of goodwill to CGUs and the provisions of IAS 36 concerning the minority interest's proportion of goodwill are dealt with in Chapter 7. That chapter also deals with IAS 36's requirements concerning the allocation and reallocation of goodwill following disposals or group reorganisations. Matters that affect the entity's CGUs arising from goodwill impairment testing are dealt with below.

IFRS 8 – *Operating Segments* – issued by the IASB in November 2006, will replace IAS 14 and will change the basis for identifying segments starting in financial statements from 1 January 2009. Under IFRS 8 an 'operating segment' is identified on the basis of internal reports that are regularly reviewed by the entity's chief operating decision maker in order to allocate resources to the segment and assess its performance.[115] As a result, IAS 36 has been amended and as from 1 January 2009, goodwill to be tested for impairment cannot be allocated to a CGU or CGU group larger than an operating segment. IFRS 8 is discussed in Chapter 30.

As the adoption of IFRS 8 might result in a change in the identification of the entity's segments, some groups or entities will have to face the issue of validating the previous goodwill allocation to CGUs or group of CGUs or of reallocating goodwill to the new operating segments it has identified when performing the impairment test. This is discussed further in Chapter 7 at 3.9.

Impairment losses on goodwill must be recognised immediately in the income statement. The losses first reduce the carrying value of the goodwill, and thereafter reduce the other assets in the CGU or group of CGUs pro-rata, as explained in more detail in 3.3.2 above.

A Timing of the goodwill impairment test and testing of CGUs

The standard requires impairment testing for goodwill as follows:

1. All CGUs or groups of CGUs to which goodwill has been allocated must be tested for impairment at least once per year and at the same time each year. Different CGUs may be tested at different times;
2. If goodwill has been allocated during the current period, the CGU or CGU group must be tested before the end of the period (not necessarily at the end of the period).[116]

The standard makes it clear that if indications of impairment necessitate an impairment test for an individual CGU or one that is part of a group to which goodwill has been allocated, this test must be performed and any impairment loss recognised first. The impairment review is carried out on the CGU or CGU group excluding goodwill.[117] Similarly, if there are any indications of impairment with respect to the assets within a CGU, to a CGU itself or to a CGU group to which goodwill has been allocated, at the time of year when the goodwill impairment test is to be performed, these 'pre-goodwill' tests are carried out first and any impairment recognised. The test on the CGU or CGU group containing the goodwill must only be performed after the individual test.[118] Therefore, the entity may have to carry out an impairment test on an individual asset or CGU at a time other than at the end of its annual period. CGUs to which goodwill has been allocated may also need to be reviewed at the end of the period if there has been an indicator of impairment even if they have been included in the goodwill test as at an earlier date.

Example 15.10: Timing of the goodwill impairment test

An entity that prepares its financial statements to December reviews its goodwill for impairment in September. Goodwill is allocated to CGUs A, B and C and any allocation at a lower level would be arbitrary. At the time of the September 2006 impairment review, an indicator of impairment is noted in CGU A. The entity is required to test CGU A for impairment in September 2006 and provide for an impairment loss, if necessary, before testing the group of CGUs with regard to the allocated goodwill.

3.5 The reversal of impairment losses

IAS 36 does not permit an impairment loss on goodwill to be reversed under any circumstances.[119] The standard justifies this on the grounds that such a reversal would probably be an increase in internally generated goodwill, rather than a reversal of the impairment loss recognised for the acquired goodwill, and that internally generated goodwill is prohibited by IAS 38.[120]

Example 15.11: Impairment of goodwill

Company A has a CGU that has a carrying value of $2,000,000 at 31 December 2005. This carrying value comprises $500,000 relating to goodwill and $1,500,000 relating to net tangible assets.

In 2006, as a result of losses, net tangible assets have decreased to $1,400,000 reducing the total carrying value of the unit to $1,900,000. Changes in the regulatory framework surrounding its business mean that the income-generating unit has a recoverable amount of $1,600,000 and has thus suffered an impairment loss of $300,000. This is charged to the profit and loss account. The carrying value of goodwill is reduced to $200,000.

In 2007 the company develops a new product with the result that the recoverable amount of the income-generating unit rises to $1,700,000. Net tangible assets have remained at $1,400,000. Despite the recoverable amount of the business unit now being $1,700,000 compared to its carrying value of $1,600,000, it is not possible to reverse $100,000 of the prior year's impairment loss of $300,000 since the reason for the increase in value of the business unit (the launch of the new product) is not the same as the reason for the original impairment loss (the change in the regulatory environment in which the business operates).

For all other assets, including intangible assets with an indefinite life, IAS 36 requires entities to assess at each reporting date whether there is any indication that an impairment loss may no longer exist or may have decreased. If there is any such indication, the entity has to recalculate the recoverable amount of the asset.[121]

Therefore if there are indications that a previously recognised impairment loss has disappeared or reduced, it is necessary to determine again the recoverable amount (i.e. the higher of FV or VIU) so that the reversal can be quantified. The standard sets out examples of what it notes are in effect 'reverse indications' of impairment.[122] These are the reverse of those set out in paragraph 12 of the standard as indications of impairment (see 3.2 above) and are, as in paragraph 12, in two categories:

External sources of information:

(a) a significant increase in the asset's market value;

(b) significant changes during the period or expected in the near future in the entity's technological, market, economic or legal environment that will have a favourable effect;

(c) decreases in market interest rates or other market rates of return on investments and those decreases are likely to affect the discount rate used in calculating the asset's value in use and increase the asset's recoverable amount materially.

Internal sources of information:

(d) significant changes during the period or expected in the near future that will affect the extent to which, or manner in which, the asset is used. These changes include costs incurred during the period to improve or enhance the asset's performance or restructure the operation to which the asset belongs;

(e) evidence from internal reporting that the economic performance of the asset is, or will be, better than expected.[123]

Compared with paragraph 12, there are two notable omissions from this list of 'reverse indicators', one external and one internal.

The external indication not included is the mirror of the impairment indicator 'the carrying amount of the net assets of the reporting entity is more than its market capitalisation'. No explanation is provided about why, if a market capitalisation below shareholders' funds is an indication of impairment, its reversal should not be an indication of a reversal. The internal omission from the list of 'reverse indicators' is that evidence of obsolescence or physical deterioration has been reversed. Once again no reason is given but it may be that the standard-setters have assumed that no such reversal could take place without the entity incurring costs to improve or enhance the performance of the asset or the CGU so that this is, in effect, covered by indicator (d) above.

The standard also reminds preparers that a reversal, like an impairment, is evidence that the depreciation method or residual value of the asset should be reviewed and may need to be adjusted, whether or not the impairment loss is reversed.[124]

A further stricture is that impairment losses should be reversed only if there has been a change in the estimates used to determine the impairment loss, e.g. a change in cash flows or discount rate (for VIU) or a change in FV. IAS 36 does not allow the mere passage of time (the 'unwinding' of the discount will increase the present value of future cash flows as they become closer) to trigger the reversal of an impairment. In other words the 'service potential' of the asset must genuinely improve if a reversal is to be recognised.[125] However, this inability to recognise the rise in value can give rise to some illogical effects, as demonstrated by the following example:

Example 15.12: Double counted losses

At the end of 2004, an entity with a single CGU is carrying out an impairment review. The discounted forecast cash flows for years 2006 and onwards would be just enough to support the carrying value of the firm's assets. However, 2005 is forecast to produce a loss and net cash outflow. The discounted value of this amount is accordingly written off the carrying value of the fixed assets in 2004 as an impairment loss. It is then suffered again in 2005 (at a slightly higher amount being now undiscounted) as the actual loss. Once that loss is past, the future cash flows are sufficient to support the original unimpaired value of the fixed assets. Nevertheless, the assets cannot be written back up through the profit and loss account to counter the double counting effect as the increase in value does not derive from a change in economic conditions or in the expected use of an asset. The entity will only 'benefit' as the assets are amortised.

If, on the other hand, the revival in cash flows is the result of expenditure by the entity to improve or enhance the performance of the asset or the CGU or on a restructuring of the CGU, there may be an obvious improvement in the service potential and the entity may be able to reverse some or all of the impairment write down.

In the event of an individual asset's impairment being reversed, the reversal may not raise the carrying value above the figure it would have stood at taking into account depreciation, if no impairment had originally been recognised.[126] Any increase above this figure would really be a revaluation, which would have to be accounted for in accordance with the standard relevant to the asset concerned.[127]

Example 15.13: Reversal of impairment losses

In 2004 an entity acquires an asset with a useful life of 10 years for $100. The asset generates net cash inflows that are largely independent of the cash inflows of other assets or groups of assets. At the end of 2006, when the carrying amount is $70, the entity recognises that there has been an impairment loss of $20. The entity writes the asset down to $50. As the useful life is not affected, the entity commences amortisation at (50 ÷ 7 = 7) $7 per annum to amortise the carrying value over the remaining useful life.

Two years later in 2008, the asset's carrying value is $36. Thanks to improvements in technology, the entity is able to increase the asset's VIU to $55 by spending $12 on parts that improve and enhance its performance.

The carrying value of the asset after the expenditure is $48. However, its depreciated historical cost (pre impairment) before charging depreciation for 2009, would have been $50. Therefore, the entity reverses an impairment loss of $2 and writes the asset back up to $50. Amortisation in 2009 and thereafter to the end of the asset's useful life is once again $10 per annum.

The reversal of the impairment loss of $2 represents the difference between the impairment loss of $20 and the cost of the expenditure of $12, to which has been added the reduction in the amortisation charge for two years based on the lower carrying amount ($10 – $7).

The Standard includes an illustration of the reversal of an impairment loss in the standard's accompanying section of illustrative examples, in Example 4.

All reversals are to be recognised in the income statement immediately, except for revalued assets which are dealt with below.[128]

If an impairment loss is reversed against an asset, its depreciation or amortisation is adjusted to allocate its revised carrying amount less residual value over its remaining useful life.[129]

A Reversals of impairments – revalued assets

If an asset is recognised at a revalued amount under another standard any reversal of an impairment loss should be treated as a revaluation increase under that other standard. Thus a reversal of an impairment loss on a revalued asset is credited directly to equity under the heading revaluation surplus. However, to the extent that an impairment loss on the same revalued asset was previously recognised as an expense in the income statement, a reversal of that impairment loss is recognised as income in the income statement.[130]

As with assets carried at cost, after a reversal of an impairment loss is recognised on a revalued asset, the depreciation charge should be adjusted in future periods to allocate the asset's revised carrying amount, less any residual value, on a systematic basis over its remaining useful life.[131]

B Reversals of impairments – cash-generating units

Where an entity recognises a reversal of an impairment loss on a CGU, the increase in the carrying amount of the assets of the unit should be allocated by increasing the carrying amount of the assets, other than goodwill, in the unit on a pro-rata basis. However, the carrying amount of an individual asset should not be increased above the lower of its recoverable amount and the carrying amount that would have resulted had no impairment loss been recognised in prior years. Any 'surplus' reversal is to be allocated to the remaining assets pro-rata, always remembering that goodwill, if allocated to an individual CGU, may not be increased under any circumstances.[132]

4 DISCLOSURES REQUIRED BY IAS 36

4.1 Introduction

This section sets out the principal disclosures required in financial statements complied under IFRS for impairment as set out in IAS 36. Any disclosures required relating to impairment by other standards are dealt with in the chapter concerned. Disclosures that may be required by other authorities such as national statutes or listing authorities are not included.

4.2 IAS 36 disclosures

The disclosures required fall into two broad categories:

(i) disclosures concerning any actual impairment losses or reversals made in the period, that are obviously only required if such a loss or reversal has occurred, regardless of the type of asset involved; and

(ii) yearly disclosures concerning the annual impairment tests required for goodwill and intangible assets with an indefinite useful life, that are required regardless of whether an impairment adjustment to these types of assets has occurred or not.

4.2.1 Disclosures required for impairment adjustments

IAS 36 defines a class of assets as 'a grouping of assets of similar nature and use in the entity's operations'.[133] For each class of assets the entity must disclose:

'(a) the amount of impairment losses recognised in profit or loss during the period and the line item(s) of the income statement in which those impairment losses are included;

(b) the amount of reversals of impairment losses recognised in profit or loss during the period and the line item(s) of the income statement in which those impairment losses are reversed;

(c) the amount of impairment losses on revalued assets recognised directly in equity during the period;

(d) the amount of reversals of impairment losses on revalued assets recognised directly in equity during the period.'[134]

These disclosures can be made as an integral part of the other disclosures, for example the property plant and equipment note reconciling the opening and closing values (as set out in Chapter 13 at 2.7) may contain the required information.[135]

Additionally, IAS 36 links disclosure of impairments with segment disclosures. Thus, if a business is subject to IAS 14 (or IFRS 8 after the implementation of that standard) then any impairments or reversals must be disclosed by primary reportable segment as follows:

(a) the amount of impairment losses recognised in profit or loss and directly in equity during the period;

(b) the amount of reversals of impairment losses recognised in profit or loss and directly in equity during the period.[136]

A Material impairments

If an impairment loss for an individual asset or an individual cash-generating unit is recognised or reversed during the period and is material to the financial statements of the reporting entity as a whole, the following disclosures are required:

(a) the events and circumstances that led to the recognition or reversal of the impairment loss;

(b) the amount of the impairment loss recognised or reversed;

(c) for an individual asset:

  (i) the nature of the asset; and

  (ii) the reportable segment (if the entity is subject to IAS 14 or IFRS 8, if that standard has been implemented) to which the asset belongs, based on the entity's primary format.

(d) for a cash-generating unit:

  (i) a description of the cash-generating unit (such as whether it is a product line, a plant, a business operation, a geographical area, a reportable segment as defined in IAS 14 or IFRS 8 if that standard has been implemented);

  (ii) the amount of the impairment loss recognised or reversed by class of assets and (if the entity is subject to IAS 14) by reportable segment based on the entity's primary format or, if IFRS 8 has been implemented, by reportable segment as defined by that standard ; and

  (iii) if the aggregation of assets for identifying the cash-generating unit has changed since the previous estimate of the cash-generating unit's recoverable amount (if any), a description of the current and former way of aggregating assets and the reasons for changing the way the cash-generating unit is identified.

(e) whether the recoverable amount of the asset or cash-generating unit is its fair value less costs to sell (FV) or its value in use (VIU);

(f) if recoverable amount is FV, the basis used to determine FV (such as whether FV was determined by reference to an active market); and

(g) if recoverable amount is VIU, the discount rate used in the current estimate and previous estimate (if any) of VIU.[137]

It is logically possible for impairment adjustments *in aggregate* to be material, yet no single one material in itself – in which case the previous requirement that relates to individual assets or CGUs could theoretically be circumvented. Therefore the following 'catch all' requirement is added:

> 'An entity shall disclose the following information for the aggregate impairment losses and the aggregate reversals of impairment losses recognised during the period for which no information is disclosed in accordance with paragraph 130:
>
> (a) the main classes of assets affected by impairment losses and the main classes of assets affected by reversals of impairment losses;
>
> (b) the main events and circumstances that led to the recognition of these impairment losses and reversals of impairment losses.'[138]

If there are any cases of impairment adjustments where intangible assets with indefinite useful life and goodwill are not involved, IAS 36 encourages the disclosure of key assumptions made in the recoverable amount calculations used to determine any impairments recognised in the period.[139] However, as set out below, if there is any impairment of a CGU containing intangible assets with an indefinite useful life or goodwill, this type of disclosure is a requirement.

4.2.2 *Annual impairment disclosures required for goodwill and intangible assets with an indefinite useful life.*

Paragraph 84 of IAS 36 accepts that following a business combination it may not have been possible to allocate all the goodwill to individual CGUs or groups of CGUs. In this case such allocation must have been completed by the end of the following period. In these circumstances the standard requires that the amount of any such unallocated goodwill be disclosed, together with the reasons why it has not been allocated.[140]

The annual disclosures are intended to provide the user with information about the types of estimates that have been used in arriving at the recoverable amounts of goodwill and intangible assets with an indefinite useful life, that are included in the assets of the entity at the period end. They are divided into two broad categories:

(i) those concerning individual CGUs or group of CGUs in which the carrying amount of goodwill or of intangible assets with an indefinite useful life is 'significant' in comparison with the entity's total carrying amount of these items. In this category disclosures are to be made separately for each significant CGU or group of CGUs; and

(ii) those concerning CGUs or groups of CGUs in which the carrying amount of goodwill or of intangible assets with an indefinite useful life is *not* 'significant' individually in comparison with the entity's total carrying amount of these items. In this case the disclosures can be made in aggregate.

No definition of 'significant' is given; but in our view it must be taken to mean significant in relation to any or all of asset values, shareholders funds, and to profit for the year if a write off were to be required.

For each cash-generating unit or group of units for which the carrying amount of goodwill or intangible assets with indefinite useful lives allocated to that unit or group of units is significant, the following disclosures are required every year:

'(a) the carrying amount of goodwill allocated to the unit (group of units);

(b) the carrying amount of intangible assets with indefinite useful lives allocated to the unit (group of units);

(c) the basis on which the unit's (group of units') recoverable amount has been determined (i.e. value in use or fair value less costs to sell);

(d) if the unit's (group of units') recoverable amount is based on value in use:

  (i) a description of each key assumption on which management has based its cash flow projections for the period covered by the most recent budgets/forecasts. Key assumptions are those to which the unit's (group of units') recoverable amount is most sensitive;

  (ii) a description of management's approach to determining the value(s) assigned to each key assumption, whether those value(s) reflect past experience or, if appropriate, are consistent with external sources of information, and, if not, how and why they differ from past experience or external sources of information;

  (iii) the period over which management has projected cash flows based on financial budgets/forecasts approved by management and, when a period greater than five years is used for a cash-generating unit (group of units), an explanation of why that longer period is justified;

  (iv) the growth rate used to extrapolate cash flow projections beyond the period covered by the most recent budgets/forecasts, and the justification for using any growth rate that exceeds the long-term average growth rate for the products, industries, or country or countries in which the entity operates, or for the market to which the unit (group of units) is dedicated;

  (v) the discount rate(s) applied to the cash flow projections.

(e) if the unit's (group of units') recoverable amount is based on fair value less costs to sell, the methodology used to determine fair value less costs to sell. If fair value less costs to sell is not determined using an observable market price for the unit (group of units), the following information shall also be disclosed:

(i) a description of each key assumption on which management has based its determination of fair value less costs to sell. Key assumptions are those to which the unit's (group of units') recoverable amount is most sensitive;

(ii) a description of management's approach to determining the value(s) assigned to each key assumption, whether those value(s) reflect past experience or, if appropriate, are consistent with external sources of information, and, if not, how and why they differ from past experience or external sources of information.

(f) if a reasonably possible change in a key assumption on which management has based its determination of the unit's (group of units') recoverable amount would cause the unit's (group of units') carrying amount to exceed its recoverable amount:

(i) the amount by which the unit's (group of units') recoverable amount exceeds its carrying amount;

(ii) the value assigned to the key assumption;

(iii) the amount by which the value assigned to the key assumption must change, after incorporating any consequential effects of that changc on the other variables used to measure recoverable amount, in order for the unit's (group of units') recoverablc amount to be equal to its carrying amount.' [141]

As set out above, there are separate disclosure requirements for those CGUs or groups of CGUs that taken individually do not have significant amounts of goodwill or of intangible assets with an indefinite useful life within their carrying values. First, an aggregate disclosure has to be made of the not significant amounts of goodwill or of intangible assets with an indefinite useful life, as follows:

> 'If some or all of the carrying amount of goodwill or intangible assets with indefinite useful lives is allocated across multiple cash-generating units (groups of units), and the amount so allocated to each unit (group of units) is not significant in comparison with the entity's total carrying amount of goodwill or intangible assets with indefinite useful lives, that fact shall be disclosed, together with the aggregate carrying amount of goodwill or intangible assets with indefinite useful lives allocated to those units (groups of units).' [142]

Secondly, if in aggregate these amounts are significant in relation to the entirety of the carrying amount of the entity's goodwill or intangible assets with an indefinite useful life, the following is required to be disclosed:

> 'In addition, if the recoverable amounts of any of those units (groups of units) are based on the same key assumption(s) and the aggregate carrying amount of goodwill or intangible assets with indefinite useful lives allocated to them is significant in comparison with the entity's total carrying amount of goodwill or intangible assets with indefinite useful lives, an entity shall disclose that fact, together with:
>
> (a) the aggregate carrying amount of goodwill allocated to those units (groups of units);

(b) the aggregate carrying amount of intangible assets with indefinite useful lives allocated to those units (groups of units);

(c) a description of the key assumption(s);

(d) a description of management's approach to determining the value(s) assigned to the key assumption(s), whether those value(s) reflect past experience or, if appropriate, are consistent with external sources of information, and, if not, how and why they differ from past experience or external sources of information;

(e) if a reasonably possible change in the key assumption(s) would cause the aggregate of the units' (groups of units') carrying amounts to exceed the aggregate of their recoverable amounts:

 (i) the amount by which the aggregate of the units' (groups of units') recoverable amounts exceeds the aggregate of their carrying amounts;

 (ii) the value(s) assigned to the key assumption(s);

 (iii) the amount by which the value(s) assigned to the key assumption(s) must change, after incorporating any consequential effects of the change on the other variables used to measure recoverable amount, in order for the aggregate of the units' (groups of units') recoverable amounts to be equal to the aggregate of their carrying amounts.' [143]

Example 9 in Appendix B of IAS 36, reproduced below, gives an indication of the types of assumptions and other relevant information the IASB envisages being disclosed under this requirement. Such detailed items as follows are envisaged by the IASB for disclosure: budgeted gross margins, average gross margins, expected efficiency improvements., whether values assigned to key assumptions reflect past experience, what improvements management believes are reasonably achievable each year, forecast exchange rates during the budget period, forecast consumer price indices during the budget period for raw materials, market share and anticipated growth in market share. It is followed by a comprehensive disclosure example from Vodafone Group plc's 2006 financial statements.

Example 15.14: Disclosures relating to impairment tests for goodwill and intangible assets

Entity M includes the following disclosure in the notes to its financial statements for the year ending 31 December 20X3.

Impairment Tests for Goodwill and Intangible Assets with Indefinite Lives

Goodwill has been allocated for impairment testing purposes to three individual cash-generating units – two in Europe (units A and B) and one in North America (unit C) – and to one group of cash generating units (comprising operation XYZ) in Asia. The carrying amount of goodwill allocated to unit C and operation XYZ is significant in comparison with the total carrying amount of goodwill, but the carrying amount of goodwill allocated to each of units A and B is not. Nevertheless, the recoverable amounts of units A and B are based on some of the same key assumptions, and the aggregate carrying amount of goodwill allocated to those units is significant.

Operation XYZ

The recoverable amount of operation XYZ has been determined based on a value in use calculation. That calculation uses cash flow projections based on financial budgets approved by management covering a five-year period, and a discount rate of 8.4 per cent. Cash flows beyond that five-year period have been extrapolated using a steady 6.3 per cent growth rate. This growth rate does not exceed the long-term average growth rate for the market in which XYZ operates. Management believes that any reasonably possible change in the key assumptions on which XYZ's recoverable amount is based would not cause XYZ's carrying amount to exceed its recoverable amount.

Unit C

The recoverable amount of unit C has also been determined based on a value in use calculation. That calculation uses cash flow projections based on financial budgets approved by management covering a five-year period, and a discount rate of 9.2 per cent. C's cash flows beyond the five-year period are extrapolated using a steady 12 per cent growth rate. This growth rate exceeds by 4 percentage points the long-term average growth rate for the market in which C operates. However, C benefits from the protection of a 10 year patent on its primary product, granted in December 20X2. Management believes that a 12 per cent growth rate is reasonable in the light of that patent. Management also believes that any reasonably possible change in the key assumptions on which C's recoverable amount is based would not cause C's carrying amount to exceed its recoverable amount.

Units A and B

The recoverable amounts of units A and B have been determined on the basis of value in use calculations. Those units produce complementary products, and their recoverable amounts are based on some of the same key assumptions. Both value in use calculations use cash flow projections based on financial budgets approved by management covering a four-year period, and a discount rate of 7.9 per cent. Both sets of cash flows beyond the four-year period are extrapolated using a steady 5 per cent growth rate. This growth rate does not exceed the long-term average growth rate for the market in which A and B operate. Cash flow projections during the budget period for both A and B are also based on the same expected gross margins during the budget period and the same raw materials price inflation during the budget period. Management believes that any reasonably possible change in any of these key assumptions would not cause the aggregate carrying amount of A and B to exceed the aggregate recoverable amount of those units.

	Operation XYZ	Unit C	Units A and B (in aggregate)
Carrying amount of goodwill	CU1,200	CU3,000	CU800
Carrying amount of brand name with indefinite useful life	–	CU1,000	–

Key assumptions used in value in use calculations *

Key assumption	Budgeted gross margins	5 year US government bond rate	Budgeted gross margins
Basis for determining value(s) assigned to key assumption	Average gross margins achieved in period immediately before the budget period, increased for expected efficiency improvements.	Yield on 5 year US government bonds at the beginning of the budget period.	Average gross margins achieved in period immediately before the budget period, increased for expected efficiency
	Values assigned to key assumption reflect past experience, except for efficiency improvements. Management believes improvements of 5% per year are reasonably achievable	Value assigned to key assumption is consistent with external sources of information.	Values assigned to key assumption reflect past experience, except for efficiency improvements. Management believes improvements of 5% per year are reasonably achievable

* The key assumptions shown in this table for units A and B are only those that are used in the recoverable amount calculations for both units

Key assumption	Japanese yen/US dollar exchange rate during the budget period	Raw materials price inflation	Raw materials price inflation
Basis for determining value(s) assigned to key assumption	Average market forward exchange rate over the budget period.	Forecast consumer price indices during the budget period for North American countries from which raw materials are purchased.	Forecast consumer price indices during the budget period for European countries from which raw materials are purchased
	Value assigned to key assumption is consistent with external sources of information.	Value assigned to key assumption is consistent with external sources of information	Value assigned to key assumption is consistent with external sources of information.

Key assumption	Budgeted market share	Budgeted market share
Basis for determining value(s) assigned to key assumption	Average market share in period immediately before the budget period.	Average market share in period immediately before the budget period, increased each year for anticipated growth in market share.
	Value assigned to key assumption reflects past experience. No change in market share expected as a result of ongoing product quality improvements coupled with anticipated increase in competition	Management believes market share growth of 6% per year is reasonably achievable due to increased advertising expenditure, the benefits from the protection of the 10year patent on C's primary product, and the expected synergies to be achieved from operating C as part of M's North American segment

An example of disclosures including key assumptions and sensitivities is given by Vodafone Group Plc.

Extract 15.1: Vodafone Group plc (2007)

Notes to the Consolidated Financial Statements [extract]

10. Impairment

The impairment losses recognised in the income statement, as a separate line item within operating profit, in respect of goodwill are as follows:

Cash generating unit:	Reportable segment:	2007 £m	2006 £m	2005 £m
Germany	Germany	**6,700**	19,400	–
Italy	Italy	**4,900**	3,600	–
Sweden	Other Europe	**–**	515	475
		11,600	23,515	475

During the year ended 31 March 2007, the increase in long term interest rates, which led to higher discount rates, led to a reduction in value of £3,700 million in Germany and Italy.

Germany

During the year ended 31 March 2007, the goodwill in relation to the Group's mobile operation in Germany was impaired by £6.7 billion following a test for impairment triggered by an increase in long term interest rates and increased price competition in the German market along with continued regulatory pressures.

The impairment loss for the year ended 31 March 2006 of £19.4 billion was determined as part of the annual test for impairment and was as a result of the intensification in price competition, principally from new market entrants, together with high levels of penetration and continued regulated reductions in incoming call rates.

The pre-tax risk adjusted discount rate used in the testing at 31 March 2007 was 10.6% (31 January 2007: 10.5%, 30 September 2006: 10.4%, 31 January 2006: 10.1%, 31 March 2005: 9.6%).

Italy

During the year ended 31 March 2007, the goodwill in relation to the Group's mobile joint venture in Italy was impaired by £4.9 billion. During the second half of the 2007 financial year, £3.5 billion of the impairment loss resulted from the estimated impact of legislation cancelling the fixed fees for the top up of prepaid cards and the related competitive response in the Italian market. At 30 September 2006, the goodwill was impaired by £1.4 billion, following a test for impairment triggered by an increase in long term interest rates.

The impairment loss for the year ended 31 March 2006 of £3.6 billion was due to competitive pressures increasing with the mobile network operators competing aggressively on subsidies and, increasingly, on price.

The pre-tax risk adjusted discount rate used in the testing at 31 March 2007 was 11.5% (31 January 2007: 11.2%, 30 September 2006: 10.9%, 31 January 2006: 10.1%, 31 March 2005: 9.2%).

Sweden

The impairment of the carrying value of goodwill of the Group's mobile operation in Sweden in the years ended 31 March 2006 and 31 March 2005 resulted from fierce competition in the Swedish market combined with onerous 3G licence obligations.

Prior to its disposal in the year ended 31 March 2006, the carrying value of goodwill was tested for impairment as increased competition provided an indicator that the goodwill may have been further impaired. The recoverable amount of the goodwill was determined as the fair value less costs to sell, reflecting the announcement on 31 October 2005 that the Group's 100% interest in Vodafone Sweden was to be sold for €953 million (£653 million). The sale completed on 5 January 2006.

In the year ended 31 March 2005, the impairment was based on value in use calculations. The pre-tax risk adjusted discount rate used in the testing at 31 March 2005 was 9.7%.

Cash generating units

The following cash-generating units, being the lowest level of asset for which there are separately identifiable cash flows, have carrying amount of goodwill that are considered significant in comparison with the Group's total goodwill balance:

	2007 £m	2006 £m
Germany	**9,355**	16,518
Italy	**11,125**	16,475
Spain	**10,285**	10,571
	30,765	43,564
Multiple units without individually significant amounts of goodwill	**9,802**	9,042
	40,567	52,606

Key assumptions used in the value in use calculations

The Group prepares and internally approves form ten years management plans for its businesses. For the year ended 31 March 2005, the Group used these plans for its value in use calculations. The plans included cash flow projections for the mobile businesses which were expected to have growth rates in excess of the long term average growth rates, beyond an initial five year period, for the markets in which they operate.

In the year ended 31 March 2006, the management plans showed the need to reflect a differing growth profile beyond an initial five year period had diminished in a number of the Group's key operating companies, as the Group revised its view of longer term trends. Accordingly, in the 2006 and 2007 financial years, only the first five years of the ten year management plans were used for the Group's value in use calculations, except for the Group's operations in India and Turkey (2006: India) where the full ten year management plans were used. For these businesses, the use of ten year management plans reflected the low penetration of mobile telecommunications in these countries and the expectation of strong revenue growth throughout the ten year period. Long term growth rates are used in the Group's value in use calculations for cash flows into perpetuity beyond the relevant five or ten year periods.

The key assumptions used in determining the value in use are:

Assumption	How determined
Budgeted EBITDA	Budgeted EBITDA, calculated as adjusted operating profit before depreciation and amortisation, has been based on past experience adjusted for the following: • Voice and messaging revenue is expected to benefit from increased usage from new customers, the introduction of new services and traffic moving from fixed networks to mobile networks, though these factors will be partially offset by increased competitor activity, which may result in price declines, and the trend of falling termination rates; • Non-messaging data revenue is expected to continue to grow strongly as the penetration of 3G enabled devices rises and new products and services are introduced; and • Margins are expected to be impacted by negative factors such as an increase in the cost of acquiring and retaining customers in increasingly competitive markets and the expectation of further termination rate cuts by regulators and by positive factors such as the efficiencies expected from the implementation of Group initiatives.
Budgeted capital expenditure	The cash flow forecasts for capital expenditure is based on past experience and includes the ongoing capital expenditure required to provide enhanced voice and data products and services and to meet the population coverage requirements of certain of the Group's licences. Capital expenditure includes cash outflows for the purchase of property, plant and equipment and computer software.
Long term growth rate	For mobile businesses where the first five years of the ten year management plan are used for the Group's value in use calculations, a long term growth rate into perpetuity has been determined as the lower of: • The nominal GDP rates for the country of operation; and • The long term compound annual growth rate in EBITDA in years six to ten of the management plan For mobile businesses where the full ten year management plans are used for the Group's value in use calculations, a long term growth rate into perpetuity has been determined as the lower of: • The nominal GDP rates for the country of operation; and • The compound annual growth rate in EBITDA in years nine to ten of the management plan. For non-mobile businesses, no growth is expected beyond management's plans for the initial give year period.

Pre-tax adjusted discount rate	The discount rate applied to the cash flows of each the Group's operations is based on the risk free rate for ten year bonds issued by the government in the respective market, adjusted for a risk premium to reflect both the increased risk of investing in equities and the systematic risk of the specific Group operating company. In making this adjustment, inputs required are the equity market risk premium (that is the required increased return required over and above a risk free rate by an investor who is investing in the market as a whole) and the risk adjustment ("beta") applied to reflect the risk of the specific Group operating company relative to the market as a whole. In determining the risk adjusted discount rate, management have applied an adjustment for the systematic risk to each of the Group's operations determined using an average of the betas of comparable listed mobile telecommunications companies and, where available and appropriate, across a specific territory. Management have used a forward looking equity market risk premium that takes into consideration both studies by independent economist, the average equity market risk premium over the past ten years and the market risk premiums typically used by investment banks in evaluating acquisition proposals.

Key assumptions for the Group's operations in Germany and Italy are disclosed below under "Sensitivity to changes in assumptions". During the year ended 31 March 2007, the most recent value in use calculation for Group's operations in Spain was based on a pre-tax risk adjusted discount rate of 9.7% (2006: 9.0%) and long term growth rate of 3.2% (2006: 3.3%).

Sensitivity to changes in assumptions

Other than as disclosed below, management believes that no reasonably possible change in any of the above key assumptions would cause the carrying value of any cash generating unit to exceed its recoverable amount.

Germany

At 31 March 2007, the fair value of the Group's operations in Germany equalled its carrying value (2006: equalled) and consequently, any adverse change in a key assumption may cause a further impairment loss to be recognised.

The most recent value in use calculation during the year ended 31 March 2007 was based on the following assumptions:

- Pre-tax risk adjusted discount rate of 10.6% (2006: 10.1%).
- Long term growth rate of 1.2% (2006: 1.1%).
- Budgeted EBITDA, expressed as the compound annual growth rates in the initial five years of the Group's approved financial plans, of (4.2)% (2006: 0.3%).
- Budgeted capital expenditure, expressed as the range of capital expenditure as a percentage of revenue in the initial five years of the Group's approved plans, of 7.5 – 7.0% (2006: 9.3-9.0%).

Italy

At 31 March 2007, the fair value of the Group's operations in Italy equalled its carrying value (2006: equalled) and consequently, any adverse change in a key assumption may cause a further impairment loss to be recognised.

The most recent value in use calculation during the year ended 31 March 2007 was based on the following assumptions:

- Pre-tax risk adjusted discount rate of 11.5% (2006: 10.1%).
- Long term growth rate of 1.0% (2006: 1.5%).
- Budgeted EBITDA, expressed as the compound annual growth rates in the initial five years of the Group's approved financial plans, of (3.8)% (2006: (1.8)%).
- Budgeted capital expenditure, expressed as the range of capital expenditure as a percentage of revenue in the initial five years of the Group's approved plans, of 11.4% – 8.7% (2006: 13.4–8.5%).

5 PRACTICAL ISSUES

5.1 Discount rates and the weighted average cost of capital

One of the rates recommended as a starting point in calculating the appropriate discount rate for a VIU calculation is the entity's weighted average cost of capital ('WACC') determined using techniques such as the Capital Asset Pricing Model.[144] Example 15.7 above explains how it may be calculated. The WACC is often used in practice. It is usually acceptable to auditors as it is supported by valuation experts and is an accepted methodology based on a well-known formula and widely available information. In addition, many entities already know their own WACC. However, it can only be used as a starting point for determining an appropriate discount rate and some of the issues that must be taken into account are as follows:

a) the WACC is a post-tax rate and IAS 36 requires VIU to be calculated using pre-tax cash flows and a pre-tax rate. Converting the former into the latter is not simply a question of grossing up the post-tax rate by the effective tax rate;

b) other tax factors may need to be considered, whether or not these will result in tax cash flows in the period covered by budgets and cash flows;

c) an entity's own WACC may not be suitable as a discount rate if there is anything atypical about the entity's capital structure compared with 'typical' market participants;

d) the WACC must reflect the risks specific to the asset and not the risks relating to the entity as a whole, such as default risk; and

e) the entity's WACC is an average rate derived from its existing business, yet entities frequently operate in more than one sector. Within a sector, different types of projects may have different levels of risk (e.g. a start-up as against an established product).

These are discussed further below.

One of the most difficult areas in practice is the effect of taxation on the WACC. In order to determine an appropriate pre-tax discount rate it is likely to be necessary to adjust the entity's actual tax cash flows.

Ultimately, the appropriate discount rate to select is one that reflects current market assessments of the time value of money and the risks specific to the asset in question, including taxation. Such a rate is one that reflects 'the return that investors would require if they were to choose an investment that would generate cash flows of amounts, timing and risk profile equivalent to those that the entity expects to derive from the asset.'[145] On the one hand, this will be a rate that takes account of some of the effects of taxation (see below); on the other, it will not necessarily be the entity's WACC.

5.1.1 Pre-and post-tax discount rates

As discussed in 3.3.2 step 4 above and explained in Example 15.7, the WACC is a post-tax rate and, when measuring VIU, IAS 36 requires pre-tax cash flows to be discounted using a pre-tax discount rate. A pre-tax WACC is not necessarily a post-tax WACC grossed up for tax.

IAS 36.BCZ85 recognises this problem and states that 'in theory, discounting post-tax cash flows at a post-tax discount rate and discounting pre-tax cash flows at a pre-tax discount rate should give the same result, as long as the pre-tax discount rate is the post-tax discount rate adjusted to reflect the specific amount and timing of the future tax cash flows. The pre-tax discount rate is not always the post-tax discount rate grossed up by a standard rate of tax.' Some may infer from this that it is appropriate to use entity's actual tax cash flows to calculate a pre-tax rate. We consider that this is not the intention of the standard because the entity's tax cash flows may be affected by matters unrelated to the asset or CGU that is being reviewed for impairment. Actual tax cash flows would not necessarily enable the calculation of either the pre-tax discount rate or the appropriate post-tax cash flows.

Grossing up the post-tax discount rate by the standard rate of tax does give the appropriate pre-tax discount rate in the following circumstances:

- no growth in cash flows;
- a perpetuity calculation; and
- tax cash flows that are a constant percentage of total cash flows.

If these criteria are met (or there is a close approximation, which may be the case for some CGUs) a simple gross up may be materially correct. The criteria are unlikely to apply to the VIU of individual assets, not least because these are rarely perpetuity calculations. If it is inappropriate to make such a gross up, an iterative calculation may be necessary to compute the appropriate pre-tax discount rate.

The only way to calculate a pre-tax WACC accurately is to calculate the VIU using a post-tax rate and apply this to post-tax cash flows. The effective pre-tax rate is calculated by removing the tax cash flows and, by iteration, one can identify the pre-tax rate that makes the present value of the adjusted cash flows equal the post tax result.

IAS 36.BCZ85 includes an example that illustrates the calculation of a pre-tax discount rate in a specific case where the cost of the asset in question is wholly deductible for taxation in the first year. However, the standard is less than clear about the general principles underlying the relationship between pre- and post-tax rates. Although the standard does not make the point explicitly, discounting post-tax cash flows at a post-tax discount rate and discounting pre-tax cash flows at a pre-tax discount rate will only ever give the same result if the tax base of the asset equals its VIU and the VIU is wholly deductible for tax purposes; this is illustrated in Example 15.15 below. Therefore in order to use a post-tax discount rate or correctly calculate the pre-tax rate, an entity's actual tax cash flows may have to be replaced by notional tax cash flows reflecting this assumption.

It is relatively straightforward to make this calculation for a single asset, whether acquired separately or as part of a business combination. It would be much more difficult for CGUs or for goodwill impairment as there is no single asset on which to base the calculation and there are often additional complications, especially if the assets have been acquired as part of a business combination. This is discussed further at 5.2 below.

The illustrations in Example 15.15 are of course simplified, and in reality it is unlikely that entities will need to schedule all of the tax cash flows and tax consequences in order to calculate a pre-tax discount rate every time they perform an impairment review. In practice it will probably not be possible to obtain a rate that is theoretically perfect – the task is just too intractable for that. The objective, therefore, must be to obtain a rate which is sensible and justifiable. Some of the following may make the exercise somewhat easier.

An entity may calculate a pre-tax rate using adjusted tax cash flows based on the assumptions that we have described and apply that rate to discount pre-tax cash flows. This pre-tax rate will only need to be reassessed when relevant market rates change, i.e. those for instruments with a period to maturity similar to the expected life of the assets being reviewed for impairment, and will not necessarily need to be recalculated every time an impairment review is carried out. Short-term market rates may increase or decrease without affecting the rate of return that the market would require on long-term assets.

Valuation practitioners often use approximations when computing tax cash flows that may also make the task more straightforward. It may often be a valid approximation to assume that the tax amortisation of assets equals their accounting depreciation. Tax cash flows will be based on the relevant corporate tax rate and the forecast earnings before interest and taxation to give post-tax 'cash flows' that can then be discounted using a post-tax discount rate. The circumstances in which this could lead to a material distortion (perhaps in the case of an impairment test for an individual asset) will probably be obvious. This approach is consistent with the overall requirement of IAS 36, which is that the appropriate discount rate to select is one that reflects current market assessments of the risks specific to the asset in question, including taxation.

As described above, some CGUs may approximate to the circumstances in which a standardised gross up will give an adequate discount rate (no growth in cash flows, a perpetuity calculation and tax cash flows that are a constant percentage of total cash flows). As long as these conditions remain unchanged, it will be straightforward to determine the discount rate for an impairment review at either the pre- or post-tax level.

However, it is unlikely that any entity can ever rely on using a post-tax discount rate and be unable to extrapolate from that to the relevant pre-tax rate. It must know the assumptions on which the post-tax rate is based in order to use it reliably.

Testing for impairment and tax losses is discussed at 5.1.2 below. A particular example when the specific tax consequences will have to be taken into account is testing assets and goodwill for impairment after an acquisition, as recognition of deferred tax, and the asset valuation methodology, may have consequences for the impairment test (see 5.2 below).

Example 15.15: Calculating the pre-tax weighted average cost of capital

Example A – Grossing up at standard rates of tax

Assume that an asset that has been acquired or constructed by the entity has a carrying value and tax base of €40,000. The tax rate is 25% and the asset is eligible for a 100% deduction in the first year. The entity's post-tax discount rate is 9%. If the cost is to be recovered in one year, the entity must generate taxable cash inflows of at least €44,800, i.e. a pre-tax rate of 12%, as follows:

	€	€
Cash inflows before taxation		44,800
tax on income at 25%	(11,200)	
tax credit at 25% of €40,000	10,000	
tax charge		(1,200)
Post-tax cash inflow		43,600

In this case, discounting the pre-tax cash flows at 12% gives the same answer as discounting the post-tax cash flows at 9% – both give the same VIU for the asset of €40,000, which is equal to its tax base.

This is also the answer if this is a calculation of the VIU of a CGU and, instead of all cash flows arising in the first year, it is a perpetuity calculation with annual pre- and post-tax cash inflows of €4,800 and €3,600. In contrast to Example A, this would have to mean different tax assumptions, for example, a higher rate of tax on profits and a lower rate of deduction for the asset so that the net tax charge (tax on income less tax deduction for the asset) has a present value of €1,200; it also assumes that capital expenditure and tax amortisation remain the same in perpetuity. Each of these inflows extended in perpetuity has a present value of €40,000 at 12% and 9% respectively. In this case the calculation meets all of the criteria outlined above as this is a perpetuity calculation with no growth in cash flows and tax cash flows that are a constant percentage of total cash flows.

However, in the case of any asset with a finite life, it will not be a perpetuity calculation and the taxation may not be a constant percentage of the cash flows. In these cases it is necessary to calculate either a pre-tax rate or the appropriate tax assumptions to enable the post-tax rate to be used.

Example B – Calculation of pre-and post-tax discount rates

The facts are as in Example A above except that the asset's cost is expected to be recovered over its five year life. The carrying value of the asset is deductible for tax in equal instalments over the five year period.

Assuming that the income arises evenly over the period, the minimum annual income necessary if the entity is to apply a post-tax rate of 9% can be calculated as €11,045. The pre-and post-tax cash flows are as follows:

	€	€	€	€	€
Cash inflows before taxation	11,045	11,045	11,045	11,045	11,045
tax on income at 25%	(2,761)	(2,761)	(2,761)	(2,761)	(2,761)
tax credit at 25% of €40,000	2,000	2,000	2,000	2,000	2,000
tax charge	761	761	761	761	761
Post-tax cash inflow	10,284	10,284	10,284	10,284	10,284
PV of post-tax cash flows at 9%	€40,000				
PV of pre-tax cash flows at 11.81%	€40,000				

The VIU of the asset is still €40,000 but the pre-tax discount rate is 11.81%, rather than 12% as in Example A – this is not a calculation of the VIU using cash flows in perpetuity.

The tax credit of €10,000 arises because the VIU of the asset, which in this example is its cost, is fully deductible for taxation.

In Example B, the cash inflow has been calculated as the minimum amount necessary to recover the cost of the asset. The next step is to consider the calculation when the cash flows are insufficient.

Example C – Calculation of pre-and post-tax discount rates when the asset is impaired

The facts are as in Example A above except that the asset is only expected to generate pre-tax cash inflows of €8,500 per annum. If the minimum amount necessary to recover the cost of the asset is €11,045, as calculated in Example B above, then if all other factors remain the same, the carrying value of the impaired asset ought to be €30,783 (8,500/11,045 × 40,000), which is also the present value of the pre-tax cash flows using the discount rate calculated above. Assume that the impairment loss is not itself tax deductible.

In order to calculate its post-tax VIU at the same amount, the 'cash flows' are as follows:

	€	€	€	€	€
Cash inflows before taxation	8,500	8,500	8,500	8,500	8,500
tax on income at 25%	(2,125)	(2,125)	(2,125)	(2,125)	(2,125)
tax credit at 25% of €30,783	1,539	1,539	1,539	1,539	1,539
tax charge	586	586	586	586	586
Post-tax cash inflow	7,914	7,914	7,914	7,914	7,914
PV of post-tax cash flows at 9%	€30,783				
PV of pre-tax cash flows at 11.81%	€30,783				

In this case, it has been assumed that neither pre- nor post-tax discount rates are affected by the fact that the asset is now impaired. Therefore, if the pre-tax cash flows and pre- and post-tax discount rates are known, the only feature of the computation that can change in order to give the same answer at both pre- and post-tax levels is the assumed tax deduction for the asset. This figure has been calculated using an iterative process and, in the table above, the post-tax value for the asset using a 9% discount rate is also €30,783. The impairment will be reflected in the entity's income statement as an impairment of €9,217, on which there will be a deferred tax asset of €2,304.

If the calculation uses the actual tax base of the asset, the tax credit in each of the five years is €2,000 (as in Example B) the annual tax charge is €125 and the post-tax income is €8,375. The present value of the pre-tax cash flows at 11.81% is €30,783 but the post-tax present value at 9% is €32,576, i.e. a difference of €1,793 between pre- and post-tax calculations.

The difference is the present value of the difference in tax of €461 (€586 – €125) in each of the five years; this difference has a gross amount of €2,304 (after taking account of rounding) and a post-tax present value, discounted at 9%, of €1,793. In order to calculate impairment, the tax credit is based on its VIU (€30,783), not its tax base (which remains €40,000). In other words, using the actual tax deduction based on the asset's actual tax base overstates the VIU calculated on a post-tax basis by the present value of the deferred tax on the actual impairment loss.

The same result would be obtained if, instead of assuming that the pre-tax discount rate is still 11.81%, the calculation starts by assuming the post-tax discount rate and uses an iterative process to arrive at the pre-tax rate and tax cash flows (both of which are unknown) that give the same present value at both pre- and post-tax level.

The calculation would be based on the post-tax cash flows of €8,375, calculated using the actual tax base, and the post-tax discount rate of 9%. As we have seen above, the present value of these cash flows is €32,576. However, in order to obtain the same answer at pre- and post-tax levels, the pre-tax rate will be calculated at 11.81% and the deduction for tax will be based on a tax-deductible amount of €30,783 as above. The pre-tax VIU at 11.81% and the post-tax VIU at 9% will both be €30,783.

It will rarely be practicable to apply this methodology to calculate a discount rate for a CGU, as so many factors need to be taken into account. Even if all assets within the CGU are individually acquired or self-constructed, they may have a range of lives for depreciation and tax amortisation purposes, up to and including indefinite lives. There are additional issues if the CGU comprises or includes assets acquired in a business combination; the fair value may or may not reflect tax benefits and there may be complications caused by deferred tax (see 5.2 below). If goodwill is being tested it has an indefinite life whilst the underlying assets in the CGU or CGU group to which it has been allocated will usually have finite lives. It is likely that a reasonable approximation to the 'true' discount rate is the best that can be achieved.

5.1.2 Determining pre-tax rates taking account of tax losses

A common problem relates to the effect of tax losses on the impairment calculation, as they may reduce the total tax paid in the period under review or even eliminate it altogether. As noted in 5.1.1 above, however, a post-tax discount rate is based on certain market assumptions about the tax-deductibility of the asset and not the actual tax cash flows. It is therefore unwarranted to assume that the post- and pre-tax discount rates will be the same if the entity pays no tax because of its own tax losses.

Any deferred tax asset arising from tax losses carried forward at the reporting date must be excluded from the assets of the CGU if the impairment review is based on VIU.

In many circumstances the past history of tax losses affects the level of risk in the cash flows in the period under review, but one must take care not to increase the discount rate to reflect risks for which the estimated cash flows have been adjusted.[146] To do so would be to double count.

5.1.3 Entity-specific WACCs and different project risks within the entity

The entity's WACC is an average rate derived from its existing business, yet entities frequently operate in more than one sector. Within a sector, different types of projects may have different levels of risk, e.g. a start-up as against an established product. Therefore, entities must ensure that the different business risks pertaining to different CGUs are properly taken into account when determining the appropriate discount rates.

It must be noted that these areas of different risk will not always coincide with the assets or CGUs that are being tested for impairment as this is a test for impairment and not necessarily a determination of business value.

Example 15.16: Different project risks and CGUS

An aircraft manufacturer makes both civilian and military aircraft. The risks for both sectors are markedly different as they are much lower for defence contractors than for the civilian market. The assembly plants for civilian and military aircraft are separate CGUs. In this sector there are entities that are based solely in one or other of these markets, i.e. they are purely defence or civilian contractors, so there will be a basis for identifying the different discount rates for the different activities.

If the entity makes its own components then the defence CGU or CGUs could include the manufacturing activity if defence is vertically integrated and components are made solely for military aircraft. Manufacturing could be a separate CGU if components are used for both activities and there is an external market for the products.

A manufacturer of soft drinks uses the same plant to produce various flavours of carbonated and uncarbonated drinks. Because the market for traditional carbonated drinks is declining, it develops and markets a new uncarbonated 'health' drink, which is still produced using the same plant. The risks of the product are higher than those of the existing products but it is not a separate CGU.

Many sectors assume a high generation of new products and a high attrition rate (pharmaceuticals and biotechnology, for example) and this is likely built into industry WACCs. If the risk of failure is not reflected in the WACC because the entity is not typical of the industry then either the discount rate or the cash flows ought to be adjusted to reflect the risk (but not so as to double count).

5.1.4 Entity-specific WACCs and capital structure

The discount rate is a pre-tax rate that reflects current market assessments of the time value of money and the risks specific *to the asset* for which the future cash flow estimates have not been adjusted.[147] An entity's own WACC may not be suitable as a discount rate if there is anything atypical about the entity's capital structure compared with 'typical' market participants. In other words, would the market assess the cash flows from the asset or unit as being riskier or less risky than the entity-wide risks reflected in the entity-wide WACC? Some of the risks that need to be thought about are country risk, currency risks and price risk.

Country risk will reflect the area in which the assets are located. In some areas assets are frequently nationalised by governments or the area may be politically unstable and prone to violence. In addition, the potential impact of physical instability such as weather or earthquakes, and the effects of currency volatility on the expected return from the asset, must be considered.

Two elements of price risk are the gearing ratio of the entity in question (if, for example, it is much more or less geared than average) and any default risk built into its cost of debt. However, IAS 36 explicitly notes that the discount rate is independent of the entity's capital structure and the way the entity financed the purchase of the asset, because the future cash flows expected to arise from an asset do not depend on these features.[148]

Example 15.17: Effect of entity default risk on its WACC

The formula for calculating the (post tax) WACC, as given in Example 15.7 above, is

$$\text{WACC} = (1 - t) \times D \times \frac{g}{(1 + g)} + E \times \left[1 - \frac{g}{(1 + g)}\right]$$

where:

t is the rate of tax relief available on the debt servicing payments

D is the pre-tax cost of debt;

E is the cost of equity

g is the gearing level (i.e. the ratio of debt to equity) for the sector

The cost of equity is calculated as follows:

Cost of equity = risk-free rate + (levered beta (β*) × market risk premium)

Assume that the WACC of a typical sector participant is as follows:

Cost of equity	
risk free rate	4%
levered beta (β)	1.1
market risk premium	6%
cost of equity after tax (market risk premium × β + risk-free rate)	10.6%
Cost of debt	
risk free rate	4%
credit spread	3%
cost of debt (pre-tax)	7%
cost of debt (post-tax)	5.25%
Capital structure	
debt / (debt + equity)	25%
equity / (debt + equity)	75%
tax rate	25%
post-tax cost of equity (10.6 × 75%)	8%
post-tax cost of debt (5.25 × 25%)	1.3%
WACC (Post tax, nominal)	9.3%

* The beta is explained in Example 15.7 above.

However, the company has borrowed heavily and is in some financial difficulties. Its gearing ratio is 75% and its actual cost of debt, based on the market price of its listed bonds, is 18% (13.5% after taking account of tax at 25%). This makes its individual post-tax WACC is 12.8% (10.6×25% + 13.5×75%). This is not an appropriate WACC for impairment purposes because it does not represent a market rate of return *on the assets.* Its entity WACC has been increased by default risk.

Ultimately it might be acceptable to use the entity's own WACC, but an entity cannot conclude on this without going through the exercise of assessing for risk each of the assets or units and concluding on whether or not they contain additional risks that are not reflected in the WACC.

5.1.5 Use of discount rates other than the WACC

IAS 36 allows an entity to use rates other than the WACC as a starting point in calculating the discount rate. These include:

(a) the entity's incremental borrowing rate; and

(a) other market borrowing rates.[149]

If borrowing rates (which are, of course, pre-tax) were used as a starting point, could this avoid some of the problems associated with adjusting the WACC for the effects of taxation? Unfortunately, this is unlikely. Debt rates reflect the entity's capital structure and do not reflect the risk inherent in the asset. A pure asset/business risk would be obtained from an entity funded solely by equity and equity risk premiums are always observed on a post-tax basis. Therefore the risk premium that must be added to reflect the required increased return required over and above a risk free rate by an investor will always have to be adjusted for the effects of taxation.

It must be stressed that the appropriate discount rate, which is the one that reflects current market assessments of the time value of money and the risks specific to the asset in question, ought to be the same whatever the starting point for the calculation of the rate.

Vodafone in its description of its pre-tax discount rate starts from the relevant bond (i.e. debt) rate (Extract 15.1 above). However, this describes many of the elements of the WACC calculation and how Vodafone has obtained these; it does not suggest that Vodafone has used anything other than an adjusted WACC as a discount rate for the purposes of the impairment test.

5.2 Impairment of assets and goodwill recognised on acquisition

There are a number of circumstances in which the fair value of assets or goodwill acquired as part of a business combination and as recorded in the consolidated accounts, may be measured at a higher amount through recognition of deferred tax or notional tax benefits. This raises the question of how to test for impairment and even whether there is, in fact, a 'day one' impairment in value. In other circumstances, deferred tax assets may or may not be recognised as part of the fair value exercise and this, too, may affect subsequent impairment tests of the assets and goodwill acquired as part of the business combination.

5.2.1 Testing goodwill 'created' by deferred tax for impairment

As described in Chapter 26 at 6.2, the requirement of IAS 12 to recognise deferred tax on all temporary differences arising on net assets acquired in a business combination may well lead to the recognition of goodwill and an increase in the net assets recognised in the consolidated accounts. This then begs the question of how to perform an impairment test on that goodwill. This is illustrated in the following example (also used to illustrate the point as Example 26.29 in Chapter 26):

Example 15.18: Apparent 'day one' impairment arising from recognition of deferred tax in a business combination

Entity A, which is taxed at 40%, acquires Entity B for €100m in a transaction that is a business combination. The fair values and tax bases of the identifiable net assets of Entity B are as follows:

	Fair value	*Tax base*
	€m	€m
Brand name	60	nil
Other net assets	20	15

This will give rise to the following consolidation journal:

	€m	€m
Goodwill (balance)	46	
Brand name	60	
Other net assets	20	
Deferred tax[1]		26
Cost of investment		100

1: 40% of (€[60m + 20m] – €15m)

The fair value of the consolidated assets of the subsidiary (excluding deferred tax) and goodwill is now €126m, but the cost of the subsidiary is only €100m. Clearly €26m of the goodwill arises solely from the recognition of deferred tax. However, IAS 36, paragraph 50, explicitly requires tax to be excluded from the estimate of future cash flows used to calculate any impairment. This raises the question of whether there should not be an immediate impairment write-down of the assets to €100m.

In our view, this cannot have been the intention of IAS 36, for the reasons described in 5.1 above. Adjustments need to be made to the post-tax discount rate in order to determine the appropriate pre-tax discount rate. This means, in effect, that as at the point of acquisition, the deferred tax liability can be offset against the goodwill that is its balancing figure in order to test that goodwill for impairment. As a result, the entity does not have to recognise an immediate loss.

This is consistent with the fact that the goodwill that is being recognised as part of this acquisition is a result of a measurement mismatch between two standards. The IASB is fully aware that this can happen. In the Basis of Conclusions to IFRS 3, it is noted that goodwill, measured as a residual, could include 'errors in measuring and recognising the fair value of either the cost of the business combination or the acquiree's identifiable assets, liabilities or contingent liabilities, or *a requirement in an accounting standard to measure those identifiable items at an amount that is not fair value*' (our emphasis).[150]

This example assumes that the entity cannot get a deduction for tax purposes for the goodwill and brand name, as is often the case for assets that arise only on consolidation. It also assumes that the fair value of the brand name does not reflect the tax deductions that might have available had it not been acquired as part of a business combination (valuations that do reflect such assumptions are considered further below). Deferred tax is measured at its full and undiscounted value and not at fair value; had it been so, it is plausible that in this case its fair value would be negligible or zero. Note that despite this 'mismatch', goodwill still has to be recognised in the financial statements and is subject to all of IAS 36's requirements.

If it is assumed that the brand name is amortised over a finite useful life then the deferred tax relating to that asset (€24m in this example) will be released over that life with the effect that the net amount charged to the income statement of €36m (€60m – €24m) will be the same as if the amortisation charge were tax deductible. Although the deferred tax liability is diminishing in line with the amortisation of the brand, the total amount of goodwill is not amortised. This does not necessarily mean that the 'mismatch' goodwill will be impaired in line with the release of the deferred tax liability as this will depend on the individual circumstances of the entity and the manner in which purchased goodwill has been allocated to CGUs or CGU groups and their post-acquisition performance.

Only deferred tax that has arisen as described in Example 15.18 above may be taken into account in considering the impairment of the related goodwill; other unrelated deferred tax, whether it arises at the same time or subsequently, will be disregarded. Entities may, of course, find it difficult to track the relevant deferred tax an ongoing basis.

If the brand name is deemed to have an indefinite life it will not be amortised. It may be possible to continue to apply the short cut method of deducting the deferred tax liability from the CGU or CGU group of which the goodwill and brand name are part, unless the intangible asset is impaired or sold. It is still a requirement for the entity to be able to track the relevant deferred tax liability. The goodwill still has to be tested annually for impairment, even though in this case the goodwill itself ought to have no net effect on the net assets of the CGU or group of CGUs to which it is allocated. The standard's disclosure requirements including the pre-tax discount rate, principally described at 4.2.2 above, will apply.

5.2.2 Assets whose fair value reflects tax benefits

This is a related area to the one described in 5.2.1 that may also affect the post-acquisition impairment test. In order to determine the fair value in an acquisition of an asset (typically an intangible asset), its value on a post-tax basis may be grossed up to take account of the tax benefits (sometimes called 'tax amortisation benefits') that the owner might have obtained if the asset had been bought separately, i.e. not as part of a business combination. Yet the asset may be one that is wholly or in part not tax-deductible by the entity. This is demonstrated in the following example:

Example 15.19: Impairment testing assets whose fair value reflects tax amortisation benefits

Assume that the entity in Example 15.18 above has acquired a brand that would be tax deductible if separately acquired but that also has a tax base of zero. The entity concludes that the fair value will reflect the tax benefit, whose gross amount is €40 (€60m × 40% / 60%) but in calculating the fair value this will be discounted to its present value – say €30m. The consolidation journal is now as follows:

	€m	€m
Goodwill (balance)	28	
Brand name (€(60 + 30))	90	
Other net assets	20	
Deferred tax[1]		38
Cost of investment		100

1: 40% of (€[90m + 20m] – €15m)

Overall, the gross assets that cost €100m will now be recorded at €138m, as against the total of €126m in Example 15.18. This increase has come about because of recognition of deferred tax of €12m, which is 40% of €30m, the assumed tax amortisation benefit.

In this example, only €8m goodwill results from the recognition of deferred tax [€28m – (€100 – (€60m + €20m))] and its treatment is discussed above at 5.2.1.

Unlike goodwill, the intangible asset will only have to be tested for impairment if there are indicators of impairment, if it has an indefinite useful life or if it has not yet been brought into use.[151] However, its 'fair value' of €90m is much in excess of the amount that the entity considers that it paid to acquire the asset and this alone could be considered an indicator of impairment. Should it be necessary to test it for impairment, the asset has been valued on the assumption that it will generate future tax inflows and it is only consistent that the impairment test takes account of the same assumptions. A discount rate is calculated using the assumptions about taxation described in 5.1.1 above (i.e. that VIU equals tax base). Whatever rate is selected, it will be one that reflects market assumptions about the availability of tax relief and the level of taxation. The implications are similar to those discussed in 5.1.1 above .

5.2.3 *Deferred tax assets and losses of acquired businesses*

Deferred tax assets arising from tax losses carried forward at the reporting date must be excluded from the assets of the CGU for the purpose of calculating its VIU. However, tax losses may not meet the criteria for recognition as deferred tax assets in a business combination, which means that their value is initially subsumed within goodwill. If the deferred tax asset is recognised at a later date goodwill is written down at that point and to the extent of the deferred tax asset at the date of acquisition – no account is taken of subsequent changes to tax rates. See also Chapter 26 at 6.2.2.

Unless and until the deferred tax asset is recognised, this raises the same problems as in 5.2.1 and 5.2.2 above. Certain assumptions regarding future taxation are built into the carrying value of goodwill. In such situations it may be appropriate to recognise the benefits of this 'contingent asset' in the VIU calculation for the CGU or CGU group.

5.3 Future capital expenditure

IAS 36 requires an asset to be tested for impairment in its current condition, excluding estimated future cash flows that may arise from a future restructuring to which the entity is not committed or future expenditure on improving or enhancing the asset's performance.[152] On the other hand, the entity is required to reflect appropriate maintenance and replacement expenditure[153] and, if the asset is incomplete, the costs necessary to make it ready for use or sale.[154]

Entities must therefore distinguish between maintenance, completion and enhancement expenditure. This is not always straightforward, as shown in the following example.

Example 15.20: Distinguishing enhancement and maintenance expenditure

Consider the situation of an entity providing fixed line, telephone, television and internet services. It must develop its basic transmission infrastructure (by overhead wires or cables along streets or railway lines etc) and in order to service a new customer it will have to connect the customer's home via cable and other equipment. It will extend its network to adjoining areas and perhaps acquire an entity with its own network. It will also reflect changes in technology, e.g. fibre optic cables replacing copper ones.

Obviously, when preparing the budgets which form the basis for testing the network for impairment, it will make assumptions regarding future revenue growth and will include the costs of connecting those customers. However, its infrastructure maintenance spend will inevitably include replacing equipment with the current technology. There is no option of continuing to replace equipment with something that has been technologically superseded. Once this technology exists it will be reflected in the entity's budgets and taken into account in its impairment tests, even though this new equipment will enhance the performance of the transmission infrastructure.

This maintenance and replacement expenditure must be distinguished from step changes in services and the technology used to provide them. BT Group plc notes the following in its 2006 Operating and financial review.

Extract 15.2: BT Group plc (2007)

Operating and financial review

Technological advances

Our continued success depends on our ability to exploit new technology rapidly.

We operate in an industry with a recent history of rapid technological changes and we expect this to continue - new technologies and products will emerge, and existing technologies and products will develop further.

We need continually to exploit next-generation technologies in order to develop our existing and future services and products.

However, we cannot predict the actual impact of these future technological changes on our business or our ability to provide competitive services.

For example, there is evidence of substitution by customers using mobile phones for day-to-day voice calls in place of making such calls over the fixed network and of calls being routed over the internet in place of the traditional switched network.

If these trends accelerate, our fixed-network assets may be used uneconomically and our investment in these assets may not be recovered through profits on fixed-line calls and line rentals.

The complexity of the 21CN programme may also result in delays to the delivery of expected benefits. Impairment write-downs may be incurred and margins may decline if fixed costs cannot be reduced in line with falling revenue.

Further examples indicate another problem area – the effects of future expenditure that the entity has identified but to which the entity is not yet committed. An entity may have acquired an asset with the intention of enhancing it in future and may, therefore, have paid for future synergies which will be reflected in the calculation of goodwill. Another entity may have plans for an asset that involve expenditure that will enhance its future performance and without which the asset may be impaired.

Examples could include:

- a TV transmission company that, in acquiring another, would expect to pay for the future right to migrate customers from analogue to digital services; or
- an aircraft manufacturer that expects to be able to use one of the acquired plants for a new model at a future point, a process that will involve replacing much of the current equipment.

In both cases the long-term plans reflect both the capital spent and the cash flows that will flow from it. There is no obvious alternative to recognising an impairment when calculating the CGU or CGU group's VIU as IAS 36 insists that the impairment test has to be performed for the asset in its current condition. This means that it is not permitted to include the benefit of improving or enhancing the asset's performance in calculating its VIU.

In the TV example above, it does not appear to matter whether the entity recognises goodwill or has a separable intangible right not yet brought into use.

An entity in this situation may attempt to avoid an impairment write down by calculating the appropriate FV, as this is not constrained by rules regarding future capital expenditure. As discussed further in 5.4 below, these cash flows can be included only to the extent that other market participants would consider them when evaluating the asset. It is not permissible to include assumptions about cash flows or benefits from the asset that would not be available to or considered by a typical market participant.

5.4 Use of fair value less costs to sell for the purposes of impairment testing

IAS 36 allows an entity to estimate FV less costs to sell of an asset even if there is no active market for assets of this type[155] and there is no binding sale agreement for the asset in question.[156]

Few assets are traded on an active market and there are no obvious examples of traded CGUs. However, it may be possible to determine fair value provided there is a basis for making a reliable estimate of the amount obtainable from the sale of the asset in an arm's length transaction between knowledgeable and willing parties.

IAS 36 permits entities to consider 'the outcome of recent transactions for similar assets within the same industry.'[157] If the entity has only recently acquired the asset or CGU in question then it may be able to demonstrate that its purchase price remains an appropriate measure of FV, although it would have to make adjustments for material costs to sell.[158]

To rely on the outcome of a recent transaction for a similar asset by a third party, the following conditions must be met:

a) the transaction should be in the same industry, unless the asset is generic and its fair value would not be affected by the industry in which the purchaser operates;

b) the assets must be shown to be substantially the same as to their nature and condition;

c) the economic environment of the entity must be similar to the environment in which the previous sale occurred (e.g. no circumstances have arisen since the earlier transaction that affect the value of the asset).

It would be unusual to be able to estimate FV reliably from a single market transaction. It is much more likely that, if reliable market assumptions are known, as discussed below, a recent market transaction would be one of the factors taken into account in the calculation of FV and used in conjunction with other valuation techniques.

If the entity cannot demonstrate that a recent transaction alone provides a reliable estimate of FV, the transaction may be one of the sources of evidence used to validate an estimate of FV using other valuation techniques. This is particularly likely to be the case if the impairment review is of a CGU or CGU group rather than an individual asset, as market transactions for individual assets are likely to be more relevant and reliable.

IAS 36 allows the use of cash flow valuation techniques such as discounted cash flows or other valuation techniques such as multiples. However, the use of these techniques and assumptions is only acceptable if it can be demonstrated that they would be used by the relevant 'market participants' i.e. other businesses in the same industry. When using a valuation technique to estimate FV, all of the following conditions must be met:

a) a relevant model must be selected – this requires consideration of industry practice, for example, a multiple of EBITDA is often used in the hotel industry to estimate fair value, while discounted cash flows are used by many manufacturing entities;

b) assumptions used in the model must only be those that other market participants would use. They cannot be based on management's uncorroborated views or information that would not be known or considered by other market participants; and

c) there must be reliable evidence showing that these assumptions would be taken into account by market participants. For this purpose, it may be necessary for the entity to obtain external advice.

If it is not possible to obtain reliable evidence regarding the assumptions and techniques that market participants would use, then fair value cannot be reliably estimated using valuation techniques and the recoverable amount of the asset must be based on its value in use.[159]

Therefore a discounted cash flow technique may be used if this is commonly used in that industry to estimate fair value. Cash flows used when applying the model may only reflect cash flows that market participants would take into account when assessing fair value. This includes the type of cash flows, for example future capital expenditure, as well as the estimated amount of cash flows. For example, an entity may wish to take into account cash flows relating to future capital expenditure, which would not be permitted for a VIU calculation (see 3.3.2 above). These cash flows can be included if, but only if, other market participants would consider them when evaluating the asset. It is not permissible to include assumptions about cash flows or benefits from the asset that would not be available to or considered by a typical market participant.

Obtaining reliable evidence of market assumptions is difficult, and unlikely to be achieved by many entities wishing to apply valuation techniques. However, Deutsche Telekom has calculated the FV of one of its CGUs and has taken a third party transaction in the same sector and geographical area into account in its valuation model, as can be seen in the following extract:

Extract 15.3: Deutsche Telekom AG (2006)

Notes to the consolidated income statement [extract]

16. **Depreciation, amortization and impairment losses** [extract]

In the 2005 financial year, Deutsche Telekom recognized an impairment loss of EUR 1.9 billion at the T-Mobile UK cash-generating unit. Telefónica announced its offer to acquire the UK group O2 at a price of 200 pence per share (approximately GBP 17.7 billion) on October 31, 2005. When determining the fair value less costs to sell, the purchase prices paid in comparable transactions must generally be given preference over internal DCF calculations. The fair value of the cash-generating unit T-Mobile UK was derived from the Telefónica offer in accordance with a valuation model based on multipliers.

5.5 Testing for impairment: group issues

5.5.1 *Associates, joint ventures and testing goodwill for impairment*

When calculating its share of an equity accounted investee's results, an investor makes adjustments to the associate's profit or loss to reflect depreciation and impairments of the associate's identifiable assets based on their fair values at the date the investor acquires its investment. This is covered in paragraph 23 of IAS 28 – *Investments in Associates* – which states that:

> 'Appropriate adjustments to the investor's share of the associate's profits or losses after acquisition are also made to account, for example, for depreciation of the depreciable assets, based on their fair values at the acquisition date. Similarly, appropriate adjustments to the investor's share of the associate's profits or losses after acquisition are made for impairment losses recognised by the associate, such as for goodwill or property, plant and equipment.'

Although this refers to 'appropriate adjustments' for goodwill impairment losses, this should not be interpreted as requiring the investor to recalculate the goodwill impairment on a similar basis to depreciation and impairment of tangible and intangible assets. The 'appropriate adjustment' is to reverse that goodwill impairment before calculating the investor's share of the investee's profit. After application of the equity method the entire equity-accounted carrying amount of the investor's investment, including the goodwill included in that carrying amount, is tested for impairment in accordance with paragraphs 31-34 of IAS 28. Note that there is no requirement to test investments in associates for impairment annually but only when there are indicators that the amount may not be recoverable. These requirements are described in detail in Chapter 8 at 4.

With joint ventures, the treatment varies depending on whether the interest is included by way of proportionate consolidation or by equity accounting. If the investor uses proportionate consolidation then it accounts for its share of the underlying assets, including goodwill, and liabilities of the investee. Therefore, the investor's share of goodwill is tested for impairment annually as described in 3.4.2 above and in Chapter 9.

If, on the other hand, the investor uses the equity method then it applies the requirements of IAS 28 as described above.

Impairment provisions made against investments in associates or joint ventures included by way of the equity method may be reversed if an impairment loss no longer exists or has decreased (see 3.5 above). IAS 36 does not allow impairments of goodwill to be reversed[160] but this is not a provision against goodwill so this prohibition does not apply. Similarly, although IAS 39 restricts the circumstances in which investments in certain financial assets may be reversed (see Chapter 20) these do not apply to interests in included in consolidated accounts using the equity method.

5.5.2 Testing investments in subsidiaries for impairment in separate financial statements

Many entities within a group prepare separate financial statements in accordance with IAS 27 – *Consolidated and separate financial statements* – either through choice or legal obligation. Of these, most probably choose to carry their investments in subsidiaries at cost, which means that they are within scope of IAS 36.[161] However, the group's CGUs may overlap individual subsidiaries so, for example, a CGU may contain more than one such subsidiary. There may be apparent indicators of impairment: the individual subsidiary may be loss-making or there may be little or no history of distributions. There are particular problems in trying to assess the investments in subsidiaries for impairment because the asset (the investment) and the underlying CGU are not the same.

The first issue is whether CGUs are different from the perspective of the parent entity compared with that of the consolidated accounts. We consider that the answer is no; once CGUs have been properly established for the group as a whole, they cannot be subdivided or differently assessed. They are defined as the *smallest* identifiable group of assets that generates cash inflows that are largely independent of the cash inflows from other assets or groups of assets. Therefore, the first challenge is to ensure that the group has set its CGUs at an appropriate level and there are no smaller identifiable groups of assets that meet the definition.

IAS 28 includes guidance on establishing the VIU of an associate that is equally applicable to other interests held by entities. It states that:

'In determining the value in use of the investment, an entity estimates:

(a) its share of the present value of the estimated future cash flows expected to be generated by the associate, including the cash flows from the operations of the associate and the proceeds on the ultimate disposal of the investment; or

(b) the present value of the estimated future cash flows expected to arise from dividends to be received from the investment and from its ultimate disposal.

Under appropriate assumptions, both methods give the same result.[162]

The recoverable amount of an investment in an associate is assessed for each associate, unless the associate does not generate cash inflows from continuing use that are largely independent of those from other assets of the entity.'[163]

Note that IAS 28 acknowledges that the associate may be part of a larger CGU. Similarly, it is the cash flows from the CGU that are, in the first instance, crucial. It is necessary to determine that the CGU itself is not impaired in value. Only then is it possible to see whether a reasonable allocation of value can be made to the interests in subsidiaries in question.

It is necessary to establish whether there is an identifiable feature that has caused the apparent impairment as that will have an impact on how the investment in the subsidiary is tested. Two common reasons are group reorganisations and issues relating to transfer pricing (on what basis intra-group charges are made or whether, indeed, they are made at all).

A Group reorganisations

A common form of group reorganisation involves the transfer to another group company of the tangible assets and trade of a subsidiary. These transactions often take place at the book value of the transferor's assets rather than at fair value. If the original carrying value was a purchase price that included an element of goodwill, the remaining shell may have a carrying value in the parent company's balance sheet in excess of its net worth. It could be argued that as the subsidiary is now a shell with no possibility in its current state of generating sufficient profits to support its value, a provision should be made by the parent to reduce its investment in the shell company to its net worth. However, the transfer of part of the group's business from one controlled entity to another has no substance from the perspective of the group and will have no effect in the consolidated accounts. There has also been no loss overall to the parent as a result of this reorganisation.

This is, of course, a transaction between companies under common control as all of the combining entities or businesses are ultimately controlled by the same party or parties both before and after the business combination, and that control is not transitory.[164] This means that the treatment by the acquirer (the transferee) is out of the scope of IFRS 3.

From the transferor entity's perspective, the transaction combines a sale of its assets at an undervalue to the transferee and a distribution of the shortfall in value (which is not reflected in its balance sheet) to its parent. The parent, in turn, could be seen as having made a capital contribution of the shortfall in value to the transferee. This is consistent with our analysis in Chapter 7 at 2.4.1 of the accounting treatments available to a transferee entity that acquires the shares in a fellow subsidiary entity from the parent. We note that there are some circumstances in which we would find it appropriate for the transferee entity to record this capital contribution in the preparation of consolidated accounts.

Briefly, we argue that in circumstances when the purchase method is acceptable, i.e. where there is substance to the transaction, the transferee may apply the purchase method of accounting as a matter of accounting policy. Having adopted such a policy, the transferee has a further choice. It may account for the transaction using only the fair value of the cash consideration or the fair value of the total consideration paid. In the latter case the difference between the cash and fair value is accounted for as a capital contribution in the consolidated accounts (see Example 7.29). Note that while the transaction described in Example 7.29 is the acquisition of a fellow subsidiary's shares, exactly the same principles apply if the transferee acquires the transferor's business. It has the same choice within its separate financial statements of applying the purchase method and, if it does, of reflecting the transaction based on the cash consideration or the fair value including the cash consideration and a capital contribution.

The transferee will not necessarily record the capital contribution even if this is an option available to it. However, the underlying principles are not affected by whether or not the transferee makes this choice – there has been a transfer of value from one subsidiary to another. This demonstrates why the business transfer alone does not result in an impairment write down of the transferor company.

What remains at issue is the effect of this transaction on the carrying amounts in the parent entity's accounts of the investments in the transferor and transferee. While there is no doubt that the carrying value of the transferor could be reduced by the deemed distribution of the shortfall in value, it is more difficult to find a mechanism for increasing the carrying value of the transferee by an equivalent amount. It does not represent an additional acquisition by the parent, who also may not wish to adopt a policy of revaluation. Again, however, it ought to make no difference whether the parent makes an actual or notional adjustment of value between the two investments.

This interpretation of the transferor's transaction (as a sale at an undervalue and a deemed distribution to the parent) is wholly consistent with a legal analysis in some jurisdictions, for example the United Kingdom, where a company that does not have zero or positive distributable reserves is unable to sell its assets at an undervalue because it cannot make any sort of distribution. However, if the above analysis is not supportable in a particular jurisdiction then an impairment write down may have to be taken.

Note that the implications of other non-arm's length transactions that may also be part of these arrangements, such as intra-group receivables and payables that are not interest-bearing, are discussed further below.

Actual circumstances may be less straightforward. In particular, the transferor and transferee entities may not be held directly by the same parent. This may make it necessary to make a provision for impairment against the carrying value of the shell company in its intermediate parent to reflect its loss in value, although there may be another, higher level within the group at which the above arguments against impairment will apply.

Example 15.21: Group reorganisations and impairment

Topco has two directly held subsidiaries, Tradeco and Shellco. It acquired Shellco for £30 million and immediately thereafter transferred all of its trade and assets to its fellow subsidiary Tradeco for book value of £10 million with the proceeds being left outstanding on intercompany account. Shellco now has net assets of £10 million (its intercompany receivable) but a carrying value in Topco of £30 million. On the other hand, the value of Tradeco has been enhanced by its purchase of the business at an undervalue.

Using the principles outlined in Chapter 7 at 2.4.1 and in Example 7.29, in our view, there are two acceptable ways in which Tradeco may account for this. The cost of the business combination may be the fair value of the cash given as consideration, i.e. £10 million and Tradeco will recognise no goodwill. Alternatively, it is the fair value of the cash given as consideration (£10 million), together with a deemed capital contribution received from Topco for the difference up to the fair value of the business of Shellco of £20 million, which will be recognised in equity, giving a total consideration of £30 million. Tradeco will recognise goodwill of £20 million.

The capital contribution measured under the second method represents the value distributed by Shellco to its parent Topco and thence to Tradeco.

If there is an intermediate holding company between Topco and Shellco but all other facts remain the same, then it would appear that a provision for impairment ought to be made against the carrying value of Shellco in its immediate parent. The argument against impairment would still apply in Topco.

B Transfer pricing

If a subsidiary is loss-making it may be because internal transfer pricing is not based on market prices for the products or services in question. The VIU of the CGU of which the loss making subsidiary is a part could therefore be apportioned between the various subsidiaries, substituting the fair values of inputs and outputs of the subsidiaries in question for the internal transfer prices. This is similar to the requirement to substitute the value on an active market for the internal transfer price when determining the VIU of a CGU, as described in 3.3.2 above.[165] Obviously, calculating the VIU of the whole CGU and apportioning it in this manner will avoid the potential pitfall of taking account of a notional increase in income to one subsidiary but neglecting to reflect the notional increase in costs to another. Individual subsidiaries may be part of more than one CGU, for example group finance, property holding or service companies, in which case the value may need to be considered by reference to a larger group of CGUs, in a manner analogous with corporate assets (see 3.3.2 Step 2 above).

Few subsidiaries can be allowed to carry on making losses in the longer term. In particular, unless they return to profitability they will eventually need the parents' support in order to be able to pay their creditors. The requirement for parental support represents a crucial difference when compared with the 'shell company' situation described above, because a parent does not need to do anything if it wishes to support indefinitely a non-trading subsidiary. This reinforces the need to understand why the subsidiary is loss-making. Only a subsidiary that is genuinely part of a larger CGU can have its value supported in this manner. If the parent is unprepared to make such a commitment, this is evidence that the investment in the subsidiary is in fact impaired.

5.5.3 Acquisitions of minority interests of a subsidiary and subsequent goodwill impairment tests

In order to test the goodwill in a non-wholly owned CGU, IAS 36 requires a notional gross-up to reflect the minority goodwill as it existed at the date of acquisition; any impairment relating to goodwill is only recognised to the extent of the group's interest. This is described in Chapter 7 at 3.4.1.

However, if the entity purchases an additional stake in the partially-owned subsidiary, it may well use a method of accounting for the acquisition of the share stake that does not result in the recognition of goodwill based on fair values, or, indeed, may not result in the recognition of any additional goodwill at all.

After such an acquisition, impairment testing of goodwill is based solely on the amount that is recorded in the consolidated accounts, regardless of the basis on which it has been calculated. There is no notional gross-up to reflect goodwill that is not recorded or recorded at an amount not based on fair value. The entity will still make a notional gross-up to the extent that there is still a minority participation. Testing goodwill for impairment in the context of minority interests is described in greater detail in Chapter 7 at 3.4.

5.5.4 Acquisitions by subsidiaries and determining the level at which the group tests goodwill for impairment

IAS 36 requires goodwill to be allocated to the lowest level within the entity at which the goodwill is monitored for internal management purposes. If a subsidiary undertakes acquisitions and recognises goodwill in its own financial statements, the level at which the subsidiary's management monitors the goodwill may differ from the level at which the parent's or group's management monitors goodwill from the group's perspective.

If a subsidiary's management monitors its goodwill at a lower level than the level at which the parent's or group's management monitors its goodwill, a key issue is whether that lower level should, from the group's perspective, be regarded as the 'lowest level within the entity at which the goodwill is monitored for internal management purposes'? The answer is no, as is demonstrated in the following example

Example 15.22: Monitoring goodwill arising from acquired by subsidiaries

A parent acquired 100% of the issued shares of a company that operates autonomously and is required to prepare IFRS-compliant financial statements. The subsidiary has acquired various businesses both before and after becoming part of the group. Those business combinations have included significant amounts of goodwill.

The subsidiary's management monitors its acquired goodwill at the level of the subsidiary's business segments. The group has assessed that these will be operating segments for the purposes of IAS 14 (or IFRS 8 on transition to that standard – see Chapter 30). However, management of the parent/group monitors its acquired goodwill at the level of the group's business segments, which is a higher level than the subsidiary's business segments. The subsidiary's operations form part of two of the group's six business segments.

The subsidiary's goodwill comprises goodwill arising on its acquisitions, some of which took place *before,* and some *after,* the subsidiary became part of the group.

In contrast, the goodwill recognised by the group comprises:

- Goodwill acquired by the parent in the acquisition of the subsidiary (some of which represents goodwill acquired and therefore recognised by the subsidiary and some of which was internally generated goodwill from the subsidiary's perspective and therefore not recognised by the subsidiary);
- Goodwill acquired by the subsidiary since becoming part of the group;
- Goodwill acquired by the parent in other business combinations (i.e. goodwill that relates to other subsidiaries and businesses that make up the group).

The goodwill acquired in the acquisition of the subsidiary that is recognised by the parent in its consolidated financial statements is therefore different from the goodwill recognised by the subsidiary (which relates only to the acquisitions made by the subsidiary and was measured at the date of the acquisition concerned).

In such circumstances the actions of the subsidiary's management in deciding the level at which it tests its goodwill for impairment will *not* cause the group to be 'locked in' to testing goodwill at the same level in the consolidated financial statements.

Rather, the group should test its goodwill for impairment at the level at which management of the parent or group monitors its various investments in goodwill, namely, in this example, at the group's business segment level (or operating segment level after the group implements IFRS 8).

6 EFFECTIVE DATE, TRANSITIONAL PROVISIONS AND FIRST-TIME ADOPTION

6.1 Transitional provisions and effective date

The transitional arrangements and effective date depend on whether an entity elects to apply IFRS 3 from any date earlier than that required by that standard. IFRS 3 required prospective application, from the beginning of the first annual period beginning on or after 31 March 2004. Any entity that elected to apply IFRS 3 to earlier business combinations also had to apply IAS 36 prospectively from that same date.[166] Otherwise, an entity was required to apply IAS 36:

(a) to goodwill and intangible assets acquired in business combinations for which the agreement date was on or after 31 March 2004; and

(b) to all other assets prospectively from the beginning of the first annual period beginning on or after 31 March 2004.[167]

6.2 First-time adoption

As far as goodwill is concerned, first time adopters of IFRS are required by IFRS 1 – *First-time Adoption of International Financial Reporting Standards* – to subject all goodwill carried in the balance sheet at the date of transition to an impairment test, regardless of whether there are any indications of impairment.

> 'Regardless of whether there is any indication that the goodwill may be impaired, the first-time adopter shall apply IAS 36 in testing the goodwill for impairment at the date of transition to IFRS and in recognising any resulting impairment loss in retained earnings (or, if so required by IAS 36, in revaluation surplus). The impairment test shall be based on conditions at the date of transition to IFRS.'[168]

For other assets, first time adopters have the benefit of a number of exemptions from the requirement for full restatement of the opening IFRS balance sheet. Given the significance of property, plant and equipment in particular in the balance sheet of most first-time adopters (and the sheer number of transactions affecting property, plant and equipment) restatement is not only extremely important but will often also involve undue cost and effort. Still, a first-time adopter needs a cost basis for the assets in its opening IFRS balance sheet. Therefore, the IASB decided to introduce the notion of a 'deemed cost' that is not the 'true' IFRS-compliant cost basis of an asset, but a surrogate that is deemed to be a suitable starting point.

The IASB argued that it is not necessary to restrict application of the exemption to classes of assets to prevent selective revaluations, because 'IAS 36 requires an impairment test if there is any indication that an asset is impaired. Thus, if an entity uses fair value as deemed cost for assets whose fair value is above cost, it cannot ignore indications that the recoverable amount of other assets may have fallen below their carrying amount. Therefore, IFRS 1 does not restrict the use of fair value as deemed cost to entire classes of asset.'[169]

If a first-time adopter recognised or reversed any impairment losses in preparing its opening IFRS balance sheet at the date of transition, it should disclose the information that IAS 36 would have required 'if the entity had recognised those impairment losses or reversals in the period beginning with the date of transition to IFRS'.[170] The purpose of this disclosure requirement is that while, as the IASB acknowledges, there is inevitably subjectivity about impairment losses, 'this disclosure provides transparency about impairment losses recognised on transition to IFRS. These losses might otherwise receive less attention than impairment losses recognised in earlier or later periods'.[171] Chapter 5 deals with first-time adoption and IFRS 1 in detail.

7 CONCLUSION

Two developments are placing increased emphasis on the part to be played by impairment within financial reporting under International GAAP. First, the regime under which goodwill is not amortised means that impairment tests will have to be applied at least annually by all entities that record goodwill in their consolidated accounts. Additionally, those entities that are adopting IFRSs for the first time will have to apply an impairment test to all goodwill carried forward at transition. Second, the policy of the IASB to extend fair value based accounting, especially fair values that are based on models and not on observable market transactions, will also increase the importance of testing for impairment.

Notwithstanding this central role, IAS 36 is not an easy standard for entities to apply in practice. To take discount rates as a case in point, an entity is required to arrive at an estimate of the rate that the market would expect on an equally risky investment.[172] This information is not readily obtainable. The standard allows a number of different methods to be used to estimate this rate; yet it gives little concrete guidance and allows as a starting point discount rates that are unlikely to be relevant, such as an entity's incremental borrowing rate. It is possible that the standard setters have attempted to deflect academic criticism by not specifying how a discount rate should be chosen; but this vagueness has left many entities unsure about how to proceed.

As a consequence, it becomes difficult to be convinced that the comparability requirement underlying IFRS is being met in practice, as entities interpret the standard's requirements in differing ways. Moreover, because assets (other than goodwill and intangible assets with an indefinite life) or CGUs are only tested for impairment if there are indicators of impairment, there must be comparability issues even within entities. There may be no indicators of impairment with regard to some assets or CGUs even though they are actually earning a sub-market rate of return, at least in the short term.

It is difficult to see how these issues can be resolved in the continuing absence of a clear underlying theoretical basis underpinning the carrying value of assets and liabilities. In the short term, it is likely that many entities will consult valuations experts in order to apply IAS 36. In the longer term it remains to be seen if the IASB will give entities the standard on impairment that they deserve, which is one that contains an unambiguous, comparable and useable impairment test.

References

1 IAS 36, *Impairment of assets*, IASB, March 2004, para. 13
2 IAS 36, paras. 138-139.
3 IAS 36, para. 1
4 IAS 36, para. 2.
5 IAS 36, para. 3.
6 IAS 36, para. 4.
7 IAS 36, para. 5.
8 IAS 36, para. 6.
9 IAS 36, para. 10.
10 IAS 36, paras. 8-9.
11 IAS 36, para. 11.
12 IAS 36, para. 15.
13 IAS 36, para. 9.
14 IAS 36, para. 13.
15 IAS 36, para. 12.
16 IAS 36, para. 14.
17 IAS 36, para. 15.
18 IAS 36, para. 16.
19 IAS 36, para. 17.
20 IAS 36, para. 18.
21 IAS 36, para. 31.
22 IAS 36, para. 19.
23 IAS 36, para. 20.
24 IAS 36, para. 21.
25 IFRS 5, para. 18.
26 IAS 36, para. 22.
27 IAS 36, para. 23.
28 IAS 36, para. 25.
29 IAS 36, para. 26.
30 IAS 36, para. 27.
31 IAS 36, para. 27.
32 IAS 36, para. 28.
33 IAS 36, para. 29.
34 IAS 36, para. 30.
35 IAS 36, para. 31.
36 IAS 36, para. 66.
37 IAS 36, para. 67.
38 IAS 36, paras. 6 and 68.
39 IAS 36, para. 68.
40 IAS 36, para. 69.
41 IAS 36, para. 70.
42 IAS 36, para. 71.
43 IAS 36, Illustrative Examples, Example 1.
44 IAS 36, paras. 72-73.
45 IAS 36, paras. 74-75.
46 IAS 36, para. 76.
47 IAS 36, para. 77.
48 IAS 36, para. 78.
49 IAS 36, para. 79.
50 IAS 36, para. 100
51 IAS 36, para. 101
52 IAS 36, para. 102
53 IAS 36, para. 102
54 IAS 36, para. 103, Illustrative Examples, Example 8
55 IAS 36, para. 30.
56 IAS 36, para. 33.
57 IAS 36, para. 34.
58 IAS 36, para. 35.
59 IAS 36, para. 38.
60 IAS 36, para. 36.
61 IAS 36, para. 37.
62 IAS 36, para. 39.
63 IAS 36, para. 40.
64 IAS 36, para. 43.
65 IAS 36, para. 41.
66 IAS 36, para. 42.
67 IAS 36, para. 44.
68 IAS 36, para. 48.
69 IAS 36, para. 49.
70 IAS 36, paras. 44-45.
71 IAS 36, paras. 46-47.
72 IAS 36, para. 47.
73 IAS 36, paras. 50-51.
74 IAS 36, para. 52-53.
75 IAS 36, para. 54.
76 IAS 21, *The Effects of Changes in Foreign Exchange Rates* , IASB, December 2003, para. 25.
77 IAS 36, para. 55.
78 IAS 36, para. 56.
79 IAS 36, para. 56.
80 IAS 36, Appendix A, para. A17.
81 IAS 36, Appendix A, para. A18.
82 IAS 36, Appendix A, para. A18.
83 IAS 36, Appendix A, para. A19.
84 IAS 36, Appendix A, para. A20.
85 IAS 36, Appendix A, para. A21.
86 IAS 36, para. 16.
87 One source of reference which may prove useful is a Digest issued by the Corporate Finance Faculty of the ICAEW – *The Cost of Capital*, Simon Pallett, ICAEW, 1999.
88 IAS 36, para. 55.
89 IAS 36, para. BCZ85.
90 IAS 36, paras. BCZ85 and BCZ94.
91 IAS 36, para. 59.
92 IAS 36, para. 60.
93 IAS 36, para. 61.
94 IAS 16, *Property, Plant and Equipment,* IASB, December 2003 (amended March 2004), para. 73(d).
95 IAS 36, para. 62.
96 IAS 36, para. 63.
97 IAS 36, para. 104.
98 IAS 36, para. 88.
99 IAS 36, para. 105.

100 IAS 36, para. 106.
101 IAS 36, para. 108.
102 IAS 36, para. 107.
103 IFRS 3, *Business Combinations*, IASB, March 2004, paras. 54-55.
104 IAS 38, paras. 89, and 107-108.
105 IAS 38, *Intangible Assets*, IASB, March 2004, para. 91.
106 IAS 38, para. 108.
107 IAS 36, para. 10.
108 IAS 36, para. 10.
109 IAS 36, paras. 10-11.
110 IAS 36, para. 89.
111 IAS 36, para. 11.
112 IAS 36, para. 89.
113 IAS 36, para. 24.
114 IAS 36, para. 80.
115 IFRS 8, *Operating Segments*, IASB, November 2006, para. 5.
116 IAS 36, para. 96.
117 IAS 36, para. 88.
118 IAS 36, paras. 97-98.
119 IAS 36, para. 124.
120 IAS 36, para. 125
121 IAS 36, para. 110.
122 IAS 36, para. 112.
123 IAS 36, para. 111.
124 IAS 36, para. 113.
125 IAS 36, paras. 114-116.
126 IAS 36, para. 117.
127 IAS 36, para. 118.
128 IAS 36, para. 119.
129 IAS 36, para. 121.
130 IAS 36, paras. 119-120.
131 IAS 36, para. 121.
132 IAS 36, paras. 122-123.
133 IAS 36, para. 127.
134 IAS 36, para. 126.
135 IAS 36, para. 128.
136 IAS 36, para. 129.
137 IAS 36, para. 130.
138 IAS 36, para. 131.
139 IAS 36, para. 132.
140 IAS 36, para. 133.
141 IAS 36, para. 134.
142 IAS 36, para. 135.
143 IAS 36, para. 135.
144 IAS 36, Appendix A, para. A17.
145 IAS 36, para. 56.
146 IAS 36, Appendix A, para. A15.
147 IAS 36, para. 55.
148 IAS 36, Appendix A, para. A19
149 IAS 36, Appendix A, para. A17.
150 IFRS 3 , para. BC130.
151 IAS 36, para. 10.
152 IAS 36, para. 44.
153 IAS 36, para. 49.
154 IAS 36, para. 42.
155 IAS 36, para. 20.
156 IAS 36, para. 25.
157 IAS 36, para. 27.
158 IAS 36, para. 28.
159 IAS 36, para. 25.
160 IAS 36, para. 124.
161 IAS 27, *Consolidated and Separate Financial Statements*, IASB, December 2003, para. 37.
162 IAS 28, *Investments in associates*, para. 33.
163 IAS 28, para. 34.
164 IFRS 3, para. 10.
165 IAS 36, para. 70.
166 IAS 36, para. 138
167 IAS 36, para. 139.
168 IFRS 1, *First-time Adoption of International Financial Reporting Standards*, IASB, June 2003 (amended March 2004), para. B2(g).
169 IFRS 1, para. BC45.
170 IFRS 1, para. 39.
171 IFRS 1, para. BC94.
172 IAS 36, para. 55.

Chapter 16 Capitalisation of borrowing costs

1 INTRODUCTION

A point of contention in determining the initial measurement of an asset is whether or not finance costs incurred during the period of its construction should be capitalised. There have always been a number of strong arguments in favour of the capitalisation of directly attributable finance costs. It is argued that they are just as much a cost as any other directly attributable cost, that expensing finance costs distorts the choice between purchasing and constructing the asset, that capitalising the costs leads to a carrying value that is far more akin to the market value of the asset and that the accounts are more likely to represent the true success or failure of the project. However, some proponents of this view have noted that there is a cost to all entities of constructing assets whether or not they have taken out borrowings for the purpose. If capitalisation were to become mandatory, in theory notional interest should also be capitalised. No standard-setter has yet taken this step.

In March 1984, the (then) IASC published IAS 23 – *Capitalisation of Borrowing Costs*. Under this original version of IAS 23, capitalisation was optional, but certain rules were laid down if a policy of capitalisation were to be adopted.[1] A revised version of IAS 23 – *Borrowing Costs* – was issued in 1993, which took a different approach. The IASC did not go so far as to ban the capitalisation of borrowing costs. Under the revised IAS 23 the benchmark treatment for borrowing costs is that they should be recognised as an expense in the period in which they are incurred regardless of how the borrowings are applied.[2] However, the revised IAS 23 incorporates capitalisation of borrowing costs as an allowed alternative treatment.

The IASB reconsidered capitalisation of interest as part of its short-term Convergence Project and as a result changed direction again. In March 2007 it issued another revised version of IAS 23 (referred to in this chapter as 'IAS 23 (revised 2007)' or 'the revised standard'), this time mandating capitalisation. The IASB has made only minor changes to the rest of the standard, principally two amendments to the scope. It now takes account of those standards that allow assets to be measured at fair value, where capitalisation will continue to be a matter of accounting policy choice and exempts inventories that are routinely manufactured or otherwise produced in large quantities on a repetitive basis (see 2.1.2 below).

The IASB notes that this eliminates the main difference between IAS 23 and FASB Statement No. 34 – *Capitalization of Interest Cost* (SFAS 34) although there remain many differences of detail that have not been addressed. The IASB has justified its change in stance by arguing that 'this will result in an improvement in financial reporting as well as achieving convergence in principle with US GAAP.[3]

The revised standard is unlikely to affect entities that have already adopted a policy of capitalisation as the requirements remain unchanged. The many entities that expense all borrowing costs as incurred will need to introduce systems and processes to capture relevant information and calculate the amount of costs to be capitalised. They will also need to consider the impact of other finance costs such as hedging activities and exchange differences on foreign currency borrowings (see 3.1.3 below).

The revised standard applies to accounting periods commencing on or after 1 January 2009 although early implementation is permitted; this is discussed at 4 below.

Except where indicated, both standards have the same requirements and in these instances references in the chapter are to both IAS 23 and IAS 23 (revised 2007).

2 THE REQUIREMENTS OF IAS 23

2.1 Scope and definitions

2.1.1 Scope

IAS 23 deals with the treatment of borrowing costs in general, rather than focusing on capitalising borrowing costs as part of the carrying value of assets.

The standard does not deal with the actual or imputed costs of equity, including preferred capital that is not classified as a liability.[4] This means that any distributions or other payments made in respect of equity instruments, as defined by IAS 32 – *Financial Instruments: Disclosure and Presentation* – are not within the scope of IAS 23; conversely, interest and dividends payable on instruments classified as financial liabilities would appear to be within the scope of the standard. See Chapter 19 regarding the classification of instruments as debt or equity.

2.1.2 Qualifying assets

IAS 23 defines a qualifying asset as 'an asset that necessarily takes a substantial period of time to get ready for its intended use or sale'.[5] Assets that are ready for their intended use or sale when acquired are not qualifying assets.[6] Examples of qualifying assets in the standard are manufacturing plants, power generation facilities and investment properties. Intangible assets have been added to this list of examples in IAS 23 (revised 2007)[7] but this should not be taken as evidence that they are not qualifying assets under the current IAS 23. For instance, IFRIC 12 – *Service Concession Arrangements* – refers to an entity capitalising borrowing costs during the construction phase when the accumulating right to be paid for construction services and the ultimate asset are both accounted for as intangible assets (see Chapter 29 at 6.4.3).[8]

Inventories are within scope as long as they meet the definition and require a substantial period of time to bring them to a saleable condition.[9] Inventories that are routinely manufactured or otherwise produced in large quantities on a repetitive basis over a short period of time are not qualifying assets under IAS 23[10] By inference, if manufacture or production took a long period of time they were qualifying assets. Presumably this is why IAS 23 (revised 2007) has a different approach to the issue. In addition, inventories that are routinely manufactured or otherwise produced in large quantities on a repetitive basis are not qualifying assets so capitalisation need not be applied.[11] This exemption has been allowed because of the difficulty of calculating and monitoring the amount to be capitalised but it will permit an entity that has chosen not to capitalise interest on such assets to continue with its existing policy. There are many examples of such inventories, including large manufactured or constructed items that take some time to complete but are basically sold a standard items, such as residential housing, aircraft or large items of equipment. Less obviously, it could also include food and drink that takes a long time to mature, such as cheeses or alcohol that matures in bottle or cask.

IAS 23 (revised 2007) does not require entities to capitalise interest in respect of assets that are measured at fair value that would otherwise be qualifying assets. If the assets are held under a full fair value model with all changes going to the income statement then capitalisation does not affect measurement in the balance sheet and is no more than a reallocation between finance costs and the fair value movement in the income statement. However, IAS 23 (revised 2007) does not restrict the exemption to assets where the fair value movement is taken to the income statement. Other assets measured at fair value, for example properties in the course of construction that fall under IAS 16's revaluation model, are also eligible for this scope exemption even though the revaluation goes to equity, not income.[12] Most such properties will be investment properties in the course of construction, currently not within scope of IAS 40 – *Investment Properties*. This will cease to be an issue if and when the proposed amendment to IAS 40 enables them to be classified as investment properties (see Chapter 14 at 2.2.5)

IAS 11– *Construction Costs* – permits borrowing costs to be capitalised when they can be attributable to contract activity and allocated to specific contracts.[13] Note that the reference to IAS 23 in this paragraph is to be deleted with the revised standard by consequential amendment because the IASB argues that it is unnecessary; attributing borrowing costs to contracts is really a matter of identifying the contract costs and does not affect the recognition of borrowing costs as specified in IAS 23.[14]

In the case of equity accounted investments, the (then) IASC considered whether or not the investor should look through to the investee's activities when applying the proposed revised Standard. However, it decided that this could involve an element of double-counting, since the investee itself would apply the Standard.[15] Accordingly,

IAS 23 states that 'other investments' (for this purpose equity accounted investments and not, for example, investment properties) should not be qualifying assets.[16] IAS 23 (revised 2007) has clarified this and now excludes all financial assets from the definition of qualifying assets.[17]

2.1.3 *Borrowing costs*

Borrowing costs are interest and other costs incurred by an entity in connection with the borrowing of funds.[18]

Borrowing costs include:

(a) interest on bank overdrafts and short-term and long-term borrowings;

(b) amortisation of discounts or premiums relating to borrowings;

(c) amortisation of ancillary costs incurred in connection with the arrangement of borrowings;

(d) finance charges in respect of finance leases recognised in accordance with IAS 17 – *Leases* – and

(e) exchange differences arising from foreign currency borrowings to the extent that they are regarded as an adjustment to interest costs.[19]

The identification and measurement of finance costs is not a matter for IAS 23 and this is an area that has changed considerably since the standard was issued in 1984. This is discussed further at 3.1 below.

2.2 Accounting policies

2.2.1 *Borrowing costs treated as an expense*

The standard's benchmark treatment is that borrowing costs should be treated as an expense in the period in which they are incurred, regardless of how the borrowings have been applied.[20] This option will not be available for periods beginning on or after 1 January 2009.

2.2.2 *Capitalisation of borrowing costs*

Borrowing costs are treated as an expense unless they meet the criteria for capitalisation. If an entity adopts the allowed alternative treatment borrowing costs should be capitalised if they are directly attributable to the acquisition, construction or production of a qualifying asset.[21] These borrowing costs are included in the cost of the asset; all other borrowing costs are recognised as an expense in the period in which they are incurred.[22]

These requirements remain unchanged in IAS 23 (revised 2007), except that references to capitalisation being the allowed alternative treatment have been removed.[23]

2.2.3 *Consistency of application of a capitalisation policy*

Because prior to revision IAS 23 allowed entities to choose whether to capitalise borrowing costs, some questioned whether an entity could choose to capitalise such costs for certain qualifying assets and not for others or whether it had to select a policy to apply to all qualifying assets. In other words, is a policy of 'selective' capitalisation permitted under IFRS? This issue was referred to the IASC's Standing Interpretations Committee (SIC), which confirmed in SIC-2 – *Capitalisation of Borrowing Costs* – that an entity must choose one or other treatment as an accounting policy and apply it consistently. Although the SIC has now been withdrawn, this does not affect the conclusion.

As a result, if an entity adopts a policy of capitalising borrowing costs, that treatment must be applied consistently to all borrowing costs that are directly attributable to the acquisition, construction or production of all qualifying assets of the entity. An entity should continue to capitalise such borrowing costs even if the carrying amount of the asset exceeds its recoverable amount. However, the carrying amount of the asset should be written down to recognise impairment losses in such cases.[24]

2.3 Capitalisation of borrowing costs

2.3.1 Directly attributable borrowing costs

In determining which borrowing costs satisfy the 'directly attributable' criterion, the standard starts from the premise that directly attributable borrowing costs are those that would have been avoided if the expenditure on the qualifying asset had not been made.[25]

The standard notes that the borrowing costs that are directly related can be readily identified if an entity borrows funds specifically for the purpose.[26] In this case, the borrowing costs eligible for capitalisation are the actual borrowing costs incurred during the period.[27] However, as entities frequently borrow funds in advance of expenditure on qualifying assets, any investment income on the temporary investment of those borrowings should be deducted and only the net amount capitalised.[28] In addition, as described in the next section, an entity that does not borrow specifically for the purpose may still be able to consider some of the borrowing costs on its general borrowings as directly attributable.

2.3.2 Capitalisation rate

IAS 23 concedes that there may be practical difficulties in identifying a direct relationship between particular borrowings and a qualifying asset and in determining the borrowings that could otherwise have been avoided. This could happen if the financing activity of an entity is co-ordinated centrally, by which the standard presumably means that the entity borrows to meet its requirements as a whole and the construction is being financed out of general borrowings. Other circumstances that may cause difficulties are identified by the standard as follows:

- an entity has a group treasury function that uses a range of debt instruments to borrow funds at varying rates of interest and lends those funds on various bases to other entities in the group; or
- loans are denominated in, or linked to, foreign currency, or the group operates in highly inflationary economies.

In any event, the standard makes allowance for the problems that arise in practice and concedes that the determination of attributable borrowing costs may be difficult and require the exercise of judgement.[29]

If funds are borrowed generally and used for the purpose of obtaining a qualifying asset, the amount of borrowing costs eligible for capitalisation should be determined by applying a capitalisation rate to the expenditures on that asset. The capitalisation rate should be the weighted average of the borrowing costs applicable to the borrowings of the entity that are outstanding during the period, other than borrowings made specifically for the purpose of obtaining a qualifying asset. The amount of borrowing costs capitalised during a period should not exceed the amount of borrowing costs incurred during that period.[30] Of course, where funds are borrowed generally, there is no question of reducing the amount of borrowing costs capitalised by interest income earned. The standard allows that the average carrying amount of the asset during a period, including borrowing costs previously capitalised, is normally a reasonable approximation of the expenditures to which the capitalisation rate is applied in that period.[31]

In some circumstances all borrowings made by the group can be taken into account in determining the weighted average of the borrowing costs. In other circumstances only those borrowings made by individual subsidiaries may be taken into account.[32] Presumably this will be largely determined by the extent to which borrowings are made centrally (and, perhaps, expenses met in the same way) and passed through to individual group companies via intercompany accounts and intra-group loans.

The capitalisation rate is discussed further at 3.2 below.

2.3.3 Impairment and capitalisation of borrowing costs

An entity that has opted for the allowed alternative in IAS 23 continues to capitalise borrowing costs that are directly attributable to the acquisition, construction or production of a qualifying asset as part of the carrying amount of the asset, even if the capitalisation causes the carrying amount of the asset to exceed its recoverable amount.

If the carrying amount of the qualifying asset exceeds its recoverable amount or net realisable value, the asset must be written down in accordance with the relevant international standard. This also applies to the asset's expected ultimate cost if the asset is incomplete.[33] The expected ultimate cost must include costs to complete and the estimated capitalised interest thereon.

IAS 36 – *Impairment of assets* – will apply if the qualifying asset is property, plant and equipment accounted for in accordance with IAS 16 – *Property Plant and Equipment*[34] – or if the asset is otherwise within scope of IAS 36. The following assets that could potentially be qualifying assets are outside the scope of IAS 36: inventories, assets arising from construction contracts, investment property that is measured at fair value and non-current assets (or disposal groups) classified as held for sale in accordance with IFRS 5 – *Non-current Assets Held for Sale and Discontinued Operations*.[35] Impairment is fully discussed in Chapter 15.

2.3.4 Capitalisation of borrowing costs in hyperinflationary economies

Paragraph 21 of IAS 29 – *Financial Reporting in Hyperinflationary Economies* – states that 'the impact of inflation is usually recognised in borrowing costs. It is not appropriate both to restate the capital expenditure financed by borrowing and to capitalise that part of the borrowing costs that compensates for the inflation during the same period. This part of the borrowing costs is recognised as an expense in the period in which the costs are incurred'.[36] IAS 23 (revised 2007) specifies that when an entity applies IAS 29, the borrowing costs that can be capitalised should be restricted and the entity must expense the part of borrowing costs that compensate for inflation during the same period. Therefore, although this is not referred to in the current version of the standard, it is not a new IFRS requirement.[37]

Issues relating to exchange differences that do not arise in hyperinflationary situations and their eligibility for capitalisation are dealt with at 3.1.1 below.

2.4 Commencement, suspension and cessation of capitalisation

2.4.1 Commencement of capitalisation

IAS 23 requires that capitalisation should commence when:

(a) expenditures for the asset are being incurred;

(b) borrowing costs are being incurred; and

(c) activities that are necessary to prepare the asset for its intended use or sale are in progress.[38]

The standard makes it explicit that only those expenditures on a qualifying asset that have resulted in payments of cash, transfers of other assets or the assumption of interest-bearing liabilities, may be included in determining borrowing costs. Such expenditures must be reduced by any progress payments and grants received in connection with the asset.[39]

The activities necessary to prepare an asset for its intended use or sale extend to more than the physical construction of the asset. Necessary activities can start before the commencement of physical construction and include, for example, technical and administrative work such as obtaining permits. Note that this does not mean that borrowing costs can be capitalised if it is unclear that permits that are necessary for the construction will be obtained. No cost could be considered 'directly attributable' prior to this point. However, interest may not be capitalised during a period in which there are no activities that change the asset's condition. For example, borrowing costs incurred while land is under development are capitalised during the period in which activities related to the development are being undertaken. However, borrowing costs incurred while land acquired for building purposes is held without any associated development activity do not qualify for capitalisation.[40] A house-builder or property developer may not capitalise borrowing costs on its 'land bank'.

2.4.2 Suspension of capitalisation

IAS 23 states that capitalisation should be suspended during extended periods in which active development is interrupted. However, the standard distinguishes between extended periods of interruption (when capitalisation would be suspended) and periods of temporary delay that are a necessary part of preparing the asset for its intended purpose (when capitalisation is not normally suspended). Capitalisation continues during periods when inventory is undergoing slow transformation – the example is given of inventories taking an extended time to mature (presumably such products as Scotch whisky or Cognac). A bridge construction delayed by temporary adverse weather conditions, where such conditions are common in the region, would also not be a cause for suspension of capitalisation.[41]

2.4.3 Cessation of capitalisation

The standard requires capitalisation to cease when substantially all the activities necessary to prepare the qualifying asset for its intended use or sale are complete.[42] An asset is normally ready for its intended use or sale when the physical construction of the asset is complete even though routine administrative work might still continue. If minor modifications, such as the decoration of a property to the purchaser's specification, are all that are outstanding, this indicates that substantially all the activities are complete.[43] In some cases there may be a requirement for inspection (e.g. to ensure that the asset meets safety requirements) before the asset can be used. 'Substantially all the activities' must have been completed before this point is reached so capitalisation will cease prior to the inspection.

Furthermore, when the construction of a qualifying asset is completed in parts and each part is capable of being used while construction continues on other parts, capitalisation should cease when substantially all the activities necessary to prepare that part for its intended use or sale are completed.[44] An example of this might be a business park comprising several buildings, each of which is capable of being fully utilised while construction continues on other parts.[45]

2.5 Disclosure requirements of IAS 23

Under the IAS 23 benchmark treatment the entity should disclose that it expenses all borrowing costs immediately.[46]

Under the IAS 23 allowed alternative treatment the following disclosures are required to be made:

(a) that the entity capitalises borrowing costs in accordance with the allowed alternative treatment;

(b) the amount of borrowing costs capitalised during the period; and

(c) the capitalisation rate used to determine the amount of borrowing costs eligible for capitalisation.[47]

IAS 23 (revised 2007) requires the disclosure of (b) and (c) above.[48]

Electrolux discloses that it expenses all borrowing costs as incurred.

Extract 16.1: Electrolux (2006)

Notes to the Consolidated Financial Statements

Borrowing costs

Borrowing costs are recognised as an expense in the period in which they are incurred.

Fortis's policy describes the period during which borrowing costs are capitalised as well as noting that it uses either an actual rate or a weighted average cost of borrowings.

Extract 16.2: Fortis (2006)

Notes to the Group Financial Statements

2.36 Borrowing costs

Borrowing costs are generally expensed as incurred. Borrowing costs that are directly attributable to the acquisition or construction of an asset are capitalised while the asset is being constructed as part of the cost of that asset. Capitalisation of borrowing costs should commence when:

- expenditures for the asset and borrowing costs are being incurred; and
- activities necessary to prepare the asset for its intended use or sale are in progress.

Capitalisation ceases when the asset is substantially ready for its intended use or sale. If active development is interrupted for an extended period, capitalisation is suspended. When construction occurs piecemeal and use of each part is possible as construction continues, capitalisation for each part ceases on substantial completion of that part.

For borrowing associated with a specific asset, the actual rate on that borrowing is used. Otherwise, a weighted average cost of borrowings is used.

AngloGold Ashanti discloses in its 'tangible assets' note its capitalisation rate used to determine its borrowing costs.

Extract 16.3: AngloGold Ashanti (2006)

Notes to the Group Financial Statements

16. Tangible assets

The capitalisation rate used to determine the amount of borrowing costs eligible for capitalisation is 8.23% (2005: 10.65%).

The amount of borrowing costs capitalised during the period (102 million rands) is disclosed within the table of movements in property, plant and equipment that precedes this narrative disclosure.

3 PRACTICAL ISSUES

3.1 Borrowing costs

At the time that IAS 23 was first implemented in 1984 there was little guidance on the measurement and accounting treatment of finance costs. Even after its revision in 1993, the standard predates the accounting rules now in IAS 32 and IAS 39.[49] In addition, in the twenty years since the standard was originally issued, financial instruments have become considerably more complex.

The standard lists various interest and other costs that may comprise part of borrowing costs, together with finance charges in respect of finance leases recognised in accordance with IAS 17. Certain exchange differences may also be capitalised; their treatment is addressed at 3.1.2 below, whilst some of the other issues are discussed in 3.1.3. The treatment of lease liabilities is addressed further in Chapter 25.

3.1.1 Exchange differences as a borrowing cost

Borrowings in one currency may have been used to finance a development the costs of which are incurred primarily in another currency, e.g. a US dollar loan financing a rouble development. This may have been done on the basis that, over the period of the development, the cost, after allowing for exchange differences, was expected to be less than the interest cost of an equivalent rouble loan.

IAS 23 defines borrowing costs as including exchange differences arising from foreign currency borrowings to the extent that they are regarded as an adjustment to interest costs.[50] The standard does not expand on this point. We consider that, as exchange rate movements are largely a function of differential interest rates, in most circumstances the foreign exchange differences on directly attributable borrowings will be an adjustment to interest costs that can meet the definition of borrowing costs. However, care will have to be taken if there is a sudden fluctuation in exchange rates that cannot be attributed to changes in interest rates. In such cases we believe that a practical approach is to cap the exchange differences taken as borrowing costs at the amount of borrowing costs on functional currency equivalent borrowings.

3.1.2 Other finance costs

Borrowing costs as identified by the standard may include interest on bank overdrafts and short-term and long-term borrowings, amortisation of discounts or premiums relating to borrowings, amortisation of ancillary costs incurred in connection with the arrangement of borrowings.

These are the costs that an entity will encounter if it has financed its development through straightforward loan from banks or similar types of organisation. In general, such financial liabilities will be accounted for at amortised cost and the finance costs calculated in accordance with IAS 39 using the effective interest method, as follows.

The *amortised cost* of a financial liability is the amount at which it was measured at initial recognition minus principal repayments, plus or minus the cumulative amortisation of any difference between that initial amount and the maturity amount. The *effective interest method* calculates amortisation using the effective interest rate of a financial instrument and allocates the interest expense over the relevant period. The *effective interest rate* is the rate that exactly discounts estimated future cash payments over the expected life of the instrument or, when appropriate, a shorter period, to the instrument's net carrying amount.[51] This is further discussed in Chapter 20 at 5.

The borrowing costs eligible for capitalisation are those that are recognised as an expense in the period using the effective interest rate. As part of the Annual Improvements Project, the IASB has proposed replacing the references to specific borrowing costs with references to interest expense calculated using the effective interest rate method as described in IAS 39.[52]

However IAS 23 does not address many of the ways in which an entity may finance its operations or other finance costs that it may incur. The standard does not, for example, address any of the following:

- the many derivative financial instruments such interest rate swaps, floors, caps and collars that are commonly used to manage interest rate risk on borrowings;
- gains and losses on derecognition of borrowings, for example early settlement of directly attributable borrowings that have been renegotiated prior to completion of an asset in the course of construction;
- dividends payable on shares classified as financial liabilities (such as certain redeemable preference shares) that have been recognised as an expense in profit or loss; and
- the unwinding of discounts that may be included within the caption 'finance costs' in an entity's income statement.

These are simply a few of the most commonly encountered examples – the list is very far from exhaustive.

We consider that IAS 23 does not preclude the classification of costs other than those that it identifies as borrowing costs that may be eligible for capitalisation. However, they must meet the basic criterion in the standard, i.e. that they are costs that are directly attributable to the acquisition, construction or production of a qualifying asset, which would therefore preclude the classification of unwinding discounts as borrowing costs. In addition, as in the case of exchange differences (see 3.1.2 above), capitalisation of such costs should be permitted only 'to the extent that they are regarded as an adjustment to interest costs'.

A Derivative financial instruments

The most straightforward and most commonly encountered derivative financial instrument used to manage interest rate risk is a floating to fixed interest rate swap, as in the following example.

Example 16.1: Floating to fixed interest rate swaps

Entity A has borrowed €4 million for five years at a floating interest rate to fund the construction of a building. In order to hedge the cash flow interest rate risk arising from these borrowings, A has entered into a matching pay-fixed receive-floating interest rate swap, based on the same underlying nominal sum and duration as the original borrowing, that effectively converts the interest on the borrowings to fixed rate. The net effect of the periodic cash settlements under the instrument is as if A had borrowed €4 million at a fixed rate of interest. Prior to IAS 39, entities simply recognised, on an accruals basis, each periodic net cash settlement in profit or loss.

Although these instruments are not addressed in IAS 23, there is no doubt that prior to IAS 39 the net costs of such 'synthetic' fixed rate debt would have been treated as a borrowing cost and therefore eligible for capitalisation if it met the criteria in the standard.

IAS 39 has complicated the situation considerably by completely changing the basis on which such instruments are recognised and measured. Briefly, a derivative financial instrument is classified by IAS 39 as held for trading and recognised initially at its fair value with changes in the fair value being taken to profit or loss (see Chapter 17 at 7.1.1) unless it is a designated effective hedging instrument (see Chapter 21), in which case the entity may be eligible to apply hedge accounting. IAS 39 describes hedge accounting as 'recognising the offsetting effects on net profit or loss of changes in the fair values of hedging instruments and related items being hedged';[53] this is achieved by taking fair value changes on hedging instruments to equity and recycling the effective element to income to match the gain or loss on the hedged item. Those elements of the changes in value of designated effective hedging instruments that are not effective in offsetting the changes in fair value of the item being hedged (e.g. changes in the counterparties' creditworthiness) are always taken to the income statement. See Chapter 21 at 4 regarding how to account for effective hedges and the conditions that these instruments must meet.

However, the net effect on income of an interest rate swap such as the above example 16.1 (a 'cash flow hedge in IAS 39 parlance because it is a hedge of the exposure to variability in cash flows) is very similar to the accruals accounting treatment under which the cash flows on the borrowing and the swap were recognised in income (see Chapter 21 at 4.2).

An entity may consider that a derivative financial instrument it has taken out, such as an interest rate swap, is directly attributable to the acquisition, construction or production or a qualifying asset. If the instrument does not meet the conditions for hedge accounting then the effects on income will be different from those if it does, and they will also be dissimilar from year to year. The question arises as to the impact of the derivative on borrowing costs eligible for capitalisation. In particular, does the accounting treatment of the derivative financial instrument affect the amount available for capitalisation? If hedge accounting is not adopted, does this affect the amount available for capitalisation?

The following examples illustrate the potential differences.

Example 16.2: Cash flow hedge of variable-rate debt using an interest rate swap

Entity A is constructing a building and expects it to take 18 months to complete. To finance the construction, on 1 January 20X8, the entity issues an eighteen month, €20,000,000 variable-rate note payable, due on 30 June 20X9 at a floating rate of interest plus a margin of 1%. At that date the market rate of interest is 8%. Interest payment dates and interest rate reset dates occur on 1 January and 1 July until maturity. The principal is due at maturity. Also on 1 January 20X8, the entity enters into an eighteen month interest rate swap with a notional amount of €10,000,000 from which it will receive periodic payments at the floating rate and make periodic payments at a fixed rate of 9%, with settlement and rate reset dates every 30 June and 31 December 31. The fair value of the swap is zero at inception.

On 1 January 20X8, the debt is recorded at €20,000,000. No entry is required for the swap on that date because its fair value was zero at inception.

During the eighteen month period, floating interest rates change as follows:

	Cash payments	
	Floating rate on principal	Rate paid by Entity A
30 June 20X8	8%	9%
31 Dec 20X8	8.5%	9.5%
30 June 20X9	9.75%	10.75%

Under the interest rate swap, Entity A receives interest at the market floating rate as above and pays at 9% on the nominal amount of €10,000,000 throughout the period.

In December 20X8 the swap has a fair value of €37,500, reflecting the fact that it is now in the money as Entity A is expected to receive a net cash inflow of this amount in the period until the instrument is terminated. There are no further changes in interest rates and the fair value of the swap declines to zero at 30 June 20X9. Note that this example excludes the effect of issue costs and discounting. In addition, it is assumed that, if Entity A is entitled to and applies hedge accounting, there will be no ineffectiveness.

The cash flows incurred by the entity on its borrowing and interest rate swap are as follows:

	Cash payments		
	Interest on principal	Interest rate swap (net)	Total
	€	€	€
30 June 20X8	900,000	50,000	950,000
31 Dec 20X8	950,000	25,000	975,000
30 June 20X9	1,075,000	(37,500)	1,037,500
Total	2,925,000	37,500	2,962,500

There are a number of different ways in which Entity A could calculate the borrowing costs eligible for capitalisation, including the following.

(i) Entity A considers that the interest rate swap meets the conditions for hedge accounting. The finance costs eligible for capitalisation as borrowing costs will be €1,925,000 in the year to 31 December 20X8 and €1,037,500 in the period ended 30 June 20X9.

(ii) Entity A does not apply hedge accounting. Therefore, it will reflect the fair value of the swap in income in the year ended 31 December 20X8, reducing the net finance costs by €37,500 to €1,887,500 and increasing the finance costs by an equivalent amount in 20X9 to €1,075,000. However, it considers that it is inappropriate to reflect the fair value of the swap in borrowing costs eligible for capitalisation so it capitalises costs based on the net cash cost on an accruals accounting basis. In this case this will give the same result as in (i) above.

(iii) Entity A does not apply hedge accounting. It considers that the interest rate swap is directly attributable to the construction and based its capitalisation on the amounts taken to income including the fair value of the interest rate swap, i.e. €1,887,500 in 20X8 and €1,075,000in 20X9.

(iv) Entity A does not apply hedge accounting and considers only the costs incurred on the borrowing, not the interest rate swap, as eligible for capitalisation. The borrowing costs eligible for capitalisation would be €1,850,000 in 20X8 and €1,075,000 in 20X9.

We consider that methods (i) and (ii) are valid interpretations of IAS 23, although in the case of (ii) it is necessary to demonstrate that the derivative financial instrument is directly attributable to the construction of a qualifying asset. Method (iii) needs to be treated with great caution as it would permit gains and losses, which are the present value of anticipated future cash flows on derivative financial instruments to be capitalised as part of the qualifying asset. It is assumed in the case of method (iii) that there will not be adequate hedge documentation but there must be clear evidence of intent. If the interest rate swap is directly attributable, as noted in connection with method (ii), this can also be an acceptable basis on which to capitalise costs. It is clearly necessary to consider the term of the derivative and the method may not be practicable if the derivative has a different term to the underlying directly attributable borrowing.

Note that these methods would not be permitted under US GAAP which prohibits the capitalisation of the gain or loss on the hedging instrument in a cash flow hedge. Instead, EITF 99-9 states that 'the amounts in accumulated comprehensive income related to a cash flow hedge of the variability of that interest should be reclassified into earnings over the depreciable life of the constructed asset, since that depreciable life coincides with the amortization period for the capitalized interest cost on the debt.'[54]

Based on the facts in this example, Method (iv) appears to be inconsistent with the underlying principles of IAS 23, which is that the costs eligible for capitalisation are those costs that could have been avoided if the expenditure on the qualifying asset had not been made.[55] However, in other circumstances, it may not be possible to argue that specific derivative financial instruments are directly attributable to particular qualifying assets, rather than being used by the entity to manage its interest rate exposure on a more general basis. In such as case method (iv) may be an acceptable treatment.

Whatever policy is chosen by the entity, it needs to be consistently applied.

B Gains and losses on derecognition of borrowings

If an entity repays borrowings early, in whole or in part, then it may recognise a gain or loss on the early settlement. This gain or loss includes amounts attributable to expected future interest rates; in other words it includes an estimated prepayment of the future cash flows under the instrument. The gain or loss is a function of relative interest rates and how the interest rate of the instrument differs from current and anticipated future interest rates. There may be circumstances in which a loan is repaid while the qualifying asset is still under construction. IAS 23 does not address the issue.

We consider that, generally, gains and losses on derecognition of borrowings are not eligible for capitalisation. It would be extremely difficult to determine an appropriate amount to capitalise and it would be inappropriate thereafter to capitalise any interest amounts (on specific or general borrowings) if to do so would amount to double counting. Decisions to repay borrowings are not usually directly attributable to the qualifying asset but to other circumstances of the entity.

C Gains or losses on termination of derivative financial instruments

If an entity terminates an interest rate swap, for example, before the end of the term of the instrument, it will usually either have to make or receive a payment, depending on the fair value of the instrument at that time. This fair value is based on expected future interest rates; in other words it is an estimated prepayment of the future cash flows under the instrument.

The treatment of the gain or loss for the purposes of capitalisation will depend on the following:

- the basis on which the entity capitalises the gains and losses associated with derivative financial instruments, described in A above; and
- whether the derivative is associated with a borrowing that has also been terminated, whose treatment is described in B above.

Entities must adopt a treatment that is consistent with their policy for capitalising the gains and losses of derivative financial instruments.

The accounting under IAS 39 will differ depending on whether the instrument has been designated as a hedge or not; in the former case, and assuming that the borrowing has not also been repaid, the entity will usually continue to account for the cumulative gain or loss on the instrument as if the hedge were still in place (see Chapter 21 at 4.2). In such a case, the amounts that are recycled from equity will be eligible for capitalisation for the remainder of the period of construction.

If the entity is not hedge accounting for the derivative financial instrument but considers it to be directly attributable to the construction of the qualifying asset then it will have to consider whether part of the gain or loss relates to a period after construction is complete.

If the underlying borrowing is also terminated then the gain or loss will not be capitalised and the treatment will mirror that applied to the borrowing, as described in B above.

D Dividends payable on shares classified as financial liabilities

An entity might finance its operations in whole or in part by the issue of preference shares and in some circumstances these will be classified as financial liabilities (see Chapter 19 at 3.2.1). It is possible that an entity might issue redeemable preference shares that are redeemable at the option of the holder (and are classified as financial liabilities) to fund the development of a qualifying asset. In this case the dividends would meet the definition of borrowing costs. This would not apply to irredeemable shares as they are not borrowings that could be avoided and hence could never be directly attributable to a qualifying asset.

E Unwinding discounts on provisions classified as finance costs in the income statement

Many unwinding discounts are treated as finance costs in the income statement. These include discounts relating to various provisions such as those for onerous leases and decommissioning costs. These finance costs will not be borrowing costs under IAS 23 because they do not arise in respect of funds borrowed by the entity that can be attributed to a qualifying asset. Therefore, they cannot be capitalised.

3.2 Borrowings and capitalisation rate

IAS 23 requires that the borrowing costs capitalised are to be those costs that would have been avoided if the expenditure on the qualifying asset had not been made. If a project has been financed from the entity's general borrowings, the standard imposes a detailed calculation method as indicated at 2.3.2 above.

The standard acknowledges that determining general borrowings will not always be straightforward. It will be necessary to exercise judgement to meet the main objective – a reasonable measure of the directly attributable finance costs.[56]

The following example illustrates the practical application of the method of calculating the amount of finance costs to be capitalised:

Example 16.3: Calculation of capitalisation rate

On 1 April 2008 a company engages in the development of a property, which is expected to take five years to complete, at a cost of £6,000,000. The balance sheets at 31 December 2007 and 31 December 2008, prior to capitalisation of interest, are as follows:

	31 December 2007	31 December 2008
	€	€
Development property	–	1,200,000
Other assets	6,000,000	6,800,000
	6,000,000	8,000,000
Loans		
5.5% debenture stock	2,500,000	2,500,000
Bank loan at 6% p.a.	–	2,000,000
Bank loan at 7% p.a.	1,000,000	1,000,000
	3,500,000	5,500,000
Shareholders' equity	2,500,000	2,500,000

The bank loan at 6% was taken out on 31 March 2008 and the total interest charge for the year ended 31 December 2008 was as follows:

	€
€2,500,000 × 5.5%	137,500
€2,000,000 × 6% × 9/12	90,000
€1,000,000 × 7%	70,000
	297,500

Expenditure was incurred on the development as follows:

	€
1 April 2008	600,000
1 July 2008	400,000
1 October 2008	200,000
	1,200,000

(a) If the bank loan at 6% p.a. is a new borrowing taken out specifically to finance the development, then the amount of interest to be capitalised is:

	€
£600,000 × 6% × 9/12	27,000
£400,000 × 6% × 6/12	12,000
£200,000 × 6% × 3/12	3,000
	42,000

(b) If all the borrowings would have been avoided but for the development then the amount of interest to be capitalised is:

$$\frac{\text{Total interest expense for period}}{\text{Weighted average total borrowings}} \times \text{Development expenditure}$$

i.e.:

$$\frac{297{,}500}{3{,}500{,}000 + (2{,}000{,}000 \times 9/12)} = 5.95\%$$

	€
€600,000 × 5.95% × 9/12	26,775
€400,000 × 5.95% × 6/12	11,900
€200,000 × 5.95% × 3/12	2,975
	41,650

If the 5.5% debenture stock were irredeemable then it would be excluded from the above calculation as it could no longer be a borrowing that could have been avoided. The calculation would be done using the figures for the bank loans and their related interest costs only.

In this example, all borrowings are at fixed rates of interest and the period of construction extends beyond the end of the period. If borrowings are at floating rates then only the interest costs incurred during that period, and the weighted average borrowings for that period, will be taken into account.

Note that the company's share capital will not be taken into account and outstanding borrowings are presumed to finance the acquisition or construction of qualifying assets.

3.3 Accrued costs

IAS 23 states that expenditures on qualifying assets include only those that have resulted in the payments of cash, transfers of other assets or the assumption of interest-bearing liabilities.[57] Therefore, costs of a qualifying asset that have only been accrued but have not yet been paid in cash should be excluded from the amount on which interest is capitalised, as by definition no interest can have been incurred on an accrued payment. It should be noted that the effect of applying this principle is often merely to delay the capitalisation of interest since the costs will be included once they have been paid in cash. In most cases it is unlikely that the effect will be material as the time between accrual and payment of the cost will not be that great. However, the effect is potentially material where a significant part of the amount capitalised relates to costs that have been financed interest-free by third parties for a long period. An example of this is retention money that is not generally payable until the asset is completed.

3.4 Assets carried in the balance sheet below cost

An asset may be recognised in the financial statements during the period of production on a basis other than cost, i.e. it may have been written down below cost as a result of being impaired. As discussed in 2.3.2 above, an asset may be impaired when its expected ultimate cost, including costs to complete and the estimated capitalised interest thereon, exceed its estimated recoverable amount or net realisable value.

The question then arises whether the calculation of interest to be capitalised should be based on the asset's cost or its carrying amount. In this case, cost should be used, as this is the amount that the company or group has had to finance.

3.5 Group financial statements

3.5.1 Borrowings in one company and development in another

A question which often arises in practice is whether it is appropriate to capitalise interest in the group financial statements on borrowings that appear in the financial statements of a different group company from that carrying out the development. Based on the underlying philosophy of IAS 23, capitalisation in such circumstances would only be appropriate if the amount capitalised fairly reflected the interest cost of the group on borrowings from third parties which could theoretically have been avoided if the expenditure on the qualifying asset were not made.

Although it may be appropriate to capitalise interest in the group financial statements, the company carrying out the development should not capitalise any interest in its own financial statements as it has no borrowings. If, however, the company has intra-group borrowings then interest on such borrowings may be capitalised.

3.5.2 Qualifying assets held by joint ventures

A number of sectors carry out developments through the medium of joint ventures – this is particularly common with property developments. In such cases, the joint venture may be financed principally by equity and the joint venture partners may have financed their participating interests by borrowings. It is not appropriate to capitalise interest in the joint venture on the borrowings of the partners as the interest charge is not a cost of the joint venture. Neither would it be appropriate to capitalise interest in the individual (as opposed to group) financial statements of the venturers because the qualifying asset does not belong to them. The investing entities have an investment as an asset, which is excluded by IAS 23 from being a qualifying asset (see 2.1.2 above). If, however, the venturer is using proportionate consolidation then arguably it can capitalise borrowing costs that relate to its share of the qualifying asset in its consolidated accounts.

3.6 Change of accounting policy

IAS 23 allowed two different treatments of borrowing costs which raised the possibility of a change in accounting policy. There was some controversy about this as the benchmark treatment was to expense all borrowing costs This is no longer an issue as an entity that wishes to change to a policy of capitalisation need only early apply IAS 23 (revised 2007).

4 TRANSITION AND FIRST-TIME ADOPTION

4.1 Effective date and transition to IAS 23 (revised 2007)

The revised standard applies to accounting periods beginning on or after 1 January 2009. Earlier application is permitted, in which case the entity must disclose that it has done so.[58] Applying IAS 23 (revised 2007) will be a change in accounting policy for those entities that currently expense borrowing costs.

The standard does not require full restatement. Instead, entities must begin to capitalise borrowing costs relating to qualifying assets for which the commencement date for capitalisation is on or after the effective date[59] – see 2.4.1 above for a discussion of the commencement date. However, an entity may designate an earlier date and capitalise borrowing costs relating to all qualifying assets for which the commencement date for capitalisation is on or after that date.[60]

This means that an entity that has incomplete qualifying assets as at its effective date has a choice. It may continue not to capitalise borrowing costs on those assets already in the course of construction, manufacture or production and only start capitalising in respect of assets whose commencement date is after the effective date. Alternatively, it can select to capitalise borrowing costs as from an earlier date, for example the date on which its incomplete construction projects commenced.

4.2 First-time adoption

Before the revision to IAS 23, IFRS 1 – *First-time Adoption of International Financial Reporting Standards* – required an entity that chose the allowed alternative treatment in IAS 23 of capitalising borrowing costs, to apply IAS 23 fully retrospectively from its date of transition.[61] This could have been problematic as, in theory, the adjustment was required in respect of all assets still held that would have satisfied the criteria adopted for capitalisation.

Now that IAS 23 (revised 2007) has been published and it is unlikely that any first-time adopter will apply a policy of expensing borrowing costs, IFRS 1's requirements have been changed. A new transitional exemption from full retrospective application has been introduced, that an entity may elect to take. This allows a first-time adopter to apply the transitional provisions set out above, i.e. to apply capitalization prospectively to new qualifying assets or retrospectively to assets whose construction, manufacture or production commenced as from an earlier specified date. The effective date is to be interpreted as 1 January 2009 or the date of transition to IFRSs, whichever is later.[62]

5 CONCLUSION

The capitalisation of finance costs is an important part of the wider issue of accounting for interest effects, about which there is no international consensus. The decision on whether or not to capitalise interest requires a discussion of the nature of finance costs and how they fit within the structure of financial reporting by a company to its stakeholders – in short, whether or not the capitalisation of finance costs is a conceptually sound basis of accounting. Until recently, the IASB has in effect adopted a holding position on the issue of capitalisation of borrowing costs, by neither banning it nor making it compulsory. The IASB has now thrown in its lot with the FASB and has decided it wants to make capitalisation compulsory. However, this is justified solely on the basis of eliminating some, but by no means all, the differences between IFRS and US GAAP in this area. There has been no attempt to argue that capitalisation gives a conceptually 'better' result than expensing borrowing costs.

At the conceptual level, there is a plausible argument for measuring the cost of financing the acquisition of qualifying assets on the basis of the entity's cost of capital, including imputed interest on equity capital as well as interest on borrowings. At the same time it must be recognised that the capitalisation of the cost of equity capital does not conform to the historical cost accounting framework, under which the cost of a resource is measured by reference to historical exchange prices. Nevertheless, to permit the capitalisation of interest only on borrowed capital is an incomplete approach.

Conversely, it may be argued that the capitalisation of borrowing costs in the context of, for example, most types of property development is an entirely logical and appropriate policy. Interest is a development cost, and is no different in this respect from the concrete and bricks. The IASB has unfortunately decided that convergence with US GAAP is a greater priority than conducting a proper debate on the issue of accounting for interest effects. Such a debate would encompass both the capitalisation of all types of finance costs as well as discounting. This debate may have to wait until the IASB overtly (rather than covertly) expresses its intentions and policy concerning the carrying values of assets and in particular whether they should be carried in the balance sheet at historical cost or whether fair value will be mandated.

References

1 IAS 23 (1984), *Capitalisation of Borrowing Costs*, IASC, March 1984, paras. 21-27.

2 IAS 23, *Borrowing Costs*, IASB, December 1993 (amended December 2003), para. 8.

3 IAS 23, *Borrowing Costs*, IASB, March 2007, para. BC3.

4 IAS 23 and IAS 23 (revised 2007), para. 3.

5 IAS 23, para. 4 and IAS 23 (revised 2007), para. 5.
6 IAS 23, para. 6 and IAS 23 (revised 2007), para. 7.
7 IAS 23 (revised 2007), para 7.
8 IFRIC 12, Service Concession Agreements, IASB, November 2006, para. IE15.
9 IAS 23, para. 6 and IAS 23 (revised 2007), para 7.
10 IAS 23 (revised 2007), para 7.
11 IAS 23 (revised 2007), para 4.
12 IAS 16, *Property, Plant and Equipment*, IASB, December 2003 (amended March 2004),, para. 31.
13 IAS 11, *Construction contracts*, IASC, December 1993, para. 18.
14 IAS 23 (revised 2007), para. BC27.
15 *Insight*, IASC, October 1991, p. 10.
16 IAS 23, para. 6.
17 IAS 23 (revised 2007), para. 7.
18 IAS 23, para. 4 and IAS 23 (revised 2007), para 5.
19 IAS 23, para. 5 and IAS 23 (revised 2007) para. 6.
20 IAS 23, paras. 7-8.
21 IAS 23, paras. 10-11.
22 IAS 23, para. 12.
23 IAS 23 (revised 2007), paras. 8 and 9.
24 SIC-2, *Consistency – Capitalisation of Borrowing Costs*, SIC, December 1997 (superseded December 2003), para. 3 and IAS 23, para. 19.
25 IAS 23, para. 13 and IAS 23 (revised 2007) para. 10.
26 IAS 23, para. 13 and IAS 23 (revised 2007) para. 10.
27 IAS 23, para. 15 and IAS 23 (revised 2007) para. 12.
28 IAS 23, paras. 15-16 and IAS 23 (revised 2007) para. 12-13.
29 IAS 23, para. 14 and IAS 23 (revised 2007) para. 11.
30 IAS 23, para. 17 and IAS 23 (revised 2007) para. 14.
31 IAS 23, para. 21 and IAS 23 (revised 2007) para. 18.
32 IAS 23, para. 18 and IAS 23 (revised 2007) para. 15.
33 IAS 23, para. 19 and IAS 23 (revised 2007) para. 16.
34 IAS 16, *Property, Plant and Equipment*, IASB, December 2003 (amended March 2004),.
35 IAS 36, *Impairment of assets*, IASB, March 2004, para. 2.
36 IAS 29, *Financial Reporting in Hyperinflationary Economies*, IASB,1989, para. 21
37 IAS 23 (revised 2007) para. 9.
38 IAS 23, para. 20 and IAS 23 (revised 2007) para. 17.
39 IAS 23, para. 21 and IAS 23 (revised 2007) para. 18.
40 IAS 23, para. 22 and IAS 23 (revised 2007) para. 19.
41 IAS 23, paras. 23-24 and IAS 23 (revised 2007) paras. 20-21.
42 IAS 23, para. 25 and IAS 23 (revised 2007) para. 22.
43 IAS 23, para. 26 and IAS 23 (revised 2007) para. 23.
44 IAS 23, para. 27 and IAS 23 (revised 2007) para. 24.
45 IAS 23, para. 28 and IAS 23 (revised 2007) para. 15.
46 IAS 23, para. 9.
47 IAS 23, para. 29.
48 IAS 23 (revised 2007) para. 26.
49 IAS 32, *Financial Instruments: Disclosure and Presentation*, IASB, December 2003 (amended March 2004); IAS 39, *Financial Instruments: Recognition and Measurement*, IASB, December 2003 (amended March 2004).
50 IAS 23, para. 5(e).
51 IAS 39, para. 9.
52 Exposure Draft, Annual Improvements To IFRSs, Proposed amendment to IAS 23 *Borrowing Costs*, IASB, October 2007.
53 IAS 39, para. 85.
54 EITF 99-9, *Effect of derivative gains and losses on the capitalisation of interest*, FASB, July 1999, para. 6.
55 IAS 23, para. 13 and IAS 23 (revised 2007) para. 10.
56 IAS 23, para. 14 and IAS 23 (revised 2007) para. 11.
57 IAS 23, para. 21 and IAS 23 (revised 2007) para. 18.
58 IAS 23 (revised 2007) para. 29.
59 IAS 23 (revised 2007) para. 27.
60 IAS 23 (revised 2007) para. 28.
61 IFRS 1, *First-time Adoption of International Financial Reporting Standards*, IASB, June 2003 (amended March 2004), paras. 7 and 9.
62 IFRS 1, paras. 13 and 25L.

Chapter 17 Financial instruments: Introduction

1 INTRODUCTION

1.1 Accounting for financial instruments – the challenge

The development of increasingly sophisticated financial markets, which permit companies to trade in newly devised contracts and thereby transform their risk profile, is perhaps the single factor in business life that poses the most searching challenge to traditional financial reporting practices. The IASC, in its newsletter of December 1996, commented on the issue in these terms:

'At the roots of the need for change in accounting for financial instruments are fundamental changes in international financial markets. … An enterprise can substantially change its financial risk profile instantaneously, requiring careful and continuous monitoring. … Alternatively, an enterprise may use derivatives as speculative tools to multiply the effects of changes in interest, foreign exchange or security or commodity prices, thus multiplying the gains if prices move advantageously or, alternatively, multiplying the losses if they move adversely. … Accounting for financial instruments has not kept pace with information needs of financial market participants.

'Existing accounting practices are founded on principles developed when the primary focus of accounting was on manufacturing companies that combine inputs (materials, labour, plant and equipment, and various types of overheads) and transform them into outputs (goods or services) for sale. Accounting for these revenue-generating processes is concerned primarily with accruing costs to be matched with revenues. A key point in this process is the point of revenue realisation – the point at which a company is considered to have transformed its inputs into cash or claims to cash (i.e. financial instruments).

'These traditional realisation and cost-based measurement concepts are not adequate for the recognition and measurement of financial instruments. Recognising this, many countries have moved part way to embrace fair value accounting for some financial instruments. ...'[1]

This lays down the challenge very clearly. Do we need a new approach to financial reporting if we are to cope with the specific characteristics of financial instruments? And indeed, does the intellectual theory behind this new approach in turn imply that we should now abandon traditional accounting methods for other areas of business activity as well? The IASC felt able to distinguish the two issues, but some of the thinking behind the developments in accounting for financial instruments has had a profound effect on work of the IASC and IASB in other areas. This has manifested itself through the IASB placing a growing emphasis on the development of its balance sheet-focused fair value model in subjects such as insurance contracts, agriculture, investment property and revenue recognition.

1.2 Publication of the original IAS 32

At the time the newsletter referred to above was issued, the IASC had been conducting a project on financial instruments for several years, initially in conjunction with the Canadian Institute of Chartered Accountants (CICA). Two attempts were made to deal comprehensively with the issue, in two successive exposure drafts (E40 in 1991 and E48 in 1994). However, the IASC then decided to lower its sights and converted E48 into a standard dealing with presentation (debt and equity classification and offset) and disclosure issues alone and the original version of IAS 32 – *Financial Instruments: Disclosure and Presentation*[2] – was published in March 1995.

1.3 Evolution of a 'full fair value' accounting model

In March 1997 – two years after the publication of IAS 32 – the IASC/CICA Steering Committee published a Discussion Paper[3] dealing extensively with the measurement and recognition issues and making proposals for a comprehensive standard on financial assets and financial liabilities. In concept, its main proposals were straightforward: all financial assets and financial liabilities should be recognised as soon as the reporting entity becomes a party to the contractual provisions that they entail;[4] thereafter they should be stated at fair value in the balance sheet;[5] and all movements in fair value thereafter should be reported in income.[6] The Discussion Paper also took a very restrictive view of hedge accounting. With two minor exceptions, it proposed that no special treatment should be accorded to financial instruments that are designated as hedges of other exposures; they should all still be carried at fair value and gains or losses reported in income.

However, later in 1997 the IASC recognised that completion of such a comprehensive standard to meet the IOSCO deadline (see Chapter 1) was not a realistic possibility and therefore committed to completing an interim international standard on recognition and measurement in 1998. Also in 1997, the IASC decided that they should join with national standard setters to develop an integrated and harmonised standard on financial instruments, building on their own Discussion Paper, existing and emerging national standards, and the best thinking and research on the subject world-wide. Thus, the Joint Working Group of standard setters (JWG) was established to perform this task. The JWG comprised representatives from the IASC, the US FASB and eight other international bodies. December 2000 saw the culmination of their work with the publication by each constituent member of its proposals in the form of a Draft Standard.[7]

The JWG proposals built on the theoretical approach of the IASC/CICA Discussion Paper. With only minor exceptions, all financial instruments would be recorded at fair value with corresponding gains and losses reported in income. This meant, for example, that the reported amount of an entity's own debt would reflect its fair value and thus take account of changes in the entity's credit risk. Likewise, even changes in the value of debt and other instruments used to hedge foreign currency net investments would be reported in income (although the basic method of accounting for foreign net investments was not altered). A corollary of this was that hedge accounting would no longer be allowed.

1.4 Publication of the original IAS 39

Following the decision in 1997, the IASC issued an exposure draft, E62,[8] in May 1998 and in December 1998 approved for publication the original version of IAS 39 – *Financial Instruments: Recognition and Measurement*[9] – its interim standard dealing with recognition and measurement of financial instruments, including rules on hedging. It was finally published in March 1999.

The origins of IAS 39 can be found in US GAAP and at a high level there are only limited differences between the two systems. Consequently, it adopted a 'mixed attribute' model, i.e. some financial instruments are measured by reference to their historical cost and some by reference to their fair value. The main ideas embodied in IAS 39 were:

- derivatives (including some embedded within other contracts) were measured at fair value;
- many financial assets were also measured at fair value;
- non-derivative liabilities were measured at amortised cost;
- hedging rules were established such that:
  - the methods of hedge accounting were defined in a way that severely curtailed existing practices in many countries;
  - hedges were tested for effectiveness; and
  - ineffectiveness was reported in income; and
- certain fair value gains and losses could be reported initially in equity before being recycled into income at a later date.

The standard had a long lead-time – although issued in 1999, adoption was only mandatory for periods commencing in 2001. At the time, some held the view (or at least the hope) that IAS 39 would never actually be implemented, and that by 2001 a 'full fair value' standard (along the lines of the JWG proposals) would have replaced it. However, this was not to be.

By dealing with most aspects of virtually all financial instruments, it was the longest, and by far the most complex, standard issued by the IASC. Because of this, and perhaps also as it became clear that a 'full fair value' standard would not be available in 2001, the IASC saw a need to help preparers, auditors and users to understand the practical implications of IAS 39. In March 2000, a process was established whereby an IAS 39 Implementation Guidance Committee (IGC) published guidance, developed to be consistent with the standard, in the form of Questions and Answers (Q&A).[10] In all, over 200 final Q&A were published under the authority of the IASC.

1.5 IASB 'improvements' project and EU adoption

In spite of the efforts that had been made in producing the implementation guidance, in 2001 the new IASB inherited a standard the implementation of which was causing great difficulty to many companies already reporting under IAS. Because of this, a project designed to clarify the application of IAS 39 based on issues identified by constituents and the IGC was included on the IASB's initial technical agenda.[11]

The project was subsequently expanded to incorporate IAS 32 and the IGC Q&A, and in June 2002 an Exposure Draft containing proposals to improve IAS 32 and IAS 39 was published.[12] In what can now be seen as the start of a trend of dissent, two (out of fourteen) members formally opposed the proposals.

The Exposure Draft was launched in an atmosphere of growing awareness of IFRS, not least by the thousands of companies that would adopt these standards for the first time in the forthcoming few years. One of the biggest concerns was the extent to which IAS 39 would allow entities to account for their risk management and hedging strategies in a manner that reflected the actual hedging practices adopted. This was especially true in the retail banking sector where entities normally manage their risk on a net basis using sophisticated techniques to balance the various exposures that exist in an entity (often referred to as 'macro-hedging'). In due course the IASB was to receive over 170 comment letters,[13] many of them critical both of the original standards and the proposed revisions.

Constituents also started to exert pressure on the IASB in other ways. With the European Union requiring all listed EU companies to apply IFRS in their consolidated accounts with effect from 2005, the EU became the IASB's most important constituency. As a result, the European Commission's 'endorsement mechanism' (see Chapter 1) provided a potentially powerful lever for the exertion of pressure on the IASB to take note of the concerns of preparers, users and auditors, the ultimate sanction being non-adoption of a standard. Various groups, particularly financial institutions, used this opportunity to ensure that the IASB entered into a constructive dialogue with their constituents and addressed their concerns – particularly with respect to fundamental issues such as derecognition, loan loss provisioning, macro-hedging and effectiveness testing. Accordingly, the IASB's revision of IASs 32 and 39 was conducted in a political, as well as a technical, arena and the non-adoption of IAS 39 became a real possibility. One of the most high profile illustrations of political pressure being exerted on the IASB was a letter written by French President Jacques Chirac to the then EC President Romano Prodi. In his letter, President Chirac expressed general reservations about IFRS, including concerns that the increasing use of fair values would lead to excessive volatility in the economy and that IASs 32 and 39 could have adverse consequences for financial stability in the EU.

As a result of the pressure, political and otherwise, publication of the revised standards was significantly delayed as the IASB took steps to demonstrate the due process it was following in the development of these standards. The most visible of these was a series of nine 'roundtable' discussions with constituents during March 2003; they were conducted in Brussels and London and over 100 organisations and individuals took part. In addition, the Board made the welcome move of entering into a formal dialogue with the financial institutions, with the result that regular meetings were held between IASB members and staff and representatives of European banks and insurers; discussions were also held with the Standards Advisory Council and liaison standard setters.[14]

The IASB's principal aim in all of this was to educate and inform constituents as to why it considered its standards to be appropriate. It certainly did not appear to intend to make any fundamental changes to the standards and, as a result, there was scepticism expressed in some quarters as to whether the Board really was conducting due process or simply going through the motions. In the meantime, the threat of eventual non-adoption of IASs 32 and 39 by the EC suddenly became greater, as it adopted all existing IASs and SICs, with the exception of these two standards and related interpretations.[15] Accordingly, the IASB was introduced to both the political reality of standard setting and the need to listen to its constituents and, without shifting significantly its overall position on amendments, started to warm to the possibility of developing compromise solutions.

The most tangible sign of progress came in August 2003, when the IASB published an Exposure Draft[16] of proposed amendments to the revised version of IAS 39 (which was at the time unpublished) dealing with macro-hedging issues for banks. However, it is telling that five (out of fourteen) IASB members voted against its publication,[17] suggesting that the IASB was only reluctantly conceding any ground in what was becoming a bruising experience on all sides.

The dialogue continued and, in December 2003, provisional final versions of IAS 32 and IAS 39 were published. Amendments to IAS 39, dealing principally with macro-hedging matters, followed in March 2004.[18] Certain members of the IASB continued to object – one opposed the publication of IAS 32, three were against IAS 39 and one against the macro-hedging proposals.[19] Unfortunately, the proposed amendments did not deal with the banks' major concerns, particularly with regard to the impact of cash flow hedging on equity volatility and the hedging of core deposits in the case of those banks that operate in a predominantly fixed interest environment. At the same time, insurers were expressing concern about the asset/liability mismatch that would result from the application of IAS 39 to their financial instruments.

In what was almost certainly an attempt to reduce the scope for confrontations of this nature in the future, concurrently with the publication of the macro-hedging amendments, the IASB announced plans to establish an international working party to assist it in developing its long-term replacement for IAS 39, which it conceded may take several years to complete. However, in a public show of conciliation, it also acknowledged that it would be willing to revise IAS 39 in the short term in the light of any solutions arising from the working party's discussions.[20] This followed a separate invitation in February 2004 from the IASC Foundation to regulators and participants in the European financial services sector to form a high level consultative group to advise the IASB on matters relating to financial instrument accounting.[21] The actual formation of the Financial Instruments Working Group was announced in September 2004.[22]

The European Central Bank, which was proving a very powerful force in the adoption process, had concerns in its role as a prudential supervisor over the unrestricted 'fair value option' (see 7.1.2 A below). Under pressure, the IASB published in April 2004 further proposed amendments to IAS 39[23] that would limit an entity's ability to measure instruments at fair value with associated gains and losses recorded in profit or loss (i.e. the full fair value option). Three Board members objected with two specifically expressing concern about the role of standard setters and prudential regulators.[24] On a different front, proposals were being considered for another macro-hedging methodology[25] and other proposed changes to the standards were being developed.

In November 2004, in what was to some a surprising move, the EC adopted a version of IAS 39 with two 'carve-outs' (i.e. with the removal of certain text from the IASB's version) which became part of European law. Essentially the carve-outs prohibited the use of fair value accounting for most non-derivative liabilities, but allowed the use of macro-hedge accounting in situations that the full version of IAS 39 would not.[26] IAS 32 was adopted the following month.

The partial endorsement of IAS 39 was accompanied by an appeal to all parties, including the IASB, the ECB as well as other regulators and banks to work intensively to find appropriately balanced solutions to the remaining outstanding issues in IAS 39 as quickly as possible.[27] In December 2004 a revised version of the proposed fair value option amendments was made available[28] and in January 2005 the IASB announced that further roundtable discussions would be held in March to discuss their new proposals.[29] Following these discussions, and further negotiations with interested parties, an amendment to IAS 39 was published by the IASB in June.[30]

This compromise document achieved its purpose in satisfying the key European constituents (even though three Board members dissented[31]) and was endorsed by the EC in November 2005 resulting in one of the carve-outs being removed. The EC emphasised again the need for the IASB and representatives of European banks to find an appropriate technical solution to allow the removal of the remaining carve-out as rapidly as possible[32] although there have been only limited signs of progress on this issue (see Chapter 21 at 8).

1.6 Conclusion

It is clear that accounting for financial instruments is likely to remain an extremely difficult area, both in the short term and for a number of years. There seems to be a high degree of consensus among the major standard setters and their representatives on the former Joint Working Group that fair valuing all financial instruments can be the only ultimate solution. In fact, as set out at 9 below the IASB and the FASB have reiterated their long-term objective of requiring all financial instruments to be measured at fair value with realised and unrealised gains and losses recognised in the period in which they occur.[33]

This remains a controversial view that continues to be met with considerable resistance. Standard setters in this area are trying to move ahead of current practice, since the proposed solution has not yet commanded acceptance in any country. This is a bold step since the traditional role of accounting standard setters has been to codify accepted best practice rather than, as now, to invent new practice.

That said, the arguments for fair value accounting seem cogent, and they were assembled very persuasively in the IASC Discussion Paper and JWG Draft Standard. But the proposals are nonetheless revolutionary; by the IASC's own admission, they would require the adoption of a new capital maintenance concept ('current-market-rate-of-return') for measuring financial instruments[34] and this would simply introduce a new inconsistency, unless it was applied to the measurement of other items in the financial statements as well. Moreover, the proposals do not sit well with generally held views on the role and meaning of financial statements, despite their elegance, and the IASB's continued move towards the use of fair values in other aspects of accounting.

In the meantime, companies have had to get to grips with IAS 39, the basic principles of which are expected to be in place for a 'considerable period'.[35] This continues to be problematic, as evidenced by the IFRIC's extensive deliberations about this standard not only by the IFRIC but also by the IASB itself. Companies also now have to deal with the requirements of IFRS 7 – *Financial Instruments: Disclosures* – which the IASB published in August 2005 to replace IAS 32's disclosure requirements by 2007.

1.7 How financial instruments are dealt with in Chapters 17 to 22

Putting these broader ramifications to one side, the subject matter of this and the next five chapters is the recognition, measurement, presentation and disclosure of financial instruments. More specifically, these chapters address the requirements of IAS 32, IAS 39 and IFRS 7.

The main text of each of IAS 32, IAS 39 and IFRS 7 is supplemented by application guidance (which is an integral part of the standard).[36] IAS 32 and IAS 39 are each supplemented by illustrative examples (which accompany, but are not part of, the standard).[37] IAS 39 and IFRS 7 are each supplemented by implementation guidance (which also accompanies, but is not part of, the standard).[38]

The objective of IAS 32 is to establish principles for presenting financial instruments as liabilities or equity and for offsetting financial assets and financial liabilities[39] whilst for IAS 39 it is to establish principles for recognising and measuring financial assets, financial liabilities and some contracts to buy or sell non-financial items.[40] The objective of IFRS 7 is to require entities to provide disclosures in their financial statements that enable users to evaluate:[41]

(a) the significance of financial instruments for the entity's financial position and performance; and
(b) the nature and extent of risks arising from financial instruments to which the entity is exposed during the period and at the reporting date, and how the entity manages those risks.

Prior to the application of IFRS 7, the objective of IAS 32 was to enhance financial statement users' understanding of the significance of financial instruments to an entity's financial position, performance and cash flows.[42]

The chapters dealing with financial instruments, and the topics covered by each, are as follows:

Chapter 17 – *Introduction*

- key definitions
- scope and exceptions
- the defining characteristics of derivatives
- derivatives embedded within other contracts
- linked and separate transactions and 'synthetic' instruments
- classification of financial assets and financial liabilities

Chapter 18 – *Recognition, derecognition and offset*

- recognition
- derecognition of financial assets
- derecognition of financial liabilities
- offset

Chapter 19 – *Classification of debt and equity*

- the classification of financial instruments by their issuer as financial liabilities or equity
- compound financial instruments (i.e. those containing both a liability and an equity component from the issuer's perspective)
- accounting for interest, dividends gains and losses
- treasury shares (i.e. shares legally owned by their issuer)
- contracts over own equity instruments

Chapter 20 – *Measurement*

- initial measurement
- subsequent measurement and recognition of gains and losses
- fair value measurement considerations
- amortised cost and the effective interest method
- impairment of financial assets
- the effect of foreign currencies

Chapter 21 – *Hedge accounting*

- hedging instruments and hedged items
- types of hedging relationships
- accounting for effective hedges
- qualifying conditions for hedge accounting
- portfolio (or macro) hedging

Chapter 22 – *Disclosure*

- disclosure requirements of IAS 32
- disclosure requirements of IFRS 7
- presentation of financial instruments and related transactions, gains and losses in the financial statements

Consequently, IAS 32 is largely dealt with in Chapters 17, 19 and 22, IAS 39 in Chapters 17, 18, 20 and 21 and IFRS 7 in Chapter 22.

2 WHAT IS A FINANCIAL INSTRUMENT?

2.1 Definitions

The main terms used are defined as follows:

A *financial instrument* is any contract that gives rise to a financial asset of one entity and a financial liability or equity instrument of another entity.

A *financial asset* is any asset that is:

(a) cash;

(b) an equity instrument of another entity;

(c) a contractual right:

  (i) to receive cash or another financial asset from another entity; or

  (ii) to exchange financial assets or financial liabilities with another entity under conditions that are potentially favourable to the entity; or

(d) a contract that will or may be settled in the entity's own equity instruments and is:

  (i) a non-derivative for which the entity is or may be obliged to receive a variable number of the entity's own equity instruments; or

(ii) a derivative that will or may be settled other than by the exchange of a fixed amount of cash or another financial asset for a fixed number of the entity's own equity instruments. For this purpose the entity's own equity instruments do not include instruments that are themselves contracts for the future receipt or delivery of the entity's own equity instruments.

A *financial liability* is any liability that is:

(a) a contractual obligation:

(i) to deliver cash or another financial asset to another entity; or

(ii) to exchange financial assets or financial liabilities with another entity under conditions that are potentially unfavourable to the entity; or

(b) a contract that will or may be settled in the entity's own equity instruments and is:

(i) a non-derivative for which the entity is or may be obliged to deliver a variable number of the entity's own equity instruments; or

(ii) a derivative that will or may be settled other than by the exchange of a fixed amount of cash or another financial asset for a fixed number of the entity's own equity instruments. For this purpose the entity's own equity instruments do not include instruments that are themselves contracts for the future receipt or delivery of the entity's own equity instruments.

An *equity instrument* is any contract that evidences a residual interest in the assets of an entity after deducting all of its liabilities.[43]

These definitions are taken from the current version of IAS 32, having been amended in December 2003 to reflect the IASB's thinking on contracts involving own shares. Essentially, part (d) was added to the definition of financial asset and part (b) to the definition of financial liability – previously such contracts were dealt with on a more piecemeal basis. These parts are not at all easy to apply and can lead to some rather counter-intuitive accounting. The implications of these particular requirements are considered further in Chapter 19 at 3 and 4.

For the purpose of these definitions, 'entity' includes individuals, partnerships, incorporated bodies, trusts and government agencies.[44]

2.2 Applying the definitions

2.2.1 The need for a contract

The terms 'contract' and 'contractual' are important to the definitions and refer to 'an agreement between two or more parties that has clear economic consequences that the parties have little, if any, discretion to avoid, usually because the agreement is enforceable at law'. Such contracts may take a variety of forms and need not be in writing.[45]

The IFRIC examined the question of what constitutes a contract in the context of gaming transactions (see 4.1.3 below). This is because, in some jurisdictions, a wager does not give rise to a contract that is enforceable under local contract law. The IFRIC staff noted that a gaming transaction constitutes an agreement between two or more parties that has clear economic consequences for both. Furthermore, in most countries, gambling is heavily regulated and only parties acting within a regulated framework are licensed to operate gaming institutions, so that such entities cannot realistically fail to pay out on a good wager and therefore the gaming institution will have little or no discretion as to whether it pays out on the bet. Consequently, the IFRIC agreed that a wager should be treated as a contract.[46]

Whilst this seems an entirely plausible analysis in context, it is a little difficult to reconcile with the conclusions of the IFRIC and the IASB concerning the existence (or otherwise) of a contractual obligation to make payments on certain preference shares and similar securities (see Chapter 19 at 3.2.1 F).

A contractual right or contractual obligation to receive, deliver or exchange financial instruments is itself a financial instrument. A chain of contractual rights or contractual obligations meets the definition of a financial instrument if it will ultimately lead to the receipt or payment of cash or to the acquisition or issue of an equity instrument.[47] Therefore it can be seen that the definitions are iterative, but not circular.

Assets and liabilities relating to income taxes that arise as a result of statutory requirements imposed by governments are not financial liabilities or financial assets because they are not contractual.[48] This is convenient because accounting for income taxes is dealt with in more detail (and not necessarily consistently with IAS 39) in another standard, IAS 12 – *Income Taxes* (see Chapter 26).

Similarly, constructive obligations as defined in IAS 37 – *Provisions, Contingent Liabilities and Contingent Assets* (see Chapter 27 at 3.1.1) do not arise from contracts and are therefore not financial liabilities.[49]

2.2.2 *Simple examples*

The application guidance to IAS 32 explains that currency (or cash) is a financial asset 'because it represents the medium of exchange and is therefore the basis on which all transactions are measured and recognised in financial statements'. A deposit of cash with a bank or similar financial institution is a financial asset because it represents the contractual right of the depositor to obtain cash from the institution or to draw a cheque or similar instrument against the balance in favour of a creditor in payment of a financial liability.[50]

The following common financial instruments give rise to financial assets representing a contractual right to receive cash in the future and corresponding financial liabilities representing a contractual obligation to deliver cash in the future:

(a) trade accounts receivable and payable;

(b) notes receivable and payable;

(c) loans receivable and payable; and
(d) bonds receivable and payable.

In each case, one party's contractual right to receive (or obligation to pay) cash is matched by the other party's corresponding obligation to pay (or right to receive).[51]

Another type of financial instrument is one for which the economic benefit to be received or given up is a financial asset other than cash. For example, a note payable in government bonds gives the holder the contractual right to receive, and the issuer the contractual obligation to deliver, government bonds, not cash. The bonds are financial assets because they represent obligations of the issuing government to pay cash. The note is, therefore, a financial asset of the note holder and a financial liability of the note issuer.[52]

Perpetual debt instruments (such as perpetual bonds, debentures and capital notes) normally provide the holder with the contractual right to receive payments on account of interest at fixed dates extending indefinitely, either with no right to receive a return of principal or a right to a return of principal under terms that make it very unlikely or very far in the future. For example, an entity may issue a financial instrument requiring it to make annual payments in perpetuity equal to a stated interest rate of 8% applied to a stated par or principal amount of $1,000. Assuming 8% is the market rate of interest for the instrument when issued, the issuer assumes a contractual obligation to make a stream of future interest payments having a net present value (or fair value) of $1,000 on initial recognition. The holder and issuer of the instrument have a financial asset and a financial liability, respectively.[53]

2.2.3 Contingent rights and obligations

The ability to exercise a contractual right or the requirement to satisfy a contractual obligation may be absolute (as in the examples at 2.2.2 above), or it may be contingent on the occurrence of a future event. A contingent right or obligation, e.g. to receive or deliver cash, meets the definition of a financial asset or a financial liability.[54]

For example, a financial guarantee is a contractual right of the lender to receive cash from the guarantor, and a corresponding contractual obligation of the guarantor to pay the lender, if the borrower defaults. The contractual right and obligation exist because of a past transaction or event (the assumption of the guarantee), even though the lender's ability to exercise its right and the requirement for the guarantor to perform under its obligation are both contingent on a future act of default by the borrower.[55]

However, even though contingent rights and obligations can meet the definition of a financial instrument, they are not always recognised in the financial statements as such. For example, the contingent rights and obligations may be insurance contracts within the scope of IFRS 4 – *Insurance Contracts* (see 3.3 below) or may otherwise be excluded from the scope of IAS 39 (see 3 below).[56]

2.2.4 Leases

In accordance with the accounting model in IAS 17 – *Leases* – a finance lease is regarded as primarily an entitlement to receive, and an obligation to make, a stream of payments that are substantially the same as blended payments of principal and interest under a loan agreement. The lessor accounts for its investment in the amount receivable under the lease contract rather than the leased asset itself.[57] The lessee accounts for its obligation to the lessor (in addition to the leased asset).

An operating lease, on the other hand, is regarded as primarily an uncompleted contract committing the lessor to provide the use of an asset in future periods in exchange for consideration similar to a fee for a service. The lessor continues to account for the leased asset itself rather than any amount receivable in the future under the contract.[58]

Accordingly, a finance lease arrangement is regarded as a financial instrument and an operating lease is not regarded as a financial instrument (except as regards individual payments currently due and payable).[59]

2.2.5 Non-financial assets and liabilities and contracts thereon

Physical assets (such as inventories, property, plant and equipment), leased assets and intangible assets (such as patents and trademarks) are not financial assets. Control of such physical and intangible assets creates an opportunity to generate an inflow of cash or another financial asset, but it does not give rise to a present right to receive cash or another financial asset.[60] For example, whilst gold bullion is highly liquid (and perhaps more liquid than many financial instruments), it gives no contractual right to receive cash or another financial asset, and so is therefore a commodity, not a financial asset.[61]

Assets such as prepaid expenses, for which the future economic benefit is the receipt of goods or services rather than the right to receive cash or another financial asset, are not financial assets. Similarly, items such as deferred revenue and most warranty obligations are not financial liabilities because the outflow of economic benefits associated with them is the delivery of goods and services rather than a contractual obligation to pay cash or another financial asset.[62]

Contracts to buy or sell non-financial items do not meet the definition of a financial instrument because the contractual right of one party to receive a non-financial asset or service and the corresponding obligation of the other party do not establish a present right or obligation of either party to receive, deliver or exchange a financial asset. For example, contracts that provide for settlement only by the receipt or delivery of a non-financial item (e.g. an option, futures or forward contract on silver and many similar commodity contracts) are not financial instruments. However, as set out at 3.9 below, certain contracts to buy or sell non-financial items are included within the scope of IAS 32 and IAS 39, essentially where they exhibit similar characteristics to financial instruments.[63]

Where payment on a contract involving the receipt or delivery of physical assets is deferred past the date of transfer of the asset, a financial instrument does arise at that date. In other words, the sale or purchase of goods on trade credit gives rise to a financial asset (a trade receivable) and a financial liability (a trade payable) when the goods are transferred.[64]

Some contracts are commodity-linked, but do not involve settlement through the physical receipt or delivery of a commodity. For example, the principal amount of a bond may be calculated by applying the market price of oil prevailing at the maturity of the bond to a fixed quantity of oil. Such a contract does constitute a financial instrument.[65]

Financial instruments also include contracts that give rise to a non-financial asset or non-financial liability in addition to a financial asset or financial liability. Such arrangements often give one party an option to exchange a financial asset for a non-financial asset. For example, an oil-linked bond may give the holder the right to receive a stream of fixed periodic interest payments and a fixed amount of cash on maturity, with the option to exchange the principal amount for a fixed quantity of oil. The desirability of exercising this option will vary over time depending on the fair value of oil relative to the exchange ratio of cash for oil (the exchange price) inherent in the bond, but the intentions of the bondholder do not affect the substance of the component assets. The financial asset of the holder and the financial liability of the issuer make the bond a financial instrument, regardless of the other types of assets and liabilities also created.[66]

2.2.6 *Equity instruments*

Examples of equity instruments include non-puttable ordinary shares, some types of preference shares and warrants or written call options that allow the holder to subscribe for or purchase a fixed number of non-puttable ordinary shares in the issuing entity, in exchange for a fixed amount of cash or another financial asset.[67] The definition of equity instruments is considered in more detail in Chapter 19 at 3.

2.2.7 *Derivative financial instruments*

As well as primary instruments such as receivables, payables and equity instruments, financial instruments also include derivatives such as financial options, futures and forwards, interest rate swaps and currency swaps. Derivatives effectively transfer the risks inherent in an underlying primary instrument between the contracting parties without any need to transfer the underlying instruments themselves (either at inception of the contract or even, where cash settled, on termination).[68]

There are important accounting consequences for financial instruments that are considered to be derivatives, and the defining characteristics of derivatives are covered in more detail at 4 below. As noted at 2.2.5 above, certain derivative contracts on non-financial items are included within the scope of IAS 32 and IAS 39, even though they are not, strictly, financial instruments as defined. These contracts are covered in more detail at 3.9 below.

On inception, the terms of a derivative financial instrument generally give one party a contractual right (or obligation) to exchange financial assets or financial liabilities with another party under conditions that are potentially favourable (or unfavourable). Some instruments embody both a right and an obligation to make an exchange and, as prices in financial markets change, those terms may become either favourable or unfavourable.[69]

A put or call option to exchange financial assets or financial liabilities gives the holder a right to obtain potential future economic benefits associated with changes in the fair value of the underlying instrument. Conversely, the writer of an option assumes an obligation to forgo such economic benefits or bear potential losses associated with the underlying instrument. The contractual right (or obligation) of the holder (or writer) meets the definition of a financial asset (or liability). The financial instrument underlying an option contract may be any financial asset, including shares in other entities and interest-bearing instruments. An option may require the writer to issue a debt instrument, rather than transfer a financial asset, but the instrument underlying the option would constitute a financial asset of the holder if the option were exercised. The option-holder's right (or writer's obligation) to exchange the financial asset under potentially favourable (or unfavourable) conditions is distinct from the underlying financial asset to be exchanged upon exercise of the option. The nature of the holder's right and of the writer's obligation (which characterises such contracts as a financial instrument) are not affected by the likelihood that the option will be exercised.[70]

Another common type of derivative is a forward contract. For example, consider a contract in which two parties (the seller and the purchaser) promise in six months' time to exchange $1,000 cash (the purchaser will pay cash) for $1,000 face amount of fixed rate government bonds (the seller will deliver the bonds). During those six months, both parties have a contractual right and a contractual obligation to exchange financial instruments (cash in exchange for bonds). If the market price of the government bonds rises above $1,000, the conditions will be favourable to the purchaser and unfavourable to the seller, and vice versa if the market price falls below $1,000. The purchaser has a contractual right (a financial asset) similar to the right under a call option held and a contractual obligation (a financial liability) similar to the obligation under a put option written. The seller has a contractual right (a financial asset) similar to the right under a put option held and a contractual obligation (a financial liability) similar to the obligation under a call option written. As with options, these contractual rights and obligations constitute financial assets and financial liabilities separate and distinct from the underlying financial instruments (the bonds and cash to be exchanged). Both parties to a forward contract have an obligation to perform at the agreed time, whereas performance under an option contract occurs only if and when the holder of the option chooses to exercise it.[71]

Many other types of derivative also embody a right or obligation to make a future exchange, including interest rate and currency swaps, interest rate caps, collars and floors, loan commitments, note issuance facilities and letters of credit. An interest rate swap contract may be viewed as a variation of a forward contract in which the parties agree to make a series of future exchanges of cash amounts, one amount calculated with reference to a floating interest rate and the other with reference to a fixed interest rate. Futures contracts are another variation of forward contracts, differing primarily in that the contracts are standardised and traded on an exchange.[72]

3 SCOPE

IAS 32, IAS 39 and, when applied, IFRS 7 apply to the financial statements of all entities that are prepared in accordance with International Financial Reporting Standards.[73] In other words there are no exclusions from the presentation, recognition, measurement, or even the disclosure requirements, of these standards, even for entities that do not have publicly traded securities or those that are subsidiaries of other entities.

The standards do not, however, apply to all of an entity's financial instruments, some of which are excluded from their scope, for example insurance contracts. Conversely, certain contracts over non-financial items that behave in a similar way to financial instruments but do not actually fall within the definition – essentially some commodity contracts – are included within the scope of the standards. These exceptions are considered in more detail below.

3.1 Subsidiaries, associates, joint ventures and similar investments

Most interests in subsidiaries, associates, and joint ventures that are consolidated, proportionately consolidated or equity accounted in consolidated financial statements are outside the scope of IAS 32, IAS 39 and, when applied, IFRS 7.[74] However, such instruments should be accounted for in accordance with IAS 39 and disclosed in accordance with IAS 32 or IFRS 7 in the following situations:

- in separate financial statements of the parent or investor if they are neither recorded at cost nor accounted for in accordance with IFRS 5 – *Non-current Assets Held for Sale and Discontinued Operations* (see Chapter 6 at 7).[75]

  It is not entirely clear whether an investment accounted for under IAS 39 that becomes classified as held for sale should continue to be accounted for under IAS 39 or be accounted for under IFRS 5 (see Chapter 4 at 2.2). The IASB has identified this issue and plans to resolve it by amending IAS 27 – *Consolidated and Separate Financial Statements* – in its annual improvements process so it is clear that IAS 39 continues to apply;[76] and

- when investments in associates or joint ventures held by venture capital organisations, mutual funds, unit trusts or similar entities are classified as 'at fair value through profit or loss' on initial recognition (see Chapter 8 at 2.1, Chapter 9 at 2.1 and 7.1.2 below).[77]

In these situations, entities should also apply the disclosure requirements in IAS 27, IAS 28 – *Investments in Associates*, or IAS 31 – *Interests in Joint Ventures* – in addition to those in IAS 32 or IFRS 7.[78] On the face of it, all disclosures set out in IAS 28 (see Chapter 8 at 5.2.1) and IAS 31 (see Chapter 9 at 4.2) should be provided in respect of investments in associates and joint ventures that are accounted for as financial assets designated at fair value through profit or loss and under IAS 39. However, such investments are excluded from the scope of IAS 28 and IAS 31 which might suggest that those disclosures should not be given (an approach commonly adopted in practice). The IASB has identified this inconsistency and plans to resolve it by deleting the requirement in IAS 32 and IFRS 7 in their annual improvements project. However, the IASB has tentatively decided that certain disclosures should be provided. These would include the nature and extent of restrictions on the ability of associates to transfer funds to the investor, information about commitments in respect of joint ventures and a listing and description of interests in significant joint ventures.[79]

IAS 32, IAS 39 and, when applied, IFRS 7 also apply to most derivatives on interests in subsidiaries, associates and joint ventures, irrespective of how the investment is otherwise accounted for. However, the requirements of IAS 39 and IFRS 7 do not apply to such derivatives if they meet the definition of an equity instrument of the entity.[80] For example, a written call option issued by a subsidiary that can be settled only by the subsidiary issuing a fixed number of its shares to the holder in exchange for a fixed amount of cash might meet the definition of equity (see 3.6 below and Chapter 19 at 3.3). Further, IAS 39 does not apply to instruments containing potential voting rights that, in substance, currently give access to the economic benefits associated with an ownership interest where that ownership interest is consolidated, proportionately consolidated or equity accounted (see Chapter 6 at 6.2, Chapter 8 at 2.2.1 D and Chapter 9 at 2.2.2 C).[81]

Sometimes strategic equity investments are made in entities that that are not controlled by the reporting entity. These are often made with the intention of establishing or maintaining a long-term operating relationship with the investee. Unless they are equity accounted as associates or proportionately consolidated or equity accounted as joint ventures, these investments are covered by IAS 39.[82]

3.2 Leases

Whilst all rights and obligations under leases to which IAS 17 applies (see Chapter 25) are within the scope of IAS 32 or, when applied, IFRS 7, they are only within the scope of IAS 39 to the following extent:

- lease receivables and payables are subject to IAS 39's derecognition provisions (see Chapter 18 at 4 and 5 respectively);
- lease receivables are subject to IAS 39's impairment provisions (see Chapter 20 at 6); and
- the relevant provisions of IAS 39 apply to derivatives embedded within leases (see 5 below).

Otherwise the applicable standard is IAS 17, not IAS 39.[83]

3.3 Insurance contracts

Although insurance contracts often satisfy the definition of a financial instrument, in general they have not, historically, been accounted for as such. In fact the IASB, and before it the IASC, has been conducting a project on accounting for insurance contracts for a number of years and the first standard on the topic, IFRS 4, was published in March 2004.

An insurance contract is defined in IFRS 4 as one 'under which one party (the insurer) accepts significant insurance risk from another party (the policyholder) by agreeing to compensate the policyholder if a specified uncertain future event (the insured event) adversely affects the policyholder'. Insurance risk is defined as 'risk, other than financial risk, transferred from the holder of a contract to the issuer' and financial risk is defined as 'the risk of a possible future change in one or more of a specified interest rate, financial instrument price, commodity price, foreign exchange rate, index of prices or rates, credit rating or credit index or other variable, provided in the case of a non-financial variable that the variable is not specific to a party to the contract.'[84] In many cases it will be quite clear whether a contract is an insurance contract or not, although this will not always be the case and IFRS 4 contains ten pages of guidance on this definition.[85]

Insurance contracts, as defined, are generally outside the scope of IAS 32, IAS 39 and, when applied, IFRS 7.[86] IAS 39 does, however, apply to derivatives that are embedded in insurance contracts if the derivative itself is not within the scope of IFRS 4.[87] IAS 32 and, when applied, IFRS 7 apply to derivatives embedded in insurance contracts if IAS 39 requires them to be accounted for separately.[88] Finally, financial guarantee contracts, which meet the definition of an insurance contract if the risk transferred is significant, are normally accounted for under IAS 39 and disclosed in accordance with IAS 32 or, when applied, IFRS 7 (see 3.4 below).[89]

The application guidance makes it clear that insurers' financial instruments, other than those that are within the scope of IFRS 4, should be accounted for under IAS 39.[90]

3.3.1 *Weather derivatives*

Some contracts require a payment based on climatic variables (often referred to as 'weather derivatives') or on geological or other physical variables. Such contracts are within the scope of IAS 39 unless they meet the definition of an insurance contract.[91] Generic or standardised contracts will rarely meet the definition of insurance contracts because the variable is unlikely to be specific to either party to the contract.[92] This is illustrated in the following example.

Example 17.1: Rainfall contract

Company E has contracted to lease a stall at an open-air event from which it plans to sells goods to people attending the event. The event will be held at a village approximately 100 km from Capital City.

Because E is concerned that poor weather may deter people from attending the event, it enters into a contract with Financial Institution K, the terms of which are that in return for a premium paid by

E on inception of the contract, K will pay a fixed amount of money to E if, during the day of the event, it rains for more than three hours at the meteorological station in the centre of Capital City.

The non-financial variable in the contract, i.e. rainfall at the meteorological station, is not specific to E. Particularly, E will only suffer loss as a result of rainfall at the village, not at Capital City. Also, because the potential payment to be received is for a fixed amount, it might not be possible to demonstrate that E has suffered a loss for which it has been compensated. Therefore, E should account for the contract as a financial instrument under IAS 39.

3.3.2 Contracts with discretionary participation features

Certain financial instruments (normally taking the form of life insurance policies) contain what are called discretionary participation features – essentially rights of the holder to receive benefits whose amount or timing is, contractually, at the discretion of the issuer[93] – and these are dealt with under IFRS 4. Accordingly, IAS 39 and the parts of IAS 32 dealing with the distinction between financial liabilities and equity instruments (see Chapter 19 at 3 and 4) do not apply to such contracts, although the disclosure requirements of IAS 32 or IFRS 7 do apply.[94]

IAS 39 does, however, apply to derivatives that are embedded in contracts containing discretionary participation features if the derivative itself is not within the scope of IFRS 4.[95]

3.4 Financial guarantee contracts

In August 2005, the IASB published amendments to IAS 39 (and IFRS 4) that changed the accounting requirements for certain financial guarantees. Where a contract meets the definition of a financial guarantee contract (see 3.4.1 below) the issuer is normally required to apply IAS 39 which now contains specific accounting requirements different from other financial liabilities – essentially the contract is measured at fair value on initial recognition and this amount is amortised to profit or loss provided it is not considered probable that the guarantee will be called (see Chapter 20 at 3.7). There are exceptions to this general requirement and these are dealt with at 3.4.2 below.

In the relatively short history of IAS 39, the accounting requirements for the issuers of financial guarantees have changed a number of times. Under the original version of IAS 39, financial guarantee contracts, including letters of credit, that provided for payments to be made if a debtor failed to make payments when due were outside its scope.[96] Such contracts continued to be outside the scope of the revised standard that was issued in December 2003, but even so, measurement requirements for those contracts were specified – these requirements were virtually identical to those in the current version.[97]

This situation was short-lived and, when IFRS 4 was issued in March 2004, IAS 39 was amended to exclude such contracts from its scope, provided that they met the definition of an insurance contract in IFRS 4 (they normally would) and the specific measurement requirements were deleted.[98] This was essentially because the measurement requirements had not been exposed for comment[99] in accordance with the IASB's own operating procedures. They were subsequently published in an exposure draft in July 2004 which led to the amendment noted above.

3.4.1 Definition

A financial guarantee contract is now defined as a contract that requires the issuer to make specified payments to reimburse the holder for a loss it incurs because a specified debtor fails to make payment when due in accordance with the original or modified terms of a debt instrument.[100] This definition is largely consistent with the descriptions of financial guarantee contracts in the previous versions of IAS 39.

A Reimbursement for loss incurred

Some credit-related guarantees (or letters of credit, credit derivative default contracts or credit insurance contracts) do not, as a precondition for payment, require that the holder is exposed to, and has incurred a loss on, the failure of the debtor to make payments on the guaranteed asset when due. An example of such a guarantee is one that requires payments in response to changes in a specified credit rating or credit index. Such guarantees are not financial guarantee contracts, as defined in IAS 39, and are not insurance contracts, as defined in IFRS 4. Rather, they are derivatives and accordingly fall within the scope of IAS 39 for the issuer.[101]

When a debtor defaults on a guaranteed loan a significant time period may elapse prior to full and final legal settlement of the loss. Because of this, certain credit protection contracts provide for the guarantor to make a payment at a fixed point after the default event using the best estimate of loss at the time. Such payments typically terminate the credit protection contract with no party having any further claim under it whilst ownership of the loan remains with the guaranteed party. In situations like this, if the final loss on the debtor exceeds the amount estimated on payment of the guarantee, the guaranteed party will suffer an overall financial loss; conversely, the guaranteed party may receive a payment under the guarantee but eventually suffer no loss on the loan. Therefore we do not believe that such a contract meets the essence of the definition.

In order for such a contract to meet the definition of a guarantee it would be necessary that the guaranteed party received only the amount lost due to the default of the debtor. Such a contract could be structured in two ways:

- the contract could require the guarantor to purchase the defaulted loan for its nominal amount instead of making a payment for the best estimate of loss; or
- on settlement of the final loss, the contract could provide for a further payment between the guarantor and guaranteed party for any difference between that amount and the initial loss estimate that was paid.

B Debt instrument

Although the term 'debt instrument' is used extensively as a fundamental part of the definition of a 'financial guarantee contract', it is not defined in IAS 32, IAS 39, IFRS 4 or IFRS 7. The term will typically be considered to include trade debts, overdrafts and other borrowings including mortgage loans and certain debt securities.

However, entities often provide guarantees of other items and analysing these in the context of IAS 39 and IFRS 4 is not always straightforward. Consider, for example, a guarantee of a lessor's receipts under a lease. As set out at 2.2.4 above, in substance a finance lease gives rise to a loan agreement and it therefore seems clear that a guarantee of payments on such a lease should be considered a financial guarantee contract.

From the perspective of the guarantor, a guarantee of a non-cancellable operating lease will give rise to a substantially similar exposure, i.e. credit risk of the lessee. Moreover, individual payments currently due and payable are recognised as financial (debt) instruments. Therefore, such guarantees would seem to meet the definition of a financial guarantee at least insofar as they relate to payments currently due and payable. It may be argued that the remainder of the contract (normally the majority) fails to meet the definition because it provides a guarantee of *future* debt instruments. However, the standard does not explicitly require the debt instrument to be accounted for as a financial instrument that is currently due and we believe a guarantee of a lessor's receipts under an operating lease could also be argued to meet the definition of a financial guarantee contract.

Where it is accepted that such a guarantee is not a financial guarantee contract, one must still examine how it should be accounted for – it is, after all, a financial instrument. The possibilities are a derivative financial instrument (accounted for at fair value through profit or loss under IAS 39) or an insurance contract (accounted for under IFRS 4 – commonly resulting only in disclosure of a contingent liability, assuming payment is not considered probable). The analysis depends on whether the risk transferred by the guarantee is financial risk or insurance risk (see 3.3 above). Credit risk sits on the cusp of the relevant definitions making the judgment a marginal one, although we believe that in many situations the arguments for treatment as an insurance contract will be credible. Of course for this to be the case the guarantee must only compensate the holder for loss in the event of default.

Other types of guarantee can add further complications – for example guarantees of pension plan contributions to funded defined benefit schemes. Where such a guarantee is in respect of discrete identifiable payments, the analysis above for operating leases seem equally applicable. However, the terms of such a guarantee might have the effect that the guaranteed amount depends on the performance of the assets within the scheme. In these cases, the guarantee seems to give rise to a transfer of financial risk (i.e. the value of the asset) in addition to credit risk, which might lend support for its treatment as a derivative.

C Form and existence of contract

The application guidance emphasises that, whilst financial guarantee contracts may have various legal forms (such as guarantees, some types of letters of credit, credit default contracts or insurance contracts), their accounting treatment does not depend on their legal form.[102]

In some cases guarantees arise, directly or indirectly, as a result of the operation of statute or regulation. In such situations, it is necessary to examine whether the arrangement gives rise to a contract as that term is used in IAS 32. For example, in some jurisdictions, a subsidiary may avoid filing its financial statements if its parent and fellow subsidiaries guarantee its liabilities by entering into a deed of cross guarantee. In other jurisdictions similar relief is granted if group companies elect to make a statutory declaration of guarantee. In the first situation it would seem appropriate to regard the deed as a contract and any guarantee made under it within the scope of IAS 39. The statutory nature of the declaration in the second situation makes the analysis more difficult. Although the substance of the arrangement is little different from the first, as set out at 2.2.1 statutory obligations are not financial liabilities and are therefore outside the scope of IAS 39.

3.4.2 *Issuers of financial guarantee contracts*

In general, issuers of financial guarantees contracts should apply IAS 32, IAS 39 and, when applied, IFRS 7 to those contracts. However, if an entity has previously asserted explicitly that it regards such contracts as insurance contracts *and* has used accounting applicable to insurance contracts, the issuer may elect to apply either IAS 39 (and IAS 32 or IFRS 7) or IFRS 4. That election may be made contract by contract, but the election for each contract is irrevocable.[103]

The IASB was concerned that entities other than credit insurers could avoid the recognition of a liability by arguing that no recognisable liability existed on inception. Consequently, it imposed the restrictions outlined in the previous paragraph.[104] The application guidance contains further information on these restrictions where it is explained that assertions that an issuer regards contracts as insurance contracts are typically found throughout the issuer's communications with customers and regulators, contracts, business documentation as well as in their financial statements. Furthermore, insurance contracts are often subject to accounting requirements that are distinct from the requirements for other types of transaction, such as contracts issued by banks or commercial companies. In such cases, an issuer's financial statements would typically include a statement that the issuer had used those accounting requirements.[105]

Nevertheless, other companies do consider it appropriate to apply IFRS 4 rather than IAS 39 to these contracts, for example as illustrated below.[106]

Extract 17.1: Diageo plc (2006)

Notes to the company financial statements [extracts]

1. **New accounting policies** [extracts]

The company has not adopted amendments … in relation to financial guarantee contracts which will apply for periods commencing on or after 1 January 2006. Where the company enters into financial guarantee contracts to guarantee the indebtedness of other companies within its group, the company consider these to be insurance arrangements, and accounts for them as such. In this respect, the company treats the guarantee contract as a contingent liability until such time as it becomes probable that the company will be required to make a payment under the guarantee. The company does not expect the amendments to have any impact on the financial statements for the period commencing 1 July 2006.

The IASB does not regard these restrictions as suitable for the long term, because they can lead to different accounting for contracts that have similar economic effects. However, it could not find a more compelling approach to resolve its concerns for the short term.[107] Consequently, the requirements are likely to be changed again, perhaps if IAS 37 is amended in line with the IASB's current proposals (see Chapter 27 at 8).

Financial guarantee contracts given in connection with the sale of goods are dealt with under IAS 18 – *Revenue*. The guarantee is likely to affect how and when the associated revenue is accounted for (see Chapter 28).[108]

3.4.3 Holders of financial guarantee contracts

In general a financial guarantee contract will meet the definition of an insurance contract in IFRS 4 if the credit risk transferred is significant.[109] Such contracts are generally outside the scope of IAS 39 (see 3.3 above) and IFRS 4 does not apply to insurance contracts that an entity holds (other than reinsurance contracts).[110] Accordingly, the holder of a financial guarantee contract will normally need to develop its accounting policy in accordance with the 'hierarchy' in IAS 8 – *Accounting Policies, Changes in Accounting Estimates and Errors* (see Chapter 3 at 4.3).[111] This is discussed further in Chapter 20 at 6.2.2.

3.4.4 Financial guarantee contracts between entities under common control

In developing these amendments, the IASB was asked by some respondents to provide an exemption from the measurement requirements of IAS 39 for guarantees issued between parents and their subsidiaries, between entities under common control and by a parent or subsidiary on behalf of a subsidiary or the parent. (A similar exemption is available under US GAAP.) They argued that the requirement to recognise these financial guarantee contracts in separate or individual financial statements would cause costs disproportionate to the likely benefits, given that intragroup transactions are eliminated on consolidation. However, to avoid the omission of material liabilities from separate or individual financial statements, the IASB decided not to create such an exemption.[112]

Therefore, for example, where a parent guarantees the borrowings of a subsidiary, the guarantee should be accounted for as a standalone instrument in the parent's separate financial statements. However, for the purposes of the parent's consolidated financial statements, such guarantees are normally considered an integral part of the terms of the borrowing (see Chapter 19 at 3.6) and therefore should not be accounted for independently of the borrowing.[113]

3.5 Loan commitments

Loan commitments are described in IAS 39 as 'firm commitments to provide credit under pre-specified terms and conditions'.[114] The term can include arrangements such as offers to individuals in respect of a residential mortgage loan as well as committed borrowing facilities granted to a corporate entity.

In the original version of IAS 39, loan commitments were dealt with no differently to other financial instruments and, in most cases, they meet the definition of a derivative financial instrument (see 2.2.7 above and 4 below). Accordingly, they were potentially subject to fair value accounting, although the IGC (see 1.4 above) did take some steps to ameliorate this by concluding that in certain circumstances loan commitments fell to be treated as 'regular way' transactions (see Chapter 18 at 3.2).[115]

To many, including the IASB, this seemed somewhat counter-intuitive, not least because the resulting assets or liabilities were normally recorded at amortised cost, and in developing the revised version of IAS 39 a pragmatic decision was taken to simplify the accounting for holders and issuers of many loan commitments.[116] Accordingly, loan commitments that cannot be settled net – in practice, most loan commitments – may be excluded from most of the scope of IAS 39. They are, however, subject to its derecognition provisions[117] (see Chapter 18 at 5) and are included within the scope of IAS 32 and, when applied, IFRS 7.[118]

Some loan commitments, however, are within the scope of IAS 39, namely:[119]

- those that are designated as financial liabilities at fair value through profit or loss (this may be appropriate if the associated risk exposures are managed on a fair value basis[120] – see 7.1.2 below);
- commitments that can be settled net in cash or by delivering or issuing another financial instrument; and
- all those within the same class where the entity has a past practice of selling the assets resulting from its loan commitments shortly after origination. The IASB sees this as achieving net settlement.[121]

In addition, commitments to provide a loan at a below-market interest rate are also within the scope of IAS 39 and for these the standard contains specific measurement requirements which are discussed in Chapter 20 at 3.7.[122] The IASB was concerned that liabilities resulting from such commitments might not be recognised in the balance sheet because, often, no cash consideration is received.[123]

The standard contains only limited guidance on what 'net settlement' means in this context. Clearly a fixed interest rate loan commitment that gives the lender and/or the borrower an explicit right to settle the value of the contract (taking into account changes in interest rates etc.) in cash would be considered a form of net settlement. However, paying out a loan in instalments (for example, a mortgage construction loan where instalments are paid out in line with the progress of construction) is not regarded as net settlement.[124]

As a matter of fact, most loan commitments could be settled net if both parties agreed, essentially by renegotiating the terms of the contract. We do not believe the IASB intended the possibility of such renegotiations to be considered in determining whether or not the commitment may be settled net. Of more relevance is the question of whether one party has the practical ability to settle net, e.g. because the terms of the contract allow net settlement or by the use of some market mechanism.

In addition, many loan commitments allow the lender to withdraw the borrowing facility in the event that there is a significant decline in the borrower's credit risk evidenced, perhaps, by the borrower breaching conventional covenants specified in the agreement. Again, we do not believe the IASB intended such terms, which are common in most facility agreements, to be considered as allowing net settlement and preventing this exception being used.

No guidance is given on what is meant by a class in this context (although the basis for conclusions makes it clear that an entity can have more than one).[125] Therefore, an assessment will need to be made based on individual circumstances.

Example 17.2: Classes of loan commitment

A banking group has two main operating subsidiaries, one in country A and the other in country B. Although they share common functions (management and information systems etc.) the two subsidiaries' operations are clearly distinct.

Both subsidiaries originate similar loans under loan commitments. In country A there is an active and liquid market for the assets resulting from loan commitments issued in that country. The subsidiary operating in that country has a past practice of disposing of such assets in this market shortly after origination. There is no such market in country B.

The fact that one subsidiary has a past practice of settling its loan commitments net (as the term is used in the standard) would not normally mean that the loan commitments issued in country B are required to be classified as at fair value through profit or loss.

The above example is relatively straightforward – in some circumstances it may be more difficult to define the class. However, there is no reason why an individual entity (say a subsidiary of a group) cannot have two or more classes of loan commitment, e.g. where they result in the origination of different types of asset that are clearly managed separately.

An issuer of loan commitments is required to apply IAS 37 if they are not subject to the requirements of IAS 39.[126] Particularly, a provision should be established if a loan commitment becomes an onerous contract as defined in that standard (see Chapter 27 at 5.3). Any associated entitlement to fees should be accounted for in accordance with IAS 18 (see Chapter 28). No accounting requirements are specified for holders of loan commitments, but they will normally be accounted for as executory contracts – essentially, this means that fees payable will be recognised as an expense in a manner that is appropriate to the terms of the commitment. Any resulting borrowing will obviously be accounted for as a financial liability under IAS 32 and IAS 39.

Although much of the discussion of loan commitments has focused on *options* to provide credit,[127] we believe it is entirely appropriate to apply the exclusion to non-optional commitments to provide credit, provided the necessary conditions above are met.

The exclusion is available only for contracts to provide credit. Normally, therefore, it will be applicable only where there is a commitment to lend funds, and certainly not for all contracts that may result in the subsequent recognition of an asset or liability that is accounted for at amortised cost. Consider, for example, a contract between entities A and B that gives B the right to sell to A a transferable (but unquoted) debt security issued by entity C that B currently owns. Even if, on subsequent acquisition, A will classify the debt security within loans and receivables (see 7.3 below), the contract would not generally be considered a loan commitment as it does not involve A providing credit to B.

3.6 Equity instruments

Financial instruments (including options and warrants) that are issued by the reporting entity and meet the definition of equity instruments in IAS 32 (see 2.1 above and Chapter 19 at 3 and 4) are outside the scope of IAS 39. However, the holder of such an instrument should apply IAS 39 unless it meets the exception at 3.1 above.[128]

From the point of view of the issuer, equity instruments are within the scope of the presentation and (until IFRS 7 is applied) disclosure requirements of IAS 32.[129] With the exception of those noted at 3.1 above, issued equity instruments are within the scope of IFRS 7. However, this is somewhat academic because IFRS 7 contains no disclosure requirements that relate to them.

From the point of view of the holder, equity instruments are within the scope of the disclosure requirements of IAS 32 or, when applied, IFRS 7.

3.7 Business combinations

3.7.1 Contingent consideration in a business combination

For the time being, IAS 32, IAS 39 and, when applied, IFRS 7, do not apply to contracts for contingent consideration in business combinations. This exemption, which applies only to the acquiror,[130] not the vendor, is perfectly sensible as the accounting for such contracts from the point of view of the acquiror is dealt with more specifically in other standards, particularly IFRS 3 – *Business Combinations* – and its predecessor IAS 22 – *Business Combinations* (see Chapter 7 at 2.3.2 E). However, the revised version of IFRS 3 (see Chapter 7 at 5) is expected to amend IAS 32, IAS 39 and IFRS 7 to remove this exemption. Accordingly, contingent consideration that meets the definition of a financial instrument will be accounted for and disclosed under these standards rather than IFRS 3.

IAS 39 does not go on to explain whether the vendor should be accounting for the contract in accordance with its provisions. This is an area that has, in the past, been considered by the IFRIC. It decided to take it no further because 'it is not pervasive in practice' and, a little unconvincingly, because the accounting for contingent consideration from the purchaser's (not vendor's) perspective is being considered in the IASB's Business Combinations Phase II project. They did add that 'one of the questions to consider is whether IAS 37 ... or IAS 39 ... applies'.[131] In most cases the vendor will have a contractual right to receive cash or another financial asset from the purchaser and, therefore, it is hard to avoid the conclusion that the contingent consideration meets the definition of a financial asset and hence is within the scope of IAS 39 not IAS 37.

3.7.2 Contracts between an acquirer and a vendor in a business combination

IAS 39 does not apply to contracts between an acquirer and a vendor in a business combination to buy or sell an acquiree at a future date.[132] Whilst a seemingly straightforward statement, it is not entirely clear how widely this exception was intended to apply, particularly because neither IAS 39 nor IFRS 3 (which introduced this exception into IAS 39 when it was published in March 2004) contain any further explanation.

The origins of the exception (for which there is no equivalent in IAS 32 or IFRS 7) lie in the fact that, during the pre-ballot process for IAS 39, a member of the IASB had suggested that when an acquirer and vendor in a business combination agree the cost of the combination before the acquisition date (i.e. before the date the acquirer obtains control of the acquiree), a forward contract arises that, at least in theory, should be accounted for under IAS 39.[133] Prior to this, the thought that such contracts might fall within the scope of IAS 39 would probably have occurred to very few people.

Following deliberations at the November 2003 meeting of the IASB, it was reported (emphasis added):

> 'The Board agreed that when an acquirer and vendor in a business combination agree the cost of the combination before the acquisition date (i.e. before the date the acquirer obtains control of the acquiree), any resulting *forward contract* should be excluded from the scope IAS 39'.[134]

The papers considered by the IASB at that meeting set out some examples of circumstances in which forward contracts might be considered to arise:[135]

- the acquirer promises to issue 5,000 of its shares in exchange for net assets that constitute a business, and the owners of those net assets promise to transfer control of the net assets to the acquirer in exchange for the 5,000 shares.

  Here, the acquirer's commitment to issue a specified number of equity instruments in exchange for the acquiree is, from the acquirer's perspective, a forward contract to sell equity. A commitment of the owners of the acquiree to transfer control of the acquiree's net assets in exchange for a specified number of equity instruments is, from the perspective of the owners of the acquiree, a forward contract to purchase equity. To the extent the financial assets and financial liabilities arising from these forward contracts are within the scope of IAS 39, they are required to be recognised on the commitment date (i.e. the agreement date in this example), at their fair values at that date, and subsequently measured at fair value, normally with changes reflected in profit or loss;[136]
- the acquirer promises to transfer fixed-rate government bonds with a face value of €1,000,000 in exchange for net assets that constitute a business, and

the owners of those net assets promise to transfer control of the net assets to the acquirer in exchange for the fixed-rate government bonds.

In this case the acquirer's promise to deliver fixed-rate government bonds with a face value of €1,000,000 in exchange for the acquiree is, from the acquirer's perspective, a forward contract that, according to the papers, gives rise to a financial liability. Similarly, a promise of the owners of the acquiree to transfer control of the net assets of the acquiree in exchange for the fixed-rate government bonds is, from the perspective of the owners of the acquiree, a forward contract that, the papers argue, gives rise to a financial asset.[137] However, it is not clear why this would always give rise to a financial *liability* for the acquirer and a financial *asset* for the owners (as opposed to a derivative, i.e. a forward contract, that could be either an asset or a liability for either party). Further, it provides no suggestion as to what the corresponding debit (or credit) might represent; and

- the acquirer promises to transfer cash of €5,000,000 in exchange for a controlling equity interest in an acquiree, and the owners of the acquiree promise to transfer that controlling equity interest to the acquirer in exchange for the €5,000,000 cash.

  The acquirer's promise in this situation to transfer cash in exchange for a controlling equity interest in the acquiree is, from the acquirer's perspective, also a forward contract that, according to the papers, gives rise to a financial liability on the agreement date. The promise of the owners of the acquiree to transfer the controlling equity interest in exchange for cash is, from the perspective of the owners of the acquirer, a forward contract that gives rise to a financial asset argue the papers.[138] Again it is unclear why the forward contract would always give rise to a liability of the acquirer and an asset of the owner.

The paper then puts forward the argument that the promise of the owners of the acquiree in the first two examples above to transfer net assets that constitute a business on a certain date in the future may also be viewed by the acquirer as forward contracts that gives rise to assets. It explains that if the business being transferred were viewed as a single non-financial item, the forward contract would not be within the scope of IAS 39. However, if the business being transferred were viewed as a number of individual assets and liabilities, some of which might be financial assets and financial liabilities, the agreement to transfer the financial assets and financial liabilities in the future would be a forward contract within the scope of IAS 39,[139] although no hint is given as to how the purchase price might be allocated between the various assets and liabilities to be acquired.

In summary, the papers do little to help clarify why that one IASB member considered that such contracts might 'theoretically' be within the scope of IAS 39 or what the consequences might be. It is worth examining the accounting treatment that might be required if the analyses above were accepted at face value and IAS 39 did not contain the exception.

Example 17.3: Accounting for forward contract to acquire a business

On 1 October 2008, Company X enters into a binding agreement to purchase from Company Y the entire share capital of Company Z, a subsidiary of Y that constitutes a business, for €1,000, its then fair value. X will obtain, and Y will relinquish, control of Z on 1 January 2009 and the consideration will be paid on this date.

As a result of positive developments in some of the main markets for its products in November and December 2008, the fair value of Z rises such that it has a fair value of €1,100 on 31 December 2008.

If X accounts for its binding agreement in its entirety as a forward contract under IAS 39 (which is covered in more detail in Chapter 20), it would make the following accounting entries:

1 October 2008

	€	€
Forward contract	–	
Cash		–

to record the forward contract at its fair value (and cost) of nil (this assumes that time value is immaterial)

31 December 2008

	€	€
Forward contract	100	
Profit or loss		100

to record the forward contract at its now fair value (calculated as the difference between the fair value of Z and the amount that will be paid for it) and the corresponding gain in profit or loss

1 January 2009

	€	€
Net assets and goodwill	1,100	
Cash		1,000
Forward contract		100

to record the business combination at its 'cost' of €1,100, being the amount of cash paid and the fair value of the forward contract that is extinguished

To most people these journal entries are extremely counter-intuitive and so it is not difficult understand why the IASB would not want contracts such as these (or at least portions of them) accounted for in accordance with IAS 39. However, it is not clear what the overriding principle is that the IASB seemed to be striving for in this exception. To the extent that there is any, it seems to be that arrangements that facilitate the consummation of a business combination should be excluded from the scope of IAS 39, but even this is a little unsatisfactory.

Given the words used to report the decision of the IASB, much of the debate on how widely this exception should apply has focused on the question of whether a contract needs to be a 'forward contract' or whether it can be, say, a 'contingent forward contract' or even an 'option' (terms are that are not formally defined within IAS 39 or IFRS 3). The issue can be illustrated by the following example.

Example 17.4: Contract for the sale and purchase of a subsidiary

Case 1

On 30 April 2008, Company A enters into a contract with Company B to purchase the entire share capital of Company C, a wholly owned subsidiary of B with a substantive business, for €100 million. The contract is binding on both parties but completion of the contract is contingent on obtaining certain regulatory approvals (e.g. from the relevant competition authorities). B will retain control of C until the contract completes which is expected to occur early in the fourth quarter of 2008.

The contract is effectively a contingent forward contract to sell (or purchase) shares in C for cash. Does that mean, in preparing their financial statements for the year ended 30 June 2008, that either of A or B should apply IAS 39 to this contract?

The contract is between an acquirer (A) and a vendor (B) in what will result in a business combination for A (the purchase of C) at a future date, assuming that regulatory approval is forthcoming. Therefore, it seems entirely appropriate that neither A nor B should apply IAS 39 in accounting for the contract.

Case 2

The facts are the same as in Case 1 except that:

- regulatory approval is not required, hence the contract contains no related contingency; and
- completion of the contract is contingent on the shareholders of A approving its acquisition of C at a general meeting to be held early in the fourth quarter of 2008.

In this case the contract is effectively a call option allowing A, as represented by its shareholders, to purchase (potentially requiring B to sell) shares in C for cash – a purchased option from A's perspective and a written option from B's perspective. Does this fact mean that this contract should be accounted for as a derivative under IAS 39?

If one believed that the exception applied only to forward contracts, then it would be difficult to conclude that this should not be accounted for under IAS 39. However, the fact remains that it is a contract between an acquirer (A) and a vendor (B) that will result in a business combination for A (the purchase of C) at a future date, assuming that shareholder approval is forthcoming. Therefore, many would argue that neither A nor B should apply IAS 39 in accounting for the contract.

Case 3

The facts are the same as in Case 2 except that no approval is required from the shareholders of A but the contract is contingent on the shareholders of B approving its sale of C at a general meeting to be held early in the fourth quarter of 2008.

In this case the contract is effectively a put option allowing B, as represented by its shareholders, to sell (potentially requiring A to purchase) shares in C for cash – a purchased option from B's perspective and a written option from A's perspective. For the same reasons as in Case 2, whilst some would view the contract as within the scope of IAS 39, many would argue that it should not be accounted for as a derivative.

In deciding to incorporate this exception in IAS 39, the IASB did not focus on what might be termed pure forward contracts. The agenda papers referred to contracts in which the parties to the business combination are committed to the transaction such that they cannot unilaterally terminate the transaction without some negative consequences (such as the payment of a break fee if one is specified in the agreement, or the high likelihood of litigation) as well as contracts that 'have the characteristics of a forward contract'[140] suggesting that a wider view might have been intended, although quite how wide is entirely unclear.

The following example illustrates another contract which some might consider to be excluded from the scope of IAS 39.

Example 17.5: Put option over shares in jointly controlled entity

Company P and Company Q established a jointly controlled entity, Company J, whereby each sold a subsidiary with a substantive business to J in exchange for 50% of J's share capital. As part of the joint venture agreement establishing J, P and Q agreed not to sell their shares in J for five years. However, because the subsidiary that P contributed to the venture was considered to have a lower fair value than the one contributed by Q, in order to retain a 50% stake in the venture, P agreed that if Q wished to sell its stake in J at the end of five years and the stake was worth less than €50 million (estimated to be its fair value on establishment) then P would buy the stake at that time for €50 million.

The agreement by P to acquire Q's holding in J for €50 million at the end of five years is a put option over an interest in a jointly controlled entity which, on the face of it, should be accounted for in accordance with IAS 39 (see 3.1 above).

However, the contract shares many common characteristics with the ones in Example 17.4 above. In particular, it is a contract between two parties that can be seen as an acquirer (P) and a vendor (Q) in a transaction that will, if completed, result in a business combination for P by obtaining control over J. Accordingly, some might argue that neither P nor Q should account for the put option under IAS 39.

In this case the argument that the put option should be excluded from the scope of IAS 39 is a little more difficult to sustain given that (a) it would highlight a potential contradiction within the standard because, as set out at 3.1 above, derivatives on jointly controlled entities are expressly said to be within the scope of IAS 39 and (b) the shares that are the subject of the put option would not in themselves represent a controlling interest in a business. However, in this case the question may be moot: the contract is a derivative over unquoted equity shares for which it is quite possible that a reliable measure of its fair value is not available and should therefore be accounted for at cost (see Chapter 20 at 4.4).

Unless some move is made to clarify these questions, it is likely that differing interpretations will be seen in practice, although there is no indication that the IASB will deal with the issue in its business combinations project.

3.8 Employee benefit plans and share-based payment

Employers' rights and obligations under employee benefit plans, which are dealt with under IAS 19 – *Employee Benefits* – are excluded from the scope of IAS 32, IAS 39 and, when applied, IFRS 7.[141] The IFRIC noted that IAS 19 indicates that employee benefit plans include a wide range of formal and informal arrangements and concluded it was clear that the exclusion of employee benefit plans from IAS 32 (and presumably IAS 39 and IFRS 7) includes all employee benefits covered by IAS 19, for example a liability for long service leave.[142]

Similarly, most financial instruments, contracts and obligations under share-based payment transactions, which are dealt with under IFRS 2 – *Share-based Payment* – are also excluded. However, IAS 32, IAS 39 and, when applied, IFRS 7 do apply to contracts to buy or sell non-financial items in share-based transactions that can be settled net (as that term is used in this context) unless they are considered to be 'normal' sales and purchases (see 3.9 below).[143] For example, a contract to purchase a fixed quantity of oil in exchange for issuing of a fixed number of shares that could be settled net would be excluded from the scope of IAS 32, IAS 39 and IFRS 7, only if it qualified as a 'normal' purchase (which would be unlikely).

In addition, IAS 32 applies to treasury shares (see Chapter 19 at 6) that are purchased, sold, issued or cancelled in connection with employee share option plans, employee share purchase plans, and all other share-based payment arrangements.[144]

3.9 Contracts to buy or sell commodities and other non-financial items

As set out at 2.2.5 above, contracts to buy or sell non-financial items do not generally meet the definition of a financial instrument. However, many such contracts are standardised in form and traded on organised markets in much the same way as some derivative financial instruments. The application guidance explains that a commodity futures contract, for example, may be bought and sold readily for cash because it is listed for trading on an exchange and may change hands many times.[145] In fact, this is not strictly true because such contracts are bilateral agreements that cannot be transferred in this way. Rather, the contract would normally be 'closed out' (rather than sold) by entering into an offsetting agreement with the original counterparty or with the exchange on which it is traded.

The ability to buy or sell such a contract for cash, the ease with which it may be bought or sold (or, more correctly, closed out), and the possibility of negotiating a cash settlement of the obligation to receive or deliver the commodity, do not alter the fundamental character of the contract in a way that creates a financial instrument. The buying and selling parties are, in effect, trading the underlying commodity or other asset. However, the IASB is of the view that there are many circumstances where they should be accounted for as if they were financial instruments.[146]

Accordingly, the provisions of IAS 32, IAS 39 and, when applied, IFRS 7 are normally to be applied to those contracts to buy or sell non-financial items that can be settled net in cash or another financial instrument or by exchanging financial instruments, effectively as if the contracts were financial instruments (see 3.9.1 below). However, there is an exception for what are commonly termed 'normal' purchases and sales or 'own use' contracts – these are considered in more detail at 3.9.2 below.[147]

Typically the non-financial item will be a commodity, but this is not necessarily the case. For example, an emission right, which is an intangible asset (see Chapter 12 at 3.3), is a non-financial item. Therefore these requirements would apply equally to contracts for the purchase or sale of emission rights if they could be settled net. These requirements will also be appropriate for determining the appropriate accounting treatment for certain commodity leases.

3.9.1 Contracts that may be settled net

IAS 39 explains that there are various ways in which a contract to buy or sell a non-financial item can be settled net, including when:

(a) the terms of the contract permit either party to settle it net;

(b) the ability to settle the contract net is not explicit in its terms, but the entity has a practice of settling similar contracts (see 3.9.2 A below) net (whether with the counterparty, by entering into offsetting contracts or by selling the contract before its exercise or lapse);

(c) for similar contracts (see 3.9.2 B below), the entity has a practice of taking delivery of the underlying and selling it within a short period after delivery for the purpose of generating a profit from short-term fluctuations in price or dealer's margin; and

(d) the non-financial item that is the subject of the contract is readily convertible to cash (see below).[148]

There is no further guidance in IAS 39 explaining what is meant by 'readily convertible to cash'. Typically, a non-financial item would be considered readily convertible to cash if it consists of largely fungible units and quoted spot prices are available in an active market that can absorb the quantity held by the entity without significantly affecting the price.

Whether there exists an active market for a non-financial item, particularly a physical one such as a commodity, will depend on its quality, location or other characteristics such as size or weight. For example, if a commodity is actively traded in London, this may have the effect that the same commodity located in, say, Rotterdam is considered readily convertible to cash as well as if it was located in London. However, if it were located in Siberia it may not be considered readily convertible to cash if more than little effort was required (often because of transportation needs) for it to be readily sold.

Like loan commitments, most contracts could as a matter of fact be settled net if both parties agreed to renegotiate terms. Again we do not believe the IASB intended the possibility of such renegotiations to be considered in determining whether or not such contracts may be settled net. Of more relevance is the question of whether one party has the practical ability to settle net, e.g. in accordance with the terms of the contract or by the use of some market mechanism.

3.9.2 Normal sales and purchases (or own use contracts)

As indicated at 3.9 above, the provisions of IAS 32, IAS 39 and, when applied, IFRS 7 are not to be applied to those contracts to buy or sell non-financial items that can be settled net if they were entered into and continue to be held for the purpose of the receipt or delivery of the non-financial item in accordance with the entity's expected purchase, sale or usage requirements (a 'normal' purchase or sale).[149]

It should be noted that this is a two-part test, i.e. in order to qualify as a normal purchase or sale, the contract needs to both (a) have been entered into, and (b) continue to be held, for that purpose. Accordingly, if a contract that was originally entered into for the purpose of delivery ceases to be held for that purpose at a later date, it should be accounted for as a financial instrument from that date. Similarly, where an entity's intentions towards a contract that was not originally held for the purpose of delivery (and was accounted for under IAS 39) subsequently change such that it is expected to be settled by delivery, the contract remains within the scope of IAS 39.

The IASB views the practice of settling net or taking delivery of the underlying and selling it within a short period after delivery as an indication that the contracts are not normal purchases or sales. Therefore, contracts to which (b) or (c) at 3.9.1 above apply cannot be subject to the normal purchase or sale exception. Other contracts that can be settled net are evaluated to determine whether this exception can actually apply.[150] The implications of this requirement are considered further at A and B below.

The implementation guidance illustrates the application of the exception as follows:

Example 17.6: Copper forward

Company XYZ enters into a fixed-price forward contract to purchase 1,000 kg of copper in accordance with its expected usage requirements. The contract permits XYZ to take physical delivery of the copper at the end of twelve months, or to pay or receive a net settlement in cash, based on the change in fair value of copper.

The contract is a derivative instrument because there is no initial net investment, the contract is based on the price of copper, and it is to be settled at a future date. However, if XYZ intends to settle the contract by taking delivery and has no history for similar contracts of settling net in cash, or of taking delivery of the copper and selling it within a short period after delivery for the purpose of generating a profit from short-term fluctuations in price or dealer's margin, the contract is accounted for as an executory contract rather than as a derivative.[151]

Sometimes a market design or process imposes a structure or intermediary that prevents the producer of a non-financial item from physically delivering it to the customer. For example, a gold miner may produce gold bars (dore) that are physically delivered to a mint for refining and, whilst remaining at the mint, the gold is credited to the producer's (or possibly a counterparty's) 'gold account'. Where a contract for the sale of gold is settled by allocating gold to the counterparty's gold account, this may constitute 'delivery' as that term is used in the standard and a contract that is expected to be settled in this way could potentially be considered a normal sale (although of course it would need to meet all the other requirements). However, if the gold is credited to the producer's account and the sale contract is settled net in cash, this would not constitute delivery – treatment as a normal sale would, in effect, link a non-deliverable contract entered into with a customer with a transaction to buy or sell through an intermediary as a single synthetic arrangement, contrary to the general requirements on linking contracts discussed at 6 below.[152]

A Net settlement of similar contracts

As set out at 3.9 above, if the terms of a contract do not explicitly provide for net settlement but an entity has a practice of settling similar contracts net, whether with the counterparty, by entering into offsetting contracts or by selling the contract before its exercise or lapse, that contract should be considered as capable of being settled net. Furthermore, as noted at 3.9.1 above, where this is the case the contract cannot be considered a normal sale or purchase and is accounted for in accordance with IAS 39.[153]

The standard contains no further guidance on what degree of past practice would be necessary to prevent an entity from treating similar contracts as own use. We do not believe that any net settlement automatically taints an entity's ability to apply the own use exception, for example where an entity is required to close out a number of contracts as a result of a major disruption arising from external events at a production facility. However, judgment will always need to be applied based on the facts and circumstances of each individual case.

Read literally, the reference to 'similar contracts' could be particularly troublesome. For example, it is common for entities in, say, the energy sector to have a trading arm that is managed completely separately from their other operations. These trading operations commonly trade in contracts on non-financial assets, the terms of which are similar, if not identical, to those used by the entity's other operations for the purpose of physical supply. Accordingly, the standard might suggest that the normal purchase or sale exemption is unavailable to any entity that has a trading operation. However, we believe that a more appropriate interpretation is that contracts should be 'similar' as to their purpose within the business (e.g. for trading or for physical supply) not just as to their contractual terms.

B Commodity broker-traders and similar entities

As set out at 3.9 above, if an entity has a practice of taking delivery of the underlying non-financial item and selling it within a short period after delivery for the purpose of generating a profit from short-term fluctuations in price or dealer's margin, all similar contracts should be considered as capable of being settled net. Furthermore, as noted at 3.9.1 above, where this is the case the contract cannot be considered a normal sale or purchase and is accounted for in accordance with IAS 39.[154]

The standard contains no further guidance on what degree of trading is necessary to make this requirement applicable, but in many cases it will be reasonably clear. For example, in our view, the presumption must be that a commodity broker-trader that measures its inventories at fair value less costs to sell in accordance with IAS 2 – *Inventories* (see Chapter 23 at 2.1) falls within the scope of this requirement. However, there will be situations that are much less clear-cut and the application of judgment will be necessary. Factors to consider in making this assessment might include:

- how the entity manages the business and intends to profit from the contract;
- whether value is added by linking parties which are normal buyers and sellers in the value chain;
- whether the entity takes price risk;
- how the contract is settled; and
- the entity's customer base.

Again the reference in the standard to 'similar contracts' in this context is troublesome for certain entities. However, as noted at A above, we believe contracts should be 'similar' as to their purpose within the business (e.g. for trading or for physical supply) not just as to their contractual terms.

C Written options that can be settled net

The IASB does not believe that a written option to buy or sell a non-financial item that can be settled net can be regarded as entered into for the purpose of receipt or delivery in accordance with the entity's expected sale or usage requirements. Essentially, this is because the entity cannot control whether or not the purchase or sale will take place. Accordingly, IAS 32, IAS 39 and, when applied, IFRS 7 apply to written options that can be settled net according to the terms of the contract or where the underlying non-financial item is readily convertible to cash (see (a) and (d) at 3.9.1 above).[155]

Example 17.7: Put option on office building

Company XYZ owns an office building. It enters into a put option with an investor, which expires in five years and permits it to put the building to the investor for £150 million. The current value of the building is £175 million. The option, if exercised, may be settled through physical delivery or net cash, at XYZ's option.

XYZ's accounting depends on its intention and past practice for settlement. Although the contract meets the definition of a derivative, XYZ does not account for it as a derivative if it intends to settle the contract by delivering the building in the event of exercise and there is no past practice of settling net.

The investor, however, cannot conclude that the option was entered into to meet its expected purchase, sale, or usage requirements – the contract may be settled net and is a written option. Regardless of past practices, its intention does not affect whether settlement is by delivery or in cash. Accordingly, the contract is accounted for as a derivative. As noted at 4 and 7.1 below, this will involve remeasuring the derivative to its fair value each reporting period with any associated gains and losses recognised in profit or loss.

However, if the contract were a forward contract rather than an option, it required physical delivery and the investor had no past practice of settling net (either in cash or by way of taking delivery and subsequently selling within a short period), the contract would not be accounted for as a derivative.[156]

D Electricity and similar 'end-user' contracts

Determining whether or not IAS 32, IAS 39 and, when applied, IFRS 7 apply to contracts to sell non-financial items (for example electricity or natural gas) to 'end-users' such as retail customers has been particularly problematic. The non-financial items will often be considered readily convertible to cash (see 3.9.1 above), at least by the supplier. Accordingly, contracts to supply such items might be considered contracts that can be settled net.

Furthermore, end-user contracts often enable the customer to purchase as much of the non-financial item as needed at a given price to satisfy its usage requirements, i.e. the supplier does not have the contractual right to control whether or not the sale will take place. This might suggest that, from the perspective of the supplier, the contract is a written option with the consequence that it could not regard it as own use (see B above).

However, many had argued that this was not necessarily the case, particularly in the following circumstances:

- the non-financial item is an essential item for the customer;
- the customer does not have access to a market where the non-financial item can be resold;
- the non-financial item is not easily stored in any significant amounts by the customer; and
- the supplier is the sole provider of the non-financial item for a certain period of time.

In circumstances such as these, the apparent optionality within the contract is not exercisable by the customer in any economic sense – instead, the customer will purchase volumes required whether the terms in the contract are advantageous or not. Such a contract can have both a positive value and a negative value for the supplier when compared with market conditions and therefore fail to exhibit one of the key characteristics of an option, i.e. that it has only a positive value for the holder (the customer) and only a negative value for the writer (the supplier). In many respects the positive value stems from an intangible, rather than financial, aspect of the contract, being the likelihood that the customer will exercise the option (an idea that is consistent with the conclusions of the JWG in their Draft Standard[157] – see 1.3 above). Accordingly, it was often argued that such contracts should not be considered written options (and therefore not within the scope of IAS 39).

Some looked to the guidance given in the standard in the context of the near-total prohibition on using written options as a hedging instrument in a hedge relationship (see Chapter 21 at 2.1.1 A), particularly to determine whether the supplier appears to receive a premium to compensate for the risk incurred of writing an option. This was often an unhelpful analogy because many customers will pay a 'standing charge' irrespective of their usage which can look very much like an option premium.

Even if contracts such as these are considered to be within the scope of IAS 39, it is common for the supplier to have the ability to increase the price charged at relatively short notice. Also, the customer may be able to cancel the contract without penalty and switch to another supplier. Features such as these are likely to reduce any fair value that the contract can have.

Only a small number of energy suppliers appeared to regard these contracts as falling within the scope of IAS 39, an accounting treatment the IASB had almost certainly not intended, and the issue reached the attention of the IFRIC. After deciding not to take the matter onto its agenda, it noted that the guidance already explains what constitutes a written option, essentially rejecting the above arguments and confirming that in this context a written option arises where a supplier does not have the contractual right to control whether or not a sale will take place.[158]

The IFRIC also noted that 'in many situations these contracts are not capable of net cash settlement' and 'would not be ... within the scope of IAS 39'. No detailed explanation was provided of why the ability of the supplier to readily realise the non-financial item for cash does not enable it to settle the contract net (as that term is used in IAS 39).[159] However, we understand the reason underlying the comment to be the inability of the counterparty to realise the non-financial item (and hence the contract) for cash which establishes a useful principle that may be applied in similar situations, i.e. when one party to the contract cannot readily realise the non-financial item for cash.

E Other contracts containing volume flexibility

It is not uncommon for other sales contracts , such as those with large industrial customers, to contain volume flexibility features. For example, a supplier might enter into a contract requiring it to deliver, say, 100,000 units at a given price as well as giving the counterparty the option to purchase a further 20,000 units at the same price. The customer might well have access to markets for the non-financial item and, following the guidance of the IFRIC, the supplier might consider such a contract to be within the scope of IAS 39 as it contains a written option. However, some would say that the supplier could split the contract into two separate components for accounting purposes: a forward contract to supply 100,000 units (which may qualify as a normal sale) and a written option to supply 20,000 units (which would not). Arguments put forward include:

- the parties could easily have entered into two separate contracts, a forward contract and a written option; and
- it is appropriate to analogise to the requirements for embedded derivatives and separate a written option from the normal forward sale or purchase contract because it is not closely related.

Although these arguments are not universally accepted, we believe that there is merit in them.

F Disclosure of normal sale and purchase contracts

IAS 32 was not developed to apply to commodity or other contracts that do not satisfy the definition of, or fall to be accounted for as, financial instruments. However, until IFRS 7 is applied it states that entities may regard it as appropriate to apply the relevant disclosure requirements to such contracts.[160] These requirements are considered in Chapter 22 at 2. IFRS 7 contains no equivalent statement.

3.10 Reimbursement rights in respect of provisions

In December 2004, the IASB published IFRIC 5 – *Rights to Interests arising from Decommissioning, Restoration and Environmental Rehabilitation Funds* – which is dealt with in more detail in Chapter 27 at 5.4.2 B.

During the development of IFRIC 5 it was recognised that certain reimbursement rights arising from decommissioning and similar funds for which provisions had been established under IAS 37 met the definition of a financial asset and were not otherwise excluded from the scope of IAS 39. Accordingly, they should have been accounted for as financial assets in accordance with IAS 39 rather than reimbursement rights under IAS 37, even though this could potentially create some accounting mismatches given the differing accounting requirements in the two standards.[161] (Most other reimbursement rights arise from insurance contracts and were previously outside the scope of IAS 39 as set out at 3.3 above).

To ensure that economically identical arrangements are accounted for in the same way, the IASB published with IFRIC 5 an amendment to IAS 39 restricting its scope.[162] Accordingly, following an entity's application of the interpretation, IAS 39 does not apply to financial instruments that are rights to payments to reimburse the entity for expenditure it is required to make to settle a liability that it recognises as a provision in accordance with IAS 37, or for which, in an earlier period, it recognised a provision in accordance with IAS 37.[163] As a result, all such rights to reimbursement are within the scope of IAS 37.[164]

However, the interpretation does note that a residual interest in a fund that extends beyond a right to reimbursement, such as a contractual right to distributions once all the decommissioning has been completed or on winding up the fund, may be an equity instrument within the scope of IAS 39.[165]

3.11 Disposal groups classified as held for sale and discontinued operations

It appears that the disclosure requirements of IAS 32 or, when applied, IFRS 7 are applicable to financial instruments within a disposal group classified as held for sale or a discontinued operation under IFRS 5. However, it is not entirely clear this was the intention of the IASB and, as set out in Chapter 4 at 2.2.2 A, practice in this area is mixed. This issue has recently come to the attention of the IFRIC which has decided to recommend to the IASB that it clarifies IFRS 5, preferably by making it clear that the disclosures in IAS 32 and IFRS 7 do not apply.[166]

4 DERIVATIVES

The question of whether an instrument is a derivative or not is an important one for accounting purposes. As noted at 7.1 below, derivatives are normally recorded on the balance sheet at fair value with any changes in value reported in profit or loss (although there are some exceptions, e.g. derivatives that are designated in certain effective hedge relationships).

For many financial instruments, it will be reasonably clear whether or not they are derivatives, but there will be more marginal cases. Accordingly, the term derivative is formally defined within IAS 39 – it is a financial instrument, or other contract within the scope of IAS 39 (see 3.9 above), with all of the following characteristics:

(a) its value changes in response to the change in a specified interest rate, financial instrument price, commodity price, foreign exchange rate, index of prices or rates, a credit rating or credit index, or similar underlying (provided in the case of a non-financial variable that it is not specific to a party to the contract);

(b) it requires no initial net investment, or one that is smaller than would be required for other types of contracts that would be expected to have a similar response to changes in market factors; and

(c) it is settled at a future date.[167]

These three defining characteristics are considered further below.

4.1 Changes in value in response to changes in underlying

4.1.1 Notional amounts

A derivative usually has a notional amount, such as an amount of currency, number of shares or units of weight or volume, but does not require the holder or writer to invest or receive the notional amount at inception. However, this is not always the case: a derivative could require a fixed payment or payment of an amount that can change (but not proportionally with a change in the underlying) as a result of some future event that is unrelated to a notional amount. For example, a contract that requires a fixed payment of €1,000 if six-month LIBOR increases by 100 basis points is a derivative, but does not have a specified notional amount[168] (at least not in the conventional sense). A further example is shown below.

Example 17.8: Derivative containing no notional amount

XYZ enters into a contract that requires payment of $1,000 if ABC's share price increases by $5 or more during a six-month period; XYZ will receive $1,000 if the share price decreases by $5 or more during the same six-month period; no payment will be made if the price swing is less than $5 up or down.

The settlement amount changes with an underlying, ABC's share price, although there is no notional amount to determine the settlement amount. Instead, there is a payment provision that is based on changes in the underlying. Provided all the other characteristics of a derivative are present, which they are in this case, such an instrument is a derivative.[169]

4.1.2 Underlying variables

A derivative will always have at least one underlying variable. The definition (see 4 above) refers to the following examples, but this is not an exhaustive list:[170]

- specified interest rate;
- financial instrument price;
- commodity price;
- foreign exchange rate;
- index of prices or rates;
- credit rating; and
- credit index.

A contract to receive a royalty, often in exchange for the use of certain property that is not exchange traded, where the payment is based on the volume of related sales or service revenues and accounted for under IAS 18 (see Chapter 28) is not accounted for as a derivative.[171]

Derivatives that are based on sales volume are not necessarily excluded from the scope of IAS 39, especially where there is another (financial) underlying, as set out in the next example.

Example 17.9: Derivative containing two underlyings

Company XYZ, whose functional currency is the US dollar, sells products in France denominated in euros. XYZ enters into a contract with an investment bank to convert euros to US dollars at a fixed exchange rate. The contract requires XYZ to remit euros based on its sales volume in France in exchange for US dollars at a fixed exchange rate of 1.00.

The contract has two underlying variables, the foreign exchange rate and the volume of sales, no initial net investment, and a payment provision. Therefore it is a derivative.[172]

However, contracts that are linked to variables that might be considered non-financial, such as an entity's revenue, can sometimes cause particular interpretative problems.

4.1.3 Non-financial variables specific to one party to the contract

The definition of a derivative (see 4 above) refers to underlyings that are non-financial variables specific to one party to the contract. This reference was introduced by IFRS 4 to help determine whether or not a financial instrument is an insurance contract (see 3.3 above) – an insurance contract is likely to contain just such an underlying, for example the occurrence or non-occurrence of a fire that damages or destroys an asset of a party to the contract. Non-financial variables that are not specific to one party to the contract might include an index of earthquake losses in a particular region or an index of temperatures in a particular city.

A change in the fair value of a non-financial asset is specific to the owner if the fair value reflects not only changes in market prices for such assets (a financial variable) but also the condition of the specific non-financial asset held (a non-financial variable). For example, if a guarantee of the residual value of a specific car exposes the guarantor to the risk of changes in the car's physical condition, the change in that residual value is specific to the owner of the car.[173]

Prima facie, it is not clear whether the reference to non-financial variables specific to one party to the contract means that all instruments with such an underlying would fail to meet the definition of a derivative or only those contracts that are insurance contracts. The IFRIC considered this issue in the context of contracts indexed to an entity's revenue or EBITDA and initially came to a tentative conclusion that the exclusion was not restricted to insurance contracts.[174] However, that conclusion was later withdrawn and the IFRIC referred the issue to the IASB, recommending that the standard be amended to limit the exclusion to insurance contracts.[175] The IASB confirmed that it did intend for the exclusion to apply only to contracts that are within the scope of IFRS 4 and it plans to amend IAS 39 to reflect this in its annual improvements project.[176] Until the standard is amended, a legitimate case can be made for interpreting IAS 39 as the IFRIC tentatively did or as the IASB originally intended.

A further issue arises in that it is not always clear whether a variable is non-financial, although this question will become redundant if the IASB amends IAS 39 as it has agreed. This uncertainty can cause particular problems in accounting for features embedded in other instruments and is considered in more detail at 5.5 below.

Whilst it is tempting to regard an entity's revenue and EBITDA as financial variables, they are driven by a number of different factors many of which are clearly non-financial in nature, for example the general business risks faced by the entity. In addition, many of the drivers of EBITDA and revenue will be specific to that business, for example the location of the business, the nature of its goods or services and management actions. Before it changed direction and asked the IASB to amend IAS 39, the IFRIC had decided it was unlikely to reach a timely consensus on the question of whether these are financial or non-financial variables.[177]

The implications of the IASB's proposed changes could be significant. Clearly many more contracts (or features within non-derivative hybrid contracts) may meet the definition of a derivative and therefore be accounted for at fair value through profit or loss under IAS 39. However, in most cases, the underlying variable will not be one for which quoted prices are available, which will make the estimate of fair value particularly challenging. Furthermore, unless the derivative is linked to, and settled by delivery of, unquoted equity instruments (which is unlikely to be the case), those fair values are deemed to be reliably estimable (see Chapter 20 at 4.4).

Contracts with non-financial variables also arise in the gaming industry where a gaming institution takes a position against a customer (rather than providing services to manage the organisation of games between two or more parties). For example, a customer will pay a stake to a bookmaker such that the bookmaker is contractually obliged to pay the customer a specified amount in the event that the bet is a winning one, e.g. if the specified horse wins a given race. The underlying variable (the outcome of the race) is clearly non-financial in nature but it is unlikely to be specific to either party to the contract. Accordingly such contracts will typically be derivative financial instruments.[178]

4.2 Initial net investment

As set out at 4 above, one of the key characteristics of a derivative is that it has no initial net investment, or one that is smaller than would be required for other types of contracts that would be expected to have a similar response to changes in market factors.[179]

An option contract meets the definition because the premium is less than the investment that would be required to obtain the underlying financial instrument to which the option is linked.[180]

The implementation guidance to the original standard suggested that the purchase of a deep in the money call option would fail to satisfy the original 'little net investment' test if the premium paid was equal *or close to* the amount required to invest in the underlying instrument.[181] A strict reading of the standard would suggest that unless the premium was at least equal (as opposed to close) to the amount required to invest in the underlying, such a contract would now be deemed to exhibit the 'no or smaller net investment' characteristic. However, the implementation guidance on which Example 17.13 below is based explains that a contract is not a derivative if the initial net investment *approximates* the amount that an entity otherwise would be required to invest.[182] This may seem a somewhat esoteric analysis, but it illustrates the problems in defining the boundaries between different classes of instrument in a mixed attribute model.

Currency swaps sometimes require an exchange of different currencies of equal value at inception as in the following example.

Example 17.10: Currency swap – initial exchange of principal

Company A and Company B enter into a five year fixed-for-fixed currency swap on euros and US dollars. The current spot exchange rate is €1 per US$. The five year interest rate in the US is 8%, while the five year interest rate in Europe is 6%. On initiation of the swap, A pays €2,000 to B, which in return pays US$2,000 to A. During the swap's life, A and B make periodic interest payments to each other without netting. B pays 6% per year on the €2,000 it has received (€120 per year), while A pays 8% per year on the US$2,000 it has received (US$160 per year). On termination of the swap, the two parties again exchange the original principal amounts.

The currency swap is a derivative financial instrument since the contract involves a zero initial *net* investment (only an exchange of one currency for another of equal fair values), it has an underlying, and it will be settled at a future date.[183]

The following examples illustrate how to assess the initial net investment characteristic in various prepaid derivatives – these can provide guidance when assessing whether what appears to be a non-derivative instrument is actually a derivative.

Example 17.11: Prepaid interest rate swap (prepaid fixed leg)

Company S enters into a €1,000 notional amount five year pay-fixed, receive-variable interest rate swap. The interest rate of the variable part of the swap resets on a quarterly basis to three month LIBOR. The interest rate of the fixed part of the swap is 10% per annum. At inception of the swap S prepays its fixed obligation of €500 (€1,000 × 10% × 5 years), discounted using market interest rates, while retaining the right to receive the LIBOR based interest payments on the €1,000 over the life of the swap.

The initial net investment in the swap is significantly less than the notional amount on which the variable payments under the variable leg will be calculated and therefore requires an initial net investment that is smaller than would be required for other types of contracts that would be expected to have a similar response to changes in market conditions, such as a variable rate bond. It therefore exhibits characteristic (b) at 4 above. Even though S has no future performance obligation, the ultimate settlement of the contract is at a future date and its value changes in response to changes in LIBOR. Accordingly, it is a derivative.[184]

Example 17.12: Prepaid interest rate swap (prepaid floating leg)

Instead of the transactions in Example 17.11, Company S enters into a €1,000 notional amount five year pay-variable, receive-fixed interest rate swap. The variable leg of the swap resets on a quarterly basis to three month LIBOR. The fixed interest payments under the swap are calculated as 10% of the notional amount, i.e. €100 per year. By agreement with the counterparty, S prepays and discharges its obligation under the variable leg of the swap at inception by paying a fixed amount determined according to current market rates, while retaining the right to receive the fixed interest payments of €100 per year.

The cash inflows under the contract are equivalent to those of a financial instrument with a fixed annuity stream since S knows it will receive €100 per year over the life of the swap. Therefore, all else being equal, the initial investment in the contract should equal that of other financial instruments consisting of fixed annuities. Thus, the initial net investment in the pay-variable, receive-fixed interest rate swap is equal to the investment required in a non-derivative contract that has a similar response to changes in market conditions. For this reason, the instrument does not exhibit characteristic (b) above and is not a derivative.[185]

Example 17.13: Prepaid forward purchase of shares

Company S also enters into a forward contract to purchase 100 shares in T in one year. The current share price is £50 per share and the one year forward price £55. S is required to prepay the forward contract at inception with a £5,000 payment.

The initial investment in the forward contract of £5,000 is less than the notional amount applied to the underlying, 100 shares at the forward price of £55 per share, i.e. £5,500. However, the initial net investment approximates the investment that would be required for other types of contracts that would be expected to have a similar response to changes in market factors because T's shares could be purchased at inception for the same price of £50. Accordingly, the prepaid forward does not exhibit characteristic (b) above and is not a derivative.[186]

The conclusions in Examples 17.11 and 17.12 above are fundamentally different for what, on the face of it, appear to be very similar transactions. The key difference is that in Example 17.11 all possible cash flow variances are eliminated and, consequently, the resulting cash flows exhibit the characteristics of a simple non-derivative instrument, i.e. an amortising loan.

Many derivative instruments, such as futures contracts and exchange traded written options, require margin payments. The margin payment is not part of the initial net investment in a derivative, but is a form of collateral for the counterparty or clearing-house and may take the form of cash, securities, or other specified assets, typically liquid assets. They are separate assets that are accounted for separately.[187]

4.3 Future settlement

The third characteristic is that settlement takes place at a future date. Sometimes, a contract will require gross cash settlement. However, as illustrated in the next example, it makes no difference whether the future settlements are gross or net.

Example 17.14: Interest rate swap – gross or net settlement

Company ABC is considering entering into an interest rate swap with a counterparty, XYZ. The proposed terms are that ABC pays a fixed rate of 8% and receives a variable amount based on three month LIBOR, reset on a quarterly basis; the fixed and variable amounts are determined based on a €1,000 notional amount; ABC and XYZ do not exchange the notional amount and ABC pays or receives a net cash amount each quarter based on the difference between 8% and three month LIBOR. Alternatively, settlement may be on a gross basis.

The contract meets the definition of a derivative regardless of whether there is net or gross settlement because its value changes in response to changes in an underlying variable (LIBOR), there is no initial net investment and settlements occur at future dates – it makes no difference whether ABC and XYZ actually make the interest payments to each other (gross settlement) or settle on a net basis.[188]

The definition of a derivative also includes contracts that are settled gross by delivery of the underlying item, e.g. a forward contract to purchase a fixed rate debt instrument. An entity may have a contract to buy or sell a non-financial item that can be settled net, e.g. a contract to buy or sell a commodity at a fixed price at a future date; if that contract is within the scope of IAS 39 (see 3.9 above) the question of whether or not it is a derivative will be assessed in the same way as a financial instrument that may be settled gross.[189]

Expiry of an option at its maturity is a form of settlement even though there is no additional exchange of consideration. Therefore, even if an option is not expected to be exercised, e.g. because it is significantly 'out of the money', it can still be a derivative.[190] Such an option will have some value, albeit small, because it still offers the opportunity for gain if it becomes 'in the money' before expiry even if such a possibility is remote – the more remote the possibility, the lower its value.

4.4 Common examples of derivatives

The following table provides examples of contracts that normally qualify as derivatives. The list is not exhaustive – any contract that has an underlying may be a derivative. Moreover, as set out at 3 above, even if an instrument meets the definition of a derivative, it may not fall within the scope of IAS 39.

Type of contract	*Main pricing-settlement underlying variable*
Interest rate swap	Interest rates
Currency swap (foreign exchange swap)	Currency rates
Commodity swap	Commodity prices
Equity swap	Equity prices (equity of another entity)
Credit swap	Credit rating, credit index, or credit price
Total return swap	Total fair value of the reference asset and interest rates
Purchased or written bond option (call or put)	Interest rates
Purchased or written currency option (call or put)	Currency rates
Purchased or written commodity option (call or put)	Commodity prices
Purchased or written stock option (call or put)	Equity prices (equity of another entity)

Type of contract	*Main pricing-settlement underlying variable*
Interest rate futures linked to government debt (treasury futures)	Interest rates
Currency futures	Currency rates
Commodity futures	Commodity prices
Interest rate forward linked to government debt (treasury forward)	Interest rates
Currency forward	Currency rates
Commodity forward	Commodity prices
Equity forward	Equity prices (equity of another entity)[191]

4.5 In-substance derivatives

The implementation guidance explains that the accounting should follow the substance of arrangements. In particular, non-derivative transactions should be aggregated and treated as a derivative when, in substance, the transactions result in a derivative. Indicators of this would include:

- they are entered into at the same time and in contemplation of one another;
- they have the same counterparty;
- they relate to the same risk; and
- there is no apparent economic need or substantive business purpose for structuring the transactions separately that could not also have been accomplished in a single transaction.[192]

The application of this guidance is illustrated in the following example.

Example 17.15: In-substance derivative – offsetting loans

Company A makes a five year fixed rate loan to Company B, while at the same time B makes a five year variable rate loan for the same amount to A. There are no transfers of principal at inception of the two loans, since A and B have a netting agreement.

The combined contractual effect of the loans is the equivalent of an interest rate swap arrangement, i.e. there is an underlying variable, no initial net investment, and future settlement. This meets the definition of a derivative.

This would be the case even if there was no netting agreement, because the definition of a derivative instrument does not require net settlement (see Example 17.14 at 4.3 above).[193]

The analysis above would be equally applicable if the loans were in different currencies – such an arrangement could synthesise a cross-currency interest rate swap and should be accounted for as a derivative if that is its substance.

4.6 Regular way contracts

A regular way purchase or sale is a purchase or sale of a financial asset under a contract whose terms require delivery of the asset within the time frame established generally by regulation or convention in the marketplace concerned.[194] Such contracts give rise to a fixed price commitment between trade date and settlement date that meets the definition of a derivative. However, because of the short duration of the commitments, they are not accounted for as a derivative but in accordance with special accounting rules. These requirements are discussed in Chapter 18 at 3.2.[195]

5 EMBEDDED DERIVATIVES

An embedded derivative is a component of a hybrid or combined instrument that also includes a non-derivative host contract; it has the effect that some of the cash flows of the combined instrument vary in a similar way to a stand-alone derivative. In other words, it causes some or all of the cash flows that otherwise would be required by the contract to be modified according to a specified interest rate, financial instrument price, commodity price, foreign exchange rate, index of prices or rates, credit rating or credit index, or other underlying variable (provided in the case of a non-financial variable that the variable is not specific to a party to the contract).[196]

The concept of embedded derivatives is one of the most difficult for many preparers and users of financial statements to understand, a fact that even the IASB has acknowledged.[197] Some may regard it as a little unfortunate, therefore, that in revising IAS 39 in 2003 the IASB's main response was to allow the greater use of fair value accounting for financial instruments containing embedded derivatives, rather than to ease the existing requirements (although there was one principle exception – see 5.1.2 A below).

The IASB introduced the concept of embedded derivatives because it believes that entities should not be able to circumvent the accounting requirements for derivatives merely by embedding a derivative in a non-derivative financial instrument or other contract, e.g. a commodity forward in a debt instrument. In other words, it is chiefly an anti-abuse measure designed to apply 'derivative accounting' to those derivatives that are 'hidden' in other contracts.[198]

Common examples of contracts that can contain embedded derivatives include non-derivative financial instruments (especially debt instruments), leases, insurance contracts as well as contracts for the supply of goods or services. In fact, they may occur in all sorts of unsuspected locations. Normal sale or purchase contracts (see 3.9 above) can also contain embedded derivatives. This is an important difference from US GAAP, under which a contract for the sale or purchase of a non-financial item that can be settled net cannot be treated as a normal sale or purchase at all if it contains an embedded pricing feature that is not clearly and closely related to the host contract – instead the whole contract would be accounted for as a derivative.[199]

In the basis for conclusions to IAS 39, the IASB asserts that, in principle, *all* embedded derivatives ought to be accounted for separately, but explains that, as a practical expedient, they should not be where they are regarded as 'closely related' to their host contracts. In those cases, it is believed less likely that the derivative was embedded to achieve a desired accounting result.[200]

Accordingly, only where the following conditions are met should an embedded derivative be separated from the host contract and accounted for separately:

(a) the economic characteristics and risks of the embedded derivative are not closely related to those of the host contract;

(b) a separate instrument with the same terms as the embedded derivative would meet the definition of a derivative; and

(c) the hybrid (combined) instrument is not measured at fair value with changes in fair value recognised in profit or loss.[201]

If any of these conditions are not met, the embedded derivative should not be accounted for separately,[202] i.e. an entity is prohibited from separating an embedded derivative that is closely related to its host contract. The process is similar, although not identical, to that applied when separating the equity element of a compound instrument under IAS 32 (see Chapter 19 at 4).

The accounting treatment for a separated embedded derivative (examples of which are included throughout this section) is the same as for a standalone derivative. As noted at 4 above, and 7.1 below, such an instrument (actually, in this case, a component of an instrument) will normally be recorded on the balance sheet at fair value with all changes in value being recognised in profit or loss (although there are some exceptions, e.g. embedded derivatives may be designated as a hedging instrument in an effective hedge relationship in the same way as standalone derivatives – see Chapter 21 at 2.1.1).

A derivative that is attached to a financial instrument but is contractually transferable independently of that instrument, or has a different counterparty from that instrument, is not an embedded derivative, but a separate financial instrument.[203]

Where an entity is unable to measure an embedded derivative that is required to be separated from its host, either on acquisition or subsequently, the entire contract is designated at fair value through profit or loss.[204] (This is a subtle change introduced by way of the fair value option amendments, covered at 7.1 below – previously such an instrument would be treated as held for trading.[205]) Even if the embedded derivative's fair value cannot be determined reliably on the basis of its terms and conditions (for example if it is based on an unquoted equity instrument – see Chapter 20 at 4.4), if the fair values of both the hybrid (combined) instrument and host can be determined, it may be determined indirectly as the difference between the two.[206]

5.1 The meaning of 'closely related'

The standard does not define what is meant by 'closely related'. Instead, it illustrates what was intended by providing a series of situations where the embedded derivative is, or is not, regarded as closely related to the host. Making this determination can prove very challenging, not least because the illustrations do not always seem to be consistent with each other. This guidance is considered in the remainder of this subsection.

5.1.1 Financial instrument hosts

Where a host contract has no stated or predetermined maturity and represents a residual interest in the net assets of an entity, its economic characteristics and risks are those of an equity instrument – therefore, an embedded derivative would need to possess equity characteristics related to the same entity to be regarded as closely related. More commonly, if the host is not an equity instrument and meets the definition of a financial instrument, then its economic characteristics and risks are those of a debt instrument.[207] The application of these principles to debt hosts is considered at A to H below and at J for equity hosts; I deals with instruments that may be debt or equity hosts.

A Foreign currency monetary items

A monetary item denominated in a currency other than an entity's functional currency is accounted for under IAS 21 – *The Effects of Changes in Foreign Exchange Rates* – with foreign currency gains and losses recognised in profit or loss. For this reason, the embedded foreign currency derivative is considered closely related to the host and is not separated. This also applies where the embedded derivative in a host debt instrument provides a stream either of principal or of interest payments denominated in a foreign currency (e.g. a dual currency bond).[208]

B Interest rate indices

Many debt instruments contain embedded interest rate indices that can change the amount of interest that would otherwise be paid or received. One of the simplest examples would be a floating rate loan whereby interest is paid quarterly based on three month LIBOR. More complex examples might include the following:

- inverse floater – coupons are paid at a fixed rate minus LIBOR;
- levered inverse floater – as above but a multiplier greater than 1.0 is applied to the resulting coupon;
- delevered floater – coupons lag overall movements in a specified rate, e.g. coupons equal a proportion of the ten year constant maturity treasuries rate plus a fixed premium; or
- range floater – interest is paid at a fixed rate but only for each day in a given period that LIBOR is within a stated range.[209]

In such cases the embedded derivative is closely related to the host debt instrument unless:

(a) the combined instrument can be settled in such a way that the holder would not recover substantially all of its recognised investment; or
(b) the embedded derivative could at least double the holder's initial rate of return on the host contract and could result in a rate of return that is at least twice what the market return would be for a contract with the same terms as the host contract.[210]

If a holder is permitted, but not required, to settle the combined instrument in a manner such that it does not recover substantially all of its recognised investment, e.g. puttable debt, condition (a) is not satisfied and the embedded derivative is not separated.[211]

To meet condition (b), the embedded derivative must be able to double the initial return *and* result in a rate of return that is at least twice what would be expected for a similar contract at the time it takes effect. If it meets only one, but not the other, part of this condition the derivative is regarded as closely related to the host. Therefore, the derivative embedded in a simple variable rate loan would be considered closely related to the host as it would not meet the second part.

C Term extension and similar call, put and prepayment options in debt instruments

The application guidance explains that a call, put or prepayment option embedded in a host debt instrument is closely related to the host instrument if, on each exercise date, the option's exercise price is approximately equal to the debt instrument's amortised cost; otherwise it is not regarded as closely related.[212] (There is no elaboration on what is meant by the term 'approximately equal' and so judgment will need to be applied.)

It also says that an option or automatic provision to extend the remaining term to maturity of a debt instrument is not closely related to the host unless, at the time of the extension, there is a concurrent adjustment to the approximate current market rate of interest.[213]

Taken in isolation the above two paragraphs appear reasonably straightforward to apply. However, in some situations, they are contradictory as set out in the following example.

Example 17.16: Extension and prepayment options

Company Z borrows €1,000 from Bank A on which it is required to pay €50 per annum interest. Under the terms of the borrowing agreement, Z is required to repay €1,000 in three year's time unless, at repayment date, it exercises an option to extend the term of the borrowing for a further two years. If this option is exercised €50 interest per annum is payable for the additional term.

Company Z also borrows €1,000 from Bank B on which it is required to pay €50 per annum interest. Under the terms of this borrowing agreement, Z is required to repay €1,000 in five year's time unless, at the end of three years, it exercises an option to redeem the borrowing for €1,000.

It can be seen that in all practical respects these two instruments are identical – the only difference is the way in which the terms of the embedded options are expressed. In the first case the guidance indicates that the (term extension) option is not closely related to the debt as there is no concurrent adjustment to market interest rates. However, in the second case the (prepayment) option *is* considered closely related provided the amortised cost of the liability would be approximately €1,000, the exercise price of the settlement option, at the end of year three (which it should be).

For put, call and prepayment options, there is a further complication that the determination as to whether or not the option is closely related depends on the amortised cost of the instrument. It is not clear whether this reference is to the amortised cost of the host instrument on the assumption that the option is separated or the amortised cost of the entire instrument on the assumption that the option is not separated – as can be seen in Chapter 20 at 5.2, the existence of such options can affect that amortised cost, especially for a portfolio of instruments. Although one trade body has published guidance explaining that where early repayment fees are included in the calculation of effective interest, the prepayment option is likely to be closely related to the loan,[214] entities are largely left to apply their own judgment to assess which appears the most appropriate in the specific circumstances.

In the context of its annual improvements project, the IASB has identified another interpretative difficulty that can arise in assessing whether prepayment options are closely related to the host debt instrument. Some loan agreements permit the borrower to prepay the loan but the borrower is charged a penalty if the option is exercised. Where the prepayment penalty compensates the lender for loss of interest, for example from origination of the loan to the exercise of the prepayment option, the guidance on interest rate indices at B above would suggest that the embedded prepayment option is closely related. However, the guidance on prepayment options would suggest it is often not closely related. The IASB plans to amend the application guidance to make it clear that these prepayment penalties are evaluated as interest rate indices thereby removing this conflict.[215]

From the perspective of the issuer of a convertible debt instrument with an embedded call or put option feature, the assessment of whether the call or put option is closely related to the host debt instrument is made before separating the equity element under IAS 32.[216] This provides a specific relaxation from the general guidance on prepayment options above because, for accounting purposes, separate accounting for the equity component results in a discount on recognition of the liability component (see Chapter 19 at 4.3) which means that the amortised cost and exercise price are unlikely to approximate each other for much of the term of the instrument.

An embedded prepayment option in an interest-only or principal-only strip is regarded as closely related to the host contract provided the host contract (i) initially resulted from separating the right to receive contractual cash flows of a financial instrument that, in and of itself, did not contain an embedded derivative, and (ii) does not contain any terms not present in the original host debt contract.[217] Again this is a specific relaxation from the general guidance on prepayment options above.

If an entity issues a debt instrument and the holder writes a call option on the debt instrument to a third party, the issuer regards the call option as extending the term to maturity of the debt instrument provided it can be required to participate in or facilitate the remarketing of the debt instrument as a result of the call option being exercised.[218] Such a component is presumably considered to represent part of a hybrid financial instrument contract rather than a separate instrument in its own right (see 5 above).

D Interest rate floors and caps

An embedded floor or cap on the interest rate on a debt instrument is closely related to the host debt instrument, provided the cap is at or above the market rate of interest, and the floor is at or below the market rate of interest, when the instrument is issued (in other words it needs to be out of the money), and the cap or floor is not leveraged in relation to the host instrument.[219]

The standard does not clarify what is meant by 'market rate of interest', or whether the cap (floor) should be considered as a single derivative or a series of caplets (floorlets) to be evaluated separately. Where the cap (floor) is at a constant amount throughout the term of the debt we would expect entities to compare the cap (floor) rate with the current floating rate at inception of the contract to determine whether the embedded derivative is closely related.

We do not believe it is necessary for both a cap *and* a floor to be present to be considered closely related. For example, a cap (or floor) on the coupon paid on a debt instrument without a corresponding floor (or cap) could be regarded as closely related to the host provided it was above (or below) the market rate of interest on origination.

E Inflation linked debt

For some entities (and governments) it is quite common to issue inflation linked debt instruments, i.e. where interest and/or principal payments are linked to, say, a consumer price index. The only guidance in IAS 39 relating to embedded inflation linked features is provided in the context of leases (see 5.1.3 B below). If that guidance is accepted as applying to finance leases, it should also apply to debt instruments because finance leases result in assets and liabilities that are, in substance, no different to debt instruments (see 2.2.4 above). Further, in much finance theory, either real (applied to current prices) or nominal (applied to inflation adjusted prices) interest rates are used, suggesting a strong link between inflation and interest rates. Finally, a government or central bank will generally raise short-term interest rates as inflation rises and reduce rates as inflation recedes, which also suggests a close relationship between the two.

Therefore, we believe it would often be appropriate to treat the embedded derivative in inflation-linked debt as equivalent to an interest rate index and apply the guidance at B above to determine whether the index is regarded as closely related to the debt. Typically, the index will be closely related to the debt where it is based on inflation in an economic environment in which the bond is issued/denominated and is not significantly leveraged in relation to the debt.

In the context of their ongoing discussions on hedging components of risk (see Chapter 21 at 2.2.1) the IFRIC staff have expressed a view on this issue. In their opinion it would be appropriate to treat the embedded derivative in inflation-linked debt as closely related in economic environments where interest rates are mainly set so as to meet inflation targets as evidenced by strong long-run correlation between nominal interest rates and inflation. In such jurisdictions they considered the characteristics and risks of the inflation embedded derivative to be closely related to the host debt contract.[220] Currently, it is unclear whether the IFRIC itself will address this question, either formally or informally.

F Commodity and equity linked interest and principal payments

Equity-indexed or commodity-indexed interest or principal payments embedded in a host debt instrument, i.e. where the amount of interest or principal is indexed to the value of an equity instrument or commodity (e.g. gold), are not closely related to the host debt instrument because the risks inherent in the embedded derivative are dissimilar to those of the host.[221] An example of such an instrument is given in Example 17.24 at 7.2.1 below.

G Credit linked notes

Credit derivatives are sometimes embedded in a host debt instrument whereby one party (the 'beneficiary') transfers the credit risk of a particular reference asset, which it may not own, to another party (the 'guarantor'). Such credit derivatives allow the guarantor to assume the credit risk associated with the reference asset without directly owning it.

Whilst the economic characteristics of a debt instrument will include credit risk, should the embedded derivative be a credit derivative linked to the credit standing of an entity other than the issuer, it would not regarded as closely related to the host debt instrument.[222]

In practice, there exists a wide variety of debt instruments that transfer the credit risk of certain referenced assets. Although many will contain an embedded derivative requiring separation, it is not necessarily correct to assume that they all will. For example, an entity (commonly a special purpose entity) may issue debt instruments that are secured on a group of assets that the entity is required to own, such as a portfolio of trade receivables, and which have recourse only to those assets. In such a case the credit risk embedded in the debt instrument is effectively that of the issuing entity through the ownership of the reference assets and accordingly is considered closely related.

H Convertible and exchangeable debt instruments

An equity conversion feature embedded in a convertible debt instrument is not closely related to the host debt instrument from the perspective of the holder of the instrument (from the issuer's perspective, the equity conversion option is often an equity instrument and excluded from the scope of IAS 39 – see Chapter 19 at 4.3).[223]

In some instances, venture capital entities provide subordinated loans on terms that they are entitled to receive shares if and when the borrowing entity lists its shares on a stock exchange, as illustrated in the following example.

Example 17.17: Equity kicker

A venture capital investor, Company V, provides a subordinated loan to Company A and agrees that, in addition to interest and repayment of principal, if A lists its shares on a stock exchange, V will be entitled to receive shares in A free of charge or at a very low price (an 'equity kicker'). As a result of this feature, interest on the loan is lower than it would otherwise be. The loan is not measured at fair value with changes in fair value recognised in profit or loss.

The economic characteristics and risks of an equity return are not closely related to those of the host debt instrument. The equity kicker meets the definition of a derivative because it has a value that changes in response to the change in the price of A's shares, requires only a relatively small initial net investment, and is settled at a future date. It does not matter that the right to receive shares is contingent upon the borrower's future listing.[224]

Similarly, the derivative embedded in a bond that is convertible (or exchangeable) into equity shares of a third party will not be closely related to the host debt instrument – in this case, both from the point of view of the holder and of the issuer.

I Puttable instruments

An example of a hybrid contract is a financial instrument that gives the holder a right to put it back to the issuer in exchange for an amount that varies on the basis of the change in an equity or commodity index (a 'puttable instrument'). Where the host is a debt instrument, the embedded derivative, the indexed principal payment, cannot be regarded as closely related to that debt instrument. Because the principal payment can increase and decrease, the embedded derivative is a non-option derivative whose value is indexed to the underlying variable (see 5.2 below).[225]

In the case of a puttable instrument that can be put back at any time for cash equal to a proportionate share of the net asset value of an entity (such as units of an open-ended mutual fund or some unit-linked investment products), the effect of separating an embedded derivative and accounting for each component is to measure the combined instrument at the redemption amount that is payable at the balance sheet date if the holder were to exercise its right to put the instrument back to the issuer.[226]

These instruments were brought into focus by a SIC project. The SIC's conclusions, which were consistent with the treatment described in the previous paragraph, resulted in the publication of a draft interpretation.[227] However, this was never finalised and the issue was subsequently absorbed into the 'improvements' project. The accounting treatment noted above is controversial because it means that under IFRS a unit trust or similar vehicle is effectively required to account for such instruments at fair value with all changes reported in profit or loss and, as a result, it may report no equity and no profit. However, the IASB has now issued proposals to amend IAS 32 such that these instruments would be classified as equity by the issuer – see Chapter 19 at 3.2.2 C.

IAS 39 is not entirely clear whether a similar treatment should apply to the holder of such an instrument. If it did it would mean that all changes in the fair value of an entity's investment in a unit trust would be recognised in profit or loss, even if it were classified as available-for-sale. However, this seems entirely wrong. To the extent that anyone has a residual interest in the net assets of a unit trust, it is the unit-holders. Consequently, a more intuitive view of the investment would be as an equity instrument host with an embedded put option, exercisable at net asset value. Further, because net asset value will approximate fair value, the embedded derivative would have little or no value.

The original SIC project dealt only with the accounting from the point of view of the issuer and, in discussing puttable instruments that vary on the basis of the change in an equity or commodity index, paragraph AG31 of IAS 39 refers only to the treatment by the issuer of such an instrument. This suggests that a different analysis is permissible when viewing the instrument from the perspective of the holder. Further support for this can be found in the definition of loans and receivables: as noted at 7.3 below, an interest in a pool of assets that are not loans or receivables (such as a mutual fund) is not considered to be a loan or receivable.[228] This also suggests the host might validly be considered an equity instrument from the point of view of the holder.

Therefore, we believe entities can account for unit trust and similar investments as available-for-sale equity investments whilst recognising fair value gains and losses in equity.

A related issue has now been considered by the IFRIC, namely the treatment by the holder of instruments that are puttable at an amount other than fair value (for example a proportion of the book value of net assets determined under IFRS or local GAAP) but which otherwise have characteristics and risks that are similar to an equity instrument, such as discretionary distributions. Although the IFRIC did not take the issue onto its agenda, it indicated that the requirement for the issuer to apply IAS 32 and the holder to apply IAS 39 means that their respective accounting treatments need not necessarily be symmetrical. Accordingly, it may be appropriate for the holder to regard the host as an equity, not debt, instrument. Of course, in this case, the put option would have a non-zero fair value and should be accounted for separately as an embedded derivative.[229]

J Callable equity instruments

An equity instrument containing an embedded call option enabling the issuer to reacquire that equity instrument at a specified price is not closely related to the host equity instrument from the perspective of the holder.[230]

The potential effect of this guidance is illustrated below.

Example 17.18: Callable preference share

Company J issues preference shares for their par value of $1,000. The shares carry the right to a discretionary 8% cumulative annual dividend, although if this is not paid J is prevented from declaring a dividend on its ordinary shares, and they are redeemable at the sole option of Company J on the fifth anniversary of issue and each fifth anniversary thereafter. The redemption amount is the par value of the shares plus any unpaid dividends. Although it is not foreseen that J will choose not to pay these dividends, from J's perspective the shares are presented as equity (see Chapter 19 at 3.2.1).

On issuance, Company R acquires the preference shares and classifies them as available-for-sale assets (rather than at fair value through profit or loss, the only other possible classification for an investment in an equity instrument). Therefore R accounts for J's embedded call (redemption) option separately as an embedded derivative. The embedded option will have a fair value that, from R's perspective, can only be negative because it is a written option. The host instrument will be equivalent to an 8% perpetual preference share with no call (or redemption) option and will have an initial fair value in excess of the $1,000 purchase price of the hybrid.

If there is no significant change in J's credit risk or the risk of J choosing not to exercise its discretion to pay dividends, a fall in interest rates will cause the value of the host instrument to increase. This results from the present value of the expected dividend payments, discounted at the lower interest rate, being higher. However, as the possible redemption date approaches, the value of the hybrid instrument as a whole should not significantly exceed the par value of the shares because J can always choose to settle the combined instrument at that par value.

Therefore, if the fair value of the host investment increases because of falls in interest rates, the negative fair value of the embedded option will also increase, especially as the redemption date approaches. Chapter 20 explains how different types of financial instrument are accounted for under IAS 39, but in simple terms, increases in the fair value of an available for sale asset are recognised and recorded in equity, whereas changes in the fair value of a derivative (including an embedded derivative) are recorded in profit or loss. In this case any such gains and losses arising on the same instrument (which in very broad terms will offset) cannot be offset in the financial statements, creating a potentially significant mismatch.

If R had designated the shares at fair value through profit or loss, it would not have accounted separately for the embedded derivative.

From the issuer's perspective, the call option is an equity instrument provided it meets the conditions for that classification under IAS 32, in which case it is excluded from the scope of IAS 39.[231] This reaffirms an important point – if a financial instrument (including its embedded features) satisfies the definition of an equity instrument from the point of view of the issuer, it cannot contain an embedded derivative requiring separation for accounting purposes.

5.1.2 Contracts for the sale of goods or services

A Foreign currency derivatives

An embedded foreign currency derivative in a contract that is not a financial instrument, such as a contract for the purchase or sale of a non-financial item where the price is denominated in a foreign currency, is closely related to the host contract provided it is not leveraged, does not contain an option feature and requires payments denominated in one of the following currencies:

(i) the functional currency of any substantial party to the contract – see I below;

(ii) the currency in which the price of the related good or service that is acquired or delivered is routinely denominated in commercial transactions around the world (such as the US dollar for crude oil transactions) – see II below; or

(iii) a currency that is commonly used in contracts to purchase or sell non-financial items in the economic environment in which the transaction takes place (e.g. a relatively stable and liquid currency that is commonly used in local business transactions or external trade) – see III below.

Therefore, in such cases the embedded foreign currency derivative is not accounted for separately from the host contract.[232]

I Functional currency of counterparty

In principle, the assessment of exception (i) above is straightforward. In practice, however, the functional currency of the counterparty to a contract will not always be known with certainty and, in some cases, can be a somewhat subjective assessment even for the counterparty's management (assuming the counterparty is a corporate entity) – see Chapter 10 at 2.5 and 3.1. Consequently, entities will need to demonstrate they have taken appropriate steps to make a reasonable judgment as to their counterparties' functional currencies. For example, it would often be appropriate to assume that an entity operating in a single country has that country's currency as its functional currency. However, if there were indicators to the contrary these would have to be taken into account.

Another practical problem that arises in applying this exception is identifying which parties to a contract are 'substantial'. IAS 39 provides no further guidance, but it is generally considered that such a party should be one that is acting as principal to the contract. Therefore if, as part of a contract, a parent provides a performance guarantee in respect of services to be provided by its operating subsidiary and the guarantee is not expected to be called upon, the parent would not normally be considered a substantial party to the contract. Particular care is necessary when assessing a contract under which one party subcontracts an element of the work to another entity under common control, say a fellow subsidiary with a different functional currency, although in most cases it will only be the primary contractor that is considered a substantial party.

II Routinely denominated in commercial transactions

For the purposes of exception (ii) above, the currency must be used for similar transactions all around the world, not just in one local area. For example, if cross-border transactions in natural gas in North America are routinely denominated in US dollars and such transactions are routinely denominated in euros in Europe, neither the US dollar nor the euro is a currency in which the good or service is routinely denominated in international commerce.[233] Accordingly, the number of items to which this will apply will be limited – in practice it will be mainly commodities that are traded in, say, US dollars throughout much of the world. Examples include crude oil, jet fuel, certain base metals (including aluminium, copper and nickel) and some precious metals (including gold, silver and platinum). One other notable item might be wide-bodied aircraft where it appears that Boeing and Airbus, the two major manufacturers, routinely denominate sales in US dollars.

III Commonly used currencies

The addition of (iii) above represented the only substantive change to the embedded derivative requirements introduced into the December 2003 version of IAS 39. The IASB noted that the requirement to separate embedded foreign currency derivatives may be burdensome for entities that operate in economies in which business contracts denominated in a foreign currency are common. For example, entities domiciled in small countries may find it convenient to denominate business contracts with entities from other small countries in an internationally liquid currency (such as the US dollar, euro or Yen) rather than the local currency of any party to the transaction. Also, an entity operating in a hyperinflationary economy may use a price list in a hard currency to protect against inflation, for example an entity that has a foreign operation in a hyperinflationary economy that denominates local contracts in the functional currency of the parent.[234] Therefore the change was welcomed by many, especially those operating in small or developing economies.

Unfortunately, however, the assessment of whether or not a particular currency meets this requirement in a particular situation has not been straightforward in practice and it has recently reached the attention of the IFRIC. Following its May 2007 meeting, the IFRIC was minded not to deal with the topic because any guidance it could provide would be more in the nature of application guidance rather than an interpretation and that judgment should be applied in each case. It did note, however, that entities should:[235]

- identify where the transaction takes place.

  This is not as straightforward as it might seem. For example, consider a Polish company that manufactures components in Poland and exports them to a third party in the Czech Republic. Should the sale of components be regarded as a transaction occurring in Poland or in the Czech Republic?[236] It is likely that the Polish company would regard it as occurring in Poland and the Czech entity in the Czech Republic, but this not entirely beyond debate; and

- identify currencies that are commonly used in the economic environment in which the transaction takes place.

  Entities need to address what the population of transactions in the economic environment is. Some might suggest that transactions to which (i) or (ii) apply should be excluded, although this is not a view shared by the IFRIC staff which considered that all transactions should be included.[237]

  Entities should also consider what an economic environment is. The guidance on which Example 17.19 below is based implies that a country could be an economic environment. The references to local business transactions and to external trade in (iii) above suggest that other examples of economic environment are the external trade or internal trade environment of the country in which the transaction takes place. The question remains as to whether there could be other economic environments, for example the luxury goods market in a country. Depending on the view taken, a different treatment could arise.[238]

In this context, the IFRIC was also asked to provide guidance on how to interpret the term 'common', but understandably was reluctant to do so.[239]

The fact that the IFRIC did not intend to address the issue was seen as a little disappointing and a number of respondents suggested the issue be referred to the IASB for clarification. At its subsequent meeting in July 2007, the IFRIC postponed making a final decision and directed the staff to perform further analysis.[240] In September 2007, the IFRIC decided to refer the matter to the IASB for clarification and directed its staff to develop proposed revisions to the standard.[241]

IV Examples and other practical issues

The application of the guidance above is illustrated in the examples below.

Example 17.19: Oil contract denominated in Swiss francs

A Norwegian company agrees to sell oil to a company in France. The oil contract is denominated in Swiss francs, although oil contracts are routinely denominated in US dollars in international commerce and Norwegian Krone are commonly used in contracts to purchase or sell non-financial items in Norway. Neither company carries out any significant activities in Swiss francs.

The Norwegian company should regard the supply contract as a host contract with an embedded foreign currency forward to purchase Swiss francs. The French company should regard it as a host contract with an embedded foreign currency forward to sell Swiss francs.[242]

The implementation guidance on which this example is based does not state in which currency the host contract should be denominated. (This will also be the currency of the second leg of the embedded forward contract). The currency should be chosen so that the host does not contain an embedded derivative requiring separation. In theory, therefore, it could be Norwegian Krone or euro (the functional currencies of the parties to the contract) or US dollars (the currency in which oil contracts are routinely denominated in international commerce). Typically, however, an entity will use its own functional currency to define the terms of the host contract and embedded derivative.

A second issue arises where, commonly, the terms of the contract require delivery and payment on different dates. For example, assume the contract was entered into on 1 January, with delivery scheduled for 30 June and payment required by 30 September. Should the embedded derivative be considered a six-month forward contract maturing on 30 June, or a nine-month forward contract maturing on 30 September? Conceptually at least, the latter approach seems more satisfactory, for example because it does not introduce into the notional terms cash flows at a point in time (i.e. on delivery) when none exist in the combined contract. In practice, however, the former approach is used far more often and is not without technical merit. For example, it avoids the recognition of an embedded foreign currency derivative between the delivery and payment dates on what would be a foreign currency denominated monetary item, something that is prohibited by IAS 39 (see 5.1.1 A above).

Example 17.20: Oil contract, denominated in US dollars and containing a leveraged foreign exchange payment

Company A, whose functional currency is the euro, enters into a contract with Company B, whose functional currency is the Norwegian Krone, to purchase oil in six months for US$1,000. The host oil contract will be settled by making and taking delivery in the normal course of business and is not accounted for as a financial instrument because it qualifies as a normal sale or purchase contract (see 3.9 above). The oil contract includes a leveraged foreign exchange provision whereby the parties, in addition to the provision of, and payment for, oil will exchange an amount equal to the fluctuation in the exchange rate of the US dollar and Norwegian Krone applied to a notional amount of US$100,000.

The payment of US$1,000 under the host oil contract can be viewed as a foreign currency derivative because the dollar is neither Company A nor B's functional currency. However, it would not be separated as the US dollar is the currency in which crude oil transactions are routinely denominated in international commerce.

The leveraged foreign exchange provision is in addition to the required payment for the oil transaction. It is unrelated to the host oil contract and is therefore separated and accounted for as an embedded derivative.[243]

In practice, all but the simplest contracts will contain other terms and features that can often make it much more difficult to isolate the precise terms of the embedded foreign currency derivative (and the host). For example, a clause may allow a purchaser to terminate the contract in return for making a specified compensation payment to the supplier – the standard offers little guidance as to whether such a feature should be included within the terms of the host, of the embedded foreign currency derivative or, possibly, of both. Other problematic terms can include options to defer the specified delivery date and options to order additional goods or services. Where an embedded foreign currency derivative is separated from a supply contract it is important to consider whether the host (which will be denominated in a different currency to the original hybrid contract) is an onerous contract under IAS 37.

B Inputs, ingredients, substitutes and other proxy pricing mechanisms

It is common for the pricing of contracts for the supply of goods, services or other non-financial items to be determined by reference to the price of inputs to, ingredients used to generate, or substitutes for the non-financial item, especially where the non-financial item is not itself quoted in an active market. For example, a provider of call centre services may determine that a large proportion of the costs of providing the service will be employee costs in a particular country. Accordingly, it may seek to link the price in a long-term contract to supply its services to the relevant wage index, effectively to provide an economic hedge of its exposure to changes in employee costs. Similarly, the producer of goods may index the price of its product to the market value of commodities that are used in the production process.

The standard contains little or no detailed guidance for determining whether or not such pricing features should be considered closely related to the host contract. However, the general requirement of the standard to assess the economic characteristics and risks would suggest that where a good link to the inputs can be established, such features will normally be considered closely related to the host unless, for example, they were significantly leveraged.

Other proxy pricing mechanisms may arise in long-term supply agreements for commodities where there is no active market in the commodity. For example, in the 1980s, when natural gas first started to be extracted from the North Sea in significant volumes, there was no active market for that gas and thus no market price on which to base the price of long term contracts. Because of this, suppliers and customers were willing to enter into such contracts where the price was indexed to the market price of other commodities such as crude oil that could potentially be used as a substitute for gas. For contracts entered into before the development of an active gas market, such features would normally be considered closely related, especially if similar pricing mechanisms were commonly used by other participants in the market.

Where there is an active market price for the non-financial items being supplied under the contract, different considerations apply. The use of the proxy pricing mechanism is a strong indication that the entity has entered into a speculative position and we would not normally consider such features to be closely related to the host.

C Inflation linked features

Apart from that related to leases (see 5.1.3 B below), there is no reference in the guidance to contracts containing payments that are linked to inflation. Many types of contracts contain inflation-linked payments and it would appear sensible to apply the guidance in respect of leases to these contracts. Consider, for example, a long-term agreement to supply services under which payments increase by reference to a general price index and are not leveraged in any way. In cases such as this, the embedded inflation-linked derivative would normally be considered closely related to the host provided the index related to a measure of inflation in an appropriate economic environment, such as the one in which the services were being supplied.

D Floors and caps

Similar to debt instruments (see 5.1.1 D above), provisions within a contract to purchase or sell an asset (e.g. a commodity) that establishes a cap and a floor on the price to be paid or received for the asset are closely related to the host contract if both the cap and floor were out of the money at inception and are not leveraged.[244]

E Fund performance fees

In the investment management industry, it is common for a fund manager to receive a fee based on the performance of the assets managed in addition to a base fee. For example, if a fund's net asset value increases over its accounting year, the manager may be entitled to a percentage of that increase. The contract for providing investment management services to the fund clearly contains an embedded derivative (the underlying is the value of the fund's assets). However, whilst not addressed explicitly in the standard, we would normally consider it appropriate to regard such features as closely related to the host contract.

5.1.3 Leases

A Foreign currency derivatives

As noted at 2.2.4 above, a finance lease payable or receivable is accounted for as a financial instrument. Therefore, a finance lease denominated in a foreign currency will not generally be considered to contain an embedded foreign currency derivative requiring separation (because the payable or receivable is a monetary item within the scope of IAS 21).

However, an operating lease is accounted for as an executory contract. Accordingly, where the lease payments are denominated in a foreign currency, the analysis at 5.1.2 A is applicable and it may be necessary to separate an embedded derivative.

B Inflation linked features

An embedded derivative in a lease is considered closely related to the host if it is an inflation-related index such as an index of lease payments to a consumer price index (provided that the lease is not leveraged and the index relates to inflation in the entity's own economic environment).[245]

The guidance does not make it clear whether or not this is intended to apply to operating leases, to finance leases or to both – in the absence of evidence to the contrary we believe it is appropriate to apply it to both types.

C Contingent rentals based on related sales

Where a lease requires contingent rentals based on related sales that embedded derivative is considered closely related to the host lease.[246] We believe this guidance also applies to both finance and operating leases.

D Contingent rentals based on variable interest rates

If a derivative embedded within a lease arises from contingent rentals based on variable interest rates it is considered closely related.[247] Again we believe this guidance applies to both finance and operating leases.

5.1.4 Insurance contracts

The guidance at 5.1.1 B, C, D and F and 5.1.2 A above also applies to insurance contracts. IFRS 4 also added two further illustrations to IAS 39 that deal primarily with insurance contracts.

A unit-linking feature embedded in a host financial instrument, or host insurance contract, is closely related to the host if the unit-denominated payments are measured at current unit values that reflect the fair values of the assets of the fund. A unit-linking feature is a contractual term that requires payments denominated in units of an internal or external investment fund.[248]

A derivative embedded in an insurance contract is closely related to the host if the embedded derivative and host are so interdependent that the embedded derivative cannot be measured separately, i.e. without considering the host contract.[249]

5.2 Identifying the terms of embedded derivatives and host contracts

The IASB has provided only limited guidance on determining the terms of a separated embedded derivative and host contract. Accordingly, entities may find this aspect of the embedded derivative requirements particularly difficult to implement. In addition to the guidance set out below, Examples 17.18 and 17.19 above also identify the terms of an embedded derivative requiring separation.

5.2.1 Embedded non-option derivatives

IAS 39 does not define the term 'non-option derivative' but suggests that it includes forwards, swaps and similar contracts. An embedded derivative of this type should be separated from its host contract on the basis of its stated or implied substantive terms, so as to result in it having a fair value of zero at initial recognition.[250]

The IASB has provided implementation guidance on separating non-option derivatives in the situation where the host is a debt instrument. It is explained that, in the absence of implied or stated terms, judgement will be necessary to identify the terms of the host (e.g. whether it should be a fixed rate, variable rate or zero coupon instrument) and the embedded derivative. However, an embedded derivative that is not already clearly present in the hybrid should not be separated, i.e. a cash flow that does not exist cannot be created.[251]

For example, if a five year debt instrument has fixed annual interest payments of £40 and a principal payment at maturity of £1,000 multiplied by the change in an equity price index, it would be inappropriate to identify a floating rate host and an embedded equity swap that has an offsetting floating rate leg. The host should be a fixed rate debt instrument that pays £40 annually because there are no floating interest rate cash flows in the hybrid instrument.[252]

Further, as noted above, the terms of the embedded derivative should be determined so that is has a fair value of zero on inception of the hybrid instrument. It is explained that if an embedded non-option derivative could be separated on other terms, a single hybrid instrument could be decomposed into an infinite variety of combinations of host debt instruments and embedded derivatives. This might be achieved, for example, by separating embedded derivatives with terms that create leverage, asymmetry or some other risk exposure not already present in the hybrid instrument.[253]

Finally, it is explained that the terms of the embedded derivative should be identified based on the conditions existing when the financial instrument was issued[254] or, presumably, following application of IFRC 9 (see 5.4.1 below) when a contract is required to be reassessed.

5.2.2 Embedded option-based derivative

As for non-option derivatives, IAS 39 does not define the term 'option-based derivative' but suggests that it includes puts, calls, caps, floors and swaptions. An embedded derivative of this type should be separated from its host contract on the basis of the stated terms of the option feature.[255]

The implementation guidance explains that the economic nature of an option-based derivative is fundamentally different from a non-option derivative and depends critically on the strike price (or strike rate) specified for the option feature in the hybrid instrument. Therefore, the separation of such a derivative should be based on the stated terms of the option feature documented in the hybrid instrument. Consequently, in contrast to the position for non-option derivatives (see 5.2.1 above), an embedded option-based derivative would not normally have a fair value of zero.

In fact, if the terms of an embedded option-based derivative were identified so as to result in it having a fair value of zero, the implied strike price would generally result in the option being infinitely out of the money, i.e. it would have a zero probability of the option feature being exercised. However, since the probability of the option feature in a hybrid instrument being exercised generally is not zero, this would be inconsistent with the likely economic behaviour of the hybrid.

Similarly, if the terms were identified so as to achieve an intrinsic value of zero, the strike price would equal the price of the underlying at initial recognition. In this case, the fair value of the option would consist only of time value. However, this may also be inconsistent with the likely economic behaviour of the hybrid, including the probability of the option feature being exercised, unless the agreed strike price was indeed equal to the price of the underlying at initial recognition.[256]

5.2.3 Nature of a financial instrument host

Consistent with the 'closely related' assessment (see 5.1 above), it is suggested that, where a financial instrument contains an embedded derivative, the host should be considered as a debt instrument 'if the hybrid instrument has a stated maturity, i.e. it does not meet the definition of an equity instrument'.[257]

The implementation guidance illustrates this by way of an example, the substance of which is reproduced below.

Example 17.21: Equity linked debt

Company A purchases a five year 'debt' instrument issued by Company B with a principal of £1,000, indexed to Company C's share price. At maturity, A will receive the principal plus or minus the change in the fair value of 100 of C's shares and no interest payments are made before maturity. On the date of acquisition, the purchase price is £1,000 and C's share price is £12. A classifies the instrument as available-for-sale.

The instrument is a hybrid instrument with an embedded derivative because of the equity-indexed principal and the host is a debt instrument (see above). The host is a zero coupon debt paying £1,200 at maturity. The embedded non-option derivative (a forward contract to purchase

100 shares of C for an amount equal to the forward price of C's shares at inception of the arrangement) is separated and will have an initial fair value of zero.[258]

A financial instrument can give rise to a residual interest in the net assets of an entity, even though IAS 32 prevents the issuing entity from classifying the instrument as equity. Where such an instrument contains an embedded derivative that requires separation, it may be appropriate to classify the host as equity rather than debt. This will commonly be the case for an investment in a unit trust (see 5.1.1 I above) and may be appropriate for some structured investments which can, in substance, give rise to a residual interest in the net assets of an entity.

Host contracts that are financial instruments should be accounted for under IAS 39. Otherwise, they are accounted for in accordance with other appropriate standards. This does not necessarily mean that the embedded derivative and host should be presented separately (or together) on the face of the financial statements (see Chapter 22 at 4.3.1).[259]

5.3 Multiple embedded derivatives

Generally, multiple embedded derivatives in a single instrument should be treated as a single compound embedded derivative. However, embedded derivatives that are classified as equity are accounted for separately from those classified as assets or liabilities (see Chapter 19 at 4). In addition, derivatives embedded in a single instrument that relate to different risk exposures and are readily separable and independent of each other should be accounted for separately from each other.[260]

For example, if a debt instrument has a principal amount related to an equity index and that amount doubles if the equity index exceeds a certain level, it is not appropriate to separate both a forward and an option on the equity index because those derivative features relate to the same risk exposure. Instead, the forward and option elements are treated as a single compound embedded derivative. For the same reason, an embedded floor or cap on interest rates should not be separated into a series of 'floorlets' or 'caplets'.[261]

In addition, if a single hybrid contains both a put option and a written call option on the hybrid instrument that require separation, e.g. callable debt with a put to the holder, those options are treated as a single embedded derivative because they are not independent of each other. Furthermore, if an investor holds callable convertible debt for which separation of the call option is required, it is not appropriate to separate an equity conversion option and a written call option on the debt instrument separately because the two embedded derivative features should not be valued independently of each other.[262]

On the other hand, if a hybrid debt instrument contains, for example, two options that give the holder a right to choose both the interest rate index on which interest payments are determined and the currency in which the principal is repaid, those two options may qualify for separation as two separate embedded derivatives since they relate to different risk exposures and are readily separable and independent of each other.[263]

5.4 Reassessment of embedded derivatives

It is clear that, on initial recognition, a contract should be reviewed to assess whether it contains one or more embedded derivatives requiring separation. However, the standard is largely silent on whether this initial assessment should be revisited throughout the life of the contract.[264]

Consider, for example, an entity that enters into a purchase contract denominated in US dollars. If, at the time the contract is entered into, US dollars are commonly used in the economic environment in which the transaction takes place, the contract will not contain an embedded foreign currency derivative requiring separation. Subsequently, however, the economic environment may change such that transactions are now commonly denominated in euros, rather than US dollars. Countries joining the European Union may encounter just such a scenario.

Clearly, in this situation, an embedded foreign currency derivative would be separated from any new US dollar denominated purchase contracts (assuming they would not otherwise be considered closely related). However, should the entity separately account for derivatives embedded within its existing US dollar denominated contracts that were outstanding prior to the change in the market?

Conversely, the entity may have identified, and separately accounted for, embedded foreign currency derivatives in contracts denominated in euros that were entered into before the economic environment changed. Does the change in economic circumstances mean that the embedded derivative should now be considered closely related and not separately accounted for as a derivative?[265]

In practice, there appeared to be differing views developing on this issue. Therefore, without further guidance, the IFRIC considered it quite possible that inconsistent practice would develop.[266] Accordingly it decided to take the issue onto its agenda and, in March 2006, published IFRIC 9 – *Reassessment of Embedded Derivatives*.

5.4.1 IFRIC 9

IFRIC 9 confirms that entities should assess whether an embedded derivative is required to be separated from the host contract and accounted for as a derivative when the entity first becomes a party to the contract and explains that subsequent reassessment is generally prohibited.[267]

The one exception is where there is a change in the terms of a contract that significantly modifies the cash flows that otherwise would be required under it, in which case reassessment is required. In order to determine whether a modification to cash flows is significant, an entity should consider the extent to which the expected future cash flows associated with the embedded derivative, the host contract or both have changed and whether the change is significant relative to the previously expected cash flows on the contract.[268]

5.4.2 *Acquisition of contracts*

IAS 39 requires an entity to assess whether an embedded derivative needs to be separated from the host contract and accounted for as a derivative when it first becomes a party to that contract. Therefore, if an entity purchases a contract that contains an embedded derivative, it assesses whether the embedded derivative needs to be separated and accounted for as a derivative on the basis of conditions at the date it acquires it, not the date the original contract was established.[269]

For example, consider an entity that purchases a debt instrument containing an embedded prepayment, put or call option some time after it was issued. In this case, the assessment of whether the exercise price of the option is approximately equal to the instrument's amortised cost (see 5.1.1 C above) will be based on the amortised cost of the acquirer (taking into account any premium or discount paid as a result of changes in value since origination), not that of the issuer or original holder.

5.4.3 *Business combinations*

From the point of view of a consolidated entity, the acquisition of a contract within a business combination is hardly different from the acquisition of a contract in general. Therefore, in principle, it would appear entirely appropriate for the guidance in 5.4.2 above to apply to business combinations too. In fact, were IFRIC 9 completely silent on the subject, the 'hierarchy' in IAS 8 (see Chapter 3 at 4.3) would leave entities with little choice but to apply this approach to contracts acquired in a business combination.

However, IFRIC 9 makes it clear that it does not address the acquisition of contracts with embedded derivatives in a business combination nor their possible reassessment at the date of acquisition.[270] Consequently, as acknowledged by the IASB staff,[271] entities would appear to have a choice of two accounting policies for such contracts: they should make their assessment of embedded derivatives either at the date of the business combination or at the date the acquired entity became party to the contract. Whichever policy is adopted should be applied consistently.

Before it finalised its interpretation, the IFRIC decided to refer this issue to its Agenda Committee[272] but ultimately decided not to deal with it as it should be addressed in the IASB's Business Combinations project (see Chapter 7 at 5).[273] The IASB has subsequently decided that the revised version of IFRS 3 will require reassessment at the date of the business combination (assuming it is accounted for using purchase accounting).[274]

5.4.4 *Remeasurement issues arising from reassessment*

IFRIC 9 does not address remeasurement issues arising from a reassessment of embedded derivatives.[275] One of the reasons cited by the IFRIC for prohibiting reassessment in general was the difficulty associated in determining the accounting treatment following a reassessment, which is explained in the following terms.

Assume that an entity, when it first became party to a contract, separately recognised a host asset, say a loan or receivable, and an embedded derivative liability. If the entity were required to reassess whether the embedded derivative was to be accounted for separately and if the entity concluded some time after becoming a party to the contract that the derivative was no longer required to be separated, then questions of recognition and measurement would arise. In the above circumstances, the entity could:[276]

(a) remove the derivative from its balance sheet and recognise in profit or loss a corresponding gain or loss. This would lead to recognition of a gain or loss even though there had been no transaction and no change in the value of the total contract or its components;

(b) leave the derivative as a separate item in the balance sheet. The issue would then arise as to when the item was to be removed from the balance sheet. Should it be amortised (and, if so, how would the amortisation affect the effective interest rate of the asset), or should it be derecognised only when the asset is derecognised?

(c) combine the derivative (which is recognised at fair value) with the asset (which is recognised at amortised cost). This would alter both the carrying amount of the asset and its effective interest rate even though there had been no change in the economics of the whole contract. In some cases, it could also result in a negative effective interest rate.

The IFRIC states that, under its view that subsequent reassessment is appropriate only when there has been a 'significant' change in the contract terms, the above issues do not arise.[277] However, it is not entirely clear that this statement is true in all circumstances, particularly where a reassessment is required. It might well be true if, under IFRS, a change of commercial substance in a contract meant that all related assets and/or liabilities were required to be derecognised and replaced with new assets and/or liabilities at specified amounts, but this is not the case.

5.5 Non-financial variables specific to one party to the contract

As set out at 5 above, in order to separate for accounting purposes an embedded feature from its host contract, that feature should meet the definition of a derivative. To be a derivative, an instrument must contain an underlying that is not a non-financial variable that is specific to one party to the contract. However, as noted at 4.1.2, it is not always clear whether a variable is financial or non-financial. This is illustrated in the following example.

Example 17.22: Borrowing with coupons linked to revenue

Company F, a manufacturing entity, issues a debt instrument for its par value of €10m. It is repayable in ten years time at par and an annual coupon is payable that comprises two elements: a fixed amount of 2.5% of the par value and a variable amount equating to 0.01% of F's annual revenues. Company F does not designate the instrument at fair value through profit or loss.

It is assumed that if F had instead issued a more conventional fixed rate borrowing for the same amount with the same maturity it would have been required to pay an annual coupon of 4% of the par value. Therefore, on the face of it, the debt contains an embedded feature that represents a swap with an initial fair value of zero whereby F receives a fixed amount annually (1.5% of €10m) and pays a variable amount annually (0.01% of its revenues).

It is very hard to argue that the economic characteristics and risks of this embedded feature are closely related to the debt instrument and the variable (F's revenue) is clearly specific to F. Therefore the key issue is whether F's revenue is a financial or non-financial variable.

It is not only contracts with payments based on revenue that can cause such problems. Some contracts may require payments based on other measures taken or derived from an entity's financial statements such EBITDA. The IFRIC has been considering this matter and agrees there is a lack of clarity within IAS 39 but believes it would be unable to reach a consensus on a timely basis and has tentatively decided not to address it further.[278]

Two companies that have faced this issue in practice are Gaz de France and Renault. They have issued liabilities on which coupons are linked to 'value added' (a measure of profit previously reported under French GAAP), revenue and net profit. As can be seen in the following extracts, Gaz de France in accounting for the entire instrument at amortised cost appears to view 'value added' as a non-financial variable whcrcas Renault clearly states that its revenue- and net profit-linked features are considered embedded derivatives.

Extract 17.2: Gaz de France S.A. (2006)

NOTES TO THE CONSOLIDATED FNANCIAL STATEMENTS [extracts]
A – SUMMARY OF SIGNIFICANT ACCOUNTING POLICIES [extracts]
2 – 24.2 IRREDEEMABLE SECURITIES [extracts]

Gaz de France issued irredeemable securities in 1985 and 1986 as authorized by law no. 83.1, dated January 1, 1983, and by law no. 85.695, dated July 11, 1985. These securities are measured at their amortized cost. As they do not meet the criteria of an equity instrument, they are classified as debt/financial liabilities.

Remuneration

The return of irredeemable securities, subject to a limit of between 85% and 130% of the average bond interest rate, comprises a fixed portion equal to 63% of the French Average Bond Rate ("TMO" in the French acronym) and a variable portion calculated on the basis of the growth in Gaz de France's "value added" in the previous year (or that of the consolidated group, Group share only, if this is more favourable).

The return on irredeemable securities according to the effective interest method is treated as a borrowing cost in interest expense.

Extract 17.3: Renault S.A. (2006)

NOTES TO THE CONSOLIDATED FNANCIAL STATEMENTS [extract]

2 – ACCOUNTING POLICIES [extract]

T – Financial liabilities and sales financing debts [extract]

Redeemable shares

Given the lack of specific guidance on the matter in IAS 39, the Group considers that the variable interest on redeemable shares is an embedded derivative …

24 – Financial liabilities and sales financing debts [extracts]

Redeemable shares [extracts]

The redeemable shares issued in October 1983 and April 1984 by Renault SA are subordinated perpetual shares. They earn a minimum annual return of 9% comprising a fixed portion (6.75%) and a variable portion that depends on consolidated revenues and is calculated based on identical Group structure and methods.

The return on Diac redeemable shares issued in 1985 comprises a fixed portion equal to the Annual Monetary Rate, and a variable portion calculated by multiplying an amount equal to 40% of the Annual Monetary Rate by the rate of increase in net consolidated profit of the Diac sub-group compared to the prior year.

6 LINKED AND SEPARATE TRANSACTIONS AND 'SYNTHETIC' INSTRUMENTS

As noted at 5 above, a derivative that is attached to a financial instrument, but is contractually transferable independently of that instrument, or has a different counterparty from that instrument, is not an embedded derivative, but a separate financial instrument.[279] This is also the case where a synthetic instrument is created by using derivatives to 'alter' the nature of a non-derivative instrument, as illustrated in the following example:

Example 17.23: Investment in synthetic fixed-rate debt

Company A acquires a five year floating rate debt instrument issued by Company B. At the same time, it enters into a five year pay-variable, receive-fixed interest rate swap with Bank C. A considers the combination of the two instruments to be a synthetic fixed rate bond and, since it has the positive intent and ability to hold them to maturity, wants to classify them as a held-to-maturity investment (see 7.2 below).

Embedded derivatives are terms and conditions that are *included in* non-derivative host contracts and it is generally inappropriate to treat two or more separate financial instruments as a single combined, or synthetic, instrument. Each of the financial instruments has its own terms and conditions and may be transferred or settled separately. Therefore, the debt instrument and the swap must be classified separately.[280]

It is asserted that these transactions differ from those discussed at 4.5 above because those had no substance apart from the resulting interest rate swap.[281] Although some might argue that the only substance of the two transactions above is the resulting synthetic fixed rate debt instrument, this interpretation is clearly not allowed under the standard.

Interestingly, the guidance does not address a much more common situation whereby a company both borrows from, and transacts a related derivative with, the same counterparty – typically the borrowing will be floating rate and the derivative a perfectly matched pay-fixed, receive-floating interest rate swap. Such transactions can offer cheaper funding than conventional fixed rate borrowings (in a perfect market this should not be true, but anecdotal evidence suggests it often is).

In fact the subject of linking transactions for accounting purposes is a difficult one, especially in the context of financial instruments. The IASB's *Framework* specifies that transactions should be reported in accordance with their substance and economic reality and not merely their legal form[282] and linking transactions can be seen as dealing with the question of how to interpret this principle.

IAS 32 and IAS 39 deal with the subject in a piecemeal way. For example, in addition to the synthetic instrument illustration above:

- two or more non-derivative contracts that are, 'in substance', no more than a single derivative are treated as a single derivative (see 4.5 above);
- derivatives that are 'attached' to a non-derivative financial instrument may sometimes be regarded as part of a single combined instrument (see 5.1.1 C above);
- in classifying an instrument in consolidated financial statements as equity or a financial liability, all terms and conditions agreed between members of the group and holders of the instrument are considered (see Chapter 19 at 3.6); and
- determining the appropriate accounting treatment for a transaction that involves the transfer of some or all rights associated with financial assets without the sale of the assets themselves inevitably involves linking separate contracts to assess whether the transaction results in derecognition of the assets. For example, there might be one contract defining the continued ownership of the asset and another obliging the owner to transfer the rights associated with the asset to a third party (see Chapter 18 at 4).

The IFRIC first considered the subject of linkage in 2002 and has, in the past, made certain recommendations to the IASB. In fact, the requirement to take account of linked terms when classifying instruments as debt or equity in consolidated financial statements was introduced into IAS 32 in December 2003 following the IFRIC's deliberations. In spite of agreeing proposed indicators for when transactions should be linked, and proposed guidance on accounting for linked transactions, these have never been published as an interpretation or standard.[283]

Consequently, in considering the borrowing and swap situation above we are left principally with the guidance in IAS 39. It is likely that the swap and the loan have their own terms and conditions and may be transferred or settled independently of each other. Therefore, the principles in Example 17.23 above would suggest separate accounting for the two instruments. Applying the guidance at 4.5 above would also suggest separate accounting in most cases. Even though the instruments are transacted with the same counterparty, there will normally be a substantive business purpose for transacting the instruments separately, namely the fact that it leads to cheaper funding.

It seems clear that in situations involving two separate legal contracts the IASB has set the bar for regarding transactions as linked very high and, in most cases, the two instruments will be regarded as separate for accounting purposes. However, in rare situations the linkage between those contracts (normally itself contractual) may be such that for accounting purposes those contracts cannot be regarded as existing independently of each other.

7 CLASSIFICATION OF FINANCIAL INSTRUMENTS

The accounting treatment for a particular financial instrument (e.g. whether it is carried at historical cost or fair value and whether any remeasurement gains are reported immediately in profit or loss or initially in equity) depends on its classification.

Four types of financial asset are defined as follows:[284]

- *Financial assets at fair value through profit or loss* – financial instruments that are either classified as *held for trading*, or are designated as such on initial recognition;
- *Held-to-maturity investments* – financial assets with fixed or determinable payments and fixed maturity, other than loans and receivables, for which there is a positive intention and ability to hold to maturity and which have not been designated 'at fair value through profit or loss' or as 'available-for-sale';
- *Loans and receivables* – financial assets with fixed or determinable payments that are not quoted in an active market, do not qualify as 'trading' assets and have not been designated 'at fair value through profit or loss' or as 'available-for-sale';
- *Available-for-sale financial assets* – financial assets that are designated as 'available-for-sale' or are not classified as 'loans and receivables', 'held-to-maturity investments' or 'at fair value through profit or loss'.

There are two main types of financial liabilities dealt with in IAS 39:

- *Financial liabilities at fair value through profit or loss* – financial instruments that are either classified as *held for trading*, or are designated as such on initial recognition;[285]
- *Other financial liabilities* are not explicitly defined but are those that are not held for trading or designated 'at fair value through profit or loss'.

In addition, IAS 39 specifies the accounting treatment for liabilities arising from certain financial guarantee contracts (see 3.4 above) and commitments to provide loans at below market rates of interest (see 3.5 above).

These definitions are covered in more detail below.

7.1 Assets and liabilities at fair value through profit or loss

This category was introduced in the December 2003 version of IAS 39. It incorporated (with some changes) the previous 'held for trading' category (see 7.1.1) but, in addition, financial instruments may be designated into it – this is often referred to as the 'fair value option' (see 7.1.2). The IASB made it clear that this new category only encompasses, and is not the same as, the former held for trading category and that trading instruments are not a separate class.[286]

It will come as no surprise that the basic accounting requirements for all instruments included in this category is that they are recorded on the balance sheet at fair value and any changes in value are reported in profit or loss (see Chapter 20 at 3).

As discussed at 1.5 above, the IASB published in June 2005 amendments to IAS 39 restricting the use of the fair value option – previously there were very few restrictions on which instruments could designated at fair value through profit or loss. These restrictions are dealt with at 7.1.2 below.

Under both versions of the standard, designation must take place on initial recognition of the instrument (subject to certain exemptions on initial application of the standard) and may not be revoked subsequently, i.e. a designated instrument will be included in this category from when it is first recognised until it is derecognised.

7.1.1 Assets and liabilities held for trading

Assets and liabilities held for trading are defined as those that are:

- acquired or incurred principally for the purpose of sale or repurchase in the near term;
- part of a portfolio of identified financial instruments that are managed together and for which there is evidence of a recent actual pattern of short-term profit-taking; or
- derivatives (except for those that are financial guarantee contracts – see 3.4 above – or are designated effective hedging instruments – see Chapter 21 at 2.1.1).[287]

It is explained that trading generally reflects active and frequent buying and selling, and financial instruments held for trading generally are used with the objective of generating a profit from short-term fluctuations in price or dealer's margin.[288] This is obviously not always true because, for example, many derivatives will be held for hedging or risk management purposes yet by default they are included in this category (unless the entity chooses to designate them as hedges and is successful in achieving hedge accounting as set out in Chapter 21 at 5).

In addition to derivatives that are not accounted for as hedging instruments, financial liabilities held for trading include:

(a) obligations to deliver financial assets borrowed by a short seller (i.e. an entity that sells financial assets it has borrowed and does not yet own);

(b) financial liabilities that are incurred with an intention to repurchase them in the near term, such as quoted debt instruments that the issuer may buy back in the near term depending on changes in fair value; and

(c) financial liabilities that are part of a portfolio of identified financial instruments that are managed together and for which there is evidence of a recent pattern of short-term profit-taking.[289]

This was a change from the original version of IAS 39 under which only liabilities within (a) would be included in the trading category. The IASB believed that the original version of IAS 39 permitted 'cherry picking' of unrealised gains or losses on liabilities within (b) and (c) and was keen to reduce the scope for this.[290] However, as before, the fact that a liability is used merely to fund trading activities does not in itself make that liability one that is held for trading[291] (even though that might give to cherry picking opportunities).

The term 'portfolio' is not explicitly defined in IAS 39, but the context in which it is used suggests that a portfolio is a group of financial assets or financial liabilities that are managed as part of that group. If there is evidence of a recent actual pattern of short-term profit taking on financial instruments included in such a portfolio, those financial instruments qualify as held for trading even though an individual financial instrument may, in fact, be held for a longer period of time.[292] In the original version of the standard, where an entity's intention was to hold an asset for a long period of time there was a prohibition on including it in within the trading category[293] but now if the asset is part of a 'trading' portfolio (as described above) it *must* be included in this category.

7.1.2 Instruments designated at fair value through profit or loss

One of the IASB's reasons for introducing the fair value option was to simplify the application of IAS 39 by mitigating some of the anomalies that result from its mixed model approach. For example, it eliminates:

- the need for hedge accounting for hedges of fair value exposures when there are natural offsets, and thereby eliminates the related burden of designating hedges, tracking and analysing hedge effectiveness;
- the burden of separating embedded derivatives; and
- problems arising from a mixed measurement model where financial assets are measured at fair value and related financial liabilities are measured at amortised cost.

In particular, it eliminates volatility in profit or loss and equity that results when matched positions of financial assets and financial liabilities are not measured consistently. It also de-emphasises interpretive issues around whether a financial instrument should be classified as trading.[294]

A The original fair value option

Prior to the June 2005 amendments to IAS 39, virtually any financial asset or financial liability within the scope of IAS 39 (and some that need not be – see 3.4

above) could be designated as a financial asset or financial liability at fair value through profit or loss. The only situation where the fair value option was not available was for investments in equity instruments that did not have a quoted market price in an active market, and whose fair value could not be reliably measured (see Chapter 20 at 4.4). Such instruments could not be designated at fair value through profit or loss, although theoretically they could be classified as trading.[295]

For entities preparing their financial statements in accordance with IFRS adopted for use by the European Union there was a further restriction in that non-derivative financial liabilities could not be designated at fair value through profit or loss (see 1.5 above).[296]

B The fair value option amendments

The June 2005 amendments to IAS 39 introduced a number of restrictions on the use of the fair value option. Following the application of these amendments, an entity may only designate a financial asset or financial liability at fair value through profit or loss if doing so results in more relevant information, because either:

- it eliminates or significantly reduces a measurement or recognition inconsistency (sometimes referred to as 'an accounting mismatch') that would otherwise arise; or
- a group of financial assets, financial liabilities or both is managed and its performance is evaluated on a fair value basis;

or if it contains an embedded derivative that meets particular conditions.[297] These are discussed further at I to III below.

The original restriction on designating certain unquoted equity instruments remained[298] and for entities preparing their financial statements in accordance with IFRS adopted for use by the European Union the restriction on designating financial liabilities was lifted (see A above).[299]

The decision to designate a financial asset or financial liability as at fair value through profit or loss is similar to an accounting policy choice (although, unlike an accounting policy choice, it is not required to be applied consistently to all similar transactions). When an entity has such a choice, IAS 8 requires the chosen policy to result in the financial statements providing reliable and more relevant information about the effects of transactions, other events and conditions on the entity's financial position, financial performance or cash flows. In the case of designation as at fair value through profit or loss, an entity needs to demonstrate that it falls within one (or both) of the two circumstances set out above.[300]

In the December 2003 version of the standard it was made clear that the option could not be applied to a portion of a financial instrument, such as a component of a debt instrument that is associated with interest rate risk but not with credit risk.[301] In response to comments raised as it developed its amendments, the IASB introduced a further clarification explaining that the fair value option could not be applied to proportions of an instrument. However, if an entity simultaneously issues two or more identical financial instruments, it is not precluded from designating only some of those instruments as being subject to the fair value option (e.g. if doing so achieves a significant reduction in an accounting mismatch). Therefore, if an entity issued a bond totalling US$100 million in the form of 100 certificates each of US$1 million, the entity could designate 10 specified certificates if to do so would meet at least one of the criteria noted above.[302]

The amendment also introduces changes to IAS 32 setting out additional disclosure requirements when the fair value option is used. These are dealt with in Chapter 22 at 2.4.4. Almost identical requirements are included in IFRS 7 and these are covered in Chapter 22 at 3.3.4 B and C.

I Designation eliminates or significantly reduces a measurement or recognition inconsistency (accounting mismatch) that would otherwise arise

The notion of an accounting mismatch necessarily involves two propositions. First, that an entity has particular assets and liabilities that are measured, or on which gains and losses are recognised, inconsistently; second, that there is a perceived economic relationship between those assets and liabilities. An accounting mismatch can arise from measuring assets or liabilities or recognising the gains and losses on them on different bases.[303]

For example, a financial asset might otherwise be classified as available for sale (with most changes in fair value recognised directly in equity) and a liability that is considered related would be measured at amortised cost (with changes in fair value not recognised). In such circumstances, the entity may conclude that its financial statements would provide more relevant information if both the asset and the liability were classified as at fair value through profit or loss.[304] It should be noted in this case that it does not matter that there is unlikely to be a significant accounting mismatch in the income statement – the fact that the mismatch arises only in the balance sheet does not prevent the use of the fair value option.

IAS 39 gives the following examples of situations in which designation at fair value through profit or loss might eliminate or significantly reduce an accounting mismatch and produce more relevant information:[305]

(a) An entity has liabilities whose cash flows are contractually based on the performance of assets that would otherwise be classified as available for sale. For example, an insurer may have liabilities containing a discretionary participation feature that pay benefits based on realised and/or unrealised investment returns of a specified pool of the insurer's assets. If the measurement of those liabilities reflects current market prices, classifying the assets as at fair value through profit or loss means that changes in the fair value of the financial assets are recognised in profit or loss in the same period as related changes in the value of the liabilities;

(b) An entity has liabilities under insurance contracts whose measurement incorporates current information (as permitted by IFRS 4), and financial assets it considers related that would otherwise be classified as available for sale or measured at amortised cost;

(c) An entity has financial assets, financial liabilities or both that share a risk, such as interest rate risk, that gives rise to opposite changes in fair value that tend to offset each other. However, only some of the instruments would be measured at fair value through profit or loss (i.e. derivatives or those classified as held for trading). It may also be the case that the requirements for hedge accounting are not met, for example because the requirements for effectiveness are not met (see Chapter 21 at 5.3);

(d) An entity has financial assets, financial liabilities or both that share a risk, such as interest rate risk, that gives rise to opposite changes in fair value that tend to offset each other and the entity does not qualify for hedge accounting because none of the instruments is a derivative. Furthermore, in the absence of hedge accounting there is a significant inconsistency in the recognition of gains and losses. For example:

   (i) the entity has financed a portfolio of fixed rate assets that would otherwise be classified as available for sale with fixed rate debentures, the changes in the fair value of each of which tend to offset each other. Reporting both the assets and the debentures at fair value through profit or loss corrects the inconsistency that would otherwise arise from measuring the assets at fair value with changes reported in equity and the debentures at amortised cost; or

   (ii) the entity has financed a specified group of loans by issuing traded bonds, the changes in the fair value of each of which tend to offset each other. If, in addition, the entity regularly buys and sells the bonds but rarely, if ever, buys and sells the loans, reporting both the loans and the bonds at fair value through profit or loss eliminates the inconsistency in the timing of recognition of gains and losses that would otherwise result from measuring them both at amortised cost and recognising a gain or loss each time a bond is repurchased.

For practical purposes, an entity need not acquire all the assets and incur all the liabilities giving rise to the measurement or recognition inconsistency at exactly the same time. A reasonable delay is permitted provided that each transaction is designated as at fair value through profit or loss at its initial recognition and, at that time, any remaining transactions are expected to occur.[306]

It is emphasised that it would not be acceptable to designate only some of the financial assets and financial liabilities giving rise to the inconsistency as at fair value through profit or loss if to do so would not eliminate or significantly reduce the inconsistency and would therefore not result in more relevant information. However, it would be acceptable to designate only some of a number of similar financial assets or similar financial liabilities if doing so does achieve a significant reduction (and possibly a greater reduction than other allowable designations) in the inconsistency.[307]

For example, assume an entity has a number of similar financial liabilities totalling €100 and a number of similar financial assets totalling €50 but are measured on a different basis. The entity may significantly reduce the measurement inconsistency by designating at initial recognition all of the assets but only some of the liabilities (for example, individual liabilities with a combined total of €45) as at fair value through profit or loss. However, because designation as at fair value through profit or loss can be applied only to the whole of a financial instrument, the entity in this example must designate one or more liabilities in their entirety. It could not designate either a component of a liability (e.g. changes in value attributable to only one risk, such as changes in a benchmark interest rate) or a proportion (i.e. percentage) of a liability.[308]

Whilst some entities can overcome measurement or recognition inconsistencies, for example by using hedge accounting, such techniques are complex and do not address all situations. Consequently, the IASB initially considered imposing conditions to limit the situations in which an entity could use the option to eliminate an accounting mismatch (e.g. by requiring entities to demonstrate that particular assets and liabilities are managed together, or that a management strategy is effective in reducing risk, as is required for hedge accounting to be used, or that hedge accounting or other ways of overcoming the inconsistency are not available). However, the IASB concluded that financial reporting was best served by providing entities with the opportunity to eliminate perceived accounting mismatches whenever that results in more relevant information. Furthermore, it concluded that the fair value option may validly be used in place of hedge accounting for hedges of fair value exposures, thereby eliminating the related burden of designating, tracking and analysing hedge effectiveness. Hence, the revised standard contains no detailed prescriptive guidance about when the fair value option could be applied (such as requiring effectiveness tests similar to those required for hedge accounting).[309]

II A group of financial assets, financial liabilities or both is managed and its performance is evaluated on a fair value basis

The second situation in which the fair value option may be used is where a group of financial assets, financial liabilities or both is managed and its performance is evaluated on a fair value basis. In order to meet this condition, it is necessary for the group of instruments to be managed in accordance with a documented risk management or investment strategy and for information, prepared on a fair value basis, about the group of instruments to be provided internally to the entity's key management personnel (as defined in IAS 24 – *Related Party Disclosures* – see Chapter 35 at 2.3.6), for example the entity's board of directors and chief executive officer.[310]

It is explained that if an entity manages and evaluates the performance of a group of financial assets, financial liabilities or both in such a way, measuring that group at fair value through profit or loss results in more relevant information. The focus in this instance is on the way the entity manages and evaluates performance, rather than on the nature of its financial instruments.[311] Accordingly, (subject to the requirement of designation at initial recognition) an entity that designates financial instruments as at fair value through profit or loss on the basis of this condition should designate all eligible financial instruments that are managed and evaluated together.[312]

An entity's documentation of its strategy need not be extensive (e.g. it need not be in the level of detail required for hedge accounting) but should be sufficient to demonstrate that using the fair value option is consistent with the entity's risk management or investment strategy. Such documentation is not required for each individual item, but may be on a portfolio basis. The IASB notes that in many cases, the entity's existing documentation, as approved by its key management personnel, should be sufficient for this purpose. For example, if the performance management system for a department (as approved by the entity's key management personnel) clearly demonstrates that its performance is evaluated on a total return basis, no further documentation is required.[313]

The IASB made it clear in its basis for conclusions that in looking to an entity's documented risk management or investment strategy, it makes no judgement on what an entity's strategy should be. However, the IASB believes that users, in making economic decisions, would find useful a description both of the chosen strategy and of how designation at fair value through profit or loss is consistent with that strategy. Accordingly, IAS 32 and IFRS 7 require these to be disclosed (see Chapter 22 at 2.2.3 and 3.3.1).[314]

The following examples show when this condition could be met. In all cases, an entity may use this condition to designate financial assets or financial liabilities as at fair value through profit or loss only if it meets the principle above:[315]

(a) The entity is a venture capital organisation, mutual fund, unit trust or similar entity whose business is investing in financial assets with a view to profiting from their total return in the form of interest or dividends and changes in fair value. IAS 28 and IAS 31 allow investments in associates and interests in joint ventures to be excluded from their scope provided they are measured at fair value through profit or loss. It is explained that an entity may apply the same accounting policy to other investments managed on a total return basis but over which its influence is insufficient for them to be within the scope of IAS 28 or IAS 31.

    In fact, in order for interests in associates and interests in joint ventures to be accounted for at fair value through profit or loss, IAS 28 and IAS 31 require them to be so 'designated ... in accordance with IAS 39'.[316] Consequently, if the investments in (a) above, both within and outside the scope of IAS 28 and IAS 31, are managed together, all of those assets should be designated at fair value through profit or loss. In other words, the fair value option could not be applied only to those investments that are associates are joint ventures;

(b) The entity has financial assets and financial liabilities that share one or more risks and those risks are managed and evaluated on a fair value basis in accordance with a documented policy of asset and liability management. An example could be an entity that has issued 'structured products' containing multiple embedded derivatives and manages the resulting risks on a fair value basis using a mix of derivative and non-derivative financial instruments. A similar example could be an entity that originates fixed interest rate loans and manages the resulting benchmark interest rate risk using a mix of derivative and non-derivative financial instruments;

(c) The entity is an insurer that holds a portfolio of financial assets, manages that portfolio so as to maximise its total return (i.e. interest or dividends and changes in fair value) and evaluates its performance on that basis. The portfolio may be held to back specific liabilities, equity or both. If the portfolio is held to back specific liabilities, this condition may be met for the assets regardless of whether the insurer also manages and evaluates the liabilities on a fair value basis. It may also be met when the insurer's objective is to maximise total return on the assets over the longer term even if amounts paid to holders of participating contracts depend on other factors such as the amount of gains realised in a shorter period (e.g. a year) or are subject to the insurer's discretion.

III Instruments containing embedded derivatives

If a contract contains one or more embedded derivatives, an entity may designate the entire hybrid (or combined) contract as a financial asset or financial liability at fair value through profit or loss unless:[317]

(a) the embedded derivative(s) does not significantly modify the cash flows that otherwise would be required by the contract; or

(b) it is clear with little or no analysis when a similar hybrid (combined) instrument is first considered that separation of the embedded derivative(s) is prohibited, such as a prepayment option embedded in a loan that permits the holder to prepay the loan for approximately its amortised cost.

As discussed at 5 above, when an entity becomes a party to a hybrid (combined) instrument that contains one or more embedded derivatives, it is required to identify any such embedded derivative, assess whether it is required to be separated from the host contract and, if so, measure it at fair value at initial recognition and subsequently. These requirements can be more complex, or result in less reliable measures, than measuring the entire instrument at fair value through profit or loss. For that reason the entire instrument is normally permitted to be designated as at fair value through profit or loss.[318]

Such designation may be used whether the entity is required to, or prohibited from, separating the embedded derivative from the host contract, except for those situations in (a) or (b) above – this is because doing so would not reduce complexity or increase reliability.[319]

Little further guidance is given on what instruments might fall within (a) and (b). The basis for conclusions explains that, at one extreme, the terms of a prepayment option in an ordinary residential mortgage is likely to mean that the fair value option is unavailable to such a mortgage (unless it met one of the conditions in I and II above). At the other, it is likely to be available for 'structured products' that contain several embedded derivatives which are typically hedged with derivatives that offset all (or nearly all) of the risks they contain irrespective of the accounting treatment applied.[320]

Essentially, the IASB explains, the standard seeks to strike a balance between reducing the costs of complying with the embedded derivatives provisions and the need to respond to concerns expressed regarding possible inappropriate use of the fair value option. Allowing the fair value option to be used for any instrument with an embedded derivative would make other restrictions on the use of the option ineffective, because many financial instruments include an embedded derivative. In contrast, limiting the use of the fair value option to situations in which the embedded derivative must otherwise be separated would not significantly reduce the costs of compliance and could result in less reliable measures being included in the financial statements.[321] Quite how this requirement will be interpreted in practice remains to be seen.

Taken at face value, IAS 39 might allow the fair value option to be applied to any contract containing a substantive embedded derivative, such as a lease accounted for under IAS 17 or a pension arrangement accounted for under IAS 19. In May 2007, the IFRIC tentatively concluded that it could be applied only to a contract that would otherwise be within the scope of IAS 39.[322] However, at its subsequent meeting in July 2007, the IFRIC did not finalise its conclusion, instead directing its staff to conduct further analysis as it had become apparent that a number of entities had taken a different view, at least as regards commodity contracts that qualify as normal purchases or sales (see 3.9.2 above).[323] In September 2007, the IFRIC decided to refer the matter to the IASB for clarification and directed its staff to develop proposed revisions to the standard.[324]

7.2 Held-to-maturity investments

As noted at 7 above, the held-to-maturity category comprises financial assets with fixed or determinable payments and fixed maturity, other than loans and receivables, for which there is a positive intention and ability to hold to maturity and which have not been designated at fair value through profit or loss or as available-for-sale.[325]

This category is viewed as an exception to be used only in limited circumstances.[326] Consequently, its use is restricted by a number of detailed conditions, largely designed to test whether there is a genuine intention and ability to hold such investments to maturity. To further restrict the use of this category, hedge accounting cannot be used if interest rate or prepayment risk associated with held-to-maturity investments is hedged,[327] for example by using a pay-fixed, receive-floating rate interest rate swap to hedge an investment that pays a fixed rate of interest (see Chapter 21 at 2.2.5).

In theory investments are not *designated* as held-to-maturity – they *must* be included in this category if they meet the appropriate conditions. However, because it is relatively easy for an entity to selectively fail any of the conditions, in practice it is effectively a voluntary classification.

7.2.1 *Instruments that may be classified as held-to-maturity*

Only assets with fixed or determinable payments and fixed maturity can be included in this category (see 7 and 7.2 above). Most equity instruments cannot be held-to-maturity investments either because they have an indefinite life (such as ordinary shares) or because the amounts the holder may receive can vary in a manner that is not predetermined (such as share options, warrants, and rights). A debt instrument with a variable interest rate generally can satisfy this condition.[328]

A perpetual debt instrument on which interest payments are made for an indefinite period cannot be classified as a held-to-maturity investment because there is no maturity date.[329] However, there is no reason why a perpetual debt instrument with fixed or determinable payments for a limited period cannot be classified as held-to-maturity. In effect, the instrument matures at the date of the last contractual payment and the amount invested is recovered through fixed or determinable payments and the rights in liquidation have no fair value (see Example 20.24 in Chapter 20 at 5.4).

A financial asset that is callable by the issuer satisfies the criteria for a held-to-maturity investment if the holder intends, and is able, to hold it until it is called, or until maturity, and if the holder would recover substantially all of its carrying amount. The call option, if exercised, simply accelerates the investment's maturity. However, if the investment is callable on a basis that the holder would not recover substantially all of its carrying amount, it cannot be classified as held-to-maturity. Any premium paid and capitalised transaction costs should be considered in determining whether the carrying amount would be substantially recovered.[330]

A financial asset that is puttable (the holder has the right to require the issuer to repay or redeem the instrument before maturity) cannot be classified as a held-to-maturity investment. Paying for a put feature is considered inconsistent with expressing an intention of holding such an instrument to maturity.[331] The previous version of IAS 39 entertained the possibility ('with great care') of classifying such an instrument as held-to-maturity.[332]

The reference to 'fixed or determinable payments and fixed maturity' in the definition means a contractual arrangement that defines the amounts and dates of payments to the holder, such as interest and principal payments. The likelihood of default is not a consideration in qualifying for this category, provided there is an intention and ability, considering the credit condition existing at the acquisition date, to hold the investment to maturity. Even if there is a significant risk of non-payment of interest and principal, for example a bond with a very low credit rating, the contractual payments on the bond may well be fixed or determinable.[333]

Where a combined instrument contains a host contract and an embedded derivative (see 5 above), the host may be classified as held-to-maturity if it has fixed or determinable payments and no other conditions are breached. This is illustrated in the following examples.

Example 17.24: Note with index-linked principal

Company A purchases a five year interest free equity-index-linked note, with an original issue price of €10, for its market price of €12. At maturity, the note requires payment of the original issue price of €10 plus a supplemental redemption amount that depends on whether a specified stock price index exceeds a predetermined level at the maturity date. If the stock index does not exceed the predetermined level, no supplemental redemption amount is paid. If it does, the supplemental redemption amount equals the product of €1.15 and the difference between the level of the stock index at maturity and original issuance divided by the level at original issuance. A has the positive intention and ability to hold the note to maturity.

The note can be classified as a held-to-maturity investment because it has a fixed payment of €10 and fixed maturity and there is the positive intention and ability to hold it to maturity. However, the equity index feature is a call option not closely related to the debt host which must be separated as an embedded derivative (see 5.1.1 F above). The purchase price (initial fair value) of €12 is allocated between the host debt instrument and the embedded derivative – the latter will have a non-zero fair value because it is an option-based derivative.[334]

Example 17.25: Note with index-linked interest

Subsequently, A purchases a note with a fixed payment at a fixed maturity date and interest payments that are indexed to the price of a commodity or equity. There is an intention and ability to hold the note to maturity.

Again the note can be classified as a held-to-maturity investment because it has a fixed payment and fixed maturity. However, the commodity-indexed or equity-indexed interest payments result in an embedded derivative that is separated and accounted for as a derivative.[335]

It is possible for the terms of the embedded derivative to breach other conditions for classifying the host as held-to-maturity. For example, an investment in a convertible bond that can be converted *before* maturity generally cannot be classified as a held-to-maturity investment. The embedded conversion feature allows the investor to settle the host investment before maturity and, as noted above, paying for such a conversion feature would be inconsistent with an intention to hold the host to maturity.[336]

7.2.2 Positive intention and ability to hold to maturity

An entity should assess its intention and ability to hold these instruments to maturity when they are initially acquired and also at each balance sheet date.[337]

If any one of the following criteria is met, a positive intention to hold an investment to maturity is deemed not to exist (and the asset cannot be classified as such):

- the intention to hold the investment is for only an undefined period;
- the holder stands ready to sell the financial asset in response to changes in market interest rates or risks, liquidity needs, changes in the availability of and the yield on alternative investments, changes in financing sources and terms, or changes in foreign currency risk (although this does not apply to situations that are non-recurring and could not have been reasonably anticipated); or
- the issuer has a right to settle the financial asset at an amount significantly below its amortised cost.[338]

Further, an investor is deemed not to have a demonstrated ability to hold an investment to maturity if:

- it does not have the financial resources available to continue to finance the investment until maturity; or
- it is subject to an existing legal or other constraint that could frustrate its intention to hold the financial asset to maturity (although as noted at 7.2.1 above, an issuer's call option does not necessarily frustrate this intention).[339]

The intention and ability to hold debt instruments to maturity is not necessarily constrained if those instruments have been pledged as collateral or are subject to a repurchase or securities lending agreements. However, an entity would not have the positive intention and ability to hold the debt instruments until maturity if it did not expect to be able to maintain or recover access to the instruments.[340]

The standard also suggest that circumstances other than those described above can indicate that an entity does not have a positive intention or ability to hold an investment to maturity.[341]

7.2.3 The tainting provisions

When an entity's actions cast doubt on its intention or ability to hold such investments to maturity, the use of amortised cost for held-to-maturity assets is precluded for 'a reasonable period of time'.[342] Consequently, no investment should be classified as held-to-maturity if, during either the current financial year or the two preceding financial years, the reporting entity has sold or reclassified more than an insignificant (in relation to the total) amount of such investments before maturity other than by those effected:

(a) close enough to maturity or call date (e.g. less than three months before maturity) so that changes in the market rate of interest did not have a significant effect on the investment's fair value;

(b) after substantially all of the investment's original principal had been collected through scheduled payments or prepayments; or

(c) due to an isolated non-recurring event that is beyond the holder's control and could not have been reasonably anticipated by the holder.[343]

Therefore, if an entity makes any 'not insignificant' sale or reclassification of a held-to-maturity investment that does not fall within (a) to (c) above, the entire remaining portfolio of such investments will have to be reclassified as available-for-sale (see 7.4 and 7.5 below) and will be remeasured to fair value for at least the following two financial years. The nature of this 'punishment' is unique within accounting standards and has become known as the 'tainting' or, by rugby followers, the 'sin-bin' provisions.

The guidance to the original version of IAS 39 explained that conditions (a) and (b) relate to situations in which an entity is expected to be indifferent whether to hold or sell a financial asset because movements in interest rates after substantially all of the original principal has been collected or when the instrument is close to maturity will not have a significant impact on its fair value. Accordingly, such a sale should not affect reported income and no price volatility would be expected during the remaining period to maturity.

It went on to say that if a financial asset is sold less than three months prior to maturity, that would generally qualify for this exception because the impact on the instrument's fair value of a difference between the stated interest rate and the market rate would generally be small for an instrument that matures in three months relative to an instrument that matures in several years. If sold after 90% or more of its original principal has been collected through scheduled payments or prepayments, condition (b) would generally be met. However, if only, say, 10% of the original principal has been collected, then that condition is clearly not met.[344]

The implementation guidance makes it clear that condition (c) does not extend to an unsolicited tender offer on economically favourable terms.[345]

The conditions must be applied to all held-to-maturity investments in aggregate and not to separate sub-categories of such assets (e.g. US dollar and euro denominated investments).[346] In consolidated financial statements they must be applied to all investments classified as held-to-maturity in those financial statements, even if they are held by different entities within the group, in different countries or in different legal or economic environments.[347]

A 'disaster scenario' that is only remotely possible, such as a run on a bank or a similar situation affecting an insurer, is not anticipated in deciding whether there is positive intention and ability to hold an investment to maturity.[348] The standard also explains that sales before maturity may satisfy condition (c) above – and therefore not trigger the tainting provisions – if they are attributable to:

- a significant deterioration in the issuer's creditworthiness (see below);
- a change in tax law that eliminates or significantly reduces the tax-exempt status of interest on the held-to-maturity investment, but not a change in tax law that revises the marginal tax rates applicable to interest income;
- a major business combination or major disposition, such as the sale of a segment, that necessitates the sale or transfer of held-to-maturity investments to maintain the holder's existing interest rate risk position or credit risk policy. Although the business combination itself is an event within the holder's control, the changes to its investment portfolio to maintain its interest rate risk position or credit risk policy may be consequential rather than anticipated;
- a change in statutory or regulatory requirements significantly modifying either what constitutes a permissible investment or the maximum level of particular types of investments, thereby causing disposal of a held-to-maturity investment;
- a significant increase in the industry's regulatory capital requirements that causes a downsizing by selling held-to-maturity investments; or
- a significant increase in the risk weights of held-to-maturity investments used for regulatory risk-based capital purposes.[349]

A sale following a downgrade in a credit rating by an external rating agency would not necessarily raise a question about the entity's intention to hold other investments to maturity if the downgrade provides evidence of a significant deterioration in the issuer's creditworthiness judged by reference to the credit rating at initial recognition.[350] However, the rating downgrade must not have been reasonably anticipated when the investment was classified as held to maturity. A credit downgrade of a notch within a class or from one rating class to the immediately lower rating class could often be regarded as reasonably anticipated.[351]

Similarly, where internal ratings are used for assessing exposures, changes in those ratings may help to identify issuers for which there has been a significant deterioration in creditworthiness, provided the approach to assigning ratings and changes therein give a consistent, reliable and objective measure of the credit quality of the issuers.[352]

If there is evidence that a financial asset is impaired (see Chapter 20 at 6), for example a rating downgrade in combination with other information, the deterioration in creditworthiness is often regarded as significant.[353]

Sales of held-to-maturity investments in response to an unanticipated significant increase by the regulator in the *industry's* capital requirements may not necessarily raise a question about the intention to hold other investments to maturity. However, in some countries, regulators may set *entity-specific* capital requirements based on an assessment of the risk in that particular entity. Therefore sales that are due to a significant increase in entity-specific capital requirements imposed by regulators *will* raise doubt over the intention to hold other financial assets to maturity unless it can be demonstrated that the sales fulfil condition (c) above. In other words, they should result from an increase in capital requirements which is an isolated non-recurring event that is beyond the entity's control and could not have been reasonably anticipated.[354]

A change in management is not identified as an exception and the guidance explains that sales in response to such a change would call into question the intention to hold investments to maturity.[355]

Example 17.26: Change of management

A company has a portfolio of financial assets that is classified as held-to-maturity. In the current period, at the direction of the board of directors, the senior management team has been replaced. The new management wishes to sell a portion of the held-to-maturity financial assets in order to carry out an expansion strategy designated and approved by the board.

Although the previous management team had been in place since the company's formation and had never before undergone a major restructuring, the sale nevertheless calls into question the company's intention to hold remaining held-to-maturity financial assets to maturity and the company may be prohibited from using the held-to-maturity classification if the amounts involved are not insignificant.[356]

7.3 Loans and receivables

At noted at 7 above, the loans and receivables category comprises financial assets with fixed or determinable payments that are not quoted in an active market, do not qualify as 'trading' assets, have not been designated at fair value through profit or loss or as available-for-sale and for which the holder may recover substantially all of its initial investment, other than because of credit deterioration.[357]

This category replaces 'originated loans and receivables' in the original version of IAS 39. Although there are some differences between the two, for most entities both comprise mainly trade receivables, other debtors and bank deposits; for banks and similar financial institutions both constitute a significant proportion (possibly more or less than previously) of their non-trading assets, in particular loans and advances to customers.[358]

Originally, to be included in this category, a loan asset had to be originated by the entity (either directly or by way of a syndication/participation arrangement). Purchased, as opposed to originated, loans and receivables were classified as held-to-maturity, available-for-sale, or held for trading, as appropriate.[359] However, in developing the December 2003 version of IAS 39 the IASB took account of respondents' concerns that:

(a) some entities typically manage purchased and originated loans together; and

(b) there are systems problems associated with segregating purchased and originated loans because any distinction between them is likely to be made only for accounting purposes.

It therefore decided to remove the requirement that loans and receivables must be originated so that if an entity purchases a portfolio of loans they may be included within this category.[360]

In response to this relaxation, the IASB decided that an asset with terms such that the holder may not recover substantially all of its initial investment (other than because of credit deterioration), for example a fixed rate interest-only strip created in a securitisation and subject to prepayment risk, should not be classified within loans and receivables. The IASB believes such instruments should be recorded at fair value,[361] probably because that value can be more volatile than that of other loans and receivables.

As noted above, instruments 'quoted in an active market' are prohibited from being included within this category and must therefore be included in one of the other three categories of financial asset.[362] Originally there was no such restriction. The IASB considered that an unrestricted ability to record an asset at amortised cost (as is the case for loans and receivables) should not apply to liquid assets. For those instruments, amortised cost accounting should only be available where there is a positive intention and ability to hold the investment to maturity.[363] Accordingly, it is likely that many originated investments in bonds are likely to be classified as available-for-sale under the revised standard. The meaning of 'quoted in an active market' is considered in more detail in Chapter 20 at 4 and 4.1.

Provided there is no intention to sell the instrument immediately or in the short term, where a bank makes a term deposit with a central or other bank it is classified within loans and receivables even if the proof of deposit is negotiable, i.e. the deposit is capable of being sold. If there was such an intention to sell, the deposit would be a trading asset.[364]

Instruments that have the legal form of equities, such as preference shares, but which under IAS 32 would be classified as liabilities in the financial statements of the issuer and have fixed or determinable payments and fixed maturity (see Chapter 19 at 3) can potentially be classified within loans and receivables, provided the instrument is not quoted in an active market. However if, under IAS 32, it would be classified as an equity instrument in the financial statements of the issuer, it could not be classified within loans and receivables by the holder.[365]

The standard explains that an interest acquired in a pool of assets that are not loans or receivables (for example, an interest in a mutual fund or a similar fund) is not a loan or receivable.[366] We believe this was added to clarify the treatment of investments in mutual funds, unit trusts and similar funds – this issue is dealt with in more detail at 5.1.1 I above.

The principal difference between loans and receivables and held-to-maturity investments is that loans and receivables are not subject to the tainting provisions (see 7.2.3 above). Consequently, loans and receivables that are not held for trading may be measured at amortised cost even if an entity does not have the positive intention and ability to hold the loan asset until maturity.[367] Financial assets that do not meet the definition of loans and receivables, e.g. because they are quoted in an active market, may be classified as held-to-maturity investments if they meet the relevant conditions.[368] However, it is important to recognise another major difference between the two classes of instrument, namely the significant restrictions on applying hedge accounting when the hedged item is a held-to-maturity investment (see Chapter 21 at 2.2.5).

On initial recognition a financial asset that would otherwise be classified as a loan or receivable may now be designated as available-for-sale or, potentially at fair value through profit or loss (see 7.4 below and 7.1.2 above respectively).[369]

7.4 Available-for-sale assets

Originally, a financial asset was classified as available-for-sale if it did not properly belong in one of the three other categories of financial assets – held for trading, held-to-maturity and loans and receivables.[370] The ability to designate instruments within certain categories means that available-for-sale is no longer quite the 'default' classification that it was.

In practice, the only type of asset that would be designated into this category on initial recognition is one that would otherwise be classified within loans and receivables (see 7.3 above).

The main interpretative issue an entity is likely to experience in respect of this classification is whether a portfolio of investments can properly be regarded as available-for-sale rather than trading. The implementation guidance provides the following example to assist in making this judgment.

Example 17.27: Portfolio balancing

Company A has an investment portfolio of debt and equity instruments. The documented portfolio management guidelines specify that the equity exposure of the portfolio should be limited to between 30% and 50% of total portfolio value. The investment manager of the portfolio is authorised to balance the portfolio within the designated guidelines by buying and selling equity and debt instruments. The instruments should be classified as trading or available-for-sale depending on Company A's intent and past practice.

If the portfolio manager is authorised to buy and sell instruments to balance the risks in a portfolio, but there is no intention to trade and there is no past practice of trading for short-term profit, the instruments can be classified as available-for-sale. If instruments are bought and sold to generate short-term profits, the financial instruments in the portfolio should be classified as held for trading.[371]

7.5 Reclassifications

To impose discipline on an entity's ability to designate items at fair value through profit or loss, financial instruments cannot be reclassified into or out of this category subsequent to initial recognition.[372] Originally there was only a prohibition on reclassifying instruments out of the trading category and it was possible to reclassify assets as trading if there was a recent pattern of short-term profit taking within the portfolio in which they were held.[373] Accordingly, if an entity starts to trade (as set out at 7.1.1 above) a portfolio of available-for-sale investments, say, all newly acquired investments will be classified as trading, but the legacy investments will continue to be classified as available-for-sale.

Taken at face value, the prohibition on reclassifying instruments into or out of 'at fair value through profit or loss' prevents an entity from (a) designating a derivative as a hedging instrument if it was previously classified as trading, and (b) revoking the designation of an effective hedge involving a derivative. However, the parts of IAS 39 dealing with hedge accounting (see Chapter 21, for example at 4.1.3, 4.2.3 and 5.3) are clear that these are not regarded as prohibited reclassifications.

Otherwise, the only reclassifications permitted are between held-to-maturity investments and available-for-sale assets. An investment will be reclassified as available-for-sale if, as a result of a change in intention or ability, it fails to meet the requirements for classification as held-to-maturity.[374] If the tainting provisions (see 7.2.3 above) are triggered, any remaining held-to-maturity investments should also be reclassified as available-for-sale.[375] Similarly if, as a result of a change in intention or ability or because the tainting period has passed, it becomes appropriate to regard an available-for-sale asset as held-to-maturity, it should be reclassified accordingly.[376] Accounting for reclassifications is dealt with in Chapter 20 at 3.6.

The IASB is considering amending IAS 39 in its annual improvements project to remove the apparent prohibition on re-designating a derivative as a hedging instrument in an effective hedge (which would effectively codify current practice). It is also considering whether the amendment should allow non-derivative instruments to be reclassified as at fair value through profit or loss if evidence arises for the first time of a recent actual pattern of short-term profit-taking in the portfolio of which they were a part, or if instruments are transferred into such a portfolio,[377] although such a change could be seen as being inconsistent with the restrictions imposed on the use of the fair value option and it is not clear whether the IASB will actually proceed with it.

7.6 Classification of financial instruments in a business combination

Neither IAS 39 nor the current version of IFRS 3 addresses how an entity should approach classifying financial assets or financial liabilities it acquires or assumes as part of a business combination. In particular, they do not deal with the question of whether the acquirer should base the classification on its strategies and intentions towards the acquired entity or whether it should look to how the acquired entity classified those instruments. This is particularly relevant for designations, e.g. at fair value through profit or loss, which can be made only on initial recognition and not revisited.

From the perspective of an acquirer applying the purchase method of accounting, it would seem logical to view the business combination as giving rise to the initial recognition of the financial instruments. The IASB staff considers this to be implied from IAS 39 already[378] and the IASB has decided that the forthcoming amendment to IFRS 3 will require this treatment.[379]

In rare cases, the pooling of interests method may be used for a business combination, for example in a transaction involving entities under common control (see Chapter 7 at 2.4). In such cases the basis of preparation involves an assumption that the acquired entities were always part of the same reporting entity and therefore it would normally be appropriate to look to the classification of the financial instruments in the financial statements of the acquired entity.

8 EFFECTIVE DATES, TRANSITIONAL PROVISIONS AND FIRST-TIME ADOPTION

This section contains information that is relevant for annual periods beginning on or after 1 January 2006. For earlier periods, equivalent requirements are dealt with in *International GAAP 2005* and *International GAAP 2007*, the predecessors to this publication.

8.1 Effective dates

The June 2005 amendments to IAS 39 relating to the fair value option (see 7.1 above) must be applied for annual periods beginning on or after 1 January 2006 and earlier application is encouraged.[380]

The August 2005 amendments to IAS 39 relating to financial guarantee contracts (see 3.4 above) must also be applied for annual periods beginning on or after 1 January 2006. Earlier application is encouraged, although entities must disclose the fact that they have done so and must also apply all of the related amendments (i.e. those to IFRS 4 as well as the consequential amendments to IAS 32 or IFRS 7) at the same time.[381]

IFRS 7 is effective for annual periods beginning on or after 1 January 2007. Entities are encouraged to apply the standard earlier, although if they do they are required to disclose this fact.[382]

IFRIC 5 (see 3.10 above) is effective for annual periods commencing on or after 1 January 2006, as is the associated amendment to IAS 39. Earlier application of IFRIC 5 is encouraged although that fact should be disclosed and the amendment to IAS 39 should be applied at the same time.[383]

IFRIC 9 (see 5.4 above) is effective for annual periods beginning on or after 1 June 2006. Earlier application is encouraged, although this fact should be disclosed.[384]

8.2 Transitional provisions

The requirements of IFRIC 9 should be applied retrospectively[385] as should the amendments to IAS 39 issued with IFRIC 5 relating to reimbursements and those relating to financial guarantee contracts. The relevant transitional provisions relating to topics covered in Chapters 18 to 22 are dealt with in those chapters.

There are transitional provisions relating to the fair value option amendments but they are not straightforward. Where the amendments are adopted for an annual period beginning on or after 1 January 2006, an entity:[386]

(a) is required to de-designate any financial asset or financial liability previously designated as at fair value through profit or loss if it does not qualify for such designation in accordance with the amended standard.

When a financial asset or financial liability will be measured at amortised cost after de-designation, the date of de-designation is deemed to be its date of initial recognition.

The fair value at the date of de-designation of any financial assets or financial liabilities de-designated, as well their new classifications, should be disclosed;

(b) is prohibited from designating as at fair value through profit or loss any previously recognised financial assets or financial liabilities.

Comparative financial statements should be restated using the new designations above provided that, in the case of a financial asset, financial liability, or group of financial assets, financial liabilities or both, designated as at fair value through profit or loss, those items or groups would have met the relevant condition at the beginning of the comparative period or, if acquired after the beginning of the comparative period, at the date of initial recognition.[387]

8.3 First-time adoption

IFRS 1 – *First-time Adoption of International Financial Reporting Standards* – is dealt with in Chapter 5. The aspects related to the topics covered in this chapter are covered in detail below. Further similar sections are included in Chapters 18 to 22.

8.3.1 Derivatives and embedded derivatives

Except for those that are designated and effective hedging instruments, all derivatives (including those that are embedded in other contracts and are required by IAS 39 to be accounted for separately) should be classified as held for trading with effect from the date of transition to IFRS.[388]

Under US GAAP, an entity was not required to account for some pre-existing embedded derivatives separately. The IASB considered this, and the fact that full retrospective accounting for embedded derivatives might be costly, but concluded 'that the failure to measure embedded derivatives at fair value would diminish the relevance and reliability of an entity's first IFRS financial statements'. Therefore, a first-time adopter should review all contracts existing at its date of transition to IFRS.[389]

IFRIC 9 states that, on first-time adoption, an entity should make an assessment of whether an embedded derivative is required to be separated from the host contract and accounted for as a derivative on the basis of conditions that existed at the later of the date it first became party to the contract and the date a reassessment is required (see 5.4.1 above).[390]

8.3.2 Other financial assets and financial liabilities at fair value through profit or loss

Although IAS 39 permits a financial instrument to be designated only on initial recognition as a financial asset or financial liability at fair value through profit or loss, exceptions apply in the following circumstances:[391]

(a) *Entities presenting their first IFRS financial statements for an annual period beginning on or after 1 September 2006*

These are permitted to designate, at the date of transition to IFRSs, any financial asset or financial liability as at fair value through profit or loss provided it meets one of the condition set out at 7.1.2 B above at that date;

(b) *Entities presenting their first IFRS financial statements for an annual period beginning on or after 1 January 2006 but before 1 September 2006*

These are permitted to designate, at the date of transition to IFRSs, any financial asset or financial liability as at fair value through profit or loss provided it meets one of the conditions set out at 7.1.2 B above at that date.

When the date of transition to IFRSs is before 1 September 2005, such designations need not be completed until 1 September 2005 and may also include financial assets and financial liabilities recognised between the date of transition to IFRSs and 1 September 2005.

Any financial assets and financial liabilities so designated that were previously designated as the hedged item in fair value hedge accounting relationships should be de-designated from those relationships at the same time they are designated as at fair value through profit or loss.

Where advantage of any of these exceptions is taken, certain additional disclosures are required which are set out in Chapter 22 at 5.3.

Different exceptions were available for entities presenting their first IFRS financial statements for earlier periods, and these depended on whether or not the fair value option amendments were adopted, but they are not covered in this publication.[392]

Other non-derivative financial instruments are included within this category if, and only if:[393]

- they were acquired or incurred principally for the purpose of selling or repurchasing it in the near term; or
- at the date of transition to IFRS were part of a portfolio of identified financial instruments that were managed together and for which there was evidence of a recent actual pattern of short-term profit taking.

These instruments would be classified as held for trading rather than being designated at fair value through profit and loss.

8.3.3 Held-to-maturity investments

The classification of investments as held-to-maturity relies, effectively, on a designation made by the entity reflecting its intention and ability to hold the investment to maturity (see 7.2 above). It is explained that sales or transfers of an entity's held-to-maturity investments before the date of transition to IFRS do not trigger the 'tainting' provisions (see 7.2.3 above) and therefore do not prevent an entity using this classification on first-time adoption.[394]

8.3.4 Loans and receivables

In assessing whether or not a financial asset can meet the definition of loans and receivables at the date of transition to IFRS the circumstances that existed when it first met the recognition criteria in IAS 39 (see Chapter 18 at 3) should be considered.[395]

8.3.5 Available-for-sale assets

Any first-time adopter is allowed to designate a non-derivative financial asset at the date of transition to IFRS as available-for-sale even though the general requirement in IAS 39 is to make such a designation on initial recognition of the instrument.[396] Where advantage is taken of this exemption, certain additional disclosures are required which are set out in Chapter 22 at 5.3.

In addition to those financial assets that are designated as available-for-sale, this category includes those assets that are not in any of the other categories above.[397]

9 FUTURE DEVELOPMENTS

The majority of the IASB's current work on financial instruments is being carried out in conjunction with the FASB as part of their Memorandum of Understanding (see Chapter 1). The boards have established three long-term objectives for simplifying and improving the accounting for financial instruments:

- to require all financial instruments to be measured at fair value with realised and unrealised gains and losses recognised in the period in which they occur;
- to simplify or eliminate the need for special hedge accounting requirements; and
- to develop a new standard for the derecognition of financial instruments.

Neither board has added projects reflecting these three objectives to its active agenda because they recognise that there are some significant impediments to attaining them, i.e. there are difficult technical and practical issues that currently exist that are likely to take time to resolve. The main issues include:

- which instruments and related assets and liabilities should be subject to the requirement;
- how to estimate fair value for instruments that are not traded or are traded in government-controlled or illiquid markets; and
- how to present the components of the net changes in fair values, and what information to disclose about past changes in fair values and exposures to future changes in market factors.

Even if these problems are resolved the boards do not expect to be in a position to require fair value measurement of all financial instruments for 'several years' and the next step envisaged by the boards is the publication before 2008 of a 'due process document' setting out possible ways to move toward their goal.[398]

Possible future developments relating to topics covered in Chapters 18 to 22, including more detail on the joint objectives noted above, are dealt with in those chapters.

References

1 *IASC Update*, IASC, December 1996.

2 IAS 32 (2005), *Financial Instruments: Disclosure and Presentation*, IASB, March 1995 to August 2005.

3 Discussion Paper, *Accounting for Financial Assets and Financial Liabilities*, IASC, March 1997.

4 Discussion Paper, Chapter 3, para. 3.1.

5 Discussion Paper, Chapter 4, para. 2.1 and Chapter 5, para. 3.1.

6 Discussion Paper, Chapter 6, para. 5.1.

7 Draft Standard, *Financial Instruments and Similar Items*, JWG, December 2000.

8 E62, *Financial Instruments: Recognition and Measurement*, IASC, June 1998.

9 IAS 39 (2000), *Financial Instruments: Recognition and Measurement*, IASC, December 1998 to October 2000.

10 *IAS 39 Implementation Guidance*, IAS 39 Implementation Guidance Committee, May 2000 and subsequently, Introduction.
11 Press Release, *IASB Announces Agenda of Technical Projects*, IASB, 31 July 2001.
12 Exposure Draft, *Amendments to IAS 32, Financial Instruments: Disclosure and Presentation, and IAS 39, Financial Instruments: Recognition and Measurement*, IASB, June 2002.
13 Press Release, *International Accounting Standards Board Issues Revised Standards on Financial Instruments*, IASB, 17 December 2003.
14 Press Release, *International Accounting Standards Board Issues Revised Standards on Financial Instruments*, IASB, 17 December 2003.
15 Press Release IP/03/1297, *Financial reporting: Commission adopts Regulation endorsing International Accounting Standards*, European Commission, 29 September 2003.
16 Exposure Draft, Amendments to IAS 39 Financial Instruments: Recognition and Measurement, *Fair Value Hedge Accounting for a Portfolio Hedge of Interest Rate Risk*, IASB, August 2003.
17 ED, para. AV1.
18 Amendment to IAS 39, Financial Instruments: Recognition and Measurement, *Fair Value Hedge Accounting for a Portfolio Hedge of Interest Rate Risk*, IASB, March 2004.
19 IAS 32, *Financial Instruments: Presentation*, IASB, para. DO1; IAS 39, *Financial Instruments: Recognition and Measurement*, IASB, para. DO1 and Amendment to IAS 39, para. DO1.
20 Press Release, *IASB Finalises Macro Hedging Amendments to IAS 39*, IASB, 31 March 2004.
21 Press Release, *European Consultative Group on Accounting Issues Affecting Financial Institutions*, IASC Foundation, 10 February 2004.
22 Press Release, *IASB announces membership of working group on financial instruments*, IASB, 21 September 2004.
23 Exposure Draft, *Amendments to IAS 39 Financial Instruments: Recognition and Measurement – The Fair Value Option*, IASB, April 2004.
24 ED, paras. AV1-AV7.
25 Press Release, *International Accounting Standards Board issues Exposure Draft of Proposed Amendment to IAS 39*, IASB, 21 April 2004.
26 Press Release IP/04/1385, *Accounting standards: Commission adopts endorses IAS 39*, European Commission, 19 November 2004.
27 Press Release IP/04/1385, *Accounting standards: Commission adopts endorses IAS 39*, European Commission, 19 November 2004.
28 Appendix to Information for Observers (17 December 2004 IASB meeting), *Amendments to IAS 39: The Fair Value Option (Preliminary First Draft of a Possible New Approach)*, IASB, December 2004.
29 Press Release, *IAS 39's Fair Value Option: Preliminary Draft of a Possible New Approach for Discussion at Public Roundtable Meetings on 16 March*, IASB, 22 January 2004.
30 Amendments to IAS 39, Financial Instruments: Recognition and Measurement, *The Fair Value Option*, IASB, June 2005.
31 Amendments to IAS 39, paras. DO1-DO4.
32 Press Release IP/05/1423, *Accounting standards: Commission endorses "IAS 39 Fair Value Option"*, European Commission, 15 November 2005.
33 *IASB Update*, IASB, October 2005.
34 Discussion Paper, *Accounting for Financial Assets and Financial Liabilities*, IASC, March 1997, Chapter 6, para. 2.4.
35 IAS 39, para. BC14.
36 IAS 32, Application Guidance, para. before para. AG1, IAS 39, Application guidance, para. before para. AG1, IFRS 7, *Financial Instruments: Disclosure*, IASB, Appendix B, Application guidance, para. after main heading.
37 IAS 32, Illustrative Examples, para. after main heading, IAS 39, Illustrative Example, para. after main heading.
38 IAS 39, Guidance on Implementing, para. before main heading Section A, IFRS 7, Guidance on implementing, para. after main heading.
39 IAS 32, para. 2.
40 IAS 39, para. 1.
41 IFRS 7, para. 1.
42 IAS 32 (2005), para. 1.
43 IAS 32, para. 11.
44 IAS 32, para. 14.
45 IAS 32, para. 13.
46 Information for Observers (May 2007 IFRIC meeting), *Gaming Transactions*, IASB, May 2007, paras. 25 to 27 and *IFRIC Update*, IASB, July 2007.
47 IAS 32, para. AG7.
48 IAS 32, para. AG12.
49 IAS 32, para. AG12.
50 IAS 32, para. AG3.
51 IAS 32, para. AG4.
52 IAS 32, para. AG5.
53 IAS 32, para. AG6.
54 IAS 32, para. AG8.

55 IAS 32, para. AG8.
56 IAS 32, para. AG8.
57 IAS 32, para. AG9.
58 IAS 32, para. AG9.
59 IAS 32, para. AG9.
60 IAS 32, para. AG10.
61 IAS 39, para. B.1.
62 IAS 32, para. AG11.
63 IAS 32, para. AG20.
64 IAS 32, para. AG21.
65 IAS 32, para. AG22.
66 IAS 32, para. AG23.
67 IAS 32, para. AG13.
68 IAS 32, paras. AG15-AG16.
69 IAS 32, para. AG16.
70 IAS 32, para. AG17.
71 IAS 32, para. AG18.
72 IAS 32, para. AG19.
73 IAS 32, para. 4, IAS 39, para. 2 and IFRS 7, para. 3.
74 IAS 32, para. 4(a), IAS 39, para. 2(a) and IFRS 7, para. 3(a).
75 IAS 27, *Consolidated and Separate Financial Statements*, IASB, paras. 37-38; IAS 28, *Investments in Associates*, IASB, para. 35; IAS 31, *Interests in Joint Ventures*, IASB, para. 46; IAS 32, para. 4(a), IAS 39, para. 2(a) and IFRS 7, para. 3(a).
76 *IASB Update*, IASB, May 2007.
77 IAS 28, para. 1; IAS 31, para. 1; IAS 32, para. 4(a) and IAS 39, para. 2(a).
78 IAS 32, para. 4(a) and IFRS 7, para. 3(a).
79 *IASB Update*, IASB, May 2007.
80 IAS 32, para. 4(a), IAS 39, para. 2(a) and IFRS 7, para. 3(a).
81 IAS 27, para. IG7.
82 IAS 39, para. AG3.
83 IAS 39, para. 2(b).
84 IFRS 4, *Insurance Contracts*, Appendix A, Defined terms.
85 IFRS 4, Appendix B, Definition of an insurance contract.
86 IAS 32, para. 4(d), IAS 39, para. 2(e) and IFRS 7, para. 3(d).
87 IAS 39, para. 2(e).
88 IAS 32, para. 4(d) and IFRS 7, para. 3(d).
89 IAS 39, para. AG4(a).
90 IAS 39, para. AG3A.
91 IAS 39, para. AG1.
92 IFRS 4, paras. B18(l) and B19(g).
93 IFRS 4, Appendix A, Defined terms.
94 IAS 32, para. 4(e), IAS 39, para. 2(e), IFRS 4, para. 2(b) and IFRS 7, para. 3.
95 IAS 39, para. 2(e).
96 IAS 39 (2000), para. 1(f); *IAS 39 Implementation Guidance*, Questions & Answers, IAS 39 Implementation Guidance Committee (IGC), May 2000 and subsequently, Q&A 1-1, Q&A 1-2, Q&A 1-5-a, and Q&A 1-5-b.
97 IAS 39 (2003), *Financial Instruments: Recognition and Measurement*, IASB, December 2003, para. 2(f).
98 IFRS 4, IASB, March 2004, Appendix C, Amendments to other IFRSs, paras. C2 and C5.
99 IFRS 4 (2004), *Insurance Contracts*, IASB, March 2004, para. BC67(d).
100 IAS 39, para. 9 and IFRS 4, Appendix A, Defined terms.
101 IAS 39, para. AG4(b) and IFRS 4, Appendix B, para. B19(f).
102 IAS 39, para. AG4.
103 IAS 32, para. 4(d), IAS 39, para. 2(e), IFRS 4, para. 4(d) and IFRS 7, para. 3(d).
104 IAS 39, para. BC23A.
105 IAS 39, para. AG4A.
106 Diageo's parent company financial statements are not prepared under IFRS but its local GAAP contains requirements for accounting for financial guarantee contracts that are equivalent to those in IAS 39.
107 IAS 39, para. BC23A.
108 IAS 39, para. AG4(c).
109 IAS 39, para. AG4(a).
110 IFRS 4, para. 4(f).
111 IFRS 4, para. IG2, Example 1.11.
112 IAS 39, para. BC23C.
113 IAS 32, para. AG29.
114 IAS 39, para. BC15.
115 IGC Q&A 30-1.
116 IAS 39, para. BC16.
117 IAS 39, para. 2(h).
118 IAS 32 (2005), para. 5 and IFRS 7, para. 4.
119 IAS 39, paras. 2(h) and 4.
120 IAS 39, para. BC17.
121 IAS 39, para. BC18.
122 IAS 39, para. 4.
123 IAS 39, para. BC20.
124 IAS 39, para. 4(b).
125 IAS 39, para. BC19.
126 IAS 39, para. 2(h).
127 IAS 39, para. BC15.
128 IAS 39, para. 2(d).
129 IAS 32 (2005), para. 5.
130 IAS 32, para. 4(c), IAS 39, para. 2(f) and IFRS 7, para. 3(c).
131 *IFRIC Update*, IASB, August 2002.
132 IAS 39, para. 2(g).
133 Information for Observers (18 November 2003 IASB meeting), *Business Combinations – Phase I*, IASB, November 2003, para. 33.
134 *IASB Update*, IASB, November 2003.
135 Information for Observers, para. 35.

136 Information for Observers, para. 36.
137 Information for Observers, para. 37.
138 Information for Observers, para. 38.
139 Information for Observers, para. 39.
140 Information for Observers, paras. 34 and 35.
141 IAS 32, para. 4(b), IAS 39, para. 2(c) and IFRS 7, para. 3(b).
142 *IFRIC Update*, IASB, November 2005.
143 IAS 32, para. 4(f), IAS 39, para. 2(i) and IFRS 7, para. 3(e).
144 IAS 32, para. 4(f)(ii).
145 IAS 32, para. AG20.
146 IAS 32, para. AG20.
147 IAS 32, para. 8, IAS 39, para. 5 and IFRS 7, para. 5.
148 IAS 32, para. 9 and IAS 39, paras. 6 and BC24.
149 IAS 32, para. 8, IAS 39, para. 5 and IFRS 7, para. 5.
150 IAS 32, para. 9 and IAS 39, paras. 6 and BC24.
151 IAS 39, para. A.1.
152 *IFRIC Update*, IASB, August 2005.
153 IAS 32, para. 9 and IAS 39, paras. 6 and BC24.
154 IAS 32, para. 9 and IAS 39, paras. 6 and BC24.
155 IAS 32, para. 10 and IAS 39, paras. 7 and BC24.
156 IAS 39, para. A.2.
157 JWG Draft Standard, paras. 92 to 94, Application Supplement, paras. 331 to 335 and Basis for Conclusions, paras. 4.18 to 4.28.
158 *IFRIC Update*, IASB, March 2007 and Information for Observers (January 2007 IFRIC meeting), *IAS 39 Financial Instruments: Recognition and Measurement – Written options in retail energy contracts (Agenda Paper 14(iv))*, IASB, January 2007, paras. 9 to 11.
159 *IFRIC Update*, IASB, March 2007 and Information for Observers (January 2007 IFRIC meeting), *IAS 39 Financial Instruments: Recognition and Measurement – Written options in retail energy contracts (Agenda Paper 14(iv))*, IASB, January 2007, para. 15.
160 IAS 32 (2005), para. AG24.
161 IFRIC 5, *Rights to Interests arising from Decommissioning, Restoration and Environmental Rehabilitation Funds*, IASB, para. BC11.
162 IFRIC 5, para. BC12.
163 IAS 39, para. 2(j).
164 IFRIC 5, para. BC13.
165 IFRIC 5, para. 5.
166 *IFRIC Update*, IASB, September 2007.
167 IAS 39, para. 9.
168 IAS 39, para. AG9.
169 IGC Q&A 10-6.
170 IAS 39, para. 9.
171 IAS 39, para. AG2.
172 IAS 39, para. B.8.
173 IAS 39, para. AG12A.
174 *IFRIC Update*, IASB, July 2006.
175 *IFRIC Update*, IASB, January 2007.
176 *IASB Update*, IASB, February 2007.
177 *IFRIC Update*, IASB, July 2006 and Information for Observers (January 2007 IFRIC meeting), *IAS 39 Financial instruments: Recognition and measurement – definition of a derivative – indexation on own EBITDA or own revenue (Agenda Paper 7)*, para. 33, IASB, January 2007.
178 *IFRIC Update*, IASB, July 2007.
179 IAS 39, para. 9.
180 IAS 39, para. AG11.
181 IGC Q&A 10-10.
182 IAS 39, para. B.9.
183 IAS 39, para. AG11 and IGC Q&A 10-3.
184 IAS 39, para. B.4.
185 IAS 39, para. B.5.
186 IAS 39, para. B.9.
187 IAS 39, para. B.10.
188 IAS 39, para. B.3.
189 IAS 39, para. AG10.
190 IAS 39, para. B.7.
191 IAS 39, para. B.2.
192 IAS 39, para. B.6.
193 IAS 39, para. B.6.
194 IAS 39, para. 9.
195 IAS 39, para. AG12.
196 IAS 39, para. 10.
197 IAS 39, para. BC76.
198 IAS 39, para. BC37.
199 Statement 133, *Accounting for Derivative Instruments and Hedging Activities*, FASB, June 1998, para. 10.
200 IAS 39, para. BC37.
201 IAS 39, para. 11.
202 IAS 39, paras. 11 and AG33.
203 IAS 39, para. 10.
204 IAS 39, para. 12.
205 IAS 39 (2003), para. 12.
206 IAS 39, para. 13.
207 IAS 39, para. AG27.
208 IAS 39, para. AG33(c).
209 Based on examples in FASB Statement 133, paras. 178-181.
210 IAS 39, para. AG33(a).
211 IAS 39, para. C.10.
212 IAS 39, para. AG30(g).
213 IAS 39, para. AG30(c).
214 *Implementation of International Accounting Standards*, British Bankers' Association, July 2004, para. 10.
215 *IASB Update*, IASB, June 2007.

216 IAS 39, para. AG30(g).
217 IAS 39, para. AG33(e).
218 IAS 39, para. AG30(c).
219 IAS 39, para. AG33(b).
220 Information for observers of March 2006 IFRIC meeting, *Hedging Inflation Risk (Agenda Paper 12)*, IASB, March 2006, para. 32.
221 IAS 39, paras. AG30(d)-(e).
222 IAS 39, para. AG30(h).
223 IAS 39, paras. AG30(f) and C.3.
224 IAS 39, para. C.4.
225 IAS 39, paras. AG30(a) and AG31.
226 IAS 39, para. AG32.
227 SIC D-34, *Financial Instrument – Instruments or Rights Redeemable by the Holder*, IASB, September 2001.
228 IAS 39, para. 9.
229 *IFRIC Update*, IASB, January 2007 and Information for Observers (November 2006 IFRIC meeting), *Financial Instruments puttable at an amount other than Fair Value (Agenda Paper 12(ii))*, IASB, November 2006.
230 IAS 39, para. AG30(b).
231 IAS 39, para. AG30(b).
232 IAS 39, para. AG33(d).
233 IAS 39, para. C.9.
234 IAS 39, para. BC39.
235 *IFRIC Update*, IASB, May 2007.
236 Information for Observers (May 2007 IFRIC meeting), *IAS 39: Financial Instruments: Recognition and Measurement AG33(d)(iii) of IAS 39 (Agenda Paper 11(v))*, IASB, May 2007, paras. 12 to 14.
237 Information for Observers, paras. 18 to 19.
238 Information for Observers, paras. 20 to 28.
239 Information for Observers, para. 44.
240 *IFRIC Update*, IASB, July 2007.
241 *IFRIC Update*, IASB, September 2007.
242 IAS 39, para. C.7.
243 IAS 39, para. C.8.
244 IAS 39, para. AG33(b).
245 IAS 39, para. AG33(f).
246 IAS 39, para. AG33(f).
247 IAS 39, para. AG33(f).
248 IAS 39, para. AG33(g).
249 IAS 39, para. AG33(h).
250 IAS 39, para. AG28.
251 IAS 39, para. C.1.
252 IAS 39, para. C.1.
253 IAS 39, para. C.1.
254 IAS 39, para. C.1.
255 IAS 39, para. AG28.
256 IAS 39, para. C.2.
257 IAS 39, para. C.5.
258 IAS 39, para. C.5.
259 IAS 39, para. 11.
260 IAS 39, para. AG29.
261 IGC Q&A 23-8.
262 IGC Q&A 23-8.
263 IGC Q&A 23-8.
264 IFRIC 9, *Reassessment of Embedded Derivatives*, IASB, March 2006, para. BC3.
265 IFRIC 9, paras. BC4 and BC5.
266 IFRIC 9, para. BC3.
267 IFRIC 9, para. 7.
268 IFRIC 9, para. 7.
269 IFRIC 9, para. BC10.
270 IFRIC 9, para. 5.
271 Information for Observers (19 April 2007 IASB meeting), *Classification and Designation of Assets, Liabilities and Equity Instruments Acquired or Assumed in a Business Combination (Agenda Paper 2B)*, IASB, April 2007, item #4, table following para. 14.
272 *IFRIC Update*, IASB, November 2005.
273 *IFRIC Update*, IASB, May 2007.
274 *IASB Update*, IASB, April 2007.
275 IFRIC 9, para. 4.
276 IFRIC 9, para. BC9.
277 IFRIC 9, para. BC9.
278 *IFRIC Update*, IASB, July 2006.
279 IAS 39, para. 10.
280 IAS 39, para. C.6.
281 IAS 39, para. C.6.
282 *Framework for the Preparation and Presentation of Financial Statements*, IASB, paras. 35 and 51.
283 *IFRIC Update*, IASB, April 2002, July 2002 and February 2003 and *IASB Update*, IASB, October 2002.
284 IAS 39, para. 9.
285 IAS 39, para. 9.
286 IAS 39, para. BC81.
287 IAS 39, para. 9.
288 IAS 39, para. AG14.
289 IAS 39, para. AG15.
290 IAS 39, para. BC82.
291 IAS 39, para. AG15.
292 IAS 39, para. B.11.
293 IGC Q&A 10-15.
294 IAS 39, para. BC74A.
295 IAS 39, para. 9.
296 IAS 39, *Financial Instruments: Recognition and Measurement*, Regulation No. 2086/2004, European Commission, 19 November 2004, para. 9.
297 IAS 39, paras. 9, 11A and AG4B.
298 IAS 39, para. 9.
299 IAS 39, *Financial Instruments: Recognition and Measurement*, Regulation No. 1864/2005, European Commission, 15 November 2005, para. 9.
300 IAS 39, para. AG4C.
301 IAS 39 (2003), paras. BC85-BC86.
302 IAS 39, paras. BC85-BC86A.

303 IAS 39, paras. 9 and BC75.
304 IAS 39, para. AG4D.
305 IAS 39, paras. AG4E and AG4F.
306 IAS 39, para. AG4F.
307 IAS 39, para. AG4G.
308 IAS 39, para. AG4G.
309 IAS 39, paras. BC75A-BC75B.
310 IAS 39, para. 9.
311 IAS 39, para. AG4H.
312 IAS 39, para. AG4J.
313 IAS 39, paras. AG4K and BC76B.
314 IAS 39, para. BC76B.
315 IAS 39, para. AG4I.
316 IAS 28, para. 1 and IAS 31, para. 1.
317 IAS 39, para. 11A.
318 IAS 39, para. AG33A.
319 IAS 39, para. AG33B.
320 IAS 39, paras. BC77A-BC78.
321 IAS 39, paras. BC77A-BC78.
322 *IFRIC Update*, IASB, May 2007.
323 *IFRIC Update*, IASB, July 2007.
324 *IFRIC Update*, IASB, September 2007.
325 IAS 39, para. 9.
326 IAS 39, para. AG20.
327 IAS 39, para. 79.
328 IAS 39, para. AG17.
329 IAS 39, para. AG17.
330 IAS 39, para. AG18.
331 IAS 39, para. AG19.
332 IAS 39 (2000), para. 82 and IGC Q&A 83-3.
333 IAS 39, para. AG17.
334 IAS 39, para. B.13.
335 IAS 39, para. B.14.
336 IAS 39, para. C.3.
337 IAS 39, para. AG25.
338 IAS 39, para. AG16.
339 IAS 39, para. AG23.
340 IAS 39, para. B.18.
341 IAS 39, para. AG24.
342 IAS 39, para. AG20.
343 IAS 39, para. 9.
344 IGC Q&A 83-1.
345 IAS 39, para. B.19.
346 IAS 39, para. B.20.
347 IAS 39, para. B.21.
348 IAS 39, para. AG21.
349 IAS 39, para. AG22.
350 IAS 39, para. AG22.
351 IAS 39, para. B.15.
352 IAS 39, para. AG22.
353 IAS 39, paras. AG22 and B.15.
354 IAS 39, para. B.17.
355 IAS 39, para. B.16.
356 IAS 39, para. B.16.
357 IAS 39, para. 9.
358 IAS 39, para. AG26.
359 IAS 39 (2000), paras. 10 and 19-20.
360 IAS 39, para. BC28.
361 IAS 39, paras. 9 and BC29.
362 IAS 39, para. 9.
363 IAS 39, paras. BC26-BC27.
364 IAS 39, para. B.23.
365 IAS 39, para. B.22.
366 IAS 39, para. 9.
367 IAS 39, para. BC25.
368 IAS 39, para. AG26.
369 IAS 39, para. 9.
370 IAS 39 (2000), para. 21.
371 IAS 39, para. B.12.
372 IAS 39, paras. 50 and BC73.
373 IAS 39 (2000), para. 107 and IGC Q&A 107-1 and Q&A 107-2.
374 IAS 39, para. 51.
375 IAS 39, para. 52.
376 IAS 39, para. 54.
377 *IASB Update*, IASB, June 2007 and Near final draft of proposed amendment to IAS 39, *Reclassifying instruments into and out of AFVTPL*, IASB website, August 2007.
378 Information for Observers (19 April 2007 IASB meeting), *Classification and Designation of Assets, Liabilities and Equity Instruments Acquired or Assumed in a Business Combination (Agenda Paper 2B)*, IASB, April 2007, item #6, table following para. 14.
379 *IASB Update*, IASB, April 2007.
380 IAS 39, para. 105A.
381 IAS 39, para. 103B and IFRS 4, para. 41A.
382 IFRS 7, para. 43.
383 IFRIC 5, para. 14 and IAS 39, para. 103A.
384 IFRIC 9, para. 9.
385 IFRIC 9, para. 9.
386 IAS 39, para. 105C.
387 IAS 39, para. 105D.
388 IFRS 1, *First-time Adoption of International Financial Reporting Standards*, IASB, para. IG56(c).
389 IFRS 1, paras. BC65-BC66.
390 IFRIC 9, para. 8.
391 IFRS 1, paras. 25A(b), (c) and (e) and IG56(d)(iii).
392 IFRS 1, paras. 25A(d) and IG56(d)(iv).
393 IFRS 1, paras. IG56(d)(i) and (ii).
394 IFRS 1, para. IG56(a).
395 IFRS 1, para. IG56(b).
396 IFRS 1, para. 25A.
397 IFRS 1, para. IG56(e).
398 *IASB Update*, IASB, October 2005 and April 2006 and Project Update, *Financial Instruments*, IASB, 18 January 2006.

Chapter 18 Financial instruments: Recognition, derecognition and offset

1 INTRODUCTION

1.1 Background

This Chapter deals with the question of when financial instruments should be included – or, to use the formal language of IFRS, 'recognised' – in financial statements. The IASB, and other national standards setters, have found this question particularly difficult to answer in the context of financial instruments. In part, this is because it is in the nature of financial instruments that there may be more separation than is usual in the case of other assets and liabilities between legal and 'economic' ownership. To take a very simple case, if an entity buys a quoted share in the financial markets, it may be entitled to all the benefits, and exposed to all the risks, inherent in owning that share somewhat earlier than the date on which it is registered as the legal owner.

The question of recognition raises the reciprocal question of derecognition – i.e. at what point should an item already recognised in financial statements cease to be included? To use the example of a traded equity share once more, if an entity sells a quoted share in the financial markets, it may cease to be entitled to all the benefits, and exposed to all the risks, inherent in owning that share somewhat earlier than the date on which it ceases to be registered as the legal owner. However, the question of derecognition goes much further than this, as it encroaches on what is commonly referred to as 'off-balance sheet' finance (see 1.2 below).

Related to recognition and derecognition is the question of offset – i.e. when, or whether, an entity may offset any of its financial assets against any of its financial liabilities. At first sight, the answer to this seems rather obvious, given the general prohibition on offsetting in IAS 1 – *Presentation of Financial Statements* (see Chapter 3 at 4.1.5). However, in the context of financial instruments, the question is more subtle. In effect, the issue is whether certain assets and liabilities, although legally separate, should be regarded as a single item from an economic perspective and reported as such in financial statements. A simple example might be where an entity has accounts in debit and in credit with the same bank.

1.2 Off-balance sheet finance

In order to understand the rationale for the requirements of IFRS for the derecognition of financial assets and financial liabilities, it is necessary to appreciate the fact that those requirements, and those in equivalent national standards, have their origins in the response by financial regulators to the growing use of off-balance sheet finance from the early 1980s onwards.

'Off-balance sheet' transactions can be difficult to define, and this poses the first problem in discussing the subject. The term implies that certain things belong on the balance sheet and that those which escape the net are deviations from this norm. The practical effect of off-balance sheet transactions is that the financial statements do not fully present the underlying activities of the reporting entity. This is generally for one of two reasons. The items in question may be included in the balance sheet but presented 'net' rather than 'gross' – for example, by netting off loans received against the assets they finance. Alternatively, the items might be excluded from the balance sheet altogether on the basis that they do not represent present assets and liabilities. Examples include operating lease commitments and certain contingent liabilities.

The result in all cases will be that the balance sheet may suggest less exposure to assets and liabilities than really exists, with a consequential flattering effect on certain ratios, such as gearing and return on assets employed. There is usually an income statement dimension to be considered as well, perhaps because assets taken off-balance sheet purport to have been sold (with a possible profit effect), and also more generally because the presentation of off-balance sheet activity influences the timing or disclosure of associated revenue items. In particular, the presence or absence of items in the balance sheet usually affects whether the finance cost implicit in a transaction is reported as such or rolled up within another item of income or expense.

Depending on their roles, different people react differently to the term 'off-balance sheet finance'. To an accounting standard setter, or other financial regulator, the expression carries the connotation of devious accounting, intended to mislead the reader of financial statements. Off-balance sheet transactions are those which are designed to allow an entity to avoid reflecting certain aspects of its activities in its financial statements. The term is therefore pejorative and carries the slightly self-righteous inference that those who indulge in such transactions are up to no good and need to be stopped.

However, there is also room for a more honourable use of the term 'off-balance sheet finance'. Entities may wish, for sound commercial reasons, to engage in transactions which share with other parties the risks and benefits associated with certain assets and liabilities. Increasingly sophisticated financial markets allow businesses to protect themselves from selected risks, or to take limited ownership interests which carry the entitlement to restricted rewards of particular assets.

In theory, it should be possible to determine what items belong in the balance sheet by reference to general principles such as those in the IASB's *Framework* and similar concepts statements. In practice, however, such principles on their own have proved a less than adequate response not only to the increasingly ingenious and aggressive structures being developed for what would generally be regarded as the less honourable forms of off-balance sheet finance, but also to what are now routine transactions such as debt factoring and mortgage securitisation.

Accordingly, standard-setters throughout the world, including the IASB, have developed increasingly detailed rules to deal with the issue. This 'anti-avoidance' aspect of the derecognition rules helps to explain why, rather unusually for IFRS, IAS 39 – *Financial Instruments: Recognition and Measurement*[1] – considers not only the economic position of the entity at the reporting date, but also prior transactions which gave rise to that position and the reporting entity's motives in undertaking them. This is sometimes referred to as a 'sticky fingers' approach – the idea being that, once an asset has become 'stuck' to the reporting entity, it is difficult to shake off. This is discussed further at 4.1.1 below.

2 DEVELOPMENT OF IFRS

2.1 General

Under IFRS:

- the recognition and derecognition of financial assets and financial liabilities is addressed in IAS 39 (see 4 and 5 below);
- the offset of financial assets and financial liabilities is addressed in IAS 32 – *Financial Instruments: Presentation*[2] (see 6 below).

The provisions of SIC-12 – *Consolidation – Special Purpose Entities*[3] – are also very relevant to certain aspects of the recognition and derecognition of financial assets and financial liabilities. Since SIC-12 is issued as an interpretation of IAS 27 – *Consolidated and Separate Financial Statements* – it is discussed principally in Chapter 6 at 3.2, but is also referred to at various points below.

IAS 32 was originally issued in March 1995 and IAS 39 in December 1998, with each standard subject to some amendment following its initial publication. However, in December 2003, the then current versions of both standards were superseded by revised versions. These new versions of IAS 32 and IAS 39 were required to be applied for annual periods beginning on or after 1 January 2005. Entities were permitted to adopt both standards in earlier periods, but required to disclose that they had done so. They were also required to adopt IAS 39 as amended in March

2004, not as originally issued, and to adopt both IAS 32 and IAS 39 (as amended) at the same time.[4]

The main text of IAS 32 is supplemented by application guidance (which is an integral part of the standard)[5] and by illustrative examples (which accompany, but are not part of, the standard).[6] Similarly, the main text of IAS 39 is supplemented by application guidance (which is an integral part of the standard)[7] and by implementation guidance and an illustrative example (both of which accompany, but are not part of, the standard).[8]

The new versions of IAS 32 and IAS 39 made no significant changes to the criteria in the previous versions for the offset of financial assets and financial liabilities, the recognition of financial assets and liabilities, or the derecognition of financial liabilities. However, the new version of IAS 39 has made significant changes to the criteria for the derecognition of financial assets (see 2.1.1 below).

2.1.1 Derecognition of assets – a mixed accounting model

Underlying these changes was the fact that the approach in the original version of IAS 39 was more than a little confusing. In part, this was because it drew on elements of different, and ultimately incompatible, concepts. To take a simple example, suppose that an entity has €100 of receivables, with an expected bad debt risk of €2. It sells these to a bank for their agreed net present value of €96. The entity also agrees with the bank that it will indemnify the bank if it fails to collect the full €100 by the due date for payment, but only up to a maximum of €10.

One analysis (sometimes referred to as a 'risks and rewards' approach) might be that the expected bad and slow payment risk was €2. In effect, the entity retains this entire risk through its €10 guarantee, and should therefore continue to recognise the entire €100 asset. An alternative analysis (sometimes referred to as a 'components' or 'control' approach) would be that either:

(a) the entire risks and rewards associated with €90 of the receivables; or

(b) the rewards, but not the risks, of the whole portfolio

have been passed to the bank and that, accordingly, either:

- at least €90 of the receivables should be considered for derecognition; or
- the whole portfolio should be derecognised and a liability recognised for the guarantee.[9]

In its 2002 exposure draft of proposed amendments to IAS 32 and IAS 39 (see Chapter 17 at 1.5), the IASB proposed that derecognition should be based on the single concept of 'continuing involvement'. However, this proposal did not find favour with many respondents to the exposure draft, including those who acknowledged the inconsistencies identified by the IASB in the original version of IAS 39. In the light of such comment from respondents, IAS 39 still retains elements of a number of derecognition concepts, but seeks to avoid conflict between them by requiring various factors to be considered in a specific order.

The main changes made by the revised IAS 39 to the derecognition provisions for assets (which are discussed in detail at 4 below) were:

- to clarify that an asset should be separated into components only in defined circumstances and otherwise regarded as a whole; and
- to require the question of derecognition to be determined by considering, in order:
  - whether the asset has been 'transferred' to another party; and
  - if so, whether the entity has also transferred substantially all the risks and rewards of the asset.

If the asset, and substantially all its associated risks and rewards, have been transferred it is derecognised.

Otherwise, the entity then determines whether or not it has retained control of the asset. If control has been retained the asset continues to be recognised. If control has not been retained, the asset is recognised only to the extent of the entity's 'continuing involvement' (see 4.8.3 below) in the asset.[10]

2.2 Definitions

The following definitions in IAS 32 and IAS 39 are generally relevant to the discussion in this Chapter.

A *financial instrument* is any contract that gives rise to a financial asset of one entity and a financial liability or equity instrument of another entity.[11]

A *financial asset* is any asset that is:

(a) cash;

(b) an equity instrument of another entity;

(c) a contractual right:

  (i) to receive cash or another financial asset from another entity; or

  (ii) to exchange financial assets or financial liabilities with another entity under conditions that are potentially favourable to the entity; or

(d) a contract that will or may be settled in the entity's own equity instruments and is:

  (i) a non-derivative for which the entity is or may be obliged to receive a variable number of the entity's own equity instruments; or

  (ii) a derivative that will or may be settled other than by the exchange of a fixed amount of cash or another financial asset for a fixed number of the entity's own equity instruments. For this purpose the entity's own equity instruments do not include instruments that are themselves contracts for the future receipt or delivery of the entity's own equity instruments.[12]

A *financial liability* is any liability that is:

(a) a contractual obligation:

  (i) to deliver cash or another financial asset to another entity; or

(ii) to exchange financial assets or financial liabilities with another entity under conditions that are potentially unfavourable to the entity; or

(b) a contract that will or may be settled in the entity's own equity instruments and is:

(i) a non-derivative for which the entity is or may be obliged to deliver a variable number of the entity's own equity instruments; or

(ii) a derivative that will or may be settled other than by the exchange of a fixed amount of cash or another financial asset for a fixed number of the entity's own equity instruments. For this purpose the entity's own equity instruments do not include instruments that are themselves contracts for the future receipt or delivery of the entity's own equity instruments.[13]

An *equity instrument* is any contract that evidences a residual interest in the assets of an entity after deducting all of its liabilities.[14]

A *derivative* is a financial instrument or other contract within the scope of IAS 39 (see Chapter 17 at 3) with all three of the following characteristics:

- its value changes in response to the change in a specified interest rate, financial instrument price, commodity price, foreign exchange rate, index of prices or rates, credit rating or credit index, or other variable, provided in the case of a non-financial variable that the variable is not specific to a party to the contract (sometimes called the 'underlying');
- it requires no initial net investment or an initial net investment that is smaller than would be required for other types of contracts that would be expected to have a similar response to changes in market factors; and
- it is settled at a future date.[15]

Fair value is the amount for which an asset could be exchanged, or a liability settled, between knowledgeable, willing parties in an arm's length transaction.[16]

3 RECOGNITION

3.1 General

IAS 39 provides that an entity must recognise a financial asset or a financial liability on its balance sheet when, and only when, the entity becomes a party to the contractual provisions of the instrument.[17] The specific application of this general rule to the particular case of 'regular way' purchases of financial assets is discussed further at 3.2 below. IAS 39 gives the following examples of the more general application of this principle.

3.1.1 Receivables and payables

Unconditional receivables and payables are recognised as assets or liabilities when the entity becomes a party to the contract and, as a consequence, has a legal right to receive or a legal obligation to pay cash.[18]

3.1.2 Firm commitments

Generally under IFRS, assets to be acquired and liabilities to be incurred as a result of a firm commitment to purchase or sell goods or services are generally not recognised until at least one of the parties has performed under the agreement. For example, an entity that receives a firm order for goods or services does not recognise an asset (and the entity that places the order does not recognise a liability) at the time of the commitment, but delays recognition until the ordered goods or services have been shipped, delivered or rendered.[19]

However, IAS 39 supplies numerous exceptions to this general rule. For example, if a firm commitment to buy or sell non-financial items is within the scope of IAS 39 (see Chapter 17 at 3), its net fair value is recognised as an asset or liability on the commitment date (see 3.1.3 below). In addition, if a previously unrecognised firm commitment is designated as a hedged item in a fair value hedge, any change in the net fair value attributable to the hedged risk is recognised as an asset or liability after the inception of the hedge (see Chapter 21 at 4.1).[20] Another exception, not noted in IAS 39, is the treatment of a gross-settled forward purchase of, or written put option over, an entity's own shares, which may require a liability to be recognised on entering into the contract (see Chapter 19 at 3.3.3 and 7).

This highlights the fundamental difference between the recognition criteria in IAS 39 and those in most other standards. Broadly speaking, under IAS 39 recognition is triggered by entering into a legal agreement, whereas under most other standards it is triggered by performance under the agreement – even though a strict application of the definitions of 'asset' and 'liability' in the IASB's *Framework* might suggest that recognition should in all cases flow from entering into, rather than performing under, a contractual agreement.

The Basis for Conclusions in IAS 39 touches on this in explaining the rationale for IAS 39's allowed treatment of hedges of firm commitments (see Chapter 21 at 3.4). The IASB argues that a firm commitment to buy or sell, say, inventory or PPE is in fact recognised when it is entered into, but at its historical cost of zero.[21] In other words, the difference (in the IASB's view) is not so much that commitments in respect of financial instruments are recognised at inception and others not, but rather that commitments in respect of financial instruments are measured at fair value, and others at historical cost.

Whatever the conceptual rationale, one suspects that the true underlying reason for the difference is simply one of practicality – or at least perceived practicality. In other words, whilst the IASB's *Framework* might in theory require all firm commitments to be recognised immediately they are entered into, the types of commitment accounted for under IAS 39 are often easier to measure than those in the scope of other IFRS. Moreover many commitments accounted for under IAS 39 can be traded, and the risks associated with them laid off, with third parties, as if they were assets or liabilities in their own right. For example, a forward contract to buy government bonds can be more objectively and reliably measured (and more readily transferred to a third party) than a contract to buy an item of PPE or a block of wood.

3.1.3 Forward contracts

A forward contract is a contract which obliges one party to the contract to buy, and the other party to sell, the asset that is the subject of the contract for a fixed price at a future date.

A forward contract within the scope of IAS 39 (see Chapter 17 at 3) is recognised as an asset or a liability at commitment date, rather than on settlement. When an entity becomes a party to a forward contract, the fair values of the right and obligation are often equal, so that the net fair value of the forward is zero. If the net fair value of the right and obligation is not zero, the contract is recognised as an asset or liability.[22]

3.1.4 Option contracts

An option contract is a contract which gives one party to the contract the right, but not the obligation, to buy from, or sell to, the other party to the contract the asset that is the subject of the contract for a fixed price at a future date (or during a longer period ending on a future date). An option giving the right to buy an asset is referred to as a 'call' option and one giving the right to sell as a 'put' option. An option is referred to as a 'bought' or 'purchased' option from the perspective of the party with the right to buy or sell (the 'holder') and as a 'written' option from the perspective of the party with the potential obligation to buy or sell. An option is referred to as 'in the money' when it would be in the holder's interest to exercise it and as 'out of the money' when it would not be in the holder's interest to exercise it.

Under IAS 39 an option is:

- 'deeply in the money' when it is so far in the money that it is highly unlikely to go out of the money before expiry;[23] and
- 'deeply out of the money' when it is so far out of the money that it is highly unlikely to become in the money before expiry.[24]

IAS 39 does not elaborate on what it means by 'highly unlikely' in this context, although the Implementation Guidance clarifies that 'highly probable' (in the context of a 'highly probable forecast transaction' subject to a hedge) indicates a much greater likelihood of happening than the term 'more likely than not'.[25] Perhaps the IASB will issue further guidance as to whether 'highly unlikely' indicates a lesser or greater probability of occurrence than 'not highly probable'!

Option contracts that are within the scope of IAS 39 (see Chapter 17 at 3) are recognised as assets or liabilities when the holder or writer becomes a party to the contract.[26]

3.1.5 Planned future transactions

Planned future transactions, no matter how likely, are not assets and liabilities because the entity has not become a party to a contract. They are therefore not recognised under IAS 39.[27] However, transactions that have been entered into as a hedge of certain 'highly probable' future transactions are recognised under IAS 39 – this raises the issue of the accounting treatment of any gains or losses arising on such hedging transactions (see Chapter 21 at 4.1 and 4.2).

3.1.6 *Treatment by transferee of transfers of financial assets not qualifying for derecognition by transferor*

IAS 39 adds that, where an asset is transferred from one party to another in circumstances where the transferor does not derecognise the asset, the transferee should not recognise the asset.[28] Instead, the transferee derecognises the cash or other consideration paid and recognises a receivable from the transferor. If the transferor has both a right and an obligation to reacquire control of the entire transferred asset for a fixed amount (such as under a repurchase agreement – see 4.7.1 below), the transferee may account for its receivable as a loan or receivable.[29]

Underlying this requirement appears to be a concern that more than one party cannot satisfy the criteria in IAS 39 for recognition of the same financial asset at the same time. In fact, however, such concern is misplaced, since it is easy for the same assets to be simultaneously recognised by more than one entity – for example if the transferor adopts settlement date accounting and the transferee trade date accounting (see 3.2 below).

3.2 'Regular way' transactions

A *regular way purchase or sale* is defined as a purchase or sale of a financial asset under a contract whose terms require delivery of the asset within the time frame established generally by regulation or convention in the marketplace concerned.[30] A contract that can be settled by net settlement (i.e. payment or receipt of cash or other financial assets equivalent to the change in value of the contract) is not a regular way transaction, but a derivative accounted for in accordance with the requirements of IAS 39 in respect of derivatives (see Chapter 20 at 3.1).[31]

Many financial markets provide a mechanism whereby all transactions in certain financial instruments (particularly quoted equities and bonds) entered into on a particular date are settled a fixed number of days after that date. The date on which the agreement is entered into is called the 'trade date' and the date on which it is settled by delivery of the assets that are the subject of the agreement is called the 'settlement date'.[32] Among other benefits, this system allows each market participant to settle all its transactions with a single net transfer of cash or other financial assets to or from a central clearing house, or a particular counterparty, rather than having to settle each transaction individually with each counterparty.

One effect of this system is that, while legal title to the assets that are the subject of the transaction passes only on or after settlement date, the buyer is effectively exposed to the risks and rewards of ownership of the assets from trade date. For example, suppose that an entity enters into a contract to purchase a financial asset but, before settlement date, decides that it no longer requires that asset and therefore enters into a second contract to sell the asset immediately it is received. The price of the second contract will be influenced, *inter alia*, by movements in the market value of the asset between the trade date of the first contract and that of the second, just as if the entity had actually owned the asset in that period.

Absent any special provisions, the accounting analysis for such transactions under IAS 39 would be that, between trade date and settlement date, an entity has a forward contract to purchase an asset (see 3.1.3 above) which, in common with all derivatives, should be recorded at fair value, with all changes in fair value recognised in profit or loss (see Chapter 20 at 3.1), unless the special rules for hedge accounting apply (see Chapter 21). This would not only be somewhat onerous but would also have the effect, in the case of an asset to be accounted for at amortised cost or as available-for-sale, that changes in its fair value between trade date and settlement date would be recognised in profit or loss, notwithstanding that any changes in fair value after settlement date would either not be recognised at all (in the case of an asset accounted for at amortised cost) or recognised in equity (in the case of an asset accounted for as available-for-sale).

To avoid this, IAS 39 permits assets subject to regular way transactions to be recognised, or derecognised, either as at the trade date ('trade date accounting') or as at the settlement date ('settlement date accounting').[33] Whichever method is used is applied consistently and symmetrically (i.e. to acquisitions and disposals) to each of the four main categories of financial asset identified by IAS 39[34] – i.e. at fair value through profit or loss, held-to-maturity, loans and receivables and available-for-sale (see Chapter 17 at 7).

3.2.1 Trade date accounting

As noted above, the trade date is the date on which an entity commits itself to purchase or sell an asset. Trade date accounting requires:

(a) in respect of an asset to be bought: recognition on the trade date of the asset and the liability to pay for it; and

(b) in respect of an asset to be sold: derecognition on the trade date of the asset, together with recognition of any gain or loss on disposal and the recognition of a receivable from the buyer for payment.

IAS 39 notes that, generally, interest does not start to accrue on the asset and corresponding liability until the settlement date when title passes.[35] However, this is in fact not necessarily the case – see 3.2.2 A below.

3.2.2 Settlement date accounting

As noted above, the settlement date is the date that an asset is delivered to or by an entity. Settlement date accounting requires:

(a) in respect of an asset to be bought, the recognition of the asset on the settlement date. Any change in the fair value of the asset to be received during the period between the trade date and the settlement date is accounted for in the same way as the acquired asset (see Chapter 20 at 2 and 3). In other words:
   - for assets carried at cost or amortised cost, the change in value is not recognised;
   - for assets classified as financial assets at fair value through profit or loss, the change in value is recognised in profit or loss; and

- for available-for-sale assets, the change in value is recognised in equity; and

(b) in respect of an asset to be sold, derecognition of the asset, recognition of any gain or loss on disposal and the recognition of a receivable from the buyer for payment on the settlement date.[36] A change in the fair value of the asset between trade date and settlement date is not recorded in the financial statements, even if the entity applies settlement date accounting, because the seller's right to changes in the fair value ceases on the trade date.[37]

A Current market practice – 'due date' accounting

In fact, IAS 39's version of 'settlement date accounting' differs from what is often understood by the term in the financial markets. A common practice among entities not subject to IAS 39 is to recognise and derecognise assets subject to regular way transactions at the due date for settlement, as opposed to the actual settlement date (which is often delayed beyond the due date due to unforeseen circumstances). This treatment is reinforced by the fact that interest on unsettled transactions in practice usually accrues from the due date, rather than the settlement date as stated by IAS 39.

3.2.3 Illustrative examples

Examples 18.1 and 18.2 below (which are based on those in the implementation guidance appended to IAS 39)[38] illustrate the application of trade date and settlement date accounting to the various categories of financial asset identified by IAS 39. The accounting treatment for these categories of asset is discussed in more detail in Chapter 20.

Example 18.1: Trade date and settlement date accounting – regular way purchase

On 29 December 2007 (trade date), an entity commits itself to purchase a financial asset for €1,000 (including transaction costs), which is its fair value on trade date. On 31 December 2007 (financial year-end) and on 4 January 2008 (settlement date) the fair value of the asset is €1,002 and €1,003, respectively. The accounting entries required to be recorded for the transaction will depend on how it is classified and whether trade date or settlement date accounting is used, as shown in the tables below:

A Financial asset accounted for at amortised cost

	Trade date accounting	€	€	Settlement date accounting	€	€
29 December 2007						
	Financial asset	1,000				
	Liability to counterparty		1,000			
	To record liability to purchase asset			*No accounting entries*		
31 December 2007						
	No accounting entries			*No accounting entries*		
4 January 2008						
	Liability to counterparty	1,000		Financial asset	1,000	
	Cash		1,000	Cash		1,000
	To record settlement of liability			*To record purchase of asset*		

B Financial asset accounted for at fair value through profit or loss

	Trade date accounting	€	€	Settlement date accounting	€	€
29 December 2007						
	Financial asset	1,000				
	Liability to counterparty		1,000			
	To record liability to purchase asset			*No accounting entries*		
31 December 2008						
	Financial Asset	2		Receivable	2	
	Income statement		2	Income statement		2
	To record change in fair value of asset			*To record change in fair value of contract*		
4 January 2008						
	Liability to counterparty	1,000		Financial asset	1,003	
	Cash		1,000	Cash		1,000
	Financial asset	1		Receivable		2
	Income statement		1	Income statement		1
	To record settlement of liability and change in fair value of asset			*To record change in fair value, and settlement, of contract*		

C *Financial asset accounted for as available-for-sale*

	Trade date accounting	€	€	*Settlement date accounting*	€	€
29 December 2007						
	Financial asset	1,000				
	Liability to counterparty		1,000			
	To record liability to purchase asset			*No accounting entries*		
31 December 2008						
	Financial Asset	2		Receivable	2	
	Equity		2	Equity		2
	To record change in fair value of asset			*To record change in fair value of contract*		
4 January 2008						
	Liability to counterparty	1,000		Financial asset	1,003	
	Cash		1,000	Cash		1,000
	Financial asset	1		Receivable		2
	Equity		1	Equity		1
	To record settlement of liability and change in fair value of asset			*To record purchase and change in fair value of asset*		

Example 18.2: Trade date and settlement date accounting – regular way sale

On 29 December 2007 (trade date) an entity enters into a contract to sell a financial asset for its then current fair value of €1,010. The asset was acquired one year earlier for €1,000 and its amortised cost is €1,000. On 31 December 2007 (financial year-end), the fair value of the asset is €1,012. On 4 January 2008 (settlement date), the fair value is €1,013. The amounts to be recorded will depend on how the asset is classified and whether trade date or settlement date accounting is used as shown in the tables below (any interest that might have accrued on the asset is disregarded).

A change in the fair value of a financial asset that is sold on a regular way basis is not recorded in the financial statements between trade date and settlement date, even if the entity applies settlement date accounting, because the seller's right to changes in the fair value ceases on the trade date.

A ***Financial asset accounted for at amortised cost***

Trade date accounting	€	€	*Settlement date accounting*	€	€
Before 29 December 2007 (cumulative net entries)					
Financial asset	1,000		Financial asset	1,000	
Cash		1,000	Cash		1,000
29 December 2007					
Receivable from counterparty	1,010				
Financial asset		1,000			
Income statement		10			
To record disposal of asset			*No accounting entries*		
4 January 2008					
Cash	1,010		Cash	1,010	
Receivable from counterparty		1,010	Financial asset		1,000
			Income statement		10
To record settlement of sale contract			*To record disposal of asset*		

B ***Financial asset accounted for at fair value through profit or loss***

Trade date accounting	€	€	*Settlement date accounting*	€	€
Before 29 December 2007 (cumulative net entries)					
Financial asset	1,010		Financial asset	1,010	
Cash		1,000	Cash		1,000
Income statement		10	Income statement		10
29 December 2007					
Receivable from counterparty	1,010				
Financial asset		1,010			
To record disposal of asset			*No accounting entries*		
4 January 2008					
Cash	1,010		Cash	1,010	
Receivable from counterparty		1,010	Financial asset		1,010
To record settlement of sale contract			*To record disposal of asset*		

C ***Financial asset accounted for at as available-for-sale***

	Trade date accounting			*Settlement date accounting*		
		€	€		€	€
Before 29 December 2007 (cumulative net entries)						
	Financial asset	1,010		Financial asset	1,010	
	Cash		1,000	Cash		1,000
	Equity		10	Equity		10
29 December 2007						
	Receivable from counterparty	1,010				
	Financial asset		1,010			
*	Equity	10				
	Income statement		10			
	To record disposal of asset			*No accounting entries*		
4 January 2008						
	Cash	1,010		Cash	1,010	
	Receivable from counterparty		1,010	Financial asset		1,010
*				Equity	10	
				Income statement		10
	To record settlement of sale contract			*To record disposal of asset*		

* The transfers between equity and retained earnings represent the 'recycling' of cumulative gains and losses required by IAS 39 on disposal of an available-for-sale asset (see Chapter 20 at 3.4). Disposal is regarded as occurring on trade date when trade date accounting applies and on settlement date when settlement date accounting applies.

A Exchanges of non-cash financial assets

The implementation guidance to IAS 39 addresses the situation in which an entity enters into a regular way transaction whereby it commits to sell a non-cash financial asset in exchange for another non-cash financial asset. This raises the question of whether, if the entity applies settlement date accounting, it should recognise any change in the fair value of the financial asset to be received arising between trade date and settlement date. A further issue is that the asset being sold may be in a category of asset to which trade date accounting is applied, while the asset being bought may be in a category of asset to which settlement date accounting is applied.

The implementation guidance essentially requires the buying and selling legs of the transaction to be accounted for independently, as illustrated by Example 18.3.[39]

Example 18.3: Trade date and settlement date accounting – exchange of non-cash financial assets

On 29 December 2007 (trade date), an entity enters into a contract to sell Note Receivable A, which is carried at amortised cost, in exchange for Bond B, which will be classified as held for trading and measured at fair value. Both assets have a fair value of €1,010 on 29 December, while the amortised cost of Note Receivable A is €1,000. The entity uses settlement date accounting for loans and receivables and trade date accounting for assets held for trading. On 31 December 2007 (financial year-end), the fair value of Note Receivable A is €1,012 and the fair value of Bond B is €1,009. On 4 January 2008, the fair value of Note Receivable A is €1,013 and the fair value of Bond B is €1,007. The following entries are made:

	€	€
29 December 2007		
Bond B	1,010	
Liability to counterparty		1,010
To record purchase of Bond B (trade date accounting)		
31 December 2007		
Loss on Bond B (income statement)	1	
Bond B		1
To record change in fair value of Bond B		
4 January 2008		
Liability to counterparty	1,010	
Note Receivable A		1,000
Gain on disposal (income statement)		10
To record disposal of receivable A (settlement date accounting)		
Loss on Bond B (income statement)	2	
Bond B		2
To record change in fair value of Bond B		

The simultaneous recognition, between 29 December and 4 January, both of the asset being bought and the asset being given in consideration for it may seem counter-intuitive. However, it is no different from the accounting treatment of any purchase of goods for credit which results, in the period between delivery of, and payment for, the goods, in the simultaneous recognition of the liability to pay the supplier and the cash that will be used to do so.

4 DERECOGNITION – FINANCIAL ASSETS

4.1 Summary

4.1.1 Background

As discussed at 1.2 above, the requirements of IAS 39 for the derecognition of financial assets are primarily designed to deal with the accounting challenges posed by various types of off-balance sheet finance. As a result, the real focus of many of the rules for the derecognition of assets is in fact the recognition of liabilities. The starting point for most of the transactions discussed below is that the reporting entity receives cash or other consideration in return for a transfer or 'sale' of all or part of a financial asset. This raises the question of whether such consideration should be treated as sales proceeds or as a liability. IAS 39 effectively answers that question by determining whether the financial asset to which the consideration relates should be derecognised (the consideration is treated as sales proceeds and there is a gain or loss on disposal) or should continue to be recognised (the consideration is treated as a liability).

This underlying objective of the derecognition criteria helps to explain why, rather unusually for IFRS, IAS 39 considers not only the economic position of the entity at the reporting date, but also prior transactions which gave rise to that position and the reporting entity's motives in undertaking them. For example, if, at a reporting date, an entity has two identical forward contracts for the purchase of a financial asset, the accounting treatment of the contracts may vary significantly if one contract relates to the purchase of an asset previously owned by the entity and the other does not.

This is because the derecognition rules of IAS 39 (like those of some other national standards) are based on the premise that, if a transfer of an asset leaves the transferor's economic exposure to the transferred asset much as if the transfer had never taken place, the financial statements should represent that the transferor still holds the asset. Thus, if an entity sells (say) a listed bond subject to a forward contract to repurchase the bond from the buyer at a fixed price, IAS 39 argues that the entity is exposed to the risks and rewards of that bond as if it had never sold it, but had simply borrowed an amount equivalent to the original sales proceeds secured on the bond. IAS 39 therefore concludes that the bond should not be removed from the balance sheet and the sale proceeds should be accounted for as a liability (in effect the obligation to repurchase the bond under the forward contract – see 4.7 below).

By contrast, if the entity were to enter into a second identical forward contract over another bond (i.e. one not previously owned by the entity), IAS 39 would simply require it to be accounted for as a derivative at fair value (see Chapter 20). This might seem a rather counter-intuitive outcome of a framework that purports to report economically equivalent transactions in a consistent and objective manner. However, the IASB would argue that the two transactions are not economically equivalent: they are distinguished by the fact that, on entering into the forward contract over the originally owned asset, the entity received a separate cash inflow (i.e. the 'sales' proceeds from the counterparty), whereas, on entering into the second contract, it did not. This reinforces the point that the real focus of IAS 39 is to determine the appropriate accounting treatment for that cash inflow and not that of the previously owned bond *per se*.

4.1.2 Decision tree

The provisions of IAS 39 concerning the derecognition of financial assets are complex, but are summarised in the flowchart opposite.[40] It may be helpful to refer to this while reading the discussion that follows.

It will be seen that the process presupposes that the reporting entity has correctly consolidated all its subsidiaries in accordance with IAS 27 (see Chapter 6). This will include any entities identified as special purpose entities (SPEs).

As discussed more fully in Chapter 6 at 3.2, the IASB (or strictly, its predecessor the IASC), like many national standard setters before it, has had to address the issue of an entity conducting its affairs through a vehicle that, though not meeting a traditional definition of a subsidiary based on ownership of equity, is still controlled by the entity. Under IFRS such an entity is referred to as a special purpose entity or SPE. SPEs are the subject of SIC-12, which requires an entity to consolidate an SPE when the substance of the relationship between them indicates that the entity controls the SPE.[41] SPEs are commonly used in transactions such as securitisations, in which a holder of a financial asset seeks to sell all or part of its interest in that asset to one or more third parties (see 4.4.3 below).

It is clearly highly significant from an accounting perspective whether an entity to which a financial asset or liability is transferred is a subsidiary or a consolidated SPE of the transferor. A financial asset (or financial liability) transferred from an entity to its subsidiary or SPE (on whatever terms) will continue to be recognised in the entity's consolidated financial statements through the normal elimination of intragroup transactions required by the consolidation procedures set out in IAS 27 (see Chapter 6 at 6.3). Thus, the requirements discussed at 4.2 to 4.6 below are irrelevant to the treatment, in an entity's consolidated financial statements, of any transfer of a financial asset by the entity to a subsidiary or SPE. Requiring consolidation of SPEs means that the same derecognition analysis applies whether the entity transfers the financial assets directly to a third party investor or to a SPE that carries out the transfer.

However, the criteria may be relevant to any onward transfer by the SPE, and to the entity's separate financial statements (see Chapter 6 at 7), if prepared. Moreover, the criteria may well be relevant to determining whether the transferee is an SPE. A transfer that leaves the entity exposed to risks and rewards through its links with the transferee similar to those arising from its former direct ownership of the transferred asset may in itself indicate that the transferee is an SPE.

Figure 18.1: *Flowchart*

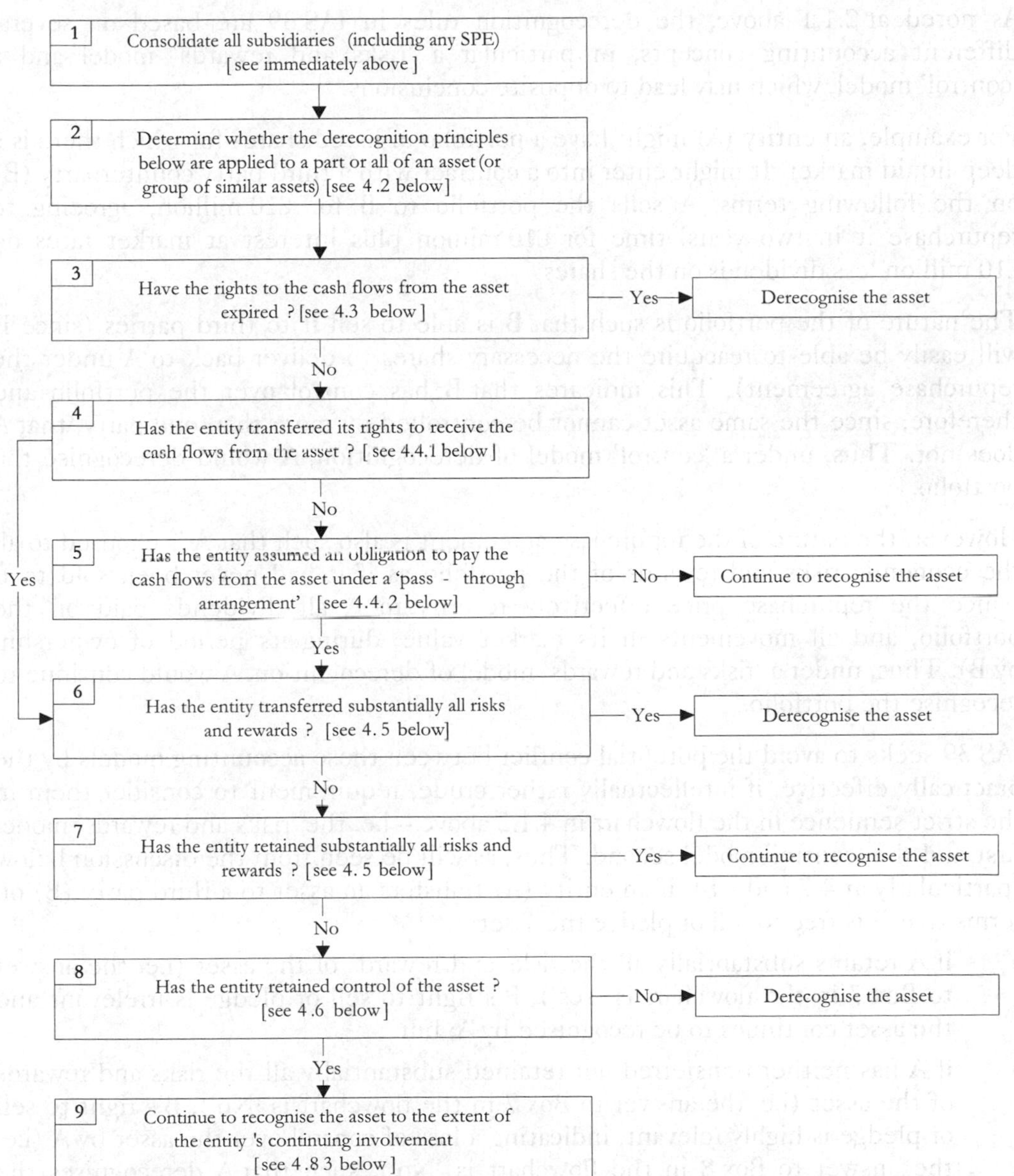

The subsequent steps towards determining whether derecognition is appropriate are discussed in 4.2 to 4.6 below. Some examples of how these criteria might be applied to some common transactions in financial assets are given in 4.7 below. The accounting consequences of the derecognition of a financial asset are discussed at 4.8 below.

4.1.3 Importance of applying tests in sequence

As noted at 2.1.1 above, the derecognition rules in IAS 39 are based on several different accounting concepts, in particular a 'risks and rewards' model and a 'control' model, which may lead to opposite conclusions.

For example, an entity (A) might have a portfolio of listed shares for which there is a deep liquid market. It might enter into a contract with a third party counterparty (B) on the following terms. A sells the portfolio to B for €10 million, agreeing to repurchase it in two years' time for €10 million plus interest at market rates on €10 million less dividends on the shares.

The nature of the portfolio is such that B is able to sell it to third parties (since it will easily be able to reacquire the necessary shares to deliver back to A under the repurchase agreement). This indicates that B has control over the portfolio and therefore, since the same asset cannot be controlled by more than one party, that A does not. Thus, under a 'control' model of derecognition, A would derecognise the portfolio.

However, the nature of the repurchase agreement is also such that A is exposed to all the economic risks and rewards of the portfolio as if it had never been sold to B (since the repurchase price effectively returns to A all dividends paid on the portfolio, and all movements in its market value, during its period of ownership by B). Thus, under a 'risks and rewards' model of derecognition, A would continue to recognise the portfolio.

IAS 39 seeks to avoid the potential conflict between those accounting models by the practically effective, if intellectually rather crude, requirement to consider them in the strict sequence in the flowchart in 4.1.2 above – i.e. the 'risks and rewards' model first and the 'control' model second. Thus, as will be seen from the discussion below (particularly at 4.7 and 4.8), if an entity (A) transfers an asset to a third party (B) on terms that B is free to sell or pledge the asset:

- if A retains substantially all the risks and rewards of the asset (i.e. the answer to Box 7 in the flowchart is 'Yes'), B's right to sell or pledge is irrelevant and the asset continues to be recognised by A; but
- if A has neither transferred nor retained substantially all the risks and rewards of the asset (i.e. the answer to Box 7 in the flowchart is 'No'), B's right to sell or pledge is highly relevant, indicating a loss of control over the asset by A (i.e. the answer to Box 8 in the flowchart is 'No'), such that A derecognises the asset.

In other words, depending on the reporting entity's position in the decision tree at 4.1.2 above, the fact that B has the right to sell the sell or pledge the asset is either irrelevant or leads directly to derecognition of the asset by A. It is therefore crucial that the various asset derecognition tests in IAS 39 are applied in the order required by IAS 39.

4.2 Are the derecognition principles applied to all or part of an asset?

The discussion in this section relates to Box 2 in the flowchart at 4.1.2 above.

IAS 39 requires an entity, before evaluating whether, and to what extent, derecognition is appropriate under the provisions discussed at 4.3 and following below, to determine whether those provisions should be applied to the whole, or a part only, of a financial asset (or the whole or, a part only, of a group of similar financial assets).

It is important to remember throughout the discussion below that these are criteria for determining at what level the derecognition rules should be applied, not for determining whether the conditions in those rules have been satisfied.

The derecognition provisions must be applied to a part of a financial asset (or a part of a group of similar financial assets) if, and only if, the part being considered for derecognition meets one of the three conditions set out in (a) to (c) below.

(a) The part comprises only specifically identified cash flows from a financial asset (or a group of similar financial assets).

For example, if an entity enters into an interest rate strip whereby the counterparty obtains the right to the interest cash flows, but not the principal cash flows, from a debt instrument, the derecognition provisions are applied to the interest cash flows.

(b) The part comprises only a fully proportionate (pro rata) share of the cash flows from a financial asset (or a group of similar financial assets).

For example, if an entity enters into an arrangement in which the counterparty obtains the rights to 90% of all cash flows of a debt instrument, the derecognition provisions are applied to 90% of those cash flows. The test in this case is whether the reporting entity has retained a 10% proportionate share of the *total* cash flows. If there is more than one counterparty, it is not necessary for each of them to have a proportionate share of the cash flows.

(c) The part comprises only a fully proportionate (pro rata) share of specifically identified cash flows from a financial asset (or a group of similar financial assets).

For example, if an entity enters into an arrangement whereby the counterparty obtains the rights to a 90% share of interest cash flows from a financial asset, the derecognition provisions are applied to 90% of those interest cash flows. The test is whether the reporting entity has (in this case) retained a 10% proportionate share of the *interest* cash flows. As in (b), if there is more than one counterparty, it is not necessary for each of them to have a proportionate share of the specifically identified cash.

If none of the criteria in (a) to (c) above is met, the derecognition provisions are applied to the financial asset in its entirety (or to the group of similar financial assets in their entirety). For example, if an entity transfers the rights to the first or the last 90% of cash collections from a financial asset (or a group of financial assets), or the rights to 90% of the cash flows from a group of receivables, but provides a guarantee to compensate the buyer for any credit losses up to 8% of the principal amount of the receivables, the derecognition provisions are applied to the financial asset (or a group of similar financial assets) in its entirety.[42]

The various examples above illustrate that the tests in (a) to (c) are to be applied very strictly. It is essential that the entity transfers 100%, or a lower fixed proportion, of a definable cash flow. In the arrangement in the previous paragraph, the transferor provides a guarantee the effect of which is that the transferor may have to return some part of the consideration it has already received. This has the effect that the derecognition provisions must be applied to the asset in its entirety and not just to the proportion of cash flows transferred. If the guarantee had not been given, the arrangement would have satisfied condition (b) above, and the derecognition provisions would have been applied only to the 90% of cash flows transferred.

The criteria above must be applied to the whole, or a part only, of a financial asset or the whole, or a part only, of a group of similar financial assets. This raises the question of what comprises a 'group of similar financial assets' – an issue recently discussed by the IFRIC and the IASB (see 4.2.2 below).

4.2.1 *Credit enhancement through transferor's waiver of right to future cash flows*

IAS 39 gives an illustrative example, the substance of which is reproduced as Example 18.18 at 4.8.4 D below, of the accounting treatment of a transaction in which 90% of the cash flows of a portfolio of loans are sold. All cash collections are allocated 90:10 to the transferee and transferor respectively, but subject to any losses on the loans being fully allocated to the transferor until its 10% retained interest in the portfolio is reduced to zero, and only then allocated to the transferee. IAS 39 indicates that in this case it is appropriate to apply the derecognition criteria to the 90% sold, rather than the portfolio as whole.

At first sight, this seems inconsistent with the position in the scenario in the penultimate paragraph of 4.2 above, where application of the derecognition criteria to the 90% transferred is precluded by the transferor's having given a guarantee to the transferee. Is not the arrangement in Example 18.18 below (whereby the transferor may have to cede some of its right to receive future cash flows to the transferee) a guarantee in all but name?

Whilst IAS 39 does not expand on this explicitly, the reasoning appears to be that the two transactions can be distinguished as follows:

(a) the transaction in Example 18.18 may result in the transferor losing the right to receive a future cash inflow, whereas a guarantee arrangement may give rise to an obligation to return a past cash inflow;

(b) the transaction in Example 18.18 gives the transferee a greater chance of recovering its full 90% share, but does not guarantee that it will do so. For example, if only 85% of the portfolio is recovered, the transferor is under no obligation to make up the shortfall.

It must be remembered that, at this stage, we are addressing the issue of whether or not the derecognition criteria should be applied to all or part of an asset, not whether derecognition is actually achieved, which is discussed at 4.3 to 4.8 below.

In many cases an asset transferred subject to a guarantee by the transferor would not satisfy the derecognition criteria, since the guarantee would mean that the transferor had not transferred substantially all the risks of the asset. For derecognition to be possible, the scope of the guarantee would need to be restricted so that some significant risks are passed to the transferee. However, if the guarantee has been acquired from a third party, there are additional issues (discussed in 4.2.2 below) to consider that may affect the derecognition of the asset and/or the guarantee.

4.2.2 Derecognition of groups of financial assets

As described above, the derecognition provisions of IAS 39 as drafted apply to the whole, or a part only, of a financial asset or a group, or a part of a group, of *similar* financial assets (our emphasis). However, transfers of financial assets, such as debt factoring or securitisations (see 4.4.3 below), typically involve the transfer of a group of assets (and possibly liabilities) comprising:

- the non-derivative financial assets (i.e. the trade receivables or securitised assets) that are the main focus of the transaction; and
- financial instruments taken out by the transferor in order to mitigate the risk of those financial assets. These arrangements may either have already been in place for some time, or they may have been entered into to facilitate the transfer.
- non-derivative financial guarantee contracts that are transferred with the assets. These are not always financial assets, e.g. mortgage indemnity guarantees which compensate the lending bank if the borrower defaults and there is a deficit when the secured property is sold and which may be transferred together with the mortgage assets to which they relate.

Financial instruments transferred with the 'main' assets typically include derivatives such as interest rate and currency swaps. The entity may have entered into such arrangements in order to swap floating rate mortgages to fixed rate, or to change the sterling cash flows receivable from financial assets into euros to match the currency of the borrowings.

Both the IFRIC and the IASB have considered whether the reference to transfers of 'similar' assets in IAS 39 is intended to require:

- a single derecognition test for the whole 'package' of transferred non-derivative assets, and any associated financial instruments, as a whole; or
- individual derecognition tests for each type of instrument (e.g. debtor, interest rate swap, guarantee or credit insurance) transferred.

This attempt to clarify the meaning of 'similar assets' was not successful. The IFRIC came to a tentative decision but passed the matter to the IASB, together with some related derecognition issues, in particular, the types of transaction that are required to be treated as 'pass through' and the effect of conditions attached to the assets that have been transferred (discussed at 4.4 below). In November 2006 the IFRIC issued a tentative decision not to provide formal guidance, based on the views publicly expressed by the IASB in the *IASB Update* for September 2006. The IFRIC's decision not to proceed was withdrawn in January 2007 on the basis of comment letters received by the IFRIC that demonstrated that the IASB's 'clarification' was, in fact, unworkable and further guidance was required after all. The IFRIC announced this as follows:

> 'In November 2006, the IFRIC published a tentative agenda decision not to provide guidance on a number of issues relating to the derecognition of financial assets. After considering the comment letters received on the tentative agenda decision, the IFRIC concluded that additional guidance is required in this area. The IFRIC therefore decided to withdraw the tentative agenda decision [not to provide further guidance] and add a project on derecognition to its agenda. The IFRIC noted that any Interpretation in this area must have a tightly defined and limited scope, and directed the staff to carry out additional research to establish the questions that such an Interpretation should address.' [43]

The next section describes the IFRIC and IASB's attempts to establish the meaning of 'similar' which demonstrated the absence of a clear principle. There is bound to be diversity in practice in the light of the failure to provide a coherent and acceptable interpretation, so it is most important that entities establish an accounting policy that they apply consistently to the derecognition of groups of financial assets.

A The IASB's view and the IFRIC's tentative conclusions

Although the IFRIC initially tended to the view that the IASB intended a single test to be undertaken,[44] the IASB itself indicated that derivatives transferred together with non-derivative financial assets were not 'similar' to non-derivative financial assets for the purposes of paragraph 16 of IAS 39. Therefore, an entity would apply the derecognition tests in IAS 39 to non-derivative financial assets (or groups of similar non-derivative financial assets) and derivative financial assets (or groups of similar derivative financial assets) separately, even if they were transferred at the same time.[45] The IASB also indicated that, in order to qualify for derecognition, transferred derivatives that could be assets or liabilities (such as interest rate swaps) would have to meet both the financial asset and the financial liability derecognition tests[46] – see the further discussion of this issue at 5.4 below.

Whilst the IASB's published decision referred only to 'derivatives' transferred with the 'main' non-derivative assets, observers of the relevant meeting reported that the IASB also took the view that the derecognition tests must also be applied separately to other financial assets, such as guarantees and credit insurance, transferred with the 'main' assets.

This could have had practical effects on many securitisations as currently structured (see 4.4.3 below). The interpretation could have made it easier to derecognise certain items (particularly non-derivative assets) than at present. Many derivatives themselves might not meet the appropriate derecognition criteria at all and would continue to be recognised. By contrast, a transaction might achieve a transfer of substantially all the risks and rewards (see Box 6 in Figure 18.1 at 4.1.2 above, and 4.5 below) of a transferred asset considered separately from any associated derivatives or guarantees, but not if the asset and the associated derivatives or guarantees are considered as a whole. However, the interpretation could well have resulted in far more arrangements falling into the category of 'continuing involvement', where the entity has neither retained nor disposed of substantially all of the risks and rewards of ownership.

Suppose that an entity transfers a loan with no prepayment risk and a credit guarantee, but retains interest rate risk through an interest rate swap with the transferee. On the view that the loan and guarantee should be considered for derecognition as a whole, there was no real credit risk prior to the transfer because of the guarantee. The entity was exposed to interest rate risk and the risk of failure by the counterparty to the guarantee. The latter risk could be considered negligible, so that the only real risk was interest rate risk. Thus, on the view that the loan and guarantee should be considered for derecognition as a whole, they would probably not be derecognised because the entity would retain the only substantial risk (interest rate risk) to which it was exposed before the transfer – i.e. the transaction would fail the test of transferring substantially all risks and rewards in Box 6 in Figure 1.

Following the IASB's decision, the implication is that the derecognition criteria would be applied separately to the loan and the guarantee. Considered individually, the loan gives rise to interest rate risk and credit risk. On this analysis, the transfer would leave the entity with only one of the two substantial risks (i.e. interest rate risk, but not credit risk) that it bore previously. This would lead to the conclusion that the entity had neither transferred nor retained substantially all the risks of the loan, and that the loan would therefore be recognised only to the extent of the entity's continuing involvement (in this example, the interest rate swap) – see Box 9 in Figure 18.1 at 4.1.2 above, and 4.8.3 below.

This may well lead to more transactions being accounted for as a continuing involvement than previously. This is unfortunate since, as discussed further at 4.8.3 below, IAS 39 gives no clear general principles to be applied in accounting for continuing involvements.

B What are 'similar assets'?

There are a number of different derivative instruments that can be transferred together with a non-derivative, including:

- hedging instruments that are always assets, e.g. interest rates caps;
- hedging instruments that are always liabilities, e.g. written options;
- hedging instruments that may be an asset or liability at any point in time, e.g. interest rate swaps;
- purchased financial guarantee contracts and insurance; and

- guarantees that are not financial guarantee contracts but are commonly accounted for as derivatives, e.g. mortgage indemnity guarantee contracts.

The IASB's interpretation would require each of the first three to meet different derecognition treatments. Derivatives that could be financial assets or financial liabilities depending on movements in market value (e.g. interest rate and credit default swaps) would need to meet both the financial asset and financial liability derecognition requirements of IAS 39 (even though at any one time they would be either an asset or a liability). The derecognition of liabilities requires *inter alia* legal release by the counterparty (see 5 below). In many securitisations there is no cancellation or discharge of swaps 'transferred' to an SPE, in which case the transferor would not be able to derecognise the instrument. This would raise issues regarding the treatment of the retained swap, as it does not actually expose the entity to risks and rewards.

The interpretation raises the difficulty of allocating the single cash flow received from the transferee to the various financial instruments transferred. This is discussed further at 4.4.1 below.

Given the withdrawal of the IFRIC 'non-interpretation', there is no underlying principle that would prevent any of the instruments described above being considered 'similar' to the main non-derivative. Therefore, an entity must make an accounting choice that it applies consistently to all transactions involving the derecognition of assets, not only to those associated with securitisation arrangements. It must bear in mind that a narrow concept of 'similar', in which instruments are treated as separate assets, may make it easier to derecognise some of them but more likely to have to engage with the problems of continuing involvement and more difficult to achieve pass through.

Once an entity has determined what is 'similar', it must consider the derecognition tests (pass through and risk and rewards) by reference to the same group of 'similar' assets (see 4.4 below).

4.2.3 *Transfer of asset (or part of asset) for only part of its life*

The examples given in IAS 39 implicitly appear to have in mind the transfer of a tranche of cash flows from the date of transfer for the remainder of the life of an instrument. This raises the question of the appropriate accounting treatment where (for example) an entity with a loan receivable repayable in 10 years' time enters into a transaction whereby all the interest flows for the next 5 years only (or those for years 6 to 10) are transferred to a third party. In our view, there is no reason why such a transaction could not be considered for partial derecognition.

4.2.4 *'Financial asset' includes whole or part of a financial asset in 4.3 to 4.8 below*

In the derecognition provisions in IAS 39, and the discussion in 4.3. to 4.8 below, the term 'financial asset' is used to refer to either the whole, or a part, of a financial asset (or a part of a group of similar financial assets).[47] It is therefore important to remember throughout the following discussion that a reference to an asset being derecognised 'in its entirety' does not necessarily mean that 100% of the asset is derecognised. It may mean, for example, that there has been full derecognition of, say, 80% of the asset to which the derecognition rules have applied separately (in accordance with the criteria above).

4.3 Have the contractual rights to cash flows from the asset expired?

The discussion in this section refers to Box 3 in the flowchart at 4.1.2 above.

The first step in determining whether derecognition of a financial asset is appropriate is to establish whether the contractual rights to the cash flows from that asset have expired. If they have, the asset is derecognised. Examples might be:

- a loan receivable is repaid;
- the holder of a perpetual debt, whose terms provide for ten annual 'interest' payments that, in effect, provide both interest and a return of capital, receives the final payment of interest; or
- a purchased option expires unexercised.

If the cash flows from the financial asset have not expired, it is derecognised when, and only when, the entity 'transfers' the asset within the specified meaning of the term in IAS 39 (see 4.4 below), and the transfer has the effect that the entity has either:

- transferred substantially all the risks and rewards of the asset (see 4.5 below); or
- neither transferred nor retained substantially all the risks and rewards of the asset (see 4.5 below), and has not retained control of the asset (see 4.6 below).[48]

4.4 Has the entity 'transferred' the asset?

An entity is regarded by IAS 39 as 'transferring' a financial asset if, and only if, it either:

(a) transfers the contractual rights to receive the cash flows of the financial asset (see 4.4.1 below); or

(b) retains the contractual rights to receive the cash flows of the financial asset, but assumes a contractual obligation to pay the cash flows on to one or more recipients in an arrangement that meets the conditions in 4.4.2 below[49] (a so-called 'pass-through arrangement')

This might be the case where the entity is a special purpose entity or trust, and issues to investors beneficial interests in financial assets that it owns and provides servicing of those assets.[50]

These conditions are highly significant for securitisations and similar transactions that fall within (b) because the entity retains the contractual right to receive cash. The requirements have the effect that, where a transaction involving a pass-through arrangement fails the strict tests in 4.4.2 below (as many such transactions may), a financial asset subject to the transaction can be derecognised under IAS 39 only if it can be shown that the contractual rights to receive the cash flows of the asset have been transferred – i.e. the transaction meets test (a) above. (see 4.4.2 and 4.4.3 below).

4.4.1 *Transfers of contractual rights to receive cash flows*

The discussion in this section refers to Box 4 in the flowchart at 4.1.2 above.

IAS 39 does not define what it means by the phrase 'transfers the contractual rights to receive the cash flows of the financial asset' in (a) in 4.4 above, possibly on the assumption that this is self-evident. However, this is far from the case, since the phrase raises a number of questions of interpretation.

There are two key uncertainties about the meaning of 'transferring' the contractual rights (which in turn determines whether a transaction falls within (a) or (b) in 4.4 above):

- whether it is a legal test – i.e. must the cash flows have been transferred as a matter of law? (see A below); and
- the effect of conditions attached to the transfers (see B below).

While both of these are of great significance to securitisations (see 4.4.3 below), they also have implications for other transactions. These issues were discussed in 2006 by both the IFRIC and the IASB. However, as described at 4.2.2 above, the IFRIC's tentative decision not to issue further guidance and the interpretation of the issues that had so far been published were both withdrawn in January 2007. There is no clear evidence that practice has changed as a result of the views that had been expressed by the IASB and the IFRIC but as this has demonstrated a lack of clear underlying principles, it would be no surprise to find that entities have divergent interpretations of the requirements.

A Meaning of 'transfers the contractual rights to receive the cash flows'

As noted above, the issue here is whether this is a 'legal' or 'economic' test – in other words:

- is it necessary that the cash flows have been transferred as a matter of law; or
- does the transfer simply have to satisfy certain minimum, and objectively determinable, economic criteria?

We have commented in previous editions of this book that the requirement to transfer 'the *contractual* rights to receive cash flows' suggests that transfer must have the effect that the transferee has a direct legal claim on those cash flows. On this interpretation, if a corporate entity securitises the future cash flows from a portfolio of trade receivables it has arguably 'transferred' them for the purposes of IAS 39 if, and only if, the finance provider could, directly and in its own name, sue the debtor for default(see 4.4.3 below). In many jurisdictions, this would simply not be possible without either:

- a tri-partite agreement between the corporate entity, the finance provider and the debtor; or

- a clause in the standard terms of trade allowing such a transfer at the sole discretion of the corporate entity without the express consent of the debtor, so that transfer can be effected by a subsequent bi-partite agreement between the corporate entity and the finance provider.

At its March 2006 meeting the IFRIC considered the issue of whether there can be a transfer of the contractual right to receive cash flows under IAS 39, if the debtor has not been notified that the transferor has entered a contract in which it is agreed that all cash flows that are collected are contractually payable to a new eventual recipient – i.e. if the debtor continues to pay the transferor, while the transferor loses the right to retain any cash collected from the debtor.[51]

The IFRIC had already concluded, in November 2005, that retaining servicing rights (i.e. continuing to administer collections and distributions of cash as agent for the transferee) does not in itself preclude derecognition.[52] However, the IFRIC then considered whether retention by the transferor of the contractual right to receive the cash from debtors for distribution on to other parties (as must inevitably happen if debtors are not notified) means that such a transaction does not meet test (a) in 4.4 above, and thus must meet test (b) (pass-through) in order to achieve derecognition. In July 2006 the IFRIC decided to refer this issue to the IASB, which considered it at its September 2006 meeting.

The IASB indicated that:

> 'a transaction in which an entity transfers all the contractual rights to receive the cash flows (without necessarily transferring legal ownership of the financial asset), would not be treated as a pass-through. An example might be a situation in which an entity transfers all the legal rights to specifically identified cash flows of a financial asset (for example, a transfer of the interest or principal of a debt instrument). Conversely, the pass-through test would be applicable when the entity does not transfer all the contractual rights to cash flows of the financial asset, such as disproportionate transfers' [53] (see 4.2 above).

The statement that such a transaction 'would not be treated as pass-through' means (in terms of the flowchart in Figure 18.1 at 4.1.2 above) that the answer to Box 4 is 'Yes', such that the pass-through test in Box 5 (see 4.4.2 below) is by-passed.

The IASB's conclusion appears to concede that the reference in IAS 39 to a transfer of the 'contractual' right to cash flows was intended to include an *equitable* transfer of those rights. A 'transaction in which an entity transfers all the contractual rights to receive the cash flows (without necessarily transferring legal ownership of the financial asset)' as referred to above would, in many jurisdictions, be a legal impossibility. The *contractual* rights to receive cash flows from a debtor cannot be legally transferred without the consent of the debtor (which is not normally obtained, or indeed practically obtainable, in many securitisations and similar transactions). We therefore assume that the IASB was seeking to indicate that the reference in IAS 39 to the transfer of the 'contractual' right to cash flows can include an agreement by A to transfer to B the cash flows it receives pursuant to a contract with C, without actually transferring the contract itself. In some jurisdictions (e.g. the UK) this is known as an 'equitable transfer'.

The IASB's comment that 'the pass-through test would be applicable when the entity does not transfer all the contractual rights to cash flows of the financial asset, such as disproportionate transfers' reinforces the derecognition hierarchy of IAS 39, as summarised in the flowchart in Figure 18.1 at 4.1.2 above. For example, if an entity transfers the rights to the first or the last 90% of cash collections from a financial asset (or a group of financial assets), or the rights to 90% of the cash flows from a group of receivables, but provides a guarantee to compensate the buyer for any credit losses up to 8% of the principal amount of the receivables, the derecognition provisions are applied to the financial asset (or a group of similar financial assets) in its entirety.[54] This means that the answer to Box 4 in the flowchart will be 'No' (since some, not all, of the cash flows of the entire asset have been transferred), thus requiring the pass-through test in Box 5 to be applied.

The IASB's interpretation gives no answer to an even more critical question. If the derecognition rules need to be applied separately to loans and derivatives or guarantees, how does this affect:

- the definition of a 'transfer' (if all the cash flows are transferred); or
- the application of the pass-through test (if the transfer is of a disproportionate share of the cash flow)?

The pass-through test would not need to be applied where the entity transfers the contractual right to receive 100% of the cash flows even if it guarantees losses up to a certain percentage of the principal. This implies that guarantees prevent a transfer only when less than 100% of the cash flows are transferred. It is not clear why a transfer of the right to 90% of the cash flows with the provision of a guarantee of losses up to a certain level would need to satisfy the pass-through test (and would probably fail), but the transfer of 100% of the cash flows with a similar guarantee could be derecognised. Indeed, it is hard to see the circumstances in which the pass-through test would ever be successfully applied to a disproportionate transfer.

In a securitisation, if the originator sells a loan and an interest rate swap to a consolidated SPE which issues a note it is the *collective* cash flows on the loan and the swap that are transferred to the note holders. If the cash flows are analysed individually:

- some of the cash flows on the loan may be passed to the note holders and some to the swap counterparty, so that not all the cash flows are transferred to the note holders, as required for a transfer (see 4.4.1 below); and
- payments on the notes may be sourced in part from the swap, so that payments to the note holders as 'eventual recipients' may not be limited to receipts from the loan as the 'original asset', as required for a pass-through arrangement (see 4.4.2 below).

Before this re-examination by the IASB of the meaning of 'transfer', it was common in some jurisdictions to apply the legal test to transfers of financial assets to a SPE in securitisation arrangements, rather than relying on an equitable transfer. After the withdrawal of the 'non-interpretation' (see 4.2.2 above), it is likely that those entities have continued to apply their previous practice. However the discussions have, yet again, highlighted the uncertainty at the heart of IAS 39's derecognition rules which means that there must be different treatments in practice. Until there is a conclusive interpretation, entities must establish an accounting policy that they apply consistently to all such transactions, whether they are transfers or pass-throughs.

I Implications for IAS 39

The implications of the IASB's discussion for securitisation transactions are discussed further at 4.4.3 E below.

B Transfers subject to conditions

An entity may transfer contractual rights to cash flows but subject to conditions. The IFRIC identified the following main types of condition:

- *Conditions relating to the existence and legal status of the asset at the time of the transfer*

  These include normal warranties as to the condition of the asset at the date of transfer and other guarantees affecting the existence and accuracy of the amount of the receivable that may not be known until after the date of transfer;
- *Conditions relating to the performance of the asset after the time of transfer*

  These include guarantees covering future default, late payment or changes in credit risk, guarantees relating to changes in tax, legal or regulatory requirements, where the buyer may be able to require additional payments if it is disadvantaged or – in some cases – reversal of the transaction, or guarantees covering future performance by the seller that might affect the recoverable amount of the debtor;
- *Offset arrangements*

  The original debtor may have the right to offset amounts against balances owed to the transferor for which the transferor will compensate the transferee. There may also be tripartite offset arrangements where a party other than the original debtor (e.g. a subcontractor) has such offset rights.[55]

All securitisations (and indeed, most derecognitions, whether of financial or non-financial assets) include express or implied warranties regarding the condition of the asset at the date of transfer. In the case of a securitisation of credit card receivables, these might include a representation that, for example, all the debtors transferred are resident in a particular jurisdiction, or have never been in arrears for more than one month in the previous two years. In our view, such warranties should not affect whether or not the transaction achieves derecognition.

It is a different matter when it comes to guarantees of post-transfer performance. In particular, one of the issues identified by the IFRIC – guarantees covering future default, late payment or changes in credit risk – links to the related debate regarding the transfer of groups of financial assets where the guarantees may have been provided by a third party (see 4.2.2 above).

In July 2006 the IFRIC decided to refer this issue to the IASB, which considered it at its September 2006 meeting. The IASB broadly confirmed our view as set out above. In its view neither conditions relating to the existence and value of transferred cash flows at the date of transfer nor conditions relating to the future performance of the asset would affect whether the entity has transferred the contractual rights to receive cash flows[56] (i.e. Box 4 in Figure 18.1 at 4.1.2 above). In other words, a transaction with such conditions that otherwise met the criteria in Box 4 would not be subject to the pass-through test in Box 5.

However, the existence of conditions relating to the future performance of the asset might affect the conclusion related to the transfer of risks and rewards (i.e. Box 6 in Figure 18.1 at 4.1.2 above) as well as the extent of any continuing involvement by the transferor in the transferred asset (i.e. Box 9 in Figure 18.1 at 4.1.2. above).[57]

These interpretations were also withdrawn by the IFRIC in January 2007 together with the views that had been expressed regarding 'similar' assets and transfers of assets (see 4.2.2 above). The entity must take a view that is consistent with its policies on these matters and, as in these other cases, hold it when considering the derecognition of any financial asset.

4.4.2 Retention of rights to receive cash flows subject to obligation to pay over to others (pass-through arrangement)

The discussion in this section refers to Box 5 in the flowchart at 4.1.2 above.

It is common in certain securitisation and debt sub-participation transactions (see 4.4.3 below) for an entity to enter into an arrangement whereby it continues to collect cash receipts from a financial asset (or more typically a pool of financial assets), but is obliged to pass on those receipts to a third party that has provided finance in connection with the financial asset.

Under IAS 39, an arrangement whereby the reporting entity retains the contractual rights to receive the cash flows of a financial asset (the 'original asset'), but assumes a contractual obligation to pay the cash flows to one or more recipients (the 'eventual recipients') is regarded as a transfer of the original asset if, and only if, all of the following three conditions are met:

(a) the entity has no obligation to pay amounts to the eventual recipients unless it collects equivalent amounts from the original asset. Short-term advances by the entity with the right of full recovery of the amount lent plus accrued interest at market rates do not violate this condition (see 4.4.3 A and B below);

(b) the entity is prohibited by the terms of the transfer contract from selling or pledging the original asset other than as security to the eventual recipients for the obligation to pay them cash flows; and

(c) the entity has an obligation to remit any cash flows it collects on behalf of the eventual recipients without material delay. In addition, the entity is not entitled to reinvest such cash flows, except in cash or cash equivalents as defined in IAS 7 – *Cash Flow Statements* (see Chapter 34 at 2.2.1) during the short settlement period from the collection date to the date of required remittance to the eventual recipients, with any interest earned on such investments being passed to the eventual recipients.[58]

These conditions are discussed further at 4.4.3 D below.

These conditions first appeared in paragraph 41 of the June 2002 exposure draft of proposed amendments to IAS 32 and IAS 39 (see Chapter 17 at 1.5), where they were referred to as a pass-through arrangement. Whilst this term does not actually appear in the revised version of IAS 39 it has become part of the language of the financial markets to refer to such transactions as pass-through arrangements. However, it should be noted that condition (c) above is slightly more onerous than that in the June 2002 exposure draft in that:

- the exposure draft proposed merely a prohibition on investment for the benefit of the transferor; but
- IAS 39 not only prohibits investment for the benefit of the transferor, but also restricts any investment made for the benefit of the transferee to cash or cash equivalents. This means that many current securitisation arrangements will fail the pass-through test – see 4.4.3 D below.

IAS 39 notes that an entity that is required to consider the impact of these conditions on a transaction is likely to be either:

- the originator of the financial asset in a securitisation transaction (see 4.4.3 below); or
- a group that includes a consolidated special purpose entity that has acquired the financial asset and passes on cash flows to unrelated third party investors.[59]

4.4.3 Securitisations

Securitisation is a process whereby finance can be raised from external investors by enabling them to invest in parcels of specific financial assets. The first main type of assets to be securitised was domestic mortgage loans, but the technique is regularly extended to other assets, such as credit card receivables, other consumer loans, or lease receivables. Securitisations are a complex area of financial reporting beyond the scope of a general text such as this to discuss in detail. However, it may assist understanding of the IASB's thinking to consider a 'generic' example of such a transaction.

A typical securitisation transaction involving a portfolio of mortgage loans would operate as follows. The entity which has initially advanced the loans in question (the 'originator') will sell them to another entity set up for the purpose (the 'issuer'). The issuer will typically be a subsidiary or SPE of the originator (and therefore consolidated – see 4.1.2 above) and its equity share capital will be small. The issuer will finance its purchase of these loans by issuing loan notes on interest terms which will be related to the rate of interest receivable on the mortgages and to achieve this it may need to enter into derivative instruments such as interest rate swaps. The swap counterparty may be the originator or a third party. The originator will continue to administer the loans as before, for which it will receive a service fee from the issuer.

The structure might therefore be as shown in this diagram:

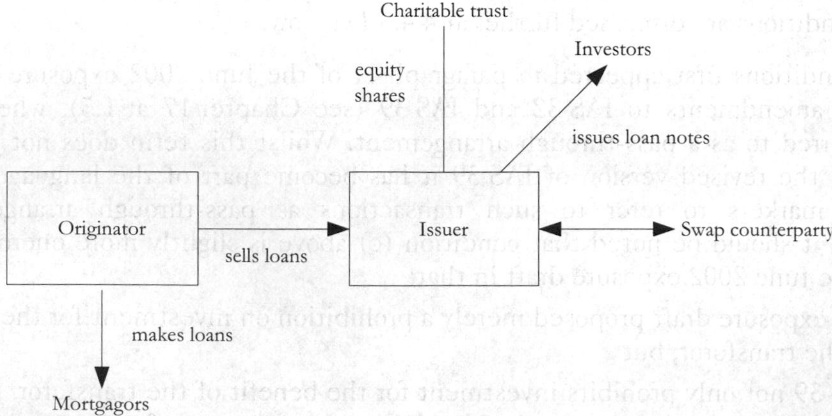

Potential investors in the mortgage-backed loan notes will want to be assured that their investment is relatively risk-free, and the issue will normally be supported by obtaining a high rating from a credit rating agency. This may be achieved by using a range of credit enhancement techniques which will add to the security already inherent in the quality of the mortgage portfolio. Such techniques can include the following:

- limited recourse to the originator in the event that the income from the mortgages falls short of the interest payable to the investors under the loan notes and other expenses. This may be made available in a number of ways; for example, by the provision of subordinated loan finance from the originator to the issuer; by the deferral of part of the consideration for the sale of the mortgages; or by the provision of a guarantee (see A below);
- the provision of loan facilities to meet temporary shortfalls as a result of slow payments of mortgage interest (see B below); or
- insurance against default on the mortgages (see C below).

The overall effect of the arrangement is that outside investors have been brought in to finance a particular portion of the originator's activities. These investors have first call on the income from the mortgages which back their investment. The originator is left with only the residual interest in the differential between the rates paid on the notes and earned on the mortgages, net of expenses; generally, this profit element is extracted by adjustments to the service fee or through the mechanism of interest rate swaps. It has thus limited its upside interest in the mortgages, while its remaining downside risk on the whole arrangement will depend on the extent to which it has assumed obligations under the credit enhancement measures.

A Recourse to originator

The conditions in 4.4.2 clearly have the effect that an arrangement that does not transfer the contractual rights to receive the cash flows but provides for direct recourse to the originator does not meet the definition of a 'transfer' for the purposes of pass-through and therefore does not qualify to be considered for derecognition. Direct recourse would include an arrangement whereby part of the consideration for the financial asset transferred was deferred depending on the performance of the asset, as illustrated by Example 18.4 below.

Example 18.4: Securitisation with deferred consideration

An originator wishes to securitise 90% of a particular portfolio of its credit card receivables. Outside investors agree to pay for 85% of the receivables immediately (with no further recourse to the originator in the event that less than 85% recovery is achieved), with the further 5% to be paid to the extent that the receivables are recovered. Under such an arrangement, IAS 39 would regard 85% of the portfolio at most as having been transferred (subject to the other conditions in 4.4.1 above having been met). This is entirely appropriate, since the originator clearly remains exposed to all the risks associated with recoveries in the range 85%-90% of the portfolio.

In our view, however, certain techniques for providing indirect recourse do not breach the conditions for transfer. These include:

(i) the originator waiving its right to receive cash flows on any retained portion of the portfolio to the extent of any losses suffered by the investors (but providing no other guarantee – see 4.2.1 above; or

(ii) the provision of certain types of insurance (see C below).

B Short-term loan facilities

Under IAS 39 (see 4.4.2 above) it is permissible to enhance a securitised asset with the provision of loan facilities to meet temporary shortfalls as a result of slow payments from the asset, but only where the loans are:

- made on a 'short-term' basis;
- repayable irrespective of whether the slow payments are eventually received; and
- bear interest at market rates.

The purpose of these restrictions is to ensure that IAS 39 allows derecognition of assets subject to such facilities only where the facilities are providing a short-term cash flow benefit to the investor, and not when they effectively transfer slow payment risk back to the originator (as would be the case if the originator made significant interest-free loans to the investor). Clearly, therefore, the circumstances in which such funds can be advanced must be very tightly defined if pass-through is to be achieved.

C Insurance protection

The conditions for 'transfer' are not, in our view, breached by the originator purchasing an insurance contract for the benefit of investors in the event of a shortfall in cash collections from the securitised assets, provided that the investors' only recourse is to the insurance policy. In other words, the originator cannot give a guarantee to investors to make good any shortfalls should the insurer become insolvent, nor can the originator provide any support to the insurer through a guarantee arrangement or a reinsurance contract.

The implications of the derecognition and pass-through requirements of IAS 39 for transfers of groups of financial assets including insurance contracts have recently been reconsidered by the IFRIC and the IASB but their tentative conclusions were withdrawn. For a discussion of the issues and the alternative interpretations of 'similar' assets, see 4.2.2 above.

D Treatment of collection proceeds

Securitisation contracts rarely require any amount received on the securitised assets to be immediately transferred to investors. This is for the obvious practical reason that it would be administratively inefficient, in the case of a securitisation of credit card receivables for example, to transfer the relevant portion of each individual, and relatively small, cash flow received from the hundreds, if not thousands, of cards in the portfolio. Instead, it is usual for transfers to be made in bulk on a periodic basis (e.g. weekly or monthly). This raises the question of what happens to the cash in the period between receipt by the issuer and onward transfer to the investors.

IAS 39 requires cash flows from transferred financial assets for which derecognition is sought to be:

- passed to the eventual recipients 'without material delay'; and
- invested only in cash or cash equivalents as defined in IAS 7 entirely for the benefit of the investors (see condition (c) in 4.4.2 above).

These requirements mean that many securitisation arrangements may well fail to satisfy the pass-through test in 4.4.2 above, as explained below.

Suppose that a credit card issuer wishes to raise five year finance secured on its portfolio of credit card receivables. The assets concerned are essentially short term (being in most cases settled in full within four to eight weeks), whereas the term of the borrowings secured on them is longer. In practice, what generally happens is that, at the start of the securitisation, a 'pool' of balances is transferred to the issuer. The cash receipts from that 'pool' are used to pay interest on the borrowings, and to fund new advances on cards in the 'pool' or to purchase other balances. Such an arrangement, commonly referred to as a 'revolving' structure, appears to breach the requirement of the pass-through tests to:

- pass on cash receipts without material delay (since only the amount of cash receipts necessary to pay the interest on the borrowings is passed on, with the balance being reinvested until the principal of the borrowings falls due); and
- only invest in cash or cash equivalents as defined in IAS 7 (since the cash not required to pay interest on the borrowings is invested in further credit card receivables, which are not cash or cash equivalents as defined in IAS 7).

Any arrangement that provides for even a small tranche of the interest from such short-term deposits to be retained by or for the benefit of the originator will not satisfy the criteria for transfer under IAS 39. Moreover, IAS 39 requires that the reporting entity 'is not entitled' to invest the cash other than as described in condition (c) in 4.4.2 above. Thus, it appears that the criteria for transfer are not satisfied merely where the entity does not in fact invest the cash in any other way – it must be contractually prohibited from doing so. In practice, this is often achieved by having the funds paid into a trustee bank account that can be used only for the benefit of the providers of finance.

The IFRIC confirmed in November 2005 that 'revolving' structures do not meet the requirements of the pass-though test for funds to be passed on without material delay and to be invested only in cash and cash equivalents.[60]

The strict requirements of IAS 39 in respect of cash received from assets subject to a pass-through arrangement raise the related, but broader, issue of the appropriate treatment under IAS 39 of client money (see 4.4.5 below).

E Transfer of a group of assets not all of which are derecognised

As discussed at 4.2.2. above, in September 2006 the IASB published its view that when a non-derivative asset (such as a securitised loan) is transferred together with other derivative assets, or a guarantee or credit insurance, the derecognition criteria must be applied to the transferred items individually rather than as a whole. In addition, transferred non-optional derivatives, such as interest swaps, which can be either assets or liabilities can be derecognised only if the derecognition criteria for both financial assets and financial liabilities are satisfied. Accordingly the IFRIC, who had originally passed the issue to the Board for consideration, concluded that no interpretation was necessary and issued a tentative 'non-interpretation' to that effect. However, this view has since been withdrawn by the IFRIC; after receiving comment letters, it has concluded that the published views cannot be sustained.

Some still consider that swaps may be derecognised only when any obligation is discharged, cancelled or expires (see 5 below), which does not occur in most securitisations. On this view, in a securitisation transaction involving the equitable transfer of an interest rate swap to an SPE, the swap would continue to be recognised by the transferor. The ongoing accounting consequences of this are less clear. The swap must clearly continue to be measured at fair value through profit or loss in accordance with the general requirement of IAS 39 for the measurement of derivatives not in a hedging relationship (see Chapter 20). However, this would have the effect that the reporting entity reflected gains and losses in the income statement for a derivative in which it no longer has a beneficial interest. In such a case, the entity should presumably recognise the notional back-to-back swap which it has effectively entered into with the transferee, so as to offset the income statement effect of the original swap.

4.4.4 'Empty' SPEs

If an entity enters into a transaction whereby:

- the entity transfers an asset to an SPE; and
- the SPE transfers the asset to noteholders on terms that satisfy the pass-through derecognition criteria in IAS 39 discussed at 4.4.2 and 4.4.3 above,

the overall effect will be that the individual financial statements of the SPE will include neither the transferred asset nor the finance raised from noteholders. This may well mean that the financial statements show nothing apart from the relatively small amount of equity of the entity and any related assets.

This, at first sight, rather strange result is perfectly consistent with SIC-12's analysis that the SPE is no more than an extension of the originating entity rather than an economic entity in its own right. Nevertheless, investors in loan notes issued by the SPE may be disturbed by the lack of any acknowledgement in the SPE's balance sheet of its liability to them!

4.4.5 Client money

A number of financial institutions and other entities hold money on behalf of clients. The terms on which such money is held can vary widely. In the case of normal deposits with a bank, the bank is free to use the client's money for its own purposes, with the client being protected by the solvency margin requirements imposed by the regulatory authorities. By contrast there are cases (e.g. in the case of certain monies held by legal advisers on behalf of their clients in some jurisdictions) where funds held on behalf of clients must be kept in a bank account completely separate from that of the depositary entity itself, with all interest earned on the account being for the benefit of clients. There are also intermediate situations where, for example:

- funds are required to be segregated in separate bank accounts but the depositary entity is allowed to retain some or all of the interest on the client accounts; or
- client funds are allowed to be commingled with those of the depositary entity, but some or all income on the funds must be passed on to clients.

This raises the question of how client monies should be accounted for in the financial statements under IFRS, and whether, in the absence of specific guidance, the rules for the treatment of funds received under a pass-through arrangement (see 4.4.3 D above) should be applied.

In our view, the types of arrangement to deal with client money are so varied that it is impossible to generalise as to the appropriate treatment. However, the analysis for the two extreme cases seems relatively straightforward. In the case of a bank deposit (or any arrangement where the entity may freely use client cash for its own benefit), the general recognition criteria of IAS 39 indicate that an asset and a liability should be recognised. Conversely, where the entity is required to hold funds held on behalf of clients in a bank account completely separate from that of the entity itself, with all interest earned on the account being for the benefit of clients, it is hard to see how such funds meet the general definition of an asset under the *Framework*. Whilst the entity controls such funds, it can derive no economic benefits from them.

The intermediate cases may be harder to deal with. Key questions are likely to include:

- which party is at risk from the failure of client assets held by the entity,
- the status of the funds in the event of the insolvency of either the reporting entity or its client, and
- which party has the benefit of income from the assets.

In general the appropriate analysis is likely to be that the depositary entity enjoys sufficient use of the client money that it should be recognised as an asset with a corresponding liability due to the client.

4.5 Has the entity transferred or retained substantially all the risks and rewards of ownership?

The discussion in this section refers to Boxes 6 and 7 in the flowchart at 4.1.2 above.

Once an entity has established that it has transferred a financial asset (see 4.4 above), IAS 39 then requires it to evaluate the extent to which it retains the risks and rewards of ownership of the financial asset.[61]

If the entity transfers substantially all the risks and rewards of ownership of the financial asset, the entity must derecognise the financial asset and recognise separately as assets or liabilities any rights and obligations created or retained in the transfer.[62] Examples of such transactions are given at 4.5.1, 4.7 and 4.8 below. If an entity determines that, as a result of the transfer, it has transferred substantially all the risks and rewards of ownership of the transferred asset, it does not recognise the transferred asset again in a future period, unless it reacquires the transferred asset in a new transaction.[63]

If the entity retains substantially all the risks and rewards of ownership of the financial asset, the entity continues to recognise the financial asset.[64] Examples of such transactions are given at 4.5.2, 4.7 and 4.8 below.

If the entity neither transfers nor retains substantially all the risks and rewards of ownership of the financial asset (see 4.5.3 below), the entity determines whether it has retained control of the financial asset[65] (see 4.6 below).

IAS 39 clarifies that the transfer of risks and rewards should be evaluated by comparing the entity's exposure, before and after the transfer, to the variability in the amounts and timing of the net cash flows of the transferred asset.[66] Often it will be obvious whether the entity has transferred or retained substantially all risks and rewards of ownership. In other cases, it will be necessary to determine this by computing and comparing the entity's exposure to the variability in the present value (discounted at an appropriate current market interest rate) of the future net cash flows before and after the transfer. All reasonably possible variability in net cash flows is considered, with greater weight being given to those outcomes that are more likely to occur.[67]

4.5.1 Transfers resulting in transfer of substantially all risks and rewards

An entity has transferred substantially all the risks and rewards of ownership of a financial asset if its exposure to the variability in the amounts and timing of the net cash flows of the transferred asset is no longer significant in relation to the total such variability. IAS 39 gives the following examples of transactions that transfer substantially all the risks and rewards of ownership:

- an unconditional sale of a financial asset;
- a sale of a financial asset together with an option to repurchase the financial asset at its fair value at the time of repurchase (since this does not expose the entity to any risk of loss or give any opportunity for profit);
- a sale of a financial asset together with a put or call option that is deeply out of the money (i.e. an option that is so far out of the money it is highly unlikely to go into the money before expiry); or
- the sale of a fully proportionate share of the cash flows from a larger financial asset in an arrangement, such as a loan sub-participation, that satisfies the criteria for a 'transfer' in 4.4.2 above.[68]

Such transactions are discussed in more detail at 4.7 below.

It is important to note that, in order for derecognition to be achieved, it is necessary that the entity's exposure to the variability in the amounts and timing of the net cash flows of the transferred asset is considered not in isolation, but 'in relation to the total such variability' (see above). Thus derecognition is not achieved simply because the entity's remaining exposure to the risks or rewards of an asset is small in absolute terms. It has also become clear, from the IFRIC and IASB's discussions described at 4.2.2 above, that derecognition also depends on the interpretation of 'asset' and of groups of similar assets that is applied by the entity.

4.5.2 Transfers resulting in retention of substantially all risks and rewards

An entity has retained substantially all the risks and rewards of ownership of a financial asset if its exposure to the variability in the present value of the future net cash flows from the financial asset does not change significantly as a result of the transfer. IAS 39 gives the following examples of transactions in which an entity has retained substantially all the risks and rewards of ownership:

- a sale and repurchase transaction where the repurchase price is a fixed price or the sale price plus a lender's return;
- a securities lending agreement;
- a sale of a financial asset together with a total return swap that transfers the market risk exposure back to the entity;
- a sale of a financial asset together with a deeply in the money put or call option (i.e. an option that is so far in the money that it is highly unlikely to go out of

the money before expiry). It will be in the holder's interest to exercise such an option, so that the asset will almost certainly revert to the transferor; and

- a sale of short-term receivables in which the entity guarantees to compensate the transferee for credit losses that are likely to occur.[69]

Such transactions are discussed in more detail at 4.7 below.

4.5.3 Transfers resulting in neither transfer nor retention of substantially all risks and rewards

IAS 39 gives the following examples of transactions in which an entity has neither transferred nor retained substantially all the risks and rewards of ownership:

- a sale of a financial asset together with a put or call option that is neither deeply in the money nor deeply out of the money.[70] The effect of such an option is that the transferor will have either (in the case of purchased call option) capped its exposure to a loss in value of the asset but have potentially unlimited access to increases in value or (in the case of a written put option) capped its potential access to increases in value in the asset but assumed potential exposure to a total loss in value of the asset; and
- a sale of 90% of a loan portfolio with significant transfer of prepayment risk, but retention of a 10% interest, with losses allocated first to that 10% retained interest.[71]

Such transactions are discussed in more detail at 4.7 and 4.8 below.

4.6 Has the entity retained control of the asset?

The discussion in this section relates to Boxes 8 and 9 of the flowchart at 4.1.2 above.

If the transferring entity has neither transferred nor retained substantially all the risks and rewards of a transferred financial asset, IAS 39 requires the entity to determine whether or not it has retained control of the financial asset. If the entity has not retained control, it must derecognise the financial asset and recognise separately as assets or liabilities any rights and obligations created or retained in the transfer. If the entity has retained control, it must continue to recognise the financial asset to the extent of its continuing involvement in the financial asset (see 4.8.3 below).[72]

IAS 39 requires the question of whether the entity has retained control of the transferred asset to be determined by the transferee's ability to sell the asset. If the transferee:

- has the practical ability to sell the asset in its entirety to an unrelated third party; and
- is able to exercise that ability unilaterally and without needing to impose additional restrictions on the transfer,

the entity has not retained control (see 4.6.1 below).

In all other cases, the entity has retained control.[73]

4.6.1 *Transferee's 'practical ability' to sell the asset*

IAS 39 clarifies that the transferee will have the practical ability to sell a transferred asset if the asset is traded in an active market, on the basis that the transferee will have the ability to repurchase the transferred asset in the market if it needs to return the asset to the entity. For example, if a transferred asset is sold subject to an option that allows the entity to repurchase it:

- the transferee may (subject to the further considerations discussed below) have the practical ability to sell the asset if it can readily obtain the transferred asset in the market if the option is exercised; but
- the transferee does not have the practical ability to sell the transferred asset if it cannot readily obtain the transferred asset in the market if the option is exercised.[74]

Moreover, the transferee has the practical ability to sell the transferred asset only if the transferee can sell the transferred asset in its entirety to an unrelated third party and is able to exercise that ability unilaterally and without imposing additional restrictions on the transfer. IAS 39 requires that to be determined by considering what the transferee is able to do in practice, rather than purely by reference to any contractual rights or prohibitions. For example, the standard notes that a contractual right to dispose of the transferred asset has little practical effect if there is no market for the transferred asset.[75]

IAS 39 goes on to point out that an ability to dispose of the transferred asset also has little practical effect if it cannot be exercised freely. Accordingly, the transferee's ability to dispose of the transferred asset must be a unilateral ability independent of the actions of others. In other words, the transferee must be able to dispose of the transferred asset without needing to attach conditions to the transfer (e.g. conditions about how a loan asset is serviced, or an option giving the transferee the right to repurchase the asset).[76]

For example, the entity might sell a financial asset to a transferee subject to the transferee having the benefit of an option to put the asset back to the entity or a performance guarantee from the entity. IAS 39 argues that such an option or guarantee might be so valuable to the transferee that the transferee would not, in practice, sell the transferred asset to a third party without attaching a similar option or other restrictive conditions. Instead, the transferee would hold the transferred asset so as to obtain payments under the guarantee or put option. Under these circumstances IAS 39 regards the transferor as having retained control of the transferred asset.[77]

However, IAS 39 notes that the fact that the transferee is simply unlikely to sell the transferred asset does not, of itself, mean that the transferor has retained control of the transferred asset.[78]

4.7 Practical application of the derecognition criteria

IAS 39 gives a number of practical examples of the application of the derecognition criteria in IAS 39, which are discussed below. In some cases, it has to be said that the guidance in IAS 39 is less than satisfactory, amounting to little more than repetition of the standard.

In order to provide a link with Figure 18.1 at 4.1.2 above we have used the following convention:

'Box 6, Yes'	The transaction would result in the answer 'Yes' at Box 6 in the flowchart
'Box 7, No'	The transaction would result in the answer 'No' at Box 7 in the flowchart

4.7.1 Repurchase agreements ('repos') and securities lending

A Agreements to return the same asset

If a financial asset is:

- sold under an agreement to repurchase it at a fixed price or at the sale price plus a lender's return; or
- loaned under an agreement to return it to the transferor,

the asset is not derecognised, because the transferor retains substantially all the risks and rewards of ownership[79] (Figure 18.1, Box 7, Yes). The accounting treatment of such transactions is discussed at 4.8.2 below.

I Transferee's right to pledge

If the transferee obtains the right to sell or pledge an asset that is the subject of such a transaction, the transferor reclassifies the asset on its balance sheet, for example, as a loaned asset or repurchase receivable.[80]

It appears that this accounting treatment is required merely where the transferee has the 'right' to sell or pledge the asset. This contrasts with the requirements for determining whether an asset subject to a transaction in which the entity neither transfers nor retains substantially all the risks and rewards associated with the asset (Figure 18.1, Box 7, No) nevertheless qualifies for derecognition because the transferee has control (Figure 18.1, Box 8, Yes). In order for the transferee to be regarded as having control for the purposes of Box 8, any rights of the transferee to sell or pledge as asset must have economic substance – see 4.6 above.

The accounting treatment of such transactions is discussed at 4.8.2 below.

B Agreements with right to return the same or substantially the same asset

If a financial asset is:

- sold under an agreement to repurchase the same or substantially the same asset at a fixed price or at the sale price plus a lender's return; or
- loaned under an agreement to return the same or substantially the same asset to the transferor,

the asset is not derecognised because the transferor retains substantially all the risks and rewards of ownership[81] (Figure 18.1, Box 7, Yes). The accounting treatment of such transactions is discussed at 4.8.2 below.

C Agreements with right of substitution

If a financial asset is the subject of:

- a repurchase agreement at a fixed repurchase price or a price equal to the sale price plus a lender's return; or
- a similar securities lending transaction

that provides the transferee with a right to substitute assets that are similar and of equal fair value to the transferred asset at the repurchase date, the asset sold or lent is not derecognised because the transferor retains substantially all the risks and rewards of ownership[82] (Figure 18.1, Box 7, Yes). The accounting treatment of such transactions is discussed at 4.8.2 below.

D Net cash-settled forward repurchase

IAS 39 gives some guidance on the treatment of net cash-settled options over transferred assets (see 4.7.2 E below), which in passing refers to net cash-settled forward contracts. This guidance indicates that the key factor for determining whether derecognition is appropriate remains whether or not the entity has transferred substantially all the risks and rewards of the transferred asset.[83] This suggests that an asset sold subject to a fixed price net-settled forward contract to reacquire it should not be derecognised (see A to C above) until the contract is settled (Figure 18.1, Box 7, Yes).

The accounting treatment of such transactions is discussed at 4.8.2 below.

E Agreement to repurchase at fair value

A transfer of a financial asset subject only to a forward repurchase agreement with a repurchase price equal to the fair value of the financial asset at the time of repurchase results in derecognition because of the transfer of substantially all the risks and rewards of ownership[84] (Figure 18.1, Box 6, Yes). The accounting treatment of such transactions is discussed at 4.8.1 below.

F Right of first refusal to repurchase at fair value

If an entity sells a financial asset and retains only a right of first refusal to repurchase the transferred asset at fair value if the transferee subsequently sells it, the entity derecognises the asset because it has transferred substantially all the risks and rewards of ownership[85] (Figure 18.1, Box 6, Yes).

IAS 39 does not address the treatment of a financial asset sold with a right of first refusal to repurchase the transferred asset at a predetermined value that might well be lower or higher than fair value (e.g. an amount estimated, at the time at which the original transaction was entered into, as the future market value of the asset). One analysis might be that, since the transferee is under no obligation to put the asset up for sale, derecognition is still appropriate. Another analysis might be that, if the asset can ultimately only be realised by onward sale, the arrangement is nearer in substance to a transferor's call option (see 4.7.2 below).

G Wash sale

A 'wash sale' is the repurchase of a financial asset shortly after it has been sold. Such a repurchase does not preclude derecognition provided that the original transaction met the derecognition requirements. However, if an agreement to sell a financial asset is entered into concurrently with an agreement to repurchase the same asset at a fixed price or the sale price plus a lender's return, then the asset is not derecognised.[86] Such a transaction would be equivalent to those in A to D above.

4.7.2 Transfers subject to put and call options

Some of the technical 'jargon' used to describe option contracts is explained at 3.1.4 above.

A Deeply in the money put and call options

If a transferred financial asset can be called back by the transferor, and the call option is deeply in the money, the transfer does not qualify for derecognition because the transferor has retained substantially all the risks and rewards of ownership (Figure 18.1, Box 7, Yes).

Similarly, if the financial asset can be put back by the transferee, and the put option is deeply in the money, the transfer does not qualify for derecognition because the transferor has retained substantially all the risks and rewards of ownership[87] (Figure 18.1, Box 7, Yes).

The accounting treatment for such transactions would be similar to that for 'repos' as set out in Example 18.12 at 4.8.2 below.

If a transferred asset continues to be recognised because of a transferor's call option or transferee's put option, but the option subsequently lapses unexercised, the asset and any associated liability would then be derecognised.

B Deeply out of the money put and call options

A financial asset that is transferred subject only to a transferee's deeply out of the money put option, or a transferor's deeply out of the money call option, is derecognised. This is because the transferor has transferred substantially all the risks and rewards of ownership[88] (Figure 18.1, Box 7, Yes).

C Options that are neither deeply out of the money nor deeply in the money

Where a financial asset is transferred subject to an option (whether a transferor's call option or a transferee's put option) that is neither deeply in the money nor deeply out of the money, the result is that the entity neither transfers nor retains substantially all the risks and rewards associated with the asset[89] (Figure 18.1, Box 7,

No). It is therefore necessary to determine whether or not the transferor has retained control of the asset under the criteria summarised in 4.6 above.

If a transferred asset continues to be recognised because of a transferor's call option or transferee's put option, but the option subsequently lapses unexercised, the asset and any associated liability would then be derecognised.

I Assets readily obtainable in the market

If the transferor has a call option over a transferred financial asset that is readily obtainable in the market, IAS 39 considers that control of the asset has passed to the transferee (Figure 18.1, Box 8, No – see 4.6 above).[90] This would presumably also be the conclusion where the transferee had a put option over a transferred financial asset that is readily obtainable in the market, although IAS 39 does not specifically address this.

II Assets not readily obtainable in the market

If the transferor has a call option over a transferred financial asset that is not readily obtainable in the market, IAS 39 considers that control of the asset remains with the transferor (Figure 18.1, Box 8, Yes – see 4.6 above). Accordingly, derecognition is precluded to the extent of the amount of the asset that is subject to the call option.[91]

If the transferee has a put option over a transferred financial asset that is not readily obtainable in the market, IAS 39 requires the transferee's likely economic behaviour to be assessed – in effect to determine whether the option gives the transferee the practical ability to sell the transferred asset (see 4.6.1 above).

If the put option is sufficiently valuable to prevent the transferee from selling the asset, the transferor is considered to retain control of the asset and should account for the asset to the extent of its continuing involvement[92] (Figure 18.1, Box 9). The accounting treatment required is discussed at 4.8.3 below.

If the put option is not sufficiently valuable to prevent the transferee from selling the asset, the transferor is considered to have ceded control of the asset, and should derecognise it[93] (Figure 18.1, Box 8, No).

The requirements above beg two questions. First the question of whether or not a put option is sufficiently valuable to prevent the transferee from selling the asset is not a matter of objective fact, but rather a function of the transferee's appetite for risk, its need for liquidity and so forth. It is not clear how the transferor can readily assess these factors.

Second, IAS 39 is not explicit as to the accounting consequences (if any) of an option that was considered at the time of the original transfer to be deeply out of the money subsequently becoming neither deeply in the money nor deeply out of the money, or even deeply in the money, (or any other of the possible permutations). This is discussed further at I below.

D Option to put or call at fair value

A transfer of a financial asset subject only to a put or call option with an exercise price equal to the fair value of the financial asset at the time of repurchase results in derecognition because of the transfer of substantially all the risks and rewards of ownership[94] (Figure 18.1, Box 6, Yes).

E Net cash-settled options

Where a transfer of a financial asset is subject to a put or call option that will be settled net in cash, IAS 39 requires the entity to evaluate the transfer so as to determine whether it has retained or transferred substantially all the risks and rewards of ownership.[95] IAS 39 comments that 'if the entity has not retained substantially all the risks and rewards of ownership of the transferred asset, it determines whether it has retained control of the transferred asset' – a repetition of the basic principles of the standard adding no clarification specific to this type of transaction.

F Removal of accounts provision

A 'removal of accounts provision' is an unconditional repurchase (i.e. call) option that gives an entity the right to reclaim transferred assets subject to some restrictions. Provided that such an option results in the entity neither retaining nor transferring substantially all the risks and rewards of ownership, IAS 39 allows derecognition, except to the extent of the amount subject to repurchase (assuming that the transferee cannot sell the assets).

For example, if an entity transfers loan receivables with a carrying amount of €100,000 for proceeds of €100,000, subject only to the right to call back any individual loan(s) up to a maximum of €10,000, €90,000 of the loans would qualify for derecognition.[96]

G Clean-up call options

A 'clean-up call' option is an option held by an entity that services transferred assets (and may be the transferor of those assets) to purchase remaining transferred assets when the cost of servicing the assets exceeds the entity's participation in their benefits. If such a clean-up call results in the entity neither retaining nor transferring substantially all the risks and rewards of ownership, and the transferee cannot sell the assets, IAS 39 precludes derecognition only to the extent of the amount of assets subject to the call option.[97]

H Same (or nearly the same) price put and call options

IAS 39 does not specifically address the transfer of an asset subject to both a transferee's option to put, and a transferor's option to call, the asset at a fixed price rather than at fair value (as discussed in D above). Assuming that:

- both options can be exercised simultaneously; and
- both the transferor and transferee behave rationally,

it will clearly be in the interest of either the transferor or the transferee to exercise its option, so that the asset will be reacquired by the transferor. This indicates that the transferor has retained substantially all the risks and rewards of ownership.

However, if the two options were exercisable on different dates or at different prices the effects of each option would need to be considered carefully.

I Changes in probability of exercise of options after initial transfer of asset

As noted at C above, IAS 39 is not explicit as to the accounting consequences (if any) of an option that was considered at the time of the original transfer to be deeply out of the money subsequently becoming neither deeply in the money nor deeply out of the money, or even deeply in the money, (or any other of the possible permutations). This is explored further in Examples 16.5 to 16.7 below.

Example 18.5: Financial asset transferred subject only to deeply out of the money call option

On 1 January 2005 an entity transferred a financial asset to a counterparty, subject only to a call option to repurchase the asset at any time up to 31 December 2009. At 1 January 2005 the option was considered deeply out of the money and the asset was accordingly derecognised (see B above).

At 31 December 2008 market conditions have changed considerably and the option is now deeply in the money. What is the accounting consequence of this change?

There are no accounting consequences since, as noted at 4.5 above, IAS 39 (paragraph AG41) specifies that an asset previously derecognised because substantially all the risks and rewards associated with the asset have been transferred (as would be the analysis for an asset transferred subject only to a deeply out of the money call – see B above) is not re-recognised in a future period unless it is reacquired. Instead the increase in the fair value of the option would be captured in the financial statements as a gain under the normal requirement of IAS 39 to account for derivatives at fair value with changes in value reflected in profit or loss (see Chapter 20).

However, if the market changes were not demonstrably beyond any reasonable expectation as at 1 January 2005, there might be an argument (given the definition of a deeply out of the money option as an option that is 'highly unlikely' to become in the money before expiry – see 3 above) that the fact that the option is now not merely in the money, but deeply in the money, indicates that the original assessment that that option was deeply out of the money was in fact an accounting error requiring correction under IAS 8 – *Accounting Policies, Changes in Accounting Estimates and Errors* (see Chapter 3).

Example 18.6: Financial asset transferred subject only to deeply in the money call option

On 1 January 2005 an entity transferred a financial asset to a counterparty, subject only to a call option to repurchase the asset at any time up to 31 December 2009. At 1 January 2005 the option was considered deeply in the money and the asset was accordingly not derecognised (see A above).

At 31 December 2008 market conditions have changed considerably and the option is now deeply out of the money. What is the accounting consequence of this change?

This is the mirror image of the fact pattern in Example 18.5. However, whereas IAS 39 makes it clear that an asset previously derecognised is not re-recognised, there is no comparable provision that an asset that previously did not qualify for derecognition on the origination of a particular transaction may not later be derecognised as a result of a subsequent change in the assessed likely impact of the transaction.

In our view, however, the original assessment as to whether or not the asset should be derecognised should not be subsequently revisited, unless (in exceptional circumstances) the original assessment was an accounting error within the scope of IAS 8. Thus, in Example 18.6 above the asset would not be derecognised. However, the fall in the value of the option indicates an impairment of the asset which is likely to be required to be reflected in the financial statements under the normal requirements of IAS 39 (see Chapter 20 at 6). This would in turn appear to require a corresponding adjustment to the liability recognised for the sale proceeds, so as to avoid recognising a net loss in the income statement that has not actually been suffered.

Example 18.7: Financial asset transferred subject to call option neither deeply in the money nor deeply out of the money

On 1 January 2005 an entity transferred a financial asset (an equity share) to a counterparty, subject only to a call option to repurchase the asset at any time up to 31 December 2009. At 1 January 2005 the option was considered to be neither deeply in the money nor deeply out of the money. However, the asset was readily marketable and freely transferable by the transferor and was accordingly derecognised because the entity, while neither transferring nor retaining substantially all the risks and rewards of the asset, no longer controls it (see C above).

At 31 December 2008 the financial asset that was the subject of the transfer ceases to be listed and is therefore not readily marketable. Had this been the case at the time of the original transfer, the entity would have been regarded as retaining control of the asset, which would not have been derecognised (see C II above). What is the accounting consequence of this change?

Again, matters are not entirely clear. The rule in paragraph AG41 of IAS 39 that a previously derecognised asset should not be re-recognised (other than on reacquisition of the asset) applies, as drafted, only where derecognition results from a transfer of substantially all the risks and rewards associated with the asset. In this case, derecognition has resulted from a loss of control over, not a transfer of substantially all the risks and rewards associated with, the asset. There is therefore some ambiguity as to whether AG41 is to be read:

- *generally* as prohibiting any re-recognition of a derecognised asset; or
- *specifically* as referring only to circumstances where derecognition results from transfer of substantially all the risks and rewards (i.e. it applies only to 'Box 6, Yes' transactions, and not to 'Box 8, No' transactions).

Again, however, we take the view that the original decision to derecognise the asset should not be revisited, unless (in exceptional circumstances) the original assessment was an accounting error within the scope of IAS 8. The fact that the asset was transferred on terms that the transferee could freely dispose of it means that the transferor did indeed lose control. This is proved by the fact that, if the transferee had exercised its right to dispose of the asset, and the transferor then exercised its call option, transferee would find it difficult, if not impossible, to deliver the actual asset (because it is not longer readily obtainable following its de-listing) and would probably be obliged to settle the option in cash. Conversely, if the asset had originally been transferred subject to conditions restricting its onward transfer by the transferee, derecognition would not have been achieved since the transferee would not have had the practical ability to dispose of the asset (see 4.6.1 above), indicating that control had been retained by the transferee.

4.7.3 Subordinated retained interests and credit guarantees

Where a financial asset is transferred, an entity may provide the transferee with credit enhancement by subordinating some or all of its interest retained in the transferred asset. Alternatively, an entity may provide the transferee with credit enhancement in the form of a credit guarantee that could be unlimited or limited to a specified amount.[98] Such techniques are commonly used in securitisation transactions (see 4.4.3 above).

IAS 39 notes that, if the entity retains substantially all the risks and rewards of ownership of the transferred asset, the asset continues to be recognised in its entirety. If the entity retains some, but not substantially all, of the risks and rewards of ownership and has retained control, derecognition is precluded to the extent of the amount of cash or other assets that the entity could be required to pay.[99] This 'guidance' is really no more than a repetition of the basic principles of the standard, adding no real clarification specific to this type of transaction.

4.7.4 Total return swaps

An entity may sell a financial asset to a transferee and enter into a total return swap with the transferee, whereby the transferor pays an amount equivalent to fixed or floating rate interest on the consideration for the transfer and receives an amount equivalent to the cash flows from, together with any increases or decreases in the fair value of, the underlying asset. In such a case, derecognition of all of the asset is prohibited,[100] since the transaction has the effect that substantially all the risks and rewards associated with the asset are retained by the transferor.

4.7.5 Interest rate swaps

An entity may transfer a fixed rate financial asset and enter into an interest rate swap with the transferee to receive a fixed interest rate and pay a variable interest rate based on a notional amount equal to the principal amount of the transferred financial asset. IAS 39 states that the interest rate swap does not preclude derecognition of the transferred asset, provided that the payments on the swap are not conditional on payments being made on the transferred asset.[101] It is interesting that this is included as guidance as it does not follow from the principles. There are situations in which the entity retains substantially all of the risks by retaining interest rate risk.

If, however, the transferor were to transfer an asset subject to prepayment risk (e.g. a domestic mortgage), and the transferor and transferee were to enter into an amortising interest rate swap (i.e. one whose notional amount amortises so that it equals the principal amount of the transferred financial asset outstanding at any point in time), the transferor would generally retain substantial prepayment risk through the swap. In this case, the transferor would (depending on the other facts of the transaction, such as the transfer or retention of credit risk) continue to recognise the transferred asset either in its entirety (Figure 18.1, Box 7, Yes) or to the extent of the transferor's continuing involvement (Figure 18.1, Box 9).[102]

Conversely, if the transferor and the transferee were to enter into an amortising interest rate swap, the amortisation of the notional amount of which is not linked to the principal amount outstanding on the transferred asset, the transferor would no longer retain prepayment risk. Therefore such a swap would not preclude derecognition of the transferred asset, provided the payments on the swap were not conditional on interest payments being made on the transferred asset and the swap did not result in the entity retaining any other significant risks and rewards of ownership on the transferred asset.[103]

4.7.6 *Factoring of trade receivables*

IAS 39 does not specifically address one of the more common forms of 'off-balance sheet finance' – the factoring of trade receivables. The common aim of all factoring structures is to provide cash flow from trade receivables quicker than would arise from normal cash collections, which is generally achieved by a 'sale' of all, or certain selected, receivables to a financial institution. However, the conditions of such 'sales' are extremely varied (which may well explain the lack of any 'generic' guidance in the standard), ranging from true outright sales and pass-through arrangements (resulting in full derecognition), to transactions with continuing involvement through guarantee or subordination arrangements.

It will therefore be necessary for an entity to consider the terms of its particular debt-factoring arrangement(s) carefully in order to determine the appropriate application of the derecognition provisions of IAS 39. Depending on circumstances, Examples 18.8 (see 4.8.1 below) 18.10 (see 4.8.1 B below), 18.13 (see 4.8.4 A below) and 18.18 (see 4.8.4 D below) may be of particular relevance.

4.8 Accounting treatment

This part of the chapter deals with the accounting consequences of the derecognition criteria for financial assets – in other words how the principles discussed in 4.1 to 4.7 above translate into accounting entries.

In order to provide a link with Figure 18.1 at 4.1.2 above we have used the following convention:

'Box 6, Yes'	The transaction would result in the answer 'Yes' at Box 6 in the flowchart
'Box 7, No'	The transaction would result in the answer 'No' at Box 7 in the flowchart

4.8.1 Transfers that qualify for derecognition

It is important to remember throughout this section that references to an asset being derecognised in its entirety include situations where a part of an asset to which the derecognition criteria are applied separately is derecognised in its entirety (see 4.2 above). In this context, IAS 39 uses the phrase 'in its entirety' in contrast to the accounting treatment applied to assets where there is continuing involvement (see 4.8.3 below) where some, but not all, of a financial asset, or part of an asset, is derecognised.

If, as a result of a transfer, a financial asset is derecognised in its entirety but the transfer results in the transferor obtaining a new financial asset or servicing asset (see B below) or assuming a new financial liability, or a servicing liability (see B below), IAS 39 requires the entity to recognise the new financial asset, servicing asset, financial liability or servicing liability at fair value.[104]

On derecognition of a financial asset in its entirety, IAS 39 requires the difference between:

(a) the carrying amount of the asset; and
(b) the sum of
   (i) the consideration received (including any new asset obtained less any new liability assumed); and
   (ii) any cumulative gain or loss that had been recognised directly in equity

to be recognised in profit or loss.[105]

The requirement in (b)(ii) above for 'recycling' of any cumulative gain or loss previously recognised directly in equity applies to assets accounted for as available-for-sale, and is discussed further in Chapter 20 at 3.4.

Example 18.8 illustrates these requirements.

Example 18.8: Derecognition of whole of financial asset in its entirety

At 1 October 2007 an entity has an available-for-sale financial asset carried at €1,400 in respect of which a cumulative gain of €200 has been recognised in equity. At that date, the asset is unconditionally sold to a third party in exchange for cash of €2,500 and a loan note issued to the third party. The loan note bears fixed rate interest below current market rates and is repayable at €1,150 but is considered to have a fair value of €1,100. The following accounting entries are made by the entity to record the disposal:

	€	€
Cash	2,500	
Equity ('recycling' of cumulative gain on asset)	200	
Gain on disposal		200
Asset		1,400
Loan note		1,100

Thereafter the loan note would be accreted up to its repayable amount of €1,150 over its expected life using the effective interest method (see Chapter 20 at 5).

If the asset had been of a type eligible for accounting using the amortised cost method, and had been so accounted for, and had a carrying amount of (say) €1,300 at the date of the transfer, the accounting entry would have been:

	€	€
Cash	2,500	
Profit on disposal		100
Asset		1,300
Loan note		1,100

A Transferred asset part of larger asset

If the transferred asset is part of a larger financial asset, for example when an entity transfers interest cash flows that are part of a debt instrument (see 4.2 above), and the part transferred qualifies for derecognition in its entirety, IAS 39 requires the previous carrying amount of the larger financial asset to be allocated between the part that continues to be recognised and the part that is derecognised. The allocation is based on the relative fair values of those parts on the date of the transfer. For this purpose, a retained servicing asset (see B below) is to be treated as a part that continues to be recognised.

IAS 39 requires the difference between:

(a) the carrying amount allocated to the part derecognised; and

(b) the sum of

  (i) the consideration received for the part derecognised (including any new asset obtained less any new liability assumed); and

  (ii) any cumulative gain or loss allocated to it previously recognised directly in equity

to be recognised in profit or loss. Any cumulative gain or loss that had been recognised in equity is allocated between the part that continues to be recognised and the part that is derecognised, based on the relative fair values of those parts.[106] The requirement in (b)(ii) above for 'recycling' of any cumulative gain or loss previously recognised directly in equity applies to assets accounted for as available-for-sale, and is discussed further in Chapter 20 at 3.4.

IAS 39 notes that the accounting treatment prescribed for the derecognition of a part (or parts) of a financial asset requires an entity to determine the fair value of the part(s) that continue to be recognised. Where the entity has a history of selling parts similar to the part that continues to be recognised, or other market transactions exist for such parts, IAS 39 requires recent prices of actual transactions to be used to provide the best estimate of its fair value. When there are no price quotations or recent market transactions to support the fair value of the part that continues to be recognised, the best estimate of the fair value is the difference between:

- the fair value of the larger financial asset as a whole; and
- the consideration received from the transferee for the part that is derecognised.[107]

The application guidance to IAS 39 requires the fair value of the part derecognised and the part retained to be determined using paragraphs AG69 to AG82 of the application guidance in IAS 39 (which deal with the determination of fair value[108] – see Chapter 20 at 4).

Example 18.9 illustrates the requirements for full derecognition of a part of an asset.

Example 18.9: Derecognition of part of financial asset in its entirety

On 1 January 2003 an entity invested €1 million in a loan with a par value of €1 million. The loan pays interest of €75,000 on 31 December annually in arrears and is to be redeemed at par on 31 December 2012. The entity accounts for the loan at amortised cost.

On 1 January 2008 it unconditionally sells the right to receive the remaining five interest payments to a bank. The derecognition provisions of IAS 39 are applied to the interest payments as an identifiable part of the asset, leading to the conclusion that they are required to be derecognised.

The consideration received for, and the fair value of, the future interest payments (based on the net present value, as at 1 January 2008, of the payments at the current market interest rate that would be available to the borrower of 5%)[109] is €324,711 (€75,000 × [$1/1.05 + 1/1.05^2 \ldots + 1/1.05^5$]). By the same methodology the fair value of the principal repayment can be calculated as €783,526 (€1,000,000 × $1/1.05^5$), giving a total fair value for the loan of €1,108,237.

In order to calculate the gain or loss on disposal, the total carrying value of the loan of €1,000,000 is allocated between the part disposed of and the part retained, based on the fair values of those parts. This allocates €292,998 (€1,000,000 × 324,711 ÷ 1,108,237) to the interest payments disposed of and €707,002 (€1,000,000 × 783,526 ÷ 1,108,237) to the retained right to the repayment of principal. This generates the accounting entry:

	€	€
Cash	324,711	
Loan (portion of carrying amount allocated to interest payments)		292,998
Gain on disposal		31,713

If the loan had instead been a quoted bond accounted for as available-for-sale, it would have already have been carried at €1,108,237, so that the basic disposal journal would simply be:

	€	€
Cash	324,711	
Bond (portion of carrying amount allocated to interest payments)		324,711

However, as the bond was accounted for as available-for-sale, it would also be necessary to recycle that portion of the cumulative revaluation gain of €108,237 that relates to the interest 'component' of the total carrying value from equity to the income statement. IAS 39 requires a pro-rata allocation of the cumulative gain or loss in equity based on the total fair value of the interest and principal – this would deem €31,713 (€108,237 × €324,711 ÷ 1,108,237) of the cumulative revaluation gain to relate to interest. This would give rise to the further journal, resulting in the same gain on disposal as above:

	€	€
Equity	31,713	
Gain on disposal (income statement)		31,713

Whilst the treatment in Example 18.9 above is what IAS 39 clearly requires, it could be argued that it does not correctly identify the true historic cost of the part of the asset being disposed of. At the original effective interest rate of 7.5% implicit in the bond at the date of issue, the current carrying value of the loan of €1,000,000 represents future interest payments of €303,441 (i.e. €75,000 × [$1/1.075 + 1/1.075^2$ … + $1/1.075^5$]) and principal of €696,559 (€1,000,000 × $1/1.075^5$). This suggests that the true profit on disposal is only €21,270, representing the difference between net present value of the interest cash flows at the current discount rate of 5% (€324,711) and at the original discount rate of 7.5% (€303,441).

B *Servicing assets and liabilities*

It is common for an entity to transfer a financial asset (or part of a financial asset) in its entirety, but to retain the right or obligation to service the asset (i.e. to collect payments as they fall due and undertake other administrative tasks) in return for a fee.

Where an entity transfers a financial asset in a transfer that qualifies for derecognition in its entirety and retains the right to service the financial asset for a fee, IAS 39 requires the entity to recognise either a servicing asset or a servicing liability for that servicing contract, as follows:

- If the fee to be received is not expected to compensate the entity adequately for performing the servicing, the entity should recognise a servicing liability for the servicing obligation at its fair value;
- If the fee to be received is expected to be more than adequate compensation for the servicing, the entity should recognise a servicing asset for the servicing right. This should be recognised at an amount determined on the basis of an allocation of the carrying amount of the larger financial asset (as described in A above).[110]

It is not immediately clear what is meant by this requirement. The application guidance expands on the point, as follows.

An entity may retain the right to a part of the interest payments on transferred assets as compensation for servicing those assets. The part of the interest payments that the entity would give up upon termination or transfer of the servicing contract is allocated to the servicing asset or servicing liability. The part of the interest payments that the entity would not give up is an interest-only strip receivable.

For example, if the entity would not give up any interest upon termination or transfer of the servicing contract, the entire interest spread is an interest-only strip receivable. Presumably, as the entity will still have a liability to service the portfolio, it will have to account for this if it allocates none of the interest spread to a servicing asset. For the purposes of applying the requirements for disposals of part of an asset discussed in A above, the fair values of the servicing asset and interest-only strip receivable are used to allocate the carrying amount of the receivable between the part of the asset that is derecognised and the part that continues to be recognised. If there is no servicing fee specified, or the fee to be received is not expected to compensate the entity adequately for performing the servicing, a liability for the servicing obligation is recognised at fair value.[111]

Unfortunately, IAS 39 does not provide an example of what exactly is meant here, but we believe that something along the lines of Example 18.10 below was intended.

Example 18.10: Servicing assets and liabilities

An entity has a portfolio of originated domestic mortgages which are accounted for at amortised cost and have a carrying amount of £10 million. The mortgages bear interest at a fixed rate of 7.5%. The average life of the mortgages in the portfolio (taking account of prepayment risk) is 12 years and the fair value of the portfolio is £11 million, representing £4.5 million in respect of future interest payments and £6.5 million in respect of the principal amounts. The entity assesses the amount that would compensate it for servicing the assets to be £0.5 million.

The entity sells the entire portfolio to a bank (on terms such that it qualifies for derecognition under IAS 39) but continues to service the portfolio. If the entity does not retain any part of the interest payments, the selling price would be the fair value of the assets of £11 million (or very close to it). It would then assume a servicing liability of £0.5 million, giving rise to the accounting entry:

	£m	£m
Cash	11.0	
Mortgage portfolio		10.0
Servicing liability		0.5
Profit on disposal		0.5

Alternatively, it retains interest payments of 1% and the right to service the portfolio. The entity estimates that the fair value of the right to receive interest payments of 1% is £0.6 million. In this case, the bank would be expected to pay fair value of £10.4 million (or very close to it).

The standard states – see above – that, if (as is the case here) the entity would not give up any interest on termination or transfer of the contract, then the whole of the interest spread is an interest-only strip receivable. In order to calculate the amount of the portfolio to be derecognised, the carrying value of £10 million is pro-rated (as in Example 18.9 above) as to £9.45 million disposed of (£10m × 10.4/11) and the part retained of £0.55 million (£10m × 0.6/11). However, as it has allocated the full amount of the interest spread to an interest-only strip receivable, it would need to recognise a servicing liability of £0.5 million in respect of its obligations under the contract. This gives rise to the following accounting entry:

	£m	£m
Cash	10.40	
Interest-only strip receivable	0.55	
Mortgage portfolio ((£9.45m disposed of plus £0.55m reclassified as interest-only strip receivable)		10.00
Servicing liability		0.50
Profit on disposal		0.45

If the entity were to retain only £0.1 million of the interest spread on termination or transfer of the servicing contract, then IAS 39 requires – see above:

- the part of the interest payments that the entity would not give up (i.e. £0.1 million) to be treated as an interest-only strip receivable; and
- the part of the interest payments that the entity would give up (i.e. £0.45 million – £0.55 million as above less £0.1 million in previous bullet) upon termination or transfer of the servicing contract to be allocated to the servicing asset or servicing liability.

This suggests that the following accounting entry would be made:

	£m	£m
Cash	10.40	
Interest-only strip receivable	0.10	
Mortgage portfolio (£9.45m disposed of plus £0.1m reclassified as interest-only strip receivable and £0.45m allocated to servicing liability)		10.00
Servicing liability (£0.5m gross cost less interest payments that would be lost on termination or transfer – £0.45m)		0.05
Profit on disposal		0.45

4.8.2 *Transfers that do not qualify for derecognition through retention of risks and rewards*

If a transfer does not result in derecognition because the entity has retained substantially all the risks and rewards of ownership of the transferred asset (see 4.5 above), IAS 39 requires the entity to continue to recognise the transferred asset in its entirety and recognise a financial liability for any consideration received. In subsequent periods, the entity recognises any income on the transferred asset and any expense incurred on the financial liability.[112] This treatment is illustrated by Examples 18.11 and 18.12 below.

It should be noted that these provisions apply only where derecognition does not occur as a result of retention by the transferor of substantially all the risks and rewards of ownership of the transferred asset (Figure 18.1, Box 7, Yes). They do not apply where derecognition does not occur as a result of continuing involvement in an asset of which substantially all the risks and rewards of ownership are neither retained nor transferred (Figure 18.1, Box 8, Yes). Such transactions are dealt with by the separate provisions discussed in 4.8.3 and 4.8.4 below.

Example 18.11: Asset not qualifying for derecognition (risks and rewards retained)

An entity holds a loan of £1,000 made on 1 January 2003, paying interest of £65 annually in arrears and redeemable at par on 31 December 2007, which it accounts for at amortised cost (see Chapter 20 at 5).

On 1 January 2007 it enters into a transaction whereby the loan is sold to a bank for its then fair value of €985, but with full recourse to the entity for any default on the loan. The guarantee provided by the entity has the effect that it retains substantially all the risks and rewards of the loan, which is therefore not derecognised (Figure 18.1, Box 7, Yes – see 4.5.2 above).[113]

The entity therefore continues to recognise the loan, and interest on it, as if it still held the loan. It accounts for the £985 proceeds as a liability which must be accreted up using the effective interest method (see Chapter 20 at 5) so that it will be equal to the carrying amount of the asset on the date on which it is expected that the asset will be derecognised.

In this case, the asset will be derecognised at maturity on 31 December 2007, when a payment of £1,065 (the final instalment of interest of £65 and return of principal of £1,000) is due. Accordingly, the liability must be accreted from £985 to £1,065 during the year ended 31 December 2007. The following accounting entries are made by the entity.

	£	£
1 January 2007		
Cash	985	
Liability		985
Consideration received from bank		
1 January–31 December 2007		
Loan (£1,065 at 31.12.05 – £1,000 at 1.1.05)	65	
Interest on loan (income statement)		65
Interest on liability (income statement)	80	
Liability (£1,065 at 31.12.05 – £985 at 1.1.05)		80
Accretion of interest income loan and liability		
31 December 2007		
Liability	1,065	
Loan receivable		1,065
'Redemption' of loan and 'discharge' of liability		

This accounting treatment recognises an overall loss of £15 in 2007, which would be expected, as representing the difference between the carrying value of the asset at the date of transfer (£1,000) and the consideration received (£985). However, IAS 39 requires the various elements of the transaction to be shown separately – it would not have been acceptable for the income statement simply to show a net loss of £15.

If the transferred asset had been accounted for at fair value through profit or loss, it would already have been carried at £985 at the date of transfer – i.e. the loss of £15 would already have been reflected in the financial statements. The accounting entries at 1 January and 31 December 2007 would be the same as above. However, the following accounting entries would then have been made during the year ended 31 December:

	£	£
1 January–31 December 2005		
Interest on liability (income statement)	80	
Liability (£1,065 at 31.12.05 – £985 at 1.1.05)		80
Loan (£1,065 at 31.12.05 – £985 at 1.1.05)	80	
Interest on loan (income statement)		65
Change in fair value of loan (income statement)		15
Recognition of interest on, and change in fair value of, loan and accretion of interest on liability		

Whilst the total amounts recorded in the income statement net to nil, they are arrived at by different methodologies – the £80 increase in the carrying value of the loan receivable is recognised as it occurs whereas the £80 interest on the liability is accrued at a constant effective rate. This means that, if the entity were to prepare financial statements at an interim date, it might well show a net gain or loss on the transaction at that date, notwithstanding that ultimately no gain or loss will be reflected.

It would presumably be possible for the entity to avoid this result by designating the liability as at fair value through profit or loss (see Chapter 17 at 7), such that changes in the fair value of the liability would be matched in line with those in the fair value of the asset.

Example 18.12: Asset not qualifying for derecognition ('repo' transaction)

An entity holds a government bond of £2,000 issued on 1 January 2003, paying interest of £50 semi-annually in arrears and redeemable at par on 31 December 2008, which it accounts for as a held-to-maturity investment at amortised cost (see Chapter 20 at 5).

A *Gross-settled transaction*

On 1 January 2007 the entity enters into a transaction whereby the bond is sold to a bank for its then fair value of £1,800, and the entity agrees to repurchase it on 1 January 2008 for £1,844. As the legal owner of the loan at 30 June 2007 and 31 December 2007, the bank will receive the £100 interest payable on the bond for the calendar year 2007. This £100, together with the £44 difference between the sale and repurchase price gives the bank £144, representing a lender's return of 8% on the £1,800 sale proceeds. Accordingly, the effect of the transaction is that the entity has retained the substantially all risks and rewards of ownership of the bond (Figure 18.1, Box 7, Yes – see 4.7.1 above).

The entity therefore continues to recognise the bond, and interest on it, as if it still held the bond. It accounts for the £1,800 proceeds as a liability which must be accreted up to £1,844 (the repurchase price due on 31 December 2007) over the period to 31 December 2007 using the effective interest method (see Chapter 20 at 5). The following accounting entries are made by the entity.

	£	£
1 January 2007		
Cash	1,800	
Liability		1,800
Consideration received from bank		
1 January–31 December 2007		
Interest on liability (income statement)	144	
Liability (£1,944 at 31.12.05 – £1,800 at 1.1.05)		144
Bond (£2,100 at 31.12.05 – £2,000 at 1.1.05)	100	
Interest on bond (income statement)		100
Accretion of income on bond and finance cost of liability		

1 January–31 December 2007		
Liability	100	
Bond		100
Notional receipt of interest on bond at 30 June and 31 December and notional transfer thereof to bank		
1 January 2008		
Liability	1,844	
Cash		1,844
Execution of repurchase contract		

The above is arguably the strict translation into accounting entries of the accounting analysis of IAS 39 that the entity still retains ownership of the bond throughout 2007. As a matter of practicality, however, the same overall result could have been obtained by the following 'short-cut' approach, which avoids recording the notional receipt and transfer to the bank of bond interest received on 30 June and 31 December:

	£	£
1 January 2007		
Cash	1,800	
Liability		1,800
Consideration received from bank		
1 January–31 December 2007		
Interest on liability (income statement)	144	
Interest on bond (income statement)		100
Liability (balance sheet)		44
Accretion of income on bond and finance cost of liability		
1 January 2008		
Liability	1,844	
Cash		1,844
Execution of repurchase contract		

If (as would be likely, given the nature of the transferred asset) the bank has the right to sell or pledge the bond during the period of its legal ownership, it would be necessary to reclassify the bond as a repurchase receivable during the period of the bank's ownership (see 4.7.1 A I above). In other words, the following additional accounting entries would be required.

	£	£
1 January 2007		
Repurchase receivable	2,000	
Bond		2,000
1 January 2008		
Bond	2,000	
Repurchase receivable		2,000

B Net-settled transaction

The entity might enter into the transaction above, but on terms that the repurchase contract was to be net-settled. In other words, on 1 January 2008, a payment would be made to or by the bank for the difference between £1,844 (the notional repurchase price) and the fair value of the bond at that date. Assuming that the fair value of the bond at 1 January 2008 is £1,860, the bank would be required to pay the entity £16 (£1,860 – £1,844).

In this case, matters are further complicated by the fact that the economic effect of the net-settled forward is the same as if the entity sold the bond on 1 January 2008. As this is before the maturity date of the bond, it is questionable whether the entity can any longer classify it as held-to-maturity. In such a case, IAS 39 requires it to be reclassified as available-for-sale (see Chapter 17). The following accounting entries would be made.

	£	£
1 January 2007		
Cash	1,800	
Liability		1,800
Consideration received from bank		
Equity	200	
Bond (£2,000 carrying amount less £1,800 fair value)		200
Restatement of bond to fair value		
Repurchase receivable	1,800	
Bond		1,800
Reclassification of bond as receivable (see 4.7.1 A I above)		
1 January–31 December 2007		
Interest on liability (income statement)	144	
Interest on bond (income statement)		100
Liability (balance sheet)		44
Repurchase receivable	60	
Equity		60
Accretion of income on bond and finance cost of liability and restatement of repurchase receivable (represented by fair value of underlying bond accounted for as available-for-sale – £1,860)		
1 January 2008		
Cash	16	
Liability	1,844	
Repurchase receivable		1,860
Loss on disposal	140	
Equity		140
Net settlement of repurchase contract and 'recycling' of cumulative losses in equity		

The loss on disposal at 1 January 2008 of £140 arises because the net-settled contract is equivalent to the entity disposing of the bond for its then fair value of £1,860, which is £140 lower than its amortised cost, at the date of reclassification from held-to-maturity to available-for-sale, of £2,000.

This illustrates the point that, where the terms of net-settled forward contract over a transferred asset are such that the original asset cannot be derecognised, the result will be that the entity's balance sheet shows a gross position – i.e. the original asset and a liability for the consideration for the transfer. This may seem a strange accounting reflection of a contract that is required to be settled net. However, the IASB is to some extent forced into this approach as an anti-avoidance measure.

It is clear from the analysis in 4.7.1 A to D above that an asset sold subject to the obligation to repurchase the same or similar asset at a fixed price should not be derecognised. If the accounting treatment were to vary merely because the contract was net-settled, it would be possible to avoid IAS 39's requirements for continued recognition of assets subject to certain forward repurchase agreements simply by altering the terms of the agreement to allow net settlement.

4.8.3 Transfers with continuing involvement – summary

If an entity neither transfers nor retains substantially all the risks and rewards of ownership of a transferred asset, but retains control of the transferred asset (see 4.6 above), IAS 39 requires the entity to continue to recognise the transferred asset to the extent of its 'continuing involvement' – i.e. the extent to which it is exposed to changes in the value of the transferred asset.[114] Such transactions fall within Box 9 of the flowchart at 4.1.2 above.

The concept of 'continuing involvement' was first introduced in the exposure draft of proposed amendments to IAS 32 and IAS 39 published in June 2002. The IASB's intention at that time was to move towards an accounting model for derecognition based entirely on continuing involvement. However, this approach (or at least the methodology for implementing it proposed in the exposure draft) received little support in the exposure period and the IASB decided to abandon it and revert largely to an accounting model for derecognition based on the transfer of risks and rewards.[115] However, the continuing involvement approach remains relevant for certain transactions – mainly transfers of assets which result in the sharing, rather than the substantial transfer, of the risks and rewards.

The accounting requirements in respect of assets in which the entity has continuing involvement are particularly complex, and are summarised at A to E below, with worked examples at 4.8.4 below. In particular, and in contrast to the treatment for transactions that do not qualify for derecognition through retention of risks and rewards (see 4.8.2 above), the associated liability is often calculated as a balancing figure that will not necessarily represent the proceeds received as the result of the transfer (see C below).

We have a general concern regarding the required accounting treatment for a continuing involvement, namely that IAS 39 provides examples of how to deal with certain specific transactions rather than clear underlying principles. It can be difficult to determine the appropriate treatment for a continuing involvement that does not correspond fairly exactly to one of the examples in IAS 39.

A Guarantees

When the entity's continuing involvement takes the form of guaranteeing the transferred asset, the extent of the entity's continuing involvement is the lower of:

- the amount of the asset; and

- the maximum amount of the consideration received that the entity could be required to repay ('the guarantee amount').[116]

An example of this treatment is given at 4.8.4 A below.

B Options

When the entity's continuing involvement takes the form of a written and/or purchased option (including a cash-settled option or similar provision) on the transferred asset, the extent of the entity's continuing involvement is the amount of the transferred asset that the entity may repurchase. However, in case of a written put option (including a cash-settled option or similar provision) on an asset measured at fair value, the extent of the entity's continuing involvement is limited to the lower of the fair value of the transferred asset and the option exercise price.[117]

Examples of this treatment are given at 4.8.4 B and C below.

C Associated liability

When an entity continues to recognise an asset to the extent of its continuing involvement, IAS 39 requires the entity to recognise an associated liability.[118] IAS 39 provides that 'despite the other measurement requirements in IAS 39', the transferred asset and the associated liability are to be measured on a basis that reflects the rights and obligations that the entity has retained. The associated liability is measured in such a way that the net carrying amount of the transferred asset and the associated liability is equal to:

- if the transferred asset is measured at amortised cost, the amortised cost of the rights and obligations retained by the entity; or
- if the transferred asset is measured at fair value, the fair value of the rights and obligations retained by the entity when measured on a stand-alone basis.[119]

The has the effect that the 'liability' is often calculated as a balancing figure that will not necessarily represent the proceeds received as the result of the transfer (see Examples 18.13 to 18.16 at 4.8.4 below). This does not fit very comfortably with the normal rules in IAS 39 for the initial measurement of financial liabilities (see Chapter 20 at 2) – hence the comment that this treatment applies 'despite the other measurement requirements in IAS 39'.

D Subsequent measurement of assets and liabilities

IAS 39 requires an entity to continue to recognise any income arising on the transferred asset to the extent of its continuing involvement and to recognise any expense incurred on the associated liability.[120] This is comparable to the requirements in respect of assets not derecognised through retention of substantially all risks and rewards (see 4.8.2 above).

When the transferred asset and associated liability are subsequently measured, IAS 39 requires recognised changes in the fair value of the transferred asset and the associated liability to be accounted for consistently with each other in accordance with the general provisions of IAS 39 for measuring gains and losses (see Chapter 20 at 3) and not offset.[121] Moreover, if the transferred asset is measured at amortised cost, the option in IAS 39 to designate a financial liability as at fair value through profit or loss (see Chapter 17 at 7.1) is not applicable to the associated liability.[122]

E Continuing involvement in part only of a larger asset

An entity may have continuing involvement in a part only of a financial asset, for example where the entity retains an option to repurchase part of a transferred asset, or retains a residual interest in part of an asset, such that the entity does not retain substantially all the risks and rewards of ownership, but does retain control.

In such a case, IAS 39 requires the entity to allocate the previous carrying amount of the financial asset between the part that it continues to recognise under continuing involvement, and the part that it no longer recognises on the basis of the relative fair values of those parts on the date of the transfer. The allocation is to be made on the same basis as applies on derecognition of part only of a larger financial asset – see 4.8.1 A and B above.

The difference between:

(a) the carrying amount allocated to the part that is no longer recognised; and

(b) the sum of:

  (i) the consideration received for the part no longer recognised; and

  (ii) any cumulative gain or loss allocated to it that had been recognised directly in equity

is recognised in profit or loss. A cumulative gain or loss that had been recognised in equity is allocated between the part that continues to be recognised and the part that is no longer recognised on the basis of the relative fair values of those parts.[123] The requirement in (b)(ii) above for 'recycling' of any cumulative gain or loss previously recognised directly in equity applies to assets accounted for as available-for-sale, and is discussed further in Chapter 20 at 3.4.

This is discussed further at 4.8.4 D below.

4.8.4 Transfers with continuing involvement – accounting examples

The provisions summarised at 4.8.3 above, even judged by the standards of IAS 39, are unusually impenetrable. However, the application guidance provides a number of clarifications and examples, the substance of which is reproduced below.

A Transfers with guarantees

If a guarantee provided by an entity to pay for default losses on a transferred asset prevents the transferred asset from being derecognised to the extent of the continuing involvement, IAS 39 requires:

(a) the transferred asset at the date of the transfer to be measured at the lower of:

  (i) the carrying amount of the asset; and

  (ii) the maximum amount of the consideration received in the transfer that the entity could be required to repay ('the guarantee amount'); and

(b) the associated liability to be initially measured at the guarantee amount plus the fair value of the guarantee (which is normally the consideration received for the guarantee).

Subsequently, the initial fair value of the guarantee is recognised in profit or loss on a time proportion basis in accordance with IAS 18 and the carrying value of the asset is reduced by any impairment losses.[124]

This is illustrated in Example 18.13 below (which is based on the circumstances in Example 18.18 below).

Example 18.13: Continuing involvement through guarantee

An entity has a loan portfolio carried at €10 million with a fair value of €10.5 million. It sells the rights to 100% of the cash flows to a third party for a payment of €10.55 million, which includes a payment of €50,000 in return for the entity agreeing to absorb the first €1 million of default losses on the portfolio. The loans are fixed rate loans with significant prepayment risk.

The guarantee has the effect that the entity has transferred substantially all the rewards, but not substantially all the risks, of the portfolio (Figure 18.1, Box 6, No). However, the prepayment risk has been transferred to the transferee, so that the entity does not retain all significant risks of the loans (Figure 18.1, Box 7, No). The portfolio is not a readily marketable asset, so that the entity retains control of the asset (Figure 18.1, Box 8, Yes – see also 4.6 above), and the continuing involvement provisions of IAS 39 apply (Figure 18.1, Box 9).

The entity turns to the requirements above. The continuing involvement in the transferred asset must be measured at the lower of:

(i) the amount of the asset transferred – i.e. €10 million; and

(ii) the maximum amount of the consideration received in the transfer that the entity could be required to repay – i.e. €1 million (the amount guaranteed).

Therefore, the entity will set up an asset that represents its continuing involvement in the transferred asset of €1 million.

The entity then considers the carrying amount of the liability. This is required to be measured at the guarantee amount (i.e. €1 million) plus the fair value of the guarantee (i.e. the €50,000 guarantee payment), a total of €1.05 million. Therefore, the entity's continuing involvement in the transaction will be reflected as follows:

	€m	€m
Cash	10.55	
Loan portfolio transferred		10.00
Continuing involvement in the transferred asset	1.00	
Liability		1.05
Profit on disposal*		0.50

* Cash received (€10.55m) less guarantee payment (€50,000) = consideration for portfolio (€10.5m) less carrying amount of portfolio (€10m).

Over the remaining life of the transaction, the €50,000 of the liability that represents the consideration received for the guarantee is amortised to the income statement on a time proportion basis. This has the effect that the income earned by the entity for entering into the guarantee arrangement is reported as revenue on a time proportion basis. This is exactly the same result as would have been obtained by simply recognising the €50,000 as a liability and amortising it (as would have been required by IAS 18).

If in a subsequent period credit losses of €0.2 million are suffered, requiring a payment under the guarantee, IAS 39 requires the following accounting entries to be made:[125]

	€m	€m
Profit or loss (loss under guarantee)	0.20	
Cash (paid to transferee)		0.20
Liability	0.20	
Continuing involvement in the transferred asset		0.20

This treatment required by Example 18.13 is problematic from several points of view. First, it results in the recognition of a liability that is actually greater than the entity's maximum potential exposure (i.e. €1 million). Second, it is recognising a contingent liability as a full liability.

In effect the accounting is something of a hybrid: the asset accounting is equivalent to a partial derecognition of 90% of the asset, but the gain on disposal is calculated on the basis of a 100% disposal. Had the rules for partial derecognition (see 4.8.1 A above) been applied, the following accounting entry would have arisen:

	€m	€m
Cash	10.55	
Loan portfolio transferred		9.00
Liability (balancing figure)		1.10
Profit on disposal*		0.45

* Cash received (€10.55m) less guarantee payment (€50,000) = consideration for whole portfolio (€10.5m). Therefore consideration for 90% of portfolio is €9.45m, less carrying amount of 90% of portfolio €9m = €0.45m

The resulting €1.1m liability represents the guarantee payment of €50,000 plus €1.05m deferred consideration for the 10% not yet derecognised (i.e. total €10.5m less €9.45 taken into account in profit on disposal above). The IASB might have been deterred from such approach on the basis that is difficult to see the €1.05m as anything other than that affront to their *Framework*, deferred income.

B Transfers of assets measured at amortised cost

If a put or call option prevents derecognition (see 4.5.3 and 4.7 above) of a transferred asset measured at amortised cost, IAS 39 requires the associated liability to be measured at cost (i.e. the consideration received) and subsequently adjusted for the amortisation of any difference between that cost and the amortised cost of the transferred asset at the expiration date of the option, as illustrated by Example 18.14 below.[126]

Example 18.14: Asset measured at amortised cost

An entity has a financial asset, accounted for at amortised cost, carried at £98. It transfers the asset to a third party in return for consideration of £95. The asset is subject to a call option whereby the entity can compel the transferee to sell the asset back to the entity for £102. The amortised cost of the asset on the option exercise date will be £100. The option is considered to be neither deeply in the money nor deeply out of the money. IAS 39 therefore requires the entity to continue to recognise the asset to the extent of its continuing involvement (Figure 18.1, Box 9 – see also 4.7.2 C above).

The initial carrying amount of the associated liability is £95. This is then accreted to £100 (i.e. the amortised cost of the asset on exercise date – *not* the £102 exercise price) through profit or loss using the effective interest method. Because the transferred asset is measured at amortised cost, the associated liability must also be accounted for at amortised cost, and not at fair value through profit or loss (see D at 4.8.3 above). This will give rise to the accounting entries:

	£	£
Date of transfer		
Cash	95	
Liability		95
After date of transfer		
Interest on liability	5	
Liability (£100 – £95)		5
Asset (£100 – £98)	2	
Income on asset		2

If the option is exercised, any difference between the carrying amount of the associated liability and the exercise price is recognised in profit or loss. This last requirement has the possibly counter-intuitive effect that the question of whether the entity records a profit or loss on exercise of the option is essentially a function of the difference between the liability (representing the amortised cost of the transferred asset) and the cash paid, not of whether it has in fact (i.e. in economic terms) made a gain or loss.

Thus, if the entity were to exercise its option at £102 it would apparently record the accounting entry

	£	£
Liability	100	
Loss	2	
Cash		102

However, the entity would not have exercised the option unless the asset had been worth at least £102 (i.e. £2 more than its carrying amount), suggesting that the more appropriate treatment would be to add the £2 to the cost of the asset.

Likewise, if instead of the entity having a call option, the transferee had a put option at £98 which it exercised, the entity would apparently record the accounting entry:

	£	£
Liability	100	
Profit		2
Cash		98

However, the transferee would not have exercised its option unless the asset had been worth less than £98 (i.e. £2 less than its carrying amount). In this case, however, the IASB's thinking may have been that the exercise of the transferee's put option suggests an impairment of the asset which is required to be recognised in the financial statements (see Chapter 20 at 6). However, this would not necessarily be the case (e.g. where a fixed-interest asset has a fair value below cost because of movements in interest rates but is not intrinsically impaired).

If the option were to lapse unexercised, the entity would simply derecognise the transferred asset and the associated liability, i.e.

	£	£
Liability	100	
Asset		100

C Transfers of assets measured at fair value

IAS 39 discusses this issue in terms of transferred assets subject to:

- a transferor's call option (see I below);
- a transferee's put option (see II below); and
- a 'collar' – i.e. a transferor's call option combined with a transferee's put option (see III below).

The way in which the rules are articulated in IAS 39 is somewhat confusing, but in general the effect is that the transferred asset is recognised at:

- in the case of an asset subject to a transferor call option, its fair value (on the basis that the call option gives the transferor access to any increase in the fair value of the asset); and
- in the case of an asset subject to a transferee put option, the lower of fair value and the option exercise price (on the basis that the put option denies the transferor access to any increase in the fair value of the asset above the option price).

This methodology summarised below is applied both on the date on which the option is written and subsequently.

I Transferor's call option

If a transferor's call option prevents derecognition (see 4.5.3 and 4.7 above) of a transferred asset measured at fair value, IAS 39 requires the asset to be continued to be measured at its fair value. The associated liability is measured:

- if the option is in or at the money, at the option exercise price less the time value of the option; or
- if the option is out of the money, at the fair value of the transferred asset less the time value of the option.

The adjustment to the measurement of the associated liability ensures that the net carrying amount of the asset and the associated liability is the fair value of the call option right, as illustrated by Example 18.15 below.[127]

Example 18.15: Asset measured at fair value subject to transferor's call option

An entity has a financial asset, accounted for at fair value through profit or loss, carried at €80. It transfers the asset to a third party, subject to a call option whereby the entity can compel the transferee to sell the asset back to the entity for €95. At the date of transfer, the call option has a time value of €5.

The option is considered to be neither deeply in the money nor deeply out of the money. IAS 39 therefore requires the entity to continue to recognise the asset to the extent of its continuing involvement (Figure 18.1, Box 9 – see also 4.7.2 C above), and to continue recording it at fair value. At the date of transfer, the call option is out of the money. IAS 39 therefore requires the liability to be measured at the fair value of the transferred asset less the time value of the option, i.e. €80 – €5 = €75. This has the result that the net of the carrying value of the asset (€80) and the carrying value of the liability (€75) equals the time value of the option (€5), i.e.:

	€	€
Date of transfer		
Cash	75	
Liability		75

A *Transferred asset increases in value*

Suppose that one year later the fair value of the asset is €100 and the time value of the option is now €3. The option is now in the money, so that the liability is measured at the option exercise price less the time value of the option, i.e. €95 – €3 = €92. This has the result that the net of the carrying value of the asset (€100) and the carrying value of the liability (€92) equals the fair value of the option (€8, representing €3 time value and €5 intrinsic value). The liability could have been more straightforwardly calculated as the fair value of the asset (€100) less the fair value of the option (€8) = €92. This gives rise to the following accounting entries:

	€	€
During year 1		
Asset (€100 – €80)	20	
Liability (€92 – €75)		17
Gain (profit or loss)		3

The €3 gain recorded in profit or loss effectively represents the increase in the fair value of the option from €5 to €8 over the period. If the entity were able to exercise the option at this point, and did so, it would record the entry:

	€	€
Liability	92	
Loss (profit or loss)	3	
Cash		95

The particular transaction results in no overall gain or loss being reflected in profit or loss (i.e. €3 gain during the year less €3 loss on exercise of option). This represents the net of the €20 gain in the fair value of the asset (€100 at the end of period less €80 at the start) and the net cash outflow of €20 (€75 in on initial transfer, €95 out on exercise of option).

B *Asset decreases in value*

Suppose instead that during the first year the fair value of the asset fell to €65 and the time value of the option at the end of the year was only €1. The liability would be measured at the fair value of the transferred asset less the time value of the option, i.e. €65 – €1 = €64. This would generate the accounting entries:

	€	€
During year 1		
Liability (€64 – €75)	11	
Loss (profit or loss)	4	
Asset (€65 – €80)		15

Again the overall loss shown in profit or loss represents the movement in the fair value of the option over the period from €5 to €1. Suppose that one year later there was no change in the fair value of the asset, and the option expired unexercised. The entity would then record the accounting entry:

	€	€
At end of year 2		
Liability	64	
Loss (profit or loss)	1	
Asset (balance sheet)		65

This results in an overall loss for the transaction as a whole of €5 (€4 in year 1 and €1 in year 2), which represents the difference between the carrying value of the asset at the date of original transfer (€80) and the proceeds received (€75).

The amount of any consideration received is in principle not relevant to the measurement of the liability. If, for example, the entity originally received consideration of €72, it would still record a liability of €75 and a 'day one' loss of €3. If it received consideration of €80, it would still record a liability of €75 and a 'day one' profit of €5. The IASB no doubt presumed that such transactions are likely to be undertaken only by sophisticated market participants such that the consideration received will always be equivalent to the fair value of the asset less the fair value of the option. However, there may well be instances where this is not the case, such as in transactions between members of the same group or other related parties.

II Transferee's put option

If a transferee's put option prevents derecognition (see 4.5.3 and 4.7 above) of a transferred asset measured at fair value, IAS 39 requires the asset to be measured at the lower of fair value and the option exercise price. The basis for this treatment is that the entity has no right to increases in the fair value of the transferred asset above the exercise price of the option. The associated liability is measured at the option exercise price plus the time value of the option. This ensures that the net carrying amount of the asset and the associated liability is the fair value of the put option obligation, as illustrated by Example 18.16 below.[128]

Example 18.16: Asset measured at fair value subject to transferee's put option

An entity has a financial asset, accounted for at fair value. On 1 January 2007 it transfers the asset, then carried at €98, to a third party, subject to a put option whereby the transferee can compel the entity to reacquire the asset for €100. The option is considered to be neither deeply in the money nor deeply out of the money. IAS 39 therefore requires the entity to continue to recognise the asset to the extent of its continuing involvement (Figure 18.1, Box 9 – see also 4.7.2 C above), and to continue recording it at the lower of (a) fair value and (b) €100 (the exercise price of the option). Assuming that the transferor pays €106 for the asset, representing €98 fair value of the asset plus €8 time value of the option, the entity would record the accounting entry:

	€	€
1 January 2007		
Cash	106	
Liability		106

A Transferred asset increases in value

Suppose that at 31 December 2007, the option has a time value of €5 and the fair value of the asset is €120. IAS 39 requires the carrying value of the asset to be restricted to €100 (the exercise price of the option). The liability is measured at the exercise price plus the time value of the option (i.e. to the transferee[129]), i.e. €100 + €5 = €105. This has the result that the net of the carrying value of the asset (€100) and the carrying value of the liability (€105) equals the fair value of the option to the transferor (–€5).

This gives the accounting entry:

	€	€
31 December 2007		
Asset (€100 – €98)	2	
Liability (€105 – €106)	1	
Gain (profit or loss)		3

The gain of €3 effectively represents the decrease in the time value of the option (an *gain* from the transferor's perspective) from €8 to €5.

If the option were then to lapse unexercised, with no further change in the fair value of the asset, the entity would record the accounting entry:

	€	€
On lapse of option		
Liability	105	
Asset		100
Gain (profit or loss)		5

The total gain on the transaction of €8 (€3 in Year 1 and €5 on lapse) represents the option premium of €8 (i.e. the difference between the total consideration of €106 and the carrying value of the asset of €98) received at the outset.

B Transferred asset decreases in value

Suppose instead that at 31 December 2007, the option has a time value of €5 but the fair value of the asset is €90. IAS 39 requires the carrying value of the asset to be measured at its fair value of €90. The liability is measured at the exercise price plus the time value of the option (i.e. to the transferee), i.e. €100 + €5 = €105.

This gives the accounting entry:

	€	€
31 December 2007		
Liability (€105 – €106)	1	
Loss (profit or loss)	7	
Asset (€90 – €98)		8

This has the result that the net of the carrying value of the asset (€90) and the liability (€105), i.e. €(-15) represents the fair value of the option to the transferor (i.e. intrinsic value €(-10) [€100 exercise price versus €90 value of asset] + time value €(-5)). The €7 loss represents the increase in the fair value of the option (a loss to the transferor) from €8 at the outset to €15 at 31 December 2007.

If the transferee were able to, and did, exercise its option at that point, the entity would record the accounting entry:

	€	€
On exercise of option		
Liability	105	
Cash		100
Gain (profit or loss)		5

The overall €2 loss (i.e. €5 gain above and €7 loss during Year 1) represents the net cash of €8 received from the transferee (€108 in at inception less €100 out on exercise) less the €10 fall in fair value of the transferred asset (€100 at inception less €90 at exercise).

III 'Collar' put and call options

Assets may be transferred in a way designed to ensure that the transferee is shielded from excessive losses on the transferred asset but has to pass significant gains on the asset back to the transferor. Such an arrangement is known as a 'collar', on the basis that it allocates a range of potential value movements in the asset to the transferee, with movements outside that range accruing to the transferor. A simple form of 'collar' would be to transfer an asset subject to a purchased call option (allowing the transferor to reacquire the asset if it increases in value beyond a certain level) and a written put option (allowing the transferee to compel the transferor to reacquire the asset if it falls in value beyond a certain level).

If a collar, in the form of a purchased call and written put option, prevents derecognition (see 4.5.3 and 4.7 above) of a transferred asset measured at fair value, IAS 39 requires the entity to continue to measure the asset at fair value. The associated liability is measured at:

- if the call option is in or at the money, the sum of the call exercise price and fair value of the put option less the time value of the call option; or
- if the call option is out of the money, the sum of the fair value of the asset and the fair value of the put option less the time value of the call option.

The adjustment to the associated liability ensures that the net carrying amount of the asset and the associated liability is the fair value of the options held and written by the entity, as illustrated by Example 18.17 below.[130]

Example 18.17: Asset measured at fair value subject to collar put and call options

An entity has a financial asset, accounted for at fair value, carried at €100. On 1 January 2007 it transfers the asset to a third party, subject to:

- a call option whereby the entity can compel the transferee to sell the asset back to the entity for €120, and
- a put option whereby the transferee can compel the entity to reacquire the asset for €80.

The options are considered to be neither deeply in the money nor deeply out of the money. IAS 39 therefore requires the entity to continue to recognise the asset to the extent of its continuing involvement (Figure 18.1, Box 9 – see also 4.7.2 C above), and to continue recording it at fair value.

At the date of transfer, the time value of the put and call are €1 and €5 respectively. At the date of transfer, the call option is out of the money, so that the associated liability is calculated as the sum of the fair value of the asset and the fair value of the put option less the time value of the call option, i.e. (€100+€1) – €5 = €96. The net of this and the fair value of the asset (€100) is €4 which is the net fair value of the two options (call €5 less put €1). Assuming that the transaction is undertaken at arm's length, the transferee would pay €96 for the asset and the entity would record the accounting entry:

	€	€
Cash	96	
Liability		96

A Transferred asset increases in value

Suppose that, at 31 December 2007, the fair value of the asset is €140, and the time value of the put and call are €0.5 and €2 respectively. The call option is now in the money, so that IAS 39 requires the entity to recognise a liability equal to the sum of the call exercise price and fair value of the put option less the time value of the call option, i.e. (€120 + €0.5) – €2 = €118.5. The net of this and the carrying value of the asset (€140) is €21.5 which is the net fair value of the two options (call €22 [time value €2 plus intrinsic value €20] less put €0.5 = €21.5). This gives the accounting entry:

	€	€
31 December 2007		
Asset (€140 – €100)	40.0	
Gain (profit or loss)		17.5
Liability (€118.5 – €96)		22.5

The gain represents the increase in fair value of the call option of €17 (€5 at outset and €22 at 31 December 2007) plus the €0.5 decrease (a gain from the transferor's perspective) in the fair value of the put option (€1 at outset and €0.5 at 31 December 2007).

If the entity were able to, and did, exercise its call option, it would record the entry:

	€	€
Exercise of call option		
Liability	118.5	
Loss (profit or loss)	1.5	
Cash		120.0

The overall gain of €16 on the transaction (€1.5 loss above and €17.5 profit recorded in 2007) represents the increase in fair value of the asset of €40 (€100 at outset, €140 at 31 December 2005) less the net €24 paid to the transferee (€120 paid on exercise of call less €96 received on initial transfer).

B Transferred asset decreases in value

Suppose instead that, at 31 December 2007, the fair value of the asset is €78, and the time value of the put and call are €0.5 and €2 respectively. The call option is now out of the money, so that IAS 39 requires the entity to recognise a liability equal to the sum of the fair value of the asset and the fair value of the put option (i.e. €2.5 – time value €0.5 plus intrinsic value €2 [€80 exercise price versus €78 fair value of asset]) less the time value of the call option, i.e. (€78 + €2.5) – €2 = €78.5.

The net of this and the carrying value of the asset (€78) is €(–0.5) which is the net fair value of the two options (call €2 less put €2.5 = €(–0.5)). This gives the accounting entry:

	€	€
31 December 2007		
Liability (€78.5 – €96)	17.5	
Loss (profit or loss)	4.5	
Asset (€78 – €100)		22.0

The loss represents the decrease in the fair value of the call option of €3 (€5 at outset and €2 at 31 December 2007) plus the €1.5 increase (a decrease from the transferor's perspective) in the fair value of the put option (€1 at outset and €2.5 at 31 December 2007).

If the transferee were able to, and did, exercise its put option, the entity would record the entry:

	€	€
Exercise of put option		
Liability	78.5	
Loss (profit or loss)	1.5	
Cash		80.0

The overall loss of €6 on the transaction (€1.5 loss above and €4.5 loss recorded in 2007) represents the decrease in fair value of the asset of €22 (€100 at outset, €78 at 31 December 2007) offset by the net €16 received from the transferee (€96 received on initial transfer less €80 paid on exercise of put).

D Continuing involvement in part only of a financial asset

IAS 39 gives the following example of the application of the continuing involvement approach to continuing involvement in part only of a financial asset.[131]

Example 18.18: Continuing involvement in part only of a financial asset

An entity has a portfolio of prepayable loans whose coupon and effective interest rate is 10% and whose principal amount and amortised cost is €10 million. It enters into a transaction in which, in return for a payment of €9.115 million, the transferee obtains the right to €9 million of any collections of principal plus 9.5% interest.

The entity retains rights to €1 million of any collections of principal plus interest at 10%, plus the remaining 0.5% ('excess spread') on the remaining €9 million of principal. Collections from prepayments are allocated between the entity and the transferee proportionately in the ratio of 1:9, but any defaults are deducted from the entity's interest of €1 million until that interest is exhausted.

The fair value of the loans at the date of the transaction is €10.1 million and the estimated fair value of the excess spread of 0.5 per cent is €40,000.

The entity determines that it has transferred some significant risks and rewards of ownership (for example, significant prepayment risk) but has also retained some significant risks and rewards of ownership because of its subordinated retained interest (Figure 18.1, Box 7, No) and has retained control (Figure 18.1, Box 8, Yes). It therefore applies the continuing involvement approach (Figure 18.1, Box 9).

The entity analyses the transaction as:

- a retention of a fully proportionate retained interest of €1 million, plus
- the subordination of that retained interest to provide credit enhancement to the transferee for credit losses.

The entity calculates that €9.09 million (90% of €10.1 million) of the consideration received of €9.115 million represents the consideration for a fully proportionate 90% share. The remainder of the consideration (€25,000) received represents consideration received by the entity for subordinating its retained interest to provide credit enhancement to the transferee for credit losses. In addition, the excess spread of 0.5% represents consideration received for the credit enhancement. Accordingly, the total consideration received for the credit enhancement is €65,000 (€25,000 received from transferee plus €40,000 fair value of excess spread).

The entity first calculates the gain or loss on the sale of the 90% share of cash flows. Assuming that separate fair values of the 10% part transferred and the 90% part retained are not available at the date of the transfer, the entity allocates the carrying amount of the asset pro-rata to the fair values of those parts (see 4.8.1 A and B and 4.8.3 E above). The total fair value of the portfolio is considered to be €10.1 million (see above), and the fair value of the consideration for the part disposed of €9.09 million. The carrying amount of the whole portfolio is €10 million. This implies a carrying amount for the part disposed of €10m × 9.09/10.1 = €9 million, and for the part retained €1 million. The gain on the sale of the 90% is therefore €90,000 (€9.09 million – €9 million).

In addition, IAS 39 requires the entity to recognise the continuing involvement that results from the subordination of its retained interest for credit losses. Accordingly, it recognises an asset of €1 million (the maximum amount of the cash flows it would forfeit under the subordination), and an associated liability of €1.065 million (the maximum amount of the cash flows it would forfeit under the subordination, i.e. €1 million, plus the consideration for the subordination of €65,000). It also recognises an asset for the fair value of the excess spread which forms part of the consideration for the subordination.

This gives rise to the accounting entry:

	€000	€000
Cash	9,115	
Asset for the subordination of the residual interest	1,000	
Excess spread received for subordination	40	
Loan portfolio		9,000
Liability for subordination		1,065
Gain on disposal		90

It is crucial to an understanding of this example that, as a result of the transaction, the original asset (the portfolio of prepayable loans) is being accounted for as two separate assets. Because the cash flows from the portfolio are split in fully proportionate (pro-rata) shares (see 4.2 above), each of these assets must be considered separately.

The first of these assets, the right to cash flows of €9 million, continues to be recognised only to the extent of the entity's continuing involvement, which in this case is via the credit enhancement. The approach is very similar to continuing involvement through guarantee (see Example 18.13 at A above), except that the liability for subordination includes the maximum cash flow that the entity might not receive from its retained share (i.e. €1 million) rather than, as in Example 18.13, a potential cash outflow (the guarantee amount, which is the maximum amount that the entity could be required to repay). This is aggregated with the fair value of the amount received in respect of the credit enhancement, in order to calculate the full liability for subordination. This is similar to the way in which the fair value of the guarantee is added to the guarantee amount in order to calculate the associated liability.[132]

The second asset is the entity's proportionate retained share of €1 million. It is, seemingly, irrelevant to the accounting analysis in IAS 39 that this has already been taken into account in calculating the entity's continuing involvement in the remaining €9 million of the portfolio.

The effect is to gross up the balance sheet with a subordination asset and liability. As IAS 39 notes, immediately following the transaction, the carrying amount of the asset is €2.04 million (i.e. €1 million part retained plus €1 million subordination asset plus €40,000 excess spread) – in respect of an asset whose fair value is only €1.01 million!

We have some reservations concerning the example above. First, we challenge whether, as a point of principle, it is appropriate to apply the derecognition criteria to part of an asset where the part that is retained provides credit enhancement for the transferee. As discussed more fully at 4.2.1 above, IAS 39 is implicitly drawing a distinction between:

- a guarantee that could result in an outflow of the total resources of the transferor, or a return of consideration for the transfer already received (which would not allow partial derecognition); and
- a guarantee that could result in the transferor losing the right to receive a specific future cash inflow, but not being obliged to make any other payment should that specific future cash inflow not materialise.

Moreover, even in the context of the analysis presented by IAS 39, we do not understand the basis of the treatment of the excess spread. The example simply asserts that this forms part of the consideration for providing the subordination, although it is not clear that it forms any more or any less of the consideration for the subordination than the interest and principal on the 10% of the portfolio retained.

In our view, a more logical analysis would have been that:

- the entity has disposed of not 90% of the whole portfolio, but 90% of the principal balances and 9.5% interest on that 90%; and
- the consideration for the subordination is still €65,000, on the basis that if:
  - the fair value of the consideration for a fully proportionate share of 90% (i.e. including 10% interest) is €9,090,000; and
  - the fair value of the excess spread of 0.5% interest is €40,000, then

  the fair value of consideration for a fully proportionate share less the excess spread is €9,050,000 (i.e. €9,090,000 less €40,000). This in turn means that the balance of the total consideration of €9,115,000 (i.e. €65,000) relates to the subordination.

In addition, of course, Example 18.18 ignores the possibility that the excess spread is retained by the transferor because it continues to service the portfolio, although this may be an attempt to avoid overcomplicating matters even further.

A further issue is that, if the excess spread is regarded as part of the asset retained, rather than the consideration received, it would seem more appropriate to recognise it on a basis consistent with the accounting treatment of the original transferred asset (typically, amortised cost) rather than at fair value.

4.8.5 Miscellaneous provisions

IAS 39 contains a number of accounting provisions generally applicable to transfers of assets, as follows.

A Offset

IAS 39 provides that, if a transferred asset continues to be recognised, the entity must not offset:

- the asset with the associated liability; or
- any income arising from the transferred with any expense incurred on the associated liability.[133]

Whilst IAS 39 does not say so specifically, this is clearly intended to apply both to assets that continue to be recognised in full and to those that continue to be recognised to the extent of their continuing involvement.

This requirement apparently over-rides the offset criteria in IAS 32[134] (see 6 below), as illustrated, for example, by the various situations highlighted in the discussion at 4.7 and 4.8.1 to 4.8.4 above where a transaction required to be net-settled (which would normally be required to be accounted for as such under IAS 32) is accounted for as if it were to be gross-settled.

B Collateral

If a transferor provides non-cash collateral (such as debt or equity instruments) to the transferee, the accounting treatment for the collateral by both the transferor and the transferee depends on:

- whether the transferee has the right to sell or repledge the collateral; and
- whether the transferor has defaulted.

If the transferee has the right by contract or custom to sell or repledge a collateral asset, the transferor should reclassify that asset in its balance sheet (e.g. as a loaned asset, pledged equity instruments or repurchase receivable) separately from other assets.

If the transferee sells collateral pledged to it, it recognises the proceeds from the sale and a liability measured at fair value for its obligation to return the collateral.

If the transferor defaults under the terms of the contract and is no longer entitled to redeem the collateral, it derecognises the collateral, and the transferee either:

- recognises the collateral as its asset initially measured at fair value or;
- if it has already sold the collateral, derecognises its obligation to return the collateral.

In no other circumstances should the transferor derecognise, or the transferee recognise, the collateral as an asset.[135]

C *Rights or obligations over transferred assets that continue to be recognised*

Where a transfer of a financial asset does not qualify for derecognition, the transferor may well have contractual rights or obligations related to the transfer, such as options or forward repurchase contracts, that are derivatives of a type that would normally be required to be recognised under IAS 39.

IAS 39 prohibits separate recognition of such derivatives, if recognition of the derivative together with either the transferred asset or the liability arising from the transfer would result in recognising the same rights or obligations twice.

For example, IAS 39 notes that a call option retained by the transferor may prevent a transfer of financial assets from being accounted for as a sale (see 4.7 above). In that case, the call option must not be separately recognised as a derivative asset.[136]

4.9 Reassessing derecognition

IAS 39 states that if an entity determines that, as a result of the transfer, it has transferred substantially all the risks and rewards of ownership of the transferred asset, it does not recognise the transferred asset again in a future period, unless it reacquires the transferred asset in a new transaction.[137] We have noted earlier that there is some ambiguity as to whether this rule in AG41 is to be read generally as prohibiting any re-recognition of a derecognised asset or specifically as referring only to circumstances where derecognition results from transfer of substantially all the risks and rewards (i.e. it applies only to 'Box 6, Yes' transactions, and not to 'Box 8, No' transactions). Our view, as expressed at 4.7.2 above, is that the broader interpretation should be applied and the requirement still applies if derecognition occurs for another reason, e.g. loss of control.

The risks and rewards of ownership retained by the entity may change as a result of market changes in such a way that, had the revised conditions existed at inception, they would have prevented derecognition of the asset. However, the original decision to derecognise the asset should not be revisited, unless (in exceptional circumstances) the original assessment was an accounting error within the scope of IAS 8.

4.9.1 Reassessment of consolidation of SPEs

The effect of SIC-12, combined with the derecognition provisions of IAS 39 is that a transaction (commonly but not exclusively in a securitisation) qualifies as a derecognised of the financial asset concerned but the 'buyer' is an SPE, so that the asset is immediately re-recognised through consolidation of the SPE. However, an entity may derecognise assets if they are transferred to a SPE that is not consolidated because, having considered all of the facts and circumstances, the entity concludes that it does not control the SPE. The conditions and criteria that indicate that the SPE is controlled by the entity are discussed in Chapter 6 at 3.2.

Changes in market conditions may affect the relationship between entity and SPE and this may raise the question of whether this should trigger a reassessment of control. SIC-12 only requires an entity to analyse whether it controls an SPE at the inception of the arrangements. It is clear that reassessment will be required if the contractual arrangements between the entity and SPE are altered, e.g. if the contractual arrangements are renegotiated in response to credit losses and the entity provides performance guarantees or additional funding to the SPE. However, there is as yet no consensus that reassessment should take place solely due to changes in risk and rewards.

5 DERECOGNITION – FINANCIAL LIABILITIES

The provisions of IAS 39 with respect to the derecognition of financial liabilities are generally more straightforward and less subjective than those for the derecognition of financial assets. However, they are also very different from the rules for derecognition of assets which focus primarily on the economic substance of the transaction. By contrast, the rules for derecognition of liabilities, like the provisions of IAS 32 for the identification of instruments as financial liabilities (see Chapter 19), focus more on legal obligations than on economic substance – or, as the IASB would doubtless argue, they are based on the view that the economic substance of whether an entity has a liability to a third party is ultimately dictated by the legal rights and obligations that exist between them.

IAS 39 contains provisions relating to:

- the extinguishment of debt (see 5.1 below);
- the substitution or modification of debt by the original lender (see 5.2 below); and
- the calculation of any profit or loss arising on the derecognition of debt (see 5.3 below).

5.1 Extinguishment of debt

IAS 39 requires an entity to derecognise (i.e. remove from its balance sheet) a financial liability (or a part of a financial liability – see 5.1.1 below) when, and only when, it is 'extinguished', that is, when the obligation specified in the contract is discharged, cancelled, or expires.[138] This will be achieved when the debtor either:

- discharges the liability (or part of it) by paying the creditor, normally with cash, other financial assets, goods or services; or
- is legally released from primary responsibility for the liability (or part of it) either by process of law or by the creditor.[139] Extinguishment of liabilities by legal release is discussed further at 5.1.2 below.

If the issuer of a debt instrument repurchases the instrument, the debt is extinguished even if the issuer is a market maker in that instrument, or otherwise intends to resell or reissue it in the near term.[140] IAS 39 focuses only on whether the entity has a legal obligation to reissue the debt, not on whether there is a commercial imperative for it to do so.

5.1.1 What constitutes 'part' of a liability?

As noted above, the requirements of IAS 39 for the derecognition of liabilities apply to all or 'part' of a financial liability. It is not entirely clear what is meant by 'part' of a liability in this context. The rules, and the examples, in IAS 39 seem to be drafted in the context of transactions that settle all remaining cash flows (i.e. interest and principal) of a proportion of a liability, such as the repayment of £25 million of a £100 million loan, together with any related interest payments.

However, these provisions are presumably also intended to apply in situations where an entity prepays the interest only (or a proportion of future interest payments) or the principal only (or a proportion of future principal payments) on a loan.

5.1.2 Legal release by creditor

As noted above, a liability can be derecognised by a debtor if the creditor legally releases the debtor from the liability. It is clear that IAS 39 regards legal release as crucial, with the effect that very similar (if not identical) situations may lead to different results purely because of the legal form.

For example, IAS 39 provides that:

- where a debtor is legally released from a liability, derecognition is not precluded by the fact that the debtor has given a guarantee in respect of the liability;[141] but
- if a debtor pays a third party to assume an obligation and notifies its creditor that the third party has assumed the debt obligation, the debtor derecognises the debt obligation if, and only if, the creditor legally releases the debtor from its obligations.[142]

The effect of these requirements can be shown by Example 18.19.

Example 18.19: Transfer of debt obligations with and without legal release

Scenario 1

Entity A issues bonds that have a carrying amount and fair value of $1,000,000. A pays $1,000,000 to Entity B for B to assume responsibility for paying interest and principal on the bonds to the bondholders. The bondholders are informed that B has assumed responsibility for the debt. However, A is not legally released from the obligation to pay interest and principal by the bondholders. Accordingly, if B does not make payments when due, the bondholders may seek payment from A.

Scenario 2

Entity A issues bonds that have a carrying amount and fair value of $1,000,000. A pays $1,000,000 to Entity B for B to assume responsibility for paying interest and principal on the bonds to the bondholders. The bondholders are informed that B has assumed responsibility for the debt and legally release A from any further obligation under the debt. However, A enters into a guarantee arrangement whereby, if B does not make payments when due, the bondholders may seek payment from A.

It is clear, in our view, that in either scenario above the bondholders are in the same economic and legal position – they will receive payments from B and, if B defaults, they will have recourse to A.

However, IAS 39 gives rise to the, in our view, anomalous result that:

- Scenario 1 is accounted for by the continuing recognition of the debt because no legal release has been obtained; but
- Scenario 2 is accounted for by derecognition of the debt, and recognition of the guarantee, notwithstanding that the effect of the guarantee is to put A back in the same position as if it had not been released from its obligations under the original bond.

IAS 39 also clarifies that, if a debtor:

- transfers its obligations under a debt to a third party and obtains legal release from its obligations by the creditor; but
- undertakes to make payments to the third party so as to enable it to meet its obligations to the creditor,

it should derecognise the original debt, but recognise a new debt obligation to the third party.[143]

5.1.3 *'In-substance defeasance' arrangements*

Entities sometimes enter into so-called 'in-substance defeasance' arrangements in respect of financial liabilities. These typically involve a lump sum payment to a third party (other than the creditor) such as a trust, which then invests the funds in (typically) very low-risk assets to which the entity has no, or very limited, rights of access. These assets are then applied to discharge all the remaining interest and principal payments on the financial liabilities that are purported to have been defeased. It is sometimes argued that the risk-free nature of the assets, and the entity's lack of access to them, means that the entity is in substance in no different position than if it had actually repaid the original financial liability.

IAS 39 regards such arrangements as not giving rise to derecognition of the original liability in the absence of legal release by the creditor.[144]

5.1.4 *Extinguishment in exchange for transfer of assets not meeting the derecognition criteria*

IAS 39 notes that in some cases legal release may be achieved by transferring assets to the creditor which do not meet the criteria for derecognition (see 4 above). In such a case, the debtor will derecognise the liability from which it has been released, but recognise a new liability relating to the transferred assets that may be equal to the derecognised liability.[145] It is not entirely clear what is envisaged here, but it may be some such scenario as the following.

Example 18.20: Extinguishment of debt in exchange for transfer of assets not meeting derecognition criteria.

An entity has a bank loan of €1 million. The bank agrees to accept in full payment of the loan the transfer to it by the entity of a portfolio of corporate bonds with a market value of €1 million. The entity and the bank then enter into a put and call option over the bonds, the effect of which will be that the entity will repurchase the bonds in three years' time at a price that gives the bank a lender's return on €1 million. As discussed further at 4 above, this would have the effect that the entity is unable to derecognise the bonds.

Under the provisions of IAS 39, the entity would be able to derecognise the original bank loan, as it has been legally released from it. However, the provisions under discussion here have the overall result that a loan effectively continues to be recognised. Strictly, however, the analysis is that the original loan has been derecognised and a new one recognised. In effect the accounting is representing that the entity has repaid the original loan and replaced it with a new one secured on a bond portfolio.

However, as the new loan is required to be initially recognised at fair value whereas the old loan may well have been recognised at amortised cost (see Chapter 20), there may well be a gain or loss to record as the result of the different measurement bases being used – see 5.2 and 5.3 below.

5.2 Exchange or modification of debt by original lender

It is common for an entity, particularly but not necessarily when in financial difficulties, to approach its major creditors for a restructuring of its debt commitments – for example, an agreement to postpone the repayment of principal in exchange for higher interest payments in the meantime, or to roll up interest into a single 'bullet' payment of interest and principal at the end of the term. Such changes to the terms of debt can be effected in a number of ways, in particular:

- a notional repayment of the original loan followed by an immediate re-lending of all or part of the proceeds of the notional repayment as a new loan ('exchange'); or
- legal amendment of the original loan agreement ('modification').

The accounting issue raised by such transactions is essentially whether there is, in fact, anything to account for. For example, if an entity owes £100 million at floating rate interest and negotiates with its bankers to change the interest to a fixed coupon of 7%, should the accounting treatment reflect that fact that:

(a) the entity still owes £100 million to the same lender, and so is in the same position as before; or

(b) the modification of the interest profile has altered the net present value of the total obligations under the loan?

IAS 39 requires an exchange between an existing borrower and lender of debt instruments with 'substantially different' terms to be accounted for as an extinguishment of the original financial liability and the recognition of a new financial liability. Similarly, a substantial modification of the terms of an existing financial liability, or a part of it, (whether or not due to the financial difficulty of the debtor) should be accounted for as an extinguishment of the original financial liability and the recognition of a new financial liability.[146]

The effect of this, as explained in more detail below, is that where a liability is treated as 'modified' under IAS 39, some of the effect of the modification is recognised immediately, whereas if the liability is not treated as modified, the effect of the modification is recognised prospectively.

IAS 39 regards the terms of exchanged or modified debt as 'substantially different' if the net present value of the cash flows under the new terms (including any fees paid net of any fees received) discounted at the original effective interest rate is at least 10% different from the discounted present value of the remaining cash flows of the original debt instrument.[147] Whilst IAS 39 does not say so explicitly, it seems clear that the discounted present value of the remaining cash flows of the original debt instrument must also be determined using the original effective interest rate, so that there is a 'like for like' comparison.

IAS 39 does not prohibit an entity from accounting for an exchange or modification of a liability where the net present value of the cash flows under the new terms is less than 10% different from the discounted present value of the remaining cash flows of the original debt instrument. Indeed, there may be situations where the modification of the debt is so fundamental that immediate derecognition is appropriate whether or not the '10% test' is satisfied. The following are examples of situations where, in our view, derecognition of the original instrument would be required:

- An entity has issued a 'plain vanilla' debt instrument and restructures the debt to include an embedded equity instrument.

  The discounted present value, at the original effective interest rate, of the cash flows of the restructured debt may not be different from the discounted present value of the remaining cash flows of the original financial liability. However, the upside and downside potential change in fair value has significantly altered, such that the modification of terms represents a substantial change in the future risk exposure of the instrument;

- An entity has issued a 5% euro-denominated debt instrument with current fair value of €100 and restructures the instrument to an 18% Turkish lire-denominated debt instrument with the same fair value at time of the restructuring.

  Even though the fair value of the restructured instrument is the same as the original debt instrument, the upside and downside potential change in fair value has significantly altered. The change in the currency exposure also represents a substantial modification in the terms as it represents a fundamental adjustment in the future economic risk exposure of the instrument. Moreover, the test under IAS 39 is any event not to compare the fair values of the old and new liability, but to compare the net present value of the original liability with the modified cash flows discounted at the effective interest rate of the original liability.

5.2.1 *Costs and fees*

An entity will almost always be required to pay fees to the lender and incur costs (such as legal expenses) on an exchange or modification of a financial liability.

If an exchange of debt instruments or modification of terms is accounted for as an extinguishment of the original debt, IAS 39 requires any costs or fees incurred to be recognised as part of the gain or loss on the extinguishment (see 5.3 below). However, if the exchange or modification is not accounted for as an extinguishment, any costs or fees incurred are an adjustment to the carrying amount of the liability and are amortised over the remaining term of the modified liability.[148]

5.2.2 *Illustrative examples*

The requirements of IAS 39 for exchanges and modifications of debt are reasonably straightforward in principle but give rise to a number of practical issues, as illustrated by Examples 18.21 and 18.22 below.

Example 18.21: Modification of debt not treated as extinguishment

On 1 January 2003 an entity borrowed £100 million on, at that time, arm's length market terms that interest of 7% was to be paid annually in arrears and the loan repaid in full on 31 December 2012. Transaction costs of £5 million were incurred. Assuming that the loan had run to term, the entity would have recorded the following amounts using the effective interest rate method. The loan is originally recorded at the issue proceeds of £100 million less transaction costs of £5 million, and the effective interest rate of 7.736% is derived by computer program or trial and error (for more detailed discussion of the effective interest rate method, see Chapter 20 at 5).

Year	Liability b/f £m	Interest at 7.736% £m	Cash paid £m	Liability c/f £m
1.1.2003	95.00			95.00
2003	95.00	7.35	(7.00)	95.35
2004	95.35	7.38	(7.00)	95.73
2005	95.73	7.40	(7.00)	96.13
2006	96.13	7.44	(7.00)	96.57
2007	96.57	7.47	(7.00)	97.04
2008	97.04	7.51	(7.00)	97.55
2009	97.55	7.55	(7.00)	98.10
2010	98.10	7.59	(7.00)	98.69
2011	98.69	7.63	(7.00)	99.32
2012	99.32	7.68	(107.00)	–

During 2007 the entity is in financial difficulties and approaches the bondholders for a modification of the terms of the bond. These are agreed on 1 January 2008 as follows. No cash interest will be paid in 2008 or 2009. From 2010 onwards interest of 9% will be paid annually in arrears, and the term of the loan will be extended for two years until 31 December 2014. Legal fees of £2 million are incurred, and paid on 1 January 2008.

The entity is required to compute the present value of the new arrangement using the original effective interest rate of 7.736%. This gives a net present value for the modified debt of £92.53 million calculated as follows.

Year	Cash flow	£m	Discount factor	£m
1.1.2008	Legal fees	2.00	1	2.00
2010	Interest	9.00	$1/1.07736^3$	7.20
2011	Interest	9.00	$1/1.07736^4$	6.68
2012	Interest	9.00	$1/1.07736^5$	6.20
2013	Interest	9.00	$1/1.07736^6$	5.75
2014	Interest and principal	109.00	$1/1.07736^7$	64.70
			Total	92.53

This represents 95.4% of the current carrying value of the debt as at the end of 2007 of £97.04 million, so that the net present value of the modified bond (discounted at the effective interest rate of the original bond) is 4.6% different from that of the original bond. This is less than 10%, so that the modification is not automatically required to be treated as an extinguishment under IAS 39.

However, the difference between the net present values of the original and the modified bonds presents a problem. Clearly, if the entity were to continue to apply the original effective interest rate to the existing carrying value of the bond a significant unamortised amount would emerge as a result of the change to the timing and quantum of the new future cash flows. In order for the numbers to 'work', either the carrying amount of the liability, or the effective interest rate, must be changed.

Here there is an apparent conflict between the specific rules of IAS 39 relating to exchanges and modification of liabilities and the general requirements for application of the effective interest method. The specific rule relating to exchanges and modifications of debt not regarded as an extinguishment is clear that:

- there should be no derecognition of the original debt, and
- any transaction costs associated with the modified debt should be amortised over the remaining term of the modified liability.

In other words, the current carrying value of £97.04 million must stand and the effective interest rate must be changed.

On the other hand, the general rules for the application of the effective interest method (see Chapter 20 at 5) are equally clear:

> 'If an entity revises its estimates of payments or receipts the entity shall adjust the carrying amount of the financial asset or financial liability (or group of financial instruments) to reflect actual and revised estimated cash flows. The entity recalculates the carrying amount by computing the present value of estimated future cash flows at the financial instrument's original effective interest rate. The adjustment is recognised as income or expense in profit or loss.'[149]

Applied in this situation, this would result in the carrying amount of the loan being restated to the £92.53 million calculated above with the recognition of a gain of £4.51 million (£97.04m current carrying value less £92.53m recalculated net present value). The £92.53 million would then be amortised at the original effective interest rate.

In our view, the specific rules dealing with derecognition of financial liabilities must take precedence. If they do not, then the exemption in IAS 39 from treating exchanges and modifications within the 10% 'band' as extinguishments would have no practical effect. The only way that the numbers can then be processed mechanically is to derive a new effective interest rate for the exchanged or modified borrowing, treating the carrying amount of the original borrowing as the issue proceeds. This was effectively the method prescribed in the guidance (in Q&A 62-1) to the original version of IAS 39 (whose requirements for derecognition of liabilities have been carried forward without major change into the current version).

Under this approach the carrying value of the of bond at the end of 2007 of £97.04 million, net of the transaction costs of £2 million, is treated as a new borrowing of £95.04 million, accounted for as follows, using the newly derived effective interest rate of 6.905%.

Year	Liability b/f £m	Interest at 6.905% £m	Cash paid £m	Liability c/f £m
2008	95.04	6.56		101.60
2009	101.60	7.01		108.61
2010	108.61	7.50	(9.00)	107.11
2011	107.11	7.40	(9.00)	105.51
2012	105.51	7.28	(9.00)	103.79
2013	103.79	7.17	(9.00)	101.96
2014	101.96	7.04	(109.00)	–

Example 18.22: Modification of debt treated as extinguishment

Assume the same facts as in Example 18.21 above, except that on 1 January 2008 the entity comes to an arrangement with the bondholders to modify the terms of the bonds as follows.

No cash interest will be paid in 2008 or 2009. From 2010 onwards interest of 12.5% will be paid annually in arrears, and the term of the loan will be extended for three years until 31 December 2015. Legal fees of £2 million are incurred, and paid on 1 January 2008.

As in Example 18.21 above, the entity is required to compute the net present value of the new arrangement using the original effective interest rate of 7.736%. This gives a net present value for the modified debt of £107.3 million calculated as follows.

Year	Cash flow	£m	Discount factor	£m
1.1.2008	Legal fees	2.00	1	2.00
2010	Interest	12.50	$1/1.07736^3$	10.00
2011	Interest	12.50	$1/1.07736^4$	9.28
2012	Interest	12.50	$1/1.07736^5$	8.61
2013	Interest	12.50	$1/1.07736^6$	7.99
2014	Interest	12.50	$1/1.07736^7$	7.42
2015	Interest and principal	112.50	$1/1.07736^8$	61.98
			Total	107.28

This represents 110.6% of the current carrying value of the debt as at the end of 2007 of £97.04 million, so that the net present value of the modified bond (discounted at the effective interest rate of the original bond) is 10.6% different from that of the original bond. This is greater than 10%, so that the modification is required to be treated as an extinguishment under IAS 39.

This will involve derecognising the existing liability and recognising a new liability. The issue is then at what amount the new liability should be recognised. It is not the £107.28 million above, since this includes the transaction costs of £2 million, which are required to be treated as integral to the cash flows of the modified bond for the purposes of comparing it with the original bond, but are then required to be expensed immediately if the test identifies an extinguishment.

Moreover, as the accounting treatment is intended to represent the derecognition of an existing liability and the recognition of a new one, the modified bond must – in accordance with the general measurement provisions of IAS 39 (see Chapter 20) – be recognised at fair value and amortised using its own effective interest rate, not that applicable to the original bond.

The difficulty is obviously in determining the fair value of the modified bonds. If the bonds were quoted, a market value might be available. Another possible approach might be to discount the cash flows of the modified bond at the interest rate at which the entity could have issued a new bond on similar terms to the modified bond. However, where (as may well be the case) the modification is being undertaken because the entity is in serious financial difficulty, it might be that no lender would be prepared to advance new finance, so that there is no readily available 'notional' borrowing rate.

If the view were taken that the fair value of the modified bond was £98 million, the accounting treatment for the modification would be (see also 5.3 below):

	£m	£m
Original bond	97.04	
Loss on extinguishment of debt (income statement)	2.96	
Modified bond		98.00
Cash (transaction costs)		2.00

In this particular case, this has the result that the actual gain or loss recognised is actually somewhat smaller than the difference calculated between the net present value of the original and modified bonds that led to the requirement to recognise the gain or loss in the first place. This differential will obviously be reflected in higher interest costs as the transaction matures.

5.2.3 Settlement of financial liability with issue of new equity instrument

A related area not specifically covered in either IAS 32 or IAS 39 is the accounting treatment to be adopted where an entity issues non-convertible debt, but subsequently enters into an agreement with the debt-holder to discharge the liability under the debt in full or in part for an issue of equity instruments. This most often occurs when the entity is in financial difficulties.

This is discussed in Chapter 19 at 4.4.5.

5.3 Gains and losses on extinguishment of debt

When a financial liability (or part of a liability) is extinguished or transferred to another party, IAS 39 requires the difference between the carrying amount of the transferred financial liability (or part of a liability) and the consideration paid, including any non-cash assets transferred or liabilities assumed, to be recognised in profit or loss.[150]

If an entity repurchases only a part of a financial liability, it calculates the carrying value of the part disposed of (and hence the gain or loss on disposal) by allocating the previous carrying amount of the financial liability between the part that continues to be recognised and the part that is derecognised based on the relative fair values of those parts on the date of the repurchase.[151] In other words, the carrying amount of the liability is not simply reduced by consideration received.

This is illustrated in Example 18.23 below.

Example 18.23: Partial derecognition of debt

On 1 January 2007 an entity issues 500 million €1 10-year bonds which are traded in the capital markets. Issue costs of €15 million were incurred and the carrying value of the bonds at

31 December 2008 is €490 million. On 31 December 2010 the entity makes a market purchase of 120 million bonds at their then current market price of €0.97. The entity records the following accounting entry:

	€m	€m
Bonds (120/500 × €490m)	117.6	
Cash (120m × €0.97)		116.4
Gain on repurchase of debt		1.2

In some cases, as discussed in 5.2 above, a creditor may release a debtor from its present obligation to make payments, but the debtor assumes an obligation to pay if the party assuming primary responsibility defaults. In such a case, IAS 39 requires the debtor to recognise:

(a) a new liability based on the fair value for the obligation for the guarantee; and

(b) a gain or loss based on the difference between

  (i) any proceeds; and

  (ii) the carrying amount of the original liability (including any related unamortised costs) less the fair value of the new liability.[152]

5.4 Derivatives that can be financial assets or financial liabilities

A potential difficulty not addressed by IAS 39 is the required treatment for the transfer of a non-optional derivative, such as a swap or forward contract, that by its nature can be either a financial asset or a financial liability at various times during its life. A literal reading of IAS 39 could suggest that the rules for derecognition of financial assets should be applied when the derivative has a positive fair value to the entity and the rules for derecognition of financial liabilities should be applied when the derivative has a negative fair value to the entity. This could lead to very different results, given the significantly different approaches underlying each set of rules (see 5 above).

In practice, however, any transfer of such derivatives is likely to require the consent of the counterparty to the entity's legal release from its obligations under the contract, and the possible payment of a fee to compensate the counterparty for the difference between the creditworthiness of the entity and that of the transferee. Such procedures are much closer to those envisaged in the derecognition rules for financial liabilities than those implicit in the derecognition rules for financial assets.

The IASB has expressed the view that a non-optional derivative that could be either an asset or liability can be derecognised only if the derecognition criteria for both assets and liabilities are satisfied (see 4.2.2 above).

6 OFFSET

IAS 1 sets out a general principle that assets and liabilities should not be offset except where such offset is permitted or required by an accounting standard or interpretation (see Chapter 3 at 4.1.5). IAS 32 provides some exceptions to this general rule applicable to financial assets and liabilities. As noted at 1.1 above, however, it is arguable that, conceptually speaking, the rules in IAS 32 are less exceptions to the general prohibition on offset than the identification of situations where an entity has separate assets and liabilities in form, but a single net asset or liability in substance.

IAS 32 requires a financial asset and a financial liability to be offset and the net amount reported in the balance sheet when, and only when, an entity:

(a) has a legally enforceable right to set off the recognised amounts; and

(b) intends either to settle on a net basis, or to realise the asset and settle the liability simultaneously.

However, in accounting for the transfer of an asset that does not qualify for derecognition, the transferred asset and any associated liability must not be offset,[153] even if they otherwise satisfy the offset criteria (see 4.8.4 above).

IAS 32 argues that offset is appropriate in the circumstances set out in (a) and (b) above, because the entity has in effect only a single cash flow and, hence, a single financial asset or financial liability. In other circumstances, financial assets and financial liabilities are presented separately from each other, consistently with their characteristics as resources or obligations of the entity.[154] Offset is not equivalent to derecognition, since no gain or loss can ever arise on offset, but may arise on derecognition.[155]

IAS 32 elaborates further on the detail of the conditions as follows.

6.1 Legal framework

IAS 32 describes a right of set-off as 'a debtor's legal right, by contract or otherwise, to settle or otherwise eliminate all or a portion of an amount due to a creditor by applying against that amount an amount due from the creditor.' The effectiveness of the right of set-off is thus essentially a legal matter, so that the specific conditions supporting the right may vary from one legal jurisdiction to another. Care must therefore be taken to establish which laws apply to the relationships between the parties.[156]

In unusual circumstances, a debtor (A) may have a legal right to apply an amount due from a third party (B) against an amount due to a creditor (C), provided that there is an agreement among A, B and C that clearly establishes A's right to set off amounts due from B against those due to C.[157]

6.2 Right and intention to settle net

IAS 32 emphasises that, in order to achieve offset of a financial asset and financial liability, it is necessary not only that the reporting entity is legally able to settle them net but also that it actually intends to do so. It is not sufficient to have the right (but not the intention) or the intention (but not the right) to settle net.

IAS 32 acknowledges that an enforceable right to set off a financial asset and a financial liability affects the rights and obligations associated with that asset and liability and may affect an entity's exposure to credit and liquidity risk. However, such a right is not, in itself, a sufficient basis for offsetting, since, in the absence of an intention to exercise the right or to settle simultaneously, the amount and timing of an entity's future cash flows are not affected. Similarly, an intention by one or both parties to settle on a net basis without the legal right to do so is not sufficient to justify offsetting because the rights and obligations associated with the individual financial asset and financial liability remain unaltered.[158]

IAS 32 notes that an entity's intentions with respect to settlement of particular assets and liabilities may be influenced by its normal business practices, the requirements of the financial markets and other circumstances that may limit the ability to settle net or simultaneously. When an entity has a right of set-off, but does not intend to settle net or to realise the asset and settle the liability simultaneously, the effect of the right on the entity's credit risk exposure is disclosed by giving the general credit risk disclosures required by IAS 32 or, where applicable, IFRS 7 – *Financial Instruments: Disclosures*[159] (see Chapter 22 at 3.4).

6.3 Simultaneous settlement

IAS 32 also clarifies that the reference to 'simultaneous' settlement in the conditions for offset above is to be interpreted literally, as applying only to the realisation of a financial asset and settlement of a financial liability at the same moment. The standard gives as an example the type of overall market settlement that occurs in a clearing house (where transactions are net- rather than gross-settled) or in a face-to-face exchange. In other circumstances, an entity may settle two instruments by receiving and paying separate amounts, becoming exposed to credit risk for the full amount of the asset or liquidity risk for the full amount of the liability. Such risk exposures, though relatively brief, may be significant, so that offset is not therefore appropriate. Accordingly, IAS 32 treats the realisation of a financial asset and settlement of a financial liability as simultaneous only when the transactions occur at the same moment.[160]

6.4 Situations where offset is not normally appropriate

IAS 32 comments that its offset criteria are not normally satisfied in the following circumstances.

6.4.1 Synthetic instruments

An entity may enter into a number of different financial instruments designed to replicate the features of a single financial instrument (referred to as a 'synthetic instrument'). For example, if an entity issues floating rate debt and then enters into a 'pay fixed/receive floating' interest rate swap, the combined economic effect is that the entity has issued fixed rate debt.

IAS 32 argues that each of the individual financial instruments that together constitute a 'synthetic instrument':

- represents a contractual right or obligation with its own terms and conditions;

- may be transferred or settled separately; and
- is exposed to risks that may differ from those to which the other financial instruments in the 'synthetic instrument' are exposed.

Accordingly, when one financial instrument in a 'synthetic instrument' is an asset and another is a liability, they are not offset and presented on an entity's balance sheet on a net basis unless they meet the criteria above.

While disclosures are provided about the significant terms and conditions of each financial instrument under IAS 32 (but not necessarily under IFRS 7), an entity may indicate in addition the nature of the relationship between the individual instruments (see Chapter 22 at 3.4).[161]

6.4.2 *Other*

Offset is also usually inappropriate where:

(a) financial assets and financial liabilities arise from financial instruments having the same primary risk exposure (e.g. assets and liabilities within a portfolio of forward contracts or other derivative instruments) but involving different counterparties;

(b) financial or other assets are pledged as collateral for non-recourse financial liabilities;

(c) financial assets are set aside in trust by a debtor for the purpose of discharging an obligation without those assets having been accepted by the creditor in settlement of the obligation (e.g. a sinking fund arrangement) – see also 5.1.3 above; or

(d) obligations incurred as a result of events giving rise to losses are expected to be recovered from a third party by virtue of a claim made under an insurance policy.[162]

6.5 Master netting agreements

It is common practice for an entity that undertakes a number of financial instrument transactions with a single counterparty to enter into a 'master netting arrangement' with that counterparty. These arrangements are typically used by financial institutions to restrict their exposure to loss in the event of bankruptcy or other events that result in a counterparty being unable to meet its obligations. Such an agreement commonly creates a right of set-off that becomes enforceable, and affects the realisation or settlement of individual financial assets and financial liabilities, only following a specified event of default or in other circumstances not expected to arise in the normal course of business.

Where an entity has entered into such an agreement, the agreement does not provide the basis for the offset of assets and liabilities unless the criteria summarised at 6 above are satisfied.[163] This will typically be the case only if the default (or other event specified in the contract) has actually occurred. When financial assets and financial liabilities subject to a master netting arrangement are not offset, the effect of the arrangement falls within the scope of the disclosure requirements of IAS 32, or (where applied) IFRS 7, relating to credit risk[164] (see Chapter 22 at 3.4).

7 TRANSITIONAL AND FIRST-TIME ADOPTION ISSUES

Except as specifically noted below, the requirements of IAS 32 and IAS 39 discussed in this chapter must be applied retrospectively, with full restatement of comparative amounts.[165] However, in the case of items subject to the requirements of IAS 39 (but not IAS 32), comparative amounts need not be restated if restatement would be impracticable, in which case the entity must disclose that fact and indicate the extent to which the information was restated.[166]

7.1 Transitional issues – derecognition of assets

The basic rule in IAS 39 is that an entity should apply the derecognition provisions for assets (discussed at 4 above) prospectively. Accordingly, if an entity derecognised financial assets under the previous IAS 39 (revised 2000) as a result of a transaction that occurred before 1 January 2004, it must not recognise those assets, even if they would not have been derecognised under the new version of IAS 39.[167]

However, notwithstanding this basic provision, an entity may apply the derecognition requirements discussed at 4 above retrospectively from any date of the entity's choosing, provided that the information needed to apply the new version of IAS 39 to assets and liabilities derecognised as a result of past transactions was obtained at the time of initially accounting for those transactions.[168]

7.2 First-time adoption issues

7.2.1 Comparative information

IFRS 1 – *First-time Adoption of International Financial Reporting Standards* – exempts an entity that adopts IFRS for the first time before 1 January 2006 from complying with IAS 32 and IAS 39 in any comparative period presented in its first IFRS financial statements. An entity taking advantage of this exemption is required to:

(a) apply its previous GAAP in the comparative information to financial instruments within the scope of IAS 32 and IAS 39;

(b) disclose this fact, together with the basis used to prepare this information; and

(c) disclose the nature of the main adjustments that would make the information comply with IAS 32 and IAS 39.

The entity need not quantify those adjustments. However, it must treat any adjustment between the balance sheet:

- at the comparative period's reporting date (i.e. the balance sheet that includes comparative information under previous GAAP); and
- at the start of the first IFRS reporting period (i.e. the first period that includes information that complies with IAS 32 and IAS 39 and IFRS 4 – *Insurance Contracts*)

as arising from a change in accounting policy and give the disclosures required by paragraph 28(a)-(e) and (f)(i) of IAS 8. Paragraph 28(f)(i) (i.e. the requirement to disclose the effect of a change of accounting policy on each line item in the financial statements) applies only to amounts presented in the balance sheet at the comparative period's reporting date.[169]

This exemption is now of significance only for entities that present more than one year of comparative information.

7.2.2 Recognition and derecognition

The basic rule in IFRS 1 is that a first-time adopter should recognise all financial assets and financial liabilities that qualify for recognition, and have not yet qualified for derecognition, under IAS 39.[170]

However, an entity should not recognise non-derivative financial assets and liabilities derecognised under its previous GAAP as a result of a transaction that occurred before 1 January 2004, unless:

(a) they qualify for recognition as the result of a later transaction or event;[171] or

(b) derecognition occurred as the result of a transfer to an entity treated as an SPE under SIC–12 (see B below).

Notwithstanding this provision, however, an entity may apply the derecognition requirements discussed at 4 and 5 above retrospectively from any date of the entity's choosing, provided that the information needed to apply the current version of IAS 39 to assets and liabilities derecognised as a result of past transactions was obtained at the time of initially accounting for those transactions.[172]

A Multiple transfers under same arrangement

IFRS 1 acknowledges that some arrangements for the transfer of assets, particularly securitisations, may last for some time, with the result that transfers might be made both before and on or after 1 January 2004 under the same arrangement. IFRS 1 clarifies that transfers made under such arrangements fall within the first-time adoption provisions only if they occurred before 1 January 2004. Transfers on or after 1 January 2004 are subject to the full requirements of IAS 39.[173]

B Transfers to SPEs

SIC-12 contains no specific transitional or first-time adoption provisions. Accordingly, its requirements with regard to the consolidation of SPEs are fully retrospective for first-time adopters. Thus if, under its previous GAAP, an entity derecognised non-derivative financial assets and liabilities as the result of a transfer to an entity treated as an SPE by SIC-12, those assets and liabilities will be re-recognised on transition to IFRS, but as the result of consolidation of the SPE rather than through application of IAS 39. Of course, if the SPE itself then subsequently achieved derecognition of the items concerned under the entity's previous GAAP (other than by transfer to a second SPE or member of the entity's group), then the items remain derecognised on transition.

References

1 IAS 39, *Financial Instruments: Recognition and Measurement*, IASB, IASB bound volume 2006.
2 IAS 32, *Financial Instruments: Presentation*, IASB, IASB bound volume 2007.
3 SIC-12, Consolidation – *Special Purpose Entities*, SIC, November 1998 (amended December 2003).
4 IAS 32, para. 96. IAS 39, para. 103.
5 IAS 32, Application Guidance, para. before para. AG1.
6 IAS 32, Illustrative Examples, para. after main heading.
7 IAS 39, Application Guidance, para. before para. AG1.
8 IAS 39, Guidance on Implementing, para. before main heading Section A; Illustrative Example, para. after main heading.
9 IAS 39, para. BC43.
10 IAS 39, paras. IN9-IN15.
11 IAS 32, para. 11.
12 IAS 32, para. 11.
13 IAS 32, para. 11.
14 IAS 32, para. 11.
15 IAS 32, para. 12 and IAS 39, para. 9.
16 IAS 32, para. 11.
17 IAS 39, para. 14.
18 IAS 39, para. AG35(a).
19 IAS 39, para. AG35(b).
20 IAS 39, para. AG35(b).
21 IAS 39, paras. BC149-BC154.
22 IAS 39, para. AG35(c).
23 IAS 39, para. AG40(d).
24 IAS 39, para. AG39(c).
25 IAS 39, para. F.3.7.
26 IAS 39, para. AG35(d).
27 IAS 39, para. 3.
28 IAS 39, paras. AG34 and AG50.
29 IAS 39, para. AG50.
30 IAS 39, para. 9.
31 IAS 39, para. AG54.
32 IAS 39, paras. AG55-AG56.
33 IAS 39, paras. AG55-AG56.
34 IAS 39, paras. 38 and AG53.
35 IAS 39, para. AG55.
36 IAS 39, paras. 57 and AG56.
37 IAS 39, para. D.2.2.
38 IAS 39, paras. D.2.1 and D.2.2.
39 IAS 39, para. D.2.3.
40 IAS 39, para. AG36.
41 SIC-12, para. 8.
42 IAS 39, para. 16.
43 *IFRIC Update*, IFRIC, January 2007.
44 *IFRIC Update*, IFRIC, May 2006.
45 *IASB Update*, IASB, September 2006.
46 *IASB Update*, IASB, September 2006.
47 IAS 39, para. 16.
48 IAS 39, para. 17.
49 IAS 39, para. 18.
50 IAS 39, para. AG37.
51 *Information for Observers*, IFRIC, March 2006.
52 *IFRIC Update*, IFRIC, November 2005.
53 *IASB Update*, IASB, September 2006.
54 IAS 39, para. 16(b).
55 *Information for Observers*, IFRIC, March 2006.
56 *IASB Update*, IASB, September 2006.
57 *IASB Update*, IASB, September 2006.
58 IAS 39, para. 19.
59 IAS 39, para. AG38.
60 *IFRIC Update*, IFRIC, November 2005.
61 IAS 39, para. 20.
62 IAS 39, para. 20(a).
63 IAS 39, para. AG41.
64 IAS 39, para. 20(b).
65 IAS 39, para. 20(c).
66 IAS 39, para. 21
67 IAS 39, para. 22.
68 IAS 39, paras. 21 and AG39.
69 IAS 39, paras. 21 and AG40.
70 IAS 39, para. AG51(g)-(h).
71 IAS 39, para. AG52.
72 IAS 39, para. 20(c).
73 IAS 39, para. 23.
74 IAS 39, para. AG42.
75 IAS 39, para. AG43.
76 IAS 39, para. AG43.
77 IAS 39, para. AG44.
78 IAS 39, para. AG44.
79 IAS 39, para. AG51(a).
80 IAS 39, para. AG51(a).
81 IAS 39, para. AG51(b).
82 IAS 39, para. AG51(c).
83 IAS 39, para. AG51(k).
84 IAS 39, para. AG51(j).
85 IAS 39, para. AG51(d).
86 IAS 39, para. AG51(e).
87 IAS 39, para. AG51(f).
88 IAS 39, para. AG51(g).
89 IAS 39, paras. AG51(h)-(i).
90 IAS 39, para. AG51(h).
91 IAS 39, para. AG51(h).
92 IAS 39, para. AG51(i).
93 IAS 39, para. AG51(i).
94 IAS 39, para. AG51(j).
95 IAS 39, para. AG51(k).
96 IAS 39, para. AG51(l).
97 IAS 39, para. AG51(m).

98 IAS 39, para. AG51(n).
99 IAS 39, para. AG51(n).
100 IAS 39, para. AG51(o).
101 IAS 39, para. AG51(p).
102 IAS 39, para. AG51(q).
103 IAS 39, para. AG51(q).
104 IAS 39, paras. 24-25.
105 IAS 39, para. 26.
106 IAS 39, para. 27
107 IAS 39, para. 28.
108 IAS 39, para. AG46.
109 In practice, other factors might be relevant to the valuation.
110 IAS 39, para. 24.
111 IAS 39, para. AG45.
112 IAS 39, para. 29.
113 IAS 39, para. AG47.
114 IAS 39, para. 30.
115 IAS 39, paras. BC44-BC52.
116 IAS 39, para. 30(a).
117 IAS 39, para. 30(b)-(c).
118 IAS 39, para. 31.
119 IAS 39, para. 31.
120 IAS 39, para. 32.
121 IAS 39, para. 33.
122 IAS 39, para. 35.
123 IAS 39, para. 27.
124 IAS 39, para. AG48(a).
125 IAS 39, para. AG52.
126 IAS 39, para. AG48(b).
127 IAS 39, para. AG48(c).
128 IAS 39, para. AG48(d).
129 The fair value of an in the money option is positive for the buyer and negative for the writer.
130 IAS 39, para. AG48(e).
131 IAS 39, para. AG52.
132 IAS 39, para. AG48(a).
133 IAS 39, para. 36.
134 IAS 32, para. 42.
135 IAS 39, para. 37.
136 IAS 39, para. AG49.
137 IAS 39, para. AG41.
138 IAS 39, para. 39.
139 IAS 39, para. AG57.
140 IAS 39, para. AG58.
141 IAS 39, para. AG57(b).
142 IAS 39, para. AG60.
143 IAS 39, para. AG60.
144 IAS 39, para. AG59.
145 IAS 39, para. AG61.
146 IAS 39, para. 40.
147 IAS 39, para. AG62.
148 IAS 39, para. AG62.
149 IAS 39, para. AG8.
150 IAS 39, para. 41.
151 IAS 39, para. 42.
152 IAS 39, para. AG63
153 IAS 32, para. 42.
154 IAS 32, para. 43.
155 IAS 32, para. 44.
156 IAS 32, para. 45.
157 IAS 32, para. 45
158 IAS 32, para. 46.
159 IAS 32 para. 47.
160 IAS 32, para. 48.
161 IAS 32, paras. 49(a) and AG39.
162 IAS 32, para. 49(b)-(e).
163 IAS 32, paras. 50 and AG39.
164 IAS 32, para. 50.
165 IAS 32, para. 96 and IAS 39, para. 103.
166 IAS 39, para. 104.
167 IAS 39, para. 106.
168 IAS 39, para. 107.
169 IFRS 1, *First-time Adoption of International Financial Reporting Standards*, IASB, June 2003 (amended March 2004), para. 36A.
170 IFRS 1, paras. 27 and IG53.
171 IFRS 1, paras. 27 and IG53.
172 IFRS 1, para. 27A.
173 IFRS 1, para. IG53.

Chapter 19 Financial instruments: Financial liabilities and equity

1 INTRODUCTION

1.1 Background

The accounting treatment of liabilities (such as loans or bonds) and equity instruments (such as shares, stock or warrants) by their issuer was not historically regarded as presenting significant problems. Essentially the accounting was dictated by the legal form of the instrument, since the traditional distinction between equity and liabilities is clear. The issue of equity creates an ownership interest in a company, remunerated by dividends, which are accounted for as a distribution of retained profit, not a charge made in arriving at the result for a particular period. Liabilities, such as loan finance, on the other hand, are remunerated by interest, which is charged in the income statement as an expense. In general, lenders rank before shareholders in priority of claims over the assets of the company, although in practice there may also be differential rights between different categories of lenders and classes of shareholders. The two forms of finance often have different tax implications, both for the investor and the investee.

In economic terms, however, the distinction between share and loan capital can be far less clear-cut than the legal categorisation would suggest. For example, a redeemable preference share could be considered to be, in substance, much more like a liability than equity. Conversely, many would argue that a bond which can never be repaid but which will be mandatorily converted into ordinary shares deserves to be thought of as being more in the nature of equity than of debt, even before conversion has occurred.

The ambiguous economic nature of such instruments, has, particularly since 1980 or so, encouraged the development of a number of complex forms of finance which exhibit characteristics of both equity and debt. The 'holy grail' is generally to devise an instrument regarded as a liability by the tax authorities (such that the costs of servicing it are tax-deductible) but treated as equity for accounting and/or regulatory purposes (so that the instrument is not considered as a component of net borrowings).

The accounting profession has not always found it easy to decide how to balance competing considerations of substance and form in accounting for these instruments, especially since the fundamental distinction between debt and equity is rooted in form to begin with.

In general, the approach both of national standards setters and of the IASB has tended towards a presumption that an instrument is a liability until proven otherwise. This stance was doubtless coloured in part by the memory of various corporate bonds issued in the 1980s which were accounted for as quasi-equity by their issuers on the basis that repayment could occur only in very remote circumstances. In reality, however, those 'very remote' circumstances (typically a fall or a lower than expected rise in the issuer's share price) did in fact occur, with the result that the entities concerned had to make significant payments to discharge liabilities that, according to their previously published financial statements, did not exist.

The accounting classification of an instrument as a liability or equity is much more than a matter of allocation – i.e. where particular amounts are shown in the financial statements. The increasing requirement of IFRS for certain liabilities, in particular derivatives, to be carried at fair value means that the classification of an item as a liability can introduce significant volatility into reported results that would not arise if the item were classified as an equity instrument (it being a fundamental principle of the IASB's *Framework* that changes in the fair value of equity are not reflected in financial statements – see Chapter 2)

1.2 Development of IFRS on classification of liabilities and equity

Under IFRS, the classification of items as liabilities or equity is dealt with mainly in IAS 32 – *Financial Instruments: Presentation* – with some cross-reference to IAS 39 – *Financial Instruments: Recognition and Measurement*.

IAS 32 was originally issued in March 1995 and subsequently amended in 1998 and 2000 as the result of the issue of, and subsequent changes to, IAS 39. However, in December 2003, the previous version of IAS 32 was withdrawn and superseded by a new version, which has itself been amended by new standards and pronouncements issued since December 2003, most notably IFRS 7 – *Financial Instruments: Disclosures* (see Chapter 22).

The main text of IAS 32 is supplemented by application guidance (which is an integral part of the standard)[1] and by illustrative examples (which accompany, but are not part of, the standard).[2]

The IFRIC has issued an interpretation of IAS 32, IFRIC 2 – *Members' Shares in Co-operative Entities and Similar Instruments* (see 3.2.2 B below), applicable to financial statements for periods beginning on or after 1 January 2005.

1.3 Possible future developments

In February 2006, the IASB and the FASB issued a joint Memorandum of Understanding – *A Roadmap for Convergence between IFRSs and US GAAP – 2006-2008.* This indicated the intention of the two boards to have issued, by 2008, one or more process documents relating to the accounting for financial instruments. In July 2006, the IASB issued a project update on its work on financial instruments. This indicated as the main objectives of the project:

- to require all financial instruments to be measured at fair value with immediate recognition of all gains and losses;
- to simplify or eliminate the need for special hedge accounting; and
- to develop a new standard on derecognition.

However, this update also noted that the FASB had an active project on the classification of items as debt or equity, and indicated that the IASB would participate in the later stages of that project.

In June 2006 the IASB published an exposure draft proposing limited amendments of the definition of 'equity' intended to address concerns raised by certain types of entity that have no equity as currently defined by IAS 32 (see 3.2.2 A below).

In addition, since late 2006, the IASB has begun to discuss other issues arising from the application of the rules in IAS 32 for classifying issued capital instruments as financial liabilities and equity. Whilst no decisions have yet been taken by the IASB, it is of interest that the IASB staff have highlighted the following broad categories of implementation issue arising from IAS 32:

- *Issues arising from specific rules in the standard*

  The specific provisions in IAS 32 were written with particular types of capital instrument in mind. Where these rules are applied to instruments that differ from those for which they were written, the result may be a classification of an item as debt or equity that does not faithfully represent the underlying instrument.

- *Counter-intuitive results*

  The classification of an instrument under IAS 32 can produce results that conflict with the generally-held perception of how the instrument should be faithfully represented. An example is the treatment of certain puttable instruments, which was the subject of the June 2006 exposure draft referred to at 1.2 above.

- *Conflicts with the conceptual framework*

  Some provisions of IAS 32 conflict with the IASB's own conceptual framework. For example, IAS 32 requires some contracts over the entity's own equity which are to be executed at a future date to be accounted for as if they had been executed on inception of the contract (in contrast to the required treatment under IFRS of nearly all other executory contracts, such as purchase orders and contracts of employment).

The IASB staff note that the first of these issues could potentially be resolved by a more principles-based revision to the drafting of IAS 32, whilst the other two issues raise more fundamental questions about the whole approach of the standard.[3]

In April 2007, the IASB reported that the FASB expects to publish a preliminary views document later this year, and that the IASB expects to publish a discussion paper based on the FASB document at around the same time.

Independently of the IASB and the FASB, task forces from the European Financial Reporting Advisory Group's PAAinE (Proactive Accounting Activities in Europe) initiative and the German Accounting Standards Board have identified a number of problems with the current approach of IAS 32, many of which are the same as those identified by the IASB staff above. The task forces are developing a model for distinguishing between liabilities and equity, based on the degree to which various holders of financial instruments issued by an entity are required to absorb losses made by the entity.[4]

2 OBJECTIVE, SCOPE AND DEFINITIONS

2.1 Objective

The objective of IAS 32 is 'to establish principles for presenting financial instruments as liabilities or equity and for offsetting financial assets and financial liabilities.' The standard addresses:[5]

- the classification of financial instruments, from the perspective of the issuer, into financial assets, financial liabilities and equity instruments (see 3 and 4 below);
- the classification of related interest, dividends, losses and gains (see 5 below); and
- the circumstances in which financial assets and financial liabilities should be offset (see Chapter 18 at 6).

IAS 32 also contains guidance on accounting for:

- treasury shares – i.e. an entity's own equity instruments held by the entity (see 6 below); and
- forward contracts or options for the receipt or delivery of the entity's own equity instruments (see 7 below).

2.2 Scope

The scope of IAS 32 is discussed in detail in Chapter 17 at 3.

2.3 Definitions

The following definitions in IAS 32 are relevant to the issues discussed in this Chapter. Further general discussion on the meaning and implications of the definitions may be found in Chapter 17 at 2.

A *financial instrument* is any contract that gives rise to a financial asset of one entity and a financial liability or equity instrument of another entity.[6]

A *financial asset* is any asset that is:

(a) cash;

(b) an equity instrument of another entity;

(c) a contractual right:

  (i) to receive cash or another financial asset from another entity; or

  (ii) to exchange financial assets or financial liabilities with another entity under conditions that are potentially favourable to the entity; or

(d) a contract that will or may be settled in the entity's own equity instruments and is:

  (i) a non-derivative for which the entity is or may be obliged to receive a variable number of the entity's own equity instruments; or

  (ii) a derivative that will or may be settled other than by the exchange of a fixed amount of cash or another financial asset for a fixed number of the entity's own equity instruments. For this purpose the entity's own equity instruments do not include instruments that are themselves contracts for the future receipt or delivery of the entity's own equity instruments.[7]

A *financial liability* is any liability that is:

(a) a contractual obligation:

  (i) to deliver cash or another financial asset to another entity; or

  (ii) to exchange financial assets or financial liabilities with another entity under conditions that are potentially unfavourable to the entity; or

(b) a contract that will or may be settled in the entity's own equity instruments and is:

  (i) a non-derivative for which the entity is or may be obliged to deliver a variable number of the entity's own equity instruments; or

  (ii) a derivative that will or may be settled other than by the exchange of a fixed amount of cash or another financial asset for a fixed number of the entity's own equity instruments. For this purpose the entity's own equity instruments do not include instruments that are themselves contracts for the future receipt or delivery of the entity's own equity instruments.[8]

An *equity instrument* is any contract that evidences a residual interest in the assets of an entity after deducting all of its liabilities.[9]

A *derivative* is a financial instrument or other contract within the scope of IAS 39 (see Chapter 17 at 3) with all three of the following characteristics:

- its value changes in response to the change in a specified interest rate, financial instrument price, commodity price, foreign exchange rate, index of prices or rates, credit rating or credit index, or other variable (sometimes called the 'underlying');

- it requires no initial net investment or an initial net investment that is smaller than would be required for other types of contracts that would be expected to have a similar response to changes in market factors; and
- it is settled at a future date.[10]

Fair value is the amount for which an asset could be exchanged, or a liability settled, between knowledgeable, willing parties in an arm's length transaction.[11]

In these definitions (and throughout IAS 32 and the discussion in this Chapter):

- *Contract* and *contractual* refer to an agreement between two or more parties that has clear economic consequences that the parties have little, if any, discretion to avoid, usually because the agreement is enforceable by law. Contracts, and thus financial instruments, may take a variety of forms and need not be in writing;[12]
- *Entity* includes individuals, partnerships, incorporated bodies, trusts and government agencies.[13]

3 LIABILITIES AND EQUITY

The most important issue dealt with by IAS 32 is the classification of financial instruments (or their components) by their issuer as financial liabilities, financial assets or equity instruments (including minority interests). The extent to which an entity funds its operations through debt or equity is regarded as highly significant not only by investors, but also by other users of financial statements such as regulators (particularly in the financial services industry) and tax authorities. This means that the question of whether a particular instrument is a liability or equity raises issues of much greater and wider sensitivity than the mere matter of financial statement classification.

Moreover, the increasing requirement of IFRS for certain liabilities, in particular derivatives, to be carried at fair value means that the classification of an item as a liability can introduce significant (and, from the perspective of many preparers, undesirable) volatility into reported results that would not arise if the item were classified as an equity instrument. As a consequence of this, the whole area remains a live battleground between the IASB (and national standard setters) and those seeking ever more ingenious loopholes in the rules.

3.1 General provisions of IAS 32

The rule in IAS 32 for classification of items as financial liabilities or equity is essentially simple. An issuer of a financial instrument must classify the instrument (or its component parts) on initial recognition as a financial liability, a financial asset or an equity instrument in accordance with the substance of the contractual arrangement and the definitions of a financial liability, a financial asset and an equity instrument (see 2.3 above).[14] The application of this principle in practice, however, is often far from straightforward.

Application of the basic definitions in IAS 32 means that an instrument is an equity instrument if and only if both the following conditions are met:

- The instrument includes no contractual obligation either:
  - to deliver cash or another financial asset to another entity; or
  - to exchange financial assets or financial liabilities with another entity under conditions that are potentially unfavourable to the issuer.
- If the instrument will or may be settled in the issuer's own equity instruments, it is either:
  - a non-derivative that includes no contractual obligation for the issuer to deliver a variable number of its own equity instruments; or
  - a derivative that will be settled only by the issuer exchanging a fixed amount of cash or another financial asset for a fixed number of its own equity instruments. For this purpose the issuer's own equity instruments do not include instruments that are themselves contracts for the future receipt or delivery of the issuer's own equity instruments.[15]

IAS 32 emphasises that a contractual obligation, including one arising from a derivative financial instrument, that will or may result in the future receipt or delivery of the issuer's own equity instruments, but does not meet the conditions above, is not an equity instrument.[16] This is discussed further at 3.3 below.

As will become apparent from the following discussion, the emphasis of IAS 32 is on the contractual rights and obligations arising from the terms of an instrument, rather than on the probability of those rights and obligations leading to an outflow of cash or other resources from the entity. Thus IAS 32 may well:

- classify as equity: an instrument that is virtually certain to result in regular cash payments by the entity, but
- treat as a liability: an instrument which
  - gives its holder a right to receive cash rather than equity which no rational holder would exercise, or
  - exposes the issuer to a liability to repay the instrument contingent on an external event so remote that no liability would be recognised if IAS 37 – *Provisions, Contingent Liabilities and Contingent Assets* – were the applicable standard.

3.1.1 Examples of equity instruments

Under the criteria above, equity instruments under IAS 32 will include non-puttable ordinary shares and some types of preference share (see 3.2 below).[17]

They also include warrants or written call options that allow the holder to subscribe for or purchase a *fixed* number of non-puttable ordinary shares in the issuing entity in exchange for a *fixed* amount of cash or another financial asset, or the *fixed* stated principal of a bond.[18] The meaning of a 'fixed amount of cash' is not as self-evident as it might appear and is discussed further at 3.3.1 below. The meaning of the 'fixed stated principal' of a bond is discussed further at 4.4.2 A below.

Conversely, an instrument would be a financial liability (or financial asset) of the issuer if it gave the holder the right to obtain:

- a *variable* number of non-puttable ordinary shares in the issuing entity in exchange for a *fixed* amount of cash or another financial asset;[19] or
- a *fixed* number of non-puttable ordinary shares in the issuing entity in exchange for a *variable* amount of cash or another financial asset.[20]

It will become apparent from the discussion later in this chapter that the effect of this is to create a rule for the definition of equity which sometimes results in instruments that expose their holders substantially to equity risk nevertheless being classified as liabilities.

An obligation for the entity to issue or purchase a fixed number of its own equity instruments in exchange for a fixed amount of cash or another financial asset is an equity instrument of the entity. However, if such a contract contains an obligation – or even a potential obligation – for the entity to pay cash or another financial asset, it gives rise to a liability for the present value of the redemption amount (which results in a reduction of equity, not an expense – see 3.3.3 below).[21] This refers only to contracts which may require the entity to gross-settle (i.e. the entity pays cash in exchange for its own shares). Contracts which can be net settled (i.e. the party for whom the contract is loss-making delivers cash or shares equal to the fair value of the contract to the other party) are generally treated as financial assets or financial liabilities. This is discussed in more detail at 7 below.

Whilst non-puttable shares are typically equity, an issuer of non-puttable ordinary shares nevertheless assumes a liability when it formally acts to make a distribution and becomes legally obliged to the shareholders to do so. This may be the case following the declaration of a dividend, or when, on a winding up, any assets remaining after discharging the entity's liabilities become distributable to shareholders.[22]

A purchased call option or other similar contract acquired by an entity that gives it the right to reacquire a fixed number of its own equity instruments in exchange for delivering a fixed amount of cash or another financial asset is not a financial asset of the entity. Moreover, any consideration paid for such a contract is deducted from equity[23] (see 7.2.1 below).

As the discussion above illustrates, in order for an instrument to be classified as an equity instrument under IAS 32, it is not sufficient that it involves the reporting entity delivering or receiving its own equity (as opposed to cash or another financial asset). The number of equity instruments delivered, and the consideration for them, must be fixed (see 3.3 below). The IASB considered that to treat any transaction settled in the entity's own shares as an equity instrument would not deal adequately with transactions in which an entity is using its own shares as 'currency' – for example, where it has an obligation to pay a fixed or determinable amount that is settled in a variable number of its own shares.[24] In such transactions the counterparty bears no share price risk, and is therefore not in the same position as a 'true' equity shareholder.

3.1.2 Comparison with IFRS 2 – Share-based Payment

The approach in IAS 32 differs from that in IFRS 2 – *Share-based Payment*. IFRS 2 essentially treats any transaction that falls within its scope and can be settled only in shares (or other equity instruments) as an equity instrument, regardless of whether the number of shares to be delivered is fixed or variable (see Chapter 31 at 2.3). There are also significant differences between the treatment of financial instruments that can be settled in either equity instruments or cash (or other financial assets) under IAS 32 (see 3.5 below) and that under IFRS 2 (see Chapter 31 at 7.2.1).

The IASB offers some (pragmatic rather than conceptual) explanation for these differences in the Basis for Conclusions to IFRS 2. First, it is argued that to apply IAS 32 to share option plans would mean that a variable share option plan (i.e. one where the number of shares varied according to performance) would give rise to more volatile (and typically greater) cost than a fixed plan (i.e. one where the number of shares to be awarded is fixed from the start), even if the same number of shares was ultimately delivered under each plan, which would have 'undesirable consequences'.[25] This serves only to beg the question of why it is not equally 'undesirable' for the same result to arise in accounting for share-settled contracts within the scope of IAS 32 rather than IFRS 2. Second, it is argued that this is just one of several inconsistencies between IFRS 2 and IAS 32 which will be addressed in the round as part of the IASB's review of accounting for debt and equity.[26]

3.2 Contractual obligation to deliver cash or other financial assets

It is apparent from the discussion in 3.1 above that a critical feature in differentiating a financial liability from an equity instrument is the existence of a contractual obligation of one party to the financial instrument (the issuer) either:

- to deliver cash or another financial asset to the other party (the holder); or
- to exchange financial assets or financial liabilities with the holder under conditions that are potentially unfavourable to the issuer.[27]

The holder of an equity instrument (e.g. a non-puttable share) is entitled to receive a pro rata share of such dividends or other distributions of equity as are made. However, since the issuer does not have a contractual obligation to make such distributions (because it cannot be required to deliver cash or another financial asset to another party), the instrument is not a financial liability of the issuer.[28]

In some entities, whether as a matter of the entity's own constitution or of general legislation in the jurisdiction concerned, the right to declare dividends and/or redeem capital is reserved for the members of the entity in general meeting. The effect of such a right may be that the members can require payment of a dividend irrespective of the wishes of management. Even where management has the right to prevent payment of such a dividend, the members will generally have the right to appoint the management, and can therefore replace a management that wishes to prevent payment of a dividend declared by members.

This could lead to the conclusion that, for example, such an entity should classify all its distributable retained earnings as a liability, on the grounds that the members could require the earnings to be distributed at any time. In our view this is not appropriate, since, where a right of an entity is reserved to the entity's shareholders in general meeting, the exercise of such a right is effectively an action of the entity itself. It is therefore at the discretion of the entity itself (as represented by the members in general meeting) that distributable retained earnings are paid out as a dividend. Accordingly, in our view, such earnings are classified as equity, not as a financial liability, until they become a legal liability of the entity.

IAS 32 requires the issuer of a financial instrument to classify a financial instrument by reference to its substance rather than its legal form, although it is conceded that substance and form are 'commonly', but not always, the same. Typical examples of instruments that are equity in legal form but liabilities in substance are certain types of preference share (see 3.2.1 below) and units in open-ended funds, unit trusts and similar entities (see 3.2.2 below).[29] Conversely, a number of entities have issued instruments which behave in all practical respects as perpetual (or even redeemable) debt, but which IAS 32 requires to be classified as equity – see 3.2.1 below.

IAS 32 further clarifies that a financial instrument is an equity instrument, and not a financial liability, not merely if the issuer has no legal obligation to deliver cash or other financial assets to the holder at the reporting date, but only if it essentially has an unconditional right to avoid doing so in all future circumstances other than an unforeseen liquidation. Thus, a financial instrument is classified as a financial liability even if:

- the issuer's ability to discharge its obligations under the instrument is restricted (e.g. by a lack of funds, the need to obtain regulatory approval to make payments on the instrument, or a shortfall of distributable profits, or other statutory restriction);[30] or
- the holder has to perform some action (e.g. formally exercise a redemption right) in order for the issuer to become obliged to transfer cash or other financial assets.[31]

Moreover, a financial instrument that does not explicitly establish a contractual obligation to deliver cash or another financial asset may nevertheless establish an obligation indirectly through its terms and conditions,[32] as illustrated by Example 19.1.

Example 19.1: Financial instrument with non-financial obligation that must be settled if, and only if, the entity fails to redeem the instrument

The reporting entity borrows €1 million from its bank for five years on terms that, at the end of five years, the entity must deliver its head office building to the bank but may instead repay the loan at €1 million plus rolled-up interest at market rates.

IAS 32 states a that financial instrument, such as that in Example 19.1 above, containing a non-financial obligation that can be avoided only by making a transfer of cash or another financial asset is a financial liability.[33]

Whilst this position seems entirely sensible, it is not entirely consistent with the definition of 'financial liability' at 2.3 above, which refers merely to an obligation to deliver cash or another financial asset or to exchange financial instruments on potentially unfavourable terms – there is no reference to an obligation that can be avoided only by a transfer of other non-financial assets.

The application guidance asserts that 'the definition of a financial instrument also encompasses a contract that gives rise to a non-financial asset or non-financial liability in addition to a financial asset or financial liability.'[34] The context of this comment is a discussion of a bond where the holder has the option of requiring settlement in a fixed amount of cash or a fixed quantity of oil. Whilst it is true that an instrument that allows the *holder* to choose settlement in cash or a non-financial asset is a financial liability, as defined in 2.3 above, of the issuer (since the issuer can always be compelled to pay cash), it is, in our view, not the case where the option to choose settlement in cash or a non-financial asset rests with the *issuer*. The definition of financial liability refers to a 'contractual obligation' to deliver *cash or other financial assets*. In Example 19.1 above the issuer clearly has no contractual obligation to pay cash, however economically irrational it might be not to do so. Nevertheless, it is clear that IAS 32 – with good reason – requires this transaction to be classified as a liability.

In our view, it would have been preferable if the IASB had dealt with this significant point in the definition of 'financial liability' rather than as something of an afterthought in the subsequent guidance. In effect, the conclusion of Example 19.1 relies on the concept of economic compulsion (i.e. the idea that no entity would rationally surrender a core asset probably worth more than €1 million rather than pay €1 million cash). However, at first sight, this is inconsistent with IAS 32's treatment of preference shares and certain similar types of capital instrument, payments on which are contractually discretionary but economically compulsory. The classification of such instruments as a liability or equity rests on a strict analysis of whether a contractual obligation exists – see 3.2.1 below.

A financial instrument is also a financial liability if it provides that on settlement the entity will deliver either:

(a) cash or another financial asset; or

(b) a number of its own shares whose value is determined to exceed substantially the value of the cash or other financial asset.

IAS 32 explains that, although the entity does not have an explicit contractual obligation to deliver cash or another financial asset, the value of the share settlement alternative is such that the entity will settle in cash. In any event, the holder has in substance been guaranteed receipt of an amount that is at least equal to the cash settlement option.[35]

IAS 32's reasoning seems slightly confused here, since any instrument that involves delivery of an amount of equity of a given value is so clearly a financial liability (see 2.3 above) that no further clarification should be necessary. Perhaps the IASB meant to refer in (b) above to a *fixed* number of the entity's own shares – the point being that an instrument which allows for repayment in a number of shares that is fixed (and therefore *prima facie* not a financial liability according to the definition), but so large as to be punitive (therefore effectively forcing the entity to choose to repay in cash) is a financial liability. However, if this was the IASB's intention, it sits rather uneasily with the reference to a 'guaranteed' amount at least equal to the cash settlement option. The right to receive a fixed number of shares, however large, can never 'guarantee' delivery of a minimum value (since the share price could collapse so much that the fixed number of shares is in fact worth less than the cash alternative).

3.2.1 Preference shares and similar instruments

Whilst some of the discussion below (and the guidance in IAS 32) is, for convenience, framed in terms of 'preference shares', it should be applied equally to any financial instrument, however described, with similar characteristics. In practice, many such instruments are not described as shares (possibly to avoid weakening any argument that, for fiscal purposes, they are tax-deductible debt rather than non-deductible equity).

Preference shares may be issued with various rights. In determining whether a preference share is a financial liability or an equity instrument, IAS 32 requires an issuer to assess the particular rights attaching to the share to determine whether it exhibits the fundamental characteristic of a financial liability.[36]

IAS 32 does this by drawing a distinction between:

- instruments mandatorily redeemable or redeemable at the holder's option (see A below);
- other instruments – i.e. those redeemable at the issuer's option or not redeemable (see B to D below).

A Instruments redeemable mandatorily or at the holder's option

A preference share (or other instrument) that:

- provides for mandatory redemption by the issuer for a fixed or determinable amount at a fixed or determinable future date; or
- gives the holder the right to require the issuer to redeem the instrument at or after a particular date for a fixed or determinable amount,

contains a financial liability, since the issuer has an obligation, or potential obligation, to transfer cash or other financial assets to the holder. This obligation is not negated by the potential inability of an issuer to redeem a preference share when contractually required to do so, whether because of a lack of funds, a statutory restriction or insufficient profits or reserves.[37]

It is more correct to say (in the words of the application guidance) that an instrument 'contains' a financial liability, rather than that (as the main body of the standard) it 'is' a financial liability. For example, if a redeemable preference share is issued on terms that any dividends paid on the share are entirely at the issuer's discretion, it is only the amount payable on redemption that is a liability. This would probably lead to a 'split accounting' treatment (see 4 below), whereby the share would, at issue, be classified as a liability to the extent of the net present value of the amount payable on redemption and as equity as to the balance of the issue proceeds.[38]

B Instruments redeemable at the issuer's option or not redeemable

A preference share (or other instrument) redeemable in cash at the option of the issuer does not satisfy the definition of a financial liability in IAS 32, because the issuer does not have a present obligation to transfer financial assets to the shareholders. In this case, redemption of the shares is solely at the discretion of the issuer. An obligation may arise, however, when the issuer of the shares exercises its option, usually by formally notifying the shareholders of an intention to redeem the shares.[39]

Likewise, where preference shares are non-redeemable, there is clearly no financial liability in respect of the 'principal' amount of the shares. In reality there may be little distinction between shares redeemable at the issuer's option and non-redeemable shares, given that in many jurisdictions an entity can 'repurchase' its 'irredeemable' shares subject to no greater restrictions than would apply to a 'redemption' of 'redeemable' shares.

Ultimately, the classification of preference shares redeemable only at the holder's option or not redeemable according to their terms must be determined by the other rights that attach to them. IAS 32 requires the classification to be based on an assessment of the substance of the contractual arrangements and the definitions of a financial liability and an equity instrument.[40] If the share establishes a contractual right to a dividend, subject only to restrictions on payment of dividends in the relevant jurisdiction, it contains a financial liability in respect of the dividends. This would lead to a 'split accounting' treatment (see 4 below), whereby the net present value of the right to receive dividends would be shown as a liability and the balance of the issue proceeds as equity. In such a case, it is quite likely that the issue proceeds would be equivalent to the fair value (at the date of issue) of dividends payable in perpetuity, such that the entire proceeds would be classified as a financial liability.

However, when distributions to holders of the preference shares, whether cumulative or non-cumulative, are at the discretion of the issuer, the shares are equity instruments. The classification of a preference share as an equity instrument or a financial liability is not affected by, for example:

- a history of making distributions;
- an intention to make distributions in the future;
- a possible negative impact on the price of ordinary shares of the issuer if distributions are not made (because of restrictions on paying dividends on the ordinary shares if dividends are not paid on the preference shares – see C below);
- the amount of the issuer's reserves;
- an issuer's expectation of a profit or loss for a period; or
- an ability or inability of the issuer to influence the amount of its profit or loss for the period.[41]

The treatment of non-redeemable preference shares, or other instruments with preferred rights, under IAS 32 is a particularly difficult issue, since such shares often inhabit the border territory between financial liabilities and equity instruments. However, the starting point is that a non-redeemable preference share whose dividend rights are simply that a dividend (whether of a fixed, capped or discretionary amount) will be paid at the issuing entity's sole discretion is equivalent to an ordinary equity share, and therefore appropriately characterised as equity.

C *Instruments with a 'dividend blocker' clause*

A number of entities have issued non-redeemable instruments (or instruments redeemable only at the issuer's option) with the following broad terms:

- a discretionary annual coupon or dividend will be paid up to a capped maximum amount; and
- unless a full discretionary coupon or dividend is paid to holders of the instrument, no dividend can be paid to ordinary shareholders.

This restriction on dividend payments to ordinary shareholders is colloquially referred to as a 'dividend blocker' clause. The economic reality is that many entities that issue such instruments are able to do so at a cost not significantly higher than that of callable perpetual debt. This indicates that the financial markets regard 'dividend blocker' clauses as providing investors with reasonable security of receiving their 'discretionary' coupon or dividend, given the adverse economic consequences for the entity of not paying it (if sufficiently solvent to do so), namely:

- the disaffection of ordinary shareholders who could not receive any dividends; and
- the fact that the entity would find it very difficult to raise any similar finance again.

These factors could admit an argument that such instruments are equivalent to perpetual debt (see 3.2.3 below) in all respects, except that the holder has no right to sue for non-payment of the discretionary dividend. However, the analysis in IAS 32 is based on the implicit counter-argument that the position of a holder of an instrument, all payments on which are discretionary, is equivalent to that of an ordinary shareholder. Ordinary shares do not cease to be equity instruments simply because an entity that failed to pay dividends to its ordinary shareholders when manifestly able to do so would be subject to adverse economic pressures from those shareholders, and might find it very difficult to raise additional share capital.

Aviva has issued instruments with 'dividend blocker' clauses that are accounted for as equity instruments.

Extract 19.1: Aviva plc (2006)

Notes to the consolidated financial statements [extract]

31 Direct capital instrument [extract]

Notional amount	2006 £m	2005 £m
5.9021% £500 million direct capital instrument	**500**	500
4.7291% €700 million direct capital instrument	**490**	490
	990	990

The euro and sterling direct capital instruments (the DCIs) were issued on 25 November 2004. They have no fixed redemption date but the Company may, at its sole option, redeem all (but not part) of the DCIs at their principal amount on 28 November 2014 and 27 July 2020 for the euro and sterling DCIs respectively, at which dates the interest rates change to variable rates, or on any respective coupon payment date thereafter. In addition, under certain circumstances defined in the terms and conditions of the issue, the Company may at its sole option:

(i) redeem all (but not part) of the DCIs at their principal amount at any time prior to 28 November 2014 and 27 July 2020 for the euro and sterling DCIs respectively;

(ii) substitute at any time all (but not some only) of the DCIs for, or vary the terms of the DCIs so that they become, Qualifying Tier 1 Securities or Qualifying Upper Tier 2 Securities;

(iii) substitute all (but not some only) of the DCIs for fully paid non-cumulative preference shares in the Company. These preference shares could only be redeemed on 28 November 2014 in the case of the euro DCIs and on 27 July 2020 in the case of the sterling DCIs, or in each case on any dividend payment date thereafter. The Company has the right to choose whether or not to pay any dividend on the new shares, and any such dividend payment will be non-cumulative.

The Company has the option to defer coupon payments on the DCIs on any relevant payment date. Deferred coupons shall be satisfied only in the following circumstances, all of which occur at the sole option of the Company:

(i) Redemption; or

(ii) Substitution by, or variation so they become, alternative Qualifying Tier 1 Securities or Qualifying Upper Tier 2 Securities; or

(iii) Substitution by preference shares.

No interest will accrue on any deferred coupon. Deferred coupons will be satisfied by the issue and sale of ordinary shares in the Company at their prevailing market value, to a sum as near as practicable to (and at least equal to) the relevant deferred coupons. In the event of any coupon deferral, the Company will not declare or pay any dividend on its ordinary or preference share capital.

D Perpetual instruments with a 'step-up' clause

Some perpetual instruments are issued on terms that they are not required to be redeemed, but that, if they are not redeemed on or before a given future date, any coupon or dividend paid after that date is increased, usually to a level that would give rise to a cost of finance higher than the entity would normally expect to incur, effectively compelling the issuer to redeem the instrument before the increase occurs. A provision for such an increase in the coupon or dividend is colloquially referred to as a 'step-up' clause. A 'step-up' clause is often combined with a 'dividend-blocker' clause (see C above).

Paragraph 22 of the version of IAS 32 in issue before its revision in December 2003 (see 1.2 above) specifically addressed 'step-up' clauses as follows:

> 'A preferred share that does not provide for mandatory redemption or redemption at the option of the holder may have a contractually provided accelerating dividend such that, within the foreseeable future, the dividend yield is scheduled to be so high that the issuer would be economically compelled to redeem the instrument.'[42]

The Basis for Conclusions to the current version of IAS 32 indicates that this example was removed because it was insufficiently clear, but there was no intention to alter the general principle of IAS 32 that an instrument that does not explicitly establish an obligation to deliver cash or other financial assets may establish an obligation indirectly through its terms and conditions (see 3.2 above).[43]

This has led some to suggest that any instrument with a 'step-up' clause is a financial liability. In our view, however, this is to misunderstand the reason for the IASB's decision to delete the old paragraph 22. The 'confusion' caused by the paragraph was that the existence of a step-up clause is in fact irrelevant to the analysis required by IAS 32. If an instrument, whether redeemable or not, contains a contractual obligation to pay a coupon or dividend, it is a liability, irrespective of the 'step-up' clause. However, if the coupon or dividend, both before and after the step-up date, is wholly discretionary, then the instrument is, absent other contractual terms that make it a liability, an equity instrument, again irrespective of the step-up clause (see B and C above).

This analysis was confirmed by the IFRIC in March 2006 in its discussion of the classification of an instrument that included a 'step-up' dividend clause that would increase the dividend at a pre-determined date in the future. The IFRIC agreed that this instrument included no contractual obligation ever to pay the dividends or to call the instrument and that therefore it should be classified as equity under IAS 32.[44]

E Relative subordination

Some have argued that instruments with 'dividend-blocker' or 'step-up' clauses (see C and D above) do not meet the definition of an equity instrument. Those that take this view point out that paragraph 11 of IAS 32 defines an equity instrument as 'any contract that evidences a residual interest in the assets of an entity after deducting all of its liabilities' (see 2.3 above) – whereas many instruments of the type described in C and D above are typically entitled only to a return of the amount originally subscribed on a winding up, rather than to any 'residual interest' in the assets. However, it is equally the case that such an instrument does not meet the definition of a liability either, for all the reasons set out above.

Moreover, as noted at 3.1 above, IAS 32 paragraph 16 indicates that, in applying the definition in paragraph 11, an entity concludes that an instrument is equity if and only if the criteria in paragraph 16 are met. In other words, an instrument is equity if it satisfies the criteria of paragraph 16, whatever construction might be placed on paragraph 11. The argument that such instruments are not equity as defined in paragraph 11 of IAS 32 simply highlights a mildly interesting, but ultimately inconsequential, inconsistency between the drafting of paragraphs 11 and 16 of the standard.

In March 2006, the IFRIC considered various issues relating to the classification of instruments under IAS 32 (see also F and G below), and agreed that IAS 32 was clear that the relative subordination on liquidation of a financial instrument was not relevant to the classification decision under IAS 32, even where the instrument ranks below an instrument classified as a liability.[45] This supports the view that an instrument can be classified as equity even if there are restrictions on participation by its holder in a liquidation or winding up.

However, in June 2006 the IASB issued an exposure draft which, in very specific circumstances, proposes that the relative subordination of an instrument should be taken into account in determining its classification as debt or equity (see 3.2.2 C below).

F Economic compulsion

The discussion in B to E above illustrates that, while IAS 32 requires the issuer of a financial instrument to classify a financial instrument by reference to its substance rather than its legal form, in reality the substance is determined, if not by the legal *form*, then certainly by the precise legal *rights* of the holder of the financial instrument concerned. Ultimately, the key determinant of whether an instrument is financial liability or an equity instrument of the issuer is whether the terms of the instrument give the holder a contractual right to receive cash or other financial assets which can be sued for at law, subject only to restrictions outside the terms of the instrument (e.g. statutory dividend controls).

By contrast, terms of an instrument that effectively force the issuer to transfer cash or other financial assets to the holder although not legally required to do so (often referred to as 'economic compulsion'), are not taken into account.

This emphasis on legal and contractual rights also helps to clarify the apparent inconsistency in the requirement of IAS 32 to take account of 'economic compulsion' in categorising financial instruments such as that in Example 19.1 at 3.2 above but to ignore the 'economic compulsion' to pay a discretionary dividend. The difference is that, in Example 19.1, if the issuer fails to deliver cash, it suffers an adverse consequence (i.e. the obligation to deliver another, probably more valuable, asset) *under the terms of the instrument*. By contrast, if an issuer of a discretionary instrument with a 'dividend blocker' clause (see C above) fails to pay any discretionary coupon or dividend, it suffers an adverse consequence (i.e. damage to its financial reputation) arising from external economic factors rather than from the holder's rights under the terms of the share. This analysis is reinforced by the fact that the matters which IAS 32 specifically requires to be ignored in assessing whether a non-redeemable share is a liability or equity (see B above) are all external economic factors and pressures, and do not arise from any legal rights or obligations inherent in the instrument itself.

In response to a submission for a possible agenda item, in March 2006 the IFRIC discussed the role of contractual and economic obligations in the classification of financial instruments under IAS 32.

The IFRIC agreed that IAS 32 is clear that, in order for an instrument to be classified as a liability, a contractual obligation must be established (either explicitly or indirectly) through the terms and conditions of the instrument. Economic compulsion, by itself, would not result in a financial instrument being classified as a liability.

The IFRIC also noted that IAS 32 restricts the role of 'substance' to consideration of the contractual terms of an instrument, and that anything outside the contractual terms is not considered for the purpose of assessing whether an instrument should be classified as a liability under IAS 32.[46]

This analysis was reinforced by the IASB itself at its meeting in June 2006,[47] following which the IFRIC formally resolved not to pursue the matter further, but agreed to draw the Board's attention to comments raised by constituents and to ask the Board whether anything could be done to achieve even greater clarity on this point.[48]

G 'Linked' instruments

An entity may issue an instrument (the 'base' instrument) that requires a payment to be made if, and only if, a payment is made on another instrument issued by the entity (the 'linked' instrument). An example of such an instrument would be a perpetual instrument with a 'dividend blocker' clause (see C above), on which the issuing entity is required to pay a coupon only if it pays a dividend to ordinary shareholders. Absent other terms requiring the perpetual instrument to be classified as liability, it is classified as equity on the basis that the event that triggers a contractual obligation to make a payment (i.e. payment of an ordinary dividend) is itself not a contractual obligation.

If, however, payments on the linked instrument are contractually mandatory (such that the linked instrument contains a liability), it is obvious that the base instrument must also contain a liability, since, in this case, the event that triggers a contractual obligation to make a payment on the base instrument (i.e. a payment on the linked instrument) is a contractual obligation that the issuing entity cannot avoid. This analysis was confirmed by the IFRIC in March 2006 following discussion of linked instruments with similar terms to these.[49]

This issue had arisen in practice in the context that the linked instrument was often very small and callable by the issuer. This would allow the issuer, with no real difficulty, to redeem the linked instrument at will and thus convert the base instrument from a liability to equity at any time. This had led some to argue that only the linked instrument should be classified as a liability.

H 'Change of control', 'taxation change' and 'regulatory change' clauses

A number of entities have issued instruments with 'dividend blocker' and 'step-up' clauses (see C and D above), which would otherwise have been treated as equity by IAS 32, but have wished to account for them as liabilities, perhaps because they can then be hedged in a way that allows the special hedge accounting of IAS 39 to be applied (see I below). Methods of achieving this have included the use of a *de minimis* linked liability instrument (see E above), or the inclusion of a clause requiring the repayment of the instrument in the event of a change of control. This raises the question of whether a change of control is within the control of the entity (such that the instrument is equity) or not (such that the instrument is debt), which is discussed in more detail at 3.4.3 below.

Another common method for attempting to convert an instrument that would otherwise be classified by IAS 32 as equity into debt is to add a clause requiring repayment of the instrument in the event of a fiscal or regulatory change (that in reality may be a remote possibility) – see 3.4.1 below.

I Hedging of instruments classified as equity

A consequence of the requirement, discussed in B to F above, to treat discretionary instruments with certain debt-like characteristics as equity is that the issuer will not be able to adopt special hedge accounting in respect of any instrument taken out as a hedge of the instrument (e.g. a receive fixed, pay floating interest rate swap taken out to hedge a fixed rate discretionary dividend on non-redeemable shares). This is because IAS 39 does not recognise a hedge of own equity as a valid hedging relationship (see Chapter 21).

Accordingly, if an issuer of an equity instrument bearing a fixed-rate discretionary coupon or dividend enters into an interest rate swap to hedge its cash outflows, the swap will be accounted for under the normal rules for derivatives not forming part of a hedging relationship – i.e. at fair value with all value changes recognised in profit or loss (see Chapter 20). Although, economically speaking, any such gains and losses are offset by equal gains and losses (due to interest rate movements) on the shares, the latter, like all movements in the fair value of own equity, are ignored for financial reporting purposes under IFRS.

3.2.2 Puttable instruments and limited-life entities

A The issue

A 'puttable instrument' is a financial instrument that gives the holder the right to put the instrument back to the issuer for cash or another financial asset.[50]

IAS 32 classifies any puttable instrument as a financial liability. This is so even when the amount of cash or other financial assets is determined on the basis of an index or other item that has the potential to increase or decrease, or when the legal form of the puttable instrument gives the holder a right to a residual interest in the assets of the issuer. The effect of the holder's option to put the instrument back to the issuer for cash or another financial asset is that the puttable instrument meets the definition of a financial liability[51] (see 2.3 above).

This analysis has what some regard as a rather startling effect on the financial statements of entities such as open-ended mutual funds, unit trusts, partnerships and some co-operative entities. Such entities often provide their unitholders or members with a right to redeem their interests in the issuer at any time for cash. Any entity whose holders have this right could have net assets of nil, or even negative net assets, under IAS 32 since what would, in normal usage, be regarded as the 'equity' of (say) a unit trust or a professional partnership (i.e. its assets less external borrowings) is classified as a financial liability under IAS 32.

The IASB believes that the accounting treatment required by IAS 32 is appropriate, but points out that the classification of members' interests in such entities as a financial liability does not preclude:

- the use of captions such as 'net asset value attributable to unitholders' and 'change in net asset value attributable to unitholders' on the face of the financial statements of an entity that has no equity capital (such as some mutual funds and unit trusts); or
- the use of additional disclosure to show that total members' interests comprise items such as reserves that meet the definition of equity and puttable instruments that do not.[52]

The illustrative examples appended to IAS 32 give specimen disclosures to be used in such cases – see Chapter 22 at 4.3.3.

The requirements of IAS 32 were implicitly drafted in the context of entities (such as investment funds) the full fair value of whose assets will typically be reflected in its financial statements. This has the end result that such entities will show net assets of zero.

However, there are entities (such as some co-operative and professional partnerships) whose owners are entitled to have their ownership interests purchased at their share of the fair value of the net assets of the entity, where the fair value of the net assets is not reflected in the financial statements. This is because a significant part of the fair value of such entities may be represented by property accounted for at cost rather than fair value or by internally generated goodwill which cannot be recognised in financial statements under IFRS.

Clearly, if such an entity were to recognise a liability for the right of its owners to be bought out at fair value, it would show net liabilities, which will increase the more the fair value of the entity increases, which is a difficult result to justify other than on rather technical grounds.

A related issue is that of limited-life entities. In some jurisdictions, certain types of entity are required to be wound up after a certain period of time, either automatically, or unless the members resolve otherwise. Some entities may also have a limited life under their own governing charter, or equivalent document. For example:

- a collective investment fund might be required to be liquidated on, say, the tenth anniversary of its foundation; or
- a partnership might be required to be dissolved on the death or retirement of a partner.

Such an entity arguably has no equity under IAS 32, since its limited life imposes an obligation, outside the entity's control, to distribute all its assets. Again, some have questioned whether it is very meaningful to show such an entity as having no equity.

In June 2006, the IASB published an exposure draft of proposed amendments to IAS 32 in order to deal with these issues (see C below).

In the meantime, the IFRIC has published IFRIC 2 which addresses the narrower issue of certain types of puttable instrument (see B below).

B IFRIC 2

The original issue that ultimately led to the issue of IFRIC 2 was the appropriate accounting for the members' contributed capital by a co-operative entity whose members are entitled to ask for the return of their investment. However, the scope of IFRIC 2 is not confined to co-operative entities, and extends to any entity whose members may ask for a return of their capital.[53]

IFRIC 2 states that the contractual right of the holder of a financial instrument (including members' shares in co-operative entities) to request redemption does not, in itself, require that financial instrument to be classified as a financial liability. Rather, the entity must consider all of the terms and conditions of the financial instrument in determining its classification as a financial liability or equity. Those terms and conditions include relevant local laws, regulations and the entity's governing charter in effect at the date of classification, but not expected future amendments to those laws, regulations or charter.[54]

Accordingly, IFRIC 2 provides that an entity should classify as equity any instrument that would be classified as equity if the holder did not have the right to request redemption where either:

- the entity has the unconditional right to refuse redemption; or
- local law, regulation or the entity's governing charter imposes an unconditional prohibition on redemption.[55]

In effect, IFRIC 2 is simply pointing out that the right of A to ask B for something that B can, or must, refuse does not impose an obligation on B – not, with hindsight, a conclusion unattainable without the aid of the IFRIC.

IFRIC 2 distinguishes between those prohibitions on redemption in local law, regulation or the entity's governing charter that are 'unconditional' (i.e. they apply at any time) and those which prohibit redemption only when certain conditions – such as liquidity constraints – are met or, as the case may be, not met. Prohibitions that apply only in certain circumstances are ignored.[56] This is consistent with the fact that under IAS 32 the classification of an instrument as debt or equity is not influenced by considerations of liquidity (see 3.2 above).

In some cases, there may be a partial prohibition on redemption. For example, redemption may be prohibited where its effect would be to reduce the number of members' shares or the amount of paid-in capital below a certain minimum. In such cases, only the amount subject to a prohibition on redemption is treated as equity. If the minimum number of members' shares or amount of paid-in capital changes, an appropriate transfer is made between financial liabilities and equity.[57]

On initial recognition, the entity is required to measure its financial liability for redemption at fair value. In the case of members' shares with a redemption feature, the entity measures the fair value of the financial liability for redemption at no less than the maximum amount payable under the redemption provisions of its governing charter or applicable law discounted from the first date that the amount could be required to be paid.[58] This is consistent with the general provisions of IAS 39 for the measurement of liabilities (see Chapter 20).

In accordance with the general provisions of IAS 32 regarding interest and dividends (see 5 below), distributions to holders of equity instruments are recognised directly in equity, net of any income tax benefits. Interest, dividends and other returns relating to financial instruments classified as financial liabilities are expenses, regardless of whether those amounts paid are legally characterised as dividends, interest or otherwise.[59]

IFRIC 2 clarifies that, where members act as customers of the entity (for example, where it is a bank and members have current or deposit accounts or similar contracts with the bank), such accounts and contracts are financial liabilities of the entity.[60]

C Possible future developments

As noted above, in June 2006, the IASB issued an exposure draft – *Proposed Amendments to IAS 32 and IAS 1 – Financial Instruments Puttable at Fair Value and Obligations Arising on Liquidation*. The principal effect of the proposals would be to require an entity to classify as equity an obligation:

- to deliver a pro-rata share of the net assets of the entity upon its liquidation, provided that all financial instruments (or components of financial instruments) in the most subordinated class of instruments with a claim to the assets of the entity impose such an obligation; or
- to redeem or repurchase a financial instrument puttable at fair value, provided that all financial instruments in the most subordinated class of instruments with a claim to the assets of the entity are financial instruments puttable at fair value.[61]

Whilst we can see the pragmatic case for these specific changes, we do not generally support piecemeal amendments as a means of addressing an issue as fundamental as the classification of items as financial liabilities or equity. It is therefore perhaps unsurprising that a number of respondents have drawn attention to other instruments with terms that might merit a similar exemption from a strict application of IAS 32. The IASB has agreed not to expand the scope of the amendment (in part to avoid the need for re-exposure), but to conduct research into other instruments for which exemption might be made.[62]

Moreover, the proposals, as tends to be the case with amendments to standards which attempt a pragmatic 'quick fix' of a more fundamental problem, could lead to some rather unexpected results. For example, an entity might have one million redeemable units in issue that, but for the redemption right, would be equity under IAS 32. Under the proposals in the exposure draft these units are equity if there is no more subordinated instrument in issue, but debt if the entity issues just one share that is either subordinated to the units or non-puttable. This highlights the essential conceptual difference between IAS 32 in general (which classifies items as debt or equity by reference only to their contractual terms) and these proposals (which also have reference to the relative subordination of the instrument, notwithstanding that this is generally irrelevant – see 3.2.1 C above).

Following requests for guidance from respondents to the exposure draft, in May 2007 the IASB agreed to clarify that:

- a general guarantee provided by the general partner in a limited partnership is considered separate from the partnership interest, and therefore does not affect subordination of partnership interests, when assessing whether an instrument falls into the most subordinated class; and
- a minority interest in the puttable instruments of a subsidiary must always be classified as a financial liability in the consolidated financial statements, even if it is classified as an equity instrument in the financial statements of the issuing subsidiary.[63]

In July 2007 the IASB had indicated that it hoped to issue a final version of this amendment to IAS 32 during the third quarter of 2007.[64] However, at its meeting in September 2007, the IASB redebated the issue further, considering a modified approach to identifying whether puttable financial instruments are the residual interest in an entity (and should therefore be classified as equity under the proposed amendment). The modified approach would assess whether the *class* of puttable instruments is the residual interest in the entity, whereas the approach in the exposure draft assessed whether the *individual* puttable instrument is a residual interest in the entity. Consideration of the class of puttable instruments as a whole would eliminate the need for the criterion in the exposure draft that each puttable instrument should be issued and redeemed at the fair value of the pro-rata share of the net assets of the entity.

The IASB also tentatively decided to make two changes to the criterion in the exposure draft that the puttable financial instrument's right to a pro rata share of the net assets of the entity is neither limited nor guaranteed, to any extent, before or at liquidation. The first change would require the total cash flows over the life of the puttable instruments to be based substantially on the earnings or change in net assets of the entity. The second change would ensure that no other contract represents the residual interest in the entity.

The IASB re-deliberated several other issues, tentatively deciding that:

- the accounting for mandatory dividends will not be addressed in the proposed amendment;
- derivatives on puttable instruments and instruments with an obligation arising on the liquidation of an entity will not be classified as equity in the proposed amendment;
- puttable instruments that are mandatorily redeemable on death or retirement will be within the scope of the proposed amendment; and
- the proposed amendment will have an effective date of 1 January 2009, with early adoption permitted.[65]

However, at its October 2007 meeting, the IASB indicated that in November 2007 there would be round-table discussions on the issue with interested parties, to be based on a staff draft of a revised proposed amendment.

3.2.3 Perpetual debt

'Perpetual debt' instruments are those that provide the holder with the contractual right to receive payments on account of interest at fixed dates extending into the indefinite future, either with no right to receive a return of principal or a right to a return of principal under terms that make it very unlikely or very far in the future. However, this does not mean that 'perpetual debt' is to be classified as equity, since the issue proceeds will typically represent the net present value of the liability for interest payments.

For example, an entity may issue a financial instrument requiring it to make annual payments in perpetuity equal to a stated interest rate of 8% applied to a stated par or principal amount of €1 million. Assuming 8% to be the market rate of interest for the instrument when issued, the issuer assumes a contractual obligation to make a stream of future interest payments having a fair value (present value) of €1 million. Thus perpetual debt gives rise to a financial liability of the issuer.[66]

3.3 Contracts settled by delivery of the entity's own equity instruments

As noted in 3.1 above, a contract is not an equity instrument solely because it may result in the receipt or delivery of the entity's own equity instruments. Where such a contract is not classified as an equity instrument by IAS 32, it will be accounted for in accordance with the general provisions of IAS 39 for derivatives – i.e. it will be measured at fair value with all changes in fair value reflected in profit or loss. In other words, entities will recognise gains and losses based on the movement of their own share price.

Broadly speaking:

- a non-derivative contract involving the issue of a fixed number of own equity instruments is an equity instrument (see 3.3.1 below);
- a non-derivative contract involving the issue of a variable number of own equity instruments is a financial liability (see 3.3.2 below);

- a derivative contract involving the sale or purchase of a fixed number of own equity instruments for a fixed amount of cash or other financial assets is an equity instrument (see 3.3.1 below);
- a derivative contract for the purchase by an entity of its own equity instruments, even if for a fixed amount of cash or other financial assets (and therefore an equity instrument) may give rise to a financial liability in respect of the cash or other financial assets to be paid. However, the initial recognition of the liability results in a reduction in equity and not in an expense (see 3.3.3 below). In other words, whilst there is a liability to pay cash under the contract, the contract itself is an equity instrument (and is therefore not subject to periodic remeasurement to fair value); and
- a derivative contract involving the delivery or receipt of:
  - a fixed number of own equity instruments for a variable amount of cash or other financial assets;
  - a variable number of own equity instruments for a variable amount of cash or other financial assets; or
  - an amount of cash or own equity instruments with a fair value equivalent to the difference between a fixed number of own equity instruments and a fixed amount of cash or other financial assets (i.e. a net-settled derivative contract)

  is a financial asset or financial liability (see 3.3.2 below).

There are also some difficulties of interpretation surrounding the treatment of certain contracts to issue equity (see 3.3.4 below) and the meaning of a 'fixed amount' of cash or other financial assets (see 3.3.1 A below).

In undertaking the analysis required by IAS 32, it is sometimes helpful, where the detailed guidance in the standard is not entirely clear, to consider whether the instrument or contract under discussion exposes the holder or the issuer to the risk of movements in the fair value of the issuer's equity. If the holder is at risk to the same degree as equity investors in the entity, it is likely that the instrument or contract should be classified as equity. If, however, the entity bears the risk of movements in the fair value of the entity's equity, or the holder bears some risk, but less than that borne by equity investors in the entity, it is likely that the contract should be classified, at least in part, as a liability.

3.3.1 Contracts accounted for as equity instruments

As noted above, a contract that will be settled by the entity delivering or receiving a fixed number of its own equity instruments in exchange for a fixed amount of cash (see A below) or another financial asset is an equity instrument, although, as noted in the summary above a liability may be recorded for any cash payable by the entity on settlement of the contract. An example would be an issued share option that gives the counterparty a right to buy a fixed number of the entity's shares for a fixed price or for a fixed stated principal amount of a bond (see 4.4.2 below).[67]

The fair value of such a contract may change due to variations in market interest rates and the share price. However, provided that such changes in fair value do not affect the amount of cash or other financial assets to be paid or received, or the number of equity instruments to be received or delivered, on settlement of the contract, the contract is an equity instrument.[68]

Any consideration received (such as the premium received for a written option or warrant on the entity's own shares) is added directly to equity. Any consideration paid (such as the premium paid for a purchased option) is deducted directly from equity. Changes in the fair value of an equity instrument are not recognised in financial statements.[69] This is consistent with the treatment of equity under the *Framework* (and as defined in IAS 32 – see 2.3 above) as a residual after deducting total liabilities from total assets rather than an item 'in its own right'.

A What is a 'fixed amount' of cash (or other financial assets)?

IAS 32 is not explicit as to how its reference to a 'fixed amount' of cash or other financial assets is to be interpreted when the amount of cash is denominated in a currency different from the reporting entity's functional currency. The problem is illustrated by the example in paragraph 24 of IAS 32 (referred to in 3.3.2 B below) of a contract being a financial asset or financial liability where the reporting entity is required 'to deliver 100 of its own equity instruments in return for an amount of cash calculated to equal the value of 100 ounces of gold'. This seems straightforward enough. If, however, one substitutes '100 US dollars' for '100 ounces of gold', the latent problem becomes apparent.

Suppose a UK entity (with the pound sterling as its functional currency) issues a £100 bond convertible into a fixed number of shares of that UK entity. As discussed in more detail at 4 below, IAS 32 requires this to be accounted for by splitting it into a liability component (the obligation to pay interest and repay principal) and an equity component (the holder's right to convert into equity). In this case the equity component is the right to convert the fixed stated £100 principal of the bond (see 4.4.2 below) into a fixed number of shares.

Suppose instead, however, that the UK entity (with the pound sterling as its functional currency) issues a US dollar bond convertible into a fixed number of shares of that UK entity. The conversion feature effectively gives the bondholder the right to acquire a fixed number of shares for a fixed stated principal (see 4.4.2 below) of $100 – is this a 'fixed amount' of cash, or is it to be regarded as being just as variable, in terms of its conversion into the functional currency of the pound sterling, as 100 ounces of gold?

The answer to this question is highly significant. If the conclusion is that the $100 is a fixed amount of cash, the conversion right is accounted for as an equity component of the bond – in other words a value is assigned to it on initial recognition and it is not subsequently remeasured (see 4.3.1 below). If, on the other hand, the conclusion is that the $100 is not a fixed amount of cash, then the conversion right (as an embedded derivative not regarded by IAS 39 as closely related to the host contract –

see Chapter 17 at 5) is accounted for as a separate derivative financial liability, introducing potentially significant volatility into the financial statements.

There is no obvious answer to this. A contention that the $100 is a fixed amount of cash is hard to reconcile with the fact that a contract to issue shares for 'as many pounds sterling as are worth $100' involves the issue of a fixed number of shares for a variable amount of cash and would therefore not be an equity instrument.

The IFRIC considered this issue at its meeting in April 2005. The IFRIC noted that although this matter is not directly addressed in IAS 32, it is clear that, when the question is considered in conjunction with guidance in other Standards, particularly IAS 39, any obligation denominated in a foreign currency represents a variable amount of cash. This is evidenced by the fact that IAS 39 allows cash flow hedge accounting for transactions denominated in a foreign currency because such transactions expose the entity to variability in cash flows (see Chapter 21 at 3.2). Consequently, the IFRIC concluded that contracts settled by an entity by delivering a fixed number of its own equity instruments in exchange for a fixed amount of foreign currency should be classified as liabilities.[70]

B Instrument issued by foreign subsidiary convertible into equity of parent

However, the conclusion that the $100 is not a fixed amount of cash apparently leads to the rather strange result that the classification of the instrument varies depending on the functional currency of the issuing entity. If, in the example in A above, the UK entity's US subsidiary (with a functional currency of US dollars) were to issue a bond convertible into its own equity, convertible in turn into the UK parent's equity, the conversion right would (from the perspective of the US subsidiary) clearly involve the issue of a fixed number of shares for a fixed amount of cash and thus be an equity instrument. Moreover, this classification would not change on consolidation since IFRS has no concept of a group functional currency (see Chapter 10).

The IFRIC discussed this issue at its meetings in July and November 2006. Specifically, it was asked to consider whether the fixed stated principal of the convertible instrument exchanged for equity of the parent on conversion can be considered 'fixed' if it is denominated in the functional currency of either the issuer of the exchangeable financial instruments (i.e. the US subsidiary in the example above) or the issuer of the equity instruments. (i.e. the UK parent in the example).

The IFRIC noted that a group does not have a functional currency. It therefore discussed whether it should add a project to its agenda to address which currency should be the reference point in determining whether the embedded conversion options are denominated in a foreign currency. The IFRIC believed that the issue was sufficiently narrow that it was not expected to have widespread relevance in practice. The IFRIC, therefore, decided not to take the issue onto its agenda.[71]

We are surprised by the IFRIC's contention that this issue is 'not expected to have widespread relevance'. Whilst the number of such arrangements may be relatively small in absolute terms, they are common, high-value, transactions in large multinational entities. We believe that the IFRIC and/or the IASB should address this issue, as there may otherwise be a divergence of practice in this area with some similar arrangements accounted for as derivative liabilities and others as equity.

In our view, given the absence of specific guidance, an entity may, as a matter of accounting policy, determine the classification, in its consolidated financial statements, of an instrument issued by a subsidiary by reference either to that subsidiary's own functional currency or to the functional currency of the parent into whose equity the bond is convertible.

The effect of this policy choice will be that, where the debt is denominated in a currency other than the designated reference functional currency, the consolidated financial statements contain no equity component (see 4 below for a more general discussion of the requirement to analyse compound financial instruments, such as convertibles, into one or more components). This policy, and its consequences under IAS 32, must be applied consistently, as illustrated by Example 19.2 below.

Example 19.2: Convertible bond issued by a subsidiary with a functional currency different to that of the parent

Suppose, as above, that a UK entity with a functional currency of the pound sterling (GBP) has a US trading subsidiary with a functional currency of the US dollar (USD). The US subsidiary issues a bond convertible, at the holder's option, into equity of the UK parent.

If the parent's functional currency (GBP) is the reference currency, the accounting treatment of the holder's conversion right in the consolidated financial statements will be as follows:

- if the fixed stated principal of the bond is denominated in GBP: equity (stated principal of bond is fixed by reference to GBP); but
- if the fixed stated principal of the bond is denominated in a currency other than GBP: derivative (stated principal of bond is variable by reference to GBP).

If, however, the subsidiary's functional currency (USD) is the reference currency, a converse analysis applies, and the accounting treatment of the holder's conversion right in the consolidated financial statements will be as follows:

- if the fixed stated principal of the bond is denominated in USD: equity (stated principal of bond is fixed by reference to USD); but
- if the fixed stated principal of the bond is denominated in a currency other than USD: derivative (stated principal of bond is variable by reference to USD).

It may be that the IFRIC's reluctance to issue guidance on this matter was influenced by consideration of the more subtle point that, in most cases, the issuing entity will not be, as in Example 19.2 above, a trading subsidiary, but rather a special purpose entity ('SPE') created for the purposes of the bond issue. IAS 21 would suggest that the functional currency of such an SPE is the same as that of the parent for whose equity the bond will be exchanged, irrespective of the currency in which the bond is denominated (see Chapter 10 at 2.5). In short, the IFRIC was perhaps hinting that, in many cases, the real problem may be the misapplication of IAS 21 rather than the interpretation of IAS 32.

C *Number of equity instruments issued adjusted for capital restructuring*

Entities, particularly larger listed companies, routinely restructure their equity capital. This may take many forms, including:

- structural changes in the issuer's ordinary shares (such as a share split, a share consolidation or a reclassification of the outstanding ordinary shares of the issuer);
- a repurchase of shares;
- a distribution of reserves or premiums, by way of extraordinary dividend;
- a payment of a dividend, or extraordinary dividend, in shares; or
- a bonus share or rights issue to existing shareholders.

Accordingly, an entity entering into financial instruments involving the purchase or delivery of its own equity generally wishes to ensure that the number of shares specified in the contract is modified in the event of such a restructuring. For example, an entity with shares with a nominal (par) value of €1 might enter into an agreement that requires it to issue '100 shares'. If, before execution of that agreement, the entity has split each €1 share into ten €0.10 shares, it must issue 1,000, not 100, shares in order to give effect to the intention of the contract.

Such adjustment formulae are most commonly seen in the terms of convertible instruments, so that the number of shares into which the bonds eventually convert will take account of any capital restructuring between issue and conversion of the bond, with the broad intention of putting the holders of the bond in the same position with respect to other equity holders before and after the restructuring.

This raises the question of whether a contract in these terms can be classified as equity under IAS 32, since the number of shares ultimately issued on conversion is not fixed at the outset, but may vary depending on whether a restructuring occurs before conversion.

In our view, an adjustment to the number of equity instruments issued in the event of a capital restructuring should not be considered to result in the issue of a variable number of shares, where its purpose is to ensure that the bondholder's equity interest is not diluted or augmented.

The effect of such an adjustment is that the risks and rewards of the bondholder are more closely aligned to those of a holder of ordinary shares. As discussed at 3.3.2 A below, IAS 32 generally treats contracts involving a variable number of equity instruments as a financial liability because the effect of the variability is that the counterparty is not exposed to any movement in the fair value of the equity instruments between the inception and execution of the contract. In this case, however, the variability is introduced so as to ensure that the counterparty remains exposed to any movement in the fair value of the equity instruments, and maintains the same interest in the equity relative to other shareholders.

3.3.2 Contracts accounted for as financial assets or financial liabilities

A Variable number of equity instruments

An entity may have a contractual right or obligation to receive or deliver a number of its own shares or other equity instruments that varies so that the fair value of the entity's own equity instruments to be received or delivered equals the amount of the contractual right or obligation.

The right or obligation may be for:

- a fixed amount – e.g. as many shares as are worth £100; or
- an amount that fluctuates in part or in full in response to changes in a variable other than the market price of the entity's own equity instruments, such as movements in interest rates, commodity prices, or the price of a financial instrument – e.g. as many shares as are worth:
  - 100 ounces of gold;
  - £100 plus interest at LIBOR plus 200 basis points;
  - 100 government bonds; or
  - 100 shares in a particular entity.

Such a contract is a financial asset or liability. Even though the contract must, or may, be settled through receipt or delivery of the entity's own equity instruments, the number of own equity instruments required to settle the contract will vary. Accordingly, the contract does not evidence a residual interest in the entity's assets after deducting all of its liabilities,[72] and is therefore a financial asset or financial liability.

B Contracts based on the price of the entity's equity instruments

There is some confusion in IAS 32 as to the treatment of contracts settled in a variable number of equity instruments where the number of equity instruments to be delivered varies with the price of the entity's own equity instruments. Paragraph 21 of the standard (summarised above) refers to a contract being a financial asset or liability where the value of shares to be delivered fluctuates in response to changes in a variable '*other than* the market price of the entity's own equity instruments'. This could lead to the inference that a contract where the value of shares to be delivered does fluctuate in response to changes in the market price of the entity's own equity instruments is not a financial asset or liability.

However, paragraph AG27(d) of the application guidance clarifies that a contract settled in a variable number of the entity's own shares is a financial asset or liability 'even if the underlying variable is the entity's own share price'.

C Fixed number of equity instruments for variable consideration

A contract that will be settled by the entity delivering or receiving a fixed number of its own equity instruments in exchange for a variable amount of cash or another financial asset is a financial asset or financial liability. An example is a contract for the entity to deliver 100 of its own equity instruments in return for an amount of cash calculated to equal the value of 100 ounces of gold,[73] or 100 government bonds. As discussed at 3.3.1 A and B above, it would also include a contract for the entity to deliver 100 of its own equity instruments in return for an fixed amount of cash denominated in a currency other than its own functional currency.

D Fixed number of equity instruments with variable value

A contract is a financial asset or financial liability if it is to be settled in a fixed number of shares the value of which will be varied (e.g. by modification of the rights attaching to them) so as to be equal to a fixed amount or an amount based on changes in an underlying variable.[74]

E Fixed amount of cash determined by reference to share price

An entity might enter into an option or forward contract to sell a fixed number of equity shares for a fixed price, where the price is determined by reference to the share price. For example, it might contract to sell 100 shares for £10 each if the share price is between £0 and £10, and for £15 each if the price is higher than £10. Considered as a whole, the contract provides for the exchange of a fixed number of equity instruments for a variable amount of cash, and is therefore a financial liability.

F Net-settled contracts over own equity

The value of a contract over an entity's own equity instruments at the date of settlement is the difference between the fixed number of equity instruments to be delivered by one party and the fixed amount of cash (or other financial assets) to be delivered by the other party. If such a contract allows for net settlement, it can then be settled, by a transfer (of cash, other financial assets, or the entity's own equity) of a fair value equal to this difference. It is inherent in the general definition of an equity instrument in IAS 32 (see 3.1 above) that a contract settled by a single net payment (generally referred to as net cash-settled or net equity-settled as the case may be) is a financial asset or financial liability and not an equity instrument, notwithstanding that an economically equivalent contract settled gross (i.e. by physical delivery of the equity instruments in exchange for cash or other financial assets) would be treated as an equity instrument (see 3.3.3 and 7 below).

3.3.3 Gross-settled contracts for the purchase of the entity's own equity instruments

The discussion that follows relates only to contracts which can be settled by the counterparty delivering equity instruments and the entity paying cash (gross-settled contracts). Contracts which will be settled net (i.e. by payment of the difference between the fair value, at the time of settlement, of the equity instruments and that of the consideration given) are accounted for as financial assets or financial liabilities[75] (see 3.5 and 7 below).

Entering into a gross-settled contract for the purchase of own shares gives rise to a financial liability in respect of the obligation to pay the purchase or redemption price[76] (but resulting, on initial recognition, in a reduction of equity rather than an expense). This treatment is intended to reflect the idea that a forward contract or written option to repurchase an equity share gives rise to a liability similar to that contained within a redeemable share (see 3.2.1 above).[77]

This is the case even if:

- the contract is an equity instrument;
- the contract is a written put option (i.e. a contract that gives the counterparty the right to require the entity to buy its own shares) rather than a forward contract (i.e. a firm commitment by the entity to purchase its own shares); or
- the number of shares subject to the contract is not fixed.[78]

The final bullet point above might refer to a put option written by the entity with a counterparty whereby the counterparty can require the entity to purchase between 1,000 and 5,000 of its own equity shares at €2 per share. In other words, the entity cannot avoid recognising a liability for the contract on the argument that it does not know exactly how many of its own shares it will be compelled to purchase.

When such a liability first arises it must be recognised, in accordance with IAS 39, at its fair value, i.e. the net present value of the redemption amount. Subsequently, the financial liability is measured in accordance with IAS 39 (see Chapter 20).[79] IAS 32 offers no guidance as to how this is to be calculated when, as might be the case with respect to a written put option such as that described in the previous paragraph, the number of shares to be purchased and/or the date of purchase is not known.

In our view, it would be consistent with the requirement of IAS 39 that liabilities with a demand feature such as a demand bank deposit should be measured at the amount payable on demand[80] (see Chapter 20 at 4.5) to adopt a 'worst case' approach. In other words, it should be assumed that the purchase will take place on the earliest possible date for the maximum number of shares. This is also consistent with IAS 32's emphasis, in the general discussion of the differences between liabilities and equity instruments, on a liability arising except to the extent that an entity has an 'unconditional' right to avoid delivering cash or other financial assets (see 3.2 above).

The treatment proposed in the previous paragraph would lead to a different accounting treatment for written 'American' put options (i.e. those that can be exercised at any time during a period ending on a future date) and written 'European' put options (i.e. those that can be exercised only at a given future date). In the case of an American option, a liability would be recorded immediately for the full potential liability. In the case of a European option, a liability would be recorded for the net present value of the full potential liability and interest accrued on that liability until the date of potential exercise. If this interpretation is correct, it has the effect that:

- a gross-settled written American put option that is an equity instrument has no effect on profit or loss (because the full amount payable on settlement would be charged to equity on inception of the contract); but
- a gross-settled European put option that is an equity instrument does affect profit or loss (because the net present value of the amount payable on settlement would be charged to equity on inception of the contract and accrued to the full settlement amount through profit or loss).

If the contract expires without delivery of the shares, the carrying amount of the financial liability is reclassified to equity. This has the rather curious effect that a share purchase contract that expires unexercised (and therefore has no impact on the entity's net assets, other than the receipt or payment of the option premium) can nevertheless give rise to a loss to the extent that interest has been recognised on the liability between initial recognition and its transfer to equity (see Example 19.18 at 7.3.2 below).

A Contracts to purchase own equity during 'close' or 'prohibited' periods

Financial markets often impose restrictions on an entity trading in its own listed securities for a given period (sometimes referred to as a 'close' or 'prohibited' period) in the run-up to the announcement of its financial results for a period. However, an entity may well wish to continue to purchase its own listed equity throughout that period, for example as part of an ongoing share-buyback programme.

One method of achieving this may be to enter into a contract with a counterparty (such as a broker) in advance of the closed period. Such a contract will give rise to a financial liability from the day that it is entered into. As discussed above, this would initially be recorded at the net present value of the amount to be paid with the unwinding of the discount on that liability recorded as a finance charge in profit or loss.

In addition, if the contract is for the purchase of a fixed number of shares for their market price (as opposed to the exchange of a fixed amount of cash for as many shares as are worth that amount), it will be necessary to remeasure the liability to reflect movements in the share price.

B Contracts to acquire minority interests

IAS 27 – *Consolidated and Separate Financial Statements* – requires minority interests to be shown within equity in consolidated financial statements (see Chapter 6 at 6.7). Accordingly, the requirements of IAS 32 relating to contacts over own equity instruments also generally apply, in consolidated financial statements, to forward contracts and put and call options over minority interests.

This analysis was confirmed by the IFRIC in November 2006, when it considered a request to clarify the accounting treatment of contracts to acquire minority interests that are put in place at the time of a business combination. It is arguable that such contracts are more appropriately accounted for under the provisions of IFRS 3 – *Business Combinations* – relating to deferred consideration. It may also be the case that such contracts have the effect that, while there is a minority interest as a matter of law, the relevant subsidiary is nevertheless regarded as wholly-owned by IAS 27, in which case IAS 32 is not relevant. Further discussion of these issues may be found in Chapters 6 and 7.

The IFRIC agreed that there was likely to be divergence in practice in how the related equity is classified, but did not believe that it could reach a consensus on this matter on a timely basis. Accordingly, the IFRIC decided not to add this item to its agenda.

However, the IFRIC noted that the requirements of IAS 32 relating to the purchase of own equity apply to the purchase of a minority interest. After initial recognition any liability to which IFRS 3 is not being applied will be accounted for in accordance with IAS 39. The parent will reclassify the liability to equity if a put expires unexercised.[81]

3.3.4 Gross-settled contracts for the sale or issue of the entity's own equity instruments

The discussion that follows relates only to contracts which must be settled by the counterparty delivering shares and the entity paying cash (gross-settled contracts). Contracts which can be settled net (i.e. by payment of the difference between the fair value, at the time of purchase, of the shares and that of the consideration given) are accounted as financial assets or financial liabilities[82] (see 3.5 and 7 below).

If an entity enters into a gross-settled contract to sell its own shares, the contract is economically the 'mirror image' of a contract for the purchase of own equity. However, there is no provision in IAS 32 that the contract gives rise to a financial asset, as compared to the specific provision that a contract to purchase own equity gives rise to a financial liability (see 3.3.3 above). Consequently, it appears that such contracts give rise to no accounting entries until settlement. This analysis is confirmed by an illustrative example in the appendix to IAS 32 (see Example 19.13 at 7.1.2 below).

Contracts for the sale or issue of own equity arise in situations such as those in Examples 19.3 and 19.4 below.

Example 19.3: Share issue payable in fixed instalments

A government intends to privatise a nationalised industry with a functional currency of euro through an initial public offering (IPO) at €5 per share. In order to encourage widespread share ownership, the terms of the issue are that shares are issued on 1 January 2007, but subscribers to the IPO are required to pay only €3 per share on 1 January 2007 followed by two further instalments of €1 per share on 1 January 2008 and 1 January 2009.

Example 19.4: Right to call for additional equity capital

A start-up technology entity with a functional currency of UK pounds sterling is unsure of its working capital requirements for the first few years of its operations. It therefore enters into an agreement with its major shareholders whereby it can require those shareholders to contribute an additional £2 per share at any time during the next seven years.

One view might be that the situation in Example 19.3 is not a contract for the future issue of equity – the share has already been issued, and so it would be quite appropriate to record a receivable for the deferred subscription payments. The exposure draft *IFRS for Small and Medium-Sized Entities* indicates that a receivable should be recognised only for shares that have been issued, but that such a receivable should be recognised as a deduction from equity, not as an asset.[83] The exposure draft states that this proposal is derived from IAS 32[84] – an assertion difficult to reconcile with the discussion above. Interestingly, an IASB staff draft of the exposure draft (as made available on the IASB's website as at September 2006) admitted, with perhaps unintended candour, that this treatment is 'not in any standard'![85] In our view, current IFRS requires any receivable recognised in respect of an issued share to be shown as an asset.

On the other hand, it is clear from IAS 32 that no receivable would be recognised if the arrangement provided for the entity actually to issue further shares (pro-rata to the shares initially issued) for €1 on 1 January 2008 and 1 January 2009, which is equivalent to the position in Example 19.4. Given that there is no clear economic difference between the transactions, it is strange that the accounting treatment for them varies simply depending on the form, but this appears to be the case.

3.4 Contingent settlement provisions

Some financial instruments (e.g. certain convertible bonds, in respect of the principal amount of the bond) may require the entity to deliver cash or another financial asset, or otherwise to settle it in such a way that it would be a financial liability, in the event of the occurrence or non-occurrence of uncertain future events (or on the outcome of uncertain circumstances) that are beyond the control of both the issuer and the holder of the instrument. These might include:

- a change in a stock market index or a consumer price index;
- changes in interest rates;
- changes in tax law; or
- the issuer's future revenues, net income or debt-to-equity ratio.[86]

IAS 32 provides that, since the issuer of such an instrument does not have the unconditional right to avoid delivering cash or another financial asset (or otherwise to settle it in such a way that it would be a financial liability), the instrument is a financial liability of the issuer unless:

(a) the part of the contingent settlement provision that could require settlement in cash or another financial asset (or otherwise in such a way that it would be a financial liability) is not genuine (see below); or

(b) the issuer can be required to settle the obligation in cash or another financial asset (or otherwise to settle it in such a way that it would be a financial liability) only in the event of liquidation of the issuer.[87]

The application guidance goes on to clarify that a requirement to settle an instrument in cash or another financial asset (or otherwise in such a way that it would be a financial liability) is not genuine (see (a) above) if the requirement would arise 'only on the occurrence of an event that is extremely rare, highly abnormal and very unlikely to occur'.[88]

Similarly, if the terms of an instrument provide for its settlement in a fixed number of the entity's equity instruments, but there are circumstances, beyond the entity's control, in which such settlement may be contractually precluded, and settlement in cash or other assets required instead, those circumstances can be ignored if there is 'no genuine possibility' that they will occur. In other words, the instrument continues to be regarded as an equity instrument and not as a financial liability.[89]

3.4.1 Terms that are 'not genuine'

The Basis for Conclusions of IAS 32 holds out the promise of guidance in the standard as to what is meant by redemption terms that are 'not genuine',[90] which is unfortunately fulfilled only by the thesaurus of synonyms ('extremely rare, highly abnormal and very unlikely to occur') noted above. It may, however, be helpful to consider the changes made by the revised version of IAS 32 to SIC-5 – *Classification of Financial Instruments – Contingent Settlement Provisions*[91] (which is now withdrawn, and its essential substance incorporated in these provisions of IAS 32). SIC-5 previously required redemption terms to be ignored if they were 'remote'. Examples given by SIC-5 were where the issue of shares is contingent merely on formal approval by the authorities, or where cash settlement is triggered by an index reaching an 'extreme' level relative to its level at the time of initial recognition of the instrument.[92]

However, the Basis for Conclusions to IAS 32 makes clear the IASB's belief that it is not appropriate to disregard events that are merely 'remote'. Accordingly, IAS 32 deliberately does not reproduce the reference to, or the examples of, 'remote' events in SIC-5.[93] Thus it is clear that, under the revised version of IAS 32, it is not appropriate to disregard a redemption term that is triggered only when an index reaches an extreme level. This suggests that it is not open to an entity to argue (for example) that a bond that is redeemed in cash only if the entity's share price falls below, or fails to reach, a certain level can be treated as an equity instrument on the grounds that there is no genuine possibility that the share price will perform in that way.

The wording in IAS 32 is presumably intended to deal with clauses inserted into financial instruments for some arcane legal or tax reason (e.g. so as to make conversion 'conditional' rather than mandatory) but having no real economic purpose or consequence.

An example of a clause that has caused some debate on this point is a 'regulatory change' clause, generally found in the terms of capital instruments issued by financial institutions such as banks and insurance companies. Such entities are generally required by local regulators to maintain certain minimum levels of equity or highly subordinated debt (generally referred to as regulatory capital) in order to be allowed to do business.

A 'regulatory change' clause will typically require an instrument which, at the date of issue, is classified as regulatory capital to be repaid in the event that it ceases to be so classified. The practice so far of the regulators in many markets has been to make changes to a regulatory classification with prospective effect only, such that any instruments already in issue continue to be regarded as regulatory capital even though they would not be under the new rules.

This has led some to question whether a 'regulatory change' clause can be regarded as a contingent settlement provision which is 'not genuine'.[94] This is ultimately a matter for the judgement of entities and their auditors in the context of the relevant regulatory environment(s).

3.4.2 Liabilities that arise only on liquidation

As noted above, IAS 32 provides that a contingent settlement provision that comes into play only on liquidation of the issuer may be ignored in determining whether or not a financial instrument is a financial liability. It should be noted that IAS 32 refers specifically to 'liquidation'. In other words, if an instrument provides for redemption on the occurrence of events that are a likely precursor of liquidation (e.g. extreme insolvency, the financial statements not being prepared on a going concern basis, or the entity being placed under the protection of Chapter 11 of the United States Bankruptcy Code) but falling short of formal liquidation, the instrument must be treated as a financial liability.

3.4.3 Liabilities that arise only on a change of control

A number of entities have issued instruments on terms that require the issuing entity to transfer cash or other financial assets only in the event of a change in control of the issuing entity. This raises the question of whether such an event is outside the control of the issuing entity, and is therefore a contingent settlement event arising other than on a liquidation for the purposes of IAS 32 (with the effect than any instrument containing such a provision would be classified as a liability to the extent of any obligations arising on a change of control).

This issue is far from straightforward. As noted at 3.2 above, we take the view that, where the power to take a decision is reserved for the members of an entity in general meeting, for the purposes of such a decision the members and the entity are one and the same. Therefore, we consider that any change of control requiring the approval of the members in general meeting should be regarded as within the control of the entity.

Conversely, in our view, a change of control is not within the control of the entity where it can be effected by one or more individual shareholders without reference to the members in general meeting, for example where a shareholder holding 40% of the ordinary equity sells its shares to another party already owning 30%.

However, we recognise that such a distinction is not as clear-cut as might at first sight appear, and indeed in some situations may give rise to what could be regarded as a purely form-based distinction, as illustrated by Example 19.5 below.

Example 19.5: Change of control

X plc is owned by:

- two wealthy individuals A and B, who own, respectively, 48% and 42% of X's equity, together with
- a number of private individuals with small shareholdings totalling 10% of the equity.

In practical terms, if A and B agree that B will sell his shares to A, thus giving A a 90% controlling stake in the entity, it makes very little difference whether this is achieved by a private sale treaty between A and B or a general meeting of the company (at which A and B would be able to cast 90% of available votes in favour of the transaction).

In a situation such as that in Example 19.5 it would seem strange to say that a sale by private treaty is not within the control of X plc, but a sale agreed in general meeting is, when in either case all that matters is the intentions of A and B.

In our view, this is an area on which it would be useful for the IASB or the IFRIC to issue guidance. It may be that such guidance would need to be based on 'rules' rather than strict principles. For example, any contention that the members in general meeting and the entity are not synonymous would have the effect, in many jurisdictions, that capital and reserves would be reclassified as a liability (on the argument the members could wind the company up at any time), which would clearly be undesirable – see 3.2 above.

3.4.4 Some typical contingent settlement provisions

The matrix below gives a number of contingent settlement provisions that we have encountered in practice – some common, some rather esoteric – together with our view as to whether they should be regarded as outside the control of the reporting entity. If a contingent settlement provision is regarded as outside the control of the issuing entity, the instrument will be classified as a liability by the issuer. If a contingent settlement provision is regarded as within the control of the reporting entity, the instrument will be classified as equity, provided that it has not other features requiring its classification as a liability and that the contingent settlement event is also outside the control of the holder.

Contingent settlement event	Within the issuer's control?
Issuer makes a distribution on ordinary shares.	Yes. Dividends on ordinary shares are discretionary (see also 3.2 above)
Upon the successful takeover of the issuer (i.e. a 'control event').	It depends. See 3.4.3 above.
Event of default under any of the issuer's debt facilities.	No.
Appointment of a receiver, administrator, entering a scheme of arrangement, or compromise agreement with creditors.	No. Whether this leads to the instrument being classified as equity or liability will depend on the respective requirements in each jurisdiction. In cases when these events do not necessarily result in liquidation of the issuer, this leads to classification as a liability, due to the requirement to ignore settlement provisions arising only on *liquidation* (see 3.4.2 above).
Upon commencement of proceedings for the winding up of the issuer.	No, but this does not lead to classification as a liability due to requirement to ignore settlement provisions arising only on liquidation (see 3.4.2 above).

Contingent settlement event	**Within the issuer's control?**
Incurring a fine exceeding a given amount, or commencement of an investigation of the issuer by, a government agency or a financial regulator.	No.
A change in accounting, taxation, or regulatory regime which is expected to adversely affect the financial position of the issuer.	No.
Upon suspension of listing of the issuer's shares from trading on the stock exchange for more than a certain number of days.	Probably not, but it will depend on the jurisdiction and whether the reasons for suspension are always within the control of the entity.
Commencement of war or armed conflict.	No.
Issue of a subordinated security that ranks equally or in priority to the securities.	Yes.
Issue of an IPO prospectus prior to the conversion date.	Yes.
Disposal of all or substantially all of the issuer's business undertaking or assets.	Yes.
Change in credit rating of the issuer.	No.

3.5 Derivative financial instruments with settlement options

A derivative financial instrument may have settlement options – in other words, it gives one party a choice over how it is settled (e.g. the issuer or the holder can choose settlement net in cash, net in shares, or by exchanging shares for cash). Where a derivative has settlement options, IAS 32 requires it to be treated as a financial asset or a financial liability unless all possible settlement alternatives would result in it being an equity instrument.[95] An example of a derivative financial instrument with a settlement option that is a financial liability is a share option that the issuer can decide to settle net in cash or by exchanging its own shares for cash.[96]

These provisions will apply mostly to contracts involving the sale or purchase by an entity of its own equity instruments. However, they will also be relevant to those contracts to buy or sell a non-financial item in exchange for the entity's own equity instruments that are within the scope of IAS 32 (rather than IFRS 2) because they can be settled either by delivery of the non-financial item or net in cash or another financial instrument. Such contracts are financial assets or financial liabilities and not equity instruments.[97]

3.6 Consolidated financial statements

In consolidated financial statements, IAS 32 requires an entity to present minority interests (i.e. the interests of other parties in the equity and income of its subsidiaries) within equity, in accordance with IAS 1 – *Presentation of Financial Statements* (see Chapter 3 at 3.1.5) and IAS 27 (see Chapter 6 at 6.7).[98]

However, when classifying a financial instrument (or a component of it) in consolidated financial statements, an entity must consider all terms and conditions agreed between all members of the group and the holders of the instrument in determining whether the group as a whole has an obligation to deliver cash or another financial asset in respect of the instrument or to settle it in a manner that results in its classification as a financial liability.[99]

For example, a subsidiary in a group may issue a financial instrument and a parent or other group entity may then agree additional terms directly with the holders of the instrument so as to guarantee some or all of the payments to be made under the instrument. The effect of this is that the subsidiary may have discretion over distributions or redemption, but the group as a whole does not.[100]

Accordingly, the subsidiary may appropriately classify the instrument without regard to these additional terms in its individual financial statements. For the purposes of the consolidated financial statements, however, the effect of the other agreements between members of the group and the holders of the instrument is to create an obligation or settlement provision, so that the instrument (or the component of it that is subject to the obligation) is classified as a financial liability.[101]

Thus it is quite possible for a financial instrument to be classified as an equity instrument in the financial statements of the issuing subsidiary but as a financial liability in the financial statements of the group.

3.7 Single entity financial statements

The corollary of the discussion in 3.6 above is that it is not uncommon for instruments that are classified as equity in the consolidated financial statements to give rise to liabilities and embedded derivatives in the financial statements of individual members of the group.

This is because a group wishing to raise finance for its operations will generally do so through a group entity specialising in finance-raising, which will then on-lend the proceeds of the finance raised to the relevant operating subsidiaries. The terms of the intragroup on-lending transactions will often be such that finance which constitutes equity from the perspective of group as a whole may be a liability in the individual financial statements of the finance-raising entity itself.

For example, the finance-raising entity might issue an irredeemable instrument with a 'dividend blocker' clause (see 3.2.1 C above), under the terms of which that entity is not required to make any payments to the holder unless the ultimate parent entity of the group pays a dividend to ordinary shareholders. Absent any other terms requiring its classification, in whole or in part, as a liability under IAS 32, the instrument will be treated as equity in the consolidated financial statements, since payments under the instrument are contingent on an event within the control of the group (payment of a dividend by the parent entity). In the finance-raising entity's single entity financial statements, however, the instrument should be classified as a liability, because the subsidiary cannot control the dividend policy of its parent and could therefore be forced to make payments to the holder of the instrument as a consequence of its parent entity paying a dividend.

Another common example is that a group may issue a convertible bond which is actually structured as a series of transactions along the following lines:

- a finance-raising company issues the bond which converts into preference shares of the finance company; and
- immediately that this conversion occurs, the parent entity is required to acquire the preference shares of the subsidiary from the holder (i.e. the previous bondholder) in exchange for equity of the parent.

Absent any other terms requiring classification as a liability under IAS 32, the instrument will be treated as having an equity component (see 4 below) in the consolidated financial statements. In the finance-raising entity's single entity financial statements, however, the instrument might be classified as a liability, if (for example) the preference shares issued on conversion by the subsidiary have terms that require them to be classified as a liability by IAS 32. In that case, the subsidiary will have issued an instrument that the holder can exchange either for cash or for a debt instrument. From the subsidiary's perspective, therefore, there is no equity component to the instrument.

Moreover, in the period prior to conversion, the parent is required to account for its contingent forward contract to acquire the preference shares in the finance company. It might be that the transaction is not an equity transaction at all in the parent's own financial statements (if for example the preference shares were not equity instruments and were denominated in a functional currency different from that of the parent – see 3.3.1 B above).

4 COMPOUND FINANCIAL INSTRUMENTS

4.1 Background

A compound financial instrument is a non-derivative financial instrument that, from the issuer's perspective, contains both a liability and an equity component.[102] Examples include:

- A bond convertible into a fixed number of equity instruments, which effectively comprises:
  - a financial liability (the issuer's obligation to pay interest and, potentially, to redeem the bond in cash); and
  - an equity instrument (the holder's right to call for shares of the issuer).

  IAS 32 states that the economic effect of issuing such an instrument is substantially the same as issuing simultaneously a debt instrument with an early settlement provision and warrants to purchase ordinary shares, or issuing a debt instrument with detachable share purchase warrants.[103] However, this analysis is questionable in the sense that, if a company did issue such instruments separately, it is extremely unlikely that one would lapse as the result of the exercise of the other (as happens on the conversion or redemption of a convertible bond);

- A mandatorily redeemable preference share with dividends paid at the issuer's discretion, which effectively comprises:
    - a financial liability (the issuer's obligation to redeem the shares in cash); and
    - an equity instrument (the holder's right to receive dividends if declared).[104]

IAS 32 requires the issuer of a non-derivative financial instrument to evaluate the terms of the financial instrument to determine whether it contains both a liability and an equity component. If such components are identified, they must be accounted for separately as financial liabilities, financial assets or equity,[105] and the liability and equity components shown separately on the balance sheet.[106]

This treatment, commonly referred to as 'split accounting', is discussed in more detail in 4.2 to 4.5 below. For simplicity, the discussion below (like that in IAS 32 itself) is framed in terms of convertible bonds, by far the most common form of compound financial instrument, but is equally applicable to other types of compound instrument.

4.1.1 Treatment by holder and issuer contrasted

'Split accounting' is to be applied only by the issuer of a compound financial instrument. The accounting treatment by the holder is dealt with in IAS 39[107] (see Chapter 17 at 5 and Chapter 20 at 3) and is significantly different. In particular:

- In the issuer's financial statements, under IAS 32:
    - the fair value of the liability component is calculated first and the equity component is treated as a residual; and
    - the equity component is never remeasured after initial recognition.
- In the holder's financial statements, under IAS 39 (see Chapter 17 at 5 and Chapter 20 at 3):
    - the equity component (from the issuer's perspective) is a derivative financial asset of the holder, the fair value of which is calculated first, with the liability component (from the issuer's perspective) treated as a residual amount; and
    - the derivative financial asset of the holder is likely to be constantly remeasured at fair value.

4.2 The components of a compound instrument

4.2.1 Determining the components of a financial instrument

Arguably the most difficult aspect of 'split accounting' is the initial determination of what the various components of the instrument actually are. In the examples in 4.1 above, these are fairly clear. However, in some instruments the analysis is far from straightforward, as illustrated by Example 19.6 below.

Example 19.6: Decomposition of compound financial instrument into components

An entity issues a bond for €100, paying an annual cash coupon of 5% on the issue price and mandatorily convertible after five years on the following terms. If, at the date of conversion, the entity's share price is €1.25 or higher, the holder will receive 80 shares. If the entity's share price is €1.00 or lower, the holder will receive 100 shares. If the entity's share price is in the range €1.00 to €1.25, the holder will receive such number of shares (between 80 and 100) as have a fair value of €100.

Any analysis must begin by determining whether the bond as whole is a non-derivative instrument. This is the case, since the issuing entity receives full consideration for its issue. The next step is to break the instrument down into its components so as to identify any equity components in the whole. At least four possible analyses suggest themselves.

I Analysis 1

The bond is a non-derivative for which the entity is obliged to deliver a variable number of equity instruments (since the number may vary between 80 and 100 shares), and therefore is in its entirety a financial liability as defined in IAS 32 (see 2.3 and 3.1 above). There is then a discussion to be had as to whether the share-price link is an embedded derivative requiring separation under IAS 39 (see Chapter 17 at 5).

II Analysis 2

The bond comprises three components:

(a) an obligation to pay interest – a financial liability;

(b) a non-derivative requiring the issuer to deliver a fixed number of shares (the 80 shares that the entity will be required to issue in any event) – an equity instrument; and

(c) an obligation to deliver up to 20 more shares depending on the ultimate share price – a derivative financial liability.

III Analysis 3

The bond comprises four components:

(a) an obligation to pay interest – a financial liability;

(b) an obligation to deliver as many shares as are worth €100 – a financial liability;

(c) a written call option, whereby the holder can require the issuer to exchange 80 shares for €100 (i.e. the fixed stated principal of the bond – see 4.4.2 below) – an equity instrument; and

(d) a purchased put option, whereby the issuer can require the holder to exchange 100 shares for €100 (i.e. the fixed stated principal of the bond – see 4.4.2 below) – an equity instrument.

However, some might argue that the reference in IAS 32 to the 'fixed stated principal' of a bond (see 4.4.2 below) is relevant only where it is a proxy for a fixed amount of 'real' cash, such as the cash that is foregone on conversion of a bond where there is no obligation to convert. In this case, it could be argued that no cash is foregone (since the bond is mandatorily convertible) and that the true consideration for the put and call options in (c) and (d) above is not €100 cash but the €100 worth of shares delivered under (b) above. This suggests Analysis 4 below.

IV *Analysis 4*

The bond comprises four components:

(a) an obligation to pay interest – a financial liability;

(b) an obligation to deliver as many shares as are worth €100 – a financial liability

(c) a written call option, whereby the holder can require the issuer to exchange 80 shares for as many shares as are worth €100 (i.e. effectively exchanging the number of shares notionally delivered under (b) above, if less than 80 shares, for 80 shares) – a derivative financial liability; and

(d) a purchased put option, whereby the issuer can require the holder to exchange 100 shares for as many shares as are worth €100 (i.e. effectively exchanging the number of shares notionally delivered under (b) above, if greater than 100 shares, for 100 shares) – a derivative financial asset.

V *Summary*

Whichever analysis is chosen will have a significant impact on the accounting treatment. Under Analyses 1 and 4, the bond would not fall within IAS 32's provisions for compound financial instruments at all, as there is no identified equity component. Under Analyses 2 and 3 by contrast, there is at least one identified equity component, so that the bond would fall within IAS 32's provisions for compound financial instruments.

We question whether Analysis 1 properly addresses the requirement of IAS 32 to separate a compound financial instrument into its component parts. To take an extreme case, suppose that the bond converted into one billion shares in some cases and one billion and one shares in others. Would it really be appropriate to classify the whole instrument as a liability on the basis of a variability of one share in a billion?

Analysis 1 might be valid if it could be shown that neither the floor of 80 shares nor the ceiling of 100 shares would ever be reached in any foreseeable scenario. However, it would be difficult to sustain such an argument in most cases. It can generally be assumed that conditions such as these are included in the terms of financial instruments because there is considered to be a real, if remote, possibility that the relevant events will occur.

Ultimately, however, we believe that Analysis 1 is flawed because it fails to identify any equity component in an instrument that clearly contains some equity features. The same objection can be made against Analysis 4.

We believe that a case can be made for either Analysis 2 or Analysis 3. However, Analysis 2 could be said not to follow the underlying principle of IAS 32 (and the IAS *Framework* in general) that equity is a residual amount, since it effectively identifies the equity component first rather than the underlying liability to deliver €100 worth of own shares.

In our view, the main conclusion to be drawn from examples such as this is that the provisions of IAS 32, which were originally drafted in the mid 1990s to deal with 'traditional' convertible instruments, are not adequate for dealing with the increasingly complex range of instruments with a link to the issuer's share price currently available in the financial markets.

4.2.2 Separated (i.e. not closely-related) embedded derivatives

As noted above, in order to qualify for split accounting, a financial instrument, when considered as whole, must be a non-derivative instrument. However, one or more of its identified components may well be embedded derivatives. Indeed, the conversion right in any convertible bond represents a holder's call option whereby the entity can be required to issue a fixed number of shares for a fixed consideration (the 'fixed stated principal' of the bond – see 4.4.2 below), which is accordingly identified as an equity component.

A bond may well contain other (non-equity) derivatives, such as options for either the issuer or the holder to require early repayment or conversion or to extend the period until conversion. On the face of things, they are subject to the normal requirement of IAS 39 for embedded derivatives to be accounted for separately if they are not considered to be closely related to the host contract (see Chapter 17 at 5).

There is, however, a certain ambiguity in the drafting of IAS 32 as to how any non-equity derivatives should be treated. The detailed guidance in IAS 32 (see 4.3 below) requires 'the fair value of any embedded non-equity derivative features [to be] determined and included in the liability component'[108] – suggesting that they are always accounted for as part of the liability component and never separated. However, this is inconsistent with the overall (bold paragraph) requirement of IAS 32 to classify the components of a compound instrument 'separately as financial liabilities, *financial assets* or equity' (see 4.1 above). Clearly, if all non-equity embedded derivatives were accounted for as part of the liability component, there would never be any recognition of financial assets.

In our view, the requirements of IAS 39 for separate accounting for certain embedded derivatives are intended to be applied to any non-equity derivatives identified in the decomposition of a compound financial instrument.

However, there are cases where over-enthusiastic trawling for embedded derivatives may dredge up results so counter-intuitive that it is hard to believe that they were really intended by the IASB, as illustrated by Example 19.7 below.

Example 19.7: Foreign currency denominated equity instrument with issuer's redemption right

An entity with a functional currency of pounds sterling issues a euro-denominated capital instrument for €145 million (equivalent to £100 million at the date of issue). Coupons on the instrument are paid entirely at the entity's discretion, subject to a 'dividend blocker' clause (see 3.2.1 C above). The entity has the right, but not the obligation, in certain circumstances to redeem the instrument (in euros) for an amount equal to the original issue proceeds.

Taken as a whole, this is an equity instrument, because it gives rise to no obligation to transfer cash or other financial assets to the holder. However, the issuer's right to redeem, if considered in isolation is not an equity instrument, but a financial asset (a call option over own equity), since it is a derivative involving the purchase of a fixed number of equity instruments for €145 million which, although fixed in euros, is variable when translated into sterling (see 3.3.1 A above). Suppose that the fair value of the call option, at the date of issue was £15 million.

This analysis would result in the following accounting entry on issue of the instrument:

	£m	£m
Cash	100	
Call option (balance sheet)	15	
Equity		115

In our view, it would be verging on the misleading to show an increase in net assets of £115 million, when the only real transaction has been the raising of £100 million of equity for cash. In this particular case, this treatment is, in our view, not in fact required since paragraph 28 of IAS 32 requires split accounting to be applied only where an instrument is determined to contain 'both a liability and an equity component'. In this case, there is no liability component, since the embedded derivative that has potentially been identified is, and can only ever be, an asset; accordingly, 'split accounting' is not required.

4.3 Initial recognition

On initial recognition of a compound instrument such as a convertible bond, IAS 32 requires the issuer to:

(a) identify the various components of the instrument;

(b) determine the fair value of the liability component (see below); and

(c) determine the equity component as a residual amount, essentially the issue proceeds of the instrument less the liability component determined in (b) above.

Thereafter the liability component (and any identified financial asset component) is accounted for in accordance with the rules for measurement of financial liabilities (and, if relevant, financial assets) in IAS 39 (see Chapter 20 at 3).[109]

The liability component of a convertible bond should be measured first, at the fair value of a similar liability (including any embedded non-equity derivative features such as an issuer's or holder's right to require early redemption of the bond) that does not have an associated equity conversion feature.

In practical terms, this will be done by determining the net present value of all potential contractually determined future cash flows under the instrument, discounted at the rate of interest applied by the market at the time of issue to instruments of comparable credit status and providing substantially the same cash flows, on the same terms, but without the conversion option. The fair value of any embedded non-equity derivative features is then determined and 'included in the liability component'[110] – see, however, the further discussion of this point at 4.2.2 above.

IAS 32 notes that:

- the equity component of a convertible bond is an embedded option to convert the liability into equity of the issuer;
- the fair value of the option comprises its time value and its intrinsic value, if any; and;
- this option has value on initial recognition even when it is out of the money.[111]

Whilst this is all true, it is actually irrelevant to the accounting, since the equity component is not (other than by coincidence) recorded at its fair value. Instead, in accordance with the general definition of equity as a residual, the equity component of the bond is simply the difference between the total issue proceeds of the bond and the liability component as determined above. Because of this 'residual' treatment, IAS 32 does not address the issue of how, or whether, the issue proceeds are to be allocated where more than one equity component is identified (as in Analysis 3 at 4.2.1 above).

This has the effect that the sum of the carrying amounts assigned to the liability and equity components on initial recognition is always equal to the fair value that would be ascribed to the instrument as a whole. No gain or loss arises from the initial recognition of the separate components of the instrument.[112]

This treatment is illustrated in Examples 19.8 and 19.9 below.

Example 19.8: Convertible bond – basic 'split accounting'[113]

An entity issues 2,000 convertible bonds. The bonds have a three-year term, and are issued at par with a face value of €1,000 per bond, giving total proceeds of €2,000,000. Interest is payable annually in arrears at a nominal annual interest rate of 6% (i.e. €120,000 per annum). Each bond is convertible at any time up to maturity into 250 ordinary shares. When the bonds are issued, the prevailing market interest rate for similar debt without conversion options is 9% per annum. The entity incurs issue costs of €100,000.

The economic components of this instrument are:

- a liability component, being a discounted fixed rate debt, perhaps with an imputed holder's put option (due to the holder's right to convert at any time), and
- an equity component, representing the holder's right to convert at any time before maturity. In effect this is a written call option (from the issuer's perspective) on American terms (i.e. it can be exercised at any time until maturity of the bond).

The practical problem with this analysis is that it is not clear what is the strike price of the holder's options to put the debt and call for shares, specifically whether it is the €2,000,000 face value of the bond or the discounted amount at which it is recorded until maturity – see the further discussion of this issue at 3.3.1 A and 4.2.1 above. Perhaps for this reason, IAS 32 does not require the true fair values of these components to be calculated.

Instead the liability component is measured first at the net present value of the maximum potential cash payments that the issuer could be required to make, and the difference between the proceeds of the bond issue and this calculated fair value of the liability is assigned to the equity component. The net present value (NPV) of the liability component is calculated as €1,848,122, using a discount rate of 9%, the market interest rate for similar bonds having no conversion rights, as shown.

Year	Cash flow	€	Discount factor (at 9%)	NPV of cash flow €
1	Interest	120,000	1/1.09	110,092
2	Interest	120,000	$1/1.09^2$	101,001
3	Interest and principal	2,120,000	$1/1.09^3$	1,637,029
			Total liability component	1,848,122
			Total equity component (balance)	151,878
			Total proceeds	2,000,000

It is next necessary to deal with the issue costs of €100,000. In accordance with the requirements of IAS 32 for such costs (see 5.1 below), these would be allocated to the liability and equity components on a pro-rata basis. This would give the following allocation of the net issue proceeds.

	Liability component €	Equity component €	Total €
Gross proceeds (allocated as above)	1,848,122	151,878	2,000,000
Issue costs (allocated pro-rata to gross proceeds)	(92,406)	(7,594)	(100,000)
Net proceeds	1,755,716	144,284	1,900,000

The €144,284 credited to equity is not subsequently remeasured (see 4.2.1 above). On the assumption that the liability is not classified as at fair value through profit or loss (see Chapter 17 at 7.1), the €1,755,716 liability component would be accounted for under the effective interest rate method (see Chapter 20 at 5). It should be borne in mind that, after taking account of the issue costs, the effective interest rate is not the 9% used to determine the gross value of the liability component, but 10.998%, as shown below.

Year	Liability b/f €	Interest at 10.998% €	Cash paid €	Liability c/f €
1	1,755,716	193,094	(120,000)	1,828,810
2	1,828,810	201,134	(120,000)	1,909,944
3	1,909,943	210,056	(2,120,000)	–
	Total finance cost	604,284		

The total finance cost can be proved as follows:

	€
Cash interest	360,000
Gross issue proceeds originally allocated to equity component	151,878
Issue costs allocated to liability component	92,406
	604,284

Example 19.9: Convertible bond – split accounting with multiple embedded derivative features[114]

The proceeds received on the issue of a callable convertible bond are £60 million. The value of a similar bond without a call or equity conversion option is £57 million. Based on an option-pricing model, it is determined that the value to the entity of the embedded call feature in a similar bond without an equity conversion option is £2 million. In this case, the value is allocated so as to reduce the liability component to £55 million (£57m – £2m) and the value allocated to the equity component is £5 million (£60m – £55m).

Unfortunately, IAS 32 does not specifically clarify on what basis the embedded call feature has been treated as a reduction of the liability component rather than as a separate asset (see 4.2.1 above). However, a convertible bond would typically be callable at par. This would lead to the conclusion under IAS 39 that the call option was not a separable derivative. IAS 39 states that a call option is generally closely related to the host debt contract if the exercise price is approximately equal to the amortised cost of the host on each exercise (which would not, *prima facie* be the case). However, in the case of a convertible bond, IAS 39 requires this assessment to be made before separating the equity component[115] – i.e. a issuer's call over a convertible bond at par is effectively deemed to be equal to amortised cost for the duration of the instrument. This is discussed further in Chapter 17 at 5.1.

A Temporary differences arising from split accounting

In many jurisdictions only the cash interest paid (and sometimes also the issue costs) is deductible for tax purposes, and may well be deductible in periods different from those in which they are recognised in the financial statements. These factors will give rise to temporary differences between the carrying value of the liability component of the bond and its tax base, giving rise to deferred tax required to be accounted for under IAS 12 – *Income Taxes* (see Chapter 26, particularly at 3.2.1 B and 4.2.5).

4.3.1 Accounting for the equity component

On initial recognition of a compound financial instrument, the equity component (e.g. the €144,284 identified in Example 19.8 above) is credited direct to equity. IAS 32 does not prescribe:

- whether the credit should be to a separate component of equity (although IFRS 1 – *First-time Adoption of International Financial Reporting Standards* – suggests that there is such a requirement – see 8.1.2 below); or
- if the entity chooses to treat it as such, how it should be described.

We imagine that the IASB deliberately allowed complete freedom in this respect so as to ensure that there was no conflict between, on the one hand, the basic requirement of IAS 32 that there should be a credit in equity and, on the other, the legal requirements of various jurisdictions as to exactly how that credit should be allocated within equity.

After initial recognition, the classification of the liability and equity components of a convertible instrument is not revised, for example as a result of a change in the likelihood that a conversion option will be exercised, even when exercise of the option may appear to have become economically advantageous to some holders. IAS 32 points out that holders may not always act in the way that might be expected because, for example, the tax consequences resulting from conversion may differ among holders. Furthermore, the likelihood of conversion will change from time to time. The entity's contractual obligation to make future payments remains outstanding until it is extinguished through conversion, maturity of the instrument or some other transaction.[116]

The amount originally credited to equity is not subsequently recycled to the income statement. Thus, as illustrated by Example 19.8 above, the effective interest rate shown in the income statement for a simple convertible bond will be equivalent to the rate that would have been paid for non-convertible debt. In effect, the dilution of shareholder value represented by the embedded conversion right is shown as an interest expense. Similarly, the dilution of shareholder value inherent in employee share options is shown as an expense under IFRS 2 (see Chapter 31), albeit using a methodology very different to that in IAS 32.

However, on conversion of a convertible instrument, it may be appropriate to transfer the equity component within equity (see 4.4.1 below).

4.4 Conversion, early repurchase and modification

4.4.1 Conversion at maturity

On conversion of a convertible instrument at maturity, IAS 32 requires the entity to derecognise the liability component and recognise it as equity. There is no gain or loss on conversion at maturity.[117]

Thus, for example, if the bond in Example 19.8 above were converted at maturity, the accounting entry required by IAS 32 would be:

	€	€
Liability	2,000,000	
Equity		2,000,000

The precise allocation of the credit to equity (e.g. as between share capital, additional paid-in capital, share premium, other reserves and so on) would be a matter of local legislation. In addition, IAS 32 permits the €144,284 originally allocated to the equity component in Example 19.8 above to be reallocated within equity.[118]

A Embedded derivatives

IAS 32 does not specifically address the treatment of any non-equity embedded derivatives outstanding at the time of conversion. The issue of principle is that when a holder exercises its right to convert, it is effectively requiring the issuer to issue equity in consideration for the bondholder ceding its rights. These may include any right to receive future payments of principal and/or interest or to require early repayment of the bond. It seems entirely appropriate that any amounts carried in respect of such rights should be transferred to equity on conversion.

Where, however, conversion has the effect of removing an issuer's right (for example, to compel early redemption or conversion), this could be seen as a loss to the issuer rather than as consideration given by the holder for an issue of equity. In our view, however, the loss of such a right by the issuer on conversion by the holder simply represents a reduction in the proceeds received for the issue of equity, and should therefore by accounted for as a charge to equity (see also 5.1 below).

4.4.2 Conversion before maturity

A 'Fixed stated principal' of a bond

The consideration given for the issue of equity instruments on conversion of a bond is the discharge by the holder of the issuer from the liability to pay any further interest or principal payments on the bond. If conversion can take place only at maturity, the amount of the liability transferred to equity on conversion will always (in Example 19.8 above) be €2,000,000. Hence, the conversion right involves the delivery of a fixed number of shares for the waiver of the right to receive a fixed amount of cash and so is clearly an equity instrument.

However, the bond in Example 19.8 allows conversion at some point before the full term. Therefore, conversion might occur at the end of year 2, when the carrying value of the bond had been accreted to only €1,909,944. Hence, the carrying amount of the liability that is forgiven on conversion can vary depending on whether conversion occurs. This begs the question as to whether the conversion right now involves the delivery of a fixed number of shares for the waiver of the right to receive a *variable* amount of cash, suggesting that it is no longer an equity instrument.

It is for this reason, in our view, that IAS 32 defines as an equity instrument one that involves the exchange of a fixed number of shares for the 'fixed stated principal' rather than the 'carrying amount' of a bond. In other words, IAS 32 regards the 'fixed stated principal' of the bond in Example 19.8 as a constant €2,000,000. The intention is to clarify that the variation in the bond's carrying amount during its term does not preclude the conversion right from being classified as an equity instrument.

B Accounting treatment

IAS 32 refers to treatment summarised in 4.4.1 above being applied on conversion 'at maturity', leaving open the question of the treatment to be adopted if a holder converts prior to maturity (as would have been possible under the terms of the bond in Example 19.8).

As noted in A above, IAS 32 concludes that the equity component of the bond is an equity instrument on the grounds that it represents the holder's right to call for a fixed number of shares for fixed consideration, in the form of the 'fixed stated principal' of the bond.

It could be argued that the logical implication of this is that, on a holder's early conversion of the bond in Example 19.8 above, the issuer should immediately recognise a finance cost for the difference between the then carrying amount of the liability component of the bond and the fixed stated principal of €2,000,000. This would create a liability of €2,000,000 immediately before conversion, so as to acknowledge that the strike price under the holder's call option is the waiver of the right to receive a fixed stated principal of €2,000,000, rather than whatever the carrying value of the bond happens to be at the time.

However, we take the view – supported by general emerging practice – that all that is required is to transfer to equity the carrying value of the liability at the date of conversion – strictly, as calculated after accrual of finance costs on a continuous basis, rather than at the amount shown in the most recently published financial statements. In such a case, the consideration for the issue of equity instruments is the release, by the bondholder, of the issuer from its liability to make future contractual payments under the bond, measured at the net present value of those payments.

Issues such as this, and those discussed at 4.2.2 above, suggest to us that the IASB needs to consider further:

- exactly what components are being accounted for in 'split accounting'; and
- whether, and why, the accounting treatment should differ from that applicable to separate instruments equivalent to those components.

4.4.3 Early repurchase

It is not uncommon for the issuer of a convertible bond to repurchase it before the end of its full term, either through exercise of rights inherent in the bond or through subsequent negotiation with bondholders. When an entity extinguishes a convertible instrument before maturity through an early redemption or repurchase in which the original conversion privileges are unchanged, IAS 32 requires the entity to allocate the consideration paid and any transaction costs for the repurchase or redemption to the liability and equity components of the instrument at the date of the transaction.[119]

It is not entirely clear what is meant by a 'redemption or repurchase in which the original conversion privileges are unchanged'. However, we assume that it is intended to imply that the repurchase must either be according to the original terms of the compound instrument, or must be at a price representing a fair value for the instrument on its original terms. A repurchase at a value implying a substantial modification of the original terms of the instrument should presumably be dealt with according to the provisions of IAS 32 for the modification of a compound instrument (see 4.4.4 below) or those in IAS 39 for the exchange and modification of debt (see Chapter 18 at 5.2).

The method used for allocating the consideration paid and transaction costs to the separate components should be consistent with that used in the original allocation to the separate components of the proceeds received by the entity when the convertible instrument was issued (see 4.2 above).[120]

Once this allocation of the consideration has been made:

- the difference between the consideration allocated to the liability component and the carrying amount of the liability is recognised in profit or loss; and
- the amount of consideration relating to the equity component is recognised in equity.[121]

The treatment of a negotiated repurchase at fair value of a convertible instrument at fair value is illustrated by Example 19.10 below, which is based on an illustrative example in IAS 32.[122]

Example 19.10: Early repurchase of convertible instrument

For simplicity this example:

- assumes that at inception the face amount of the instrument was equal to the carrying amount of its liability and equity components in the financial statements – i.e. there was no premium or discount on issue; and
- ignores transaction costs and tax.

On 1 January 2008, an entity issued a convertible bond with a face value of €100 million maturing on 31 December 2017, at which point the holder may opt for repayment of €100 million or conversion into 4 million shares. Interest is paid half-yearly in arrears at a nominal annual interest rate of 10% (i.e. €5m per half year). At the date of issue, the entity could have issued non-convertible debt with a ten-year term bearing interest at 11%. On issue, the carrying amount of the bond was allocated as follows:

	€m
Present value of the principal – €100m payable at the end of ten years[1]	34.3
Present value of the interest – 20 6-monthly payments of €5m[2]	59.7
Total liability component	94.0
Equity component (balance)	6.0
Proceeds of the bond issue	100.0

The amounts above are discounted using a semi-annual rate of 5.5% (11%/2) as follows

1 $€100m/1.055^{20}$

2 $€5m \times (1/1.055 + 1/1.0552 + 1/1.0553 + \ldots 1/1.055^{20})$

On 1 January 2013, the entity makes a tender offer to the holder of the bond to repurchase the bond at its then fair value of €170 million, which the holder accepts. At the date of repurchase, the entity could have issued non-convertible debt with a five-year term with interest payable half-yearly in arrears at an annual coupon interest rate of 8%.

At the time of repurchase, the carrying amount of the liability component of the bond, discounted at the original semi-annual rate of 5.5% is as follows.

	€m
Present value of the principal – €100m payable at the end of five years[1]	58.5
Present value of the interest – 10 6-monthly payments of €5m[2]	37.7
Carrying value of liability component	96.2

1 $€100m/1.055^{10}$

2 $€5m \times (1/1.055 + 1/1.055^2 + 1/1.055^3 + \ldots 1/1.055^{10})$

The fair value of the liability element of the bond, discounted at the current semi-annual rate of 4% (8%/2) is as follows.

	€m
Present value of the principal – €100m payable at the end of five years[1]	67.6
Present value of the interest – 10 6-monthly payments of €5m[2]	40.5
Carrying value of liability component	108.1

1 $€100m/1.04^{10}$

2 $€5m \times (1/1.04 + 1/1.04^2 + 1/1.04^3 + \ldots 1/1.04^{10})$

The fair value calculation indicates that, of the repurchase price of €170 million, €108.1 million is to be treated as redeeming the liability component of the bond, and €61.9 million as redeeming the equity component. This gives rise to the accounting entry:

	€m	€m
Liability component of bond	96.2	
Equity	61.9	
Debt settlement expense (income statement)	11.9	
Cash		170.0

The debt settlement expense represents the difference between the carrying value of the debt component (€96.2m) and its fair value (€108.1m).

Any costs of the repurchase would have been allocated between the income statement and equity in proportion to the fair value of the liability and equity components at the time of redemption.

4.4.4 Modification

An entity may amend the terms of a convertible instrument to induce early conversion, for example by offering a more favourable conversion ratio or paying other additional consideration in the event of conversion before a specified date. The difference, at the date the terms are amended, between:

- the fair value of the consideration the holder receives on conversion of the instrument under the revised terms and,
- the fair value of the consideration the holder would have received under the original terms

is recognised as a loss in profit or loss.[123] IAS 32 illustrates this treatment, as shown in Example 19.11 below.[124]

Example 19.11: Modification of terms of bond to induce early conversion

Suppose that the entity in Example 19.10 above wished, on 1 January 2009, to induce the bondholder to convert the bond early. The original terms of the bond allowed for conversion into 4 million shares. The entity offers the bondholder the right to convert into 5 million shares during the period 1 January-28 February 2009. The market value of the entity's shares is €40 per share.

The enhanced conversion terms offer the bondholder the right to receive an additional 1 million shares. Accordingly, the entity recognises a cost of €40m (1m shares × share price €40/share).

We are far from convinced by the approach taken in Example 19.11. It appears to be based on the premise that the only additional benefit being given is the right to 1 million additional shares. However, in our view, this misses the point that there is a significant difference between the right to call for 4 million shares in nine years' time embedded in the original bond and the right to call for those shares within the next two months embedded in the proposed early conversion terms.

In our view, an approach more consistent with that in Example 19.10 above would have been to say that the entity is proposing to purchase, in exchange for 5 million shares, the holder's right to receive:

(a) interest for the next nine years; and
(b) in nine years' time, either:
    (i) a repayment of principal; or
    (ii) the right to convert the principal into 4 million shares.

The entity would then (as in Example 19.10 above) determine the fair value of the liability component by reference to current market rates and allocate the fair value of the consideration given of €200 million (i.e. 5 million shares at €40 per share) between the liability and equity component. The carrying value of the liability component at the end of 2008 would be €94.34 million, as shown below.

	€m
Liability component at 1.1.00 (see above)	94.00
Finance charge (94 × 11%)	10.34
Interest paid – 2 6-monthly payments of €5m	(10.00)
Liability component at 1.1.01	94.34

Suppose that the current fair value of the liability component at 1 January 2009 was determined to be €105 million; the implication must be that €95 million of the total €200 million consideration must relate to the equity component. That would suggest the accounting entry:

	€m	€m
Liability component of bond	94.3	
Debt settlement expense (income statement) – note 1	10.7	
Equity – note 2		105.0

1 Fair value of consideration given for liability component (€105m) less carrying value of liability component (€94.3m).
2 Fair value of equity issued (€200m) less cost of settling existing conversion right (€95m).

However, this raises two questions not specifically addressed by IAS 32:

- the accounting treatment to be applied when a financial liability is settled with a new equity instrument (i.e. not pursuant to the original terms of the liability) – see 4.4.5 below); and
- the accounting treatment to be applied when an equity instrument is settled at an amount different from its fair value, as might well be occurring in Example 19.11 above (see 6.1 below).

For the avoidance of doubt, our 'preferred' treatment as set out above cannot be applied in practice, since it conflicts with the explicit requirements of IAS 32, as set out in Example 19.11 above.

4.4.5 Settlement of financial liability with new equity instrument

An issue not specifically covered in IAS 32, or IAS 39, is the accounting treatment to be adopted where an entity issues non-convertible debt, but subsequently enters into an agreement with the debt-holder to discharge the liability under the debt in full or in part for an issue of equity. This most often occurs when the entity is in financial difficulties, as shown in Example 19.12 below.

Example 19.12: Discharge of liability for fresh issue of equity

During 2003 an entity issued £100 million bonds due to be repaid in 2013. By 2008 the entity is in some financial difficulty and reaches an agreement with the holders of the bonds whereby they will accept equity shares in the entity with a fair value of £60 million in full and final settlement of all amounts due under the bonds. How should this transaction be accounted for?

The basic rules in IAS 39 for derecognition of financial liabilities (see Chapter 18 at 5) provide that, where a liability is extinguished, the difference between the carrying amount of that liability and the 'consideration paid' must be recognised in profit of loss. This raises the issue of whether an issue of equity instruments constitutes 'consideration paid'. It would, in our view be difficult to argue that it does not, given the requirements of other standards such as IFRS 2 and IFRS 3.

It may also be in point that, if there has been an event of default under the terms of the original loan, this is now due on demand, given the explicit requirement of IAS 39, paragraph 49, that the fair value of an on-demand liability is (effectively) its face value (see Chapter 20 at 4.5). This could support the argument that, although there is no specific guidance on the treatment of a liability settled for the issue of an equity instrument, the transaction above is equivalent to:

- the entity redeeming the original liability at £60 million (thereby giving rise to a gain of £40 million – see Chapter 18 at 5); and
- the former bond holders using that £60 million to subscribe for new shares in the entity at market value.

Another argument for recognition of a gain might be that IAS 39 requires a gain or loss to be recognised on any significant modification of the terms of a debt (see Chapter 18 at 5.2), and the conversion of previously repayable debt into equity is a significant modification.

However, a counter-argument might be that the rules in IAS 32 governing the conversion of convertible debt simply require the carrying value of the liability component at the time of conversion to be transferred into equity (see 4.4.2 above), irrespective of the fact that this may not be equivalent to the fair value of the debt at that time. On this analogy, the £100 million carrying amount of the debt should be transferred to equity.

In our view, absent further guidance from IFRIC or the IASB, either approach can be argued to be acceptable, provided that it is applied consistently. This lack of clarity arises from a more general problem – the absence in IFRS of any general accounting rules for the recording of an issue of equity instruments. IFRS 3 generally requires shares issued in a business combination to be recorded at their fair value (see Chapter 7). However, IFRS 2 broadly requires shares issued for share-based payment transactions to be recorded at the fair value of the goods or services received in the case of transactions with non-employees, but at the fair value of the shares issued in the case of transactions with employees (see Chapter 31).

The IASB would no doubt respond that to have a general rule would be inconsistent with the general principle of IFRS that equity is a residual and should therefore be measured by reference to the movements in assets and liabilities that give rise to it rather than 'in its own right'. Interestingly, the exposure draft *IFRS for Small and Medium-Sized Entities* proposes that an entity should measure an issue of equity at the fair value of the cash or other resources received or receivable, net of direct costs of issuing the equity shares'.[125] The ED asserts that this proposal derives from IAS 32,[126] but the reality is, as was conceded in the staff draft of the exposure draft previously available on the IASB's website, that this treatment, 'is not in any standard'.[127]

4.5 Issuer cash settlement options

As discussed as 3.5 above, IAS 32 requires a derivative with two or more settlement options to be treated as a financial asset or a financial liability unless all possible settlement alternatives would result in it being an equity instrument. Many convertible bonds currently in issue contain a provision whereby, if the holder exercises its conversion option, the issuer may instead pay cash equal to the fair value of the shares that it would otherwise have been required to deliver. This is to allow for unforeseen circumstances, such as an inability to issue the necessary number of shares to effect conversion at the appropriate time.

Where a bond has such a term, the conversion right is a derivative (in effect, a written call option over the issuer's own shares) which may potentially be settled in cash, such that there is a settlement alternative that does not result in it being an equity instrument. This means that the 'equity component' of a bond with an issuer cash settlement option is not in fact an equity instrument, but a financial liability. The financial reporting implication of this is that the conversion right must be accounted for as a derivative at fair value, with changes in value included in profit or loss – in other words the financial statements will reflect gains and losses based on the movement of the reporting entity's own share price.

It was for this reason that in 2005 Man Group changed the terms of its guaranteed exchangeable bonds to remove the cash settlement alternative so as to avoid this treatment.

Extract 19.2: Man Group plc (2005)

Notes of the Group Financial Statements [extracts]

4. Exceptional items [extract]

Year ended 31 March 2005

Fair value gain on exchangeable bonds

The exceptional gains of $202 million for the year ended 31 March 2005 related to the £400 million exchangeable bonds, issued in November 2002.

22. Borrowings [extract]

Forester Limited, a special purpose entity (…), has issued guaranteed exchangeable bonds of £400 million at par value, guaranteed by Man Group plc and which mature in November 2009. The bonds have the following features: (1) a coupon of 3.75%, paid semi-annually; (2) holders have the option at any time to exchange for Man Group plc ordinary shares at an initial exchange price of £12.82 (the exchange price is subject to adjustment in accordance with the terms of the bonds); (3) Forester Limited can redeem the bonds early (at their principal amount together with accrued interest) at any time on or after 15 days after the fifth anniversary of the issue of the bonds if on not less than 20 days out of a period of 30 consecutive days the Man Group plc share price exceeds 130% of the then current exchange price or at any time if less than 15 % of the total issue remains outstanding; and (4) Forester Limited has the option to redeem (either on maturity or early redemption) the bonds for a fixed number of shares. On 5 November 2004, the terms and conditions of the exchangeable bonds were amended to remove the option, which Forester Limited had, to settle in cash rather than shares, upon exercise of an exchange right by a bond holder.

36. Transition to IFRS [extract]

Exchangeable bonds (IAS 32/39)

Under IFRS, the exchangeable bonds are compound financial instruments as defined by IAS 32. As such, the debt and conversion option components have to be separately classified and measured. As at 12 November 2002, the date of issue, the fair value of the exchangeable bonds in US dollar terms was $735 million, the debt component being $598 million with the remaining $137 million allocated to the conversion option. The fair value of the debt component was determined on the issue date using a market interest rate for an equivalent non-exchangeable bond. This amount is recorded as a liability on an amortised cost basis until extinguished on conversion or maturity of the bonds. The finance costs charged to the income statement includes the discount (…), interest coupon and issue costs. The remainder of the proceeds received on issue was allocated to the conversion option. From 5 November 2004, when the cash settlement alternative option that existed on issue was revoked …, the conversion option was recognised as an equity instrument as part of equity (included in other capital reserves) and not subsequently remeasured. Before this date, the conversion option was classified as a derivative within liabilities and fair valued through the income statement. As a result of movements in Man Group plc's share price during the period between 12 November 2002 and 5 November 2004, under IFRS the fair value gains and losses on the conversion option posted to the income statement are significant in the comparative year to 31 March 2005, but will not reoccur in future periods.

4.6 Other issues

The following issues discussed earlier in this Chapter are of particular relevance to convertible bonds:

- the treatment, in consolidated financial statements, of instruments denominated in a currency different from the functional currency of the issuing entity or that of the entity into whose equity the bond will be converted (see 3.3.1 B above)

- the treatment of instruments settled with equity instruments the number of which varies to reflect major capital restructurings before settlement (see 3.3.1 C above)

These and other issues noted at various points above reinforce an increasing concern that the 'split accounting' rules in IAS 32 are implicitly based on a bond with terms much more straightforward than those of many bonds actually in issue.

It is to be hoped that the joint FASB and IASB project on financial liabilities and equity will lead to a future standard that takes due account of the typical features of the generality of bonds actually in issue.

5 INTEREST, DIVIDENDS, GAINS AND LOSSES

The basic principle of IAS 32 is that inflows and outflows of cash (and other assets) associated with equity instruments are recognised in equity and the net impact of inflows and outflows of cash (and other assets) associated with financial liabilities is ultimately recognised in the income statement. Accordingly, IAS 32 requires:

- interest, dividends, losses and gains relating to a financial instrument or a component that is a financial liability to be recognised as income or expense in profit or loss;
- distributions to holders of an equity instrument (net of any related income tax benefit) to be debited directly to equity; and
- the transaction costs of an equity transaction (net of any related income tax benefit) to be accounted for as a deduction from equity, other than the costs of issuing an equity instrument that are directly attributable to the acquisition of a business (which are accounted for under IFRS 3 – see Chapter 7 at 2.3.2 D).[128]

The treatment of the costs and gains associated with instruments is determined by their classification in the financial statements under IAS 32, and not by their legal form. Thus dividends paid on shares classified as financial liabilities (see 3.2.1 above) will be recognised as an expense in profit or loss, not as an appropriation of equity. Gains and losses associated with redemptions or refinancings of financial liabilities are recognised in profit or loss, whereas redemptions or refinancings of equity instruments are recognised as changes in equity.[129]

Similarly, gains and losses related to changes in the carrying amount of a financial liability are recognised as income or expense in profit or loss, even when they relate to an instrument that includes a right to the residual interest in the assets of the entity in exchange for cash or another financial asset (see 3.2.2 above). However, IAS 32 notes that IAS 1 requires any gain or loss arising from the remeasurement of such an instrument to be shown separately on the face of the income statement where it is relevant in explaining the entity's performance.[130]

Changes in the fair value of an equity instrument are not recognised in the financial statements.[131]

IAS 32 permits dividends classified as an expense to be presented in the income statement either with interest on other liabilities or as a separate item. The standard notes that, in some circumstances, separate disclosure is desirable, because of the differences between interest and dividends with respect to matters such as tax deductibility. Disclosure of interest and dividends is required by IAS 1 (see Chapter 3), IAS 32 or IFRS 7 as applicable (see Chapter 22), and IAS 30 – *Disclosures in the Financial Statements of Banks and Similar Financial Institutions* (not covered in detail in this book). Disclosures of the tax effects are made in accordance with IAS 12 (see Chapter 26).[132]

5.1 Transaction costs of equity transactions

An entity typically incurs various costs in issuing or acquiring its own equity instruments, such as registration and other regulatory fees, amounts paid to legal, accounting and other professional advisers, printing costs and stamp duties. The transaction costs of an equity transaction are accounted for as a deduction from equity (net of any related income tax benefit), but only to the extent they are incremental costs directly attributable to the equity transaction that otherwise would have been avoided. The costs of an equity transaction that is abandoned are recognised as an expense.[133]

IAS 32 requires that it is only the costs of 'issuing or acquiring' equity that are recognised in equity. Accordingly, in our view, the costs of listing shares already in issue should not be set off against equity, but recognised as an expense. It may well be that, in an initial public offering ('IPO'), an entity simultaneously lists its existing equity and additional newly-issued equity. In that situation the total costs of the IPO should, in our view, be allocated between the newly issued shares and the existing shares on a rational basis (e.g. by reference to the ratio of the number of new shares to the number of total shares).

Transaction costs that relate to the issue of a compound financial instrument are allocated to the liability and equity components of the instrument in proportion to the allocation of proceeds (see Example 19.8 at 4.3 above). Transaction costs that relate jointly to more than one transaction (for example, costs of a concurrent offering of some shares and a stock exchange listing of other shares) are allocated to those transactions using a basis of allocation that is rational and consistent with similar transactions.[134]

The amount of transaction costs accounted for as a deduction from equity in the period is required to be disclosed separately under IAS 1 (see Chapter 3 at 3.3 and Chapter 22 at 4.2). Any related tax relief recognised directly in equity is included in the aggregate amount of current and deferred income tax credited or charged to equity disclosed under IAS 12 (see Chapter 26 at 8).[135]

6 TREASURY SHARES

Treasury shares are shares issued by an entity that are held by the entity itself, or by a subsidiary of the entity, or by another entity controlled by the entity[136] (see 6.1 below).

Holdings of treasury shares may arise in a number of ways. For example:

- The entity holds the shares as the result of a direct transaction, such as a market purchase, or a buy-back of shares from shareholders as a whole, or a particular group of shareholders;
- The entity is in the financial services sector with a market-making operation that buys and sells its own shares along with those of other listed entities in the normal course of business, or holds them in order to 'hedge' issued derivatives;
- In consolidated financial statements:
  - the shares were purchased by another entity which subsequently became a subsidiary of the reporting entity, either through acquisition or changes in financial reporting requirements;
  - the shares have been purchased by an entity that is a consolidated SPE of the reporting entity.

The circumstances in which an entity is permitted to hold treasury shares are a matter for legislation in the jurisdiction concerned.

Treasury shares do not include own shares held by an entity on behalf of others, such as when a financial institution holds its own equity on behalf of a client. In such cases, there is an agency relationship and as a result those holdings are not included in the entity's balance sheet, either as assets or as a deduction from equity.[137]

If an entity reacquires its own equity instruments, IAS 32 requires those instruments to be deducted from equity. They are not recognised as financial assets, regardless of the reason for which they are reacquired. No gain or loss is recognised in profit or loss on the purchase, sale, issue or cancellation of an entity's own equity instruments. Accordingly, any consideration paid or received in connection with treasury share must be recognised directly in equity.[138]

IAS 1 requires the amount of treasury shares to be disclosed separately either on the face of the balance sheet or in the notes (see Chapter 3 at 3.1.6 and Chapter 22 at 4.3). In addition IAS 24 – *Related Party Disclosures* – requires an entity to make disclosures where it reacquires its own equity instruments from related parties (see Chapter 35 at 2.5.5 and Chapter 22 at 6.2).[139]

As in the case of the requirements for the treatment of the equity component of a compound financial instrument (see 4 above), IAS 32 does not prescribe precisely what components of equity should be adjusted as the result of a treasury share transaction. This may have been to ensure that there was no conflict between, on the one hand, the basic requirement of IAS 32 that there should be an adjustment to equity and, on the other hand, the legal requirements of various jurisdictions as to exactly how that adjustment should be allocated within equity.

As literally drafted, IAS 32 appears to require not only that the cost of purchasing treasury shares be charged to equity, but also that the treasury shares themselves be deducted from equity. However, this would yield a 'three-legged' accounting entry which cannot have been the IASB's intention. It is clear from the illustrative examples in the Appendix to IAS 32 (see 7 below) that the true intention of the standard is simply that the cost of purchasing treasury shares should be charged, and the proceeds of reissuing them credited, directly to equity.

6.1 Entities 'controlled' by the entity

IAS 32 does not include specific guidance on what constitutes an entity controlled by the reporting entity (such that any shares in the reporting entity by that other entity are treated as treasury shares).

In practical terms, a controlled entity will include any entity consolidated as a subsidiary or special purpose entity under IAS 27 and SIC-12 – *Consolidation – Special Purpose Entities* – including any employee benefit trust consolidated under SIC-12, or treated as an extension of the reporting entity (see Chapter 31 at 10.5). It will not therefore generally include shares held by:

- any associates; or
- the entity's pension fund.

However, IAS 1 requires disclosure of own shares held by associates,[140] and IAS 19 – *Employee Benefits* – requires disclosure of own shares held by defined benefit plans.[141]

6.2 Comparison with IFRS 2 – *Share-based payment*

The apparently unequivocal requirement of IAS 32 that no profits or losses should ever be recognised on transactions in own equity instruments is inconsistent with IFRS 2. If an employee share award is characterised as an equity instrument under IFRS 2 (a 'share-settled' award) and settled in cash (or other assets) at more than its fair value, the excess of the consideration over the fair value is recognised as an expense (see Chapter 31 at 4.10, 5.5.2 and 7.2.2).

It is not clear whether or not the IASB specifically considered transactions in own equity other than at fair value in the context of IAS 32, particularly since the relevant provisions of IAS 32 essentially reproduce requirements previously contained in SIC-16 – *Share Capital – Reacquired Own Equity Instruments (Treasury Shares)* – which was implicitly addressing market purchases and sales at fair value. In other words, the provision can be seen merely as clarifying that, if an entity buys one of its own shares in the market for £10 which it later reissues in the market at £12 or £7, it has not made, respectively, a profit of £2 or a loss of £3.

This is slightly different to the situation where an entity purchases an equity instrument for more than its fair value – i.e. if the original purchase had been for £11 when the market price was £10. Such a transaction could occur, for example where the entity wishes to rid itself of a troublesome shareholder or group of shareholders. In this case, the entity might have to offer a premium specific to the holder over and above the 'true' fair value of the equity instruments concerned. There could be an argument that such a transaction does not fall within the type of transaction envisaged by the rules for treasury shares, such that the holder-specific premium should be accounted for in profit or loss, not equity. In our view, this is an area which the IASB might wish to consider further, but without rushing to judgement.

7 CONTRACTS OVER OWN EQUITY INSTRUMENTS

A significant change made to IAS 32 as a result of its revision in December 2003 was the addition of a number of detailed examples of the accounting treatment required, under the provisions of revised IAS 32 and IAS 39, to be adopted by an entity for contracts in its own equity instruments. Examples are given of each of the main possible permutations, namely:

- a forward purchase (see 7.1.1 below);
- a forward sale (see 7.1.2 below);
- a purchased call option (see 7.2.1 below);
- a written call option (see 7.2.2 below);
- a purchased put option (see 7.3.1 below); and
- a written put option (see 7.3.2 below).

All such contracts can be either:

(a) net cash-settled (i.e. the contract provides that the parties will compare the fair value of the shares to be delivered by the seller to the amount of cash payable by the buyer and make a cash payment between themselves for the difference);

(b) net share-settled (i.e. the contract provides that the parties will compare the fair value of the shares to be delivered by the seller to the amount of cash payable by the buyer and make a transfer between themselves of as many of the entity's shares as have a fair value equal to the difference);

(c) gross settled (i.e. the contract provides that the seller will deliver shares to the buyer in exchange for cash); or

(d) subject to various settlement options, whereby the manner of settlement is not predetermined, and instead one or other party can choose the manner of settlement (i.e. gross, net cash or net shares).

Each example considers the options above in turn.

7.1 Forward contracts

7.1.1 Forward purchase

In a forward purchase transaction, the entity and a counterparty agree that on a given future date the counterparty will sell a given number of the entity's shares to the entity. Such a contract is illustrated in Example 19.13 below.[142]

Example 19.13: Forward purchase of shares

The reporting entity (A), which has a year end of 31 December, and another party (B) enter into a forward contract for the purchase of A's shares by A, for which the following are the major assumptions.

Contract date	1 February 2008
Maturity date	31 January 2009
Market price per share on 1 February 2008	€100
Market price per share on 31 December 2008	€110
Market price per share on 31 January 2009	€106
Fixed forward price to be paid on 31 January 2009	€104
Present value of forward price on 1 February 2008	€100
Number of shares under contract	1,000
Fair value of forward to A on 1 February 2008	€0
Fair value of forward to A on 31 December 2008	€6,300
Fair value of forward to A on 31 January 2009	€2,000

For simplicity, it is assumed that no dividends are paid on the underlying shares (i.e. the 'carry return' is zero) so that the present value of the forward price equals the spot price when the fair value of the forward contract is zero. The fair value of the forward has been computed as the difference between the market share price and the present value of the fixed forward price. At settlement date this is €2,000 representing 1000 shares at €2, being the difference between the market price of €106 and the contract price of €104

A Net cash settlement

If the contract is entered into as cash-settled, on 1 February 2008, A enters into a contract with B to pay, or receive as the case may be, on 31 January 2009 a cash payment for the difference between the fair value, at 31 January 2009, of 1,000 of A's own shares and €104,000 (i.e. 1000 shares at the forward price of €104 per share). IAS 32 classifies this derivative contract as a financial asset or liability (see 3.3.2 D and 3.5 above), which IAS 39 requires to be accounted for at fair value (see Chapter 20). A records the following accounting entries.

	€	€
1 February 2008		
No entry is required because the fair value of the contract is zero at inception and no cash is paid or received		
31 December 2008		
Forward contract (balance sheet)	6,300	
Gain on forward (income statement)		6,300
To record increase in fair value of forward		
31 January 2009		
Loss on forward (income statement)	4,300	
Forward contract (balance sheet)		4,300
To record decrease in fair value of forward		
Cash	2,000	
Forward contract (balance sheet)		2,000
To record settlement of forward		

B Net share settlement

If the contract is entered into as net share-settled, on 1 February 2008, A enters into a contract with B to pay, or receive as the case may be, on 31 January 2009 a payment of as many of A's shares as have a fair value equal to the difference between the fair value, at 31 January 2009, of 1,000 of A's own shares and €104,000 (i.e. 1000 shares at the forward price of €104 per share). IAS 32 classifies this derivative contract as a financial asset or liability (see 3.3.2 D and 3.5 above), which IAS 39 requires to be accounted for at fair value (see Chapter 20). A records the following accounting entries.

	€	€
1 February 2008		
No entry is required because the fair value of the contract is zero at inception and no cash is paid or received		
31 December 2008		
Forward contract (balance sheet)	6,300	
Gain on forward (income statement)		6,300
To record increase in fair value of forward		
31 January 2009		
Loss on forward (income statement)	4,300	
Forward contract (balance sheet)		4,300
To record decrease in fair value of forward		
Equity	2,000	
Forward contract (balance sheet)		2,000
To record net settlement of forward by transfer of €2,000 worth of A's shares by B to A. This is shown as a deduction from equity in accordance with IAS 32's requirements for treasury shares (see 6 above).		

C Gross settlement

If the contract is entered into as gross-settled, on 1 February 2008, A enters into a contract with B to pay B, on 31 January 2009, €104,000 in exchange for 1,000 of A's own shares. IAS 32 classifies this derivative contract as an equity instrument giving rise to a financial liability for the purchase price (see 3.3.3 above). On the assumption that A accounts for this liability under the effective interest method in IAS 39 (see Chapter 20), A records the following accounting entries.

	€	€
1 February 2008		
Equity	100,000	
Forward contract (balance sheet)		100,000
To record net present value of liability on forward contract		
31 December 2008		
Interest expense	3,660	
Forward contract (balance sheet)		3,660
To record accrual of interest on liability to settle forward contract		

31 January 2009

Interest expense	340	
Forward contract (balance sheet)		340
To record further accrual of interest on liability		
Forward contract (balance sheet)	104,000	
Cash		104,000
To record settlement of liability		

D Settlement options

If there are settlement options (such as net in cash, net in shares or by an exchange of cash and shares), the forward contract is a financial asset or a financial liability – see 3.3.4 and 3.5 above. If one of the settlement alternatives is to exchange cash for shares, A recognises a liability for the obligation to deliver cash. Otherwise, A accounts for the forward contract as a derivative.

7.1.2 Forward sale

In a forward sale transaction, the entity and a counterparty agree that on a given future date the entity will sell (or issue) a given number of the entity's shares to the counterparty. Such a contract is illustrated in Example 19.14 below.[143]

Example 19.14: Forward sale of shares

The reporting entity (A), which has a year end of 31 December, and another party (B) enter into a forward contract for the purchase of A's shares by B, for which the following are the major assumptions.

Contract date	1 February 2008
Maturity date	31 January 2009
Market price per share on 1 February 2008	€100
Market price per share on 31 December 2008	€110
Market price per share on 31 January 2009	€106
Fixed forward price to be paid on 31 January 2009	€104
Present value of forward price on 1 February 2008	€100
Number of shares under contract	1,000
Fair value of forward to A on 1 February 2008	€0
Fair value of forward to A on 31 December 2008	€(6,300)
Fair value of forward to A on 31 January 2009	€(2,000)

For simplicity, it is assumed that no dividends are paid on the underlying shares (i.e. the 'carry return' is zero) so that the present value of the forward price equals the spot price when the fair value of the forward contract is zero. The fair value of the forward has been computed as the difference between the market share price and the present value of the fixed forward price. At settlement date this is negative €2,000 representing 1000 shares at €2, being the difference between the market price of €106 and the contract price of €104.

A Net cash settlement

If the contract is entered into as cash-settled, on 1 February 2008, A enters into a contract with B to pay, or receive as the case may be, on 31 January 2009 a cash payment for the difference between the fair value, at 31 January 2009, of 1,000 of A's own shares and €104,000 (i.e. 1000 shares at the forward price of €104 per share). IAS 32 classifies this derivative contract as a financial asset or liability (see 3.3.2 D and 3.5 above), which IAS 39 requires to be accounted for at fair value (see Chapter 20). A records the following accounting entries.

	€	€
1 February 2008		
No entry is required because the fair value of the contract is zero at inception and no cash is paid or received.		
31 December 2008		
Loss on forward (income statement)	6,300	
Forward contract (balance sheet)		6,300
To record decrease in fair value of forward		
31 January 2009		
Forward contract (balance sheet)	4,300	
Gain on forward (income statement)		4,300
To record increase in fair value of forward		
Forward contract (balance sheet)	2,000	
Cash		2,000
To record net settlement of forward by payment of €2,000 cash by A to B		

B ***Net share settlement***

If the contract is entered into as net share-settled, on 1 February 2008, A enters into a contract with B to pay, or receive as the case may be, on 31 January 2009 a payment of as many of A's shares as are equal to the difference between the fair value, at 31 January 2009, of 1,000 of A's own shares and €104,000 (i.e. 1000 shares at the forward price of €104 per share). IAS 32 classifies this derivative contract as a financial asset or liability (see 3.3.2 D and 3.5 above), which IAS 39 requires to be accounted for at fair value (see Chapter 20). A records the following accounting entries.

	€	€
1 February 2008		
No entry is required because the fair value of the contract is zero at inception		
31 December 2008		
Loss on forward (income statement)	6,300	
Forward contract (balance sheet)		6,300
To record decrease in fair value of forward		
31 January 2009		
Forward contract (balance sheet)	4,300	
Gain on forward (income statement)		4,300
To record increase in fair value of forward		
Forward contract (balance sheet)	2,000	
Equity		2,000
To record net settlement of forward by issue of €2,000 worth of A's shares to B		

C ***Gross settlement***

If the contract is entered into as gross-settled, on 1 February 2008, A enters into a contract with B whereby B will pay A, on 31 January 2009, €104,000 in exchange for 1,000 A's own shares. IAS 32 classifies this contract as an equity instrument (see 3.3.4 above); therefore no entries are recorded, other than on settlement of the contract:

	€	€
31 January 2009		
Cash	104,000	
Equity		104,000
To record settlement of forward contract		

D ***Settlement options***

If there are settlement options (such as net in cash, net in shares or by an exchange of cash and shares), the forward contract is a financial asset or a financial liability – see 3.3.4 and 3.5 above. A accounts for the forward contract as a derivative (as in A and B above), with the accounting entry made on settlement determined by the manner of settlement (i.e. equity or cash).

7.1.3 'Back-to-back' forward contracts

The accounting treatment in 7.1.1 and 7.1.2 produces rather strange results when applied to 'back-to-back' forward contracts, such as might be entered into by a financial institution with two different clients. Example 19.15 below illustrates the point.

Example 19.15: 'Back-to-back' forward contracts

Suppose that a bank entered into the forward purchase contract in Example 19.13 above with a client and laid off its risk by entering into the reciprocal forward sale contract in Example 19.14 above with a second client. If both contracts are required to be settled gross, the overall effect of the accounting entries required to be made by the bank (assuming that the bank was the reporting entity in Examples 19.12 and 19.13) can be summarised as set out below. Note that these are not the actual entries that would be made, but the arithmetical sum of all the entries:

	€	€
Income statement (interest expense on liability for purchase contract)	4,000	
Equity (€104,000 on sale less €100,000 on purchase)		4,000

If the purchase contract is required to be settled gross, but the sale contract net in cash, the required accounting entries (again, not the actual entries, but the arithmetical sum of all the entries) can be summarised as:

	€	€
Income statement (loss on sale contract €2,000 plus interest on liability for purchase contract €4,000)	6,000	
Equity (purchase contract)	100,000	
Cash (€104,000 on purchase, €2,000 on sale)		106,000

If the purchase contract is required to be settled net in cash, but the sale contract gross, the required accounting entries (again, not the actual entries, but the arithmetical sum of all the entries) can be summarised as:

	€	€
Cash (€104,000 in on sale, €2,000 in on purchase)	106,000	
Income statement (gain on purchase contract)		2,000
Equity (sale contract)		104,000

If both contracts are net settled, no net gain or loss arises.

Some might argue that this exposes a flaw in the requirements of IAS 32. Self-evidently, these contracts are matched and should therefore, if both run to term, give rise to no economic profit or loss, irrespective of how they are settled. However, IAS 32 requires three different results to be shown depending on whether both contracts are settled gross, or one gross and the other net. This is less understandable in the case where both contracts are settled gross. However, in cases where one contract is settled net and that contract gives rise to an initial receipt or payment of cash, then some difference is bound to occur due to interest effects.

7.2 Call options

7.2.1 *Purchased call option*

In a purchased call option, the entity pays a counterparty for the right, but not the obligation, to purchase a given number of its own equity instruments from the counterparty for a fixed price at a future date. The accounting for such a contract is illustrated in Example 19.16 below.[144]

Example 19.16: Purchased call option on shares

The reporting entity (A), which has a year end of 31 December, purchases a call option over its own shares from another party (B), for which the following are the major assumptions.

Contract date	1 February 2008
Exercise date (European terms – i.e. can be exercised only on maturity)	31 January 2009
Market price per share on 1 February 2008	€100
Market price per share on 31 December 2008	€104
Market price per share on 31 January 2009	€104
Fixed exercise price to be paid on 31 January 2009	€102
Number of shares under contract	1,000
Fair value of option to A on 1 February 2008	€5,000
Fair value of option to A on 31 December 2008	€3,000
Fair value of option to A on 31 January 2009	€2,000

The fair value of the option would be computed using an option pricing model and would be a function of a number of factors, principally the market value of the shares, the exercise price, and the time value of money.

A Net cash settlement

If the contract is entered into as cash-settled, on 1 February 2008 A enters into a contract with B whereby A can require B, on 31 January 2009, to make a cash payment to A of any excess of the fair value, at 31 January 2009, of 1,000 of A's own shares over €102,000 (i.e. 1000 shares at the option price of €102 per share). IAS 32 classifies this derivative contract as a financial asset (see 3.3.2 D and 3.5 above), which IAS 39 requires to be accounted for at fair value (see Chapter 20). A records the following accounting entries.

	€	€
1 February 2008		
Call option asset	5,000	
Cash		5,000
Payment of option premium (equal to fair value of option) to B		
31 December 2008		
Loss on option (income statement)	2,000	
Call option asset		2,000
To record decrease in fair value of option		
31 January 2009		
Loss on option (income statement)	1,000	
Call option asset		1,000
To record decrease in fair value of option		
Cash	2,000	
Call option asset		2,000
To record net settlement of option by payment of €2,000 cash by B to A		

B Net share settlement

If the contract is entered into as net share-settled, on 1 February 2008, A enters into a contract with B, whereby A can require B, on 31 January 2009, to deliver to A as many of A's own shares as have a fair value equal to any excess of the fair value, at 31 January 2009, of 1,000 of A's own shares over €102,000 (i.e. 1000 shares at the option price of €102 per share). IAS 32 classifies this derivative contract as a financial asset (see 3.3.2 D and 3.5 above), which IAS 39 requires to be accounted for at fair value (see Chapter 20). A records the following accounting entries.

	€	€
1 February 2008		
Call option asset	5,000	
Cash		5,000
Payment of option premium (equal to fair value of option) to B		
31 December 2008		
Loss on option (income statement)	2,000	
Call option asset		2,000
To record decrease in fair value of option		

31 January 2009

Loss on option (income statement)	1,000	
Call option asset		1,000
To record decrease in fair value of option		
Equity	2,000	
Call option asset		2,000
To record net settlement of option by transfer of €2,000 worth of A's shares by B to A. This is shown as a deduction from equity in accordance with IAS 32's requirements for treasury shares (see 6 above).		

C ***Gross settlement***

If the contract is entered into as gross-settled, on 1 February 2008, A enters into a contract with B whereby A can require B, on 31 January 2009, to deliver 1,000 of A's shares in return for a payment by A of €102,000. IAS 32 classifies this derivative contract as an equity instrument (see 3.3.3 above); therefore no entries are recorded, other than to record the cash flows arising under the contract:

	€	€
1 February 2008		
Equity	5,000	
Cash		5,000
Payment of option premium (equal to fair value of option) to B		
31 January 2009		
Equity	102,000	
Cash		102,000
To record gross settlement of option by payment of €102,000 cash to B in exchange for 1,000 own shares.		

If the option had lapsed unexercised, because the market price of A's shares had fallen below €102 as at 31 January 2009, the £5,000 premium would remain in equity, even though it is, from an economic perspective, clearly a loss rather than an amount paid to repurchase A's own shares. This is because IFRS regards any holder of an instrument classified as equity under IAS 32 as an 'owner'.

It should be noted that, in contrast to the treatment of a gross-settled forward purchase (see 7.1.1 above) and a gross-settled written put option (see 7.3.2 below), which also require a gross outflow of cash on settlement, there is no requirement to record a liability at the outset of the contract on which interest is accrued during the period of the contract. This is because:

- in a gross-settled forward purchase or written put option, the entity can be required to make a payment of cash, but
- in a purchased call option, there is no liability, since the entity has no obligation to exercise its right to call for the shares even if the option is 'in the money' and it is in the entity's interest to do so.

D Settlement options

If there are settlement options (such as net in cash, net in shares or by an exchange of cash and shares), the option is a financial asset. A accounts for the forward contract as a derivative (as in A and B above), with the accounting entry made on settlement determined by the manner of settlement (i.e. equity or cash).

7.2.2 Written call option

In a written call option, the entity receives a payment from a counterparty for granting to the counterparty the right, but not the obligation, to purchase a given number of the entity's own equity instruments from the entity for a fixed price at a future date. The accounting for such a contract is illustrated in Example 19.17 below.[145]

Example 19.17: Written call option on shares

The reporting entity (A), which has a year end of 31 December, writes a call option over its own shares with another party (B), for which the following are the major assumptions.

Contract date	1 February 2008
Exercise date (European terms – i.e. can be exercised only on maturity)	31 January 2009
Market price per share on 1 February 2008	€100
Market price per share on 31 December 2008	€104
Market price per share on 31 January 2009	€104
Fixed exercise price to be paid on 31 January 2009	€102
Number of shares under contract	1,000
Fair value of option to A on 1 February 2008	€(5,000)
Fair value of option to A on 31 December 2008	€(3,000)
Fair value of option to A on 31 January 2009	€(2,000)

The fair value of the option would be computed using an option pricing model and would be a function of a number of factors, principally the market value of the shares, the exercise price, and the time value of money.

A Net cash settlement

If the contract is entered into as cash-settled, on 1 February 2008, A enters into a contract with B whereby B can require A, on 31 January 2009, to make a cash payment to B of any excess of the fair value, at 31 January 2009, of 1,000 of A's own shares over €102,000 (i.e. 1000 shares at the option price of €102 per share). IAS 32 classifies this derivative contract as a financial liability (see 3.3.2 D and 3.5 above), which IAS 39 requires to be accounted for at fair value (see Chapter 20). A records the following accounting entries:

	€	€
1 February 2008		
Cash	5,000	
Call option liability		5,000
Receipt of option premium (equal to fair value of option) from B		

	€	€
31 December 2008		
Call option liability	2,000	
Gain on option (income statement)		2,000
To record decrease in fair value of option		
31 January 2009		
Call option liability	1,000	
Gain on option (income statement)		1,000
To record decrease in fair value of option		
Call option liability	2,000	
Cash		2,000
To record net settlement of option by payment of €2,000 cash to B		

B ***Net share settlement***

If the contract is entered into as net share-settled, on 1 February 2008, A enters into a contract with B, whereby B can require A, on 31 January 2009, to deliver to B as many of A's own shares as have a fair value equal to any excess of the fair value, at 31 January 2009, of 1,000 of A's own shares over €102,000 (i.e. 1000 shares at the option price of €102 per share). IAS 32 classifies this derivative contract as a financial liability (see 3.3.2 D and 3.5 above), which IAS 39 requires to be accounted for at fair value (see Chapter 20). A records the following accounting entries.

	€	€
1 February 2008		
Cash	5,000	
Call option liability		5,000
Receipt of option premium (equal to fair value of option) from B		
31 December 2008		
Call option liability	2,000	
Gain on option (income statement)		2,000
To record decrease in fair value of option		
31 January 2009	1,000	
Call option liability		1,000
Gain on option (income statement)		
To record decrease in fair value of option		
Call option liability	2,000	
Equity		2,000
To record net settlement of option by issue of €2,000 worth of A's shares to B		

C Gross settlement

If the contract is entered into as gross-settled, on 1 February 2008, A enters into a contract with B whereby B can require A, on 31 January 2009, to deliver 1,000 of A's shares in return for a payment by B of €102,000. IAS 32 classifies this derivative contract as an equity instrument (see 3.3.3 above); therefore no entries are recorded, other than to record the cash flows arising under the contract:

	€	€
1 February 2008		
Cash	5,000	
Equity		5,000
Receipt of option premium (equal to fair value of option) to B		
31 January 2009		
Cash	102,000	
Equity		102,000
To record gross settlement of option by receipt of €102,000 cash to B in exchange for 1,000 own shares.		

If the option had lapsed unexercised, because the market price of A's shares had fallen below €102 as at 31 January 2009, the £5,000 premium would remain in equity, even though it is, from an economic perspective, clearly a gain rather than an amount received from an owner. This is because IFRS regards any holder of an instrument classified as equity under IAS 32 as an 'owner'.

D Settlement options

If there are settlement options (such as net in cash, net in shares or by an exchange of cash and shares), the option is a financial liability. A accounts for the forward contract as a derivative (as in A and B above), with the accounting entry made on settlement determined by the manner of settlement (i.e. equity or cash).

7.3 Put options

7.3.1 Purchased put option

In a purchased put option, the entity makes a payment to a counterparty for the right, but not the obligation, to require the counterparty to purchase a given number of the entity's own equity instruments from the entity for a fixed price at a future date. The accounting for such a contract is illustrated in Example 19.18 below.[146]

Example 19.18: Purchased put option on shares

The reporting entity (A), which has a year end of 31 December, purchases a put option over its own shares from another party (B), for which the following are the major assumptions.

Contract date	1 February 2008
Exercise date (European terms – i.e. can be exercised only on maturity)	31 January 2009
Market price per share on 1 February 2008	€100
Market price per share on 31 December 2008	€95
Market price per share on 31 January 2009	€95
Fixed exercise price to be paid on 31 January 2009	€98
Number of shares under contract	1,000
Fair value of option to A on 1 February 2008	€5,000
Fair value of option to A on 31 December 2008	€4,000
Fair value of option to A on 31 January 2009	€3,000

The fair value of the option would be computed using an option pricing model and would be a function of number of factors, principally the market value of the shares, the exercise price, and the time value of money.

A Net cash settlement

If the contract is entered into as cash-settled, on 1 February 2008, A enters into a contract with B whereby A can require B, on 31 January 2009, to make a cash payment to A of any excess, at 31 January 2009, of €98,000 (i.e. 1000 shares at the option price of €98 per share) over the fair value of 1,000 of A's own shares. IAS 32 classifies this derivative contract as a financial asset (see 3.3.2 D and 3.5 above), which IAS 39 requires to be accounted for at fair value (see Chapter 20). A records the following accounting entries.

	€	€
1 February 2008		
Put option asset	5,000	
Cash		5,000
Payment of option premium (equal to fair value of option) to B		
31 December 2008		
Loss on option (income statement)	1,000	
Put option asset		1,000
To record decrease in fair value of option		
31 January 2009		
Loss on option (income statement)	1,000	
Put option asset		1,000
To record decrease in fair value of option		
Cash	3,000	
Put option asset		3,000
To record net settlement of option by receipt of €3,000 cash from B		

B Net share settlement

If the contract is entered into as share-settled, on 1 February 2008, A enters into a contract with B, whereby A can require B, on 31 January 2009, to deliver to A as many of A's own shares as have a fair value equal to any excess of €98,000 (i.e. 1000 shares at the option price of €98 per share) over the fair value, at 31 January 2009, of 1,000 of A's own shares. IAS 32 classifies this derivative contract as a financial asset (see 3.3.2 D and 3.5 above), which IAS 39 requires to be accounted for at fair value (see Chapter 20). A records the following accounting entries.

	€	€
1 February 2008		
Put option asset	5,000	
Cash		5,000
Payment of option premium (equal to fair value of option) to B		
31 December 2008		
Loss on option (income statement)	1,000	
Put option asset		1,000
To record decrease in fair value of option		
31 January 2009		
Loss on option (income statement)	1,000	
Put option asset		1,000
To record decrease in fair value of option		
Equity	3,000	
Put option asset		3,000
To record net settlement of option by receipt of €3,000 worth of A's shares from B. This is shown as a deduction from equity in accordance with IAS 32's requirements for treasury shares (see 6 above).		

C Gross settlement

If the contract is entered into as gross-settled, on 1 February 2008, A enters into a contract with B whereby A can require B, on 31 January 2009, to take delivery 1,000 of A's shares in return for a payment by B of €98,000. IAS 32 classifies this derivative contract as an equity instrument (see 3.3.4 above); therefore no entries are recorded, other than to record the cash flows arising under the contract:

	€	€
1 February 2008		
Equity	5,000	
Cash		5,000
Payment of option premium (equal to fair value of option) to B		

31 January 2009

Cash	98,000	
Equity		98,000

To record gross settlement of option by delivery of 1,000 own shares to B in exchange for €98,000.

If the option had lapsed unexercised, because the market price of A's shares had risen above €98 as at 31 January 2009, the £5,000 premium would remain in equity, even though it is, from an economic perspective, clearly a loss rather than an amount paid to repurchase A's own shares.

D Settlement options

If there are settlement options (such as net in cash, net in shares or by an exchange of cash and shares), the option is a financial asset. A accounts for the forward contract as a derivative (as in A and B above), with the accounting entry made on settlement determined by the manner of settlement (i.e. equity or cash).

7.3.2 Written put option

In a written put option, the entity receives a payment from a counterparty for granting to the counterparty the right, but not the obligation, to sell a given number of the entity's own equity instruments to the entity for a fixed price at a future date. The accounting for such a contract is illustrated in Example 19.19 below.[147]

Example 19.19: Written put option on own shares

The reporting entity (A), which has a year end of 31 December, writes a put option over its own shares with another party (B), for which the following are the major assumptions.

Contract date	1 February 2008
Exercise date (European terms – i.e. can be exercised only on maturity)	31 January 2009
Market price per share on 1 February 2008	€100
Market price per share on 31 December 2008	€95
Market price per share on 31 January 2009	€95
Fixed exercise price to be paid on 31 January 2009	€98
Number of shares under contract	1,000
Fair value of option to A on 1 February 2008	€(5,000)
Fair value of option to A on 31 December 2008	€(4,000)
Fair value of option to A on 31 January 2009	€(3,000)

The fair value of the option would be computed using an option pricing model and would be a function of a number of factors, principally the market value of the shares, the exercise price, and the time value of money.

A Net cash settlement

If the contract is entered into as cash-settled, on 1 February 2008, A enters into a contract with B whereby B can require A, on 31 January 2009, to make a cash payment to B of any excess of €98,000 (i.e. 1000 shares at the option price of €98 per share) over the fair value, at 31 January 2009, of 1,000 of A's own shares. IAS 32 classifies this derivative contract as a financial liability (see 3.3.2 D and 3.5 above), which IAS 39 requires to be accounted for at fair value (see Chapter 20). A records the following accounting entries.

	€	€
1 February 2008		
Cash	5,000	
Put option liability		5,000
Receipt of option premium (equal to fair value of option) from B		
31 December 2008		
Put option liability	1,000	
Gain on option (income statement)		1,000
To record increase in fair value of option		
31 January 2009		
Put option liability	1,000	
Gain on option (income statement)		1,000
To record increase in fair value of option		
Put option liability	3,000	
Cash		3,000
To record net settlement of option by payment of €3,000 cash to B		

B Net share settlement

If the contract is entered into as net share-settled, on 1 February 2008, A enters into a contract with B, whereby B can require A, on 31 January 2009, to deliver to B as many of A's own shares as have a fair value equal to any excess of €98,000 (i.e. 1000 shares at the option price of €98 per share) over the fair value, at 31 January 2009, of 1,000 of A's own shares. IAS 32 classifies this derivative contract as a financial liability (see 3.3.2 D and 3.5. above), which IAS 39 requires to be accounted for at fair value (see Chapter 20). A records the following accounting entries.

	€	€
1 February 2008		
Cash	5,000	
Put option liability		5,000
Receipt of option premium (equal to fair value of option) from B		
31 December 2008		
Put option liability	1,000	
Gain on option (income statement)		1,000
To record increase in fair value of option		

31 January 2009

Put option liability	1,000	
Gain on option (income statement)		1,000
To record increase in fair value of option		
Put option liability	3,000	
Equity		3,000
To record net settlement of option by issue of €3,000 worth of own shares to B		

C Gross settlement

If the contract is entered into as gross-settled, on 1 February 2008, A enters into a contract with B whereby B can require A, on 31 January 2009, to take delivery of 1,000 of A's shares in return for a payment by A of €98,000. IAS 32 classifies this derivative contract as an equity instrument giving rise to a financial liability for the purchase pricc (see 3.3.3 and 3.5 above). On the assumption that A accounts for this liability under the effective interest method in IAS 39 (see Chapter 20), A records the following accounting entries.

	€	€
1 February 2008		
Cash	5,000	
Equity	90,000	
Liability (net present value of €98,000 potentially payable under option)		95,000
Receipt of option premium (equal to fair value of option) from B and recording of potential liability to settle option		
31 December 2008		
Interest (income statement)	2,750	
Liability		2,750
To accrue interest on the liability		
31 January 2009		
Interest expense (income statement)	250	
Liability		250
To accrue interest on the liability		
Liability	98,000	
Cash		98,000
To record gross settlement of option by delivery of by B of 1,000 shares in A in exchange for €98,000		

If the option had lapsed unexercised, because the market price of A's shares had risen above €98 as at 31 January 2009, the economic consequence is clearly that A has made a profit of €5,000 – the premium that it received from B, for which it has ultimately had to give nothing in return. However the overall effect of the treatment that would be required by IAS 32 can be summarised as follows:

	€	€
Cash	5,000	
Income statement (interest on potential liability to pay cash)	3,000	
Equity (€98,000 carrying amount of liability transferred at date of lapse less €90,000 debited on 1.2.07)		8,000

To some, to record a loss on a transaction that makes a profit (on any natural meaning of the word) might seem a distortion of economic reality; to the IASB, it is merely an inexorable consequence of its *Framework*.

D Settlement options

If there are settlement options (such as net in cash, net in shares or by an exchange of cash and shares), the option is a financial liability. A accounts for the forward contract as a derivative (as in A and B above), with the accounting entry made on settlement determined by the manner of settlement (i.e. equity or cash). If one of the settlement alternatives is to exchange cash for shares, A recognises a liability for the obligation to deliver cash (as in C above). Otherwise, Entity A accounts for the put option as a derivative liability.

The requirement for A to recognise a liability 'if one of the settlement alternatives is to exchange cash for shares', as drafted, applies whether the choice of settlement rests with A or B. This seems curious since, where A had the choice of settlement there would be no obligation to deliver gross settle. We assume that the example is written on the presumption that the choice of settlement of an option would normally rest with the buyer rather than the writer of the option.

7.4 Dissenting opinion

Certain aspects of IAS 32's required accounting treatment for transactions in own equity prompted one IASB member (James J Leisenring) to dissent from the standard. Specifically, Mr Leisenring believes that:

- the requirement to record a liability for the amount payable under a gross-settled forward contract to purchase own equity (see 7.1.1 above) is inconsistent with the accounting for other forward contracts;
- the liability recorded in accounting for a gross-settled written put option (see 7.3.2 above) does not represent a present obligation of the entity, and is therefore not consistent with the IASB's *Framework*. It is a derivative which should be accounted for like any other derivative. Mr Leisenring also believes that an instrument such as a redeemable preference share (classified by IAS 32 as a liability) should instead be accounted for as an equity instrument with the redemption feature accounted for as a derivative; and
- the conclusion of IAS 32 that a purchased put or call option on a fixed number of an issuer's equity instruments is not an asset is not correct. The rights created by these contracts meet the definition of an asset and should be accounted for as assets and not as a reduction in equity. These contracts also meet the definition of derivatives that should be accounted for as such in accordance with IAS 39.[148]

8 TRANSITIONAL AND FIRST-TIME ADOPTION PROVISIONS

There are no transitional provisions in IAS 32.

The discussion below deals only with the first-time adoption provisions for periods beginning on or after 1 January 2006. Specific requirements for earlier periods were addressed in *International GAAP 2005* and *International GAAP 2007*.

IFRS 1 contains two general provisions in respect of the classification of financial instruments on first-time adoption of IFRS.

IFRS 1 requires the entity to apply the criteria in IAS 32 to classify financial instruments issued (or components of compound instruments issued) as either financial liabilities or equity instruments in accordance with the substance of the contractual arrangement when the instrument first satisfied the recognition criteria in IAS 32, without considering events after that date (other than changes to the terms of the instruments). IFRS 1 draws particular attention to the requirement of IAS 32 that, following initial recognition, the classification of the liability and equity components of a compound financial instrument is not revised (for example to reflect an increased or decreased probability of conversion) – see 4.3.1 above.[149]

In other words, if an entity has issued a compound financial instrument, for which IAS 32 requires 'split accounting' (see 4 above), and some or all of the liability component of which is outstanding at the date of transition to IFRS, the entity must determine the carrying amount of the liability and equity components at transition at the amounts at which they would have been carried if 'split accounting' had been adopted from the date of issue of the bond. The fair value of the liability component of the bond should therefore be determined by reference to the interest rate which would have been applicable to a non-convertible bond issued by the entity at the original issue date and not the (potentially significantly different) rate at the date of transition.[150]

IFRS 1 also contains the following transitional provision in respect of compound financial instruments, where none of the liability component is outstanding at the date of transition:

> 'IAS 32 *Financial Instruments: Disclosure and Presentation* requires an entity to split a compound financial instrument at inception into separate liability and equity components. If the liability component is no longer outstanding, retrospective application of IAS 32 involves separating two portions of equity. The first portion is in retained earnings and represents the cumulative interest accreted on the liability component. The other portion represents the original equity component. However, under this IFRS, a first-time adopter need not separate these two portions if the liability component is no longer outstanding at the date of transition to IFRSs.'[151]

This is slightly curious in that it refers to a 'requirement' in IAS 32 to credit the equity component arising on initial recognition of a compound instrument to a separate component of equity. We are unable to identify such a requirement –

IAS 32 requires merely that the amount be credited to equity (see 4.3.1 above). Moreover, the concession granted by IFRS 1 implies a further requirement that the amount originally credited to the equity component must remain in that separate component permanently. However, this is arguably contradicted by the application guidance to IAS 32 which, on conversion of a convertible bond, allows a transfer within equity of the amount originally credited there in respect of the equity component (see 4.4.1 above). Thus, even if, on initial recognition of a compound instrument, the entity had been required to credit the equity component to a separate component of equity, on final conversion or settlement it could, on subsequent conversion of the instrument, notionally have transferred the separately recognised component of equity to another component of equity (e.g. retained earnings), so that no further adjustment would be required on transition to IFRS.

References

1 IAS 32, 2007 IASB bound volume of standards, Application Guidance, para. before para. AG1.
2 IAS 32, Illustrative Examples, para. after main heading.
3 *Overview of IAS 32 (Agenda paper 12B)*, Information for Observers, IASB meeting, January 2007, para. 48.
4 *IASB Update*, IASB, April 2007.
5 IAS 32, para. 2.
6 IAS 32, para. 11.
7 IAS 32, para. 11.
8 IAS 32, para. 11.
9 IAS 32, para. 11.
10 IAS 32, para. 12 and IAS 39, *Financial Instruments: Recognition and Measurement*, IASB 2007 bound volume, para. 9.
11 IAS 32, para. 11.
12 IAS 32, para. 13.
13 IAS 32, para. 14.
14 IAS 32, para. 15.
15 IAS 32, para. 16.
16 IAS 32, para. 16.
17 IAS 32, para. AG13.
18 IAS 32, paras. 22 and AG13.
19 IAS 32, para. 21.
20 IAS 32, para. 24.
21 IAS 32, para. AG13.
22 IAS 32, para. AG13.
23 IAS 32, para. AG14.
24 IAS 32, para. BC21.
25 IFRS 2, *Share-based Payment*, IASB 2007 bound volume, para. BC109.
26 IFRS 2, para. BC110.
27 IAS 32, para. 17.
28 IAS 32, para. 17.
29 IAS 32, para. 18.
30 IAS 32, paras. 19 and AG25.
31 IAS 32, para. 19.
32 IAS 32, para. 20.
33 IAS 32, para. 20.
34 IAS 32, para. AG23.
35 IAS 32, para. 20.
36 IAS 32, para. AG25.
37 IAS 32, paras. 18(a) and AG25.
38 IAS 32, para. AG37.
39 IAS 32, para. AG25.
40 IAS 32, para. AG26.
41 IAS 32, para. AG26.
42 IAS 32 (pre-2003 version – issued March 1995 and revised December 1998 and October 2000), para. 22.
43 IAS 32, para. BC9.
44 *IFRIC Update*, IASB, March 2006.
45 *IFRIC Update*, IASB, March 2006.
46 *IFRIC Update*, IASB, March 2006.
47 *IASB Update*, IASB, June 2006
48 *IFRIC Update*, IASB, November 2006.
49 *IFRIC Update*, IASB, March 2006.
50 IAS 32, para. 18(b).
51 IAS 32, para.18(b).
52 IAS 32, paras. 18(b) and BC7-BC8.
53 IFRIC 2 – *Members' Shares in Co-operative Entities and Similar Instruments*, IASB 2007 bound volume, paras. 1-4.
54 IFRIC 2, para. 5.
55 IFRIC 2, paras. 6-8.
56 IFRIC 2, para. 8.
57 IFRIC 2, para. 9.

58 IFRIC 2, para. 10.
59 IFRIC 2, para. 11.
60 IFRIC 2, para. 6.
61 Exposure draft – *Proposed Amendments to IAS 32 and IAS 1 – Financial Instruments Puttable at Fair Value and Obligations Arising on Liquidation*, IASB, June 2006, revision to IAS 32, para. 11.
62 *IASB Update*, IASB, April 2007.
63 *IASB Update*, IASB, May 2007.
64 IASB Work Plan as published on IASB website July 2007.
65 *IASB Update*, IASB, September 2007.
66 IAS 32, para. AG6.
67 IAS 32, para. 22.
68 IAS 32, para. 22.
69 IAS 32, paras. 22 and AG27(a).
70 *IFRIC Update*, IASB, April 2005.
71 *IFRIC Update*, IASB, July 2006.
72 IAS 32, paras. 21 and AG27(d).
73 IAS 32, para. 24.
74 IAS 32, para. AG27(d).
75 IAS 32, para. AG27(c).
76 IAS 32, paras. 23 and AG27(a)-(b).
77 IAS 12, para. BC12.
78 IAS 32, paras. 23 and AG27(a)-(b).
79 IAS 32, paras. 23 and AG27(b).
80 IAS 39, para. 49.
81 *IFRIC Update*, IASB, November 2006.
82 IAS 32, para. AG27(c).
83 Exposure draft *IFRS for Small and Medium-Sized Entities*, IASB, February 2007, ('SME ED') para. 21.2
84 SME ED, Derivation Table.
85 IASB staff draft of proposed exposure draft *International Financial Reporting Standard for Small and Medium-Sized Entities* (as made available on the IASB's website as at September 2006) ('SME staff draft ED') paras. 22.2-22.4.
86 IAS 32, para. 25.
87 IAS 32, para. 25.
88 IAS 32, para. AG28.
89 IAS 32, para. AG28.
90 IAS 32, para. BC19.
91 SIC-5, *Classification of Financial Instruments – Contingent Settlement Provisions*, SIC, May 1998 (superseded December 2003).
92 SIC-5, para. 9.
93 IAS 32, paras. BC16-BC17.
94 *Agenda item 12B*, Information for Observers, IASB meeting, January 2007, para. 39.
95 IAS 32, para. 26.
96 IAS 32, para. 27.
97 IAS 32, para. 27.
98 IAS 32, para. AG29.
99 IAS 32, para. AG29.
100 IAS 32, para. AG29.
101 IAS 32, para. AG29.
102 IAS 32, paras. 28 and AG30.
103 IAS 32, para. 29.
104 IAS 32, para. AG37.
105 IAS 32, para. 28.
106 IAS 32, para. 29.
107 IAS 32, para. AG30.
108 IAS 32, para. 31.
109 IAS 32, paras. 31-32.
110 IAS 32, para. 31.
111 IAS 32, AG31(b).
112 IAS 32, para. 31.
113 Based on Example 9 in IAS 32, paras. IE34-IE36.
114 Based on Example 10 in IAS 32, paras. IE37-IE38.
115 IAS 39, para. AG30(g).
116 IAS 32, para. 30.
117 IAS 32, para. AG32.
118 IAS 32, para. AG32.
119 IAS 32, para. AG33.
120 IAS 32, para. AG33.
121 IAS 32, para. AG34.
122 Based on example in IAS 32, paras. IE39-IE46.
123 IAS 32, para. AG35.
124 IAS 32, paras. IE47-IE50.
125 SME ED, para. 21.3.
126 SME ED, Derivation Table.
127 SME staff draft ED, paras. 22.3-22.4.
128 IAS 32, para. 35.
129 IAS 32, para. 36.
130 IAS 32, para. 41.
131 IAS 32, para. 36.
132 IAS 32, para. 40.
133 IAS 32, para. 37.
134 IAS 32, para. 38.
135 IAS 32, para. 39.
136 IAS 32, para. 33.
137 IAS 32, para. AG36.
138 IAS 32, paras. 33 and AG36.
139 IAS 32, para. 34.
140 IAS 1, *Presentation of Financial Statements*, IASB 2007 bound volume, para. 76(a)(vi).
141 IAS 19, *Employee Benefits*, IASB 2007 bound volume, para. 120(d)(i).
142 IAS 32, paras. IE2-IE6.
143 IAS 32, paras. IE7-IE11.
144 IAS 32, paras. IE12-IE16.
145 IAS 32, paras. IE17-IE21.
146 IAS 32, paras. IE22-IE26.
147 IAS 32, paras. IE27-IE31.
148 IAS 32, paras. DO1-DO3.
149 IFRS 1, IASB 2007 bound volume, para. IG35.
150 IFRS 1, para. IG36.
151 IFRS 1, para. 23.

58 IFRIC 2, para. 10.
59 IFRIC 2, para. 11.
60 IFRIC 2, para. 6.
61 Exposure draft – *Proposed Amendments to IAS 32 and IAS 1 – Financial Instruments Puttable at Fair Value and Obligations Arising on Liquidation*, IASB, June 2006, revision to IAS 32, para. 11.
62 *IASB Update*, IASB, April 2007.
63 *IASB Update*, IASB, May 2007.
64 IASB Work Plan as published on IASB website, July 2007.
65 *IASB Update*, IASB, September 2007.
66 IAS 32, para. AG6.
67 IAS 32, para. 22.
68 IAS 32, para. 22.
69 IAS 32, paras. 22 and AG27(a).
70 *IFRIC Update*, IASB, April 2005.
71 *IFRIC Update*, IASB, July 2005.
72 IAS 32, paras. 21 and AG27(d).
73 IAS 32, para. 21.
74 IAS 32, para. AG27(d).
75 IAS 32, para. AG27(c).
76 IAS 32, paras. 22 and AG27(a)-(b).
77 IAS 32, para. BC12.
78 IAS 32, paras. 23 and AG27(a)-(b).
79 IAS 32, paras. [illegible] and AG27(b).
80 IAS 39, para. 49.
81 *IFRIC Update*, IASB, November 2006.
82 IAS 32, para. AG27(c).
83 Exposure draft *IFRS for Small and Medium-sized Entities*, IASB, February 2007 ('SME ED'), para. 22.2.
84 SME ED, Derivation Table.
85 IASB staff draft of proposed exposure draft *International Financial Reporting Standard for Small and Medium-sized Entities* (as made available on the IASB's website in August/September 2006) ('SME staff draft'), paras. 22.2-22.[illegible].
86 IAS 32, para. 25.
87 IAS 32, para. 25.
88 IAS 32, para. AG28.
89 IAS 32, para. AG28.
90 IAS 32, para. BC19.
91 SIC-5, *Classification of Financial Instruments – Contingent Settlement Provisions*, SIC, May 1998 (superseded December 2003).
92 SIC-5, para. 5.
93 IAS 32, paras. BC16-BC17.
94 *Board meeting – Information for Observers*, IASB meeting January 2007, para. 30.
95 IAS 32, para. 26.
96 IAS 32, para. 27.
97 IAS 32, para. 27.
98 IAS 32, para. AG29.
99 IAS 32, para. AG29.
100 IAS 32, para. AG29.
101 IAS 32, para. AG29.
102 IAS 32, paras. 28 and AG30.
103 IAS 32, para. 29.
104 IAS 32, para. AG37.
105 IAS 32, para. 28.
106 IAS 32, para. 29.
107 IAS 32, para. AG30.
108 IAS 32, para. 31.
109 IAS 32, paras. 31-32.
110 IAS 32, para. 31.
111 IAS 32, AG31(b).
112 IAS 32, para. 31.
113 Based on Example 9 in IAS 32, paras. IE34-IE36.
114 Based on Example 10 in IAS 32, paras. IE37-IE38.
115 IAS 39, para. AG30(g).
116 IAS 32, para. 30.
117 IAS 32, para. AG32.
118 IAS 32, para. AG32.
119 IAS 32, para. AG33.
120 IAS 32, para. AG33.
121 IAS 32, para. AG34.
122 Based on example in IAS 32, paras. IE39-IE46.
123 IAS 32, para. AG35.
124 IAS 32, paras. IE47-IE50.
125 SME ED, para. 22.[illegible]
126 SME ED, Derivation Table.
127 SME staff draft ED, paras. 22.3-22.[illegible]
128 IAS 32, para. 35.
129 IAS 32, para. 36.
130 IAS 32, para. 41.
131 IAS 32, para. 36.
132 IAS 32, para. 40.
133 IAS 32, para. 37.
134 IAS 32, para. 28.
135 [illegible]
136 [illegible]
137 IAS 32, para. AG36.
138 IAS 32, paras. 33 and AG36.
139 IAS 32, para. 34.
140 IAS 1, *Presentation of Financial Statements*, IASB 2007 bound volume, para. 76(a)(vi).
141 IAS 23, *Borrowing Costs*, IASB 2007 bound volume, para. 20(d)(i).
142 IAS 32, paras. IE2-IE6.
143 IAS 32, paras. IE7-IE11.
144 IAS 32, paras. IE12-IE16.
145 IAS 32, paras. IE17-IE21.
146 IAS 32, paras. IE22-IE26.
147 IAS 32, paras. IE27-IE31.
148 IAS 32, paras. DO1-DO3.
149 IFRS 1, IASB 2007 bound volume, para. IG35.
150 IFRS 1, para. IG36.
151 IFRS 1, para. 23.

Chapter 20 Financial instruments: Measurement

1 INTRODUCTION

The Introduction to Chapter 17 provides a general background to the development of accounting for financial instruments. It explains that the long-term goal of most standard setters, particularly the IASB, remains a 'full fair value' accounting model for financial instruments. Under such a model all financial instruments would be recognised in the balance sheet at their fair value with changes in value recorded in the period in which they arise.

Notwithstanding the IASB's desires, the current accounting requirements for financial instruments (which are largely set out in IAS 39 – *Financial Instruments: Recognition and Measurement*) are more accurately described as a 'mixed attribute' model. In other words, financial instruments are generally accounted for using either historical cost or fair value measures. However, even this is something of a simplification. Depending upon its nature and the decisions of management, an instrument will rarely be accounted for on a pure historical cost, or a pure fair value, basis, e.g. as a result of one or more of the following:

- all financial instruments are subject to the general requirements of IAS 21 – *The Effects of Changes in Foreign Exchange Rates* – so that monetary financial instruments denominated in foreign currencies are retranslated at closing rates with gains and losses normally recognised in the income statement;
- similarly, financial instruments held by foreign entities are retranslated at closing rates, along with the entities' other assets and liabilities, but associated gains and losses are recognised in equity;
- financial assets that are measured at cost or amortised cost are subject to review for impairment and impaired assets are written down, normally to an amount derived using net present value techniques;

- some financial assets (those classified as available-for-sale) are measured at fair value in the balance sheet but are, effectively, accounted for at cost or amortised cost in profit or loss – the residual gains and losses are temporarily recognised in equity pending their subsequent recognition in profit or loss by way of 'recycling' adjustments; and
- the prescribed methods of hedge accounting involve the over-ride of other general accounting requirements, including those applicable to financial instruments.

It is this mixture of historical cost and fair value accounting bases that causes much of the complexity within IAS 39. This is particularly true in the case of hedge accounting, which depends to a large extent on management intent, which the IASB has reluctantly accepted, despite its general belief that management intent should not, in principle, influence accounting. However, in finalising the amendments to IAS 39 in December 2003 arising from its 'improvements project', the IASB conceded that the basic principles of IAS 39 already established will be in place for a considerable period.[1] In fact the IASB continues to admit that it does not expect to be in a position to require fair value measurement of all financial instruments for 'several years'.[2]

Therefore, in the improvements project, the scope of the amendments to IAS 39 was restricted to improving the existing requirements, rather than making any fundamental change to the underlying approach. Notwithstanding this, the improvements project (and a subsequent amendment to the standard)[3] resulted in some important changes to the main building blocks of measurement, specifically the requirements surrounding the estimation of fair values, recognition of impairment losses and, to a lesser extent, calculation of amortised cost using the effective interest method.

In what was described as a further attempt to simplify the accounting requirements under the mixed attribute model, the IASB also decided to allow any financial instrument to be designated as 'at fair value through profit or loss'. Such instruments are effectively accounted for as if in a 'full fair value' model. In spite of the official explanation, this move was probably inspired as much by a desire to allow entities to experiment with such a model to assist the standard setters in their project research. However, as discussed in Chapter 17 at 1.5, following some intensive lobbying within the EU, IAS 39 was amended to impose a number of restrictions on the use of the 'fair value option' (as the IASB refers to it).

This chapter deals only with the basic measurement requirements of IAS 39. The special form of accounting that is allowed for instruments within designated effective hedging relationships is dealt with in Chapter 21.

2 INITIAL MEASUREMENT

2.1 General requirements

At a conceptual level, a significant change to the initial measurement basis for financial assets and financial liabilities was introduced into IAS 39 in December 2003. Previously all financial instruments recognised under IAS 39 were measured by reference to their cost; now they are measured by reference to their fair value. More precisely, on initial recognition, financial assets and financial liabilities at fair value through profit or loss are normally measured at their fair value on the date they are initially recognised. The initial measurement of other financial instruments is also based on their fair value, but adjusted in respect of any transaction costs that are directly attributable to the acquisition or issue of the instrument.[4]

For most entities this change made little, if any, practical difference – not least because the previous implementation guidance explained that if the apparent cost differed from the instrument's fair value then part of the cost was deemed to relate to something other than the instrument itself.[5] It did, however, represent an important shift of emphasis and was a further demonstration of the increasing use of fair value measures in accounting for financial instruments. It also has important implications for those entities that actively trade in financial instruments as discussed at 4.7 below.

2.2 Initial fair value

IAS 39 contains a formal definition of the term 'fair value' and requirements for determining the fair value of financial instruments, which are considered in detail at 4 below. This subsection deals with those aspects of fair value measurement that are particularly applicable on initial recognition.

2.2.1 *Interest-free and low-interest loans*

The initial fair value of a financial instrument will normally be the transaction price, i.e. the fair value of the consideration given or received. IAS 39 assumes the transaction price is the best evidence of fair value, however this will not always be the case. The standard explains that if part of the consideration given or received is for something other than the financial instrument, the fair value of the instrument should be estimated using a valuation technique (see 4.2 below). For example, the fair value of a long-term loan or receivable that carries no interest can be estimated as the present value of all future cash receipts discounted using the prevailing market rate(s) of interest for instruments that are similar as to currency, term, type of interest rate, credit risk and other factors. Any additional amount advanced is an expense or a reduction of income unless it qualifies for recognition as some other type of asset.[6]

Example 20.1: Interest-free loan to supplier

Company A lends €1,000 to Company B for five years and classifies the resulting asset within loans and receivables. The loan carries no interest and, instead, A expects (or possibly contracts) to receive other future economic benefits, such as a right to receive goods or services at favourable prices or an implicit right to exert influence over the activities of B.

On initial recognition, the market rate of interest for a similar five year loan with payment of interest at maturity is 10% per year. The initial fair value of the loan is the present value of the future payment of €1,000, discounted using the market rate of interest for a similar loan of 10% for five years. This equates to €621.

Rationally, A would also expect to obtain other future economic benefits that have a fair value of €379 (the difference between the total consideration given of €1,000 and the loan's initial fair value of €621). The difference is not a financial asset, since it is paid to obtain expected (or possibly contracted) future economic benefits other than the right to receive payment on the loan asset. A recognises that amount as an expense unless it qualifies for recognition as an asset, for example under IAS 38 – *Intangible Assets* (see Chapter 12).[7]

What this approach is trying to do is isolate a 'pure' financial instrument from the remainder of an arrangement. In practice, however, identifying the financial instrument component of an arrangement like this is not always so simple. Often the financial and non-financial elements of an arrangement are interlinked, making separation more difficult. This problem is illustrated in the following example.

Example 20.2: Interest-free loan to employee

As part of their remuneration package, employees of Company F may borrow up to €1,000 from F on interest-free terms. These loans are repayable only in the event that employment ceases (which may be at the option either of the employee or of F, subject to relatively short contractual notice periods and perhaps certain statutory requirements). F determines that the average service life of an employee is five years and the market rate of interest for a five year loan with payment of interest at maturity is 10% per year. Accordingly, when an employee joins and borrows €1,000, as in Example 20.1 above, F may calculate that the initial fair value of the loan is €621.

However, if this approach is adopted, the question arises as to what the 'spare' €379 represents. There is often a high degree of scepticism expressed at the recognition of prepaid employment costs as it is often questionable whether such costs can ever be recovered. However, in this case, it is clear that the €379 will be recoverable in the event that the employee leaves, so this is clearly one alternative.

The €379 may also be seen as representing the value of a contract whereby F has the choice of receiving cash (repayment of the loan, say in the event that F was to terminate the employee's service contract) or employment services. In a similar way to the oil-linked bond considered in Chapter 17 at 2.2.5 this element might also be considered a financial instrument. Because it is also a financial instrument, there appears to be no reason why this part of the contract should be accounted for separately from the remainder of the financial instrument (unless it is considered an embedded derivative).

One could also view F's ability to terminate the employment contract and force settlement of the loan at face value as an embedded call option that is not closely related to the host instrument because the strike price, €1,000, is significantly different from the loan's amortised cost, initially €621 (see Chapter 17 at 5.1.1 C). This would be another form of financial instrument, in this case a derivative, although it is again hard to see why this should be accounted for separately.

Finally, notwithstanding its expected life based on average service lives, there is an argument to be made that the fair value of the loan is approximately €1,000 if F can demand payment of €1,000 within a short space of time (albeit by terminating the employment contract), suggesting there is no (significant) spare debit.

In practice, the impact is unlikely to be material in most such cases. Where it is, a number of approaches might be considered acceptable but it is hard to say which is the more appropriate under the standard and will depend on the specific circumstances of the entity and the judgment of management.

Bayer articulates its accounting policies for interest-free and low-interest receivables as shown in the following extract.

> *Extract 20.1: Bayer AG (2006)*
>
> **Notes to the Consolidated Financial Statements** [extracts]
>
> **4.3 Basic recognition and valuation principles** [extracts]
>
> **Financial assets** [extracts]
>
> Financial assets comprise receivables, acquired equity and debt instruments, cash and cash equivalents and derivative financial instruments with positive fair values.
>
> Financial assets are initially recognised at fair value plus transaction costs. ... Interest-free and low-interest receivables are stated at the present value of expected future cash flows.

Similar issues often arise from transactions between entities under common control. For example, parents commonly lend money to subsidiaries on an interest-free or low-interest basis. Where, in its separate financial statements, the parent (or subsidiary) is required to record a receivable (or payable) on initial recognition at a fair value that is lower than cost, the additional consideration will normally represent an additional investment in the subsidiary (or equity contribution from the parent).

IAS 20 – *Accounting for Government Grants and Disclosure of Government Assistance* – requires the benefit of a loan received from a government that has a below-market rate of interest not to be quantified by the imputation of interest.[8] This appears to conflict with the requirement discussed above to measure the loan on initial recognition at fair value and, in practice, a number of entities have followed IAS 20 in preference to IAS 39. The IASB has now decided to amend IAS 20 as part of its annual improvements project to require the imputation of interest to below-market rate loans received from governments. The excess of the consideration received over the initial fair value of the loan would be accounted for as a government grant.[9]

If a financial instrument is recognised where the terms are 'off-market' (i.e. the consideration given or received does not equal the instrument's fair value) but instead a fee is paid or received in compensation, the instrument should still be recognised at its fair value, i.e. net of the fee received or paid.[10]

Example 20.3: Off-market loan with origination fee

Bank J lends $1,000 to Company K. The loan carries interest at 5% and is repayable in full in five years' time, even though the market rate for similar loans is 8%. To compensate J for the below market rate of interest, K pays J an origination fee of $120. There are no other directly related payments by either party.

The loan is recorded at its fair value of $880 (net present value of $50 interest payable annually for five years and $1,000 principal repaid after five years, all discounted at 8%). This equals the net amount of cash exchanged ($1,000 loan less $120 origination fee) and hence no gain or loss is recognised on initial recognition of the loan.[11]

Again, applying the requirements of IAS 39 to the simple fact pattern provided by the IASB is a relatively straightforward exercise. In practice, however, it may be more difficult to identify those fees that are required by IAS 39 to be treated as part of the financial instrument and those that should be dealt with in another way, for example under IAS 18 – *Revenue*. Particularly, it may be difficult to determine the extent to which fees associated with a financial instrument that is not quoted in an active market represents compensation for off-market terms or for the genuine provision of services.

2.2.2 *Short-term receivables and payables*

A degree of pragmatism is introduced when accounting for short-term receivables and payables with no stated interest rate. The standard explains that these may be measured at the original invoice amount if the effect of discounting is immaterial. The alternative would be to discount the invoice amount for the time value of money over the expected or contractual settlement period and accrue interest on this amount.[12]

In connection with this, the IFRIC has considered the accounting for extended payment terms, such as six month's interest-free credit and concluded that the accounting treatment under IAS 39 was clear. In such circumstances, the effect of the time value of money should be reflected when this is material. It was noted that a different conclusion might be drawn from reading IAS 18 in isolation, but the IFRIC considered the wording in IAS 18 lacked clarity and needed to be improved.[13]

2.2.3 *Equity instruments reclassified as liabilities following modification of contractual terms*

The IFRIC has also considered the accounting treatment to be applied when the contractual terms of an issued equity instrument are modified such that it is subsequently classified as a financial liability. Some had argued that the financial liability should be measured at the amount recorded in equity on the basis that it was akin to a non-substantive modification to the terms of a financial liability (see Chapter 18 at 5.2) However, the IFRIC concluded that the financial liability should be measured at its fair value on the date it is initially recognised *as a financial liability*, with any difference between this amount and the amount recorded in equity being dealt with in equity.[14] Consequently, a number of companies revised their accounting treatment as illustrated in the following extract from the financial statements of Royal and SunAlliance.

Extract 20.2: Royal & SunAlliance Insurance Group plc (2006)

Notes to the financial statements [extracts]

19. **Loan capital** [extracts]

	2006 £m	Restated 2005 £m
Subordinated guaranteed perpetual notes	519	526

The subordinated guaranteed perpetual notes have a nominal value of £450m and pay an annual coupon of 8.50% with an option to call the notes, or if not called for the coupon rate to be reset, on 8 December 2014 and every five years thereafter.

During 2005, the terms of the subordinated guaranteed perpetual notes were revised with the effect that their classification under IFRS changed from being equity instruments to debt instruments. In the 2005 financial statements, the reclassification was accounted for as an exchange transaction as the underlying terms of the notes were not substantially impacted by the variation in terms and there were no changes in the holders of the notes immediately before and immediately after the change. During 2006, the International Financial Reporting Interpretations Committee (IFRIC) provided guidance on its understanding of accounting for such a change in terms. The directors have considered the IFRIC's deliberations and concluded that the Company should change its accounting treatment. The accounting treatment now recognises the impact of the revision of the terms of the notes as if the revision had given rise to a redemption of the equity instruments in exchange for a debt instrument, which is measured at the fair value of the notes at the date of the revision. The carrying value of the notes included in the 2005 results has been increased by £81m …. Opening shareholders' funds have been restated ….

2.2.4 Financial guarantee contracts and off-market loan commitments

The requirement to measure financial instruments at fair value on initial recognition also applies to issued financial guarantee contracts that are within the scope of IAS 39 as well as to commitments to provide a loan at a below-market interest rate (see Chapter 17 at 3.4 and 3.5).

When issued to an unrelated party in a stand-alone arm's length transaction, the fair value of a financial guarantee contract at inception is likely to equal the premium received, unless there is evidence to the contrary.[15] There is likely to be such evidence where, say, a parent provided to a bank a financial guarantee contract in respect of its subsidiary's borrowings and charged no fee. As when an off-market loan is provided to an entity's subsidiary (see 2.2.1 above), a 'spare debit' arises in the separate financial statements of the parent as a result of the recognition of the guarantee at fair value. Again, it is normally appropriate to treat this as an additional cost of investment in the subsidiary.

2.2.5 'Day 1' profits

Aside from the situations discussed above, e.g. where part of the consideration given or received is for something other than the financial instrument, it is theoretically possible to make a profit on initial recognition of a financial instrument, typically a derivative, (often called a 'day 1' profit). This will only be the case if there is sufficient evidence to demonstrate that the amount paid or received is different to the fair value of the instrument and the circumstances in which this can arise will be rare for most entities. This issue is considered in further detail at 4.7 below.

2.3 Transaction costs

As noted at 2.1 above, the initial carrying amount of an instrument that is not classified at fair value through profit or loss should be adjusted for transaction costs. Consequently, these costs will reduce (increase) the amount of interest income (expense) recognised over the life of the instrument (for interest-bearing items) or increase the amount of profit or loss on disposal or impairment (for non-interest bearing assets). Transaction costs relating to the acquisition or incurrence of financial instruments at fair value through profit or loss are recognised in profit or loss as they are incurred.

Transaction costs are defined as incremental costs that are directly attributable to the acquisition, issue or disposal of a financial asset or liability. An incremental cost is one that would not have been incurred had the financial instrument not been acquired, issued or disposed of.[16] Expenses that would be incurred on the subsequent transfer or disposal of a financial instrument are not transaction costs.[17]

Example 20.4: Transaction costs – initial measurement

Company A acquires an equity security that will be classified as available-for-sale. The security has a fair value of £100 and this is the amount A is required to pay. In addition, A also pays a purchase commission of £2. If the asset was to be sold, a sales commission of £3 would be payable.

The initial measurement of the asset is £102, i.e. the sum of its initial fair value and the purchase commission. The commission payable on sale is not considered for this purpose.[18]

Transaction costs include fees and commissions paid to agents (including employees acting as selling agents), advisers, brokers, and dealers. They also include levies by regulatory agencies and securities exchanges, transfer taxes and duties. Debt premiums or discounts, financing costs and allocations of internal administrative or holding costs are not transaction costs.[19]

Payments to sales staff, and employees acting as such, are common in the insurance industry and many bodies of GAAP require these payments to be deferred and recognised in profit or loss over the life of the related contracts. Following the publication of IFRS 4 – *Insurance Contracts* – many instruments that might previously have been considered insurance contracts now fall within the scope of IAS 39. In order for this legacy accounting treatment to be preserved, an amendment was made so that these payments are now considered transaction costs.

Treating internal costs as transaction costs could open up a number of possibilities for abuse by allowing entities to defer expenses inappropriately. However, it is made clear that internal costs should be treated as transaction costs only if they are incremental and directly attributable to the acquisition, issue or disposal of a financial asset or financial liability.[20] Therefore, it will be rare for internal costs (other than, say, commissions paid to sales staff in respect of an instrument sold) to be treated as transaction costs.

In connection with the creation or acquisition of a financial asset that is not classified at fair value through profit or loss, the appendix to IAS 18 acknowledges that an entity may incur 'related direct costs' that are accounted for in a similar way to transaction costs.[21] IAS 18 does not contain a definition of such costs; particularly it does not refer to the need for them to be 'incremental'. However, it would appear inappropriate to apply a wider definition of transaction costs than is contained in IAS 39 to determine whether such an expense should be accounted for in this way. The IASB has now decided, in the context of its annual improvements project, to align the wording in the appendix to IAS 18 with IAS 39 to remove this inconsistency.[22]

2.4 Bid-ask spreads

In some markets, dealers or market makers charge minimal or no explicit transaction costs, but instead quote differential prices for purchases and sales. Such prices are often referred to as 'bid' and 'asking' (or offer) prices (see 4.1 below). The standard states that the term bid-ask spread (normally interpreted as the difference between quoted bid and asking prices) is used to include only transaction costs and not other adjustments to arrive at fair value such as for counterparty credit risk.[23] Nevertheless, the guidance in IAS 39 seems to imply that in practice the entire bid-ask spread is deemed to be a transaction cost as illustrated in the following example.

Example 20.5: Bid-ask spread – initial measurement

As in Example 20.4 above, Company A acquires an equity security which will be classified as available-for-sale. In this case A purchases the asset in an active market where no explicit transaction costs are charged, but separate bid and offer prices are quoted. On acquisition the security has an asking price of £102, which is the amount A is required to pay, and a bid price of £97, which is what A would receive were it to sell the asset.

The fair value of a quoted asset is deemed to be its bid price (see 4.1 below) and this suggests that A should initially measure the asset at £97. This would result in an immediate loss of £5, the difference between the initial fair value of the asset and the cash paid. What is more, this loss would be recognised in the income statement as it does not arise on remeasurement of the asset (see 3.4 below).

However, what the standard appears to be saying is that the £5 'loss' (i.e. the bid-ask spread) is deemed to be a transaction cost and, therefore, should be included in the initial measurement of the asset. The asset would then be initially measured at £102 (which happens to be what was paid for it) with no immediate loss recognised in the income statement.

If, instead, the security had been classified at fair value through profit or loss, the accounting treatment on initial recognition would have been significantly different. For such assets, transaction costs are recognised in profit or loss and A *would* have recorded a £5 loss.

Consequently, under this interpretation, the initial measurement requirements do not appear to depend on how a particular market operates, i.e. whether transaction costs are charged explicitly by dealers or market makers or are included within a bid-ask spread. Although this is what might be expected, it is interesting to contrast this with the subsequent measurement requirements shown in Examples 20.10 and 20.11 at 4.1 below.

2.5 Embedded derivatives and financial instrument hosts

In Chapter 17 at 5.2, it was explained that the terms of an embedded derivative that is required to be separated and the associated host should be determined so that the derivative is initially recorded at its fair value and the host as the residual (at least for an optional derivative – a non-option embedded derivative will have a fair value and initial carrying amount of zero).[24]

The standard does not clarify what it is that entities are meant to be determining the residual of. In two separate instances, the implementation guidance suggests that a host financial instrument should be recognised as the residual of the *purchase price* after adjusting for the fair value of the embedded derivative.[25] This does not correctly reflect the revisions to IAS 39 (which require measurement to be based on the instrument's fair value, not its purchase price – see 2.1 above) but this could be seen as little more than an oversight on the part of the IASB. We suspect the IASB's most likely intention was that the host should initially be measured based on the residual of the *fair value* of the hybrid instrument (which, admittedly, will normally equal its purchase price – see 4.7 below) adjusted for any transaction costs and also after adjusting for the fair value of the embedded derivative.

2.6 Regular way transactions

When settlement date accounting is used for regular way transactions (see Chapter 18 at 3.2) and those transactions result in the recognition of assets that are subsequently measured at amortised cost or (very rarely) cost, there is an exception to the general requirement at 2.1 above.

The standard explains that, in such circumstances, rather than being initially measured by reference to their fair value on the date they are first recognised, i.e. settlement date, these financial instruments are initially measured by reference to their fair value on the trade date.[26] Or, as some would say, those assets that are to be subsequently measured at cost or amortised cost should initially be measured at their cost!

In practice, the difference will rarely be significant because of the short time scale involved between trade date and settlement date, the main reason the IASB tolerates this special accounting treatment for these 'derivatives'.[27]

2.7 Assets and liabilities arising from loan commitments

Loan commitments are a form of derivative financial instrument, although for pragmatic reasons the IASB decided that certain loan commitments could be excluded from the requirements of IAS 39 (see Chapter 17 at 3.5). This exclusion creates a degree of confusion over how assets and liabilities arising from such arrangements should be measured on initial recognition, as illustrated in the following example.

Example 20.6: Drawdown under a committed borrowing facility

Company H obtains from Bank Q a committed facility allowing it to borrow up to €10,000 at any time over the following five years, provided certain covenants specified in the facility agreement are not breached. Interest on any drawdowns is payable at LIBOR plus a fixed margin, representing Q's initial assessment of H's credit risk. Any such borrowings can be repaid at any time at the option of H, but must be repaid at the end of five years unless the facility is renegotiated and extended. They also become repayable immediately in the event that H breaches the covenants. For the purposes of this illustration, any other amounts payable by H to Q (such as non-utilisation fees) have been ignored.

Both H and Q choose to exclude the commitment from the requirements of IAS 39 and any asset or liability arising from drawdowns under the facility will be classified within loans and receivables by Q and within other liabilities by H. Q applies IAS 37 – *Provisions, Contingent Liabilities and Contingent Assets* – and assesses whether the facility is an onerous contract (effectively by assessing the probability of H's default following a future drawdown). If it were, Q would recognise a provision.

After one year, no drawdowns have been made and H's credit risk has increased (although it has not breached any of the covenants and there is no expectation of default, i.e. it is not an onerous contract as defined in IAS 37). As a result of this change in credit risk, the fair value of the facility is, say, €200 (positive value to H, negative value to Q). Because the commitment is not accounted for under IAS 39 and because it is not onerous, nothing is recognised in the accounts of either Q or H in respect of the facility.

Shortly afterwards H draws down the maximum €10,000 available under the facility. Because of the change in credit risk the drawdown results in the recognition of an asset (liability) by Q (H) that has a fair value at that date of, say, €9,800.

The €200 difference between the €9,800 fair value of the financial instrument created and the €10,000 cash transferred effectively represents the change in fair value of the commitment arising from the change in H's credit risk.

Should Q (H) initially measure the resulting asset (liability) at its €9,800 fair value or at €10,000, being the amount of cash actually exchanged? If it is recognised at €9,800, how is the 'spare' €200 accounted for, particularly does Q (H) recognise it as a loss (profit)?

The general requirement noted at 2.1 above would imply that the asset (liability) should initially be measured at €9,800. Consequently a loss (profit) of €200 would be recognised – this is because the spare €200 does not represent any other asset or liability arising form the transaction.

However, the Basis for Conclusions to IAS 39, explains that the effect of the loan commitment exception is that, consistent with the likely measurement basis of the resulting loan, the fair value of these commitments from changes in market interest rates or credit spreads will not be recognised or measured.[28] This is exactly what the 'spare' €200 represents so, in accordance with the underlying rationale and objective of allowing loan commitments to be excluded from the scope of IAS 39, it seems appropriate to initially measure the asset or liability arising in this case at €10,000.

Such treatment is also consistent with that for similar assets arising from regular way transactions recognised using settlement date accounting (see 2.6 above). This is relevant because the IASB introduced the loan commitment exception as a result of issues identified by the IGC and the only solution the IGC could identify at the time involved treating loan commitments as regular way transactions and using settlement date accounting.[29]

If, in the above example, Q (H) accounted for the loan commitment at fair value through profit or loss this issue would not arise. At the time the loan was drawn down the commitment would be recognised as a €200 liability (asset) and an equivalent loss (profit) would have been recorded in the income statement. The loan would be recognised at its fair value of €9,800 and the €200 balance of the cash movement over this amount would be treated as the settlement of the loan commitment liability (asset). Therefore, no further gain or loss would need to be recognised at this point.

3 SUBSEQUENT MEASUREMENT AND RECOGNITION OF GAINS AND LOSSES

As set out in Chapter 17 at 7, IAS 39 classifies financial assets into one of the following four categories:

- at fair value through profit or loss;
- held-to-maturity investments;
- loans and receivables; and
- available-for-sale assets.

Most financial liabilities that are within the scope of IAS 39 are classified either at fair value through profit or loss or as other financial liabilities (as that term is used in Chapter 17).

Following the initial recognition of financial assets and financial liabilities, their subsequent accounting treatment depends principally on the classification of the instrument, although there are a small number of exceptions.[30] These requirements are summarised in the following table and are considered in more detail in the remainder of this section.

Classification	Instrument type	Balance sheet	Fair value gains and losses	Interest and dividends	Impairment	Foreign exchange
At fair value through profit or loss (including derivatives that are not designated in effective hedges)	Debt, Equity or Derivative	Fair value	Profit or loss*	Profit or loss*	Profit or loss* (assets)	Profit or loss*
	Equity or equity derivative: not reliably measurable	Cost	–	Profit or loss: dividends receivable	Profit or loss (assets)	–
Held-to-maturity investments	Debt	Amortised cost	–	Profit or loss: effective interest rate	Profit or loss	Profit or loss
Loans and receivables	Debt	Amortised cost	–	Profit or loss: effective interest rate	Profit or loss	Profit or loss
Available-for-sale assets	Debt	Fair value	Equity †	Profit or loss: effective interest rate	Profit or loss	Profit or loss
	Equity	Fair value	Equity †	Profit or loss: dividends receivable	Profit or loss	Equity †
	Equity: not reliably measurable	Cost	–	Profit or loss: dividends receivable	Profit or loss	–
Other financial liabilities	Debt	Amortised cost	–	Profit or loss: effective interest rate	–	Profit or loss

* Little guidance is given on how gains and losses should be disaggregated – see Chapter 22 at 4.1.1.
† Recycled to profit or loss on disposal or impairment.

In addition, IAS 39 sets out the accounting treatment for certain financial guarantee contracts (see Chapter 17 at 3.4) and commitments to provide a loan at a below market interest rate (see Chapter 17 at 3.5).

3.1 Financial assets and financial liabilities at fair value through profit or loss

After initial recognition, financial assets and financial liabilities that are classified at fair value through profit or loss (including derivatives that are not designated in effective hedging relationships) should, in general, be measured at fair value, with no deduction for sale or disposal costs. Associated gains and losses should, not surprisingly, be recognised in profit or loss.[31] Section 4 below deals with the requirements of IAS 39 relating to the determination of fair values.

Investments in equity instruments whose fair value cannot be reliably measured and derivatives that are linked to, and must be settled by delivery of, such instruments (see 4.4 below) are measured at cost less (for assets) any impairment (see 6.4 below).[32] If a reliable measure of fair value subsequently becomes available, the instrument should be remeasured at that fair value, and the gain or loss reported in profit or loss.[33] If a reliable measure ceases to be available, it should thereafter be measured at 'cost', which is deemed to be the fair value carrying amount on that date.[34]

3.2 Held-to-maturity investments

The basic requirement for held-to-maturity investments is that they are measured at amortised cost using the effective interest method, although they are also subject to review for impairment.[35] Gains and losses are recognised in the income statement when the instrument is derecognised or impaired, as well as through the amortisation process.[36]

This effective interest method of accounting is dealt with in Section 5 below and Section 6 deals with the impairment requirements of IAS 39.

3.3 Loans and receivables

Loans and receivables are also measured at amortised cost using the effective interest method and are subject to review for impairment with gains and losses recognised in the income statement when the instrument is derecognised or impaired, as well as through the amortisation process.[37] However, in contrast to the treatment for held-to-maturity investments, this method of accounting applies to *all* loans and receivables without regard to whether they are intended to be held until maturity.[38]

3.4 Available-for-sale assets

Accounting for available-for-sale assets is slightly more complex. They should, in general, be measured at fair value, with no deduction for sale or disposal costs.[39] Gains and losses arising from changes in fair value (after adjusting for interest accruals and foreign exchange gains and losses on monetary items) are initially recognised directly in equity and reported in the statement of changes in equity (see Chapter 3 at 3.3). When an asset is derecognised, often by way of sale, or is impaired, the cumulative gain or loss previously recognised in equity is recycled and recognised in profit or loss.[40] For example, consider an equity security that is purchased for its fair value of €100, has a fair value of €120 at the end of the year and is sold subsequent to the year-end for €130. In the first year a gain of €20 is recognised in equity as a result of remeasuring the security at its fair value. In the second year a profit of €30 is recognised in the income statement – this effectively represents the €10 difference between the proceeds received (€130) and the previous carrying amount of the asset (€120) and the recycling of the €20 gain previously recognised in equity.

Where appropriate, interest receivable on available-for-sale assets is recognised in the income statement using the effective interest method (see 5 below), and dividends receivable are recognised in profit or loss when a right to receive payment is established (see Chapter 28). Impairment and foreign currency retranslation are covered in more detail at 6 and 7 respectively,[41] although it should be recognised that foreign exchange gains and losses arising on monetary available-for-sale investments, such debt instruments, are normally recognised in profit or loss, not in equity.

The accounting requirements for available-for-sale assets are further illustrated in the examples below.

Example 20.7: Gain or loss on available-for-sale shares in takeover target

Company S holds a small number of shares in Company T. The shares are classified as available-for-sale. On 20 December 2008, the fair value of the shares is $120 and the cumulative gain recognised in equity is $20. On the same day, Company U, a large public company, acquires T. As a result, S receives shares in U in exchange for those it had in T of equal fair value.

The transaction qualifies for derecognition (see Chapter 18 at 4), therefore the cumulative gain of $20 that has been recognised in equity should now be recognised in the income statement.[42]

Example 20.8: Available-for-sale asset – determination of interest

A company acquires a zero coupon bond at the end of 2008 for £760, its fair value, which matures at the beginning of 2012 at £1,000. It is classified as an available-for-sale asset and, accordingly, associated fair value gains and losses are reported in equity. Its fair value at the end of 2009, 2010 and 2011 is £850, £950 and £1,000 respectively and it can be determined that the effective interest rate is 9.6% (the effective interest method is discussed in more detail at 5 below).

The financial statements would therefore include the accounting entries set out in the following table (amortised cost is memorandum information used to determine interest).

Year	Amortised cost at start of year £		Interest – income statement £		Gains and losses – equity £		Cash flow £	Fair value B/S £
2008	–		–		–		–	760
2009	760		73	*[=760 × 9.6%]*	17	*[=850 {760 + 73}]*	–	850
2010	833	*[=760 + 73]*	80	*[=833 × 9.6%]*	20	*[=950 – {850 + 80}]*	–	950
2011	913	*[=833 + 80]*	87	*[=913 × 9.6%]*	(37)	*[=1,000 – {950 + 87}]*	–	1,000
2012	1,000	*[=913 + 87]*	–		–		1,000	–

The standard does not specify the cost basis to be used for fungible available-for-salc assets (or, indeed, for any other fungible financial instrument). This is in contrast to, say, IAS 2 – *Inventories* – which specifies the use of a weighted average cost or FIFO (first in first out) basis in most circumstances.[43]

On a theoretical level, an asset-by-asset approach is arguably the most technically pure. This would, for example, prevent the offsetting of an impairment arising on one asset against an unrealised gain on another. However, it could also allow entities to manipulate their earnings. For example, when selling an asset an entity could choose to sell one with a low (or high) cost base in order to maximise (minimise) the profit on disposal. In practice, average cost bases are typically used (perhaps applied to individual portfolios within the entity), although others may be acceptable provided they are applied consistently (e.g. both to disposals and impairment).

The financial statements of UBS disclose that it uses an average cost method.

Extract 20.3: UBS AG (2006)

Note 1 Summary of Significant Accounting Policies [extract]

8) Financial investments available-for-sale [extract]

Financial investments available-for-sale are carried at fair value. Unrealized gains or losses on available-for-sale investments are reported in Equity, net of applicable income taxes, until such investments are sold, collected or otherwise disposed of, or until any such investment is determined to be impaired. On disposal of an investment, the accumulated unrealized gain or loss included in Equity is transferred to Net profit or loss for the period and reported in Other income. Gains and losses on disposal are determined using the average cost method.

The standard does not address the situation when there is a change in the relationship between the reporting entity and the entity holding the assets. For example, consider the disposal of a subsidiary. Should the gains and losses recorded in equity in respect of the assets held by that subsidiary be recycled at the date of disposal? This issue is covered in more detail in Chapter 6 at 6.6.

Available-for-sale equity investments whose fair value cannot be reliably measured (see 4.4 below) are measured at cost less any impairment (see 6.4 below).[44] If a reliable measure of fair value subsequently becomes available, the asset should be remeasured at that fair value, and the gain or loss reported in equity (provided it is not impaired).[45] If a reliable measure ceases to be available, it should thereafter be measured at 'cost', which is deemed to be the fair value carrying amount on that date. Any gain or loss previously recognised in equity should be left there until the asset has been sold, otherwise disposed of or impaired, at which time it should be recycled into profit or loss.[46]

3.5 Other financial liabilities

Other financial liabilities, as that term is used in Chapter 17 at 7, are measured at amortised cost using the effective interest method with gains and losses recognised in the income statement when the instrument is derecognised as well as through the amortisation process.[47]

3.6 Reclassifications

As set out in Chapter 17 at 7.5, the standard restricts the scope for reclassifying instruments between the main categories, although reclassifications between available-for-sale assets and held-to-maturity investments are possible.

Where a held-to-maturity investment is reclassified as available-for-sale (for example as a result of triggering the 'tainting' provisions – see Chapter 17 at 7.2.3), the asset should be remeasured to fair value and any associated gain or loss recognised in equity.[48]

If an available-for-sale asset is reclassified as held-to-maturity, the fair value carrying amount of the financial asset on that date becomes its new amortised cost. Any previous gain or loss on that asset that has been recognised in equity should be amortised over the remaining life of the investment using the effective interest method. Any difference between the new amortised cost and maturity amount should be similarly amortised, akin to the amortisation of a premium or discount.[49]

Example 20.9: Debt instrument reclassified as held-to-maturity

Company Y acquires a debt instrument that it classifies as available-for-sale. The purchase price equals the fair value of the instrument, £110. Its terms are such that it pays a fixed coupon for ten years and a principal payment of £100. Subsequently, when the fair value of the instrument is £120, a gain of £12 has been recognised in equity, and £2 of the initial cost has been amortised to profit or loss, Y reclassifies the debt instrument as held-to-maturity.

The £120 fair value carrying amount becomes the new amortised cost of the instrument thereby giving rise to an effective premium of £20 that is amortised over the remaining term to maturity using the effective interest method. In addition, the £12 gain in equity is also amortised to profit or loss over the remaining period to maturity.

In effect, the income statement should be broadly the same as if the instrument had not been reclassified (or had always been classified as held-to-maturity).

If the asset subsequently becomes impaired, any gain or loss remaining in equity should be recognised in profit or loss.[50]

3.7 Financial guarantees and commitments to provide a loan at a below-market interest rate

Financial guarantees and commitments to provide a loan at a below-market interest rate should be measured on initial recognition at their (negative) fair value and subsequently at the higher of:

- the amount recognised under IAS 37 (see Chapter 27); and
- the amount initially recognised less, where appropriate, cumulative amortisation recognised in accordance with IAS 18 (see Chapter 28).

This assumes that the instrument is not classified at fair value through profit or loss (in which case 3.1 above applies) and, in the case of a financial guarantee contract, does not arise from a 'failed derecognition' transaction (see 3.8.3 below).[51]

For financial guarantee contracts within the scope of IAS 39, this requirement applies only to entities that have adopted the amendments to IAS 39 published in August 2005 (see Chapter 17 at 3.4). Prior to this such contracts would normally have been accounted for as insurance contracts under IFRS 4.

3.8 Other exceptions

3.8.1 Hedging relationships

Financial assets and financial liabilities that are designated as hedged items are subject to measurement under the hedge accounting requirements of IAS 39[52] and these can over-ride the general accounting requirements discussed above. Also, monetary financial instruments may be designated as hedging instruments (in hedges of foreign currency risk), which can affect whether exchange gains and losses are recognised in the income statement or initially in equity.[53] Hedge accounting is covered in Chapter 21.

3.8.2 Regular way transactions

Where settlement date accounting is used for regular way transactions (see Chapter 18 at 3.2), any change in the fair value of the asset to be received arising between trade date and settlement date is not recognised for those assets that will be measured at cost or amortised cost (see also 2.6 above). For assets that will be recorded at fair value, such changes in value are recognised:

- in the income statement for assets to be classified at fair value through profit or loss; and
- initially in equity (except for impairments and certain foreign exchange gains and losses as above) for available-for-sale assets.[54]

On disposal, changes in value of such assets between trade date and settlement date are not recognised because the right to changes in fair value ceases on the trade date.[55] This illustrated in Chapter 18 at 3.2.

3.8.3 Liabilities arising from 'failed derecognition' transactions

There are special requirements for financial liabilities (including financial guarantee contracts) that arise when transfers of financial assets do not qualify for derecognition, or are accounted for using the continuing involvement approach.[56] These are dealt with in Chapter 18 at 4.8.3.

4 FAIR VALUE MEASUREMENT CONSIDERATIONS

Consistent with the original version of IAS 39, and various other standards, fair value is defined as 'the amount for which an asset could be exchanged, or a liability settled, between knowledgeable, willing parties in an arm's length transaction.'[57] However, the guidance supporting the application of that definition to financial instruments was amended significantly in the December 2003 version of the standard as well as by a subsequent amendment published in December 2004. These changes are of limited relevance to many entities but are extremely important to banks and similar institutions that actively trade in financial instruments.

Underlying the definition is a presumption that an entity is a going concern without any intention or need to liquidate, curtail materially the scale of operations, or undertake a transaction on adverse terms. Fair value is not, therefore, the amount that would be received or paid in a forced transaction, involuntary liquidation, or distress sale. It does, however, reflect an instrument's credit quality.[58] This may be obvious for a financial asset but, more controversially, it applies equally to financial liabilities. The IASB's reasons for adopting this requirement are considered further at 4.8 below.

For the purpose of determining an instrument's fair value, the application guidance distinguishes between two main types of instrument – those for which there exist quoted prices in an active market and all others. As ever, there is no clear bright line between the two and judgment will be necessary at the margins. This distinction takes on a particular significance in the classification of instruments. As explained in Chapter 17 at 7.3, a financial asset cannot be classified within loans and receivables if it is quoted in an active market. It can also make a difference as to whether an immediate gain or loss can be recognised on the initial recognition of a financial instrument (see 4.7 below).

The requirements to be followed in determining the fair value of financial instruments for which no quoted market price is available were significantly expanded compared to those included in the original standard (see 4.2 to 4.4 below). The IASB decided it was desirable to provide clear and reasonably detailed guidance about the objective and use of valuation techniques to achieve reliable and comparable fair value estimates when financial instruments are measured at fair value.[59]

4.1 Quoted prices in an active market

The standard explains that the existence of published price quotations in an active market is the best evidence of fair value.[60] Therefore, such prices are to be used even if the entity believes valuation techniques are more appropriate for measuring fair value, even if valuation models are consistent with industry best practice (e.g. for pricing contracts) and even where they are accepted for regulatory capital purposes.[61]

This requirement received a good deal of attention during the improvements project, but the IASB reaffirmed (and strengthened slightly) the position in the previous standard that quoted prices are the best indicator of fair value because:

- in an active market, the best evidence of fair value is the quoted price, given that fair value is defined in terms of a price agreed by a knowledgeable, willing buyer and a knowledgeable, willing seller;
- it results in consistent measurement across entities; and
- fair value as defined does not depend on entity-specific factors.[62]

Additional guidance is now included explaining what the term 'quoted in an active market' means: quoted prices should be readily and regularly available from an exchange, dealer, broker, industry group, pricing service or regulatory agency, and those prices should represent actual and regularly occurring market transactions on an arm's length basis.[63] In practice, this will encompass instruments traded on most regulated exchanges, although a quoted price does not necessarily mean there is an active market in a particular instrument. For example, some debt securities may have a 'technical' listing on an exchange, often for credit rating purposes, even though the instrument is rarely traded. Conversely, the existence of a formal exchange is not always necessary to satisfy this term. Prices reflecting an active market may be quoted in many different ways, e.g. in trade journals or on websites.

As noted at 3.1 above, fair value should be measured without any deduction for transaction costs that may be incurred on sale or disposal. This is illustrated in the following example.

Example 20.10: Transaction costs – subsequent measurement

In Example 20.4 at 2.3 above, Company A acquired an available-for-sale equity security that was initially measured at £102 – fair value of £100 plus £2 purchase commission; no account was taken of £3 sales commission that would be paid in the event of disposal.

If Company A had a balance sheet date immediately after purchase, assuming the fair value had not changed, A would measure the security at £100 (again ignoring potential transaction costs) and recognise a loss of £2 in equity.[64]

The standard uses the terms 'bid price' and 'asking price' ('current offer price' or 'offer price') in the context of quoted market prices.[65] In the context of an asset an entity would receive the bid price if it sold the asset; it would have to pay the asking price to acquire the asset.

The appropriate quoted market price for an asset held, or liability to be issued, is usually the current bid price; for an asset to be acquired or liability held, the current asking (or offer) price. Using bid rather than, say, mid-market price (average of bid and asking prices) is a controversial requirement, although there is one situation when mid-market prices may be used, namely when assets and liabilities with offsetting market risks are held (e.g. within a portfolio of interest rate swaps).[66]

As noted at 2.4 above, the term 'bid-ask spread' is used to include only transaction costs.[67] Whilst this appears to eliminate accounting anomalies on initial recognition, it still leaves inconsistencies in the subsequent measurement of instruments. Consider the following extension of Example 20.5 at 2.4 above.

Example 20.11: Bid-ask spread – subsequent measurement

Company A has acquired an available-for-sale equity security that was initially measured at £102 – fair value (bid price) of £97 plus £5 bid-ask spread deemed to be a transaction cost.

If A had a balance sheet date immediately after purchase, assuming the quoted prices had not changed, A would measure the security at £97 (bid price) and recognise a loss of £5 in equity.

Comparing this outcome to that in Example 20.10 above, it becomes apparent that instruments may be measured differently in the balance sheet depending on whether dealers and market makers charge transaction costs explicitly or include them within a bid-ask spread. For many companies the amounts involved are unlikely to be significant (and will normally be recognised outside of income for available-for-sale assets). However, at a conceptual level, the IASB does not appear to have fully resolved this issue.

Rules applicable to some investment funds require net asset values to be reported to investors based on mid-market prices. However, the existence of such regulations does not justify a departure from the general requirement to use the current bid price in the absence of a matching liability position. Therefore, in its financial statements, an investment fund should normally measure its assets at current bid prices and, in reporting its net asset value to investors, it may wish to provide a reconciliation between the fair values reported on its balance sheet and the prices used for the net asset value calculation.[68]

The IASB has acknowledged that some entities operate in different markets and that the prices in those markets may be different. For example, a trader may originate derivatives with its corporate clients in an active 'retail' market and offset these by taking out derivatives in an active dealers' 'wholesale' market where prices may be more favourable. Accordingly, the standard now clarifies that the objective of determining fair value is to arrive at the price at which a transaction in a particular instrument would occur in the *most advantageous* active market to which the entity has immediate access. However, the price in the more advantageous market should be adjusted to reflect any differences in counterparty credit risk between instruments actually traded in that market and those being valued.[69]

The fair value of a portfolio of financial instruments is always the product of the number of units of the instrument held and its quoted market price.[70] Often quoted prices only reflect the price a dealer or market maker is prepared to pay for a maximum deal size. In transactions involving large holdings, a buyer may be prepared to pay a higher price, or a seller may need to accept a lower price, than the one quoted. However, no adjustment is made in these circumstances as illustrated in the following example based on the implementation guidance to IAS 39.

Example 20.12: Valuing publicly quoted shares at other than market price

Company X holds 15% of the share capital in Company Y. The shares are publicly traded in an active market, the currently quoted price is €100, and daily trading volume is 0.1% of outstanding shares. Because X believes that the fair value of the shares it owns, if sold as a block, is greater than the quoted market price, it obtains several independent estimates of the price it would obtain if it were to sell its holding. These estimates indicate that it would be able to obtain a price of €105, a 5% premium above the quoted price.

The published price quotation in an active market is the best estimate of fair value. Therefore, the published price quotation (€100) should be used. X cannot depart from the quoted market price solely because independent estimates indicate that it would obtain a higher (or lower) price by selling the holding as a block.[71]

The use of the words 'solely because' suggest there is some scope for not using the quoted price. However, this is not the case as these words are simply a hangover from the original version of the implementation guidance. Under the original version of the standard it was acknowledged that the quoted price could be adjusted to reflect the existence of objective reliable evidence, such as a contract to sell the asset to a third party for an amount different to the quoted price.[72] Nevertheless, entities are prohibited from taking account of such evidence.

We share the IASB's concern with applying a *premium* to the quoted price, such as in the situation described in Example 20.12 above, or where a portfolio of equities is said to command a 'control premium'. In the absence of an actual transaction, it is hard to verify the value of such premiums. However, in the case of a large holding of debt instruments, disposals are commonly made at a discount to the prevailing quoted price. It therefore seems imprudent to defer the inherent loss until the disposal actually takes place.

If quoted prices do not exist for an instrument in its entirety, but active markets exist for its component parts, fair value should be determined on the basis of the prices for the component parts.[73] An example might be a debt instrument containing an embedded forward based on a stock market index where active markets exist for similar debt instruments and similar forward contracts, but not for the combined instrument itself.

If a rate (rather than a price) is quoted in an active market, that market-quoted rate should be used as an input into a valuation technique to determine fair value. If the market-quoted rate does not include credit risk or other factors that market participants would include in valuing the instrument, adjustments should be made for those factors.[74] Valuation techniques are discussed in more detail at 4.2 and 4.3 below.

When current prices are unavailable, the most recent transaction price should be used in determining the current fair value, provided there has been no subsequent change in economic circumstances. If circumstances have changed, the fair value should reflect the change in conditions by reference to current prices (or rates) for similar instruments as appropriate. For example, a change in the risk-free interest rate following the most recent price quote for a corporate bond should be reflected in determining the fair value of that bond. Similarly, if it can be demonstrated that the last quoted transaction did not take place at fair value, e.g. because it reflected the amount paid or received in a forced transaction, involuntary liquidation or distress sale, that price should also be adjusted.[75]

4.2 Valuation techniques where there is no active market

In the June 2002 exposure draft that preceded the December 2003 amendments, a rigid measurement hierarchy was proposed under which the fair value of instruments not quoted in an active market would normally be determined by reference to recent market transactions. Only if there were no recent market transactions would valuation techniques be used. However, this hierarchy was simplified and the fair value of all instruments that are not quoted in active markets is to be determined on the basis of valuation techniques. It is acknowledged that such techniques include, where available, the use of recent market transactions between knowledgeable, willing parties in arm's length transactions.[76]

There are many other valuation techniques available – including discounted cash flow analyses and option pricing models, as well as making reference to the current fair value of other instruments that are substantially the same. However, if there is a valuation technique that is commonly used by market participants to price an instrument, and that technique has been demonstrated to provide reliable estimates of prices obtained in actual market transactions, that technique should be used.[77]

It is explained that the objective of using a valuation technique is to establish what the transaction price would have been, on the measurement date, in an arm's length exchange motivated by normal business considerations. A valuation technique that makes maximum use of market inputs, and relies as little as possible on entity-specific inputs, is considered more likely to meet this objective. Also, the technique should reasonably reflect how the market could be expected to price a particular instrument. Accordingly, the inputs should represent, so far as possible, market expectations and measures of the risk-return factors inherent in the instrument.[78]

In other words, valuation techniques should incorporate all factors that market participants would consider in setting a particular price and be consistent with accepted economic methodologies for pricing financial instruments. They should also be calibrated and tested for validity using prices from any observable current market transactions in the same instrument (without modification or repackaging) or based on any available observable market data. Market data should be obtained from the same market in which the instrument was originated or purchased.[79]

The best evidence of fair value at initial recognition is taken to be the transaction price (i.e. the fair value of the consideration given or received) unless fair value is evidenced by comparison with other observable current market transactions in the same instrument (without modification or repackaging) or based on a valuation technique whose variables include only data from observable markets.[80] This single sentence is very important to those entities that trade in financial instruments. Its effect is to prevent the immediate recognition of a profit on initial recognition of most financial instruments that are not quoted in active markets – see 4.7 below.

The transaction price arising from a market transaction is said to provide a 'foundation' for estimating fair value. For example, the fair value of a loan can be determined by reference to the transaction price at acquisition or origination as well as current market conditions or interest rates currently charged (by the originator or by others) for instruments that are similar as to remaining maturity, cash flow pattern, currency, credit risk, collateral and interest basis. Alternatively, provided there has been no change in the debtor's credit risk and applicable credit spreads, an estimate of the current market interest rate may be derived by using a benchmark interest rate reflecting a better credit quality than the underlying instrument, holding the credit spread constant and adjusting for the change in the benchmark interest rate. However, if conditions have changed since the most recent market transaction, corresponding changes in fair value are determined by reference to current prices or rates for similar instruments, adjusted as appropriate for any differences from the one being valued.[81]

The same information may not be available each time an instrument is measured. For example, at the date a loan is made (or debt instrument acquired) there is a transaction price that is also a market price. At the next measurement date, although updated general market interest rates are likely be available, there may be no information from new or recent transactions to determine the level of, say, credit risk that market participants would now consider in pricing the instrument. In the absence of evidence to the contrary, it would be reasonable to assume that no changes have taken place from the original spread, although reasonable efforts should be made to determine whether there is any such evidence. When evidence of a change exists, the effects of the change should be considered in determining an instrument's fair value.[82]

In applying discounted cash flow analyses, the discount rate(s) used should equal the prevailing rates of return for instruments with substantially the same terms and characteristics, including currency, credit quality and the remaining term(s) for interest rate resets and principal repayments. As for initial measurement, short-term receivables and payables with no stated interest rate may be measured at the original invoice amount if the effect of discounting is immaterial (see 2.2 above).[83]

4.3 Inputs to valuation techniques

Appropriate techniques for estimating fair value should incorporate observable market data about the market conditions and other factors that are likely to affect the fair value of an instrument. The standard explains that one or more of the following factors (and perhaps others) will need to be incorporated into the valuation technique.

(a) *The time value of money (i.e. interest at the basic or risk-free rate)*. Basic interest rates can usually be derived from observable government bond prices and are often quoted in financial publications. These rates typically vary with the expected dates of the projected cash flows. For example, the annual interest rate applicable to a cash flow occurring in five years will be different to that applicable to one occurring in ten years. These interest rates can be plotted against different time horizons to form what is often known as a 'yield curve'.

For practical reasons, a well-accepted and readily observable general rate, such as LIBOR or a swap rate, may be used as the benchmark rate. However, because such rates are not the risk-free interest rate, any credit risk adjustment is determined in relation to the credit risk in this benchmark rate rather than the risk-free rate.

In some countries, central government bonds may carry a significant credit risk and may not provide a stable benchmark basic interest rate for instruments denominated in that currency. In fact, some entities in these countries may have a better credit standing and a lower borrowing rate than the central government. In such cases, basic interest rates may be more appropriately determined by reference to the highest rated corporate bonds issued in the currency of that jurisdiction;

(b) *Credit risk*. The effect on fair value of credit risk (i.e. the premium over the basic interest rate for credit risk) may be derived from observable market prices for traded instruments of different credit quality or from observable interest rates charged by lenders for loans of various credit ratings;

(c) *Foreign currency exchange prices*. Active currency exchange markets exist for most major currencies, and prices are quoted daily in financial publications;

(d) *Commodity prices*. There are observable market prices for many commodities;

(e) *Equity prices*. Prices (and price indices) of traded equity instruments are readily observable in some markets. Present value based techniques may be used to estimate the current market price of equity instruments for which there are no observable prices;

(f) *Volatility (i.e. the magnitude of expected future changes in price of the financial instrument or other item)*. Measures of the volatility of actively traded items can normally be reasonably estimated on the basis of historical market data or by using volatilities implied in current market prices;

(g) *Prepayment risk and surrender risk*. This is the risk that an option to settle a debt instrument before its maturity will be exercised – rationally, such an option may be expected to be exercised by a borrower paying a fixed rate of interest if interest rates fall. Expected prepayment patterns for financial assets and expected surrender patterns for financial liabilities can be estimated on the basis of historical data. However, the fair value of a financial liability that can be surrendered by the counterparty cannot be less than the present value of the surrender amount – see 4.5 below;

(h) *Servicing costs for a financial asset or a financial liability*. Costs of servicing can be estimated using comparisons with current fees charged by other market participants. If the costs of servicing a financial asset or liability are significant and other market participants would face comparable costs, the issuer would consider them in determining the fair value of that financial asset or financial liability. It is likely that the fair value at inception of a contractual right to future fees equals the origination costs paid for them, unless future fees and related costs are out of line with market comparables.[84]

4.4 Unquoted equity instruments and related derivatives

There are special accounting requirements for certain equity instruments that do not have a quoted market price in an active market and derivatives that are linked to, and must be settled by delivery of, such unquoted equity instruments. Specifically, they should be measured at cost, less impairment, if their fair value cannot be reliably measured (see 3.1 and 3.4 above).

The fair value of these instruments is deemed to be reliably measurable if:

- the variability in the range of reasonable fair value estimates is not significant for that instrument; or
- the probabilities of the various estimates within the range can be reasonably assessed and used in estimating fair value.[85]

It is explained that there are many situations in which the variability in the range of reasonable fair value estimates of such investments is likely not to be significant and that, normally, it is possible to estimate the fair value of a financial asset that has been acquired from a third party. However, if the range of reasonable fair value estimates is significant and the probabilities of the various estimates cannot be reasonably assessed, such instruments are precluded from fair value measurement.[86]

It is not stated explicitly that the fair value of any other type of financial instrument is deemed to be reliably measurable, although there was such a statement in the original standard[87] and the original implementation guidance contained the following example to illustrate the point.

Example 20.13: Complex stand-alone derivative – no unquoted equity underlying

Company Z acquires a complex stand-alone derivative that is based on several underlying variables, including commodity prices, interest rates, and credit indices. There is no active market or other price quotation for the derivative and no active markets for some of its underlying variables.

The presumption that the derivative's fair value can be reliably determined cannot be overcome because it is not linked to, or required to be settled by delivery of, an unquoted equity instrument. It cannot, therefore, be carried at cost.[88]

However, the IFRIC has addressed this in the context of certain principal-to-principal derivatives designed to fix the price of a supply of electricity. Here, valuation issues include the fact that the derivative can have a variable notional amount (often depending on one party's usage requirements) and that the term of the derivative may extend well beyond the period for which there is any observable market data. The IFRIC confirmed that the only exception in IAS 39 from the requirement to fair value derivatives after initial recognition relates to instruments that are linked to, and must be settled by delivery of, unquoted equity instruments.[89]

The presumption that the fair value of all such instruments can be reliably measured is controversial. In fact, in our experience, even professional valuation specialists can be reluctant to provide valuation services in respect of some complex instruments, explaining that any estimate is likely to be purely speculative. Nevertheless, the standard contains no relaxation from its requirement to determine an estimate of fair value in these circumstances.

Where a financial instrument contains an embedded derivative whose fair value cannot be reliably measured (see Chapter 17 at 5) the relaxation may apply to the hybrid (or combined) contract if it contains a link to an unquoted equity instrument.

Example 20.14: Embedded derivative cannot be reliably measured

A company enters into a contract containing an embedded derivative that requires separation. However, the derivative cannot be reliably measured because it will be settled by delivery of an unquoted equity instrument whose fair value cannot be reliably measured. An example of such an instrument might be a convertible bond issued by a company whose shares are unquoted.

The entire combined contract is designated as a financial instrument at fair value through profit or loss (see Chapter 17 at 5). If the fair value of the combined instrument can be reliably measured, it is measured at fair value. However, the equity component of the combined instrument may be sufficiently significant to preclude the reliable estimation of its fair value. In this case, the combined contract is measured at cost less impairment.[90]

4.5 Demand deposits and similar liabilities

Financial institutions often manage risk on the assumption that demand liabilities paying no interest (such as many current accounts) or lower than market interest rates (some deposit accounts) will remain outstanding for long periods of time. Such assumptions are normally borne out by empirical evidence, including the historical behaviour of similar instruments. Accordingly, it might be argued that the fair value of such instruments is less than the demand amount (discounted if it cannot be called immediately). The price at which portfolios of such instruments are transferred in genuine third party transactions normally supports this assertion.

The IASB disagreed with this argument. Although reasonably predictable, at least at a point in time for a particular portfolio, the value to the financial institution of a customer choosing not to demand repayment at the earliest opportunity, thereby continuing to receive a low rate of interest, is not considered part of the contract that gives rise to the financial liability. Rather, it is value reflecting the 'economically irrational' behaviour of the customer. This value may be recognised as an intangible asset in certain circumstances[91] but should not be taken into account in measuring the financial liability. Recognition criteria for intangible assets (such as core deposit intangibles, i.e. the difference between the value of a portfolio of deposits measured under IAS 39 and the amount that would actually be transferred to acquire or assume the portfolio) are covered in Chapter 7 and Chapter 12.

It is explained that, in many cases, the market price observed for such financial liabilities is the price at which they are originated between the customer and the deposit-taker, i.e. the demand amount, and recognising such a liability at less than the demand amount would give rise to an immediate gain on origination, which the IASB believed inappropriate (see 4.7 below).[92] Accordingly, the standard states that the fair value of a financial liability with a demand feature is not less than the amount payable on demand, discounted from the first date that the amount could be required to be paid.[93]

It is not the direct effect of this decision that worries most banks – it is unlikely that any such institution would ever consider recognising an immediate profit on acceptance of a deposit. However, it has serious implications for those wishing to use the provisions of the March 2004 macro-hedging amendments to IAS 39, although this concern has, for the time being, been ameliorated for European banks (see Chapter 17 at 1.5 and Chapter 21 at 6).

Some financial liabilities can become repayable on demand in certain circumstances that could, theoretically, occur shortly after issuance. For example, an entity may have issued a long-term loan note that becomes payable on demand in the event that a covenant is breached. It would not normally be appropriate to regard such an instrument as a demand liability.

4.6 Negative assets and liabilities

The standard helpfully points out that if the fair value of a financial asset falls below zero it becomes a financial liability (assuming it is measured at fair value).[94] The only real alternative would be treatment as a negative asset which would not be sensible. It does not go on to explain what happens if the fair value of a financial liability become positive, but it is safe to assume that it becomes a financial asset not a negative liability.

4.7 'Day 1' profits

Historically, dealers in financial instruments recognised an amount of profit on (or just after) origination of an instrument – this is often referred to as recognising a 'day 1' profit. The profit effectively represents the margin that has been 'locked in' as a result of the differential between the price charged to a customer and prices available to the dealer in wholesale markets.

The practice of recognising day 1 profits continued under the original version of IAS 39. Although instruments were initially recognised at cost, the guidance on determining fair value allowed remeasurement to a different fair value very shortly after origination (provided there was adequate supporting evidence), thereby resulting in the immediate recognition of profit. However, the December 2003 version of the standard somewhat restricted the scope for recognising day 1 profits.

As noted at 4.1 above, if an instrument is quoted in an active market and the dealer has access to another, more favourable, active market in (virtually) the same instrument, the instrument's initial fair value is determined by reference to the more advantageous market (appropriately adjusted for any differences between the instruments, e.g. in credit risk). The use of the more advantageous price may give rise to a day 1 profit.

For instruments that are not quoted in an active market, the initial fair value should be determined by reference to a valuation technique, the starting point for which is the transaction price. Only if supported by prices of other transactions in the same instrument, or the use of a valuation technique in which all inputs include data from observable markets (see 4.2 above), can an immediate profit be recognised. The IASB concluded that these conditions were necessary and sufficient to provide reasonable assurance that fair value was actually different to the transaction price for the purpose of recognising day 1 profits or losses. In other cases, the transaction price is deemed to give the best evidence of fair value, an approach that achieves convergence with US GAAP.[95]

A disingenuous reading of these requirements might have suggested that, although recognition of a day 1 profit in these circumstances was prohibited, there was nothing to prevent the recognition of a profit on 'day 2'. This was obviously not the intention of the IASB and they moved quickly to clear this up with amendments to the standard being published in December 2004. It is now explained that the subsequent measurement of the financial asset or financial liability and the subsequent recognition of gains and losses should be consistent with the other requirements of IAS 39. Where an entity is prevented from recognising a day 1 profit, gains and losses should be recognised subsequently only to the extent that it arises from a change in a factor (including time) that market participants would consider in setting a price.[96]

Consequently, locked in profits will emerge over the life of the instrument, although precisely how they should emerge is not at all clear. The IASB was asked to clarify that straight-line amortisation was an appropriate method of recognising the day 1 profits but decided not to do so. Somewhat unhelpfully, it stated (without further explanation) that although straight-line amortisation may be an appropriate method in some cases, it will not be appropriate in others.[97]

Given the emphasis that the standard now puts on active market price quotations, comparing the following two situations can give rise to a slightly counter-intuitive outcome.

- Where an instrument is quoted in an active market, it may be measured by reference to a similar (but not identical) instrument that is quoted in a different active market;
- However, where the instrument is not quoted in an active market, it is the inactive market in which it is originated that is deemed to provide the most

reliable information as to the instrument's fair value. This is the case even if a similar (but not identical) instrument *is* quoted in an active market.

In voting against publication of the December 2003 version of the standard, one of the IASB members disagreed with the principle of using a market in which an instrument has not been traded, noting that there were many related issues that needed addressing.[98] We tend to agree.

Another situation in which day 1 profits (or losses) appear to arise is on the acquisition of a large holding of instruments that are quoted in an active market. Consider the following extension of Example 20.12 at 4.1 above.

Example 20.15: Valuing publicly quoted shares at other than market price

Company Z acquires from Company X its 15% holding in the share capital of Company Y for €105 when the quoted price in an active market is €100. It intends to hold the shares as a strategic investment and they are classified as available-for-sale.

It appears that there is no scope for overcoming the presumption that a published price quotation in an active market is the best estimate of fair value. Therefore, the shares should be recorded at €100 resulting in a loss on initial recognition of €5 per share. Moreover, because the loss arises on initial recognition, not remeasurement, of an available-for-sale asset, it appears that the loss should be recognised in the income statement.

We are not entirely convinced that this was the IASB's intention in these circumstances and, in practice, price volatility and the market's reaction to such a transaction may make it difficult to isolate and measure such a loss accurately. However, the above treatment appears to flow from the requirements of the standard, at least in theory.

4.8 Own credit risk

One of the more controversial aspects of the fair value option is that in determining the fair value of a financial liability, the credit risk associated with the instrument should be taken into account. This can result in the rather counter-intuitive result of a financially distressed entity reporting significant gains as the fair value of its debt deteriorates (and vice versa). For example, in its 2003 financial statements, Marconi disclosed the following information on the book and fair value of its financial liabilities.

Extract 20.4: Marconi Corporation plc (2003)

28 **Financial instruments** [extracts]

d **Fair value of financial assets and liabilities** [extracts]

The book values and fair values of the Group's financial assets and liabilities at 31 March 2003 and 31 March 2002 were:

	Book value		**Fair value**	
	2003 £million	2002 £ million	**2003 £ million**	2002 £ million
Short-term financial liabilities and current portion of long-term borrowings	**(4,745)**	(2,436)	**(1,068)**	(2,436)
Long-term borrowings and long-term financial liabilities	**(30)**	(2,208)	**(30)**	(707)

The fair values of the traded outstanding long-term borrowings … have been determined by references available from the markets on which the instruments are traded. … [O]ther fair values have been calculated by discounting cash flows at prevailing interest rates.

Had Marconi been accounting for its debt instruments under the fair value option, it would have measured these financial liabilities at approximately £1.1 billion at 31 March 2003, rather than £4.8 billion, and recorded a cumulative additional profit in its income statement of £3.7 billion. Based on the book and fair values disclosed above, approximately £2.2 billion of this additional profit would have been recorded in the year to 31 March 2003 alone.[99] This is, of course, an extreme example, but it illustrates the issue very well.

In the Basis for Conclusions to IAS 39, the IASB states that it considered responses to the exposure draft that suggested, in effect, that fair value should exclude the effects of changes in the credit risk of a liability.[100] However, the IASB decided that because financial statements are prepared on a going concern basis, credit risk affects the value at which liabilities could be repurchased or settled. Accordingly, the fair value of a financial liability does, in fact, reflect the credit risk relating to that liability. Therefore, it was decided to include credit risk relating to a financial liability in the fair value measurement of that liability for the following reasons:

- entities realise changes in fair value, including fair value attributable to the credit risk of a liability, for example, by renegotiating or repurchasing liabilities or by using derivatives;
- changes in credit risk affect the observed market price of a financial liability and hence its fair value;
- it is difficult from a practical standpoint to exclude changes in credit risk from an observed market price; and
- the fair value of a financial liability (i.e. the price of that liability in an exchange between a knowledgeable, willing buyer and a knowledgeable, willing seller) on initial recognition reflects its credit risk and the IASB believes that it is inappropriate to include credit risk in the initial fair value measurement of financial liabilities, but not subsequently.[101]

The IASB also considered whether the component of the fair value of a financial liability attributable to changes in credit quality should be specifically disclosed, separately presented in the income statement, or separately presented in equity. It decided that, whilst separately presenting or disclosing such changes might be difficult in practice, disclosure of such information would be useful to users of financial statements and would help alleviate the concerns expressed. Therefore, it was decided to require disclosure that helps identify those changes in the fair value of a financial liability that arise from changes in the liability's credit risk. The IASB believes that this is a reasonable proxy for the change in fair value that is attributable to changes in the liability's credit risk, in particular when such changes are large, and will provide users with information with which to understand the profit or loss effect of such a change in credit risk.[102] In addition, entities are also required to disclose the difference between the carrying amount of such a liability and the amount it would be contractually required to pay at maturity to the holder of the obligation.[103] These disclosures are considered further in Chapter 22 at 2.4.4 B and 3.3.4 B.

Finally, the IASB clarified that this issue relates only to the credit risk of the financial liability, rather than to the creditworthiness of the entity, because this was considered to describe more appropriately the objective of what is included in the fair value measurement of financial liabilities.[104] Of course the two are very closely related, but the deterioration of an issuer's creditworthiness may not, of itself, result in a corresponding deterioration in the credit risk of all of its liabilities. For example, the fair value of liabilities secured by valuable collateral, guaranteed by third parties or ranking ahead of virtually all other liabilities is generally unaffected by changes in the entity's creditworthiness.[105]

5 AMORTISED COST AND THE EFFECTIVE INTEREST METHOD

IAS 39 contains three key definitions relating to this method of accounting, which are set out below.

The *amortised cost* of a financial instrument is defined as the amount at which it was measured at initial recognition minus principal repayments, plus or minus the cumulative amortisation using the 'effective interest method' of any difference between that initial amount and the maturity amount, and minus any write-down (directly or through the use of an allowance account) for impairment or uncollectability. The *effective interest method* is a method of calculating the amortised cost of a financial instrument (or group of instruments) and of allocating the interest income or expense over the relevant period.

The *effective interest rate* is the rate that exactly discounts estimated future cash payments or receipts over the expected life of the instrument or, when appropriate, a shorter period, to the instrument's net carrying amount. The calculation of the effective interest rate should include all fees and points paid or received between the contracting parties to the extent they are an integral part of the effective interest rate. The definition refers to IAS 18 for further guidance on what should and should not be considered integral (see Chapter 28). The calculation should also include transaction costs, and all other premiums or discounts, but not the effect of future credit losses,[106] a point reiterated by the IFRIC.[107]

It is important to note that the effective interest rate is normally based on estimated, not contractual, cash flows and there is a presumption that the cash flows and the expected life of a group of similar financial instruments can be estimated reliably. However, in those rare cases when it is not possible to estimate reliably the cash flows or the expected life of a financial instrument (or group of instruments), the contractual cash flows over the full contractual term of the financial instrument (or group of instruments) should be used.[108]

During the improvements project, the IASB considered whether the effective interest rate for all financial instruments should be calculated on the basis of *estimated* cash flows, or whether *contractual* cash flows should be used for individual financial instruments with the use of estimated cash flows being restricted to groups of financial instruments. The position adopted was chosen because the IASB believes it achieves consistent application of the effective interest method throughout the standard.[109]

As set out in Chapter 19 at 4, a compound financial instrument such as a convertible bond is accounted for as a financial liability component and an equity component. In accounting for the financial liability at amortised cost, the expected cash flows should be those of the liability component only and the estimate should not take account of the bond being converted.

The application guidance explains that, in some cases, financial assets are acquired at a deep discount that reflects incurred (as opposed to expected or future) credit losses. Therefore, in accordance with the definition above, *incurred* credit losses should be included in the estimated cash flows when computing the effective interest rate[110] (otherwise higher interest income than that inherent in the price paid for the instrument would be recognised). However, expected future defaults should not be included in estimates of cash flows because this would be a departure from the incurred loss model for impairment recognition.[111] Unfortunately, as set out at 6 below, the distinction between incurred, expected and future losses is not entirely clear.

The IASB acknowledged that it was not always clear how to interpret the requirement in the original standard that the effective interest rate must be based on discounting cash flows through maturity or the next market-based repricing date. In particular, it was not always clear whether fees, transaction costs and other premiums or discounts should be amortised over the period until maturity or the period to the next market-based repricing date.[112] For consistency with the estimated cash flows approach, it was decided to clarify that the effective interest rate is calculated over the expected life of the instrument or, when applicable, a shorter period. A shorter period is used when the variable (e.g. interest rates) to which the fee, transaction costs, discount or premium relates is repriced to market rates before the expected maturity of the instrument. In such a case, the appropriate amortisation period is the period to the next such repricing date.[113] The application of this requirement is considered in more detail at 5.3 below.

5.1 Fixed interest, fixed term instruments

The effective interest method is most easily applied to instruments that have fixed payments and a fixed term. The following examples (as well as Example 20.8 at 3.2 above) illustrate this.

Example 20.16: Effective interest method – amortisation of premium or discount on acquisition

At the end of 2008 a company purchases a debt instrument with five years remaining to maturity for its fair value of US$1,000 (including transaction costs). The instrument has a principal amount of US$1,250 and carries fixed interest of 4.7% payable annually (US$1,250 × 4.7% = US$59 per year). In order to allocate interest receipts and the initial discount over the term of the instrument at a constant rate on the carrying amount, it can be shown that interest needs to be accrued at the rate of 10% annually. The table below provides information about the amortised cost, interest income, and cash flows of the debt instrument in each reporting period.[114]

Year	*(a)* Amortised cost at start of year (US$)	*(b = a × 10%)* Interest income (US$)	*(c)* Cash flows (US$)	*(d = a + b – c)* Amortised cost at end of year (US$)
2009	1,000	100	59	1,041
2010	1,041	104	59	1,086
2011	1,086	109	59	1,136
2012	1,136	113	30	1,190
2013	1,190	119	1,250 + 30	–

Example 20.17: Effective interest method – stepped interest rates

On 1 January 2008, Company A acquires a debt instrument for its fair value of £1,250 (including transaction costs). The principal amount is £1,250 which is repayable on 31 December 2013. The rate of interest is specified in the debt agreement as a percentage of the principal amount as follows: 6% in 2008 (£75), 8% in 2009 (£100), 10% in 2010 (£125), 12% in 2011 (£150) and 16.4% in 2012 (£205). It can be shown that the interest rate that exactly discounts the stream of future cash payments to maturity is 10%. In each period, the amortised cost at the beginning of the period is multiplied by the effective interest rate of 10% and added to the amortised cost. Any cash payments in the period are deducted from the resulting balance. Accordingly, the amortised cost, interest income and cash flows of the debt instrument in each period is as follows:

Year	*(a)* Amortised cost at start of year (£)	*(b = a × 10%)* Interest income (£)	*(c)* Cash flows (£)	*(d = a + b – c)* Amortised cost at end of year (£)
2008	1,250	125	75	1,300
2009	1,300	130	100	1,330
2010	1,330	133	125	1,338
2011	1,338	134	150	1,322
2012	1,322	133	1,250 + 205	–

It can be seen that, although the instrument is issued for £1,250 and has a maturity amount of £1,250, its amortised cost does not equal £1,250 at each balance sheet date.[115]

Methods for determining the effective interest rate for a given set of cash flows (as in the examples above) include simple trial and error techniques as well as more methodical iterative algorithms. Alternatively, many spreadsheet applications contain 'goal-seek' or similar functions that can also be used to derive effective interest rates.

5.2 Prepayment, call and similar options

The standard explains that when calculating the effective interest rate, all contractual terms of the financial instrument, for example prepayment, call and similar options, should be considered.[116] The following simple example illustrates how this principle is applied.

Example 20.18: Effective interest rate – embedded prepayment options

Bank ABC originates 1,000 ten year loans of £10,000 with 10% stated interest. Prepayments are probable and it is possible to reasonably estimate their timing and amount. ABC determines that the effective interest rate including loan origination fees received by ABC is 10.2% based on the *contractual* payment terms of the loans as the fees received reduce the initial carrying amount.

However, if the *expected* prepayments were considered, the effective interest rate would be 10.4% since the difference between the initial amount and maturity amount is amortised over a shorter period.

The effective interest rate that should be used by ABC for this portfolio is 10.4%.[117]

5.2.1 Revisions to estimated cash flows

The standard contains an explanation of how changes to estimates of payments or receipts (e.g. because of a reassessment of the extent to which prepayments will occur) should be dealt with.

Where estimates change, the carrying amount of the financial instrument (or group of instruments) should be adjusted to reflect actual and revised estimated cash flows. More precisely, the carrying amount should be calculated by computing the present value of estimated future cash flows at the instrument's original effective interest rate. Any consequent adjustment should be recognised immediately in profit or loss.[118]

This creates an apparent inconsistency with the requirements of IAS 39 for instruments accounted for using the effective interest method that have been the subject of a fair value hedge (see Chapter 21 at 4.1.2). IAS 39 requires the original effective interest rate of such an instrument to be recalculated at the date of commencement of amortisation of hedge accounting adjustments to the carrying value of the asset. It seems clear that in these circumstances the reference in the previous paragraph to the 'original effective interest rate' should be read as being to the recalculated rate. The IASB has acknowledged this inconsistency and decided to remove it by way of its annual improvements project.[119]

The IASB considers this approach to have the practical advantage that it does not require recalculation of the effective interest rate, i.e. an entity simply recognises the remaining cash flows at the original rate. Consequently, a possible conflict with the requirement to discount estimated cash flows using the original effective interest rate when assessing impairment is avoided.[120]

This requirement is illustrated in the following example taken from the implementation guidance to IAS 39.

Example 20.19: Effective interest method – revision of estimates

At the end of 2008 a company purchases a debt instrument with the same terms as the instrument in Example 20.16 at 5.1 above, except that the contract also specifies that the borrower has an option to prepay the instrument and that no penalty will be charged for prepayment (i.e. any prepayment will be made at the principal amount of US$1,250 or a proportion thereof).

At inception, there is an expectation that the borrower will not prepay and so the information about the instrument's effective interest rate, amortised cost, interest income and cash flows in each reporting period would be the same as that in Example 20.16.

On the first day of 2011 the investor revises its estimate of cash flows. It now expects that 50% of the principal will be prepaid at the end of 2011 and the remaining 50% at the end of 2013. Therefore, the opening balance of the debt instrument in 2011 is adjusted to an amount calculated by discounting the amounts expected to be received in 2011 and subsequent years using the original effective interest rate (10%). This results in the new opening balance in 2011 of US$1,138. The adjustment of US$52 (US$1,138 – US$1,086) is recorded in profit or loss in 2011.

The table below provides information about the amortised cost, interest income and cash flows as they would be adjusted taking into account this change in estimate.

	(a)	*(b = a × 10%)*	*(c)*	*(d = a + b – c)*
Year	Amortised cost at start of year (US$)	Interest and similar income* (US$)	Cash flows (US$)	Amortised cost at end of year (US$)
2009	1,000	100	59	1,041
2010	1,041	104	59	1,086
2011	1,086	114 + 52	625 + 59	568
2012	568	57	30	595
2013	595	60	625 + 30	–

*the standard and related guidance do not state whether the catch-up adjustment (US$52 in 2011 in this case) should be classified within the income statement as interest income or as some other income or expense, but simply that it should be recognised in profit or loss.

This amortised cost calculation would be applicable whether the instruments were classified as held-to-maturity or available-for-sale.[121]

5.2.2 Interaction with the requirements for embedded derivatives

Although not explained in the standard, for hybrid instruments containing terms such as prepayment and similar options that are accounted for separately as embedded derivatives (see Chapter 17 at 5.1.1 C) those terms should not be taken into account in applying the effective interest method. It is only the host (not the hybrid) instrument that is being accounted for at amortised cost and the deemed terms of the host will not normally contain those terms. If a prepayment option, say, were accounted for as an embedded derivative at fair value, it would effectively be accounted for twice if it was also taken into account in determining the effective interest rate of the host.

In Example 20.19, which is based on the implementation guidance to IAS 39, it is not clear why the prepayment option has *not* been separately accounted for as an embedded derivative. The exercise price is US$1,250 and the option may be exercised at any time, yet the amortised cost is initially only US$1,000. Therefore, unless these two figures were considered approximately equal, the option would not be regarded as closely related to the host (see Chapter 17 at 5.1.1 C). We find it hard to believe that the IASB considers two numbers, one of which is 25% larger than the other, to be approximately equal. More likely, the requirements regarding embedded derivatives were overlooked when developing the above example as it is intended, primarily, to illustrate the new accounting requirements for estimate revisions.

This actually raises other questions with regards to the issue of whether prepayment and similar options should be regarded as closely related to the host instrument. In assessing whether the exercise price is approximately equal to the amortised cost at each exercise date, should one consider the amortised cost of the hybrid on the assumption the option is regarded as closely related, or the amortised cost of the host on the assumption that it is not? This conundrum is illustrated in the following simple example (which also provides further illustrations of the application of the effective interest method to instruments containing prepayment options).

Example 20.20: Embedded prepayment option

Company P borrows €1,000 on terms that require it to pay annual fixed rate coupons of €80 and €1,000 principal at the end of ten years. The terms of the instrument also allow P to redeem the debt after seven years by paying the principal of €1,000 and a penalty of €100.

The debt instrument can be considered to comprise the following two components:

- a host debt instrument requiring ten annual payments of €80 followed be a €1,000 payment of principal; and
- an embedded prepayment option, exercisable only at the end of seven years with an exercise price of €1,100.

If, at inception, the prepayment option was expected *not* to be exercised, the effective interest rate of the *hybrid* would be 8%. This is the rate that would discount the expected cash flows of €80 per year for ten years plus €1,000 at the end of ten years to the initial carrying amount of €1,000. The table below provides information about the amortised cost, interest income and cash flows using this assumption.

Year	(a) Amortised cost at start of year (€)	(b = a × 8%) Interest and similar income (€)	(c) Cash flows (€)	(d = a + b – c) Amortised cost at end of year (€)
1	1,000	80	80	1,000
2	1,000	80	80	1,000
3	1,000	80	80	1,000
4	1,000	80	80	1,000
5	1,000	80	80	1,000
6	1,000	80	80	1,000
7	1,000	80	80	1,000
8	1,000	80	80	1,000
9	1,000	80	80	1,000
10	1,000	80	80 + 1,000	–

However if, at the outset, the option *was* expected to be exercised, the effective interest rate of the *hybrid* would be 9.08% as this is the rate that discounts the expected cash flows of €80 per year for seven years, plus €1,100 at the end of seven years, to the initial carrying amount of €1,000. The table below provides information about the amortised cost, interest income and cash flows using this alternative assumption.

Year	(a) Amortised cost at start of year (€)	(b = a × 9.08%) Interest and similar income (€)	(c) Cash flows (€)	(d = a + b – c) Amortised cost at end of year (€)
1	1,000	91	80	1,011
2	1,011	92	80	1,023
3	1,023	93	80	1,036
4	1,036	94	80	1,050
5	1,050	95	80	1,065
6	1,065	97	80	1,082
7	1,082	98	80 + 1,100	–

On the face of it, therefore, comparing the amortised cost of the hybrid with the exercise price of the option at the date it could be exercised suggests the prepayment option might be considered closely related if it was likely to be exercised but not if exercise was unlikely.

However, even this is not the whole story. If the option (on inception) was not expected to be exercised, but at a later date exercise became likely, the amortised cost carrying amount would be revised so that it represented the expected future cash flows discounted at the original effective interest rate. For example, if at the end of Year 5, it became likely that the option would be exercised, the carrying amount would be revised so that it represented €80 discounted for one year at 8% plus €1,180 discounted for two years at 8% – in other words, €1,086 rather than €1,065. The difference of €21 would be recognised in profit or loss immediately and the amortised cost carrying amount would subsequently accrete so that it represented the final cash outflow (option exercise price of €1,100 plus coupon of €80) at the end of Year 7. So even in this situation there is an argument to suggest that the prepayment option should not be separated as the exercise price will always equal the amortised cost (at least to the extent that the option is expected to be exercised).

If the assessment was performed based on the amortised cost of the *host*, the initial fair value of the prepayment option is needed. From P's perspective it will have a positive fair value and for the purpose of this example this is assumed to be €50. Therefore, the initial value of the host will be €1,050 (€1,000 + €50). The effective interest rate of the host can be demonstrated to be 7.28% and the amortised cost each year would be as follows:

Year	(a) Amortised cost at start of year (€)	(b = a × 7.28%) Interest and similar income (€)	(c) Cash flows (€)	(d = a + b – c) Amortised cost at end of year (€)
1	1,050	76	80	1,046
2	1,046	76	80	1,042
3	1,042	76	80	1,038
4	1,038	76	80	1,034
5	1,034	75	80	1,029
6	1,029	75	80	1,024
7	1,024	75	80	1,019
8	1,019	74	80	1,013
9	1,013	74	80	1,007
10	1,007	73	80 + 1,000	–

In this case, the amortised cost at the date the option can be exercised is €1,019. Comparing this with the exercise price of €1,100 suggests the option may not be considered closely related in this case.

In fact if this analysis were applied to prepayment options for which there was no associated penalty (i.e. the instrument would always be redeemed at its principal amount), separating the embedded derivative in this way would artificially create a difference between the amortised cost of the *host* and the exercise price. However, we are entirely unconvinced it would be appropriate to separate an embedded derivative from such a simple instrument.

Unfortunately, the standard is silent on these issues and preparers of accounts will be required to exercise judgment as to the most appropriate method to use in their individual circumstances, although as noted in Chapter 17 at 5.1.1 C, one trade body has published guidance explaining that where early repayment fees are included in the calculation of effective interest, the prepayment option is likely to be closely related to the loan.[122]

5.3 Floating rate instruments

When the estimated cash flows for a floating rate instrument are revised, application of the requirements at 5.2.1 above could produce some surprising results, as shown in the following example.

Example 20.21: Effective interest method – variable rate loan

At the start of July 2008, Company G originates a floating rate debt instrument. Its fair value is equal to its principal amount of $1,000 and no transaction costs are incurred. The instrument pays, in arrears at the end of June, a variable rate coupon, determined by reference to 12 month LIBOR at the start of each previous July. It has a term of five years and is repayable at its principal amount at the end of June 2013.

On origination, 12 month LIBOR is 5% and this establishes the first payment, to be made in June 2009, at $50. Based on a market-derived yield curve, G estimates that the subsequent floating rate payments will be $60, $70, $80 and $90 (yield curve rises steeply). It can be demonstrated that the interest rate that exactly discounts these estimated coupon payments and the $1,000 principal at maturity to the current carrying amount of $1,000 is 6.87% (the definition does not acknowledge the possibility of more than one effective interest rate that would be reflective of a yield curve that is not flat).

In this situation, recognising interest at 6.87% in the first year would seem entirely counter-intuitive and is inconsistent with traditional notions of interest recognition for floating rate instruments, which even the IASB agrees with. Therefore the standard contains additional guidance for applying the effective interest method to floating rate instruments.

Normally, the effective interest rate remains constant over the life of an instrument. However, for floating rate instruments, it is stated that periodic re-estimation of cash flows to reflect movements in market interest rates *does* alter the effective interest rate. The standard goes on to explain that where such an instrument is initially recognised at an amount equal to the principal repayable on maturity, re-estimating the future interest payments normally has no significant effect on the carrying amount of the instrument.[123]

Further, whilst payments, receipts, discounts and premiums included in the effective interest method calculation are normally amortised over the expected life of the instrument, there may be situations when they are amortised over a shorter period (see 5 above). This will be the case when the variable to which they relate reprices to market rates before the instrument's expected maturity. In such cases, the appropriate amortisation period is to the next repricing date.[124]

For example, if a premium or discount on a floating rate instrument reflects interest that has accrued since interest was last paid, or changes in market rates since the floating interest rate was reset to market rates, it will be amortised to the next date when the interest rate is reset to market rates. If, however, it results from a change in the credit spread over the floating rate specified in the instrument, or other variables that are not reset to market rates, it is amortised over the expected life of the instrument.[125]

The following examples illustrate the requirements of applying a discount resulting from a credit downgrade and accrued interest.

Example 20.22: Effective interest method – amortisation of discount arising from credit downgrade

A twenty year bond is issued at £100, has a principal amount of £100, and requires quarterly interest payments equal to current three month LIBOR plus 1% over the life of the instrument. The interest rate reflects the market-based required rate of return associated with the bond issue at issuance. Subsequent to issuance, the credit quality of the bond deteriorates resulting in a rating downgrade. It therefore trades at a discount, although there is no objective evidence of impairment. Company A purchases the bond for £95 and classifies it as held-to-maturity.

The discount of £5 is amortised to income over the period to the maturity of the bond and not to the next date interest rate payments are reset as it results from a change in credit spreads.[126]

Example 20.23: Effective interest method – amortisation of discount arising from accrued interest

At the start of November 2008, Company P acquires the bond issued by Company G in Example 20.21 above – current interest rates have not changed since the end of July 2008 and G's credit risk has not changed since origination so P pays $1,016.

The premium of $16 paid by P relates to interest accrued since the last reset date and so is amortised to income over the period to the next repricing date, June 2009; further, the $50 cash flow received at the end of June 2009 is also 'amortised' over this period.

Consequently, for the eight months ended June 2009, P will record interest of $34 ($50 – $16), which is also the approximate equivalent of eight months interest at current rates (5%) earned on P's initial investment.

This treatment is consistent with the requirements of IAS 18 that apply when unpaid interest has accrued before the acquisition of an interest-bearing investment. In such cases, it is explained (in more traditional terms) that the subsequent receipt of interest should be allocated between pre-acquisition and post-acquisition periods and only the post-acquisition portion should be recognised as revenue.[127] In fact for many floating rate instruments, it will often be appropriate to apply a simplistic method of accounting – for example, by amortising transaction costs on a straight line basis over the life of the instrument combined with a simple time apportionment approach to the floating rate coupons.

5.4 Perpetual debt instruments

Where perpetual debt instruments are originated and interest is paid either at a fixed or variable rate, the amortised cost (the present value of the stream of future cash payments discounted at the effective interest rate) equals the principal amount in each period and the difference between the initial consideration and zero ('the maturity amount') is not amortised.[128]

However, where the stated rate of interest on perpetual debt decreases over time, some or all of the interest payments are, from an economic perspective, repayments of the principal amount as illustrated in the following example.[129]

Example 20.24: Amortised cost – perpetual debt with decreasing interest rate

On 1 January 2008 Company A subscribes £1,000 for a debt instrument which yields 25% interest for the first five years and 0% in subsequent periods. The instrument is classified as a loan. It can be determined that the effective yield is 7.9% and the amortised cost is shown in the table below.[130]

Year	(a) Amortised cost at start of year (£)	(b = a × 7.9%) Interest income (£)	(c) Cash flows (£)	(d = a + b – c) Amortised cost at end of year (£)
2008	1,000	79	250	829
2009	829	66	250	645
2010	645	51	250	446
2011	446	36	250	232
2012	232	18	250	–
2013	–	–	–	–

5.5 Acquisition of impaired debt instruments

As noted at 5 above, incurred (but not expected or future) credit losses should be included in the estimated cash flows when computing the effective interest rate. This is illustrated in the following example.

Example 20.25: Purchase of impaired debt

On 1 January 2002, Company D issued a debt instrument that required it to pay an annual coupon of €800 in arrears and to repay the principal of €10,000 on 31 December 2011. By 2007, D was in financial difficulties and was unable to pay the coupon due on 31 December 2007. On 1 January 2008, Company V estimated that the holder could expect to receive a single payment of €4,000 at the end of 2009 following a financial restructuring and acquired the debt instrument at an arms length price of €3,000.

It can be shown that using the contractual cash flows (including the €800 overdue) gives rise to an effective interest rate of 70.1% (the net present value of €800 now and annually thereafter until 2011 and €10,000 receivable at the end of 2011 is €3,000 when discounted at 70.1%). However, because the debt instrument has clearly incurred a credit loss, V should calculate the effective interest rate using the estimated cash flows on the instrument. In this case, the effective interest rate is 15.5% (the net present value of €4,000 receivable in two years is €3,000 when discounted at 15.5%).

All things being equal, interest income of €464 (€3,000 × 15.5%) would be recognised on the instrument during 2008 and its carrying amount at the end of the year would be €3,464 (€3,000 + €464). However if at the end of the year the cash flow expected to be generated by the instrument had increased to €4,250 (still to be received at the end of 2009), an adjustment to the asset would be made as set out at 5.2.1 above. Accordingly, its carrying amount would be increased to €3,681 (€4,250 discounted over one year at 15.5%) and a further €217 income would be recognised in profit or loss. Of course, there would need to be a substantive and supportable basis for revising the cash flow estimates.

5.6 Other, more complex, instruments

The application of the effective interest method to instruments with unusual embedded derivatives that are deemed closely related to the host, or other embedded features that are not accounted for separately, is not always straightforward or intuitive. Specifically it is not always clear how to deal with changes in the estimated cash flows of the instrument and in any given situation one needs to assess which of the approaches set out at 5.2.1 and 5.3 above is more appropriate.

Consider an entity that issues a debt instrument for its par value of €10m which is repayable in ten years' time on which an annual coupon is payable comprising two elements: a fixed amount of 2.5% of the par value and a variable amount equating to 0.01% of the entity's annual revenues (see Example 17.22 in Chapter 17). The instrument is not designated at fair value through profit or loss and it is judged that the embedded feature is not a derivative.

The two approaches set out at 5.2.1 and 5.3 above could give rise to significantly different accounting treatments. In the former case, F would need to estimate the amount of payments to be made over the life of the bond (which will depend on its estimated revenues for the next ten years) in order to determine the effective interest rate to be applied. Any changes to these estimates would result in a catch-up adjustment to profit or loss and the carrying amount of the bond which, potentially, could give rise to significant volatility. In the latter case the annual coupon would simply be accrued each year and changes in estimated revenues of future periods would have no impact on the accounting treatment until the applicable year.

In this situation we believe that it would be appropriate to apply the former approach, principally because the entity's revenue does not represent a floating rate that changes to reflect movements in market rates of interest.

For other instruments, the decision as to which approach to use is less clear. For example, it might be argued that simple inflation-linked bonds are similar enough to floating rate instruments to apply the latter approach. Some might go further and apply it more exotic instruments, for example to an 'inverse floater' where coupons on an otherwise simple debt instruments are paid at a fixed rate minus LIBOR (subject to a floor of zero) – they would say that this is similar to a floating rate instrument because any re-estimation of cash flows will only reflect movements in market interest rates.

6 IMPAIRMENT

The impairment requirements of IAS 39 might appear somewhat over-engineered for what is a relatively simple subject for many entities, i.e. making appropriate provisions for bad and doubtful debts. The reason for this complexity is that IAS 39 is designed for use by all entities, including financial institutions for which impairment losses are often highly material. Accordingly, the IASB has tried to lay down clear guidelines as to when impairment losses should (and should not) be recognised in order to ensure that a consistent approach is taken both from period to period for individual entities and from entity to entity.

The topic is one in which different, and hard to reconcile, views are held by many, especially those setting the standards. This manifested itself under the original standard when the IGC attempted to issue guidance interpreting the original impairment requirements. A number of draft Q&A were issued but never finalised and it became apparent that the IASB would need to address the topic as part of its improvements project. The revised approach set out in the June 2002 exposure draft did not convince all IASB members and one even felt the need to formally dissent on the subject of impairment.[131] The proposals in the exposure draft were amended somewhat before the current standard was published, but this time three IASB members, citing impairment as an area of disagreement, voted against publication.[132]

The two most controversial issues related to impairment are (a) whether an individual asset that has been reviewed for impairment and found not to be impaired can then be included in a portfolio of assets that are subject to a collective impairment assessment and (b) how to deal with losses arising on available-for-sale equity instruments. These are covered in the remainder of this section.

Further, the IASB explains that the accounting model adopted is based on 'incurred losses' (rather than, say, expected losses and certainly not on future losses). It believes that such a model, which does not take account of future events or transactions, is more consistent with an amortised cost basis of accounting.[133] Accordingly, lengthy guidance explaining what is meant by 'incurred' is included in the standard. Whether this achieves what was intended remains to be seen as the detailed requirements may potentially be subject to somewhat different interpretations.

6.1 Impairment reviews

All financial assets, except for those measured at fair value through profit or loss, are subject to review for impairment.[134] Assessments should be made at each balance sheet date as to whether there is any objective evidence that a financial asset or group of assets is impaired. If such evidence exists, the requirements set out at 6.2, 6.3 or 6.4 below should be followed to determine the amount of any impairment loss.[135]

A financial asset or a group of assets is impaired (and impairment losses are incurred) if, and only if, there is objective evidence of impairment as a result of one or more events that occurred after initial recognition (a 'loss event') and that loss event (or events) has an impact on the estimated future cash flows of the financial asset or group of assets that can be reliably estimated.[136]

Therefore, an entity should recognise an impairment loss on a group of loans if the loss expectation at initial recognition of the loans had not changed, but it could be estimated reliably, based on past history, that loss events had occurred after initial recognition, but before the reporting date.[137]

It may not be possible to identify a single, discrete event that caused the impairment; rather, the combined effect of several events may have caused the impairment. However, losses expected as a result of future events, no matter how likely, are not recognised.[138] Similarly, an impairment loss may not be recognised at the time an asset is originated (i.e. before a loss event can have occurred) as illustrated in the following example.[139]

Example 20.26: Immediate recognition of impairment

Bank B lends $1,000 to Customer M. Based on historical experience, B expects that 1% of the principal amount of loans given will not be collected, but an immediate impairment loss of $10 cannot be recognised.[140]

Objective evidence that a financial asset or group of assets is impaired includes observable data that comes to the attention of the holder about the following loss events:

- significant financial difficulty of the issuer or obligor;
- breach of contract, such as a default or delinquency in interest or principal payments;
- the lender, for economic or legal reasons relating to the borrower's financial difficulty, granting to the borrower a concession that would not otherwise be considered;

- it becoming probable that the borrower will enter bankruptcy or other financial reorganisation;
- the disappearance of an active market for that asset because of financial difficulties (but not simply because the asset is no longer publicly traded[141]); or
- observable data indicating that there is a measurable decrease in the estimated future cash flows from a group of financial assets since initial recognition, although the decrease cannot yet be identified with the individual assets in the group, including:
  - adverse changes in the payment status of borrowers in the group (e.g. an increased number of delayed payments or an increased number of credit card borrowers who have reached their credit limit and are paying the minimum monthly amount); or
  - national or local economic conditions that correlate with defaults on the assets in the group (e.g. an increase in the unemployment rate in the geographical area of the borrowers, a decrease in property prices for mortgages in the relevant area, a decrease in oil prices for loan assets to oil producers, or adverse changes in industry conditions that affect the borrowers in the group).[142]

A downgrade of an entity's credit rating is not, of itself, evidence of impairment, although it may be when considered with other available information.[143] Other factors that would be considered in determining whether an impairment has been incurred include information about the debtors' or issuers' liquidity, solvency and business and financial risk exposures, levels of and trends in delinquencies for similar financial assets, national and local economic trends and conditions, and the fair value of collateral and guarantees.[144] A decline in the fair value of a financial asset below its cost or amortised cost is not necessarily evidence of impairment – for example, the fair value of a debt instrument may decline only from an increase in the risk-free interest rate.[145] Therefore, it is possible that an 'available-for-sale reserve' in equity can be negative.

The original standard did not include guidance about impairment indicators that are specific to investments in equity instruments and consequently questions had been raised about when, in practice, such investments become impaired.[146] The IASB acknowledged that, for marketable equity investments, any impairment trigger other than a decline in fair value below cost is likely to be arbitrary to some extent. If markets are reasonably efficient, today's market price is the best estimate of the discounted value of the future market price. However, it was considered important to provide guidance to address the questions raised in practice.[147]

Accordingly, the standard now explains that the following are objective evidence of impairment of an equity investment:

- information about significant changes with an adverse effect that have taken place in the technological, market, economic or legal environment in which the issuer operates, and indicates that the cost of the investment in the equity instrument may not be recovered; and

- a significant or prolonged decline in the fair value of an investment in such an instrument below its cost.[148]

The meaning of the terms 'significant' and 'prolonged' are not defined or explained further. For example, if the price of Company A's shares is significantly more volatile than that of shares in Company B, can a decline of, say, 10% be significant for the purposes of investments in B but not in A? Clearly judgment will be necessary in applying this part of the standard, but any revaluation below cost is likely to be viewed with some suspicion.

These triggers apply in addition to those specified earlier, which focus on the assessment of impairment in debt instruments.[149]

Sometimes, the observable data required to estimate an impairment loss may be limited, or no longer fully relevant to current circumstances, for example when a borrower is in financial difficulties and there are few available historical data relating to similar borrowers. In such cases, judgement and experience should be used to estimate the amount of any impairment loss and to adjust observable data for a group of financial assets to reflect current circumstances. The fact that an impairment loss is difficult to measure is not a reason for not recognising a loss that has been incurred. The use of reasonable estimates is an essential part of the preparation of financial statements and does not undermine their reliability.[150]

6.2 Financial assets carried at amortised cost

6.2.1 *Individual and collective assessments*

The standard requires that impairment assessments should be performed as follows:

- for assets that are individually significant, assessment should be made on an individual basis;
- other assets may also be assessed individually, although such an assessment is not necessarily required;
- assets that have been individually assessed, but for which there is no objective evidence of impairment, should be included within a group of assets with similar credit risk characteristics and collectively assessed for impairment;
- assets that are individually assessed for impairment and for which an impairment loss is (or continues to be) recognised cannot be subject to a collective impairment assessment; and
- any other assets, i.e. those that have not been individually assessed, should also be the subject of a collective assessment.[151]

The above requirements might be read as allowing an asset that is not individually significant, but known to be impaired, to be included in a collective assessment thereby avoiding the recognition of a loss if, say, the fair value of other assets in the group exceed their amortised cost. However, the implementation guidance clearly states that in such a case the impairment loss should be recognised.[152]

As noted at 6 above, the ability to include individual assets that have been reviewed for impairment in a collective assessment is a controversial one and two IASB members cited this as a reason for them voting against publication of the standard.[153] The Basis for Conclusions contains an extensive discussion of the arguments for and against the proposal[154] but it essentially boils down to whether or not one believes a loan can actually be impaired even if a review has not identified it as such.

If, in performing an individual review, the lender had access to all relevant information about the loan and the borrower, it might seem quite reasonable to conclude that there is no need to perform an additional collective review. However, in practice, not all information is going to be readily available on a timely basis, and any individual assessment is likely to be incomplete. Therefore, in our view, it is entirely appropriate to require an additional collective review.

6.2.2 Measurement – general requirements

If there is objective evidence that an impairment loss has been incurred on loans and receivables or held-to-maturity investments, that loss should be measured as the difference between the asset's carrying amount and the present value of estimated future cash flows. Those cash flows, which should exclude future credit losses that have not been incurred, should be discounted at the original effective interest rate of the financial asset, i.e. the effective interest rate computed at initial recognition.[155] The original effective interest rate is used because discounting at the current market interest rate would, in effect, impose fair-value measurement on assets that would otherwise be measured at amortised cost.[156]

The standard allows the carrying amount of an impaired asset to be reduced, either directly or through use of an allowance account, but emphasises that the loss should always be recognised in profit or loss.[157]

If the terms of an instrument are renegotiated or otherwise modified because of the borrower's financial difficulties, impairment should be measured using the original effective interest rate before the modification of terms. For variable rate assets, the discount rate for measuring the impairment loss is the current effective interest rate(s) determined under the contract. As a practical expedient, impairment may be measured based on an instrument's fair value using an observable market price.[158] In the original standard, this concession was allowed only for floating rate assets,[159] but it may now be used for fixed rate assets too. There is little conceptual merit in this, but it aligns IAS 39 more closely with US GAAP.[160]

The implementation guidance makes it clear that recognition of impairment losses in excess of those that are determined based on objective evidence (either at an individual asset or collective group level) is not permitted.[161]

These basic principles are illustrated in the following example.

Example 20.27: Impairment – changes in amount or timing of payments

A bank is concerned that, because of financial difficulties, five customers, Companies A to E, will not be able to make all principal and interest payments due on originated loans in a timely manner.

It negotiates a restructuring of the loans and expects the customers will meet their restructured obligations. The restructured terms are as follows:

- A will pay the full principal amount of the original loan five years after the original due date, but none of the interest due under the original terms;
- B will pay the full principal amount of the original loan on the original due date, but none of the interest due under the original terms;
- C will pay the full principal amount of the original loan on the original due date but with interest at a lower interest rate than the interest rate inherent in the original loan;
- D will pay the full principal amount of the original loan five years after the original due date and all interest accrued during the original loan term, but no interest for the extended term;
- E will pay the full principal amount of the original loan five years after the original due date and all interest, including interest on all outstanding amounts for both the original term of the loan and the extended term.

An impairment loss has been incurred if there is objective evidence of impairment – this is assumed to be the case here because of the customers' financial difficulties. The amount of the impairment loss for a loan measured at amortised cost is the difference between the loan's carrying amount and the present value of future principal and interest payments, discounted at the loan's original effective interest rate.

For A to D, the present value of the future principal and interest payments discounted at the loan's original effective interest rate will be lower than the carrying amount of the loan. Therefore an impairment loss is recognised in those cases. For E, even though the timing of payments has changed, the bank will receive interest on interest, so that the present value of the future principal and interest payments, discounted at the loan's original effective interest rate, will equal the carrying amount of the loan. Therefore, there is no impairment loss. However, this fact pattern is unlikely given Company E's financial difficulties.[162]

Consistent with the initial measurement requirements (see 2.2 above), cash flows relating to short-term receivables are not discounted if the effect of discounting is immaterial.[163] This does not mean that such instruments are not, as a matter of principle, discounted, as illustrated in the following example.

Example 20.28: Impairment of short-term receivable

A construction company, K, agrees to build a new stadium for a professional football club, L. The project takes approximately six months and payment of €10 million is due six weeks after completion. On completion, K has recognised revenue and a corresponding receivable of €10 million because the effect of discounting at the current annualised rate of 5% is immaterial.

Shortly after completion, it becomes apparent that L is in financial difficulties and is unlikely to be able to settle the €10 million debt. In order to avoid formal insolvency proceedings, L attempts to restructure its financial obligations and offers to pay K €1 million per year for the next 10 years. Because it believes this arrangement appears to offer the best prospects for the recovery of its debt, K accepts.

On the face of it (and assuming no defaults on the rescheduled debt are expected), it might be argued that K need not recognise an impairment loss because it will receive all of the money owed and the debt's original effective interest rate was 0%. However, the original receivable was, in principle, discounted – it is just that the effects of discounting were not reflected in the financial statements as they were not material. Therefore, the effect of discounting the rescheduled payments at 5% per annum (approximately €2.28 million) should be recognised as an impairment loss.

It is common practice for companies to determine bad debt provisions using a provisioning matrix or similar formula based on the number of days a loan or debt is overdue, e.g. 0% if less than 90 days, 20% if 90 to 180 days, 50% if 180 to 365 days and 100% if more than 365 days overdue. This will be acceptable only if the formula can be demonstrated to produce an estimate sufficiently close to one determined under the methodology specified in IAS 39.[164]

In measuring the impairment of a collateralised or secured loan, the cash flows used should reflect those that may result from foreclosure less costs for obtaining and selling the collateral, whether or not foreclosure is probable.[165] The collateral itself should not be recognised as a separate asset unless it meets the recognition criteria for an asset in another international standard.[166]

To a lender, guarantees provided by a third (sometimes related) party such as a parent, other shareholder or fellow subsidiary, are little different to collateral – they provide a source of funds in the event that the debtor defaults. In the original implementation guidance it was made clear that guarantees should be taken into account in determining the amount of an impairment loss.[167] Unfortunately, most of this guidance has been removed from the standard and, on a pure technical level, it is not clear that the accounting treatment should remain the same.

The guarantee is clearly a financial instrument (see Chapter 17 at 2.2.3). Based on the analysis in Chapter 17 at 6, it will normally be considered a separate financial instrument, even if it cannot be transferred independently from the loan. This is because there will almost certainly be a substantive business purpose for structuring the arrangement in this way, i.e. to reduce the lender's exposure to default. The guarantee is likely to satisfy the definition of an insurance contract in IFRS 4[168] but will be excluded from the scope of that standard because it is a direct insurance contract not held by a cedant.[169] (A cedant is an insurer that is the policyholder under a reinsurance contract.[170]) If the guarantee satisfies the definition of an insurance contract in IFRS 4 it is outside the scope of IAS 39[171] irrespective of whether it is within the scope of IFRS 4 (see Chapter 17 at 3.3 and 3.4). Therefore it is hard to avoid the conclusion that the guarantee is a contingent asset within the scope of IAS 37 because it is not 'covered' by another standard[172] (see Chapter 27 at 2.2.1 B).

What this means is that the guarantee can only be recognised as an asset when it is 'virtually certain' that a recovery will be made. In conceptual terms this seems a more onerous test than that for recognising an impairment loss on the associated loan asset. Therefore, it might seem necessary to recognise an impairment loss on the asset (that would be fully recovered under the guarantee) but without being able to recognise an offsetting recovery from the guarantee. This seems entirely wrong.

There is more than one counter-argument to this analysis. For example, it might be considered that the guarantee and the loan should be accounted for as a single 'synthetic' instrument, irrespective of what is said in Chapter 17 at 6, especially where the two parties are related. A degree of support for this treatment can be found in the Basis for Conclusions to IAS 39 where it is stated that 'the fair value of liabilities ... guaranteed by third parties ... is generally unaffected by changes in the entity's creditworthiness'.[173] This suggests that the IASB considers a third party guarantee of a borrowing to be an integral part of the borrowing arrangement rather than a separate instrument. Further, where the guarantor is a member of the same group as the borrower, IAS 32 – *Financial instruments: Disclosure and Presentation* – requires both elements of the transaction to be considered together when determining the appropriate classification of the instrument from the point of view of the group's consolidated financial statements (see Chapter 19 at 3.6).

Even if it is considered that IAS 37 should apply to the guarantee, some might argue that it is more appropriate to characterise it as a 'reimbursement' in respect of the impairment loss, rather than as a standalone contingent asset. As set out in Chapter 27 at 4.4, a reimbursement is recognised as an asset when it is virtually certain that the reimbursement will be received if the obligation for which a provision has been established is settled. By analogy, therefore, the guarantee would be recognised as an asset to the extent it is virtually certain a recovery could be made if the lender suffered the impairment loss on the loan.

Finally, following the application of the amendments to IAS 39 dealing with financial guarantee contracts (see Chapter 17 at 3.4), IFRS 4 explains that the holder of a financial guarantee contract will normally need to develop its accounting policy in accordance with the 'hierarchy' in IAS 8 – *Accounting Policies, Changes in Accounting Estimates and Errors* – (see Chapter 3 at 4.3)[174] suggesting an entity does not automatically apply IAS 37.

6.2.3 Measurement – detailed requirements

The standard contains a significant amount of detailed application guidance on the processes to be used for the assessment and calculation of impairment losses within groups of financial assets carried at amortised cost. In practice, this will be of limited relevance to entities that are determining a bad debt provision in respect of a portfolio of short-term trade receivables. However, for banks and other financial institutions with significant portfolios of loans and receivables, these detailed requirements will be highly relevant and could have a major impact on the way that loan impairments are assessed. This guidance might also be more relevant for entities providing goods or services on deferred settlement terms, such as retailers operating their own store-cards.

The guidance explains that the process for estimating impairment should consider all credit exposures, not only those of low credit quality. For example, if an internal credit grading system is used, all credit grades should be considered, not only those reflecting a severe credit deterioration.[175] In other words, the possibility of an impairment existing in a portfolio of high quality assets that contain a low risk of default should not be ignored.

Whatever process is used to estimate an impairment loss, it may produce either a single amount or a range of possible amounts. In the latter case, the best estimate within the range should be recognised as the impairment loss. This estimate should take into account all relevant information about known conditions that existed at the balance sheet date. The standard cross-refers to IAS 37 for guidance on selecting the best estimate in a range of possible outcomes (see Chapter 27 at 4.1).[176]

When performing a collective evaluation of impairment, assets should be grouped on the basis of similar credit risk characteristics that are indicative of the debtors' ability to settle according to the contractual terms of the instruments concerned. For example, this may be done on the basis of a credit risk evaluation or grading process that considers some or all of the following characteristics depending on their relevance: asset type, industry, geographical location, collateral type, past-due status as well as other factors.[177]

It is stated that loss probabilities and other loss statistics differ at a group level between (a) assets that have been individually evaluated for impairment and found not to be impaired, and (b) assets that have not been individually evaluated for impairment, with the result that a different amount of impairment may be required.[178] In practice, the extent of the difference in approach to these groups will depend on the quality of the individual assessments – i.e. the less detailed or accurate they are, the less the loss probabilities should differ from those not individually assessed.

Further, it is explained that if an entity does not have a group of assets with similar risk characteristics, it should not make any additional assessment over and above that performed at an individual level.[179] It is this situation that the two dissenting IASB members found hard to accept. If one entity owned 50% of a loan asset for which there was no evidence of impairment when assessed on an individual basis, but it owned no similar assets, then it would recognise no impairment loss. However, if another entity owned the other 50% of the loan asset and also owned a number of similar assets, that entity may end up recognising an impairment loss in respect of its identical asset.[180]

This anomaly may be rationalised in a number of ways. For example, if a company owned only one significant asset, rather than a group of similar assets, it is quite likely to assess impairment of that asset in a more detailed manner than a company with a group of similar assets. Also, this situation is not dissimilar to the treatment of warranty claims under IAS 37 (at least the current version of that standard). If there was a small probability, say 1%, of a warranty claim arising on each sale made, a company that had sold one unit would not normally recognise a provision. However, a company that had sold thousands of identical units would almost certainly recognise a provision.

It is explained that impairment losses recognised on a group basis represent an interim step pending the identification of impairment losses on individual assets in the group. Accordingly, as soon as information is available that specifically identifies losses on individually impaired assets, those assets should be removed from the group.[181]

Estimates of future cash flows for a group of financial assets should be based on historical loss experience for assets with credit risk characteristics similar to those in the group. Entities that have no, or insufficient, entity-specific loss experience, should use peer group experience for comparable groups of assets. Historical loss experience should be adjusted on the basis of current observable data to reflect the effects of current conditions that did not affect the period on which the historical loss experience is based, and to remove the effects of conditions in the historical period that do not exist currently. Estimates of changes in future cash flows should reflect, and be directionally consistent with, changes in related observable data from period to period (such as changes in unemployment rates, property prices, commodity prices, payment status or other factors that are indicative of incurred losses in the group and their magnitude). The methodology and assumptions used for estimating future cash flows should be reviewed regularly to reduce any differences between loss estimates and actual loss experience.[182]

As an example of this approach, historical experience may demonstrate that one of the main causes of default on credit card loans is the death of the borrower. Although the death rate may be unchanged since the previous year, some of the group of borrowers could have died in the year. This would indicate that an impairment loss has occurred, even if it was not possible to identify which specific borrowers had died at the year-end, and it would be appropriate for an impairment loss to be recognised for these 'incurred but not reported' losses. However, it would not be appropriate to recognise an impairment loss for deaths that are expected to occur in a future period. In that case the necessary loss event (the death of the borrower) has not yet occurred.[183]

When using historical loss rates in estimating future cash flows, it is important that information about historical loss rates is applied to groups that are defined in a manner consistent with the groups for which the historical loss rates were observed. Therefore, the method used should enable each group to be associated with information about past loss experience in groups of assets with similar credit risk characteristics and relevant observable data that reflect current conditions.[184]

Formula-based approaches or statistical methods may be used to determine impairment losses in a group of financial assets (e.g. for smaller balance loans) as long as they are consistent with the general requirements of the standard. Therefore any model used should incorporate the effect of the time value of money, consider the cash flows for all of the remaining life of an asset (not only the next year), consider the age of the loans within the portfolio and not give rise to an impairment loss on initial recognition.[185]

6.2.4 Impairment of assets subject to hedges

Where an asset with fixed interest rate payments is hedged against the exposure to interest rate risk by a receive-variable, pay-fixed interest rate swap, the carrying amount of the asset will include an adjustment for fair value changes attributable to movements in interest rates (see Chapter 21 at 4.1.1). As a result, in accounting for the asset, the original effective interest rate and amortised cost of the loan are adjusted to take into account these recognised fair value changes and the adjusted effective interest rate is calculated using the adjusted carrying amount of the loan.[186]

In order to take account of the hedge effects on the carrying amount of the asset, any impairment loss on the hedged loan should be calculated as the difference between its carrying amount *after* adjustment for fair value changes attributable to the risk being hedged and the expected future cash flows of the loan discounted at the *adjusted* effective interest rate.[187]

When a loan is included in a portfolio hedge of interest rate risk (see Chapter 21 at 6) the change in the fair value of the hedged portfolio should be allocated to the loans (or groups of similar loans) being assessed for impairment on a systematic and rational basis.[188]

6.2.5 *Reversal of impairment losses*

If, in a subsequent period, the amount of the impairment or bad debt loss decreases and the decrease can be objectively related to an event occurring after the write-down (such as an improvement in the debtor's credit rating), the previously recognised impairment loss should be reversed, either directly or by adjusting an allowance account. The reversal should not result in a carrying amount of the asset that exceeds what its amortised cost would have been at the date of reversal, had the impairment not been recognised. The amount of the reversal should be recognised in the income statement.[189]

6.3 Available-for-sale assets measured at fair value

6.3.1 *Recognition of impairment*

When a decline in the fair value of an available-for-sale asset has been recognised directly in equity and there is objective evidence that the asset is impaired (see 6.1 above), the cumulative loss in equity should be recycled into profit or loss even though the asset has not been derecognised.[190]

The amount of the loss that should be recycled is the difference between its acquisition cost (net of any principal repayment and amortisation for assets measured using the effective interest method) and current fair value, less any impairment loss on that asset previously recognised in profit or loss.[191]

For non-monetary assets, such as equity instruments, the cumulative net loss included in equity will include any portion attributable to foreign currency changes. It follows that this element of the loss should also be recognised in the income statement if the asset becomes impaired.[192]

6.3.2 *Reversals of impairment*

If, in a subsequent period, the fair value of an available-for-sale *debt* instrument increases, and the increase can be objectively related to an event occurring after the loss was recognised in the income statement, the impairment loss should be reversed and recognised in profit or loss.[193] However, in the case of *equity* instruments, impairments cannot be reversed through the income statement.[194] This restriction on the reversal of impairments of available-for-sale equity instruments represented a significant change from the original version of the standard.

The Basis for Conclusions includes an explanation for the difference in treatment. In particular, in the context of the reversal of impairments on available-for-sale debt securities, it is noted that:

- the reversal of impairment losses of non-financial assets (e.g. inventories, property, plant and equipment and intangible assets) is required if circumstances change;
- the treatment provides consistency with the requirement to reverse impairment losses on loans and receivables and on assets classified as held-to-maturity; and
- determining an increase in fair value attributable to an improvement in credit standing is more objectively determinable than for equity instruments.[195]

The IASB, however, could not find an acceptable way to distinguish reversals of impairment losses from other increases in fair value of available-for-sale equity instruments. Therefore, it decided that precluding such reversals was the only appropriate solution, even though a number of other approaches were considered.[196] In the end this approach probably seemed most expedient as it is comparable to US GAAP under which reversals of impairment losses on equity instruments are not permitted.[197] One IASB member formally disagreed with the approach adopted, not because he considered it appropriate to reverse an impairment loss but because he would have preferred all losses below original cost to be recognised as impairments,[198] i.e. in profit or loss, an even more draconian approach.

6.3.3 *Further declines in the fair value of impaired equity instruments*

The question has arisen as to what the accounting treatment should be if, following an impairment, the fair value of an available-for-sale equity instrument declines further. This is illustrated in the following example.

Example 20.29: Decline in the fair value of an impaired available-for-sale equity investment

Company A acquired 100 shares in Company X on 1 January 2007, for their fair value of €10,000. On 31 December 2007, A's year end, the fair value of the shares in X had fallen to €6,000 and A concluded the shares were impaired. Accordingly, in its 2007 financial statements, A reported an impairment loss of €4,000 in its income statement.

On 31 December 2008, the fair value of the shares in X had fallen a little further to €5,900. In its 2008 financial statements, should A automatically regard the loss of €100 as a further impairment (to be recognised in profit or loss) or should it regard it as a normal revaluation to be recognised in equity?

The implementation guidance to the standard suggests that any further declines in the fair value of an impaired available-for-sale equity instrument should be recognised in profit or loss, although only in the context of explaining the treatment of portions of fair value movements arising from foreign currency changes.[199]

However, perhaps because the accounting treatment is said to be comparable to US GAAP (see 6.3.2 above), some considered that, once impaired, the asset acquired a new 'cost base' equal to the fair value at the date of impairment. Consequently, the €100 decline in fair value would be assessed for impairment as if the asset had been acquired on 31 December 2007 for €6,000. This approach would not necessarily result in the €100 being characterised as an impairment loss.

The IFRIC has addressed this issue and took the view that impairments do not establish a new cost basis. Therefore, for an equity instrument for which a prior impairment loss has been recognised, in applying the indicators discussed at 6.1 above, 'significant' should be evaluated against the original cost at initial recognition and 'prolonged' should be evaluated against the period in which the fair value of the investment has been below original cost at initial recognition.[200]

6.3.4 Timing of impairment tests and interaction with interim reporting

The standard does not discuss how frequently an available-for-sale equity instruments should be assessed for impairment, only that it should be done 'at each balance sheet date'.[201] It might seem sensible to perform such reviews at the end of both interim and annual periods. However, this could give rise to what some see as anomalous results.

Consider, for example, an entity that purchases an equity share for €100 at the start of its reporting period. If the fair value of the share had fallen to €60 at the end of the half-year, it is very likely to conclude that the share had become impaired. Consequently, a €40 loss would be recognised in profit or loss. However, if the share price had recovered to €100 by the end of the full financial year, should this loss be reversed? The introduction to IAS 34 – *Interim Financial Reporting* – states that 'The frequency of an entity's reporting – annual, half-yearly, or quarterly – should not affect the measurement of its annual results.'[202] This might suggest that the impairment loss recognised at the half-year could be reversed at the year-end.

On the other hand, the guidance that accompanies IAS 34 states that the same impairment testing, recognition, and reversal criteria that would be applied at the year end should be applied at an interim date.[203] Further, the accounting requirements of IAS 39 are generally applied on a continuous basis and it might be argued that ignoring losses between balance sheet dates (whatever their frequency) fails to apply properly the requirements of the standard.

This is an issue that has reached the IFRIC's agenda. Early on in their deliberations it was made clear that the IFRIC did not support an approach that would require entities to review for impairment on a continuous basis, leaving the apparent conflicts within IAS 34 and between IAS 34 and IAS 39 to be dealt with.[204]

In July 2006, the IFRIC published an interpretation, IFRIC 10 – *Interim Financial Reporting and Impairment* – setting out how to resolve the conflicts. The IFRIC took the view that the more specific requirements in IAS 39 should take precedence and, therefore, that impairments of available-for-sale equity instruments recognised in an interim period should not be reversed.[205] IFRIC 10 also deals with a similar conflict in the treatment of goodwill impairments but it contains a prohibition on extending by analogy its consensus to other areas of potential conflict between IAS 34 and other standards.[206]

6.4 Financial assets carried at cost

As set out at 3.1 and 3.4 above, unquoted equity instruments and derivative assets that are linked to and must be settled by delivery of such instruments whose fair value cannot be reliably measured, are measured at cost.

If there is objective evidence that an impairment loss has been incurred on such an asset, the amount of the impairment loss is measured as the difference between the carrying amount of the financial asset and the present value of estimated future cash flows, discounted at the current market rate of return for a similar financial asset (see 4.3 above).[207] There is something a little inconsistent in the requirement to determine and include in the financial statements such a net present value when, supposedly, the fair value of the instrument cannot be reliably measured. However, this is not explicitly addressed or even acknowledged.

Consistent with the treatment for other available-for-sale equity securities, any such impairment losses may not be reversed.[208] IFRIC 10 addresses these assets as well as available-for-sale assets measured at fair value.[209]

6.5 Interest income after impairment recognition

Once a financial asset, or group of similar assets, has been written down as a result of an impairment loss, interest income is thereafter recognised based on the rate of interest that was used to discount the future cash flows for the purpose of measuring the impairment loss.[210]

It is not clear how this requirement should be applied to a fixed interest rate debt instrument that is measured at amortised cost and has been written down to its fair value (rather than its net present value using the original effective interest rate of the instrument – see 6.2.2 above). Using an appropriate long-term interest rate at the date of the impairment would seem consistent with the measurement basis adopted, although this is not strictly in accordance with the standard.

7 FOREIGN CURRENCIES

7.1 Foreign currency instruments

The provisions of IAS 21 apply to transactions involving financial instruments in just the same way as they do for other transactions, although the manner in which certain hedges are accounted for can over-ride its general requirements.

Consequently, the balance sheet measurement of a foreign currency financial instrument is determined as follows:

- firstly, it is recorded and measured in the foreign currency in which it is denominated, whether it is carried at fair value, cost, or amortised cost;
- secondly, that amount is retranslated to the entity's functional currency using:
    - closing rate, for all monetary items (e.g. a debt security) and for non-monetary items (e.g. an equity share) carried at fair value; or

- an historical rate, for non-monetary items carried at cost because their fair value cannot be reliably measured.

Therefore, for a foreign currency denominated monetary asset carried at amortised cost under IAS 39, amortised cost is calculated in the currency in which it is denominated. That foreign currency amount is then retranslated into the entity's functional currency at the closing rate.

As an exception, if the financial instrument is designated as a hedged item in a fair value hedge of foreign currency exposure, it is remeasured for changes in foreign currency rates even if it would otherwise have been reported using a historical rate (see Chapter 21 at 4.1).

The reporting of changes in the carrying amount of a financial instrument in the income statement or in equity depends on a number of factors, including whether it is an exchange difference or other change in carrying amount, whether the instrument is a monetary or non-monetary item and whether it is designated as part of a foreign currency cash flow hedge or hedge of a net investment.

Profit and loss items associated with financial instruments, e.g. dividends receivable, interest payable or receivable and impairments, are recorded at the spot rate ruling when they arise (although average rates may be used when they represent an appropriate approximation to spot rates throughout the period). Exchange differences arising on retranslating monetary items are generally reported in profit or loss, although they may be recognised in equity for instruments designated as hedges of future foreign currency transactions or net investments in foreign entities (see Chapter 21 at 4.2 and 4.3). All other fair value changes (e.g. the change in value of a debt instrument as a result of interest rate movements) are reported in profit or loss if the instrument is classified at fair value through profit or loss, or equity if it is available-for-sale.

In cases where some portion of the change in carrying amount is reported in profit or loss and some in equity, e.g. if the fair value of a bond has increased in foreign currency and decreased in the measurement currency, those two components cannot be offset for the purposes of determining gains or losses that should be recognised in profit or loss and equity.[211]

These principles are illustrated in the following example.

Example 20.30: Available-for-sale foreign currency debt security

On 31 December 2008 Company A, whose measurement currency is the euro, acquires a dollar bond for its fair value of $1,000. The bond is the same as the one in Example 20.16 at 5.1 above, i.e. it has five years to maturity and a $1,250 principal, carries fixed interest of 4.7% paid annually ($1,250 × 4.7% = $59 per year), and has an effective interest rate of 10%.

A classifies the bond as available-for-sale. The exchange rate is $1 to €1.50 and the carrying amount of the bond is €1,500 ($1,000 × 1.50).

	€	€
Bond	1,500	
Cash		1,500

On 31 December 2009, the dollar has appreciated and the exchange rate is $1 to €2.00. The fair value of the bond is $1,060 and therefore its carrying amount is €2,120 ($1,060 × 2.00). Its amortised cost is $1,041 (or €2,082 = $1,041 × 2.00) and the cumulative gain or loss to be included in equity is the difference between its fair value and amortised cost, i.e. a gain of €38 (€2,120 – €2,082; or, alternatively, [$1,060 – $1,041] × 2.00).

Interest received on the bond on 31 December 2009 is $59 (or €118 = $59 × 2.00). Interest income determined in accordance with the effective interest method is $100 ($1,000 × 10%) of which $41 ($100 – $59) is the accretion of the initial discount.

It is assumed that the average exchange rate during the year is $1 to €1.75 and that the use of an average exchange rate provides a reliable approximation of the spot rates applicable to the accrual of interest during the year. Therefore, reported interest income is €175 ($100 × 1.75) including accretion of the initial discount of €72 ($41 × 1.75).

The exchange difference reported in profit or loss is €525, which comprises three elements: a €500 gain from the retranslation of the initial amortised cost ($1,000 × [2.00 – 1.50]); a €15 gain from the retranslation of interest income received ($59 × [2.00 – 1.75]) and a €10 gain on the retranslation of the interest income accreted ($41 × [2.00 – 1.75]).

	€	€
Bond	620	
Cash	118	
Interest income (P&L)		175
Exchange gain (P&L)		525
Fair value change (equity)		38

On 31 December 2010, the dollar has appreciated further and the exchange rate is $1 to €2.50. The fair value of the bond is $1,070 and therefore its carrying amount is €2,675 ($1,070 × 2.50). Its amortised cost is $1,086 (or €2,715 = $1,086 × 2.50) and the cumulative gain or loss to be included in equity is the difference between its fair value and the amortised cost, i.e. a loss of €40 (€2,675 – €2,715; or, alternatively, [$1,070 – $1,086] × 2.50). Therefore, there is a debit to equity equal to the change in the difference during 2010 of €78 (€40 + €38).

Interest received on the bond on 31 December 2010 is $59 (or €148 = $59 × 2.50). Interest income determined in accordance with the effective interest method is $104 ($1,041 × 10%), of which $45 ($104 – $59) is the accretion of the initial discount.

Using the same assumptions as in the previous year, interest income is €234 ($104 × 2.25) including accretion of the initial discount of €101 ($45 × 2.25).

The exchange difference reported in profit or loss is €547, which again comprises three elements: a €521 gain from the retranslation of the opening amortised cost ($1,041 × [2.50 – 2.00]); a €15 gain from the retranslation of interest income received ($59 × [2.50 – 2.25]) and an €11 gain on the retranslation of the interest income accreted ($45 × [2.50 – 2.25]).[212]

	€	€
Bond	555	
Cash	148	
Fair value change (equity)	78	
Interest income (P&L)		234
Exchange gain (P&L)		547

It is worth repeating that the treatment would be different for available-for-sale equity instruments. Under IAS 21, these are not considered monetary items and exchange differences would form part of the change in the fair value of the instrument, which would be reported in equity.

7.2 Foreign entities

IAS 39 does not amend application of the net investment method of accounting for foreign entities set out in IAS 21 (see Chapter 10 at 2.7). Therefore, for the purpose of preparing its own accounts for inclusion in consolidated accounts, a foreign entity that is part of a group applies the principles at 7.1 above by reference to its own functional currency. Consequently, the treatment of gains and losses on, say, trading assets held by a foreign entity should follow the treatment in the example below.

Example 20.31: Interaction of IAS 21 and IAS 39 – foreign currency debt investment

Company A is domiciled in the US and its functional currency and presentation currency is the US dollar. A has a UK domiciled subsidiary, B, whose functional currency is sterling. B is the owner of a debt instrument which is held for trading and is therefore carried at fair value.

In B's financial statements for 2008, the fair value and carrying amount of the debt instrument is £100. In A's consolidated financial statements, the asset is translated into US dollars at the spot exchange rate applicable at the balance sheet date, say 2.0, and the carrying amount is US$200 (£100 × 2.0).

At the end of 2009, the fair value of the debt instrument has increased to £110. B reports the trading asset at £110 in its balance sheet and recognises a fair value gain of £10 in profit or loss. During the year, the spot exchange rate has increased from 2.0 to 3.0 resulting in an increase in the fair value of the instrument from US$200 to US$330 (£110 × 3.0). Therefore, A reports the trading asset at US$330 in its consolidated financial statements.

Since B is classified as a foreign entity, A translates B's income statement 'at the exchange rates at the dates of the transactions'. Since the fair value gain has accrued through the year, A uses the average rate of 2.5 (= [3.0 + 2.0] ÷ 2) as a practical approximation. Therefore, while the fair value of the trading asset has increased by US$130 (US$330 – US$200), A recognises only US$25 (£10 × 2.5) of this increase in profit or loss. The resulting exchange difference, i.e. the remaining increase in the fair value of the debt instrument of US$105 (US$130 – US$25), is classified as equity until the disposal of the net investment in the foreign entity.[213]

8 EFFECTIVE DATES, TRANSITIONAL PROVISIONS AND FIRST-TIME ADOPTION

This section contains information that is relevant for annual periods beginning on or after 1 January 2006. For earlier periods, equivalent requirements are dealt with in *International GAAP 2005* and *International GAAP 2007*, the predecessors to this publication.

8.1 Effective dates

The June 2005 amendments to IAS 39 that imposed restrictions on the use of the fair value option (see 1 above) and the August 2005 amendments to IAS 39 relating to financial guarantee contracts (see 3.7 above) must be applied for annual periods beginning on or after 1 January 2006.[214]

Application of IFRIC 10 (see 6.3.4 above) is required for periods commencing on or after 1 November 2006. Earlier adoption is encouraged, although entities should disclose the fact that they have done so.[215]

8.2 Transitional provisions

Where the amendments relating to the fair value option are adopted for an annual period beginning on or after 1 January 2006, an entity:[216]

(a) is required to de-designate any financial asset or financial liability previously designated as at fair value through profit or loss only if it does not qualify for such designation in accordance with the amended standard (see Chapter 17 at 7.1.2).

    When a financial asset or financial liability will be measured at amortised cost after de-designation, the date of de-designation is deemed to be its date of initial recognition.

    The fair value at the date of de-designation of any financial assets or financial liabilities de-designated, as well their new classifications, should be disclosed;

(b) is prohibited from designating as at fair value through profit or loss any previously recognised financial assets or financial liabilities.

Comparative financial statements should be restated using the new designations above provided that, in the case of a financial asset, financial liability, or group of financial assets, financial liabilities or both, designated as at fair value through profit or loss, those items or groups would have met the relevant condition at the beginning of the comparative period or, if acquired after the beginning of the comparative period, at the date of initial recognition.[217]

The amendments in respect of financial guarantee contracts should be applied retrospectively.

For investments in available-for-sale equity instruments and financial assets measured at cost, IFRIC 10 should be applied prospectively from the date from which the measurement criteria of IAS 39 were first applied.[218]

8.3 First-time adoption

IFRS 1 – *First-time Adoption of International Financial Reporting Standards* – is dealt with in Chapter 5. The aspects related to the topics covered in this chapter are covered in detail below. Further similar sections are included in Chapters 17 to 19, 21 and 22.

The general requirement in IFRS 1 is for a first-time adopter to use the same accounting policies in its opening IFRS balance sheet and throughout all periods presented in its first IFRS financial statements and those accounting policies should comply with each IFRS effective at the reporting date for its first IFRS financial statements, although there are a number of exceptions.[219] For financial instruments, an entity should, in preparing its opening IFRS balance sheet, apply the criteria in IAS 39 to identify those that are measured at fair value and those that are measured at amortised cost (see Chapter 17 at 8.3).[220] The implications of these general requirements are discussed below.

8.3.1 Assets and liabilities measured at amortised cost

For those financial instruments measured at amortised cost in the opening IFRS balance sheet their cost should be determined on the basis of circumstances existing when they first satisfied the recognition criteria in IAS 39. However, if they were acquired in a past business combination, their carrying amount under the entity's previous GAAP immediately following the business combination should be taken as their deemed cost under IFRS at that date.[221]

To determine amortised cost using the effective interest method, it is necessary to determine the transaction costs incurred when the instrument was originated. During the development of IFRS 1, some argued that determining these transaction costs could involve undue cost or effort for financial instruments originated long before the date of transition to IFRS and argued for concessions to be made, e.g. by allowing transaction costs to be ignored.[222] However, the IASB believes that the unamortised portion of transaction costs at the date of transition to IFRS is unlikely to be material for most financial instruments. Further, even where the unamortised portion may be material, reasonable estimates are believed possible. Therefore, no exemption was created in this area.[223]

8.3.2 Loan impairments

It is explained that estimates of loan impairments at the date of transition to IFRS should be consistent with estimates made for the same date under previous GAAP (after adjustments to reflect any difference in accounting policies), unless there is objective evidence that those assumptions were in error. Consequently, the impact of any later revisions to those estimates should be treated as impairment losses (or, if the criteria in IAS 39 are met, reversals of impairment losses) of the period in which revisions are made.[224]

In the context of the detailed requirements for loan impairments, it is very unclear where the dividing line between estimates and accounting policies lies. Therefore, for entities where loan impairment provisions are highly material, such as banks and similar financial institutions, this requirement overlooks a very important point of detail and, consequently, appears to include a rather glib statement.

8.3.3 Derivatives and other instruments classified at fair value through profit or loss

It almost goes without saying that all derivative financial instruments should be measured at fair value at the date of transition but the implementation guidance does make this clear.[225]

However, first-time adopters are given some transitional relief in respect of the day 1 profit requirements – in fact this is the same was available to existing IFRS reporters. Consequently, those that choose not to apply the requirements retrospectively are allowed to apply them prospectively to transactions entered into after 25 October 2002 (the effective date of equivalent US GAAP requirements) or 1 January 2004 (the date of transition to IFRS for many entities).[226] It is important to note that the latter date is fixed and does not change according to an entity's date of transition.

8.3.4 Embedded derivatives

Under IAS 39, some embedded derivatives are accounted for separately at fair value. Some argued that retrospective application of this requirement would be costly and suggested either an exemption from retrospective application of this requirement, or a requirement or option to use the fair value of the host instrument at the date of transition to IFRS as the deemed cost of the instrument at that date should be introduced.[227]

Although the IASB recognised that an option not to account separately for some pre-existing embedded derivatives was provided when the equivalent US GAAP requirements became mandatory, it concluded that the failure to measure embedded derivatives at fair value would diminish the relevance and reliability of an entity's first IFRS financial statements. It also observed that IAS 39 addresses an inability to measure an embedded derivative and the host contract separately (in such cases, the entire combined contract is measured at fair value).[228] Accordingly, no exception was created in this area.

Accordingly, when an entity is required to separate an embedded derivative from a host contract, the initial carrying amounts of the components at the date when the instrument first satisfied the recognition criteria in IAS 39 should reflect circumstances at that date. If the initial carrying amounts of the embedded derivative and host contract cannot be determined reliably, the entire combined contract should be designated at fair value through profit or loss.[229]

8.3.5 Transition adjustments: available-for-sale assets

Retrospective application of IAS 39 to available-for-sale financial assets requires a first-time adopter to recognise the cumulative fair value changes in a separate component of equity in the opening IFRS balance sheet and transfer those fair value changes to the income statement on subsequent disposal or impairment of the asset.[230]

During the development of IFRS 1, some suggested that the cost of determining the amount to be included in a separate component of equity would exceed the benefits. However, the IASB noted that these costs would be minimal if a first-time adopter carried the available-for-sale financial assets under previous GAAP at cost or the lower of cost and market value. They acknowledged that these costs might be more significant if they were carried at fair value, but in that case those assets might well be classified as held for trading. Therefore, the requirement that a first-time adopter should apply IAS 39 retrospectively to available-for-sale financial assets was retained in the standard.[231]

Given the requirements in respect of impairments of available-for-sale equity instruments (see 6.3 above) full retrospective application in this area may not be as straightforward as the IASB thinks. However, this does not change the fact that no exceptions have been made in this respect.

8.3.6 Transition adjustments: other instruments

With the exception of hedges (which are dealt with in Chapter 21) other adjustments to the carrying amount of financial assets or liabilities that arise from the adoption of IAS 39 should be recognised in the opening balance of retained earnings.[232]

9 FUTURE DEVELOPMENTS

As set out in the Future Developments section of Chapter 17, the majority of the IASB's current work on financial instruments is being carried out in conjunction with the FASB as part of their joint Memorandum of Understanding. Although this is expected to be a very long-term exercise, there is one joint project, Fair Value Measurement, which may in the slightly nearer term lead to a change in the way the fair value of some financial instruments is determined.

This project is expected to result in the publication of a standard that amends the way in which fair value is determined. The standard would not attempt to address when fair value is used but would apply whenever another international standard requires an asset or a liability (financial and otherwise) to be measured at fair value. The FASB published Statement of Financial Accounting Standards No. 157 – *Fair Value Measurements* – in September 2006 and the IASB published a discussion paper in November 2006 setting out its preliminary views on the principal issues contained in the FASB document with a view to issuing an exposure draft by early 2008.[233]

This project is likely to be of particular interest to those entities that actively trade in financial instruments, especially those affected by the requirements of IAS 39 regarding day 1 profits because the requirements in IAS 39 are more restrictive than those set out in SFAS 157, a matter specifically identified by the IASB in its discussion paper.[234]

References

1 IAS 39, *Financial Instruments: Recognition and Measurement*, IASB, para. BC14.
2 *IASB Update*, IASB, October 2005 and Project Update, *Financial Instruments*, IASB, 18 January 2006.
3 Amendment to IAS 39, Financial Instruments: Recognition and Measurement, *Transition and Initial Recognition of Financial Assets and Financial Liabilities* IASB, December 2004.
4 IAS 39, para. 43.
5 *IAS 39 Implementation Guidance*, Questions & Answers, IAS 39 Implementation Guidance Committee (IGC), May 2000 and subsequently, May 2000 and subsequently, Q&A 66-3.
6 IAS 39, para. AG64.
7 IGC, Q&A 66-3.
8 IAS 20, para. 37.
9 *IASB Update*, IASB, June 2007.
10 IAS 39, para. AG65.
11 Extrapolated from example in IAS 39, para. AG65.
12 IAS 39, para. AG79.
13 *IFRIC Update*, IASB, July 2004.
14 *IFRIC Update*, IASB, November 2006.
15 IAS 39, para. AG4(a).
16 IAS 39, para. 9.
17 IAS 39, para. E.1.1.
18 IAS 39, para. AG67.
19 IAS 39, para. AG13.
20 IAS 39, para. BC222(d).

21 IAS 18, *Revenue*, IASB, Appendix, para. 14(a)(i).
22 *IASB Update*, IASB, June 2007.
23 IAS 39, para. AG70.
24 IAS 39, para. AG28.
25 IAS 39, paras. C.3 and C.5.
26 IAS 39, para. 44.
27 IAS 39, para. AG12.
28 IAS 39, para. BC16.
29 IGC Q&A 30-1.
30 IAS 39, paras. 45 and 47.
31 IAS 39, paras. 46 and 55(a).
32 IAS 39, paras. 46(c)-47(a).
33 IAS 39, para. 53.
34 IAS 39, para. 54(b).
35 IAS 39, para. 46.
36 IAS 39, para. 56.
37 IAS 39, paras. 46 and 56.
38 IAS 39, para. AG68.
39 IAS 39, para. 46.
40 IAS 39, para. 55(b).
41 IAS 39, para. 55(b).
42 IAS 39, para. E.3.1.
43 IAS 2, *Inventories*, IASB, para. 25.
44 IAS 39, paras. 46(c).
45 IAS 39, para. 53.
46 IAS 39, para. 54(b).
47 IAS 39, paras. 47 and 56.
48 IAS 39, paras. 51-52.
49 IAS 39, para. 54(a).
50 IAS 39, para. 54(a).
51 IAS 39, paras. 47(c) and (d) and AG4(a).
52 IAS 39, paras. 46, 47 and 56.
53 IAS 39, paras. 72, 95 and 102.
54 IAS 39, paras. 55 and 57.
55 IAS 39, para. D.2.2.
56 IAS 39, paras. 47(b) and (c) and AG4(a).
57 IAS 39, para. 9.
58 IAS 39, para. AG69.
59 IAS 39, para. BC95.
60 IAS 39, para. AG71.
61 IAS 39, paras. BC96-BC97.
62 IAS 39, paras. BC96-BC97.
63 IAS 39, para. AG71.
64 IAS 39, para. AG67.
65 IAS 39, para. AG70.
66 IAS 39, para. AG72.
67 IAS 39, para. AG70.
68 IAS 39, para. E.2.1.
69 IAS 39, paras. AG71 and BC98.
70 IAS 39, para. AG72.
71 IAS 39, para. E.2.2.
72 IAS 39 (2000), *Financial Instruments: Recognition and Measurement*, IASB, December 1998 to October 2000, para. 98 and IGC Q&A 100-1.
73 IAS 39, para. AG72.
74 IAS 39, para. AG73.
75 IAS 39, para. AG72.
76 IAS 39, paras. AG74 and BC102-BC103.
77 IAS 39, para. AG74.
78 IAS 39, para. AG75.
79 IAS 39, para. AG76.
80 IAS 39, para. AG76.
81 IAS 39, para. AG77.
82 IAS 39, para. AG78.
83 IAS 39, para. AG79.
84 IAS 39, para. AG82.
85 IAS 39, para. AG80.
86 IAS 39, para. AG81.
87 IAS 39 (2000), para. 70.
88 IGC Q&A 70-1.
89 *IFRIC Update*, IASB, November 2006.
90 IAS 39, para. C.11. Following application of the fair value option amendments, such instruments should be designated at fair value through profit or loss whereas previously they would have been treated as held for trading (see Chapter 17 at 5). However, the implementation guidance has not been updated to reflect this amendment.
91 IAS 39, para. F.2.3.
92 IAS 39, paras. BC93-BC94.
93 IAS 39, para. 49.
94 IAS 39, para. AG66.
95 IAS 39, para. BC104.
96 IAS 39, para. AG76A.
97 IAS 39, para. BC222(v)(ii).
98 IAS 39, para. DO6.
99 These financial statements were not prepared under IFRS, but the accounting principles for simple borrowing arrangements, and the requirements to disclose fair values, under Marconi's local GAAP were very similar to the requirements under IFRS.
100 IAS 39, para. BC88.
101 IAS 39, para. BC89.
102 IAS 39, para. BC90.
103 IAS 32 (2005), *Financial Instruments: Disclosure and Presentation*, IASB, March 1995 to August 2005, para. 94(h)(ii) or IFRS 7, *Financial Instruments: Disclosure*, IASB, para. 10(b).
104 IAS 39, para. BC91.
105 IAS 39, para. BC92.
106 IAS 39, para. 9.
107 *IFRIC Update*, IASB, October 2004.
108 IAS 39, para. 9.
109 IAS 39, para. BC30.
110 IAS 39, para. AG5.
111 IAS 39, para. BC32.
112 IAS 39, para. BC34.
113 IAS 39, para. BC35.
114 IGC Q&A 73-1.
115 IAS 39, para. B.27.

116 IAS 39, para. 9.
117 IGC Q&A 10-19.
118 IAS 39, para. AG8.
119 *IASB Update*, IASB, June 2007.
120 IAS 39, para. BC36.
121 IAS 39, para. B.26.
122 *Implementation of International Accounting Standards*, British Bankers' Association, July 2004, para. 10.
123 IAS 39, para. AG7.
124 IAS 39, para. AG6.
125 IAS 39, para. AG6.
126 IGC Q&A 76-1.
127 IAS 18, para. 32.
128 IAS 39, para. B.24.
129 IAS 39, para. B.25.
130 Based on the example in IAS 39, para. B.25.
131 Exposure Draft, *Amendments to IAS 32, Financial Instruments: Disclosure and Presentation, and IAS 39, Financial Instruments: Recognition and Measurement*, IASB, June 2002, para. D6.
132 IAS 39, paras. DO2, DO4, DO7 and DO12-DO14.
133 IAS 39, paras. BC108-BC110.
134 IAS 39, para. 46.
135 IAS 39, para. 58.
136 IAS 39, para. 59.
137 *IFRIC Update*, IASB, October 2004.
138 IAS 39, para. 59.
139 IAS 39, para. E.4.2.
140 IAS 39, para. E.4.2.
141 IAS 39, para. 60.
142 IAS 39, para. 59.
143 IAS 39, para. 60.
144 IAS 39, para. E.4.1.
145 IAS 39, paras. 60 and E.4.10.
146 IAS 39, para. BC105.
147 IAS 39, para. BC106.
148 IAS 39, para. 61.
149 IAS 39, para. BC107.
150 IAS 39, para. 62.
151 IAS 39, para. 64.
152 IAS 39, para. E.4.7.
153 IAS 39, paras. DO2, DO4 and DO7.
154 IAS 39, paras. BC108-BC121.
155 IAS 39, para. 63.
156 IAS 39, para. AG84.
157 IAS 39, para. 63.
158 IAS 39, para. AG84.
159 IGC Q&A 113-3.
160 IAS 39, para. BC221(f).
161 IAS 39, para. E.4.6.
162 IAS 39, para. E.4.3.
163 IAS 39, para. AG84.
164 IAS 39, para. E.4.5.
165 IAS 39, para. AG84.
166 IAS 39, para. E.4.8.
167 IGC Q&A 113-1.
168 IFRS 4, *Insurance Contracts*, IASB, Appendix A (Defined terms).
169 IFRS 4, para. 4(f).
170 IFRS 4, Appendix A (Defined terms).
171 IAS 39, para. 2(e).
172 IAS 37, *Provisions, Contingent Liabilities and Contingent Assets*, IASB, paras. 1(c) and 5(e).
173 IAS 39, para. BC92.
174 IFRS 4, para. IG2, Example 1.11.
175 IAS 39, para. AG85.
176 IAS 39, para. AG86.
177 IAS 39, para. AG87.
178 IAS 39, para. AG87.
179 IAS 39, para. AG87.
180 IAS 39, para. DO4.
181 IAS 39, para. AG88.
182 IAS 39, para. AG89.
183 IAS 39, para. AG90.
184 IAS 39, para. AG91.
185 IAS 39, para. AG92.
186 IAS 39, para. E.4.4
187 IAS 39, para. E.4.4
188 IAS 39, para. E.4.4
189 IAS 39, para. 65.
190 IAS 39, para. 67.
191 IAS 39, para. 68.
192 IAS 39, para. E.4.9.
193 IAS 39, para. 70.
194 IAS 39, para. 69.
195 IAS 39, para. BC128.
196 IAS 39, para. BC130.
197 IAS 39, para. BC221(g).
198 IAS 39, para. DO13.
199 IAS 39, para. E.4.9.
200 *IFRIC Update*, IASB, June 2005.
201 IAS 39, para. 58.
202 IAS 34, *Interim Financial Reporting*, IASB, para. 28.
203 IAS 34, para. B36.
204 *IFRIC Update*, IASB, August 2005.
205 IFRIC 10, *Interim Financial Reporting and Impairment*, IASB, July 2006, paras. 8 and BC9.
206 IFRIC 10, para. 9.
207 IAS 39, para. 66.
208 IAS 39, para. 66.
209 IFRIC 10, para. 6.
210 IAS 39, para. AG93.
211 IAS 39, paras. AG83 and E.3.4.
212 IAS 39, para. E.3.2.
213 IAS 39, para. E.3.3.
214 IAS 39, paras. 103B and 105B.
215 IFRIC 10, para. 10.
216 IAS 39, para. 105C.
217 IAS 39, para. 105D.
218 IFRIC 10, para. 10.

219 IFRS 1, paras. 7, 13 and 26.
220 IFRS 1, para. IG56.
221 IFRS 1, paras. B2(e) and IG57.
222 IFRS 1, para. BC72.
223 IFRS 1, para. BC73.
224 IFRS 1, paras. 31 and IG58.
225 IFRS 1, para. IG56(c).
226 IFRS 1, para. 25G.
227 IFRS 1, para. BC65.
228 IFRS 1, para. BC65.
229 IFRS 1, para. IG55. Following application of the fair value option amendments, such instruments should be designated at fair value through profit or loss whereas previously they would have been treated as held for trading (see Chapter 17 at 5). However, IFRS 1 has not been updated to reflect this amendment.
230 IFRS 1, paras. IG59 and BC81.
231 IFRS 1, para. BC83.
232 IFRS 1, para. IG58A.
233 Discussion Paper, *Fair Value Measurements*, IASB, November 2006, paras. 1 to 5.
234 Discussion Paper, *Fair Value Measurements*, IASB, November 2006, paras. 25 to 31.

Chapter 21 Financial instruments: Hedge accounting

1 INTRODUCTION

1.1 Background

The Introduction to Chapter 17 provides a general background to the development of accounting for financial instruments and notes the fundamental changes that have been experienced in international financial markets. The markets for derivatives, especially, have seen remarkable and continued growth over the past two to three decades. This reflects the increasing use of such instruments by businesses, commonly to 'hedge' their financial risks. Accordingly, the accounting treatment for derivatives and hedging activities has taken on a high degree of importance. Historically, however, the accounting guidance has struggled to keep up with business practices and, at best, issues were dealt with very much on a piecemeal basis. Therefore, until recently, entities were left largely to their own devices in developing accounting policies for hedges so that their financial statements reflected the objectives for entering into such transactions.

'Hedging' itself is a much wider topic than hedge accounting and is *not* the primary subject of this chapter. It is an imprecise term although standard setters frequently describe hedging in terms of designating a hedging instrument that has a value that is expected, wholly or partly, to offset changes in the value or cash flows of a 'hedged position'.[1] In this context, hedged positions normally include those arising from recognised assets and liabilities, contractual commitments and expected, but uncontracted, future transactions. Whilst this may be an appropriate description for many hedges, it does not necessarily capture the essence of all risk management activities involving financial instruments. Nevertheless, it forms the basis for the hedge accounting requirements under IFRS.

1.2 What is hedge accounting?

Hedge accounting is often seen as 'correcting' deficiencies in the accounting requirements that would otherwise apply to each leg of the hedge relationship. Typically, it involves recognising gains and losses on a hedging instrument in the same period(s) and/or in the same place in the financial statements as gains or losses on the hedged position. It may be used in a number of situations, for example to correct for:[2]

- *Measurement differences*

  These might arise where the hedge is of a recognised asset or liability that is measured on a different basis to the hedging instrument. An example is an investment in shares that is recorded in the financial statements at cost (not that this would be permissible under IAS 39), but whose value is hedged by a put option that enables shares of the same class to be sold at a predetermined price. In this case, both the hedging instrument and the hedged position exist and are recognised in the financial statements, but they are likely to be measured on different bases.

  In this situation hedge accounting could be achieved in a number of ways. Unrealised gains and losses on the put option might simply not be recognised and realised gains and losses could be deferred (e.g. separately as assets or liabilities or by including them within the carrying amount of the investment) until the investment is sold. Alternatively, if unrealised gains and losses on the put option were recognised in profit or loss, the measurement basis of the investment could be changed to reflect changes in its fair value in profit or loss;

- *Performance reporting differences*

  Even if the measurement bases of the hedging instrument and hedged item are the same, performance reporting differences might arise if gains and losses are reported in a different place in the financial statements. In the example above, the investment and the put option may both be measured at fair value. However, if gains and losses on the investment were recognised in equity (or its equivalent) whilst those on the put option were recognised in profit or loss, there would be a mismatch in the income statement. Similarly, gains and losses on retranslating the net assets of a foreign operation are normally recorded in equity (or its equivalent) whilst retranslation gains and losses on a borrowing used to hedge that net investment would generally be recorded in profit or loss.

  In the case of the investment and the put option, hedge accounting might involve reporting gains and losses on the investment in profit or loss, or gains and losses on the put option in equity. For the foreign operation, hedge accounting normally involves reporting the retranslation gains and losses on the borrowing in equity;

- *Recognition differences*

  These might arise where the hedge is of contractual rights or obligations that are not recognised in the financial statements. An example is a foreign currency denominated operating lease where the unrecognised contractual commitment to pay lease rentals in another currency is hedged by a series of forward currency contracts (i.e. each payment is effectively 'fixed' in functional currency terms).

In this case, hedge accounting might involve treating the lease as a 'synthetic' functional currency denominated lease. A similar outcome would be obtained if unrealised gains and losses on each forward contract remained unrecognised until the accrual of the lease payment it was hedging;

- *Existence differences*

  These might arise where the hedge is of cash flows arising from an uncontracted future transaction, i.e. a transaction that does not yet exist. An example is a foreign currency denominated sale expected next year that is hedged by a forward currency contract.

  Again, hedge accounting might involve treating the future sale as a 'synthetic' functional currency sale or it might involve deferring the gain or loss on the forward contract until the sale is recognised in profit or loss.

1.3 Development of hedge accounting standards

Hedge accounting does not sit well with the standard setters' desired goal for financial instrument accounting, i.e. a full fair value model (see Chapter 17 at 1.3). Only in the case of measurement differences, and some performance reporting differences, would the accounting treatment under the full fair value model reflect a degree of offset within the income statement (and then only if the hedge were of a financial instrument rather than, say, an item of inventory).

Further, hedge accounting relies on management intent to link (for accounting purposes) what the standard setters see as two or more separate transactions. It also overrides accounting requirements that would otherwise apply to those transactions when viewed separately. Although accounting for such transactions separately is likely to result in mismatches in the income statement, many standard setters do not see this as an accounting recognition or measurement problem. In their view, separate accounting is the best way to 'tell it as it is' and, instead, might prefer a more comprehensive analysis of an entity's gains and losses combined with a detailed explanation from management of what those gains and losses mean in the context of their overall risk management strategy.

In spite of the standard setters' long term ambitions, it became clear that the wider financial reporting community could not be persuaded to accept the abolition of hedge accounting (at least for the time being). Therefore, to address some of their more fundamental concerns about hedge accounting, the standard setters needed another approach. Eventually, the FASB published SFAS 133 – *Accounting for Derivative Instruments and Hedging Activities* – in June 1998, the first accounting standard to deal comprehensively with hedge accounting. To a large extent, SFAS 133 was used as the basis for most of the hedge accounting requirements of the original version of IAS 39 – *Financial Instruments: Recognition and Measurement* – which was approved for publication in December of the same year.

These standards have established requirements that mean hedge accounting is available only for certain hedge relationships. Particularly, formal documentation of the hedge is required and it must be demonstrated (both at inception and on an ongoing basis) that the hedge is 'highly effective'. An important corollary of these requirements is that hedge accounting may not be available for every arrangement an entity considers a hedge. In fact, because hedge accounting requires additional action by management, it is essentially voluntary.

The methods of hedge accounting were also defined by these standards, although they had to fit within a new accounting model for derivatives. Whilst a full fair value model was some way off, the standard setters had concluded that the only relevant balance sheet measure for derivatives was fair value. Further, because gains and losses from remeasuring derivatives to fair value do not meet the standard setters' definition of assets or liabilities they should not be recorded in the balance sheet as if they do. As a result, hedge accounting mostly involves:

- where the hedge reduces the risk of variability in cash flows associated with a future transaction (a cash flow hedge), the gain or loss arising on the hedging instrument is initially reported in equity and subsequently recycled to profit or loss as the hedged transaction affects profit or loss;
- where the hedge offsets the risk of volatility in the fair value of a recognised asset or liability (a fair value hedge), the gain or loss on the hedging instrument is recognised in profit or loss, together with a broadly offsetting gain or loss as a result of adjusting the hedged item to reflect certain changes in its fair value; or
- where the hedge is of a net investment in a foreign operation (a net investment hedge), the gain or loss arising on the hedging instrument is initially reported in equity and subsequently recycled to profit or loss on disposal of that foreign operation.

Further, to the extent that a *highly* effective hedge is not *perfectly* effective, the degree of ineffectiveness should be identified and recognised in profit or loss. For a fair value hedge this will automatically follow from the accounting treatment noted above. For a cash flow hedge, the amount of the gain or loss recognised in equity must be adjusted.

Although this topic accounts for some of the most complex and controversial aspects of IAS 39, few changes were proposed as a result of the IASB's improvements project (see Chapter 17 at 1.5). However, commentators raised several concerns in this area and before publishing the revised standard (and subsequently) the IASB revisited a number of the detailed aspects of the hedge accounting requirements, but not the overall approach. Most notably, as discussed at 6 below, amendments were made to make it easier for banks and similar financial institutions to obtain hedge accounting for portfolio (or macro) hedges of interest rate risk. Even so, these concessions were not sufficient to allay all concerns and in Europe an amended version of IAS 39 is now in use.

2 HEDGING INSTRUMENTS AND HEDGED ITEMS

In the terminology of IAS 39, the two main ingredients of a hedge are the hedging instrument and the hedged item. The definition of these and related terms are as follows:

- *Hedging instrument:* a designated derivative or (for a hedge of the risk of changes in foreign currency exchange rates only) a designated non-derivative financial asset or non-derivative financial liability whose fair value or cash flows are expected to offset changes in the fair value or cash flows of a designated hedged item;
- *Hedged item:* an asset, liability, firm commitment, highly probable forecast transaction or net investment in a foreign operation that (a) exposes the entity to risk of changes in fair value or future cash flows and (b) is designated as being hedged;
- *Firm commitment:* a binding agreement for the exchange of a specified quantity of resources at a specified price on a specified future date or dates.

  In addition to simple agreements to purchase a given quantity of units on a given date for a given amount of money, other arrangements may also be firm commitments, for example construction contracts under which payments are made periodically based on documented progress or achievement of milestones; and
- *Forecast transaction:* an uncommitted but anticipated future transaction.[3]

The standard contains one other definition related to hedge accounting, i.e. of 'hedge effectiveness' and this is covered at 5.3 below.

2.1 Hedging instruments

There are a number of restrictions on what type of item may be used as the hedging instrument in a 'valid' hedge, i.e. one that can qualify for hedge accounting, and these operate on many levels as set out below. One of these restrictions stems from the definition of a hedging instrument and requires an entity to have an expectation that its fair value or cash flows will offset changes in the fair value or cash flows of the hedged item attributable to the hedged risk. This requirement principally manifests itself in the provisions on hedge effectiveness, which are dealt with at 5.3 below.

2.1.1 *Derivative financial instruments*

The distinction between derivative and non-derivative financial instruments is covered in Chapter 17 at 4. With the exception of certain written options (see below), the circumstances in which a derivative may be designated as a hedging instrument are not restricted, provided the conditions for hedge accounting set out at 5 below are met.[4] Those conditions mean that a derivative that is not carried at fair value because it is linked to and must be settled by delivery of an unquoted equity instrument whose fair value cannot be reliably measured (see Chapter 20 at 4.4) cannot be designated as a hedging instrument.[5]

In order to be able to qualify as a hedging instrument, the derivative must be accounted for as such under IAS 39. Therefore, an embedded derivative that is accounted for separately from its host contract (see Chapter 17 at 5) can be used as a hedging instrument. However, a contract that is considered a normal sale or purchase, and is therefore accounted for as an executory contract (see Chapter 17 at 3.9), could not.[6]

Example 21.1: Hedging with a sales commitment

Company J has the Japanese yen as its functional currency. J has issued a fixed rate debt instrument with semi-annual interest payments that matures in two years with principal due at maturity of US$5 million. It has also entered into a fixed price sales commitment for US$5 million that matures in two years and is not accounted for as a derivative because it qualifies for the normal sales exemption.

Because the sales commitment is accounted for as a firm commitment rather than a derivative instrument it cannot be a hedging instrument in a hedge of the foreign currency risk associated with the debt instrument. However, if the foreign currency component of the sales commitment was required to be separated as an embedded derivative (essentially a forward contract to buy US dollars for yen) that component could be designated as the hedging instrument in such a hedge.[7]

Similarly, a forecast transaction or planned future transaction cannot be the hedging instrument as it is not a recognised financial instrument,[8] and is therefore not a derivative.

A Options and collars

It is explained that an option an entity writes is not effective in reducing the profit or loss exposure of a hedged item. In other words, the potential loss on a written option could be significantly greater than the potential gain in value of a related hedged item. Therefore, a written option is prohibited from qualifying as a hedging instrument unless it is designated as an offset to a purchased option, including one that is embedded in another financial instrument. An example of this might be a written call option that is used to hedge a callable liability. In contrast, a purchased option has potential gains equal to or greater than losses and therefore has the potential to reduce profit or loss exposure from changes in fair values or cash flows. Accordingly, a purchased option can qualify as a hedging instrument.[9]

It follows that a derivative such as an interest rate collar that includes a written option cannot be designated as a hedging instrument if it is a net written option. However, a derivative instrument that includes a written option may be designated as a hedging instrument if it is a net purchased option or zero cost collar.[10]

The following factors, taken together, indicate that an instrument is not a net written option:

- no net premium is received, either at inception or over the life of the instrument – the distinguishing feature of a written option is the receipt of a premium to compensate for the risk incurred;
- except for the strike prices, the critical terms and conditions of the written and purchased option components are the same, including underlying variable(s), currency denomination and maturity date; and

- the notional amount of the written option component is not greater than that of the purchased option component.[11]

The application of these requirements is illustrated in the following two examples.

Example 21.2: Foreign currency collar (or 'cylinder option')

Company E, which has sterling as its functional currency, has forecast that it is highly probable it will receive €1,000 in six months time in respect of an expected sale to a customer in France.

E is concerned that sterling might have appreciated by the time the payment is received and wishes to protect the profit margin on the sale without paying the premium that would be required with an ordinary currency option. E also wishes to benefit from some of the upside in the event that sterling depreciates, so would prefer not to use a forward contract.

Accordingly, E enters into an instrument under which it effectively:

- purchases an option that allows it to buy sterling for €1,000 from the counterparty at €1.53:£1.00; and
- sells an option that allows the counterparty to sell sterling to E for €1,000 at €1.47:£1.00.

In the foreign currency markets, such an instrument is often called a 'cylinder option' rather than a 'collar' and it operates as follows. If, in six months time, the spot exchange rate exceeds €1.53:£1.00, E will exercise its option to sell €1,000 at €1.53:£1.00, effectively fixing its minimum proceeds on the sale (in sterling terms) at £654. Similarly, if the rate is below €1.47:£1.00, the counterparty will exercise its option to buy €1,000 at €1.47:£1.00, effectively capping E's maximum proceeds on the sale at £680. If the rate is between €1.47:£1.00 and €1.53:£1.00, both options will lapse unexercised and E will be able to sell its €1,000 for sterling at the spot rate, generating between £654 and £680.

The premium that E would pay to acquire the purchased option equals the premium it would receive to sell the written option and therefore no premium is paid or received on inception. The critical terms and conditions, including the notional amounts, of the written and purchased option components are the same except for the strike price. Therefore, E concludes that the instrument is not a net written option and, consequently, it may be used as the hedging instrument in a hedge of the foreign currency risk associated with the future sale.

It is possible that the counterparty might, instead, have offered E a variation on the instrument described above. If the notional amount on E's purchased option component had been reduced, say to €500, the counterparty could have offered a better rate on that component, say €1.51. However, in this case, the notional amount on the written option component is twice that of the purchased option component and the instrument would be seen as a net written option. Accordingly, even if E had very good business reasons for using such an instrument to manage its foreign exchange risk, it could not qualify as a hedging instrument under IAS 39. Therefore, hedge accounting would be precluded.

Example 21.3: 'Knock-out' swap

Company Y has a significant amount of long-dated floating rate borrowings. In order to hedge the cash flow interest rate risk arising from these borrowings, Y has entered into a number of matching pay-fixed, receive-floating interest rate swaps that effectively convert the interest rates on the borrowings to fixed rate.

Under the terms of one of these swaps, on each fifth anniversary of its inception until maturity the swap counterparty may choose to simply terminate the swap at no cost. This is often referred to as a knock-out feature. In return for agreeing to this, Y benefits by paying a lower interest rate on the fixed leg of the swap than it would on a conventional swap. In other words, Y receives a premium for taking on the risk of the counterparty cancelling the swap.

This instrument contains a net written option, i.e. the knock-out feature, and therefore cannot be used as a hedging instrument unless it is used in a hedge of an equivalent purchased option. (In practice, it is somewhat unlikely that the hedged borrowings will contain such an option feature.)

B Credit break clauses

It is not uncommon for certain derivatives (e.g. interest rate swaps) to contain terms that allow the counterparties to settle the instrument at 'fair value' in certain circumstances. Such terms, often called 'credit break clauses', enable the counterparties to manage their credit risk in markets where collateral or margin accounts and master netting agreements are not used. They are particularly common where a long-duration derivative is transacted between a financial and non-financial institution. For example, the terms of a twenty-year interest rate swap may allow either party to settle the instrument at fair value on the fifth, tenth and fifteenth anniversary of its inception.

These terms can be seen as options on counterparty credit risk. However, provided the two parties have equivalent rights to settle the instrument at fair value, the credit break clause will generally not prevent the derivative from qualifying as a hedging instrument. Particularly, in assessing whether a premium is received for agreeing to the incorporation of such terms into an instrument, care needs to be exercised. For example, marginally better underlying terms offered by one potential counterparty (as a result of market imperfections) should not be mistaken for a very small option premium.

2.1.2 Cash instruments

In contrast to the position for derivatives, there are significant restrictions over the use as hedging instruments of non-derivative financial assets and liabilities, or 'cash instruments' as the IASB sometimes refer to them.[12] Essentially, a cash instrument may be designated as a hedging instrument only for a hedge of foreign currency risk.[13]

This would allow, say, a held-to-maturity investment carried at amortised cost to be designated as a hedging instrument in a hedge of foreign currency risk[14] as well as other instruments such as loans and receivables, available for sale debt instruments and borrowings. However, an investment in an unquoted equity instrument that is not carried at fair value because its fair value cannot be reliably measured (see Chapter 20 at 4.4), cannot be designated as a hedging instrument.[15]

The following two examples illustrate the types of permitted hedge relationships where the hedging instrument is a non-derivative.

Example 21.4: Hedging with a non-derivative liability

In Example 21.1 above, Company J had issued a fixed rate debt instrument with principal due at maturity in two years of US$5 million. J had also entered into a fixed price sales commitment, accounted for as an executory contract, for US$5 million that matured in two years as well.

J could not designate the debt instrument as a hedge of the exposure to *all* fair value changes of the fixed price sales commitment because the hedging instrument is a non-derivative. However, J could designate it as a hedge of the foreign currency exposure associated with the future receipt of US dollars on the fixed price sales commitment.[16]

Example 21.5: Hedge of foreign currency bond

Company J has also issued US$5 million five year fixed rate debt and owns a US$5 million five year fixed rate bond, which is classified as available for sale.

J's bond has exposure to changes in both foreign currency and interest rates, as does the liability. However, the liability can only be designated as a hedge of the bond's foreign currency, not interest rate, risk because it is a non-derivative instrument.

In fact in this case, hedge accounting is unnecessary because the amortised cost of the hedging instrument and the hedged item are both remeasured using closing rates with differences reported in profit or loss as required by IAS 21 – *The Effects of Changes in Foreign Exchange Rates.*[17]

In principle, there is no reason why a non-derivative financial instrument cannot be a hedging instrument in one hedge (of foreign currency risk) and a hedged item in another hedge (for example in a hedge of interest rate risk).

In revising IAS 39 in 2003, the IASB considered whether to allow cash instruments to qualify as hedging instruments in less restrictive circumstances. However, although it was acknowledged that some entities did actually use non-derivatives to manage risks other than foreign currency risk, for various reasons it was concluded that the existing prohibition should be retained.[18]

2.1.3 Combinations of instruments

Two or more derivatives, or proportions of them (see 2.1.4 below) may be viewed in combination and jointly designated as a hedging instrument. This is the case even when the risk(s) arising from some derivatives offset(s) those arising from others. However, an interest rate collar or other derivative instrument that combines a written option and a purchased option cannot qualify as a hedging instrument if it is, in effect, a net written option (for which a net premium is received).[19]

Similarly, two or more instruments (or proportions of them) may be designated as a hedging instrument only if *none of them* is a written option or a net written option.[20] Under the original version of the standard, two or more derivatives, or proportions thereof could be viewed in combination and jointly designated as the hedging instrument, provided the *combination* was not a net written option.[21]

In practice, many zero cost collars are transacted as legally separate written and purchased options. On the face of it, therefore, such transactions can not be treated as a combined hedging instrument. However, we are not at all convinced the IASB intended such a prohibition to take effect in practice. This is especially the case if the reason the collar takes the legal form of two options is for the seller's administrative ease, which would in many cases be irrelevant to the entity purchasing the collar. In fact, if it can be demonstrated that the only substantive business purpose for entering into such an arrangement is to purchase a zero cost collar to hedge an underlying exposure, the logic in some of the implementation guidance would *require* these contracts to be treated as a single instrument for this purpose (see 2.3.3 below and Chapter 17 at 4.5 and 6).

In the case of a hedge of foreign currency risk, the standard also allows two or more non-derivatives, or proportions of them, to be viewed in combination and designated as a hedging instrument. Further, in what seemed like a significant change (or at least a major clarification) from the original standard, a combination of derivatives and non-derivatives, or proportions of them, may now be similarly combined.[22]

Unlike for combinations of derivatives, the standard does not clarify whether it is acceptable for these combinations to contain offsetting terms although in the absence of an indication to the contrary we believe it is. For example, an entity with the euro as its functional currency may have issued a yen denominated floating rate borrowing and entered into a matching receive-yen floating (plus principal at maturity), pay-US dollar floating (plus principal at maturity) cross-currency interest rate swap. These instruments, which effectively synthesise a US dollar floating rate borrowing, contain offsetting terms, i.e. the whole of the borrowing and the yen leg of the swap. The entity could designate the combination of these two instruments in a hedge of the entity's foreign currency risk arising from, say, an asset with an identifiable exposure to yen/US dollar exchange rates.

2.1.4 Portions and proportions of hedging instruments

In contrast to the position for hedged financial items (see 2.2.1 below), there are significant restrictions on what components of an individual financial instrument can be carved out and designated as a hedging instrument. It is explained that there is normally a single fair value measure for a hedging instrument in its entirety and the factors that cause changes in its fair value are co-dependent. Normally, therefore, a financial instrument (or proportion thereof – see B below) can only be designated as a hedging instrument in its entirety.[23]

Example 21.6: Combination of written and purchased options

Company Y transacts a combination of a written option and purchased option (such as an interest rate collar) as a single instrument with one counterparty. Y cannot split the derivative instrument into its written and purchased option components and designate the purchased option component as a hedging instrument.[24]

Similarly, the 'knock-out swap' in Example 21.3 above could not be split into a conventional interest rate swap, to be used as a hedging instrument, and the knock-out feature (a written swaption, i.e. an option for the counterparty to enter into an offsetting interest rate swap with the same terms as the conventional swap).

However, there are a number of exceptions to this general rule:

- the time and interest elements of options and forwards may be separated (see A below);
- a proportion only of a hedging instrument may be designated in a hedging relationship (see B below);
- the spot rate retranslation risk of a foreign currency instrument may be separated (see C below); and
- a derivative may be separated into notional component parts when each part is designated as a hedge and qualifies for hedge accounting (see D below).

A Time and interest elements of options and forwards

IAS 39 permits an entity to separate:

- the intrinsic value and time value of an option contract and designating as the hedging instrument only the change in intrinsic value of the option and excluding changes in its time value; and
- the interest element and spot price of a forward contract.

These separations are permitted because, the standard explains, the intrinsic value of the option and the premium on the forward can generally be measured separately.[25] However, this explanation is slightly hollow as the same would apply to the type instrument discussed in Example 21.6 above.

There are a number of reasons an entity may wish to take advantage of these exceptions. For example, excluding these portions may be consistent with the entity's overall hedging strategy, such as where the interest element of forward contracts are managed with the rest of the entity's interest rate exposures rather than in conjunction with the associated spot rate exposures. Excluding these components may also make it administratively easier to process the hedges and it can certainly improve a hedge's effectiveness (especially when using an option – see 5.3.11 below).

However, the use of these exceptions is not mandatory. For example, a dynamic hedging strategy that assesses both the intrinsic value and time value of an option contract can qualify for hedge accounting (see 5.1.2 below).[26]

B Proportions of instruments

In addition to the above exceptions, a proportion of the entire hedging instrument, such as 50% of the notional amount, may also be designated in a hedging relationship. However, a hedging relationship may not be designated for only a portion of the time period in which the hedging instrument is outstanding.[27]

C Cash instruments

There is one further situation where a portion of an instrument may be designated as a hedging instrument (in fact, is required to be). In the case of a cash instrument used as a hedge of foreign currency risk, it is essentially only the spot rate retranslation risk of, say, a borrowing that is used as the hedging instrument and not the other components, such as its changes in fair value arising from interest rate risk.

D Notional decomposition

We also believe it is acceptable to split a derivative (or allowable portion thereof) into component parts provided all of those components are designated and qualify for hedge accounting. For example a 'functional currency leg' could be introduced into a derivative that is denominated in two currencies (such as a forward contract or cross-currency interest rate swap). In fact, the implementation guidance effectively contains examples of just such an approach – see Examples 21.7 and 21.8 at 2.1.6 below – and the IFRIC has recently confirmed that it considers such an approach to be acceptable.[28]

E Restructuring of derivatives

An entity may exchange a derivative that does not qualify as a hedging instrument (say, the knock-out swap in Example 21.3 above) for two separate derivatives that, together, have the same fair value as the original instrument (say, a conventional interest rate swap and a written swaption). Such an exchange is likely to be motivated by a desire to obtain hedge accounting for one of these new instruments, perhaps in preparation for transition to IFRS.

In order to determine whether the new arrangement can be treated as two separate derivatives, rather than a continuation of the original derivative, we believe it is necessary to determine whether the exchange transaction has any substance, which is clearly a matter of judgement.

For example, in the case of the knock-out swap, if the two new contracts had the same counterparty and, in aggregate, the same terms as the original contract this would not necessarily lead to the conclusion that the exchange lacked substance. However if, in addition, the swaption would be settled by delivery of the conventional interest rate swap in the event that it was exercised, this is a strong indicator that the exchange does lack substance.

2.1.5 Reduction of risk

The implementation guidance explains that risk exposures should be assessed on a transaction basis and, therefore, a hedging instrument need not reduce risk at an entity-wide level. For example, if an entity has a fixed rate asset and a fixed rate liability, each with the same principal terms, it may enter into a pay-fixed, receive-variable interest rate swap to hedge the fair value of the asset even though the effect of the swap is to create an interest rate exposure for the entity that previously did not exist.[29]

However, a hedging instrument does need to reduce risk at the transaction level. Consider a 'basis swap' that effectively converts one variable interest rate index (say a central bank base rate) to another (say LIBOR). Instruments of this nature would not normally qualify as a hedging instrument because they do not reduce or eliminate risk in any meaningful way. Unless they are used in a hedge of offsetting asset and liability positions (see 2.1.6 below) they simply convert one risk to another similar risk.

A basis swap or similar instrument may also qualify as a hedging instrument when considered in combination with another instrument (see 2.1.3 above). For example, the basis swap described above and a pay-fixed, receive-LIBOR interest rate swap may qualify as a hedging instrument in a hedge of a borrowing that pays interest based on a central bank rate.

2.1.6 Hedging different risks with one instrument

A single hedging instrument may be designated as a hedge of more than one type of risk, provided that:

- the risks hedged can be identified clearly;
- the effectiveness of the hedge can be demonstrated (see 5.3 below); and
- it is possible to ensure that there is specific designation of the hedging instrument and different risk positions.[30]

The implementation guidance provides the following example to illustrate this point.

Example 21.7: Foreign currency forward hedging positions in two foreign currencies

Company J, which has Japanese yen as its functional currency, issues five year floating rate US dollar debt and acquires a ten year fixed rate sterling bond. The principal amounts of the asset and liability, when converted into Japanese yen, are the same. J enters into a single foreign currency forward contract to hedge its foreign currency exposure on both instruments under which it receives US dollars and pays sterling at the end of five years.

Designating a single hedging instrument as a hedge of multiple types of risk is permitted if three conditions are met:

- the hedged risks can be clearly identified.

  In this case the risks are exposures to changes in the US dollar/yen and yen/sterling exchange rates respectively;
- the effectiveness of the hedge can be demonstrated.

  For the sterling bond, effectiveness can be measured as the degree of offset between the fair value of the principal repayment in sterling and the fair value of the sterling payment on the forward exchange contract.

  For the US dollar liability, effectiveness can be measured as the degree of offset between the fair value of the principal repayment in US dollars and the US dollar receipt on the forward exchange contract.

  Even though the bond has a ten year life and the forward only protects it for the first five years, hedge accounting is permitted for only a portion of the exposure (see 2.2.1 A below); and
- it is possible to ensure that there is a specific designation of the hedging instrument and the different risk positions.

  The hedged exposures are identified as the principal amounts of the liability and the bond in their respective currency of denomination.

The hedging instrument satisfies all of these conditions and J can designate the forward as a hedging instrument in a cash flow hedge against the foreign currency exposure on the principal repayments of both instruments and qualify for hedge accounting.[31]

In this example, the hedging instrument is effectively decomposed and viewed as two forward contracts, each with an offsetting position in yen, i.e. J's functional currency.

By analogy with Example 21.7 above, we believe it would be acceptable to use a basis swap as a hedge of relevant asset and liability positions. For example, an entity may have made a $1m loan that earns LIBOR based interest and a $1m liability that pays interest based on the central bank rate. In this case it may use as a hedging instrument an interest rate swap under which it pays LIBOR based interest and receives interest based on the central bank rate on a notional amount of $1m.

The implementation guidance also explains that a single hedging instrument may be designated in both a cash flow hedge and a fair value hedge, provided the above conditions are met (section 3 covers the three different types of hedge recognised by IAS 39). For example, entities may use a combined interest rate and currency swap to convert a variable rate position in a foreign currency to a fixed rate position in the functional currency. Such a swap could be designated separately as a fair value hedge of the currency risk and a cash flow hedge of the interest rate risk.[32]

The IASB's implementation guidance takes the concept of hedging different risks a little further, as set out in the following example.

Example 21.8: Cross-currency interest rate swap hedging two foreign currency exchange rate exposures and fair value interest rate exposure

Company J now issues five-year floating rate US dollar debt and acquires a ten-year fixed rate sterling bond and wishes to hedge the foreign currency exposure on both the bond and the debt as well as the fair value interest rate exposure on the bond. To do this it enters into a matching cross-currency interest rate swap to receive floating rate US dollars, pay fixed rate sterling and exchange the US dollars for sterling at the end of five years.

Hedge accounting is permitted for components of risk, provided effectiveness can be measured (see 2.2.1 below) and a single hedging instrument may be designated as a hedge of more than one type of risk if the risks can be identified clearly, effectiveness can be demonstrated, and specific designation of the hedging instrument and the risk positions can be ensured.

Therefore, the swap may be designated as a hedging instrument in a fair value hedge of the sterling bond against exposure to changes in its fair value associated with the interest rate payments on the bond until year five and the change in value of the principal payment due at maturity to the extent affected by changes in the yield curve relating to the five years of the swap (see Example 21.9 at 2.2.1 A below) as well as the exchange rate between sterling and US dollars.

The mechanics of hedge accounting for fair value hedges is discussed at 4.1 below. In summary, the swap would be measured at fair value with changes in fair value reported in profit or loss. The carrying amount of the receivable would be adjusted for changes in its fair value caused by changes in UK interest rates for the first five-year portion of the yield curve. Both the receivable and payable are remeasured using spot exchange rates under IAS 21 and the changes to their carrying amounts recorded in profit or loss.[33]

Taken literally, the designation set out above takes no account of the existence of the US dollar liability and thereby suggests that the exchange rate between sterling and US dollars (the hedged risk) is seen as a component of the risk associated with the sterling bond (the hedged item). Mathematically this is clearly true from the point of view of a yen functional entity – together, the sterling/US dollar rate and the US dollar/yen rate give the sterling/yen exchange rate, i.e. the true foreign currency risk arising on the sterling bond. However, without considering the US dollar liability (which does not appear to be part of the designated hedge relationship) the hedge provides no real offset against the currency risk of the sterling liability. Instead it simply converts one foreign currency risk (exposure to sterling) to another (exposure to US dollars) and, as set out at 2.1.5 above, this would not normally be considered an acceptable hedging relationship. The IASB obviously sees the existence of the US dollar liability as important (otherwise it would not have been introduced into the example) but the point it is trying to articulate is not perfectly clear. In all likelihood, their failure to refer to the US dollar liability in the description of the hedge designation was simply an oversight.

The guidance above discussed combinations of (a) different cash flow hedges, (b) different fair value hedges and (c) a cash flow hedge and a fair value hedge. However, there appears to be no reason why a single instrument could not, in theory, be designated in other combinations of hedges, for example a cash flow hedge and a hedge of a net investment.

When a single hedging instrument is designated as a hedge of more than one type of risk, the IFRIC has confirmed that effectiveness testing (see 5.3 below) may be carried out for the total hedged position, i.e. incorporating all risks identified, if these risks are inextricably linked in the hedging instrument.[34]

2.1.7 *Own equity instruments*

An entity's own equity instruments are not financial assets or liabilities of the entity and, therefore, cannot be hedging instruments.[35] This prohibition would also apply to instruments that give rise to minority interests in consolidated financial statements – under IFRS it is clear that minority interests are part of a reporting entity's equity.

2.1.8 *Pension scheme assets*

An entity may wish to enter into transactions to hedge the risk associated with assets held by a pension or other long-term employee benefit fund. We consider that, for many reasons, plan assets are unlikely to qualify as hedged items under IAS 39. For example, a pension scheme is, in many respects, a non-financial asset or liability and, therefore, the portion of the risk associated with only the assets could not be a hedged item (see 2.2.2 above).

2.2 Hedged items

The basic requirement for a hedged item is for it to be one of the following:

- a recognised asset or liability;
- an unrecognised firm commitment;
- a highly probably forecast transaction; or
- a net investment in a foreign operation,

and it should expose the entity to the risk of changes in fair value or future cash flows.[36]

Recognised assets and liabilities can include financial items and non-financial items such as inventory. They can also include recognised firm commitments that are not routinely recognised as assets or liabilities absent the effects of hedge accounting for such items (see 3.4 below). Most internally generated intangibles (e.g. for a bank, a core deposit intangible – see 2.2.8 below) are not recognised assets and therefore cannot be hedged items.[37]

Financial assets and liabilities need not be within the scope of IAS 39 to qualify as hedged items. For example, finance lease payables or receivables could be hedged items in a hedge of interest rate or foreign currency risk.

In the case of a financial asset or liability containing an embedded derivative (see Chapter 17 at 5), if the embedded derivative is accounted for separately from the host instrument, the hedged item would be the host instrument or cash flows from the host; otherwise it would be the hybrid instrument (i.e. the instrument including the embedded derivative) or cash flows from the hybrid.

2.2.1 Financial items: portions and proportions

If the hedged item is a financial asset or liability, the standard contains a general principle that it may be a hedged item with respect to the risks associated with only a portion of its cash flows or fair value, such as one or more selected contractual cash flows or portions of them or a percentage of the fair value (i.e. a proportion of the asset or liability).[38]

A Portions of interest rate risk

As an example of the general principle above, an identifiable and separately measurable portion of the interest rate exposure of an interest-bearing asset or liability may be designated as the hedged risk. Such a portion might be a risk-free interest rate or benchmark interest rate component of the total interest rate exposure of a hedged financial instrument. This is always subject to the proviso that effectiveness can be measured (see 5.3 below).[39]

This has the effect that a hedge can be designated for part of the term that a hedged item remains outstanding as illustrated in the following example.

Example 21.9: Partial term hedging

Company A acquires a 10% fixed rate government bond with a remaining term to maturity of ten years and classifies it as available-for-sale. To hedge against the fair value exposure on the bond associated with the first five years' interest payments, it acquires a five year pay-fixed receive-floating swap.

The swap may be designated as hedging the fair value exposure of the interest rate payments on the government bond until year five and the change in value of the principal payment due at maturity to the extent affected by changes in the yield curve relating to the five years of the swap.[40]

In finalising the 'portfolio hedge' amendments to IAS 39, the IASB received comments that demonstrated the meaning of a 'portion' was unclear. Accordingly, the following guidance on what may, or may not, be designated as a hedged portion, was added to the standard to explain this concept further.[41]

In general, if a portion of the cash flows of a financial asset or liability is designated as the hedged item, that designated portion must be less than its total cash flows. For example, in the case of a liability whose effective interest rate is below LIBOR, designating the following components is not permitted:

- a portion of the liability equal to the principal amount plus interest at LIBOR; and

- a negative residual portion.[42]

This is unlikely to be of major concern to many companies outside of the financial services sector. In contrast to banks and similar financial institutions that take deposits from customers (who often accept a return that is lower than prevailing market rates) many such entities cannot access variable-rate funding at below LIBOR rates. However, those entities with a particularly strong credit rating are sometimes able to borrow at sub-LIBOR rates, even in the capital markets.

In these cases, all of the cash flows of the entire financial asset or liability may be designated as the hedged item in a hedge of only one particular risk (e.g. only for changes that are attributable to changes in LIBOR). For example, an entire financial liability whose effective interest rate is 100 basis points (1%) below LIBOR (i.e. the principal plus interest at LIBOR minus 100 basis points) can be designated as the hedged item in a hedge of the change in the fair value or cash flows of that entire liability that is attributable to changes in LIBOR. Nevertheless, some ineffectiveness will occur and, in order to improve the effectiveness of the hedge, a hedge ratio of other than one-to-one may be chosen (see 2.2.2 below).[43]

The guidance goes on to explain that, if a fixed rate financial instrument is hedged some time after its origination, and interest rates have changed in the meantime, a portion equal to a benchmark rate that is actually higher than the contractual rate paid on the item *can* be designated as the hedged item. This is provided that the benchmark rate is less than the effective interest rate calculated on the assumption that the instrument had been purchased on the day it was first designated as the hedged item.[44] This is illustrated below.

Example 21.10: Hedge of a portion of an existing fixed rate financial asset following a rise in interest rates

Company B originates a fixed rate financial asset of €100 that has an effective interest rate of 6% at a time when LIBOR is 4%. B begins to hedge that asset some time later when LIBOR has increased to 8% and the fair value of the asset has decreased to €90.

B calculates that if it had purchased the asset on the date it first designated it as the hedged item for its then fair value of €90, the effective yield would have been 9.5%. Because LIBOR is less than this effective yield, the entity can designate a LIBOR portion of 8% that consists partly of the contractual interest cash flows and partly of the difference between the current fair value (€90) and the amount repayable on maturity (€100).[45]

It is not uncommon for entities to have borrowed money when prevailing rates were low and decide, at a later date after rates have increased, to 'convert' that low fixed rate borrowing into a floating rate borrowing. The guidance illustrated in Example 21.10 above will assist such entities in designating these hedges in a way that significantly reduces ineffectiveness. In fact, as noted at 5.3.9 below, the ability to designate a portion of a financial instrument as the hedged item can enable many hedges to be designated in a way that minimises or even eliminates ineffectiveness.

B Foreign currency risk associated with publicly quoted shares

The implementation guidance explains that the foreign currency risk associated with a holding of publicly traded shares may be hedged if they give rise to a clear and identifiable exposure to changes in foreign exchange rates. It is asserted that this will be the case if:

- the shares are not traded on an exchange, or other established market, in which trades are denominated in the same currency as the holder's functional currency; and
- dividends on the shares are not denominated in that currency.

Consequently, if the share trades in multiple currencies, one of which is the holder's functional currency, hedge accounting would not be permitted.[46] However, this does not stand up to close scrutiny, as illustrated in the following example.

Example 21.11: Foreign currency risk associated with equity shareholding

ABC plc, a UK company whose functional currency is sterling, acquires a small shareholding in IJK Limited. IJK is a South African company whose operations are based solely in that country and whose income, expenditure and dividends are all denominated in South African rand. IJK's shares are listed on the Johannesburg Stock Exchange where trades are denominated in rand.

The implementation guidance suggests that, potentially, ABC could hedge the foreign currency risk arising from the sterling/rand exchange rate on its IJK holding, which appears quite sensible. If, on day 1, the shares trade at R50 and the exchange rate is R10 to £1, the shares would have a sterling value of £5.00 (= R50 ÷ 10). If, on day 2, the exchange rate moves to R8 to £1, all other things being equal, the rand value of IJK should not change, but its sterling value would be £6.25 (= R50 ÷ 8), exactly mirroring the exchange rate movement.

If IJK subsequently obtained a secondary listing on the London Stock Exchange where trades were denominated in sterling, but its business fundamentals were unchanged, in the scenario outlined above ABC's foreign exchange exposure would be exactly the same. In fact, the operation of the markets should ensure that share price in London on days 1 and 2 is £5.00 and £6.25 respectively. However, the guidance suggests that because of the secondary listing, ABC no longer has a clear and identifiable exposure to changes in foreign exchange rates on the IJK shares.

C IFRIC and IASB deliberations

The question of what constitutes a portion of financial risk was under discussion by the IFRIC for some time. Initially, the issue was debated in the context of whether inflation qualifies as a risk associated with a portion of the fair value or cash flows of an interest bearing financial asset or liability (a proposition that the IFRIC staff found unconvincing[47]). However, the debate widened and the IFRIC started to examine portions in general.

The IFRIC agreed that, while IAS 39 permits hedging of some portions of risk for financial assets or liabilities, there are intended to be some restrictions, i.e. a portion cannot be simply anything. It also noted that IAS 39 requires a hedged portion to have an effect on the price of the hedged item or transaction that is separately measurable from the hedged item or transaction itself. Consequently, a portion cannot be a residual; i.e. an entity is not permitted to designate as a portion the residual fair value or cash flows of a hedged item or transaction if that residual does not have a separately measurable effect on the hedged item or transaction.

The IFRIC also discussed whether a qualifying portion is required to have a predictable effect on the price of the hedged item or transaction (as implied by the guidance for non-financial items considered at 2.2.2 below) and, if so, what is meant by the term 'predictable effect'. However, it tentatively concluded that the current wording of the standard does not provide a strong enough basis to interpret the meaning of that term. Consequently, in July 2006, it referred the issue to the IASB.[48]

The IASB decided that it, rather than the IFRIC, should address the issue and that it would do this by way of a separate project to amend IAS 39 rather than through the annual improvements project. Consequently, in September 2007, the IASB published an exposure draft of proposed amendments to IAS 39 which specifies the risks that would qualify for designation as a hedged risk when an entity hedges its exposure to a financial instrument, as follows:[49]

- market interest rate risk.

  For example, this would permit an entity to designate as a hedged item changes in the fair value of a fixed rate sterling financial asset attributable to changes in sterling LIBOR or the Bank of England base rate;
- foreign currency risk;
- credit risk;
- prepayment risk; and
- the risks associated with the contractually specified cash flows of a recognised financial instrument.

  For example, if an entity held a financial asset on which it received interest of 3% plus inflation and an inflation embedded derivative was not required to be separated, the entity would be permitted to designate as a hedged item changes in the cash flows of the financial asset attributable to inflation. However, it would not be permitted to designate as a hedged item changes in the fair value of a fixed rate financial asset attributable to inflation.

In addition, the proposed amendments specify the portions that would qualify for hedge accounting (other than partial term hedges, hedges of a proportion of the cash flows of an item and hedges of one-sided risks which the standard clearly permits). These 'other portions' are:[50]

- any contractually specified cash flows of a financial instrument that are independent from the other cash flows of that instrument (for example, the first four interest payments on a floating rate financial liability);
- the portion of the cash flows of an interest-bearing financial instrument that is equivalent to a financial instrument with a risk-free rate; and
- the portion of the cash flows of an interest-bearing financial instrument that is equivalent to a financial instrument with a quoted fixed or variable inter-bank rate, for example LIBOR.

Finally, an entity would not be permitted to specify as the hedged item a cash flow that does not exist in the financial instrument as a whole. For example, in designating a one-sided risk (such as the decrease in the fair value of a financial asset) as a hedged portion, an entity would not be able to include any cash flows that are imputed or inferred in the designated hedged portion. For example, the cash flows arising from the time value of a hypothetical written option should not be inferred into a non-derivative financial asset[51] (an issue the IFRIC has been addressing – see 5.3.11 below).

The IASB has emphasised that it does not intend to change existing practice significantly and has consulted its Financial Instruments Working Group and other constituents to provide assurance that this will be the case.[52]

2.2.2 Non-financial items: portions

It is explained that changes in the price of an ingredient or component of a non-financial asset or liability generally do not have a predictable, separately measurable effect on the price of the item that is comparable to the effect of, say, a change in market interest rates on the price of a bond. Therefore, because of the difficulty of isolating and measuring the appropriate portion of cash flows or fair value changes attributable to specific risks (other than foreign currency risks) a non-financial asset or liability can be designated as a hedged item only:

- in its entirety for all risks; or
- for foreign exchange risks.[53]

A number of commentators disagree with this assertion, at least in certain situations, and some urged the IASB in revising IAS 39 to reconsider this restriction. For example, Swiss International Air Lines, in responding to the June 2002 exposure draft, wrote the following:

> 'Like any airline SWISS is short of jet fuel. The Company is exposed to the daily price fluctuations of crude oil and the prices of inter product spreads (cracks, differentials) that convert crude oil into gas oil and finally into jet fuel.
>
> There is more liquidity in crude oil for positions beyond two years. Therefore, it is part of SWISS' fuel risk management strategy to do long-term hedges with crude oil. These positions are then rolled into gas oil and jet fuel as they move closer to the settlement dates.
>
> Paragraphs 129-130 [of the Exposure Draft] state that non-financial assets and liabilities can only be hedged in their entirety or separately with respect to foreign exchange risk.
>
> Crude oil hedges therefore must be designated as hedging the risk of price movements of jet fuel in its entirety. The critical terms of the hedging instrument and the hedged item therefore do not perfectly match – frequently a certain ineffectiveness will result. Even if the hedge can be expected to be highly effective due to a high historical correlation of the price movements of crude and jet fuel, actual effectiveness might fall outside the 80-125% range in some periods and the hedge will have to be dedesignated.

> We believe that due to the special properties of jet fuel prices, it should be allowed to designate the price changes of a jet fuel component such as crude oil as the hedged risk.
>
> The reason given in paragraphs 129 and 130 is that risk components of non-financial instruments generally do not have a predictable, separately measurable effect on the price of the entire item. This is a generalization that does not account for the special properties of jet fuel pricing.
>
> Jet fuel is a derivative of crude oil. Crude oil is then converted into gas oil. The difference of the crude and the gas oil price is called gas oil crack. Gas oil is finally converted into jet fuel, the price difference being called jet differential.
>
> It is not difficult to isolate and measure the portion of the changes of jet fuel prices attributable to the price risk of these components. Crude, gas oil crack, and jet differential are separately traded and market prices are available through market information systems such as Platt's as for jet fuel itself. The price of jet fuel actually is calculated from the prices of its components.
>
> Changes in the price of the components of jet fuel do have a predictable, separately measurable effect on the price of jet fuel. This effect can be compared to the effect of a change in the market interest rates on the price of a bond.'[54]

However, in spite of protestations such as this, the IASB noted that, in many cases, changes in the cash flows or fair value of a portion of a non-financial hedged item *are* difficult to isolate and measure and therefore the restriction was retained largely unchanged.[55] This was much to the disappointment of various airlines and entities with similar fuel requirements who would have preferred the standard to adopt a different approach, e.g. to establish a 'rebuttable presumption' that components could not be identified and separately hedged. In fact, it appears that this message had not been fully appreciated because, in October 2004, it was reiterated by the IFRIC.[56]

This does not prevent an entity hedging a specified range of absolute values of a non-financial item. For example, an entity may hedge the risk that its gold inventory will fall in value by purchasing a cash-settled at-the-money put option that allows (but does not require) the entity to sell a fixed amount of gold for a price that is fixed at its market value at inception of the contract – in this case the hedged risk is the risk that the value of the gold inventory will fall below a specified price.

The IASB also considered whether the interest rate risk portion of loan servicing rights could be designated as the hedged item on the grounds that this portion can be separately identified and measured, and that changes in market interest rates have a predictable and separately measurable effect on the value of such rights. In fact the possibility of treating loan servicing rights as financial assets rather than non-financial assets, perhaps on an elective basis, was also considered. However, it was concluded that no exceptions should be permitted for this matter either.[57]

It seems reasonably clear from the logic of the above restriction that an entity may hedge a non-financial exposure for all risks *except* foreign currency risk (even if it is not clear from the standard itself), as illustrated in the following example.

Example 21.12: Hedge of foreign currency denominated commodity risk

Company P has the FC as its functional currency. It has forecast, with a high probability, the need to purchase a fixed quantity of crude oil for US Dollars in twelve months time. To hedge part of its exposure to the price risk inherent in this purchase P enters into an exchange traded twelve-month cash-settled crude oil forward contract. The strike price of the forward is denominated in US dollars (there is no active market in FC denominated crude oil futures) and P therefore fixes the US dollar price of the oil to be purchased. P chooses not to hedge the risk associated with FC to US dollar exchange rates. This might be because of illiquidity in the foreign currency markets for FCs or, perhaps, because P has forecast US dollar inflows that provide a natural hedge of the foreign exchange risk.

P may designate the forward contract as the hedging instrument in a hedge of the exposure to the US dollar denominated price risk associated with its forecast purchase of crude oil.

In many cases it will be difficult to identify a separately measurable effect on non-financial assets, even for foreign currency risk, as illustrated in the following example from the implementation guidance.

Example 21.13: Foreign currency borrowings hedging a ship

A Danish shipping company, D, has a US subsidiary that has the same functional currency as the parent, the Danish krone. Accordingly in D's consolidated financial statements, ships owned by the subsidiary, which are carried at depreciated historical cost, are reported in Danish krone using historical exchange rates. To hedge the potential currency risk on the disposal of the ships in US dollars, purchases of ships are normally financed with loans denominated in US dollars.

US dollar borrowings cannot be classified as fair value hedges of a ship because ships do not contain any separately measurable foreign currency risk even if their purchase was, and sale is likely to be, denominated in US dollars.

The proceeds from the anticipated sale of the ship may, however, be designated in a cash flow hedge, provided all the hedging criteria are met (see 5 below). Those conditions require that the sale is highly probable, which is only likely if the sale is expected to occur in the immediate future.[58]

Unfortunately, the statement that a ship does not contain any separately measurable foreign currency risk is not explained any further, which makes it difficult to apply this guidance in other situations. For example, it is hard to argue that a commodity such as crude oil, which is traded throughout the world in US dollars, does not contain a measurable exposure to US dollars. If another commodity is regularly traded and quoted both in US dollars and in euro (the implementation guidance suggests this might be the case for natural gas – see Chapter 17 at 5.1.2 A) it might seem sensible to treat that commodity as containing both US dollar and euro exposures. However, by analogy with the guidance on quoted shares (see 2.2.1 B above), a commodity that is traded and quoted in more than one currency would probably be deemed to have no measurable currency exposure from the perspective of an entity whose functional currency is one of those currencies.

Inevitably, for many hedges of non-financial items there will be a difference between the terms of the hedging instrument and the hedged item (as well as the restriction on hedging portions of the non-financial item, there may simply be no perfectly matching hedging instruments). For example, a forward contract to purchase Colombian coffee might be used as a hedge of the forecast purchase of Brazilian coffee on otherwise similar terms. Such a hedge may, nonetheless, qualify as a hedge relationship, provided all the conditions at 5 are met.[59]

To meet these conditions, it must be expected that the hedge will be highly effective. For this purpose, the amount of the hedging instrument may be greater or less than that of the hedged item if this improves the effectiveness of the hedging relationship. For example, a regression analysis could be performed to establish a statistical relationship between the hedged item (e.g. a transaction in Brazilian coffee) and the hedging instrument (e.g. a transaction in Columbian coffee). If there is a valid statistical relationship between the two variables (i.e. between the unit prices of Brazilian coffee and Columbian coffee), the slope of the regression line can be used to establish the hedge ratio that will maximise expected effectiveness. For example, if the slope of the regression line is 1.02, a hedge ratio based on 0.98 quantities of hedged items to 1.00 quantities of the hedging instrument maximises expected effectiveness. However, the hedging relationship may result in ineffectiveness that is recognised in profit or loss during the term of the hedging relationship.[60] This idea is a recurring theme in the standard and is referred to a number of times.

Current tax receivable (payable) is a non-financial asset (liability). Therefore it is not possible to designate a portion of current tax as a hedged item except for foreign exchange risk. This is the case even where the portion arises indirectly from foreign exchange risk. For example, an entity may be taxed at, say, 30% on exchange gains or losses arising on a specified monetary item but the portion of the tax payable or receivable arising on those gains and losses may not be a hedged item. Consequently, gains and losses on the hedging instrument (which in some cases will offset the corresponding portion of the tax charge or credit in the right period without the need for hedge accounting) could not be offset against the tax charge in the income statement (see Chapter 22 at 4.1.3).

2.2.3 Groups of items as hedged items

The standard explains that a hedged item can be a single item or a group of such items with similar risk characteristics.[61] To aggregate and hedge similar assets or liabilities as a group, the individual items need to share the risk exposure for which they are hedged. Further, the standard requires that fair value changes attributable to the hedged risk for each individual item should be approximately proportional to the equivalent fair value change of the entire group.[62]

For example, a group of mortgage loans may be considered a hedged item with respect to interest rate risk as long as the changes in fair value attributable to changes in the hedged risk for each loan are expected to be approximately proportional to the overall change in fair value of the entire group of loans due to the hedged risk. However, the risk characteristics of the individual shares in a portfolio designed to replicate a share index will be different from each other and from the portfolio as a whole. Therefore, the portfolio could not be hedged with respect to movements in the index[63] even though, in economic terms, the portfolio of shares may well be perfectly (or near perfectly) hedged. In situations like this, an entity may be able to designate the assets within the portfolio at fair value through profit or loss so that gains and losses from the hedging instrument and hedged items should offset in the income statement (but of course designation could only take place on initial recognition – see Chapter 17 at 7.1.2).

As discussed at 5.3 below, hedge effectiveness is assessed by comparing the change in value or cash flow of hedging instruments and of hedged items. Therefore, comparing a hedging instrument to an overall net position, e.g. the net of all fixed rate assets and fixed rate liabilities with similar maturities, rather than to a specific hedged item, cannot qualify for hedge accounting.[64] Similarly, the net cash flows arising from a portfolio of floating rate assets and liabilities cannot be designated as the hedged item.[65]

However, approximately the same effect on profit or loss can be achieved by designating part of the underlying items as the hedged position. For example, a European company with firm commitments to make purchases and sales of US$100 and US$90 respectively could hedge the net exposure by acquiring a derivative and designating it as a hedging instrument associated with purchases of US$10. Similarly, a bank with €100 of assets and €90 of liabilities with risks and terms of a similar nature could hedge the net exposure by designating €10 of those assets as the hedged item.[66]

2.2.4 Hedges of general business risk

To qualify for hedge accounting, the hedge must relate to a specific identified and designated risk, and not merely to the entity's general business risks; also, it must ultimately affect profit or loss. Therefore, a hedge of the risk of obsolescence of a physical asset or the risk of expropriation of property by a government is not eligible for hedge accounting (effectiveness cannot be measured because those risks are not measurable reliably).[67] Similarly, the risk that a transaction will not occur is an overall business risk that is not eligible as a hedged item.[68]

A firm commitment to acquire a business in a business combination cannot be a hedged item, except for foreign exchange risk, because the other risks being hedged cannot be specifically identified and measured. These other risks are also said to be general business risks.[69] However, transactions of the business to be acquired (for example floating rate interest payments on its borrowings) may potentially qualify as hedged items. For this to be the case, it would need to be demonstrated that, from the perspective of the acquirer, those transactions are highly probable which may not be straightforward because it would require both the business combination and the transactions to occur.

2.2.5 Held-to-maturity investments

Unlike loans and receivables, a held-to-maturity investment (whether it pays fixed or floating interest rates) cannot be a hedged item with respect to interest rate risk or prepayment risk. This is because designating an investment as held-to-maturity requires an intention to hold the investment until maturity without regard to changes in the fair value or cash flows of such an instrument attributable to changes in interest rates (see Chapter 17 at 7.2).[70]

However, a held-to-maturity investment (or related cash flows) can be a hedged item in the following circumstances:

- the investment may be a hedged item with respect to risks from changes in foreign currency exchange rates and credit risk;[71]
- the forecast purchase of such an investment may be a hedged item, say to lock in current interest rates – this is because an investment is not given an IAS 39 classification until it is actually recognised;[72] and
- the forecast reinvestment of fixed or variable interest receipts can be hedged items with respect to the risk of interest rate changes.[73]

  It should be noted that this hedge relationship is significantly different from a hedge of the interest rate risk on the held-to-maturity investment itself. This is most commonly used as a building block in the cash flow macro-hedging model (see 6 below).

2.2.6 *Derivatives*

Unless they are designated and effective hedging instruments, derivative financial instruments are always deemed held for trading and measured at fair value with gains and losses recognised in profit or loss. Therefore, a derivative cannot normally be a hedged item. However, as noted at 2.1.1 above, there is an exception where a written option is used to hedge a purchased option.[74]

This has the effect that cash flows from a forecast derivative transaction cannot be hedged items. For example, a company with the euro as its functional currency that expects to issue floating rate debt in three months time may wish to enter into a forward starting euro denominated pay-fixed receive-floating interest rate swap to fix the cash flows on that debt before it is issued, and those cash flows could qualify as hedged items. However, it may be that the entity expects to issue US dollar denominated debt and, immediately after issuance, swap it into floating rate euro debt by way of a cross currency interest rate swap. In this case, the floating rate euro interest payments arise from a derivative contract and are not valid hedged items.

2.2.7 *Own equity instruments*

Transactions in an entity's own equity instruments (including distributions to holders of such instruments) are generally recognised directly in equity by the issuer (see Chapter 19) and do not affect profit or loss. Therefore, such instruments cannot be designated as a hedged item. However, a declared dividend that qualifies for recognition as a financial liability, e.g. because the entity has become legally obliged to make the payment, may qualify as a hedged item. For example, a recognised liability to pay a dividend in a foreign currency would give rise to foreign exchange risk. Similarly, a forecast transaction in an entity's own equity instruments or a forecast dividend payment cannot qualify as a hedged item.[75]

2.2.8 Recognised core deposit intangibles

The term 'core deposit intangible' is often used to represent the difference between:

(a) the fair value of a portfolio of core deposits (e.g. current or deposit accounts); and

(b) the aggregate of the individual fair values of the liabilities within the portfolio, normally calculated in accordance with the requirements of IAS 39 (see Chapter 20 at 4.5).

It was noted at 2.2 above that an internally generated core deposit intangible cannot be a hedged item because it is not a recognised asset. If a core deposit intangible is acquired together with a related portfolio of deposits, it is required to be recognised separately as an intangible asset (or as part of the related acquired portfolio of deposits) if it meets the recognition criteria in IAS 38 – *Intangible Assets*.[76]

Theoretically, therefore, a recognised core deposit intangible asset could be designated as a hedged item. However this will only be the case if it meets the conditions for hedge accounting, including the requirement that the effectiveness of the hedge can be measured reliably (see 5.3 below). The implementation guidance explains that, because it is often difficult to measure reliably the fair value of a core deposit intangible asset other than on initial recognition, it is unlikely that this requirement will be met.[77] In fact, this probably understates the difficulty.

2.3 Internal hedges and other group accounting issues

One of the most pervasive impacts that IAS 39 can have on groups, especially those operating centralised treasury functions, is the need to reassess hedging strategies that involve intra-group transactions. To a layman this might come as something of a surprise because the standard does little more than reinforce the general principle (established many years ago in accounting standards such as IAS 27 – *Consolidated and Separate Financial Statements*) that transactions between different entities within a group should be eliminated in the consolidated financial statements of that group. Nevertheless, a significant amount of the standard and related implementation guidance is devoted to this subject.

2.3.1 Internal hedging instruments

The starting point for this guidance is the principle of preparing consolidated financial statements in IAS 27 that requires that 'intragroup balances, transactions, income and expenses shall be eliminated in full'.[78]

Although individual entities within a consolidated group (or divisions within a single legal entity) may enter into hedging transactions with other entities within the group (or divisions within the entity), such as internal derivative contracts to transfer risk exposures between different companies (or divisions), any such intra-group (or intra-entity) transactions are eliminated on consolidation. Therefore, such hedging transactions do not qualify for hedge accounting in the consolidated financial statements of the group[79] (or in the individual or separate financial statements of an entity for hedging transactions between divisions of the entity). Effectively, this is because they do not exist in an accounting sense.

As a consequence, IAS 39 makes it very clear that for hedge accounting purposes only instruments that involve a party external to the reporting entity (i.e. external to the group, segment (see below) or individual entity that is being reported on) can be designated as hedging instruments.[80]

The implementation guidance explains that IAS 39 does not specify how an entity should *manage* its risk. Accordingly, where an internal contract is offset with an external party, the external contract may be regarded as the hedging instrument. In such cases, the hedging relationship (which is between the external transaction and the item that is the subject of the internal hedge) may qualify for hedge accounting.[81] The following example illustrates this.

Example 21.14: Internal derivatives

The banking division of Bank A enters into an internal interest rate swap with A's trading division. The purpose is to hedge the interest rate risk exposure of a loan (or group of similar loans) in the loan portfolio. Under the swap, the banking division pays fixed interest payments to the trading division and receives variable interest rate payments in return.

Assuming a hedging instrument is not acquired from an external party, hedge accounting treatment for the hedging transaction undertaken by the banking and trading divisions is not allowed, because only derivatives that involve a party external to the entity can be designated as hedging instruments. Further, any gains or losses on intragroup or intra-entity transactions should be eliminated on consolidation. Therefore, transactions between different divisions within A cannot qualify for hedge accounting treatment in Bank A's financial statements. Similarly, transactions between different entities within a group cannot qualify for hedge accounting treatment in A's consolidated financial statements.

However, if, in addition to the internal swap in the above example, the trading division entered into an interest rate swap or other contract with an external party that offset the exposure hedged in the internal swap, hedge accounting would be permitted. For the purposes of IAS 39, the hedged item is the loan (or group of similar loans) in the banking division and the hedging instrument is the external interest rate swap or other contract.

The trading division may aggregate several internal swaps or portions of them that are not offsetting each other (see 2.3.2 below) and enter into a single third party derivative contract that offsets the aggregate exposure. Such external hedging transactions may qualify for hedge accounting treatment provided that the hedged items in the banking division are identified and the other conditions for hedge accounting are met. It should be noted, however, that hedge accounting is not permitted where the hedged items are held-to-maturity investments and the hedged risk is the exposure to interest rate changes.[82]

It follows that internal hedges may qualify for hedge accounting in the individual or separate financial statements of individual entities within the group, as well as in segment reporting (see below), provided they are external to the individual entity or segment that is being reported on.[83]

The implementation guidance contains the following summary of the application of IAS 39 to internal hedging transactions:

- IAS 39 does not preclude an entity from using internal derivative contracts for risk management purposes and it does not preclude internal derivatives from being accumulated at the treasury level or some other central location so that risk can be managed on an entity-wide basis or at some higher level than the separate legal entity or division;

- Internal derivative contracts between two separate entities within a consolidated group can qualify for hedge accounting by those entities in their individual or separate financial statements, even though the internal contracts are not offset by derivative contracts with a party external to the consolidated group;
- Internal derivative contracts between two separate divisions within the same legal entity can qualify for hedge accounting in the individual or separate financial statements of that legal entity only if those contracts are offset by derivative contracts with a party external to the legal entity;
- Internal derivative contracts between separate divisions within the same legal entity and between separate entities within the consolidated group can qualify for hedge accounting in the consolidated financial statements only if the internal contracts are offset by derivative contracts with a party external to the consolidated group;
- If the internal derivative contracts are not offset by derivative contracts with external parties, the use of hedge accounting by group entities and divisions using internal contracts must be reversed on consolidation.[84]

The premise on which the restriction on internal hedging instruments is based is not completely true. As noted at 2.3.4 below, foreign currency intra-group balances may well give rise to gains and losses in profit or loss that are not eliminated on consolidation. However, this does not change the fact that internal transactions, even those that affect consolidated profit or loss, cannot be used as a hedging instrument in consolidated financial statements.

Although the improvements project did not explicitly address this topic (essentially, it retained the existing requirements unchanged) the IASB received a great deal of comment on it. Particularly, many constituents argued that internal hedges should be allowed to qualify for hedge accounting. They often pointed to US GAAP, which allows internal derivative contracts to be designated as hedging instruments in hedges of some forecast foreign currency transactions. However, the only changes made were to clarify that intra-group transactions could qualify for hedge accounting in segment reporting or in the individual financial statements of entities or segments, provided they were external to the segment or entity.[85]

The references above to segment reporting make sense in the context of IAS 14 – *Segment Reporting* – which requires segment information to be prepared in accordance with IFRS (see Chapter 30 at 2.4.1). However, IFRS 8 – *Operating Segments* – requires disclosure of information that is reported to the chief operating decision maker even if this is on a non-GAAP basis (see Chapter 30 at 4.2.2 and 4.4). On the face of it, therefore, IAS 39 and IFRS 8 appear to be in conflict. The IASB has identified this problem (essentially an oversight when it published IFRS 8) and, as part of its annual improvements project, has decided to remove the references to segment reporting in IAS 39.[86]

2.3.2 Offsetting internal hedging instruments

As noted at 2.3.1 above, if an internal contract used in a hedging relationship is offset with an external party, the external contract may be regarded as a hedging instrument and the hedge may qualify for hedge accounting.[87] The implementation guidance elaborates on this further in the context of both interest rate and foreign currency risk management, particularly in the situation where the internal derivatives are offset before being laid off with a third party.

A Interest rate risk

As set out in Example 21.14 above, central treasury functions sometimes enter into internal derivative contracts with subsidiaries and, perhaps, divisions within the consolidated group to manage interest rate risk on a centralised basis. If, before laying off the risk, the internal contracts are first netted against each other and only the net exposure is offset in the marketplace with external derivative contracts, the internal contracts cannot qualify for hedge accounting in the consolidated financial statements.[88]

An internal contract designated at the subsidiary level, or by a division, as a hedge results in the recognition of changes in the fair value of the item being hedged in profit or loss (for a fair value hedge – see 4.1.1 below) or in the recognition of the changes in the fair value of the internal derivative in equity (for a cash flow hedge – see 4.2.1 below). On consolidation, there is no basis for changing the measurement attribute of the item being hedged in a fair value hedge unless the exposure is offset with an external derivative. Similarly, on consolidation, there is no basis for including the gain or loss on the internal derivative in equity for one entity and recognising it in profit or loss by the other entity unless it is offset with an external derivative.[89]

Where two or more internal derivatives used to manage interest rate risk on assets or liabilities at the subsidiary or division level are offset at the treasury level, the effect of designating the internal derivatives as hedging instruments is that the hedged non-derivative exposures at the subsidiary or division levels would be used to offset each other on consolidation. Accordingly, since IAS 39 does not permit designating non-derivatives as hedging instruments (except for foreign currency exposures) the results of hedge accounting from the use of internal derivatives at the subsidiary or division level that are not laid off with external parties must be reversed on consolidation.[90]

It should be noted, however, that there will be no effect on profit or loss and equity of reversing the effect of hedge accounting in consolidation for internal derivatives that offset each other at the consolidation level if they are used in the same type of hedging relationship at the subsidiary or division level and, in the case of cash flow hedges, where the hedged items affect profit or loss in the same period. Just as the internal derivatives offset at the treasury level, their use as fair value hedges by two separate entities or divisions within the consolidated group will also result in the offset of the fair value amounts recognised in profit or loss. Similarly, their use as cash flow hedges by two separate entities or divisions within the consolidated group will also result in the fair value amounts being offset against each other in equity.[91]

However, there may be an effect on individual line items in both the consolidated income statement and the consolidated balance sheet, for example when internal derivatives that hedge assets (or liabilities) in a fair value hedge are offset by internal derivatives that are used as a fair value hedge of other assets (or liabilities) that are recognised in a different balance sheet or income statement line item. In addition, to the extent that one of the internal contracts is used as a cash flow hedge and the other is used in a fair value hedge, the effect on profit or loss and equity would not offset since the gain (or loss) on the internal derivative used as a fair value hedge would be recognised in profit or loss and the corresponding loss (or gain) on the internal derivative used as a cash flow hedge would be recognised in equity.[92]

Notwithstanding this, under the principles set out at 2.2.3 above, it may be possible to designate the external derivative as a hedge of *some* of the underlying exposures as illustrated in the following example.

Example 21.15: Internal contracts offset on a net basis

Company A uses what it describes as internal derivative contracts to document the transfer of responsibility for interest rate risk exposures from individual divisions to a central treasury function. The central treasury function aggregates the internal derivative contracts and enters into a single external derivative contract that offsets the internal derivative contracts on a net basis.

On one particular day the central treasury function enters into three internal receive-fixed, pay-variable interest rate swaps that lay off the exposure to variable interest cash flows on variable rate liabilities in other divisions and one internal receive-variable, pay-fixed interest rate swap that lays off the exposure to variable interest cash flows on variable rate assets in another division. It enters into an interest rate swap with an external counterparty that exactly offsets the four internal swaps.

A hedge of an overall net position does not qualify for hedge accounting. However, designating a part of the underlying items as the hedged position on a gross basis is permitted (see 2.2.3 above). Therefore, even though the purpose of entering into the external derivative was to offset internal derivative contracts on a net basis, hedge accounting is permitted if the hedging relationship is defined and documented as a hedge of a part of the underlying cash inflows or cash outflows on a gross basis and assuming that the hedge accounting criteria are met.[93]

B Foreign exchange risk

Although much of the discussion at A above applies equally to hedges of foreign currency risk, there is one important distinction between the two situations. As set out at 2.1.2 above, IAS 39 does allow non-derivative financial instruments to be used as the hedging instrument in the hedge of foreign currency risk. Therefore, in this case, internal derivatives may be used as a basis for *identifying* external transactions that qualify for hedge accounting provided that the internal derivatives represent the transfer of foreign currency risk on underlying non-derivative financial assets or liabilities. However, for consolidated financial statements, it is necessary to *designate* the hedging relationship so that it involves only external transactions.[94]

Furthermore, as set out at 2.1.1 above, forecast transactions and unrecognised firm commitments cannot qualify as hedging instruments under IAS 39. Accordingly, to the extent that two or more offsetting internal derivatives represent the transfer of foreign currency risk on such items, hedge accounting cannot be applied. As a result, if any cumulative net gain or loss on an internal derivative has been included in the initial carrying amount of an asset or liability (a 'basis adjustment') or deferred in equity (see 4.2.1 and 4.2.2 below), it would have to be reversed on consolidation if it cannot be demonstrated that the offsetting internal derivative represented the transfer of a foreign currency risk on a financial asset or liability to an external hedging instrument.[95]

The following example illustrates this principle – it also illustrates the mechanics of accounting for cash flow hedges and fair value hedges, which are discussed in more detail at 4.1 and 4.2 below.

Example 21.16: Using internal derivatives to hedge foreign currency risk[96]

In each of the following cases, 'FC' represents a foreign currency, 'LC' represents the local currency (which is the entity's functional currency) and 'TC' the group's treasury centre.

Case 1: Offset of fair value hedges

Subsidiary A has trade receivables of FC100, due in 60 days, which it hedges using a forward contract with TC. Subsidiary B has payables of FC50, also due in 60 days, which it hedges using a forward contact with TC.

TC nets the two internal derivatives and enters into a net external forward contract to pay FC50 and receive LC in 60 days.

At the end of month 1, FC weakens against LC. A incurs a foreign exchange loss of LC10 on its receivables, offset by a gain of LC10 on its forward contract with TC. B makes a foreign exchange gain of LC5 on its payables, offset by a loss of LC5 on its forward contract with TC. TC makes a loss of LC10 on its internal forward contract with A, a gain of LC5 on its internal forward contract with B and a gain of LC5 on its external forward contract.

Accordingly, the following entries are made in the individual or separate financial statements of A, B and TC at the end of month 1. Entries reflecting intra-group transactions or events are shown in italics.

A's entries

	LC	LC
Foreign exchange loss	10	
Receivables		10
Internal contract (TC)	*10*	
Internal gain (TC)		*10*

B's entries

	LC	LC
Payables	5	
Foreign exchange gain		5
Internal loss (TC)	*5*	
Internal contract (TC)		*5*

TC's entries

	LC	LC
Internal loss (A)	*10*	
Internal contract (A)		*10*
Internal contract (B)	*5*	
Internal gain (B)		*5*
External forward contract	5	
Foreign exchange gain		5

Both A and B could apply hedge accounting in their individual financial statements provided all necessary conditions were met. However, because gains and losses on the internal derivatives and the offsetting losses and gains on the hedged receivables and payables are recognised immediately in profit or loss without hedge accounting, hedge accounting is unnecessary (see 3.3 for further information on hedges of foreign currency denominated monetary items).

In the consolidated financial statements, the internal derivative transactions are eliminated. In economic terms, B's payable hedges FC50 of A's receivables. The external forward in TC hedges the remaining FC50 of A's receivable. In the consolidated financial statements, hedge accounting is again unnecessary because monetary items are measured at spot foreign exchange rates under IAS 21 irrespective of whether hedge accounting is applied.

The net balances, before and after elimination of the accounting entries relating to the internal derivatives, are the same, as set out below. Accordingly, there is no need to make any further accounting entries to meet the requirements of IAS 39.

	LC	LC
Receivables	–	10
Payables	5	–
External forward contract	5	–
Gains and losses	–	–
Internal contracts	–	–

Case 2: Offset of cash flow hedges

To extend the example, A also has highly probable future revenues of FC200 on which it expects to receive cash in 90 days. B has highly probable future expenses of FC500 (advertising cost), also to be paid for in 90 days. A and B enter into separate forward contracts with TC to hedge these exposures and TC enters into an external forward contract to receive FC300 in 90 days.

As before, FC weakens at the end of month 1. A incurs a 'loss' of LC20 on its anticipated revenues because the LC value of these revenues decreases and this is offset by a gain of LC20 on its forward contract with TC. Similarly, B incurs a 'gain' of LC50 on its anticipated advertising cost because the LC value of the expense decreases and this is offset by a loss of LC50 on its transaction with TC.

TC incurs a gain of LC50 on its internal transaction with B, a loss of LC20 on its internal transaction with A and a loss of LC30 on its external forward contract.

Both A and B complete the necessary documentation, the hedges are effective and both A and B qualify for hedge accounting in their individual financial statements. A defers the gain of LC20 on its internal derivative transaction in a hedging reserve in equity and B does the same with its loss of LC50. TC does not claim hedge accounting, but measures both its internal and external derivative positions at fair value, which net to zero.

Accordingly, the following entries are made in the individual or separate financial statements of A, B and TC at the end of month 1. Entries reflecting intra-group transactions or events are shown in italics.

A's entries

	LC	LC
Internal contract (TC)	*20*	
Equity		*20*

B's entries

	LC	LC
Equity	*50*	
Internal contract (TC)		*50*

TC's entries

	LC	LC
Internal loss (A)	*20*	
Internal contract (A)		*20*
Internal contract (B)	*50*	
Internal gain (B)		*50*
Foreign exchange loss	30	
External forward contract		30

IAS 39 requires that, in the consolidated financial statements, the accounting effects of the internal derivative transactions must be eliminated.

If there were no hedge designation for the consolidated financial statements, the gains and losses recognised in equity and profit or loss on the internal derivatives would be reversed. Consequently, a loss of LC30 would be recognised in profit or loss in respect of the external forward contract held by TC.

However, for the consolidated financial statements, TC's external forward contract on FC300 *is* designated, at the beginning of month 1, as a hedging instrument of the first FC300 of B's highly probable future expenses. Therefore, LC30 of the gain recognised in equity by B may remain in equity on consolidation, because it involves an external derivative. Accordingly, the net balances, before and after elimination of the accounting entries relating to the internal derivatives, are as set out below and there is no need to make any further accounting entries in order for the requirements of IAS 39 to be met.

	LC	LC
External forward contract	–	30
Equity	30	–
Gains and losses	–	–
Internal contracts	–	–

Case 3: Offset of fair value and cash flow hedges

The example is extended further and it is assumed that the exposures and the internal derivative transactions are the same as in Cases 1 and 2. In other words, Subsidiary A has trade receivables of FC100, due in 60 days, and highly probable future revenues of FC200 on which it expects to receive cash in 90 days. Subsidiary B has payables of FC50, due in 60 days, and highly probable future expenses of FC500 to be paid for in 90 days. Each of these exposures is hedged using forward contacts with TC. However, in this case, instead of entering into two external derivatives to hedge separately the fair value and cash flow exposures, TC enters into a single net external derivative to receive FC250 in exchange for LC in 90 days.

Consequently, TC has four internal derivatives, two maturing in 60 days and two maturing in 90 days. These are offset by a net external derivative maturing in 90 days. The interest rate differential between FC and LC is minimal, and therefore the ineffectiveness resulting from the mismatch in maturities is expected to have a minimal effect on profit or loss in TC.

As in Cases 1 and 2, A and B apply hedge accounting for their cash flow hedges and TC measures its derivatives at fair value. A defers a gain of LC20 on its internal derivative transaction in equity and B does the same with its loss of LC50.

Accordingly, the following entries are made in the individual or separate financial statements of A, B and TC at the end of month 1. Entries reflecting intra-group transactions or events are shown in italics.

A's entries

	LC	LC
Foreign exchange loss	10	
Receivables		10
Internal contract (TC)	*10*	
Internal gain (TC)		*10*
Internal contract (TC)	*20*	
Equity		*20*

B's entries

	LC	LC
Payables	5	
Foreign exchange gain		5
Internal loss (TC)	*5*	
Internal contract (TC)		*5*
Equity	*50*	
Internal contract (TC)		*50*

TC's entries

	LC	LC
Internal loss (A)	*10*	
Internal contract (A)		*10*
Internal loss (A)	*20*	
Internal contract (A)		*20*
Internal contract (B)	*5*	
Internal gain (B)		*5*
Internal contract (B)	*50*	
Internal gain (B)		*50*
Foreign exchange loss	25	
External forward contract		25

The gains and losses recognised on the internal contracts in A and B can be summarised as follows:

	A	B	Total
	LC	LC	LC
Income (fair value hedges)	10	(5)	5
Equity (cash flow hedges)	20	(50)	(30)
Total	30	(55)	(25)

In the consolidated financial statements, IAS 39 requires the accounting effects of the internal derivative transactions to be eliminated.

If there were no hedge designation for the consolidated financial statements, the gains and losses recognised in equity and profit or loss on the internal derivatives would be reversed. Consequently, a loss of LC30 would be recognised in profit or loss in respect of the external receivable and payable held by A and B respectively and the external forward contract held by TC.

However, for the consolidated financial statements, the following designations are made at the beginning of month 1:

- the payable of FC50 in B is designated as a hedge of the first FC50 of the highly probable future revenues in A.

  Therefore, at the end of month 1, the following entries are made in the consolidated financial statements: Dr Payable LC5; Cr Equity LC5;
- the receivable of FC100 in A is designated as a hedge of the first FC100 of the highly probable future expenses in B.

  Therefore, at the end of month 1, the following entries are made in the consolidated financial statements: Dr Equity LC10, Cr Receivable LC10; and
- the external forward contract on FC250 in TC is designated as a hedge of the next FC250 of highly probable future expenses in B.

  Therefore, at the end of month 1, the following entries are made in the consolidated financial statements: Dr Equity LC25; Cr External forward contract LC25.

Combining these entries produces the total net balances as follows:

	LC	LC
Receivables	–	10
Payables	5	–
External forward contract	–	25
Equity	30	–
Gains and losses	–	–
Internal contracts	–	–

Case 4: Offset of fair value hedges with adjustment to carrying amount of inventory

Similar transactions to those in Case 3 are assumed except that the anticipated cash outflow of FC500 in B relates to the purchase of inventory that is delivered after 60 days. It is also assumed that the entity has a policy of basis-adjusting hedged forecast non-financial items (see 4.2.2 below).

To recap, Subsidiary A has trade receivables of FC100, due in 60 days, and highly probable future revenues of FC200 on which it expects to receive cash in 90 days. Subsidiary B has payables of FC50, due in 60 days, and a highly probable future purchase of inventory for FC500, to be delivered in 60 days and paid for in 90 days. Each of these exposures is hedged using forward contacts with TC, and TC enters into a single net external derivative to receive FC250 in exchange for LC in 90 days.

At the end of month 2, there are no further changes in exchange rates or fair values. At that date, the inventory is delivered and the loss of LC50 on B's internal derivative, deferred in equity in month 1, is adjusted against the carrying amount of inventory in B. The gain of LC20 on A's internal derivative is deferred in equity as before.

In the consolidated financial statements, there is now a mismatch compared with the result that would have been achieved by unwinding and redesignating the hedges. The external derivative (FC250) and the receivable (FC50) offset FC300 of the anticipated inventory purchase. There is a natural hedge between the remaining FC200 of anticipated cash outflow in B and the anticipated cash inflow of FC200 in A. This relationship does not qualify for hedge accounting under IAS 39 and this time there is only a partial offset between gains and losses on the internal derivatives that hedge these amounts.

Accordingly, the following entries are made in the individual or separate financial statements of A, B and TC at the end of month 1. Entries reflecting intra-group transactions or events are shown in italics.

A's entries (all at the end of month 1)

	LC	LC
Foreign exchange loss	10	
Receivables		10
Internal contract (TC)	*10*	
Internal gain (TC)		*10*
Internal contract (TC)	*20*	
Equity		*20*

B's entries (at the end of month 1)

	LC	LC
Payables	5	
Foreign exchange gain		5
Internal loss (TC)	*5*	
Internal contract (TC)		*5*
Equity	*50*	
Internal contract (TC)		*50*

B's entries (at the end of month 2)

	LC	LC
Inventory	50	
Equity		50

TC's entries (all at the end of month 1)

	LC	LC
Internal loss (A)	*10*	
Internal contract (A)		*10*
Internal loss (A)	*20*	
Internal contract (A)		*20*
Internal contract (B)	*5*	
Internal gain (B)		*5*
Internal contract (B)	*50*	
Internal gain (B)		*50*
Foreign exchange loss	25	
External forward contract		25

The gains and losses recognised on the internal contracts in A and B can be summarised as follows:

	A LC	B LC	Total LC
Income (fair value hedges)	10	(5)	5
Equity (cash flow hedges)	20	–	20
Basis adjustment (inventory)	–	(50)	(50)
Total	30	(55)	(25)

Combining these amounts with the external transactions (i.e. those not marked in italics above) produces the total net balances before elimination of the internal derivatives as follows:

	LC	LC
Receivables	–	10
Payables	5	–
External forward contract	–	25
Equity	–	20
Basis adjustment (inventory)	50	–
Gains and losses	–	–
Internal contracts	–	–

For the consolidated financial statements, the following designations are made at the beginning of month 1:

- the payable of FC50 in B is designated as a hedge of the first FC50 of the highly probable future revenues in A.

  Therefore, at the end of month 1, the following entry is made in the consolidated financial statements: Dr Payables LC5; Cr Equity LC5.

- the receivable of FC100 in A is designated as a hedge of the first FC100 of the highly probable future inventory purchase in B.

  Therefore, at the end of month 1, the following entries are made in the consolidated financial statements: Dr Equity LC10, Cr Receivable LC10; and at the end of month 2, Dr Inventory LC10; Cr Equity LC10.

- the external forward contract on FC250 in TC is designated as a hedge of the next FC250 of highly probable future inventory purchase in B.

  Therefore, at the end of month 1, the following entry is made in the consolidated financial statements: Dr Equity LC25; Cr External forward contract LC25; and at the end of month 2, Dr Inventory LC25; Cr Equity LC25.

The total net balances after elimination of the accounting entries relating to the internal derivatives are as follows:

	LC	LC
Receivables	–	10
Payables	5	–
External forward contract	–	25
Equity	–	5
Basis adjustment (inventory)	35	–
Gains and losses	–	–
Internal contracts	–	–

These total net balances are different from those that would be recognised if the internal derivatives were not eliminated, and it is these net balances that IAS 39 requires to be included in the consolidated financial statements. The accounting entries required to adjust the total net balances before elimination of the internal derivatives are as follows:

- to reclassify LC15 of the loss on B's internal derivative that is included in inventory to reflect that FC150 of the forecast purchase of inventory is not hedged by an external instrument (neither the external forward contract of FC250 in TC nor the external payable of FC100 in A); and
- to reclassify the gain of LC15 on A's internal derivative to reflect that the forecast revenues of FC150 to which it relates is not hedged by an external instrument.

The net effect of these two adjustments is as follows:

	LC	LC
Equity	15	
Inventory		15

It is apparent that extending the principles set out in this relatively simple example to the more complex, and higher volume, situations that are likely to be encountered in practice is not going to be straightforward.

2.3.3 Offsetting external hedging instruments

The implementation guidance explains that where two offsetting derivatives are transacted at the same time, it is generally not permitted to designate one of them as a hedging instrument in a (fair value) hedge unless:

- the second swap was not entered into in contemplation of the first; or
- there is a 'substantive business purpose' for structuring the transactions separately.

It is emphasised that judgement should be applied in determining what is a substantive business purpose. For example, a centralised treasury company may enter into third party derivative contracts on behalf of other subsidiaries to hedge their interest rate exposures and, to track those exposures within the group, enter into internal derivative transactions with those subsidiaries. It may also enter into a derivative contract with the same counterparty during the same business day with substantially the same terms as a contract entered into as a hedging instrument on behalf of another subsidiary as part of its trading operations, or because it wishes to rebalance its overall portfolio risk. In this case, there is a valid business purpose for entering into each contract. However, a desire to achieve fair value accounting for the hedged item is deemed not to be a substantive business purpose.[97]

The following example, based on the implementation guidance, explores this issue a little further.

Example 21.17: External derivative contracts settled net

A company uses internal derivative contracts to transfer interest rate risk exposures from individual divisions to a central treasury function. For each internal derivative contract, the central treasury function enters into a derivative contract with a single external counterparty that offsets the internal derivative contract. For example, if the central treasury function has entered into a receive-5% fixed, pay-LIBOR interest rate swap with another division that has entered into the internal contract with central treasury to hedge the exposure to variability in interest cash flows on a pay-LIBOR borrowing, central treasury would enter into a pay-5% fixed, receive-LIBOR interest rate swap on the same principal terms with the external counterparty.

Although each external derivative contract is formally documented as a separate contract, only the net of the payments on all of the external derivative contracts is settled since there is a netting agreement with the external counterparty.

Even though the external derivatives are settled on a net basis the individual external derivative contracts, such as the pay-5% fixed, receive-LIBOR interest rate swap above, can generally be designated as hedging instruments of underlying gross exposures, such as the exposure to changes in variable interest payments on the pay-LIBOR borrowing above.

External derivative contracts that are legally separate contracts and serve a valid business purpose, such as laying off risk exposures on a gross basis, qualify as hedging instruments even if those external contracts are settled on a net basis with the same external counterparty, provided the hedge accounting criteria in IAS 39 are met.[98]

In the context of interest rate instruments, the facts in this example appear a little unlikely. This is because most master netting agreements have a practical effect only in the event of default by, or insolvency of, one of the counterparties – otherwise payments tend to be made gross. The above situation seems possible only where the instruments are settled through a clearing house (or where the clearing house is the counterparty).

For foreign currency instruments, a number of financial institutions provide services that are broadly analogous to the one described in Example 21.17. Under these arrangements a treasury function will transact, say, legally separate forward exchange contracts with the financial institution to offset each individual intra-group derivative it has entered into with a subsidiary or division. These contracts will be administered under a centralised facility with settlements being made on a net basis. Further, the financial institution will often price these contracts to reflect the reduced credit risk and administrative burden associated with the arrangements so that the cost of transacting individual contracts is significantly reduced.

Some may express surprise that the guidance explains that arrangements such as those illustrated in Example 21.17 above may qualify for hedge accounting. In substance, they are little different from the entity offsetting its internal contracts before entering into an offsetting external transaction, which as explained at 2.3.2 above, would not permit hedge accounting to be applied for each item hedged using an internal contract. However, this is nothing compared to what follows. The implementation guidance considers an extension to the arrangement set out above:

> 'Treasury observes that by entering into the external offsetting contracts and including them in the centralised portfolio, it is no longer able to evaluate the exposures on a net basis. Treasury wishes to manage the portfolio of offsetting external derivatives separately from other exposures of the entity. Therefore, it enters into an additional, single derivative to offset the risk of the portfolio.'[99]

The guidance explains that the purpose of structuring the external derivatives like this is consistent with the entity's risk management policies and strategies and, generally, hedge accounting may still be used. Even if this final external derivative is effected with the same counterparty under the same netting arrangement, and notwithstanding the fact that all exposures with that counterparty will, as a result, net to zero, it is implied that this constitutes a substantive business purpose as described at the start of this sub-section.[100]

In essence, the guidance appears to suggest that the use of internal derivatives for hedge accounting is allowed, provided that an agreement is reached with a third party to give the appearance of laying off the exposure even though the risk is immediately taken back again. This seems a long way from what the standard requires and, in fact, begs the question of why an entity should even go to the trouble of creating such an artificial external agreement that appears to lacks any commercial substance. We have serious reservations over this part of the guidance, particularly we question whether it really would be possible to demonstrate the existence of a valid business purpose for such an arrangement. It remains to be seen to what extent this becomes accepted practice.

2.3.4 Internal hedged items

Only assets, liabilities, firm commitments or highly probable forecast transactions that involve a party external to the entity can be designated as hedged items. It follows that hedge accounting can be applied to transactions between entities or segments (see 2.3.1 above) in the same group only in the individual or separate financial statements of those entities or segments and not in the consolidated financial statements of the group. However, there are two exceptions – intragroup monetary items and forecast intragroup transactions, discussed at A and B below.[101]

A Intragroup monetary items

IAS 39 allows the foreign currency risk of an intra-group monetary item (e.g. a payable or receivable between two subsidiaries) to qualify as a hedged item in the consolidated financial statements if it results in an exposure to foreign exchange rate gains or losses that are not fully eliminated on consolidation under IAS 21. Under IAS 21, foreign exchange gains and losses on such items are not fully eliminated on consolidation when they are transacted between two group entities that have different functional currencies (see Chapter 10 at 2.7.2 A)[102] as illustrated in the following example.

Example 21.18: Intra-group monetary items that will affect consolidated profit or loss

Company A has two subsidiaries, Company B and Company C. A and B have the euro as their functional currencies, while C has the US dollar as its functional currency. On 31 March, C purchases goods from B for US$110, payable on 30 June.

In this case, the intra-group monetary item of US$110 may be designated as a hedged item in a hedge of foreign currency risk both by B in its separate financial statements and by A in its consolidated financial statements.

While B's foreign currency receivable is eliminated against C's foreign currency payable on consolidation, the exchange differences that arise for B cannot be eliminated since C has no corresponding exchange differences.

Thus, the intra-group monetary item results in an exposure to variability in the foreign currency amount of the intra-group monetary item that will affect profit or loss in the consolidated financial statements. Therefore, the intra-group monetary item may be designated as a hedged item in a foreign currency hedge.[103]

B Forecast intragroup transactions

Under the original version of IAS 39, a *forecast* intra-group transaction could also be designated as a hedged item if, on occurrence, it would give rise to an intra-group monetary item that itself could qualify as a hedged item.[104] The IASB considered that this concession had little conceptual merit and, in the version of the standard published in December 2003, it was removed. Essentially, until the forecast transaction has occurred, there is no real exposure to the group.[105] However, following the publication of that version of the standard, constituents raised the following concerns:[106]

- it is common practice for entities to designate a forecast intra-group transaction as the hedged item;

- some entities using IFRS and entities that were planning to adopt IFRS in 2005 had established a practice of designating forecast intragroup transactions as hedged items and had entered into derivative instruments to hedge the resulting exposures; and
- the revised standard created a difference from US GAAP, which permits hedge accounting for foreign currency risk on forecast intra-group transactions.

After considering the issue further the IASB published an exposure draft of proposed amendments to IAS 39 in July 2004. An amendment to the standard followed in April 2005.[107]

As a result, IAS 39 now contains a second exception allowing the foreign currency risk of a highly probable forecast intragroup transaction to qualify as a hedged item in consolidated financial statements in certain circumstances. The transaction must be denominated in a currency other than the functional currency of the entity (parent, subsidiary, associate, joint venture or branch) entering into that transaction and the foreign currency risk must affect consolidated profit or loss (otherwise it cannot qualify as a hedged item).[108]

Normally, royalty payments, interest payments and management charges between members of the same group will not affect consolidated profit or loss unless there is a related external transaction. However, a forecast sale or purchase of inventory between members of the same group will affect profit or loss if there is an onward sale of the inventory to a party external to the group. Similarly, a forecast intragroup sale of plant and equipment from the group entity that manufactured it to a group entity that will use it in its operations may affect consolidated profit or loss. This could occur, for example, because the plant and equipment will be depreciated by the purchasing entity and the amount initially recognised for the plant and equipment may change if the forecast intragroup transaction is denominated in a currency other than the functional currency of the purchasing entity.[109]

These provisions, which are similar (but not identical) to those contained in the original standard, are markedly different from the approach set out in the exposure draft. That approach would not have allowed intragroup transactions to be hedged items. Instead it would have allowed entities to designate as a hedged item in their consolidated financial statements a highly probable forecast external transaction denominated in the functional currency of the entity entering into the transaction, provided the transaction gave rise to an exposure that would have an effect on the consolidated profit or loss (i.e. was denominated in a currency other than the group's presentation currency). However, the IASB concluded that allowing a forecast transaction to be designated as the hedged item in consolidated financial statements would not be consistent with the functional currency framework in IAS 21 if the transaction was denominated in the functional currency of the entity entering into it.[110]

Although the standard refers exclusively to forecast intragroup transactions we believe there is no reason why these provisions should not also apply to intragroup firm commitments.

2.3.5 Hedged item and hedging instrument held by different group entities

The implementation guidance explains that, in a group, it is not necessary for the hedging instrument to be held by the same entity as the one that has the exposure being hedged in order to qualify for hedge accounting in the consolidated financial statements (at least in the context of cash flow hedges).[111] This is illustrated in the following example.

Example 21.19: Subsidiary's foreign exchange exposure hedged by parent

Company S is based in Switzerland and prepares consolidated financial statements in Swiss francs. It has an Australian subsidiary, Company A, whose functional currency is the Australian dollar and is included in the consolidated financial statements of S. A has forecast purchases in Japanese yen that are highly probable and S enters into a forward contract to hedge the change in yen relative to the Australian dollar.

Because A did not hedge the foreign currency exchange risk associated with the forecast purchases in yen, the effects of exchange rate changes between the Australian dollar and the yen will affect A's profit or loss and, therefore, would also affect consolidated profit or loss. Therefore that hedge may qualify for hedge accounting in S's consolidated financial statements provided the other hedge accounting criteria in IAS 39 are met.[112]

3 TYPES OF HEDGING RELATIONSHIPS

There are three types of hedging relationship defined in IAS 39:

- *fair value hedge:* a hedge of the exposure to changes in the fair value of a recognised asset or liability or an unrecognised firm commitment, or an identified portion of such an asset, liability or firm commitment, that is attributable to a particular risk and could affect profit or loss;
- *cash flow hedge:* a hedge of the exposure to variability in cash flows that:
  - (i) is attributable to a particular risk associated with a recognised asset or liability (such as all or some future interest payments on variable rate debt) or a highly probable forecast transaction; and
  - (ii) could affect profit or loss; and
- *hedge of a net investment in a foreign operation*: as defined in IAS 21 (see Chapter 10 at 2.3).[113]

These definitions are considered further in the remainder of this section.

3.1 Fair value hedges

An example of a fair value hedge is a hedge of the exposure to changes in the fair value of a fixed rate debt instrument as a result of changes in interest rates – if interest rates increase, the fair value of the debt decreases and vice versa. Such a hedge could be entered into either by the issuer or by the holder[114] (provided, in the case of the holder, it was not classified as held-to-maturity – see 2.2.5 above).

On the face of it, if a fixed rate loan that is classified within loans and receivables is held until it matures (as is the case for many such loans), changes in the fair value of the loan would not affect profit or loss. However, the implementation guidance explains that such assets may be hedged items in a fair value hedge because the loan *could* be sold, in which case fair value changes *would* affect profit or loss.[115] The same would be true of a fixed rate borrowing for which settlement before maturity is very unlikely.

A variable rate debt may be the hedged item in a fair value hedge in certain circumstances. For example, the fair value of such an instrument will change if the issuer's credit risk changes. There may also be changes in its fair value relating to movements in the market rate in the periods between which the variable rate is reset. For example, if a debt instrument provides for annual interest payments reset to the market rate each year, a portion of the debt instrument has an exposure to changes in fair value during the year.[116]

The exposure to changes in the price of inventories that are carried at the lower of cost and net realisable value may also be the subject of a fair value hedge because their fair value will affect profit or loss when they are sold or written down. For example, a copper forward may be used as the hedging instrument in a hedge of the copper price associated with copper inventory.[117]

An equity method investment cannot be a hedged item in a fair value hedge because the equity method recognises in profit or loss the investor's share of the associate's profit or loss, rather than changes in the investment's fair value. For a similar reason, an investment in a consolidated subsidiary cannot be a hedged item in a fair value hedge because consolidation recognises in profit or loss the subsidiary's profit or loss, rather than changes in the investment's fair value.[118]

3.2 Cash flow hedges

An example of a cash flow hedge is the use of an interest rate swap to change floating rate debt to fixed rate debt, i.e. a hedge of a future transaction where the future cash flows being hedged are the future interest payments.[119]

As noted at 3.1 above, a hedge of the exposure to changes in the fair value of a fixed rate debt instrument as a result of changes in interest rates could be treated as a fair value hedge. This could not be a cash flow hedge because changes in interest rates will not affect the cash flows on the hedged item, only its fair value.[120]

It was also noted at 3.1 above that a copper forward, say, may be used in a fair value hedge of copper inventory. Alternatively, the same hedging instrument may qualify as a cash flow hedge of the future sale of the inventory.[121]

The following example from the implementation guidance explains how a company might lock in current interest rates by way of a cash flow hedge of the anticipated issuance of fixed rate debt.

Example 21.20: Hedge of anticipated issuance of fixed rate debt

Company R periodically issues new bonds to refinance maturing bonds, provide working capital, and for various other purposes. When R decides it will be issuing bonds, it sometimes hedges the risk of changes in long-term interest rates to the date the bonds are issued. If long-term interest rates go up (down), the bond will be issued either at a higher (lower) rate, with a higher (smaller) discount or with a smaller (higher) premium than was originally expected. The higher (lower) rate being paid or decrease (increase) in proceeds is normally offset by the gain (loss) on the hedge.

In August 2008 R decides it will issue £2m seven-year bonds in January 2009. Historical correlation studies suggest that a seven-year treasury bond adequately correlates to the bonds R expects to issue, assuming a hedge ratio of 0.93 futures contracts to one debt unit (adjusting the hedge ratio to maximising expected effectiveness is discussed further at 2.2.2 above). Therefore, it hedges the anticipated issuance of the bonds by selling ('shorting') £1.86m worth of futures on seven-year treasury bonds.

From August 2008 to January 2009 interest rates increase and the short futures positions are closed on the date the bonds are issued. This results in a £120,000 gain, which offsets the increased interest payments on the bonds and, therefore, will affect profit or loss over the life of the bonds. The hedge may qualify as a cash flow hedge of the interest rate risk on the forecast debt issuance (assuming all other conditions for hedge accounting are met).[122]

Similarly, the forecast reinvestment of interest cash flows from a fixed rate asset can be the subject of a cash flow hedge using, say, a forward rate agreement to lock in the interest rate that will be received on that reinvestment.[123]

3.3 Hedges of foreign currency monetary items

A foreign currency monetary asset or liability that is hedged using a forward exchange contract may be treated as a fair value hedge because its fair value will change as foreign exchange rates change. Alternatively, it may be treated as a cash flow hedge because changes in exchange rates will affect the amount of cash required to settle the item (as measured by reference to the entity's functional currency).[124]

3.4 Hedges of firm commitments

A hedge of a firm commitment (e.g. a hedge of the change in fuel price relating to an unrecognised contractual commitment by an electricity utility to purchase fuel at a fixed price) is considered a hedge of an exposure to a change in fair value. Accordingly, such a hedge is a fair value hedge.[125] This is a change from the original version of IAS 39 under which hedges of firm commitments were treated as cash flow hedges.[126]

There was widespread support for the original requirement and this change proved to be controversial. The differences in opinion can be seen to arise as a result of different philosophical views as to the basis of financial reporting. The standard setters see a firm commitment as an asset or liability (as defined) that is accounted for at historical cost (which, for the most part, just happens to be zero). The more traditional view of a firm commitment is that it is something that simply does not belong in the financial statements until performance has taken place; and that applies whether or not the transaction that arises from the commitment is the subject of a hedge. However, in spite of these objections, the IASB saw this change as an opportunity to reduce the differences between IAS and US GAAP and, ultimately, this is likely to have been a key factor in its decision.[127]

Nevertheless, a hedge of the foreign currency risk of a firm commitment may be accounted for as a cash flow hedge.[128] This is because foreign currency risk affects both the cash flows and the fair value of the hedged item. Accordingly, a foreign currency cash flow hedge of a forecast transaction need not be redesignated as a fair value hedge when the forecast transaction becomes a firm commitment.[129]

3.5 All-in-one hedges

There are situations where an instrument that is accounted for as a derivative under IAS 39 is expected to be settled gross by delivery of the underlying asset in exchange for the payment of a fixed price. The implementation guidance states that such an instrument can be designated as the hedging instrument in a cash flow hedge of the variability of the consideration to be paid or received in the future transaction that will occur on gross settlement of the derivative contract itself. It is explained that this is acceptable because there *would* be an exposure to variability in the purchase or sale price without the derivative.[130]

For example, consider an entity that enters into a fixed price contract to sell a commodity and that contract is accounted for as a derivative under IAS 39. This might be because the entity has a practice of settling such contracts net in cash or of taking delivery of the underlying and selling it within a short period after delivery for the purpose of generating a profit from short-term fluctuations in price or dealer's margin. In this case, the fixed price contract may be designated as a cash flow hedge of the variability of the consideration to be received on the sale of the asset (a future transaction) even though the fixed price contract is the contract under which the asset will be sold.[131]

Similarly, an entity may enter into a forward contract to purchase a debt instrument that will be settled by delivery, but the forward contract is a derivative. This will be the case if its term exceeds the regular way delivery period in the marketplace (see Chapter 18 at 3.2). In this case the forward may be designated as a cash flow hedge of the variability of the consideration to be paid to acquire the debt instrument (a future transaction), even though the derivative is the contract under which the debt instrument will be acquired.[132]

It might come as a surprise to many entities that such contracts are, in fact, derivatives as defined. Therefore, the use of an 'all-in-one hedge' strategy for such instruments could prove useful in keeping fair value gains and losses, on what might be considered little more than purchase or sale orders, from being recognised immediately in profit or loss.

However, it seems best to accept the all-in-one hedge for what it is, i.e. a pragmatic concession, rather than trying to determine how it is derived from the principles of the standard. For example, the hedged item in each of the above two paragraphs, i.e. the spot price payment on the future purchase or sale of the asset, appears to be a cash flow that will never happen because the asset will be purchased or sold for the fixed price specified in the contract. Further, the hedged item also appears to be accounted for as a derivative, which is generally prohibited (see 2.2.6 above).

3.6 Hedges of net investments in foreign operations

From the perspective of an investor (e.g. a parent) it is clear that an investment in a foreign operation is likely to give rise to a degree of foreign currency exchange rate risk. However, as noted at 3.1 above, equity method investments and consolidated subsidiaries cannot be hedged items in a fair value hedge but they may be designated in a net investment hedge relationship. A hedge of a net investment in a foreign operation is said to be different because it is a hedge of the foreign currency exposure, not a fair value hedge of the change in the value of the investment.[133]

Unfortunately, IAS 39 provides very little guidance on what may or may not be considered a valid net investment hedge relationship. In particular, it is not clear precisely what should be regarded as the hedged foreign currency exposure. In practice, there appear to be two broad views, namely that it is the risk associated with translating the net assets of an entity from its functional currency to either:

- the presentation currency of the reporting entity in whose consolidated financial statements it is included (referred to hereafter as a 'presentation currency approach'); or
- the functional currency of another entity in those consolidated financial statements (a 'functional currency approach').

In many circumstances it would not matter which approach is adopted. For example, consider a parent with the euro as its functional and presentation currency that uses a US dollar borrowing to hedge its net investments in a subsidiary that has the US dollar as its functional currency. Under either approach this could be a valid net investment hedge relationship. However, there are other situations where a hedge would be considered valid under one approach and be prohibited under the other. These two approaches, and some of the secondary issues associated with them, are considered in more detail below.

3.6.1 Presentation currency approach

As noted above, this approach views the hedged exposure as being the risk associated with translating the net assets of an entity from its functional currency into the presentation currency of the reporting entity in which it is included. In other words, it defines the hedged risk by reference to the accounting entry that is recorded in equity using the translation process set out in Chapter 10 at 3.3.5.

The significant secondary issue associated with this approach is how to assess the effectiveness of the hedging instrument. This is illustrated using the following example.

Example 21.21: Hedging instrument held by subsidiary with a functional currency that is different to the presentation currency

Company A's functional currency is the US dollar and it presents its consolidated financial statements in US dollars. It has a 100% investment in Company B, the functional currency of which is the euro. B has a 100% investment in Company C, the functional currency of which is the pound sterling. Also, B has issued borrowings that are denominated in pound sterling, Each company has substantive operations and no other relevant transactions.

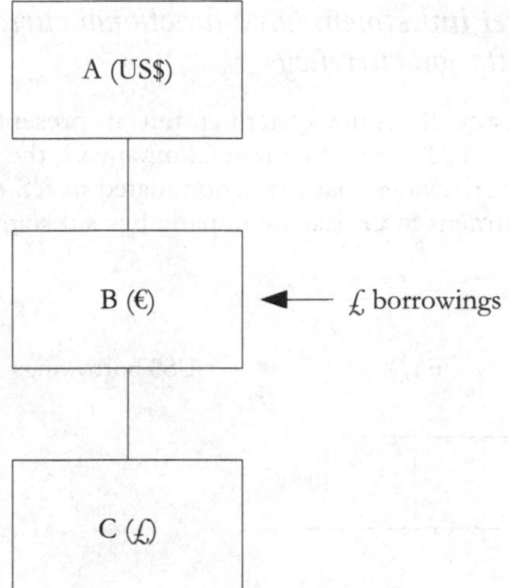

Accordingly, from the perspective of A's consolidated financial statements, the exposure relating to the net investment in Company C that is being hedged is the £/US$ exchange rate. Is it possible for B's sterling denominated loan to be designated, for the purposes of A's consolidated financial statements, as a hedge of the group's exposure to its net investment in C?

In practice there again seems to be two views. First, there is the view that one can look only at the transactional exposure that the hedging instrument gives rise to. Consequently, the entity holding the hedging instrument would look at its exposure relative to its functional currency and compare that to the hedged risk. In the example above, the validity of the hedge would be assessed by comparing the €/£ exchange risk (transactional exposure in Company B) to the £/US$ exchange risk (translational exposure in Company A's consolidated financial statements). This is unlikely to be considered an effective hedge unless it can be demonstrated that the two exchange rates move in tandem.

The second view would also take into account in assessing the effectiveness of the hedge the additional foreign currency exposure associated with retranslating the hedging instrument into the presentation currency of the group. The hedge relationship in the example above would be considered a valid one under this view because the risk associated with both the hedging instrument and the hedged item is defined by reference to the £/US$ exchange rate.

The first view can give rise to significant difficulties in obtaining net investment hedge accounting where treasury functions are decentralised. In fact a corollary of this view is that, in general, net investment hedge accounting can only be achieved by using as a hedging instrument one that is held by an entity with a functional currency that is the same as the group's presentation currency.

The conclusion under the second view is more permissive and it would remain true if the group structure was slightly different, for example if Company C was a direct subsidiary of Company A. However, there are situations under this second view where net investment hedge accounting would be prohibited, as illustrated using the following example.

Example 21.22: Hedged net investment has a functional currency that is the same as the presentation currency

Company F's functional currency is pounds sterling but it presents its consolidated financial statements in US dollars. It has a 100% investment in Company G, the functional currency of which is the US dollar. F has issued borrowings that are denominated in US dollars which are viewed as a hedge of the group's net investment in G, Each company has substantive operations and no other relevant transactions.

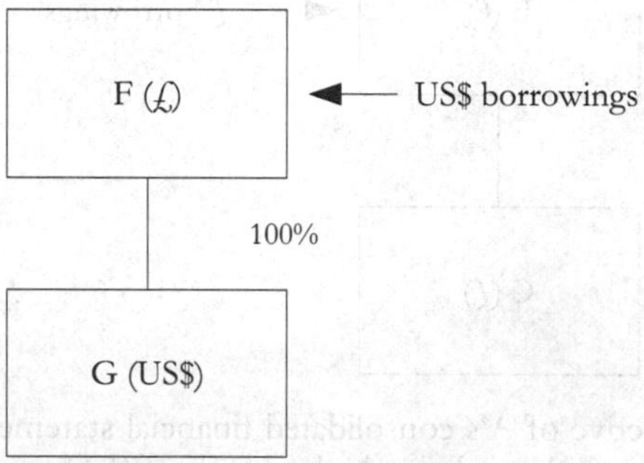

It is clear that from the perspective of Company F in its separate financial statements there should be an offset between the hedged item and the hedging instrument as they are both denominated in the same currency, US dollars. In those financial statements this could be achieved by accounting for it as a fair value hedge. However, as discussed in Chapter 10 at 3.3.4 and 3.3.5, IAS 21 has the effect that, when F prepares consolidated financial statements, it does not first prepare a consolidation in sterling and then translate that consolidation into dollars for presentation purposes. Rather the results and net assets of G are included 'directly' into the US Dollar consolidation. Accordingly, because F's net investment in G has a functional currency that is the same as the presentation currency of the group, it gives rise to absolutely no foreign currency translation exposure in F's consolidated financial statements. Accordingly hedge accounting would not, in our opinion, be permitted in the consolidated financial statements under a presentation currency approach.

3.6.2 Functional currency approach

This approach ignores the presentation currency and defines the hedged risk as the risk associated with translating the net assets of an entity from its own functional currency to the functional currency of another entity included in the same consolidated financial statements as the entity. In general that other entity will be a parent of (or, in the case of associates or jointly controlled entities, an investor or venturer in) the hedged net investment. In accounting for the hedging instrument, this approach normally focuses only on the transactional exposure that it creates in the entity holding it.

Under a functional currency approach, the hedge relationship in Example 21.22 above would be seen as perfectly acceptable because it views the hedged net investment and the hedging instrument from the perspective of Company F, i.e. using the pound sterling (F's functional currency) as a reference point.

The key issues that tend to arise using this approach are:

- by reference to which entity the hedged risk should (or could) be defined; and

- the necessary proximity of the entity holding the hedging instrument to the entity that is the subject of the hedge.

US GAAP, which adopts a functional currency approach to hedges of net investments, is somewhat restrictive on these issues. Either the operating unit that has the foreign currency exposure or another member of the consolidated group that has the same functional currency as that operating unit (provided there is no intervening subsidiary with a different functional currency) should be party to the hedging instrument.[134] Accordingly, the following relationships would be acceptable, irrespective of the presentation currency chosen:

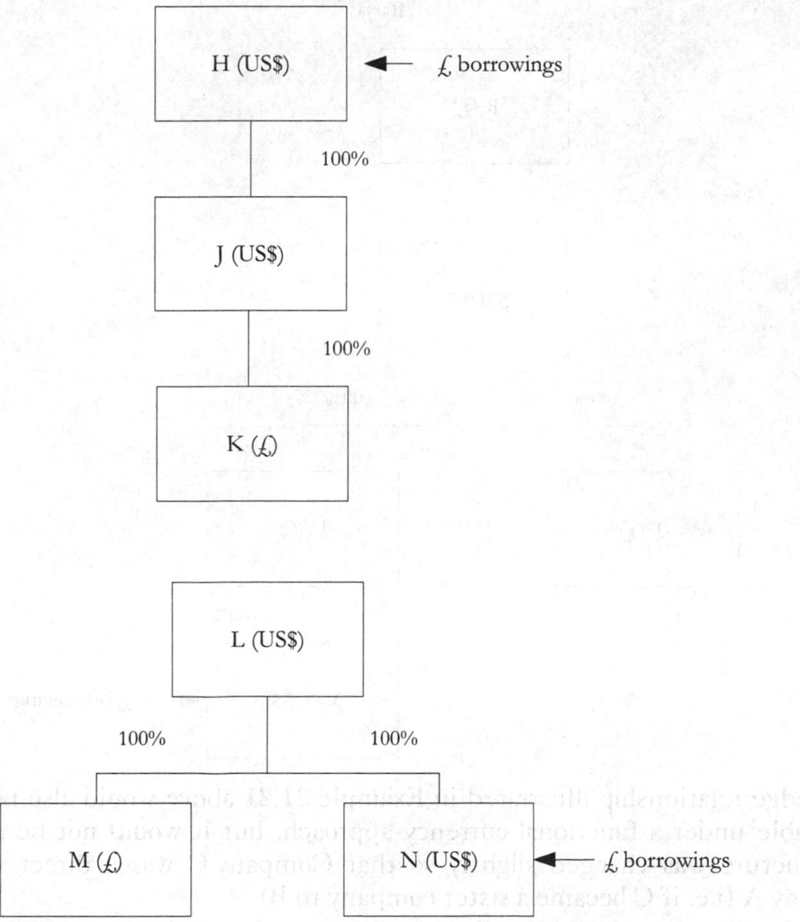

but the following would not:

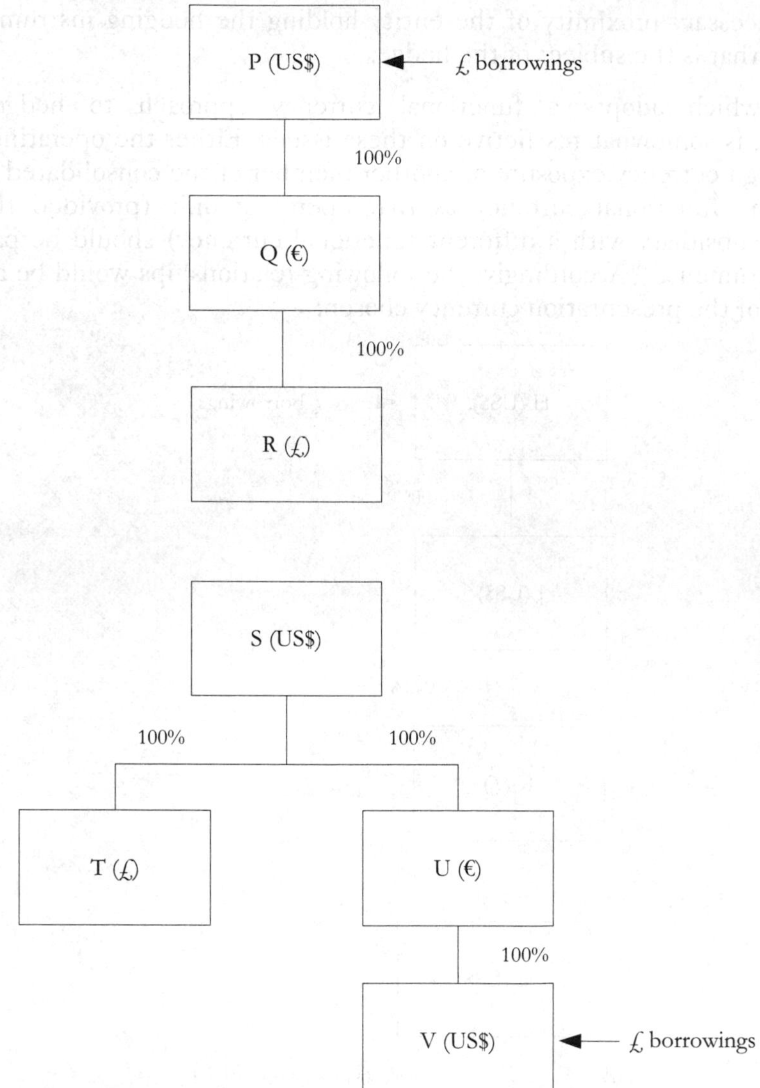

The hedge relationship illustrated in Example 21.21 above would also be considered acceptable under a functional currency approach, but it would not be acceptable if the structure was changed slightly so that Company C was a direct subsidiary of Company A (i.e. if C became a sister company to B).

However, it is not clear how strong an analogy may be drawn with US GAAP because there are some important differences of detail for foreign currency hedges, in particular:

- US GAAP applies the restrictions noted above to all foreign currency hedges[135] whereas IAS 39 does not, certainly not for cash flow hedges[136] (see 2.3.5 above); and

- US GAAP allows the use of intragroup hedging instruments (where they are offset by an external transaction)[137] whereas IAS 39 would require the external transaction to be designated as the hedging instrument (see 2.3.1 above).

Accordingly, some might argue that a more flexible form of functional currency approach is acceptable under IFRS. For example, some might argue that the hedged risk may be defined by reference to any parent of the hedged net investment within the group and, therefore, that the net investment hedge relationship involving Companies P, Q and R illustrated above is a valid one under IFRS.

3.6.3 IFRIC deliberations

The subject of net investment hedges was taken onto the IFRIC's agenda in November 2006 and the following key principles were agreed:

- a hedged risk should represent an economic exposure and this can arise only between functional currencies, rather than between an elective presentation currency and a functional currency;[138]
- the hedged functional currency risk is that between the identified net investment and any specified parent, whether its immediate parent, an intermediate parent or the ultimate parent entity;[139]
- a hedging instrument, whether a derivative or non-derivative, may be held by any entity within the group, whatever its functional currency or proximity to the hedged net investment. Furthermore, effectiveness would be assessed by reference to the functional currency of the parent entity hedging its risk, effectively ignoring the exchange gains and losses accounted for, whether recorded in profit or loss or equity.[140]

Under these principles, every arrangement illustrated at 3.6.1 and 3.6.2 above could qualify for hedge accounting (although the precise designation and documentation may need to change). In fact, we expect there will be few relationships likely to arise in practice that could not qualify for hedge accounting.

Also considered by the IFRIC was the question of whether an entity should look through its directly held net investment to consider the full extent of its foreign currency exposure at the lowest possible level of net investment. This is best illustrated by way of an example:

- a parent, Company X, has sterling as its functional currency;
- X has a subsidiary, Company Y, with US dollars as its functional currency;
- Y has a subsidiary, Company Z, with the euro as its functional currency;
- Y's net investment in Z is £30m worth of euro net assets; and
- X's overall net investment in Z is £100m comprising £70m worth of US dollar net assets in Y and Y's net investment in Z.

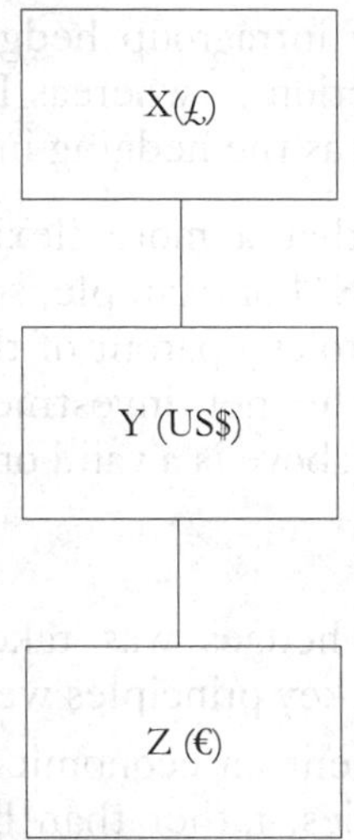

In considering X's maximum exposure to its US dollar net investment that may be hedged, can the investment in Y be considered an exposure to US dollars of £100m or should it be viewed as a £70m exposure to US dollars and a £30m exposure to euro? The IFRIC concluded that either approach is possible provided the same exposure is not hedged twice.

Finally, the IFRIC has decided that any interpretation should be applied prospectively, rather than requiring application from the start of the earliest period for which comparative information under IFRS is presented.[141]

In July 2007, IFRIC Draft Interpretation D22 – *Hedges of a Net Investment in a Foreign Operation* – was published containing the proposals set out above.

3.6.4 Summary

Conceptually, net investment hedging is somewhat unsatisfactory, mixing as it does foreign currency translation risk (largely an accounting exposure) with transactional risk (much more an economic exposure). Nevertheless, it is allowed by IAS 39, so that the basis on which it can be applied needs to be considered, and it has become clear that there has evolved a wide range of views of what does (and does not) constitute a valid hedging relationship. In the light of all this, the work of the IFRIC in attempting to draw together these almost incompatible concepts and differing views is to be applauded. It seems unlikely that many preparers will take offence at these proposals given the wide array of arrangements that could qualify as valid net investment hedges, although some technical purists may question whether they do anything other than endorse all manner of 'inappropriate' practices.

4 ACCOUNTING FOR EFFECTIVE HEDGES

If there is a designated hedging relationship between a hedging instrument and a hedged item as described at 3 above and it meets the conditions set out at 5 below, the accounting for the gain or loss on the hedging instrument and the hedged item will be as set out in the remainder of this section.[142] This is referred to as 'hedge accounting' and is said to recognise the offsetting effects on profit or loss of changes in the fair values of the hedging instrument and the hedged item.[143]

4.1 Fair value hedges

4.1.1 Ongoing fair value hedge accounting

If a fair value hedge meets the conditions set out at 5 below during the period, it should be accounted for as follows:

- the gain or loss from remeasuring the hedging instrument at fair value (for a derivative hedging instrument) or the foreign currency component of its carrying amount measured in accordance with IAS 21 (for a non-derivative hedging instrument) is recognised in profit or loss; and
- the carrying amount of the hedged item is adjusted for the change in its value attributable to the hedged risk and the gain or loss is recognised in profit or loss. This applies if the hedged item is an available-for-sale financial asset (and that gain or loss would otherwise be recognised in equity) or if it is otherwise measured at cost.[144]

It will be rare for the change in fair value of the hedging instrument (or, for non-derivative hedging instruments, foreign exchange gains or losses) to be exactly the same as the change in fair value of the hedged item attributable to the hedged risk, even for highly effective hedges. To the extent these amounts differ, a net profit or loss will be recognised in the income statement. The recognition of this difference is commonly referred to as the measurement of hedge ineffectiveness.

The following simple example illustrates how the treatment above might apply to a hedge of fair value interest rate risk on an investment in fixed rate debt.

Example 21.23: Fair value hedge

During Year 1 an investor purchases a fixed rate debt security for £100 and classifies it as available-for-sale. At the end of Year 1, the fair value of the asset is £110. To protect this value, the investor enters into a hedge by acquiring a derivative with a nil fair value. By the end of Year 2, the derivative has a fair value of £5 and the debt security has a corresponding decline in fair value (its fair value does not change as a result of any factors other than interest rates).

The investor would record the following accounting entries:

Year 1

	£	£
Debt security	100	
Cash		100

To reflect the acquisition of the security.

	£	£
Debt security	10	
Equity		10

To reflect the increase in the security's fair value.

Year 2

	£	£
Derivative	–	
Cash		–

To record the acquisition of the derivative at its fair value of nil.

	£	£
Derivative	5	
Profit or loss		5

To record the increase in the derivative's fair value.

	£	£
Profit or loss	5	
Debt security		5

To record the decrease in the security's fair value.[145]

The example is taken from the original version of the standard and was not carried forward into the December 2003 version of the standard, although it is not entirely clear why not. Even if it was considered too simplistic to be a useful practical example (it does not deal, for example, with net cash settlements on the derivative, coupon payments on the debt or the subsequent impact on the recognition of interest under the effective interest method) it does illustrate the basic mechanics of fair value hedge accounting quite well.

The standard explains that if only particular risks attributable to a hedged financial instrument are hedged, recognised changes in the fair value of the hedged item that are unrelated to the hedged risk should be recognised as set out in Chapter 20 at 3.[146] Therefore, for instruments measured at amortised cost, these other gains and losses would generally not be recognised; for available-for-sale assets those gains and losses would generally be recognised in equity. Exceptions to this would include foreign currency retranslation gains or losses on monetary items and impairment losses, which would be recognised in profit or loss in any event. The following example illustrates this.

Example 21.24: Hedging foreign currency risk of publicly traded shares

Company C, whose functional currency is sterling, acquires 100,000 shares in a listed US corporation for US$1m, which it classifies as available-for-sale. It is assumed the shares gives rise to a clear and identifiable exposure to changes in the US dollar/sterling exchange rate and to protect itself from changes in this exchange rate, C enters into a forward contract to sell US$0.75m which it intends to roll over for as long as the shares are held.

A portion of an exposure may be designated as a hedged item, and so the forward contract may be designated as a hedge of part of the shareholding. It could be a fair value hedge of the foreign exchange exposure of US$0.75m associated with the shares (alternatively it could be a cash flow hedge of a forecast sale of the shares but only if the timing of the sale is identified with sufficient certainty). Any variability in the fair value of the shares in US dollars would not affect the assessment of hedge effectiveness unless their fair value fell below US$0.75m.[147]

Gains and losses on the forward contract would be reported in profit or loss. Gains and losses arising from remeasuring the dollar value of the hedged proportion of the shares to sterling would also be reported in profit or loss and the remainder would be reported in equity (as would all of the foreign currency amount were it not for the hedge relationship).

The basic hedge accounting treatment above applies equally to fair value hedges of unrecognised firm commitments. Therefore, where an unrecognised firm commitment is designated as a hedged item in a fair value hedge, the subsequent cumulative change in its fair value attributable to the hedged risk should be recognised as an asset or liability with a corresponding gain or loss recognised in profit or loss. Thereafter, the firm commitment would be a *recognised* asset or liability (albeit that its carrying amount will not represent either its cost or, necessarily, its fair value). The changes in the fair value of the hedging instrument would also be recognised in profit or loss.[148]

4.1.2 Dealing with adjustments to the hedged item

In general, adjustments to the hedged asset or liability arising from the application of hedge accounting as described at 4.1.1 above are dealt with in accordance with the normal accounting treatment for that item. For example, copper inventory might be the hedged item in a fair value hedge of the exposure to changes in the copper price. In this case, the adjusted carrying amount of the copper inventory becomes the cost basis for the purpose of applying the lower of cost and net realisable value test under IAS 2 – *Inventories* (see Chapter 23).[149]

Where the hedged item is a financial instrument for which the effective interest method of accounting is used, the adjustment should be amortised to profit or loss. Amortisation may begin as soon as the adjustment exists and should begin no later than when the hedged item ceases to be adjusted for changes in its fair value attributable to the hedged risk. The adjustment should be based on a recalculated effective interest rate at the date amortisation begins and should be fully amortised by maturity.[150]

When an entity enters into a firm commitment to acquire an asset or assume a liability that is a hedged item in a fair value hedge, the initial carrying amount of the asset or liability that results from the entity meeting the firm commitment is adjusted to include the cumulative change in the fair value of the firm commitment attributable to the hedged risk that was recognised in the balance sheet.[151]

Example 21.25: Hedge of a firm commitment to acquire equipment

Company X has the euro as its functional currency. It has chosen to treat all hedges of foreign currency risk associated with firm commitments as fair value hedges. In January 2008 it contracts with a US supplier (with the US dollar as its functional currency) to purchase an item of machinery it intends to use in its business. The machine will be delivered at the start of July 2008 and the contracted price, payable on delivery, is US$1,000.

X has no appetite to take on foreign currency exchange risk in relation to euro/US dollar exchange rates and so contracts with a bank to purchase US$1,000 at the start of July in exchange for €900 (six month forward exchange rate is US$1:€0.90). In other words, X has effectively fixed the price it will pay for the machine (in euro terms) at €900.

If the fair value of the forward contract at the end of March 2008 (X's year end) is €30 positive to X, on delivery is €50 positive to X (spot exchange rate is US$1:€0.95) and assuming the hedge is perfectly effective (this might be the case if the hedged risk is identified as the forward exchange rate rather than the spot rate – see 5.3.3 and 5.3.9 below) and meets all the requirements for hedge accounting, the journal entries to record this hedging relationship would be as follows:

January 2008

No entries are required as the firm commitment is unrecognised, the forward contract is recognised but has a zero fair value and no cash is paid or received.

March 2008

	€	€
Forward contract	30	
Profit or loss		30

To record the change in fair value of the forward contract.

	€	€
Profit or loss	30	
Firm commitment		30

To record the change in fair value of the (previously) unrecognised firm commitment in respect of changes in forward exchange rates.

July 2008

	€	€
Forward contract	20	
Profit or loss		20

To record the change in fair value of the forward contract.

	€	€
Profit or loss	20	
Firm commitment		20

To record the change in fair value of the (now recognised) firm commitment in respect of changes in forward exchange rates.

	€	€
Cash	50	
Forward contract		50

To record the settlement of the forward contract at its fair value.

	€	€
Machine	950	
Cash		950

To record the settlement of the firm commitment at the contracted price of US$1,000 at the spot rate of US$1:€0.95.

	€	€
Firm commitment	50	
Machine		50

To remove the carrying amount of the firm commitment from the balance sheet and adjust the initial carrying amount of the machine that results from the firm commitment.

In summary, the result of these accounting entries is as follows:

	€	€
Machine	900	
Cash		900

which is somewhat reassuring given the starting presumption, i.e. that X had effectively fixed the purchase price of its machine at €900.

However, to some, the route to get to this position may seem slightly convoluted. This is especially so when one considers that, in addition to the above net entry in the balance sheet, both a profit and a loss of €50 have been recognised in the income statement and, as the balance sheet at the end of March 2008 illustrates, an asset or liability representing part of the fair value (or change in fair value) of X's commitment to purchase the item of machinery is also recognised temporarily.

4.1.3 Discontinuing fair value hedge accounting

The ongoing fair value hedge accounting set out at 4.1.1 above should be discontinued prospectively if any one of the following occurs:

- the hedging instrument expires or is sold, terminated, or exercised.

  For this purpose, the replacement or a rollover of a hedging instrument into another is not an expiration or termination if that is part of the documented hedging strategy;
- the hedge no longer meets the criteria for hedge accounting in 5 below; or
- the designation is revoked.[152]

If the reason the hedge no longer meets the criteria for qualification for hedge accounting is that it does not meet the hedge effectiveness criteria, hedge accounting should be discontinued from the last date on which compliance with hedge effectiveness was demonstrated. However, if the event or change in circumstances that caused the hedging relationship to fail the effectiveness criteria can be identified, and it can be demonstrated that the hedge was effective before the event or change in circumstances occurred, the hedge accounting should be discontinued from the date of the event or change in circumstances.[153]

Example 21.26: Hedge of foreign exchange risk from currency pegged to the US dollar

Company Z has the euro as its functional currency and prepares annual financial statements for the year ended 31 December. It also prepares interim financial statements for the six months ended 30 June and, in general, assesses the effectiveness of hedges at these dates.

In January 2008, Z acquires an equity instrument issued by a company whose functional currency is the FC. It is assumed the investment has a clear and identifiable exposure to changes in the FC/euro exchange rate and is classified as available-for-sale. For many years the value of the FC has been has pegged to the US dollar and historical studies show that during this time the FC/US dollar exchange rate has never moved outside of a corridor representing 2.5% of the mean rate. Furthermore, there is no evidence to suggest that the peg will not continue for the foreseeable future.

Accordingly, in January 2008, Z is able to designate a US dollar denominated borrowing as a highly effective hedge of the foreign currency risk associated with part of the equity instrument.

At the end of June 2008, Z performs an effectiveness assessment and determines that the hedge has been highly effective and, therefore, changes in the value of the equity instrument attributable to changes in the FC/euro exchange rate are recognised in profit or loss rather than equity, together with the exchange differences on the US dollar borrowing.

At the beginning of October 2008, there is an unexpected financial crisis, the peg ceases and the FC is devalued by 25% relative to the US dollar.

When Z assesses the effectiveness of the hedge in December 2008 it concludes that, because of the cessation of the peg and consequent devaluation, the hedge can no longer be regarded as highly effective and that hedge accounting should cease.

However, Z is able to determine that the failure of the hedge arose because of the cessation of the FC/US dollar peg and subsequent devaluation at the beginning of October 2008. Therefore, it is able to apply hedge accounting for the first three months of its second interim period. Thus, changes in the value of the equity instrument attributable to changes in the FC/euro exchange rate for that period will be recognised in profit or loss, but thereafter will be reflected in equity when accounting for the available-for-sale asset at fair value.

In other cases, hedge accounting should be discontinued from the date the hedging instrument expires or is sold, terminated or exercised, or the hedge designation is revoked. For example, if the forward contract in Example 21.25 above were settled (or the hedge designation was revoked) at the end of March 2007, no further adjustments to the carrying value of the firm commitment (€30) would be made after that date.

4.2 Cash flow hedges

4.2.1 Ongoing cash flow hedge accounting

If a cash flow hedge meets the conditions in 5 below, it should be accounted for as follows:

- the portion of the gain or loss on the hedging instrument that is determined to be an effective hedge should be recognised directly in equity; and
- the ineffective portion should be reported immediately in profit or loss.[154]

More specifically, the accounting should be as follows:

- the separate component of equity associated with the hedged item is adjusted to the lesser of the following (in absolute amounts):
  (i) the cumulative gain or loss on the hedging instrument from inception of the hedge; and
  (ii) the cumulative change in fair value (present value) of the expected future cash flows on the hedged item from inception of the hedge;
- any remaining gain or loss on the hedging instrument or designated component of it (that is not an effective hedge) is recognised in profit or loss; and

- if the documented risk management strategy for a particular hedging relationship excludes from the assessment of hedge effectiveness a specific component of the gain or loss or related cash flows on the hedging instrument, that excluded component of gain or loss is recognised as set out in Chapter 20 at 3 (effectively in profit or loss for a derivative hedging instrument).
- Those excluded components can include the time value of an option, the interest element of a forward contract or a proportion of an instrument (see 2.1.4 above).[155]

This is illustrated in the following examples.

Example 21.27: Cash flow hedge of anticipated commodity sale

On 30 September 2008, Company A hedges the anticipated sale of 24 tonnes of pulp on 1 March 2008 by entering into a short forward contract. The contract requires net settlement in cash, determined as the difference between the future spot price of 24 tonnes of pulp on a specified commodity exchange and £1m. A expects to sell the pulp in a different, local market.

A determines that the forward contract is an effective hedge of the anticipated sale and that the other conditions for hedge accounting are met. It assesses hedge effectiveness by comparing the entire change in the fair value of the forward contract with the change in the fair value of the expected cash inflows. On 31 December 2008, the spot price of pulp has increased both in the local market and on the exchange, although the increase in the local market exceeds the increase on the exchange. As a result, the present value of the expected cash inflow from the sale on the local market is £1.1m and the fair value of the forward is £85,000 negative. The hedge is determined to be still highly effective.

The cumulative change in the fair value of the forward contract is £85,000, while the fair value of the cumulative change in expected future cash flows on the hedged item is £0.1m. Ineffectiveness is not recognised in the financial statements because the cumulative change in the fair value of the hedged cash flows exceeds the cumulative change in the value of the hedging instrument. The whole of the fair value change in the forward contract would be recognised in equity.

However if A concluded that the hedge was no longer highly effective, it would discontinue hedge accounting prospectively as from the date the hedge ceased to be highly effective (see 4.2.3 below).[156]

Example 21.28: Cash flow hedge of a floating rate liability

Company A has a floating rate liability of £1m with five years remaining to maturity. It enters into a five year pay-fixed, receive-floating interest rate swap with the same principal terms to hedge the exposure to variable cash flow payments on the floating rate liability attributable to interest rate risk.

At inception, the swap's fair value is £nil. Subsequently, there is an increase of £49,000 which consists of a change of £50,000 resulting from an increase in market interest rates and a change of minus £1,000 resulting from an increase in the credit risk of the swap counterparty. There is no change in the fair value of the floating rate liability, but the fair value (present value) of the future cash flows needed to offset the exposure to variable interest cash flows on the liability increases by £50,000.

Even if A determines that the hedge of interest rate risk is 'highly effective' (simplistically, the offset ratio is 49,000/50,000 or 98%, so this is quite likely) it is not fully effective if part of the change in the fair value of the derivative is due to the counterparty's credit risk (see 5.3.9 below). However, because the hedge relationship is still 'highly effective', A credits the effective portion of the swap's fair value change, £49,000, to equity. There is no debit to profit or loss for the change in fair value of the swap attributable to the deterioration in the credit quality of the swap counterparty because the cumulative change in the present value of the future cash flows needed to offset the exposure to variable interest cash flows on the hedged item, £50,000, exceeds the cumulative change in value of the hedging instrument, £49,000. If A concluded that the hedge was no longer highly effective, it would discontinue hedge accounting prospectively as from the date the hedge ceased to be highly effective (see 4.2.3 below).

Alternatively, if the fair value of the swap increased to £51,000 of which £50,000 results from the increase in market interest rates and £1,000 from a decrease in the counterparty's credit risk, there would be a credit to profit or loss of £1,000 for the change in the swap's fair value attributable to the improvement in the counterparty's credit quality. This is because the cumulative change in the value of the hedging instrument, £51,000, exceeds the cumulative change in the present value of the future cash flows needed to offset the exposure to variable interest cash flows on the hedged item, £50,000. The difference of £1,000 represents the excess ineffectiveness attributable to the swap, and is reported in profit or loss.[157]

It can be seen that the measurement of hedge ineffectiveness differs for a cash flow hedge when compared to a fair value hedge. In a cash flow hedge, if the fair value of the derivative increases by €10 and the present value of the hedged expected cash flows change by only €8, the €2 difference is reflected in profit or loss (as would be the case for a fair value hedge). However, if the present value of the hedged expected cash flows changes by €10, but the fair value of the derivative changes by only €8, this €2 of hedge ineffectiveness is *not* reflected in profit or loss (which would not be the case for a fair value hedge).

Because of this, an entity might consider deliberately under-hedging an exposure in a cash flow hedge. It might do this by targeting an offset of, say, 85% to 90%, which would keep it within the prescribed 80% to 125% range (see 5.3.1 below) but avoid the need to recognise ineffectiveness in profit or loss. However, as discussed at 5.3.7 below, this is not permitted.

As an exception to the general accounting requirements set out at the start of this sub-section, if there is a hedging relationship between a non-derivative monetary asset and a non-derivative monetary liability, changes in the foreign currency component of both those financial instruments should be recognised in profit or loss.[158] This might be the case if a foreign currency denominated receivable is designated as the hedging instrument in a cash flow hedge of the repayment of the principal of a foreign currency denominated borrowing[159] (although hedge accounting would be unnecessary for this relationship).

4.2.2 Recycling gains and losses from equity

If a hedged forecast transaction subsequently results in the recognition of a *financial* asset or liability, the associated gains or losses that were recognised directly in equity should be recycled into profit or loss in the same period(s) during which the asset acquired or liability assumed affects profit or loss, e.g. in the periods that interest income or interest expense is recognised. However, if it is expected that all or a portion of a loss recognised directly in equity will not be recovered in one or more future periods, the amount that is not expected to be recovered should be recycled into profit or loss immediately.[160]

If a hedged forecast transaction subsequently results in the recognition of a *non-financial* asset or liability (or a forecast transaction for a *non-financial* asset or liability becomes a firm commitment for which fair value hedge accounting is applied) then a choice of accounting policies is available. In these circumstances, an entity should either:

- recycle the associated gains and losses that were recognised directly in equity into the income statement in the same period(s) during which the asset acquired or liability assumed affects profit or loss, e.g. in the periods that depreciation expense or cost of sales is recognised. However, if it is expected that all or a portion of a loss recognised directly in equity will not be recovered in one or more future periods, the amount that is not expected to be recovered should be recycled into profit or loss. Essentially this is the same treatment as for hedges of financial items; or
- remove the associated gains and losses that were recognised directly in equity and include them in the initial cost or other carrying amount of the asset or liability[161] as a 'basis adjustment'.

An entity should adopt one of these as its accounting policy and apply it consistently to all relevant hedges.[162] These treatments are illustrated in the following example.

Example 21.29: Hedge of a firm commitment to acquire equipment

Consider a variation of the situation in Example 21.25 at 4.1.2 above whereby Company X has chosen to treat all hedges of foreign currency risk associated with firm commitments as cash flow hedges, rather than as fair value hedges, as permitted by the standard (see 3.4 above). In the first case, X's accounting policy is to apply a basis adjustment to cash flow hedges that result in the recognition of non-financial assets or liabilities; in the second case it does not. Otherwise, the underlying facts and assumptions are the same. The accounting entries made at the end of March 2008 have not been shown separately (as they were in Example 21.25) because they are not relevant to the issue being illustrated.

Case 1: Basis adjustment

The journal entries to record this hedging relationship would be as follows:

January 2008

No entries are required as the firm commitment is unrecognised, the forward contract is recognised but has a zero fair value and no cash is paid or received.

July 2008

	€	€
Forward contract	50	
Equity		50

To record the change in fair value of the forward contract and, because no ineffectiveness arises, the whole of this change is recognised in equity.

	€	€
Cash	50	
Forward contract		50

To record the settlement of the forward contract at its fair value.

	€	€
Machine	950	
Cash		950

To record the settlement of the firm commitment at the contracted price of US$1,000 at the spot rate of US$1:€0.95.

	€	€
Equity	50	
Machine		50

To recycle the gain recognised in equity and adjust the carrying amount of the machine that results from the hedged transaction by this amount.

In summary, the result of these accounting entries is as follows:

	€	€
Machine	900	
Cash		900

which again reflects the starting presumption, i.e. that X had effectively fixed the purchase price of its machine at €900. However, the route to get to this position may also seem slightly convoluted.

Case 2: No basis adjustment

The journal entries to record this hedging relationship would be as follows:

January 2008

No entries are required as the firm commitment is unrecognised, the forward contract is recognised but has a zero fair value and no cash is paid or received.

July 2008

	€	€
Forward contract	50	
Equity		50

To record the change in fair value of the forward contract and, because no ineffectiveness arises, the whole of this change is recognised in equity.

	€	€
Cash	50	
Forward contract		50

To record the settlement of the forward contract at its fair value.

	€	€
Machine	950	
Cash		950

To record the settlement of the firm commitment at the contracted price of US$1,000 at the spot rate of US$1:€0.95.

In summary, the result of these accounting entries is as follows:

	€	€
Machine	950	
Cash		900
Equity		50

The gain deferred in equity would be recycled into profit or loss as the machine affects profit or loss, e.g. as it is depreciated, impaired or derecognised. If the machine has a very long useful economic life, this might involve tracking this adjustment for many years. The result might be considered less intuitive than before.

Under the original version of the standard, the 'basis adjustment' accounting treatment was required for all cash flow hedges where the hedged transaction resulted in the recognition of an asset or liability.[163] This was irrespective of whether the asset or liability was financial or non-financial. This was another controversial amendment to the standard, with many commentators supporting the retention of the original approach and most of the IASB wanting a prohibition on basis adjustments.

The IASB sees basis adjustments as 'contaminating' the carrying amount of a hedged asset or liability with gains and losses arising on a completely separate transaction (i.e. the hedging instrument), which results in a lack of comparability. For example, it believes that two identical assets that are purchased at the same time and in the same way (except for the fact that one was hedged) should be recognised at the same amounts. Commentators expressed pragmatic as well as conceptual concerns about the removal of basis adjustments. For example, without a basis adjustment, tracking the effects of cash flow hedges after the asset or liability is acquired could be complicated and could require systems changes[164] and, as demonstrated in Example 21.29 above, gains and losses in equity could take many years to recycle.

What we are left with is a political fudge that effectively allows preparers to choose whether or not to move a little closer to US GAAP (under which all basis adjustments are prohibited). Three IASB members formally objected to this change, essentially because they disagree with basis adjustments, but also because they saw the introduction of this choice into IAS 39 as a retrograde step.[165]

For all other cash flow hedges (i.e. those that do not result in the recognition of an asset or a liability), amounts that had been recognised directly in equity should be recycled into the income statement in the same period or periods during which the hedged forecast transaction affects profit or loss, e.g. when a forecast sale occurs[166] or when variable rate interest income or expense is recognised. In fact, when instruments such as conventional interest rate swaps are used as a hedging instrument in a cash flow hedge, it is common for entities to simply recognise, on an accruals basis, each periodic cash settlement in profit or loss. Strictly, however, each cash settlement simply represents a realisation of the fair value of the swap, i.e. in a fair value model using continuous (or real-time) accounting, they simply represent balance sheet movements between cash and the carrying value of the swap. In principle, therefore, the amount that is recycled into profit or loss should be completely independent of the swap accruals. Nevertheless, for most simple hedges of interest rate risk, this treatment is likely to result in income statement entries that are sufficiently precise.

Following adoption of the April 2005 amendment to IAS 39 (see 2.3.4 B above), if a hedge of a forecast intragroup transaction qualifies for hedge accounting, any gain or loss that is recognised directly in equity should be reclassified into profit or loss in the same period(s) during which the foreign currency risk of the hedged transaction affects consolidated profit or loss.[167]

It was stated at 3.3 above that using a forward exchange contract to hedge a foreign currency payable or receivable could be treated either as a fair value hedge, or a cash flow hedge, under IAS 39. In a fair value hedge, the gain or loss on remeasurement of the forward contract and the hedged item are recognised immediately in profit or loss. However, in a cash flow hedge, the gain or loss on remeasuring the forward contract is initially recognised in equity and recycled into profit or loss when the payable or receivable affects profit or loss. Because the payable or receivable is remeasured continuously in respect of changes in foreign exchange rates, the gain or loss on the forward contract will be recycled to profit or loss as the payable or receivable is remeasured, not when the payment occurs.[168] This should be very similar, if not identical, to the fair value hedge treatment. Indeed, it is similar to the accounting required if hedge accounting is not adopted for such transactions.

Where a forward exchange contract is used as a hedging instrument in a cash flow hedge, the discount or premium in the contract (i.e. the difference between the spot and forward rates, which is normally referred to in IAS 39 as the interest element) cannot be amortised to profit or loss over the contract term (which may have been an entity's accounting policy prior to the adoption of IAS 39). This is because derivatives are always measured at fair value. Where cash flow hedge accounting is applied, the effective portion of the gain or loss on the forward contract should initially be included in equity pending recycling into profit or loss. The interest element of the fair value of a forward may be excluded from the designated hedge relationship (see 2.1.4 A above) although in this case changes in the fair value of the interest element would be recognised immediately in profit or loss.[169] This could produce very different results to amortising the net premium or discount as illustrated in Example 21.33 at 5.3.3 below.

4.2.3 Discontinuing cash flow hedge accounting

Cash flow hedge accounting should be discontinued prospectively in any of the following circumstances:

(a) the hedging instrument expires or is sold, terminated, or exercised.

For this purpose, the replacement or a rollover of a hedging instrument into another hedging instrument is not an expiration or termination if such replacement or rollover is part of the documented hedging strategy.

In this case the cumulative gain or loss that was recognised directly in equity in the period when the hedge was effective should remain in equity until the forecast transaction occurs. Thereafter, it is required to be dealt with as set out at 4.2.2 above.

The standard does not entertain the possibility that, subsequently, the hedged forecast transaction might not occur. However, it would seem appropriate to deal with this situation in the same way as for hedges where the hedged instrument has not been terminated, i.e. as in (c) below;

(b) the hedge no longer meets the criteria for hedge accounting at 5 below.

In this case, the cumulative gain or loss that was recognised directly in equity is dealt with in same way as in (a) above;

(c) the forecast transaction is no longer expected to occur.

In this case, the cumulative gain or loss on the hedging instrument that was recognised directly in equity should be recognised in profit or loss. However, a forecast transaction that is no longer highly probable (and therefore the hedge no longer meets the criteria for hedge accounting at 5 below) may still be expected to occur, in which case (b) above will apply, not (c);

(d) the designation as a hedge is revoked.

In this case, the cumulative gain or loss that remains in equity is dealt with in same way as in (a) above. However, if the transaction is no longer expected to occur, (c) applies.[170]

As for fair value hedges, if the reason the hedge no longer meets the criteria for qualification for hedge accounting is that it does not meet the hedge effectiveness criteria, hedge accounting should normally be discontinued from the last date on which compliance with hedge effectiveness was demonstrated. However, if the event or change in circumstances that caused the hedging relationship to fail the effectiveness criteria can be identified, and it can be demonstrated that the hedge was effective before the event or change in circumstances occurred, the hedge accounting should be discontinued from the date of the event or change in circumstances.[171]

4.2.4 Acquisitions and disposals

Where a reporting entity acquires a subsidiary that is applying cash flow hedge accounting, additional considerations arise. In applying the purchase method of accounting in its consolidated financial statements, the reporting entity does not inherit the subsidiary's existing cash flow hedge reserve, since this clearly represents cumulative pre-acquisition gains and losses.[172] This has implications for the assessment of hedge effectiveness and the measurement of ineffectiveness because, so far as the group is concerned, it has effectively started a new hedge relationship with a hedging instrument that is likely to have a non-zero fair value (see 5.1.1 and 5.3.5 below).

The standard does not address the situation when the hedge relationship ceases because there is a change in the relationship between the reporting entity and the entity that is holding the hedging instrument and/or is exposed to the hedged transaction, for example when a subsidiary is disposed of. This issue is covered in more detail in Chapter 6 at 6.6.

4.3 Accounting for hedges of a net investment in a foreign operation

Hedges of a net investment in a foreign operation, including a hedge of a monetary item that is accounted for as part of the net investment (see Chapter 10 at 3.4.1), should be accounted for in a similar way to cash flow hedges:

- the portion of the gain or loss on the hedging instrument that is determined to be an effective hedge should be recognised directly in equity through the statement of changes in equity; and
- the ineffective portion should be recognised in profit or loss.[173]

The gain or loss on the hedging instrument relating to the effective portion of the hedge that has been recognised directly in equity should be recognised in profit or loss on disposal of the foreign operation (see Chapter 10 at 2.7.3).[174]

Unfortunately, this is pretty much all of the guidance there is on accounting for net investment hedges. Even the meaning of 'similarly to cash flow hedges' is unclear. For example, is it simply a reference to the fact that gains and losses are recognised initially in equity (as they are for cash flow hedges)? Or does it mean that ineffectiveness should be measured in the same way, i.e. no ineffectiveness is recognised in profit or loss if the gain or loss on the hedging instrument is less, in absolute terms, than the gain or loss on the hedged item (see 4.2.1 above)?

Although it is clear that ineffectiveness should be recorded for under-hedges as well as over-hedges under US GAAP,[175] this does not necessarily define the accounting treatment under IFRS. Therefore, whilst there is a case to be made for the US GAAP treatment (and we can see that companies with secondary reporting requirements will use this argument), an equally strong case can be made for the alternative interpretation.

5 QUALIFYING CONDITIONS FOR HEDGE ACCOUNTING

A hedging relationship qualifies for hedge accounting as set out at 4 above if, and only if, all of the following conditions are met:

(a) at the inception of the hedge there is formal designation and documentation both of the hedging relationship and the entity's risk management objective and strategy for undertaking the hedge;

(b) the hedge is expected to be highly effective in achieving offsetting changes in fair value or cash flows attributable to the hedged risk, consistently with the originally documented risk management strategy for that particular hedging relationship;

(c) a forecast transaction that is the subject of a cash flow hedge must be highly probable and must present an exposure to variations in cash flows that could ultimately affect net profit or loss;

(d) the effectiveness of the hedge can be reliably measured, i.e. the fair value or cash flows of the hedged item that are attributable to the hedged risk and the fair value of the hedging instrument can be reliably measured (see Chapter 20 at 4 for guidance on determining fair value); and

(e) the hedge is assessed on an ongoing basis and determined actually to have been highly effective throughout the financial reporting periods for which the hedge was designated.[176]

These conditions are considered in further detail in the remainder of this section.

5.1 Documentation and designation

The documentation supporting the hedge should include identification of:

- the hedging instrument;
- the hedged item or transaction;
- the nature of the risk being hedged; and
- how the entity will assess the hedging instrument's effectiveness in offsetting the exposure to changes in the hedged item's fair value or cash flows attributable to the hedged risk.[177]

Designation of a hedge relationship takes effect prospectively from the date all of the criteria at 5 are met. In particular, hedge accounting can be applied only from the date all of the necessary documentation is completed. Therefore, hedge relationships cannot be designated retrospectively.[178]

Where an ongoing hedge relationship fails the retrospective effectiveness test (see 5.3.1 below) an entity is not precluded from redesignating the hedging instrument in a hedge of the same financial asset or liability. Therefore, hedge accounting may be obtained for a subsequent period in which the hedge is effective provided the hedge meets the requirements set out at 5 above.[179] Similarly, an instrument that has been dedesignated as a hedging instrument may be redesignated in a hedge of the same or a different exposure provided all other conditions for hedge accounting are met.

Hedge designation need not take place at the time a hedging instrument is entered into. For example, a derivative contract may be designated and formally documented as a hedging instrument any time after entering into the derivative contract. Hedge accounting will apply prospectively from designation, provided all other conditions are met.[180] However, there is often a hidden danger when designating a derivative as a hedging instrument subsequent to its inception. For non-option derivatives, such as forwards or interest rate swaps, any fair value is likely to create 'noise' in a hedge effectiveness assessment that may not be fully offset by changes in the hedged item, especially in the case of a cash flow hedge. Consequently, there is likely to be more ineffectiveness recognised and, in extremis, could cause the hedge not be regarded as highly effective (see 5.3.5 below). Only by coincidence will a derivative still have a fair value that is zero, or close to zero, which would minimise this problem.

5.1.1 Business combinations

In a business combination accounted for using the purchase method of accounting where the acquired business has designated hedging relationships, the question arises of whether the acquirer should:

- be permitted to continue to apply the hedge accounting model to hedge relationships designated previously by the acquiree, assuming it is consistent with the acquirer's strategies and policies; or
- be required to re-designate hedge relationships at the acquisition date.[181]

Redesignating the hedge relationships at the acquisition date means that if the hedging instrument has a fair value other than zero, it is likely that ineffectiveness will be introduced in a hedge that may have been nearly 100% effective prior to the acquisition. In fact it is possible that a hedge relationship that would continue to be effective for the acquiree had the business combination not occurred will fail to qualify for hedge accounting in the acquirer's consolidated financial statements if the hedging instrument has a significant fair value at the acquisition date, particularly for cash flow hedges (see 5.3.5 below). To mitigate this, the acquirer may, subsequent to the combination, choose to settle the hedging instruments and replace them with more effective ones.[182]

The IASB has decided that, following adoption of the revised version of IFRS 3 – *Business Combinations* (see Chapter 7 at 5), in order to obtain hedge accounting in their consolidated financial statements acquirers will be required to redesignate the acquiree's hedges.[183] IFRSs are silent on whether acquirers should adopt this approach currently,[184] although we consider that the acquired hedge relationships should at least be 'reaffirmed' and that, consistent with the IASB's plans, assessments of effectiveness should take account of the fair value of the hedging instruments at the date of acquisition.

5.1.2 Dynamic hedging strategies

As noted at 2.1.4 A above, the standard explains that a dynamic hedging strategy that assesses both the intrinsic value and time value of an option contract can qualify for hedge accounting.[185] The implementation guidance explains that this allows the use of a delta-neutral hedging strategy as well as other dynamic hedging strategies under which the quantity of the hedging instrument is constantly adjusted in order to maintain a desired hedge ratio (e.g. to achieve a delta-neutral position, insensitive to changes in the fair value of the hedged item), to qualify for hedge accounting. For example, a portfolio insurance strategy that seeks to ensure that the fair value of the hedged item does not drop below a certain level, while allowing the fair value to increase, may qualify for hedge accounting.[186]

For a dynamic hedging strategy to qualify for hedge accounting, the documentation must specify how the hedge will be monitored and updated and how effectiveness will be measured. In addition, the entity must be able to track properly all terminations and redesignations of the hedging instrument, in addition to demonstrating that all other criteria for hedge accounting are met. Also, it must be demonstrated that the hedge is expected to be highly effective for a specified short period of time during which adjustment of the hedge is not expected.[187]

5.2 Forecast transactions

In the case of a hedge of a forecast transaction, the documentation should identify the date on, or time period in which, the forecast transaction is expected to occur. This is because, in order to qualify for hedge accounting:

- the hedge must relate to a specific identified and designated risk;
- it must be possible to measure its effectiveness reliably; and
- the hedged forecast transaction must be highly probable.

To meet these criteria, entities are not required to predict and document the exact date a forecast transaction is expected to occur. However, the time period in which the forecast transaction is expected to occur should be identified and documented within a reasonably specific and generally narrow range of time from a most probable date, as a basis for assessing hedge effectiveness. To determine that the hedge will be highly effective, it is necessary to ensure that changes in the fair value of the expected cash flows are offset by changes in the fair value of the hedging instrument and this test may be met only if the timing of the cash flows occur within close proximity to each other.[188]

If a forecast transaction such as a commodity sale is properly designated in a hedge and, subsequently, its expected timing changes to an earlier period, this does not affect the validity of the original designation. The entity can conclude that this transaction is the same as the one designated as being hedged. However, this may well affect the assessment of the hedge's effectiveness, especially as the hedging instrument will be designated for the remaining period of its existence, which will exceed the period to the forecast sale.[189]

Further, hedged forecast transactions must be identified and documented with sufficient specificity so that when the transaction occurs, it is clear whether the transaction is, or is not, the hedged transaction. Therefore, a forecast transaction may be identified as the sale of the first 15,000 units of a specific product during a specified three-month period, but it could not be identified as the last 15,000 units of that product sold because they cannot be identified when they occur. For the same reason, a forecast transaction cannot be specified solely as a percentage of sales or purchases during a period.[190]

Finally, the standard requires a forecast transaction that is the subject of a cash flow hedge to be 'highly probable'. The implementation guidance explains that this term indicates a *much* greater likelihood of happening than the term 'more likely than not' (a term used throughout the IASB's work to describe, or define, 'probable').[191] The implementation guidance to the original version of the standard referred to a '*significantly* greater likelihood'[192] although it is very difficult to know whether or not to read anything into this subtle change of words, even for someone whose first language is English. In fact, we can claim no originality in pointing out that there is a serious risk that non-native English speakers will be unable to distinguish the important nuances of meaning within phrases such as these that are used extensively by the IASB.[193]

Before returning to the matter in hand, it is interesting to note that 'highly probable' is defined in IFRS 5 – *Non-current Assets Held for Sale and Discontinued Operations* – a standard published only a few weeks after the December 2003 version of IAS 39. It may come as a surprise, therefore, that the relevant test when applying IFRS 5 is the seemingly outdated term '*significantly* more likely'.[194] Furthermore, in the basis for conclusions to IFRS 5, it is explained that in the equivalent US GAAP requirements, the phrase 'likely to occur' describes the term 'probable' and that the IASB regards 'highly probable' as implying the same probability as 'likely to occur'.[195] Taking this wordplay to its logical conclusion, one might be tempted to deduce that the IASB regards probable as meaning 'significantly (or much) more likely than probable'!

Concerns about the precise meaning of words aside, the guidance does add some slightly more practical pointers. It states that probability should be supported by observable facts and attendant circumstance and should not be based solely on management intent, because intentions are not verifiable. In making this assessment, consideration should be given to the following circumstances:

- the frequency of similar past transactions;
- the financial and operational ability to carry out the transaction;
- substantial commitments of resources to a particular activity, e.g. a manufacturing facility that can be used in the short run only to process a particular type of commodity;
- the extent of loss or disruption of operations that could result if the transaction does not occur;
- the likelihood that transactions with substantially different characteristics might be used to achieve the same business purpose, e.g. there are several ways of raising cash ranging from a short-term bank loan to a public share offering; and
- the entity's business plan.[196]

The length of time until a forecast transaction is projected to occur is also a consideration in determining probability. Other factors being equal, the more distant a forecast transaction is, the less likely it is to be considered highly probable and the stronger the evidence that would be needed to support an assertion that it is highly probable. For example, a transaction forecast to occur in five years may be less likely to occur than a transaction forecast to occur in one year. However, forecast interest payments for the next 20 years on variable-rate debt would typically be highly probable if supported by an existing contractual obligation.[197]

In addition, other factors being equal, the greater the physical quantity or future value of a forecast transaction in proportion to transactions of the same nature, the less likely it is that the transaction would be considered highly probable and the stronger the evidence that would be required to support such an assertion. For example, less evidence would generally be needed to support forecast sales of 100,000 units in the next month than 950,000 units when recent sales have averaged 950,000 units for each of the past three months.[198]

The implementation guidance uses the following example to elaborate on this:

Example 21.30: Hedge of foreign currency revenues

An airline operator uses sophisticated models based on past experience and economic data to project its revenues in various currencies. If it can demonstrate that forecast revenues for a period of time into the future in a particular currency are 'highly probable', it may designate a currency borrowing as a cash flow hedge of the future revenue stream.

However it is unlikely that 100% of revenues for a future year could be reliably predicted. On the other hand, it is possible that a portion of predicted revenues, normally those expected in the short-term, will meet the 'highly probable' criterion.[199]

It is also explained that cash flows arising after the prepayment date on an instrument that is prepayable at the issuer's option may be highly probable for a group or pool of similar assets for which prepayments can be estimated with a high degree of accuracy, e.g. mortgage loans, or if the prepayment option is significantly out of the money. In addition, the cash flows after the prepayment date may be designated as the hedged item if a comparable option exists in the hedging instrument.[200]

The implementation guidance states that a history of having designated hedges of forecast transactions and then determining that the forecast transactions are no longer expected to occur, calls into question both the ability to accurately predict forecast transactions and the propriety of using hedge accounting in the future for similar forecast transactions.[201] This is clearly common sense, however the standard contains no prescriptive 'tainting' provisions in this area akin to those applied to held-to-maturity investments (see Chapter 17 at 7.2.3). Therefore, entities are not automatically prohibited from using cash flow hedge accounting if a forecast transaction fails to occur. Instead, whenever such a situation arises the particular facts, circumstances and evidence should be assessed to determine whether doubt has, in fact, been cast on an entity's ongoing hedging strategies.

5.3 Assessing hedge effectiveness

One of the fundamental requirements of IAS 39 is that to use hedge accounting, the hedge must be an effective one. To this end, hedge effectiveness is defined as:

> 'the degree to which changes in the fair value or cash flows of the hedged item that are attributable to a hedged risk are offset by changes in the fair value or cash flows of the hedging instrument.'[202]

There is little doubt that demonstrating the effectiveness of a hedge can be one of the most challenging aspects of IAS 39. The assessment of a hedge's effectiveness has the potential to be an extremely difficult exercise, involving the use of complex statistical techniques and valuation models of which many accountants have, at best, only limited experience. All of this is not helped by the fact that the IASB has provided very limited practical guidance on how to go about testing effectiveness and the IFRIC has shied away from developing application guidance in this area.[203] Accordingly, it is possible that differing interpretations as to what is an acceptable method for assessing effectiveness will develop in practice.

5.3.1 Basic requirements

As noted at 5 above, three of the qualifying conditions for hedge accounting involve hedge effectiveness as follows:

- the entity should expect the hedge to be highly effective in achieving offsetting changes in fair value or cash flows attributable to the hedged risk, consistently with the originally documented risk management strategy for that particular hedging relationship;
- the effectiveness of the hedge can be reliably measured, i.e. the fair value or cash flows of the hedged item that are attributable to the hedged risk and the fair value of the hedging instrument can be reliably measured; and
- the hedge should be assessed on an ongoing basis and determined actually to have been highly effective throughout the financial reporting periods for which the hedge was designated.[204]

Qualification for hedge accounting is based on an expectation of future (prospective) effectiveness, the objective of which is to ensure there is firm evidence to support an expectation of high effectiveness, and an evaluation of actual (retrospective) effectiveness.[205] The application guidance explains that a hedge is regarded as highly effective only if both of the following conditions are met:

(a) at the inception of the hedge, and in subsequent periods, the hedge is expected to be highly effective in achieving offsetting changes in fair value or cash flows attributable to the hedged risk during the period for which the hedge is designated.

Such an expectation can be demonstrated in various ways, including a comparison of past changes in the fair value or cash flows of the hedged item that are attributable to the hedged risk with past changes in the fair value or cash flows of the hedging instrument, or by demonstrating a high statistical correlation between the fair value or cash flows of the hedged item and those of the hedging instrument. A hedge ratio of other than one to one may be chosen in order to improve the effectiveness of the hedge (see 2.2.2 above); and

(b) the actual results of the hedge are within a range of 80% to 125%.

For example, if actual results are such that the loss on the hedging instrument is €120 and the gain on the cash instrument is €100, offset can be measured by 120 ÷ 100, which is 120%, or by 100 ÷ 120, which is 83%. In this example, assuming the hedge meets the condition in (a), it would be concluded that the hedge has been highly effective.[206]

Effectiveness should be assessed, at a minimum, at the time annual or interim financial reports are prepared.[207] However, there is nothing to prevent effectiveness assessments being performed more frequently. In fact this might be desirable if there is a risk of the hedge ceasing to be considered highly effective (although the prospective test should ensure such a risk is actually very low). The sooner an ineffective hedge is identified, the sooner the accounting volatility that results from a failure to obtain hedge accounting can be managed. For example, following a failure, it might be possible to redesignate the hedge (perhaps with some adjustment to the hedging instrument) but hedge accounting for that new hedge relationship will be available only prospectively.

No single method for assessing hedge effectiveness is specified by IAS 39 – the method used will depend on the entity's risk management strategy adopted. For example, if the risk management strategy is to adjust the amount of the hedging instrument periodically to reflect changes in the hedged position, it needs to be demonstrated that the hedge is expected to be highly effective only for the period until the amount of the hedging instrument is next adjusted.[208]

Hedge effectiveness may also be assessed on a pre-tax or after-tax basis. If effectiveness is to be assessed on an after-tax basis, this should be designated at inception as part of the formal documentation of the hedging strategy.[209]

In some cases, an entity will adopt different methods for different types of hedges. The documentation of its hedging strategy should include its procedures for assessing effectiveness and those procedures should state whether the assessment will include all of the gain or loss on a hedging instrument or whether the time value of the instrument is excluded (see 2.1.4 above).[210]

The appropriateness of a given method will depend on the nature of the risk being hedged and the type of hedging instrument used. The method must be reasonable and consistent with other similar hedges unless different methods are explicitly justified. An entity is required to document, at the inception of the hedge, how effectiveness will be assessed and then to apply that effectiveness test on a consistent basis for the duration of the hedge. Several mathematical techniques can be used including ratio analysis, i.e. a comparison of hedging gains and losses to the corresponding gains and losses on the hedged item at a point in time, and statistical measurement techniques such as regression analysis (see 5.3.6 below). If regression analysis is used, the entity's documented policies for assessing hedge effectiveness must specify how the results of the regression will be assessed.[211]

Expected hedge effectiveness may be assessed on a cumulative basis if that is how the hedge is designated and that condition is reflected in the hedging documentation. Therefore, even if a hedge is not expected to be highly effective in a particular period, hedge accounting is not precluded if effectiveness is expected to remain sufficiently high over the life of the hedging relationship.[212]

Example 21.31: Cumulative hedge effectiveness

A company designates an interest rate swap linked to LIBOR as a hedge of a borrowing whose interest is a UK base rate plus a margin. The UK base rate changes, perhaps, once each quarter or less, in increments of 25 to 50 basis points, while LIBOR changes daily. Over a one to two year period, the hedge is expected to be almost perfect. However, there will be quarters when the UK base rate does not change at all while LIBOR has changed significantly. This would not necessarily preclude hedge accounting.[213]

The time value of money will generally need to be considered in assessing the effectiveness of a hedge. The fair value of an interest rate swap derives from its net settlements and the fixed and variable rates on a swap can be changed without affecting the net settlement if both are changed by the same amount. In other words, a pay-7% fixed, receive-LIBOR swap should have the same fair value as a pay-6% fixed, receive-LIBOR minus 1% swap with otherwise identical terms. Consequently, the fixed rate on a hedged item need not exactly match the fixed rate on a swap designated as a fair value hedge. Nor does the variable rate on an interest-bearing asset or liability need to be the same as the variable rate on a swap designated as a cash flow hedge.[214]

In the case of interest rate risk, it is suggested that hedge effectiveness may be assessed by preparing a maturity schedule for financial assets and liabilities that shows the net interest rate exposure for each time period, provided that the net exposure is associated with a specific asset or liability (or a specific group of assets or liabilities or a specific portion of them) giving rise to the net exposure, and hedge effectiveness is assessed against that asset or liability.[215] The macro-hedging models (see 6 below) have their origins in just such an approach.

An important point to note is that the method used in the *assessment* of hedge *effectiveness* need not be the same as that used in the *measurement* (i.e. recognition in profit or loss) of hedge *ineffectiveness*. Therefore, even if the calculations used to measure ineffectiveness would not support a retrospective hedge effectiveness test performed using the 'dollar-offset' method (see 5.3.2 below), hedge accounting would not necessarily be precluded, provided the hedge passed the originally documented retrospective hedge effectiveness test, for example regression analysis (see 5.3.6 below).[216]

5.3.2 The 'dollar-offset' method

As noted at 5.3.1 above, one method that may be used to assess hedge effectiveness is a comparison of hedging gains and losses to the corresponding gains and losses on the hedged item at a point in time.[217]

This method essentially uses the mechanics of *measuring* hedge ineffectiveness set out at 4.1.1 and 4.2.1 above as a basis for *assessing* effectiveness. In other words, it compares the monetary amounts of the change in fair value of the hedging instrument with the monetary amount of the change in fair value or cash flows of the hedged item or transactions attributable to the hedged risk over the assessment period. To the extent that dividing these monetary amounts results in a fraction between 0.80 and 1.25, the hedge will be seen as highly effective on a retrospective basis. Largely because of the terminology used under US GAAP, this has become known as the 'dollar-offset' method.

The dollar-offset method is commonly used as a basis for assessing hedge effectiveness on an ongoing basis because it uses the calculations that have to be performed for determining the hedge accounting bookkeeping entries, and therefore requires limited additional effort.

Example 21.32 below contains a very comprehensive illustration of the dollar-offset method for a cash flow hedge that is based on the implementation guidance to IAS 39. Although it is somewhat esoteric, and many accountants will find the calculations difficult to follow, it is an important example. Particularly, it establishes two relatively practical methods of measuring ineffectiveness, and assessing effectiveness, for cash flow hedges. They are normally referred to as the 'hypothetical derivative method' and the 'change in fair value method' (which is what they are called under US GAAP).

As its name suggests, the hypothetical derivative method involves establishing a notional derivative that would be the ideal hedging instrument for the hedged exposure (normally an interest rate swap or forward contract with no unusual terms and a zero fair value at inception of the hedge relationship). The fair value of the hypothetical derivative is then used as a proxy for the net present value of the hedged future cash flows against which changes in value of the actual hedging instrument are compared to assess effectiveness and measure ineffectiveness.

It is also worth noting that, because this example is as close as one can get to a perfect hedge, it may seem to do little more than demonstrate what was evident at the outset, i.e. that absolutely no ineffectiveness will arise. However, by setting out in longhand the calculations, it provides a useful model to apply in other, less straightforward, situations.

Example 21.32: Measuring effectiveness for a hedge of a forecast transaction in a debt instrument

A forecast investment in an interest-earning asset or forecast issue of an interest-bearing liability creates a cash flow exposure to interest rate changes because the related interest payments will be based on the market rate that exists when the forecast transaction occurs. The objective of a cash flow hedge of the exposure to interest rate changes is to offset the effects of future changes in interest rates so as to obtain a single fixed rate, usually the rate that existed at the inception of the hedge that corresponds with the term and timing of the forecast transaction. However, during the period of the hedge, it is not possible to determine what the market interest rate for the forecast transaction will be at the time the hedge is terminated or when the forecast transaction occurs.

During this period, effectiveness can be measured on the basis of changes in interest rates between the designation date and the interim effectiveness measurement date. The interest rates used to make this measurement are the interest rates that correspond with the term and occurrence of the forecast transaction that existed at the inception of the hedge and that exist at the measurement date as evidenced by the term structure of interest rates.

Generally it will not be sufficient simply to compare cash flows of the hedged item with cash flows generated by the derivative hedging instrument as they are paid or received, since such an approach ignores the entity's expectations of whether the cash flows will offset in subsequent periods and whether there will be any resulting ineffectiveness.

It is assumed that Company X expects to issue a €100,000 one-year debt instrument in three months. The instrument will pay interest quarterly with principal due at maturity. X is exposed to interest rate increases and establishes a hedge of the interest cash flows of the debt by entering into a forward starting interest rate swap. The swap has a term of one year and will start in three months to correspond with the terms of the forecast debt issue. X will pay a fixed rate and receive a variable rate, and it designates the risk being hedged as the LIBOR-based interest component in the forecast issue of the debt.

Yield curve

The yield curve provides the foundation for computing future cash flows and the fair value of such cash flows both at the inception of, and during, the hedging relationship. It is based on current market yields on applicable reference bonds that are traded in the marketplace. Market yields are converted to spot interest rates ('spot rates' or 'zero coupon rates') by eliminating the effect of coupon payments on the market yield. Spot rates are used to discount future cash flows, such as principal and interest rate payments, to arrive at their fair value. Spot rates also are used to compute forward interest rates that are used to compute variable and estimated future cash flows. The relationship between spot rates and one-period forward rates is shown by the following formula:

Spot-forward relationship

$$F = \frac{(1 + SR_t)^t}{(1 + SR_{t-1})^{t-1}} - 1$$

where F = forward rate (%)

SR = spot rate (%)

t = period in time (e.g. 1, 2, 3, 4, 5)

It is assumed that the following quarterly-period term structure of interest rates using quarterly compounding exists at the inception of the hedge.

Yield curve at inception (beginning of period 1)

Forward periods	*1*	*2*	*3*	*4*	*5*
Spot rates	3.75%	4.50%	5.50%	6.00%	6.25%
Forward rates	3.75%	5.25%	7.51%	7.50%	7.25%

The one-period forward rates are computed on the basis of spot rates for the applicable maturities. For example, the current forward rate for Period 2 calculated using the formula above is equal to $[1.0450^2 \div 1.0375] - 1 = 5.25\%$. The current one-period forward rate for Period 2 is different from the current spot rate for Period 2, since the spot rate is an interest rate from the beginning of Period 1 (spot) to the end of Period 2, while the forward rate is an interest rate from the beginning of Period 2 to the end of Period 2.

Hedged item

In this example, X expects to issue a €100,000 one-year debt instrument in three months with quarterly interest payments. X is exposed to interest rate increases and would like to eliminate the effect on cash flows of interest rate changes that may happen before the forecast transaction takes place. If that risk is eliminated, X would obtain an interest rate on its debt issue that is equal to the one-year forward coupon rate currently available in the marketplace in three months. That forward coupon rate, which is different from the forward (spot) rate, is 6.86%, computed from the term structure of interest rates shown above. It is the market rate of interest that exists at the inception of the hedge, given the terms of the forecast debt instrument. It results in the fair value of the debt being equal to par at its issue.

At the inception of the hedging relationship, the expected cash flows of the debt instrument can be calculated on the basis of the existing term structure of interest rates. For this purpose, it is assumed that interest rates do not change and that the debt would be issued at 6.86% at the beginning of Period 2. In this case, the cash flows and fair value of the debt instrument would be as follows at the beginning of Period 2.

Issue of fixed rate debt (beginning of period 2) – no rate changes (spot based on forward rates)

	Total					
Original forward periods		*1*	*2*	*3*	*4*	*5*
Remaining periods			*1*	*2*	*3*	*4*
Spot rates			5.25%	6.38%	6.75%	6.88%
Forward rates			5.25%	7.51%	7.50%	7.25%
	€		€	€	€	€
Cash flows:						
Fixed interest at 6.86%			1,716	1,716	1,716	1,716
Principal						100,000
Fair value:						
Interest*	6,592		1,694	1,663	1,632	1,603
Principal*	93,408					93,408
	100,000					

* cash flow discounted at the spot rate for the relevant period, e.g. fair value of principal is calculated as €100,000 ÷ $(1 + [0.0688 \div 4])^4$ = €93,408

Since it is assumed that interest rates do not change, the fair value of the interest and principal amounts equals the par amount of the forecast transaction. The fair value amounts are computed on the basis of the spot rates that exist at the inception of the hedge for the applicable periods in which the cash flows would occur had the debt been issued at the date of the forecast transaction. They reflect the effect of discounting those cash flows on the basis of the periods that will remain after the debt instrument is issued. For example, the spot rate of 6.38% is used to discount the interest cash flow that is expected to be paid in Period 3, but it is discounted for only two periods because it will occur two periods after the forecast transaction.

The forward interest rates are the same as shown previously, since it is assumed that interest rates do not change. The spot rates are different but they have not actually changed. They represent the spot rates one period forward and are based on the applicable forward rates.

Hedging instrument

The objective of the hedge is to obtain an overall interest rate on the forecast transaction and the hedging instrument that is equal to 6.86%, which is the market rate at the inception of the hedge for the period from Period 2 to Period 5. This objective is accomplished by entering into a forward starting interest rate swap that has a fixed rate of 6.86%. Based on the term structure of interest rates that exist at the inception of the hedge, the interest rate swap will have such a rate. At the inception of the hedge, the fair value of the fixed rate payments on the interest rate swap will equal the fair value of the variable rate payments, resulting in the interest rate swap having a fair value of zero. The expected cash flows of the interest rate swap and the related fair value amounts are shown as follows.

Interest rate swap

	Total					
Original forward periods		*1*	*2*	*3*	*4*	*5*
Remaining periods			*1*	*2*	*3*	*4*
	€		€	€	€	€
Cash flows:						
Fixed interest at 6.86%			1,716	1,716	1,716	1,716
Forecast variable interest*			1,313	1,877	1,876	1,813
Forecast based on forward rate			*5.25%*	*7.51%*	*7.50%*	*7.25%*
Net interest			(403)	161	160	97
Fair value						
Discount rate (spot)			*5.25%*	*6.38%*	*6.75%*	*6.88%*
Fixed interest	6,592		1,694	1,663	1,632	1,603
Forecast variable interest	6,592		1,296	1,819	1,784	1,693
Fair value of interest rate swap	0		(398)	156	152	90

* forecast variable rate cash flow based on forward rate, e.g. €1,313 = €100,000 × (0.0525 ÷ 4)

At the inception of the hedge, the fixed rate on the forward swap is equal to the fixed rate X would receive if it could issue the debt in three months under terms that exist today.

Measuring hedge effectiveness

If interest rates change during the period the hedge is outstanding, the effectiveness of the hedge can be measured in various ways.

Assume that interest rates change as follows immediately before the debt is issued at the beginning of Period 2 (this effectively uses the yield curve existing at Period 1 with a 200 basis point (2%) shift).

Yield curve assumption

Forward periods	*1*	*2*	*3*	*4*	*5*
Remaining periods		*1*	*2*	*3*	*4*
Spot rates		5.75%	6.50%	7.50%	8.00%
Forward rates		5.75%	7.25%	9.51%	9.50%

Under the new interest rate environment, the fair value of the pay-fixed at 6.86%, receive-variable interest rate swap that was designated as the hedging instrument would be as follows.

Fair value of interest rate swap

	Total					
Original forward periods		*1*	*2*	*3*	*4*	*5*
Remaining periods			*1*	*2*	*3*	*4*
	€		€	€	€	€
Cash flows:						
Fixed interest at 6.86%			1,716	1,716	1,716	1,716
Forecast variable interest			1,438	1,813	2,377	2,376
Forecast based on new forward rate			*5.75%*	*7.25%*	*9.51%*	*9.50%*
Net interest			(279)	97	661	660
Fair value						
New discount rate (spot)			*5.75%*	*6.50%*	*7.50%*	*8.00%*
Fixed interest	6,562		1,692	1,662	1,623	1,585
Forecast variable interest	7,615		1,417	1,755	2,248	2,195
Fair value of interest rate swap	1,053		(275)	93	625	610

In order to compute the effectiveness of the hedge, it is necessary to measure the change in the present value of the cash flows or the value of the hedged forecast transaction. There are at least two methods of accomplishing this measurement.

Method A – Compute change in fair value of debt

	Total					
Original forward periods		*1*	*2*	*3*	*4*	*5*
Remaining periods			*1*	*2*	*3*	*4*
	€		€	€	€	€
Cash flows:						
Fixed interest at 6.86%			1,716	1,716	1,716	1,716
Principal						100,000
Fair value:						
New discount rate (spot)			*5.75%*	*6.50%*	*7.50%*	*8.00%*
Interest	6,562		1,692	1,662	1,623	1,585
Principal	92,385					*92,385
Total	98,947					
Fair value at inception	100,000					
Difference	(1,053)					

* €100,000 ÷ $(1 + [0.08 \div 4])^4$

Under Method A, a computation is made of the fair value in the new interest rate environment of debt that carries interest that is equal to the coupon interest rate that existed at the inception of the hedging relationship (6.86%). This fair value is compared with the expected fair value as of the beginning of Period 2 that was calculated on the basis of the term structure of interest rates that existed at the inception of the hedging relationship, as illustrated above, to determine the change in the fair value. Note that the difference between the change in the fair value of the swap and the change in the expected fair value of the debt (€1,053) exactly offset in this example, since the terms of the swap and the forecast transaction match each other.

Method B – Compute change in fair value of cash flows

	Total					
Original forward periods		*1*	*2*	*3*	*4*	*5*
Remaining periods			*1*	*2*	*3*	*4*
Market rate at inception			6.86%	6.86%	6.86%	6.86%
Current forward rate			5.75%	7.25%	9.51%	9.50%
Rate difference			1.11%	(0.39%)	(2.64%)	(2.64%)
Cash flow difference (principal × rate)			€279	(€97)	(€661)	(€660)
Discount rate (spot)			*5.75%*	*6.50%*	*7.50%*	*8.00%*
Fair value of difference	(€1,053)		€275	(€93)	(€625)	(€610)

Under Method B, the present value of the change in cash flows is computed on the basis of the difference between the forward interest rates for the applicable periods at the effectiveness measurement date and the interest rate that would have been obtained if the debt had been issued at the market rate that existed at the inception of the hedge. The market rate that existed at the inception of the hedge is the one-year forward coupon rate in three months. The present value of the change in cash flows is computed on the basis of the current spot rates that exist at the effectiveness measurement date for the applicable periods in which the cash flows are expected to occur. This method also could be referred to as the 'theoretical swap' method (or 'hypothetical derivative' method) because the comparison is between the hedged fixed rate on the debt and the current variable rate, which is the same as comparing cash flows on the fixed and variable rate legs of an interest rate swap.

As before, the difference between the change in the fair value of the swap and the change in the present value of the cash flows exactly offset in this example, since the terms match.

Other considerations

There is an additional computation that should be performed to compute ineffectiveness before the expected date of the forecast transaction that has not been considered for the purpose of this illustration. The fair value difference has been determined in each of the illustrations as of the expected date of the forecast transaction immediately before the forecast transaction, i.e. at the beginning of Period 2. If the assessment of hedge effectiveness is performed before the forecast transaction occurs, the difference should be discounted to the current date to arrive at the actual amount of ineffectiveness. For example, if the measurement date were one month after the hedging relationship was established and the forecast transaction is now expected to occur in two months, the amount would have to be discounted for the remaining two months before the forecast transaction is expected to occur to arrive at the actual fair value. This step would not be necessary in the examples provided above because there was no ineffectiveness. Therefore, additional discounting of the amounts, which net to zero, would not have changed the result.

Under Method B, ineffectiveness is computed on the basis of the difference between the forward coupon interest rates for the applicable periods at the effectiveness measurement date and the interest rate that would have been obtained if the debt had been issued at the market rate that existed at the inception of the hedge. Computing the change in cash flows based on the difference between the forward interest rates that existed at the inception of the hedge and the forward rates that exist at the effectiveness measurement date is inappropriate if the objective of the hedge is to establish a single fixed rate for a series of forecast interest payments. This objective is met by hedging the exposures with an interest rate swap as illustrated in the above example. The fixed interest rate on the swap is a blended interest rate composed of the forward rates over the life of the swap. Unless the yield curve is flat, the comparison between the forward interest rate exposures over the life of the swap and the fixed rate on the swap will produce different cash flows whose fair values are equal only at the inception of the hedging relationship. This difference is shown in the table below.

	Total					
Original forward periods		*1*	*2*	*3*	*4*	*5*
Remaining periods			*1*	*2*	*3*	*4*
Forward rate at inception			5.25%	7.51%	7.50%	7.25%
Current forward rate			5.75%	7.25%	9.51%	9.50%
Rate difference			(0.50%)	0.26%	(2.00%)	(2.25%)
Cash flow difference (principal × rate)			(€125)	€64	(€501)	(€563)
Discount rate (spot)			*5.75%*	*6.50%*	*7.50%*	*8.00%*
Fair value of difference	€1,055		(€123)	€62	(€474)	(€520)
Fair value of interest rate swap	€1,053					
Ineffectiveness	(€2)					

If the objective of the hedge is to obtain the forward rates that existed at the inception of the hedge, the interest rate swap is ineffective because the swap has a single blended fixed coupon rate that does not offset a series of different forward interest rates. However, if the objective of the hedge is to obtain the forward coupon rate that existed at the inception of the hedge, the swap is effective, and the comparison based on differences in forward interest rates suggests ineffectiveness when none may exist. Computing ineffectiveness based on the difference between the forward interest rates that existed at the inception of the hedge and the forward rates that exist at the effectiveness measurement date would be an appropriate measurement of ineffectiveness if the hedging objective is to lock in those forward interest rates. In that case, the appropriate hedging instrument would be a series of forward contracts each of which matures on a repricing date that corresponds with the date of the forecast transactions.

It also should be noted that it would be inappropriate to compare only the variable cash flows on the interest rate swap with the interest cash flows in the debt that would be generated by the forward interest rates. That methodology has the effect of measuring ineffectiveness only on a portion of the derivative, and IAS 39 does not permit the bifurcation of a derivative for the purposes of assessing effectiveness in this situation (a point reiterated recently by the IFRIC[218]) – see 2.1.4 above. It is recognised, however, that if the fixed interest rate on the interest rate swap is equal to the fixed rate that would have been obtained on the debt at inception, there will be no ineffectiveness assuming that there are no differences in terms and no change in credit risk or it is not designated in the hedging relationship.[219]

5.3.3 Dollar-offset: comparison of spot rate and forward rate methods

It was explained at 2.1.4 above that the spot and interest elements of a forward contract could be treated separately for the purposes of hedge designation. The next example, based on the implementation guidance, contrasts two variations of the dollar-offset method. Case 1 can be used when the whole of a forward contract is treated as the hedging instrument and the hedged risk is identified by reference to changes attributable to the forward rate (forward rate method). Case 2 can be used when the interest component is excluded and the hedged risk is identified by reference to changes attributable to the spot rate (spot rate method).

To demonstrate these methods, the implementation guidance uses a type of hedge that is very common in practice, the hedging of foreign currency risk associated with future purchases using a forward exchange contract. The example also illustrates the difference in the accounting for such hedges depending on whether the spot and interest elements of a forward contract are treated separately for the purposes of hedge designation.

Example 21.33: Cash flow hedge of firm commitment to purchase inventory in a foreign currency

Company A has the Local Currency (LC) as its functional and presentation currency. A's accounting policy is to apply basis adjustments to non-financial assets that result from hedged forecast transactions and it chooses to treat hedges of the foreign currency risk of a firm commitment as cash flow hedges.

On 30 June 2008, A enters into a forward exchange contract to receive Foreign Currency (FC) 100,000 and deliver LC109,600 on 30 June 2009 at an initial cost and fair value of zero. On inception, it designates the forward exchange contract as a hedging instrument in a cash flow hedge of a firm commitment to purchase a certain quantity of paper for FC100,000 on 31 March 2009 and, thereafter, as a fair value hedge of the resulting payable of FC100,000, which is to be paid on 30 June 2009. It is assumed that all hedge accounting conditions in IAS 39 are met.

On 30 June 2008, the spot exchange rate is LC1.072 to FC1, while the twelve-month forward exchange rate is LC1.096 to FC1. On 31 December 2008, the spot exchange rate is LC1.080 to FC1, while the six-month forward exchange rate is LC1.092 to FC1. On 31 March 2009, the spot exchange rate is LC1.074 to FC1, while the three-month forward rate is LC1.076 to FC1. On 30 June 2009, the spot exchange rate is LC1.072 to FC1. The applicable yield curve in the local currency is flat at 6% per annum throughout the period. The fair value of the forward exchange contract is negative LC388 on 31 December 2008 ($\{[1.092 \times 100{,}000] - 109{,}600\} \div 1.06^{(6/12)}$), negative LC1,971 on 31 March 2009 ($\{[1.076 \times 100{,}000] - 109{,}600\} \div 1.06^{(3/12)}$), and negative LC2,400 on 30 June 2009 (1.072 × 100,000 – 109,600).

This is summarised in the following table:

Date	Spot rate	Forward rate to 30 June 2009	Fair value of forward contract
30 June 2008	1.072	1.096	–
31 December 2008	1.080	1.092	(388)
31 March 2008	1.074	1.076	(1,971)
30 June 2008	1.072	–	(2,400)

Case 1: Changes in the fair value of the forward contract are designated in the hedge

The hedge is expected to be fully effective because the critical terms of the forward exchange contract and the purchase contract and the assessments of hedge effectiveness are based on the forward price.

The accounting entries are as follows.

30 June 2008

	LC	LC
Forward	–	
Cash		–

To record the forward exchange contract at its initial fair value, i.e. zero.

31 December 2008

	LC	LC
Equity	388	
Forward – liability		388

To record the change in the fair value of the forward contract between 30 June 2008 and 31 December 2008, i.e. 388 – 0 = LC388, in equity. The hedge is fully effective because the loss on the forward exchange contract, LC388, exactly offsets the change in cash flows associated with the purchase contract based on the forward price $\{([1.092 \times 100{,}000] - 109{,}600) \div 1.06^{(6/12)}\} - \{([1.096 \times 100{,}000] - 109{,}600) \div 1.06\} = -LC388$. The negative figure denotes a reduction in the net present value of cash outflows and, therefore, effectively represents a 'gain' to offset the loss on the forward in equity.

31 March 2009

	LC	LC
Equity	1,583	
Forward – liability		1,583

To record the change in the fair value of the forward contract between 1 January 2009 and 31 March 2009, i.e. 1,971 – 388 = LC1,583, in equity. The hedge is fully effective because the loss on the forward exchange contract, LC1,583, exactly offsets the change in cash flows associated with the purchase contract based on the forward price $\{([1.076 \times 100{,}000] - 109{,}600) \div 1.06^{(3/12)}\} - \{([1.092 \times 100{,}000] - 109{,}600) \div 1.06^{(6/12)}\} = -LC1{,}583$. The negative figure denotes a reduction in the net present value of cash outflows and, therefore, effectively represents a 'gain' to offset the loss on the forward in equity.

	LC	LC
Paper (purchase price)	107,400	
Paper (hedging loss)	1,971	
Equity		1,971
Payable		107,400

To record the purchase of the paper at the spot rate (1.074 × 100,000) and remove the cumulative loss on the forward reported in equity, LC1,971, and include it in the initial measurement of the purchased paper. Accordingly, the initial measurement of the purchased paper is LC 109,371 consisting of a purchase consideration of LC 107,400 and a hedging loss of LC 1,971.

30 June 2009

	LC	LC
Payable	107,400	
Cash		107,200
Profit or loss		200

To record the settlement of the payable at the spot rate (100,000 × 1.072 = LC107,200) and the associated exchange gain of LC200 = 107,400 – 107,200.

	LC	LC
Profit or loss	429	
Forward – liability		429

To record the loss on the forward exchange contract between 1 April 2009 and 30 June 2009, i.e. 2,400 – 1,971 = LC429) in profit or loss. The hedge is considered to be fully effective because the loss on the forward exchange contract, LC429, exactly offsets the change in the fair value of the payable based on the forward price [1.072 × 100,000] – 109,600 – {([1.076 × 100,000] – 109,600) ÷ $1.06^{(3/12)}$} = –LC429. The negative figure denotes a reduction in the net present value of the payable and, therefore represents a gain to offset the loss on the forward contract.

	LC	LC
Forward – liability	2,400	
Cash		2,400

To record the net settlement of the forward exchange contract.

Although this arrangement has been set up to be a 'perfect hedge', the loss on the forward in the last three months is significantly different from the gain recorded on retranslating the hedged payable. The principal reason for this is that the change in the fair value of the forward contract includes changes in its interest element, as well as its currency element. The interest element of the payable is generally not accounted for (even on an amortised cost basis) because it is immaterial (see Chapter 20 at 2.2).

Case 2: Changes in the spot element of the forward contract only are designated in the hedge

The hedge is expected to be fully effective because the critical terms of the forward exchange contract and the purchase contract are the same and the change in the premium or discount on the forward contract is excluded from the assessment of effectiveness.

30 June 2008

	LC	LC
Forward	–	
Cash		–

To record the forward exchange contract at its initial fair value, i.e. zero.

31 December 2008

	LC	LC
Profit or loss (interest element of forward)	1,165	
Equity (spot element)		777
Forward – liability		388

To record the change in the fair value of the forward contract between 30 June 2008 and 31 December 2008, i.e. 388 – 0 = LC388. The change in the present value of spot settlement of the forward exchange contract is a gain of LC777 = {([1.080 × 100,000] – 107,200) ÷ $1.06^{(6/12)}$} – {([1.072 × 100,000] – 107,200) ÷ 1.06}), which is recognised directly in equity. The change in the interest element of the forward exchange contract (the residual change in fair value) is a loss of LC1,165 = 388 + 777, which is recognised in profit or loss. The hedge is fully effective because the gain in the spot element of the forward contract, LC777, exactly offsets the change in the purchase price at spot rates {([1.080 × 100,000] – 107,200) ÷ $1.06^{(6/12)}$} – {([1.072 × 100,000] – 107,200) ÷ 1.06} = LC777. The positive figure denotes an increase in the net present value of cash outflows and, therefore, effectively represents a 'loss' to offset the gain on the forward in equity.

31 March 2009

	LC	LC
Equity (spot element)	580	
Profit or loss (interest element)	1,003	
Forward – liability		1,583

To record the change in the fair value of the forward contract between 1 January 2009 and 31 March 2009, i.e. 1,971 – 388 = LC1,583. The change in the present value of spot settlement of the forward exchange contract is a loss of LC580 = $\{([1.074 \times 100{,}000] - 107{,}200) \div 1.06^{(3/12)}\} - \{([1.080 \times 100{,}000] - 107{,}200) \div 1.06^{(6/12)}\}$, which is recognised in equity. The change in the interest element of the forward contract (the residual change in fair value) is a loss of LC1,003 = 1,583 – 580), which is recognised in profit or loss. The hedge is fully effective because the loss in the spot element of the forward contract, LC580, exactly offsets the change in the purchase price at spot rates $\{([1.074 \times 100{,}000] - 107{,}200) \div 1.06^{(3/12)}\} - \{([1.080 \times 100{,}000] - 107{,}200) \div 1.06^{(6/12)}\}$ = –LC580. The negative figure denotes a reduction in the net present value of cash outflows and, therefore, effectively represents a 'gain' to offset the loss on the forward in equity.

	LC	LC
Paper (purchase price)	107,400	
Equity	197	
Paper (hedging gain)		197
Payable		107,400

To recognise the purchase of the paper at the spot rate (= 1.074 × 100,000) and remove the cumulative gain on the spot element of the forward contract that has been recognised in equity (777 – 580 = LC197) and include it in the initial measurement of the purchased paper. Accordingly, the initial measurement of the purchased paper is LC107,203 consisting of a purchase consideration of LC107,400 and a hedging gain of LC197.

30 June 2009

	LC	LC
Payable	107,400	
Cash		107,200
Profit or loss		200

To record the settlement of the payable at the spot rate (100,000 × 1.072 = LC107,200) and the associated exchange gain of LC200 (= – [1.072 – 1.074] × 100,000).

	LC	LC
Profit or loss (spot element)	197	
Profit or loss (interest element)	232	
Forward – liability		429

To record the change in the fair value of the forward between 1 April 2009 and 30 June 2009, i.e. 2,400 – 1,971 = LC429). The change in the present value of spot settlement of the forward exchange contract is a loss of LC197 = $\{[1.072 \times 100{,}000] - 107{,}200 - \{([1.074 \times 100{,}000] - 107{,}200) \div 1.06^{(3/12)}\}$, which is recognised in profit or loss. The change in the interest element of the forward contract (the residual change in fair value) is a loss of LC232 = 429 –197, which is recognised in profit or loss. The hedge is fully effective because the loss in the spot element of the forward contract, LC197, exactly offsets the gain on the payable reported using spot rates = $\{[1.072 \times 100{,}000] - 107{,}200 - \{([1.074 \times 100{,}000] - 107{,}200) \div 1.06^{(3/12)}\}$ = –LC197. The negative figure denotes a reduction in the net present value of the payable and, therefore represents a gain to offset the loss on the forward contract.

	LC	LC
Forward – liability	2,400	
Cash		2,400

To record the net settlement of the forward exchange contract.

The following table provides an overview of the components of the change in fair value of the hedging instrument over the term of the hedging relationship. It illustrates that the way in which a hedging relationship is designated affects the subsequent accounting for that hedging relationship, including the assessment of hedge effectiveness and the recognition of gains and losses.[220]

Period ending	Change in spot settlement LC	Fair value of change in spot settlement LC	Change in forward settlement LC	Fair value of change in forward settlement LC	Fair value of change in interest element LC
30 June 2008	–	–	–	–	–
31 December 2008	800	777	(400)	(388)	(1,165)
31 March 2009	(600)	(580)	(1,600)	(1,583)	(1,003)
30 June 2009	(200)	(197)	(400)	(429)	(232)
Total	–	–	(2,400)	(2,400)	(2,400)

In each case, the hedge is perfectly effective because of the way effectiveness is measured, but there is a significant difference on profit or loss. In part (a) all gains and losses on the forward are initially deferred in equity whereas in part (b) changes in the fair value of the interest element of the forward are immediately recognised in profit or loss. The example also sets out how a single hedge can initially be a cash flow hedge of the future sale and then become a fair value hedge of the associated payable, provided it is documented as such.

5.3.4 Law of small numbers

As set out at 5.3.2 above, the dollar-offset method of assessing effectiveness is commonly used because it requires limited additional effort over and above that required to determine the amount of ineffectiveness to be recorded in profit or loss. However, there can be significant problems in achieving high correlation, particularly when the actual movements in fair value or cash flows of the hedging instrument and hedged item are small.

Consider a fair value hedge of a fixed interest rate bond where interest rates barely change in the period. The change in fair value of the hedging instrument for the period might be €1,000 and the corresponding change in fair value of the hedged item €2,000, being an increase from €1,000,000 to €1,002,000. This would indicate that the hedging relationship was only 50% effective and would therefore not qualify for hedge accounting. However, the changes in fair value are very small in relation to the fair value of the contract being hedged. In fact it might be possible to demonstrate that had interest rates moved by a more noticeable amount, the change in value of the hedged item and the hedging instrument would have been, say, €50,000 and €49,000 respectively, i.e. the strategy would actually have been highly effective. This scenario is often described as 'the law of small numbers' problem. Although well documented, the standard does not address this phenomenon and certainly offers no insight as to how an entity might deal with it.

A common approach, for the purposes of *assessing* hedge effectiveness, is simply to ignore changes in fair value that are below a given fixed limit (strictly, for the purpose of *measuring* ineffectiveness, these amounts should be recorded but they will not be material). This limit should be established at the inception of the hedge and should be included in the hedge documentation. Care should be taken in setting this limit – too high and the entity could be accused of not establishing an appropriate method of assessing effectiveness; too low and the risk of failing the assessment is increased.

5.3.5 Hedging using instruments with a non-zero fair value

The application guidance to IAS 39 states that a hedge of a highly probable forecast purchase of a commodity with a forward contract is likely to be highly effective if, among other things, the fair value of the forward contract at inception is zero (see 5.3.9 below). A non-optional derivative, such as a forward or swap contract, that has a non-zero fair value is unlikely to be a perfectly effective hedging instrument, especially in a cash flow hedge. This is because the derivative contains a 'financing' element (the initial fair value), gains and losses on which will not be replicated in the hedged item and therefore the hedge contains an inherent source of ineffectiveness. In extreme cases it may not be possible to determine that the hedge will be highly effective. This situation can arise when a derivative is designated or redesignated in a hedging relationship subsequent to its initial recognition or in a business combination (see 5.1.1 above).[221]

5.3.6 Regression analysis and other statistical methods

The use of regression analysis is referred to in the standard in the context of optimising the ratio of hedging instrument quantities to hedged item quantities in order to improve the effectiveness of a hedge.[222] The implementation guidance also explains (as noted at 5.3.1 above) that statistical measurement techniques such as regression analysis may also be used for assessing hedge effectiveness.[223] This section sets out the basic concepts underlying linear regression analysis, together with guidelines and considerations that we believe are appropriate when determining whether a hedge relationship can be considered highly effective when using this approach to test effectiveness.

A Basic concepts of regression

Linear regression is a method of identifying and describing the relationship between variables, for example y and x; linear refers to the assumption of a straight-line relationship between the variables. Regression analysis identifies a line of 'best fit' through a swarm of data using least squares analysis to minimise the total squared distances of the plotted points from the line. Some regression analyses will indicate a wider scatter of data points around the regression line than others; these wider scatters indicate a relationship between the variables that is less strong than a regression with a narrow scatter.

The regression is represented by the algebraic formula:

$$y = \alpha + \beta x + \varepsilon$$

In this equation, y is the dependent variable, x is the independent variable, α is the intercept, β is the slope of the regression line, and ε is the residual, or error term. In the context of hedge effectiveness, it is convenient to define y as the change in the fair value of the hedged item, and x as the change in fair value of the hedging instrument.

The following example of a regression describes the formula's terms in more detail:

Figure 21.1: The line of best fit, drawn through a series of correlated observations of changes in the x and y variables (such a line is likely to incorporate a non-zero intercept, if only due to random error)

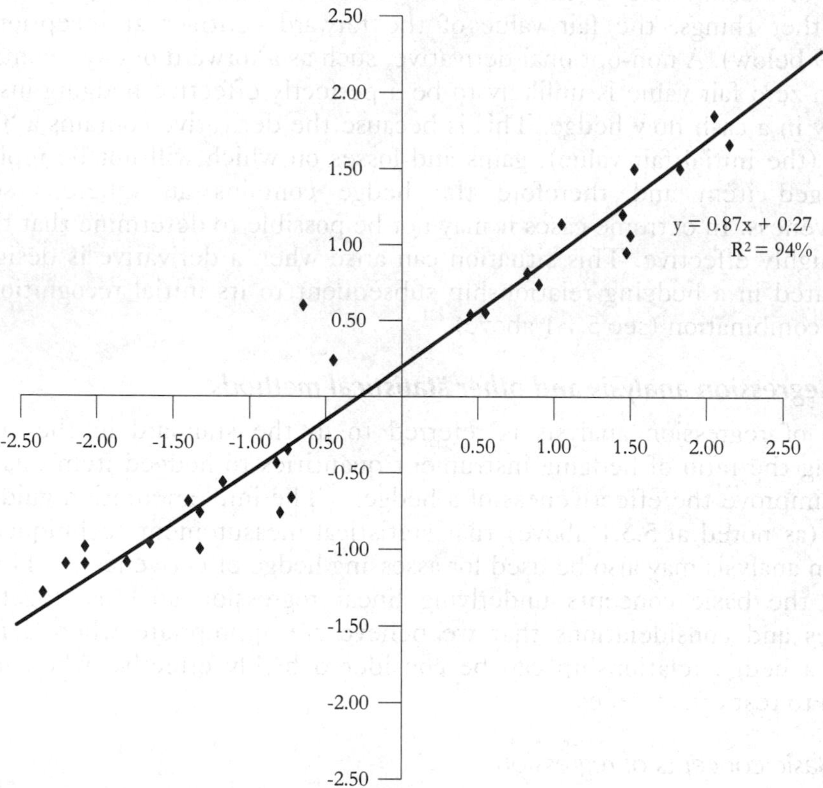

The coefficient of determination, R^2, is the percentage of the variance in y that is 'explained' by x, and is a measure of the tightness of the distribution around the regression line. In the example above, an R^2 value of 94% indicates that 94% of the variance in y can be explained by x. When assessing hedge effectiveness, the closer the line is to the actual results, the less ineffectiveness there will be. Higher R^2 values indicate a stronger relationship. The square root of this value, R, is often referred to as the coefficient of correlation. We consider that the value of R^2 should be at least 80% in order to indicate an effective hedge relationship.

The slope of the regression line is known as β or beta. In Figure 21.1 above, the slope of 0.87 indicates that, given an increase in x of 1, we would expect an increase in y of 0.87.

As noted at 2.2.2 above, IAS 39 describes a situation in which expected hedge effectiveness is maximised if the ratio between the hedging instrument and the hedged item is set at a level other than 1.00. In such circumstances it may be easier to demonstrate hedge effectiveness by multiplying the y observations by the hedge ratio so as to bring the slope closer to 1.

The intercept is the point at which the regression line crosses the y-axis – the expected value of y when x is 0. In Figure 21.1 above, the intercept is 0.27. The presence of a non-zero intercept increases the likelihood of hedge ineffectiveness, as it implies that y will change even when there is no change in x. While a small y intercept will not necessarily invalidate a hedging relationship, it is easier to demonstrate that a hedge is effective by forcing the line of regression to have a y intercept of zero, although this will reduce the value of R^2, and may also alter the slope. The chart below illustrates the impact of forcing the regression line through the origin. The effect is a reduction of the R^2 to 88% but (as described further below) an increase in the 'confidence' of the estimate.

Figure 21.2: The line of best fit, drawn through a series of correlated x and y movements so that it passes though the origin

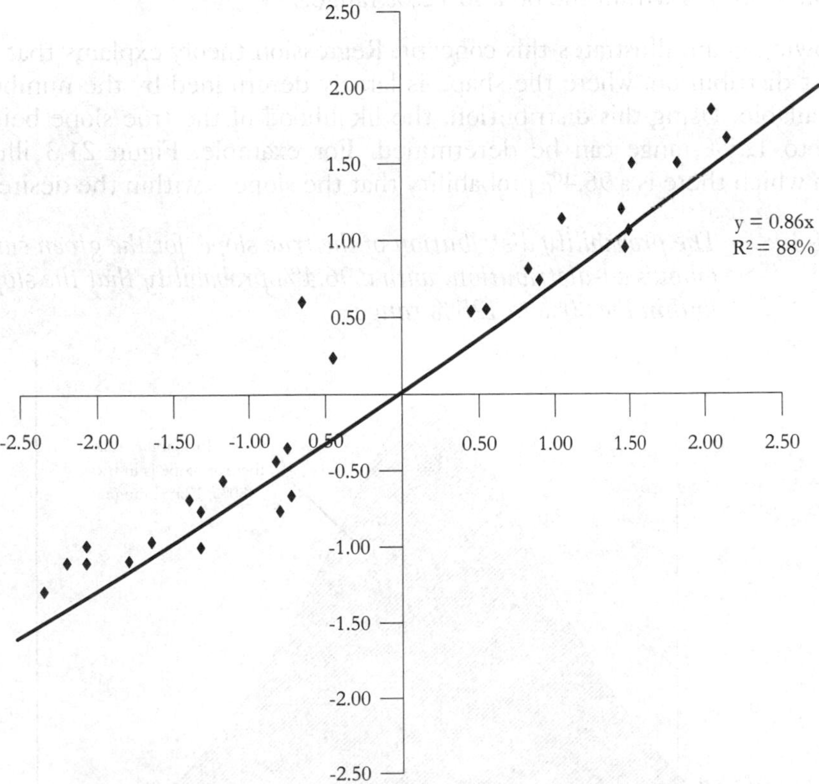

When performing regression analysis, an important notion is the concept of the sample as opposed to the population. The sample represents observations, whereas the population is the relationship between the variables that we are attempting to find. Estimates of the parameters of the population are based on the parameters of the sample. Statistical techniques can be used to express the confidence in the estimate.

For this reason, it is important to consider the statistical significance of the sample regression parameters: the degree to which the sample will provide an indication of the true (population) regression parameters. This will largely be driven by the number of data points sampled and the consistency between these points. Without some consideration of the confidence in the regression analysis, it is possible that a high R^2 could be calculated and an appropriate slope based on the sample (implying that a hedge will be highly effective), even though the sample is not a fair reflection of the population as a whole. If this were the case, it would not be appropriate to conclude that the hedge relationship will be highly effective, and there is a higher possibility of the hedge relationship failing to satisfy a retrospective test of effectiveness in future periods.

There are a number of methods that can be used to assess the significance of the regression, including the sample size, T tests, F tests and P statistics. While these tests, when performed appropriately, are largely consistent, we recommend incorporating all tests into a single methodology to ensure sufficient statistical significance e.g. a 95% confidence that the actual population slope (as compared to the sample slope) is within the 80% to 125% range.

The following graph illustrates this concept. Regression theory explains that the slope follows a t-distribution, where the shape is largely determined by the number of data points available. Using this distribution, the likelihood of the true slope being within the 80% to 125% range can be determined. For example, Figure 21.3 illustrates a sample in which there is a 96.4% probability that the slope is within the desired range.

Figure 21.3: *The probability distribution of the true slope, for the given sample, follows a t-distribution, with a 96.4% probability that the slope is within the 80% to 125% range*

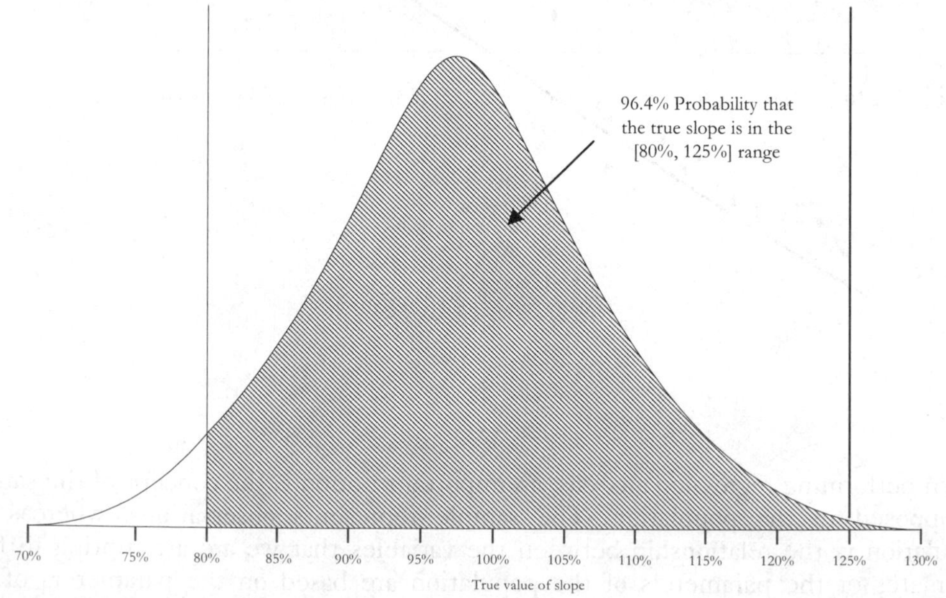

The error term ε represents the unpredicted or unexplained variation in the hedged item. In a perfectly valid regression, the error terms should be normally distributed, with constant variance, and should be independent of each other (i.e. should have no 'autocorrelation'[224]). This is an impossible expectation for real market data as financial markets almost always incorporate autocorrelation of some sort. However the imperfections most likely to invalidate regression conclusions, such as significant trends, are less likely to occur in financial price data due to the existence of arbitrage activities that take advantage of such inefficiencies.

Finally, when considering whether to use regression analysis, we believe that there must be a logical, a priori, expectation of a relationship between the relevant variables. It would be inappropriate to establish a hedge relationship based solely on statistics, as there is a greater possibility of the hedge relationship being coincidental or temporary, and so breaking down in the future if it has no ongoing economic or intuitive rationale.

B Summary

In order to assess a hedge relationship as highly effective (either on a prospective or retrospective basis) using regression analysis, we believe that all of the following criteria should normally be met:

- the line of best fit passes through the origin;
- the value of R^2 is at least 80%;
- there is at least 95% confidence that the true population slope of the line is within the 80% to 125% range; and
- there is an intuitive economic rationale for the hedge relationship.

Whilst a regression analysis that does not comply with these guidelines is not necessarily invalid, in such circumstances, consideration should be given so that inappropriate reliance on the regression analysis is avoided.

Finally, as noted at 5.3.1 above, the IFRIC concluded that if regression analysis, as the originally documented method for assessing hedge retrospective hedge effectiveness, demonstrated that a hedge had been effective but a 'dollar-offset' test would have fallen outside of the 80-125% range, hedge accounting would not necessarily be precluded.[225] However, in such instances, care should be taken to ensure that the regression analysis remains valid, especially if the dollar-offset comparison regularly falls outside of the range.

5.3.7 'Almost fully offset' and under-hedging

In the original version of the standard, the prospective test was expressed as 'almost fully offset', whereas the retrospective test was 'within a range of 80% to 125%'.[226] This requirement appeared to be significantly more onerous than the equivalent test under US GAAP, which is described in terms of 'highly effective' expectations. Consequently, during the improvements project, many commentators suggested that the IASB amend IAS 39 to be more consistent with US GAAP in this respect.

However, the IASB was concerned that, without this requirement, entities might wish to purposely hedge, say, 85% of the total exposure and designate this as a hedge of 100% of the exposure. For a cash flow hedge, this could reduce the amount of ineffectiveness recognised (see 4.2.1 above) and the previous implementation guidance explained that under-hedging in this way was not permitted because such a hedge would fail the 'almost fully offset' aspect of the prospective test.[227] Therefore, the original wording was initially retained in order to prevent entities from under-hedging, but this was not the end of the issue.[228]

When finalising the requirements for portfolio hedges of interest rate risk (see 6 below), the IASB received further representations that many hedges would fail the 'almost fully offset' test in IAS 39, including some that would qualify for the short-cut method in US GAAP (see 5.3.8 below) and thus be assumed to be 100% effective. This time, the IASB was persuaded and decided to remove the words 'almost fully offset' from the prospective test requirements (see 5.3.1 above).[229]

In order to address their concerns about under-hedging, the standard states that if an entity hedges less than 100% of the exposure on an item, such as 85%, it should designate the hedged item as being 85% of the exposure and measure ineffectiveness based on the change in that designated 85%. However, when hedging the designated 85% exposure, a hedge ratio of other than one to one may be used if that improves the expected effectiveness of the hedge, as explained at 2.2.2 above.[230]

5.3.8 'Short-cut method'

Under US GAAP, an entity is allowed to assume that there will be no ineffectiveness in a hedge of interest rate risk using an interest rate swap as the hedging instrument, provided specified criteria are met. This is known as the 'shortcut method' for assessing hedge effectiveness.[231] The original version of IAS 39 precluded such an approach and during the improvements project many commentators urged the IASB to permit the use of the short-cut method under IAS 39.[232] However, one of the general principles of IAS 39 is that ineffectiveness in a hedging relationship is measured and recognised in profit or loss and the IASB did not want to make an exception to this principle. Therefore, IAS 39 was not amended to permit the short-cut method.[233] Nevertheless, as set out at 5.3.9 below, an approach to assessing effectiveness may be adopted in some situations that requires only a little more effort than the short-cut method.

5.3.9 'Critical terms match' approach

The application guidance explains that if the principal terms of the hedging instrument and of the hedged asset, liability, firm commitment or highly probable forecast transaction are the same, the changes in fair value and cash flows attributable to the risk being hedged may be likely to offset each other fully, both when the hedge is entered into and afterwards. For example, a hedge of a highly probable forecast purchase of a commodity with a forward contract is likely to be highly effective if:

- the forward contract is for the purchase of the same quantity of the same commodity at the same time and location as the hedged forecast purchase;
- the fair value of the forward contract at inception is zero; and
- either the change in the discount or premium on the forward contract is excluded from the assessment of effectiveness and included directly in profit or loss or the change in expected cash flows on the forecast transaction is based on the forward price for the commodity (see 5.3.3 above).[234]

Similarly, an interest rate swap is likely to be an effective hedge if the notional and principal amounts, term, repricing dates, dates of interest and principal receipts and payments, and basis for measuring interest rates are the same for the hedging instrument and the hedged item.[235] However, if the fair value of the swap at inception of the hedge was not zero, a presumption that no ineffectiveness will arise would be as inappropriate in this case as it would for the forecast purchase of a commodity (see 5.3.5 above).

Sometimes the hedging instrument offsets only part of the hedged risk. For example, if the hedging instrument and hedged item are denominated in different currencies that do not move in tandem, the hedge would not be fully effective. Also, a hedge of interest rate risk using a derivative would not be fully effective if part of the change in the fair value of the derivative is attributable to the counterparty's credit risk.[236] Therefore, when assessing effectiveness, both at inception and thereafter, the risk of counterparty default should be considered. In a cash flow hedge, if default becomes probable the hedging relationship is unlikely to achieve offsetting cash flows and hedge accounting would be discontinued. In a fair value hedge, if there is a change in the counterparty's creditworthiness, the hedging instrument's fair value will change, which affects its effectiveness and hence whether it qualifies for continued hedge accounting.[237]

In deciding not to permit the short-cut method, the IASB noted that IAS 39 permits the hedging of portions of financial assets and liabilities in cases where US GAAP does not. Therefore, an entity may hedge a portion of a financial instrument (e.g. interest rate risk or credit risk – see 2.2.1 above) and if the critical terms of the hedging instrument and the hedged item are the same, the entity will, in many cases, recognise no ineffectiveness.[238] The implementation guidance continues with this theme and explains that, to improve hedge effectiveness, an entity may designate only certain risks in an overall exposure as being hedged. For example, if an interest rate swap issued by a counterparty with a AA credit rating is used to hedge the fair value of a fixed interest rate debt instrument, designating only the exposure in the debt related to AA rated interest rate movements will reduce the impact on effectiveness of market changes in credit spreads.[239] It is not clear that this technique would be permitted by the IASB's amendments dealing with 'portions' of hedged items – see 2.1.1 C above.

Therefore it can be seen, at least for hedges of financial items, that the designation of the hedge can be tailored to reduce significantly the ineffectiveness that can feasibly occur. However, because ineffectiveness may still arise because of other attributes (e.g.

liquidity of the hedging instrument or its credit risk), hedge effectiveness cannot be assumed throughout the life of the hedge even if the principal terms of the hedging instrument and hedged item are the same.[240] Consideration should also be given to the issues covered at 5.3.10 below, particularly the frequency with which variable interest rates are reset on an instrument such as an interest rate swap.

It is clear from the guidance discussed above that IAS 39 acknowledges a method of assessing *prospective* hedge effectiveness that involves comparing the critical terms of the hedging instrument and the hedged item, supplemented by a qualitative review of counterparty credit risk and other factors such as liquidity of the hedging instrument (a 'critical terms match' approach). What is less clear from the standard is whether such an approach should be considered acceptable for the ongoing *retrospective* test. Under US GAAP, SFAS 133 allows a 'critical terms match' approach to be used for retrospectively assessing the effectiveness of cash flow hedges,[241] leading some to believe that it is equally acceptable under IFRS. However, some would say that the lack of any equivalent guidance in IAS 39 means that a quantitative assessment is always necessary.

In many ways the extent of testing that is required in order to qualify for hedge accounting is not an accounting question, but a regulatory issue, and we have seen evidence of some regulators setting their own benchmarks as to what they consider to be appropriate methods to use in practice.

In fact the use of the critical terms match approach under US GAAP has recently come under close regulatory scrutiny. In December 2006 an SEC staff member indicated that a difference of 'a few days' between the settlement date of a forecasted transaction and the hedging instrument would prevent the use of the critical terms match approach.[242] This caused a great deal of uncertainty for those entities that had been using the approach for hedges of, say, the foreign currency risk associated with forecast transactions occurring in a given month, although the SEC ameliorated its stance slightly where it could be demonstrated by way of a quantitative analysis that the amount of ineffectiveness was de minimis.[243] Subsequently, after noting that 'many preparers are frustrated and have expressed the view that good-faith efforts to comply with Statement 133 are being second-guessed by auditors and regulators', the FASB initiated a project to resolve practical issues and simplify the accounting for hedging activities.[244]

In the light of these risks, entities need to carefully evaluate the use of seemingly simple methods of assessing effectiveness and, in general, a quantitative method is likely to give rise to a lower risk of challenge than a qualitative method. The risk is heightened because, if it is determined that the selected method of assessing effectiveness is inappropriate, then hedge accounting should arguably never have been applied even if the hedge was demonstrably effective by other means such as a simple dollar-offset calculation (an approach the SEC endorses).[245]

Nevertheless, we believe that qualitative methods may be justified in certain circumstances. For example, if the principal terms of a hedged forecast transaction and a hedging instrument *exactly* matched as noted above, a qualitative assessment would seem to offer no less assurance about the hedge's effectiveness than a dollar-offset calculation using a hypothetical derivative. However, we would expect the hedge documentation to identify a quantitative methodology (e.g. dollar-offset using a hypothetical derivative) to be used in the event that the critical terms ceased to match. In addition, an ongoing qualitative assessment should be performed and documented at least every reporting date to ensure that:

- the principal terms continue to match;
- and that there has been no change in any factors which would affect the fair value of the hedging instrument, such as a deterioration of the counterparty's credit rating; and
- there has been no change in the terms of the hedged item, such as the expected timing of cash flows.

If this review identifies any potential source of ineffectiveness, the quantitative assessment identified in the hedge documentation should be performed to determine whether the hedge remains highly effective. Finally, it should be remembered that hedge ineffectiveness should always be measured and recognised in profit or loss.

5.3.10 Interest accruals and 'clean' vs. 'dirty' values

Another problem that entities can face when assessing the effectiveness of hedging instruments such as interest rate swaps, is the fair value 'noise' that is generated between interest rate reset dates. The payments on an interest rate swap are typically established at the beginning of a reset period and paid at the end of that period. Between these two dates the swap is no longer a pure pay-fixed receive-variable (or vice versa) instrument because both the next payment and the next receipt are fixed. Accordingly, the corresponding changes in the fair value of the hedged item (e.g. fixed rate debt) will not strictly mirror that of the swap. This problem becomes more acute the less frequent it is that variable interest rates reset to market rates.

The IASB does not seem to see this as a potential source of ineffectiveness. For example, it is stated in IAS 39 that 'an interest rate swap is likely to be an effective hedge if the notional and principal amounts, term, repricing dates, dates of interest and principal receipts and payments, and basis for measuring interest rates are the same for the hedging instrument and the hedged item.'[246] Further, given the IASB's statements (see 5.3.9 above) regarding the decision not to permit the short-cut method, which is only available for hedge relationships involving interest rate swaps, it seems safe to assume that they do not normally expect ineffectiveness from interest rate repricings to arise on such relationships where the hedge is 'perfect'. In fact, it is interesting to note that the one comprehensive example showing the measurement of effectiveness of an interest rate swap (see Example 21.32 at 5.3.2 above) completely avoids this issue.

Entities are therefore left with little practical guidance in dealing with the apparent ineffectiveness that can result even from hedges that seem perfectly effective. A common approach to avoid much of this noise is to use 'clean' fair values (which effectively ignore the effects of the next net settlement or interest payment) rather than 'dirty' fair values (which includes them). The mathematics of an effectiveness assessment using this approach should mean there is a much lower likelihood of the hedge failing the test. This approach is likely to prove acceptable in many situations, especially where the interval between repricings is frequent enough, e.g. quarterly rather than yearly, so as to minimise the changes in fair value from the fixed net settlement or next interest payment. However, in principle, ineffectiveness should always be measured and recognised in profit or loss.

5.3.11 Effectiveness of options

It was explained at 2.1.4 A above that the time value of an option may be excluded from the hedge relationship and, in many cases, this may make it easier to demonstrate the effectiveness of a hedge. In such cases, if the documented hedged risk is appropriately customised there will, in many cases, be no ineffectiveness to record, as set out in the following example.

Example 21.34: Out of the money put option used to hedge an equity share

Company A has an investment in one hundred shares of Company Z. The share is classified as available-for-sale, therefore associated fair value gains and losses are recognised initially in equity. The shares have a quoted price of £100 each and to partially protect itself against decreases in the share price, A acquires a put option, which gives it the right to sell one hundred shares in Z for £90 each.

A is permitted to designate changes in the option's intrinsic value as the hedging instrument. The changes in the intrinsic value of the option provide protection against the risk of variability in Z's share price below or equal to the strike price of the put of £90. For prices above £90, the option is out of the money and has no intrinsic value. Accordingly, gains and losses on the shares in Z for prices above £90 are not attributable to the hedged risk for the purposes of assessing hedge effectiveness and recognising gains and losses on the hedged item.

Therefore, changes in the fair value of the shares in Z are recognised in equity if associated with variations in share price above £90. Changes in the fair value of the shares in Z associated with price declines below £90 form part of the designated fair value hedge and are recognised in profit or loss. Assuming the hedge is effective, those changes are offset by changes in the intrinsic value of the put, which are also recognised in profit or loss (see 4.1.1 above).

Changes in the time value of the put are excluded from the designated hedging relationship and recognised in profit or loss as they arise.[247]

The downside associated with designating the hedge in this way is that changes in the time value of the option are recognised in profit or loss, resulting in some inescapable volatility.

Under US GAAP, subsequent to the publication of SFAS 133, an interpretation was issued that set out a method of assessing effectiveness and measuring ineffectiveness of an entire option (i.e. including its time value) in certain cash flow hedges, which normally resulted in the measurement of no ineffectiveness.[248] This allows entities to defer all changes in the fair value of an option (including the time value) in equity until the hedged transaction affects profit or loss. Prior to this, the conventional wisdom was that the only way to assess effectiveness of a purchased option (or zero-cost collar) designated in a cash flow hedge was to focus on changes in the intrinsic value of the option.

From the perspective of IAS 39, this interpretation is problematic. The current consensus – to the extent there is one – appears to be that it is an exception to, rather than an interpretation of, the general principles of hedge accounting under US GAAP. Consequently, the use of this method has, to date, been seen by many as incompatible with IAS 39. Whilst the topic was brought to the attention of the IFRIC's Agenda Committee in July 2006,[249] it was first addressed by the IFRIC only in May 2007. At that time, the IFRIC tentatively agreed with the consensus view,[250] although it subsequently softened the way in which it expressed this view whilst noting that the IASB's project on 'portions' would make it clear that such an approach is not allowed by IAS 39 (see 2.2.1 C above).[251]

5.3.12 Net investment hedges

As discussed at 3.6 above, there can be a number of issues surrounding what constitutes a valid net investment hedge and the remainder of this section deals with some of the practical aspects of such hedges on the assumption that the hedge relationship is considered valid in those terms.

A Non-derivative liabilities used as the hedging instrument

It seems quite clear that a foreign currency denominated non-derivative financial liability, such as a borrowing, can be used as the hedging instrument in a hedge of a net investment in a foreign operation. This can be seen as a pure 'accounting' hedge, i.e. the retranslation gain or loss on the borrowing (an accounting entry representing a part of its change in fair value that is accounted for on a continuous basis) can offset the retranslation gain or loss on the net investment (another accounting entry). In fact, if the liability is:

- denominated in the same currency as the functional currency of the hedged net investment;
- has an amortised cost that is lower than the net investment in the foreign operation; and
- is designated appropriately,

the hedge is likely to be perfectly effective in terms of the offsetting retranslation gains and losses on the liability and the hedged proportion of the net investment.

If a borrowing or similar liability is denominated in a different currency to the functional currency of the net investment, it may still be possible to designate it as the hedging instrument. However, it will need to be demonstrated that the two currencies are sufficiently correlated so that the hedging instrument is expected to result in offsetting gains and losses over the period that the hedge is designated. This might be the case if the two currencies are formally pegged or otherwise linked to one another or if the relevant exchange rates move in tandem because of, say, similarities in the underlying economies.

Even if such a hedge is highly effective, it is likely to result in some ineffectiveness (unless the link between the two currencies is near-perfect). Under US GAAP it is suggested that the retranslation gains and losses on the actual instrument should be compared to those on a hypothetical non-derivative (e.g. a borrowing in the correct currency) with any difference reported in profit or loss.[252] This approach should normally be acceptable under IAS 39.

B Derivatives used as the hedging instrument

It is harder to determine what types of derivative may be used in a hedge of a net investment. The same definition of effectiveness applies to such hedges (see 5.3 above), but what are the changes in the fair value or cash flows of the hedged item that are attributable to the hedged risk that are to be offset by changes in the fair value or cash flows of the hedging instrument? In many respects it is only an accounting entry that it being hedged but, unlike in A above, the hedging instrument will be accounted for at fair value. Even for the simplest derivative that fair value is likely to reflect factors other than changes in the spot exchange rate.

Under US GAAP a number of interpretations to SFAS 133 have been issued setting out what types of derivative may be designated in a net investment hedge and how changes in the value of those derivatives should be accounted for. This guidance is summarised in the following table:[253]

	Method of assessing effectiveness*	
Type of derivative	**Spot rate method**	**Forward rate method**
Forward contract	Changes in value attributable to spot rate changes recorded in equity Changes in value of interest element recorded in profit or loss	All changes in value (including interest element) recorded in equity
Purchased option	Changes in intrinsic value recorded in equity Changes in time value recorded in profit or loss	All changes in value (including time value) recorded in equity
Cross-currency interest rate swap: both legs floating rate	Interest settlements accrued in profit or loss All other changes in value recognised in equity	All changes in value (including interest settlements) recorded in equity
Cross-currency interest rate swap: both legs fixed rate	Changes in value from retranslating notional at spot exchange rates recorded in equity Interest settlements accrued in profit or loss Other changes in value (e.g. from changes in interest rates) recorded in profit or loss	All changes in value (including interest settlements) recorded in equity
Cross-currency interest rate swap: one floating rate leg, one fixed	Hedge accounting not available	Hedge accounting not available

* one method to be applied consistently for all derivatives designated as hedges of a net investment.

This table assumes the contracts are denominated in the same currency as the functional currency of the hedged net investment and that there are no other sources of ineffectiveness. The applicability of this guidance to IAS 39 is considered below.

I Forward currency contracts

It is very common for forward currency contracts to be used as the hedging instrument in a hedge of a net investment – in fact this is the one example that is acknowledged in the implementation guidance. Therefore, applying the US GAAP guidance under IAS 39 seems relatively uncontroversial. However, as noted at 4.2.2

above, where the spot rate method is used (i.e. the interest element of the forward is excluded from the hedge relationship) the premium or discount cannot be amortised to profit or loss.[254] Inevitably, therefore, some income statement volatility will arise and the longer the term of the forward, the greater is the potential volatility.

Some may wonder why entities might choose the spot rate method over the forward rate method. Prior to the development of standards such as IAS 39, the interest element of a forward contract (and similar instruments) was commonly recognised as interest on an accruals basis. Depending on the relative interest rates of the two currencies in the forward, accounting for the interest element in this way could potentially result in a credit to the income statement, which is clearly desirable from the perspective of preparers of the financial statements. Where an entity is prepared to accept the volatility associated with this method, a similar effect on the income statement (over time) may be achieved by using the spot rate method.

If the forward contract is denominated in a different currency to the functional currency of the net investment it is likely that, at best, some ineffectiveness will arise (unless the link between the two currencies is near-perfect). Under US GAAP a comparison of the forward contract with a hypothetical derivative (a forward contract in the right currency) would be made to measure the amount of ineffectiveness[255] and this approach would normally be acceptable under IAS 39.

II Purchased options

The spot rate method involves designating the intrinsic value of a purchased option as the hedging instrument (i.e. its time value is excluded from the hedge relationship). This is clearly acceptable under IAS 39 (see 2.1.4 A and 5.3.11 above), although this will always result in an expense being recorded in profit or loss as the time value decays.

Under the forward rate method, the whole option would be designated as the hedging instrument. However, as discussed at 5.3.11 above, there are currently believed to be conceptual problems in designating the entire value of a purchased option as the hedging instrument under IAS 39 and recording all changes in value in equity.

III Cross-currency interest rate swaps

Like forward contracts, these instruments are commonly used as hedging instruments in net investment hedges. At a conceptual level, it is easy to see that the changes in value of a cross-currency swap with two floating-rate legs are likely to offset the retranslation gains and losses of a net investment, provided the floating rate resets sufficiently frequently. It is also reasonably easy to see that a swap with one floating-rate leg and one fixed-rate leg is unlikely to provide the necessary offset because the fixed rate leg will give rise to changes in the swap's value that are unrelated to changes in exchange rates.

It is less easy to see that a swap with two fixed-rate legs will provide a good hedge against the retranslation gains and losses (again the fixed-rate legs will give rise to changes in the swap's value that are unrelated to changes in exchange rates).

However, such an instrument may be viewed as a combination of forward contracts, each of which could be designated in a hedge of a net investment (see I above). Using the forward rate method, this interpretation makes a good deal of sense. The 'spot rate' treatment under US GAAP, however, is generally considered to have limited technical merit although it is unlikely that entities would want to apply this method because it may result in significant income statement volatility.

C Combinations of derivative and non-derivative instruments used as the hedging instrument

It is not uncommon for entities to hedge their net investments using synthetic foreign currency debt instruments. For example, consider a parent with the euro as its functional currency that has a net investment in a Japanese subsidiary with yen as its functional currency. Such an entity might borrow in US dollars and enter into a pay-Japanese yen, receive-US dollar cross-currency interest rate swap. In this way the two instruments might be considered a synthetic Japanese yen borrowing (although under IAS 39 they will be accounted for separately – see Chapter 17 at 6).

As noted at 2.1.3 above, a combination of derivatives and non-derivatives may now be viewed in combination and jointly designated as a hedging instrument under IAS 39.[256] This would appear to permit the synthetic Japanese yen borrowing described above to be designated as a hedge of the net investment in the Japanese subsidiary (assuming all other conditions for applying hedge accounting are met), although this would often not result in a good degree of offset in cases where one or both legs of the cross-currency swap carries fixed rate coupons.

In fact it may well be easier to demonstrate hedge effectiveness if the cross-currency interest rate swap was notionally decomposed by introducing an interest bearing functional currency denominated leg and designating one part as a hedge of the borrowing and the other as a hedge of the net investment (see 2.1.4 D).

D Unrecognised assets

In many cases the full economic value of a net investment will not be recognised in the financial statements. The most common reason will be the existence of assets such as goodwill that are either not recognised or measured at an amount below their current value. In these situations, if an investor hedges the entire economic value of its net investment (or, more commonly, the original purchase price) it will not be able to obtain hedge accounting for the proportion of the hedging instrument that exceeds the recognised net assets.

E Individual or separate financial statements

It is common for an entity with an investment in a subsidiary, associate or joint venture to be party to a financial instrument (a borrowing, say) that in the entity's consolidated financial statements is designated as the hedging instrument in a hedge of its net investment in the subsidiary, associate or joint venture. However, in the entity's individual or separate financial statements, the investment will generally be accounted for as an asset measured at cost or as a financial asset in accordance with

IAS 39.[257] In other words, it will not be accounted for by way of consolidation, the equity method or proportional consolidation.

Accordingly, from the perspective of the individual or separate financial statements, the reporting entity will not have a net investment in a foreign operation. Therefore, the borrowing could not be designated as the hedging instrument in a net investment hedge for the purposes of the separate financial statements. However, if hedge accounting is desirable, it may be possible to designate the borrowing as the hedging instrument in another type of hedge. Typically, this would be a fair value hedge of the foreign currency risk arising from the investment. This will be an independent hedge relationship, separate from the net investment hedge in the consolidated financial statements. Therefore, all of the other hedge accounting criteria (including the documentation requirements) will need to be met for this hedge too. Of course, the effects of this hedge accounting will need to be reversed when preparing the group's consolidated financial statements (otherwise those financial statements will reflect as an asset or liability certain changes in the fair value of a parent's investment in its subsidiary which would be contrary to the general principles of IAS 27).

6 PORTFOLIO (OR MACRO) HEDGING

At a detailed level, the topic of portfolio (or macro) hedging for banks and similar financial institutions is beyond the scope of a general financial reporting publication such as this. However, no discussion of hedge accounting would be complete without an overview of the high level issues involved and an explanation of how thc standard setters have tried to accommodate these entities.

The underlying philosophy of IAS 39's approach to hedge accounting is that individual hedging instruments are designated as hedging individual assets, liabilities or other risk exposures. However, banks and similar financial institutions typically manage their interest rate risk exposures on a portfolio (or macro) level. Accordingly, there is a fundamental difference between the hedging activities of the financial institution and the hedge accounting requirements of the standard. This can serve as a significant impediment to obtaining hedge accounting treatment for such entities.

Following the publication of the original version of IAS 39, a number of financial institutions worked with the Implementation Guidance Committee to develop a model under which cash flow hedge accounting could be achieved where interest rate risk is managed over a whole portfolio on a net basis. As a result of this effort, some of the most complex implementation guidance to the standard was published.[258] This was a significant achievement, although it did not necessarily provide a low cost solution. In fact, it was sometimes easier for entities to develop a parallel system, completely separate from their primary risk management systems, solely to manage their IAS 39 hedge accounting requirements.

Further, the cash flow hedge accounting model was not sufficient to satisfy many of the banks that would be required to adopt IAS 39 in 2005, particularly those in Europe. One of the problems is that banks were not just concerned with minimising volatility in their earnings, the primary focus for many entities preparing to adopt IAS 39, but also to reduce volatility in their equity.

Notwithstanding this growing opposition from an important part of the IASB's constituency, in revising IAS 39, the basic principles of hedge accounting were not immediately readdressed and no attempt was made to address the banks' concerns. In fact, when the revised standard was finally published in December 2003, the original guidance for macro cash flow hedges was simply incorporated as guidance to the standard and was largely unchanged.[259]

However, as set out in Chapter 17 at 1.5, this is not the whole story. In August 2003, the IASB published an exposure draft of proposed amendments to the revised version of IAS 39 (which was, at the time, unpublished) dealing with macro-hedging issues for banks.[260] The exposure draft proposed a number of limited amendments to IAS 39 that would make it easier for banks to apply fair value hedge accounting to portfolios of fixed interest assets and liabilities, particularly those assets that were subject to prepayment risk. The key advantage of such an accounting model is that it could reduce the volatility in a bank's equity: although derivative hedging instruments would be recorded on the balance sheet at fair value, equivalent changes in the fair value of the hedged assets and liabilities would also be recognised on the balance sheet within assets or liabilities.

IAS 39 was eventually amended in March 2004 along the lines set out in the exposure draft.[261] Unfortunately, the banks' concerns were not addressed. In particular, as set out in Chapter 20 at 4.5, there is a significant restriction on the fair value measurement requirements for liabilities with a demand feature and this effectively prevents banks from applying fair value hedge accounting to the majority of their current and deposit accounts. The EC's response to this was to endorse a version of IAS 39 with certain parts 'carved out'[262] thereby allowing the use of hedge accounting in situations that the full version of IAS 39 would not. The possibility of future developments in this area is considered at 8 below.

7 EFFECTIVE DATES, TRANSITIONAL PROVISIONS AND FIRST-TIME ADOPTION

This section contains information that is relevant for annual periods beginning on or after 1 January 2006. For earlier periods, equivalent requirements are dealt with in *International GAAP 2005* and *International GAAP 2007*, the predecessors to this publication.

7.1 Effective dates

The April 2005 amendments to IAS 39 allowing certain forecast intragroup transactions to qualify as hedged items (see 2.3.4 B and 4.2.2 above) should be applied for annual periods beginning on or after 1 January 2006 and earlier application is encouraged.[263]

7.2 Transitional provisions

The April 2005 amendments relating to cash flow hedges of intragroup transactions (see 2.3.4 B and 4.2.2 above) include some transitional requirements. Where an entity has designated as the hedged item an external forecast transaction that:

- is denominated in the functional currency of the entity entering into the transaction;
- gives rise to an exposure that will have an effect on consolidated profit or loss (i.e. is denominated in a currency other than the group's presentation currency); and
- would have qualified for hedge accounting had it not been denominated in the functional currency of the entity entering into it,

it may apply hedge accounting in the consolidated financial statements in the period(s) before the date of application of the amendments.[264] Essentially this provides some relief for entities that adopted the approach set out in the exposure draft (see 2.3.4 B above).

In addition, the amended requirement to recycle gains and losses from equity when the foreign currency risk of a hedged forecast intragroup transaction affects consolidated profit or loss (see 4.2.2 above) need not be applied in comparative information to periods before the date of application of the amendment.[265] For example, an entity may have designated a forecast intragroup transaction as a hedged item at the start of an annual period beginning on or after 1 January 2005 (or, for the purpose of restating comparative information, the start of an earlier comparative period) in a hedge that would qualify for hedge accounting in accordance with IAS 39 as amended. That entity may use that designation to apply hedge accounting in consolidated financial statements from the start of the annual period beginning on or after 1 January 2005 (or the start of the earlier comparative period) and shall also apply the amendment in full from the start of the annual period beginning on or after 1 January 2005. However, it need not apply the requirement to recycle gains and losses from equity when the foreign currency risk of a hedged forecast intragroup transaction affects consolidated profit or loss to comparative information for earlier periods.[266]

7.3 First-time adoption

IFRS 1 – *First-time Adoption of International Financial Reporting Standards* – is dealt with in Chapter 5. The aspects related to hedge accounting are summarised below. Further similar sections are included in Chapters 17 to 20 and 22.

7.3.1 Cumulative translation differences and related hedges

As set out in Chapter 5 at 2.7.2, IFRS 1 contains a concession for the treatment of cumulative translation differences arising on net investments in foreign operations accounted for under IAS 21. Accordingly, an entity is not required to identify such differences prior to the date of transition to IFRS and classify them in a separate component of equity. Instead, it may 'reset' this separate component of equity to zero at this date.

Unfortunately, IFRS 1 is not entirely clear whether this concession extends to similar gains and losses arising on related hedges. Paragraph 22, which contains the concession, explains that a first-time adopter need not comply with 'these requirements'.[267] The requirements referred to are those summarised in paragraph 21 which explain that IAS 21 requires an entity

(a) to classify some translation differences as a separate component of equity; and

(b) on disposal of a foreign operation, to transfer the cumulative translation difference for that foreign operation (*including, if applicable, gains and losses on related hedges*) to the income statement as part of the gain or loss on disposal.[268]

The problem arises because paragraph 21 does not refer to the initial recognition of hedging gains or losses in a separate component of equity (only the subsequent recycling thereof). Accordingly, a very literal reading of the standard might suggest that an entity *is* required to identify historical gains and losses on such hedges. However, even if this position is accepted, on what basis this might be done is not at all clear. For example, it is quite likely that such hedges would not have met the conditions for hedge accounting in IAS 39 and, other than in paragraph 21, IFRS 1 does not specifically address net investment hedges at all.

It is clear that the reasons cited by the IASB for including this concession apply as much to related hedges as they do to the underlying exchange differences. The fact that IFRS 1 can be read otherwise might be seen as little more than poor drafting. In fact there is already clear evidence that paragraph 21 was not subject to the most rigorous scrutiny before publication – it is IAS 39, not IAS 21, that deals with the recycling of gains and losses taken to equity in a net investment hedge. Accordingly, we believe it is entirely appropriate for this concession to be applied to net investment hedges as well as the underlying gains and losses.

7.3.2 Hedge accounting: prohibition on retrospective application

IFRS 1 explains that entities are prohibited from applying retrospectively some of the hedge accounting provisions of IAS 39.[269] In the basis for conclusions, it is explained that:

> '... it is unlikely that most entities would have adopted IAS 39's criteria for (a) documenting hedges at their inception and (b) testing the hedges for effectiveness, even if they intended to continue the same hedging strategies after adopting IAS 39. Furthermore, retrospective designation of hedges (or retrospective reversal of their designation) could lead to selective designation of some hedges to report a particular result.[270]
>
> 'To overcome these problems, the transitional requirements in [the original version of] IAS 39 require an entity already applying IFRS to apply the hedging requirements prospectively when it adopts IAS 39. As the same problems arise for a first-time adopter, the IFRS requires prospective application by a first-time adopter.'[271]

Unfortunately, there is only a limited amount of guidance in IFRS 1 regarding hedge accounting and therefore it is not entirely clear what applying these requirements of IAS 39 'prospectively' actually involves, especially insofar as the opening IFRS balance sheet is concerned. However, the basis for conclusions continues:

> 'ED 1 – *First-time Application of International Financial Reporting Standards* – included a redrafted version of the transitional provisions in IAS 39 and related Questions and Answers (Q&As) developed by the IAS 39 Implementation Guidance Committee. The Board confirmed in the Basis for Conclusions published with ED 1 that it did not intend the redrafting to create substantive changes. However, in the light of responses to ED 1, the Board decided in finalising IFRS 1 that the redrafting would not make it easier for first-time adopters and others to understand and apply the transition provisions and Q&As. However, the project to improve IAS 32 and IAS 39 resulted in certain amendments to the transition requirements. In addition, this project incorporated selected other Q&As (i.e. not on transition) into IAS 39. The Board therefore took this opportunity to consolidate all the guidance for first-time adopters in one place, by incorporating the Q&As on transition into IFRS 1.'[272]

This indicates that the transitional provisions set out in the original version of IAS 39 and IGC Q&As, ED 1 and IFRS 1 are intended to be broadly consistent. Consequently, the fact that all three sources are expressed in different ways can be useful in interpreting this aspect of IFRS 1. These documents are referred to at 7.3.3 below where they assist in understanding the requirements set out in IFRS 1.

7.3.3 Hedge accounting: opening IFRS balance sheet

A Measurement of derivatives and elimination of deferred gains and losses

Under its previous GAAP an entity's accounting policies might have included a number of accounting treatments for derivatives that formed part of a hedge relationship. For example, accounting policies might have included those where the derivative was:

- not explicitly recognised as an asset or liability (e.g. in the case of a forward contract used to hedge an expected but uncontracted future transaction);
- recognised as an asset or liability but at an amount different from its fair value (e.g. a purchased option recognised at its original cost, perhaps less amortisation; or an interest rate swap accounted for by accruing the periodic interest payments and receipts); or
- subsumed within the accounting for another asset or liability (e.g. a foreign currency denominated monetary item and a matching forward contract or swap accounted for as a 'synthetic' functional currency denominated monetary item).

Whatever the previous accounting treatment, a first-time adopter should isolate and separately account for all derivatives in its opening IFRS balance sheet as assets or liabilities measured at fair value.[273]

The implementation guidance explains that all derivatives, other than those that are designated and effective hedging instruments, are classified as held for trading. Accordingly, the difference between the previous carrying amount of a derivative (which may have been zero) and its fair value should be recognised as an adjustment of the balance of retained earnings at the beginning of the financial year in which IFRS 1 is initially applied (other than for a derivative that is a designated and effective hedging instrument).[274]

Hedge accounting policies under an entity's previous GAAP might also have included one or both of the following accounting treatments:

- derivatives were measured at fair value but, to the extent they were regarded as hedging future transactions, the gain (or loss) arising was reported as a liability (or asset) such as deferred (or accrued) income;
- realised gains or losses arising on the termination of a previously unrecognised derivative used in a hedge relationship (such as an interest rate swap hedging a borrowing) were included in the balance sheet as deferred or accrued income and amortised over the remaining term of the hedged exposure.

In all cases, an entity is required to eliminate deferred gains and losses arising on derivatives 'that were reported under previous GAAP as if they were assets or liabilities'.[275] Essentially, this is because deferred gains and losses do not meet the definition of assets or liabilities under the IASB's *Framework*. In contrast to adjustments made to restate derivatives at fair value, the implementation guidance does not specify in general terms how to deal with adjustments to eliminate deferred gains or losses, i.e. whether they should be taken to retained earnings or a separate component of equity.

The requirement to eliminate deferred gains and losses does not appear to extend to those that have been included in the carrying amount of other assets or liabilities that will continue to be recognised under IFRS. For example, under an entity's previous GAAP, the carrying amount of non-financial assets such as inventories or property, plant and equipment might have included the equivalent of a basis adjustment (i.e. hedging gains or losses were considered an integral part of the asset's cost). In fact, carrying forward this treatment into an entity's first set of IFRS financial statements would be consistent with the transitional provisions of the December 2003 version of IAS 39 (see 7.2 above). Of course, entities should also consider any other provisions of IFRS 1 that apply to those hedged items.

The way in which an entity accounts for these adjustments will, to a large extent, dictate how its existing hedge relationships will be reflected in its ongoing IFRS financial statements. Particularly, an entity's future results will be different depending on whether the adjustments are taken to retained earnings or to a separate component of equity – in the latter case they would be recycled to profit or loss at a later date but would not in the former. Similarly, its future results would be affected if the carrying amount of related assets or liabilities are changed to reflect these adjustments (as opposed to the adjustments being made to retained earnings).

For short-term hedges (e.g. of sales and inventory purchases) these effects are likely to work their way out of the IFRS financial statements relatively quickly. However, for other hedges (e.g. of long term borrowings) an entity's results may be affected for many years. The question of which hedge relationships should be reflected in an entity's opening IFRS balance sheet is dealt with at B to D below.

B Hedge relationships reflected in the opening IFRS balance sheet

The standard states that a first-time adopter *should not* reflect a hedging relationship in its opening IFRS balance sheet (or the balance sheet at the beginning of its first IFRS reporting period, if comparatives are not restated) if that hedging relationship is of a type that *does not* qualify for hedge accounting under IAS 39. As examples of this it cites many hedging relationships where the hedging instrument is a cash instrument or written option; where the hedged item is a net position; or where the hedge covers interest risk in a held-to-maturity investment.[276]

However, if an entity had designated a net position as a hedged item under its previous GAAP, the IASB decided that an individual item within that net position *may* be designated as a hedged item under IFRS, provided that it does so no later than the date of transition to IFRS (or the beginning of the first IFRS reporting period, if comparatives are not restated).[277] In other words, such designation could allow the hedge relationship to be reflected in the opening IFRS balance sheet (or the balance sheet at the beginning of its first IFRS reporting period, if comparatives are not restated).

Further, a first-time adopter is not permitted to designate hedges retrospectively in relation to transactions entered into before the date of transition to IFRS (or the beginning of the first IFRS reporting period, if comparatives are not restated).[278] This would appear to prevent an entity from reflecting hedge relationships in its opening balance sheet that it did not identify as such under its previous GAAP.

It might seem to follow that a hedge relationship designated under an entity's previous GAAP *should* be reflected in its opening IFRS balance sheet (or the balance sheet at the beginning of its first IFRS reporting period, if comparatives are not restated) if that hedging relationship *is* of a type that *does* qualify for hedge accounting under IAS 39. In fact, if an entity was allowed not to reflect such a hedge in its opening IFRS balance sheet (or the balance sheet at the beginning of its first IFRS reporting period, if comparatives are not restated) this would effectively allow the retrospective reversal of the hedge designation. As noted at A above, this is something the IASB has sought to avoid.[279] However, while such a 'principle' seems to be implied by the implementation guidance (see C and D below), the IASB has not actually articulated it in these terms.

There are, perhaps, a number of reasons for the IASB's reticence. For example, under an entity's previous GAAP, it might not have been clear whether a derivative instrument was actually designated as a hedge. Further, even if it were clear that a derivative had previously been designated as a hedge, the hedged item might not have been identified with sufficiently specificity to allow the effects of the hedge to be reflected in the opening IFRS balance sheet and/or, thereafter, to be 'unwound' at the appropriate time.

C Reflecting cash flow hedges in the opening IFRS balance sheet

The implementation guidance to IFRS 1 explains that a first-time adopter may, under its previous GAAP, have deferred gains and losses on a cash flow hedge of a forecast transaction. If, at the date of transition to IFRS (or the beginning of the first IFRS reporting period, if comparatives are not restated) the hedged forecast transaction is not highly probable, but is expected to occur, the entire deferred gain or loss should be recognised in equity.[280] To be consistent, this would be included in the same component of equity an entity would use to record future gains and losses on cash flow hedges.

This raises the question of how to deal with such a hedge if, at the date of transition to IFRS (or the beginning of the first IFRS reporting period, if comparatives are not restated), the forecast transaction *was* highly probable. It would make no sense if the former was required to be reflected in the opening IFRS balance sheet, but the latter (which is clearly a 'better' hedge) was not. Therefore, it must follow that a cash flow hedge should be reflected in the opening IFRS balance sheet in the way set out above if the hedged item is a forecast transaction that is highly probable. Similarly, it follows that a cash flow hedge of the variability in cash flows attributable to a particular risk associated with a recognised asset or liability (such as all or some future interest payments on variable rate debt) should also be reflected in the opening balance sheet.

If, at the date of transition to IFRS (or the beginning of the first IFRS reporting period, if comparatives are not restated), the forecast transaction was *not* expected to occur, this would be a relationship of a type that does not qualify for hedge accounting under IAS 39. Therefore, the hedging relationship should not be reflected in the opening IFRS balance sheet. In fact ED 1 was explicit on this point.[281]

There are various ways in which gains or losses might have been deferred under an entity's previous GAAP. ED 1 explained that, in this context, deferral included:

- treating deferred gains as if they were liabilities and deferred losses as if they were assets; and
- not recognising changes in the fair value of the hedging instrument.[282]

Even though this explanation was not incorporated into IFRS 1, at a conceptual level there is scarce reason why it should not apply under the standard. However, it is possible to read parts of the implementation guidance as preventing this treatment if the hedge has not been designated in an effective hedge under IAS 39 by the date of transition (or the beginning of the first IFRS reporting period, if comparatives are not restated). The following example highlights this issue.

Example 21.35: Unrecognised gains and losses on existing cash flow hedge

Company T has the euro as its functional currency. In September 2006 it entered into a forward currency contract to sell dollars for euros in twelve months to hedge dollar denominated sales it forecasts are highly probable to occur in September 2007. T will apply IAS 39 from 1 January 2007, its date of transition to IFRS. The historical cost of the forward contract is €nil and at the date of transition it had a positive fair value of €100.

Case 1: Gains and losses deferred

Under T's previous GAAP, until the sales occurred the forward contract was recognised in the balance sheet at its fair value and the resulting gain or loss was deferred in the balance sheet as a liability or asset. When the sale occurred, any deferred gain or loss was recognised in profit or loss as an offset to the revenue recognised on the hedged sales.

Case 2: Gains and losses unrecognised

Under T's previous GAAP, the contract was not recognised in the balance sheet. When the sale occurred, any unrecognised gain or loss was recognised in profit or loss as an offset to the revenue recognised on the hedged sales.

In Case 1 the relationship can clearly be reflected in T's opening IFRS balance sheet whether or not it is designated as an effective hedge in accordance with IAS 39 at the date of transition: there is no restriction on transferring the deferred gain to a separate component of equity and there is no adjustment to the carrying amount of the forward contract.

Case 2 is slightly more problematical. As noted at A above, the implementation guidance explains that the difference between the previous carrying amount of a derivative and its fair value should be recognised as an adjustment of the balance of retained earnings (other than for a derivative that is a designated and effective hedging instrument).[283] Read literally, this implementation guidance could prevent the relationship from being reflected in T's opening IFRS balance sheet, unless T had designated the relationship as an effective hedge in accordance with IAS 39 at the date of transition. This is because the adjustment to the carrying amount of the forward would be recorded in retained earnings rather than a separate component of equity.

Such an interpretation would allow T to choose not to designate (in accordance with IAS 39) certain cash flow hedges, say those that are in a loss position, until one day after its date of transition, thereby allowing associated hedging losses to bypass profit or loss completely. However, this would effectively result in the retrospective dedesignation of hedges to achieve a desired result, thereby breaching this general principle of IFRS 1. Arguably, this general principle of the standard should take precedence over the implementation guidance.

D Reflecting fair value hedges in the opening IFRS balance sheet

The implementation guidance to IFRS 1 explains that a first-time adopter may, under its previous GAAP, have deferred or not recognised gains and losses on a fair value hedge of a hedged item that is not measured at fair value. For such a fair value hedge, the entity should adjust the carrying amount of the hedged item at the date of transition to IFRS (or the beginning of the first IFRS reporting period, if comparatives are not restated). The adjustment, which is essentially the effective part of the hedge that was not recognised in the carrying amount of the hedged item under the previous GAAP, should be calculated as the lower of:

(a) that portion of the cumulative change in the fair value of the hedged item that reflects the designated hedged risk and was not recognised under previous GAAP; and

(b) that portion of the cumulative change in the fair value of the hedging instrument that reflects the designated hedged risk and, under previous GAAP, was either (i) not recognised or (ii) deferred in the balance sheet as an asset or liability.[284]

This requirement is consistent with the requirement in the original version of IAS 39 (and the proposals in ED 1) under which any balance sheet positions in fair value hedges of existing assets and liabilities would be accounted for in the opening balance sheet in (broadly) the same manner as above.[285]

Available-for-sale assets are measured at fair value so the guidance above would not appear to apply to fair value hedges of such instruments. However, it would be logical to apply an equivalent adjustment to the cost or amortised cost of such assets.

7.3.4 *Hedge accounting: subsequent treatment*

The implementation guidance explains that hedge accounting can be applied prospectively only from the date the hedge relationship is fully designated and documented. Therefore, if the hedging instrument is still held at the date of transition to IFRS (or the beginning of the first IFRS reporting period, if comparatives are not restated), the designation and documentation of a hedge relationship must be completed on or before that date if the hedge relationship is to qualify for hedge accounting on an ongoing basis from that date.[286]

An entity may, before the date of transition to IFRS (or the beginning of the first IFRS reporting period, if comparatives are not restated), have designated a transaction as a hedge that does not meet the conditions for hedge accounting in IAS 39. In these cases it should following the general requirements in IAS 39 for discontinuing hedge accounting – these are dealt with at 4.1.3 for fair value hedges and at 4.2.3 for cash flow hedges.[287]

For cash flow hedges, any net cumulative gain or loss that was reclassified to equity on initial application of IAS 39 (see 7.3.3 C above) should remain in equity until:

(a) the forecast transaction subsequently results in the recognition of a non-financial asset or non-financial liability;

(b) the forecast transaction affects profit or loss; or

(c) subsequently circumstances change and the forecast transaction is no longer expected to occur, in which case any related net cumulative gain or loss that had been recognised directly in equity is recognised in profit or loss.[288]

The requirements above do little more than reiterate the general requirements of IAS 39, i.e. that hedge accounting can only be applied prospectively if the qualifying conditions are met, and entities should experience few interpretative problems in dealing with this aspect of the hedge accounting requirements.

7.3.5 Hedge accounting: examples

The following examples illustrate the guidance considered at 7.3.2 to 7.3.4 above.

Example 21.36: Pre-transition cash flow hedges

Case 1: All hedge accounting conditions met from date of transition and thereafter

In 2000 Company Q borrowed €10m from a bank. The terms of the loan provide that a coupon of 3 month LIBOR plus 2% is payable quarterly in arrears and the principal is repayable in 2015. In 2003, Q decided to 'fix' its coupon payments for the remainder of the term of the loan by entering into a twelve-year pay-fixed, receive-floating interest rate swap. The swap has a notional amount of €10m and the floating leg resets quarterly based on 3 month LIBOR.

In Q's final financial statements prepared under its previous GAAP, the swap was clearly identified as a hedging instrument in a hedge of the loan and was accounted for as such. The fair value of the swap was not recognised in Q's balance sheet and the periodic interest settlements were accrued and recognised as an adjustment to the loan interest expense. On 1 January 2007, Q's date of transition to IFRS, the loan and the swap were still in place and the swap had a positive fair value of €1m and a €nil carrying amount. In addition, Q met all the conditions in IAS 39 to permit the use of hedge accounting for this arrangement throughout 2007 and 2008.

In its opening IFRS balance sheet Q should:

- recognise the interest rate swap as an asset at its fair value of €1m; and
- credit €1m to a separate component of equity, to be recycled as the hedged transactions (future interest payments on the loan) affect profit or loss.

In addition, hedge accounting would be applied throughout 2007 and 2008.

Case 2: Hedge terminated prior to date of transition

The facts are as in Case 1 except that in April 2006 Q decided to terminate the hedge and the interest rate swap was settled for its then fair value of €1.5m. Under its previous GAAP, Q's stated accounting policy in respect of terminated hedges was to defer any realised gain or loss on terminated hedging instruments where the hedged exposure remained. These gains or losses would be recognised in profit or loss at the same time as gains or losses on the hedged exposure. At the end of December 2006, Q's balance sheet included a liability (unamortised gain) of €1.4m.

IFRS 1 does not explicitly address hedges terminated prior to the date of transition but we see no reason why these relationships should not be reflected in an entity's opening IFRS balance sheet in the same way as other cash flow hedges that are reflected in an entity's closing balance sheet under its previous GAAP. Accordingly, in its opening IFRS balance sheet Q should:

- remove the deferred gain of €1.4m from the balance sheet; and
- credit €1.4m to a separate component of equity, to be recycled as the hedged transactions (future interest payments on the loan) affect profit or loss.

Example 21.37: Existing fair value hedges

Case 1: All hedge accounting conditions met from date of transition and thereafter (1)

On 15 November 2006, Company Y entered into a forward contract to sell 50,000 barrels of crude oil to hedge all changes in the fair value of certain inventory. Y will apply IAS 39 from 1 January 2007, its date of transition to IFRS. The historical cost of the forward contract is $nil and at the date of transition the forward had a negative fair value of $50.

In Y's final financial statements prepared under its previous GAAP, the forward was clearly identified as a hedging instrument in a hedge of the inventory and was accounted for as such. The contract was recognised in the balance sheet as a liability at its fair value and the resulting loss was deferred in the balance sheet as an asset. In the period between 15 November 2006 and 1 January 2007 the fair value of the inventory increased by $47. In addition, Y met all the conditions in IAS 39 to permit the use of hedge accounting for this arrangement throughout 2007 until the forward expired.

In its opening IFRS balance sheet Y should:

- continue to recognise the forward contract as a liability at its fair value of $50;
- derecognise the $50 deferred loss on the forward contract;
- recognise the crude oil inventory at its historical cost plus $47 (the lower of the change in fair value of the crude oil inventory, $47, and that of the forward contract, $50); and
- record the net adjustment of $3 in retained earnings.

In addition, hedge accounting would be applied throughout 2007 until the forward expired.

Case 2: All hedge accounting conditions met from date of transition and thereafter (2)

In 2000 Company Z borrowed €10m from a bank. The terms of the loan provide that a coupon of 8% is payable quarterly in arrears and the principal is repayable in 2015. In 2003, P decided to alter its coupon payments for the remainder of the term of the loan by entering into a twelve-year pay-floating, receive-fixed interest rate swap. The swap has a notional amount of €10m and the floating leg resets quarterly based on 3 month LIBOR.

In Z's final financial statements prepared under its previous GAAP, the swap was clearly identified as a hedging instrument in a hedge of the loan and accounted for as such. The fair value of the swap was not recognised in Z's balance sheet and the periodic interest settlements on the swap were accrued and recognised as an adjustment to the loan interest expense.

On 1 January 2007, Z's date of transition to IFRS, the loan and the swap were still in place and the swap had a negative fair value of €1m and a €nil carrying amount. The cumulative change in the fair value of the loan attributable to changes in 3 month LIBOR was €1.1m, although this change was not recognised in Z's balance sheet because the loan was accounted for at cost. In addition, Z met all the conditions in IAS 39 to permit the use of hedge accounting for this arrangement throughout 2007 and 2008.

In its opening IFRS balance sheet Z should:

- recognise the interest rate swap as a liability at its fair value of €1m; and
- reduce the carrying amount of the loan by €1m (the lower of the change in its fair value attributable to the hedged risk, €1.1m, and that of the interest rate swap, $1m).

In addition, hedge accounting would be applied throughout 2007 and 2008.

Case 3: Hedge terminated prior to date of transition

The facts are as in Case 2 above except that in April 2006 Z decided to terminate the hedge and the interest rate swap was settled for its then negative fair value of €1.5m. Under its previous GAAP, Z's stated accounting policy in respect of terminated hedges was to defer any gain or loss on the hedging instrument as a liability or an asset where the hedged exposure remained and this gain or loss was recognised in profit or loss at the same time as the hedged exposure. At the end of December 2006 the unamortised loss recognised as an asset in Z's balance sheet was €1.4m. In 2006 the cumulative change in the fair value of the loan attributable to changes in 3 month LIBOR that had not been recognised was €1.6m.

In its opening IFRS balance sheet Z should:

- remove the deferred loss of €1.4m from the balance sheet; and
- reduce the carrying amount of the loan by €1.4m (the lower of the change in its fair value attributable to the hedged risk, €1.6m, and the change in value of the interest rate swap that was deferred in the balance sheet, €1.4m).

The €1.4m adjustment to the loan would be amortised to profit or loss over its remaining term (see 4.1.2 above).

Case 4: Documentation completed after the date of transition

The facts are as in Case 2 above except that, at the date of transition, Z had not prepared documentation that would allow it to apply hedge accounting under IAS 39. Hedge documentation was subsequently prepared as a result of which the hedge qualified for hedge accounting with effect from the beginning of July 2007 and throughout 2008.

As in Case 2, in its opening IFRS balance sheet Z should:

- recognise the interest rate swap as a liability at its fair value of €1m; and
- reduce the carrying amount of the loan by €1m (the lower of the change in its fair value attributable to the hedged risk, €1.1m, and that of the interest rate swap, €1m).

For the period from January 2007 to June 2007, hedge accounting would not be available. Accordingly, the interest rate swap would be remeasured to its fair value and any gain or loss would be reported in profit or loss with no offset from remeasuring the loan. With effect from July 2007 hedge accounting would be applied prospectively.

8 FUTURE DEVELOPMENTS

As discussed in Chapter 17 at 1.5, the majority of the IASB's current work on financial instruments is being carried out in conjunction with the FASB as part of their Memorandum of Understanding. Although the boards have as part of this a joint objective to simplify or eliminate the need for hedge accounting, this is a long term project and whilst there have been regular discussions, there has been limited tangible progress so far. The next step envisaged by the boards is the publication before 2008 of a 'due process document' setting out possible ways to move toward their goal.[289]

In Europe the issue of the IAS 39 'carve out' (see 6 above) remains and there have been continuing discussions between representatives of the IASB and the Fédération Bancaire de l'Union Européenne ('FBE') in order to try and resolve some of the more contentious aspects of the hedge accounting requirements as they apply to portfolio (or macro) hedging of interest rate risk.

The main focus of these discussions is FBE's proposal that a new type of hedge accounting should be developed for hedges of interest rate margin. In May 2004, the IASB acknowledged that the goal was for FBE, as soon as possible, to develop its proposal to the point that it would be appropriate for presentation to the IASB. The

IASB would then consider whether an exposure draft, based on this proposal, should be issued.[290]

Although the IASB was seen to embrace FBE's work (the issue was put on the IASB's research agenda), there was little doubt that the IASB retained a good degree of scepticism about the proposals.[291] In the meantime the EC continued to emphasise the need for an appropriate and speedy solution to be found,[292] but by January 2006 little appeared to have changed when the IASB Chairman addressed the European parliament. He explained that, in spite of a team of IASB Board members and staff having had extensive technical discussions with FBE, a number of their important questions had still not been answered.[293]

In June 2006 there were some signs of progress when FBE published a document setting out their proposals[294] and a summary of these proposals was presented by FBE representatives to the IASB in December 2006. Whilst the IASB clearly remained unconvinced of the need for a new hedge accounting model, it nevertheless reported that a way forward had been agreed whereby FBE would prepare a list of specific paragraphs perceived as preventing some banks from using the existing cash flow hedge accounting model, and the IASB would analyse those paragraphs to determine whether any clarifications to IAS 39 were necessary and appropriate.[295]

An update was presented to the IASB in June 2007 following a meeting between representatives of the IASB and FBE at which the possible clarifications to IAS 39 that had been raised at the December 2006 meeting had been discussed again. It was noted that that some IASB members and staff intend to hold discussions with some banks currently using the cash flow hedge accounting model set out in IAS 39 in order to understand the application issues faced by those banks and to help establish whether clarifications to IAS 39 are necessary.[296]

References

1 For example, see IAS 39 (2000), *Financial Instruments: Recognition and Measurement*, IASC, December 1998 to October 2000, para. 10.
2 Based, in part, on Discussion Paper, *Derivatives and Other Financial Instruments*, ASB, June 1996, Summary of issues and the Board's initial conclusions, paras. 34-38.
3 IAS 39, *Financial Instruments: Recognition and Measurement*, IASB, para. 9.
4 IAS 39, para. 72.
5 IAS 39, para. AG96.
6 IAS 39, para. F.1.2.
7 IAS 39, para. F.1.2.
8 IAS 39, paras. AG35(e) and F.1.6.
9 IAS 39, para. AG94.
10 IAS 39, para. F.1.3.
11 IAS 39, para. F.1.3.
12 IAS 39, para. BC144.
13 IAS 39, para. 72.
14 IAS 39, para. AG95.
15 IAS 39, para. AG96.
16 IAS 39, para. F.1.2.
17 IAS 39, para. F.1.1.
18 IAS 39, paras. BC144-BC145.
19 IAS 39, para. 77.
20 IAS 39, para. 77.
21 *IAS 39 Implementation Guidance*, Questions & Answers, IAS 39 Implementation Guidance Committee (IGC), May 2000 and subsequently, Q&A 122-1.
22 IAS 39, para. 77.
23 IAS 39, para. 74.

24 IAS 39, para. F.1.8.
25 IAS 39, para. 74.
26 IAS 39, para. 74.
27 IAS 39, para. 75.
28 *IFRIC Update*, IASB, July 2007.
29 IAS 39, para. F.2.6
30 IAS 39, para. 76.
31 IAS 39, para. F.1.13.
32 IAS 39, para. F.1.12.
33 IAS 39, para. F.2.18.
34 *IFRIC Update*, IASB, October 2004.
35 IAS 39, para. AG97.
36 IAS 39, para. 9.
37 IAS 39, para. F.2.3.
38 IAS 39, para. 81.
39 IAS 39, para. 81.
40 IAS 39, para. F.2.17.
41 IAS 39, para. BC135A.
42 IAS 39, para. AG99C.
43 IAS 39, para. AG99C.
44 IAS 39, para. AG99D.
45 IAS 39, para. AG99D.
46 IAS 39, para. F.2.19.
47 Information for observers of March 2006 IFRIC meeting, *Hedging Inflation Risk (Agenda Paper 12)*, IASB, March 2006, para. 27.
48 *IFRIC Update*, IASB, July 2006.
49 Exposure Draft (ED), *Amendments to IAS 39, Financial Instruments: Recognition and Measurement – Exposures Qualifying for Hedge Accounting*, IASB, September 2007, para. 80Y.
50 ED, para. 80Z.
51 ED, para. AG99E.
52 Information for Observers of April 2007 Financial Instruments Working Group meeting, *IAS 39 Financial Instruments: Recognition and Measurement, Identification of 'other portions' of an exposure eligible for hedge accounting*, IASB, April 2007 and *IASB Update*, IASB, June 2007.
53 IAS 39, paras. 82 and AG100.
54 *Comments of Swiss International Air Lines Ltd. on Paragraphs 129 and 130 of the "Exposure Draft of Proposed Amendments to IAS 39 Financial Instruments: Recognition and Measurement"*, Swiss International Air Lines Ltd, October 2002.
55 IAS 39, paras. BC137-BC138.
56 *IFRIC Update*, IASB, October 2004.
57 IAS 39, paras. BC140-BC143.
58 IAS 39, para. F.6.5.
59 IAS 39, para. AG100.
60 IAS 39, para. AG100.
61 IAS 39, para. 78.
62 IAS 39, para. 83.
63 IAS 39, para. F.2.20.
64 IAS 39, para. 84.
65 IAS 39, para. F.2.21.
66 IAS 39, para. AG101.
67 IAS 39, para. AG110.
68 IAS 39, para. F.2.8.
69 IAS 39, para. AG98.
70 IAS 39, paras. 79 and F.2.9.
71 IAS 39, para. 79.
72 IAS 39, para. F.2.10.
73 IAS 39, para. F.2.11.
74 IAS 39, para. F.2.1.
75 IAS 39, para. F.2.7.
76 IAS 39, para. F.2.3.
77 IAS 39, para. F.2.3.
78 IAS 27, *Consolidated and Separate Financial Statements*, IASB, para. 24 and IAS 39, para. F.1.4.
79 IAS 39, paras. 73 and F.1.4.
80 IAS 39, para. 73.
81 IAS 39, para. F.1.4
82 IAS 39, para. F.1.4.
83 IAS 39, para. 73.
84 IAS 39, para. F.1.4.
85 IAS 39, paras. BC165-BC172.
86 *IASB Update*, IASB, March 2007.
87 IAS 39, para. F.1.4.
88 IAS 39, para. F.1.5.
89 IAS 39, para. F.1.5.
90 IAS 39, para. F.1.5.
91 IAS 39, para. F.1.5.
92 IAS 39, para. F.1.5.
93 IAS 39, para. F.2.15.
94 IAS 39, para. F.1.6.
95 IAS 39, para. F.1.6.
96 IAS 39, para. F.1.7.
97 IAS 39, para. F.1.14.
98 IAS 39, para. F.2.16.
99 IAS 39, para. F.2.16.
100 IAS 39, para. F.2.16.
101 IAS 39, para. 80.
102 IAS 39, para. 80.
103 IGC Q&A 137-13.
104 IGC Q&A 137-14.
105 Exposure Draft (ED), *Amendments to IAS 39, Financial Instruments: Recognition and Measurement – Cash flow Hedge Accounting of Forecast Intragroup Transactions*, IASB, July 2004, para. BC7.
106 ED, Background, para. 3.
107 Amendment to IAS 39, Financial Instruments: Recognition and Measurement, *Cash Flow Hedge Accounting of Forecast Intragroup Transactions*, IASB, June 2005.
108 IAS 39, paras. 80 and AG99A.
109 IAS 39, para. AG99A.
110 IAS 39, para. BC222(s).
111 IAS 39, para. F.2.14.
112 IAS 39, para. F.2.14.
113 IAS 39, para. 86.

114 IAS 39, para. AG102.
115 IAS 39, para. F.2.13.
116 IAS 39, para. F.3.5.
117 IAS 39, para. F.3.6.
118 IAS 39, para. AG99.
119 IAS 39, para. AG103.
120 IAS 39, para. F.3.1.
121 IAS 39, para. F.3.6.
122 IAS 39, para. F.2.2.
123 IAS 39, para. F.3.2.
124 IAS 39, paras. F.3.3 and F.3.4.
125 IAS 39, para. AG104.
126 IAS 39 (2000), para. 140.
127 See IAS 39, paras. BC149-BC154 and BC221(h).
128 IAS 39, paras. 87 and AG104.
129 IAS 39, para. BC154.
130 IAS 39, para. F.2.5.
131 IAS 39, para. F.2.5.
132 IAS 39, para. F.2.5.
133 IAS 39, para. AG99.
134 Statement 133, *Accounting for Derivative Instruments and Hedging Activities*, FASB, May 2003, paras. 40 and 42 and Statement 133 Implementation Issue H1, *Foreign Currency Hedges: Hedging at the Operating Unit Level*, FASB (Derivatives Implementation Group), September 2000.
135 Statement 133, *Accounting for Derivative Instruments and Hedging Activities*, FASB, May 2003, paras. 40 and 42 and Statement 133 Implementation Issue H1, *Foreign Currency Hedges: Hedging at the Operating Unit Level*, FASB (Derivatives Implementation Group), September 2000.
136 IAS 39, para. F.2.14.
137 Statement 133, *Accounting for Derivative Instruments and Hedging Activities*, FASB, May 2003, paras. 40 and 42 and Statement 133 Implementation Issue H1, *Foreign Currency Hedges: Hedging at the Operating Unit Level*, FASB (Derivatives Implementation Group), September 2000.
138 *IFRIC Update*, IASB, January 2007.
139 *IFRIC Update*, IASB, March 2007.
140 *IFRIC Update*, IASB, May 2007.
141 *IFRIC Update*, IASB, May 2007.
142 IAS 39, para. 71.
143 IAS 39, para. 85.
144 IAS 39, para. 89.
145 IAS 39 (2000), para. 154.
146 IAS 39, para. 90.
147 IAS 39, para. F.2.19.
148 IAS 39, para. 93.
149 IAS 39, para. F.3.6.
150 IAS 39, para. 92.
151 IAS 39, para. 94.
152 IAS 39, para. 91.
153 IAS 39, para. AG113.
154 IAS 39, paras. 95 and F.4.5.
155 IAS 39, para. 96.
156 IAS 39, para. F.5.3.
157 IAS 39, para. F.5.2.
158 IAS 39, para. AG83.
159 IAS 39, para. F.5.1.
160 IAS 39, para. 97.
161 IAS 39, para. 98.
162 IAS 39, para. 99.
163 IAS 39 (2000), para. 160.
164 See IAS 39, paras. BC155-BC164.
165 See IAS 39, paras. BC164, BC221(i)-(j), DO2, DO5 and DO8-DO11.
166 IAS 39, para. 100.
167 IAS 39, para. AG99B.
168 IAS 39, paras. F.3.3 and F.3.4.
169 IAS 39, para. F.6.4.
170 IAS 39, para. 101.
171 IAS 39, para. AG113.
172 Information for Observers (February 2007 IASB meeting), *Business Combinations II: Reassessments (Agenda Paper 2B)*, IASB, February 2007, para. 28 and Information for Observers (April 2007 IASB meeting), *Classification and Designation of Assets, Liabilities and Equity Instruments Acquired or Assumed in a Business Combination (Agenda Paper 2B)*, IASB, April 2007, item #5, table following para. 14.
173 IAS 39, para. 102.
174 IAS 39, para. 102.
175 Statement 133 Implementation Issue H8, *Foreign Currency Hedges: Measuring the Amount of Ineffectiveness in a Net Investment Hedge*, FASB (Derivatives Implementation Group), February 2001.
176 IAS 39, para. 88.
177 IAS 39, para. 88(a).
178 IAS 39, para. F.3.8.
179 *IFRIC Update*, IASB, June 2005.
180 IAS 39, para. F.3.9.
181 Information for Observers (February 2007 IASB meeting), *Business Combinations II: Reassessments (Agenda Paper 2B)*, IASB, February 2007, para. 25.
182 Information for Observers (February 2007 IASB meeting), *Business Combinations II: Reassessments (Agenda Paper 2B)*, IASB, February 2007, paras. 26 and 27.
183 *IASB Update*, IASB, April 2007.
184 Information for Observers (February 2007 IASB meeting), *Business Combinations II: Reassessments (Agenda Paper 2B)*, IASB, February 2007, para. 29 and Information for Observers (April 2007 IASB meeting), *Classification and Designation of Assets, Liabilities*

and Equity Instruments Acquired or Assumed in a Business Combination (Agenda Paper 2B), IASB, April 2007, item #5, table following para. 14.
185 IAS 39, para. 74.
186 IAS 39, para. F.1.9.
187 IAS 39, para. F.1.9.
188 IAS 39, para. F.3.11.
189 IAS 39, para. F.5.4.
190 IAS 39, para. F.3.10.
191 IAS 39, para. F.3.7.
192 IGC Q&A 142-1.
193 For example, see *Uncertain terms*, Ron Paterson, Accountancy, September 2003.
194 IFRS 5, *Non-current Assets Held for Sale and Discontinued Operations*, IASB, March 2004, para. BC81.
195 IFRS 5, Appendix A (Defined terms).
196 IAS 39, para. F.3.7.
197 IAS 39, para. F.3.7.
198 IAS 39, para. F.3.7.
199 IAS 39, para. F.2.4.
200 IAS 39, para. F.2.12.
201 IAS 39, para. F.3.7.
202 IAS 39, para. 9.
203 *IFRIC Update*, IASB, September 2006.
204 IAS 39, para. 88.
205 IAS 39, paras. BC136 and BC136B.
206 IAS 39, para. AG105.
207 IAS 39, para. AG106.
208 IAS 39, para. AG107.
209 IAS 39, para. F.4.1
210 IAS 39, para. AG107.
211 IAS 39, para. F.4.4.
212 IAS 39, para. F.4.2.
213 IAS 39, para. F.4.2.
214 IAS 39, para. AG112.
215 IAS 39, para. AG111.
216 *IFRIC Update*, IASB, November 2006.
217 IAS 39, para. F.4.4.
218 *IFRIC Update*, IASB, March 2007.
219 IAS 39, para. F.5.5.
220 IAS 39, para. F.5.6.
221 IAS 39, para. AG108, *IFRIC Update*, IASB, March 2007, Information for Observers (January 2007 IFRIC meeting), *IAS 39 Financial Instruments: Recognition and Measurement – Assessing Hedge Effectiveness of an Interest Rate Swap in a Cash Flow Hedge (Agenda Paper 14(v))*, IASB, January 2007, Information for Observers (February 2007 IASB meeting), *Business Combinations II: Reassessments (Agenda Paper 2B)*, IASB, February 2007, para. 29 and Information for Observers (April 2007 IASB meeting), *Classification and Designation of Assets, Liabilities and Equity Instruments Acquired or Assumed in a Business Combination (Agenda Paper 2B)*, IASB, April 2007, item #5, table following para. 14.
222 IAS 39, para. AG100.
223 IAS 39, para. F.4.4.
224 Autocorrelation is the correlation of a variable with itself (i.e. the risk of repeating patterns in the error term).
225 *IFRIC Update*, IASB, November 2006.
226 IAS 39 (2000), para. 146.
227 IGC Q&A 146-3 and IAS 39, para. F.4.6 (deleted, March 2004).
228 IAS 39, paras. BC136 and BC136A.
229 IAS 39, para. BC136A.
230 IAS 39, para. AG107A.
231 IAS 39, para. BC132.
232 IAS 39, para. BC133.
233 IAS 39, para. BC134.
234 IAS 39, para. AG108.
235 IAS 39, para. AG108.
236 IAS 39, para. AG109.
237 IAS 39, para. F.4.3.
238 IAS 39, para. BC135.
239 IAS 39, para. F.4.7.
240 IAS 39, para. F.4.7.
241 Statement 133, *Accounting for Derivative Instruments and Hedging Activities*, FASB, May 2003, para. 65.
242 Speech by SEC Staff, *Remarks Before the 2006 AICPA National Conference on Current SEC and PCAOB Developments by Timothy S. Kviz*, U.S. Securities and Exchange Commission, December 2006.
243 *Minutes of the March 15, 2007 Meeting of the FASB Emerging Issues Task Force*, FASB, March 2007.
244 *Minutes of the May 23, 2007 Board Meeting: Agenda Decision: Hedging*, FASB, May 2007, para. 8 and *Project Update: Accounting for Hedging Activities*, FASB, July 2007.
245 Speech by SEC Staff, *Remarks Before the 2006 AICPA National Conference on Current SEC and PCAOB Developments by Timothy S. Kviz*, U.S. Securities and Exchange Commission, December 2006.
246 IAS 39, para. AG108.
247 IAS 39, para. F.1.10.
248 Statement 133 Implementation Issue G20, *Cash Flow Hedges: Assessing and Measuring the Effectiveness of a Purchased Option Used in a Cash Flow Hedge*, FASB (Derivatives Implementation Group), August 2001.
249 *IFRIC Update*, IASB, July 2006.
250 *IFRIC Update*, IASB, May 2007.
251 *IFRIC Update*, IASB, September 2007.
252 Statement 133 Implementation Issue H8, *Foreign Currency Hedges: Measuring the Amount of Ineffectiveness in a Net Investment Hedge*, FASB (Derivatives Implementation Group), February 2001, Question 2.

253 Statement 133 Implementation Issue H8, Question 1 and Statement 133 Implementation Issue H9, *Foreign Currency Hedges: Hedging a Net Investment with a Compound Derivative That Incorporates Exposure to Multiple Risks*, FASB (Derivatives Implementation Group), December 2000.
254 IAS 39, para. F.6.4.
255 Statement 133 Implementation Issue H8, Question 2.
256 IAS 39, para. 77.
257 IAS 27, para. 37.
258 IGC Q&As 121-1 and 121-2 and Appendix to Q&A 121-2.
259 IAS 39, paras. F.6.1, F.6.2 and F.6.3.
260 Exposure Draft, *Amendments to IAS 39, Financial Instruments: Recognition and Measurement, Fair Value Hedge Accounting for a Portfolio Hedge of Interest Rate Risk*, IASB, August 2003.
261 See particularly, IAS 39, paras. 78, 81A, 89A, 92, AG114-AG132, IE1-IE31, DO1 and DO2.
262 IAS 39, *Financial Instruments: Recognition and Measurement, Regulation* No. 2086/2004, European Commission, 19 November 2004, paras. 35, AG107A, AG124(a) and AG130 and parts of paras. 81A, AG31, AG99C, AG99D, AG114(c) and (g), AG118, AG119(d), (e) and (f), AG121, AG122, AG124(d), AG126, AG127 and AG129.
263 IAS 39, para. 108A.
264 IAS 39, para. 108A.
265 IAS 39, para. 108B.
266 IAS 39, para. AG133.
267 IFRS 1, para. 22.
268 IFRS 1, para. 21.
269 IFRS 1, para. 26(b).
270 IFRS 1, para. BC75.
271 IFRS 1, para. BC76.
272 IFRS 1, para. BC77.
273 IFRS 1, para. 28.
274 IFRS 1, para. IG58A.
275 IFRS 1, para. 28.
276 IFRS 1, para. 29.
277 IFRS 1, para. 29.
278 IFRS 1, para. 30.
279 IFRS 1, para. BC75.
280 IFRS 1, para. IG60B.
281 ED 1, *First-time Application of International Financial Reporting Standards*, IASB, July 2002, para. C3(c)(i).
282 ED 1, para. C4.
283 IFRS 1, para. IG58A.
284 IFRS 1, para. IG60A.
285 IAS 39 (2000), para. 172(e) and ED 1, para. C3(b).
286 IFRS 1, paras. IG60 and IG60B.
287 IFRS 1, para. 30.
288 IFRS 1, para. IG60B.
289 *IASB Update*, IASB, October 2005 and April 2006 and Project Update, *Financial Instruments*, IASB, 18 January 2006.
290 *IASB Update*, IASB, May 2004.
291 For example, see *Written Statement of Sir David Tweedie, Chairman, International Accounting Standards Board, to the Committee on Economic and Monetary Affairs of the European Parliament*, IASB, 22 September 2004.
292 For example, see Press Release IP/05/1423, *Accounting standards: Commission endorses "IAS 39 Fair Value Option"*, European Commission, 15 November 2005.
293 *Prepared statement of Sir David Tweedie, Chairman of the International Accounting Standards Board before the Economic and Monetary Affairs Committee of the European Parliament*, IASB, 21 January 2006.
294 *Interest Margin Hedging: FBE Proposal*, FBE, 1 June 2006.
295 *IASB Update*, IASB, December 2006.
296 *IASB Update*, IASB, June 2007.

Chapter 22 Financial instruments: Disclosures

1 INTRODUCTION

The Introduction to Chapter 17 provides a general background to the development of accounting for, and disclosure of, financial instruments. It notes that, currently, disclosure of financial instruments is largely dealt with in IAS 32 – *Financial Instruments: Disclosure and Presentation* – or, when applied, IFRS 7 – *Financial Instruments: Disclosures*.

1.1 IAS 32

The original version of IAS 32 was published in March 1995 and was subject to subsequent minor revisions, particularly to make it more consistent with IAS 39 – *Financial Instruments: Recognition and Measurement* – following approval of that standard in December 1998. A more fundamental review took place as part of the IASB's 'improvements' project, which resulted in the publication of a revised standard in December 2003 as a result which, all disclosure requirements relating to financial instruments in IAS 39 were moved to IAS 32.

There have been a number of consequential amendments since then, notably as IFRS 4 – *Insurance Contracts* – the amendment to IAS 39 restricting the use of the fair value option (see Chapter 17 at 7.1.2) as well as other new standards have been published.

In IAS 32 it is explained that the objective of the standard is to enhance financial statement users' understanding of the significance of financial instruments to an entity's financial position, performance and cash flows.[1] The standard identifies the information that should be disclosed about financial instruments and requires disclosure of information about factors that affect the amount, timing and certainty of an entity's future cash flows relating to financial instruments as well as the accounting policies applied to those instruments. Disclosure of information about the nature and extent of an entity's use of financial instruments, the business purposes they serve, the risks associated with them, and management's policies for controlling those risks are also required.[2] The principles in IAS 32 are designed to complement the recognition and measurement principles in IAS 39 which are covered in Chapters 17 to 21.[3]

The basic disclosure requirements in IAS 32 are no different for banks or other financial institutions, although a flexible approach is allowed to suit an entity's particular circumstances. In addition, IAS 30 – *Disclosures in the Financial Statements of Banks and Similar Financial Institutions* – contains further disclosure requirements which complement, and sometime overlap with, those in IAS 32, although a standard as specialised as IAS 30 is beyond the scope of this publication.

IAS 32 also contains requirements regarding the presentation of financial instruments. These requirements apply to the classification of financial instruments, from the perspective of the issuer, into financial assets, financial liabilities and equity instruments; the classification of related interest, dividends, losses and gains; and the circumstances in which financial assets and financial liabilities should be offset.[4] These requirements are principally covered in Chapters 18 and 19.

1.2 IFRS 7

In 2001 the IASB inherited from the IASC a project principally focused on revising IAS 30 which, in the light of the IASC's work in other areas, was becoming somewhat outdated. This was also seen as an important topic because fundamental changes were taking place in the financial services industry and in the way in which financial institutions managed their activities and risk exposures. This made it increasingly difficult for users of the financial statements of banks to assess and compare their financial position and performance, their associated risk exposures, and their processes for measuring and managing those risks.[5]

The project was taken onto the IASB's initial technical agenda and soon evolved into a comprehensive review of all disclosure requirements related to financial instruments, not just for banks and similar financial institutions. An exposure draft of a new standard, ED 7 – *Financial Instruments: Disclosures*[6] – was published in July 2004, followed by IFRS 7 in August 2005.

The application of IFRS 7 will, for most entities, require the inclusion of additional disclosures in their financial statements (remembering that the standard is not industry specific and applies to all entities – see 3.1.1 below). However, it need not be applied in financial statements for annual periods commencing before 1 January 2007 (see 5.1 below) so entities will have some time to prepare.

The objective of IFRS 7 is to require entities to provide disclosures in their financial statements that enable users to evaluate:[7]

- the significance of financial instruments for the entity's financial position and performance; and

- the nature and extent of risks arising from financial instruments to which the entity is exposed during the period and at the reporting date, and how the entity manages those risks.

Its principles are designed to complement those for recognising, measuring and presenting financial assets and financial liabilities in IAS 32 and IAS 39 which are covered in Chapters 17 to 21.[8] When IFRS 7 is applied, IAS 30 is superseded and the disclosure requirements of IAS 32 are deleted (its title is changed too, to IAS 32 – *Financial Instruments: Presentation*).[9]

2 IAS 32

2.1 General matters

2.1.1 Scope

Section 3 of Chapter 17 contains a detailed explanation of the scope of IAS 32. It is important to recognise that the scope of IAS 32 is somewhat wider than that of IAS 39. Therefore IAS 32 can apply to instruments that are not subject to the recognition and measurement provisions of IAS 39, for example finance leases, certain loan commitments, and an entity's issued equity instruments.

Although IAS 32 was not developed to apply to commodity or other contracts that do not satisfy the definition of a financial instrument or are otherwise within the scope of the standard (see Chapter 17 at 3.9), it may be regarded as appropriate to apply the relevant disclosure requirements to such contracts.[10]

2.1.2 Risks arising from financial instruments

The standard explains that transactions in financial instruments may result in the assumption or transfer of one or more of the following types of financial risk:

(a) *Market risk*, of which there are three types:

  (i) *Currency risk*, the risk that the value of a financial instrument will fluctuate because of changes in foreign exchange rates;

  (ii) *Fair value interest rate risk*, the risk that the value of a financial instrument will fluctuate because of changes in market interest rates;

  (iii) *Price risk*, the risk that the value of a financial instrument will fluctuate as a result of changes in market prices whether those changes are caused by factors specific to the individual instrument or its issuer or factors affecting all instruments traded in the market.

  The term 'market risk' embodies not only the potential for loss but also the potential for gain;

(b) *Credit risk* is the risk that one party to a financial instrument will fail to discharge an obligation and cause the other party to incur a financial loss;

(c) *Liquidity risk*, also referred to as funding risk, is the risk of encountering difficulty in raising funds to meet commitments associated with financial instruments. Liquidity risk may result from an inability to sell a financial asset quickly at close to its fair value;

(d) *Cash flow interest rate risk* is the risk that future cash flows of a financial instrument will fluctuate because of changes in market interest rates. In the case of a floating rate debt instrument, for example, such fluctuations result in a change in the effective interest rate of the financial instrument, usually without a corresponding change in its fair value.

The required disclosures are intended to provide information that assists users in assessing the extent of risk related to an entity's financial instruments, particularly those risks noted above.[11]

2.1.3 Format, location and degree of aggregation

Neither the format of the disclosures, nor their location within the financial statements, is prescribed by the standard. Therefore, management will need to consider the most appropriate method of presenting the information required by the standard. This information will include a combination of narrative descriptions and specific quantified data, as appropriate to the nature of the instruments and their relative significance to the entity.[12]

The standard emphasises that judgement should be exercised in determining the level of detail to be disclosed, taking into account the relative significance of the particular instruments concerned. A balance should be maintained between providing excessive detail and obscuring important information in aggregated disclosures. Summarised information by reference to particular classes of instrument will be appropriate when dealing with large homogenous groups whilst specific information about an individual instrument may be important when, for example, that instrument represents a material component in an entity's capital structure.[13]

Financial instruments should therefore be grouped into classes that are appropriate to the nature of the information disclosed, taking into account matters such as the characteristics of the instruments and the measurement basis applied. In general, classes should distinguish items carried at cost or amortised cost from items carried at fair value and there should be sufficient information to permit a reconciliation to relevant balance sheet line items,[14] although information presented on the face of the financial statements need not be repeated in the notes.[15]

Financial instruments that are not within the scope of IAS 32 (see Chapter 17 at 3) constitute a class or classes of financial assets or liabilities separate from those within the scope of the standard. Disclosures about these instruments are also dealt with by other standards.[16]

2.2 Narrative disclosures

2.2.1 Risk management policies

Entities are required to describe their financial risk management objectives and policies, including their policies for hedging each major type of forecasted transaction for which hedge accounting is used.[17]

Not only should this description provide specific information about particular balances and transactions related to financial instruments but it should also include a discussion of:

- the extent to which financial instruments are used;
- the business purposes served by those instruments; and
- the associated risks.

It should also include a discussion of management's policies for controlling those risks including policies on matters such as:

- hedging risk exposures;
- avoidance of undue concentrations of risk; and
- requirements for collateral to mitigate credit risk.

The standard explains that such a discussion should provide a valuable additional perspective that is independent of the specific instruments held or outstanding at a particular time.[18]

2.2.2 Hedging Activities

The following should be disclosed separately for designated fair value hedges, cash flow hedges and hedges of a net investment in a foreign operation (see Chapter 21):

- a description of the hedge;
- a description of the financial instruments designated as hedging instruments and their fair values at the balance sheet date;
- the nature of the risks being hedged; and
- for cash flow hedges:
  - the periods in which the cash flows are expected to occur;
  - when the cash flows are expected to enter into the determination of profit or loss; and
  - a description of any forecast transaction for which hedge accounting had previously been used but which is no longer expected to occur.[19]

Such disclosures may be integrated with the narrative disclosures covered at 2.2.1 above and, perhaps, with the numerical disclosures covered at 2.3.3 A below.

2.2.3 Accounting policies

For each class of financial asset, financial liability and equity instrument, disclosure should be made of all significant accounting policies, including the general principles adopted and the method of applying those principles to transactions, other events and conditions arising in the business. These should include:[20]

- the criteria applied in determining when to recognise and derecognise financial assets and liabilities;
- the measurement basis applied on initial recognition and subsequently;
- the basis on which associated income and expenses are recognised and measured; and
- for financial assets and financial liabilities designated at fair value through profit or loss:
  - the criteria for so designating such financial assets or financial liabilities on initial recognition; and
  - how the conditions in IAS 39 for such designation have been satisfied.

    For instruments designated to eliminate or significantly reduce a measurement or recognition inconsistency, this should include a narrative description of the circumstances underlying the inconsistency that would otherwise arise.

    For groups of instruments that are managed and the performance evaluated on a fair value basis, this should include a narrative description of how designation at fair value through profit or loss is consistent with the entity's documented risk management or investment strategy.

  These disclosures are introduced following application of the amendment to IAS 39 in respect of the fair value option.

They should also include, for each of the four categories of financial assets (see Chapter 17 at 7), an explanation of whether regular way purchases and sales are accounted for at trade date or settlement date (see Chapter 18 at 3.2).[21]

For some items, entities will have a choice of accounting policies (or bases of applying a policy) and such policies (or bases) should be disclosed where they have a material effect on the financial statements. For example, Extract 20.2 in Chapter 20 at 3.4 illustrates UBS' disclosure of the costing formula applied to its available-for-sale assets.

2.2.4 Terms and conditions

The contractual terms and conditions of an instrument affect the amount, timing and certainty of associated cash receipts and payments. Therefore, when financial instruments are significant to the financial position or future operating results, either individually or as a class, their terms and conditions should be disclosed.[22] Unlike many other disclosure requirements of IAS 32, this information is also required for each class of equity instrument (which will include minority interests) issued by an entity.[23] This is in addition to the information about share capital, required by IAS 1 – *Presentation of Financial Statements* (see 4.3.3 below).

More specifically, for each class of financial asset, financial liability and equity instrument, information should be disclosed about the extent and nature of those instruments, including significant terms and conditions that may affect the amount, timing and certainty of future cash flows.[24] If no single instrument is individually significant, the essential characteristics of the instruments should be described by reference to appropriate groupings of like instruments.[25]

When financial instruments held or issued, either individually or as a class, create a potentially significant exposure to the risks described at 2.1.2 above, terms and conditions that warrant disclosure include:

(a) the principal, stated, face or other similar amount, which for some derivatives might be the notional amount;

(b) the date of maturity, expiry or execution;

(c) early settlement options held by either party to the instrument, including the period in which, or date at which, the options can be exercised and the exercise price or range of prices;

(d) options held by either party to convert the instrument into, or exchange it for, another financial instrument or some other asset or liability, including the period in which, or date at which, the options can be exercised and the conversion or exchange ratio(s);

(e) the amount and timing of principal repayments, including instalment repayments and any sinking fund or similar requirements;

(f) the stated rate or amount of interest, dividend or other periodic return on principal and the timing of payments;

(g) any collateral held or pledged;

(h) the currency in which cash flows are denominated, where this is not the entity's functional currency;

(i) in the case of an instrument that provides for an exchange, information described in (a) to (h) for the instrument to be acquired in the exchange; and

(j) any condition or associated covenant that, if contravened, would significantly alter any of the other terms (for example, a maximum debt-to-equity ratio in a bond covenant that, if contravened, would make the full principal amount of the bond due and payable immediately).[26]

When the balance sheet presentation of a financial instrument differs from its legal form, the standard indicates that it is desirable for the nature of the instrument to be explained.[27] This could be the case for preference shares that are classified as liabilities.

The standard states that the usefulness of this information is enhanced when it highlights any relationship between individual instruments that can significantly affect the amount, timing or certainty of the future cash flows. For example, it may be important to disclose hedging relationships such as might exist when an investment in shares is held for which a put option has been purchased. The extent to which a risk exposure is altered by the relationship among the assets and liabilities may be apparent to financial statement users from information of the type described in (a) to (j) above but in some circumstances further disclosure will be necessary.[28]

In practice, some of the most comprehensive disclosures can be found in respect of an entity's capital. This is illustrated in the following extracts from the financial statements of Jardine Matheson and Roche (showing information about their borrowings) and Zurich Financial Services (showing information about its minority interests).

Extract 22.1: Jardine Matheson Holdings Limited (2005)

Notes to the Financial Statements [extract]

29. Borrowings [extract]

	2005		2004	
	Carrying amount US$m	**Fair value US$m**	Carrying amount US$m	Fair value US$m
Current				
– bank overdrafts	**42**	**42**	37	37
– other bank advances	**613**	**613**	426	426
	655	**655**	463	463
Current portion of long-term borrowings				
– Bank	**894**	**882**	29	30
Mandarin Oriental Convertible Bonds	**–**	**–**	15	16
– Astra Sedaya Finance III Bonds	**16**	**16**	–	–
– Astra Sedaya Finance IV Bonds	**26**	**25**	–	–
– Astra Sedaya Finance V Bonds	**52**	**49**	–	–
– Astra Sedaya Finance VI Bonds	**21**	**20**	–	–
Federal Int. Finance II Bonds	**29**	**28**	–	–
Federal Int. Finance III Bonds	**10**	**10**	–	–
Federal Int. Finance IV Bonds	**7**	**6**	–	–
Federal Int. Finance V Bonds	**40**	**39**	–	–
– Serasi Autoraya I Bonds	**5**	**5**	–	–
– Others	**33**	**33**	–	–
	1,133	**1,113**	44	46
	1,788	**1,768**	507	509

Long-term borrowings				
– Bank	**2,439**	**2,436**	1,554	1,555
Jardine Matheson Guaranteed Bonds	**526**	**545**	513	560
Jardine Strategic Guaranteed Bonds	**296**	**327**	296	345
– Astra Sedaya Finance III Bonds	**4**	**4**	–	–
– Astra Sedaya Finance IV Bonds	**23**	**22**	–	–
– Astra Sedaya Finance V Bonds	**61**	**57**	–	–
– Astra Sedaya Finance VI Bonds	**76**	**74**	–	–
– Federal Int. Finance II Bonds	**7**	**7**	–	–
– Federal Int. Finance III Bonds	**20**	**19**	–	–
– Federal Int. Finance IV Bonds	**18**	**17**	–	–
– Federal Int. Finance V Bonds	**55**	**54**	–	–
– Serasi Autoraya I Bonds	**15**	**15**	–	–
– Astra Graphia I Bonds	**12**	**12**	–	–
– Others	**84**	**81**	19	19
	3,636	**3,670**	2,382	2,479
	5,424	**5,438**	2,889	2,988

	2005 US$m	2004 US$m
Secured	1,877	1,039
Unsecured	3,547	1,850
	5,424	2,889
Due dates of repayment:		
Within one year	1,788	507
Between one and two years	1,633	236
Between two and five years	1,611	1,405
Beyond five years	392	741
	5,424	2,889

	Fixed rate borrowings				
Currency:	Weighted average interest rates %	Weighted average period outstanding Years	US$m	Floating rate borrowings US$m	Total US$m
2005					
Euro	5.9	2.7	14	–	14
Chinese Renminbi	4.7	–	–	13	13
Hong Kong Dollar	4.2	2.6	372	239	611
Indonesian Rupiah	11.6	1.2	2,208	97	2,305
Japanese Yen	1.3	0.3	13	19	32
Malaysian Ringgit	4.9	1.4	126	24	150
New Taiwan Dollar	2.3	1.6	17	17	34
Singapore Dollar	3.3	0.8	72	500	572
Swiss Franc	3.4	26.0	2	21	23
Thailand Baht	4.7	–	–	5	5
United Kingdom Sterling	5.9	1.1	81	82	163
United States Dollar	6.4	3.2	901	601	1,502
			3,806	1,618	5,424

2004					
Euro	6.0	3.7	17	–	17
Chinese Renminbi	4.7	–	–	13	13
Hong Kong Dollar	2.3	2.8	313	356	669
Malaysian Ringgit	3.8	1.9	26	61	87
New Taiwan Dollar	1.8	1.8	11	17	28
Singapore Dollar	2.0	1.4	64	546	610
Swiss Franc	3.0	27.0	2	26	28
Thailand Baht	4.0	–	5	–	5
United Kingdom Sterling	5.8	2.1	91	134	225
United States Dollar	6.1	4.4	826	381	1,207
			1,355	1,534	2,889

All borrowings were within subsidiary undertakings.

The Jardine Matheson Guaranteed Bonds with nominal value of US$550 million and bearing interest at 4.75% were issued by a wholly-owned subsidiary undertaking and are guaranteed by the Company. The Bonds are exchangeable, at the option of the holders, into shares of common stock of J.P. Morgan Chase on the basis of 15.83 shares for each US$1,000 principal amount of the bonds from 6th September 2001 until 30th August 2007. The bonds will mature on 6th September 2007.

The Jardine Strategic Guaranteed Bonds with nominal value of US$300 million and bearing interest at 6.375% were issued by a wholly-owned subsidiary undertaking of Jardine Strategic and are guaranteed by Jardine Strategic. The bonds will mature on 8th November 2011.

The Asta Sedaya Finance III, IV, V and VI Bonds, with nominal values of Rp380 billion, Rp650 billion, Rp1,200 billion, and bearing interest at 13.5%, 11.88% to 12.88%, 8.3% to 11.25% and 8% to 11% respectively were issued by a partly-owned subsidiary undertaking of Astra and are collateralized by fiduciary guarantee over customer financing debtors of the subsidiary undertaking amounting to 60% of the total principal of the bonds (refer note 14). The bonds will mature in 2007, from 2006 to 2008, from 2006 to 2008 and from 2006 to 2010 respectively.

The Federal International Finance II, III, IV and V Bonds, with nominal values of Rp500 billion, Rp300 billion and Rp300 billion, and Rp1,000 billion, and bearing interest at 13.19% to 13.5%, 12% to 12.75%, 10.75% to 11.75% and 8.38% to 10.75% respectively were issued by a wholly-owned subsidiary undertaking of Astra and are collateralized by fiduciary guarantee over consumer financing debtors of the subsidiary undertaking amounting to 80%, 60%, 60% and 60% of the total principal of the bonds respectively (refer note 14). The bonds will mature from 2006 to 2007 except for the V Bonds which will mature from 2006 to 2008.

The Serasi Autoraya I Bonds with nominal value of Rp300 billion and bearing interest at 13.88% were issued by a partly-owned subsidiary undertaking of Astra and are collateralized by fiduciary guarantee over transport equipment of the subsidiary undertaking (refer note 8). The bonds will mature in 2008.

The Astra Graphia I Bonds with nominal value of Rp150 million and bearing interest at 13.38% were issued by a partly-owned subsidiary undertaking of Astra and are collateralized by specific collateral equal to 75% of nominal value in the form of land use rights, buildings and trade debtors of the subsidiary undertaking (refer notes 7, 8 and 19). The bonds will mature in 2008.

By 23rd February 2005, US$76 million of Mandarin Oriental's 6.75% Convertible Bonds, including US$61 million held by Jardine Strategic, had been converted into 113 million ordinary shares of the company.

Secured borrowings at 31st December 2005 included Mandarin Oriental's bank borrowings of US$362 million (2004: US$485 million) which were secured against its tangible fixed assets, Astra's bonds of US$497 million (2004: *nil*) which were secured against its various assets as described above and bank borrowings of US$487 million (2004: nil) which were secured against its various assets, and Jardine Matheson's Guaranteed Bonds of US$256 million (2004: US$513 million). Secured borrowings at 31st December 2004 also included Jardine Cycle & Carriage's bank borrowings of US$40 million which were secured against its assets.

The weighted average interest rates and period of fixed rate borrowings are stated after taking into account hedging transactions.

Extract 22.2: Roche Holding Ltd (2005)

Notes to the Roche Group Consolidated Financial Statements [extracts]

30. Debt [extracts]

Debt: recognised liabilities *in millions of CHF*

	2005	2004
Debt instruments	**8,564**	6,602
Amounts due to banks and other financial institutions	**934**	1,643
Capitalised lease obligations	**31**	701
Other borrowings	**141**	144
Total debt	**9,670**	9,090
Reported as		
– Long-term debt	**9,322**	7,077
– Short-term debt	**348**	2,013
Total debt	**9,670**	9,090

Debt: repayment terms *in millions of CHF*

	2005	2004
Within one year	**348**	2,013
Between one and two years	**2,526**	688
Between two and three years	**2,799**	2,297
Between three and four years	**690**	2,823
Between four and five years	**645**	618
More than five years	**2,662**	651
Total debt	**9,670**	9,090

The 'LYONs' zero coupon US dollar exchangeable notes (see below) are reflected as due the first year that the holders of the notes can request the Group to purchase the notes.

The fair value of the debt instruments is 9.2 billion Swiss francs (2004: 6.9 billion Swiss francs) and the fair value of total debt is 10.3 billion Swiss francs (2004: 9.4 billion Swiss francs). This is calculated based on the observable market prices of the debt instruments or the present value of the future cash flows on the instruments, discounted at a market rate of interest for instruments with similar credit status, cash flows and maturity periods.

There are no pledges on the Group's assets in connection with debt.

Amounts due to banks and other financial institutions

Interest rates on these amounts, which are primarily denominated in euros, average approximately 3.0% (2004: 3.5%). Repayment dates are up to three years. 224 million Swiss francs (2004: 683 million Swiss francs) are due within one year.

Debt instruments

Recognised liabilities and effective interest rates of debt instruments in millions of CHF

	Effective interest rate	2005	2004
European Medium Term Note programme			
4% bonds due 9 October 2008, principal 750 million euros	4.16%	1,193	1,196
5.375% bonds due 29 August 2023, principal 250 million pounds sterling	5.46%	557	536
3.25% bonds due 2 October 2007, principal 750 million US dollars	3.28%	984	848
Swiss franc bonds			
'Rodeo' 1.75% due 20 March 2008, principal 1 billion Swiss francs	3.00%	1,001	1,003
US dollar bonds			
'Chameleon' 6.75% due 6 July 2009, principal 487 million US dollars	6.77%	681	611
Zero coupon US dollar exchangeable notes			
'LYONs V' due 25 July 2021, principal 2.051 billion US dollars	4.14%	1,528	1,264

Japanese yen exchangeable bonds			
'Sumo' 0.25% due 25 March 2005, principal 104.6 billion Japanese yen	–	–	1,123
Genentech Senior Notes			
4.40% Senior Notes due 15 July 2010, principal 500 million US dollars	4,53%	644	–
4.75% Senior Notes due 15 July 2015, principal 1 billion US dollars	4.87%	1,314	–
5.25% Senior Notes due 15 July 2035, principal 500 million US dollars	5.39%	657	–
Japanese yen convertible bonds issued by Chugai			
'Series 6 Chugai Pharmaceutical Unsecured Convertible Bonds' 1.050% due 30 September 2008, principal amount of 0.45 billion Japanese yen (1.86 billion Japanese yen in 2004)	1.05%	5	21
Total debt instruments		**8,564**	**6,602**

Terms of outstanding convertible debt instruments

'LYONs V': The notes are exchangeable for Non-voting Equity Securities (NES) or American Depositary Shares (ADS) at an exchange ratio of 5,33901 NES or 10.67802 exchange ADSs per USD 1,000 principal amount at maturity of the notes. The Group will purchase any note for cash, at the option of the holder, on 25 July 2007, 25 July 2011 and 25 July 2016 for a purchase price per USD 1,000 principal amount of the notes of USD 604.74, USD 698.20 and USD 835.58, respectively. In addition, the notes will be redeemable at the option of the Group in whole or in part at any time after 25 July 2007 at the issue price plus accrued original issue discount (OID). If the notes outstanding at 31 December 2005 were all exchanged it would require 10,947,634 non-voting equity securities to meet the obligation.

'Series 6 Chugai Pharmaceutical Unsecured Convertible Bonds': Each bond of JPY 1,000,000 par value is convertible for 1,311 shares of Chugai. Conversion is at the option of the bondholder and may be made at any time up to the due date of 30 September 2008. The bonds will be redeemable at maturity at the issue price. If the bonds outstanding at 31 December 2005 were all converted it would require 586,229 Chugai shares to exactly meet the obligation. The Group's percentage ownership in Chugai would not be affected by any conversion, as the Group has bonds convertible into Chugai shares that mirror those that Chugai has outstanding with third parties.

Extract 22.3: Zurich Financial Services Group (2005)

Notes to the Consolidated Financial Statements [extract]

24. Preferred securities and minority interests

in USD million, as of December 31	**2005**	2004
Preferred securities	355	407
Minority interests	459	433
Total	**814**	**840**

Minority interests include third-party equity interests, preferred securities and similar instruments issued by consolidated subsidiaries of the Group in connection with the provision of structured financial solutions to its customers.

In December 1999, Zurich Financial Services (Jersey) Limited, a subsidiary of Zurich Group Holding (formerly Zurich Financial Services), issued 12,000,000 perpetual non-voting, non-cumulative Series A Preference Shares on the Euromarket with a par value of EUR 25 (EUR 300,000,000). The securities benefit from a subordinated support agreement from Zurich Group Holding and carry a fixed coupon of 7.125% payable quarterly. The securities are, subject to certain conditions, redeemable at the option of the issuer in whole, but not in part, from time to time on or after five years from the issue date. Proceeds from the issue were used to refinance existing intercompany debt and for general corporate purposes. With this issue, the Group was able to reinforce its capital base while raising equity-like but non-dilutive long-term funds.

Novartis provides the following information in respect of derivative instruments to which it is party.

Extract 22.4: Novartis AG (2005)

Notes to the Novartis Group Consolidated Financial Statements [extract]

15. Marketable securities and derivative financial instruments[extract]

DERIVATIVE FINANCIAL INSTRUMENTS

The following tables show the contract or underlying principal amounts and fair values of derivative financial instruments analyzed by type of contract at December 31, 2005 and 2004. Contract or underlying principal amounts indicate the volume of business outstanding at the balance sheet date and do not represent amounts at risk. The fair values are determined by the markets or standard pricing models at December 31, 2005 and 2004.

	Contract or underlying principal amount		Positive fair values		Negative fair value	
	2005 USD millions	2004 USD millions	2005 USD millions	2004 USD millions	2005 USD millions	2004 USD millions
Currency related instruments						
Forward foreign exchange rate contracts	9 536	5 771	149	65	–223	–281
Over the counter currency options	44	3 987	1	6		–3
Cross currency swaps	1 092	1 236	231	296	–18	
Total of currency related instruments	**10 672**	**10 984**	**381**	**367**	**–241**	**–284**
Interest rate related instruments						
Interest rate swaps	2 479	3 820	3	11	–3	–7
Forward rate agreements	1 386	9 219		6	–1	–6
Interest rate options		100				
Total of interest rate related instruments	**3 865**	**13 139**	**3**	**17**	**–4**	**–13**
Options on equity securities	9	268		15		
Total derivative financial instruments included in marketable securities and in current financial debt	**14 546**	**24 391**	**384**	**399**	**–245**	**–297**

The contract or underlying principal amount of derivative financial instruments at December 31, 2005 are set forth by currency in the table below.

	CHF USD millions	EUR USD millions	USD USD millions	JPY USD millions	Other Currencies USD millions	Total 2005 USD millions	Total 2004 USD millions
Currency related instruments							
Forward foreign exchange rate contracts	1 818	2 211	4 194	956	357	9 356	5 771
Over the counter currency options			1	43		44	3 987
Cross currency swaps		1 068	24			1 092	1 226
Total of currency related derivatives	**1 818**	**3 279**	**4 219**	**999**	**357**	**10 672**	**10 984**
Interest rate related instruments							
Interest rate swaps	381	1 898	200			2 479	3 820
Forward rate agreements		1 186	200			1 386	9 219
Interest rate options							100
Total of interest rate related derivatives	**381**	**3 084**	**400**			**3 863**	**13 139**
Options on equity securities			**9**			**9**	**268**
Total derivative financial instruments	**2 199**	**6 363**	**4 628**	**999**	**357**	**14 546**	**24 391**

AMVESCAP provides detailed information regarding its banking covenants.

Extract 22.5: AMVESCAP PLC (2005)

Notes to the Financial Statements [extract]

17. Long-Term Debt [extract]

The credit facility provides for borrowings of various maturities and contains certain conditions. Financial covenants under the credit agreement include the quarterly maintenance of a debt/EBITDA ratio of not greater than 3.25:1.00 and a coverage ratio of not less than 4.00:1.00 (EBITDA/interest payable for the four consecutive fiscal quarters ended before the date of determination). Interest is payable on the credit facility based upon LIBOR, Prime, Federal Funds or other bank-provided rates in existence at the time of each borrowing.

2.3 Principal numerical disclosures

2.3.1 Interest rate risk disclosures

Changes in interest rates can have a direct effect on the cash flows associated with some financial instruments and on the fair value of others. Therefore IAS 32 requires disclosure of information concerning interest rate exposure.[29] This information should include, for each class of financial asset and financial liability:

- contractual repricing or maturity dates, whichever dates are earlier; and
- effective interest rates, when applicable.[30]

Maturity dates, or repricing dates when earlier, indicate for how long interest rates are fixed; effective interest rates indicate the levels at which they are fixed. This provides a basis for evaluating the exposure to interest rate fair value risk and the associated potential for gain or loss. For instruments that reprice to a market rate before maturity, the period until the next repricing is more important for this purpose than the period to maturity.[31]

To supplement this, information about *expected* repricing or maturity dates may be given when those dates differ significantly from the contractual dates. Such information may be particularly relevant when, for example, it is possible to predict with reasonable reliability the amount of fixed rate mortgage loans that will be repaid before maturity and this information is used as the basis for managing interest rate risk exposure. Such information should explain that it is based on management's expectations and include an explanation of the assumptions used and how they differ from the contractual dates.[32]

An indication should be given of which instruments are:

- exposed to fair value interest rate risk, such as fixed rate instruments;
- exposed to cash flow interest rate risk, such as floating rate instruments that reset as market rates change; and
- not directly exposed to interest rate risk, such as some investments in equity instruments.[33]

Effective interest rates should be disclosed for bonds, notes, loans and similar instruments that create a return and a cost reflecting the time value of money. This requirement does not apply to those instruments that do not bear a determinable effective interest rate such as investments in equity instruments and derivatives – whilst interest rate swaps, forward rate agreements and options are exposed to fair value or cash flow risk from changes in interest rates, disclosure of an effective interest rate is not required. However, when providing such information, the effect of hedging transactions such as interest rate swaps should be disclosed.[34]

Where an instrument has been issued that contains both a liability and an equity component and the instrument has multiple embedded derivative features whose values are interdependent, such as a callable convertible debt instrument (see Chapter 19 at 4.3) the effective interest rate on the liability component (excluding any embedded derivatives that are accounted for separately) should be disclosed. Together with the disclosure of the existence of these features, this information means their impact on the amounts reported as liabilities, equity and interest expense will be highlighted. The IASB sees this as important given what they recognise is an arbitrary allocation of the joint value attributable to this interdependence under the revised version of IAS 32. Hence they have added these new disclosure requirements.[35]

Interest rate risk can arise from transactions in which no financial instrument is recognised and information should be provided to explain the nature and extent of these exposures. In the case of a commitment to lend funds, this information will normally include the stated principal, interest rate and term to maturity of the amount to be lent and any other significant terms of the transaction.[36]

The nature of an entity's business and the extent of its activity in financial instruments will determine whether interest rate risk information is presented in narrative form, in tables, or by using a combination of the two. The standard suggests that one or more of the following approaches may be used:

- Tables showing the carrying amounts of instruments exposed to interest rate risk, grouped by those that will mature or be repriced in the following periods after the balance sheet date:
  - in one year or less;
  - in more than one year but not more than two years;
  - in more than two years but not more than three years;
  - in more than three years but not more than four years;
  - in more than four years but not more than five years; and
  - in more than five years.[37]
- When performance is significantly affected by interest rate exposure, more detailed information is desirable, for example banks may use the following additional groupings:
  - in one month or less after the balance sheet date;
  - in more than one month but not more than three months after the balance sheet date; and

- more than three months but not more than twelve months after the balance sheet date.

- Similarly, tables aggregating the carrying amount of floating rate instruments maturing within various future time periods give an indication of cash flow interest rate risk;
- Information may be disclosed for individual instruments; alternatively weighted average rates or a range of rates may be presented for each class. Instruments denominated in different currencies or having substantially different credit risks may be grouped into separate classes when these factors result in substantially different effective interest rates.[38]

Examples of interest rate risk disclosures given in practice can be seen in Extracts 22.4 and 22.5 at 2.2.4 above.

The standard suggests that indicating the effect of a hypothetical change in market rates on the fair value of financial instruments and future earnings and cash flows may provide useful information. Such information may be based on an assumed one percentage point (100 basis points) change in rates occurring at the balance sheet date. The effects should include changes in interest income and expense relating to floating rate financial instruments and gains or losses resulting from changes in the fair value of fixed rate instruments, but may be restricted to the direct effects on interest-bearing instruments recognised at the reporting date because the indirect effects of a rate change on financial markets and individual entities cannot normally be predicted reliably. When disclosing interest rate sensitivity information, the basis on which the information has been prepared should be indicated, including any significant assumptions.[39] For example, the disclosures would normally include an explanation of how hedging contracts had been dealt with.

2.3.2 *Credit risk*

A failure by counterparties to discharge their obligations could reduce the amount of future cash inflows from financial assets recognised at the balance sheet date or require a cash outflow from other credit exposures (such as a credit derivative or an issued guarantee of the obligations of a third party) thereby giving rise to a recognised loss. Consequently, to allow an assessment of the extent of such failures, IAS 32 requires disclosure of information relating to credit risk.[40]

For each class of financial assets and other credit exposures, information about credit risk exposure should be disclosed, including:

- the amount that best represents the maximum credit risk exposure at the balance sheet date in the event of other parties failing to perform their obligations, without taking account of the fair value of any collateral; and
- significant concentrations of credit risk.[41]

This information need not include an assessment of the probability of losses arising in the future.[42]

The reasons given for ignoring potential recoveries from the realisation of collateral are to provide a consistent measure of credit risk exposure for financial assets and other credit exposures and to take into account the possibility that the maximum exposure may differ from the carrying amount of financial assets recognised at the balance sheet date.[43]

The carrying amount of a financial asset, net of any applicable provisions, usually represents the credit risk exposure at a particular point in time. For example, the maximum exposure to loss for an interest rate swap carried at fair value is normally its carrying amount as this represents its current replacement cost in the event of default. In these circumstances, no additional disclosure beyond that provided on the balance sheet is necessary.[44] Consequently, the required disclosures in respect of credit risk for many entities could be minimal.

Depending on an entity's particular circumstances, however, the maximum potential loss from some financial instruments may differ significantly from their carrying amount and from other disclosed amounts such as their fair value or principal amount. In such circumstances, additional disclosure is necessary.[45]

For example, financial assets subject to legally enforceable rights of set-off against financial liabilities are not presented net unless settlement is intended to take place net or simultaneously (see Chapter 18 at 6). However, where a legal right of set-off exists, a loss can be avoided in the event of default if the receivable is due before a payable of equal or greater amount. When a liability is due to be settled before an asset, credit risk exposure may also be mitigated if default is known about before the liability is settled. On the other hand, if the likely response to default is the extension of the asset's term, an exposure would exist if collection is deferred beyond the date the liability is due. Therefore the existence of legal rights of set-off should normally be disclosed to explain the maximum potential loss, but only when the relevant asset is expected to be collected in accordance with its terms.[46]

Master netting arrangements can mitigate credit risk but do not always meet the offset criteria. When such arrangements significantly reduce credit risk, additional information about the arrangement should be provided, indicating that:

- credit risk is eliminated only to the extent that amounts due to the same counterparty will be settled after the assets are realised; and
- the extent to which overall credit risk is reduced may change substantially within a short period because the exposure is affected by each transaction subject to the arrangement.

The standard states it is also desirable to disclose the terms of master netting arrangements that determine the extent of the reduction in credit risk.[47]

An entity may be exposed to credit risk as a result of a transaction in which no financial asset is recognised on its balance sheet, such as a financial guarantee or credit derivative contract (see Chapter 17 at 3.4). Guaranteeing an obligation of another party creates a liability and exposes the guarantor to credit risk that should be taken into account in making the credit risk disclosures.[48] An entity is likely to conclude that credit risk information in respect of guarantees should be disclosed separately from similar information regarding recognised financial assets (see 2.1.3 above).

Significant credit risk concentrations should be disclosed when they are not otherwise apparent. These concentrations may represent exposures to a single debtor or to groups of debtors whose ability to meet their obligations is expected to be affected by similar changes in economic or other conditions.[49] The information disclosed should include a description of the shared characteristic that identifies each concentration and the amount of the maximum credit risk exposure associated with all financial assets sharing that characteristic.[50]

Characteristics that may give rise to a concentration of risk include the nature of the debtors' activities, such as the industry in which they operate, the geographical area in which activities are undertaken and the level of creditworthiness of groups of borrowers. For example, a manufacturer of equipment for oil and gas producers will normally have debtors for which the risk of non-payment is affected by economic changes in the energy industry. A bank that lends internationally may have many loans outstanding to less developed nations, which may be adversely affected by local economic conditions.[51]

The standard acknowledges that identification of significant concentrations is a matter of judgement and suggests using the guidance in IAS 14 – *Segment Reporting* – to identify industry and geographical segments within which concentrations may arise (see Chapter 30 at 2.3).[52]

2.3.3 Fair values

Given the long-term goal of the standard setters to record all financial instruments in the balance sheet using measures based on fair value rather than historical cost, it is not surprising that, in the interim, the IASB sees the disclosure of information about their fair value as being an important requirement. It is explained in the following terms:

'Fair value information is widely used for business purposes in determining an entity's overall financial position and in making decisions about individual financial instruments. It is also relevant to many decisions made by users of financial statements because, in many circumstances, it reflects the judgement of the financial markets about the present value of expected future cash flows relating to an instrument. Fair value information permits comparisons of financial instruments having substantially the same economic characteristics, regardless of why they are held and when and by whom they were issued or acquired. Fair values provide a neutral basis for assessing management's stewardship by indicating the effects of its decisions to buy, sell or hold financial assets and to incur, maintain or discharge financial liabilities.'[53]

Therefore, when financial assets or liabilities are not measured on a fair value basis, information on fair values should be given by way of supplementary disclosures.[54] The detailed disclosure requirements have changed a little in the revised standard, mainly to align them with the accounting requirements in the revised version of IAS 39, and the principal amendments are highlighted below.

A General disclosure requirements

Except as set out at B below, the fair value of each class of financial assets and liabilities should be disclosed in a way that permits comparison with the corresponding carrying amounts in the balance sheet. Guidance on determining fair values is included in IAS 39 and is covered in Chapter 20 at 4.[55] In providing this disclosure, instruments should be offset only to the extent that their related carrying amounts are also offset in the balance sheet.[56]

In addition, the following information should be disclosed:

(a) the methods and significant assumptions applied in determining fair values, separately for significant classes of financial assets and liabilities.[57]

For example, this might include information about the assumptions relating to prepayment rates, rates of estimated credit losses and interest or discount rates if they are significant;[58]

(b) whether those fair values are determined directly, in full or in part, by reference to published price quotations in an active market or are estimated using a valuation technique;

(c) whether financial instruments are measured at fair values determined in full or in part using a valuation technique based on assumptions that are not supported by observable market prices or rates.

If changing any such assumption to a reasonably possible alternative would result in a significantly different fair value, this fact should be stated and the effect on the fair value of a range of reasonably possible alternative assumptions should be disclosed. For this purpose, significance shall be judged with respect to profit or loss and total assets or total liabilities;

(d) the total amount of the change in fair value estimated using a valuation technique that was recognised in profit or loss during the period.[59]

These disclosures are applicable equally to all classes of financial instruments with the exception of (d) which is clearly not applicable to financial instruments that are not measured at fair value through profit or loss. The extent to which these disclosures are presented separately for those instruments that are measured at fair value, and those for which fair values are only disclosed, will depend on an entity's specific circumstances.

In order to provide a sense of the potential variability of fair value estimates, information about the use of valuation techniques should be disclosed, for example the sensitivities of fair value estimates to the main valuation assumptions. The IASB considered the view that disclosure of sensitivities could be difficult, in particular when there are many valuation assumptions to which the disclosure would apply and these assumptions are interdependent. However, it noted that a detailed quantitative disclosure of sensitivity to all valuation assumptions was not required, only those that could result in a significantly different estimate of fair value. Also, the standard does not require all interdependencies between assumptions to be reflected when making the disclosure.[60] Rather, the sensitivity disclosure is required only if:

- the fair value is sensitive to a particular assumption;
- reasonably possible alternatives for that assumption would result in a significantly different result; and
- that assumption is not supported by observable market prices or rates.[61]

The IASB also considered view that such disclosure might imply that a fair value established by a valuation technique is less valid than one established by other means. However, it was noted that fair values that are estimated by valuation techniques are more subjective than those established from an observable market price, and concluded that users should be given information to help them in assessing this subjectivity.[62]

As set out at 2.2.2 above, the fair values of financial instruments designated as hedging instruments should be disclosed separately for designated fair value hedges, cash flow hedges and hedges of a net investment in a foreign operation.[63] It will often be possible to combine those disclosures within the general fair value disclosures. However, a single hedging instrument may be simultaneously designated in a cash flow and a fair value hedge (see Chapter 21 at 2.1.6), in which case the instrument in question would need to be included in the disclosures for both cash flow hedges and fair value hedges.[64]

B Exceptions

Pragmatically, disclosure of fair values is not required for instruments such as short-term trade receivables and payables when their carrying amount reasonably approximates fair value.[65]

To align with the measurement provisions of IAS 39, fair values need not be given for investments in unquoted equity instruments, or derivatives linked to such instruments, that are measured at cost because their fair value cannot be measured reliably (see Chapter 20 at 4.4). However, these instruments are singled out for additional disclosure. This is to assist users of the financial statements in making their own judgements about the extent of possible differences between the carrying amount of such financial assets and liabilities and their fair value.[66] Particularly, disclosure should be made of the fact that they are measured at cost because their fair value cannot be reliably measured together with:

- a description of the instruments;
- their carrying amount;
- an explanation of why fair value cannot be measured reliably; and
- if possible, the range of estimates within which fair value is highly likely to lie.[67]

  Where such a range is provided, there is no explicit requirement to disclose the methods and significant assumptions applied in determining those fair values, or other information equivalent to that set out at 2.3.3 A above. However, such information is likely to be useful and relevant.

This information should include an explanation of the principal characteristics of the instruments that are pertinent to their value as well as information about the market for the instruments. The standard acknowledges that, in some cases, the disclosed terms and conditions (see 2.2.4 above) may provide sufficient information.[68]

Also, when it has a reasonable basis for doing so, management may indicate its opinion on the relationship between the instruments' fair value and carrying amount.[69] For example, management might have a reasonable basis for stating that the fair value of an investment or portfolio of investments is 'likely to be in excess' or 'significantly in excess' of cost.

If financial assets whose fair value previously could not be reliably measured are sold, that fact should be disclosed as well as:

- the carrying amount of such financial assets at the time of sale; and
- the amount of gain or loss recognised.[70]

As set out in Chapter 17 at 3.3.2 some instruments (normally life insurance policies) contain a discretionary participation feature. If the fair value of that feature cannot be reliably measured, that fact should be disclosed together with a description of the contract, its carrying amount, an explanation of why fair value cannot be measured reliably and, if possible, the range of estimates within which fair value is highly likely to lie.[71]

For all other financial instruments, the IASB believes it is reasonable to expect that fair value can be determined with sufficient reliability within constraints of timeliness and cost. It therefore concluded that there should be no exception from the requirement to disclose fair value information for these instruments.[72]

2.3.4 Income, expenses, gains and losses

IAS 32 requires disclosure of material items of income and expense and gains and losses resulting from financial assets and liabilities that are included in the income statement. It goes on to state that these items should include at least the following:[73]

- total interest income, calculated using the effective interest method, for financial assets that are not at fair value through profit or loss;
- total interest expense on financial liabilities on the same basis;
- the amount of any gain or loss that was removed from equity in respect of available-for-sale financial assets and recognised in the income statement for the period; and
- the amount of interest income accrued on impaired financial assets.

In addition, the amount of any impairment loss recognised in the income statement in respect of financial assets should be disclosed, separately for each significant class of financial asset, together with an indication of the nature of the loss.[74]

Material gains and losses that are included in equity should be disclosed, including at least the following:

- for available-for-sale financial assets:[75]
  - the amount of any gain or loss recognised directly in equity during the period; and
  - the amount that was removed from equity and recognised in the income statement for the period; and
- for cash flow hedges:[76]
  - the amount of gains or losses on designated hedging instruments recognised in equity during the period;
  - the amount removed from equity during the period and reported in the income statement; and
  - the amount removed from equity during the period and included in the initial measurement of the acquisition cost or other carrying amount of hedged non-financial assets or liabilities.

2.4 Other disclosures

2.4.1 Derecognition

Where certain arrangements in respect of financial assets have been entered into that do not qualify as a transfer of those assets and they continue to be recognised, or are recognised to the extent of the entity's continuing involvement, the following should be disclosed for each class of financial asset:

- the nature of the assets;
- the nature of the risks and rewards of ownership to which the entity remains exposed;
- when the entity continues to recognise all of the asset, the carrying amounts of the asset and of the associated liability; and
- when the entity continues to recognise the asset to the extent of its continuing involvement, the total amount of the asset, the amount of the asset that the entity continues to recognise and the carrying amount of the associated liability.[77]

Although not clear from the standard, it would seem sensible for entities to disclose the carrying amount of the original assets at the date of derecognition and the amount of assets and associated liabilities that continue to be recognised at the balance sheet date.

This disclosure requirement is included because the IASB considers it will help users to evaluate the significance of transactions that are subject to the derecognition provisions of IAS 39. The types of arrangement for which such disclosures are required are discussed in Chapter 18 at 4. This disclosure may be required, for example, if an entity sells a portfolio of receivables and provides a limited guarantee of only one risk – the amount of the transferred receivables the transferor continues to recognise may be much riskier than the amount it derecognises.[78]

2.4.2 Defaults and breaches

With respect to defaults of principal, interest, sinking fund or redemption provisions during the period on loans payable recognised as at the balance sheet date, and any other breaches during the period of loan agreements when those breaches can permit the lender to demand repayment, the following information should be disclosed:

- details of those breaches;
- the amount recognised as at the balance sheet date in respect of the loans payable on which the breaches occurred; and
- with respect to these amounts, whether the default has been remedied or the terms of the loans payable renegotiated before the date the financial statements were authorised for issue.[79]

However, disclosure is not required for breaches that are remedied, or in response to which the terms of the loan are renegotiated, on or before the balance sheet date.[80]

For these purposes, loans payable include issued debt instruments and financial liabilities other than short-term trade payables on normal credit terms.[81]

When such a breach has occurred during the period, and the breach was not remedied or the terms of the loan payable were not renegotiated by the balance sheet date, the standard includes a reminder that the effect of the breach on the classification of the liability as current or non-current is determined under IAS 1 (see Chapter 3 at 3.1.4).[82] These requirements are considered to provide relevant information about an entity's creditworthiness and its prospects of obtaining future loans.[83]

2.4.3 Reclassifications

Where a financial asset has been reclassified as one measured at cost or amortised cost rather than at fair value (see Chapter 17 at 7.5) the reason for that reclassification should be disclosed.[84]

2.4.4 Financial instruments at fair value through profit or loss

IAS 32 contains a large number of disclosure requirements for financial instruments at fair value through profit or loss, many of which apply only to those that are in this category by designation (i.e. those that are not classified as held for trading). These are summarised below.

A Balance sheet and income statement

Separate disclosure should be made of the carrying amounts of:[85]

- financial assets that are classified as held for trading;
- financial liabilities that are classified as held for trading;

- financial assets that, upon initial recognition, were designated as financial assets at fair value through profit or loss (i.e. those that are not classified as held for trading); and
- financial liabilities that, upon initial recognition, were designated as financial liabilities at fair value through profit or loss (i.e. those that are not classified as held for trading).

The amendments to IAS 39 in respect of the fair value option introduce a requirement to disclose separately net gains or net losses on financial assets or financial liabilities that are designated by the entity as at fair value through profit or loss.[86]

B Financial liabilities designated at fair value through profit or loss

The decision by the IASB to allow financial instruments to be designated at fair value through profit or loss was not uncontroversial, particularly insofar as it related to non-derivative liabilities. In fact, the most common concern is not that such liabilities may be designated at fair value through profit or loss, it is the fact that the IASB's definition of fair value takes into account the instrument's credit risk which, depending on the terms of the instrument, will be based to a greater or lesser degree on the creditworthiness of the issuing entity.

Some commentators argued that recognising a gain or loss when there is a change in an entity's own creditworthiness results in potentially misleading information and that users may misinterpret the profit or loss effects of changes in credit risk, especially in the absence of disclosures.[87]

The IASB was not persuaded by any arguments to exclude changes in credit risk from the measurement of liabilities, (although it eventually introduced restrictions on the use of the option) but agreed that disclosure of the change in fair value of the financial liability that is caused by changes in its credit risk would help alleviate the concerns expressed. However, it noted that this would often not be practicable because it may not be possible to identify and measure reliably that part of the change in fair value separately. Consequently, IAS 32 calls for a 'reasonable proxy' of this information to be disclosed to provide users with information with which to understand the profit or loss effect of such a change in credit risk.[88]

Therefore, where a (non-derivative) financial liability has been designated at fair value through profit or loss, i.e. it is not classified as trading, the amount of change during the period and cumulatively in its fair value that is attributable to changes in credit risk should be disclosed.[89]

Unless an alternative method more faithfully represents this amount, it should be determined as the amount of change in the fair value of the liability that is not attributable to changes in market conditions that give rise to market risk. Changes in market conditions that give rise to market risk include changes in a benchmark interest rate, commodity price, foreign exchange rate or index of prices or rates. For contracts that include a unit-linking feature, changes in market conditions include changes in the performance of an internal or external investment fund. If the only relevant changes in market conditions for a financial liability are changes in an observed (benchmark) interest rate, the amount to be disclosed can be estimated as follows:

(a) first, the liability's internal rate of return at the start of the period is computed using the observed market price and contractual cash flows at that time and from this is deducted the observed (benchmark) interest rate at the start of the period, to arrive at an instrument specific component of the internal rate of return;

(b) next, the present value of the cash flows associated with the liability is calculated using the liability's contractual cash flows at the start of the period and a discount rate equal to the sum of the observed (benchmark) interest rate at the end of the period and the instrument-specific component of the internal rate of return at the start of the period as determined in (a);

(c) the amount determined in (b) is then adjusted for any cash paid or received on the liability during the period and increased to reflect the increase in fair value that arises because the contractual cash flows are one period closer to their due date; and

(d) the difference between the observed market price of the liability at the end of the period and the amount determined in (c) is the change in fair value that is not attributable to changes in the observed (benchmark) interest rate and this is the amount to be disclosed.

This assumes that changes in fair value other than those arising from changes in the instrument's credit risk or from changes in interest rates are not significant. If the instrument contained an embedded derivative, the change in fair value of the embedded derivative would be excluded in determining the amount to be disclosed.[90]

If another method more faithfully represents the amount of change in the fair value of the liability that is attributable to changes in credit risk, that method should be used.[91]

Whatever the chosen method(s), it (they) should be disclosed. Further, if the disclosure is not considered to represent faithfully the change in the fair value of the financial liability attributable to changes in credit risk, the reasons for reaching this conclusion and the factors believed to be relevant should also be disclosed.[92]

These disclosures were refined by the fair value option amendments to IAS 39 – previously only one method of calculation was prescribed and no account was to be taken of embedded derivatives and similar changes in market conditions that would affect the fair value of the instrument.

In addition, the IASB concluded that the difference between the carrying amount of such a liability and the amount the entity would be contractually required to pay at maturity to the holder of the obligation should also be disclosed.[93] The fair value may differ significantly from the settlement amount, particularly for liabilities with a long duration when the entity has experienced a significant deterioration in creditworthiness subsequent to issuance.[94]

C Loans and receivables designated at fair value through profit or loss

The fair value option amendments to IAS 39 introduced additional disclosure requirements into IAS 32 for loans and receivables (or groups of such assets) that are designated at fair value through profit or loss. These disclosures are as follows:

- the maximum exposure to credit risk (see 2.3.2 above) at the reporting date of the loan or receivable (or group of loans or receivables);
- the amount by which any related credit derivative or similar instrument mitigates that maximum exposure to credit risk;
- the amount of change during the period and cumulatively in the fair value of the loan or receivable (or group of loans or receivables) that is attributable to changes in credit risk (see below); and
- the amount of change in the fair value of any related credit derivative or similar instrument that has occurred during the period and cumulatively since the loan or receivable was designated.

Calculating the change in fair value attributable to changes in credit risk is approached in the same way as for financial liabilities (see B above). It may be determined either as the amount of change in its fair value that is not attributable to changes in market conditions that give rise to market risk or by using an alternative method that more faithfully represents the amount of change in its fair value that is attributable to changes in credit risk.[95] The chosen method(s) should be disclosed and if the disclosure is not considered to represent faithfully the change in the fair value of the financial liability attributable to changes in credit risk, the reasons for reaching this conclusion and the factors believed to be relevant should be disclosed.[96]

2.4.5 Collateral

The carrying amount of financial assets pledged as collateral for liabilities and for contingent liabilities should be separately disclosed, along with any material terms and conditions relating to those assets.[97] There is no explicit requirement to disclose the fair value of such assets, although entities may conclude that pledged assets constitute a separate class (see 2.1.3 above) in which case information about the fair value of such assets could be derived from the disclosures at 2.3.3 above.

When collateral has been accepted by an entity that it is permitted to sell or repledge in the absence of default by the owner, the following should be disclosed:

- the fair value of the collateral accepted (both financial and non-financial assets);
- the fair value of any such collateral sold or repledged and whether there is an obligation to return it; and
- any material terms and conditions associated with the use of this collateral.[98]

3 IFRS 7

As noted at 1.2 above, IFRS 7 was published in August 2005 and must be adopted for annual periods commencing on or after 1 January 2007. In most cases, IFRS 7 will require more disclosure than was previously required under IAS 32, although there are exceptions. The main differences between IAS 32 and IFRS 7 are as follows:

- IFRS 7 requires additional disclosure about assets and liabilities and income statement and equity items, including detailed numerical information about hedging gains and losses and day 1 profits (see 3.3.2, 3.3.3, 3.3.4 A and 3.3.5 B below);
- additional guidance is provided in IFRS 7 setting out the type of accounting policies an entity might need to disclose and what information it might need to explain its approach to financial risk management (see 3.3.1 and 3.4.1 below);
- additional disclosures concerning credit risk exposures are required by IFRS 7, including information about impairment allowance accounts (bad debt provisions), overdue financial assets and collateral held (see 3.3.4 G and 3.4.2 B below);
- to provide information about liquidity risk a maturity analysis of financial liabilities in a prescribed form should be given when IFRS 7 is applied (see 3.4.2 C below);
- extensive qualitative and quantitative information about an entity's exposure to market risk, including sensitivity analyses, is required by IFRS 7 (see 3.4.2 D below); and
- the disclosures of terms and conditions of financial instruments required by IAS 32 (see 2.2.4 above) are largely withdrawn.

As set out at 1.2 above, the objective of IFRS 7 is to require entities to provide disclosures in their financial statements that enable users to evaluate:[99]

- the significance of financial instruments for the entity's financial position and performance; and
- the nature and extent of risks arising from financial instruments to which the entity is exposed during the period and at the reporting date, and how the entity manages those risks.

These objectives manifest themselves in two disclosure principles, to the effect that an entity should disclose information that enables users of its financial statements to evaluate:

- the significance of financial instruments for its financial position and performance (see 3.3 below); and
- the nature and extent of risks arising from financial instruments to which the entity is exposed at the reporting date (see 3.4 below).

3.1 Scope

3.1.1 *Entities required to comply with IFRS 7*

Although IFRS 7 evolved from a project to update IAS 30 (which applies only to banks and similar financial institutions) it applies to all entities preparing their financial statements in accordance with IFRS that have financial instruments.[100] The IASB considered exempting certain entities, including insurers, subsidiaries and those that are small or medium-sized (SMEs), but decided that IFRS 7 should apply to all entities whilst keeping the decision in respect of SMEs under review in its related project.[101] The IASB has now issued an exposure draft of an IFRS for SMEs that would require reduced disclosures about financial instruments.

3.1.2 *Financial instruments within the scope of IFRS 7*

Section 3 of Chapter 17 contains a detailed explanation of the scope of IFRS 7. It is important to recognise that the scope of IFRS 7 is somewhat wider than that of IAS 39. Therefore IFRS 7 can apply to instruments that are not subject to the recognition and measurement provisions of IAS 39, for example finance leases and certain loan commitments.[102]

The scope of IFRS 7 is the same as that of IAS 32 with one exception, namely that IFRS 7 does not apply to derivatives based on interests in subsidiaries, associates or joint ventures that meet the definition of an equity instrument in IAS 32. The standard explains this is because equity instruments are not remeasured and hence do not expose the issuer to balance sheet and income statement risk. Also, the disclosures about the significance of financial instruments for financial position and performance are not considered relevant for equity instruments.[103]

Given the reasons quoted, it is not entirely clear why the IASB did not exclude *all* instruments meeting the definition of equity in IAS 32 from the scope of IFRS 7, e.g. non-puttable ordinary shares issued by the reporting entity. However, this is of largely academic interest only because IFRS 7 specifies no disclosure requirements for issued equity instruments.

3.2 Structuring the disclosures

The main text of IFRS 7 is supplemented by application guidance, which is an integral part of the standard,[104] and by implementation guidance, which accompanies, but is not part of, the standard.[105] The implementation guidance suggests possible ways of applying some of the requirements of the standard but, it is emphasised, does not create additional requirements.[106]

Although the implementation guidance discusses each disclosure requirement in IFRS 7 separately, disclosures would normally be presented as an integrated package and individual disclosures might satisfy more than one requirement. For example, information about concentrations of risk might also convey information about exposure to credit or other risk.[107] This section of the chapter follows a similar approach whereby each topic is considered individually in the context of the requirements of the standard as well as related application and implementation guidance.

3.2.1 Level of detail

Entities need to decide, in the light of their circumstances, how much detail to provide to satisfy the requirements of IFRS 7, how much emphasis to place on different aspects of the requirements and how information is aggregated to display the overall picture without combining information with different characteristics. It is necessary to strike a balance between overburdening financial statements with excessive detail that may not assist users of financial statements and obscuring important information as a result of too much aggregation. For example, important information should not be obscured by including it among a large amount of insignificant detail. Similarly, information that is so aggregated that it obscures important differences between individual transactions or associated risks should not be disclosed.[108]

This means that not all of the information suggested, say, in the implementation guidance is necessarily required.[109] On the other hand, there is a reminder that IAS 1 requires additional disclosures when compliance with the specific requirements in IFRSs is insufficient to enable users to understand the impact of particular transactions, other events and conditions on the entity's financial position and financial performance (see Chapter 3 at 4.1.1 A).[110]

3.2.2 Materiality

The implementation guidance to IFRS 7 draws attention to the definition of materiality in IAS 1 (see Chapter 3 at 4.1.5 A):[111]

> 'Omissions or misstatements of items are material if they could, individually or collectively, influence the economic decisions of users taken on the basis of the financial statements. Materiality depends on the size and nature of the omission or misstatement judged in the surrounding circumstances. The size or nature of the item, or a combination of both, could be the determining factor.'[112]

It then notes that a specific disclosure requirement need not be satisfied if the information is not material[113] and draws attention to the following explanation in IAS 1:[114]

> 'Assessing whether an omission or misstatement could influence economic decisions of users, and so be material, requires consideration of the characteristics of those users. The *Framework for the Preparation and Presentation of Financial Statements* states ... that 'users are assumed to have a reasonable knowledge of business and economic activities and accounting and a willingness to study the information with reasonable diligence.' Therefore, the assessment needs to take into account how users with such attributes could reasonably be expected to be influenced in making economic decisions.'[115]

The inclusion of such guidance could be seen as curious given that it is no more or less applicable to IFRS 7 than any other standard. However, what it amounts to is a degree of reassurance that entities with few financial instruments and few risks (for example a manufacturer whose only financial instruments are accounts receivable and accounts payable) will give few disclosures, something that is borne out in other references within the standard and accompanying material.[116]

3.2.3 Classes of financial instrument

Certain disclosures should be provided by class of financial instrument. For these, entities should group financial instruments into classes that are appropriate to the nature of the information disclosed and take into account the characteristics of those instruments.[117]

It is emphasised that these classes should be determined by the entity and are, thus, distinct from the categories of financial instruments specified in IAS 39 (which determine how financial instruments are measured and where changes in fair value are recognised – see Chapter 17 at 7 and Chapter 20 at 3).[118] However, in determining classes of financial instrument an entity should, as a minimum, distinguish instruments measured at amortised cost from those measured at fair value and treat as a separate class or classes those financial instruments outside the scope of IFRS 7.[119]

3.2.4 Reconciliation to balance sheet

Sufficient information should be provided to permit the disclosures by class of asset to be reconciled to the line items presented in the balance sheet.[120]

3.3 Significance of financial instruments for an entity's financial position and performance

The IASB decided that the disclosure requirements in this area should result from the following disclosure principle:

> 'An entity shall disclose information that enables users of its financial statements to evaluate the significance of financial instruments for its financial position and performance.'

Further, they concluded that this principle could not be satisfied unless other specified disclosures (which are dealt with at 3.3.1 to 3.3.5 below) are also provided.[121]

3.3.1 Accounting policies

The main body of IFRS 7 contains a reminder of IAS 1's requirement to disclose, in the summary of significant accounting policies, the measurement basis (or bases) used in preparing the financial statements and the other accounting policies used that are relevant to an understanding of the financial statements.[122]

Further details are included in the application guidance, which is more detailed than the equivalent provisions in IAS 32 (see 2.2.3 above). For financial assets or financial liabilities designated at fair value through profit or loss (see Chapter 17 at 7.1.2), such disclosure may include:[123]

- the nature of the financial assets or financial liabilities designated at fair value through profit or loss;
- the criteria for so designating such financial assets or financial liabilities on initial recognition; and
- how the conditions in IAS 39 for such designation have been satisfied.

  For instruments designated to eliminate or significantly reduce a measurement or recognition inconsistency, this should include a narrative description of the circumstances underlying the inconsistency that would otherwise arise.

  For groups of instruments that are managed and the performance evaluated on a fair value basis, this should include a narrative description of how designation at fair value through profit or loss is consistent with the entity's documented risk management or investment strategy.

Other policies that might be appropriate include:[124]

- the criteria for designating financial assets as available for sale;
- whether regular way purchases and sales of financial assets are accounted for at trade date or at settlement date (see Chapter 18 at 3.2);
- how net gains or net losses on each category of financial instrument are determined, for example whether the net gains or net losses on items at fair value through profit or loss include interest or dividend income;
- the criteria the entity uses to determine that there is objective evidence that an impairment loss has occurred; and
- when the terms of financial assets that would otherwise be past due (see 3.4.2 B I) or impaired have been renegotiated, the accounting policy for financial assets that are the subject of renegotiated terms.

  In contrast to its specific requirements for the derecognition of financial liabilities (see Chapter 18 at 5.2), IAS 39 does not explicitly address whether or in what circumstances a financial asset whose terms are subject to renegotiation should be derecognised by the holder or whether it should be regarded as a continuation of the existing asset. Therefore, this could be an important accounting policy for banks and other financial institutions if they frequently renegotiate the terms of their loans and receivables.

When an allowance account (such as a bad debt provision) is used to reduce the carrying amount of financial assets impaired by credit losses, the accounting policies may need to indicate:[125]

- the criteria for determining when the carrying amount of impaired financial assets is reduced directly (or, in the case of a reversal of a write-down, increased directly) and when the allowance account is used; and
- the criteria for writing off amounts charged to the allowance account against the carrying amount of impaired financial assets (as set out at 3.3.4 G above, a reconciliation of changes in the allowance account should be given);

The application guidance also contains a reminder that IAS 1 requires entities to disclose the judgements, apart from those involving estimations, that management has made in the process of applying the entity's accounting policies and that have the most significant effect on the amounts recognised in the financial statements (see Chapter 3 at 5.1.1 B).[126]

3.3.2 *Income, expenses, gains and losses*

Under IFRS 7, entities are required to disclose various items of income, expense, gains and losses. The disclosures below may be provided either on the face of the financial statements or in the notes.[127]

A Gains and losses by measurement category

The IASB concluded that disclosure of the following net gains or net losses is necessary to understand the financial performance of an entity's financial instruments given the different measurement bases in IAS 39:[128]

- financial assets or financial liabilities at fair value through profit or loss, showing separately those on financial instruments designated as such upon initial recognition, and those on financial instruments classified as held for trading;
- available-for-sale financial assets, showing separately the amount of gain or loss recognised directly in equity during the period and the amount removed from equity and recognised in profit or loss for the period;
- held-to-maturity investments;
- loans and receivables; and
- financial liabilities measured at amortised cost;

These disclosures, which are designed to complement the balance sheet disclosure requirement described at 3.3.4 A below,[129] are more extensive than those in IAS 32 (see 2.3.4 above).

Some entities include interest and dividend income in gains and losses on financial assets and financial liabilities held for trading and others do not. To assist users in comparing income arising from financial instruments across different entities, entities are required to disclose how the income statement amounts are determined. For example, an entity should disclose whether net gains and losses on financial assets or financial liabilities held for trading include interest and dividend income (see 3.3.1).[130]

B Interest income and expense

Just as under IAS 32 (see 2.3.4 above), for financial assets or financial liabilities that are not at fair value through profit or loss, total interest income and total interest expense (calculated using the effective interest method) should be disclosed, as should interest income on impaired financial assets (accrued as described in Chapter 20 at 6.5).[131]

Financial instruments containing discretionary participation features fall within the scope of IFRS 4 rather than IAS 39 (see Chapter 17 at 3.3.2). However, IFRS 7 does apply to such instruments and IFRS 4 acknowledges that the interest expense disclosed need not be calculated using the effective interest method.[132]

Similarly, finance lease payables and receivables are within the scope of IFRS 7 (see Chapter 17 at 3.2) but are not accounted for using the effective interest method. However, there is no equivalent acknowledgement either in IAS 17 or IAS 39 that the disclosed interest income and interest expense should be made on the basis of the finance cost and finance revenue recognised under IAS 17. Nevertheless, this seems little more than an oversight and we consider it appropriate to include in the disclosure the amounts actually recognised rather than amounts calculated in accordance with the effective interest method.

C Fee income and expense

IFRS 7 introduces new disclosure requirements for fees (excluding amounts included in the effective interest rate calculation). Accordingly, entities should disclose fee income and expense arising from:[133]

- financial assets or financial liabilities that are not at fair value through profit or loss; and
- trust and other fiduciary activities that result in the holding or investing of assets on behalf of individuals, trusts, retirement benefit plans, and other institutions.

This information is said to indicate the level of such activities and help users to estimate possible future income of the entity.[134]

D Impairment losses

Finally, like under IAS 32 (see 2.3.4 above), the amount of any impairment loss should be disclosed for each class of financial asset.[135]

3.3.3 Hedge accounting

When hedge accounting is applied (see Chapter 21) entities are required to disclose the following, separately for each type of hedge (i.e. fair value hedges, cash flow hedges, and hedges of net investments in foreign operations):[136]

- a description of each type of hedge;
- a description of the financial instruments designated as hedging instruments and their fair values at the reporting date; and
- the nature of the risks being hedged.

A single hedging instrument may be simultaneously designated in a cash flow and a fair value hedge (see Chapter 21 at 2.1.6), in which case the instrument in question would need to be included in the disclosures both for cash flow hedges and fair value hedges.[137]

For cash flow hedges, entities are also required to disclose:[138]

- the periods when the cash flows are expected to occur and when they are expected to affect profit or loss;

- a description of any forecast transaction for which hedge accounting has previously been used, but which is no longer expected to occur;
- the amount that was recognised in equity during the period;
- the amount that was removed from equity and included in profit or loss for the period, showing the amount included in each line item in the income statement; and
- the amount that was removed from equity during the period and included in the initial cost or other carrying amount of a non-financial asset or non-financial liability whose acquisition or incurrence was a hedged highly probable forecast transaction.

With the exception of identifying the amount of gains and losses on cash flow hedges recycled into the income statement by line item (which is a new requirement in IFRS 7), the disclosures above are substantially the same as those required by IAS 32 (see 2.2.2, 2.3.3 A and 2.3.4 above). IFRS 7 also requires the following to be disclosed, for which there is no explicit requirement in IAS 32:[139]

- in fair value hedges, gains or losses:
  - on the hedging instrument; and
  - on the hedged item attributable to the hedged risk;
- the ineffectiveness recognised in profit or loss that arises from cash flow hedges; and
- the ineffectiveness recognised in profit or loss that arises from hedges of net investments in foreign operations.

The financial statements of Deutsche Telekom include the following disclosure about hedges.

Extract 22.6: Deutsche Telekom AG (2006)

Notes to the consolidated balances sheet [extract]

43. Risk management and financial derivatives [extract]

Hedge accounting.

Fair value hedges.

To hedge the fair value risk of fixed-interest liabilities, Deutsche Telekom used interest rate swaps and forward interest rate swaps (receive fixed, pay variable) denominated in EUR, GBP, and USD in the 2006 and 2005 financial years. Fixed-income bonds denominated in EUR, USD, and GBP were designated as hedged items. The changes in the fair values of the hedged items resulting from changes in the Euribor, USDLibor, or GBPLibor swap rate are offset against the changes in the value of the interest rate swaps. The aim of this hedging is to transform the fixed-income bonds into variable-interest debt, thus hedging the fair value of the financial liabilities. Credit risks are not part of the hedging.

The effectiveness of the hedging relationship is prospectively tested using the critical terms match method set out in IAS 39.AG108. An effectiveness test is carried out retrospectively at each balance sheet date using either the dollar-offset method or statistical methods in the form of a regression analysis. The dollar-offset method compares past changes in the fair value of the hedged item expressed in currency units with past changes in the fair values of the interest rate swaps expressed in currency units. The changes in the fair value of the two transactions are calculated on the basis of the outstanding cash flows at the beginning and end of the test period and are adjusted for accrued interest. All hedging relationships were effective within the range of the ratios of the two past changes in value (between 80 and 125 percent) as specified in IAS 39. When the effectiveness was being measured, the change in the credit spread was not taken into account for calculating the change in the fair value of the hedged item. The statistical method involves defining the performance of the hedged item as the independent variable and the performance of the hedging transaction as the dependent variable. A hedging relationship is classified as effective, when $R^2>0.96$ and, depending on the actual realization of R^2, factor b has a value between –0.85 and –1.17. All hedging relationships, with their effectiveness having been treated using statistical methods, were effective at the reporting date.

As the list of the fair values of derivatives shows (see table in the Derivatives section), Deutsche Telekom had designated interest rate derivatives in a net amount of EUR –1 million (2005: EUR +149 million) as fair value hedges as of December 31, 2006. The remeasurement of the hedged items results in gains of EUR 124 million being recorded in other financial income in the 2006 financial year (2005: EUR 68 million); the changes in the fair values of the hedging transactions result in losses of EUR 126 million (2005: EUR 67 million) being recorded in other financial income.

Cash flow hedges – interest rate risks.

In the 2006 financial year, Deutsche Telekom entered into a variable-interest EUR bond EUR forward payer interest rate swap (receive variable, pay fixed) to hedge the cash flow risk. Variable-interest bonds denominated in EUR were designated as the hedged items. The changes in the cash flows of the hedged items resulting from changes in the Euribor swap rate are offset against the changes in the cash flows of the interest rate swaps. The aim of this hedging is to transform the variable-interest bonds into fixed-income debt, thus hedging the cash flows of the financial liabilities. Credit risks are not part of the hedging.

The following table shows the contractual maturities of the payments, i.e. when the hedged item will be recognized in profit or loss:

Start	End	Nominal volume million of €	Reference rate
January 5, 2007	March 5, 2009	100	3-month Euribor
January 8, 2007	December 8, 2009	500	3-month Euribor
January 17, 2007	August 17, 2009	500	3-month Euribor

The effectiveness of the hedging relationship is prospectively tested using the critical terms match method set out in IAS 39,AG 108. An effectiveness test is carried out retrospectively at each balance sheet date using statistical methods in the form of a regression analysis. This involves defining the performance of the hedged item as the independent variable and the performance of the hedging transaction as the dependent variable. The hedged item used is a hypothetical derivative in accordance with IAS 39.IG F.5.5. A hedging relationship is classified as effective when $R^2>0.96$ and, depending on the actual realization of R^2, factor b has a value between – 0.85 and 1.17. All hedging relationships of this nature were effective as of the reporting date.

As the list of the fair values of derivatives shows (see table in the Derivatives section), Deutsche Telekom had designated interest rate derivatives amounting to EUR 13 million as hedging instrument in cash flow hedges as of December 31, 2006. The recognition directly in equity of the change in the fair value of the hedging transactions resulted in gains of EUR 13 million being recorded in the revaluation reserve in the 2006 financial year.

Cash flow hedges – currency risks.

In 2006 and 2005, Deutsche Telekom designated some "forward purchase U.S. dollar/sell in EUR" currency derivatives as cash flow hedges to hedge the amount translated into EUR payable for contractually fixed payments denominated in U.S. dollars.

These are hedges of unrecognized firm commitments against foreign-currency risks arising from spot rate changes. The hedged items designated in 2006 and 2005 were highly probably U.S. dollar payments for software licenses.

The following table shows the contractual maturities of the payments, i.e. when the hedged item will be recognized in profit or loss:

Nominal amount (millions of USD)	Maturity
10	January 15, 2007
8	February 1, 2007
10	January 15, 2008
8	February 1, 2008
36	

Additionally, the Company in 2006 and 2005 entered into hedges of future interest payments denominated in U.S. dollars resulting from recognized liabilities against foreign-currency risks arising from spot rate changes. The hedged items designated were interest payments from bonds denominated in U.S. dollars.

The following table shows the contractual maturities of the payments, i.e. when the hedged item will be recognized in profit or loss:

Nominal amount (millions of USD)	Maturity
115	2007 – 2009
100	2010 – 2015
74	2016 – 2020
74	2021 – 2025
67	2026 – 2030
430	

In 2006, the Company also entered into hedges of other future interest payments denominated in U.S. dollars resulting from recognized liabilities against foreign-currency risks arising from spot rate changes. The hedged items designated were interest payments from bonds denominated in U.S. dollars.

The following table shows the contractual maturities of the payments, i.e. when the hedged item will be recognized in profit or loss:

Nominal amount (millions of USD)	Maturity
164	2007 – 2009
360	2010 – 2015
271	2016 – 2020
271	2021 – 2025
280	2026 – 2030
1,346	

The objective of this hedging is to eliminate the risk from payment fluctuations as a result of exchange rate movements. Any unused amounts will be rolled forward to the next interest payment date.

The effectiveness of the hedging relationship is determined prospectively using the critical terms match method set out in IAS 39.AG108. An effectiveness test is carried out retrospectively using the cumulative dollar-offset method. For this, the changes in the fair values of the hedged item and the hedging instrument attributable to spot rate changes are calculated and a ratio is created. If this ratio is between 80 and 125 percent, the hedge is effective.

In the 2006 financial year, losses totaling EUR 66 million (2005: gains of EUR 106 million) resulting from the change in the fair values of currency derivatives were taken directly to equity (hedging reserve). These changes constitute the effective portion of the hedging relationship. Gains amounting to EUR 7 million (2005: EUR 29 million; losses of EUR 1 million) recognized in shareholders equity in 2005 were transferred to other financial income/expense in the 2006 financial year. Deutsche Telekom expects that, within the next 12 months, gains recognized in equity (hedging reserve) in the amount of EUR 1 million will be transferred to the income statement when payments are made. There was no material ineffectiveness of these hedges recorded as of the balance sheet date.

As the list of the fair values of derivatives shows (see table in the Derivatives section), Deutsche Telekom had currency forwards in a net amount of EUR –55 million (2005: EUR –32 million) designated as hedging instruments for cash flow hedges as of December 31, 2006.

Net investment hedge.

Deutsche Telekom hedged repayable preferred stock of T-Mobile USA amounting to USD 5,000 million against foreign-currency risks in 2006 and 2005 using fixed-income U.S. dollar bonds and currency derivatives. The interests in T-Mobile USA (hedged item) constitute a net investment in a foreign operation. The aim of the hedging was to eliminate the risk from a potential repayment of the interests resulting from exchange rate fluctuations.

The effectiveness of the hedging relationship was tested using prospective and retrospective effectiveness tests. In a retrospective effectiveness test, the changes in the fair value of the U.S. dollar bonds since the inception of the hedge resulting from spot rate changes are compared with the proportionate changes in the value of the interests due to changes in the spot rate. The prospective effectiveness test is carried out using the critical terms match method set out in IAS 39.AG 108. As both the nominal volumes and currencies of the hedged item and the hedging transaction were the same, a high level of effectiveness was expected from the hedging relationship.

In 2006 gains from spot rate changes of the U.S. dollar bonds of EUR 432 million (2005: losses of EUR 584 million) were taken directly to equity (hedging reserve). The U.S. dollar bonds designated as hedging instruments for net investment hedges had a market value of EUR 5,232 million as of December 29, 2006 (market value as of December 31, 2005: EUR 4,945 million). On December 29, 2006, the repayable preferred stock was converted into ordinary shares and the hedging relationship de-designated at the same time. In accordance with IAS 39.102, the amount of EUR 1,292 million recorded in shareholders' equity (hedging reserve) as of December 31, 2006 will not be reclassified to the income statement until the investment in T-Mobile USA is sold.

Furthermore, loans amounting to a nominal volume of USD 4,030 million were designated as hedging instruments in the 2005 financial year as part of the hedging of the net investment in T-Mobile USA. The prospective and retrospective effectiveness was determined in line with the method described above. Losses of EUR 59 million (hedging reserve) were charged to equity in connection with this hedge; this amount will be transferred to other financial income or expense upon discontinuation of the hedged item. This hedge was de-designated as of April 30, 2005.

Derivatives.

The following table shows the fair values of the various derivatives carried. A distinction is made depending on whether these are part of an effective hedging relationship as set out in IAS 39 (fair value hedge, cash flow hedge, net investment hedge) or not. Other derivatives can also be embedded (i.e. a component of a hybrid instruction that contains a non-derivatives host contract).

millions of €	Net carrying amounts Dec. 31, 2006	Net carrying amounts Dec. 31, 2005
Assets		
Interest rate swaps		
– Held for trading	100	205
– In connection with fair value hedges	64	151
– In connection with cash flow hedges	13	0
Currency forwards/currency swaps		
– Held for trading	3	18
– In connection with cash flow hedges	3	0
Cross-currency swaps held for trading	176	53
Embedded derivatives	0	18
Liabilities and shareholders' equity		
Interest rate swaps		
– Held for trading	154	311
– In connection with fair value hedges	65	2
Currency forwards/currency swaps		
– Held for trading	20	14
– In connection with cash flow hedges	58	32
Cross-currency swaps held for trading	245	308
Embedded derivatives	20	11

3.3.4 *Balance sheet*

A *Categories of financial assets and financial liabilities*

The carrying amounts of each of the following categories of financial instrument should be disclosed, either on the face of the balance sheet or in the notes:[140]

- financial assets at fair value through profit or loss, showing separately:
  - those designated as such upon initial recognition; and
  - those classified as held for trading;
- held-to-maturity investments;
- loans and receivables;
- available-for-sale financial assets;
- financial liabilities at fair value through profit or loss, showing separately:
  - those designated as such upon initial recognition; and
  - those classified as held for trading; and
- financial liabilities measured at amortised cost.

Although accounted for identically, the carrying amounts of financial instruments that are classified as held for trading and those designated at fair value through profit or loss are shown separately because designation is at the discretion of the entity.[141]

The IASB concluded that such disclosure would assist users in understanding the extent to which accounting policies affect the amounts at which financial assets and financial liabilities are recognised.[142] This represents something of an extension of IAS 32's disclosure requirements, although it is likely that an entity will have provided many of these disclosures as a result of complying with the more general requirements of IAS 1 (see 4.3.1 below).

A derivative that is designated as a hedging instrument in an effective hedge relationship does not fall within any of the above categories and should not be included in these disclosures. Disclosure requirements for hedges are set out at 3.3.3 above.

B Financial liabilities designated at fair value through profit or loss

Where a (non-derivative) financial liability has been designated at fair value through profit or loss, i.e. it is not classified as trading, the amount of change during the period and cumulatively in its fair value that is attributable to changes in credit risk should be disclosed.

Unless an alternative method more faithfully represents this amount, it should be determined as the amount of change in the fair value of the liability that is not attributable to changes in market conditions that give rise to market risk. Changes in market conditions that give rise to market risk include changes in a benchmark interest rate, commodity price, foreign exchange rate or index of prices or rates. For contracts that include a unit-linking feature, changes in market conditions include changes in the performance of an internal or external investment fund.[143] If the only relevant changes in market conditions for a financial liability are changes in an observed (benchmark) interest rate, the amount to be disclosed can be estimated as follows:

(a) first, the liability's internal rate of return at the start of the period is computed using the observed market price and contractual cash flows at that time and from this is deducted the observed (benchmark) interest rate at the start of the period, to arrive at an instrument specific component of the internal rate of return;

(b) next, the present value of the cash flows associated with the liability is calculated using the liability's contractual cash flows at the end of the period and a discount rate equal to the sum of the observed (benchmark) interest rate at the end of the period and the instrument-specific component of the internal rate of return at the start of the period as determined in (a); and

(c) the difference between the observed market price of the liability at the end of the period and the amount determined in (c) is the change in fair value that is not attributable to changes in the observed (benchmark) interest rate and this is the amount to be disclosed.

This assumes that changes in fair value other than those arising from changes in the instrument's credit risk or from changes in interest rates are not significant. If the instrument contained an embedded derivative, the change in fair value of the embedded derivative would be excluded in determining the amount to be disclosed.[144] This method is illustrated in the following example.[145]

Example 22.1: Estimating the change in fair value of an instrument attributable to its credit risk[146]

On 1 January 2008, Company J issues a 10-year bond with a par value of €150,000 and an annual fixed coupon rate of 8%, which is consistent with market rates for bonds with similar characteristics. J uses LIBOR as its observable (benchmark) interest rate. At the date of inception of the bond, LIBOR is 5%. At the end of the first year:

- LIBOR has decreased to 4.75%; and
- the fair value of the bond is €153,811, consistent with an interest rate of 7.6% [the remaining cash flows on the bond, i.e. €12,000 per year for nine years and €150,000 at the end of nine years, discounted at 7.6% equals €153,811].

J assumes a flat yield curve, that all changes in interest rates result from a parallel shift in the yield curve, and that the changes in LIBOR are the only relevant changes in market conditions.

The amount of change in the fair value of the bond that is not attributable to changes in market conditions that give rise to market risk is estimated as follows:

Step (a)

The bond's internal rate of return at the start of the period is 8%. Because the observed (benchmark) interest rate (LIBOR) is 5%, the instrument-specific component of the internal rate of return is 3%.

Step (b)

The contractual cash flows of the instrument at the end of the period are:

- interest: €12,000 [€150,000 × 8%] per year for each of years 2009 to 2017.
- principal: €150,000 in 2017.

The discount rate to be used to calculate the present value of the bond is thus 7.75%, which is the 4.75% end of period LIBOR rate, plus the 3% instrument-specific component calculated as at the start of the period which gives a notional present value of €152,367 [=€12,000 × $(1 - 1.0775^{-9})$ / 0.0775) + €150,000 × 1.0775^{-9}], on the assumption that there has been no change in the instrument-specific component.

Step (c)

The market price of the liability at the end of the period (which will reflect the real instrument-specific component at the end of the period) is €153,811, therefore J should disclose €1,444 [€153,811 – €152,367] as the increase in fair value of the bond that is not attributable to changes in market conditions that give rise to market risk.

If another method more faithfully represents the amount of change in the fair value of the liability that is attributable to changes in credit risk, that method should be used.[147]

Whatever the chosen method(s), it (they) should be disclosed. Further, if the disclosure is not considered to represent faithfully the change in the fair value of the financial liability attributable to changes in credit risk, the reasons for reaching this conclusion and the factors believed to be relevant should also be disclosed.[148] This second requirement is somewhat curious and, where provided, could be regarded as undermining the entity's compliance with the requirements above.

In addition, the IASB concluded that the difference between the carrying amount of such a liability and the amount the entity would be contractually required to pay at maturity to the holder of the obligation should also be disclosed.[149] The fair value may differ significantly from the settlement amount, particularly for liabilities with a long duration when the entity has experienced a significant deterioration in creditworthiness subsequent to issuance and the IASB concluded that knowledge of this difference would be useful. Also, the settlement amount is important to some financial statement users, particularly creditors[150] – in other words a creditor might be more interested in knowing how much is owed, not how much the debt is worth.

These disclosures are very similar to those required by IAS 32 following application of the fair value option amendments to IAS 39 (see 2.4.4 B above).

C Loans and receivables designated at fair value through profit or loss

Additional disclosure requirements apply to loans and receivables (or groups of such assets) that are designated at fair value through profit or loss. These are:

- the maximum exposure to credit risk (see 3.4.2 B below) at the reporting date of the loan or receivable (or group of loans or receivables);
- the amount by which any related credit derivatives or similar instruments mitigate that maximum exposure to credit risk;
- the amount of change during the period and cumulatively in the fair value of the loan or receivable (or group of loans or receivables) that is attributable to changes in credit risk (see below); and
- the amount of change in the fair value of any related credit derivative or similar instrument that has occurred during the period and cumulatively since the loan or receivable was designated.

Calculating the change in fair value attributable to changes in credit risk is approached in the same way as for financial liabilities (see B above). It may be determined either as the amount of change in fair value that is not attributable to changes in market conditions that give rise to market risk or by using an alternative method that more faithfully represents the amount of change in its fair value that is attributable to changes in credit risk.[151] The chosen method(s) should be disclosed and if the disclosure is not considered to represent faithfully the change in the fair value of the financial asset attributable to changes in credit risk, the reasons for reaching this conclusion and the factors believed to be relevant should be disclosed.[152]

Although this is not addressed explicitly within the standard, we believe that the disclosure requirements above apply to financial assets that would, absent the designation, be accounted for as a loan or receivable and a separate embedded derivative, not just those financial assets that meet the definition of loans and receivables in their entirety.

These disclosures are also very similar to those required by IAS 32 following application of the fair value option amendments to IAS 39 (see 2.4.4 C above).

D Reclassification

As set out at Chapter 17 at 7.5, there are circumstances in which a financial asset is reclassified as one measured:

- at cost or amortised cost, rather than at fair value; or
- at fair value, rather than at cost or amortised cost

Where this occurs, the amount reclassified into and out of each category should be disclosed, together with the reason for that reclassification.

In addition to financial assets that are reclassified from available-for-sale to held-to-maturity or vice versa, this disclosure should be provided for those unquoted equity instruments and related derivative assets that cease to be measured at cost or at fair value because a reliable measure of fair value becomes available or ceases to be available (see Chapter 20 at 3.1 and 3.4).[153] Strictly, this requirement does not appear to apply to similar derivative liabilities whose measurement basis changes from cost to fair value or vice versa, although it would seem sensible to make equivalent disclosures.

The equivalent disclosure under IAS 32 (see 2.4.3 above) applied only to the first category of reclassifications, i.e. financial assets that were reclassified as measured at cost or at amortised cost rather than at fair value, and did not include any disclosure of the amounts reclassified. The additional information is regarded by the IASB as useful because the categorisation of financial instruments has a significant effect on their measurement.[154]

E Derecognition

Where financial assets have been transferred in such a way that part or all of those assets do not qualify for derecognition (see Chapter 18 at 4), the following should be disclosed for each class of such financial assets:[155]

- the nature of the assets;
- the nature of the risks and rewards of ownership to which the entity remains exposed;
- when the entity continues to recognise all of the assets, the carrying amounts of the assets and of the associated liabilities; and
- when the entity continues to recognise the assets to the extent of its continuing involvement, the total carrying amount of the original assets, the amount of the assets that the entity continues to recognise and the carrying amount of the associated liabilities.

Although not clear from the standard, it would seem sensible for entities to disclose the carrying amount of the original assets at the date of derecognition and the amount of assets and associated liabilities that continue to be recognised at the balance sheet date.

This required disclosure, which is virtually identical to that contained in IAS 32 (see 2.4.1 above), assists in evaluating the significance of the risks retained from such transactions.[156]

Fiat, which applied IFRS 7 in 2005, included in its financial statements the following disclosure about transfers of financial assets that did not qualify for derecognition.

Extract 22.7: Fiat S.p.A. (2006)

Notes to the Consolidated Financial Statements [extract]
Significant Accounting Policies [extract]
Sales of receivables [extract]

The Fiat Group sells a significant part of its financial, trade and tax receivables through either securitisation programs or factoring transactions.

A securitisation transaction entails the sale of a portfolio of receivables to a securitisation vehicle. This special purpose entity finances the purchase of the receivablcs by issuing asset-backed securities (i.e. securities whose repayment and interest flow depend upon the cash flow generated by the portfolio). Asset-backed securities are divided into classes according to their degree of seniority and rating: the most senior classes are placed with investors on the market; the junior class, whose repayment is subordinated to the senior classes, is normally subscribed for by the seller. The residual interest in the receivables retained by the seller is therefore limited to the junior securities it has subscribed for. In accordance with SIC-12 – *Consolidation – Special Purpose Entities* (SPE), all securitisation vehicles are included in the scope of consolidation, because the subscription of the junior asset-backed securities by the seller entails its control in substance over the SPE.

Furthermore, factoring transactions may be with or without recourse to the seller; certain factoring agreements without recourse include deferred purchase price clauses (i.e. the payment of a minority portion of the purchase price is conditional upon the full collection of the receivables), require a first loss guarantee of the seller up to a limited amount or imply a continuing significant exposure to the receivables cash flow. These kinds of transactions do not meet IAS 39 requirements for asset derecognition, since the risks and rewards have not been substantially transferred.

Consequently, all receivables sold through both securitisation and factoring transactions which do not meet IAS 39 derecognition requirements are recognised as such in the Group financial statements even though they have been legally sold; a corresponding financial liability is recorded in the consolidated balance sheet as "Asset-backed financing". Gains and losses relating to the sale of such assts are not recognised until the assets are removed from the Group balance sheet.

Balance sheet [extract]
19. Current receivables [extract]

At December 31, 2006, Current receivables include receivables sold and financed through both securitisation and factoring transactions of 7,717 millions of euros (10,123 millions of euros at December 31, 2005) which do not meet IAS 39 derecognition requirements. These receivables are recognised as such in the Group financial statements even though they have been legally sold; a corresponding financial liability is recorded in the consolidated balance sheet as Asset-backed financing.

F Collateral

Where an entity has pledged financial assets as collateral for liabilities or contingent liabilities it should disclose the carrying amount of those assets and the terms and conditions relating to its pledge. This also applies to transfers of non-cash collateral where the transferee has the right, by contract or custom, to sell or repledge the collateral (see Chapter 18 at 4.8.5 B).[157]

When an entity holds collateral (of financial or non-financial assets) and is permitted to sell or repledge the collateral in the absence of default by the owner of the collateral, it should disclose:[158]

- the fair value of the collateral held;
- the fair value of any such collateral sold or repledged, and whether the entity has an obligation to return it; and
- the terms and conditions associated with its use of the collateral.

Although some respondents to ED 7 argued for an exemption from this disclosure in cases where it is impracticable to obtain the fair value of the collateral held, the IASB concluded that it is reasonable to expect an entity to know the fair value of collateral that it holds and can sell even where there is no default.[159]

These disclosures are not significantly different to those required by IAS 32 (see 2.4.5 above).

C Allowance account for credit losses

IFRS 7 introduces new disclosure requirements when impairments of financial assets are recorded in a separate account (for example, an allowance account used to record individual impairments or a similar account used to record a collective impairment of assets) rather than directly reducing the carrying amount of the asset. In such cases an entity should disclose a reconciliation of changes in that account during the period for each class of financial assets.[160] The components of the reconciliation are not specified, thereby allowing entities flexibility in determining the most appropriate format for their needs.[161]

Equivalent information is not required for entities that do not use an allowance account. The IASB believes that IAS 39's requirement to consider impairment on a group basis (see Chapter 20 at 6) necessitates the use of an allowance or similar account for virtually all entities. The disclosures required by IFRS 7 in respect of accounting policies (see 3.3.1 above) also include information about the use of direct adjustments to carrying amounts of financial assets.[162]

This requirement applies to all entities, not just financial institutions, and the following extracts from the financial statements of Deutsche Telekom and the Nationwide Building Society show how this requirement has been dealt with in practice.

Extract 22.8: Deutsche Telekom AG (2006)

Notes to the consolidated balance sheet [extracts]

18 Trade and other receivables [extract]

The following table shows the development of allowances on receivables:

millions of €	**2006**	2005
Allowances as of January 1	**1,108**	1,045
Currency translation adjustments	**(29)**	23
Additions (allowances recognized as expense)	**534**	541
Use	**(425)**	(396)
Reversal	**(40)**	(105)
Allowance as of December 31	**1,148**	1,108

Extract 22.9: Nationwide Building Society (2007)

Notes to the Accounts [extract]

13 Impairment provisions on loans and advances to customers [extracts]

2007	**Loans fully secured on residential property**		**Loans fully secured on land**		**Other loans**		**Total**	
	Individual	Collective	Individual	Collective	Individual	Collective	Individual	Collective
Group	£m	£m	£m	£m	£m	£m	£m	£m
At 5 April 2006	1.8	30.1	9.6	23.2	–	91.9	11.4	145.2
Charge/(credit) for the year	1.0	(0.8)	0.4	(0.1)	–	133.1	1.4	132.2
Amounts written off during the year	(1.4)	(0.9)	(0.5)	–	–	(86.2)	(1.9)	(87.1)
Amounts recovered during the year	0.8	–	(0.2)	–	–	9.0	0.6	9.0
Unwind of discount of provision	(0.2)	–	(1.8)	–	–	(5.0)	(2.0)	(5.0)
At 4 April 2007	2.0	28.4	7.5	23.1	–	142.8	9.5	194.3

2006	**Loans fully secured on residential property**		**Loans fully secured on land**		**Other loans**		**Total**	
	Individual	Collective	Individual	Collective	Individual	Collective	Individual	Collective
Group	£m	£m	£m	£m	£m	£m	£m	£m
At 5 April 2005	0.4	30.7	9.7	21.4	–	82.8	10.1	134.9
Charge/(credit) for the year	1.2	(0.3)	0.2	1.8	–	73.7	1.4	75.2
Amounts written off during the year	(0.9)	(0.3)	(0.5)	–	–	(67.6)	(1.4)	(67.9)
Amounts recovered during the year	1.1	–	0.8	–	–	6.5	1.9	6.5
Unwind of discount of provision	–	–	(0.6)	–	–	(3.5)	(0.6)	(3.5)
At 4 April 2006	1.8	30.1	9.6	23.2	–	91.9	11.4	145.2

H Compound financial instruments with multiple embedded derivatives

Where an instrument has been issued that contains both a liability and an equity component and the instrument has multiple embedded derivatives whose values are interdependent, such as a callable convertible debt instrument (see Chapter 19 at 4.3), the existence of these features should be disclosed.[163] Accordingly, the impact on the amounts reported as liabilities and equity will be highlighted, something the IASB sees as important given the acknowledged arbitrary nature of the allocation under IAS 32 of the joint value attributable to this interdependence.[164]

This disclosure is similar to that required under IAS 32 (see 2.3.1 above), although IFRS 7 requires no disclosure about the effective interest rate of such instruments.

I Defaults and breaches of loans payable

Loans payable are defined as 'financial liabilities other than short-term trade payables on normal credit terms.'[165] It is considered that disclosures about defaults and breaches of loans payable and other loan agreements provide relevant information about the entity's creditworthiness and its prospects of obtaining future loans.[166]

Accordingly, for any loans payable recognised at the reporting date, an entity is required to disclose:[167]

- details of any defaults during the period of principal, interest, sinking fund, or redemption terms;
- the carrying amount of the loans payable in default at the reporting date; and
- whether the default was remedied, or the terms of the loans payable were renegotiated, before the financial statements were authorised for issue.

If, during the period, there were breaches of loan agreement terms other than those described above, the same information should be disclosed if those breaches permitted the lender to demand accelerated repayment (unless the breaches were remedied, or the terms of the loan were renegotiated, on or before the reporting date).[168]

It is noted that any defaults or breaches may affect the classification of the liability as current or non-current in accordance with IAS 1 (see Chapter 3 at 3.1.4).[169]

These requirements are substantially the same as those required by IAS 32 (see 2.4.2 above).

3.3.5 Fair values

Given the long-term goal of the standard setters to record all financial instruments in the balance sheet using measures based on fair value rather than historical cost, it is not surprising that, in the interim, the IASB sees the disclosure of information about their fair value as being an important requirement. It is explained in the following terms:

> 'Many entities use fair value information internally in determining their overall financial position and in making decisions about individual financial

instruments. It is also relevant to many decisions made by users of financial statements because, in many circumstances, it reflects the judgement of the financial markets about the present value of expected future cash flows relating to an instrument. Fair value information permits comparisons of financial instruments having substantially the same economic characteristics, regardless of why they are held and when and by whom they were issued or acquired. Fair values provide a neutral basis for assessing management's stewardship by indicating the effects of its decisions to buy, sell or hold financial assets and to incur, maintain or discharge financial liabilities.'

Therefore, when financial assets or liabilities are not measured on a fair value basis, information on fair values should be given by way of supplementary disclosures to assist users in comparing entities on a consistent basis.[170] With the exception of information on 'day 1' profits (see B below), the detailed disclosure requirements are not significantly different to those in IAS 32.

A General disclosure requirements

Except as set out at C below, the fair value of each class of financial assets and liabilities should be disclosed in a way that permits comparison with the corresponding carrying amounts.[171] In providing this disclosure, instruments should be offset only to the extent that their related carrying amounts are also offset in the balance sheet.[172] Guidance on determining fair values is included in IAS 39 and is covered in Chapter 20 at 4.

In addition, the following information should be disclosed:[173]

(a) the methods and, when a valuation technique is used, the assumptions applied in determining fair values of each class of financial assets or financial liabilities.

For example, this might include information about the assumptions relating to prepayment rates, rates of estimated credit losses and interest or discount rates;

(b) whether the fair values are determined directly, in whole or in part, by reference to published price quotations in an active market or are estimated using a valuation technique;

(c) whether the fair values, recognised or disclosed, are determined in whole or in part using a valuation technique based on assumptions that are not supported by prices from observable current market transactions in the same instrument (i.e. without modification or repackaging) and not based on available observable market data.

For fair values that are recognised in the financial statements, if changing one or more of those assumptions to reasonably possible alternatives would change fair value significantly, this fact should be stated and the effect of those changes disclosed. For this purpose, significance should be judged with respect to profit or loss and total assets or total liabilities or (when changes in fair value are recognised in equity) total equity; and

(d) where (c) applies, the total amount of the change in fair value estimated using such a valuation technique that was recognised in profit or loss during the period.

In order to provide a sense of the potential variability of fair value estimates, information about the use of valuation techniques should be disclosed, in particular the sensitivities of fair value estimates to the main valuation assumptions. The IASB considered the view that disclosure of sensitivities could be difficult, in particular when the disclosure would apply to many valuation assumptions which are interdependent. However, it noted that a detailed quantitative disclosure of sensitivity to all valuation assumptions was not required, only those that could result in a significantly different estimate of fair value. Also, the standard does not require interdependencies between assumptions to be reflected when making the disclosure.[174]

The IASB also considered whether such disclosure might imply that a fair value established by a valuation technique is less reliable than one established by other means. However, it was noted that fair values that are estimated by valuation techniques are more subjective than those established from an observable market price, and concluded that users need information to help them assess the extent of this subjectivity.[175]

B Day 1 profits

If the market for a financial instrument is not active, fair value should be established using a valuation technique (see Chapter 20 at 4.2 and 4.3). Nevertheless, as set out in Chapter 20 at 4.7, the best evidence of fair value at initial recognition is the transaction price (i.e. the fair value of the consideration given or received), unless certain conditions are met. It follows that there could be a difference between the fair value at initial recognition and the amount that would be determined at that date using the valuation technique (a day 1 profit).[176] In these circumstances, the difference will be recognised in profit or loss in subsequent periods in accordance with IAS 39 and the entity's accounting policy.[177]

Where such a difference exists, IFRS 7 introduces a requirement to disclose, by class of financial instrument:[178]

- the accounting policy for recognising that difference in profit or loss to reflect a change in factors (including time) that market participants would consider in setting a price; and
- the aggregate difference yet to be recognised in profit or loss at the beginning and end of the period and a reconciliation of changes in the balance of this difference.

In other words, disclosure is required of the profits an entity might think it has made but which it is prohibited from recognising, at least for the time being. This disclosure is illustrated in the following example based on the implementation guidance. It is rather curious in that it illustrates a day 1 *loss*.[179]

Example 22.2: Disclosure of deferred day 1 profits

On 1 January 2008 Company R purchases financial assets that are not traded in an active market for €15 million which represents their fair value at initial recognition. After initial recognition, R applies a valuation technique to establish the fair value of the financial assets. This valuation technique includes variables other than data from observable markets. At initial recognition, the same valuation technique would have resulted in an amount of €14 million, which differs from fair value by €1 million. R has only one class of such financial assets with existing differences of €5 million at 1 January 2008. The disclosure in R's 2009 financial statements would include the following:

Accounting policies

R uses the following valuation technique to determine the fair value of financial instruments that are not traded in an active market: [insert description of technique, not included in this example]. Differences may arise between the fair value at initial recognition (which, in accordance with IAS 39, is generally the transaction price) and the amount determined at initial recognition using the valuation technique. Any such differences are [description of the R's accounting policy].

In the notes to the financial statements

As discussed in note X, [insert name of valuation technique] is used to measure the fair value of the following financial instruments that are not traded in an active market. However, in accordance with IAS 39, the fair value of an instrument at inception is generally the transaction price. If the transaction price differs from the amount determined at inception using the valuation technique, that difference is [description of R's accounting policy].

The differences yet to be recognised in profit or loss are as follows:

	2009 €m	2008 €m
Balance at beginning of year	5.3	5.0
New transactions	–	1.0
Recognised in profit or loss during the year	(0.7)	(0.8)
Other increases	(0.1)	(0.1)
Balance at end of year	4.5	5.3

UBS, which has not yet applied IFRS 7, discloses the following information about recognition of day 1 profits within its accounting policies.

Extract 22.10: UBS AG (2006)

Accounting Standards and Policies [extract]
Critical accounting policies [extract]
Recognition of deferred Day 1 profit and loss

A closely related issue to determining fair value of financial instruments is the recognition of deferred Day 1 profit and loss. We have entered into transactions, some of which will mature in the long term, where we determine fair value using valuation models for which not all inputs are market observable prices or rates. We initially recognize such a financial instrument at the transaction price, which is the best indicator of fair value, although the value obtained from the relevant valuation model may differ. Such a difference between the transaction price and the model value is commonly referred to as "Day 1 P/L". We do not immediately recognize that initial difference, usually a gain, in profit and loss because the applicable accounting literature prohibits immediate recognition of Day 1 profit. The accounting literature does not, however, address its subsequent recognition prior to the time when fair value can be determined using market observable inputs or by reference to prices for similar instruments in active markets. It also does not address subsequent measurement of these instruments and recognition of subsequent fair value changes indicated by the model.

> Our decisions regarding recognizing deferred Day 1 profit are made after careful consideration of facts and circumstances to ensure we do not prematurely release a portion of the deferred profit to income. For each transaction, we determine, individually, the appropriate method of recognizing the Day 1 profit amount in the income statement. It may be amortized over the life of the transaction, or deferred until fair value can be determined using market observable inputs, or realized through settlement. In all instances, any unrecognized Day-1 profit is immediately released to income if fair value of the financial instrument in question can be determined either by using market observable model inputs or by reference to a quoted price for the same product in an active market.
>
> Changes in fair value after Day 1 resulting from changes in observable parameters or otherwise indicated by the model are recognized immediately in the income statement independently of the release of deferred Day 1 profits.

C *Exceptions*

Pragmatically, disclosure of fair values is not required for instruments whose carrying amount reasonably approximates their fair value, for example short-term trade receivables and payables.[180]

Fair values need not be given for investments in unquoted equity instruments, or derivatives linked to such instruments, that are measured at cost because their fair value cannot be measured reliably (see Chapter 20 at 4.4). As set out in Chapter 17 at 3.3.2 some instruments (normally life insurance policies) contain a discretionary participation feature. If the fair value of that feature cannot be reliably measured, disclosures of fair value are not required.[181] However, such instruments are singled out for additional disclosure. This is to assist users of the financial statements in making their own judgements about the extent of possible differences between the carrying amount of such financial assets and financial liabilities and their fair value. Particularly, the following should be disclosed:[182]

- the fact that fair value has not been disclosed because it cannot be reliably measured;
- a description of the instruments, their carrying amount, and an explanation of why fair value cannot be measured reliably;
- information about the market for the instruments;
- information about whether and how the entity intends to dispose of the instruments; and
- for instruments whose fair value previously could not be reliably measured that are derecognised:
  - that fact;
  - their carrying amount at the time of derecognition; and
  - the amount of gain or loss recognised.

For all other financial instruments, the IASB believes it is reasonable to expect that fair value can be determined with sufficient reliability within constraints of timeliness and cost. It therefore concluded that there should be no exception from the requirement to disclose fair value information for these instruments.[183]

3.4 Nature and extent of risks arising from financial instruments

IFRS 7 establishes a second key principle, namely:

> 'An entity shall disclose information that enables users of its financial statements to evaluate the nature and extent of risks arising from financial instruments to which the entity is exposed at the reporting date.'[184]

Again this is supported by related disclosure requirements (which are covered at 3.4.1 and 3.4.2 below) and these focus on the risks arising from financial instruments and how those risks have been managed.[185]

These risks typically include, but are not limited to, credit risk, liquidity risk and market risk, which are defined as follows:[186]

(a) *Credit risk*, the risk that one party to a financial instrument will cause a financial loss for the other party by failing to discharge an obligation;

(b) *Liquidity risk*, the risk that an entity will encounter difficulty in meeting obligations associated with financial liabilities;

(c) *Market risk*, the risk that the fair value or future cash flows of a financial instrument will fluctuate because of changes in market prices. It comprises three separate types of risk:

  (i) *Currency risk*, the risk that the fair value or future cash flows of a financial instrument will fluctuate because of changes in foreign exchange rates.

  Currency risk (or foreign exchange risk) arises on financial instruments that are denominated in a foreign currency, i.e. in a currency other than the functional currency in which they are measured. For the purpose of IFRS 7, currency risk does not arise from financial instruments that are non-monetary items or from financial instruments denominated in an entity's functional currency.[187] Therefore if a parent with the euro as its functional and presentation currency owns a subsidiary with the pound sterling as its functional currency, monetary items held by the subsidiary that are denominated in sterling do not give rise to any currency risk in the consolidated financial statements of the parent;

  (ii) *Interest rate risk*, the risk that the fair value or future cash flows of a financial instrument will fluctuate because of changes in market interest rates.

  It is explained that interest rate risk arises on interest-bearing financial instruments recognised in the balance sheet (e.g. loans and receivables and debt instruments issued) and on some financial instruments not recognised in the balance sheet (e.g. some loan commitments).[188] This is true but not the whole story because so far as fair values are concerned interest rate risk will arise on virtually all financial instruments;

  (iii) *Other price risk*, the risk that the fair value or future cash flows of a financial instrument will fluctuate because of changes in market prices (other than those arising from interest rate risk or currency risk), whether those changes are caused by factors specific to the individual financial

> instrument or its issuer, or factors affecting all similar financial instruments traded in the market.
>
> Other price risk arises on financial instruments because of changes in, for example, commodity prices, equity prices, prepayment risk (i.e. the risk that one party to a financial asset will incur a financial loss because the other party repays earlier or later than expected), and residual value risk (e.g. a lessor of motor cars that writes residual value guarantees is exposed to residual value risk).[189]
>
> Two examples of financial instruments that give rise to equity price risk are a holding of equities in another entity, and an investment in a trust, which in turn holds investments in equity instruments. Other examples include forward contracts and options to buy or sell specified quantities of an equity instrument and swaps that are indexed to equity prices. The fair values of such financial instruments are affected by changes in the market price of the underlying equity instruments.[190]

The specified disclosures can be provided either in the financial statements or may be incorporated by cross-reference from the financial statements to some other statement that is available to users of the financial statements on the same terms and at the same time, such as a management commentary or risk report (preparation of which might be required by a regulatory authority). Without the information incorporated by cross-reference, the financial statements are incomplete.[191]

Consistent with the approach outlined at 3.2 above, it is emphasised that the extent of these disclosures will depend on the extent of an entity's exposure to risks arising from financial instruments.[192] Therefore, entities with many financial instruments and related risks should provide more disclosure and those with few financial instruments and related risks may provide less extensive disclosure.[193]

The IASB recognised that entities view and manage risk in different ways and that some entities undertake limited management of risks. Therefore, disclosures based on how risk is managed are unlikely to be comparable between entities and, for some entities, would convey little or no information about the risks assumed. Accordingly, whilst at a high level the disclosures are approached from the perspective of information provided to management (see 3.4.2), certain minimum disclosures about risk exposures are specified to provide a common and relatively easy to implement benchmark across different entities. Obviously, those entities with more developed risk management systems would provide more detailed information.[194]

It is explained that the implementation guidance, which illustrates how an entity might apply IFRS 7, is consistent with the disclosure requirements for banks developed by the Basel Committee (known as Pillar 3), so that banks can prepare, and users receive, a single co-ordinated set of disclosures about financial risk.[195]

In developing the standard, the IASB considered various arguments that risk disclosures should not be included within the financial statements (even by cross-reference). For example, concerns were expressed that the information would be difficult and costly to audit and that it did not meet the criteria of comparability, faithful representation and completeness because it is subjective, forward-looking and based on management's judgement. It was also suggested that the subjectivity involved in the sensitivity analyses could undermine the credibility of the fair values recognised in the financial statements. However, the IASB was not persuaded and these arguments were rejected.[196]

3.4.1 Qualitative disclosures

For each type of risk arising from financial instruments, an entity is required to disclose:[197]

(a) the exposures to risk and how they arise; and

(b) its objectives, policies and processes for managing the risk and the methods used to measure the risk.

Any changes in either (a) or (b) above compared to the previous period, together with the reasons for the change, should be disclosed. These changes may result from changes in exposure to risk or the way those exposures are managed.[198]

The type of information that might be disclosed to meet these requirements includes, but is not limited to, a narrative description of:[199]

- the entity's exposures to risk and how they arose, which might include details of exposures, both gross and net of risk transfer and other risk-mitigating transactions;
- the entity's policies and processes for accepting, measuring, monitoring and controlling risk, which might include:
  - the structure and organisation of the entity's risk management function(s), including a discussion of independence and accountability;
  - the scope and nature of the entity's risk reporting or measurement systems;
  - the entity's policies for hedging or mitigating risk, including its policies and procedures for taking collateral; and
  - the entity's processes for monitoring the continuing effectiveness of such hedges or mitigating devices; and
- the entity's policies and procedures for avoiding excessive concentrations of risk.

It is noted that information about the nature and extent of risks arising from financial instruments is more useful if it highlights any relationship between financial instruments that can affect the amount, timing or uncertainty of an entity's future cash flows. The extent to which a risk exposure is altered by such relationships might be apparent from other required disclosures, but in some cases further disclosures might be useful.[200]

At a high level, these disclosures are similar to those required by IAS 32 (see 2.2.1 above), although the guidance in IFRS 7 is more detailed.

The following extract from the financial statements of Origin Energy shows the type of disclosure that can be seen in practice.[201]

Extract 22.11: Origin Energy Limited (2006)

Notes to the Financial Statements [extracts]

29. Financial instruments [extracts]

Financial risk management

Financial risk factors

The consolidated entity's activities expose it to a variety of financial risks: market risk (including foreign exchange risk, interest rate risk and price risk), credit risk and liquidity risk. The consolidated entity's overall risk management programme focuses on the unpredictability of financial markets and seeks to minimise potential adverse effects on the consolidated entity's financial performance. The consolidated entity uses a range of derivative financial instruments to hedge these risk exposures.

Risk management is carried out by Group Treasury for interest rate and foreign exchange exposures. Risk management activities in respect of the commodity exposures are undertaken by the Energy Risk Management Group (ERM). Both Group Treasury and ERM operate under policies approved by the Board of Directors. Group Treasury and ERM identify, evaluate and hedge the financial risks in close co-operation with the consolidated entity's operating units. The consolidated entity has written policies covering specific areas, such as foreign exchange risk, interest rate risk, electricity price risk, oil price risk, credit risk, use of derivative financial instruments and non-derivative financial instruments, and the investment of excess liquidity.

(a) Market risk [extracts]

(i) Foreign exchange risk [extracts]

The consolidated entity operates internationally and is exposed to foreign exchange risk arising from various currency exposures, primarily with respect to the New Zealand dollar and US dollar. Foreign exchange risk arises from future commercial transactions (including interest payments on long-term borrowings, the sale of oil, the sale and purchase of LPG and the purchase of capital equipment), recognised assets and liabilities (including foreign receivables and borrowings) and net investments in foreign operations.

To manage the foreign exchange risk arising from future commercial transactions the consolidated entity uses forward foreign exchange contracts transacted by Group Treasury. To manage the foreign exchange risk arising from the future principal and interest payments required on foreign currency denominated long-term borrowings, the consolidated entity uses cross currency interest rate swaps (both fixed to fixed and fixed to floating) which convert the foreign currency denominated future principal and interest payments into the functional currency for the relevant entity for the full term of the underlying borrowings.

The consolidated entity has certain investments in foreign operations whose net assets are exposed to foreign currency translation risk. Currency exposure arising from the net assets of the consolidated entity's foreign operations is managed primarily through borrowings denominated in the relevant foreign currencies. The consolidated entity's risk management policy is to manage foreign currency exposures using Profit at Risk and Value at Risk methodologies on 95% confidence levels. Exposure limits are set to ensure that the consolidated entity is not exposed to excess risk from foreign exchange exposures.

(ii) Price risk [extract]

The consolidated entity is exposed to commodity price risk from a number of commodities, including electricity, oil and related commodities associated with the purchase and/or sale of these commodities. The consolidated entity is also exposed to equity securities price risk because of investments held by the consolidated entity and classified on the consolidated balance sheet as available-for-sale and fair value through profit or loss. To manage its commodity price risks in respect to electricity and oil, the consolidated entity utilises a range of derivative instruments including fixed priced swaps, options and futures. The consolidated entity's equity investments subject to price risk are all publicly traded.

The consolidated entity's risk management policy for commodity price risk is to hedge forecast future transactions for up to 5 years into the future. ERM has a risk management policy framework that manages the exposure arising from its commodity based activities. The policy permits the active hedging of price and volume exposure arising from the retailing, generation and portfolio management activities, within prescribed risk capacity limits. The policy prescribes the maximum risk exposure permissible over any two-day period for the full commodity portfolio, under defined worse case scenarios. The full portfolio is tested daily against this limit, and reported monthly to management.

(b) Credit risk [extract]

The consolidated entity manages its exposure to credit risk via credit risk management policies which allocate credit limits based on the overall financial and competitive strength of the counterparty. Publically available credit information from recognised providers is utilized for this purpose where available. Credit policies cover exposures generated from the sale of products and the use of derivatives instruments. Derivative counterparties are limited to high-credit-quality financial institutions and other organisations in the relevant industry. The consolidated entity has Board approved policies that limit the amount of credit exposure to each financial institution and derivative counterparty. The consolidated entity also utilises ISDA agreements with all derivative counterparties in order to limit exposure to credit risk through the netting of amounts receivable from and amounts payable to individual counterparties. At balance date, the only significant concentration of credit risk with any single counterparty is to the NSW Government in relation to electricity derivatives undertaken in accordance with the consolidated entity's hedging and risk management activities.

(c) Liquidity risk [extract]

Prudent liquidity risk management implies maintaining sufficient cash and marketable securities, the availability of funding through an adequate amount of committed credit facilities and the ability to close out market positions. Due to the dynamic nature of the underlying businesses, Group Treasury aims to maintain flexibility in funding by keeping committed credit lines available.

(d) Interest rate risk (cash flow and fair value) [extract]

The consolidated entity's income and operating cash flows are substantially independent of changes in market interest rates. The consolidated entity's interest rate risk arises from long-term borrowings. Borrowings issued at variable rates expose the consolidated entity to cash flow interest rate risk. Borrowings issued at fixed rates expose the consolidated entity to fair value interest rate risk. The consolidated entity's risk management policy is to manage interest rate exposures using Profit at Risk and Value at Risk methodologies on 95% confidence levels. Exposure limits are set to ensure that the consolidated entity is not exposed to excess risk from interest rate volatility. The consolidated entity manages its cash flow interest rate risk by using floating-to-fixed interest rate swaps. Such interest rate swaps have the economic effect of converting borrowings from floating rates to fixed rates. Under the interest rate swaps, the consolidated entity agrees with other parties to exchange, at specified intervals (mainly quarterly), the difference between fixed contract rates and floating rate interest amounts calculated by reference to the agreed notional principal amounts.

3.4.2 Quantitative disclosures

A General matters

For each type of risk arising from financial instruments (see 3.4 above), entities are required to disclose summary quantitative data about their exposure to that risk at the reporting date. It should be based on the information provided internally to key management personnel of the entity as defined in IAS 24 – *Related Party Disclosures* – (see Chapter 35 at 2.3.6), for example the board of directors or chief executive officer.[202]

This 'management view' approach was adopted by the IASB because it was considered to:[203]

- provide a useful insight into how the entity views and manages risk;
- result in information that has more predictive value than information based on assumptions and methods that management does not use, for instance, in considering the entity's ability to react to adverse situations;
- be more effective in adapting to changes in risk measurement and management techniques and developments in the external environment;
- have practical advantages for preparers of financial statements, because it allows them to use the data they use in managing risk; and
- be consistent with the approach used in IAS 14 (see Chapter 30).

When several methods are used to manage a risk exposure, the information disclosed should use the method(s) that provide the most relevant and reliable information. It is noted, in this context, that IAS 8 – *Accounting Policies, Changes in Accounting Estimates and Errors* – discusses relevance and reliability (see Chapter 3 at 1.2.2).[204]

Where the quantitative data disclosed as at the reporting date are unrepresentative of an entity's exposure to risk during the period, further information that is representative should be provided.[205] For example, if an entity typically has a large exposure to a particular currency, but at year-end unwinds the position, the entity might disclose a graph that shows the exposure at various times during the period, or it might disclose the highest, lowest and average exposures.[206]

In developing IFRS 7, the IASB considered whether quantitative information about average risk exposures should be given in all cases. However, this is more informative only if the year end risk exposure is not representative of the exposure during the period and would be onerous to prepare and, consequently, they decided that disclosure by exception was appropriate.[207]

The disclosures set out at B to D below should be provided in all cases unless the risk is not material. In this situation reference is made to the guidance in IAS 1 dealing with materiality and aggregation (which is considered in Chapter 3 at 4.1.5 A), not to the definition and guidance from IAS 1 considered at 3.2.2 above.[208]

B Credit risk

Many of the credit risk disclosures are to be given by class and it is noted that financial instruments in the same class should reflect shared economic characteristics with respect to the risk being disclosed, credit risk in this case (see 3.2.3). Therefore, a lender might determine that residential mortgages, unsecured consumer loans, and commercial loans each have different economic characteristics.[209] Although IAS 32 required some disclosure about credit risk (see 2.3.2 above), those under IFRS 7 are likely to be much more extensive.

For each class of financial instrument, entities should disclose the amount that best represents its maximum exposure to credit risk at the reporting date without taking account of any collateral held or other credit enhancements (e.g. netting agreements that do not qualify for offset in accordance with IAS 32).[210] For a financial asset, this is typically the gross carrying amount, net of any amounts offset in accordance with IAS 32 (see Chapter 18 at 6) and any impairment losses recognised in accordance with IAS 39 (see Chapter 20 at 6).[211] This disclosure is required even if there are no identified problems in, say, a loan portfolio.[212]

Activities that give rise to credit risk and the associated maximum exposure to credit risk include, but are not limited to:[213]

- granting loans and receivables to customers and placing deposits with other entities. In these cases, the maximum exposure to credit risk is the carrying amount of the related financial assets;
- entering into derivative contracts, e.g. foreign exchange contracts, interest rate swaps and credit derivatives. When the resulting asset is measured at fair value, the maximum exposure to credit risk at the reporting date will equal the carrying amount;

  It is recognised that this disclosure does not always reflect potential *future* exposure to credit risk (because fair value could increase), but the disclosure requirement is for the exposure *at the reporting date*;[214]
- granting financial guarantees. In this case, the maximum exposure to credit risk is the maximum amount the entity could have to pay if the guarantee is called on, which may be significantly greater than the amount recognised as a liability; and
- making a loan commitment that is irrevocable over the life of the facility or is revocable only in response to a material adverse change. If the issuer cannot settle the loan commitment net in cash or another financial instrument, the maximum credit exposure is the full amount of the commitment. This is because it is uncertain whether the amount of any undrawn portion may be drawn upon in the future. This may be significantly greater than the amount recognised as a liability.

The following extracts from the financial statements of Deutsche Telekom and HSBC illustrate how these disclosures may be provided in practice – clearly credit risk is much more significant to an entity such as HSBC.

Extract 22.12: Deutsche Telekom AG (2006)

Notes to the consolidated balance sheet [extract]

Other disclosures [extract]

43. Risk management and financial derivatives [extract]

Credit risks [extract]

The maximum exposure to credit risk is partly represented by the carrying amounts of the financial assets that are carried in the balance sheet, including derivatives with positive market values. Except for the collateral agreements mentioned in Note 24, no significant agreements reducing the maximum exposure to credit risk (such as contractual netting) had been concluded as of the reporting date. In addition, Deutsche Telekom is exposed to credit risk through the granting of financial guarantees. Guarantees amounting to a nominal total of EUR 216 million had been pledged as of the reporting date.

Extract 22.13: HSBC Holdings plc (2006)

Report of the Directors: The Management of Risk [extracts]

Maximum exposure to credit risk *(Audited)* [extracts]

The following table presents the maximum exposure to credit risk of balance sheet and off balance sheet financial instruments, before taking account of any collateral held or other credit enhancements unless such credit enhancements meet offsetting requirements as set out in Note 2(m) on the Financial Statements. For financial assets recognised on the balance sheet, the exposure to credit risk equals their carrying amount. For financial guarantees granted, the maximum exposure to credit risk is the maximum amount that HSBC would have to pay if the guarantees are called upon.

For loan commitments and other credit related commitments that are irrevocable over the life of the respective facilities, the maximum exposure to credit risk is the full amount of the committed facilities.

	Maximum exposure	
	2006 US$m	2005 US$m
Items in course of collection from other banks	**14,144**	11,300
Trading assets	**300,998**	212,706
Treasury and other eligible bills	**21,759**	12,746
Debt securities	**155,447**	117,659
Loans and advances	**123,792**	82,301
Financial assets designated at fair value	**9,971**	6,513
Treasury and other eligible bills	**133**	53
Debt securities	**9,449**	5,705
Loans and advances	**389**	755
Derivatives	**103,702**	73,928
Loans and advances to banks	**185,205**	125,965
Loans and advances to customers	**868,133**	740,002
Financial investments	**196,509**	174,823
Treasury and other eligible bills	**25,313**	25,042
Debt securities	**171,196**	149,781
Other assets	**22,846**	18,954
Endorsements and acceptances	**9,577**	7,973
Other	**13,269**	10,981
Financial guarantees	**62,014**	66,805
Loan commitments and other credit related commitments[1]	**714,630**	654,343
At 31 December 2005	**2,478,152**	2,085,339

1 *The amount of the loan commitments shown above reflects, where relevant, the expected level of take-up of pre-approved loan offers made by mailshots to personal customers. In addition to those amounts, there is a further maximum possible exposure to credit risk of US$464,984 million (2005: US$313,629 million), reflecting the full take-up of such irrevocable loan commitments. The take-up of such offers is generally at modest levels. 2005 data have also been adjusted to ensure consistency with 2006 data for this disclosure.*

In respect of the maximum credit risk exposure by class, entities should provide a description of collateral held as security and other credit enhancements.[215] This requirement may be met by disclosing:[216]

- the policies and processes for valuing and managing collateral and other credit enhancements obtained;
- a description of the main types of collateral and other credit enhancements (examples of the latter being guarantees and credit derivatives, as well as netting agreements that do not qualify for offset in accordance with IAS 32);
- the main types of counterparties to collateral and other credit enhancements and their creditworthiness; and
- information about risk concentrations within the collateral or other credit enhancements.

Entities should also provide information about the credit quality of financial assets that are neither past due (see I below) nor impaired.[217] The IASB believes this gives a greater insight into the credit risk of assets and helps users assess whether such assets are more or less likely to become impaired in the future. Because this information will vary between entities, no particular method for giving this information is specified. Rather, each entity should devise a method that is appropriate to its circumstances.[218] This might include:[219]

- an analysis of credit exposures using an external or internal credit grading system;

  When external ratings are considered when managing and monitoring credit quality, information might be disclosed about:[220]

  - the amounts of credit exposures for each external credit grade;
  - the rating agencies used;
  - the amount of an entity's rated and unrated credit exposures; and

  When internal credit ratings are considered when managing and monitoring credit quality, information might be disclosed about:[221]

  - the internal credit ratings process;
  - the amounts of credit exposures for each internal credit grade; and

  In each case information might be provided explaining the relationship between internal and external ratings.[222]
- the nature of the counterparty;
- historical information about counterparty default rates; and
- any other information used to assess credit quality.

It should be noted that the above disclosures do not need to include the fair value of all collateral held (something that was proposed in ED 7). The IASB recognised that such information would often be onerous to collect and may sometimes be misleading (for example if information about over- and under-collateralised assets is aggregated). Of more relevance will be the extent of under-collateralised loans (see 3.3.4 above).[223]

Finally, the carrying amount of financial assets that would otherwise be past due or impaired whose terms have been renegotiated should be disclosed.[224]

The Nationwide Building Society includes the following disclosures about credit risk in its financial statements.

Extract 22.14: Nationwide Building Society (2007)

Notes to the Accounts [extract]

48 Financial instruments [extract]

Credit risk – Loans and advances to customers [extract]

a) Personal Financial Services (PFS)

The PFS portfolio is predominantly made up of £95.3 billion loans fully secured on residential property (2006 – £84.3 billion) with £3.0 billion unsecured consumer lending (2006 – £2.6 billion). By their nature, our PFS lending books are comprised of a large number of smaller loans, have low volatility of credit risk outcomes and are intrinsically highly diversified.

In respect of its PFS book, the Group operates across the whole of the UK but lending is biased towards the south east of England reflecting the concentration of branches in that region and asset growth trends. As at 4 April 2007 around 44% (2006 – 46%) of the residential mortgage book was in respect of the south east.

In its specialist mortgage lender, UCB, the Group sells loans in the markets of self-certification and buy-to-let distributed through intermediaries. UCB balances outstanding at the year end were £6.6 billion (2006 – £6.0 billion) of which £2.7 billion (2006 – £1.7 billion) were in respect of buy-to-let.

The average loan to value (LTV) ratio of the Group's PFS loan portfolio is estimated at 39% (2006 – 39%) whilst the average LTV of new residential mortgage lending was 58% (2006 – 55%). Further LTV information on the Group's PFS loan portfolio is set out as follows:

	2007	2006
	%	%
Loan to value analysis:		
Total book		
<70%	**87**	88
70% – 80%	**7**	6
80% – 90%	**5**	5
>90%	**1**	1
Average loan to value of stock (indexed)	**39**	39
Average loan to value of new business	**58**	55
New business profile:		
First-time buyers	**19**	15
Home movers	**31**	25
Remortgagers	**46**	57
Buy-to-let	**4**	3

Nationwide Group asset quality continues to significantly outperform both the secured and unsecured lending markets. The proportion of residential lending cases currently more than 3 months in arrears is 0.24 % (2006 – 0.28%) against an industry average of 0.87% (CML figure as at 31 March 2007) (2006 – 0.97%). For consumer lending, the value of personal loans over 30 days in arrears as a percentage of total loans is 6.2% (2006 – 4.6%) around 25% lower than the average of the members of the Finance and Leasing Association (February 2007) (March 2006 – 40%). For credit card accounts, the value of loans over 30 days in arrears as a percentage of total card accounts is 7.3% (2006 – 6.9%) and are approximately 30% better than the industry benchmark.

The table below provides further information on PFS loans and advances by payment due status as at 4 April 2007.

	2007		2006	
	£bn	**%**	£bn	%
Not impaired:				
Neither past due nor impaired	**96.6**	**98**	85.2	98
Past due up to 3 months but not impaired	**1.4**	**2**	1.4	2
Impaired:				
Past due 3 to 6 months	**0.2**	**–**	0.2	–
Past due 6 to 12 months	**0.1**	**–**	0.1	–
Past due over 12 months (£37.1 million)	**–**	**–**	–	–
Possessions* (£13.5 million)	**–**	**–**	–	–
	98.3	**100**	86.9	100

* Against possession case, £13.0 million (2006 – £10.6 million) of collateral is held.

£49.1 million (2006 – £44.4 millio) of loans that would be past due or impaired have had their terms renegotiated.

Loans in the analysis above which are less than 3 months past due have collective impairment allowances set aside to cover credit losses on loans which are in the early stages of arrears.

I Financial assets that are either past due or impaired

A financial asset is defined as 'past due' when a counterparty has failed to make a payment when contractually due.[225] For example, consider an entity that enters into a lending agreement that requires interest to be paid every month. On the first day of the next month, if interest has not been paid, the loan is past due. Past due does not mean that the counterparty will never pay, but it can trigger various actions such as renegotiation, enforcement of covenants, or legal proceedings.[226]

When the terms and conditions of financial assets that have been classified as past due are renegotiated, the terms and conditions of the new contractual arrangement should be applied to determine whether the financial asset remains past due.[227]

To provide information about financial assets with the greatest credit risk, entities are required to disclose the following for each class of financial asset (including trade receivables):[228]

- an analysis of the age of financial assets that are past due as at the reporting date but not impaired (essentially to identify those financial assets that are more likely to become impaired and help users to estimate the level of future impairment losses[229]).

  Judgement should be used to determine an appropriate number of time bands. For example, the following time bands might be considered appropriate:[230]

  - not more than three months;
  - more than three months and not more than six months;
  - more than six months and not more than one year; and
  - more than one year;

- an analysis of financial assets that are individually determined to be impaired as at the reporting date, including the factors the entity considered in determining that they are impaired.

  This analysis might include:[231]

  - the carrying amount, before deducting any impairment loss; and
  - the amount of any related impairment loss.

  It might also include an analysis of such assets by factors other than age, such as the nature of the counterparty or a geographical analysis of the impaired assets;[232] and

- for the amounts disclosed above, a description of collateral held as security and other credit enhancements (which might indicate their nature[233]) and, unless impracticable, an estimate of their fair value.

The analysis of the 'age' of financial assets that are past due implied by a literal reading of IFRS 7 could be completely meaningless and in most cases it will be appropriate to analyse the assets by reference to the period of time the asset has been past due. For example, if a borrower had missed only the most recent interest payment due 20 days before the lender's year end, the fact that the payment is 20 days past due seems far more relevant to assessing its credit risk than the date the asset was originated which could be many years earlier.

Deutsche Telekom provides in its financial statements the following analysis of trade receivables that are past due but not impaired.

Extract 22.15: Deutsche Telekom AG (2006)

Notes to the consolidated balance sheet [extracts]

18 Trade and other receivables [extracts]

millions of €	**Carrying amount**	Of which: not impaired on the reporting date and past due in the following periods					
		less than 30 days	between 31 and 60 days	between 61 and 90 days	between 91 and 180 days	between 181 and 360 days	more than 360 days
	As of Dec. 31, 2006						
Trade receivables	7,577	872	130	89	69	131	28
	As of Dec. 31, 2005						
Trade receivables	7,328	705	107	63	55	161	31

Extract 22.14 above (Nationwide) contains another example of how this disclosure requirement has been dealt with in practice.

II Collateral and other credit enhancements obtained

When an entity obtains financial or non-financial assets during the period by taking possession of collateral it holds as security, or calling on other credit enhancements such as guarantees, and these assets meet the recognition criteria in other standards, it should disclose the nature and carrying amount of the assets obtained and, when the assets are not readily convertible into cash, its policies for disposing of such assets or for using them in its operations.[234] This disclosure is intended to provide information about the frequency of such activities and the entity's ability to obtain and realise the value of the collateral.[235]

C Liquidity risk

IAS 32 contained no explicit disclosure requirements about liquidity risk, although some information was normally necessary to describe the terms and conditions of financial instruments (see 2.2.4 above) and the requirements under IFRS 7 are more prescriptive and comprehensive.

I Maturity analysis

To illustrate liquidity risk, the principal disclosure required is a maturity analysis for financial liabilities that shows their remaining contractual maturities.[236] The time bands to be used in the maturity analysis are not specified. Rather, entities should use their judgement to determine what is appropriate. For example, an entity might determine that the following are appropriate:[237]

- not later than one month;
- later than one month and not later than three months;
- later than three months and not later than one year; and
- later than one year and not later than five years.

When a counterparty has a choice of when an amount is paid, the liability should be included on the basis of the earliest date on which the entity can be required to pay. For example, financial liabilities such as demand deposits that an entity can be required to repay on demand should be included in the earliest time band.[238] This means that the disclosure shows a worst case scenario, even if there is only a remote possibility that the entity could be required to pay its liabilities earlier than expected[239] (although the disclosures at II below may be relevant in these circumstances). No guidance is given on how to deal with instruments where the issuer has a choice of when an amount is paid. For example, borrowings containing embedded call or prepayment options might be included in the analysis based on the earliest, latest or expected contractual payment dates.

When an entity is committed to make amounts available in instalments, each instalment should be allocated to the earliest period in which the entity can be required to pay. For example, an undrawn loan commitment would be included in the time band containing the earliest date it could be drawn down.[240]

The amounts that should be disclosed in the maturity analysis are the contractual undiscounted cash flows, for example:

- gross finance lease obligations (before deducting finance charges);
- prices specified in forward agreements to purchase financial assets for cash;
- net amounts for pay-floating/receive-fixed interest rate swaps for which net cash flows are exchanged;
- contractual amounts to be exchanged in a derivative financial instrument (e.g. a currency swap) for which gross cash flows are exchanged; and
- gross loan commitments.

These undiscounted cash flows will differ from the amount included in the balance sheet because the balance sheet amount is based on discounted cash flows.[241] Quite how perpetual debt obligations will be dealt with in this analysis remains to be seen because the amount the standard requires in the latest maturity category is infinity!

When the amount payable is not fixed, the amount disclosed should be determined by reference to the conditions existing at the reporting date. For example, if the amount payable varies with changes in an index, the amount disclosed may be based on the level of the index at the reporting date.[242] The standard does not explain whether the amount should be based on the spot or forward price of the index and, in practice, both approaches are likely to be used.

The following example illustrates the cash flows that it appears should be included in the maturity analysis for a simple floating rate borrowing.

Example 22.3: Maturity analysis: floating rate borrowing

On 1 January 2008, Company P borrowed €100 million from a bank on the following terms: coupons are payable on the entire principal on 30 June and 31 December each year at the annual rate of LIBOR plus 1% as determined on the previous 1 January and 1 July; the principal is repayable on 31 December 2011.

At the end of 2008, P's year end, LIBOR is 5%. Accordingly, P would include the following cash flows in its maturity analysis:

	€ million
30 June 2009	3
31 December 2009	3
30 June 2010	3
31 December 2010	3
30 June 2011	3
31 December 2011	103
Total	118

If appropriate, entities should disclose in the maturity analysis derivative financial instruments separately from non-derivative financial instruments. For example, it would be appropriate to distinguish cash flows from derivative financial instruments and non-derivative financial instruments if the cash flows arising from the derivative financial instruments are settled gross. This is because the gross cash outflow may be accompanied by a related inflow.[243]

In practice, the treatment of derivatives in the analysis can be particularly troublesome. For example, in the case of derivatives that are settled by a gross exchange of cash flows, it is not entirely clear whether the IASB intended entities to disclose the related cash inflow as well as the cash outflow, although such information might be considered useful. Further, because the analysis is of financial liabilities, it seems clear that, strictly, cash outflows from a derivative *asset* that is settled by a gross exchange of cash should not be included. However, the contractual cash flows on these instruments would appear to be no less relevant than on those that have a negative fair value.

Further issues can arise in the case of a derivative liability settled by exchanging net cash flows in a number of future periods. For example, the relevant index for a long-term interest rate swap might predict that in some periods the entity could have cash inflows. It is entirely unclear whether these inflows should be included within the analysis.

The treatment of financial guarantee contracts is not addressed by the standard and they can be included in the analysis in one of at least two ways. On the one hand, they can be seen as akin to loan commitments whereby the total exposure is included in the analysis based on the earliest date the guaranteed debt instrument could default. On the other hand, they can be seen as contracts under which the payment is not fixed and the amount included in the analysis is determined by reference to the index at the reporting date – in this case the index is defined as the expected default (or otherwise) of the guaranteed debt instrument, so that an amount would be included in the analysis only if default were considered probable. A similar approach may be taken for other contracts with similar characteristics such as credit default swaps or written options to purchase financial assets for cash.

The following extract from the financial statements of National Grid shows a maturity analysis that identifies inflows and outflows from derivative contracts separately and includes derivative assets as well as derivative liabilities.

Extract 22.16: National Grid plc (2007)

Notes to the Accounts [extract]
23. Financial risk factors [extract]
(c) Liquidity analysis

We manage our liquidity requirements by the use of both short and long-term cash flow forecasts. These forecasts are supplemented by a financial headroom position which is used to demonstrate funding adequacy for at least a 12 month period.

The following is an analysis of the contractual undiscounted cash flows payable under financial liabilities and derivative assets and liabilities as at the balance sheet date:

At 31 March 2007	**Due within 1 year £m**	**Due between 1 and 2 years £m**	**Due between 2 and 3 years £m**	**Due 3 years and beyond £m**	**Total £m**
Non derivative financial liabilities					
Borrowings, excluding finance lease liabilities	**(776)**	**(1,865)**	**(1,013)**	**(12,283)**	**(15,937)**
Interest payments on borrowings (i)	**(686)**	**(612)**	**(548)**	**(6,489)**	**(8,335)**
Finance lease liabilities	**(17)**	**(17)**	**(12)**	**(113)**	**(159)**
Other non interest-bearing liabilities	**(1,525)**	**(214)**	**–**	**–**	**(1,739)**
Derivative financial liabilities					
Derivative contracts – receipts	**382**	**608**	**299**	**2,116**	**3,405**
Derivative contracts – payments	**(443)**	**(571)**	**(318)**	**(1,910)**	**(3,242)**
Commodity contracts	**(56)**	**(55)**	**(38)**	**(240)**	**(389)**
Total at 31 March 2007	**(3,121)**	**(2,726)**	**(1,630)**	**(18,919)**	**(26,396)**

At 31 March 2006	Due within 1 year £m	Due between 1 and 2 years £m	Due between 2 and 3 years £m	Due 3 years and beyond £m	Total £m
Non derivative financial liabilities					
Borrowings, excluding finance lease liabilities	(2,569)	(404)	(1,317)	(8,948)	(13,238)
Interest payments on borrowings (i)	(572)	(488)	(439)	(3,892)	(5,481)
Finance lease liabilities	(20)	(26)	(22)	(124)	(192)
Other non interest-bearing liabilities	(1,528)	(324)	–	–	(1,906)
Derivative financial liabilities					
Derivative contracts – receipts	1,170	87	248	1,225	2,730
Derivative contracts – payments	(1,046)	(122)	(209)	(1,011)	(2,388)
Commodity contracts	(113)	(114)	(112)	(439)	(778)
Total at 31 March 2006	(4,732)	(1,391)	(1,851)	(13,279)	(21,253)

(i) The interest on borrowings is calculated based on borrowings held at 31 March without taking account of future issues. Floating-rate interest is estimated using a future interest rate curve as at 31 March.

II *Management of associated liquidity risk*

In addition to the maturity analysis for financial liabilities, the entity should provide a description of how it manages the liquidity risk inherent in that analysis.[244] Factors that might be considered when making this disclosure include, but are not limited to, whether the entity:[245]

- expects some of its liabilities to be paid later than the earliest date on which the entity can be required to pay (as may be the case for customer deposits placed with a bank);
- expects some of its undrawn loan commitments not to be drawn;
- holds financial assets for which there is a liquid market and that are readily saleable to meet liquidity needs;
- has committed borrowing facilities (e.g. commercial paper facilities) or other lines of credit (e.g. stand-by credit facilities) that it can access to meet liquidity needs;
- holds financial assets for which there is not a liquid market, but which are expected to generate cash inflows (principal or interest) that will be available to meet cash outflows on liabilities;
- holds deposits at central banks to meet liquidity needs;
- has very diverse funding sources; or
- has significant concentrations of liquidity risk in either its assets or its funding sources.

If an entity manages liquidity risk on the basis of *expected* maturity dates, it might disclose a maturity analysis of the expected maturity dates of both financial liabilities and financial assets. Where an entity does this, the disclosure might clarify that expected dates are based on estimates made by management, explain how the estimates are determined and highlight the principal reasons for differences from the *contractual* maturity analysis.[246]

D *Market risk*

Under IFRS 7 entities are required to provide disclosure of their sensitivity to market risk in one of two ways which are set out at I and II below. The sensitivity analyses should cover the whole of an entity's business but different types of sensitivity analysis may be provided for different classes of financial instruments.[247] This is considered by the IASB to be simpler and more suitable than the 'terms and conditions' disclosure required by IAS 32 (see 2.2.4 above) which are effectively withdrawn.[248]

No sensitivity analysis is required for financial instruments that an entity classifies as equity instruments. Such instruments are not remeasured so that neither profit or loss nor equity will be affected by the equity price risk of those instruments.[249]

With the possible exception of interest rate risk (see 2.3.1), IAS 32 required little or no disclosure of market risk information – any such information would normally be provided in order to meet the 'terms and conditions' disclosure (see 2.2.4 above).

I 'Basic' sensitivity analysis

Except where the disclosures set out at II below are provided, entities should disclose:[250]

- a sensitivity analysis for each type of market risk to which the entity is exposed at the reporting date, showing how profit or loss and equity would have been affected by changes in the relevant risk variable that were reasonably possible at that date.

  The sensitivity of profit or loss (which arises, for example, from instruments classified as at fair value through profit or loss and impairments of available-for-sale financial assets) should be disclosed separately from the sensitivity of equity (which arises, for example, from instruments classified as available for sale).[251]

  The term 'profit or loss' is used in IAS 1 to mean profit after tax. Therefore, it might well be argued that the amounts disclosed should take account of any related tax effects, a view corroborated by the illustrative disclosures in the implementation guidance to IFRS 7 (see Example 22.5 below). However, as noted below, the application guidance suggests this requirement should (and the implementation guidance might suggest it could) be met by disclosing the impact on interest expense, a pre-tax measure of profit. Given this conflicting guidance, it is difficult to say that a pre-tax approach fails to comply with the standard and, in practice, both approaches are seen.

  Where a post-tax figure is disclosed, it will not always be straightforward to determine the related tax effects, especially for a multinational group, and it may be appropriate to use the guidance in Chapter 26 at 6 which deals with the allocation of income tax between profit or loss and equity;
- the methods and assumptions used in preparing the sensitivity analysis; and
- changes from the previous period in the methods and assumptions used, and the reasons for such changes.

The standard contains a reminder of the general guidance at 3.2.1 above and explains that an entity should decide how it aggregates information to display the overall picture without combining information with different characteristics about exposures to risks from significantly different economic environments. For example, an entity that trades financial instruments might disclose this information separately for financial instruments held for trading and those not held for trading. Similarly, an entity would not aggregate its exposure to market risks from areas of hyperinflation with its exposure to the same market risks from areas of very low inflation. However, an entity that has exposure to only one type of market risk in only one economic environment, would not show disaggregated information.[252]

Risk variables that are relevant to disclosing market risk include, but are not limited to:[253]

- the yield curve of market interest rates.

  It may be necessary to consider both parallel and non-parallel shifts in the yield curve (yield curves are considered further in Chapter 20 at 4.3);

- foreign exchange rates.

  The standard requires a sensitivity analysis to be disclosed for each currency to which an entity has significant exposure;[254]
- prices of equity instruments; and
- market prices of commodities.

When disclosing how profit or loss and equity would have been affected by changes in the relevant risk variable, there is no requirement to determine what the profit or loss for the period would have been if the relevant risk variables had been different *during the year*. The requirement is subtly different because the effect that is disclosed assumes that a reasonably possible change in the relevant risk variable had occurred *at the balance sheet date* and had been applied to the risk exposures in existence *at that date*. For example, if an entity has a floating rate liability at the end of the year, the entity would disclose the effect on profit or loss (i.e. interest expense) for the current year if interest rates had varied by reasonably possible amounts. Further, this disclosure is not required for each change within a range of reasonably possible changes, only at the limits of the reasonably possible range.[255] The following example illustrates how this requirement might be applied – for simplicity, tax effects are ignored.

Example 22.4: Sensitivity analysis

Company X, which has the euro as its functional currency, is party to the following instruments at 31 December 2008, X's balance sheet date:

- a €100m floating rate loan;
- a forward contract to sell US$10m in July 2009 that is designated in an effective hedge of a highly probable forecast sale that is denominated in US dollars;
- a short-term loan of £10m made to a related party;
- an interest rate swap that is not designated as a hedge;
- investments in fixed rate debt securities that are classified as held-to-maturity
- investments in similar securities that are classified as available-for-sale; and
- investments in a portfolio of US equities with a fair value of US$50m.

Floating rate loan

Changes in interest rates will result in this instrument impacting on X's profit or loss. If X concludes that a reasonably possible change in interest rates is 50 basis points (0.5%), €0.5m [€100m × 0.5%] would be included in the amount disclosed as the impact on profit or loss of this reasonably possible change.

Forward contract

Changes in exchange rates will have an impact on the fair value (and carrying value) of this instrument, but this would be recognised in equity, not profit or loss (assuming ineffectiveness is insignificant). If a reasonably possibly change in exchange rates would change the value of the contract by €0.3m, this would be included in the amount disclosed as the impact on equity of this reasonably possible change.

Foreign currency loan

Changes in spot exchange rates will have an impact on the carrying amount of this asset with changes recognised in profit or loss as a result of the application of IAS 21. If a reasonably possible change in the exchange rate would alter the carrying value of the contract by €1.0m, this would be included in the amount disclosed as the impact on profit or loss of this reasonably possible change.

If the loan were made to a subsidiary of X that had sterling as its functional currency, the loan itself would eliminate on consolidation but the impact of retranslating it into euros in X's own financial statements would remain in consolidated profit or loss. Therefore, in these circumstances, the loan would still be included in the sensitivity analysis for X's consolidated financial statements.

Interest rate swap

Changes in interest rates will have an impact on the fair value (and carrying value) of this instrument and such changes would be recognised in profit or loss. If a reasonably possible change of 50 basis points in interest rates would change the value of the contract by €0.4m, this would be included in the amount disclosed as the impact on profit or loss of this reasonably possible change.

Fixed rate debt securities

Changes in interest rates will have an impact on the fair value of all these instruments. However, because those classified as held-to-maturity are measured at amortised cost, the carrying amount only of those that are classified as available-for-sale will change as interest rates move and such change will normally be recognised in equity. Therefore, if a reasonably possible 50 basis point change in interest rates would change the fair value of each group of instruments by €0.5m, only the amount in respect of the available-for-sale securities would be included in the sensitivity disclosure as an impact on equity. Of course there would be nothing to preclude disclosure, as additional information (if considered relevant), of the sensitivity of the fair value of held-to-maturity investments to changes in interest rates.

US equity securities

Changes in exchange rates might be considered to impact the fair value of these investments. However, as noted at (c)(i) at 3.4 above, financial instruments that are non-monetary items do not give rise to foreign currency risk for the purposes of IFRS 7 – essentially the foreign currency risk is seen as part of the market price risk associated with such instruments. Therefore, X should take no account of these investments when disclosing its sensitivity to changes in the euro/US dollar exchange rate. However, this information may be provided as additional disclosure where it is considered relevant.

Relevant risk variables for the purpose of this disclosure might include:[256]

- prevailing market interest rates, for interest-sensitive financial instruments such as a variable-rate loan; or
- currency rates and interest rates, for foreign currency financial instruments such as foreign currency bonds.

For interest rate risk, the sensitivity analysis might show separately the effect of a change in market interest rates on:

- interest income and expense;
- other line items of profit or loss (such as trading gains and losses); and
- when applicable, equity.

An entity might disclose a sensitivity analysis for interest rate risk for each currency in which the entity has material exposures to interest rate risk.[257]

In determining what a reasonably possible change in the relevant risk variable is, the economic environment(s) in which the entity operates and the time frame over which it is making the assessment should be considered. A reasonably possible change should not include remote or 'worst case' scenarios or 'stress tests'. Moreover, if the rate of change in the underlying risk variable is stable, the chosen reasonably possible change in the risk variable need not be altered.

For example, assume that interest rates are 5 percent and an entity determines that a fluctuation in interest rates of ±50 basis points is reasonably possible. It would disclose the effect on profit or loss and equity if interest rates were to change to 4.5 percent or 5.5 percent. In the next period, interest rates have increased to 5.5 percent. The entity continues to believe that interest rates may fluctuate by ±50 basis points (i.e. that the rate of change in interest rates is stable). The entity would disclose the effect on profit or loss and equity if interest rates were to change to 5 percent or 6 percent. The entity would not be required to revise its assessment that interest rates might reasonably fluctuate by ±50 basis points, unless there is evidence that interest rates have become significantly more volatile.

The time frame is defined by the period until these disclosures will next be presented. This will normally coincide with the next annual reporting period,[258] although in some jurisdictions such information may be included in interim reports.

Because the factors affecting market risk will vary according to the specific circumstances of each entity, the appropriate range to be considered in providing a sensitivity analysis of market risk will also vary for each entity and for each type of market risk.[259]

Where an entity has exposure to other price risk, it might disclose the effect of a decrease in a specified stock market index, commodity price, or other risk variable. For example, if residual value guarantees that are financial instruments are given, the disclosure could include an increase or decrease in the value of the assets to which the guarantee applies.[260]

The following example from the implementation guidance illustrates the type of disclosure that might be provided.

Example 22.5: Disclosure of sensitivity analyses

Interest rate risk

At 31 December 2008, if interest rates at that date had been 10 basis points lower with all other variables held constant, post-tax profit for the year would have been €1.7 million (2007: €2.4 million) higher, arising mainly as a result of lower interest expense on variable borrowings, and other components of equity would have been €2.8 million (2007: €3.2 million) higher, arising mainly as a result of an increase in the fair value of fixed rate financial assets classified as available for sale.

If interest rates had been 10 basis points higher, with all other variables held constant, post-tax profit would have been €1.5 million (2007: €2.1 million) lower, arising mainly as a result of higher interest expense on variable borrowings, and other components of equity would have been €3.0 million (2007: €3.4 million) lower, arising mainly as a result of a decrease in the fair value of fixed rate financial assets classified as available for sale.

Profit is more sensitive to interest rate decreases than increases because of borrowings with capped interest rates. The sensitivity is lower in 2008 than in 2007 because of a reduction in outstanding borrowings that has occurred as the entity's debt has matured (see note X).

Foreign currency exchange rate risk

At 31 December 2008, if the euro had weakened 10 percent against the US dollar with all other variables held constant, post-tax profit for the year would have been €2.8 million (2007: €6.4 million) lower, and other components of equity would have been €1.2 million (2007: €1.1 million) higher.

Conversely, if the euro had strengthened 10 percent against the US dollar with all other variables held constant, post-tax profit would have been €2.8 million (2007: €6.4 million) higher, and other components of equity would have been €1.2 million (2007: €1.1 million) lower.

The lower foreign currency exchange rate sensitivity in profit in 2008 compared with 2007 is attributable to a reduction in foreign currency denominated debt. Equity is more sensitive in 2008 than in 2007 because of the increased use of hedges of foreign currency purchases, offset by the reduction in foreign currency debt.

Deutsche Telekom included the following sensitivity analysis in its financial statements.

Extract 22.17: Deutsche Telekom AG (2006)

Notes to the consolidated balance sheet [extract]
Other disclosures [extracts]
42. Risk management and financial derivatives [extracts]
Currency risks [extract]

For the presentation of market risks, IFRS 7 requires sensitivity analyses that show the effects of hypothetical changes of relevant risk variables on profit or loss and shareholders' equity. In addition to currency risks, Deutsche Telekom is exposed to interest rate risks and price risks in its investments. The periodic effects are determined by relating the hypothetical changes in the risk variables to the balance of financial instruments at the reporting date. It is assumed that the balance at the reporting date is representative for the year as a whole.

Currency risks as defined by IFRS 7 arise on account of financial instruments being denominated in a currency that is not the functional currency and being of a monetary nature; differences resulting from the translation of financial statements into the Group's presentation currency are not taken into consideration. Relevant risk variables are generally non-functional currencies in which Deutsche Telekom has financial instruments.

The currency sensitivity analysis is based on the following assumptions:

Major non-derivative monetary financial instruments (liquid assets, receivables, interest-bearing securities and/or debt instruments held, interest-bearing liabilities, finance lease liabilities, liabilities arising from ABS transactions, non-interest-bearing liabilities) are either directly denominated in the functional currency or are transferred to the functional currency through he use of derivatives. Exchange-rate fluctuations therefore have no effects on profit or loss, or shareholders' equity.

Non-interest-bearing securities or equity instruments held are of a non-monetary nature and therefore are not exposed to currency risk as defined by IFRS 7.

Interest income and interest expense from financial instruments are also either recorded directly in the functional currency or transferred to the functional currency by using derivatives. For this reason, there can be no effects on the variables considered in this connection.

In the case of fair value hedges designed for hedging currency risks, the changes in the fair value of the hedged item and the hedging instruments attributable to exchange rate movements balance out almost completely in the income statement in the same period. As a consequence, these financial instruments are not exposed to currency risks with an effect on profit or loss, or shareholders' equity either.

Cross-currency swaps are always assigned to non-derivative hedged items, so these instruments also do not have any currency effects.

Deutsche Telekom is therefore only exposed to currency risks from specific currency derivatives. Some of these are currency derivatives that are part of an effective cash flow hedge of hedging payment fluctuations resulting from exchange rate movements in accordance with IAS 39. Exchange rate fluctuations of the currencies on which these transactions are based affect the hedging reserve in shareholders' equity and the fair value of these hedging transactions. Others are currency derivatives that are neither part of one of the hedges defined in IAS 39 nor part of a natural hedge. These derivatives are used to hedge planned transactions. Exchange rate fluctuations of the currencies, on which such financial instruments are based, affect other financial income or expense (net gain/loss from remeasurement of financial assets to fair value).

If the euro had gained 10 percent against the U.S. dollar at December 31, 2006, the hedging reserve in shareholders' equity and the fair value of the hedging instruments would have been EUR 125 million lower (higher) (December 31, 2005: EUR 68 million higher (lower)).

If the euro had gained 10 percent against all currencies at December 31, 2006, other financial income and the fair value of the hedging instruments would have been EUR 29 million higher (lower) (December 31, 2005: EUR 3 million lower (higher)). The hypothetical effect on profit or loss of EUR +29 million results from the currency sensitivities EUR/USD: EUR –14 million; EUR/AED: EUR +1 million; EUR/GBP: EUR +8 million; EUR/HUF: EUR +8 million; EUR/PLN EUR: +22 million; EUR/SKK: EUR +4 million.

Interest rate risks [extract]

Interest rate risks are presented by way of sensitivity analyses in accordance with IFRS 7. These show the effects of changes in market interest rates on interest payments, interest income and expense, other income components and, if appropriate, shareholders' equity. The interest rate sensitivity analyses are based on the following assumptions:

Changes in the market interest rates of non-derivative financial instruments with fixed interest rates only affect income if these are recognized at their fair value. As such, all financial instruments with fixed interest rates that are carried at amortized cost are not subject to interest rate risk as defined in IFRS 7.

In the case of fair value hedges designed for hedging interest rate risks, the changes in the fair values of the hedged item and the hedging instrument attributable to interest rate movements balance out almost completely in the income statement in the same period. As a consequence, these financial instruments are also not exposed to interest rate risk.

Changes in the market interest rate of financial instruments that were designated as hedging instruments in a cash flow hedge to hedge payment fluctuations resulting from interest rate movements affect the hedging reserve in shareholders' equity and are therefore taken into consideration in the equity-related sensitivity calculations.

Changes in market interest rates affect the interest income or expense of non-derivative variable-interest financial instruments, the interest payments of which are not designated as hedged items of cash flow hedges against interest rate risks. As a consequence, they are included in the calculation of income-related sensitivities.

Changes in the market interest rate of interest rate derivatives (interest rate swaps, cross-currency swaps) that are not part of a hedging relationship as set out in IAS 39 affect other financial income or expense (net gain/loss from remeasurement of the financial assets to fair value) and are therefore taken into consideration in the income-related sensitivity calculations.

Currency derivatives are not exposed to interest rate risks and therefore do not affect the interest rate sensitivities.

If the market interest rates had been 100 basis points higher (lower) at December 31, 2006, profit or loss would have been EUR 254 million (December 31, 2005: EUR 158 million) lower (higher). The hypothetical effect of EUR –254 million on income results from the potential effects of EUR –206 million from interest rate derivatives and EUR –48 million from non-derivative, variable-interest financial liabilities. If the market interest rates had been 100 basis points higher (lower) at December 31, 2006, shareholders' equity would have been EUR 27 million higher (lower).

Other price risks

As part of the presentation of market risks, IFRS 7 also requires disclosures on how hypothetical changes in risk variables affect the price of financial instruments. Important risk variables are stock exchange prices or indexes.

As of December 31, 2006, Deutsche Telekom did not hold any material investments to be classified as "available for sale".

II Value-at-risk and similar analyses

Where an entity prepares a sensitivity analysis, such as value-at-risk, that reflects interdependencies between risk variables (e.g. interest rates and exchange rates) and uses it to manage financial risks, it may disclose that analysis in place of the information specified at I above.[261] If this disclosure is given, the effects on profit or loss and equity at I above need not be given.[262]

In these cases the following should also be disclosed:[263]

- an explanation of the method used in preparing such a sensitivity analysis, and of the main parameters and assumptions underlying the data provided; and
- an explanation of the objective of the method used and of limitations that may result in the information not fully reflecting the fair value of the assets and liabilities involved.

This applies even if such a methodology measures only the potential for loss and does not measure the potential for gain. Such an entity might comply with the disclosure requirements above by detailing the type of value-at-risk model used (e.g. whether the model relies on Monte Carlo simulations), an explanation about how the model works and the main assumptions (e.g. the holding period and confidence level). Entities might also disclose the historical observation period and weightings applied to observations within that period, an explanation of how options are dealt with in the calculations, and which volatilities and correlations (or, alternatively, Monte Carlo probability distribution simulations) are used.[264]

Syngenta has included in its financial statements the following disclosures pursuant to these requirements.

Extract 22.18: Syngenta AG (2006)

Notes to the Syngenta Group Consolidated Financial Statements [extracts]

32. Financial instruments [extracts]

Financial Risk Assessment

The residual risk exposure post hedging is assessed using a variety of "Value-at-Risk" (VaR) methods. The exact method selected depends on the underlying risk itself. All VaR approaches try to recognize that holding different assets/liabilities or future cash flow exposures may actually reduce portfolio risk through the de-correlation benefits of diversification. This benefit is captured within the calculation and thus aims to holistically present portfolio risk.

Syngenta uses three difference approaches to measuring exposure to market risk, and operates within pre-defined risk levels.

a) the VaR variance-covariance method as introduced by RiskMetrics Group

b) the Earnings-at-Risk (EaR) Monte Carlo method – a variant of VaR

c) the Earnings-at-Risk (EaR) historical simulation method

The particular method selected is dependent on the data distribution characteristics for the risk exposure being measured.

VaR – Variance-Covariance (or Parametric) Approach

This method measures within what ranges the value of respective assets or liabilities may fluctuate with a certain probability over a certain time period (holding period).

Transaction Risk-Committed

Syngenta uses a 95% confidence interval (i.e. there is a 5% probability that the impact from market fluctuations exceeds the level calculated) over a 30 day holding period. This is applied to the committed foreign currency balance sheet exposure. The holding period reflects the monthly review period and use of the variance/covariance approach is suited to the linear nature of instrument protection.

The statistical measure takes 252 days of past price data and implicitly assumes that the value changes in the recent past are indicative of value changes in the future. The measure is performed monthly and a 30 day maximum risk limit is in place. Thus there is a 5% probability of market fluctuations affecting the Group Income Statement by more than the calculated net VaR in the 30 days following measurement.

Interest Charge-at-Risk

Syngenta calculates an Interest Charge-at-Risk as applied by the RiskMetrics Group based on a variance-covariance approach, using a 95% confidence interval and a 12 month holding period in order to estimate its Interest Rate Risks for its forecasted debt levels. Syngenta uses a 12 month time horizon given the seasonality of cash flows and duration of cash forecasts. This measure is performed quarterly. Syngenta does not hold any interest rate instruments with optionality, so this is not addressed in the model.

EaR – Monte Carlo Approach

Syngenta also uses an Earning-at-Risk (EaR) approach which is a similar methodology to VaR but rather than measuring ranges within which the value of assets/liabilities may fluctuate it measures the potential changes to profits/losses from a series of future exposures over a certain time period and with a certain probability.

Again a 95% confidence interval is used but with a 1 year holding period in order to estimate the foreign exchange risk on forecast operating income exposure.

The Monte Carlo simulation computation uses parameters estimated from historical data and applies a randomiser to generate possible future exchange rate paths. Syngenta considers this a good method of assessing operating income risk when non linear derivative instruments have been traded.

The measure is performed monthly and a risk limit is in place over a 12 month holding period.

Thus there is a 5% chance that the impact to reported operating income as a result of foreign exchange rate fluctuations within a year following the measurement date will be more than the calculated net EaR.

Commodity EaR – historical simulation

Syngenta has adopted the historical simulation method as a basis for assessing commodity risk EaR. Again this is measuring the potential changes to profits/losses from a series of future exposures over a certain time period and with a certain probability.

One year of historical prices are used to calculate the daily return. From this the process generates 252 scenarios for future price movements. The movements are then used to value the portfolio of underlying transactions and hedges and by selecting the twelfth of 252 portfolio value changes the 95% EaR is produced.

This measure is performed monthly and a risk limit for both hard commodities (oil and gas) and soft commodities (agricultural produce) over a 12 month holding period is in place.

Risk Calculation Summary Table (Net Impact)

(US$ million)	Time horizon (Months)	31 December 2006	31 December 2005
Foreign Exchange Risks:			
Transaction Risk uncommitted – Earnings-at-Risk	12	**26**	45
Transaction Risk committed – Value-at-Risk	1	**3**	7
Translation Risk – Value-at-Risk	1	**90**	109
Interest Rate Risks – Interest Charge-at-Risk	12	**8**	6
Other Price Risks – Earnings-at-Risk	12	**36**	34

Foreign Exchange Risks – Explanation and Risk Sensitivity Analysis

Syngenta uses US dollars as its reporting currency and is therefore exposed to foreign exchange movements in a wide range of currencies. Consequently, it enters into various contracts, such as forward contracts and options, which represent agreements to exchange a defined amount in one currency for an amount in another currency at a defined exchange rate on a defined settlement date in the future. These contracts change in value as foreign exchange rates change, to preserve the value of assets, commitments and anticipated transactions.

To cover existing balance sheet exposures, and to hedge committed foreign currency transactions, Syngenta uses forward contracts.

To hedge anticipated foreign currency cash flows Syngenta uses currency options and forward contracts. In a forward contract, Syngenta and its counterparty must exchange these amounts on the settlement date. In its option contracts, Syngenta normally pays its counterparty a premium amount at the start of the contract in exchange for the right to make the exchange on the settlement date if it is beneficial to do so at that date (a "purchased" option). In certain circumstances, Syngenta may receive a premium amount from its counterparty in exchange for giving the counterparty the right to make a similar exchange (a "written" option). Syngenta has only options, or combinations of options, where a net premium was paid (a "net purchased" option).

The following table demonstrates the sales and operating cost foreign currency exposures. The primary net foreign currency exposures against the US dollar include the Swiss franc, the British pound and the Euro.

The split of sales and operating costs by currency for the years 2006 and 2005 was as follows:

Currency	Sales in % 2006	Sales in % 2005	Operating costs in % 2006	Operating costs in % 2005
US dollar	**36**	37	**33**	33
Euro	**22**	24	**19**	20
Swiss franc	**1**	1	**19**	17
British pound sterling	**2**	2	**11**	11
Other	**39**	36	**18**	19
Total	**100**	100	**100**	100

"Other" includes over 46 currencies. However, none accounts for more than 10% of total sales or total operating costs.

Transaction Risk – Uncommitted

Syngenta collects information about anticipated cash flows for major currencies at Group level and hedges material mismatches in currency flows for a 12 month benchmark horizon using options and forward contracts to reduce operating income volatility. The approach is designed to hedge the year on year earnings transaction risk for the main currencies. The transactional flows and derivative financial instruments required to operate the program are analyzed on an ongoing basis. The remaining currency exposures are closely monitored and additional protection can, with appropriate authorization, be purchased.

The remaining currency risk occurs across numerous emerging markets, and the diversification offers protection – however, these unhedged currencies are also strictly monitored and managed against clearly defined risk limits.

(US$ million)	December 31, 2006 Earnings-at-Risk			December 31, 2005 Earnings-at-Risk		
	Gross impact	**Net impact**	**Risk reduction**	**Gross impact**	**Net impact**	**Risk reduction**
Swiss franc	**87**	**11**	**87%**	65	50	23%
Euro	**34**	**25**	**26%**	25	24	4%
British pound	**31**	**11**	**65%**	25	21	16%
Other core currencies	**27**	**11**	**59%**	30	25	17%
Rest of World	**58**	**58**	**–%**	54	54	–%
Total undiversified	**237**	**116**	**51%**	**199**	**174**	**13%**
Diversification	**(183)**	**(90)**	**51%**	**(139)**	**(129)**	**7%**
Net EaR	**54**	**26**	**52%**	**60**	**45**	**25%**

The Earnings-at-Risk calculation is performed for anticipated net transactional currency flows for 2007 taking into account related currency hedges. As of December 31, 2006, the total potential adverse movement for 2007 net transactional flows after hedges relative to year-end spot levels, at the 95% confidence level, was US$26 million (December 31, 2005: US$45 million).

From the Earning-at-Risk table above the Swiss franc stands out as a major exposure. This risk arises from having a significant cost base in Switzerland with no material offsetting sales. This exposure is monitored continuously by the risk management team and by senior finance management.

The actual movement on transaction flows due to currency movements in 2006 was adverse. This arose due to weak European currencies in the first half of the year – a period when the majority of European sales are made. It has been compounded by a weak US dollar in the second half and the impact of that on the Swiss franc cost base.

Transaction Risk-Balance Sheet

Committed foreign currency exposures are largely generated by the routing of products from central manufacturing sites to foreign affiliates. They are normally fully covered and are in the majority of cases managed by the use of forward contracts. There are a number of currencies for which either no forward market exists or where the cost of hedging that currency is deemed too costly. These instances thus give rise to VaR. These net committed transactional currency exposures are determined by identification and monthly reporting by business units. The Value-at-Risk calculations for committed exposures related to the revaluation of exposures relative to spot rates over a monthly period. The impact of interest differentials and other factors is not included in these calculations.

(US$ million) Income Currency (1 month holding period)	December 31, 2006 Value-at-Risk			December 31, 2005 Value-at-Risk		
	Gross impact	**Net impact**	**Risk reduction**	**Gross impact**	**Net impact**	**Risk reduction**
Swiss franc	**7**	**–**	**100%**	48	–	100%
Euro	**1**	**1**	**–%**	13	–	100%
British pound	**33**	**2**	**94%**	60	7	88%
Other core currencies	**3**	**1**	**67%**	8	1	88%
Rest of World	**23**	**6**	**74%**	21	6	71%
Total undiversified	**67**	**10**	**85%**	**150**	**14**	**91%**
Diversification	**(34)**	**(7)**	**79%**	**(42)**	**(7)**	**83%**
Net VaR	**33**	**3**	**91%**	**108**	**7**	**94%**

The Value-at-Risk calculation was performed for net committed transactional currency flows existing at December 31, 2006 taking into account related currency hedges. As of December 31, 2006, the total 30-day Value-at-risk, after hedges, at the 95% confidence level was US$3 million (December 31, 2005: US$7 million). Maximum and minimum levels of risk through the year were US$8 million and US$2 million.

The largest exposures arise in the Swiss franc and the British pound. These countries house large research and manufacturing sites.

Translation Risk – Balance sheet

Translation exposure arises from the consolidation of the foreign currency denominated financial statements of the Group's subsidiaries. This translation effect is visible as currency translation movement in the consolidated equity of Syngenta. The table below demonstrates the 1 month translation Value-at-Risk:

(US$ million)	**December 31, 2006 Value-at-Risk**			**December 31, 2005 Value-at-Risk**		
Income Currency (1 month holding period)	**Gross impact**	**Net impact**	**Risk reduction**	**Gross impact**	**Net impact**	**Risk reduction**
Swiss franc	24	24	–%	46	46	–%
Euro	18	10	44%	23	15	35%
British pound	56	29	48%	57	30	47%
Other core currencies	10	10	–%	10	10	–%
Rest of World	69	69	–%	53	53	–%
Total undiversified	177	142	20%	189	154	19%
Diversification	(57)	(52)	9%	(49)	(45)	8%
Net VaR	120	90	25%	140	109	22%

Balance sheet translational exposures in subsidiaries are, where appropriate, hedged by the use of foreign denominated debt and in exceptional circumstances, foreign exchange forward contracts. The latter focuses on risk reduction for monetary items.

The translation risk can be significant, however, Syngenta believes over the longer-term mean reversion tendency of currencies reduces the risk to acceptable levels. The Syngenta equity base is also deemed to be of sufficient magnitude to absorb the short to medium-term impact of exchange rate movements.

The large investments and operations in Switzerland and the UK lead to the most significant risk.

Interest Rate Risks

Syngenta is exposed to fluctuations in interest rates on its borrowings.

Syngenta monitors its interest rate exposures and analyzes the potential impact of interest rate movements on net interest expense through an Interest Charge-at-Risk approach.

As of December 31, 2006, the 12 month Interest Charge-at-Risk at the 95% confidence level was US$8 million (December 31, 2005: US$6 million).

III Other market risk disclosures

When the sensitivity analyses discussed at I and II above are unrepresentative of a risk inherent in a financial instrument, that fact should be disclosed together with the reason for believing the sensitivity analyses are unrepresentative.[265]

This can occur when the year-end exposure does not reflect the exposure during the year[266] or a financial instrument contains terms and conditions whose effects are not apparent from the sensitivity analysis, e.g. options that remain out of (or in) the money for the chosen change in the risk variable.[267] Additional disclosures in this second case might include

- the terms and conditions of the financial instrument (e.g. the options);
- the effect on profit or loss if the term or condition were met (i.e. if the options were exercised); and
- a description of how the risk is hedged.

For example, an entity may acquire a zero-cost interest rate collar that includes an out-of-the-money leveraged written option (e.g. the entity pays ten times the amount of the difference between a specified interest rate floor and the current market interest rate if that current rate is below the floor). The entity may regard the collar as an inexpensive economic hedge against a reasonably possible increase in interest rates. However, an unexpectedly large decrease in interest rates might trigger payments under the written option that, because of the leverage, might be significantly larger than the benefit of lower interest rates. Neither the fair value of the collar nor a sensitivity analysis based on reasonably possible changes in market variables would indicate this exposure. In this case, the entity might provide the additional information described above.[268]

Where financial assets are illiquid, e.g. when there is a low volume of transactions in similar assets and it is difficult to find a counterparty, additional disclosures might be requircd,[269] for example the reasons for the lack of liquidity and how the risk is hedged.[270]

A large holding of a financial asset that, if sold in its entirety, would be sold at a discount or premium to the quoted market price for a smaller holding could also require additional disclosure.[271] This might include:[272]

- the nature of the security (e.g. entity name);
- the extent of holding (e.g. 15 percent of the issued shares);
- the effect on profit or loss; and
- how the entity hedges the risk.

E Concentrations of risk

Concentrations of risk should be disclosed if not otherwise apparent.[273] This should include:

- a description of how management determines concentrations;
- a description of the shared characteristic that identifies each concentration (for example, counterparty, geographical area, currency or market).

  For example, the shared characteristic may refer to geographical distribution of counterparties by groups of countries, individual countries or regions within countries;[274] and
- the amount of the risk exposure associated with all financial instruments sharing that characteristic.

Concentrations of risk arise from financial instruments that have similar characteristics and are affected similarly by changes in economic or other conditions. It is emphasised that the identification of concentrations of risk requires judgement taking into account the circumstances of the entity.[275] For example, they may arise from:

- Industry sectors.

  If an entity's counterparties are concentrated in one or more industry sectors (such as retail or wholesale), it would disclose separately exposure to risks arising from each concentration of counterparties;
- Credit rating or other measure of credit quality.

  If an entity's counterparties are concentrated in one or more credit qualities (such as secured loans or unsecured loans) or in one or more credit ratings (such as investment grade or speculative grade), it would disclose separately exposure to risks arising from each concentration of counterparties;
- Geographical distribution.

  If an entity's counterparties are concentrated in one or more geographical markets (such as Asia or Europe), it would disclose separately exposure to risks arising from each concentration of counterparties;
- A limited number of individual counterparties or groups of closely related counterparties.

Similar principles apply to identifying concentrations of other risks, including liquidity risk and market risk. For example, concentrations of liquidity risk may arise from the repayment terms of financial liabilities, sources of borrowing facilities or reliance on a particular market in which to realise liquid assets. Concentrations of foreign exchange risk may arise if an entity has a significant net open position in a single foreign currency, or aggregate net open positions in several currencies that tend to move together.[276]

Under IAS 32, information on concentrations of risk was only required explicitly for credit risk (see 2.3.2 above).

F *Operational risk*

In developing IFRS 7, the IASB considered whether disclosure of information about operational risk should be required by the standard. However, the definition and measurement of operational risk were considered to be in their infancy and were not necessarily related to financial instruments. Also, such disclosures were believed to be more appropriately located outside the financial statements. Consequently, this issue was deferred for consideration in the management commentary project (see Chapter 3 at 2.3).[277]

G *Capital disclosures*

The IASB considers that the level of an entity's capital and how it is managed are important factors for users of financial statements to consider in assessing the risk profile of an entity and its ability to withstand unexpected adverse events. It might also affect an entity's ability to pay dividends. Consequently, ED 7 contained proposed disclosures about capital.[278]

However, some commentators questioned the relevance of the capital disclosures in a standard dealing with disclosures relating to financial instruments and the IASB noted that an entity's capital does not relate solely to financial instruments and, thus, they have more general relevance. Accordingly, whilst these disclosures were retained, they were included in IAS 1, rather than IFRS 7.[279] The IASB also decided that entities should be able to adopt the amendments to IAS 1 independently of IFRS 7, something which the publication of separate amendments facilitates.[280] The amendments to IAS 1 are dealt with in Chapter 3 at 6.2.

4 PRESENTATION ON THE FACE OF THE FINANCIAL STATEMENTS AND RELATED DISCLOSURES

Although they require certain minimum disclosures, IAS 32 and IFRS 7 provide little guidance as to where financial instruments and related gains and losses should be presented on the face of the financial statements nor how such items should be disaggregated. Further, the disclosures required by those standards need not always reflect how items are presented on the face of the statements. Therefore, for the time being at least, management must use its judgement in deciding how best to present much of the information relating to financial instruments, taking account of the minimum requirements of IAS 32, IFRS 7 and other related standards (including, for relevant entities, IAS 30) as well as the provisions of IAS 1 (see Chapter 3 at 3).

4.1 Income statement

4.1.1 Presentation on the face of the income statement

The effects of an entity's various activities, transactions and other events (including those relating to financial instruments) differ in frequency, potential for gain or loss and predictability. Accordingly, IAS 1 explains, disclosing the components of financial performance assists in providing an understanding of the financial performance achieved and in making projections of future results.[281]

IAS 1 prescribes minimum requirements for inclusion on the face of the income statement but only one caption, 'finance costs', clearly relates to financial instruments.[282] The implementation guidance to IFRS 7 explains that this caption includes total interest expense (see 3.3.2 B above) but may also include amounts that arise on non-financial items, for example the unwinding of the discount on long-term provisions (see Chapter 27 at 4.2.4).[283]

Rather confusingly, the guidance also suggests that finance costs include total interest income (and similar amounts that arise on non-financial assets and liabilities).[284] This might imply that it is permissible to present a line item 'net finance costs' (or a similar term) on the face of the income statement without showing the finance costs and finance revenue composing it. This was an issue the

IFRIC had discussed prior to the publication of IFRS 7 and had concluded that such a treatment was prohibited by IAS 1 (although the presentation of finance revenue followed immediately by finance costs and a subtotal, e.g. 'net finance costs', on the face of the income statement was allowed).[285] This matter was revisited in the light of the guidance in IFRS 7 and the IFRIC confirmed its earlier conclusion (although it acknowledged that the guidance may result in confusion and the IASB subsequently decided to amend IFRS 7 in its annual improvements project to remove this confusion).[286]

Additional line items, headings and subtotals should be presented on the face of the income statement when such presentation is relevant to an understanding of the elements of an entity's financial performance. Factors that should be considered include materiality and the nature and function of the components of income and expenses. For example, a bank should amend the descriptions to apply the more specific requirements in IAS 30, at least until IFRS 7 is applied (thereafter a financial institution may amend the descriptions to provide information that is relevant to the operations of a financial institution, although this change in wording is unlikely to have any significant change in practice).[287]

The following items should also be disclosed on the face of the income statement as allocations of profit or loss for the period:

- profit or loss attributable to minority interest; and
- profit or loss attributable to equity holders of the parent.[288]

The amount of dividends recognised as distributions to equity holders during the period, and the related amount per share, may be disclosed on the face of the income statement. Alternatively, this information can be disclosed on the face of the statement of changes in equity or in the notes.[289]

4.1.2 Further analysis of gains and losses recognised in the income statement

As noted at 2.3.4 and 3.3.2 B above, entities are required to disclose total interest income and total interest expense, calculated using the effective interest method, for financial assets and financial liabilities that are not at fair value through profit or loss. Whilst finance leases are included within the scope of IAS 32 and IFRS 7, strictly they are not accounted for using the effective interest method (although for most leases the method prescribed in IAS 17 – *Leases* – results in a very similar treatment). Accordingly, where material, finance income (charges) arising on finance leases should be shown separately from the interest income (expense) shown above. IAS 18 – *Revenue* – also requires separate disclosure of interest income arising on assets that do not arise from leases.[290] In fact, it will often be appropriate to include such items within the same caption on the face of the income statement and include a sub-analysis in the notes.

Dividends classified as an expense (for example those payable to holders of redeemable preference shares) may be presented either with interest on other liabilities or as a separate item. Such items are subject to the requirements of IAS 1 (and, for relevant entities, IAS 30). In some circumstances, because of the differences between interest and dividends with respect to matters such as tax deductibility, it is desirable to disclose them separately in the income statement.[291]

The following gains and losses reported in the income statement should also be disclosed:

- the amount of revenue arising from dividends;[292]
- changes in fair value that relate to instruments at fair value through profit or loss.

  The implementation guidance to IAS 39 explains that IAS 32 and IFRS 7 neither require nor prohibit disclosure of components of the change in fair value by the way items are classified for internal purposes. For example, the change in fair value of those derivatives that IAS 39 classifies as held for trading but the entity classifies as part of risk management activities outside of the trading portfolio may be disclosed separately.[293]

  Little guidance is given on other aspects of disaggregating gains and losses from instruments classified as at fair value through profit or loss. For example, the components of the change in fair value of a debt instrument can include:

  - interest accruals;
  - foreign currency retranslation;
  - movements arising from changes in the issuer's credit risk; and
  - changes in market interest rates.

  An entity is neither required to disaggregate, nor prohibited from disaggregating, these components on the face of the income statement provided the minimum disclosure requirements are met (e.g. see 2.4.4 and 3.3.2 above). Accordingly, the interest accrual component, say, may be included separately within an interest receivable caption or it may be included within the same caption as other components of the gain or loss such as dealing profit. As noted at 3.3.1 above, whatever the entity's approach, it should be explained in its accounting policies;
- changes in fair value that relate to hedging instruments.[294]

  Taken at face value, this particular disclosure will include, in aggregate, gains and losses on derivative hedging instruments that are part of a fair value hedge relationship and ineffectiveness recognised in the income statement in respect of hedging instruments that are part of either a cash flow hedge or a hedge of a net investment. In practice such an analysis will mean little and even those entities not applying IFRS 7 can be expected to disaggregate these amounts in a more appropriate manner (as set out at 3.3.3 above, entities adopting IFRS 7 are required to make such disclosures).

  Further, until IFRS 7 is applied, there is no explicit requirement to disclose changes in the fair value of assets or liabilities that are a hedged item in a fair value hedge. However, entities may choose to disclose such gains and losses in order to assist users to understand the effect of these hedges on their financial statements. As set out at 3.3.3 above, this disclosure is required by IFRS 7; and

- the amount of exchange differences recognised in the income statement under IAS 21 – *The Effects of Changes in Foreign Exchange Rates* – except for those arising on financial instruments measured at fair value through profit or loss.[295]

In IAS 1 it is explained that when items of income and expense are material, their nature and amount are required to be disclosed separately.[296] Circumstances that can give rise to separate disclosure include the disposal of investments[297] (e.g. available-for-sale assets) and the early settlement of liabilities. However, gains and losses should not be reported as extraordinary items, either on the face of the income statement or in the notes.[298]

4.1.3 Offsetting and hedges

IAS 1 explains that income and expenses should not be offset unless required or permitted by another standard. This is because offsetting detracts from the ability of users to understand fully the transactions, other events and conditions that have occurred and to assess the entity's future cash flows (except where it reflects the substance of the transaction or other event).[299] It goes on to explain that gains and losses on the disposal of non-current investments (such as many available-for-sale assets) are reported by deducting the carrying amount of the asset and related selling expenses from the proceeds on disposal rather than showing gross proceeds as revenue[300] – in the case of available-for-sale assets the profit or loss on disposal will also include any gains and losses that are recycled from equity. It also explains that gains and losses arising from groups of similar transactions should be reported on a net basis, for example gains and losses arising on financial instruments held for trading or foreign exchange differences. The individual transactions should, however, be reported separately if they are material.[301]

Whilst IAS 32 prescribes when financial assets and liabilities should be offset in the balance sheet (see Chapter 18 at 6) it contains no guidance on when related income and expenses should be offset. IAS 39 is largely silent on the subject too, but it does state that hedge accounting 'recognises the offsetting effects on profit or loss of changes in the fair values of the hedging instrument and the hedged item.'[302] This is a little short of an explicit requirement or permission for showing income or expenses net of related hedging gains and losses. However, it is entirely consistent with the objective of hedge accounting to include within an income statement caption related hedging gains and losses even if that results in a degree of offset. Further support for this position is found within IAS 30, which explains that income and expense items 'shall not be offset except for those relating to hedges and to assets and liabilities that have been offset… .'[303]

Example 22.6: Hedge of a forecast sale

Company K has the euro as its functional currency. On 1 January 2008 it forecasts the sale of certain goods in dollars in six months and, to hedge that exposure, enters into a forward foreign exchange contract maturing on 1 July 2008. The hedge is designated as a cash flow hedge and meets the conditions for hedge accounting throughout the term of the hedge.

On 1 July 2008 the forecast sale occurs and is recorded using the prevailing spot rate resulting in, say, €1,000 being recognised in revenue. The forward contract is settled on this date at which point a related loss of, say, €100 has been recognised in equity.

The mechanics of cash flow hedge accounting require the €100 loss to be recycled out of equity and into the income statement on 1 July 2008. Using the analysis above, K presents the €100 loss as a deduction from revenue resulting in the hedged sale being recognised at a net amount of €900.

Although the €100 loss recycled out of equity is being offset in the income statement it will, however, be disclosed in the statement of changes in equity (see 4.2 below) or notes thereto.

4.1.4 Embedded derivatives

IAS 39 states that it does not address whether embedded derivatives should be presented separately on the face of the financial statements.[304] In practice, it will depend on the nature both of the hybrid and the host whether related profits and losses are included in the same or separate income statement captions.

For example, an investment in a credit linked note that is accounted for as a debt instrument host and an embedded credit derivative might give rise to interest income and credit losses respectively that could well be reported in separate income statement captions. Alternatively, changes in the fair value of an embedded prepayment option in a host debt instrument that is accounted for separately may be included in the same income statement caption as interest on the debt instrument if the value of the option varies largely as a result of change in interest rates.

4.1.5 Entities whose share capital is not equity

Gains and losses related to changes in the carrying amount of a financial liability are recognised as income or expense in profit or loss even when they relate to an instrument that includes a right to the residual interest in the assets of the entity in exchange for cash or another financial asset, such as shares in mutual funds and co-operatives (see Chapter 19 at 3.2.2). Any gain or loss arising from the remeasurement of such an instrument should be presented separately on the face of the income statement when it is relevant in explaining the entity's performance.[305]

The following example illustrates an income statement format that may be used by entities such as mutual funds that do not have equity as defined in IAS 32, although other formats may be acceptable.

Example 22.7: Income statement format for a mutual fund

Income statement for the year ended 31 December 2008[306]

	2008 €	2007 €
Revenue	2,956	1,718
Expenses (classified by nature or function)	(644)	(614)
Profit from operating activities	2,312	1,104
Finance costs		
– other finance costs	(47)	(47)
– distributions to members	(50)	(50)
Change in net assets attributable to unit holders	2,215	1,007

Although it may not be immediately clear, the final line item in this format is an expense. Therefore the entity's 'profit or loss' (as that term is used in IAS 1) for 2008 is €2,312 – €47 – €50 – €2,215 = €nil.

The next example illustrates an income statement format that may be used by entities whose share capital is not equity as defined in IAS 32 because the entity has an obligation to repay the share capital on demand, for example co-operatives, but which do have some equity. Again, other formats may be acceptable.

Example 22.8: Income statement format for a co-operative

Income statement for the year ended 31 December 2008[307]

	2008 €	2007 €
Revenue	472	498
Expenses (classified by nature or function)	(367)	(396)
Profit from operating activities	105	102
Finance costs		
– other finance costs	(4)	(4)
– distributions to members	(50)	(50)
Change in net assets attributable to members	51	48

In this example, the line item 'Finance costs – distributions to members' is an expense and the final line item is equivalent to 'profit or loss'.

Corresponding balance sheet formats for both of these examples are shown at 4.3.4 below.

4.2 Statement of changes in equity

IAS 1 requires the presentation of a statement of changes in equity that includes the profit or loss for the period as well as other items of income and expense not recognised within profit or loss.[308] Material items of income and expense and gains and losses that result from financial assets and liabilities and are included in equity are required to be disclosed separately and should include at least the following:

- changes in fair value of available-for-sale financial assets,[309] including:[310]
  - the amount of any gain or loss recognised directly in equity during the period; and
  - the amount that was removed from equity and recognised in the income statement for the period; and
- for cash flow hedges:[311]
  - the amount of gains or losses on designated hedging instruments recognised in equity during the period;
  - the amount removed from equity during the period and reported in the income statement; and
  - the amount removed from equity during the period and included in the initial measurement of the acquisition cost of hedged non-financial assets or liabilities.

The implementation guidance to IAS 39 states that disclosure should be provided of changes in the fair value of hedging instruments that are recognised in equity.[312] This will include, in aggregate, gains and losses on hedging instruments in both cash flow hedges and hedges of net investments. However, this may often be dealt with by presenting for hedges of net investments similar information to that noted above for cash flow hedges.

The following information in respect of transactions in equity instruments should be shown either on the face of the statement of changes in equity or in the notes:

- the amounts of transactions with equity holders acting in their capacity as equity holders, showing distributions separately; and
- a reconciliation between the carrying amount of each class of contributed equity and each reserve at the beginning and the end of the period, separately disclosing each change.[313]

In addition, IAS 32 notes that IAS 1 requires the amount of transaction costs accounted for as a deduction from equity in the period to be disclosed separately.[314]

If an entity reacquires its own equity instruments from related parties disclosure should be provided in accordance with IAS 24 (see Chapter 35).[315]

If an entity such as a mutual fund or a co-operative has no issued equity instruments, it may still need to present a statement of changes in equity. For example, such an entity may have gains or losses arising on available-for-sale assets that are recognised in equity.

4.3 Balance sheet

4.3.1 Assets and liabilities

IAS 1 does not prescribe the order or format in which items are to be presented on the face of the balance sheet, but states that the following items relating to financial instruments, are sufficiently different in nature or function to warrant separate presentation:

- trade and other receivables;
- cash and cash equivalents;
- other financial assets;
- trade and other payables;
- provisions; and
- other financial liabilities.[316]

However, additional line items, headings and subtotals should be presented on the face of the balance sheet when the size, nature or function of an item or aggregation of similar items is such that separate presentation is relevant to an understanding of the entity's financial position.[317] The judgement on whether additional items are presented separately should be based on an assessment of:

- the nature and liquidity of assets;
- the function of assets within the entity; and
- the amounts, nature and timing of liabilities.[318]

The descriptions used and the ordering of items or aggregation of similar items may be amended according to the nature of the entity and its transactions, to provide information that is relevant to an understanding of the entity's financial position. For example, banks should amend the captions and apply the more specific requirements in IAS 30, at least until IFRS 7 is applied (thereafter a financial institution may amend the descriptions to provide information that is relevant to the operations of a financial institution, although this change in wording is unlikely to have any significant change in practice).[319]

Although, for measurement purposes, IAS 39 classifies financial assets into four categories (see Chapter 17 at 7), other descriptors for these categories or other categorisations may be used when presenting information on the face of the financial statements.[320]

However, the use of different measurement bases for different classes of assets suggests that their nature or function differs and, therefore, that they should be presented as separate line items.[321] For example, loans and receivables measured at amortised cost would often be presented separately from available-for-sale assets measured at fair value.

As noted at 4.1.4 above, IAS 39 states that it does not address whether embedded derivatives should be presented separately on the face of the financial statements[322] and this applies to the balance sheet as much as to the income statement. Although the guidance in the previous paragraph suggests that embedded derivatives will often be presented separately on the face of the balance sheet, this will not always be the case, e.g. for the 'puttable instruments' shown in Example 22.9 below, which is based on IAS 32.

Further sub-classifications of the line items presented should be disclosed, either on the face of the balance sheet or in the notes, classified in a manner appropriate to the entity's operations.[323] The detail provided in sub-classifications will depend on the size, nature and function of the amounts involved and will vary for each item. For example, receivables should be disaggregated into amounts receivable from trade customers, receivables from related parties and other amounts. Assets included within receivables that are not financial instruments, such as many prepayments, should also be shown separately.[324]

4.3.2 *The distinction between current and non-current assets and liabilities*

For entities presenting a balance sheet that distinguishes between current and non-current assets and liabilities, the requirements for determining whether items are classified as current or non-current are dealt with in Chapter 3 at 3.1.1 to 3.1.4. This section deals with two interpretive issues that have arisen in applying those requirements to financial instruments.

A Derivatives

Where a derivative is not designated as a hedging instrument in an effective hedge it is classified by IAS 39 as 'held-for-trading' (see Chapter 17 at 7.1.1).[325] Where assets and liabilities are held 'primarily for the purpose of being traded' IAS 1 requires them to be classified as current.[326] Some had concluded from these requirements, together with some slightly loose drafting in IAS 1, that any derivative not designated as a hedging instrument in an effective hedge must always be classified as current.

The IFRIC has considered this issue and, whilst noting that IAS 1 might be read as implying the treatment noted above, implicitly concluded that derivatives should be classified according to the general requirements in IAS 1. In other words, the IAS 39 classification should be ignored and the maturity of the derivative would be the principal determinant of its classification (unless it was held primarily for the purpose of being traded, in which case current classification would be required).[327] The IASB has subsequently resolved to amend IAS 1 to remove any confusion.[328]

B Convertible loans

The IFRIC was also asked to consider a situation in which an entity issued convertible financial instruments that were accounted for as an equity component (i.e. the holders' rights to convert the instruments into a fixed number of the issuer's equity instruments) and a liability component (i.e. the entity's obligation to deliver cash to holders at the maturity date). Furthermore, the maturity date was more than one year after the balance sheet but the conversion option could be exercised at any time before maturity. The issue is whether the liability component should be classified as current or non-current.

The IFRIC considered that the requirements in IAS 1 and the Framework were in conflict and that there were valid arguments to support both current and non-current classification, although it noted that non-current classification was most common in practice.[329] The IASB subsequently decided that IAS 1 should be amended through its annual improvements project so that it would require non-current classification of the liability component in these circumstances.[330]

4.3.3 Equity

IAS 1 explains that, as a minimum, the face of the balance sheet should include line items that present the following amounts within equity:

- minority interest, presented within equity; and
- issued capital and reserves attributable to equity holders of the parent.[331]

As for assets and liabilities, additional line items, headings and subtotals should be presented on the face of the balance sheet when such presentation is relevant to an understanding of the entity's financial position[332] and further sub-classifications of the line items presented should be disclosed, either on the face of the balance sheet or in the notes, classified in a manner appropriate to the entity's operations.[333] The detail provided in the sub-classifications will depend on the size, nature and function of the amounts involved and will vary for each item. For example, equity capital and reserves should be disaggregated into various classes, such as paid-in capital, share premium and reserves.[334] A description of the nature and purpose of each reserve within equity should also be provided.[335]

For each class of share capital, the following information should be disclosed, either on the face of the balance sheet or in the notes:

- the number of shares authorised;
- the number of shares issued and fully paid, and issued but not fully paid;
- par value per share, or that the shares have no par value;
- a reconciliation of the number of shares outstanding at the beginning and at the end of the period;
- the rights, preferences and restrictions attaching to that class including restrictions on the distribution of dividends and the repayment of capital;
- shares in the entity held by the entity or by its subsidiaries (treasury shares[336]) or associates; and
- shares reserved for issue under options and contracts for the sale of shares, including the terms and amounts.[337]

An entity without share capital, such as a partnership or trust, should disclose equivalent information, showing changes during the period in each category of equity interest, and the rights, preferences and restrictions attaching to each category of equity interest[338] (assuming of course it has actually issued instruments that meet the definition of equity).

4.3.4 Entities whose share capital is not equity

Continuing Examples 22.7 and 20.8 at 4.1.5 above, the following examples illustrate corresponding balance sheet formats that may be used by entities such as mutual funds that do not have equity as defined in IAS 32, or entities such as co-operatives whose share capital is not equity as defined in IAS 32 because the entity has an obligation to repay the share capital on demand.

Example 22.9: Balance sheet format for a mutual fund

Balance sheet at 31 December 2008[339]

	2008		2007	
	€	€	€	€
ASSETS				
Non-current assets (classified in accordance with IAS 1)	91,374		78,484	
Total non-current assets		91,374		78,484
Current assets (classified in accordance with IAS 1)	1,422		1,769	
Total current assets		1,422		1,769
Total assets		92,796		80,253
LIABILITIES				
Current liabilities (classified in accordance with IAS 1)	647		66	
Total current liabilities		(647)		(66)
Non-current liabilities excluding net assets attributable to unit holders (classified in accordance with IAS 1)	280		136	
		(280)		(136)
Net assets attributable to unit holders		91,869		80,051

As for the equivalent income statement format, it may not be immediately clear what the final line item in this format represents. It is, in fact, a liability and therefore the entity's 'equity' (as that term is used in IAS 1) at the end of 2008 is €92,796 – €647 – €280 – €91,869 = €nil.

Example 22.10: Balance sheet format for a co-operative

Balance sheet at 31 December 2008[340]	2008		2007	
	€	€	€	€
ASSETS				
Non-current assets (classified in accordance with IAS 1)	908		830	
Total non-current assets		908		830
Current assets (classified in accordance with IAS 1)	383		350	
Total current assets		383		350
Total assets		1,291		1,180

LIABILITIES				
Current liabilities (classified in accordance with IAS 1)	372		338	
Share capital repayable on demand	202		161	
Total current liabilities		(574)		(499)
Total assets less current liabilities		717		681
Non-current liabilities (classified in accordance with IAS 1)	187		196	
		187		196
RESERVES*				
Reserves, e.g. revaluation reserve, retained earnings	530		485	
		530		485
		717		681
MEMORANDUM NOTE				
TOTAL MEMBERS' INTERESTS				
Share capital repayable on demand		202		161
Reserves		530		485
		732		646

*In this example, the entity has no obligation to deliver a share of its reserves to its members.

The line item 'Share capital repayable on demand' is part of the entity's liabilities and the items within 'Reserves' represent its equity.

Although not required by IAS 1, an entity adopting this type of balance sheet format may choose to present an analysis of movements in (or reconciliation of) total members' interests (often defined as equity plus share capital repayable on demand, perhaps adjusted for other balances with members) if this is considered to provide useful information; this would not remove the need to present a statement of changes in equity.

4.4 Cash flow statement

The implementation guidance to IAS 39 acknowledges that the terminology in IAS 7 – *Cash Flow Statements* – was not updated to reflect the publication of IAS 39 but does explain that the classification of cash flows arising from hedging instruments within the cash flow statement should be consistent with the classification of these instruments as hedging instruments. In other words, such cash flows should be classified as operating, investing or financing activities, on the basis of the classification of the cash flows arising from the hedged item.[341]

5 EFFECTIVE DATE, TRANSITIONAL PROVISIONS AND FIRST-TIME ADOPTION

This section contains information that is relevant for annual periods beginning on or after 1 January 2006. For earlier periods, equivalent requirements are dealt with in *International GAAP 2005* and *International GAAP 2007*, the predecessors to this publication.

5.1 Effective date

The June 2005 amendments to IAS 39 relating to the fair value option (which included consequential amendments to IAS 32 – see 2.2.3 and 2.4.4 B and C above) must be applied for annual periods beginning on or after 1 January 2006 and earlier application is encouraged.[342]

IFRS 7 is effective for annual periods beginning on or after 1 January 2007. Entities are encouraged to apply the standard earlier, although if they do they are required to disclose this fact.[343]

5.2 Transitional provisions

Certain disclosures can be required when applying the amendment to IAS 39 relating to the fair value option and these are noted in Chapter 17 at 8.2.

IFRS 7 contains no transitional concessions for annual periods beginning on or after 1 January 2006 and therefore comparative information should be given in accordance with IAS 1.[344]

5.3 First-time adoption

IFRS 1 – *First-time Adoption of International Financial Reporting Standards* – is dealt with in Chapter 5. The aspects related to the topics covered in this chapter are noted below. Further similar sections are included in Chapters 17 to 21.

As set out in Chapter 17 at 8.3.2 and 8.3.5, first time adopters may designate previously recognised financial assets or financial liabilities at fair value through profit or loss or financial assets as available-for-sale. Where this is done the following should be disclosed for each of those categories:[345]

- the fair value of any financial assets or financial liabilities designated into it; and
- the classification and carrying amount in the previous financial statements.

IFRS 1 contains many other disclosure requirements that apply to financial instruments as well as other items in the financial statements, such as reconciliations designed to assist a user of the financial statements understand how the transition to IFRS has been effected. These requirements are covered in Chapter 5.

6 FUTURE DEVELOPMENTS

It was noted in Chapter 17 at 9 that the majority of the IASB's current work on financial instruments is being carried out in conjunction with the FASB. One of their objectives is to require all financial instruments to be measured at fair value with realised and unrealised gains and losses recognised in the period in which they occur.

However, the boards recognise that there are some significant impediments to attaining their objectives, i.e. there are difficult technical and practical issues that currently exist that are likely to take time to resolve. One of the main issues identified was how to present the components of the net changes in fair values, and what information to disclose about past changes in fair values and exposures to future changes in market factors. For example, is interest relevant information in a fair value model and, if so, should it be measured on an historical cost basis or some form of fair value basis (taking account of current interest rates)?

As part of their research into the issue, in March 2006 a questionnaire was posted to the boards' websites seeking views of users on the types of information related to financial instruments measured at fair value that would be relevant to their analysis. Responses to the questionnaire indicated that users need information on certain factors that cause fair value to change such as changes in contractual cash flows and expected collections. Other information received indicated that there is little demand for interest income and interest expense on a fair value basis and there is a lack of consistency between entities in the reporting of fair value changes in the income statement.[346]

Whilst disclosure requirements are considered important by the boards, it seems unlikely that any major changes will be forthcoming in the near term as they focus on their overall strategy in addressing the measurement of financial instruments, their derecognition and the distinction between financial liabilities and equity instruments.

References

1 IAS 32 (2005), *Financial Instruments: Disclosure and Presentation*, IASB, March 1995 to August 2005, para. 1.
2 IAS 32 (2005), para. 2.
3 IAS 32 (2005), para. 3.
4 IAS 32 (2005), para. 2.
5 IFRS 7, *Financial Instruments: Disclosures*, IASB, paras. BC2 and BC6.
6 Exposure Draft ED 7, *Financial Instruments: Disclosures*, IASB, July 2004.
7 IFRS 7, para. 1.
8 IFRS 7, para. 2.
9 IFRS 7, paras. 45 and C2.
10 IAS 32 (2005), para. AG24.
11 IAS 32 (2005), para. 52.
12 IAS 32 (2005), para. 53.
13 IAS 32 (2005), para. 54.
14 IAS 32 (2005), para. 55.
15 IAS 32 (2005), para. 53.
16 IAS 32 (2005), para. 55.
17 IAS 32 (2005), para. 56.
18 IAS 32 (2005), para. 57.
19 IAS 32 (2005), para. 58.
20 IAS 32 (2005), paras. 60 and 66.
21 IAS 32 (2005), para. 61.
22 IAS 32 (2005), para. 62.
23 IAS 32 (2005), para. 60.
24 IAS 32 (2005), para. 60.
25 IAS 32 (2005), para. 62.
26 IAS 32 (2005), para. 63.
27 IAS 32 (2005), para. 64.
28 IAS 32 (2005), para. 65.
29 IAS 32 (2005), para. 68.
30 IAS 32 (2005), para. 67.
31 IAS 32 (2005), para. 69.
32 IAS 32 (2005), para. 70.
33 IAS 32 (2005), para. 71.
34 IAS 32 (2005), para. 72.
35 IAS 32 (2005), paras. 94(d) and BC42.
36 IAS 32 (2005), para. 73.
37 IAS 32 (2005), para. 74.
38 IAS 32 (2005), para. 74.
39 IAS 32 (2005), para. 75.
40 IAS 32 (2005), para. 77.

41 IAS 32 (2005), para. 76.
42 IAS 32 (2005), para. 77.
43 IAS 32 (2005), para. 78.
44 IAS 32 (2005), para. 79.
45 IAS 32 (2005), para. 79.
46 IAS 32 (2005), para. 80.
47 IAS 32 (2005), para. 81.
48 IAS 32 (2005), para. 82.
49 IAS 32 (2005), paras. 83-84.
50 IAS 32 (2005), para. 85.
51 IAS 32 (2005), para. 84.
52 IAS 32 (2005), para. 83.
53 IAS 32 (2005), para. 87.
54 IAS 32 (2005), para. 87.
55 IAS 32 (2005), para. 86.
56 IAS 32 (2005), para. 89.
57 IAS 32 (2005), para. 92.
58 IAS 32 (2005), para. 93.
59 IAS 32 (2005), para. 92.
60 IAS 32 (2005), para. BC36.
61 IAS 32 (2005), para. BC49(i).
62 IAS 32 (2005), para. BC36.
63 IAS 32 (2005), para. 58(b).
64 IAS 39, *Financial Instruments: Recognition and Measurement*, IASB, para. F.1.12.
65 IAS 32 (2005), para. 88.
66 IAS 32 (2005), para. 91.
67 IAS 32 (2005), para. 90.
68 IAS 32 (2005), para. 91.
69 IAS 32 (2005), para. 91.
70 IAS 32 (2005), para. 90.
71 IAS 32 (2005), para. 91A.
72 IAS 32 (2005), para. BC35.
73 IAS 32 (2005), para. 94(k).
74 IAS 32 (2005), para. 94(l).
75 IAS 32 (2005), para. 94(k).
76 IAS 32 (2005), para. 59.
77 IAS 32 (2005), para. 94(a).
78 IAS 32 (2005), para. BC38.
79 IAS 32 (2005), para. 94(m).
80 IAS 32 (2005), para. 94(m).
81 IAS 32 (2005), para. 95.
82 IAS 32 (2005), para. 95.
83 IAS 32 (2005), para. BC48.
84 IAS 32 (2005), para. 94(j).
85 IAS 32 (2005), para. 94(e).
86 IAS 32 (2005), para. 94(f).
87 IAS 32 (2005), para. BC45.
88 IAS 32 (2005), paras. BC44 and BC46.
89 IAS 32 (2005), para. 94(h)(i).
90 IAS 32 (2005), para. AG40.
91 IAS 32 (2005), para. 94(h)(i).
92 IAS 32 (2005), para. 94(i).
93 IAS 32 (2005), para. 94(h)(ii).
94 IAS 32 (2005), para. BC47.
95 IAS 32 (2005), para. 94(g).
96 IAS 32 (2005), para. 94(i).
97 IAS 32 (2005), para. 94(b).
98 IAS 32 (2005), para. 94(c).
99 IFRS 7, para. 1.
100 IFRS 7, para. BC6.
101 IFRS 7, para. BC9 to BC11.
102 IFRS 7, para. 4.
103 IFRS 7, para. BC8.
104 IFRS 7, Appendix B, Application guidance, para. after main heading.
105 IFRS 7, Guidance on implementing, para. after main heading.
106 IFRS 7, para. IG1.
107 IFRS 7, para. IG2.
108 IFRS 7, para. B3.
109 IFRS 7, para. IG5.
110 IFRS 7, para. IG6.
111 IFRS 7, para. IG3.
112 IAS 1, *Presentation of Financial Statements*, IASB, para. 11.
113 IFRS 7, para. IG3.
114 IFRS 7, para. IG4.
115 IAS 1, para. 12.
116 IFRS 7, paras. IN4 and BC10.
117 IFRS 7, para. 6.
118 IFRS 7, para. B1.
119 IFRS 7, para. B2.
120 IFRS 7, para. 6.
121 IFRS 7, paras. 7 and BC13.
122 IFRS 7, para. 21.
123 IFRS 7, para. B5(a).
124 IFRS 7, paras. B5(b), (c) and (e) to (g).
125 IFRS 7, para. B5(d).
126 IFRS 7, para. B5.
127 IFRS 7, para. 20.
128 IFRS 7, paras. 20(a) and BC33.
129 IFRS 7, para. BC33.
130 IFRS 7, para. BC34.
131 IFRS 7, paras. 20(b) and (d).
132 IFRS 4, para. 35(d).
133 IFRS 7, para. 20(c).
134 IFRS 7, para. BC35.
135 IFRS 7, para. 20(e).
136 IFRS 7, para. 22.
137 IAS 39, para. F.1.12.
138 IFRS 7, para. 23.
139 IFRS 7, para. 24.
140 IFRS 7, para. 8.
141 IFRS 7, para. BC15.
142 IFRS 7, para. BC14.
143 IFRS 7, para. 10(a).
144 IFRS 7, para. B4.
145 IFRS 7, para. IG7.
146 IFRS 7, paras. IG8 to IG11.
147 IFRS 7, para. 10(a)(ii).
148 IFRS 7, para. 11.
149 IFRS 7, para. 10(b).
150 IFRS 7, para. BC22.

151 IFRS 7, para. 9.
152 IFRS 7, para. 11.
153 IFRS 7, para. 12.
154 IFRS 7, para. BC23.
155 IFRS 7, para. 13.
156 IFRS 7, para. BC24.
157 IFRS 7, para. 14.
158 IFRS 7, para. 15.
159 IFRS 7, para. BC25.
160 IFRS 7, para. 16.
161 IFRS 7, para. BC26.
162 IFRS 7, para. BC27.
163 IFRS 7, para. 17.
164 IFRS 7, para. BC31.
165 IFRS 7, Appendix A, Defined terms.
166 IFRS 7, para. BC32.
167 IFRS 7, para. 18.
168 IFRS 7, para. 19.
169 IFRS 7, para. IG12.
170 IFRS 7, para. BC36.
171 IFRS 7, para. 25.
172 IFRS 7, para. 26.
173 IFRS 7, para. 27.
174 IFRS 7, para. BC38.
175 IFRS 7, para. BC38.
176 IFRS 7, para. 28.
177 IFRS 7, para. IG14.
178 IFRS 7, para. 28.
179 IFRS 7, para. IG14.
180 IFRS 7, para. 29(a).
181 IFRS 7, paras. 29(b) and (c).
182 IFRS 7, para. 30.
183 IFRS 7, para. BC37.
184 IFRS 7, para. 31.
185 IFRS 7, para. 32.
186 IFRS 7, Appendix A.
187 IFRS 7, para. B23.
188 IFRS 7, para. B22.
189 IFRS 7, paras. B25 and IG32.
190 IFRS 7, para. B26.
191 IFRS 7, para. B6 and BC46.
192 IFRS 7, para. BC41.
193 IFRS 7, para. BC40(b).
194 IFRS 7, para. BC42.
195 IFRS 7, para. BC41.
196 IFRS 7, paras. BC43 to BC46.
197 IFRS 7, paras. 33(a) and (b).
198 IFRS 7, paras. 33(c) and IG17.
199 IFRS 7, para. IG15.
200 IFRS 7, para. IG16.
201 Origin Energy prepares its financial statements in accordance with Australian-IFRS including AASB 7 which contains requirements that are identical to those in IFRS 7.
202 IFRS 7, para. 34(a).
203 IFRS 7, para. BC47.
204 IFRS 7, para. B7.
205 IFRS 7, para. 35.
206 IFRS 7, para. IG20.
207 IFRS 7, para. BC48.
208 IFRS 7, para. 34(b).
209 IFRS 7, para. IG21.
210 IFRS 7, para. 36(a).
211 IFRS 7, para. B9.
212 IFRS 7, para. BC49.
213 IFRS 7, para. B10.
214 IFRS 7, para. BC50.
215 IFRS 7, para. 36(b).
216 IFRS 7, para. IG22.
217 IFRS 7, para. 36(c).
218 IFRS 7, para. BC54.
219 IFRS 7, para. IG23.
220 IFRS 7, para. IG24.
221 IFRS 7, para. IG25.
222 IFRS 7, paras. IG 24 and IG25.
223 IFRS 7, paras. BC51 to BC53 and BC73(c).
224 IFRS 7, para. 36(d).
225 IFRS 7, Appendix A.
226 IFRS 7, para. IG26.
227 IFRS 7, para. IG27.
228 IFRS 7, paras. 37 and BC55.
229 IFRS 7, para. BC55(a).
230 IFRS 7, para. IG28.
231 IFRS 7, para. IG29.
232 IFRS 7, para. BC55(b).
233 IFRS 7, para. IG29(c).
234 IFRS 7, para. 38.
235 IFRS 7, para. BC56.
236 IFRS 7, para. 39.
237 IFRS 7, para. B11.
238 IFRS 7, para. B12.
239 IFRS 7, para. BC57.
240 IFRS 7, para. B13.
241 IFRS 7, para. B14.
242 IFRS 7, para. B16.
243 IFRS 7, para. B15.
244 IFRS 7, para. 39.
245 IFRS 7, para. IG31.
246 IFRS 7, para. IG30.
247 IFRS 7, para. B21.
248 IFRS 7, para. BC59.
249 IFRS 7, para. B28.
250 IFRS 7, para. 40.
251 IFRS 7, para. B27.
252 IFRS 7, para. B17.
253 IFRS 7, para. IG32.
254 IFRS 7, para. B24.
255 IFRS 7, para. B18.
256 IFRS 7, para. IG33.
257 IFRS 7, para. IG34.
258 IFRS 7, para. B19.
259 IFRS 7, para. IG35.
260 IFRS 7, para. B25.

261 IFRS 7, para. 41.
262 IFRS 7, para. BC61.
263 IFRS 7, para. 41.
264 IFRS 7, para. B20.
265 IFRS 7, para. 42.
266 IFRS 7, para. 42.
267 IFRS 7, para. IG37(a).
268 IFRS 7, para. IG38.
269 IFRS 7, para. IG37(b).
270 IFRS 7, para. IG39.
271 IFRS 7, para. IG37(c).
272 IFRS 7, para. IG40.
273 IFRS 7, para. 34 (c).
274 IFRS 7, para. IG19.
275 IFRS 7, para. B8.
276 IFRS 7, para. IG18.
277 IFRS 7, para. BC65.
278 IAS 1, para. BC42.
279 IAS 1, para. BC44.
280 IAS 1, para. BC45.
281 IAS 1, para. 84.
282 IAS 1, para. 81(b).
283 IFRS 7, para. IG13.
284 IFRS 7, para. IG13.
285 *IFRIC Update*, IASB, October 2004.
286 *IFRIC Update*, IASB, November 2006 and *IASB Update*, IASB, November 2006.
287 IAS 1, paras. 83-84.
288 IAS 1, para. 82.
289 IAS 1, para. 95.
290 IAS 18, *Revenue*, IASB, paras. 6(a) and 35(b)(iii).
291 IAS 32, *Financial Instruments: Presentation*, IASB, para. 40.
292 IAS 18, para. 35(b)(iv).
293 IAS 39, para. G.1.
294 IAS 39, para. G.1.
295 IAS 21, *The Effects of Changes in Foreign Exchange Rates*, IASB, para. 52(a).
296 IAS 1, para. 86.
297 IAS 1, para. 87.
298 IAS 1, para. 85.
299 IAS 1, paras. 32-33.
300 IAS 1, para. 34.
301 IAS 1, para. 35.
302 IAS 39, para. 85.
303 IAS 30, *Disclosures in the Financial Statements of Banks and Similar Financial Institutions*, IASB, August 1990 to December 2003, para. 13.
304 IAS 39, para. 11.
305 IAS 32, para. 41.
306 IAS 32, para. IE32.
307 IAS 32, para. IE33.
308 IAS 1, paras. 8 and 96.
309 IAS 39, para. G.1.
310 IAS 32 (2005), para. 94(k), IFRS 7, para. 20(a)(ii).
311 IAS 32 (2005), para. 59, IFRS 7, para. 20(c), (d) and (e).
312 IAS 39, para. G.1.
313 IAS 1, para. 97.
314 IAS 32, para. 39.
315 IAS 32, para. 34.
316 IAS 1, paras. 68 and 71.
317 IAS 1, paras. 69 and 71(a).
318 IAS 1, para. 72.
319 IAS 1, para. 71(b).
320 IAS 39, para. 45.
321 IAS 1, para. 73.
322 IAS 39, para. 11.
323 IAS 1, para. 74.
324 IAS 1, para. 75(b).
325 IAS 39, para. 9.
326 IAS 1, paras. 57 and 60.
327 *IFRIC Update*, IASB, May 2007.
328 *IASB Update*, IASB, June 2007.
329 *IFRIC Update*, IASB, November 2006.
330 *IASB Update*, IASB, November 2006.
331 IAS 1, paras. 68(o)-(p).
332 IAS 1, para. 69.
333 IAS 1, para. 74.
334 IAS 1, para. 75(e).
335 IAS 1, para. 76(b).
336 IAS 32, para. 34.
337 IAS 1, para. 76(a).
338 IAS 1, para. 77.
339 IAS 32, para. IE32.
340 IAS 32, para. IE33.
341 IAS 39, para. G.2.
342 IAS 39, para. 105A.
343 IFRS 7, para. 43.
344 IFRS 7, para. 44.
345 IFRS 1, *First-time Adoption of International Financial Reporting Standards*, IASB, para. 43A.
346 Project Update, *Financial Instruments*, IASB, 7 July 2006.

Index of extracts from financial statements

Index of standards

Framework for the Preparation and Presentation of Financial Statements

IFRS 1, First-time Adoption of International Financial Reporting Standards

IFRS 2, Share-based payment

IFRS 3, Business Combinations

IFRS 3 Revised (this edition discusses the proposed revisions to IFRS 3, Business combinations, on the basis of the near-final draft of the revised IFRS 3 published by the IASB in June 2007, to which the following refer).

IFRS 4, Insurance Contracts

IFRS 5, Non-current Assets Held for Sale and Discontinued Operations

IFRS 6, Exploration for and Evaluation of Mineral Resources

IFRS 7, Financial Instruments Disclosures

IFRS 8, Operating Segments

IAS 1, Presentation of Financial Statements

IAS 1 Revised 2007

IAS 2, Inventories

IAS 7, Cash Flow Statements

IAS 8, Accounting Policies, Changes in Accounting Estimates and Errors

IAS 10, Events After the Balance Sheet Date

IAS 11, Construction contracts

IAS 12, Income taxes

IAS 14, Segment Reporting

IAS 16, Property, plant and equipment

IAS 17, Leases

IAS 18, Revenue

IAS 19, Employee Benefits

IAS 20, Accounting for Government Grants and Disclosure of Government Assistance

IAS 21, The Effects of Changes in Foreign Exchange Rates

IAS 23, Borrowing Costs

IAS 24, Related Party Disclosures

IAS 27, Consolidated and Separate Financial Statements

IAS 27 Revised (this edition discusses the proposed revisions to IAS 27, Consolidated and separate financial statements, on the basis of the near-final draft of the revised IAS 27 published by the IASB in June 2007, to which the following refer).

IAS 28, Investments in Associates

IAS 29 Financial Reporting in Hyperinflationary Economies

IAS 31, Interests in joint ventures

IAS 32 Financial Instruments Disclosure and Presentation

IAS 33, Earnings per Share

IAS 34, Interim financial reporting

IAS 36, Impairment of assets

IAS 37, Provisions, Contingent Liabilities and Contingent Assets

IAS 38, Intangible Assets

IAS 39, Financial Instruments Recognition and Measurement

IAS 40, Investment property

IAS 41 Agriculture

Index

Notes

Notes

Notes

Notes

Notes

Notes

Notes